The Pennsylvania Railroad

Volume 1

The Pennsylvania Railroad

Volume 1   Building an Empire, 1846–1917

Albert J. Churella

PENN

University of Pennsylvania Press

Philadelphia

American Business, Politics, and Society

SERIES EDITORS:
Richard R. John, Pamela Walker Laird, and Mark H. Rose

Books in the series American Business, Politics, and Society explore the relationships over time between governmental institutions and the creation and performance of markets, firms, and industries large and small. The central theme of this series is that public policy—understood broadly to embrace not only lawmaking but also the structuring presence of governmental institutions—has been fundamental to the evolution of American business from the colonial era to the present. The series editors are especially interested in publishing books that explore developments that have enduring consequences.

Published by

University of Pennsylvania Press
Philadelphia, Pennsylvania 19104-4112

www.upenn.edu/pennpress

Printed in the United States of America on acid-free paper

10 9 8 7 6 5 4 3 2 1

Library of Congress Cataloging-in-Publication Data

Churella, Albert J.
    The Pennsylvania Railroad /Albert J. Churella. — 1st ed.
        v. cm. — (American business, politics, and society)
    Includes bibliographical references and index.
    Contents: v. 1. Building an empire, 1846-1917
    ISBN 978-0-8122-4348-2 (hardcover : alk. paper)
    1. Pennsylvania Railroad—History.   I. Title.
    II. Series: American business, politics, and society.
    HE2791.P43C48   2011
    385.09748—dc23

                            2011043921

Contents

Introduction

My earliest memories are of the Pennsylvania Railroad. As I grew up in Columbus, Ohio, the PRR interrupted more than one family dinner, as my parents helped me to walk unsteadily outside to see a train lurch even more unsteadily down the little-used branch line to Mount Vernon, abandoned just a few years later. I am a product of the last year of the baby boom, born as the Standard Railroad of the World was dying. The Pennsylvania Railroad merged itself out of existence, becoming the Penn Central Transportation Company in 1968, shortly before I rode my first train. On more than one occasion, my parents would bring me to Union Station in Columbus, then less than a decade away from demolition. I could stand by the concourse windows and look down—an uncommon perspective for a small child—on the slowly spinning cooling fans on the Penn Central diesels that idled below. But on one particular day, the station was more crowded than it had been in years, as the United Aircraft TurboTrain was open for public viewing. It was Tuesday, May 25, 1971. I am certain of the date, because I still have the yellowed newspaper clipping, tucked in a box, forgotten through several moves, and serendipitously rediscovered less than a year before I finished writing this volume.[1] An announcement that the train was offering a free one-way trip to Pittsburgh later that evening induced my

father, in a world still innocent of automatic teller machines, to take every cent my mother had in her purse, leaving her behind to explain to an understanding teacher why I would not be in school the next day.

The Pan Handle route to Pittsburgh was now part of the Penn Central, but for all intents and purposes it still looked like the PRR, with the equipment, buildings, and people unchanged since the merger. The track was sound enough that my father could escort me to the glass partition aft of the upper-level engineman's compartment, watching as the speedometer briefly touched a hundred miles an hour. At Pittsburgh, we transferred to a local train, operated by the newly formed National Railroad Passenger Corporation, better known as Amtrak. The train was still purely Penn Central, and probably consisted of a tired old E-8 locomotive pulling a few equally worn out coaches. We traveled through the night to Altoona, where it was too dark to see the Horseshoe Curve, arriving in the small hours of the morning, too late for a hotel, too early for rental cars to be available, just right for a restless nap on a hard wooden bench in the waiting room. Come morning, my father rented a car and we drove past the half-deserted buildings of what had once been the greatest railroad shops in the world. Climbing through hills that the Pennsylvania Railroad had drained of coal, we went to visit relatives in

Ebensburg and Patton, a town named for a family that was closely connected with the PRR.

The Pennsylvania Railroad had once provided passenger service to Ebensburg, Patton, and countless other small towns, but those links to the wider world had long since disappeared, and even the freights called at increasingly infrequent intervals. My father's brother was born, grew up, still lived, and later died in Patton, amid first- and second-generation Poles, Czechs, and Slovaks. For many decades, most people in Patton dug coal from the surrounding hills and loaded it into PRR hopper cars. Just after the dawn of the twentieth century, they were digging underneath Patton, at the same moment as their countrymen, along with Irish, Italians, and African Americans, were burrowing through the muck and mire underneath the Hudson River, pushing the PRR one last mile into Manhattan, at almost the same moment that my uncle came into the world, in 1909.

My uncle's first memory was of an early day in school, lessons interrupted by a continuous wailing whistle, the teacher leaving briefly, then returning, telling the children to go to their homes, the school emptying as men ran uphill to the entrance of the mine. Explosions, fires, and cave-ins (he could not remember which one happened that day) were common enough during the early years of the twentieth century, but that incident soured him on a career in the mines. Years later, a stint at the Patton Clay Manufacturing Company, home of the renowned "Patton Pavers," so filled his mouth and nostrils with red dust that he worked for one day, went home, and never returned. For more than half a century, he ran a store and meat market, the last link in a chain of distribution in which the PRR brought the necessities and luxuries of life to yet another small town. The railroad yards were once filled with the PRR's cars, bringing in those supplies, and ready to carry away the coal and the bricks that made the town prosper. On later trips to Patton, I wandered through those yards, virtually deserted, and past the closed mines and the abandoned brickworks, full of the ghosts of the Pennsylvania Railroad.

The years passed and the spirits faded, but never fully disappeared. I spent four years at Haverford College, the alma mater of David Bevan, chief financial officer and perhaps the most despised executive, and

unfairly so, on the Pennsylvania Railroad. The surrounding suburb had once been home to one of the PRR's most respected executives, Alexander J. Cassatt, an individual with whom I share a monogram, if not necessarily the same wealth or managerial predilections. Haverford was an affluent bedroom community on the Main Line, one of the nation's first railroad suburbs, made possible and indeed planned by the Pennsylvania Railroad. At the small station nearly a century old, there was still a chance to see the *Broadway Limited,* at that time operated by Amtrak, but now extinct, go flashing past. And the opposite perspective, glimpsing the Haverford station from a sleeping car window on the *Broadway,* the only proper way, I thought, to travel from central Ohio to Philadelphia. The *National Limited* route from St. Louis had long since disappeared, and I was not about to rely on a car, bus, or airplane to reach my parents' home in Columbus. My post-Christmas trip back to college thus began on a frigid January night on the deserted platform at Crestline, Ohio, waiting for a train that offered transportation, warmth, companionship, the scenery of a nation transected. Minutes after flashing through Haverford, the train arrived at a far grander edifice than the one that I had left the night before. A magnificent structure, 30th Street Station had somehow escaped the sad fate of so many great train stations, and it uplifted the soul of many a weary long-distance traveler. The nearby and contemporaneous Suburban Station seemed conversely designed to crush the spirits of the commuters who daily trudged through its rabbit warren of underground passageways. And on numerous occasions, I traveled to both Philadelphia stations on the SEPTA Silverliner cars that had only recently replaced the last of the red rattletrap PRR MP-54 commuter equipment.

My connection to the Pennsylvania Railroad, perhaps tenuous, is hardly unique. It has become a routine experience, on telling someone that I am writing a book "about trains," to hear in response a story of an ancestor who worked for a railroad, or even worked for *the* railroad. The ancestral recollections, and particularly the reminiscences of those who earned a PRR paycheck, now nearly a lifetime ago, rarely paint a rosy picture of their employer. Railroading has always been, and remains, a brutally dangerous occupation, one that wears down men and women with the same steady predictability as it erodes rail, ties, locomotives, and cars. Many people gave their lives while serving the Pennsylvania Railroad, scalded in boiler explosions, crushed between cars, victims of momentary carelessness or simple bad luck. Others lost fingers, hands, arms, legs, or eyesight. The trauma was hardly confined to the ranks of labor, and even top executives succumbed to the strain of managing the world's largest transportation corporation. "Railroad service has become like that of the army and navy—in effect, service of the public, and . . . the work is more arduous than in civil life," one PRR executive noted in 1912.[2] Variants of the phrase "retired owing to ill health" appeared with deplorable frequency in PRR personnel records and managerial biographies. The incessant demands associated with running a railroad caused some executives to collapse under the strain, to request a transfer to less arduous duties, to suffer a complete nervous breakdown. Or worse. Of the first eight presidents of the Pennsylvania Railroad, four died in office, and two others lived less than a year into their retirement. Many other executives died at their desks, felled by a heart attack or a stroke. In 1882, a writer for the trade journal *Railroad Gazette* portrayed the burden of management in starkly accurate terms. "The responsibilities and duties of this officer [the president] are almost too great to be borne by any one man who desires faithfully to fulfil them and not die an early death."[3]

Employment at all levels of the company was demanding and dangerous in large measure because the PRR stood at the apex of industrial America. By 1875, it operated more miles of track, carried more tons of freight, reflected a larger concentration of investment capital, and generated more revenues than any other railroad in the United States.[4] For two decades, beginning in 1881, the Pennsylvania Railroad was the largest privately owned business corporation in the world.[5] At its height, the Pennsylvania Railroad controlled nearly 13 percent of all the capital invested in the American railroad network, and operated a tenth of the locomotives and a seventh of the freight cars in service in the United States. Nearly half of the electrified mainline track in the country belonged to the Pennsylvania Railroad. Its trains rumbled and roared across a four-track main line that stretched from New York to Pittsburgh, and over thirty thousand miles of track on eleven thousand miles of route, scattered across thirteen states and the District of Columbia.[6] The Pennsylvania Railroad operated more miles of railroad than any other *country* in the world, with the exception of Britain and France. It manufactured far more steam locomotives than any other railroad. And, it built some of the most monumental civil engineering works and some of the grandest railway terminals in the country.

"The Company" (internal corporate documents routinely used the upper case, as if there were no other) employed more people than any other railroad in the United States. At peak employment levels, in 1919, more than 280,000 people worked for the PRR. That was more than twice the number of soldiers who were enlisted in the United States Army at the beginning of World War I. The company's senior executives enjoyed access to the highest levels of political and economic power, and they helped to shape the political economy of the nation. For many years the president of the Pennsylvania Railroad served as an industrial statesman, speaking on behalf of the railway industry and the values of capitalism. In the commonwealth of Pennsylvania, the phrase "the President" could just as easily mean the occupant of the PRR's executive suite in Philadelphia as the individual who lived in the White House. "Do not think of the Pennsylvania Railroad as a business enterprise," *Forbes* magazine informed its readers in May 1936. "Think of it as a nation."[7]

Like the works of any nation, the legacy of the Pennsylvania Railroad endures. The size and the scope of the company's operations have left an indelible imprint on the physical and human geography of the United States. From the brutally truncated remains of Penn Station in New York, through the tunnels under the Hudson River, south to the grander edifices at Philadelphia, Baltimore, and Washington, and west across the Rockville Bridge and the Horseshoe Curve, the PRR's engineering works—many of them more than a century old—endure.

The Pennsylvania Railroad was, and still is, intertwined with the lives of a great many people. The company shaped the destinies of millions of Americans, from the train crews that moved millions of passengers and countless tons of freight, to the shop forces that labored at Altoona and other facilities, to the Irish, Italian, African American, and Hispanic track workers for whom the Pennsylvania Railroad represented both an income and an opportunity for social mobility. In 1914, an anonymous writer for the trade journal *Railway Age Gazette*, the successor to the *Railroad Gazette*, emphasized that a job with the PRR represented more than a paycheck. "To be a Pennsylvania employee," he observed, "is to have a fixed position, the assurance of fair treatment, and a certain respect and prestige in the social and business life of the community."[8]

The Pennsylvania Railroad had its share of critics, which included many of its employees, passengers, and shippers—to say nothing of legislators, presidents, and an often-hostile press. Some of that criticism was justified, to be sure, but much was also the result of the PRR's status as the largest railroad—and the biggest target—in the world. For all of the criticism, however, most Americans respected the Pennsylvania Railroad and its beneficent influence on the maturing American industrial economy. In an era of weak national governance, the PRR was a highly developed bureaucracy. In an era of relatively modest federal budgets, the Pennsylvania Railroad had a budget larger than any other company in the United States, second only to that of the national government itself. In an era of sharply limited social welfare programs, the PRR provided benefits to its employees and to the communities that it served. "There was a time," the 1914 author continued, "when the farmers and storekeepers along the lines of the Pennsylvania Railroad preferred to take Pennsylvania pay checks in payment of bills rather than United States greenbacks."[9]

The sheer size of the Pennsylvania Railroad ensured that the research, writing, and above all the organization of its corporate history would be a daunting task. Simply listing the name of every employee who worked for the PRR in 1919 would generate a document nearly the length of this book. What was originally envisioned as a one-volume work has, with the kind indulgence of the publisher, grown to two rather lengthy volumes. The division between the two is set around 1917, at a time when the completion of the link to Manhattan, a changing regulatory environment, American

entry into World War I, and looming highway competition significantly altered the PRR's course. Still, to keep this project within somewhat manageable limits, I had to downplay, or even discard, some elements of the PRR's history and emphasize others. To some degree, the choices are obvious. After all, how could one *not* discuss the building of Penn Station, the development of what was once the most sophisticated organizational bureaucracy in the world, or the application of extraordinarily complex technological systems? In other areas, I have pursued more esoteric topics that I have found of interest, or that foreshadowed significant future developments. Even though several key issues, most notably locomotive development, passenger service, and labor policies, were of considerable importance in the nineteenth century, I have nonetheless elected to postpone a discussion of those topics, largely omitting them from Volume 1. Instead, I will include them in their entirety in the second volume, covering the period since 1917. Those issues transcend the division between the two halves of the PRR's history, and it seems appropriate to discuss the long sweep of such topics in a single integrated chapter.

This volume covers the antecedents of the Pennsylvania Railroad, the company's formation, and its rapid growth during the last third of the nineteenth century and the first decades of the twentieth. The first two chapters offer an overview of transportation patterns in Pennsylvania prior to the 1846 incorporation of the PRR. Some readers might be tempted to skip forward to Chapter 3, but the railroad's history really began well before 1846. Commercial rivalries between the great port cities of New York, Philadelphia, and Baltimore shaped the political and economic circumstances that created massive public investments in the transportation infrastructure—most notably Pennsylvania's Main Line of Public Works. That state-owned transportation system was largely a failure, but it established at least a portion of the route that the Pennsylvania Railroad would later follow. The next four chapters describe the contentious and politically constructed chartering of the PRR, as well as equally divisive debates over the company's finances and management. The turmoil led to the presidency of J. Edgar Thomson, one of the first professional managers in the history of American business, and someone who was capable of wresting governing power away from the individuals who owned the company. Thomson and his fellow managers reshaped the PRR's corporate structure while confronting the realities of competition within an industry that was far more capital-intensive than any that had previously existed.

As described in Chapter 7, during the 1850s Thomson moved aggressively to establish friendly connections in the Midwest, while keeping the PRR's financial exposure in that process to a minimum. The midwestern connections became far more important, as the Civil War greatly accelerated the scope and complexity of the PRR's operations—as shown in Chapter 8. The following chapter details the intense postwar rivalry between the trunk lines amid a period of rapid expansion in the railway industry. During the eight years that followed 1865, Thomson and other executives developed the PRR's route structure along the Atlantic seaboard and in the Midwest, solidifying the company's status as a major east-west trunk line, and creating the most powerful railroad corporation in the United States. Thomson and his protégé, Thomas A. Scott, simultaneously endeavored to extend the PRR's reach even farther afield, deep into the South, and as far west as the Pacific Ocean. Those efforts, described in Chapter 10, fell victim to the diseconomies of scale associated with the creation of vast railway systems, as well as to the severe economic depression that followed the Panic of 1873. The depression of the 1870s imposed severe limits on PRR executives, detailed in Chapter 11, as they confronted adversaries such as oil magnate John D. Rockefeller and beat back protests emanating from their own labor force. During the 1880s, as Chapter 12 suggests, railway executives attempted to impose order on their industry, at first through largely unsuccessful efforts to control competition, and ultimately by building large, integrated systems. That decade also featured the ascendency of federal railroad regulation, as a long history of state control over transportation policy yielded to the inescapable reality that the PRR and its competitors were engaged in interstate commerce.

As shown in Chapter 13, PRR officials also attempted to impose order on the railroad industry through the creation of efficient technological systems. The company's engineer-managers engaged in a desperate race to make the railroad's operations more efficient and to stay ahead of the continually increasing demand for transportation services. This chapter is probably the least conventional of any of those in Volume 1. It begins early in the PRR's corporate existence and continues into the 1920s, and even beyond, well after the ostensible chronological limits of the first volume of this work. The topical rather than chronological treatment seems appropriate, however. The functional specialists who addressed complex technical problems never operated in isolation from the rest of the company, but they did follow an agenda that was largely separate from the day-to-day procedures associated with running a railroad. They, like the chapter, pursued technical dilemmas wherever they might lead, and over a considerable span of time.

The final two chapters of Volume 1 return to a more conventional organization, covering the implications of the rapid growth in bituminous coal production, the creation of a "community of interest" that brought together the PRR and some of its competitors, the evolution of government regulation at the turn of the century, and finally the enormous improvement projects that occurred after 1899, when Alexander Cassatt assumed the presidency. The volume culminates with what many people regard as the greatest achievement of the Pennsylvania Railroad and its new president—the construction of the New York Improvements, including Penn Station.

Volume 2 officially begins in 1917, but it harkens back a decade earlier to 1907, the last good year for the Pennsylvania Railroad. Although the PRR remained a strong company for decades to come, a combination of diminishing productivity gains, increased regulatory oversight, intensified labor-management confrontations, dissipated executive talent, and motor-vehicle competition all conspired to erode the company's fortunes. The first chapter describes changes within the PRR's organizational structure, set amid the traffic crisis of World War I and the period of federal government control over the railroads. The next chapter details labor relations, focusing largely on the interwar period but reaching back to the late nineteenth century antecedents of conflicts between workers and managers. That interwar period was largely one of stagnation, as railroad executives and government regulators attempted to resolve the "railroad problem," only to discover that there was no easy—or politically expedient—solution. During the 1920s PRR executives also pursued major engineering works, including the beginnings of a new terminal complex at Philadelphia, a worthy rival to the facilities in New York. Yet, the Philadelphia Improvements also marked the end of large-scale construction projects and, with them, the closing of one of the most promising routes for upward mobility within the ranks of senior management.

Two further chapters in Volume 2 deviate once again from the generally chronological focus of the book, with one describing motive power and the other, passenger service. Each chapter reaches back into territory covered in the first volume. As with the development of any technological system, however, an analysis of the creation and application of motive-power technology and the movement of people demands the long view. Another chapter revisits labor-management relations during World War II and the years that followed, with particular emphasis on the growing schism between executives and their most highly skilled employees. The next chapter details the ongoing and often frustrating efforts by PRR managers, throughout much of the twentieth century, to mix railways with other modes of transport, on highways, over water, and even in the air. In addition to serving as a precursor to modern intermodal operations, the PRR's innovations offered a possible—although ultimately illusory—solution to the long, slow decline in demand for rail transport. Illusions appear in a subsequent chapter, as well, with a discussion of the changing ways in which PRR executives have promoted their railroad, as well as the manner in which the public has viewed the Pennsylvania Railroad, and its place in American culture. The final chapter details the steady postwar decline of the PRR and efforts by its managers to find salvation in a merger with its longtime rival, the New York Central. While the corporate existence of the Pennsylvania Railroad came to an end in 1968, an epilogue carries the story through the dismal years of the Penn Central and the brighter prospects associated with Conrail.

The unhappy fate of the Penn Central has forever colored analyses of the Pennsylvania Railroad. Failure

has been an all-too-common occurrence in the history of American railroading, but not for *the* railroad. The PRR never suffered a significant financial embarrassment in its entire 122-year history, and the company paid dividends in good times and bad. Yet, its merger into the Penn Central helped trigger what was at that time the largest bankruptcy in American history. It was a financial disaster of cataclysmic proportions, one that sent shock waves through corporate boardrooms and union halls, through Washington and Wall Street. The crisis not only fundamentally reshaped the American railroad network, but also helped bring about a redefinition of the role of government in the economy and the role of labor in industry.

This book stands at the threshold of bankruptcy day, June 21, 1970, looking backward in an attempt to determine what went wrong. That is admittedly a dangerously presentist approach, inasmuch as we know what happened, but not even the most prescient observer could have sensed the impending crisis until it was far too late to alter the course of events. Likewise, it strains the bounds of credulity to imagine that an employee, executive, shipper, passenger, regulator, or politician ever rose from bed in the morning determined to bring the Pennsylvania Railroad to its knees. Yet, the cumulative actions of a great many talented and dedicated individuals produced precisely that effect. It would be tempting to succumb to the sort of journalistic finger-pointing that occurred in the aftermath of the bankruptcy, singling out one cause for the Penn Central debacle. Some have blamed the Penn Central's management team, consisting of chief financial officer David Bevan, chairman of the board Stuart Saunders, and president Alfred Perlman. Others condemned unionized labor and arcane rules that protected jobs but nearly destroyed an industry. Still others found fault with the actions of the Interstate Commerce Committee and with the regulatory state in general. More dispassionate observers suggested that the steady postwar decline of the industrial Northeast, particularly the coal and steel industries, contributed to the long descent of the Pennsylvania Railroad. So too did the development of competing modes of transportation during the 1920s and 1930s.

All of the arguments pertaining to the PRR's demise have merit. Yet, to fully understand the birth, life, and death of the greatest railroad in the United States, it is necessary to examine four broad issues that overarch the company's existence. Throughout both volumes, those four grand themes—organization, labor, technology, and government—frame much of the history of the Pennsylvania Railroad. The first concerns the development of one of the most innovative and sophisticated organizational systems in the history of American business. Railroads were large, sprawling, and capital-intensive enterprises, and the managerial strategies that were appropriate for a turnpike or a textile mill simply would not work for them. As the biggest of the railroads, the PRR was of necessity a leader in the development of management practice. The creation of statistical controls, the implementation of a line-and-staff operating system, the cultivation of adept managers, and corporate centralization and decentralization all appeared on the Pennsylvania Railroad, in many cases establishing a model for other businesses to follow. The truly remarkable aspect of the company's organization, moreover, was its flexibility and the willingness of executives to repeatedly alter the corporate structure in order to suit the unique talents of the individuals who were indispensible to the PRR's operations. At heart, the PRR was a collection of people who shaped a bureaucracy rather than allowing a bureaucracy to shape them.

Managers, however, constituted a distinct minority of the hundreds of thousands of individuals who built, maintained, and operated the Pennsylvania Railroad. The labor force was the company's greatest strength, yet ultimately became one of its greatest concerns. PRR managers were never able to develop a satisfactory solution to the labor "problem" that became apparent in the aftermath of the 1877 strikes. Skilled operating employees ultimately had recourse to pension and insurance funds, a savings society, company-sponsored medical care, and the other trappings of welfare capitalism. They were also secure in the knowledge that their sons could follow in their footsteps and be guaranteed a job that was difficult and often dangerous, but that nonetheless carried with it high pay and considerable prestige. Other workers, particularly shop forces, were far less able to enjoy security and autonomy. During the 1920s, managerial efforts to dampen down their militancy produced disastrous

consequences. By then, as the railway industry began its long period of contraction, even operating employees were beginning to wonder whether their careers would continue into the next generation, as whatever solidarity labor might have forged with management had long since vanished.

If managers were frustrated at their inability to control and routinize the output of labor, they were likewise increasingly concerned at their diminishing ability to employ technology in order to ensure efficient and profitable operations. Railroads were the great engineering works of their age, and the Pennsylvania Railroad was greater than most. The company depended on a dedicated cadre of professional engineers who established the PRR's reputation, first as the Standard Railroad of America, then as the Standard Railroad of the World. The two monikers, the first enticingly flamboyant, the second even more so, were in the end little more than testaments to the Pennsylvania Railroad's flair for public relations. As students of the transportation industry soon discover, the PRR was idiosyncratic in technology, tradition, and managerial style. In the words of noted railway author David P. Morgan, "The Standard Railroad of the World did many nonstandard things."[10]

Few railroads, few companies, few bureaucratic entities of any kind imitated the Pennsylvania Railroad to any degree, and none ever surpassed it. The PRR was the Standard Railroad of the World, not because its personnel established a pattern for others to follow, but because they set a standard that no other railroad in the world could match. Within a few years after the company was established, engineers dominated the executive ranks of the Pennsylvania Railroad and retained that authority for the next century. As managers, they proved superbly equipped to develop machinery and to create technological systems. Yet, by the early twentieth century, those engineer-managers could not escape a growing frustration that—despite their skills and the technology that their expertise had created—they were becoming less and less successful at the core business of moving freight and passengers in a timely and efficient manner. They confronted the law of diminishing returns, and could no longer achieve the rapid productivity gains and the equally impressive rate reductions that had become commonplace during the final third of the nineteenth century. In addition to affecting corporate profitability, that situation brought into starker relief the discriminatory practices that had always been a part of railway economics. By the early twentieth century, shippers and passengers felt deprived of a better—or at least a cheaper—transportation future, and they increasingly sought redress through the political process.

There is thus a fourth overarching theme, concerning the relationship between the PRR and federal, state, and local governments, and ultimately involving the broader issue of the interaction of the private and public sectors of the economy. To many, the history of the PRR still symbolizes the contrast between virtuous private enterprise and stifling governmental bureaucracy. In the past, and today, the PRR's defenders have drawn a stark contrast between the presumed ineptitude of publicly financed internal improvements and the efficiency of a private corporation operating in a free market, encumbered only by ill-conceived governmental regulations.

The PRR's reputation as a bastion of free enterprise bears little relation to reality. From its birth in 1846 until its death in 1968, the Pennsylvania Railroad was fundamentally a creature of public policy. Indeed, the PRR owed its very existence to political decisions made in Washington, in state legislatures, and in city halls. The publicly owned Main Line of Public Works dictated much of the path that the Pennsylvania Railroad was to follow and provided critical early links in the PRR's route between Philadelphia and Pittsburgh. The Pennsylvania legislature awarded the Pennsylvania Railroad its corporate charter and protected the company that they had brought into being from incursions by the Baltimore & Ohio and other rivals. The PRR received more than half of its initial financing from local governments in Philadelphia and Pittsburgh. Legislation and the threat of additional, unwelcome regulation shaped the PRR's use of technology, in applications as diverse as automatic signals, air brakes, electrification, and the erection of huge termini in such cities as New York, Philadelphia, and Chicago. PRR executives embraced regulation in an effort to control competition, speaking out against it only when rival

modes of transportation threatened the very premise of the regulatory state.

Just as public policy shaped the formation and growth of the Pennsylvania Railroad, so, too, was it a factor in the company's steady downward slide. While historians have long debated whether or not the railroads were able to "capture" the Interstate Commerce Commission, it appears that the regulatory apparatus, particularly the ICC and the United States Railroad Administration, actually captured the railroad, altering the ways in which PRR executives framed their decisions, changing even the language they used. In myriad ways, ICC officials set the boundaries of the American railroad industry, circumscribing the realm of what PRR executives could achieve. As the structure of the privately owned railroad network threatened to disintegrate, and when the PRR itself failed, the company's executives again called on the government, this time to assist in picking up the pieces of an empire that had come crashing down around them. Government was always and forever a part of the PRR's existence. In the words of historian Colleen A. Dunlavy, it was a "structuring presence" that delineated the contours of the world in which the Pennsylvania Railroad operated.[11]

Whatever grand themes or theories many be present in this book, this is first and foremost a biography of a company and of the individuals who shaped its existence. There is a tendency, in all biographies, for the biographer to glorify his or her subject. I have endeavored to avoid that failing, even when it has seemed necessary to refute earlier, and largely unjustified, criticisms of the PRR's personnel and their conduct. Readers may judge for themselves the degree to which I have succeeded in my efforts to maintain objectivity. In the interests of full disclosure, however, I acknowledge that I have spent countless hours over many years doing my best to learn about virtually every aspect of the PRR's operations, warts and all. I have explored business practices, organizational culture, technology, labor relations, public policy, urban history, finance, competition, and war. After all of those years, after all of the research, and after all of the writing, I remain in awe of what the men and women associated with the Pennsylvania Railroad were able to accomplish.

Today, long after the bankruptcy of the Penn Central, and longer still after the chartering of the Pennsylvania Railroad, hundreds of freight and passenger trains travel each day along the routes that the PRR's engineer-executives established, rounding the Horseshoe Curve, crossing the Susquehanna River on the Rockville Bridge, pausing underneath the majestic 30th Street Station in Philadelphia, delivering commuters to Bryn Mawr, Paoli, and other destinations on the Philadelphia Main Line, and traveling through the tunnels under the Hudson River and into Manhattan. The Pennsylvania Railroad is still interwoven into the very fabric of American society, just as it is inextricably connected with the events, great and small, of American history. It is the past, but it is also the present, and the future. Even as those who created it have gone, the Standard Railroad of the World endures.

Abbreviations

A&GW	Atlantic & Great Western	CTC	Centralized traffic control
ACL	Atlantic Coast Line	CTUA	Commercial Telegraphers' Union of America
AFTO	Association of Freight Traffic Officers		
AIME	American Institute of Mining Engineers	GE	General Electric
		GR&I	Grand Rapids & Indiana
AREA	American Railway Engineering Association	HML	Hagley Museum & Library
		HPMJ&L	Harrisburg, Portsmouth, Mount Joy & Lancaster
AREMWA	American Railway Engineering and Maintenance of Way Association		
		ICC	Interstate Commerce Commission
ASCE	American Society of Civil Engineers	IRT	Interborough Rapid Transit
ASTM	American Society for Testing Materials	KP	Kansas Pacific
ATC	Automatic train control	LCL	Less than carload lot
ATO	Association of Transportation Officers	LIRR	Long Island Rail Road
ATS	Automatic train stop	MCBA	Master Car-Builders' Association
B&O	Baltimore & Ohio	N&W	Norfolk & Western
B&P	Baltimore & Potomac	NP	Northern Pacific
BLE	Brotherhood of Locomotive Engineers	NYC	New York Central
BLF	Brotherhood of Locomotive Firemen	NYP & N	New York, Philadelphia & Norfolk
BRSA	Brotherhood of Railroad Signalmen of America	ORT	Order of Railway Telegraphers / Order of Railroad Telegraphers
BRT	Brooklyn Rapid Transit	ORTDAS	Order of Railroad Telegraphers, Dispatchers, Agents, and Signalmen
BRT	Brotherhood of Railroad Trainmen		
C&O	Chesapeake & Ohio	P&E	Philadelphia & Erie
CC&C	Cleveland, Columbus & Cincinnati	PFW&C	Pittsburgh, Fort Wayne & Chicago
CC&IC	Columbus, Chicago & Indiana Central	PHMC	Pennsylvania Historical & Museum Commission
CH&D	Cincinnati, Hamilton & Dayton		
CP&I	Columbus, Piqua & Indiana	PRR	Pennsylvania Railroad

PSC	New York Public Service Commission	TU	Trainmen's Union
PV&C	Pittsburgh, Virginia & Charleston	UMW	United Mine Workers
PW&B	Philadelphia, Wilmington & Baltimore	UP	Union Pacific
RF&P	Richmond, Fredericksburg & Potomac	UPED	Union Pacific, Eastern Division
S&I	Steubenville & Indiana	US&S	Union Switch & Signal
SAL	Seaboard Air Line	USMRR	United States Military Rail Roads
SIC	South Improvement Company	USRA	United States Railroad Administration
SRSC	Southern Railway Security Company	W&LE	Wheeling & Lake Erie
T&P	Texas & Pacific	WC&A	Wilmington, Columbia & Augusta
TH&I	Terre Haute & Indianapolis	WSS	Women's Service Section

Chapter 1

The Way West

1682–1826

Philadelphia, the city founded by William Penn in 1682 as a religious refuge for Quakers, lay atop a narrow strip of land separating the Delaware River from the Schuylkill. For the next hundred years, most of the settlement in the town—it could hardly yet be called a metropolis—clustered along the broad river that ran south toward the Delaware Bay, the Atlantic Ocean, and the wider world. By the end of the colonial period, Philadelphia was the leading commercial center in the mid-Atlantic region, surpassing New York and Boston. The merchants who dominated the economic, political, and intellectual life of the city collected raw materials from the surrounding hinterland while distributing to more rural locales the manufactured goods of an industrializing Britain.

The rising tide of capitalism did as much as the increasing demands for political liberty to sever the ties that bound Britain to its most valued colonial possession. The revolution that began in Boston soon spread to Philadelphia, a city that played a role second to none in shaping the destiny of the early republic. The authors of the Declaration of Independence, meeting in Philadelphia, did not advocate a rebellion against government, but instead demanded that governments be responsive to the will of the people, particularly those prosperous white men of property who chafed under British trade policies.

After the Revolution, mercantile elites insisted that economic growth would ensure the survival of the new nation while simultaneously promoting the public good. In 1787, the Constitution, also crafted in Philadelphia, created a system of political federalism, in which the central government and the states shared both the protection of the commonweal and the oversight of business activity. The Constitution included a commerce clause that gave the national government, and the national government alone, the power to oversee trade among the states. It would take many decades, and a great many cases before the U.S. Supreme Court, to delineate the parameters of federal and state involvement in the economy and in the affairs of business corporations. From the protection of individual physical and intellectual property rights to the creation of a stable national government, however, the Constitution gave notice that business and government would operate as allies rather than as enemies.

A great war had raged in the decade that separated the Declaration of Independence from the Constitution. The British had occupied Philadelphia, ready to hang anyone who had betrayed king and empire by affixing their name to Thomas Jefferson's document. The Continental Congress had fled west in 1777, across the gently rolling landscape, past the farms of the German Anabaptists who had been drawn to the

1

Figure 1. Jack's Narrows, near Mt. Union, Pennsylvania, provided an excellent illustration of the role of geography in shaping the Main Line of Public Works—whose location in turn dictated much of the route of the Pennsylvania Railroad. From right to left are the Juniata River (which the commonwealth's General Assembly had decreed to be a free waterway, open to navigation by all); the Juniata Division Canal and adjacent towpath, a part of the state-owned Main Line of Public Works; and the Pennsylvania Railroad, which mixed private and public ownership.
Pennsylvania Historical and Museum Commission, Pennsylvania State Archives.

area by Penn's experiment in religious tolerance. The Congress settled in Lancaster, and then in York, anxious to escape the wrath of the king's men. In the years following independence, both the national and state capitals resided in Philadelphia, yet they too soon migrated, one going north to New York and then south again to Washington, and the other moving progressively west, by 1812 reaching the site of the ferry that trading-post operator John Harris, Sr., had established in 1733, on the banks of the Susquehanna River.

Cities such as Lancaster, York, and Harrisburg were geographically proximate to Philadelphia, but their residents were more apt to look southward, along the Susquehanna River, to Baltimore. On the journey from western Pennsylvania and upstate New York, the wide, shallow Susquehanna, Algonquin for "muddy water," and the longest river in the eastern United States, passed Harrisburg, then split Lancaster and York counties before entering Maryland and flowing onward to Chesapeake Bay. As an artery of commerce, the river proved far superior to the local roads and did much to divert Pennsylvania's trade away from Philadelphia.

To the north and west of Harrisburg, the Juniata carried the clear, cold waters of the Appalachians down to the Susquehanna River. Above the headwaters of the Juniata lay the summit of the Alleghenies. Later generations of Pennsylvania Railroad train crews—brakemen standing atop swaying boxcars, their ability to leap from one to the other their only protection against death, and their skill with a brake club the only defense against catastrophe, enginemen straining to make out the signals cloaked by the fog that rose, wraithlike, from the hollows—would refer to this area simply as "The Mountain," but for now the great gray-green mass lay still and silent, pristine in its wildness. For generations, those mountains constituted a serious impediment to westward expansion, but they also concealed some of the world's richest deposits of coal, the essential fuel for the first industrial revolution.

West of the summit, some of the waters flowed down the valley of the Conemaugh and eventually toward the Allegheny River. They went past Johnstown, barely a clearing in the woods before the Western Division of the Pennsylvania Canal and then the Pennsylvania Railroad accelerated settlement there, building a community that would one day be obliterated by the most catastrophic flood in American history.[1] The Allegheny joined the Monongahela River, forming the Ohio, whose waters flowed down the Mississippi to the Gulf of Mexico, two thousand river miles away. That too was a natural trade route that long predated the arrival of the railroad, as flatboats set off from Pittsburgh, bound for New Orleans. The city that saw them depart had once been

Fort Duquesne, where an overconfident and inexperienced George Washington, a colonel in the Virginia militia, failed to take the French stronghold, surrendered his own garrison at Fort Necessity, and started the Seven Years' War. In that conflict, General Edward Braddock, in charge of a British army that, in 1755, was very much still allied with the colonials, traveled through the same area before leading his Redcoats to their slaughter at the hands of the French and their Indian allies.

A hundred years later, the French, the Indians, and the British had all been driven from the land between Philadelphia and Pittsburgh. In their place lay the burnished iron rails of the Pennsylvania Railroad, a company that would soon become the mightiest railroad in the United States and, by some measures, the largest business corporation in the world. The geography of Pennsylvania shaped that state's history and likewise dictated the path that the Pennsylvania Railroad would follow across the mountains. But geography alone was not destiny, and the people of Pennsylvania shaped their own course and that of the Pennsylvania Railroad. They did so not merely by creating a "private" company, but by blending the public and private spheres into a mixed enterprise, one that was shaped as much by the government as by the marketplace.

In 1846, Philadelphia's merchant elite brought the Pennsylvania Railroad into existence. They were able to do so, however, only within the public policy framework that the Constitution had established in 1787. The federal government had provided the political and legal structure in which the company operated, and it had made states the primary incubators of internal improvements and economic growth. Legislators who gathered at the state capital in Harrisburg had ushered into existence turnpikes, canals, and railroads that delineated Pennsylvania's economic landscape. They also granted the corporate charter that created the PRR and made that railroad the commonwealth's economic champion.

The PRR was by no means the first attempt to employ internal improvements to bind together the people and the places of the commonwealth. Before there was the Pennsylvania Railroad, there was the Main Line of Public Works, the peoples' thoroughfare that linked Philadelphia and Pittsburgh. The development of the Main Line, and of the other components of Pennsylvania's vast system of internal improvements, was a product of geography, but even more so of government. The resulting artery of commerce was far from ideal, but it largely established the spatial, economic, and political parameters that shaped the early development of the Pennsylvania Railroad. In 1846, when Philadelphians obtained a legislative charter for the PRR, they were the inheritors of many decades of public policy. The route that they subsequently followed, between Philadelphia and Pittsburgh, had been laid out before them.

Improving the New Republic

By the time of the Early Republic, a broad spectrum of the new nation's residents supported the federal government's role in the process of national improvement. Such zeal for expanding the reach of government was hardly inconsistent with the republican tendencies of the revolutionary generation. Instead, it represented a widespread belief that government should play a critical role in safeguarding hard-won freedoms by enhancing transportation, commerce, defense, and education in order to promote the well-being of the body politic. By the early years of the nineteenth century, however, internal improvements had increasingly come to mean transportation improvements, both to ensure national security and to promote commercial development.[2]

In the years immediately following the American Revolution, private enterprise promised to deliver the economic rewards associated with improved transportation. Such was the case with the Patowmack (Potomac) Company, established in 1785 as a mechanism for improving navigation along its namesake river. At a time when private investors possessed little basis for evaluating a company's worth, the naming of George Washington as the president of the enterprise afforded the project substantial public respect. Washington suggested that the company would provide great benefits for the new nation, yet Washington's native state of Virginia and his lands in the Ohio Valley were certain to receive the largest reward. Even though Washington's love of country seemed above suspicion, Marylanders harbored grave doubts about his fellow Virginians, and they did their best to postpone a canal that would benefit one state more than another.

Most of the early privately sponsored postwar internal improvement projects—including the Potomac Company—were unsuccessful. The newness of the nation, shortages of capital, and a scarcity of skilled canal engineers undoubtedly contributed to the failures. However, many Americans saw through the noble republican rhetoric of internal-improvement promoters and believed that the elites, and the federalists in particular, had supported these projects solely for personal gain. Improved transportation was too important to a vibrant economy and national security, they argued, to be left to private enterprise. It was likewise a national goal, and the rights of states should not be allowed to interfere, as had been the case with the long-standing feud between Virginia and Maryland over the right to improve the Potomac River. Thus, where local private enterprise had failed, they assumed that national government would set things right.[3]

Curiously, the desire of many Americans to safeguard transportation from the elites conflicted with their other goal of formulating a national internal-improvement policy. Alexander Hamilton, scion of the federalists, drew considerable criticism for his insistence that the future of the United States must be tied to the economic welfare of the moneyed gentry. In addition to his efforts to restore the nation's tarnished credit, through the federal assumption of state debts and the creation of a national bank, Hamilton favored industrialization and internal improvements, following the British model. In his 1791 *Report on Manufactures*, he suggested that tariffs could be used to subsidize domestic production, and to finance a network of roads and canals that would tie the nation together.[4]

Thomas Jefferson, one of Hamilton's most ardent critics, disagreed with most of the recommendations contained in the *Report on Manufactures*, including federal support for road and canal construction. Yet Jefferson and his allies were not ideologically opposed to internal improvements, or to public support for such ventures. After all, Albert Gallatin, secretary of the treasury to both Jefferson and James Madison, became the best-known advocate of federally sponsored internal improvements. Although he was a

Jeffersonian republican, Gallatin overcame his initial opposition to Hamiltonian federalism and soon came to appreciate the need for government-fostered economic growth. Unlike Europe, he noted, the United States suffered from a low population density and a scarcity of capital. Those two characteristics retarded commercial development and constituted a serious obstacle to the nation's success. The federal government could circumvent such problems through support for transportation improvements, thus underwriting economic growth and in effect magnifying the efforts and resources of a small national population. In 1808, Gallatin presented his comprehensive internal-improvement plan to Congress, in the form of a *Report of the Secretary of the Treasury on the Subject of Roads and Canals.* Among other projects, Gallatin called for four isthmian canals: at Cape Cod, between the Hudson and Delaware rivers in New Jersey, across the Delmarva Peninsula, and connecting the Chesapeake Bay in Virginia and Albemarle Sound in North Carolina. More ambitiously, Gallatin envisioned several routes from the Atlantic seaboard to the interior, including one along the Susquehanna, Juniata, and Allegheny rivers in Pennsylvania, to be composed of river improvements, canals, and turnpikes.[5]

Gallatin's report was in part an innovative agenda for an integrated national transportation network, and in part a compilation of local infrastructure proposals. By the time that Gallatin issued his recommendations, near the end of Jefferson's second term, it was apparent that the local orientation had triumphed over the national perspective. There was the practical matter that—despite Gallatin's optimistic budget predictions—the federal treasury lacked the money to pay for such an ambitious slate of projects, but the principal objections were constitutional, not financial. The Constitution did not explicitly grant the federal government the authority to undertake transportation improvements, or for that matter to levy tariffs for any purpose other than to raise revenue. During the administrations of Jefferson and his successors, members of Congress were engaged in often-rancorous debate as to whether they possessed the authority to fund any internal-improvement projects at all. Furthermore, many Americans worried that federal aid would unavoidably give preference to some states and

locales above others, leading to divisiveness that the young republic could ill afford. Such largess, they believed, would also spawn corruption, as unscrupulous promoters would feed at the public trough, enriching themselves at the expense of the people. They perceived the potential for endless debates, favoritism, corruption, and influence peddling, attendant to the allocation of federal funds to particular local interests, making a mockery of the republican ideals associated with the Revolution. Reflecting widespread mistrust of a large standing army, some insisted that a more efficient transportation system could extend the reach of federal power, although Gallatin's supporters argued that rapid deployments would enable a smaller and less threatening military to guard national borders.[6]

Concerns over the limits of federal authority paralyzed Congress, ensuring that only a few select types of internal improvements received national aid. Congress established the constitutionality of assistance for lighthouses and harbor improvements, based on the clear constitutional prerogatives of commerce and national defense. Federal oversight of post offices and post roads was deemed acceptable, because a postal system provided immediate and tangible benefits to virtually every citizen, and because one locale did not benefit at the expense of another. Although a series of prominent political leaders spoke out in favor of federal support for other internal improvements, claiming to be acting for the good of the nation and all of its people, their altruistic rhetoric often thinly camouflaged personal motivations and local orientations. In that context, citizens were inclined to be suspicious of any proposal to unite disparate locales through internal improvements, particularly if those projects promised to confer the bulk of their benefits on a small group of elites.[7]

Ultimately, however, federal government support for internal improvements, such as it was, occurred because the people wanted better transportation. They instructed their elected officials to get what they could from the federal treasury, confident that they would be the winners, and other locales the losers. With the federalists out of power, the national government seemed less despotic and more of a resource, with funds to be withdrawn as needed. Naturally, virtually every politician who advocated a local project sought to connect that work to some grand scheme of national betterment, but most people understood that that rhetoric only made the exploitation of government more palatable, and more in keeping with republican ideals.[8]

As such, relatively few projects truly offered the potential for interregional transportation. Chief among them was the National Road, seen as a mechanism for binding the Northwest Territories to the existing states. The 1802 Enabling Act, in addition to granting statehood to Ohio, specified that a portion of public land sales be set aside for road construction, relieving the federal treasury of any financial burden. The choice of route was nonetheless highly politicized, with members of Congress from both Pennsylvania and Virginia voicing displeasure at the decision to build westward through Maryland. Pennsylvanians demanded and received an alteration in the route to include the settlements of Uniontown and Washington, confirming the fears of those who believed that sectional rivalries would take precedence over the national good whenever federal funding was involved. In any event, the March 1806 act that authorized the building of the National Road lay dormant until 1811, when construction finally commenced.[9]

The War of 1812 created deep political divisions in the United States while exposing the embarrassing weaknesses of American coastal defenses and the difficulty of moving troops and supplies with any degree of speed. By the time peace returned in 1815, Americans were anxious to use the power of the federal government to rectify each of those problems. The federalists, those who would be most likely to support nationally sponsored public works, had by that time lost much of their influence. The Hartford Convention, which met in December 1814 and January 1815, illustrated the depths of New England's opposition to the war, with some federalist delegates suggesting secession from the Union. In the aftermath of Andrew Jackson's victory at the Battle of New Orleans, the views expressed at the Hartford Convention made the federalists seem little better than traitors. What followed was the "Era of Good Feelings," nearly a decade marked by what was ostensibly one-party republican governance. Yet, even in the midst of peace, prosperity, and relative political harmony, regional rivalries and political discord conspired to undermine federal support for internal improvements.

In 1816, John C. Calhoun of South Carolina sponsored the Bonus Bill, designed to allocate $1.5 million in surplus revenue from the recently chartered Second Bank of the United States to fund a national system of internal improvements. In part, the act was a revival of Gallatin's 1808 plan for internal improvements, but it also embodied efforts by Calhoun and his allies to bring the regions of the United States into closer contact with one another in order to repair the political schism that had emerged as a result of the War of 1812. Wisely, Calhoun did not recommend any specific routes, leading everyone to believe that their pet project was certain to receive funding. In March 1817, almost at the end of his presidency, James Madison—who had earlier spoken favorably on the use of federal resources in support of better transportation—unexpectedly vetoed the legislation. The Constitution's "power to regulate commerce among the several States," Madison noted, "cannot include a power to construct roads and canals, and to improve the navigation of water-courses, in order to facilitate, promote, and secure such a commerce."[10] Despite his invocation of strict constructionism, Madison was more concerned with the vague nature of the bill. To simply assert that the federal government had the authority to spend money on internal improvements, without a specific list of projects, Madison believed, would fail to produce a comprehensive transportation system, yet it would invariably create political divisiveness and even outright corruption.[11]

Madison's veto of the Bonus Bill did not by any means end federal support for internal improvements, but it did send a clear message that the national government had absolved itself of all responsibility for coordination and planning, and that the states were on their own, each responsible for undertaking whatever projects they saw fit. The devolution of responsibility for transportation to the states did not by any means signify that private enterprise had taken charge of the planning and construction of internal improvements. Instead, state and local governments competed vigorously in order to gain a commercial advantage over rival locales, and they invested public resources accordingly.[12] At the level of the state and the region, moreover, it was and remains difficult to argue convincingly that government played but a small role in the economy. To the contrary, the revolutionary generation's reaction against perceived British tyranny had the paradoxical effect of diffusing, rather than eliminating, governmental authority over business and the economy.

Particularly in the antebellum period, most Americans led intensely local lives, with their economic and political activities extending no further than the county seat. At least through the time of the Civil War, most Americans harbored grave misgivings regarding centralized political authority, and their primary identification lay with region, state, and community rather than with the nation. As such, federal and even state actors played but peripheral roles within the narrowly circumscribed community. Government touched the people not through the president or the governor, but rather through selectmen, judges, road commissioners, and a whole host of other local officials, each of them minor to the great course of American history, but collectively of immense importance in the everyday lives of ordinary citizens. To the extent that Americans rebelled against government, they did so by chopping it up into myriad tiny pieces, scattering them all over the new nation, and keeping political power close to the people while ensuring that governmental entities could compete against one another. Political power as if a departing mist cleared from the national government and settled over a vast landscape composed of local legislators, jurists, and others whose cumulative actions—no matter how seemingly mundane and insignificant—nonetheless set the parameters for economic development in the United States.[13]

For two decades, between Madison's veto of the Bonus Bill and the onset of the Panic of 1837, state governments engaged in a systematic program to foster internal improvements. Pennsylvania was in the forefront of state-sponsored highway, canal, and railroad development, but virtually every state, from Massachusetts to Georgia, committed public funds to improve transportation. More than any other type of interaction among people, state, and markets—with the possible exception of banking—internal improvements aroused the political and economic passions of the citizenry. Roads, river improvements, canals, and railroads offered physical mobility that, as everyone knew, translated into economic and social mobility. Everyone wanted better transportation for themselves and their communities, and all understood that in a world of finite resources, the awarding of internal-improvement funding to some meant its withholding from others. Once the pathways to economic success had been built, they conferred a permanent advantage on certain groups. Unlike laws, highways and canals could not be readily repealed.[14]

Such widespread and sustained public support for internal improvements belies the notion that early nineteenth-century governments were weak and ineffectual, and refutes the assumption that citizens, suspicious of all political authority, permitted the laissez-faire marketplace to sort out economic development. Likewise, the development of internal improvements in the immediate aftermath of the War of 1812 does not comport with the widely held belief that political parties oversaw the distribution of spoils by granting their supporters favors such as corporate charters and subsidies, thus ensuring that transportation arteries passed through certain communities while permitting weeds to grow in the streets of others. Such an analysis fails on two counts.

For one thing, parties in the early republic were amorphous and highly localized. Even though history textbooks often describe the post-1815 Era of Good Feelings as a time of one-party rule, there was neither unity nor harmony in the ranks of the republicans. There was in fact some confusion as to whether many Pennsylvania politicians even identified themselves as republicans or democrats.[15] As one member of the Pennsylvania legislature observed in 1820, "When I say parties, I mean a division in the Democratic ranks."[16] After 1815, Pennsylvania politicians cleaved into a dizzying number of factions. "New School Democrats" favored a national bank, protective tariffs, and public support for internal improvements—agendas typically supported by the now-discredited federalists, whose members often threw in their lot with the "Old School Democrats," largely out of opposition to Governor Simon Snyder. During the early 1820s, the New School Democrats evolved into the Family Party (so called because all of their key leaders were related by blood or marriage), which drew most of its strength from Philadelphia and Pittsburgh. Their opponents became the Amalgamation Party, strongest in rural areas. In the 1824 election, the Amalgamationists took to calling themselves the "Jackson–Clay men," while the members of the Family Party (who favored a slate that would unite their interests with South Carolina) were styled the "Calhoun–Jackson men," or the "Eleventh-Hour men." Confusingly, neither party really wanted Jackson in office, but when his nomination became inevitable, each group supported him in the hope of federal patronage. Jackson lost to John Quincy Adams, and by the time that the contest was restaged in 1828, the remnants of both the Family and Amalgamation parties were pro-Jackson, while many former federalists supported his opponent, and the ballots generally read simply "Jackson Party" or "Adams Party." Jackson's victory led to additional realignments, with a succession of Wolfites, Muhlenberg Men, and many others. The development of internal improvements in Pennsylvania thus took place amid a remarkably fluid political landscape that was much more attuned to local rivalries than national contests. There was no coherent "party" available to dispense spoils with predictable regularity.[17]

An explanation that suggests that political parties served as the primary generators of internal improvements fails on another count, in that many of the key actors in the development process were neither politicians nor legislators. During the 1820s, in particular, a diverse range of individuals—from merchants to professional iconoclasts—attempted to create a more orderly economic landscape in Pennsylvania.[18] Improved transportation was one of their primary goals, but it was by no means their only objective. In northeastern Pennsylvania, they used public policy to ensure abundant and inexpensive supplies of anthracite. They provided clean drinking water to the citizens of Philadelphia. Across the state, they encouraged economic growth through the formation of banks, while establishing schools, orphanages, and mental institutions to safeguard the welfare of the populace. They also constructed a vast network of roads, river improvements, canals, and railroads. None of these initiatives were strictly public, or strictly private. Rather, state and marketplace were connected and hotly contested arenas.[19]

Public and private actors, working in tandem, devised numerous mechanisms for promoting economic development and the general welfare, particularly with respect to the construction of internal improvements. State legislatures, not Congress, possessed the authority to shape the economic landscape through the selective granting of corporate charters.[20] Such charters grew out of a long-standing tradition of chartering activities that were clearly public in nature, ranging from the formation of municipalities to building almshouses.[21] At their most basic level, corporate charters embodied a grant of public privileges to private individuals, in the expectation of public as well as private benefit.[22] Incorporation diffused the benefits of a growing economy to ever-larger segments of the population by providing better access to transportation, commodities, and credit. In the process, however, corporations sharply narrowed public control over such functions, transferring political and economic authority from the electorate to a few well-positioned investors.[23] Most corporate charters followed a standard format in that they provided a combination of limited liability and unlimited life and, for transportation enterprises, the power of eminent domain. Until 1874, when Pennsylvania adopted a comprehensive general incorporation law, many corporate charters required specific acts of the General Assembly, thus giving legislators a powerful tool to direct the economic energies of the commonwealth and its citizenry.[24]

Prior to the Civil War, the bulk of Pennsylvania's corporate charters were related to transportation, banking, or mining. Of the 2,333 acts of incorporation in Pennsylvania between 1790 and 1860, nearly two-thirds—1,497 in all—were for turnpikes, bridge companies, canals, railroads, or other transportation improvements. In 1821 alone, the legislature chartered 146 turnpikes, resulting in 1,800 miles of planned road construction. In addition to bolstering the finances of the state government, state-chartered banks often underwrote the construction of internal improvements, as both a financial and a political investment.[25] Mining charters were likewise vitally important to the development of better transportation. In a few instances, legislators issued charters that permitted one company to engage in both the mining and transportation of anthracite. More commonly, however, mining charters encouraged the rapid exploitation of coal, which quite naturally stimulated the incorporation of separate canal and railroad companies to serve northeastern Pennsylvania.[26]

More notably, the Commonwealth of Pennsylvania, in common with virtually every other state, provided substantial direct financial support for the development of internal improvements. In some cases, particularly involving turnpike construction, the legislature subsidized private companies.[27] In other instances, legislators provided more than $100 million in public funds and created an administrative mechanism that would build and operate nearly a thousand miles of canals and railroads. Later generations would decry what they labeled a waste of public resources and gross mismanagement by public officials. With the benefit of hindsight, and particularly with the knowledge that canals would succumb to railroads, many of their claims ring true. At the time, however, both ordinary citizens and their elected officials generally agreed that state government should play a role in the promotion of improved transportation and mobility.[28]

If the people of Pennsylvania were foolish in their choice to involve government so intimately in the promotion of improved transportation, then they were not alone. To varying degrees, residents of every state demanded that their government participate in the process of economic development. Madison's 1817 veto of the Bonus Bill ensured that individual states would each be responsible for regulating the economic landscape. The actions of the federal government thus unleashed a vigorous contest for commercial supremacy among the states of the Chesapeake and mid-Atlantic regions, and within each of those states, as well. Geography dictated that there would be one winner, and the prize went to the state that possessed the easiest route between tidewater and the west.[29]

"Erie Fever"

Of all of the state-sponsored internal-improvement projects, the Erie Canal was by far the most successful, enriching the Empire State and contributing to the status of New York City as the nation's commercial center and leading port. Yet, even before July 4, 1817, the ceremonial beginning of work on the Erie Canal, New York was far ahead of such rival seaports as Boston, Philadelphia, and Baltimore. In that context, the new waterway only made a strong state even stronger.

For a start, New York possessed one of the greatest natural harbors in the world. The turbulent meeting of the Hudson River and the salt-laden Atlantic Ocean kept the area's waters virtually ice free. The city thrived on a legacy established by Dutch merchants, at a time when the community was known as New Amsterdam. New York's commercial ascendancy may have begun in the late colonial period, thanks to the military contracting system employed by the British during the French and Indian (Seven Years') War. In 1797, largely owing to the effects of the French Revolutionary Wars, New York surpassed Philadelphia as the nation's leading port. The city possessed a vibrant regional economy, integrated with that of New England and facilitated by superior coastal and transatlantic transportation connections. Between 1790 and 1800, the population of greater New York increased by more than 80 percent, and by 1810 it was the most populous city in the country. During the early years of the nineteenth century, however, Philadelphia and Boston were not far behind, and merchants in those two cities might have harbored a realistic expectation of reestablishing their earlier commercial supremacy.[30]

The War of 1812 temporarily slowed New York's population growth, but the conflict and its immediate aftermath catapulted the city into a position of unassailable dominance. By 1815, the city's foreign commerce was double that of either Philadelphia or Baltimore, with Boston lagging even farther behind. In the immediate aftermath of the Treaty of Ghent, the British selected New York as the principal port that would receive the arrearage of manufactured goods held back owing to the wartime blockade. In April 1817, on the same day that it approved the construction of the Erie Canal, the New York state legislature liberalized the rules pertaining to auction sales at the port.[31] In January of the following year, the Black Ball line established the first regularly scheduled packet service between New York and Liverpool, England. New York soon became the principal arrival point for British textiles and other European products that poured into the United States. By the early 1820s, New York had emerged as the only true commercial entrepôt in the United States—that is, the principal location where merchants received shiploads of European manufactured goods, repackaging them for transshipment to ports in other nations, as well as to other American coastal cities and the interior.[32]

During the early years of the nineteenth century, New York's economic and political elites developed plans to link the Hudson River, at Albany, with Lake Erie, at Buffalo, creating an all-water route to the west. Albert Gallatin, in his 1808 report on internal improvements, noted that the New York route, with an elevation difference of no more than six hundred feet, offered perhaps the only opportunity to build a practicable canal between the east coast and the west. Surveys began as early as 1808, although the War of 1812 delayed construction. The intervening decade proved valuable, for it allowed the development of new building techniques and gave engineering experts ample time to debunk impractical designs, including one that would have allowed water to flow on a steady downgrade all the way from Buffalo to Albany.[33]

New Yorkers initially petitioned for federal assistance for the canal, but they adapted readily to the devolution of internal improvement responsibilities to the states. As early as 1811, the state's politicians were actively lobbying for federal funds. They supported the 1816 Bonus Bill, but Madison's veto early the following year caused them to rethink their strategy. In April 1817, only a month after Madison's veto message, the New York legislature gave its approval to the funding and construction of the Erie Canal. With canal-building techniques already established in England and, to a lesser extent, in the United States, the most innovative part of the project was its financing and organization. The Commissioners of the Canal Fund, a body comprised entirely of public officials, generally yielded to the demands of the project's engineers, and for the most part avoided political partisanship. In addition to selling canal bonds, backed by the state's sterling credit, they supported a series of taxes on auction sales and on items as diverse as salt and steamboats. Governor DeWitt Clinton turned the first shovelful of earth on July 4, 1817, and by the autumn of 1819, the canal was in service between Rome and Utica and was open along its entire 363-mile length in October 1825.[34]

Even before its completion, the Erie Canal had become one of the most successful transportation improvements in the history of the United States. Prior to opening the entire canal for traffic, toll keepers had already collected $1 million in revenues, equivalent to one-seventh of the cost of construction. With the canal in full operation, an inrush of settlers, producing crops for sale, quickly supplanted the small number of subsistence farmers who had previously eked out an existence in the region. In 1835, the commissioners authorized the first of several efforts to enlarge the waterway, and by the following year they were able to retire all of the initial construction debt. With the expansion of agriculture in Ohio, Indiana, and Illinois, a torrent of grain flowed eastward over the Erie Canal toward New York City. Finished goods traveled in the opposite direction, $10 million worth in 1836 and $94 million in 1853—equivalent to almost $2.5 billion in 2010 dollars.[35] Even though the completion of a parallel rail route—the New York Central—had by 1853 diverted the bulk of the westbound shipments of manufactured goods, the canal remained a vital transportation artery for the movement of bulk cargoes to tidewater, with that traffic not peaking until 1880.[36]

By reinforcing the already established dominance of New York City as the nation's leading port, the Erie Canal served as a powerful argument in favor of state-directed efforts to encourage economic development. Its success engendered an envious "Erie Fever" among residents of neighboring states, who attempted to mimic New York's link to the West regardless of the constraints imposed by geography. None of those efforts were as successful as their inspiration, and many proved financially ruinous to the states that sponsored them.[37]

The Battle for Second Place

Even before the completion of the Erie Canal, most Philadelphians had accepted that their community would never regain its status as the nation's largest city. With the bulk of transatlantic shipping heading to and from New York, moreover, they confronted the loss of their city's status as an entrepôt in the United States. Instead, they would have to be content with the coastal trade. Their commercial success would accordingly be based on the size of Philadelphia's hinterland—that is, the geographic region where they could collect raw goods for processing and outward shipment and in turn distribute finished products. Unfortunately for Philadelphians, geography had endowed them with a small hinterland. In an era of extraordinarily expensive overland transportation, Philadelphia merchants were unlikely to handle much of the agricultural and mineral bounty generated in central Pennsylvania. In 1816, for instance, it cost as much to transport a bushel of wheat 218 miles by road as that crop would bring in the city's markets. For corn, the distance was far shorter, at 135 miles. In other words, any farmer who lived in York, 104 miles to the west of Philadelphia, would have had to have been willing to sell his crop for only twenty-six cents a bushel if he wished to remain competitive in the city. Westbound shipments were equally problematic, with the authors of an 1816 United States Senate Committee report suggesting that it cost as much to move cargoes thirty miles inland by road as it had been to transport them across the Atlantic from Britain.[38]

In comparison with New York, with its ready access to the Hudson River, Philadelphia possessed relatively poor water connections to the interior. The Schuylkill and Delaware rivers, which passed to either side of the city, possessed modest catchment basins, and the former was not suitable for commercial navigation. At the far western extremity of the commonwealth, the Allegheny and Monongahela rivers came together at Pittsburgh (a town of fewer than five thousand inhabitants in 1810) to form the Ohio River. Pittsburgh quickly became a break-of-bulk point, where workers transferred cargoes from overland transportation routes to the boats that traveled along the Mississippi River and its many tributaries. Those rivers guaranteed Pittsburgh's rapid growth but they were of little benefit to Philadelphia. With the spine of the Alleghenies interposed between the two cities, it was easier and far less expensive to send goods down the Ohio and Mississippi rivers, through the Gulf of Mexico, and then out into the Atlantic. The development of river steamboats during the 1810s only accelerated that

trading pattern, tying Pittsburgh more closely to the burgeoning cotton kingdom of the South.[39]

Pennsylvania's great watercourse east of the Alleghenies was the Susquehanna River. The North Branch of the Susquehanna began in central New York, then snaked southeast and then southwest through Pennsylvania, to Northumberland. There it met the smaller West Branch, with its source in northwestern Pennsylvania. From Northumberland, the river ran almost due south some ninety miles to Harrisburg, after 1812 the capital of Pennsylvania. The broad Susquehanna flowed on to the southeast, bisecting the rich farmlands of York and Lancaster counties. The Susquehanna was by no means ideally suited to navigation, and it is today the longest river system in the nation without any commercial boat traffic. It nonetheless enabled boatmen to transport cargoes of grain, flour, whisky, salt pork, pelts, lumber, coal, and iron from the interior of Pennsylvania to the river's mouth.

And that, for Philadelphians, was precisely the problem. The Susquehanna River flowed south, into Maryland, before meeting the waters of Chesapeake Bay at Havre de Grace. Prior to the construction of a canal linking Chesapeake Bay with Delaware Bay—a project long supported by Philadelphia merchants—there was little likelihood that traffic flowing off of the Susquehanna River would continue on to the Quaker City. Instead, it would more likely reach Baltimore, some forty miles to the southwest of Havre de Grace. Lancaster, which by 1830 was the second largest city in Pennsylvania, was as close to Baltimore as it was to Philadelphia, and the distance between York and Chesapeake Bay was far shorter than that to the Delaware River. Therefore, it was hardly surprising that few farmers in York and other communities to the west of the Susquehanna River shipped their crops to Philadelphia. Although they were geographically proximate to the city, residents of south-central Pennsylvania evinced little commercial or political loyalty to Philadelphia. While they generally received high-value manufactured goods from Philadelphia along a network of turnpikes that radiated through Lancaster, bulkier agricultural and mineral cargoes often went down the Susquehanna River, toward Chesapeake Bay and Baltimore.[40]

The inability of Philadelphia merchants to tap into the Susquehanna River trade was only one of several factors that contributed to the city's growing commercial malaise. Philadelphia lay nearly a hundred miles upriver from the Atlantic Ocean—a day's sail even in the best of conditions, and far longer in adverse weather. Captains would also have to wait for the best tidal conditions to carry their ships over a series of bars.[41] In the colder months, ice choked the Delaware River, and in exceptionally cold years the port was closed for extended periods.

Several crises exacerbated Philadelphia's geographic limitations. During the American Revolution, the British had blockaded and occupied the city. In 1793, yellow fever swept across Philadelphia, killing some five thousand people, nearly a tenth of the city's population. Frightened sailors, teamsters, and merchants diverted their cargoes to other ports. In the aftermath of the perhaps understandable panic that accompanied the epidemic, local officials routinely imposed strict quarantines that impeded access to the city and thus diverted considerable commerce to Baltimore. Jefferson's Embargo Acts of 1807 and 1808 caused considerable damage, as did the War of 1812. [42]

Even after trade resumed, the fees charged by Delaware River pilots were among the highest in the nation. Residents in areas outside of Philadelphia supported a commonwealth tax of one-half of one percent on auction sales—almost all of which took place in Philadelphia—apparently viewing the commercial metropolis as a vast untapped pool of wealth.[43] Philadelphia merchant Thomas Pim Cope reminisced that "the inhabitants of the [outlying] counties generally treat [the city] as a fat goose to be plucked & roasted for their sustenance."[44] "When any project for the partial benefit of any country district is on the tapis," Cope noted, "these countrymen are not backward in asking our aid, & millions, many millions, of Philadelphia capital have been expended on such unproductive schemes of local policy. We now pay directly & indirectly nearly half of the public burdens, but from envy or other causes we command but little rural sympathy & have to make our way as we can."[45]

Cope and his fellow merchants watched in dismay as Philadelphia's fortunes plummeted. Exports from Pennsylvania, most of which flowed through Philadel-phia, peaked at $17 million in 1806 and then declined steadily. By 1814, the state's exports were practically nil. They rose again following the war, reaching $8 million in 1817, $9 million in 1822, and $11 million in 1825. Exports plunged again thereafter, and not until 1854 would they again exceed $8 million. The city might have recovered had not many of the first generation of entrepreneurial shipping magnates either retired or died, taking their expertise with them.[46]

Barely ninety miles to the south and west, Baltimore merchants reveled in the expectation that their city would soon supplant Philadelphia as the nation's second-most important port. Baltimore's success began early. The city was positioned much farther to the west than either New York or Philadelphia, ensuring the least distance between the Atlantic seaboard and the western waters—fifty miles shorter than the distance between Philadelphia and the Ohio River, at Pittsburgh, and a hundred and fifty miles less than the route between New York City and Lake Erie, at Buffalo. Although poorly positioned to capture the transatlantic trade and inconveniently sited relative to New York, Baltimore possessed an ice-free harbor, one that enabled ready access to the rapidly growing economies of the Carolinas, Georgia, and the Caribbean. During the American Revolution, Baltimore remained open to trade, and it likewise escaped the ravages of the 1793 yellow fever epidemic. Between 1798 and 1800, therefore, Baltimore outpaced Philadelphia in the value of exports.[47]

Baltimoreans lacked good water access to the west, and in compensation underwrote the construction of a network of roads that expanded their city's hinterland. By 1770, eight highways connected Baltimore with York County, to the west of the Susquehanna River. In 1804 and 1805, Maryland legislators chartered several turnpike companies to build toward Pennsylvania, and their Keystone State counterparts responded by incorporating companies that would soon provide service to communities such as York, Carlisle, Gettysburg, and Chambersburg. The construction of the National Road, which began in 1811, extended Baltimore's reach from the upper limit of the Potomac River navigation at Cumberland, west toward the Ohio River.[48]

The decline of tobacco production in the upper South proved paradoxically beneficial to Baltimore, as wheat took root in the Chesapeake and Piedmont regions. European demand for grain and flour stagnated following the end of the Napoleonic Wars, but that circumstance benefited Baltimore. American agricultural products were generally competitive only in Caribbean markets, and Baltimore was the port best positioned to exploit that trade. Between 1810 and 1820, Baltimore grew more rapidly than any other port in the nation as entrepreneurs took advantage of the area's abundant water power and erected a series of flour mills.[49] The quantity of flour inspected annually at Baltimore rose steadily, interrupted only by the War of 1812, from 273,000 barrels in 1800 to 577,000 barrels in 1820. Philadelphia was well behind, with 400,000 barrels exported in 1820, but its residents could still take great comfort that New York ranked a distant third, at 267,000 barrels. By 1825, the story was very different, however. Baltimore's exports had fallen slightly, to 510,000 barrels, but New York had surged ahead to 446,000 and Philadelphia had dropped to third place, with 351,000. By 1828, with the Erie Canal in service, New York shipped 722,000 barrels of flour, easily surpassing Baltimore's 546,000 and Philadelphia's anemic 333,000 barrels.[50]

From the early 1790s onward, as Philadelphia merchants read the latest trade and population statistics from Baltimore, their reactions ranged from concern to panic. For the next fifty years, they warned their friends and neighbors of the danger, called on their elected officials to take action, and predicted dire consequences should Pennsylvania fail to fund the construction of internal improvements that would draw the trade of the Susquehanna Valley and the west away from Baltimore. Their fears were understandable, but misplaced, as a more careful assessment of economic and demographic data revealed that Baltimore was at best an anemic rival.

Baltimore did indeed grow at a rapid rate, particularly between 1785 and the implementation of the Embargo Act of 1807, but that growth was relative to a small base. The city, founded in 1729, was far younger, and far smaller, than New York or Philadelphia. And, with the general constriction of trade that began in 1807, Baltimore's rapid rise slowed considerably. Between 1790 and 1800, furthermore, both Philadelphia and Baltimore grew more slowly than the nation as a whole. The reason for that seeming anomaly is that the incorporated city Philadelphia occupied a fairly small geographic area, and tightly packed inhabitants were spilling over into suburbs like Kensington, the Northern Liberties, Spring Garden, and Southwark. Not until 1854 would municipal consolidation create the City of Greater Philadelphia. The situation was quite the reverse in Baltimore, which lacked suburbs until 1840.

Between 1810 and 1820, therefore, Philadelphia proper grew by only 18.8 percent, but the greater city experienced a population increase of 24.6 percent—still well below Baltimore's growth of 34.8 percent, but not catastrophically so. Furthermore, slaves and free blacks composed a large proportion of Baltimore's population increase—in 1820, for example, 4,357 slaves and 10,326 free blacks resided in the city, equivalent to 23.4 percent of all residents.[51] Many persons of color practiced skilled trades, but their ability to participate fully in Baltimore's economic development was substantially curtailed. The depression that began in 1819, moreover, affected Baltimore with particular severity, and even though trade rebounded in 1821, the city's rapid expansion was over. More broadly, in 1810, Baltimore boasted 53.3 percent of the population of greater Philadelphia, increasing to only 57.7 percent in 1820. In those terms, Baltimore's advance on the economic power of Philadelphia was at best glacial.[52]

The difference between the growth of Pennsylvania and that of Maryland was even more striking. The Keystone State's population grew by 34.5 percent between 1800 and 1810, and by 29.5 percent during the following decade—well below New York, but also well above Maryland, where the comparable figures indicated only 11.4 and 7.0 percent growth, respectively. The first decade of the nineteenth century was in fact the only ten-year period, between 1790 and 1840, when Maryland's population growth exceeded 10 percent. The population of Pennsylvania, in contrast, quadrupled during that period, with growth of at least 25 percent in each of those decades. Much of Pennsylvania's expansion thus occurred in the hinterland rather than in the metropolis. Between 1800 and 1810, the population of Pennsylvania, outside of Philadelphia, grew by 34.8 percent, while the population of Maryland, exclusive of Baltimore, increased only 6.0 percent. During the following decades, the divergence was even more apparent, at 30.3 percent and 3.2 percent, respectively.[53]

With the benefit of hindsight, all of the trade and population statistics boiled down to one unassailable conclusion. Philadelphia merchants had little to fear from their rivals in Baltimore. At the time, however, they could be forgiven for believing that they had to take swift and decisive action to save themselves by redirecting the western agricultural trade to Philadelphia. Urban merchants—those who expected to benefit the most from improved mobility—lacked the financial wherewithal to develop a route between the Atlantic seaboard and the Ohio River. The post-1817 devolution of transportation projects to the state level, moreover, ensured that they could not count on the federal government for assistance. Even within their own state, farmers and merchants in south-central Pennsylvania, who were economically tied to Baltimore, were unlikely to have much sympathy for efforts to protect Philadelphia merchants. Yet, if those merchants labored under the strictures of federalism, they were also astute enough to take advantage of the rhetoric of the Revolution, and its emphasis on republican values, to justify the intervention of state government in the business of transportation. The Constitution of the United States might not permit the national government to invest in internal improvements, they conceded, but the public good of the commonwealth and all of its citizens demanded that the state government take over where federal responsibilities had faltered.

Early Internal Improvements in Pennsylvania

Even before the American Revolution, prominent Philadelphians were anxious to improve access to the west, typically by reaching the Susquehanna River. As early as 1690, William Penn had recommended the construction of a canal that would link the Susquehanna River with the Schuylkill, by way of the Tulpehocken and Swatara creeks. By 1762, late in the colonial era, explorers and surveyors had identified a viable route between the Schuylkill River, at Reading, and the southernmost limit of reliable Susquehanna River navigation, at Middletown. Their line through the Lebanon Valley was in fact the only one lying entirely within Pennsylvania that required but a single summit crossing to secure passage between Philadelphia and the Susquehanna. In 1766, Benjamin Franklin, future governor Thomas Mifflin, scientist David Rittenhouse, and Thomas Gilpin, a Delaware native who had recently moved to Philadelphia, helped to establish the American Society for Promoting Useful Knowledge. One of their principal goals was improved transportation in the colony, and they generally supported a 1771 law that declared the colony's major rivers to be public highways. The same year, the members of the American Philosophical Society solicited funds, through private subscription, for a survey for a canal between the Schuylkill and Susquehanna rivers.[54]

During the years immediately following the Revolution, Pennsylvanians endeavored to use both public and private funds to improve transportation in the new commonwealth. In 1791, a group of prominent Philadelphians, most of whom were staunch Hamiltonian federalists, established the Pennsylvania Society for Promoting the Improvement of Roads and Inland Navigation, with preeminent wartime financier Robert Morris serving as the organization's president. Morris and his allies were deeply concerned about two projects that threatened Philadelphia's commercial interests. One was the Potomac Company, chartered in Virginia six years earlier. The more immediate threat, much closer to home, involved efforts by Baltimoreans to improve navigation on the lower Susquehanna River. In 1783, the Maryland legislature issued a charter to the Proprietors of the Susquehanna Canal to build along the east bank of the river, from Chesapeake Bay north to the Pennsylvania state line. The Proprietors lacked the authority to build northward into Pennsylvania, but their allies in York County were certain to demand corresponding charter rights from the Pennsylvania legislature. In founding the Pennsylvania Society, Morris and other Philadelphians were hoping that they could divert much of the Susquehanna River trade to their city before it could be irretrievably lost down a canal to Chesapeake Bay. On February 7, 1791, Morris presented a detailed memorial to the General Assembly, replete with maps and detailed cost estimates. In an astute attempt to gain the broadest possible political support, and to disguise their personal economic motivations that were tied to the plans, the society's members urged the General Assembly "to combine the interests of all parts of the state and to cement them into a perpetual commercial and political union" through the creation of better roads and waterways.[55]

In his 1790 annual message, Governor Thomas Mifflin had called on the members of the Pennsylvania General Assembly to support internal improvements and, to no one's surprise, he seconded the recommendations of the society in which he held membership. By April of 1791, legislators had agreed to accept proposals for more than a dozen river and canal projects, and twice that many turnpikes. The most spectacular plan involved a series of river improvements and canals that would provide an all-water route from Philadelphia to Pittsburgh. The proposed canal would cross the isthmus that separated the Delaware and the Schuylkill rivers, and then follow the Schuylkill north to Reading. From there, the Tulpehocken, Quittapahilla, and Swatara creeks would carry traffic westward to Middletown, on the Susquehanna River. A short distance to the north, the Juniata River led west to the foothills of the Alleghenies, where a short portage over the summit would provide access to the Conemaugh, Kiskiminetas, and Allegheny rivers and so on to Pittsburgh. Society members claimed that it would be possible to create the cross-state route at a cost of no more than $2 million, but most conceded that only the easternmost portion was immediately practicable.[56]

While legislators provided relatively modest sums for a variety of river improvements, they were less willing to bear the expense of a canal across the state, or even as far west as the Susquehanna River. Instead, in 1791 and 1792, they chartered two private firms, the Schuylkill & Susquehanna Navigation Company and the Delaware & Schuylkill Navigation Company, to build a waterway between Philadelphia and Middletown. Robert Morris, president of both firms, and the other incorporators probably intended to use the two companies as much to increase the value of their landholdings in southeastern Pennsylvania as to generate a profit from the provision of transportation services. The project soon faltered, despite access to a state lottery, implemented in 1795. It mattered little, in any event, as the speculative real estate bubble burst in 1797, with the unfortunate Morris landing in debtor's prison and the two companies fading from the scene. In 1806, the commonwealth purchased four hundred shares of stock in the Schuylkill & Susquehanna Navigation, to little benefit. Five years later, legislators merged the two firms into the Union Canal Company, but the results were scarcely better. The route linking Norristown and the Delaware River had been abandoned, and little work took place on the line between Reading and Middletown.[57]

Members of the Pennsylvania Society for Promoting the Improvement of Roads and Inland Navigation enjoyed considerably more success in their efforts to promote turnpike construction. Roads could be constructed far more easily and cheaply than canals, and in this instance modest infusions of public funds soon brought many of the society's plans to fruition. Turnpike construction proceeded at a rapid rate, particularly along routes that led west from Philadelphia. In 1792, Philadelphians established the Philadelphia & Lancaster Turnpike Road Company, under the leadership of president William Bingham. By 1795, the sixty-two-mile-long road, the first macadamized highway in the United States, was in operation. Beginning in 1806, the members of the General Assembly gave their financial support to improved highways, allowing the governor to purchase up to a fifth of shares in turnpike companies. By 1820, the commonwealth had invested over $1 million in turnpikes. Five years later, public investments in fifty-six turnpikes totaled $1.8 million, as compared with private investments of $4 million.[58]

Such investments produced visible results, and in 1822, more than 1,800 miles of road were complete and in service. By 1830, the General Assembly had chartered more than two hundred turnpike companies, responsible for constructing more than three thousand miles of highways. It has often been suggested that Pennsylvania possessed more miles of turnpikes than any other state in the nation. That may not have been the case, because many proposed and even chartered projects never came to fruition. Nevertheless, thanks to the extensive and rapidly growing turnpike system, overland transportation rates decreased from between thirty and sixty cents per ton-mile before 1819 to perhaps thirteen cents in 1824. Yet, despite the fondest hopes of the Philadelphians who dominated the Pennsylvania Society for Promoting the Improvement of Roads and Inland Navigation, turnpikes did not protect Philadelphia from the commercial ambitions of Baltimoreans. For the most part, the roads that lay to the east of the Susquehanna River, particularly those that centered on the regional transportation hub of Lancaster, enabled high-value goods to proceed overland from Philadelphia. In York County and in other areas to the west of the Susquehanna, highways were more apt to follow the shorter distance to Baltimore. Settlers in Pittsburgh were also likely to rely on road connections to Baltimore, particularly after the National Road reached Brownsville, on the Monongahela River, in 1817.[59]

Anthracite

Despite the threat that Baltimore posed to Philadelphia's commercial interests, the extensive anthracite

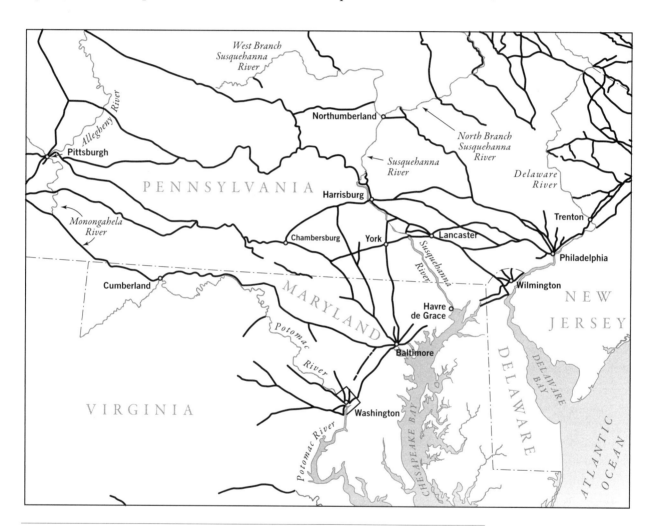

Figure 2. By 1830, Pennsylvania possessed one of the most extensive turnpike networks in the United States. The turnpikes enabled high-value goods to travel from tidewater to Lancaster, York, Chambersburg, Bedford, Pittsburgh, and other inland towns, but considerable commerce from western Pennsylvania also went down the Ohio River to New Orleans. Philadelphians could count on trade as far west as Lancaster. Beyond the Susquehanna River, York and other western communities were as likely to fall within the influence of Baltimore.

Map based on research by Christopher T. Baer, Hagley Museum and Library.

coal reserves that underlay much of northeastern Pennsylvania provided a far stronger motivation for the development of internal improvements. Even after the Revolution, Americans continued to import bituminous (soft) coal from Britain, made affordable because it arrived as ships' ballast. Additional coal came from bituminous deposits in the vicinity of Richmond, Virginia, sent north in coastal schooners.[60]

Another source lay closer to hand, however. Since the late 1760s, Pennsylvania's colonists had been aware of deposits of anthracite (hard) coal in an area that today comprises Luzerne County, in the Wyoming Valley, along the North Branch of the Susquehanna River. During the 1780s, similar discoveries took place in what are now Carbon and Schuylkill counties.[61] Until the 1840s, charcoal remained the fuel of choice for iron smelting, but anthracite was well suited to the reheating of pig iron and the subsequent manufacture of finished goods. Despite some local use, however, high overland transportation costs precluded the widespread use of hard coal.[62]

The War of 1812 temporarily curtailed imports of British coal and suddenly made Pennsylvania anthracite a far more attractive proposition. By 1814, there were severe coal shortages in Philadelphia and other eastern cities. Jacob Cist, a Wilkes-Barre businessman, and his brother-in-law George M. Hollenback were among the first to take advantage of the crisis. In tandem with other investors, they began a venture to send anthracite down the Lehigh River on rafts. It was a difficult business, as the Lehigh was navigable only during periods of high water, and even then was strewn with rocks and other hazards. The return of peace in 1815 caused coal prices to plummet, and spelled the end of Cist's ambitions in the region.[63]

An even more pervasive problem with anthracite was that the substance was difficult to ignite and almost impossible to burn properly. Haphazard experiments with anthracite combustion, some intentional, others accidental, enabled foundrymen to master the intricacies of the new fuel. Around 1811, Josiah White and Erskine Hazard established a rolling mill and wire factory at the falls of the Schuylkill River, fueling their furnaces with Virginia bituminous coal. By late 1812 or early 1813, their workmen accidentally discovered that anthracite ignited best when starved of oxygen. As

early as December 1812, White was promoting plans to improve navigation along the Schuylkill River, in order to ensure access to anthracite supplies. In 1815, the legislature chartered the Schuylkill Navigation Company (not to be confused with the 1791 Schuylkill & Susquehanna Navigation, which had become part of the Union Canal Company in 1811). Differences of opinion regarding engineering matters soon caused both White and Hazard to distance themselves from that venture.[64]

In 1818, after abandoning the Schuylkill River route, White and Hazard moved on to the Lehigh River, the same watercourse that had frustrated Jacob Cist. The two entrepreneurs established the Lehigh Coal Company and the Lehigh Navigation Company (soon consolidated as the Lehigh Coal & Navigation Company), in order to both mine and transport anthracite. By 1820, their construction crews had completed a system of dams that enabled operators to pond and then release water. Although traffic could move in only one direction, the Lehigh Navigation nonetheless funneled substantial cargoes of coal toward the Delaware River and Philadelphia. The company soon built the Mauch Chunk Railroad, the first permanent line in the anthracite region, to more efficiently move coal from the mines to the waterway. By 1829, construction crews had sufficiently improved the Lehigh River so as to permit navigation upstream as well as down.[65]

Even as White and Hazard were experiencing considerable success with the Lehigh Navigation, the Schuylkill River project that they had once supported did not fare too badly, either.[66] By 1818, the Schuylkill Navigation Company (the same firm that White and Hazard had helped to found three years earlier) opened the first in a series of canals and river improvements. Unlike the Lehigh Coal & Navigation Company, however, the owners of the Schuylkill Navigation operated only a toll transportation route, and their charter forbade them from engaging in mining. By 1825, a combination of slackwater navigation and canals enabled boats traveling on the Schuylkill Navigation to reach Port Carbon, in the heart of anthracite country. At Port Clinton, the Little Schuylkill Navigation, Railroad & Coal Company, another pioneering railroad, chartered in 1826, headed north toward the coalfields near Tamaqua, reaching that location in 1832. At the northern edge of the anthracite region, the Delaware & Hudson Canal, opened in 1828, and its associated railroad moved coal to New York markets.[67]

From Commerce to Manufacturing in Philadelphia

The Lehigh and Schuylkill navigations lowered transportation costs and induced a period of rampant speculation in coal properties. Entrepreneurs drove up the cost of anthracite lands, but they also increased production and lowered prices, to the obvious benefit of consumers. By 1821, anthracite from the Schuylkill River Valley cost only eighteen cents a bushel, with a similar product from the Lehigh Valley available in New York for thirty cents—well below the cost of imported British anthracite, which sold for nearly fifty cents a bushel. Reduced costs generated additional demand, and production soared. In 1820, Pennsylvania mines had produced a mere 2,000 long tons of anthracite, an amount that reached 38,500 tons in 1825 and 592,200 tons by 1833. Much of that coal was destined to flow through Philadelphia, transported by coastal shipping to other cities along the Atlantic seaboard—particularly New York and Boston, which lacked any locally available coal deposits.[68]

Philadelphia became the nexus of a growing interregional anthracite trade. In 1816, the city imported more than $60,000 worth of coal from other parts of the United States, with the vast majority of that originating in Virginia. That pattern changed in 1822, with the first exports of coal. By 1837, Philadelphia was shipping more than $2.6 million worth of coal to other regions, dwarfing the $338,469 in outbound flour shipments. Even though the city never regained its status as a major transatlantic port, the anthracite trade caused coastal maritime traffic to triple during the first half of the nineteenth century.[69]

The rapid growth of anthracite production in northeastern Pennsylvania sparked a remarkable transformation in Philadelphia. As merchants declined in importance, relative to their counterparts in other seaboard cities, its manufacturers were in the ascendency. In many respects, Philadelphia was well positioned for the anthracite-induced manufacturing boom that began in the 1820s and continued for much

of the remainder of the century. Although the city had lost its status as a national capital, it retained many important government institutions, including the Navy Yard, the United States Mint, the Frankford Arsenal, and the Schuylkill Arsenal, all of which supported a cadre of technically proficient workers. Many of Philadelphia's leading citizens, as products of the Enlightenment and the scientific revolution, enthusiastically supported the mechanical arts. As early as 1787, they formed the Pennsylvania Society for the Encouragement of Manufactures and the Useful Arts. Six years later, Benjamin Rush, Caspar Wistar, Tench Coxe, and others revived the faltering organization and secured for it a charter.[70]

The embargo that began in December 1807 and the War of 1812 that followed greatly increased the opportunities associated with manufacturing. With Philadelphia already losing ground to New York, the suspension of virtually all maritime trade threatened to drive merchants into ruin. The economic disaster nonetheless provided its own solution. So long as Americans were unable to purchase European manufactured goods, they would have to make do with locally produced items, regardless of their price or quality. To the north, Francis Cabot Lowell and his fellow members of the so-called Boston Associates became manufacturers, and perhaps the best-known beneficiaries of the changed commercial conditions that accompanied the war.[71]

Yet, it was Philadelphia and not Boston that became the nation's new manufacturing hub. Many merchants—Stephen Girard foremost among them—invested heavily in mining and manufacturing enterprises, and profited handsomely as a result. By 1812, Girard had abandoned the West Indian trade as hopeless. Girard established a bank in 1812, taking advantage of both the wartime industrial boom and of the 1811 expiration of the charter of the Bank of the United States. He augmented his considerable wealth with investments in coal lands, canals, and eventually railroads, and accordingly constituted a powerful force in Philadelphia's emerging industrial economy. With access to capital, fuel, and skilled labor, Philadelphia soon excelled in such industries as textiles, leather, machine tools, paper, printing and publishing, and many others.[72]

For the most part, Philadelphia's new industrial elites simply did not need much in the way of state intervention. Girard, White, Hazard, and their fellow industrialists were by no means isolated from local and state governments. To the contrary, they relied on the orderly commercial framework established by the courts and by state-chartered banks. Yet, their orientation was regional and even national in scope, as it was not limited to the narrow political parochialism contained within the boundaries of the city or the commonwealth. They invested heavily in projects like the Lehigh Coal & Navigation Company and the Schuylkill Navigation, which offered a certain opportunity for profit and a clear benefit to the region's manufacturers. They were far less committed to such nebulous and often highly politicized goals as the betterment of the commonweal, the rights of the common man, or the commercial struggle against New York and Maryland. By the early 1820s, the rising generation of Philadelphia manufacturers was poised to challenge the fading mercantile elite for economic, political, and social dominance. That confrontation of necessity embodied radically different visions of the development of transportation improvements in Pennsylvania, and of the state's role in that process.[73]

For all of the success of the new generation of Philadelphia manufacturers, however, there were many others who believed that unaided private enterprise could not generate widespread economic growth, secure the prosperity of communities far removed from Philadelphia, or advance the personal fortunes of those who were not intimately connected with Philadelphia's industries, or with transportation along the Lehigh and Schuylkill rivers. Farmers in south-central Pennsylvania, shippers along the upper reaches of the Susquehanna River, and frontiersmen in the western part of the state all looked with some suspicion at the growing economic and political power of the new industrial elite. So, too, did Philadelphia's merchants, who felt simultaneously threatened by their rivals in other seaport cities, by manufacturers in their own community, and by the residents of the commonwealth's other, smaller communities.

Many of the resulting confrontations between merchants and manufacturers, and between the metropolis and the hinterland, related to the development of trade along the Susquehanna. Jacob Cist and other residents of the Wyoming Valley, who had pioneered the use of anthracite, ironically suffered from poor transportation that rendered them uncompetitive against the dominant producers in Schuylkill County to the south and east. After failing in his initial efforts to send coal to tidewater, along the Lehigh River, Cist turned to the North Branch of the Susquehanna River, the watercourse that transected the Wyoming Valley. Cist and his allies were keenly interested in navigation improvements along the Susquehanna, particularly those that would enable coal to travel south to Chesapeake Bay.[74]

Despite its potential as a conduit for the transportation of anthracite to tidewater, the Susquehanna River suffered from serious defects. The river was wide but was in places strewn with rock ledges, often referred to as "riffles," that threatened to snag boats with even the shallowest of drafts. During exceptionally dry summers, the river was virtually un-navigable. The more serious impediment, however, was at the Conewago Falls, near Middletown, Pennsylvania, a community just to the south of Harrisburg. A series of rapids, caused as the river descended more steeply toward sea level, made downstream navigation a difficult and dangerous proposition and rendered upriver travel essentially impossible.[75]

A short canal, less than a mile in length, opened in 1797, bypassing the Conewago Rapids and permitting boats to travel upriver. Yet, despite the completion of the Conewago Canal, Susquehanna River navigation was still problematic, especially to the south of Columbia, Pennsylvania. That community soon became a regional transportation hub, as many high-value cargoes, sent overland from Philadelphia, were transferred to watercraft for the river journey north. Farther to the south, efforts to improve navigation along the Susquehanna experienced little success. In 1783, the Proprietors of the Susquehanna Canal received their charter from the Maryland legislature, in part triggering the formation of the Pennsylvania Society for Promoting the Improvement of Roads and Inland Navigation eight years later. In 1802, they completed their canal along the Susquehanna River, as far north as the Pennsylvania state line, but it was little more than a badly maintained shallow ditch, and the lightly patronized waterway fell victim to creditors in 1817.[76]

Enterprising and daring rivermen, anxious to avoid tolls on the Conewago and Susquehanna canals, constructed large, rugged flat-bottom scows, which they referred to as "arks." During spring freshets, the arks were capable of descending the Susquehanna River to its mouth. By the early 1820s arks loaded with Wyoming Valley anthracite were transiting the Susquehanna and continuing on through the Chesapeake and Delaware bays to Philadelphia. Additional traffic, principally lumber, came down from the West Branch of the Susquehanna. Salt pork, flour, whiskey, iron, and other commodities added to the Susquehanna River trade. In 1821, for example, more than nine hundred lumber rafts braved the rapids, while the following year nearly five hundred arks descended the river, carrying $1.5 million in goods toward Chesapeake Bay. During 1827, 1,370 arks and 1,631 rafts floated past the state capital in Harrisburg. It was a hazardous business, however, with many arks and their cargoes lost en route. The boatmen who survived and reached Chesapeake Bay, at Havre de Grace, often found little reward for their efforts—sufficient water was available for navigation for only a few weeks during the year, producing a temporary glut in the marketplace and hence low prices on the Baltimore docks. Even with the development of the steamboat, beginning in the 1810s, it was virtually impossible to ship goods north against the river's current. As such, small, high-value manufactured goods still flowed through Philadelphia, reaching the interior over a network of turnpikes that radiated from Lancaster. Agricultural products and other bulk cargoes followed the river south to Havre de Grace and Baltimore, often continuing north to Philadelphia, in a regionalized version of the triangle trade.[77]

Efforts to further improve navigation along the Susquehanna River confronted political impediments that proved at least as intractable as shallow water and rapids. Before reaching Chesapeake Bay, the river transited a portion of Maryland. Even though Havre de Grace lay near the northern end of Chesapeake Bay, the absence of direct water access across the neck of the Delmarva Peninsula ensured that Susquehanna River commerce would be drawn toward Baltimore rather than Philadelphia. As such, Baltimore interests were anxious to improve navigation along the Susque-

hanna River, yet they lacked the authority to do so, north of the Pennsylvania state line. Periodic efforts to improve the section of the river that lay between Columbia and the border—a project supported by Marylanders and also by many residents of southern Pennsylvania—met with a frosty reception from a majority of the legislators in the Keystone State.[78]

Given the hydrological and political impediments to transportation on the Susquehanna, Wyoming Valley anthracite producers and others who had settled along the river looked for alternate access to tidewater. They were keenly interested in the progress, or lack thereof, of the Union Canal Company, the product of an 1811 consolidation of the Schuylkill & Susquehanna Navigation Company and the Delaware & Schuylkill Navigation Company. Since the early 1790s, Robert Morris and other promoters associated with the two companies had tried, and thus far failed, to connect the Susquehanna River with Philadelphia. The project might have succeeded admirably had its incorporators been able to build along the entire intended distance, from Philadelphia through Reading, to Middletown. The 1815 Schuylkill Navigation had established control over the more lucrative portion of the route, however, depriving the Union Canal of anthracite revenues. Absent that income, private investors were reluctant to commit funds to the venture. Unlike the Schuylkill Navigation, which relied solely on private funds, the struggling Union Canal required significant public assistance. Beginning in 1819, legislators permitted another lottery, agreed to guarantee a 6 percent dividend to investors, and finally subscribed to a substantial block of stock, under the terms of the March 26, 1821, Improvement Act.[79] Construction resumed soon thereafter.[80]

Workers completed the canal in December 1827, and it opened to traffic the following March. In common with many of the waterways built in the wake of the Erie Canal, the Union Canal was hardly the financial success that its public and private backers had hoped. The waterway was neither as well engineered nor as heavily patronized as the Schuylkill Navigation. Much of the route lay over limestone bedrock, causing seepage and ensuring chronic water-supply problems. Even though engineers were soon able to correct that situation, they faced a design failure that was not so easily remedied. In the interest of more economical construction, the canal had been designed with small locks and a narrow and shallow cross-section, or "prism," that precluded the use of large boats. A massive improvement project carried out during the 1840s and 1850s increased the canal's capacity. Until then, however, the Union Canal was a poor conduit for the transportation of anthracite to tidewater.[81]

Given the slow pace of construction on the Union Canal, individuals who lived along the main stem of the Susquehanna River, and its northern and western branches, hoped for better results from another canal project, one that lay entirely outside Pennsylvania. The construction of a canal across the narrow northern neck of the Delmarva Peninsula, connecting Chesapeake and Delaware bays, promised a convenient method for routing the commerce of the Susquehanna Valley toward Philadelphia. The city's merchants were thus strong supporters of the Chesapeake & Delaware Canal, which would give them a commercial advantage over Baltimore. Surveys for a canal across the isthmus had been conducted as early as the 1760s, and the route seemed a logical choice for the first great rush of internal improvement proposals that emerged in the immediate aftermath of the American Revolution. As with so many other projects, interstate rivalries intervened. Not until 1799 did Maryland grant a charter for its portion of the route, and then only after Pennsylvania legislators agreed to remove obstructions in their portion of the lower Susquehanna River. Construction began in 1804, but a shortage of capital and persistent opposition from Maryland legislators brought the project to a halt two years later. Not until the early 1820s did Marylanders give their approval to the project, in exchange for promises from the Pennsylvania legislature to further improve navigation along the Susquehanna River.[82]

By the early 1820s, and in light of the slow pace of the various internal-improvement projects, many Pennsylvanians had ample reason to be disenchanted with transportation routes in the Keystone State. Jacob Cist and other anthracite interests in the Wyoming Valley lacked ready access to tidewater, as did the loggers and homesteaders along the West Branch of the Susquehanna. Settlers in the western portions of the commonwealth, and particularly residents of Pitts-

burgh, were constantly demanding better links to the east in order to overcome the high overland transportation costs that made it impossible to compete with eastern producers. Many Philadelphia merchants also sought improved access to the Susquehanna Valley and the areas to the west in order to gain a commercial advantage over Baltimore. Virtually everyone acknowledged that improved transportation was a necessity. Few agreed as to the location of those internal improvements, and fewer still could articulate a comprehensive plan for a coordinated statewide transportation system.

Saving the Commonwealth

By the early 1820s, many Pennsylvanians, particularly those merchants who resided in Philadelphia, were understandably concerned that their state was about to be boxed in by its commercial rivals, north, south, and west. On July 4, 1817, construction began on the Erie Canal, solidifying New York's role as the nation's dominant port. West of Cumberland, Maryland, the National Road was making steady progress toward Wheeling, to the obvious benefit of Baltimore. In January 1824, Virginians incorporated the Chesapeake & Ohio Canal Company, acquired the assets of the 1785 Potomac Company, and vowed to dig a canal west from Washington, following the Maryland side of the Potomac River as far west as they could before somehow reaching the Ohio. The Pennsylvania legislature promptly blocked any possibility of using the Monongahela River to provide access to Pittsburgh. Despite some initial opposition, Marylanders elected to support the project anyway, even though construction did not begin until 1828.

To the west, the steamboat *Washington* became the first vessel to ascend the Mississippi and Ohio rivers, under its own power, from New Orleans to Louisville. With the exception of the falls of the Ohio, at Louisville, an obstacle not overcome until 1830, Pittsburgh and other downriver cities possessed an unimpeded all-water conduit to the cities of the Northeast. Despite its great length, it was far cheaper to send bulk cargoes along that route, rather than overland across Pennsylvania. There seemed little likelihood that either the expanding grain production of the Old Northwest or the booming cotton output of the western South would ever go the other direction, passing through Pittsburgh on its way to Philadelphia. By 1825, the situation had become even more critical. Only July 4, the customary date for the commencement of great new civil engineering works, dignitaries initiated construction on the Ohio & Erie Canal, a waterway that was designed to connect the Ohio River with Lake Erie. When complete, the canal would intercept eastbound shipments of grain and other agricultural commodities, sending them south toward New Orleans or, more likely, north and east to New York, in conjunction with the Erie Canal. It was no coincidence that New York governor DeWitt Clinton, the father of the Erie Canal, joined his Ohio counterpart at the festivities, for New Yorkers welcomed the Ohio & Erie Canal as a logical extension of their state's waterway.[83]

During the same period, the United States suffered through a decline in farm prices, brought about by the end of the Napoleonic Wars, the mismanagement of the Second Bank of the United States, and the subsequent onset of a financial panic in 1819. The resulting economic depression was particularly severe in Pennsylvania, with the price of flour in Philadelphia falling from $14 a barrel in 1817 to $4 in 1821. Many Pennsylvanians, naturally if somewhat unfairly, blamed Baltimore for this disaster, and they became increasingly strident in their calls for a transportation artery similar to the Erie Canal. In that context, entrepreneurs—including Philadelphia merchants and Wyoming Valley anthracite producers—who lacked the transportation that they thought essential to their individual business opportunities now sensed a great opportunity. Through skillful manipulation, they employed the rhetoric of crisis to equate their private needs with the public good of the commonwealth.

The solution to Pennsylvania's problems, stressed the economically afflicted, lay in the construction of a new transportation artery across Pennsylvania—what came to be known as the "Main Line of Public Works." The project, they hoped, would capture the western grain trade, fend off the challenge from Baltimore, and revive Philadelphia's commercial fortunes. To those who suggested that much of the territory that separated Philadelphia and Pittsburgh was too sparsely

settled to support a canal, internal-improvement advocates argued that the new transportation link would generate its own demand, by stimulating economic development and population growth. Fallow lands would become valuable once improved transportation had made them accessible to the plow, they argued, with increases of 50 to 500 percent all but certain. At the same time, internal-improvement advocates suggested, a route across between Philadelphia and Pittsburgh would bind together the diverse interests of the commonwealth and end regional rivalries. Some politicians went so far as to assert that improved transportation would "consolidate the varied population of Pennsylvania into one great mass, influenced by the same interests and pointing its active energies to the same objects."[84]

The claims of ardent canal advocates quickly rose from the sublime to the ridiculous. Their economic arguments made the most sense, particularly their assertion that tolls from coal shipments would recoup construction costs and even cross-subsidize other types of traffic. Loftier and less plausible rhetoric suggested that internal improvements would reduce unemployment, idleness, and "pauperism"; improve the moral character of every Pennsylvanian; and advance the course of civilization. By removing heavy freight wagons from the turnpikes, canals could preserve those vital roads from destruction, with the attendant savings in repair expense apparently serving as more than adequate compensation for the loss of business suffered by turnpike owners. Teamsters would not become unemployed and destitute, they insisted, because the legislature could always assist them in finding work in more remote areas of the state—until, presumably, an expanding canal network would reach even the darkest corners of Pennsylvania. In 1825, in perhaps the most outlandish and oft-quoted example of hyperbole, some members of the state legislature asserted that canal tolls "will support the government, and educate every child in the commonwealth," without subjecting the populace to the burden of taxation.[85]

Most Pennsylvanians were not so easily fooled, however, and they recognized this rhetoric for what it was—an attempt by fading economic elites to maintain their power. Most Philadelphia merchants were too poor, too frugal, and too wise to risk their own funds on a Main Line of Public Works. Because no sane investor would have pledged funds to support an enterprise of such dubious profitability, construction of the Main Line would have to depend on a substantial allocation of governmental funds. The Main Line would be no mixed enterprise, blending public and private capital. Instead, it would be entirely built, owned, and operated by the Commonwealth of Pennsylvania.

To those who argued that private enterprise had already demonstrated its ability to construct canals, turnpikes, and other internal improvements, Philadelphia merchants insisted that only the state could ensure that every citizen received a consistent level of benefits from such projects. In 1825, Philadelphia attorney John Sergeant noted that private companies "would make [i.e., build] the parts of the line that were least expensive, and at the same time would be most productive of toll, while difficult parts would be left undone, and thus the main object would be frustrated."[86] In a republican society, the "main object" of the state was to provide everyone with equal access to economic development, and private enterprise threatened to erode that goal. Private entrepreneurs had succeeded admirably in providing transportation in areas where it was in their economic self-interest to do so. But, Sergeant asked, what of everyone else? Economic fairness and republican values dictated that the state should achieve "the main object" of equitable access to transportation by partly or completely subsidizing canal construction in areas where investors did not think it profitable.

In their often-strident advocacy for a Main Line of Public Works, however, Philadelphia merchants alienated the vast majority of Pennsylvania's citizenry, and in many instances they found it difficult to command the allegiance of even a modest percentage of their fellow Philadelphians. Few Pennsylvanians were ideologically opposed to the commingling of public and private funds in mixed enterprises, or even to outright governmental ownership of internal improvements. Virtually all Pennsylvanians supported local transportation improvements that would link their community to an expanding, if small, hinterland and were perfectly willing to accept any legislative subsidies that might facilitate construction. However, few of those who resided in the hinterlands favored the public financing of roads or canals that would bring them under the commercial sway of Philadelphia, depriving them of the local monopolies that they had long enjoyed. Regardless of their geographic orientation, most Pennsylvanians argued that the commonwealth's resources would be better spent on a series of local transportation improvements, rather than on an east-west link of doubtful utility.[87]

Connecting Philadelphia to the West

In 1817, the commencement of construction on the Erie Canal shocked many Pennsylvania legislators into action. Unlike their counterparts in New York, however, they were badly divided by partisan disputes. For a few years, nervous Philadelphians could find solace in the hope that financial or technical difficulties might prevent the Erie Canal from ever being completed. As gangs of laborers made steady progress across upstate New York, that hopeful pessimism rapidly transformed into fear. The opening of the National Road to Wheeling, Virginia, in August 1818 caused them further anxiety. In 1821 the members of the legislature responded rather cautiously to those developments, passing an Internal Improvement Act and allocating state funds to finance turnpike and canal construction—although most of the monies went to pay off the debts of established turnpike routes, and not to generate new projects. In November 1822, Jacob Cist and his father-in-law, Matthias Hollenbeck, along with other influential Wyoming Valley residents, gathered in Wilkes-Barre in an effort to build political support for improved transportation along the Susquehanna River. Cist saw the Erie Canal as an opportunity rather than a threat, and he envisioned a link from the Wyoming Valley northward into New York, with access to the nation's largest city. His vision included a "National Canal" from Washington, along the North Branch into New York, and eventually to the Great Lakes.[88] In November 1823, the project's supporters participated in a national canal convention in Washington, D.C., but the absence of federal support for internal improvements precluded such grand plans.[89]

Many Philadelphians were echoing Cist's calls for improved transportation, although without reliance on the Erie Canal. During the 1822 and 1823 legislative sessions, William Lehman, a Philadelphia pharmacist, introduced resolutions calling for the appointment of commissioners to oversee a statewide system of transportation improvements. In March 1824, and after years of inaction, the General Assembly passed a bill sponsored by Lehman, instructing the governor to appoint three commissioners for the "Purpose of Promoting the Internal Improvement of the State."[90]

Governor John Andrew Shulze soon appointed Colonel Jacob Holgate, James Clarke, and Charles Treziyulney to the Internal Improvements Commission. The first two were politicians, but Treziyulney, a Polish émigré, was an accomplished surveyor who now possessed both the experience and the authority to survey a canal route across Pennsylvania. In their February 2, 1825, report to the governor, Holgate and Clarke favored a direct route across Pennsylvania, from Middletown (the western terminus of the Union Canal), up the Susquehanna to Duncan's Island, then west along the Juniata River and over the Alleghenies. They suggested that a four-mile tunnel underneath the summit, which they estimated would cost nearly half a million dollars, could carry canal boats to the Conemaugh River, with the Kiskiminetas and Allegheny rivers providing onward access to Pittsburgh. At the time they issued their recommendation, there was precisely one transportation tunnel in North America, on the Schuylkill Navigation, that had entered service less than four years earlier. Engineers on the Union Canal were about to begin construction of a longer tunnel, near Lebanon, Pennsylvania—but, at 729 feet in length, it was far shorter than the summit tunnel that Holgate and Clarke proposed. The two commissioners nonetheless expressed little concern at the technical difficulties involved. Wells were commonplace, they argued and, after all, what was a tunnel except a very deep well, turned on its side?[91]

Treziyulney begged to differ. In a dissenting report to the governor, on February 21, he insisted that a tunnel of such magnitude and complexity would be virtually impossible, in an environment where "mountains are thrown together, as if to defy human ingenuity, and baffle the engineer."[92] With a summit that lay

2,322 feet above sea level, a canal across the Alleghenies would constitute a far more difficult proposition than the Erie Canal, much of which lay on virtually level terrain, and which rose to no more than 650 feet in elevation. Even if a summit tunnel could be built, Treziyulney doubted that sufficient water would be available, at such a high elevation, to keep a canal in service. The only feasible route, he suggested, would follow the West Branch of the Susquehanna River, before intersecting the Allegheny River well to the north of Pittsburgh. In spite of the imminent completion of the Erie Canal and the anticipated construction of the Ohio & Erie Canal, the members of the Internal Improvements Commission were paralyzed by indecision, imperiling the commonwealth's efforts to respond.[93]

Promoting Internal Improvements

The dissension with the Internal Improvements Commission ensured that civic boosterism and political activism would shape the contours of Pennsylvania's public works. While the three commissioners debated the best method to cross the Alleghenies, private advocacy groups began pressuring the legislature to begin canal construction as quickly as possible. On October 11, 1824, a few months before the internal improvement commissioners issued their sharply divided report, forty-eight prominent Philadelphians chartered the Pennsylvania Society for the Promotion of Internal Improvements in the Commonwealth.[94] They were well known to one another, through shared memberships on the boards of banks (particularly the Second Bank of the United States), in scientific groups such as the American Philosophical Society and the Franklin Institute, and in charitable organizations. All of the society's members were prosperous—and needed to be, with an initiation fee of $100 and dues set at $10 per year. Few were in the top tier of Philadelphia's economic and political elite, however, as members of that august group had developed a fairly hardheaded and realistic appraisal of the society's limited chances for success and accordingly preferred to concentrate on more lucrative mining and manufacturing endeavors.[95]

The membership of the society hardly reflected either the general populace of Philadelphia, its largely

Figure 3. Mathew Carey (1760–1839) settled in the United States and became a journalist and political agitator. A successful publisher, printer, and bookbinder, Carey was widely respected in Philadelphia, yet he also made numerous enemies, thanks to his dogged defense of his principles. He believed strongly in Kentucky Senator Henry Clay's American System and its attendant call for internal improvements—and he was one of the first Pennsylvanians to warn his fellow citizens of the danger that the Erie Canal and the Baltimore & Ohio Railroad posed to their economic well-being.

Portrait by John Neagle, 1825, courtesy of the Library Company of Philadelphia.

mercantile past, or its increasingly industrial future.[96] Some members were merchants who had not been able to make the transition to manufacturing. Others were dabbling in the business of internal improvements, hoping that public funds would improve transportation in the commonwealth, yet were unwilling to commit substantial amounts of their own money on the society's financially dubious proposals. More than a few joined because it seemed socially respectable to be associated with the idea of progress through transportation. Most of those who belonged to the organization were boosters who were genuinely anxious to improve Philadelphia's commercial fortunes, but few believed that the forging of better transportation connections with the interior was the only, or indeed the best, method of achieving that end. They spoke piously of employing the resources of government to build a

stronger and more united commonwealth, tied together by public works, yet most privately acknowledged that their words were but a smokescreen, concealing their desire for personal aggrandizement. Ultimately, they proved extraordinarily effective in mobilizing local and statewide political support, in furtherance of their internal-improvement agenda, but their actions ultimately proved detrimental to the commonwealth's finances.[97]

Although he possessed few commercial motives for his support of a Main Line of Public Works, Mathew Carey quickly became the society's most tireless organizer and primary spokesman. He was an iconoclast and agitator, someone who delighted in rattling the establishment, tilting at windmills, and serving as the proverbial fly in the ointment. Born in Dublin in 1760, Carey apprenticed as a printer and a bookseller. He also wrote stinging social critiques, including a 1779 pamphlet that called for tolerance for Catholicism in Ireland. That work so alarmed British authorities that Carey found it expedient to move to Paris, where he spent time with both Benjamin Franklin and the Marquis de Lafayette. He returned to Ireland in 1784, but his spirited defense of Irish Catholic rights, in the form of the *Volunteer Journal*, made his stay there a brief one. After serving a short sentence in a Dublin prison, he emigrated later that year to Philadelphia.[98]

Carey switched allegiances, parties, and causes as easily as he changed countries. Once an ardent Hamiltonian, Carey was so emboldened by the French Revolution that he joined forces with the Jeffersonian republicans, and in 1812 he was rewarded with a directorship of the partisan Bank of Pennsylvania. Over the next three decades, Carey remained on the board, while periodically railing at the purported incompetence and mismanagement of his fellow directors. Carey's access to Philadelphia's financial elite served him well in his business interests. With Lafayette's support, Carey had established a newspaper, the *Pennsylvania Herald*. After suffering near-fatal wounds in a duel with the editor of a rival newspaper, Carey went on to establish the *Columbian Magazine* and *Carey's American Museum*.

Finding few financial rewards in the newspaper business, Carey abandoned his commitment to journalism and set up shop as a book dealer, printer, and bookbinder. His most famous employee was undoubtedly Mason Locke "Parson" Weems, the originator of so many virtuous myths regarding George Washington and other American patriots. Carey's primary staple was the Bible, and he kept the book set in type, ready for additional copies at a moment's notice. In 1814, Carey published *The Olive Branch or, Faults on Both Sides, Federal and Democratic. A Serious Appeal on the Necessity of Mutual Forgiveness and Harmony*, in which he called on Americans to unite during a time of war. The book proved extraordinarily popular, on par with the Bible and Thomas Paine's *Common Sense*. Like his son Henry Charles Carey, Mathew Carey was a strong supporter of both high protective tariffs and Henry Clay's American System, with its call for federally sponsored internal improvements. Carey was active in social reform issues, commented

on politics, and was one of the founders of the Hibernian Society. As industrialization transformed working and living conditions in his native city, he published invectives against the new economic order, including *Essays on Public Charities of Philadelphia* (1830) and *A Plea for the Poor* (1836). Beginning in 1821, he agitated for the construction of the Chesapeake & Delaware Canal, but he was generally suspicious of privately financed internal improvements. The chronic failures of the Schuylkill & Susquehanna canal, Carey believed, occurred largely because speculators had subscribed most of the company's stock and then had refused to pay the periodic assessments on their shares.[99]

Because private enterprise had failed, Carey suggested, it was up to government to build a canal across the commonwealth. To that end, and in addition to helping to found the Society for the Promotion of Internal Improvements, he published memorials in the *United States Gazette* and generally hounded Philadelphia merchants into submission. Under the guidance of Carey and his associates, the society embodied a threefold purpose—to study canals and railways elsewhere in the United States and in Europe, to raise public awareness of the necessity of internal improvements, and to place pressure on the General Assembly to fund them. By December 1824, the members of the society's Acting Committee had prepared a memorial to the legislature, requesting the establishment of a "Board of Public Works."[100]

In their efforts to promote a trans-Pennsylvania canal, the members of the society developed an effective grassroots organization, creating committees in each county and mobilizing virtually every newspaper editor in the commonwealth. The society's initial target audience was the citizenry of Philadelphia, who stood to benefit more than anyone from a Main Line of Public Works. On January 24, 1825, Carey and his fellow society member, attorney John Sergeant, presided over a meeting at the Philadelphia County Courthouse, designed to raise public support. They introduced a resolution calling for the state to construct a canal between the Allegheny and Susquehanna rivers, relying on the Union Canal and the Schuylkill Navigation to carry traffic eastward to Philadelphia. The following day, the Acting Committee, which consisted of Carey, Stephen Duncan, Joseph Hemphill, Richard Peters,

Jr., and William Strickland, sponsored "An Address to the Citizens of Philadelphia" in all of the city's newspapers. The missive reinforced their assertion that the project was too complex, and too important to the state's welfare, to be placed under the control of private individuals or corporations.[101]

By February, the society had organized rallies in several other counties that were likely to benefit from the proposed canal. One of the most significant took place in Wilkes-Barre, where Jacob Cist and his allies again demanded improved transportation for Wyoming Valley anthracite. The plethora of meetings resulted in a flood of petitions to the General Assembly, from Philadelphia and other regions to the west.[102]

At the same time, the recently released majority report of internal improvement commissioners Holgate and Clarke, along with Treziyulney's scathing dissent, goaded the society's members into further action. Adopting the pseudonym "Fulton," Carey employed his publishing house to issue eight pamphlets covering various aspects of turnpike, canal, and railway construction, printing and distributing a thousand copies of each. The members of the Acting Committee and of the Committee of Twenty-four (convened in January 1825) warned the legislature, the commercial elite, the common folk, and anyone else who would listen that Philadelphia's exports were declining and that the internal-improvement projects sponsored by New York, Maryland, and Virginia were already well under way. The society's organizers pledged to "place established facts before the public in an impartial form," including an "investigation of the merits and advantages of *canals and railways*, and of other modes of communication."[103] They also asserted that it was "the duty of the Committee to abstain from the expression of preference for any plans of improvement," suggesting an awareness that a detailed discussion of transportation routes would likely create significant disagreements among residents of various parts of the state.[104]

Canals and Railroads

Very soon, however, the Society for the Promotion of Internal Improvements confronted severe dissent in matters pertaining to both engineering and politics.

The first crisis stemmed from ongoing debates regarding the relative merits of canals and railroads. In hindsight, and particularly given the mountains that lay athwart the route from Philadelphia to Pittsburgh, rail transportation held obvious advantages over waterways. At the time, however, the issue was not so straightforward. Two waterways—the Schuylkill Navigation and the still-incomplete Union Canal—already spanned more than a third of the distance between Philadelphia and Pittsburgh. Under those circumstances, railroad construction to the west of the Susquehanna River seemed likely to create an inefficient hybrid transportation system.

Railways nonetheless offered advantages that merited consideration. In mountainous terrain, where canals required numerous locks, railways were less expensive to construct. They were also easier to maintain, particularly when the rivers that typically paralleled the canals and supplied them with water overran their banks during springtime floods. Because they did not require a reliable water supply, trains could go virtually anywhere and generally followed a much straighter path. Railroads also allowed for faster travel than canals.[105] Yet, many Pennsylvanians questioned whether such speeds were necessary. There might be some benefit in rushing passengers and small, high-value shipments across the state, they admitted, but they asserted that most traffic would consist of grain, coal, and other bulk cargoes. For such low-value commodities, speed hardly mattered. In the final analysis, people living in well-watered lowland areas, with ready access to rivers, favored the proven design of the canal, while settlers in more rugged areas, where topography precluded canal construction, supported the railroad.[106]

Partisans on both sides looked to Britain for advice and support, but Britain offered only limited guidance in that context. The earliest British colliery railroads existed because many mines were situated along hillsides, out of reach of canals. They served as adjuncts to canals, which had long since proven their ability to handle coal and other bulk cargoes. They typically exploited gravity, using the weight of loaded coal cars to descend hills, and often to pull empty cars back up to the mines. In other cases, they relied on horses to provide motive power, and horses could move rail cars scarcely faster than canal boats.

Only later would steam locomotives provide railroads with a significant advantage over canals. In 1821, the British Parliament had chartered the Stockton & Darlington, the first true railway in the world, only three years before Carey and his associates founded the Society for the Promotion of Internal Improvements. The Stockton & Darlington was a horse-drawn line, however, and would remain so until September 1825. The famous Rainhill Trials on the Liverpool & Manchester Railway, which conclusively demonstrated the superiority of steam locomotives to horses, at least under British operating conditions, did not take place until October 1829. In the United States, the first test of a steam locomotive occurred in August 1829, on track belonging to the Delaware & Hudson Canal Company, but the results were disappointing.[107]

With railroads still in their infancy, the members of the Pennsylvania Society for the Promotion of Internal Improvements seemed initially convinced of the superiority of canals. On January 24, 1825, when the society held its organizational meeting in Philadelphia, most of the assembled delegates favored a canal across the state. The recently organized Committee of Twenty-four soon petitioned the General Assembly for support for a "Grand Pennsylvania Canal," with no mention of railroads.[108]

There were nonetheless several dissident society members who believed that railroads merited serious consideration. While in the minority, their very public opinions cast troubling doubts on the efficacy of canals. In December 1824, Stephen Duncan, a federalist who had recently been selected to represent Philadelphia in the Pennsylvania Senate, asked Nicholas Biddle to provide information about the recently chartered Liverpool & Manchester Railway. Biddle responded with enthusiastic support for the new mode of transport. The small group of railway advocates soon coalesced around Charles J. Ingersoll, the society's vice president and the United States District Attorney for Pennsylvania. Even Carey was initially sympathetic to railways, and by February 16 he had published a pamphlet entitled *Canals and Railroads*, an evenhanded exposition of the merits and potential of each.

The first ominous rumblings of protest against railways appeared soon after, by Pennsylvanians who in-

sisted that it was impossible to assess their worth without taking the time to accumulate additional data. On February 18, and probably in response to *Canals and Railroads*, the editor of the *United States Gazette* sharply criticized railroad supporters, claiming that their "narrow prejudices and selfish views" were threatening to override prudence and caution.[109]

A similar debate was taking place in the General Assembly. On February 5, 1825, the Senate created a committee to investigate the possibility of constructing a railroad between Philadelphia and Pittsburgh. Commissioner Treziyulney issued his minority report, on February 21, suggesting that a four-mile-long summit tunnel was impracticable, and that too little water would be available to maintain a canal route over the Alleghenies. Treziyulney was not in favor of a railroad, either, but his doubts about the practicability of a canal gave considerable ammunition to the supporters of a rail route. A week later, the members of the House Committee on Inland Navigation and Internal Improvements concluded that the matter should be delayed until the next legislative session, in order to collect additional information, but acknowledged that railways were worthy of consideration.[110]

Treziyulney and his supporters were in the minority, but his doubts regarding a canal invigorated railroad advocates within the Society for the Promotion of Internal Improvements. In an effort to settle the issue, on January 19, 1825, the members of the society resolved to dispatch a representative to Europe, to perform an objective evaluation of canals and railways. On March 20, William Strickland, the only trained engineer among the society's members, departed for Liverpool.[111] Strickland appears to have traveled across the Atlantic with an open mind, but he had not been in Britain more than a few weeks before he reached a firm conclusion in favor of trains. Early in his visit, he saw several colliery railways in action, and in his June 5 report to the society he insisted that "although much wealth and commercial greatness have been produced by numerous canals, still railroads offer greater facilities for the conveyance of goods, with more *safety, speed,* and *economy.*"[112] In September, when the Stockton & Darlington first tested *Locomotion No. 1,* Strickland was in attendance. The locomotive's success banished any lingering doubts regarding the potential of the new technology. In an October 20, 1825, letter to the society, Strickland advocated the construction of a double-track railroad between Philadelphia and Pittsburgh. In December 1825, Strickland completed his research visit to the British Isles, his engineering expertise giving him confidence in the superiority of railroads over canals—but by the time he returned to Philadelphia, the debate was over, and the canals had won.[113]

Mathew Carey was horrified at the growing public interest in Strickland's writings. He had devoted many years to his quest to draw western trade to Philadelphia, but no sooner had he organized an improvement society that could help translate his dream into reality than the unexpected emergence of a new form of transport threatened to destroy all of his efforts. It was not that Carey possessed any innate dislike for railroads. His fear, rather, was that the canal-railroad debate would paralyze both the society and the legislature into inaction, with each day of delay representing just that many more shovels full of earth on the Erie Canal as that commercial artery neared completion.[114]

Carey believed that the conflict could be resolved only through the intervention of a body of expert engineers, but he was astute enough to make certain that that group followed his wishes. Even before Strickland reached Britain, Carey and the society's other pro-canal members were lobbying for a canal-only route. The General Assembly approved legislation, signed by Governor Shulze on April 11, 1825, that dissolved the three-member Internal Improvements Commission. In its stead was a five-member Board of Canal Commissioners, specifically tasked with the construction of a canal across the commonwealth. Shulze declined to nominate Treziyulney, with his troublesome doubts about the viability of a canal. The governor instead offered a seat on the Canal Commission to former treasury secretary Albert Gallatin, whose 1808 report on internal improvements certainly qualified him for the post. Gallatin declined to serve, however, citing "the situation . . . of my family at this moment."[115] Shulze then appointed John Sergeant, the president of the Society for the Promotion of Internal Improvements, and a strong canal supporter, to chair the new commission. Sergeant, as a director of the Schuylkill Navigation, had some experience with canal construction and operation, but his real strengths

lay in his political connections and in his ability to moderate Carey's often inflammatory rhetoric. The governor selected the remaining members of the commission in order to ensure that different political factions and various geographic regions were appropriately represented. Although not engineers themselves, the five commissioners would be responsible for hiring personnel and authorizing and evaluating the surveys that would determine the location of the commonwealth's internal improvements.[116]

The legislation that created the Board of Canal Commissioners ordered its members to begin a new round of surveys, in order to resolve the issues associated with the work that Holgate, Clarke, and Treziyulney had undertaken in 1824. The two most important prospects were along the Juniata River (the route that Clarke and Holgate had suggested) and the West Branch of the Susquehanna (Treziyulney's preference). Yet, the two proposed routes bypassed great swaths of Pennsylvania, areas whose residents were certain to plea for additional canals.

Even before the surveyors were in the field, Carey was already organizing a statewide canal convention, designed to bring together individuals representing virtually all of the political factions and regions of the commonwealth. Some members of the Committee of Twenty-four dissented, fearing that the convention might reinvigorate the debate between canal and railroad partisans, and that residents from outlying counties would flock to the convention, each arguing for a branch canal to their own isolated section of the commonwealth. Carey dismissed those concerns, feeling that the need for publicity outweighed the risk, and his views ultimately prevailed.[117]

Between August 4 and August 6, 1825, barely a month after the ceremonial groundbreaking on the Ohio & Erie Canal, more than a hundred delegates attended the state Internal Improvement Convention in Harrisburg. Many of them had read the pamphlet *Facts and Arguments in Favour of Adopting Railways in Preference to Canals in the State of Pennsylvania*, published anonymously on July 20. Carey immediately—and incorrectly—suspected Strickland of authoring this plea for the consideration of railways, and his hatred for the engineer only increased. As the convention opened, Carey and his allies succeeded in appointing Sergeant as chairman of the Philadelphia delegation, and secured him a seat on the policy committee. Sergeant played an important role in steering the convention toward a single, cross-state canal route. The convention attendees considered and rejected a motion by Charles Ingersoll and William J. Duane in support of a railroad, seemingly bringing the argument over the proper mode of transportation to an end. Less than a week later, however, Philadelphia newspapers published William Strickland's preliminary report, sent from Britain several weeks earlier, and his enthusiastic support for railroads reinvigorated the debate.[118]

Carey, who envisioned Philadelphia falling further and further behind New York and Baltimore with each passing month, cautioned against any additional delays. He sought to end the debate by discrediting railways, and the reports of William Strickland. Under Carey's direction, the society's Acting Committee responded coolly to Strickland's preliminary report, warning him on September 19 that his support for railroads would "divide the friends of the cause of internal improvement, and postpone, if not prevent the commencement of the great work."[119] Strickland ignored the advice, but could do little about Carey's determination to censor his findings. Society members, and Carey in particular, compiled Strickland's reports into a single volume, using editorial discretion in the process. In August 1826, when the publishing house of Carey & Lea issued Strickland's *Reports on Canals, Railways, Roads and Other Subjects*, it retained many of Strickland's illustrations, but eliminated his ringing endorsement of railroads—including his assertion that "railroads offer greater facilities for the conveyance of goods, with more *safety*, *speed*, and *economy*."[120] Instead, Carey continued to emphasize his demand, most forcefully articulated in November 1825, that his fellow Pennsylvanians must "abandon the idea of railroads for such general traffic as may be expected between Philadelphia and Pittsburg, and all unite to promote the success of a canal."[121]

Main Line and Branch Lines

Even as Mathew Carey was attempting to stifle support for railroads, a second debate emerged in the General Assembly, pitting the "Main Liners" against the "Branch Men." The former, typically residents of Philadelphia, sought to concentrate all of the commonwealth's resources on the formidable task of building a canal across the state to Pittsburgh. The latter, representing outlying districts, saw little in the proposal to benefit their constituents, and demanded a complex network of feeder canals that would crisscross Pennsylvania. The creation of the Board of Canal Commissioners, in April 1825, generated further support for a widespread internal-improvements network, with political considerations dictating Governor Shulze's choice of five commissioners from different parts of the state.[122]

The members of the Pennsylvania Society for the Promotion of Internal Improvements did their best to contain the scope of the project, but to no avail. In January 1825, when the society's Committee of Twenty-four petitioned the legislature for a "Grand Pennsylvania Canal," they made clear their preference for a single route, without expensive branches to outlying areas. When the state Internal Improvement Convention met at Harrisburg that August, John Sergeant, as head of the Philadelphia delegation and a member of the policy committee, informed the delegates that their task was limited to the development of a main transportation artery. Delegates from Philadelphia and Pittsburgh, as well as from some of the communities along the route that lay between them, were emphatic in their support for a cross-state canal, along with a possible link between the Susquehanna River and Lake Erie. In the aftermath of the convention, Mathew Carey printed a memorial to the "Citizens of the Commonwealth of Pennsylvania." He highlighted the report of commissioners Holgate and Clarke, and emphasized their intent that "The state should make these great primary canals on her own account, and may accomplish all in 12 or 15 years, leaving to companies and individuals to construct the numerous lateral canals and side cuts, that will necessarily be connected with them."[123]

Despite the calls for restraint, coal bound together the interests of the Main Liners and the Branch Men and ensured the construction of a widespread canal network.[124] The numerous residents of southern Pennsylvania were opposed to the Main Line, and their political strength in the legislature was almost equal to that of Philadelphia and the central counties that stretched west to Pittsburgh. As such, Carey, Sergeant, and their allies desperately needed the allegiance of legislators from the northern part of the state. They sought the favor of Jacob Cist, the Wyoming Valley anthracite producer who served as the Luzerne County delegate to the 1825 canal convention in Harrisburg. He was ready to make a deal with the Main Liners in order to gain better transportation for his anthracite. Temporarily abandoning his plans for a link to the Erie Canal, Cist indicated his support for a canal in the opposite direction, south along the Susquehanna River, in order to connect with the proposed Main Line of Public Works. To achieve that end, he was prepared to use his influence in the legislature to deliver votes from northeastern Pennsylvania. In March 1825, less than a month after Cist suggested his plan to the leaders of the Society for the Promotion of Internal Improvements, Mathew Carey's publishing house began churning out pamphlets suggesting that revenues from Wyoming Valley anthracite shipments could be used to pay construction costs and offset unremunerative tariffs on the Main Line of Public Works.[125]

Cist was by no means the only one who sought to attach his local economic self-interest to plans for state-funded canals. People living along the West Branch of the Susquehanna River noted that Treziyulney had insisted that their watercourse constituted the only feasible mechanism for reaching the Allegheny River. Even if the Main Line were to follow a different route, they thought it only fair that they should have a canal as well. Those who dwelled along the upper reaches of the Allegheny, as well as residents of the Erie Triangle, demanded better transportation in a chronically underdeveloped area of the commonwealth, and particularly coveted access to supplies of inexpensive bituminous coal. To the south, some Pittsburghers suggested a canal linking their city to the Potomac River, even if such a project was bound to be of far more benefit to Baltimore than to Philadelphia. To the east, anthracite producers demanded a canal along the Delaware River—a project that as events transpired became the only commercially viable segment of Pennsylvania's massive system of internal improvements.[126] Across the commonwealth, virtually everyone who lacked

ready access to a canal considered himself ill-used, and most were convinced that a small addition to the list of proposals could end their isolation and make them competitive in the regional economic marketplace. Aside from a few naysayers—most of whom lived in south-central Pennsylvania, an area that was tied to Baltimore—the average Pennsylvania citizen accepted Carey's publicity and was convinced that a cornucopia of tolls would fund the construction of endless miles of canal. In that context, the most politically expedient method of securing the votes necessary to fund the Main Line of Public Works was to give all of the Branch Men exactly what they wanted.[127]

Canals for the Commonwealth

In a climate of optimism tinged with hysteria, political considerations mattered far more than engineering ones. In that context, the suggestions of engineers and surveyors, as well as politicians who urged restraint, largely fell on deaf ears. In his December 1825 message to the legislature, Shulze had proposed "waiting for full and perfect information before any irretrievable steps shall be taken," but to no avail.[128] A few weeks later, the canal commissioners hired William Strickland, recently returned from England, to evaluate the surveys that had been conducted that summer. Strickland had little difficulty in agreeing with Charles Treziyulney's assessment, in the aftermath of the 1824 surveys, that a summit tunnel was not feasible. Instead, Strickland recommended a series of inclined planes, similar to those employed on British colliery railroads, to lift traffic over the Alleghenies. Strickland's recommendations could hardly come as a shock to Pennsylvanians, for by that time even Mathew Carey had acknowledged that a canal could not be built through the mountains. The cost of the inclined-plane railroad, more than $3 million, nevertheless caused considerable consternation within the legislature, but it failed to stop the momentum of the internal-improvements supporters. On February 8, 1826 the Board of Canal Commissioners issued their initial report to the General Assembly, recommending the immediate construction of canals at the eastern and western ends of the route, and suggesting that the matter of crossing the Alleghenies be resolved at a later date.[129]

Legislators moved quickly to authorize and fund a portion of the Main Line canal. John Sergeant and William Lehman were largely responsible for guiding the internal-improvement bill through the General Assembly. Sergeant apparently did not perceive any conflict of interest in his simultaneous roles as a legislator, as chairman of the Board of Canal Commissioners, and as president of the Society for the Promotion of Internal Improvements. Nor did Lehman, who was also a society member. Sergeant, who was privy to the as-yet unreleased survey data that had been generated during the summer and autumn of 1825, refused to disclose the commission's preferred route for the Main Line canal—ensuring that residents of northern Pennsylvania would continue to support the project, secure in their vain hope that they would be on the principal route to Pittsburgh. Lehman stifled legislative opposition to a bill that would permit the Chesapeake & Ohio Canal to build into southwestern Pennsylvania, a move that ensured him the support of residents of Pittsburgh and the surrounding areas.[130]

On January 16, 1826, three weeks before the commissioners issued their report, the House Committee on Inland Navigation and Internal Improvements introduced "An Act to Provide for the Commencement of a Canal, to be constructed at the Expense of the State, and to be styled 'The Pennsylvania Canal.'" It passed the House by a comfortable majority of sixty-one to thirty-two, and the Senate by a much narrower margin, nineteen votes to fourteen. On February 25, 1826, Governor Shulze, despite his reservations regarding the nebulous nature of the proposed route, signed the bill into law. The members of the General Assembly had appropriated $300,000 to begin work on canals linking Philadelphia to Pittsburgh and Lake Erie. The bill, a product of adroit political compromise, provided only three specific indications of where the canals would actually be located. The Eastern Division of the Pennsylvania Canal, along the Susquehanna River between Middletown and Duncan's Island, would link the western terminus of the Union Canal with the mouth of the Juniata River, and it would be used regardless of whether the ultimate route followed

the Juniata or the West Branch of the Susquehanna. The Western Division, from Pittsburgh to Freeport, at the mouth of the Kiskiminetas River, was likewise vital to the Main Line, no matter whether it continued east toward the Conemaugh or followed a more northerly route, in order to connect with the West Branch of the Susquehanna. A short, disconnected section of canal in northwestern Pennsylvania, known as the French Creek Feeder, would likewise be useful, regardless of the choice between two possible routes linking Pittsburgh and Lake Erie, one via the Allegheny River and the other via the Beaver and Shenango rivers. Neither the legislators nor the canal commissioners had made any provision for filling in the gaps between the sections, largely because engineers had not yet agreed on a route through the area. A few weeks later, on April 1, 1826, the General Assembly passed the Internal Improvement Fund Act, which provided an administrative mechanism for collecting and distributing the monies necessary to undertake construction. The act empowered the commonwealth to issue $300,000 in bonds, with the expectation that canal revenues would be sufficient to pay the interest on the debt and eventually to retire the principal.[131]

To the disappointment of the Branch Men, the General Assembly did not initially include funds for the construction of the feeder canals. Legislators emphasized the danger posed by Baltimore and insisted that Pennsylvania's resources should be concentrated on a single transportation artery. The Branch Men soon insisted upon their share of the commonwealth's largess and reminded the canal commissioners of their obligations, under the 1825 act, to conduct a series of surveys throughout Pennsylvania. On April 10, barely six weeks after the passage of the internal improvement bill, the General Assembly increased the number of canal commissioners from five to nine. The additional appointees were all Branch Men who soon put pressure on legislators for additional construction. Almost precisely a year later, on April 9, 1827, Governor Shulze signed a bill that provided the additional funding necessary to continue construction on the Main Line of Public Works—and to do so very much more.[132]

The 1827 bill committed the commonwealth to a massive system of internal improvements, well before the Main Line of Public Works could be completed and before any of its tolls could flow into the state treasury. Legislators authorized the issuance of a further $1 million in state bonds, allocated to additional construction at numerous locations. On the Main Line of Public Works, the projects included forty-five miles of the Juniata Division, paralleling its namesake river, westward from Duncan's Island to Lewistown, as well as forty-four miles of the Western Division, from the junction of the Kiskiminetas and Allegheny rivers to Blairsville. Legislators also funded numerous projects that played no role in a grand east-west canal across the commonwealth. They included the Susquehanna Division, from Duncan's Island thirty-nine miles north to Northumberland, where the river split into its East and West Branches. Although Jacob Cist had died in December 1825, at the age of forty-three, his fellow Wyoming Valley anthracite producers had collected the political debt associated with their earlier support of the Main Line of Public Works. The legislation also provided for a plethora of surveys across the length and breadth of the commonwealth, placating the interests of the Branch Men. Some of the survey parties explored routes that possessed at least some commercial potential, while a great many more merely satisfied local constituents who saw no reason why they, too, should not have access to a canal.[133]

Thereafter, the canal projects multiplied with astonishing rapidity. On March 24, 1828, the General Assembly funded the extension of the Juniata Division, as far west as Huntingdon, and the Western Division nearly to Johnstown. Legislators also approved surveys for two rail lines, the Allegheny Portage Railroad and the Philadelphia & Columbia Railroad, the first reflecting the impossibility of constructing a canal over the summit of the Alleghenies, and the second as a substitute for the Union Canal, a waterway now deemed inadequate for the volume of traffic expected to flow across the Main Line. The Delaware Division, the most sensible portion of the entire system of publicly funded internal improvements, would provide access to the anthracite region north of Philadelphia, intersecting the Lehigh Navigation at Easton, and running sixty miles south along the Pennsylvania

side of the Delaware River to Bristol. Other projects included the new West Branch and North Branch divisions along the two arms of the Susquehanna River, as well as numerous local feeder canals and navigation improvements.[134]

In common with many other states, Pennsylvania's internal-improvement expenditures mushroomed during the late 1820s and into the 1830s. When Andrew Jackson emerged victorious in the 1828 presidential election, a large number of Jacksonians rode his coattails into the Pennsylvania legislature. In April 1829, the new majority purged the incumbent canal commissioners and appointed party loyalists to take their place. They were mostly Branch Men from rural areas, and they intensified the pressure to blanket the commonwealth with a network of canals of doubtful utility. The legislature's accompanying internal-improvement bill proved so extravagant that Governor Shulze elected to veto the measure. A compromise limiting funding to a still-substantial $2.2 million mattered little. Through the summer, the commonwealth failed to place the new bonds and was in danger of defaulting on those that had been issued earlier. That October, Jacksonian democrat George Wolf won the race for governor, while urging fiscal restraint. Once in office, however, Wolf bowed to political realities and vowed to expand the system of public works. He supported modest tax increases and benefited from a generally prosperous economy, so much so that Pennsylvania's bond issues sold at premiums of up to 15 percent—enough to offset interest payments and make it seem that the projects could be constructed for less money than anticipated. In March 1831, legislators funded initial construction on the Allegheny Portage Railroad and the Philadelphia & Columbia Railroad, a southward extension of the Eastern Division, from Middletown to Columbia, necessary now that a railroad was to substitute for the Union Canal. The Wyoming Line of the North Branch Division would continue a canal past Wilkes-Barre and on toward the New York state line.[135] Money also became available for the completion of the Juniata Division to its western terminus at Hollidaysburg. Residents of northwestern Pennsylvania would benefit from the Beaver Division, part of a plan to link the Ohio River to Lake Erie. Nor was that the limit of as-

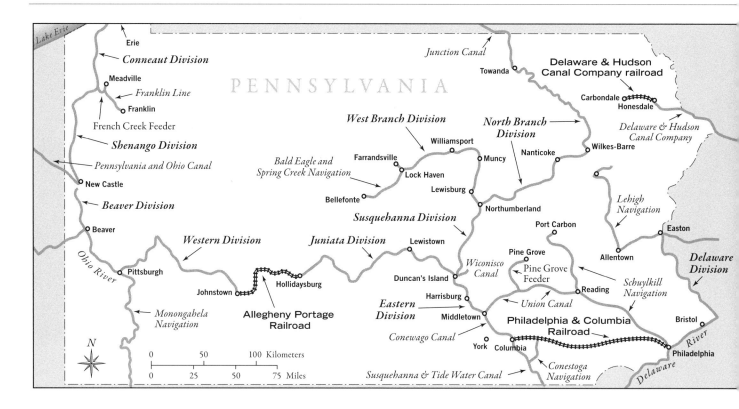

sistance for the latest round of canal and road projects, which would be paid for by almost $2.5 million in new state bonds.[136]

Loan followed loan, until by 1835, the commonwealth had spent $12 million on the 395-mile route linking Philadelphia and Pittsburgh, and an additional $6.5 million on 134 miles of local canals. The goal of building a cross-state transportation link had swollen to include proposals for 934 miles of canals, railways, and river improvements, equivalent to the distance between Philadelphia and a point nearly fifty miles to the west of St. Louis, Missouri. The compromise between the Main Liners and the Branch Men, far from offering victory for both sides, instead portended doom for Pennsylvania's now overly ambitious and exceedingly costly public works program. In 1831, with construction well under way, the energetic instigator Mathew Carey had wisely excused himself from further involvement with a project that had grown out of control and had exceeded even his most enthusiastic recommendations. "This system," he warned, "was moulded by the prevalence of local interests, in violation of the plain dictates of sound policy," and he wanted no more part of it.[137]

While some of the canal proposals never proceeded beyond the planning stages, the commonwealth nevertheless spent $53.4 million on internal improvements between 1826 and 1842—an amount of money that was nearly thirty times the state's debt at the beginning of 1826. That was more money than New York—indeed more money than any other state—had committed to the development of its transportation infrastructure. Unlike their counterparts in New York, moreover, Pennsylvania legislators refused to levy new taxes in order to fund construction. Instead, they issued state bonds to banks, and the banks in turn used the bonds to underwrite the issuance of bank notes. Everyone involved in the process expected that revenues from canal traffic—which, in hindsight, were based on overly optimistic traffic projections—would pay the interest on the loans. The Board of Canal Commissioners would construct the most important part of the system—the Main Line of Public Works—under a funding mechanism that would not generate any income until the entire route was essentially complete. It was, in short, a recipe for disaster.[138]

Figure 4. During the 1820s and into the 1830s, the Pennsylvania legislature developed and began to implement plans for an elaborate system of canals, railroads, and river improvements, designed largely to placate both the "Main Liners" and the "Branch Men." The Main Line of Public Works, spanning the state between Philadelphia and Pittsburgh, included the Philadelphia & Columbia Railroad; the Eastern Division, Juniata Division, and Western Division of the Pennsylvania Canal; and the Allegheny Portage Railroad. Other important state projects included the Susquehanna Division (built between 1827 and 1830), from a connection with the Eastern Division, at Duncan's Island, along the west bank of the Susquehanna River to Northumberland. The West Branch Division (built between 1828 and 1835), followed the west branch of the Susquehanna River from Northumberland as far as Farrandsville, although plans to extend the canal to the upper reaches of the Allegheny River were never implemented. Work on the North Branch Division began in 1828, with subsequent extensions not finished until 1856, carrying traffic along the north branch of the Susquehanna River between Northumberland and a connection with the Junction Canal at the New York state line. The Wiconisco Canal (begun by the state, and completed by private investors) followed the east bank of the Susquehanna River, between Duncan's Island and Millersburg. In the western part of the state, the Beaver Division, the Shenango Division, and the Conneaut Division linked the Ohio River to Lake Erie. The three canals were collectively known as the Beaver & Erie Canal, with the northernmost section completed by a private firm, the Erie Canal Company. The French Creek Feeder supplied water to the Beaver & Erie Canal, while the Franklin Line began just north of Meadville, intersected the French Creek Feeder, and continued southward to the Allegheny River, at Franklin. The Delaware Division, an important anthracite carrier, paralleled its namesake river from Easton to Bristol. With the exception of the Delaware Division, none of the state's canals would be as successful as their privately owned counterparts, which included the Schuylkill Navigation, the Lehigh Coal & Navigation Company's canal (often referred to simply as the Lehigh Navigation), and the Delaware & Hudson Canal. The Union Canal, also privately owned, carried traffic between the Schuylkill Navigation at Reading, and the Susquehanna River (and the Eastern Division Canal) at Middletown, a short distance south of Harrisburg. The Susquehanna & Tide Water Canal, built between 1836 and 1840, carried substantial traffic from Columbia south to Chesapeake Bay, to the benefit of Baltimore. Following the completion of the Chesapeake & Delaware Canal (not shown on this map) in 1829, water traffic could continue on to Philadelphia, transforming both the Susquehanna River and the Susquehanna & Tide Water Canal from liabilities to assets for Philadelphia.

Chapter 2

Commonwealth

1826–1846

On January 3, 1842, Charles Dickens and his wife, Catherine Hogarth Dickens, boarded the steamship *Britannia*, bound for the United States. Not yet thirty years old, Dickens was already a celebrity on both sides of the Atlantic, made famous by the publication of such early works as *The Pickwick Papers* and *Oliver Twist*. Dickens received a warm welcome from the pillars of American society, yet he seemingly preferred to spend a good portion of his time in the United States mingling with the ordinary folk whose growing political power had been reflected in Andrew Jackson's presidency. Dickens's *American Notes*, published in October 1842, mercilessly skewered the manners and morals of ordinary Americans, so much so that he found it advisable to note in the preface, "Prejudiced, I am not, and never have been, otherwise than in favour of the United States." While in many respects critical of the American experience, *American Notes* nonetheless reflected Dickens's respect for the potential of the United States, its people, and their technological and political achievements.[1]

It was hardly surprising that Dickens traveled over Pennsylvania's Main Line of Public Works, a route that simultaneously embodied the skill of some of the best civil engineers and surveyors in the United States, while reflecting the extraordinary confluence of politi-

cal forces that became necessary to bring the project to fruition. By diffusing the economic benefits associated with improved transportation, Pennsylvania had created the Main Line for the universal benefit of the commonweal, or so many of the project's supporters had claimed. Yet, Dickens's presence on canal boats and on the cars of the Allegheny Portage Railroad was indicative of the disappointing results associated with that monumental civil engineering project. Dickens traveled west on the Main Line of Public Works because he was a curious tourist, not because he wanted to reach Pittsburgh efficiently. Most other travelers, particularly those as affluent as Dickens, preferred to travel other routes, bypassing large portions—or even the entirety—of the Main Line of Public Works. Furthermore, the scenes that Dickens observed bespoke the failure of the state system to direct commerce toward Philadelphia, or to generate the economic prosperity that its promoters had envisioned.

Dickens had earlier visited Washington, D.C., and Virginia—he had thought it imperative to see a slave state—and he reached the state capital in Harrisburg by stagecoach from Baltimore, bypassing the Philadelphia & Columbia Railroad. He "emerged upon the streets of Harrisburg, whose feeble lights, reflected dismally from the wet ground, did not shine out upon a very cheerful city," before boarding "a barge with a little

Figure 5. The Main Line of Public Works linked Philadelphia and Pittsburgh, and the Pennsylvania Railroad would later follow much of that route. A combination of political and engineering considerations prevented the construction of a canal between Philadelphia and the Susquehanna River, at Columbia. Instead, the Commonwealth of Pennsylvania constructed the Philadelphia & Columbia Railroad, the longest double-track railroad in the world at the time of its completion. Engineers built inclined planes at each end of the route in order to lift cars out of the valleys of the Schuylkill and Susquehanna rivers. After departing the eastern terminus, freight and passengers crossed the Schuylkill River on the Columbia Bridge (visible at upper center), then gained 187 feet in elevation by traversing the 2,805-foot-long Belmont inclined plane. By the end of 1850, the completion of the West Philadelphia Railroad and the extension of the City Railroad across the Schuylkill Permanent Bridge enabled the Philadelphia & Columbia to abandon the plane. Philadelphia's West Fairmount Park occupies the site today.

J. C. Wild, From the Inclined Plane near Philadelphia, 1838, Temple University Libraries, Urban Archives, Philadelphia.

house in it," as Dickens described the canal boat. Departure was delayed until the arrival of travelers who had come by train from Philadelphia, along the Philadelphia & Columbia and the Harrisburg, Portsmouth, Mount Joy & Lancaster railroads. The new passengers boarded the canal boat, adding "a great many boxes, which were bumped and tossed upon the roof, almost as painfully as if they had been deposited on one's own head." A steady rain beat down as the boat moved slowly toward Hollidaysburg, giving Dickens the chance to examine closely his fellow travelers, as if he and they were in "one of those . . . museums of penny wonders."

Dickens had ample opportunity to comment at length on the coarseness and vulgarity of the Americans who were his traveling companions—a common theme that ran throughout *American Notes*. His bemusement at the behavior of his rustic American cousins only increased with nightfall, as he confronted "three long tiers of hanging bookshelves, designed apparently for volumes of the small octavo size," that turned out to be sleeping berths. After appropriating "a sort of microscopic sheet and blanket," the Englishman settled into a bunk "just the width of an ordinary sheet of Bath post letter-paper." He noted that some attempts had been made to observe sexual propriety, with a red curtain separating the men from the sleeping area assigned to the women—"though as every cough, or sneeze, or whisper, behind this curtain, was perfectly audible before it, we had still a lively consciousness of their society." Dickens spent an anxious night staring upward at the sagging bulk of "a very heavy gentleman above me, whom the slender cords seemed quite incapable of holding; and I could not help reflecting upon the grief of my wife and family in the event of his coming down in the night." Sleep was impossible, in any event, as "All night long, and every night, on this canal, there was a perfect storm and tempest of spitting." Dickens's account of his travails was not, strictly speaking, accurate—the boat's captain had graciously given up his quarters in order to ensure the comfort of his distinguished guest—but such passages nonetheless reflected the inconvenience and irritation that most passengers experienced.

The next day's trip along the Allegheny Portage Railroad proved even more unnerving. As he traveled over the spine of the Appalachians, Dickens described the inclined planes and "the comparatively level spaces between, being traversed, sometimes by horse, and sometimes by engine power, as the case demands." Dickens nonetheless emphasized the pastoral, with each "valley full of light and softness" as he rode "onward, high above them, like a whirlwind." Even the steam locomotive seemed less like a mechanical monster than "a great insect, its back of green and gold so shining in the sun." There were still terrors aplenty,

however, particularly when "the rails are laid upon the extreme verge of a giddy precipice; and looking from the carriage window, the traveler gazes sheer down, without a stone or scrap of fence between, into the mountain depths below."

Once at Johnstown, safely out of the mountains, Dickens experienced the vagaries of the service provided on the Main Line of Public Works. He had earlier traveled along the Juniata Division Canal on the Express Line, at Hollidaysburg catching up to the passengers who had purchased tickets on the cheaper and slower Pioneer Line, and riding with them over the mountains. Once on the Western Division Canal, the more fortunate Express Line passengers had been promised their own boat to Pittsburgh, yet more than forty-five people were unceremoniously herded onto the same vessel with their poorer brethren. As a visitor to the United States, Dickens was willing to endure such mistreatment, but a Mississippian so browbeat the vessel's operators that they returned to the canal basin and forced a goodly number of Pioneer Line passengers to disembark and wait for the next boat.

Yet, Dickens relished his canal ride: "The fast, brisk walk upon the towing-path, between that time and breakfast, when every vein and artery seemed to tingle with health; the exquisite beauty of the opening day, when light came gleaming off from everything; the lazy motion of the boat, when one lay idly on the deck, looking through, rather than at, the deep blue sky; the gliding on at night, so noiselessly, past frowning hills, sullen with dark trees, and sometimes angry in one red, burning spot high up, where unseen men lay crouching round a fire; the shining out of the bright stars undisturbed by noise of wheels or steam, or any other sound than the limpid rippling of the water as the boat went on: all these were pure delights."

Pittsburgh offered a gritty contrast to the pastoral idyll that characterized rural Pennsylvania. Dickens noted that the city was "like Birmingham in England; at least its townspeople say so," but his first view was of "that ugly confusion of backs of buildings and crazy galleries and stairs, which always abuts on water." After a delay of three days, Dickens departed for Cincinnati on the steamboat *Messenger*, leaving the Keystone State in his wake.

In his journey across Pennsylvania, Dickens acknowledged the grandness of the American landscape and the character of its people—even if many of the latter became subjects for his satirical humor—but he also observed that the economic prosperity that the Main Line of Public Works was supposed to generate had proven elusive. Mile after mile, he floated by "cab-ins with simple ovens, outside, made of clay; and lodgings for the pigs nearly as good as many of the human quarters; broken windows, patched with worn-out hats, old clothes, old boards, fragments of blankets and paper; and home-made dressers standing in the

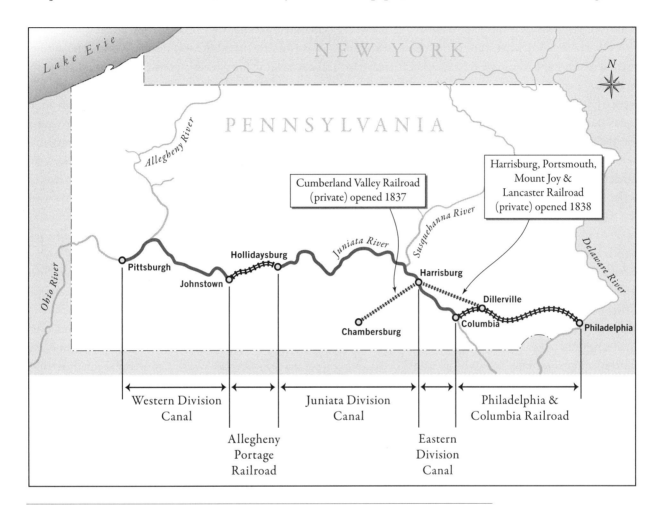

Figure 6. The Main Line of Public Works was the central spine of Pennsylvania's widespread network of internal improvements. The Philadelphia & Columbia Railroad traversed Chester and Lancaster Counties. The Eastern Division Canal followed the Susquehanna River, linking Columbia with the mouth of the Juniata River at Duncan's Island, a short distance north of Harrisburg. The Juniata Division followed its namesake river as far west as Hollidaysburg, at the foot of the Alleghenies. Horses and eventually locomotives drew trains over the level sections of the Allegheny Portage Railroad, while inclined planes raised and lowered cars on the steeper sections. West of Johnstown, the Western Division Canal paralleled the Conemaugh and Kiskimine-tas rivers to Freeport, on the Allegheny River. The canal then followed the north bank of the river to Allegheny City, with an aqueduct carrying boats across the river into Pittsburgh. During the 1830s, entrepreneurs built two private railroads, the Harrisburg, Portsmouth, Mount Joy & Lan-caster, between Dillerville (Lancaster) and Harrisburg, and the Cumberland Valley, between Har-risburg and Chambersburg. In conjunction with the state-owned Philadelphia & Columbia, they offered all-rail service from Philadelphia to the state capital and west toward a turnpike connec-tion to Pittsburgh, offering stiff competition for the Main Line of Public Works.

open air without the door." Observing the destruction associated with slash-and-burn agriculture, Dickens lamented that "The eye was pained to see the stumps of great trees thickly strewn in every field of wheat, and seldom to lose the eternal swamp and dull morass, with hundreds of rotten trunks and twisted branches steeped in its unwholesome water."

Even though Dickens and many other travelers praised the engineering marvels associated with the Main Line of Public Works, Pennsylvania residents were increasingly concerned that the canals and railroads had not produced adequate economic benefits for the commonwealth. The Main Line never competed effectively against the Erie Canal, and never fulfilled the expectations of publisher Mathew Carey and other Philadelphia boosters who had hoped to divert the western trade to their city. Debt piled upon debt, as the state struggled to build, maintain, and operate a poorly conceived transportation network. The public system of internal improvements drove the commonwealth to the brink of bankruptcy and suggested to many people that the government was unable to manage a transportation enterprise. During the 1840s, their arguments would provide a powerful incentive for the supporters of the privately owned Pennsylvania Railroad, a new transportation artery that largely paralleled the discredited Main Line of Public Works.

The Pennsylvania Canal

On Independence Day 1826, sixteen years before Charles Dickens glided slowly across Pennsylvania, construction began on the transportation artery that had made possible his voyage. Not far from the capitol building in Harrisburg, Governor John Andrew Shulze ceremoniously turned over the first spade of earth to begin construction of the Eastern Division Canal, paralleling the Susquehanna River. After years of often-acrimonious debate, work had finally begun on the three sections of the Pennsylvania Canal. The Eastern, Juniata, and Western divisions, in conjunction with rail links in the eastern and western parts of the state, were to form the Main Line of Public Works, Pennsylvania's most ambitious attempt at internal improvement.[2]

The timing was perfect, as the completion of the Erie Canal the year before made available a plethora of highly trained engineers and surveyors. In December 1825, the canal commissioners had asked William Strickland, one of the best in the business, to serve as a consultant and to evaluate the initial canal surveys, made earlier that year. Strickland had no experience on the Erie Canal, but he was a supremely talented engineer and, of considerable political importance, he was well respected in his native Philadelphia. By the following March, the commissioners had hired Strickland, at the princely salary of $3,000 per year, to locate portions of the canal. Other key personnel included Nathan S. Roberts, designer of the flight of locks that carried the Erie Canal up the Niagara Escarpment; James Geddes, who had been one of the earliest advocates of the Erie Canal and one of its leading construction experts; Major David B. Douglass, a West Point–trained engineer and veteran of the War of 1812; and Canvass White, who had established a reputation as one of the best canal engineers in the United States. His talented protégé, Sylvester Welch, likewise obtained work with the Board of Canal Commissioners. John Randel, Jr., best known for his imposition of a grid plan on Manhattan Island, had conducted surveys on both the Delaware & Raritan Canal and the Chesapeake & Delaware Canal, and he also brought his considerable expertise to bear on the project. DeWitt Clinton, Jr., the son of the man widely hailed as the "Father of the Erie Canal," took charge of the Juniata Division.[3]

Yet, the cost-conscious members of the General Assembly soon alienated their most experienced employees. In April 1827, less than a year after construction commenced, legislators sharply reduced the salaries of their engineers (from $3,000 to $2,000 per year) and imposed an absolute prohibition on outside consulting. Roberts, Geddes, Douglass, and most of the others departed for greener pastures.[4] Strickland protested, resigned his post, and was willing to serve only as an unpaid consultant, presumably with little interest in the success of the project. The few engineers who remained, and the legion of new hires, proved less adept than their predecessors. More important, the transition and the resultant loss of the initial knowledge base slowed construction and greatly increased the likelihood of engineering errors.[5]

Some five thousand laborers, many of them recent Irish immigrants, faced substantial hardships as they dug their way across Pennsylvania. Mathew Carey, who had become something of a social reformer, informed his fellow citizens that canal workers were virtually destitute, unable to earn enough to support their families. "It is almost certain, that among the whole number employed, five percent return to their families in the winter," he protested, "with broken constitutions, by fevers and agues, one half of whom are carried off to an untimely grave."[6] The greatest horror appeared during the summer of 1832, as a cholera epidemic swept through Pennsylvania, killing nearly a thousand people in Philadelphia and many more along the nearly complete Pennsylvania Canal.[7]

Despite such hardships, construction proceeded with considerable speed. Workers excavated a shallow ditch, four feet deep, twenty-eight feet wide at the base, and forty feet wide at the waterline—a prism that was essentially identical to that of the Erie Canal.[8] Each lock—and there were 162 of them over the 274 miles of canal—was ninety feet long and between fifteen and seventeen feet in width, with an average lift of about seven feet. The original plans called for substantial stone locks, but the enormous expense of the project—compounded by the political necessity of building a plethora of canals to satisfy the demands of the Branch Men—induced significant cost-cutting measures. Wooden locks predominated, and the canal commissioners hoped that the Main Line, once in service, would generate enough revenue to replace the locks before they rotted away.[9]

The Eastern Division, which entered service in April 1833, paralleled the Susquehanna River for forty-three miles. Initially, the Board of Canal Commissioners envisioned a route between Middletown, at the western end of the Union Canal, some twenty-four miles north to the mouth of the Juniata River, at Duncan's Island. By 1828, however, the decision to bypass the Union Canal and the Schuylkill Navigation in favor of the Philadelphia & Columbia Railroad had forced construction crews to begin much farther to the south, at Columbia. Even with the added length, however, the gradual descent of the Susquehanna River ensured that only fourteen locks were necessary. At the canal's northern extremity, a dam at Clark's

Ferry impounded sufficient water to enable boats to cross to the west bank of the Susquehanna River and enter the Juniata Division Canal. Once on the west side of the Susquehanna River, boats could also proceed northward, along the Susquehanna Division to Northumberland.[10]

The Juniata Division followed its namesake river almost due west to Hollidaysburg, at the base of the Allegheny Mountains. Construction began in 1827, and by November 1832 all 127 miles were in service. The route began on the north side of the Juniata River, where an aqueduct carried boats to the south bank. They then headed west, along a combination of canals and slackwater navigation. A series of eighty-eight locks—one every mile and a half, on average, lifted boats a total of 582 feet en route to Hollidaysburg.[11]

On the other side of the Allegheny Mountains, more than thirty miles to the west of Hollidaysburg, the Western Division carried traffic another 104 water miles, and through an additional sixty locks, to Pittsburgh. From the canal basin at Johnstown, the Conemaugh River provided a route out of the mountains. Once joined by Loyalhanna Creek, at Saltsburg, the Conemaugh became the Kiskiminetas River, which led boats to the Allegheny River at Freeport. Along the way, the canal passed through a ridge at the aptly named site of Tunnelton. The 817-foot tunnel, which workers completed in 1829, was only the third in the United States, and its portal opened onto a spectacular 412-foot-long viaduct over the Conemaugh River. Further west, canal engineers chose the north bank of the Allegheny River, disappointing Pittsburgh residents who had initially demanded that the canal follow the south shore, directly to their city. At Allegheny City, canal engineers constructed a massive aqueduct—one of sixteen on the Western Division—to carry boats to Pittsburgh's canal basin, at 11th Street between Liberty Street and Penn Avenue. By May 1831, the Western Division was complete, from Pittsburgh to Johnstown—and was soon wrecked by floods that kept long stretches of the canal out of service for most of the remainder of the navigation season. In August 1832, workers finished a tunnel under Grant's Hill, providing canal boats with expensive and infrequently used access to the Monongahela River.[12]

The Philadelphia & Columbia Railroad

The canal commissioners initially envisioned that canals would make up virtually the entire route across Pennsylvania, save for a railroad that would span the short distance over the summit of the Alleghenies. Yet, a combination of engineering and political considerations ensured that the state would build a second railroad, between Philadelphia and Columbia, vastly increasing the difficulty and expense associated with shipping goods along the Main Line of Public Works. East of the Susquehanna River, the Schuylkill Navigation and the Union Canal were already in service between Philadelphia and Middletown, and most early supporters of internal improvements assumed that they would constitute a critical portion of a cross-state route. However, while the Schuylkill Navigation route between Philadelphia and Reading had proven itself capable of handling considerable quantities of traffic, the Union Canal was another matter entirely. Initially, it was prone to seepage and difficult to keep filled with water. The more significant problem was that its locks were far too narrow and incapable of accommodating large boats.[13]

Still, the extant Union Canal could have been improved and pressed into service as part of the Main Line of Public Works. In fact, it *was* improved, between 1841 and 1858, and carried considerable traffic until it was finally abandoned in 1884. Even after the completion of the Main Line of Public Works, respectable quantities of freight continued to flow along the two canals, between Philadelphia and Middletown, bypassing the more expensive tariffs of the Philadelphia & Columbia Railroad.[14]

Politics, as much as engineering considerations, precluded the use of the Schuylkill Navigation and the Union Canal. Residents of prosperous and densely populated Chester and Lancaster counties demanded access to the Main Line of Public Works, and their representatives refused to support the project unless it followed a more southerly alignment. By the spring of 1827, the Canal Commission had abandoned the possibility of employing the Schuylkill and Union canals, and instead resolved to construct a new canal from Philadelphia to Columbia.[15]

The Board of Canal Commissioners assigned to Major John Wilson the task of locating a southerly canal route between Philadelphia and the Susquehanna River. Wilson was born in Scotland, the son of an engineering officer in the 71st Regiment (Highlanders) of the British Army. The American Revolution soon sent the family across the Atlantic, with the elder Wilson posted at Savannah and Charleston. The father was seriously wounded at Charleston and remained there for a time, marrying the daughter of another Scotsman who was residing in the city. The family returned to Scotland, where his son received formal engineering training at the University of Edinburgh. John Wilson, Sr., died in 1807, probably as a result of his wartime injuries, and his widow moved the family back to Charleston. Ten years later, Secretary of War John C. Calhoun recommended the younger Wilson for the job of improving the harbor fortifications at Charleston. When the Army reassigned Wilson to a new post at Nashville, he resigned his commission, perhaps because he disapproved of his new commanding officer, General Andrew Jackson, or perhaps because he preferred not to move his family to an isolated frontier outpost. Wilson worked on a variety of civil engineering projects, serving for a time as chief engineer of the South Carolina Board of Public Works, yet the exposure to tropical diseases ruined his health. In 1826, Wilson moved his family north, in a vain attempt to recuperate, and was willing to accept work from the Pennsylvania Board of Canal Commissioners. He never fully recovered, and he died in 1833, on board a ship anchored in the harbor at Matanzas, Cuba.[16]

The summer of 1827 had just begun when Wilson led his fifteen-year-old son, along with a surveyor, a leveler, a rodman, two chainmen, and a pair of axmen, west out of Philadelphia.[17] They traveled past the battlefield at Valley Forge and into the broad uplands of Chester County, paralleling the great Lancaster Turnpike that had ushered so many Conestoga wagons and their cargoes toward the western frontier. The axmen had little to do at first, as the party passed through one of the richest and most densely populated agricultural regions in the United States. The two chainmen presumably had plenty to do, regardless of the topography, as they worked their way, sixty-six feet at a time, across Pennsylvania. The pair included a young John Edgar Thomson, who obtained a very practical indoctrination into the mysteries of civil engineering while learning the route in intimate detail, a quarter-century before he became the president of the Pennsylvania Railroad.[18]

By the time the party reached the Lancaster County community of Gap, the aptly named divide between the Chester and Conestoga valleys, the chief engineer had realized that a canal was impracticable. The terrain was hillier than expected, but the fatal problem stemmed from the absence of a reliable water source. The surveyors touched the Susquehanna River at Middletown, about ten miles downstream from Harrisburg, then worked their way eighteen miles farther south to Columbia, more convinced than ever that a railway offered the only practical solution to the constraints imposed by both geography and politics. By December 1827, Wilson had presented his findings to the Canal Commission, emphasizing that a canal would be costly and difficult to construct, would be impeded by numerous locks, would be forced to bypass the city of Lancaster, and could only reach the Delaware River at a point approximately ten miles to the south of Philadelphia, and then only by traversing the state of Delaware.[19]

Three months later, on March 24, 1828, the members of the General Assembly abandoned any possibility of building a canal through southeastern Pennsylvania and instead adopted "An act relative to the Pennsylvania Canal, and to provide for the commencement of a railroad" between Philadelphia and Columbia.[20] The canal commissioners divided the eighty-two-mile route into mile-long contract sections, as they had done on the Pennsylvania Canal. They appointed J. Edgar Thomson as the principal assistant engineer for the line, in charge of the Eastern Division and responsible for overseeing the work of the contractors who built each section of the route. By December 1829, however, the commonwealth was finding few takers for its improvement bonds, and called a halt to further construction. Both Thomson and Wilson departed for the Camden & Amboy Rail Road, a line that would itself eventually become a part of the PRR system. By early 1831, the funding crisis had eased somewhat, enabling the canal commissioners to order crews back into the field.[21]

By September 1832, construction crews had managed to lay only twenty miles of track. Their pace quickened thereafter, and crews completed the line through to the canal basin at Columbia in April 1834.

On Tuesday, April 15, 1834, the canal commissioners, legislators (most of whom were returning home after the end of the session), and other invited guests traveled south from Harrisburg on the canal boat *Washington*. When they reached Columbia, the locomotive *Black Hawk* was waiting to convey them to Lancaster. At eight o'clock the following morning, the party left Lancaster and continued east, all the way to Philadelphia, in eight and a half hours.[22]

Even with the completion of the Philadelphia & Columbia Railroad, travel between Philadelphia and the Susquehanna River was far from easy. At its eastern end, the Philadelphia & Columbia stopped at the boundary of Philadelphia, with several other lines carrying traffic to the city center and to the docks that lined the Delaware River. The privately owned Northern Liberties & Penn Township Railroad, incorporated in April 1829, by 1835 had constructed a line along Noble and Willow streets, east to the wharves that lined the Delaware River, to the north of the city. Many Philadelphians expressed grave concerns that the Northern Liberties & Penn Township would divert trade away from the city proper. In January 1833, under pressure from merchants, the Philadelphia City Councils approved the construction of the publicly owned City Railroad. That line, completed in December, began at Cedar (later, South) Street, at the city's southern boundary, and followed Broad Street north to Vine Street, the northern border of the city and the beginning of the Philadelphia & Columbia route. In 1837, and despite pressure from some storeowners to halt work and tear up the tracks, workers completed an extension of the City Railroad, from Broad Street along Market, Third, and Dock streets, to the Delaware River waterfront. A third carrier, the Southwark Rail-Road, chartered in 1831 and completed in 1835, followed Broad Street from Philadelphia's southern boundary at Cedar Street south to Prime Street (today's Washington Avenue) and then ran along Prime Street east to the docks along the Delaware River, south of the city.[23]

Most passengers began their westward journey on the City Railroad. There was no central freight or passenger station, however. Many passenger lines that offered service over the Northern Liberties & Penn Township Railroad used as their station a tavern at the intersection of Third Street and Willow. The City

Railroad also operated a facility along Market Street. Horses pulled passenger and burden (freight) cars through city streets, joining Philadelphia & Columbia tracks at Broad and Vine. The cars continued north on Broad Street to Noble Street, then west, and northwest, past the future site of East Fairmount Park and the Philadelphia Museum of Art. Well to the northwest of the city, the tracks crossed the Schuylkill River on the 1,040-foot-long Columbia Bridge, completed in 1834.[24]

At the western end of the Columbia Bridge, the Philadelphia & Columbia connected with a prosperous railway that would later become a significant regional competitor of the Pennsylvania Railroad. By the early 1830s, many prominent residents of southeastern Pennsylvania, including attorney Thomas Sergeant and banker Nicholas Biddle, had concluded that the Schuylkill Navigation was no longer adequate for the supply of anthracite to Philadelphia. In April 1833, they obtained a charter for the Philadelphia & Reading Rail Road. The first stockholders' meeting took place on November 22, 1834, and on the same day the Reading's directors chose Moncure Robinson as chief engineer. Robinson designed a superb route, ensuring that southbound coal trains did not face any adverse grades along their entire journey from the anthracite fields to Philadelphia.[25] At Port Richmond, to the north of Philadelphia's city limits, he laid out what was to become a massive facility for transferring coal to ships and barges.[26] In December 1839, the line between Reading and Philadelphia opened for business, and the Reading Rail Road was soon funneling traffic from the anthracite regions to tidewater. The Reading's timing was propitious, as the first successful use of anthracite in a blast furnace took place in October 1839, two months prior to the railroad's completion. Soon thereafter, anthracite replaced charcoal as the preferred fuel for the smelting of iron. The Reading's traffic increased rapidly and so too did revenues, outstripping even the most optimistic projections of the company's investors.[27]

A short distance west of the junction with the Reading, the Philadelphia & Columbia relied on the 2,805-foot-long Belmont inclined plane, in what is today West Fairmount Park, that elevated cars 187 feet out of the Schuylkill River Valley, on a one-in-fifteen grade. The tracks headed west, following the Lancaster Turnpike (later the Lincoln Highway) to the summit of the South Valley Ridge, 543 feet higher in elevation than the city of Philadelphia. After surmounting the South Valley Ridge, west of Paoli, the line traveled downgrade, into the rich farming country of the Chester Valley. Residents of West Chester had demanded that the Philadelphia & Columbia pass directly through their community but their pleas were unsuccessful.[28]

After swinging to the northwest, the tracks reached Gap. Despite a deep cut through the unstable rock strata of Mine Ridge, the area possessed the steepest grades on the entire route. The railroad then again turned west and descended onto the Lancaster Plain. The original Philadelphia & Columbia surveys bypassed Lancaster, the largest city en route, in favor of easier grades to the north. Unlike their counterparts in West Chester, the inhabitants of Lancaster were successful in their demands for direct access to the railroad. Bowing to political considerations, the canal commissioners ordered that the railroad pass through the center of the community, a decision that entailed many years of operating difficulties.[29] To the west of Lancaster, the Philadelphia & Columbia reached the bluffs above the Susquehanna River, where a second incline, 1,800 feet long, lowered cars 90 feet to the Columbia canal basin, at the southern terminus of the Eastern Division of the Pennsylvania Canal.[30]

The Allegheny Portage Railroad

Mathew Carey, like most other early proponents of internal improvements in Pennsylvania, initially envisioned an all-water route, akin to the Erie Canal, that would span the entire distance between Philadelphia and Pittsburgh. The topography along the Erie Canal's route between Albany and Buffalo was radically different from that of western Pennsylvania, however. Boats traversing the Erie Canal rose about 600 feet in elevation, along the 360 miles that separated Albany and Buffalo. The total vertical distance between tidewater at Philadelphia and the crest of the Alleghenies was an astonishing 2,585 feet. Even worse, it was not a slow, steady ascent, but rather a gradual rise, followed

Figure 7. A steam locomotive moves through Lancaster during the early years of the Philadelphia & Columbia Railroad. Any citizen with sufficient capital and ambition could purchase a wagon and a team of horses, similar to the one traveling down North Queen Street. Steam locomotives, however, represented a complex and expensive investment that was clearly beyond the reach of an individual—a situation that concentrated economic and political power in the railroad, and in the government that built, owned, and operated it. Legislators echoed those concerns by permitting independent companies—like the Pioneer Line, with its two buildings at the right of the illustration—to control freight and passenger transportation on both the Philadelphia & Columbia Railroad and the Allegheny Portage Railroad, just as they did on the Pennsylvania Canal. At the left edge of the picture, a type of motive power even more basic than the horse is shifting a freight car. The artist has correctly depicted the Philadelphia & Columbia as a double-track railroad, but with the two tracks sharing a center rail—an obvious technological impossibility indicative of limited public familiarity with the new mode of transportation.

Pennsylvania Historical and Museum Commission, Pennsylvania State Archives.

by a short, steep climb over the mountains. From Hollidaysburg, the western terminus of the Juniata Division of the Pennsylvania Canal, freight and passengers would ascend 1,399 vertical feet to reach the summit. To the west lay a descent of 1,172 feet to the Western Division canal basin at Johnstown.

The earliest surveys over the summit of the Alleghenies, conducted by Charles Treziyulney under the auspices of the Commissioners for the Purpose of Promoting the Internal Improvements of the State, offered little hope that a canal could be built through the area, even with a long tunnel. Those concerns prompted a new round of surveys, and by June 1826, both Governor Shulze and the members of the Canal Commission had acknowledged that the canal tunnel was impossible. The commissioners then debated at length whether a conventional turnpike or a railroad would be the preferred alternative. Their indecision gave an edge to canal supporters in the General Assembly, which by April 1827 had once again ordered the Canal Commission to study the feasibility of a transmountain canal. By December 1827 the canal commissioners had described such a waterway as "utterly impracticable," but legislators remained unconvinced.[31] The following year saw a new set of surveys, under the direction of Nathan S. Roberts. His report, issued on December 1, 1828, acceded to political concerns if not necessarily engineering ones by recommending the construction of both a turnpike and a railroad alongside each other. Roberts and his fellow Erie Canal veterans resigned a week later in protest of the Canal Commission's ban on consultancy fees, consigning their recommendations to obscurity.[32]

In December 1828, Moncure Robinson replaced the departing engineers. He was the individual who would have the greatest influence over the route of what would become the Allegheny Portage Railroad. His stunning success in establishing the alignment of the Philadelphia & Reading Rail Road lay several years in the future, but he had already acquired a reputation as an expert surveyor. A native of Virginia, he had observed the Erie Canal before returning to his home state in order to assist in the development of the James River Canal. Beginning in 1825, he spent more than two years in Europe, studying with eminent engineers and observing the newest transportation innovations. While in Britain, Robinson met Philadelphians Henry Seybert and Nathaniel Chauncey. The two men later provided Robinson the letters of introduction that enabled him to secure a position with the Board of Canal Commissioners.[33]

When Robinson went into the mountains in the spring of 1829, he carried with him the unshakable conviction that a railroad represented the best option for constructing the shortest possible line at the lowest possible summit crossing. As canal proponents had repeatedly observed, however, early railway locomotives were weak and unreliable. Even the most enthusiastic supporters of railways were unwilling to suggest that those underpowered machines would be able to pull trains up a grade of much more than 1 percent. To achieve such a modest ascent over the summit would require an exceptionally long railroad that would loop its way up the sides of hills. The cost of such a line would be inconceivable, and its operation a nightmare. Robinson conceded that a series of inclined planes would be a necessary, if unwelcome, part of the route.[34] On November 21, 1829, in his report to the Board of Canal Commissioners, he proposed a rail tunnel a mile long, in tandem with a series of inclined planes and level sections.[35]

Canal supporters expressed their outrage, both at the introduction of complex inclined planes and at Robinson's support of a tunnel—particularly as the difficulty of its construction was ostensibly the reason for rejecting a canal through the mountains. In March 1830, legislators approved yet another survey. The party included Robinson; an Army surveyor, Lieutenant-Colonel Stephen Harriman Long; and Major John Wilson, the same engineer who had earlier recommended the construction of the Philadelphia & Columbia Railroad in lieu of a canal. The necessity of establishing a connection with the Juniata Division of the Pennsylvania Canal sharply restricted their ability to choose the optimal route over the Allegheny Mountains. Of the seventeen passes in the region, only one—Blair's Gap—was sufficiently proximate to Hollidaysburg to be suitable for the rail route to Johnstown. The three engineers were unanimous in their preference for a railroad, yet they differed substantially as to the route. Robinson continued to favor the summit tunnel that he had first advocated in 1829, while the Army engineers proposed increasing both the distance (by five miles) and the number of inclined planes, while eliminating the summit tunnel and replacing it with a far shorter one, at a lower elevation. The final proposal included ten inclined planes, with the shortest just over 1,600 feet long, and the longest, well over three thousand. Elevation gains ranged from 130 feet to 307 feet, with the steepest incline at slightly less than a 10 percent grade. The eleven intervening level stretches were often quite short—in one case, only 0.15 miles—with the longest at just over thirteen miles. Despite the nomenclature, the levels were not precisely level—they possessed grades of up to one-half of 1 percent—but such mild ascents were well within the capabilities of horses and early steam locomotives.[36]

By the summer of 1830 the situation was becoming desperate, as the canals were nearing completion and no one had reached a decision on how to get people and freight over the mountains. The members of the General Assembly insisted that something be done as quickly as possible, warning that Pennsylvania was in danger of economic ruin. The Main Line of Public Works and the citizens of Pennsylvania paid the price for the initial delay and subsequent panic, for there was too little time left to develop an alternate engineering profile that might have eliminated the inclined planes. On March 21, 1831, five years after his predecessor authorized the construction of the Main Line of Public Works, Governor George Wolf signed into law "An Act to continue the Improvement of the State by Canal and Railroads," providing for a rail route along the lines that Long and Wilson had recommended. Finally, after years of often acrimonious debate, the Board of Canal Commissioners now had the authority to begin construction of a double-track railroad linking the eastern canal basin at Hollidaysburg with its western counterpart at Johnstown.[37]

Some of the most talented surveyors and engineers in the United States were soon at work, supervising the construction of the Allegheny Portage Railroad. Samuel Jones served as superintendent, based on his established responsibilities for the Western Division of the Pennsylvania Canal. Moncure Robinson was a consulting engineer, in cooperation with principal engineer Sylvester Welch, an accomplished veteran of the Erie Canal. Welch had been the principal assistant to chief engineer Canvass White, as part of the Engineer Corps on the Lehigh Canal. Their staff included a young surveyor, Edward Miller, who had graduated from the University of Pennsylvania, with a Mathematical Honor, at the age of seventeen. When Welch accepted the position of principal engineer on the Western Division of the Pennsylvania Canal, in 1829, Miller followed, as his assistant. Miller, only twenty years of age, took charge of the surveys for the Portage Railroad and in 1831 he went to England and Scotland on a fact-finding mission. By the summer of 1832, Miller was the principal assistant engineer and superintendent in charge of machinery on the Allegheny Portage, responsible for designing the stationary steam engines at the top of each inclined plane. Two other principal assistant engineers, both recent veterans of the Lehigh Canal, oversaw the construction and operation of the remainder of the Portage Railroad. William Milnor Roberts was in charge of the area between Hollidaysburg and the summit, and Solomon White Roberts (the two men were not related) possessed oversight of the line from the summit west to Johnstown.[38]

The engineers designed two complex and expensive engineering works. The first was the Staple Bend Tunnel, nineteen miles west of the summit, a double-track, nine-hundred-foot bore necessary to cut off a bend in the Conemaugh River and one of the first railroad tunnels built in the United States.[39] The other was a massive stone arch viaduct, often referred to as the Conemaugh Viaduct or simply as the Big Viaduct, across the Little Conemaugh River at Horseshoe Bend, some eight miles east of Johnstown. The elegant structure, designed by Solomon Roberts, reduced the length of the Allegheny Portage Railroad by fully two miles. A masterpiece of stone arch construction, it later served the Pennsylvania Railroad until 1889, when the Johnstown Flood swept it to oblivion. Those two projects alone cost the commonwealth more than $90,000, consuming nearly 10 percent of the initially estimated $936,000 expense of the Allegheny Portage Railroad. In addition, sixty-eight culverts required the attention of stonemasons, indicative of both the expense and the high quality of initial construction.[40]

On March 18, 1834, the Allegheny Portage Railroad opened for service, with the second track on the levels completed during the latter half of that year.[41] Miller had done a superb job of supervising the construction of the massive steam-powered hoisting engines that lifted cars along the inclined planes.[42] The stationary engines pulled a three-and-a-half-inch-diameter hemp rope across a series of rollers, incrementally dragging cars up one side of the summit and carefully easing them down the other. Even though ropes were changed every season, they still broke with some frequency. Fortunately, railroad officials soon employed single-axle braking cars, typically known as "bucks," that stopped the cars within a few feet, before they could run away down an incline. Experienced travelers nonetheless tended to walk up or down the inclines at a respectable distance from the tracks while the hoisting engines raised or lowered the empty cars.[43]

Unfortunately, the complications associated with the railroad's construction paled in comparison with those associated with its operation. The design of the Allegheny Portage Railroad entailed particularly severe operating difficulties. The disconnected nature of the inclined planes and levels ensured that the movement of one car between Hollidaysburg and Johnstown required the services of fifty-four people (ten stationary engineers and eleven locomotive engineers, twenty-one firemen, and twelve teamsters), operating eleven locomotives, twelve horse teams, and ten stationary engines. Even though cars could cover the thirty-six miles over the mountains in as few as four

hours, traffic often backed up at the inclined planes, which could only accommodate three cars at a time. Freight cars typically required three days to make the round trip between Hollidaysburg and Johnstown. Service was simply unavailable during the winter, when the railroad suspended operations, to match the navigation season on the Pennsylvania Canal.[44]

Pennsylvania legislators, the canal commissioners, and the popular press tended to laud the Allegheny Portage Railroad as a stunning success.[45] Professional engineers were not so certain. Franz Anton Ritter von Gerstner, an Austrian civil engineer who was one of Europe's leading experts on the subject of internal im-

Figure 8. At the time of their construction, the ten inclined planes on the Allegheny Portage Railroad constituted a marvel of civil engineering, but they soon became the weakest link in the Main Line of Public Works. When trains reached the base of the incline, workers would uncouple the cars from horses, or from steam locomotives, for the ascent to the next level section. The three cars shown here represented the maximum capacity of the ropes used on the planes, perhaps twenty-one thousand pounds in all.

Pennsylvania Historical and Museum Commission, Pennsylvania State Archives.

provements, visited the Allegheny Portage Railroad and promptly dubbed it a failure. His was a cautionary tale, and he warned his European audience that the Canal Commission's surveyors had been too economical and too careless in their work, missing completely an alternate low-grade route between Huntingdon and Johnstown. "So the ten inclined planes of the Portage Railroad were unnecessary and could have been avoided easily!" Gerstner observed, noting that the line offered "a striking proof of the fact that a railroad survey can never be carried out with too much care or attentiveness and that much more time and expense should be devoted to studying the terrain than is usually the case."[46]

"They Must Number over One Hundred": The Role of the Freight Forwarders

Far from constituting Pennsylvania's transportation system of the future, the Main Line of Public Works, including the Allegheny Portage Railroad and the Philadelphia & Columbia Railroad, was a throwback to an earlier era. The route functioned much like a turnpike, with commonwealth employees maintaining the infrastructure and private individuals owning and operating the canal boats and railroad cars. Both railroads employed steam locomotives, but horses and mules remained in service as late as December 1850. The legislature did not authorize the Canal Commission to purchase either passenger or freight cars, nor could state employees sell tickets to travelers.[47] Instead, on both railroads, the canal commissioners contracted with the companies that were responsible for freight and passenger transportation. That was indeed an odd state of affairs, as Governor David Rittenhouse Porter noted in his January 1842 message to the legislature. "No railroad in the United States could sustain itself if it were to relinquish the carrying of passengers," Porter complained, "yet, on that road [the Philadelphia & Columbia], this strange condition of things is exhibited. The State has expended in its construction over four millions of dollars, while the capital employed by those carrying the passengers, is, perhaps thirty thousand dollars. The State on her immense outlay, is reaping about 3 per cent. while the individual carriers on

their thirty thousand dollars, are clearing nearly 200 per cent."[48]

The presence of highly profitable private transportation firms on the largely profitless system of public works was a legacy of the open-access policies that had long applied to highway, river, and canal navigation. On both the Philadelphia & Columbia and the Allegheny Portage Railroad, the canal commissioners charged a "wheel toll" of a cent or two per mile, while transferring to the railroads the existing laws pertaining to turnpike travel. Such rules ensured that no teamster could impose his will on another or demand preferential access to a section of track. Some horse-drawn rail cars traveled at a leisurely pace, others more briskly. Teamsters started, stopped, and fed their horses at intervals that suited their own schedules.[49] Independent teamsters on the Portage Railroad proved extraordinarily intractable. They answered to no one but themselves, complained principal assistant engineer Solomon Roberts. They were a "rough set of fellows, and sometimes very stubborn and unmanageable." They refused to work according to any sort of a timetable, he noted, "and the officers of the railroad had no power to discharge them." Roberts, who had helped build the Portage Railroad and stayed on to run it, recalled that the only solution in cases where a teamster refused to yield the right of way "was to have the man arrested, and taken before a magistrate, perhaps many miles off, to have him fined according to the law, a copy of which I used to carry in my pocket."[50]

For those who could not afford a horse and teamster, the Canal Commission provided both motive power and operating employees. That service entailed a charge ranging between six mills and four cents per ton-mile on freight, and a cent per mile for each passenger, in addition to the wheel tolls. The commissioners provided only a small number of cars for that service—twenty-five on the Allegheny Portage Railroad, for example. They soon increased the roster to eighty, but even that complement was woefully inadequate for the demand. Small wonder, then, that most shippers provided their own equipment, or else bypassed the railroad entirely, in favor of wagon haulage between Hollidaysburg and Johnstown.

An organized corps of freight forwarders rapidly replaced the individual teamsters who operated over

Figure 9. Initially, many proponents of the Main Line of Public Works envisioned the creation of an open-access transportation system, with any citizen industrious enough to afford a freight car or canal boat possessing the right to haul freight or passengers, as had been the case on turnpikes. Rather quickly, however, the complex operational procedures associated with the Philadelphia & Columbia Railroad and the Allegheny Portage Railroad precluded free access to those routes. Even on the canals, few shippers could afford to maintain the elaborate organizational structure—with clerks at locations such as Philadelphia, Columbia, Harrisburg, Hollidaysburg, Johnstown, and Pittsburgh—necessary to move people and cargoes across the breadth of Pennsylvania. As such, a small number of transporters, or freight forwarders, solicited business, bundled small shipments, sold tickets, and billed shippers. They also publicized their services, as with this advertisement from the Reliance Transportation Company, circa 1840. The advertisement illustrates a steam locomotive pulling a sectionalized canal boat on carrier trucks.

Pennsylvania Historical and Museum Commission, Railroad Museum of Pennsylvania.

the Main Line of Public Works. The freight forwarders, often referred to as "transporters," were not so much shippers as consolidators who solicited freight and passengers, loaded them on board railroad cars or canal boats, and handled all transshipment operations. Most of the freight forwarders were grain or dry-goods merchants who engaged in the transportation business as a secondary occupation in order to ensure the safe and timely delivery of their merchandise. In addition to transporting cargoes for others, they often acted as jobbers, buying goods at wholesale in cities such as Philadelphia and selling them to shopkeepers farther west. Freight forwarders often hired or formed partnerships with their counterparts in Philadelphia and Pittsburgh and employed commission freight and passenger agents in every significant city in between. Furthermore, the transporters—unlike the lone teamsters—could afford to maintain agents, warehouses, and other ancillary facilities at Philadelphia and Pittsburgh, as well as at such important transshipment points as Columbia, Hollidaysburg, and Johnstown.[51]

On his tour of the Philadelphia & Columbia, Gerstner observed that "numerous contractors for freight transportation are found. They must number over one hundred."[52] Gerstner's count was probably correct, yet it ignored the dominant position enjoyed by a half-dozen of the dominant freight forwarders. The largest transporters, companies such as the Pioneer Line, the Western Transportation Company (also known as David Leech & Company), the Reliance Transportation Company, Bingham's Line, the Union Line, and the Pittsburgh Transportation Line either owned or contracted for substantial fleets of freight and passenger cars, as well as canal boats and even river steamboats.[53] The partnerships were quite fluid, with transporters first competing against and later cooperating with one another. Most specialized in the transportation of either freight or passengers, although David Leech and his various partners appear to have accommodated both types of traffic. The Pittsburgh-based partnership of Clarke & Thaw (also known as the Pennsylvania & Ohio Line) was located at the western extremity of the Main Line, and it accordingly operated steamboats along the Ohio River, as far west as Louisville.[54]

In addition to handling both passengers and freight, David Leech was unusual in that he was an entrepreneur with little previous experience in either wholesaling or transportation. Yet, he soon operated what was by far the most extensive freight forwarder network on the Main Line of Public Works. Originally from Mercer County, in the far northwestern part of Pennsylvania, Leech arrived in 1827 at a bend in the Kiskiminetas River, five miles upstream from its junction with the Allegheny River, at Freeport. He possessed a state contract to build a dam along the river, some 36 feet high and 574 feet long. Leech reasoned that the dam could be used for things other than providing water for the Western Division of the Pennsylvania Canal, and he soon carved out a millrace. In 1828, he founded a town, Leechburg, and by the following year he was the postmaster, as well as the owner of a sawmill, a flourmill, and a woolen factory, all powered by water from the Kiskiminetas. His sawmills produced lumber, and it was not long before Leech had become a boat builder. He then began operating those boats along the length-

ening Western Division Canal. His was the second boat to reach Pittsburgh, and he soon had a total of eight vessels in service. As he expanded what amounted to a vertically integrated manufacturing and transportation firm, Leech became a freight forwarder. Leech and his son Addison, occasionally in partnership with others, solicited shipments moving along some portion of the Main Line of Public Works.[55] They then employed canal boats, wagons, and eventually railroad cars and steamboats to consolidate shipments and move them to their destination. By May 1829, Leech's boats were moving salt from Saltsburg to Pittsburgh. Two months later, the extension of the canal to Blairsville enabled Leech to initiate service west to Pittsburgh and east over the mountains. By the end of the decade, Leech had attained a substantial first-mover advantage as the dominant transporter in western Pennsylvania, with more than sixty cars operating over the Portage Railroad alone. Following the incorporation of the Pennsylvania Railroad in 1846, that company's executives would find a deeply entrenched Leech, an entrepreneur who held the potential to become a formidable foe, but an even more valuable ally.[56]

The same was true of William Thaw, who later served as an important PRR executive. In 1834, at the age of sixteen, Thaw began his business career in his father's bank, located in Pittsburgh. A year later, he became a clerk in the mercantile house of McKee, Clarke & Company. By 1842 he had established himself as a transporter over the Main Line, in partnership with his brother-in-law, Thomas S. Clarke. Their Pennsylvania & Ohio Line soon offered service by railroad, canal, and river steamer, from Philadelphia through to New Orleans. In later years, Thaw would also throw in his lot with the Pennsylvania Railroad.[57]

Restricting an Open-Access Thoroughfare

Solomon Roberts, one of the principal assistant engineers on the Allegheny Portage Railroad, recalled traveling slowly along the Philadelphia & Columbia, with horses pulling a solitary passenger car toward Harrisburg. Roberts, in the presence of an unnamed state senator from Chester County, suggested that steam locomotives might be employed to speed them on their way, but he received a frosty response. "The reply being," Roberts recalled, "that the people were taxed to make the railroad, and that the farmers along the line should have the right to drive their own horses and cars on the railroad, as they did on the Lancaster turnpike, to go to market in Philadelphia; and that, if they were not permitted to do it, the railroad would be a nuisance to the people of Lancaster and Chester counties."[58] Roberts's experience reflected more than a disagreement as to whether the canal commissioners should employ steam locomotives on the Philadelphia & Columbia. It also embodied a fundamental transformation in the operation of the railroad portions of the Main Line of Public Works.

Most of the opposition to the use of steam power along the Philadelphia & Columbia came from the residents of communities along the route. Teamsters were concerned that locomotives would put them out of work. Many shippers objected to the supplemental haulage charge, in addition to the wheel toll, that the canal commissioners would have to levy in order to purchase and maintain the engines. Some politicians, including Thaddeus Stevens, asserted that the right of the canal commissioners to operate such complex and expensive equipment would be a harbinger of the unbridled growth of arbitrary governmental power. Such concerns reflected the republican value of rugged individualism, inasmuch as any hard-working entrepreneur could afford to buy a horse and railcar to transport their goods a short distance, often to markets in nearby towns. Once the canal commissioners assumed responsibility for motive power, however, individual Pennsylvanians would be at their mercy. Only the large freight forwarders, with their ample resources and their cozy political connections, would be able to use the railroad that the people had funded.[59]

However, there were others, individuals who typically possessed a regional rather than a local orientation, who advocated even more forcefully for the use of steam locomotives. The larger freight forwarders, in particular, were less concerned with republican individualism than they were with the speedy and efficient movement of their cargoes over long distances. They were increasingly responsible for generating the revenue necessary to sustain the Main Line of Public

Works, and their political influence rose in tandem with their growing economic authority. The canal commissioners were well aware that the transporters could divert eastbound freight off of the Main Line, at Columbia, and send it southward to Chesapeake Bay. As such, the commissioners were anxious to improve service on the Philadelphia & Columbia, and they placed pressure on the General Assembly to authorize the use of locomotives on that railroad. The slow pace of travel on the Allegheny Portage Railroad likewise annoyed the freight forwarders, and suggested that steam locomotives were a necessity on that route, as well.

Change came slowly, nonetheless. As early as March 1833, Moncure Robinson had recommended that the commonwealth purchase locomotives and, as a consequence, end the turnpike model of operations in favor of a long-term lease to a private operator. A Select Committee of the legislature had commented favorably on his advice, but the canal commissioners ignored it. In October 1833, Edward F. Gay, the chief engineer of the Philadelphia & Columbia, recommended that the canal commissioners employ locomotives on his railroad in order to accommodate the traffic generated by the freight forwarders. In December, members of the Senate ordered the canal commissioners to investigate the use of locomotives. The following January, the commissioners agreed that locomotives were feasible on the Philadelphia & Columbia and at least some of the level sections of the Allegheny Portage Railroad. Finally, on April 15, 1834, legislators authorized the canal commissioners to purchase steam locomotives and to develop regulations for their use. The vote was one of the last acts of the legislative session, for later that day many legislators began their eastward journey to Philadelphia, inaugurating service on the Philadelphia & Columbia.[60]

The *Black Hawk*, the locomotive that hauled the legislators' train between Columbia and Philadelphia, was hardly the best advertisement for the advantages of steam power over horses. A product of the Philadelphia machine shop of Stephen H. Long and Edward S. Norris (later the Norris Locomotive Works), the *Black Hawk* steamed so badly that the members of its crew were forced to stop en route to replenish their wood supply by appropriating the slats from split-rail fences. In any event, the *Black Hawk* was merely a demonstration model, and the canal commissioners sensibly declined to purchase it for regular use on the Philadelphia & Columbia. By February 1835, the legislature had nonetheless appropriated $144,900 for locomotives and, in June 1836, stipulated that they could be purchased only from American manufacturers.[61]

Other Long & Norris locomotives performed more successfully. Chief among them was the *George Washington*, which on July 10, 1836, pulled a loaded train up the Belmont plane at the eastern end of the railroad. Although some skeptics who doubted the *George Washington's* pulling power and adhesion initially dismissed the report as propaganda, a second trial, held nine days later, removed any doubt that locomotives could surmount substantial grades—a finding that came just too late to prevent the inclusion of inclined planes on the Allegheny Portage Railroad and the Philadelphia & Columbia.[62]

The *George Washington* benefited greatly from the earlier design of the *Lancaster*, the first locomotive purchased by the Board of Canal Commissioners. The *Lancaster* was the third locomotive produced in the Philadelphia workshops of Matthias Baldwin, and embodied many of the characteristics that would make the Baldwin Locomotive Works the preeminent manufacturer of steam locomotives in the United States. While roughly the same size as a British locomotive, the *Lancaster* possessed a single driving axle and a two-axle lead, or pony, truck that guided the wheels through curves, switches, and undulating track. The design owed a great deal to the influence of Edward Miller, principal assistant engineer on the Allegheny Portage Railroad. In 1833, acting on Miller's suggestion, Baldwin had observed a similar locomotive in operation on the Mohawk & Hudson Railroad in New York. Baldwin's second locomotive, and its first of the 4-2-0 wheel arrangement, was accordingly named the *E. L. Miller*, before being dispatched to the South Carolina Railroad. The virtually identical *Lancaster* was originally intended for the Philadelphia & Trenton Railroad but, with that line still incomplete, was diverted to the Philadelphia & Columbia, and entered service in June 1834. Although weighing a mere 7¼ tons, the *Lancaster* generated thirty horsepower and routinely pulled thirty-five tons. According to some accounts, the locomotive was able to haul a sixteen-car train weighing seventy-five tons, ten times the locomotive's weight.[63]

Other locomotives, particularly those destined for the Allegheny Portage Railroad, proved somewhat less successful. The *Boston*, built in 1834, came from the workshops of the Mill Dam Foundry Company in Boston (hence its distinctly un-Pennsylvania name), with the Canal Commissioners intending to use it as a prototype for other locomotives. They included the *Delaware*, and the *Allegheny*, built in 1835 by Edward A. G. Young, in New Castle, Delaware. In common with many early locomotives, they were built in machine shops that had not yet begun to specialize in railway equipment and, as such, were quite primitive machines (having wooden driving wheels a mere four feet in diameter, as one example). Young's locomotives were particularly disappointing, in part because he deviated from the template provided by the *Boston*. The *Delaware* lasted only four days in service before breaking its crank axle, while the *Allegheny* managed to operate for two weeks before suffering a similar fate. Not surprisingly, Miller and other officials turned to another builder when they purchased their fourth locomotive for the Allegheny Portage Railroad. It was the *Pittsburgh*, from McClurg, Wade & Company, in its eponymous city, delivered later in 1835. In 1836, the same builder produced the *Backwoodsman*, a copy of the *Boston*. The canal commissioners intended to employ the new locomotive on the Philadelphia & Columbia, but diverted it to one of the level sections on the Portage Railroad. By the fourth operating season in 1837, seventeen locomotives were in service, four at Hollidaysburg, three on the level section between Planes Four and Five, and the remainder along the two longest levels east of Johnstown.[64]

The steam locomotives proved only marginally successful at alleviating the operating problems on both railroads, particularly the Philadelphia & Columbia. At the most basic level, horses and locomotives traveled at incompatible speeds, but the more pervasive problem was that the canal commissioners initially lacked the authority to coordinate the two types of traffic. Teamsters, who were well aware that steam engines were a threat to their livelihoods, periodically stopped on the line to feed or water their horses, deliberately impeding the progress of locomotive-hauled trains. Such actions of civil disobedience slowed traffic to a crawl. More serious problems erupted when teamsters and locomotive engineers confronted each other from opposing directions. While built as a double-track railroad, deferred maintenance ensured that long stretches of the Philadelphia & Columbia were reduced to a single track for extended periods. Rather than allocate the funds to restore both tracks to service, commonwealth personnel adopted a more frugal approach, setting up posts midway between two sidings. Whichever teamster arrived at the post first would be able to proceed, with later arrivals from the opposite direction forced to retreat to the nearest siding or double-track section. While sensible in theory, in practice that method of operations caused drivers to race toward the center post from opposite directions, in one instance causing a fatal head-on collision.[65]

When a locomotive did encounter a horse or mule, the probable outcome was that the teamster would unhitch the animal from its burden car, which the locomotive-hauled train would then push or pull to the nearest siding or functioning section of double track. And even at such slow speeds, given the primitive braking techniques of the day, many thrilling incidents occurred when an iron horse rounded a curve, only to chance upon its flesh-and-blood counterpart plodding along the tracks just ahead. One historian accurately summarized the problems, when he noted "the profanities, the inconvenience and loss caused by the use of uncontrolled mixed power."[66] Furthermore, the bridges that spanned the Philadelphia & Columbia tracks had been designed to permit the passage of horses, not the more ample height of steam locomotives. As one traveler observed in 1835, "The chimneys of the steam-tugs are jointed, and in passing a viaduct the upper part is turned down, which allows the smoke to rush out at so small a height, as to envelope [sic] the whole train in a dense and noisome cloud of smoke and cinders."[67]

The mixing of mechanical and animal power, along with other inefficient operating practices, restricted maximum speeds to no more than fifteen miles per hour, and an express passenger train would often take seven hours to travel the eighty-two miles between Philadelphia and Columbia. Gerstner observed that, despite the double track, "The *speed* of travel on the Philadelphia & Columbia is lower than on many other American railroads."[68] Low speeds and poor maintenance ensured that, in 1836, the Philadelphia & Columbia could only accommodate about three hundred tons of freight per day—the equivalent of perhaps five canal boats.[69]

As many local entrepreneurs had feared, locomotives helped end the open-access turnpike model of operations on the Philadelphia & Columbia and, to a lesser extent, the Allegheny Portage Railroad. The canal commissioners, anxious to employ locomotives as efficiently and safely as possible, pressured legislators to give them the authority to regulate—and eventually to eliminate—the horse-drawn traffic that was under the control of the independent teamsters. On April 15, 1834, when legislators authorized the Canal Commission to buy locomotives, they also gave the commissioners the power to employ agents to coordinate traffic. In June of that year the board replaced the turnpike rules with regulations more suitable for a railroad. Steam locomotives would move all freight cars at a uniform speed, ten miles per hour for burden cars and fifteen miles per hour for passenger equipment. Locomotive-drawn trains had absolute superiority over their horse-drawn counterparts. The regulations also established a class system for trains, with preference to trains hauling the mail, followed by passenger trains, and lastly freight trains. In developing the new operating methods, the commissioners on December 2, 1834, conceded that "These [rail] roads, either as regards revenue, facilities to trade, or general accommodation, will not answer public expectation if thrown open like highways to be used indiscriminately."[70]

Despite the growing use of locomotives, horses held their own for quite some time. It was not until April 1844 that the canal commissioners banned animal power, between Columbia and the top of the Belmont plane. That policy finally brought down the curtain on the operation of the Philadelphia & Columbia as an open-access, "turnpike" railroad. In the future, all shippers would have the right to use the line, but only on schedules dictated by the commonwealth. Given Philadelphia's ban on the operation of steam locomotives within city limits, however, horses still moved cars through city streets. On the Allegheny Portage

Railroad, horses remained in use until December 1850, particularly on the shortest of the levels.[71]

Public Operation on Pennsylvania's Public Works

The Main Line of Public Works was a creature of state government. As soon as the transportation artery entered service, however, that same government became its greatest enemy. The engineers who designed the canals and railroads did the best that they could, given the state of transportation practice during the 1820s and 1830s. The canals, despite the employment of such economies as wooden locks, generally functioned well, and problems with leakage and low water supply were steadily corrected. Even educated observers, such as Gerstner, who suggested that the inclined planes could have been avoided, acknowledged that the Philadelphia & Columbia and Allegheny Portage railroads were of sound construction. No one, however, had anything good to say about the management of the state works. Every element of their construction and ongoing operation was intensely politicized, and the resulting errors and inefficiencies retarded the performance of the Main Line of Public Works. Other publicly owned internal improvement projects, including the Erie Canal, were hardly immune from political machinations, and Pennsylvania's problems, if worse than those in some states, were nonetheless better than in others. Furthermore, even if the Main Line had been blessed with supremely enlightened personnel, the hybrid canal and rail system could not have competed against the Erie Canal. By themselves, politics and geography each conspired to undermine the performance of the Main Line. Together, their effects were catastrophic.

Public operation of the canals and railroads (as distinct from public ownership) created several problems. The Main Line of Public Works was governed by the Board of Canal Commissioners rather than by a board of directors chosen from among stockholders in a private corporation. Unlike corporate directors, the canal commissioners could not dictate policy. Rather, they could only implement the instructions provided by the legislature. The canal commissioners had assumed responsibility for the most complex and by far the most expensive governmental function in Pennsylvania's history. Yet, the members of the General Assembly were determined that the Canal Commission should not possess either legislative or executive authority. The commissioners were rarely able to develop long-term plans to improve the Main Line, as they were dependent on the vagaries of the legislature's intensely politicized annual budgeting process. While the elected legislature appropriated the funds for each segment of the commonwealth's internal improvements, it was up to the appointed canal commissioners to negotiate contracts and approve the hiring of employees. The delegation of legislative authority to the Canal Commission was not absolute, and legislators curried favor with local constituents by overturning or modifying the commission's awards for eminent domain property confiscations and damages caused by construction. Moreover, the commissioners repeatedly called on the legislature to enact, with the force of law, what private companies might have considered to be routine administrative matters.[72]

Those administrative matters in turn were almost inevitably framed by politics, and not by operating requirements or by the discipline imposed by competing transportation arteries. Political patronage offered choice positions for party loyalists, and none were better than that of canal commissioner. The governor appointed the members of the Canal Commission until that power shifted to the legislature in 1829. That system lasted only a year before Governor Wolf regained control over appointments, while reducing the size of the commission from nine to three. Regardless of who chose the canal commissioners, however, the post continued to be based on patronage, with the customary purges to be expected each time power changed hands in the state capitol or the governor's mansion. Not until 1843 were the canal commissioners subject to popular election.

The many employees who were under the supervision of the canal commissioners created another set of difficulties. Competent personnel were always in short supply, especially given the novelty of canal and rail transportation and the near-simultaneous development of projects in many parts of the United States. When construction on the Main Line began, the commissioners were able to hire some of the most talented civil engineers in the United States, many of whom were veterans of the Erie Canal and other major projects. Because the legislature elected to build myriad canals at virtually the same time, funding constraints limited the ability of even the most talented engineers.[73] Legislative frugality combined with the ban on consulting, caused engineers to look with envy at other, better funded privately owned canal and railroad projects. Once construction was completed, therefore, the expert canal engineers usually left in order to apply their highly marketable skills in some other part of the country.[74]

The people in charge of ongoing operations and maintenance were generally far less qualified, and they were typically patronage employees. Most were party loyalists who lived—and voted—in the county where they sought work. The best jobs on the Main Line of Public Works, including stationary engineers and lock tenders, offered both prestige and good pay—as much as two dollars per day, plus a company house. The partisan canal commissioners who had secured the appointments of those chosen few naturally expected something in return, in the form of enthusiastic support on election day. The members of the General Assembly empowered canal commissioners to evaluate the "moral character and religious principles" of prospective contractors and employees, and everyone understood that this was but a thinly veiled reference to political affiliation.[75]

Every political party participated in the circle of patronage politics.[76] Democrats had been in power during the construction and early operating phases of the Main Line of Public Works, and their adherents benefited accordingly. Yet, purges could be expected whenever the legislature shifted parties, followed by the wholesale replacement of toll collectors, operating and maintenance personnel, and other commonwealth employees who worked on the canal. The first turnover occurred in 1835, when a coalition of Whigs and Anti-Masons came to power. In 1839, when the Democrats gained control of the General Assembly and the governorship, they unleashed an even more comprehensive round of terminations, eliminating most of the engineers on the public works, including several whose tenure dated to the earliest days of the Pennsylvania Canal.[77]

The politicized nature of employment on the Main Line of Public Works created a sense of uncertainty that precluded the development of consistent construction or operating standards. Furthermore, the party that was out of favor was likely to call for a legislative investigation into alleged malfeasance by patronage employees. Because there were rarely sufficient posts available for all of those who sought them, there was also continual infighting even within the ranks of the party in power, leading to further accusations. "Not a session of the Legislature passes without harassing the Commissioners with investigations," Governor Porter complained in 1842, stating, "the whole State is ransacked for accusers—every act is questioned and misrepresented, and after all, the result is fruitless."[78] The charges ran the gamut from dereliction of duty to alcoholism and moral turpitude to embezzlement. Such charges were in some cases justified, but in most instances not. Yet, the allegations were often sufficient to ruin careers, or at least to convince competent employees to search for less-politicized positions in the private sector.[79]

Political partisanship also ensured that the managerial structure of the Main Line of Public Works was predicated on the desire to prevent fraud rather than to maximize revenue or minimize expenses. Virtually all employees, from construction contractors to toll collectors, were in positions to divert state funds into their own pockets, particularly under circumstances where they worked in isolated locations with minimal supervision. In 1844, for example, the commonwealth filed suit against seventeen toll collectors, part of a group of fifty-five who had failed to remit more than $11 million in tolls to the treasury.[80] Fraud was a continual problem in privately owned business as well, but it took on a political significance when connected to the public works. In addition to enriching themselves, state employees might divert some of their ill-gotten gains to their favored political representatives. Legislators were acutely sensitive to the possibility that misappropriated funds might aid their political opponents, and they were as concerned with uncovering and punishing fraud in order to settle political scores as they were with protecting the financial integrity of the public works.

Politics therefore conditioned the development of the accounting methods employed on the Main Line of Public Works. Because the commonwealth's system of record keeping was to a substantial degree predicated on the desire to ensure financial integrity, it was less well able to generate the kinds of data that might improve operating efficiency or allow the canal commissioners to set tolls at a level that might attract additional business. The canal commissioners mandated extensive record keeping for every employee who came into contact, no matter how briefly, with even a small portion of toll revenues. The commonwealth's auditor general maintained a reasonably accurate accounting of the receipts and disbursements associated with the entirety of Pennsylvania's public works. His subordinates, the superintendents of each division, likewise knew approximately the amount of tolls that had been collected, as well as the allocation of the legislature's annual appropriation. The accuracy of that data rested in turn on the reports of the toll collectors. In an effort to prevent fraud, the legislators prohibited lock tenders from collecting tolls, requiring a separate set of toll collectors and greatly increasing the number of operating employees.[81]

Furthermore, many of the patronage employees were utterly unfamiliar with the procedures necessary to operate and repair a canal, much less a railroad. To the uninitiated, a canal was little more than a big ditch filled with water. In reality, however, a canal was a complex engineering system that demanded attention from highly trained personnel with a knowledge of at least the basic techniques of surveying and hydrology. Leaks, floods, and even something as seemingly innocuous as a family of burrowing muskrats could wreak havoc if not attended to promptly and competently. Problems on the Philadelphia & Columbia and the Allegheny Portage Railroad held the potential for much more serious consequences, including derailments, a runaway on one of the inclined planes, injury, or death. Without a basic knowledge of accounting, supervisory personnel would have found it very difficult to keep track of boats and cargoes, collect tolls, and forward monies to the state treasury. The assignment and repair of steam locomotives—the most complex mechanisms in existence at that time—required substantial mechanical expertise. In short, the successful operation of the Main Line of Public Works demanded a great deal more skill and attention than

such traditional bastions of patronage as the Customs House or the Post Office. Such skills were often beyond the abilities of the local party boosters. Even if they were honest—and many were—they lacked the managerial expertise necessary to coordinate the operation of a complex transportation system. The truly gifted employees often found better opportunities elsewhere. When they resigned, retired, or died, there was no bureaucratic structure in place that could select, hire, promote, and reward a successor.[82]

Moreover, it was exceedingly difficult to organize and discipline commonwealth employees in a manner conducive to safe and efficient operations. In 1873, more than fifteen years after the closure of the Allegheny Portage Railroad, civil engineer Solomon W. Roberts insisted that "For the proper management of a railroad, strict discipline is necessary, and the power of discharging employés [sic] is needed to ensure prompt obedience. In the service of a corporation this is understood, but in that of the State other considerations are apt to interfere."[83]

Lines of authority were blurred, and few employees had a clear concept of their precise duties. Even though division and section superintendents had theoretical control over the operation of their assigned portion of the Main Line of Public Works, the Canal Commission was a highly centralized body that severely restricted their authority. There were few channels for conveying information downward to the employees or upward to the Canal Commission. In 1833 a Grand Committee of the General Assembly recommended that supervisory authority be geographically decentralized, but the close of the legislative session ended discussion of that proposal. The members of the legislature were nonetheless perplexed by a situation in which "strange as it may sound . . . as we descend in the rank of officers, the amount of power vested in each increases."[84] Three years later, a committee of the legislature noted, "A great want of subordination appears to exist among the officers, few of their duties seem clearly defined or understood," and lamented, "What one approves another condemns, and the management of the works is, therefore, in a state of constant uncertainty and fluctuation."[85]

Construction and repair contracts required legislative approval, and funding depended on the annual appropriations process. Particularly given the disappointing earnings of the Main Line of Public Works, there was never enough money available for every project that required attention. Private companies rarely possessed sufficient capital to fully satisfy the requirements of construction, maintenance, and betterments, but their directors could at least allocate those limited resources with minimal input from either the government or the electorate. The members of the Pennsylvania legislature, however, favored certain projects based on political pressure and power brokering rather than the sort of economic rationality that attended a cost-benefit analysis. One of the contractors who worked on the Philadelphia & Columbia complained, "There was so much jealousy in regard to the distribution of appropriations of money by the State, that it was impossible to get an appropriation through the Legislature for any one piece of work, without including others of doubtful utility."[86] Inadequate allocations for ongoing maintenance, along with the misappropriation of funds, severely curtailed repair work, which was usually just enough to keep the system barely operational. In desperation, many superintendents extended their meager maintenance budgets by paying workers and contractors in scrip, often redeemable only when the next legislative session had selected a replacement manager. The annual appropriations process was also ill suited to the resolution of one-time crises, such as the disastrous floods of June 1838. Repairs proved extraordinarily difficult and expensive and, thanks in part to sluggishness and parsimony on the part of legislators, were not completed until the third week in November, almost at the end of the annual navigation season.[87]

On the Allegheny Portage Railroad, the situation was even worse. Until 1845, commonwealth employees performed all maintenance on the inclined planes, while contracting out those responsibilities on the level sections—a practice that increased expenditures and greatly impeded coordination and efficiency. By 1839 the wooden rails on the inclines had rotted so badly that they had to be replaced. While the superintendent favored more durable iron T-rails, legislators did not appropriate sufficient money for that purpose, forcing the installation of yet another set of obsolete wooden stringers. By the late 1840s, in desperation,

Portage Railroad crews were siphoning money from their motive power fund to pay for repairs to the physical plant, a move that hampered operations still further when worn-out locomotives failed on the road with increasing frequency.[88]

It was hardly surprising, then, that in 1854, as members of the Pennsylvania legislature were contemplating the disposition of the commonwealth's investments in internal improvements, a Select Committee of the Senate issued a report sharply critical of the mismanagement and political favoritism associated with the construction and operation of the Main Line of Public Works. "Had the object of this anomalous system been to destroy and not to build up the revenues and the morals of the state," noted the members of the committee, "it could not have been more ingeniously devised."[89]

New Routes West: The Harrisburg, Portsmouth, Mount Joy & Lancaster Railroad and the Cumberland Valley Railroad

The Main Line of Public Works was not the only transportation artery designed to funnel commerce toward Philadelphia. One privately financed railroad linked Lancaster with the state capital, while another continued into the Cumberland Valley, a rich agricultural area to the west of the Susquehanna River, a region that had long been tied to Baltimore. Neither carrier altered trade patterns to an appreciable degree, but each became a part of the PRR system—one served as an integral part of the railroad's main line, while the other would eventually provide a link to the coal fields of West Virginia.

In 1832, the General Assembly chartered the Portsmouth & Lancaster Rail-road Company, a privately funded enterprise that would link Lancaster to the terminus of the Union Canal, at Middletown. The next year, the incorporators—who included two prominent Lancaster residents, future President James Buchanan and future Secretary of War Simon Cameron—renamed the company as the Harrisburg, Portsmouth, Mount Joy & Lancaster Railroad and changed its western terminus from Middletown to Harrisburg. Although a tunnel at Elizabethtown—

the third to be built in the United States—slowed construction, the single-track line entered service in 1838, permitting all-rail travel between Philadelphia and Harrisburg. The faster and more direct route soon drew traffic away from the southernmost portion of the Eastern Division Canal, justifying the addition of a second track in 1842. Despite opposition from Columbia businessmen and the canal commissioners alike, the new railroad interchanged considerable traffic with the Philadelphia & Columbia at Dillerville, near Lancaster, and freight forwarders operated through cars between the state's political and commercial capitals.[90]

The Cumberland Valley Railroad, another private enterprise, extended the reach of the iron horse farther to the west. Its route stretched from Bridgeport (since renamed Lemoyne), opposite the Susquehanna River from Harrisburg, south and west to Chambersburg. By the 1820s, like much of Pennsylvania to the west of the Susquehanna River, the Cumberland Valley was well connected to Baltimore via turnpike. In 1828, however, a new competitor emerged in the form of the Baltimore & Susquehanna Railroad, whose promoters envisioned a direct rail link between Baltimore and York. On March 26, 1828, and in response to the threat emanating from Baltimore, the canal commissioners ordered two surveys through the region, one from Wrightsville to Gettysburg, and a second from Bridgeport through the Cumberland Valley toward Chambersburg. By January 1829, civil engineer William R. Hopkins had reported that a railroad could not be constructed over the first route, but that a link to Chambersburg was possible. His report inspired local residents who, on April 2, 1831, obtained a Pennsylvania charter for the Cumberland Valley Railroad Company.[91]

The Cumberland Valley charter lapsed in 1835, but the area's residents persuaded the General Assembly to bring the project back to life. While the new company enjoyed strong local support, the Philadelphians who represented most of the large shareholders subscribed 60 percent of the stock. In 1836, the Cumberland Valley received $200,000 in additional capital, thanks to Nicholas Biddle's willingness to invest in transportation companies, in exchange for the legislative approval of the charter of the United States Bank of Pennsylvania. Under the leadership of chief engineer William

Milnor Roberts, construction proceeded rapidly down the broad Cumberland Valley. In 1837, despite the effects of a credit crisis, the company's organizers were able to complete tracks to Chambersburg. Two years later, crews finished a railroad bridge across the Susquehanna River at Harrisburg, enabling the Cumberland Valley Railroad; the Harrisburg, Portsmouth, Mount Joy & Lancaster Railroad; and the Philadelphia & Columbia Railroad to offer through service between Philadelphia and Chambersburg.[92]

Baltimore and the Valley of the Susquehanna

Baltimoreans did not sit idly by as their competitors to the north built and operated routes that promised to link central Pennsylvania more closely with Philadelphia. Since the early nineteenth century, Marylanders had built turnpikes into the area of south-central Pennsylvania that lay to the west of the Susquehanna River, often relying on the support of local residents to steer the necessary charters through the Pennsylvania legislature. As a result, many of the Pennsylvania communities located west of the Susquehanna were more closely tied to Baltimore than to Philadelphia. The Main Line of Public Works; the Harrisburg, Portsmouth, Mount Joy & Lancaster; and the Cumberland Valley threatened the longstanding connection between Baltimore and south-central Pennsylvania.

By the 1820s, the growing population and increased commercial importance of the Susquehanna River corridor—particularly the anthracite deposits of the Wyoming Valley, along the river's North Branch—encouraged Baltimoreans to develop improved transportation routes. Since 1802, the Proprietors of the Susquehanna Canal had operated a short waterway, along the east bank of the Susquehanna River, as far north as the Pennsylvania state line. That canal was largely a failure, owing to poor design, damage from periodic floods, and above all by the inability of traffic to continue into Pennsylvania. In February 1823, members of the Maryland legislature approved plans to construct a canal linking Baltimore to the Conewago Falls at York Haven, a short distance downstream from the western terminus of the Union Canal at Middletown. Even though many residents of south-central

Pennsylvania favored that project, most Pennsylvania legislators were steadfast in their opposition to any improvements to the Susquehanna River between Columbia and the Maryland state line. However, many Pennsylvanians, particularly Philadelphia merchants, were also strong supporters of the Chesapeake & Delaware Canal, a project that had been on hiatus since 1806. Marylanders were as reluctant to support its construction as their Pennsylvania counterparts were to improve the Susquehanna, for they suspected, rightly, that a canal linking the Chesapeake and Delaware bays would direct much of the commerce of the Susquehanna Valley away from Baltimore and toward Philadelphia.[93]

The situation was ideally suited for political compromise. Marylanders agreed to support the Chesapeake & Delaware Canal, while Pennsylvania legislators pledged to fund improvements along their portion of the Susquehanna River. Work on the Chesapeake & Delaware Canal resumed in 1824, and it opened to traffic five years later. The canal soon drew traffic away from Baltimore, a trend that accelerated after the establishment of the Philadelphia Steam Tow-Boat Company, in 1835, enabled steamships to tow canal boats and barges through Chesapeake Bay and up the Delaware River. The other half of the compromise, to build a canal along the Susquehanna River, proved less successful. In March 1826, the Maryland legislature incorporated the Susquehanna & Patapsco Canal Company, whose promoters planned to build along the Susquehanna River, as far as York Haven, on the west bank of the river, a few miles north of Columbia. Despite generous financial support from the Maryland legislature, the Susquehanna project soon ground to a halt and remained in stagnation for nearly a decade.[94]

The completion of the Main Line of Public Works encouraged Baltimoreans to revive efforts to build a canal along the Susquehanna. In April 1835, Pennsylvania legislators gave their grudging assent to the plans to extend the canal into their state, as part of the quid pro quo for Maryland's support for the Chesapeake & Delaware Canal. Despite objections from some elected officials, who were anxious to prevent the diversion of traffic from the Main Line of Public Works, the General Assembly chartered the Susquehanna Canal Company, covering the Pennsylvania portion of the route. The moribund Susquehanna & Patapsco Canal Company became the Tide Water Canal Company of Maryland, merging with the Susquehanna Canal Company of Pennsylvania to form the Susquehanna & Tide Water Canal Company. Promoters initially intended to incorporate the work completed in 1802 by the Proprietors of the Susquehanna Canal as part of their route, but the largely abandoned waterway was in extremely poor condition and its owners demanded an exorbitantly high price. As a result, the Susquehanna & Tide Water Canal followed the opposite (west) bank of the Susquehanna. It entered service in April 1840, yet its effects on Philadelphia were not as severe as many of that city's residents had feared. In addition to the Philadelphia Steam Tow-Boat Company, a new firm, the Philadelphia & Havre-de-Grace Steam Tow Boat Company, established in 1841, shuttled the commerce of the Susquehanna Valley to and from Philadelphia, to the detriment of Baltimore.[95]

Railroads offered Baltimoreans an alternative means of reaching the Susquehanna Valley, although they too depended on the willingness of Pennsylvania legislators to grant corporate charters. On February 13, 1828, well before the revival of efforts to build a canal along the Susquehanna River, the Maryland legislature incorporated the Baltimore & Susquehanna Railroad.[96] Unlike the Susquehanna River, which emptied into Chesapeake Bay at Havre de Grace, almost forty miles northeast of Baltimore, the proposed railway paralleled the route of the Baltimore & York Turnpike, following a direct path toward York and then to York Haven on the Susquehanna. Yet, the company's Baltimore backers faced the customary unwillingness of Pennsylvania legislators to permit access to the Keystone State. There followed many years of political gamesmanship, pitting Philadelphians against the pro-Baltimore interests of the south-central portions of the state—a process that greatly strengthened the hold of the Anti-Masonic Party in the region.[97]

The logjam finally broke in December 1831 when Governor Wolf, in his annual message to the Pennsylvania General Assembly, asked legislators to grant a charter that would enable the Baltimore & Susquehanna to extend its route into Pennsylvania. Ultimately, on March 14, 1832, the Pennsylvania legislature incorporated the York & Maryland Line Railroad, permitting the construction of a rail link between Baltimore and York, in conjunction with the Baltimore & Susquehanna. Work on the two railroads proceeded slowly, hobbled by labor disputes, shortages of funds, and critics who argued that the rail line would not be competitive against the Susquehanna & Tide Water Canal. In 1835, the Maryland legislature provided a $1 million loan, which helped matters considerably. The first Baltimore & Susquehanna train arrived in York in August 1838. Two years later, a third company, the Wrightsville, York & Gettysburg Railroad, connected the Baltimore route with Wrightsville, across the Susquehanna River from Columbia.[98] Rails laid on the Columbia-Wrightsville Bridge provided a connection with the Philadelphia & Columbia Railroad, as well as the Eastern Division Canal.[99]

The three companies, all of which operated under the aegis of the Baltimore & Susquehanna, were far more effective than the Susquehanna & Tide Water Canal at diverting commerce from central Pennsylvania away from Philadelphia and toward Baltimore. The Cumberland Valley Railroad and the Harrisburg, Portsmouth, Mount Joy & Lancaster often hauled commodities as far east as the junction with the Philadelphia & Columbia at Dillerville (Lancaster). From there, they sent their produce back west to Columbia, and then across the river to Wrightsville and south by rail or canal to Baltimore. More distant western shippers employed the Main Line as far east as Columbia and then routed their goods south to Baltimore—a considerably shorter route than the one to Philadelphia. Likewise, few travelers endured the long journey across Pennsylvania on the railroads, canals, and inclined planes that constituted the Main Line of Public Works. Rather, they typically rode by rail as far west as Chambersburg and then transferred to stagecoaches operated by the Good Intent Mail Line and the Swiftsure Opposition Line for the remainder of the journey to Pittsburgh. On that route, the commonwealth collected revenue only along the short segment between Philadelphia and Dillerville. The journey over the Harrisburg, Portsmouth, Mount Joy & Lancaster; the Cumberland Valley; and the stagecoach lines was admittedly more expensive than traveling on the Main Line. Most travelers were willing to pay a premium for speed, however, and had little use for canal boats that

moved no more than five miles in an hour.[100] In 1842, when Charles Dickens traveled west over the Main Line, he was not a typical passenger. By and large, the people who traveled with Dickens were those who accompanied bulk shipments, or were too poor to afford the higher charges associated with rail and stage travel. When he wrote of "that class of society who travel in these boats," Dickens was by no means being complimentary.[101]

What made the situation all the more galling to Philadelphians was that portions of the Main Line of Public Works—which they had supported and helped to finance—were now being used to move traffic away from their city and toward Baltimore. Yet, that concern paled in comparison to the threat that they saw looming farther to the south and west. The Baltimore & Susquehanna was dangerous enough to the commercial ambitions of Philadelphia merchants. Far more frightening was another Baltimore railroad route that was to connect the Chesapeake Bay with the Ohio River and the west.[102]

Baltimore & Ohio

While there had long been talk of connecting Baltimore to the west, the completion of the Erie Canal and the imminent construction of the Pennsylvania Main Line of Public Works galvanized Baltimore merchants and Maryland legislators into action. In December 1825, only months after the Erie Canal entered service, a group of prominent citizens, meeting at the Baltimore Exchange, issued a resolution in favor of a canal route into the interior. Promoters soon began to argue the relative merits of canals and railroads in a discussion that mimicked the debates occurring in Pennsylvania at the same time. At first, it appeared that canal advocates had the upper hand. In March 1826, the Maryland legislature authorized public support for the Chesapeake & Ohio Canal, established two years earlier as a resurrection of the 1785 Potomac Company. Maryland's participation was vital, as Potomac Company investors had failed to extend their canal along the Virginia side of the Potomac River, and their successors on the Chesapeake & Ohio Canal would need to follow the opposite shore. Even though the canal would be located in Maryland, Baltimore residents were not entirely certain how they would get access to it—either via a cross-cut canal west to the Potomac Valley, or else south down Chesapeake Bay to Washington. It was not long, moreover, before Maryland had abandoned its plans for a canal network in favor of a railway linking Baltimore to the Ohio River. In making that decision, which in hindsight seemed so much more sensible than Pennsylvania's commitment to the hybrid Main Line of Public Works, Marylanders possessed two advantages over their northern rivals.[103]

First, while Pennsylvanians looked to the north, taking as their inspiration the relatively easy construction of the Erie Canal, Marylanders had a more sobering example of canal construction much closer to home. The Chesapeake & Ohio Canal served as a cautionary lesson of what Maryland might endure if, as railway proponents argued, they were foolish enough to build a canal through the state's western mountains. During the summer of 1824, surveyors from the Army Corps of Topographical Engineers, under the direction of Major John J. Abert, began surveying the route of the Chesapeake & Ohio Canal. Had Major Abert paused in his labors and walked fifty miles north, he would have met Charles Treziyulney and his survey crew, performing precisely the same tasks for the Pennsylvania Canal Commission. By the end of that summer, Treziyulney had concluded that a railway would offer the surest way to link Pittsburgh with the east, but Pennsylvania built a canal. Correspondingly, as survey followed survey, Abert and his colleagues concluded that a canal along the north bank of the Potomac was practicable, but Maryland built a railroad.[104]

The reason for that seeming incongruity was that the Maryland locating engineers had erred on the side of caution when estimating the cost of the proposed canal. Newspapers, particularly the *Baltimore American*, did not wait for the surveyors' report to become public, but instead relied on inaccurate information to issue wildly inflated figures in March 1826. It would cost $30 million, the *American* predicted, a sum that staggered even the most ardent canal advocates. The official report, issued in December 1826, provided little solace. It lowered the estimate to $22.5 million, but it included plans for a 2,500-foot summit tunnel and nearly four hundred locks along the proposed 341-mile

route. Construction on the Chesapeake & Ohio Canal went forward nonetheless, with John Quincy Adams presiding at the groundbreaking ceremonies, held in Georgetown on July 4, 1828. In 1850, work finally ground to a halt at Cumberland, with barely half of its length completed. Long before then, however, Baltimoreans had decided that a canal—particularly one that began in Washington—was too closely tied to Virginia and would not preserve their city's commercial fortunes.[105]

The Baltimore merchants who craved better access to the west possessed a second key advantage over their Philadelphia rivals. That was the virtue of patience. The Pennsylvania Society for the Promotion of Internal Improvements had dispatched William Strickland to Britain in order to evaluate the relative merits of canals and railways, yet Mathew Carey and other society members, nervously watching the Erie Canal move toward completion, were too impatient to wait for his report or to endure the debate that it was certain to engender. On April 11, 1825, while Strickland was still in Britain, the members of the Pennsylvania General Assembly for all intents and purposes chose canals over railways, dissolving the Internal Improvements Commission and replacing it with the Board of Canal Commissioners. Four months later, on August 15, the *Baltimore American* reprinted excerpts from Strickland's first report to the society, now some two months old. When Strickland published his *Reports on Canals, Railways, Roads and Other Subjects* in August 1826, the Commonwealth of Maryland purchased ten copies, and at least four prominent engineers who would later be associated with the Baltimore & Ohio bought the book as well. Despite the editorial changes made by Carey and other society members, Strickland's *Reports* contained valuable data on British railway practices, information that soon influenced the Maryland debate over the proper mode of transportation to the west. By the end of the year, Baltimoreans, already aghast at the estimated cost of the Chesapeake & Ohio Canal, were asserting that only a railroad could meet their transportation requirements. By February 1827, under the leadership of prominent banker George Brown, Baltimore's commercial elite had chartered the Baltimore & Ohio Railroad. During a twelve-day period, some 23,000 Baltimore residents enthusiastically subscribed to almost 42,000 shares of B&O stock.[106]

Unlike the Erie Canal and the Main Line of Public Works, which were purely state projects, the Baltimore & Ohio mixed public and private support. Baltimoreans were by no means hostile to government involvement in transportation, however, and they called upon their city to facilitate and direct the city's economic growth by contributing to the construction of the B&O and seven other railroads. The first support was in the form of a $500,000 stock subscription to the Baltimore & Ohio. Beginning in 1827, and for nearly sixty years thereafter, municipal authorities invested $20 million in internal improvements, more than any other city in the United States, save Cincinnati.[107] Based on Baltimore's 1850 population of 169,000, the city's public investments represented an average per capita contribution to public improvements in excess of $118—equivalent to perhaps six months' wages for a day laborer. Bolstered by public assistance, construction on the B&O began on July 4, 1828. Workers progressed haltingly westward as engineers struggled with inadequate financing, primitive construction methods, and limited familiarity with the most efficient methods of constructing the railway track.[108]

The B&O's promoters had adopted a time-honored strategy associated with internal improvements, asserting that the tracks would soon reach the Ohio River, but without specifying precisely where. Regardless of the railroad's western terminus, the railroad's backers confronted a major problem in that Maryland did not touch the Ohio River. As a result, the B&O would have to cross either Virginia or Pennsylvania. B&O officials prepared for either possibility. In March 1827, they persuaded Virginia legislators to permit construction through their state, so long as the tracks met the Ohio River somewhere above the mouth of the Little Kanawha.[109]

Pittsburgh was also a tempting target for the B&O, but efforts to reach that city were likely to rouse the ire of many Pennsylvanians, particularly those residing in Philadelphia, and who had long harbored fears of Baltimore's commercial power. However, the B&O also inspired many Pittsburghers, who chafed at the ongoing legislative debate regarding the construction of the Main Line of Public Works. Following an August 1827

convention, Pittsburgh residents called on the General Assembly to grant the B&O access to the southwestern portion of the commonwealth. In 1828, and despite the still-unresolved plans for their own canal system, Pennsylvania legislators placated residents in the western part of the state by permitting the B&O to reach Pittsburgh, provided that the line would be completed within the next fifteen years.[110] Three years later, Pittsburgh residents organized the Washington & Pittsburgh Railroad, which would function as an extension of the B&O, north of the Maryland state line.[111]

The projected B&O connection to Pittsburgh languished for several years, until it was reawakened by completion of Pennsylvania's Main Line of Public Works. In November 1835, an internal-improvement convention met at Brownsville, Pennsylvania, where the National Road crossed the Monongahela River, south of Pittsburgh. Most of the delegates judged the Main Line to be a disappointing failure and sought a better transportation alternative. The following May, a second convention was held in Baltimore, with many of the attendees conversely suggesting that the Main Line, if not perfect, was at least successful enough to threaten Baltimore's commercial interests. The resulting political pressure was sufficient to persuade the Baltimore city government to subscribe to $3 million in B&O stock, ensuring the continuing construction of a company that was experiencing severe financial difficulties.[112]

In addition to generating municipal support for the B&O, the 1835 internal-improvement convention at Brownsville encouraged residents of southwestern Pennsylvania to agitate for a connection between their city and the B&O. As a result of their lobbying, the February 1836 charter of the United States Bank of Pennsylvania required that financial institution to take $200,000 in B&O stock. In April 1837, the legislature chartered the Pittsburgh & Connellsville Railroad as another mechanism whereby the B&O could continue north and west into Pennsylvania, and to the Ohio River at Pittsburgh. Some of the most prominent residents of southwestern Pennsylvania supported the venture, including banker William Larimer, Jr., and William Robinson, Jr., soon to be mayor of Allegheny City. In May 1838, another political convention called on the Pittsburgh City Council to subscribe to $1 million in Baltimore & Ohio stock, with the expectation that the B&O would fund construction in western Pennsylvania. Their pleas were unsuccessful, capital was in short supply, and not a mile of track was laid on the Pittsburgh & Connellsville route through Pennsylvania.[113]

By 1839, moreover, construction crews on the B&O were still struggling through the mountains west of Harpers Ferry, and it was obvious that the line would not reach Pittsburgh by 1843, the time that its 1828 Pennsylvania charter would expire. In an adroit act of political compromise, Pennsylvania legislators representing the state's western counties extended the B&O charter until 1847, thus placating their constituents, while eastern representatives protected that region's interests by loading the recharter act with stipulations designed to protect the Main Line of Public Works. B&O officials, faced with a choice between losing their right to build into Pennsylvania and acceding to legislative authority to levy taxes on freight and to set rates (biased in favor of Philadelphia-bound traffic), chose the former course and refused to accept the charter. For a time, at least, the Baltimore & Ohio remained little more than a potential threat to Pennsylvania's Main Line of Public Works.[114]

Improving the Public Works

The development of competing transportation routes—including the Harrisburg, Portsmouth, Mount Joy & Lancaster; the Cumberland Valley; the Baltimore & Susquehanna; and the Baltimore & Ohio—all threatened the future of Pennsylvania's Main Line of Public Works. In response to the danger, the legislature and the canal commissioners improved and expanded the commonwealth's internal improvements. The Main Line of Public Works constituted the crown jewel in the Pennsylvania system of public works, but the Allegheny Portage Railroad was the weak link in the chain. By 1836, even before it was possible to travel by rail between Philadelphia and Chambersburg, legislators were contemplating the replacement of the Allegheny Portage Railroad. Had they been able to do so, the next logical step would have been to lay tracks along the route of the Pennsyl-

vania Canal, creating an unbroken rail link between Philadelphia and Pittsburgh. There was a real possibility that the Commonwealth of Pennsylvania, and not the Pennsylvania Railroad, might have completed the first rail link between the two largest cities in the commonwealth.[115]

But, it was not to be. As with so many other aspects of the Main Line of Public Works, politics both created and ultimately destroyed the opportunity for a new route over the mountains. The October 1835 elections swept many Democrats from office and empowered a coalition of Whigs and Anti-Masons. When he took office the following January, Governor Joseph Ritner purged the Board of Canal Commissioners of Democratic loyalists, and the new appointees in turn fired most of the patronage employees—from engineers to lock tenders—hired by the previous administration. Initially, Ritner cautioned against a rapid and ill-conceived expansion of the commonwealth's system of public works. His greatest act of restraint occurred in April 1837, when he vetoed a massive internal-improvements bill. The proposed expenditure of more than $3 million, Ritner argued, included needless construction and was more than the treasury could afford. Ritner was first and foremost a politician, however, and his desire to win reelection transformed his caution into enthusiastic support for an even larger expansion program. The catalyst for the change was the Bank War.[116]

Andrew Jackson had long harbored an antipathy to the Second Bank of the United States, an institution that he regarded as a bastion of wealth and privilege. On July 10, 1832, he vetoed a bill to recharter the bank, and his action became an issue in the presidential election that fall. Jackson won a narrow victory, but he interpreted his success as a public mandate to destroy the bank. When Treasury Secretary Louis McLane proved reluctant to tamper with such a critical element of the national economy, Jackson reassigned him as secretary of state—one of the last government positions that McLane would hold before becoming president of the Baltimore & Ohio Railroad. The final blow came in October 1833, when Jackson removed all federal funds from the bank.

With the bank's charter due to expire on March 4, 1836, its president, Nicholas Biddle, was desperate for any means of survival. One of his key allies was Thaddeus Stevens, a Gettysburg attorney and a member of the Pennsylvania House of Representatives who saw the rescue of Biddle's bank as a mechanism to extort internal-improvement funds from the harried financier. Stevens, the newly inaugurated leader of the Anti-Masonic forces, was acutely sensitive to charges that the public works were unfairly burdening Pennsylvania taxpayers. Many of the commonwealth's residents were displeased with a slate of new taxes that the General Assembly had introduced in March 1831, not long after legislators agreed to fund the Allegheny Portage Railroad and the Philadelphia & Columbia Railroad.

On February 18, 1836, Governor Ritner signed "An Act to Repeal the State Tax on Real and Personal Property, and To Continue and Extend the Improvements of the State by Railroads and Canals, and To Charter a State Bank To Be Called the United States Bank." The new law eliminated any use of taxes to pay for the commonwealth's internal improvements. Instead, the legislature granted a charter to the new United States Bank of Pennsylvania in exchange for a promise by Biddle and other bank officials to pay $2 million into the commonwealth treasury, to lend as much as $6 million to the government in support of internal improvements, and to subscribe liberally to any private canal or railroad project favored by legislators in the General Assembly. Many states, including Pennsylvania, had routinely required that banks provide financial support for transportation projects, as a condition of their corporate charters. The Bank Act, however, took such policies to an unprecedented level.[117]

Biddle, for one, had no illusions regarding the 1836 Bank Act or the role of Stevens in arranging what amounted to little better than political and financial blackmail. "They call Mr. Stevens an inquisitor," Biddle lamented, and "he is certainly very expert at the rack."[118] Biddle likewise acknowledged that his bank would henceforth constitute the chief source of funds that were vital to the operation and expansion of Pennsylvania's public works. The newly chartered bank, he observed, was to be "made the channel by which capital to any extent may be brought in to aid our Pennsylvania improvements."[119] For better or worse, the survival of the United States Bank of Penn-

sylvania and that of the Pennsylvania system of public works were inextricably tied to one another.

The Bank Act facilitated a rapid expansion of the scope of the internal-improvement program in Pennsylvania. Legislators provided the money necessary to complete the Philadelphia & Columbia Railroad and the Allegheny Portage Railroad, while authorizing surveys for several other, privately organized rail lines. One of those private companies, the Gettysburg Extension Railroad, was little better than a pet project of Stevens. He claimed that a western extension of the Wrightsville, York & Gettysburg Railroad, in which he was heavily invested, would eventually provide a connection between the Baltimore & Ohio and the city of Philadelphia, by way of the Philadelphia & Columbia Railroad. The project's many critics disparaged the convoluted route of the Gettysburg Extension—necessary, Stevens insisted, to accommodate the local topography—and promptly dubbed it the "tapeworm" line. They asserted, with considerable justification, that it would serve no useful purpose other than to provide access to Stevens's Caledonia Iron Works in Adams County.[120]

With the United States Bank of Pennsylvania providing a seemingly limitless source of funding, members of the legislature did not neglect canal construction. To the contrary, they authorized surveys or other funding for a plethora of projects—including many that Mathew Carey and his supporters had proposed more than a decade earlier, in their effort to maximize support for the Main Line of Public Works. The North Branch Extension Canal was to carry traffic ninety-four miles farther along the North Branch of the Susquehanna River, from Pittston to the New York state line. The Shenango Division would extend the Beaver Division of the Beaver & Erie Canal sixty-one miles to the north, from Pulaski to Conneaut Lake, enabling boats from Pittsburgh to travel within forty-five miles of Lake Erie.[121] Supporters of the Beaver & Erie Canal (also known as the Erie Extension) insisted that the project was certain to generate substantial tolls, enabling bituminous coal from western Pennsylvania to reach the Great Lakes, an area where fuel was in chronically short supply.[122]

In the wake of the 1836 Bank Act, the commonwealth's massive commitment to internal improvements also affected the existing elements of the Main Line of Public Works. In June 1836, legislators directed the Canal Commission to undertake surveys to eliminate all of the inclined planes along the Main Line of Public Works. The planes at each end of the Philadelphia & Columbia were the easiest to bypass. In March 1840, six and a half miles of new line led down to the Susquehanna River, replacing the Columbia plane. The Belmont plane at the eastern end of the line lasted a decade longer. During the initial planning stages for the Philadelphia & Columbia, Senator John Hare Powel had lobbied, unsuccessfully, for a route through his "Powelton" estate in West Philadelphia. Powel was a strong supporter of the West Philadelphia Railroad, incorporated in 1835, in an effort to construct a bypass line between central Philadelphia and a location known today as Ardmore. The company's promoters were unable to complete construction, however, and in 1850 the commonwealth took over the project. Construction crews extended the City Railroad west along Market Street to the Schuylkill River. Local bridge builder Daniel Stone strengthened and added rails to the Schuylkill Permanent Bridge, built between 1800 and 1805 as a private toll bridge, but now owned by the city.[123] The tracks continued northwest to 52nd Street, where a connection with the old roadbed of the West Philadelphia Railroad led to the original main line of the Philadelphia & Columbia, at Ardmore. On January 1, 1850, the Philadelphia & Columbia officially abandoned the now-useless Belmont plane and shifted traffic to the West Philadelphia route that later became the Pennsylvania Railroad's main line out of the city.[124]

The elimination of inclined planes along the Allegheny Portage Railroad would prove far more difficult, however. In September 1836, the canal commissioners ordered principal engineer Charles DeHaas to develop an alternate path across the mountains. In October, DeHaas and his two surveying crews began work, searching for a lower route through the mountains than that used by the Portage Railroad, through Blair's Gap. At Sugar Run Gap, they found a crossing that was nearly forty feet lower, but they spent considerable time locating approaches at an acceptable grade. At fifty-eight miles, the proposed route would be much longer than the existing Allegheny Portage

Railroad and it would require a new, mile-long summit tunnel, but it eliminated the inclined planes in favor of moderate grades in both directions.[125] By the time that DeHaas reported his findings to the canal commissioners in January 1837, he had laid out several alternate routes, one of which called for the extension of the western end of the new railroad to Blairsville, along with the abandonment of the easternmost portion of the Western Division Canal.[126]

DeHaas's proposals garnered little support, however. The canal commissioners were anxious to preserve as many of the existing level stretches as possible, along with the Staple Bend Tunnel, the Big Viaduct across the mouth of the Little Conemaugh River, and the canal basins at Hollidaysburg and Johnstown. Moreover, Andrew Jackson's withdrawal of federal funds from the Second Bank of the United States was one of several factors that led to a credit crisis. On May 10, 1837, after British bankers began pulling money out of the United States, New York banks refused to redeem their paper notes for hard currency. The contagion spread to Philadelphia the following day, affecting the United States Bank of Pennsylvania. Under the circumstances, and despite the terms of the 1836 Bank Act, little money was available for internal improvements.[127]

The commonwealth's support for indiscriminate canal and railroad construction reappeared in April 1838, when legislators passed another massive internal-improvements bill. The economy had temporarily rebounded from the credit crisis commonly referred to as the Panic of 1837, and an influx of British capital ensured that money was again available. Legislators appropriated nearly $2 million, augmenting funding for many of the projects that they had proposed in the aftermath of the 1836 Bank Act. Governor Ritner nevertheless harbored no illusions about the value of most of the initiatives, and he warned of the unwise extension of the commonwealth's credit. Yet, he was desperate to hold together his crumbling coalition of Whigs and Anti-Masons in the face of resurgent Democratic power, and he was becoming concerned about his chances for reelection in October. Accordingly, he simply backed away from the bill and permitted it to become law, without his signature.[128]

The feast of projects that accompanied the 1838 internal-improvement bill raised the possibility that the

Canal Commission might build a railroad across the commonwealth. On March 6, 1838, representatives from twenty-nine counties had attended a convention in Harrisburg, presided over by Robert Thomas Conrad, and called for an all-rail route between Harrisburg and Pittsburgh. Legislators obligingly folded Conrad's proposals into the 1838 bill, in the form of a survey for a road or railroad linking Pittsburgh with Chambersburg, the western terminus of the recently completed Cumberland Valley Railroad.[129]

In May 1838, the canal commissioners hired Hother Hagé as principal engineer and instructed him to survey the route. Hagé was no stranger to the rugged uplands of western Pennsylvania. Born in Copenhagen, Denmark, in 1800, he graduated, at the age of fourteen, from the Royal University of Copenhagen. He came to the United States five years later and spent the next nine years in Clearfield County, homesteading a plot of land given to him by his father. A skilled surveyor and civil engineer, Hagé worked for the Canal Commission in 1832, and later served as the chief engineer of the West Feliciana Railroad in Louisiana. He also surveyed the Franklin Railroad, a line from Chambersburg south to Hagerstown, Maryland, and on to the Potomac River at Williamsport, Maryland. In carrying out his 1838 orders from the canal commissioners, Hagé plotted a route through Franklin, Bedford, Somerset, Westmoreland, and Allegheny counties. From Cumberland, the line went west through Bedford and Greensburg, roughly paralleling what would eventually become the route of the Lincoln Highway and, later, the Pennsylvania Turnpike. In November 1838, Hagé presented his findings to the canal commissioners. His timing could not have been worse.[130]

Six months earlier, Ritner had rewarded his Whig and Anti-Masonic supporters, appointing Thaddeus Stevens, John Dickey, and Elijah F. Pennypacker to the Board of Canal Commissioners. As the head of the Canal Commission, Stevens proved particularly adept at alienating Pennsylvania Democrats by naming Whigs and Anti-Masons to important patronage posts, demanding in return their support in the October 1838 elections. In perhaps the most egregious example of patronage politics, during the summer of 1838 the canal commissioners embarked on a grand tour of the public works. Along the way, they awarded

jobs to staunch Whigs and Anti-Masons, informing everyone who worked for the commonwealth that their continued employment depended on maintaining Ritner as governor.[131] Lancaster native Thomas H. Burrowes, secretary of the commonwealth and the head of Ritner's cabinet, likewise exercised considerable influence over the Canal Commission, at a time when a spate of new construction projects portended an increase in patronage jobs and lucrative construction contracts. "By the end of Ritner's administration," the *New York Times* later observed, "the political machinery of the Public Works was all in the hands of Stevens, Ritner, and Burrowes."[132]

The elections on October 9, 1838, were among the most hotly contested in the history of Pennsylvania. Despite Ritner's best efforts to play the patronage card, he narrowly lost to Democrat David R. Porter, who promised fiscal restraint and the curtailment of internal improvements. Porter presided over a badly divided Democratic Party, however, and had little influence with either the faction that supported internal improvements or the one that opposed them. More ominously, the coalition of Whigs and Anti-Masons claimed electoral fraud.[133]

The disputed election led to the so-called Buckshot War, with the *New York Times* later suggesting that the "campaign was the fiercest and bitterest, politically and personally, in the history of parties in the State."[134] Disgruntled Anti-Masons and Whigs, unwilling to accept defeat, attempted to retain control of the House through chicanery, while infuriated Democrats allegedly recruited Spring Garden butcher "Balty" Sowers and a gang of thugs to murder Stevens, Burrowes, and Whig Speaker of the Senate Charles Biddle Penrose. After unsuccessfully begging President Martin Van Buren for federal troops, the outgoing Governor Ritner mobilized the Pennsylvania militia in a desperate attempt to maintain order. A rumor soon circulated that a Democratic legislator from Bedford County, Thomas B. McElwee, had procured three barrels of powder, intending to blow up the Philadelphia & Columbia train carrying the troops westward—a plan that he abandoned after learning that most of the members of the militia were fellow Democrats. Tempers eventually cooled, and the threat of violence subsided. Porter took the oath of office on January 15, and

Joseph Ritner retired from public life. All three of the presumptive victims of "Balty" Sowers survived, even if they did have to flee the Senate chamber through a back window in order to do so. McElwee, whose purported attempt to demolish a portion of the Philadelphia & Columbia Railroad apparently caused him no lasting political harm, was later expelled from the General Assembly "for grossly insulting a fellow-member while drunk."[135]

Hother Hagé and his rail route across the southern part of the state were the biggest casualties of the 1838 election, the Buckshot War, and the subsequent political infighting within the Pennsylvania legislature. To no one's great surprise, the newly inaugurated governor expelled his Whig and Anti-Masonic enemies from the Canal Commission. Stevens was the first to go, replaced by Democratic loyalist James Clarke. Democrats Edward B. Hubley and William F. Packer soon joined Clarke on the Canal Commission. The new commissioners halted all work on the Gettysburg Extension, Stevens's pet project.[136] They vowed to continue construction on the West Branch Division and the North Branch Extension, but the former had halted at Farrandsville, and went no farther, and the latter did not reach the New York border until 1856.

The new commissioners systematically purged the Main Line of Public Works of Whig and Anti-Masonic patronage employees. William Hasell Wilson, one of the engineers who had worked on the Philadelphia & Columbia, was unceremoniously dismissed. So too was Hother Hagé, effectively marking the end of any serious possibility that the Canal Commission would authorize the construction of a railroad from Chambersburg west to Pittsburgh. Herman Haupt, the principal assistant engineer of the Gettysburg line, also lost his job. The young West Point–trained engineer spent much of the next decade looking for work equal to his talents and nursing a grudge against the canal commissioners who had dismissed him.[137]

The political upheavals associated with the 1838 election had done nothing to improve the performance of the Main Line of Public Works. To the contrary, the patronage battles, combined with Governor Porter's critical appraisals of the state's financial obligations, increased the calls for a replacement for the

canals and for the inclined planes associated with the Allegheny Portage Railroad. On July 19, 1839, the legislators authorized the Canal Commission to survey an all-rail route between Harrisburg and Pittsburgh that would make most of the Main Line canals effectively redundant. The commissioners in turn appointed Charles L. Schlatter as principal engineer to select a route. Schlatter, along with a crew that included future bridge engineer John A. Roebling, ran more than a thousand miles of surveys. The complexity of the project stemmed in part from Schlatter's innate sense of thoroughness, and in part from political considerations, inasmuch as virtually every community between Harrisburg and Pittsburgh expected to be included. He also confronted the limitations of 1830s steam locomotive design, which meant that the ruling grade could be no more than forty-five feet per mile, equivalent to a modest 0.85 percent.[138]

By 1840, Schlatter had identified three possible routes. The southern route was essentially the one that Hother Hagé had surveyed in 1838, and was thus sometimes referred to as "Mr. Hagé's Route." The terrain to the west of Chambersburg was hardly conducive to railroad construction, however. In January 1839, the newly appointed Democratic Board of Canal Commissioners dismissed Hagé's proposals as being too expensive and impracticable. Conditions had not changed, and Schlatter, despite making some minor modifications to Hagé's surveys, could find no way to reduce the ruling grade below sixty feet per mile, as the line surmounted three summit crossings, the highest at 2,677 feet above sea level. The substitution of a turnpike over the ninety miles between Fort Loudon and Laughlintown, along a route well to the north of the Hagé survey, would eliminate the gradient issue and reduce construction costs substantially, but such a hybrid arrangement would be no better than the existing Main Line of Public Works.[139]

The northern route ran almost due north along the Susquehanna River and the Susquehanna Division of the Pennsylvania Canal, as far as Northumberland. From there, it headed west along the West Branch of the Susquehanna River, paralleling the West Branch Division of the Pennsylvania Canal, through Williamsport and Lock Haven, almost as far as the canal's terminus in Farrandsville. The surveys continued in a southwesterly direction toward Tyrone, along Bald Eagle Creek, almost due west across the summit of the Alleghenies at Emigh's Gap, and then south along Clearfield Creek. Near Ebensburg, it joined the middle route for the remaining distance west toward Pittsburgh. The northern route took advantage of the great westward reach of the West Branch of the Susquehanna River and enjoyed the virtue of the lowest crossing of the Alleghenies, at little more than two thousand feet. However, there were two summits to surmount, and the route was by far the longest of the three.

The middle route was the most attractive. It followed the Susquehanna River and the Eastern Division of the Pennsylvania Canal, from Harrisburg north to Duncan's Island. It then swung west, paralleling the route of the Juniata Division Canal along the Juniata River as far as Lewiston. The alignment then followed the Kishacoquillas Creek to Huntingdon, where it again met the Juniata. West of Huntingdon, the route owed its virtues to principal assistant engineer Stephen Moylan Fox, who was completing part of the survey. Slogging his way through the dense forests of the Alleghenies, Fox located a superb route with grades no greater than forty-five feet to the mile, across Sugar Run Gap, at a point about two miles north of the Portage Railroad crossing, down the Black Lick Creek valley to Blairsville, and then west to Pittsburgh. The line across the summit was only four miles longer than the existing Portage Railroad, yet it dispensed with the need for inclined planes and kept the gradient to an acceptable 44.88 feet per mile. Even better, it would allow the use of eight miles of the existing Portage Railroad.[140]

In January 1842, Schlatter made his final report to the canal commissioners, recommending the middle route as the most practicable. It promised to connect Harrisburg and Pittsburgh with an iron band 229.5 miles long, sixty-two miles shorter than the southern route and ninety-one miles less than the northern route. Schlatter estimated that a railroad along the middle route would cost $9.5 million to construct, compared with $10.9 million for the north and $11.1 million for the south.[141]

Schlatter's surveys lay untouched for nearly another decade, as economic malaise settled over Pennsylvania and the nation. The recovery that followed the Panic of 1837 proved short lived, and a far more severe depression began in 1839. Nicholas Biddle, operating largely on his own account, although using the United States Bank of Pennsylvania as a base, had spent the years after 1837 engaged in cotton speculation. The 1839 harvest was far larger than Biddle had anticipated, and he struggled in vain to maintain cotton prices. Nicholas Biddle resigned the bank presidency on March 29, 1839, and in October, bank officials suspended specie payments, refusing to redeem notes for gold. The bank reopened, as it had in 1837, but in this instance Biddle's bank was mortally wounded. In January 1841, the Commonwealth of Pennsylvania required the state's banks to redeem notes for specie, under the terms of the Bank Act of 1840, and bank officials were unable to comply. On February 4, 1841, the United States Bank of Pennsylvania suspended specie payments for the third and final time, destroying an institution that had contributed more than $8 million to the state's public works projects. The resulting financial crisis was serious enough to merit mention in John Tyler's state of the union address the following year, when the President spoke of "the utter and disastrous prostration of the United States Bank of Pennsylvania."[142] When Charles Dickens passed through Philadelphia, he saw from the window of his hotel a ghostly white marble edifice, which he later discovered to be "the tomb of many fortunes, the Great Catacomb of investment, the Memorable United States Bank."[143]

The banking crisis that began in 1839 was far more severe than the Panic of 1837. Many states, particularly those in the west, had helped bring about the overextension of credit that contributed to the severity of the crisis and they soon fell victim to it as well. Legislators in Indiana and Illinois, two states that had succumbed to the siren song of internal improvements, repudiated debts, while their counterparts in Ohio came to the brink of insolvency. Even New York was in danger, thanks in part to the construction of feeder canals that proved far less successful than the Erie Canal. By the end of 1842, nine states had defaulted on their financial obligations.[144]

The list of failures included Pennsylvania, where the legislature's attempts to maintain payment of the state's debts greatly exacerbated the crisis. For the commonwealth, the most immediate effect of the panic was the rapid reduction in the value of its stock-holdings in various banks, the dividends on which had traditionally generated the largest source of annual revenue. For more than a year, the Pennsylvania legislature struggled to keep pace with the interest obligations on its massive public debt while endeavoring to shed the unprofitable portions of the Main Line of Public Works. In May 1841, despite Governor Porter's veto, the legislature passed a Relief Act designed to extract $3 million from the state's financial institutions. The banks were able to issue small-denomination notes, redeemable only in state stock, in $100 increments. The Whigs who supported the measure intended it to aid the banks, especially the stricken United States Bank of Pennsylvania, and to restore the commonwealth's credit, but the law was unsuccessful on both counts. "After having borrowed as much as she could in the old-fashioned way from banks and brokers, and domestic and foreign capitalists," one contemporary financial writer noted, the Commonwealth of Pennsylvania "resolved to extort a loan of a dollar a head from every washerwoman and woodsawyer and everybody else within her limits who had a dollar to lend."[145]

The crisis deepened in January 1842, with a run on Philadelphia's Girard Bank, which promptly failed. In March, legislators debated and subsequently passed a bill requiring banks to resume specie payments, while considering and ultimately rejecting an amendment that would have exempted banks from the requirements of the Relief Act. Investor concerns over the creditworthiness of the relief notes caused their value to plummet. On July 27, 1842, in a last-ditch effort to save the state from financial disaster, legislators authorized the sale of the Main Line of Public Works, as well as many of the commonwealth's other internal-improvement investments.[146] It was all in vain, however, and on August 1, 1842, the commonwealth declined to pay its interest obligations, offering scrip in lieu of cash. With its credit ruined, the Commonwealth of Pennsylvania was no longer in a position to construct a railroad along Schlatter's middle route between Harrisburg and Pittsburgh, nor to build much of anything else.[147]

In April 1843, with his political influence virtually nil, Governor Porter lost a battle with the legislature to retain control over the Board of Canal Commissioners. Henceforth, those former plums of political patronage would be elected officials, on staggered three-year terms—ensuring that political divisions within the commonwealth would inevitably devolve onto the Canal Commission. With no money, and no political solidarity, there was little that the canal commissioners could do to remedy the imperfections of the Main Line of Public Works. Between 1836 and 1843, Charles DeHaas, Hother Hagé, and Charles Schlatter had demonstrated that it was possible to build an all-rail line across Pennsylvania. Henceforth, however, private rather than public enterprise would guide the project forward.[148]

The Main Line of Public Works in Retrospect

Beginning in 1843, in the midst of a severe economic crisis, the commonwealth began to dispose of its investments in public works. In March, legislators voted to simply give away the still-incomplete Beaver & Erie Division in an effort to encourage private investors to complete the canal from the Ohio River north to Erie.[149] A massive divestment of additional public holdings in mixed-enterprise banks, turnpikes, canals, and bridge companies occurred later that year. In 1844, Pennsylvanians voted 149,748 to 124,598 to sell the Main Line of Public Works, a process that was not finally consummated until 1857.[150] In that year, when the privately owned Pennsylvania Railroad purchased the publicly owned Main Line, Governor James Pollock accused the commonwealth's grand experiment in internal improvements of exhibiting a "reckless disregard of the public interests as exhibited in the extravagant, useless and fraudulent expenditures of the public moneys for selfish or partisan purposes."[151]

From the 1830s onward, most accounts have described the Main Line of Public Works as a dismal failure.[152] Such criticisms, although valid, reflect the perspective of contemporary observers and historians who were closely connected to—or even employed by—the Pennsylvania Railroad, the company that put the commonwealth's system of internal improvements out of business.[153] Other scholars, in contrast, have suggested that state governments were inherently more successful than business partnerships and infant corporations, in terms of their ability to generate capital and manage complex projects, such as the Pennsylvania Canal and the Philadelphia & Columbia and Allegheny Portage railroads.[154] Still others have explored the perplexing disconnect between the ability of the canal commissioners to construct massive public works and their failure to manage them effectively.[155]

Despite the mismanagement and the dismal financial results associated with the Main Line of Public Works, the Board of Canal Commissioners managed to plan, construct, and operate a transportation system through some of the most rugged terrain in the eastern United States, linking Pennsylvania's two largest cities and connecting the Ohio River to the Atlantic seaboard. At the time of its completion, the Philadelphia & Columbia was the longest double-track railroad in the United States. The railroad was also built to high engineering standards, even if large stretches of second track were out of service indefinitely owing to a shortage of repair funds. The Allegheny Portage Railroad constituted a remarkable engineering achievement, despite the fact that the route was soon obsolete.[156]

Pennsylvania nonetheless paid a substantial price for the limited economic benefits associated with the Main Line of Public Works. The commonwealth spent in excess of $100 million, more than any other state, and equivalent to more than $2.1 billion in 2010 dollars, to build and operate an internal improvement system that included more than 800 miles of canals and 117 miles of railroad.[157] Even with the employment of wooden locks and other economies, construction costs for each segment were far higher than the canal commissioners had predicted, and the final expenditure was in some cases nearly double the initial estimate. By the time the entire Main Line of Public Works opened in the spring of 1834, the state had invested between $14.36 million and $15.6 million in that project alone, representing roughly half of the $33.5 million expended on the construction of all of the publicly funded internal improvements.[158] Once completed, the Main Line earned a profit (in the sense that revenues exceeded expenditures) every year, save for 1840. The annual operating surpluses, however, barely made a dent in the enormous capital costs required to build the line in the first place, particularly when most of the branch canals were hemorrhaging funds.[159]

The legislature's support for canals and other transportation improvements largely accounted for Pennsylvania's massive debt, greater than that of any other state in the union. It should be noted, moreover, that Pennsylvania's population in 1830 was not much more than a tenth of that in 2010, putting a considerable strain on the financial resources of the government and the populace alike. Between 1820 and 1838, the Keystone State issued nearly $27.3 million in bonds, almost $5 million greater than the next most profligate state, New York.[160] In their entirety, the Main Line of Public Works and other internal improvements represented more than $22 million of the commonwealth's $24.6 million debt in 1835. Interest payments on the internal-improvement debt totaled almost $1.2 million in 1835, far exceeding the $684,357 in tolls collected that year. Results in subsequent years were no better. By the time that the General Assembly disposed of the public works in 1857, the Main Line's cumulative deficit stood at $6.7 million. When Pennsylvania exited the transportation business, late in the 1850s, the commonwealth received $43.8 million from the sale of various portions of the public works. Given their $100 million cost, the public treasury had suffered a net loss of more than $56 million. It was hardly surprising, then, that both contemporaries and historians have branded the Main Line of Public Works as a failure.[161]

Yet, it would be a mistake to ignore the successes associated with the Main Line of Public Works and the other internal improvements. The primary benefit lay in the reduction of transportation costs within regions of Pennsylvania along comparatively small segments of the Main Line. Freight that had traveled by wagon for thirteen cents per ton-mile in 1824 moved along the Main Line canals at an average rate of 2.7 cents per ton-mile in 1853—although that figure was still well above the tariffs of the Erie Canal, where rates in 1853 ranged between .57 and 1.34 cents. The cost to move a ton of merchandise between Hollidaysburg and Blairsville decreased from as high as $16 to only $4. In 1829, with construction just beginning on the Main Line of Public Works, it could cost as much as $56.25 to ship a ton of wheat from Pittsburgh to

Philadelphia. By 1838, the expense had fallen to $15.00 via the Main Line, well below the rates of $19.00 to $21.00 by way of New Orleans.[162]

The public works accordingly stimulated the growth of communities along the route.[163] Hollidaysburg, where the Juniata Division Canal met the Allegheny Portage Railroad, grew from fewer than a hundred people in the early 1820s to more than 1,200 by 1838, and 3,000 in 1846. Pittsburgh experienced rapid expansion, thanks in part to the Pennsylvania Canal. The city's population swelled from fewer than 5,000 in 1810 to more than 46,000 in 1850. By decade, the greatest growth occurred during the 1840s, when the population increased by more than 120 percent. The production of coal, salt, ironwork, machinery, and other commodities experienced similarly impressive increases. Many factors contributed to Pittsburgh's development, including the removal of Britain's presence in the Old Northwest following the War of 1812, the completion of turnpike connections to Philadelphia (in 1820) and Erie (in 1823), the construction of river steamboats, and improvements along the Monongahela and Youghiogheny rivers. Nevertheless, the Western Division Canal greatly facilitated the ability of Pittsburgh's manufacturers to draw raw materials toward their factories.[164]

The new transportation system did not create an artery of commerce flowing across Pennsylvania, however, largely because the Allegheny Portage Railroad retarded movement between the eastern and western portions of the system. Between 1834 and 1849, shipments of coal from Pittsburgh, over the Western Division Canal, never exceeded 2,656 tons annually, well below the levels that traveled south along the Ohio and Mississippi rivers toward New Orleans, and a trickle compared to the torrent that moved to tidewater along the Lehigh Coal & Navigation Company's canal and the Schuylkill Navigation.[165] Figures for total coal shipments over the Main Line are available for only one year—1836—and indicate the movement of a paltry 24,151 tons, well below the 113,647 tons of anthracite that traveled along the privately owned northeastern anthracite canals. Most of that western soft coal moved only a short distance to Pittsburgh, for the idea of sending heavily laden coal cars over the Allegheny Portage Railroad and toward eastern markets

would have been absurd in the extreme.[166] In general, respectable quantities of high-value merchandise traveled west across the commonwealth, although bulk commodities tended to avoid the Main Line, instead following established water routes, such as the Ohio and Susquehanna rivers, and the Union and Schuylkill canals.[167] The predominance of westbound traffic would have dismayed Mathew Carew and the other Philadelphia boosters associated with the Pennsylvania Society for the Promotion of Internal Improvements in the Commonwealth, who had envisioned a steady parade of canal boats moving grain toward their city.

The Main Line of Public Works failed utterly to redirect shipments of western grain and other agricultural commodities off of the Erie Canal and toward Philadelphia. The cost of shipping a barrel of flour from Pittsburgh to Philadelphia admittedly fell by 90 percent between 1800 and 1835, but this was as much the result of the development of competing transportation arteries—including river steamboats and the Erie Canal—as it was the product of any efficiencies generated by Pennsylvania's internal improvements. Proponents of the Main Line of Public Works could point with pride to the twenty thousand hogsheads of tobacco that traveled east over the route each year. By the early 1850s, some estimates suggested that nearly as much pork went east over the Alleghenies as south down the Ohio River. Nonetheless, the predominant direction of trade was from tidewater to the west, and not the other way around.[168]

Despite the most optimistic assertions of Carey and his allies, the Main Line of Public Works was never able to compete effectively against the Erie Canal. Located farther south, Pennsylvania's canals were in operation for a few additional weeks each year, and the early spring and late fall accordingly witnessed brief surges of traffic that could not pass through New York. Yet, David Leech and the other private freight forwarders largely negated that advantage by charging exorbitant rates during the few weeks when they possessed a monopoly over east-west transportation, keeping the resulting profits for themselves, rather than passing them on to the state treasury.[169] Even during the period when the Erie Canal was in service, overall rates on the Main Line of Public Works remained quite high. The canal commissioners had begun to implement reduced tariffs as early as 1831, and experimented with rebates and volume discounts over the years that followed, largely in an effort to fend off the Susquehanna & Tide Water Canal and other competitors. Yet, the low levels of traffic ensured that a small number of shipments had to bear the fixed costs of building the Main Line, as well as the variable costs associated with keeping it in operation. In New York, revenues from tolls, augmented by the taxes that had underwritten the construction of the Erie Canal in the first place, enabled periodic betterments that increased capacity, generated greater transportation efficiency, and permitted lower rates. Pennsylvanians needed every cent of toll revenues, and then some, just to pay the interest on the multitude of internal-improvement loans. There was never enough money to improve the canals, or even to keep them in good repair, so traffic remained low and tolls stayed high.[170]

Nature and topography also did the canal commissioners no favors. The Erie Canal rose only 655 feet in 350 miles, while the canal portion of the Main Line of Public Works—exclusive of the Philadelphia & Columbia and Allegheny Portage railroads—rose and fell 1,168 feet over 274 miles. The Pennsylvania Canal was considerably shorter than the Erie Canal, yet the first had more than twice as many locks as the second. From the perspective of impatient boatmen, that meant that they encountered a lock every five miles or so in New York, on average, but every one and two-thirds miles in Pennsylvania—to say nothing of the delays associated with transferring cargoes between boats and railroad cars.[171]

Much of the explanation for the inadequacy of the Main Line of Public Works lay in the defects associated with its construction. Engineers and surveyors designed and built the Main Line of Public Works at a time when civil engineering was still in its infancy in the United States. Late in his life, Solomon Roberts acknowledged as much, as he recalled his role in selecting the route of the Allegheny Portage Railroad. "Railroad construction was a new business, and much had to be learned from actual trial," he recalled, "but it was known at the time, that the location was too much hurried, which arose from the great impatience of the public."[172] Construction crews failed to create proper

angles of repose along the line, so embankments collapsed and periodic landslides covered the tracks with earth, boulders, and mud. Each spring, the poorly constructed track on the Philadelphia & Columbia and Allegheny Portage railroads heaved and buckled with the thawing ground, obligating crews to perform arduous maintenance work. Natural disasters played a role as well, and in June 1838 floodwaters swept down the Juniata River, virtually obliterating the Main Line canal system between Huntingdon and Hollidaysburg, and leaving the Portage Railroad almost deserted west of that location.[173]

The hybrid nature of the Main Line of Public Works, a product both of Pennsylvania's geography and the haste of Mathew Carey and his associates to begin construction as quickly as possible, constituted a chronic impediment to efficient operation. Any freight that moved across the state required three transshipments, from rail to canal at Columbia, from canal to railroad at Hollidaysburg, and back to a canal boat at Johnstown. Those transshipment costs, which were not reflected in published tolls, constituted a significant expense for the private transporters who operated over the route, with one testifying before the Pennsylvania House of Representatives that they increased his expenses by $15,000 per year compared with operations on the Erie Canal.[174]

In the final analysis, the Main Line of Public Works did not—and could not—restore Philadelphia's role as the nation's leading port, and neither did it resurrect the commercial fortunes of the city's merchants. The merchant class was literally dying out, with sons abandoning their fathers' footsteps in favor of manufacturing, politics, or indulgence in their inheritances. By the 1830s, the smart money was in manufacturing rather than trade. Under those circumstances, the drawing of commerce away from New York and Baltimore, and toward Philadelphia, seemed distinctly less important than it had a few decades earlier.

By the early 1840s, coal and iron created an economic landscape that the charter members of the Society for the Promotion of Internal Improvements could not have imagined. From its inauspicious beginnings as a fuel that no one knew how to burn, anthracite quickly became the dominant energy source for ironworking. The growing iron output attracted private investment in canals and railroads, reducing transportation costs and stimulating additional investor interest in ironworks. Companies such as the Schuylkill Navigation, the Lehigh Coal & Navigation, and the Philadelphia & Reading Rail Road helped to create a flourishing iron trade and a vibrant regional economy along the Schuylkill River, while the Monongahela Navigation had much the same effect in the area around Pittsburgh. Those carriers established a virtuous cycle that generated additional investment in manufacturing, which in turn induced further privately financed transportation improvements.

Enterprising Philadelphians, those who accepted that their city could no longer compete with New York for ocean-going commerce, broke from their mercantile roots and became industrialists. Philadelphia's manufacturers both contributed to and benefited from an economic "take-off" that occurred during the late 1830s and early 1840s as the United States recovered from the Panic of 1837. By that time, both Philadelphia and its hinterland had experienced substantial economic expansion. Much of that growth had occurred as a result of improved transportation, although it came in the form of anthracite canals, not the Main Line of Public Works. At a time when many of Pennsylvania's residents delighted in complaining about the inefficiencies of a government-managed system of internal improvements, the private transportation companies generated healthy profits.[175] That dichotomy caused many prominent merchants and manufacturers to suggest that direct public control was unnecessary to secure either better transportation or a robust economy.[176]

In 1846, amid a period of rapid economic growth, escalating sectional tensions, and a war with Mexico, a new generation of Philadelphians called on their government to support another transportation link to the west. Like their predecessors in the Pennsylvania Society for the Promotion of Internal Improvements in the Commonwealth, they were hardly representative of their state, or even of the city in which they resided. They were merchants, manufacturers, scientists, and dilettantes, near but not in the top tier of Philadelphia society. Their audacious plan for a railroad across the entirety of Pennsylvania seemed so financially dubious that few of the city's industrial moguls wanted any part of it. Despite the confident predictions of its promoters that it would bring unity and prosperity to the entire commonwealth, few people outside Philadelphia wanted anything to do with it, either. They had heard this refrain before, in the siren song that had accompanied the publicity, promotion, and political pressure associated with the Main Line of Public Works. They had seen the results, and they were not pretty. As such, the city's leading industrialists were reluctant to support a project that did not appear to be commercially viable in its own right, that threatened to disrupt long-established patterns of trade, and that promised to use public funds to enhance the welfare of the few at the expense of the many.

The first generation of enthusiastic if inexperienced Philadelphia boosters had so skillfully finessed the political process in pursuit of their personal interests that they had brought into being the Main Line of Public Works, a morass that for generations to come served to discredit the very idea of public involvement in business enterprise. The second generation of enthusiastic if inexperienced Philadelphia boosters nonetheless proceeded apace in their efforts to employ politics in a similar manner, again claiming that they could ensure economic advancement for all. When they finished, they had created the Pennsylvania Railroad.

At seven o'clock on the morning of November 3, 1842, a train crept out of Baltimore's Pratt Street Station, heading west. That evening, the dignitaries who had undertaken the trip were celebrating their arrival in Cumberland, Maryland. Baltimoreans were ecstatic, even though the greatest part of their work—the construction of a railroad across the Appalachian Mountains that blocked their path to the Ohio River—lay before them. For more than a decade following its incorporation, the Baltimore & Ohio had posed little more than a potential threat to the commercial interests of Philadelphia. A combination of inadequate financing, legal disputes with the promoters of the Chesapeake & Ohio Canal, the novelty of railway engineering, and unexpectedly difficult construction conditions had retarded work on the B&O. Many Pennsylvanians, and even many residents of Maryland, expressed serious doubts as to whether the railroad would ever reach the Ohio River. Yet, the inaugural trip to Cumberland shattered the complacency of many Philadelphia merchants and reawakened long-standing fears that Pennsylvania would be surpassed by rival states.

The new route to Cumberland certainly did no favors for Pennsylvania's Main Line of Public Works. Before 1842, most savvy travelers had proceeded westward along the Philadelphia & Columbia; the

Harrisburg, Portsmouth, Mount Joy & Lancaster; and the Cumberland Valley Railroad to Chambersburg, where a stagecoach would convey them west to Pittsburgh. By avoiding both the Pennsylvania Canal and the Allegheny Portage Railroad, those intrepid voyagers deprived the commonwealth of virtually all revenue on the Main Line, save for the relatively short rail journey between Philadelphia and Lancaster. After 1842, the canal commissioners watched in dismay as even that revenue began to slip away. Now, passengers could head south from the Quaker City along the Philadelphia, Wilmington & Baltimore Railroad. The B&O carried them west to Cumberland, and from there a stage journey of some seventy-five miles along the National Road brought them to the Monongahela River, at Brownsville. Pittsburgh was but a short steamboat ride to the north. In a desperate effort to win back business on the Main Line of Public Works, the Pennsylvania canal commissioners cut rates between Pittsburgh and Philadelphia by 25 percent. The strategy proved only modestly successful, particularly as B&O officials responded with similar tariff reductions. The commissioners did, however, succeed in driving the Main Line even deeper into the red, without appreciably quieting the clamor of Pittsburghers for better transportation to the east.

Figure 10. This is the Philadelphia that would have been intimately familiar to the promoters of the Pennsylvania Railroad. The view, looking southwest from the Delaware River in the mid-1850s, suggests the compact nature of the city, illustrates the effects of steam power (as indicated by the ship in the lower center, probably just arriving from Trenton, New Jersey), and gives a good impression of the bustling commerce at one of the nation's most important ports. Appearances could be deceiving, however, and by the 1790s Philadelphia had lost its status as the leading port in the United States—a trend accelerated by the War of 1812 and the construction of the Erie Canal. The westward progress of the Baltimore & Ohio Railroad threatened to accelerate Philadelphia's commercial decline, and it was that threat, as much as the inadequacies of the Pennsylvania Main Line of Public Works, that spurred Philadelphia merchants into action.

John Bachmann, Birds Eye View of Philadelphia [Looking West from the Delaware River]*, ca. 1850, used by permission of the Rare Book Department, Free Library of Philadelphia.*

To the north were other threats to Pennsylvania's commercial interests, particularly to the welfare of Philadelphia merchants. New Yorkers were building not one, but two railroads toward Lake Erie, the New York & Erie and a series of companies that would later become the New York Central. The New York & Erie Rail Road, chartered in 1832, was by far the least serious of the threats. Its supporters hoped that the line would provide economic benefits to the counties of southern New York that the Erie Canal had bypassed.

The project lagged for many years, the victim of investor disinterest and the active political opposition of the counties to the north. Construction on the rail line began in 1835, creeping west from Piermont, on the Hudson River. The company's engineers chose an unusually broad gauge of six feet, ostensibly for reasons of stability and safety, but in reality as a thinly disguised attempt to prevent the diversion of freight traffic to other railroads or other states. Less compelling was the decision to lay the tracks atop thousands of wooden piles to forgo the expense of more conventional graded roadbed. The piles proved unworkable and had to be completely replaced. In January 1841, the Pennsylvania legislature granted the company the right to transit the far northeastern corner of the state in exchange for a $10,000 annual fee, greatly simplifying the engineering challenges in what was fairly rugged terrain. The concession could do little to save the company, particularly with the economic crisis that followed the collapse of the United States Bank of Pennsylvania. That fall, work ground to a halt at Goshen, New York, and would not resume until August 1846.[1]

Farther north, the Erie Canal had stimulated an economic boom along its route. As cities such as Syracuse and Rochester grew in population and economic importance, many local boosters advocated the construction of rail lines that would link them together. There was little chance that those early, disconnected lines could take away the eastbound grain traffic that was the underpinning of the Erie Canal. Passengers and high-value westbound merchandise traffic were another matter, however. The first company to compose part of the route was the Mohawk & Hudson Railroad, which was chartered in 1826 and designed to bypass a lock-infested section of the Erie Canal at its eastern end. The New York legislature chartered the Utica & Schenectady Railroad in 1833, two years after the Mohawk & Hudson opened to traffic. The Syracuse & Utica Railroad (1836), the Auburn & Syracuse Railroad (1834), the Auburn & Rochester Railroad (1836), the Tonawanda Railroad (1832), and the Attica & Buffalo Railroad (1836) pieced together the remainder of the route. By 1841, it was possible to travel by rail from the Hudson River to Lake Erie, with the exception of a short interval at Rochester. That gap closed in 1844, two years after

the Commonwealth of Pennsylvania passed on its debt obligations, and just as Philadelphia merchants were beginning to think seriously about constructing a route west to the Ohio River. It would be another nine years before Albany businessman Erastus Corning welded the lines together into the New York Central Railroad, but no one had to explain to Philadelphia merchants the value of that route to their Manhattan rivals.[2]

Baltimore Redux

While few Philadelphians relished New York's rapidly expanding railroad network, most were astute enough to realize that they could not hope to match the economic power of the Empire State. As in earlier years, their main adversary was Baltimore. The city on Chesapeake Bay could not sustain the burst of rapid growth that it had enjoyed during the quarter-century that followed the end of the American Revolution, and by the end of the 1820s it was clear that the city would not displace Philadelphia as the second-largest port in the nation. Baltimore merchants nonetheless remained formidable rivals, particularly as the city experienced a resurgence during the 1840s and into the 1850s. As the Baltimore & Ohio built steadily westward, civic boosters anticipated the benefits associated with the city's location, farther west than any other major Atlantic seaport. Even though the B&O had not reached the Ohio River, it had already tapped coal deposits in the western part of Maryland. The Chesapeake Bay region boomed, with fruit and vegetable farms and oyster beds contributing to Baltimore's growth. Burgeoning trade with South America also increased activity at the city's docks.[3]

Baltimore's growth during the 1840s occurred at a time of economic and political crisis in Pennsylvania. Commonwealth legislators had borrowed heavily in order to finance a massive system of internal improvements, only to fall victim to the depression that followed the Panic of 1837. On August 1, 1842, state officials issued scrip rather than cash on a bonded debt that had reached $37,319,395. With its credit shattered, many members of the General Assembly were anxious to wash their hands of the public works by selling them to private investors. They were certainly not in a position to improve or replace the Main Line in order to create a transportation artery that could compete with the Baltimore & Ohio or the canal and railroad routes in New York State.[4]

Just as the oversight of internal improvements had passed from the federal government to the states after 1817, the economic crisis of 1842 caused it to devolve still further, to the level of the municipality. During the 1840s, a new generation of Philadelphia merchants simultaneously confronted Baltimore's resurgence, the steady progress of the B&O, the evident failure of the Main Line of Public Works, and Pennsylvania's fiscal crisis. Responsibility for Philadelphia's commercial salvation, they believed, now rested with them. The Main Line and its network of feeder canals had generated the vast majority of the commonwealth's debt and therefore represented a public policy experiment never to be repeated. The insertion of patronage politics into virtually every aspect of operations and management had likewise helped to doom the Main Line, and Philadelphia merchants acknowledged that state ownership and management of internal improvements was no longer tenable. Instead, they hoped that the old hybrid system of canals and railroads—a situation conditioned by Pennsylvania's geography and by the early state of railway technology—would be replaced with an all-rail system.

Philadelphians made a virtue out of necessity, however, and developed a solution for the problems of technology, ownership, and management. Now that the technological superiority of the railroad had been proven, they argued, only a private corporation could be entrusted with the construction and operation of the new system. Several decades of experience had demonstrated that the open-access model, so typical of turnpike and canal traffic, simply would not work on a railroad. Even the canal commissioners had ultimately acknowledged that they would need to restrict public access to the commonwealth's railroads. In that context, Philadelphia merchants insisted, it made no sense for "the people" to own and operate a railroad as if it were a turnpike or a canal.

The only feasible solution to the new operational parameters of railroads, the prospective entrepreneurs suggested, was to adopt a new organizational model, in which a private corporation would manage the system. That private firm would have to possess a state-sanctioned monopoly on all rail transportation across Pennsylvania, they explained—to do otherwise would be to deprive investors of the just returns on their capital. In practical terms, promoters of the new private corporation insisted that legislators keep the Baltimore & Ohio from providing service to Pittsburgh, a demand that was certain to infuriate residents in the southwestern part of the state. Those in the south-central region, with their strong commercial ties to Baltimore, likewise opposed efforts to interfere with the B&O, or with Maryland. As had been the case with the Main Line, most of those who lived outside of Philadelphia correctly perceived the proposed new railroad as a project that would provide benefits for a select group of the city's merchants, and no one else. By the 1840s, the interstate rivalry between Maryland and Pennsylvania had thus been augmented by an even more internecine struggle within the commonwealth, pitting Philadelphians against the residents of Pittsburgh and the southwestern regions surrounding Allegheny County.

To make matters worse, the Philadelphians who launched what became the Pennsylvania Railroad were hardly representative of their state, or even of the city in which they operated. Like Mathew Carey and others who, a generation earlier, had founded the Pennsylvania Society for the Promotion of Internal Improvements in the Commonwealth, the new generation of promoters was close to, but not in, the circle of elite Philadelphians who dominated the city's commercial life. Their greatest business achievements had predated the new anthracite-driven industrial economy, or else they had failed in their attempts to master the new economic order. Those in the top tier wisely preferred to concentrate on profitable manufacturing ventures, often connected with the Schuylkill Navigation, the Philadelphia & Reading Rail Road, and other links to the anthracite regions. Individuals like shipbuilder William Cramp, machine-tool expert William Sellers, and even locomotive manufacturer Matthias W. Baldwin were more attuned to national and even international business trends. They saw considerable risk, and little profit, in constructing a railroad across the Alleghenies merely to salvage Philadelphia's commercial dignity.

The promoters of the new railroad enterprise thus had to choose their words with extreme care. They chose to mimic their predecessors in the Society for the Promotion of Internal Improvements, haranguing their fellow Pennsylvanians, and especially their fellow Philadelphians, about the economic and political benefits that the new railroad was certain to bring to the Keystone State. It would be a tough sell, in part because many of the state's residents had clear and bitter memories of the remarkably similar language that the earlier generation of boosters had used. In that context, it was hardly surprising that the next generation refrained from reciting the inadequacies associated with the Main Line of Public Works, as the two projects bore many discomforting similarities.

Philadelphia merchants sensed that many people would not take kindly to their efforts to link the commonwealth's economic future to a privately owned, monopolistic corporation possessing the sole right to build a transportation artery across the state. In their efforts to overcome opposition within their community and from across the commonwealth, they creatively turned the monopoly argument on its head. State government, once heralded as the guarantor of the rights of the people against monopolistic special interests, in their view became the enemy of the citizenry. The Main Line had failed because politicians—who were the elected representatives of the people, after all—had focused too narrowly on the interests of their constituents, to the detriment of the greater good of the commonwealth. How fair was it, they asked the people of Pennsylvania, to be shackled to a Board of Canal Commissioners that had monopolized transportation across the state and had managed that vital artery so ineptly? What was needed, they argued, was a private corporation that could allocate resources according to sound business principles, and not political whims. That corporation, far from enslaving the people of Pennsylvania, would underwrite the state's economic growth and thus guarantee the public good.

Yet, even as they emphasized the inherent superiority of private enterprise over the public sphere, Philadelphia's merchants without a hint of irony sought to manipulate public policy to serve their own ends. They demanded a charter from the legislature, a document that transferred substantial public authority to a private corporation, yet insisted that no other company could receive the corresponding privilege to build a rail line to Pittsburgh. By shielding them from the competitive pressures of the rival Baltimore & Ohio, legislators employed politics to structure economic development. Ultimately, Philadelphia's railroad promoters succeeded because the Pennsylvania General Assembly anointed them as the commonwealth's economic champions. The supporters of what became the Pennsylvania Railroad won their political battle against the allies of the B&O by the narrowest of margins, but their victory in the charter fight guaranteed the company's economic and political dominance over its native state for generations.

The charter was not enough. The railroad's promoters demanded, and received, substantial public support for their "private" project. Their company, in its earliest years, was not so much a private corporation as a mixed enterprise, one that was able to generate the capital necessary to begin construction only because municipal governments had purchased half of the outstanding stock.[5] In that sense, the project was not a revolutionary departure from public involvement in the economy, but was instead part of a continuum that encompassed many types of corporations, all designed to provide some measure of public benefit.[6] In that context, the new railroad emerged in an antebellum American economy that reflected coordinated, collective action that combined public good with private profit, and not in a theoretical world of laissez-faire individualism.

From the beginning, therefore, government was intimately involved in the creation of the Pennsylvania Railroad, as it had been with the Main Line of Public Works. The transition from one enterprise to another did not represent a battle between the public and the private sectors. Rather, it reflected different entrepreneurial visions, regarding precisely how the government could provide order and structure to the process of economic development. There was a substantial difference between the public Main Line and the new private corporation, however. The state government issued a corporate charter and local communities provided significant financial support, yet they did not exert a corresponding measure of control. Unlike the Main Line, business executives rather than politicians would create and manage the new enterprise.

Preparing for Battle

The significance of the first Baltimore & Ohio train to reach Cumberland was not lost on the residents of Pittsburgh, only 148 miles away. Many of the city's merchants and industrialists longed for a railroad link to Baltimore, as an alternative to the slow, unreliable, seasonal, and expensive Main Line of Public Works. They were also desperate to prevent the B&O from essentially following the route of the National Road, which passed south of Pittsburgh and reached the Ohio River at Wheeling. Pittsburgh merchants knew full well that two-thirds of the eastbound commerce that passed through their city originated along the Ohio River, to the south of Wheeling. Should the B&O connect Wheeling to Baltimore with a route that was far more efficient than the Main Line of Public Works, then Pittsburgh, they feared, was likely to wither and die.[7]

Pittsburgh residents had long sought to draw the B&O to their city. In February 1828, Pittsburghers had persuaded Pennsylvania legislators to grant the B&O the right to build through Pennsylvania, to reach the Ohio River at Pittsburgh. The charter carried a fifteen-year time limit, however, and it would expire long before the B&O could extend rails from Cumberland to the Pennsylvania state line. Nine years later, in April 1837, several Pittsburgh businessmen, chief among them William Larimer, Jr., and William Robinson, Jr., obtained a charter for the Pittsburgh & Connellsville Railroad. During the 1830s Larimer operated a freighting business, transporting cargoes between Philadelphia and Pittsburgh. Robinson was one of the first white residents of Pittsburgh, eventually became the mayor of Allegheny City, and was likewise heavily involved in transportation enterprises. They hoped that the proposed railroad, following the Monongahela and Youghiogheny rivers, would bring coal to Pittsburgh and generally improve transportation in the region. However, it could not have escaped the notice of residents of either Pennsylvania or Maryland that the line might someday offer the B&O access to Pittsburgh. Such plans lay in the future, however, and the Pittsburgh & Connellsville charter lapsed, without any construction taking place.[8]

Unfortunately for Pittsburgh's commercial interests, the B&O's Pennsylvania charter expired just as the railroad reached Cumberland. The railroad's supporters accordingly adopted two complimentary strategies. Their long-term goal was to secure legislative approval for a new charter that would allow the B&O to build into Pennsylvania. Their more immediate objective was to revive the charter of the moribund Pittsburgh & Connellsville Railroad, as a mechanism to reach the B&O's tracks at Cumberland. They hoped that that company's name, encompassing two communities that lay within the commonwealth of Pennsylvania, would be less likely to attract the scrutiny of the Philadelphians who were alert for any activity on the part of the B&O. In April 1843, promoters of the Pittsburgh & Connellsville shepherded through the Pennsylvania legislature "an act for the relief of the overseers of the poor of the borough of Erie, and for other purposes." Those "other purposes" included the reestablishment of the Pittsburgh & Connellsville, as well as its extension from Connellsville to a connection with the B&O line at Cumberland. Philadelphia interests discovered the subterfuge before the bill reached the governor's desk, however, and had the re-charter provisions stricken from the legislation.[9]

The issue of a rail connection between Pittsburgh and Baltimore lay dormant for several years, but it resurfaced at the beginning of the 1845 legislative session. The General Assembly adjourned in April without acting on a proposal to revive the Pittsburgh & Connellsville charter. The bill's presence on the legislative calendar was nonetheless sufficient to excite alarm in Philadelphia—eventually. Philadelphians received news of the threat from an unlikely source, a canal boat operator named "Captain" Samuel D. Karns. During the winter months, when the Main Line canals were closed to navigation, Karns resided in Harrisburg, where he supplemented his income by acting as a political lobbyist. According to Senator Alexander K. McClure, that "jolly and companionable" man "did not pretend to debauch legislators, but gave such attention to little matters of personal legislation as made parties willing to pay him the small fee he demanded." He was, in short, part of a class of "borers," who earned their unsavory nickname by relentlessly lobbying elected officials for favors large and small in exchange for appropriate compensation from those seeking corporate charters or desiring resolution of other matters requiring legislative attention. They often acted without pay, simply because they maintained a strong personal interest in the proposed legislation, but others, such as the versatile "Captain" Karns, arranged political favors, for a fee, for individuals who found it difficult to attend the legislative sessions in Harrisburg.[10]

During the 1845 session, supporters of the Baltimore & Ohio retained Karns to represent their interests in the legislature. The captain, untroubled by conflicts of interest or other abstract ethical concepts, reasoned that he could collect double fees by persuading Philadelphians to hire him to promote a competing railroad, in opposition to the B&O. Karns was apparently the first person to inform Philadelphia residents of the proposed B&O charter, and he was disappointed when his warnings did not initially induce the panic (and the payout) that he had anticipated.[11]

By the autumn of 1845, however, Philadelphians were at last sensible of the danger that the Baltimore & Ohio posed to their city and its merchants. On January 6, 1846, when Senator George Darsie, representing Allegheny County, introduced a bill that would authorize the B&O to build a line to Pittsburgh, Philadelphia residents were prepared. Seven years earlier, Darsie had been one of the organizers of the Chambersburg & Pittsburgh Railway, which he saw as part of an ambitious plan to link Philadelphia to St. Louis by rail. That scheme would be successful only if Pittsburgh enjoyed a reliable rail link to the east coast. Now, with Democrats controlling both chambers of the legislature, Darsie, a Whig, ostensibly possessed little political influence. His resolution nevertheless touched off a firestorm of debate. Western Pennsylvanians insisted that a connection to the B&O was indispensible for the future of their region, while their eastern counterparts claimed that such a link would drag Philadelphia into ruin.

Few people had a better understanding of Philadelphia's precarious and declining fortunes, or were in a better position to do something about it, than Thomas Pim Cope.[12] Born in Lancaster in 1768, Cope had been apprenticed at age eighteen to his uncle's dry goods store in Philadelphia. By 1803, he was a partner in the mercantile house of Cope & Thomas, and in 1807 he became part owner in the *Lancaster*, a ship that was soon engaged in the China trade. He acquired a reputation as something of a maverick for refusing to insure any of his ships or their cargoes, asserting that the savings in premiums offset the rare possibility of a catastrophic loss. In 1821, he founded the Cope Line, one of the first regularly scheduled packet services, operating once a month between Philadelphia and Liverpool. The company lasted until the time of the Civil War, but Cope suffered financially, particularly between 1828 and 1830, as the China and India trades shifted from Philadelphia to New York and Boston.[13]

Cope was as interested in the betterment of his native city as he was in advancing his personal wealth. In 1838, Cope helped to establish the Philadelphia Board of Trade, serving as its president for the next twenty-two years. As fellow Board of Trade member Richard D. Wood asserted, Cope was "liberal and prompt in assisting public works, and better deserves the name of patriot than all the soldiers who have ever shed blood."[14] When the backers of the Chesapeake & Delaware Canal were struggling to raise enough money to continue construction, Cope pledged a substantial portion of his personal fortune to the venture. He was also active in the city's political and intellectual affairs, serving in both the Select Council and the state legislature, and helping to found the Mercantile Library and the Franklin Institute, the city's preeminent center for the dissemination of scientific knowledge. His support for a wide variety of municipal betterments—ranging from the Philadelphia waterworks to the almshouse, Fairmount Park, and the Zoological Society—indicated his desire to improve life in the city. As a Quaker, he was both a pacifist and an abolitionist, strongly opposed to the Mexican War, and suspicious of the growing political power of the slave-owning South. His faith also brought him into close contact with many other Quakers, giving him access to the political and economic resources that he would need in order to help establish a new railroad that could compete against the B&O.[15]

By the mid-1840s, Cope was tired of the stress associated with global shipping sans insurance. His diaries reflected his concern about the dangers of maritime commerce, including an incident involving a ship belonging to another merchant: "The New York & Liverpool packet Columbia was visited on her outward passage by a sea that washed her captain, Rathbone, his two mates, five seamen & a boy, overboard—the remaining crew pillaged the cabin, broke open trunks & mutinied."[16] Such tragic events could affect his commercial interests as well, hardly making for a quiet, stress-free retirement.

Cope was no less concerned with the potential pitfalls associated with railway construction. He sensed the danger associated with the British "Railway Mania," a speculative bubble that would soon collapse amid rampant speculation, fraud, and overbuilding. "The rage for Rail Roads in Great Britain is astonishing," he wrote in the summer of 1845. "May not these speculations terminate in the ruin of unwary adventurers—& and [sic] may not many of our people suffer from the same mania."[17]

Cope might never have engaged in railroad promotion had not Philadelphia so desperately needed the wealth and influence of the Quaker merchant. By the time that Senator Darsie introduced his January 1846 resolution authorizing the B&O to build to Pittsburgh, Cope was an old man (he died in November 1854, at the age of eighty-six), ready to withdraw from active involvement in business matters. "My desire is rather to retire from bustle & contention, than to enter more deeply into embarrassing concerns," he wrote in March 1847, "& were it not my conscientious belief that the future prosperity of the City depends on the completion of this Railroad, it had not met my personal support." Cope admittedly had no great love for the "vulgar herd" that he thought composed the bulk of the city's population, but he was anxious to preserve the status of the city and likewise to enable his peers to continue to fund the scientific and cultural pursuits that he believed were essential to enlightened progress.[18]

Cope's social prominence made him the logical choice to promote a trans-Pennsylvania railroad, and it was his sense of duty that persuaded him to accept that role. On October 29, 1845, in the Board of Trade Room at the Philadelphia Merchants' Exchange, he presided over a meeting of prominent merchants who were anxious to blunt the proposed B&O incursion into Pennsylvania. He spoke in reaction to the editors of western Pennsylvania newspapers, such as the *Indiana Republican*, who hinted that they would support the B&O's entrance into Pittsburgh unless Philadelphians discarded their "Quaker conservatism" and funded an all-rail route across the state.[19] Cope's diary reflected the feeling of many Philadelphians when he closed out the year 1845 by noting that he was "in favour of a road through our own State, & under our own control, in preference to one passing to a rival City, & under the management of persons having no Pennsylvania interest. After providing for ourselves, it will be time enough to be generous to others, & not put a staff in an enemies hand, to break our own head."[20]

The only way to protect the city, Cope and his associates reasoned, was to build a railroad from Harrisburg to Pittsburgh. That all-rail route, variously called the Central Railroad or the Pennsylvania Central Railroad, would make use of the existing Philadelphia & Columbia and replace the remainder of the Main Line of Public Works with a parallel continuous rail line, using the Allegheny Portage Railroad as a temporary expedient to speed construction. The cost, they estimated, would be but $7.5 million, while the benefits would be enormous. An efficient transportation artery to Pittsburgh, they insisted, would capture the western grain trade from the Erie Canal and the Baltimore & Ohio Railroad, redirect it to the wharves and warehouses of Philadelphia, and once again enable the city to flourish.

Philadelphia merchants were quick to support the Pennsylvania Central project. In November 1845 a petition signed by 513 prominent Philadelphians warned of "the magnitude of the interests at stake," including "the loss of our most valuable trade," and called for a railroad convention in their city.[21] Yet, those elites recognized that widespread public and municipal support would be essential for such a complex and expensive endeavor. Accordingly, the members of the group empowered Cope to call a town meeting on December 10, 1845, at the Chinese Museum in Philadelphia, where the issue would be publicly debated.[22] The timing was hardly auspicious, with news reaching the United States in late November that the speculative British market for railway securities (which Cope suggested "surpasses the Tulip Lunacy & falls little short of the South Sea bubble") had collapsed.[23]

Figure 11. Thomas Pim Cope (1768–1854) was a successful Philadelphia merchant and ship owner, part of a small body of affluent Quakers who dominated the city's economic and intellectual life. The references to his shipping activities and to his role in founding the Mercantile Library Company of Philadelphia are evident. More than any other individual, he was responsible for creating the Pennsylvania Railroad. He served on its board and would have been named its first president had not advanced age and ill health forced him to decline that position.

Engraving by John Sartain, from a portrait by John Neagle, ca. 1848, Print Collection, Miriam and Ira D. Wallach Division of Art, Prints and Photographs, The New York Public Library, Lenox and Tilden Foundations.

Joseph R. Chandler called the meeting to order. Chandler was a Whig, like most other Philadelphia elites, a member of the Philadelphia Select Council, the editor of the *United States Gazette*, and a future U.S. representative. George Darsie was present and, as a state senator and as a resident of Pittsburgh, he emphasized that neither he nor his fellow westerners harbored any animosity to the project—but that he was also compelled to support the interests of his local constituents and the B&O route. Also prominent among the attendees was Henry D. Gilpin, a former U.S. attorney general who, like Cope, was a Quaker, was a member of the American Philosophical Society, and had held a seat on the board of directors of the Second Bank of the United States. William M. Meredith, president of the Select Council, spoke enthusiastically of the Pennsylvania Central project. He had served in the General Assembly and later as the United States district attorney for the Eastern District of Pennsylvania. He possessed extensive political connections in the Whig Party (he would become secretary of the treasury in March 1849) and was a valuable asset to the group. Colonel John McCahan represented the Northern Liberties, the area north of the Center City district of Philadelphia, from Vine Street to Kensington. George Washington Toland, a Whig and former U.S. congressman whose district had included Philadelphia, insisted that Cope chair the meeting.[24]

Facing the "immense crowd," Cope emphasized, "The necessity of immediate & effective action, every man in the community, from the day labourer to the man of wealth, the dealer in stocks, the mortgage holder, the owner of Real Estate, are all interested in the success of this great undertaking." Cope warned of the danger posed by the Erie Canal and especially the Baltimore & Ohio Railroad, even as he "wished success to that spirited Company." He likewise espoused no animosity for the Main Line of Public Works, and he claimed that the construction of a new, privately held line would offer "a certainty of passage at all seasons" and might even quadruple traffic on the state system. Placing the burden of Pennsylvania's future squarely on the shoulders of his audience, Cope ended the meeting with a dramatic flourish worthy of the oratory of the age. "Nature has done much for us," he declared. "Let us now see what we can do for ourselves."[25]

The Battle for the Charter

Cope and his fellow Philadelphians knew what they had to do for themselves. They would have to convince the members of the legislature—who but a decade earlier had financed the construction of the Main Line of Public Works, and for which public debt it was still legally liable—to grant a charter to a competing private corporation. That new company, the proposed Pennsylvania Central Railroad, would monopolize rail transportation across the commonwealth. Such circumstances were likely to arouse the ire of many legislators, as well as their constituents.

Cope and his allies expected that the state legislature would charter their railroad, while denying corresponding privileges to the Baltimore & Ohio. As such, their assurances to "disclaim all intention or desire . . . of throwing obstacles or restraints in the way of improvements proposed to be made, within this State, by companies incorporated by other States," rang somewhat hollow.[26] The Pennsylvania Central Railroad's principals offered three counterarguments to anyone who accused them of possessing a double standard. First, they maintained that the Pittsburgh market could not support two competing railway routes, noting that it was "obvious there is to be *one* great line of trade and travel between the Atlantic and the West, and wherever this line shall strike the Ohio, it will be met and continued indefinitely, through the valleys and the prairies of the vast region beyond."[27] Second, they demanded reciprocal treatment and decried the unwillingness of the Maryland legislature to permit railroads incorporated in Pennsylvania to enter that state. Finally, in a rather crass and disingenuous effort to deflect criticism from those who suggested that their company would destroy the Main Line of Public Works, the Pennsylvania Central Railroad's supporters insisted that the B&O would achieve that unhappy result by siphoning away all traffic moving across the commonwealth, but that the Pennsylvania Central Railroad would attract the western trade and induce an "increase of business on the State Canal . . . augmenting in proportion the revenue, and diminishing more and more, every year, the burden of taxation."[28]

Furthermore, by 1845 a strong anti-charter movement had developed in the United States. Many citizens

Figure 12. The Old State Capitol in Harrisburg was built in 1822 and destroyed by fire in 1896. It was here that Whigs battled Democrats, and Philadelphians argued with Pittsburghers, over the twin charters of the Pennsylvania Central and the Baltimore & Ohio.

Pennsylvania Historical and Museum Commission, Pennsylvania State Archives.

believed that charters, with their grant of unlimited life and implied monopoly power, enabled the few to accumulate vast sums of wealth while tyrannizing the many. The anti-charter argument asserting that corporations fostered corruption may have had little traction given the rampant nepotism and mismanagement associated with the Main Line of Public Works. In their quest for a charter, however, Cope and his allies could not argue, as had earlier proponents of publicly funded internal improvements, that the Pennsylvania Central Railroad was designed to benefit equally all residents of Pennsylvania.[29] At the December 10 town meeting, Colonel McCahan, whom Cope described as "a hackenied [sic] stump orator [and] a thorough going demagogue," was understandably pessimistic regarding the willingness of Harrisburg legislators to grant the Pennsylvania Central what amounted to a trans-

portation monopoly within the commonwealth. "He said the Legislature regarded Corporations with great distrust," Cope noted, and "that we should accept from them such a charter as we could get."[30]

Politically, much had changed since the 1820s, when Mathew Carey and his allies had persuaded the members of the General Assembly to fund the Main Line of Public Works. The charter battle occurred during a time of flux in Pennsylvania politics. The constitution of 1838 had increased the number of elective offices and drastically reduced the governor's authority. Voters ratified that constitution by an extraordinarily slim margin, of barely a thousand votes out of more than 225,000 cast, with the greatest support coming from the rural northern and western parts of the commonwealth, and the greatest opposition from the urban southeast—something that did not bode well for the

Philadelphia Quakers who sought to exercise power under the new system of governance. Prior to the 1850s, party organizations remained relatively weak, affording legislators considerable autonomy in responding to political pressure—not all of which came from the constituents in their districts. At the same time, the members of the General Assembly considered relatively few bills (they passed 132 laws in 1815, and 191 in 1830, representing approximately half of the bills under consideration) enabling legislators to consider carefully the merits of each act and making it difficult to shield bribery or other acts of political malfeasance from the light of public scrutiny.[31]

The proliferation of public and private internal-improvement projects during the 1830s greatly increased the scope and complexity of the legislature's activities. The ventures, along with the banks that helped to finance them, required some form of legislative approval, and the number of laws passed ballooned to 358 in the 1845 session, and 725 in 1860. Under such circumstances, legislators often assented to bills without even reading them, as a professional courtesy to the member who had sponsored them. Lobbyists exploited that situation through the practice of "logrolling," by creating omnibus bills that ostensibly covered some minor matter of purely local interest, but which also included a corporate charter that might have caused considerable controversy, had anyone bothered to study carefully the full text of the bill. Even though it was relatively easy to slip a provision through the legislature, largely unnoticed, it was also a simple matter to bury any bill that had even a few enemies. As few as two legislators could argue for postponement until late in the session, when chances for passage were substantially reduced, delaying or defeating a corporate charter with surprisingly little opposition. Legislators intended to use their authority as much to promote the interests of their constituencies as to safeguard the economic survival of Pennsylvania. Under those circumstances, the Philadelphia merchants who supported the railroad would need to resort to intense political lobbying and deal making, as well as outright corruption, to secure a charter and deny one to the Baltimore & Ohio.[32]

The B&O was likely to find favor with many Pennsylvania legislators. It was an established company, ef-fectively organized and adequately capitalized, and its supporters could point to steady, if slow, progress toward the west. Because the B&O was based in Baltimore and its strongest Pennsylvania supporters resided in the southwestern part of the state, the company thus avoided the elitist overtones that often attached to the affluent Quaker Whigs of Philadelphia. The B&O was also well positioned to influence the General Assembly by means both fair and foul. Cope recalled that several years before the charter debate, a B&O stockholder had said to him, "Mr. Cope we can do anything with your Legislature."[33] Other Philadelphians darkly suggested that the B&O's promoters were ready to distribute whatever funds they thought necessary in order to secure the cooperation of the Pennsylvania legislators.

Cope had good reason to believe such accusations. Many years earlier, during the War of 1812, American privateers had seized one of his ships, the *Susquehanna*, and he had retained a young Wilmington, Delaware, attorney, Louis McLane, to secure its return. According to Cope, McLane had conspired with the local district attorney to demand a $1,000 bribe in order to settle the case in an amicable manner. Cope was outraged, and refused on principle to pay so much as a cent in aid of corruption. The two men parted on poor terms, the years passed, and, in 1837, Louis McLane became president of the Baltimore & Ohio Railroad. The fact that McLane was not even in the United States at the time (he was serving as minister to Britain in order to negotiate the Oregon boundary dispute) seemed to matter little, and Cope, for one, believed that he would stop at nothing to secure a Pennsylvania charter for his company.[34]

The Pennsylvania Central faced far more serious threats that were much closer to home. Charles Gibbons, a youthful and irascible Whig, and one of the two state senators representing Philadelphia, became an extremely dangerous adversary to Cope and to the Pennsylvania Central Railroad. Gibbons originally hailed from Wilmington, Delaware. "The inhabitants of that City have never shown any particular attachment to Philadelphia," Cope mused, largely because the Philadelphia merchants who had financed the Chesapeake & Delaware Canal had chosen to bypass Wilmington.[35] Like Cope, Gibbons was an abolitionist Quaker, but his unwillingness to uphold his city's interests earned him many enemies. Cope certainly agreed with one newspaper's assessment, which he thought characterized Gibbons as "tricky, malignant & traitorous."[36] Gibbons was not opposed to the new railroad in and of itself, but he insisted that it should not receive legislative sanction to create a transportation monopoly in Pennsylvania. Following his election to the Senate in 1844, and his elevation to speaker two years later, he had supported the B&O, because at that time he had sincerely believed that it was the only viable alternative to the Main Line of Public Works. He felt disinclined to retreat from that position, and he insisted that the western trade could support two routes running through Pittsburgh, without detriment to Philadelphia.[37] By December 1845, Gibbons had already published a series of essays in the *United States Gazette* praising the B&O route and condemning the Pennsylvania Central project.[38]

John Bannister Gibson, chief justice of the Pennsylvania Supreme Court, was also particularly vociferous in his opposition to the Pennsylvania Central charter. He had long-standing personal and professional connections to communities in the Susquehanna River Valley, as well as to Hagerstown, Maryland—all areas that were likely to benefit from the success of the B&O—and held that Cope and his allies were "prejudiced" in favor of a route through central Pennsylvania. Gibson was the grand master of a Masonic Lodge in Lancaster that counted among its members Treasury Secretary James Buchanan and Molton C. Rogers, Buchanan's former law partner. Rogers, who also held a seat on the state supreme court, was more restrained in his criticism of the Pennsylvania Central but nonetheless insisted that the B&O provided the surer access to Pittsburgh and the west. His fellow justice (and former state senator and U.S. congressman) Thomas Burnside was, however, cautiously optimistic about the Pennsylvania Central's prospects. "Burnside entertained more of a Pennsylvania view," Cope recalled, "reprobating the [Baltimore & Ohio] connection as injurious to the state." In addition to promising his own support, Burnside offered that of his son, James, a state legislator who had been instrumental in defeating the B&O's attempts to obtain a Pennsylvania charter less than a year earlier.[39]

The Pennsylvania Central had even stronger allies. One of the most important was William A. Crabb, who in 1841 had served as speaker of the State House of Representatives, and was now the other state senator representing Philadelphia. He was a Whig, like Charles Gibbons, but unlike Gibbons, Crabb was an enthusiastic supporter of the cross-state route. Charles B. Trego, a Philadelphia delegate to the State House of Representatives and another Pennsylvania Central advocate, was well placed to emphasize the feasibility of railroad construction through western Pennsylvania and the potential for agricultural and mineral traffic along the new line. As a geologist, he had tramped through much of the area west of Harrisburg, he had been the instigating force behind the commonwealth's first geological survey, conducted in the late 1830s, and he later declined Governor Ritner's invitation to serve as state geologist. It was Trego who cautioned that the Pennsylvania Central's organizers should not choose a specific route, lest such an announcement excite political jealousies and inflate real estate prices.[40]

John Sergeant, who had been a member of the United States House of Representatives, the legal counsel for the Second Bank of the United States, and the chairman of the Board of Canal Commissioners, came out in support of the Pennsylvania Central, as did his brother Thomas Sergeant, a former state attorney general and a justice on the state supreme court. The promoters of the Pennsylvania Central also enlisted the aid of Richard Rush, a noted statesman and former attorney general and treasury secretary, who wrote a cogent editorial in the *North American*. Cope promptly mailed copies of the journal to each member of the General Assembly, to the entire Pennsylvania delegation in Congress, to Treasury Secretary James Buchanan, and to Vice President George M. Dallas.[41]

Two sets of lobbyists—one representing the Pennsylvania Central, and the other, the Baltimore & Ohio—descended on Harrisburg for the beginning of the 1846 legislative session. On January 6, 1846, in the first act of the new legislature, Senator George Darsie, representing Allegheny County, introduced a bill to permit the Baltimore & Ohio to build to Pittsburgh. Less than a week later, at a railroad convention in Harrisburg, James Clarke, president of the Board of Canal Commissioners, made a rousing speech in favor of the

Pennsylvania Central. Supporters of the B&O packed the convention, however, overwhelming those who favored a Pennsylvania route. The situation soon degenerated into political chaos, as the latter group boycotted the meeting and then proceeded to establish a rival convention. Back in Philadelphia, on the evening of January 19, 1846, the Board of Trade unanimously adopted a resolution, introduced by George Toland's brother, Robert, calling on the state's legislators to charter a railway between Harrisburg and Pittsburgh.[42]

Three days later, on January 22, Philadelphia representative William H. Haley strode into the House chamber and introduced "An Act to Incorporate the Pennsylvania Railroad Company," giving it the authority to build a line across the state. The House took no action, however, and waited for the Senate Committee on Internal Improvement to consider its own version of the bill, which it sent to the full chamber on January 26. On February 18, the Senate voted against adding a provision to Darsie's bill for the B&O charter, making it void in the event that the Pennsylvania Central were incorporated, and then narrowly defeated the entire bill, sixteen votes to fifteen.[43]

That same day, Cope, George Toland, George N. Baker, and James A. Bayard, Jr., departed for Harrisburg, determined, in Cope's words, "to oppose the scheme of the Baltimore & Ohio Rail Road Company in their attempt to rob us on our own soil of the western trade."[44] The fireworks began almost immediately. Governor Francis Rawn Shunk, who was dying of tuberculosis, greeted the delegation courteously, but made few promises. He was a Democrat, as were a majority of the state senators, and he harbored a deep mistrust of the Pennsylvania Central and the Whigs who promoted it. More ominously, he was opposed to the very idea of corporate charters, believing such grants of monopoly power more in keeping with the traditions of monarchical Britain than those of American democracy. In his January 5, 1848, message to the General Assembly, a few months before his death, Shunk would insist that "in this age and country, under our free system, where the people are sovereign, to grant special privileges, is an invertion [sic] of the order of things."[45] Under that view, the supporters of the Pennsylvania Central charter were not merely threat-

ening the commercial interests of western Pennsylvania—they were threatening the very idea of democracy itself.

Of more immediate concern to Cope, even Philadelphians were divided over the merits of the charter. Of Philadelphia's two Whig senators, Charles Gibbons and William A. Crabb, the former supported the B&O and the latter, the Pennsylvania Central, increasing the political discord. By February 21, three days after the delegation arrived in Harrisburg, Gibbons's steadfast opposition to the Pennsylvania Central, which had already cost him the support of his fellow Philadelphians, nearly cost him his life as well. He had become so incensed at the pro-Pennsylvania Central writings of Judge Robert T. Conrad, the Whig editor of the *North American*—editorials that defamed him personally—that he threatened to shoot the judge, and only the timely intervention of Charles J. Biddle (the son of Nicholas Biddle) prevented a duel from taking place.[46]

The histrionics involving Charles Gibbons were but a sideshow to the battle in the state Senate, where legislators from southwestern Pennsylvania were doing their best to give the B&O access to Pittsburgh. They received strong encouragement from B&O investors, yet the Baltimore company was at something of a disadvantage. President Louis McLane, serving as minister to Britain, was out of the country between July 1845 and October 1846, and he was thus unable to coordinate the B&O's lobbying efforts. On February 19, the senators listened to the second reading of the Pennsylvania Central bill, while a majority declined to reconsider the B&O charter. Western Pennsylvanians were livid. The editor of the *Pittsburgh Chronicle* protested, "We, in connection with a larger portion of the State, have long suffered under the domineering diction of the Philadelphians."[47] Pittsburgh attorney and former Treasury Secretary Walter Forward had little use for a Pennsylvania Railroad charter that would "usurp our natural rights, and render us serfs and slaves to Philadelphia."[48] William McCandless, from Clarion County, was proud to be counted among the "hard-fisted people who would not bow down to the Golden Calf which the Chinese of Chestnut Street had set up."[49] More radical residents of the southwestern counties threatened to cease payment of all state taxes, secede from Pennsylvania, and join Maryland should the B&O bill fail to become law. Philadelphia newspaper editors had little patience with what they called the "Pittsburgh Lunacy," but both the governor and members of the legislature were anxious to contain the growing political chaos.[50]

Legislators from southern and western Pennsylvania were not the only ones who supported the B&O. Representatives from other areas expressed their concern that a trans-Pennsylvania railroad would render the Main Line of Public Works worthless. Legislators representing southwestern Pennsylvania were aghast that the commonwealth's residents should continue to repay the construction cost of the Pennsylvania Canal, which the railroad would soon put out of business. Such concerns were in part genuine and in part a thin disguise for yet another political stratagem to favor the B&O over the Philadelphia company.

On February 20, Senator William Bigler, a Democrat from Clearfield County in west-central Pennsylvania, attempted to overcome fears that the Pennsylvania Central would deprive the state system of revenue by proposing a "tonnage tax" of five mills per ton-mile, to be collected only from March until December, the months when the canals were open to traffic. Supporters of the tonnage tax argued that the surcharge was necessary to protect the commonwealth's substantial investment in the Main Line of Public Works. More precisely, a portion of the increased efficiency generated by rail transportation would be used to offset the resulting loss in value of the canals.[51] The proposed tonnage tax represented a strong assertion of the state's power to shape economic development, yet the stipulation ultimately benefited the Pennsylvania Central's promoters. The tonnage tax assured legislators that the new railroad would generate sufficient tax revenue to pay the interest on the commonwealth's outstanding internal improvement bonds, and removed the last impediment to its charter.

On February 24, the Senate, by an overwhelming majority of twenty-six to five, agreed to incorporate the Pennsylvania Central. The following day, in response to intense political pressure from the western part of the commonwealth, the Senate agreed to reconsider the B&O charter and passed the bill, by a vote of seventeen to thirteen, on February 27. Both

charters now moved to the House, where the contest was more closely divided. On March 19, 1846, the House passed the Pennsylvania Central charter bill. Additional votes in the Senate (on March 25) and in the House (on March 27) were required to reconcile the two versions of the charter. Yet Shunk refused to sign the bill, pending the outcome of the debate regarding the B&O legislation.[52]

The B&O charter seemed likely to succeed as well, but supporters of the Pennsylvania Central devised a stratagem that would allow the bill to pass while rendering its provisions ineffective. They issued an amendment to the B&O charter stipulating that the Philadelphia company should generate at least $3 million in stock subscriptions, with 10 percent paid in, and award construction contracts for a minimum of thirty miles of railroad. If that were to occur prior to July 30, 1847, then the B&O charter would be suspended. In the meantime, the B&O would be unable to build into Pennsylvania. On March 20, with a razor-thin vote of fifty to forty-eight, the House approved the amendment. Pittsburgh interests later retaliated by introducing an amendment to the amendment, requiring that at least fifteen of the first thirty miles be on the western end of the railroad, and raising the amount of paid-in capital to $1 million.[53] In another effort to strike back at the Pennsylvania Central, B&O partisans on April 3 resurrected the charter of the Pittsburgh & Connellsville Railroad, enabling it to build from Pittsburgh south to a connection with the B&O at the Pennsylvania state line. The provisions were little more than a minor inconvenience for the supporters of the Pennsylvania Central. Despite the efforts of Pittsburghers, the March 20 vote effectively rendered useless any charter granted to the B&O and, of greater importance, cleared the political logjam by providing legislators and Governor Shunk with a safe mechanism for supporting both bills.[54]

Shunk nonetheless continued to express concerns about some of the terms of the Pennsylvania Central legislation. He was particularly opposed to the provision that would have enabled the state to repurchase the railroad, but only at the par value of what some suspected to be watered stock. Legislators accordingly modified the Pennsylvania Central charter, inserting a provision enabling the state to buy the railroad for the actual cost of construction, a fairly standard provision that states rarely exercised.[55] On April 11 the House approved the final changes, followed by the Senate on April 13. Later that day, April 13, 1846, Governor Shunk signed the bill that created a new corporation that was known simply as the Pennsylvania Railroad.[56]

In granting a charter to the Pennsylvania Railroad, legislators attempted, as they had in the past, to ensure that the private company would operate in the public interest. While authorized to build between Harrisburg and Pittsburgh, as well as a second route to Erie, there were nonetheless substantial constraints on the railroad's geographic reach. The company lacked the authority to build west of Pittsburgh, a stipulation designed to ensure that that city would remain a key transfer point for any freight or passengers connecting with riverboats or other railroads reaching farther to the west. The PRR could not construct branch lines outside the counties traversed by its main line. In order to protect the freight forwarders who operated over the Main Line of Public Works, legislators permitted any individual or company who owned a railroad car to operate it on PRR rails. The General Assembly also established maximum freight and passenger rates, a move that gave the state extraordinary control over the railroad's operations and management—or would have, had not steadily declining transportation costs rendered the issue moot.

Despite those restrictions, legislators had granted the Pennsylvania Central an exceedingly favorable corporate charter. The act of incorporation listed 198 "commissioners," from the city of Philadelphia and twenty-nine outlying counties, although only a dozen of those individuals possessed the authority "to act in the premises."[57] The commissioners had considerable time to organize their company, and pledged to begin construction within two years and to complete the entire route within a decade. As a common carrier, the railroad possessed the right of eminent domain, yet it was precluded from "passing through any burying-ground, or place of public worship, or any dwelling house, without the consent of the owner."[58] In order to make the project more attractive to investors during the critical construction phase, members of the General Assembly authorized the commissioners to begin payment of 5 percent annual dividends on paid-in cap-

ital, beginning when the railroad had completed fifteen miles of track at each end of the line, and ending when construction crews had laid fifty miles at each end. Inasmuch as the railroad, at that stage, could not have been expected to generate much income, the company was to pay those guaranteed dividends (which were referred to as "interest" payments) from the capital account rather than treat them as a charge against earnings. In simple terms, the railroad's directors would borrow money in order to pay the interest charges on money that they had already borrowed.[59]

During the week that followed the signing of the Pennsylvania Central charter, debate continued over the Baltimore & Ohio's access to Pittsburgh. On April 17, the House passed the final version of the B&O charter, fifty-one votes to forty-five, while the Senate gave its assent the following day, by a slim majority of sixteen to fifteen. On April 21, Governor Shunk signed the bill into law. The General Assembly chartered two railroads almost simultaneously, but the supporters of the B&O had been decisively defeated. Legislators had given the incorporators of the Pennsylvania Railroad a fifteen-month head start on the B&O. The directors of the Baltimore company would have to wait until the end of July 1847 to see if their Philadelphia rivals could raise capital and begin construction. To make good on their lead, Thomas Pim Cope and the other Philadelphians who backed the Pennsylvania Railroad would nonetheless need to act quickly in order to take advantage of the opportunities that the legislature had offered to them.

A New Mixed Corporation

From its creation, the Pennsylvania Railroad was a creature of state and local politics. The state legislature provided the corporate charter, with its attendant advantages to the PRR coming at the expense of the "foreign" Baltimore & Ohio, a corporation that had been chartered in Maryland. The members of the General Assembly were nonetheless reluctant to provide direct financial support to the PRR, in large measure because they had bitter memories of the problems associated with the earlier state-funded system of internal improvements. Just as the construction of the Main Line of Public Works indicated that responsibility for internal improvements had shifted from the federal government to the states, the incorporation of the Pennsylvania Railroad marked a further devolution of responsibility, to local government. Much of the money needed to construct the Pennsylvania Railroad came not from the commonwealth, but from Philadelphia and Pittsburgh, the two communities that stood to benefit the most from the new railroad. Once incorporated, the PRR received critical financial support from those locales, which were themselves incorporated, as municipalities.

Governmental funding for the PRR differed markedly from earlier state support for the Main Line. It was not merely because private funding underwrote approximately half of the cost of the railroad's construction. Instead, and in marked contrast to the state management of the Main Line, the railroad's organizers were able to take money from those municipal corporations without ceding any significant degree of organizational control to them. In brief, the government paid half of the bills but exerted none of the corresponding authority.

The Philadelphia merchants who organized the PRR were determined to preclude any form of governmental oversight of the railroad's construction or operations. They were well aware of the long history of mismanagement associated with the Main Line, and they had no desire to repeat that experience. In December 1845, on the eve of the charter battle, Colonel John McCahan, representing the interests of the Northern Liberties, had suggested that the company raise funds (and placate legislative fears regarding monopoly power) by offering the commonwealth half ownership in the new venture, along with half of the resulting profits. Cope, and others, sensed the danger of that plan. "Should his doctrine of connecting the State in the management of the Road & dividing the income, be carried out," he confided to his diary, "there must be a speedy end to our hopes, [for] few men will be inclined to venture their money in a scheme, the whole hazard of which is to be at their expense—& if successful others are to pocket half the profits, besides these politicians have so mismanaged the public works that prudent men will little incline to them."[60]

Initially, there seemed little need for any sort of direct governmental involvement in the new enterprise. On the evening of April 27, 1846, local citizens assembled in the Chinese Museum, overfilling even the largest salon in that building, to learn about the progress of their railway. Rumors of war with Mexico could do little to dim their celebratory mood. They had much to celebrate. The Pennsylvania Railroad was precisely two weeks old, and ecstasy over the success of the charter bill had not yet given way to debates over routes, construction methods, and financing. Thomas Cope chaired the meeting, and he was careful to maintain "the harmony & good feeling which were exclusively prevalent throughout all our proceedings" by judiciously avoiding such troublesome questions. The gathering approved the appointment of a Committee of Seven, consisting of Job R. Tyson (Cope's son-in-law), David S. Brown, John Grigg, Thomas Sparks, George N. Baker, Richard D. Wood, and James Magee, each of them responsible for promoting the railroad and organizing stock subscriptions.[61] Frederick Fraley, the recently appointed president of the Schuylkill Navigation and one of the founders of the Franklin Institute, spoke for more than an hour. Senators William Bigler and William Crabb received an enthusiastic reception, as did House members Victor E. Piolett (Bradford County) and Benjamin Hill (Montgomery County). Conspicuous by his absence was "the traitor Charles Gibbons," for to include him, Cope suggested, "would have been beneath the dignity of the meeting."[62]

Cope and his associates soon discovered that Philadelphians' public encouragement for the Pennsylvania Railroad did not necessarily translate into financial support, and that they would need to rely on the government to a far greater degree than they had anticipated. On June 22, 1846, Thomas Cope presided at the Philadelphia Merchants' Exchange as the PRR commissioners opened the railroad's stock register for public subscriptions. Cope demonstrated his continuing support for the project by personally buying four hundred shares. It was just as well that he did so, because only 6,180 shares had been subscribed by the time that the company's books closed at 3:00 P.M. The majority of the subscriptions—some 60 percent— were for five or fewer shares. Those figures offered a fairly clear indication of the great public support that Philadelphian merchants maintained for the railroad, but also of the fact that few large investors were willing to risk their capital in the venture. Among the small investors were 169 craftsmen employed at the Philadelphia manufactory of Matthias W. Baldwin, who each subscribed to one or two shares. Baldwin had doubtless encouraged his employees to support the PRR, but their willingness to do so signified both their awareness of the increased locomotive orders that the railroad's success would engender, and the privileged status that skilled craftsmen held in their community. By the time that the subscription books closed on July 2, Baldwin employees had purchased 264 shares, and their counterparts at the Norris Locomotive Works had bought seventy-six.[63] At least one woman subscribed, beginning a long tradition of the Pennsylvania Railroad as a company that was amenable to female investors.[64]

Cope considered the first day of subscriptions to be "a pretty good beginning," but even his optimism could not disguise the fact that the number of new subscribers declined precipitously on the following day. By June 27, pledges had reached barely twelve thousand shares, with two thousand additional shares placed over the next two days. Sales were so slow that the railroad's backers formulated a plan under which twenty-five prominent Philadelphians would each endeavor to place a thousand shares with their friends, neighbors, or business associates, as best they could. Cope, the persuasive septuagenarian Quaker, even attended a meeting of the Insurance Company of North America for no purpose other than to foist a hundred shares of PRR stock on its directors. The aggressive marketing tactics helped, but they were not enough.[65]

The Pennsylvania Railroad suffered from excruciatingly poor timing during that pivotal summer of 1846, as the commissioners attempted to translate its charter into construction funds. Three years earlier, Congress reinstated a high protective tariff on railway iron, absent since 1830, greatly increasing construction costs and capital requirements. The United States was at war with Mexico, a war that Philadelphia Quakers opposed politically, as an opportunity for the South to extend slavery, and on moral grounds, as an act of unprovoked violence. Early, conflicting battlefield reports

alternately filled Americans with joy and despair, and the resulting uncertainty dampened investor confidence. Across the Atlantic, on June 25, Parliament repealed the Corn Laws, which had restricted importation of all types of grain, and thus gave American farmers access to British markets.[66] Word of the repeal, and of the collapse of Sir Robert Peel's government, did not reach Philadelphia until July 20.[67] Only then, after the Pennsylvania Railroad had struggled for nearly a month to place its shares, did investors learn that the export grain market would provide a lucrative source of revenue to any line that could link Philadelphia with the west.[68]

Had the PRR made its initial stock offering six months earlier, or a month later, the results might have been very different. As it was, however, when the subscription books closed on July 2, the railroad had sold only seventeen thousand shares. At $50 par value apiece, that theoretically yielded only $850,000. That was far below the level necessary to finance construction, particularly given that subscribers did not pay cash for their shares but instead pledged themselves liable for periodic assessments on their stock.[69] More important, it was well below the $1 million in paid-in capital that the legislature had established as the threshold to prevent the B&O from building to Pittsburgh.

Even before July 2, the promoters of the Pennsylvania Railroad (who continued to refer to themselves as "commissioners" because they did not yet possess the legal authority to incorporate the company or select a board of directors) acknowledged that public funding would be essential to the survival of the project. Their greatest chance for success would come from the areas that stood to gain the most from the railroad—the city of Philadelphia, represented by Mayor John Swift and the Select and Common Councils, as well as the nearby districts of Spring Garden and the Northern Liberties.[70]

Philadelphia's councilmen, united in their support of the railroad in principle, nonetheless balked at committing public funds to the actual project. On June 4, the Common Council, by a vote of twelve to eight, assigned the matter to its finance committee, which was known to be averse to municipal assistance. Later that day, the Select Council split evenly on the issue, six votes to six, and the tie caused the measure to be tabled. Even Select Council President William Meredith, who had opened the December 10, 1845, meeting with a rousing speech in support of the railroad, voted in favor of burying the measure in committee. Cope decried that "strange lack of public spirit" and noted bitterly that "these self same Councilmen, when the subject was pending before the Legislature, passed a resolution unanimously recommending the passage of the Bill creating this very line of Railroad."[71]

Other prominent Philadelphians were overtly hostile to the extension of public funds to the PRR, believing such an act to lie outside the legitimate parameters of municipal governance. Chief among them was Horace Binney, best known for establishing the legality of charitable trusts through his brilliant arguments before the United States Supreme Court in the 1844 case *Vidal v. Girard's Executors*. He acted in concert with his son, Horace Binney, Jr., a member of the Common Council whose chief claim to fame was that he was the motivating force behind the issuance of perforated postage stamps in the United States. Together, the Binneys used their legal acumen and political influence to argue against public funding for the Pennsylvania Railroad. Writing under the pseudonym "A Voter," the elder Binney, in collaboration with his nephew Horace Binney Wallace and Wallace's brother-in-law, John L. Riddle, sent a series of letters to the *United States Gazette*, denying the legality of the public purchases and attacking the reputations of the railroad's promoters. "A Voter" did not deny the authority of the Select and Common Councils to fund internal improvements—nor could he, given a long tradition of local public support for bridges, gas lighting, and waterworks—but argued that their authority extended only to the city limits. The PRR's supporters considered such attitudes hopelessly antiquated and provincial. "If all our citizens had been Binneys," Cope noted caustically, "Philadelphia would now be but a village."[72]

Binney, however, was not so resolutely antithetical to Philadelphia's interests as Cope might have suspected. Binney had long supported transportation improvements that might benefit his native city. In 1823, after New Jersey shipping magnate John Stevens organized a company that planned an all-rail route between Philadelphia and Pittsburgh, Binney was one of the incorporators. Binney had nothing against the Pennsylvania Railroad, but he was disturbed at the efforts of Cope and the other PRR commissioners to intimidate the Select and Common Councils into investing money in the venture. Binney believed that such public funding would erode the willingness of investors to commit private capital to that and other commercial ventures. He acknowledged the authority of the councils to invest public monies for the public good, but only within city limits, and he noted that the vast majority of the railroad's assets, employees, and operations would be outside those boundaries. Binney was also dismayed that Cope and the other PRR promoters had asked him to play a leading role at the December 10, 1845, town meeting in order to whip public enthusiasm into an emotional and economically irrational frenzy. He had declined to participate, explaining that he had no intention of talking people into investing in the railroad against their better judgment, or of casting aspersions on those who wanted nothing to do with the project. According to his grandson and principal biographer, Charles Chauncey Binney, such tactics were "all the more to be condemned because the leaders in the campaign of coercion were men who stood high in the community and should not have condescended to use such methods."[73]

In July 1846, Horace Binney defended himself against his detractors by publishing a pamphlet in which he drew a distinction between Philadelphia's "corporate duty" and what "may be alleged by the majority to be convenient or to promote the welfare of the inhabitants." He emphasized that public funding would create a dangerous precedent in which "the inhabitants of this city and their property are not under the protection of the Legislature of the State, but at the mercy of a majority of the City Councils whenever they are satisfied by a speculative inquiry that the money, whenever and upon whatever expended, will promote the welfare of the city."[74]

John Price Wetherill joined the Binneys in their opposition to public funding. Wetherill was a geologist and chemist, a partner in his family's drug and paint business, and a member of both the Academy of Natural Sciences and the American Philosophical Society. Like most other Philadelphia elites, he was a Whig, elected to the Common Council in 1829 and to

Figure 13. Former U.S. Representative Horace Binney, Sr. (1780–1875), in tandem with his son, Common Council member Horace Binney, Jr., supported the Pennsylvania Railroad but argued vigorously that the City of Philadelphia lacked both the authority and the resources necessary to support the company.

Thomas Sully portrait, 1833, courtesy of Jenkins Law Library, Philadelphia.

the Select Council two years later. Wetherill was a Quaker, as were many of the PRR's supporters, but his religious affiliation may have accounted for some of his animosity toward the project. Decades earlier, in 1781, his father, Samuel Wetherill, had been expelled from the Quaker church in response to his willingness to swear an oath of loyalty to the United States and to bear arms in a defensive war. Along with other like-minded individuals, Samuel Wetherill had established the Society of Free Quakers, often referred to as the "Fighting Quakers."[75] John Price Wetherill inherited some of his father's obstinacy, and one of his biographers noted that "neither argument, opposition, nor ridicule could move him. He rarely abandoned a position, but fought on until the last."[76] As such, he made a formidable adversary to Cope and the other supporters of the Pennsylvania Railroad.[77]

However, as the PRR commissioners and public officials alike expressed disappointment at the slow pace of stock sales to private individuals, the reluctance of councilmen to purchase PRR shares began to dissolve. On July 1, the Joint Committee of the Philadelphia

City Councils consulted three attorneys, Thomas I. Wharton, former canal commissioner John Sergeant, and Judge Thomas McKean Pettit, the United States district attorney for the Eastern District of Pennsylvania, regarding the legality of public subscriptions to the new company. All three replied in the affirmative, ironically basing their arguments in part on a legal precedent established by Horace Binney, Sr., in *Vidal v. Girard's Executors*. The general public weighed in as well, with nearly six thousand petitioners calling on the Select and Common Councils to purchase PRR stock, and only 133 united in opposition to the proposal.[78]

Based on their advice, on July 2 the majority members of the Joint Committee of the Philadelphia City Councils proposed a resolution calling on Mayor Swift and the City of Philadelphia to subscribe ten thousand shares of PRR stock as soon as the company had been able to place fifty thousand shares with private owners. Under the terms of the resolution, the city would acquire a further ten thousand shares after the PRR had placed 125 miles of track in service, and a final block of ten thousand shares once 200 miles had been completed. In their report, the members of the Joint Committee invoked the familiar specter of Baltimore and its counterparts, cautioning against the "immediate losses which Pennsylvania sustains by the diversion of a trade which is naturally her own to points on the North and the South, near and around her, as well as those more remote."[79]

Dissenters on the Joint Committee were equally forceful in their warnings, with "regard to the calling into existence of a great railroad corporation by the power and money of this city as an utter deviation from her true public policy." Even if the Commonwealth of Pennsylvania would benefit, they saw no reason why "the narrow strip between Vine and South Streets is alone to bear the burden."[80] On July 16, the deadlocked members of the Common Council voted nine to nine over the issue, and the tie vote precluded public funding for the PRR.[81]

With the incumbent councilmen deadlocked over the funding issue, the fate of the Pennsylvania Railroad now hung on the October 13 municipal elections. Cope and the other PRR commissioners, almost all of whom were Whigs, were nonetheless opposed to the existing Whig ticket. By the end of September, George W. Toland and Benjamin M. Hinchman had drawn up what Cope described "a strictly Rail Road whig [sic] ticket"—one that attempted to appeal to the widest possible cross-spectrum of voters by including candidates from other parties.[82] Richard Wood took charge of raising funds for the pro-railroad Whigs and distributing them to the various wards.[83]

Horace Binney, Sr., formed an anti-railroad slate, also composed of multiple parties. Binney's son, and his allies on the Select and Common Councils, then began to pressure the tax assessors (who were elected officials, but who nonetheless preferred to retain the incumbents in office) to use their knowledge of the local citizenry to influence public opinion against municipal funding. On October 10, three days prior to the election, Binney and sixty-seven of his supporters blanketed the city with broadsides inimical to the railroad. Advocates of the PRR retaliated by characterizing Binney as a man opposed to all progress, resurrecting his 1833 memorial in which he had claimed that municipally funded gas lighting would envelop the city in fireballs while killing all of the fish in the Delaware and Schuylkill rivers. Binney denied that he had ever been "anti-gas," but he acknowledged that he could not precisely remember everything that he had said or written nearly two decades earlier. As pro- and anti-railroad Whigs threatened to eviscerate each other, candidates from other parties, including radical "Locofoco" Democrats and anti-immigrant Know-Nothings, stood by in eager anticipation. Cope was putting the situation mildly when he predicted, "The election will be one of some novelty."[84]

The results of the elections, published in the Philadelphia papers on the morning of October 14, were far less satisfactory than Cope and the other PRR commissioners might have hoped. As Richard Wood lamented, "The railroad ticket failed, owing to the extreme anxiety of the Whigs for their whole ticket."[85] The principal issue turned out to be not the railroad, but instead matters of sectionalism and tariff policy. In 1842 congressional Whigs had succeeded in legislating a high protective tariff, one that was certain to benefit northern manufacturing interests. Four years later, in July 1846, southern Democrats secured passage of the Walker Tariff, which substantially reduced import duties and plunged the commerce and manufacturing of the Northeast into an economic malaise. By October, infuriated Pennsylvanians were determined to make the Democrats pay for that transgression against their interests, and they did so by voting the Whig ticket. Whigs swept both the Select and Common Councils (as well as the state legislature and the congressional delegation), and most of the Whig incumbents retained their seats regardless of their position on public funding. The backlash against the Walker Tariff constituted a stroke of luck for the PRR commissioners because it prevented rival parties from exploiting the discord between pro- and anti-funding Whigs, and it allowed the party most closely identified with the Philadelphia elites to solidify its position in the city and throughout the commonwealth. Cope was nonetheless disappointed that pro-railroad Whigs did not gain a clear majority, but he found considerable solace in the fact that the election had the desired result. Several anti-funding candidates had won re-election by narrow margins, and thus now saw the precariousness of their position.[86]

On the evening of November 5, the Common Council, by a vote of twelve to eight, agreed to use city funds to purchase PRR securities. Eight days later, on November 13, 1846, at a meeting that lasted until nearly 1:00 in the morning, the Select Council followed suit, eight votes to four. Select Councilman Charles Gilpin, whose ancestor Thomas Gilpin had in 1766 pledged his support for internal improvements by helping to establish the American Society for Promoting Useful Knowledge, voted against the measure. So, too, did John Price Wetherill and William Meredith, but to no avail. The City of Philadelphia would purchase thirty thousand shares of PRR stock, at $50 a share, representing fully a fourth of the Pennsylvania Railroad's initially authorized capitalization. To pay for the purchases, the city would borrow $2.5 million, at 6 percent interest. If PRR dividends proved insufficient to fund the interest on the loan, then Philadelphia residents would make up the difference through increased tax assessments. There was an important stipulation, however. The PRR's opponents on the Select Council had inserted a clause requiring the members of the Pennsylvania legislature to approve the use of public funds in that manner.[87]

The willingness of the Select and Common Councils to endorse the PRR project by purchasing the railroad's shares did not immediately boost private sales to the extent that Cope and other promoters had hoped. "Subscriptions small," he noted on November 27, admitting that the PRR's allies "will have to beat up the wards by calls."[88] On December 4, Cope and his resourceful allies accordingly divided the city into districts along the lines of the existing political wards. Commissioners representing each ward assigned persuasive salesmen to go from door to door exhorting the advantages of the new company.[89]

At first, the railroad's supporters experienced considerable difficulty in soliciting stock subscriptions. Cope suggested that canvassers arrange their subscription books according to the number of shares purchased, "On one part to read 'Subscriptions of 100 shares & upwards'—On another for 50 shares & upwards—then 25—10 & 5—& again for any less sum, so that the collector might show the largest column first—& if the party called on would'nt [sic] go that—to turn him to the next [page] & the next until he was suited," but the

other railroad commissioners nixed that proposal.[90] An overly enthusiastic Elliott Cresson (whom Mayor Swift referred to as "the Magnus Apostle") initially served as a "forward man" in attempting to place shares, but owing to "his injudicious zeal & impudence, persons [in order] to avoid him keep away."[91] Wood harangued his fellow directors of the Philadelphia Bank to subscribe to two hundred shares, but the measure passed by only one vote, over the vigorous opposition of the bank's president. In Harrisburg, former Governor David Rittenhouse Porter presided at a rally to sell PRR stock, but with scant results.[92]

One piece of good news came on December 16, when the commissioners of Spring Garden, the location of such railroad-related manufactories as the Baldwin and Norris, agreed to subscribe to two thousand PRR shares.[93] Other municipal corporations provided aid as well. In return for a subscription by the Northern Liberties of Philadelphia of five thousand shares of PRR stock, the railroad agreed to transport "flour & grain upon the same terms & for the same charges" regardless of their location in the city—and irrespective of differences in the cost of transportation to those locations.[94]

Despite the additional municipal subscriptions, sales to individuals remained sluggish, and by the end of 1846 the Pennsylvania Railroad was teetering on the verge of collapse. Cope criticized his affluent neighbors, whom he sarcastically referred to as "patriots," individuals "who ought to subscribe liberally, [but] act when called on, as if you were soliciting a favour." He also bemoaned his colleagues' refusal to support his marketing plan, noting that "some of our collectors began with 10, 5 & even 1 share, and seldom got beyond. All see it now when too late."[95]

By the time that the PRR closed its subscription books in February 1847, only 2,634 people had invested in the railroad. Two-thirds of them owned fewer than ten shares apiece, and only twenty-two held more than a hundred shares. Their composition indicated the extent to which the PRR was a Philadelphia enterprise, with little support in the western part of the state. "Beyond Philadelphia we have no subscriptions as yet worth recording," Cope had noted on December 31, and "not a single share west of the Susquehanna River."[96] Even if the legislature had blocked the B&O from reaching Pittsburgh, that city's residents were enthusiastic in their support of the next best alternative, the B&O-allied Pittsburgh & Connellsville. That company placed 6,325 shares during the first two days of subscriptions, while sales for the PRR in Pittsburgh over six months amounted to zero. Statewide, the PRR commissioners sold 30,570 shares to private individuals. At $50 par value, that netted $1,528,500, only a small fraction of which had actually been paid into the company.[97] Cope may have boasted that the sale of more than thirty thousand shares "places us on velvet" and that the company had succeeded in "accomplishing by private means in Philadelphia alone, a subscription of one million five hundred thousand dollars towards that great work," but that amount represented barely half of the $3 million minimum subscription established by the act of incorporation.[98] In the midst of all the gloom, there was but one piece of good luck. State Attorney General John Meredith Read, Sr., whom Cope described as "a violent opponent of the Road," had planned to intervene in order to halt the city's subscription. He resigned in December 1846 to pursue private practice, and his successor was much more amenable to the project.[99]

Construction could not proceed until Philadelphia made good on its pledge to purchase PRR shares. Cope and the other PRR commissioners confronted two difficulties as they continued to press municipal officials for support. Despite the votes in the Select and Common Councils, several key representatives of Philadelphia's government were hesitant to commit the city to a massive and risky loan that would provide funds to a private corporation. On the morning of February 11, Cope and Joseph Toland, representing the railroad, met with Mayor Swift, the city solicitor, the city treasurer, and representatives from both the Select and Common Councils. Swift was the first popularly elected mayor of Philadelphia and, as such, might well have doubted his authority to carry out the will of the people.[100] Neither the solicitor nor the treasurer was particularly disposed to invest city funds in the railroad, and the former reminded the mayor (who was poised over the subscription book, pen in hand), that the councils had not yet voted to disburse the necessary funds. The procedural glitch in turn induced a

new round of debates, revolving around the issue of whether the councils had specifically directed or merely authorized the purchase of PRR stock. Late that night the Select and Common Councils voted to give the mayor the necessary authority.[101]

The only remaining obstacle to the city subscription was the clause, inserted in the enabling legislation, that required the state's General Assembly to approve the expanded use of municipal powers. In early 1847, nearly a year after the charter battle, many politicians representing western Pennsylvania still bore a grudge against the Pennsylvania Railroad. By that time, however, the Baltimore & Ohio's directors had committed a serious strategic blunder, one that rebounded to the interests of the Pennsylvania Railroad. The previous autumn, B&O officials had responded to the conditions imposed by the Pennsylvania legislature, delaying and perhaps annulling their chances of building into Pennsylvania. As such, they sought permission from the Virginia assembly to construct its main line west to a junction with the Ohio River at Parkersburg, well to the south and east of Pittsburgh. Following the decision, Pittsburghers who had formerly been in the B&O camp, including banker William McCandless, informed the Philadelphia mayor and the councils that they "now perceived that their *ugly Cousin* Baltimore, had been coquetting with them, & that a great change of feeling towards [us] had taken place in Pittsburg, and that they were now disposed to cultivate a good understanding with their *Fair Sister* Philadelphia & to help us along with our *Central* railroad."[102]

The B&O's willingness to bypass Pittsburgh helped erode resistance to the PRR, and to the provision of municipal funding for the company. On January 15, 1847, a committee of the PRR commissioners traveled to Harrisburg to lobby for a bill allowing the City of Philadelphia, and other municipal corporations, to purchase stock in the railroad. When the 1847 session had opened a week earlier, Governor Shunk, in his annual message to the legislature, emphasized that the Pennsylvania Railroad did not constitute a threat to the Main Line of Public Works; in contrast, it was likely to increase traffic over the Philadelphia & Columbia and the Allegheny Portage Railroad, without doing damage to the canals.[103] On February 20, 1847, a supplement to the Pennsylvania Railroad charter passed the House, forty-seven to thirty-seven, confirming the city subscription, and stipulating that municipal bonds paid to the PRR in exchange for stock could be treated by the railroad as cash.[104]

Municipal authorities interpreted the February 20 House vote as a signal to commit public funds to the Pennsylvania Railroad. Two days after the House vote, the city placed the first installment of its loan, enabling Mayor Swift to subscribe for thirty thousand shares of Pennsylvania Railroad stock. The City of Philadelphia's contribution nearly doubled the number of shares that had been sold and finally enabled the PRR to surpass the critical threshold of $3 million in subscribed capital stock. Thomas Pim Cope, for one, was inordinately pleased. "The commencement of another volume of facts & reflections lucubrations [sic] of my own Mirror," he noted as he began the ninth volume of his diary, "is attended with at least one very pleasant & inspiring circumstance." The successful vote in the House was "a glorious event, & a proud day for the prosperity of Philadelphia & the State at large." Our next step," he wrote on February 22, "is to secure the Charter, for which we are now prepared."[105] Three days later, the PRR commissioners attained that goal when Governor Shunk issued the letters patent that formally incorporated the Pennsylvania Railroad Company.

Although Mayor Swift had pledged to buy PRR stock, the city could not yet legally pay for it, as the Senate had not yet given its approval. Senators Gibbons and Darsie predictably spoke out against the bill.[106] Senator James Lisle Gillis chaired a convention that called for the PRR to pass through Sunbury, more than a hundred miles out of its way, in order to increase the value of land that he and his associates owned in north-central Pennsylvania, and he also threatened to oppose the railroad's interests in the legislature.[107] "The enemies of the Railroad abated nothing of their violence," Cope noted on March 12, as he criticized "the same reckless hostility [that] is persisted in by Gibbons in the Senate. Who would, if he could, rouse Heaven & Earth against us." Cope was undoubtedly frustrated at the tactics of Gibbons and his allies, including Speaker of the House James Cooper, a Whig who was "hand & glove with Gibbons."[108] They were attempting to delay consideration of the Pennsylvania Railroad bill until

the legislative session expired, accounting for Cope's frustration with "these curs in the manger [who] will neither eat themselves nor let others eat."[109]

Senator Gibbons, although a Whig, tapped into the antigovernment and antimonopoly rhetoric that was often a part of Jacksonian Democracy. He called the PRR's efforts to secure public funding a swindle, on par with that of the Second Bank of the United States, and he was quick to point out that many of the same people—including Cope—had been involved in both ventures. Gibbons even went so far as to purchase five shares of PRR stock, on credit, and then requested a receipt of ownership that he could allege was a bribe from the railroad's supporters in order to secure his cooperation.[110] By the time that the legislature disbanded in the middle of March, the supplement was still buried in a Senate committee, and its supporters, while in the majority, lacked the two-thirds vote necessary to bring the bill to the floor. In the months that followed, Gibbons and his allies proposed several strategies for denying municipal funds to the railroad, ranging from an injunction against the company to a lawsuit to prevent the Philadelphia Select and Common Councils from employing tax money to support a private corporation. The political maneuverings even began to test Cope's Quaker pacifism, and he reflected, "I sometimes fear I shall never attain that self-possession & equanimity which philosophy & religion demand."[111]

The PRR commissioners nevertheless acted as if the funds were in hand, selecting a board of directors, which elected Samuel Vaughan Merrick as president, creating an organizational structure, hiring personnel, and authorizing construction. By August 12, 1847, the company had secured $1 million in paid-in capital and had placed the first fifteen miles on both the east and west ends of the route under contract. As Cope noted, with a certain amount of malevolent satisfaction, "This puts an end to the Balt. & O. right of way."[112] In November, when Merrick suggested that the board request that the legislature confirm the city's subscription, Cope cautioned that "this appeared too much like rousing the Lyon from his den. . . . To indicate, at this time, any doubt would be to invite the enemies of the Compy. to renewed opposition."[113]

By the following January, as the 1848 legislative session began, the issue of public financing had still not been resolved. On January 5, the PRR commissioners again prepared a memorial to the General Assembly, calling on it to permit the Philadelphia Select and Common Councils and other municipalities to subscribe to its stock. In the Senate the bill encountered stiff opposition from William Williamson, a Whig representing Chester and Delaware Counties who believed that the B&O/Pittsburgh & Connellsville route should be completed, and then extended to Chicago. Democrat William F. Packer, a resident of Lycoming County in north-central Pennsylvania, led opposition in the House. In 1837 Packer, along with Thomas Cope, Job Tyson, and many others, had been one of the original incorporators of the Sunbury & Erie Railroad, an as-yet unfulfilled plan to link Philadelphia to Lake Erie. A decade later, however, Packer had distanced himself from Cope, Tyson, and the PRR interests. In January 1847 a Philadelphia convention to promote the construction of the Sunbury & Erie appointed Packer to a Committee of Correspondence, charged with negotiating an agreement with the Pennsylvania Railroad commissioners in order to construct twin routes to both Pittsburgh and Erie. Philadelphia interests balked at the proposal, however, largely because they believed that insufficient capital would be available to construct the two lines simultaneously and that too little traffic existed to support them both. Packer, nursing a grudge and more determined than ever to protect the interests of his native locale, constituted a formidable foe to the Pennsylvania Railroad.[114]

By the middle of March 1848, at an informal meeting of the PRR's supporters, Cope bemoaned that the "supplement drags heavily through the Legislature, & it is hinted that a majority could easily be obtained by the rise of a little money among the members, which several present said was not unusual."[115] Both the PRR minute book and Cope's diary decline to mention whether any money actually changed hands, but by the end of the month the bill had passed both houses of the General Assembly, and Governor Shunk soon affixed his signature. The bill permitted municipal corporations, including Allegheny County, the Philadelphia Select and Common Councils, and the Northern Liberties to purchase stock in the Pennsylvania Railroad, with each increment of ten thousand shares entitling those entities to appoint an additional direc-

tor—provided that public representatives make up no more than 49 percent of the board. The bill offered additional financial relief to the beleaguered railroad. In lieu of the five-mill tonnage tax, to be collected during the navigation season on the canals, the legislators substituted a year-round tax of three mills, increasing the PRR's ability to compete against the Main Line of Public Works. In order to stimulate additional stock subscriptions, the members of the General Assembly raised the maximum permissible dividend rate from 5 to 6 percent. Finally, the bill contained a provision that would be far more important in the long run, in that it allowed the company to undertake loans, raising capital through debt as well as stock equity.[116]

With the legality of public subscriptions finally established, Pittsburgh interests lent their financial support to the Pennsylvania Railroad. "The Company is growing more into popular favour," Cope noted, and "The Pittsburgers [sic] even are opening their eyes to their true interest, & have ceased courting & coquetting with the Baltimorians [sic]."[117] Angered at the B&O's decision to bypass their city, and resigned to the inevitability of the Pennsylvania Railroad, in June 1848 the commissioners of Allegheny County agreed to purchase twenty thousand shares of PRR stock, provided "that the terminus of the said rail road shall be permanently and finally established within the City of Pittsburgh."[118] That language was no more restrictive than the PRR's legislative charter, however, a document that prevented the railroad from building beyond the western border of Allegheny County. During 1850 and 1851, as the PRR pursued the heavy and expensive construction in the mountains, the City of Philadelphia subscribed an additional $2.5 million in stock, while the adjacent Northern Liberties and Spring Garden contributed a further $750,000. By the end of 1851, the various cities and counties had subscribed $5,750,000 in PRR stock, more than double the $2,356,000 pledged by private individuals.[119]

Such stock ownership carried with it a measure of control, which nonetheless fell well short of public ownership. Even though shares owned by various government entities were more than twice as numerous as those held by individual investors and private companies, both the Select and Common Councils and the Allegheny County commissioners initially declined to appoint any directors to the PRR board. The first of those public directors, Morris L. Hallowell and George Howell (representing Philadelphia) and John H. Shoenberger and William Wilkins (representing Allegheny County) did not take office until December 4, 1848.[120] Eventually, the City of Philadelphia held three of the fourteen seats on the board of directors, while the Allegheny County commissioners appointed a further two. Municipal corporations were grossly underrepresented on the board, relative to their proportion of stock ownership, reflecting the prevailing belief that public investment should yield to private management. By law, private investors were entitled to elect a majority of the railroad's directors, even if governmental entities owned a majority of the company's stock.[121] The issue soon became moot, as the railroad's enormous capital requirements forced the PRR to issue additional stock, much of which went to construction contractors in lieu of cash. As a result, the percentage of public share ownership steadily declined.[122]

It would not have mattered much, in any event, as there did not seem to be a divergence in policies between publicly and privately appointed directors. State legislators at least paid lip service to the need to protect the public interest by controlling the private corporations that they had chartered. In contrast, municipal directors often thought only about the welfare of the Pennsylvania Railroad, and the positive results that that company might have for the commercial interests of Philadelphia and Pittsburgh. Should the PRR produce deleterious effects in other parts of the state, then that was not really their problem.[123]

Aftermath

The battles that occurred between 1845 and 1848, particularly those that took place in the Pennsylvania General Assembly and in the Philadelphia Select and Common Councils, shaped the destiny of the Pennsylvania Railroad. The state legislature transferred public authority to a private corporation, granting a charter to the PRR while effectively denying one to the Baltimore & Ohio. The discord that existed between supporters of those two railroads ensured that, even with the promise of a monopoly that the charter

offered, the PRR commissioners could raise little money outside of Philadelphia, too little to fund construction. Municipal corporations, most notably the City of Philadelphia, provided the critically necessary financial support through their purchase of PRR stock. Legislators again weighed in, this time to determine whether such financial support lay within the legitimate parameters of local political authority. The answer was in the affirmative, yet the General Assembly also imposed conditions—most notably the year-round tonnage tax—that the railroad's directors found onerous. Their successful efforts to repeal that tax, under the leadership of future president Thomas A. Scott, would lead to allegations that the PRR engaged in corrupt business practices and controlled the Pennsylvania legislature. Those battles lay in the future, however, and as the 1840s drew to a close, it was the legislature that had created the Pennsylvania Railroad, and not the other way around.

Yet it would be difficult to minimize the individual contributions that Cope and his fellow commissioners had made to the success of the new enterprise. They were a small, elite group, mostly Whigs, and mostly Quakers. They conducted business together, socialized together, supported the same charitable institutions, shared wonderment at the same scientific discoveries, and raised children who intermarried with one another and who followed in their parents' footsteps. Although they were not at the pinnacle of success, and had largely missed the opportunities associated with industrialization, they still commanded considerable economic and social power. Their staunchest adversaries were people from outside the city, and even those Philadelphians who opposed the PRR—individuals such as Charles Gibbons—were originally from somewhere else.[124]

In an era when states' rights were in the ascendancy, these merchants were first and foremost loyal not to their state, but to their city. They cared as deeply for Philadelphia's future as for their own commercial fortunes, and they were troubled at their city's rapid decline during the early decades of the nineteenth century from America's preeminent port to an also-ran. Cope and his associates possessed both social capital and a synergistic network of personal and professional networks, with all of their attendant economic advantages.

As such, they were well positioned to organize a state-wide, yet Philadelphia-based transportation company and to call on local political elites to provide critically necessary financing.[125]

During the 1840s, they accomplished something truly remarkable, for in chartering the Pennsylvania Railroad they cast aside their traditional Quaker conservatism, embracing instead a radically different type of business activity. During and after the War of 1812, many Philadelphia merchants made the challenging transition to manufacturing enterprises. In many respects, the shift from mercantile activity to transportation reflected as substantial a transformation, and relatively few Philadelphians were anxious to take part in this new realm of economic activity. Individuals such as Thomas Cope had many supporters, but relatively few close allies, members of elite society who were willing to engage in the difficult labor of organizing a company, soliciting subscriptions, and mobilizing political support. A time would come, not many years hence, when professional managers such as Herman Haupt and J. Edgar Thomson would clash with, and ultimately supplant, the merchants who had attempted to master the art of transportation. That too lay in the future, and for now, those who did join forces with Cope, those who fought for the Pennsylvania Railroad instead of against it, solidified their reputations as guardians of Philadelphia's commercial interests.[126]

Most of those who opposed the Pennsylvania Railroad did not fare nearly so well. Far from being antithetical to progress or modernity, they acted for a variety of politically and economically defensible motives. Many in western Pennsylvania remembered the seemingly endless debates and interminable delays associated with the construction of the Main Line of Public Works, and they hardly relished what they envisioned might be a repeat of that experience. The Baltimore & Ohio was an established company, one that was building, albeit slowly, toward them, while the Philadelphia company existed only on paper, and in the minds of its commissioners. Others, particularly in the northern part of the commonwealth, saw no reason why the General Assembly should charter a railroad that would do little to address their transportation needs. Fiscally responsible members of the legislature recalled what the 1842 repudiation of the commonwealth's debt had done to its economic fortunes, and to its credit rating. They had little desire to support a private corporation that might—despite Governor Shunk's confident pronouncements—destroy the earning potential of the Main Line of Public Works, without erasing the public debt incurred to create it. Even in Philadelphia, individuals with no particular antipathy toward the Pennsylvania Railroad envisioned a dangerous precedent in using municipal funds to create a company in which the vast majority of its economic activity would take place outside of city limits.

The opposition of Horace Binney, Sr., to municipal support for the PRR did little to reduce his considerable wealth or to tarnish his reputation as one of the leading attorneys in the United States. Philadelphians soon realized that Binney's repeated warnings against committing public funds that "whenever and upon whatever expended, will promote the welfare of the city" represented not so much conservatism as foresight. The July 1846 minority report of the Joint Committee of the Philadelphia City Councils had warned that as a result of public funding "the city, in undertaking this immense work of State improvement, will leave the quiet orbit in which she has hitherto revolved to rush into a wild and eccentric path in which she was never designed to move."[127] And so she did. Within a decade following the funding debate, the City of Philadelphia had invested $10 million in the securities of various railroad corporations. Following the Panic of 1857, half of those shares were worthless.

The residents of southwestern Pennsylvania faced much the same problem. In addition to Allegheny County's $1 million PRR stock subscription, the county and the cities of Pittsburgh and Allegheny together had pledged $4.5 million in direct assistance to several other railroads, including the Pittsburgh & Connellsville. Much of that aid was in the form of Allegheny County bonds, which the railroads could then sell in order to raise cash. After the panic, however, few investors wanted government bonds, and the commissioners of Allegheny County permitted the Pittsburgh & Connellsville to sell their county bonds at a steep 25 percent discount, reflecting the ruination of the county's credit. Even worse, Allegheny County had guaranteed the bond interest of several of the carriers serving Pittsburgh, and when those companies tottered on the brink of insolvency, it was up to the county commissioners to make good their promises. In June 1857, they acknowledged that the necessity of assuming the railroads' interest payments required them to implement a substantial tax increase. That October, furious voters, led by Pittsburgh attorney and politician Thomas Williams and banker Thomas Mellon (who held a seat on the PRR board), elected a new slate of commissioners.[128] The "Repudiationists," as their name suggested, forestalled a tax increase through the simple, although illegal, expedient of refusing to honor the county's interest guarantees on railroad bonds. The resulting lawsuits did not affect the Pennsylvania Railroad, but the commissioners elected to use their PRR stock to help pay off owners of Allegheny County government bonds. After 1858, therefore, the Allegheny County directors left the PRR board, and that government entity no longer had a say in the management of the Pennsylvania Railroad. The entire affair, particularly the bond interest guarantees afforded to the other railroads, caused much resentment among the residents of Pittsburgh and surrounding communities. "The people groaned under the enormous burden," wrote one historian, forty years later, and the "railway indebtedness hung like a millstone around the neck of this community."[129]

The public and private sectors shared the blame for the overly enthusiastic expansion of the railroads, but voters could only vent their rage on the first group, and not the second. By the autumn of 1857, Pennsylvanians had voted, 112,658 to 13,653, to amend their Constitution, limiting the commonwealth's debt to $150,000 and stipulating that "the legislature shall not authorize any city, county, borough or township, or unincorporated district, by virtue of a vote of its citizens, or otherwise to become a stockholder in any company."[130]

The toxic effects of the links between the city and the PRR remained, however. According to Binney's grandson, "The worst result of these investments in railroad stock by Philadelphia and other communities in the State was not the loss of many millions of the taxpayers' money, but the close association and alliance thereby created between certain powerful corporations and the various municipal governments, an association and alliance which is generally thought to be . . . one of the leading causes of the misgovernment long so manifest throughout the state, and especially in Philadelphia."[131] Resentment lingered as late as 1890, when opponents of the PRR suggested that the city's "subscription was the birth of a railroad, but the death of our city."[132] Horace Binney, Sr., was not alive to hear those words, but he lived until 1875, long enough to feel vindicated. He also lived long enough to suffer the deaths of two of his key allies: in 1852 his nephew Horace Binney Wallace, and in 1870 his son, Councilman Horace Binney, Jr.[133]

George Darsie survived the public disapprobation that had initially attached to anyone opposed to the PRR, but only because he had upheld the interests of his constituents in Allegheny County. The Whigs lost control of the Pennsylvania Senate in the 1849 election, and Darsie, the senior member of the party, retained his seat but lost the post of speaker. In 1854, Darsie ran again for a seat on the Canal Commission, but the Whigs were a spent force, and he suffered a resounding defeat at the hands of his Democratic opponent. Councilman Charles Gilpin, who in November 1846 had voted against public funding for the PRR, ran for Philadelphia mayor in 1849, and lost. Despite the statewide drubbing that the Whigs suffered in 1849, the following year Gilpin won election as the next-to-last Whig mayor of Philadelphia. He served four terms. His successor was Robert T. Conrad, editor of the *North American* and the man who had once challenged Charles Gibbons to a duel. In 1854, Conrad became the first mayor of a united Philadelphia, after the state legislature consolidated the city and county governments, eliminating such political entities as Spring Garden and the Northern Liberties. William Meredith suffered little lasting damage from his unwillingness to commit public funds to the PRR; he retained his seat on the Select Council until 1849, when his fellow Whig, President Zachary Taylor, selected him to be the secretary of the treasury. William Packer, the House Democrat who had attempted to block municipal funding for the PRR, was elected governor of Pennsylvania in 1857. While in office he helped to dismember what little remained of Pennsylvania's publicly owned internal improvements. After an 1850 constitutional amendment to subject judicial appointments to a popular vote, John Bannister Gibson was forced to resign from the Pennsylvania Supreme Court, was easily elected to his old post, and remained the chief justice until his death in 1853. Despite his opposition to public funding for the PRR, John Price Wetherill remained on the Philadelphia Select Council until his death in 1853. His son, John Price Wetherill, Jr., represented the City of Philadelphia on the board of directors of the Pennsylvania Railroad from 1878 until 1888.[134]

Perhaps no one suffered more for his opposition to the Pennsylvania Railroad than Charles Gibbons. In February 1846, Cope had met privately with the state senator, cautioning him "that not one of his constituents . . . could in my opinion be found in the City or County, who did not disapprove of his advocating the right of way to the Baltimore Company," and warned him, with considerable prescience, that "the retribution will come."[135] And so it did. On February 28, a delegation from the town meeting informed Gibbons that he must either vote against the B&O charter, or resign from the Senate. With a stubborn "disregard of the known unanimous will of constituents," Gibbons refused to follow either suggestion.[136] Reviled as a traitor to Philadelphia, he was defeated in the 1847 Senate race. His political career at an end, he virtually retired from public life. He became an ardent abolitionist, and in 1855 he gained at least partial redemption in the eyes of his fellow Quakers. He defended five African Americans who had helped liberate runaway slave Jane Johnson and her two children from their owner, Ambassador John Hill Wheeler, following a scuffle at the Camden & Amboy ferry terminal in Philadelphia. Gibbons was a Republican and a strong Unionist, and after Fort Sumter he advocated a vigorous suppression of the rebellion. Following the Civil War, he sought reelection to the Pennsylvania legislature, and in a bitterly contested election, he was denied office following a judicial ruling.[137]

The Baltimore & Ohio route to Pittsburgh was not quite dead, but, thanks to the efforts of the Pennsylvania Railroad, it lingered for decades in a state of suspended animation. In 1843, several years before the great charter battle in Harrisburg, Pittsburghers had

engaged in logrolling, shepherding through the Pennsylvania legislature "an act for the relief of the overseers of the poor of the borough of Erie, and for other purposes" in an unsuccessful attempt to revive the charter of the Pittsburgh & Connellsville Railroad. In early April 1846, shortly before the PRR charter became law, those who sought an alliance with the B&O adopted a similarly disingenuous tactic. Buried in "an act to authorize the court of quarter sessions of Allegheny county to vacate Delaware lane in said county, and for other purposes" was another provision for the Pittsburgh & Connellsville charter. Advocates of the Pennsylvania Central, who were presumably too involved in their own charter battle to appreciate the full scope of their rivals' actions, overlooked the bill, which Governor Shunk signed into law. The *North American* broke the story in early May, and Cope was outraged at "a deed of fraud & infamy . . . [and] a trick worthy of the perpetrators [that] has been played on the Legislature & the Governor."[138]

During the autumn of 1846, the backers of the Pittsburgh & Connellsville conducted surveys along the proposed route, requesting financial support from the B&O. It was not forthcoming, however, as that railroad's directors had elected to concentrate their resources on the completion of a route to Wheeling, a city that had offered to purchase $1 million in B&O securities.[139] In 1853, after the B&O had reached Wheeling, PRR officials considered building west into Ohio, along a route than ran well to the south of Pittsburgh. Enraged Pittsburghers, recalling that they had been cheated out of a rail route once before, were determined to resurrect the Pittsburgh & Connellsville link to the B&O. The slumbering company received $500,000 in bonds from the City of Pittsburgh and another $750,000 from Allegheny County, along with a bond guarantee from the City of Baltimore. When computed on a mile-for-mile basis, that support was far in excess of what the PRR had received in 1847 and 1848. Despite a massive embezzlement scheme perpetrated by Pittsburgh & Connellsville president William J. Larimer, the line opened for service in January 1857, relying in part on trackage rights on the Pennsylvania Railroad between Turtle Creek and Pittsburgh. PRR officials did not object to that arrangement because their now-complete main line offered considerably better access to the west, and because the Pittsburgh & Connellsville did not yet reach the B&O main line.[140]

The Pittsburgh & Connellsville would not receive a direct connection to the Baltimore & Ohio for many more years. By the mid-1850s, the credit of Allegheny County was so poor that the Pittsburgh & Connellsville was unable to sell its quota of public bonds, even at a 25 percent discount. In 1859, in response to the financial panic that had begun two years earlier, Pittsburgh and Allegheny County each repudiated their bonds. The Civil War nonetheless demonstrated the advantages of a direct connection between Pittsburgh and western Maryland, and by 1864 the Pittsburgh & Connellsville was ready to join forces with the B&O to construct a line south to Cumberland, Maryland.

PRR executives by that time exerted considerable influence over the Pennsylvania legislature, and the company's representatives reacted swiftly to the proposed route. They sponsored two bills, one stripping the Pittsburgh & Connellsville of its right to build the connection with the B&O, and the other chartering a PRR subsidiary, the Connellsville & Southern Pennsylvania Railroad Company, to build a parallel line that would drive the Pittsburgh & Connellsville out of business.[141] Years of political maneuvering and judicial action followed, until the Pennsylvania State Supreme Court, in January 1868, finally resolved the issue in favor of the Pittsburgh & Connellsville.[142]

The bruising battle over the Pittsburgh & Connellsville charter finally brought to an end the legislature's power to anoint a state economic transportation champion. Three months later, in April 1868, Pennsylvania enacted a free incorporation law, prohibiting the legislature from denying a railroad charter to any legitimately organized company. The internecine struggle

between eastern and western Pennsylvania for political and economic supremacy had not ended—it would reappear in a quite vicious form during the labor unrest of 1877, for example—but it had reached a temporary stasis. Likewise, the battle between the B&O and the PRR for access to Pittsburgh, a conflict that had begun in the 1830s, before convulsing the General Assembly and the Philadelphia Select and Common Councils in 1845, 1846, and into 1847, was temporarily over.

In the quarter century that followed 1846, executives from the PRR and the B&O would do battle time and time again as they competed for local and regional traffic. For the moment, however, the PRR had achieved a narrow but complete victory. Dedicated advocates like Thomas Cope had played a role in that success, as did fortuitous circumstance and blind luck. Much of the company's critical early lead also stemmed from political factors, including the charter provisions conferred by the General Assembly and the funding provided by the City of Philadelphia. In the two decades that followed, the PRR established an insurmountable lead over every other rival railroad in the commonwealth—that is, through skillful manipulation of the political process, the railroad's supporters had gained what economists refer to as a first-mover advantage. The PRR's initial success enabled the company to influence the legislature and, if not prevent, at least delay incursions by the B&O and its affiliates. In June 1871, the Pittsburgh & Connellsville line to Cumberland, Maryland, entered service, and Pittsburgh finally gained a connection to the east coast over the Baltimore & Ohio. But by then, the Pennsylvania Railroad was the largest and most powerful transportation enterprise in the United States, and was on the verge of becoming the largest corporation in the world.[143]

Chapter 4

Enterprise

1846–1852

On March 30, 1847, a group of prominent Philadelphia merchants gathered at the Board of Trade in the Philadelphia Exchange and created the Pennsylvania Railroad. Thomas Pim Cope was the elder statesman among the railroad's directors, one of the last survivors of the group fortunate enough to come of age in the heady days following the end of the American Revolution and the ratification of the Constitution. He had done as much, if not more, than anyone else to secure the PRR's charter and subsequent municipal funding. Cope was also nearly eighty, exhausted from his already considerable exertions on behalf of the railroad, and when his fellow board members proposed to anoint him as president, he refused the honor. Cope was not even certain he possessed the energy to serve on the board, but he felt that refusal would send a poor signal to the Philadelphians who had invested in the venture. "After an effort to excuse myself," Cope "was constrained reluctantly to assent, with the understanding that I could be at liberty to resign hereafter," which he did on April 26, 1848.[1] "This company is destined to fight its way through many obstacles to a happy issue," Cope wrote, adding nostalgically, "In younger life, I should fearlessly have wrestled with them all. Not so now. My health is giving way."[2]

Cope was not the only one proposed for the presidency. In all probability the offer first went to Charles Ellet, the president of the Schuylkill Navigation Company, who declined the post.[3] The next choice was William Bigler, whose impressive political connections (he was elected governor of Pennsylvania in 1851) would have proved valuable to the PRR. He, too, refused to serve.[4] Cope himself favored Richard Rush, the former secretary of the treasury and son of physician and signer of the Declaration of Independence Benjamin Rush. Only a week earlier, however, President James K. Polk had appointed Rush as minister to France, precluding any possibility that he might take the reins of the Pennsylvania Railroad. Instead, the presidency went to the board's fourth choice, Samuel Vaughan Merrick.

Merrick was the first of two PRR presidents who were merchant managers, individuals who were ignorant of even the most basic principles of civil engineering and railway operations. Yet they were sufficiently aware of their limitations to hire some of the nation's best professional engineers in order to construct the railroad. Merrick and his colleagues soon discovered, however, that those engineers insisted that they be given the authority to run the railroad that they had helped to build. As professional railroaders, moreover,

Figure 14. A Pennsylvania Railroad locomotive pauses adjacent to the Gallitzin House, a station at the west entrance to the summit tunnel at Gallitzin, Pennsylvania, circa 1858. The tunnel was a critical element in the PRR's line through the Alleghenies, bypassing the complex system of inclined planes and levels that constituted the Allegheny Portage Railroad. Chief engineer J. Edgar Thomson was determined to complete the route over the mountains, between Altoona and Johnstown. He recommended that the board of directors issue bonds in order to finance construction, triggering a dispute that left him in control of the PRR. During this upheaval, and in a desperate attempt to rectify the deficiencies of its original line, the Commonwealth of Pennsylvania built the New Portage Railroad on a route that closely paralleled that of the PRR—its summit tunnel was located just yards to the south, off of the right edge of the photograph.

Pennsylvania Historical and Museum Commission, Railroad Museum of Pennsylvania.

the engineer-managers sought to apply the latest techniques of railroad operation in order to maximize efficiency and profitability, even if those policies worked to the detriment of Philadelphia's mercantile interests. Very soon, the merchants and the engineers would battle for control of the Pennsylvania Railroad. The outcome of that struggle would determine whether the company would become the commercial servant of the Quaker City, or a stand-alone corporation attuned to expansion and profitability.

Merchant Managers

Most of the Philadelphians who sat on the board of the Pennsylvania Railroad were merchants rather than manufacturers. They were economically, politically, and socially prominent in their community, but they ranked well below Cope in terms of their influence and stood a distinct tier below the city's richest "first families."[5] The initial thirteen directors were closely tied to Philadelphia's commercial interests, and they were far more concerned with protecting their city's trade with the west than they were with mastering the complexities of a large-scale transportation enterprise. Most possessed little knowledge of railroad operations, or indeed of any aspect of transportation or manufacturing.

Despite being the fourth choice for the presidency, Samuel Vaughan Merrick was the most prominent individual on the board, and an eminently logical choice for the railroad's top executive office. He was also one of the few directors who possessed some experience in manufacturing. If Cope was the embodiment of Philadelphia's rapidly vanishing mercantile aristocracy, then Merrick represented the nexus of science, technology, and production that was rapidly transforming the city into an industrial powerhouse.[6] Born in 1801 to a prominent Philadelphia family, at the age of fifteen Merrick apprenticed in his uncle's mercantile house. The War of 1812, with its attendant disruption to transatlantic trade, encouraged many merchants to specialize in manufacturing, and Merrick was one of those who benefited. His uncle gave him control of a fire-engine manufacturer that was teetering on the verge of bankruptcy.[7] Merrick made the business a success. He later co-founded the Southwark Iron Foundry, one of the city's largest machine shops, and built the Philadelphia Gas Works. In 1824, after Merrick and William H. Keating had been denied membership in a mechanics' guild, they joined forces to establish the Franklin Institute, in tandem with Mathew Carey and future locomotive builder Matthias Baldwin. As a merchant and then a manufacturer, Merrick exemplified the economic changes that revolutionized Philadelphia during the first half of the nineteenth century. As an individual who was well connected to the city's

scientific and business communities, Merrick's prominence and connections increased the likelihood that the PRR would attract sufficient private subscriptions to allow the company to begin work. As board member Richard Wood confided to his diary, "Several inquiries made in relation to S. V. Merrick satisfy me that the public approve his nomination, as the best man to be obtained for the making of the road."[8]

Aside from Merrick, the initial board of directors for the Pennsylvania Railroad included only three industrialists, and two of them were in the iron trade. Stephen Colwell was a lawyer and one of the most important iron manufacturers in Philadelphia. He was a close political and intellectual ally of Henry Charles Carey (Mathew Carey's son), now retired from his work at the publishing firm of Carey & Lea. Colwell remained on the PRR board only until 1850—which was just as well, for in the following year he published *New Themes for the Protestant Clergy*, a work that attacked traditional religious mores and so scandalized Philadelphia society that Colwell became something of a pariah. Although the PRR's incorporation documents listed David S. Brown as a "merchant," he did possess some manufacturing expertise, albeit in connection with his primary business as a commission broker for cotton and woolen goods. In 1817, he had joined the family firm, J. & M. Brown, and he established Hacker, Brown & Co. four years later. In 1830, Brown changed the company's name to David S. Brown & Co. and by 1844 he had become president of a Gloucester, New Jersey, textile firm, the Washington Manufacturing Company. James Magee, the other director with manufacturing expertise, was more familiar with horses than with iron horses. In 1824, Magee had formed a partnership with George Taber, and the two men had purchased Peter Dickson & Company, a saddlery manufacturer with a shop at Fourth and Market Streets. He retired from the successor firm of Magee, Taber & Company in 1847, the same year that he became a PRR director.[9]

The other nine directors, including Cope, owed their livelihoods to trade, and not to industry. William C. Patterson, who would eventually replace Merrick as president, was a merchant and the owner of warehouses along the Philadelphia waterfront.[10] Henry C. Corbit operated a dry goods business, Corbit, Davis & Co., which he had established in 1838 at the southeast corner of Second and Market Streets. Thomas Tatnall Lea, related to the proprietors of the publishing house of Carey & Lea, was a merchant and a director of the Bank of North America. Although his extended family had invested in flour mills and textile factories in Philadelphia and along the Brandywine River in Delaware, he was nonetheless primarily a merchant. George W. Carpenter was an amateur mineralogist, a member of the Academy of Natural Sciences, and a wholesale druggist, in competition against John Price Wetherill, one of the leading opponents of municipal funding for the PRR. Director Christian Spangler, in partnership with his brother Levi, operated coal mines near Tremont, Pennsylvania, in Beaver County. Robert Toland was a merchant and a director of the Girard Bank and three insurance companies, and in the 1820s he had established the Franklin Fire Insurance Company. His brother was the proprietor of grocery wholesalers Henry Toland & Son. John A. Wright was also a merchant, although he later entered the iron business, largely as a result of his association with the Pennsylvania Railroad.[11]

Another director, Richard Davis Wood, hailed from a prominent Quaker family in New Jersey. At the age of twenty-one, he established a dry-goods store in Salem, New Jersey. A leaky ship caused extensive water damage to a consignment sent from England. He turned the potential disaster into opportunity by offering the merchandise at reduced prices, attracting many new customers. Wood moved to Philadelphia during the 1820s, and in 1823 he established a wholesale dry-goods business, Wood, Abbott & Wood (later Wood, Abbott & Company). He became a director of the Girard Bank in 1831, and he also served as a director of the Schuylkill Navigation Company, the Philadelphia National Bank, the Allentown Iron Works, and the Insurance Company of North America. In 1844, he joined his half-brother, David C. Wood, at the Cumberland Furnace, a thirty-one-year-old pipe manufacturer. He was the treasurer of the Philadelphia Board of Trade and was well acquainted with the organization's president, Thomas Cope. To a greater degree than perhaps any other individual, save Cope, Wood had been instrumental in securing financing

and political support for the Pennsylvania Railroad. In addition to subscribing to $20,000 of the company's initial stock offering, he used his connections with the Philadelphia National Bank and the Insurance Company of North America to solicit additional investments. As such, he merited a seat on the board, as well as on the PRR's finance committee.[12]

Although some of the PRR board members—Merrick in particular—were embedded in Philadelphia's emerging industrial economy, most were more closely connected to the bygone era of the diversified merchant. They believed that their mission, and the mission of the Pennsylvania Railroad, was to divert the western grain trade away from Baltimore and toward Philadelphia. The success of the Pennsylvania Railroad, as a business enterprise in its own right, was a secondary concern. Even President Merrick, the most modern of the lot, hewed to the vision of Philadelphia's merchant-managers. He reminded the board that they had committed themselves to rescuing Philadelphia's mercantile fortunes and should not be content merely to earn a profit on their investment. "The road is being built by the business community for the benefit of trade," Merrick asserted in the company's *Second Annual Report*. "This was the main object of their organization, and must never be lost sight of."[13]

Organizing the Company

In addition to their local, and largely mercantilist, orientation, the PRR's directors embodied the state of management practice at that time. Most of the city's commercial firms were partnerships, with a small initial capitalization and limited managerial requirements. Clerks and bookkeepers handled a steady stream of routine transactions, freeing the partners to solicit business, usually on the basis of personal trust. The basic techniques of double-entry bookkeeping, dating to the Renaissance, generally sufficed, and proprietors often learned whether their business had made or lost money only when the books were balanced at the end of each fiscal year. Early manufacturing enterprises were scarcely more complex. The largest factories, mainly New England textile mills, were likewise operated as partnerships, with a fairly small initial investment. Production processes were both routine and uncomplicated. Two or three foremen gave orders to no more than a few hundred employees, many of them women and children, who performed rote tasks. Independent middlemen, often referred to as "jobbers," took on many of the firm's marketing functions. The partners or directors of such companies exercised minimal oversight, and they met with the foremen or toured the facility perhaps once a week.[14]

The PRR's initial organizational structure reflected the management practices that were more properly associated with counting houses and cotton mills than with railroads. Even though Merrick possessed some technical expertise, he became president because he was socially prominent, not because he had mastered the fundamentals of railway construction and operation. Merrick employed his wisdom and sagacity in resolving interpersonal conflicts within the board, with the expectation that the directors would make decisions by consensus. The railroad's other initial directors likewise drew heavily on their mercantile experience in the city of Philadelphia.

Commerce and railroading were two very different sorts of enterprises, however. Railroads required far more capital, far greater willingness to assume investment risk, and above all far greater delegation of authority to salaried managers than characterized the familial merchant banking houses. Merrick and the other directors had proved proficient at raising large sums of capital, yet they lacked the engineering expertise that would be critical if the PRR was to complete its main line in a timely and efficient manner. Furthermore, they woefully underestimated the complexity associated with railroad operations and with the pricing of transportation services. Their scant knowledge, combined with the necessity of making many decisions, ensured that board meetings were far more contentious than the genteel Philadelphia merchants had expected.[15]

When the directors established the company's first organizational structure, on April 21, they were initially attuned to the management of a construction project and only later began to implement operating methods. The PRR's executive staff was extraordinarily small, consisting initially of President Merrick, Secretary Oliver Fuller, and Treasurer George Vaux

Bacon. Board members also established three standing committees: Road, Accounts, and Finance. The Committee on Accounts existed solely to act as a check on the expenditures authorized by the board, while the Finance Committee was responsible for the management of the railroad's investment capital. The Road Committee was by far the most important of the three. The PRR's bylaws indicated that its function was to oversee construction, but its duties soon expanded to include all aspects of running the company. Although not named as such, the Road Committee functioned as an executive committee, advising the president and the board on matters relating to construction, real estate acquisition, the development of yard and station facilities, rates, and negotiations with other railroads. The Road Committee also exercised authority over the employees of the engineer corps who would build the railroad. In practice, however, the responsibilities of the Road Committee were poorly defined, and in many instances neither the bylaws nor the board specified which officer possessed ultimate authority over key aspects of the company's operations.[16]

Merrick and the other board members possessed little experience with engineering matters, and they accordingly resolved to hire a chief engineer and numerous subordinates—none of whom were shareholders—to oversee construction. Once the railroad was complete, however, the directors believed that its ongoing operation would be far less complicated, and that they would have little need for a cadre of high-paid, independent, and powerful executives.

Within a very short time, however, both the directors and the president had demonstrated their inability to manage a large and complex corporation, particularly one that had to almost immediately resolve thorny issues pertaining to routes, surveys, construction contracts, and negotiations with the Commonwealth of Pennsylvania regarding the Main Line of Public Works. The external struggles of the PRR commissioners to secure a charter and then to obtain municipal funding were but a prelude to the internal conflicts that wracked the railroad during the first years of its corporate life. Within five years of the railroad's incorporation, a small group of salaried managers had successfully challenged the prerogatives of the conservative owners on the board of directors, creating distinctive operating and financial strategies to suit their unique needs. As construction costs mounted, and as the company's operations increased in complexity, the salaried executives used their engineering skills—and their considerable political acumen—to unseat first Merrick, and then his successor and fellow merchant William C. Patterson from the presidency. There followed a wholesale purge of all directors with the temerity to believe that they might run the company. In their place came generation after generation of engineer-managers, individuals who attempted, usually with considerable success, to apply the principles of their profession to the operation of an increasingly complex hierarchical bureaucratic organization. They would transform the company's managerial elite from merchants to engineers.

"We Think They Will Form a Strong Corps"

In early April 1847, only days after the PRR's initial board meeting, the directors began to discuss the proper organizational structure and personnel for the engineer corps that would survey and build the railroad. Merrick called for the hiring of an engineer-in-chief and two assistants, with all three subject to his direct authority. His choice for the senior engineering position was probably Herman J. Lombaert, a thirty-year-old veteran of the Philadelphia & Trenton and the Philadelphia, Wilmington & Baltimore railroads.[17] Lombaert had recently returned from Colombia, where he had surveyed a canal linking Cartagena with the Río Magdalena. Although he was a competent engineer, he lacked the age and experience necessary to manage such a complex project as the Pennsylvania Railroad. He did, however, have in his favor the not inconsequential fact that he was a relative of director James McGee. Thomas Cope was not impressed, and suggested that "although accomplished, respectable & honest, [Lombaert] is believed to lack industry and energy." He thought that all three of the proposed "engineers in nomination are about equal in age & experience" and warned that "it is questionable should either be chosen Chief, [that the] other two among them would consent to be subordinate."[18]

Rather than establish a hierarchy within the engineer corps, Cope recommended that the board divide the route into three sections—the Eastern, Middle, and Western Divisions—each under the charge of a co-equal engineer who would report directly to the president, but who could be relieved of his duties only by the board. The tripartite structure, Cope believed, was essential because the entire railroad was "a long & intricate line for one man, who must of necessity occupy much time in his closet with plans, calculations, etc."[19] On April 8, Merrick, Cope, and several other directors argued over what Cope considered the "vexed question" of the structure of the engineer corps.[20] Cope believed that a substantial majority of the board would support his proposal, but he was reluctant to press for a vote. In an effort to achieve consensus, Cope felt that "harmony was desirable" but difficult to achieve, with a "President who was immovable & I hope right."[21] At last, they reached a compromise. Cope accepted Merrick's proposal for an engineer-in-chief, while the president assented to the establishment of two engineering sections, the Eastern Division and the Western Division. Merrick also conceded that the engineer corps should report to the board, and not to him.

Given its scope and importance, the Pennsylvania Railroad garnered considerable interest within the engineering community. A weak economy and a badly depressed job market made the project an even more attractive prospect. As director Richard Wood noted, with a certain degree of understatement, there were "many applications for positions on the Pennsylvania Central Railroad."[22] The directors could afford to be choosy, and they selected some of the most talented engineers in the United States. Within a matter of days, as Wood observed, the PRR possessed "one company of engineers organized and ready for the field, and another forming."[23] On April 9, the board established the engineer corps for the Western Division. By April 18, the engineering organization for the Eastern Division was in place. Cope, for one, was pleased with the personnel that the board had obtained. "We think they will form a strong corps," he predicted.[24]

Edward Miller took charge of the PRR's Western Division. An 1828 graduate of the University of Pennsylvania, Miller soon joined Canvass White and

Sylvester Welch on the construction of the Lehigh Navigation. The next year, he accompanied Welch to the Western Division Canal, but by 1830 he was at work on the surveys for the Allegheny Portage Railroad. Miller spent much of 1831 in Britain, observing railway technology that might be applied to Pennsylvania. Based on his experience, the canal commissioners appointed him as the principal assistant engineer on the Allegheny Portage Railroad. He was therefore responsible for designing the inclined planes and hoisting equipment that lifted cars over the mountains. With construction completed, Miller accepted a number of other engineering posts. They included the chief engineer of the Sunbury & Erie Railroad, intended to link Philadelphia and Lake Erie. He was responsible for the first thorough surveys of the route, but he chose an unnecessarily circuitous and steeply graded alignment—probably at the insistence of investors who desired that the railroad should pass through their extensive landholdings. The project faltered, and in 1840, Miller became first a consulting engineer and later the chief engineer of the New York & Erie Rail Road, as part of that company's early, failed effort to construct a line between the Hudson River and Lake Erie. In 1843, with a recession well under way, he was fortunate to find work as the president of the Harrisburg, Portsmouth, Mount Joy & Lancaster. Two years later, he became chief engineer of the Schuylkill Navigation, in charge of the enlargement of that profitable anthracite carrier to better meet competition from the Philadelphia & Reading Rail Road. The organization of the PRR's engineer corps coincided with the completion of major engineering work along the Schuylkill, and Miller was anxious for new employment. The PRR directors were happy to get him, for he had a close personal knowledge of the terrain that lay across much of the commonwealth of Pennsylvania.[25]

William B. Foster, Jr., became the associate engineer for the Eastern Division. He was the son of William Barclay Foster, a state legislator and a strong supporter of internal improvements, particularly the Pennsylvania Canal. A chance meeting with Nathan S. Roberts, who was surveying the canal's route along the Allegheny River, won young William a job as one of the party's axmen. He rose rapidly to the position of assistant engineer and then, after the canal was in ser-

vice, traveled widely, practicing his craft. By March 1839, he was the principal engineer of the North Branch Division. Four years later, he was elected to the Board of Canal Commissioners. Foster was outraged at the mismanagement of the commonwealth's transportation projects, and did his best to eliminate corruption and nepotism. He may have paid a steep price for his integrity, for he, like many of his fellow Democrats, lost his seat in the Whig tidal wave that characterized the October 1846 elections. Less musically inclined than his younger brother, composer Stephen C. Foster, William Foster was eager to find work with the Pennsylvania Railroad.[26]

"An Intelligent Cautious Energetic Man"

When Cope yielded to Merrick's suggestion to appoint an engineer-in-chief, the compromise permitted the hiring of an individual who was to have more of an influence over the railroad's destiny than any other. Cope knew exactly who he wanted for the post. His choice was thirty-nine-year-old John Edgar Thomson. When the Pennsylvania Railroad commissioned a centennial history of the company, authors George H. Burgess and Miles C. Kennedy typically prefaced their accounts of each president's administration with a brief biographical sketch. Their account of Thomson's activities on the PRR consumes fully a third of their massive volume, but background information is almost nonexistent, as if Thomson simply sprang into being, godlike, ready to lead the Pennsylvania Railroad to glory.

Thomson was nonetheless fully human, and prone to frailties. He possessed considerable intellect and talent. However, as a writer for the trade journal *Railroad Gazette* later observed, "Mr. Thomson was a man not without errors"—perhaps one of the mildest and most diplomatic criticisms on record.[27] Historian James A. Ward, Thomson's only modern biographer, has referred to the engineer as "among the least personable of nineteenth-century American businessmen, a man difficult to know, often characterized as cold and aloof, and, as befitted his Quaker background, one of few words."[28] A brilliant civil engineer, Thomson was an enormously dedicated and hardworking individual, one who said little, kept his thoughts to himself, and did not make friends easily—although, once made, those friendships could last a lifetime.[29] Isaac Jones Wistar, the son-in-law of PRR organizer Robert Toland, noted that Thomson's "judgements were deliberate and his words few, but he was an attentive and able listener. . . . So slowly were his conclusions formed as sometimes to try the patience of more ardent spirits; but once fixed, they remained unchangeable and were but consolidated and strengthened under opposition and hostility."[30] Cope described him more succinctly as "an intelligent cautious energetic man."[31]

Thomson was born on February 10, 1808, on a farm some ten miles distant from Philadelphia. His father, John Thomson, embodied the heady potential of upward economic and social mobility that was inherent in the new republic. His ancestors had arrived from England in the company of William Penn, and had been present at the founding of the Pennsylvania colony. As a surveyor for the Holland Land Company, John Thomson was intimately familiar with the western frontier. In 1793, Thomson and an assistant found themselves at Presque Isle (Erie) with only a small collection of hand tools. They nonetheless managed to build a schooner, the *White Fish*, and they sailed off in the direction of Philadelphia. At Niagara Falls, Thomson hired an ox team to drag the ship around the cascade and into Lake Ontario. Upon reaching Oswego, New York, the two men sailed to Oneida Lake and again portaged their vessel to the headwaters of the Mohawk River, which they followed to the Hudson. When they arrived in Philadelphia, they became the first individuals to have reached that city by water from Lake Erie. Enthusiastic local residents dragged the *White Fish* from the waterfront to Independence Square, where it remained on display until it rotted away. In 1809, when John Edgar was barely a year old, his father helped build a short tramway for stone haulage, making it one of the first antecedents of the railway in the United States. The elder Thomson also conducted many of the surveys for the Chesapeake & Delaware Canal, one of the great early engineering works in the United States. In 1830, in tandem with Enoch Lewis, Thomas Baird, and Charles L. Schlatter (the last being the same individual who

had surveyed a series of rail routes across Pennsylvania between 1839 and 1842), Thomson completed an extraordinarily thorough survey of a large tract of anthracite coal lands purchased by Stephen Girard. By the time he died in 1842, John Thomson had afforded his son an example of a skilled and highly respected civil engineer who had an extraordinary sense of adventure.[32]

As the younger Thomson came of age, he apparently harbored a burning desire to attend West Point, and his father's relative affluence and political connections would have made him a strong candidate for appointment. His father was also a Quaker, however, which meant he opposed warfare and held a low opinion of formal classroom instruction. As a result, the young Thomson stayed away from West Point, and indeed received very little formal education. Instead, his father used his political connections to secure a job for his son. In 1827, the young Thomson became a surveyor on the Main Line of Public Works, working with Major John Wilson to locate a canal between Philadelphia and Columbia. He soon came to agree with Wilson that a railroad represented a far better alternative than a canal over the rough and poorly watered terrain. By 1829 Wilson had promoted Thomson to principal assistant engineer, in charge of constructing one of the most difficult sections of the entire route of the Philadelphia & Columbia Railroad—from Philadelphia, across the Schuylkill River, along the base of Fairmount Hill, and then up the Belmont Plane.

During the spring of 1830, the commonwealth's inability to sell its internal-improvement bonds brought work on the Philadelphia & Columbia to a halt, forcing Thomson to seek alternate employment. He worked on several other transportation projects in the region—including a never-built extension of the state-owned Delaware Division Canal between Philadelphia and Bristol and the proposed Oxford Railroad, intended to connect the Susquehanna River at Port Deposit, with a location on the Philadelphia & Columbia, about forty miles west of Philadelphia.

Thomson might well have remained in his native state had it not been for the untimely death of his friend and mentor, Major John Wilson. In the winter of 1832, after fewer than four years as the chief engineer for the Board of Canal Commissioners, Wilson became seriously ill. During a leave of absence, he surveyed portions of the Camden & Amboy Railroad, again assisted by Thomson. Wilson's health did not improve, and he headed for the warmer climes of Matanzas, Cuba. He died there on February 27, 1833, just shy of his forty-fourth birthday. Absent Wilson's guidance, a distraught Thomson looked to the American South for a fresh start.[33]

In 1834 the directors of the Georgia Rail Road (after 1836, the Georgia Rail Road & Banking Company) hired Thomson as chief engineer. Although later generations of Yankees decried the antebellum South as a feudalistic bastion of agrarian stagnation, slave-state entrepreneurs in fact eagerly embraced the most modern railway developments and created considerable opportunity for talented engineers like Thomson. Georgia was hardly a backwater, and Thomson's presence did not sever his ties to the northern engineering community.[34]

Thomson's immediate task was to locate a line from Augusta west to Athens, Macon, and, ultimately, to a junction with the Western & Atlantic Railroad. He soon acquired larger executive responsibilities, a circumstance that was in keeping with the evolution of the engineering profession. During the 1820s, people in charge of state-sponsored public works, in states such as New York and Pennsylvania, attempted to segregate construction from strategic decision-making.[35] Their efforts proved problematic because managers frequently made decisions involving engineering, an area where many of them lacked even basic expertise, while engineers in the field sometimes took on policy issues. The directors of the Georgia Rail Road, like their contemporaries at several other companies, sought to avoid such conflicts by concentrating engineering and management responsibilities in one person. Thus, Thomson's full title was "Chief Engineer and General Agent." Thomson and other senior engineers found considerable promise in the commingling of responsibilities, for it offered them the opportunity to run the railroad that they had built rather than move on to yet another project once construction was complete.[36]

Thomson's interest in management extended to his efforts to encourage solidarity among engineers and turn them into a community of skilled technical practitioners. Beginning in December 1838, Thomson at-

tempted to organize a Society of Civil Engineers in the United States. In February of the following year, he attended an initial meeting of the society in Baltimore, along with Edward Miller, the future associate engineer in charge of the PRR's Western Division. Other pioneers in railway operation and management, including George W. Whistler and Benjamin H. Latrobe, Jr., were also present at the meeting, but Miller wrote the constitution and was the person most committed to the organization. Thomson found it extraordinarily difficult to establish consensus among strong-willed engineers, particularly as the aftereffects of the Panic of 1837 heightened competition for jobs. Many prospective members were scattered across the country at isolated construction sites, and the consequent travel difficulties did not help matters. Military engineers declined to participate. The members of the society developed an utterly unworkable organizational structure. The group soon dissolved, but the experience taught Thomson that without proper organization, it would be impossible to harness the activities of skilled individuals to suit a common purpose.[37]

During the twelve years that he spent in Georgia, Thomson learned two valuable lessons, which he would later put to good use on the PRR. First, he developed a keen appreciation for the need to manage interpersonal conflicts among the owners and senior managers, a skill that was often more important than engineering expertise. To a far greater extent than any other mid-nineteenth-century enterprise, railroads required cooperation and teamwork, and Thomson was well positioned to achieve those goals. Second, Thomson perceived, far better than the railroad's promoters, that local business alone could not support a line in sparsely settled territory, and that through traffic was correspondingly essential to profitability.[38]

While in Georgia, Thomson experienced many of the difficulties that he would later confront on the PRR, including financial crises, hostile legislators, and conservative shareholders who saw no reason to expend any more of the railroad's financial resources than was absolutely necessary. By the summer of 1839, the directors of the Georgia Rail Road were attempting to reduce Thomson's salary (which, as chief engineer, had been twice that of the line's president), as well as parsimoniously denying him reimbursement for even minor expenditures. Thomson went so far as to resign, on July 1, 1841, but by the following February he was back at work. By 1845 the Georgia Rail Road offered service to its connection with the Western & Atlantic at a junction named simply "Terminus"—a location that Thomson, according to popular opinion, dubbed Atlanta. With construction essentially complete, Thomson could anticipate few additional engineering responsibilities. At the same time, the shareholders and the directors of the railroad increasingly challenged Thomson's authority within the company and dismissed his suggestions on how to operate the line. In February 1847 he resigned a second and final time.[39]

Thomson was certainly pushed out of Georgia, thanks to both the completion of the Georgia Rail Road and to his conflicts with its directors, but he was also pulled north to Pennsylvania by the lure of what the engineering community was already acknowledging as one of the great works of the age. Thomas Cope and other PRR directors were well aware of Thomson's considerable reputation as an engineer and as a manager. Thomson was clearly their first choice for chief engineer, and on April 9, 1847, over Merrick's initial objections, the board offered him the job. The directors agreed to pay Thomson $4,000 a year, well above the $3,208 that represented the mean yearly earnings for "engineers of the first rank" in 1847—but a thousand dollars less than his peak 1839 salary as the chief engineer of the Georgia Rail Road. Each of Thomson's immediate subordinates received the smaller, but still impressive, sum of $3,000 annually.[40] Cope dismissed the high cost of their salaries, suggesting, "If we have first rate men, we must pay for them, it is poor economy to employ inferior persons to conduct a work of such magnitude."[41] Thomson accepted the board's offer with alacrity, and by the middle of April 1847, he was on his way to Philadelphia.

The Work Begins

By 1847, the techniques of railway construction had changed significantly from Thomson's early days on the Philadelphia & Columbia and the Georgia Rail Road. The early decades of the nineteenth century constituted a period of experimentation, as fledgling American railroads struggled to adapt British equipment and operating practices to local geography and demographics. Britain was generally more densely populated than the United States, and a widespread canal network had established trade routes and construction methods well before the railroads arrived. In the United States, however, a more dispersed population, more rugged terrain, a shortage of investment capital, and higher labor costs mitigated against such features of British construction as low grades, double tracks, and substantial masonry bridges. The more demanding operating conditions forced American mechanics to make substantial modifications to imported British locomotives. This situation in turn established the conditions of American railway practice: single track, grades as steep as 2.2 percent (the practical limit for reasonably efficient mainline operation), sharp curves, cheaply built timber bridges and lineside structures, and rugged and easily repaired locomotives and rolling stock, all presided over by a core of inventive and pragmatic machinists. As the railroad network expanded, the operating men had little choice but to rebuild large parts of their lines, replacing wood and iron with steel and masonry, straightening curves, filling in trestles, lowering grades, and adding additional tracks.

The PRR's route was by no means fixed, and Thomson's first and most important responsibility was to choose the optimal line between Harrisburg and Pittsburgh, one that possessed the lowest possible grade for predominately eastbound grain traffic. Thomson reexamined the 1839–42 surveys conducted by Charles Schlatter, but he quickly dismissed two of the three routes.[42] Even though the northern route possessed the lowest crossing of the Alleghenies, Thomson found its location along the West Branch of the Susquehanna River to be indefensibly long. The chief engineer was intrigued by the more direct southern route, which would permit the employment of the existing Cumberland Valley Railroad as far west as a point near Shippensburg. The fatal defect in such a plan, Thomson noted, was "the rugged character of the country, and the high gradients necessary to overcome the numerous summits upon it"—the same problem that Hother Hagé had encountered a few years earlier.[43] Thomson readily chose Schlatter's middle route along the Juniata River, close to the line of the Juniata Division Canal. That was the most logical path, for it allowed him to construct a reasonably direct route, with one summit to surmount, while enabling the PRR to take advantage of the commercial development that had grown up along the Main Line of Public Works.

Thomson also suggested, and the directors quickly agreed, that the Allegheny Portage Railroad could be employed as a temporary passage through the Appalachians, saving both time and money. The PRR's chief engineer accordingly concluded that, with "the middle, or mountain division, not having been provided for," it would be most appropriate to extend the remaining two divisions to meet the eastern and western ends of the commonwealth's route over the Alleghenies.[44]

Once he had selected the route, Thomson saw little reason to deviate from it. When a delegation from Perry County approached Thomson, anxious to have the county's communities included on the new line, the chief engineer was courteous enough, and curious enough, to survey an alternate route. After discovering that the alteration would increase the length of the line by four miles and impose heavier grades, Thomson would have nothing more to do with the delegation from Perry County.[45]

Thomson nonetheless made some changes to the Schlatter survey. Schlatter, confronted with the poor performance and low horsepower of early locomotives, had attempted to keep the rate of ascent as low as possible, with a maximum grade of no more than 0.85 percent. He had recommended a long, continuous moderate climb from Lewistown west, following the curving contours of the Juniata River Valley and zigzagging up the sides of the mountains, while minimizing the assault on the summit itself. Schlatter also located numerous sharp curves, some no more than four hundred feet of radius, which were better suited to short trains pulled by horses or early and primitive locomotives.

Thomson was the beneficiary of nearly a decade's worth of improvements in steam locomotive design, and those more powerful engines enabled him to modify Schlatter's route. His engineering expertise told him that such a side-hill route would require numerous cuts, fills, and bridges, and that tight curves would constitute an ongoing impediment to efficient operations. Thomson instead chose a moderate, steady climb from Harrisburg along the Juniata, as far west as the foothills of the Alleghenies. The westbound grade ranged from a maximum of 0.3 percent between Harrisburg and Lewistown to no more than 0.4 percent from Lewistown west to the mountains. Given the expected role of the PRR in moving grain from west to east, the eastbound ruling grade was far more significant, and that was no more than 0.2 percent. Thomson likewise reduced the maximum curvature to no more than 995 feet of radius, save for the eastern approach to the Rockville Bridge across the Susquehanna River, where an 880-foot radius curve proved necessary.[46]

In June 1848, with his surveys complete and construction already under way, Thomson presented his first annual report to the board, and the directors finally learned what their railroad would cost. In his 1842 report to the canal commissioners, Schlatter had suggested that the middle route would require just under $1.5 million to build. In 1845, the promoters of what had originally been called the Pennsylvania Central Railroad claimed that $7.5 million would be sufficient to lay tracks between Harrisburg and Pittsburgh. Thomson thought that figure adequate, but only if he were willing to increase grades, curvature, and overall distance to unacceptable levels. He presented the board with several estimates, each based on the assumption that his crews would grade a double-track line but, for the moment, lay only a single track with passing sidings. A reasonable expenditure for the physical plant over the entire distance between Harrisburg and Pittsburgh would probably be on the order of $9,150,000, he suggested. Reliance on the Allegheny Portage Railroad would lower the cost to $6,970,000. The provision of depots ($475,000), shop facilities ($185,000), locomotives ($510,000), and passenger and freight cars ($820,000) would add an additional $1,990,000 to the cost. Thomson informed the board that it would cost $8,960,000 to complete a rail route between Harrisburg and Pittsburgh.

The PRR's chief engineer was nonetheless sensitive that the cost of nearly $9 million might well discomfit the PRR's directors, as it vastly exceeded the $1,017,725 of paid-in capital in the corporate treasury. Thomson accordingly took great pains to emphasize that the eastern portions of the railroad would begin to generate revenue almost as soon as they were complete, stating "It will not be necessary to expend the whole of this amount until some time after the Road is in use."[47] Additional economies, including the reduction of cuts and fills to the width of a single track, might bring the total cost to a more manageable $7,860,000.[48]

A New Route West

Of the four major lines between tidewater and the west, the PRR was the last to begin. Yet, thanks in large measure to Thomson's engineering skill, a rapid pace of construction ensured that it reached the western waters at virtually the same time as its rivals, the Baltimore & Ohio, the Erie, and the collection of railroads that later became the New York Central. Even before Thomson arrived in Philadelphia, much less determined the railroad's final alignment and calculated the cost of construction, survey crews were working their way east from Pittsburgh and west from Harrisburg. On June 8, the board authorized Thomson to negotiate the first grading contracts, for fifteen miles on both the eastern and western ends of the line, as required by the corporate charter. A month later, on Wednesday, July 7, 1847, officials gathered at the intersection of Market Street and Meadow Lane in Harrisburg to turn the first ceremonial shovel of earth. On the same day, the directors of the Harrisburg, Portsmouth, Mount Joy & Lancaster Railroad agreed to connect their tracks with those of the PRR, ultimately enabling through service east to Dillerville and a junction with the Philadelphia & Columbia Railroad.[49]

By the end of July, with work on the eastern end of the line well under way, the directors approved the first grading contracts on the Western Division. The work at the western end of the route was something of a distraction to Thomson, but it was necessary to fulfill the conditions attached to the PRR's 1846 corporate charter as an appeasement to Pittsburgh residents who would otherwise have favored the Baltimore & Ohio. The flurry of activity occurred just in time, days ahead of the July 30 deadline imposed by the charter. On August 2, with construction clearly under way, Governor Shunk declared the Baltimore & Ohio charter null and void, ensuring that the PRR would have a

virtual monopoly over Pittsburgh traffic for the next quarter of a century. The Philadelphia company had taken full advantage of the head start that the state legislature had conferred.[50]

The awarding of construction contracts secured the future of the Pennsylvania Railroad, but they were only a minor prelude to the difficult work of building the line. Thomson, Foster, and Miller subdivided the railroad's two divisions into thirty-mile segments. A principal assistant engineer oversaw each section and in turn superintended the sub-assistants who were in charge of ten-mile construction segments.[51] The western slope of the Alleghenies proved the most problematic. Contractors on the Western Division badly underestimated the cost and complexity of construction, and soon went bankrupt. Thomson and the PRR's directors were not overly concerned, as the limited amount of work that had been done was sufficient to satisfy the provisions of the charter. To the dismay of many Pittsburghers, construction crews concentrated their energies on the eastern portion of the line, between Harrisburg and a temporary connection with the Allegheny Portage Railroad at Duncansville, near Hollidaysburg.

On the eastern end of the PRR route, workmen faced an immediate obstacle in the Susquehanna River, which required a 3,680-foot bridge at Rockville. Beyond the Rockville Bridge, the line followed the west bank of the Susquehanna River for a short distance, through Marysville to Duncannon, at the mouth of the Juniata River. The tracks turned west, up the south side of the Juniata Valley, following the Juniata Division Canal, on the opposite side of the river. The tracks climbed gradually from an elevation of 310 feet at Harrisburg to 480 feet at Lewistown, sixty-one miles away.[52]

Construction was more difficult west of Lewistown, where the Juniata Valley became narrower and more sinuous. The river turned to the southwest, and so too did the Pennsylvania Railroad, passing between Blue Mountain and Jack's Mountain. Thomson continued to follow the general outlines of the Schlatter survey, yet made minor changes to reduce distance and curvature, particularly in the vicinity of the Kishacoquillas Valley. Numerous bridges, necessary to maintain the best route, took the line back and forth across

Figure 15. In August 1849, construction crews completed the Rockville Bridge, which spanned the Susquehanna River, a few miles north of Harrisburg. Its lightweight construction entailed certain problems—a cyclone destroyed a large portion of the bridge before the first train had even crossed it, and heavy traffic levels forced the PRR's engineers to replace the bridge in 1877 and again in 1902. The original bridge, however insubstantial, was inexpensive and did not delay the PRR's westward progress.

Pennsylvania Historical and Museum Commission, Railroad Museum of Pennsylvania.

the Juniata. At Newton Hamilton, the railroad cut through a great horseshoe bend in the river, requiring a deep excavation that was for years afterward plagued by slides. At Mount Union, eighty-five miles from Harrisburg, the tracks entered Jack's Narrows, a steep defile that gave railroad, canal, and river alike passage through the foothills of the Alleghenies.[53]

Beyond Jack's Narrows, all three arteries of transportation turned to the northeast. The railroad followed the north bank of the Juniata to Huntingdon, ninety-seven miles from Harrisburg, and three hundred feet higher in elevation. After cutting through Warrior Ridge, the tracks reached Petersburg and the mouth of the Little Juniata River. Here, the railroad and the canal diverged from one another. The canal turned to the southwest, along the Frankstown Branch of the Little Juniata. The tracks followed the main stem of the Little Juniata to the northwest, crossing the narrowing watercourse more than a dozen times in order to maintain the best grade, the easiest curvature, and the lowest construction costs. A 1,200-foot tunnel, the first along the route, took tracks through a shoulder of Tussey's Mountain. West of the tunnel the grade stiffened from 16 to 21 feet per mile (from 0.3 percent to 0.4

percent). By the time the tracks reached Tyrone, 21 miles from Huntingdon, they had gained an additional 276 feet in elevation. The community of Tyrone, at the mouth of the Little Bald Eagle Creek, quickly became a major coal and iron-producing center.

West of Tyrone, Thomson broke with the Schlatter survey. The line now went to the southwest, roughly paralleling—but at a considerable distance from—the Juniata Division Canal. The tracks diverged from the Little Juniata and entered the Tuckahoe Valley, with Brush Mountain to the east and the spine of the Alleghenies to the west. On one side of the three-mile-wide valley lay rich reserves of iron ore and limestone, while the other slope boasted deposits of bituminous coal—all of which would generate considerable traffic for the PRR. The small community of Tipton provided a connection with a plank road over the Alleghenies, while Blair's Furnace was proximate to high-yield iron ore deposits.

Three miles beyond Blair's Furnace lay Robinson's Summit, the point at which the grade became far more severe. The tracks had climbed 858 feet in the 132 miles that separated Robinson's Summit from Harrisburg, and they confronted an even greater rise of 992 feet in order to crest the top of the Alleghenies. That last push over the mountains would entail a maximum grade of 1.5 percent—steep, but well below the 2.2 percent that engineers generally considered the optimal maximum for railway operations. At Robinson's Summit, PRR crews would nonetheless need to add additional motive power solely for the relatively short climb to the top of the mountains, a short distance to the west. Here, too, however, the grade was decidedly in favor of eastbound traffic. Trains laden with grain and other bulk commodities could coast downhill, while lightly laden westbound traffic would be far easier to drag upgrade. Furthermore, Thomson noted that high-quality bituminous coal was readily available nearby, greatly reducing the cost of fueling the many helper locomotives that would be necessary to push trains over the mountain.[54]

The critical location where the grade stiffened and the Pennsylvania Railroad met the Allegheny Mountains soon blossomed into the company town of Altoona—a community that Thomson may have named after Allatoona Pass in northern Georgia, where he had once worked as a surveyor. The town did not exist before the coming of the Pennsylvania Railroad, but it would become the single most important point on the system, an iconic location not only in the operations of the PRR, but in the history of all of American railroading.[55]

By the end of 1848, contractors were at work on the 117 miles of line west of Harrisburg, as far as Logan's Narrows. Construction proceeded rapidly, despite the failure of inexperienced contractors, epidemics of disease, labor shortages, and disputes over pay. Work on the Rockville Bridge began in the fall of 1847, with the task of erecting the piers assigned to contractors who had proven their expertise on the Philadelphia & Reading. Thomson's confidence in their abilities was misplaced, and they soon failed. Heavy flooding in the spring of 1848 caused further delays. By December 1848, the stone piers were ready for the twenty-three wooden Howe trusses. Daniel Stone, an experienced bridge builder who had recently completed the reconstruction of the Market Street Bridge across the Schuylkill River in Philadelphia, took charge of the erection of the superstructure. In March 1849, a severe windstorm (often described as a cyclone or a tornado) destroyed six trusses of the incomplete bridge, forcing workers to rebuild a portion of the structure. Despite those delays, the Rockville Bridge opened to traffic in August 1849.[56]

By early 1849, the roadbed and bridges between Harrisburg and Lewistown were largely complete, awaiting only rails. On August 30, 1849, PRR officials made a ceremonial first trip as far west as Lewistown. Regular service began two days later, with the locomotive *Mifflin* having the honor of pulling the first revenue-generating trip in the history of the Pennsylvania Railroad. On Christmas Eve, 1849, crews reached McVeytown, at milepost 72. Mount Union saw its first train on April 1, 1850, with service to Huntingdon beginning on June 10. By September, construction crews had reached Robinson's Summit, more than half way to Pittsburgh, and they quickly began work on the yard and shop facilities at the new company town of Altoona. Thomson had already developed plans to push west from Altoona, building over the summit and then downgrade toward Johnstown, but he delayed construction in favor of a temporary alliance with the Allegheny Portage Railroad. PRR construction crews therefore continued to build six miles farther south from Altoona, to a connection with the Allegheny Portage tracks at Duncansville. On September 16, 1850, the first trains ran between Harrisburg and Duncansville.

East of Harrisburg, PRR officials soon established control over the vitally important Harrisburg, Portsmouth, Mount Joy & Lancaster Railroad. On April 5, 1848, the PRR board appointed a special committee to negotiate a lease of the HPMJ&L, and by the end of September the PRR directors had agreed to operate the line, using it as its exclusive route between Dillerville (Lancaster) and Harrisburg. The level of through freight and passenger traffic determined the rental, paid in semimonthly installments. The larger railroad had the absolute authority to set through freight and passenger rates, although the HPMJ&L retained the rights to establish rates for local traffic. In return, the HPMJ&L agreed to "keep their road in good order . . . and relay the flat bar portion with H Rail, or lay another track along side thereof on or before the First day of January A.D. 1850, and also lay a Second track on the river route [along the Susquehanna between Columbia and Royalton, a short distance to the south of Harrisburg] as soon as the trade shall require the same." The PRR's investors also gained control over the HPMJ&L's locomotives, cars, structures, and shops, ensuring that through traffic would not be disrupted by poorly maintained equipment.[57]

PRR officials soon inaugurated service to the west in conjunction with the Philadelphia City Railroad, the Philadelphia & Columbia, and the Harrisburg, Portsmouth, Mount Joy & Lancaster. By October 1850, a month after construction crews completed the link with the Allegheny Portage Railroad, the PRR operated daily fast passenger, slow passenger, and freight trains over the entire route between Philadelphia and Duncansville. For a few weeks, westbound travelers could continue west to Pittsburgh along the Main Line of Public Works. From Johnstown, at the western end of the Allegheny Portage Railroad, freight reached Pittsburgh on the Western Division Canal, while passengers were more likely to ride by stagecoach. In early December, however, commonwealth employees drained the Western Division Canal in preparation for winter, and, as they had done in the past, they shut down the Allegheny Portage Railroad as well.

During the 1851 navigation season on the public works, the PRR offered through freight and passenger service between Philadelphia and Pittsburgh. Through did not mean convenient, however. East of Dillerville, PRR traffic was at the mercy of the Philadelphia City Railroad and the Philadelphia & Columbia. The close spacing of the Philadelphia & Columbia tracks and the restrictive clearances in the sole tunnel on the Harrisburg, Portsmouth, Mount Joy & Lancaster precluded the through operation of more capacious PRR equipment. The poor condition of the Allegheny Portage Railroad caused further delays and difficulties.

To the great annoyance of the inhabitants of southwestern Pennsylvania, the PRR's link between Pittsburgh and Johnstown lagged well behind the eastern portion of the route. In July 1847, the PRR's engineers had completed negotiations with local contractors for the first fifteen miles of line, barely enough to satisfy the terms of the corporate charter. Some work had taken place, but an epidemic of fever created a labor shortage, and by the following year most of the contractors had abandoned their sections as unprofitable. Merrick and the other members of the board were growing increasingly concerned about the lack of progress. They were hoping that residents of Pittsburgh and nearby communities would subscribe to as much as $2 million in PRR stock—a possibility that was contingent on resuming work on the Western Division as quickly as possible. In March 1848, the engineer corps began a new set of surveys, designed in part to placate residents of western Pennsylvania. On June 4, 1848, when the Allegheny County commissioners agreed to take $1 million in PRR stock, their offer required the timely commencement of work on the Western Division.

In August 1849, with construction well under way on the line between Harrisburg and Duncansville, Thomson asked that work be resumed on the Western Division. The directors were hardly averse to his suggestions, but they were concerned at the steady drain on the corporate treasury. In response to his pleas, the board authorized several construction contracts to the west of Johnstown. Additional sections followed through the remainder of the summer and into the fall, but it was not until November 1849 that the entire line from Johnstown toward Pittsburgh was under contract.[58]

It was indeed fortunate that the board acted when it did. By 1850, the managers of four companies were engaged in a race for the west. Since reaching Cumberland, Maryland, in November 1842, Baltimore & Ohio construction crews had continued to push onward. Three acts of the Virginia legislature, in 1845, 1846, and 1847, granted the company the right to build across the narrow strip of land that separated Maryland from the Ohio River. During the spring and summer of 1847, with the PRR having precluded the Pittsburgh & Connellsville route to Pittsburgh, B&O president Louis McLane and his shareholders set the B&O's Ohio River terminus at Wheeling. Throughout the summer of 1848, survey crews worked their way through the rugged terrain of western Maryland. On November 14, 1849, during the same month that the PRR negotiated many of the construction agreements on the Western Division, the directors of the Baltimore & Ohio approved contracts for the route between Cumberland and Wheeling, Virginia. By June 1851, construction crews had surmounted the summit of the Alleghenies and continued west, toward the Ohio River.[59]

The situation to the north looked equally grim. Throughout the 1830s and 1840s, workers from numerous railroads were incrementally piecing together a route from Albany to Buffalo, paralleling the Erie Canal. In 1844, they closed the last link in the chain. In order to protect the Erie Canal, the New York legislature imposed restrictions similar to Pennsylvania's tonnage tax on freight transported over the route, but with little effect. Bulk cargoes were naturally drawn to the low-cost waterway, while passengers and merchandise went by rail. Initially, many passengers connected at Albany with the fast Hudson River steamboats operated by Cornelius Vanderbilt. After October 1851, however, they also had the option of riding along the Hudson River Railroad, from New York to East Albany, across the Hudson from the state capital.

The New York & Erie posed a threat that was only slightly less serious. Since 1840, construction crews had been laboring westward from Piermont, on the Hudson River. By October 1841, the tracks reached Goshen, New York, and for a time, the financially destitute company could push them no farther. The respite ended in August 1846, with construction resuming only a few months after the bruising charter bill in the Pennsylvania General Assembly. By December 1848, the railhead was at Binghamton. In May 1851, well before Thomson had completed the PRR's Western Division, the Erie opened its line to Dunkirk, on Lake Erie.

Given the intensity of the competition, Thomson could brook no further delays in the construction of the Western Division. In the summer of 1850 work recommenced, as a new group of presumably wiser contractors pushed west up Two Mile Run, Turtle Creek, and Brush Creek. The work proved relatively straightforward, thanks to the growing expertise of the engineer corps. Thomson also benefited from the geography of the Eastern Continental Divide. On the east side of the Allegheny Mountains, the terrain rose rapidly toward the summit, making it difficult to avoid steep grades. To the west, the terrain descended more gradually. Pittsburgh, at an elevation of 1,224 feet, was far higher than Harrisburg and many of the other communities on the eastern portion of the route. Of even greater value to Thomson, the tributaries of the Allegheny and Monongahela rivers had cut deep valleys in the western slope of the mountains, allowing engineers to locate a gradually descending line along their flanks. This accident of topography was a blessing for the Pennsylvania Railroad, for it enabled heavily laden eastbound trains to cross the mountains with relative ease.[60]

Western Division associate engineer Edward Miller and his staff nonetheless had their work cut out for them. The route east from Pittsburgh began near the basin of the Western Division Canal, ran along Liberty Street, and then swung east, parallel to and a few blocks away from the Allegheny River. The tracks curved back to the southeast, following an ancient bed of the Monongahela River, through Millvale, East Liberty, Homewood, and Swissdale (later, Swissvale). A line along the modern riverbank would have been shorter and yielded lower grades, Thomson acknowledged, but he emphasized that his alignment "presented the only apparently feasible route by which a connexion could be formed with a road extending toward the great West."[61] What Thomson did not mention was that Pittsburghers, still furious with the PRR interests for denying the Baltimore & Ohio access to their city, continued to hope that the Pittsburgh & Connellsville might be resurrected and had reserved for it the better route.[62]

The Pennsylvania Railroad finally reached the Monongahela River at Braddock (sometimes referred to as Braddock's Field), the location where British general Edward Braddock had met his end during the Seven Years' War. At Brinton's Station, a short distance east of Braddock, the Monongahela River turned to the south, while the Pennsylvania Railroad continued east. The stop was a convenient transfer point for passengers headed up the Monongahela and Youghiogheny rivers and, in the early years of construction, for those transferring to the plank road linking Pittsburgh to the eastern part of the state. The location, near the mouth of Turtle Creek, presented Thomson with several possible routes. He initially favored a variant of the Schlatter survey, following Turtle Creek northeast and then east, through Murrysville and New Alexandria, and then diverging into two possible routes to the summit. Thomson considered locations as far north as Ebensburg before settling on a modification to Schlatter's southern route, one that would take the tracks through Greensburg and on to Latrobe. Thomson's grade ascended Brush Run, where fourteen small bridges over that watercourse brought the tracks to Barclay Summit. While that section provided few construction difficulties, it possessed an undulating profile that plagued Pennsylvania Railroad dispatchers and train crews for the remainder of the company's existence—particularly as traffic between Pittsburgh and Johnstown soon became heavy in both directions.[63]

Well into the mountains now, the track passed through two tunnels, a three-hundred-foot one underneath Greensburg, the seat of Westmoreland County, and the other, twice as long, between Crabtree and Fourteen Mile Run, followed by a deep cut half a mile in length. At Beatty's Station, the tracks crossed the Stoystown–Greensburg Turnpike (also known as the Southern Turnpike), one of the main routes over the mountains to Pittsburgh. Alternating

cuts and fills characterized the next few miles to Latrobe, where the railroad left the valley of the Loyalhanna for that of the Conemaugh.[64] Along the way, crews blasted their way through Packsaddle Narrows, where the Conemaugh River had carved a narrow passage through Chestnut Ridge. Once in the Conemaugh Valley, the tracks paralleled the Main Line of Public Works, hugging the hillside well above the Western Division Canal on the opposite side of the river. The two routes followed the Conemaugh through gaps in Chestnut Ridge and Laurel Hill, past Lockport and on to Johnstown. Rather than make a connection with the Allegheny Portage Railroad at Johnstown, Thomson chose to continue construction farther to the east, closely paralleling the commonwealth's line to a point just to the west of the Big Viaduct over the Little Conemaugh River. The additional construction was well worth it, however, as it enabled traffic to avoid both the westernmost inclined plane on the Allegheny Portage Railroad as well as the Staple Bend Tunnel, while using the Long Level that the state had constructed nearly twenty years earlier.[65]

Construction on the Western Division proceeded apace, despite labor shortages and worker unrest. At one point, a frustrated Edward Miller sought warrants to arrest striking Irish workers, complaining to Thomson that "the laborers are in open rebellion."[66] Although problems continued, on August 25, 1851, PRR crews had completed some twenty miles of track between the connection with the Allegheny Portage Railroad at the Big Viaduct and the Western Division Canal at Lockport. Passengers and cargoes could then continue their journey to Pittsburgh along the Western Division Canal, although most travelers chose the faster stage route. By December 10, track had reached Beatty's Station and the Stoystown–Greensburg Turnpike.[67]

On January 27, 1852, four and a half years after construction began at Harrisburg, the PRR first offered through service between Philadelphia and Pittsburgh. The route actually consisted of seven distinct segments: from Philadelphia to Dillerville along the tracks of the Philadelphia & Columbia; from Dillerville to Harrisburg along the Harrisburg, Portsmouth, Mount Joy & Lancaster; from Harrisburg to Duncansville along its own rails; from Duncansville to the

Figure 16. Between Bolivar and Torrance, Pennsylvania, the PRR main line passed along the side of Chestnut Ridge, the westernmost Appalachian ridge in Pennsylvania. The tracks were perched a terrifying 160 feet above the Conemaugh River and the Western Division Canal. The canal continued west along the Conemaugh and Kiskiminetas rivers, but the PRR's tracks curved to the southwest, reaching Latrobe before heading west for Greensburg and Pittsburgh. Packsaddle Narrows afforded the railroad a narrow passage through the mountains and soon became a landmark for photographers and tourists.

Pennsylvania Historical and Museum Commission, Railroad Museum of Pennsylvania.

Big Viaduct via the Allegheny Portage Railroad; then on its own rails again from the Big Viaduct to Beatty's Station; then a twenty-eight-mile gap covered by wagons and stagecoaches; and finally by PRR tracks from Turtle Creek to Pittsburgh.[68]

Slowly, the gap closed. On July 15, 1852, construction crews connected Brinton's Station and Radebaugh. Finally, on November 29, 1852, workers finished laying track between Beatty's Station and Radebaugh. The first westbound train arrived in Pittsburgh that evening. After three decades of acrimonious debates, extraordinary feats of engineering, and the expenditure of colossal sums by both the commonwealth and the corporation, Pennsylvanians could at long last travel more than 350 miles between their two largest cities on a single mode of transportation.[69]

By the time that rails spanned the breadth of Pennsylvania, a radical transformation had taken place on the Pennsylvania Railroad. The merchants who had willed the company into being, fought for its corporate charter, and begged both private citizens and elected officials for stock subscriptions were no longer in control of the enterprise that they had created. Their most highly prized employee, chief engineer Thomson, had displaced them and had seized control of the Pennsylvania Railroad.

Herman Haupt

The conflict that would eventually enable Thomson to become the president of the Pennsylvania Railroad largely centered on his chief deputy, Herman Haupt. A brilliant but combative individual, and someone who did not suffer fools gladly, Haupt was almost completely lacking in political finesse. He was largely responsible for developing the PRR's early organizational structure, and his management methods later diffused throughout the railroad industry. Haupt nonetheless seemed utterly unable to function in the type of hierarchical corporate organization that he had created, and his time with the PRR was both contentious and brief.

Haupt was born in Philadelphia on March 26, 1817, the son of a merchant. His father died in 1828, making it unlikely that his son, then only twelve years old, would follow the same career. Further, owing to the intercession of Congressman John B. Steriger, President Andrew Jackson appointed Haupt as a cadet at West Point. He was still only thirteen, a year younger than the earliest possible age for admission, so his commission was simply postdated. Like many of his classmates, Haupt saw his West Point education as a means to establish his engineering credentials rather than remain in the less promising employ of the military. In September 1835, three months after graduation, he resigned his commission in order to assist in the surveying of a railroad in eastern Pennsylvania linking Norristown and Allentown. By the fall of 1836, he was the principal assistant engineer of the Gettysburg Railroad, the "tapeworm" line that owed its unhappy existence to the political influence of Thaddeus Stevens. Haupt soon fell victim to one of the political purges that periodically roiled the Board of Canal Commissioners, and he was unceremoniously dismissed—a circumstance that no doubt accounted for his later enmity toward the commonwealth's management of the Main Line of Public Works.

With few engineering jobs in the offing following the Panic of 1837 and the subsequent 1841 collapse of the United States Bank of Pennsylvania, Haupt spent much of the next decade in search of remunerative work. For six years, he was a professor of mathematics and civil engineering at Pennsylvania College (later Gettysburg College), an institution that Thaddeus Stevens had founded in 1832. Haupt was particularly fascinated with bridges, and between 1839 and 1847 he became one of the world's leading authorities on the subject. By 1840, he was serving as an engineer for the Wrightsville, York & Gettysburg. Haupt noticed weaknesses in the design of the company's bridges, and rather than attempt to rectify the deficiencies himself, he wrote to eminent engineers, requesting their advice. With the exception of the Baltimore & Ohio's Benjamin H. Latrobe, however, no one had ever bothered to make detailed and systematic calculations of bridge stresses and load factors. The energetic and determined Haupt developed his own methods. In 1841 he published, anonymously, a short pamphlet called "Hints on Bridge Construction," while continuing to work on his magnum opus, *The General Theory of Bridge Construction*. He spent five years attempting to find a publisher, but his theories were so far ahead of the state of the profession that no eminent engineer would endorse the work. The book finally appeared in 1851, was an immediate success, and served as a repository of the best engineering knowledge of the day.[70]

Like many other talented engineers, Haupt was drawn to the opportunities offered by the Pennsylvania Railroad. He sought work from President Merrick but received a cold reception, an assertion that "engineers were as plentiful as blackberries," and no job offer.[71] Merrick was a manufacturer who possessed considerable mechanical aptitude, but he was not an engineer. Those who were engineers, however, and were well acquainted with Haupt, either personally or by reputation, encouraged him to apply to Thomson directly. The chief engineer was at first no more impressed with Haupt than Merrick had been; the professor's quiet demeanor appeared to him to be arrogance.

Thomson nonetheless needed Haupt's expertise in surveying and bridge construction. By the time that Thomson settled into his duties as chief engineer, associate engineers Foster and Miller had already prepared preliminary surveys over portions of the route. Both men were highly experienced, but that knowledge paradoxically impaired their ability to prepare the alignment that Thomson favored. Foster and his assistants, in particular, seemed habituated to the lessons that they had learned while associated with the

Figure 17. Herman Haupt (1817–1905) was an extraordinarily talented civil engineer who quite literally wrote the book on bridge construction in the United States. Under the tutelage of J. Edgar Thomson, Haupt soon took charge of all aspects of the PRR's operations, helping to develop many of the practices that enabled employees to cope with rising traffic levels and an expanding route structure. While those who knew him praised his talents, they also acknowledged that he could be arrogant, stubborn, and confrontational. This photograph, taken when Haupt was thirty-four, shows some of the determination that enabled him to excel in his profession.

Manuscripts and Archives, Yale University Library.

commonwealth's public works. Much as if they were designing a canal, they favored a less abrupt attack on the summit of the Alleghenies. More problematically, they countenanced sharp curves and undulating profiles that were generally associated with early, horse-powered railways.[72]

In July 1847, three months after he accepted the post of chief engineer, Thomson walked along much of the route between Harrisburg and Lewistown, and he soon demanded that it be resurveyed. Eastern Division principal assistant engineer Samuel W. Mifflin recommended Haupt for the job, and Thomson—either unaware or unconcerned that Merrick had refused him employment—placed him on the payroll. In remedying the problems associated with Foster's work, Haupt received something of a baptism by fire. He assisted Thomson in relocating the line between Millerstown and Lewistown to a more suitable route, even though the board had already issued grading contracts. Haupt managed to locate in a matter of days sections of line that had taken earlier surveyors weeks of effort. Thomson was suitably impressed by this display of professional expertise, and even more so by Haupt's familiarity with bridge design. By January 1848, at Thomson's insistence, the board had promoted Haupt to principal assistant engineer, in charge of both the Harrisburg–Lewistown line and the Rockville Bridge across the Susquehanna River. In the spring of 1848, Thomson created a new position for Haupt, assistant to the chief engineer.[73]

Thomson and Haupt soon became close friends as well as professional colleagues. Each was a skilled engineer, at the top of his profession. They knew far more about railroad construction and operations than any member of the board of directors, and they were not content to accept orders that they believed to be misguided. Decades earlier, canal and railroad engineers had exercised their authority with impunity, as business owners yielded to their superior knowledge of a complex and mysterious craft. By the late 1830s, however, the mystique of the all-knowing engineer had begun to fade. The Panic of 1837 added to the diminution of engineering expertise and authority, as cost-conscious owners kept a tighter control on construction costs and on operating methods.[74]

But Thomson and Haupt were not willing to accept efforts by the railroad's owners to control their actions or to dictate corporate policy. Rather, as PRR construction crews worked their way across Pennsylvania, Thomson and Haupt discussed what they would do once the major engineering work had been completed. Rather than move on to another project, both men chose to stay with the company and take on management responsibilities. Thomson, befitting his experience on the Georgia Rail Road, wanted to focus on long-term strategic decision-making, as the PRR made the transition from construction to routine operations. Haupt, with his passion for detail, believed himself to be ideally suited to oversee the railroad's day-to-day operations. They sensed that their respective talents complemented each other, and were convinced that only their intervention could save the railroad that they had helped to create from the meddling and mismanagement of the company's directors. In the process, they each chose a course that would provoke open conflict with the owners of the Pennsylvania Railroad.

Initially, the PRR's directors were willing to defer to the expertise of Thomson and Haupt, at least where engineering matters were concerned. Management of the company was another matter, however, and most board members would not countenance any interference with what they considered to be their absolute prerogative to run the Pennsylvania Railroad as they saw fit. The marriage between experts who lacked authority and authorities who lacked expertise would be brief and unhappy.

Confrontation

The owners of the newly chartered Pennsylvania Railroad were keenly aware that they would be building and operating one of the first large railroads in the United States. That cognizance had induced them to assemble a superbly talented engineer corps, staffed with individuals who were well suited to a task of such magnitude. From the perspective of some board members, however, Thomson and his colleagues may have been *too* talented, too knowledgeable about railroad operations, too headstrong, and far too willing to challenge seemingly arbitrary authority, whenever and wherever it interfered with engineering pragmatism. By 1850, with the PRR in transition from a construction project to an operating railroad, those interpersonal conflicts threatened to tear the company apart.

As Philadelphians, the directors had become increasingly uncomfortable with the notion that the Pennsylvania Railroad had developed in ways that they had not anticipated. The intent of both the Main Line of Public Works and the privately owned Pennsylvania Railroad was essentially the same—to protect the commercial interests of Philadelphia by drawing western traffic to that city rather than to Baltimore, New York, or the competing port of some other state. To the canal commissioners and to the first two presidents of the PRR—Samuel Vaughan Merrick and William C. Patterson—that goal transcended considerations of efficiency and even profitability.

Even though Thomson shared the directors' concern for Philadelphia's future as a center of commerce, he had little patience with the board's policies. Thomson's loyalty lay with his company and above all with his commitment to the preeminence of engineering principles as guidelines for efficient construction and operating practices. He saw Philadelphia primarily as a generator of traffic, not as a commercial center to be protected in its own right. As such, he was perfectly content to allow trade to flow along developed channels of commerce. If that commerce was destined for Baltimore, or to New York, then so be it; he would lay tracks to those places, confident in the knowledge that the most efficiently operated railroad would take the business and the profits. Thomson's focus was thus on the financial health of the Pennsylvania Railroad and not necessarily on the well-being of Philadelphia or of that city's merchants—not even if they happened to be on the company's board of directors.

Almost from the very beginning of their employment on the Pennsylvania Railroad, both Thomson and Haupt were at odds with the president and the more conservative members of the board of directors. To a certain degree, the conflict between Philadelphia merchants and professionally trained engineers was a microcosm of the difficult transition that occurred in countless locations across the United States, as the intensely local interests of civic boosters clashed with the

system-building tendencies of professional managers. In that sense, Thomson's 1852 ascent to the presidency offered an early example of the emergence of railroads as big-business enterprises in their own right. Yet, upon closer examination, conservative owners such as Samuel Merrick and William Patterson were not wholly antithetical to Thomson's vision of an efficiently built and operated transportation artery—nor were they so resolutely localist in their outlook that they were blinded to the railroad's long-term strategic interests.

Rather, Philadelphia's merchant-railroaders chafed at the manner in which their company would become part of a regional transportation enterprise. In particular, they believed that Thomson's incessant calls for construction funds threatened to undermine public confidence in the venture and thus jeopardized the PRR's ability to generate additional investment capital. Furthermore, many board members were aghast that Thomson and Haupt—even if they were highly paid and supremely talented, they were still merely employees, after all—would deign to repeatedly challenge their authority. It was the resulting battle of wills and personalities, more than a conflict between local and regional orientations, that led to a profound change in the management of the Pennsylvania Railroad.

The schism that would ultimately split the board of directors and elevate the chief engineer to the presidency began well before Thomson left Georgia to return to his native Pennsylvania. In early April 1847, as the directors were establishing an organizational structure for the Pennsylvania Railroad, Merrick had argued that the chief engineer should be subject solely to his authority. Western Division associate engineer Edward Miller seconded that view, and he suggested that the chief engineer should request money directly from the president for disbursement to the engineers and construction contractors.[75]

Thomas Cope and his allies on the board were reluctant to yield such control solely to the president of the company. Cope believed that "the love of power" explained Merrick's attempt to have sole control over the chief engineer, and he at least privately chastised the PRR president for attempting to dictate policy matters that were rightly beyond his proper scope of authority.[76] As a result, the PRR's organization provided that the chief engineer should report directly to the board, not to the president. Thanks in large part to Cope's persuasiveness, Thomson would possess the right to attend any and all board meetings and to have his comments entered into the minutes. Rather than allowing Merrick to filter and perhaps misrepresent the chief engineer's views, Cope's organizational structure gave Thomson the opportunity to appeal directly to dissident directors and to take full political advantage of inevitable splits within the board.

After he assumed his new responsibilities as chief engineer, Thomson apparently believed that the board had accorded him equal status with Merrick, particularly where matters of construction and operation were concerned. Thomson had scarcely arrived in Philadelphia when he began to assert his authority. He attended his first board meeting on April 28, 1847, and explained to the directors how he thought that the engineer corps should be organized, based on his experience with the Georgia Rail Road. The next day, Thomson demanded—and received—the authority to dismiss any engineer under his supervision. That request was certainly in keeping with the requirements of a major construction project, but it must have seemed to Merrick and some of his fellow directors that the chief engineer, and not the board, was in charge of personnel policy.[77]

The directors, who lacked even the most rudimentary understanding of the principles of railway construction and operation, soon ceded additional authority to Thomson. The chief engineer continued to attend board meetings and, even though he could not vote, his expertise frequently swayed the opinions of those who did. The Road Committee was particularly susceptible to Thomson's blandishments inasmuch as it was not clear whether the chief engineer, the president, or the committee had jurisdiction over the railroad's construction. To cite but one example, in October 1849, Thomson signed contracts worth $230,000 for construction on the Western Division—and only then informed the board what he had done.[78]

Thomson had many enemies on the board, however. They were conservative Philadelphia merchants who resented his authority and who opposed his seemingly endless calls for more money. In October 1847, Merrick apparently believed that the chief engineer

was usurping a portion of his authority, and he urged the members of the Road Committee to clarify the precise nature of the relationship between Thomson and the board. By January 1848, barely nine months after assuming his duties, Thomson was already embroiled in a power struggle with Merrick. On January 8, Merrick called fellow board member Thomas Cope to his office to show him correspondence with the chief engineer, "from which," Cope noted, "it appears that jealousies exist as to their relative powers prerogatives & rights." Thomson, Merrick claimed, was "disrespecting his orders," as well as spending money and signing contracts without the board's notification or approval.[79]

The tempest was part of a larger struggle to determine control over the board and the company. Merrick believed that three members of the board (James Magee, Robert Toland, and John A. Wright) were trying to unseat him, with Toland angling to serve as the new president. Cope emphasized that both Merrick's leadership and Thomson's engineering expertise were critical to the PRR's success. He counseled restraint, lest there be "an open rupture which might end in the resignation of either of them [and] would prove most disastrous to the Company." The dispute subsided, but tensions remained. "Jealousy still exists between the Engineer & President in the exercise of power," Cope noted at the end of March, "the latter being sufficiently stately & fond of supreme control, while Thomson does not incline to wear the yoke wantonly thrust upon his neck."[80]

While Merrick continued to heed Cope's advice that he dare not antagonize the chief engineer, the president nonetheless contended that Magee and Toland were determined to destroy him. By the end of May, board member Richard Wood lamented that "there was much personal feeling manifested by some of the board toward the president."[81] On June 5, 1848, the PRR's secretary, Oliver Fuller, went so far as to beg Cope to reconsider his resignation from the board, complaining that "jealousies and bickerings have crept into their counsels" and claiming that the aged Quaker was the only person who could keep the peace among the warring factions.[82]

While the precise circumstances are unclear, the feud consumed all three men. Robert Toland resigned from the board, effective July 19, 1848, followed by

James Magee on December 4. Merrick, after quarreling again with Thomson in the spring of 1849, and again accusing the chief engineer of insubordination, yielded the presidency to William Patterson. Merrick submitted his resignation to the board in late August, ostensibly to oversee his interests in the Southwark Foundry, after John Henry Towne, his business partner in that venture, retired from the business.[83] Thomson was largely unaffected by the troubles of 1848 and 1849. He produced results and was careful not to make any political blunders. For his first five years in the railroad's employ, he was virtually untouchable.

Haupt was another matter, however, and his relationship with Thomson virtually shattered the PRR's board of directors. Haupt was a supremely skilled engineer. As well, he could be brusque, opinionated, and condescending, certain that his course of action was the correct one and convinced that those who stood in his way were at best stupid, and at worst corrupt. He was a social introvert, a man who did not make friends easily, but who made enemies quickly. Haupt was also steadfast in the defense of his principles. Even though the board considered Haupt "petulant" and "determined to have the uncontrolled government not only of the conduct of his own department, but of the policy of the Company," Haupt was in fact an early proponent of the separation of ownership and management.[84] He believed, to a far larger degree than the Philadelphia merchants who dominated the board, that it was imperative to run the railroad as an efficient, high-volume, low-margin operation. Even more than Thomson, Haupt grounded the PRR's management in a solid foundation of financial and operational statistics.

An Army of Railroaders

Haupt attracted controversy based in large measure on his development of an organizational model for the Pennsylvania Railroad. Those efforts in turn brought three interrelated issues to the fore. The most immediate effect was to turn the conflict between Thomson and the board of directors into open warfare. Another had to do with the establishment of a managerial foundation that would, with continual modifications, serve the PRR well into the next century—and that,

by extension, would contribute to the development of management principles on other railroads, and in industry. Finally, given Haupt's West Point pedigree, his organizational model invited suggestions that he was heavily influenced by the structure of the United States Army.

Historians have long disagreed about the extent to which military training influenced management practices on the PRR and other railroads.[85] Yet most acknowledge that the interaction between the military and transportation firms emerged incrementally during the late eighteenth and early nineteenth centuries. At that time, even the most ardent proponents of states' rights conceded that military engineers possessed the constitutional authority to construct fortifications that were necessary in order to provide for the common defense. From that basis, many Americans argued that the federal government could lawfully fund the construction of lighthouses and harbor improvements, particularly if they were designed by military engineers.[86]

Following the War of 1812, many in Congress hoped that military surveyors would resolve the tension, associated with the American federal system, between national and state support for internal improvements. Even those who opposed outright federal funding for local projects were often willing to countenance the loan of army engineers—who were already trained and often underemployed during peacetime. Such sentiments grew stronger during the 1820s, as sectional tensions increasingly divided North, South, and West. In 1819, a severe financial panic and depression ended the economic prosperity that had characterized the Era of Good Feelings. Northerners demanded customs duties to protect emerging industries, while their southern counterparts denounced protective (as opposed to revenue-generating) tariffs as a threat to their economic survival and as an unconstitutional expansion of federal authority. The simultaneous debate regarding whether Missouri should be admitted to the Union as a free state or a slave state caused further regional polarization. Whig politician Henry Clay, whose conciliatory attitudes earned him the nickname of the "Great Compromiser," was desperate to restore harmony. In addition to orchestrating the Missouri Compromise of 1820, Clay revived Treasury Secretary

Alexander Hamilton's 1791 call for a network of internal improvements, not in order to restore the nation's credit, but rather as a mechanism to alleviate sectionalism. Clay also drew heavily from the writings of Henry Charles Carey, Mathew Carey's son and one of the nation's greatest early economists. Clay supported an "American System" that would enable each of the three regions of the United States, North, South, and West, to engage in economic specialization by pursuing the law of comparative advantage. Clay suggested that high tariffs would support domestic manufacturing, while providing the funds necessary to construct internal improvements.[87]

Clay's first official public announcement of the "American System" occurred in 1829, but his ideas were in circulation many years earlier. In 1822, the House Committee on Roads and Canals explored the possibility of creating a national transportation infrastructure. Many of the old doubts resurfaced, particularly fears that the federal government lacked the necessary resources and that the allocation of funds would arouse the sectional tensions that Clay was trying to dampen down. Congressman Joseph Hemphill, who would soon become a member of the Acting Committee of the Pennsylvania Society for the Promotion of Internal Improvements in the Commonwealth, suggested that the federal government could improve transportation, at minimal cost, by assigning West Point surveyors to local infrastructure projects. By providing advice rather than money, such a plan possessed the additional virtue of minimizing jealousies among states. It was also eminently constitutional, as it merely embodied an extension of the responsibilities of the existing Board of Engineers for Fortifications. Two years later, Congress passed the General Survey Act of 1824, which permitted the president to authorize surveys for internal improvement projects deemed to have national importance. The definition for such undertakings was fairly elastic, and promoters of roads, canals, and later railroads quickly emphasized the value of their projects to national security and the movement of troops, with commerce constituting an ostensibly insignificant afterthought.[88]

When members of Congress gave Army engineers the authority to survey, although not to construct, internal improvements, they drew on an institution that was in the process of transforming its engineering curriculum and indeed the entire engineering profession. The War of 1812 had demonstrated the necessity of improved coastal fortifications, as well as a better-managed military. John C. Calhoun took charge of the War Department in October 1817, and he soon attempted to reform the Army's organizational structure and training methods. One key goal was to create a system of staff officers who could undertake military engineering projects whenever and wherever needed, and who were responsible for coordinating information flows between a central command and various units. Those staff officers thus possessed quite different duties from the line officers who commanded specific units and issued battlefield commands down through a hierarchy of direct subordinates.

Massachusetts native Sylvanus Thayer, a West Point graduate and a veteran of the War of 1812, became the key architect of Calhoun's plan to transform the military. After 1817, when President James Monroe appointed him as superintendent of the United States Military Academy at West Point, Thayer established an engineering curriculum. Having spent the years immediately following the war studying in France, Thayer based the academy's instructional methods, and even its textbooks and exams, on those employed by the French École Polytechnique. Thayer initially emphasized a combination of military and civil engineering, but by 1822 the focus had shifted to civil engineering, a trend that was even more apparent by 1830. Furthermore, between 1826 and 1832, Thayer pioneered a rigid code of discipline based on the awarding of demerits. By applying numbers to conduct, as well as to academic grades, Thayer attempted to create an objective system whereby officers could accurately evaluate and rank cadets—a concept that would later prove of considerable importance to railroad management. West Point was ideally suited to produce a cadre of practical engineers who could design fortifications and supervise harbor improvements. The surveying of canal and railroad routes constituted a logical extension of their duties.

Army surveyors were not the only ones responsible for determining the alignments of roads, canals, and railroads, however. Between the 1820s and the 1840s, more than half of the field engineers associated with internal improvements were civilians who had never received any military training. They were civil engineers, a nomenclature based in part on their status as civilians and not merely their oversight of non-military infrastructure projects. Some had received formal training at schools such as the Rensselaer School (later the Rensselaer Polytechnic Institute), co-incidentally established in 1824, the same year as the adoption of the General Survey Act. A large number had apprenticed with older and more highly skilled mentors. Many engineers had cut their teeth on the greatest engineering project of the age, the Erie Canal. After the canal opened in 1825, members of the Erie Canal school, along with other civil engineers, drifted from project to project, including the Pennsylvania state system, working themselves ragged during times of prosperity and hanging on during the depressions that halted many undertakings. They oversaw both public and private projects, and saw no real distinction between the two.[89]

By the time that the Erie Canal was in operation, and certainly by the time that the PRR was under construction, the methods of the civil engineer were quite well developed. Some engineers had been to West Point, but all had been in the field, conducting surveys and supervising construction. Each survey party consisted of a small band of men, working in unison, away from the rest of society, amid shared hardships and dangers, almost as if they were in a military campaign. Significantly, however, civilian engineers developed their methods incrementally, in response to local conditions, and those techniques only coincidentally mimicked military practice. Engineers were in many cases a breed apart, and the requirements of their profession bred a unique esprit de corps, an influence that was similar to, and perhaps stronger than, military training. The members of an engineering party were generally well educated and possessed a highly marketable set of skills. As such, they enjoyed an elite status within their local communities, much as a bemedaled Army officer would gain the respect of others. As in the military, advancement took place hierarchically. As junior engineers demonstrated ability and achievement, they could expect promotion to more senior positions.[90]

In most surveys, a chief engineer or his assistant would command rodmen, chainmen, axmen, and the teamsters who handled supplies. The engineer would then send the raw survey data to a draftsman, who possessed particular functional skills in drawing and arithmetic, for conversion into maps and profiles. When construction began, a chief engineer would oversee the entire process, while delegating authority to a hierarchy of subordinates, from associate engineers to principal assistant engineers to assistant engineers—much as a military commander would issue orders to his line officers. Ultimately, the members of the engineering fraternity would give orders to the noncommissioned officers (the construction contractors) and to the foot soldiers (the day laborers) who were an indispensible part of the grand army of railway construction.[91]

Whether their training was military or civilian, engineers responsible for the construction of canals and early railroads usually moved on to other projects once the route was in service. Operations on the Main Line of Public Works, for example, were so routine as to present few engineering challenges.[92] As a result, the canal commissioners and the engineers who worked for them were never able to develop any significant managerial innovations on the Main Line of Public Works. Commonwealth employees were more concerned with preventing fraud and maintaining their patronage jobs than they were with effective management—and the wheel of patronage further complicated matters by precluding the development of the stability and continuity that lay at the base of every effective bureaucratic organization. Whatever the cause, the absence of managerial control on behalf of the canal commissioners permitted the independent freight forwarders to develop many of the organizational innovations related to the management of traffic on the Main Line of Public Works and, in conjunction with Ohio River steamboats, to points west of Pittsburgh.

Managers on many of the railroads that predated the PRR fared significantly better in their efforts to incrementally build up the organizational capabilities of their companies. Pennsylvania's earliest railroads transported anthracite, and the primary difficulty that their executives faced was to move heavy trains in one direction while returning empty cars to the mines. Many early colliery lines, in Pennsylvania as in Britain, relied on gravity to propel loaded cars downgrade, with horses or locomotives employed at set times to drag the empties back uphill. Such methods reached their apex with the Philadelphia & Reading. While not, strictly speaking, a gravity railway, it nonetheless benefited from a steady descending grade all the way from the anthracite fields to the Delaware River waterfront north of Philadelphia. Although a double-track line, it boasted what was, for the time, an extraordinarily high traffic density, and so required close and careful coordination.

As railroad and even canal operations increased in scope and complexity, both military and civilian engineers found themselves taking on management responsibilities, above and beyond routine repairs. The conversion of engineers into executives was in many respects a logical continuation of the development of both professions. For many decades, after all, owners and proprietors had exercised surveying and engineering functions in order to keep track of and improve their dominions, with George Washington being perhaps the most famous example. During the early 1800s, many internal improvements entered service incrementally, so that construction and operation were proceeding simultaneously, and it made sense to have the same person in charge of both. Even after work had been completed, engineers were well equipped to assume executive responsibilities—after all, no one knew more about the inner workings of a canal or railroad than the person who had designed and built it. The commissioners and directors of many canals and railroads, both publically and privately operated, believed that they could reduce expenses by combining engineering and supervisory functions in one manager—such was Thomson's experience as chief engineer and general agent on the Georgia Rail Road. Engineers often possessed excellent computational skills, making them equally adept at calculating operating as well as construction costs. Finally, many engineers claimed that they possessed professional objectivity that enabled them to manage a transportation enterprise more effectively than individuals who held a personal financial stake in the project, or who favored a particular community or geographic region.[93]

Significantly, the commingling of engineering and managerial responsibilities occurred on both public and private transportation projects, and in the personages of both civilian and military engineers. Those circumstances strongly suggest that it was the nature of the transportation business, and not the source of training or financing, that encouraged engineers to become managers. To be sure, some engineers refused executive responsibility, often arguing that their profession could not be sullied by corporate caretakers who cared only about the balance sheet. Particularly after the Panic of 1837, however, directors and commissioners looked with greater favor upon any engineer who demonstrated a willingness to be a team player and a company man, particularly if he proved adept at controlling both construction and operating costs. Engineers were often eager to accept managerial responsibilities in lieu of the nomadic and uncertain life of wandering from project to project. Many also viewed management status as signifying membership in the engineering aristocracy.[94]

The willingness of both civilian and military engineers to participate in management did not by any means eliminate tensions between representatives of the two groups, a situation that was readily apparent on the Baltimore & Ohio. The Maryland legislature chartered the B&O in the spring of 1827, less than three years after Congress passed the General Survey Act. Accordingly, the B&O was the first railroad to receive a contingent of Army surveyors. Under the direction of Lieutenant Colonel Stephen Harriman Long and Captain William Gibbs McNeill, they soon applied their military expertise to more efficiently organize the railroad's construction. At West Point, military engineers had learned to calculate precisely the design of bridges and the other elements of the physical plant, employing the minimum quantity of material and favoring the lowest possible cost.

Far from being welcomed for their logistical skills, Long and his colleagues soon came into conflict with civilian engineers over the B&O's construction and operating requirements. Their civilian counterparts on the B&O, including Jonathan Knight and Caspar W. Wever, had constructed highways, including the extension of the National Road, west of Wheeling, Virginia. Such projects were relatively simple and did not require extensive engineering skill. Faced with the more rigorous demands of building a railroad through some of the most mountainous country in the eastern United States, they compensated for their lack of formal engineering training by overbuilding bridges and other structures. Wever in particular argued that considerations of both safety and aesthetics mandated massive masonry viaducts, exasperating Long and his dozen or so West Point–trained assistants. To make matters worse, Long and Knight possessed equal authority, so that neither could overrule the other's decisions.[95]

The civilians won the first round, contributing to a schism within the ranks of company management in 1829 and the reassignment of the army engineers the following year. The new construction regulations that followed represented a pragmatic blending of army methods and the specific circumstances that applied to railroads. As B&O construction crews proceeded west, and as the cost of building a mountain railroad drained the corporate treasury, the company's directors found little difficulty in authorizing the erection of lightly built wooden bridges, precisely as the army surveyors had earlier advocated. Many of the B&O's earliest bridges, built solidly of stone, remain in service even today, while later bridges to the west were replaced time and time again. Yet, the disagreements between civil and military engineers exerted relatively little influence on the B&O's management, for the simple reason that the railroad, still in its infancy, possessed too little track, and too little traffic, to warrant any managerial innovations over and above the methods employed by canals and early railways.[96]

Some of the earliest railroad management practices emerged in New England. Train movements were both complicated and dangerous, and managers often prevented accidents by dispatching trains only at predetermined times of the day and holding them at intermediate points until opposing trains had arrived. Such was the early policy of the Western Railroad, which linked Albany, New York, to Worcester, Massachusetts, with the Boston & Worcester Railroad providing service eastward to Boston. On October 5, 1841, the Western Railroad's dispatching practices provoked a serious accident and a public outcry. The task of preventing future catastrophes fell to chief engineer George Whistler. He had a definite West Point pedigree, having graduated in 1819 and then returned to serve as a drawing instructor in 1821 and 1822. Major William McNeill (Whistler's brother-in-law) and Captain William Swift, also West Pointers, assisted Whistler in developing an operating system

for the railroad. By the end of November, barely six weeks after the accident, Whistler had produced a "Report on Avoiding Collisions and Governing the Employees." The speed with which Whistler developed the new operating procedures indicated that he responded with commendable alacrity to public pressure—or, more likely, that he had developed a preliminary reorganization plan even before the tragedy.[97]

The new organization of the Western Railroad has been hailed, and rightly so, for its contributions to safety. Uppermost in the minds of Whistler and his colleagues, however, was the importance of efficient operation that would enable the railroad to employ its resources more profitably. The master of transportation (who was the railroad's chief operating officer) supervised the actions of three assistant masters of transportation (later renamed division superintendents), one for each of the railroad's three geographic divisions. They were in turn responsible for the safe and efficient movement of trains on their respective divisions and for issuing orders down the line of authority to the personnel involved in train operations. Each assistant master of transportation supervised a roadmaster who was responsible for the maintenance of the tracks, bridges, and other elements of the physical plant on his division. Senior mechanics on each division took charge of maintaining locomotives and cars, but they reported to the master of transportation at company headquarters rather than the division superintendents.

The new organization on the Western Railroad pioneered two important elements of management practice. First, it divided the railroad's personnel into three main functions: controlling transportation (the assistant master of transportation), maintenance of way (the roadmaster), and maintenance of equipment (the senior mechanic). Second, the system differentiated between line officers—those who possessed a functional specialty in some area, such as operations, and passed their orders down a chain of command—and staff officers, who advised and assisted the president, the master of transportation, and other central office personnel in the management of the entire company.[98]

The incipient line-and-staff structure certainly resembled the military's separation of combat officers and support staff. As former army staff officers, McNeill, Whistler, and Swift were certainly familiar with the distinction between the two sets of responsibilities, and the management structure of the Western Railroad would have seemed quite natural to them. There is little evidence, however, to suggest that those practices were transmitted, largely intact, to other companies. In 1838, Congress repealed the General Survey Act, and by the time of the PRR's incorporation, the army was no longer assigning surveyors to nongovernmental infrastructure projects. Many military engineers were still in the field, as several hundred West Point–trained engineers had cut short their military careers to work for privately owned railroad companies. As the railroad industry matured, however, they confronted an increasingly sophisticated set of operational requirements that proved ever more divergent from army practices. By the time the PRR began construction, army models had been greatly diluted and filtered through the managerial cadres of established railways. The Western Railroad was thus something of an exception to the rule, and executives on other carriers, including the Baltimore & Ohio and the PRR, certainly developed managerial techniques that were only coincidentally based on military practice.

The Baltimore & Ohio moved away from the army methods that had caused so much dissent during the initial construction phase. President Louis McLane and chief engineer Benjamin H. Latrobe, Jr., adopted elements of the Western Railroad system, while adding their own innovations. To a far greater degree than military surveyors, they were concerned with the generation and allocation of funds. McLane and Latrobe established two departments, one for operations and the other for the "collection and disbursement of revenues." The operating functions included the three basic categories (running trains, maintaining equipment, and maintaining the physical plant) contained in the Western Railroad's 1842 structure. The innovative nature of the B&O organization came instead from the second department and the accounting controls that its personnel developed.[99]

Herman Haupt Manages the Pennsylvania Railroad

As a West Point graduate, Herman Haupt was the most logical candidate for transmitting army practice to the railroad industry. As he developed an organizational structure for the PRR, however, he only coincidentally incorporated military methods and instead relied much more heavily on innovations developed on other railroads. Even those he adjusted, in order to conform to the unique operating requirements of his employer. PRR workers began laying track nearly twenty years after their counterparts on the B&O and construction proceeded with lightning speed compared with the slow progress of the Baltimore company. Operating practices likewise developed far more quickly. Furthermore, the tonnage tax increased the cost of moving freight on the PRR and placed a premium on efficient operations. For all of those reasons, Haupt confronted issues for which neither his military training nor his previous railroad experience had left him fully prepared.

It was in the context of organizational implementation, rather than organizational innovation, that Haupt most likely applied his West Point experience. While he did not develop any of the basic principles of railroad operations or management, Haupt was well equipped to collect and interpret the data necessary to justify new and unfamiliar operating methods. That data became a powerful weapon, as Haupt could unleash a blizzard of information on anyone who resisted his suggestions. Such adversaries generally yielded, particularly if they were not especially knowledgeable about railroad technology.

In many respects, Haupt's military career had been both brief and disappointing, and it had ended long before he joined the Pennsylvania Railroad. When he began his studies at West Point, he was a cocky and arrogant teenager, and he believed he could game the conduct system that superintendent Sylvanus Thayer had established. Instead, he came within one demerit of dismissal and, after failing an exam, believed that he would be expelled. The experience shocked him out of his complacency. Chastened, he saw the error of his ways and developed a deep appreciation for the importance of objective performance measures. He had loathed Thayer's complex system of demerits, but he now came to understand them as a precise, orderly, and eminently fair mechanism for regulating human behavior. Haupt internalized that lesson and applied it to all of his subsequent endeavors. Yet, his newfound zeal for self-improvement served him no better than a rank of twenty-nine out of fifty-six graduates. He was only eighteen when he graduated in 1835, and he quickly resigned his military commission. During the twelve years before he joined the PRR—one of the most formative periods in the history of railway engineering—he was very much a civilian, and not a soldier.[100]

Haupt's brief military experience convinced the engineer that a managerial system would be successful only if all of its participants clearly understood what was expected of them, knew how their performance would be measured, and above all were persuaded that their successes would be rewarded and that their offenses would be fairly punished. Haupt's passion for order and method was important, but it was not in and of itself an organizational structure. To develop one for the PRR, Haupt looked to managerial practices on other railroads, rather than to the United States Army. He nonetheless found it difficult to copy wholesale the methods that other railroaders had devised. In part, Haupt was frustrated by the primitive nature of management on most other companies. Many carriers were so short as to have little need for a codified organization. Others—including the New York & Erie Rail Road, later heralded as an organizational innovator—were during the late 1840s so badly managed as to offer Haupt few insights. The Baltimore & Ohio and the Western Railroad served as better models, but there too the potential for knowledge transfer was somewhat limited.[101]

The Pennsylvania Railroad, Haupt and Thomson knew, was different from any other carrier in the United States. The problem was not so much its length, but rather its disjointed structure. The wholly independent and publicly owned Philadelphia & Columbia formed the eastern portion of the route, with the independent City Railroad providing crucial access to Philadelphia. The Harrisburg, Portsmouth, Mount Joy & Lancaster, which carried traffic from Dillerville to Harrisburg, was likewise an independent company, although it was closely allied with the PRR. From Harrisburg, the PRR's own rails extended only as far west as Duncansville, a temporary terminus that provided a connection with another state work, the Allegheny Portage Railroad. Only at Johnstown did PRR traffic again reach its own rails, for the last leg to Pittsburgh—a city where there was certain to be a substantial interchange of traffic with other railroads and

with steamboats. Somehow, Haupt would have to devise a structure that would allow PRR managers to oversee all of the constituent elements of that route—while they were still building parts of it. The Baltimore & Ohio took a quarter of a century to reach the Ohio River, giving managers ample time to incrementally manage the transition from construction to operation. The PRR reached the Ohio in a fifth of the B&O's time, giving Haupt much less flexibility, and much more reason to innovate quickly.

Thomson made certain that Haupt, whom he was grooming to oversee day-to-day operations on the PRR, would be the principal architect of the PRR's new organization. Late in December 1848, Thomson informed the Road Committee that he needed more information regarding organizational methods, but could not spare the time to investigate practices of other companies. The directors concurred and on January 2, 1849, asked President Merrick to investigate the matter. Merrick, who had virtually no knowledge of railroad operations, threw the matter back at Thomson, who then ordered Haupt to tour New England railroads. Haupt's most fruitful visit was to the Western Railroad, where he studied the operating methods and corporate structure that Whistler, McNeill, and Swift had developed. Haupt went north at a propitious time, for a global recession (induced by the same bursting British railway bubble that accounted for much of Thomas Cope's hesitancy to become involved with the PRR) had caused New England investors to demand more rigorous operating and financial controls.[102]

Haupt returned to the PRR in the late spring of 1849, ready to implement his (or, more precisely, Whistler's) ideas. In early March, Thomson informed the board of his proposed plan of organization, one that drew on his own experience on the Georgia Rail Road, on Haupt's fact-finding tour, and probably on the B&O system as well. Thomson identified four types of financial accounts, including "maintenance of way," "maintenance of cars," "motive power," and, most important of all, "conducting transportation." In that respect, the 1849 organization closely resembled the system that Thomson had introduced on the Georgia Rail Road and that was in use on most other large carriers.[103]

Haupt introduced one more critical element, based on his favorable impression of the accounting methods developed by the New England railroads and Thomson's experience in Georgia. The four broad categories would be of little value in the absence of reliable real-time information flows. A carefully devised system of accounts, Haupt realized, would enable Thomson and other managers to control costs and thus ensure efficient operation, while simultaneously providing the data required for long-term planning. As such, Haupt advocated the establishment of a set of statistical measures that he labeled the "Accounts of the General Office," segregated from the collection and disbursement of monies. Personnel would submit daily, weekly, and monthly reports to a central location, the "General Transportation Office" in Harrisburg. At Harrisburg, initially the base for the PRR's day-to-day operations, the information would create standard statistical measures of the company's day-to-day performance. The resulting information could then be sent to the corporate headquarters in Philadelphia, where it would enable senior executives and members of the board of directors to make reliable long-term strategic decisions.[104]

In early June 1849, the board of directors adopted the basic outlines of Haupt's plan and approved the railroad's first organization manual. Merrick again intervened, eliminating portions that he found objectionable and blocking the creation of a freight department under Thomson's control. By late August, however, the board had ceded additional authority to the chief engineer, allowing him to set freight and passenger rates—a responsibility that he probably assigned to Haupt.[105]

The success of the PRR's transportation organization would depend on the selection of the proper personnel, and particularly on the ability of the company's chief operating officer, Thomson, to delegate down the line of authority. Thomson knew about as much as anyone in the United States about railway operating practices, yet he was not ideally suited for the job of running the railroad. The PRR's main line was still under construction, and Thomson's time and talents as chief engineer were very much in demand. Furthermore, Thomson's thoughts ran to broad concepts, and he seems to have had little interest in the minutiae of operating data. He believed that Haupt, with his knowledge of statistics and operating methods, would be the ideal choice for general superintendent in charge of managing day-to-

day operations—a post that was likely to entail ever-increasing responsibilities, as each newly constructed section of track entered revenue service. Thomson wanted to provide Haupt with considerable autonomy in order to function effectively, by insulating him and his staff from meddling by the directors.[106]

Merrick and other members of the board saw no reason why Haupt should have sole authority over transportation, the right to hire and fire employees at will, and the power to design forms and promulgate rules for the railroad's operations. By early June, given Merrick's opposition to Haupt, Thomson had agreed to serve as general superintendent, while retaining his existing duties as chief engineer. The expanded duties, without any corresponding increase in pay, theoretically afforded Thomson the opportunity to supervise both the construction and the operation of the Pennsylvania Railroad, and to create the company's organizational structure. In practice, however, Thomson concentrated on engineering matters and long-term corporate strategy, with Haupt unofficially in charge of all day-to-day operations. For all intents and purposes, therefore, Haupt was general superintendent in all but name.

On September 1, 1849, Merrick resigned from the presidency (although not from the board), but his successor, William C. Patterson, was equally unwilling to defer to the expertise of hired engineers. At that time, the PRR was complete as far west as Lewistown, and Patterson organized an excursion train to celebrate the event, which coincided with his first day as the company's president. Patterson wished to pause during the trip, and on his own authority he ordered the train to halt on the main line. Only Haupt's timely intervention prevented a head-on collision with another locomotive, reinforcing his view that the merchant managers on the board were little better than incompetent. It is not clear whether the incident shocked Patterson into an awareness of his own limitations. However, on September 5 the board selected Haupt as superintendent of transportation, effectively approving the recommendation that Thomson had made three months earlier. By the end of September, Haupt, presumably with Thomson's blessing, had issued the first set of rules for the governance of operating employees, designed in part to substitute order and method for the haphazard and cavalier approach to train movements that Patterson's actions had illustrated.[107]

Haupt was not the only one who was aghast at Patterson's lack of familiarity with railroad construction and operations. The December 3, 1849, shareholders' meeting proved extraordinarily contentious, as some directors gave their approval to the methods developed by Haupt and Thomson while challenging Patterson's authority. Director James Magee (who in 1854 would join with Haupt and others associated with the PRR in establishing the Westmoreland Coal Company) had already criticized Merrick's performance as president, and now he lashed out at Patterson. He resolved that the president's salary should be reduced to $2,500—far less than what Thomson earned, and not much above Haupt's $2,000 annual pay—unless he should be a "qualified engineer" who would be capable of serving as superintendent or general agent. On December 24, Magee amended his resolution, offering to set Patterson's salary at $3,000, but the stockholders defeated it resoundingly nonetheless.[108]

The dawning of the new year did little to soothe tensions between the aggrieved parties, as the board was increasingly split into a faction supporting Patterson and another siding with Thomson and Haupt. In January 1850, the Road Committee (which Merrick and later Patterson had typically dominated) prevented either engineer from participating in negotiations with the Harrisburg, Portsmouth, Mount Joy & Lancaster Railroad and decreeing that such matters be left solely to the board's discretion. Haupt observed that his input was essential, given that the PRR would soon have to operate the railroad that the board was in the process of acquiring, yet his protests were in vain. He was now second-in-command to Thomson, yet he lacked his mentor's ability to influence the board on matters of long-term corporate policy. Whereas the chief engineer had used his professional expertise as a pretext to invite himself to board meetings, the directors simply asked Haupt to leave, and not return unless summoned.[109]

The conflict that erupted as the result of the 1849 organization probably marked the understandable reluctance of the owners of the Pennsylvania Railroad to cede authority to hired executives with little ownership stake in the company. Haupt undoubtedly contributed to the tension with his brusque, authoritative demeanor and his often arrogant and condescending dismissals of the directors and their ignorance of railroad matters. The disputes, while increasingly acrimonious, nonetheless served a useful function. Thomson rarely disagreed with Haupt's policies, and he usually deferred to his assistant's knowledge of accounting and operational matters. Thomson nonetheless protected his own position within the company, as well as his ability to effectively manage the railroad, by permitting the directors to focus all of their criticisms on Haupt. In addition to preserving Thomson's freedom of action, Haupt's role as a scapegoat also enabled the railroad's growing cadre of middle managers to quietly develop and implement the procedures associated with day-to-day operations, free of undue interference from the board.[110]

By April 1850, however, the quality of PRR service had deteriorated markedly, owing largely to poor coordination with the independent transporters and the employees of the Main Line of Public Works, as well as to the inexperience of company personnel. As the individual principally in charge of the railroad's operations, Haupt bore much of the blame, and he and Thomson were in turn critical of the board's restrictions on their authority. By October, the operating difficulties had become so severe that the board created a committee, which included Thomson and Patterson, to compare the PRR's operating procedures with those of other northeastern railroads. As discussed above, Haupt had made a similar trip eighteen months earlier, and the new excursion probably had little point other than to suggest that he had singularly failed to learn any useful lessons. The committee members were to travel west on the Baltimore & Ohio and return over their own line, to evaluate the strengths and weaknesses of each. They also intended to go north, to examine the Erie, the predecessor companies to the New York Central, as well as other carriers, and to poach skilled railway employees wherever they could find them.[111]

It is not clear whether this inspection trip ever took place (in all probability it did not), but its proposal represented a clear message by Patterson, Merrick, and their supporters that they intended to rein in both Haupt and Thomson. Many board members assumed that Thomson's oversight of both engineering and operating matters had overtaxed his abilities, contributing to the PRR's operating difficulties. Accordingly, on November 7, 1850, the board proposed to separate the offices of chief engineer, responsible for matters of engineering policy and construction, and of general superintendent, in charge of routine operations. For several months, however, the board deferred the implementation of this policy in order to ensure that the proper personnel were in place. In December, the board appointed Herman J. Lombaert, who quite possibly had been one of the early contenders for the position of chief engineer, as an assistant to Haupt.[112]

On January 8, 1851, Thomson resigned his post as general superintendent, retaining only his duties as chief engineer. The board abolished Haupt's office of superintendent of transportation and appointed him the new general superintendent, with Lombaert as his assistant. In fulfilling the organizational plan that they had established two months earlier, the directors enabled Thomson to concentrate on equipping the main line and building the railroad's route over the Alleghenies. Haupt took charge of day-to-day operations, including the selection of PRR freight and passenger agents, who worked with the independent transporters to coordinate traffic at major shipping points. The newly bifurcated responsibilities eased some of the strain on Thomson, while transforming Haupt from the de facto to the actual general superintendent. In addition, as Thomson became ever more involved in construction matters, as well as increasingly anxious to avoid conflict with the board, Haupt aired his mentor's views before the directors.[113]

Haupt's new authority over the PRR's operations did not sit well with Patterson, Merrick, and their allies on the board, and they soon retaliated. In December 1850, Haupt had selected Joseph L. Elliott for the job of passenger agent, but the Road Committee blocked the appointment on the grounds that the new post was unnecessary. A month later, Haupt attempted to appoint Elliott as a bookkeeper and tariff collector at the railroad's Philadelphia freight station, but the board again refused, selecting George W. Mears for that position. Members of the Road Committee questioned Haupt's decision to transfer Thomas A. Scott, the PRR's agent at Duncansville, to Philadelphia, where he

was slated to become the new general agent. The board also resolved that at least two directors should inspect the line every month—but, as none of them possessed any experience in the construction or operation of railways, the policy was solely a mechanism for increasing control over Haupt.[114]

A more serious crisis erupted in February 1851 when Haupt discussed operating arrangements with the canal commissioners. He was the logical person for the job, inasmuch as he was based in the state capital, and he understood the details associated with the coordination of ongoing traffic along the PRR, the Philadelphia & Columbia, and the Allegheny Portage Railroad. Despite his limited familiarity with the operations of either the PRR or the Main Line of Public Works, Patterson insisted that such negotiations were a strategic matter that could be undertaken only by the president. Haupt suggested that Patterson's edict, in addition to jeopardizing the PRR's relationship with the Commonwealth of Pennsylvania, violated corporate policy. After all, he asserted, the general superintendent, the chief engineer, and the president were all appointed by and answerable to the board, suggesting that none of the three could give orders to any of the others. Haupt was willing to make "a ready compliance with any *request*," but he emphasized that he "would not permit an acknowledgement of [Patterson's] . . . *right* to command."[115]

The conflict between Haupt and his allies and the Merrick/Patterson faction escalated throughout 1851. In May, the board took advantage of Thomson's absence (he was in Georgia, resolving some matters relating to his railroad work there) to implement changes to the organization designed to bring both the chief engineer and especially the general superintendent under their control. The 1851 organization divided the company into two units, one pertaining to operating personnel, and the other to money. The First Department included "all that pertains to the maintenance of the Road, the care of all the Real Estate & business of the Company on the line of the Road, the charge of all the Cars, Machinery, Tools, Furniture and other personal property" on both the PRR and the Harrisburg, Portsmouth, Mount Joy & Lancaster. The general superintendent (Haupt, in this instance) was the primary liaison between the board and the day-to-day operations of the railroad, providing regular reports on the traffic levels and the condition of the line. He also had the authority to purchase locomotives and cars, as well as other items necessary for the railroad's operation. In addition, he supervised the freight agent and the passenger agent (new positions, created earlier that year), as well as transportation, real estate, and maintenance-of-way functions. The board retained the right to examine the general superintendent's accounts at any time and held the ultimate authority in staff appointments. The responsibilities of the Second Department were far more circumscribed. Its only function was to "have charge of the receipt and disbursement of money."[116] The funds in question included freight and passenger revenues, as well as wages and invoices—but not the stocks that funded the capital account, which were under the control of the board's finance committee.[117]

The board's 1851 plan was quite different from the organizational structure of either the Georgia Rail Road or the Western Railroad. Its primary purpose was ostensibly to ensure honesty in the collection of the PRR's revenues, much like the two-department system that Louis McLane and Benjamin H. Latrobe had created for the B&O in 1846 and 1847. Furthermore, the basic subdivision of the railroad into two units—one for operations and the other for finance—soon became standard practice across the United States.[118]

Patterson and his allies had more Machiavellian motives, however. The detailed description of the First Department consisted mainly of regulations designed to curtail the power of the general superintendent and thus limit Haupt's authority to operate the railroad. In response to Haupt's insistence that he and Thomson would obey orders from the board and the board alone, the 1851 organization specified that the president possessed the authority to issue commands to anyone in the company, unless the directors instructed him otherwise. The plan also stripped Haupt of the ability to hire personnel or to create new offices. Patterson, as president, held the right to specify all regulations governing transportation, pending the approval of the board.[119]

Finally, the new policies required Haupt to submit detailed reports regarding virtually every aspect of the railroad's performance, and to estimate expenditures a month in advance. Haupt himself recognized the importance of rapid information flows, but he apparently considered the types of data requested by the directors to be utterly irrelevant to the railroad's operations. Merely collecting the data would be a burden so severe that it would imperil his ability to manage the railroad. Haupt, often inclined to be pugnacious, made an elaborate show of providing all of the information that Patterson had demanded—and then some. Haupt's associated compendium of figures was so detailed that Patterson characterized Haupt as "a man whose communications to the Board were a perfect diarrhea of words with a constipation of ideas."[120]

Sabbath Day

Haupt's assertion that the railroad should eliminate, or at least sharply curtail, its Sunday operations further antagonized many board members. His attitudes reflected the emergence of the Second Great Awakening and the development of a powerful Sabbatarian movement, whose adherents took literally the biblical injunction against labor on the Sabbath. Many feared that transportation improvements had allowed the intrusion of both commercial enterprise and the coercive power of government into a day reserved for the most personal and private matters of introspection. Sabbatarianism soon came into conflict with other religious traditions, with the federal government (in the form of the Post Office), and with increasingly routinized and systematized railroad operating methods.[121]

In earlier years, the Canal Commission and its employees had treated Sunday as they did any other day. "Little regard is here paid to the Sabbath," noted one traveler, while passing through Columbia in 1836, and "there is no cessation of business on railroad or canal."[122] The Sabbatarian movement soon gained strength in the United States and by January 1852 even the canal commissioners had voted to suspend Sunday operations, with the exception of passenger packets.[123]

The newfound religious fervor permeated Pennsylvania communities, as well as the ranks of PRR stockholders. The Quakers who were instrumental in the establishment of the Pennsylvania Railroad injected their religious beliefs into the company's management.

Some board members chafed at a section of the company's legislative charter that required the railroad to transport troops and war materiel at half the regular rate. "Besides being unjust," noted pacifist Quaker and PRR board member Thomas Cope, "the U.S. contributing nothing towards the construction of the Road— it is especially onerous to Friends—& is understood to be unexampled."[124]

A few years later, a debate emerged within the PRR over the issue of Sunday operations, as pragmatic managers clashed with powerful Sabbatarian interests. Yet, even railroad officials who were disinclined to mix religion and business acknowledged that there were economically defensible reasons for exempting employees from work on Sunday. In 1849, the directors requested that Thomson suspend Sunday operations in the interest of greater efficiency and safety, arguing that "universal experience shows the necessity of occasional rest."[125]

During the earliest years of the PRR's existence, the directors could do little to curtail Sunday operations, because the Post Office required the company to operate mail trains seven days a week. In July 1838, Congress had declared the railways to be post routes and had empowered the postmaster general to establish mail contracts with each carrier. As early as 1841, however, Postmaster General Charles Wickliffe had realized that the Post Office could save considerable money, with little effect on revenues, by discontinuing Sunday service. A later postmaster general, Nathan Hall, elected to suspend Sunday mail trains on the PRR, effective at the beginning of 1850, and that decision provided the directors with the impetus to discuss the total suspension of Sunday operations.[126]

In November 1849, in anticipation of the change in Post Office policy, the directors "Resolved That the General Superintendent be instructed to discontinue . . . all operations on the road upon the sabbath and . . . to relieve all persons in the service of the Company from duty on that day."[127] Haupt supported that policy, for he detested Sunday operations, emphasizing his "hope to see the day when the Sabbath will cease to be desecrated in Penna. by Sunday trains."[128] At the annual meeting on December 3, the stockholders appointed a committee to investigate the matter. By the end of the month, the company's investors had voted to suspend all Sunday activities, including repair work, effective January 1, 1850.

Not all directors agreed with the new policy, however. While traffic on the Sabbath was generally low relative to the other days of the week, the individuals who controlled competing transportation routes might choose to operate on that day, drawing business away from the PRR. Furthermore, some directors were philosophically opposed to the Sabbatarian movement and insisted that a few high-priority trains continue to operate on Sundays. William M. Kennedy, a major stockholder, called the ban an unconstitutional endorsement of a particular religious tradition and demanded a stockholders' poll on the issue. In March 1850, PRR stockholders voted to overturn the board's ban on Sunday service, much to Haupt's dismay.[129]

Traffic and Rates

As an experienced railroader, Haupt was certainly aware of some basic principles of transportation economics. He possessed a clear understanding of economies of scale in transportation—namely, that larger shipments were generally more profitable than smaller ones. He also recognized the importance of balancing shipments in each direction in order to minimize the unproductive backhauling of empty cars. Those concepts were not new. During the 1840s, other railroad executives and even the canal commissioners had experimented with flexible rates and volume discounts. Yet Haupt faced a problem that most of his colleagues did not, in the form of the tonnage tax that the legislature had included in the PRR's corporate charter, as a mechanism for protecting the Main Line of Public Works. By raising rates on long-distance shipments, the tax reduced the PRR's attractiveness to shippers. As Thomson noted in November 1849, the PRR's rates "are as low as the very high rates and onerous conditions imposed on the Columbia Rail-road, and the State [tonnage] taxes will permit us to fall to."[130] Despite frequent criticism of the tax by Haupt, Thomson, and other PRR officials, there seemed little immediate prospect for its repeal—particularly as the commonwealth was still paying off the enormous debt associated with the public works.

If the PRR were to remain competitive, Haupt realized, the only option was to contain rates by minimizing operating costs and to maximize revenues by adjusting tariffs with an infinite degree of precision. Such efforts would, in turn, depend on the employment of innovative cost accounting methods. The engineering profession demanded a solid grounding in mathematics and a thorough attention to detail, but Haupt had mastered those skills better than most. He emphasized the role that statistical data could play in the railroad's pricing and cost-containment policies, efforts that ran counter to the rather more cavalier attitude of the PRR's directors.

Haupt's analysis of the minutest details of the railroad's operations began in March 1849, contemporaneous with the development of the PRR's first system of organization. He had the authority to design all of the blanks (forms) that were the first step in data collection and management. From there, it was a natural progression to analyze the information contained on those forms. By the end of the year, he was assisted by a bookkeeper and two clerks, one of whom was his brother, Lewis L. Houpt.[131] The result was an impressive array of information that enabled Haupt, Thomson, and other PRR executives to establish objective performance measures that would maximize efficiency.

It took some time, however, for Haupt to develop his cost accounting methods and put them into practice. He prepared the "Report of the Superintendent of Transportation" for the PRR's *Fourth Annual Report*, covering the company's activities in 1850. His summary contained four pages of tabular data, one of which was no more than a listing of the twenty-six steam locomotives then in service. Two other pages provided monthly statements of the number of passengers who boarded at each station along the route—data that were not notably different from what the canal commissioners had collected even decades earlier. The only page that was of real value, for cost accounting purposes, provided a breakdown of the railroad's expenses, divided into the basic categories, established in 1849, of Maintenance of Way, Motive Power, Maintenance of Cars, and Conducting Transportation.[132]

Haupt's detailed analysis of the PRR's costs began sometime in late 1850, about a year after he became general superintendent. In any event, the full flower-

ing of his methods appeared in his January 1, 1852, "Report of the General Superintendent," published in the following month's *Fifth Annual Report* and based on data that he had collected during 1851. The number of pages of data doubled compared with the previous report, with additional cost categories in each of the company's four basic areas of performance. More significant was a detailed "Report of tonnage of articles sent from and received at Philadelphia," listing everything from fresh meats to tobacco to pig iron.[133]

Yet, it was the following year's *Sixth Annual Report*—the first report prepared while Thomson was president, albeit for less than the entire year—that demonstrated Haupt's growing mastery of statistics and cost accounting. Twenty-one pages of data provided detailed monthly statements of receipts and expenditures. It was now possible to disaggregate costs in the four basic areas of activity, by month and by division. Figures on the number of passengers boarding at each station had yielded to precise measures of the revenue that each station generated, from Philadelphia ($15,455.51 in the month of January, and $43,693.73 two months later) to Mountville (total receipts in May, twenty-five cents).

Haupt's figures were particularly useful for the purpose of setting freight rates. Tables in the *Sixth Annual Report* showed the quantities of through and local freight—enabling Haupt to establish the basis of long-haul/short-haul price differentiation. Much of the freight was listed as "Subject to State [tonnage] tax," providing objective evidence of the cost to the railroad and giving Haupt and Thomson valuable evidence in their attempts to repeal that portion of the PRR's corporate charter.[134]

Between 1849 and 1852, Haupt labored mightily to establish a sound statistical basis for ratemaking. He pioneered many of the cost accounting techniques that later generations of railroad executives took for granted. The key, as Haupt and his successors always emphasized, was to establish an objective basis for the analysis and comparison of costs. PRR officials needed to know—and did know—which engineer used the most wood or tallow, and which division transported freight at the lowest cost per ton-mile. Those performance criteria in turn provided the basis whereby PRR personnel would be promoted or demoted. The canal commissioners had failed to properly manage the Main Line of Public Works in part because they relied on nepotism and political cronyism as a basis of selection. The statistics that they collected, designed primarily to ensure at least the appearance of honesty by the commonwealth's employees, had little value in goading personnel to excel at the often difficult work of cutting costs, eliminating waste, and maximizing efficiency. Haupt's statistics, in contrast, sent a clear message to every PRR employee that results produced rewards, and that their own futures were accurately indexed to their personal roles in ensuring the profitability of their company.

Well before 1852, moreover, the data that Haupt and his colleagues collected indicated the inability of the PRR's owners to establish remunerative rates. When Merrick issued a set of freight charges in August 1850, Haupt saw instantly that the tariffs did not take into account many of the costs associated with transportation, and he prevented them from taking effect. Infuriated board members summoned Haupt, determined, he believed, to humiliate him. Instead, it was Haupt who humiliated the directors, showing them that the railroad was losing money on much of its traffic. The turnabout reflected the directors' limited understanding of the sheer volume of statistics that were required to run a railroad. They were essentially mercantile in their orientation, while Haupt pursued policies that later generations of managers in transportation and industrial enterprises would have found quite familiar.

During the summer of 1851, Haupt further confounded the PRR's directors with his decision to adjust rates in response to the emergence of a new rail transportation artery. For many decades, Baltimoreans had sought better access to central Pennsylvania. In 1828, they had chartered the Baltimore & Susquehanna Railroad, but it would be another decade before its subsidiary, the York & Maryland Line Rail Road, reached the city of York, west of the Susquehanna River. Thirteen years later, in February 1851, the York & Cumberland Railroad connected York with Bridgeport (later, Lemoyne), on the west bank of the Susquehanna River, opposite Harrisburg. It then became a simple matter for eastbound freight and passengers to travel over the PRR and then head south to Baltimore, bypassing Philadelphia.[135]

Haupt immediately sensed the advantage of cooperation with the Baltimore & Susquehanna route. Favorable rates for Baltimore-bound traffic, he argued, would allow the railroad "to get all of this business that we can conveniently accommodate, and charge upon it as much as it will bear; thus using it as a means to cheapen tolls [on other shipments headed] to Philadelphia."[136] The canal commissioners were naturally displeased that such rates would divert traffic from the Philadelphia & Columbia, enriching the PRR (and the Baltimore & Susquehanna) at their expense.

Haupt's rates, which would divert traffic from Philadelphia, also struck many board members as heresy. After all, their investment rested largely on the rationale that the PRR would further the commercial success of the Quaker City. In the PRR's *First Annual Report*, Merrick emphasized that the company's initial stock offering "was considered by many as a patriotic endeavor to retain and extend a trade which legitimately belonged to this city, and which was about to be wrested from her grasp by her enterprising rivals."[137] He echoed those comments the following year when he asserted that "the [Pennsylvania Rail] road is being built by the business community for the benefit of trade."[138]

Haupt cared little for the consequences of his rate policies on either the state works or on Philadelphia. "The discovery was made that business operations of life, and especially the requirements of trade, cannot be made to conform to arbitrary regulations," he observed early in 1852, "but that these regulations must conform to them, and must be varied to accommodate the changing phases which competition or other circumstances may produce."[139] That was about as clear an assertion as Haupt could make that the financial interests of the PRR, dictated in large measure by geography and established trade patterns, must take precedence over the well-being of Philadelphia merchants. Haupt nonetheless acknowledged the motives of the PRR's founders, but he did attempt to steer the board members in a different direction. "It cannot be denied that a principal object in the construction of the Pennsylvania Railroad was the promotion of the mercantile interests of Philadelphia," he wrote in 1852, in defense of his actions, but he had "never yet been able to perceive that the mercantile interests of Philadelphia and the pecuniary interests of the stockholders were incompatible with one another."[140]

Despite the objections of Merrick, Patterson, and some other board members, Haupt's rate policies were very much in keeping with emerging investor attitudes toward railways. In brief, those who owned railway stocks and bonds, and their representatives, argued that only those who had invested capital in a business enterprise were eligible to determine corporate policy. The number of stakeholders might be quite large, as it included passengers, shippers, workers, and residents of cities served by the railroad. Yet the new view held that stakeholder interest should yield to shareholder control, with the implicit claim that such practices would maximize corporate performance to the betterment of all.

Investment analyst Henry Varnum Poor, a lifelong advocate of sound management and full financial disclosure, was one of the most forceful spokesmen for the rights of investors. Railroads should be "merely *commercial* enterprises," Poor insisted in 1852, "and are to be conducted upon commercial principles, which never sanction an enormous sacrifice for a contingent good."[141] That philosophy meant that the PRR's operating officials should set rates in a manner that would maximize net income regardless of their effects on the trade of Baltimore or Philadelphia. Yet, such ratemaking flexibility would come only later, after Thomson became president. In the meantime, the Merrick/Patterson faction on the board systematically blocked Haupt's efforts to generate new sources of traffic and thus paradoxically reinforced his commitment to accurately measure and thereby contain costs. "Unable to effect a change in the policy of the Board in regard to revenue," he emphasized, "my suggestions and representations being viewed as acts of insubordination, I confined my attention to a watchful supervision of the expenditures."[142]

Intriguingly, both Merrick and Patterson had already provided some indication that they agreed with Haupt's fundamental point—that the PRR should be a profit-maximizing entity in its own right, not merely an enabler for Philadelphia's commerce. In the same *First Annual Report* in which he discussed the PRR's role as a "patriotic endeavor," Merrick acknowledged that many investors, particularly those who had purchased but a few shares of stock, had a different motive for their support of the venture. "Since the period when this enterprise was first undertaken a marked change has manifested itself in the public mind with respect to its feasibility and prospects of profit," he observed. "As an investment, this work is now viewed in a very different light from what it was a year ago," he continued. "That the Pennsylvania Railroad must yield an immediate profit on the investment is generally admitted by all well informed persons, and we may now look to capital seeking investment, and not patriotism to furnish it."[143]

Four years later, in the PRR's *Fifth Annual Report*—the last he would oversee as president—Patterson suggested that the Pennsylvania Railroad could benefit Philadelphia by benefiting itself. "Great as have been the reductions made through the instrumentality of this Company, the people of Pennsylvania have yet to learn what low prices are," he predicted. Noting that Boston merchants had enacted a low-rate/high-volume policy on the railroads that they managed, Patterson insisted, "It is for the Pennsylvania Railroad to perform the same office for Philadelphia on the one hand, or to fall with her into a state of premature decrepitude on the other."[144]

The Battle for the Presidency

In time, the PRR's directors might have found themselves in full agreement with Haupt's ratemaking policies. Yet during the autumn of 1851, as a result of Haupt's incessant demands for higher volumes and lower rates, his relationship with the board deteriorated rapidly. In response to their concern regarding Haupt's actions, the directors convened a special investigating committee. Its chair was flour merchant Alexander J. Derbyshire, but the real authority lay with Haupt's nemesis, Samuel Merrick.[145]

The resulting criticisms of the investigating committee transformed the simmering hostility between Haupt and Patterson into open warfare. Incident after incident illustrated the chasm that separated the two sides. When the board elected to delay the departure of westbound passenger trains until sufficient travelers had boarded to fill the cars, Haupt countermanded the order. He insisted that adherence to regularly scheduled departures was vital to the safe and efficient operation of the railroad, but some directors were displeased that "many passengers have been left while paying their fares in the [ticket] office."[146] The board had not approved the contracts that Haupt *had* negotiated in a timely manner, and Haupt complained that he was accordingly "placed in the ridiculous position of appearing to perform duties for which [he] was not authorized."[147] In early October 1851, Patterson produced two letters that Haupt had written—one to the president and the other to passenger agent Thomas Moore, as well as a third, from Lombaert to Haupt. He claimed that the documents offered proof "that Mr. Haupt neglects or refuses to obey the instructions of the Board unless they correspond with his own views of policy."[148]

Patterson, Merrick, and their allies were infuriated that Haupt—and, by extension, Thomson—dared to participate in strategic planning. They developed "the conviction that Mr. Haupt is determined to have the uncontrolled government not only of the conduct of his own department, but the policy of the Company."[149] On October 15, the members of the investigating committee demanded that Haupt be charged with insubordination, convinced that, had they not done so, "The insubordination of this officer will without doubt soon communicate itself throughout the ranks & unless the Board firmly asserts its supremacy confusion and disaster are sure to follow."[150]

The committee's report touched off a fierce debate among the board members, with Merrick, Patterson, Thomas T. Lea, and David S. Brown in agreement that both Haupt and Thomson had to be brought into line. Derbyshire was undecided, but was sympathetic to Merrick's position. George W. Carpenter, Christian E. Spangler, and George Howell (one of the two directors representing the City of Philadelphia) united in opposition to the Merrick/Patterson faction. The other three directors—Washington Butcher, John Yarrow, and Edward M. Davis, the other Philadelphia city director—professed support for Haupt. In the end, however, they sided with Merrick, and the board voted eight to three to call Haupt to account.[151]

When he appeared before the board on October 22, Haupt defended himself with far more eloquence than

might have been expected from a notoriously reticent and soft-spoken engineer. "No single individual now before me has ever been able to appreciate the difficulties by which I have been surrounded," Haupt told the board, "or the extremely trying circumstances in which I have been placed."[152] He also suggested that Merrick had fabricated evidence against him by altering his correspondence. Haupt insisted that he should be insulated from Patterson's presidential oversight, inasmuch as "the duties of the Chief Engineer in regard to location and construction and of the [General] Superintendent in reference to the management of transportation were of a professional character and that those of the President were executive and financial and that the first named officers derived their powers not from the President immediately but from the Board."[153]

After Haupt had delivered his litany of complaints, Patterson could do no better than stammer "that Mr. Haupt's memory was entirely at fault with regard to most of the transactions mentioned in connection with himself," and proceeded to recall several instances in which "Mr. Haupt had omitted or misstated material facts."[154] Several members of the board were outraged at Haupt's temerity and considered his statements to be "more accurately characterized as an attack than a defence."[155] Other directors were more conciliatory. After Haupt departed, John Yarrow, one of those who had originally voted against Haupt, now thought him vindicated. Turning on Merrick, Yarrow accused him of outright dishonesty and insinuated that the former president was little better than a thief.[156]

During the next few weeks, however, Haupt's opponents gave nearly as good as they got. At the next board meeting, Merrick complained that in return for his "courtesy" in permitting Haupt to appear before the board, the general superintendent had "presented a paper with an attempt at explanation, the main object of which appears to be to throw odium upon individual members and to excite the sympathy of other members of the Board by attempting to show that the [investigating committee's] report was the result of individual hostility."[157] Merrick retaliated by introducing a resolution to remove Haupt from the company, but it failed by one vote. The former president vowed to resign from the board in protest, but the other directors persuaded him to remain. Merrick was no more successful in his efforts to convince the board to maintain absolute secrecy at meetings, with only directors entitled to possess information regarding the topics that were under discussion. George Howell, a strong supporter of Haupt and Thomson, privately informed the embattled general superintendent of what had occurred.[158]

Haupt's opponents complained of "a wide and apparently irreconcilable diversity of opinion [that] has from the outset existed among the members of this Board as to the general policy which should govern its councils." That was something of an understatement, as the board was virtually paralyzed by indecision. Patterson insisted that he and his allies had "labored unremittingly to perfect an organization which should compel a strict adherence to a system of rigid accountability and subordination," a system that Haupt's alleged insubordination had now undermined.[159]

At the November 5 board meeting, Merrick again pledged to resign, in tandem with Patterson, Lea, and Brown, rather than to submit to Haupt's policies. They also noted that the railroad would need to fund a half-million dollars worth of short-term notes, due within the next thirty days, a situation that would certainly be made more difficult by a mass defection. The threat had the desired effect, and the board voted eight to three to demand Haupt's resignation rather than lose the services of the PRR's president and three of its directors. Only Spangler, Carpenter, and Howell sided with Haupt and Thomson.

Haupt complied with the board's request, noting that he would "willingly surrender myself as a sacrifice to gratify those who have made this the sole condition of their continuance on the Board."[160] His letter of resignation included a detailed account of the dispute, emphasizing the efforts of the Merrick/Patterson faction to destroy his career. Haupt also saw to it that the letter was published in the Philadelphia newspapers. While the controversy was not entirely unknown to the city's residents, the resulting publicity indicated that a major fracas was likely to occur at the shareholders' meeting the following February. On November 26, the day after the letter became public, the board resolved, by a six-to-five vote, that Haupt withdraw his resignation. He agreed, but promised to remain with

the company only until replaced by a qualified individual. Two days later, whatever conciliation that Haupt might have exhibited disappeared when he published an open letter to the shareholders. Already, several major stockholders who were not on the board were demanding a full accounting of the dispute. Haupt's two letters amplified their concerns and energized the opponents of Merrick and Patterson.[161]

Until that point, Thomson had been sympathetic to Haupt's plight but had refrained from participating directly in the increasingly contentious debates among the board members. By the end of 1851, however, the financial conservatism of the Patterson faction threatened to do more than deprive the chief engineer of the services of his general superintendent. Far worse, they threatened the survival of the Pennsylvania Railroad, as well as Thomson's professional future.

Eighteen months earlier, in early June 1850, Thomson had appeared before the directors bearing bad news. At least $2 million would be needed to complete the line along the Juniata River and up the valley of the Little Juniata to the connection with the Portage Railroad at Duncansville—money that the PRR's treasury did not possess. By the end of 1850, with work on the Western Division far from complete, the PRR had redeemed the subscribers' pledges on most of the initial $7.5 million stock offering. On December 9, 1850, and in keeping with the provisions of the 1846 charter, the board voted to raise the equity ceiling to $10 million. The Philadelphia investment market was still soft, however. Following the collapse of their country's railway boom, in 1847, British iron manufacturers had dumped their products in the United States, undermining Pennsylvania's manufacturing base and souring financial markets. Thomson therefore warned that construction would soon grind to a halt unless the directors were willing to augment the company's equity with debt, through bank loans or mortgage bonds.[162]

The directors were disinclined to issue bonds, however. As merchant bankers, they were fiscally conservative and unwilling to burden the company with long-term debt obligations. Board members emphasized that all of the railroads built in Massachusetts, save one, had been constructed solely through stockholders' equity. Companies that relied on bonds, they emphasized, had not been treated kindly either by the financial press or by investors. Based on the experience of other firms, they claimed, bonded indebtedness "has been almost universally a disappointment. The property of the stockholders has, in many cases, been sacrificed to pay an interest to loanholders. Money has been raised at usurious interest by the sale of bonds below their par value." The directors were referring to bonds sold at a discount (that is, a bond with a face value of $100 being sold for $90), which raised the effective interest rate on the funds actually collected, often well above the 6 percent considered customary on government bonds and the securities of reliable corporations. The end result, they stressed, was that the PRR would "labor under an accumulation of debt, which absorbs all the profit of the concern to pay the interest."[163] In other words, the absolute necessity of paying interest to bondholders would force a reduction in dividends to the point where few investors would be willing to buy the railroad's stock. Far better, many directors argued, that "the profits of the enterprise, instead of being diverted to its creditors, would be reaped by its shareholders."[164]

Thomson had little patience with the board's refusal to raise additional funds through bond sales. As he repeatedly informed the president, the directors, and anyone else who would listen, the greater danger lay in undercapitalization. Parsimony during the initial construction phase would be a false economy, Thomson insisted, for it would produce an inadequate line that would burden the railroad with inefficient operations for decades to come. More ominously, as the chief engineer emphasized, three other railroads were racing toward the west, and the PRR could not afford to finish last.

By the autumn of 1851, as Haupt was defending his actions before the directors, the PRR's financial condition had gone from bad to worse. A year had elapsed since the board had approved the issuance of an additional $2.5 million worth of stock, and the company had sold most of those shares. With the capital ceiling set at $10 million, the corporate treasury had collected $8.1 million and spent all but $125,000 of that. The PRR's earnings over the course of 1851 amounted to 4¼ percent on capital, with no provision for depreciation. Under those circumstances, prospective investors were understandably anxious regarding the value of the PRR's stock. Even worse, the directors coped with a worsening

cash-flow problem, delaying the payment of invoices, offering promises of payment rather than cash, and taking out short-term loans, all in a desperate attempt to keep the company solvent. The unsecured floating debt increased steadily, with no end in sight.[165]

Several board members recognized the danger of financial ruin. In December 1851, Haupt and dissident director Christian Spangler traveled west to Lewistown to intercept Thomson, who was returning to the east after supervising construction on the Western Division. They met at the home of ironmaker John Armstrong Wright, a former director of the Pennsylvania Railroad, and the individual chiefly responsible for organizing the company town at Altoona.[166] The four men could look out across the snow-covered fields of central Pennsylvania, toward the properties of the Greenwood Furnace and the adjacent Freedom Iron Works, which Wright had recently purchased—and which now supplied many of the PRR's metallurgical needs. To the south, over the summit of Jack's Mountain, lay the Juniata Division Canal, drained of water and lifeless, and adjacent to it the Pennsylvania Railroad, still open for business and poised to deliver coal and iron ore wherever and whenever needed.[167]

Yet, Spangler and Wright emphasized, the Pennsylvania Railroad could never reach its full potential as long as cautious, ignorant directors such as Patterson and Merrick remained in charge. Such men did not appreciate the PRR's need for capital, they stressed, nor did they understand the complex technological requirements associated with efficient and profitable operations. Only Thomson, they claimed, could save the Pennsylvania Railroad. Thomson agreed, but to agree in private was one thing, to take action in public quite another. He feared, understandably, that if he sought the presidency and failed, then Patterson and his allies would exact their revenge and find a new chief engineer.

In his memoirs, Haupt claimed that he, along with Wright and Spangler, characterized Patterson, Merrick, and the other conservative Philadelphia merchants on the board as a "silk stocking aristocracy," men of inherited wealth and easy privilege, who understood neither a hard day's work, nor the most basic engineering principles.[168] That, apparently, was what did it. As chief engineer, Thomson believed that he

Figure 18. John Armstrong Wright (1820–1891) had been a surveyor, was one of the organizers of the Pennsylvania Railroad, and served on its board for a brief period between March 1847 and December 1848. The meeting that persuaded J. Edgar Thomson to run for the presidency took place at Wright's home near Lewistown. By the time that this photograph was taken, circa 1865, he had begun to experiment with the Bessemer process—earning him the respect of steel magnate Andrew Carnegie, whom he employed to run the operation, but bankrupting himself in the process. When Congress established the Interstate Commerce Commission in 1887, Wright served as one of its first commissioners.

Greenwood Furnace State Park, Pennsylvania Bureau of State Parks.

alone comprehended the grand design of how the railroad should be built and operated. In that context, the board's reluctance to borrow funds to complete the line across the Alleghenies represented not so much a directorial prerogative as an inexcusable failure to do the engineering work that had to be done. Thomson was not one to allow the board to dictate corporate policy on such a critical issue. Moreover, the perennial battles between Thomson, Haupt, and the board—and within the board itself—over personnel issues threatened the efficiency of the entire enterprise. The disagreements echoed the patronage politics that many years earlier had bedeviled Thomson's efforts to

secure steady employment on the Philadelphia & Columbia Railroad, and that even now were poisoning relations between the PRR and the Main Line of Public Works.[169]

Strong personal motives also lay behind Thomson's anger at the conduct of the "silk stocking aristocracy." The salaries of American civil engineers exhibited a high degree of variance in the fifteen years following 1835. As railroads became more commonplace and routinized, engineers who focused solely on technical issues found themselves consigned to a secondary rank within their profession. In an increasingly bifurcated market, top salaries went to those who took on managerial and administrative responsibilities. Thomson feared that he would find himself in the first, low-paid group, unless he could offer the Pennsylvania Railroad something more than mere engineering expertise. By insisting on his right to command, therefore, Thomson was fighting for his own professional life.[170]

Now thoroughly incensed, Thomson brought his considerable political skills to the fore, going well beyond the level of authority usually accorded to salaried managers. As 1851 drew to a close, Thomson began to openly solicit support from members of the PRR's board of directors. His task became considerably easier on December 26, when the board appointed the final two directors to fill the unclaimed seats held for the representatives of Allegheny County. With the backing of Haupt's supporters, the directors chose one individual, William Robinson, Jr., who was firmly opposed to Merrick and Patterson. Five days later, on New Year's Eve, the board defeated an effort by Merrick to publish some of his correspondence with Haupt in order to bolster his side of the argument.[171]

The conflict accelerated in the first weeks of the New Year. On January 3, the *Philadelphia Evening Bulletin* described the controversy in detail, serving to increase support for Thomson and his allies on the board. Thomson undoubtedly gave his private blessing to an open letter by Haupt published on January 20, 1852. Haupt insisted that the Merrick/Patterson faction was woefully ignorant of the Pennsylvania Railroad's costs, and of their consequent effect on rates. Always in command of his data, Haupt calculated precisely how much that ineptitude had cost the railroad. The first two presidents, he argued, had also prevented the implementation of more efficient managerial techniques that might have further reduced expenses and increased profits.[172]

On January 27, a week after Haupt released his latest remarks to the press, the first passengers embarked on the PRR's through service between Philadelphia and Pittsburgh. As they traveled west, they must surely have been aware that the company that had made their trip possible was on the verge of implosion. A few days later, on February 1, board member James Magee informed Thomson that Haupt's indecorous remarks— correct though they may have been—were unlikely to win the chief engineer much support at the upcoming shareholders' meeting.

Thomson responded to Magee's insinuations and the escalating public controversy with a letter to the *North American*, published on the morning of February 2, 1852, the date of the annual stockholders' meeting. He defended the general superintendent, after a fashion, insisting that Haupt would refuse reelection to the company. That concession was irrelevant, however, as Haupt had never been elected to any office on the Pennsylvania Railroad. He was instead appointed at the discretion of the president, whose job Thomson hoped to take. Thomson also offered a detailed argument in favor of the bond sales, pointing out that the board had failed in its efforts to raise money through stock subscriptions. That method of finance had by that time netted $8.3 million, far below the $12.5 million that Thomson estimated would be required to complete and equip the railroad. That was a shame, he concluded, because the PRR, even in its incomplete state, had shown enormous revenue potential and provided "an unusually broad basis to found credit upon."[173]

A certain amount of tension characterized the stockholders' meeting that occurred later that day. Haupt observed that the conflict between Thomson and the board "agitated the city of Philadelphia as much as a presidential election."[174] Like any presidential election, there was politicking aplenty. Magee insisted that his relative, Herman Lombaert, be installed as chief engineer in Haupt's place in exchange for his support of the Thomson camp. The commissioners of Spring Garden resolved to vote their shares in favor of Thomson, and when Merrick and his allies attempted to contact them in order to change their minds, Thomson's allies placed them under guard, out of Merrick's reach.[175]

It probably would not have mattered in any case, since there was a general consensus that Patterson and his allies had to go, not so much to save Haupt, but rather to rescue the PRR's precarious finances. At the meeting, stockholders bombarded Patterson with grievances, some more damaging than others. They objected to his decision to purchase several large tracts of land in West Philadelphia and in Pittsburgh at what they considered to be exorbitant prices—parcels that would eventually prove critical to the railroad's operations in those two cities. And, according to one source, they believed that they could make further economies by eliminating Thomson's salary as chief engineer (which by now had risen to $5,000 a year) and combining his existing duties with those of the president. The underlying issue, however, was always the assertion that Haupt and Thomson could manage the Pennsylvania Railroad far more effectively than the existing president.[176]

The February 2, 1852, election of a new slate of directors resulted in a resounding victory for Thomson and his allies. Howell, Spangler, and Carpenter all retained their seats on the board, as did William Robinson, Jr., the recently appointed pro-Thomson director from Allegheny County. The shareholders purged the board of its more conservative members, including Patterson and Merrick, electing five new, pro-Thomson directors to take their places. Thomas Lea and David Brown, strong critics of Haupt and Thomson, were reelected by a narrow margin. They were now powerless, however, and they resigned from the board two days later. The new board met on February 3, unanimously electing Thomson the new president of the Pennsylvania Railroad.[177]

From Engineer to President

Thomson's election to the presidency marked more than a personal victory. His success ensured that the railroad would develop into a stable, effectively managed, profit-maximizing entity. For the next fifty years, all of the PRR's presidents adhered to Thomson's—and Haupt's—belief that the railroad should undertake massive capital investments in the physical plant and equipment in order to move the highest volume of traffic at the lowest possible rates. Now that he had won the battle to control the Pennsylvania Railroad, Thomson would need to move with considerable speed in order to develop the railroad's traffic, improve its operating efficiency, and manage relations with city and state governments.

The defeat of the Merrick/Patterson faction also marked the ascendancy of a new corporate managerial style on the Pennsylvania Railroad. Thomson's engineering ethos dominated the company, as virtually all of the PRR's presidents, and many of their

subordinates, were thoroughly versed in the railroad's operations. With his seemingly endless capacity for work, Thomson for most of his presidency served as the chief executive officer and oversaw every aspect of the company's transportation business. He became a coordinating force and was the ultimate mediator of disputes within the company. Whereas Merrick and Patterson, with their limited knowledge of engineering and operating matters, had lacked the credibility to successfully serve as arbiters, Thomson was one of the most experienced railroaders in the world. For all intents and purposes, his word was law, and it was final.

Even though he was a salaried executive who never owned more than a relatively small portfolio of PRR stock, Thomson dictated policy to the board, based in large measure on his managerial expertise. Whereas Merrick and Patterson had used their positions on the board as a basis for winning election to the presidency, Thomson and all of his successors employed their role as president as justification for taking a seat on the board. Beginning in 1853, first one and eventually four vice presidents were on the board, as well. The board also met less and less frequently after 1852, and the directors who were not also salaried managers exerted progressively less influence over the company's long-term corporate strategy. The number of board meetings fell from seventy-one in 1852 to forty by 1854. In the decade that separated 1856 and 1865—a period that included the unprecedented operational problems associated with the Civil War—the board met, on average, only thirty times per year. In 1872, there were only sixteen board meetings. After October 1882, the president was chairman of the board. By 1896, the president possessed the authority to appoint no fewer than thirty-eight senior officers, subject only to a pro forma confirmation by the board.[178]

By the late nineteenth century, the growing power of Thomson and his successors represented an increasingly common pattern in American business. As corporations grew in size and complexity, most boards relinquished authority for day-to-day operations to salaried managers. The outside directors, few of whom had any particular experience in railroading, were generally involved in numerous other business enterprises, from banking to steel, and lacked the time and expertise required to assume an active role in the PRR's management.

The PRR's directors by no means relinquished all of their power. Some board members, particularly those who were members of the Road Committee, were involved in special projects that did not relate directly to the railroad's routine operations. Furthermore, the directors could and did assert their authority whenever they suspected that salaried managers were jeopardizing the considerable capital that they had invested in the company. Their approval was still required for such weighty matters as the issuance of new stocks or bonds, the acquisition of other railroads, major construction projects, and large real estate purchases. In that sense, the board continued to influence the railroad's long-term corporate strategy. Directors and other large shareholders were also willing to restrain what they considered to be inappropriate actions on the part of salaried executives. In 1874, they were sharply critical of Thomson's involvement in such projects as allied fast freight lines and affiliated railroads outside of the territory traditionally served by the PRR. Thirty years later, the directors were likewise involved in a sweeping investigation of links between PRR officials and colliery owners.[179]

Generally, however, the directors had little to complain about. For the most part, Thomson and his fellow executives managed the Pennsylvania Railroad wisely and well. Thomson's policies ensured that professional managers would retain control over the PRR, and that the company would not fall under the sway of financial speculators or nepotistic family members. Thomson's prudent and professional management of the railroad stood in sharp contrast to the actions of financiers who batted the Erie around Wall Street like a football. After 1858, when John W. Garrett became president of the Baltimore & Ohio, he and later his son managed that company as a personal and family enterprise, to the eventual detriment of investors. In 1867, the New York Central came under the control of Cornelius Vanderbilt, and several generations of his family ran the company—generally with great effectiveness, but nonetheless in a manner that delayed the NYC's control over its allied lines in the Midwest.

Thomson's rise to power, and his ability to professionalize the management of the Pennsylvania Railroad, coincided with the emergence of a new generation of Philadelphia businessmen. Schooled in the ways of the industrial revolution, they were more attuned to the needs of their profession than to those of their community. While individuals such as Thomas P. Cope and Richard D. Wood had established and joined civic associations, their successors belonged to professional business and engineering societies. They were urban businessman rather than civic boosters, and they were attuned to regional, national, and international markets rather than to the parochial welfare of their community.[180] Thomson and his colleagues and successors were never isolated from the political and social environment of their native city. Yet, their civic involvement was largely the means to an end, designed to protect the multimillion-dollar corporation that they managed. In that sense, then, Thomson's election to the presidency indicated that the Pennsylvania Railroad was a valued corporate entity in its own right, and not just the handmaiden to commercial interests in Philadelphia.

Chapter 5

Executive

1852–1857

Accidents have been a part of railroading almost from the first day that wheels began to roll along rails. Destruction of property, injuries, and loss of life have occurred with such grim regularity that individual incidents became almost unnoticeable, buried in the gruesome torrent of statistics. The accident that occurred near Duncansville, Pennsylvania, on a warm summer day in early August 1852 nonetheless stood apart from the rest. It remains today one of the most unusual, even bizarre catastrophes to befall the Pennsylvania Railroad, or indeed any company in the transportation business. On that day a runaway canal boat demolished a Pennsylvania Railroad freight train.

At the time of the accident, PRR construction crews had not yet completed the railroad's Western Division between Johnstown and Pittsburgh. Even when they closed that gap in late November, freight and passengers continued to rely on the Allegheny Portage Railroad between Duncansville and Johnstown. The commonwealth's railway hauled other cargo as well, including the sectionalized canal boats of the Reliance Portable Boat Company, mounted on special flatcars for the trip over the mountains. The brakes on the car carrying one of the sections of the canal boat had malfunctioned, and the boat, moving far faster than it ever had before, or would afterward,

careened toward the bottom of the incline. One of the workers sensed something amiss, heard a sound, paused, and then looked up the nearby hillside in mute horror before yelling a warning to his comrades. By the time the dust had cleared, the canal boat and the cars that had transported it were a total loss. So too were three brand-new cars belonging to the Pennsylvania Railroad, en route from Philadelphia to the end of track west of Beatty's Station, but destined never to complete their journey.[1]

Despite some sensationalistic contemporary accounts, there were few such disasters on the inclined planes, but accidents were common enough to cause concern for PRR managers.[2] In 1847, well before the company's tracks reached Duncansville, the cars containing the section boat *Sam'l P. Funk* had come loose on the same grade. Andrew Cassady, a passenger on board the boat, was badly bruised and lost the fingers on one hand. The PRR's *Fifth Annual Report* indicated that accidents at Plane Number 4 had claimed two boxcars and two passenger cars. PRR officials stationed at Duncansville complained repeatedly to the board of directors about the ordinary inadequacies of the Portage Railroad and the limited cooperation that they had received from its employees. President J. Edgar Thomson was certainly aware that any attempt to acquire or bypass the Portage Railroad would entail con-

Figure 19. J. Edgar Thomson was the third president of the Pennsylvania Railroad, serving from 1852 until his death in 1874—longer than any other person in that office. During his lifetime, and after, fellow railway executives, the popular press, and historians praised Thomson's devotion to his profession and to his company, in sharp contrast to such financiers as Jay Gould. Yet Thomson could be manipulative, as well, and he was certainly willing to use the Pennsylvania Railroad as a base to advance his own personal fortunes as well as those of his business associates.

Pennsylvania Historical and Museum Commission, Pennsylvania State Archives.

siderable costs, both economically and politically. Yet, he and his directors were rapidly coming to the conclusion that the only way to protect their railroad—quite literally, in that instance—from the destructive effects of their rival would be to buy it outright.[3]

For fifty years after its inception in 1846, the PRR's owners and managers struggled to define the company's organizational parameters, debating which functions could be safely externalized and which were so important that the railroad must bear the heavy cost of internalization. Time after time the PRR's executives persuaded the board to choose the latter course. Investors agreed that the railroad had little choice but to protect its already enormous capital investment through additional massive investments in the physical plant, building or acquiring new lines and improving existing ones through the construction of bridges, tunnels, junctions, and additional tracks. The PRR's equipment needs mandated the construction of extensive workshops at Altoona, and elsewhere, to build and repair locomotives and cars. By 1881, the PRR had become the world's largest railroad in part because its directors had acceded to managerial demands to internalize so many aspects of its operations, rather than risk the company's fortunes on the vagaries of outside firms.

Many of the PRR's stockholders and board members criticized the additional expense incurred by Thomson and other senior executives, but in the end they usually followed his advice. Director George W. Carpenter was one of the strongest supporters of Thomson's vision for massive investments in the Pennsylvania Railroad. Born in Germantown, Pennsylvania, in 1802, Carpenter was a successful merchant, operating a wholesale drug business in Philadelphia, and he was an amateur geologist and a member of the Academy of Natural Sciences. On March 30, 1847, when the original thirteen directors of the Pennsylvania Railroad convened their first board meeting, Carpenter was among them. When poor health forced his resignation from the board on January 6, 1858, he was the last of the initial thirteen, but he remained steadfast in his loyalty to Thomson and his fellow executives.

When Thomson demanded vast sums of money to bypass the Allegheny Portage Railroad, and then to buy the entire Main Line of Public Works, Carpenter

readily agreed. When the president wanted even more money to improve and equip the line across Pennsylvania, Carpenter acquiesced to the additional cost. "How much greater the censure ought to have been if they had not created this debt," he reminisced on his final day as a director, "and after expending Twenty Millions of dollars in building a road to have allowed it to languish in an unfinished state, and to allow the immense amount of produce and other tonnage waiting at Western Depots destined for the East to go to other Atlantic Cities by rival lines for want of rolling stock and other facilities to do the business on our road, which is the natural channel, it being the shortest and most direct route from the West."[4]

As Carpenter recognized, the disagreements that had taken place in 1851 and 1852, regarding whether the PRR should issue construction bonds, represented only one facet of a broader transformation in management strategy. Samuel Merrick, William Patterson, and the other conservative merchants of the PRR board had sought to husband the railroad's resources, spending only the bare minimum necessary to create a viable transportation route across the commonwealth. Their goal was first and foremost to protect Philadelphia and the merchants who resided there.

Thomson possessed a much broader vision, one that saw the PRR expanding in response to shippers' demands and the competition from other railroads. His loyalty was to his company, not his city, and he was willing to protect the interests of the former, even if it meant harming those of the other. Since joining the Pennsylvania Railroad in 1847, he had become progressively more frustrated with the merchant-managers who had constrained his policies. Upon assuming the presidency less than five years later, he gave clear notice that things would be different. "This short era of Public Benevolence lasted only until 1852," wrote novelist Nathaniel Burt, more than a century later. "It was followed by a thirty-year-long and very different era of Hard-Boiled Railroading."[5] For the remainder of his presidency, the most hard-boiled of Thomson's policies were conditioned by his belief that the only way to protect the monies already invested in the PRR was to spend more money, and that his firm must either expand or die.

The Pennsylvania Railroad in 1852

In February 1852, when Thomson became president of the Pennsylvania Railroad, he inherited what could only charitably be described as a composite route across the commonwealth. Passengers leaving Philadelphia for Pittsburgh faced a particularly arduous journey. With the Portage Railroad suspending operations at nightfall, passengers had to leave Philadelphia well before dawn if they hoped to reach Pittsburgh the same day. They first rode over the tracks of the municipally owned City Railroad. Horses pulled the passenger cars along Market Street and across the Schuylkill Permanent Bridge, which had been created as a private toll bridge nearly fifty years earlier and later adapted for railroad use. When the cars reached the West Philadelphia yards on the opposite bank of the Schuylkill River, crews attached locomotives so that the barely awake passengers could continue their trip west to Dillerville (Lancaster).

With its narrowly spaced tracks, the state-owned Philadelphia & Columbia could not accommodate the wider passenger cars employed on the PRR and its Harrisburg, Portsmouth, Mount Joy & Lancaster subsidiary. At Dillerville, passengers did their best to retain a sense of humor as they crossed from one set of cars to another by traversing a twelve-inch-wide board—an adventure that they commonly referred to as "walking the plank."[6] Once travelers reached the state capital, they proceeded westward along PRR rails, but only as far west as the junction with the Allegheny Portage Railroad at Duncansville. From there, passengers enjoyed the benefit of steam locomotives on the level sections (the last horses had been put out to pasture in December 1850), but they still endured the slow and dangerous trip up and down the inclined planes. Their trials continued, however, for the Western Division of the PRR was still under construction. The gap between the railheads shrank daily, but travelers nonetheless faced an arduous stagecoach ride before they could rejoin the PRR's tracks for the last leg of the journey into Pittsburgh.

A trip that was inconvenient and exhausting for passengers was inefficient and costly for freight, with a veritable army of teamsters lumping cargoes across the roads to the west of Johnstown. To the east, the Philadelphia & Columbia was unable to efficiently accommodate the PRR's freight traffic. Small wonder, then, that General Superintendent Herman Haupt complained, "The business of the Pennsylvania Rail Road in its unfinished condition, with the additions from the other roads centering at Harrisburg, and the canal, has already taxed the Columbia Rail Road to its full capacity, and the most serious delays and inconveniences have been experienced."[7] Even before he had become president, Thomson had warned the board that those problems would prevent the PRR from competing against rival carriers, such as the Baltimore & Ohio. As president, he emphasized that the PRR could survive only if it owned its own rails and controlled its own operations, from the center of Philadelphia to Pittsburgh and beyond. For the first five years of his long administration, Thomson sought to internalize the railroad's freight and passenger operations, bypass the outmoded Allegheny Portage Railroad, and establish control over the Philadelphia & Columbia. In each of those goals, he succeeded admirably.

Taming the Transporters

One of Thomson's earliest goals was to establish control over the independent freight forwarders that operated on the PRR. The freight forwarders, commonly known as transporters, dominated the carriage of freight and passengers on the Main Line of Public Works, and they soon made the transition to the privately owned Pennsylvania Railroad and its connections. During the 1846 charter battle in the General Assembly, many legislators had endeavored to maintain some vestige of open access to transportation services in order to preclude the possibility that PRR executives might establish a transportation monopoly and set indefensibly high rates. The company's charter specified that the railroad "shall be esteemed a public highway, for the conveyance of passengers and the transportation of freight," giving PRR managers "exclusive control of the motive power." Under that arrangement, not markedly different from that which applied on the state-owned Philadelphia & Columbia and Allegheny Portage railroads, the PRR was entitled to "such rates of toll or other compensation, for the use of the said road, and of said motive power." In granting the charter, legislators did not specify the maximum rates that PRR officials could charge on their own operations. They did, however, establish maximum "rates of toll and motive power charges . . . when the cars used for such conveyance or transportation are owned or furnished by others." PRR officials were thus free to levy whatever rates they wished when offering freight and passenger service using their own equipment, but the existence of the transporter alternative acted as a check on their rate-making flexibility. The terms of the PRR charter also afforded a powerful advantage to the established freight forwarders. PRR executives could not prohibit their cars from the railroad, nor could they charge them confiscatory rates.[8]

To a certain degree, the use of transporters was a necessary expedient prior to the completion of the route between Harrisburg and Pittsburgh. In 1848, President Merrick acknowledged that "it was the intention of the Company, on the completion of the road, to conduct transportation by their own machinery as much as possible, consistently with the rights reserved to individuals in the charter; but until the road is finished to Pittsburgh arrangements would be made with private individuals engaged in the business to act in concert with them in carrying the trade through."[9]

In the spring of 1849, Thomson, then the chief engineer, worked with principal assistant engineer Herman Haupt to create the PRR's first organization manual. They recommended that the company establish a system of freight agents, but President Merrick overruled that suggestion. He elected to rely on established transporters, with Craig & Bellas (formerly the proprietors of the Citizens Portable Boat Line) handling freight service and the Eagle Line accommodating passengers. Thomson was hardly pleased, but at least he retained the right to specify freight and passenger rates.[10]

Thomson saw the danger that the transporters posed to both efficient operation and profitability, and he continually advocated that they be brought under his managerial control. He had good reason to be concerned, for the transporters soon interfered with the

efficiency of the PRR's operations, particularly on through traffic. Craig & Bellas owned too few freight cars, delaying service. In February 1850 a PRR agent at Elizabethtown, a station on the Harrisburg, Portsmouth, Mount Joy & Lancaster, complained to the board, accusing S. A. Cook, a baggage agent for the Eagle Line, of "neglecting or refusing to deliver the Ledger [of passenger receipts] at that place."[11] Later that year, Thomson insisted that the Philadelphia & Columbia's "present system of Collectors & Conductors [the former employed by transporters, the latter by the state] does not answer a good purpose."[12] In 1852, he complained bitterly about "the want of attention on the part of contractors for transportation of our freight between Lockport and Pittsburgh" and condemned "the utter confusion into which their business had been thrown by allowing their agent at Pittsburgh to receive freight without stint or system."[13] Even after a complete rail line was in place between Philadelphia and Pittsburgh, PRR officials continued to rely on transporters for the two sections of its route that the company did not control—the Philadelphia & Columbia and the Allegheny Portage Railroad.

The independent forwarding companies caused further problems by exposing passengers and train crews to the evils of alcohol. Transporters operated many stations along the route, often leasing a portion of an inn or tavern rather than building a separate structure. By March 1854, PRR regulations prohibited train employees from stopping trains "at any public house or other place where spirituous, vinous or malt liquors are sold or kept as a beverage."[14] That policy in part reflected the growing temperance sentiments of the era of reform that followed the second Great Awakening—Haupt, in particular, took a very dim view of alcohol, although he saw to it that any employee caught drinking on the job would be allowed to take the pledge and not merely fired. The members of the Road Committee nonetheless reported that unless the railroad acquired its own station facilities, it would be difficult to bypass the inns, taverns, and other locations where patrons were accustomed to boarding trains.[15]

To prevent such problems from disrupting the railroad's operations, PRR officials began to evict the transporters from the lines that the PRR owned and operated. One mechanism for doing so was simply to price them out of existence. The PRR's charter set an upper limit on the rates that the railroad charged independent freight forwarders. That ceiling, however, was based on the tariffs that applied to the Main Line of Public Works and not to the vastly more efficient Pennsylvania Railroad. Thomson and his associates could set the forwarders' rates at a level that was within the range allowed by the charter yet were far higher than what the PRR might charge, in order to earn a profit on the same service. In June 1850, in response to a request from the proprietors of Dutilh, Humphreys & Company, the board prepared a toll sheet for the movement of transporters' cars from Philadelphia to Duncansville. The rate schedule was so high that Dutilh and other forwarders balked at the cost and refused to do business with the railroad.

Thomson was also willing to use a carrot as well as a stick, offering to buy out the freight forwarders at a favorable price. In September 1850, the PRR purchased the assets of the Eagle Line, including its lucrative mail contract over the Philadelphia & Columbia. The following spring, the railroad paid $6,700 for the equipment that the Board of Canal Commissioners employed to transport passengers over the Allegheny Portage Railroad. Thereafter, the PRR managed all passenger traffic over the Portage Railroad, paying the commonwealth a dollar for each through passenger in lieu of a wheel toll.[16]

PRR officials did not so much destroy the established freight forwarders, however, as to co-opt them and incorporate their equipment and personnel into the railroad's operations. In August 1850, Craig & Bellas became the PRR's freight agent rather than an independent forwarder.[17] Yet, it was David Leech & Company that ultimately became more closely connected with the PRR's operations. Throughout the 1840s, Leech had been the most important transporter operating over the Main Line of Public Works, in part because the company employed agents at Cincinnati and other points in order to coordinate shipments with Ohio River steamboats. By 1848, Leech was one of the few forwarders to operate express cars on the Philadelphia & Columbia's passenger trains. In March 1850, Leech began offering through passenger and express service between Philadelphia and Pittsburgh, traveling over the PRR for part of the route.

Leech contributed several of its agents to the PRR, individuals who proved exceptionally valuable at managing traffic at critical locations along the railroad. One was future PRR president Thomas A. Scott, who began his career in 1849 as a Leech agent at Columbia. Given his experience in managing the transfer of cargoes from rail to water, he was a natural choice for a similar post at Duncansville. Appointed as an agent in the fall of 1850, he was only at Duncansville a short time before Haupt asked that he be moved to Philadelphia. The board, still dominated by the Merrick/Patterson faction that attempted to control Haupt's authority, blocked that move, but Scott was soon on his way to Pittsburgh as the agent there.

In January 1851, Henry Howard Houston, another Leech employee, became the PRR's freight agent at Philadelphia. Houston, a native of York County, of Irish stock, was distantly related to Sam Houston, well known for his role in the independence of Texas. During his teen years, Henry Houston served as a clerk in a general store in Wrightsville, Pennsylvania, the northern terminus of both the Susquehanna & Tide Water Canal and the Baltimore & Susquehanna Railroad. He amassed a detailed knowledge of transportation costs, as well as the characteristics of a wide variety of products. During the early 1840s, he was involved in iron production, adding to his varied expertise. He joined Leech & Company in 1847.[18]

In 1852, the PRR board expanded the railroad's traffic capabilities by creating the posts of general freight agent and general ticket agent. By December 1852, Houston had been promoted to general freight agent, with supervision over the newly constituted Freight Department. He possessed the authority to set rates, pay damage claims, and operate freight terminals, as well as solicit business. Houston's staff included George C. Franciscus, who had worked for Leech at the Columbia canal basin and at Baltimore before joining the PRR as the freight agent at Pittsburgh. Another Leech veteran, E. J. Sneeder, became the corresponding freight agent at Philadelphia.[19]

As PRR managers took charge of freight and passenger operations on their own lines, they began to purchase the necessary equipment. As early as April

1848, the board ordered seventy-five freight cars and six passenger cars to be operated directly by the railroad. The roster continued to grow in the years that followed, and by the end of 1851 the PRR owned 439 freight cars and 71 passenger cars. Freight equipment included 23 platform (flat) cars, 96 stock cars, and 220 box cars, all of them with four axles apiece, along with 100 of the nearly obsolete two-axle boxcars.[20] The remaining equipment was a varied lot, with passenger cars, emigrant cars, mail cars, and baggage cars scattered between the Eastern Division, the Western Division, the Allegheny Portage Railroad, and the Philadelphia & Columbia. The last of those cars were the only ones that could operate between Philadelphia and Dillerville, owing to the exceptionally narrow spacing between the commonwealth's two tracks.[21]

The additional equipment was of little value, however, without traffic to fill it. During 1851, Haupt's insistence on high volumes and low rates had caused repeated confrontations with President Patterson and his allies on the board. By early 1852, with Thomson ensconced in the president's office, Haupt had much freer rein to develop the PRR's traffic. In May 1852, he began authorizing rate reductions for large freight shipments.

Haupt's cost-accounting expertise had also demonstrated that passenger traffic was roughly twice as profitable as freight, and he did what he could to appeal to the traveling public. In May 1852, probably at Haupt's insistence, the board commissioned a guidebook for travelers featuring evocative pictures of the PRR route—the first of many that would appear over succeeding decades. At a time when most passenger traffic was from west to east, Haupt tried to fill empty westbound seats with immigrants. The only difficulty was that most immigrants arrived in New York, a city that the PRR did not serve, and then proceeded west by either the Erie or the companies that later became the New York Central. Haupt persuaded independent ticket agents in New York to send immigrants south on the Camden & Amboy Rail Road, one of two cooperatively managed lines linking New York to Philadelphia. From there, they would travel west via the Philadelphia & Columbia and the PRR. By July 1852, he had established a PRR ticket office in New York to sell tickets directly to new arrivals.[22]

Despite those innovative marketing efforts, the Board of Canal Commissioners impeded Haupt's efforts to establish greater control over traffic and rates. Haupt had a particularly strong reason to dislike the canal commissioners, given that their predecessors had fired him in 1839 for no reason other than that he owed his job to the rival Anti-Masonic Party. Whether motivated by personal enmity or frustration with the inefficient operations of the Main Line of Public Works, his ongoing communications with state officials were generally more than a little tactless. Haupt's diatribes threatened to undermine the PRR's efforts to cooperate with the canal commissioners regarding the interchange of traffic with the Philadelphia & Columbia and the Allegheny Portage Railroad.[23]

By the summer of 1852, tensions had escalated between PRR officials and the canal commissioners, threatening to undo many of Haupt's efforts to secure additional traffic. In May 1852 the canal commissioners solicited bids for the exclusive right to accommodate passengers traveling over the Philadelphia & Columbia. Haupt had submitted several bids on behalf of the PRR, but each involved setting passenger fares at a level that the canal commissioners considered exorbitant. Instead, the commissioners granted to Bingham & Dock, one of the long-standing transporters operating over the Main Line, the exclusive right to carry passengers via the Philadelphia & Columbia. Even though Bingham & Dock did not initially possess sufficient passenger equipment to operate the service on which they had successfully bid, the canal commissioners were convinced that they were prepared "to afford every possible comfort to passengers." That comfort included what the canal commissioners judged to be "a splendid depot in Philadelphia," at Eighteenth and Market Streets.[24]

Despite the improved facilities offered by Bingham & Dock's Commonwealth Passenger Station, their arrangement with the canal commissioners reeked of nepotism. John Bingham's partner, Jacob Dock, was the uncle of Governor William Bigler, a man who had named one of his sons William Dock Bigler. In 1851, Jacob Dock's brother, William Dock, had been the chairman of the state Democratic convention that had nominated Bigler for governor. Under such circumstances, it was hardly surprising that when Haupt subsequently offered to renegotiate the PRR's bid, the canal commissioners rejected the offer and later denied that Haupt had been willing to discuss amended terms.[25]

The Bingham & Dock monopoly soon placed Haupt and Thomson in a vulnerable position. In the summer of 1852, the Canal Commission refused to accept PRR passenger cars at West Philadelphia, forcing passengers to transfer to those used by Bingham & Dock and essentially rendering valueless the PRR's $20,000 investment in the Eagle Line. Bingham & Dock also refused to sell PRR passenger tickets at its Commonwealth Passenger Station in Philadelphia, forcing through passengers to purchase a second set of tickets at a PRR facility, seven blocks away.

The larger concern that lay at the center of the dispute was the decision of the canal commissioners to discourage passengers who traveled along the Philadelphia & Columbia from transferring to the PRR at Dillerville. Like their counterparts on the PRR and other railroads, the commissioners wished to avoid short-hauling their railroad, by allowing traffic to escape their tolls at Dillerville. Instead, the commissioners intended to carry passengers straight through to Columbia, leaving them to reach PRR tracks at Harrisburg by whatever means they could. That meant a trip north on the Eastern Division Canal or, more likely, along the "River Branch" of the Harrisburg, Portsmouth, Mount Joy & Lancaster, completed in 1850, which connected Columbia with the main line at Royalton.[26]

The extra eleven miles of transportation between Dillerville and Columbia would net the commonwealth an additional twenty-two cents per passenger but caused added inconvenience and expense for any PRR passengers traveling between Philadelphia and western Pennsylvania. However, even though the Bingham & Dock passenger equipment that operated over the Philadelphia & Columbia no longer stopped in Dillerville, there was nothing that the commonwealth could do to prevent passengers from detraining at Lancaster. Accordingly, PRR officials organized an armada of stagecoaches to ferry travelers from Lancaster to the eastern extremity of the Harrisburg, Portsmouth, Mount Joy & Lancaster.

The commonwealth's insistence on ticketing passengers through to Columbia nonetheless threatened

to undo many of Haupt's efforts to solicit additional passenger traffic, particularly with respect to the immigrant trade. The Pennsylvania Railroad could still transport immigrants between Harrisburg and Duncansville, as well as between Johnstown and Pittsburgh, but by the time that the Camden & Amboy, the Philadelphia & Columbia, Bingham & Dock, and the Allegheny Portage Railroad had each taken their cut of the proceeds, the PRR retained only $1.55 of each $5.25 ticket sold.[27]

There followed during the summer of 1852 a series of furious exchanges between PRR officials and the canal commissioners. Thomson attacked the problem on two fronts. He began by playing the political card, writing directly to Governor Bigler to complain of the PRR's unjust treatment. PRR officials also appealed to the public. They were responsible for numerous anonymous letters, printed in Philadelphia newspapers, all of which were highly critical of the canal commissioners. The campaign emphasized that the canal commissioners had not given sufficient public notice of the bidding process, that the Bingham & Dock monopoly was destructive of competition, and that the arrangement would reduce rather than augment the commonwealth's revenues. The PRR's attacks culminated in mid-August, following an emergency meeting of the board of directors. With their blessing, Thomson published a letter "To the People of Pennsylvania," criticizing the commonwealth for its inefficient policies and condescendingly insinuating that the canal commissioners were little short of incompetent.

The canal commissioners defended themselves with considerable vigor, accusing Thomson and Haupt of having treated them "with duplicity and arrogance." Thomson's alleged "duplicity" was in consequence of his demand for access to the Philadelphia & Columbia and the Allegheny Portage Railroad, even as he endeavored to bar independent freight forwarders from the PRR. The "arrogance" was apparently linked to the president's strident criticism of the commonwealth's plans to build a New Portage Railroad without inclined planes and his willingness to build a separate PRR line rather than use the state's new route. Even at that late date, as the PRR was about to bury the Main Line of Public Works once and for all, the commissioners stressed that they did "not view the

Pennsylvania Railroad, if its affairs are managed in a liberal and enlightened spirit, as a rival of the State improvements." They were, however, incensed at the PRR's competitive practices, which meant "that the revenues which should properly be applied to relieve a heavily-burdened tax paying community should go into their own private coffers."[28]

Already facing considerable public criticism for the expense associated with the New Portage Railroad, the canal commissioners soon fell victim to the PRR's onslaught. Even though the state supreme court ruled that the commonwealth possessed the right to exclude the PRR from the Philadelphia & Columbia, by the end of December, the canal commissioners agreed to give the PRR the right of access. During the spring of 1853, Governor Bigler brokered a compromise between the warring parties. Thomson agreed to purchase a half interest in Bingham & Dock in return for a guarantee of half of the profits generated by the transportation of passengers along the Philadelphia & Columbia. As part of the arrangement, PRR passengers were able to use the Bingham & Dock Commonwealth Passenger Station at Eighteenth and Market Streets. More important, the PRR would "have the exclusive and entire control of the line, appointment of all officers &c. without any interference from Bingham & Dock."[29] Finally, on March 3, 1853, the General Assembly issued its approval, decreeing "that the Pennsylvania Railroad Company be, and that they are hereby authorized to run . . . their cars over the railroads belonging to this commonwealth, for the transportation of freight, passengers, their baggage, and the United States mails with the right of attachment to the motive power of the State."[30]

Through Freight Service

The 1852 dispute between the PRR, the canal commissioners, and Bingham & Dock coincided with Thomson's efforts to establish through freight service between Philadelphia and Pittsburgh. With his superb knowledge of rates and operating costs, Haupt probably laid most of the groundwork. However, he resigned his post as general superintendent, effective November 1, 1852, just weeks before construction crews completed the Western Division. Thereafter, Thomson was in charge of the PRR's freight and passenger traffic, but he relied quite heavily on the personnel and facilities provided by the transporters, particularly David Leech & Company and Bingham & Dock. When through freight service began in January 1853, it was the transporters, and not the railroad, who provided most of the necessary organizational capabilities.

Thanks in some measure to the influence of the freight forwarders, the locations of Philadelphia's earliest freight depots changed with dizzying frequency. In 1850, as construction crews were pushing the PRR's tracks westward, the railroad established its first Philadelphia freight service in cooperation with Craig & Bellas and employed that firm's depot at Broad and Cherry Streets. By the spring of 1851, however, Craig & Bellas had left the transportation field, and PRR officials relied principally on Bingham & Dock for freight originating or terminating in Philadelphia. Workers loaded and unloaded cars at the Bingham & Dock freight house at Eighth and Market, ten blocks east of the Bingham & Dock's Commonwealth Passenger Station.

As construction crews completed the PRR's route across Pennsylvania, and as through freight business seemed certain to expand, the directors were less willing to rely on Bingham & Dock's facilities. In May 1852, the Philadelphia, Wilmington & Baltimore Railroad opened a new terminal at Broad and Prime Streets and abandoned service to their old facility at Eleventh and Market, sometimes referred to as the Mansion House. With tracks already in place, the building was certainly adequate for the PRR's freight service. The PRR leased the station and suspended freight operations at the Bingham & Dock building at Eighth and Market. The Bingham & Dock Commonwealth Passenger Station, ten blocks away, continued to host PRR passenger service for another two years.[31]

The Mansion House was barely large enough for the PRR's freight business, and the transfer of passenger service there, as well, would have overwhelmed the small facility. In June 1852, just weeks after leasing the Mansion House, the PRR board laid plans for a new freight terminal in Philadelphia. The directors elected to buy land along the south side of Market Street, between Thirteenth and Juniper, for the new freight de-

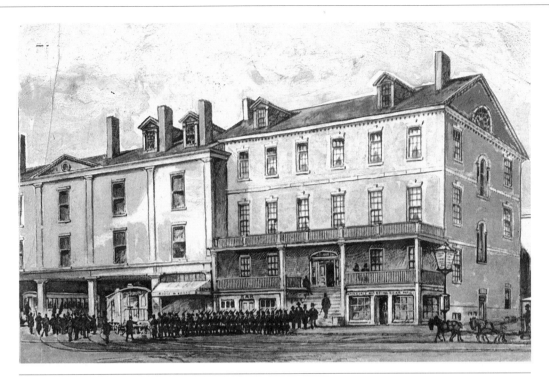

Figure 20. The small building to the left was not the first railway station in Philadelphia, but it was the first that the PRR owned outright. In 1852, the PRR leased the former Philadelphia, Wilmington & Baltimore station (known as the Mansion House) for use as a freight depot, and then bought the property, transferring passenger service there in May 1854. Use of the new facility permitted the abandonment of the former Bingham & Dock freight depot at Eighth and Market as well as the sale of the Commonwealth Passenger Station at Eighteenth and Market to the West Chester & Philadelphia Railroad. In 1853 and 1854, the PRR transferred freight service to a new building, at Thirteenth and Market Streets, but passengers used the Mansion House until 1864. To the right is the Bingham House, named for Philadelphia native and U.S. Senator William Bingham. Around the time of the Civil War, it was extensively remodeled and renamed the United States Hotel.

Temple University Libraries, Urban Archives, Philadelphia.

pot. Service began at that location in April 1853, although the structure was not finished until December of the following year. The gradual shift of freight traffic to the new facility permitted the use of the former PW&B Mansion House station for passengers. Beginning in May 1854, and for the next ten years, travelers bound for Harrisburg and points west boarded the cars at the Mansion House, at Eleventh and Market. By 1860, the PRR had expanded the freight house at Thirteenth and Market to encompass more than ninety thousand square feet. Horses drew loaded cars east on Market Street and south on Broad before turning east again to reach a freight platform adjacent to Kelley Street. Once unloaded, the cars

spun ninety degrees on a small turntable, ready to be loaded on platforms, parallel to Broad Street, before heading back west along Market.[32]

The completion of the PRR's Philadelphia freight station did not by any means relieve Thomson from the influence of the freight forwarders. The key personnel, equipment, and operating methods were essentially passed down, largely intact, into the railroad's operations. Furthermore, even though Thomson had internalized traffic solicitation and billing functions on the PRR itself, the independent transporters retained their influence to the east of Philadelphia and to the west of Pittsburgh. PRR managers initially had little interest in developing traffic capabilities beyond

Figure 21. During the earliest years of its operation, the PRR had relied on Philadelphia freight facilities maintained by the transporters Bingham & Dock, and later leased a depot vacated by the Philadelphia, Wilmington & Baltimore. In anticipation of through freight service between Philadelphia and Pittsburgh, which began on January 1, 1853, the PRR board elected to build an entirely new freight station, at the corner of Market and Thirteenth Streets. The first part of the building entered service in April 1853, and the remainder of the structure was completed in December 1854. The PRR used the facility until 1874, and shortly afterward it became the home of John Wanamaker's first department store.

Temple University Libraries, Urban Archives, Philadelphia, Pennsylvania.

the geographic limits of their company. Instead, they elected to retain control of the movement of freight on their own lines, while permitting closely affiliated firms to manage shipments that entered or left the PRR system.

Since about 1850, the Pennsylvania & Ohio Transportation Company (also known as Clarke & Thaw and as Lewis & Butler, or simply as Clarke & Company) had taken responsibility for PRR shipments that connected with Ohio River steamboats at Pittsburgh. Established in 1843, under the direction of Thomas S. Clarke and his brother-in-law William Thaw, the Pennsylvania & Ohio line was one of the largest shipping firms on the western rivers, with steamboat service to Cincinnati, Louisville, St. Louis, and New Orleans.[33] A competing firm, David Leech & Com-

pany (sometimes operating as the Western Transportation Company or as Harris & Leech), had performed a similar function east, north, and south of Philadelphia.[34] During 1853, the principals of both firms had attempted to secure preferential rates on the PRR, but the board had refused. Finally, in May 1855, Clarke and Thaw dissolved the Pennsylvania & Ohio company, selling off the Ohio River steamboat operations and indicating their willingness to sell their equipment and operations east of Pittsburgh to the PRR.

The sale caused a rapid realignment of the various partnerships and overcame the enmity between Leech and the Clarke/Thaw interests. Within weeks after selling their assets, David Leech oversaw the reconstitution of Leech & Company, with the sole right to solicit business on traffic bound for all points east of

Philadelphia and west of Pittsburgh.[35] Clarke joined forces with Leech, and with two secondary partnerships, Leech & Harris and Black & Clarke, establishing offices at the railroad's termini, the first in Philadelphia and the second in Pittsburgh. Under the new system, Leech & Company employees solicited business for the railroad, offering whatever rate necessary to attract business. That rate, however, could not be lower than a floor specified by the PRR's general freight agent—who, it should be noted, was Henry Houston, a former employee of David Leech & Company. Leech took a percentage of the tariff as a fee for his services, and the freight then traveled in PRR equipment, under the supervision of PRR employees. In return, the transporters received commissions ranging from 6 to 10 percent of the rate. The resulting profits were split six ways, with one share to each of the four partners, and the remaining third set aside for the PRR. By 1856, George Black had withdrawn from the Black & Clarke partnership. In his place was William Thaw, who would soon play an important role in Thomson's efforts to expand the PRR's influence into Ohio and Indiana.[36]

In May 1857, the Road Committee of the board of directors instructed Henry Houston, the general freight agent, to perform a cost-benefit analysis to determine whether the company should retain its association with Leech & Company, or whether it should employ independent agents for the solicitation of off-line freight. In August 1857, based on Houston's recommendations, the PRR retained the basic outlines of its western freight operations but reorganized the partnerships, with westbound freight assigned to William F. Leech and George W. Harris, of Leech & Company, and eastbound traffic under the control of William Thaw, Thomas S. Clarke, and Charles J. Clarke of the newly constituted firm of Clarke & Company.[37]

The firm of Bingham & Dock likewise continued to influence the PRR, albeit in a much-modified form. John Bingham and Jacob Dock had obtained exceedingly favorable terms for their capitulation to the Pennsylvania Railroad. Jacob Dock used his share of the proceeds to ensure a comfortable retirement, with no further connection to the transportation of people or property. After taking a brief hiatus from the trans-portation business, John Bingham in 1859 became the superintendent of the Adams Express Company, a firm that had developed close ties to the Pennsylvania Railroad.[38]

Adams Express dated to 1839, when Boston merchant Alvin Adams launched a package-delivery service, Adams & Company. The business thrived, soon expanding to include New York and Philadelphia, and eventually as far west as California. In some respects, Adams offered similar services to the transporters that operated over the Main Line of Public Works and the Pennsylvania Railroad, in that he accepted responsibility for shipments and then forwarded them to their destinations over transportation routes that he did not own. The forwarders, however, operated their own equipment and often handled shipments in bulk, much like a modern trucking company. Adams concentrated on letters and smaller, high-value packages, a system similar to that developed by United Parcel Service and FedEx, late in the twentieth century.[39]

By the early 1850s, Adams was offering service between Philadelphia and the west, over the Main Line of Public Works and, west of Pittsburgh, in conjunction with an enterprising steamboat and stage operator, George Washington Cass. In the spring of 1851, with the completion of the PRR's original main line imminent, Adams officials made plain their desire to shift their business to the new route. The PRR Road Committee approved a contract to carry express shipments on passenger trains in return for 40 percent of gross receipts. In exchange, Adams received a monopoly on the express business over the PRR, one that it retained for many decades. By October 1851, with the main line still incomplete and stages required for part of the journey, Adams was advertising thirty-eight-hour service to Pittsburgh. Packages were guaranteed to reach Cincinnati in three and a half days, Louisville in four, and St. Louis in seven.

The links between Adams and the PRR increased in 1854, when the original Adams & Company partnership became a joint-stock company. Among the incorporators were John Bingham and George Cass, who became a key figure in Thomson's efforts to extend PRR tracks into Ohio and Indiana. In order to secure the continued cooperation of PRR executives, Adams officials provided them with large blocks of the company's stock, either for free or at a steeply discounted price. As Pennsylvania Railroad executives extended their network throughout the Northeast and Midwest, Adams Express expanded right along with it. Adams profited handsomely from its PRR monopoly and reinvested its profits in the railroad that nurtured it. In addition, PRR managers frequently tapped Adams Express as a source for additional capital, and by the beginning of the twentieth century, Adams was the PRR's second-largest shareholder.[40]

Refining the Organization

Over its 122-year history, the organizational structure of the Pennsylvania Railroad exhibited a remarkable degree of fluidity. The process of developing that structure began in 1847 and continued with the modifications that Herman Haupt developed two years later. There were major reorganizations in 1852, 1858, 1863, 1873–74, 1881, 1920, and 1955, along with numerous other smaller changes. There was never one best system of management practices, but rather an ongoing series of experimentations and adjustments.

Two major factors stimulated the recurring changes in the PRR's organization. First, the construction or acquisition of new lines, changing traffic patterns, and the general growth in business challenged existing organizational methods. Altered conditions, external to the firm, gave PRR officials a powerful incentive to modify the railroad's organization. Economic recessions, such as those that began in 1857 and 1873, increased the need for efficiency and heightened competition with rival carriers. Ultimately, the PRR, like most other corporations, adapted its corporate structure to suit its business strategy—a process that was continually influenced by the actions of shippers, passengers, competing railroads, and local, state, and national governments.[41]

Yet, the PRR was more than a bureaucratic organization. It was, like all bureaucracies, composed of people who did not readily conform to predetermined slots on an organization chart. Therefore, PRR officials adapted the corporate structure to suit its personnel, creating and eliminating offices, reassigning responsibilities, and altering chains of command in order to match the orga-

nizational framework to individual talents and abilities.[42] In his lengthy, unpublished history of the PRR, corporate insider J. Elfreth Watkins emphasized, "Modifications of the organization caused by the death or resignation of an officer occupying a place of great responsibility has [sic] been somewhat different from that pursued by other corporations, inasmuch as it has been found to be good policy to make the organization fit the special abilities of the *personnel* of the available administrative staff, which is always possible, rather than to select new men to perform certain duties strictly specified, which latter method is oft-times found impracticable."[43] In other words, as Watkins explained, "The organization has been so modified that the valued services of the men advanced in position should be retained in the particular fields for which they have become specially fitted by extended service or inherent ability."[44]

On November 1, 1852, the PRR temporarily lost the valued services of one of the men advanced in position when Haupt resigned as general superintendent to take a job as the chief engineer of the Southern Railroad of Mississippi. His assistant, Herman J. Lombaert, who had been serving since July as superintendent of transportation, took his place. Haupt had been badly bruised by the fight for the presidency, and he probably sensed that even the dissident directors who had supported Thomson were far less entranced with his own role in the PRR. Furthermore, with the PRR's operating structure and accounting methods already reasonably well established, Haupt may have relished the opportunities associated with building a new railroad. As early as January 1852, with the outcome of the battle for the presidency still in doubt, Haupt had informed the PRR's stockholders, "The drudgery is to a great extent now over; the task of organization has been performed; the numerous parts which constitute the complicated mechanism of a railway system have been brought into harmonious action; a complete code of regulations, applicable to almost every possible contingence, has been established; subordinates, who entered the service of the Company without experience, are now competent and efficient officers; every wheel in the machine is now in order. The work of the pioneer is now over. My successor will find the highway prepared for him."[45] Eight months later, in his letter of resignation to his friend, ally, and now president, Haupt nonetheless stated that he had delayed his departure because "no other officer was familiar with the details of the business of the road, and I could not then withdraw without causing difficulties which I felt it my duty to avoid. . . . The time has now arrived when I can retire from the management of the road with less embarrassment to its operations than at any previous period."[46] In that sense, the PRR's 1852 organization manual might well have represented the distillation of Haupt's methods, codified for his successor. Yet it was Lombaert who implemented one of the more significant changes in the corporate structure.[47]

On December 1, the same day that the PRR first offered all-rail passenger and mail service across the breadth of Pennsylvania, the new organizational structure took effect, with Thomson becoming the railroad's chief executive officer as well as its president. The chief engineer and the superintendent of transportation, the individuals who were ultimately responsible for construction and operation, respectively, reported directly to him, rather than to the board of directors.[48] In his history of the Pennsylvania Railroad, William Bender Wilson suggested, "When the engineering difficulties which surrounded the physical features of the road ceased to be problems, and had been practically overcome, Mr. John Edgar Thomson, the Chief Engineer, whose genius had produced the result, leaving the field, took the Presidential chair for the purpose of organizing the financial, commercial and transportation features of the line."[49] In other words, Thomson elected to concentrate on matters of corporate policy and long-term strategy, leaving routine operational matters in the hands of others.

The December 1852 reorganization reflected the current best practices in railroad operations. In particular, it mimicked the February 1852 organization manual of the New York & Erie, but it also reflected the concepts that Thomson, Haupt, and others had developed since 1849. The new system established four departments—Treasury, Auditor's, Construction, and Transportation—but it retained the basic subdivision, established in May 1851, between the First Department, affecting people, plant, and equipment, and the Second Department, in charge of money. The Treasury Department (in effect the re-

named Second Department) handled all external financial transactions, including freight and passenger receipts, the payment of invoices, and the disbursement of dividends and interest on the PRR's outstanding stocks and bonds.[50]

The Auditor's Department did not come from the Second Department. Instead, it embodied the oversight functions that had been a part of the Operating Department since 1849. Personnel within the Auditor's Department (renamed the Accounting Department at the beginning of 1858) processed real-estate transactions and oversaw internal financial matters, transferring funds from one unit of the company to another and auditing the records provided by the Treasury Department. Cost accounting, which determined the expenses associated with the various classes of transportation, remained under the control of the personnel in the Transportation Department. Because cost accounting measured the efficiency of day-to-day operation and provided senior managers with the information that they needed in order to make long-term strategic decisions, it was logically separate from both the Financial Department and the Auditor's Department, units that processed routine transactions that were not directly connected with operations. The position of auditor went to William B. Foster, Jr., who in earlier years had begun engineering work on the Eastern Division, even before Thomson had arrived from Georgia. With the completion of the line from Harrisburg to Duncansville, Foster had left the PRR for a job as principal engineer on the North Branch Extension Canal. Although Foster possessed little knowledge of accounting practices, the former canal commissioner was a highly competent individual with impeccable political connections. Thomson accordingly brought him back into the PRR family—and into his own family, as the PRR president had married Lavinia Francis Smith, Foster's sister-in-law.[51]

A far more significant change reflected the complexity associated with building and operating a railroad that stretched between Pittsburgh and Harrisburg, with connections to Philadelphia. In dissolving the First Department, the board created two distinct functions, one associated with new work and the other with routine operations. The engineer corps became the Construction Department, a system-wide office responsible for new projects, under the direction of chief engineer Edward Miller.

The more important unit was the Transportation Department (the former Operating Department), responsible for the movement of trains and other routine matters. The board promoted Herman Lombaert from superintendent of transportation to superintendent (the title "general superintendent" was temporarily discontinued, and not resurrected until 1858). As president, Thomson was the head of the Transportation Department, but Superintendent Lombaert was the chief operating officer and the top middle manager, exercising responsibility over day-to-day operations. The board moved Lombaert and the headquarters of the Transportation Department from Harrisburg to Altoona, to be closer to the center of the PRR's operations and to facilitate both the interaction with the Allegheny Portage Railroad and, with the pending completion of the PRR's route, the helper operations necessary to lift trains over the summit.[52]

The Transportation Department was in turn geographically subdivided into three operating segments: the Eastern Division, between Dillerville and Mifflin; the still-incomplete Middle Division, between Mifflin and Conemaugh; and the Western Division, linking Conemaugh and Pittsburgh. They were not true operating divisions in the manner that would soon become commonplace in the railroad business. Instead, they were the legacy of the construction divisions that dated to the formation of the PRR.

Lombaert oversaw four assistant superintendents, whose status varied according to their abilities and the PRR's needs. The first assistant superintendent was in charge of the Maintenance of Way Department, along the portion of the PRR that lay to the east of the junction with the Allegheny Portage Railroad at Duncansville. Also classified as the resident engineer, his office was in Altoona. The second assistant superintendent, also based in Altoona, oversaw the Motive Power Department, including the cars, locomotives, and shop facilities, and would serve as acting superintendent in the event that Lombaert were unavailable. From his office in Pittsburgh, the third assistant superintendent controlled operations on the Western Division and the Allegheny Portage Railroad, as well as the company's affairs in Pittsburgh. The fourth assistant superin-

tendent, stationed at Harrisburg, held authority over the Harrisburg, Portsmouth, Mount Joy & Lancaster, the portion of the Eastern Division that lay east of the state capital. His responsibilities included supervision of the interchange traffic with the Philadelphia & Columbia, and he additionally acted as a sort of troubleshooter and ad hoc transportation coordinator who could tackle problems on an as-needed basis.[53]

To the untrained observer, the four assistant superintendents represented a strange admixture of geographic and functional responsibilities. The structure nonetheless reflected the ongoing construction taking place west of Altoona, as well as the continued reliance on both the Allegheny Portage Railroad and the Philadelphia & Columbia. The first assistant superintendent controlled maintenance, but not new construction on the westernmost portion of the line. The third and fourth assistants oversaw critical transfer points. The only assistant superintendent who possessed authority over the entire railroad was the one in charge of equipment, which he could allocate to various locations as needed. As such, he was the logical choice to fill the role of acting superintendent. Finally, it should be emphasized that the numerical designations reflected seniority, and had nothing to do with the relative importance of each position. They were staff offices, reporting only to Lombaert, the president, and the board of directors, and none of the assistant superintendents possessed any direct supervisory authority over the others. The first assistant superintendent was simply the first of the four assistant superintendents who had found employment with the Pennsylvania Railroad.

Most significantly, Thomson and the board followed the long-standing PRR policy of tailoring the duties of the assistant superintendents to suit the temperaments and abilities of the individuals who filled each office. First assistant superintendent George R. Mowry was well suited to oversee the maintenance of the PRR's physical plant east of Duncansville, inasmuch as he had helped to build much of it. He had already acquired a reputation as a hydrological engineer, and in 1845, at the request of Illinois governor Thomas Ford and Secretary of the Navy George Bancroft, he had worked to improve navigation along the Illinois River. Beginning in 1847, Mowry had served as an as-

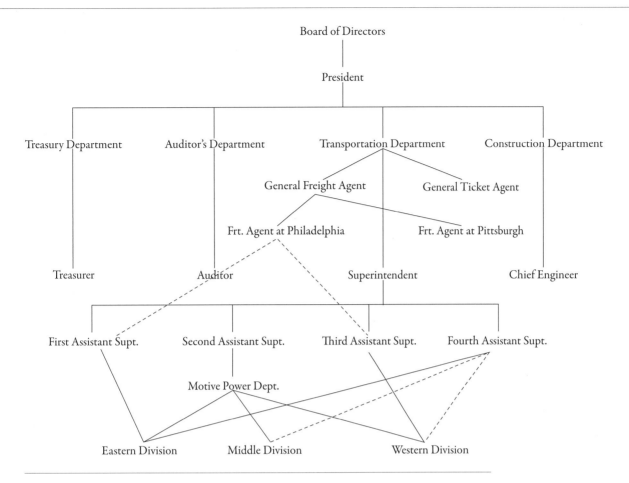

Figure 22. On December 1, 1852, the Pennsylvania Railroad unveiled a new corporate organization, in conjunction with the initiation of all-rail service between Philadelphia and Pittsburgh. The new structure also reflected the unique requirements caused by reliance on both the Philadelphia & Columbia Railroad and the Allegheny Portage Railroad. As president, J. Edgar Thomson held control over the PRR's transportation and traffic functions, assisted by staff officers. The four principal departments were Treasury, Auditor's, Construction, and Transportation, with the division between the first two and the last two reflecting a modification of the 1851 organizational division between the units responsible for managing money and for overseeing people and property. The Transportation Department, under superintendent Herman Lombaert, was the most significant of the four. Lombaert oversaw four assistant superintendents, whose duties varied both functionally and geographically. That odd mix was quite different from earlier organizational models on other railways, such as the Western Railroad of Massachusetts. Traffic functions were the responsibility of the general ticket agent and the general freight agent, and his deputies at Philadelphia and Pittsburgh. They were within the Transportation Department, subordinate to Lombaert and ultimately to Thomson.

sistant engineer on the Pennsylvania Railroad's Eastern Division. He later surveyed the community of Mifflin, in Juniata County, and considered locating the PRR's shop facilities there.[54]

Even at the age of thirty-two, Second Assistant Superintendent Enoch Lewis had already acquired a reputation as a highly skilled master mechanic. In 1835, as a bored Philadelphia office boy, he had been staring aimlessly out of a window. He caught sight of a locomotive, built by Matthias Baldwin and destined for the Philadelphia & Germantown Railroad, being skidded along the street. Entranced, he soon obtained an apprenticeship at the Garrett & Eastwick machine shop (later the locomotive builders Eastwick & Harrison), where he learned the crafts of mechanical engineering and locomotive design. In 1844, he traveled to Russia and spent nearly two years supervising a machine shop on the railroad linking St. Petersburg and Moscow—a project on which Major George W. Whistler, a veteran of the Western Railroad of Massachusetts, served as a consulting engineer. After his return to the United States, Lewis worked at machine shops in New Jersey and Massachusetts. In the autumn of 1850, he became the second of the four future assistant superintendents to join the PRR, obtaining work in the Mifflin shops. He was there barely a year before Lombaert noticed his ability and plucked him as his assistant. With the implementation of the December 1852 organization, Lombaert and Lewis moved from Harrisburg to Altoona and continued their earlier practice of sharing an office. In keeping with their close association, it was Lewis, and not the first assistant superintendent, who took control of the Transportation Department in Lombaert's absence.[55]

The third assistant superintendent, still young and inexperienced, was destined to make an imprint on the Pennsylvania Railroad almost as great as that of Thomson himself. Thomas Alexander Scott was born on December 28, 1824, in Loudon, a small town near Chambersburg, in south-central Pennsylvania. He was the son of a tavern owner, and Scots-Irish as well, in both respects worlds away from the genteel Quakers who dominated commercial affairs in Philadelphia. In 1835 his father died, and the tragedy did not bode well for the young boy's future. Tom Scott was nonetheless blessed with a fortuitous family connection. His older sister's husband, Major James Patton, was the toll collector for the Main Line of Public Works at Columbia, where the Philadelphia & Columbia Railroad met the Pennsylvania Canal. In 1841, Patton took on Scott as his personal assistant, and the young man was soon busy learning the intricacies of freight transfer between railroad cars and canal boats, at one of the most congested locations on the entire state system. The wheel of patronage turned against him, and he soon lost his position. Yet he was not totally isolated from the commonwealth's largess, as he soon found a partner and established a sawmill at Columbia, supplying the state system with lumber. In July 1844, the Canal Commission appointed Scott the inspector of cargoes at Columbia. By the spring of 1847, he was an assistant to the collector of tolls at West Philadelphia. In 1849 he found employment with the independent transporter David Leech & Company as their agent at Columbia.[56]

Scott's service with Leech & Company soon vaulted him into the highest ranks of the Pennsylvania Railroad. By 1850, Haupt was desperate for talented individuals to manage the PRR's operations, and he listened attentively when independent contractor John Ott Rockafeller spoke highly of Scott. Haupt recommended Scott as the station agent at Duncansville, the critically important point of interchange between the PRR and the eastern end of the Allegheny Portage Railroad. The board approved the appointment that November. By January 1851, Haupt had moved Scott to Pittsburgh. In 1853, frustrated at slow communication with the east, Scott worked to implement telegraphic train dispatching, poaching talented young operators, including Andrew Carnegie, from the Atlantic & Ohio Telegraph Company. From there, Scott rose swiftly up the corporate hierarchy, thanks in large measure to his intelligence, his affable personality, and his considerable political skills.

As third assistant superintendent in charge of the Western Division at Pittsburgh, Scott was responsible for coordinating transportation over the unfinished Western Division, with freight dodging construction trains and riding in wagons for part of the journey. However, Scott's duties in Pittsburgh were as much political as organizational. He was by all accounts an extraordinarily personable and charismatic individual who could charm many of his opponents into submission. Scott worked assiduously to soothe the tempers of local residents, still angry that the PRR had blocked the construction of the Pittsburgh & Connellsville (B&O) into their city. Scott also helped to placate Pittsburgh commercial interests by offering rapid service to the east, as well as fares that were competitive with those of the Main Line of Public Works.[57]

General Augustus Louis Roumfort had perhaps the most varied career of the PRR's early management corps, and he was ideally suited for his responsibilities as fourth assistant superintendent. He was born in

France, emigrated to the United States, and graduated from West Point in 1817, just before the arrival of superintendent Sylvanus Thayer. After resigning his commission as a Navy lieutenant, Roumfort was the director of the Mount Airy Academy near Philadelphia, military storekeeper at Philadelphia, a member of the Pennsylvania legislature, and a general in the state militia. In 1846, Governor Shunk appointed him harbormaster at Philadelphia, and in 1849 Roumfort became the superintendent of motive power on the Philadelphia & Columbia. He joined the PRR in 1852, the beneficiary of a wealth of military, political, and business experience.[58]

As a West Point graduate, Roumfort employed his military experience on the PRR. He probably had little effect on the railroad's managerial practices, both because he had received his training before the revolutionary changes that had transformed the Military Academy and because, by the time he joined the PRR, Haupt and Thomson had already established the basis of the PRR's organization. Instead, Roumfort applied the no-nonsense discipline that he had mastered in the military to the railroad's day-to-day operations.

Roumfort's most immediate concern upon taking office was to arrange for the efficient transportation of what PRR personnel euphemistically referred to as "baggage." In addition to suitcases and steamer trunks, that baggage included all of the possessions and purchases of the river boatmen who had come down the Susquehanna and its tributaries, and who then used the railroad and the canals to return home. Confronted with piles of cargo belonging to what PRR officials considered to be a surly lot of ignorant and often drunken rustics, Roumfort was ideally suited to restore a semblance of order. A great bear of a man, six feet tall and massively built, Roumfort soon imposed military discipline on employees and passengers alike. "His very appearance commanded respect and demanded obedience," PRR historian William Bender Wilson noted, "and he got it."[59]

Roumfort was also the first manager to demand that employees adhere to professional standards, particularly when they interacted with the public. He required passenger service employees to wear uniforms—for conductors, black pants, a tan vest, and a blue coat with brass buttons, and for brakemen, a solid gray suit. Train crews hated the new military-style clothing and likewise despised Roumfort's habit of sitting on a porch on the second story of the PRR station in Harrisburg, scrutinizing every move his employees made. Nevertheless, as one excessively laudatory chronicler later suggested, Roumfort was the ideal "choice of a man to establish that discipline and esprit de corps for which the Pennsylvania Company is so famous that to this day it is held up as the apotheosis of all that is desirable in a railroad staff."[60]

The PRR's 1852 organization represented a hybrid between older (1849 and 1851) models and what would become the characteristic line-and-staff management structure of the railroads. The assistant superintendents were assigned to several different locations, and they had responsibilities that varied geographically as well as functionally. They operated in an advisory capacity to the superintendent (one of the characteristics of staff officers), yet also stood near the top of the downward line of authority in the Transportation Department. The central office staff in Philadelphia, such as it was, consisted of the secretary, treasurer, auditor, general freight agent, and general ticket (that is, passenger) agent, all of whom reported to the president and the general superintendent.[61]

The number of staff officers increased in 1853, as Thomson began to extend the PRR's influence into Ohio, and as the board authorized the construction of branch lines in Pennsylvania. In March 1853, the Pennsylvania legislature amended the PRR's corporate charter, permitting the company to invest in other railroads. The supplement also gave the railroad the right to appoint a vice president, who would undertake whatever tasks were needed to relieve the president's workload. In May, William B. Foster, Jr., became vice president and, like Thomson, took a seat on the board of directors. Haupt returned to the PRR in April 1853 as chief engineer, responsible for new construction projects throughout the system. He was particularly well equipped to evaluate possible PRR alliances in the west.

The completion of major construction work on the PRR's route over the Alleghenies in February 1854 caused the board to create the post of fifth assistant superintendent (Thomas W. Seabrook), who oversaw maintenance-of-way functions west of Altoona. The

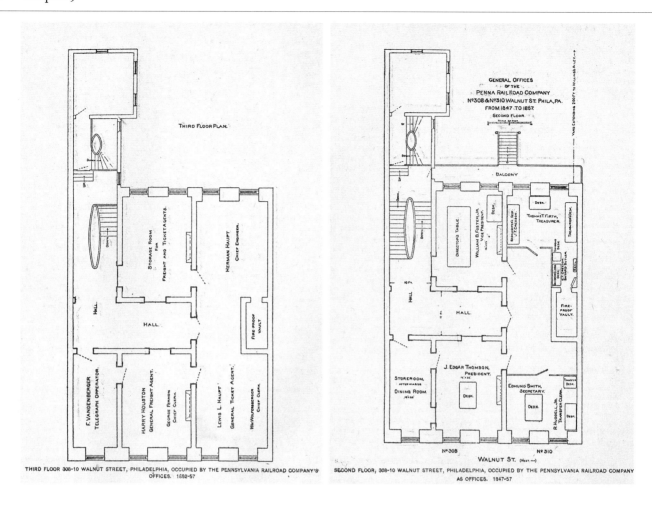

THIRD FLOOR 308-10 WALNUT STREET, PHILADELPHIA, OCCUPIED BY THE PENNSYLVANIA RAILROAD COMPANY'S OFFICES. 1852-57

SECOND FLOOR, 308-10 WALNUT STREET, PHILADELPHIA, OCCUPIED BY THE PENNSYLVANIA RAILROAD COMPANY AS OFFICES. 1847-57

Figure 23. In May 1847, the management of the Pennsylvania Railroad moved into offices on the second floor of the American Fire Insurance Building, at 308–10 Walnut Street. Five years later, not long after J. Edgar Thomson became president, the PRR leased the third floor of the building as well. These plan views must date to the period after May 1853, when William B. Foster, Jr., became the company's first vice president, and before July 1855, when Herman Haupt resigned the post of chief engineer. PRR officials were able to receive and transmit information on a moment's notice—note the office of telegraph operator F. Vandenberger on the third floor—but the PRR did not complete its own telegraph line between Philadelphia and Harrisburg until April 1856. Yet, most routine operating decisions were made by local operating personnel, and the central office was accordingly quite small. The second floor housed President Thomson, secretary Edmund Smith, Vice President Foster (whose desk was in the boardroom), treasurer Thomas T. Firth, a bookkeeper, and two clerks. On the floor above resided Chief Engineer Haupt, along with his brother Lewis (who was the general ticket agent), a clerk, the telegraph operator, and general freight agent Henry H. Houston and his clerk, George W. Fernon. In September 1857, the PRR moved to new office facilities at 238–40 South Third Street.

From J. Elfreth Watkins, Pennsylvania Railroad Company, 1846–1896, in its Relation to the Pennsylvania State Canals and Railroads and the Consolidated System East and West of Pittsburgh, *"The Administration of Samuel V. Merrick," 245, Courtesy of the Pennsylvania Historical and Museum Commission, Railroad Museum of Pennsylvania.*

growing importance of through freight and passenger service between Philadelphia and Pittsburgh justified an expansion of the PRR's legal staff. Prior to January 1854, the PRR had kept legal counsel on retainer, beginning with Thomas Cope's brother-in-law, Job R. Tyson. After that time, however, the directors appointed a solicitor at Pittsburgh and, beginning in September 1854, another solicitor at Harrisburg, in close proximity to the capitol.[62]

A New Route over the Mountain

As chief engineer, Thomson had employed the existing Allegheny Portage Railroad as a temporary expedient in order to reduce costs and speed the completion of an all-rail route across Pennsylvania. PRR equipment used the commonwealth's route between Duncansville and the Big Viaduct over the Little Conemaugh River, east of Johnstown. Thomson nonetheless shared the concern of the PRR's directors, who suspected that the Portage Railroad would be inadequate for the task. Accordingly, on September 29, 1847, the directors resolved "to address a letter to the Board of Canal Commissioners, urging the necessity of taking measures to put the Portage Road in a condition to receive the trade of the Penna. Rail Road."[63]

By the spring of 1850, as the PRR's route to Duncansville was nearing completion, Thomson became increasingly concerned that the Board of Canal Commissioners had allowed the line to become unsafe, as well as inefficient. In April, he provided an explanation for "the many complaints which have been made against the management of our road," emphasizing that "the difficulty lies on each side of us [on the Portage Railroad and the Philadelphia & Columbia] and can only be remedied by Legislative action."[64] At the end of May, the directors noted that "Mr. T. calls the attention of the Board to the matter of running our Cars over the State Road & thinks it requires early attention"—in part because the cables and hoisting machinery were so worn, and in part because the track gauge had spread to such an alarming extent that it was quite possible that PRR cars might simply fall between the rails.[65]

The PRR reached Duncansville in September 1850, and subsequent events soon proved Thomson's worst

fears correct. The increased traffic taxed the decrepit Portage Railroad to its limit, especially when Thomson demanded that the planes operate until midnight in order to clear the traffic backlog. The extra work displeased the state patronage employees, who suspected that the PRR would soon put them out of a job. It was hardly surprising, therefore, that Haupt complained to the PRR directors, regarding "sundry petty annoyances from Agents on state road and that sundry fines had been put upon us for various alleged offences & violation of their numerous rules."[66]

In October 1850, the canal commissioners suspended nighttime operations over the Allegheny Portage Railroad, requiring PRR cars to arrive in Duncansville before 5:00 P.M. Inasmuch as it took at least ten hours to travel from Philadelphia to Duncansville, the commonwealth's restrictions forced through trains to leave Philadelphia in the wee hours of the morning. Even then, many passengers suffered considerable delays. During 1851 the PRR built a hotel, the Mountain House, at Duncansville in order to accommodate the hundreds of travelers who were often stranded for the night. Thomson was also exasperated that the Portage Railroad suspended operations on December 1, coincident with the seasonal closing of the Main Line canals. He insisted that the planes operate year round in order to accommodate PRR traffic. The canal commissioners refused Thomson's request in 1850, but relented the following year—while increasing tolls by a third.[67]

The conflict between the two railroads also revealed profound differences in their operating methods. The commonwealth had gone to considerable expense to construct both the Portage Railroad and the Philadelphia & Columbia with two tracks, facilitating operations by ensuring that each track carried trains in only one direction. The commonwealth's operating methods were correspondingly informal, haphazard, and inefficient. As the managers of a private corporation answerable to its investors, PRR executives initially sought to minimize costs by building a single track, with strict operating rules to govern the resulting bidirectional traffic. In a scathing letter, Thomson reminded William S. Campbell, the superintendent of the Portage Railroad, "That we have a single track and must run one way at least to schedule or we would delay all of the trains on the road, so as to cause indescribable confusion." Thomson also emphasized that problems on either the Portage Railroad or the Philadelphia & Columbia would "derange all our trains" by rendering their schedules meaningless.[68]

By December 1850, both Thomson and the directors agreed that the PRR would need to complete its own route across the Appalachians as quickly as possible. "Experience has made it evident that the existing Rail Road over the Allegheny Mountains will soon be inadequate to the transmission of all freight and passengers that may be expected from the State Canal & the Pennsylvania Rail Road," the directors noted, "and that the delays incident to that road render the immediate substitution of a line without inclined planes of the 1ust [first] importance to the trade of Pennsylvania & necessary to enable us to compete on equal footing with rival public improvements."[69]

That December, at Samuel Merrick's suggestion, PRR officials offered to cooperate with the Board of Canal Commissioners in order to construct a single, shared line across the summit. Under Merrick's proposal, the legislature would purchase forty thousand shares of PRR stock, the proceeds from which would "be applied immediately and exclusively to the construction of a double track rail road on the best practicable grades" between Hollidaysburg and Johnstown.[70] In April 1852, Thomson, as the newly elected president, made another, similar offer to the Board of Canal Commissioners. Should the state be willing to abandon the Portage Railroad, its traffic could travel on PRR's new route in exchange for discounted rates for PRR traffic on the Philadelphia & Columbia. The canal commissioners pointed out that Thomson was proposing something of a double standard, as they considered the rates that the PRR would pay on the Philadelphia & Columbia to be far too low, and the charges that the PRR would levy on its new route to the west far too high. Even worse, they argued, if Thomson had his way, "the main line of our improvements would thus be severed into two grand divisions, and the intermediate link be placed in the hands of a company owning a rival improvement."[71] The canal commissioners had little interest in assisting the PRR under those terms. In a desperate attempt to maintain the viability of the Main Line of Public Works, they had already decided to build a second Portage Railroad over the Allegheny Mountains.

A New Route over the Mountain, Times Two

The early years of the 1850s witnessed a remarkable surge of activity in the mountains east of Johnstown, as surveyors and construction crews raced to build two new rail routes across the spine of the Alleghenies. Some worked for the Pennsylvania Railroad, endeavoring to give that company control of the entire distance between Harrisburg and Pittsburgh, free of the inefficiencies associated with the Allegheny Portage Railroad. The others took their orders from the canal commissioners, who were desperately trying to preserve the viability of the Main Line of Public Works against the onslaught of rail competition. The Allegheny Portage Railroad, they knew, had always constituted a weak link in the system. If they could replace the inclined planes with a line constructed to modern engineering standards, then they might be able to save the state-funded system of internal improvements.

The Pennsylvania Railroad struck first, as company engineers and carefully selected contractors chose the best workers. During the summer of 1849, surveyors located the route between Altoona and Gallitzin. The initial surveys provided for westbound grades of 1.74 percent, but at the expense of a 3,750-foot tunnel at the summit. In 1850, Thomson ordered a new set of surveys, which he hoped would reduce the amount of tunneling that would be necessary. He got his wish, but only by allowing the maximum grade to increase to 1.8 percent.[72] That was not a trivial change, but it would likely have little effect on operations given that the predominant direction of traffic would be eastbound. Furthermore, Thomson wisely followed the practice of other railroads and reduced grades on curves to a much more modest 1.55 percent. Aside from that compensation, Thomson provided a steady westbound grade to the summit. He thus avoided the undulating profiles common to other mountain railroads that caused severe operating difficulties.[73]

In June 1850, the PRR board approved the construction contracts for the first segment of the former Middle Division, referred to for construction purposes as the Mountain Division. Over the next eighteen months, the board was embroiled in conflict, as the directors debated the speed with which construction should take place and whether or not the com-

Figure 24. One of the earliest known views of the Horseshoe Curve, probably recorded during the 1870s. From Altoona, trains bound for Pittsburgh ascended along the north bank of Burgoon Run, traveling west and slightly to the north, in front of the photographer. They then crossed a massive fill over Kittanning Run (visible to the lower right of the photo), reversed direction, traversed another fill over Glen White Run (in the left center) and then continued to head upgrade, now traveling southeast before swinging back to the west and continuing to climb toward the summit tunnel at Gallitzin, six miles away.

Pennsylvania Historical and Museum Commission, Railroad Museum of Pennsylvania.

pany should issue bonds to pay for the work. By the beginning of 1852, however, Thomson and the board had awarded the first grading contracts along the route that would eventually stretch between Altoona and Johnstown.

In his efforts to extend the PRR's tracks west of Altoona, Thomson faced an immediate obstacle in the east slope of the Allegheny Mountains. While he considered numerous options, in the end he selected a route that required the construction of the Horseshoe Curve, the PRR's most notable civil engineering achievement in the region and a symbol of the railroad's geographic presence in Pennsylvania. At Altoona, the tracks split from the original line leading to the connection with the Allegheny Portage Railroad at Duncansville and headed southwest, climbing steadily. The new line turned sharply to the west, along the north side of Burgoon Run. After bridging Scotch

Run on a fill, the tracks reached Kittanning Point, where they crossed Kittanning Run and curved sharply to the south, around the apex of the horseshoe. Then, after traversing Glen White Run, the line headed briefly east, then south, and then west again, into Sugar Run Gap and toward the summit at Gallitzin. By doubling back on itself, the line gained 122 feet in elevation, while maintaining the 1.8 percent grade.[74]

To the west of the Horseshoe Curve, the tracks hugged the bluff along the north side of Sugar Run Gap. At Allegrippus, they crossed a high fill, followed by another at Bennington Curve. To the west lay the summit, at Gallitzin. In 1851, construction began on the Summit Tunnel, later known as the Allegheny Tunnel, under the direction of Haupt and Western Division assistant engineer Thomas W. Seabrook. Crews sped construction on the tunnel by working from both ends, and from four intermediate shafts. Workers in each shaft battled groundwater that gushed forth at more than a hundred gallons per minute, as well as shale so unstable that virtually the entire tunnel had to be lined with bricks.[75] Built at a cost of nearly half a million dollars, the 3,612-foot tunnel was completed on January 21, 1854, and was in continual use by the middle of February. Even then, frequent repairs were necessary, as the remaining unlined sections of the tunnel were prone to collapse.[76]

The tracks between the summit and Johnstown enjoyed moderate grades, less steep than those on the eastern slope. That fortuitous circumstance favored eastbound traffic, expected to constitute the bulk of the PRR's business. Just to the east of the Big Viaduct, PRR rails paralleled those of the Allegheny Portage Railroad, following them a short distance west, where the existing Western Division continued on to Johnstown and Pittsburgh. On February 15, 1854, construction crews completed work on the Horseshoe Curve, the last remaining obstacle on the Mountain Division, and the Pennsylvania Railroad finally possessed its own route between Harrisburg and Pittsburgh.

"The Most Radical and Perfect Remedy"

PRR surveyors and construction crews were not the only ones at work in the Allegheny Mountains during the early 1850s. When the commonwealth completed the Portage Railroad in 1834, it was widely hailed as a civil engineering triumph. However, the line was neither popular nor remunerative. Each day in 1834, on average, eleven passenger cars traveled over the inclined planes. They carried a total of sixty-six paying passengers, yielding an abysmal $4.68 in revenue. Traffic then began to decline, with twenty thousand passengers traveling over the Allegheny Portage Railroad in 1835, four thousand fewer than the year before. During 1835, a paltry fifty thousand tons of freight moved over the Portage Railroad, an amount that in 1836 fell to little more than 45,000 tons—29,740 tons westbound and 15,439 tons eastbound, with a directionality inverse of what promoters of the Main Line of Public Works had originally envisioned.[77]

Since 1836, despite the efforts of engineers such as Charles DeHaas, Hother Hagé, and Charles L. Schlatter, the General Assembly had done little to remedy the defects of the Allegheny Portage Railroad. The political infighting associated with the Buckshot War in 1838 and 1839 and the collapse of the United States Bank of Pennsylvania in 1841 had effectively paralyzed the entire state system of public works. With the commonwealth's credit ruined, legislators were reluctant to fund even routine maintenance, much less improvements. Some positive changes did take place, including the installation of wire ropes on the inclined planes, completed in 1849, and the elimination of the last horses and mules used on the level sections, in 1850. Years of deferred maintenance had taken their toll, however. The enormous weight of steam locomotives and section boats, along with all of the other traffic, had caused the rails to spread out of gauge and resulted in frequent derailments. Operating personnel repeatedly requested that the legislature provide funds to replace the iron-strap rail with modern T-rail, but no money was forthcoming. By 1850 and 1851 the Portage Railroad was reaching the breaking point, with accidents claiming the lives of eight people in each of those years.[78]

As PRR construction crews progressed steadily westward along the Juniata River, inching ever closer to the base of the Alleghenies, many Pennsylvania politicians feared that the new enterprise would soon force the existing system of inclined planes out of business. The closure of the Portage Railroad would in turn sever the Main Line of Public Works, ensuring that the PRR would possess a virtual transportation monopoly across Pennsylvania—and, more importantly, ending the flow of canal revenues into the state treasury. On the first day of 1850, in his message to the General Assembly, Governor William F. Johnston accused the Portage Railroad, once hailed as an engineering marvel, of constituting "a serious obstacle to the business of the community and the occasion of trade seeking other channels to the Atlantic markets."[79] Less than six months later, on May 10, 1850, legislators authorized the construction of the New Portage Railroad, to cross the mountains between Hollidaysburg and Johnstown without inclined planes. In August, the Board of Canal Commissioners selected Robert Faries as its principal engineer and ordered him to begin work.

They had waited too long. After the PRR reached Duncansville in September 1850, Thomson had quickly laid claim to the best route over the mountain, a variant of the one that Charles Schlatter and Stephen Moylan Fox had surveyed through Sugar Run Gap more than a decade earlier. The PRR's presence in the mountains required Faries to undertake additional survey work. In February 1851, Faries issued his report to the Board of Canal Commissioners, and construction began soon afterward.[80] Legislators nonetheless balked at the cost associated with replacing all of the planes, and in May 1852 they appointed William Milnor Roberts (who had worked on the original Allegheny Portage Railroad and had also been responsible for the construction of the Cumberland Valley Railroad between 1835 and 1837) and Edward F. Gay to reexamine the survey work that Faries had completed.[81] After additional delay, Roberts and Gay agreed entirely with the route that Faries had chosen. "Sound policy, as well as true economy," they asserted, "dictate that the Commonwealth should, without the unnecessary delay of a single day, apply the most radical and perfect remedy," by completing the New Portage Railroad as quickly as possible.[82]

From Hollidaysburg, the forty-five-mile-long New Portage route employed the existing Allegheny Portage Railroad tracks for some two miles before diverging to the south and climbing along the bank of Dry Run. Along its path to the summit, the tracks skirted around seven ravines, with Faries adding curve after curve in order to keep grades to a minimum. After crossing a branch of Blair Gap Run, the line passed near the summit of Plane Number 10, continued to climb along the slope, and crossed the original line again in a sharp mule shoe curve above Plane Number 9. Still climbing, now to the north of Blair Gap Run, it cut through a low ridge to gain access to Fetter's Run, then traversed another gap, one that led to a three-mile grade along Sugar Run. At Sugar Run Gap, workers drove a new 1,800-foot tunnel through the mountain, only a few hundred yards to the south and twenty-five feet higher in elevation than the PRR's bore. Heading west, downgrade, the New Portage route paralleled the PRR for more than five miles, creating both an un-

necessary duplication of expense and an operational nightmare, as the two lines crossed each other at least eight times. The two sets of tracks again diverged slightly before they reached the stone viaduct over the Little Conemaugh River. Both railroads shared the structure and the four miles of track that led west to Conemaugh Station, just short of Johnstown, the terminus of the soon-to-be-obsolete Western Division Canal.[83]

As contractors built their assigned portions of the New Portage Railroad, their crews often labored within sight of PRR workers constructing the Mountain Division. The ominous duplication of effort did not deter the Canal Commission, and most of the grading on the New Portage Railroad had been completed by the end of the 1853 construction season. The canal commissioners eagerly anticipated a growing volume of traffic, both from the canals and—they hoped—from the Pennsylvania Railroad. Rather naively, they believed that PRR employees might fail in their efforts to build the Horseshoe Curve route, or that those tracks would be inadequate to accommodate all of the PRR traffic that moved over the Alleghenies.

The PRR shattered those expectations on February 15, 1854, when its new line entered service, bypassing both the inclined planes of the Portage Railroad and the still-incomplete grade of the New Portage Railroad. Revenue on the existing Allegheny Portage Railroad immediately declined by two-thirds. In desperation, the commissioners suggested that the New Portage Railroad could survive without PRR traffic and even compete against the newer enterprise. They put on a show of optimism when, on July 1, 1855, the New Portage Railroad opened to traffic, replacing the last of the inclined planes.[84]

The confidence of the canal commissioners was sorely misplaced. The PRR route ascended the eastern slope of the Allegheny Mountains at a 1.8 percent grade, steeper than the 1.6 percent used on the longer New Portage line. The difference was of little consequence, however, as most of the PRR's traffic was eastbound, descending rather than ascending that slope. More important, the PRR's tracks were part of an unbroken rail line across Pennsylvania, while the New Portage connected with canals at each end. By 1857 state revenues on the New Portage were barely 8 percent of what the original Allegheny Portage Railroad had earned prior to the completion of the Pennsylvania Railroad.[85]

Money for the Railroad

The PRR had decisively defeated the Canal Commission in the Allegheny Mountains, but the construction of the Horseshoe Curve route had pushed the limits of the railroad's credit. By the winter of 1852, as contractors were putting the finishing touches on the Western Division, the company was already in serious financial trouble. At the same February 2 stockholder meeting that had deposed the Merrick/Patterson faction from the board, investors agreed to issue an additional $2.5 million in common stock. The City of Philadelphia and the Northern Liberties soon subscribed to $1 million of those shares. That brought the PRR's total outstanding common stock to just under $10 million (the PRR had no preferred stock), but not all of those funds had yet reached the corporate treasury. Investors had made only an initial payment for their shares, and they were not required to contribute more than an additional 10 percent every sixty days. Even if they had paid in full, the total stock authorization was well below the $12.5 million that would be necessary to complete and equip the railroad. On March 1, 1852, barely a month after selecting Thomson to replace Patterson as president, the stockholders convened a second meeting and approved the board's call for a committee to investigate the railroad's finances.[86]

The members of the committee were shocked by what they found, for they uncovered a capital shortage far more severe than the previous annual report had revealed. Their findings, issued on April 5, showed that the balance sheet listed total assets of $1.6 million, with immediate and projected liabilities estimated at $12.5 million. The committee estimated that no more than $9.75 million could be raised through the sale of additional stock, and even that figure seemed overly optimistic. Even worse, the railroad had accumulated a substantial floating debt in the form of promissory notes and short-term loans, and unsecured by any physical assets.

The directors, shaken by the committee's report, recommended that the railroad issue additional securities in order to fund the completion of the Mountain Division. On April 23, the legislature authorized a $3 million increase in the company's capital stock, followed only two weeks later by another $1 million authorization. More significantly, in late May the PRR's directors for the first time authorized the issuance of mortgage bonds, with $3 million to be put on the market immediately and an additional $2 million held in reserve for future construction requirements. The bonds carried an interest rate of 6 percent, fairly typical for the time, and were convertible to stock, another common feature.[87] The thirty-year bonds would constitute a first mortgage and a lien on the PRR's assets. The shareholders voted their overwhelming approval, vindicating Thomson's financial agenda. Yet, issuing stocks and bonds was one thing. Selling them was quite another.[88]

The Evolution of Railway Finance

The incorporation of the Pennsylvania Railroad in 1846 coincided with the rapid development of American capital markets. The ratification of the Constitution, coupled with the financial agenda of Treasury Secretary Alexander Hamilton and his fellow federalists, brought stability and predictability to national financial markets. As a result, federal bonds became extraordinarily safe and popular investments. So, too, were shares in the First and Second Banks of the United States. Perhaps as early as the War of 1812, and certainly by the 1830s, the United States had developed an integrated securities market of remarkable sophistication. Contrary to some contemporary assertions of the nation as a rustic backwater, Americans possessed a larger equity market than Britain, or indeed any country in Europe. That enormous reservoir of capital, coupled with the contributions of European investors, proved crucial to American economic development, particularly to the construction of internal improvements. Furthermore, the multiplicity of state-funded canal and railroad projects, and the ease with which entrepreneurs could secure legislative charters for private corporations, flushed loose a torrent of additional capital.[89] Prudent investors, risk-taking speculators, and local boosters who were eager do their part to bring better transportation to their isolated communities all contributed their motes to the reservoir of capital.[90]

By the late 1820s, several states had funded their often-lavish internal-improvement programs primarily through the sales of bonds, rather than through taxation or other politically sensitive means. The bonds sold well, both in the United States and in Europe, in large measure because investors were more familiar with the states than they were with private corporations. They equated state governments with the federal government, and thus generally assumed that the risk of default would be extraordinarily low. Bond sales peaked in the mid-1830s, with the states issuing more bonds between 1836 and 1838 than they had in all the previous decades of their existence. Those years coincided with a general expansion of long-term capital markets in Europe, especially in Britain. The bonds accordingly found buyers at home and overseas, despite clear evidence that many states, including Pennsylvania, had embraced overly ambitious internal-improvement agendas.[91]

The crash, when it came, was severe. Following the Panic of 1837, nine states repudiated their debts, although several later made good their obligations. The legislatures of three states—Michigan, Arkansas, and Mississippi—and the territory of Florida abandoned all responsibility for debts that totaled nearly $14 million. Pennsylvania paid investors with scrip, in lieu of cash. Several other states, including the economic powerhouse of New York, came perilously close to insolvency. European investors learned that state bonds could indeed prove worthless. Creditors foreign and domestic called on Congress to make good the state debts, but to no avail. In disgust, Europeans turned away from state securities and instead invested directly in private corporations, principally railroads. Even if they had retained any lingering desire to invest in the public sector, they would have found it difficult to do so, as the people of nineteen states, including Pennsylvania in 1857, eventually adopted constitutional amendments that either prohibited or sharply restricted the issuance of state, county, and municipal bonds for internal improvements.[92]

The first half of the nineteenth century also witnessed a migration of the nation's primary capital market from Philadelphia north to Boston, and then south again to New York. During the years that immediately followed the American Revolution, Philadelphia had been the nation's financial capital, as exemplified by the formation of the Philadelphia Board of Brokers in 1790, the first stock exchange in the United States, predating its counterpart in New York by two years. Philadelphia was also home to the First Bank of the United States, chartered in 1791, as well as its 1816 successor. Philadelphia bankers, most notably the house of Thomas Biddle & Company, played an instrumental role in placing state internal-improvement bonds with domestic and foreign investors. During the late 1830s and into the 1840s, however, the Bank War, the withdrawal of federal funds from the Second Bank of the United States, and the formation and subsequent collapse of the United States Bank of Pennsylvania badly damaged Philadelphia's financial primacy.[93] Nonetheless, even though states increasingly turned to Boston or New York, or abroad, for the capital needed to finance massive internal-improvement projects, representatives from many smaller privately financed canals and railroads continued to depend on Philadelphia investors.[94]

Philadelphia's banking and commercial decline enabled Boston investors to finance the initial wave of railroad construction that occurred during the 1830s and early 1840s. Bostonians, who suffered comparatively little damage from the Panic of 1837, invested heavily in railroads during the decade that followed, helping to fund the construction of many lines, particularly in New England and the Midwest. The Philadelphia, Wilmington & Baltimore, for example, was initially a Philadelphia enterprise, but the need for additional capital caused control to pass into the hands of Boston capitalists during the 1840s. Boston financiers likewise controlled the Philadelphia & Reading Rail Road, although that company would later be dominated by British investors.[95]

In 1847, however, the collapse of the British railway boom helped trigger a worldwide recession, and Boston was more seriously affected than any other American city. The resulting downturn permitted New York capitalists to capture a larger share of the market for railway securities. The development of the New York Stock Exchange, dating to 1792 and assuming a more modern form in 1817, symbolized the emergence of the nation's new financial capital.[96] As with the commercial development of New York in general, the financing of the Erie Canal accelerated but did not itself create the city's dominance in capital markets. Yet, New York's role as the nation's entrepôt enhanced the close personal connections among merchant bankers that were essential to the importation of capital as well as goods from abroad. By the time that railroads supplanted canals, New York was well positioned to provide financing for the new form of transportation. In 1830, the Mohawk & Hudson Railroad, later a component of the New York Central, became the first railroad stock traded on the exchange. Particularly after 1845, New York investment bankers became quite active in the financing of railway securities. The leading firm was Winslow, Lanier & Company, established in 1849, specializing in western railroads.[97]

The PRR was a Philadelphia company, and accordingly relied on a network of Philadelphia financiers for much of its capital. Initially, railroad officials personally marketed securities to their peers. At times, senior executives, such as Thomson and chief engineer Edward Miller, traveled to Europe to place bonds with established banking houses and their customers. After the Civil War, Philadelphia developed a small but respectable financial community of its own, largely under the leadership of Anthony J. Drexel, who, on his own account and in partnership with J. P. Morgan and others, handled a significant share of the PRR's securities.

In any event, the PRR's initial reliance on Philadelphia capital markets generated some unique investment features. One of the more notable was that a share of PRR stock possessed a par value of $50, half of the face value of most New York securities. The low par value of PRR stock made the company a relatively safe investment. At a time when investors were subjected to periodic assessments on their stock, par represented the limit of what they would be required to pay. As a result, the asset value of a company, as listed on the balance sheet, was simply the par value of the stock, not the firm's earning potential. Under limited-liability law, moreover, investors in a failed firm could lose no more than the value of their cumulative invest-

ment, valued at par, in the company's stock. During much of the nineteenth century, newspaper reporters and financial advisers warned investors of the dangers of "watered" stock, where the aggregate par value of the stock greatly exceeded the actual value of the company—a situation that typically occurred when corporate officials issued stock without making a commensurate increase in the value of assets. Should the firm fail, investors might be liable for their share of the difference between actual value and par value. As a result, investment analysts advised their clients to buy stock with a low par value, and the PRR certainly fit the bill. Ultimately, securities are worth what investors are willing to pay for them, and the PRR's stock almost always sold well above par.[98]

Soliciting Capital in European Markets

The vast American railway network could not have been constructed without a continual influx of capital from Europe. Throughout its history, the size and evident earning potential of the PRR rendered it less dependent on foreign financing than many other railroads. Nevertheless, British investors in particular contributed mightily to the PRR's growth, enabling Thomson and his successors to create traffic capacity and underwrite the development of the railroad's western subsidiaries. Many of those Ohio and Indiana carriers likewise benefited from overseas investments, before and after they became tied to the PRR system.

Despite the sophistication of antebellum financial markets in the United States, they were quite different from their counterparts in London and on the Continent in one crucial respect. New York in particular served as a vast conduit for the importation of funds into a nation that was chronically starved for investment capital. As the most capital-intensive businesses around, railroads both caused and were particularly severely affected by the capital shortfall. Federalism, with its attendant commercial rivalry between and within states, coupled with the trading of political favors, known as logrolling, ensured that legislatures chartered a plethora of companies, all of which competed vigorously for a limited pool of capital. The resultant capital shortages were largely responsible for the importance of debt financing, with bond sales reaching and in some cases exceeding stockholder equity.[99]

During the antebellum period, European investors developed something of a love-hate relationship with American railway securities. Many had been badly stung by the repudiation of state internal-improvement debts following the Panic of 1837, and had thereafter resolved to avoid state bonds that had financed much of the canal and railroad construction. Railroads were equally risky, particularly when investors possessed little information on the bewildering array of companies that lay across the Atlantic. Some of them were already in operation, some under construction, and others were proposed and never built.[100] For that reason, European investors generally preferred bonds to stock, reasoning that they could always foreclose on the railroad's physical assets in the event of financial disaster. Investors also valued the fixed rate of return on bonds, as well as the frequent availability of discounts below par on the initial purchase price.[101]

For all of their risks, however, American railway securities held out the lure of high rates of return, sometimes double what a supposedly safer European investment might provide. Britain was reducing its national debt, freeing capital for investment in American railroads. Industrialization spawned a generation of middle-class savers who were able to pool their resources in new exchanges in Aberdeen, Edinburgh, Glasgow, Liverpool, and Manchester, all established between 1843 and 1845 in response to the British "railway mania." In 1848, the political upheavals that roiled Europe convinced many foreign investors to look to the United States for investment opportunities. Their first choice was generally the federal government securities issued to finance the 1846–48 war with Mexico. That pattern continued through 1850, but the increased demand for government bond issues ensured that bonds sold at very small discounts, or even at a premium, thus driving down the effective rate of return.[102]

The increased demand for government bonds in turn made railway securities more attractive investments. By the early 1850s, as the PRR and its competitors were seeking the capital needed to complete their main lines, Europeans began investing directly in railway companies. A brief economic downturn in April and May of 1851 soured the bond markets and provided ammunition for the PRR's more conservative directors, who preferred to continue reliance on equity financing. By September, however, the economy had recovered, and demand for bonds was on the increase—precisely at the time when Thomson was on the verge of unseating the Merrick/Patterson faction from the board. In December 1851, a coup d'état temporarily removed Napoleon III from power in France, and the resulting turmoil drove even more investment capital from Europe to the United States. The following spring, the Bank of England lowered its interest rate to a mere 2 percent, and the 6 or even 7 percent interest rates offered by American railroad securities generated considerable investor interest. The years that followed saw a surge in European investment in American railroads, at first from Germany, Switzerland, and France, and later from Great Britain. At least half a dozen major European investment houses began to actively participate in the market for American railway securities. Thomson thus assumed the presidency and authorized the PRR's initial complement of bonds at a particularly fortuitous time.[103]

Pennsylvania Railroad officials generally experienced little difficulty in marketing their securities in Europe, at least during times of economic prosperity. For one thing, the PRR existed in reality, and not merely on paper, and it was the only company to offer service between two of the most important commercial centers in the United States. For that reason, the PRR possessed a good measure of name recognition, and its activities were reported frequently in financial chronicles, newspapers, engineering journals, and travelers' accounts. Thomson, in particular, was widely regarded as a capable, prudent, and conscientious executive who was unlikely to pursue personal gain at the expense of investors. As a result, even though PRR securities generally offered a standard 6 percent interest rate, they frequently sold at or near par.[104]

Selling Stocks and Bonds

During the summer of 1852, when Thomson added bonds to the PRR's repertoire of financial instruments, he for the first time enabled European investors to make substantial contributions to the railroad's finances. In June, only weeks after the board of directors authorized the initial $3 million bond issue, they dispatched chief engineer Edward Miller to Europe to market the securities in London, Paris, and Amsterdam. Miller possessed extraordinary discretionary authority, including the ability to negotiate such terms as the discount rate and the date at which the bonds might be convertible to stock. Miller began negotiations with the London firm of Overend, Gurney & Company, whose principals expressed some interest in handling the distribution of the new issue. In the end, however, the winning bid for the entire $3 million in bonds went to Philadelphia businessman Charles Henry Fisher, who paid $103.20 per hundred, well above par. Fisher, in turn, apparently transferred most of the bond issue to the well-known European financial houses of Baring Brothers and N. M. Rothschild & Son for sale in the London market. As a result, by 1853 foreign investors owned fully $2.5 million of the $3 million worth of PRR bonds.[105]

In June 1853, with work on the Mountain Division proving more expensive than anticipated, the board authorized the issuance of the remaining $2 million in first mortgage bonds. They did not sell well in the United States, and on September 7 Thomson left Philadelphia for Liverpool, bearing with him more than a million dollars in unsold securities. Thomson arrived in Europe just as the Crimean War was beginning. Perversely, the same crisis that accelerated overseas demand for American grain also made it vastly more difficult for Thomson to raise the funds necessary to complete a railroad that could transport that grain to market. The European depression that accompanied the Crimean War caused investors on both sides of the English Channel to be wary of new financial offerings. As such, Thomson managed to place a mere $230,000 worth (denominated in pounds sterling), at just 90 percent of par. Other firms experienced similar difficulties. Yet by 1853 ten American railways had been able to place more than $1 million worth of securities in European markets, a good result under the circumstances.[106]

The PRR's capital demands, coupled with the tight European markets, encouraged Thomson to rely again on equity financing. In March 1853, the General Assembly authorized another amendment to the PRR charter, increasing the amount of capital stock by $4 million. Even though that legislative action was essentially pro forma, PRR officials explained that they expected that the resulting funds would be used to benefit Pennsylvania, and Philadelphia in particular. They intended to use a large share of the money to support railroad development in Ohio and Indiana to ensure that midwestern grain reached Philadelphia, and not New York or Baltimore.[107]

Meanwhile, bond sales continued to be unpromising. In April 1854, the legislature authorized the PRR to increase its bonded debt up to the amount of capital stock, which at that time equaled $18 million. Within weeks, the board approved a second mortgage in the amount of $5 million. Like the first mortgage bonds issued two years earlier, the new securities bore 6 percent interest and were convertible to common stock. In order to place the first million-dollar allotment with the London firm of Timothy Wiggin & Company, the directors again showed extraordinary discretion, permitting the payment of interest in London, and in pounds sterling—concessions that caused the chairman of the Finance Committee to resign in protest. It mattered little, in any event—the escalation of the Crimean conflict soured European markets, and the overseas investment-banking firms were able to place only a few of the PRR's bonds.[108]

The situation in the United States was scarcely better. In 1854, even with American sales added to those in Europe, the PRR had managed to place only about $1.5 million of the $5 million second mortgage bond issue. In addition to the sluggish bond sales, the price of PRR stock declined considerably, reaching a low of 40½ in December 1854. With funds in short supply, Thomson reluctantly ordered the postponement of further work on double-tracking the main line. In May 1855, the legislature again amended the PRR's charter, permitting the company to issue an additional $2 million worth of stock. Given the sluggish economy, however, most of the shares went unissued.

By 1855 and 1856, securities markets in both Europe and the United States began to recover, with overseas investors concentrating their attention on the PRR and a few other large carriers. The prosperity proved to be short lived, and the Panic of 1857 played havoc with financial markets in the United States and Europe. In

November, even though earnings held steady, the board elected not to pay the 3 percent semiannual dividend. By the end of the year, the PRR had sold perhaps $6.5 million of its first and second mortgage bonds, and had issued only $12.4 million of the $20 million in stock permitted by its amended charter. The disappointing results, coupled with declining revenues, forced Thomson to curtail expenses, cutting wages, salaries, and dividends, and again temporarily halting the installation of a second track on the main line. Dividend payments, as well as new track work, did not resume until 1859. At that time, the board established a sinking fund for the PRR's second mortgage bonds, setting aside a reserve in part to reassure investors that sufficient money would be available for redemption.[109] Otherwise, the PRR's finances changed little until after 1860, when the Civil War both accelerated the railroad's demand for capital and revolutionized the world of finance.[110]

Buying the Main Line of Public Works

After attaining the presidency in 1852, Thomson was determined to gain control over the Philadelphia & Columbia Railroad, by far the most useful portion of the Main Line of Public Works. He indicated his willingness to construct a parallel line, but had no real intention of doing so. Instead, he sought a mechanism for pressuring the commonwealth into selling the Main Line to the PRR. Promoters had chartered several local railroads in southeastern Pennsylvania, and both Thomson and his directors believed that some of them had the potential to provide the PRR with alternate access to Philadelphia. Thomson considered, and soon rejected, involvement with either the West Chester Railroad or the Columbia & Octoraro Railroad, neither of which offered any real potential.[111]

The Lancaster, Lebanon & Pine Grove Rail Road was quite another matter, however. Local interests incorporated the company in 1852, planning a line between Norristown, linked to Philadelphia by the Norristown Railroad, through Phoenixville, and west to a junction with the Harrisburg, Portsmouth, Mount Joy & Lancaster. Most of the promoters were residents of Lebanon and Lancaster counties, although some

hailed from Philadelphia and one—Christian Spangler—was a commissioner of the new company, as well as a director of the PRR. If completed, the Lancaster, Lebanon & Pine Grove would allow the PRR to bypass the Philadelphia & Columbia, which lay a dozen or so miles to the south, and thus complete a route from Philadelphia to Pittsburgh on its own rails. As Thomson realized, however, the PRR's construction crews would not need to lay so much as a single rail along the route of the Lancaster, Lebanon & Pine Grove. The mere threat of a parallel line, especially one built to modern engineering standards, might well frighten the Board of Canal Commissioners into selling the Philadelphia & Columbia to the PRR on extremely favorable terms.[112]

With the PRR's support, the Lancaster, Lebanon & Pine Grove gave every appearance of beginning construction. Spangler became president of the new line. The Lancaster road's board meetings must have given him a certain sense of déjà vu, as four of the remaining board members also served simultaneously as PRR directors. During the spring of 1853, survey crews were in the field, between Lebanon and Cornwall. By the end of April, the company's supporters were calling on the Philadelphia City Councils to subscribe to a million dollars' worth of stock. In June, the PRR's directors voted to pay for additional surveys along the new route. By the beginning of September, a special committee of the board recommended that the PRR lease the company, and the directors approved that plan on December 21. Yet Thomson, who would have vastly preferred to acquire the extant Philadelphia & Columbia on his terms, was reluctant to begin work on the Lancaster, Lebanon & Pine Grove. In February 1854, the PRR board agreed to spend as much as $500,000 on the railroad's construction, but only to the minimum extent necessary to prevent forfeiture of its charter.[113]

Even though Thomson did not proceed with the construction of the Lancaster, Lebanon & Pine Grove, he held that company's charter, like a sword of Damocles, over the heads of the canal commissioners. In May 1856, some three years after the PRR had first made a token effort to build the line, Thomson indicated that he was prepared to begin construction. The board then appointed a special committee with instructions to initiate negotiations with Governor James Pollock and the

Board of Canal Commissioners. Their task was to convince the commonwealth's representatives to part with the most valuable segment of the Main Line of Public Works.[114]

There was really very little to discuss. To the east, the Harrisburg, Portsmouth, Mount Joy & Lancaster was under PRR control, funneling traffic away from the Philadelphia & Columbia at Dillerville. With the stroke of a pen, the PRR board of directors could authorize the construction of the Lancaster, Lebanon & Pine Grove, bypassing the entire state-owned route between Philadelphia and Harrisburg.[115] To the west, PRR trains sped past the canal boats that moved at no better than a walking pace. The PRR's line over the Alleghenies, in service since 1854, had consigned the Allegheny Portage Railroad to oblivion. The recently opened New Portage Railroad, built at great public expense, could do little to stem the loss of traffic to the PRR so long as it was tied to the waterborne transportation on the canals. With all of the dignity, decorum, and diplomacy that the occasion demanded, the PRR's representatives informed the governor and the canal commissioners that the Main Line of Public Works was finished.

As Thomson placed ever more pressure on the General Assembly to sell the entire Main Line of Public Works, legislators proved increasingly receptive to his arguments.[116] The only portion of the state system that interested Thomson was the seventy-mile section of the Philadelphia & Columbia between Dillerville and Philadelphia. Neither the Pennsylvania Canal nor either version of the Portage Railroad had any value to the PRR, but the canal commissioners were likely to insist that everything be sold as a package, for—absent the Philadelphia & Columbia—the remainder of the Main Line was essentially useless.

Thomson's criticism of the Main Line of Public Works found a ready audience in the state capital, as by the early 1850s, state-sponsored internal improvements had very nearly brought Pennsylvania to the brink of financial disaster. The commonwealth had invested more than $22 million in the Main Line system at the time of its completion in 1835, accounting for virtually all of its $24.6 million debt. Indiana, Illinois, and other western states had engaged in a similar orgy of politically motivated internal improvements,

only to see both their dreams and their financial stability come crashing down in the wake of the Panic of 1837 and the collapse, four years later, of the United States Bank of Pennsylvania. The Panic of 1837 claimed a great many private partnerships and corporations, but the citizenry was most broadly aware of its effects on public and mixed enterprise.

The financial catastrophes of the 1830s coincided with the maturation of railroad technology and its clear ascendency over canals. To a certain degree, railroad operating practices—most notably the need to combine the ownership of the right of way with control over all traffic—required the abandonment of the open-access policies that had characterized state-owned canals and turnpikes. Yet, there was no inherent reason why a publicly owned railroad could not incorporate such restrictive practices into its operations. After all, the canal commissioners had banned individual access to the Philadelphia & Columbia Railroad after they replaced horses with steam locomotives. In the aftermath of the Panic of 1837, however, entrepreneurs could easily claim that publicly owned canals had failed, and that privately owned railroads offered both the technological and the organizational systems necessary to move the nation's economy forward.[117]

Pennsylvania had an added burden, not only shouldering the operating losses associated with the Portage Railroad—more than a hundred thousand dollars in the 1840 season alone—but also the cost of upgrading railroad tracks and purchasing additional locomotives and cars. The commonwealth effectively went bankrupt in August 1842, when it defaulted on its debt obligations, destroying its creditworthiness in the process. Voters had also read numerous accounts of mismanagement associated with the system's operation, and they blamed the Board of Canal Commissioners for the problems. In 1843, therefore, the legislature stripped the governor of the authority to appoint the canal commissioners and placed that power in the hands of the voters.[118]

In 1844, a year after the commonwealth gave away the Erie Extension Canal rather than bear the expense of its completion and operation, legislators resolved to sell most of the Main Line for $20 million. The members of the General Assembly sought public approval for the sale, placing the issue before the voters in a general referendum. Voters in areas that depended heavily on canal traffic, such as Susquehanna County, voted overwhelmingly to keep the state system in operation, as did residents of more remote areas that were, or might soon be, served by internal improvements. Their numbers were too few to overcome the heavily populated eastern regions, such as Philadelphia City and County (where the vote was two to one in favor of the sale) and Lancaster County (twelve to one), and the measure passed by a plurality of more than 25,000 votes, out of almost 275,000 cast. The suggested price, however, was roughly what it had cost to build the system, and far more than it was worth. Furthermore, the terms required the purchaser to maintain all of the canals and railways as public thoroughfares, irrespective of their economic viability. Potential buyers balked at the prohibition against abandoning unprofitable segments of the state system, and no offers were forthcoming. The vote nonetheless encouraged the canal commissioners to implement administrative reforms. In tandem with improving economic conditions, those changes temporarily dampened public enthusiasm for disposing of the state system.[119]

During the final decade before the Civil War, however, political developments, set amid growing sectionalism, played to the PRR's advantage. In 1851, Whig governor William F. Johnston paid dearly for his refusal to enforce the 1850 federal Fugitive Slave Act, and Democrat William Bigler swept him from office. The Democrats gained control of the General Assembly in October 1853, and under Bigler's leadership they resurrected the proposal to sell the Main Line. The following April, legislators authorized the sale for $10 million, precisely half of the asking price a decade earlier.[120] The bill included a provision permitting the purchaser to build a railroad between Columbia and Pittsburgh. The charter provision would be a direct threat to the PRR's interests, and the legislature was in effect making the PRR an offer that it could not refuse. Yet Thomson and the board did refuse, both because they believed the price to be too high and because they balked at provisions that set maximum rates on the Philadelphia & Columbia while requiring the purchaser to maintain the canals. A month later, in May 1854, PRR stockholders likewise rejected the purchase—like Thomson, gambling that no other com-

pany would be in a position to purchase the Main Line.[121]

It was not much of a gamble. During the last years before the Civil War, sectional tensions had begun to disintegrate the national political parties, and the PRR used the ensuing statewide chaos to its advantage. In 1854 Governor Bigler made much the same mistake that Johnston had committed a few years earlier, in this instance supporting the popular sovereignty provisions of the Kansas-Nebraska Act and raising the possibility that slavery would spread into the northern Great Plains. That October, Whig James Pollock unseated Bigler and won the gubernatorial race. The Whig Party was on the verge of collapse, however, and could govern only by forming a coalition with the American ("Know-Nothing") Party. That faction, best known for its nativist attitudes, was also opposed to state ownership of the Main Line. In that same election, Know-Nothing votes ensured that a Democrat, Henry S. Mott, defeated Whig candidate and Scottish immigrant George Darsie for the post of canal commissioner. Now that they no longer controlled the Canal Commission, the Whigs had an additional motivation to share the antipathy of their Know-Nothing allies toward state ownership of the Main Line of Public Works.[122]

For the next three years, legislators made a pretense of demanding what they considered to be a fair price for the Main Line, while Thomson simply bided his time, waiting for an offer that he considered acceptable. In May 1855, the General Assembly proposed to sell the Main Line for $7.5 million, a 25 percent reduction from the 1854 price, but with the customary stipulation that it be kept in service, in its entirety. PRR officials assessed the state works, and concluded "that the highest prospective value that can be placed upon the Main Line is less than $7,000,000." The canals could be repaired, and would generate some income, they suggested, but they believed that "the Portage Rail Road would be of no value to this Company except for the material upon it." In its current condition, the Philadelphia & Columbia was worth perhaps $3.5 million, and it would require an additional expenditure of $4 million in order to be put in proper shape. All told, the PRR would spend at least $11 million to buy and repair the Main Line—"to say nothing," the directors lamented, "of the additional expense of forever maintaining the unprofitable portions of the line." The board had little difficulty rejecting the state's latest offer. In July, the commonwealth attempted to auction off the Main Line, but no one was willing to meet the $7.5 million minimum bid.[123] When two of the Cameron brothers, Simon and William, pooled their resources with transporters John and James Bingham and offered $3 million for the Philadelphia & Columbia Railroad, it did not take long for the canal commissioners to reject the bid.[124]

Thomson, still waiting for the right offer, benefited from a sea change in public attitudes regarding the propriety of public ownership of transportation enterprises. By 1856, no sane Pennsylvanian could justify the commonwealth's continued operation of the Main Line on economic grounds alone. Instead, opponents of the sale focused on two principal concerns. First, they understandably demanded as high a price as possible in order to offset the enormous debt that the legislature had authorized to construct the internal improvements in the first place. Representatives of each major political party, the Democrats and the Whigs, called for the sale of the Main Line of Public Works; yet, each party excoriated the other for failing to negotiate sufficiently remunerative terms.

Second, those who opposed the sale emphasized that the PRR, a privately held company, would eliminate its publicly owned competition, depriving the people of free and open access to transportation and allowing a handful of wealthy Philadelphians to monopolize the carriage of passengers and freight. To counteract those fears, Thomson and other PRR officials revisited many of the same arguments employed by those who had supported the construction of the Main Line of Public Works some three decades earlier. The PRR's supporters emphasized that only private enterprise could protect Pennsylvania's commercial interests against rival entrepreneurs in New York and Maryland. Public works were inherently tainted with patronage and inefficiency, they suggested, and were sure to waste the people's money while leading the state into an economic disaster.

By the mid-1850s, antipathy toward private ownership of the Main Line was fading rapidly, replaced by a growing public belief that the state had no business being involved in business. The earlier indictments against public ownership, based on specific acts of malfeasance by the canal commissioners and their party loyalists, had evolved into a more pervasive belief that the patronage system stifled individual initiative, draining promising young men of their talent and ambition and turning them into political hacks. That broad-gauged criticism was strikingly similar to the abolitionist rhetoric of the age, much of which argued that slavery was evil—not because it caused African Americans to suffer but because that institution tainted white society and led good southern Christian white men down the path to sin and depravity. Indeed, the very idea that a government could not manage a business enterprise mimicked public fears that corrupt and self-aggrandizing politicians were incapable of saving the American republic from disintegration. Even those who still believed in the innate goodness of government found reason to support the sale of the Main Line of Public Works, asserting that association with the "sordid matters of commerce" should not sully that purity.[125] "The separation of politics and trade would do much to restore our government to its original purity," emphasized the members of a Senate committee, "and would be hailed by every virtuous citizen as the dawn of a brighter day."[126]

Given the climate of public opinion, few Pennsylvanians sought to hold on to the state system, few disputed the price, and fewer still cared that the Pennsylvania Railroad was likely to be the only bidder. The PRR directors, sensing that the commonwealth was at their mercy, suggested the terms of new legislation that would lower the asking price. The timing was again propitious, since the Whig Party had disintegrated, the Democrats were severely weakened by sectional issues, and in March 1857 the last remnants of the Know-Nothings joined forces with the new Republican Party, a political organization whose principal members were closely allied with the PRR. The company had other allies, as well, in the independent freight forwarders who had once depended on the publicly owned Main Line of Public Works, but who had recently shifted their allegiance to the Pennsylvania Railroad.[127]

On May 16, 1857, legislators began the final act in the sale of the Main Line of Public Works, with a bill authorizing the sale to any interested parties for $7.5 million. That was the same as the 1855 asking price, but without the stipulation that the purchaser keep the entire Main Line of Public Works in service. The legislation also included what amounted to a bribe for the PRR, offering the railroad the opportunity to pay an additional $1.5 million in exchange for a repeal of the tonnage tax and a permanent exemption from all other state taxes on stocks, bonds, or property. The canal commissioners were outraged at the elimination of their authority and, led by commissioner Henry S. Mott, took Governor Pollock to court in an attempt to block the sale. In June 1857 the Pennsylvania Supreme Court ruled, in *Mott v. Pennsylvania Railroad Company*, that the legislature had the authority to sell the Main Line, but not to permanently abrogate the commonwealth's power to impose a tax on the railroad. The battle to eliminate the tonnage tax would have to wait for another day.[128]

At 7:30 on the evening of June 24, 1857, Thomson walked into the Merchants' Exchange building in Philadelphia and offered $7.5 million of the Pennsylvania Railroad's money for the entire Main Line of Public Works. To no one's surprise, he was the only bidder. The commonwealth received payment in PRR bonds, bearing 5 percent interest and secured by a lien on the property that it had just sold to the railroad. On August 1, 1857, the PRR took possession of the Philadelphia & Columbia, the New Portage Railroad, and the Eastern, Juniata, and Western Division canals.[129]

Within a few months, the remainder of the commonwealth's massive investment in public works had disappeared as well. In January 1858, in his annual message to the General Assembly, Governor Pollock recommended the sale of the state's other canals. With the Main Line of Public Works now in private hands, he faced little opposition. Legislators agreed to sell the Delaware, Susquehanna, North Branch, and West Branch Divisions to the Sunbury & Erie Railroad, in the hope that they would facilitate the completion of that company's rail route to Lake Erie. In April 1858, the General Assembly approved the transaction. The Sunbury & Erie took control of the canals on May 19 and promptly resold them in order to raise additional construction funds. In January 1859, the legislature

eliminated the office of canal commissioner. The Commonwealth of Pennsylvania was out of the canal business.[130]

The Main Line of Public Works and much of the rest of the state's internal-improvement network lived on, however, under the control of the Pennsylvania Railroad. The Philadelphia & Columbia was by far the most valuable component of the new acquisition. William Hasell Wilson, who as a teenager had assisted his father, Major John Wilson, in surveying the Philadelphia & Columbia, became the resident engineer of the PRR's new Philadelphia Division. Wilson had his work cut out for him. During the early 1850s, in response to pressure from PRR executives and Philadelphia merchants, commonwealth employees had installed modern iron T-rails in place of the original strap-iron and Clarence rails, while replacing stone blocks and sills with wooden crossties. In many locations, crews had also moved the tracks a foot farther apart, permitting the passage of wider equipment. Later in the decade, however, the track again deteriorated as the Board of Canal Commissioners suspended virtually all maintenance during the long period of negotiations involving the sale of the public works. During 1856 and 1857, the PRR had funded improvements to the Philadelphia & Columbia, even before taking control of the line. After the purchase, engineers and track crews soon swarmed over virtually the entire distance between Philadelphia and Lancaster, upgrading the tracks to the same standards as the remainder of the PRR system.[131]

The other pieces of the line between Philadelphia and Harrisburg soon fell into place. In early 1858, construction crews increased the clearances in the Elizabethtown tunnel on the Harrisburg, Portsmouth, Mount Joy & Lancaster.[132] Even though the PRR still did not own an entrance into Center City Philadelphia, or a route to the Delaware River waterfront, the Philadelphia Select and Common Councils approved an ordinance providing for increased spacing on the tracks of the City Railroad, again at the PRR's expense. On July 18 a PRR passenger train operated over the entire distance between Philadelphia and Pittsburgh, marking the first time in the history of Pennsylvania that a passenger could travel across the state without changing vehicles.[133]

The New Portage Railroad, whose operating losses exceeded $70,000 in the first eight months of 1857 alone, was of little value. On November 1, Thomson ordered the abandonment of the route, which had cost well over $2 million to construct and had been in service barely a year. By 1858, PRR employees were stripping the rails off of the line and sending them west to construction crews in Indiana. That action convinced many skeptics that Thomson had purchased the Main Line just so he could eliminate his competition. Yet, while the governor made a weak attempt to prevent the abandonment, he was more incensed at the state's wasted investment than at the possibility of a transportation monopoly.[134]

The commonwealth's canals, far from being mere relics of a bygone age of transportation, lasted longer than did the New Portage Railroad. During the summer of 1857, the PRR board created a Canal Department, under the direction of chief engineer and general superintendent T. Haskins Du Puy, to oversee the continued operation and maintenance of the newly acquired Eastern Division, Juniata Division, and Western Division canals. While administratively a part of the Pennsylvania Railroad, the Canal Department was organizationally separate from the rail operations. Du Puy had evaluated the condition of the canals prior to the PRR's purchase of the Main Line, and he was not impressed. He was particularly pessimistic about the future of the Western Division Canal, which was badly maintained and carried little traffic. That section was the first to go, closed incrementally between 1861 and 1865. The PRR sold the right of way to the Western Pennsylvania Railroad, then an independent carrier, but later a part of the PRR system. The remaining canals, particularly the Eastern Division, fared somewhat better, thanks to the traffic demands of the Civil War and the PRR's rather limited early carrying capacity. In February 1863, for example, PRR directors suggested that "the day is not far distant when that portion of our road from Duncans Island [at the mouth of the Juniata River] to Philadelphia will be crowded to its utmost capacity and create the necessity of throwing on to the Canals such heavy materials as Coal particularly as it is generally admitted that Canals when of sufficient capacity and well maintained can transport Coal at a cheaper rate than can be done by rail."[135] That year just over a million tons of cargo floated along the PRR's canals, only a little less than half of what the railroad carried. In 1867, the PRR transferred the Eastern and Juniata Division canals to a newly incorporated subsidiary, the Pennsylvania Canal Company.[136]

Competition

During the 1850s, as Thomson and his associates pieced together a railroad that linked Philadelphia with Pittsburgh, they were preparing to do battle with a host of competitors. Before the decade was even half over four rail routes, often referred to as trunk lines, connected the east coast with the western waters, with two leading to the Ohio River and the others to Lake Erie. For the next century, those four carriers—the Pennsylvania Railroad, the Baltimore & Ohio, the New York Central, and the Erie—would divide the traffic that flowed across the nation's industrial and agricultural heartland. Within Pennsylvania, the Philadelphia & Reading Rail Road was a strong regional competitor to the PRR, even if that company never attained trunk-line status. To some extent, the construction of myriad rail lines stimulated economic growth and ensured rising traffic levels for all. In the near term, however, and from the perspective of PRR officials, railroad competition was very much a zero-sum game. Whatever markets and whatever traffic fell to the PRR's competitors represented that much less revenue for Thomson's company.

For nearly a decade after 1846, the most serious threat to the PRR's interests emanated from the Philadelphia & Reading. By the time that the Pennsylvania legislature issued the PRR's charter, the Reading had been in existence for more than a decade. Well capitalized and capably managed, the Reading enjoyed a secure traffic base, ferrying anthracite from northeastern Pennsylvania to tidewater. Its tracks connected Philadelphia and Harrisburg, shortly after Thomson was able to establish control over the Philadelphia & Columbia. During the antebellum period, the Reading endangered the PRR's ability to control the western traffic that flowed into Philadelphia, and the company remained a threat even after the Civil War. Its managers, schooled in the ongoing, decades-old rivalry with the PRR, readily formed alliances with other carriers, continuing to block the ambitions of PRR executives.

The Reading was by no means the first railroad to penetrate the anthracite county of northeastern Pennsylvania, but it was the first to link that region to Philadelphia by rail. In 1833, the General Assembly granted the company a charter to build, between Philadelphia and Reading, the gateway to the anthracite coal-mining region of northeastern Pennsylvania. From a connection with the Philadelphia & Columbia, construction crews built northward along the valley of the Schuylkill River, paralleling the Schuylkill Navigation. They reached Norristown in 1838 and Reading late the following year. By 1842, the Reading offered service to Mount Carbon in the heart of anthracite country. At its eastern extremity workers completed a branch to Port Richmond, on the Delaware River, north of Philadelphia. There, as many as a hundred ships at a time could load anthracite. In 1851, after the state abandoned the Belmont plane, the Reading gained access to Philadelphia on its own rails by purchasing the short portion of the original Philadelphia & Columbia route, including the Columbia Bridge, from the base of the plane east to the junction of Broad and Vine Streets.

The Lebanon Valley Railroad offered the Reading the opportunity to complete a route between Philadelphia and Harrisburg, in competition with the Philadelphia & Columbia and, ultimately, the PRR. In April 1836, many of the same individuals who had invested in the Reading Rail Road obtained a charter to build a line from the city of Reading some fifty-four miles west to Lebanon and Harrisburg, along a route that roughly paralleled the Union Canal. There was little local interest in the line, stock subscriptions proved disappointing, and the project faded into obscurity.[137]

The Lebanon Valley charter nonetheless posed several threats to the PRR. Should the route be constructed, it would draw traffic away from the Harrisburg, Portsmouth, Mount Joy & Lancaster. More ominously, if the Reading gained control of the Lebanon Valley, it would be a simple matter to link that line to the Cumberland Valley Railroad, extending the anthracite carrier's reach west of the Susquehanna River. As early as

May 1850, Thomson (then serving as chief engineer and general superintendent) was acutely aware of the possibility that the Lebanon Valley might harm the interests both of the PRR and of Philadelphia. He warned the board that "the Lebanon Valley Rail Rd. stock should be looked after to prevent it being controlled by New York influence to divert the trade towards New York," but the members of the Road Committee declined to take action on the matter.[138]

In 1853, Reading interests revived and reorganized the Lebanon Valley Railroad, partly as a response to the growing involvement of PRR officials in the competing Lancaster, Lebanon & Pine Grove Rail Road. The activities of the Reading supporters in turn goaded PRR executives into providing additional assistance to the Lancaster, Lebanon & Pine Grove. The following year, work began on the Lebanon Valley, under the direction of Richard Boyse Osborne, a talented and experienced civil engineer who had also been involved in building the Dauphin & Susquehanna Coal Company's railroad. The Reading provided most of the capital necessary to complete the line, which reached Harrisburg in January 1858. Later that year, the Reading acquired outright control over the Lebanon Valley. The Reading & Columbia Railroad, chartered in 1857, soon constructed a line from Sinking Spring, in the Lebanon Valley just west of Reading, southwest, across the route of the PRR-controlled Harrisburg, Portsmouth, Mount Joy & Lancaster, and to the Susquehanna River at Columbia. Thus began what was to be a long period of direct competition between the Reading and the PRR.[139]

The Cumberland Valley Railroad offered the Reading a logical westward extension and, even more ominously, the possibility of a connection with the Baltimore & Ohio, one that would virtually encircle the eastern portion of the PRR's operations. In 1856 and again in 1857, the Pennsylvania legislature had authorized the Cumberland Valley Railroad to buy the Chambersburg, Greencastle & Hagerstown Railroad (the former Franklin Railroad). The Cumberland Valley board declined to purchase its southern extension, which was little more than a poorly built branch line to the isolated terminus of Hagerstown, Maryland. Should it fall under the control of the Reading, however, that company could have rehabilitated the tracks and extended its rails to the B&O main line, little more than twenty miles to the south. In August 1857, several investors purchased the Pennsylvania portion of the Chambersburg, Greencastle & Hagerstown. They were fronting financier Jay Cooke and his banking house, E. W. Clark & Company. The new owners rebuilt the line, again named the Franklin Railroad and operated by the Cumberland Valley.

Thomson was now determined to prevent the Cumberland Valley route from falling under the control of his rival. In July 1859, a year and a half after the Reading's Lebanon Valley subsidiary reached Harrisburg, the PRR purchased a controlling interest in the Cumberland Valley, removing the line from the management of its local proprietors. Three years later, a merger of the Cumberland Valley and the Franklin Railroad gave the PRR a route south, into Maryland. After 1859, when the Cumberland Valley came under PRR control, the Reading no longer had a realistic chance to reach Pittsburgh, the Great Lakes, and the West.[140]

Even though Thomson frustrated early efforts by Reading officials to extend the scope of their railroad's operations, the company remained far stronger than the youthful Pennsylvania Railroad. Since its incorporation in 1833, the Reading grew rich from an ever-increasing floodtide of anthracite bound for the wharves at Port Richmond. In 1846, the same year that the legislature chartered the PRR, the Reading hauled nearly 1.2 million tons of coal, twenty-four times its traffic of only six years earlier. Revenues in 1846 were in excess of $1.9 million, with a net income of $402,292. In 1847, the year that PRR officials broke ground at Harrisburg, the Reading carried more tons of freight than the Erie Canal, and at a far lower cost per ton mile. By 1855, the Reading's receipts totaled nearly $4.3 million ($3.6 million of which came from the shipment of 2.2 million tons of coal), generating a net income of more than $2.3 million. Despite the propensity of the Reading's managers to reinvest earnings in the property, the company's investors nonetheless received more than a million dollars in dividends that year, at a healthy rate of 12 percent—all in all, not a bad performance for a railroad only ninety-eight miles long.[141]

The Pennsylvania Railroad in 1855 had the advantage of mileage (259) and total capitalization, but little else. The PRR's total freight traffic stood at just 365,000 tons, compared with the Reading's 2.9 million tons. Given the disparity in mileage, those figures indicated that the Reading moved nearly 30,000 tons annually per mile of road, while the PRR managed only 1,409 tons per mile of track, less than one-twentieth of the Reading's volume. The Pennsylvania Railroad's receipts were just under $4.3 million, nearly the same as those of the Reading, but net income was far less, at just over $1.8 million. The PRR began to overtake its rival later in the decade, as poor economic conditions reduced the demand for anthracite, but the Reading remained a formidable competitor.[142]

Thomson perceived an even greater threat from the two northern trunk lines that funneled traffic to New York City, now firmly established as the nation's center of commerce. The New York & Erie Rail Road was struggling, yet the company had the potential to deny the PRR access to the west. By May 1851, months before the PRR was open to Pittsburgh, the Erie reached the shores of Lake Erie, at Dunkirk, New York, creating what was then the longest railroad in the United States, under one management.[143]

The other New York trunk line posed an even more proximate threat to the PRR's interests. In March 1853, partly in response to the arrival of the PRR into Pittsburgh the year before, Erastus Corning welded together the eight railroads that formed the route between Albany and Buffalo into the New York Central Railroad.[144] The Hudson River Railroad, completed in 1851, provided a secure connection from Albany to New York City. In February 1852, the Buffalo & State Line Railroad (a company later allied with the New York Central) completed a route between Buffalo and the Pennsylvania border. In Ohio, the Cleveland, Painesville & Ashtabula Railroad built east from Cleveland, reaching the Ohio state line in November.

For a time, Thomson and other PRR executives hoped that the General Assembly could protect the PRR from the New York Central and the Erie. The owners of the two New York roads set their sights on the rich farmlands of Ohio and Indiana and the booming city of Chicago. To reach them, however, they would need to lay rails through the Erie Triangle, at the one small place where the commonwealth of Pennsylvania touched Lake Erie. That narrow strip of land gave Pennsylvania legislators a pronounced geographic advantage in that they could block the western extension of the two New York carriers. Their counterparts in Virginia did much the same, delaying the B&O route to the Ohio River and, later, blocking the PRR's efforts to gain access to southern Ohio. Other states followed similar policies, jealously guarding the right to protect their corporations and their communities from "foreign" competition. Few locales, however, produced results as spectacular as the conflict that erupted in the streets of Erie, Pennsylvania. The resulting fracas bemused and dismayed railroaders and the general public alike, but it did little to slow down the westward progress of the two New York trunk lines.

The Erie, Pennsylvania, "gauge war" of 1853 and 1854 ranks as one of the oft-told stories of confrontation between railroads and the local communities that they served. Far more than a mere antiquarian anecdote, however, the events in Erie reflected the struggle by the eastern trunk lines, including the PRR, to obtain an outlet to the west. The gauge war also indicated the deep ambivalence that the residents of many cities felt toward the railroads. While they valued access to other regions of the country, they also feared that the iron rails would divert traffic away from their businesses and their communities, plunging them into commercial ruin.

During the early 1850s, Pennsylvania legislators gradually abandoned their efforts to rebuff corporations chartered in other states, such as New York. The growing economic liberalization placated many voters in Erie, who did not yet have rail access to the east coast. More significantly, it reflected the growing regional and even national organization of Philadelphia businessmen, who were active in many states, not just Pennsylvania. Prior to 1851, the General Assembly did not permit any railroad to build across the Erie Triangle, blocking the westward advance of the New York trunk lines. In March 1851, however, legislators relented and allowed east–west railroads to pass through Erie. To the delight of PRR interests and Erie residents, the General Assembly required that all railroads east of Erie were to be constructed to either the New York & Erie's broad gauge (6′) or to standard gauge (4′ 8¼″), while rails were to be set to 4′ 10″ Ohio

gauge west of the city. The artificial impediment to commerce, more typical of railroads in the South, required freight to be transshipped from one set of cars to another, to the obvious benefit of Erie's workforce and its commercial interests. The legislation also proved beneficial to the PRR because it acted as an impediment to the efficient movement of trains on the Erie and the New York Central.[145]

The Pennsylvania gauge law resulted in a complex tangle of corporate entities competing for the right to build across the narrow strip of land between New York and Ohio. One company was the Erie & North East Railroad, chartered in 1842 to link Erie with the town of North East, Pennsylvania, near the New York border. By January 1852, the line was complete, providing a western extension for the Buffalo & State Line Railroad. Yet, in conformity with the Pennsylvania gauge law, it was laid to six-foot gauge, not to the standard gauge employed from the New York border to the east.

The saga of the Franklin Canal Company's railroad was somewhat more complex. In 1844, the General Assembly chartered the firm, giving its owners the right to rehabilitate the old Franklin Line slackwater navigation and convert the route to a canal. That project was essentially hopeless, however, and in April 1849 legislators permitted the Franklin Canal Company to build a railroad along what was to have been the route of the canal towpath from Franklin to Meadville, with extensions south to Pittsburgh and north to Erie. That provision soon caught the attention of the New York financiers who were associated with the Cleveland, Painesville & Ashtabula, the Ohio ally of the railroads that would soon become the New York Central. In August 1850, they agreed to revive the Franklin Canal Company and to use its charter to lay tracks, set to Ohio gauge, between Erie and the Pennsylvania-Ohio state line. By November 1852, construction crews had laid track across the western portion of the Erie Triangle, much to the consternation of PRR officials.[146]

The nearly simultaneous westward expansion of the New York & Erie Rail Road also gave Thomson and his fellow PRR executives cause for concern. Since 1851, commercial interests in New York, Pennsylvania, and Ohio had been planning a western extension to the Erie. In March 1851, the Ohio legislature approved a charter for the Franklin & Warren Railroad (after September 1853, the Atlantic & Great Western Railroad), linking the far northeastern corner of Ohio, at the Pennsylvania state line, with Dayton. A few months later, in June 1851, residents of Jamestown, New York, organized the Erie & New York City Railroad, to connect their community with the Erie's main line at Salamanca, New York. Neither company was directly affiliated with the Erie, but both were to be built to the Erie's six-foot gauge. Together, the Franklin & Warren and the Erie & New York City would create an unbroken broad gauge line from New York to Dayton, with the exception of a small segment through the Erie Triangle. That segment, however, ran afoul of the Pennsylvania gauge law.

Accordingly, proponents of the broad-gauge route adopted a bit of legal subterfuge. In April 1846, barely a week after authorizing the incorporation of the PRR, the Pennsylvania legislature had chartered the Pittsburgh & Erie Railroad Company. The charter had been something of a pacifier for the western Pennsylvania interests who had supported the B&O's efforts to reach Pittsburgh. It was also based on the assumption that the PRR would not complete its first thirty miles of track by July 30, 1847—in which case the B&O would be allowed to construct a line to Pittsburgh. In that event, the Pittsburgh & Erie would be authorized to connect with the B&O, providing that company a route from Baltimore to Lake Erie, via Pittsburgh. Even though the PRR's success temporarily denied the B&O access to Pittsburgh, the Pittsburgh & Erie's supporters began construction in 1849. They accomplished little useful work, however. In addition to the right to build a line between its namesake cities, the Pittsburgh & Erie held the authority to construct a branch line to the Ohio border. In October 1852, at a meeting held in Cleveland, Ohio, the broad-gauge A&GW interests resolved to negotiate an agreement with the owners of the Pittsburgh & Erie. By August 1853, work was under way at Meadville, Pennsylvania, but financial and political problems soon brought construction to a halt.[147]

In April 1853, Pennsylvania legislators repealed the gauge law, leading to allegations that the representatives of the New York trunk lines had secured their victory through bribery. In November, officials of the broad-gauge Erie & North East Railroad announced plans to convert their line between Erie and the New York state line to Ohio gauge. The difference between Ohio gauge and standard gauge was only one and a half inches, thus allowing compromise-gauge cars to pass unimpeded from New York through Buffalo to Cleveland.[148]

The announcement infuriated local commercial interests, who had long assumed that Erie was destined to become the western terminus of both the New York Central and the New York & Erie. The city's mayor, Alfred King, the city council, community leaders, and an enraged mob blocked efforts at conversion, ripping up sections of track and threatening railroad workers. Governor Bigler, along with most of the members of the legislature, openly applauded the actions of Erie's citizens. The General Assembly supported Bigler's call to repeal the charter of the Franklin Canal Company, ending its right to serve as the connection between the Erie & North East and the Cleveland, Painesville & Ashtabula. Although the courts initially questioned the right of the Franklin Canal Company to construct a railroad that only tangentially fulfilled the terms of its 1844 corporate charter, a series of court rulings upheld the repeal of the gauge law and enjoined the citizens of Erie from doing any other mischief with the tracks that ran through their city.[149] The "rippers" managed to delay the conversion of the line to Ohio gauge until February 1854, but the trains eventually rolled through Erie nonetheless.[150]

The repeal of the gauge law and the quelling of the violence in Erie represented a serious setback for the Pennsylvania Railroad. The gauge war occurred just as the PRR was completing its own line across the Alleghenies, bypassing the inclined planes of the Allegheny Portage Railroad. To the east, the PRR had not yet established control over the Philadelphia & Columbia. To the west, commercial interests in Pittsburgh, already predisposed to be hostile to the PRR's railroad monopoly in the region, waged their own campaign against the railroad. More restrained than their counterparts in Erie, Pittsburghers nonetheless were determined to retain their status as a break-of-bulk point. They retarded Thomson's efforts to forge a direct connection between the PRR and its allied railroads in Ohio and Indiana.

Another serious threat to the PRR's interests loomed to the south. Since 1828, the Baltimore & Ohio had been building westward, at first sluggishly, and then with accelerating speed. Its arrival in Cumberland, Maryland, in November 1842 helped to trigger the battle of the charters that erupted in the Pennsylvania legislature less than four years later. The Pennsylvania legislature, at the behest of Philadelphia mercantile interests, had prevented the B&O from building toward Pittsburgh. Despite the setback, Baltimore & Ohio construction crews continued to push west into Virginia. On January 1, 1853, the first B&O train reached the Ohio River at Wheeling. The PRR had already inaugurated service between Philadelphia and Pittsburgh, but over a line cobbled together from new construction, the Philadelphia & Columbia, and the Allegheny Portage Railroad. Baltimore, in contrast, enjoyed a continuous line of railroad, under a single ownership, stretching to the west.

While all three rival trunk lines constituted a serious threat to the PRR's interests, it was another transportation artery that prevented the company from attaining the goals that its promoters had envisioned. The continued success of the Erie Canal reflected the development of transportation patterns during the decade prior to the Civil War. By 1860, canals carried the majority of the nation's freight, by weight, but the railroads held the larger share by shipment value. On the Erie Canal, westbound traffic in manufactured goods peaked in 1853 and had been cut in half by 1860. Speed clearly mattered in the case of high-value shipments and passenger traffic, and the railroads, including the PRR, had little difficulty in seizing that business from the canals.[151]

Grain was another matter entirely. Neither the New York Central nor any of the other eastern trunk lines had crippled the Erie Canal, and that waterway continued to be the dominant transporter of grain between the Great Lakes and the Atlantic seaboard. While passengers had largely deserted the canal packets in favor of more rapid locomotion, grain was a low-value commodity, well suited to water transport. Accordingly, the New York canals in 1855 accommodated more than four million tons of traffic, with well over half of that amount traveling on the Erie Canal, by far the state's most important manmade waterway.

More than a million tons of agricultural products, principally grain, crossed New York that year. Total revenues for the state system were in excess of $2.6 million.[152]

By comparison, the Pennsylvania Railroad had singularly failed to funnel western grain toward Philadelphia, or to rebuild the mercantile preeminence of the Quaker City. The PRR's $4.2 million in gross earnings compared favorably with toll receipts on the New York canals, indicative of the premium that many passengers and shippers were willing to pay for speed. Flour, partly a natural and partly a manufactured commodity, was only slightly more likely to travel by water than by rail—although the PRR obtained relatively little of that traffic, given Buffalo's prominence as a milling center. Grain traffic was negligible, however, and would always remain so. Together, the PRR, the Erie, and the New York Central competed for a pool of eastbound traffic that was perhaps half of what the Erie Canal carried on its own. The tremendous growth of agriculture in the Old Northwest during the 1850s and 1860s saved the PRR and its rail competitors. The cornucopia of grain taxed the capacity of Great Lakes shipping and the Erie Canal, and made attractive every avenue of transportation.[153]

The PRR's limited success in capturing the western trade persisted for the remainder of the company's history. In 1886, a report prepared by the Senate Committee on Interstate Commerce noted that three of the four U.S. trunk lines generated as much as 90 percent of their revenues from through traffic. The exception was the Pennsylvania Railroad, where more than half of total tonnage originated along the route between Pittsburgh and Philadelphia.[154] Even as late as 1955, more than a century after the PRR's incorporation, most products exported out of Philadelphia originated in a small area, barely larger than the state of Pennsylvania, with virtually no traffic coming from the region west of Youngstown, Ohio.[155] Furthermore, the PRR did scarcely better than the Main Line of Public Works at diverting to Philadelphia the traffic from the Susquehanna River Valley that had traditionally flowed through Baltimore. Ever since the completion of the Pennsylvania state system, shippers had dispatched a large share of eastbound traffic down the Susquehanna River to the Chesapeake Bay. That option became even more convenient in 1840 with the completion of the Baltimore & Susquehanna Railroad, and the PRR could do little to stop the leakage out of the Keystone State. By 1955, moreover, Baltimore, New York, and Philadelphia each shared roughly a third of the export traffic originating in central Pennsylvania. Never in its history was the PRR able to capture the western trade, as its promoters had intended.

As Thomson soon discovered, however, the PRR's salvation lay in short-haul freight traffic. That was particularly true so long as the tonnage tax was in place on longer shipments. As Thomson informed his shareholders, in the PRR's *Seventh Annual Report*, "It is to the local business that we must look for the most reliable source of revenue."[156] Of the 365,000 tons of freight that traveled over the PRR in 1855—less than a tenth of the amount that followed the New York canals—well over half was local in nature. The PRR's reliance on local traffic would only increase in the decades to come, and by the 1880s it constituted some 90 percent of total shipments. During the middle years of the nineteenth century, the local carriage of coal, metallurgical products, and other commodities would more than compensate for the disappointingly low levels of grain traffic, greatly benefiting the PRR, if not necessarily its headquarters city. Local traffic generated the revenues that enabled Thomson and his successors to withstand repeated rate wars and to finance new construction, betterments, and expansion into Ohio, Indiana, and Illinois.[157]

From Regional Railroad to Trunk Line

In April 1856, as Thomson looked back over the decade that had elapsed since the PRR's incorporation, he doubtless took great satisfaction at his accomplishments. He had triumphed over considerable adversity, wresting control away from the merchants who had dominated the PRR board and placing power in the hands of civil engineers. He had overseen the construction of a new line of railroad from Harrisburg to Pittsburgh and had then completed one of the engineering wonders of the world, designing a new route over the Allegheny Mountains in order to replace the antiquated Allegheny Portage Railroad. By incurring

bonded debt, he had made provision for the financial integrity that would be the PRR's hallmark for more than a century. While often critical of the lax management of the Main Line of Public Works, he had wisely refrained from constructing a direct alternative to the Philadelphia & Columbia, and he had skillfully maneuvered the commonwealth into selling that railroad, and the remainder of the Main Line of Public Works, on exceedingly favorable terms. Thomson did not merely incorporate the tracks of the Philadelphia & Columbia into the PRR system, however. He also co-opted the independent freight forwarders who had operated over the Main Line, using their equipment and their experienced personnel to develop the PRR's initial, embryonic freight and passenger traffic capabilities.

Given the magnitude of the engineering work involved, the Pennsylvania Railroad had completed its route with astonishing swiftness. In October 1850, PRR directors were able to travel by train from Philadelphia as far west as Duncansville and the interchange with the Allegheny Portage Railroad. By December 1852, the Western Division was open to traffic between Johnstown and Pittsburgh. The completion of the Horseshoe Curve and the Summit Tunnel allowed the intervening Middle Division to enter service on February 15, 1854, giving the PRR complete control over the route between Harrisburg and Pittsburgh. By the beginning of 1856, the Pennsylvania Railroad operated 118 locomotives, 119 passenger cars, and 1,635 freight cars over that route, 136 miles of which were already double-tracked. With the purchase of the Main Line of Public Works the following year, the PRR controlled an unbroken rail route from Philadelphia to Pittsburgh and had attained the status of a trunk line between east and west.[158] Now in the fifth year of his presidency, Thomson undoubtedly agreed with a comment that Herman Haupt had made several years earlier. "The Penna. RR," Haupt had written, "will soon be ready for a race in which no competitor can distance her."[159]

Yet, there was much that remained to be done. Iron rails for an additional forty miles of second main line were ready for installation. Temporary wooden trestles required either fills or the erection of more substantial structures. Particularly on the Middle Division, cuts and fills that had not yet reached their angle of repose were prone to slides, blocking some tracks and undermining others. Applying the finishing touches to the new main line of private works constituted the least of Thomson's worries, however. The president and his fellow executives and employees struggled to develop efficient operating routines, fend off competition, add branches to the PRR's newly established trunk line, and establish outlets to the west.

Those concerns paled in comparison with a deteriorating national economy, and the political balkanization of the nation itself. The Panic of 1857, set amid the growing sectional tensions between North and South, shattered investor confidence and brought to an end the heady days of antebellum railway expansion in the Northeast. Of the four emerging trunk lines, the Erie and its western connections were perhaps the most seriously affected. Yet, the New York Central and the Baltimore & Ohio also felt the effects of the economic crisis. So, too, did the Pennsylvania Railroad. By September 25, PRR shares, with a par value of fifty, had

declined to thirty-six. The board suspended work on double-tracking the main line, and the railroad's employees, and all but a few of its officers, suffered steep pay cuts.[160]

By the autumn of 1857, whatever satisfaction that Thomson may have taken from his past accomplishments had yielded to his conviction that two changes were necessary to secure the future of the Pennsylvania Railroad. First, he would need to recreate the company's organizational structure, yielding control to local managers while using carefully collected statistical data to monitor their performance. Second, he would have to find a way to persuade the General Assembly to repeal the tonnage tax that had placed the PRR at a competitive disadvantage against the other three trunk lines. And, he would have to achieve both of those goals while maintaining harmonious relations with allied railroads to the north, south, and west, all of which funneled traffic into the PRR system. In each of those efforts, he succeeded.

Chapter 6

Coordination

1857–1860

In September 1857, a hurricane raged off the coast of the Carolinas. Of all the ships trapped in its maelstrom, none suffered a more tragic fate than the SS *Central America*. A week earlier, the ship had left Colón, Panama, for New York. On board were passengers and cargo that had traveled from California, south along the Pacific Coast, and then across the isthmus by the recently completed Panama Railroad. With them came the treasure of the California goldfields, perhaps twenty tons of the yellow metal. Their wealth now helped to seal their doom, as the waterlogged ship began to founder in heavy seas. On the morning of Friday, September 11, water began pouring into the hull, through the paddlewheel housings, and all hands were set to bailing. The effort was futile, and at eight o'clock the next evening, the ship sank off of Cape Hatteras. More than four hundred passengers and crew went to the bottom, along with the many tons of gold.[1]

The sinking of the *Central America* was part of a much larger tragedy that affected far more than the souls on board and their families. The Panic of 1857 was well under way by the time that the ship disappeared, but the loss of its golden cargo helped strike a crippling blow to the American economy. The railroad network was badly overbuilt, with the trunk lines in particular possessing far more capacity than they

could use in the near term. Grain prices had fallen, depressing land values and causing great hardship for farmers. Declining property prices in turn ruined many land speculators. British capitalists, concerned about the soundness of American investment banking houses, began to withdraw funds from the economy. The ongoing horrors of "Bleeding Kansas," the caning of Senator Charles Sumner (in May 1856), and the Supreme Court's decision in the *Dred Scott* case (announced in March 1857) convinced many Americans that their nation was on the edge of disintegration.

On August 24, 1857, the New York branch of the Ohio Life Insurance & Trust Company suspended specie payments, amid swirling rumors of rampant embezzlement. Within days, the principals of other New York investment houses curtailed lending in a desperate effort to save their firms. By early September, values on the New York Stock Exchange plummeted. The loss of the *Central America,* and the gold that might have underwritten new loans, added to the chaos. The failure of the Bank of Pennsylvania on September 25 compounded the misery, particularly within its namesake state. The crisis peaked on October 14 when virtually all of the banks in New York and New England suspended payments. Both commerce and industrial output declined sharply, with perhaps one hundred thousand people unemployed. The economy

Figure 25. In 1830, the New Jersey legislature chartered the Camden & Amboy Rail Road and the Delaware & Raritan Canal—two attempts to improve transportation between New York and Philadelphia, on the most heavily trafficked corridor in the United States. In 1836, the two companies established an alliance with the Philadelphia & Trenton Railroad and the New Jersey Rail Road & Transportation Company. Bordentown, shown here, was the southern terminus of the Delaware & Raritan Canal, as well as the site of a junction between the original Camden & Amboy line and a short branch that connected to Trenton, and the Philadelphia & Trenton right of way. Steamboat travel on the Delaware River was fast, comfortable, and convenient, and many travelers—including those seen here disembarking from the *William Penn*—boarded the Camden & Amboy at Bordentown, and rode the thirty-four miles across New Jersey, where another steamboat was waiting to convey them to New York. By the time that the Pennsylvania Railroad leased the New Jersey lines, in 1871, most people preferred to ride via the Philadelphia & Trenton and the New Jersey Rail Road, in part because of the more convenient northern terminus, located in Jersey City.

The Camden and Amboy Railroad with the Engine "Planet" in 1834, *by Edward Lamson Henry, 1904, Frye Art Museum, Seattle, Washington.*

struggled to recover, but the crisis did not finally end until the onset of the Civil War.[2]

The Panic of 1857 brought to an end the first great period of railway expansion in the United States. In 1853 and 1854, construction crews had almost simultaneously completed work on the four great eastern trunk lines—the PRR, the New York Central, the Erie, and the Baltimore & Ohio. All four had been in

some measure built to tap the western grain trade, yet all four shared roughly as much traffic as that transported by the Erie Canal alone. For a very few years, an expanding economy and the overtaxed carrying capacity of the canal had permitted each carrier to capture a respectable amount of business. After 1857, however, each company competed for a much smaller traffic base. To make matters worse, the State of New York was steadily enlarging the Erie Canal. Although construction of what was essentially an entirely new waterway was not completed until 1862, the effects of the increased carrying capacity on the railroads were apparent well before that date.

The depression fell hardest on the Baltimore & Ohio and the Erie. By November 1858, the B&O's private investors were thoroughly disgusted with the mismanagement and political cronyism associated with the public directors. In a rebellion similar to what had occurred on the PRR, more than six years earlier, they chose John W. Garrett as the new president of the B&O. Like J. Edgar Thomson, Garrett would remain in power for decades, shaping the company to suit his will. The changes on the B&O were nonetheless mild in comparison to those on the New York & Erie. In August 1859 that company plunged spectacularly into bankruptcy, marking the first time that a trunk line had failed.

The Pennsylvania Railroad was well equipped to withstand the financial catastrophe. In January 1852, shortly before Thomson became president, general superintendent Herman Haupt had boasted that "the expenses on the Pennsylvania Railroad, *proper*, fall below the usual average of fifty per cent. of the receipts; but the most gratifying result is shown in the whole cost of running the trains per mile, which has been less than on any other railroad in the United States; less than on any of the best managed roads in New England; [and] less than on the Georgia Railroad."[3] By 1854, and thanks in large measure to the rigorous statistical controls that Haupt had developed, the PRR posted some of the lowest expenses in the railroad business. Its average operating costs, per mile, were just 7.05 cents, compared with 8.97 cents on the B&O and an astronomical 10.30 cents on the Erie. When the depression that began in 1857 caused revenues to plummet, the PRR was well positioned to weather the storm.

The Pennsylvania Railroad nonetheless faced several problems, each of which placed the company at a competitive disadvantage against the other three trunk lines. First, unlike the Erie and the New York Central, the PRR lacked secure access to New York, the most important market in the United States. Instead, Thomson relied on the interchange of traffic at Philadelphia, with two separate but administratively coordinated

carriers, the Philadelphia & Trenton Railroad and the Camden & Amboy Rail Road. To make matters worse, there was no direct rail connection between the PRR and either of its New York outlets, mandating the costly and time-consuming transfer of freight and passengers at Philadelphia. Perhaps most vexingly, the tonnage tax imperiled Thomson's ability to compete against other railroads. The legislature had added the tax to the PRR's corporate charter in an effort to protect the Main Line of Public Works, but in June 1857 the PRR bought the Main Line, and soon dismantled parts of it, leaving little to protect.

The economic malaise that followed the Panic of 1857 encouraged Thomson to make four major changes to the Pennsylvania Railroad. First, he became more sympathetic to Haupt's incessant pleas for lower rates and higher volumes of traffic, even if such policies threatened to destabilize the northeastern railroad network. Second, Thomson oversaw a radical reorganization of the PRR's corporate structure, a move designed in large measure to increase the company's operational efficiency in difficult economic times. Third, he sought closer cooperation with the independent railroads that moved much of the PRR's traffic along the Atlantic seaboard. Finally, the president became more determined than ever to lift the burden of the tonnage tax from the Pennsylvania Railroad. In each case, Thomson had planned the broad outlines of those policies well before the failure of the Ohio Life & Trust Company. The economic crisis nonetheless accelerated Thomson's ambitious agenda.

Organizing a Statewide Railroad

As PRR executives expanded the company's organizational capabilities, they continued to make corresponding adjustments to their system of corporate governance. By the autumn of 1857, three factors had induced a sweeping transformation in the PRR's organizational structure. On August 1, the PRR began operating the Main Line of Public Works, greatly increasing the scope and complexity of the company's activities. Less than a month earlier, the North Pennsylvania Railroad (a separate company from the PRR, and later a part of the Philadelphia & Reading) suffered a horrific accident at Fort Washington, Pennsylvania. The disaster killed sixty people, many of them children, and led to an immediate public outcry for more precisely controlled operating methods. Most important, however, was the Panic of 1857, which caused a sharp downturn in business and exacerbated the already severe competition among the eastern railroads. By November, Thomson had suspended the double-tracking of the main line, as well as most other new construction, and employees suffered steep pay cuts. In that context, he saw administrative reforms as essential to the company's survival.[4]

A rival eastern railroad, the New York & Erie, greatly influenced the PRR's new organizational structure. The Erie was by far the longest railroad in the United States under continuous management. Rising expenditures, a high rate of accidents, and a crippling strike by engine crews further complicated the railroad's operations. Since 1849, civil engineer Daniel C. McCallum had been building bridges for the Erie, and in 1853 the company's officials hired him as superintendent of the Susquehanna Division. McCallum soon developed a set of operating rules that precisely delineated the responsibilities for each employee and that showed little mercy for incompetency or even simple error.[5] He attempted to control expenses and maximize efficiency by developing a mechanism for comparing one set of executives with another. Rather than mimic the functional specializations of a traditional business, McCallum divided the Erie into five operating divisions, decentralizing authority into the hands of regional managers.[6]

McCallum's ideas were not precisely new. More than a decade earlier, George Washington Whistler had employed a similar divisional strategy on the Western Railroad of Massachusetts, although he lacked the statistical data and the information flows necessary to fully coordinate and comparatively evaluate each division's personnel. On the PRR, Haupt in 1849 implemented a revised version of the Whistler plan, and he also developed many of the statistical measures necessary to accurately assess performance. Soon afterward, the PRR board established the Eastern, Middle, and Western Divisions as part of the 1852 reorganization. At that time, however, the duties of the four assistant superintendents varied both geographically and functionally,

and it was accordingly impossible to compare them against each other.[7]

McCallum's original contribution lay in his efforts to facilitate the flow of information among the personnel on each division, the line officers who were responsible for safe and efficient operation, and the managerial staff at the central office who coordinated the activities of the entire company. The need for effective communication and clear delineation of authority in turn mandated the creation of one of the first organizational charts in the history of American business. Unlike more recent charts, it was a literal rendition of a tree, with departments depicted as branches, and personnel as individual leaves.[8] Henry Varnum Poor, the editor of the *American Railroad Journal*, offered lithographed copies of McCallum's schema for sale, at a dollar apiece. Thomson and other PRR executives were certainly aware of McCallum's ideas. Yet, Poor seems to have given Haupt and Thomson little credit for developing, on their own, ideas that were remarkably similar to McCallum's—probably because of a long-running feud between the editor and the PRR president.[9]

Rather than give preference to McCallum, Haupt, or any other individual for the organizational revolution that characterized the railroads during the 1850s, it would be more apt to credit a small and closely connected network of senior executives, each of whom was familiar with the innovations generated by the others. On the PRR, general superintendent Herman J. Lombaert was probably responsible for many of the details of the company's new organization, developed during the autumn of 1857.[10] By September 1857, and probably at Lombaert's suggestion, the board had copied the divisional structure that Whistler, McCallum, and others had developed. With the PRR directly serving Philadelphia, the board subdivided the Transportation Department into the Philadelphia, Eastern, Middle, and Western Divisions. In December, the board approved the other details associated with the PRR's new organization manual.[11]

In developing the new organizational structure, which took effect on January 1, 1858, both Lombaert and Thomson desired to free Transportation Department personnel from all of the basic support functions—particularly those associated with transportation accounting—that were not directly related to the day-to-day operation of trains. The relatively short length of each division enabled operating personnel to concentrate their efforts on a small portion of the railroad's operations. Thomson and Lombaert also sought a mechanism for evaluating and promoting promising junior executives, grooming them for positions of greater responsibility.[12]

The result was a decentralized operating structure. Each division resembled a company within a company, with clearly demarcated lines of authority that would allow information to be passed up the chain to supervisory personnel, and that would in turn allow supervisors to pass orders down the line to their subordinates. Division superintendents governed each division, and they possessed full control over routine operating matters on their divisions, equivalent to the authority that the general superintendent held over the company as a whole. The responsibilities of each division superintendent included the supervision of train scheduling and movements; communications affecting his division; the purchase and distribution of fuel and other supplies; repairs to the tracks, bridges, buildings, locomotives, and freight and passenger cars; the hiring and discipline of employees; and the enforcement of both divisional and system rules.[13]

The relative autonomy of the PRR's division superintendents stood in sharp contrast to the departmental structure employed on many other railroads. Even on Daniel McCallum's Erie, the heads of the various company-wide departments were in charge of such functional duties as the maintenance of locomotives, rolling stock, and the physical plant. Their role was not to serve the divisional personnel, but rather to tell them what to do. A similar situation applied on the New York Central, even though that company possessed a fairly small central office staff, with most administrative duties carried out by the railroad's constituent corporate entities.[14]

The PRR's decentralization of authority to the division superintendents was by no means the only innovation associated with the 1858 reorganization. The new rules created a direct line of authority in the Transportation Department, from the president, through the general superintendent, to the division superintendents and their personnel, who managed routine transporta-

tion functions on each section of the railroad. Yet, Thomson and Lombaert depended on another group of executives for functions that were not directly associated with daily operations. Staff officers were in charge of coordinating activities across the entire railroad, ensuring that the division superintendents worked in harmony with one another. As such, they reported directly to Thomson and the board of directors. In addition to coordinating transportation functions, system staff personnel were responsible for setting rates and schedules, resolving legal matters, purchasing real estate, and establishing standards for the construction and repair of locomotives, rolling stock, and the right of way. As each division was in some respects a company within a company, each of the division superintendents likewise supervised a compliment of divisional staff officers.

The 1858 organization, marked by a combination of line officers in the Transportation Department and staff officers at both the company and the divisional levels, launched the Pennsylvania Railroad's line-and-staff corporate structure.[15] At the central staff level, the new system reflected the organic changes that had taken place since 1852. By 1856, with construction on the main line essentially complete, the centralized engineer corps had been dissolved. Instead, two company-wide resident engineers, each of whom reported to the general superintendent, oversaw the small number of new construction projects and developed engineering standards for the railroad as a whole. One resident engineer was based in Altoona and assigned to the Western Division, and the other was responsible for the comparatively less problematic matters on the remainder of the railroad. Routine maintenance-of-way matters were in the hands of the division superintendents and their staffs.

The Legal Department, which the board had established in January 1854, went through several reorganizations. Beginning on January 1, 1858, the railroad briefly employed three solicitors, one each at Philadelphia, Harrisburg, and Altoona. A few months later, Thomson impressed on the directors the need to mount a full-scale assault on the tonnage tax. At the same meeting, the board adopted plans for reorganizing the Legal Department—no doubt the two events were connected. Effective July 1, 1858, the PRR fielded eleven district solicitors, based at the state capital and in various county seats across the system. They were located in close proximity to courts, well positioned to challenge the legality of the tonnage tax and to respond rapidly to other legal matters.[16]

The more significant changes affected the Auditor's Department. Before 1858, the auditor possessed a quite limited role, functioning primarily to ensure honesty and integrity in the management of the railroad's receipts and disbursements. Since 1849, when Haupt had first emphasized the value of operating data to control costs and set rates, the general superintendent assumed responsibility for collecting and interpreting that information. Subsequent increases in the railroad's length, the volume of its traffic, and the types of data collected soon overwhelmed the general superintendent and interfered with his ability to keep the trains moving.[17]

The 1858 organization manual made sweeping changes to the Transportation Department, which was the most important component of the railroad. The Transportation Department employed the bulk of the PRR's personnel, and it thus constituted the principal downward line of authority that extended from the president to the lowliest laborer. Under the new system, the board divided the Transportation Department into two units. One, by far the largest, managed transportation and traffic functions, under the direction of the general superintendent. The other embodied a radical revision of the Auditor's Department, now renamed the Accounting Department. The person in charge of the Accounting Department, given the title "controller and auditor," supervised the collection and dissemination of statistics pertaining to the railroad's operations. Effective January 1, 1858, Lombaert became controller and auditor, in charge of the PRR's transportation accounts. He yielded the position of general superintendent to Tom Scott, who had proven himself as third assistant superintendent, in charge of the Western Division. The bifurcation of the Transportation Department worked to the benefit of both Scott and Lombaert, as well as the company. As an energetic and charismatic problem-solver, Scott kept traffic moving, while Lombaert—diligent, fastidious, scrupulously honest, and according to Thomson possessed with an unrivaled knowledge of costs—kept close watch on the company's operating statistics.[18]

As general superintendent, Scott had the responsibility for day-to-day operations, assisted by the master of machinery (after 1863, the superintendent of motive power and machinery) in the Motive Power Department (established in October 1857), the general foreman of the Car Department, and the two resident engineers.[19] As controller and auditor, Lombaert advanced many of the techniques that Haupt had pioneered relating to the collection and interpretation of statistical data.[20] Because they required real-time knowledge of every aspect of the railroad's operations, PRR accountants collected data monthly, weekly, or even daily, rather than yearly. Within little more than a decade after the founding of the Pennsylvania Railroad, its managers had access to the most advanced set of data ever used in the history of business. That information was vitally important for the efficient management of daily operations in terms of controlling costs and in pricing the railroad's services so as to maximize revenues. The numbers also enabled Thomson and other senior managers to make appropriate long-term strategic decisions.[21]

Lombaert and his staff relied on two different types of accounts.[22] Financial accounts tracked the railroad's traffic and revenues, as well as expenditures on every aspect of operation and maintenance. By 1855, the railroad's accountants were keeping track of more than two hundred specific commodities, bundled into four separate rate classifications.[23] With the 1858 reorganization, the PRR maintained 144 types of accounts, of which 33 related to passenger traffic, 25 to freight, 26 to motive power, 22 to the maintenance of way, and 21 to construction and equipment. That data enabled managers to develop the operating ratio, a performance measure that indicated the percentage of gross revenue that was consumed by operating costs.[24]

PRR officials also paid close attention to capital accounting, which involved the allocation of expenses pertaining to such major assets as locomotives, rolling stock, and the physical plant. In general terms, the accountants charged the purchase of a new item, such as a locomotive, as a betterment (capital improvement) cost, and classified its replacement as an operating cost. Beginning in 1855, the PRR board had established a contingency fund to help offset the inevitable wear-and-tear—estimated at $110,000 annually for the physical plant, and $40,000 for equipment. That was not a depreciation account, per se. Rather, the board calculated the PRR's net income and paid the customary 6 percent annual dividend. Any monies left over went into a fund that could be tapped for new capital expenditures. In practice, the contingency fund was merely an accounting device, and its assets were folded into the railroad's expense account and, in some instances, used to fund investments in subsidiary and affiliated lines.[25]

Rates, Revisited

Herman Haupt returned to the PRR in April 1853, following a brief stint on the Southern Railroad of Mississippi. In his new post as the PRR's chief engineer, he again addressed the cost of transportation and its effects on rates. His ever more detailed cost and revenue estimates reinforced his commitment to a low-rate, high-volume pricing strategy. Given the extraordinary expense of railway construction, Haupt argued, it was vital that the PRR spread those costs over as large a traffic base as possible. Haupt was aware that most of the expenditures associated with the PRR—from real estate to rails to bridges to locomotives and cars—constituted fixed costs that would be present regardless of how much freight the railroad transported. Unlike other antebellum industries, variable costs—fuel, wages, repairs, and the like—were relatively insignificant. Once the PRR had incurred its fixed costs, and was obligated to pay interest charges on that investment, additional tons of freight could be accommodated with only a modest increase in variable costs. Under those circumstances, Haupt argued, the customary practice of simply dividing the railroad's total costs by the quantity of freight transported (yielding an expense of roughly two cents per ton-mile) offered a far too simplistic depiction of the effects of revenue and cost on net income. The better method, he insisted, was to ensure that freight charges covered at least their associated variable costs. Once that had occurred, any excess of revenues over variable costs would buy down some of the high fixed costs that the railroad had already incurred.[26]

In delineating the low marginal costs of the railroad industry, Haupt was one of the first people to articulate a principle that would become second nature to a later generation of transportation economists. During the early 1850s, however, the conventional wisdom suggested that rates must be kept high, and that revenues should be generated through markup, not through volume. That approach made sense at a time when the railroads generally carried only passengers and small quantities of high-value freight, leaving haulage of grain, coal, and other undifferentiated bulk commodities to the water carriers. Before 1852, moreover, PRR directors were resolutely opposed to low rates, and even after Thomson assumed the presidency, many doubted the wisdom of Haupt's proposals.

Even though Thomson supported Haupt in almost all instances, he was reluctant to sanction a low-rate, high-volume policy. Thomson had some experience with cost accounting from his days as the chief engineer of the Georgia Rail Road. In the South, however, Thomson had observed a railroad with limited traffic potential, serving lightly populated rural areas.[27] He concluded that any carrier operating under those conditions would have to charge high rates in order to earn a profit on a low volume of traffic. Thomson may have operated under the mistaken belief that the principles he had developed in Georgia were equally applicable to the far more industrialized and densely populated regions of central Pennsylvania. What was more likely, however, was that during the early 1850s Thomson regarded with horror the prospect of moving large quantities of freight across Pennsylvania, in conjunction with the City Railroad, the Philadelphia & Columbia, and the Allegheny Portage Railroad—to say nothing of the wagon haulage across the gap that separated the two halves of the Western Division.[28]

By the time that Haupt returned to the PRR, the company had established through freight service between Philadelphia and Pittsburgh, and was poised to complete a new route between Altoona and Johnstown, bypassing the cumbersome inclined planes of the Allegheny Portage Railroad. By 1854, the PRR's physical plant was finally capable of hosting the kind of low-rate, high-volume traffic that Haupt envisioned. In February 1854, Haupt issued his most forceful call yet for low rates and high volumes. The "increase of trade, activity of business, and the extension of our great cities," he insisted, "constitute objects of greater importance than large profits on transportation."[29] Haupt was not asserting that the PRR should move traffic at cost in order to benefit Philadelphia. Instead, he argued that low rates would permit a satisfactory profit based on volume, rather than markup. In addition, he believed that favorable rates would encourage commercial development along the route of the PRR, creating a virtuous cycle of additional traffic, which would permit a further reduction in rates and so create additional economic development.

The key, Haupt insisted, was to fill the PRR's tracks to capacity. At the time, they were anything but full, as the railroad had transported just under 160,000 tons of freight in 1853. Haupt suggested that the PRR could and should move at least a million tons of freight per year, a third of the eastbound volume on the Erie Canal, and half that of the Reading. Perhaps half of that amount would consist of bituminous coal. At such volumes, rates could be lowered to six mills (0.6 cents) per ton-mile east of the Alleghenies, and seven mills per ton-mile to the west—well below the two cents per ton-mile that many industry observers suggested was the minimum level to guarantee profitability. In order to ensure that the PRR would be "an instrument of incalculable good to the citizens of the State," Haupt argued, "*low rates*, with *moderate dividends*, must indicate the settled policy upon which the operations of the road are to be conducted."[30]

Haupt's demands for low rates and high volumes became even more strident after June 1855, when he essentially became a consultant for the PRR while working on other engineering projects.[31] A month earlier, the General Assembly had repealed the tonnage tax on coal and lumber shipments, increasing traffic volumes and for the first time making coal an important category of freight. Perhaps more than any other individual associated with the PRR, Haupt perceived that the railroad was well positioned to move ever-larger coal shipments. In February 1857, Haupt addressed a plea "to the Stockholders as well as to the President and Directors, because the opinion is prevalent amongst them that no profit can be derived from the transportation of coal on the Pennsylvania Railroad."[32] Haupt begged to differ. With his typical attention to detail, the PRR's former chief engineer analyzed the costs associated with local and long-distance transportation,

and insisted that the railroad could accommodate an additional fifty thousand tons of coal traffic annually, without the need to purchase additional equipment. Haupt's assertion that "a moment's reflection must satisfy any person of ordinary intelligence" that a rate of three mills per ton-mile would prove profitable revealed both his impressive command of statistics and the arrogant condescension that earned him many enemies.[33]

Haupt soon saw evidence that his predictions were coming true. Between 1855 and 1859, thanks in large measure to the partial repeal of the tonnage tax, freight traffic on the PRR increased by two-thirds, from 102,171,312 ton-miles to 170,255,033. The total tonnage of freight handled more than doubled, from 365,006 to 754,354 tons, coming ever closer to the magical million-ton mark that Haupt had envisioned in 1854. More important, net earnings (gross earnings less operating expenses) rose from $167,208 in 1850 to $1,829,277 in 1855 and $2,231,617 in 1859.[34]

Excess Competition

Although relations between Haupt and Thomson were generally amicable, the PRR's president initially resisted Haupt's calls for low rates and high volumes. During his first period of employment on the PRR, between 1847 and 1852, Haupt's agenda had foundered, thanks to the incomplete state of the Western Division and the inadequacies of the Philadelphia & Columbia and the Allegheny Portage Railroad. Even after Haupt returned to the PRR, Thomson was reluctant to implement his suggestions. The completion of the line west of Harrisburg, the acquisition of the Main Line of Public Works, and the partial repeal of the tonnage tax had eliminated some of Thomson's objections, to be sure. Still, with the bulk of the tonnage tax in place and with much of the main line not yet double-tracked, Thomson hesitated to radically increase the PRR's traffic.

Furthermore, as Thomson may have suspected, there was a dark side to Haupt's high-volume, low-rate philosophy. Haupt was not the only individual who was gradually uncovering the underlying principles of railway economics. Executives from all of the trunk lines confronted extraordinarily high fixed costs and comparably low variable costs. Under those circumstances, they all possessed a strong incentive to maximize volume by lowering rates. Such a strategy would work, however, only so long as there was enough freight to transport. Prior to the Panic of 1857, with the Erie Canal essentially at capacity, the four trunk lines were able to garner sufficient shares of what traffic remained. Falling traffic levels, such as those that prevailed after 1857, were another matter entirely. In the face of intense competition between rival trunk lines, executives slashed long-haul rates below the fully allocated cost of service—that is, set rates so low that each ton of freight would barely meet variable costs, and thus contribute little or nothing to offsetting its share of fixed costs.

In order to avoid bankruptcy, managers raised rates on captive local traffic to exceedingly high levels, in effect assigning a disproportionately large share of fixed costs to local shippers. That fundamental principle of competitive ratemaking was certain to benefit the PRR, as its ratio of local to through traffic was higher than that of any of the other trunk lines. Such discriminatory practices might generate Haupt's promised "increase of trade, activity of business, and the extension of our great cities," but they were hardly conducive to the success of the smaller communities that lined the PRR's route. Pittsburgh residents in particular suffered under the higher rates generated by the PRR's monopoly on rail transportation, a situation made all the more galling by the fact that their local government had helped to pay for the construction of the railroad in the first place. It was not uncommon for a shipment between Chicago and New York to travel at a cost no higher than one from Pittsburgh to Philadelphia. Angry Pittsburghers charged that "the Pennsylvania railroad, instead of helping the city to which it is in part indebted for existence, steps in and takes away from us this advantage, at the same time making us pay, through our local trade, the loss the road sustains in doing us the injury."[35]

The PRR's rate policies, many Pittsburgh merchants alleged, were benefiting western cities at the expense of residents of their own state. They spoke of "the decaying engine shops, the silent and deserted boat yards, the idle steamers, and ruined millers, the produce business banished to western points, the shipping business monopolized by a corporation, and merchants and manufacturers of all kinds leaving Pennsylvania for other States." As a result, even "the City of Philadelphia, by aiding the Pennsylvania railroad to transfer its termini from Philadelphia to New York and Boston, at the east, and from Pittsburgh to Cleveland, Chicago, St. Louis, Cincinnati, and elsewhere, at the west, is encompassing her own ruin with ours."[36]

The protestors did not mention that Philadelphia's commercial decline, relative to New York, began long before the PRR had received its corporate charter, and that Pittsburgh's problems were largely the result of continuing westward migration, coupled with the effects that impending secession and civil war would have on the Mississippi River trade. Nevertheless, their frustration was evident in their insistence that "the Pennsylvania railroad becomes what the Legislature never meant it to be, an oppressor of the citizen—wronging the home shipper by making him pay double as much as the foreign."[37] The local shippers who faced what they perceived as unfairly high rates soon forgot that the PRR was a far better transportation option than the Main Line of Public Works and instead argued that their grievances demanded legislative or judicial remedy.[38]

The chaotic railway situation in the Midwest created further instability. All four trunk lines competed for western traffic, brought to the three key gateway cities (Buffalo, Pittsburgh, and Wheeling) by an expanding network of railroads in Ohio and Indiana. Even though Thomson provided various forms of financial assistance to several of those midwestern lines, they were independent and often poorly coordinated carriers whose executives were generally free to route traffic at will.

Midwestern railroads were fundamentally different from their trunk-line counterparts, and they followed very different pricing strategies. The railroads in Ohio and Indiana were far more local in their orientation, collecting small quantities of grain from as many farm communities as possible, generally for delivery to ports along the Great Lakes or the Ohio River. As such, they charged relatively high ton-mile rates, to compensate for the lower traffic densities on their lines.

The nature of railway ratemaking further complicated Thomson's efforts to maximize traffic and revenues on the PRR. During the navigation season on the Great Lakes, through grain rates plummeted, owing to the greater efficiency of water carriers. Lake freighters and barges operating along the Erie Canal set the rate on eastbound grain, forcing railroad traffic officials and independent freight agents to offer the lowest possible rates in order to secure the business. Significantly, shippers could specify only the origin and destination points, as well as the identity of the originating carrier—and sometimes not even that, if they contracted for haulage services with an independent traffic solicitor. Until passage of the Mann-Elkins Act in 1910, which strengthened government control over the railroads, shippers could not dictate the route that their cargoes would follow, nor could they choose which subsequent carriers would handle the traffic. Because the originating carriers determined both the route and the rate for the entire distance, their executives were anxious to keep for themselves the longest haul. Few traffic managers were willing to short-haul their own railroads by relinquishing traffic any sooner than was absolutely necessary. In many cases, therefore, that meant sending shipments on a circuitous path that deviated from a straight-line route by dozens or even hundreds of miles. Moreover, traffic officials on midwestern feeder routes determined the through rate without even bothering to consult their counterparts on the trunk lines. Each midwestern carrier would offer large grain shipments to the four eastern trunk lines, playing them off against one another in an effort to obtain the highest rate division—that is, the originating carrier would keep the largest possible share of the rate for itself, while the trunk line would receive a relatively small proportion of the overall rate for the much longer haul to the east.

Eastern trunk lines specialized in bulk haulage at low per-ton rates, requiring substantial volumes of traffic in order to maintain high throughput. The most financially troubled carriers—and the Erie was a chronic offender—had little choice but to accept the grain rates that midwestern railroads had established. In order to remain competitive, managers on the PRR and the other trunk lines matched the low rates that the weakest among them had established. The result was a combination of low rates and the inefficient use of the railway infrastructure, as grain

made its way to tidewater over a multitude of indirect routings.[39]

The presence of independent, commission freight agents increased Thomson's difficulty in securing remunerative rates on long-haul traffic. Railroad executives did not control through routes between major transportation hubs such as Philadelphia and Chicago—and, even if they had, they assumed that such a large system was far too complex to be managed effectively. Many through routes involved breaking bulk (that is, shifting cargo from one vehicle to another), owing to a change in gauge, a river crossing, or some other chokepoint. Such impediments, which often required supervision of the transfer process at intermediate points, provided considerable power to independent freight agents. Those agents, akin to the wholesalers, or jobbers, who were responsible for placing a wide variety of manufactured goods in a geographically dispersed market, aggressively solicited traffic in exchange for a small commission. Unlike the freight forwarders who had operated over the Main Line of Public Works and, for a time, the PRR as well, these agents generally did not assume responsibility for the shipment from origin to destination. Instead, they functioned more as brokers, consolidating small units of grain into carload or trainload lots. As such, they possessed the specialized expertise and the geographical reach to coordinate shipments over multiple carriers. Their survival depended on their ability to quote the lowest possible rates on grain shipments to the east coast. Because they lacked any innate loyalty to a particular railroad, independent agents took advantage of the trunk lines' incessant demand for higher volumes of traffic, and they could and did route shipments to whichever carrier proved most cooperative. Agents offered large lots of freight to the trunk lines on a "take it or leave it" basis. Any trunk-line executive who refused to accept the rate was likely to see a large quantity of traffic go to a rival carrier.[40]

During the early 1850s, Thomson began to internalize many of the PRR's traffic functions, often by acquiring the facilities and personnel once employed by freight forwarders such as David Leech, Thomas Clarke, and William Thaw. Accordingly, Thomson was able to minimize reliance on independent agents. In 1854, for instance, the president assured his shareholders that "the expediency and utility of maintaining an army of noisy drummers throughout the West, has always been doubted by this Company, and practiced only to a limited extent." Despite such reassurances, however, Thomson could hardly deny that those independent agents were exerting a destabilizing influence on rates. In the final analysis, it did not matter whether the PRR was able to set rates directly. So long as commission agents were able to divert shipments to other railroads, Thomson would be forced to match their through rates.[41]

Even before the Panic of 1857, Thomson and his fellow trunk-line executives sought to end the combined problems associated with rate cutting and with independent freight agents. The solution to ruinously low rates was, in theory, extraordinarily simple. The representatives of all of the railways serving a particular market could agree to establish a cartel, with fixed, remunerative rates. Such cartels frequently took the form of traffic pools, with each railroad assigned a particular share of the business between city pairs. While simple in conception, however, cartels and pools were extraordinarily difficult to maintain in practice. Each party to the agreement had a strong incentive to cheat, by offering a hidden rate (usually in the form of a drawback or rebate) that was below the cartel price, yet above the variable cost of providing service.[42] Furthermore, particularly in the Midwest, a plethora of railroads provided an extraordinary variety of routings, making it difficult to allocate traffic, and even more difficult to assess when cheating was taking place.[43]

The first cooperative efforts to control rates began during the summer of 1854. By then, all four trunk lines had completed their routes between tidewater and the gateway cities of Buffalo, Pittsburgh, or Wheeling, creating an intense competition for through traffic. In August 1854, the trunk-line representatives, including Thomson, met at the St. Nicholas Hotel in New York. In their efforts to maintain equitable competition, the executives pledged to restrict advertising and the issuance of free passes. Further, by restricting both the number and the speed of trains, they hoped to reduce their collective transportation capacity and maintain higher rates thereby. After much debate, the attendees agreed to eliminate the employment of independent agents for the solicitation of freight. "Instead of an army

of drummers and runners, spread over the country, and paid by each Company," Thomson observed, "an agent is now maintained at the joint expense of the four [trunk] lines, at all important points in the West, to distribute bills and give unbiased information to the traveler."[44]

More significantly, the agreement ensured that the railroads would levy charges based on the value rather than the cost of transportation, creating a policy that was to characterize the railroad business for many years to come. The representatives from the carriers agreed to establish a system of uniform freight classifications, based largely on the categories that the PRR had recently developed, with the expectation that such standardization would facilitate the issuance of common tariff schedules. Rates were to be equal from each of the western gateways to the tidewater cities of Philadelphia, New York, and Baltimore. That provision disturbed Thomson, for it required shipments to Philadelphia to bear the additional cost of transportation to New York, in addition to the standard through rate. He was in a very weak bargaining position, however, as the tonnage tax limited his ability to cut rates to match those of the two New York trunk lines.[45]

The pooling arrangements established in August 1854 were not illegal, but neither were they enforceable under American law. Since well before the advent of the railroads, Americans had developed a strong aversion to monopolistic business practices, and their elected officials and judges refused to countenance anything that undermined competition or suggested collusive efforts to raise the rates charged to shippers. Unlike their counterparts in most European countries, where pools generally carried the force of law, railway executives in the United States operated under a political system that made it far more difficult to rationalize competition, and that provided strong incentives for suicidal rate reductions that would destabilize the entire railroad business.[46]

The delegates were anxious to gain legal sanction for pooling, and they vowed, unsuccessfully, to pressure their respective state legislatures to enact some sort of enforcement mechanism. In the meantime, they made vague references to the creation of a "General Railroad Association of the Eastern, Middle, and Central States," in order to ensure compliance. Like most traffic pools and rate agreements, the 1854 conference came to naught, as trunk-line executives continued to rely on independent agents and set rates at will.[47]

The events of 1857 made rate stability a critical matter to the PRR and to the other trunk lines. In August, the PRR took control of the Philadelphia & Columbia. A month later, construction crews completed a bridge across the Allegheny River at Pittsburgh. The new connection between the PRR and its primary western outlet, the Pittsburgh, Fort Wayne & Chicago Rail Road, enabled Thomson to compete effectively for the midwestern grain trade. More generally, the greater efficiency that accompanied integrated operations gave Thomson greater latitude in terms of rate reductions. The deepening economic crisis that followed the Panic of 1857 induced further rate cutting by all the trunk lines.

By the time that Tom Scott became general superintendent, on January 1, 1858, the situation had become critical. Scott gained his new post as part of a general reorganization of the Transportation Department, a move induced by both the acquisition of the Main Line of Public Works and the difficult economic conditions. According to Haupt, it was Scott who finally persuaded Thomson to embrace lower rates on high-volume traffic, but in reality none of them had much choice in the matter. Thomson complained that "the competition which the Pennsylvania Rail Road Company could not control or ignore without serious injury to the trade of the City and State has not only led to the adoption of unremunerative tariffs, but has entailed upon each line the heavy cost of maintaining high speeds, and the employment of numerous agents and drummers for the soliciting of freight and travel, materially enhancing the expense of operating each road, while the rates of transportation have been reduced below public requirements."[48]

There followed a seemingly interminable series of conferences, as executives struggled to maintain rates by allocating pieces of a shrinking pool of traffic. In May 1858, representatives from the eastern trunk lines met in Philadelphia, intending to reestablish 1857 rates. Officials from the Hudson River Railroad declined to participate, however, and absent their cooperation, the agreement collapsed. In July, following another meet-

ing at the St. Nicholas Hotel, B&O and New York Central officials reached an accord on rates, but with representatives from the Erie and the Hudson River refusing to take part, Thomson and Scott both declined. Another convention, held later that month in Cleveland, produced similarly disappointing results.[49]

In September 1858, a series of meetings—first at Philadelphia's Girard House and then at the St. Nicholas Hotel in New York—failed to generate lasting rate stability, but it did lay the foundation for the basic rate structure that the railroads were to follow for the next century. For the first time, Thomson was in a strong bargaining position relative to the New York trunk lines. He had made considerable progress in integrating the allied freight forwarders into the PRR's operations. More important, Thomson had every reason to believe that the tonnage tax would soon be eliminated. In January, Governor Pollack had called for its repeal, and representatives of commercial interests in Philadelphia and Pittsburgh soon followed suit. Later that year, the PRR board resolved to stop paying the tax, as part of a determined effort to see it abolished. As such, Thomson enjoyed a freer hand in setting rates.

In particular, Thomson wanted to rectify the PRR's competitive disadvantage against the New York Central and the Erie, the only two trunk lines that directly served New York. In compensation for the PRR's geographic situation, Thomson sought correspondingly lower rates to Philadelphia. On September 25, when trunk-line representatives signed the latest rate accord, Thomson emerged victorious. In order to offset Philadelphia's status as a secondary port, the PRR received a rate reduction of twenty cents per ton, while the B&O garnered a thirty-cent reduction on traffic moving to Baltimore. The disparity, often referred to as a port differential (because it was based on the destination port for eastbound shipments) reflected the added cost of transportation, typically by water, from Philadelphia or Baltimore north to New York. Thanks to the port differentials, the PRR's traffic and revenues surged by some $234,000, while the New York Central and the Erie each experienced the loss of more than $400,000 in revenue.[50]

The 1858 agreement collapsed after barely six months. The managers of the New York trunk lines were aghast at their shrinking revenues. Their anxiety increased when, in December 1858, the Pittsburgh, Fort Wayne & Chicago extended its tracks to the Windy City. From that point onward, the PRR and its western ally were well positioned to move grain from Chicago directly to tidewater. New York commercial interests were likewise displeased with the 1858 rate accord. They saw no reason why they should pay higher rates, effectively subsidizing their rivals in Philadelphia and Baltimore.

A conference in June 1859 preserved the port differentials but forbade the PRR from exploiting its advantage on Philadelphia traffic by offering lower through rates than the New York Central or the Erie on any traffic that continued onward to New York. Despite periodic modifications, including significant changes in 1877, the port differentials established in 1858 persisted for more than a century. They did not end until 1963, when the United States Supreme Court affirmed a lower court ruling abolishing them. Until then, courts and regulatory agencies accepted the price discrimination inherent in the rate differentials that the trunk-line executives had established during the 1850s.[51]

By the autumn of 1859, the competitive situation had become far more chaotic. In August, the Erie declared bankruptcy, in part as a result of the rate wars. Absent the fixed costs associated with funding its now worthless debt, the Erie's managers had little to lose and much to gain by slashing through rates. The same year, the Grand Trunk Railway of Canada created what amounted to a fifth trunk line, linking Portland, Maine, west through Montreal and Toronto to Port Edward, Ontario, across the St. Clair River from Port Huron, Michigan. With little traffic in the offing, the Grand Trunk cut rates while teetering on the brink of bankruptcy, further destabilizing the railroad system.

Between July and October 1860, in a series of meetings held in New York City and at Saratoga Springs, the executives of the now five trunk lines desperately attempted to maintain rates. They reaffirmed the principle of rate differentials but, more importantly, agreed to curtail the independent freight solicitors and the lowball rates that they so often quoted. Their efforts bore little fruit, however, particularly because officials from the New York Central—the carrier that benefited the most from the independent jobbers—were reluctant to make concessions to the other trunk lines. On

the eve of the Civil War, independent freight agents still abounded, particularly in Ohio and Indiana.[52]

The Civil War temporarily restored a measure of rate stability, but that did not immediately bring to an end the practices of the independent freight agents. Military traffic generated substantial additional business for all the carriers, while fighting periodically suspended operations over the Baltimore & Ohio and thus reduced available transportation capacity. More importantly, the war encouraged many midwestern farmers to abandon subsistence agriculture in favor of commodity production for U.S. and overseas markets. The resulting torrent of grain made possible the low-rate strategy that Haupt had long advocated. Between 1864 and 1873, the PRR's freight traffic increased from 421 million to 1.4 billion ton-miles. During the same period, the average cost of transportation fell from 1.87 cents to 0.857 cents. As a result, even though expenditures on freight service increased (from $7.9 million in 1864 to $11.9 million in 1873), net freight earnings increased by an even larger amount, from $2.5 million to $7.7 million.[53]

Haupt, the earliest advocate for a high-volume, low-rate pricing strategy, had long since departed from the Pennsylvania Railroad. He left the PRR for the second and final time in 1856, apparently because he felt that the now-complete railroad would never again be able to offer him an engineering challenge worthy of his abilities. Haupt had played a critical role in the development of organizational and operating methods on the PRR, yet that success had come at considerable cost. He incurred the enmity of many PRR officials and he continued to be embroiled in controversy, later in his career. Even though they had disagreed on the matter of freight rates, Haupt and Thomson remained friends, with each respecting the engineering ability of the other.[54]

Yet, even though the steady decline in transportation costs reflected the PRR's increasing efficiency, it also indicated Thomson's inability to mediate volatile railroad rates. In meeting after meeting, representatives of the trunk lines had agreed on the importance of maintaining remunerative freight and passenger tariffs, yet could not long adhere to any mechanism for implementing their agenda. Haupt could take some satisfaction that the PRR was bringing to life his vision of a low-rate, high-volume carrier, but such policies owed far more to the internecine rivalry among the trunk lines, than they did to any desire to advance the greater good of the railroad, its Philadelphia owners, or the commonwealth of Pennsylvania.

Destroying the Tonnage Tax

Perhaps more than any other issue in the Pennsylvania Railroad's early history, the tonnage tax exemplified the shifting nature of the relationship between private enterprise and the public welfare. Thomson's efforts to repeal the tax tarnished his reputation, and that of his company, and not until each provided heroic service in the Civil War were their images redeemed. Despite public scorn, however, Thomson's actions were born out of desperation, not corporate malice or blatant disregard for the government of Pennsylvania. The elimination of the tonnage tax was a vital step in the protection of the PRR against rivals such as the New York Central, the Erie, and the Baltimore & Ohio. By lowering transportation rates across the commonwealth, moreover, Thomson protected the PRR while also guarding the commercial interests of Pennsylvania against rivals in New York and Maryland.

In 1846, when the General Assembly had granted the Pennsylvania Railroad its corporate charter, legislators imposed the tonnage tax as a surcharge on the company's established rates. PRR officials were to pay to the commonwealth five mills per ton-mile on all freight traveling over PRR rails between March 10 and December 1, the navigation season on the canals. The tax applied to all freight loaded at Harrisburg, Pittsburgh, or intermediate points destined to travel more than twenty miles. A supplement to the charter declared the tonnage tax to be a first lien on the railroad, to take precedence over all other debts. In March 1848, the legislature lowered the tonnage tax to three mills, but stipulated that it apply year round.[55]

The tonnage tax represented far more than an inconvenient added expense; instead, it was a threat to the business strategy that lay at the core of the PRR's operations. Even though they were often at odds over the interrelated issues of rates and traffic volumes, Thomson and Haupt were in complete agreement on the deleterious effects of the tonnage tax. Haupt noted that the supplement added a dollar to the cost of moving a ton of freight between Pittsburgh and the junction with the Philadelphia & Columbia, at Dillerville.[56] Thomson agreed with Haupt's assessment. "The operation of the tax," he noted, "seems to have been intended to limit the Company to a small tonnage carried at high rates, instead of permitting it to encourage a large tonnage by low rates."[57]

In order to maintain competitive through rates, Thomson shifted the burden of the tonnage tax to noncompetitive shipments within Pennsylvania. In other words, the tax exacerbated the tendency, created by trunk-line competition, to move long-haul traffic at little more than the variable cost of transportation, while allowing local traffic to bear the bulk of the PRR's fixed costs. Legislative enactment of the tonnage tax, combined with the economics of railway competition, had created that discriminatory pricing structure, but many Pennsylvanians simply blamed the PRR for unfair and prejudicial behavior against its native state.[58]

Even before he became president, Thomson attempted to persuade the legislators, and the voters, that the health of the Pennsylvania economy should take precedence over the narrow interests of the Main Line of Public Works. He contended that the effect of the tonnage tax was not to protect the state canals, but rather to drive freight traffic north to New York City over the rails of the New York Central and the Erie, and south to Baltimore via the Baltimore & Ohio. The situation became so severe, Thomson and Haupt noted, that Philadelphians could purchase imported British coal at a lower rate than the products of their own state, thanks to the rate surcharge imposed by the tonnage tax. Haupt accordingly insisted that the tax be modified to encourage shipments of coal and other bulk commodities. He also demanded that the members of the General Assembly reduce the tonnage tax, while making it applicable to all railroads in the commonwealth, and use the proceeds to retire the debt for the Main Line of Public Works, which would then be largely abandoned. On May 7, 1855, in response to relentless pressure from PRR officials and from shippers, legislators eliminated the tax on coal and lumber shipments in an attempt to determine whether or not the move would increase freight traffic. It did, giving further encouragement to Haupt's low-rate strategy and making Thomson more determined than ever that the tonnage tax should be eliminated in its entirety.[59]

By 1857, as legislators became increasingly anxious to dispose of the entire Main Line system, Thomson realized that he was in an exceptionally strong position to demand a repeal of the tonnage tax as part of the agreement. In January 1857, the board authorized Thomson to prepare a bill for introduction to the legislature, offering an extra million dollars for the Main Line of Public Works, subject to the repeal of the tonnage tax. By the time that the General Assembly approved the act, in May 1857, Thomson had agreed to contribute an additional $1.5 million to the state treasury in consideration for a suspension of the tonnage tax on both the PRR and the Harrisburg, Portsmouth, Mount Joy & Lancaster.[60] His plans were stymied by the canal commissioners, who took legal action to block the proposed sale. Although the Pennsylvania Supreme Court ruled that the legislature could legally sell the Main Line, the justices struck down the provision of the act freeing the PRR from future state taxation, including the tonnage tax.[61]

Thomson's opponents were quick to point out that even if the commonwealth no longer owned the Main Line, it was still obliged to fund the debt that it incurred to build it. In addition, they asserted that the tax was an ongoing obligation on the part of the PRR in return for the legislature's 1846 promise to prevent the B&O from reaching Pittsburgh. More broadly, the tax contributed substantially to the state's coffers, allowing the legislature to provide services while minimizing the burden of taxation on individual citizens. Governor James Pollock acknowledged that the "continuance [of the tax] can only be justified as a revenue measure."[62] Amid the Panic of 1857, many Pennsylvanians were desperate to preserve the tonnage tax, which they saw as a guaranteed source of revenue in difficult economic times.

The panic also imperiled the railroad's finances, making repeal imperative and inducing Thomson to adopt a three-pronged strategy to achieve that goal. First, in appealing to legislators and the public, he invoked the argument of economic fairness, but in a manner that would have been unfamiliar to those who still remembered the original justification for the Main Line of Public Works. In an earlier generation,

"fairness" meant that the commonwealth would take action to guarantee economic development by providing citizens with access to cheap and reliable transportation. Open access to roads, canals, and even railroads would foster entrepreneurship, while protecting the rugged republicanism that was so crucial to the maintenance of a democratic society. A large and heavily capitalized private enterprise (read "monopoly") threatened both the narrowly construed goal of individual economic self-sufficiency and the more abstract notion of political virtue.

In the new era, however, many citizens saw private enterprise as more efficient than public works. Companies such as the PRR were better managed, more efficient, less prone to the vagaries of politics and patronage, and better equipped to lift the economy of the state above those of its rivals. If that rising tide lifted some boats faster and higher than others, then so be it. Far better that situation, Thomson argued, than one in which New York or Maryland rose to a greater height than Pennsylvania, simply because an "unfair" tax had hobbled the corporation that was the commonwealth's economic champion. Governor Pollock said as much on January 6, 1858, in his opening address to the General Assembly. "It is virtually a tax upon the trade and commerce of the Commonwealth," Pollock emphasized. "The produce of the west is forced upon the competing railroads of other States and to other markets than our own."[63] Pollock was not the only person to voice that sentiment. Thanks to persistent lobbying by Thomson and other PRR officials, the Philadelphia City Councils, the Pittsburgh Board of Trade, and the directors of the Pittsburgh, Fort Wayne & Chicago all issued public statements supporting the repeal of the tonnage tax. William A. Stokes published a *Letter . . . on the Subject of the Tonnage Tax*, in which he argued that social intercourse was the key marker of civilized behavior. Because the tax interfered with commercial intercourse (essentially the same concept as social intercourse, in Stokes's opinion), it was antithetical to the interests of civilization. Stokes was hardly an objective observer—he was the solicitor for the PRR's Western Division—but many legislators found persuasive his assertion that "each person being the best judge of his own interests, untrammeled effort must be most effective."[64]

Second, Thomson worked with the Legal Department to undermine the tonnage tax in the courts. In February 1858, the directors established a committee to investigate a mechanism for challenging the constitutionality of the tonnage tax. Three months later, the board reorganized the Legal Department in anticipation of the tonnage tax fight. At the same meeting, the directors gave Thomson the authority to unleash the PRR's formidable legal talents on the Commonwealth of Pennsylvania.[65]

Thomson and the PRR's attorneys developed an attack that illustrated the changing nature of transportation in the United States. Since the collapse of the federal government's initial, modest efforts to develop a coordinated national transportation system, early in the 1800s, the residents of individual states had taken it upon themselves to protect their own economic interests. State legislatures had chartered turnpike, canal, and railroad companies that could, by definition, operate only within state boundaries. Transportation patterns were more apt to conform to geography than to political divisions, however. Railroad traffic, in particular, soon traveled across state lines. In that context, the policies of one state legislature—such as Pennsylvania's tonnage tax—invariably affected interstate commerce, an activity that was under the control of the federal government.

The PRR's attorneys invoked the Commerce Clause of the U.S. Constitution, arguing that Congress alone possessed the authority to regulate trade "among the several states." Beginning in December 1858, the railroad's executives provoked a test case, through the simple expedient of refusing to pay the tax. The commonwealth filed suit to collect the $87,000 that the railroad withheld, an amount that had swollen to more than $661,000 by 1861. In 1860, the Pennsylvania Supreme Court, in *Pennsylvania Railroad Company v. The Commonwealth of Pennsylvania*, rejected the PRR's Commerce Clause argument. The justices noted that the tax applied only to intrastate traffic, and further ruled that because the tax affected shippers, rather than the railroad, they should be the ones to advocate its repeal. The PRR's attorneys appealed to the United States Supreme Court, but Chief Justice Roger B. Taney remanded it to the state court, on a writ of error. It would be some years before the federal government would fully assert its authority over interstate commerce.[66]

With the outcome of the PRR's legal campaign still in doubt, Thomson embarked on a third strategy to secure repeal of the tonnage tax. His use of political favoritism, outright bribery, and other behind-the-scenes appeals to legislators proved far more important than either the public-relations or the legal campaigns. When he assumed the presidency, in 1852, Thomson had done his best to maintain the moral high ground, convincing the board that it was inappropriate to continue the policy of his predecessor, William Patterson, of allocating some $2,500 per year in payments to state legislators. In the face of persistent failures to secure the repeal of the tonnage tax, however, Thomson's scruples soon began to erode. In 1858 he authorized the distribution of PRR funds to legislators, along with free railway passes to the governor, the canal commissioners, and influential newspaper editors.[67]

Despite his acceptance of bribery, and long before the Pennsylvania Supreme Court ruled against the Pennsylvania Railroad, Thomson had ceased his efforts to directly influence the outcome of the tonnage tax battle. He stopped attending legislative sessions in order to better attend to corporate business, sending other PRR executives and hired lobbyists in his place. Initially, his point man was vice president and treasurer William B. Foster, Jr., an individual who surpassed Thomson in both charisma and political skill. However, on March 4, 1860, Foster died unexpectedly, at the age of fifty-two. Having lost his chief lobbyist at that critical juncture, Thomson was anxious to find someone who was as politically savvy and skillful as Foster had been. The man he chose was Tom Scott.

Tom Scott

In many popular accounts of the history of the Pennsylvania Railroad, Thomson emerges as the dedicated and selfless hero, and Scott the antihero, arrogant, self-absorbed, egomaniacal, and dishonest, the opposite of everything good that Thomson represented. In his autobiography, Andrew Carnegie noted that Scott was both a political genius and perhaps the most personable man in America. A reporter for the *New York*

Figure 26. Thomas A. Scott (1824–1881) lacked any engineering training or experience, but he possessed a keen understanding of the details of railroad operations and cost accounting methods. J. Edgar Thomson was the quiet, introverted strategist and Scott was the outgoing, charismatic man of action. The strengths of each individual complemented those of the other, and they formed a strong team. Yet, while Thomson was often hailed as the sage founder of the Pennsylvania Railroad, many chroniclers have been critical of Scott—perhaps because he was often more brazen in his efforts to curry favor for the Pennsylvania Railroad and its policies.

Pennsylvania Historical and Museum Commission, Pennsylvania State Archives.

Times seconded that assessment, and perhaps made a sly reference to a work by Niccolò Machiavelli, when he called Scott "a railroad prince."[68] John D. Rockefeller, who knew a thing or two about Machiavellian behavior, initially thought that Scott was the most unscrupulous man he had ever met—but, once mellowed with age, the oil magnate conceded that Scott was "a great railroad man, and he was a great man."[69] Western railroad mogul Collis P. Huntington suggested that Scott and Jay Gould were "two of the worst men in the country"—although it should be noted that Huntington's Southern Pacific and Scott's Texas & Pacific were at that time engaged in a fearsome contest for the right to build the first railroad across the southwestern United States, and each man was doing his best to destroy the reputation of the other.[70] The abolitionist orator Wendell Phillips commented that "there is no power in one State to resist such a giant as the Pennsylvania road. We have thirty-eight one-horse legislatures in this country; and we have a man like Tom Scott with three hundred and fifty millions in his hands, and if he walks through the States they have no power."[71] Shortly after the Civil War, a PRR employee shared an inside joke with Thomson's personal assistant, William Jackson Palmer, suggesting that "Scott has been at Hbg. [Harrisburg] during the last week running the state."[72] The best-known, and most darkly humorous, manifestation of Scott's tactics occurred in February 1867, in an incident, perhaps apocryphal. Following the PRR's successful efforts to prevent the General Assembly from chartering the rival Pittsburgh & Connellsville, one senator purportedly expressed his relief at the cessation of the PRR's intense lobbying efforts by asking, "Mr. Speaker, may we now go Scott free?"[73]

Tom Scott was nothing if not adaptable, and he played whatever roles were necessary to benefit both the Pennsylvania Railroad and his own welfare.[74] Although he was undoubtedly an intelligent and capable individual, he was primarily an organizer and a promoter, and he lacked training in engineering. Instead, he possessed a superb understanding of transportation logistics and was extraordinarily adept at coordinating the movement of trains and traffic. Nevertheless, his greatest assets seemed to be his charm and the force of his personality, which perhaps accounts for some of the enmity that the more introverted engineers who otherwise dominated the railroad felt toward him. What was undeniable, however, was that, for nearly twenty years, Thomson and Scott enjoyed an unusually close working partnership. The president was the skilled yet taciturn engineer, uncomfortable in social circles, while his deputy was the charismatic and outgoing dealmaker who thrived on his ability to interact with others.[75] General Isaac Jones Wistar, the longtime head of the PRR's canal operations, was probably thinking of Scott when he recalled, "Thomson's experience and knowledge of men, no less than his calm mental processes and changeless imperturbability of temperament . . . could not fail to moderate the faults of his associates less endowed by nature with those priceless qualities."[76]

Scott joined the PRR in November 1850 as the station agent at Duncansville, where the PRR met the Allegheny Portage Railroad. Thomson apparently had a chance conversation with John S. Given, a former toll collector on the Main Line of Public Works, who recommended Scott for the job. According to an oft-told account that has assumed legendary proportions in the history of the Pennsylvania Railroad, then–Chief Engineer Thomson was unimpressed with the young man that he interviewed for the position. Scott's pants were tucked into his boots, and his mane of golden hair was likewise stuffed into a slouch hat. He radiated charm and—according to a writer for the *New York Times*—"an exhaustless flow of animal spirits," something that the more staid Thomson was probably never able to achieve. Thomson told Scott that the Pennsylvania Railroad did not require his services, whereupon the young man disdainfully suggested that he had only been willing to work for the company for a month or so, to determine if it suited his ambitions. Thomson was impressed by Scott's assertiveness and hired him on the spot. It is unlikely that the encounter took place in precisely that manner. The account, however fanciful, nonetheless symbolized the synergistic relationship that developed between two wildly different, but complementary, individuals.[77]

Thereafter, Scott rose through the ranks with astonishing rapidity. The December 1852 reorganization of the Transportation Department afforded Scott the post of third assistant superintendent in charge of the Western Division at Pittsburgh. On January 1, 1858, with the debut of the initial line-and-staff organization, the board appointed the thirty-five-year-old Scott as the general superintendent. When expanding the PRR's influence in the Midwest, Thomson accepted responsibility for the region to the northwest of Pittsburgh, while delegating to Scott the area to the southwest. On March 4, 1860, Scott's career advanced considerably, thanks to the untimely death of Vice President Foster. Later that month, the directors appointed Scott as vice president and a director of the Pennsylvania Railroad.[78]

Scott soon demonstrated his worth in the tonnage tax fight. He was even more aggressive than Foster had been, and unlike Foster—who had been a Democrat—Scott was well connected to the rapidly rising Republican Party. Defeated in the courts, and with Thomson purposefully avoiding any personal efforts to exercise untoward influence over legislators, Scott accelerated the PRR's campaign to win over the General Assembly. That was destined to be a difficult proposition, with the 1860 elections sweeping anti-PRR legislators into office, particularly in the Pittsburgh area. Scott proved tenacious, however, and far less scrupulous than either Thomson or Foster had been.

By the 1860s, a new generation of professional lobbyists had replaced the earlier "borers" who had descended seasonally upon the state capital, at the beginning of each legislative session. They proliferated, in part, because the PRR had greatly improved access to Harrisburg, enabling lobbyists to routinely shuttle back and forth to other cities. Scott worked with some of the most influential lobbyists in the commonwealth, including John B. Beck, James Burns, and Charles Frailey, to influence the tonnage tax legislation. He also relied on his good friend Alexander K. McClure, a Chambersburg native, a member of the Pennsylvania senate, and chairman of the Republican State Committee.[79]

Scott maintained an office in the capitol building, conveniently located adjacent to the legislative chambers. Under Scott's direction, the PRR placed advertisements in newspapers throughout the state, taking whatever measures he deemed necessary to secure favorable editorials. He promised the Pittsburgh Board of Trade that he would do his best to lower rates to that city, and to finance the construction of feeder lines in the area. He persuaded the governor, William Fisher Packer, to support the repeal of the tonnage tax in his January 1861 annual message to the General Assembly. Scott met personally with many legislators in order to convince them of the value of supporting the PRR.

Scott also resorted to outright bribery. Thomson undoubtedly authorized the payments, but it was up to Scott to make the actual arrangements. On one occasion, a legislator innocently (or so he claimed) walked into Scott's hotel room, only to discover an envelope, stuffed with $500 in cash, with his name on it, lying conspicuously on a table. Scott and the PRR thus played a crucial role in replacing the "logrolling" that had characterized an earlier era of lobbying with rather more direct and ignoble efforts to influence the course of politics in Pennsylvania.[80]

Scott and his legislative allies drafted a bill that resembled few others that legislators had ever considered, for it was phrased as a contract rather than as a law. In 1855, when the General Assembly had exempted coal and lumber from the tonnage tax, that body retained "the right to repeal this act at any time, and to re-enact the several acts hereby repealed."[81] Scott knew that the legislature could likewise rescind any subsequent commutation of the tonnage tax. A contract, however, was a binding legal agreement that could not be abrogated or modified without the consent of both parties.[82]

In February 1861, as Abraham Lincoln headed for his inauguration in Washington, and as the nation disintegrated, the Pennsylvania legislature began debates on "An Act for the commutation of Tonnage duties." The bill included two provisions that helped persuade legislators to repeal the tonnage tax. Both were designed to placate western Pennsylvania voters, yet each ultimately rebounded to the PRR's benefit. The first condition obliged the PRR to reduce rates on westbound traffic by an amount corresponding to the cost of the tonnage tax. Charges for local traffic between Philadelphia and Pittsburgh would be no higher than the through rate between those two cities, and likewise would be no higher than a rate from any point west of Pittsburgh to tidewater. In essence, the bill prohibited the PRR from charging shippers a higher rate for a shorter distance, probably the first time that any legislature in the United States enacted such a long-haul/short-haul provision.[83]

The second stipulation required the PRR to use the taxes that Thomson had withheld from the commonwealth to subsidize the construction of local railroads in western Pennsylvania. The Panic of 1857 had halted work on some of those projects, while others had not progressed beyond the planning stage. Influential legislators had promoted many of those lines, and they were anxious to see their pet projects through to completion. Many of those commutation lines (so called because they were linked to the commutation of the tonnage tax) offered substantial advantages to the Pennsylvania Railroad. They included the Pittsburgh & Steubenville Railroad, whose route across the Virginia panhandle would soon offer the PRR access to the southern regions of Ohio and Indiana. The Western Pennsylvania Railroad, with a route paralleling the old Western Division Canal, would form a useful northern bypass of Pittsburgh, as well as a shortcut to the oilfields of northwestern Pennsylvania. The Tyrone & Clearfield Railroad, the Tyrone & Lock Haven Railroad, the Ebensburg & Cresson Railroad, the Mifflin & Centre County Railroad, the Chartiers Valley Railroad, and the Bedford Railroad eventually offered valuable branch lines into the rich coal country of western Pennsylvania.[84] Thus, the PRR would have constructed most of the commutation lines in due course, and the provisions of the repeal legislation merely enabled the company to benefit financially from Thomson's refusal to pay the tonnage tax.[85]

While the two concessions were not enough to satisfy many of the PRR's critics, Scott's political skills and his personal connections overcame all opposition. His timing was impeccable, as the final debate over repeal of the tonnage tax coincided almost precisely with the secession of the southern states and the dissolution of the union. Democrats, a minority in the General Assembly, suffered from the schism that had split their party into northern and southern wings. Some Republicans, particularly those representing Allegheny County, were opposed to repeal, but they were soon overwhelmed by Alexander McClure's skillful management of his party. "But for the fact that the ap-

palling advent of civil war became the paramount question with the people generally and throughout the state, and measurably diverted attention from the tonnage tax issue," McClure reminisced, many decades later, "it is reasonably certain that Scott would have failed."[86]

On February 18, 1861, with five southern states already out of the union, the Pennsylvania House passed the bill, sixty votes to thirty. Ten days later, the Senate gave its approval, by a vote of eighteen to fifteen. Governor Andrew Curtin, a Republican, had been in office little more than a month, and he was reluctant to alienate his western constituents by affixing his signature. He waited more than a week after the legislative session had ended before signing the bill into law. Curtin's caution was hardly misplaced, and it was fortunate that he did not have to face the voters that fall. Those legislators who did fared badly. Of the seventy or so House and Senate members who voted in favor of the repeal of the tonnage tax and stood for reelection, the only ones who retained their seats were those representing Philadelphia, along with a solitary survivor from Warren County. Senator Jeremiah "Pap" Shindel, a Lutheran minister from Lehigh County, must have felt particularly ill used. He had spent much of the tonnage-tax battle ferrying messages between the legislative chamber and Scott's adjacent office, and he proved his loyalty to the PRR by voting for the repeal of the surcharge. In the aftermath of the election, the now-former state senator joined the Union army as a chaplain, not for reasons of faith or patriotism, but rather, McClure noted, as "a place of rescue" from his enraged constituents.[87]

Thanks in large measure to Scott's efforts, the PRR had succeeded in gaining control over rates, but at a considerable cost. The provisions of the bill enabled the PRR to withstand rate cutting by executives on the other trunk lines, largely by using captive local traffic to cross-subsidize long-distance shipments. By holding rates on short-haul traffic sent from intermediate stations along the route from Philadelphia and Pittsburgh to no more than the through rate *between* those two cities, the tonnage tax bill effectively redirected tonnage tax revenues from the commonwealth treasury to shippers in western Pennsylvania in the form of lower rates. However, residents of Pittsburgh and surrounding areas quickly forgot that their rates had declined, and that they would generally continue to decline in the decades that followed. Instead, they calculated rates on a strict mileage basis and compared them against the tariffs paid by through shippers. They were not pleased that cargoes traveling between Philadelphia and Pittsburgh often traveled at rates higher than those applying to the entire distance between the New York and Chicago, communities that were *beyond* the Philadelphia–Pittsburgh axis established by the tonnage tax bill. In 1866 and again in 1868, shippers petitioned the General Assembly for legislation to equalize rates, but without success.[88]

In the decades that followed, moreover, the PRR developed a reputation as a company whose officers—particularly Scott—would stop at nothing in their efforts to manipulate the political process. The PRR's lobbying efforts, corrupt though they may have been, nonetheless guaranteed the company's long-term survival. At a time when the rate wars of the late 1850s were pitting the eastern trunk lines against each other, the tonnage tax constituted a burden on the PRR that the Baltimore & Ohio, the New York Central, and the Erie did not share. By any means necessary, Thomson and Scott reasoned, they had to secure repeal of the tonnage tax. They succeeded just at the moment when Thomson secured access to Chicago and other western gateways, enabling the PRR to compete equally for long-haul traffic. The timing of the victory in the tonnage tax battle was even more fortuitous, as it enabled Thomson to maximize the PRR's earnings during the traffic boom that accompanied the Civil War.[89]

Carnegie

Scott's steadily increasing involvement in the repeal of the tonnage tax, as well as other administrative matters, provided valuable opportunities for one of his chief assistants. Andrew Carnegie began his involvement with the Pennsylvania Railroad as a telegrapher and an intelligent but essentially insignificant errand boy, someone who could be counted on to quietly hold select investments undertaken by senior executives such as Thomson and Scott. By the end of the Civil War, however, Carnegie had proved his worth as a

PRR executive in his own right, and had further demonstrated a degree of financial skill, daring, and unscrupulousness that Thomson, in particular, found increasingly troubling. In his *Autobiography*, published in 1920, a year after his death, Andrew Carnegie fondly recalled his years of employment on the Pennsylvania Railroad. It was a period in his young life that brought him into contact with the telegraph and the railroad, the great communication and transportation technologies of the age, and enabled him to demonstrate his resolute work ethic to others, particularly Scott. Under Scott's guidance, Carnegie parlayed his railroad experience into a uniquely American success story.

Carnegie's *Autobiography* was as much a work of fiction as it was of thoughtful and accurate introspection. It shared much in common with a literary tradition, best exemplified in the novels of Horatio Alger, that a combination of pluck and luck would enable any hardworking and self-sacrificing young American (assuming that he were white and male) to achieve great success. Luck certainly appeared in the *Autobiography*, particularly as Carnegie recounted an incident on the PRR that nearly ended his career. Riding on a locomotive, Carnegie allowed the railroad's payroll to slip from his grasp, yet persuaded the engineer to back slowly along the tracks, until he located the vital package. "'All right, my boy!'" Carnegie reminded himself, "'the gods were with you, but don't do it again!'"[90] Yet, it was the pluck that was most in evidence in Carnegie's autobiography, as he told one story after another of his talent, his initiative, and his dedication to the Pennsylvania Railroad.

The truth was somewhat different. Carnegie's family was hardly destitute, as his father was a skilled handloom weaver in Dunfermline, Scotland. The mechanization of textile production destroyed William Carnegie's career, and in 1848 the family emigrated to the United States. They settled in Allegheny City, where Andrew, aged thirteen, took a job as a bobbin boy in a textile mill. In 1850 his uncle recommended him to David Brooks, who managed the local office of the Atlantic & Ohio Telegraph Company, one of several firms owned by entrepreneur Henry O'Rielly. Hired as a messenger boy, Carnegie soon became friends with David McCargo and Robert Pitcairn, two coworkers of Scottish ancestry. Carnegie learned telegraphy and gained a promotion to telegraph operator, at the princely salary of a dollar a day.[91]

The Pennsylvania Railroad had just reached Pittsburgh, and it provided Carnegie with ample possibilities for advancement. Effective December 1, 1852, Scott took charge of the Western Division, headquartered in Pittsburgh. Scott soon encountered Carnegie, in many respects a younger version of himself, working at the Atlantic & Ohio office. In February 1853, Scott hired the eighteen-year-old as his personal assistant at a salary of $35 a month. Carnegie discovered that "the change at first was far from agreeable," largely because railroad work put him "at once into the company of coarse men"—an example of the moralizing that made Carnegie's *Autobiography* something of a jeremiad.[92]

Carnegie soon took considerable initiative, and received commensurate rewards from Scott. At Carnegie's urging, both Pitcairn and McCargo quit the telegraph company for the greater opportunities afforded by the PRR. Both did well, with Pitcairn spending much of his subsequent career overseeing the PRR's operations in Pittsburgh, and McCargo serving as the president of several PRR-affiliated companies, until felled by a stroke in 1898.[93]

Yet, neither individual apparently possessed Carnegie's drive and ambition. The young Scotsman dispatched trains on his own authority, forging Scott's name in order to grant himself the necessary approval. He meted out discipline to errant employees and insisted, erroneously, that appeal to a higher authority was impossible. In 1856, when a group of PRR employees threatened to strike, Carnegie sent Scott a list of the names of the ringleaders, each of whom was subsequently fired. In an anonymous article in the *Pittsburgh Journal*, he lambasted local commercial interests for their opposition to Scott's plan to expand terminal facilities in that city. For all of that, his star rose in Scott's estimation.[94]

In January 1858, when Scott became general superintendent, he moved to Altoona, Carnegie in tow. As a recent widower, Scott made few friends in Altoona, and he spent much of his time with Carnegie. Over the next several years, Scott shuttled back and forth between Philadelphia, Harrisburg, and Washington, securing the repeal of the tonnage tax, assisting with the Union war effort, and generally promoting the PRR's political interests. His repeated absences enabled Carnegie to take on many of the general superintendent's responsibilities.[95]

Effective December 1, 1859, the board promoted Carnegie to superintendent of the Western Division. Carnegie moved back to Pittsburgh, retaining the services of his brother, Tom, as his personal assistant.[96] As Carnegie himself admitted, he expected as much from his employees as he did from himself, and he drove his workers relentlessly.[97] Carnegie nevertheless reveled in the authority associated with his position, and in particular with the opportunity to increase efficiency by maximizing traffic volume and cutting operating costs. He favored round-the-clock operations, with telegraph offices open twenty-four hours a day.[98] In an oft-quoted story, Carnegie was informed of a wreck that blocked the PRR's main line. Rather than wait for work crews to laboriously clean up the mess, Carnegie simply ordered that the cars be set afire, with the resulting debris pushed to the side. Although other PRR executives were apparently astonished at the destruction of the railroad's property, they soon came to appreciate that the cost of the burned equipment was insignificant, compared to the lost revenue associated with an inoperable line.[99] Carnegie's determination to achieve high throughput induced his support for more capacious freight cars. His advocacy of lower rates to attract higher volumes resembled Haupt's strategies, and Carnegie in fact called Haupt "the first 'great man' I ever knew."[100]

It would be a mistake however, to suggest that Carnegie dictated the PRR's business strategy. Much of the evidence for Carnegie's innovative ideas has derived from his own self-serving autobiographical writings, all of which bent the truth to a substantial degree. Haupt and Thomson had accumulated a wealth of practical railroading experience before Carnegie had even entered adulthood. The two older men had laid the foundations for a system of low-rate, high-volume transportation prior to Carnegie joining the railroad. Scott certainly sensed that Carnegie's abilities were well suited to the efficient transportation enterprise that he, Thomson, and Haupt were attempting to establish. He gave free rein to Carnegie's undoubted abilities. In return, Carnegie eagerly implemented the ideas that his more experienced mentors had developed.

Rather than the PRR executives learning from Andrew Carnegie, it would be more apt to suggest that Carnegie learned from the PRR. He copied methods that were already firmly established on the Pennsylvania Railroad, appreciated their value, and applied those lessons to his later business endeavors. Those activities included the opening of the Edgar Thomson Steel Works in 1875 and culminated in 1892, with the incorporation of the Carnegie Steel Company. Each of Carnegie's many projects demonstrated his desire both to know and to control costs, ranging from wages to ore prices to transportation. His zeal, particularly in the latter case, would eventually put him at odds with the railroad that had once employed him.

Connections to the North and South of Philadelphia

In 1846, the incorporators of the Pennsylvania Railroad had envisioned their new company as a mechanism for bringing the western grain trade to Philadelphia, and away from Baltimore and New York. As such, they had built to the west, but they saw little reason to connect the Quaker City to rival ports to the north or the south. By the end of the 1850s, with a route to Chicago under Thomson's control, the PRR barely penetrated the city of Philadelphia and could reach the docks along the Delaware River only by transferring cars—drawn by horses—to the City Railroad, the Northern Liberties & Penn Township Railroad, or the Southwark Rail-Road. The Pennsylvania Railroad likewise did not possess tracks leading north or south out of Philadelphia, and it lacked an adequate connection to either New York or Baltimore.

Instead, independent carriers forwarded freight and passengers arriving in Philadelphia from the west to other destinations along the Atlantic seaboard. To the north, three allied carriers, the Camden & Amboy Rail Road, the New Jersey Rail Road & Transportation Company, and the Philadelphia & Trenton Railroad, offered service to New York Harbor but—owing to obvious geographical constraints—not all the way to Manhattan. To the south, the Philadelphia, Wilmington & Baltimore Railroad connected its namesake

cities and, in conjunction with the Baltimore & Ohio, provided a route to the nation's capital. For the first decade of the PRR's existence, executives were content to rely on those independent connections for the small quantities of traffic that moved across the PRR main line and then north to New York, and the even smaller amount that went south toward Washington.

By the eve of the Civil War, however, PRR executives became more reliant on their connections along the east coast. The process of extending control over those independent lines evolved gradually and was not fully implemented until 1881. By then, the PRR had established convenient connections through Philadelphia, acquired two separate routes to Baltimore, and extended service south to Washington and north to New York. The development of the PRR's easternmost lines nonetheless depended heavily on the contributions of predecessor companies, including some of the oldest railways to operate in the United States.

Even before the American Revolution, there had been considerable demand for improved transportation between Philadelphia and New York. The first through service between the two cities, by boat and stagecoach, began in 1755. By the early nineteenth century, the United States Mail Coach operated same-day stage service, open to all who could afford the fare and who were willing to depart at 5:00 A.M. The trip became considerably easier in January 1806, when the Trenton-Delaware Bridge Company opened a bridge across the Delaware River. The preferred route was nonetheless largely by water, up the Delaware River to Trenton, then by land to the Raritan River, and by water again to its mouth and across New York Harbor.[101]

John Stevens, a native of Hoboken, New Jersey, soon dominated service between Philadelphia and New York. Early in the nineteenth century, he had tried, and failed, to break the monopoly on Hudson River traffic that Robert R. Livingston and Robert Fulton had established. Stevens soon transferred his attentions to the Delaware River, and by 1823 he was in control of the Union Line, a successful stage and steamboat service between Philadelphia and New York. Stevens was also an early proponent of railways, in New York, Pennsylvania, and New Jersey. In 1812, he published *Documents Tending to Prove the Superior Advantages of Railway and Steam Carriages over Canal Navigation.*[102] He proposed an elevated rail line over the Erie Canal, built on pilings. In 1823 he secured a charter for the Pennsylvania Rail Road Company, a company unconnected with the later Pennsylvania Railroad, with the intention of building a line between Philadelphia and Columbia. Both projects came to naught, but Stevens had more success with his plan to replace the overland stage portion of the New York–Philadelphia journey with a railroad. As early as 1811, he had first petitioned the New Jersey legislature for the authority to construct a railroad between Trenton and New Brunswick, on the Raritan River. He finally prevailed in 1815, receiving the first railroad charter issued in the United States, for the New Jersey Railroad Company. Stevens was ahead of his time, however, and could find few investors.[103]

A decade later, growing interest in railways, in both Britain and the United States, revived Stevens's efforts to lay tracks across New Jersey. In 1825 he constructed a small steam locomotive that puffed along a short circular track at his estate in Hoboken. Later that year, the opening of the Stockton & Darlington Railway in England and William Strickland's fact-finding mission to Britain, on behalf of the Pennsylvania Society for the Promotion of Internal Improvements, generated additional support for Stevens's project. In 1827, after resigning his position as an engineer for the Pennsylvania Canal Commission following a dispute over consulting fees, Strickland surveyed a rail route through New Jersey. He determined that construction was feasible, and he endorsed railroads over canals. So too did noted canal engineer Canvass White. Their reports provided much fodder for discussion at two internal-improvement conventions held in Princeton in 1827 and 1828. Railway supporters used the Strickland survey as evidence of the ease of construction, but opponents were equally vociferous in their insistence that a canal between the two cities, first proposed in 1804, with an unsuccessful attempt at resurrection in 1820, would be a more certain undertaking. Many prominent individuals favored the canal, including Governor Isaac H. Williamson and Robert F. Stockton, on temporary hiatus from what was destined to be a stellar career in the United States Navy. The organizers of the People's Line, the primary competitor of the Union Line, were also behind the waterway.[104]

During the 1827–28 session, New Jersey legislators debated the merits of three plans to link New York and Philadelphia. John Stevens and his sons Robert and Edwin introduced a proposal to build a rail line between Trenton and New Brunswick. They were in competition with two other groups, one that favored a railroad between Camden and South Amboy, with the other supporting a canal between the Delaware and Raritan rivers. All three proposals went down to defeat, causing Stevens to join forces with the entrepreneurs who were promoting the Camden–South Amboy line. Bickering between the railroad and canal partisans continued unabated until January 1830, when New York investors requested a New Jersey charter to build the New Jersey Atlantic Railroad across the state.[105]

The possibility that a New York railroad might dominate transportation in New Jersey galvanized the warring parties into action. According to popular lore, in January 1830, John Stevens and his son Robert bumped into Robert Stockton at a New York theater. Each entrepreneur admitted that the ongoing hostility would benefit no one, and they agreed to set aside their differences. What was more likely, however, is that both sides were prepared to unite in the face of a common enemy, and that New Jersey legislators were prepared to be exceedingly accommodating in order to exclude the New Jersey Atlantic Railroad. Whatever the reason, on February 4, 1830, the legislature chartered both the Camden & Amboy Rail Road & Transportation Company and the Delaware & Raritan Canal Company, giving each the opportunity to span the New Jersey portion of the route between Philadelphia and New York. The charter prohibited the construction of competing transportation routes within five miles of either line and permitted the Camden & Amboy to charge high fares—eight cents per ton-mile and ten cents per passenger mile. In return, representatives from both companies agreed to pay the state a "transit duty" on passenger and freight traffic—a provision that served as a model for the tonnage tax that the Pennsylvania legislature would later levy on the PRR.[106]

Contemporary investors considered the railroad to be the more promising of the two companies. Within ten minutes they had subscribed all of the Camden & Amboy's $1 million worth of stock—much to the delight of President Robert L. Stevens and Treasurer

Edwin Stevens. Even after several days, however, the canal company barely managed to place a tenth of that amount, and it would probably have faltered had not Stockton volunteered a substantial subscription, resulting in his election to the presidency. By October 1830, moreover, the promoters of the Delaware & Raritan Canal were concerned that the Camden & Amboy would put their water route out of business. Legislators refused their request to amend the charter, to build a railroad instead of a canal. Ultimately, however, Delaware & Raritan directors concluded that the only realistic alternative to what they called "suicidal competition" would be to pool their resources with the Camden & Amboy.[107] The Stevens family was reluctant to subsidize the canal, but they were also frightened that Stockton might join forces with the supporters of the New Jersey Atlantic.[108]

With the creation of an alliance between the Camden & Amboy Rail Road and the Delaware & Raritan Canal, construction began on both routes. Camden & Amboy officials hired Major John Wilson, a veteran of the Main Line of Public Works, to undertake surveys between Camden and South Amboy. He had served as something of a mentor to Thomson when they worked together on the Philadelphia & Columbia, and Wilson subsequently employed the young engineer to head one of the Camden & Amboy survey parties.[109] In December 1830 construction crews began work, at Bordentown, New Jersey. The railroad's promoters selected a track gauge of 4′ 10″ between the rails, slightly broader than the standard (4′ 8½″) gauge employed on the Philadelphia & Columbia and the PRR. That choice probably stemmed from a decision to use rails with a one-inch-wide head, with the outside edges spaced five feet apart. Whatever the reason, it would be some years before tracks set to New Jersey gauge physically connected with lines in Pennsylvania. The slight difference in width would eventually cause problems, however, particularly when railroads in Ohio and Indiana also adopted 4′ 10″ as their standard. Crews spiked down lengths of rail to stone blocks supplied by the inmates at Sing Sing Prison. Camden & Amboy president Robert L. Stevens is given credit for being the first to use wooden ties in place of the stone blocks (the insufficiently industrious inmates apparently could not match the railroad's ambitious con-

struction timetable), but engineers on other railroads seem to have experienced a similar epiphany on their own. Stevens also developed the T-section rail profile, one that would soon become standard on railroads across North America.[110]

While in England to arrange for the rolling of rails to his novel design, Stevens also placed an order with the Newcastle-upon-Tyne firm of Robert Stephenson for the fifth locomotive that that company delivered to the United States. Completed on June 18, 1831, the *John Bull* pulled an inspection train along a short stretch of track on November 12 of that year. The excursion was a considerable success in that it persuaded the passengers, many of whom were members of the New Jersey legislature, that the railway constituted a reliable form of transportation. Stevens and machinist Isaac Dripps, later the Camden & Amboy's master mechanic, soon added such improvements as a tender, a pilot, and a two-wheel pilot truck. Unlike most other early locomotives, the *John Bull* escaped the scrap yard, and it remains the oldest motive power employed on the PRR or any of its subsidiaries.[111]

By December 1832 the Camden & Amboy was in service between South Amboy and Bordentown, on the Delaware River, a few miles south of Trenton. Passengers could then take a steamboat from New York City to South Amboy, transfer to the steam cars, and finish their journey on a Union Line riverboat linking Bordentown with Philadelphia.[112] In September 1834, the Camden & Amboy completed its original main line, linking its two namesake cities. As there was no bridge across the Delaware River, passengers arriving in Camden boarded ferries for the crossing to Philadelphia. However, except for the winter months, when the Delaware River might be choked with ice, few through passengers chose to ride the railroad to the end of the line. The steamboats between Bordentown and Philadelphia were faster and considerably more comfortable.[113]

By May 1834, the Delaware & Raritan Canal Company had also completed construction. Its route included a forty-four-mile-long waterway from New Brunswick to Bordentown and a twenty-two-mile-long feeder canal along the east bank of the Delaware River, from Trenton north to Bull's Island. The newly opened Delaware & Raritan Canal boasted a generous prism (cross-section)—seventy-five feet wide and eight feet deep, as opposed to little more than forty feet wide and five feet deep on Pennsylvania's Delaware Division—and could accommodate heavily laden anthracite barges that were robust enough to survive the open waters of Chesapeake Bay, the Hudson River, and Long Island Sound. Initially, canal revenues were barely a tenth of those on the railroad. By the 1850s, however, increased anthracite traffic, much of it destined for New England, ensured the Delaware & Raritan Canal about half the earnings generated by the Camden & Amboy. The canal carried substantial bulk tonnage through the 1870s, well after most of the Pennsylvania canal system had fallen into disuse. Commercial traffic ended in 1932, but much of the canal remains open today for recreational use and as a water-supply channel.[114]

A Transportation Monopoly in New Jersey

During the construction of the Camden & Amboy Rail Road and the Delaware & Raritan Canal, officials from both companies petitioned the New Jersey legislature for greater protection from competition. In February 1831, the Camden & Amboy donated one thousand shares of stock to the state in exchange for a nine-year moratorium on the construction of a parallel rail line. In exchange, the state stipulated that the transit duties would apply only to through traffic—ensuring that the tax would affect outsiders, not New Jersey residents. The Stevens family also solidified its alliance with Robert Stockton and his fellow Delaware & Raritan investors rather than risk the possibility that the canal would fall under the sway of the New Jersey Atlantic Railroad. Officials from the Camden & Amboy and the Delaware & Raritan Canal negotiated a cooperative agreement that stopped just short of an outright merger, with a joint board of directors and pooled income, but separate financial accounts. On February 15, 1831, and with some reluctance, legislators gave their assent to an Act of Union. The two firms, known until 1867 as the "Joint Companies," now had a virtual monopoly on transportation across New Jersey. The popular press may have jocularly referred to the arrangement as the "Marriage Act," but that attempt at humor did little to dampen public fears that the "marriage" was merely a ruse to build one line without offering the competitive benefits of the other.[115]

The New Jersey legislature provided additional benefits to the Camden & Amboy, solidifying the company's rail transportation monopoly across the state. Legislators asserted that the existing traffic levels did not justify the construction of more than one line, and that the chartering of the New Jersey Atlantic, or any other competing railroad, would only imperil the finances of both. Therefore, in March 1832 New Jersey legislators passed the Protection Act, prohibiting any other railroad from building within three miles of the Camden & Amboy's termini. In practical terms, the Protection Act prevented any competing company from building a railroad across the state or from carrying freight or passengers traveling between Philadelphia and New York—provisions that remained in place until 1869.[116]

The monopoly provisions gave investors in the Camden & Amboy Rail Road and the Delaware & Raritan Canal an extraordinarily high rate of return. Almost from its inception, the Joint Companies paid steady dividends of between 6 and 12 percent per year, something that was virtually unheard of in the railroad business, while disbursing numerous supplemental dividends and accumulating a substantial reserve fund. As railroad analyst Henry Varnum Poor noted in 1860, the "extraordinary revenues are in a great measure due to the monopoly it enjoys of the right of way between the cities of New York and Philadelphia."[117] Small wonder, then, that contemporaries frustrated at the absence of competitive transportation referred to New Jersey as "The State of Camden and Amboy."[118]

The monopoly came at a significant price, however. In order to ensure passage of the Protection Act, Joint Companies officers donated an additional one thousand shares of stock to the state. They also agreed that the transit duties, when combined with the dividends on the two thousand shares of stock, would funnel at least $30,000 per year into the state treasury. By the 1850s, the transit duties actually amounted to some $200,000 annually, contributing more than half of New Jersey's revenues, with additional income earned from the dividends on the state's allotment of Camden & Amboy stock.[119]

The Protection Act created a partnership between the New Jersey legislature and the Camden & Amboy, one that retarded the development of rail travel between New York and Philadelphia. To the delight of Garden State property owners, who enjoyed the lowest real estate taxes in the nation, the alliance with the Camden & Amboy exploited out-of-state shippers and passengers to subsidize New Jersey's residents. As Poor noted, "The State became a willing party to the [monopoly] scheme, under the idea that it could thereby draw the means for supporting its government from citizens of other States, relieving its own from the burdens of taxation."[120] Poor, who was far more loyal to the railroad industry than to any state government, railed against the arrangement, which he saw as a drag on commerce. During the Civil War, Massachusetts Senator Charles Sumner relentlessly attacked the transit duties, which he believed to be an impediment to the Union military effort. He echoed the sentiments of many passengers and shippers when he suggested that "New Jersey is the Valley of Humiliation through which all travelers north and south from the city of New York to the city of Washington must pass; and the monopoly, like Apollyon, claims them all as 'sub-jects,' saying 'for all that country is mine, and I am the prince and god of it.'"[121]

A New Competitor in New Jersey

The Stevens brothers and the Joint Companies had no sooner established their canal, rail, and steamboat empire in New Jersey than other companies challenged their near-monopoly on transportation between Philadelphia and New York. In February 1832, in the midst of the flurry of rail and canal construction, the promoters of the Philadelphia & Trenton Railroad Company obtained a charter from the Pennsylvania legislature to build a line between its namesake cities. By November 1834, the company had completed its line from Kensington, barely four miles north of Center City Philadelphia, to Morrisville, Pennsylvania, across the Delaware River from Trenton.

The Joint Companies also faced a measure of competition to the north. For several years, supporters of the New Jersey Atlantic Railroad had attempted, in vain, to obtain a New Jersey charter. The Protection Act had finally ended their hopes, but the legislation had likewise increased resentment toward the Camden & Amboy. In an effort at compromise and reconciliation, five days

Figure 27. Since 1830, the Camden & Amboy Rail Road possessed a virtual monopoly on transportation in New Jersey, particularly along the lucrative route between New York and Philadelphia—the most heavily traveled transportation corridor in the United States. The service, in conjunction with steamboats in New York Harbor and along the Delaware River, was fast and convenient, but also extremely expensive, owing to the transit duties authorized by the New Jersey legislature. The competing Philadelphia & Trenton Railroad ran through Pennsylvania, paralleling the west bank of the Delaware River to a point opposite Trenton, but could not offer service into New Jersey. Nor did it enter Center City Philadelphia, as a series of riots halted plans to extend the line south of Kensington. The New Jersey Rail Road & Transportation Company, chartered as a local carrier, extended from Jersey City as far south as New Brunswick, but its promoters soon made plans to connect with the Philadelphia & Trenton. In response, Camden & Amboy officials negotiated an agreement with the New Jersey Rail Road and built a connection between New Brunswick and Trenton, as well as a short link between Trenton and the Camden & Amboy main line, at Bordentown. Initially, the original Camden & Amboy tracks between South Amboy and Camden (with ferries continuing across the Delaware River to Philadelphia) constituted the principal link between New York and Philadelphia. By the time of the Civil War, however, the New Jersey Rail Road and Philadelphia & Trenton route assumed far greater importance.

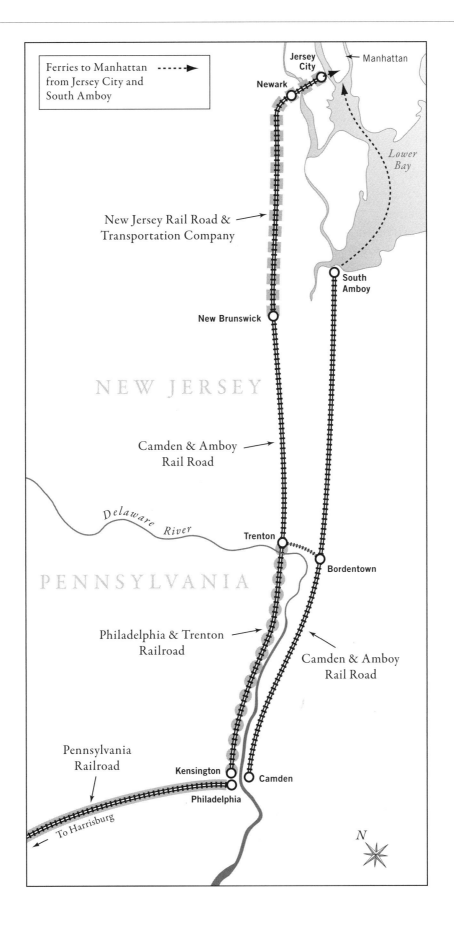

after adopting the Protection Act the legislature chartered the New Jersey Rail Road & Transportation Company. In order to protect the Camden & Amboy, however, the new company was to be a purely local line between Jersey City and New Brunswick, and it would not offer through services to the Delaware River at Trenton. The company's limited prospects dampened enthusiasm for stock subscriptions. What little money the company raised it soon spent within sight of New York, cutting through Bergen Hill and building a fill across the boggy ground that constituted the New Jersey Meadowlands. The Panic of 1837 caused still more difficulties, and it was not until 1838 that the line reached New Brunswick, little more than thirty miles from Jersey City.[122]

Of greater concern to Stockton, the Stevens brothers, and their fellow Joint Companies investors, the Philadelphia & Trenton had acquired a controlling interest in two key firms. One was the Trenton-Delaware Bridge Company with its 1806 span across the Delaware River between Trenton and Morrisville. The other was the Trenton & New Brunswick Turnpike Company, a New Jersey corporation that in 1804 had completed a road, often known as the "Straight Turnpike" (today's U.S. Route 1), across central New Jersey. The promoters of the Philadelphia & Trenton asserted that the turnpike possessed the authority to lay rails along its right of way. Joint Companies officials naturally disputed that claim, and 1835 witnessed a series of political and legal battles over the issue.[123]

Stockton and the Stevens brothers were uncertain as to the outcome, and fearful that the federal courts might intervene to resolve the issue, perhaps stripping away the Joint Companies' monopoly privileges in the process. Beginning in late 1834, they accordingly began efforts to buy out their rivals, first acquiring stock in the Trenton-Delaware Bridge Company and charging extraordinarily high tolls for anyone wishing to cross the span in order to transfer to the Philadelphia & Trenton. Camden & Amboy managers then set their sights on the Philadelphia & Trenton itself. In November 1835, negotiations between Philadelphia & Trenton and Joint Companies officials led to a tentative consolidation agreement, which Philadelphia & Trenton shareholders approved the following April. The arrangement was not a merger, nor could it be,

given the status of the Philadelphia & Trenton as a Pennsylvania corporation. Likewise, the board of directors of the Joint Companies did not contain any representatives from the Philadelphia & Trenton. The three firms nonetheless coordinated their operations and pooled revenues and profits.[124]

The inclusion of the Philadelphia & Trenton in the Joint Companies family permitted the development of an alternate rail route to New York. By September 1836, Joint Companies officials had agreed to build a line between New Brunswick and Trenton, connecting the New Jersey Rail Road and the Philadelphia & Trenton. The following year, the Philadelphia & Trenton laid tracks across the Delaware River bridge, at Trenton. The Camden & Amboy then built a short connection between Bordentown and Trenton, linking its line with that of the Philadelphia & Trenton. In 1838, construction crews continued northeast from Trenton, along the Delaware & Raritan Canal, through Kingston and Princeton, to Millstone Junction, a short distance southwest of New Brunswick, where they met the tracks of the New Jersey Rail Road.[125] During 1839, construction crews widened the Philadelphia & Trenton's gauge from standard to 4' 10", to match that of the Camden & Amboy.[126]

As the decade of the 1830s came to an end, three carriers—the Joint Companies, the Philadelphia & Trenton, and the New Jersey Rail Road—operated two parallel rail routes between New York and Philadelphia, but that hardly qualified as through service. The ferry trip across the Hudson River constituted the most serious impediment, but it would be many decades before that part of the journey could be eliminated. The New Jersey Rail Road quickly acquired a reputation as a safer and more efficient carrier than the Camden & Amboy, and its Jersey City terminal was much closer to Manhattan than the South Amboy facility. As such, most southbound passengers rode the New Jersey Rail Road to Trenton, as the connecting steamboat service to Philadelphia was more convenient, and considerably more comfortable, than the extended rail journey to Kensington. Those who wished to continue on by rail faced another obstacle, one engendered by law rather than geography. The transit duties taxed all passengers from Pennsylvania and other states who crossed through New Jersey. Southbound passenger trains halted at Trenton, requiring through passengers to disembark, cross over the Delaware & Raritan Canal on a footbridge, and board a second train in order to continue their journey across the Delaware River into Pennsylvania, on the tracks of the Philadelphia & Trenton. People traveling north to New York endured a similar process, but in reverse. The transfer was an inconvenience, but it exempted through passengers from the requirements of the transit duties—or so claimed Joint Companies officials.[127]

To their undoubted chagrin, travelers on the Philadelphia & Trenton discovered that that railroad's title was something of a misnomer. They could travel by train no farther south than Kensington, several miles from Center City Philadelphia. In 1840, the state legislature granted the railroad the right to lay tracks down the center of Front Street, to provide a connection with the Northern Liberties & Penn Township Railroad, the City Railroad, and the Philadelphia & Columbia. Local teamsters were concerned that they would lose the business associated with the transfer of freight and passengers. They joined forces with residents, many of whom were handloom weavers, who feared that the trains would endanger public safety and set fire to the mostly wooden buildings along Front Street. They argued that their street was a public highway and could not be given over to a private, monopolistic corporation. Their tactics included public demonstrations, political pressure, lawsuits, and ultimately mob violence. The Kensington riots began in July 1840 and recurred sporadically for the next two years. Townsmen tore up the tracks, burned ties, and rained stones down on railroad workers who attempted to repair the damage. In 1842, the legislature repealed the charter, preventing the Philadelphia & Trenton from connecting with the other railroads that served Philadelphia. In response, the Joint Companies withdrew most of their trains from Kensington and generally routed freight and passengers into Camden. As a result, most of the passengers who did not take advantage of the steamboats at Trenton continued south on the Camden & Amboy to the railroad's ferry terminal, across the Delaware River from Philadelphia. The railroad never did go through Kensington, and it would take the Civil War to induce the construction of a di-

rect connection between the Philadelphia & Trenton and the PRR, farther to the west.[128]

South to Baltimore

During the antebellum years, Thomson and other PRR officials had little reason to pursue expansion south of Philadelphia. Baltimore was dominated by the B&O, and the nation's capital was little more than a village along the Potomac, with scant traffic potential. The South generated considerable agricultural produce, but most of that flowed along rivers and early railways to the nearest seaport. During the Civil War, and in the decades that followed, the territory south of Philadelphia would assume greater importance to the PRR. For the time being, however, Thomson was content to exchange limited quantities of passengers and freight with the Philadelphia, Wilmington & Baltimore Railroad—a company that linked the eastern ends of two great trunk lines, but whose managers were determined to show no preference to either.

Prior to the completion of the Chesapeake & Delaware Canal in 1829, the neck of the Delmarva Peninsula constituted an impediment to travel between Baltimore and Philadelphia. In January 1809, the promoters of the New Castle & Frenchtown Turnpike Company secured a turnpike charter from the Delaware legislature, followed by a corresponding Maryland charter a year later. The New Castle Turnpike Company, established in 1811, also built a portion of the route. Together, the companies constructed a road between the upper reaches of Chesapeake Bay, at Frenchtown Landing, Maryland, and the Delaware Bay, at New Castle, Delaware. Passengers from Baltimore could travel by water to the headwaters of Chesapeake Bay, endure a short stage ride, and follow the Delaware River for the remainder of their journey to Philadelphia.[129]

Railway development occurred somewhat later but nonetheless long antedated the incorporation of the Pennsylvania Railroad. The ninety-four miles that separated Philadelphia and Baltimore spanned the territories of three states and required separate corporate charters. Six companies were involved, although four of them soon pooled their efforts. The owners of the two turnpike companies feared that the imminent opening of the Chesapeake & Delaware Canal would drain away much of their business unless they upgraded their facilities. In March 1828, the Maryland legislature permitted the New Castle & Frenchtown Turnpike Company to change its name to the New Castle & Frenchtown Turnpike & Rail Road Company and to lay rails along its right of way. The Delaware legislature also gave its assent to a railroad in February 1829. At the same time, the New Castle Turnpike Company, which controlled a short section of the route in Delaware, became the New Castle Turnpike & Railroad Company. A year later, the new company merged into the Newcastle & Frenchtown Turnpike & Rail Road Company. Most of the railroad construction took place during 1831, and by 1832 the Newcastle & Frenchtown was offering regular services along the sixteen miles of track that separated those two cities, at first with horsecars and soon thereafter with steam locomotives. Steamboat routes at each end of the line provided connecting service to Philadelphia and Baltimore.[130]

Promoters soon sought to at least partially substitute rail travel for the steamship voyage. In 1831, the Pennsylvania General Assembly chartered the Philadelphia & Delaware County Railroad Company to build a seventeen-mile line between Gray's Ferry (on the west bank of the Schuylkill River, opposite South Philadelphia) and the Delaware state line. In January 1832, the Delaware legislature chartered a similar corporation, the Wilmington & Susquehanna Rail Road Company, with the intent to build from the Pennsylvania state line south through Wilmington to the Maryland border. A third company, the Delaware & Maryland Rail Road, in March 1832 received a Maryland corporate charter, authorizing its promoters to build a line from the border with Delaware to some point along the Susquehanna River. The fourth company, the Baltimore & Port Deposit Rail Road, chartered in Maryland in March 1832, possessed the authority to build a line between Baltimore and the Susquehanna River, at Port Deposit, Maryland.[131] Together, the four companies would create an all-rail route between Philadelphia and Baltimore (with the exception of the crossing of the mile-wide Susquehanna River), in competition with both the New Cas-

tle & Frenchtown and the Chesapeake & Delaware Canal.[132] In April 1836 the two Maryland companies agreed to pool their efforts, selecting Havre de Grace, just downstream from Port Deposit, as a meeting place and the site of a railroad ferry across the Susquehanna River. Construction on both lines began in the early summer of 1835. The first trains reached Wilmington in May 1837, and construction crews extended the line south to Baltimore in July of that year.[133]

In March 1836 the Pennsylvania legislature authorized the Philadelphia & Delaware County Railroad Company to increase its capitalization and change its name to the Philadelphia, Wilmington & Baltimore Railroad. Legislators also exempted the company from an earlier prohibition against constructing any bridge across the Schuylkill River that might constitute a hazard to navigation, enabling work to begin on a crossing at Gray's Ferry. In 1836 the Delaware & Maryland Rail Road merged into the Wilmington & Susquehanna, and by February 1838 the four remaining companies (the Philadelphia, Wilmington & Baltimore, the Wilmington & Susquehanna, the Baltimore & Port Deposit, and the Newcastle & Frenchtown) were operating as one unit.[134]

Matthew Newkirk, a prominent Philadelphia merchant, played a key role in the new cooperative enterprise. Born in New Jersey in 1794, at the age of sixteen Newkirk moved to Philadelphia and clerked with J. & C. Cooper, wholesale dry goods merchants. Along with Thomas Cope, Newkirk had been instrumental in the establishment of the Philadelphia Board of Trade in 1833. He had also invested heavily in the various railroad companies and, later in his life, in metallurgy—by 1854 he was an investor in the Cambria Iron Works in Johnstown, Pennsylvania, a firm that was closely tied to the Pennsylvania Railroad. After 1838, Newkirk served as president of two of the nominally independent companies, and as a director of the others.[135]

In July 1837 workers completed the rail route between Baltimore and Wilmington, with the exception of the Susquehanna River crossing at Havre de Grace. The following January, service was extended as far north as Gray's Ferry. For a short time, the PW&B provided a connecting ferry to Philadelphia, followed by an omnibus ride to a ticket office and waiting area at the intersection of Market and Third Streets. Construction on the Gray's Ferry Bridge, also known as the Newkirk Viaduct, had begun on July 4, 1836, and the span was completed on Christmas Day, 1838. Designed as a combined railroad and highway bridge, the wooden structure was probably not strong enough to support steam locomotives, which posed an additional fire hazard. Until 1852, when the PW&B rebuilt and strengthened the bridge to accommodate locomotives, horses pulled the cars across the bridge and into central Philadelphia. On the east side of the Schuylkill River, PW&B tracks continued along Prime Street (now known as Washington Avenue) to a junction with the Southwark Rail-Road, at the intersection of Broad and Prime Streets. PW&B cars proceeded north to Cedar Street, where they could continue north along Broad Street on the City Railroad, to a connection with the Philadelphia & Columbia at Broad and Vine. After 1842, they would more likely travel a short distance west on Market Street, to the new PW&B station at Eleventh and Market Streets.[136]

By 1840, the Joint Companies and the Philadelphia, Wilmington & Baltimore offered through service between New York and Baltimore, by way of Philadelphia. Rail operations were neither seamless nor convenient, however. Southbound passengers left Manhattan early in the morning, taking a ferry to Jersey City. The New Jersey Rail Road took them south to New Brunswick, where they confronted three options, none of them ideal. The Philadelphia & Trenton line to Kensington required an omnibus ride to the Philadelphia, Wilmington & Baltimore station. The more popular Camden & Amboy route would get them closer, to a terminal in Camden opposite downtown Philadelphia, but they still faced a ferry crossing of the Delaware River. Many passengers avoided the railcars south of Trenton in favor of the steamboats that proceeded down the Delaware River to Philadelphia.

Once in Philadelphia, travelers would make their way to the PW&B station at Eleventh and Market. From there, horses would draw the passenger cars west, across the Gray's Ferry Bridge over the Schuylkill River. Locomotives powered the train south to the Baltimore city limits, a journey interrupted only by the ferry crossing of the Susquehanna River at Havre de Grace. When the trains reached the PW&B President Street Yard on the outskirts of Baltimore, the locomotives could proceed no farther. Thanks to a Baltimore city ordinance banning the use of steam locomotives within city limits, horses pulled each car for a mile, along Pratt Street, to the Baltimore & Ohio's Charles Street station. That was as far as a southbound passenger could travel in one day, as the last onward train for Washington had already departed. The next day, the intrepid voyager would endure another mile along Pratt Street, behind a plodding horse, before reaching the B&O's Mount Clare yard, where locomotives completed the trip to Washington.[137]

During the 1840s the Philadelphia, Wilmington & Baltimore connected two of the largest cities along the eastern seaboard, yet the resulting railroad was woefully undercapitalized, with unballasted track, few depots or service facilities, and an inadequate number of locomotives and rolling stock. Company directors compounded their financial problems by regularly voting themselves substantial dividends. During 1846 and 1847 a consortium of Boston capitalists, led by the banking house of John E. Thayer & Brother, reorganized the PW&B's bloated debt structure and gained control over the company. The new owners began to rebuild the property, replacing the original strap-iron rail with modern T-section rail, and providing new cars and locomotives. Their investments included the construction of new passenger stations in both Baltimore (on President Street, opened in 1850) and Philadelphia (at Broad and Prime Streets, opened in 1852).[138]

In 1851, the Bostonians selected a new president to run the PW&B. Samuel Morse Felton had been the superintendent of the Fitchburg Railroad in Massachusetts, and he was well acquainted with the operational and financial innovations of the early New England railroads. In the summer of 1854, Felton persuaded Henry Fletcher Kenney to resign from the Fitchburg Railroad and contribute his considerable mechanical and organizational skills as the PW&B's master of transportation. By June 1856, Felton had assumed the duties of superintendent, as well as those of president. Like the PRR, the PW&B suffered through severe interpersonal conflicts during the 1850s, particularly involving chief engineer and general superintendent Isaac R. Trimble. Felton and Trimble barely tolerated one another, perhaps because each considered himself indispensible to the company's operations. The situation came to a head in 1854, when the PW&B board dismissed Trimble for mismanagement of the railroad and for using the company's resources in his personal business endeavors.[139]

Felton attempted to avoid such difficulties, as well as reduce operating costs, by outsourcing virtually all of the constituent functions of the Philadelphia, Wilmington & Baltimore, the first time that any railroad had done so to such an extent. Many observers suggested that Felton's "contract system" offered an opportunity to separate ownership from management and would thus prevent the types of conflicts that had paralyzed the PRR's board during 1851 and the PW&B a few years later. The Bostonians who owned the PW&B believed that the contract system would enable them to cede day-to-day operating matters to professional railroaders, while they could continue to set long-term corporate strategy. The PW&B's contract system began on a trial basis during the second half of 1855. Very quickly, as Pennsylvania Railroad officials later observed, "responsible parties had submitted offers, for one year, to supply, under contract, all wood, oil and waste; to keep engines in repair and furnish men to run them; to furnish labor to keep the road in repair; to lay new track and turnouts not exceeding seven miles; to furnish all labor in the Freight Department and clerical hire; and to take all risk and damage to freight in transit, and all loss on freight in collection."[140]

By August 1856, the PW&B had become in essence a shell corporation, with all of the company's operations carried out, under contract, by the partnership of Henry Kenney, A. J. Barrett, George Stearns, Jr., and William Stearns. The contract system saved the PW&B more than $33,000 in 1855 alone, and may have saved the company itself from bankruptcy. Outsourcing paid its greatest benefits during the early years of the Civil War, unintentionally and in a manner that brought the contract system to an end. Wartime inflation threatened to bankrupt the outside contractors, who had negotiated fixed-price agreements with the railroad, but who had to purchase their own labor and supplies on the open market, at a time of rapid price increases. That discontinuity lowered the PW&B's 1862 operating ratio (the percentage of earnings consumed by operating expenses) to 29 percent, but sup-

pliers thereafter refused to negotiate any further contracts. The disputes caused such ill feeling that PW&B officials never again employed the contract system. PRR managers likewise exhibited an aversion to contracting, and it would not be used on the PRR system until the 1920s.

Connections North and South

During the 1850s, Thomson had little reason to worry about the PRR's connections to the south of Philadelphia. Under Felton's guidance, the Philadelphia, Wilmington & Baltimore became a reasonably efficient carrier, even if it was burdened by the absence of a bridge over the Susquehanna River and by inadequate connections in Baltimore and Philadelphia. While the primary goal of both the Pennsylvania Railroad and the Baltimore & Ohio was to funnel western traffic to their respective tidewater ports, the two rival trunk lines did forward some freight and passengers to other east coast destinations. The Boston capitalists who controlled the PW&B were perfectly happy to accept traffic from both trunk lines, without prejudice toward either.

The situation to the north was somewhat more worrisome. The New York financial interests who oversaw the operation of the Joint Companies opened their lines to all traffic on an equal basis. The 1832 Protection Act, with its legislatively mandated monopoly protection for the Camden & Amboy, complicated the situation, however. In order to pay the transit duties and maintain a steady stream of dividends to investors (including the state of New Jersey), Camden & Amboy officials had little choice other than to set high rates, at a time when competition was inducing rapid rate reductions in other parts of the United States. By 1848, for example, fares on the Camden & Amboy were the highest in the United States, and double the average for railroads in the Northeast. Those high rates infuriated through travelers and shippers, particularly those whose businesses were located in New York or Philadelphia. Many New Jersey residents, especially those in the southern part of the state, complained that monopolistic railroad rates made their products uncompetitive in New York or Philadelphia markets. The Stockton and Stevens families—and, in particular, Camden & Amboy treasurer Edwin A. Stevens—were determined to use the Joint Companies to augment their personal fortunes rather than to improve service or increase transportation efficiency. The high profits associated with the monopoly likewise made New Jersey a tempting target for railroad promoters who could find a way around the legislative restrictions and build a railroad that could compete with the Joint Companies. From the perspective of Thomson and other PRR officials, the transit duties hampered their ability to compete for New York traffic, and they accordingly sought other routes to the nation's largest city.[141]

Thomson, occupied with efforts to extend the PRR's influence west into Ohio and Indiana, saw little reason to attempt to control the PW&B or the Joint Companies, nor did he have the resources to do so. Given the small amount of freight and passenger business passing through Philadelphia, he was likewise unconcerned with the indirect and laborious nature of interchange operations in that city. By the end of the 1850s, however, Thomson was beginning to rethink his strategy. What concerned Thomson on the eve of the Civil War was the development of two alternate routes to the east coast. One followed the traditional transportation corridor along the Susquehanna River, improving Baltimore's access to central Pennsylvania. The other was a relatively new route, through Reading and Allentown, that promised better service to New York. Together, they threatened to draw the western grain trade away from Philadelphia, and toward its rival port cities—a situation that would have horrified the Quaker City merchants who had first proposed the Pennsylvania Railroad. Of more concern to Thomson, however, the Northern Central Railway and the Allentown Route drew traffic away from PRR tracks at Harrisburg, depriving the company of the full rail haul to the east coast, and greatly reducing the value of the recently acquired Philadelphia & Columbia Railroad.

Rails Along the Susquehanna

Efforts to connect Baltimore to the Susquehanna River Valley began well before the incorporation of the Pennsylvania Railroad. Beginning in 1828, Baltimoreans and their allies in York County organized a series of railroads (the Baltimore & Susquehanna, the York & Maryland Line, and the Wrightsville, York & Gettysburg) that by 1840 offered service to York and to Wrightsville, across the Susquehanna River from Columbia. By 1851, those entrepreneurs had completed yet another railroad, the York & Cumberland, north to Bridgeport (Lemoyne), on the west bank of the Susquehanna. A connection with the Cumberland Valley Railroad provided access to Harrisburg. Despite the completion of an extensive rail network, owners of the Baltimore & Susquehanna and its affiliated companies were disappointed in the results of their investment. Traffic was less lucrative than expected, particularly after the 1840 opening of the Susquehanna & Tide Water Canal.[142]

In an attempt to improve the finances of their various companies, the Baltimore investors eyed covetously the vast anthracite deposits that lay along the east side of the Susquehanna, as distant as the Wyoming Valley region around Wilkes-Barre. In April 1851, two months after the completion of the York & Cumberland, the General Assembly chartered the Susquehanna Railroad, with rights to build from Bridgeport north along the Susquehanna River to Sunbury, Pennsylvania. From there, branches were to continue northeast along the North Branch of the Susquehanna River to Wilkes-Barre and along the West Branch of the Susquehanna to Williamsport. The owners of the Susquehanna & Erie Railroad, chartered one day after the Susquehanna Railroad, possessed the authority to construct a line from Williamsport to Erie. The promoters of the more southerly Susquehanna Railroad soon organized their company, selecting future governor William Packer as their president. By November 1852, Packer and his associates had signed construction contracts, and crews were at work early the following year.[143]

In 1853, a financial panic brought construction to a standstill and induced the reorganization and consolidation of the four railroads that connected Baltimore to central Pennsylvania. In December 1854, the Susquehanna Railroad, the Baltimore & Susquehanna, the York & Maryland Line, and the York & Cumberland merged into the Northern Central Railway Company.[144] A year later, construction resumed on the line north to Sunbury. From Bridgeport, the railroad followed the west bank of the Susquehanna River, intersecting the PRR main line at Marysville. Just to the north of the PRR's bridge over the Susquehanna, the Northern Central crossed the river on its own nineteen-span, 3,880-foot-long structure, known as the Marysville Bridge. Construction crews then followed the east bank of the Susquehanna, reaching Sunbury on August 1, 1858.[145]

North to Erie

The Northern Central provided Thomson with two opportunities—first, to reach Lake Erie, and, second, to gain direct access to Baltimore. The PRR president, and his associates, pursued both of those opportunities more or less simultaneously. The link to Baltimore was the first to enter service, and the first to fall under the PRR's influence. The corresponding route to Erie, however, brought to fruition a decades-old dream to connect Philadelphia to the Great Lakes.

Since 1792, when the Commonwealth of Pennsylvania purchased the small triangle of land adjacent to Presque Isle (Erie), boosters had advocated for a transportation route that would connect Philadelphia to that small band of Lake Erie shoreline.[146] In the years that followed, internal-improvement advocates suggested that turnpike, canal, and railroad routes linking Philadelphia to Erie were comparable in importance to those running west to Pittsburgh.

Erie was not wholly isolated from the rest of the state, although its citizens were probably more closely tied to Buffalo and the western terminus of the Erie Canal than they were to Harrisburg or Philadelphia. By the 1820s, Erie nonetheless enjoyed turnpike access to Pittsburgh, Harrisburg, and Philadelphia.[147] Still, with the Erie Canal gathering the bulk of the traffic on the Great Lakes, many Pennsylvanians hoped that a canal to Erie could capture some of that trade. In 1825, when legislators established the Board of Canal Commissioners, they assigned to that body the responsibility for developing a route to Erie. The canal commissioners, legislators, community boosters, and promoters advocated a variety of schemes for canals between Harrisburg and Erie (along the Susquehanna River) and Pittsburgh and Erie (along the Allegheny River). Most of those proposals died a quick death,

owing to a lack of funds. Not until 1844 did canal boats reach Erie, traveling north from the Ohio River, and not west from the Susquehanna.[148]

Railroad construction between Philadelphia and Erie likewise lagged, although not for want of effort. One of the first meetings to rally support took place in March 1836, in Jersey Shore, Pennsylvania. Eight months later, more than two hundred delegates, many from Philadelphia, traveled to Williamsport to attend a convention in support of a railroad between Erie and Sunbury, near the confluence of the North and West Branches of the Susquehanna River. In addition to calling on the General Assembly for financial support, the delegates chose as vice presidents future Secretary of War Simon Cameron, future Governor William Packer, Erie merchant and shipowner Rufus S. Reed, and pioneering Erie resident Thomas King. For the post of president of the convention, they selected Philadelphia financier Nicholas Biddle.

Biddle and his cousin, Edward R. Biddle, were the driving force behind efforts to build a railroad to Erie, as part of their broader interests in banking, mining, and transportation in New York and Pennsylvania. Nicholas Biddle was well connected to the world of finance. He served as the president of the Second Bank of the United States between 1822 and 1836. Following the Bank War (President Andrew Jackson's attempt to destroy the Second Bank), Biddle oversaw the formation of the United States Bank of Pennsylvania and served as president of the new enterprise until 1839. He was also responsible for chartering a branch of the United States Bank of Pennsylvania in Erie. Biddle believed the bank to be overcapitalized, and he eagerly sought investment opportunities, particularly those that would benefit him personally.[149]

The Biddles and their fellow investors intended to establish routes that would tie New York to the anthracite fields of northeastern Pennsylvania, with additional links to Philadelphia, south-central Pennsylvania, and Lake Erie. Edward Biddle served as a director of the Morris Canal & Banking Company, the easternmost portion of the route. Opened in 1831, the Morris Canal connected Phillipsburg, New Jersey (across the Delaware River from Easton, Pennsylvania) and Newark, with an extension to Jersey City entering service in 1836. To gain access to the anthracite lands that lay to the west of the Delaware River, the Lehigh Canal would serve as a temporary expedient, pending the completion of the Beaver Meadow Railroad & Coal Company's tracks to the future site of Black Creek Junction. There, investors intended to connect with a branch of the Little Schuylkill & Susquehanna Railroad, which was in turn linked to one of the oldest railroads in the United States.[150]

Between 1829 and 1831, the Little Schuylkill Navigation, Railroad & Coal Company built a line from a junction with the Schuylkill Navigation (and later the Philadelphia & Reading Rail Road), at Port Clinton, uphill to Tamaqua. In March 1831, a consortium of investors incorporated the Little Schuylkill & Susquehanna Railroad as an extension of the initial route.[151] The tracks skirted the northern edge of the anthracite fields, but the promoters hoped to forge links to both the east and the west. A connection with the Beaver Meadow Railroad & Coal Company would facilitate the shipment of anthracite to New York. In the opposite direction, the line ascended to the headwaters of the Little Schuylkill Creek, and then descended to the west, down the banks of Catawissa Creek, along a route that Moncure Robinson had surveyed in 1828. The Little Schuylkill & Susquehanna reached the North Branch of the Susquehanna River at Catawissa. From there, supporters projected that the line would eventually continue to the Great Lakes, by way of Williamsport, Pennsylvania, and Elmira, New York. In addition to providing the Biddle interests with a route between New York and Lake Erie, by way of the anthracite fields, the project was certain to benefit the Philadelphia & Reading, in which Nicholas Biddle was heavily invested.[152]

The Pennsylvania General Assembly soon gave Nicholas and Edward Biddle and their allies the legal mechanism to extend their rail network to the west. On April 3, 1837, Governor Joseph Ritner signed legislation chartering the Sunbury & Erie Railroad, the Pittsburgh & Susquehanna Railroad, and the Harrisburg & Sunbury Railroad.[153] In return for their charters, promoters of the three companies promised to provide Erie with rail access east to Sunbury, Harrisburg, and Philadelphia, as well as a second route from Erie south to Pittsburgh. Nicholas Biddle became the first president of the Sunbury & Erie, which was by far the most important of the three companies. He also arranged for the United States Bank of Pennsylvania to purchase six thousand shares of Sunbury & Erie stock.[154]

In April 1838, Sunbury & Erie chief engineer Edward Miller began survey work. Miller, the same individual who would later serve as the PRR's assistant engineer for the Western Division, soon located a route through the towns of DuBois and Franklin, with moderate grades. In his January 1839 report, Miller nonetheless recommended a more northerly course, through Warren, one that possessed substantially steeper grades. As justification, he emphasized that the new alignment offered a more direct route between Sunbury and Erie. Despite Miller's rationalizations, there were other, non-engineering forces at work. Thomas Struthers and Jacob Ridgway had invested in the Sunbury & Erie, and they lobbied vigorously for the northern route, one that would provide access to their large landholdings in the vicinity of Warren. In early 1840, Miller made a second report in which he set the cost of a double-track railroad between Sunbury and Erie at just under $9 million.[155]

Chief engineer Miller's reports spent the next decade gathering dust, as the Sunbury & Erie fell victim to the Panic of 1837 and the financial machinations that surrounded the United States Bank of Pennsylvania. The Little Schuylkill & Susquehanna was the first element of the Biddles' plan to collapse. Construction stopped in 1838, even though most grading was complete, and a locomotive purchased. Worse was to follow. Nicholas Biddle, as it turned out, was not the only one who valued the capital that the bank could provide. When the General Assembly chartered the bank in February 1836, legislators forced Biddle to fund much of the state's debt, as well as bear the cost of their ambitious internal-improvements program. The propensity of both Biddle and the commonwealth's legislators to regard the United States Bank of Pennsylvania as a bottomless well of capital produced predictably unfortunate results, and the bank failed in 1841. At the same time, Edward Biddle was forced out of the Morris Canal & Banking Company. Work on the Sunbury & Erie soon came to a halt, after an expenditure of some $1.5 million.[156]

The excitement generated by the incorporation of the Pennsylvania Railroad paradoxically delayed construction of the Sunbury & Erie. In January 1847, for example, a convention in Philadelphia in support of the Sunbury & Erie disintegrated amid allegations that it was nothing more than a plot to draw scarce capital away from the PRR. By the spring of 1851, however, the possibility that a rival carrier might seize control of the Sunbury & Erie route goaded that company's supporters into action. In February, the York & Cumberland Railroad, the northernmost extension of the series of rail lines linking Baltimore to the Susquehanna River, reached Bridgeport, opposite Harrisburg. A month later, the Pennsylvania legislature chartered the Susquehanna Railroad, with the authority to build from Bridgeport to Sunbury and Williamsport, and the Susquehanna & Erie Railroad, from Williamsport to Erie. The two new companies threatened to duplicate much of the Sunbury & Erie route, but they would direct commerce toward Baltimore rather than Philadelphia.

The threat posed by the Susquehanna Railroad and the Susquehanna & Erie Railroad reinvigorated the supporters of the Sunbury & Erie. Many of the Philadelphians who had been reluctant to simultaneously fund both the Sunbury & Erie and the PRR now blanched at the possibility of a direct connection between Baltimore and the Great Lakes. In May 1851, supporters of the project gathered in St. Mary's, Pennsylvania. A week later, a ceremonial groundbreaking took place at Farrandsville, the terminus of the West Branch Division canal. Construction nonetheless took place in a rather desultory fashion, as there was little money in the corporate treasury.

In September, a Philadelphia convention in favor of the Sunbury & Erie authorized thirty-five prominent individuals to lobby in support of the project. They included William M. Meredith, Job R. Tyson, and Judge James L. Gillis, each of them closely connected to the PRR. A second Philadelphia convention took place in January 1852 at the Chinese Museum, the same facility that had witnessed the organization of the Pennsylvania Railroad. By the end of the month, Thomson had conferred his blessing on the project by buying shares in the company and by reassuring his fellow Philadelphians that he did not consider the Sunbury & Erie to be competing against the PRR, for either traffic or investment capital. Thomson also lent Edward Miller, the newly appointed chief engineer of

the PRR, to serve the same function on the Sunbury & Erie—a route that he knew well, based on his surveys more than a decade earlier.[157]

As with the Pennsylvania Railroad, Philadelphia entrepreneurs could not raise sufficient private capital to begin construction on the Sunbury & Erie, so they relied on the assistance of local government. In February 1852, following numerous extensions to the Sunbury & Erie's charter, legislators gave local governments the authority to invest in the company. Six years earlier, the City of Philadelphia had invested heavily in the Pennsylvania Railroad. Now, the members of the Select and Common Councils promised to subscribe $2 million in the Sunbury & Erie, even though it took them nearly two years to make good on their offer.[158] The City of Erie, Erie County, Warren County, Elk County, Clinton County, Lycoming County, and the Boroughs of Lock Haven, Milton, Northumberland, and Sunbury also invested in the project, in amounts ranging from $25,000 to $300,000.[159]

Officials of the reinvigorated Sunbury & Erie did their best to block the Susquehanna Railroad. By June 1852, both companies were competing for the same alignment along the Susquehanna River, north of Harrisburg. Susquehanna Railroad officials promptly requested and received an injunction from the Pennsylvania Supreme Court, halting construction by Sunbury & Erie crews. Following their defeat in the courts, Sunbury & Erie executives favored negotiations over further conflict. They permitted construction to proceed on the Susquehanna Railroad in exchange for the right to use that company's tracks between Sunbury and a junction with the PRR at Marysville.

The battle for the Susquehanna River corridor was not the only right-of-way dispute that embroiled the Sunbury & Erie. In March 1853, Robert Faries replaced Miller as chief engineer, inheriting Miller's two surveys across western Pennsylvania. As Miller had discovered, one route possessed more favorable gradients, while the other appealed to the railroad's investors. Faries postponed a decision as long as possible, even as the pace of construction accelerated. Although Faries preferred the easier grades to the south, pressure from land speculators again forced the railroad's officials to adopt a more northerly alignment, via Emporium and Ridgway.[160]

Despite disagreements over the route, tracklayers made steady progress. In December 1854, the first section of the new line, between Williamsport and Milton, opened to traffic. In September 1855, the tracks from Milton south to Northumberland entered service. A few months later, in January 1856, construction crews bridged the Susquehanna River to Sunbury. Under the terms of the agreement with the Susquehanna Railroad, operations went no farther south than Northumberland. It was not until June 1858 that the Northern Central Railway (the successor company to the Susquehanna Railroad) reached Northumberland, completing a through route to Baltimore.[161]

With the Sunbury & Erie already short of funds, the company was in no position to extend rails from Williamsport west and north to Erie. President William Bigler, recently unseated as Pennsylvania's governor, failed to manage the firm effectively or, more importantly, to attract additional capital. In February 1856, he exchanged the presidency for a seat in the United States Senate. Bigler's successor was none other than Samuel Vaughan Merrick, the first president of the Pennsylvania Railroad. Merrick, who probably nursed some bitter memories of his unceremonious departure from the PRR board, initially declined the offer to manage the Sunbury & Erie. He soon received a letter from twenty-one prominent Philadelphians, no doubt worried that their city's investment in the project would disappear without producing any appreciable commercial benefits. Merrick did his best to rebuild the Sunbury & Erie, purging the board of directors and renegotiating many of the dubious construction contracts that his predecessors had undertaken. The Panic of 1857 swept over the nation not long after Merrick began his efforts to reorganize the railroad. The financial crisis exhausted Merrick's abilities, and he resigned the presidency in December. William G. Moorhead, the brother-in-law of financier Jay Cooke, took Merrick's place.

Despite the Sunbury & Erie's chronic financial problems, many members of the General Assembly were determined to prevent the company from going bankrupt. A few years earlier, Philadelphians had assisted the company in order to prevent Baltimore interests from controlling access to Erie. By the late 1850s, however, there emerged a far more serious threat in the form of the Catawissa Route, a new rail connection to New York that bypassed Philadelphia entirely.

The development of the Catawissa Route occurred quite gradually, largely as the result of efforts to reach the Pennsylvania anthracite fields. In March 1849, more than a decade after the panic of 1837 brought construction on the Little Schuylkill & Susquehanna Railroad to a standstill, the company's promoters renamed the project the Catawissa, Williamsport & Erie Railroad. They retained their goal of connecting the Little Schuylkill Navigation, Railroad & Coal Company, near Tamanend, Pennsylvania, with the North Branch of the Susquehanna River, at Catawissa. Such a connection would, for the first time, provide an all-rail route from the anthracite fields of the Wyoming Valley to the East Coast. In June 1854, construction crews reached Catawissa and then continued westward along the North Branch of the Susquehanna River. They passed to the north of Sunbury and Northumberland, cutting across the top of the fork created by the two branches of the Susquehanna. In September they built a connection with the Sunbury & Erie at Milton, on the West Branch of the river.

The junction at Milton created a somewhat haphazard route between Philadelphia and Buffalo, one that offered some potential benefit to the Quaker City. From Philadelphia, traffic could move north along the Reading to Port Clinton. It then traveled north to Tamanend, along the route built by the Little Schuylkill Navigation, Railroad & Coal Company. The Catawissa, Williamsport & Erie dispatched the traffic west to Milton, while the Sunbury & Erie continued north and west to Williamsport. From Williamsport, three railroads—the Williamsport & Elmira, the Canandaigua & Elmira, and the Canandaigua & Niagara Falls—provided access to North Tonawanda, New York, and the Niagara Falls Bridge, as well as the main lines of the Erie and the New York Central.[162] Service began in December 1854, and the directors of the Reading soon authorized the purchase of new passenger equipment for a "through route to the Lakes." The connection could not have been all that convenient, however. Until 1853, the Erie had operated the line between Elmira and Canandaigua, and the tracks west of Elmira were still laid to broad gauge. The indirect routing and the break of bulk proved fatal to efforts at coordinated operation, and through passenger service ended in 1857.[163]

Very shortly, however, new railway construction offered a route that threatened to drive traffic away from Philadelphia, and toward New York. In September 1855, the completion of the Lehigh Valley Railroad Bridge across the Delaware River, linking Easton, Pennsylvania, and Phillipsburg, New Jersey, permitted eastbound traffic to flow off of the Catawissa and onto the Reading, and then onto the Lehigh Valley and the Jersey Central, in order to reach New York. The route was a bit circuitous, however. A far greater peril arose from the Quakake Railroad, which intersected the Catawissa line near Tamanend. After the Quakake Railroad entered service in September 1858, eastbound Great Lakes traffic that reached Williamsport could follow the Sunbury & Erie to Milton, the Catawissa, Williamsport & Erie to Tamanend, the Quakake to Black Creek Junction, the Beaver Meadow Railroad & Coal Company to Mauch Chunk (today, Jim Thorpe), the Lehigh Valley to Phillipsburg, New Jersey, and the Jersey Central to Elizabethport. Despite the multiplicity of carriers involved, the "Catawissa Route" provided an excellent connection between the Sunbury & Erie and New York.[164]

The Catawissa, Williamsport & Erie entered receivership in 1859, and was reorganized the following year as the Catawissa Railroad, but those administrative matters did little to remove the threat posed by the Catawissa Route. PRR officials were concerned that it would draw traffic away from their main line, while Philadelphians were worried that it would accelerate the loss of the western trade to New York. Sunbury & Erie investors were also nervous, as the owners of the Catawissa Railroad were planning on building west from Milton, using the charter of a closely allied company, the Williamsport & Erie Railroad. If such a project came to fruition, the Williamsport & Erie route would roughly parallel the still-incomplete Sunbury & Erie and probably put the latter company out of business. Yet the full potential of the Catawissa Route would not emerge until the end of the Civil War, with the oil boom in northwestern Pennsylvania.

Over the next several years, Pennsylvanians worked assiduously to ensure that the Sunbury & Erie, and not the Catawissa, would be the first to reach the Great Lakes. Philadelphians, including many of the PRR's

KEY TO RAILROADS (in circles, on map)

APC	Auburn & Port Clinton Railroad (not completed)
AR	Allentown Railroad (not completed)
BD	Belvidere Delaware Railroad
BO	Baltimore & Ohio Railroad
BS	Baltimore & Susquehanna Railroad*
CA	Camden & Amboy Rail Road
CNJ	Central Railroad of New Jersey (Jersey Central)
CV	Cumberland Valley Railroad
CWE	Catawissa, Williamsport & Erie Railroad (after 1860, the Catawissa Railroad)
DS	Dauphin & Susquehanna Coal Company (after 1859, the Schuylkill & Susquehanna Railroad)
EP	East Pennsylvania Railroad
LV	Lehigh Valley Railroad
LVR	Lykens Valley Railroad & Coal Company
NJ	New Jersey Rail Road & Transportation Company
PRR	Pennsylvania Railroad
PT	Philadelphia & Trenton Railroad
PWB	Philadelphia, Wilmington & Baltimore Railroad
Q	Quakake Railroad
RDG	Reading Rail Road
SE	Sunbury & Erie Railroad (as of 1860)
SR	Susquehanna Railroad*
SV	Shamokin Valley & Pottsville Railroad (before 1858, Danville & Pottsville Railroad)
WE	Williamsport & Elmira Railroad
WYG	Wrightsville, York & Gettysburg Railroad
YC	York & Cumberland Railroad*
YM	York & Maryland Line Railroad*

*After 1854, part of the Northern Central Railway

KEY TO TOWNS AND CITIES

A	Allentown
Ba	Baltimore
Bel	Belvidere
Bo	Bordentown
Br	Bridgeport (Lemoyne)
Cam	Camden
Ch	Chambersburg
Col	Columbia/Wrightsville
D	Dauphin
E	Erie
El	Elmira
EP	Easton, Pennsylvania/Phillipsburg, New Jersey
H	Harrisburg
HG	Havre de Grace
JC	Jersey City
La	Lancaster
Ma	Marysville
MC	Mauch Chunk
Phi	Philadelphia
Pit	Pittsburgh
QJ	Quakake Junction
R	Reading
SA	South Amboy
Su	Sunbury
Tr	Trenton
W	Williamsport
Y	York

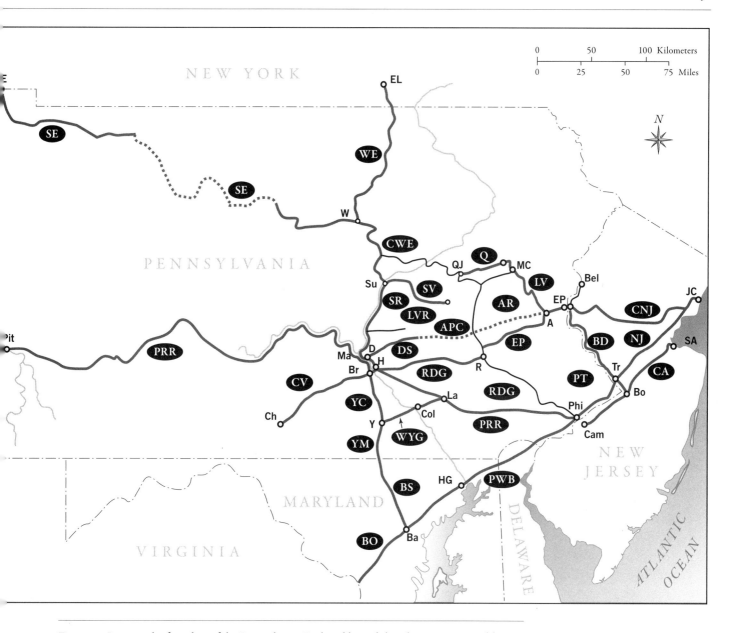

Figure 28. In 1846, the founders of the Pennsylvania Railroad hoped that the company would capture some of the traffic that flowed down along the Susquehanna Valley, toward Baltimore. Yet, Baltimoreans proved resilient, building a series of railroads (the Baltimore & Susquehanna, the York & Maryland Line, the York & Cumberland, and the Susquehanna) that captured much of the anthracite traffic generated in the Wyoming Valley, along the North Branch of the Susquehanna River. PRR executives also worried about the powerful Philadelphia & Reading Rail Road, whose main line along the Schuylkill River was a virtual conveyor belt for funneling anthracite to the Delaware River at Port Richmond, just north of Philadelphia. By the 1850s, moreover, several companies were promoting railroads that would span the mountainous terrain between the Schuylkill and Susquehanna Rivers, in order to more efficiently bring anthracite to New York markets. To the dismay of PRR executives, who lacked a convenient route through Philadelphia, the new lines offered superior service from the west to tidewater. As such, J. Edgar Thomson was forced to extend PRR tracks to the Delaware River waterfront and to cooperate with the Reading and other carriers on the new "Allentown Route" to New York, bypassing Philadelphia. By the 1860s, Thomson had also moved aggressively to acquire the lines along the Susquehanna River (consolidated in 1854 as the Northern Central Railway), as well as the incomplete Philadelphia & Erie Railroad (renamed the Sunbury & Erie Railroad in 1861), with a route west to Erie, Pennsylvania.

officers and investors, pressured their legislators to provide financial encouragement for the local champion, the Sunbury & Erie. As a Williamsport native who was closely associated with the Sunbury & Erie, Governor Packer possessed both personal and political motives for aiding the enterprise. Members of the General Assembly were determined to rescue the faltering company, despite a provision in the 1857 constitution that prohibited direct public assistance to private corporations. Convinced of the urgency of the situation, they soon discovered a mechanism for undermining the intent of the law. In April 1858 they authorized the Sunbury & Erie to issue an additional $7 million in bonds. Sunbury & Erie officials would doubtless find those securities difficult to sell, given the state of the economy and the company's shaky finances. As such, legislators accepted $3.5 million of those bonds, in exchange for the leftover portions of the state canal system that had not already been promised to the PRR. The expectation was that the Sunbury & Erie would then sell the canals, keeping a quarter of whatever profit resulted (over and above the $3.5 million purchase price), while ceding the remainder to the state. A month later, the Sunbury & Erie bought the Susquehanna, West Branch, North Branch, and Delaware divisions, and soon resold them.[165] The sale of the canals netted the Sunbury & Erie a modest profit of $375,000, three-quarters of which ($281,250) the company still owed to the commonwealth.[166] When added to the remaining $3.5 million of the bond issue, however, the company had enough cash to resume construction.[167]

In the summer of 1859, and with the new injection of capital, Sunbury & Erie construction crews reached Lock Haven and then crept slightly farther up the West Branch of the Susquehanna. Between May and December 1859, the Sunbury & Erie also completed the westernmost portion of its route, the sixty-six miles between Erie and Warren. The onset of the Civil War tightened credit and created shortages of both material and labor, bringing construction to a standstill. With almost 140 miles of partly graded roadbed separating the two disconnected halves of the route, the completion of the Sunbury & Erie between Philadelphia and Lake Erie seemed a distant if not impossible dream.[168]

Between the Schuylkill and the Susquehanna

Along its route between Bridgeport and Sunbury, the Susquehanna Railroad (after 1854, the Northern Central Railway) connected with several companies that fed anthracite from northeastern Pennsylvania down to the banks of the Susquehanna River. During the 1830s and 1840s, the primitive nature of railway construction ensured that rail lines, many of them powered by gravity or by horses, were barely adequate to move coal downgrade to the nearest navigable waterway or adjacent canal. With the steady improvement of railway engineering practices, however, it was possible for local investors and mine operators to construct routes that spanned the entire distance between the Schuylkill and the Susquehanna. When completed, coal traffic could flow with equal facility to the western tracks of the Northern Central, or to the more easterly routes developed by the Philadelphia & Reading and the other major anthracite carriers. That situation exacerbated the already intense rivalry between the PRR and the Reading until executives from the two companies reached a truce of sorts, on the eve of the Civil War. Of equal significance, the opening of through routes posed a serious problem for Thomson and his colleagues in that they allowed all manner of traffic—including western grain—to leave PRR rails at Harrisburg and follow a reasonably direct route to New York. The lost New York traffic deprived the PRR of significant revenue and threatened to place Philadelphia at an even greater disadvantage against Manhattan as a commercial center.

One significant generator of traffic was the Danville & Pottsville Railroad, incorporated in 1826, and one of the first attempts to connect the Schuylkill and Susquehanna river valleys by rail. The project, in conjunction with the Schuylkill Navigation, was part of an ambitious plan by Philadelphia's Stephen Girard to gain access to his coal lands on Broad Mountain. Many Philadelphians also saw it as a mechanism for diverting the commerce of the upper Susquehanna Valley away from Baltimore. Moncure Robinson, at that time in charge of building the Little Schuylkill Railroad, was responsible for much of the engineering work. Construction began shortly after Girard's death in December 1831, with funds allocated by the executors of his estate. Although promoters intended to span the distance between the Schuylkill and the Susquehanna, their immediate goal was to bring anthracite down to both rivers, along two disconnected sections of the same railroad. On the eastern segment, workers built a short tunnel and six inclined planes and associated levels, similar to those employed on the Allegheny Portage Railroad. The single-track line carried coal traffic for more than twelve miles, over Broad Mountain, linking the Mahanoy Valley to the Schuylkill Navigation at Wadesville, near Pottsville. In August 1837, construction crews completed the western portion of the railroad, laying twenty miles of track between anthracite mines at Shamokin and the Susquehanna River and the Susquehanna Division Canal, at Sunbury. Despite the initial application of steam power, the line was so poorly constructed that horses soon were used to pull cars laden with coal. Plans to connect the two halves of the route fell victim to the Panic of 1837, and by 1838, the company's officials had even abandoned service on the eastern portion.[169]

In 1845, local interests sought to extend the western portion of the Danville & Pottsville along the Susquehanna River to Williamsport, and then into New York State. Nothing came of those efforts, and the line went bankrupt. Following foreclosure and subsequent sale, its new owners in 1851 reorganized the project as the Philadelphia & Sunbury Railroad. Work crews rebuilt the line with T-rail, reintroduced steam locomotives, and extended service from Shamokin to Mount Carmel and other nearby mining communities. The company again went bankrupt in 1857 and was reorganized the following year as the Shamokin Valley & Pottsville Railroad. The Northern Central soon invested in the railroad and its affiliated coal lands—the first in a long series of acquisitions that would provide traffic for the route south to Baltimore. The Shamokin Valley & Pottsville was never able to complete a Schuylkill–Susquehanna route, and that company's chronic financial problems imperiled the Northern Central's finances.[170]

Farther to the south, the Lykens Valley Railroad & Coal Company provided another valuable source of traffic. Organized in 1831—with Thomas Pim Cope serving as president—by 1834 horses were hauling carloads of coal from the mines at Bear Run some sixteen

miles to the Susquehanna River at Millersburg. The legislature's massive 1838 internal-improvements bill provided for the construction of the Wiconisco Canal along the east bank of the Susquehanna River, covering the dozen miles between Millersburg and a connection with the northern terminus of the Eastern Division Canal, at Clark's Ferry (near Duncan's Island). Work on the canal stopped in 1841, thanks to the commonwealth's growing financial problems. Within a decade, furthermore, the primitive rail line inland to the mines was worn out and abandoned. In 1845, however, investors reestablished the Lykens Valley Railroad & Coal Company and began rebuilding the route with modern iron rail, suitable for steam locomotives. They also revived and completed the commonwealth's Wiconisco Canal as a private venture.[171]

Although the Wiconisco Canal remained in service until 1890, Northern Central officials made rail access to the Lykens Valley coal traffic one of their top priorities. By December 1856, coal trains were running from Millersburg south to Dauphin, where the railroad operated by the Dauphin & Susquehanna Coal Company spanned the short distance to PRR tracks at the east end of the Rockville Bridge.[172] Thomson was no doubt keenly interested in the new connection, which promised additional traffic for the PRR. He also stood to benefit personally, as in February 1851 he had joined with other investors, including PRR stalwart Job Tyson (Cope's son-in-law), forming the Short Mountain Coal Company, in order to exploit coal reserves in the Lykens Valley.[173]

By the mid-1850s, it was not clear which railroad, or which city, would gain the most from the expansion of the transportation network in the western part of anthracite country. The Baltimoreans who controlled the Northern Central Railway believed that they could capture much of the coal traffic generated by the Philadelphia & Sunbury Railroad, the Lykens Valley Railroad & Coal Company, and the Dauphin & Susquehanna Coal Company. Once Northern Central construction crews reached Sunbury, in 1858—and assuming that the Sunbury & Erie completed its route—anthracite could flow with equal facility north to Lake Erie or south to Baltimore. Both destinations bypassed Philadelphia, as well as the tracks of the Pennsylvania Railroad.

Pennsylvania Railroad officials were nonetheless optimistic that they could capture some of the anthracite trade, divert it onto PRR rails at Harrisburg, and then dispatch it east to Philadelphia. The involvement of Thomson and Tyson in the Short Mountain Coal Company and other similar ventures was bound to generate additional coal traffic for the PRR. Perhaps, as Jacob Cist had suggested, many years earlier, the anthracite from the Wyoming Valley, around Wilkes-Barre, could travel down the North Branch and then the main stem of the Susquehanna River, before crossing overland to Philadelphia. If PRR officials could influence or gain control over the Northern Central, then they would likewise be in a strong position to demand that traffic moving south along the Susquehanna would go to Philadelphia rather than Baltimore.

By 1860, however, PRR officials had conceded defeat, at least where anthracite traffic was concerned. The victor in the anthracite trade was neither the Northern Central nor the PRR but the Philadelphia & Reading. The Reading was for all intents and purposes a conveyor belt that funneled anthracite between northeastern Pennsylvania and tidewater. Much of its success was attributable to its capacious and modern coal terminal at Port Richmond, on the Delaware River just north of Philadelphia. The most readily accessible anthracite deposits lay along the Schuylkill and Delaware rivers. They were easy pickings for the Reading and a host of smaller railroads, most of which moved the coal to New York markets. Anthracite production along the Susquehanna River and in the Wyoming Valley remained at low levels until well after the Civil War. Even then, the Reading was in a strong position to capture a share of that market as well. In addition to an expanding network of branch lines that eventually encompassed most of the mining areas in northeastern Pennsylvania, the Reading in 1858 acquired the Lebanon Valley Railroad, providing a connection between Harrisburg and Philadelphia. While the Lebanon Valley never lived up to the expectations of Reading officials (in some measure because the PRR gained control over its logical western extension, the Cumberland Valley Railroad), they nonetheless used the line to move coal from the Susquehanna Valley east to Philadelphia.

In contrast, the PRR was primarily an east–west railroad, poorly positioned for the anthracite trade and without direct access to the Delaware River waterfront. Few shippers were willing to forgo the Reading's Port Richmond terminal for the distinctly inferior facilities offered by the PRR. Following the Civil War, PRR officials undertook substantial investments in anthracite coal lands, mining operations, and transportation facilities. Yet, even though the PRR grew rich from the transportation of bituminous coal in western Pennsylvania, the company never played a significant role as a carrier of anthracite.

In western Pennsylvania, by the late 1850s the PRR dominated the small yet steadily increasing transportation of bituminous coal, at least as far east as the Susquehanna River. Yet, western Pennsylvania mine owners, who also appreciated the efficiency of Port Richmond, were likely to demand that that traffic be transferred to the Reading's Lebanon Valley line at Harrisburg, or perhaps sent down the Northern Central to Baltimore. Either routing deprived the PRR of badly needed traffic over the recently purchased Philadelphia & Columbia Railroad. More ominously, farmers in Ohio and Indiana were increasingly resistant to shipping their grain east over the PRR. New York was the nation's commercial center, and they saw little reason to send their products to Manhattan by way of Philadelphia. Instead, they were more likely to employ the New York Central or the Erie for the entire distance. Thomson responded to the impending loss of business on two fronts. First, he worked with his adversaries on the Reading to develop better connections with New York. The cooperative Allentown Route bypassed Philadelphia and caused eastbound traffic to leak from the PRR at Harrisburg, but it at least preserved the railroad's traffic west of that point. Second, Thomson began to improve the PRR's facilities and connections in Philadelphia, a process that continued through the Civil War.[174]

The Allentown Route

Four factors conspired against Thomson's efforts to gain a share of eastbound traffic. For one thing, the PRR did not directly serve the Delaware River waterfront. Even after gaining access to West Philadelphia as a result of the 1857 purchase of the Main Line of Public

Works, cargoes faced an arduous horse-drawn transfer through the streets of Center City Philadelphia. The resulting cost and inconvenience made New York Harbor a more attractive option to many shippers. Here, too, Thomson faced problems. The PRR main line dipped to the south between Harrisburg and Philadelphia, adding extra distance and cost to shipments that then went north to New York. Furthermore, there was no direct rail connection in Philadelphia between the PRR and either the Philadelphia & Trenton or the Camden & Amboy. The actions of the New Jersey legislature compounded those physical impediments, as the state's transit duties increased freight and passenger rates to non-competitive levels.

Thomson could do nothing to alter Philadelphia's location in the southern extremity of Pennsylvania. Nor, it seemed, could he avoid the transit duties, although not for want of effort. Pennsylvania Railroad officials, Philadelphia business owners, and the city's politicians were all outraged at New Jersey's impediments to the flow of rail traffic through Philadelphia and on to New York. As early as 1848, members of the Philadelphia Board of Trade protested the onerous conditions and prepared a petition to Congress calling for federal intervention. A decade earlier, Congress had declared that all railroads would be federal post roads, suggesting the possibility that congressional action could override restrictive charter provisions imposed by state legislatures. Now Philadelphians wanted the federal government to charter a company that would operate as a post road and thus break the state-sanctioned Joint Companies' stranglehold on New Jersey commerce. Their efforts came to naught, however, and the PRR still lacked good access to New York.[175]

On the eve of the Civil War, Pennsylvania Railroad managers developed a route to New York, one that bypassed the Joint Companies and the transit duties—although not in precisely the manner that Thomson might have wished. The creation of a new link between New York City and the west began in February 1849, when New York interests merged the Elizabethtown & Somerville Railroad and the Somerville & Easton Railroad into the Central Railroad of New Jersey, more commonly referred to as the Jersey Central. By 1852, the Jersey Central had constructed a line from Elizabeth, New Jersey, west to Phillipsburg on the Delaware River. In September 1855, after a three-year delay, the Lehigh Valley Railroad completed a bridge linking Phillipsburg and Easton, Pennsylvania. The Lehigh Valley connection enabled anthracite from Mauch Chunk, at the eastern edge of the Southern Anthracite Field, to reach New York markets. The Lehigh Valley line to Mauch Chunk passed through Allentown, before turning sharply to the north.

Allentown lay almost due east of Dauphin, the Susquehanna River terminus of the railroad operated by the Dauphin & Susquehanna Coal Company. The owners of that firm had steadily extended their tracks eastward, reaching a junction with the Reading, at Auburn, in early 1853. What remained was a gap of some forty miles, between Allentown and Auburn. In April 1853, the owners of the Jersey Central and the Dauphin & Susquehanna Coal Company obtained a charter for the Allentown Railroad, designed to link the Lehigh Valley at Allentown with Port Clinton. At Port Clinton, the Allentown Railroad would connect with the Reading main line, permitting a roundabout journey between New York and Philadelphia, independent of the Joint Companies in New Jersey.

The collection of railroads offered an even more tantalizing possibility, in the form of a connection west to the Susquehanna River. The Auburn & Port Clinton Railroad, chartered in March 1854, would carry trains from Port Clinton a short distance west to Auburn and a junction with the Dauphin & Susquehanna. The Dauphin & Susquehanna line met the Susquehanna River just to the north of Harrisburg. From there, it was a simple matter to connect with either the Northern Central to Baltimore or, of greater value, with the PRR west to Pittsburgh. Work began on the Allentown Railroad in 1855, but the Panic of 1857 soon ended construction. By 1859, the Dauphin & Susquehanna Coal Company had gone bankrupt, and its line between Dauphin and Auburn was reorganized as the Schuylkill & Susquehanna Railroad (not to be confused with the Little Schuylkill & Susquehanna Railroad, the predecessor of the Catawissa, Williamsport & Erie Railroad).[176]

Another project, backed by the Reading Rail Road, precluded the completion of either the Allentown Railroad or the Auburn & Port Clinton. Commercial interests in the city of Reading were displeased that the route through Allentown and Port Clinton would bypass their community. In March 1856, and despite concerted opposition from PRR officials and residents of Philadelphia, they secured a charter for the Reading & Lehigh Railroad. The following year, they renamed the company the East Pennsylvania Railroad. By May 1859, construction crews had completed a thirty-five-mile line from Reading northeast to Allentown.[177]

The completion of the East Pennsylvania Railroad link established the "Allentown Route," the first direct line between Pittsburgh and New York. From Pittsburgh, eastbound trains followed the PRR to Harrisburg, where they transferred to the Reading's former Lebanon Valley Railroad line to the city of Reading. At Reading, trains continued east on the East Pennsylvania Railroad to Allentown. The Lehigh Valley then dispatched trains to Phillipsburg, New Jersey, and the Jersey Central handled them on the final stretch into Elizabethport, on Newark Bay.[178]

Despite the number of carriers involved, the Allentown Route was by far the shortest and fastest way to move trains from Pittsburgh and points west toward New York City. Time-sensitive passenger traffic and livestock shipments were particularly good candidates for the new connection. Prior to the opening of the Allentown Route, a passenger traveling from Pittsburgh to New York could proceed by locomotive-hauled train only as far as the PRR's West Philadelphia yards. There, a horse would draw the cars across the Permanent Bridge and into Center City Philadelphia. Travelers might ride a horsecar over the Philadelphia City Railroad to the Delaware River at Dock Street, then take a ferry ride to Camden followed by a trip north on the Camden & Amboy. Or, passengers could make their way through the city to the Philadelphia & Trenton terminal in Kensington and then ride in relative comfort to Jersey City. Cattle bound for New York, while less likely to complain, also faced an inconvenient route through Philadelphia. Drovers unloaded the cattle at Fifty-Second Street in West Philadelphia and herded them through city streets until the animals reached the Delaware River. There, they boarded a ferry for Trenton and the stock cars of the Camden & Amboy. Although the cattle probably found both the walk and the boat ride salubrious, it was an inconvenient and inefficient method of funneling traffic

through the city. Along the Allentown Route, however, passengers both human and bovine could remain in the same cars from Pittsburgh all the way to the Hudson River.[179]

Given the convenience of the Allentown Route, western shippers soon pressured PRR executives to divert traffic along that line. So too did the managers of the PRR's western connections, including George Washington Cass, president of the Pittsburgh, Fort Wayne & Chicago. PRR officials were naturally reluctant to allow that traffic to leave their tracks at Harrisburg. With merchant-managers such as Samuel Vaughan Merrick and William C. Paterson long gone from the company, Thomson's hesitation had relatively little to do with concern for Philadelphia's mercantile economy. Instead, he was opposed to short-hauling his railroad—that is, he would have preferred to send shipments on the longer haul east to Philadelphia, where they could be sent north by water or turned over to the independent Joint Companies.

Yet PRR executives had little choice other than to cooperate in the Allentown Route, lest they lose a large proportion of their western traffic to the New York Central or the Erie. Livestock trains began operating along the Allentown Route in March 1860, followed by passenger trains that May. Through Pittsburgh–Jersey City sleeping cars began running a short time later. Traffic increased substantially during the Civil War years, at least until the PRR built better connections, in Philadelphia, with the Joint Companies and with the Philadelphia, Wilmington & Baltimore.[180]

With the Allentown Route drawing traffic away from the Pennsylvania Railroad, and away from Philadelphia, Thomson increased his efforts to improve the PRR's access to the Delaware River waterfront. As early as January 1852, General Superintendent Haupt had emphasized the need for a link to the river, but both he and Thomson were in the final stages of their battle to wrest control of the PRR from Patterson and his allies, and nothing was done. Two years later, Haupt, at that time the chief engineer, reiterated the call for action. Thomson echoed Haupt's complaints that the municipally owned City Railroad, designed for lightly loaded horsecars, could not accommodate the PRR's traffic, especially when seasonal grain and coal shipments became heavy. "The road now leading to the Delaware front is so much out of repair that it is difficult to use it," he informed the members of the Select and Common Councils in October 1855, "and it must with the heavy business which should be done on it during the next few months, if not repaired, become impassible."[181]

Finally, in January 1856, Thomson announced that the PRR would shoulder the expense of reaching the Delaware River. In April, he persuaded the Pennsylvania legislature to amend the PRR's charter to permit the construction of a line to the waterfront at Prime Street, near the old Philadelphia Navy Yard—one that would be temporarily isolated from the rest of the system, as the PRR had not yet purchased the Philadelphia & Columbia. The negotiations to acquire the Main Line of Public Works and the Panic of 1857 prevented construction of the Delaware River Extension for several years.[182]

In January 1859, with the railroad's finances recovering and with the Allentown Route nearing completion, the PRR board of directors authorized the construction of the Delaware Extension. Work began the following year. Thomson's plan to reach the Delaware River depended on the cooperation of three companies: the Philadelphia, Wilmington & Baltimore, the Southwark, and the West Chester & Philadelphia.[183] The Delaware Extension ran southward from Market Street in West Philadelphia, sharing the West Chester & Philadelphia's tracks to a point just north of the PW&B's Gray's Ferry Bridge. Rather than make use of that antiquated structure, Jacob H. Linville, the assistant resident engineer of the PRR's Middle Division at Altoona, oversaw the fabrication of a new cast-iron bridge. The eastern end of the PRR bridge was adjacent to the Schuylkill Arsenal and was thus known as the Arsenal Bridge. On the east side of the Schuylkill, the PRR used the PW&B and Southwark tracks to reach the Delaware River. The extension entered service in January 1862. The next year, the PRR completed the Point Breeze Branch to the Philadelphia Gas Works and opened a grain warehouse at the foot of Prime Street, in a largely futile attempt to increase the company's share of the grain trade. During the years that followed, the construction of additional tracks improved the PRR's access to the docks and industrial facilities in South Philadelphia, while permitting the withdrawal of most freight traffic from the City Railroad tracks on Market Street. The Delaware Extension did not eliminate the importance of the Allentown Route, but it did make the PRR more competitive against the Reading, while enabling Philadelphia to gain a portion of the traffic that might otherwise have gone to New York.[184]

The Northern Central to Baltimore

In addition to completing the Delaware Extension to the Philadelphia waterfront, Thomson also sought better access to Baltimore. That goal offered clear evidence of the changes that had occurred in the political economy of Pennsylvania during the first half of the nineteenth century. Unlike many of the individuals who had supported the Main Line of Public Works— and even many of those who had helped to establish the Pennsylvania Railroad—Thomson was not so naive as to believe that he could redirect long-established patterns of commerce away from the Susquehanna Valley and toward Philadelphia. The PRR's eventual acquisition of the Northern Central Railway ensured that Philadelphia's company—although not necessarily the city of Philadelphia—would benefit from economic development along the Susquehanna River. In particular, Thomson hoped that the Northern Central would enable the PRR to increase its share of the anthracite trade while providing a terminal in Baltimore that might provide some relief for the overburdened facilities in Philadelphia. In his search for revenue, and in his efforts to protect his company against competitors, Thomson had little choice other than to offer service to Philadelphia's traditional rival, Baltimore.

Pennsylvania Railroad officials were not the only ones who coveted the Northern Central. During the 1850s, executives from both the Baltimore & Ohio and the Reading acquired substantial blocks of Northern Central stock. By 1859, however, the Reading was largely out of the race to capture the Northern Central. Thomson's control of the Cumberland Valley Railroad had effectively confined the Reading to the territory east of the Susquehanna River. At the same time, the Sunbury & Erie, which offered the Reading the possibility of expansion west to the Great Lakes, was in danger of foundering. The diversion of PRR traffic to the Allentown Route and the concomitant routing of coal shipments to the Reading's terminal at Port Richmond constituted what amounted to a temporary truce between the two carriers. Under those circumstances, Reading officials were willing to yield the Northern Central to the PRR.

Baltimore & Ohio executives were more determined to maintain control over the Northern Central. Thirty years earlier, they had opposed the construction of its earliest predecessor, the Baltimore & Susquehanna Railroad, reasoning that the line might eventually offer a competing route between Baltimore and the Ohio River. B&O officials were also concerned that the route north to the Susquehanna Valley would bring cheap anthracite to Baltimore, reducing demand for bituminous coal from western Maryland. By the 1850s, however, B&O executives coveted the Northern Central's access to central Pennsylvania, as well as the possibility that it might be joined to the Sunbury & Erie route to Lake Erie. More significantly, they were determined to keep the line away from the influence of the PRR.[185]

United States Senator Simon Cameron was ultimately responsible for delivering the Northern Central to the Pennsylvania Railroad. Cameron was for the most part an ally of the PRR. However, unlike the board members who had invested in the Northern Central and its predecessors, Cameron's ambitions transcended both the PRR and its native state. He possessed national aspirations, in both business and politics, briefly challenging Abraham Lincoln for the 1860 Republican nomination for President. Although Pennsylvania was the base of Cameron's power, his interest in the Northern Central reflected his desire to turn a quick profit, regardless of the consequences that might accompany a diversion of trade away from Philadelphia. Cameron owned the construction companies that had built most of the Pennsylvania rail lines that were allied with the Baltimore & Susquehanna Railroad. As one example, the financially troubled Susquehanna Railroad, while struggling to complete its route north of Bridgeport, paid Cameron and his associates with $300,000 in bonds. Cameron was closely involved in the 1854 consolidation of railroads to form the Northern Central, and he took a seat on the board of directors of the new company. His brother-in-law Anthony B. Warford, the former chief engineer of the Susquehanna Railroad, soon became

chief engineer of the Northern Central, and later became that company's president.[186]

In June 1860, Cameron urged Thomson and Scott to join forces with him in an effort to gain control of the Northern Central by purchasing stock on the open market. Pennsylvania state law did not yet permit the PRR to own the stock of another railroad that did business within the commonwealth.[187] The two PRR executives would have to risk their own resources in the project, and they blanched at the thought. Yet, they had little choice but to participate, as they feared losing the Northern Central to either the Reading or the B&O, and because they desperately needed Cameron's political support during the legislative battle over the repeal of the tonnage tax.[188]

The effort of Cameron, Thomson, and Scott to buy control of the Northern Central was no mere raid by a group of Pennsylvania capitalists on a Maryland corporation. To the contrary, Thomson benefited greatly from local investors in Baltimore. His allies included Baltimore capitalists Benjamin Franklin Newcomer, William Thompson Walters, and John Sterett Gittings. Newcomer's ancestors originally hailed from southeastern Pennsylvania. At age eighteen, he took over his father's flour mills, and he later went on to co-found the Baltimore Corn & Flour Exchange. He would eventually count four PRR presidents (Scott, George B. Roberts, Frank Thomson, and Alexander J. Cassatt) as close personal friends, and his loyalties clearly lay with the Pennsylvania Railroad. Walters also traced his roots to Pennsylvania. He was born in the small town of Liverpool on the west bank of the Susquehanna River, midway between Harrisburg and Sunbury. After receiving training as a civil and mining engineer, he developed considerable experience in the iron business. In 1849, Walters moved to Baltimore, where he became a commission merchant, specializing in trade with Philadelphia. There he joined Newcomer in establishing a local bank, the Safe Depository Company.[189]

John S. Gittings, the president of the Northern Central, was a particularly valuable ally. He began his career at age sixteen as a clerk. He later became a stock broker and in 1835 was elected president of the Chesapeake Bank. The following year, the governor of Maryland appointed Gittings as commissioner of loans, in charge of efforts to secure state funding for the Baltimore & Ohio. He held numerous public offices and was for many years a member of the Baltimore City Council and chairman of the Finance Committee. Gittings was also a director of the Baltimore & Ohio, but he despised the authority of president John W. Garrett.[190]

Newcomer, Walters, and Gittings valued the B&O's links to the west, yet they were unwilling to depend solely on that company for transportation. Instead, they sought to connect Baltimore to several rail lines, ranging from the B&O to Wheeling to the Northern Central/PRR route to Pittsburgh, and potentially including the Sunbury & Erie extension to the Great Lakes. During the 1850s, for example, Walters served as a director of the Baltimore & Susquehanna, which in conjunction with the PRR offered a link between Baltimore and the west, free of the B&O. As the Northern Central's president, Gittings was particularly anxious to retain his company's independence from the B&O, even if that meant a closer alliance with the PRR.

During the summer of 1860, the investors allied with the PRR began to purchase Northern Central shares. Baltimore & Ohio president John W. Garrett begged Reading officials for help, offering to share the Northern Central with them, but to no avail. The PRR interests soon benefited from fortuitous timing. On November 1, the Commonwealth of Maryland began foreclosure proceedings against the Northern Central, ostensibly to force repayment of state loans to the company. The move was in reality a cooperative effort between the state and the B&O to prevent the PRR from gaining control of the Northern Central. The plan backfired, however, as the foreclosure proceedings left the Northern Central strapped for funds and sent its stock prices into a downward spiral. To save the Northern Central, Gittings advanced funds from his banking house, John S. Gittings & Company, and the rescue increased the control of the PRR forces over the company. Less than a week after the filing of the foreclosure suit, Abraham Lincoln was elected to the presidency. Maryland voters had favored southern Democrat John C. Breckenridge, and Lincoln's victory in the national contest depressed the Northern Central's stock prices still further, reducing the financial burden on the members of the PRR investment consortium. The impending secession of the southern

states contributed to an economic curtailment that forced both the B&O and the Reading to dump most of their Northern Central shares on the market. The PRR consortium snapped them up at bargain prices.[191]

By February 1861, the PRR interests gained control over the Northern Central and were able to elect a majority of its directors.[192] Each of the Baltimore capitalists accepted a seat on that railroad's board, with Newcomer serving as chairman of the Finance Committee. The new slate of officers included President Anthony B. Warford, Simon Cameron's brother-in-law, and James Donald Cameron, the senator's son. Two months later, on April 23, 1861, the General Assembly permitted any railroad incorporated in Pennsylvania to own the securities of any other carrier that operated in the commonwealth. As a result, Thomson was able to abandon the legal subterfuge of relying on personal ownership of Northern Central stock, and he and his allies soon sold most of their shares to the PRR.

On April 12, 1861, less than two weeks before the General Assembly gave the PRR the authority to own the Northern Central, Confederate artillery opened fire on Fort Sumter. The war that followed badly damaged the B&O and forced Garrett and his allies to sell their remaining Northern Central holdings, ending any possibility that the B&O might regain control over the line. The PRR bought the shares, but only to the extent necessary to maintain control, and the PRR never owned more than about 55 percent of the Northern Central.[193]

As the wartime military buildup intensified, troops and war materiel poured into Washington, and much of the traffic arrived on the Northern Central. With the B&O out of service for extended periods, the PRR and the Northern Central offered by far the best route from the west to the nation's capital. The Joint Companies/Philadelphia, Wilmington & Baltimore route along the Atlantic seaboard was often filled to capacity, and the Northern Central, in conjunction with the Allentown Route, offered an alternate path from New York to Washington. Despite suffering depredations at the hands of Confederates, the Northern Central benefited enormously from the Civil War, with high traffic levels justifying additional tracks, locomotives, and cars. Even though Thomson did not initially integrate the company into the PRR's corporate structure—it remained a separate entity until leased by the PRR in 1914—the Northern Central soon became an integral part of the Pennsylvania Railroad system.

Coordinating a Railroad

In the spring of 1861, as secession threatened to give way to civil war, Thomson could take some comfort in his accomplishments. He had consolidated the impressive gains that he had made since assuming the presidency in 1852, and was well prepared for the upcoming conflict. The Pennsylvania Railroad had survived the Panic of 1857, in far better shape than the Erie, and probably in far better shape than any other trunk line. The depression, combined with overcapacity on all of the routes linking the Midwest to tidewater, had forced Thomson to aggressively pursue the low-rate, high-volume pricing strategy that Haupt had long advocated. Economic conditions also led him to participate in numerous pooling arrangements, generally with scant success.

More significantly, the PRR's tightening finances led to a comprehensive reorganization of the Transportation Department, creating the line-and-staff corporate structure that, with numerous modifications, persisted for the remainder of the company's history. As part of that process, the PRR benefited from the contributions of Tom Scott, Andrew Carnegie, and numerous other talented executives. Some of those individuals would leave the railroad and continue their careers elsewhere, while others would remain with the PRR until the end of their lives, but all helped to shape the company's organizational structure.

The depression of the late 1850s indicated substantial weaknesses at the eastern end of the PRR system, and here, too, Thomson did his best to protect the PRR against its competitors. To the south of Philadelphia, he was willing to rely on the Philadelphia, Wilmington & Baltimore to carry modest quantities of PRR traffic to Baltimore. On the eve of the Civil War, he gained control over the Northern Central, wresting it free from the Baltimore & Ohio and the Reading. His goal was not to protect Philadelphia by preventing shipments from being lost to Baltimore, but rather to protect the PRR by avoiding the loss of traffic to rival carriers.

New York presented a rather more serious problem. Given the burdensome nature of the transit duties and the absence of a direct connection between the PRR and either the Philadelphia & Trenton or the Camden & Amboy, Thomson experienced considerable difficulty in competing for business in the nation's largest market. The development of two backdoor lines to New York—the Allentown Route and the Catawissa Route—bore witness to the PRR's vulnerability. Thomson countered the first of those threats by pushing the Pennsylvania Railroad as far east as it was possible to go, all the way to the Delaware River waterfront. Even that was not enough, and the Allentown Route continued to divert traffic away from Philadelphia, and away from the PRR. The Catawissa Route was, for the moment, less of a threat, given the incomplete state of the Sunbury & Erie. Thomson was nonetheless concerned enough, and sufficiently attracted to the traffic potential of northwestern Pennsylvania, to move cautiously forward with plans to link Philadelphia and Erie by rail.

Even as he was coordinating the PRR's operations and its connections to the east, Thomson was waging an even more intense battle in the west. The Philadelphia merchants who had promoted the "Pennsylvania Central Railroad" had always envisioned a route that would carry western grain toward Philadelphia, keeping it away from such carriers as the Baltimore & Ohio and the Erie Canal. Yet, they had made scant provision for ensuring that that grain would reach the end of the tracks at Pittsburgh, rather than flow toward Wheeling, Buffalo, or some other rival western gateway, where it would be lost to them forever. The PRR's initial complement of directors accordingly showed little interest in expansion to the west of Pittsburgh. Seemingly myopic, that conservative policy was in fact rooted in pragmatism, as the completion of the main line across the commonwealth was sufficient to consume whatever energies, money, organizational abilities, and political capital the directors had at their disposal. Once he became president, however, Thomson acted aggressively, extending the PRR's influence into the vast, fertile lands of Ohio, Indiana, and Illinois. Thomson had no doubt that such decisive action was necessary. He was less certain about how to make it work.

Chapter 7

Expansion
1850–1868

Throughout the spring and summer of 1850, heavy rains bucketed down along the lower reaches of the Ohio River. The fifty-four and a half inches that fell on Cincinnati set a record, as did the more than fifty-seven inches at Portsmouth. Springdale, Kentucky, received more than sixty-seven inches of precipitation. It was a wet year along the eastern seaboard as well, but curiously, not in Pittsburgh, or along the upper portion of the Ohio River. The normal autumn rise on the Ohio did not occur until the end of October, weeks behind schedule, but that anomaly was merely a precursor to the drought that began in 1851 and continued for the next eight years. With levels falling in wells and formerly reliable springs reduced to trickles, people drank water wherever they could find it, and cases of dysentery skyrocketed. Of greater concern to J. Edgar Thomson and his fellow PRR executives, traffic along the upper Ohio River had quite literally dried up and could no longer supply freight to the PRR's facilities at Pittsburgh. Even before he assumed the presidency, Thomson had supported expansion beyond Pennsylvania. Now, as the drought continued, he was more determined than ever to secure a reliable railway outlet to the west.[1]

The rich agricultural lands of Ohio, Indiana, and Illinois were critical to the success of the Pennsylvania Railroad. By 1850, farmers had settled large areas of the Old Northwest and had established a flourishing agrarian economy. Grain exports increased steadily, thanks to the 1846 repeal of the British Corn Laws, the effects of the Irish Potato Famine, the growing industrialization of western Europe, and the price increases triggered by the 1853–56 war in the Crimea. While cotton cultivation in the South had largely underwritten previous economic booms, the rising prosperity of the 1850s owed its source mostly to the grain trade.[2]

The PRR's promoters envisioned a steady stream of grain and flour flowing eastward, over the Alleghenies, through Pittsburgh, and to Philadelphia. With the PRR terminating at Pittsburgh, however, there was no guarantee that western grain would not follow some other channel to Baltimore or New York. Beginning in the late 1830s, an improving canal network in Ohio had greatly expanded the Erie Canal's catchment basin, slowly redirecting the grain trade away from the Mississippi River and its tributaries, and toward the east coast. By the middle of the 1840s, the change in the direction of commerce was much more pronounced, thanks in large measure to improved transportation in the Midwest. In 1847, for the first time in its history, the Erie Canal carried more eastbound traffic from the Old Northwest than it did from New York State. While PRR officials generally conceded

Figure 29. During the 1850s and 1860s, PRR president J. Edgar Thomson (third from left, seated) negotiated alliances with local railroad entrepreneurs in Ohio and Indiana in order to extend the PRR's reach to the west of Pittsburgh. His most important connection was the Pittsburgh, Fort Wayne & Chicago, under the leadership of George Washington Cass (fifth from the left, with the white beard). Between 1860 and 1862, Thomson and Cass oversaw the financial reorganization of the Fort Wayne, in tandem with James F. D. Lanier (seventh from the left, and, like Cass, holding his top hat) and attorney and future presidential candidate Samuel J. Tilden (standing in the center of the group). This composite photo, pieced together from individual portraits, shows the Fort Wayne's directors in 1865, a time when the Civil War had made their railroad a very valuable property. This photo was originally published in William J. Watt, *The Pennsylvania Railroad in Indiana* (Bloomington: Indiana University Press, 1999), p. 27, with the author providing valuable insights into the individuals depicted here.

Allen County–Fort Wayne Historical Society.

that the grain trade on the Great Lakes would probably continue east on the Erie Canal for the foreseeable future, and trade moving along the Ohio River might flow south to New Orleans or east on the Baltimore & Ohio, they could nonetheless contend for the great middle swath of territory that lay between the Ohio River and the Lakes.[3]

As early as June 1847, the PRR directors dispatched a delegation of board members and other investors to Ohio "in order that they might understand the interests that would probably be brought to bear upon their future prospects."[4] With construction of the Pennsyl-

vania Railroad barely begun, they had neither the funds nor the inclination to pursue expansion west of Pittsburgh. Within five years, however, the situation had changed dramatically. The drought had stunted the flow of eastward commerce through Pittsburgh, even as construction crews completed the first iteration of the PRR route across the commonwealth. The subsequent completion of the new line around the Horseshoe Curve and over the Allegheny Mountains gave further reason for the solicitation of western traffic. Most importantly, in 1852, Thomson became president of the Pennsylvania Railroad.

"Commerce Is a Strife for Conquest Without Bloodshed"

In the spring of 1852, only a few months after he had gained control over the Pennsylvania Railroad, Thomson met with a very useful and well-connected man. Thomas Sargent Fernon, who had just completed a term as a Democratic state senator, representing Philadelphia, was a long-standing advocate for railways. He had been president of the North Pennsylvania Railroad, and he would later serve as the editor of a trade journal, the *United States Railroad & Mining Register*.[5] During the years following the Civil War, Fernon would become sharply critical of the PRR's executives, Tom Scott in particular. At the time, however, Fernon was an unabashed supporter of the PRR and its management, believing that the company could help maintain Philadelphia's commercial status as a grain port. In June 1852 Fernon received an official letter from Thomson asking him to "take a trip through all the West, north of the Ohio River," and report on the commercial possibilities of the region.[6] Fernon spent months traveling through the Midwest, accumulating a mass of data. In December, he submitted a glowing report, emphasizing the rapid growth of cities such as Cincinnati, Chicago, and Cleveland. He had seen the point where the Allegheny and Monongahela rivers joined to form the Ohio and had compared them to an even more momentous waterway that lay half a world away, and nearly two thousand years in the past. Railroad development in the west would continue to benefit New York, he warned, "*until* Philadelphia shall cross the rubicon [*sic*], and lend her aid to hasten the completion of connecting roads on and beyond the banks of the Ohio River."[7]

Fernon predicted, "The time is not remote when competition among rival lines will compel a consolidation of interests on through routes."[8] That statement, made with considerable prescience, was couched in the language of system building. It was also precisely what Thomson wanted to hear, for it justified his efforts to provide assistance to railroads west of Pittsburgh. Fernon's report nonetheless reflected the civic loyalties of Samuel Vaughan Merrick, William C. Patterson, and other recently discredited and evicted members of the board. "How important is it, then," Fernon wrote,

in the classic language of a civic booster, "that Philadelphia should keep fully up with the events of to-day, and fortify her interests by a system of wise measures. . . . A city's plans for commercial defence and conquest should be laid down with a view to permanent future results, and not be compressed into miniature limits for temporary ends. . . . Commerce is a strife for conquest without bloodshed."[9]

Thomson adopted a more realistic assessment of the probable results of the "strife for conquest." He was under no illusions that Philadelphia's economy would again rival that of New York. Well before 1850, most transatlantic commerce flowed through New York, with Philadelphia's trade dominated by coastal shipments of anthracite coal and locally manufactured goods. Thomson, in common with many Philadelphia merchants, nonetheless hoped that he could bolster the fortunes of both his city and his company by redirecting western grain traffic—much of which continued to flow east over the Erie Canal—to the Quaker City.

While the new president and the recently deposed Merrick-Patterson faction on the board had agreed on strategy, however, they differed widely in tactics. The Philadelphia merchants who had founded the PRR had envisioned a *Pennsylvania* railroad, a carrier whose operations would be confined to its native state, and whose function would be to prevent rival cities, particularly Baltimore, from drawing away western trade.

As a chief engineer and later as president, Thomson espoused a different rationale. Rather than employ the Pennsylvania Railroad as a means to an end, he envisioned it as an end unto itself. The PRR's survival, Thomson reasoned, demanded vigorous competition against rival carriers. The mere provision of transportation at Pittsburgh, Thomson asserted, was insufficient to draw in grain and other traffic, particularly when rival eastern trunk lines were expanding rapidly into Ohio, Indiana, and Illinois. Unless he matched their efforts, he would preside over a Pennsylvania Railroad that would be forever confined to its namesake state.

Thomson's successful 1852 coup against the conservative mercantile interests who had dominated the board did not render the new president all-powerful, however. The PRR's owners, as represented by the board, had not completely capitulated to his managerial expertise, either in day-to-day operational matters or in long-term corporate strategy. In particular, many board members were hesitant to invest the PRR's scarce resources in speculative ventures and in unproven railroad properties far removed from Philadelphia.

Public policy imposed additional limitations on the PRR's expansionist policies. The company, chartered in Pennsylvania, had no legal right to conduct business in any other state. Many political interests were reluctant to cede additional authority to what was already one of the largest companies in the commonwealth. Near the end of his career, Thomson recalled that he had long been "sensible of the prejudice against large corporations since the failure of the United States Bank [of Pennsylvania]."[10] The PRR's 1846 corporate charter reflected that public disapprobation. The charter prohibited any construction outside of the counties lining the route between Harrisburg and Pittsburgh, limiting Thomson's ability to establish traffic-generating branch lines. PRR officials were likewise prohibited from building west of the western border of Allegheny County—a provision that the Allegheny County commissioners reinforced in 1848 when they agreed to subscribe to PRR stock only on the condition that the PRR's terminus be fixed at Pittsburgh. More problematically, the charter prohibited PRR officials from investing in the securities of other railroads, including those lying outside Pennsylvania.

Pennsylvania legislators, fearing that their state was losing ground to New York and Maryland, liberalized the PRR's charter. In March 1853, under intense pressure from Thomson and other PRR officials, legislators permitted the PRR's directors to issue an additional $4 million in stock and to invest up to 15 percent of the company's outstanding shares in out-of-state lines, so long as those purchases would help draw the western trade toward Philadelphia. That change by no means removed the legal obstacles to westward expansion, however. Although the courts never tested the issue, PRR accountants and attorneys believed that if the railroad operated as a chartered corporation in locations such as Ohio and Indiana, those states would levy taxes on the entire value of the company's capital.[11]

More ominously, money was always in short supply, particularly during the troubled economic times of the late 1850s. After 1853, Thomson possessed the legal authority to fund the construction of western rail lines. However, any substantial direct investment would have necessitated the creation of a third mortgage, inferior to the existing PRR first mortgage and general mortgage bonds. Such a weak security would be unlikely to attract many investors, and would accordingly be marketed at a steep discount. Efforts to buy the stocks of existing western railroads on the open market would likely induce a bidding war with the other major trunk lines, further straining the PRR's resources.

Despite all of those obstacles, Thomson succeeded in obtaining access to such key gateway cities as Cincinnati, Chicago, and St. Louis, and he did so without spending much money. Instead, he negotiated a complex web of purchases, leases, personal investments, joint ventures, interlocking directorates, and traffic agreements, all designed to acquire control of western lines without actually owning them. The PRR's president asserted that "the policy of this Company was first directed to the procuring of those connections by securing the organization of independent railway companies, and their construction by such pecuniary assistance as was required to effect this necessary object." That indirect support, Thomson suggested, would minimize legislative opposition, and "would meet the objects desired without [involving] this Company in the direct management of distant enterprises."[12] Such views meshed well with those of chief engineer Herman Haupt, who noted in 1854 that the western trade "can be secured more readily by intimate relations between business men, than by building branch rail roads."[13]

As they pursued their "intimate relations," Thomson and his counterparts of the midwestern railroads had much to offer each other. Allied lines in Ohio and Indiana could funnel an ever-increasing torrent of grain to the PRR's rails at Pittsburgh, and receive in return a somewhat smaller quantity of manufactured goods and westward-moving passengers. In return, the PRR could provide the capital necessary for expansion. That might take the form of direct investments, but even the PRR's guarantee of a bond issue could lift a local carrier out of the obscurity induced by financial uncertainty, and into the heady realms of the international capital markets. Once European investors knew that those railroads were connected to the PRR through leases and traffic guarantees, they assumed—rightly or wrongly—that Thomson and his fellow executives would keep them safe from mismanagement and financial embarrassment.[14]

Thomson and his associates possessed two basic mechanisms for extending their influence into Ohio and Indiana. First, they could subscribe to the stock of a promising western connection. While that method gave PRR representatives leverage over the company's board of directors, it entailed substantial up-front costs. Furthermore, should the firm fail, the investment would be worth little or nothing. As an alternative, Thomson could employ the PRR's sterling credit to guarantee the mortgages of struggling western carriers. If those western lines succeeded, he would have a friendly connection to the west. If they failed, he could either seize the property in foreclosure proceedings, or else dictate the terms of reorganization.

Both strategies depended on Thomson's ability to forge alliances with western entrepreneurs and the companies that they promoted, while persuading them that they could help themselves while helping the Pennsylvania Railroad. The men who worked with the PRR in the regions to the west of Pittsburgh were a remarkably homogeneous lot. During the early 1800s, they were among the first settlers in what was still largely a frontier. They took an early interest in transportation, either by river, canal, or road. From there, they branched out into related enterprises, such as milling, ironworking, warehousing, and contracting. A large proportion practiced law, and many were judges. Most held political office and were among the leading figures in their communities. By the late 1840s, with the feasibility of railroads proven beyond all doubt, they began to invest a portion of their wealth in local projects that would enhance the connectivity of their communities and the value of their businesses and landholdings. Geographically, they stood at the nexus of East and West, and at the intersection of land and water routes. Socially, they were at the juncture of economic and political power born of the exploitation of previously unavailable opportunities. Because they occupied positions of political authority, as mayors, governors, judges, and state legislators, they were well positioned to seek state aid for their commercial ventures.

That group of midwestern railway entrepreneurs possessed strong first-mover advantages—they were born at exactly the right time, and in exactly the right place, and could accomplish what neither the preceding nor the succeeding generations could. They were often fiercely independent, and determined to retain control over the mini-empires that they had created. Yet, they were also willing to cooperate closely with the Pennsylvania Railroad, or any of its competitors, whenever they sought additional investment capital, traffic guarantees, or other perquisites. As Haupt observed in 1854, many of those executives were experts at "avoiding entangling alliances while cultivating friendly relations with all these [trunk-line] roads."[15] Thomson would have his work cut out for him as he endeavored to reconcile their interests with those of the Pennsylvania Railroad.

Thomson's reliance on those upwardly mobile entrepreneurs left him open to charges that he placed his investment schemes ahead of the interests of the Pennsylvania Railroad and its stockholders—yet, it was a necessary cost of doing business in that manner. More problematically, Thomson's western allies were anxious to pursue their own interests, and they could and did turn against him. Finally, the alliances depended on the ability of the PRR's subsidiaries to generate traffic and profits, something that was by no means guaranteed. Issues of loyalty and profitability would ultimately force Thomson and the PRR board to establish firmer control over western lines.

Those difficulties notwithstanding, Thomson's methods proved remarkably effective. Of the great networks of lines that interlaced the economically burgeoning Northeast and Midwest, the Pennsylvania Railroad itself had constructed only 249 miles, along the original route linking Harrisburg and Pittsburgh. By the time of Thomson's death in 1874, the PRR had nonetheless established two routes to St. Louis, and two to Chicago, along with lines to Cleveland, Cincinnati, and Columbus, Ohio; Indianapolis; and Louisville, Kentucky, with thousands of miles of track and an empire that stretched from Jersey City to Washington, D.C., and west to the Mississippi. The carriers that operated through Ohio, Indiana, and Illinois were not under the direct control of the Pennsylvania Railroad, yet the structure of those routes was as much a part of the railroad's corporate strategy as the tracks, trains, and personnel that were resident within the commonwealth of Pennsylvania.

Into the Old Northwest

While Thomson intended the PRR to be primarily an east-west railroad, he soon confronted a very different transportation pattern in Ohio and Indiana. To a substantial extent, most of the established routes in those two states ran north to south, connecting Lake Erie to the Ohio River. Given the natural advantages of waterborne transportation, any trade that reached Lake Erie was likely to continue east over the Erie Canal or perhaps one of the New York roads, while commerce along the Ohio River might well proceed south to New Orleans or connect with the B&O at Wheeling. Thomson and his allies were determined to break traditional transportation routes and to draw as much traffic as possible to the center of those two midwestern states. Once freed from the pull of Lake Erie and the Ohio River, the grain and other cargoes might logically flow east over the PRR.

Of all of the states in the Old Northwest, Ohio had the best-developed transportation infrastructure and the most significant complement of local entrepreneurs. As Thomson told his stockholders in the PRR's *Sixth Annual Report*, "The geographical position of the State of Ohio makes her the transit ground, where the commercial contest for the trade of the West must be waged between the great northern Atlantic cities."[16] In 1822, the Ohio legislature had first addressed the development of canals in the state, creating a canal commission and selecting James Geddes—associated with both the Erie Canal and the Main Line of Public Works—to prepare a set of surveys. Three years later, legislators funded an ambitious program of internal improvements. Construction began more or less simultaneously on two routes. The Ohio & Erie Canal, completed in 1832, linked Cleveland and Portsmouth.[17] The other important north-south connection lay in the western portion of the state, eventually linking Toledo and Cincinnati. By 1830, the Miami Canal connected Cincinnati with Dayton. That route, renamed the Miami & Erie Canal, reached Lake Erie in 1845, rein-

forcing the north-south orientation of commerce in the region. Both canals enabled Ohio's agricultural produce to leave the Ohio River and flow north to Lake Erie, and eventually east over the Erie Canal.

The situation in Indiana was much the same. The Wabash & Erie Canal, some 460 miles in length, was a truly spectacular—and spectacularly unsuccessful—project. In 1827, Congress provided a federal land grant for the canal. The following January, Indiana legislators established a canal commission, but work did not begin until February 1832, at Fort Wayne. In January 1836, the legislature passed the so-called Mammoth Internal Improvement Act, providing funds for a plethora of canal, turnpike, and railroad projects, most of which were never completed. The financial panic that began in 1837 mandated the curtailment of most of the legislature's ambitious public works program, and in 1841 it forced the state into bankruptcy. Work on the Wabash & Erie Canal went forward nonetheless. The canal entered service in 1843, but it would be another decade before boats were able to travel the entire distance from Evansville, on the Ohio River, to Lake Erie, at Toledo. Traffic levels never matched the ambitious predictions of the project's sponsors, and some portions of the canal remained in use for less than a decade.[18]

The early railways in Ohio and Indiana were generally built as feeders to the canal network, reinforcing the north-south orientation that the canals had helped to establish. As early as 1826, representatives from communities that had been left off the list of proposed canal routes, for reasons of either geography or politics, demanded railroads as consolation prizes. Their pleas became stronger after President Andrew Jackson gave a clear indication that he thought that internal improvements should be largely a state responsibility. In 1830, when Congress approved the investment of public funds in a private company chartered to build a turnpike between Maysville and Lexington in Kentucky, Jackson vetoed the bill. Jackson insisted, inaccurately, that the road was "a measure of purely local character," and asserted that the "taxes [that] have borne severely upon the laboring and less prosperous classes of the community" did not entitle local interests to demand "irregular, improvident, and unequal appropriations of public funds."[19]

In Ohio, as in so many other states, the development of early railroads occurred amid a landscape structured by public policy. Andrew Jackson's veto of the Maysville Road bill prompted a flurry of local activity. The state legislature chartered twelve transportation corporations during the 1831–32 legislative session, and seventy-seven by 1840. Virtually all of the principal Ohio railroads were, in one form or another, descended from those pioneers. The 1837 Ohio Loan Law promised that the state treasury would fund up to a third of the cost of private rail, canal, and turnpike projects. The bill was enacted in March, only weeks before the May 10 suspension of specie payments that marked the beginning of the Panic of 1837. In light of the subsequent economic crisis, the legislative support for internal improvements seemed foolish in the extreme, and the act soon became known as the "Plunder Law." Particularly in the aftermath of the panic, which sharply curtailed revenues on the state-owned canals, many Ohioans adopted similar rhetoric to their Pennsylvania contemporaries, arguing that privately owned railroads were innately superior to public waterways. Yet, that did not stop entrepreneurs and local boosters from demanding state and municipal support for railroad construction, nor did it prevent the state government from shaping transportation policy.[20]

Internal-improvement advocates had initially recommended a canal connecting the Ohio River to Lake Erie, at Sandusky, but adverse topography and a lack of water stymied their efforts. In January 1832, therefore, Ohio legislators chartered the Mad River & Lake Erie Railroad, which they intended to link Sandusky to the Miami & Erie Canal. Construction did not begin until September 17, 1835, when General William Henry Harrison and Governor Joseph Vance turned the first shovels of earth at Sandusky. The railroad's owners chose a gauge of 4′ 10″ (the same as in New Jersey), probably owing to the possibility that the New York & Erie would use that width for its route west. Although the Erie was subsequently built to six-foot gauge, the Mad River & Lake Erie's choice became the de facto standard for railroads built in Ohio—made official by an 1848 state law, not modified until 1852. That "Ohio gauge," slightly wider than the 4′ 8½″ gauge used on the PRR, would later create difficulties for the exchange of freight at Pittsburgh. In light of the depressed economic conditions that began in 1837, the Mad River & Lake Erie probably would not have made much progress had it not been for $70,000 in aid, under the terms of the Loan Law. Work proceeded south from Sandusky, but tracks did not reach Springfield, Ohio, until September 1848.[21]

At Springfield, the Mad River & Lake Erie connected with the Little Miami Railroad, the first carrier to enter Cincinnati. The Little Miami had received its charter in 1836, but its promoters experienced considerable difficulty in beginning construction. The 1837 Ohio Loan Law permitted the state to subscribe to $115,000 in Little Miami stock, while the governments of Greene County and the city of Cincinnati provided additional support. Work began in February 1839, and thereafter proceeded in fits and starts. The Little Miami's line between Cincinnati, Xenia, and Springfield opened in August 1846. With the completion of the Mad River & Lake Erie two years later, Ohio possessed its first through rail route between the Ohio River and Lake Erie.[22]

In addition to serving as the southern extension of the Mad River & Lake Erie, the Little Miami also anchored the southern end of a chain of railroads that composed a second link between the Ohio River and Lake Erie, by way of the state capital. The Columbus & Xenia Railroad received a charter in 1844. Construction began the following year, but soon halted. Work resumed in 1847, with the first trains running two years later. By February 1850, the tracks were finished as far north as Columbus, awaiting the southbound progress of the construction crews laboring to complete the third link in the chain, the Cleveland, Columbus & Cincinnati Railroad.[23]

As its name suggested, the promoters of the Cleveland, Columbus & Cincinnati Railroad intended to connect the three cities of its corporate title. Chartered in 1836, the CC&C sat lifeless for nearly a decade. In 1845, the moribund charter was revived, largely under the influence of the Neil brothers, Robert and William. Originally from Kentucky, and the son of Scottish immigrants, Robert Neil moved to Ohio early in the nineteenth century to clerk in a Champaign County mercantile establishment. In 1815, he sent for his older brother to join him. Three years later, William Neil moved from Urbana to Columbus, where he soon became a clerk at the Franklin Bank, owned by his future father-in-law and business partner, William Sullivant. By 1825, the older Neil brother operated a foundry and coachworks, William Neil & Company. Another Neil enterprise, the Ohio Stage Line, served more than 1,500 route miles and included a link from Wheeling to Columbus and on to Cincinnati. William Neil also helped to establish one of the leading banks in Columbus, as well as the city's most luxurious hotel, the Neil House. The brothers invested in several railroad enterprises—which was just as well, as their stage service succumbed to rail competition in 1854. Their influence extended to the development of the route between Xenia and Cleveland, with William Neil serving as president of the Columbus & Xenia, and treasurer of the CC&C. His son, Robert E. Neil, and son-in-law, William Dennison, Jr., were also closely associated with both companies.[24]

Under the supervision of the Neil brothers, construction on the Cleveland, Columbus & Cincinnati occurred during a period of considerable transition in Ohio. By the early 1840s, both the state and the nation were recovering from the Panic of 1837. Settlers continued to pour into the region, and eastern capitalists became enthusiastic about investment opportunities in the trans-Appalachian west. The steady westward progress of several trunk lines—a group that would soon include the Pennsylvania Railroad—likewise whetted the appetites of eastern investors. In 1845, for the first time, the owners of three Ohio carriers, including the Mad River & Lake Erie and the Little Miami, successfully placed securities in eastern markets.

The new capital arrived at a particularly propitious time, as demand for additional rail lines coincided with the drying up of state aid. Ohioans wanted railroads more than ever, and they still wanted the government to help pay for them, but widespread outrage over the "Plunder Law" ensured that the state legislature would not be in a position to provide much assistance. As a result, entrepreneurs turned to their local governments, arguing that county and municipal subsidies would constitute a form of seed capital that would help convince eastern and overseas investors that those railroads were a good credit risk. State legislators, engaged in the customary political practice of logrolling, authorized some $10 million in local bonds,

to be used to subsidize railroad construction. Until 1850, county and municipal governments contributed almost half of all of the capital devoted to railway construction in Ohio. As was the case in Pennsylvania, therefore, the locus of transportation policy had shifted from the federal to the state to the local level.[25]

The Panic of 1847 soured many Ohioans on local support for internal improvements, just as the crisis ten years earlier had caused them to excoriate the "Plunder Law." In part, they were reacting to the financial problems of the railroads, including some that were probably built in advance of demand, and others that were subsidized but never built at all. The more pervasive problem, however, was that railroads were the most visible scapegoat for Ohio's economic problems, particularly when newspaper editors were quick to decry the malevolent influences of eastern capital. The railroads tended to concentrate wealth and political power in the cities, and many rural farmers, particularly in areas where trains had not yet arrived, refused to commit additional public funds to feather someone else's nest. A number of local governments accordingly rescinded or reassigned their financial aid packages.

In 1850, Ohioans decided to replace the original state constitution of 1802, and the constitutional convention soon entailed a substantial dose of railroad-bashing. The slate of delegates was largely Democratic, and tilted heavily toward rural areas. A cholera epidemic forced the proceedings to be relocated from the state capital to the small town of Chillicothe, reinforcing the rural bias. Many delegates believed that the legislature, under the 1802 constitution, possessed far too much authority, and that unwise aid to canals and railroads was a clear indication of the need to reduce its power. When S. J. Kirkwood addressed the convention, expressing his outrage that "a company should have the right to push a railroad thro' a man's farm—through his house, that they might plow up the very bones of his father which he had buried on his soil, against his consent," the supporters of the railroads must have known that they were in serious trouble.

The only delegates who favored a continuation of government funding were from districts where there were no railroads—suggesting that any philosophical objections to the role of the state in the economy would surface only after they had obtained what they considered their fair share of the spoils. Virtually everyone who had received the aid that they had wished for was now determined to put a stop to further funding. "Are farmers less important than the railroad that carries their produce?" asked Charles Reemelin, a Hamilton County resident who was himself a farmer. E. B. Woodbury, an attorney from Ashtabula, demanded to know, "Who created this debt? and what have we got for it? What is our duty to the generation that shall come after us? Shall we send down this debt of nineteen millions to them[?] . . . What more?"[26] No more, according to the delegates at the constitutional convention. The new constitution, adopted in March 1851, prohibited all government entities in the state of Ohio from lending money to private companies.[27]

Despite the caustic rhetoric at the 1850–51 constitutional convention, Ohioans remained strongly supportive of railroad development. Like many citizens of Pennsylvania, Ohio residents chose to interpret the depression of the late 1840s as an indication that the public sector should facilitate, but not manage, railroad development. Just as railroads had demonstrated their clear superiority over canals, the belief went, private entrepreneurs were demonstrably the ones best qualified to control the new form of transportation. In that context, government could best serve the people by creating a protected space—often referred to, inaccurately, as the laissez-faire "market"—in which private enterprise could flourish.

In the difficult financial circumstances that accompanied the Panic of 1847, Ohio legislators favored economic liberalization over the provision of public funds. In February 1848, they passed a general railroad incorporation law that eliminated the need for legislative charters. On March 3, 1851, exactly one week prior to the ratification of the new constitution, the legislature permitted Ohio railroads to invest in other state-chartered railroad companies—a move that was certain to spark a round of consolidations. In 1856, legislators copied provisions of Indiana's 1852 General Railroad Law, allowing companies to issue preferred stock in order to finance construction. Much of that stock, it should be noted, later came under the control of the Pennsylvania Railroad, as Thomson and his fellow executives bought control of midwestern subsidiary companies.[28]

Although the political developments of the late 1840s and early 1850s ultimately placed far more authority in the hands of railroad managers, the immediate effect of the 1851 constitution was to curtail access to capital. With local governments no longer able to support railroad construction, owners sought other forms of financing. In particular, they were anxious to secure the services of executives who could forge physical and financial connections with the eastern trunk lines. One such individual was Alfred Kelley. In 1810, Kelley had set up a practice as the first attorney in Cleveland. He soon became one of that city's leading citizens and its first mayor, in 1815. He was elected to the state legislature in 1814, became a Whig, and soon attained leadership over that party. Kelley was an ardent supporter of canal construction, Ohio's answer to New York's DeWitt Clinton, and he served as a state canal commissioner from 1825 to 1834. Kelley was a vocal, if unsuccessful, opponent of the 1837 Loan Law, as he believed that the money should be used to charter a state bank rather than to fund politically motivated infrastructure projects. In 1847, investors in the Columbus & Xenia and the CC&C persuaded Kelley to become the president of both companies, temporarily displacing the Neil interests in the process.

Fortunately for Kelley and his allies, the recent repeal of the Corn Laws and the more general growth of agriculture in the Ohio Valley soon revived the fortunes of the two faltering railroads. In February 1851, Kelley drove the ceremonial last spike on the CC&C, at Iberia, Ohio, completing the second route between Lake Erie and the Ohio River. Under Kelley's leadership, the prosperous CC&C soon began to subsidize numerous feeders, including the Columbus & Xenia, that were designed to draw traffic toward its main line. Kelley was also responsible for negotiating a series of traffic agreements and consolidations that tied together the various elements of his Ohio rail empire.[29]

Alfred Kelley's entrepreneurship portended serious problems for the Pennsylvania Railroad. Although Kelley eventually settled in Columbus to be near the statehouse, he was more closely connected to Cleveland. Given the south-to-north orientation of the CC&C, he naturally believed that most of the region's traffic should go north to Lake Erie, rather than east toward Pittsburgh. As such, he was keenly interested in the construction of a series of rail lines that extended the New York Central's reach west from Buffalo, through Cleveland, and on to Chicago. The Cleveland, Painesville & Ashtabula Railroad, incorporated in 1848, was part of that chain of railroads, connecting Cleveland with the Pennsylvania state line. In conjunction with the Franklin Canal Company's railroad, the Erie & North East Railroad, and the Buffalo & State Line Railroad, it would provide a connection to the NYC's tracks at Buffalo. In 1851, Kelley accepted the presidency of the Cleveland, Painesville & Ashtabula, and during the summer of 1852, he had little difficulty negotiating a joint operating agreement between that railroad and the CC&C.

Kelley also helped to extend tracks west to Chicago. The owners of the Toledo, Norwalk & Cleveland Railroad, incorporated in March 1850, planned to build a line between Toledo and Grafton, on the Cleveland, Columbus & Cincinnati main line, and they soon received the support of CC&C officials, including a bond guarantee. With the completion of the Toledo, Norwalk & Cleveland, in January 1853, the CC&C, between Cleveland and Grafton, became an integral part of a route that stretched between New York and Chicago.

With Kelley's ambitious agenda targeted toward New York, PRR officials had little reason to hope that they could draw on traffic from the CC&C or its Columbus & Xenia and Little Miami connections. Nonetheless, beginning in January 1852, it was possible for freight and passengers to follow the CC&C from Cincinnati north to Cleveland, and then proceed southeast to Pittsburgh, via the PRR-allied Cleveland & Pittsburgh and Ohio & Pennsylvania railroads. That route, although indirect, reflected some of Thomson's first efforts to extend the PRR into Ohio and toward Lake Erie.[30]

From Pittsburgh to Lake Erie

Many of the Pennsylvanians who had supported a comprehensive statewide program of internal improvements during the 1820s and 1830s had confidently predicted the imminent completion of canal or rail routes linking Philadelphia and Erie. Those who were still alive more than a generation later might well have been surprised that the PRR first reached the Great Lakes at Cleveland, and not Erie. As early as the spring of 1836, the Ohio legislature incorporated the Cleveland, Warren & Pittsburgh Railroad, but nearly another decade passed before construction began. The company lay dormant until 1845, when the legislature revived the charter, modifying it to specify that the line, now known as the Cleveland & Pittsburgh Rail Road, be constructed along any practicable route to the Ohio River.[31]

Clevelanders initially showed little interest in the Cleveland & Pittsburgh project, particularly after Alfred Kelley and other prominent local citizens gained control over the Cleveland, Columbus & Cincinnati route to the state capital. In 1846, however, the simultaneous chartering of the PRR and the B&O by the Pennsylvania legislature raised the possibility that Pittsburgh might be the western terminus of not one, but two great trunk lines, making Clevelanders long for a rail connection to that city. In April 1847, Cleveland residents called on city officials to rescind the funds that they had pledged to the CC&C and transfer the stock subscription to the Cleveland & Pittsburgh. Allegheny County provided additional financial support. The following year, Cleveland & Pittsburgh construction crews began building south and east from Cleveland.

Their original destination was Wellsville, Ohio, but by the beginning of 1850 the company's promoters had elected to continue east from Wellsville, along the Ohio River to Pittsburgh. In February 1850, the Ohio legislature permitted the Cleveland & Pittsburgh to build east into Pennsylvania. Two months later, the Pennsylvania legislature issued a corporate charter, permitting construction in that state. The tracks stretched to Hudson in February 1851, and a month later they reached Ravenna and a connection with the Pennsylvania & Ohio Canal. By November, the railhead was at Hanover (later, Kensington), seventy-five miles from Cleveland. The following March, the line reached Wellsville, creating another north–south link between the Ohio River and Lake Erie. In October 1856 tracklayers reached Rochester, Pennsylvania, at the junction of the Ohio and Beaver rivers, some twenty-five miles northwest of Pittsburgh. At Rochester, a connection with the recently formed Pittsburgh, Fort Wayne & Chicago Rail Road (the former Ohio & Pennsylvania Railroad) created a through route between Cleveland and Allegheny City, across the Allegheny River from Pittsburgh.[32]

Even before the Cleveland & Pittsburgh reached Rochester, that company was a valuable western connection for the PRR. The tracks of the Cleveland & Pittsburgh passed through Alliance, Ohio, a town that was also on the route of the Ohio & Pennsylvania Railroad, whose workers were then building from Allegheny City westward toward Crestline, Ohio. The Ohio & Pennsylvania reached Alliance in January 1852, and a junction with the Cleveland & Pittsburgh enabled traffic to flow between Pittsburgh and Cleveland. When PRR construction crews completed the Western Division a few months later, therefore, a complete rail link existed between Philadelphia and Lake Erie, via Pittsburgh. However, the Ohio & Pennsylvania offered a much greater benefit to the PRR than a connection to Cleveland. The goal of its promoters, one that Thomson shared, was to reach the city that was the gateway to the Great Plains.[33]

West to Chicago

During the first half of the nineteenth century, Chicago was rapidly emerging as the new commercial center in the west. In 1830, as Thomson was supervising the construction of his assigned section of the Philadelphia & Columbia Railroad, Chicago had a population of barely a hundred. A decade later, as Pennsylvanians were struggling to remedy the difficulties associated with the Allegheny Portage Railroad, the population had grown to more than four thousand. In 1850, as Thomson was on the verge of taking control of the PRR, Chicago housed nearly thirty thousand people, and by the eve of the Civil War, its population had swollen to well over one hundred thousand. Even before he assumed the PRR presidency, Thomson was determined to gain access to what would soon become the nation's most important railroad hub.[34]

But he had to hurry. In 1851, the Ohio legislature granted the Franklin & Warren Railroad a charter to build southwesterly across Ohio, with a terminus in

Dayton that would allow easy access to Cincinnati. By 1853, the company had been renamed the Atlantic & Great Western Railroad and served as a friendly connection with the Erie. Farther to the north, a series of railroads hugged the southern shore of Lake Erie before heading west to Chicago. On February 20, 1852, the Northern Indiana & Chicago Railroad finished a route between Toledo and Chicago, with the Michigan Central completing a line from Detroit a few months later. By November 1852, the Cleveland, Painesville & Ashtabula Railroad had linked Erie with Cleveland. The following January, construction crews building the Toledo, Norwalk & Cleveland Railroad closed the gap between Cleveland and Toledo. In conjunction with the CC&C route through Cleveland, there was now a continuous rail route from New York to Chicago, via Buffalo—albeit one that included a gauge break and a ferry crossing of the Hudson River. Many years would pass before the companies involved would be consolidated into the Lake Shore & Michigan Southern Railway, and ultimately into the New York Central. There could be little doubt, however, that their tracks were destined to carry freight to New York, not to Philadelphia.

Thomson gained his coveted through route to Chicago by stitching together three struggling independent lines. The first to receive PRR support was the Ohio & Pennsylvania Railroad, a company that was linked to the PRR through the personage of William Robinson, Jr. His father had been one of the first permanent settlers at the junction of the Allegheny and Monongahela rivers, a barely inhabited location then known as Fort Pitt. The elder Robinson operated a ferry across the Allegheny River, and the son, who claimed to be the first white infant born in the area, was likewise involved in transportation. Shortly after the War of 1812, he was a commissioner for a bridge over the Allegheny River—his fellow Pittsburgher, John Thaw (the father of Main Line freight forwarder and PRR ally William Thaw), held a corresponding position for a span over the Monongahela. By 1818, Robinson was a local agent for the Pittsburgh Transporting Company, in conjunction with William B. Foster, Sr., and the next year he became one of the commissioners of the proposed Pittsburgh & Butler Turnpike Road Company. In 1819, Robinson also helped establish the

Western Navigation & Insurance Company (soon renamed the Pittsburgh Navigation & Insurance Company), with no less an intent than to control commerce on the Ohio River and all of its tributaries. In 1827, he was a passenger on board the *Albion*, the first steamship to attempt an ascent of the Allegheny River. Robinson was an early advocate of railways, and in 1831 he was one of the promoters of a failed railroad project intended to link Pittsburgh to the Ohio & Erie Canal. He tried again in 1837, but was likewise unsuccessful. In addition to his support for internal improvements, Robinson was a prominent area industrialist, with a rolling and slitting mill established in 1818 under the name of the Pittsburgh Steam Engine Company. In 1840, Robinson became the first mayor of Allegheny City.[35]

Robinson's involvement in Ohio railroads stemmed from his association with the Pittsburgh & Connellsville Railroad, incorporated in 1837. The company's charter subsequently expired, but it became a key element in the 1846 charter battle between allies of the B&O and supporters of what would soon become the Pennsylvania Railroad. Robinson and his associates, including fellow Pittsburgh businessman William Larimer, Jr., were stung by legislative efforts to hobble the B&O. They surreptitiously guided through the legislature a bill restoring the charter of the Pittsburgh & Connellsville and permitting the railroad to build south and east to the Maryland border, where it could connect with the B&O.

Officials of the newly incorporated Pennsylvania Railroad, outraged at what they considered the duplicity of the Pittsburgh interests, for many years used their influence in the legislature to delay construction on the Pittsburgh & Connellsville. As part of that strategy, Samuel Merrick gave Robinson an attractive offer. The PRR's president informed Robinson that the contest between the PRR and the Pittsburgh & Connellsville was likely to be long, difficult, and expensive, and its outcome uncertain. It would be far better, Merrick suggested, if Robinson could be an ally rather than an adversary of the Pennsylvania Railroad, and if he could extend the PRR's interests north and west of Pittsburgh, rather than heading south and east to meet the B&O. In return, Merrick promised that the PRR would aid the new line. Accordingly, Robin-

son favored transferring the stock subscriptions of the Pittsburgh & Connellsville to a new company that would build from Pittsburgh into Ohio. The proposal divided the shareholders of the Pittsburgh & Connellsville, with Robinson's longtime associate, William Larimer, Jr., strongly in opposition to the PRR's aims. Nonetheless, in December 1847, Pittsburgh & Connellsville investors approved the arrangement. In February 1848 the Ohio legislature incorporated the Ohio & Pennsylvania Railroad in that state, with the Pennsylvania General Assembly providing a corresponding corporate charter two months later.

Robinson certainly profited from his alliance with Merrick. He became the first president of the Ohio & Pennsylvania. In 1851, the commissioners of Allegheny County appointed Robinson as one of the directors of the Pennsylvania Railroad, a position that he retained until 1856. He was a member of the Road Committee, the PRR's equivalent of an executive committee. Robinson was ideally positioned to be a point man for the PRR, safeguarding the railroad's interests in Pittsburgh and to the west.

Robinson and his associates originally intended to build from Pittsburgh west to the Indiana state line. At their September 18, 1850, meeting, the Ohio & Pennsylvania's board of directors agreed to terminate the railroad at Crestline, rather than push on to the Indiana border. The truncated route nonetheless promised valuable connections with the Cleveland & Pittsburgh Rail Road (at Alliance, Ohio, and after October 1856 at Rochester, Pennsylvania), the Mansfield & Sandusky City Railroad (at Mansfield), and the Cleveland, Columbus & Cincinnati Railroad (at Crestline). As such, the completed route would enable the PRR to gather traffic from two Lake Erie ports (Cleveland and Sandusky), as well as Columbus and Cincinnati. The depressed economic conditions that followed the Panic of 1847 slowed construction on the Ohio & Pennsylvania. By 1851, the company had managed to build a line from Allegheny City only as far west as Salem, Ohio, before running out of money.[36]

The financial difficulties experienced by the Ohio & Pennsylvania caused PRR officials to escalate their involvement with that company—although not without some dissent. Job Tyson, along with George Howell and Edward M. Davis (the two directors appointed by the Philadelphia Select and Common Councils), saw little reason to aid a railroad so far removed from Philadelphia and unconnected with the PRR's corporate charter. While generally conservative, locally oriented, and opposed to the issuance of bonds, Merrick nonetheless recalled his 1847 pledge to support a link between Pittsburgh and the west, and he therefore urged the PRR to honor that promise. In September 1851 the PRR board agreed to trade unissued PRR securities for $250,000 worth of stock in the Ohio & Pennsylvania, pending shareholder approval. The following February, at the annual shareholders' meeting, the assembled investors demanded that a financial committee investigate the proposed funding, but they were probably more concerned about Thomson's proposal to issue bonds in order to bypass the Allegheny Portage Railroad.[37]

Thomson emerged victorious over the Merrick/Patterson faction, and that outcome validated his expansionist vision. Many of the newly installed directors, while more reluctant than the new president to spend lavishly in the west, were nonetheless willing to extend aid to companies like the Ohio & Pennsylvania. So, too, were the stockholders, and on April 22, 1852, they approved the purchase of the Ohio & Pennsylvania stock, as well as an additional $150,000 investment to build a bridge across the Allegheny River and install tracks to connect the two railroads at Pittsburgh. Political officials in Pittsburgh and Allegheny City, anxious to improve the region's role as a transportation hub, authorized $600,000 in aid to the chain of railroads that ultimately stretched toward Chicago.[38]

The proposed injection of PRR funds encouraged the Ohio & Pennsylvania to build farther west, reaching Alliance in January 1852. At Alliance, a connection with the Cleveland & Pittsburgh Rail Road gave access to Cleveland. On April 11, 1853, tracklayers reached their destination of Crestline, Ohio, where the Cleveland, Columbus & Cincinnati Railroad provided links to the state capital and the Ohio River. Four miles southwest of Crestline, along the CC&C route to Columbus, lay the town of Galion, and a junction with the Bellefontaine & Indiana Railroad, part of a still-incomplete route to Indianapolis.[39]

A second western line, the Ohio & Indiana Railroad, allowed the PRR to extend its influence even closer to Chicago. Incorporated in Ohio in 1850 and in Indiana in 1851, its promoters envisioned advancing the Ohio & Pennsylvania's route by building from Crestline to Fort Wayne, Indiana. Local interests predominated, with five counties along the route subscribing to a total of $450,000 in stock. One of the most enthusiastic supporters of the project was Samuel Hanna, a miller, banker, judge, and state senator from Fort Wayne who became a director of the Ohio & Indiana in 1851. The following September he participated in a convention held in Warsaw, Indiana, to rally support for an extension of the Ohio & Indiana to Chicago.[40] The attendees quickly organized the Fort Wayne & Chicago Railroad, electing Hanna as president of the new company.[41]

The Fort Wayne & Chicago Railroad became the third of the three allied carriers that composed the route between Pittsburgh and Chicago. In September 1852, many of the promoters involved in the Ohio & Indiana took advantage of an Indiana general railroad law, barely five months old, to file articles of association to construct a line from Fort Wayne in a northwesterly direction to the Illinois state line. The Illinois legislature granted a corresponding charter the following February, allowing construction on the last few miles into Chicago. From the beginning, the Fort Wayne & Chicago shared many officers with the Ohio & Indiana, and depended on that company for financial support.[42]

While he was determined to oversee the construction of a route to Chicago, Hanna's more pressing problem was to ensure the completion of the Ohio & Indiana Railroad. The Pennsylvania Railroad was one potential source of funds to achieve that objective. George H. Hart and Thomas S. Fernon had attended the Warsaw convention, curious about the benefits that the link to Chicago might offer the PRR. They must have made some strong promises, for Haupt later noted that "the Fort Wayne and Chicago Rail Road Company expect assistance from Philadelphia in the completion of their road, and claim it as a right, in consequence of assurances given by delegates from Philadelphia at a convention held at Warsaw" in 1852.[43]

Some aid was indeed forthcoming, and in April 1853, PRR shareholders decisively approved the board's recommendation to purchase $300,000 in Ohio & Indiana stock. The investment was on the condition, however, that the company would select the same 4′ 10″

track gauge as the Ohio & Pennsylvania, permitting the convenient interchange of traffic. In return, the directors of the Ohio & Indiana promised to "run through trains in connection with those of the Pennsa. & Ohio [*sic*] and Pennsa. Rail Roads and form equitable arrangements for through passengers and freights."[44] PRR directors were less willing to support the Fort Wayne & Chicago, however, and in August 1853 they refused to subscribe to $200,000 worth of that company's stock.[45]

By the autumn of 1854, the energetic Hanna was serving as both the president of the Ohio & Indiana and as a construction contractor along the line, but even he was beginning to doubt the project's chances for success. The relatively minor Panic of 1853 had dampened investor confidence. An unusually severe drought during the summer of 1854 had ruined many midwestern farmers, leaving them unable to pay installments on their small stock subscriptions in local railroads. The Ohio & Pennsylvania Railroad board approved emergency aid, but in insufficient quantities. In desperation, Hanna traveled to Philadelphia to beg Thomson for additional assistance.

Hanna and his fellow Ohio & Indiana investors did not confine their supplication to the PRR, however. To the contrary, they negotiated a tentative agreement with their counterparts on the Cleveland, Columbus & Cincinnati, who were anxious to establish a route between Cleveland and Chicago, via Crestline. CC&C officials proposed to buy or place with other investors $400,000 of Ohio & Indiana bonds, to guarantee $250,000 in Fort Wayne & Chicago bonds, to buy $100,000 of that company's stock, and to implement coordinated operations between Cleveland and Chicago.[46]

As president of the Ohio & Pennsylvania, William Robinson, Jr., was doubly alarmed at the CC&C's offer of alliance with the Ohio & Indiana. First, all of the western trade would head northeast at Crestline, leaving Robinson's Ohio & Pennsylvania starved for traffic. Second, that traffic would pass well to the north of Pittsburgh, depriving his native city of commerce. By unhappy coincidence, both the Pennsylvania Railroad and the city of Philadelphia would be harmed as well—a situation that Robinson did not hesitate to emphasize to his colleagues on the PRR board of directors. There was considerable risk, he

warned, in "throwing the Indiana and Ohio Company, with all of its prospective advantages, into the arms of *interests* hostile to our lines of travel and trade for all time to come." Rather than allow even a portion of the Chicago route to fall into "the hands of enemies," Robinson recommended decisive action.[47]

Robinson used his investments in—and his influence over—the Ohio & Indiana to block the link with the CC&C. He persuaded the Ohio & Indiana directors to delay acceptance of the proposal, and then frantically sent word to Thomson of the danger. Thomson in turn instructed Chief Engineer Haupt, recently returned to the PRR following a stint on the Southern Railway of Mississippi, to travel west to examine both the Ohio & Indiana and the Fort Wayne & Chicago. Haupt inspected the route and attended a board meeting. He investigated the books of both companies and cautioned that their "financial condition . . . differs materially from that presented to the [PRR] Board at the time of subscription."[48]

Yet, Haupt was less concerned about what he regarded as innocent financial errors than he was at the possibility that either of the New York roads might draw away the commerce of the west. "The Lake trade, if secured at all to Philadelphia, must be diverted before it reaches the Lakes," he observed, "and this can only be effected by a trunk line, sufficiently far south of the Lake shore to be removed from New York influence, and of the same gauge as the north and south lines connecting with it."[49] Those connecting lines—twenty-five feeder railroads that were completed, under construction, or in the planning stages between Pittsburgh and Chicago—would gather in the traffic of Ohio and Indiana and forward it to Pittsburgh and Philadelphia before it could fall under the grasp of the New York Central, the Erie, or the Erie Canal.

Ohio & Pennsylvania chief engineer Solomon W. Roberts was even more blunt in his assessment of the PRR's ability to compete against the three transportation routes that ran through New York. "I have come to the conclusion," he stressed, "that Philadelphia cannot contend successfully for any large share of the trade and travel of the West, upon the shores of Lake Erie. . . . Such lines may be very important for other reasons, but in this object they will fail."[50] Philadelphia and the PRR were certain to gain the trade along the Ohio

River, Roberts predicted, just as the New York carriers would always hold sway over the Great Lakes. In between, however, the rich belt of farmland that stretched west through Ohio and Indiana and into Illinois was up for grabs, and the PRR possessed a rare opportunity to capture that middle ground. Robinson, Haupt, and Roberts urged the PRR board to break with the more cautious practices of the past and to provide the financial support necessary to finish the line to Chicago, in the amount of $737,701. "The Road, when finished, must be one of the most profitable in the United States," Haupt suggested.[51]

In May 1854, William Neil and the PRR vice president, William B. Foster, Jr., met in Chicago with Ohio & Indiana and Fort Wayne & Chicago executives. Foster, whose father had once been a business partner of William B. Robinson, Jr., was doubtless sympathetic to the plight of the two railroads. Foster and Neil nonetheless recommended to Thomson and the board that they not undertake any additional direct investments in the stock of connecting railroads. Instead, they suggested that the PRR guarantee the bonds of the two companies, to the amount of half a million dollars apiece.[52]

PRR stockholders and conservative board members, concerned at their company's growing indebtedness, were initially reluctant to extend additional money or credit to either company. Despite a worsening economy, the Ohio & Indiana was able to begin service between Crestline and Fort Wayne in November 1854. Absent the PRR's assistance, however, the Fort Wayne & Chicago managed to lay only nineteen miles of track west from Fort Wayne. In 1856, workers reached Columbia City, Indiana, and there construction stopped.[53]

By 1855 the PRR had subsidized the construction of the Ohio & Pennsylvania and the Ohio & Indiana to the tune of $300,000 apiece in stock subscriptions, yet had comparatively little to show for its efforts. Neither railroad carried much traffic, and both were physically isolated from the PRR by the absence of a bridge across the Allegheny River at Pittsburgh. The Fort Wayne & Chicago had stalled well short of its goal. All three western lines suffered from a combination of crushing debts, initially estimated at $800,000, but which ultimately totaled almost $1.4 million. Absent a through route from Chicago to the east coast, local revenues could barely cover operating costs and were certainly insufficient to fund expansion or improvements.[54]

Those difficulties did not diminish the potential value of the three lines as a western extension of the PRR, but they did increase the likelihood that a rival trunk line might acquire any or all of them at a bargain price. To safeguard the Pennsylvania Railroad's interests, Thomson insisted that he and the board would need to play a more active role in the fortunes of the three struggling carriers. His point man was William Hasell Wilson, the son of the man who had surveyed the original route of the Philadelphia & Columbia Railroad. The younger Wilson followed in his father's footsteps, starting as a rodman on the project. By 1831 he was the principal assistant engineer responsible for building the forty miles at the eastern end of the railroad. Between 1841 and 1852, Wilson was a farmer and absent from the engineering profession. For the next few years, he was involved in several projects associated with the PRR, including surveys of the Lancaster, Lebanon & Pine Grove Rail Road, Thomson's proposed bypass of the Philadelphia & Columbia. Before becoming the resident engineer of the PRR's Philadelphia Division (the former Philadelphia & Columbia Railroad) in September 1857, Wilson was available to examine several connecting railroads that might be valuable to the PRR. In February 1856, Thomson sent Wilson west to evaluate both the Ohio & Indiana and the Fort Wayne & Chicago. The following month, Wilson recommended to the board of directors that the PRR provide financial assistance to the two companies. Both Thomson and the board complied, with the PRR's president even pledging a portion of his personal fortune to the project.[55]

As a condition for additional support, Thomson insisted that the three railroads be merged into one and brought firmly under the PRR's control. In June 1856, PRR officials began negotiating a contract "for close running connections and for favorable terms in regard to freight and passengers" interchanged with the Ohio & Pennsylvania and its two western connections.[56] A month later, the new Pittsburgh, Fort Wayne & Chicago Rail Road Company subsumed the Ohio & Pennsylvania, the Ohio & Indiana, and the Fort Wayne & Chicago. The PRR now owned a considerable quantity of the new company's stock, as well as $650,000 in first mortgage bonds. Thomson took a seat on the board of directors, as well as on the PFW&C's finance committee. There was one small setback for the PRR interests, however, in that Tom Scott, who had been a director of the Ohio & Pennsylvania, failed to win a seat on the board of the new company—that smallish plum would have to wait until 1860.

George Washington Cass served as the first president of the Pittsburgh, Fort Wayne & Chicago. Cass, a remarkably industrious entrepreneur, was destined to play an important role in the history of the Fort Wayne, as well as that of the Pennsylvania Railroad. He was born in Dresden, Ohio, the son of New Englanders who had migrated west. At age fourteen, he moved to Detroit to continue his education, lodging with his uncle, Michigan Territorial Governor Lewis Cass. In 1832, he graduated from West Point and was immediately assigned as a surveyor, for improvements to the harbor at Provincetown, Massachusetts. For the next few years, he worked in Ohio, on the westward extension of the National Road. Impressed with the potential of the west, he established a mercantile business in Brownsville, Pennsylvania, where the National Road crossed the Monongahela River, and where passengers bound for Pittsburgh boarded boats for the short trip downriver. He established the first steamboat line on the Monongahela, as well as stage connections to the east. As early as 1828, the Pennsylvania legislature had authorized surveys for improvements along the river. With little public action forthcoming, however, local interests formed the Monongahela Navigation Company in 1836, and Cass was extensively involved in its operations.

In 1849, Cass and his business associates bought out the interests of a Baltimore firm, Green & Company, which operated an express line along the Ohio River. Cass soon came to the attention of the president of the Madison & Indianapolis Railroad, who permitted the entrepreneur to move packages between the Ohio River and the Indiana state capital. Taking advantage of the best available transportation alternatives, Cass developed a route between Cincinnati and Indianapolis, using steamboats to Madison and then railcars to Indianapolis. He styled his operation "Adams & Company," even though he apparently did not yet possess any formal connection to the firm established by Bos-

tonian Alvin Adams. That defect was soon rectified, as Adams later employed Cass as his western agent. Between 1855 and 1857, Cass served as the second president of the recently established Adams Express Company and was instrumental in organizing and systematizing the firm's operations.[57]

By the early 1850s, Cass had invested in railroads leading west out of Pittsburgh, principally the Ohio & Pennsylvania. In January 1856, he joined that company's board of directors. A few months later, he helped to arrange the Pittsburgh, Fort Wayne & Chicago merger and by August he was president of that company. While he would later step aside temporarily, in favor of Thomson, Cass continued to exert a substantial influence over the Fort Wayne well into the 1860s, keeping that company closely allied with, yet still independent of, the Pennsylvania Railroad.

Under the joint oversight of Cass and Thomson, the PRR poured resources into the Fort Wayne, including a guarantee of $3.5 million in construction mortgage bonds, a $250,000 bond issue to complete the Allegheny River bridge, $239,000 in direct contributions, and even the iron rails and hardware ripped up from the recently abandoned New Portage Railroad. The PRR also ensured substantial traffic for the Fort Wayne by dispatching shipments destined for Cincinnati over the line as far as Crestline, and then southwest over the Cleveland, Columbus & Cincinnati. In the process, Thomson drained traffic from the Steubenville & Indiana Railroad, a central Ohio route that he was also supporting, while greatly inconveniencing passengers traveling between Pennsylvania and the Midwest. In return for that munificence, Thomson insisted that he be appointed chief engineer for the PFW&C, effective January 5, 1858, with full authority to select locations and prepare construction contracts for the remaining eighty-five miles to Chicago. By July he had temporarily replaced Cass as the railroad's president.[58]

With the infusion of PRR credit, the Fort Wayne rapidly upgraded its physical plant and equipment, straightening and ballasting track and purchasing hundreds of new locomotives and cars. By 1856, rails extended as far west as Plymouth, Indiana, where a connection with the Michigan Southern & Northern Indiana Railroad provided access to Chicago. In the autumn of 1858 the tracks reached the Rock Island Railroad line at Englewood, Illinois, only seven miles south of Thomson's goal. On Christmas Day, 1858, Pittsburgh, Fort Wayne & Chicago construction crews gave Thomson and the Pennsylvania Railroad quite a present when they spiked down the last rails leading to Van Buren Street in Chicago.[59]

By the time the Fort Wayne's tracks reached Chicago, construction crews had already completed work on the last link of an unbroken rail line that stretched west from Philadelphia. Since 1852, Thomson had been actively pursuing a Pittsburgh connection between the PRR and the Ohio & Pennsylvania. The engineering challenges were considerable, and they included a bridge, nearly a thousand feet long, between Pittsburgh and Allegheny City, at the site of the viaduct that had once carried the final leg of the Western Division Canal.

The political issues were more difficult to address. Pittsburghers had not forgotten the efforts of PRR supporters to deny them access to the B&O, and they continued to chafe at discriminatory short-haul freight rates. They were also unimpressed by what they considered to be the substandard terminal facilities that the PRR provided for their city. In January 1851, Thomson had selected Tom Scott as the PRR's agent at Pittsburgh, owing to the young man's winning personality and his established relationship with local shippers and transportation firms. Scott's immediate task was to locate a site for permanent freight and passenger facilities that would fulfill the 1848 stipulation of the Allegheny County commissioners that the PRR's terminus be located within city limits, yet still provide for a junction with the Ohio & Pennsylvania route that began across the river, in Allegheny City. Scott chose a temporary location along Liberty Street (later, Liberty Avenue) near the Western Division Canal basin. The temporary facilities lasted far longer than anyone had anticipated, however, as PRR and city officials became embroiled in a battle over the railroad's connection to the west.[60]

Pittsburgh's commercial interests had long benefited from the city's status as a break-of-bulk point, with cargoes shifted among canal boats, steamboats, and railroad cars, and they strenuously objected to the loss of that trade. In January 1854, the Pittsburgh City Council nonetheless granted the Ohio & Pennsylvania Railroad the right to build the Allegheny River bridge, and construction began a few months later. Workers completed the structure in September 1857, but it would be another year before through service was possible. Pennsylvania Railroad interests had been working to secure the right to lay tracks through Pittsburgh, initially without success. Their task became easier in January 1856, when William Bingham—a freight forwarder who was closely affiliated with the PRR—was elected mayor. In February 1858, a city ordinance permitted the Ohio & Pennsylvania, by now merged into the Pittsburgh, Fort Wayne & Chicago, to complete the short link with the PRR. Despite continued attempts by city officials to prevent construction crews from installing tracks in city streets, the work was finished by early March.[61]

With the connection issue resolved, PRR officials were finally able to complete a new (and also temporary) passenger station near the intersection of Grant and Liberty Streets for use by both the PRR and the Fort Wayne. The first "permanent" union station was not finished until September 1865. Even then, many Fort Wayne trains continued to originate and terminate at that railroad's station in Allegheny City. In the meantime, PRR personnel showed considerably more alacrity in opening freight yards at the foot of Liberty Street along the Monongahela River, near its confluence with the Allegheny. The first facilities opened in December 1852, and by February 1855 the PRR had completed the Duquesne Freight Depot—an edifice that was much larger, and considerably more grand, than the nearby passenger station.[62]

The collective efforts of Scott and others to secure a route through Pittsburgh were to have profound consequences for both the railroad and the city. The Pittsburgh connection was by no means ideal, for it included more than a mile of track located on Liberty Street. A more serious problem resulted from the incompatibility between the standard gauge employed on the PRR and the Ohio gauge used west of Pittsburgh, which often required freight to be transshipped from one set of cars to another.

Thomson nonetheless possessed a substantial advantage over the Baltimore & Ohio in that it would be more than a decade before that railroad completed its bridge across the Ohio River at Wheeling. For Pittsburgh, the consequences were no less momentous. As many Pittsburghers had feared, the bridge across the Allegheny River and, more generally, the PRR's growing network of feeder lines to the west reduced the city's importance as a break-of-bulk point. Undeterred, many local entrepreneurs redirected their efforts into the iron and steel industries, helping to transform the city from a distribution center into one of the nation's leading industrial regions.[63]

Refinancing the Fort Wayne

Despite the assistance provided by the PRR, the expense associated with building a line to Chicago, coupled with the recession of the late 1850s, soon bankrupted the PFW&C. With many different classes of securities outstanding, Fort Wayne officials began refusing payment on some of the company's obligations as early as the autumn of 1857, with the first mortgage bonds entering default in July 1859. The bankruptcy increased the involvement of New York investors in the Fort Wayne, a situation that did not bode well for the PRR. Thomson nonetheless found a way to benefit from the financial crisis, and in the process he enhanced the PRR's control over the company.

New York capitalists were initially not well represented on the Fort Wayne's board, a situation that benefited Thomson and the PRR. At the company's inception, only one New York financier, Theodore T. Moran, served as a director. That state of affairs made it more difficult for the New York roads to influence the Fort Wayne, while concomitantly increasing Thomson's effectiveness in protecting the PRR's access to Chicago.

James F. D. Lanier played a critical role in increasing the control of New York investors over the Fort Wayne, as well as many other midwestern railroads. He began his career as a lawyer and a banker in Indiana before moving to New York and establishing the banking house of Winslow, Lanier & Company. Lanier specialized in the securities of western railroads at a time when other bankers typically considered them too uncertain to constitute a worthwhile investment. After the Fort Wayne fell victim to the Panic of 1857, Lanier and his fellow New Yorkers attempted to

sort out the mess. In March 1858, Lanier's partner, Robert H. Winslow, became a Fort Wayne director. After the Fort Wayne defaulted on its first mortgage bonds, on July 1, 1859, Lanier convened a meeting of the company's principal creditors at his New York offices. Thomson attended in an effort to protect the PRR's $650,000 share of Pittsburgh, Fort Wayne & Chicago bonds, as well as its substantial investments in Fort Wayne stock. The most important figure present was undoubtedly Samuel J. Tilden. An accomplished attorney and a veteran of the New York state legislature, Tilden had developed a reputation as an expert at railroad reorganization. The Fort Wayne would be one of his thorniest problems, and one of his greatest triumphs.[64]

The obstacles that confronted those individuals—now constituted as a reorganization committee—were indeed formidable. As the *New York Times* noted, ten years after the fact, "To give some idea of the chaos existing in the affairs of the company, we may state that there were outstanding, at the time, nine different classes of bonds, secured in one way or another upon the different portions of the road; two classes secured by real estate belonging to the company, and several issued in the funding of coupons. . . . The Company also owed more than $2,000,000 of floating debt, portions of it in the form of judgments recovered in the State courts."[65] Despite the PRR's support, the Fort Wayne was also in a sorry physical condition, still with some unballasted track and worn-out equipment.

Lanier, Tilden, and their associates proved quite successful in reorganizing the Fort Wayne route. Thomson apparently wanted to substitute preferred stock for some of the railroad's bonds, a system that he had suggested to financial analyst Henry Varnum Poor during the autumn of 1859.[66] Thomson did not prevail, and it was Lanier who handled the financial arrangements, wiping out the Fort Wayne's debt in favor of $12.3 million in new bonds. Tilden managed the political intricacies, simultaneously shepherding through the Pennsylvania, Ohio, Indiana, and Illinois legislatures the charter amendments necessary to make the reorganization possible. Then, on October 24, 1861, the members of the reorganization committee purchased the assets of the Pittsburgh, Fort Wayne & Chicago Rail *Road*. The following February, they organized the new Pittsburgh, Fort Wayne & Chicago Rail*way*, with Cass as president.[67]

The reorganization lulled PRR officials into a false sense of security, as they believed that the Fort Wayne was safely in their camp. After relinquishing the presidency of the PFW&C, Thomson resumed his role as a director, overseeing the PRR's investments in the company. Under the terms of the reorganization, the Fort Wayne was authorized to issue $6.5 million in stock, of which only $816,050 went to the PRR. That amount was far short of a majority, and insufficient to give Thomson control over his Chicago outlet. The PRR also received more than $1 million in Fort Wayne bonds, but those debt instruments hardly increased Thomson's influence. By 1864, moreover, Thomson needed funds to complete a route across the West Virginia Panhandle, and he authorized the sale of most of the PRR's holdings in the Fort Wayne. The PRR's shareholders were delighted at the profit that their company realized on the transaction, and relieved that they were no longer responsible for such a significant investment in another railroad. Within a few years they would regret Thomson's decision, as George Cass demonstrated his lack of loyalty to the Pennsylvania Railroad.[68]

For the moment, however, Thomson could be pleased with the results of the Fort Wayne reorganization. Thanks to the restructuring of the Fort Wayne's debt and to the traffic demands of the Civil War, the PFW&C quickly became both prosperous and profitable. Freight ton-miles increased from 58 million in 1858 to 166 million in 1863, and to 194 million by 1865. Revenues increased from $2.3 million in 1860 to $8.5 million in 1865. By 1869, the holders of Fort Wayne stock reaped a 12 percent dividend each year.[69]

Yet, that railroad's prosperity also made it an attractive target for the executives of the New York roads. The Fort Wayne offered the most direct route between Philadelphia and Chicago, but its connection with the Cleveland, Columbus & Cincinnati Railroad at Crestline made it possible to move traffic toward Buffalo and Dunkirk, the termini of the New York Central and the Erie. Even the Baltimore & Ohio, whose president, John W. Garrett, was still attempting to complete the Pittsburgh & Connellsville, offered the remote chance of serving as the Fort Wayne's outlet to tidewater. What was worse, from Thomson's perspective, Cass seemed insufficiently grateful for the role that the PRR had played in stabilizing the Fort Wayne. During the 1860s, Cass would attempt to protect the interests of his railroad as best he could. In the process, he would court the executives of several trunk lines, jeopardizing Thomson's vision of a secure route to Chicago.

Through the Heart of Ohio

Even as they were facilitating the construction of railroads north and west from Pittsburgh and toward Chicago, Thomson and his PRR associates were establishing another route west, through central Ohio. Their initial intent was to reach Cincinnati. By the mid-1850s, they achieved that goal, along a route that was indirect and not entirely under their control. In time, they would remedy those deficiencies and establish multiple links to Cincinnati. Their more important achievement, however, lay in the creation of the nucleus of the southwestern part of the PRR system, extending the PRR's reach westward to the vitally important gateway city of St. Louis.

Ultimately, PRR executives joined together more than sixty separate railroads to form the corporate entity known as the Lines West of Pittsburgh and Erie. The vast majority of those predecessor companies carried trains along the central route through Ohio and Indiana. Needless to say, their collective corporate histories were extraordinarily convoluted. There would in fact be two essentially separate routes between Columbus, Ohio, and Richmond, Indiana, and then diverging, one northwest to Chicago, and the other west to St. Louis—along with a second line (between Bradford, Ohio, and Logansport, Indiana) that carried Chicago traffic, plus branches to Madison, Indiana; Louisville, Kentucky; and Vincennes, Indiana, among others.[70]

The Queen of the West

Cincinnati, larger even than Pittsburgh, was the dominant commercial center on the Ohio River. Between

Northwest System

Pittsburgh, Fort Wayne & Chicago Railway (1860–71)
  Pittsburgh, Fort Wayne & Chicago Rail Road (1856–60)
    Ohio & Pennsylvania Railroad (1848–56)
    Ohio & Indiana Railroad (1850–56)
    Fort Wayne & Chicago Railroad (1853–56)

Cleveland & Pittsburgh Railroad (1853–71)

Erie & Pittsburgh Railroad (1858–71)
  Erie Canal Company (of Pennsylvania) (1843–71)
  Erie & North East Rail Road Company (1842–67)
    –to New York Central
  Pittsburgh & Erie Railroad (1846–57)[a]

4th Grand Rapids & Indiana Railroad (1884–96)
  Bay View, Little Traverse & Mackinaw Railroad (1879–88)
  3rd Grand Rapids & Indiana Railroad (1857–84)
    2nd Grand Rapids & Indiana Railroad (1855–57)
      Grand Rapids & Southern Railroad (1855)
      1st Grand Rapids & Indiana Railroad (1854–55)
    Grand Rapids & Mackinaw Railroad (1857)
    Grand Rapids & Fort Wayne Railroad (1857)
    Grand Rapids, Indiana & Mackinaw Railroad (1881–84)

[a] A portion of the Pittsburgh & Erie Railroad was sold to the Meadville Railroad in 1860, and became part of the Erie. The remainder sold in 1860 to the Erie & Pittsburgh Railroad, only the portion from Clarksville to Sharpsville placed in service.

1810 and 1820, Cincinnati's population nearly tripled, from 2,540 to 9,642. The sluggish national economy that characterized much of the 1820s had little effect on the city, whose population reached 24,831 by the end of the decade. In 1840, 46,338 people resided there. A decade later, the city boasted some 115,000 inhabitants—two and a half times the number who lived in Pittsburgh. By the 1830s, slaughterhouses in Cincinnati butchered more hogs than those in any other city in the nation, gaining the community the unflattering nickname "Porkopolis." The poet Henry Wadsworth Longfellow gave a kinder assessment, with his 1854 ode "to the Queen of the West, in her garlands dressed, on the banks of the Beautiful River."[71]

Much of Cincinnati's economic growth was based on its location on the Ohio River, which permitted ready access to Pittsburgh, Louisville, St. Louis, and New Orleans. Until the Civil War, river steamers, like canal boats, were the most efficient carriers of bulk cargoes. Yet, the Ohio River wound a serpentine course on its way from the Alleghenies to the Mississippi. Steamboats leaving Cincinnati faced an upriver run of 470 miles to Pittsburgh. Railroads could provide a more direct route that was 154 miles shorter. Furthermore, shippers who relied on independent freight forwarders to handle steamboat cargoes at break-bulk points were pleased to discover that rail-

Southwest System, Railroads Between Pittsburgh and Indianapolis
(Consolidated in 1890 as the Pittsburgh, Cincinnati, Chicago & St. Louis Railway)

Pittsburg, Cincinnati & St. Louis Railway (1868–90)
  Pan Handle Railway (1861–68)
    Pittsburg & Steubenville Railroad (1851–67)
    Holliday's Cove Rail Road (1860–68)
    Steubenville & Indiana Railroad (1848–68)
    Little Miami Railroad (1836–69)[b]
      Dayton, Xenia & Belpre Railroad (1851–65)
      Columbus & Xenia Railroad (1844–68)
      Dayton & Western Railroad (1846–69)
  Columbus, Chicago & Indiana Central Railway (1868–83)
    Columbus & Indiana Central Railway (1867–68)
      Columbus & Indianapolis Central Railway (1864–67)
        Indiana Central Railway (1851–64)
          Terre Haute & Richmond Railroad (East of
            Indianapolis) (1850–51)
        Columbus & Indianapolis Railroad (1863–64)
          Columbus, Piqua & Indiana Railroad (1849–63)
          Richmond & Covington Railroad (1862–64)
      Union & Logansport Railroad (1863–67)
        2nd Marion & Mississinewa Valley Railroad (1854–63)
          1st Marion & Mississinewa Valley Railroad (1852–54)
          Marion & Logansport Railroad (1853–54)
      Toledo, Logansport & Burlington Railway (1862–67)
        Toledo, Logansport & Burlington Railroad (1858–62)
          Logansport, Peoria & Burlington Railway (1854–58)
            Logansport & Pacific Railway (1853–54)
              Logansport & Pacific Railroad (1853)
    4th Chicago & Great Eastern Railway (1865–68)
      Cincinnati & Chicago Air-Line Railroad (1860–65)
        2nd Cincinnati & Chicago Railroad (1854–60)
          Cincinnati, Logansport & Chicago Railway (1853–54)
            New Castle & Richmond Railroad (1848–53)
          1st Cincinnati & Chicago Railroad (1854)
          Cincinnati, Cambridge & Chicago Short Line Railway
            (1853–54)
            Cincinnati, New Castle & Michigan Railroad (1853–54)
      3rd Chicago & Great Eastern Railway (1865)
        Chicago & Cincinnati Railroad (1857–65)
        2nd Chicago & Great Eastern Railway (1863–65)
          Galena & Illinois River Railroad (1857–63)
          1st Chicago & Great Eastern Railway (1863)
  Cincinnati, Richmond & Chicago Railroad (1866–90)
    2nd Eaton & Hamilton Railroad, in Ohio (1854–66)

Richmond & Miami Railway (1862–90)
  2nd Eaton & Hamilton Railroad, in Indiana (1854–62)
    1st Eaton & Hamilton Railroad (1847–54)
    Richmond & Miami Railroad (1846–54)

Jeffersonville, Madison & Indianapolis Railroad (1866–90)
  Indianapolis & Madison Railroad (1862–66)
    Madison & Indianapolis Railroad (1854–62)
    Madison, Indianapolis & Peru Railroad (1854–55)[c]
      Madison & Indianapolis Railroad (private, 1842–54)
        Madison & Indianapolis Railroad (public, 1838–42)
          Madison, Indianapolis & Lafayette Railroad
            (public, 1836–38)
            Madison, Indianapolis & Lafayette Railroad,
              (private, 1832–36)
      Peru & Indianapolis Railroad (1846–54)
  Jeffersonville Railroad (1849–66)
    Ohio & Indianapolis Railway (1832–49)

[b] After January 1865, owned in partnership by the Little Miami Railroad and the Columbus & Xenia Railroad. After November 1868, the Little Miami Railroad leased the Columbus & Xenia Railroad and the Dayton, Xenia & Belpre Railroad.

[c] The Peru & Indianapolis Railroad regained control of property from the Madison, Indianapolis & Peru Railroad in 1855, reorganized as the (3rd) Peru & Indianapolis Railroad in 1864, and then as the Lake Erie & Western Railroad, then as the New York, Chicago & St. Louis Railroad (the Nickel Plate Road).

Other Railroads Between Pittsburgh and Indianapolis
(Not Consolidated in 1890 into the Pittsburgh, Cincinnati, Chicago & St. Louis Railway)

Cleveland, Akron & Cincinnati Railway (1911–24)
  Cincinnati & Muskingum Valley Railroad (1898–1911)
    Cincinnati & Muskingum Valley Railway (1864–98)
      Cincinnati & Zanesville Railroad (1864–90)
        Cincinnati, Wilmington & Zanesville Railroad (1851–64)
  Cleveland, Akron & Columbus Railway (1885–1911)
    Cleveland, Mt. Vernon & Delaware Railroad (1869–86)
      Pittsburgh, Mt. Vernon, Columbus & London Railroad (1869)
      Cleveland, Zanesville & Cincinnati Railroad (1853–69)
        Akron Branch of the Cleveland & Pittsburgh Railroad (1851–53)
      Springfield, Mt. Vernon & Pittsburgh Railroad (1852–69)
        Springfield & Mansfield Railroad (1850–52)

Southwest System, Railroads West of Indianapolis
(Consolidated in 1905 as the Vandalia Railroad)

St. Louis, Vandalia & Terre Haute Railroad (1865–1905)

Terre Haute & Indianapolis Rail Road (1865–1905)
  Terre Haute & Richmond Railroad (1850–65)
    Terre Haute & Richmond Rail Road (1847–50)

Terre Haute & Logansport Railway (1898–1905)
  Terre Haute & Logansport Railroad (1879–98)
    Logansport, Crawfordsville & South Western Railway (1871–79)
      Crawfordsville & Rockville Railroad (1869–71)
      Frankfort & Crawfordsville Railroad (1869–71)
      Logansport, Camden & Frankfort Railroad (1869–71)

Logansport & Toledo Railway (1901–05)
  Eel River Railroad (1877–1901)
    Detroit, Eel River & Illinois Rail Road (1868–77)
      Detroit, Logansport & St. Louis Rail Road (1869–70)
        Toledo, Logansport & Northern Indiana Rail Road (1869)
          Logansport & Northern Indiana Railroad (1853–63)
            Auburn & Eel River Valley Rail Road (1853)

Indianapolis & Vincennes Railroad (1865–1905) [d]

[d] The Cairo & Vincennes Railroad (1867–80) served as the western connection for the Indianapolis & Vincennes Railroad, but was never part of the PRR system. Reorganized as Cairo & Vincennes Railway in 1880, as the Wabash, St. Louis & Pacific Railway in 1881, as the Cairo, Vincennes & Chicago Railway in 1889, as the Cleveland, Cincinnati, Chicago & St. Louis Railway (Big Four) in 1890, and then as the New York Central in 1906.

Other Companies

Affiliated with PRR (friendly connections):
Toledo, Peoria & Western Railway (1887–1926) [e]
  Toledo, Peoria & Western Railroad (1879–87)
    2nd Toledo, Peoria & Warsaw Railway (1865–80)
      1st Toledo, Peoria & Warsaw Railway (1864–65)
        Logansport, Peoria & Burlington Railroad (1861–64)
          Peoria & Oquawka Railroad (1849–61)
          Mississippi & Wabash Railroad (1853–65)

Principal lines affiliated with the Baltimore & Ohio Railroad:
Central Ohio Railroad (1847–66)

Baltimore & Ohio Southwestern Railroad (1889–1900)
  Cincinnati, Washington & Baltimore Railroad (1882–89)
    Marietta & Cincinnati Railroad (1851–82)
      Belpre & Cincinnati Railroad (1845–51)
  Ohio & Mississippi Railway (1867–93)
    Ohio & Mississippi Rail Road (1854–67)

Principal lines affiliated with the Lake Shore & Michigan Southern Railway/New York Central:
Cleveland, Columbus, Cincinnati & Indianapolis Railway (1868–89)
  Bellefontaine Railway (1864–68)
    Indianapolis, Pittsburgh & Cleveland Railroad (1855–64)
      Indianapolis & Bellefontaine Railroad (1848–55)
    Bellefontaine & Indiana Railroad (1846–64)
  Cleveland, Columbus & Cincinnati Railway (1836–68)

Principal lines affiliated with the New York & Erie Rail Road (1832–61)/Erie Railway (1861–78)/New York, Lake Erie & Western Railroad (1878–95)/Erie Railroad (1895–1960):
New York, Pennsylvania & Ohio Railroad (1880–96) [f]
  Atlantic & Great Western Railway (1865–80) [g]
    Atlantic & Great Western Railroad (1853–65)
      Franklin & Warren Railroad Company (1851–53)
      Cleveland & Mahoning Railroad (1848–63)
    Atlantic & Great Western Railroad Company of Pennsylvania (1858–65)
      Meadville Railroad (1857–58)
    Atlantic & Great Western Railroad Company of New York (1859–65)
      Erie & New York City Railroad (1851–59)

Independent lines, offering connections for the Baltimore & Ohio and the Erie:
Cincinnati, Hamilton & Dayton Railway (1895–1917)
  Cincinnati, Hamilton & Dayton Railroad (1847–95)
  Cincinnati, Dayton & Ironton Railroad (1891–95)

Cincinnati, Dayton & Chicago Railroad (1891–95)

[e] Owned jointly by PRR (Pennsylvania Company) and by Chicago, Burlington & Quincy Railroad, between 1893 and 1927, with control relinquished following the line's bankruptcy. The company was eventually reorganized as the Toledo, Peoria & Western Railroad in 1952, with joint ownership by the PRR and the Atchison, Topeka & Santa Fe Railway, 1960–68.

[f] Sold to the Erie Railroad in 1896, merged into the Erie Railroad in 1941.

[g] Leased by Erie Railway, 1868–74.

Note: So far as can be determined, the spellings of the corporate names listed above are those that appeared on the original corporate charters, with the most common deviation from modern practice being the use of "Pittsburg" rather than "Pittsburgh." In the text of this book, modern spellings have been used in place of the archaic versions.

roads could offer uninterrupted through service. Despite the presence of two rail routes between Lake Erie and the Ohio River, Cincinnati lacked a rail connection to tidewater, and the city became a magnet for all four of the trunk lines, particularly the Pennsylvania Railroad and the Baltimore & Ohio.[72]

The Baltimore & Ohio won the race to the Queen of the West. As B&O construction crews made steady progress toward the Ohio River, the Ohio legislature chartered several companies whose promoters promised to continue the Baltimore route farther west. One of those companies was the Central Ohio Railroad, incorporated in February 1847. Its promoters, most of

whom were from Zanesville, Ohio, received the right to build as far west as the Indiana state line. The Central Ohio's eastern terminus was something of a mystery, however, as B&O officials had not yet decided whether

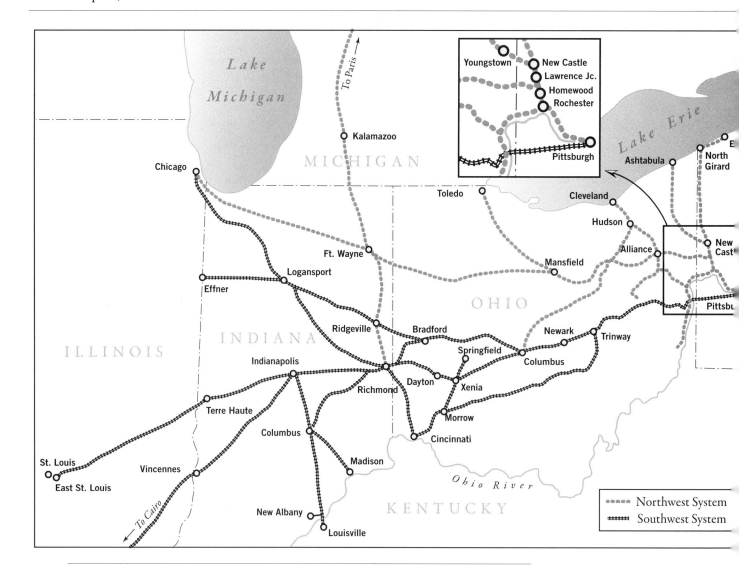

Figure 30. During the 1850s, local railroad entrepreneurs and civic boosters in Ohio and Indiana promoted routes that they hoped would link their communities to the Ohio River, Lake Erie, or one of the eastern trunk lines. After the Civil War, some of those promoters would contribute mightily to the development of the PRR's Lines West of Pittsburgh and Erie, while others would create financial difficulties that would take decades to resolve. By 1870, the PRR had established one group of lines, based on George W. Cass's Pittsburgh, Fort Wayne & Chicago Railway (referred to as the Northwest System, after 1890), and another, tied to the faltering companies pieced together by Benjamin E. Smith (after 1890, the Southwest System). The network provided the PRR with access to such key cities as Chicago, St. Louis, Louisville, Cleveland, and Cincinnati, but traffic densities never reached the levels of the PRR's key eastern routes.

their line would reach the Ohio River at Pittsburgh (a temporary possibility, until the terms of the PRR's 1846 charter took effect), at Wheeling, or farther south, at Parkersburg, Virginia. In June 1847, B&O officials traveled to Columbus and met with Alfred Kelley and other prominent local politicians, in order to

solicit their opinions on the best rail route across Ohio. Kelley favored an alignment that led more or less due west from Wheeling. On July 16, B&O officials seconded Kelley's suggestions and recommended Wheeling as the B&O's western terminus. Hard on the heels of the B&O delegation came representatives from the

PRR, also expressing interest in a connection with the line, but experiencing a less enthusiastic welcome. Within days, now that they knew where they would be constructing their railroad, the promoters of the Central Ohio began soliciting stock subscriptions. Central Ohio's supporters suggested that two trunk lines were interested in their company, and accordingly experienced little difficulty in raising funds. Late in 1852, B&O rails finally reached the Ohio River. By November 1854, the Central Ohio Railroad linked Bellaire, Ohio (opposite Benwood, Virginia, a location on the B&O, four miles south of Wheeling), to Columbus. From there, the Little Miami Railroad provided access to Cincinnati. It was a roundabout route, however, that was further handicapped by the absence of a bridge across the Ohio River, which the B&O did not complete until 1871. The Central Ohio also experienced severe financial difficulties and entered receivership in 1859.[73]

With the Central Ohio aligned with the B&O, PRR officials turned instead to the Marietta & Cincinnati Railroad. However, their efforts to reach Cincinnati by that route fell victim to that company's poor financial prospects, as well as Thomson's inexperience as president. The Ohio legislature chartered the Marietta & Cincinnati in 1845, as the Belpre & Cincinnati Railroad. Its incorporators hoped to build east to Belpre, Ohio, opposite Parkersburg, at a time when no one, not even B&O officials, was entirely certain where the Baltimore road would strike the Ohio River. In 1850, the owners of the Belpre & Cincinnati secured an amendment to the charter, shifting the meeting point with the Ohio River to Marietta, Ohio, and permitting construction to continue north to Bellaire, opposite Benwood (Wheeling), soon to be the terminus of the B&O. In 1851, they changed the company's name to the Marietta & Cincinnati to better reflect their goals.[74]

In February 1851, however, Virginia legislators chartered the Northwestern Virginia Railroad, abandoning their earlier refusal to permit the B&O access to the Ohio River south of Wheeling. When complete, its tracks would leave the B&O main line at Grafton and head due west to Parkersburg, south of the Marietta & Cincinnati line. Civic interests in Wheeling, afraid that their city would no longer be the B&O's preferred terminus, instead began to ally themselves with the PRR. So, too, did Marietta & Cincinnati officials, such as President William Parker Cutler, a native of Marietta and a former member of the Ohio House of Representatives. There was still a substantial gap between the Marietta & Cincinnati's proposed northern terminus at Bellaire and the end of PRR rails in Pittsburgh. Supporters of the PRR affiliation accordingly placed their faith in the Hempfield Railroad, a company chartered in May 1850, to build a line from Wheeling to Greensburg, Pennsylvania, on the PRR main line east of Pittsburgh.[75]

As early as 1851, Cutler had solicited funds from both the City of Wheeling and the Pennsylvania Railroad. The board was unimpressed with the Marietta & Cincinnati's prospects and dispatched Thomson, then serving as chief engineer, to inspect the property. Nothing happened, however, until Thomson ascended to the PRR presidency in January 1852. By June, representatives from the Marietta & Cincinnati had requested that the PRR subscribe to $750,000 of their stock, and their counterparts on the Hempfield, not wanting to be left out, asked for $500,000. Soon thereafter, acting on Thomson's instructions, Thomas Fernon traveled through Pittsburgh on his way west. He evaluated the prospects of the Marietta & Cincinnati and gave the project his endorsement. By January 1852, PRR chief engineer Edward Miller also recommended that the PRR support the Hempfield/Marietta & Cincinnati route.[76]

The two reports were enough to convince Thomson that the PRR needed to move quickly to secure a connection to Cincinnati. He had to tread cautiously, however, particularly with respect to the Hempfield Railroad. Pittsburghers, already displeased that the PRR had denied the B&O the right to build to their city, were doubly livid at the thought that the PRR's main line to the west would bypass them. In September 1852, Thomson urged the board to invest $750,000 in the Marietta & Cincinnati, but he wisely made no mention of the Hempfield. In any event, the board refused the new president's request, forcing Thomson to issue an appeal directly to the shareholders. In February 1853, the board reversed its earlier decision and cautiously approved aid to the Marietta & Cincinnati, but only on the condition that the agreement be approved by a majority of shareholders.[77]

In his efforts to help the Marietta & Cincinnati, Thomson confronted the PRR's status as a mixed enterprise, one that was financed in large part with public monies and governed by several public directors. William Wilkins and William Robinson, Jr., the two Allegheny County directors, opposed any support for the Hempfield and Marietta & Cincinnati route, which they thought would undermine Pittsburgh's position as a river port. Wilkins was a close personal friend of Lewis Cass, the uncle of George W. Cass, and both he and Robinson were strong supporters of the Fort Wayne route. As such, they were anxious to prevent the construction of a competing rail link along a more southerly alignment. Their fellow Pittsburghers responded to the Hempfield threat by increasing their efforts to revive the moribund Pittsburgh & Connellsville, the B&O's planned extension into their city. However, Wilkins's resignation from the board, on February 7, 1853 undermined their effectiveness.[78]

In contrast, many Philadelphians and their representatives on the PRR board welcomed the proposed link to Cincinnati. On February 3, 1853, the Select and Common Councils instructed the PRR's city directors to support Thomson's plan to invest in the Marietta & Cincinnati. For good measure, the councils also agreed to a $500,000 municipal subscription to the Hempfield, something that the PRR president had not been able to accomplish with his own board. That decision, made on the same day that the councilmen agreed to subscribe to twenty thousand shares of Sunbury & Erie stock, indicated the desire of municipal leaders to invest large amounts of money for the protection of Philadelphia's mercantile interests. "These sums," former PRR board member Richard D. Wood suggested, "will enable the companies to make these roads, absolutely essential to the commercial prosperity of our city."[79]

Not everyone shared Wood's optimistic assessment of municipal investment in the Hempfield Railroad. In 1846, when Thomas P. Cope and the other Pennsylvania Railroad commissioners had lobbied the Philadelphia Select and Common Councils for aid, they had faced formidable opposition. Horace Binney and his allies had argued against a stock subscription, on the grounds that the city charter did not provide the councils with the authority to invest in a private com-

pany. The matter was not resolved until March 1848, when the state legislature amended the PRR's charter to permit municipal subscriptions. Even then, opponents of municipal aid did not give up. Their opportunity came when the city councils elected to support the Hempfield (as well as the Philadelphia, Easton & Water-Gap Railroad, a company that eventually became part of the Reading and was not connected with the PRR). Four Philadelphians took the matter to the Pennsylvania Supreme Court, arguing that legislative actions to aid private corporations were in violation of the state constitution. City and county governments were local corporations, they argued, and as such their actions were constitutionally limited to their locales. By no measure was the Hempfield, a railroad based in southwestern Pennsylvania, within the legitimate sphere of Philadelphia's municipal influence. Moreover, in a novel and complex argument, opponents of funding argued that forced taxation to support public investment in private industries violated the rights of citizens to their property. In short, the plaintiffs in *Sharpless v. the Mayor of Philadelphia* were doing nothing less than challenging the constitutionality of mixed enterprise.

The majority of the justices had little patience with such arguments. They agreed with railroad attorneys that what mattered was whether duly elected municipal officials believed that their investment, no matter where applied, would benefit their constituents. "The right to tax depends on the ultimate use, purpose and object for which the fund is raised," they ruled, "and not on the nature or character of the person or corporation whose immediate agency is to be used in applying it."[80] The *Sharpless* case thus preserved the broad right of municipal corporations to invest in private companies—ironically, at a time when a growing public dissatisfaction with such mixed enterprises was rendering the argument moot.[81]

Even as his Hempfield allies were prevailing in the state supreme court, Thomson was doing his best to convince Pennsylvania legislators that the PRR's support of the Marietta & Cincinnati was in the best economic interest of the commonwealth. In January 1853 he asked legislators to introduce a bill allowing the PRR to increase its capital stock to $4 million and to acquire the securities of railroads outside of Pennsylvania, up to 15 percent of the PRR's total capitalization. A favorable Act of Assembly followed on March 23, 1853, and the PRR immediately gave notice of its intent to use the $750,000 that the board had allocated to purchase thirteen thousand shares of Marietta & Cincinnati stock. The outcome of the shareholders' vote, held in April 1853, was a foregone conclusion. Aside from the Allegheny County directors, virtually every PRR investor lived in or near Philadelphia, and they put the future of their company ahead of the concerns of Pittsburgh boosters.[82]

During 1853, construction began on both the Marietta & Cincinnati and the Hempfield, but the efforts soon ran afoul of a business recession that lasted well into the following year. In 1854, Winslow, Lanier & Company attempted to place a consignment of Marietta & Cincinnati bonds. Their efforts were unsuccessful, however, and construction soon ground to a halt. Thomson had insisted that the Marietta & Cincinnati employ the bulk of the PRR subscription to advance construction, but the financial crisis caused the company's managers to defy those instructions and use most of the money to retire existing debts. In the autumn of 1856, the PRR board nonetheless supported a plan to merge the Marietta & Cincinnati and the Hempfield into an "Ohio Valley Rail Road Company," thus creating "a short route of uniform gauge from the City of Philadelphia to the City of Cincinnati."[83] A traffic agreement with the broad-gauge Ohio & Mississippi Rail Road would provide onward service to St. Louis, but the entire proposal came to naught. Despite its financial hardships, the Marietta & Cincinnati completed its main line in April 1857, but the company went bankrupt in November. The PRR's $750,000 investment was now effectively worthless.[84]

In January 1858 the PRR board dispatched one of its members, John Hulme, to determine what, if anything, the company could salvage from the debacle. His report was not encouraging. Concerning "the assets, liabilities, and conditions of the Marietta and Cincinnati Rail Road Company," Hulme wrote, it was "very evident that its financial as well as working condition is decidedly bad, [and] that its future prospects are no better." He thought it his duty to "warn the Pennsylvania Rail Road Company against rendering

another cent of aid to the Marietta and Cincinnati."[85] In the aftermath of Hulme's report, the PRR wrote off its entire investment in the Marietta & Cincinnati Railroad.

Even worse, the loss of the Marietta & Cincinnati rebounded to the interests of the B&O. In 1857 the B&O completed the Northwestern Virginia Railroad to Parkersburg, and from there, a thirteen-mile river transfer led to Marietta. Following a transit of Marietta & Cincinnati rails, a friendly connection with the Ohio & Mississippi provided secure access to St. Louis. That route, and not the indirect and financially troubled Central Ohio Railroad, became the B&O's access to the west.[86]

For Thomson, the Marietta & Cincinnati escapade was little short of an unmitigated disaster. The PRR president might have consoled himself that he had delayed the B&O's efforts to acquire the company, at least until after the Civil War had helped to weaken his southern rival. Aside from that, the only good to arise from the situation concerned William Jackson Palmer, a seventeen-year-old who in 1853 joined the surveying corps on the Hempfield Railroad. Following the completion of work on the Hempfield line, Palmer's uncle, Francis H. Jackson, provided him with a job as secretary of the Westmoreland Coal Company. Jackson sent his nephew to Britain, to study coal mines and railroads. Upon his return, Palmer worked with Westmoreland's president, James Magee, an individual who was a business associate of J. Edgar Thomson and who had briefly served as a PRR director. It was that connection, probably more than his work on the Hempfield, that brought Palmer to Thomson's attention, and by 1857 Palmer was the private secretary to the president of the Pennsylvania Railroad.[87]

Even though he must have been despondent at John Hulme's damning 1858 report on the condition of the Marietta & Cincinnati, Thomson took to heart Hulme's final kernel of advice: "It is utterly useless to afford financial aid to any of the railroads running west from Pittsburgh or Wheeling unless they are first relieved of a great portion of their enormous load of liabilities and then placed under the full control and management of the Pennsylvania Rail Road Company."[88] In the future, Thomson would employ precisely that strategy.

Having failed to capture the Marietta & Cincinnati Railroad's admittedly imperfect route to Cincinnati, Thomson next turned his attention to an even more unlikely prospect, the Springfield, Mt. Vernon & Pittsburgh Railroad. The Ohio legislature had chartered the company in March 1850 as the Springfield & Mansfield Railroad. The ambitions of its incorporators were fairly modest, to build a regional line linking Springfield to Mansfield (where the future Ohio & Pennsylvania route to Crestline connected with the Mansfield & Sandusky City line to Lake Erie), or to a location along the Cleveland, Columbus & Cincinnati Railroad. Less than a year later, an amendment to the company's charter changed the northern terminus to Loudonville, Ohio, or some other point on the Ohio & Pennsylvania Railroad.[89]

The seemingly minor change of destination was more than sufficient to arouse Thomson's interest. By sending traffic from Allegheny City west over the Ohio & Pennsylvania, the proposed line could provide a route south to Springfield. At Springfield, a connection could be made with the Little Miami Railroad for access to Cincinnati. Even though the route was longer than that of the Marietta & Cincinnati, it offered easier grades and broader curves. Accordingly, in January 1853, the shareholders of both the Ohio & Pennsylvania and the Little Miami indicated their willingness to support the project. A few weeks later, at the same time that they purchased $750,000 in Marietta & Cincinnati stock, PRR stockholders agreed to buy $100,000 of Springfield, Mt. Vernon & Pittsburgh shares.[90]

The PRR's contribution to the Springfield, Mt. Vernon & Pittsburgh was a colossal waste of money. The company suspended work in 1854, after completing a line from Delaware, Ohio, southeast to Springfield. When officials again begged the PRR for assistance, Thomson had had enough. In June 1855, the PRR board declined any additional stock subscriptions. Early the following year, however, and even as their counterparts on the Ohio & Pennsylvania board gave up the cause as hopeless, the PRR directors reconsidered. They promised additional aid to the Springfield line, but only if the railroad was in acceptable financial shape. It was not, and by the end of 1856 officials of both the PRR and the Little Miami had concluded that the provision of additional support would be un-

wise. In 1858, the PRR wrote off as worthless its investments in the Springfield, Mt. Vernon & Pittsburgh. Without continued PRR support, the railroad was bankrupt by 1860, and the following year it came under the control of the Cleveland, Columbus & Cincinnati.[91]

Spanning the Panhandle

Some good did come out of the Springfield, Mt. Vernon & Pittsburgh Railroad fiasco, however. The project ultimately enabled the PRR to establish a route almost due west from Pittsburgh, through central Ohio and Indiana and ultimately to St. Louis. Like many of the PRR's western endeavors, the link began with local boosters. Community leaders in Steubenville, Ohio, feared that railroads would soon supplant much of the traffic that moved past their town, along the Ohio River. Steubenville was some sixty-five river miles downstream from Pittsburgh, but only forty miles directly west of that city, and boosters asserted that a rail link between the two communities was destined for success. Their first priority was to push rails westward, toward Columbus and the Indiana border. In February 1848, they received a charter for the Steubenville & Indiana Railroad Company, allowing them to build from Steubenville to the Indiana state line, with the city of Steubenville pledging to subscribe to $100,000 in the company's stock.[92]

Promoters waited until early 1850 to organize the Steubenville & Indiana, with Daniel Kilgore, a banker, judge, and former member of Congress, serving as president. Thomas L. Jewett, a Steubenville attorney and judge, became treasurer and, along with his brother Hugh, was destined to play an important role in the development of Ohio railroads. In an effort to appeal to the PRR, the incorporators ordered the rails laid to standard gauge, rather than the 4′ 10″ Ohio gauge that the legislature had initially specified. Under the leadership of President James Wilson, grandfather of future U.S. President Woodrow Wilson, the company secured additional concessions from the Ohio legislature. They included the right to build to Columbus and, more importantly, to bridge the Ohio River at Steubenville.[93]

As their counterparts on so many other railroads had done, Steubenville & Indiana investors turned to the Pennsylvania Railroad for assistance. Once again, Thomson faced the prospect of aiding a hapless local carrier, rather than risk the possibility that it fall under the control of a rival trunk line. In the fall of 1853, Thomas Jewett asked the PRR board of directors to guarantee a $500,000 bond issue. The members of the Road Committee approved the arrangement but demanded a substantial security deposit—$500,000 in S&I stock, a $1 million indemnity bond, and mortgages on the company's physical plant. In February 1854 the PRR's stockholders gave their assent. The PRR also provided equipment to the Steubenville & Indiana. In 1855, with that assistance, the S&I completed its line between Steubenville and Newark, Ohio.[94]

Initially, Steubenville & Indiana officials planned to continue west toward the Indiana border. The Steubenville & Indiana was undercapitalized, however, and its directors soon contemplated ways to shorten their route. Their opportunity came in the form of the Central Ohio Railroad, the carrier, allied with the B&O, whose executives planned to reach the Ohio River at Bellaire. From Bellaire, the Central Ohio's route extended west through Zanesville and Newark to Columbus. As early as 1851, representatives from the Steubenville & Indiana and the Central Ohio had been attempting to form a cooperative agreement in order to avoid the construction of duplicate lines through eastern Ohio. By 1852, with the support of the Columbus & Xenia Railroad, the Central Ohio had completed its line between Zanesville and Newark, and tracks reached Columbus in early 1853. At the same time, a series of cooperative agreements with officials from the Columbus & Xenia and the Little Miami ensured that traffic could flow south and west to the Ohio River.[95]

The cooperation between the Central Ohio and the Steubenville & Indiana depended on the willingness of the Central Ohio's directors to relocate the eastern terminus from Bellaire north to Steubenville—a decision that would make it far more difficult to connect with the Baltimore & Ohio. Central Ohio officials were not about to let the opportunity of linking to the B&O slip from their grasp, and they proceeded with their original intentions, with construction crews

reaching Bellaire in November 1854. A month later, they nonetheless permitted the Steubenville & Indiana to use their tracks between Newark and Columbus. That conciliatory attitude probably owed a great deal to the substantial investments that the Jewett brothers held in both companies, with Hugh J. Jewett serving as president of the Central Ohio as well as the Little Miami. The physical linking of the tracks of the Central Ohio and the Steubenville & Indiana did not take place until 1857, but thereafter traffic could flow from Steubenville to Columbus—and to Cincinnati, as well, via the Columbus & Xenia/Little Miami route.[96]

More than any other person associated with the Steubenville & Indiana, Thomas Jewett prospered from the PRR's support. He joined the S&I board in August 1854 and became the company's president in June of the following year. Thereafter, he served as the primary liaison between his company and the Pennsylvania Railroad, a position that would become extraordinarily important as Thomson sought to close the final gap in the route to Columbus.

The completion of the Steubenville & Indiana/Central Ohio line to Columbus gave Thomson access to Cincinnati, but nonetheless left the PRR in a vulnerable position in east-central Ohio. On January 1, 1853, the first B&O train arrived in Wheeling and, as expected, that railroad employed the Central Ohio as its western outlet, with connections to Dayton, Cincinnati, and Indianapolis. The absence of a bridge across the Ohio River, between Wheeling and Bellaire, constituted a relatively minor inconvenience. The PRR faced a far bigger gap in its route, the forty miles that separated Pittsburgh and Steubenville.

The PRR was not completely isolated from the Steubenville & Indiana, to be sure. Since the late 1840s, construction crews on the Cleveland & Pittsburgh Rail Road had been laying tracks south from Cleveland to Wellsville, and then east along the Ohio River, reaching Rochester, Pennsylvania, in October 1856. By the end of 1856, the Cleveland & Pittsburgh had constructed a branch line from Wellsville west along the Ohio River, as far south as Bellaire, with service beginning early the following year. In response, and at the insistence of PRR officials, construction crews widened the tracks of the Steubenville & Indiana from standard gauge to Ohio gauge, to match the Cleveland & Pittsburgh. Eastbound traffic could follow the Central Ohio to Newark; the Steubenville & Indiana Mingo Junction (Steubenville); the Cleveland & Pittsburgh to Rochester, Pennsylvania; and the Pittsburgh, Fort Wayne & Chicago (the former Ohio & Pennsylvania) to Allegheny City and PRR tracks at Pittsburgh. The resulting journey was indirect, about twenty-five miles longer than a straight-line route across the Virginia Panhandle.[97]

Building a direct line between Pittsburgh and Steubenville presented few engineering challenges. Nonetheless, more than fifteen years would elapse before trains ran along a route that a reasonably healthy person could cover on foot in two days. The saga began in March 1849, when the Pennsylvania legislature chartered the Pittsburgh & Steubenville Railroad as the eastern extension of the Steubenville & Indiana. Although some construction took place the following year, the project lapsed into obscurity. The incorporation of the Hempfield Railroad in May 1850 jolted Pittsburghers out of their complacency. They had already been bypassed by the B&O and had no desire to see the completion of the Hempfield route, which would run well south of their city. In July 1851, they convened in a desperate effort to develop an alternative to the Hempfield Railroad.[98]

The Pittsburgh boosters soon revived and organized the Pittsburgh & Steubenville. The presidency initially went to Harmar Denny, an attorney, politician, son of the first mayor of Pittsburgh, and nephew of PRR board member William Wilkins. He was soon replaced by James Kennedy Moorhead, a Pittsburgh resident with long experience in transportation and manufacturing. Born in 1806, by 1828 he was superintendent of the Juniata Division Canal. In 1835, he established the first packet boat service to operate on the Main Line of Public Works. During the late 1830s he had been one of the contractors responsible for building the Northern Liberties Bridge across the Allegheny River and then oversaw the construction of the Monongahela Navigation, serving for twenty-one years as that company's president. In 1844 he established the Pittsburgh Brownsville Packet Company in conjunction with George Cass and other investors. He later operated an ironworks, Moorhead & Company, established in 1859,

and he served in Congress and as president of the Atlantic & Ohio Telegraph Company.[99]

Despite the affluence and prominence of Denny, Moorhead, and other investors, work on the Pittsburgh & Steubenville proceeded haphazardly. Beginning in 1853, Allegheny County subscribed to $150,000 in the company's stock, part of an aid package that would eventually reach half a million dollars. The City of Pittsburgh provided an additional $550,000 in assistance. Pennsylvania Railroad officials were less eager to offer support, largely because they had already decided to invest in the Marietta & Cincinnati, and they balked at the additional expenditure. In February 1853, Ohio & Pennsylvania president William Robinson, Jr., failed to persuade his fellow PRR directors to subscribe to $500,000 of Pittsburgh & Steubenville stock. Robinson later appeared to have his doubts as well. By February 1854, he cautioned the PRR board against guaranteeing the bonds of the more westerly Steubenville & Indiana. If that railroad faced such poor prospects and was, as Robinson suggested, likely to default on its obligations, then circumstances did not bode well for the Pittsburgh & Steubenville, either.[100]

Even worse, the organizers of the Pittsburgh & Steubenville lacked the legal authority to build west of the Pennsylvania state line. A narrow strip of land, barely seven miles wide, separated the border from the Ohio River, but crossing it would require the assent of the Virginia legislature. Legislators meeting in far-off Richmond, Virginia, had many reasons to refuse the request. Baltimore & Ohio officials, anxious to protect their westward ambitions, were determined to block the Pittsburgh & Steubenville. Residents of Wheeling, Virginia, opposed the venture on the grounds that the line would bypass their city. They, and others in the eastern part of the state, placed sufficient pressure on the Virginia legislators that they denied a charter for the Pittsburgh & Steubenville.[101]

Given the unwillingness of the Virginia legislature to grant a charter to the organizers of the Pittsburgh & Steubenville, local residents took matters into their own hands. Jesse Edgington was one of the pioneer residents of the Virginia Panhandle region, and his father claimed to have built the first cabin along Ohio's eastern border. The younger Edgington became a lawyer, served as the prosecuting attorney for Brooke

County, Virginia, spent four years in the state Senate, and was a political intimate of Henry Clay of Kentucky. Nathaniel Wells could boast a remarkably similar life story. His grandfather, Richard "Gray Beard" Wells, was a native of Baltimore County, Maryland, who procured a large tract of land in Brooke County. In 1773, after recruiting a party of recently arrived Irish indentured servants, he hacked his way west. His house along the Ohio River was in reality a trading post and a fort, designed to resist attack by Native Americans. In 1799, Wells initiated a ferry service across the Ohio and, in conjunction with a business associate, established the town of Steubenville. In 1836, at the age of twenty-seven, Nathaniel Wells took charge of his grandfather's ferry. He also operated a hotel, a sawmill, a lumberyard, granaries, and warehouses, and speculated in farmlands. Between 1849 and 1852, he too served in the Virginia legislature, representing Brooke and Hancock Counties.[102]

Jesse Edgington and Nathaniel Wells typified the growing restlessness of western Virginians. They desperately sought internal improvements, but confronted an eastern Virginia establishment that cared mainly about the interests of tidewater planters. Given Virginia's limitations on popular voting—far more restrictive than in Pennsylvania—it was unlikely that they could muster the necessary political support from their relatively poor and disenfranchised fellow westerners. Wells was the chief sponsor of repeated efforts to gain a Virginia charter for the Pittsburgh & Steubenville (the issue came up at each legislative session between 1847 and 1853). Each attempt failed, he believed, because his fellow legislators were so outraged at growing northern abolitionist sentiment that they were unwilling to allow Pennsylvanians to build across their native soil.

Unable to secure a charter, Wells and Edgington joined forces to purchase the necessary parcels of land across the Virginia Panhandle. In so doing, they could operate as a private, unincorporated railroad, one that lacked either the benefits or the restrictions associated with common-carrier status. The process was not difficult and involved only thirty-six landowners, most of whom welcomed the prospect of a railroad and were happy to sell at the inflated prices that Edgington and Wells were prepared to offer. The actual funding came from the Pittsburgh & Steubenville Railroad, with that company holding a $300,000 mortgage on the trans-Panhandle line.

Construction began in August 1853, but soon encountered legal difficulties. The Virginia attorney general, in an attempt to halt the work, filed suit against the two entrepreneurs in the Ohio County Circuit Court and in the Brooke County Circuit Court. Edgington and Wells had access to some excellent legal counsel in their own right, and they soon dispensed with the nuisance. They did, however, find it necessary to travel to Richmond to lobby against a bill that would have made the construction of a railroad in Virginia, without a legislative charter, an imprisonable offense.[103]

In 1854, construction crews completed work on the line, logically if unofficially known as the Edgington & Wells Railroad, linking the Pennsylvania state line and the Ohio River. Because the members of the Virginia legislature refused to permit a bridge across the Ohio River to Steubenville, the tracks ended at the water's edge, at the Holliday's Cove ferry landing operated by Jesse Edgington. The Pittsburgh & Steubenville had not yet reached the Pennsylvania/Virginia state line, however, and absent that critical connection, the private railway closed within six months.

During the summer of 1856, Thomson looked with dismay at the efforts of local entrepreneurs to connect Pittsburgh and Columbus. By May 1, construction contractors had abandoned work on the Pittsburgh & Steubenville, having accomplished little. The isolated Edgington & Wells Railroad had failed, and there was no bridge across the Ohio River. The Steubenville & Indiana possessed only an indirect connection to Pittsburgh, and did not even reach the Ohio capital directly. Despite the PRR's $500,000 bond guarantee, it was also in desperate financial shape. Thomson accordingly assigned Tom Scott and William Thaw to bring order out of the wreckage.

The Steubenville & Indiana was perhaps the lowest-hanging fruit. In August 1856, Thomson indicated that the PRR would buy $100,000 in S&I stock in exchange for assurances that that railroad would widen its gauge from standard to the 4' 10" that its Ohio charter had originally specified—and be compatible with both the Cleveland & Pittsburgh and the Pittsburgh, Fort Wayne & Chicago. Such a large investment in a financially precarious company might have seemed unwise, but Thomson was not actually risking any of the Pennsylvania Railroad's money. Instead, he traded the PRR's holdings in the Springfield, Mt. Vernon & Pittsburgh Railroad for a like amount of S&I stock. By that time, Thomson believed that the combined S&I/Central Ohio route to Columbus was far superior to the hapless Springfield, Mt. Vernon & Pittsburgh. If that carrier should fall into the hands of a rival railroad, then so be it—and it did in fact later become part of the New York Central—but Thomson had chosen his champion. The PRR's equity stake in the S&I enabled Thomson to demand Scott's appointment as a director and as a vice president of that company. Thus empowered, Scott proceeded to destroy the company that his superior had so recently supported. He poured money into new construction and betterments—extravagantly and needlessly so, according to his critics—and authorized other questionable expenditures. Absent the completion of the connection between Pittsburgh and Steubenville, the company could rely only on local traffic, and there was precious little of that. A casualty of the Panic of 1857, the Steubenville & Indiana went bankrupt in 1859, and PRR executives soon picked up the pieces.[104]

Thomson proceeded to demonstrate that a railroad bankruptcy was not necessarily a bad thing. Under the terms of the December 1853 agreement to endorse the Steubenville & Indiana's bonds, the PRR had received liens on the railroad's entire right-of-way, from Steubenville to Newark. When the S&I defaulted, the PRR in effect owned that company.[105]

Thomson's control over the Steubenville & Indiana counted for little so long as the gap remained between Steubenville and Pittsburgh. In the spring of 1856, the PRR president oversaw the incorporation of the Western Transportation Company in order to see the Pittsburgh & Steubenville through to completion. Its officers were all closely tied to the PRR, including Thomson, Herman J. Lombaert, Thomas S. Clarke, Henry H. Houston, Joseph D. Potts, and Thomson's personal secretary, William Jackson Palmer. The individuals bought 165 shares of Western Transportation stock, at $1,000 a share, although the money undoubtedly came from the PRR's treasury. Grading resumed in October, but halted again the following February. The PRR had been regularly contributing money to

the Pittsburgh & Steubenville in exchange for third mortgage bonds, and in April 1857, board members agreed to a further loan of $50,000. The additional support revived the company. In August, work began on a bridge across the Monongahela River at Pittsburgh, and by the end of December the Western Transportation Company had secured a new construction contractor. Thomson's problems were far from over, however. The decade-long evolution of the Pittsburgh & Steubenville, involving the failure of two construction contractors and disputes between local and PRR interests, triggered lawsuits that delayed construction until December 1862.[106]

During 1863, Thomson signaled his indication to finally complete the link between Pittsburgh and Steubenville. He allocated $160,000 to the Pittsburgh & Steubenville, as provided by the terms of the March 1861 Commutation Act, which abolished the commonwealth's tonnage tax on PRR freight. The PRR board also purchased most of the shares in the Western Transportation Company from the original, PRR-allied investors, ensuring Thomson direct control over the project. Delays and difficulties continued nonetheless. Legislators in the General Assembly issued a special dispensation, enabling construction crews to tunnel through Grants Hill, on the south side of the city, and underneath a church. Pittsburgh officials attempted to prevent the completion of the mile-long Steubenville Extension, the easternmost portion of the line that crossed the Monongahela River to a connection with the PRR's tracks in the center of the city. The Pennsylvania Supreme Court resolved the issue in favor of the Pennsylvania Railroad, and by October 1865, both the Monongahela River Bridge and the remainder of the route were in service.[107]

Fortunately for the PRR, Thomson had little difficulty resolving the issues associated with building across the Virginia Panhandle. In August 1856, the Pittsburgh & Steubenville had purchased the Edgington & Wells Railroad for $100,000. On March 30, 1860, and in order to complete the route across Virginia, Thaw and his associates at Western Transportation secured a charter for the Holliday's Cove Railroad to rebuild the Edgington & Wells Railroad and, more importantly, complete a bridge across the Ohio River. Virginia legislators abandoned their earlier opposition to the PRR route across the Panhandle and to the bridge at Steubenville. In return, they demanded assurances that, prior to the completion of the Pittsburgh & Steubenville, the Western Transportation Company would build an extension south to Wheeling and a bridge across the Ohio River at that location—hence, the incorporation of the Wheeling Railroad Bridge Company on March 31.[108]

Thomson had little interest in underwriting the construction of the Wheeling Bridge—a structure that would be useful primarily to the B&O—before he could open the line through Steubenville. Some time earlier, in the spring of 1858, he had instructed Scott to secure the assistance of Senator Simon Cameron, always a loyal supporter of the PRR. In July 1862, Cameron sponsored legislation that declared the proposed Steubenville Bridge, and others along the Ohio River, part of the federal system of post roads, removing the matter from the jurisdiction of the Virginia legislature. By that time, Virginia had seceded from the Union, and counties in the western part of the state had in turn seceded from Virginia. Even before the region gained statehood, in June 1863, the provisional government of West Virginia had abandoned opposition to a rail line across the Panhandle—emblematic of the accelerated development of the region's internal improvements that took place after the influence of eastern planters had been silenced. In January 1863, the West Virginia legislature allowed construction to proceed on the Steubenville Bridge, regardless of the progress made on its downstream counterpart at Wheeling. By October 1865, the first trains crossed the Ohio River at Steubenville, giving the PRR unfettered access to a direct route between Pittsburgh and Columbus.[109]

During and immediately following the Civil War, Thomson and other PRR executives took steps to ensure that the Pittsburgh & Steubenville and the Holliday's Cove were organizationally and operationally integrated with the Steubenville & Indiana and with the rest of the PRR system. By 1863, the PRR had secured ownership of the Pittsburgh & Steubenville and presided over that company's default on its first mortgage bonds, in August 1865, and the orderly bankruptcy that followed. In November 1867, PRR assistant secretary William J. Howard (who would soon be named the PRR's general solicitor) purchased the line for $1.96 million. In January 1868, Howard and his PRR associates in turn transferred the Pittsburgh & Steubenville to a shell organization, the Pan Handle Railway Company. In May, the PRR merged the Pan Handle, the Holliday's Cove, and the Steubenville & Indiana into the Pittsburgh, Cincinnati & St. Louis Railway, commonly referred to as the "Pan Handle" route.[110]

Those corporate reorganizations did little to affect the operation of through trains over the line between Pittsburgh and Columbus. Thomas Jewett, the onetime president and then receiver of the Steubenville & Indiana, appears to have been the primary coordinator. With the completion of the Steubenville Bridge in October 1865, Jewett oversaw the operations of both the S&I and the Western Transportation Company (Pittsburgh & Steubenville and Holliday's Cove) properties. In tandem with the Columbus & Xenia Railroad and the Little Miami Railroad, he was able to advertise through service between Pittsburgh and Cincinnati, by way of Steubenville and Columbus. By the late 1860s, the PRR had invested $5.6 million in its share of the through route between Pittsburgh and Columbus. That link would soon assume much greater importance as local railway entrepreneurs continued to build lines through western Ohio and into Indiana.[111]

From One State Capital to Another

Indianapolis, due west of Columbus, Ohio, offered another tempting target for the Pennsylvania Railroad, as well as the possibility of extensions farther west to St. Louis, north to Chicago, and south to Louisville. Prior to the Civil War, however, PRR officials were hesitant to provide financial assistance, either in the form of stock purchases or bond guarantees, as they had for the lines east of Columbus. That reluctance accordingly gave greater license to local promoters and their efforts to build small transportation empires. Their autonomy would eventually create some difficulties for the PRR, but generally not until well after the war ended. Fifty or so companies contributed to the development of the PRR network west of Columbus. Given the relative absence of direct PRR involvement, as well as the extraordinary complexity of the corporate histories of all these carriers, the following is merely a brief overview.

The Columbus, Piqua & Indiana Railroad formed the principal link from Columbus west to the Indiana border. In February 1849, the Ohio legislature granted the company a charter to build a standard-gauge line from the capital through Urbana, due west to the Indiana line. William Neil, the largest investor, was also heavily involved in the Columbus & Xenia, the Cleveland, Columbus & Cincinnati, and other area railroads. In 1851, an amendment to the CP&I charter permitted Neil and his associates to modify the route west of Covington, Ohio, running northwesterly to Union City, Indiana. There, CP&I officials intended to connect with the Indianapolis & Bellefontaine Railroad, a standard-gauge line chartered in May 1848 that would provide a route southwest to Indianapolis. Under the terms of a June 1852 agreement, the two railroads would offer through service between Indianapolis and Columbus, with the Steubenville & Indiana carrying traffic east to the Ohio River, without a break of gauge. In January 1854, the directors of the Steubenville & Indiana (having already abandoned their own intentions to build west to Indiana) recommended that shareholders endorse a CP&I bond issue, provided that their PRR counterparts made the same guarantee.[112]

Thomson appreciated the value of the route to Indianapolis, but he was unwilling to provide much help to the Columbus, Piqua & Indiana. PRR officials spoke favorably of the road's prospects, encouraging more than a hundred Philadelphians to purchase that company's bonds. Yet, when Neil and his associates asked the PRR for a loan, the members of the railroad's Finance Committee declined their support. In February 1854, the PRR directors also resoundingly rejected the proposed Steubenville & Indiana guarantee of CP&I bonds.[113]

Absent PRR assistance, the CP&I suffered severe financial distress before temporarily falling into the distant orbit of the New York Central. The Cleveland, Painesville & Ashtabula, the NYC's primary western outlet, made a friendly connection at Cleveland with the CC&C line to Columbus. At Galion, Ohio, a few miles to the south of Crestline, the CC&C connected with the Bellefontaine & Indiana Railroad, an Ohio-gauge line running southwest to Union City, where it connected with the standard-gauge Indianapolis &

Bellefontaine Railroad. The route between Cleveland and Indianapolis entered service in August 1853, but the gauge break at Union City retarded its effectiveness. At that time, the Columbus, Piqua & Indiana line, from Union City southeast to Columbus, was far from completion. Despite the terms of the 1852 agreement with the CP&I, the directors of the Indianapolis & Bellefontaine soon changed their tracks from standard gauge to Ohio gauge to match those of the Bellefontaine & Indiana and the Cleveland, Columbus & Cincinnati. In February 1855, the Indianapolis & Bellefontaine (the Indiana company) changed its name to the Indianapolis, Pittsburgh & Cleveland Railroad. By the following year, the two companies were effectively operating as one between Galion and Indianapolis, over a route frequently referred to as the "Bee Line."[114]

During the development of the Bee Line route between Galion and Indianapolis, the Columbus, Piqua & Indiana largely fell by the wayside. The CP&I's investors struggled to complete their tracks to Union City, giving little indication that their railroad would be of any practical use to the PRR. When the directors of the Indianapolis & Bellefontaine elected to convert their line from standard gauge to Ohio gauge, the CP&I was bereft of a same-gauge connection at its western terminus. During the autumn of 1853, CP&I personnel filed a lawsuit against the Indianapolis & Bellefontaine but failed to prevent the conversion from taking place.[115]

Far from preventing the Indianapolis & Bellefontaine from being drawn into the Cleveland orbit, the CP&I was itself brought into the Ohio-gauge camp. In February 1854, only a week after the PRR board rejected the bond guarantee package first proposed by Steubenville & Indiana officials, the directors of the CP&I threw in their lot with William Neil and his son-in-law, William Dennison, Jr. Neil was well known to PRR officials, and Dennison would eventually become a key player in Thomson's efforts to control railroads in Ohio and Indiana. Born in 1815, Dennison began to practice law in 1840, and he soon became a successful entrepreneur—even more so when he married the daughter of one of the wealthiest and most influential residents of Columbus. Dennison was president of the Exchange Bank in Columbus and of the Columbus & Xenia Railroad. He was elected to the state senate in 1848, was one of the first to abandon the Whig Party in favor of the Republicans, and in 1859 capped his political career with election to the governor's office. Given his business and political connections, Dennison would prove of immense value for the PRR.[116]

Even though Dennison would later be an ally of Thomson and Scott, his involvement in the Columbus, Piqua & Indiana was distinctly antithetical to the PRR's interests. Dennison and Neil pledged to complete the CP&I in exchange for a combination of cash and CP&I bonds, guaranteed by three railroads in which they held substantial investments—the Cleveland, Columbus & Cincinnati, the Bellefontaine & Indiana, and the Indianapolis & Bellefontaine. In accepting the arrangement, CP&I directors agreed to widen their tracks to match those of the Indianapolis & Bellefontaine. That decision merely transferred the gauge break from Union City to Columbus, ensuring that the PRR's allied (and standard-gauge) Steubenville & Indiana would be unable to easily dispatch through freight west of that point. Instead, CP&I freight would move eastward over the Ohio-gauge Central Ohio Railroad to Bellaire, where it would be handed over to the B&O.[117]

Despite the potential loss of traffic to the B&O, Thomson and the PRR board were nonetheless wise to minimize their direct involvement with the CP&I. In October 1855, the still-incomplete CP&I went bankrupt, saddling the CC&C with the cost of the bond guarantee and reducing the value of its CP&I stock effectively to zero. In February 1856, a new slate of directors took charge of the reorganized CP&I, including such familiar names as William Neil and the Steubenville & Indiana's Thomas Jewett. Also on the board was Benjamin E. Smith, a prominent Columbus banker and railroad contractor who was involved in a great many projects, mainly to the south and west of the state capital.[118]

During the summer of 1858, John Brough, a newspaper editor and future governor of Ohio, emerged victorious in the battle to gain control of the CP&I. Brough was president of both the Indianapolis, Pittsburgh & Cleveland (the former Indianapolis & Bellefontaine) and the Bellefontaine & Indiana, and the CP&I seemed a logical extension to his empire. Brough

pushed the CP&I through to completion in the spring of 1859. His interests lay more with the New York Central–affiliated Cleveland, Painesville & Ashtabula Railroad than with the PRR, however, as symbolized by his decision to move from Cincinnati to Cleveland shortly before the Civil War.[119]

Aside from its financial difficulties, the principal problem associated with the Columbus, Piqua & Indiana was that it offered at best an indirect route between Columbus and Indianapolis, with a looping detour north to Union City. Efforts to develop a more convenient link between the two capitals typified the complexity associated with early midwestern railway development.

The Indiana Central Railway provided a direct line from the state line at Richmond west to Indianapolis. The origins of that carrier dated to January 1847, when Terre Haute, Indiana, entrepreneur Chauncey Rose oversaw the incorporation of the Terre Haute & Richmond Rail Road. A successful miller and real estate speculator, Rose had long sought improved transportation for his community, located near Indiana's western border. He proposed to build east, through Greencastle and Indianapolis, and on to Richmond. Given the magnitude of the task, it was hardly surprising that barely a year elapsed before Rose and his associates curtailed their ambitions and divided the project into two sections. In 1849 Rose began construction on the line between Terre Haute and Indianapolis, the Terre Haute & Richmond. In May 1850, residents of eastern Indiana incorporated the Terre Haute & Richmond Railroad (east of Indianapolis), to build between the state capital and the Ohio border. The following January, they dropped the cumbersome title in favor of the Indiana Central Railway. A month later, the Ohio legislature permitted the Indiana Central to pool its efforts with the Dayton & Western Railroad, a company chartered in February 1846. By 1854, the Indiana Central route was open, permitting through service between Indianapolis and Richmond, with the Dayton & Western, completed in October 1853, carrying traffic east to Dayton.[120]

At Dayton, a number of transportation alternatives were available, but the most important was the Cincinnati, Hamilton & Dayton Railroad, the second carrier to enter Cincinnati from the north. By September 1851, the CH&D spanned the sixty miles separating Cincinnati and Dayton, where it made a connection with the Springfield & Dayton Railroad and its northern continuation, the Mad River & Lake Erie Railroad route leading to Sandusky. As such, the CH&D was an integral part of the more westerly route between the Ohio River and Lake Erie, in competition with the Little Miami/Columbus & Xenia/Cleveland, Columbus & Cincinnati chain that ran farther to the east.[121]

The Cincinnati, Hamilton & Dayton route offered a number of important connections with other railroads. As such, the representatives of that short carrier attempted to extend their influence west into Indiana and they were in turn courted by executives from several of the eastern trunk lines. At Dayton, the Dayton, Xenia & Belpre Railroad, incorporated in 1851 and opened in June 1854, covered the short distance east to Xenia. Despite its small size, Xenia was an important rail hub, with the Little Miami Railroad offering service to Cincinnati and the Columbus & Xenia Railroad heading northeasterly to Columbus and (via the CC&C) to Cleveland. A more significant connection was at Hamilton, midway between Dayton and Cincinnati. The Cincinnati, Hamilton & Dayton was closely allied with a chain of railroads that stretched from Hamilton north and west toward Chicago. The Eaton & Hamilton Railroad, incorporated in February 1847, possessed the authority to build from Hamilton to Eaton, Ohio, and thence to Neels, on the Indiana border. In Indiana, investors in the even shorter Richmond & Miami Railroad received a January 1846 charter to connect the western terminus of the Eaton & Hamilton, at the Ohio/Indiana border with Richmond, Indiana. By the summer of 1853, both routes were in service, with the Eaton & Hamilton possessing trackage rights on the Cincinnati, Hamilton & Dayton south into Cincinnati. The following year, the Richmond & Miami was merged into the Eaton & Hamilton, temporarily losing its corporate identity.[122]

Despite the rich array of railroads that crisscrossed southeastern Indiana and southwestern Ohio, there was still no direct route between Indianapolis and Columbus. The Indiana Central spanned half the distance, but it lacked an Ohio counterpart that would carry traffic east to Columbus. The traffic demands associated with the Civil War led to a rapid resolution of that situation. In March 1862, Greenville, Ohio, attorney Evan Baker joined forces with William Dennison, Benjamin E. Smith, and others associated with the Columbus, Piqua & Indiana and the Indiana Central. They incorporated the Richmond & Covington Railroad, designed to link the Columbus, Piqua & Indiana at Bradford with the Indiana state line, just west of New Paris, Ohio. The new line enabled traffic to flow between Columbus and Indianapolis by way of Richmond, without dependence on the Indianapolis, Pittsburgh & Cleveland/Bellefontaine & Indiana "Bee Line" connection at Union City. By the end of 1863, Dennison and Smith had reorganized the Columbus, Piqua & Indiana as the Columbus & Indianapolis Railroad, and the newly constituted company devoted substantial resources to the completion of the Richmond & Covington. Construction presented few difficulties, and the route between Bradford and New Paris entered service in 1863. The Richmond & Miami Rail*road* of 1846, which had been folded into the Eaton & Hamilton eight years later, reappeared in the guise of the Richmond & Miami Rail*way*, as the reorganized Indiana portion of the Eaton & Hamilton. The reborn company constructed a short branch between New Paris and Richmond, completing the direct link between Columbus and Indianapolis.[123]

The growing influence of the Erie Railway in Ohio soon tightened the bonds linking many of the area's railroads.[124] During the fall of 1863, the broad-gauge Atlantic & Great Western Railroad, the Erie's primary western connection, employed the Cincinnati, Hamilton & Dayton as an entrance into Cincinnati. By the summer of 1864, after construction crews laid a third rail on the Cincinnati, Hamilton & Dayton, the Erie and its western allies possessed a uniform-gauge route between Jersey City and East St. Louis, beating the PRR and other rival trunk lines to that vital western gateway. The Atlantic & Great Western endured chronic financial difficulties, and in 1869 it failed in its attempts to lease the Cincinnati, Hamilton & Dayton.

The short-lived alliance between the Atlantic & Great Western and the Cincinnati, Hamilton & Dayton nonetheless induced a new round of construction and consolidations, with Benjamin Smith managing much of that process. In January 1864, officials representing the Indiana Central, the Richmond & Covington, and the Columbus & Indianapolis created the "Great Central Line," with service between Columbus and Indianapolis, by way of the Columbus & Indianapolis to Bradford, the Richmond & Covington to New Paris, the Richmond & Miami to Richmond, and the Indiana Central west from there—thus reducing the former Columbus, Piqua & Indiana Union City main line to the status of a branch, west of Bradford.[125] The operating agreements soon became a more formal consolidation. In June 1864, officials representing the Columbus & Indianapolis agreed to purchase the Richmond & Covington. That autumn, the Columbus & Indianapolis and the Indiana Central merged to form the Columbus & Indianapolis Central Railway, with Smith as the company's first president.[126]

Southern Routes to Chicago

Even as he was consolidating the carriers linking Columbus and Indianapolis, Benjamin Smith was working to develop a route from central Ohio north and west to Chicago, in competition with George Cass's Pittsburgh, Fort Wayne & Chicago. During the late 1860s, Smith negotiated a complex series of lease agreements and bond guarantees that brought a chain of Ohio and Indiana railroads rather tenuously under his control and laid the foundations for what later became the southwestern portion of the Pennsylvania Railroad's Lines West of Pittsburgh and Erie. Unfortunately, he built his empire on a structure of generally weak railroads, achieving his vision through extraordinarily creative financing. He created a morass that would for decades plague the efforts of PRR executives to bring stability to those companies.

Logansport, Indiana, was the nexus of Smith's plans to gain access to the western gateways of Chicago and Keokuk, Iowa. The process of linking Richmond to Logansport began in February 1848, with the incorporation of the New Castle & Richmond Railroad. The company's president, Wayne County merchant John T. Elliott, and his associates initially planned to build from Richmond, northwest to New Castle, but soon secured a charter amendment extending the route to Lafayette and a junction with the north–south Lafayette & Indianapolis Railroad. Construction on the New Castle &

Richmond began in 1851, but proceeded slowly. In February 1853, the company became the Cincinnati, Logansport & Chicago Railway, with its destination correspondingly changed from Lafayette to the more northerly community of Logansport. There, promoters hoped to connect with the Logansport & Pacific Railway, which would carry traffic farther west, to the Illinois state line.[127] The route between Richmond and New Castle opened in December 1853, but construction on the remainder of the line soon faltered.[128]

In October 1854, the Cincinnati, Logansport & Chicago merged into the Cincinnati & Chicago Railroad. The new company's president, Caleb B. Smith, an Indiana attorney, journalist, and politician, was able to attract additional financing.[129] In July 1857, Cincinnati & Chicago construction crews completed the route between Richmond and Logansport. Like so many other companies, the Cincinnati & Chicago fell victim to the Panic of 1857, going bankrupt the following year. Smith relinquished the railroad's presidency in 1859 and would soon become Abraham Lincoln's secretary of the interior. The railroad itself emerged from receivership in July 1860, as the Cincinnati & Chicago Air-Line Railroad.[130]

At Logansport, the Cincinnati & Chicago Air-Line connected with the Chicago & Cincinnati Railroad, a company incorporated in September 1857, to build between Logansport and a junction with the Pittsburgh, Fort Wayne & Chicago at Valparaiso, Indiana. The company's first president was John W. Wright, a Logansport attorney, judge, banker, and speculator who would later become heavily involved in the Kansas Pacific Railway. Construction began in 1858, and the route opened in 1861. The completion of a bridge across the Wabash River at Logansport (in September 1861) permitted through service between Cincinnati and Chicago, over a series of closely allied railroads, led by the Cincinnati, Hamilton & Dayton and also including the Eaton & Hamilton, the Richmond & Miami, the Cincinnati & Chicago Air-Line, the Chicago & Cincinnati, and the Fort Wayne.

In June 1863, New York investors established the Chicago & Great Eastern Railway, originally intending to build between Logansport and the Illinois state line. They soon acquired the charter of the Galena & Illinois River Railroad, which would have permitted them to continue west to the Mississippi River, at Galena, Illinois. The promoters of the Chicago & Great Eastern soon approached James McHenry, a London banker who was the principal backer of the broad-gauge Atlantic & Great Western. They hoped that McHenry would use the Chicago & Great Eastern as the western outlet for the Atlantic & Great Western (and, by extension, the Erie), giving those two companies access to Chicago. By that time, however, the Erie and the Atlantic & Great Western were firmly allied with the Cincinnati, Hamilton & Dayton, and the two broad-gauge roads could rely on that company's connections through Richmond and Logansport to Valparaiso and Chicago.

After failing to reach an accord with the Atlantic & Great Western, the New Yorkers who controlled the Chicago & Great Eastern joined forces with the carriers allied with the Cincinnati, Hamilton & Dayton that operated the route between Cincinnati and Valparaiso. The process of consolidation began in January 1865, when the owners of the Chicago & Cincinnati first mortgage bonds agreed to exchange their holdings for Chicago & Great Eastern securities. Soon afterward, investors in the Cincinnati & Chicago Air-Line agreed to merge their company into the Chicago & Great Eastern. By March, the completion of the Chicago & Great Eastern route between La Crosse and Chicago enabled the abandonment of the section of Chicago & Cincinnati track between La Crosse and the junction with the Fort Wayne, at Valparaiso. In May, the Chicago & Cincinnati joined the Air-Line as part of the enlarged Chicago & Great Eastern.[131]

By the autumn of 1864, Ben Smith had consolidated the route between Columbus and Indianapolis (as the Columbus & Indianapolis Central Railway), and he looked for new worlds to conquer. His entrepreneurial spirit encouraged him to find a use for the tracks between Bradford and Union City, built by the Columbus, Piqua & Indiana, and now controlled by that company's successor, the Columbus & Indianapolis Railroad. The construction of the Richmond & Covington had relegated the route to the status of a little-used branch. As a mere branch line, the rump end of the old CP&I possessed little value, but it angled tantalizingly in the direction of Logansport and Chicago.

In his efforts to reach Chicago, Smith took advantage of the work of earlier entrepreneurs. In January 1853, Judge John M. Wallace had presided over the incorporation of the Marion & Mississinewa Valley Railroad, intending to build between Union City and Marion, Indiana. Like most prewar midwestern railroad entrepreneurs, Wallace was determined to improve transportation and stimulate economic development in his community. He was also politically well connected—his brother was Indiana governor David Wallace, and his nephew was Lewis "Lew" Wallace, who later served as governor of the New Mexico Territory and is perhaps best remembered as the author of *Ben Hur*. By June 1853, Judge Wallace and his fellow investors had persuaded the directors of the Columbus, Piqua & Indiana to operate the line to Marion as an extension of their route from Columbus to Union City. The interested parties had also determined to extend the line from Marion, northwest to Chicago. Logansport made a logical intermediate destination—hence the incorporation of the Marion & Logansport Railroad, organized in April 1853, which was folded into the Marion & Mississinewa Valley some eighteen months later. The project lagged for nearly a decade, however, during which time it seemed that Union City was destined to be the end of the line for the Columbus, Piqua & Indiana.[132]

In January 1863, James H. Goodman attempted to revive the Marion & Mississinewa Valley route, but—as so often happened in that part of the Midwest—Benjamin Smith ultimately attained control. A native of Marion, Ohio, Goodman had been the president of the defunct Marion & Mississinewa Valley and a director of the Bellefontaine & Indiana. He incorporated the Union & Logansport Railroad and served as its first president, intending to complete the line from Union City to Logansport. In May 1866, his company awarded Smith the contract to lay rails to the northwest of Union City. With the completion of the Chicago & Great Eastern route between Richmond and Chicago, there was little reason to build a duplicate line between Logansport and Chicago. Construction crews accordingly laid tracks only as far as a connection with the Chicago & Great Eastern at Anoka Junction, a few miles southeast of Logansport.[133]

From Logansport, a valuable branch stretched due west to the Illinois border at State Line, a location later known as Effner, Indiana. The route's origins dated to March 1853 and the incorporation of the ambitiously named Logansport & Pacific Railway, with Logansport merchant William Chase serving as the company's first president. From the Indiana border, the Peoria & Oquawka Railroad was to extend the tracks into Illinois, creating a route to the west that would bypass Chicago.[134] During the next few years, the Logansport & Pacific went through multiple reorganizations, with attendant changes in name. Tracklaying began in July 1859 under the corporate title of the Toledo, Logansport & Burlington Railroad, and the route between Logansport and State Line opened to traffic by the end of the year. The near-simultaneous completion of the Peoria & Oquawka enabled traffic to continue west to the Mississippi River, opposite Burlington, Iowa. In May 1858, the sponsors of the Indiana portion of the project (at that point named the Logansport, Peoria & Burlington Railway) attempted to sell some of the company's bonds to the Pennsylvania Railroad. The PRR board "respectfully declined"—which was probably just as well, as the successor company entered bankruptcy in December 1860.[135]

By September 1867, Benjamin Smith was poised to assemble all of the elements associated with his plan to link Ohio with the west, at Chicago and Keokuk. Using the Columbus & Indianapolis Central Railway as a nucleus, Smith added by merger the Union & Logansport Railroad and the Toledo, Logansport & Burlington Railway, forming the Columbus & Indiana Central Railway. Although construction would not be completed until March 1868, its tracks would soon stretch from Columbus through Union City and Anoka Junction (Logansport) and then west to State Line. Another route, to Indianapolis, diverted from the Logansport line at Bradford, Ohio, before continuing southwest to Richmond, Indiana, and on to the state capital.[136]

Only a few months later, in February 1868, Smith's corporate fiefdom expanded still further. After the New York promoters of the Chicago & Great Eastern Railway failed to join forces with the Atlantic & Great Western, they were willing to sell Smith their company, and the Ohio financier soon merged it with the Columbus & Indiana Central Railway. The resulting company, the Columbus, Chicago & Indiana Central Railway, gave Smith access to Indianapolis by way of Bradford and Richmond, two parallel routes to Logansport, and tracks from there due west to State Line and northwest to Chicago.[137]

In a remarkably short time, Benjamin Smith had welded together a railroad empire that appeared impressive, but that was built on a foundation of sand. He had orchestrated the mergers largely through the swapping of securities and the provision of bond guarantees, and it would take a legion of attorneys several decades to determine who owned precisely what portions of the system. Furthermore, he presided over a ramshackle line with poor-quality roadbed and a continual shortage of equipment. For the moment, Smith and the Columbus, Chicago & Indiana Central offered Thomson and his fellow Pennsylvania Railroad executives a useful mechanism to collect and distribute traffic through Ohio and Indiana. Smith was by no means loyal to the PRR, however, if for no other reason than that shippers along his lines demanded the best and cheapest access to the east coast, particularly New York—a city that Thomson's company did not yet serve directly. Within a short time, therefore, Thomson would have little choice other than to bring Benjamin Smith and his railroad more decisively under PRR control.

Indianapolis to St. Louis

During the 1830s, Indiana legislators were zealous in their efforts to employ public policy in the furtherance of better transportation and economic development. During the 1831–32 legislative session, they chartered eight railroads in various parts of the state. As was the case in Pennsylvania, at about the same time, local boosters demanded transportation arteries through their communities, with scant regard for the development of a comprehensive and integrated statewide system. The politicized nature of Indiana's internal improvements was reflected in the near-simultaneous chartering of lines to Lawrenceburg and Jeffersonville, a product of the strong commercial rivalry between the two river towns.

Investors in some of the earliest Indiana rail lines were anxious to connect the state capital with the Ohio River. They favored two routes, and began work on both in 1832. The promoters of the Lawrenceburg & Indianapolis Railroad, incorporated in February 1832, promised to build from Indianapolis to the river town of Lawrenceburg, in the southeastern corner of the state, within striking distance of Cincinnati.[138] The pathetic wood-rail and horse-carriage line made scant progress, and took more than two decades to reach its destination. Indianans hoped for better results from the Ohio & Indianapolis Railroad. The company's promoters, who obtained their charter only one day after their Lawrenceburg rivals, intended to lay rails almost due south to Jeffersonville, across the river from Louisville.[139]

Many residents of Indianapolis opposed both routes, however, on the grounds that they would enrich the already booming cities of Louisville (across the Ohio River from Jeffersonville) and Cincinnati (just upriver from Lawrenceburg), at the expense of the state capital. They accordingly pinned their hopes on a compromise route that would reach the Ohio River at the small community of Madison, about midway between Lawrenceburg and Jeffersonville. In February 1832, they too chartered a new company, the Madison, Indianapolis & Lafayette Railroad. The project lay dormant for several years, until the passage of the Mammoth Internal Improvement Act in January 1836. By March, the members of the newly constituted Indiana Board of Internal Improvements had elected to pursue the compromise route to the Ohio River. Topographical considerations precluded canal construction, so they agreed to an initial expenditure of $1.3 million in state funds to construct the railroad, now publically owned, and renamed the Madison & Indianapolis Railroad in 1838 to better reflect its intended route. Work began in September 1837, but soon encountered a serious problem. The town of Madison lay at the base of a high bluff overlooking the Ohio River, requiring the use of an inclined plane, similar to the ones employed on each end of the Philadelphia & Columbia. From the floor of the Ohio River Valley, trains traveled 7,012 feet, on a 5.89 percent grade, rising 413 vertical feet to the level of the relatively flat land that lay to the north.[140]

Despite the difficulties associated with the Madison incline (which required nearly five years to complete), construction proceeded apace. On November 28, 1838, Indiana Governor David Wallace celebrated the opening of the first portion of the line. Work ground to a halt in November 1839, owing to the state's financial problems, and by the summer of 1842 the state legislature had agreed to privatize the line, along with most of the rest of Indiana's public works. In February 1843, the incorporators of the now-private Madison & Indianapolis Railroad took control. They received quite a bargain, paying little more than $65,000 for a railroad that had cost the state more than $1.6 million. The new owners experienced considerable difficulty in securing financing, but by 1847 the entire route was complete. Regular service began the following January on what would become, by date of incorporation, the oldest segment of the Pennsylvania Railroad west of the Appalachians.[141]

Even before the Madison & Indianapolis Railroad opened for service, critics were deploring the line's poor construction, as well as its lack of access to Louisville. In January 1846, the Indiana legislature resurrected the 1832 charter of the Ohio & Indianapolis Railroad. The company, subsequently renamed the Jeffersonville Railroad, had by the fall of 1852 completed a sixty-seven-mile line linking Jeffersonville to the Madison & Indianapolis main line at Columbus, Indiana. The owners of the Jeffersonville Railroad soon made plans to continue north to Indianapolis, paralleling the much weaker Madison & Indianapolis virtually the entire distance.[142] Officials from the two companies soon worked out a settlement, permitting joint operation of the existing line north of Columbus, Indiana. In June 1866, the two companies merged into the Jeffersonville, Madison & Indianapolis Railroad, with the route due south from the state capital continuing to carry most of the traffic.[143]

In 1847, the same year that the Madison & Indianapolis Railroad completed its link between the Ohio River and the state capital, Terre Haute entrepreneur Chauncey Rose organized the Terre Haute & Richmond Rail Road. Rose, who served as the company's first president, was determined to ensure that his western Indiana hometown would be on a rail line connecting the east coast to St. Louis. In 1850, as noted earlier, he curtailed his ambitions by calving off the Terre Haute & Richmond Railroad (east of Indianapolis), soon to be renamed the Indiana Central Railway. That separation left Rose free to concentrate his efforts in the western part of the state. In February 1852, the company completed tracklaying between Terre Haute and Indianapolis, where freight and passengers would soon be able to reach the Ohio River via the Madison & Indianapolis or the Jeffersonville Railroad. From Indianapolis, Terre Haute residents could also reach Columbus, Ohio, via the Indiana Central and the Columbus, Piqua & Indiana; Cincinnati via the Indiana Central, the Dayton & Western and other carriers; and Cleveland via the Bee Line.[144]

Rose controlled a railroad that acted as the neck of a funnel, accommodating traffic from the PRR, the New York Central, the B&O, and their Ohio affiliates, and directing it toward St. Louis. The Terre Haute & Richmond nonetheless required a reliable western outlet that would allow traffic to continue west to that gateway city. Rose initially sought an alliance with the Mississippi & Atlantic Railroad, which commercial interests in southern Illinois had incorporated in August 1850. John Brough, who at various times had served as the president of the Madison & Indianapolis, the Indianapolis & Bellefontaine, and the Steubenville & Indiana, was one of the staunchest supporters of the proposed link from Terre Haute to St. Louis.[145] Chicagoans objected bitterly to the thought that the railroad might draw traffic away from their city, and to St. Louis and New Orleans. They repeatedly delayed the chartering of the Mississippi & Atlantic, whose supporters succeeded only after the passage of an Illinois general railway incorporation law in November 1849. Even then, the railroad's opponents hired a crack team of attorneys, including Abraham Lincoln, to fight the Mississippi & Atlantic charter, all the way to the state supreme court. Thanks in large measure to the spirited opposition, the supporters of the Mississippi & Atlantic were never able to complete their railroad.[146]

Temporarily stymied by the Mississippi & Atlantic's legal battles, Rose oversaw the construction of the Evansville & Crawfordsville Railroad, due south from

Terre Haute. By October 1854, that carrier linked Terre Haute and Vincennes, Indiana, providing a connection with the Ohio & Mississippi Rail Road. By July 1855, despite the efforts of many of the same interests that continued to oppose the Mississippi & Atlantic, the owners of the Ohio & Mississippi were able to connect Vincennes to Illinoistown (East St. Louis). Although there was a break-of-bulk point at Vincennes, where the Evansville & Crawfordsville met the broad-gauge Ohio & Mississippi, eastern traffic could now flow directly to St. Louis, through Indianapolis and Terre Haute.[147]

The indirect route to St. Louis was not what Rose had in mind, and he soon sought better access to the Mississippi River. He obtained it, ironically, as a result of the same forces that had crippled his efforts to support the Mississippi & Atlantic Railroad. Influential citizens in Alton, Illinois, were determined to ensure that their community, and not East St. Louis, would constitute the Mississippi River terminus of a line across Illinois. In January 1851, in response to the danger that the Mississippi & Atlantic posed to their commercial interests, they secured an Illinois charter for the Terre Haute & Alton Railroad. A month later, they obtained an Indiana charter for the short distance between the Illinois–Indiana line and Terre Haute. Despite efforts by Alton boosters to protect their town, it would have been foolish to ignore the far larger commercial potential of St. Louis. The result was the 1852 incorporation of the Belleville & Illinoistown Railroad. By 1854, its tracks spanned the short distance south along the Mississippi River to East St. Louis, and in 1856 the company merged with the Terre Haute & Alton to form the Terre Haute, Alton & St. Louis Railroad.[148]

By the spring of 1856, tracklayers had completed work between Terre Haute and East St. Louis, a community that—much to the dismay of the Alton boosters who had chartered the Terre Haute & Alton—soon became the principal railroad terminus on the east bank of the upper Mississippi. From East St. Louis, passengers and freight could travel over the Terre Haute, Alton & St. Louis; the Terre Haute & Richmond; the Indiana Central; the Indianapolis & Bellefontaine; the Bellefontaine & Indiana; the Cleveland, Columbus & Cincinnati; and the Cleveland, Painesville & Ashtabula to reach the New York Central at Buffalo. Similar service between East St. Louis and Philadelphia was far more problematic, as it would be another three years before the Columbus, Piqua & Indiana Railroad completed its tracks between Union City and a connection with the Steubenville & Indiana, at Columbus. Beginning in October 1859, however, through freight service was available between East St. Louis and the respective termini of the PRR, the NYC, the Erie, and the B&O, at Pittsburgh, Buffalo, Dunkirk, and Wheeling. For the first time, traffic could flow between St. Louis and the east coast without breaking bulk, in cars with broad-tread "compromise" wheels.[149]

Thomson and other PRR officials soon demonstrated interest in the new through route to St. Louis. In September 1859 Thomson dispatched his assistant, William Jackson Palmer, to inspect the line, as well as the Fort Wayne link to Chicago. Palmer traveled to Keokuk, Iowa and Hamilton, Illinois, on opposite sides of the Mississippi River, where Thomson and his associates planned on building a bridge. He also visited St. Louis and St. Charles, Missouri, near the junction of the Mississippi and Missouri rivers, an area where Thomson owned large tracts of land. It was a "pleasant" experience, he wrote his parents, as "I find the name of J. Edgar Thomson a passport wherever I go—and believe, with his letter of credit, I could travel from Maine to Texas without the unpleasant necessity of putting my hand in my pocket for the pewter."[150]

The potential of St. Louis and the West remained largely unrealized until after the Civil War, however. Despite the steady stream of through traffic that traversed central Indiana, the Terre Haute, Alton & St. Louis experienced financial difficulties, succumbing to the Panic of 1857. The company went bankrupt in December 1859, sparking the transfer of the railroad out of local control and into the hands of New York bankers. By June 1862, such "foreign" interests as Samuel Tilden, Russell Sage, and other New Yorkers completed the reorganization of the Terre Haute, Alton & St. Louis into the St. Louis, Alton & Terre Haute Railroad, in a complex transaction that engendered years of legal battles. By the time that Tilden and his associates reorganized the company, the Civil War had closed the Mississippi River, greatly increasing the

value of both the St. Louis, Alton & Terre Haute and the connecting Terre Haute & Richmond. Traffic from the west poured across the single line linking East St. Louis, Terre Haute, and Indianapolis.[151]

The surge in business, coupled with the poor condition of the St. Louis, Alton & Terre Haute, convinced Rose that the Terre Haute & Richmond required an alternate outlet to St. Louis. Still smarting from the failure of the Mississippi & Atlantic Railroad, Rose attempted to resurrect a variant of that project. In February 1865, he helped to incorporate the St. Louis, Vandalia & Terre Haute Railroad, to connect its namesake cities along a route that ran south of the St. Louis, Alton & Terre Haute. A month later, Rose and his associates renamed their original Terre Haute & Richmond, giving it the more accurate title of the Terre Haute & Indianapolis Railroad and securing the right to build from Terre Haute east to the Illinois state line.[152]

Chauncey Rose's line to St. Louis—often called the Vandalia Route—finally opened to traffic in April 1870. His Terre Haute & Indianapolis was seemingly in an unimpeachable position as the key link between a host of railroads to the east and two lines—one of which he controlled—leading to St. Louis. By early 1867, however, a series of events led the Pennsylvania Railroad to become much more actively involved in the development of railroad lines west of Indianapolis, ensuring that neither Rose nor his successor, William Riley McKeen, would remain fully in control of the companies that they had helped to establish.

Connections, North and South

By 1867, the year in which Thomson and the PRR became far more actively involved in the railroads of Ohio and Indiana, Benjamin Smith and George Cass had each assembled a rail empire in the Midwest. There the comparisons stopped, however. Cass's Fort Wayne was a solidly built and well-managed carrier that had benefited enormously from the traffic growth associated with the Civil War. While Cass was not wholly committed to the welfare of the Pennsylvania Railroad, at least Thomson could count on the Fort Wayne to collect grain and other traffic from the upper Midwest and funnel it efficiently and expeditiously to Pittsburgh.

To the south, Benjamin Smith's Columbus, Chicago & Indiana Central Railway (as it was known after February 1868) was a weak company with a byzantine debt structure, continually teetering on the brink of financial insolvency. The company was burdened with a route structure that was far less robust than the one that Cass had established. CC&IC tracks followed an indirect path to Chicago and were no match for the Fort Wayne. To the east of Columbus, Smith depended on the Steubenville & Indiana, and he was essentially at the mercy of Chauncey Rose and the Terre Haute & Indianapolis west of the Indiana capital. Traffic on the St. Louis route, although swollen by war, never kept pace with the torrent of commerce that flowed through Chicago. Still, those factors hardly excused Smith's poor management of the CC&IC, or that carrier's broken-down physical plant and worn-out equipment. During the years that followed the end of the Civil War, Thomson and his associates would experience some difficulty with Cass and the Fort Wayne, but that was nothing compared with the disaster that was Benjamin Smith and the Columbus, Chicago & Indiana Central Railway.

The End of an Era

On Monday, October 3, 1859, a small group of Pennsylvania Railroad officials departed Philadelphia on a triumphal procession, a grand tour of all that they had accomplished in the preceding decade. The highest-ranking officer was vice president William B. Foster, Jr., who brought along his two nieces, Ada Thomson and Harriet Buchanan. As a family biographer noted, "it was William's farewell view of the great enterprise he helped to establish."[153] Foster already suffered from a painful infection at the base of his skull, and he would die five months later, at age fifty-two. Other executives on the train included general freight agent Henry H. Houston, treasurer Thomas T. Firth, and resident engineer William Hasell Wilson. Nine PRR directors were present, including George W. Cass, soon to be president of the Pittsburgh, Fort Wayne & Chicago Rail Road. Including family members, forty-seven people were "making a tour of the great and growing west," headed for the gateway cities of Chicago and St. Louis. They were undertaking the journey "for the purpose of acquainting themselves, by personal observation, with the condition and capacity of those of the Western Railways having intimate business relations with the Pennsylvania Rail Road Company, and of procuring such general information as to the trade and resources of the country traversed and reached by them."[154]

The inspection party would follow the Pennsylvania Railroad for the outbound leg of their journey and return via their rival, the Baltimore & Ohio. They headed west across the long-settled farmlands of Lancaster County, along the rails of the recently acquired Philadelphia & Columbia Railroad. Traveling northwest from Dillerville, Pennsylvania, over the Harrisburg, Portsmouth, Mount Joy & Lancaster—another recent acquisition—they soon arrived at the state capital. There, they joined the tracks that had originally been constructed by the PRR, following the east bank of the Susquehanna River for a short distance before crossing the shallow waters via the bridge that Herman Haupt had designed. Along the Juniata River, they saw evidence of Thomson's wise decision to minimize grades until the railroad reached the foothills of the Alleghenies. They saw, too, the last gasp of the Main Line of Public Works, and the redundant Juniata Division Canal they now owned. After passing Altoona, a town that was just beginning its career as the preeminent shop facility in the United States, they rounded the Horseshoe Curve along a route that replaced both the inclined planes of the Allegheny Portage Railroad and the commonwealth's wasted expenditure on the New Portage Railroad. Pacing the waters of the Little Conemaugh River, they proceeded through Johnstown, and on to Pittsburgh.

The town at the junction of the Allegheny and Monongahela rivers had grown enormously during the previous decade, thanks in no small measure to the PRR's presence there. Local residents demonstrated considerable hostility to the railroad, to be sure, as indicated by their support of the Pittsburgh & Connellsville Railroad, their protests over the PRR's rate structure, and their reluctance to permit construction of a bridge linking the PRR with the Fort Wayne. Yet that connection had been built with little delay, a tribute to Thomson's skill in forming alliances with at least some influential figures in Pittsburgh.

The inspection party passed over the Allegheny River, off of the tracks owned by the Pennsylvania Railroad, and onto those of the Fort Wayne. Farther west, deep into Ohio and on into Indiana, lay a land in transition. Subsistence farmers, until recently deprived of access to reliable transportation, had eked out an existence as best they could. Now, with the railroad close to hand, they were beginning to specialize and to produce crops for market. Day by day the country filled up, with immigrants and migrants alike, with each trip across the Fort Wayne's tracks seemingly revealing more farms, more houses, and more inhabitants. As they neared Chicago, the travelers rode over some of the rails wrenched from the New Portage Railroad, symbolic of the ascendancy of private enterprise over state-sponsored internal improvements.

The PRR party reached Chicago on October 6, less than ten months after construction crews had spiked down the last rails at Van Buren Street. The city's rapid ascent was based on its role as an intermediary between the still sparsely populated agricultural lands that lay to the west and the rail and water routes that stretched to the east. That, surely, was a prize worth fighting for, worth every penny that Thomson had invested in the stocks of Ohio and Indiana railroads, worth all of the bond guarantees, worth even the iron rails donated to the original Fort Wayne & Chicago Railroad.

The remainder of the trip must have been something of an anticlimax. The excursionists left Chicago on the morning of October 8, via the Chicago, Alton & St. Louis Rail Road, and reached St. Louis at midnight. St. Louis was second only to Chicago as a western gateway, yet the city's prosperity testified to the still powerful influence of the steamboat trade, more than to the role of railroads. Three days later, the travelers moved on to Cincinnati, along the Ohio & Mississippi Rail Road, a route that had been completed only two years earlier. On October 14, they left the Queen of the West along the tracks of the Little Miami Railroad, a company that would later become a part of the PRR system. From the Ohio capital, the Central Ohio Railroad carried them east to Wheeling, along a route that was under the influence of the Baltimore & Ohio, and not the

Pennsylvania Railroad. As they traveled past Wheeling and toward tidewater, they saw a formidable competitor. The western portions of the B&O resembled a typical American railroad, with wooden bridges and curves that were sharper than desirable. The farther east that they went, however, the more they encountered the original vision of the B&O's promoters—a beautifully engineered and solidly built route through some of the most formidable topography in the eastern United States.

The procession was forced to stop temporarily at Martinsburg, Virginia, thanks to the actions of an uncompromising abolitionist determined to purge with blood the sins of slavery. John Brown's raid on Harpers Ferry, a town that lay alongside the B&O tracks at the junction of the Potomac and Shenandoah rivers, did not itself cause the Civil War. The roots of that carnage lay much deeper. Along with the election of Abraham Lincoln to the presidency a year later, the raid nonetheless marked the beginning of cataclysmic changes, both for the nation and for the Pennsylvania Railroad. The excursionists undoubtedly sensed that the raid was a portent of truly evil days ahead. They passed through Harpers Ferry on October 18, only hours after Marines stormed the fire engine house where Brown and his followers had taken refuge, then crossed the bridge that had brought those soldiers, under the command of Colonel Robert E. Lee, into town. Saddest of all may have been Harriet Buchanan, the eighteen-year-old niece of Vice President Foster—her other uncle, President James Buchanan, was already being reviled for his indecisive and ineffectual efforts to prevent the United States from disintegrating.

Despite the delays that John Brown had induced, the PRR visitors arrived in Baltimore on the afternoon of October 18. That city showed few ill effects from the completion of the Pennsylvania Railroad, or from the broader vision of Philadelphia merchants to outpace their more southerly rivals. The arks, flatboats, and scows that had once descended the Susquehanna River had largely disappeared, replaced first by the Susquehanna & Tide Water Canal to Chesapeake Bay, and then by the Northern Central Railway that led directly to Baltimore. Flour exports at Baltimore remained healthy, showing no signs of diminishing. If the trip across the PRR main line and over the Fort

Wayne had demonstrated the PRR's maturation as a major corporation, the scenes on the Baltimore docks offered evidence that the company had failed in its mission to restore Philadelphia's commercial glory.[155]

The exhausted travelers departed for Philadelphia on October 19 along the same route that John Brown's body would follow six weeks later. They rode in the cars of the Philadelphia, Wilmington & Baltimore Railroad, a company whose owners were willing to serve the interests of both the PRR and the B&O. Back in the Quaker City, the voyagers were probably too exhausted to care that the PW&B did not make a direct connection with the PRR, and that considerable difficultly would be involved in transferring passengers and freight between the two lines. And, had they continued north to New York along the tracks of the Joint Companies, they would have experienced much the same problem. The excursionists had already suffered through ferry crossings at St. Louis, Wheeling, and Havre de Grace—although the last instance had gone so smoothly that they thanked PW&B officials "for their kind consideration in arranging so comfortable a passage between Baltimore and Philadelphia, by transporting our car over the Susquehanna, avoiding the necessity of a change of seats at that place."[156] In sixteen days, they had traveled 2,180 miles over the routes of eight railroads with three incompatible track gauges. Clearly, much work remained to be done before the ribbons of iron linking east and west could be called an integrated transportation network.

When the PRR officials returned to Philadelphia, it had been less than eight years since Thomson had dispatched Thomas Fernon to the Midwest in order to protect the PRR's interests in the region. In that time, Thomson and his associates had done more than justice to Fernon's recommendations. Working with local entrepreneurs in Ohio and Indiana, PRR executives had created a network of allied lines that provided access to Cincinnati, Chicago, and other important cities along routes that traveled through some of the most productive farmland in the world. In 1852, Fernon had correctly anticipated that officials from all of the eastern trunk lines would soon scramble to create through routes to the west. He had also been correct in his assertion that the ensuing struggle would lend credence to the maxim that "commerce is a strife for conquest without bloodshed."

A decade later, however, the nation was engaged in a very different strife for conquest, in which there was bloodshed almost beyond imagining. The Civil War and its aftermath did not by any means halt efforts by the trunk lines to expand to the west. Rather, the war provided all four companies with the opportunity to forge a new set of alliances, both with other railroads and—of even greater importance—with key figures in the national government. Thomson and his fellow PRR executives would exploit those political alliances far more effectively than their counterparts on other railroads. During the war years, Thomson, Scott, and other PRR officials were able to protect their company's interests while laying the foundation for a period of extraordinary growth during the late 1860s and early 1870s.

Chapter 8

Conflict

1860–1868

The Civil War was the greatest and most destructive war on U.S. soil. It was also the first modern industrial war, and it revolutionized the strategic and tactical methods of combat for generations to come. For the first time in history, entire armies could reposition themselves with astonishing speed, quickly enough to influence the outcome of campaigns and even individual battles while they were raging. Yet, if the railroads made possible modern industrial war, the war did not create the modern railroad network.[1] Instead, the war acted as a catalyst, accelerating the coordination and system building that had been under way since the completion of the four eastern trunk lines in the early and mid-1850s.

The effects of that acceleration on the Pennsylvania Railroad were profound. Close to the Mason-Dixon Line, yet northerly enough to be spared the destruction heaped upon the rival Baltimore & Ohio, the PRR earned considerable sums moving passengers and freight toward the ever-shifting points of collision between Union and Confederate forces. The intensified wartime demand for manufactured products placed a premium on efficient transportation, especially along the vital corridor that linked New York, Philadelphia, Baltimore, and Washington. With the Mississippi River closed to commercial traffic, western commerce had little alternative but to reach tidewater by rail. A torrent of agricul-

tural products from the Midwest headed east along the PRR, to fill the bellies of blue-coated troopers. Europe suffered from a series of poor harvests during the war years, further stimulating demand for American grain and accelerating the transformation of Ohio and Indiana from a land of subsistence farms to an interconnected agrarian market economy. Farmers in those states demanded—and received—more efficient through transportation to the east, in the form of additional routes, fast freight lines, and new equipment. The Civil War years also witnessed the development of the oil industry, as wells located in the PRR's home state brought forth gushers of black gold. Finally, the war enabled PRR officials to contribute their considerable engineering and executive talents to the military effort. Company managers received a commensurate benefit in return, establishing valuable contacts in Washington and on other railroads. Those who survived to hear news of Robert E. Lee's surrender at Appomattox saw a very different Pennsylvania Railroad than the one that had existed at the time hostilities began at Fort Sumter.[2]

A Management Forged in the Crucible of War

The executives of the PRR had no doubts about their loyalties, and many were early and enthusiastic sup-

Figure 31. During the early 1860s, northwestern Pennsylvania became a battlefield, albeit one far less bloody than those in Virginia and elsewhere in the South. That fight was over oil, and it involved three of the four trunk lines, as well as refiners in the cities of Pittsburgh and Cleveland. The prize was the Oil Creek Valley, shown here with the Phillips Well to the right and the Woodford Well to the left.

Pennsylvania Historical and Museum Commission, Drake Well Museum Collection, Titusville.

porters of the Union war effort. President J. Edgar Thomson seems to have shared little of the abolitionist sentiment that characterized his distant Quaker ancestry, but his unwillingness to condemn slavery did not prevent him from furiously criticizing Southerners, whose irresponsible political ambitions he blamed for the crisis.[3] His faith had likewise taught him to reject acts of violence, yet neither his religious principles nor his time spent in Georgia blinded him to the obvious role that the Pennsylvania Railroad could play in transporting the war materiel that the Union would

employ in crushing the Confederacy. In a symbolic gesture, he offered the PRR's Logan House Hotel in Altoona as the site for a September 1862 meeting of several Northern governors, political leaders who were desperately attempting to revive popular support for a war that the North was at that time in danger of losing. The greatest contribution that the PRR made to the war effort, however, lay in its ability to move soldiers and civilians, materiel and merchandise, south toward the nation's capital and the battlefields that lay beyond.[4]

The Baltimore & Ohio, the PRR's southern rival, suffered mightily on account of its proximity to the Confederacy. For much of the Civil War, the B&O was in no position to deliver much freight to Baltimore, or anywhere else, for that matter. In November 1858, a young John W. Garrett had assumed the presidency of the B&O, marking the end of municipal government influence over that company. He had barely settled into his new position when the Civil War tore across his railroad. The resulting hardships included the demolition of the bridge at Harpers Ferry, the destruction of other bridges, structures, and parts of the right-of-way, and a spectacular raid on Harpers Ferry by Colonel Thomas J. Jackson (who had not yet earned either his rank of general or his nickname "Stonewall") that netted dozens of B&O locomotives and hundreds of freight cars. The B&O main line between Baltimore and Wheeling was frequently closed to service.

The Pennsylvania Railroad proper suffered little physical damage during the war, but the same could not be said for the Northern Central Railway and the Philadelphia, Wilmington & Baltimore Railroad.[5] Both of those companies experienced substantial physical and organizational changes, and the ripple effects extended to the PRR as well. The Civil War vastly increased the value of the Northern Central Railway route linking Baltimore to the PRR main line. Accordingly, Thomson and Tom Scott took advantage of their political connections in order to bring that line more firmly under PRR control. In March 1861, President Abraham Lincoln named Simon Cameron as his first secretary of war and, a month later, the staunch PRR ally persuaded the Pennsylvania legislature to lift the restrictions on inter-corporate stock ownership. Thomson was then able to transfer the shares that he owned in his own name directly to the PRR. Thomson continued to buy Northern Central stock during the war years, and by January 1863 the PRR owned nearly 34 percent of the company. That was not a majority, but it enabled the PRR to dictate policy to the Northern Central, inasmuch as Cameron still held a large block of Northern Central shares, which he was happy to assign to Thomson.[6]

Unlike the Northern Central, the Philadelphia, Wilmington & Baltimore was independent of the PRR, and would remain so until 1881. Even though Thomson utilized the Northern Central route to Baltimore, he also relied on the PW&B to expedite shipments from New York and Philadelphia south toward the national capital. As such, he was deeply concerned at the possibility that the war might sever the PRR's connection from Philadelphia to Baltimore. Samuel Morse Felton, the president of the PW&B had problems of his own, as his railroad, although untouched by the Confederate army, suffered at the hands of Southern sympathizers. As a Northerner and a staunch Unionist who headed a railroad that operated through two slave states, Felton was understandably nervous, even before the shelling of Fort Sumter. He received credible reports of a plot by those loyal to the South to sabotage his railroad, particularly the long and vulnerable wooden trestles over the watercourses that emptied into Chesapeake Bay. Felton responded by hiring Alan Pinkerton, who in February 1861 arrived from Chicago accompanied by both male and female detectives. Pinkerton claimed to have uncovered evidence that Southern sympathizers were prepared to assassinate president-elect Lincoln as he traveled through Baltimore—although some cynics suggested that the detective fabricated the plot in order to enhance his own reputation. Initially, Lincoln had planned to travel south from Harrisburg on the Northern Central to Baltimore, and then follow the B&O to Washington. Instead, on the evening of February 22, Lincoln boarded a PW&B train in Philadelphia. The most anxious moments occurred in the wee hours of the next morning as Lincoln traveled, secretly and excruciatingly slowly, through the darkened streets in a horse-drawn railroad car. Lincoln survived the ordeal physically unscathed, but his reputation suffered as his opponents quickly branded him a coward.[7]

Whatever their level of involvement in the plot against Lincoln, Baltimoreans were far more resolute in their efforts to keep Northern soldiers from reaching the South. On April 19, 1861, seven hundred troops from the Sixth Massachusetts Regiment arrived at the PW&B President Street Station and prepared for the ten-block transfer to the B&O Camden Station. Southern sympathizers formed a mob, blocked the tracks, and forced the soldiers to leave their horse-drawn cars and proceed by foot. The ensuing Pratt

Street Riot left four soldiers and a dozen civilians dead. Mayor George W. Brown endeavored to prevent further violence by halting the movement of troops through the city. By the next morning, mobs had severed the telegraph lines connecting the city to the north and set fire to the bridges along the Northern Central, as well as the long trestles over the Back, Bush, and Gunpowder rivers on the PW&B. The pyrotechnics were organized by Isaac R. Trimble, an ardent supporter of the Southern cause and future Confederate general. In addition to striking a blow for the South, Trimble was exacting a measure of revenge against the PW&B, the company that had fired him from his post as chief engineer and general superintendent some seven years earlier. President Felton, whose relationship with Trimble had never been good, was hardly surprised at the actions of his former subordinate. Nevertheless, he was probably exaggerating when he accused Mayor Brown and Police Marshall George Proctor Kane of inciting and planning the incendiary acts. Yet, given Baltimore's reputation as home to numerous Confederate loyalists, he could not afford to take chances.[8]

Although PRR and PW&B executives were hardly close allies, the rapidly escalating conflict forced them to work together. Thomson cooperated with Felton to develop an alternate route to Washington, one that would avoid the chaos in Baltimore. Trains bypassed the burned bridges north of the city by following the PW&B south as far as Perryville, where the train ferry *Maryland* conveyed the cars to Annapolis. From there, a routing over the Annapolis & Elk Ridge Railroad and the Baltimore & Ohio provided access to Washington. PRR and PW&B officials planned the operation in conjunction with General Benjamin Butler and Admiral Samuel Francis Du Pont, yet they lacked any formal federal authorization for their actions. Thomson nonetheless relied on Secretary of War Simon Cameron, a fellow investor in the Northern Central, to impose military control over the Annapolis & Elk Ridge in order to protect that vital link in the new route. Cameron, sensitive to the urgency of the situation and aware that Thomson was for all intents and purposes already operating the line as his own, placed the PRR president in command of the federal government's first military railroad. Thomson, exhausted from

his efforts to repeal the tonnage tax, soon collapsed under the strain, leaving Vice President Scott to carry on in his place. On April 27, Scott took charge of the railway and telegraph lines between Washington and Annapolis, and he soon selected Andrew Carnegie, the superintendent of the PRR's Western Division, as his principal assistant.[9]

On May 13, 1861, the PW&B reopened the line through Baltimore and dispatched its first train from Philadelphia south to Washington. In later years, Carnegie recalled riding in the cab of the locomotive, scanning the tracks ahead for signs of sabotage. At one location, just north of the Capital District, Carnegie spotted a telegraph wire that Southern sympathizers had pulled taught across the tracks. He paid the price for his vigilance, for when the train crew severed the wire, it sprung back into his face, cutting him badly.[10] It was a thrilling story, but like so many other aspects of the Carnegie mystique, it was a complete fabrication. His fellow telegraphers knew better, but were disinclined to contradict their former colleague merely for the sake of historical accuracy. Carnegie biographer David Nasaw nonetheless determined that there was no telegraph wire across the tracks, that Carnegie never suffered any facial trauma, and that he was not on the first train into Washington, in the locomotive or in the cars, nor had he even made it as far as Maryland.[11]

Despite that embellishment, during the early days of the war, Carnegie and several of his young PRR associates did employ their telegraphic expertise to facilitate the movement of trains. At the request of Governor Andrew Curtin, Scott established a telegraph office in the PRR depot at Harrisburg, primarily to prepare the commonwealth's defense and to coordinate the movement of state militia. Scott assigned Carnegie the task of safeguarding communications with the capital. Someone—perhaps Carnegie, perhaps Scott, or perhaps Secretary of War Cameron—in turn ordered PRR Superintendent of Telegraph David McCargo to impress into federal service four PRR telegraph operators and dispatch them to Washington. McCargo created the first military telegraph corps in the United States, yet he was wholly reliant on the independent, and private, American Telegraph Company for transmission facilities. McCargo and his associates likewise retained their civilian status, were never eligible for military pensions, and were supported in later years by Carnegie's munificence—perhaps explaining why they failed to contradict the industrialist's inaccurate account of his arrival in Washington.[12]

On May 23, 1861, Cameron placed Scott in charge of all railroads and telegraph lines in the Washington area. As a recently commissioned colonel of volunteers, however, Scott possessed little power to command, and military officers frequently overrode his policies. Robert Patterson, a major general of Pennsylvania Volunteers and an aged and indecisive veteran of both the War of 1812 and the Mexican-American War, was particularly obdurate. Cameron accordingly persuaded Congress to appoint Scott as his assistant secretary of war, effective August 3, 1861. Not surprisingly, one of Scott's first acts was to take control of the equipment and operations of the American Telegraph Company.[13]

Scott's relationship with Cameron, however, soon proved the downfall of both. PRR executives were not averse to exploiting the intense wartime demand for transportation to their advantage, although to a far smaller extent than many of the purveyors who supplied food, clothing, and equipment to the military. Cameron was willing to bypass the direct Joint Companies/PW&B route between New York and Baltimore in favor of the Allentown Route and the PRR-controlled Northern Central.[14] War Department officials also dispatched western traffic destined for Washington via the PRR main line and onto the Northern Central at Harrisburg. That routing proved especially problematic with cattle shipments. Pennsylvania Railroad personnel billed them as two separate high-rate local hauls (Pittsburgh to Harrisburg and Harrisburg to Baltimore) rather than levying much lower through rates, arguing that the PRR and the Northern Central were nominally separate companies. A more serious scandal erupted after July 12, 1861, when Scott issued a rate schedule that charged the military substantially higher rates than those paid by commercial shippers—40 percent higher on the PRR, and double on the Northern Central. When called to account before the Congressional Committee on Government Contracts, Scott pleaded that those only been the maximum applicable rates and that it was hardly his fault if the military had automatically paid the full amount without negotiating a lower price. While there was no way to determine the validity of those accusations, one way or another, by January 1862 Lincoln was under sufficient political pressure to demand Cameron's resignation, appointing him minister to Russia and assigning Edwin Stanton to take his place in the War Department.[15]

Scott rebounded quickly from his widely criticized association with Simon Cameron and soon made himself indispensable to the War Department. In January 1862, Scott provided Stanton with a set of recommendations that crystallized into the Railways and Telegraph Act and the creation of the United States Military Rail Roads. The new law gave Lincoln the authority to impress into military service any railway deemed necessary to the war effort. Lincoln refrained from federalizing the northern lines, as those companies operated efficiently under private management, and as their owners possessed the political influence necessary to retain control. As such, the USMRR confined its operations to railroads seized from the Confederacy, and to new tracks installed to support the advancing Union armies. The USMRR initially extended only from Washington to Annapolis, Maryland, but expanded rapidly as the Union army increased its strength and captured ever-larger swaths of Confederate territory.

Because so few military personnel understood anything about railway operations, civilians soon took charge of the USMRR. Former Erie general superintendent Daniel C. McCallum was commissioned a brigadier general and served as the director of the USMRR. McCallum and his staff were responsible for the construction, repair, and operation of a fairly small network of railroads south of Washington that had been seized from the Confederacy. Because USMRR personnel had little direct authority over northern railroads, such as the PRR, they instead worked to coordinate and mediate relations between federal officials, military officers, railway executives, shippers, and equipment suppliers.[16]

It was Herman Haupt who actually kept the trains running. In April 1862, Secretary of War Stanton asked Haupt to rebuild the Richmond, Fredericksburg & Potomac Railroad between Aquia Creek and Fredericksburg, a route that was critical to the success of General George B. McClellan's Peninsula Campaign. Haupt was happy to take the opportunity, if for no other reason than he was able to escape from the seemingly endless series of disasters that accompanied his supervision of the construction of the Hoosac Tunnel in Massachusetts.[17]

As the chief of construction in the Department of the Rappahannock, Haupt quickly established work crews that consisted of skilled white workers and former slaves who either had escaped or else had been captured by federal troops.[18] Haupt succeeded in reopening the line, enabling strings of freight cars to travel by water from Washington to Aquia Creek Landing, where they could proceed by rail to Fredericksburg. His ability to design replacement bridges and the ability of his men to build them virtually overnight with whatever material could be obtained locally never failed to impress observers—including Lincoln, who praised Haupt with his legendary comment that "that man Haupt has built a bridge across Potomac Creek, about 400 feet long and nearly 100 feet high, over which loaded trains are running every hour, and, upon my word, gentlemen, there is nothing in it but beanpoles and cornstalks."[19] Haupt's crews rebuilt shattered railroads so quickly that European railway experts, accustomed to a slower pace of construction, routinely if inaccurately dismissed accounts of Haupt's successes as exaggerated Union propaganda.[20]

However, career military officers denigrated Haupt's accomplishments amid a growing conflict between the army and the Military Rail Roads. In June 1862, General John Pope, the recently appointed commander of the new Army of Virginia, insisted that military quartermasters, not railroaders, be given control over the movement of supplies. The results were little short of disastrous. Freight cars sat parked on the main line while civilian laborers, often escaped or captured slaves pressed into service, unloaded their cargoes. By August, a chastened Pope had returned control over the USMRR to Haupt, with a promise that military personnel would no longer interfere with civilian railway managers. The effects of direct military operation lingered, however, and during the September 1862 Antietam campaign, Haupt investigated the cause of slow traffic on the USMRR and found six trains blocking the tracks, with the army quartermaster refusing to use soldiers to unload their cargoes.[21]

With Haupt's administrative talents acknowledged, if not necessarily appreciated, by the military, in September 1862 he received a promotion to brigadier general of volunteers, and served as the chief of construction and transportation in the Virginia theater. He soon developed a new organizational structure for the USMRR, based in considerable measure on his experience on the Pennsylvania Railroad. Under the new system, which took effect on January 1, 1863, Haupt created two divisions—a construction corps and a transportation corps—to ensure that tracks were repaired and that trains continued to run over them. The members of the transportation corps were typically composed of civilian railroaders employed by the USMRR. Many of his key personnel were PRR employees, lent to him by Scott. A large proportion of the ten-thousand-strong construction corps consisted of former slaves, often working alongside white engineers and surveyors. The personnel of the construction corps confronted racial animosity, catastrophic damage, and the limited familiarity of many workers with railway building techniques. Yet, they performed with extraordinary effectiveness, rebuilding railroads needed to supply Union forces and wrecking those that might prove valuable to the Confederacy. Haupt's abilities were certainly apparent during the Gettysburg campaign in June and July 1863, when USMRR construction forces managed repairs and operations on the Northern Central Railway, the Baltimore & Ohio Railroad, the Western Maryland Railroad, the Cumberland Valley Railroad, and the Franklin Railroad, funneling 1,500 tons of supplies a day toward Union forces and evacuating 16,000 wounded soldiers.[22]

At the same time, Haupt engendered as much friction within the ranks of the military as he had within the executive corps of the PRR. Most career officers assumed that railroad construction and operation should be subordinated to their authority. As a PRR executive, Haupt had developed many of the strict policies and procedures that governed railroad operation, and he expected everyone to obey those regulations. Unfortunately, many officers did not appreciate Haupt's detailed requirements, his often brusque and dismissive manner, or his blistering condemnation of their actions. Instead, they regarded him as a martinet and an obstructionist. On September 14, 1863, Stanton relieved Haupt of command, to the undoubted relief of many in the military.[23]

Scott was more personable than Haupt, and politically far more astute, yet he too faced intense criticism for his role in the war effort. Scott survived the furor over military transportation rates, and he might have remained Stanton's assistant had not his past—in the form of the tonnage tax—come back to haunt him. Shortly after assuming his duties as secretary of war, Stanton requested that Scott undertake a survey of the transportation capabilities of various western railroads. Scott traveled more than five thousand miles between January 29 and March 26, 1862, accumulating knowledge that was of considerable use to the War Department—and would soon be vital to the PRR's postwar expansion plans. On March 14, Scott returned briefly to Washington, but at Stanton's request, he was soon on his way west again.

As a close friend of Baltimore & Ohio president John Garrett, Stanton was doubtless reluctant to give Scott additional insights into the western railroad network and to thereby provide the PRR with such an obvious advantage over its rivals. However, Republican Party politics gave the new secretary of war little choice other than to shield Scott from his critics. On January 17, the Pennsylvania House had appointed a special committee to investigate allegations that Scott had resorted to bribery in his efforts to influence the members of the legislature to repeal the tonnage tax. Leading the attack were Thomas Williams, a Republican from Allegheny County who had saved his political career by voting against the elimination of the tonnage tax, and William Hopkins, a Democrat from Washington County who in 1861 had replaced a Republican incumbent who had voted in favor of repeal. Williams persuaded the investigative committee to issue a subpoena, compelling Scott to testify under oath. The sergeant-at-arms was unable to locate Scott in Philadelphia, or in Washington, probably because he was secretly loyal to the PRR's vice president. Williams demanded that Stanton inform him as to Scott's whereabouts, threatening to travel to Washington to personally issue the subpoena.

Stanton alerted Scott to the situation, and probably informed Lincoln, as well. At the same time, Senator David Wilmot reminded the president of the danger that the controversy posed to the Republican Party, both in Pennsylvania and nationally. Scott was a Republican, not so much out of strong conviction as out of a realization that the Republican Party was—and was likely to remain—the dominant political force in Pennsylvania for some time to come.[24] In 1860, in an effort to demonstrate his loyalty, Scott had obligingly issued more than three hundred free passes on the PRR to allow party loyalists to attend the Chicago convention that nominated Lincoln for the presidency. Lincoln obviously found Scott to be a useful ally, and he accordingly ordered Stanton to get the PRR executive out of Washington, lest he be compelled to testify. Scott's only practicable route lay along the PRR and through Harrisburg, where he had many political enemies. Scott thus mimicked Lincoln's ride along the streets of Baltimore the year before, transiting the state capital in the middle of the night. Williams attempted to extend the investigative committee's powers into the recess that followed the end of the legislative session, but his inability to do so ended efforts to compel Scott's testimony.[25]

The ruse protected Scott from the investigative committee but did little to improve his relations with Stanton, or his standing in the government. The creation of the United States Military Rail Roads had reduced the importance of Scott's role as an ad hoc transportation coordinator, and signaled that PRR executives would no longer be in sole control of federal transportation operations. Many of the members of the House Committee on Government Contracts were still not entirely convinced of Scott's innocence in the matter of military freight and passenger rates, and they continued to investigate allegations that Scott's relationship with both the PRR and the War Department constituted an unacceptable conflict of interest. Under the mounting pressure, Scott resigned his post as assistant secretary of war and returned to the PRR on June 1, 1862.[26]

Later that year, the PRR itself came under the most severe threat yet from Confederate forces. In October 1862, cavalry troops led by Confederate General J. E. B. Stuart laid waste to the Cumberland Valley shops and yards in Chambersburg, Pennsylvania, destroying the passenger station and engine house, along with three locomotives and numerous freight cars. General

George Pickett finished the job in late June and early July of the following year, shortly before leading his troops to disaster at Gettysburg. During Lee's 1863 invasion of the North, Confederate troops, including Stuart's cavalry, destroyed thirty-three bridges along the Northern Central. The biggest casualty, on June 28, was the Northern Central Railway bridge across the Susquehanna River at Wrightsville, deliberately burned by Pennsylvania soldiers in order to deny its use to Confederate troops under the command of General John Gordon. The real prize escaped Gordon's troops, however—even though a small contingent of Confederate soldiers reached Camp Hill, Pennsylvania, they were forced to retreat before they had a chance to seize or destroy the PRR bridge across the Susquehanna at Rockville, less than ten miles away.[27]

Such forays were the exception, however, and the PRR suffered most from the ongoing burden of wartime traffic. Locomotives and cars were in short supply, and the physical plant deteriorated faster than it could be repaired. Wartime inflation tripled the cost of some supplies. Lincoln's call for a federal draft—the first in the nation's history—further complicated the PRR's operations. The War Department quickly exempted telegraph operators from conscription, but that protection did not extend to enginemen, firemen, or other skilled occupational categories. Conscription produced such outrage over discriminatory treatment that train service employees were on the verge of striking, rioting, or both. Both Scott and Pittsburgh, Fort Wayne & Chicago president George Washington Cass wrote to Stanton, warning him that the draft would threaten railroad operations. The draft ultimately exempted enginemen, but not other equally vital occupations, causing crew shortages and a 40 percent increase in wages. The PRR incurred additional expenses by hiring substitutes to fight in place of skilled employees. Sunday operations and double shifts—some as long as thirty hours on duty—left enginemen and firemen asleep in the cabs of their locomotives.[28]

Stanton ultimately conceded that he did not care whether skilled PRR employees were drafted so long as Pennsylvania fulfilled its allotted troop quotas. Rising to the challenge, Scott devoted his energies to the recruitment of troops, as much to save his railroad as to bolster the might of the Union armies. Following

General Lee's first incursion into the North, in September 1862, Scott hurriedly recruited fifty thousand Pennsylvanians to participate in an expected defense of the commonwealth. The railroad paid for uniforms for the chronically underequipped Philadelphia-based Second Regiment of the Pennsylvania Militia (the Blue Reserves). By April 1864, the PRR was also providing significant financial support to the Free Military School for Applicants for the Command of Colored Troops, an institution that trained white officers to lead a growing number of African-American soldiers. Although federal officials refused to train African-American officers, and initially specified that United States Colored Troops would receive less pay and a lower uniform allowance than white soldiers, the PRR board of directors nonetheless insisted "that the same regulations in reference to the military transportation of black recruits will be observed as are now in force in regard to the white recruits."[29]

Scott's logistical abilities soon overcame both Stanton's antipathy and the lingering criticisms associated with his links to Simon Cameron. In September 1863, with Confederate forces threatening General William S. Rosecrans's army at Chattanooga, Tennessee, Stanton welcomed Scott back in the military, with the rank of colonel. Scott coordinated the transfer of the Union Eleventh and Twelfth Corps, from their arrival in Louisville to their ultimate destination in Chattanooga. His greatest challenge would be to assemble sufficient equipment that could operate on the southern railroads, most of which were set to a five-foot gauge. Scott imperiously ordered that all locomotive manufacturers in the United States work around the clock to convert their existing orders to the southern gauge and deliver them as soon as they were operational, even if incomplete, to the United States Military Rail Roads. Between September 25 and October 6, 1863, Scott supervised the movement of twenty-three thousand soldiers nearly 1,300 miles, relieving the beleaguered Union garrison. With that triumph behind him, Scott retired again—this time permanently—from military service.[30]

Even though Scott and his colleagues were heavily invested in government service, they were nonetheless able to orchestrate significant technological, organizational, and managerial changes on the Pennsylvania

Railroad. With the best-quality iron being forged into the weapons of war, new iron rails quickly wore out, and accidents occurred with depressing frequency. Thomson, desperate to keep the PRR's tracks in service, in 1863 ordered 150 tons of British steel rails, although difficulties in securing the appropriate hardware delayed their installation until the following summer. The steel was of such poor quality, however, that the rails would have shattered under the stress of heavy mainline traffic, and their use was restricted to yard tracks at Altoona and Pittsburgh. Similarly, a test of "Doddized" composite rails with an iron base and a steel head, developed by British inventor Thomas Dodd, produced disappointing results. The PRR nonetheless continued to install steel rails in critical areas, as did the Fort Wayne. By 1866, Thomson was sufficiently persuaded as to the merits of steel rail that he supported the incorporation of the Pennsylvania Steel Company for the domestic manufacture of steel rails.[31]

Intense wartime traffic also led Thomson to authorize the installation of additional double track. By the beginning of 1863, two tracks were in place over the entire distance between Altoona and Pittsburgh, except for the bridge over the Conemaugh River at Johnstown. At year's end, the only remaining stretch of single track was a twenty-one-mile-long section between Lewistown and Mill Creek, and only a shortage of labor prevented Thomson from eliminating that bottleneck. Double-tracking continued even after the war was over, and by 1869 a second track was in place over the entire distance between Philadelphia and Pittsburgh, except for the bridge over the Susquehanna River, and two other short lengths of track at Mount Union and at Manayunk. Work crews also installed stretches of double track on the Northern Central and the Pittsburgh, Fort Wayne & Chicago.[32]

The war also accelerated improvements to the PRR's equipment. One of the most notable changes involved the conversion of locomotives from wood burners to coal burners, a process that had begun in 1853. By 1862, all freight locomotives burned coal, and shop forces had converted the remainder of the fleet by 1864. Many new locomotives joined the roster as well, as PRR officials cemented their long-standing relationship with the Baldwin Locomotive Works—helped, no doubt, by Baldwin's willingness to secretly under-

cut any other manufacturer's bid by $250 in exchange for large and predictable orders. Equipment improved, too, as more and more eight-wheel (double-trucked) freight cars replaced the small, hard-riding, four-wheel coal "jimmies" and the like. PRR officials also made considerable efforts to utilize existing rolling stock more efficiently. In April 1864, superintendent of transportation John Reilly created a Car Record Office at Altoona, centralizing the collection of data pertaining to car allocations. Yet, the PRR suffered from chronic equipment shortages, with grueling wartime service and the need to transfer motive power to its subsidiaries causing the locomotive roster to decrease from 229 in 1861 to 225 in 1864.[33]

The Pennsylvania Railroad benefited enormously from the Civil War, despite the contentious nature of its relationship with the federal government and shortages of equipment and personnel. During the war, the PRR transported nearly a million soldiers and their supplies.[34] Freight traffic nearly doubled between 1861 and 1865, from 1.5 million to 2.8 million tons. The PRR's revenues jumped from $5.9 million in 1860 to $19.5 million in 1865, while net income rose from $2.3 million to $4.6 million during the same period—substantial increases, even accounting for the wartime inflation that caused overall prices to more than double between 1860 and 1865. Earnings would have been even higher than the balance sheet indicated had not Thomson and the board disguised millions of dollars in profits, by treating many capital improvements as business expenses.[35]

The war produced its greatest benefit in the intangible realm of networking. In Ohio and Indiana, executives on the PRR's western connections faced unprecedented traffic levels and began to work more closely with one another to coordinate service. After 1865, that cooperation would greatly facilitate Thomson's efforts to transform those allies into a comprehensive network of subsidiary lines. PRR executives were tested under the most extreme circumstances, as they worked with government officials and colleagues from other railroads. While Thomson, Scott, and Haupt were certainly the best-known individuals who parlayed their PRR experience into wartime service, many others did so, as well. One example was Joseph N. Du Barry, superintendent of the Northern

Central. It was his responsibility to move troops and supplies through the critical Baltimore gateway on their way to Washington, over a route that was periodically demolished by Confederate raiders. In September 1862, Du Barry helped to make possible the movement of Union troops to the battlefield at Antietam. That logistical feat contributed to his rapid rise through the PRR hierarchy, and in January 1872 he became superintendent of the Baltimore & Potomac, the PRR's extension to Washington. Du Barry later served the PRR in a variety of executive capacities.[36]

And there were many others as well. William H. Brown served under Herman Haupt on the United States Military Rail Roads, joined the PRR after the war, and rose to the rank of chief engineer. John Pugh Green fought in the Army of the Potomac for much of the war, taking part in General William Tecumseh Sherman's March to the Sea. Captain Green later became Scott's private secretary and was eventually promoted to a PRR vice president in charge of matters relating to accounting and finance. Telegrapher William Bender Wilson did not participate in anything so dramatic as Sherman's march, but he was so bedazzled by meeting Lincoln and other key leaders that he became one of the PRR's most prolific chroniclers, and his output included a two-volume history of the railroad and its officers. Frank Thomson, one of Scott's early assistants, was a veteran of both the eastern and western theaters and played a critical role in the transportation of reinforcements to aid General Rosecrans. In 1862, Thomson became the superintendent of the Eastern Division of the Philadelphia & Erie Railroad (the former Sunbury & Erie) and soon began the development of track and roadbed standards that were essential to the efficient movement of traffic. He later oversaw the creation of the PRR's Association of Transportation Officers, bringing together some of the railroad's most talented engineering and operating officials. As general manager and as vice president, he was instrumental in systematizing the PRR's operations—a contribution that led to his appointment as president in 1897. In many respects, then, the Civil War provided the PRR and its executives with the knowledge, the contacts, and the resources necessary to dominate transportation in the Northeast and Midwest for decades to come.[37]

Tom Scott benefited more from the economic and political aspects associated with the Civil War than any other executive on the Pennsylvania Railroad. His wartime service freed him from the haunting legacy of the tonnage tax, enabling him to elude a legislative subpoena and, more importantly, allowing him to recast his public image from unscrupulous political manipulator to heroic savior of the Union. Scott expanded his already impressive network of personal contacts among local, state, and federal government officials, executives associated with railroad and telegraph companies, and military officers who in the aftermath of the Civil War would command the highest levels of power in both the public and private spheres. Even the disgraced and exiled Simon Cameron, who campaigned successfully for reelection to the Senate in 1867, asked for and received Scott's support—and returned that loyalty with more than one favor for the PRR. Based on his wartime travels, Scott knew more about the midwestern railroad network than any of his contemporaries. That knowledge, gained through government service, would provide important strategic advantages in the years following the Civil War, as PRR executives expanded the railroad's influence into Ohio, Indiana, Illinois, the far west, and the southeast.[38]

Wartime Organizational Changes

The Civil War generated considerable changes in the PRR's organizational structure as officials responded to the increasing scope and complexity of operations. For the first decade of its existence, the PRR was a relatively small and uncomplicated corporate entity, operating only the 249 miles of track linking Harrisburg and Pittsburgh. Many key functions, including the solicitation of traffic, were accommodated by individuals who were connected with, but not organizationally a part of, the PRR. By 1860, with the acquisition of the Main Line of Public Works, the railroad had grown to 423 miles, including branches. While that was not an insubstantial increase, more significant changes accompanied such developments as the growth of traffic, especially from the west, the increased interaction with federal officials, and new construction projects, particularly those designed to speed freight and passengers through Philadelphia.

During the spring of 1863, the board further refined and decentralized the line-and-staff corporate structure within the Transportation Department, first established in the 1858 organization manual. Since January 1, 1858, the PRR had maintained lines of authority that cascaded downward from the president through the general superintendent, and then to the division superintendents and their personnel. Most of the PRR's employees, and therefore most of its supervisory authority, resided in the Transportation Department. As the company grew, however, senior managers became correspondingly less able to directly supervise personnel in the field. At the same time, the line managers required far more support services from individuals with expertise in such matters as accounting and the law. Therefore, the board began to create additional staff positions to advise and assist the line executives, helping them to operate trains with greater efficiency. Even though their primary responsibility was to support Transportation Department executives, staff officers held considerable authority over their line counterparts, particularly where legal issues were concerned.

As a preliminary step, the board balanced both the geographic boundaries and the executive responsibilities associated with each operating division. With the purchase of the Main Line of Public Works in 1857, the PRR had in effect inherited a structure of four operating units—the Philadelphia (the former Philadelphia & Columbia Railroad), Eastern (which included the leased Harrisburg, Portsmouth, Mount Joy & Lancaster Railroad), Middle, and Western divisions. A new organization manual, which took effect in February 1863, eliminated the historically conditioned division point at Dillerville in favor of the Philadelphia Division, between Philadelphia and Harrisburg; the Middle Division, between the state capital and Altoona; and the Pittsburgh Division, stretching west to Pittsburgh. All three divisions were collectively supervised by the PRR's general superintendent, assisted by a staff that included the reestablished position of superintendent of transportation (Robert Pitcairn), the superintendent of motive power and machinery, the chief engineer, the general freight agent, and the gen-

eral ticket agent.[39] After the PRR leased the Philadelphia & Erie Railroad in January 1862, that carrier was divided into eastern and western divisions. Operated essentially as a separate railroad, the Philadelphia & Erie also possessed a general superintendent, with an associated staff.[40]

The reorganization of the Transportation Department, in 1863 and again in 1866, gave the three division superintendents greater flexibility and autonomy. The authority of division personnel was generally limited to local matters that affected only their divisions, not the entire railroad. On their respective divisions, however, each possessed the powers equivalent to those exercised by the general superintendent over the railroad as a whole. As in the 1858 organization, each division superintendent had full authority over the downward line of Transportation Department employees on his division, including all matters of personnel policy. Like the general superintendent, the division superintendents had a full complement of staff officers to oversee the basic functions of conducting transportation, fielding locomotives and cars, and maintaining the right of way. They supervised a trainmaster, a resident engineer (beginning in 1863), and a master mechanic and foreman of the Car Shop (beginning in 1866), with additional staff positions added at later dates.[41]

Even as they gave more authority to the division superintendents, Thomson and the directors were careful to augment the staff capabilities at the company level in order to more effectively manage matters affecting the entire system. Even though division superintendents were responsible for the movement of cars within their respective divisions, the PRR's assistant superintendent coordinated the allocation of rolling stock, and possessed the authority to issue special rates. Also significant was the appointment of John B. Collin in July 1866 as the PRR's first mechanical engineer, a system officer who was soon in charge of standardizing motive-power designs.

An increasingly important function involved the purchase of supplies for company use. Initially, department heads bought whatever they needed and subtracted the cost from divisional revenues. Under the organization of May 1851, the board had placed the assistant superintendent, based in Harrisburg, in charge of supplies, but also enabled the freight agent and the passenger agent, in Philadelphia, to make purchases for their departments. In 1857, the board specified that the general superintendent would process all supply requests, although he could delegate that authority to the division superintendents, the resident engineers, or the master of machinery. All requests would nonetheless be entered in a single "Order Book," and the supplies themselves placed under the watchful eye of a keeper of stores at a central location. In May 1863, the board created the position of supply agent as part of the Transportation Department. Less than three years later, in February 1866, the directors established a centralized Supplying Department, under the direction of the purchasing agent, who reported directly to the general superintendent.[42]

As the 1866 organization manual made clear, the general superintendent was no longer merely the chief operating officer—he was also responsible for mediating interactions between the divisional line officers and the company staff officers. However, the general superintendent lacked authority over most traffic matters—a characteristic that had been true of the 1858 organization, as well. The general freight agent and the general ticket agent (after May 1869, the general passenger and ticket agent) were responsible for setting rates and soliciting business, but they reported directly to the president. However, the general superintendent possessed the authority to negotiate special rates for local freight, a situation that produced a certain amount of tension within the PRR organization.[43]

Authority over engineering personnel varied considerably over time. Each division superintendent was responsible for routine engineering matters, pertaining to the maintenance of the physical plant. The 1858 reorganization had provided for two resident engineers (for the Eastern and Western Divisions), but by the end of the year the reassignment of Eastern Division Resident Engineer Thomas W. Seabrook left his counterpart, William Hasell Wilson, as the sole remaining resident engineer, in charge of maintenance of way for the entire railroad. In 1862, in recognition of the increased demands caused by wartime traffic, the board promoted Wilson to chief engineer and gave him a staff that included an engineer of bridges and buildings, as well as line authority over three resident engineers, one for each division. Chief Engineer Wilson and his resident engineers were part of the Transportation Department, with the former answering to the general superintendent and the latter to their respective division superintendents. The Philadelphia & Erie also possessed a chief engineer—William Hasell Wilson's son, John A. Wilson—and two resident engineers, one for each of that railroad's divisions.

Although day-to-day maintenance requirements remained relatively constant over the years, new construction projects waxed and waned according to the availability of new traffic opportunities, the threat from competing carriers, and the state of the economy. As such, PRR's engineering functions went through a bewildering array of reorganizations during the remaining decades of the nineteenth century. In late 1867, in light of the expansionist period that followed the end of the war, the board reestablished the Engineer Department as a stand-alone entity, answering to the president, the first vice president, and the board, but not to the general superintendent or the division superintendents. Beginning in January 1868, William Hasell Wilson became the chief engineer of construction and consulting engineer, in charge of new construction, and the existing office of chief engineer was eliminated. John A. Wilson made something of a lateral move, trading his supervision over routine maintenance on the Philadelphia & Erie for a comparable post on the PRR as chief engineer of maintenance-of-way. By the summer of 1874, as new construction virtually ground to a halt, the Engineer Department was again abolished, with William Hasell Wilson transferred to the new Real Estate Department. For some time thereafter, most engineering work was of the routine variety.[44]

With the division superintendents responsible for day-to-day operations as well as routine construction and maintenance, the central office increasingly concentrated on long-term corporate strategy. The members of the board acknowledged that the increasing complexity of the PRR's operations had badly taxed the abilities of Thomson, Scott, and other senior executives. In March 1863, a supplement to the corporate charter permitted the PRR to add a second vice president. Thereafter, the vice president was no longer a deputy who provided whatever assistance that the president might require. Instead, the first vice president (Scott) managed political matters and relations with connecting railroads—an important responsibility after the Civil War stimulated the growth of through traffic. The second vice president (Herman J. Lombaert) was the controller, with authority in all accounting matters. Thomson remained in command of the Transportation Department, as he had since 1852, and could call on the services of an assistant who was required to possess experience in engineering.

A few months later, in May 1863, the board created a new General Office Department, which encompassed the PRR's senior executives and was responsible for the management of the company's Philadelphia headquarters. It consisted of the president, the two vice presidents, the secretary, the treasurer, and their assistants. While not a member of the General Office Department, the new general agent at Philadelphia, filling a position created at the beginning of 1866 in response to the completion of the Junction Railroad and the Connecting Railway, was responsible for all Transportation Department matters within the city.[45]

The number of executives soon increased further, thanks to a March 1869 Pennsylvania law that permitted the state's corporations to select additional vice presidents from among their directors. Thereafter, until the abolition of the system of numbered vice presidencies in 1912, the PRR maintained at least three and sometimes as many as six vice presidents, three of whom, along with the president, were members of the board of directors. Initially, the first vice president continued his responsibilities pertaining to relations with connecting lines, the second vice president retained his accounting functions while relinquishing some of his authority to a separate controller, the third vice president oversaw leases and other financial arrangements with subsidiaries, and the fourth vice president controlled the Engineer Department, while serving as an engineering adviser to the president (for projects on the PRR) and the first vice president (for projects on connecting lines). Aside from the increase in the number of vice presidents, the key change was that after 1869 a vice president served as an intermediary in the line of authority, between the president and the general superintendent. That vice president could therefore oversee Transportation Department matters, such as rates and the solicitation of traffic, that did not directly relate to the general superintendent's responsibilities for the safe and efficient operation of trains.[46]

The president could call upon the services of one or more assistants, who handled work that lay outside the normal chain of command. Because the assistants worked closely with the president and oversaw projects that crossed jurisdictional boundaries, they were frequently being groomed for rapid advancement up the executive ladder, often bypassing several rungs in the process. Any expansion projects would likely be overseen by Joseph N. Du Barry, who in 1875 became the assistant to the president in matters pertaining to new construction. Strickland Kneass performed much the same role, but he generally specialized in the complex Philadelphia area. John Pugh Green was an adviser on financial and organizational matters to the companies that composed the Lines West of Pittsburgh and Erie.

During the next five decades, the number of vice presidents, and their job descriptions, changed with a frequency that rivaled the alterations in the structure of the company's engineering functions. Despite the changing titles, four vice presidents—Alexander J. Cassatt, Frank Thomson, Charles E. Pugh, and William Wallace Atterbury—were in charge of the Transportation Department between 1874 and 1924.[47] The reason for that seeming schizophrenia was simply that the vice presidential designations had little to do with executive responsibilities. The numerical designation was merely a reflection of the seniority system that was so much a part of railway employment. That is, the first vice president attained that title solely because he was the longest serving vice president on the railroad. He did not possess any direct supervisory authority over the other vice presidents, each of whom was answerable only to the president and the board of directors. On more than one occasion, vice presidents were promoted over the heads of those in a more direct line of succession, as any vice president who lacked experience in engineering or transportation—no matter how senior or how competent—could never be put in charge of the Pennsylvania Railroad.[48] The key to the vice-presidential system was that duties followed the individual rather than the position. Through some combination of aptitude and experience, certain executives were well suited to certain responsibilities, and the board of directors repeatedly and routinely adjusted the PRR's corporate structure in order to accommodate their abilities.

The PRR's organizational flexibility made the company's management structure somewhat different from that of other railroads in the United States. In 1880, the editor of the *Railroad Gazette* suggested that "an essential element in a system of railway management is that it should be calculated to train persons competent to fill places of responsibility and authority; it will not do to rely on chance for supplying fit persons. The system should form them, and it will, if properly organized."[49] The PRR's management system may well have formed legions of junior executives. At the higher levels, however, it was the organization that altered to fit the individual, and not the individual that altered to fit the organization.

Finally, it should be emphasized that the PRR's executives functioned with remarkable effectiveness for a great many decades, largely because they were embedded in an organizational culture that adapted easily to rapidly changing circumstances. Much of that evolution was accidental, brought about by the unique abilities of a particularly talented manager, by the necessity of putting out to pasture someone who was too old or too overwhelmed to fulfill his duties, by the acquisition of executive talent from subsidiary railroads, and, regrettably, by untimely death. In 1882, when an observer from the *Railroad Gazette* reflected on the development of the PRR organization, he opined that "all wise things are not done on purpose; but nevertheless the soundest principles, on this as on other occasions, were incorporated into the organization by accidents of circumstance about which it is difficult to say whether the occasion only served a purpose, or a purpose took advantage of an occasion."[50]

Breaking the Philadelphia Bottleneck

The Civil War generated unprecedented levels of traffic along the Atlantic seaboard, but the tracks between New York and Washington were not well prepared to accommodate the additional business. Four cooperating carriers (the Camden & Amboy Rail Road, the Delaware & Raritan Canal, the Philadelphia & Trenton Railroad, and the New Jersey Rail Road & Transportation Company) operated a canal and two parallel rail lines across New Jersey. For years, they had relied on the monopoly profits associated with the 1832 Protection Act, and the absence of competition had undermined incentives to improve service. The route between New Brunswick and Trenton was single-track, in poor condition, and prone to accidents.

In addition to the fairly minor damage caused by Confederate sympathizers, the Philadelphia, Wilmington & Baltimore line south of Philadelphia suffered from a major impediment. Despite some desultory attempts at construction, there was still no bridge across the Susquehanna River at Havre de Grace, forcing the PW&B to continue its reliance on the train ferry *Maryland*. As a result, considerable traffic flowed along the Allentown Route/Northern Central alignment between New York and Baltimore.

Perhaps the most serious bottleneck lay in Philadelphia, as PRR tracks did not connect directly with either the PW&B or the Joint Companies. Civilians, soldiers, and supplies headed south on the Philadelphia & Trenton route could go no farther than Kensington, well north of Center City Philadelphia. Alternatively, they could travel on the Joint Companies Camden & Amboy line to Camden, New Jersey, and then cross the Delaware River to Philadelphia by ferry. Once in the city, they faced a slow transit of the City Railroad to a junction with either the PRR to the west or the PW&B to the south.[51]

The traffic congestion between New York and Philadelphia sharpened criticism of the Joint Companies transportation monopoly in New Jersey. As early as December 1861, members of the New York Chamber of Commerce petitioned Congress to override the Protection Act by issuing a federal charter that would compel New Jersey to permit the construction of a competing railroad. The creation of a National Air-Line Railroad between New York and Washington, they argued, would ease both commercial and military travel. Their pleas took on greater urgency as the war raged on. Massachusetts Senator Charles Sumner, still recovering from his savage beating at the hands of South Carolina Congressman Preston Brooks, was particularly strident in his advocacy for improved transportation along the Atlantic seaboard. Sumner suggested that "the present pretension of New Jersey belongs to the same school with that abhorred and blood bespattered pretension of South Carolina," the seedbed of the rebellion.[52] Many entrepreneurs echoed Sumner's call for a new rail line between New York and Washington, although they typically acted for reasons of parochialism, not the national good. Simon Cameron, a faithful ally of the PRR, was likewise a strong supporter of the Air-Line, which he hoped would provide the Northern Central with direct access to Washington.[53]

By early 1864, members of a House committee were ready to meet with officials from the Joint Companies, the PW&B, and the B&O—the three carriers that composed the New York–Washington route—and had requested that representatives from the Post Office and the War Department describe their difficulties in securing transportation between those cities. For PW&B president Samuel Morse Felton, this was too much to bear. He was already resentful that traffic was surging along the indirect Allentown Route, and he was further annoyed that he had to pay for repairs to his railroad, while the federal government shouldered the expense of rebuilding the Northern Central after each Confederate raid. The poor operating conditions on the Joint Companies route through New Jersey were hardly his fault, nor could he be held responsible for the taxes that the New Jersey and Maryland legislatures had levied on rail traffic north of Philadelphia and south of Baltimore. In frustration, and in a desperate effort to prevent the construction of another competing carrier, Felton published *The Impolicy of Building another Railroad between Washington and New York*. Although the House, in July 1866, passed a bill to charter the National Railway Company as a mechanism to construct the new Air-Line, the end of the war and the impending expiration of the Camden & Amboy monopoly (on January 1, 1869) had removed much of the urgency, and the project faded, temporarily, from the scene.[54]

During the war, however, the agitation for the Air-Line had frightened Joint Companies and PW&B officials into closer cooperation with each other, and with the PRR, in order to facilitate transportation along the east coast. Joint Companies officials autho-

rized the rapid double-tracking of much of their route. In 1862, they solidified and extended their cooperative agreement with the New Jersey Rail Road—although a more formal consolidation would not take place until 1867. Joint Companies and PW&B officials met repeatedly in an effort to coordinate service between New York and Washington. The more significant accomplishment was the construction of two short yet exceedingly important lines—the Junction Railroad and the Connecting Railway—that enabled the PRR to speed traffic through and around Philadelphia.[55]

To the south of Philadelphia, the PW&B, the PRR, and the Reading jointly constructed a three-and-a-half-mile railroad that would link their lines into the city. On May 3, 1860, the Pennsylvania legislature chartered the Junction Railroad, with each of the three companies maintaining a one-third ownership interest. Construction did not begin until December 1862, as the various parties negotiated for the necessary right of way. On November 23, 1863, the northern portion of the Junction Railroad opened for traffic, connecting the Reading's line at the base of the now-abandoned Belmont Plane with the PRR's tracks at Thirty-Fifth Street in West Philadelphia. From Thirty-Fifth Street south almost to Market Street, the Reading and the PW&B operated trains over approximately a mile of existing PRR track, included as a part of the Junction Railroad.[56]

The northern segment of the Junction Railroad enabled north–south traffic to travel through Philadelphia by rail for the first time, although the route was a bit circuitous. Southbound traffic would travel over the Philadelphia & Trenton to Kensington, where it would intersect the Reading's Port Richmond Branch, which terminated at the massive anthracite terminal on the Delaware River waterfront. Cars could then follow the Reading for a short distance to the north and west (against the southbound flow of coal traffic that had originated in Schuylkill County), across the Schuylkill River, and then south to Belmont. The new section of the Junction Railroad led south to the PRR's Delaware Extension, which ran east over the Arsenal Bridge across the Schuylkill River. Cars then reached the PW&B station at Broad and Prime Streets. From there, they followed the PW&B back west, crossing the Schuylkill River for a third time (at the Gray's Ferry Bridge) before turning southward.

The southern section of the Junction Railroad, from Market Street in West Philadelphia to the PW&B tracks at Gray's Ferry took somewhat longer to complete. The line paralleled the West Chester & Philadelphia Railroad, a local carrier, and disputes over the right of way delayed construction. The link opened in December 1864, eliminating the need to cross and re-cross the Schuylkill River at the Arsenal and Gray's Ferry bridges. The final details were not completed until July 1866, but the more serious impediment to the expeditious movement of trains through Philadelphia lay to the north of the city.[57]

The gap between the Philadelphia & Trenton Railroad at Kensington and PRR tracks in West Philadelphia had long interfered with travel between New York and Washington. In 1862, as the agitation for the National Air-Line Railroad was gaining momentum, representatives from the PRR and the Joint Companies/Philadelphia & Trenton began planning a route that would skirt northwestern Philadelphia. As with many such agreements, the competitive arrangements were as important as the engineering details. Thomson guaranteed $1 million of the bonds of the new rail link, and he agreed to deliver all of the western commerce destined for New York to the Joint Companies at Philadelphia—eliminating the need to transfer traffic to the Reading at Harrisburg, as part of the prewar Allentown Route. Thomson also promised the Joint Companies access to the PRR's West Philadelphia yards. In return, Joint Companies officials pledged to send their traffic west via the PRR and not the B&O, and to provide adequate terminal facilities at Jersey City and South Amboy in order to accommodate the anticipated increase in business.

In April 1863 the Pennsylvania legislature chartered the Connecting Railway. The route began at a junction with the PRR main line at Mantua Station, a mile and a half northwest of West Philadelphia. From that connection (renamed Mantua Junction and, later, Zoo Tower), the tracks curved to the northeast, crossing the Schuylkill River. They crossed over the Reading line into Center City Philadelphia, the tracks that had once belonged to the Philadelphia & Columbia. The Connecting Railway passed through Germantown Junction (later, North Philadelphia) and terminated at a connection with the Philadelphia & Trenton at Frankford, a short distance north of that company's station at Montgomery Avenue and Front Street in Kensington.[58]

Work began in 1864, and the Connecting Railway entered service in July 1867. Traffic could now flow from Harrisburg, Pittsburgh, and points west through Philadelphia and north to New York—although the transition between the standard gauge on the PRR and the 4' 10" gauge on the New Jersey lines still constituted an impediment to efficient operations. Of equal importance, passengers and freight moving along the Atlantic seaboard could travel easily through West Philadelphia, bypassing the congestion in the city proper. Traffic levels soon rose precipitously along the critical link that the Connecting Railway provided as the route grew from its original two tracks to become a four- and then a six-track main line. On a value-per-mile basis, therefore, that 6.4-mile line proved to be the most important segment of the vast Pennsylvania Railroad empire.[59]

With the completion of the Junction Railroad and the Connecting Railway, PRR officials abandoned service to Center City Philadelphia. Surface-street congestion and municipal restrictions on the use of steam locomotives had long complicated operations east of the Schuylkill River. In May 1851, a decade before the Civil War began, President Patterson had persuaded the board to spend $350,000 to purchase the ninety-three-acre West Philadelphia estate of John Hare Powel, in the hopes of locating station facilities there.[60] Many of the PRR shareholders who opposed the Merrick/Patterson faction on the board criticized the purchase of that property—later the site of many of the PRR's most important terminal facilities—as an impecunious extravagance.[61] Within a few months, the PRR had purchased even more land in the area, along Chestnut Street and on Market Street. In November 1851, Thomson, then the PRR's chief engineer, trod through West Philadelphia in the company of several directors, attempting to identify a suitable location for passenger and freight depots. By 1858, PRR workers had constructed a small station in West Philadelphia near the site of a West Chester & Philadelphia facility at Thirty-First and Chestnut Streets. The loca-

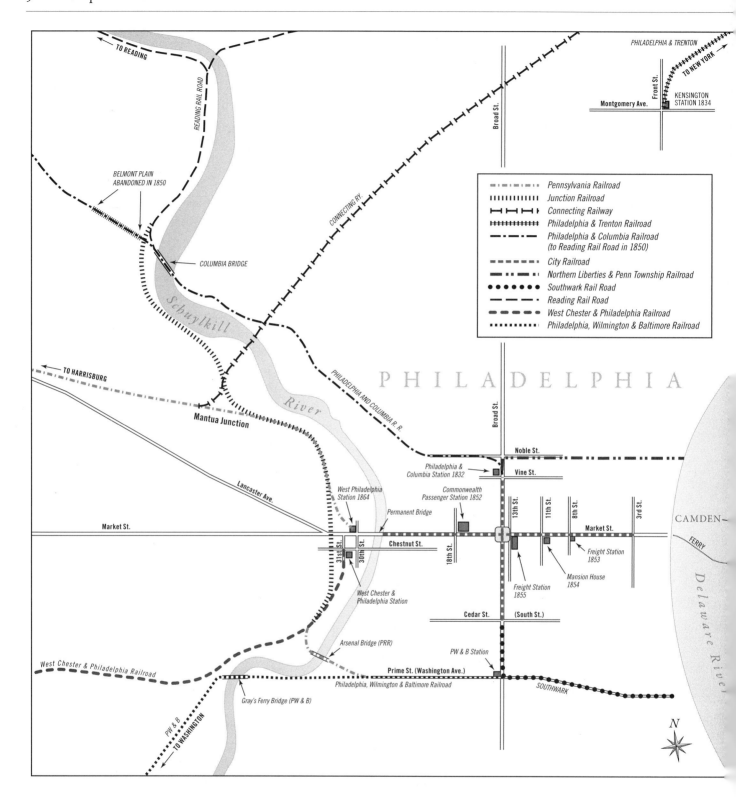

tion was as far east as trains on either railroad could travel without switching to horses. In October 1864, with the Junction Railroad completed, the PRR closed its Center City station at Eleventh and Market, and terminated all eastbound passenger trains at a new depot at Thirtieth and Market Streets in West Philadelphia. The PRR maintained a freight station at that location, along with two passenger depots, one for passengers bound for New York, and the other for those heading toward Pittsburgh.[62]

Once the Connecting Railway and the Junction Railroad were in service, the West Philadelphia location was ideally suited for trains traveling over the Joint Companies and the Philadelphia, Wilmington & Baltimore, as well as those operated by the PRR. However, many of Philadelphia's residents were not happy at the extra distance that they had to travel before they could board their train. The members of the Select and Common Councils had once expressed their displeasure at the rail traffic that clogged city streets. Yet, they were also determined to preserve Philadelphia's role as a connection point between the PRR, the Joint Companies, and the PW&B. During the war, despite the federal government's desperate need for troops and supplies, councilmen attempted to block the construction of the Junction Railroad and the Connecting Railway, but to no avail. By 1869, with the war over and with traffic flowing smoothly through West Philadelphia, workers had ripped up much of the trackage of the City Railroad along Market and Broad Streets.[63]

The Civil War also demonstrated the inadequacy of terminal arrangements in Baltimore as thousands of Union troops funneled through the city on their way to southern battlefields. Efforts to remove tracks from city streets would have to wait until well after the war, thanks in part to a determined campaign by the Baltimore & Ohio to prevent the PRR from expanding into its territory.[64]

The final gap in the route between Philadelphia and Baltimore was not closed until 1866. As early as 1851, PW&B officials discussed the possibility of building a bridge across the mouth of the Susquehanna River, at Havre de Grace, and in 1854 and 1855 they authorized surveys and preliminary site preparation. A combination of engineering challenges and a shortage of funds soon brought work to a halt. In 1862, a surge in wartime traffic prompted PW&B officials to authorize the resumption of construction. Crews sank masonry piers into the riverbed and then erected thirteen Howe truss spans—made of wood, but sheathed in iron, so as to be fireproof. On July 25, 1866, as the bridge was nearing completion, a tornado destroyed most of the superstructure. Undaunted, company officials ordered the damage rebuilt and the remainder of the project brought to completion, and the bridge opened to traffic in November.[65]

One War Ends, and Another Begins

Even before the battlefields of the Civil War had grown quiet, the executives who represented the PRR and the other major northeastern trunk lines—the New York Central, the Erie, and the Baltimore & Ohio—were preparing for another sort of battle, to determine who would control lucrative sources of traffic. With its physical plant and its balance sheet strengthened by the war, the Pennsylvania Railroad was well positioned to fend off the expansionist efforts

Figure 32. Beginning in 1836, trains traveling north on the Philadelphia, Wilmington & Baltimore Railroad approached Philadelphia from the southwest, and then swung sharply east at Gray's Ferry and crossed over the Schuylkill River. They followed Prime Street (today's Washington Avenue) east as far as Broad Street, where they joined the tracks of the Southwark Rail-Road. Moving north along Broad Street, they reached the northern extremity of the Southwark line at Cedar Street (South Street, today). From there, the City Railroad continued north to Vine Street and the beginning of the Philadelphia & Columbia Railroad. The PRR's Delaware Extension, built between 1859 and 1862, employed an existing section of PW&B track, along with the new Arsenal Bridge over the Schuylkill River, for access to the Delaware River waterfront. The Junction Railroad, completed in 1864, enabled PW&B trains to reach PRR tracks in West Philadelphia. The Connecting Railway, completed in 1867, provided ready access to the Philadelphia & Trenton route to New York.

Figure 33. (top left) John W. Garrett (1820–1884) attained
the presidency of the Baltimore & Ohio in 1858. After the
Civil War, he was determined to establish western outlets at
St. Louis and Chicago, as well as to Virginia and points
south. (top right) Cornelius Vanderbilt (1794–1877) earned
a substantial fortune while operating steamboats along the
Hudson River between Manhattan and Albany. In 1867 he
established control over the chain of railroads that paralleled
the Hudson River and the Erie Canal between New York and
Buffalo, as part of the New York Central system. (right) Jay
Gould (1836–1892) outmaneuvered Vanderbilt and gained
control over the Erie Railway, a chronically weak carrier
recently emerged from bankruptcy. Gould's tactics in that
fight helped cement his reputation in the eyes of the public
as an unscrupulous speculator. Once ensconced as the Erie's
president, however, Gould invested heavily in the company,
turning it into an efficient, high-volume, low-rate carrier
capable of accommodating substantial quantities of traffic.
All three executives, and the railroads that they managed,
represented a serious threat to the Pennsylvania Railroad.

*(top left) Library of Congress Prints & Photographs Division,
LC-B2-5332-12;(top right) George Grantham Bain Collection,
Library of Congress Prints & Photographs Division,
LC-USZ62-100652; (right) George Grantham Bain Collection,
Library of Congress Prints & Photographs Division,
LC-B2-785-1.*

of rival carriers. Yet, executives like Thomson and Scott would face severe challenges in the immediate postwar period, particularly as they fought for the oil traffic that originated in their home state of Pennsylvania.

The Baltimore & Ohio, badly damaged in the war, was perhaps the least serious of those threats. Yet, even the B&O's president, John W. Garrett, was able to extend the railroad's influence south into Virginia, while in 1866 authorizing the construction of a line, the Metropolitan Branch, that would improve access between Washington, D.C., and the west. More ominously, in November 1866, Garrett leased the Central Ohio Railroad, with a line from Wheeling west to Columbus, Ohio. In May 1868, workers began construction on a bridge across the Ohio River at Wheeling. The next year, the Central Ohio leased the Sandusky, Mansfield & Newark Railroad, giving the B&O access to Lake Erie. At virtually the same time, work began on another bridge across the Ohio River, at Parkersburg, that when completed would provide the B&O with a direct link with the still independent but nonetheless closely allied Marietta & Cincinnati Railroad. No one, least of all Thomson, could doubt that Garrett coveted access to Chicago.[66]

Under the leadership of former Hudson River steamboat operator Cornelius Vanderbilt, the New York Central was rapidly emerging as the PRR's most significant competitor and its chief rival for access to the west. With a substantial fortune at his disposal, Vanderbilt bought the two railroads that paralleled the Hudson River and competed with his steamboats—the New York & Harlem Railroad in 1863 and the Hudson River Railroad in 1864. Three years later, when he became president of the New York Central Railroad, Vanderbilt presided over an all-rail route between New York and Buffalo. In late 1867 and early 1868, Vanderbilt attempted to gain control of the Erie, as well, but failed to match the financial manipulations of Daniel Drew, the Erie's treasurer. In November 1869 Vanderbilt merged his holdings into the New York Central & Hudson River Railroad.[67]

With the New York Central under his control, Vanderbilt became more interested in establishing alliances in Ohio, Indiana, and Illinois. Between 1867 and 1869, a series of mergers combined the Buffalo & Erie Railroad; the Cleveland, Painesville & Ashtabula Railroad; the Cleveland & Toledo Railroad; and the Michigan Southern & Northern Indiana Railroad, forming the Lake Shore & Michigan Southern Railway, with a continuous route between Buffalo and Chicago. Vanderbilt did not gain control over the Lake Shore & Michigan Southern until 1873, but even before then the line functioned as a western extension to the New York Central, and constituted a serious threat to the interests of the PRR.

The New York & Erie Rail Road, financially weaker than the New York Central, was only marginally less dangerous. In 1859, the Erie was the first major American railroad to enter bankruptcy, emerging in 1861 as a reorganized but scarcely healthier company, the Erie Railway. Yet, the Erie held considerable promise, should it have the benefit of better management and additional capital. New York financier Jay Gould recognized that potential. In cooperation with fellow investors Daniel Drew and James Fisk, Gould invested heavily in the Erie, and in 1867 he gained a seat on the Erie's board of directors. By early 1868, through his adroit use of what even his allies admitted was financial chicanery, Gould managed to deflect Vanderbilt's efforts to seize control of the railroad. By July 1868, after unceremoniously dumping his ally, Daniel Drew, Gould was president of the Erie. Belying his reputation as someone who was little better than an unscrupulous financial manipulator, Gould invested heavily in the company.[68] The installation of steel rails, double tracking, and the provision of new locomotives and cars helped transform the Erie from a ramshackle line into an efficient, high-volume, low-rate carrier. That transformation would prove vital to efforts by the Erie and its western connection—the Atlantic & Great Western Railroad—to gain control over a lucrative source of traffic that flowed out of the hills of northwestern Pennsylvania.[69]

Drake's Well

The Civil War coincided with a monumental economic transformation in northwestern Pennsylvania, one that exerted profound effects on the Pennsylvania Railroad. Crude oil, a product valuable for lubrication and illumination, although not yet for propulsion, sparked a fierce competition among the trunk lines for business. The resulting oil wars, which continued long after the Civil War ended, led to the construction of additional routes, the development of a new generation of transportation firms, and the reestablishment of cartels, in order to control rates. Despite the advantages possessed by the PRR—not the least of which was that the oil originated in the company's home state—Thomson and Scott experienced one setback after another in their efforts to control the oil trade. The story that began at Drake's well ended badly for the PRR and, to a substantial degree, ended badly for the railroad industry as a whole.

In 1859, just as the Erie entered bankruptcy and construction on the Sunbury & Erie Railroad lurched to a halt, the first great oil strike in world history upset the competitive balance of the railroad network in the eastern United States. Native Americans had long known of the oil that seeped from the ground in that region. By the late 1700s white settlers were collecting small amounts of oil and tar, initially as a form of medicine, and later to lubricate machinery and burn for illumination. In 1854, Jonathan G. Eveleth and George H. Bissell, partners in a New York law firm, incorporated the Pennsylvania Rock Oil Company, and purchased more than a hundred acres of land in Venango County. The following year, Benjamin Silliman, Jr., a chemist from Yale University, analyzed a sample of oil taken from that land, and said that it could be successfully refined into kerosene and other commercially viable products. Bissell and Eveleth hired former railroader Edwin Drake to drill oil wells in the vicinity of Titusville. On August 27, 1859, at a depth of less than seventy feet, Drake struck oil.[70]

Drake's well, and the others that soon sprouted nearby, created a freewheeling economic boom in northwestern Pennsylvania, in communities such as Titusville, Oil City, and Franklin. With minimal efficiency and with scant regard for the environmental consequences, drillers rushed to extract as much oil from the ground as possible. The oil that gushed from the earth went first into large holding tanks, and then into various sizes of wooden barrels. There was, as yet, no railroad transportation into the oil region, and barges ferried the barrels down the Allegheny River. In their wake came tub-like scows, filled with oil and covered over with canvas tarps, all bound for Pittsburgh.[71]

Rails to the Oilfields

The Atlantic & Great Western Railroad was the first carrier to reach the oilfields. During the 1850s, entrepreneurs in southwestern New York, northwestern Pennsylvania, and northeastern Ohio chartered three separate companies in order to construct a six-foot gauge line that, although independent of the Erie, would serve as a westward extension of that company's route.[72] An 1857 New York charter enabled the promoters to consolidate the three railroads under cooperative ownership as the Atlantic & Great Western. The company's backers soon headed for Europe to raise capital and procure iron rails. They succeeded, thanks in large measure to the efforts of a Spanish nobleman, Don José de Salamanca, who placed $1 million in A&GW bonds. The infusion of capital enabled construction crews to build west from a junction with the Erie at Salamanca, New York, reaching Jamestown in September 1860. On May 15, 1861, the tracks reached Corry, Pennsylvania, and a junction with the old Sunbury & Erie, a railroad that had been renamed the Philadelphia & Erie barely two months earlier. With most of the A&GW's capital exhausted, however, the company remained stalled at Corry for the next year.[73]

Corry lay little more than twenty miles to the north of Titusville, within striking distance of the heart of the oil fields. In October 1862, six months after the A&GW reached its temporary western terminus, the Oil Creek Railroad became the first carrier to penetrate the region, linking Corry and Titusville. By the following year, construction crews had extended the tracks farther south, to Petroleum Centre. The Oil Creek was an independent, locally controlled company, but it was constructed to broad gauge, ensuring that oil would begin to flow to New York over the Erie. During the summer of 1863, the Atlantic & Great Western completed a branch line linking Meadville to Franklin, giving the company another route into the oil region, this time from the west.[74] In October 1863, the A&GW leased the Cleveland & Mahoning Railroad. Within a month, construction crews had converted the Cleveland & Mahoning into a dual-gauge line, capable of routing shipments from Cleveland to Jersey City, via the Erie, and it was not long before the city on the lake became a major refining center.[75]

Thomson and his fellow executives had every reason to be concerned at the progress of the Atlantic & Great Western. In cooperation with the Erie, the A&GW had established the first uniform-gauge rail line between the oil region and the east coast. Exploiting that advantage, A&GW and Erie managers elected to maximize throughput, shipping large quantities of freight to the east by keeping rates as low as possible. By the summer of 1864, that low rate/high volume strategy, even more ambitious than the one Herman Haupt had first recommended for the PRR a decade earlier, enabled the A&GW to dominate the rapidly expanding oil trade.

More ominously, in the spring of 1862, construction had resumed on the A&GW main line, and it seemed only a matter of time before the broad-gauge rails would reach the grain-growing regions of the Midwest. Indeed, by June 1864 the company had opened a route, angling in a southwesterly direction across Ohio, to Dayton. There, a connection with the Cincinnati, Hamilton & Dayton Railroad and the Ohio & Mississippi Rail Road provided an unbroken line of broad-gauge track between St. Louis and New York. The new route held the potential to deprive the PRR of much of its western traffic.[76]

Fortunately for the PRR, both the Atlantic & Great Western and the Erie were in poor physical and financial condition. The Erie was in bankruptcy between 1859 and 1861, and it limped along for several years after emerging from receivership. The two companies operated a single-track railroad, at a time when the PRR was almost entirely double-tracked between Pittsburgh and Philadelphia. Capital shortages and wartime inflation had drastically curtailed equipment purchases. Conditions on the Erie were so poor that, during the winter of 1864, managers on the A&GW had little choice other than to turn away fully 80 percent of the eastbound business offered to them.[77]

Thomson was nonetheless caught off guard by the unexpectedly rapid progress of the Atlantic & Great Western. He was, after all, busily engaged in fending off efforts by competing carriers to control routes through southeastern Pennsylvania, along the Susquehanna River, and in anthracite country. At the same time, he was expanding the PRR's interests in Ohio and Indiana, while overseeing efforts to repeal the tonnage tax, refine the PRR's corporate structure, and raise additional capital during a period of economic uncertainty. Yet, the inability of A&GW and Erie officials to cope with the rapid rise in oil traffic negated much of their initial advantage over the PRR, and gave Thomson room to maneuver.

Thomson counterattacked quickly, once he realized the danger posed by the Atlantic & Great Western and the Erie to both the PRR's oil revenues and its share of the western grain trade. He employed three basic strategies in his effort to protect the PRR from the A&GW/Erie combination, as well as from an increasingly powerful New York Central. First, Thomson supported the development of new lines, either controlled by or closely allied with the PRR, which gave him better access to the oilfields. Second, he exploited new equipment, particularly tank cars and pipelines, which promised to increase transportation efficiency. Finally, Thomson, Scott, and their PRR colleagues reconceptualized the role of the prewar transportation firms, transforming them into a new generation of freight forwarders. While such methods helped stem the loss of oil traffic to rival carriers, they could not prevent the decline of Pittsburgh as a refining center, as that city yielded to Cleveland. In the long run, therefore, and despite Thomson's best efforts, the PRR failed to dominate the oil trade. Furthermore, many of the tactics that Thomson, Scott, and others employed generated considerable opposition, as much from the oilmen and the politicians who represented them as from the executives of the other trunk lines.

New Routes to the Oilfields I:
The Western Pennsylvania Railroad

During the early years of the oil boom, the low transportation costs afforded by the Allegheny River ensured that Pittsburgh became the leading refining center in the United States. In addition to enjoying a convenient water route to the oilfields, the city also benefited from an established support structure that included machine shops, foundries, engine builders, and barrel makers. In 1861, Pittsburgh received more than one hundred thousand barrels of oil, and by the spring of the following year, the city had the largest storage capacity in the United States. Oil receipts peaked at 1,250,000 barrels in 1866, with storage and refinery capacity increasing as well. By the end of the Civil War, Pittsburgh possessed eighty-six refineries processing crude oil. The bulk of the resulting kerosene and other products, along with much of the remaining crude, continued east over the Pennsylvania Railroad.[78]

Even though the PRR dominated the oil trade that flowed through Pittsburgh, Thomson sought a more direct connection to the oilfields. His opportunity came in the form of the North Western Rail Road Company, incorporated in February 1853. Its promoters, mainly residents of Butler and Lawrence Counties, had envisioned a line connecting the PRR at some point near Johnstown with Cleveland, by way of Butler, and a junction with the Cleveland & Mahoning Railroad, near New Castle. Unlike the companies that would eventually become part of the Pittsburgh, Fort Wayne & Chicago (which used Ohio-gauge track), the North Western project promised a standard-gauge route between Philadelphia and Chicago. Political and economic interests in Philadelphia perceived the benefits of such a link, and the Select and Common Councils subscribed to $750,000 of the company's stock. Pittsburghers were far less supportive, however, as the line would allow western trade to flow to tidewater without passing through their city. Construction began in 1854, but financial problems and the disinterest of the Cleveland & Mahoning investors brought the project to a halt a few years later. In 1859, the PRR board considered purchasing the tattered remnants of the company, but by then they had already reached agreement with George Cass and the Pittsburgh, Fort Wayne & Chicago and had little use for an alternate route through northern Ohio.[79]

The Civil War and the oil boom reinvigorated the North Western. In 1860, the company reorganized as the Western Pennsylvania Railroad, and its promoters were soon asking the PRR for assistance. In May 1862,

the PRR directors approved aid, under the terms of the Commutation Act, but soon rescinded their support. Soon after, however, the board agreed to purchase some Western Pennsylvania bonds, and to sell to the company Western Division Canal. Construction resumed in 1863, with track crews laying rail along the bed of the abandoned canal. By the summer of 1865, they reached the Allegheny River at Kiskiminetas (Kiski) Junction, near Freeport. The PRR soon leased the Western Pennsylvania, with Thomson envisioning the route as a low-grade bypass around congested trackage at Pittsburgh. By November 1866, the PRR had extended the line from Kiski Junction along the west side of the Allegheny River (again using the right-of-way of the abandoned Western Division Canal) to a connection with the Fort Wayne in Allegheny City.[80]

The Western Pennsylvania Railroad offered the PRR an excellent mechanism for moving oil directly to tidewater, bypassing the Pittsburgh refineries. By 1865, in addition to hauling refined petroleum east from Pittsburgh, the PRR transported some 1,500 barrels of crude oil directly to the east coast each day, representing more than sixty cars. Pittsburgh refiners reacted with alarm to the Western Pennsylvania Railroad. As they perceived the situation, Thomson and Scott, not content with their monopoly over transportation in southwestern Pennsylvania, were willing to cast adrift the city and one of its leading industries.[81]

New Routes to the Oilfields II: The Philadelphia & Erie Railroad

Oil revenues gave a new sense of urgency to the decades-old dream of connecting Philadelphia and Erie by rail. The organizers of the hapless Sunbury & Erie had spent a quarter of a century trying to complete the line, yet they had little to show for their efforts, save a financially crippled corporation and two disconnected segments of railroad track—one between Sunbury and Williamsport and the other linking Erie and Warren. The isolated Western Division was dependent on a connection with the Erie & North East Railroad (later the Buffalo & Erie Railroad, then the Lake

Shore & Michigan Southern Railway and, ultimately, the New York Central), and another with the Atlantic & Great Western at Corry. Corry was also the northern gateway to the oil region, and the Sunbury & Erie held the potential to funnel oil traffic toward Philadelphia. Yet, the line was of little practical value so long as the 142-mile gap remained, between Warren and Williamsport.[82]

Thomson's first priority was to ensure the completion of the Sunbury & Erie, and he assigned that task to Scott. In March 1861, two months before the A&GW reached Corry, the Pennsylvania General Assembly had amended the Sunbury & Erie charter, renaming it the Philadelphia & Erie Railroad. The legislation also authorized the new company to issue $5 million in first mortgage bonds, for sale to the public, and an additional $4 million in second mortgage bonds. The latter securities, which constituted an inferior lien on the property, were given to the commonwealth in exchange for the $3.5 million in Sunbury & Erie bonds that had been tied to the sale of portions of the state's canal network. A month later, on a plea of urgent wartime necessity, Scott shepherded through the legislature a bill permitting railroads incorporated in Pennsylvania to acquire the securities of any other railroad chartered in the state, so long as they made a physical connection.

The new law enabled the PRR to control the Philadelphia & Erie directly, subject to stockholder approval. That was not difficult, as the PRR was the largest single stockholder in the Philadelphia & Erie, with the City of Philadelphia a close second, and other interests very much in the minority. PRR officials informed investors in both companies that the Philadelphia & Erie route was bound to be completed, "by some other Company, if not by this, at no very distant period." Should a hostile carrier complete the line, they continued, a rate war between the Philadelphia & Erie and the PRR would be inevitable. PRR control over the Philadelphia & Erie, however, "forever sets at rest efforts to obtain traffic by reduced rates which have been invariably resorted to upon the completion of all new competing lines." That statement offered a fairly clear indication that the consolidation of the two railroads would reduce competition—a circum-

stance that some Pennsylvanians might construe as running counter to the public interest. Making a virtue out of a necessity that they themselves had helped to create, PRR executives argued that the combination of public and private financing that underwrote the construction of both the PRR and the Philadelphia & Erie mandated consolidation, for the good of the people. "The ownership of nearly one half of both railways is in the same party, the City of Philadelphia," they explained, "while under the provisions of the Charters of the respective Companies, they [the Philadelphia Select and Common Councils] cannot interpose any effectual check to the injury which the Managers of those works might inflict upon each other's revenues, without a corresponding benefit to any interest within this Commonwealth." That statement ignored any possibility that competition, and hence lower rates, might constitute "a corresponding benefit to any interest within this Commonwealth." More significantly, the rationale of PRR executives indicated how readily they exploited public funding for their enterprise, without yielding a corresponding degree of control to the government that had provided that money. PRR officials ignored an obvious solution to the problem of suicidal competition—namely, that the Select and Common Councils, through their representatives on each company's board of directors, should coordinate operations between the two carriers. They instead insisted that an increase in the corporate power of private managers such as Thomson, with the possibility of an attendant decline in competition, constituted the only realistic method of protecting the city's investment in two companies.[83]

The members of the Select and Common Councils, as well as the few private investors who were not connected to the PRR, probably needed little prodding. The ample investment opportunities associated with the Civil War ensured that few speculators were interested in the Philadelphia & Erie first mortgage bond issue. On June 27, with no other options available, Philadelphia & Erie stockholders agreed to lease their company to the PRR—an action that would have been a violation of state law only a few months earlier. In November, six months after the A&GW had reached Corry, PRR shareholders approved the

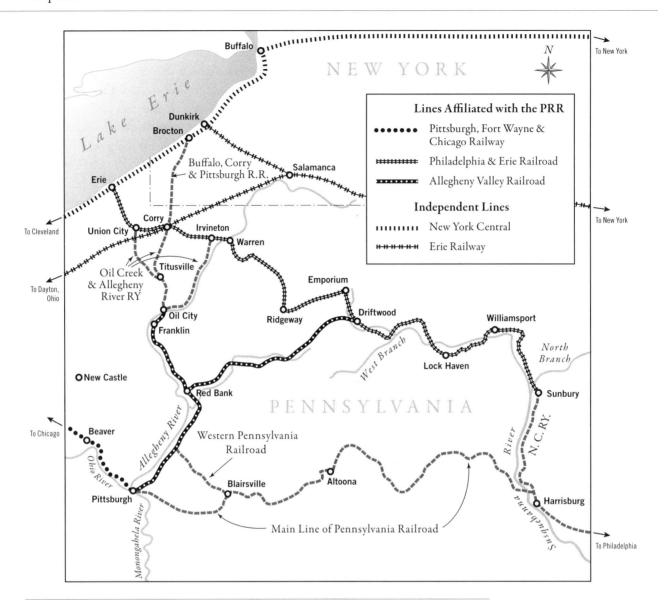

Figure 34. During the 1860s and into the early 1870s, J. Edgar Thomson attempted to increase the PRR's share of the northwestern Pennsylvania oil trade by constructing better routes into the region. The northernmost line, finished in 1864, was the Philadelphia & Erie Railroad (the former Sunbury & Erie). The Allegheny Valley Railroad, completed in 1867, linked Pittsburgh to Oil City. Under Thomson's guidance, the Philadelphia & Erie and the Allegheny Valley cooperated on the construction of a low-grade line between Driftwood and Red Bank, opened in 1874. The southernmost route was the Western Pennsylvania Railroad. In 1865, its tracks connected Blairsville to Kiskiminetas (Kiski) Junction (Freeport) on the Allegheny River. The Western Pennsylvania reached Pittsburgh in 1866, paralleling the Allegheny Valley route on the opposite bank of the river. Pittsburgh refiners, who had built their initial dominance of the oil trade on the advantages that the Allegheny River had provided, could not help but be concerned that most of the new PRR routes, while well suited for the movement of oil to tidewater, nonetheless bypassed their city.

terms of a 999-year lease, effective on January 1, 1862, bringing the Philadelphia & Erie under the control of Thomson and Scott. By October 1864, and with the resources of the Pennsylvania Railroad at their disposal, construction crews closed the gap between Williamsport and Warren, uniting the two segments of the Philadelphia & Erie. In conjunction with the Northern Central Railway, controlled by the PRR since 1861, Thomson possessed a direct route between Erie and Philadelphia.[84]

The Philadelphia & Erie helped Thomson compete more effectively against the New York trunk lines, but the route did not live up to expectations. Aside from oil, very little freight flowed along the Philadelphia & Erie, a railroad that transected a sparsely populated region. Some lumber moved eastbound, and some anthracite westbound, but the Great Lakes grain traffic that Philadelphians so eagerly sought continued to travel by the slower but cheaper Erie Canal. Despite the completion of the Philadelphia & Erie and its associated branches, the Atlantic & Great Western still transported far more oil than did the Pennsylvania Railroad. Oil shipments on the PRR's northwestern Pennsylvania route increased from a mere 325 barrels in 1859 (on what was then the Western Division of the Sunbury & Erie) to 300,000 in 1864 and 400,000 the following year. Yet, that paled in comparison to the more than 750,000 barrels shipped on the A&GW during 1865, not to mention the nearly 700,000 barrels that moved to Pittsburgh along the Allegheny River.[85]

Thomson and his associates embraced several interrelated strategies for improving the performance of the Philadelphia & Erie. The first involved the development of yet more rail links, in both western and eastern Pennsylvania. During the summer of 1864, Scott pulled the Oil Creek Railroad out of the orbit of the Atlantic & Great Western, negotiating an agreement with the New York Central to jointly own the line and share its traffic.[86] The owners of the Oil Creek had already converted their line to dual gauge in anticipation of a connection with the Philadelphia & Erie. Its new owners ordered the outermost rail ripped up, denying its usefulness to the broad-gauge Atlantic & Great Western. Also in 1864,

the PRR established control over a local line, chartered in May 1861 as the Warren & Tidioute Railroad, and in 1865 renamed the Warren & Franklin Railway (not to be confused with the Franklin & Warren Railroad, one of the broad-gauge predecessors of the Atlantic & Great Western). By 1866, construction crews had completed the Warren & Franklin between Oil City and Irvineton, a station on the Philadelphia & Erie.[87]

Although executives from the trunk lines competed vigorously for long-haul oil traffic, in northwestern Pennsylvania they generally favored cooperation over confrontation, maintaining a sort of open access arrangement to the oilfields. In September 1865, a group of investors closely linked to the PRR, and led by Scott, acquired sole control of the Oil Creek Railroad from the New York Central. In January 1868, the Warren & Franklin gained control of the Farmers Railroad, a line that connected Oil City and Petroleum Centre. A month later, the merger of the Oil Creek Railroad and the Warren & Franklin Railway, forming the Oil Creek & Allegheny River Railway, gave PRR and NYC control over the main routes into the oilfields.[88] The crucial element of the cooperative management lay in a fixed rate of fifty cents for every barrel of oil transported to either the Atlantic & Great Western at Corry or to the Philadelphia & Erie at Irvineton.[89] Oil producers considered that rate to be far too high, but they could at least console themselves with predictable transportation costs.[90]

The PRR also became involved in a much more extensive construction project in western Pennsylvania, in the form of a low-grade freight line along Red Bank Creek. That endeavor brought the Philadelphia & Erie and the PRR into a closer association with the Allegheny Valley Railroad, a company that enabled oil to reach Pittsburgh's refineries. A further strategy for improving the performance of the Philadelphia & Erie depended on the Catawissa Railroad as a shortcut between the Philadelphia & Erie and New York. That plan entailed not the construction of additional tracks, but rather a transformation of the traffic that ran over them, in the form of the fast freight lines.

Figure 35. Since its incorporation in 1837, the Sunbury & Erie Railroad had made slow progress toward the goal of linking Philadelphia and Lake Erie. The discovery of oil in northwestern Pennsylvania increased the value of the line to the Pennsylvania Railroad. In 1861, the company was renamed the Philadelphia & Erie Railroad, and the PRR's lobbyists persuaded the members of the General Assembly to pass legislation permitting the PRR to lease the line. In addition to providing financial support, the PRR assigned some of its most promising young engineers and surveyors, in order to complete the route to Erie. Many of the individuals relaxing at Renovo, Pennsylvania, in 1864 later achieved considerable renown on the PRR itself, none more so than Alexander J. Cassatt (second from left). He had just been appointed resident engineer on the Middle Division of the Philadelphia & Erie, and in 1899 he became the PRR's seventh president. Like Cassatt, Robert Neilson (far right) was a graduate of Rensselaer Polytechnic Institute. In 1863, he was hired as a rodman, and he was promoted to resident engineer only two years later. He died in office in 1896, as the general superintendent of the Philadelphia & Erie Railroad Division and the Northern Central Railway. Henry R. Campbell, in the center, was a veteran civil engineer and locomotive designer who had once mentored Herman Haupt, and in 1864 he took responsibility for laying out the Philadelphia & Erie shops at Renovo. Albert Hewson, right of center, later served as an assistant to senior executive George Brooke Roberts and held administrative posts on a number of PRR subsidiaries.

Pennsylvania Historical and Museum Commission, Pennsylvania State Archives.

New Routes to the Oilfields III: The Allegheny Valley Railroad and the Low-Grade Line

Pittsburgh refiners reacted with alarm to the ability of the Atlantic & Great Western, as well as the PRR's Western Pennsylvania Railroad, to draw traffic away from their city. Anxious to preserve their city's status as the nation's leading refining center, Pittsburghers resurrected a moribund railroad that paralleled the Allegheny River, from Pittsburgh north toward the oil-fields. Originally incorporated in April 1837 as the Pittsburgh, Kittanning & Warren Railroad, its pro-moters envisioned a company that would reach to the New York state line, with other carriers extending the route to Buffalo. However, financial crises delayed construction for the next fifteen years. In April 1852, the investors secured an amendment to the original charter so that the company, renamed the Allegheny Valley Railroad, could build a broad-gauge line that would connect Pittsburgh to the New York & Erie Rail Road at Olean, New York, with access from there to Buffalo. Construction began in March 1854, and by January 1856, tracklaying progressed as far as Kittan-ning, forty-four miles north of Pittsburgh, before the company again ran out of capital.[91]

The oil boom reawakened interest in the Allegheny Valley Railroad. Work resumed in 1863, and by January 1865 the company's board of directors had autho-rized the completion of the line to Oil City. The following year, Colonel William Phillips, a partner in the refinery of Phillips & Frew, assembled a new slate of directors and ordered that construction proceed with all possible speed. By December 1867, tracks reached Venango City, on the east bank of the Alle-gheny River, opposite Oil City. A pipeline laid across the river enabled the Allegheny Valley to capture a siz-able share of the oil traffic. The Allegheny Valley pro-vided Pittsburgh with direct rail access to the oilfields, but the new line was not sufficient to ensure that the city's refiners would retain their dominant position in the refinery business.[92]

As the decade of the 1860s neared its end, the Allegheny Valley remained independent of the PRR, although the two companies interchanged consid-erable traffic at Kiski Junction and at Pittsburgh. Very quickly, however, the Allegheny Valley came under PRR influence. That development was in part a re-sponse to the construction of a route, affiliated with the New York Central, between Corry and Brocton on Lake Erie, and convenient to both Cleveland and Buffalo.[93] An even more significant factor was Thom-son's vision of a new freight line across western Penn-sylvania, one that would remedy the defects of the Philadelphia & Erie while easing congestion on the original PRR main line.

The increased traffic that accompanied the Civil War and the period of economic prosperity that fol-lowed taxed the PRR's main line to its capacity. The installation of a second track ensured that trains could move efficiently in opposite directions, with few delays caused by meets and little danger of collision. How-ever, the double-track main line was ill-suited to cope with trains that traveled at different speeds. The need to pass fast passenger trains around slow-moving freights created almost as many difficulties as the op-eration of trains in two directions over a single-track railroad. "A line possessing a large mixed traffic, such as commanded by the Pennsylvania Railroad," Thom-son emphasized in the PRR's 1867 *Annual Report*, "cannot fully meet this requirement without the con-struction of a third track throughout its length, by which trains can be moved at a low rate of speed with-out serious interruption to the traffic that will pay the cost of a more rapid movement."[94]

Thomson believed that he could avoid the need to lay additional tracks along the PRR's original main line by building a direct, low-grade line that would ex-peditiously move vast quantities of grain and other bulk commodities over long distances, at rates that would finally undercut both competing railroads and the Erie Canal. West of Driftwood, Pennsylvania, lay the lowest summit crossing of the Alleghenies, with such a gradual ascent that, decades earlier, surveyors had contemplated using the route as part of the com-monwealth's canal system. Because the route bypassed Pittsburgh and other large urban areas, it held little potential for the development of passenger or local freight traffic. However, the low grades and absence of congestion made it ideally suited for long-distance through freight traffic. Thomson envisioned a parade of long freight trains, traveling at a steady six miles per hour, slowly hauling grain, coal, oil, and other bulk commodities, unimpeded by grades, passenger trains, or local traffic. Like sailors on ships at sea, crewmen would live on board, continually rotating on twelve-hour shifts, as the trains ground slowly across the landscape of northern Pennsylvania.[95]

In no sense, however, did Thomson envision a low-grade bypass across northwestern Pennsylvania as a substitute for the route that he had designed some twenty years earlier. Any attempt "to supersede the present lines" of the PRR would starve them of traffic, Thomson noted, and "can only end in disastrous failure wherever tried."[96] Thomson was nonetheless steadfast in his belief that increased traffic on an efficient, low-grade route could generate high enough throughput to drive down rates to unprecedented levels, in some instances at least. At present, Thomson noted, there was precisely one efficient, low-speed, high-volume carrier in the United States, and that was the Erie Canal. The proposed low-grade line would be another; as he stated, "No route in Pennsylvania or elsewhere between the seaboard and the West affords equal facilities for the introduction of this system as the line occupied by the Eastern portion of the Philadelphia and Erie Railroad."[97]

Thomson envisioned that the new route might be extended west into Ohio, and to a connection with the allied Pittsburgh, Fort Wayne & Chicago. "A railroad operated on this plan," he suggested, "will ultimately be extended to the Mississippi River across the table lands of Ohio, Indiana, and Illinois . . . [and] will afford a medium of transportation at all seasons of the year as cheap and more expeditious than *via* the Lakes and the Erie Canal, without materially interfering with the prospects of existing lines."[98] At that time, the Erie Canal moved more grain to tidewater than did the PRR, and it would be at least another decade before the railroads could compete successfully for the bulk of that traffic. Thomson nevertheless suggested that the new low-grade route could compete successfully against the water carriers.

Thomson's plan was simple in conception, yet it proved extraordinarily difficult to implement. At the instigation of PRR officials, the directors of the Philadelphia & Erie agreed to build the line between Driftwood (a junction on the Philadelphia & Erie, midway between Williamsport and Warren) and Red Bank.

Under the terms of its corporate charter, however, they did not possess the right to build west of the Jefferson County border. The authority to construct the rest of the route lay with the independent Allegheny Valley Railroad. The owners of the Allegheny Valley, which had never been a terribly prosperous railroad, realized that the PRR's plans had offered them an extraordinary opportunity to extract the best possible terms for the sale of their company. PRR executives had little choice other than to acquire partial ownership in the Allegheny Valley, and by December 1868 they owned twenty-five thousand shares of that company's stock. Protracted negotiations resulted in a plan whereby the PRR would provide money to its subsidiary, the Philadelphia & Erie, to allow that railroad to buy back $7.5 million of its own bonds from the Allegheny Valley; they were the same securities that the commonwealth had purchased in order to aid the Philadelphia & Erie's construction, and they were now in effect traded for $3.5 million in Allegheny Valley second-mortgage bonds.[99]

Surveys for the low-grade route began in 1868, but construction proved more difficult than anticipated. Completed in May 1874, the 110-mile line entered service the following month as the Low Grade Division of the Allegheny Valley Railroad. The directors' initial concern about the project's expense had certainly been justified, as the cost had ballooned to nearly $13 million, more than twice the initial estimates. Even worse, the Allegheny Valley was still nominally an independent company, not subject to full oversight by PRR officials. When the Allegheny Valley's president, William Philips, died unexpectedly in 1874, an inspection of the company's books revealed gross mismanagement, as well as financial irregularities. Under those circumstances, PRR personnel believed that increased control offered the only way to safeguard the Allegheny Valley's finances and to protect their investment in the company. Pittsburgh businessman John Scott, a PRR director (no relation to Tom Scott, and not to be confused with Senator John Scott, later the PRR's general solicitor), became the president of the Allegheny Valley. Thomas Scott and fellow PRR executive George B. Roberts served on the Allegheny Valley board of directors.[100]

Despite the PRR's increasing control over the Allegheny Valley, Thomson's low-grade route never fulfilled his expectations. Even after the oil boom ended, the low-grade line continued to serve as a useful freight route to and from Pittsburgh. However, the great ships on rails never materialized, and most through traffic continued to travel east over the original main line. The route might have been more valuable to the PRR, had Thomson been able to fulfill his vision of a westward extension, across northern Ohio, northern Indiana, and on to Chicago. For the next sixty years several of his successors had similar aspirations, until the Great Depression and the decline in freight traffic finally put an end to such ambitious plans for expansion. Had it been completed, however, the route would have bypassed Altoona, the Horseshoe Curve, Pittsburgh's notorious traffic congestion, and the curving trackage to the west of that city, creating the shortest and fastest route between the East and the Midwest. While Thomson never succeeded in fully implementing his ideas, the dream of a route that would serve as a merchandise conveyor belt between the Midwest and tidewater would linger for generations.[101]

The Fast Freight Lines: An Intermediate Step in System-Building

The construction of new rail routes—from the Philadelphia & Erie to the Allegheny Valley and its associated low-grade line—were not sufficient to increase the PRR's share of the oil trade. PRR officials concluded that the loss of oil revenues to the A&GW and the Erie could be countered only by creating a system of fast freight lines that were closely associated with, but organizationally separate from, the Pennsylvania Railroad. As the PRR's general freight agent, Henry H. Houston, emphasized, the arrival of the Atlantic & Great Western in northwestern Pennsylvania constituted "the point at which the necessity of Fast Freight Lines on the Pennsylvania Railroad became a fixed fact."[102] Aside from their importance in oil transportation, fast freight lines increased operating efficiency during a critical surge in wartime traffic, while increasing the PRR's ability to acquire traffic from the Midwest.

The fast freight lines created during the Civil War represented an intermediate step in the progression from the prewar use of independent transporters and freight agents toward a traffic department that was wholly a part of the corporation—a process that was not completed until the 1880s. The earlier transporters, such as Clarke & Thaw and David Leech & Company, typically began their operations on the Main Line of Public Works. They had been responsible for coordinating shipments that moved across Pennsylvania and, often, onto Ohio River steamboats. They had long since been incorporated into the PRR's organization, with their equipment, facilities, and personnel becoming part of the Freight Department. In the Midwest, particularly during the 1850s, independent freight agents had solicited grain shipments and dispatched them east over whichever route offered the lowest transportation costs—and they accordingly helped to destabilize the rate structure of the railroad industry, despite efforts by Thomson and other executives to bring them under control.

In place of the transporters and the commission agents arose a new generation of freight forwarders—the Star Union Line, the Empire Line, and the Anchor Line. The companies were outwardly similar to the prewar transportation firms that had operated over the Main Line of Public Works but, in their new incarnation, they were far more closely connected to the PRR's management. The fast freight lines were effectively freight forwarders, or consolidators, soliciting, bundling, and billing shipments, often over multiple railroads. They were particularly important for the transportation of eastbound agricultural traffic, as their agents directed grain from Ohio, Indiana, and farther west onto PRR lines in Pennsylvania. Correspondingly, the freight lines disaggregated shipments of westbound manufactured goods, diffusing them from the PRR into various locales in the Midwest. The freight lines provided warehouses and other storage facilities, and their clerical staff handled most paperwork, relieving the PRR of that burden. Freight-line personnel issued through bills of lading, eliminating the need for shippers to negotiate with each of the railroads that composed a segment of the route, and likewise denying independent commission freight agents the authority to negotiate rates and terms of service at break-of-bulk points. Once they had consolidated shipments into freight-car-sized lots, the fast freight lines paid the PRR a haulage fee, at a rate considerably lower than the sum of the tariffs that the forwarders assigned to the individual, smaller shipments. The difference between the forwarder rate and the PRR rate, less overhead costs, constituted the freight forwarder's profit.

Fast freight lines enabled the PRR and its trunk-line competitors to coordinate services over long distances, without the necessity of owning and managing midwestern connections. By the time of the Civil War, the managers of the eastern trunk lines had developed reasonably effective mechanisms for moving cargoes across Pennsylvania, New York, and Maryland. West of cities such as Pittsburgh, Buffalo, and Wheeling, however, the PRR and its rivals confronted myriad carriers and routes interlacing Ohio and Indiana. Executives on many of those companies maintained an affiliation with a particular trunk line, interchanging traffic and offering through freight and passenger services. Midwestern railway entrepreneurs nonetheless exhibited considerable independence and rarely allowed executives such as Thomson, Scott, Vanderbilt, or Gould to dictate rates and terms of service to them. Some midwestern railway executives simply refused to interchange freight with one or more of the eastern trunk lines. In a few instances, moreover, charter restrictions prohibited certain types of interchange traffic.[103]

Fast freight lines offered an expedient solution to charter restrictions and to the relative independence of the midwestern lines. Or, as Thomson succinctly described the situation in 1867, "In competing with other organizations for the transportation of through traffic, these lines are more efficient than a combination effected among railway companies to secure the same object."[104] In essence, the freight lines were an intermediate step in the efforts of trunk-line executives to integrate the railway network, a form of low-cost system building. Of equal importance, they enabled PRR officials to undermine some of their rivals' advantages in the oil trade without resorting to unenforceable rate agreements or to the construction of expensive new rail lines.

The Pennsylvania Railroad was by no means a pioneer in the development of the new generation of fast freight lines. Kasson's Despatch was one of the earliest, dating to 1855. Beginning in 1856, the United States Express Company's Great Western Despatch accommodated shipments on the Erie, with Merchants Despatch, owned by the American Express Company, offering similar services on the New York Central.[105]

During the trunk line rate conferences in 1858, 1859, and 1860, Thomson had unsuccessfully called on his colleagues on the New York railroads to curtail the early fast freight companies, which were skimming away much of the PRR's long-distance, high-value freight. Thomson failed to dissuade his rivals, and so resolved to mimic the efforts of the companies that operated over their lines. His timing was propitious. The Civil War created a shortage of freight equipment, yet capital constraints precluded new car purchases. Even worse, many of those cars would likely be redundant once the war was over. The increased wartime traffic created a particular problem at Pittsburgh, where the PRR met its principal western subsidiary, the Pittsburgh, Fort Wayne & Chicago. Even though the two railroads exchanged considerable traffic with one another, their tracks were laid to two different gauges (standard 4' 8½" to the east and "Ohio gauge" 4' 10" to the west), forcing most freight to be laboriously transferred between cars at one of the most congested locations on the system.[106]

PRR executives responded quickly to wartime congestion and the growth of forwarders on other railroads by establishing proprietary freight lines. In early 1862, PRR officials attempted to incorporate the Philadelphia & Eastern Transportation Company, yet they faced stiff opposition from Philadelphia commercial interests who feared that its operations would draw freight away from their city. PRR personnel waited another year, and in April 1863 they secured a charter for the Western Insurance & Transportation Company. In August, PRR officials changed the firm's name to the Union Transportation & Insurance Company. Each corporate title was something of a ruse, with the word "Insurance" included in order to comply with the terms of an 1856 Pennsylvania law permitting the incorporation of companies that provided insurance but were also able to pursue other functions. Because the company never offered insurance, in January 1865 the title changed again, to the Union Railroad & Transportation Company, with service offered as the Star Union Line, or, simply, the Union Line.[107]

Thanks in part to public policy, the Union Line and other fast freight companies were kept organizationally separate from the PRR. Under Pennsylvania law, the PRR was able to own the securities of other railroads, but it did not (and would not, until 1868) possess the authority to own a company that was not a railroad. As a result, the Union Line was not officially a part of the PRR system, but individuals with close ties to the railroad nonetheless controlled the firm. General Freight Agent Houston, who had been an operative for Leech & Company before joining the PRR in 1851, was among the founders of the Union Line. So, too, were Thomas Clarke, William Thaw, and William F. Leech, other veterans of the prewar transportation firms. Tom Scott's presence among the incorporators guaranteed that the new company would work closely with the PRR. Midwestern railroad entrepreneurs George Washington Cass (representing the Pittsburgh, Fort Wayne & Chicago Railway) and Thomas L. Jewett (president of the Steubenville & Indiana Railroad) ensured that the Union Line would have access to railroads in Ohio and Indiana.[108]

In addition to satisfying the dictates of Pennsylvania law, the separate nature of the fast freight lines exempted them from many of the rate policies that applied to the PRR proper. According to William Thaw, the Union Line worked to "solicit and obtain all our business from the public, through our own officers and agents, issue our own bills of lading, furnish the whole clerical labor of the business . . . receive and deliver our freights, and settle with consignees." Under the terms of its contract with the PRR, the Union Line retained all of the tariffs that its agents collected. Between Pittsburgh and tidewater, the company paid the PRR a flat haulage fee per car, of $72 to either Philadelphia or Baltimore, and $110 to New York, between December 1 and May 1. The rate dropped substantially during the summer and fall to enable the Union Line to compete against water carriers on the Great Lakes and the Erie Canal. West of Pittsburgh, the PRR paid the Union Line two cents per car-mile, as a kind of finder's fee for generating business for the railroad and keeping it away from rival trunk lines. As employees of a nominally independent company, Union Line solici-

tors set rates at whatever level they thought appropriate in order to maximize revenues. However, PRR Freight Traffic Department officials could exercise veto power over those tariffs, particularly in instances where they threatened to draw business away from the PRR proper.[109]

By the spring of 1864, the Union Line was offering six-day through service between Chicago and New York, as well as more localized services along branch and secondary lines. The Union Line owned and maintained its own equipment, emblazoned with a distinctive star-in-a-circle emblem. In order to permit through operations, most of those cars were equipped with compromise-gauge trucks. That innovation, in use at least as early as 1860, employed wheels with an exceedingly wide (five-inch) tread that could accommodate gauges ranging from 4′ 8½″ to 4′ 10″. Despite the obvious dangers associated with such coarse standards, compromise cars were a relatively low-cost solution to incompatible track gauges. By the summer of 1864 the Union Line had a thousand compromise-gauge boxcars in service, eliminating the need to transfer cargoes at Pittsburgh.[110]

The Empire Line was in many respects similar to the Union Line, but it possessed a far more specific mandate as a mechanism for rescuing the Philadelphia & Erie Railroad. In 1864, when the PRR leased the Philadelphia & Erie, that company possessed very little freight equipment. Not that there was much freight to transport, in any event, inasmuch as the city of Erie was oriented toward New York, with most traffic flowing east over the Erie, the New York Central, or the Erie Canal. Thomson and his PRR associates hoped that a new fast freight line would divert the Great Lakes grain traffic away from the Erie Canal and onto the rails of the Philadelphia & Erie. Furthermore, they intended that the Empire Line would possess sufficient ratemaking flexibility to exploit the Catawissa Route to New York, capturing the bulk of the oil trade.[111]

In May 1865, William H. Barnes oversaw the incorporation of the Pennsylvania Transportation & Insurance Company, soon renamed the Empire Transportation Company, commonly known as the Empire Line.[112] Other incorporators included individuals who possessed long experience as independent transporters before joining the PRR family—William F. Leech, Henry S. Leech, David E. Leech, Henry H. Houston, William Thaw, Thomas S. Clarke, and the partnership of Clarke & Company. The Fort Wayne's George W. Cass matched his involvement in the Union Line with participation in the Empire Line. In September 1865, Joseph D. Potts resigned his post as general manager of the Philadelphia & Erie and replaced Barnes as president of the Empire Line. The choice of Potts as president was certainly understandable given that the Empire Line shipped primarily over the Philadelphia & Erie.[113]

The Empire Line offered service to Harrisburg, Philadelphia, and Baltimore, but its competitive energies were directed more to the New York market, and its headquarters were in fact located in Manhattan. Grain and other bulk freight rode in boxcars with a distinctive arrow logo—hence the common name of the "Arrow Line." Beginning with an initial complement of 200 boxcars, by 1875 the Empire Line had 3,400 grain-carrying cars in service. Many of those cars ferried grain from Erie toward the east coast along the Philadelphia & Erie. Others traveled farther afield, however, into Ohio, Indiana, and Illinois, as Empire Line agents solicited business from the granger railroads that stretched west of Chicago. The Empire Line's service originally reached both Chicago and St. Louis, and it was later extended as far west as Burlington, Iowa, and Omaha, Nebraska. Until the eastbound grain and other shipments reached Pennsylvania, the trains traveled along whichever route Empire Line officials thought to be the fastest and most economical. As such, they relied heavily on a collection of railroads that would soon be consolidated into the Lake Shore & Michigan Southern—carriers that were wholly outside of the PRR's sphere of influence, and which would later become part of the New York Central. The one caveat was that the Empire Line could not poach traffic that would otherwise flow over the PRR's Pittsburgh–Philadelphia main line.[114]

The Empire Line on the Lakes

Even though the Empire Line developed elaborate organizational capabilities and exerted substantial con-

trol over rates, the PRR's affiliate could not overturn a basic principle of transportation economics. Quite simply, it was more efficient, and therefore more economical, to ship grain and other bulk cargoes by water than by rail. The willingness of Union Line and Empire Line agents to implement reduced summertime rates could only do so much to wrest traffic away from lake boats. Unable to beat that competition, Empire Line officials elected to join in it, by establishing a Great Lakes water carrier subsidiary. Their goal was not to dominate the Lakes trade, per se, but rather to ensure that a steady stream of eastbound commerce would flow from Empire Line boats to Empire Line freight cars. Those cars would continue east on the Philadelphia & Erie and the PRR—and would not be lost to the Erie Canal or one of the New York trunk lines.

In June 1865 a group of dummy incorporators, mainly Empire Line personnel, established the Erie & Western Transportation Company. Not until early 1869 did the true ownership become apparent as key PRR executives took control of the company, with Scott elected as president and William Thaw and Henry H. Houston serving as directors. Approximately a year earlier, in February 1868, Erie & Western officials negotiated a contract with the PRR's Philadelphia & Erie subsidiary. Under the terms of the agreement, the shipping line established offices at Chicago, Detroit, and Milwaukee to solicit freight that would be delivered to the Philadelphia & Erie, at Erie, in exchange for 5 percent of the Philadelphia & Erie's revenue on that traffic. In return, the Philadelphia & Erie provided free dock facilities at Erie, as well as a 20 percent discount on coal delivered to Erie & Western ships at that port. The Empire Line guaranteed the terms of the contract, and the Erie & Western operated as a de facto subsidiary of that fast freight line.[115]

The Erie & Western in turn contracted the steamship service to an established operator based in Buffalo. The Evans Line, whose origins traced back to 1832, was a large and progressive shipping company that in 1862 placed in service the first iron-hulled ship to operate on the Great Lakes. Now under the leadership of James C. Evans and his son Edwin T. Evans, the company furnished nine boats to the Erie & Western. Those vessels, and their successors, operated over three Great Lakes routes, under the name of the Anchor

Figure 36. The Civil War greatly accelerated shipments of grain and other products between the Midwest and the Atlantic seaboard, at a time when incompatible track gauges retarded the development of through traffic. The Union Line and the Empire Line operated fleets of cars with compromise-gauge trucks, suitable for use on standard and Ohio-gauge tracks. Of equal importance, clerks on the fast freight lines oversaw the routing of shipments over multiple railroads, including the Pittsburgh, Fort Wayne & Chicago. A Fort Wayne locomotive is shown here, pulling a string of Union Line boxcars, probably loaded with grain, and easily recognizable by the distinctive star-in-a-circle logo.

Pennsylvania Historical and Museum Commission, Pennsylvania State Archives.

Line. By the end of the nineteenth century, the Anchor Line operated seventeen ships carrying passengers and freight. Anchor Line elevators at Buffalo and Erie stored vast quantities of grain, much of which then flowed east over the Philadelphia & Erie. Yet, the Anchor Line also interchanged considerable freight with the Erie Canal, and even operated some barges along that waterway.[116]

For a brief period, the Anchor Line enabled PRR officials to forge links with carriers in the western

United States. Both freight and passenger vessels provided service between Erie and Duluth, Minnesota. At Duluth, Anchor Line ships interchanged traffic with the Lake Superior & Mississippi Railroad, which offered service west to St. Paul. During the late 1860s and early 1870s, Thomson, Scott, and other PRR associates invested in that carrier, as well as in Jay Cooke's Northern Pacific Railroad—the junction between the two carriers was initially named Thomson in recognition of that influence. In January 1872, the first cargo of Pennsylvania coal, shipped from Erie on the Anchor Line, made its way to Duluth and then west to Moorhead, Minnesota—the precursor of many more to come. In May 1872, the Northern Pacific leased the Lake Superior & Mississippi, but Jay Cooke's financial empire collapsed the following year. That ended the PRR's involvement in the construction of a route to Puget Sound on the Pacific Ocean, finally completed in 1883.[117]

Despite the problems associated with the Northern Pacific, the Anchor Line remained an important part of the PRR's operations. For some sixty years, Anchor Line ships linked PRR rails at Buffalo, Erie, and Cleveland to such off-line ports as Detroit; Mackinac, Michigan; Chicago; Milwaukee; Sault Ste. Marie; Marquette, Michigan; and Duluth. In the process, the PRR's Great Lakes subsidiary greatly expanded the PRR's catchment basin, sending cargoes of grain, lumber, and other bulk cargoes toward the cars operated by the Empire Line and the Pennsylvania Railroad.[118]

The Empire Line and the Oil Trade

Despite the Empire Line's involvement in grain traffic and in Great Lakes shipping, its most important initial function was to increase the PRR's share of the oil trade. At the same time, the development of the tank car greatly increased the efficiency of crude oil transportation, while complicating the mission of the Empire Line and engendering additional instability among the eastern trunk lines. The Empire Line gave the PRR a crucial advantage against the New York Central and the Erie, in both the ownership of tank cars and in the pricing flexibility that those cars generated.

From the beginning of the oil boom in 1859, producers typically loaded oil into wooden barrels of various sizes for transportation to the refineries. The barrels were expensive to produce and prone to leakage, with one oilman estimating that between 50 and 75 percent of the oil disappeared en route. Under those circumstances, the bulk shipment of oil offered obvious benefits to the railroads. In 1865, PRR employees experimented with a "rotary oil car," which consisted of two massive hollow axles, each filled with five hundred gallons of oil, attached to wheels five feet in diameter, and fixed to a wooden platform that could carry additional freight. That particular experiment, if successful, was never put into general use.[119]

Brothers James and Amos Densmore, oil producers and brokers from Miller's Farm, Pennsylvania, experienced more success with the vat car. Simple in design, the vat car consisted of two large wooden tubs, each holding between forty and forty-five barrels of oil, mounted atop a conventional flatcar. In the late summer of 1865, the Densmores employed vat cars to ship oil to New York along the Atlantic & Great Western and the Erie, with virtually no leakage in transit. The Densmore brothers neglected to patent their invention until 1866, by which time the cars had become commonplace. Despite missing out on the financial rewards associated with their efforts, they continued their inventive streak and in later years played a role in the development of the familiar QWERTY typewriter keyboard.[120]

Empire Line personnel were quick to adopt Amos Densmore's innovative vat car, with Charles P. Hatch, an Empire Line agent at Titusville, going so far as to claim that he had developed the design himself in 1866. Hatch was probably referring to a disastrous experiment in which PRR officials attempted to ship oil in a conventional boxcar, operating under the assumption that it could be returned to regular merchandise service once emptied of its liquid cargo. Crews installed three oil vats inside the car, yet made no provision for filling them. Hatch improvised as best he could, chopping holes in the roof of the car and instructing his employees to fill the tanks with oil. When they did so, oil seeped from the joints between the boards composing the vats, and then flowed out of the sides and the floor of the surrounding boxcar as

Figure 37. Officials from the Philadelphia & Erie Railroad and the Empire Line, both PRR subsidiaries, sought better methods for transporting crude oil to refineries. Flat cars loaded with barrels gave way to "Densmore Cars" consisting of round wooden tanks mounted atop flat cars. Like the barrel cars, they were prone to leakage and fire. By the late 1860s, railroads were using cylindrical iron tanks, resting horizontally on a flatcar or a simple wooden underframe—the same basic design employed by tank cars today. In this view, discarded Densmore tanks litter the foreground, superseded by the more efficient design seen in the middle distance.

Pennsylvania Historical and Museum Commission, Drake Well Museum Collection, Titusville.

well. There was no convenient access to the partly filled tanks, so stopping the leaks was almost impossible. As Hatch later admitted, in language that any recent veteran of the Civil War would understand, the

boxcar "looked as though it had been subjected to a cannonading and it was practically ruined."[121] PRR train crews nonetheless dispatched the shipment east, the car dripping oil as it went. Hatch eventually received "a letter of earnest inquiry" from his Empire Line superiors, but he apparently explained himself well enough to retain his job. With that experiment never to be repeated, Empire personnel instead copied Densmore's basic design.[122]

The vat cars were at best a stopgap solution, however, as they were prone to both leakage and fire. In the autumn of 1865, not long after the first vat cars had entered service, Pittsburgh resident J. F. Keeler constructed a large, U-shaped iron tank atop a flatcar. Virtually leakproof, with baffles to prevent sloshing and airspace to allow for the expansion of the petroleum vapors, Keeler's design was the progenitor of modern tank cars.[123]

Of the railroads that served the oil fields, only the PRR's Empire Line owned large numbers of costly tank cars. In May 1865, at the same time that they created the Arrow Line for grain and merchandise traffic, Empire officials established another subsidiary, the "Pennsylvania Railroad & Allegheny Valley Railroad Oil Line." To the undoubted relief of calligraphers in the paint shop, it was soon shortened to simply the "Green Line," with a distinctive if somewhat impractical emerald color scheme. The first shipments to New York began in June. By the end of the year, the Green Line possessed three hundred vat cars, along with an equal number of barrel cars.[124] In 1867, the Green Line introduced the first true tank cars, consisting of a single horizontal, iron cylindrical tank, soon to become the design standard. By 1875, Empire owned more than 1,300 oil tank cars, along with 400 older, barrel-carrying, flatcars. The Empire Line's equipment gave the PRR an advantage over the other trunk lines, as the Erie owned only a very small number of tank cars, and the NYC none at all.[125]

While tank cars undoubtedly increased the efficiency of oil transportation, their utility may have had more to do with rates than with the new equipment. Many of the PRR officials who oversaw the transportation of oil in fact preferred the older barrel cars. For example, the PRR's general freight agent complained that tank cars could be used for no other application than petroleum products, and they offered no offsetting backhaul on their return to the oilfields.[126] Furthermore, he suggested, in the event of a wreck, it might be possible to salvage at least some oil barrels,

while the cargo of a derailed tank car was likely to be a total loss. Tank cars were also quite expensive at about $700 apiece, perhaps twice the cost of a boxcar.[127]

Despite their cost and operational limitations, tank cars did enable PRR managers to provide hidden rebates to Standard Oil and other large refiners, and to hobble Standard's smaller competitors. Railroad managers routinely granted tank car rates that were far lower than what the enhanced efficiency of the new equipment would justify. A large portion of the spread between tank car rates and barrel rates constituted a hidden rebate. Less favored shippers found it extraordinarily difficult to prove price discrimination, as PRR managers could simply make vague references to a generic claim of the efficiency of tank car operations. Furthermore, operating officials on the PRR, as well as the PRR's competitors, allocated scarce tank cars to favored shippers, while withholding them from competing firms.[128]

The Catawissa Connection

The Empire Line's tank cars, in and of themselves, could do little to increase the PRR's share of the oil trade, largely because New York and later Cleveland displaced Pittsburgh as a refining center. For a brief period during the 1850s, several New York firms had extracted oil from cannel coal, a type of hydrogen-rich oil shale. It was a relatively simple matter to convert their facilities and expertise into petroleum distillation. New York was also the dominant port for trade with Europe, and overseas demand for American kerosene likewise helped to advance the city's refining capabilities. Despite its port status, Philadelphia was not a serious contender for the oil business, as the PRR still lacked convenient access to the Delaware River, and areas suitable for refineries were typically occupied, often by residential development.[129]

The growing importance of the New York market created a serious problem for Thomson and Scott, threatening to undermine both the value of the Philadelphia & Erie and the PRR's share of the oil trade. From northwestern Pennsylvania, crude destined for New York traveled over what could charitably be described as a circuitous route—southeast over the Philadelphia & Erie to Sunbury, then due south on the Northern Central to Harrisburg, then east over the PRR main line to Philadelphia. Prior to 1867, there was no direct connection in Philadelphia between the PRR and the railroads that continued north to Jersey City and South Amboy. Even after the completion of the Connecting Railway, through traffic still faced a gauge break, between the 4′ 8½″ employed on the PRR and the 4′ 10″ used in New Jersey. The existence of a transit duty on through freight, imposed in 1832 by the New Jersey legislature, increased rates and contributed to the unattractive nature of the route. Because the Erie and the New York Central possessed more direct routes to New York, while avoiding the New Jersey transit duties, they were certain to garner the bulk of the oil business.[130]

Thomson and Scott soon established a more direct link between the oilfields and New York, one that came at the expense of the city of Philadelphia. In 1831, in the midst of the anthracite boom in northeastern Pennsylvania, the legislature had chartered the Little Schuylkill & Susquehanna Railroad to build a line connecting the Little Schuylkill Navigation, Railroad & Coal Company line, at a point near Tamanend, with Catawissa, a town on the North Branch of the Susquehanna River. By 1854, construction crews had extended the line from Catawissa west to Milton and a junction with the Sunbury & Erie (later, the Philadelphia & Erie). The company went through several name changes, becoming the Catawissa Railroad in 1860. The Catawissa served primarily as a bridge route between the Schuylkill and Susquehanna rivers. Of greater significance, following the completion of the Philadelphia & Erie in 1864, northwestern Pennsylvania oil traffic possessed a direct path to New York.[131]

In April 1865, Thomson and his board agreed to cooperate with the Catawissa Railroad, in order to create a link to tidewater that, much like the prewar Allentown Route, short-hauled the PRR. From northwestern Pennsylvania, oil followed the Philadelphia & Erie to Milton, a short distance north of Sunbury. Operating under a lucrative haulage contract, the Catawissa moved the traffic east to a connection with the Lehigh Valley Railroad at Quakake Junction, just north of Tamanend. From there, it traveled through Allentown to Easton and across the Delaware River to Phillips-burg, where it transferred to the Jersey Central for the remainder of the trip to Jersey City. Despite the number of carriers involved, the Catawissa Route was considerably shorter than the more circuitous route offered by the PRR main line or, more significantly, either of the New York trunk lines. The distance between the oilfields and New York, via the Catawissa Railroad, was sixty-four miles less than over the Erie, the carrier that possessed the shortest trunk-line route from the oilfields to the east coast—equivalent to 15 percent of the total journey. Thomson naturally would have preferred that oil traffic stay on PRR rails for the entire journey to Philadelphia. That was unrealistic, however, so long as the Erie and the New York Central possessed more direct connections with New York. Thanks to the Catawissa Route, eastbound oil traffic would leave PRR (Philadelphia & Erie) rails at Milton, but Thomson concluded that that was a better option than yielding all oil revenue to the two New York carriers.[132]

The shortcut was of such immense value that PRR executives were willing to go to substantial lengths to keep the Catawissa out of unfriendly hands. That was never more true than in 1865 and 1866. In the autumn of 1865, the A&GW's traffic contract with the Erie expired, leaving the A&GW without a secure route to tidewater. At the same time, A&GW officials welcomed to the United States a group of British investors led by financier S. Morton Peto. Suitably impressed by their tour of the company's facilities, the British capitalists poured money into the broad-gauge railroad's physical plant and equipment. In addition, the investors planned to construct a new route between the oilfields and a connection with the Catawissa at Milton. While many railroads would be involved, the Catawissa was to serve as the critical link between the oilfields and New York. Accordingly, on November 1, 1865, A&GW officials leased the Catawissa, for the substantial sum of $1,000 a day. Philadelphia & Reading executives were eager to participate in the new route, and in January 1866 they signed a ninety-nine-year traffic agreement with the A&GW, agreeing to construct additional trackage leading to a new crossing of the Delaware River, at Easton.[133]

Thomson and his colleagues feared that the Atlantic & Great Western lease of the Catawissa would prevent them from competing for the transportation of oil to the New York market. What made the situation even more galling was that A&GW officials proposed to route trains over the PRR's newly acquired Philadelphia & Erie subsidiary between Williamsport and Milton until their new line across Pennsylvania could be completed.[134]

With considerable legal acumen, PRR attorneys attempted to persuade the Pennsylvania Supreme Court to invalidate the lease on a technicality.[135] They were unsuccessful, but the PRR's tactics delayed the lease, and therefore the construction of a competing connecting line across Pennsylvania, just long enough for Sir Morton Peto's financial empire to collapse. In 1867, Peto's bankruptcy helped plunge the A&GW into receivership. The following April, Atlantic & Great Western officials terminated the Catawissa lease, ending any possibility that that railroad would further invade the PRR's territory.[136]

With the Catawissa safely isolated from the Atlantic & Great Western, Thomson attempted to exploit the distance advantage that that route afforded relative to the New York trunk lines. The Empire Line provided the organizational mechanism for soliciting business, billing shippers, negotiating through freight service, and delivering oil to its final destination. Initially, much of the oil went to the Jersey Central yards at Elizabethport, where barges transported it across Upper New York Bay to refineries in Brooklyn. In 1867, Empire established a subsidiary, the National Storage Company, to build a freight and oil terminal at Communipaw, adjacent to the Jersey Central yards and close to Manhattan and Brooklyn.[137]

While the Communipaw terminus undoubtedly increased the ability of Empire—and the PRR—to compete in the New York market, it was the fast freight line's rate structure that provided a critical advantage over the New York Central and the Erie. In 1865 and 1866, a series of agreements among the Empire Line, the PRR, the Philadelphia & Erie, and the Catawissa spelled out the details. While the contract provisions were extraordinarily complex, they provided both the PRR and the Empire Line with enormous opportunities for profit. The same could not be said for the Philadelphia & Erie, however, a company that seemed destined for perennial financial disap-

pointment. Those vagaries in fortune arose because the PRR, while heavily invested in Philadelphia & Erie securities, did not own that company outright. The City of Philadelphia controlled a substantial block of Philadelphia & Erie shares, which it had purchased in the expectation of funneling the Great Lakes trade to the Quaker City. There were many small investors as well, Philadelphians who either had shared the boosterism of the Select and Common Councils or else lived along the route, in towns that they expected would flourish with the coming of the railroad. To their collective chagrin, the Empire Line received the sole right to ship oil over the Philadelphia & Erie—and that traffic would benefit neither on-line communities nor the City of Philadelphia.

The fact that the PRR leased, rather than owned, the Philadelphia & Erie led Thomson and his associates to the inescapable conclusion that it would be far better to shift whatever profits the oil trade generated away from that struggling carrier and toward the PRR and its close affiliate the Empire Line. The Empire Line profited primarily from the spread between the rate that Empire charged to the shipper and the tariff that Empire paid to the Philadelphia & Erie and the other railroads that participated in the Catawissa Route. With Empire charging producers $3.07 a barrel, between the oilfields and New York, a car carrying forty barrels of oil would generate $122.80 in revenue. Yet, Empire paid the participating railroads only $67 in haulage fees, yielding a profit of $55.80. Even better, from the perspective of Empire Line officials, was that the Philadelphia & Erie paid them a drawback equivalent to a third of the rate over the distance between the oilfields and the connection with the Catawissa at Milton. Even accounting for overhead cost, Empire's profit was considerable—and much of that profit went into the accounts of that company's investors, who were also closely connected with the PRR.[138]

The Pennsylvania Railroad also profited handsomely from the Empire Line's use of the Catawissa Route. The haulage contracts specified that the Empire Line would ship solely on the Philadelphia & Erie and the PRR, wherever possible, eliminating any chance that the freight forwarder might divert traffic to competing trunk lines. The real plum, however, reflected the difference in distance via the Catawissa Route and via Philadelphia. Even though the Catawissa Route was some ninety miles shorter from the oilfields to New York, the PRR billed Empire as if its cars ran the far longer distance through Philadelphia. In effect, Empire paid for an additional ninety miles of transportation on the PRR that it did not actually use. For each car, the billing system was equivalent to an additional $12.12 in needless expense—or, from the PRR's perspective, a bonus of $12.12 in additional, if unearned, revenue.[139]

In 1870, the Empire Line and its shareholders gained additional benefits at the expense of investors in the Philadelphia & Erie. In April, state legislators freed all transportation companies operating on the Philadelphia & Erie from the maximum rate provisions that the General Assembly had implemented in 1849. Three months later, PRR officials orchestrated a crucial modification to the terms of their 1862 lease of the Philadelphia & Erie.[140] Originally, the PRR had agreed to pay the Philadelphia & Erie's shareholders an annual rental equivalent to 30 percent of gross earnings. The new arrangements specified the same percentage, but only on whatever net earnings remained after deducting operating and maintenance expenditures, including a 7 percent return on the cost of equipment. By shifting the basis of the rental from gross receipts to net receipts, the PRR possessed a strong incentive to maximize the traffic and the revenues generated by the Empire Line (which would count as an expense against the Philadelphia & Erie, and thus reduce that carrier's earnings). As such, the Philadelphia & Erie, and not the Empire Line or the PRR, would bear the brunt of any destructive competition.[141]

Such accounting practices were by no means unusual in the railroad business, but they did attract attention from government officials, shippers, and investors. The gist of their complaints was that the Union Line, the Empire Line, and similar organizations constituted a sort of unholy cabal, enabling a handful of privileged investors to manipulate terms of service, rates, and profits at will. Many Philadelphia politicians complained bitterly that the city's investment in the Philadelphia & Erie, intended to promote economic development, had now been subordinated to the financial interests of the Pennsylvania Railroad. Legislative committees in both Pennsylvania and Ohio singled out the PRR's fast freight lines for further scrutiny. Although Ohio legisla-

tors lambasted the PRR's traffic policies, their Pennsylvania counterparts were more sympathetic, presumably because they appreciated the ability of the Union and Empire Lines to divert traffic away from the New York Central, the Erie, and the Baltimore and Ohio.

Shippers likewise complained that freight line service over multiple railroads made a mockery of interfirm competition. As they observed, the fast freight lines were hardly independent of the railroads over which they operated. Shippers accordingly had little patience with the traffic solicitors who attempted to delude them into believing that they were receiving the best possible rates. Executives from competing railroads asserted that the PRR had given preferential treatment to Union Line and Empire Line equipment, had repaired that equipment without charge at PRR facilities, had provided those forwarders with free warehouse and terminal facilities, and had given free passes to Union and Empire employees. According to the Reading's general freight agent, the Pennsylvania had abrogated a cooperative traffic arrangement between the two railroads when, short of motive power, crewmen had removed from trains cars belonging to the Reading and other railroads and replaced them with equipment owned by the Union Line and the Empire Line.[142]

Some Pennsylvania Railroad investors shared the critical assessment of the fast freight lines. They alleged that the Union Line and the Empire Line were skimming off the PRR's high-value traffic, leaving them with the dregs.[143] In 1873, for example, the Empire Line transported 414,076 tons of freight (318,352 tons, mostly grain and oil, eastbound, and 95,724 tons westbound). That represented only 4.5 percent of the total tonnage of the Pennsylvania Railroad that year, but a far higher percentage of total freight receipts. PRR stockholders who anxiously awaited their dividends were concerned that a carload of oil generated $85 in revenue for the Empire Line and only $67 for the Pennsylvania Railroad itself. In addition, the flat haulage rate that the PRR charged to the fast freight lines encouraged those companies to overload cars, placing additional stress on the PRR's track and bridges. Investors in the Philadelphia & Erie were particularly angry as, despite the PRR lease, their company failed to show any sort of a profit at all, while the owners of the Empire Line cars that trundled across their railroad were raking in double-digit returns.[144]

A few PRR shareholders attributed darker motives to the organizers of the fast freight lines, asserting that they were merely a mechanism for transferring revenues from the PRR to a small group of privileged inside investors. Colonel James Page, who delighted in being a gadfly to Thomson and his fellow executives, was the chief critic of the fast freight lines—although, it should be noted, Page was a vocal opponent of virtually every policy undertaken by the PRR's managers. Page was a longtime Philadelphia attorney who served as the city's postmaster, the county treasurer, and the collector for the Port of Philadelphia. At the 1862 shareholders' meeting, Page excoriated Thomson and his associates for their alleged financial extravagances, and for their rate policies. "The history of the decline of Philadelphia trade," Page inaccurately asserted, "may be written in a few words—adverse discriminations, and sacrifice of all other interests to the coal business."[145]

Beginning in 1861 and continuing through 1867, Page repeatedly demanded that special investigative committees, composed of stockholder representatives, investigate virtually every aspect of the PRR's affairs, including the railroad's connections to the fast freight lines. One such committee made a thorough investigation of the PRR's finances and operations, before issuing a report in January 1863. Six of the seven committee members agreed "that the present system and regulations for the freight and forwarding business are calculated to promote the interests of the Stockholders and the accommodation of the public."[146] Only Page refused to sign the report.[147]

Similar investigations, in 1867 and again in 1874, likewise cleared Thomson, Scott, and other executives of allegations that they were lining their own pockets by diverting premium freight from the PRR to the fast freight lines. Page was not involved in the 1874 committee report, and that document, while critical of some aspects of the PRR's management, nonetheless asserted that the fast freight lines were both necessary and beneficial. Particularly during the Civil War, the report concluded, the PRR had lacked the capital and the organizational sophistication necessary to capture freight from rival trunk lines. Even though the investi-

gating committee found everything to be in order, the cumulative effect of the widespread criticism of the PRR's association with fast freight lines led to changes in that relationship. Thomson and Scott yielded to propriety and soon divested their holdings in the Union Line. Thereafter, they were generally careful to use "dummy" incorporators to disguise their participation in such endeavors.[148]

Despite the problems associated with the fast freight lines, they enabled Thomson and Scott to capture a substantial quantity of freight for the Pennsylvania Railroad. The average Union Line shipment traveled a little less than a thousand miles, far longer than PRR's main line, indicating that much of the freight was being gathered from locales west of Pittsburgh and diverted onto home rails.[149] The freight companies made great progress in overcoming the gauge differential at Pittsburgh, undermining the authority of independent freight agents, and establishing through traffic arrangements with western carriers. In 1871, for example, the *New York Commercial Bulletin* reported that, thanks to the Empire Line, the PRR's profit on oil traffic was above that of grain, and second only to livestock transportation. Some of the proceeds generated by the Union Line and the Empire Line may have lined the pockets of privileged PRR managers, at some cost to the PRR. Yet, the expense would have been much greater had the fast freight lines not existed, for Thomson and his fellow executives would have found it necessary to make even more substantial investments in midwestern carriers to prevent losing traffic to rival trunk lines.[150]

In Pursuit of Empire

The Civil War had been good to the Pennsylvania Railroad. Trains swollen with merchandise, soldiers, and civilians lumbered across Pennsylvania, taxing the physical plant and testing the endurance of employees. They had also contributed mightily to the company's bottom line, in the form of profits and—what was perhaps even more important—rapid improvements to tracks, bridges, locomotives, and cars. The war had induced closer cooperation among the PRR, the Joint Companies, and the Philadelphia, Wilmington &

Baltimore, with the Connecting Railway and the Junction Railroad finally establishing a smooth flow of rail traffic through Philadelphia.

The expansion of oil and grain shipments had proven especially gratifying to Thomson and his fellow executives. The burgeoning production of the northwestern Pennsylvania oilfields had caught the PRR's president off guard, but he had responded quickly. New construction, the acquisition of existing carriers, and the establishment of the Empire Line ensured the PRR a stake in the oil trade. To the west, farmers responded to high wartime grain prices by rapidly increasing production. The resulting flood of grain benefited the Erie Canal more than any other transportation artery, and it would be at least another decade before the railroads were efficient enough to overtake it. During the Civil War, the Erie Canal carried twice as much freight as the New York Central and the Erie combined and, as late as 1872, 85 percent of the freight moving between Chicago and Philadelphia traveled by water.[151] Yet, the growing grain traffic convinced Thomson that he had been wise to negotiate prewar alliances with railway entrepreneurs in Ohio and Indiana. After Appomattox, he intended to solidify those arrangements in order to guarantee the PRR an adequate supply of western traffic.

Thomson was not the only railroad executive to see the value of western connections. John W. Garrett presided over a company that had been thoroughly wrecked by the Civil War, yet the Baltimore & Ohio remained a formidable competitor. Cornelius Vanderbilt and Jay Gould had spent a fair portion of the immediate postwar period sparring with one another, but they were shrewd executives, and both the powerful New York Central and the weaker Erie posed a danger to the Pennsylvania Railroad. All of those entrepreneurs pursued the same goal as Thomson—control over the traffic of the Midwest.

In the years immediately following the Civil War, Thomson could not have envisioned either the magnitude or the variety of the traffic that would one day flow over the railroad network that he had helped to assemble. Nor could he have imagined that that system would soon be in danger of disintegration. During the first decade of his presidency, in order to conserve scarce capital, Thomson had had little choice other than to provide funds to struggling local carriers and then withdraw the PRR's investments when it appeared that the railroads could survive on their own. Thomson reasoned, or at least hoped, that he could then keep those companies loyal to the Pennsylvania Railroad through favorable traffic interchange agreements and through alliances with those erstwhile allies as they pursued a variety of off-the-books investment opportunities. When that stratagem worked, it worked haphazardly, at best. When it failed—and it all too often did—the owners and executives of the affiliated lines demonstrated their weak loyalty to the PRR and their willingness to secure a better deal elsewhere.

With the other three trunk lines arrayed against him, Thomson could no longer afford to maintain the loose affiliations that he had established between the Pennsylvania Railroad and its western connections. The rapid expansion and specialization of midwestern agriculture, a process driven as much by wartime demand as by the presence of the local railroads that interlaced the region, promised a wealth of traffic to be funneled to the east. Four carriers would battle for that traffic, and each would compete against the low commodity rates offered by water carriers operating over the Great Lakes and the Erie Canal. Every trunk-line executive was willing to go to great lengths to garner as much traffic as possible, even at exceedingly low rates, in order to offset the extraordinarily high fixed costs that were an inevitable part of railroading. Confronted by ruinous rate wars and the expansionist visions of Garrett, Vanderbilt, and Gould, Thomson had reached the limits of what he could accomplish through indirect influence. Regardless of the cost, he would henceforth seek to control his western affiliates. He succeeded, and he created a railroad empire.

Chapter 9

Empire

1868–1876

For all of its success, the Pennsylvania Railroad in 1865 was not the preeminent transportation enterprise in the United States. Over the previous few decades, numerous other companies had laid more serious claim to that title. The Baltimore & Ohio, launched two decades before the PRR, marched steadily westward as Philadelphians argued over the construction and operation of the Main Line of Public Works. The New York & Erie, while slower to get under way, made more rapid progress. In 1851, it became the longest railroad in the United States, and the first link between the east coast and the western waters, under one management. Two years later, before PRR construction crews had completed their bypass of the Allegheny Portage Railroad, Erastus Corning stole a march on the Erie. When he created the New York Central, Corning placed himself in command of the longest railroad and the largest commercial enterprise, as measured by asset value, in the United States.

Even within Pennsylvania, J. Edgar Thomson could not count himself the dominant force in railroading. By 1847, when PRR officials broke ground at Harrisburg, the Philadelphia & Reading was carrying more freight than any other railroad in the nation, and more tonnage than even the Erie Canal. Through the 1850s, Thomson struggled to complete the PRR's main line, fought for control over the company, and worked to

develop more efficient management systems. Yet, as the Civil War broke over the nation, the Reading remained far more powerful than the Pennsylvania Railroad.[1] In 1860, the Reading moved nearly two million tons of coal to its docks at Port Richmond, representing nearly half of the coal traffic into Philadelphia. A decade later, the Reading was still the wealthiest corporation in the world. Until 1875, the Reading hauled more tons of freight than any other railroad in the United States, and only then did the PRR take the lead.[2]

One by one, however, the PRR's competitors fell by the wayside. Thomson's acquisition of the Cumberland Valley Railroad and the Northern Central Railway boxed the Reading into eastern Pennsylvania, ensuring that that company would forever after be known primarily as an anthracite carrier, and not as a trunk line. The Baltimore & Ohio might have started too early, and the primitive nature of early railway finance and construction techniques blunted its early lead. The Civil War helped wreck the B&O's physical plant and its finances, and the B&O would never again have the opportunity to meet the PRR on an equal basis. The Erie was in miserable condition, and in 1859 it imploded into the first of a series of spectacular bankruptcies. The New York Central was a far more serious rival, but it too faltered after 1865. While Thomson

Figure 38. When the Pennsylvania Railroad was chartered in 1846, it was a Philadelphia company, organized by Quaker City merchants and designed to bring grain from the Midwest to their community. Thirty years later, when this photograph was taken in West Philadelphia, the PRR was a far-flung railroad empire, controlling routes as far west as Chicago and St. Louis. The company's organizational structure reflected its regional orientation, with its managers committed to protecting the railroad's strategic interests, even at the expense of the city that had given it birth.

Library of Congress Prints & Photographs Division, LC-USZ62-57212.

moved aggressively to cement control over the PRR's midwestern affiliates, Cornelius Vanderbilt and his successors maintained a system of loose affiliations with their western allies. The members of the Vanderbilt family, and their close associates, served to interlock the boards of directors of the many carriers that were part of the larger NYC system. Not until the early years of the twentieth century would a new generation of bankers and professional managers solidify their oversight of the New York Central and bring lines in Ohio, Indiana, and Illinois more firmly under the NYC's control.

During the fifteen years that followed the end of the Civil War Thomson and his associates transformed the Pennsylvania Railroad and made it the undisputed leader of the transportation sector of the economy.

Thomson's successor, Tom Scott, followed the lead of his mentor and built the PRR into the largest corporation in the world. In a five-year period, from the late 1860s into the early 1870s, the PRR grew from 491 route miles to nearly six thousand miles. In 1869 alone, Thomson tripled the size of the Pennsylvania Railroad, establishing control over the Pittsburgh, Fort Wayne & Chicago Railway; the Columbus, Chicago & Indiana Central Railway; and other connections in the Midwest. Two years later, Thomson presided over the lease of the United New Jersey Railroad & Canal Companies, providing the PRR with two routes linking Philadelphia to New York. By 1873, Thomson and his associates had assembled a formidable railroad empire, with secure connections to Erie, Ashtabula, Cleveland, Toledo, Chicago, St. Louis, Louisville, Cincinnati, and

New York. Of equal importance, PRR managers had developed new organizational structures that enabled them to coordinate both routine operations and long-term corporate strategy across their far-flung empire.

As the 1850s ended, Thomson had ensured that the PRR would be a major eastern trunk line. Little more than a decade later, as the 1870s began, Thomson and his allies made certain that their company would be a dominant force in regional transportation. By May 1874, when Thomson died in office, exhausted by his labors, the PRR controlled 8 percent of the railway mileage in the United States and almost 13 percent of the total capitalization. With the notable exceptions of Britain and of France, no nation operated as much railway mileage as did the Pennsylvania Railroad.[3]

An Empire in the West

The end of the Civil War unleashed a new round of competition between the eastern trunk lines. Yet, some of the most serious threats to Thomson's expansionist vision came from within his growing empire, from his erstwhile allies in Ohio and Indiana. Since attaining the presidency in 1852, Thomson had built relationships with midwestern railway entrepreneurs such as George Washington Cass and Samuel J. Tilden on the Fort Wayne, Benjamin E. Smith and former Ohio governor William Dennison on the Columbus & Indianapolis Central, and Thomas Jewett of the Steubenville & Indiana. Those entrepreneurs were attuned to their local communities and to regional transportation demands, yet they valued their connections to the PRR and the other eastern trunk lines. Without their help, Thomson could not have extended the PRR's influence to the west of Pittsburgh. He was too busy with other matters—including the purchase of the Main Line of Public Works, the repeal of the tonnage tax, and the Civil War—to devote much time to the direct management of enterprises in the Midwest. Thomson's board of directors, while generally supportive of his expenditures along the PRR proper, were nonetheless dubious at the prospect of investing heavily in unproven western affiliates. They accordingly adopted a policy of limiting the railroad's direct investments to only those lines that operated solely within Pennsylvania. Legal restrictions also hampered Thomson's efforts to establish direct control over railroads that operated outside of the commonwealth. Under such circumstances, direct PRR ownership of lines in Ohio and Indiana was out of the question.

Midwestern railroad executives maintained an uneasy alliance with the Pennsylvania Railroad. Their companies, no matter how well constructed or how well managed, were of little value so long as they lacked access to the Atlantic seaboard. The PRR and the other trunk lines provided that access, but only at a significant cost. Trunk-line executives demanded steady traffic flows from the Midwest, as well as convenient connections to gateway cities like Chicago and St. Louis. While they often professed loyalty to their midwestern allies, managers on the PRR, the New York Central, the Erie, and the Baltimore & Ohio were also perfectly willing to join forces with whichever affiliate offered the best connections and the most traffic. Should midwestern managers refuse to cooperate, trunk-line executives possessed ample resources to purchase or build a competing local carrier.

Railroad executives in Ohio and Indiana were hardly powerless against the onslaught of the trunk lines, however. Cass, Smith, Dennison, and Jewett controlled the routes that generated the traffic that the eastern carriers so desperately needed. Particularly during slack economic times, they could play one trunk line off against another, especially with eastward grain shipments. In the end, local entrepreneurs were willing to work with Thomson and other PRR executives only so long as it benefited their corporations, their communities, and their personal fortunes. They were eager to pursue more lucrative deals elsewhere, irrespective of the effect that those arrangements might have on the Pennsylvania Railroad.

The growing integration of the eastern and midwestern railroads exerted a profound effect on transportation patterns within the region. Since the 1830s, local entrepreneurs and community boosters had laid tracks through the relatively flat, agriculturally rich lands of Ohio and Indiana. As investment analyst Henry Varnum Poor observed, those local lines made money almost immediately, as they transported crops to market. That rapid profitability in turn stimulated still more railroad construction. While easterners confronted a small number of transportation options (one railroad between Philadelphia and Pittsburgh, and two between New York and Buffalo, for example), the Midwest was crisscrossed with a web of railroad lines. By the time of the Civil War, virtually every midwestern town and village was connected to the wider world of commerce. Throughout the region, individuals residing in each locale, no matter how small, were convinced that their community was destined to be a crossroads of commerce, a new Cincinnati, Louisville, or Chicago.

The dreams of most of those community boosters never became reality, as the postwar expansion of the trunk lines favored a few communities at the expense of most. As the PRR and the other trunk lines gained control over the best routes through the Midwest, a few key junctions did indeed become centers of trade. Most towns were left off of the main lines, destined to stagnate. They never achieved the glory that their residents had envisioned when they had first promoted their rail link to the wider world. As a result, many Midwesterners complained bitterly that local railway entrepreneurs had sold out to big businesses such as the PRR, and that eastern capital had seized control over local affairs.

At the same time, farmers in Ohio and Indiana confronted the increased uncertainty that accompanied their integration into the national and indeed the international economy. By the late 1860s, farmers in Xenia, Ohio, were no longer shipping to Cincinnati or Columbus, but to Philadelphia and New York. Grain prices in other parts of the world increasingly affected farmers in the Midwest. Yet, rather than attribute their fluctuating fortunes to the international commodities market or the law of comparative advantage, farmers blamed the railroads—and particularly the eastern trunk lines—for the resulting economic dislocations. Even though short-haul rates continued to decline steadily, in what was generally a deflationary period, they were often higher, on a ton-mile basis, than the through rates assessed by the trunk lines. Thunderstruck farmers watched as carloads of grain rolled from Chicago to Philadelphia, at far lower per-mile rates than they paid to send their hard-earned bounty to the nearest competitive shipping point. Trunk-line managers had ample economic evidence to demonstrate

the necessity of allocating a large share of fixed costs to local transportation, producing those attendant high rates. To farmers, who were losing their advantage in distance to their rivals on the Great Plains, such pricing policies were unfair, and an abomination. They often expected their local railroad owners to protect them against that type of exploitation by the trunk lines. Instead, they believed, their community leaders sold them out to the enemy.

After 1865, midwestern railway entrepreneurs possessed numerous opportunities to relinquish local control, as executives from all four trunk lines sought greater dominance over their western outlets. The Erie struck first, thanks largely to Jay Gould's efforts to solidify his connections in Ohio and Indiana, and PRR officials soon responded in kind. The Baltimore & Ohio, still recovering from the Civil War, struggled to gain access to western gateways. The New York Central lagged far behind the others, largely because Cornelius Vanderbilt and his heirs maintained a small central management structure, and made relatively few efforts to administratively consolidate their western connections with the corridor linking New York and Buffalo.

During the postwar scramble for western outlets, Thomson felt that he had little choice other than to bring the PRR's midwestern connections more tightly under his control. In doing so, he followed much the same model that he had used during the 1850s when he transformed the independent transporters into the nucleus of the PRR's Freight Department. Thomson did not impose his will on the midwestern affiliates so much as incorporate those companies and their personnel into the PRR's operations. In the end, Thomson left the corporate structures of the western lines largely intact, grouping most of them into a separate organization—the Pennsylvania Company—that was only loosely affiliated with the Pennsylvania Railroad itself.

Thomson's decision to co-opt the midwestern railroads was a product of necessity, lest they fall under the control of his rivals, but his strategy was one that would produce considerable difficulties for the PRR. While there were many railroads in Ohio and Indiana, competition among the trunk lines for the best routes was intense. Thomson, Scott, and their associates had to think several moves ahead, endeavoring not merely to acquire the lines that they sought, but also preventing rival trunk lines from obtaining access to competing routes. Such policies were extraordinarily expensive, requiring PRR executives to commit large sums of money or agree to extraordinarily remunerative leases. They also left the PRR vulnerable to deceit, and to the unanticipated actions of strong-willed actors, many of whom proved thoroughly unreliable. Several demonstrated their willingness to betray their PRR allies, one proved as incompetent in the field of railways as he had been on the field of battle, and another suffered repeated nervous breakdowns before dying in an insane asylum. Building a midwestern railroad empire on the backs of such individuals would offer Thomson and Scott a formidable challenge.

Problems on the Fort Wayne

During the 1860s, Thomson continued to labor under the fiscal conservatism of the PRR board, and in the process he nearly lost control over the Fort Wayne's vital link to Chicago. Despite the support provided by the Pennsylvania Railroad, the expenditures associated with reaching Chicago had thrown the Pittsburgh, Fort Wayne & Chicago Rail Road into receivership on December 7, 1859. PRR executives suggested a reorganization plan that led to the creation of the new Pittsburgh, Fort Wayne & Chicago Railway in October 1861. New York attorney Samuel J. Tilden hammered out the details of the reorganization, and as a result solidified his considerable reputation in financial circles. Thomson yielded the presidency of the new Fort Wayne to George Cass, who effectively ran the company for many years afterward. The PRR settled for more than a million dollars in new Fort Wayne bonds, but had received only $816,050 worth of the $6.5 million in stock that the reorganized Fort Wayne had issued, far too little to exercise effective control over the company. The Fort Wayne issued an additional $3.5 million in stock in April 1864 and another $1.5 million in May 1867, further diluting the PRR's ownership stake.[4]

During 1864 Thomson sold most of the PRR's investments in the Fort Wayne. The president was anxious to finance the construction of the Pittsburgh &

Steubenville Railroad and he was likewise under pressure from PRR shareholders who preferred not to invest in companies outside the PRR system. The sale was a serious strategic blunder, inasmuch as the Fort Wayne was by no means utterly dependent on the Pennsylvania Railroad. Cass and his Fort Wayne associates had repeatedly demonstrated their weak loyalty to the PRR. During the late 1850s, Cass had pressured Thomson and his colleagues to send traffic over the Allentown Route, despite the attendant loss in revenue for the PRR. The alternative, as Cass made quite clear, was for the Fort Wayne to divert traffic to either of the New York roads. In 1858 Cass went so far as to organize a fast freight line between Chicago and Buffalo, a service that was tailor-made to benefit the New York Central, the Erie, and even the Erie Canal, but one that could only draw business away from the PRR. Particularly during the Civil War, Cass routinely complained that the PRR was unable to accommodate all of the Fort Wayne's interchange traffic at the Pittsburgh gateway. New York financiers, especially Tilden and Louis H. Meyer, who owned large blocks of Fort Wayne securities and occupied seats on its board of directors, reinforced Cass's independence from the PRR. They encouraged Cass to direct the Fort Wayne's traffic toward New York, rather than to Philadelphia. In short, the Pennsylvania Railroad needed the Fort Wayne more than the Fort Wayne needed the Pennsylvania Railroad.[5]

The immediate postwar period presented Cass with a multitude of options for bypassing the Pennsylvania Railroad. At Mansfield, Ohio, the Fort Wayne crossed the broad-gauge Atlantic & Great Western Railway, the western outlet for the Erie. The Fort Wayne's interchange with the independent Cleveland, Columbus & Cincinnati Railroad at Crestline allowed traffic to move north toward the Lake Shore & Michigan Southern and the New York Central. Cass preferred not to short-haul his railroad, and he refrained from turning over traffic at either Mansfield or Crestline when he could route shipments east as far as Pittsburgh. In 1864, however, interests connected with the Baltimore & Ohio had attempted to revive the construction of the Pittsburgh & Connellsville Railroad. Four years later, the justices of the Pennsylvania Supreme Court overturned the last of the legal challenges to construction. Also in 1868, members of the Pennsylvania General Assembly enacted a new railroad incorporation law, based in part on concerns that the PRR had monopolized transportation in southwestern Pennsylvania. Construction began almost immediately on the line that would connect Pittsburgh to the B&O and to the port of Baltimore. Cass cared little whether he handed over his traffic to the PRR or the B&O at Pittsburgh, and he suspected that he could play one eastern trunk line against the other.

Cass was not invincible, however. After construction crews completed work on the Pittsburgh & Steubenville Railroad in October 1865, the PRR no longer needed the Fort Wayne and its ally, the Cleveland & Pittsburgh Rail Road, for access to Columbus and Indianapolis. The new, direct route between Pittsburgh and Columbus included the Pittsburgh & Steubenville, the Holliday's Cove Railroad, and the Steubenville & Indiana Railroad, with Benjamin Smith's Columbus & Indianapolis Central Railway providing onward service to the Indiana state capital. Cass was understandably apprehensive at Smith's plans for expansion, which threatened to provide the PRR with an alternate route to Chicago. In 1865, Cass's fears began to come true as the newly merged Chicago & Great Eastern Railway laid tracks between Valparaiso, Indiana, and Chicago, creating a route to the Windy City that was entirely free of the Fort Wayne. In September 1867, Smith transformed his company into the Columbus & Indiana Central Railway and shortly thereafter signed a traffic agreement with the Chicago & Great Eastern. A few months later, in February 1868, Smith merged the two companies into the Columbus, Chicago & Indiana Central Railway, with a route between Columbus and Chicago via Logansport, Indiana. Within a month, the company placed a second and even more direct route in service, by way of Bradford, Ohio, and Union City, Indiana.

Benjamin Smith's efforts to promote his new railroad empire transformed Cass's concern into fury. Smith was desperate for additional capital to finance his expansion projects, and he sought to attract investors by falsely claiming that the PRR would use the Columbus, Chicago & Indiana Central as its exclusive route to Chicago. Cass was outraged, vowing to construct his own line through Pennsylvania, and to the

east coast. He also explored the possibility of an alliance between his Pittsburgh, Fort Wayne & Chicago and the Baltimore & Ohio and its affiliated Pittsburgh & Connellsville Railroad. A consolidation between those three companies would produce disastrous consequences, depriving Thomson of the PRR's most direct access to Chicago and giving that great prize to his rival, B&O president John W. Garrett.

Thomson attempted to placate Cass as best he could. In April 1868, the PRR board appointed a committee to come to terms with the Fort Wayne, and negotiations began a few months later. By December, Thomson had promised Cass that the Fort Wayne would carry all of the PRR's traffic to Chicago. That agreement, negotiated just as financier Jay Gould was consolidating his control over the Erie Railway, was to have enormous consequences for the development of a Pennsylvania Railroad empire in Ohio, Indiana, and Illinois.[6]

The Pan Handle Railway and the Columbus, Chicago & Indiana Central

The completion of the Pittsburgh & Steubenville route across the West Virginia Panhandle, in October 1865, encouraged PRR officials to increase their control over routes in central Ohio and Indiana. In the process, they worked closely with entrepreneurs such as Ben Smith and, farther west, William Riley McKeen. While McKeen was a stable and capable railroad manager, the same could not be said for Smith. Ben Smith was always more of a promoter than a railroader, and his companies—culminating with the Columbus, Chicago & Indiana Central—were badly constructed, poorly maintained, and built on a nightmare of dubious financial interests. Of all of the PRR's allies in the Midwest, Smith was the least reliable and the most troublesome. His inaccurate boast that his roundabout and rundown route would carry the PRR's traffic to Chicago had nearly cost Thomson control over the Fort Wayne. Yet, the possibility that Smith might ally himself with Jay Gould was sufficiently alarming to cause Thomson to bring the CC&IC into the PRR system. Despite its problems, Smith's railroad would be an integral part of a southwestern main line stretching from Pittsburgh through Columbus and Indianapolis, and on to St. Louis.

The CC&IC was not the only weak carrier in central Ohio. The Pittsburgh & Steubenville had at long last succeeded in crossing the West Virginia Panhandle, but the cost of construction had exhausted the P&S's resources, and it was soon bankrupt. The bankruptcy allowed the PRR to purchase the company and reorganize it as the Pan Handle Railway Company in January 1868.[7] Four months later, in May 1868, the PRR consolidated the lines linking Pittsburgh and Columbus (the Pan Handle Railway, the Holliday's Cove Railroad, and the Steubenville & Indiana Railroad) into the Pittsburgh, Cincinnati & St. Louis Railway. The new company, still widely if unofficially known as the Pan Handle, thereafter functioned as a useful administrative structure that would allow PRR managers to coordinate operations southwest of Pittsburgh. The Pan Handle also facilitated Thomson's efforts to establish access to St. Louis and, indirectly, to Chicago. In the process, the repercussions of the 1868 Pan Handle merger produced a rapid consolidation of the rail network in Ohio and Indiana.[8]

Thomson was quick to appreciate the value of Benjamin Smith's Columbus, Chicago & Indiana Central. The Pan Handle system, created within weeks of the CC&IC merger, linked Pittsburgh to Newark, Ohio, with half-ownership in a segment of the Central Ohio Railroad allowing traffic to continue west to Columbus. Once in Columbus, the CC&IC's managers could route traffic to Indianapolis. Two CC&IC lines—one angling northwest from Columbus and the other from Richmond, Indiana—intersected at Logansport, Indiana, providing links from Columbus and Cincinnati to Chicago, and enabling traffic moving between Pittsburgh and Chicago to bypass the more direct Fort Wayne route.

The Pan Handle/CC&IC route offered Thomson, Scott, and their midwestern associates a chance to establish a new gateway to the trans-Mississippi West. Smith's CC&IC included a branch from Logansport west to State Line (later, Effner) on the Illinois border. Once in Illinois, the tracks of the Toledo, Peoria & Warsaw Railway provided access to Keokuk, Iowa, on the west bank of the Mississippi River, just north of the mouth of the Des Moines River. Enticingly,

Keokuk lay more or less due east of Omaha, the western terminus of the Union Pacific Railroad. Any connection with the still-incomplete transcontinental railroad was certain to be lucrative for both the CC&IC and the PRR. In anticipation of such a connection, the PRR associates planned to construct a bridge across the Mississippi River, at Keokuk. In December 1868, five months before dignitaries from the Union Pacific and Central Pacific drove the golden spike at Promontory Point, Utah, representatives from the Columbus, Chicago & Indiana Central, the Toledo, Peoria & Warsaw, the Des Moines Valley Railroad, and the Wabash & Western Railway organized the Keokuk & Hamilton Bridge Company. The PRR was not officially a party to the agreement, but Thomson and Scott invested in the project. As such, they were anxious to maintain a close relationship with the CC&IC, both to augment the PRR's western traffic and to safeguard their personal investments.[9]

Smith's financial empire was something of a house of cards, however, and that vulnerability made the Columbus, Chicago & Indiana Central a tempting target for the heads of the other trunk lines. The February 1868 merger that had joined the Chicago & Great Eastern and the Columbus & Indianapolis Central had vaulted Smith from a local to a regional railway entrepreneur. In the process, however, Smith had diluted his influence and considerably weakened his control over the CC&IC. Ultimately, some 40 percent of that railroad's stock was in the hands of New York investors. The weakest component of his system, the Chicago & Great Eastern, carried considerable debt, placing Smith's entire empire in jeopardy. The newspapers of the mid-1800s often referred to the financial "embarrassment" of such overextended companies, but that word did not begin to describe the magnitude of the calamity that threatened to overtake the Columbus, Chicago & Indiana Central.[10]

From the perspective of Thomson and the board of directors of the Pennsylvania Railroad, the CC&IC's financial problems, and Smith's loss of control over that company, could not have occurred at a worse possible time. Jay Gould, president of the Erie, soon perceived both the potential and the weakness of Smith's CC&IC, and he made plans to add that railroad to his growing sphere of influence. Gould served as an *agent provocateur*, inciting a cascading series of corporate re-alignments that forced Thomson to gain control over the PRR's midwestern affiliates. In his efforts to extend his railroad empire to the west, Gould attempted to control all four of the principal routes linking New York and Pennsylvania to the Midwest. One was the collection of lines between Buffalo and Chicago, along the southern shore of Lake Erie, generally allied with the New York Central.[11] Another was the Atlantic & Great Western to Dayton, with onward connections over the Cincinnati, Hamilton & Dayton to Cincinnati, and over the Ohio & Mississippi Railway to St. Louis, all broad-gauge routes that were tied to the Erie. Two others, the Fort Wayne and the Pan Handle/Columbus, Chicago & Indiana Central, served the needs of the PRR. Once in charge of the Erie, Gould audaciously sought to control all four of those routes, in an attempt to sever the other eastern trunk lines, including the PRR, from their western outlets.[12]

Gould's first and most obvious acquisition was the Atlantic & Great Western, the Erie's traditional western conduit. With the A&GW in receivership and the Erie deeply in debt, neither company could be considered a prize. In December 1868, Gould leased the A&GW, agreeing to pay exceedingly high rental charges. The arrangement nonetheless guaranteed Gould a large share of the oil trade—vital if he wished to make good the rental payments on the A&GW and carry out his high-volume, low-rate policies for the Erie. Unfortunately for Gould, the Ohio & Mississippi Railway, which offered broad-gauge service from Cincinnati as far west as St. Louis, soon came under the influence of the B&O, depriving the Erie of access to Indiana and Illinois.[13]

Gould also cast a covetous eye on the financially weak and therefore exceedingly vulnerable Columbus, Chicago & Indiana Central. At Urbana, Ohio, Gould's Atlantic & Great Western connected with the eastern end of the CC&IC, offering the New York financier a valuable, if somewhat indirect route to Chicago. Smith and associates were still reeling from Thomson's December 1868 decision to withdraw all of the PRR's traffic from the CC&IC in favor of the Fort Wayne, and they saw Gould as a potential savior. The same month, the CC&IC board of directors, heavily influenced by

that railroad's New York investors, agreed to lease their line to the Erie. Gould pledged that the Erie would pay CC&IC investors 30 percent of gross receipts, with a minimum rental of $1.8 million annually—an indication of his desperation to secure additional western outlets. Construction crews were poised to install a third rail enabling the Erie's broad-gauge equipment to proceed westward to Chicago.[14]

The Erie's control over the Columbus, Chicago & Indiana Central would have disastrous consequences for the PRR, not merely allowing the Erie to reach Chicago, but also preventing the PRR from using the CC&IC line between Columbus and Indianapolis and blocking entry into St. Louis, as well. Even worse, Cass was still so enraged at what he perceived as Thomson's duplicity that he might conceivably negotiate an exclusive traffic agreement with either Gould or Vanderbilt, denying the PRR access to Chicago via the Fort Wayne.[15]

And all of those developments took place amid a ruinous rate war between the PRR and the other eastern trunk lines. Since the collapse of the last, prewar traffic pool in 1861, relative harmony had existed between the carriers. The Civil War had largely removed the Baltimore & Ohio from contention, and there was ample wartime traffic to fill the tracks of the three remaining trunk lines. As the economy contracted after the war, and as construction crews repaired the destruction along the B&O, the railroads began to compete more vigorously for western traffic.

Trouble began in October 1869 with a dispute that pitted managers on the Erie and the New York Central against the independent freight agents who quoted rates over those two roads. Both companies slashed their fares, and PRR officials had little choice but to follow suit. Thomson and the PRR had weathered earlier rate wars. This time, however, he sensed that something was different. Over the previous decade, through the adroit use of financial assistance, leases, and fast freight lines, Thomson had captured the freight of the PRR's western connections without actually owning them. Now, it appeared that Gould, Vanderbilt, and Garrett wanted those affiliates for themselves, if for no other reason than to deny them to the PRR. Under such circumstances, Thomson insisted, Gould in particular wanted nothing less than "to get control of our connecting lines; and by this means divert business from its natural channels to *their* circuitous route to the seaboard."[16]

Thomson's actions over the next few months would determine whether the Pennsylvania Railroad would remain one of the great eastern trunk lines, or whether it would be reduced to the status of a regional carrier, serving only Pennsylvania. The editors of London newspapers were some of the most interested spectators in the ensuing contest. They were nonpartisan, yet anxious to provide British investors with the best possible analysis of the situation. They judged Vanderbilt to be the ablest of the trunk-line presidents, but they commented favorably on Gould's tenacity and quick intellect. The Pennsylvania Railroad, they emphasized, enjoyed the greatest capitalization and the best physical plant. They predicted that Thomson and Scott would put up a strong fight, but that the New York Central would probably prevail in the end. They seem not to have appreciated that the PRR possessed one crucial advantage over all of the other trunk lines in that it earned the bulk of its revenues from local traffic within Pennsylvania, including the transportation of bituminous coal. Thomson and Scott could set high rates on that captive traffic, and then use the resulting revenues to cross-subsidize non-remunerative long-haul competitive traffic, allowing the PRR to ride out even the most severe rate wars.[17]

Thomson's first priority was to persuade the PRR directors to abandon their earlier reticence to invest directly in lines outside of Pennsylvania. They needed little convincing. They were as shocked as Thomson at Gould's maneuvers, and they gave their president the freedom to respond as he saw fit. Board members acceded to Thomson's policies not only to secure the Fort Wayne, but also to take whatever steps might be necessary to guarantee access to St. Louis and the southwestern United States, and to protect the PRR's eastern flank with routes to New York and Washington.[18]

Thomson demonstrated his willingness to pay any price to break the Gould lease of the CC&IC. Even though the CC&IC directors had agreed to Gould's generous terms, the stockholders had not yet ratified the contract. Before they could do so, Thomson matched the Erie's offer, suggesting that the Pittsburgh, Cincinnati & St. Louis (a.k.a., the Pan Handle) should lease the CC&IC. Like Gould, he offered a rental payment equivalent to 30 percent of gross earnings, to be applied to the interest charges on the CC&IC's massive $22 million debt. After paying the bondholders, any excess would be distributed as dividends to stockholders. The proposal was slightly less lucrative than the Gould offer, but Smith and the CC&IC's other investors-well aware of the Erie's shaky financial reputation—considered the PRR to be the more reliable partner.[19]

News of Thomson's offer caused CC&IC stock to more than double, from $40 to $90 a share. The CC&IC stockholders had little difficulty in agreeing to those extraordinarily favorable terms, and the lease took effect on February 1, 1869. Thomson had acted so quickly that neither he nor anyone else had made a careful inspection—indeed, any inspection—of Ben Smith's railroad. PRR officials soon experienced something of buyers' remorse once they discovered that they had leased a company that was in extraordinarily poor condition. As Thomson admitted in the PRR's *Annual Report* for 1868, "The lease of these lines will require additional capital, to be applied especially to an increase of their Rolling Stock."[20] The PRR board had little choice other than to issue additional stock in order to fund emergency repairs. The expense associated with leasing and rehabilitating the CC&IC was essentially irrelevant, however, as Thomson had to protect the PRR's access to Chicago and the Midwest by any means necessary.[21]

Controlling the Fort Wayne

Thomson had much more elaborate goals than merely controlling the Columbus, Chicago & Indiana Central, however. His acquisition of that line gave him the mechanism that he needed to safeguard an even better route to Chicago, via the Fort Wayne. For all of his bluster, George Cass knew that Thomson's success in leasing the Columbus, Chicago & Indiana Central had left the Fort Wayne in an extremely vulnerable position. Now that he had a secure route to Chicago, by way of Columbus, Thomson could withdraw all of the PRR's traffic from the Fort Wayne. Such a move would cripple Cass's railroad, and he would have had little choice other than to seek the shelter of another of the eastern trunk lines—with the most obvious candidate, the Erie, essentially being able to name its price. At the same time, a series of mergers, beginning in 1867 and culminating in June 1869, created the Lake Shore & Michigan Southern Railway. The consolidated company—independent but nonetheless closely allied with the New York Central—possessed a route between Buffalo and Chicago, and its executives were no longer interested in conveying the Fort Wayne's traffic to the east coast.

Cass, perhaps mollified by reassurances that Benjamin Smith, and not Thomson, had been behind the CC&IC's pledge to divert through traffic off of the Fort Wayne, acquiesced to a PRR takeover. Working through the investment-banking house of Winslow, Lanier & Company, the Fort Wayne board appointed a committee to develop a strategy for denying Gould control over the company. The committee's members—including Thomson and Samuel Tilden—decided that the most likely scenario for an Erie takeover would involve a Gould acquisition of a large block of Fort Wayne stock. In that case, the New York financier could appoint a majority of the Fort Wayne's board, with the new directors immediately voting to lease their company to the Erie. By February, their worst fears seemed to be coming true when Gould announced that he had acquired sufficient stock proxies to elect his own slate of directors.[22]

Thomson possessed a crucial advantage over Gould, one that had far more to do with politics than with finance or operating efficiency. The Pennsylvania legislature had chartered the Fort Wayne, and that body could make any changes that it deemed fit to the original articles of incorporation. Gould may have been a master manipulator on Wall Street, but he was no match for Thomson's influence in Harrisburg. Scott was well versed in such matters, as well, and he took responsibility for explaining the gravity of the situation to the state's legislators. The Pennsylvania Railroad was a Pennsylvania company, he explained, and would funnel western traffic through the state, while a foreign usurper, like the Erie, would divert that western trade to New York. That was an argument that almost precisely echoed the one that promoters of the Main Line of Public Works had articulated, decades earlier, when they called for commonwealth support for internal improvements, lest the western trade be drawn off by the Erie Canal. There were no commonwealth funds involved this time—just the request that Fort Wayne's charter be modified so that no more than a quarter of its directors could be replaced in any one year. Under those circumstances, it would take Gould three years to secure control. On February 3, 1869, the legislature readily acquiesced, and the entire process, from the introduction of the bill to its passage, occupied precisely thirty-four minutes.[23]

The amended charter blunted Gould's attempt to acquire the Fort Wayne and left Thomson and Cass free to negotiate terms. Cass drove a hard bargain, receiving a $1.3 million annual rental, equivalent to a 12 percent return on the Fort Wayne's outstanding stock. On July 1, 1869, the PRR took control of the Fort Wayne main line between Pittsburgh and Chicago, as well as its branches, under the terms of a 999-year lease. Construction crews were soon at work, re-laying the Fort Wayne's Ohio-gauge tracks to a slightly narrower 4′ 9½″. At the same time, the PRR widened the tracks on its main line between Philadelphia and Pittsburgh from standard gauge to 4′ 9″. As a result, freight and passenger cars could pass directly from Philadelphia to Chicago without requiring either transshipment or the use of potentially dangerous compromise-gauge equipment.[24]

While Thomson was negotiating the lease of the Fort Wayne, its allied company, the Cleveland & Pittsburgh Rail Road, nearly slipped from his grasp. In January 1869, Jay Gould obtained control over the Cleveland & Pittsburgh, both to gain access to the Cleveland refineries and as a part of his larger effort to control the Fort Wayne and its connections. Scott arranged to be appointed as a Cleveland & Pittsburgh director and he quickly rallied his allies on the board. George Cass and Samuel Tilden held substantial blocks of Cleveland & Pittsburgh stock, and they further safeguarded the PRR's interests. In November 1871, effectively defeated in his efforts to control the Cleveland & Pittsburgh, Gould acquiesced to a PRR lease of the company. Gould's Erie allies departed the Cleveland & Pittsburgh's board in January 1873, but the New Yorker remained a director for an additional year.[25]

Thomson's control over the Fort Wayne and the Cleveland & Pittsburgh came at a hefty price. In addition to shouldering the rental fees and guaranteed dividends, the PRR covered the bonded indebtedness for the Fort Wayne and its subsidiaries, including some that were of little value to the PRR. That provision, in keeping with an Ohio law passed in March 1869, saddled the PRR with some $58 million in debt. By 1874, moreover, the PRR's guaranteed payments to the Fort Wayne had more than doubled, to just over $2.6 million. The economic depression that began the previous year cut sharply into revenues, making the fees all the more painful for PRR officials. In later years, the economy rebounded, as did traffic on the Fort Wayne. Once again, Thomson's strategic vision had cost the PRR dearly in the short term, but established the basis for its long-term success.[26]

Two Routes to St. Louis

Even as he was solidifying the PRR's control over the Columbus, Chicago & Indiana Central and the Fort Wayne, Thomson was working to extend the PRR's influence to St. Louis. That city had once been the gateway to the west, but by 1860 had lost that role to Chicago. The Windy City was ideally located on Lake Michigan and in close proximity to the headwaters of the Mississippi River. Chicago also benefited from the tireless activities of municipal boosters, who emphasized their city's advantages and encouraged the development of a wide-ranging transportation infrastructure.[27]

As Chicago rose, St. Louis declined in relative importance. The Civil War increased traffic between St. Louis and the east, but it dealt a serious blow to navigation on the Mississippi River, from which the city never fully recovered. While the four eastern trunk lines developed their own routes to Chicago (with the Baltimore & Ohio the last to arrive, via an indirect route, in November 1874), there was simply too little traffic to merit four parallel railroads to St. Louis. As such, Thomson and his fellow trunk-line executives would have preferred to maintain a single route to St. Louis, to be shared by all. As events transpired, however, two railroads would connect Indianapolis and St. Louis, and the Pennsylvania Railroad would control a portion of each.

The Terre Haute & Indianapolis Railroad became the key link that would allow the trunk lines access to St. Louis. Decades earlier, Chauncey Rose, a Terre Haute merchant and civic booster, had desired to connect his community to the expanding midwestern railroad network. In 1847, he obtained a charter for the Terre Haute & Richmond Railroad, and by 1852 the line was in service between Terre Haute and Indianapolis. East of the Indiana capital, the Indiana Central Railway opened in 1853, carrying traffic toward Ohio.

It was not long before two rail lines carried traffic west across Illinois. In 1856, the Terre Haute, Alton & St. Louis Railroad linked the western end of the Terre Haute & Richmond to the Mississippi River, at both Alton and at Illinoistown (East St. Louis), Illinois. The following spring, the broad-gauge Ohio & Mississippi Rail Road opened its line between Cincinnati and Illinoistown.[28] The near-simultaneous completion of the Marietta & Cincinnati Railroad across southern Ohio offered the B&O a mediocre sort of access to St. Louis. The Ohio & Mississippi also held considerable potential to serve as the Erie's outlet to the southwest, following the completion of the Atlantic & Great Western Railroad to Dayton, Ohio, in 1864. Neither line was a stunning success, however, with the Ohio & Mississippi entering receivership in 1860, and with the Terre Haute, Alton & St. Louis Railroad reorganized in 1862 as the St. Louis, Alton & Terre Haute Railroad (the "Alton Route").[29]

Despite those financial setbacks, the Civil War stimulated increased interest in the St. Louis gateway. Rose and his associates, flush with wartime revenues, were determined to establish their own link between Terre Haute and St. Louis. In February 1865, after several false starts, they chartered the St. Louis, Vandalia & Terre Haute Railroad. The new company was empowered to build a line across southern Illinois through Vandalia, south of the St. Louis, Alton & Terre Haute, and north of the Ohio & Mississippi. A month later, the Terre Haute & Richmond assumed a new name—the Terre Haute & Indianapolis Railroad—that more accurately reflected its eastern terminus in the Indiana capital. Rose and his backers made little progress on the St. Louis, Vandalia & Terre Haute, however, and two years passed without any significant construction taking place. In the meantime,

Rose and his fellow investors in the Terre Haute & Indianapolis continued their reliance on the Alton Route to St. Louis.[30]

The managers of the eastern trunk lines reacted with great interest to the developments in southern Illinois. The Baltimore & Ohio was never a serious contender for the St. Louis market, leaving the field to Thomson, Gould, and Vanderbilt, and the railroads allied with them. The Erie bypassed Indianapolis in favor of the broad-gauge Atlantic & Great Western/ Cincinnati, Hamilton & Dayton/Ohio & Mississippi route through Cincinnati and southern Indiana, and Gould accordingly had little use for Chauncey Rose's Terre Haute & Indianapolis/Alton Route combination. The two remaining trunk lines each relied on a railroad connection from the east into Indianapolis, although neither owned their affiliate outright. Vanderbilt and the New York Central utilized the Cleveland, Painesville & Ashtabula Railroad (after 1869, the Lake Shore & Michigan Southern Railway) for access to Cleveland. From there, the Cleveland, Columbus & Cincinnati Railroad reached Bellefontaine, Ohio, with the Bellefontaine Railway (colloquially known as the "Bee Line") covering the remaining distance to Indianapolis.[31] Following the completion of the Pittsburgh & Steubenville Railroad in October 1865, and its subsequent incorporation into the Pan Handle route, the Pennsylvania Railroad maintained a direct link from Pittsburgh almost due west through Columbus, Ohio, and Richmond, Indiana, with PRR traffic entering Indianapolis over the Columbus & Indianapolis Central Railway. In September 1867, that line became a part of Benjamin Smith's Columbus & Indiana Central Railway, and in February 1868 it became a key component of the Columbus, Chicago & Indiana Central Railway. A year later, the PRR's lease of the CC&IC gave Thomson a secure link to the Indianapolis, and a connection with the railroad lines that led west to St. Louis.

Cincinnati attorney and investor Henry C. Lord precipitated the rapid realignment of the routes linking Indianapolis, Terre Haute, and St. Louis. By the time of the Civil War, Lord controlled the Indianapolis & Cincinnati Railroad, which extended only as far east as Lawrenceburg, Indiana. On the eastern end of the line, Lord relied on trackage rights over the Ohio

& Mississippi in order to reach Cincinnati proper. That was more than a minor inconvenience, as the terms of the agreement prohibited Lord from soliciting any traffic to or from St. Louis. Lord asked Rose and his allies to pay for the construction of a new entrance into Cincinnati, which would free him from reliance on the Ohio & Mississippi. They complied, and received in exchange Lord's guarantee that he would serve as an eastern conduit for Rose's lines between Indianapolis and St. Louis.[32]

During the second half of 1866, Lord sought to expand his small railroad empire by gaining control of Rose's Terre Haute & Indianapolis line through western Indiana. Upon hearing of that maneuver, investors in the New York Central–affiliated Bellefontaine Railway, fearful of losing their access to St. Louis, likewise attempted to purchase a controlling interest in the Terre Haute & Indianapolis. George Cass, president of the Fort Wayne, was understandably concerned that, should Chauncey Rose accept either offer, his railroad might be denied access to St. Louis.

Afraid of exacerbating what was already shaping up to be a bidding war for the line, Cass declined to provide a third offer, instead working with Thomson and the PRR to develop six-party control of both the TH&I and the St. Louis, Alton & Terre Haute. In April 1867, a month after he had overseen the merger of the Indianapolis & Cincinnati into the Indianapolis, Cincinnati & Lafayette Railroad, Lord met with representatives from the PRR; the Fort Wayne; the Cleveland, Columbus & Cincinnati Railroad; the Cleveland, Painesville & Ashtabula Railroad; the Bellefontaine Railway; and the Indianapolis, Cincinnati & Lafayette (the latter three of which were aligned with the Vanderbilt system). On May 17, they offered to buy the TH&I, using that company to lease the Alton Route—a lease that would be guaranteed by the six railroads in the consortium. The New York investors who controlled the Alton Route readily assented to the arrangement, which now depended solely on the willingness of the TH&I's owners to sell their railroad to representatives of the eastern trunk lines.[33]

The members of the consortium soon confronted the intense regionalism associated with local boosters anxious to protect their communities from the economic dislocations that so often accompanied the system-building efforts of the trunk lines. Edwin J. Peck, president of the TH&I, strongly supported the proposal and promised to secure the support of the company's other investors. The directors of the TH&I, however, preferred to retain local control of their railroad, both because they valued their autonomy and because they feared that the trunk lines might implement rates and terms of service that would adversely affect Terre Haute and other communities along the line. They refused to sell their company to the six-party consortium and reviled Peck as a sellout. Demonstrating their independence, they abrogated the proposed lease of the St. Louis, Alton & Terre Haute. A few days later, on June 18, Peck resigned and the TH&I board elected Terre Haute banker William Riley McKeen as the company's new president.[34]

McKeen vowed that the TH&I would not come under the control of eastern interests, yet he soon allied himself with Thomson and his fellow PRR associates. With the opening of the Pan Handle/Columbus & Indiana Central route westward to Indianapolis, the PRR offered the most direct route between Philadelphia and St. Louis. By the summer of 1867, Thomson, Scott, and their allies were heavily involved in efforts to bridge the Mississippi River at St. Louis and to influence railroad development farther west. Under those circumstances, Thomson was disinclined to share the St. Louis market with the other five railroads in the consortium. Instead, he withdrew from the agreement and sought sole control of the Terre Haute & Indianapolis.

There was only one difficulty associated with Thomson's plans: without simultaneous control over the St. Louis, Alton & Terre Haute, PRR traffic could travel as far west as Terre Haute, but no farther. The five railroads that remained in the consortium had problems of their own, as they possessed a link between Terre Haute and East St. Louis, but no connection between Indianapolis and Terre Haute. Their managers were prepared to bypass the obstinate McKeen, and in August 1867 they incorporated the Indianapolis & St. Louis Railroad, to link the Illinois state line to Indianapolis. By September, the new company had leased the St. Louis, Alton & Terre Haute.[35] Lord's Indianapolis, Cincinnati & Lafayette held a one-third share in the lease, as did Cass's Fort Wayne. The remaining

third was held collectively by the Bellefontaine Railway; the Cleveland, Columbus & Cincinnati Railroad; and the Cleveland, Painesville & Ashtabula Railroad. The money to build the new Indianapolis & St. Louis line came in equal measure from the PRR-affiliated Fort Wayne and the New York Central's western connection, the Cleveland, Columbus & Cincinnati. The PRR was conspicuous by its absence, but Thomson had no need for the Indianapolis & St. Louis. Instead, he had pledged his support to McKeen, and to McKeen's efforts to extend the Terre Haute & Indianapolis west to the Mississippi River.[36]

McKeen, who was determined to provide his railroad with secure access to St. Louis, now found himself in the unusual, if highly enviable position of being able to dictate policy to the PRR. When Thomson attempted to negotiate a through traffic agreement over the TH&I, McKeen informed the PRR president that he could not countenance such an arrangement unless the PRR constructed a western extension to his railroad. The mechanism to build such a connection had been in place for more than two years, in the form of the charter for the St. Louis, Vandalia & Terre Haute Railroad. Thomson, who was equally anxious that the PRR should reach St. Louis, had little choice other than to accede to McKeen's demands. In December 1867, the PRR president agreed to fund construction of the "Vandalia Route" between Terre Haute and St. Louis, providing both the PRR and the TH&I with a western outlet.[37]

With the PRR providing indirect financial support for the Vandalia Route, construction began in earnest. In April 1868 George Brooke Roberts took charge of the project. Officially, Roberts was a PRR locating engineer and assistant to Thomson. More significantly, he was Thomson's chief protégé, on the fast track to the presidency, and his involvement in the St. Louis, Vandalia & Terre Haute gave him valuable experience in overseeing a major engineering challenge. By April 1870, construction crews had built from East St. Louis to the Indiana state line, where they connected with the Terre Haute & Indianapolis. Meanwhile, the competing Indianapolis & St. Louis, backed by the remaining five companies in the May 1867 agreement, extended its tracks from Terre Haute east to the Indiana capital. The new line, in conjunction with the Alton Route, created two parallel railroads through a territory that could barely support one.[38]

The Pennsylvania Railroad soon owned a portion of both routes to St. Louis, thanks to Thomson's rapid moves in 1869 to control his western connections. When the PRR leased the Fort Wayne, Thomson assumed that railroad's interest in the joint operation of the Indianapolis & St. Louis, as well as that company's lease of the St. Louis, Alton & Terre Haute. That placed the PRR in the rather unusual position of operating two competing carriers across central Illinois. One, the Vandalia Route, had been financed largely by the PRR and its affiliates, but it was leased to an independent friendly connection, the Terre Haute & Indianapolis. The Fort Wayne had an interest in the other combination, having paid for half the cost of building the Indianapolis & St. Louis, and having guaranteed a third of that company's lease of the Alton Route.

The more northerly Alton Route was of limited use to the PRR, however, and it eventually drifted under the influence of the New York Central. Five railroads had agreed to build the Indianapolis & St. Louis and lease the St. Louis, Alton & Terre Haute, but, one by one, the signatories exempted themselves from the consortium. In May 1868, the Bellefontaine Railway merged with the Cleveland, Columbus & Cincinnati to form the Cleveland, Columbus, Cincinnati & Indianapolis Railway, still known as the Bee Line. By April 1869, the Cleveland, Painesville & Ashtabula Railroad had become a part of the Lake Shore & Michigan Southern Railway. Of the two remaining independent companies, the Indianapolis, Cincinnati, & Lafayette Railroad was bankrupt by 1871, unable to pay its share of the annual rentals on the Indianapolis & St. Louis.[39] As a result, the PRR and the Cleveland, Columbus, Cincinnati & Indianapolis shared the expense of maintaining the Indianapolis & St. Louis route. That line was of little practical value to the PRR, however, as its 1868 lease of the Terre Haute & Indianapolis required the PRR to route all St. Louis traffic over that railroad and its western extension, the St. Louis, Vandalia & Terre Haute.[40]

William Riley McKeen, president of the Terre Haute & Indianapolis, probably won the most from the complex series of negotiations that had taken place during the late 1860s. To his dismay, the construction of the Indianapolis & St. Louis had shattered his monopoly on traffic moving between Indianapolis and Terre Haute. In compensation, he had ensured that the PRR's growing stream of St. Louis business would pass over his railroad, at extremely remunerative rates. At the same time, he had preserved his company's independence, preventing it from falling under the dominance of any of the trunk lines.

McKeen's independence, underwritten by revenues from PRR traffic, encouraged his expansionist visions, particularly in northern Indiana. By 1871, local investors had consolidated several existing railroads into the Logansport, Crawfordsville & South Western Railway. The incorporators suggested that the resulting north–south route would bring tobacco and cotton from the South to the Great Lakes. The line subsequently went bankrupt, and in September 1879 representatives of the TH&I bought it for a pittance. They reincorporated the company as the Terre Haute & Logansport Railway. Tracklayers pushed north from Logansport, and by 1884 they reached South Bend, Indiana, followed by St. Joseph, Michigan, in 1890. Coal from southern Illinois could travel north to Benton Harbor, Michigan, and the waiting holds of lake boats. McKeen's efforts to reach Lake Michigan proved something of a disappointment, undermined the financial health of the TH&I, and helped to end that company's independence from the PRR. For the moment, however, William Riley McKeen was an ally, and not a subject, of the Pennsylvania Railroad.[41]

Ohio River Gateways

While Thomson was creating a route to St. Louis, the PRR finally gained access to Cincinnati over its own rails. The line was part of the original route between Columbus and Cincinnati, via the Columbus & Xenia Railroad (chartered in 1844 and completed in 1850) and the Little Miami Railroad (incorporated in 1836 and opened nine years later). The two railroads coordinated their operations, serving as a southern extension for the Cleveland, Columbus & Cincinnati Railroad, whose tracks extended only as far south as the state capital. By 1863, the three companies were pooling traffic between Cleveland and Cincinnati.

As described above, in May 1868, the Cleveland, Columbus & Cincinnati merged with the Bellefontaine Railway, forming the Cleveland, Columbus, Cincinnati & Indianapolis Railway. The new company, allied with the New York Central, caused the directors of the Little Miami and the Columbus & Xenia to join forces with the PRR. They ended the Cleveland–Cincinnati traffic pool that they had established in 1863. In March 1869, the Little Miami leased the Columbus & Xenia, bringing the two companies under joint ownership. Within weeks, the creation of the Lake Shore & Michigan Southern gave the directors of the Little Miami additional cause for concern. They suspected that the Cleveland, Columbus, Cincinnati & Indianapolis, in cooperation with the Lake Shore, might build its own line to Cincinnati.

The owners of the Little Miami faced another threat from the west in the form of the Cincinnati & Zanesville Railroad. Originally incorporated in 1851 as the Cincinnati, Wilmington & Zanesville Railroad, its promoters harbored the grandiose vision that their company would serve as the western outlet for the Baltimore & Ohio. The completion of the Marietta & Cincinnati Railroad in 1857 put an end to those dreams, but the promoters of the Zanesville line persevered nonetheless. By 1869, the company had already declared bankruptcy (twice), yet had managed to establish a route between Zanesville and a junction with the Little Miami, at Morrow. By the time of the second bankruptcy, the PRR had acquired $807,000 worth of the company's bonds and retained control over the line, now reconstituted as the Cincinnati & Muskingum Valley Railway. Thomson and his associates reasoned that sixteen miles of new construction, from Zanesville north to Trinway, Ohio, would provide the company with access to the Pittsburgh, Cincinnati & St. Louis (Pan Handle) route. At the western end of the line, traffic would travel the short distance from Morrow to Cincinnati over the Little Miami.

The Little Miami's owners perceived the precariousness of their position. With the Cleveland, Columbus, Cincinnati & Indianapolis prepared to construct a parallel line between Columbus and Cincinnati, there was also a strong possibility that the PRR would build a similar duplicate route between Morrow and Cincinnati—reducing the Little Miami's traffic to a trickle. The company's owners sought protection with the PRR's Pan Handle subsidiary, hoping that Thomson and his associates would be interested in a more direct access to Cincinnati. In February 1870, the PRR gained control over the Little Miami, by virtue of a ninety-nine-year lease to the Pittsburgh, Cincinnati & St. Louis. Eight months later, when construction crews finished the short link between Trinway and Zanesville, the PRR possessed two routes to Cincinnati—a roundabout, poor-quality line that meandered through the hills of southern Ohio, and a far superior alignment over the former Columbus & Xenia and Little Miami, southwest from the state capital.[42]

The city of Louisville, a hundred miles west of Cincinnati, offered far more potential for the PRR. Louisville was the western gateway to the South, with access to several important carriers, most notably the Louisville & Nashville Railroad. In 1871, the Pan Handle leased the Jeffersonville, Madison & Indianapolis Railroad. The new acquisition gave the PRR a route from Indianapolis to Jeffersonville, Indiana, across the Ohio River from Louisville. Also included was a branch from Columbus, Indiana, to the Ohio River town of Madison, a section of track that was the oldest in the PRR system west of the Appalachians. The line also boasted another historical curiosity in that it contained the steepest grade on the PRR, descending to the riverbank at Madison. That characteristic, combined with the absence of a bridge across the Ohio River at Madison, ensured that most traffic would continue to flow south to Jeffersonville.[43]

By the time that the PRR took control of the lines in southern Indiana, they were connected to the southern railway network. In February 1867, the Jeffersonville, Madison & Indianapolis had joined forces with the Louisville & Nashville to build a bridge across the Ohio River at Louisville, under the auspices of the Louisville Bridge Company. The bridge carried its first trains in February 1870. After the PRR established control over the Jeffersonville, Madison & Indianapolis, it gained part ownership in the Ohio River crossing as well. Within a few years, however, the Panic of 1873 curtailed the development of traffic through a region that still felt the effects of the Civil War. The Louisville gateway never reached the potential that Thomson had envisioned for it.[44]

Thomson's efforts to establish yet another Ohio River gateway, at Cairo, Illinois, were even more disappointing. Cairo, where the Ohio joined the Mississippi River, was to be the most southwesterly point of the PRR system. The city was a logical destination for PRR traffic, as it offered a connection with a chain of railroads linking Chicago to New Orleans. In angling for Cairo, Thomson overreached badly, and suffered a rare rebuke from his shareholders as a result. Yet, the failure of the Cairo gateway had less to do with his failings than with the uncertainties associated with reliance on outside actors. The financial malaise of the 1870s, combined with the missteps of individuals such as railroad promoter Colonel Henry S. McComb, severely limited Thomson's freedom of action.[45]

While most railways built in the United States linked east to west, the Mississippi River provided a natural transportation corridor that was amenable to rail as well as water traffic. A line between Chicago and Cairo, built by the Illinois Central between 1851 and 1856, was one of the oldest mainline railroads in the western part of the United States. Farther south, the New Orleans, Jackson & Great Northern Railroad by 1858 connected New Orleans to Canton, Mississippi. Two years later, construction workers—many of them enslaved African Americans—completed the Mississippi Central Railroad between Canton and Jackson, Tennessee. The two railroads consolidated their operations, relying on a connection with the Mobile & Ohio Railroad from Jackson north to Columbus, Kentucky, a short distance below the mouth of the Ohio River at Cairo.

Under Scott's guidance, the PRR attempted to exert influence over the lines along the Mississippi River, employing Colonel McComb as an intermediary. McComb was a self-made Wilmington, Delaware, leather goods manufacturer. He earned his fortune during the Civil War by supplying more than $2 million worth of tents and wagon covers to the Union Army. By 1864, McComb was affiliated with the Union Pacific Railroad, and he was among the original stockholders of Crédit Mobilier, the construction company responsible for building the line.

The Civil War provided McComb the opportunity to expand into the South. The war had virtually destroyed the combined New Orleans, Jackson & Great Northern/Mississippi Central/Mobile & Ohio route between New Orleans and Columbus, Kentucky. In September 1865, former Civil War general Absolom W. West took charge of rebuilding the Mississippi Central, and he appointed McComb as his agent in Washington, D.C. By 1868, McComb had overseen the creation of the Southern Railroad Association, an early version of the holding company. Working through that entity, McComb attempted to connect New Orleans with Cairo, Illinois, and to create a rail network through the western portion of the former Confederacy. He became president of the New Orleans, Jackson & Great Northern Railroad, and he moved that railroad's shops from New Orleans to the company town of McComb, Mississippi.[46]

PRR executives saw considerable potential in McComb's Mississippi River rail corridor. At a time when Thomson and Scott were attempting to use the Southern Railway Security Company to establish a route between Washington and New Orleans, via Atlanta, McComb's companies offered alternate, more westerly access to the Crescent City. Thomson and Scott cautiously arranged to provide limited financial support for McComb's Southern Railroad Association, purchasing approximately $1.3 million in Mississippi Central and New Orleans, Jackson & Great Northern securities.[47]

To reach the McComb route, Thomson relied on two railroads, the Indianapolis & Vincennes and the Cairo & Vincennes. General Ambrose Burnside, who was associated with the Illinois Central and who had once served as that company's treasurer, promoted both lines. Burnside, widely reviled for his military incompetence during the Civil War, proved equally ill starred as a railroad promoter. He became president of the Indianapolis & Vincennes in 1867, two years after its incorporation, about the time that construction crews began laying track through southwestern Indiana. Benjamin Smith's Columbus, Chicago & Indiana Central provided some of the capital, and so did the Pan Handle and the NYC-affiliated Indianapolis, Cincinnati & Lafayette Railroad. By July 1868, the Indianapolis & Vincennes was in service between Indianapolis and Martinsville, Indiana.

By the time trains entered Vincennes, in November 1869, Thomson had solidified the PRR's control over the CC&IC, and the Indianapolis & Vincennes was part of the bargain. By 1870, the PRR board had guaranteed a portion of the bonds of both the Indianapolis & Vincennes and the Cairo & Vincennes, the Illinois extension of the route. The control over the Indianapolis & Vincennes was particularly strong, with such PRR stalwarts as Scott, George Brooke Roberts, Herman J. Lombaert, Hugh J. Jewett, William Thaw, and Henry H. Houston at one time or another serving on the company's board of directors, and with the Pan Handle operating the line as an extension of its route to Indianapolis.

In December 1872, construction crews completed the Cairo & Vincennes, enabling PRR traffic to flow between Indianapolis and Cairo. From there, it could follow the McComb roads south to New Orleans. Or, once across the Mississippi River, it might travel west on the Cairo, Arkansas & Texas Railroad (the former Cairo & Fulton Railroad) to Poplar Bluff, Missouri, and then north on the St. Louis, Iron Mountain & Southern Railway to St. Louis, or else south to Texarkana.[48] There, it would connect with the still-incomplete Texas & Pacific, a railroad in which both Thomson and Scott had invested.

The Panic of 1873 soon destroyed the ambitious plans of Thomson and other PRR executives. McComb was also badly overextended, and by 1877 the Illinois Central had taken control over his companies. By the spring of 1874, the Cairo & Vincennes was bankrupt, with Burnside and PRR officials accusing each other of acting in bad faith. Drexel, Morgan & Company had arranged much of the financing for the line, and J. P. Morgan soon displaced Ambrose Burnside and supervised the company's affairs. After undergoing several reorganizations and mergers, ultimately costing the Morgan interests more than $2 million, the Cairo & Vincennes became a part of the New York Central. The PRR retained control over the Indianapolis & Vincennes, wrote off most of its investment in the company, and in 1905 incorporated it into its Vandalia Railroad subsidiary.[49]

Western Routes to Lake Erie

After Thomson established the Fort Wayne as the PRR's principal route to Chicago, he and his successors used that relationship to gain control over additional lines to the Lake Erie ports. The routes included a connection between Pittsburgh and Erie, as well as links to Ashtabula and Toledo. In conjunction with the established connection to Cleveland, the PRR was well positioned to tap into the trade of the Great Lakes. The three new routes provided access to the rich agricultural lands of northern Ohio, while enhancing the PRR's ability to compete against the high-volume, low-rate water carriers that plied the Great Lakes.

The New Castle & Beaver Valley Railroad, although barely fifteen miles long, provided the PRR with access to Ashtabula and to Erie, Pennsylvania, as well as with an alternate route to Cleveland. On February 6, 1862, the Pennsylvania General Assembly incorporated the company, with the rights to construct a railroad from Homewood (later, Homewood Junction), along the Fort Wayne's main line, some thirty-five miles northwest of Pittsburgh, to New Castle, Pennsylvania. By April of the following year, the PRR and the Fort Wayne had pledged their support for the venture, and they jointly acquired $100,000 of New Castle & Beaver Valley bonds.[50]

At New Castle, two routes diverged, one to Erie, and the other to Ashtabula. The link to Erie had a long and checkered history. In 1846, a week after they failed to block the incorporation of the Pennsylvania Railroad, representatives from southwestern Pennsylvania guided through the General Assembly a bill to charter the Pittsburgh & Erie Railroad. Their aim was to provide added incentive for the B&O to build to Pittsburgh, and from there north to Erie, in the hope that PRR supporters would be unable to raise the funds necessary to begin construction. With the success of the PRR, however, the B&O did not build into southwestern Pennsylvania, and the Pittsburgh & Erie charter remained moribund. In 1853, the residents of Crawford County subscribed to $200,000 worth of the Pittsburgh & Erie's securities, but to no avail.[51]

The Erie "gauge war" that took place in December 1853 and January 1854 helped to resurrect the Pittsburgh & Erie. By the autumn of 1852, the promoters of the Erie & North East Rail Road and the Cleveland, Painesville & Ashtabula had employed subterfuge in their efforts to build across Pennsylvania by acquiring the rights originally assigned to the Franklin Canal Company to build a branch line from Erie east to the

New York state line. They completed their route, which later became a part of the Lake Shore & Michigan Southern (New York Central), but in the process antagonized local interests in Erie. Their representatives in the legislature were able to exact a measure of retribution against the company, and in October 1855 they revoked the charter of the Erie & North East. Some six months later, legislators restored the charter rights, but there were strings attached. The April 1856 recharter bill required the company to divert $400,000 to the Pittsburgh & Erie, either by purchasing that company's stock or by performing the equivalent amount of engineering and construction work. As a result, the Erie & North East located the portion of the Pittsburgh & Erie between Girard Junction and Jamestown.[52]

In April 1858, relying on the tribute that the legislature had extracted from the Erie & North East, investors in Erie chartered the Erie & Pittsburgh Railroad, replacing the earlier Pittsburgh & Erie Railroad. The chief figure in the venture was William Lawrence Scott (no relation to Tom Scott). By 1850, Scott had established himself as a coal and iron merchant, whose ownership of coal lands was second only to those of the PRR and the Reading. He operated both anthracite and bituminous mines, with many of the latter located along the Erie & Pittsburgh right of way. He was a staunch Democrat who served as the mayor of Erie and in the United States House of Representatives.[53]

The new company was organized in September, 1858, but soon ran into difficulties. A month later, attorneys representing Crawford County prevailed in the court battle to withdraw their subscription to the older Pittsburgh & Erie, throwing the charter rights of the new company into doubt as well. Those difficulties were quickly resolved, and by August 1864, crews had completed work on the line. From New Castle and a junction with Fort Wayne–controlled New Castle & Beaver Valley Railroad, the tracks ran almost due north to Girard Junction and a connection with the Cleveland, Painesville & Ashtabula Railroad (later, the Lake Shore & Michigan Southern). Trackage rights over that New York Central–affiliated line provided PRR trains with access to Erie and to a short, PRR-owned branch to the city's docks. On March 1, 1870, under Scott's supervision, the Pennsylvania Railroad leased

the Erie & Pittsburgh for 999 years, officially bringing the company into the PRR system.[54]

During the years following the Panic of 1873, PRR executives built additional connections to Lake Erie ports. In doing so, they laid tracks across the main lines of the Erie and the New York Central, invading the territory of rival trunk lines. It was not much of an invasion, however, as the PRR could hardly compete against its two more advantageously located competitors, hauling freight between the Great Lakes ports and the east coast.

After Cleveland and Erie, Ashtabula was the third Lake Erie port to be connected with the PRR system. During the 1850s, the organizers of the Ashtabula & New Lisbon Rail Road had proposed to build from Ashtabula south to (New) Lisbon, Ohio, but suspended operations after completing some thirty miles of grading. By 1870, the right to construct the line had passed to the Ashtabula, Youngstown & Pittsburgh Railroad. In May 1871 PRR officials established the Granite Improvement Company to construct the railroad between Ashtabula and Youngstown. In March of the following year, they leased the Ashtabula, Youngstown & Pittsburgh. At Youngstown, the new line would connect with the Lawrence Railroad, a Fort Wayne subsidiary, for the remaining distance to New Castle and thence to Pittsburgh. Representatives from both the Erie-allied Atlantic & Great Western and the NYC-affiliated Lake Shore & Michigan Southern did their best to block construction of the line. However, the railroad was complete and in operation by May 1873. The first inbound shipments of ore, and the first outbound shipments of coke, began the following month. By 1888, Ashtabula was the largest iron-ore port on the Great Lakes, with the PRR handling a significant share of that traffic.[55]

The line to Toledo was the last to be completed. The construction and subsequent operation of the route between Toledo and Mansfield, on the Fort Wayne, occupied the energies of eighteen subsidiary companies, the oldest of which dated to 1867. Initially, Cass and his PRR allies were anxious to connect the Fort Wayne's main line at Mansfield, Ohio, with an alignment that angled northwesterly through Tiffin, Ohio, and Battle Creek, Michigan to Allegan, near the shore of Lake Michigan. In the spring of 1871, they oversaw the formation of the Mansfield, Coldwater & Lake Michigan Railroad, and construction soon began at both ends of the route.[56] Disputes with contractors, a sobering assessment of the region's traffic potential, and the depression that began in 1873 ensured that the project would never be completed. Instead, PRR interests elected to use the route only as far west as Tiffin. From there, the Toledo, Tiffin & Eastern Railroad ran north to Toledo, on Lake Erie. The last leg into Toledo was via the municipally owned Toledo & Woodville Railroad, leased to the two PRR-affiliated carriers in March 1873. Service between Mansfield and Toledo began in April 1873. The depression forced both companies into bankruptcy and provided managers associated with the PRR with the opportunity to solidify their control over the route.[57]

All of the links to Lake Erie provided the PRR with substantial additions to its traffic base, but only in the fullness of time. Initially, the grain trade constituted the most important revenue generator for the PRR in that region. However, the opening of such rich iron ore deposits as Michigan's Marquette Range (after 1847) and Menominee Range (after 1866) ensured that the new lines would play an increasingly important role in transporting iron ore from Great Lakes steamers to the mills around Youngstown and Pittsburgh. In 1853, the Cleveland Iron Mining Company moved a scant 152 tons of iron ore from Marquette to Erie. Two years later, the completion of the St. Marys Falls Canal enabled ore boats to bypass the rapids at Sault Ste. Marie, Michigan, avoiding an expensive portage. On the docks, the first steam-powered unloading hoists appeared in 1867, quickly displacing horse-drawn winches. Over the following decade, steamships replaced less capacious sail-powered schooners, with the first iron ship entering service in 1882, followed by the first of the "whaleback" ore boats in 1889. By the end of the nineteenth century, iron ore shipments accounted for a third of the PRR's total freight tonnage on its lines to the west of Pittsburgh and Erie. Massive freighters, heavily laden with the rich iron ores of northern Minnesota, lumbered along Lake Superior, past Sault Ste. Marie, into Lake Huron, and then down the Detroit River into Lake Erie. They frequently ended their journey by disgorging their cargoes into Pennsylvania Railroad ore cars, generating a steady source of revenue as they carried their raw materials onward to the steel mills of Cleveland, Youngstown, and the Monongahela Valley.[58]

Holding Companies and the End of the Era of Personal Capitalism on the Pennsylvania Railroad

Holding companies represented one of the many ways in which public policy helped to define the contours of the Pennsylvania Railroad. Like many early American railroads, the PRR began its corporate life in April 1846, thanks to a specific corporate charter granted by the Pennsylvania legislature. Over the next dozen years, the General Assembly handed down thirteen supplements to the PRR charter, along with thirty-two Acts of Assembly that in some manner affected the PRR's operations.[59] Legislators simplified the process in February 1849 when they passed the commonwealth's first railway incorporation law, modified in 1854. That legislation merely codified and standardized the legal framework for the organization of railway companies, and still required "a special act of the general assembly . . . authorizing the incorporation of a company for the construction of a railroad within this commonwealth."[60] The creation of affiliated corporations likewise required a special legislative act. Even for a company that was as politically well connected as the PRR, the process of obtaining charters was fraught with pitfalls, ranging from hostile amendments to gubernatorial vetoes.[61]

States like Pennsylvania lacked the authority to grant charters for rail lines outside their borders, yet by the 1850s railroads routinely crossed state lines. Moreover, Pennsylvania legislators were generally reluctant to grant carriers the authority to engage in other forms of economic activity, such as mining—in large measure the legacy of fears that a few large firms would monopolize the production, distribution, and sale of anthracite.[62] As such, PRR executives found it difficult to develop a regional railroad system or to internalize long-distance freight forwarding, Great Lakes shipping, the development of coal and timber lands, and other activities that were not directly a part of the company's core transportation capabilities.

To overcome charter and other legal restrictions—and, as critics were quick to point out, to camouflage their involvement in various financial endeavors—PRR executives pioneered the development of a new form of corporate organization, the holding company. As the name suggested, holding companies enabled

PRR officials to manage firms that held a variety of assets and charter rights. Holding companies, many of which were short lived, others of which persisted for decades, were a response to the rapid growth of the railroads, as well as the relative immaturity of the corporate form of organization and the absence of state general-incorporation laws. By employing holding companies, Thomson and his associates could acquire real estate, oversee construction projects, invest in other railroads and shipping concerns, and implement mechanisms for controlling rates. Holding companies greatly facilitated the acquisition of independent railroads, inasmuch as organizers could purchase an established line without petitioning a state legislature for re-incorporation and a new corporate charter.

In most instances, holding companies fulfilled their assigned function with little fanfare. In a few cases, however—most notably the South Improvement Company and the Southern Railway Security Company—the PRR's investment vehicles generated considerable controversy. In the public mind, holding companies represented nothing less than a vast hidden behemoth, with the Pennsylvania Railroad ensnaring all types of business activity, and not merely the railways, in its tentacles. Newspaper editors expressed dismay at the mysterious nature of holding companies, something that they often equated with a conspiracy against the public interest. Politicians fulminated at what they labeled a legal subterfuge that obfuscated the true ownership of those firms. Many of those same legislators, it should be noted, had also favored the kinds of restrictions on the PRR's corporate charter that had made the holding companies a virtual necessity. Thomson, Scott, and their PRR associates may have appreciated the irony, but if so, they found little solace therein. Instead, they seemed genuinely shocked at the depth of public hostility to the few holding companies that might threaten the public interest. For all of their apparent and asserted faults, however, holding companies enabled PRR executives to manage an increasingly complex railroad empire.

During the early nineteenth century, investors in the anthracite fields of northeastern Pennsylvania were pioneers in the development of holding companies, often styled as "improvement companies." Mining obviously depended on the ownership of land and the rights to the coal that lay beneath it. Under Pennsylvania law, and in reaction to the British practice of primogeniture, it was both possible and commonplace for individuals to inherit fractional shares of what had once been large estates. Improvement companies enabled landowners to incorporate, and to assign shares to each investor, depending on the acreage that the investor controlled.

The prospect of land control was even more daunting for New York or other "foreign" capitalists. The charter of the Forest Improvement Company, dating to 1839, was a pioneering example of the entrepreneurial ability to invest across state lines. New York investors had purchased some ten thousand acres of coal lands, yet their 1823 New York charter did not give them the authority to carry out mining operations in another state. Even worse, the Pennsylvania legislature did not permit the company to own any lands within the commonwealth. The new holding company gave the New Yorkers the authority to oversee all of the activities associated with anthracite mining while disguising their out-of-state affiliations.

Over the next fifteen years, investors from inside and outside Pennsylvania established similar organizations in the mining business. Improvement companies could issue securities to fund the construction of such investments as mineshafts, tipples, breakers, and company towns. They in turn leased the actual mining operations to ostensibly independent contractors, separating land ownership from mining. In the years that followed, developers extended the improvement company model to encompass the construction and operation of industrial districts, freight terminals, and docks. Improvement company charters became more commonplace after 1854, when the Pennsylvania legislature standardized the incorporation process. Within a few years, however, the Civil War had eliminated most lingering resentment to out-of-state investors, and improvement companies became largely unnecessary.[63]

Railroads were somewhat slower to adopt the improvement-company model. Under some special circumstances, state legislatures permitted carriers to acquire other firms that were directly related to their core mission of transportation. In 1833, for example, the Maryland legislature had permitted the Baltimore & Ohio to buy two-thirds of the stock of the

Washington Branch Road. In March 1853, the Pennsylvania legislature amended the PRR's charter, permitting the PRR to invest as much as 15 percent of its stock in the securities of western railroads that promised to funnel traffic into the Keystone State. Eight years later, as Thomson sought control over the Northern Central and the Philadelphia & Erie, the General Assembly permitted the PRR to purchase the securities of other railroads that operated in Pennsylvania. In 1864, the Chicago & North Western Railway gained similar powers in Illinois. Those acquisitions were atypical, however, and control was vested directly in the owning railroad rather than through the intermediary of a holding company. Furthermore, the PRR was still barred from making direct investments in companies not engaged in transportation. As a result, PRR officials chartered ancillary companies—most notably the Empire Line and the Star Union Line—to accommodate various traffic functions. Those companies were closely tied to the PRR, but they were not a part of its corporate structure.[64]

After the Civil War, the PRR's rapid expansion into the Midwest encouraged executives to apply the holding company structure to some of the railroad's activities. Their first effort, in April 1868, involved the construction of the Grand Rapids & Indiana Railroad. As was typical of midwestern lines, local boosters with grandiose visions projected a major regional railroad, in this instance one that would link the Straits of Mackinac to the Ohio River. They incorporated the company in 1854 and, two years later, laid claim to roughly a third of the three million acres of public lands that the federal government had allocated to Michigan—making the railroad the only segment of the PRR to have ever received land grants. The Panic of 1857 brought construction to a halt, and the project languished for more than a decade. In February 1867, the Michigan legislature demanded that the GR&I's promoters begin work immediately, or else forfeit the land grants. The company possessed enough money to begin construction, but not to complete the line, and its owners soon requested aid from the Pittsburgh, Fort Wayne & Chicago.[65]

Fort Wayne officials coveted the land grants associated with the Grand Rapids & Indiana, and likewise hoped that the new line would generate considerable lumber traffic. In April 1868, President Cass and his associate William Thaw incorporated the Continental Improvement Company. In the process, they brought Tom Scott and other PRR officials into the arrangement. Under an agreement dated May 1, 1869, Continental agreed to complete the GR&I and make good the GR&I's $600,000 debt. In return, Continental received $8 million in GR&I bonds and the entirety of the land grant. Continental's risk was minimal, as Cass arranged for the Fort Wayne to guarantee half of the $8 million GR&I bond issue. In exchange for the bond guarantee, the Fort Wayne received trusteeship of a majority of the GR&I's stock—a mechanism of control over the company that Cass soon assigned to the PRR.[66]

Continental was little different from the myriad firms that enabled investors to earn significant profits from the construction of a new railroad—the most infamous being Crédit Mobilier, the firm that built the Union Pacific, but also was involved in the scandalous trading of stock for political favors in 1872. While Continental's owners profited from their construction contract, the same could not be said for the Grand Rapids & Indiana, a company that was already in receivership. Construction went forward nonetheless, and work crews reached Little Traverse Bay (Petoskey) in November 1873. Once the area's timber reserves had been exhausted, however, the line generated little traffic, save for tourists headed north to summer resorts.[67]

Continental was little more than a variant on the traditional construction subsidiary, but it awakened PRR executives to the potential of the holding-company structure. From 1868 to 1872, PRR officials, and Scott in particular, shepherded through the General Assembly a series of bills to charter various holding companies. To this day, it is not precisely clear how many holding companies they established. The muckraking journalist Ida Tarbell placed the number at thirteen, but she found it difficult to obtain an exact count because Scott altered the names of some of the companies, and because several incorporations (including that of the South Improvement Company) were only published in the commonwealth's legislative proceedings after a delay of more than a year. In their 1932 history of the holding company, economists James C. Bonbright and Gardiner C. Means set the number much higher, at forty-one between 1868 and 1872, with twenty-three of those firms connected with the PRR.[68]

Regardless of their precise number, however, all of the Scott holding companies shared common characteristics. The charters listed "dummy" incorporators who were only tangentially associated with top PRR management. They included William Thaw, recently retired general freight agent Henry H. Houston, and Scott's private secretaries, Richard D. Barclay and Samuel S. Moon. Scott's name rarely appeared, for its inclusion would constitute an obvious signal of the PRR's involvement. While chartered in Pennsylvania, the companies' operations transcended state borders. Even though their primary function usually involved the construction, acquisition, or ongoing management of one or more railways, the names of the holding companies did not include the word "railroad." Had that specific language been included, the 1849 Pennsylvania General Railroad Law would have mandated legislative approval for the issuance of mortgage bonds and the selection of routes. Holding-company titles were generally vague and imprecise, and could readily be changed at the behest of stockholders—that is, of Scott and his fellow executives. As an added benefit, the names of the charters rarely revealed their true function, so they were far less likely to create opposition in the Pennsylvania legislature or draw the attention of the press. In addition, the vague and generic titles helped camouflage the plans of PRR executives from their rivals on competing railroads. The imprecision also enabled Scott and his associates to create holding companies and then preserve their charters in a kind of suspended animation, ready to be resurrected quickly whenever and however required. Several of the charters were never used; they slumbered away their corporate life, existing solely on paper.

In 1869 and into the spring of 1870, not long after the PRR leased the Columbus, Chicago & Indiana Central and the Fort Wayne, Scott flooded the General Assembly with holding company charters. Legislators approved five charters in 1869, with the most notable being the Union Improvement Company, the entity responsible for building the Denver & Rio Grande Railroad under the stewardship of Thomson's former personal assistant, William Jackson Palmer. In April 1870 came the Occidental Improvement Company, the Central Improvement Company, the Morgan Improvement Company, and several others. Central Improvement was responsible for building the

Shenandoah Valley Railroad, under the supervision of Herman Haupt, while Morgan Improvement financed the construction of an Illinois railroad, the Gilman, Clinton & Springfield (later part of the Illinois Central). In March 1871, Scott oversaw the incorporation of the Empire Contract Company and the American Improvement Company. By June 1871, the legislature had also granted charters for the Duquesne Contract Company and the Madison Improvement Company. Some holding companies, such as the Manor Real Estate & Trust Company (an 1886 renaming of the Morgan Improvement Company), served as shadow organizations that enabled PRR officials to quietly purchase real estate without inducing speculation and increased prices. Others, such as the American Improvement Company (subsequently renamed the American Contract & Trust Company), oversaw a variety of non-rail investments, including oceangoing shipping. Its responsibilities became even broader during the 1920s, when a new generation of PRR executives became involved in truck and bus operations.[69]

Nor was the Pennsylvania Railroad the only firm to employ the holding company model. Philadelphia & Reading president Franklin B. Gowen was anxious to stabilize anthracite prices and to prevent excess railway construction in northeastern Pennsylvania. By 1871, he was convinced that the Reading should match some of its competitors by integrating mining and transportation activities. The Reading was at a disadvantage, however, in that its charter prevented the company from owning coalfields or engaging in mining. In order to circumvent that restriction, Gowen created the Laurel Run Improvement Company, later renamed the Philadelphia & Reading Coal & Iron Company. PRR officials objected strongly to Gowen's tactics, but they could hardly complain, nor could they ask the courts to intervene. After all, they had pioneered the development of the holding company in the first place, and had given Gowen a model to emulate.[70]

The Pennsylvania Company

Of all of the holding companies, the Pennsylvania Company was by far the most significant. As Thomson and his fellow PRR executives shifted from influence to outright control over the lines that lay west of

Pittsburgh and Erie, they encountered the challenges of oversight. The process of supervision would not be easy. It involved directing the actions of more than fifty thousand employees, who operated trains over more than four thousand miles of track.[71] Because the PRR had acquired most of the lines west of Pittsburgh and Erie through stock purchases and interest guarantees, rather than new construction or outright purchase, the company confronted a complex tangle of leases, partial ownership, traffic guarantees, and rental payments on dozens of subsidiaries that ranged from the vitally important Pittsburgh, Fort Wayne & Chicago to the marginally significant Massillon & Cleveland Railroad. Some companies, such as George Cass's Fort Wayne, were well maintained and well managed and held considerable traffic potential. Others, most notably Benjamin Smith's Columbus, Chicago & Indiana Central, were marginal carriers at best, burdened with years of dubious financing and deferred maintenance.

The development of what came to be known as the Pennsylvania Company was contemporaneous with efforts by PRR executives to gain control over the Fort Wayne and the Columbus, Chicago & Indiana Central. Early in the 1870 legislative session, PRR interests sought a charter for the National Improvement Company, to manage the PRR's western subsidiaries. National Improvement was to have far broader powers than the PRR's other holding companies, and the bill aroused considerable opposition. Scott bided his time and submitted a similar bill, under a different name. The ruse was successful, and on April 7, 1870, the General Assembly chartered the Pennsylvania Company.

The Pennsylvania Company possessed the authority "to build, construct, maintain or manage any work or works, public or private, which may tend or be designed to improve, increase, facilitate, or develop trade, travel, or transportation and conveyance of freight, live stock, passengers, and any other traffic, by land or water, from or to any part of the United States or the territories thereof." The provision that the Pennsylvania Company "shall also have the power to make purchases and sales of or investments in the bonds and securities of other companies" permitted it to acquire the assets of virtually any company connected to rail-

road construction or operation. The Pennsylvania Company lacked confiscatory powers, but the charter enabled it "to aid, co-operate and unite with any other company, person or firm" and thus exploit the power of eminent domain exercised by the PRR and its subsidiaries. The 1870 charter also allowed the Pennsylvania Company "to fix or regulate the tolls or charges to be charged or demanded for any freight, property or passengers," subject to any regulations established by state governments.[72]

The formal organization of the Pennsylvania Company took place in Philadelphia on June 1, 1870. The organization's principal incorporators included William Thaw, an investment banker, a major shareholder in the PRR, and one of the principals of the Union Railroad & Transportation Company, better known as the Star Union Line. Thaw became the first president of the Pennsylvania Company. George B. Edwards, Thaw's son-in-law, was the manager for the Union Line's operations east of Pittsburgh and Erie. Henry H. Houston, the PRR's former general freight agent, had left the direct employment of the PRR in 1867 to help establish the Union Line. George B. Bonnell was Houston's longtime business partner. William H. Barnes began work with the PRR Engineer Department in March 1848, became the assistant superintendent of the Pittsburgh, Fort Wayne & Chicago a decade later, and was active as a manager for both the Union Line and the Empire Line; he became the Pennsylvania Company's treasurer. By early 1871, additional subscribers included Scott (who soon replaced Thaw as president of the Pennsylvania Company) and future PRR presidents George B. Roberts and Alexander J. Cassatt.[73]

Pennsylvania Company officials soon made arrangements to consolidate the PRR's western subsidiaries. The Pennsylvania Company issued $8 million in preferred stock, an offering that went a long way toward establishing that class of securities as a legitimate investment.[74] Shortly afterward, the Pennsylvania Company issued another $4 million in common stock. On April 1, 1871, the PRR's board of directors traded most of the Pennsylvania Railroad's investments in its western subsidiaries to the Pennsylvania Company in exchange for the entire allotment of preferred shares.[75]

The Pennsylvania Company was not the western equivalent of its parent firm, the Pennsylvania Railroad, nor did Pennsylvania Company officials exercise a level of administrative oversight that matched that of their PRR counterparts. Instead, the Pennsylvania Company was an administrative mechanism for consolidating the PRR's stock and bond ownership, leases, and traffic agreements with its lines in Ohio, Indiana, and Illinois. It directly managed several important carriers—most notably the Fort Wayne—through interlocking directorates. Other Lines West subsidiaries were to a large extent governed independently from the Pennsylvania Company, with the Columbus, Chicago & Indiana Central and the Grand Rapids & Indiana being the most important examples.

For all of its organizational complexity, the creation of the Pennsylvania Company essentially divided the PRR system into three components. The Pennsylvania Railroad formed the core of what was generally known as the Lines East of Pittsburgh and Erie. It was by far the most important component of the PRR empire, as its routes generated the greatest proportion of traffic and the highest percentage of revenues.[76] The Lines West of Pittsburgh and Erie constituted the remainder of the system. As its name suggested, Lines West included all mileage west of Pittsburgh and Erie that was operationally or organizationally connected to the PRR system. While Lines West included numerous carriers, most were grouped into two units. One encompassed the Pittsburgh, Fort Wayne & Chicago and its affiliates and the other the Pan Handle and the Columbus, Chicago & Indiana Central.

With a direct route between Pittsburgh and Chicago, the lines historically associated with the Fort Wayne were operationally and financially the most important component of Lines West. These companies, after 1890 grouped into the Northwest System of Lines West, linked Pittsburgh to Crestline, Fort Wayne, and Chicago, with additional routes to Erie, Cleveland, and eventually to Ashtabula and Toledo. In 1871 the Pennsylvania Company assumed responsibility for the PRR's 1869 lease of the Fort Wayne and its two subsidiaries, the New Castle & Beaver Valley Railroad and the Lawrence Railroad, as well as the lease of the Erie & Pittsburgh Railroad and the 1862 operating agreement with the Cleveland & Pittsburgh Rail Road. The Fort Wayne's guarantee of bonds issued by the Grand Rapids & Indiana brought that carrier into the system, although the GR&I operated essentially as a separate company until well into the twentieth century. Given the nature of the lease arrangements, as well as the importance of the Fort Wayne to the PRR system, Pennsylvania Company officials directly managed most of these lines, with tight control over both day-to-day operations and long-term strategy.

Most of the other components of Lines West—what became known as the Southwest System, beginning in 1890—had evolved outside of direct PRR influence, prior to the formation of the Pennsylvania Company. The routes extended from Pittsburgh to Columbus, Cincinnati, Louisville, Indianapolis, and Chicago, with a secure connection to St. Louis. The southwestern lines were under the Pennsylvania Company corporate umbrella, but they operated as independent, although coordinated firms. Managerial oversight rested primarily with the Pittsburgh, Cincinnati & St. Louis Railway (the Pan Handle) and its executives, who simultaneously held corresponding managerial posts on various other Pennsylvania Company subsidiaries. The Pan Handle was not operated directly by the Pennsylvania Company, although the two entities had overlapping directorates. Benjamin Smith and his associates retained considerable authority over the CC&IC and they were responsible for that company's routine operations and management. To the west, the Pennsylvania Company controlled but did not operate the St. Louis, Vandalia & Terre Haute Railroad. The intervening Terre Haute & Indianapolis was still firmly under the leadership of William Riley McKeen, tied to the Pennsylvania Company and the PRR only by virtue of a traffic contract, as well as the shared commitment to build the Vandalia Route.

A number of other, less important lines were tied to either the Pan Handle or the CC&IC, and they were thus included in what later became the Southwest System. The Little Miami Railroad, with access to Cincinnati, was leased and controlled by the Pan Handle, not directly by the Pennsylvania Company. The Jeffersonville, Madison & Indianapolis, and its line to Louisville, was also supposed to conform to that pattern, but that company's investors demanded that the lease be transferred from the Pan Handle to the Pennsylvania

Company. Many of the Pennsylvania Company's other investments in the region bordered on the useless, including the Indianapolis & Vincennes and the half share in the Indianapolis & St. Louis—which carried no PRR traffic whatsoever, serving instead primarily to provide the New York Central with access to St. Louis. The Indianapolis & St. Louis, moreover, was geographically associated with the southwestern lines, but was organizationally under the control of the Fort Wayne.[77]

The formation of the Pennsylvania Company enabled PRR officials to dispense with the PRR's principal western fast freight line. Since 1863, the Union Railroad & Transportation Company (a.k.a. the Star Union Line) had fielded traffic agents and operated a fleet of compromise-gauge boxcars, designed to funnel grain onto the PRR at Pittsburgh. Within a few years, however, the importance of freight forwarders such as the Union Line had begun to wane. In 1866, in response to traffic congestion that had occurred during the Civil War, Congress compelled all common carriers to issue through bills of lading, eliminating the possibility that one of the PRR's western connections might refuse to interchange traffic. By the early 1870s, the modest change of gauge at Pittsburgh had been eliminated, Thomson had secured control over the PRR's principal western outlets, and some dissident stockholders were criticizing the ties between senior PRR managers and the fast freight lines. More important, the Pennsylvania Company now offered a mechanism to coordinate traffic functions across the entire PRR system. In July 1873, Thomson arranged for William Thaw, Henry Houston, and the other major investors in the Union Line to trade their holdings for $3 million worth of previously authorized but unissued Pennsylvania Company common stock. The Pennsylvania Company then operated its acquisition, including its nearly three thousand box cars, as the Union Line Bureau.[78]

Given the breadth and diversity of the carriers on Lines West, Thomson and his successors could not possibly have maintained direct oversight of the affairs of each company. Subsidiaries carried out routine operations as if they were separate from the PRR, a situation that was particularly true on the southwestern lines. The Fort Wayne and the Pan Handle maintained shops at Fort Wayne and Columbus, each of which

dated to 1857. Their personnel designed and built motive power and rolling stock independently of the PRR shop forces at Altoona. Ultimately, officials on the various Lines West subsidiaries, and not their PRR counterparts in Philadelphia, were responsible for the overall financial performance of their companies. So long as executives on the PRR's western affiliates operated their firms with a reasonable degree of efficiency and profitability, the senior PRR executives in Philadelphia largely left them to their own devices.

The primary function of the Pennsylvania Company was to implement long-term corporate strategy and to coordinate system-wide traffic functions. Aside from a few through passenger trains (such as the *New York & Chicago Limited*, inaugurated in 1881), traffic rarely flowed uninterrupted between Lines East and Lines West.[79] Instead, Pennsylvania Railroad officials wanted to ensure that through rates would be both remunerative and competitive. As Thomson had once confided to Virginia railroad developer William Mahone, "The advantage of a single management is seen in the reduction of the general expenses of management but chiefly in the increase of business by the power to give through rates for traffic to meet every changing circumstance."[80] Furthermore, as Thomson emphasized in the PRR's annual report for 1872, his goal was "to secure, by a single management of these works, harmonious action throughout the entire system of railways that we control, and at the same time to obtain the best results from the large amount of rolling stock upon them, by transferring, as occasions may require, portions of that of one line to another, where the demand for its use was more urgent and important to the interests of the Company and the public."[81]

In order to achieve coordination between Lines East and Lines West, key personnel often held comparable posts on the PRR, the Pennsylvania Company, and its principal subsidiaries, especially the Fort Wayne and the Pan Handle. Beginning in 1874, the president of the PRR was also the president of the Pennsylvania Company, ensuring continuity of management.[82] The Pennsylvania Railroad and the Pennsylvania Company maintained separate, although interlocking, boards of directors, with the former meeting in Philadelphia and the latter in Pittsburgh.

The "Philadelphia directors" of the Pennsylvania Company were also members of the PRR board. For the most part, the "Pittsburgh directors" did not hold a comparable rank on the PRR. The Pennsylvania Company board oversaw the issuance of stocks and bonds, major capital investments, and the development of new routes, always in close collaboration with PRR officials.[83]

In many respects, the organizational structure of the Pennsylvania Company resembled that of the PRR a decade earlier, although there was less similarity in the backgrounds of the managers who filled the posts. Senior PRR executives tended to be career railroaders who had spent many years in the commonwealth of Pennsylvania. With the notable exception of Tom Scott, they also tended to be skilled engineers. On Lines West, executives were more likely to be from the Midwest; to have backgrounds in finance, politics, or law rather than engineering; and to have been inherited from the predecessor corporations that were folded into the Pennsylvania Company. As such, their influence over the PRR's western operations reflected the company's tradition of tailoring positions to fit the talents and personalities that were available at the time, rather than attempting to mold individuals to fit a precisely delineated corporate structure.

The first vice president of the Pennsylvania Company was the chief executive officer for Lines West, responsible for coordinating the activities of the various subsidiaries with each other, with Lines East, and with non-PRR carriers. Jacob N. McCullough, the Pennsylvania Company's longtime first vice president, was born in Ohio, but spent his early career in New Orleans as a trader. He later moved to Pittsburgh and then to Wellsville, Ohio, where he was a wholesale grocer and a banker. Middle-aged, and with no previous experience in the railroad business, McCullough in 1858 invested in the Cleveland & Pittsburgh Rail Road. The company was at that time suffering from the effects of the Panic of 1857, and its stock was available at extraordinarily low prices. McCullough bought a substantial number of shares, joined the Cleveland & Pittsburgh board, and became president in 1859. It was a shrewd investment, as McCullough tripled his money and eventually possessed wealth variously estimated at between $6 and $14 million. He soon par-

layed his newfound railroad experience into a position as the general superintendent of the Cleveland & Pittsburgh and the Pittsburgh, Fort Wayne & Chicago—two companies that were governed by a joint executive committee, beginning in April 1863. He worked closely with Cass and PRR officials to deflect Jay Gould's attempt to take over the Cleveland & Pittsburgh, and he was rewarded with a promotion to general manager of the Fort Wayne. Following the creation of the Pennsylvania Company, he became a director of that entity, as well as its general manager. On January 1, 1874, McCullough became the first vice president of the Pennsylvania Company, with control over transportation and traffic functions. He was simultaneously the president of the Cleveland & Pittsburgh, the vice president and general manager of the Fort Wayne, and the third vice president of the Pan Handle, ensuring continuity with those important subsidiaries. McCullough attained considerable expertise in financial matters, and he was particularly adept at securing traffic and setting rates. In addition to managing the Pennsylvania Company and its holdings, McCullough was typically the Lines West representative at various trunk-line rate conferences in Saratoga Springs and similar locations, coordinating his activities with senior PRR executives. He retained his post as the Pennsylvania Company's first vice president until his death in 1891, when he was succeeded by James McCrea, the first of two Lines West executives who eventually became president of the Pennsylvania Railroad.[84]

The first vice president in turn supervised the general manager, who was in charge of the Transportation Department.[85] The downward line of authority consisted of three assistant general managers, each overseeing a division superintendent, for the Cleveland & Pittsburgh Division, the Eastern Division (essentially the Fort Wayne route between Pittsburgh and Crestline, Ohio, with associated branches), and the Western Division (Crestline to Chicago). The line officers in the Transportation Department could call on the services of various staff, including a general counsel, a general freight agent, a general passenger and ticket agent, a purchasing agent, and a chief engineer.

The two other Pennsylvania Company vice presidents were also interlinked with various Lines West subsidiaries. William Thaw was the second vice president of the Pennsylvania Company, in charge of finance. He was also the second vice president of the Pan Handle and the vice president of the Indianapolis & Vincennes, thus connecting the Pennsylvania Company with the southwestern lines. Thaw was a long-time PRR associate who had gained his transportation expertise as a freight forwarder on the Main Line of Public Works. After joining the PRR and helping to build that company's traffic capabilities, Thaw had taken charge of the Union Line. He had considerable knowledge of transportation in Ohio and Indiana and, prior to the Civil War, he had offered his assessment of the PRR's investment opportunities in the region. By 1874, both Thaw and the Union Line were a part of the Pennsylvania Company.

Hugh J. Jewett was the Pennsylvania Company's third vice president, assisting First Vice President McCullough with traffic matters. Jewett also served as the general counsel of the Pennsylvania Company, as well as the first vice president of the Pan Handle and the general manager of the Indianapolis & Vincennes. During the 1850s, Hugh Jewett had worked closely with his brother Thomas to develop a network of rail lines in central and southern Ohio. At various times, Thomas Jewett was president of the Steubenville & Indiana and the Pan Handle, and was also involved in state and national politics. In 1871, just as PRR officials were overseeing the formation of the Pennsylvania Company, Jewett withdrew from active involvement in railroading, possibly after suffering a debilitating stroke.[86] Hugh Jewett, who had served as president of the Central Ohio Railroad and who had also been one of the organizers of the Pan Handle, took on many of the responsibilities that might otherwise have gone to his brother. He remained associated with the Pennsylvania Company for only a few years, before attaining great renown as the president of the Erie.

Unlike the earlier vice presidents, Thomas D. Messler was a career railroader, but one whose specialty was accounting rather than engineering. In 1876, he was promoted to third vice president of the Pennsylvania Company, although (unlike Jewett) his primary responsibilities had to do with corporate accounts, rather than traffic. Messler apprenticed on the Erie before moving west and imposing financial controls on the

Fort Wayne. With the formation of the Pennsylvania Company, Messler took charge of accounting matters on the various Lines West subsidiaries. In addition to his vice-presidential duties, he was the comptroller of the Pennsylvania Company as well as (at various times) the comptroller of the Fort Wayne, the Pan Handle, and the Indianapolis & Vincennes.[87]

While McCullough, Thaw, Jewett, Messler, and others were represented on the various Lines West affiliates, they exerted relatively little control over the Columbus, Chicago & Indiana Central, the largest component of the southwestern lines. Benjamin Smith had orchestrated the consolidation of the various routes linking Columbus, Indianapolis, Logansport, and Chicago, and he remained president of the company. His fellow Ohioan, William Dennison, was also on the CC&IC board, along with a substantial contingent of New York investors. During the 1870s, PRR and Pennsylvania Company officials attempted to rein in an increasingly unstable Ben Smith, but with scant success. It all ended very badly for both the entrepreneur and his railroad, with the CC&IC entering bankruptcy in 1883 and Smith committed to an insane asylum two years later.[88]

Benjamin Smith was the most extreme example of the problems associated with efforts by Thomson, Scott, and other PRR executives to employ the Pennsylvania Company as an oversight mechanism for the Lines West of Pittsburgh and Erie. His instability illustrated the dangers associated with continued reliance on the midwestern entrepreneurs who had brought into being some of the constituent elements of the PRR's western routes. Yet, Smith and his counterparts constituted something of a necessary evil. At the time that they created the Pennsylvania Company, PRR executives had pursued the best available option for integrating the disparate elements of a vast and diverse railroad empire. During the years immediately following the Civil War, the Pennsylvania Railroad lacked the financial resources necessary to own its western subsidiaries outright. For the moment, it was better to allow Ohio and Indiana entrepreneurs, with their knowledge of local markets and political systems, to manage routine operations, subject to the Pennsylvania Company's oversight. While some of those executives were unreliable—Benjamin Smith being the most obvious example—the others were generally competent and capable of delivering adequate results. By leaving them in charge of the PRR's western affiliates, the officers of the Pennsylvania Railroad could concentrate on their core transportation enterprise east of Pittsburgh, while coordinating traffic functions and long-term corporate strategy with the Pennsylvania Company.

Breaking Free from Philadelphia: An East–West Railroad Becomes a North–South Railroad

Even though Thomson had protected the PRR's western gateways by securing routes to Chicago, Cincinnati, and St. Louis, the eastern portion of the system was still exceedingly vulnerable. New York was the nation's financial and commercial center, as well as its dominant port. The Baltimore & Ohio lacked direct access to New York, but both the Erie and the New York Central reached the city well before the PRR. The Erie opened its Jersey City terminal in 1861, but it stopped on the west bank of the Hudson, short of New York City. The activities of Cornelius Vanderbilt caused Thomson far greater concern. By 1864, the former riverboat king had acquired both the New York & Harlem Railroad and the Hudson River Railroad, providing direct access to Manhattan. Five years later, Vanderbilt consolidated his empire, which already offered a formidable challenge to the PRR, into the New York Central & Hudson River Railroad. In addition to its route into Manhattan, the New York Central enjoyed the best access to New England of any of the four trunk lines, thanks to its connection at Albany with carriers that later merged to form the Boston & Albany Railroad. The Pennsylvania Railroad, however, reached only to Philadelphia on its own rails. With shippers demanding through service to New York, and with rival railroads augmenting their access to that city, Thomson was determined to expand the PRR in the Northeast. Thomson's masterstroke, perhaps more important than even his lease of the Fort Wayne, brought the PRR to the doorstep of New York.

Since the 1830s, four companies had dominated transportation in New Jersey. The owners of the Camden & Amboy Rail Road and the Delaware & Raritan

Canal Company, linked together as the "Joint Companies," controlled the Philadelphia & Trenton Railroad through stock ownership and maintained an operating agreement with the New Jersey Rail Road & Transportation Company. Together, the three railroads maintained two parallel lines that linked Camden, New Jersey and Kensington, Pennsylvania with Jersey City and South Amboy. In 1832, the New Jersey legislature had provided the Joint Companies with a virtual transportation monopoly in New Jersey, in exchange for transit duties that filled the public treasury—necessitating freight and passenger rates that were among the highest in the nation. The monopoly had made Joint Companies executives wealthy but not popular, and they were constantly vigilant in their efforts to prevent an aroused public from voiding one of their principal assets. During the Civil War, they had narrowly avoided congressional efforts to charter the National Air-Line Railroad as a mechanism for superseding state charter stipulations. That project never came to fruition, but other threats took more tangible form. In September 1862, for example, the Raritan & Delaware Bay Railroad had joined forces with the Camden & Atlantic Railroad, offering coordinated rail-steamship service between Camden and New York via the piers at Port Monmouth, New Jersey. Thomson had not offered his direct support of those two upstart companies. He nonetheless gave his blessing to the erosion of the Joint Companies transportation monopoly in New Jersey, and the PRR's freight forwarders soon began routing traffic over the new lines. The courts eventually concluded that the Raritan & Delaware Bay lacked the legal authority to carry through traffic, and the line ultimately went bankrupt in March 1867. Three months later, construction crews completed work on the Connecting Railway, linking the PRR to the Philadelphia & Trenton. The Connecting Railway, which was leased to the P&T, ensured that Thomson would be more dependent than ever on the Joint Companies and their affiliates, if he wished reliable access to New York.[89]

During the immediate postwar period, a confluence of events further increased cooperation among the New Jersey carriers. Robert F. Stockton and Edwin A. Stevens had been the two chief creators of the Joint Companies, but Stockton died in 1866 and Stevens in

1868. They had been content to collect the profits associated with the monopoly, but their successors were more concerned with developing an efficient and competitive transportation enterprise. They had to be, for the monopoly provisions expired on January 1, 1869. Two months later, on March 4, 1869, the New Jersey legislature repealed the transit duties in favor of a provisional tax on every railroad operating in the state. As events transpired, the expiration of the monopoly provision had little immediate effect. Until April 1873, when New Jersey adopted a general railroad incorporation law, any company that attempted to build across New Jersey would have to secure a charter from the state legislature. Lawmakers, influenced by Joint Company lobbyists and anxious to protect the state's investment in Camden & Amboy stock, were unlikely to comply. Nevertheless, given Thomson's concerns at the inefficiency and the expense associated with forwarding PRR freight across New Jersey, Joint Companies officials had good reason to suspect that absent the monopoly, the PRR might establish a competing route to New York.

In January 1867, the owners of the Joint Companies attempted to better safeguard their interests through a more formal consolidation. Relations between the Joint Companies and the New Jersey Rail Road had always been somewhat contentious, with chronic disputes regarding the division of traffic and revenues. By March, representatives from both parties had established the Joint Board of Directors of the United Canal & Railroad Companies of New Jersey, more commonly referred to simply as the "United Companies." As with the earlier agreements that had established the Joint Companies, the United Companies consolidation was not a true merger. Rather, the three companies involved (the Camden & Amboy, the Delaware & Raritan Canal, and the New Jersey Rail Road) agreed to pool their earnings and to pay dividends to all stockholders at the same rate. The Philadelphia & Trenton was, as before, under the control of the United Companies, but was organizationally a separate entity.

From Thomson's perspective, the creation of the United Canal & Railroad Companies was not sufficient to guarantee the PRR's access to the greater New York area. The formation of the United Companies actually made the situation worse, as much of the traffic that had formerly gone to South Amboy was now dispatched over the New Jersey Rail Road, before being dumped on the overcrowded piers at Jersey City. United Companies officials purchased a large parcel of land at Harsimus Cove, New Jersey, yet they lacked sufficient resources to develop the property as a major rail-marine terminal. Accordingly, PRR representatives worked closely with their United Railroads counterparts to develop new freight facilities at that location.[90]

The cooperation of the two railroads on the design of the Harsimus Cove facility soon led to negotiations regarding the establishment of a more formal connection between the PRR and the United Companies. Thomson's efforts to gain control over the western end of the PRR system had drained the corporate treasury, so outright purchase of the United Companies was not an option. Thomson initially preferred to lease trackage rights over the New Jersey lines, in conjunction with a performance guarantee for terminal operations at Harsimus Cove.

The directors of the United Companies were in a strong bargaining position, however, and they demanded much more. Thanks to the monopoly provision granted by the New Jersey legislature and to the traffic boom of the Civil War, the Joint Companies had enjoyed substantial profits. The owners of what was now the United Companies expected those profits to continue. After the war, a 10 percent annual return exceeded the performance of all but the most prosperous corporations, yet that was precisely what they demanded of the PRR. Although Thomson technically referred to the payments as "rentals," many PRR directors balked at the 10 percent dividend guarantee (which, after all, exceeded the dividends that *they* were receiving from the PRR). Several directors voted against the lease, but Thomson prevailed. On December 1, 1871, a 999-year lease gave the PRR control of the United Companies, including the Philadelphia & Trenton, encompassing 172 miles of railroad and 66 miles of canals.[91]

Workmen soon swarmed over the route, narrowing the tracks in New Jersey by an inch to conform to the unusual 4' 9" gauge that the PRR had adopted in 1869 after leasing the Columbus, Chicago & Indiana Central and the Pittsburgh, Fort Wayne & Chicago. Iron rails quickly gave way to steel. After the Civil War and the completion of the Connecting Railway, the Philadelphia & Trenton, rather than the Camden & Amboy, became the dominant United Companies route between Philadelphia and New York, a trend that continued following the 1871 PRR lease. In 1876, in anticipation of additional traffic for the Centennial Exhibition, PRR crews began widening the Philadelphia & Trenton to four tracks at critical locations. In 1874, the Keystone Bridge Company replaced the original wooden span across the Delaware River at Trenton with a new iron bridge.[92]

The United Companies lease enhanced the PRR's commitment to Harsimus Cove and, by the summer of 1874, the PRR had poured some $1.3 million into the facility. Those direct investments in land and trackage nonetheless paled in comparison to the funds expended by various companies that were affiliated with the PRR. The Central Stock Yard & Transit Company leased a portion of the site for the construction of a stockyard and slaughterhouse. When completed in early 1874, the PRR rerouted most livestock traffic away from the PRR-Reading's Allentown Route, and onto PRR rails for the entire eastbound journey. The New Jersey Warehouse & Guaranty Company made a similar arrangement with the PRR for the construction of a granary at Harsimus Cove. So too did the Berwind-White Coal Mining Company, which possessed the exclusive right to process coal at the Harsimus Cove docks. Farther inland, the PRR constructed Meadows Yard, located in Kearney, New Jersey, between the Hackensack and Passaic rivers, at a junction with the Delaware, Lackawanna & Western. With the completion of the various yards, docks, and warehouses, the PRR downgraded the South Amboy terminal, ending its direct freight and passenger service to Manhattan and reserving the facilities there primarily for coal traffic.[93]

Thomson had gained access to New York, but at considerable cost. The PRR's directors had good reason to be concerned about the generous terms of the lease, as the guaranteed rental payments cost the PRR more than $3 million per year regardless of the amount of traffic that the line carried. As the postwar prosperity gave way to the depression of the 1870s, the 10 percent dividend guarantee appeared lavish in the extreme. With one exception—the centennial year of 1876—the PRR lost money on the United Companies every year until 1889.[94]

In the long run, however, the lease of the United Companies turned out to be one of the best investments that Thomson ever made. The integration of the New Jersey lines into the Pennsylvania Railroad system nullified the allure of the Reading's Allentown Route and ensured that eastbound traffic would remain on PRR tracks all the way to New York Harbor. Thomson enabled a later generation of PRR executives and engineers to match the New York Central by taking the PRR's rails into the heart of Manhattan. In tandem with the construction of the Connecting Railway and the Junction Railroad, and the establishment of a route from Philadelphia south to Washington, Thomson linked the nation's commercial and political capitals and afforded the PRR a north–south as well as an east–west orientation. As a later PRR president accurately observed, the United Companies were "vital to its [the PRR's] future as an Eastern Trunk Line, and . . . the indirect benefits more than compensated for its losses."[95]

From Baltimore to Washington

South of Philadelphia, the Pennsylvania Railroad possessed reasonably efficient access to Baltimore. The Boston capitalists who owned the Philadelphia, Wilmington & Baltimore Railroad did not discriminate between the PRR and the Baltimore & Ohio, and accommodated the traffic of both. The PRR possessed even more secure access to Baltimore thanks to the Northern Central Railway line south from Harrisburg. Traffic along both routes grew substantially during the Civil War, leading PRR officials to authorize significant capital improvements. The projects included the double-tracking of the Northern Central and the construction of the Junction Railroad, which provided direct access between the PRR's tracks in West Philadelphia and those of the PW&B.[96]

Access to Washington was far more problematic, however, as the Baltimore & Ohio held a monopoly on rail traffic moving into the national capital. In 1831, B&O officials had secured a charter from the Maryland legislature, authorizing the construction of a railroad between Baltimore and Washington. In March 1833, the Maryland legislature agreed to purchase

$500,000 in B&O stock (placed in a separate category from the remainder of the company's securities), as soon as private investors had contributed $1 million. In return, the B&O was to pay 20 percent of the gross passenger receipts on the Washington Branch into the state treasury. While there was nothing to prevent the Maryland legislature from chartering a competing line between Baltimore and Washington, the combination of the B&O's political influence, the presence of the half-million-dollar stock subscription, and the monies generated by the state's one-fifth share of passenger revenues all mitigated against such a course of action.[97]

By 1835, B&O construction crews had completed the Washington Branch, linking Baltimore to the District of Columbia. The route diverged from the B&O mainline at Washington Junction (Relay), Maryland, seven miles southwest of Baltimore, and ran south and west to the capital. A converted boardinghouse at Pennsylvania Avenue and Second Street N.W., near the site of today's Capitol Reflecting Pool, served as a temporary station. In 1851, the B&O replaced the ramshackle facility with a much larger, purpose-built station at New Jersey Avenue and C Street.

Prior to the Civil War, Washington, D.C., was a sleepy town along the Potomac with modest traffic potential. The war transformed the city as soldiers and supplies poured into the region. Military traffic virtually ceased after 1865, but Thomson, Scott, and other PRR executives perceived immense potential in the shattered railways of a defeated Confederacy. In 1871, they chartered the Southern Railway Security Company as part of an ambitious agenda to extend the PRR's influence as far south as New Orleans. Yet, their investments in southern railways would amount to little, so long as they lacked access to Washington, the gateway to the South.

Baltimore & Ohio president John W. Garrett was also interested in the South's railroads, and he was particularly anxious to maintain his monopoly on service to the national capital. Garrett peremptorily—PRR officials would say arrogantly—refused to cooperate with the Pennsylvania Railroad on through freight and passenger service. B&O traffic agents arranged schedules to make it as difficult as possible for Northern Central passengers to connect with B&O trains at Baltimore,

and they refused to sell through tickets or handle baggage between Washington and cities along the PRR and its affiliates. Exasperated Northern Central officials made a point of continuing to ticket passengers through to Washington. Each passenger received an envelope containing a Northern Central ticket to Baltimore, the money necessary to buy a B&O ticket, and a slip of paper containing an explanation of why travelers had to be inconvenienced.[98]

The intolerable nature of disruptions to through passenger and freight service made it essential for Thomson to establish an independent line between Baltimore and Washington. After the war, however, ever-vigilant representatives from the Baltimore & Ohio were determined to preserve their sole access to Washington from the north. Inasmuch as the B&O exerted considerable influence over the Maryland Legislature, Thomson, Scott, and other PRR executives suspected that they would not be able to secure a new charter to construct a line from Baltimore to the edge of the District of Columbia. B&O attorneys were also alert for any efforts by the PRR to acquire a previously chartered company, one that possessed legislative authority to build between Baltimore and Washington.

Oden Bowie, a leading member of one of the most prominent political dynasties in Maryland, provided PRR officials with a mechanism to outwit Garrett and his B&O allies. For many years, the Bowies had consistently inveighed against the B&O's monopolistic powers in Maryland, and had likewise advocated for the construction of improved railroad facilities in the state. One of their projects involved the Baltimore & Potomac Railroad, a line that proposed to link Baltimore with a nearly deserted backwater tobacco port at Popes Creek, Maryland. First chartered in 1853, with numerous extensions, the project languished for more than a decade. In 1860, Oden Bowie became the company's president, but a shortage of capital and the onset of the Civil War hamstrung his efforts to begin construction. After the war ended, Bowie solicited the support of John Garrett, but received no assistance. Rebuffed, Bowie next attempted to shop the Baltimore & Potomac charter to Scott and the PRR.[99]

The key element of the Baltimore & Potomac charter, as Scott quickly realized, was the provision authorizing the company to build branch lines up to twenty miles in length—and such a branch would be just long enough to reach the nation's capital. In August 1866, the PRR guaranteed a portion of the Baltimore & Potomac's bonded debt, and in return that railroad signed a construction contract with a group of associates that included Scott, George Cass, president of the Northern Central James Donald Cameron (the son of Simon Cameron), and president of the Empire Line Joseph D. Potts (who was also the former general manager of the Philadelphia & Erie).[100]

B&O officials, realizing they had been had, frantically attempted to persuade the Maryland legislature to somehow block the Baltimore & Potomac's progress toward Washington. They faced a formidable foe in the man they had earlier jilted, Oden Bowie. He began his political career in 1849, when he was elected to the Maryland House of Delegates. He served briefly in the state Senate, where he became chairman of the Committee on Federal Relations and Executive Nominations, as well as a member of the Committee on Internal Improvements. He was elected governor in 1867, although he did not take office until 1869, owing to a change in the Maryland constitution. Bowie did his best to deflect any bill that had any chance of stifling the railroad that he and his father, William Duckett Bowie, had helped to establish. As governor, he enriched the treasury—and also perhaps took a great deal of malevolent personal satisfaction—by forcing Garrett to pay several hundred thousand dollars, which represented the state's 20 percent share of passenger revenues on the Washington Branch that the B&O had kept for itself. Bowie was not alone in his support for the PRR. Several of the PRR's allies in the battle to acquire the Northern Central Railway—including Benjamin Franklin Newcomer and William Thompson Walters—again threw in their lot with the PRR, hoping to use the Baltimore & Potomac as a means to obtain access to their railroad investments in the South.[101]

In September 1868, construction began in earnest on the Baltimore & Potomac. The company did indeed build to Popes Creek, as its charter demanded, yet the southernmost portion of that route saw little service. At Bowie, Maryland (a town named for Oden Bowie), a "branch" line effectively became the main line to the northern border of the District of Colum-

bia. In order to obtain access to the Capital District, Thomson and Scott relied on the political influence of their wartime ally Simon Cameron. After resigning his post as secretary of war, in disgrace, Cameron had served as minister to Russia. In 1866 the Pennsylvania legislature returned him to the United States Senate. In February 1867, Cameron helped to guide through Congress a bill permitting the Baltimore & Potomac to enter the District of Columbia, so long as it had completed construction within four years. Another act of Congress in March 1869 specified the route that the Baltimore & Potomac would follow through the district. The Baltimore & Potomac accordingly approached Washington from the east, crossed the Anacostia River, and followed Virginia Avenue into the city before turning north along Sixth Street, S.W. In March 1871, Congress and the mayor and Boards of Aldermen and Common Council offered the Baltimore & Potomac a station site. When the location proved inadequate, they obligingly granted the company the right, gratis, to lay tracks across the Mall and to construct a station at Sixth and B Streets, N.W., near the present-day site of the National Gallery of Art. The B&P terminus was centrally located, making it particularly convenient for travelers bound for the Capitol, yet it also represented the most blatant of many intrusions on the city's premier public space. By early July 1872, however, most Washingtonians were delighted that the PRR was able to establish through service between Harrisburg and Washington, over its own rails, and to participate in joint service from Jersey City to the nation's capital.[102]

By the summer of 1872, the city of Baltimore constituted the one remaining impediment to the Pennsylvania Railroad's operations south of Philadelphia. In addition to the B&O, four railroads served the city. All were interconnected to a certain degree, but not in a manner that would permit efficient through freight or passenger service. The Philadelphia, Wilmington & Baltimore was a neutral connection for all the other carriers, while the Northern Central and the Baltimore & Potomac were under the control of the PRR. The remaining company was oriented toward the coalfields in the western part of Maryland, but its operations nonetheless shaped the development of Baltimore's railroad infrastructure. In May 1852, the

Maryland legislature chartered the Baltimore, Carroll & Frederick Rail Road Company to lay rails from a junction with the terminus of the Green Spring branch of the Baltimore & Susquehanna (later the Northern Central) west to Hagerstown, Maryland. A year later, the company changed its name to the Western Maryland Railroad, and by 1872 its tracks had reached Hagerstown. The following year, the Western Maryland completed its own route into Baltimore, and it no longer relied on the Green Spring branch. Although it was never a strong carrier, and lacked access to the Baltimore harbor, the Western Maryland nonetheless competed against the B&O in eastern Maryland.[103]

All PRR traffic that moved between Philadelphia and Washington endured the same slow, horse-drawn trip through Baltimore city streets that more than a decade earlier had placed President-elect Lincoln's life in such peril. Northern Central traffic was at a particular disadvantage as the company lacked a site suitable for the construction of a deepwater port comparable to the B&O's facilities at Locust Point in Baltimore. That situation impeded efforts by Northern Central officials to develop anthracite traffic along the main stem and the North Branch of the Susquehanna River, north and east of Harrisburg. As a result, Northern Central officials cooperated with the Canton Company, an independent real estate development corporation established in 1828. The Canton Company's promoters intended to develop new terminal facilities in the southeastern part of Baltimore, away from the congestion of the Inner Harbor. In 1850, the directors of the Baltimore & Susquehanna, the Northern Central's predecessor, had approved construction of a short extension to Canton. Work soon stopped, owing first to opposition from property owners, and then to the Civil War.[104] In 1866, the owners of the Canton Company oversaw the incorporation of the Union Railroad. They intended to resume construction of the link to the waterfront, at Canton, with the line open to all of the railroads that served Baltimore. Because the B&O already possessed good facilities at Locust Point, President Garrett declined to participate. Baltimore city government officials likewise declined to provide assistance to the company and, as a result, the PRR underwrote a share of the construction.[105]

During the early 1870s, as Baltimore & Potomac construction crews built the line south to Washington, the Union Railroad project took on new urgency for the PRR. In addition to providing access to the Canton docks, the line would also create a north–south route through Baltimore. In May 1871, construction began on the Union Railroad, with the work completed by July 1873 at a cost of $3 million. The tracks of the Union Railroad resembled the letter "T" with a truncated eastern arm. The route ran due north from the Canton waterfront to a point just north of Monument Street. Along the way, the tracks crossed the original main line of the Philadelphia, Wilmington & Baltimore at Canton Crossing. More significantly, a short connection near Monument Street linked the Union Railroad with the PW&B's tracks at Bay View Junction, at the point where they turned southwest toward Baltimore's Inner Harbor. At the apex of the T, the Union Railroad turned sharply west. The tracks passed through the 3,410-foot-long Union Tunnel north of the city center. Immediately after emerging from the west portal of the tunnel, trains crossed onto the PW&B main line at Union Junction before reaching a Union Depot that was shared by the PRR's Northern Central and Baltimore & Potomac subsidiaries, as well as by the PW&B. Just west of the Union Depot, at B&P Junction, the route connected with the Northern Central's link into the city, down the Jones Falls Valley. A short distance farther west, trains transited the B&P Tunnels, collectively 7,669 feet long, in three sections separated by short open cuts. Immediately west of the tunnels lay Fulton Junction and the connection with the Western Maryland route to Hagerstown.[106]

By July 1873, construction crews had completed work on the Union Tunnel and the B&P Tunnels, permitting through service between Philadelphia and Washington. The tunnels conformed to Baltimore's congested geography and soon became an operating bottleneck. From Union Depot, southbound trains negotiated a sharp curve, followed by a long uphill climb out of the city. Their northbound counterparts faced much the same problem, in the form of a 1.2 percent grade out of Baltimore, along the Union Railroad. The use of steam locomotives through the long tunnels presented severe ventilation problems. Despite their limitations, the tunnels nonetheless offered a marked improvement over the earlier practice of following city streets. In conjunction with the completion of the Baltimore & Potomac, they gave the PRR convenient access to Washington and the South. The PRR's annual report for 1871 noted that when the tunnels were complete, "there will be an unbroken railroad from our terminus opposite New York, from Philadelphia, and from Baltimore, to all points of importance in the South Atlantic and Gulf States operated continuously by locomotive power, and with the single object in view, to promote the internal commerce between the North and South."[107] The Civil War was over, and the road to the South was open.

Trunk-Line Competition for the Oil Trade

During the late 1860s, PRR officials struggled to cope with the economic and political ramifications associated with radical transformations in the petroleum business. The shift of refining capacity from Pittsburgh to Cleveland, the growing dominance of John D. Rockefeller in the oil trade, and increased opposition to the organizational mechanisms afforded by holding company charters each limited the ability of Scott and his fellow PRR executives to stabilize rates and acquire a larger share of the oil traffic that flowed to tidewater. Cartels were not legally enforceable, so PRR executives and their counterparts on other railroads could do little to maintain the stability of oil rates through traffic pools. Because Pennsylvania law prohibited the PRR and its competitors from direct ownership of oil wells and refineries, executives could not establish or regulate integrated production and transportation capabilities. As Scott and others concluded, the only way to bypass public policy restrictions was to rely on a holding company.

The postwar oil trade involved a battle between regions as well as railroads. Refining capacity first emerged in the oilfields of northwestern Pennsylvania and in Pittsburgh. Early refining methods were quite primitive and extracted only a small portion of useable product (typically kerosene) from each gallon of crude oil. As a result, there was considerable economic logic in refining oil near the wellhead and then transporting only the saleable commodity to distant markets. Large Pittsburgh refineries enjoyed considerable economies of scale, however, and their greater efficiency more than compensated for the relatively modest cost of moving crude oil south along the Allegheny River. By the early 1860s, large quantities of oil went by barge to Pittsburgh refineries, with refined petroleum sent east via the PRR.

By the late 1860s, however, Pittsburgh was rapidly losing its advantage as a refining center. The completion of the Philadelphia & Erie Railroad in 1864 and the opening of the Western Pennsylvania Railroad the following summer gave the PRR two new routes to the oilfields, each of which bypassed Pittsburgh and its refineries. The Pennsylvania Railroad could then move both crude oil and locally refined kerosene from northwestern Pennsylvania directly to east coast markets. The Atlantic & Great Western/Erie also possessed a route from the oilfields to tidewater, and the resulting competition between the two trunk lines kept rates low.

In order to compensate for low rates on the competitive traffic moving from the oilfields directly to tidewater, PRR officials authorized far higher charges on Pittsburgh traffic. Until 1871, the PRR possessed a virtual monopoly on rail transportation at Pittsburgh, to the dismay of the city's refiners. They were eighty-six miles closer to Philadelphia than were the producers in the oilfields. Yet, their refined petroleum rate was precisely the same as the rate on crude moving from the oil regions to Philadelphia. In addition to erasing the distance advantage of the Pittsburgh refiners, the PRR in effect required them to shoulder the additional cost of moving crude oil from the wells to their refineries, via either the Allegheny Valley Railroad or barges along the Allegheny River. The same situation applied with respect to the New York market. In 1867, for example, one Pittsburgh oilman vented his spleen to the members of a Pennsylvania Senate investigating committee. Under the PRR rate structure, he complained, the cost to ship refined petroleum to New York was the same whether it had originated in Pittsburgh or in the oil region, with the latter distance being 114 miles greater than the former. Despite the refiners' complaints, PRR officials initially had scant reason to change their rate policies. They possessed good routes to Pittsburgh, to the oilfields, and (thanks to the Connecting Railway and the Catawissa Route) to New York as well. Therefore, it mattered little to them whether oil was refined in the oilfields, in Pittsburgh, or in New York.[108]

By the late 1860s, however, Cleveland was challenging Pittsburgh's dominance as a refining hub, and that transformation had serious consequences for the PRR's competitive position in the oil trade. The city at the mouth of the Cuyahoga River seemed an unlikely location for a refinery center. Cleveland was situated approximately as far to the northwest of the oil region as Pittsburgh lay to the south, yet it was more distant from tidewater markets. Prior to 1863, a year after the first refinery began operations, the city lacked direct rail access to the oilfields. Even then, the cost to transport crude by rail from northwestern Pennsylvania to Cleveland greatly exceeded the expense of floating it down the Allegheny River to Pittsburgh. By 1865, Cleveland processed only about eight hundred barrels of oil per day, barely a third as much as Pittsburgh.[109]

Over the next five years, Cleveland became a force to be reckoned with in the oil trade, for reasons that had more to do with railway competition than with geography. Cleveland, in contrast to Pittsburgh, enjoyed several highly competitive transportation options. After 1863, the Atlantic & Great Western offered convenient service between the oil region and Cleveland and, in conjunction with the Erie, on to tidewater. For a short period, the A&GW enjoyed a monopoly on the Cleveland oil trade, with its agents free to charge exorbitant rates. During the second half of the 1860s, the Atlantic & Great Western garnered between 95 and 97 percent of all of the oil traffic destined for Cleveland. In 1863 the company carried more than 530,000 barrels of oil. A year later, the total had increased to 675,000 barrels, with Cleveland generating an average of $1,200 per day in oil revenues.[110]

The New York Central's western allies soon shattered the A&GW monopoly, to the immense benefit of Cleveland's refiners. In March 1864, the Cleveland, Painesville & Ashtabula Railroad leased the incomplete Jamestown & Franklin Railroad. By 1870, construction crews had extended the line to Oil City, giving Cleveland competitive rail access to the oilfields. The Cleveland, Painesville & Ashtabula—after 1869 a part of the Lake Shore & Michigan Southern

Railway—also dispatched traffic to the east coast, in competition with the A&GW/Erie route. Between 1867 and 1870, oil traffic along the Lake Shore increased more than fivefold, from 150,000 to 786,150 barrels. With the loss of their railroad's monopoly over the Cleveland oil trade, A&GW agents lowered the average shipping charge east by nearly 40 percent. The Erie Canal, in conjunction with steamer service on Lake Erie, offered Cleveland refiners a third transportation option. While canal rates on oil traffic were not generally competitive with the railroads, they did provide an upper limit to what either the Erie or the New York Central could charge.[111]

The presence of so much competition had a salubrious effect on the rates paid by Cleveland refiners, and proved equally detrimental for their Pittsburgh counterparts. Cleveland refiners were quick to pressure the New York railroads for lower posted rates, often coupled with rebates (an up-front reduction in the posted rate, offered at the time of shipment) or drawbacks (a periodic refund of a portion of the revenues that the railroad had already collected), and parlayed cheaper transportation costs into dominance over the oil trade. In 1867, for example, a Pittsburgh refiner paid $1.75 to send a barrel of oil to Philadelphia, while his competitors in Cleveland spent but $1.53 to ship a barrel to New York—even though the latter journey was 274 miles longer, representing a 77 percent greater distance. Thanks to favorable rates, between 1865 and 1870 crude oil shipments to Cleveland increased nearly ninefold, from 225,000 barrels to 2,000,750 barrels. By 1869, Cleveland had surpassed Pittsburgh as the nation's leading oil processing center.[112]

Organizational inefficiencies plagued the Cleveland refineries, but provided an opportunity for John D. Rockefeller to dominate the oil trade. Pittsburgh refiners coordinated their activities through brokerage firms, which maintained offices in Philadelphia in order to better distribute products in east coast markets. No such coordination existed in Cleveland, however, enabling Rockefeller considerable scope to consolidate the disorganized markets. He began his career as a partner in a produce firm, Clark & Rockefeller. In 1862, he entered the oil business and helped to finance a refinery operation, and he founded Clark, Andrews & Company the following year. Rockefeller demonstrated an early appreciation for increased efficiency and economies of scale, and by 1865 Clark, Andrews & Company was regarded as one of the best-managed refineries in the city. By the late 1860s, Rockefeller had begun to integrate vertically, establishing an export sales office in New York and assigning to his brother, William, the task of buying oil at the wellhead. In 1867, Rockefeller joined forces with another produce merchant, Henry M. Flagler, as a partner in Rockefeller, Andrews & Flagler. In the years to come, Flagler would assume responsibility for negotiating with the railroads in an effort to obtain rebates and other types of favorable rates. In January 1870, when Rockefeller established the Standard Oil Company of Ohio, he was the dominant refiner in Cleveland. On the first day of January 1872, Rockefeller persuaded the Standard Oil executive committee to buy refineries in Cleveland, and by the end of March he had control of twenty-two of the twenty-six independent refineries operating in the city.[113]

The two New York trunk lines competed for Cleveland's oil traffic, yet neither was a match for Rockefeller. He probably obtained his first rate concessions in 1867, but was not the only Cleveland refiner to do so. In 1868, in tandem with two other refinery companies, Rockefeller, Andrews & Flagler bought a share of a pipeline in the oil region operated by the Allegheny Transportation Company. As part of the deal, Rockefeller gained access to Allegheny Transportation's traffic agreement with the Atlantic & Great Western—a $5.00 per car drawback on oil destined for Cleveland, and a $12.00 consideration on cars sent to tidewater. Numerous other rate concessions followed. In 1870, they culminated in a contract between Standard Oil and the Atlantic & Great Western in which Rockefeller received a rebate of five cents per barrel for all shipments from the oilfields to Cleveland, in return for a promise that he would employ the A&GW as his sole transportation conduit along that route. Following the completion of the Lake Shore & Michigan Southern's link to the oilfields in 1870, representatives from that company soon demonstrated a willingness to grant comparable rate concessions to Standard Oil.[114]

Rockefeller's success, and Cleveland's rapid growth as a refining center, did not bode well for the PRR's involvement in the oil trade. The PRR's only access to

Cleveland was through the Cleveland & Pittsburgh Rail Road, but the roundabout route between the oilfields and Rockefeller's refineries could not compete with the far more direct access provided by the A&GW and the Lake Shore. By the late 1860s, PRR officials were concerned that much of the nation's refining capacity might shift from Pittsburgh north to Cleveland, a city where they could not possibly offer competitive service. Accordingly, PRR managers became quite solicitous of their Pittsburgh customers, lowering rates so that the refiners might remain in business. During the spring of 1868, the members of the Committee of the Coal Oil Refiners of Pittsburgh approached Vice President Scott, hopeful that they might secure rebates similar to those that Rockefeller had recently received from the New York trunk lines. As an inducement, the refiners offered to nearly double oil traffic on the PRR—from 550,000 to one million barrels per year. In an effort to gain that extra business, Scott recommended that oil rates from northwestern Pennsylvania to Philadelphia, by way of Pittsburgh and the PRR main line, should be forty cents per barrel below New York rates. The board of directors agreed, even though such a policy would require the PRR to "concede" between five and thirty-six cents per barrel relative to posted rates. As the directors acknowledged, it was nonetheless imperative that "rates from Oil City to New York shall be as low by way of Pittsburgh as by Cleveland or other rail route."[115] To do otherwise would be to put all of the Pittsburgh refineries at risk, while seriously imperiling the PRR's share of the oil trade.

In addition to their efforts to protect Pittsburgh refiners (and thus traffic on the PRR main line), PRR officials were increasingly concerned that the growth of Cleveland's refining capacity was threatening their investment in the Philadelphia & Erie. As such, they offered substantial rate reductions to the oilfield independents, just as they had to refiners in Pittsburgh. In 1869, in the midst of a particularly vicious trunk-line rate war, PRR officials slashed the Philadelphia & Erie's rates between the oilfields and the east coast, causing the region's refiners to crow that "Cleveland was to be wiped out as a refining center as with a sponge."[116]

The residents of northwestern Pennsylvania soon discovered that it was their region that was to be wiped out as a refining center. The final blow came not from Pittsburgh, or even from Cleveland, but from New York. For the first decade of oil production, inefficient refining techniques had shielded northwestern Pennsylvania refiners from east coast competitors. With high wastage rates, it had made little sense to transport crude oil to New York for processing. During the late 1860s, however, rapid improvements in refining techniques greatly reduced waste. With a far larger percentage of useable crude in each barrel, it was now economically feasible to transport oil to distant refining centers that were ideally positioned to serve east coast and overseas markets. With three of the four trunk lines willing to cut rates to tidewater, crude oil shipments to New York area refineries increased substantially—to the obvious detriment of Cleveland, Pittsburgh, and the oil region itself.

What frightened those oilfield refiners even more was that New York was the gateway to Europe. Traditionally, most of the petroleum that traveled across the Atlantic consisted of kerosene and other refined products, rather than crude, but public policy accelerated the development of a European refining capability. In the United States, Congress imposed a ten-cent-per-gallon tax on kerosene as an 1862 wartime revenue measure, yet declined to tax crude oil. As a result, it became more profitable to ship untaxed oil to Europe and refine it there. In 1871, after a disastrous defeat in the Franco-Prussian War, France attempted to strengthen and industrialize its economy. The French National Assembly encouraged the development of a domestic refining capacity by placing prohibitively steep import duties on refined petroleum, but not crude oil. Even absent that nationalistic rationale, other European nations began to increase their imports of American crude oil, while decreasing their imports of kerosene and other refined products.[117]

As the 1860s came to an end, massive changes were sweeping over the nation's four leading oil centers and the three railroad systems that served them. Increases in both output and production efficiency led to a rapid decline in the price of refined petroleum products. The various refining centers—Cleveland, New York, Pittsburgh, and the oil region—vied for dominance. Substantial overcapacity plagued the oil business, with refineries collectively able to process twice as much oil

as the drillers could supply—a situation that forced many small refiners into bankruptcy. With overcapacity inducing a brutal shakeout of the weaker firms, refiners sought to preserve their businesses by reducing transportation costs. The larger refiners—Rockefeller in particular—put intense pressure on the railroads for lower posted rates, drawbacks, and rebates. Executives responded with rate cuts that further destabilized the railroads.[118]

The South Improvement Company and the Oil Wars

The year 1871 was an *annus horribilis* for the American petroleum industry and for the railroads that served it. Refiners in Pittsburgh and the oilfields were losing ground to Rockefeller and his Cleveland juggernaut. Oilmen in all three regions were fearful of the growth of New York's refining capacity, and of the possibility that New York City would funnel crude oil to Europe, away from domestic refineries. Overcapacity had driven kerosene prices to ruinously low levels. Transportation costs had also declined, thanks to zealous competition among the trunk lines, but the low rates threatened to drive some railroads into insolvency.

And then, in May, the Baltimore & Ohio entered Pittsburgh. Its affiliate, the Pittsburgh & Connellsville Railroad, had endured a quarter century of efforts by PRR officials to retain their monopoly in southwestern Pennsylvania. Yet, the interloper had ultimately bested the PRR in the courts and benefited from Pennsylvania's general railway incorporation law, and the company's tracks finally connected with the B&O, at Cumberland, Maryland. With Pittsburgh in play for the first time since the sale of the Main Line of Public Works, PRR officials suddenly became far more solicitous of the city's oil refiners. They also lost much of their ability to use rates on local traffic in southwestern Pennsylvania to subsidize traffic from the oilfields to tidewater, much of which did little more than cover its variable cost of transportation.

Even as PRR managers began to compete actively for the Pittsburgh oil trade, they possessed a valuable weapon in their battle against the New York trunk lines. In May 1871, the same month that the B&O entered Pittsburgh, the directors of the PRR approved a lease of the United New Jersey Railroad & Canal Companies. Now that the PRR controlled the entire route between the oilfields and New York, executives were willing to offer substantial rebates and drawbacks in order to encourage producers in northwestern Pennsylvania to ship crude oil directly to New York City, bypassing both Pittsburgh and Cleveland. In early May 1871, Empire Line managers authorized a substantial rate cut on crude oil moving from northwestern Pennsylvania to the New York area, from $1.90 to $1.50 per barrel.[119]

The PRR's new rates helped undermine some of Cleveland's advantages in the oil trade. It was not long, however, before the Erie and the NYC, and their affiliates, authorized matching rate reductions. The ongoing rate wars threatened to cripple all of the trunk lines, while perpetuating the instability in the oil business.

Scott took the lead in devising a solution to the problem, one that would benefit the railroads and many—although by no means all—of the refiners. As 1871 drew to a close, Scott endeavored to maximize the PRR's share of the oil traffic that flowed from northwestern Pennsylvania directly to New York, while arresting the further decline of Pittsburgh as a refining center. To do so, he oversaw the creation of the South Improvement Company, perhaps the most controversial of all of the holding companies chartered under the aegis of the Pennsylvania Railroad.

The South Improvement Company was a cartel with a twist. Since the late 1850s, executives associated with the trunk lines had agreed, time and time again, to inevitably short-lived traffic pools, or other efforts to shore up rates. Oilmen in northwestern Pennsylvania had negotiated similar efforts to control supplies and prices, ranging from the 1867 Oil Buyers' Association to the 1869 Petroleum Producers' Association. Unlike the earlier efforts at coordination, however, the South Improvement Company was a cartel that included interests associated with both the shippers *and* the railroads.[120]

As its critics were quick to emphasize, the origins of the South Improvement Company were, and remain, shrouded in mystery. The records of the Pennsylvania legislature contain references to three separate iterations of a *Southern* Improvement Company, the first dating to April 1870. In all three cases, the proposed

incorporators were closely connected to the PRR. The 1871 session of the legislature approved a similar charter, this time for the South Improvement Company, and on May 6 Governor John White Geary signed the bill into law. Scott's personal secretary, Richard D. Barclay, was listed in the articles of incorporation, as was Samuel Moon, who had replaced Scott as the PRR's principal lobbyist, and who would soon become owner of the journal *The Railway World*.

The South Improvement Company remained moribund until the second half of 1871, when Scott grew increasingly concerned about the situation in the refining sector and its effects on the Pennsylvania Railroad. He soon made use of the South Improvement Company charter, and was the individual chiefly responsible for its methods. John D. Rockefeller, who would never escape scathing public criticism for his role in the cartel, spent his later years insisting that the South Improvement Company was a "Tom Scott Scheme" and that it "represented the views of Thomas A. Scott and some of our Pennsylvania [Railroad] friends as a way of equalizing the oil business and improving the freight rates."[121]

Scott recruited Peter H. Watson, a former patent lawyer from Ashtabula, Ohio. In January 1862, Watson had served for less than a week as assistant secretary of war, succeeding Scott in that office. During the early stages of the oil boom, Watson had invested in the oilfields near Franklin, Pennsylvania, as well as several railroads that served the region. Watson was a business associate of John D. Rockefeller. Of equal importance to Scott, Watson was also a close friend of Horace F. Clark, president of the Lake Shore and the son-in-law of NYC president Cornelius Vanderbilt.[122]

Given his connections to Standard Oil, the New York Central, and the PRR, Watson was the ideal person to mediate a settlement among the oilmen and the railroaders. He initially received the support of Pittsburgh refiners, who thought the scheme drastic and impracticable, but nonetheless welcomed any plan that might restore their companies to prosperity. Rockefeller proved more hesitant, as he was apparently already developing his own ideas for bringing stability to the oil markets by creating a trust around Standard Oil. By the end of 1871, however, Rockefeller had agreed to join the cartel, if for no other reason than to use its anticipated failure as an excuse to bully his fellow oilmen into accepting his consolidation plan. Rockefeller in turn persuaded or pressured many of the other major Cleveland refiners to participate.

The South Improvement Company united the interests of the trunk lines with most of the major refiners in both Pittsburgh and Cleveland, although not those in New York or the oil region. On January 2, 1872, refiners and railroaders gathered in Philadelphia in order to formally organize the South Improvement Company, with Watson serving as president. The largest shareholders were Pittsburgh oilmen William G. Warden and Orville T. Waring, and five of their fellow Pittsburghers were likewise involved in the company. Several of the city's major refineries, including Lockhart, Frew & Company, were represented, as was that company's Philadelphia ally, Warden, Frew & Company. Another Philadelphia firm, the Atlantic Refining Company, also took part. Henry Flagler and the Rockefeller brothers were not among the original incorporators, but they later took a large portion of the company's shares. So too did Oliver Hazard Payne (a partner in Clark, Payne & Co., and until 1872 Rockefeller's most significant competitor in Cleveland) and New York refiner Jabez A. Bostwick. Most of the other New York refiners (including Charles Pratt & Company) refused to join, a situation that would soon help to undermine the cartel's chances for success. Two of the largest refiners in northwestern Pennsylvania, Jacob J. Vandergrift and John D. Archbold, likewise refused to join.[123]

The first contract between the members of the South Improvement Company and the PRR, the Erie, and the New York Central revealed the salient features of the new cartel. At its heart was a traditional traffic pool, in which the PRR received 45 percent of the available business, with the New York Central and the Erie's subsidiary, the Atlantic & Great Western, each allocated 27.5 percent. The refiners, Standard Oil foremost among them, would act as "eveners," allocating traffic as necessary to maintain the agreed-upon percentages and preventing any railroad from gaining increased traffic by lowering rates. Rockefeller would later emphasize his role as a mediator of the cartel, asserting that his preferential rates constituted "a proper consideration to the Standard Oil Company for the

service which it rendered to all the interests."[124] The members of the South Improvement Company possessed the right to examine each railroad's traffic reports and financial statements, ensuring that any preferential treatment would be quickly uncovered. The PRR and the other railroads associated with the cartel sent daily reports to South Improvement Company secretaries, indicating the amount of oil that they handled and permitting the refiners to allocate shipments in order to maintain the agreed-upon percentages and prevent one railroad from poaching traffic from the others.

The railroads' uniform rate structure certainly benefited Pittsburgh and Cleveland refiners, at the expense of their competitors in the oil region. Rates from those two cities remained at $2.00 a barrel to New York, while the rate on the shorter distance between the oilfields and New York City rose to $2.56. More notably, the posted rates doubled the cost of shipping crude oil to either Pittsburgh or Cleveland, to eighty cents a barrel. Under the new tariff structure, Standard Oil officially paid $2.80 per barrel in transportation costs—eighty cents from the oilfields to Cleveland, and another $2.00 to New York. That was well above the $1.65 overall rate that Flagler had negotiated in 1870, and seemingly indicated that Rockefeller had been unwise to participate in the South Improvement Company cartel.[125]

Rockefeller and the other cartel members were hardly that foolish, and they knew full well that the posted rate and the actual rate were two very different things. As Scott and other railroad executives had long since recognized, most traffic pools and similar arrangements to control competition failed because shippers had been able to negotiate discounted rates with railroads that were willing to shave down the cartel price. Scott and his colleagues were determined to keep the cartel intact by relying on two time-tested methods of price discrimination, the rebate and the drawback. Officially, all shippers faced the posted rate. Members of the South Improvement Company received a rebate—in the form of an immediate reduction in the rate that they paid to the railroads. The rebates were substantial, ranging from 40 to 50 percent on crude oil, and from 25 to 50 percent on refined products. On the trip from the oilfields to Cleveland, for example, the rebate lowered the cost to Standard Oil and other SIC members from eighty cents to forty cents per barrel—the same as it had been prior to the implementation of the new rate structure. Shippers outside the cartel received no such rebate, and paid the full, posted rate. The rebate reduced Standard Oil's transportation costs to $1.90 a barrel—more than the 1870 rate, but still a decided advantage over producers and refiners who were not associated with the South Improvement Company.[126]

There was another component to the cartel, however, based on the difference between the posted rate charged to ordinary shippers and the rebated cost assessed to SIC members. At the end of each month, SIC officials calculated the additional revenues generated by non-members, thanks to the spread between the regular and the cartel rates. They then distributed that amount to the various shippers who were part of the SIC, in the form of a drawback. The drawback on shipments from the oilfields to Cleveland alone amounted to forty cents a barrel. In other words, Standard Oil was billed at eighty cents a barrel, actually paid the rebated price of forty cents a barrel, and at the end of each month received a drawback of forty cents a barrel, courtesy of its non-SIC competitors. Assuming that each group shipped an identical quantity of crude to Cleveland, Rockefeller's crude oil transportation costs to its refineries would be zero, while outside firms would pay eighty cents a barrel. While the actual arithmetic did not work out that precisely, the drawbacks on the route between the oilfields and Cleveland alone reduced Standard's overall transportation costs to well below the $1.65 rate that Flagler had negotiated in 1870.[127]

Although many of the independent oilmen complained bitterly at the doubly discriminatory nature of the South Improvement Company's rate structure, the system was of vital importance in regulating output and maintaining the cartel. SIC officials controlled the distribution of the drawbacks, and would not allocate those funds to any shipper who attempted to negotiate a lower rate (that is, secure a higher rebate) from any of the railroads. Furthermore, the drawbacks were intended to generate between $5 million and $6 million annually for the members of the South Improvement Company. That revenue would constitute a

kind of war chest that could be used to underwrite predatory pricing strategies and other attacks against any refinery or railroad that attempted to bypass the cartel.[128]

The South Improvement Company negated the distance, and therefore the price, advantage that New York refineries had previously enjoyed. Under the new rate structure, favored refiners could ship crude to Cleveland or Pittsburgh, and then dispatch refined petroleum to New York, all for less money than it would cost outsiders to send their crude directly to New York City. Scott, Rockefeller, and the other organizers of the South Improvement Company emphasized that price discrimination against New York refiners was vital to their efforts to restore stability, while preventing the loss of refining business to European firms. By concentrating refining at Cleveland and Pittsburgh, the members of the cartel reduced the possibility that crude oil, if sent to New York, would simply be transshipped to Europe for processing.[129]

The South Improvement Company was certain to cause severe problems for the New York refiners, as well as for oil-region producers and refiners who were not part of the cartel, yet it is not clear whether they were to be excluded. At the January 2 organization meeting, all of the parties agreed that any refiner should be permitted to join, regardless of location. Pittsburgh refiner and SIC member William G. Warden later testified, "It never entered into my head that the refineries would not all be brought in," and New York firms might have indeed joined, had the cartel lasted a bit longer.[130] Crude oil producers were another matter, however. Rockefeller insisted that the inclusion of producers in the oil region would undermine the cartel's efforts to control output and prices. Scott, who was far more interested in controlling rates than the level of oil production, apparently suggested that all producers be eligible to join the South Improvement Company.[131]

The membership issue was still unresolved when word of the cartel began to leak out. As early as February 24, 1872, newspapers such as the *Cleveland Plain Dealer* were intimating that a sophisticated new railroad freight pool was in effect. Then, on February 25, 1872, an employee of the Lake Shore & Michigan Southern inadvertently released the new rate schedule.

Drillers and refiners in the oil region were both horrified and outraged, and their angry reactions against the South Improvement Company eliminated any possibility that the cartel's membership might be expanded.[132]

Ida Tarbell, at the time the teenage daughter of an independent oil producer, recalled that "for weeks the whole body of oil men abandoned regular business and surged from town to town intent on destroying the 'Monster,' the 'Forty Thieves,' the 'Great Anaconda,' as they called the mysterious South Improvement Company."[133] The independent oilmen, Archbold and Vandergrift among them, railed against the new cartel. They formed the Petroleum Producers' Union (which, ironically, was itself a cartel), whose members vowed not to sell any oil to the South Improvement Company. They issued a "Black List" that included the names of Rockefeller, South Improvement Company president Peter H. Watson, and the Pennsylvania Railroad. More radical activists ripped up tracks and punctured Watson's oil tanks, spilling thousands of gallons of crude onto the ground near Franklin, Pennsylvania. With protestors naming Watson as the head of the "Anaconda," he had little choice other than to resign the presidency of the South Improvement Company, in a vain attempt to dampen the hysteria.[134]

Those outside the cartel, particularly the independent producers and refiners in northwestern Pennsylvania, initially directed their anger against Standard Oil and the other members of the cartel rather than the Pennsylvania Railroad. "Curiously enough," recalled Ida Tarbell, "it was chiefly against the combination which had secured the discrimination from the railroads—not the railroads which had granted it—that their fury was directed. They expected nothing but robbery from the railroads, they said. They were used to that; but they would not endure it from men in their own business."[135]

It was not long, however, before the independents began to uncover the full extent of the PRR's complicity in the formation of the cartel. They were outraged that an anonymous legislator had introduced the bill that had chartered the South Improvement Company, that no record had been kept of the vote on the measure, and that the proceedings of the Pennsylvania General Assembly had carried no mention of the legislation's passage—all hallmarks of what Tarbell referred to as "that interesting body known as the Tom Scott legislature."[136]

The independents adopted a variety of tactics to undermine the South Improvement Company. For the previous seven years, pipelines had offered at least a theoretical opportunity for independent oilmen to increase competition among the railroads. The pipeline saga began with the development of railroad vat and tank cars, which vastly increased the efficiency associated with the transportation of oil. Tank cars ensured that the movement of oil from well to railhead became a reverse salient—a choke point in the flow of petroleum. There seemed little reason to pour oil into barrels at the well, only to drain them at the nearest railroad siding, a few miles away.

Short pipelines offered a far better alternative. In the summer of 1865, oil broker Samuel Van Syckel built a line from Pithole to Miller's Farm, a shipping point on the Oil Creek Railroad. Within a short time, more and more lines snaked their way through the oil region. In 1867, William H. Abbott and Henry Harley established the Western Transportation Company, consolidating an established network of short-haul pipelines. Western possessed an extraordinarily valuable asset in that it was the only company chartered by the legislature to deliver oil directly to a rail line.

At that time, executives from all three trunk lines were anxious to avoid overbuilding and the creation of excess capacity in the oilfields. Therefore, they had established a flat fee of fifty cents per barrel for all oil transported on any oilfield railroad, between the railhead and any carrier's main line, regardless of distance. The flat-rate policy ensured that producers would move oil to the nearest local rail line, and that all rate competition would occur on the trunk-line portion of the route. Even though pipelines were still in their infancy, and incapable of transporting oil over long distances, Western Transportation enabled the independents to break the railroads' local transportation monopoly. By delivering the oil to a trunk line railroad, pipelines allowed shippers to avoid the fifty-cent local rail charge, while gaining access to competitive through rates.[137]

Officials from the PRR and the Erie were determined to maintain the uniform local access rail charge and avoid any possibility that improvements in pipelines might give oil producers access to more distant markets or shipping points. Jay Gould and his Erie associates soon acquired control of Western Transportation, which they renamed the Allegheny Transportation Company. Harley was president of the new company, while serving as general oil agent for the Atlantic & Great Western and the Erie. During the summer of 1869, the Erie constructed a new oil terminal at Pen Horn, near Jersey City, ready to accommodate the oil that would travel through Allegheny Transportation pipelines to the railhead, and then via the Atlantic & Great Western and the Erie to the east coast. In 1872, Gould arranged for Harley to acquire the competing Commonwealth Oil & Pipe Company, soon combined with Allegheny Transportation to form the Pennsylvania Transportation Company. Very quickly, however, Scott moved to neutralize the threat, buying a substantial interest in Pennsylvania Transportation. As such, the PRR and Erie interests maintained their monopoly over local traffic in the oilfields, by both rail and pipeline.[138]

The ability of the Erie and the PRR interests to integrate local delivery pipelines with their rail operations prevented the independents from pitting the trunk lines against each other. Their only recourse, they believed, was to charter a new series of pipelines, extending as far south as the B&O at Pittsburgh, or even north to the Great Lakes. Absent the passage of a free pipeline incorporation bill, however, the independents would have to obtain a charter for any new pipeline, from a state legislature dominated by the PRR. Likewise, they would lack the power of eminent domain, ensuring that the PRR could simply buy key parcels of land that lay along the pipeline's proposed right of way.[139]

On April 2, 1872, the independents achieved partial success when the General Assembly adopted a free pipeline bill. Thanks to the efforts of PRR lobbyists, however, the legislation's power of eminent domain was restricted to an eight-county area immediately surrounding the oilfields. Under those circumstances, there was no possibility that the independents could have constructed a pipeline to the Pittsburgh or to the Great Lakes, much less to tidewater. It would not have mattered much, in any case, as pipelines were not yet practicable over long distances, nor would they be until the 1880s.[140]

Although pipelines initially yielded few results, the producers and refiners left out of the South Improvement Company cartel experienced far more success through economic pressure. The boycott organized by the Petroleum Producers' Union was proving remarkably effective at starving the refineries at Cleveland and Pittsburgh. Between February and March, shipments of crude dispatched from the oil region dropped from 400,000 barrels to 276,000 barrels. Cleveland's receipts of crude oil fell from 73,000 barrels to 15,415, while Pittsburgh's share declined from 92,000 barrels to 39,000 barrels. With little oil to transport, and little to refine, the members of the South Improvement Company were willing to concede defeat.[141]

By the middle of March, the independent producers in the oilfields had found common cause with the New York refiners, with members of both groups charging that the practices of the South Improvement Company would spell their ruin. A delegation of twelve independent oilmen headed east to meet with New York refiners and the representatives of the railroads associated with the cartel. Given Scott's pivotal role in organizing the South Improvement Company, it was hardly surprising that it was to his office that they went first. On March 18, 1872, Scott welcomed them warmly, expressing his surprise at the uproar. He had always assumed that the South Improvement Company had represented the entire oil industry, he told the delegation, and disingenuously suggested that Rockefeller, and not he, had developed and managed the cartel for the benefit of the refiners, and not the railroads. Now that he realized that some important interests had been inadvertently left out of the South Improvement Company, he purred, he was fully prepared to offer the independents rates over the PRR that matched those awarded to Standard Oil and other favored refiners. The members of the delegation, won over either by Scott's personality or by his rather transparent explanation, assumed that they had made the PRR vice president finally see reason. One even suggested, without a hint of facetiousness, that Scott should run for the presidency (of the United States) that autumn.[142]

In reality, Scott had already decided that the South Improvement scheme was unsalvageable well before the independent oilmen walked into his office. His fellow railway executives were much less sanguine regarding the outcome, however, and were determined to preserve the cartel as long as possible. By March 25, the independents' delegation had met with representatives from the New York Central and the Erie, who remained steadfast in their support of the South Improvement Company. Demonstrating considerably more loyalty to the South Improvement Company than to his own family, Cornelius Vanderbilt was quick to assign blame for the fiasco to his son. Regardless of William Henry Vanderbilt's competence or complicity, however, the future of the cartel depended to a large degree on Scott.[143]

Two other events further undermined Scott's willingness to continue the pool. By March 12, the British investors who controlled the Atlantic & Great Western had succeeded in gaining control over the Erie, deposing Jay Gould in the process. Their representatives, including former Civil War general George B. McClellan, intended to launch a new fast freight line over the Erie/A&GW route, similar to the Empire Line, in an effort to draw traffic away from the South Improvement Company. A week later, on March 19, the New York legislature authorized the City of Buffalo to sell bonds in order to finance a new railroad to Titusville, deep in the oil region.[144] If completed, that line would free the independents from the authority of the cartel to a far greater degree than any pipeline.[145]

Despite their initial loyalty to the South Improvement Company, the traffic statistics collected during March horrified NYC and Erie officials into abandoning the pool. The boycott arranged by the independent oilmen had reduced traffic on all three trunk lines, but had affected the New York roads the most. During March, the Lake Shore captured $13\frac{1}{2}$ percent of the oil business, while the Erie scraped by with $4\frac{1}{4}$ percent, and the remainder, 82 percent, went to the PRR. Under those circumstances, a continuation of the war with the independents would only give more power to the Pennsylvania Railroad.[146]

On March 26, the three railroads officially announced an end to the rebates and drawbacks—although Standard Oil continued to receive a rate concession until November 15. On April 2, on the same day that they passed the limited free pipeline bill,

and a week after the announced end to the traffic pool had made the South Improvement Company irrelevant, legislators voted to suspend its charter. Rockefeller may have been exaggerating when he later insisted that "the South Improvement Company never existed as a business organization," but his comment nonetheless attested to its exceedingly brief lifespan.[147]

Thereafter, railroad executives reverted to their traditional efforts to establish traffic pools. Officially, at least, the trunk lines equalized the rates between any of the three shipping points—Pittsburgh, Cleveland, and the oil region—and New York. Refiners in Cleveland and Pittsburgh bore an additional fifty cents per barrel in transportation costs compared with their competitors in northwestern Pennsylvania, reflecting the cost of transporting crude oil to refineries in those cities. In consequence, newspaper editors in Cleveland and Pittsburgh were soon as vitriolic in their condemnation of the end of the traffic pool as their counterparts in the oilfields had been of its creation.[148]

The termination of the cartel seemed certain to reignite the rate war between the three trunk lines, and in the resulting contest the PRR was likely to emerge victorious. For one, Scott's railroad was transporting nearly as much oil as the railroads of his two competitors combined, and it still enjoyed the well-honed organizational structure of the Empire Line, as well as exclusive control over the Catawissa route. Of perhaps greater importance, the original northwestern Pennsylvania oil fields were drying up, and production was shifting farther south, away from the New York Central and the Erie, but toward the PRR's main line. As such, the PRR's acquisition of the Allegheny Valley and the completion of the Low Grade Division in the spring of 1874 offered Scott an excellent opportunity to solidify his dominance of the oil trade.[149]

The Pennsylvania Railroad was better positioned than the NYC to accommodate shipments by independent producers and refiners, which, despite Rockefeller's influence, still composed more than half of the total traffic. During 1872 and 1873, thanks in large measure to the ability of the PRR's Empire Line affiliate to offer favorable rates to the petroleum interests, the PRR maintained at least a 60 percent share of the oil traffic moving to tidewater. While the PRR and the

NYC vied for dominance of the oil trade, the Erie fell by the wayside, handling barely fifty-three thousand barrels a month, compared with three hundred thousand on the PRR. The Pennsylvania Railroad won the oil war, with the New York Central finishing a close second, and the Erie out of the running, and headed for a second receivership, in 1875.[150]

Rockefeller and the railroads continued to negotiate rates of oil transportation. As the South Improvement Company collapsed, Rockefeller protected the interests of Standard Oil, securing substantial rebates from the New York Central in exchange for a guarantee that he would ship at least one hundred thousand barrels a month. With their recent lease of the United New Jersey Railroad & Canal Companies, PRR officials were in an excellent position to counter the NYC rates. In December 1872, the Pennsylvania Railroad's freight agents sharply reduced the rate on refined petroleum moving to New York, benefiting refiners in Pittsburgh and in the oilfields. Standard Oil executives demanded that Vanderbilt offer matching reductions in the New York Central's rates, lest Cleveland be crippled as a refining center. Thereafter, rates continued to fluctuate, with sub rosa rebates and drawbacks further complicating the tariff situation.[151]

Rockefeller suffered little from the collapse of the South Improvement Company. He claimed to have been deeply wronged by the PRR interests, and he suggested that Scott had bullied him into participation in the pool. While that self-serving recollection seems hardly credible, Rockefeller nonetheless was quick to pursue other mechanisms for controlling output, more secure than the South Improvement Company had been able to provide. By April 1872, Rockefeller had acquired five of the biggest Cleveland refineries, as well as a major New York refining and brokerage firm. By August, Rockefeller had overseen the creation of the National Refiners' Association, with the support of leading producers and refiners in the oilfields and at Pittsburgh. In the years that followed, he gained control of 90 percent of the refining capacity in the United States, and in 1882 created the Standard Oil trust—a landmark in the development of large, vertically integrated business enterprises.[152]

In the final analysis, it was Standard Oil's John D. Rockefeller, and not Scott of the PRR, who shouldered the blame for the unsavory ratemaking practices associated with the South Improvement Company. Scott's ability to deflect criticism and disguise his role in the cartel's operations was so successful that in November 1877, when the members of the Petroleum Producers' Union lobbied for bills that would ban rate discrimination and create an open-access pipeline across the commonwealth, they had apparently forgotten that Scott and the PRR were largely responsible for the rate structure that they found so objectionable. With Rockefeller controlling the oil trade, they argued, PRR officials were little more than "slaves without voice or power in the oil trade, except as their master may will."[153]

The Aftermath of the Oil Wars

The oil wars in northwestern Pennsylvania lasted only forty days, and the South Improvement Company was in existence for less than a year, but the effects of the controversy lingered for decades. In the realm of railroad regulation, the national government was still quite weak, relative to the states, and did little to resolve the crisis. In March 1872, members of the U.S. House of Representatives called on the Commerce Committee to investigate the South Improvement Company and its developers. The congressional hearings began on March 30 and lasted until April 17. Yet, when the committee issued its report on May 7, it could do little more than label the now-defunct South Improvement Company "one of the most gigantic and dangerous conspiracies ever attempted." Within a few years, the Commerce Committee would again investigate the PRR's role in the oil trade but, for the moment, the matter was closed.[154]

The political consequences at the state level were equally mild. In January 1873, less than ten months after the collapse of the South Improvement Company, delegates convened for the purpose of writing a new state constitution, the first since 1838. The actions of the PRR and the South Improvement Company generated considerable discussion, as well as calls for regulation and reform. However, the convention was not directly a product of the oil wars, and its delegates did not interfere with the PRR in any substantive way. To the contrary, support for a new constitution had begun in the late 1860s, well before the development of the South Improvement Company, and had far more to do with the presumed evils of the legislature than with those of the Pennsylvania Railroad. Influential leaders in the Republican Party and, to a lesser extent, in the ranks of the Democrats believed that the customary political practice of logrolling had become uncontrollable. With more than two thousand bills introduced in the General Assembly every year, legislators rarely bothered to read the measures that they were approving and instead provided their assent as a courtesy to the sponsor of the legislation. Political leaders and newspaper editors in many communities asserted that such practices abrogated local political autonomy. That was the position of the publishers of the Philadelphia *Public Ledger*, following the 1870 legislative session, but their indictment of legislative malfeasance assigned blame to the General Assembly, and not to the railroads.[155]

By August, however, the Republican Convention of Allegheny County had adopted a resolution calling for railroad regulation, in order to ensure that the PRR and other carriers operated in the public interest. It was hardly surprising that such a statement originated in Pittsburgh, where merchants and industrialists had long complained of the PRR's monopoly on rail transportation. The agenda of the Allegheny County Republicans added to the pressure for a constitutional convention, but there were many other factors at work, including concerns that the electoral system underrepresented Republicans in traditionally Democratic counties in northeastern Pennsylvania. In October, 1870, the Union League of Philadelphia—a staunchly Republican and impeccably pro-business organization—endorsed a constitutional convention but avoided a specific indictment against the railroads. Instead, the organization's position was that logrolling had enabled corporations to buy political favors from corrupt legislators, to the detriment of the people. The Union League nonetheless called for reform of the legislature, and not regulation of the railroads.

The involvement of the *Public Ledger*, the Republican Party of Allegheny County, and the Union League indicated that the calls for a new constitution arose from the elites rather than from the masses. Under such circumstances, attacks on the Pennsylvania Rail-

road were more apt to be symbolic than substantive. While many reporters churned out sensationalistic accounts of the alleged evils perpetrated by the Pennsylvania Railroad and the South Improvement Company, there was no widespread call for punishment or reform. The independent oilmen in northwestern Pennsylvania were among the strongest critics of the railroad and the cartel, but their outrage had more to do with their specific economic circumstances than with opposition to big business, railroads, or capitalism in general. Some older Pennsylvanians, aged veterans of the Jacksonian era, continued to manifest a philosophical distaste for the monopoly provisions inherent in corporate charters. They recalled the ongoing efforts by PRR officials to prevent the B&O and the Pittsburgh & Connellsville from reaching Pittsburgh. Scott's unscrupulous, if successful efforts to repeal the tonnage tax also appeared to them as an affront to the will of the people. Their criticism struck a chord with many shippers in the southwestern part of the commonwealth, who disliked the PRR's rate structure. Yet, the anti-charter and anti-monopoly voices were relatively muted, and failed to resonate with most Pennsylvanians. Most of the state's residents, in contrast, were well aware of the PRR's accomplishments in increasing travel speeds and in lowering overall rates. The general consensus, then, was that the company had done far more good than ill, and that many of its peccadilloes could be overlooked or safely forgiven.[156]

There were nonetheless some delegates to the constitutional convention who lashed out at the PRR and the other railroads in the state. Chief among them was Thomas E. Cochran, who was an attorney, newspaper editor, and state senator, first a staunch Whig and later an equally dedicated Republican, and former auditor general of the commonwealth of Pennsylvania. Jeremiah S. Black was likewise an attorney from York County but, aside from his place of residence and his opposition to the PRR, he had little in common with Cochran. A lifelong Democrat, he served as President James Buchanan's attorney general. In February 1861, weeks before Buchanan left office, Black faced a Senate confirmation hearing for a seat on the Supreme Court. His bid failed, almost certainly owing to the political rancor that accompanied secession. In later years, Black opposed what he considered to be the unfairly harsh terms associated with the postwar Reconstruction plan supported by radical Republicans in Congress. Thomas Howard and T. H. Baird Patterson were both Republican attorneys from Allegheny County. Significantly, each hailed from a region where shippers maintained commercial ties with Baltimore, favored the B&O, and correspondingly exhibited antipathy toward the PRR. All but Black were members of the Committee on Railroads and Canals. However, their calls for increased regulation, most forcefully articulated by Cochran, instead related to their assertion that the railroads were public utilities, and so should operate for the good of the people, rather than a small number of privileged investors. Those views notwithstanding, few ordinary Pennsylvanians possessed either the time or the money necessary to take part in the constitutional convention, and Cochran and his allies hardly spoke for them.[157]

Thomson, Scott, and other PRR officials were anxious to control the proceedings at the 1873 constitutional convention, and they succeeded remarkably well. The PRR contributed three delegates, board member Edward C. Knight, chief counsel Theodore Cuyler, and Philadelphia & Erie president (and former Pennsylvania governor) William Bigler. Wayne MacVeagh, the son-in-law of Simon Cameron and later the PRR's general counsel, was also a staunch supporter of the railroads. Franklin B. Gowen, the president of the Philadelphia & Reading, also served as a delegate. He manifested an intense rivalry with the PRR, but in this instance, at least, he was willing to join forces with Scott, Thomson, and their associates. None of these individuals were members of the Committee on Railroads and Canals, but they certainly shared their transportation expertise with other attendees. Furthermore, senior PRR managers undoubtedly influenced the actions of many of the other prominent business executives who attended the convention, and whose careers and corporations depended on steadfast loyalty to their transportation lifeline.

PRR officials could also count on the support of delegates who were anti-regulation, if not necessarily pro-railroad. They included George Washington Woodward, like Black a Democrat and a failed Supreme Court nominee. Woodward had served briefly in the U.S. House of Representatives, from a district

around Johnstown and Latrobe, before moving to Philadelphia—all areas where many residents were loyal to the PRR. Hugh Nelson McAllister also hailed from PRR country, as he was born in Juniata County and later became a judge in Centre County. George Lear was from Bucks County, just north of Philadelphia. J.W.F. White was a Republican attorney from Pittsburgh, but he disagreed with Howard and Patterson on the necessity of railroad regulation. None of the four were willing to give PRR executives complete freedom of action, but all believed that regulation might do more harm than good. McAllister, in particular, doubted that railroads and canals were public utilities, and insisted that those companies be regulated in the same manner as other corporations. Some, including Lear, recalled the problems associated with the antebellum mixing of public and private control over internal improvements, and asserted that governmental regulation of corporate affairs had become passé.[158]

The pro-railroad forces possessed a key psychological advantage, in that the convention met in Philadelphia, the headquarters city of the Pennsylvania Railroad. The proceedings began with a letter of welcome from the Philadelphia Select and Common Councils, the body that had helped to finance the PRR a quarter of a century earlier. The delegates met in a building provided by the city's government, the same political entity that still owned a substantial block of PRR stock.[159]

For a time, it appeared that the pro-regulation delegates to the constitutional convention were in control of the proceedings. Whether it was by accident or by design, the PRR's officers and their allies allowed the reformers to draft a constitution that included severe restrictions on the railroads. Various iterations of the draft prohibited the issuance of free passes; prevented railroads or their executives from maintaining an ownership in fast freight lines, mines, or forest lands; permitted any interested party (later amended to any stockholder) to examine the books of a railroad corporation at will; eliminated drawbacks and long-haul/short-haul rate discrimination; and afforded the commonwealth secretary of internal affairs broad regulatory powers over the railroads. Following months of debate, the convention had no sooner approved those provisions than MacVeagh and other PRR allies orchestrated a vote to reconsider the entire section of the proposed constitution that pertained to railroad regulation. The PRR's stunned and exhausted opponents were left reeling, unable to articulate a coherent response or—more important—muster the votes necessary to block reconsideration. The pro-railroad delegates then substituted provisions that were considerably milder than the original version. It was that language that appeared in the final draft of the proposed constitution.

The voters approved the document in December 1873, and it became effective on the first day of January 1874, but the changes had little effect on the PRR. Perhaps the most burdensome restriction associated with the new constitution involved a repudiation of the 1861 act that had enabled railroad companies to buy or lease a parallel or competing line—although end-to-end mergers remained permissible. However, the new constitution did little to affect the PRR's reliance on cartels and rate differentiation as weapons against rival trunk lines. It prohibited rates that were clearly discriminatory, a provision that seemingly precluded the use of drawbacks, but it did not define what constituted discrimination, leaving that matter to the legislature and the courts, two bodies known to be heavily influenced by the PRR. Moreover, the constitution exempted the railroads from rate regulation and permitted the continued use of holding companies.[160]

In April 1874 the same elitist pressure for political reform that produced the constitutional convention also encouraged legislators to adopt a general incorporation law. In this instance, however, the South Improvement Company scandal, combined with ongoing resentment at the PRR's treatment of the Pittsburgh & Connellsville, colored their actions. Nonetheless, the merchants and industrialists who supported the new incorporation act were not primarily concerned with punishing the PRR. Instead, they hoped that the law would encourage the formation of additional railroads that could compete against the PRR, the Reading, and other established carriers, and thus reduce rates. Their position dovetailed with the largely Republican concerns about legislative misconduct, as the law would systematize the incorporation process, reduce the number of bills that came before the overbur-dened legislature, and prevent corporate lobbyists from interfering with economic development.[161]

Neither the Constitution of 1874 nor the general incorporation act exerted much of an influence on the Pennsylvania Railroad. In part, that was because PRR officials were extraordinarily adroit at influencing the courts and, to an even greater degree, the legislature. The supporters of the 1874 Constitution attempted to dilute the power of companies like the PRR, or at least make their machinations more costly, by doubling the size of the General Assembly. However, the expansion brought to Harrisburg a plethora of naive and inexperienced junior legislators, readily susceptible to the blandishments of PRR lobbyists.

The PRR's officials also took advantage of the hardening of party lines that had accompanied the Civil War. Both Republicans and Democrats were more likely to vote as a bloc than had been the case with their antebellum counterparts, and PRR executives generally aligned themselves with the former, and typically more powerful, group. Alexander K. McClure, the Republican who had so ably assisted Scott in the prewar effort to repeal the tonnage tax, was still a useful ally, even if he had left the mainstream Republican Party in favor of the Liberal Republicans. Other politicians proved even more valuable to the PRR, at both the state and the national levels. Simon Cameron served in the United States Senate until 1877, safeguarding the PRR's interests in the Capitol. He was also a leading power broker in Pennsylvania politics, and ensured that the PRR's executives and lobbyists enjoyed favorable treatment in Harrisburg as well as Washington. James Donald Cameron followed very much in his father's footsteps. Between 1866 and 1874, he served as president of the Northern Central Railway. He was secretary of war in 1876 and 1877, resigning that post after his father demanded that the Pennsylvania legislature appoint him as his successor in the Senate. The younger Cameron controlled the Republican Party in Pennsylvania and ensured that House Speaker E. Reed Myer (elected in 1877) and his successor Henry M. Long (elected in 1879) were sympathetic to the PRR. Democratic Speaker Samuel F. Patterson was equally amenable to the PRR's interests, meeting frequently with Scott.

Republican Senator John Scott was the other United States senator from Pennsylvania (he served between 1869 and 1875), and he was the PRR's staunchest ally in Congress. The son of a tanner, at the age of eighteen he began the study of law with Alexander Thomson, the father of future PRR president Frank Thomson. He established a legal practice based in Huntingdon, Pennsylvania. In 1857, he assisted PRR officials in Cambria County, where he came to the attention of Thomson and Tom Scott. They soon selected him as a PRR special counsel for Cambria, Huntingdon, and Blair Counties, with the added responsibility of resolving any legal issues associated with the PRR's purchase of the Pennsylvania Canal. He resigned those responsibilities in 1869 when the members of the commonwealth's General Assembly elected him to the United States Senate, but he remained connected with several PRR subsidiaries. In addition to being a senator, he was also general counsel of the Pittsburgh, Cincinnati & St. Louis Railway (the Pan Handle). When he left the Senate in 1875, he became general counsel for the Pennsylvania Company. He joined the PRR proper in 1877, first as general counsel at Pittsburgh and shortly afterward as general solicitor and head of the Legal Department. Democrat William A. Wallace occupied the Senate seat that John Scott had vacated, and he was also a close associate of PRR executives, particularly Scott.[162]

In addition to maintaining friendly relationships with influential politicians, PRR officials apparently continued to bribe individual politicians. As one example, the PRR's opponents claimed that the company had disbursed $870,000 to state legislators in order to secure Wallace's appointment to the U.S. Senate. More commonly, the PRR offered lucrative positions, especially in the Legal Department, for individuals, like John Scott, who were energetic, loyal, and politically well connected.[163]

Access to Anthracite

Even as Scott was trying in vain to impose order on the oil trade, Thomson and other executives were engaged in the development of a more traditional energy source. For at least the first half of the nineteenth century, anthracite (hard) coal from the northeastern part of the state was the fuel of choice, far exceeding the importance of the commonwealth's oil reserves or, for that matter, its more westerly bituminous deposits. The anthracite lay in three fairly narrow bands, running from southwest to northeast. The Southern Field was centered around Pottsville, extending from Mauch Chunk (today, Jim Thorpe) on the Lehigh River to Dauphin on the Susquehanna River. The Middle Field was actually two distinct regions, one around Mount Carmel and the other to the east, at Hazleton, separated from one another by Lehigh Mountain. Regional carriers dominated the transportation of anthracite from the Southern and Middle Fields to tidewater. By 1820, well before even the construction of the Main Line of Public Works, the Lehigh Coal & Navigation Company was shipping anthracite to Philadelphia, initially by damming and releasing water on the Lehigh River, and later by canal. The Delaware & Hudson Canal Company likewise brought anthracite to New York, relying in part on one of the first railways in the United States to do so. So, too, did the Lehigh Valley; the Delaware, Lackawanna & Western; the Jersey Central; and others. However, the Philadelphia & Reading was the preeminent anthracite carrier, with its main line from the coalfields to Port Richmond serving as a veritable conveyor belt for coal traffic.[164]

The Northern Field, largest of the three, surrounding Wilkes-Barre and Scranton, lay generally along the Wyoming Valley of the North Branch of the Susquehanna River. During the 1820s, those deposits had encouraged Jacob Cist and other Wilkes-Barre entrepreneurs to press the General Assembly for an expansion in the commonwealth's internal-improvement network, helping to trigger a conflict between the "Main Liners" and the "Branch Men." Despite the construction of the North Branch Division of the Pennsylvania Canal and the subsequent expansion of Wyoming Valley anthracite production during the 1840s, the area did not live up to its potential. While anthracite could easily reach canal ports on the main stem of the Susquehanna River, the Union Canal provided a poor route eastward. The Philadelphia & Columbia Railroad was no better, as—particularly during the period of state control—rates were far too high to permit the economical transportation of coal to tide-water. The completion of the Susquehanna & Tide Water Canal in 1840 helped matters considerably, but it was not until the period immediately following the Civil War that production surged in the Wyoming Valley. That was the area that captured the interest of Thomson and other PRR executives.[165]

The PRR never matched the Reading's share of the anthracite traffic, but after the Civil War the PRR's managers did gradually increase their involvement in both the mining and transportation of hard coal. The PRR's 1857 purchase of the Main Line of Public Works had included the Eastern, Juniata, and Western Division canals, under the control of a newly established Canal Department. The Western Division carried little traffic and was incrementally abandoned, with much of the right of way sold to the Western Pennsylvania Railroad in 1867. The Juniata and Eastern Divisions remained in service, however, with the former accommodating local business and the latter serving principally to transport Wyoming Valley coal along the independent Susquehanna & Tide Water Canal to Chesapeake Bay, and on to Philadelphia by way of the Chesapeake & Delaware Canal. However, the owners of the two principal independent feeders to the PRR's Eastern Division Canal, the West Branch & Susquehanna Canal Company and the Wyoming Valley Canal Company, along the West and North Branches of the Susquehanna River, often failed to keep their properties in an adequate state of repair. As such, the PRR's efforts to increase depths and lengthen locks on PRR-owned canals were of little value, and the railroad's canal traffic suffered accordingly. After the Civil War, with the expectation of booming anthracite production in the Wyoming Valley, PRR officials elected to bring the entire regional canal system under their control. They hoped to standardize canal capacity, improve efficiency, rationalize tolls, and facilitate competition with the regional anthracite railroads.[166]

In May 1866, Thomson oversaw the incorporation of the Pennsylvania Canal Company and served briefly as its president—a move that indicated his determination to expand the PRR's involvement in waterborne transportation. Thomson's front man was General Isaac Jones Wistar, a Philadelphia attorney and veteran of the Civil War. Wistar left the Union Army in May 1864, his early departure partly the result of battlefield injuries, and partly because of allegations of incompetence. He invested heavily in the Union Canal Company and became the president of the run-down transportation artery linking the Schuylkill and Susquehanna rivers. In order to raise funds for badly needed improvements, Wistar attempted to sell to either the Reading or the PRR the company's charter rights to build a railroad through the upper Swatara Valley (essentially the moribund Dauphin & Susquehanna/Auburn & Port Clinton route that dated to the early 1850s). Wistar, whose father-in-law, Robert Toland, had been one of the principal organizers of the Pennsylvania Railroad, had little trouble gaining an audience with Thomson. The PRR president declined to purchase the franchise, but he helped Wistar sell it to the Reading, and he seemed impressed with Wistar's business acumen and his knowledge of canal operations.[167]

In June 1867, Thomson recalled Wistar to his office. There, the former brigadier general encountered such other luminaries as Scott, former governor William F. Packer, and Senator Simon Cameron. Thomson asked Wistar to covertly study the traffic potential of the West Branch & Susquehanna Canal. Wistar apparently believed that Thomson was interested only in determining whether the West Branch company might generate appreciable interchange traffic for the PRR, and he was therefore astonished to learn that Thomson had already leased the property through the Pennsylvania Canal Company. Wistar was even more shocked when Thomson asked him to become president of the PRR's canal subsidiary.[168]

Wistar soon oversaw an expansion in the Pennsylvania Canal Company's operations. By leasing the West Branch & Susquehanna Canal Company, the PRR's canal subsidiary gained access to the lumber trade along the West Branch of the Susquehanna River. The acquisition of the Wiconisco Canal Company and the Wyoming Valley Canal Company extended the PRR's reach into anthracite country, at Wilkes-Barre.[169] In New Jersey, the 1871 lease of the United Companies netted the PRR the Delaware & Raritan Canal, operating under a resurrected Canal Department rather than as part of Wistar's Pennsylvania Canal Company. By the end of 1873, Wistar had authorized nearly $2 million worth of improvements, particularly along the route into the Wyoming Valley, between Northumberland and Wilkes-Barre. When privately owned canal boats proved inadequate to accommodate the anthracite traffic, Wistar in 1872 ordered the construction of more than two hundred coal barges.[170]

Very quickly, however, Reading officials began to block the PRR's water routes. Reading president Franklin B. Gowen, like his colleagues and competitors, confronted an anthracite market where demand, production, and prices fluctuated wildly. Gowen sensed that stability would require coordinated management of both mining and transportation, in order to regulate anthracite price and output. Gowen was equally anxious to undermine union activity, soon finding a way to combine those two goals. He persuaded the members of the fledgling Workingmen's Benevolent Association to tie their wages to anthracite prices, ensuring that labor costs rose or fell in tandem with colliery revenues. Although miners were shocked to discover that the new arrangement had reduced rather than increased their pay, Gowen had succeeded admirably in his efforts to develop a mechanism to control hard coal prices. In May 1871, he created the Laurel Run Improvement Company, quickly renamed the Philadelphia & Reading Coal & Iron Company, as a subsidiary of the Philadelphia & Reading Rail Road. In the process, Gowen managed to skirt the prohibition against the company's direct ownership in coal lands, a feature that the Pennsylvania legislature had inserted in the Reading's 1833 corporate charter, although not in the charters issued to the Reading's competitors. Gowen quickly invested some $50 million in his new subsidiary, buying nearly one hundred thousand acres of coalfields, along with mines and ironworks.[171]

With the establishment of this early holding company, Gowen now held a powerful advantage in his attempts to control both the rates on anthracite traffic and the price of the coal itself. At virtually the same time, Scott had failed miserably in his efforts to use the South Improvement Company to bring stability to the oil business. Gowen fared rather better. He began by taking control of anthracite marketing, particularly at the Reading's vast Port Richmond terminal, where

he displaced the independent brokers who had negotiated coal prices. Gowen also did his best to prevent the Pennsylvania Railroad and its subsidiaries from bringing their coal to market. The Reading ceased interchanging traffic with the Delaware & Raritan Canal, causing rapid declines in business on the New Jersey route. More problematic, in 1872 the Reading leased the Susquehanna & Tide Water Canal, in effect bottling up the PRR's boats and preventing them from reaching Chesapeake Bay.[172]

In retaliation, Wistar recommended that the Pennsylvania Canal Company acquire anthracite fields as a mechanism for guaranteeing traffic for the North Branch Canal. Surreptitiously, and apparently in a manner known only to himself and Thomson, Wistar began buying parcels totaling six thousand acres of coal lands. In 1869, the PRR and the Pennsylvania Canal Company jointly acquired the Pittston Railroad & Coal Company, located in the Northern Field near Nanticoke, Pennsylvania, and renamed it the Susquehanna Coal Company. Shortly thereafter, Thomson and his PRR associates snapped up the Lykens Valley Coal Company. By 1873, the PRR's holdings had expanded to include some twenty-eight thousand acres of property in the western portions of the anthracite region, acquired and developed at a cost of more than $3.8 million. The PRR's investments included the Mineral Railroad & Mining Company (near Shamokin, in the Western Middle Field) and the Summit Branch Railroad Company (later, the Summit Branch Mining Company, in the Lykens Valley, at the very western end of the Southern Field). While corporate charter restrictions precluded the combination of the firms into a single corporate entity, Wistar was president of all of them, with the Susquehanna Coal Company serving as the de facto umbrella organization.[173] The PRR extended tracks along the North Branch of the Susquehanna River into the anthracite fields near Hazleton and Wilkes-Barre, augmenting its canal into the region.[174]

The anthracite reached tidewater over a variety of routes. Despite the problems associated with the Susquehanna & Tide Water Canal, the Pennsylvania Canal Company continued to transport a respectable share of coal. Much of the anthracite that was destined for New York followed the Lehigh Valley and the PRR-controlled Belvidere Delaware Railroad to Coalport, a loading station on the Delaware & Raritan Canal near Trenton. Shortly after the Civil War, construction crews had built a short connecting line, between Monmouth Junction and Jamesburg, enabling the coal to reach South Amboy, over the original Camden & Amboy Railroad route. In May 1872, the PRR board of directors authorized the construction of an anthracite coal facility at South Amboy. New terminal facilities at Greenwich Point in South Philadelphia included an anthracite pier, completed in 1874, that handled much of the coal from the Lykens Valley. Farther south, the 1873 completion of the Canton Branch ensured that anthracite shipments on the Northern Central could easily reach the Baltimore harbor.[175]

Throughout the remainder of the 1870s, the PRR's mining subsidiaries produced between one million and two million tons of hard coal per year, representing roughly 5 percent of the state's total anthracite output. While the Lykens Valley ran chronic deficits, the other concerns generally showed a respectable profit, even during the depression of the 1870s. In 1880, for example, Susquehanna Coal generated $2.3 million in revenues and contributed $209,806 in profit to its parent company. Profit and loss was not terribly relevant, however, as the anthracite concerns served primarily to generate traffic for the Pennsylvania Railroad and its Pennsylvania Canal Company subsidiary.[176]

The PRR's investments were nonetheless insufficient to make the company a significant factor in either the mining or transportation of hard coal. Even though the PRR and its subsidiaries owned large tracts of coal land, the mines were scattered over the Northern, Middle, and Southern Fields, with little possibility of integration. The Reading owned nearly one hundred thousand acres, more than three times the PRR's holdings, and most of them were concentrated in one fairly compact area. In contrast to the role of Franklin Gowen in establishing the Philadelphia & Reading Coal & Iron Company and its associated cartels, PRR executives were never able to coordinate anthracite production and marketing. After 1872, Reading control over the Susquehanna & Tide Water Canal greatly reduced the usefulness of the Pennsylvania Canal Company as a transportation artery, and the PRR lacked good rail connections between the anthracite fields and east coast markets. As a result, most

of the PRR's anthracite shipments went west toward Pittsburgh or Lake Erie, leaving the Reading and the other regional carriers to compete for the tidewater traffic.

Finally, the provisions of Pennsylvania's 1874 Constitution, adopted in the aftermath of the South Improvement Company scandal, prohibited railroads from acquiring coal lands.[177] Even though a grandfather clause protected the PRR's existing operations—and, for that matter, such integrated companies as the Lehigh Coal & Navigation, the Delaware & Hudson Canal, and the Delaware, Lackawanna & Western Railroad—further expansion had become impossible. The constitutional prohibition also frightened some conservative shareholders into believing that the PRR should leave the coal business. By October 1874, as the effects of a catastrophic depression swept over the Pennsylvania Railroad, some of the PRR's dissident shareholders emphasized that the ownership of anthracite properties "is not only of doubtful propriety . . . but involves financial problems that may confuse and confound the wisest of managers."[178]

The Port Road

The PRR's involvement in the anthracite business instigated the development of a new rail route, paralleling the lower reaches of the Susquehanna River and augmenting the Northern Central line to Baltimore. After the Civil War, PRR officials supported the construction of the Columbia & Port Deposit Railroad to Chesapeake Bay. The "Port Road," as it was often known, was initially of limited value to the PRR, but it increased the level of cooperation between the PRR and the independent Philadelphia, Wilmington & Baltimore Railroad, and eventually facilitated the efficient movement of freight traffic.

During the early 1850s, farmers and other local boosters living in Oxford and other towns in Chester County, Pennsylvania, attempted to build a rail line through the area. Officials from the Philadelphia, Wilmington & Baltimore regarded Chester County as their territory, and temporarily succeeded in blocking the plans. In 1853, however, the promoters secured a charter for the Philadelphia & Baltimore Central

Railroad.[179] Over the next decade, construction crews slowly built through Chester County. The railroad relied on a connection with the West Chester & Philadelphia Railroad at Baltimore Junction (Wawa) to provide an outlet to the Quaker City. In 1861, the Philadelphia & Baltimore Central suffered the fate of many rural short lines, and entered receivership.

The Civil War greatly increased the volume of traffic flowing between Philadelphia and Baltimore and suggested the possibility that the West Chester & Philadelphia/Philadelphia & Baltimore Central route could be extended to form a competitor to the Philadelphia, Wilmington & Baltimore, the dominant carrier in the region. Samuel Morse Felton and other PW&B officials were accordingly anxious to gain control over their two smaller rivals, if for no other reason than to eliminate the threat of a parallel line. In March 1862, however, Philadelphia & Baltimore Central shareholders rejected consolidation with either the PW&B or the West Chester & Philadelphia. Felton kept up the pressure, and in August he gained control over the Philadelphia & Baltimore Central. The PW&B soon began construction on the Chester Creek Railroad, completed in 1869, providing a connection with its new acquisition. West Chester & Philadelphia officials were then in an extremely vulnerable position, as the Chester Creek Railroad had rendered their company essentially redundant. For the moment, neither PW&B nor PRR officials were concerned about the fate of that small and seemingly insignificant company. Within a decade, however, the owners of the West Chester & Philadelphia would be involved in a series of events that ultimately brought the Philadelphia, Wilmington & Baltimore under the control of the Pennsylvania Railroad.[180]

During the late 1850s, as the promoters of the Philadelphia & Baltimore Central were struggling to build their route through Chester County, another group of local entrepreneurs was involved in the construction of a similar line, a few miles to the west. Between Columbia, Pennsylvania, and Port Deposit, Maryland, the Susquehanna River passed through a steep gorge, with little settlement on the eastern shore. Jacob Tome, a Port Deposit entrepreneur who became a self-made millionaire and noted philanthropist, supported the construction of a railroad that would end the community's isolation. Beginning in April 1857, Tome and his associates organized a series of companies that became the Columbia & Port Deposit Railroad.[181] By happy coincidence, a route along the Susquehanna River, south of Columbia, would facilitate the transportation of anthracite to the lower reaches of the Delaware River. From Port Deposit, an extension of the Junction & Breakwater Railroad would send coal east, relying in part on a section of roadbed recently abandoned by the New Castle & Frenchtown Rail Road. Ships calling at Lewes, Delaware, could then load anthracite, without making the trek upriver to Philadelphia, and avoiding the ice that often choked the upper reaches of the Delaware River. A number of established carriers, most notably the Reading, dominated the transportation of anthracite to tidewater, and few investors were interested in the project. Inadequate financing and the disruptions caused by the Civil War prevented more than a token effort at construction.

After the Civil War, as the PRR began investing millions of dollars in coal lands and anthracite mines, executives faced the problem of getting that coal to tidewater markets. Under the direction of Isaac Wistar, the PRR's Pennsylvania Canal Company subsidiary had greatly increased capacity as far south as Columbia. However, the independent Susquehanna & Tide Water Canal controlled access to Chesapeake Bay, and that company was ill equipped to accommodate the PRR's waterborne coal traffic. The PRR could of course transfer coal to railroad cars, at either Harrisburg or Columbia, for the trip east to Philadelphia. That route, over the old Philadelphia & Columbia Railroad, followed an undulating profile that impeded the efficient transportation of bulk commodities. It was certainly no match for the steadily descending grade of the Reading along the Schuylkill River. The Northern Central route to Baltimore was scarcely better. Since the 1830s, the promoters of what was then the Baltimore & Susquehanna Railroad had envisioned a rail line that could send anthracite to Baltimore rather than Philadelphia or New York. Unfortunately, their railroad suffered from adverse grades against southbound traffic. A more pervasive problem was that Baltimore was never a strong market for anthracite. The city on Chesapeake Bay was oriented to the southern states, where there was little demand for the fuel—in part because of the warm climate, in part because of the scarcity of manufacturing, and in part because of the presence of readily accessible bituminous coal reserves in the vicinity of Richmond, Virginia.

The proposed Columbia & Port Deposit line along the lower Susquehanna River promised a more efficient mechanism for sending the PRR's coal to tidewater. As early as January 1866, representatives for the PRR and its Northern Central subsidiary were elected to the board of directors of the Columbia & Port Deposit. However, the PRR's plans soon confronted the Philadelphia, Wilmington & Baltimore's efforts to gain control over the Philadelphia & Baltimore Central, and more generally to expand its influence through the territory between Philadelphia and the Susquehanna River. In December 1866, the Philadelphia, Wilmington & Baltimore completed a short branch, less than five miles in length, linking the main line at Perryville (across the Susquehanna River from Havre de Grace) with Port Deposit, the terminus of the proposed Columbia & Port Deposit Railroad. PW&B officials planned to build farther north to the mouth of Octoraro Creek, near Conowingo. From there, a route along Octoraro Creek would provide a second connection with the Philadelphia & Baltimore Central, at Rising Sun, Maryland.

With the support of PRR and Northern Central officials, the directors of the Columbia & Port Deposit elected to build the short stretch of track between Octoraro and Port Deposit rather than permit the PW&B to occupy the east bank of the Susquehanna River. In January 1867, the PRR pledged $100,000 to support the project. Construction on the Columbia & Port Deposit began in the spring of 1868. By January 1869, the first trains had reached Octoraro. For the moment, the line went no farther north. It was operated by the Philadelphia, Wilmington & Baltimore, as its only function was to serve as the western connection to the tracks of the Philadelphia & Baltimore Central.[182]

The depression of the 1870s was only one of many developments that delayed construction of the remainder of the Columbia & Port Deposit. In 1872 and 1873, the PRR built a series of coal piers at Greenwich Point in South Philadelphia, reducing the importance of a terminal at the mouth of Delaware Bay. In 1873, the Pennsylvania & Delaware Railway, another locally promoted line, opened for service. It linked Pomeroy, on the PRR main line, just west of Coatesville, Pennsylvania, with Newark, Delaware, and Delaware City, offering access to the lower reaches of the Delaware River and the eastern entrance to the Chesapeake & Delaware Canal.

By the late 1870s, PRR executives were ready to resume construction on the Columbia & Port Deposit. The Pennsylvania & Delaware Railway had proven a failure, eliminating the possibility that anthracite might move to the Delaware River along that route. In 1872, the Reading Rail Road leased the Susquehanna & Tide Water Canal, jeopardizing the Pennsylvania Canal Company's access to Chesapeake Bay and making a parallel, PRR-owned, rail line a more attractive proposition. Still, the route along the Susquehanna remained a low priority. Not until the summer of 1877 did construction crews finish laying rail all the way north to Columbia. From Columbia, traffic continued north on an existing line (the old "River Branch," completed in 1850 by the Harrisburg, Portsmouth, Mount Joy & Lancaster) to Royalton and Harrisburg.

The Port Road served few communities or industries of any consequence, and there were several factors that limited through traffic, as well. Until the PRR purchased the Philadelphia, Wilmington & Baltimore, in 1881, there was little incentive to route traffic toward Philadelphia or Baltimore via Port Deposit. In addition, the PRR owned barely enough Northern Central stock to guarantee control of the company, and the Northern Central's independent investors resisted any plans to transfer freight from their line to the Columbia & Port Deposit. That situation did not change until the PRR leased the Northern Central in 1914. By that time, the Port Road had become a useful low-grade freight line, allowing southern traffic to bypass the congestion around Philadelphia.[183]

Postwar Finance

Empires do not come cheap. The Civil War and its aftermath created unprecedented financial demands on the Pennsylvania Railroad. Wartime traffic required the construction and maintenance of tracks and bridges, the laying of steel rail, and the purchase of new locomotives and cars. The oil boom in northwestern Pennsylvania led to the construction of additional facilities, ranging from the completion of the Philadelphia & Erie Railroad to the building of the Allegheny Valley Railroad's Low Grade Division. In the decade after 1865, Thomson, Scott, and their associates moved quickly to solidify the PRR's control of the routes west of Pittsburgh and Erie, and to provide access to New York. They had built most of their empire on the back of leases, bond guarantees, and traffic agreements, minimizing the drain on the PRR's treasury. Yet many of the lines, particularly Benjamin Smith's Columbus, Chicago & Indiana Central Railway, were in such poor shape that they needed immediate infusions of capital. All across the system, technically proficient engineers struggled to remove impediments to the rapid and efficient movement of freight and passenger traffic. In the postwar era, gauge differences, weak bridges, underpowered locomotives, and small-capacity freight cars yielded to a new generation of motive power, equipment, and physical facilities.

There was no denying that efforts to modernize the Pennsylvania Railroad, and to extend its influence, would consume enormous amounts of money. Between 1869 and 1873, when the expansion boom came to an end, the Pennsylvania Railroad had placed $87 million in stocks and bonds. The par value of the PRR's outstanding stock nearly tripled, from $27.0 million to $68.1 million. That was more money than any business had ever raised, anywhere in the world, in such a short span of time.[184]

After 1865, as both the PRR's capital needs and the complexity of its operations increased, the company's executives were no longer able to devote their time to personally assist in marketing securities in American or European financial markets. Nor were they prepared to maintain a staff of securities brokers. Although PRR executives internalized many of the railroad's operations, they asserted that they "could not justify the cost of creating and maintaining our own organization and Nation-wide relations with investors and institutions . . . especially since we are in the railroad and not the banking business."[185] PRR officials further noted, "There is an advantage in having

an established relationship with reputable investment bankers with adequate capital, which is continually in touch with World-wide economic and financial conditions," inasmuch as those specialized investment-banking firms possessed "full knowledge of the investment laws of various States as well as the Federal statutes . . . and, by reason of a long experience and record of fair dealings, command the confidence of investors."[186] Accordingly, PRR managers came to rely on the services of as many as forty-eight independent investment-banking firms.[187]

The massive expansion in the PRR's capital requirements coincided with equally sweeping changes in the world of finance. The Civil War vastly increased the size of domestic capital markets, as well as the scope of American financiers, and concentrated both in New York City. The federal government financed about two-thirds of its war costs through borrowing, and issued more than $3 billion in bonds. Individual states, including Pennsylvania, borrowed many millions more. A series of laws permitted the federal government to levy income taxes, print paper currency, and grant charters for national banks, empowering those financial institutions to issue notes based on their holdings of government bonds. Federal regulations, particularly a tax on bank notes, greatly curtailed the activities of state banks. Rather than create another central bank, along the lines of the First and Second Banks of the United States, Congress in 1864 designated New York as the primary repository for credit. As a result, interest rates were generally lower in New York (and in Philadelphia, as well) than they were in the rural regions to the west. During the immediate postwar period, the federal government redeemed war bonds as quickly as the Treasury's resources would allow, injecting substantial quantities of capital into the New York markets. A steady deflationary trend worked to the benefit of creditors and made American railway securities particularly attractive to overseas investors. Each of those developments proved a boon to fledgling American investment bankers and provided a seemingly inexhaustible supply of credit for railroad promoters.[188]

Of all the financiers in the United States, the one who gained the most immediate benefit from the war was undoubtedly Jay Cooke. He began his career in

1839, in E. W. Clark & Company, and became a partner in 1843. In 1861, he established Jay Cooke & Company in partnership with his brother-in-law, William G. Moorhead, president of the Philadelphia & Erie. In March 1862, Treasury Secretary Salmon P. Chase appointed Cooke's banking house as the sole agent for a massive federal loan. Over the months that followed, Cooke became the dominant force in wartime banking, placing $1.6 billion in loans, representing more than a quarter of the debt that the Union government incurred during the war. He also marketed numerous state loans, including a $3 million Commonwealth of Pennsylvania issue during the summer of 1861. The Pennsylvania Railroad purchased 10 percent of that amount, in a show of support for the Union cause. Yet, Jay Cooke was by no means the only financier affected by the Civil War. Many others had gained valuable experience through the marketing of wartime government securities. After 1865, American investment-banking houses came to rival the financial strength and the organizational expertise of their European counterparts.[189]

By the late 1860s, investment bankers benefited from the growing availability and reliability of financial information. In 1841, Lewis Tappan had begun to collect financial information for businesses in New York City. Eight years later, Benjamin Douglass took control of the business, and began issuing credit reports. In the same year, in Cincinnati, Ohio, John M. Bradstreet established a similar credit-reporting firm, which a decade later came under the management of his brother-in-law, Robert Dun. In the decades that followed the Civil War, railway executives and investors alike had access to reliable financial data, and no longer depended on the private, specialized knowledge of market insiders.[190]

Publisher and business analyst Henry Varnum Poor played an equally important role in the dissemination of railway information. During the 1850s, Poor was editor of the *American Railroad Journal*. While he reprinted stories from newspapers and other items submitted to him—as was common practice for trade journals at that time—he was also one of the first in the financial sector to undertake statistical analyses of railway operations and finances. One of his greatest contributions to investor confidence lay in his meticulous listings of all of the railway stock and bond issues in the United States. In 1860, Poor published the first volume of the *History of the Railroads and Canals of the United States of America*, a massive compilation of data on virtually every aspect of transportation development north of Virginia and east of Ohio. He never completed the remaining two volumes, but he continued to serve investors in other ways. In connection with his son, Henry William, he established H. V. & H. W. Poor Company, the forerunner of Standard & Poor's. Beginning in 1868, he began publishing his yearly *Manual of the Railroads of the United States*, providing still more data about operating and financial conditions.[191]

Despite the regularized nature of Poor's statistics, however, he was still dependent on information supplied by railway executives—information that could be accurate, misleading, or utterly fraudulent. There were nonetheless a growing number of periodicals whose editors and readers expected timely and accurate information from the nation's railroad executives. Newspapers and journals such as *Hunt's Merchants' Magazine*, the *Bankers' Magazine*, *Railway World*, *Railway Review*, *Railway Age*, the *Railroad Gazette*, and the *Commercial and Financial Chronicle* greatly facilitated the ability of bankers and investors to evaluate the value of stock and bond offerings.[192]

Money for Expansion

As in so many other aspects of the PRR's existence, government, principally at the state level, established the parameters of executive efforts to fund construction and operation. In granting the 1846 charter, legislators had set the PRR's capitalization at $7.5 million, although the total could be raised to $10 million, at the discretion of the railroad's shareholders—an act that took place in December 1850. As the PRR's capital needs increased, its executives repeatedly requested that the legislature raise the equity ceiling, twice in 1852, and again in 1853 and 1855, with further supplements permitting an increase in bonded debt in 1854 and 1863. The supplements conformed to the conventional wisdom that suggested that a properly financed company's capitalization should be divided equally between stocks and bonds. Because bonds accounted for virtually all of the PRR's long-term debt, such a policy indicated a debt-to-equity ratio that approached one to one. Today, such a ratio could be construed as a sign of extraordinarily conservative capitalization, with very little leverage. At the time, however, Thomson's recommendations were in keeping with the evolving nature of railroad finance.[193] As financial analysts such as Henry Varnum Poor had observed, unscrupulous railroad executives possessed considerable temptation to "water" their stock by allotting large numbers of shares to construction contractors. An overabundance of equity, as a percentage of total capitalization, indicated the possibility that speculators, and not local managers, were in control of a railroad's affairs. Likewise, bond issues that were not linked to readily identifiable construction or betterment expenditures raised suspicions that railway executives were assigning routine operating costs to the capital account, thus artificially inflating net earnings. Parity between debt and equity was a sign of a conservatively managed company, and therefore indicative of a relatively safe investment.[194]

Through their decision to pour $9 million in retained wartime earnings back into the physical plant, the PRR's directors demonstrated their ongoing commitment to financial conservatism. The installation of a second track along virtually the entire main line, at a cost of $7 million, was funded entirely through reinvested earnings, as were a number of other smaller projects. As a result, the 1867 book value of the much-improved route was listed at $13.4 million, virtually the same as when the original line was completed in 1854. In later years, investment analysts and government regulators would find fault with the low capitalization of the PRR's physical plant. At the time, however, the funding of improvements through reinvestment, rather than through the issuance of new securities, greatly reduced the PRR's fixed charges. During the postwar years, that tendency would give the PRR an important advantage over rival trunk lines, such as the Erie, that possessed more bloated capital structures.[195]

Despite the use of retained earnings, Thomson and his fellow executives were in desperate need of additional capital. As in the antebellum period, Europeans showed considerably more interest in the PRR's mort-

gage bonds than in the company's stock. Yet, the Pennsylvania Railroad remained something of an anomaly in European financial circles. The Crédit Mobilier scandal of 1872–73, the economic depression that followed the Panic of 1873, and the labor unrest of 1877 discouraged Europeans from seeking investment opportunities in the United States. Thus, as late as 1878, the PRR was one of only six U.S. railroads whose stocks were widely traded in London, a privileged status that was based on the railroad's skilled management and conservative capitalization. Even so, the London branch of the Rothschild family showed little interest in American railroad securities, and it was not until after the death of Lionel N. Rothschild, in 1879, that his heirs began to invest heavily in the PRR.[196]

Thanks to the hesitancy of European investors, the PRR's bond sales were temporarily sluggish. Beginning in 1865, the directors authorized a £100,000 issue of 6 percent bonds. The following January, the board increased the amount to £500,000, equivalent to $2.5 million, with Foster & Braithwaite and the London, Asiatic & American Company jointly handling a £200,000 consignment. The bonds sold poorly, however, and by June the PRR was offering an additional $1 million in bonds to the American financial markets. By the end of 1866, the PRR had placed scarcely more than $1.5 million of the $3.5 million on offer.[197]

As in the prewar period, PRR officials readily augmented the company's bonded debt with additional stock, particularly when bond sales proved slow. However, European investors were even more averse to American railroad stocks than they were to bonds, believing that equity investments were both volatile and risky. In 1861, for example, Americans held more than 92 percent of PRR stock, with only 6.93 percent in the hands of 116 foreign investors, mainly in Britain. A decade later, the numbers had barely changed, with 206 foreign stockholders owning 7.36 percent of the PRR's total shares. Not until the late nineteenth century would Europeans own greater equity in the PRR— and then only because they had earlier purchased bonds that they were able to convert to stock.[198]

The issuance of additional stock required legislative approval, but that step was generally less of a problem than was vocal opposition from a few malcontent investors. In May 1855, the Pennsylvania legislature had permitted the board to raise the PRR's stock from $18 million to $20 million. Despite the expense associated with Thomson's assistance to western railroads, much of the stock had gone unissued, and by the end of 1863 only $13.4 million was outstanding. The total rose substantially during 1864, thanks to Thomson's determination to fund the completion of the subsidiary Philadelphia & Erie. In March 1866 the PRR received yet another charter supplement, raising the authorized amount of stock to $30 million. The provision also raised the debt ceiling to the same level, continuing the maxim of keeping debt and equity obligations in parity with one another. However, the same economic forces that dampened investor enthusiasm for the PRR's bonds also affected stock sales. In addition, the members of the Philadelphia Select and Common Councils were strongly opposed to the issuance of additional shares (which they could no longer legally purchase), arguing that it would dilute the city's influence over the PRR's policies. As a result, PRR officials relinquished the rights contained in the 1866 charter supplement. Then, in March 1867 they accepted in its stead a second, similar proposal, raising the maximum level of stocks and of bonds to $35 million apiece.[199]

The willingness of the PRR board to issue additional securities did not by any means mark the end of Thomson's problems, for he soon faced dissent from a few energetic shareholders. A similar dispute had erupted during the early 1850s, as conservative board members disputed Chief Engineer Thomson's suggestions that bonds would be necessary to complete the main line. The postwar controversy was far less serious in its consequences. The chief instigator was Colonel James Page, a longtime critic of PRR management. During the Civil War, Page had opposed the links between Thomson, Scott, and their associates and freight forwarders such as the Union Line and the Empire Line. During the years that followed, Page criticized the PRR's rate structure, the disposition of the tonnage tax commutation funds, the PRR's aid to western railroads, and its dividend policies. By the time of the 1867 shareholders' meeting, he was fixated on the PRR's increased capitalization, and somehow managed to persuade his fellow investors to appoint an investigating committee to look into the matter. Based on his long and tiring experience with Page's rants, Thomson calculated that the

committee would provide his opponent with a forum in which Page would discredit himself. Such was the case and, with the sole exception of Page, members of the investigating committee concluded that Thomson had been appropriately managing the railroad, and that the president's expansionist vision did indeed merit the issuance of additional securities.[200]

Beginning in 1867, as Thomson moved aggressively to counter Jay Gould's strategic moves in Ohio and Indiana, the PRR experienced a rapid increase in capitalization. In April, a month after the General Assembly raised the PRR's debt limit, the board approved a $35 million consolidated mortgage bond issue, maturing in 1910. Investors shied away from the bonds, which were inferior to the existing first and second mortgages. By 1870, less than half the amount had been subscribed. The bonds also sold at between 90 and 93 percent of par—a steep discount for an established railroad in a time of general prosperity. Once again, the board responded to the slow pace of bond sales by relying on equity financing. Between 1868 and 1873, following additional charter amendments, the PRR's outstanding stock increased by 224 percent, from $21 million to $68 million.[201]

By the late 1860s, many American railroads had established exclusive relationships with banking houses, but the PRR changed allies more often than most. The railroad's executives initially worked with Jay Cooke, and his banking house was instrumental in providing access to European financial markets. In March 1870 Cooke organized the first truly large underwriting syndicate in the United States in order to guarantee placement of the PRR's bonds, at 90 percent of par. Under that arrangement, the PRR received its money immediately, regardless of whether Cooke had sold his full allotment of bonds to third parties. In return, PRR officials promised that they would not market any of the company's bonds until after Cooke had sold to investors all of the securities in his firm's portfolio.[202]

After 1870, PRR officials placed less reliance on Cooke, in part because the financier was increasingly involved in western railroads such as the Northern Pacific. That involvement triggered the Panic of 1873, which brought a swift end to Cooke's influence. Even before that disaster, however, Thomson, Scott, and their associates were depending more heavily on the services of three closely related individuals—Junius Spencer Morgan, his son John Pierpont Morgan, and Anthony J. "Tony" Drexel—each of them at the pinnacle of transatlantic financial markets.

Before the Civil War, Junius Morgan had made his reputation as a partner in the London banking house of Peabody & Company. Peabody retired in 1854, and the firm became J. S. Morgan & Company. In 1857, J. Pierpont Morgan briefly joined his father's firm before moving to New York to take a position with Duncan, Sherman & Company, the American ally of Peabody & Company. In 1864, he joined forces with Charles H. Dabney, forming Dabney, Morgan & Company. In the process, J. P. Morgan gained from his father and his other business associates a comprehensive knowledge of railway finance, along with a wealth of business connections.

In conjunction with Tony Drexel, Junius Morgan handled several issues that financed improvements to Harsimus Cove and other terminal facilities opposite New York City. In April 1869, J. S. Morgan & Company, in cooperation with Drexel & Company, secured a £360,000 loan for the United Companies. Junius Morgan placed another £500,000 ($2.5 million) loan in January 1871, in tandem with Drexel and the Philadelphia-based J. & W. Welsh & Company. Following the PRR lease of the United Companies, J. S. Morgan & Company placed two £300,000, 6 percent bond issues, in cooperation with his Philadelphia allies. Pierpont Morgan informed his father that the bonds had sold very quickly, earning handsome commissions for the house of Morgan. In February 1875, a subsequent United Companies bond issue, for £460,000 ($2.3 million), sold equally well.[203]

J. P. Morgan proved extraordinarily useful in a variety of projects that were only indirectly related to the PRR's operations. It is not clear precisely how Morgan became involved in the western ambitions of Thomson, Scott, and other executives. It may have come through the intermediary efforts of Tony Drexel. At the same time, however, former PRR executive Andrew Carnegie was helping to bring together such financial partners as Thomson, Scott, and Morgan. In any event, by early 1872, J. P. Morgan was handling much of the financing for the Cairo & Vincennes Railroad, the PRR's ill-starred link to the Southwest. When

that company went bankrupt early in 1874, Morgan supervised the reorganization and replaced the hapless former Union general Ambrose Burnside as the company's president. In association with Carnegie, Morgan also marketed bonds for the St. Louis Bridge Company, a project that PRR officials regarded as a key element in their access to the trans-Mississippi West.

Closer to home, the most evident link between Morgan, Carnegie, and the PRR involved financing for two of the PRR's subsidiaries, the Philadelphia & Erie and the Allegheny Valley. Carnegie, who had learned much from Thomson, now turned the tables on his former mentor and, unasked, offered advice on the placement of PRR securities. In 1871, Carnegie persuaded Thomson to trade $5 million worth of Philadelphia & Erie 6 percent gold bonds for a like amount of 7 percent Allegheny Valley bonds—which, because they offered interest payable in U.S. paper currency, were unlikely to find buyers in the British market. With the Philadelphia & Erie bonds in hand, Carnegie traveled to London and negotiated an agreement with Baring Brothers to sell the securities at par. A crisis in the European financial markets caused Baring Brothers to withdraw from the arrangement, and a frantic Carnegie placed the entire matter before Junius Morgan. The investment banker drove a hard bargain, agreeing to find buyers for the bonds at 87 percent of par, and then selling them all, in tandem with Drexel & Company, at considerable profit. In December 1871, the elder Morgan made arrangements to place another $2 million in Philadelphia & Erie securities, followed in the spring of 1873 by a $2 million consignment of Allegheny Valley bonds to fund the construction of the Low Grade Line. Carnegie was apparently not involved in those transactions.[204]

By the late 1870s, however, PRR officials were placing far less reliance on the Morgans for their capital needs. Part of the difficulty lay with Junius Morgan, who was reluctant to yield authority to rival investment banking houses. Junius Morgan routinely cooperated with other investment bankers, but he generally demanded that his firm be given top billing. Furthermore, he would not permit Thomson to stipulate which investment banking houses should be his allies, and he refused to take part in the transaction.[205]

More important, J. P. Morgan's growing association with the New York Central led him away from the PRR, while establishing his reputation as one of the most innovative and successful investment bankers on either side of the Atlantic. William H. Vanderbilt, heir to Cornelius Vanderbilt's New York Central system, desperately needed capital in order to fend off Jay Gould's efforts to create yet another railroad empire.[206] Vanderbilt was also anxious to avoid inquiries by the Hepburn Committee of the New York state legislature, regarding pooling arrangements and rate differentials. He elected to dispose of a substantial portion of his family holdings, and Morgan organized a consortium of investment bankers to place the shares. In addition to collecting a whopping $3 million commission, Morgan could take immense pride in having disposed of the securities without creating a glut on the market and eroding their worth. Morgan established himself as *the* investment banker representing the interests of the New York Central and became a member of that company's board. Despite his ties to the NYC, however, his leadership role in the investment-banking community ensured that he would also be involved in the marketing of PRR securities.[207]

Morgan remained in New York, a city that had long since surpassed Philadelphia as the nation's financial center. Because the PRR was a Philadelphia corporation, Morgan employed Anthony J. Drexel as a useful front man in the Quaker City. Tony Drexel was a Philadelphia native and the son of investment banker Francis Martin Drexel. In 1847, at only twenty-one years of age, he became a partner in his father's business. The timing was propitious, as Drexel & Company benefited from the borrowing associated with the Mexican–American War, the California Gold Rush, and the Civil War. Even though they were a Philadelphia firm, the Drexels were represented on Wall Street, after the formation of VanVleck, Read, Drexel & Company in 1855. When Francis Drexel died in 1863, his son was the most respected financier in Philadelphia, even if Jay Cooke was more widely known. In 1870, Tony Drexel landed the PRR account, the ripest plum on the biggest tree in the orchard.[208]

Tony Drexel's ties to the PRR soon attracted the attention of the Morgans, then on the way to becoming the preeminent banking family in the United States,

and all three cooperated to a significant extent. Generally speaking, Tony Drexel was most closely connected to the world of Philadelphia finance, J. P. Morgan to Wall Street, and Junius Morgan to the London exchange. More accurately, however, each of those three individuals, and their associates, moved with considerable fluidity through the realms of transatlantic finance. Drexel valued Morgan's New York affiliations, and as a carrot could offer a share of the PRR's business. Drexel depended on Morgan's sense of loyalty and fairness, did what Morgan told him to do, and in return collected substantial commissions that involved little work and a low degree of risk. In 1871, the two men formed Drexel, Morgan & Company, but the partnership was based in New York, not Philadelphia, and Morgan was clearly the dominant partner.[209]

Drexel, Morgan was well positioned to take advantage of the further increases in the PRR's capitalization that occurred during the early, expansionist years of the 1870s. In December 1869, the General Assembly allowed all corporations chartered in the commonwealth to raise their stock and bond capitalization by 50 percent above their existing limits, which in the case of the PRR permitted an increase in both shares and bonds from $35 million to $52.5 million. Yet, even that was not enough, given the need to rebuild the PRR's midwestern subsidiaries (particularly the Columbus, Chicago & Indiana Central) and improve operating conditions on the Northern Central, the Philadelphia & Erie, and the leased United Companies.[210]

In February 1873, the General Assembly again permitted Thomson to increase the PRR's capitalization. The new limit stood at $151.7 million, although it would be 1901 before that many shares were actually in the hands of investors. Even more sweeping changes affected the PRR's bonded debt. In March 1873 the board approved a consolidated mortgage of $100 million. That was a staggeringly large amount, given that the market value of the PRR was approximately $94 million, with the value on the balance sheet only a little more than half of that amount. PRR officials had no intention of issuing $100 million in bonds, however. Under the provisions of the mortgage authorization, the board reserved the right to release bonds in increments, and under varying terms—a common practice that reduced the number of times that the

PRR's lobbyists would have to request state legislators to increase the railroad's debt ceiling.[211]

The PRR offered the bonds in two initial lots, in July 1873 and again in July 1874. The timing of the new consolidated mortgage was extraordinarily poor, given the depressed economic conditions of the 1870s. As a result, the bonds went overseas, primarily to Britain. Moreover, the level of borrowing began to raise concerns among investors. In February 1872, PRR stock had peaked at nearly $65 a share, and then it began to decline steadily as financial analysts expressed increasing reservations at the PRR's spiraling debt obligations. Although dividends remained quite high, at 10 percent, the PRR's directors were increasingly concerned that there was too little cash available to pay them—and in November 1873 they voted to satisfy the promised 5 percent semiannual dividend with scrip. Despite some doubts regarding the security of the new consolidated mortgage, the first consignment of 7 percent bonds sold well. The London, Asiatic & American Company took the entire allotment of £2 million ($10 million), at 90 percent of par, and quickly placed the bonds with investors.[212]

By 1874, as the economic recession deepened, Tony Drexel became more intimately involved in the PRR's financing. In May, the railroad issued an additional £3 million of the consolidated mortgage bonds, at 6 percent, using much of the proceeds to retire the company's second mortgage, due to mature the following year. Drexel, Morgan took the lead in organizing a consortium of three banking houses (Drexel & Company, Philip Speyer & Company, and the London, Asiatic & American Company) to market the bonds. In August 1875, when the board authorized another $5 million general mortgage bond issue, Tony Drexel struggled to sell the securities in the United States. Philadelphia investors purchased only $2 million of the offering, although at a respectably modest discount of 96 percent of par. The remainder of the bonds sold on the London exchanges, at a far less satisfactory 90 percent.[213]

Yet, Morgan and Drexel did far more than raise capital for the PRR. Tony Drexel helped to mediate rate agreements between the PRR and the other trunk lines—a function that J. P. Morgan would more famously embrace a decade or so later. Drexel was also a useful intermediary for some of the PRR's real-estate transactions, including the 1875 purchase of the prime waterfront real estate at the old Philadelphia Navy Yard. Even before his death in 1893, however, Drexel's ties to the PRR began to fade. During the 1880s and into the 1890s, the New York firm of Kuhn, Loeb & Company increasingly served as the PRR's financial outlet.[214]

Even though the PRR's executives became steadily more dependent on Jay Cooke, the Morgans, Tony Drexel, and other investment bankers for infusions of capital and other services, they did not permit those financiers to dictate corporate policy. Thomson, Scott, and their fellow managers borrowed heavily, yet always for productive purposes. They invested the newly acquired capital, along with a large dose of retained earnings, to increase the capacity and the operating efficiency of the PRR system. While Thomson and Scott engaged in a few speculative ventures, they did so with their own money, and they rarely used the PRR itself as a vehicle for personal financial gain. That fiscal restraint, coupled with the healthy net income that accompanied judicious investments in the physical plant and in equipment, reassured domestic and overseas investors that the PRR was a safe haven for their capital. The high level of investor confidence ensured that investment bankers would rarely experience serious difficulties in placing PRR securities, so long as the economy was reasonably robust. The ready market for the PRR's stocks and bonds meant that those bankers possessed far less leverage over the railroad than they exerted over weaker carriers with more speculative financing. Investment bankers became increasingly important as purveyors of capital, but the Pennsylvania Railroad was run by engineers, and not by financiers.

Reorganizing the Empire

The early 1870s witnessed a second great period of organizational transformation on the Pennsylvania Railroad. During the 1850s, Thomson, Herman Haupt, and Herman J. Lombaert had made numerous refinements to the PRR's corporate structure, often borrowing liberally from developments on other railroads.

Yet, the PRR's managerial structure remained both small and highly centralized. At first, and with the company's business largely restricted to the distance between Harrisburg and Pittsburgh, there seemed little need for a large and layered corps of management. Within little more than a decade of its incorporation, however, the PRR had greatly broadened the scope of its operations. The PRR acquired the Harrisburg, Portsmouth, Mount Joy & Lancaster Railroad, and then the Philadelphia & Columbia and the remainder of the Main Line of Public Works. Investments in the Northern Central and the Philadelphia & Erie soon followed. West of Pittsburgh, Thomson negotiated alliances with connecting lines, investing in their securities and developing agreements for the interchange of traffic. The Civil War accelerated the connectivity between the PRR and other carriers.

As the PRR expanded, its management grew incrementally, and syncretically. The prevailing assumption among Thomson's contemporaries—one that was not limited to the PRR, or for that matter to business enterprise in general—was that a large and complex management system would prove unwieldy. Problems of communication and coordination, managers believed, would outweigh any benefits associated with greater executive control over a multifaceted business enterprise. As such, Thomson and his fellow PRR associates developed a wide variety of unofficial managerial functions. Freight forwarders accommodated many of the PRR's shipments, and their personnel coordinated the railroad's traffic functions, particularly those involving relations with western affiliates. Holding companies enabled Scott to oversee a wide variety of projects, ranging from railroad construction and acquisition to efforts to control rates.

The accretive management structure proved remarkably successful, but by the early 1870s it was no longer adequate for the PRR's needs. Quite simply, the PRR had outgrown the system that Thomson and others had devised to manage it. During the decade that followed the end of the Civil War, American railroads had experienced a second great period of expansion and combination, mimicking the one that had taken place during the 1850s. In short order, the maximum length of a system that could be effectively operated under one management grew from a few hundred

miles to several thousand miles. The PRR was in the forefront of that process. During the 1860s, the booming oil trade greatly increased the importance of the Philadelphia & Erie. The events of 1869 had given the PRR an instant western rail empire. The most important lines to the west of Pittsburgh and Erie soon became part of the Pennsylvania Company, and were not under the direct, day-to-day management of the Pennsylvania Railroad. The growth of the western part of the system nonetheless increased the responsibility of PRR officials, both to coordinate the interchange of traffic and to ensure that the strategic goals of Lines West meshed with those of Lines East. In 1871, the lease of the United Companies gave the PRR a secure route to New York, but it also greatly increased the complexity of the PRR's operations. By the end of the 1870s the PRR had attained a system length of about four thousand miles, and accordingly required a more sophisticated management structure.[215]

More broadly, by 1870 the PRR, in common with other railroads, had become part of an integrated system of transportation. PRR engineers had largely eliminated the physical barriers to integrated operations, by constructing new lines (most notably the Connecting Railway and the Junction Railroad in Philadelphia), building bridges, and standardizing track gauge, ensuring the free flow of traffic. With the elimination of engineering impediments came a corresponding increase in the level of traffic moving from one railroad to another. As a result, railroad managers redirected their efforts from the construction and operation of their own lines to the development of cooperative relationships with other carriers.[216] Efforts to coordinate interline service and to resolve the administrative (as opposed to technological) problems that such shipments entailed created new layers of oversight. The presence of multiple transportation arteries, particularly between Chicago and the east coast, forced railroad executives to develop a system of rate differentials that accounted for the value of the commodity and the route that it followed. As more and more shipments transited multiple railroads, managers needed to determine the allocation of the proper portion of the rate to the various carriers involved, and not merely the total tariff that applied to a particular cargo. They developed documents and other administrative procedures that facilitated the calculation of interline rates, and kept track of the increasing number of cars that strayed from PRR rails. Such paperwork included waybills (records that traveled with a shipment, specifying the type of cargo, origin and destination, and consignor and consignee) and bills of lading (documents issued to the shipper that transferred the ownership and responsibility of the cargo to the carrier). By the late 1870s, those new inter-firm traffic and rate agreements, as well as through billing arrangements, had largely superseded the semi-autonomous fast freight lines such as the Union Line and the Empire Line.[217]

During and immediately after the Civil War, as operational complexity grew and as PRR executives developed more formal relations with other railroads, the board refined the company's incipient line-and-staff organization. By May 1869, the board added a third and a fourth vice president, with the numerical designations again reflecting seniority rather than job description. In general, however, one of the vice presidents oversaw relations with connecting railroads, one had jurisdiction over issues pertaining to accounting, one kept track of the finances of the PRR's subsidiaries, and one coordinated engineering matters.[218] The president and the four vice presidents, along with their assistants and the PRR secretary composed the General Office Department. By 1869, the directors maintained six other departments—the Transportation Department, the Accounting Department, the Treasury Department, the Supplying Department, the Legal Department, and the Engineer Department.

As always, the Transportation Department was the most important single unit on the railroad, representing perhaps 95 percent of the company's employees. As he had throughout his long presidency, Thomson remained in charge of the Transportation Department. Three of the other departments (General Office, Accounting, and Treasury) continued the same basic functions as in the 1858 reorganization. The Supplying Department, which dated to 1866, centralized purchasing functions under the direction of a purchasing agent.[219]

The Legal Department traced its origins to 1854, and the appointment of a solicitor at Pittsburgh, to augment the work of the Philadelphia staff. By the summer of 1858, there were eleven district solicitors on the PRR, with an additional four on the Philadelphia & Erie, once the PRR gained control over that company. As the railroad's legal functions grew in size and complexity, the board accorded its attorneys departmental status. Effective May 3, 1869, the board created the Legal Department, under the authority of William J. Howard, who became the PRR's first general solicitor. Huntingdon County attorney John Scott exerted considerable influence over the postwar Legal Department. The railroad first used his services in 1857, and for the next eight years Scott was a PRR special counsel, working on retainer. In 1868, the Pennsylvania legislature appointed him to the United States Senate, where he served until 1875. He then returned to Pittsburgh as general counsel for the Pennsylvania Company and was responsible for organizing the complex legal issues associated with the Lines West of Pittsburgh and Erie. On July 1, 1877, he became the PRR's general counsel at Pittsburgh and almost immediately faced a trial by fire, in the form of the riots that roiled the city later that month. In October, the board promoted him to the position of general solicitor for the Pennsylvania Railroad and head of the Legal Department. Over the next eighteen years, he was largely responsible for developing the organizational structure of the Legal Department and for coping with the thousands of cases that his attorneys prosecuted in any given year.[220]

Over the course of the nineteenth century, the makeup of the PRR's engineering functions varied more than any other aspect of the company's organization. It was typical for the PRR to maintain a large central engineering staff during times of growth, which entailed extensive new construction and the rebuilding of existing and newly acquired lines. When the pace of expansion slowed, particularly during economic depressions, the central engineering staff shrank accordingly. William Hasell Wilson had worked for the PRR since 1856, and as the railroad expanded, so did his duties. By January 1859, he was resident engineer for the entire main line, between Philadelphia and Pittsburgh, with associated branches. In addition to overseeing the track, roadbed, bridges, and buildings, Wilson was responsible for acquiring real estate, providing water and fuel for the railroad's locomotives, and purchasing the supplies necessary for maintenance functions. In 1862, Wilson's title changed from resident engineer to chief engineer, although his duties remained essentially the same, as the individual responsible for all system-wide engineering matters. With wartime traffic placing additional demands on the physical plant, Wilson received the assistance of an engineer of bridges and buildings, as well as the services of resident engineers on the Eastern, Middle, and Pittsburgh divisions. Effective January 1, 1868, the board responded to the anticipated postwar growth in railway construction by separating major new projects from routine engineering matters. With the office of chief engineer abolished, Wilson took charge of the Engineer Department, as chief engineer of construction, based in Philadelphia. His son, John A. Wilson, became the chief engineer of maintenance-of-way, part of the Transportation Department, with his headquarters located at the site of the PRR's shops at Altoona.[221]

The lease of the United Companies, in 1871, induced a significant change in the PRR's organizational structure. It was no longer possible for a single individual to coordinate routine operations across the entire system east of Pittsburgh and Erie. The solution was to decentralize operational control, in effect creating three companies within the PRR. Beginning in December 1871, and culminating with the organization manual introduced on March 1, 1873, the board divided the Lines East of Pittsburgh and Erie into three "Grand Divisions," one for the PRR itself (with headquarters in Altoona), one for the United Railroads of New Jersey (based in Jersey City), and one for the Philadelphia & Erie (based in Williamsport). Those three Grand Divisions encompassed the PRR's most important and most heavily trafficked routes, linking Philadelphia to, respectively, Pittsburgh, New York, and Erie.

Other, less important routes were left out of the Grand Division structure, generally because they were controlled through stock ownership rather than through lease or purchase. One example was the Northern Central Railway, with its route from Baltimore north to Sunbury. Many of the other shareholders were Baltimore natives who were more anxious to increase the value of their investment than they were to accede to the dictates of PRR corporate strategy. They were often able to argue, convincingly, that a lease to the PRR would enable that Philadelphia corporation to discriminate against Baltimore. One of the chief impediments was John Hulme, who served on the PRR board from 1857 until 1867. Hulme also owned a substantial block of Northern Central stock and accused PRR managers of exploiting its control of the company. He was a strong opponent of leasing the Northern Central to the PRR, and he even used the Maryland courts to block further negotiations. In April 1874, only weeks before Hulme's death, the Northern Central's independent stockholders rejected a lease to the PRR. In December, a frustrated J. Donald Cameron, an individual closely aligned with the PRR, resigned the presidency of the Northern Central, along with several directors. With the Northern Central essentially bereft of leadership, and with lease negotiations bogged down in the worsening economic crisis, all of the parties involved agreed on a compromise. The Northern Central would remain a nominally independent corporation, with its headquarters in Baltimore, but it would be operated by the PRR, as if it were a Grand Division.[222]

Several other important carriers lay outside the Grand Division structure. They included the Baltimore & Potomac Railroad, between Baltimore and Washington, a route that connected with the Northern Central but that relied on the independent Philadelphia, Wilmington & Baltimore for direct access to the Quaker City. The West Jersey Railroad (after 1896, the West Jersey & Seashore Railroad) was composed of nearly a dozen local lines that branched off of the main Camden & Amboy and Philadelphia & Trenton routes across New Jersey. Many had been built with the support, or at least the acquiescence, of the Joint Companies and its successor, the United Companies, whose officials were anxious to placate local interests and avoid any legislative interference with their cross-state transportation monopoly.[223] Like the Northern Central, both the Baltimore & Potomac and the West Jersey possessed their own boards of directors and a small-scale line-and-staff corporate structure. They fielded senior officers (who coordinated each company's activities with the rest of the PRR system) and middle managers (who ran the trains on their railroad).

The top-level managers of the PRR's General Office Department were ultimately responsible for overseeing the long-term corporate strategy affecting the Grand Divisions and affiliated companies to the east of Pittsburgh and Erie. President Thomson was the chief executive officer, and he also served as head of the Transportation Department. He possessed ultimate authority over all traffic matters, including rates. First Vice President Scott continued his existing duties associated with maintaining strategic (as opposed to daily operating) relationships among the PRR and its connections, particularly the Pennsylvania Company lines in Ohio, Indiana, and Illinois. Second vice president Herman J. Lombaert had charge of PRR correspondence, accounting matters, the appointment of senior personnel on Lines West, and, for a short time, traffic and rates. The third vice president kept watch on the financial condition of the PRR's subsidiaries. Beginning in 1872, as the PRR began to invest in coal lands, he took responsibility for those properties, as well. As was the case throughout the postwar period, however, the duties assigned to each vice president changed with considerable frequency, according to the PRR's strategic requirements and in response to the promotion, retirement, or death of key individuals.[224]

The decentralization of authority to the Grand Divisions in turn led the board to create an executive tier, below the level of the General Office Department, to coordinate day-to-day operations across the routes to the east of Pittsburgh and Erie. In December 1871, the board established the office of general manager to oversee transportation and traffic functions on all three Grand Divisions, as well as the other lines that were outside of the Grand Division structure. The general manager was the PRR's chief operating officer, reporting directly to Thomson, the chief executive officer. The general manager possessed full authority over personnel and purchasing matters, collected and interpreted operating statistics, and calculated the capital needs of each Grand Division. Typically, the PRR's general manager and his staff filled the same role on subsidiaries such as the Northern Central, the Baltimore & Potomac, and the West Jersey, ensuring coordinated operation across the system. He was also responsible for ensuring smooth traffic flows between Lines East and Lines West, as well as with other railroads.

Alexander J. Cassatt, superintendent of transportation on the PRR, was the ideal candidate for the general manager's job. In December 1871, shortly before establishing the United Railroads of New Jersey Grand Division, the board promoted Cassatt to general manager. His former position of general superintendent on the PRR was left vacant—indicating that Cassatt was in effect the chief operating officer both for the PRR main line west to Pittsburgh and, as general manager, for all of Lines East. In addition to holding supervisory line authority over each of the Grand Divisions, Cassatt relied on the assistance of his staff officers, including the superintendent of transportation, the superintendent of motive power, the chief engineer of maintenance-of-way, the engineer of bridges and buildings, the superintendent of telegraph, and the purchasing agent for the Supplying Department.[225]

For a time, Cassatt had control over both transportation and traffic functions, in collaboration with Thomson. In April 1872, however, an overworked Thomson relinquished his authority over traffic and rates. Direct supervision over the general freight agent and the general passenger agent and their staffs then went to Second Vice President Lombaert. Unfortunately, Lombaert was in poor health, both physically and mentally, and in all likelihood Cassatt and Thomson continued to set traffic policy within the Transportation Department. For a very brief period (between March and June 1873) Cassatt was in charge of all traffic personnel, as well as train operations. Thereafter, the creation of the Freight Department divided traffic oversight between Cassatt and second vice president George Brooke Roberts (who had replaced Lombaert in March 1873).[226]

Scott's election to the presidency in June 1874 coincided with the onset of the depression that followed the Panic of 1873. As such, PRR executives were anxious to capture as much business as possible, and at the most remunerative rates. For the first time in the PRR's history, Scott and his fellow executives began to refine the company's traffic functions. Until 1874, there was scant coordination between those who set rates and those who incurred the expense of providing transportation—or, as one PRR executive noted, "no office of the company found its ambition and *principal*

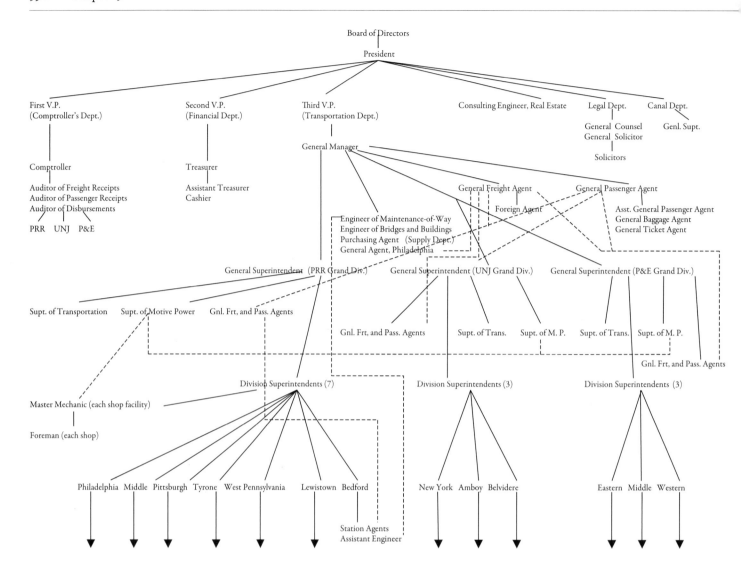

duty in earning not a revenue merely, but a profit, by rates."[227]

Although Thomson had been in charge of the Transportation Department, Scott and all of his successors relinquished that authority to whichever vice president possessed the responsibility for conducting transportation. In July 1874, shortly after Scott became president, the board promoted Cassatt from general manager to third vice president, in charge of all transportation and traffic functions. The new general manager, Frank Thomson, shared with Cassatt supervision of the Freight Department and the newly created Passenger Department, but—unlike his predecessor—he had no power to set rates. Beginning in 1881, the general manager lost his remaining authority over traffic functions, and thereafter concentrated solely on the running of trains.[228]

The July 1, 1874, reorganization that accompanied Scott's election to the presidency also produced changes in the PRR's engineering functions. With the deepening recession ensuring that little new construction would be taking place, the board dissolved the central Engineer Department, leaving the remaining routine maintenance-of-way functions in the hands of the assistant engineers on each division. William Hasell Wilson, chief engineer of construction since 1868, became a consulting engineer and possessed sufficient spare time to serve briefly as president of the Philadelphia & Erie. An engineer of maintenance-of-way (a post established in 1870) and an engineer of bridges and buildings (established in 1863), reporting to the general manager, were the principal remaining individuals responsible for developing standards for track, roadbed, and structures on Lines East.[229]

As part of the 1874 reorganization, Wilson resigned the presidency of the Philadelphia & Erie to take charge of the new Real Estate Department, exercising some of the same functions that he had undertaken, first as resident engineer and then as chief engineer.[230] On many western railroads, particularly those that had received large land grants, real estate department personnel encouraged settlement by migrants and immigrants. On the PRR, however, the primary purpose of the Real Estate Department was to acquire the land and the buildings that the PRR required for its operations, including the wharf facilities at the site of the old Philadelphia Navy Yard. However, Real Estate De-

partment personnel also attended to developmental projects such as the residential suburb of Bryn Mawr, west of Philadelphia. The new Real Estate Department blended the surveying and mapping responsibilities formerly undertaken by the Engineer Department with the deed and tax functions that had earlier been a part of the Legal Department. Despite their reduced responsibilities, Legal Department personnel were kept quite busy, and by the end of the century its seventy local solicitors were endeavoring to resolve some two thousand pending cases on Lines East alone.[231]

Below the first-tier executives in the General Office Department and their subordinates (the general

Figure 39. By the mid-1870s, PRR officials had developed a full-fledged decentralized line-and-staff corporate structure. This simplified 1874 organization chart reflects the changes that took place in 1873 and 1874, in response to the 1871 lease of the United New Jersey Railroad & Canal Companies, the recession that followed the Panic of 1873, and the death of J. Edgar Thomson in 1874. The line of authority flowed from the president (who was the chief executive officer but, after 1874, no longer the head of the Transportation Department), to the vice president in charge of the Transportation Department (who was at that time the third vice president, Alexander J. Cassatt), to the general manager (the chief operating officer), and then to the general superintendents of each of the three Grand Divisions—the Pennsylvania Railroad (PRR), the United Railroads of New Jersey (UNJ), and the Philadelphia & Erie (P&E). From each general superintendent, the line flowed down to the division superintendents (seven on the PRR, three on the UNJ, and three on the P&E). Each division superintendent was responsible for the safe and efficient movement of trains on his division, assisted by a staff that accommodated the basic functions of conducting transportation, maintaining the right of way, maintaining locomotives and cars, and soliciting business. The master mechanics and foremen who maintained equipment at each shop facility reported to their respective division superintendents, as well as to the superintendent of motive power. Likewise, the assistant engineers in charge of divisional maintenance-of-way functions were under the supervision of the division superintendents, as well as the engineer of maintenance-of-way, who in turn reported to the general manager of Lines East. With little new construction taking place, there was no separate Engineer Department, as there had been during the late 1860s and into the early 1870s. By 1874, the PRR had developed a traffic function, reflected by the presence of a general freight agent and a general passenger agent, and their staffs. Yet, they reported to the general manager and the third vice president, not to a separate vice president in charge of traffic (after 1881, the general manager no longer had authority over traffic functions, and he concentrated solely on operating matters). In addition, most of the key traffic personnel—in the form of the station agents on each division—reported to the division superintendents, as well as to the general freight and passenger agents. Not included on this chart are the leased lines outside those three Grand Divisions, including the Northern Central and the Baltimore & Potomac, which the PRR operated together as a de facto Grand Division. Likewise, the Lines West of Pittsburgh and Erie, most of which were controlled by the Pennsylvania Company, were part of a separate organizational structure that shared only a common president and several overlapping board members with the PRR proper.

Organization chart based on J. Elfreth Watkins, Pennsylvania Railroad Company, 1846–1896 *(unpublished ms., 1896), vol. 2, "Organization and Departments," 12.*

manager and his staff) lay a third tier of managers. Each Grand Division was under the authority of a general superintendent, a line officer who reported to the general manager. The general superintendent of each Grand Division was assisted by a superintendent of transportation, a superintendent of motive power, a principal assistant engineer, a general freight agent, and a general ticket agent.

Organizationally, every Grand Division was of equal status, but some were more equal than others. The superintendent of transportation for the Pennsylvania Railroad Grand Division maintained equipment records and was in charge of car distribution on Lines East. His counterpart, the superintendent of motive power on the PRR Grand Division, oversaw motive power and equipment matters affecting all of Lines East—a necessary arrangement at a time when PRR officials were moving rapidly toward standardized locomotive designs. That arrangement persisted until 1882, when the board established a general superintendent of motive power with responsibility for Lines East. In addition, many of the PRR personnel who were responsible for coordinating activities across Lines East (such as the general freight agent, the general passenger agent, and the purchasing agent) held comparable positions on the PRR subsidiaries that lay outside the Grand Division Structure. As a rule of thumb, then, officials associated with each Grand Division or subsidiary handled all of the day-to-day operations that were confined to their territories. Any functions that required coordination (for example, traffic functions) or could be more efficiently spread across the company as a whole (such as purchasing) ensured that a PRR Grand Division officer and his staff would oversee the entirety of Lines East.[232]

All of the Grand Divisions, along with most of the associated lines, were divided into multiple divisions, each of which replicated in miniature the organizational structure of the Grand Divisions. The length of a division was generally dictated by the distance that a slow-moving freight train could cover in a day, perhaps a hundred miles. The number of divisions varied considerably over the years, with the system total peaking at forty-nine in 1920. By 1874, the three original divisions on the PRR (Eastern, Middle and Western) had grown to seven: the Philadelphia, Middle, Pittsburgh,

Tyrone, West Pennsylvania, Lewistown, and Bedford Divisions. The Philadelphia & Erie Grand Division was divided into the Eastern, Middle, and Western Divisions, and the United Railroads of New Jersey Grand Division included the New York, Amboy, and Belvidere Divisions. The other subsidiaries that were a part of Lines East added more divisions to the mix, and there were numerous divisions on the various railroads that made up Lines West.[233]

Each division was under the supervision of a division superintendent, a line officer who reported to the general superintendent. Every division superintendent relied on a staff, including a trainmaster (who was in charge of transportation) and a master mechanic (in charge of locomotives and cars). Each division employed a resident engineer (assistant engineer after 1873, and engineer of maintenance-of-way after 1881) and associated staff. Regardless of title, the divisional engineering employees were in charge of routine maintenance matters, adhering to Lines East standards that were first developed in 1872 by Philadelphia & Erie Eastern Division Superintendent Frank Thomson. In addition, the division superintendent had full authority over personnel matters—unlike railroads such as the Erie, the PRR lagged in the development of centralized personnel policies, which did not come into force until 1920.[234]

The divisional structure was common to all North American railroads of any size, but it proved particularly valuable on the PRR as a mechanism for selecting talented managers from the ranks of the Transportation Department. Because divisions varied considerably in the intensity of their operations, they offered a proving ground for aspiring junior executives, as well as an opportunity for the members of the General Office Department to evaluate comparatively each division's senior personnel. While most of the PRR's senior executives possessed strong engineering backgrounds, relatively few proved themselves solely on the basis of new construction projects. Instead, most began their careers at the bottom of the line in the Maintenance-of-Way Department, as rodmen or chainmen on various divisions. The more able among them earned promotion to resident engineers or assistant engineers (the duties were equivalent, but the titles varied over time). They were ultimately responsible for ensuring that the track in their division was adequately maintained for safe and efficient operation, according to standards developed by Frank Thomson in collaboration with the engineer of maintenance-of-way for Lines East. One of the surest ways to determine their capabilities was simply to ride over the track. In 1876, the PRR's shop forces fabricated a track inspection car, and they built another one in 1880, with further improvements in 1882 and 1883. Every year, senior PRR personnel would ride around Lines East, observing the condition of the right of way. At Thomson's suggestion, they awarded "premiums," bonuses for the smoothest ride and best appearance.[235]

More important, highly capable assistant engineers soon found themselves transferred to more demanding divisions. Should they succeed there, a promotion to the central office would likely follow. Conversely, any sign of ineptitude was likely to result in banishment to a marginal division, if not outright dismissal. Once they had gained routine maintenance-of-way engineering experience on several divisions, the best assistant engineers would become division superintendents. Those who proved themselves in that more comprehensive and more demanding capacity could again expect to be shunted between divisions, with a chosen few promoted to high-traffic, high-stress divisions. Some then joined the staff of the general manager, perhaps as principal assistant engineer. They might eventually become senior staff officers, attached to one of the vice presidents or to the president.[236] Those who demonstrated a particular finesse for transportation functions would become the general superintendent of a Grand Division. Worthy candidates could become the general manager on Lines East, the chief operating officer at the head of the downward line of authority. The next step was promotion to a vice presidency in charge of Transportation, and ultimately to the top job in the company.

Individuals who followed that career path possessed a thorough knowledge of the physical structure of the PRR, as well as virtually every aspect of the company's operations. Yet, they could also be somewhat myopic, more focused on immediate issues than on long-term strategy. Furthermore, as a writer for the *Railroad Gazette* observed in 1882, "The Pennsylvania Railroad has an individuality of method and official

conduct which is more easily taken on [by] a young and less experienced mind than by men already trained in other types of organization."[237] The experience of Transportation Department personnel—which, of necessity, involved conformity to a rigid system of rules and procedures—could blunt their creativity.[238]

Not all senior executives rose through the ranks of the Transportation Department, however, and some avoided prolonged tenures as assistant engineers and division superintendents. Major engineering projects offered an excellent test of an individual's capabilities, as they included responsibility for real estate acquisition and other legal issues, track work, bridges, buildings, relations with government officials, and interactions with other railroads. Design and construction engineering (as opposed to routine maintenance-of-way engineering) attracted some of the most talented and ambitious professionals available. Unlike their counterparts at the divisional level, they were more likely to possess a perspective that encompassed the system as a whole. Exceptional ability in project management could lead to rapid advancement to the General Office Department, as an assistant to the president on engineering matters, as principal assistant engineer, or as a vice president in charge of the construction of new lines. Those who followed that path to the executive suite were often experts at seeing the big picture and at interacting comfortably with their counterparts on other railroads.[239] In contrast, they were less likely than their Transportation brethren to have mastered routine operating procedures, and less likely to have made the varied contacts within the ranks of the PRR that often proved so vital to a successful corporate culture. In addition, economic contractions and the maturation of the American railway network periodically curtailed new construction and restricted the supply of engineers who had cut their teeth on major projects.

The dichotomy between the two paths to the top—one through the Transportation Department and the divisions, and the other through system engineering projects—reflected the unique relationship between the third and the fourth presidents of the Pennsylvania Railroad. As an engineer-manager, J. Edgar Thomson began the process. He had risen rapidly from chief engineer of the Georgia Railroad to the same post on the PRR. Between June 1849 and January 1851, he was both chief engineer and general superintendent, controlling both engineering and transportation functions. After he assumed the presidency in 1852, Thomson was both chief executive officer and head of the Transportation Department. His assistant and successor, Vice President Scott, had little knowledge of engineering but possessed a superb understanding of transportation logistics, dating from his work as a freight forwarder along the Main Line of Public Works. Therefore, Thomson and Scott each advocated a different promotion process. Thomson mentored individuals who, much like himself, had proven their merits through engineering expertise, new construction, and the oversight of subsidiary lines, and not through day-to-day operations.[240] Scott's protégés were more likely to have risen through the ranks of the Transportation Department as division personnel.[241] Members of the second generation of senior executives likewise chose successors much like themselves, ensuring the perpetuation of the two advancement tracks, at least until the 1930s.[242] Each path to the presidency possessed its strengths and weaknesses for the Pennsylvania Railroad. Yet, for more than three-quarters of a century, that duality produced a remarkably talented executive corps.[243]

It should be emphasized, moreover, that the vast majority of PRR employees, even at a comparatively senior level, never left the division where they began their careers. Locations such as New York, Philadelphia, and Pittsburgh generated considerable traffic and possessed extraordinarily intricate operating patterns. It would often take many years for a division superintendent and his ancillary personnel to master that complexity and to develop a comfortable relationship with shippers and other important local interests. Once a division superintendent had proven himself in such a high-pressure environment, he was often far too valuable there to be promoted to a more senior position, even though he might be worthy of assignment to corporate headquarters.

Robert Pitcairn best exemplified the tendency of competent PRR executives to remain for decades at a single post. A highly capable officer, he was the superintendent of the Western Division (later the Pittsburgh Division) for virtually his entire career. Pitcairn

was a native of Scotland whose parents had emigrated to the United States when he was just a child. In 1848, he became a messenger for the Atlantic & Ohio Telegraph Company. He soon worked with two fellow Scotsmen—David McCargo, who signed on the following year, and Andrew Carnegie, who joined in 1850. In July 1853, Pitcairn became a telegraph operator on the PRR, first at the Mountain House, near Hollidaysburg, and soon thereafter at Altoona, where he clerked for Superintendent Herman J. Lombaert. Pitcairn demonstrated superb judgment in both his timing and his choice of superiors, for he was at Altoona precisely when Lombaert was taking the lead in the development of the PRR's basic operating routines.[244]

Pitcairn's knowledge of both telegraphy and railway operating procedures served him well. On August 1, 1860, while still in his early twenties, Pitcairn was appointed superintendent of the Middle Division, headquartered at Altoona. His skill at managing the crush of wartime transportation resulted in his rapid promotion to superintendent of transportation in April 1862. Three years later, the board named him superintendent of the Pittsburgh Division, replacing his former fellow telegrapher, Andrew Carnegie. There Pitcairn remained for the remainder of his career, until he retired in June 1906 at the mandatory retirement age of seventy. His title changed—with the additional responsibilities of general agent at Pittsburgh (in 1874) and resident assistant to the president at Pittsburgh (in 1902)—but his duties did not. Over a span of more than forty years, he weathered increased traffic flows, the riotous strikes of 1877, and the effects of the worst flood in the history of the United States.

While Pitcairn was undoubtedly a technically proficient railroader, his greatest skill was in building consensus among PRR personnel on both Lines East and Lines West, and with shippers, other transportation officials, and local politicians and businessmen. Soon after he began his tenure at Pittsburgh, he instituted a series of weekly staff meetings, designed as much to allow his subordinates to educate him on the latest conditions as to enable the superintendent to issue orders to his staff. As general agent, Pitcairn was well positioned to interact with all of the industrialists who called Pittsburgh home and to develop close working relationships with the executives from the other rail-

Figure 40. Robert Pitcairn (1836–1909) spent most of his long Pennsylvania Railroad career as superintendent of the Pittsburgh Division. He excelled at coordinating traffic moving between Lines East and Lines West, and he was equally adept at maintaining cordial relationships with other railroad executives and local industrialists. Pitcairn won the accolades of his peers, and amassed a considerable fortune besides. Yet, he might well have ascended to even higher office had the PRR possessed a better mechanism for moving him back into the ladder of corporate promotion.

Pennsylvania Historical and Museum Commission, Pennsylvania State Archives.

roads serving the city. His connections also enabled him to invest in mining and manufacturing enterprises, earning him a fortune of some $20 million.

Robert Pitcairn possessed a unique set of talents, ideally suited to the task of meshing the operations on the eastern and western halves of the Pennsylvania Railroad System. His competence and tact smoothed the flow of people and products through a gateway that, by the time of his retirement, processed more freight cars than any other city in the world. Yet, despite his success, Pitcairn was to a certain degree trapped at Pittsburgh. He was outside the customary promotional pathways that characterized the PRR. Despite his status as a division superintendent, high up on the line of authority in the Transporta-

tion Department, he was effectively a staff officer, unable to rise to the executive suite. Although Pitcairn's career could hardly be considered a failure, it did represent one of the failings of the PRR's organizational structure.

Despite the willingness of senior PRR executives to tailor elements of the company's organization to fit the unique talents of key individuals, however, the names and the personalities of the division superintendents and their personnel were largely irrelevant. The PRR was a bureaucracy, not so much in the commonly accepted, pejorative sense of the term, but rather in the manner described by economist and social scientist Max Weber. He defined a bureaucracy as a self-perpetuating entity, one that would outlast the individuals who had created it. Those people, and their successors, adhered to a carefully articulated and commonly accepted set of rules, defining themselves according to their status in a clearly delineated organizational hierarchy. While twentieth-century critics condemned the stultifying effects of endless rules and regulations on the emasculated "organization man," Weber and many of his contemporaries advocated the creation of a meritocracy, where deserving individuals could succeed on the basis of their talents rather than on family pedigree, patronage, graft, or luck.

In a broad sense, the Pennsylvania Railroad, with its carefully crafted organization charts, its thick rulebooks, and its legions of technically proficient middle managers, conformed to the Weberian ideal. In 1882, a writer from the trade journal *Railroad Gazette* indicated as much—although his comments could have been made at almost any time in the PRR's history. "One quality of the Pennsylvania Railroad Company as an organization is strength, that is to say, such a division of duty and responsibility as enables it to use the ability of all its officers without dependence upon any one of them."[245]

A system of overlapping responsibilities ensured managerial continuity and reduced the likelihood that one person could make a quick but erroneous decision, without any check on his authority. During the Civil War, many generals had made horrific mistakes, or had simply refused to commit their troops to battle, and PRR executives were determined to circumvent similar failings. J. Elfreth Watkins, who was beginning a promising career as a PRR engineer until an on-the-job injury relegated him to a post as company historian, emphasized the difference between military and PRR practices. "Unlike the Army and the Navy, where the highest encomium that can be paid to officers and men is that orders are promptly obeyed and to the letter," Watkins observed, "the various departments and branches of the Pennsylvania Railroad interlock and thus secure more complete unification of operation."[246] The station agents on each division processed shipments and interacted with the railroad's customers, under the supervision of the division superintendents. Yet, they were ultimately answerable to the general freight agent and the general passenger agent on each Grand Division, and through them to

the vice president in charge of transportation and traffic functions (although not to the general manager, who oversaw only transportation). Each division's assistant engineers maintained the right of way, independently of their colleagues on other divisions, but according to standards established by the engineer of maintenance-of-way for Lines East. That engineer, who was on the staff of the general manager, had direct authority over the principal assistant engineers, who were on the staffs of the general superintendents on each Grand Division. Similarly, the superintendent of motive power on each Grand Division supervised the master mechanics and shop foremen—individuals who were also under the authority of their respective division superintendents. Thus, staff officers injected their influence at multiple layers of the organization.

While the development of a Weberian managerial bureaucracy undoubtedly reduced friction within the organization, there were nonetheless many tensions that characterized the PRR's line-and-staff organization. Those problems were not unique to the Pennsylvania Railroad, but its executives were among the first to address them. As PRR officials clearly recognized, decentralization created enormous potential for conflicts between local officials and the central office. Such disputes were particularly evident in the area of budgeting. Freight and passenger traffic could originate or terminate on or off of the PRR system. It might move within a division, or across several divisions. Division superintendents were responsible for moving trains across their division, but not for soliciting the traffic that filled the freight and passenger cars. They shouldered the expense of operations and routine maintenance, yet relied on system shops, most notably the ones at Altoona, for the construction of new locomotives and cars, and for major repairs. While some expenses, such as coal and trainmen's wages, were clearly attributable to specific divisions, others—principally long-term betterments—were more properly a cost incurred by the PRR as a whole.

The key to preventing conflicts between divisional and system personnel, as many PRR officials and outside observers emphasized, was to delineate lines of authority clearly. Thomson, in particular, was careful not to intrude into established areas of responsibility. "He organizes the company, and makes this theoretical organization a fact by respecting the positions in which he places his subordinates," the *Railroad Gazette* observed. "He would uphold a trusted officer to almost any degree, whatever this involved; and the strength of the Pennsylvania organization lies to-day in the development of the principle, that control must flow through the organization, reaching subordinates only by the acts and words of their own immediate officers."[247] The principle of rigidly delineated authority was hardly a new development on the PRR; it could be found in the company's 1858 organizational manual, as well as the New York & Erie Rail Road 1852 corporate structure, upon which it was based.[248]

What made the PRR's organization particularly successful was that decision making proceeded along informal as well as formal lines. Many observers noted that the great strength of the PRR's organization lay in the less formal linkages that connected personnel up as well as down lines of authority. The PRR's organization of the 1850s bore scant relation to Army practice, and the reorganizations of the 1870s moved the company even farther away from the military model. In 1882, when an observer from the trade journal *Railroad Gazette* reflected on the development of the PRR organization, he acknowledged that, to some degree, "The present working corps may be likened to an army." The resemblance was coincidental rather than causal, however, and the author noted that the PRR "organization cannot be said to be military.... There is a freedom for suggestion and mutual consultation and for independence of action not found in an army."[249] In other words, on the PRR, superior officers acted on the recommendations of their subordinates, and did not merely order them around.

By the 1870s, PRR executives had developed a variety of mechanisms to solicit input from middle managers across all of Lines East. Once a year, typically in March, all of the division superintendents would meet in order to discuss issues of mutual concern and coordinate their activities for the coming year. One of those meetings, held in 1879, addressed a long-standing concern regarding colorblindness among operating personnel. From that meeting emerged the Association of Transportation Officers of the Pennsylvania Railroad, initially an organization of little consequence, but by the 1890s a vital mechanism for coordinating construction and operational matters on Lines East.

PRR personnel also relied on a large number of ad hoc committees, consisting of whichever personnel were best suited to resolve a specific, and often unique problem and drawn from across the system. Committee members tackled issues ranging from accident prevention and the provision of benefits to workers, to the purchase and management of everything from coal lands to suburban real estate to steamships, to the construction and acquisition of new rail lines. Some of those informal collaborative efforts later evolved into standing committees, on par with (although less important than) the Road Committee and the Finance Committee. They included the Committee on Supplies and the Committee on Insurance, both established during the late 1870s. In the process many of the committees recommended changes to the PRR's corporate structure, ranging from the reorganization of the Purchasing Department to the board's decision to self-insure the company by creating an Insurance Bureau.

One key responsibility involved the design and publication of the hundreds of blanks (forms) that regulated every aspect of the PRR's operations, from train movements, to billing, to employee discipline. In December 1877, for example, the members of the Committee of Superintendents recommended the standardization of all of the 1,815 blanks used on Lines East, reducing their number by more than a third. Such paperwork was—and remains—one of the least-loved elements of any organizational bureaucracy. For railroads such as the PRR, however, those forms represented a careful codification of the rules and regulations that were vital to the maintenance of safe and efficient operations. Their use, however unpleasant, prevented the petty tyranny associated with junior officers who would otherwise be required to issue an unending number of instructions, many of them arbitrary, capricious, and contradictory.[250]

A small group of staff officers played an important role in resolving tensions between line and staff authority. They possessed functional authority, also known as limited line authority, with the ability to dictate policy in matters pertaining to their areas of expertise. Those functional specialists were part of a growing cadre of middle managers whose areas of responsibility lay somewhere between the division superintendents who ran the trains and the senior executives who formulated corporate policy. Their primary responsibility was to ensure efficient and economical operation.[251] The individuals who possessed functional authority were railroading's point men, attending conferences, contributing to engineering journals, and participating in a wide variety of professional organizations that included representatives from virtually every major carrier. While many of those technically proficient middle managers had worked their way up through the ranks, learning by experience, the more senior among them possessed formal academic training. Their number included George Brooke Roberts, who in 1880 became the first PRR president with a college degree. They regarded themselves as profes-

sionals, and not mere employees, and were often more closely identified with their field than with their company. Nevertheless—and this was particularly true on the Pennsylvania Railroad—they retained a high degree of loyalty to their employer, and movement from company to company was almost unheard of. The growing influence of those functionally specialized middle managers constituted one of the most important developments on the Pennsylvania Railroad—and, indeed, in American business—during the last decades of the nineteenth century.[252]

Yet there remained much for those middle managers to do in the two decades that followed the Civil War. During the 1870s, the PRR's mechanical engineers were just beginning to develop standards for brakes, couplers, signaling systems, rails, and equipment. Whenever those devices passed from one railroad to

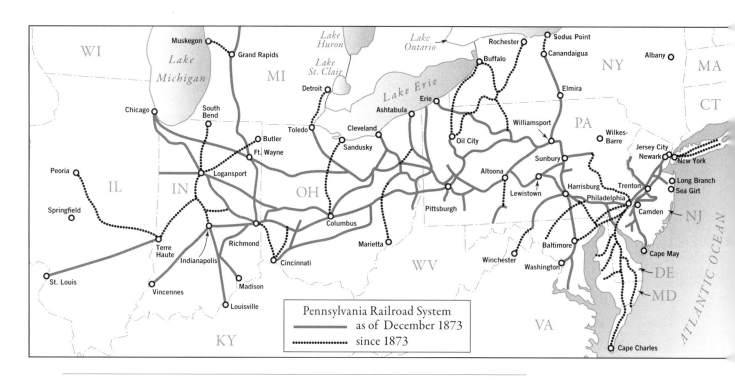

Figure 41. By 1873, J. Edgar Thomson, Tom Scott, and other PRR executives had established an impressive railway empire, one that included access to the western gateways of St. Louis and Chicago; the Ohio River towns of Louisville, Cincinnati, Wheeling, and Pittsburgh; the Great Lakes ports of Toledo, Cleveland, and Erie; the nation's capital; and the tidewater ports of Baltimore, Philadelphia, and New York. In the years to follow, their successors would extend that empire to include Buffalo, Detroit, and the port of Cape Charles, at the tip of the Delmarva Peninsula. Based on George H. Burgess and Miles C. Kennedy, *Centennial History of the Pennsylvania Railroad Company, 1846–1946* (Philadelphia: Pennsylvania Railroad, 1949), 318–19.

another—particularly when they were attached to freight cars—the development of uniform standards took on far greater importance and complexity. However, the management of a truly integrated and interchangeable system of railroad equipment would not emerge until the early years of the twentieth century, as executives struggled to accommodate the surge in traffic that followed the nation's recovery from the depression of the 1890s.

Forging an Empire

During the final six years of his life, J. Edgar Thomson had achieved something truly remarkable, not merely by fending off challenges by rival trunk lines, but also by dramatically increasing the size, the geographic reach, and the organizational complexity of the Pennsylvania Railroad. Between 1868 and 1873, the PRR expanded its holdings west of Pittsburgh more than fifteen-fold, from 191 to 2,943 route miles. The first, anemic line from Pittsburgh to Columbus, Ohio, grew to a system that included two separate routes to Chicago, along with arteries to St. Louis, Cincinnati, Louisville, Toledo, Cleveland, and Indianapolis.[253]

Thomson changed the PRR from a regional trunk-line railroad to one with national scope; effectively creating the PRR system that persisted until the Penn Central merger in 1968. Thomson had taken the PRR

out of Pennsylvania, as far west as Chicago and the Mississippi River, as far south as the Ohio River, and as far to the north and east as the shores of the Hudson River. Yet, the PRR went that far, and no farther. Aside from a few short extensions, the PRR never expanded beyond the territorial limits that Thomson had established.

PRR executives nonetheless possessed much grander territorial ambitions. During the early 1870s, before the Panic of 1873 brought an end to their efforts, Thomson and Scott were associated with railway projects that promised to extend the PRR's influence as far west as California and as far south as Florida. While such endeavors involved PRR personnel and in many cases PRR funding, they were not directly part of the railroad's corporate strategy or core mission. Instead, they represented a common theme in nineteenth-century capitalism, in that they blended executive responsibilities with opportunities for personal gain. Tom Scott became particularly adept at exploiting his connections with the PRR, quite possibly to the detriment of his employer. Even if he never matched the excesses of a Jim Fisk or a Jay Gould, Scott nonetheless proved more willing than Thomson to use his position and his contacts to advance his own fortunes, to the chagrin of many who had once admired the restraint of the PRR's corporate executives. Had Scott's plans come to fruition, however, he would have forged a series of connections linking the PRR to a railroad network that spanned the continent.

Chapter 10

Connections

1865–1873

On November 19, 1871, Russia arrived in the United States, in the personage of Grand Duke Alexei Alexandrovich. Grand Duke Alexis, as he was generally known, was the fourth son of Tsar Alexander II, a reformer responsible for abolishing serfdom, reorganizing and westernizing the army and the navy, restricting corporal punishment, and improving the quality of education. Less than a decade after the firing on Fort Sumter, many northerners appreciated the Tsar's support for the Union during the early days of the Civil War. They also saw parallels to Lincoln's role in ending slavery. "Emperor Alexander, in 1861, before our act of emancipation took place, set free twenty-three million serfs," observed former Wisconsin senator James Rood Doolittle. "Our emancipation came in blood. His came in peace." In Boston, Robert C. Winthrop, the one-time speaker of the United States House of Representatives, made plain the grand duke's role as an abolitionist. "It is now hardly more than ten or eleven years since there was common to large masses of the population of both nations a deplorable condition of serfdom or slavery. We thank God this night, in presence of each other, that from both lands that dark spot has disappeared forever."[1]

The 1867 purchase of Alaska, by Secretary of State William H. Seward, enhanced the ties between Russia and the United States. While many Americans saw little immediate need for the vast new territory (Harvard University professor and famed Romantic poet James Russell Lowell made a rather poor pun when he noted that "Russia has given to us Alaska and made us keeper of her seals"), they appreciated Alexander's willingness to relinquish his last claims in the western hemisphere. As such, Grand Duke Alexis could expect a warm welcome in the United States, particularly as many Americans were starstruck by his noble lineage, his foreign presence, and his imposing stature.

Given the grand duke's desire to see as much of the United States and Canada as possible, rail travel would be essential, and Pennsylvania Railroad officials were responsible for making most of the arrangements. President J. Edgar Thomson delegated the matter to vice president Tom Scott, who in turn selected Frank Thomson, then the superintendent of the Eastern Division of the PRR's Philadelphia & Erie subsidiary. Scott knew Frank Thomson well from their wartime experience. Since Appomattox, Thomson had demonstrated keen abilities as an organizer and a logistician. He was a superbly talented civil engineer who developed most of the track standards employed on the Philadelphia & Erie—criteria that he later applied to the PRR proper. As events transpired, only a small portion of Alexis's journey would take place on PRR

Figure 42. Although far distant from the verdant Alleghenies, the Great Plains near the 100th meridian in Nebraska were briefly a part of the Pennsylvania Railroad's sphere of influence. J. Edgar Thomson, Tom Scott, and other PRR officials attempted to capture additional traffic by investing in more than a dozen railroads west of the Mississippi River and south of the Mason-Dixon Line. Had it not been for the depression that began in 1873, Thomson and Scott might well have created the first truly transcontinental railroad empire in the United States. In this photo, an unidentified individual—perhaps Thomas C. Durant—stands along the uncompleted Union Pacific right of way near Cozad, Lincoln County, Nebraska Territory, in October 1866.

Westward, the Monarch Capital Makes Its Way: Union Pacific Rail Road, Excursion to the 100th Meridian, October 1866, *John Carbutt photo, Library of Congress Prints & Photographs Division, LC-USZ6-294.*

rails. Nonetheless, as an executive of the nation's largest railroad, Thomson was responsible for arranging national train and telegraph operations. He worked with other carriers and the Pullman Company to provide equipment for the grand duke's use and made available J. Edgar Thomson's private car *Pennsylvania*—a logical choice, given that its adjustable wheels enabled it to accommodate a multiplicity of track gauges.

On November 19, 1871, the grand duke arrived off of Sandy Hook, New Jersey, on board the *Svetlana*, the flagship of the Russian fleet. The United States revenue cutter *Northerner* steamed out to meet the vessel and escort it into New York, accompanied by a phalanx of American and Russian warships. Two days later, Alexis crossed the Hudson River on a ferry, to Jersey City, and traveled south on the rails of the New Jersey Rail Road & Transportation Company, part of the United Companies, at almost precisely the same instant that Pennsylvania Railroad officials were completing the final details associated with their lease of that critical transportation artery. "The fact that the distinguished visitor was on the train," one account noted, "was known to only a few of the employés, and no demonstration of any kind was made." Thanks to the construction of the Connecting Railway and the Junction Railroad, the grand duke passed smoothly through Philadelphia. Had he arrived just a few years later, his journey through Baltimore would have been equally convenient. As it was, however, the PRR's Baltimore & Potomac route through the city and on to Washington was still under construction. Alexis stood on the rear platform of the sleeping car *Kearsarge*, waving to the cheering crowds at the B&O's Camden Street Station. Then, like countless travelers before him, he sat as horses towed the cars through the streets of Baltimore. In Washington, Alexis met with the customary complement of dignitaries, including Maryland governor Oden Bowie, the individual who had helped make possible Thomson's efforts to break the B&O's monopoly on rail access to the nation's capital. The host was President Ulysses S. Grant, his victory in the 1868 election largely the result of his conquest of the Confederacy.

During the days that followed, the grand duke made a visit to Annapolis, before returning to New York for more receptions, and trips to the Navy Yard and to West Point. He thoroughly enjoyed a review of the Metropolitan Fire Brigade, and used a call box to dispatch firefighters to an imaginary conflagration. He again traveled to Philadelphia, remaining there long enough to visit Girard College, Independence Hall, the Navy Yard, and the Baldwin Locomotive Works. At a ball held at the Academy of Music, he took the first dance with Margaret Butler Meade, the never-married daughter of the hero of Gettysburg. On December 4, Alexis went back to New York, along the route of the Philadelphia & Trenton, whose stockholders had only recently voted to lease their company to the PRR. The train paused at Bristol, Pennsylvania, midway along its journey, and the grand duke and his party disembarked. They stood trackside while the train thundered past, and Alexis, with a wave of his arm, brought the mass of machinery to a halt, through the application of the recently developed Westinghouse air brake.

From New York, Alexis rode north toward Boston. At Bridgeport, Connecticut, he toured the Union Metallic Cartridge Company, and then he stopped at the Smith & Wesson factory in Springfield, Massachusetts. Both companies symbolized the growing industrial prowess of the United States, and each was producing munitions for the Russian government. He later crossed into Canada, and then north to Montreal, and west to Ottawa and Toronto, before continuing south to Niagara Falls and Buffalo, and then Detroit. The trip west from Detroit, via the Lake Shore & Michigan Southern, was slightly delayed as the result of an earlier train wreck at Jackson, Michigan—one of the seemingly unavoidable consequences of the new transportation age. The grand duke arrived in Chicago to cheering crowds assembled amid "the sickening devastated forests of walls and chimneys," mute survivors of the Great Chicago Fire that had swept across the city less than three months earlier. Alexis toured the ruins, expressing his sympathy for the victims and his admiration for their resiliency in rebuilding the city.

The grand duke headed west onto the Great Plains, for what he considered the most exciting and enjoyable portion of the tour. On January 12, 1872, the grand duke's train arrived at Council Bluffs, Iowa, and Alexis disembarked while the cars were hauled across the frozen Missouri River. The transcontinental railroad had just been completed (although the Union Pacific bridge to Omaha would not enter service until later that year), settlers were taking advantage of the 1862 Homestead Act, and Native Americans were being systematically starved, slaughtered, and dispossessed of their lands. The frontier was by no means closed, but American attitudes toward the West were changing rapidly, from fear of the unknown wilderness to a romantic nostalgia for a vanishing way of life. Alexis, a man from a country as vast and as wild as the United States, simply had to see all of the iconic elements of the western frontier. He watched war dances and hunting demonstrations arranged by Spotted Tail, the war chief of the Lower Brulé Sioux.

At the request of General Philip H. Sheridan, the head of the Department of the Missouri and the man in charge of pacifying the Plains Indians, William "Buffalo Bill" Cody staged a buffalo hunt for the entertainment of the grand duke. Like many others, Alexis wished to "enjoy pleasing seclusion, and indulge in the unrestrained sport of hunting and slaying the noble buffalo in untold numbers." At "Camp Alexis" on Red Willow Creek, some forty miles southeast of North Platte, Nebraska, Buffalo Bill, Alexis, and their associates prepared to sally forth. They were accompanied by General George Armstrong Custer, the flamboyant cavalryman who would soon meet his end at the Battle of the Little Bighorn. Frank Thomson lacked a horse, but the avid hunter and fisherman refused to be left behind. Cody graciously loaned the PRR executive his prized horse, "Buckskin Joe," and permitted Thomson to kill a buffalo. The two men remained friends for the rest of their lives. At first, Alexis "availed himself of Custer's experience, asked many questions, and practiced running and shooting at imaginary buffaloes as he went." They eventually found a herd of the massive animals, who stood motionless as the grand duke slaughtered them. Later, while on horseback, he used his pistol to bring down a cow, and then killed its calf for good measure. They dragged the newborn back to camp in its entirety, but took only the head and the tail of its mother.

A few days later, Alexis and his party traveled along the Union Pacific to Cheyenne, Wyoming, where another accident—this one involving their train— delayed their southward progress over the Denver Pacific Railway to Denver. They then returned east to

Kansas City, along the Kansas Pacific Railway. Alexis and Custer, stationed in a baggage car, shot still more buffalo while the train toiled along the Kansas prairies. The rest of the trip was somewhat less memorable, as Alexis traveled by rail to St. Louis, Louisville (including a visit to Mammoth Cave), and Memphis. Then, he headed down the Mississippi River by steamboat to New Orleans, where he was the guest of honor at Mardi Gras. On February 22, 1872, Alexis sailed out of Pensacola, Florida, on the *Svetlana*, leaving the United States behind.

At 9:00 A.M. on Thursday, February 26, 1874—two years, almost to the day, after Grand Duke Alexis had departed from Pensacola—"there stood upon the rails of the Pennsylvania railroad at Jersey City, a miniature dwelling house, capable of accommodating a family of twenty-three, ready to receive its occupants and to roll away from the Hudson to the St. John—from the wintery blasts of the North to the orange groves of Florida." The car was in fact the *Pennsylvania*, officially the perquisite of the ailing President Thomson, but by that time primarily used by Scott. The facilities were luxurious but presumably a bit cramped, as there really were twenty-three guests on board, along with a cook and a steward. They were in fact too numerous for the single dining-room table, and had to eat in shifts.

The official host was Newark banker Alfred L. Dennis, president of the PRR's leased New Jersey Rail Road & Transportation Company. He had joined forces with J. Edgar Thomson in numerous other business arrangements, including the Poughkeepsie Bridge Company and its ill-starred attempt to span the Hudson River.[2] Most of the others on board the *Pennsylvania* were in some way associated with transportation or finance, or both. They included his brother Martin R. Dennis (a Newark streetcar magnate), his son and future business partner Samuel S. Dennis, William D. Bishop (one of the promoters of the New York, New Haven & Hartford Railroad), and Nehemiah Perry (a cloth manufacturer, former member of Congress, and a director of the New Jersey Rail Road). Philadelphia merchant Josiah Bacon was a PRR director. Newspaperman Thomas T. Kinney owned the *Newark Advertiser* and was also a stockholder in the Morris & Essex Railroad and the Delaware, Lackawanna & Western Railroad. Anthony Q. Keasbey, the United States district attorney for the District of New Jersey and an attorney for several mainline and street railway companies, was still shaken from an incident that had occurred the previous November, when his yacht, anchored off of Seabright, New Jersey, was accidently rammed and sunk by the coastal steamer *Twilight*.

The most powerful financier among them was undoubtedly Moses Taylor, whose wealth vastly exceeded that of either Scott or Thomson. Taylor was a confidant of John Jacob Astor, and he had skillfully parlayed the Panic of 1837 into the foundation of his fortune. He later controlled substantial interests in the National City Bank of New York, as well as the Delaware, Lackawanna & Western, and was a director of the Lackawanna Coal & Iron Company, the Chicago & North Western Railway, the Michigan Central Railroad, and the Western Union Telegraph Company, among many other firms. Several years earlier he had been one of the owners of the lands at Harsimus Cove, soon to become the PRR's primary New York area freight facility.

Taylor was traveling south largely in order to assess the investment possibilities available in the defeated Confederacy. During the 1870s, he invested heavily in southern railroads, including the Central Railroad & Banking Company of Georgia, the South Carolina Railroad, and the Atlanta & Richmond Air Line Railroad. The others could not command the same level of resources, and most were just along for the ride. Like Taylor, however, they were interested in real estate development and tourism in Florida. They experienced little success, but their efforts prefigured those of Henry M. Flagler, the Standard Oil associate who was primarily responsible for negotiating shipping arrangements with the PRR and its competitors. Little more than a decade later, Flagler and his Standard Oil fortune would develop St. Augustine and Palm Beach into flourishing resort towns.

In 1874, Alfred Dennis, Moses Taylor, and the others were a few years ahead of their time, traveling south before the maturation of the southern railway system. The party began their journey in a snowstorm. Like later generations of travelers, they were happy to be snug in their berths, headed for a warmer clime. During the initial portion of their trip, they fared somewhat better than Duke Alexis, as the Baltimore & Potomac route was open through Baltimore and on to Washington. From there, they crossed into Virginia, continuing south on two PRR subsidiaries, and then on the rails of the independent Richmond, Fredericksburg & Potomac Railroad. South of the Virginia and former Confederate capital, they followed a chain of railroads that in 1889 would be consolidated into the Atlantic Coast Line, one of the great systems of the New South. Before the Civil War, the principal southern railroads had connected the coast to the interior, and north–south routes were slower to develop. Their progress was accordingly both indirect and leisurely, and they did not reach Charleston, South Carolina, until March 5. They toured the battered remains of Fort Sumter, escorted by General Quincy Adams Gillmore, a skilled engineer whose wartime annihilation of Fort Pulaski, Georgia, had demonstrated the obsolescence of such brick fortifications. Continuing south, the party halted at Savannah, where there was as yet no bridge across the city's namesake river. The guests enjoyed southern hospitality, while the *Pennsylvania* followed a long inland detour, in order to reach the south bank of the watercourse. The intrepid travelers continued into Florida, but the state's primitive rail system ensured that they spent most of their time on steamboats that cruised along the St. Johns River.[3]

The two journeys—one to the mythic West and the other through a reborn South—reflected the continental ambitions of American railway promoters, including J. Edgar Thomson and Tom Scott. The Pennsylvania Railroad was, at heart, a Pennsylvania company, and it depended on a complex system of leases and securities ownership to maintain access to such out-of-state destinations as New York, Baltimore, Washington, Cincinnati, St. Louis, and Chicago. The United Companies, the Baltimore & Potomac, the Northern Central, the Pan Handle, the Fort Wayne, and many other carriers funneled crucial traffic to the main stem of the Pennsylvania Railroad. Without their contributions, the PRR could not have survived.

By the early 1870s, with the PRR's eastern and western connections secured, Thomson and Scott began to extend their vision farther west and south. Settlement on the Great Plains promised rapid railroad development and considerable agricultural and merchandise traffic. The Civil War had wrecked the railroads of the South, but tremendous opportunities existed for anyone who could rebuild the shattered lines and integrate the isolated carriers into a comprehensive regional system. Thomson, Scott, and their PRR associates plunged headlong into the national railroad arena, both as a chance for personal gain and as a mechanism for increasing the PRR's traffic catchment basin. They influenced, albeit briefly, the development of many of the routes followed by Grand Duke Alexis, and by Moses Taylor and his coterie of northern developers. The wandering private car *Pennsylvania* was not so far from home rails as it might at first appear.

Success largely eluded Thomson and Scott, however. They faced, on a grand scale, the problems of coordination and personal mistrust that had plagued their efforts to control affiliates in Ohio, Indiana, and Illinois only a few years earlier. They lacked the time, the financial resources, and the level of oversight that they possessed closer to home, and that were necessary to keep their far-flung interests in line. In the aftermath of the Panic of 1873, the entire house of cards came tumbling down, and the PRR's stockholders made clear their determination to restrict the involvement of company executives to the area north of the Ohio River and east of the Mississippi.

At the time, and in the decades since, many critics have excoriated Thomson, Scott, and the others for their presumed ability to extend the PRR's tentacles into every corner of the United States and to make unsavory backroom political deals that ruined investors, bilked the federal government, and destroyed local political and economic patrimony. Some malfeasance did take place, to be sure. To the extent that PRR officials were involved, it merely indicated that they were no different than their counterparts on other railroads and in other businesses.[4] More commonly, however, Thomson, Scott, and their contemporaries shouldered the blame for wide-ranging economic changes that they facilitated, particularly in the Reconstruction South, but which would have occurred eventually, even without their involvement.

Personal and Corporate Capitalism

When J. Edgar Thomson died, on May 27, 1874, he left a wife, no biological children, and an estate valued at a little under a million dollars.[5] While that was a considerable sum for the time, it had been sharply reduced as a result of the Panic of 1873 and unwise investments late in his life. His holdings paled in comparison to the fortunes amassed by other railroaders, bankers, and industrialists. Thomson's financial portfolio held only 1,400 shares of the PRR's stock, and he had no son to inherit even that modest legacy—a situation quite different from the family control that the Vanderbilts exercised over the New York Central, or the Garretts over the Baltimore & Ohio. Yet, Thomson's relatively modest means did not indicate an aversion to speculation. He had spent decades buying and selling securities for himself, for his friends and business associates, and on behalf of the Pennsylvania Railroad, representing more than eighty-eight thousand shares in dozens of companies.

What was astonishing, at the end, was the extraordinary diversity of his holdings. They included the West Branch Boom Company, a log-floating operation on the Susquehanna River that was part of the PRR-controlled Pennsylvania Canal Company. Others, such as the Karthaus Coal & Lumber Company, the Volcanic Oil Company, the Horse Creek Oil & Manufacturing Company, the Kinzua Petroleum Company, the Bright Oil Company, and the Westmoreland Coal Company, were linked to the PRR's long-standing reliance on the transportation of natural resources. The Foster Coal & Iron Company was part of Thomson's efforts to provide support for the family of vice president William B. Foster, Jr., following his untimely death in March 1860. The Susquehanna Gold Company and the Live Oak Copper Company exploited natural resources, as well, but they—like many of Thomson's other minor holdings—constituted extraordinarily poor investments. Other speculative ventures were more promising, including those in the Lake Superior & Mississippi Railroad, the Hope Mutual Insurance Company, and the Astor House Hotel Company. In prior years, Thomson had owned securities in Andrew Carnegie's Keystone Bridge Company and such prominent American railroads as the Union Pacific, the Northern Pacific, and the Texas & Pacific, along with enough land to establish a small fiefdom—two million acres in Maine, three thousand acres at the junction of the Mississippi and Missouri rivers, and other parcels scattered here and there, many of them rich in coal.[6]

Thomson's colleague and eventual successor, Tom Scott, likewise possessed a far-ranging investment portfolio, worth some $17 million at the time of his death. According to the conventional wisdom, Thomson invested in order to guarantee a modicum of stability for himself and to create a stronger Pennsylvania Railroad, while Scott relished the risk and the thrill of financial manipulation. Scott made himself wealthy through his investments in companies—like Keystone Bridge—that depended largely on the PRR for business. He plunged into speculation in railroads far removed from the PRR's traditional territory, from Georgia to Texas, and north to the Great Plains. In the process, he allegedly depleted Thomson's investment portfolio, helped to ruin his health, and caused serious harm to the Pennsylvania Railroad. The actions of Scott, and to a lesser extent those of Thomson, seemingly raised serious conflict-of-interest issues and called into question the integrity of those two executives.[7]

The reality was somewhat more complex. Despite the varied nature of their investments, most of Thomson's and Scott's activities were closely connected to their core mission of managing the Pennsylvania Railroad. Many of their holdings were in companies that served as suppliers to the PRR, or else depended on the railroad for the timely shipment of coal, timber, or other natural resources. The ships that plied the Great Lakes and the Atlantic Ocean, funded in part with PRR assistance, extended the reach of the Pennsylvania Railroad. Investments in western rail lines, while unlikely to create a true transcontinental line under unified ownership, nevertheless ensured that the PRR would garner traffic from a wide swath of the continent, as far away as the distant Pacific shores.[8]

Those investments were integral to the managerial strategies of PRR executives. Thomson was one of the most accomplished engineers and one of the most talented managers in the American business community, while Scott was a superb logistician who also provided the charisma and political clout that enabled the PRR to flourish within the complex environment of local, regional, and national politics. Yet, they drew small official salaries, far below those of managers during the early twenty-first century, even when adjusted for in-

flation. They gained additional compensation by way of their status as PRR executives, exalted positions that gave them access to an extraordinary range of financial opportunities. Other railroad officials observed the connection between the PRR and outside investment opportunities, with the Southern Pacific's David D. Colton writing to Collis P. Huntington, "If it were not that he [Scott] had the great Pen. Central Railroad behind him he would go out of sight in six months, but he keeps up by reason of his position in that great railroad."[9]

For Thomson, Scott, and others, that relationship worked both ways, and it offered considerable benefit to the Pennsylvania Railroad. Their involvement in a wide variety of enterprises provided them with connections that were immensely valuable to the Pennsylvania Railroad, and that correspondingly gave the two executives greater authority over the PRR board. Directors who might have been inclined to oppose executive decisions found it difficult to rally support from outside the company, primarily because investors assumed that Thomson and Scott *were* the Pennsylvania Railroad, and that their policies were the railroad's policies. As everyone on the board knew, Thomson and Scott possessed the ultimate weapon inasmuch as their financial empires afforded them the opportunity to desert the railroad should the directors prove recalcitrant. Many of the owners who sat on the board of directors rankled at that arrangement, which enabled managers such as Thomson and Scott to dictate corporate strategy, but the end result was a prosperous and well-run company.[10]

The financial empire that Thomson and Scott created both expanded and protected the Pennsylvania Railroad. Their investments extended the PRR's reach from coast to coast, and even to Europe, ensuring the collection of more traffic, and furthering the development of a high-volume, low-rate transportation policy. The two executives relied heavily—perhaps too heavily—on a network of close and trusted associates, during an era when sophisticated investment data were difficult to obtain, and when the most reliable information came from personal connections. Finally, in an era when financiers frequently battled for control over even powerful trunk-line carriers, the multilayered investments that Thomson and Scott established constituted barrier after barrier against attack. Because Thomson and Scott dominated the PRR's board of directors, it was virtually impossible for outsiders to gain control of the company. During the PRR's entire history, corporate raiders were never able to attack it, in part because a thicket of outlying corporations protected the company itself.[11]

As the prosperity of the postwar decade gave way to the severe depression of the 1870s, many of the investments undertaken by executives such as Thomson and Scott proved quite disappointing, both to them personally and to the company that they represented. With the benefit of hindsight, journalists and politicians—and even some of the PRR's investors—criticized the involvement of PRR managers in railroad projects thousands of miles removed from Pennsylvania. While acknowledging that other railroaders had committed far worse offenses—and they frequently invoked the name of Jay Gould in that context—critics charged PRR officials with being involved in conflicts of interest. Most of those accusations, it should be noted, emanated from those who had battled the Pennsylvania Railroad, and lost. Furthermore, the term "conflict of interest" had a very different meaning during the middle years of the nineteenth century than it does today. As entrepreneurs, investors, and managers were navigating the transition from personal to corporate capitalism, the good of the individual and that of the company were often closely intertwined.[12] Thomson and Scott certainly intended to profit from their projects in the south and west, but they also expected that the Southern Railway Security Company, the Texas & Pacific Railway, and other ventures would funnel traffic to the Pennsylvania Railroad. That their strategy failed was less an indictment of conflicting interests than of the unpredictable cycles of nineteenth-century capitalism, coupled with the inability of any manager, no matter how skilled, to oversee a truly national railroad system.

A Bridge to the West

St. Louis was the gateway city for the central and southern West, the source for the railway traffic that would flow east over PRR rails. Of equal importance to Thomson and Scott, it was the focal point for potentially lucrative investments in the construction and operation of western railroads. Reaching the city from the east, however, would require two very different sorts of bridges. The first was a conventional, if extraordinarily complex work of civil engineering, the work of the St. Louis Bridge Company chief engineer James Buchanan Eads. Yet, the St. Louis Bridge (or Eads Bridge, as it was later known) would have mattered little had it not been for a very different sort of bridge, one that linked the political and organizational connections of PRR executives—as well as their ability to guarantee a steady flow of rail traffic over the structure—to Andrew Carnegie's financial acumen.

During the Civil War, Carnegie had parted company with the Pennsylvania Railroad, but the young financier continued to benefit from his experiences as a railway telegrapher, a personal assistant to Scott, and a PRR executive. He had learned the importance of efficiency as a prerequisite for generating a high volume of output at the lowest possible price, a lesson that he would ultimately employ to great effect in the steel industry. That came later, however. In the immediate aftermath of the Civil War, Carnegie, like many Americans, believed that the railroads provided the greatest technological, organizational, and financial challenges and opportunities of his generation. He also knew that the PRR, as the nation's preeminent railroad, offered more potential than any other company in the United States. Carnegie had left the Pennsylvania Railroad not because he thought it unimportant, but because he suspected that he could earn far higher rewards through independent action in concert with the PRR. By exploiting his personal and professional connections to Thomson, Scott, and other PRR executives, Carnegie could enrich himself—and them—by serving as a supplier and a contractor for the railroad.

Given their complex construction and high cost, bridges offered an unparalleled source of investment opportunity, particularly to someone who, like Carnegie, understood a thing or two about metal. As was typical of American railway construction, most of the early bridges on the PRR were built from wood, quickly and relatively inexpensively. By 1858, PRR resident engineer Thomas Seabrook had concluded that many of those original wooden bridges were badly decayed and weakened. They were also at considerable risk, on a railroad that operated steam locomotives. By the time of the Civil War, the PRR had lost two smaller wooden bridges to fire, despite a precautionary coating of "fireproof" paint. Because such bridges could be expected to last only nine years in normal service, Seabrook asserted, it was time to invest in more durable iron replacements.[13]

Engineers on the Baltimore & Ohio, anxious to avoid the enormous expense of the stone viaducts that were used on the eastern end of the route, sought a cheaper way to build bridges. In 1839 Benjamin Latrobe made use of bridge components fabricated from cast iron (which is strongest in compression and weakest in tension) and wrought iron (which is strongest in tension but comparatively weak in compression). In 1840, engineers designed the first iron truss road bridge, followed in 1845 by the first all-iron railway bridge.

The PRR was not an early adopter of iron, but the delay fortuitously enabled engineers such as Herman Haupt to assess its merits in bridge construction. In 1848, Thomson had hired Haupt as his principal assistant engineer, based largely on his abilities as a bridge designer. Haupt had gone on to establish the basis of the PRR's operations, with his superb command of statistics proving essential to efficient, low-cost operation. He did not abandon his love of bridges, however, and he soon came to appreciate the advantages of cast and wrought iron. Perhaps with the assistance of Western Division associate engineer Edward Miller, Haupt prepared designs for four composite bridges that blended elements of iron and timber construction, although only three of them were ever built.[14]

Based on his previous experience, in 1851 Haupt felt confident enough to design a single-track bridge at Johnstown. At Altoona, crews fabricated the all-iron superstructure of the Pratt deck truss, and assembled the components at the bridge site. When completed, its five spans stretched 380 feet across the Conemaugh River. A reporter for the *Johnstown Mountain Echo* called it "the most beautiful structure in the world."[15]

Haupt was an acknowledged expert in the mathematical analysis of stresses and, unlike many other pioneering designs, the Haupt bridge at Johnstown, and those modeled on it, proved more than adequate for the loads that he intended them to carry. His most important insight did not stem from the use of iron, but rather from his decision to divide the Conemaugh River bridge into a series of standardized panels. The length of the bridge determined the number of spans, with the two Haupt trusses that composed each span likewise made up of fourteen, sixteen, or eighteen panels, depending on the length required. Once fabricated, the panels could be stored at Altoona and quickly assembled into bridge trusses whenever the need arose.[16]

Haupt was by no means the only talented bridge designer to work for the PRR. One of the best was Jacob Hays Linville, who joined the company in 1857 as assistant resident engineer on the Middle Division, under William Hasell Wilson. Linville, a Quaker from Lancaster County, followed a rather atypical career path. Determined to be a lawyer, he clerked for William M. Meredith, who as Philadelphia Select Council president in 1846 had supported the Pennsylvania Railroad but had been reluctant to commit city funds to the project. Abandoning the law after less than a year, Linville became a surveyor for the unbuilt Lancaster, Lebanon & Pine Grove Railroad, which Thomson had once envisioned as an alternate route to the state-owned Philadelphia & Columbia.

Linville rose rapidly on the PRR. He soon earned a promotion to Middle Division assistant resident engineer and in 1863 to engineer of bridges and buildings. Given the PRR's territorial expansion, and with traffic levels on the rise, Linville had his work cut out for him. "I went to Altoona with a young wife, with everything new to me," he recalled. "The bridges on the line were nearly all a wreck; I knew nothing of bridges, and had at my disposal nothing but Haupt's old book, all wrong." Linville had some cause to denigrate Haupt's 1851 magnum opus, *The General Theory of Bridge Construction*, as it was now more than a decade old in a rapidly changing profession. The young upstart's first major work was the design of the Arsenal Bridge, which carried the PRR's Delaware Extension across the Schuylkill River and gave the PRR access to South Philadelphia and the Delaware waterfront.[17]

To the west, the construction of the Pittsburgh & Steubenville Railroad provided Linville with the opportunity to design bridges across the Monongahela

River at Pittsburgh and across the Ohio River at Steubenville. Steamboat interests, concerned that the new route would erode their traffic, demanded that the bridge across the Ohio River offer a clear span of three hundred feet between piers in order to provide unobstructed navigation. They were certain that such a bridge could not be built, but Thomson, equally confident in Linville's abilities, agreed to the stipulation without hesitation. His trust was not misplaced, and the Steubenville Bridge opened to traffic on October 9, 1865. As part of the Steubenville Bridge project, Linville developed a machine to test bridge components, in collaboration with the Philadelphia machine shops of William Sellers & Company—one of many examples of the benefits that the tightly knit community of technological practitioners in the Quaker City provided for the Pennsylvania Railroad.

By the end of the Civil War, thanks largely to his association with the Pennsylvania Railroad, Linville had established a reputation as one of the best bridge engineers in the United States. Linville left the PRR and established his own consulting business, and he secured the PRR as one of his major clients.

Linville's ability to design iron bridges soon attracted the attention of Andrew Carnegie. As early as 1856, Carnegie, then a twenty-one-year-old assistant to Scott, expressed a keen interest in Herman Haupt's iron truss bridges, but it would be several more years before Carnegie would be in a position to enter the bridge-building field. During the Civil War, the interests of Andrew Carnegie and those of the Pennsylvania Railroad were increasingly divergent. Carnegie still depended on Thomson, Scott, and the PRR, principally because he had an ironclad rule that he would never undertake any investments without reliable inside information—and his connections to the PRR provided some of the best inside information available. Yet his interests were those of an investor, not a manager, and his annual PRR salary of $2,400 represented no more than 5 percent of his total income. During the war, Carnegie invested in the oilfields of northwestern Pennsylvania, and by the summer of 1863 his holdings in the Columbia Oil Company had made him exceedingly wealthy.

After spending barely four months in Washington during 1861, assisting Scott with the military's transportation needs, Carnegie returned to his position as superintendent of the Western Division (which became the Pittsburgh Division in a February 1, 1863, reorganization). His employees struggled to cope with weak and deteriorating wooden bridges, suggesting to Carnegie the possibility of a lucrative postwar market for replacement structures made of iron.

In short order, Carnegie made the transition from railroader to bridge builder, and then to steel manufacturer. Each of those enterprises was critically dependent on the railroads, and on the PRR in particular. In February 1862, six years after he first observed workers fabricating iron bridge panels at Altoona, Carnegie established the partnership of Piper & Shiffler. His associates were John Piper, the PRR's chief mechanic at Altoona, Aaron Shiffler, the PRR's bridge supervisor, and Jacob Linville, at that time the PRR's Middle Division assistant resident engineer. For an investment of $1,250, Carnegie maintained a one-fifth share in the new company. His major client, the Pennsylvania Railroad, was also his employer.[18]

In April 1865, Carnegie resigned his job on the Pennsylvania Railroad in order to manage Piper & Shiffler, as well as his other investments. On May 1, 1865, Carnegie and Linville incorporated the Piper & Shiffler partnership as the Keystone Bridge Company. Scott matched Carnegie's $40,000 investment in the new firm, and the future steel magnate reciprocated by holding Scott's shares, disguising his investment from PRR shareholders. Thomson likewise invested heavily in Keystone Bridge, registering the stock in his wife's name.[19]

By 1868, Thomson had increased his stake in Keystone Bridge, and in that year he authorized the PRR's Engineer Department to install iron bridges in place of the existing wooden ones all along the main line. The contracts went to the Keystone Bridge Company. Thomson and Scott thus enriched themselves, apparently at the expense of PRR stockholders. However, as bridge designer Washington A. Roebling noted when he visited the Keystone Bridge fabrication yard, that type of interlocking ownership enabled the PRR to maintain control over the quality and delivery dates of bridge materials. It also allowed PRR officials to pay relatively low salaries to their bridge engineers, primarily because those individuals hoped that a probationary period on the railroad would lead to a more lucrative career at Keystone Bridge.[20]

Thomson and Scott found many ways to benefit from their association with the Keystone Bridge Company. They participated in the profit generated by the orders that the PRR placed with Keystone. Carnegie's Union Iron Mills, in which Thomson and Scott were investors, sold iron to Keystone, offering further opportunities for gain. The greatest rewards, however, came not from the bridges themselves, but rather from the new railroad lines that the bridges made possible. Thomson and Scott, often with Carnegie in tow, invested heavily in the development of western railroads, in the construction companies that built them, and in the railway equipment that ran over them.[21]

Congress provided the opportunity for Thomson, Scott, and Carnegie to profit from their association with the Keystone Bridge Company. On July 25, 1866, President Andrew Johnson signed Senate Bill No. 236, authorizing the construction of eight bridges across the Mississippi River—at Winona, Minnesota; Prairie du Chien, Wisconsin; Dubuque, Iowa; Burlington, Iowa; Keokuk, Iowa; Quincy, Illinois; Hannibal, Missouri; and St. Louis.

The bridge at Keokuk quickly attracted the attention of Carnegie, who in turn interested Thomson and Scott in the project. Keokuk lay at virtually the same latitude as the eastern end of the transcontinental railroad at Council Bluffs, Iowa, and any company that controlled a bridge across the Mississippi at that location could easily build a rail line due west across southern Iowa, benefiting from land grants, tapping into rich agricultural traffic, and controlling rail access to California. In December 1868 representatives from several railroads that might connect with the proposed bridge—including Benjamin Smith's Columbus, Chicago & Indiana Central Railway—organized the Keokuk & Hamilton Bridge Company.[22] Carnegie, Thomson, and Scott invested in the company as well. The two PRR executives sought personal financial gain from the project, but they also appreciated that the bridge, in conjunction with the CC&IC, might well generate additional traffic for the PRR. To no one's surprise, the Keystone Bridge Company secured the contract to build the span across the river, while another Carnegie enterprise, Carnegie, Kloman & Company, manufactured the basic components. By

Eastern Lines affiliated with the Pennsylvania Railroad

PFW	Pittsburgh, Fort Wayne & Chicago Railway (Chicago to Pittsburgh)
CC	Columbus, Chicago & Indiana Central Railway (Illinois state line (Effner) to Logansport and Richmond, Indiana and Columbus, Ohio)
THI	Terre Haute & Indianapolis Rail Road / St. Louis, Vandalia & Terre Haute Railroad (St. Louis to Indianapolis)
V	Indianapolis & Vincennes Railroad / Cairo & Vincennes Railroad (Indianapolis to Cairo, Illinois)
MC	Memphis & Charleston Railroad (Memphis to Stevenson, Alabama, with connections to Chattanooga)
EW	Erie & Western Transportation Company (Anchor Line, steamship service connecting Chicago, Duluth, Cleveland, Erie, Buffalo, and other Great Lakes ports)

Western Lines affiliated with the Pennsylvania Railroad

UP	Union Pacific Railroad (Omaha, Nebraska to Ogden, Utah)
KP	Leavenworth, Pawnee & Western Railroad / Union Pacific, Eastern Division / Kansas Pacific Railway (Kansas City to Denver)
I	Iowa Contracting Company (Keokuk, Iowa to Kearney, Nebraska, not built)
DSP	Davenport & St. Paul Construction Company / Davenport & St. Paul Railway (never completed)
NP	Northern Pacific Railroad (Duluth to St. Paul, Minnesota, and Duluth to Tacoma Washington—complete to Bismarck, Dakota Territory, at the time of its 1874 bankruptcy)
AP	Atlantic & Pacific Railroad (Springfield, Missouri west along the 35th Parallel, largely incomplete at the time of the Panic of 1873, most of route eventually built by several companies, without any PRR involvement)
IM	St. Louis & Mountain Railroad (St. Louis to Texarkana)
CF	Cairo & Fulton Railroad (Birds Point, Missouri/ Cairo, Illinois to Arkansas state line)
TP	Texas & Pacific Railway (Texarkana to Marshall, Texas and west to San Diego, California, largely incomplete at the time of the Panic of 1873, western terminus later established at Sierra Blanca, Texas)

Western Lines, not affiliated with the Pennsylvania Railroad

CNW	Chicago & North Western Railroad
CP	Central Pacific Railroad
DP	Denver Pacific Railway
SP	Southern Pacific Railroad

the summer of 1871, trains were crossing the Mississippi River at Keokuk, but the bridge remained primarily a Carnegie project, and not one that was critical to the interests of Thomson, Scott, or the Pennsylvania Railroad.[23]

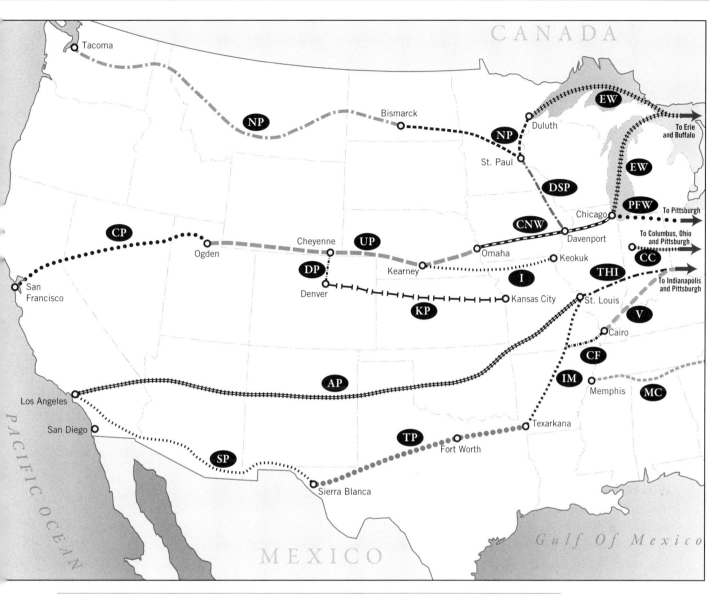

Figure 43. The Pacific Railroad Act of 1862 provided federal support for a transcontinental railroad, and anointed the Union Pacific and the Central Pacific as the two companies that would lay rails between Omaha, Nebraska, and Sacramento, California. A provision in the legislation offered the Leavenworth, Pawnee & Western Railroad (later the Union Pacific, Eastern Division, and later still the Kansas Pacific) the chance to garner federal bond guarantees for a parallel line west. J. Edgar Thomson, Tom Scott, and other investors associated with the PRR soon became involved in the Union Pacific Railroad, as well as the Union Pacific, Eastern Division, a proposed link across Iowa, and two bridges over the Mississippi River, one at St. Louis, and the other at Keokuk, Iowa. There were also investments in the Northern Pacific Railway, west from Duluth, Minnesota, and in the Atlantic & Pacific Railroad in the Southwest. The St. Louis, Iron Mountain & Southern Railway angled southwestward toward Tom Scott's most notorious investment, the Texas & Pacific Railway. This map shows all of those projects at their greatest promised extent, even though many were barely under way at the time of the PRR's involvement, and several would never be completed. Had the plans of Thomson and Scott come to fruition, the PRR would have established friendly connections with railroads leading to San Diego, San Francisco, and Puget Sound, through gateways such as Cairo, Illinois, St. Louis, and Keokuk. The ships of the PRR's Anchor Line subsidiary, plying the Great Lakes, would have provided additional links between east and west. The Panic of 1873 ended those dreams and restricted the PRR's operations to the lands east of the Mississippi.

St. Louis was another matter entirely. While the Keokuk bridge offered the PRR the possibility of a connection to the transcontinental railroad, the corresponding river crossing at St. Louis provided something far more valuable—access to one of the key gateway cities to the West. On July 20, 1868, Congress authorized the Illinois & St. Louis Bridge Company to build across the Mississippi River at St. Louis. The timing was fortuitous for the PRR. In April, the PRR board of directors had consolidated several of its subsidiaries, including the Steubenville & Indiana Railroad and the Pan Handle Railway, into the Pittsburgh, Cincinnati & St. Louis Railway, the core component of the PRR's Southwest System. Two months earlier, in February 1868, representatives of those companies had agreed to finance jointly the construction of the St. Louis, Vandalia & Terre Haute Railroad. By the summer of 1870, the completed Vandalia Route offered the PRR a secure connection with the Mississippi River.

The PRR did not invest directly in the Illinois & St. Louis Bridge Company, but by 1871 Thomson and Scott, along with Carnegie, had a considerable personal stake in the venture. They intended for the company to earn a profit, but they also believed that the greatest returns would arise from building the bridge, and not its operation. The three executives arranged a construction contract for cost plus 20 percent with the Keystone Bridge Company. Half of the surcharge was a commission to the three executives for negotiating the arrangement, and the remainder a constituted guaranteed profit for Keystone (largess that would ultimately trickle down into the pockets of Carnegie, Thomson, Scott, and other investors). Thomson and Scott also assisted Carnegie in securing financing for the bridge, and their personal endorsement of the Illinois & St. Louis Bridge Company provided Carnegie with considerable leverage as he attempted to place bonds with Junius S. Morgan's investment banking house.[24]

The pending completion of the St. Louis Bridge (it opened for traffic in 1874) induced PRR executives to demand adequate facilities for the handling of passengers and freight in St. Louis. In June 1870, Thomson assigned PRR chief assistant engineer Joseph M. Wilson to evaluate the designs for the new St. Louis Grand Union Passenger Depot. Four years later, in May 1874, Scott helped to organize the Union De-

pot Company of St. Louis, and served as that firm's vice president. Several railroads affiliated with the PRR, including the Pittsburgh, Cincinnati & St. Louis and the St. Louis, Vandalia & Terre Haute, owned shares representing $600,000 of the Union Depot Company's $1.5 million capitalization. Bridge designer Eads initially persuaded Scott to advocate a union depot site at the western end of the bridge, with the station itself suspended on pilings forty-five feet in the air. Carnegie dissuaded Scott from such an impractical plan, and the station, which opened on June 11, 1875, was subsequently located south of the bridge and some ten blocks away from the river.[25]

Ever Westward

The bridges at Keokuk and St. Louis were but the leading edge of what Thomson and Scott envisioned as a multi-pronged incursion into the West. Once again, public policy provided Thomson and Scott with unprecedented opportunities to extend the westward reach of the Pennsylvania Railroad, while creating potentially profitable investment opportunities. During the 1850s, in a decade rife with sectional tension, Congress had authorized a series of Pacific Railroad Surveys. A combination of engineering and political considerations ensured that there would not be one route to the Pacific, but five. Four ran east to west, while the fifth, along the Pacific coast, explored the possibility of uniting San Diego and Seattle by rail. Between 1853 and 1855, and acting under instructions from Secretary of War Jefferson Davis, teams of surveyors scoured the West, attempting to locate viable crossings of the Rocky Mountains and the Sierra Nevada.

America at mid-century offered substantial opportunities for the ambitious young men who led the surveying teams across half a continent. It could be a time of great risk, as well, and only three of the five principal surveyors were destined to live out the full measure of their natural lives. John W. Gunnison, assigned to a route bounded by the 38th and 39th parallels, lived barely long enough to send back word of a horror of ridges and canyons before dying at the hands of Ute Indians. Isaac Stevens, responsible for the northern route, between the 47th and 49th parallels, survived his work but not the Civil War; in September 1862 he perished at the Battle of Chantilly. A few years after Amiel Whipple supervised a southern survey along the 35th parallel, he fell at Chancellorsville. John Parke and John Pope, the only surveyors to die of old age, explored the territory along the 32nd parallel—a particular favorite of Davis's, owing to its southern location.[26]

The individuals who carried out the Pacific Railroad Surveys did their work well. As the nation recovered from the war that had killed Stevens, Whipple, and thousands of others, promoters, engineers, and laborers constructed railroads that roughly followed all four of the east–west routes. It was a testament to the thoroughness of Thomson, Scott, and other Pennsylvania Railroad executives that they became involved in efforts to build and control railroads along all four routes. West of the Mississippi, several carriers—most notably the Union Pacific, the Kansas Pacific, the Northern Pacific, and the Texas & Pacific—offered a mechanism for directing west coast traffic to PRR rails. They also provided Thomson, Scott, and their associates considerable opportunity for personal profit, through speculative transactions, access to government aid, and lucrative construction contracts. Even before dignitaries drove the golden spike at Promontory Point, Utah, on May 10, 1869, Thomson, Scott, and other railway executives hoped to capture a substantial portion of the California traffic that was certain to flow along the new transcontinental railroad. If that route would connect to the western end of the Pennsylvania Railroad system, then so much the better. If it funneled additional profits into the pockets of Thomson and Scott, then better still. Yet, the West was a long way from the familiar territory of Pennsylvania, and PRR executives time and time again encountered serious impediments to their efforts to influence the railroads that lay beyond the Mississippi.

Union Pacific and Kansas Pacific

While Thomson, Scott, and their PRR associates pursued several western railroad projects more or less simultaneously, their earliest investments were in two parallel lines, the Union Pacific and the Union Pacific, Eastern Division, known after 1869 as the Kansas Pacific Railway. During the 1850s, sectional rivalries had delayed the construction of a transcontinental railroad, with northerners and southerners each arguing in favor of alignments that best served their commercial and political interests. Secession resolved that issue in favor of the North. On July 1, 1862, President Abraham Lincoln signed the Pacific Railroad Act, empowering the Union Pacific Railroad and the Central Pacific Railroad to construct a transcontinental line along the 38th parallel route, funded in part by a subsidy of government bonds and land grants. The law authorized the construction of another, more southerly, route west from the Missouri River, also underwritten by federal aid. That project, eventually known as the Kansas Pacific Railway, soon attracted the attention of Thomson and Scott, and only later did they turn their attentions to the Union Pacific itself.

In 1855, local boosters in Leavenworth, Kansas, had incorporated the Leavenworth, Pawnee & Western Railroad, hoping to connect their community to Kansas City, to the south and east along the Missouri River, and to the expanding eastern rail network. Within two years, the company had passed into the hands of outside speculators, but the prairie sod remained untouched. The 1862 Pacific Railroad Act suddenly made the hapless Leavenworth, Pawnee & Western a very valuable property. Its promoters now had the right to build west from Kansas City, Kansas, to Fort Riley and then northwest to meet the Union Pacific at the 100th meridian. In 1863, its incorporators renamed the company the Union Pacific, Eastern Division, in an effort to convince investors that it was destined to be *the* transcontinental railway. After persistent lobbying by UPED promoters, a second Pacific Railroad Act stipulated that should the company arrive at the 100th meridian ahead of the Union Pacific, it could continue west to meet the Central Pacific. Success eluded the UPED and its promoters, however.[27]

Had the events of the mid-1860s taken place a half-century later, observers would probably have suggested that the Keystone Cops had been turned loose to build a railroad. Samuel Hallett, a New York promoter who had attained resoundingly modest success by attempting to interest European investors in the rights to the Nautilus Diving-Bell Submarine, bullied his way into the organization as a construction contractor. He had been involved with the Atlantic & Great Western, and so presumably knew something about railroads. Hallett nonetheless did an abysmally poor job of building his allotted section of roadbed. He was also involved in chronic disputes with his subordinates and on July 27, 1864, one of his subcontractors shot him to death. Hallett's former partner, John C. Frémont, was also involved in the company, but he was already in over his head. Frémont, whose earlier western explorations had earned him the sobriquet of "The Pathfinder," found financial matters rather more difficult to manage, and he began searching for a way to withdraw from the project. Thomas C. Durant, who was already heavily involved in building the Union Pacific, then attempted to take charge of the UPED. John D. Perry, the president of the Exchange Bank of St. Louis, had lent Hallett money to construct the UPED, and he now challenged Durant's control of the company. In the process, he enlisted the aid of Ann Hallett, the promoter's widow, and what little assistance Frémont could provide.[28]

By late November 1864, in his efforts to gain control over the UPED, Perry also recruited Columbus, Ohio, banker Benjamin E. Smith, former Ohio governor William Dennison, and Steubenville, Ohio, lawyer Thomas L. Jewett. All three were closely connected with the Pennsylvania Railroad, and to Thomson and Scott personally, and all three had played an important role in enabling the PRR to establish western connections at Chicago and St. Louis. Dennison, Jewett, and Smith were apparently the ones who approached Thomson and Scott and encouraged them to invest in the venture. Early in 1865, Thomson, along with Scott and locomotive builder Matthias Baldwin, paid a million dollars for a half-interest in the company, although Thomson had the authority to appoint one additional director, giving him effective control. Perry and his fellow St. Louis investors were delighted with the new infusion of capital and equally pleased that someone of Thomson's sterling reputation was associated with the company—proof, they insisted, the UPED would never attempt to defraud the federal government by failing to abide by the terms of the Pacific Railroad Act.[29]

In June 1865, Thomson and the other investors associated with the UPED formed a construction consortium, Robert M. Shoemaker & Company. Shoemaker, a native of Cincinnati, was an accomplished civil engineer and promoter who had worked on the Mad River & Lake Erie Railroad. As such, he was well acquainted with fellow Ohioans Smith, Dennison,

and Jewett.[30] The Shoemaker firm was similar to the 1864 Crédit Mobilier scheme that Durant and George Francis Train had organized to build the Union Pacific, but it was, in the words of an accountant employed by the federal government's Pacific Railway Commission, "more cleverly done."[31]

In August 1865, William Jackson Palmer, Thomson's onetime personal assistant, became secretary and treasurer of the UPED, serving as the liaison between the PRR interests and their St. Louis allies while overseeing the building of the railroad. Palmer, whose loyalty to the United States and hatred of slavery overcame his Quaker pacifism, had served with distinction during the Civil War. He earned both a Medal of Honor and a promotion to brigadier general, thanks in part to Tom Scott's influence. By March 1867, Thomson was anxious for greater control over the UPED, and he insisted that the board appoint Palmer vice president. The attempt failed and Thomson, whose authority on the PRR was by now almost unchallenged, must have been stung by the UPED board's refusal to carry out his instructions. With increasing frequency, moreover, the St. Louis investors were challenging or overriding the policies that Thomson and his PRR associates had established.[32]

During those struggles for control, westward construction on the UPED proceeded at a plodding pace. Initially, the Union Pacific itself did no better, but that company soon outdistanced the UPED, beating it to the 100th meridian and ensuring that it would be the first transcontinental line. After that disheartening defeat, both the PRR and the St. Louis factions were in agreement that they should no longer attempt to link up with the Union Pacific, but instead build west to Denver and a connection with the Denver Pacific Railway. In 1869, they abandoned the UPED moniker in favor of the more accurate Kansas Pacific Railway, and Palmer took charge of the Denver extension. At the same time, Perry was attempting to negotiate an agreement with the Central Pacific's Collis P. Huntington to form a through route to the Pacific Ocean, one that would draw traffic away from the Union Pacific and funnel it toward PRR rails at St. Louis, rather than Chicago. Scott apparently used his most persuasive lobbying skills, but he was unable to convince members of Congress to support a plan that would undermine the eastern end of the transcontinental railroad that they had only recently established.[33]

By 1870, when the Kansas Pacific reached Denver, the PRR associates had withdrawn from active participation in the company. PRR executives had never enjoyed adequate control over the Kansas Pacific, as demonstrated by Thomson's inability to elevate Palmer to the vice presidency in 1867. Following the 1868 elections, moreover, the federal government began to economize, threatening to suspend the lavish subsidies that western railroads had enjoyed only a few years earlier. Palmer was so pessimistic about the future of the Kansas Pacific that he left the company and began planning a railroad route along the Front Range of the Rocky Mountains, what in 1870 would become the Denver & Rio Grande Railroad. Both Thomson and Samuel Morse Felton, the former president of the Philadelphia, Wilmington & Baltimore Railroad, were associated with the venture, as trustees for the railroad's first mortgage bonds.[34]

After 1869, control over the Fort Wayne had given the PRR secure access to Chicago, the likely destination of much of the traffic flowing east over the Union Pacific.[35] In short, the PRR interests no longer needed the Kansas Pacific and were too busy to pay much attention to it. More important, Thomson was exhausted from his efforts to consolidate the PRR's properties in Ohio, Indiana, and Illinois; to establish control over the lines in New Jersey; to construct the Baltimore & Potomac to Washington; and to survive a seemingly unending series of rate wars. When Palmer briefly considered a final attempt to gain control over the Kansas Pacific and invited the PRR president to join forces with him, Thomson quickly declined. "I have reflected upon your suggestions in relationship to the Kansas Pacific," he wrote in January 1869, "but have come to the conclusion that if I attempt to increase my labours and responsibilities, that I will soon break down. In view of this, I have concluded that nothing but an overwhelming necessity shall induce me to extend our control of Railways beyond Chicago on the North and the Mississippi River on the South."[36] Thereafter, Scott, and not Thomson, would be the principal actor in the West.[37]

Thomson, Scott, and their associates experienced even greater disappointment from their association with the Union Pacific. Thomson had been a strong supporter of the Pacific Railroad Act, and during the Civil War he had served briefly on the Union Pacific's board of directors before shifting his attentions to the Kansas Pacific. He reacquainted himself with the Union Pacific in December 1870, after the federal government's requirement that the carrier begin paying interest on its subsidy bonds drastically reduced the value of its stock. The weakened condition of the Union Pacific soon attracted three rival sets of investors—New Yorkers under the leadership of Cornelius Vanderbilt; Bostonians led by John Murray Forbes, James F. Joy, and Oliver and Oakes Ames; and a group that orbited around the PRR.[38]

The PRR consortium began to form early in 1871, when sleeping car magnate George Pullman, an investor in the Union Pacific, told Carnegie that the UP needed an emergency infusion of $600,000 in cash. Pullman suggested that Carnegie talk the matter over with Scott and Thomson, hinting that Vanderbilt and other New York Central associates might take advantage of the situation to establish a close relationship with the eastern half of the transcontinental railroad. Thomson and Scott quickly agreed to supply Carnegie with sufficient PRR securities to underwrite the loan, with the proviso that all three men, along with Pullman, be elected to the UP board of directors at the March 1871 annual meeting, with Scott serving as president of the company. Also on the board was General Grenville M. Dodge, whose command of the Department of the Missouri had awakened him to the possibilities associated with a transcontinental railroad. Dodge had laid out much of the UP's initial route, but he repeatedly clashed with Thomas Clark Durant, the major shareholder in the railroad, who saw the company in largely speculative terms. Dodge—who, it should be noted, was a speculator and a lobbyist in his own right—soon formed an alliance with Scott, as the PRR vice president attempted to impose reforms on the Union Pacific. Scott moved the UP's executive office to New York and improved the carrier's operating efficiency by implementing the same administrative structures used on the PRR. A writer for the *Railroad Gazette* suggested that such tactics ensured that the PRR would "be likely to control all the transcontinental traffic for many years to come."[39]

The *Railroad Gazette*'s prediction turned out to be monumentally incorrect, and Scott and his fellow PRR associates lost control over the Union Pacific almost as quickly as they had gained it. With the PRR providing both operating talent and a guaranteed eastern outlet for the Union Pacific, investors bid up the price of UP securities. The stock soon surpassed $30 a share—more than it was worth, according to Carnegie. The Union Pacific had supplied the PRR with thirty thousand shares of stock, valued at something like a million dollars, as collateral for the $600,000 loan. The temptation proved too much for Carnegie, who, like Thomson, Scott, and Pullman, held those shares in trust, with options to buy them at market price. As the UP's stock rose in value, Carnegie began to sell his allotment of shares (which he did not yet legally own) anticipating that he could buy them back at some future date, after the speculative frenzy had subsided and the market price of the UP stock had declined. Word of the scheme leaked out, ruining the investors' plans. By the time of the next UP annual meeting, in March 1872, Thomson, Scott, and Carnegie no longer owned any Union Pacific securities, and they accordingly lost their seats on the UP's board of directors. To add insult to injury, New York Central interests, under the leadership of Horace F. Clark, Cornelius Vanderbilt's son-in-law, gained control over the UP, albeit only for an equally short period.[40]

In his *Autobiography*, Carnegie absolved himself of all responsibility in the fiasco, insisting that someone had removed the UP securities from a Boston bank vault while he was innocently abroad, selling Missouri River bridge bonds in London. "The idea that these [securities] should be sold, or that our party should lose the splendid position we had acquired in connection with the Union Pacific, never entered my brain," Carnegie reminisced.[41] He insisted that Pullman was likewise blameless, and suggested that it was all Scott's fault. In truth, Carnegie was ultimately responsible for the collapse of the PRR investment pool. His actions deeply affected Thomson's sensitive constitution and, according to his wife, caused his death two years later. To Scott, Carnegie's actions constituted both a public humiliation and a private betrayal. He learned that even the most trustworthy of individuals could not always be trusted, and that personal speculation by one business associate could have disastrous effects on the PRR's corporate policy.[42]

Transcontinental Opportunities to the North and to the South

Even as they were attempting, with scant success, to bring the Kansas Pacific and the Union Pacific into the PRR's sphere of influence, Thomson and Scott were also involved in a more northerly transcontinental project. Like the other two ventures, their association with the Northern Pacific Railroad owed much to the Pacific Railroad Surveys. In 1853, President Franklin Pierce appointed Isaac I. Stevens, an experienced engineer trained at West Point, as the first governor of the Washington Territory, and the young man set off for Olympia. Stevens may well have set a record for the longest yet simultaneously most productive crossing of the continent since the Lewis and Clark Expedition half a century earlier. On his way west, Stevens and his colleagues surveyed a railroad route through a region bounded by the 47th and 49th parallels. More than a decade passed before Congress, in July 1864, chartered the Northern Pacific Railroad, with the attendant promise of large land grants. The route to Puget Sound ran through rugged and remote country, however, and few investors were interested in the project.

The Northern Pacific, in conjunction with the PRR's existing routes to the Great Lakes, offered Thomson, Scott, and other executives associated with the PRR additional opportunities to extend their company's reach and to earn a profit for themselves. Much of the assistance came through an intermediary, the Pittsburgh, Fort Wayne & Chicago, a company that the PRR would lease in the summer of 1869. As early as April 1867, the directors of the Fort Wayne agreed to subscribe to a one-twelfth interest in the Northern Pacific securities being offered by Winslow, Lanier & Company and, a month later, resolved to provide up to $10,000 in direct aid to the new railroad.

The Northern Pacific project nonetheless lay dormant until May 1869, when the banking house of Jay Cooke & Company issued $100 million in NP first mortgage bonds. Thomson was in large measure responsible for Cooke's involvement in the Northern

Pacific venture. During the summer of 1868, Thomson had worked with Cooke to finance the Lake Superior & Mississippi River Railroad, with a route between St. Paul and Duluth. Cooke was already involved in real estate speculation in the region and, while complying with Thomson's request, he became intrigued with the financial possibilities associated with the Northern Pacific.

Thomson, Scott, and other PRR principals invested in the Northern Pacific, yet undertook little direct involvement in the railroad's financing, construction, or operation. Thomson's personal share was an eighth of the Fort Wayne's one-twelfth interest. Samuel Morse Felton, elected to the NP's board of directors in 1870, was particularly well placed to represent the PRR's interests on the Northern Pacific, as in 1869 President Grant had appointed him a commissioner to inspect the various Pacific railroads. Felton relinquished his NP directorship in 1873, at almost the same time that he was elected to the board of the PRR. Of more significance to the PRR associates, Fort Wayne president George Cass became the NP's president in 1872.[43]

In February 1870, thanks to the infusion of capital provided by Cooke and his associates, construction crews began work on the Northern Pacific. They headed west from a junction with the Lake Superior & Mississippi at Thomson, Minnesota, a site now known as Carlton, located just west of Duluth; the original name was a clear indication of the Northern Pacific's ties to the Pennsylvania Railroad. There was a serious problem, however, in that the nearest PRR rails ended at Chicago, more than four hundred miles away. Undaunted, Thomson and Scott developed at least two plans to connect the lines.

One of the projects was directly connected to the Keokuk Bridge Company, and indirectly associated with the Northern Pacific. Thomson, Scott, and Carnegie organized the Iowa Contracting Company to build a railroad that would stretch from Keokuk, across Iowa and through Nebraska City and Lincoln, before connecting with the Union Pacific at Fort Kearney, Nebraska. Like the Kansas Pacific, the line would have provided the PRR with access to California traffic flowing off of the Central Pacific and the Union Pacific. The resulting financial arrangements were so Byzantine in their complexity that, as one

Carnegie biographer has noted, "even Carnegie's closest associates lost track of him in the maze."[44] Thomas Carnegie, Andrew's brother, was not even aware that the Iowa Contracting Company was part of the family's business empire. In any event, the project never came to fruition.[45]

The Iowa Contracting Company in turn owned a share of another consortium, one that was much more closely linked to the Northern Pacific. On May 17, 1871, Thomson, Scott, and Carnegie incorporated the Davenport & St. Paul Construction Company. Joining them were some familiar faces. They included Union Pacific investors Oakes Ames and his son Oakes A. Ames, and Benjamin E. Smith and William Dennison, who had worked closely with Thomson and Scott in Ohio and Indiana, as well as on the Union Pacific, Eastern Division. Their goal was to connect Davenport, Iowa, to St. Paul by way of Rochester, Minnesota, along a route that was roughly parallel to, but well inland from the Mississippi River, affording the PRR a direct connection to the Northern Pacific. The consortium acquired the charter rights of the Davenport & St. Paul Railway, originally organized in May 1868, and construction proceeded, albeit at a sluggish pace. In 1872, crews built from Davenport ninety miles north to Delaware, Iowa. In 1873, the rails crept to Fayette, another thirty-nine miles closer to their goal, and there they stopped. By 1876, bondholders were suing the railroad, claiming that the money had been raised under false pretenses and misappropriated.[46] The railroad went bankrupt and was sold at foreclosure proceedings in March 1876. The assessment of the Iowa Board of Railroad Commissioners, that they had "never been able to find the records of this company," summarized the sad history of that moribund railroad.[47] In 1880, what there was of the Davenport & St. Paul came under the control of the Chicago, Milwaukee & St. Paul Railway, a company that in later years would pursue its own ill-advised transcontinental ambitions.[48]

With the failure of the Davenport & St. Paul project, the PRR obtained access to the Northern Pacific by water, rather than land. In 1870, the Erie & Western Transportation Company (the Anchor Line) established through service linking Erie, Pennsylvania, and Duluth, Minnesota. The ships used on the Great Lakes were named the *China*, the *Japan*, and the *In-*

dia, in anticipation of transpacific trade with Asia. The Lake Superior & Mississippi Railroad, completed in 1870 and leased to the Northern Pacific the following year, provided rail access at Duluth. By January 1872 the NP and the PRR were shipping Pennsylvania coal by rail to Erie, then by Erie & Western ship to Duluth, and then again by train to the western railhead of Moorhead, Minnesota. In the years that followed, the Anchor Line ferried coal and eastern manufactured goods to Lake Superior, for onward movement by rail, while grain and lumber made the trip in reverse. By the 1880s, ever-increasing quantities of iron ore were moving out of northern Minnesota, bound for eastern steel mills. The Anchor Line did not compete for that traffic, and PRR officials were content to transport the ore by rail from lake ports such as Cleveland, Ashtabula, and Erie to the mills.

Well before the development of the ore deposits in northern Minnesota, however, the Northern Pacific was in serious trouble, and so too were the PRR's ties to that company. By January 1871, thanks in part to inaccurate surveys by chief engineer W. Milnor Roberts, a veteran of Pennsylvania's Main Line of Public Works, the railroad was on the verge of bankruptcy. In desperation, Cooke begged Scott to use his political connections to persuade Congress to guarantee the Northern Pacific's bonds. Scott did his best, but in the aftermath of the Crédit Mobilier scandal, few elected officials were willing to support a federal subsidy for another struggling western railroad. Without federal aid, the Northern Pacific collapsed, as did the banking house of Jay Cooke & Company. When Cooke's bank failed on September 18, 1873, it sparked the Panic of 1873, which in turn plunged eighty-nine railroads into bankruptcy and led to one of the most severe depressions in American history. After the NP defaulted on its bond interest in 1874, Cass relinquished the presidency and became receiver of the bankrupt company. The collapse wiped out the relatively trivial sums that Thomson, Scott, and others had invested in the Northern Pacific venture, but the PRR investors nonetheless exerted considerable influence over the NP's reorganization. Their input continued until 1881, when financier and journalist Henry Villard acquired control of the NP. Under his leadership, the Northern Pacific reached the Pacific coast in 1883, but the PRR was not a part of that success.[49]

Even as the Northern Pacific was faltering, Thomson and Scott pursued more southerly routes to the Pacific, building on their investments in the St. Louis Bridge Company. On March 12, 1849, local entrepreneurs incorporated the Pacific Railroad Company of Missouri to build west from St. Louis, toward the Kansas state line. By 1852, tracks had reached Franklin (later renamed Pacific), Missouri, a short distance southwest of St. Louis. In June 1852 Congress permitted the state of Missouri to award federal lands to encourage railroad construction. The Missouri legislature in turn chartered the Southwest Branch of the Pacific Railroad and empowered the new company to receive federal land grants. From a junction with the Pacific Railroad at Franklin, the Southwest Branch, as its name suggested, would angle toward the southwestern portion of the state. Over the following two years, as part of the Pacific Railroad Surveys, Lieutenant Amiel Weeks Whipple mapped out a transcontinental route along the 35th parallel, from Fort Smith, Arkansas, west to the Pacific. Fort Smith, situated in northwestern Arkansas, was not that far from the destination of the Southwest Branch, suggesting that that carrier could constitute the easternmost portion of yet another transcontinental railroad. In an effort to speed construction, the railroad's managers hired some of the best available talent, including former PRR chief engineer Edward Miller. Nevertheless, by 1861, the Southwest Branch had managed to complete only a short stretch of track linking the Missouri towns of Franklin and Rolla. The lavish aid provided by the state of Missouri did little to help matters, and in 1866 the state government seized the railroad for nonpayment of debts.[50]

In June 1866, John C. Frémont purchased the Southwest Branch (although not the earlier Pacific Railroad) in order to secure both the land grants and a possible St. Louis connection for his Union Pacific, Eastern Division, project. He reorganized his new acquisition as the Southwest Pacific Railroad.[51] A month later, Congress incorporated the Atlantic & Pacific Railroad, enabling Frémont to build from Springfield, Missouri, west to California, and gain nearly fifty million acres of federal land grants in the process. Thomson and Scott were among the initial incorporators of the Atlantic & Pacific. So too was James Eads, who envisioned the company as a mechanism for funneling western traffic over the St. Louis Bridge Company's crossing at St. Louis. The two PRR executives likewise concluded that the Atlantic & Pacific would constitute a superb western outlet for the PRR's traffic, moving through the secure gateway at St. Louis.[52]

For Thomson and Scott personally, as well as for the Pennsylvania Railroad, the foray into the Atlantic & Pacific was a disappointment. Much of the problem stemmed from the decision to build across Indian Territory (Oklahoma), where federal land grants were not available. Frémont's involvement lasted barely a year, owing to his failure to pay the state of Missouri for the purchase of the Southwest Pacific Railroad. By 1872, work had ground to a halt, with tracks extending only as far west as Vinita, near the eastern border of Indian Territory. During 1873, Thomson, Scott, and their PRR associates increased their involvement in the company, probably as part of an attempt to build south to a connection with the Texas & Pacific at the 104th meridian. Both Thomson and Scott were on the board of directors of the Atlantic & Pacific, with Scott serving a brief stint as president between the summer of 1873 and August 1874. Yet the company continued to stagnate, thanks in large measure to the Panic of 1873 and the collapse of Jay Cooke's banking house. Repeated efforts to petition the federal government for assistance proved unsuccessful.[53] In November 1875, the Atlantic & Pacific went bankrupt, ending any further PRR involvement. The eastern portion of the Atlantic & Pacific eventually became part of the St. Louis–San Francisco Railway, while a section to the west formed a key component of the Atchison, Topeka & Santa Fe main line. The middle portion, composing much of the proposed route, was never completed.[54]

Texas & Pacific

The Texas & Pacific Railway offered the PRR yet another possible route to the Pacific coast, but its turbulent history taxed Scott's ability to his utmost, and nearly destroyed him. To an even greater extent than any other western venture, the Texas & Pacific offered large potential rewards to Scott, to Thomson, and to the Pennsylvania Railroad. If completed, the railroad would guarantee the PRR access to the Pacific coast through its gateway city of St. Louis. For Scott person-

ally, the land grants that accompanied the project held far greater allure, as did the possibility of a federal construction subsidy. Finally, as with other western projects, Scott, Thomson, and their associates could anticipate lavish profits associated with the construction of the new railroad. As events transpired, however, all of those avenues of opportunity remained closed to PRR officials, in large measure because they faced an extraordinarily formidable adversary in the person of Collis Potter Huntington, one of the principal backers of the Central Pacific Railroad.

Of the four transcontinental routes identified by the 1853–1855 Pacific Railroad Surveys, the one farthest to the south ran roughly along the 32nd parallel, from the eastern border of Texas to San Diego, California. Although the proposed railway would traverse arid and largely uninhabited country, it would cross the Continental Divide at the lowest elevation of any of the transcontinental routes and was the only one that offered the certainty of year-round operation, free of snow and ice. It was also a particular favorite of Secretary of War Jefferson Davis, the Mississippi planter who headed the surveys, and his fellow southerners, as it afforded the South unimpeded access to the Pacific. Unfortunately, part of the route lay in Mexico, a problem not resolved until April 1854, when the Senate temporarily overcame sectional animosities and ratified the Gadsden Purchase. The secession of the southern states a few years later, however, ensured that a northern-dominated Congress would support the construction of a transcontinental railroad on the more northerly route occupied by the Union Pacific and the Central Pacific.

Even before the driving of the golden spike in 1869, the Central Pacific's organizers were beginning to expand their rail empire into southern California, and then east along the 32nd parallel route. The Central Pacific's "Big Four" (president Leland Stanford, vice president Huntington, treasurer Mark Hopkins, and construction contractor Charles Crocker) obtained control of several railroads south of Sacramento. The most important carrier was the Southern Pacific Railroad, incorporated in November 1865, with the rights to build from San Francisco south to Los Angeles and San Diego, and east to the Arizona territorial line. The Central Pacific acquired the Southern Pacific in 1868, and by September 1876, its rails had reached Los Angeles. Under Huntington's direction, Southern Pacific construction crews were soon working their way east through the San Gorgonio Pass, headed for the Colorado River at Fort Yuma, California.[55]

By the early 1870s, however, Huntington and Scott were contending for the right to connect Fort Yuma to the east. They were not the first to advocate a railroad along that route. Prior to the Civil War, the Texas legislature had chartered railroad corporations that would permit the construction of as many as five transcontinental railroads through the state. One project dated to February 1852, with the incorporation of the "Vicksburg & El Paso Railroad Company, or Texas Western Railroad Company," to build from Vicksburg, Mississippi, west to El Paso, by way of Shreveport, Louisiana, and Marshall and Fort Worth, Texas. In 1853, Texas legislators authorized a parallel line, the Memphis, El Paso & Pacific Railroad. Both the Texas Western (renamed the Southern Pacific Railroad in 1856, and an entirely separate entity from the later Southern Pacific of California) and the Memphis, El Paso & Pacific tempted investors with substantial state land grants, but by 1862 the Civil War had halted construction on both lines. In 1867, Frémont became associated with the Memphis, El Paso & Pacific and, using that railroad's land grants as collateral, sold more than $5 million in dubious bonds, mostly to French investors. The bonds were barely worth the paper that they were printed on, particularly after the Texas legislature rescinded the company's land grants. The resulting international financial scandal cost Frémont dearly, besmirching his reputation and making it politically impossible for Congress to provide aid for the Memphis, El Paso & Pacific. By July 1870, as part of a plan to restore the land grants, the Texas legislature had rechartered the Memphis, El Paso & Pacific as the Southern Trans-Continental Railway Company, but that did little to help the railroad's finances.[56]

A parallel transcontinental route gave Frémont a chance to rebuild his reputation and, of perhaps even greater importance, to recoup some of his effort by selling the rights of the Memphis, El Paso & Pacific/Southern Trans-Continental to other parties. The new project also offered Scott the opportunity to extend the PRR's influence westward and to advance his own investment interests. On March 3, 1871, Congress chartered the Texas Pacific Railroad Company to build a transcontinental line along the 32nd parallel route, resurrecting the old Memphis, El Paso & Pacific/Southern Trans-Continental. The Texas legislature authorized its own contribution of $6 million in state bonds and allowed the Texas Pacific to acquire the Southern Trans-Continental Railway Company and the Southern Pacific of Texas, along with their associated state land grants. The Texas Pacific project thus offered the triple inducement of state bonds, state land grants, and ultimately federal land grants, as well.[57]

Frémont and Scott were among the incorporators of the new Texas Pacific Railroad (renamed the Texas & Pacific Railway in May 1872), as was Scott's ally from the Union Pacific, Grenville M. Dodge. Working closely with Scott, Dodge soon became an indispensible spokesman, promoter, and lobbyist for the railroad, and for a federal subsidy to build it. Five of the Texas Pacific's directors were associated with the PRR. In addition to Scott, they included future PRR president Alexander J. Cassatt; Albert Hewson, a clerk to future president George B. Roberts and later secretary of several PRR subsidiaries; Pennsylvania Company secretary Joseph Lesley; and Thomson's private secretary, Henry C. Spackman. In February 1872, the Texas Pacific's board of directors elected Scott to the presidency.[58]

Scott and the other principals in the Texas & Pacific intended to profit from the construction of the railroad as much as from the bonds and the land grants. Scott's association with Grenville Dodge proved particularly valuable in that regard, because during the 1860s Dodge had helped to organize Crédit Mobilier, the construction company that built the Union Pacific. By June 1, Scott had assigned the Texas & Pacific construction mortgage to Thomson and Samuel Morse Felton. Little more than two weeks later, Thomson, Scott and his private secretary (and future PRR vice president) John P. Green, George B. Roberts, Henry H. Houston, and Baldwin Locomotive Works executive Matthew Baird met in Philadelphia to form the Domain Land Company, soon renamed the California & Texas Railway Construction Company, a firm that closely resembled both Crédit Mobilier and the PRR's 1868 Continental Improvement Company. Scott persuaded Thomson to invest half a million dollars in the enterprise. Scott also endeavored to soothe relations with French investors in the Memphis, El Paso & Pacific by promising that he would make good their losses, even though he was not legally required to do so. The pledge went unfulfilled, however, a lapse that later cost Scott dearly, when he attempted to obtain a federal construction subsidy for the Texas & Pacific. Under the terms of the August 1872 construction contract, engineers were ready to move beyond the Texas border and survey a line from El Paso west to San Diego, roughly paralleling Huntington's Southern Pacific of California. In early 1873, construction began in earnest, with 251 miles of track laid by the end of the year.[59]

There was a problem, however, in that the eastern extremity of the Texas & Pacific route was at Texarkana, nearly five hundred miles from the nearest PRR-affiliated rails at St. Louis. To bridge that gap, Scott intended to rely on the St. Louis & Iron Mountain Railroad, linking St. Louis to the Arkansas state line, and often known simply as the "Iron Mountain." The Cairo & Fulton Railroad, a company that the Iron Mountain absorbed in 1874, provided a terminus on the Mississippi River opposite Cairo, Illinois. From Cairo, the PRR-affiliated Cairo & Vincennes/Indianapolis & Vincennes route provided another connection to the Pennsylvania Railroad system.[60] Had Scott's ambitions come to fruition, the Iron Mountain would have offered the PRR access to California, by way of the Texas & Pacific. The Iron Mountain also provided a connection, at Little Rock, with two other lines—the Memphis & Little Rock Railroad and the Memphis & Charleston Railroad—that linked with the Southern Railway Security Company that Thomson and Scott were establishing in the southeast.[61]

Scott's ambitious plans soon confronted the harsh realities of railway building in the southwestern United States. Much of the Texas & Pacific route ran through sparsely settled territory that could generate little revenue, and the rapid construction schedule soon drained the assets of Scott's California & Texas Railway Construction Company. Few American investors were interested in the project, so Scott turned to Europe. He was away from the United States between July and October 1873 in a largely fruitless effort

to sell Texas & Pacific bonds, and in an attempt to recuperate from the stress and exhaustion associated with his PRR responsibilities. Unable to place the company's bonds either in the United States or in Europe, Scott relied even more heavily on his connections with the Pennsylvania Railroad. Apparently without Thomson's knowledge or consent, Scott asked the PRR board to trade $2 million worth of Pittsburgh, Cincinnati & St. Louis Railway (Pan Handle) bonds for $4 million of Texas & Pacific construction bonds, which at that point were practically worthless. The directors agreed in August 1873, but the collapse of Jay Cooke's banking empire a month later threatened both the Texas & Pacific and the California & Texas Railway Construction Company. Carnegie, who had about $250,000 in the Texas & Pacific, wrote his investment off as a dead loss and refused to contribute any additional funds to resuscitate the venture. He likewise declined to rescue Thomson and Scott by endorsing their request for a loan from investment banker Junius Morgan. Both Thomson and Scott, among others, risked their personal fortunes to bolster the two companies, but to no avail.[62]

Scott appears to have accepted the disaster with a certain degree of equanimity, but Thomson, whom he had persuaded to invest in the venture, was furious at Scott's cupidity and at his own gullibility. On November 3, 1873, Thomson again begged Carnegie for financial assistance, offering what was perhaps an undeservedly restrained and charitable assessment of Scott's role in the fiasco. "The scheme itself was good enough," Thomson suggested, "but it has been most woefully mismanaged financially, Scott having acted upon his faith in his guiding star, instead of sound discretion."[63] The next day, the California & Texas Railway Construction Company defaulted on $300,000 worth of its securities, and Scott offered his resignation to the board of directors of the Pennsylvania Railroad. At Thomson's insistence, the board declined to accept the resignation, but the two executives remained on poor terms. The break with Carnegie was even more abrupt. By refusing to lend his name to the efforts of Thomson and Scott to obtain emergency financing, the steelmaker wisely avoided further losses, but in the future he would no longer be part of the investment schemes developed by PRR executives.[64]

As the Texas & Pacific imploded, Thomson and Scott suffered personal losses that compounded the damage that they had done to the Pennsylvania Railroad. According to one of the PRR's official corporate histories, Scott was able to continue his executive duties, unaffected by the course of events in the West.[65] The same could not be said of Thomson, who lost more than $400,000 in the venture. The crisis contributed to a heart attack in April 1874, and to a second, fatal one a month later. It also seems likely that Scott neglected his responsibilities to the PRR to some extent, for he spent a good portion of the next four years attempting to arrange for the federal government to rescue both the California & Texas Railway Construction Company and the Texas & Pacific Railway.[66]

Scott, now president of the Pennsylvania Railroad, turned to Congress in an attempt to save his disintegrating Texas & Pacific project. In December 1874 Senator John Scott, at Tom Scott's request, introduced a petition to provide a federal subsidy, in the form of $100 million in government bonds (later reduced to $40 million), in exchange for Texas & Pacific bonds. For the next five years, various iterations of Texas & Pacific subsidy bills appeared in Congress. Tom Scott's adversary was Collis Huntington, who was determined to retain the Central Pacific's monopoly on California rail traffic, while preserving his right to build and control the Southern Pacific as the only other transcontinental route. He estimated that the Texas & Pacific, if completed, would drain away as much as $1 million per year in Central Pacific revenues, and he believed that Scott's access to Los Angeles would be a blow every bit as severe as if the PRR president had built a railroad directly to San Francisco.[67]

Scott and his close ally, Grenville Dodge, appealed to public opinion and attempted to sway votes in Congress by portraying themselves as crusaders against the Huntington monopoly. A federal subsidy for the Texas & Pacific, they argued, was a small price to pay to achieve equitable freight and passenger rates, and to free California from the tyranny of the Central Pacific. Huntington counterattacked by emphasizing Scott's reputation as a corrupt and unscrupulous speculator whose willingness to bribe legislators tainted the democratic process. Surely, Huntington asserted,

it would be the height of folly for the federal government to subsidize such a venal enterprise as the Texas & Pacific.[68]

With millions of dollars at stake, the two sides prepared to do battle in Congress. Huntington possessed a key advantage, in that he merely needed to defeat a subsidy bill—always an easier task than promoting a new piece of legislation. Both parties employed dozens of advocates, in what was the largest sustained lobbying campaign in the history of the United States until that time. In January 1877, during the key debates on the Texas & Pacific subsidy bill in the House of Representatives, the area set aside for lobbyists was filled to overflowing, until, a reporter noted, "the sleek solicitors of Congressmen's votes were incontinently turned out." Even though some of Scott's advocates "made violent protests," in the end "the Texas-Pacific crew and some minor vultures" were at least temporarily expelled.[69] Huntington was probably accurate when he alleged that Scott had assembled the "largest lobby in Washington ever known, two hundred men, many of them ex-members of railroad committees of [the] Senate and [the] House." Given the formidable political forces arrayed against him, Huntington was perhaps being more realistic than paranoid when he suggested, "It looks as though the devil, the commissioners, and the Pennsylvania Railroad had united against us."[70] And, both sides resorted to outright bribery to influence the political process.[71]

In his fight to prevent passage of the Texas & Pacific subsidy bill, Huntington benefited from what was, for him, extraordinarily good timing. During the autumn of 1872, newspaper reporters had begun to uncover the sordid details of the Crédit Mobilier scandal, demonstrating how a good portion of the public's money had enriched the Union Pacific's promoters while producing a poor-quality transcontinental railroad. Grenville Dodge, whose association with both the Union Pacific and the Texas & Pacific had made him something of an expert in shoddy railway construction, cautioned Scott that under no circumstances could a government investigating committee be allowed to inspect the ramshackle Texas & Pacific line. Dodge had good reason to be concerned, for by February 1875, Charles A. Dana, the acerbic editor of the *New York Sun*, had published a blistering retrospective on the Texas & Pacific project, going all the way back to the days of the discredited Memphis, El Paso & Pacific. In case anyone missed the point, he helpfully titled the piece "Crédit Mobilier Eclipsed."[72]

Huntington was quick to criticize the subsidy bill, and his assertion that he was prepared to build along the route without the benefit of subsidies or land grants found a receptive audience in Congress and in the press. The *New York Times* was set against the subsidy bill, so much so that Scott wrote an editorial (which he signed as the president of the Texas & Pacific, although not of the PRR), criticizing the paper's "misstatements" and a "perversion" of the "facts spread before Congress and the public generally."[73] In February 1875, a month after those comments appeared in the *Times*, the Texas & Pacific subsidy bill went down to defeat in the House of Representatives. Scott and his allies would have to wait for the 44th Congress to convene, on March 4, 1875.[74]

The new Congress was certain to be less favorable to the Texas & Pacific subsidy bill than its predecessor had been. Scott was able to exploit his connections to the Republican Party to ensure the GOP's support, but the Democrats were another matter. By 1874, Redeemers (native white southerners who sought to regain control of the region) were reestablishing themselves in positions of power, and they were anxious to promote the political and economic renaissance of the South. Many northerners were likewise growing weary of Reconstruction, and they turned against the Republicans who supported it. In the 1874 elections, Democrats gained 94 seats in the House of Representatives, giving them control of that body for the first time since before the Civil War. Scott, whose influence in the Republican Party had become more of a liability than an asset, began to appeal to the southern Democrats who had enjoyed a political resurgence. Scott distanced himself from allegations of corruption associated with a massive federal subsidy for the Texas & Pacific and its well-placed investors. Instead, he emphasized that the South deserved to have a transcontinental railroad, to match the one that a wartime Congress had routed through the northern territories. Far from representing a corrupt bargain between railroaders and politicians, Scott argued, the Texas & Pacific was the fulfillment of the prewar vision of

Secretary of War Jefferson Davis. In the aftermath of the war, Scott insisted, the South needed—indeed, deserved—that railroad more than ever.[75]

Grenville Dodge also appealed to southern interests. He orchestrated a series of editorials in southern newspapers suggesting that the Texas & Pacific was essential to the region's economic development, and that a resurgent South should not permit carpetbaggers and northern Republican politicians to deprive southerners of their lifeline to the Pacific Ocean. Southern legislatures, chambers of commerce, and boards of trade passed resolutions in support of the enterprise. In November 1875, the public relations campaign culminated in a National Railroad Convention in St. Louis, where southern delegates called for "An Acceptable Route to the Pacific" over the Texas & Pacific. Scott arranged for a special PRR train to carry forty Pennsylvania delegates directly to the convention so that they might demonstrate their support for the struggling company. Former Confederate president Jefferson Davis, the original advocate of a southern transcontinental, attended the meeting, but declined a seat on the platform. Scott was the true guest of honor, however, and he delivered a rousing speech, demonstrating the benefits of the Texas & Pacific to the South, and insisting that the line would help to break Huntington's railway stranglehold on the west coast.[76]

By December 1875, Scott and Dodge had shifted their attention from a public relations campaign in the South to a full-scale lobbying effort in Washington. Scott supporters dominated the Pacific Railroad Committee of the House of Representatives, but Huntington and his allies soon stymied all attempts to secure a congressional subsidy for the Texas & Pacific. Scott fared somewhat better in the Senate. In January 1876 he came before the Senate Committee on Railroads, and "said he only asked an indorsement of $85,000,000, so that he could get money cheap and build as cheap." A reporter noted that Scott "painted a beautiful picture about the development of the country, and argued that this road would be a godsend to the whole land." Huntington, in contrast, spent more than an hour reading a prepared speech. Even though the Central Pacific had received millions in subsidies, helping make Huntington a very rich man, he claimed poverty, saying "his road was poor and did not pay at the rate charged for freight." Scott clearly won that round, publically humiliating his adversary while retaining his temper. "Huntington was excited and Scott cool and taunting," the *New York Times* observed.[77]

The arguments and counterarguments dragged on for the remainder of the year, but in December 1876, Huntington proposed a truce, offering to drop his opposition to a Texas & Pacific subsidy if Scott in turn agreed not to build the line into California. The arrangement made a mockery of Scott's claims that he intended to rescue California from a Central Pacific–Southern Pacific monopoly, and encouraged reporters from the *New York Times* and other newspapers to suspect that Huntington and Scott had joined forces in order to monopolize transportation in the southwest.[78]

In January 1877, with Scott and Huntington no longer blocking each other's actions, the Pacific Railroad Committee was finally able to report a bill for subsidizing the Texas & Pacific. The measure authorized the Texas & Pacific to build to a point one hundred miles east of El Paso, where it would join the Southern Pacific line being built east from California. The bill's financial terms were extraordinarily generous, with the federal government proposing to guarantee the interest on construction bonds issued by the Texas & Pacific and its various branches. Newspapers reported that the potential liability would be a staggering $223,675,000, more than double the total of all federal internal-improvement spending from 1789 to 1873—or, as the *New York Times* suggested, "a sum nearly large enough to build the canal connecting the Atlantic and Pacific by the Nicaragua route."[79] Reporters for the *Times* and other newspapers, who routinely referred to the subsidy bill as "the great subsidy swindle," were nonetheless exaggerating the scope of the legislation. Had the bill become law, the federal government would have done no more than guarantee the interest on the accumulated debt—a sum that in turn reflected the construction costs associated with a vast web of railroads connecting Cairo, Illinois, St. Louis, Memphis, and New Orleans to Los Angeles and San Diego. Furthermore, the supporters of the Texas & Pacific adopted the classic political tactic of asking for far more than they needed or could reasonably assume to receive, and then steadily and incrementally conceding that they might be able to accept a smaller subsidy.[80]

The bill was generous nonetheless, and its generosity proved its undoing. Northern Democrats, including some representing Pennsylvania, balked at a massive infusion of public monies into a private corporation—particularly one whose spokesmen proudly proclaimed would help to redeem the South. Some northern Republicans, lacking any particular loyalty to Scott or the Pennsylvania Railroad, likewise saw no reason to subsidize a southern transcontinental route. Despite the public relations campaign that Scott and Dodge had orchestrated, southern Democrats lost interest in the project when they realized that Scott intended for the Texas & Pacific to funnel traffic northeast to St. Louis, and thence over PRR rails. Many southerners also recoiled at the prospect of the federal government giving the people's money to Tom Scott and Grenville Dodge, two northerners who were infected with the taint of corruption.[81]

Under normal political circumstances, and given the intensity of the opposition to the Texas & Pacific subsidy bill, Scott might well have conceded defeat. These were not normal political circumstances, however, as the nation was embroiled in one of the most serious political crises in its history. In the midst of widespread allegations of fraud, New York Democrat Samuel J. Tilden won the popular vote in the 1876 presidential election and came within one electoral vote of capturing the presidency, with some twenty more in dispute. In January 1877, in an attempt to resolve the crisis, Congress passed the Electoral Commission Act, establishing a fifteen-member panel to allocate the disputed electoral votes. Five members of the Electoral Commission were senators (three Republicans and two Democrats), five were representatives (two Republicans and three Democrats), and the remainder were Supreme Court justices, two of whom were Republicans and two of whom were Democrats. In order to maintain some semblance of impartiality, the commission included one independent, Justice David Davis. Davis's election to the Senate, as a Democrat, forced him to withdraw from the commission. His replacement was Justice Joseph P. Bradley, a New Jersey Republican and former chief legal counsel for the Camden & Amboy Rail Road and the Delaware & Raritan Canal Company, two firms that were by now subsidiaries of the PRR.

Even though Tilden had probably won the popular vote in Louisiana, the commission awarded that state's electoral votes to Republican Rutherford B. Hayes, thanks to Bradley's deciding vote. With that, Democrats anticipated the likely outcome of the process and began to negotiate a compromise with Republicans. In exchange for conceding the presidency, Tilden supporters requested certain rewards, ranging from the removal of the last federal troops in the South to Democratic control over patronage jobs in the Post Office. They also wanted Hayes's support for the Texas & Pacific subsidy.[82]

Scott's quest for a Texas & Pacific subsidy soon became intertwined with one of the great back-room political deals in the history of American politics, one that brought an end to Reconstruction and the federal military occupation of the former Confederacy. There undoubtedly was a "Compromise of 1877," but what is less clear is the role that Scott and the Texas & Pacific Railway played in that process. Historian C. Vann Woodward, perhaps the foremost expert on that period, has argued that Scott brokered an arrangement that enabled Hayes to win the election in exchange for the new president's promise to support the Texas & Pacific subsidy bill. Under that scenario, Scott likewise persuaded James A. Garfield, the ranking Republican on the Pacific Railroad Committee, to drop his initial opposition to the Texas & Pacific subsidy in exchange for Scott's promise of southern support for Garfield's bid to become speaker of the House. Woodward in fact routinely referred to the Compromise of 1877 as the "Scott Plan," and there is some merit in that argument. It was certainly true that Hayes learned that he would be the next president of the United States while traveling on Scott's private office car, the *Pennsylvania*, and it is equally true that the two men—one at the pinnacle of political power, the other economic—could prove extraordinarily useful to one another.[83]

The arrangement might not have been so crass, however. Scott had after all served as assistant secretary of war only a few years earlier, was used to moving in the highest of political circles, and as a staunch unionist was well aware of the dangers associated with political discord. He also believed that the political divisiveness associated with the Hayes-Tilden controversy threatened the nation's economic stability, as well as that of the Pennsylvania Railroad—at a time when the company faced both an economic recession and a ruinous rate war. Scott may simply have been endeavoring to

open up the South to the PRR, because he knew that the full flowering of the southern economy, and of the southern infrastructure, depended on allowing southern Redeemers to move past what they viewed as the humiliation of Reconstruction. In addition, as Woodward's critics have observed, northern Republicans had ample reason to settle the disputed 1876 election in their favor, even without the subsidy issue. At the same time, the growing power of the Redeemers in the South divided the Democratic Party, making its members unable to resist a negotiated Republican victory.[84]

Finally, even though Scott and his fellow PRR executives were staunch Republicans and expected that party and its presidential candidate to support the railroad's interests, they were not hostile to Tilden and the Democrats. To the contrary, Tilden was closely associated with the Pittsburgh, Fort Wayne & Chicago, and was therefore intimately connected with Scott's business dealings. In 1860, in a masterpiece of financial wizardry, Tilden had overseen all of the legal matters associated with the reorganization of the Fort Wayne, a prelude to its later acquisition by the Pennsylvania Company. Scott and the PRR would have benefited no matter which candidate won the disputed election.[85]

The greatest defect of the purported "Scott Plan," however, was that Hayes did not offer his political support to the Texas & Pacific, and that neither the railroad nor Scott ever received direct federal assistance. Despite his sometime truce with Scott, Huntington continued to push the Southern Pacific out of California. In 1877, that company's tracks crossed the Colorado River at Fort Yuma and continued east. Beyond Fort Yuma, Huntington simply appropriated the Texas & Pacific right of way, precipitating a further round of legal battles. Huntington's success—without any federal subsidy, he was quick to point out—presented a stark contrast with Scott, who was demanding millions for a railroad that was demonstrating lackluster progress at best.

After suffering a stroke in October 1878, and having long since abandoned all hope of a federal subsidy for the Texas & Pacific, Scott elected to withdraw from any additional involvement in the project. In December 1879, Jay Gould organized a consortium of investors to acquire the company, and they took control in August of 1880.[86] Scott apparently remained on the board of directors of the Pacific Improvement Company, the successor to the California & Texas Railway Construction Company, until April 12, 1881, some months after he had resigned the presidency of the Pennsylvania Railroad.[87]

Amid the subsidy battles, Texas & Pacific construction crews had slowly built westward, and by July 1876 the line was complete as far west as Fort Worth. Finally, in November 1881, Gould and Huntington agreed to abide by the compromise that the members of the Pacific Railroad Committee had first considered in January 1877. The two railroaders agreed to join their tracks at a location some one hundred miles east of El Paso. On December 16, 1881, the two railroads met at the tiny hamlet of Sierra Blanca, Texas, creating a second transcontinental railroad route from St. Louis to the Pacific coast.[88]

In the final analysis, the Texas & Pacific was a considerable disappointment for all of the parties involved. Thomson lost money on the project, but Scott, by persevering in the face of Huntington's determined efforts, preserved much of the value of the Texas & Pacific charter. He was then able to sell his interests to Gould, either for a minimal loss, or perhaps even for a small profit. The stress associated with the Texas & Pacific was severe, however, and undoubtedly contributed to the deaths of both PRR presidents.

When he sold the Texas & Pacific to Gould, Scott must have realized that that railroad would not be a western outlet for the PRR and would instead be tied to the rest of the Gould railway empire, including the Wabash and the Missouri Pacific. The Texas & Pacific, once completed, also disappointed Gould and its other investors. Although entitled to more than 12.4 million acres of state land grants, for the construction of 972 miles of track within Texas, the Texas & Pacific actually received only 5.1 million acres, for the track built to the west of Fort Worth, and even a portion of that was rescinded by the state. The company was theoretically eligible for more than 14.3 million acres of federal land grants, had it built all the way to the Pacific coast, yet it became the only eligible railroad that utterly failed to receive any national lands. The Texas & Pacific failed to generate adequate traffic and entered receivership in 1885, only four years after completing its main line.[89]

Pennsylvania Railroad and affiliates:

PRR	Pennsylvania Railroad
NC	Northern Central Railway (Baltimore to Harrisburg and Sunbury, Pennsylvania)
BP	Baltimore & Potomac Railroad (Baltimore to Washington)
AF	Alexandria & Washington Railroad / Alexandria & Fredericksburg Railway (Washington to Quantico, Virginia)
CV	Cumberland Valley Railroad (Harrisburg to Hagerstown, Maryland)
SV	Shenandoah Valley Railroad (Hagerstown to Roanoke, Virginia, incomplete)
PFW	Pittsburgh, Fort Wayne & Chicago Railway (Pittsburgh to Chicago)
PH	Pan Handle Route (Pittsburgh to Indianapolis)
V	Indianapolis & Vincennes Railroad / Cairo & Vincennes Railroad (Indianapolis to Cairo, Illinois)

Southern Railway Security Company holdings:

RP	Richmond & Petersburg Railroad (Richmond to Petersburg)
P	Petersburg Railroad (Petersburg to Weldon)
WCA	Wilmington, Columbia & Augusta Railroad
	Wilmington & Weldon Railroad (Wilmington to Weldon, North Carolina)
	Wilmington & Manchester (Wilmington to Manchester, North Carolina)
	Northeastern Railroad (Florence to Charleston)
CD	Cheraw & Darlington Railroad (Florence to Cheraw, South Carolina)
CC	Charlotte, Columbia & Augusta Railroad (Charlotte to Columbia, South Carolina, and Augusta, Georgia)
RD	Richmond & Danville Railroad (Richmond to Charlotte, North Carolina, by way of Danville, Virginia)
	Piedmont Railroad (Danville to Greensboro, North Carolina, leased to the Richmond & Danville in 1868)
	North Carolina Railroad (Greensboro to Charlotte, leased to the Richmond & Danville in 1871)
AR	Atlanta & Richmond Air-Line Railway (Charlotte to Atlanta)
ETV	East Tennessee, Virginia & Georgia Railroad (Bristol, Tennessee to Dalton, Georgia, and Cleveland, Tennessee to Chattanooga)
WA	Western & Atlantic Railroad (Atlanta to Chattanooga)
MC	Memphis & Charleston Railroad (Memphis to Stevenson, Alabama)
WRA	Western Railroad of Alabama (West Point, Georgia and Ophelika, Alabama to Selma, Alabama, by way of Montgomery)
MM	Mobile & Montgomery Railroad
	Alabama & Florida Railroad (Montgomery to Pensacola, Florida)
	Mobile & Great Northern Railroad (Pollard to Tensas, Alabama / Mobile)

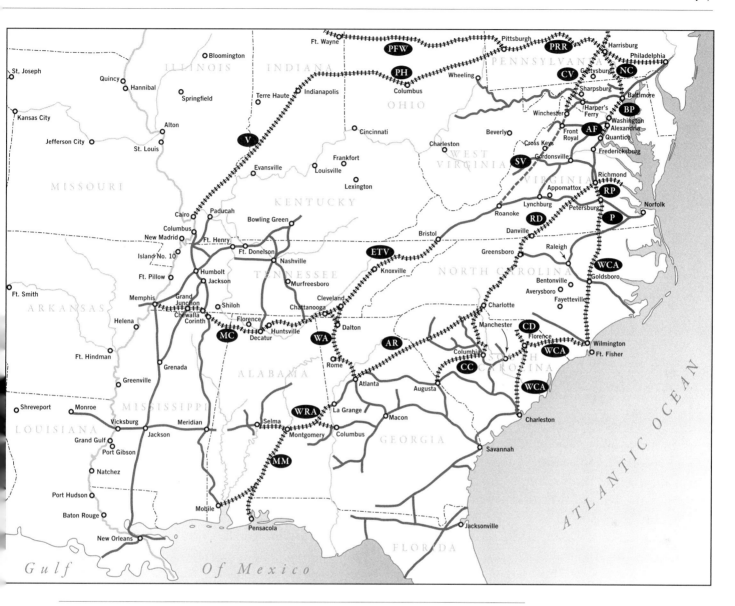

Figure 44. The Civil War shattered the South's railroads, but the conflict also created considerable opportunity for Thomson, Scott, and others connected with the PRR. In an area that had long been dominated by local carriers, the Southern Railway Security Company served as a useful investment vehicle for the consolidation of numerous southern railroads into regional systems. Along with other PRR-influenced southern lines, such as the Cumberland Valley Railroad and the Shenandoah Valley Railroad, the SRSC gave the PRR access to many of the key cities of the South. Even though southern capitalists participated in the SRSC, rival local entrepreneurs and civic leaders charged that the consortium was basically a front for corrupt northern carpetbaggers. While the PRR interests may have been able to overcome that opposition, they could not stop the economic crisis that followed the Panic of 1873. The SRSC collapsed, and PRR officials retrenched in the South, as they had in the West. By the end of the nineteenth century, the SRSC lines contributed to the formation of some of the great railway systems in the Southeast—including the Atlantic Coast Line and the Southern Railway—but the PRR had long since retreated to its traditional territory, north of the Potomac River.

Huntington probably benefited the most from the complex political maneuvering. The Southern Pacific continued building east from Sierra Blanca toward New Orleans, while a subsidiary, the Galveston, Harrisburg & San Antonio Railway, worked its way west. On January 12, 1883, near the Pecos River, construction crews joined the rails of a third transcontinental line, established in conjunction with another subsidiary, the Texas & New Orleans Railroad. Henceforth, Huntington and his successors on the Central Pacific and the Southern Pacific would be among the dominant forces in western railroading. Julius Grodinsky, in his masterful study of the development of the western railways, aptly described Huntington's adroit management of a complex chess game. "Of all the transcontinental railroad men of the early 1870's," Grodinsky observed, "he alone survived."[90]

Southern Gateways

The efforts of PRR executives to influence the southeastern railway network proved as disappointing, and as politically contentious, as was the case in the West. There was in the South little need to construct rail lines in advance of demand, and most of the PRR's affiliates were either already in operation, under construction, or planned for routes that could generate a reasonable amount of traffic. The difficulties lay instead in the coordination and integration of a largely localized rail network, and of applying the same system-building techniques that Herman Haupt, Thomson, and Scott had used to such great advantage on the PRR. Those executives were northerners, even though Thomson had begun his career in Georgia and Haupt had worked in the South as well. Southerners, still smarting from their defeat in the Civil War, were unlikely to welcome such presumed outsiders with open arms, particularly when they intended to destroy the isolated local markets that many of the region's railroads and communities had developed. In extending their reach into the South, PRR executives were astute enough to work closely with southerners, or at least with financiers who moved comfortably and repeatedly across the Mason-Dixon Line. Despite that economic rapprochement, however, southern Redeemers

accused Scott and other so-called carpetbaggers of indulging in the very worst of political, entrepreneurial, and moral corruption in order to deprive the South of its transportation and economic patrimony. Such accusations were both inaccurate and unfair, but their legacy lingered for many decades to come. Yet, as with so many other aspects of the PRR's operations, it was ultimately the depression of the 1870s, and not local opposition, that shattered Scott's dreams for a southern rail empire.

The economic geography of the South dictated that its railroads would develop distinct regional characteristics. Yet, the differences between North and South were mostly a matter of degree, with the latter region exhibiting far more intense local rivalries. Since colonial days, economic elites in the Tidewater region of Virginia had specialized in the cultivation of staple crops, mainly tobacco. Their counterparts farther to the south oversaw the production of rice and indigo. Cotton would not become a significant crop until the early 1800s, and then only to the west, away from the Atlantic seaboard. Enslaved African Americans performed much of the cultivation, but large numbers of poor whites also toiled in the fields, often alongside slaves and free blacks. Regardless of what they produced, workers typically loaded agricultural commodities onto small boats for a trip downstream, and a rendezvous with coastal or oceangoing ships. The plantation economy created a chain of tiny shallow-water ports along the southern seaboard. Few had any economic importance, yet residents of every quayside village with a harbor large enough to accommodate a two-masted schooner dreamed that they could establish one of the South's great commercial entrepôts, if only they possessed better transportation to the interior.

Southern states, Virginia in particular, accordingly funded a plethora of internal improvements. In 1816, the Virginia legislature created a Board of Public Works, and during the remainder of the antebellum period the state invested more than $14 million in turnpikes, canals, and railroads, shouldering $850,000 in annual interest payments in the process. Other states followed the same model, although on a smaller scale. During the 1840s, the State of Georgia spent nearly $5 million to construct the Western & Atlantic Railroad between Atlanta and Chattanooga. South Carolina lent $100,000 to the South Carolina Canal & Railroad Company (better known as the Charleston & Hamburg Railroad) and invested heavily in other railroad companies throughout the state. When it opened its line between Charleston and Hamburg in 1833, the company possessed the longest route in the world. It would be a mistake, therefore, to disparage the accomplishments of the southern states in developing a railway system.[91]

Nevertheless, southerners typically considered railroads to be part of their local economy, rather than components of a larger regional system.[92] Most southern railroads traversed sparsely settled agrarian lands, with barely enough traffic to sustain a single carrier. In order to cover operating expenses, railway proprietors had little choice other than to set high rates—a reality that Thomson had experienced during the years that he was chief engineer for the Georgia Rail Road. High rates were only possible with a local transportation monopoly, and the promoters and owners of each local railroad were accordingly deeply resentful of any efforts by "outsiders," even fellow southerners, to construct a rival line into their sovereign territory. Through lines were likewise anathema because they carried long-distance traffic at rates well below the level at which local carriers could survive. Promoters constructed railroads to differing gauges in a deliberate attempt to prevent one railroad from invading or establishing a through route traversing another railroad's region. Much of the South's rail network was laid to 5' gauge, but by 1871 there were nearly two dozen track gauges in use. Not until 1886, in a massive and carefully coordinated effort, would the southern railroads be brought into conformity with their northern counterparts. The gauge issue notwithstanding, many communities refused to permit two railroads to physically connect their track. In so doing, local boosters ensured that their town would always remain a transfer point and would never be consigned to commercial oblivion. As such, the southern railroad network, which by the 1850s appeared on paper to be reasonably integrated and robust, actually consisted of a patchwork of independent and isolated carriers, linked by connections that failed to connect.[93]

The southerners who did become involved in railroad promotion encountered considerable obstacles. Most southern capital was invested in land and slaves, with little left over for other pursuits. The nation's largest banking houses were located in the North, and their principals were closely tied to the northern urban-industrial economy. Europeans were likewise reluctant to invest in the poorly developed southern transportation system, and their aversion increased in proportion to strengthening abolitionist sentiments in Great Britain and on the Continent. Finally, even though a skilled and dependable corps of independent, professional railroad construction contractors had emerged in the North as early as the 1850s, no such body existed in the South. The South's reliance on agriculture and slavery had left skilled labor in short supply, with most engineers and mechanics imported from the North. Although the antebellum South possessed several talented railroad entrepreneurs, none were as skilled as Thomson, Scott, Vanderbilt, Garrett, or Gould at putting together a railroad empire.

The Civil War left the southern railway network in ruins, with shattered track, burned bridges, and locomotives that had been overworked, badly maintained, destroyed, or confiscated by Union forces. Little capital was available to repair the damage, particularly as the South had lost both its investment in slaves and its Confederate war debt. State governments, which had funded a considerable portion of railroad construction during the antebellum period, were no longer in a position to provide money for rebuilding or expansion.

Some southern railroad owners attempted to generate funds by mimicking what their northern counterparts had done during the 1850s, creating trunk lines for through traffic. The increased volume of business would enable executives from the dominant carrier in each region to rebuild the physical plant, acquire additional equipment, and pay a profit to investors. As they pursued long-distance routes, railway developers shattered the comfortable local monopolies that had characterized the antebellum period. Carriers that were not able to participate in the creation of trunk lines were almost certain to experience a decline in traffic and revenues. Local elites often bitterly opposed the entrance of outside interests into their territory, particularly if those outsiders, although fellow southerners, were in any way tied to northern financial interests.[94]

As the decade of the 1860s drew to a close, Virginia whites in particular had ample reason to be uneasy, for reasons that went beyond their military defeat at the hands of Ulysses S. Grant and his Union armies. New inventions, such as the deep-draft steamship and the telegraph, reduced regional variations in commodity prices and shifted agricultural exports to northern cities. Northern banks, as well as European investors, expressed concern at the economic and political chaos of the Reconstruction South and were less willing to provide credit to planters. Those trends affected not merely the planters but their local mercantile allies as well—individuals who had once supported railroad construction when it promised to mix local control with regional economic benefits, but who saw no reason why the transportation infrastructure should fall under the control of northern capitalists and their allies, men who presumably wanted nothing less than to drain the economic lifeblood from the South. Those attitudes, augmented with simmering sectional resentments, racial discord, and the political upheavals associated with the creation of Reconstruction-era governments, ensured that when Thomson, Scott, and their associates became involved in southern railroading on behalf of the PRR, they would be walking into a hornets' nest.[95]

Washington to Richmond

In 1872, thanks to the use of the Baltimore & Potomac charter, the PRR had reached Washington, D.C. For Thomson and Scott, Washington was not so much the end of the line as the gateway to the South. Just beyond the Potomac River lay a railroad network, never as extensive as in the North, and now shattered by war, yet offering enormous potential. More to the point, the Pennsylvania Railroad desperately needed southern traffic. After Appomattox, Washington settled back into its prewar slumber, with little passenger and even less freight traffic. The capital, and the territory from there north to Baltimore, could barely support one railroad, much less two. Yet, with the Baltimore & Ohio and the PRR's Baltimore & Potomac now vying

for what little traffic there was, Thomson and Scott considered it vital that their company have access to the South and its commerce.

If Washington was the gateway to the South, then Richmond was its hub, with railroads radiating to all points of the compass. Petersburg, only a few miles to the south of Richmond, possessed the better port facilities, as well as the first railroad. Built between 1830 and 1833, the Petersburg Railroad connected its namesake city with the north bank of the Roanoke River, opposite Weldon, North Carolina. The project proved so successful that the Virginia Board of Public Works developed plans to extend that line from Petersburg north to Richmond and the Potomac River. The Richmond & Petersburg Railroad, built between 1836 and 1838, connected Petersburg to the state capital. In 1834, the legislature chartered the Richmond, Fredericksburg & Potomac Railroad, and the state subscribed to something less than two-fifths of the company's stock.[96] By January 1837, the line was in service as far north as Fredericksburg. Rather than build due north to Washington, however, the company's owners chose the far easier course of a fourteen-mile extension from Fredericksburg to the lower reaches of the Potomac River estuary, at Aquia Creek (sometimes spelled Acquia Creek), with construction completed in 1842. North of Aquia Creek, the western shore of the Potomac River was heavily indented with tributary creeks and would have required extensive engineering work to bridge the deeply cut valleys.

In March 1851, the Virginia legislature chartered the Alexandria & Fredericksburg Railroad, to extend the RF&P route to the north and west, to a junction with the Orange & Alexandria Railroad. The new company would have completed an indirect route between Richmond and Alexandria, bypassing the rugged terrain along the Potomac, but construction was not forthcoming. Five years later, Virginia legislators granted the RF&P the authority to follow much the same alignment, but work likewise faltered. By the time of the Civil War, the only through rail route was along the Virginia Central Railroad, linking the RF&P at Hanover Junction to the Orange & Alexandria at Gordonsville—a path so indirect as to render it almost useless, particularly for passenger travel. Accordingly, freight and passengers continued to transfer to steamboats at Aquia Creek for the fifty-five-mile upriver journey to Washington, where they could connect with the Baltimore & Ohio.[97]

Thanks to the efforts of local capitalists, the Richmond, Fredericksburg & Potomac remained an independent line, beholden to neither the PRR nor the Baltimore & Ohio. Moncure Robinson, who had performed one of the surveys for the Allegheny Portage Railroad, was from a prominent Richmond family, although he spent most of his later years in Philadelphia. Between 1834 and 1842, he had been largely responsible for building the route from the state capital north to Aquia Creek. His son, John Moncure Robinson, followed in his footsteps and assembled a rail and water empire that included the RF&P, the Seaboard & Roanoke Railroad line between Hampton Roads and Weldon, North Carolina, with connections to Wilmington and Raleigh, as well as the Baltimore Steam Packet Company. The Robinsons were opposed to any actions by either the PRR or the B&O that might challenge their profitable local transportation network in eastern Virginia or their links to Baltimore.[98]

During the 1850s, the Baltimore & Ohio established connections with the southern railroad network, but the Civil War and its immediate aftermath afforded the PRR the opportunity to surpass its rival. A key point of contention, one that in many respects symbolized the struggle between the two trunk lines, was the Long Bridge, the easternmost rail crossing of the Potomac River, at the site of today's Fourteenth Street Bridge. In 1809, the Washington Bridge Company, a private corporation, had opened the first incarnation of the Long Bridge. During the years that followed, the wooden structure was repeatedly damaged by fire or flood, and after one such disaster, Congress purchased the rights to build and maintain a bridge at that location.

The Alexandria & Washington Railroad, chartered in 1854, offered a possible mechanism to link the B&O's tracks in Washington to northern Virginia. The company did not initially live up to its potential, largely because of opposition from local residents and PRR allies. Many Washingtonians were aghast at the possibility that through traffic for points south might travel along city streets. At most, only local horsecar service operated over the Washington portion of the

route, delivering travelers and workers to various hotels and businesses. There were no rails on the Long Bridge, which was restricted to pedestrian and vehicular traffic. The company thus operated as two distinct sections, on opposite sides of the Potomac. In 1860, Baltimore & Ohio president John W. Garrett requested permission from Congress to build a railroad bridge at the site, but staunch PRR ally Simon Cameron, then a senator, blocked the measure.[99]

The Alexandria & Washington operated tracks linking the south end of the bridge to Alexandria, but the absence of rails on the Long Bridge and the lack of a direct connection in Alexandria with any other railroad ensured that the line south of the Potomac probably would not carry any significant degree of traffic. The portion of the Alexandria & Washington that lay south of the Potomac River had been part of an experimental line, built to test a novel railway design pioneered by James F. French. The French system employed sets of rollers, akin to small locomotive driving wheels, that gripped the underside of an extra-wide, flat iron bar, fastened to the top of wooden longitudinal stringers and hanging out over their edges. Virginia legislators concluded that the design was a great success, but its use was short lived. It had no lasting effect on the development of railway technology.[100]

At the beginning of the Civil War, French and the other Alexandria & Washington Railroad personnel, as future Southern Railway president Fairfax Harrison noted, "retired within the Confederate lines, taking their rolling stock with them."[101] The newly constituted, pro-Union government that had recently been installed in Alexandria promptly took possession of what was left of the company's Virginia operations as war contraband. The war funneled a torrent of men and materiel from the North into Virginia, and the Long Bridge quickly became a serious bottleneck. In 1862, Congress authorized the laying of rails on the Long Bridge, as a matter of military necessity, and cars from the B&O were soon running across the Potomac, through Alexandria, and to a connection with the Orange & Alexandria Railroad.

The Virginia portion of the Alexandria & Washington promptly fell under the control of a consortium of speculators who were also associated with the Union Pacific and the passage of the 1862 Pacific Railroad Act. In May 1862, a month after the foreclosure of the Washington & Alexandria's second mortgage, they formed a new company, the Washington, Alexandria & Georgetown Railroad, and obtained a charter from Virginia's Union government in Wheeling. During the summer of 1864, construction crews completed a new Long Bridge, a hundred feet downstream of the original, but the structure was as yet innocent of rails. In February 1865, the weight of a locomotive collapsed one of the spans of the decrepit original bridge. The United States Military Rail Roads Construction Corps promptly seized the newer Long Bridge, laid rails, and made it the conduit for trains passing from Washington to Alexandria. Six months later, the federal government restored the property of the Washington, Alexandria & Georgetown, including the new Long Bridge, to the northern investors who had reorganized the company.[102]

Soon after the Civil War, Garrett was eager to develop a network of southern connections, which he hoped to link with the B&O's Washington Branch via the Long Bridge. In 1866, Garrett began investing in the Orange & Alexandria Railroad, with a route that stretched southwest to Charlottesville and Lynchburg, Virginia, along a line completed in 1860. In February 1866, the Virginia legislature incorporated a southern extension of the route, the Lynchburg & Danville Railroad. Five months later, with Garrett's blessing, the Orange & Alexandria merged with the Manassas Gap Railroad, forming the Orange, Alexandria & Manassas Railroad.

Garrett's ambitious plans to dispatch Virginia's traffic to Baltimore soon aroused the alarm of a local, and extremely influential, entrepreneur. Virginia's primary east–west route was under the control of former Confederate Major General William Mahone, an individual who was lionized by southerners for leading the defense of "The Crater" at the Battle of Petersburg. Before the war, he had been a railway engineer and executive, and was largely responsible for the construction of the Norfolk & Petersburg Railroad. After Appomattox, Mahone set about rebuilding the wrecked line. He believed that it was imperative that Virginia consolidate and rehabilitate its railway network so that trade could funnel through the port cities along Hampton Roads rather than be lost to northern rivals, such as Baltimore or Philadelphia. Within a

year after the end of the war, he gained control of the Norfolk & Petersburg and the South Side Railroad (linking the James River port of City Point with Petersburg, and then west to Lynchburg, Virginia). The independent Virginia & Tennessee Railroad extended the South Side farther west, through Big Lick (Roanoke) to Bristol, Tennessee. West of Bristol, another independent carrier, the East Tennessee & Virginia Railroad, led to Knoxville, with onward connections to locations as far distant as New Orleans.

The Orange & Alexandria route, allied with the B&O, threatened Mahone's rebuilt railroad empire. At Lynchburg, most traffic from western Virginia flowed northeast toward Washington and Baltimore, rather than east to Richmond and Hampton Roads. Thomson, never one to pass up an opportunity to hobble the B&O, was soon advising Mahone on how to resolve the situation. The obvious solution was to force a merger of all three companies along the route between Norfolk and Bristol. Yet, the directors of the Virginia & Tennessee (the line west of Lynchburg) refused to divert freight to the Mahone roads or to merge with them. Worse news was to follow. In March 1867, Virginia provisional governor Francis H. Pierpont, a staunch Unionist and the key instigator of the formation of the state of West Virginia, informed Mahone that Garrett planned to construct a line (the Valley Railroad of Virginia) through the Shenandoah Valley, parallel to and in competition with the PRR-allied Shenandoah Valley Railroad. If completed, the B&O route would intersect the Virginia & Tennessee at Salem (near Big Lick/Roanoke), and divert still more traffic away from the Mahone roads.[103]

In response to the B&O threat, Mahone persuaded his allies in the Virginia legislature to give him the authority to consolidate the Norfolk & Petersburg, the South Side, and the Virginia & Tennessee into one company. He and his supporters purchased enough Virginia & Tennessee stock to enable him to become the company's president, but his opponents nonetheless continued to block the merger. The orientation of the Virginia & Tennessee depended on whether Mahone or Garrett could gain control of the 60 percent of the company's stock owned by the Virginia Board of Public Works. The disposition of the stock was in turn the responsibility of three individuals—the treasurer, the auditor, and most importantly the governor.[104]

Mahone's future, as well as the competitive positions of the PRR and the B&O in the postwar South, was heavily influenced by political developments in Reconstruction Virginia. In 1867, thanks to the efforts of Radical Republicans in Congress, African Americans were eligible to vote for delegates to the convention tasked with drafting the state's new constitution. In a gesture of either protest or resigned apathy, many white southerners boycotted the constitutional convention, ensuring that Radical Republicans would dominate the proceedings. After the election, native white Virginians, many who had once been Democrats, Whigs, or Constitutional Unionists, joined forces to form the Virginia Conservative Party, dedicated to stripping political power from African Americans, local scalawags, and northern carpetbaggers.

Radical Republicans, under the leadership of John C. Underwood, dominated the constitutional convention held in Richmond between December 1867 and April 1868. The Underwood Convention—or the "Mongrel Convention," as it was dubbed by many white Virginians—guaranteed black male suffrage, while disenfranchising as many Conservatives as possible. In addition, delegates confronted the state's massive public debt, in excess of $40 million, much of which had been devoted to prewar internal improvements. As their counterparts in Pennsylvania had done a decade earlier, Virginians barred public aid to private corporations. They were so desperate to reduce the debt, moreover, that they planned to sell most of Virginia's investments in public works.[105]

The three principal actors—Mahone, Garrett, and Thomson—each sought to exploit the political transformations for his own advantage. Henry H. Wells, who succeeded Pierpont as provisional governor, came close to ending Mahone's plans and thereby awarding pride of place to Garrett and the Baltimore & Ohio. In October 1868, a B&O representative offered to purchase the state's share of the Virginia & Tennessee Railroad. Wells assented, but state treasurer George Rye and General George Stoneman, the military commander of Virginia, blocked the proposal. In the process, Wells earned Mahone's enmity and likewise infuriated Virginians who saw no reason to transfer the state's resources to a Baltimore company that had greatly assisted the Union in its defeat of the Confederacy.[106]

The 1869 gubernatorial race, the first since the ratification of the new constitution, provided the Conservatives with a path to power and installed in the Governor's Mansion an individual who would prove quite receptive—some would say suspiciously so—to the interests of the Pennsylvania Railroad. To no one's surprise, Mahone backed the "True Republican" candidate, Gilbert C. Walker, against Wells, the Radical Republican. Walker was a northerner, born in Pennsylvania and a longtime resident of Binghamton, New York. He did not spend any appreciable amount of time in the South until 1864, when he became president of the Exchange National Bank in Norfolk, Virginia. He was a Democrat, but in the 1860 presidential campaign he had strongly supported the party's northern candidate, Stephen A. Douglas, rather than southerner John C. Breckinridge. Walker pledged to support civil rights, but he also spoke out forcefully against the disenfranchisement of white Conservatives. He was therefore the ideal candidate, someone with substantial appeal to moderate whites and even to some African American voters. While the future of the Virginia & Tennessee probably mattered little to most voters, whites possessed ample reason to dislike Wells. Walker gained broad Conservative support, as well as most of the white vote, and he won an easy victory.[107]

In office, Walker faced a host of difficulties that temporarily transcended the political conflicts between the Conservatives and the Radicals. Virginia had borne the brunt of the fighting in the Eastern Theater of the Civil War, and much of Richmond, like the countryside from the state capital north to the Potomac River, lay in ruins. The commonwealth's antebellum system of internal improvements, which had never lived up to expectations, was particularly hard hit, with Union and Confederate troops alike ripping up rails, burning bridges, and confiscating or demolishing locomotives and rolling stock. In 1863, a third of Walker's state had simply disappeared, as Unionists in the western counties had formed West Virginia. In so doing, they had cheerfully expropriated all of the state-funded internal improvements that lay within their new domain, yet saw no reason to contribute to the repayment of the debts that Virginia had incurred many years earlier in order to pay for those projects. Quite simply, Virginia was a fiscal and a physical wreck.

At the end of March 1871, Walker and the Conservative-dominated state legislature attempted to resolve many of Virginia's financial problems, including its outstanding debt, its relationship to West Virginia, and the sorry state of its internal improvements. In the so-called Funding Act, legislators unilaterally assigned a third of the state's debt to West Virginia and authorized the issuance of "indebtedness certificates" to cover that amount, under the assumption that the new state would be responsible for repayment. In order to cover its two-thirds' share of the debt, Virginia issued more than $12.7 million in bonds to repay its creditors. The legislature then ordered the Board of Public Works to sell the state's internal-improvement investments, stipulating that private investors in each of those companies could buy out the state's interest by purchasing the equivalent amount of newly issued bonds.[108]

In the near term, the Funding Act caused few problems for William Mahone. In November 1870, he had finally succeeded in combining the Norfolk & Petersburg, the South Side, and the Virginia & Tennessee into the Atlantic, Mississippi & Ohio Railroad, keeping the line from Lynchburg to Bristol safely away from the Baltimore & Ohio. More broadly, however, Mahone was deeply concerned that the Funding Act would enable both the B&O and the PRR to purchase competing rail lines, to his detriment. He had supported Walker's gubernatorial bid, and he now felt betrayed. Mahone broke with his former ally, exploiting popular resentment over the Funding Act and creating considerable political conflict within Virginia. The Conservative Party split into two factions. The Funders, composed mainly of affluent and commercially oriented urban residents, favored the full payment of the commonwealth's debts, with interest. The other faction, the short-lived Readjuster Party, embraced a form of pseudo populism and demanded the redistribution of economic and political power, in part through increased support for public education and a repudiation of the commonwealth's debts. By the late 1870s, Mahone had become one of the leading Readjusters, and in 1877 he ran, unsuccessfully, for the governorship. Well before then, however, he had given notice that he was ready to do battle with any company that proposed to invade his territory. By the autumn of 1871, with the Virginia & Tennessee safely under his con-

trol, Mahone was convinced that the PRR would be the primary beneficiary of the Funding Act and that he had far more reason to fear Thomson and Scott than he did John Garrett and the B&O.[109]

After March 1871, under the terms of the Funding Act, the Commonwealth of Virginia disposed of all of its railroad investments, save those in the Richmond, Fredericksburg & Potomac, at exceedingly low prices. "This Act marks an era in the railroad history of the South," observed Fairfax Harrison, "for, while it was only one of similar and contemporaneous determinations on the part of the several Southern States, which opened the way to that control of Southern railroads by Northern capital which has been their most remarkable phenomenon in their recent history, its immediate effect was to project into Virginia the rivalry and competition of the Pennsylvania Railroad Company and the Baltimore and Ohio."[110] Or, to put the matter in more colloquial terms, the Virginia legislature had let loose a flock of chickens, directly in front of two skilled and very determined foxes.[111]

As Harrison suggested, the B&O and the PRR were the two leading contenders for the railroads of the South, with each company possessing a unique set of advantages and disadvantages. The Pennsylvania Railroad was by far the stronger of the two companies, with more modern equipment and a superior physical plant capable of producing annual dividends of 8 to 10 percent. At a time when the B&O was struggling to reach Chicago, the PRR enjoyed secure access to that city, as well as St. Louis and New York. Coal and grain traffic generated substantial revenues, funding further expansion and improvements. PRR officials had comparatively little trouble raising investment capital, and Thomson's name alone was often sufficient to entice investors into supporting whatever venture he advocated. The PRR's outstanding capital was a fourth that of the railroads in all of the former states of the Confederacy, save Texas. In 1871, the PRR had almost as many freight cars as the entire railroad fleets in ten of the eleven states of the former Confederacy combined. By 1872, the PRR's gross earnings were half those of the combined total of the seventy largest railroads in the South. Yet, Thomson and Scott in particular had their fingers in a great many pies, ranging from the lease of the United Companies to the control and the consolidation of the carriers that composed the Pennsylvania Company, to investments in several western transcontinental railroad projects. To those undertakings, they added efforts to influence state and national legislatures, and to cope with a seemingly endless series of rate wars.[112]

The Baltimore & Ohio was hardly powerless against the PRR onslaught. Under the leadership of John W. Garrett, the company operated the most southerly route of the four eastern trunk lines and lay athwart any path that the PRR might take to reach the South. It was the first railroad to reach Washington and to acquire the rights to cross the Potomac River. Yet, the B&O's southerly location, most of it below the Mason-Dixon Line, proved costly during the Civil War. Postwar rebuilding consumed much of the B&O's scarce capital, as did the reconstruction of the line through the Patapsco River Valley following a flood in 1868. The B&O devoted additional resources to reaching Pittsburgh in 1871 and Chicago three years later. Even though the coal mines located along the B&O generated considerable traffic, the resulting revenues were far less than those that the PRR received. While Thomson and Scott possessed ample resources to devote to improvements in the PRR's physical plant and to the construction of new lines, Garrett lacked the wherewithal to fund substantial betterments. That discrepancy, in turn, ensured that the B&O would have the higher operating costs of the two railroads, further retarding expansion and improvements. Finally, at a time when the symbiotic pairing of Thomson and Scott was enjoying stunning success, Garrett had lost much of his earlier skill, and he exhibited increasing signs of mental instability.[113]

In 1871, Garrett became one of the beneficiaries of the Funding Act, when he persuaded his fellow investors in the Orange, Alexandria & Manassas Railroad to buy Virginia's interest in that company. Under a September 1871 agreement, the B&O paid the commonwealth just over $1 million and received in exchange a controlling interest in the newly privatized carrier. In 1873, the chain of B&O-allied railroads south of the Potomac merged into the Washington City, Virginia Midland & Great Southern Railroad, better known simply as the Virginia Midland. By the early 1870s, Garrett could point with pride to a route affiliated with the B&O that formed an awkwardly shaped "H," with north–south legs linking Alexandria

to Danville and Harpers Ferry to Lexington, tied together by an east–west crossbar, between Manassas Junction and Harrisonburg, Virginia.[114]

Yet, even as Garrett gathered railroads together, his PRR adversaries were blocking his efforts. Garrett faced one very small, or more precisely, one very short problem, in the form of the seven-mile-long Alexandria & Washington Railroad, which provided a critical link between B&O rails and those of the Orange, Alexandria & Manassas. As noted above, in 1862 northerners had appropriated the Alexandria & Washington, reorganizing and renaming it as the Washington, Alexandria & Georgetown Railroad. After the Civil War, the Virginians who had originally owned the Alexandria & Washington returned to the area, determined to reclaim their property. They were nonplussed to discover that their company had been confiscated, and they filed suit to recover their investment. In 1870, the Military Court of Appeals of Virginia restored the company to its original prewar owners, but the ruling applied only to Virginia—that is, to the trackage south of the southern end of the Long Bridge. The District of Columbia courts, in contrast, held that the Alexandria & Washington Railroad that owned the remainder of the tracks was a *different* Alexandria & Washington Railroad than the Virginia company and that neither the Long Bridge nor the trackage north of the Potomac River should revert to the Virginians who had just regained the southern portion of the line.[115]

For both the Pennsylvania Railroad and the Baltimore & Ohio, the consequences of that legal hairsplitting were enormous. In June 1870, and in anticipation of the completion of the Baltimore & Potomac route into Washington, PRR officials worked with the ever-reliable Pennsylvania senator Simon Cameron, and likewise relied on the support of Representative Calvin W. Gilfillan, a Republican from the Venango County oil region. Their aim was to guide through Congress a bill allowing the PRR's subsidiary to extend its tracks along Maryland Avenue to the Potomac River. More controversial was a provision to give the Baltimore & Potomac the sole possession of the government-owned Long Bridge, particularly as another two years would pass before the company completed its route into the District of Columbia. Representative Lewis McKenzie, a Conservative from Alexandria, Virginia, wondered "why should such an important franchise as this be given to a railroad that is not yet within twenty miles of this city?"[116] Ohio Republican Martin Welker was in accord with that sentiment, and suggested that all of the railroads serving Washington and Alexandria should have equal right of access. Gilfillan argued against an amendment to that effect, as it would make it impossible to determine which company was responsible for the maintenance of the Long Bridge. Gilfillan and his PRR backers were open to compromise, however, and almost everyone was anxious to save the federal government the $20,000 annual upkeep on the bridge. In its final form, the bill provided that the Baltimore & Potomac would have the authority to use the 1865 Long Bridge in perpetuity, while giving "other railroad companies the right to pass over said bridge upon such reasonable terms as may be agreed upon or as Congress may prescribe."[117] The open access provision was vague and meaningless, and of little value to any company that the PRR might wish to exclude from the crossing. A few days later, with a stroke of President Grant's pen, the PRR deprived the B&O of its principal link to the South and, for the moment, the Orange, Alexandria & Manassas Railroad might just as well have been on the far side of the moon.[118]

The final blow came in November 1872, thanks to Alexander R. Shepherd, the head of the District of Columbia Board of Public Works, and soon to be governor of the district. Shepherd was passionately committed to improving the city's infrastructure. When Shepherd approved the elevation of several city streets by eighteen inches, he required the B&O to raise its trackage by a similar amount. B&O officials refused to bear the expense of raising the rails in conformity with the city's road improvement project. An Irish city road building crew accordingly proceeded to bury the tracks under eighteen inches of dirt, while African American railroaders with equal fortitude shoveled away the soil. In that confrontation, described as "a case of Ireland against Africa," the railway workers prevailed—although local residents were apparently quite disappointed that the anticipated race riot failed to materialize. Garrett, who was no longer able to use the Long Bridge, even if B&O trains could have reached it, abandoned his resistance to Shepherd's civic improvements, and his link to the South was severed.[119]

In desperation, Garrett authorized the construction of a roundabout, twelve-mile line that sent B&O trains looping in a huge slanted "U," from the Washington station northeast through Bladensburg, and then south and southwest to the north bank of the Potomac River at Shepherd's Landing (also known as Marbury Point, and later renamed East Alexandria), south of central Washington. The cost of a bridge at that location would have been enormous, but that was a moot point—the War Department considered the Potomac to be a navigable waterway south of Washington, and refused permission for a crossing. The B&O instead ferried cars across the river, to the Orange, Alexandria & Manassas tracks on the west shore. Despite the ferry service (which complemented the long-established steamship route between Washington and the Richmond, Fredericksburg & Potomac at Aquia Creek), the B&O's link to northern Virginia was greatly inferior to the one operated by the PRR and the Baltimore & Potomac. The B&O retained its interest in the Virginia Midland until 1881, but by then the PRR had effectively blocked any possibility that Garrett and his successors might play a significant role in the South.[120]

After the Civil War, and in anticipation of the completion of the Baltimore & Potomac, Thomson and Scott were anxious to establish a direct rail connection from Alexandria south to Richmond. Despite the 1851 charter of the Alexandria & Fredericksburg Railroad and the 1856 charter supplement of the RF&P, neither company had been able to construct a line between Aquia Creek and a connection with the Orange & Alexandria at Manassas Junction. In February 1864, the Unionist government that met in Alexandria had chartered the Alexandria & Fredericksburg Rail*way*, giving the northerners who controlled the Washington, Georgetown & Alexandria the authority to extend their line directly south, along the Potomac River, to a connection with the RF&P at Aquia Creek. They were no match for the undulating terrain, and were not even able to begin construction before the charter expired in February 1869.[121]

In February 1870, the owners of the Alexandria & Fredericksburg Railway agreed to sell their interests to the PRR. That June, the compliant members of the Virginia legislature restored the company's lapsed charter, and the PRR affiliate again possessed rights to build south, as far as Quantico. George Roberts, at that time the PRR's fourth vice president, became the president of the newly acquired company, with PRR stalwarts Tom Scott, Albert Hewson, and John P. Green serving on the board of directors. Two years later, in April 1872, the PRR purchased a controlling interest in the Virginia portion of the Alexandria & Washington, a company that was essentially useless to any other railroad now that the PRR had established control over the Long Bridge. When construction contractors built the northernmost portion of the Alexandria & Fredericksburg, they simply condemned and appropriated a portion of the Alexandria & Washington right of way, between the southern end of the Long Bridge and Alexandria, touching off a round of litigation that would not be resolved for another decade. Construction moved swiftly forward nonetheless. On May 1, 1872, the RF&P completed a short northerly extension, from Aquia Creek to Quantico. Two months later, construction crews finished work on the thirty-two-mile Alexandria & Fredericksburg line to Quantico, enabling through rail service between Baltimore & Richmond in conjunction with the recently completed Baltimore & Potomac route into Washington.[122]

There was now a direct rail link between Philadelphia and Richmond, yet it was of little immediate value to the Pennsylvania Railroad. The Alexandria & Fredericksburg was quickly and poorly constructed, parts of it over an oily clay that allowed tracks to shift after the passage of every train. In desperation, crews ripped much of the lumber off of the old Long Bridge and used it to shore up the tracks. Other problems were not so easily remedied, however. In the early years of the railroad's operation, many Virginians deeply resented the PRR's northern influence in the line, so they performed small acts of sabotage and, in one case, even attempted to remove spikes and rails in order to trap a locomotive stopped at Alexandria.[123]

Local animosities subsided over time (as did the track bed, apparently), but the larger problem was the contentious relations between the PRR and the Richmond, Fredericksburg & Potomac. Each company controlled half of the link between Washington and Richmond. Each company depended on the other, yet neither wanted to be dependent on the other. The Robinsons controlled two routes to the North—the

first along the RF&P and its subsidiary Potomac Steamboat Company ships to Washington, and the second via their Baltimore Steam Packet Company (also known as the Old Bay Line), which offered overnight service between Norfolk and Baltimore. They had little interest in accepting a short haul by turning traffic over to the Alexandria & Fredericksburg (PRR) at Quantico. As a result, the owners of the RF&P allowed only a single through passenger train to travel each night between Richmond and Washington, forcing daytime passengers to travel by rail and water.[124]

The Robinsons' obstinacy undermined the value of the Alexandria & Fredericksburg and, more important, threatened the viability of the Baltimore & Potomac as well. In addition, much of the freight traffic from the PRR's growing network of affiliated lines south of Richmond had to be offloaded at the James River and carried north to Baltimore by water—a situation that perversely placed the PRR, the only company with a rail route through Washington to the South, at a distinct disadvantage against the B&O, a company that lacked such a direct connection. In disgust, the PRR's managers complained to their stockholders, in the *Annual Report* for 1870, that "On reaching the Richmond, Fredericksburg and Potomac Railway [*sic*], however, we unexpectedly meet the restrictive policy which has heretofore governed most of the Seaboard Railroads south of New York, a policy which belongs in the past and which we trust will soon be abandoned as inconsistent with the interests of the public and the permanent interests of the shareholders of that company, and traffic will be permitted to reach its destination and market whenever it will leave margin of profit to the transporter."[125] There was certainly no "margin of profit" for the Alexandria & Fredericksburg, however. In November 1872, George Roberts informed the PRR board that their subsidiary had lost at least $10,000 since it opened, owing to the restrictive traffic policies of the RF&P. The company entered receivership a month later, although with little effect on ownership or operations.[126]

During the 1870s, PRR and RF&P officials continued their efforts to outmaneuver each other. In March 1871, in response to concerted lobbying by PRR interests, Virginia legislators permitted the Alexandria & Fredericksburg to build from Quantico south to Richmond. Yet, the persistent efforts of William Mahone, who was as anxious to protect his Atlantic, Mississippi & Ohio as the Robinsons were to safeguard the RF&P, ensured that the bill contained so many restrictions that it would be of little value to the PRR. Two months later, RF&P forces counterattacked by organizing the Potomac Railroad Company, a carrier that had been incorporated in 1867. Initially, the Potomac Railroad consisted of a short connection, little more than a mile long, between the tracks of the RF&P and the Alexandria & Fredericksburg at Quantico. However, RF&P officials threatened to extend the route of the Potomac Railroad all the way north to Alexandria, paralleling the Alexandria & Fredericksburg.

The sparring between PRR and RF&P executives continued into the next decade. In 1880, RF&P and B&O managers attempted to establish a cooperative car-ferry service between Quantico and the terminus of the B&O's Alexandria Branch at Shepherd's Landing. As soon as PRR officials learned of the plan, they threatened to divert virtually all of the Baltimore & Potomac's southern traffic to the Virginia Midland at Alexandria, essentially abandoning their own Alexandria & Fredericksburg line, in order to starve the RF&P of revenues. RF&P managers, suitably chastened, cancelled plans for the car-ferry operations. Thereafter, the two rivals began to cooperate more closely with one another. By the beginning of the twentieth century the RF&P would become a reliable conduit between Washington and Richmond, conveying the traffic of the PRR and five other railroads.[127]

The Southern Railway Security Company

For a brief period during the 1870s, Scott and his associates outmaneuvered the B&O by stringing together a network of connecting lines throughout the South, under the aegis of the Southern Railway Security Company. The SRSC was yet another PRR-sponsored holding company, designed to integrate, coordinate, and stabilize the southern railroad network, in much the same way that the South Improvement Company was to regulate freight rates, or the Pennsylvania Company was to unify the railroads west of Pittsburgh and Erie. Created in 1871, within two years the SRSC had thirteen railroads under its control, encompassing 2,131 miles of track, and providing the PRR with several routes connecting Richmond to such cities as Augusta, Georgia; Atlanta; and Charleston, South Carolina. Yet, the height of its power also marked the beginning of its decline. The collapse of Jay Cooke's banking empire in September 1873 so destabilized the railroad business that PRR officials had little choice other than to withdraw from their financial participation in the South. By 1880, it was all over.

Tom Scott was the guiding force behind the creation of the SRSC and—perhaps not surprisingly, given his reputation for political deviousness—he has often been characterized as an individual bent on capturing the southern railway network, bending it to his will, disenfranchising local managers, and funneling the wealth of the South into the coffers of the Pennsylvania Railroad. That description was more stereotype than reality, however. It was largely the product of Scott's adversaries, who employed every weapon at their disposal—including efforts to sway public opinion—in order to undermine his plans. In truth, Scott knew relatively little about the South, and possessed far less political clout in the region than he enjoyed in Harrisburg or in Washington. As such, he depended heavily on southern railway promoters and managers. He identified promising local lines and noteworthy executives, brought them together, coordinated their activities, and provided them with sufficient capital to modernize and expand their railroads. In that sense, Scott was following essentially the same policies that Thomson had developed during the 1850s and 1860s, when he arranged for the PRR to provide support for the Ohio and Indiana railways that later became part of the Pennsylvania Company. Those southern entrepreneurs, not Scott and the PRR, were the primary beneficiaries of the postwar realignment of the southern railroad network.

Of all the talented and well-connected southerners who would play a role in the organization and operation of the Southern Railway Security Company, the two most promising were Benjamin Franklin Newcomer and William Thompson Walters. Scott was closely connected with the two Baltimore bankers, as they had worked together to wrest control of the Northern Central from the Baltimore & Ohio in 1861.

Newcomer and Walters were anxious to improve Baltimore's transportation connections and to increase the traffic that moved through their city. To that end, after the Civil War they underwrote efforts by Robert R. Bridgers, the president of the Wilmington & Weldon Railroad, to rehabilitate his line and link it to the Wilmington & Manchester Railroad. The first of those companies offered service between Wilmington, North Carolina, and Weldon, where a connection with the Petersburg Railroad funneled traffic north toward Petersburg and Richmond. The second, still under construction, would link Wilmington with Columbia, South Carolina, and ultimately continue to Augusta, Georgia.[128]

Newcomer and Walters believed that the two Wilmington-based carriers held the potential to become one of the great trunk lines of the South, but that considerable capital would be required to bring those plans to fruition. Accordingly, on September 14, 1868, at Barnum's Hotel in Baltimore, the two bankers presided over a meeting in which thirty-eight subscribers pledged $1.2 million to enable the Wilmington & Weldon to acquire the Wilmington & Manchester. Most of the participants were from Baltimore, but no one at the meeting could have missed the presence of Thomson, Scott, and J. Donald Cameron, Simon Cameron's son. Nor could they have failed to appreciate that the PRR was willing to invest substantial funds in order to ensure a traffic source for the still incomplete Baltimore & Potomac route that stretched south to Washington. Yet, it was Baltimoreans Newcomer and Walters, and not Scott or his PRR associates, who took charge of matters in Wilmington. They were the point men who were chiefly responsible for placing inexpertly managed and locally oriented southern railways on a sound business footing, and for integrating them into a larger national network.[129]

The meeting at Barnum's Hotel was the genesis of the Southern Railway Security Company. On April 26, 1870, the members of the investment syndicate met again at Barnum's, where Scott presented his ideas for widespread participation in the railroad network of the South. The PRR needed traffic for its Baltimore & Potomac subsidiary, Scott explained, and the Wilmington & Weldon and other southern railroads could

provide it. When connected to various Pennsylvania Railroad affiliates west of the Mississippi, those lines could also funnel PRR traffic to the southwest. Southern carriers required capital, and the PRR, with revenues on Lines East roughly thirty-five times those of the Wilmington & Weldon, could supply all that was required. Everyone would benefit, Scott argued persuasively, for the listless southern railroads, if adequately capitalized, managed, and coordinated, were certain to become profitable.[130]

In March 1871, Scott used his influence in the Pennsylvania legislature to obtain a charter for the Overland Contract Company, its rather bland and innocuous name typical of the PRR's holding companies. A month later, the subsidiary changed its name to the Southern Railway Security Company, revealing its true function. The holding company was a necessity in order to operate across state lines and to coordinate the activities of railroads chartered by several different legislatures. The SRSC's charter made clear that interstate orientation, in order "to secure the control of such Southern railroads as may be essential to the formation of through lines between New York, Philadelphia, Baltimore, Washington City, and the principal cities of the South, by ownership of the capital stock of said companies, by leases and by contract relations."[131] The SRSC was capitalized at $10 million, although it probably issued shares for no more than half that amount, with the PRR owning approximately $2.6 million of its assets.[132]

PRR officials participated actively in the SRSC, although without exercising complete control. Scott's private secretaries, Samuel S. Moon and Richard D. Barclay, were the original incorporators of the company, but they were simply placeholders who represented the interests of more senior PRR officials. Several of the PRR members of the 1868 syndicate, including Scott and J. Donald Cameron, held seats on the SRSC board. Longtime PRR ally George Washington Cass served as the president. Thomson suggested that Herman Haupt be appointed as vice president, but when the directors decided not to create that position, the PRR's former general superintendent was assigned as the general manager of the Richmond & Danville Railroad, a carrier that was under the SRSC's corporate umbrella.[133]

Scott was the best-known individual to be associated with the company, and it was perhaps inevitable that many southerners referred to the SRSC as "the Tom Scott." He provided further access to capital by inviting New York investment bankers, including Morris K. Jessup, D. Willis James, and James Roosevelt (the father of Franklin Delano Roosevelt) to join the Southern Railway Security Company, but Scott was hardly in a position to demand that those individuals obey his orders, or look solely to the interests of the Pennsylvania Railroad. Banker Richard T. Wilson was also listed as a New Yorker, albeit one who had been born in Georgia and who had served as commissary general of the Confederate Army. Despite the presence of PRR associates, however, it was up to southerners such as Newcomer and Walters to manage properties such as the Wilmington & Weldon. Overall, Baltimore capital dominated the SRSC, as the editors of the *Railroad Gazette* acknowledged, and southerners were the ones principally in charge.[134]

Once constituted, the Southern Railway Security Company proceeded to buy or lease numerous southern railroads. It was a good time to go shopping, as local carriers were suffering severe financial problems, while state governments were anxious to part with their internal improvement investments, often at bargain prices. In the process, the members of the consortium made excellent progress toward establishing three southern trunk lines that, Scott hoped, would provide important routes for PRR traffic.

Newcomer and Walters were largely responsible for the creation of a north–south trunk line along the Atlantic seaboard, through Weldon and Wilmington to Charleston, with a branch continuing through South Carolina from Florence to Columbia and then to Augusta, Georgia. The two Baltimore capitalists brought together the Wilmington & Weldon and the Wilmington & Manchester, consolidated between 1870 and 1872 as the Wilmington, Columbia & Augusta Railroad. The Northeastern Railroad gave access to Charleston, while the Richmond & Petersburg Railroad and its southern extension, the Petersburg Railroad, linked with the Wilmington & Weldon and guaranteed a secure connection to Richmond from the south.[135]

William Mahone did his best to prevent the Virginia Board of Public Works from selling the Richmond & Petersburg. He informed Norfolk residents that the SRSC, once in control of the company, would shift traffic away from that port—and, incidentally, away from his Atlantic, Mississippi & Ohio. Not for the first time, Thomson regretted his efforts to educate Mahone on the intricacies of railroad strategy in the immediate aftermath of the Civil War. During the late 1860s, Thomson's advice had helped Mahone keep the Virginia & Tennessee Railroad away from the B&O, and to make it part of the Atlantic, Mississippi & Ohio. By the early 1870s, however, Mahone had honed his skills, and he demonstrated more antipathy toward the PRR than he had ever harbored toward the Baltimore road. He was even willing to join forces with the B&O in order to block the SRSC's acquisition of the Richmond & Petersburg. His efforts were in vain, however, and the PRR's allies gained control.[136]

A second trunk route, often referred to as the Piedmont Air Line, connected Richmond and Atlanta by way of Danville, Greensboro, and Charlotte, North Carolina, with onward connections to Montgomery and Mobile, Alabama, as well as Pensacola, Florida. Algernon S. Buford, president of the Richmond & Danville Railroad, controlled a route linking Richmond to Greensboro, North Carolina. He also possessed grand ambitions for a railroad to Atlanta, even New Orleans, yet lacked the necessary resources. In 1869, Buford had supported construction of the Atlanta & Richmond Air-Line, between Charlotte and Atlanta, but funding soon ran out. His cooperation with the SRSC worked to his advantage, as well as that of northern investors. In August 1871, based on legislation enacted in March, the SRSC acquired the Virginia government's interest in the Richmond & Danville, blocking Garrett's efforts to extend the Lynchburg & Danville route (soon to become the Virginia Midland) into North Carolina. Of equal importance, the Richmond & Danville and the Air-Line promised a direct connection with Atlanta and a region that was rapidly becoming associated with the economic transformations of the New South.[137]

Mahone again lobbied against the transaction. He made reference to the emblems of early Pennsylvania militia units, labeling the sale of the railroad to Scott as the "Bucktail Swindle," but to no avail. Within months, construction crews were hard at work, completing the Air-Line to Atlanta. The North Carolina

Railroad filled the gap between Greensboro and Charlotte, and it too came into the SRSC fold. The Richmond & York River Railroad, another leased line, carried traffic from Richmond to tidewater, where Baltimore, Chesapeake & Richmond Steamboat Company ships conveyed it onward to Baltimore. The Charlotte, Columbia & Augusta Railroad linked Charlotte with Augusta, Georgia. Other SRSC investments created a route between Atlanta and the Gulf of Mexico, at Mobile and Pensacola, through the Western Railroad of Alabama and the Mobile & Montgomery Railroad.[138]

The story was much the same with Henry B. Plant, who provided the nucleus for a third route, through Bristol, Knoxville, and Chattanooga, Tennessee, to Memphis. Plant was a Connecticut Yankee, but a longtime resident of the South. He began his career as a messenger for Alvin Adams on the New York & New Haven Railroad. In 1854, Adams assigned Plant as his superintendent for the Southern Territory, based in Augusta, Georgia. During the war, Plant had organized the southern properties of the Adams Express Company into the Southern Express Company, in order to prevent their confiscation by the Confederacy, and he served as the first president of the new firm.[139]

Plant brought the Western & Atlantic Railroad into the SRSC, providing a route from Atlanta north to Chattanooga. Richard T. Wilson, another southerner who lived north of the Mason-Dixon Line, joined the syndicate in November 1871. His East Tennessee, Virginia & Georgia Railroad extended the Western & Atlantic route from junctions at Dalton and Chattanooga, farther north to Bristol, Tennessee (and a connection with Mahone's rival Atlantic, Mississippi & Ohio), with the ultimate goal of Cincinnati. By March of 1872, the SRSC had leased the Memphis & Charleston Railroad, with a line between Memphis, Tennessee and Stevenson, Alabama, at the far northeastern corner of the state. A connection with the Nashville & Chattanooga Railroad covered the last few miles into Chattanooga, and offered the Pennsylvania Railroad, through the SRSC, its first secure connection to one of the southern gateways to the trans-Mississippi West, at Memphis.[140]

Scott was not content to stop there. He also intended to create a route, independent of the SRSC, south through the Appalachian Valley, toward Birmingham, Alabama. Coal from West Virginia, iron ore from the Shenandoah Valley, forest products from Virginia, and cotton from the Gulf states all promised to feed valuable traffic into the Pennsylvania Railroad. The PRR's Cumberland Valley Railroad provided a line from Harrisburg to Hagerstown, Maryland. Farther south, Wilson's East Tennessee, Virginia & Georgia linked Bristol, Tennessee, to the Western & Atlantic tracks at Dalton.

In order to close the gap between Hagerstown and Bristol, Scott relied on the Shenandoah Valley Railroad, in effect a southern extension of the Cumberland Valley Railroad.[141] Incorporated in February 1867, the company soon fell under Scott's influence. In July 1870, Scott oversaw the organization of the Central Improvement Company, with his secretary, Richard Barclay, serving as president. Alexander K. McClure—for decades a staunch political supporter of the PRR interests—acted as legal counsel for the Central Improvement Company. Herman Haupt returned to the PRR family to serve as the chief engineer for the project, and by April 1871, Scott was president of the Shenandoah Valley. By September 1873, construction crews building south from Hagerstown had crossed the Potomac River and laid rails as far south as Martinsburg, West Virginia. They went no farther, however, as the Panic of 1873 brought construction to a halt.[142]

By the summer of 1873, PRR officials had undertaken the establishment of an integrated system of allied railroads throughout the South. With a relatively small investment (probably not much more than $4 million) and in a remarkably short span of time, the SRSC had united thirteen railroads and had made substantial progress toward creating three southern trunk lines—along the Atlantic seaboard, through the Piedmont to Atlanta, and from the Blue Ridge west to the Mississippi.[143] The coal lands of the southern Appalachians, the cotton fields of the Deep South, and the timber of the Piedmont all lay within reach. The PRR had rail links to almost every large southern city, with connections to western railroad affiliates at St. Louis, Cairo, and Memphis. It was an impressive network, to be sure, and helped to explain why the editor of a Memphis newspaper considered the PRR to be "the most powerful and effective organization of its kind in existence. It seeks, and is rapidly obtaining, control of the entire railroad system of the country."

Or, as the editor of the *New York Herald* suggested, Scott, "the Pennsylvania Napoleon, has been ambitious to take possession of the republic under a nine hundred and ninety-nine years' lease."[144]

And then, everything fell apart. Scott and his associates on the PRR and the SRSC could not control every southern railroad, and executives on independent lines such as the South Carolina Railroad, the Georgia Rail Road, the Seaboard & Roanoke, and the Atlantic, Mississippi & Ohio reacted to the growing competitive threat by pushing forward their own expansion projects. The result was a frenzy of overbuilding, which in turn depressed rates and weakened all of the southern carriers. Furthermore, much of the increased revenues that promoters expected to accompany the creation of the southern trunk lines simply did not materialize. Western grain shipments did not come flooding into southern distribution centers along the new railroads, for example. It proved far cheaper to move the grain along one of the northern trunk lines to New York, Philadelphia, or Baltimore, and then send it south by water.

The commercial disruptions that attended the development of the new southern trunk lines were not all that different from those that had earlier affected the North—and, for that matter, California, following completion of the transcontinental railroad in 1869. The postwar South was already in a weakened condition, however, and could ill afford the additional shock. The region's railroads, and the SRSC, might well have recovered had it not been for the economic calamities of 1873. Jay Cooke's failure soon induced the collapse of the Southern Railway Security Company, spelling an end to the PRR's efforts to influence the railways of the South.[145]

On November 21, 1873, barely two months after the downfall of Jay Cooke & Company, participants in the Southern Railway Security Company met in New York to assess the full scope of the disaster. Scott had made it clear that neither he nor the Pennsylvania Railroad would continue to participate in the syndicate. Absent the PRR's support, the remaining members had little choice other than to retrench. By the spring of 1874, the SRSC had either sold or else terminated the leases of many of its key assets, including the East Tennessee, Virginia & Georgia and the Rich-

mond & Danville. Yet, Thomson still considered the Richmond & Danville to be a valuable property, in part because of his decades-old connections to Georgia railroading, and in part because the company's route to Atlanta constituted one of the key transportation corridors in the postwar South. Furthermore, while the coastal lines were under the control of Walters and Newcomer, and reasonably secure, Thomson was not willing to risk the possibility that the Richmond & Danville might fall into unfriendly hands. Accordingly, when the PRR cashed out its interest in the SRSC, Thomson acquired many of the securities of the Richmond & Danville (and its leased North Carolina Railroad), along with those of the Atlanta & Richmond Air-Line, the Western Railroad of Alabama, and the Mobile & Montgomery.

Of the remaining companies under SRSC control, the Wilmington, Columbia & Augusta was soon in serious trouble. In April 1878, that railroad, still under the control of Newcomer and Walters, entered receivership. Absent the securities of the WC&A, the Southern Railway Security Company was little more than a shell corporation. The Commonwealth of Pennsylvania seized the SRSC charter for nonpayment of taxes and, in a remarkable display of recycling, sold it to some of the individuals involved in Standard Oil. They in turn renamed the firm the National Transit Company and used it to oversee Standard's pipelines—which, like railroads, inconveniently crossed state lines.[146]

Most of the railroads associated with the Southern Railway Security Company went on to greater glory, although without the PRR's participation. In 1880, the PRR sold its interests in the Richmond & Danville and related lines to a consortium of investors, including such familiar faces as Newcomer, Walters, Plant, and Wilson. The real motivating force, however, came from Philadelphians Thomas and William Clyde, who had made their fortunes in the steamboat business. The Clydes and their associates made the Richmond & Danville and the other companies that composed the Piedmont Air Line part of the Richmond & West Point Terminal Railway & Warehouse Company, which in turn went bankrupt in 1893. New York investment banker J. P. Morgan reorganized the firm in 1894, creating the Southern Railway. The East Tennessee, Virginia & Georgia and the Memphis & Charleston also became part of the Southern system. So too, did the Virginia Midland, the B&O's entry to the South, which had been leased to the Richmond & Danville in 1886. The Mobile & Montgomery became part of the Louisville & Nashville Railroad. In 1890, the Western & Atlantic eventually passed to the Nashville, Chattanooga & St. Louis Railway, which itself had been leased by the Louisville & Nashville a decade earlier. Despite the collapse of the SRSC and the bankruptcy of the Wilmington, Columbia & Augusta, Newcomer and Walters were survivors, and they managed to hold on to their railway investments in the region. During the late 1880s, they folded their investments into a new holding company, the Atlantic Coast Line. In later years, their sons, Waldo Newcomer and Henry Walters, served on the board of the Northern Central and the Baltimore & Potomac, continuing the close affiliation with the Pennsylvania Railroad.[147]

The railroads promoted by William Mahone, the Robinsons, and the other opponents of the SRSC did not fare too badly either. The Seaboard & Roanoke survived, despite the competition from the SRSC roads, and became the Seaboard Air Line Railroad. As a competitor to the Atlantic Coast Line, its access to Richmond helped to spark one final confrontation between the PRR and the Richmond, Fredericksburg & Potomac, at the beginning of the twentieth century. Mahone's Atlantic, Mississippi & Ohio also underwent substantial changes that would transform it into one of the nation's preeminent coal-hauling railroads. During the summer of 1879, Philadelphia banker Clarence H. Clark, representing the Philadelphia banking house of E. W. Clark & Company, bought the PRR's interest in the unbuilt Shenandoah Valley Railroad for ten cents on the dollar. He established the Shenandoah Valley Construction Company and resumed construction on the line. By June 1882 trains were running along a route connecting the PRR main line at Harrisburg with the Atlantic, Mississippi & Ohio Railroad at Roanoke. More than a year earlier, in February 1881, Clark had purchased Mahone's railroad. Working through another family business, Clark, Dodge & Company, and with the assistance of Drexel, Morgan & Company, he soon reorganized the property into the Norfolk & Western Railroad. The Pennsylvania Railroad eventually acquired a large

share of the Norfolk & Western Railway (as it was known following an 1896 reorganization) and in later years used the profitable Pocahontas coal-hauler as a cash cow. In the end, the railroads of Tom Scott and William Mahone acted in concert, even if their managers had never been able to do the same.[148]

The Southern Railway Security Company in Retrospect

During its short existence, the Southern Railway Security Company made more than its share of enemies. The PRR's involvement in the SRSC continues to distort interpretations of the PRR's history, as well as Scott's career. By the late nineteenth century, Scott and his allies on southern railroads had become the scapegoats for the concerns of southerners, individuals who were aware that their economic world was changing for the worse, but who were not precisely sure what to do about it. Their fears were evident in the nature of their attacks on Scott, and on the Pennsylvania Railroad. Southerners saw Scott and his ilk as intruders and carpetbaggers who would corrupt southern governments. As a citizen of Pennsylvania, a staunch Republican, and the business partner of the former secretary of war, Scott was the ultimate outsider, a persona non grata in the political economy of the Reconstruction South.

Southern newspaper editors distilled the amorphous fears of their subscribers into a concerted and vitriolic attack against Scott, the Pennsylvania Railroad, and northern, "outside" interests. Scott, they suggested, had secured passage of Virginia's 1871 Funding Act by bribing Governor Walker with two thousand shares of PRR stock. Scott was a Republican, newspaper editors argued, and so southern Republicans must have fallen under his sway—even though very few were associated with the PRR. Scott's plans would benefit black Republicans more than any other group, they argued—even though there was no evidence to suggest that Scott expressed any concern for the political or economic rights of African Americans in the South. Rumors spread like wildfire. Scott, part of the northern inner circle that had freed southern slaves without compensation, that had repudiated the

Confederate debt, and that had seized southern cotton as war contraband, was now so flush with his ill-gotten gains that he sponsored galas to seduce southerners that could be of use to him—complete with punchbowls full of complimentary currency. Even worse, southerners suggested, Scott and his minions were corrupting pure southern womanhood, providing prostitutes for southern politicians and other influential individuals for whom monetary bribes were apparently insufficient.[149]

Well before the formation of the Southern Railway Security Company, Scott had acquired a reputation as a scoundrel and a swindler, and many southerners were determined to keep him as far away as possible. "Take, for instance, the Pennsylvania Central Railroad, which has and is daily encircling with extended arms the smaller roads and railway corporations throughout the Union," charged an incensed Florida legislator in 1872. "Look what a stretch of power and authority is placed within the hands of Thomas Scott, the president [sic] of that railroad. We, who are in Florida, cannot conceive of the vastness of his schemes . . . but I am credibly informed that, by means of the power that he and his board of directors possess, they carry everything desired throughout the State of Pennsylvania." That must not happen in Florida, he continued, for "We want no *Tom Scotts*, *Jim Fisks* or *Vanderbilts* in this State to govern us."[150]

The sustained condemnation of Scott came from the mouth of John W. Wyatt, an African Methodist Episcopal minister from Tallahassee who owed his seat in the legislature to the Reconstruction agenda of northern Radical Republicans—a situation that indicated the extraordinary complexity of the postwar South. It is doubtful that Scott was aware of the irony associated with two nearly simultaneous accusations against him. One, emanating from the Conservative Party in Virginia, suggested that Scott was cooperating with African Americans in the "Mongrel Convention" in order to acquire the state's public works. The other involved allegations that he was in league with white racists in a conspiracy to deprive African Americans in Florida of their rights. The incongruity nonetheless bespoke the extent to which Scott and his SRSC associates had become scapegoats for the contentious reconfiguration of race relations in the postwar South. Conservative whites were aghast that individuals who

had only recently been slaves now possessed political rights, thanks to northern Republicans. Particularly in Virginia, Scott benefited from that political transformation and even if he did not actively support it he nonetheless was assigned responsibility for it. Farther south, Florida possessed more than twice as much public land as any other state, and many African Americans hoped that the equitable distribution of that resource would establish the foundation for their economic emancipation. The possibility that the state legislature might give away the public patrimony, not to freedmen but to railroads, seemed the worst sort of sellout. It was not difficult for southern blacks, and even some recent historians, to suggest that Scott was willing to make deals with the Democrats who sought to redeem the South from the influences of scalawags and black freedmen. In that assessment, Scott used the SRSC's treasury to provide bribes for the Redeemers and employed his influence in Washington to encourage the federal government to be less stringent in its protection of civil rights in the South. In that view, Scott may not have directly aided the Ku Klux Klan and other white supremacist groups, but he certainly tolerated them and facilitated their activities.[151]

Race relations constituted only one facet of the postwar South, and here too Scott and the SRSC shouldered the blame for transformations that no one could control. One allegation was that SRSC officials had bought control of most of the South's leading newspapers, ensuring that the editors who in the late 1860s had so vociferously criticized the PRR's "foreign" intervention had become strangely silent on the issue. The SRSC also allegedly encouraged the development of a system of debt peonage in the South, to grow crops, principally tobacco and cotton, that offered a guaranteed source of bulk traffic for the railroads that were a part of that holding company. SRSC officials relied on the contributions of southern prison systems (to guarantee a ready supply of convict labor) and of state agricultural societies (to encourage farmers to make extensive use of fertilizer, which was brought in—at considerable expense—in SRSC freight cars). In the process, the SRSC set freight rates so as to encourage the cultivation of traditional staples and to discourage manufacturing and economic diversification supported by promoters of the New South movement.[152]

In truth, the actions of Scott and the SRSC were considerably more benign. The SRSC rarely purchased southern newspapers outright. Instead, railroaders helped to fund entrepreneurial journalists, asking in return that they receive generally favorable editorials, and that train schedules and fares be published at regular intervals. Such practices may have run afoul of twentieth-century standards of journalistic ethics, but they were common practice at the time. By January 1875, for example, Scott had helped his business associate and lobbyist Samuel S. Moon purchase Thomas S. Fernon's *United States Railroad & Mining Register.* Moon's paper, known afterward as *Railway World,* was generally friendly to Scott, particularly in matters relating to the Texas & Pacific, but it was by no means a propaganda arm for the PRR. The same could be said for the *New York World,* a general-circulation paper managed by William Henry Hurlburt that Scott also owned for a time, during the 1870s. Never an appendage of the PRR, it passed outside the PRR's orbit after Scott's death.[153]

A more nuanced view suggests that Scott, the Pennsylvania Railroad, and the Southern Railway Security Company were part of the integration of the national railroad network, but that it would be a mistake to attribute solely to them the broad social, economic, and political changes that were sweeping through the postwar South. Between 1870 and 1900, more and more of the directors of the southern railroads listed their address as New York, Boston, Philadelphia, or some other northern city. Postwar railway promoters were a footloose lot, however. Northerners moved to the South, southerners moved north, and the Mason-Dixon Line became a permeable membrane to self-interested capitalists who cared more about profit than about lingering sectional animosities. In that context, location mattered little. The real change was that investors' paternalistic stewardship for local communities gave way to corporate and individual self-interest. In turn, that self-interest became a nationwide phenomenon, overriding the localized concerns of ordinary southerners. Tied to their place of origin, and still smarting from the wounds of the Civil War, they were understandably concerned at the willingness of southern promoters to abandon their charges and to disrupt regional economies. It was likewise reasonable

that, rather than label elite southerners as traitors to their communities, local residents would channel their resentment toward Scott, the PRR, and other readily identifiable northern interests.[154]

The railroads that composed the SRSC—and, for that matter, all southern railroads—did set low rates on staple crops, such as tobacco and cotton, but not in order to stifle other economic activities. Unlike perishables and manufactured goods, staple crops possessed a low value-to-weight ratio, were not subject to spoilage, and did not entail significant inventory-in-transit costs. As such, they inherently commanded low rates. The managers of southern railroads undoubtedly encouraged better farming techniques, ranging from crop rotation to the use of fertilizer, but the intent of such educational outreach programs was to increase shipments through improved crop yields, not to force southern farmers to remain locked into an antebellum agrarian economy. It should be noted, moreover, that western railroads were funding similar agricultural outreach programs and earned widespread praise for doing so.

The structural characteristics of the southern economy proved far more important than the short period of PRR and SRSC involvement in the South. Coastal Virginia and the Carolinas were suited for the cultivation of fruits and vegetables, while the Piedmont excelled in textile production.[155] Aside from those two regions, however, the North and the West maintained a high degree of comparative advantage in manufacturing and food crops, perpetuating the South's reliance on staples. The South possessed substantial reserves of coal and iron ore, particularly in the Cumberland Valley and the Birmingham region, but they were too remote and ultimately noncompetitive with northern steel production. Finally, the growing regional specialization of southern agriculture, and its attendant disruptions, occurred because the southern railroad network became more integrated during the 1870s and 1880s, and increasingly tied to the national economy. It would be a mistake, therefore, to attribute to Scott the long-term structural changes in the transportation and agricultural sectors of the southern economy.[156]

In the final analysis, it was the South, and not Scott or the PRR, that benefited the most from northern involvement in the region. In the aftermath of the Civil

War, only the North possessed the resources to rebuild the southern railroad infrastructure. Northern investors, working closely with their southern allies, provided both the economic resources and the organizational expertise necessary to rescue the southern railways, and to integrate formerly isolated lines into a national transportation network.

For Scott and the PRR, the results were less encouraging, but not disastrous. The Southern Railway Security Company played an active role in the southern railroad network for less than five years, between 1871 and 1876, and was out of business by 1880. The PRR was able to recoup most of its $2.6 million to $2.7 million investment in southern railway lines, a generally more satisfactory result than what the Baltimore & Ohio was able to accomplish.

More important, by investing in the South, and by blocking the B&O's efforts to do likewise, Thomson, Scott, and their associates ensured that, for decades to come, the Pennsylvania Railroad would be the primary conduit for traffic moving between the northeast and the southeast. For the last third of the nineteenth century, the B&O was largely shut out of the South, defeated by both Scott's maneuverings and John W. Garrett's missteps. Not until 1906, with the completion of the Washington Union Station and the sprawling Potomac Yard to the south of its namesake river, did the B&O again enjoy a convenient connection with the Richmond, Fredericksburg & Potomac, the Southern, and other southeastern railroads. Most southern freight traveled over the PRR, and the 1910 opening of Pennsylvania Station in New York ensured that passenger trains destined for Richmond, Miami, Atlanta, New Orleans, and other southern destinations would also use PRR tracks north of Washington. Throughout much of the twentieth century, the *Silver Meteor*, the *Crescent*, and myriad other streamliners sailed along PRR tracks to the national capital before heading off to all parts of the South, their routes in part a legacy of Tom Scott and the Southern Railway Security Company.[157]

In February 1886, twenty years before the opening of Potomac Yard, railroad officials who were members of the Southern Time Convention began planning the conversion of the South's railroads to a uniform gauge. While some southern lines chose standard gauge, others selected the 4' 9" gauge of their principal northern connection, the Pennsylvania Railroad. That difference of half an inch, largely inconsequential in matters of operation, symbolized the PRR's ongoing influence in the American South.[158]

Retrenchment

The depression of the 1870s put an end to the efforts of PRR executives, Scott in particular, to extend the railroad's influence into the South and West. Scott and his colleagues probably never intended that locomotives lettered for the Pennsylvania Railroad should ever pass through the Louisiana bayous, cross the Continental Divide, or feel the salt spray of the Pacific Ocean. In that sense, there was little chance that the PRR would become the first truly transcontinental railroad in the United States. Instead, Scott merely sought to establish reasonably secure connections with railroads that might extend the PRR's reach. Eastern coal and manufactured products might flow west over the Northern Pacific, the Union Pacific, the Kansas Pacific, and the Texas & Pacific. More important, grain production from the rapidly populating Great Plains would reach tidewater via PRR gateways at St. Louis and Chicago, without contributing to the revenues of the Baltimore & Ohio, the New York Central, or the Erie. Grain traffic might likewise move through the South, and to southern ports, over the network of railroads coordinated by the Southern Railway Security Company. The SRSC could potentially divert the agricultural bounty of a recovering South to the PRR's Baltimore & Potomac tracks at Washington, validating what was initially a profitless link to the nation's capital.

But, it was not to be. Thomson, Scott, and other PRR executives failed to exert the same degree of influence over the western lines as they had over the Pittsburgh, Fort Wayne & Chicago and other routes through Ohio and Indiana. Most spectacular of all, the Texas & Pacific fiasco proved an acute financial and political embarrassment, and perhaps hastened Thomson's path to the grave. Scott's involvement in the Texas venture ensured that he would bear the blame for most of the PRR's failures in the West, and hasten his own death as a result. His actions on behalf of the Texas & Pacific bordered on the corrupt and unethical, although they were less audacious than those of Jay Cooke, Thomas C. Durant, and many other Gilded Age railway promoters.

In the West, there were two, more systemic, problems. First, Thomson and Scott associated with individuals such as Cooke and Durant, who turned out to be financially insecure or devious to the point of unreliability. PRR executives had encountered disappointments in Ohio and Indiana also—the insanity of Benjamin Smith and the incompetence of Ambrose Burnside certainly come to mind. Yet, western railway construction coupled lavish government subsidies with construction that may have outstripped demand. It attracted risk takers and speculators, and undoubtedly contributed to the high percentage of untrustworthy allies. Second, the presence of a large number of transcontinental routes through the sparsely populated West ensured that no carrier would be as well funded, as well managed, or as successful as the eastern trunk lines. The halcyon days of the western lines did not begin until late in the nineteenth century, well after Thomson and Scott had departed the scene, when a new generation of empire builders—including James Jerome Hill and Edward Henry Harriman—rebuilt their companies into respectable carriers of passengers and freight.

In the South, Thomson and Scott were plagued neither by untrustworthy allies nor by speculative ventures in advance of demand. Individuals such as Benjamin Newcomer and William Walters were skilled and reliable financiers whose involvement with the Northern Central had proven both their expertise and their loyalty to the Pennsylvania Railroad. Likewise, an ample and growing demand for transportation existed in the South, even if Wilmington, Charleston, and Savannah never developed their full potential as port cities. The difficulties lay rather in the nature of geography, business, politics, and race in the South. Even as late as the 1870s, two decades after the development of integrated northern railway systems, many southerners were anxious to protect their community and their region. As such, they were understandably hostile to any endeavor, such as the Southern Railway Security Company, that threatened to shatter their local monopolies. That insularity was soon translated into political opposition to the SRSC. Although most of those connected with the SRSC had southern roots, Scott found it impossible to disguise his role in the project. Southerners therefore experienced little difficulty in tapping into a deep well of resentment toward the Yankees who had so recently shattered the Confederacy's dreams of independence, and of portraying northern capitalists as money-grubbing carpetbaggers in league with traitorous southern scalawags.

It the end, however, it was simple economics that put an end to the PRR's national reach. The depression that began in 1873 caused many casualties, from the Northern Pacific Railroad, to the California & Texas Railway Construction Company, to the Southern Railway Security Company. Conditions were hardly ideal on the Pennsylvania Railroad, either. Even if there was little danger of bankruptcy, Thomson and Scott still fought vigorously to protect the PRR's finances and to fend off seemingly interminable challenges from the other eastern trunk lines. Under the circumstances, PRR executives possessed neither the time nor the money to go beyond the PRR's established territory, which lay to the north of the Ohio River and to the east of the Mississippi. In 1874, Pennsylvania Railroad shareholders said as much when they insisted that their managers refrain from additional expansion.

The stockholders' revolt, the first serious challenge to PRR management in more than two decades, was one of the factors that helped to limit executive flexibility. At virtually the same time, powerful shippers, John D. Rockefeller foremost among them, asserted their authority in ways unimaginable even a decade earlier. The Panic of 1873 spawned one of the great economic and social catastrophes of the nineteenth century, a recession that sparked the riots of 1877, damaged the PRR's physical plant, and left the organizational confidence of executives badly shaken. Scott proved even more willing than Thomson to preserve the PRR's future by whatever means he deemed necessary, whether that involved the suppression of the violence or attempts to control rates. The events of the 1870s nonetheless alerted PRR managers that they faced stronger constraints than ever before, from shippers, government officials, and organized labor. Even as they celebrated the 1876 Centennial, when the United States entered the second century of its independence, the Pennsylvania Railroad and its new generation of executives were about to enter an age of limits.

Chapter 11

Limits

1874–1877

In 1776, the city of Philadelphia had played host to the Second Continental Congress, and to the distinguished individuals who had drafted the founding document of American independence. A hundred years later, the United States had been transformed from thirteen new states clinging to the Atlantic seaboard to a nation that spanned a continent, from a minor player in the international arena to an emerging world power.

More than any other event, the Centennial Exhibition, held in West Philadelphia, marked the changes that a century had wrought in the affairs of the United States. For the exhibition, twenty-four participating states erected buildings that reflected popular conceptions of regional identities. The Rhode Island building was among the smallest, Michigan's was a forest of ornate woodwork from its timberlands, and the structure provided by Kansas resembled a barn in a frontier town. Mississippi supplied a log cabin, dripping with Spanish moss, while Virginia furnished what looked much like a plantation home. Most southern states chose not to participate, however, a sign that the wounds of the Civil War had not yet healed.

Many of the exhibits reflected the expansionist and increasingly international vision of the American people. Eleven nations erected pavilions, and more than a dozen more maintained exhibits. Despite America's

progress, Great Britain remained the world's leading industrial economy. Germany, a nation still in formation, was making rapid advances in transportation and industrialization. Only recently brought into close contact with the West, Japan was on the verge of a transformation from agrarian feudalism to an industrial economy. Liberia, a nation envisioned as a destination for former slaves, was one of only two participants from Africa. Fifty-three years earlier, under the terms of the Monroe Doctrine, the United States had anointed itself the protector of Latin America, and exhibition visitors who saw displays from Mexico, Nicaragua, Guatemala, Honduras, Colombia, and other nations may well have congratulated themselves on how well they were treating those "backward" peoples.

For most Americans, particularly those who lived in the Northeast, the greatest alteration over the previous century had little to do with faraway states or exotic foreign lands. It was instead the transformation of their communities, and their lives, from a rural pastoral world, filled with farms and small towns, to an industrial society, where factories and the railroads had produced an almost unimaginable increase in standards of living and the speed of peoples' lives. It was not surprising, then, that the exhibition was a hagiography in steel of inventors and industrialists, of technology and what was, to many, an unalloyed faith in progress and a con-

Figure 45. In 1877, only a year after the nation's centennial celebrations, railway workers across the United States went on strike. The resulting violence shocked Americans into a realization that class conflict, once thought to be solely a European problem, had arrived on their shores. It also caused extensive damage to the PRR facilities at Pittsburgh, shown here, and shattered confident managerial assumptions that PRR workers were part of a small and interdependent family. The strike was the greatest single blow to the psyche of PRR managers at any time in the railroad's history, and it conditioned the company's personnel policies for decades to come.
Pennsylvania Historical and Museum Commission, Railroad Museum of Pennsylvania.

stantly brighter future. The most popular exhibits celebrated the new economic virtues of capitalism and individual initiative—with all of their attendant possibilities for seemingly endless abundance, prosperity, and progress. The huge Corliss steam engine, the iconic symbol of the exhibition, physically dominated and provided power for the main exhibit hall, leaving visitors with a commingled sense of awe and self-satisfied pride at their nation's prowess.

In 1846, the span of a human lifetime beyond the Declaration of Independence, Philadelphia and its resi-

dents had ushered the Pennsylvania Railroad into being. The PRR had been a uniquely Philadelphia enterprise, one that had garnered little support from western Pennsylvanians, and less still from residents of other states. The railroad was wholly and inexorably linked to the Quaker City, the birthplace of American independence.

Three decades later, as the nation approached the Centennial, PRR executives saw the event as a chance to showcase their railroad, its achievements, and the benefits that it had brought to the city of Philadelphia, the commonwealth of Pennsylvania, and to the United States. In J. Edgar Thomson, the Pennsylvania Railroad had its own founding father, whose death in 1874 ensured his deification and did much to shelter him from the innuendo that attended his multifarious financial endeavors. His successor, Tom Scott, was publicly reviled for his financial schemes and for his attempts to influence state and national politics, but Scott could at least show Americans that his tactics produced results.

When the members of the General Assembly balked at a $1 million appropriations bill to underwrite the cost of the Centennial Exhibition, Scott took charge of the situation. He instructed his personal assistant and legislative liaison, Samuel S. Moon, to travel to Harrisburg in order to alter the votes of parsimonious legislators. "Well, Moon, see that the bill is passed; the Centennial must be made a great success," Scott allegedly told his subordinate—and, whether or not he used those precise words, it was obvious that the PRR's president expected the commonwealth to fund a substantial portion of an exhibition that was certain to benefit the Pennsylvania Railroad.[1]

The PRR contributed its own resources as well. In preparation for the exhibition, PRR crews created the nation's most extensive block signaling system, designed to move traffic more efficiently and—so PRR executives asserted—so safely that the possibility of accident was remote indeed. From central Philadelphia, construction workers completed a fourth mainline track as far west as Merion—the beginnings of what would eventually be a four-track main line to Pittsburgh. In order to accommodate the traffic associated with the exhibition, shop forces at Altoona designed whole new classes of passenger cars.

The board of directors authorized the construction of two new passenger stations, one at West Philadelphia and the other farther west, at the site of the exhibition grounds. The West Philadelphia Station, popularly known as "Centennial Station," sat at the corner of Thirty-Second Street and Lancaster Avenue, and it faced Market Street, the main thoroughfare leading into the heart of Philadelphia. Two train sheds spanned the twelve tracks serving the station, while elaborate public spaces provided evidence that the PRR was catering to Centennial crowds with the finest passenger

terminal yet constructed along the entire system. During the summer of 1876, the West Philadelphia facility alone accommodated more than twenty thousand trains and more than 2.3 million passengers.[2]

At the site of the exhibition, a massive new station sat at the corner of Belmont and Elm Avenues. With four corner towers and a 100- by 130-foot waiting room, it was designed in the same popular "stick" style that characterized the other exhibition buildings. A set of circular balloon tracks allowed trains from any direction to pull into the station, disgorge their passengers, and just as quickly depart again. The PRR also built a freight yard, solely to handle the forty thousand tons of merchandise destined for the exhibit halls. In a portent of the system-wide congestion to come, the space was inadequate, and soon overwhelmed, which contributed to severe delays in setting up the exhibits.[3]

Travelers destined for the exhibition, many of whom boarded PRR trains at points as far west as Chicago or St. Louis, taxed the capacity of what was already the world's largest railroad. Between May 10 and November 10, 1876, the PRR accommodated nearly five million passengers (and 730,000 pieces of their baggage), who traveled in some 270,000 cars attached to 42,600 trains. On October 19, 1876, Maryland and Delaware Day, the PRR station at the Centennial accommodated the heaviest traffic density ever seen in the United States, far surpassing anything that had occurred during the Civil War, with 245 trains carrying nearly 56,000 passengers, with more than 17,000 of them entraining between 4:20 P.M. and 6:00 P.M.[4]

In addition to transporting goods and people to the exhibition, the Pennsylvania Railroad was itself on display. Shop forces had restored the oldest locomotive on the system, the Camden & Amboy's *John Bull*, as a tribute to the great advancements in locomotive design that had occurred since 1831. Other exhibits awaited inside the Machinery Hall, a massive structure designed by Joseph Miller Wilson, the PRR's engineer of bridges and buildings.[5] The Empire Line provided working models of a grain elevator, an Anchor Line Great Lakes steamship, and an oil well with pipelines and storage tanks.

Even after the exhibition closed in the autumn of 1876, traces of the PRR's involvement remained. The passenger station and associated trackage, built on

PRR property, became the site of a massive freight yard that stretched six blocks, from Forty-Sixth Street to Fifty-Second Street. The Empire Line reused portions of the dismantled Machinery Hall as a warehouse for its National Storage Company subsidiary, at Communipaw, New Jersey. One of the most enduring legends of survival, however, involved the Japanese Building. With commendable frugality, according to some accounts, PRR crews appropriated the small, ornate structure, hauled it fourteen miles west to Wayne, and used it as a commuter station. During the late 1880s, crews moved the building to the next stop to the west, a location then known as Eagle, and today as Strafford, where it still stands.[6]

For both the nation and the Pennsylvania Railroad, the Centennial Exhibition was both a triumphant celebration of the decade of sustained economic growth that had marked the North's recovery from the disruptions of the Civil War and a portent of the grimmer realities of the new industrial age, including depression and class conflict. Not everyone benefited equally from the changes wrought by industrialization, mass production, and the railroads. As the nation's wealth increased, standards of living rose faster for some than for others. The working poor, recent immigrants in particular, endured long and exhausting workdays, dangerous working conditions, low pay, and poor-quality housing. The skilled artisans of an earlier generation—the cobblers, printers, coopers, and blacksmiths—found their skills devalued by mass production and their lives transformed from autonomous entrepreneurs to wage laborers, under the constant supervision of the boss and the clock. For all workers, a job was no more secure than the state of the economy, and rapid fluctuations in the business cycle in turn forced breadwinners to endure periods of unrelenting toil followed by long stretches of unemployment and penury.

Since 1846, the Pennsylvania Railroad had done as much as any other company, and far more than most, to bring into being that new industrial order. Yet, like even the smallest of businesses, it was not immune to the cycles of prosperity and depression. The enthusiastic celebrations that accompanied the Centennial festivities in Philadelphia did little to mask serious problems in the United States, and on the Pennsylvania Railroad. Less than three years earlier, in September 1873, the badly overextended banking house of Jay Cooke & Company failed—a collapse induced in large measure by Cooke's involvement in the construction of the Northern Pacific Railroad. By itself, Cooke's financial embarrassment might not have crippled the American economy. In combination with the passage of the Coinage Act of 1873 (which demonetized silver and devastated the western silver mines), the aftereffects of the Great Chicago Fire of 1871, and even a severe strain of equine influenza that struck the following year, the nation settled into a deep and lingering depression. Northeastern manufacturers, desperate to cut costs, pressured the railroads for lower rates. To the west, farmers became increasingly vocal in their opposition to long-haul/short-haul price discrimination.

The economic malaise that followed the Panic of 1873 predictably triggered yet another round of trunk-line rate wars, which began in January 1874 and continued through December of the following year. The perpetually weak Erie had initiated the confrontation, but it was made far more severe by the expansionist vision of John W. Garrett, the president of the Baltimore & Ohio. In January 1871, construction crews completed work on a bridge across the Ohio River at Parkersburg, West Virginia, providing the B&O with a direct connection to the independent Marietta & Cincinnati Railroad. Three months later, the Pittsburgh & Connellsville Railroad entered service, giving the B&O its long-sought access to Pittsburgh and breaking the PRR's rail monopoly in that city. In June, the completion of another bridge across the Ohio River, at Wheeling, enabled the B&O to connect with the Central Ohio Railroad, leased since 1866, and its line to Columbus. Construction crews quickly converted the Central Ohio from Ohio gauge to standard, facilitating the westward extension of B&O traffic. By November 1874 the B&O had reached Chicago. The B&O's movement into the Midwest caused overall rates to decline, as trunk-line executives competed more intensely for traffic.[7]

After the exhibition closed, the PRR board of directors voted nearly $30,000 in bonuses to the senior Transportation Department managers who had handled the temporary surge of freight and passengers so expeditiously—while announcing layoffs in response to the worsening depression and the cessation of Centennial traffic. During the year following the Centennial, some of the remaining employees, who had delivered visitors in safety, without a single injury, while losing only twenty-six pieces of luggage, engaged in a strike that convulsed the railroad. Within a year of the exhibition, the full-scale versions of the oil wells that the Empire Line had on display threatened the PRR's competitive position in western Pennsylvania. Within fifteen years, the tracks that had carried five million passengers to Philadelphia were clogged with freight traffic, with the PRR's managers engaged in a race to engineer their way out of congestion. During the last decades of the nineteenth century, the efforts of PRR executives to control competition and prevent ruinous rate wars failed repeatedly. By 1876, at the end of a decade of remarkable growth in railroad traffic and revenues, the managers of the Pennsylvania Railroad confronted the limits of their power.[8]

The Empire Line and the Second Oil War

The depression of the 1870s and the destabilizing influence of the B&O soon spilled over into the oil region of northwestern Pennsylvania. During the late 1860s, the development of the tank car, combined with improvements in drilling and refining methods, had increased output while lowering production costs, creating a deflationary spiral that proved detrimental to producers, refiners, and railroads alike. In the ensuing rate wars, the Pennsylvania Railroad had more than held its own, thanks in part to the PRR's control of the Philadelphia & Erie, its affiliation with the Empire Line, and its access to the Catawissa route. Cleveland refiner John D. Rockefeller likewise thrived, based on his ability to buy out his competitors and rationalize production. In concert with other refiners in Cleveland and Pittsburgh, Rockefeller had participated in Scott's South Improvement Company, a short-lived effort to stabilize both railroad rates and oil prices.

While the collapse of the South Improvement Company did not engender chaos on the railroads or in the oilfields, it was likely that Rockefeller and Scott would soon confront new challenges to their respective companies. For Rockefeller, the problems came in the spring of 1873, in the form of the dissolution of his Petroleum Producers' Agency, ending its efforts to control price and output levels. Further difficulties emerged with the opening of new oilfields in Butler, Armstrong, and Clarion Counties, to the south of the original strike at Titusville. Surging production played havoc with an industry already burdened by excess capacity.[9]

Empire Line president Joseph D. Potts responded aggressively to the changes that were taking place in the petroleum business, and his actions soon brought

Figure 46. Empire Line president Joseph D. Potts unwisely attempted to enter the oil refining business, in direct competition with John D. Rockefeller. Even though Thomson, Scott, and other PRR executives had formerly cooperated with Potts, they made him a sacrificial lamb in their attempts to placate Rockefeller and prevent the oil magnate from taking all of his business to other railroads.

University Archives and Records Center, University of Pennsylvania.

him into conflict with John D. Rockefeller. Born in Downingtown in 1829, Potts went to work for the Pennsylvania Railroad as a civil engineer. By the eve of the Civil War, he had succeeded Scott as superintendent of the Western Division. He was well connected politically, inasmuch as his wife, Mary, was the niece of former governor James Pollock. Like Thomson, Potts was from a Quaker family. He nonetheless felt detached enough from that denomination's pacifist traditions to participate in the Civil War as an aide to Governor Curtin, with responsibilities for telegraph services, and he attained the rank of colonel. When the Philadelphia & Erie opened for service in 1864, Potts became that railroad's first superintendent.[10]

In September 1865, Potts resigned as the Philadelphia & Erie's general manager in order to devote all of his attention to the presidency of the Empire Line. Under his leadership, the Empire Line soon garnered a substantial share of the oil trade, based on Potts's ability to offer favorable rates to shippers while enjoying a lucrative haulage contract with the Pennsylvania Railroad. In the process, the Empire Line acquired hundreds of barrel cars, vat cars, and ultimately tank cars in order to transport the oil. Empire also established another subsidiary, the National Storage Company, to provide the facilities necessary to accommodate the surge in oil traffic. Under his supervision, the company also diversified into grain elevators and Great Lakes steamships, establishing the Erie & Western Transportation Company, better known as the Anchor Line.

Along with his fellow PRR executives, Potts recognized the importance of local pipelines as feeders for the railroads that interlaced the oil region. Under Potts's direction, Empire purchased the Titusville Pipe Company in 1866. In 1871, Potts and five other PRR executives established the Enterprise Transit Company (after 1908, the Kewanee Oil & Gas Company), intending to move oil by pipeline to the tracks of the Philadelphia & Erie for transfer into Empire Line tank cars. The opening of new fields in Bradford County afforded Empire the opportunity of expanding its pipeline network. In April 1872, Empire acquired the Mutual Transportation Company, followed in September by the Union Pipe Line. Within a year, a greatly expanded Union Pipe Line operated 300 route miles, capable of funneling 26,400 barrels a day into storage tanks that collectively held 300,000 barrels. In 1875, the Empire Line gained control of the Olean Petroleum Company, Limited, a 14¼-mile line linking northern Pennsylvania wells to the Buffalo, New York & Philadelphia Railroad at Olean, New York.[11]

Rockefeller was not about to allow Empire's pipeline network to expand unchallenged, particularly given the danger that the company might come under the control of one of Standard Oil's competitors. He invested in the United Pipe Line Company and the American Transfer Company, soon possessing a pipeline network that rivaled the one that Potts had established.[12]

Scott had worries of his own, chiefly related to the effects that pipelines and the Panic of 1873 would have on the fragile pooling arrangements for oil traffic. Few rail lines served the new oilfields, with the PRR enjoying better access than any of the other trunk lines. A burst of new pipeline construction threatened to negate that advantage by directing oil to the Atlantic & Great Western (Erie) and the Lake Shore & Michigan Southern (New York Central). Many of those new pipelines served wells that produced a large initial flow of oil, followed by a sharp reduction in output—a geological constraint that led to the creation of excess pipeline capacity, perhaps twice what was needed to handle the region's total output. The existence of that overcapacity led to pipeline rate wars, mimicking the situation on the railroads. Such indiscriminate rate cutting unnerved PRR executives, who feared that producers would be able to inexpensively dump large quantities of oil at the railheads of the New York roads, with the downward pressure on rates inevitably spilling over into rail as well as pipe transportation. Even worse, from Scott's perspective, was the possibility that oilmen might build a pipeline to Pittsburgh, providing access to the recently arrived Baltimore & Ohio.[13]

The depression that began in 1873 soon exacerbated the problems associated with the production, refining, and transportation of petroleum products, whether by pipe or by rail. During the summer of 1874, pioneer pipeline builder Henry Harley joined forces with Potts to develop a comprehensive plan that would prevent destructive competition in all aspects of oil production and distribution. Given the potentially deleterious effects of pipeline competition on railroad

Figure 47. As president of the Empire Line, Joseph Potts was anxious to capture waterborne traffic on the Great Lakes, by diverting it to the PRR's Philadelphia & Erie Railroad. He oversaw the establishment of the Erie & Western Transportation Company, a firm better known as the Anchor Line. Many of the facilities at Erie, shown here early in the twentieth century, were tied to the operations of the PRR and its rail and water subsidiaries, including a coal dock, freight and passenger termini, and a grain elevator. Virtually all of the cars are directly or indirectly owned by the PRR, but they are lettered for a variety of companies—the Pennsylvania Railroad; the Pennsylvania Lines (that is, the Lines West of Pittsburgh and Erie); the Pittsburgh, Fort Wayne & Chicago (also a part of Lines West); the Northern Central Railway; the Union Line; and the Empire Line—an indication of the many administrative entities that PRR officials employed in order to capture traffic and circumvent legal restrictions on common ownership.

Detroit Publishing Company Photograph Collection, Library of Congress, Prints & Photographs Division, LC-D4-12893.

revenues, Scott and other executives were receptive to their proposals. The PRR's president was particularly anxious to bring the Erie into line, as that carrier had recently agreed to haul Standard Oil traffic at rock-bottom rates—so low that the NYC's Cornelius Vanderbilt thought them profitless. In August 1874 trunk-line representatives met at Saratoga Springs in an effort to control rates, but the agreement had not addressed oil traffic, enabling the Erie to continue its low-rate policies.[14]

In September, Potts and Harley, in concert with trunk-line executives, orchestrated a solution to the competition for oil traffic. The PRR received the exclusive right to transport oil to Philadelphia and Baltimore, to the extent of 37.5 percent of total petroleum production. The remaining 62.5 percent of the oilfields' output would be directed to New York, with the PRR and the two New York roads sharing equally in that traffic. Standard Oil and the other large refiners would act as eveners, ensuring that the available oil traffic would be allocated according to those percentages. The agreement for the first time specified that rates from the oil region to tidewater would remain constant, regardless of whether crude was first shipped to Cleveland or Pittsburgh, and then refined and sent east. That is, refiners in Pittsburgh and Cleveland were in effect able to ship crude from the oilfields to their refineries for free. The rate structure primarily benefited Standard Oil and its allies, and there was little doubt that Rockefeller had pressured Potts, Harley, and the trunk-line executives into approving the arrangement.

To prevent pipeline owners from dumping oil at railheads, destabilizing the pool, the railroads included nine of the largest oil-region pipelines in the new rate agreement. They included the Empire Line's Union Pipe Line subsidiary and the two Standard Oil affiliates, United Pipe Lines and the American Transfer Company. The rate war that erupted between the PRR and the B&O that November shook, but did not destroy, the joint rail-pipeline pooling arrangements, which provided a temporary respite in the oil wars.[15]

Additional pipeline construction soon shattered the fragile truce between the trunk lines and pitted Standard Oil against the Pennsylvania Railroad. In 1874, patent-medicine manufacturer and Pittsburgh resident David Hostetter gained control of the Columbia Conduit Company, intending to build a pipeline from the newly established Butler County oilfields south to Pittsburgh. By some means, Hostetter secured an amendment to the charter, permitting Columbia Conduit to build into Allegheny County, outside the eight-county limit established in the 1872 free pipeline bill. Although Hostetter possessed the right of eminent domain and the authority to lay pipe under railway lines, PRR officials fought his project at every turn. In Butler County, along the line between Dilken and Delano, PRR crews twice ripped out the Columbia Conduit pipe that passed under the railroad's right of way. Much the same thing happened in Allegheny County, where the pipeline was to follow Powers Run, underneath the PRR tracks. Despite that opposition, in April 1875, a group of oilmen, David McKelvy, Robert E. Hopkins, and Byron D. Benson, leased Columbia Conduit. They soon completed the line to Pittsburgh—except for the still-disputed crossing of the PRR right of way, which required the oil to be lugged across the tracks in wagons.[16]

By 1875, President Garrett of the B&O was becoming increasingly aggressive in his efforts to siphon off the PRR's business at Pittsburgh. Even though the Columbia Conduit line offered at best an imperfect method of achieving that end, Garrett did have other options. One of the most destabilizing was his ability to tap a small oilfield southwest of Pittsburgh. Garrett's competitive instincts soon diverted oil shipments away from the PRR and Philadelphia, toward Baltimore. When representatives from the Philadelphia Board of Trade examined that city's export statistics, they were horrified to discover that oil exports had declined from 94,561 barrels during the first three weeks of 1874 to 35,550 barrels during the same period in 1875—a loss of 62 percent—while Baltimore's exports had risen more than tenfold, from 3,315 to 37,331 barrels. In the spring of 1875, PRR officials responded to the B&O incursion by drastically lowering their rates on refined petroleum moving between Pittsburgh and tidewater. The perhaps inevitable rate war led to another conference, and an agreement that assigned 51 percent of the eastbound oil traffic to the PRR, 20 percent each to the NYC and the Erie, and the remaining 9 percent to the upstart B&O.[17]

Rockefeller was equally concerned, as both the southwestern Pennsylvania fields and the Pennsylvania Railroad posed a serious threat to his attempts to control petroleum markets. By 1875, Rockefeller had developed a business strategy that hinged on control over local transportation in the oilfields, the rationalization of refining facilities in Cleveland, and the forward integration into distribution and marketing facilities in New York, coupled with a rate policy dependent on playing the two New York roads against one another. To a large degree, Rockefeller's business plan required the suppression of independent producers and refiners, as well as establishing control over the crude and refined products that they moved to tidewater. To deal with the new interlopers, the oil magnate responded much as he had in the past, by allying himself with some of the leading refiners in southwestern Pennsylvania. In the process, he developed access to the B&O, a potentially useful weapon in his effort to extract more favorable rates from the other three trunk lines.[18]

Of more concern to PRR and Empire Line officials, Rockefeller began to develop an east coast refining and distribution capacity. During the summer of 1873, representatives from the Erie, anxious to increase that company's pitifully small share of the oil trade, offered to match the New York Central's rates on Standard Oil traffic moving to New York. Rockefeller was interested, but complained that the Erie's Weehawken, New Jersey, terminal was small, inefficient, and no match for the NYC facility at Hunter's Point, along the East River. The Erie officials offered to sell the Weehawken facility to Standard, enabling Rockefeller to reorganize its operations. Rockefeller accordingly pledged to modernize the facility, agreeing to ship at least half of his oil over the Erie. In April 1874, when the Erie agreed to cede its Weehawken terminal to Standard Oil, the struggle between Potts and Rockefeller began in earnest. Thereafter, Rockefeller chose to negotiate primarily with representatives from the Erie and the New York Central, to the obvious detriment of the Empire Line.[19]

The Pennsylvania Railroad and the Empire Line threatened to disrupt Rockefeller's strategy. More than two-thirds of the Empire Line's oil shipments belonged to the independents, affording them an outlet to tidewater, free from Rockefeller's influence. Conversely, Rockefeller was far less able to dictate terms to the PRR than to the New York or the Erie, railroads that depended heavily on his oil traffic. Unlike the New York lines, the PRR remained largely independent of Standard Oil.[20]

Alexander J. Cassatt, the PRR's third vice president, in charge of transportation and traffic, was quick to appreciate Rockefeller's desire to establish control over the remaining holdout. Acknowledging that Standard Oil was "getting very strong," Cassatt suggested that "if we wanted to retain our full share of the business and get fair rates on it, it would be necessary to make arrangements to protect ourselves."[21] A few years earlier, when Scott had organized the South Improvement Company, he had cooperated with Rockefeller in order to control the independents. Now, PRR executives were to rely on the independents in order to protect themselves from Rockefeller.

The front man in the PRR's battle against Standard Oil was not Cassatt or Scott, but Empire Line president Joseph D. Potts. Although both Potts and his company existed solely at the sufferance of the PRR, since 1865 he had demonstrated considerable competence and had accordingly won enormous independence. Potts was ultimately responsible for virtually every aspect of oil transportation on the PRR, from the provision of cars, pipelines, and storage facilities to ratemaking and billing operations—in fact, everything short of actually hauling the trains. Through the Erie & Western Transportation Company (the Anchor Line), Potts extended his reach to the Great Lakes, operating the only long-distance water carrier directly connected with the Pennsylvania Railroad. Prior to 1875, Potts's Empire Line had been the sole recipient of the PRR's rebates and drawbacks, which it had then passed to Standard and other shippers, at his discretion. Through repeated rate wars involving oil, grain, and other types of traffic, Potts envisioned that he, as head of a semiautonomous fast freight line, was ideally positioned to allocate traffic between competing carriers and end the interminable cycles of pooling and rate cutting.[22]

John D. Rockefeller likewise relished his role as an "evener." His authority shattered Potts's visions, as well as the relationship between the Empire Line and the Pennsylvania Railroad. The rate conferences that took place during the summer of 1875 had awarded the PRR a 51 percent share of the oil trade. More disturbing to Potts, the new arrangement offered rebates directly to Standard Oil, in recognition of Rockefeller's role in overseeing the allocation of shipments among the trunk lines. Potts considered the agreement to be an ominous precedent, and an insult to his honor, and he soon took steps to protect the Empire Line.[23]

Potts had good reason to be nervous as Standard Oil gained ground. The Empire Line president knew full well that the oil business was divided into three basic endeavors—drilling, transportation, and refining—and logically concluded that if Rockefeller controlled one of those aspects, the other two must inevitably fall under his sway as well. The oil magnate had already dominated refining operations and was putting pressure on producers. The newly acquired Weehawken terminal had increased the level of integration in his New York operations. Under Rockefeller's direction, Standard had also acquired refineries in New York, Philadelphia, Pittsburgh, and the oil region. Completing the encirclement, Standard's investments in the United Pipe Line challenged Empire's Union Pipe Line Network, portending difficulties for both the Empire Line and the Pennsylvania Railroad.[24]

Potts concluded that he had little choice but to follow Rockefeller's lead into east coast refining, lest the oil traffic be drawn away from the Empire Line's fleet of more than a thousand tank cars. Given Rockefeller's rapidly increasing dominance over the oil business, Potts and Scott had little choice other than to continue to depend on one another. Under the arrangement, Potts would significantly expand the Empire Line by moving from transportation into refining. With Rockefeller threatening to rely solely on the NYC and the Erie to transport oil to his New York facilities, Potts's east coast refineries would provide both the Empire Line and the PRR with a guaranteed source of traffic. The PRR was to play no part in Empire's acquisition of east coast refining capacity, but Scott did retain the right to buy those properties, just as he could exercise the existing provisions that enabled the PRR to purchase all of Empire's assets. The independent oilfield producers would be eager to sell to the Empire Line, as they would be freed from Rockefeller's efforts

to set oil prices at the wellhead. Potts may well have been emboldened as much by his self-appointed role as a savior of the independents as by his desire to earn a profit.[25]

In January 1877, Potts signed a contract with the Pennsylvania Railroad, promising to ship exclusively over the PRR in return for preferential rates. Should a rate war develop, Potts agreed to reimburse the PRR for any and all losses. His agreement with the PRR in hand, Potts invested in refining capacity. Empire Line provided funding to the Kings County Oil Works in Brooklyn, allowing the former partnership to expand and to incorporate as the Sone & Fleming Manufacturing Company. In Philadelphia, Empire purchased the Philadelphia Refining Company. Potts consolidated his various pipeline holdings under the banner of the Empire Pipe Company (in Pennsylvania) and the Olean Petroleum Company (in New York).[26]

This was a very dangerous game indeed. The new strategy undermined Rockefeller's cartel and infuriated the oilman who, despite his reliance on the New York roads, still generated a substantial share of the PRR's oil traffic. Rockefeller later suggested that Potts and his PRR allies "bethought them that they could combine the transporting and refining, and thus secure an advantage over the other railroad companies who were willing to keep to their legitimate business of transporting."[27] By the end of January 1877, Rockefeller had personally called upon president Scott and vice president Alexander Cassatt, demanding that they bring Potts into line. True to form, Scott attempted to brazen it out, professing ignorance of the precise relationship between the PRR and the Empire Line. Cassatt seems to have been badly shaken by the encounter—or he perhaps had developed a more realistic assessment of the probable outcome of a rate war with Rockefeller—and he pleaded with Potts to sell Empire's refineries to Standard Oil. Empire's status as an affiliate, rather than a subsidiary, of the PRR now became painfully apparent, as Potts refused to back down.

Rockefeller, his diplomatic overtures having failed, now attempted to crush the Empire Line and, if need be, the Pennsylvania Railroad. In March 1877, he refused to ship via the Empire Line and even closed his refineries in Pittsburgh so that he would not be forced to route traffic over the PRR. Much of the business withdrawn from the Empire Line went instead to the Star Tank Line, established in 1866 by Jacob J. Vandergrift, and made a part of the Standard Oil corporate empire in 1873. The Star Tank Line soon acquired six hundred new tank cars for service on the New York Central and the Erie.[28]

Potts responded by purchasing oil from the independents, at any price, while the PRR lowered its tariffs to the east coast. The reduction naturally triggered a war with the two New York roads, as Rockefeller forced those two carriers to match the PRR's discounts. In a futile effort to compete against the Standard Oil colossus, PRR officials agreed to transport the independents' oil at rock-bottom rates, as low as anything that the New York roads might offer. By April, the Empire Line's oil rates were below the variable cost of transportation. Its services in the Midwest were severely disrupted, as Rockefeller persuaded New York Central officials to bar Empire Line equipment from their routes.

The Pennsylvania Railroad and the Empire Line were fighting a losing battle. During the 1877 rate war, the PRR's share of oil traffic fell from 52 percent to 30 percent. The railroad suffered huge losses, perhaps as high as a million dollars in three months, as its executives endeavored to shore up the Empire Line. The New York Central and the Erie suffered, too, but Standard Oil made good a large part of their losses. PRR investors had no such savior, and they chafed at the board's willingness to subsidize the Empire Line, which many regarded as little better than a lucrative investment scheme for well-connected PRR insiders. As the economic depression deepened, the rate war caused the PRR to forgo dividend payments and to cut wages in a manner that soon resulted in labor unrest and, in July, a riot that destroyed a significant portion of the PRR's facilities in Pittsburgh.[29]

Under the circumstances, Potts and Scott had little choice but to settle with Rockefeller. By September, Scott had conceded to Rockefeller's demands, with the most important condition being that Empire would leave the oil business. Under the terms of the October 17, 1877, settlement, Rockefeller agreed to pay $3.4 million for the bulk of the Empire Line's assets, including its interest in the Sone & Fleming Manufacturing Company, the Philadelphia Refining Company,

the Empire Pipe Company, and the Olean Petroleum Company. Most of the funds—$2.5 million in all—were due immediately, forcing Rockefeller to make the rounds of Cleveland banks demanding whatever cash they had on hand. Rockefeller thought highly of the speed and dignity with which Scott had capitulated, later recalling that the PRR executive "very graciously recognized the situation and proceeded to the removal of the parasite, and in so doing one of the important obstacles to permit peace and harmony respecting this feature of the railroad traffic."[30]

Rockefeller's "parasite" was Empire Line president Joseph Potts, who did not yield so easily. Even at this late stage, Potts obstinately refused to accept the arrangement, but he was now a considerable liability to Scott, and to the PRR, and his opinions no longer mattered. Exercising a clause from the original 1865 Empire Line charter, Pennsylvania Railroad officials bought out all of Empire Line's assets that were directly related to rail transportation, for $2.5 million in cash and $2.1 million in bonds. Given the railroad's cash-flow problems, Scott borrowed most of the money from Rockefeller. The PRR then took possession of the bulk of the Empire Line's equipment, including more than 3,400 Empire Line freight cars (mostly boxcars) and more than 1,300 Green Line tank cars, all of which were incorporated into the PRR's operations. Empire Line investors retained only the company's cash and short-term securities, as well as the Erie & Western Transportation Company (Anchor Line) subsidiary.[31]

Joseph Potts was distraught and bitter at what he saw as a betrayal by Scott and other PRR executives. When the sale became final, and Scott gave Rockefeller's check to the Empire Line's treasurer, Potts sat at his desk, sobbing. He was a survivor, however. Since 1874, he had been the managing director of the National Storage Company, which owned and operated Empire's terminal at Communipaw, New Jersey. The company had not been part of the settlement with Standard Oil, and Potts retained control, even after 1877. In May 1881, Potts sold the firm to Standard Oil. Rockefeller valued Potts's abilities and offered him the presidency of the new National Transit Company, the holding company that managed Standard Oil's pipelines. Potts refused that office, but agreed to serve as a board member and as an adviser to the firm, the final remnant of his dreams to play mediator to the railroads.[32]

Although the Green Line name persisted until 1903, as part of the Allegheny Valley Railway, PRR executives soon lost interest in tank cars. During the 1880s, the northwestern Pennsylvania oil fields began to dry up, and production soon shifted west into Ohio and Indiana. Many tank cars still traveled over the PRR, carrying crude oil, refined petroleum products, chemicals, and other liquids, but most were not owned by the railroad. Tank cars represented a specialized type of equipment, one that changed so rapidly that much of the investment was obsolete long before it was worn out. By the early 1900s, private tank car lines, owned by consortiums of shippers, provided most of the cars that carried liquids on the PRR and other American railroads.[33]

The 1877 agreement enabled Rockefeller to establish absolute dominance over the oil business. On October 17, the same day that Standard Oil took over Empire's pipelines, Rockefeller purchased those of the Columbia Conduit Company, giving Standard a virtual monopoly over local oil shipments. More important, Standard's acquisition of Empire's refineries meant that the independent producers had nowhere to ship their oil, unless they were willing to sell it to Rockefeller, at Rockefeller's price. His control over rates proved equally gratifying. The October 17 settlement included a new traffic pool, with the PRR receiving 47 percent, the Erie and the New York Central receiving 21 percent each, and the B&O allocated the remaining 11 percent. Standard Oil received a 10 percent rebate for its role in maintaining the cartel. Within months, Rockefeller had negotiated separate rebate agreements with trunk-line executives, with concessions ranging from 22¼ cents per barrel of crude on the PRR to 20 to 35 cents on the Erie, with the two New York roads providing a whopping 80-cent-per-barrel discount on kerosene moving from Cleveland to New York.[34]

The independent producers continued to resist Rockefeller's efforts to dominate the oil business through his control over transportation. In 1874, Henry Harley, president of the Pennsylvania Transportation Company, had joined forces with Joseph Potts and trunk-line railroad executives, helping to forge a combined rail and pipeline traffic cartel. By 1876, Harley was convinced that a pipeline to tidewater would free the independents from reliance on either Rockefeller or the railroads. He hired PRR veteran Herman Haupt as the company's chief engineer on an unprecedented project that would span more than three hundred miles. The plan faltered, however, and Pennsylvania Transportation entered bankruptcy in 1877.[35]

A year later, Byron D. Benson resurrected the idea of a long-distance pipeline. He was a partner in Benson, McKelvy & Hopkins, the firm that had purchased David Hostetter's interest in the Columbia Conduit Company, and he was a periodic annoyance to John D. Rockefeller.[36] Benson intended to build a line right through to the east coast, at Baltimore, and acquired the charter rights of the Seaboard Pipe Line Company in order to accomplish that goal. The cost was staggering, however, and he quickly scaled back the plans. Under the banner of the Tide Water Pipe Company, Limited, Benson again awarded Haupt the post of chief engineer. Given the absence of a statewide free pipeline bill, opponents of the pipeline project could have brought work to a halt by acquiring key parcels of land along the proposed route. Haupt perplexed his adversaries by running dozens of surveys, making it impossible for anyone to predict which route he might finally select. By 1879 Haupt had overcome numerous engineering challenges and extended the line to a connection with the Philadelphia & Reading at Williamsport, Pennsylvania. Reading president Franklin B. Gowen, who was resolutely hostile to both Standard Oil and the Pennsylvania Railroad, agreed to ship the oil to New York and Philadelphia by tank car.[37]

Pennsylvania Railroad executives recognized the danger that the Tide Water line posed to their share of the oil trade. They endeavored to prevent the line from crossing under the Philadelphia & Erie and, when that failed, retaliated by authorizing steep increases to the fees charged to the Reading, for access to Philadelphia via the Junction Railroad. The opening of the Tide Water route in May 1879 initiated another rate war, this time pitting the PRR and the New York roads against the Reading. Over the next six months, the three trunk lines lost perhaps $1.2 million, with the Reading sacrificing some $500,000—and increasing

Gowen's already substantial dislike of the Pennsylvania Railroad.[38]

Once again, Rockefeller's control over so much of the oil business helped bring an end to the rate war. Rockefeller purchased the New Jersey refineries that received the oil, forcing Tide Water to capitulate and settle for a one-sixth share of the eastbound oil traffic. In October 1880, when the PRR's new president, George Brooke Roberts, courted the independents by cutting oil rates and encouraging the development of new refineries along the railroad's lines, Rockefeller retaliated by cutting Standard's shipments. The PRR's share of the oil trade immediately dropped from a quarter to an eighth of the market.

Rockefeller also authorized the construction of a competing pipeline network, with routes linking the oilfields to Cleveland, Buffalo, Pittsburgh, Philadelphia, and Bayonne, New Jersey. By 1881, under the auspices of the newly formed National Transit Company, Rockefeller controlled virtually all of the oil pipelines in the United States, with the exception of the Tide Water Pipe Company. Even then, Tide Water executives were willing to work with Rockefeller in order to stabilize oil rates.[39] Such arrangements did little to benefit the independent producers, the individuals that Byron Benson had claimed to be protecting. As the *New York Times* noted, Benson, "the man who is credited with being the producers' friend, and the Standard Company's most implacable enemy, had endeavored to sell out his friends and his company to the rival corporation."[40]

The greater transportation efficiency associated with pipelines, more than Rockefeller's aggressive business tactics, eroded the PRR's oil traffic. In August 1884, National Transit guaranteed the PRR a 26 percent share of the oil trade, but the pool was shrinking rapidly.[41] By 1888, in areas served by pipelines, the railroads collectively managed no better than a 28 percent share of the oil traffic. PRR executives were reasonably content with that situation because, under the terms of the 1884 agreement, they would receive payments from National Transit, even for oil that they did not transport. The efficiency and cost savings inherent in pipeline transportation were so large that Rockefeller could afford to maintain high rates on pipeline traffic (which would help force the remaining independent oilmen out of business) and use the resulting profits on pipeline shipments to offset Standard's large (on paper) transportation costs, while effectively bribing the PRR not to lower rail rates on oil traffic. Such arrangements aside, the Pennsylvania Railroad had lost the major portion of one of the company's most lucrative traffic segments, and would regain it only for a brief period during World War II, when German U-boats interfered with coastal shipping.[42]

The conflict with Standard Oil offered PRR executives an object lesson as to the limits of their power, and it also triggered a new round of politically motivated investigation and legislation at the state and the federal levels. During the summer of 1876, with memories of the 1872 oil war still very much in evidence, the United States House Commerce Committee reconvened hearings on discriminatory freight rates, and the investigation soon delved into abusive and monopolistic practices in the oil business. Opponents of Standard Oil produced evidence to support their assertion that the trunk lines had granted unfairly low rates to Cleveland. The independents claimed that "this investigation, if earnestly prosecuted, will prove as interesting to railroad stockholders as to oil-producers and refiners, as it will show that the discriminations practiced are in the interest of companies composed of officers of the railroad companies, whose profits are swelled at the expense of the stockholders of the railroads." The relationship between the PRR and the Empire Line was Exhibit A, and the members of the committee subpoenaed Alexander Cassatt, as well as several other railway executives. They also asked for copies of "all contracts or agreements, public or private, with individuals, organizations, or corporations, relating to the transportation of petroleum, crude or refined."[43] Cassatt was the only one who actually obeyed the subpoena. He was extraordinarily frank in his testimony, acknowledging that the PRR and its competitors routinely adjusted rates for favored shippers. Cassatt declined to supply the requested data, however, asserting that because Congress lacked any authority to regulate railroad rates, it did not have the power to investigate rate discrimination. Scott was even less cooperative. He sent a terse statement to Representative Frank Hereford (Dem., W.Va.), the chairman of the committee, asserting that any suggestions of rate discrimination in favor of Standard Oil were "villainous and unwarranted."[44]

The hearings ended with little accomplished, but the issue of discriminatory freight rates soon resurfaced. In 1878, Congressman John H. Reagan (Dem., Texas) first introduced a bill that would prohibit rebates and long-haul/short-haul rate discrimination. That legislation appealed more to the interests of western farmers, but similar developments were occurring in the east. In February 1879, the New York legislature appointed Alonzo B. Hepburn to head a committee investigating allegations that the trunk lines—especially the NYC and the Erie—had granted preferential rates to Standard Oil. By January 1880, the Hepburn Committee had recommended that the New York legislature establish a regulatory agency with the power to set rates. Within a very few years, the efforts of Reagan, Hepburn, and others to regulate the railways would come to fruition in the form of the federal 1887 Act to Regulate Commerce.[45]

At the state level, the consequences for the PRR were far less severe. In 1878, western Pennsylvania representatives introduced another free pipeline bill in the General Assembly, as well as a bill to prohibit discrimination in railroad rates. Both failed. It was no wonder, then, that the social reformer Wendell Phillips protested, "There is no power in one State to resist such a giant as the Pennsylvania road," or that a reporter from the New York Times asserted that "the Pennsylvania Railroad Company controls the Legislature, and the member who votes contrary to the dictation of that corporation will be shelved at no distant day."[46]

Pennsylvania Railroad executives might not have been as conspiratorial as those and other critics alleged. When the bill attempting to ban discrimination and equalize rates came up for a House roll call, it failed by a vote of sixty-three to sixty-four, indicating that any efforts by Scott and other PRR executives to dictate policy to the members of the legislature succeeded by only the narrowest of margins. More tellingly, forty-four of the forty-five legislators representing districts west of the Alleghenies voted for the bill, and fifty-one of the fifty-seven eastern representatives voted against it, with central Pennsylvania districts almost evenly divided, thirteen to twelve in favor. Such

statistics indicated either that the Pennsylvania Railroad succeeded brilliantly in buying the votes of eastern Pennsylvanians while failing miserably at precisely the same effort where westerners were involved, or else that most legislators simply voted their regional economic loyalties, regardless of pressure from Scott and his ilk.[47]

Western Pennsylvanians, Pittsburgh residents in particular, had ample reason to despise the PRR's rate policies, which in the context of the conflicts between the four major trunk lines were necessarily biased in favor of through traffic and against local and intrastate business. They were able to voice that outrage in the legislature nonetheless, and the mere fact that they did not prevail in their efforts to equalize rates does not offer conclusive evidence that the Pennsylvania Railroad controlled Pennsylvania politics. The railroad had many supporters from eastern and central Pennsylvania, after all, individuals who benefited from low through rates and who in many instances owed their livelihood to the PRR. That company constituted the largest business enterprise in the commonwealth, indeed in the entire United States, and was responsible for the generation of jobs, economic growth, and tax revenue. Even the most ardent opponent of the Pennsylvania Railroad, moreover, had to confront the company's salubrious effect on oil transportation rates. Thanks to increased efficiency and to competition between the PRR and the other trunk lines, the cost to ship a barrel of oil to seaboard had fallen from perhaps $11.00 in 1860 to between $1.06 and $1.70 per barrel in 1878. In that context, most Americans—who now enjoyed far greater access to cheap kerosene and other refined products—wondered what the fuss over rates was all about.[48]

Efforts to Control Interfirm Competition

The depression of the 1870s transformed the always-intense competition for the eastbound grain trade into something far more brutal. While lake boats retained a dominant position in the grain business, the railroads were finally winning their battle against the Erie Canal. In 1851, the canal accommodated 83 percent of the grain shipments in the United States, but that figure had declined to only 30 percent twenty years later. In 1874, for the first time, more grain traveled by the New York Central than the Erie Canal. By the late 1870s, moreover, the surge in wheat shipments threatened to overtax the Erie Canal, at a time when increased efficiency was rapidly lowering the cost of rail transport. Grain was a valuable prize for the railroads, accounting for three-quarters of the tonnage bound for the east coast. Prior to 1870, relatively little of that grain had been sent abroad, but that situation soon changed. Within a decade, grain exports had nearly quadrupled. A particularly sharp increase occurred in 1879, when a disastrous harvest in Europe was fortuitously coupled with abundant output in the United States. Perhaps three-fourths of the export traffic was in the form of flour, rather than raw wheat—a situation that promised great benefit for the NYC and the Erie, the two carriers that served the milling center of Buffalo.[49]

Yet, the grain trade was not without its problems. Most of that traffic originated from a relatively small area, in Ohio, Indiana, and Illinois. The lands to the west of the Mississippi River were not yet well integrated into the national economy, with Wisconsin and Iowa together composing perhaps 10 percent of total eastbound tonnage. Similarly, less than a third of all westbound traffic passed beyond the Illinois border. The narrow geographic confines of the grain belt posed particular problems for the trunk lines, whose western connections were sandwiched between the Ohio River and Lake Erie. Lake boats were particularly disruptive, for they could deliver grain to tidewater far more efficiently than could the railroads of that era. Some of the lakers that arrived in Buffalo transferred their cargoes to boats operating along the Erie Canal, while others filled boxcars bound by rail for New York—something known as the "ex-lake trade," of great value to the New York Central, but not so for the PRR. Overall, however, waterborne shipping set the rate on eastbound grain, with tariffs falling precipitously at the beginning of the navigation season, and rising just as rapidly when the lakes iced over in the autumn.[50]

So long as the economy was robust, the PRR and the other trunk lines could flourish off of the surplus that water carriers could not accommodate, but the depression changed that situation. Ship owners slashed their rates to no more than the variable cost of transportation and, as one transportation economist emphasized, "the lake boats were prepared to carry grain for almost nothing."[51] Trunk-line officials had little choice but to respond in kind. By 1874, for the first time, the PRR and other eastern trunk lines began to routinely undercut their own grain rates, offering rebates to large shippers.

A truce, signed at Saratoga Springs in August 1874, provided only temporary relief. Scott traveled to Saratoga Springs to meet with representatives of the Erie and the New York Central. Hugh J. Jewett, the recently appointed president of the Erie, was especially receptive to negotiations, as his poorly maintained and financially mismanaged railroad was in no position to take on the PRR or the New York Central. Representatives from the PRR and the New York roads did their best to restore rates, and, Thomson emphasized, "to abolish all commissions, drawbacks, and agencies of every kind."[52]

The attendees also agreed to establish a Western Railroad Bureau to set rates from common points—the precursor to the rate bureaus that became common during the 1880s and into the 1890s. According to railroad executives, the purpose of the new organization was to allow a disinterested body of traffic experts to determine rates administratively, by use of appropriate statistical measures, and not through wasteful and destructive cutthroat competition. In practice, however, the rate bureaus represented another attempt to maintain traffic pools. The Western Rate Bureau, collectively managed by the trunk-line carriers, possessed the authority to establish uniform tariffs and to fire any railroad employee who violated the agreed-upon rates. The agreement was more honored in the breach than in the observance, however, and independent commission agents continued to set whatever rates they thought necessary to secure business.[53]

The Baltimore & Ohio soon helped to undermine the new rate agreements. B&O officials had not attended the Saratoga meeting, but they did agree to abolish independent freight agents. In November 1874, however, the completion of the Baltimore, Pittsburgh & Chicago Railroad gave the B&O access to Chicago and a share in the grain trade. From Wheeling, the route headed almost due west to Newark, along the Central Ohio route to Columbus. At Newark, the Sandusky, Mansfield & Newark Railroad ran north to Chicago Junction, a short distance south of Sandusky. From there, the tracks angled to the northwest before reaching the Windy City. Garrett boasted that the distance between Baltimore and Chicago over the new line was only 795 miles, compared with the 899 miles that separated Chicago and Philadelphia, over the PRR, with even longer distances facing the New York roads. Furthermore, as the southernmost trunk line, the B&O was least affected by competition from the Great Lakes, giving Garrett a powerful weapon, particularly against the NYC and its Lake Shore affiliate. Baltimore did not enjoy the rail or the maritime connections associated with either Philadelphia or New York, a situation that forced Garrett to make rate concessions in order to secure through traffic for the B&O. The growing export grain trade placed Baltimore at a further disadvantage, as that port was considerably more distant from Europe than either Philadelphia or New York.[54]

To gain a share of the grain trade, the B&O would have to offer substantial rate reductions, in order to compensate for the disadvantages of Baltimore's location. Garrett relished his role as an underdog, pledging that he would act "like another Samson, . . . [and] pull down the temple of rates around the heads of these other trunk lines."[55] He quickly abrogated the terms of the three-month-old Saratoga Compact (which he had never formally signed, unlike Scott), slashing rates on tidewater traffic. By February 1875, PRR officials had responded by cutting the rates on traffic between Baltimore and Chicago nearly in half. In 1873, grain traveled from Chicago to New York at a rate of sixty cents per hundredweight, but the charges fell to forty cents in 1874, thirty cents in 1875, and twenty-five cents by March 1876. As fares spiraled downward, both the B&O and the PRR suffered financially, with Garrett publicly laying the blame solely at the feet of Tom Scott. Not until June of 1875 did representatives from the two companies agree to raise rates, set tariffs cooperatively, and end rebates. Even then, the intransigence of New York Central and Erie executives ensured that rates remained quite low through the end of the year.[56]

The concord between the PRR and the B&O could not restore the financial health of the railroads, as the poor economic conditions induced further competitive rate cutting. In 1875, the Grand Trunk Railway Company of Canada negotiated traffic agreements with the Michigan Central and the Vermont Central, and attained access to New York, Boston, and Chicago. Grand Trunk officials, who were desperate to obtain as much traffic as possible, slashed rates on eastbound grain and other commodities. The rate war that followed peaked in April 1876, cutting passenger fares between Boston and Chicago almost in half, while grain rates from Chicago to New York dropped from fifty to eighteen cents per hundredweight. The trunkline managers did not reach a truce until December 1876, and the resulting agreement primarily benefited the New York Central.[57]

Cornelius Vanderbilt died only a few weeks after the signing of the rate settlement, leaving the New York Central in the hands of his son, William Henry Vanderbilt. The transition proved less disruptive than many had feared, and William generally proved himself a capable manager. More ominous, in February 1877, was the expiration of the previous year's rate accord. As economic conditions worsened, the new president of the NYC was amenable to compromise, and he encouraged another round of negotiations among the eastern trunk lines.

In April 1877, Scott, third vice president Alexander J. Cassatt, and other trunk-line executives gathered in the stately splendor of New York's Brevoort House in order to form yet another pool. The difficulty, as always, was how to allocate traffic at the agreed-upon percentages while minimizing the incentive of rogue carriers to cheat on the cartel. Over the years, a number of entities—ranging from independent freight forwarders to traffic executives on western connections to the managers of the fast freight lines to eveners such as Standard Oil—had all endeavored to allocate traffic. Each effort had ultimately failed. In 1877, however, trunk-line executives implemented a radically new method of preserving the pool.[58]

Their solution lay in a series of rate differentials, so called because eastbound rates to tidewater varied according to the length of each carrier's route. Variants of the differential system had existed as early as the late

1850s, with an 1869 rate agreement listing what was probably the first instance on record of differentials in their modern form. A Pennsylvania Railroad rate clerk, one Mr. MacGraham, articulated the two key elements of the full-fledged differential system, in a rate agreement that went into effect in December 1871. The MacGraham system employed the 920-mile route between Chicago and New York (via the Lake Shore to Dunkirk, New York, and the Erie from there eastward) as the standard unit of measurement, referred to as a 100 percent basis or a New York basis. Shorter distances, such as Fort Wayne to Philadelphia, commanded correspondingly lower rates. Traffic from points to the west of Chicago moved at higher rates, such as a 110 percent basis. Water carrier tariffs set the base railroad rate, which primarily affected the NYC and the Erie, the two carriers that were the closest to the Erie Canal and the Great Lakes. Railroads farther removed from the Great Lakes—particularly the PRR and the B&O—correspondingly lowered their charges to match those already in place on the New York trunk lines.[59]

The second, crucial element in the MacGraham system took advantage of a geographic coincidence. The two railroads serving the nation's dominant port—the NYC and the Erie—possessed the longest mainline distance between Chicago and the east coast, 960 and 998 miles, respectively. The PRR served the less-robust port of Philadelphia, via a route that, at 899 miles, was shorter than either of the New York trunk lines. Baltimore, the weakest of the three major east coast ports, was also the closest to Chicago, 795 miles by way of the B&O. The progressively shorter distances compensated the PRR and the B&O for the rate reductions necessary to bring their charges in line with the New York basis, while giving Garrett a strong incentive to avoid further, destabilizing rate cutting. Regardless of the carrier, all rates consisted of a through charge coupled with a local tariff, with the proviso that the most direct route to tidewater would also command the lowest rate—preventing the roundabout movement of cargoes, as the traffic managers of local feeder railroads attempted to play one trunk line against another. Railroads that fed traffic to the trunk lines, at Chicago or intermediate points, collected a pro-rated percentage of the total haul. Because the B&O route was shorter

than those of the two New York roads, its feeders accordingly collected a larger percentage of the total tariff. In a hypothetical example, wheat shipped from Chicago to New York via either the NYC or the Erie would travel at a 100 percent New York basis of thirty cents per hundredweight. Midwestern railroads such as the Chicago, Burlington & Quincy collected grain from points such as Sterling, Illinois, 145 miles west of Chicago, for shipment east, corresponding to a 116 percent basis, and adding perhaps 4.7 cents to the total tariff. A hundred pounds of grain destined for New York over the NYC would contribute 4.6 cents to the CB&Q's coffers: $(145 \div [145 + 960]) \times (0.30 + 0.047) = 0.0455$. The same shipment, sent east over the B&O, would yield 5.4 cents for the CB&Q: $(145 \div [145 + 795]) \times (0.30 + 0.047) = 0.0535$.[60] That seemingly insignificant difference of less than a cent on a hundred-pound shipment, when multiplied by thousands of carloads of grain, provided CB&Q traffic managers with a powerful incentive to route commodities over the B&O and reduced Garrett's propensity to break the pool. Because Baltimore was the least developed of the major east coast ports, Garrett would never be able to capture all of the business, however. Furthermore, executives representing the PRR and the New York lines pledged to withhold westbound traffic from the CB&Q and other midwestern carriers, should they refuse to allocate fairly grain shipments moving east to tidewater.[61]

In April 1877, railroad executives codified the MacGraham system when they established a new cartel under the terms of the Seaboard Differential Agreement. As the name suggested, the compact primarily affected rates on traffic from the Midwest, bound for the east coast and often intended for export. As such, the trunk lines were but one component in a transportation chain that stretched, by rail and water, for thousands of miles. New York was the closest port to Europe, yet the farthest, by rail, from Chicago. As such, the New York trunk lines supposedly possessed higher operating costs than either the PRR or the B&O, and thus deserved higher rates. Philadelphia was the next-closest port to Europe, followed by Baltimore. The PRR merited somewhat lower rates than the New York roads, with the B&O charging still-lower tariffs. Yet, because of their greater distance from Europe, the overall transportation charges from the Midwest to Europe would theoretically be the same, regardless of which port garnered the shipment. Thus, shippers would not care which trunk line received their business, as overall rates between the Midwest and Europe would be the same, regardless of whether the grain traveled over the NYC, the Erie, the PRR, or the B&O.[62]

Because New York freight commanded the highest rates, it set the basis for the other trunk lines. On the PRR, eastbound cargoes destined for Philadelphia merited a two-cent-per-hundredweight reduction relative to New York. Westbound traffic tended to consist of higher-value merchandise, and garnered a six-cent-per-hundredweight differential out of Philadelphia. Because Baltimore was farther from Europe, the B&O received a three-cent differential on eastbound traffic and eight cents on westbound freight. The differentials were more modest on the all-important eastbound shipments of grain, as well as for iron and steel products—a one-cent reduction at Philadelphia and 1.5 cents at Baltimore, relative to New York. The differential on flour was one and two cents, respectively. In theory, the shorter routes and thus lower overall operating costs of the PRR and the B&O, relative to the New York roads, would compensate the more southerly carriers for the reduced rates.[63]

In reality, the professed rationale for the port differentials was little more than an effort to provide a palatable justification for the latest trunk-line cartel. Because terminal costs constituted the greatest single item of expense associated with a typical shipment, the difference of a few dozen miles on the line haul were of little consequence—certainly not enough to justify such deep discounts for Philadelphia and Baltimore traffic. Furthermore, New York's proximity to Europe had little effect on transatlantic shipping rates. By the late 1880s, if not before, eastbound grain rates from all Atlantic ports to Europe were essentially equal. Instead, the port differentials served primarily as an evener, to ensure that shippers allocated eastbound grain traffic according to percentages that the carriers had negotiated.[64]

While the B&O gained as a result of the differential system, the greatest winner was probably the PRR. Between 1860 and 1880, Philadelphia increased

its share of exports from 11 to 20 percent of the national total. Much of that gain came at the expense of southern ports, with Baltimore and New York retaining essentially the same share. The differentials were not solely responsible for Philadelphia's good fortune. Improvements in the PRR's physical plant had greatly increased the company's transportation efficiency—investments that, in the aftermath of the collapse of the Southern Railway Security Company, southern carriers were unable to match. Nor was the PRR the only carrier to serve the port of Philadelphia. Nonetheless, the Quaker City's gain could not help but rebound to the interest of the Pennsylvania Railroad.[65]

While the basic MacGraham system remained in use for decades, it required constant adjustment in response to economic conditions and changing commodity flows. In June 1877, the trunk-line representatives again gathered in New York to allocate westbound freight shipments. Scott agreed that the PRR would receive a quarter of the traffic, while the New York Central and the Erie would each receive a third. The Baltimore & Ohio garnered a paltry 9 percent, owing to its lack of a direct rail route into New York. The Grand Trunk joined later, at least temporarily ending the latest rate wars.[66]

More significantly, the June 1877 agreement created a rate bureau, the Eastern Trunk Line Association (also referred to as the Trunk Line Commission), as a mechanism to enforce the traffic agreements. Given the highly competitive nature of the northeastern railroads and the inherent complexity of railroad rates, traffic pools could function effectively only if managed by an individual with a comprehensive knowledge of railway rate classifications and possessed of the political skills necessary to keep the participants in line.[67]

Albert Fink was a superb fit on both counts. A graduate of the Polytechnic Institute in Darmstadt, Germany, he emigrated to the United States in 1849 and soon became an office assistant to Benjamin Henry Latrobe, Jr., a civil engineer on the Baltimore & Ohio. Fink was intimately involved in the construction of the B&O between Cumberland and Wheeling, and he supervised the erection of the some of the first iron railway bridges in the United States. In 1865, with his engineering skills beyond dispute, Fink became the general manager of the Louisville & Nashville Railroad, and was promoted to vice president five years later.

During the late 1860s, Fink began to develop the principles of railway cost accounting, adding that measure to the financial and capital accounting techniques that Herman Haupt and others had developed prior to the Civil War. While associated with the Louisville & Nashville, Fink determined the costs of moving different types of commodities, under varying conditions, and wrote several influential pamphlets on the subject of rate control. In particular, Fink was obsessed with efforts to determine precisely the ton-mile cost associated with transporting freight. He developed new cost accounting categories based on the type of expense rather than the operating unit that had incurred them.[68]

The rate wars of the early 1870s convinced Fink that some sort of secure cartel arrangement was necessary to prevent cutthroat competition. In October 1875, Fink helped to organize the Southern Railway & Steamship Association, and he became its general agent, beating out Herman Haupt for the job. The PRR never joined the association, which lay outside of its traditional territory. However, given the PRR's involvement in the Southern Railway Security Company, Scott in particular must have been familiar with Fink's abilities, and the other trunk-line executives certainly knew of him as well. In June 1877, Fink stopped briefly in New York on his way to a vacation in his native Germany. There, four of the most powerful railroad executives in the United States—Scott, William Henry Vanderbilt, John W. Garrett, and Hugh Jewett—descended upon him, begging him to impose order and stability on the trunk lines.[69]

Fink soon accepted a post as head of the Joint Executive Committee of the Eastern Trunk Line Association, with the authority to approve or disallow all rates suggested by the PRR and the other member railroads. He maintained a staff of sixty people in the association's New York offices, continually establishing, checking, and reevaluating posted rates. Only the association's board of arbiters had the authority to override Fink's rulings. That body consisted of Charles Francis Adams, generally considered the originator of the weak, or "sunshine," form of railroad regulation, an economist, David A. Wells, and Philadelphia resident and PRR board member John A. Wright.[70]

At least superficially, Fink had created a powerful mechanism for determining rates administratively rather than through competition. He was in charge of what he called an "executive department," presiding over a "legislative department" made up of trunk-line executives, and a "judiciary department," in the form of the board of arbiters. "You have thus formed a complete government," he told the other members of the Joint Executive Committee in December 1879, "over this large competitive traffic over which it has heretofore been found impractical to exercise intelligent control."[71]

To many shippers, that sort of formal collusion seemed to promise nothing less than rates that would imperil their ability to earn a living. The idea that Fink presided over a "complete government" did not sit well with many people, either. As Fink—and PRR executives—emphasized, however, the cutthroat competition that accompanied unenforceable traffic pools did no one any favors. Railroad investors suffered because their companies, with rates cut to the bone, were not profitable. Underfunded carriers were susceptible to bankruptcy and, more typically, lacked the resources necessary to increase capacity, improve efficiency, and drive down rates.

High rates, as most people recognized, were not the problem. Between 1865 and 1890, eastbound grain rates fell from 38.6 cents per bushel to 14.3 cents—a decline of 63 percent. The average rate per ton-mile was cut more than in half, from 1.925 cents to .941 cents. For many shippers, the difficulty was instead that rates were uneven, and that the railroads were willing to modify tariff structures to which they had grown accustomed. The 1870s depression fanned the fury of midwestern farmers toward long-haul/short-haul discrimination, and they convinced legislators in Illinois, Iowa, Minnesota, and Wisconsin to create strong state railroad commissions, in order to rectify such problems. New York businessmen were angry, too, after the 1877 Seaboard Differential Agreement eroded much of the competitive advantage that their city had once enjoyed. After 1877, members of the New York Board of Trade demanded that the New York Central protect their interests, scrapping the differentials if need be. William Henry Vanderbilt stood by Fink and the Eastern Trunk Line Association, and disgruntled

New Yorkers showed a keen interest in legislation, sponsored by Congressman John Reagan, that would ban pooling arrangements.[72]

For the PRR and the other eastern trunk lines, the more immediate problem was that Fink was incapable of holding the railroads to their agreed-upon rates. Within the PRR and the other carriers, middle managers were always under pressure to maximize throughput, something that could be done only by gathering as much traffic as possible and keeping it out of the reach of competitors. As such, Traffic Department personnel always possessed a strong incentive to negotiate lower rates, offer rebates, or otherwise cheat on the cartel. In an effort to secure additional shipments, many railroad traffic managers deliberately misstated weight, classification, or the distance that a shipment had traveled. In response, the association in 1882 began assigning auditors to major shipping points to ensure that local freight agents adhered to published tariffs, but this had little effect.[73]

Senior PRR officials also possessed ample reason to yield to pleas of their traffic managers for lower rates. The cartel price that Fink and his associates had established was, by definition, above the market price. Therefore, each carrier's representatives knew that they could boost revenues and profits by offering a sub rosa rate that was below the cartel rate but above the increased variable cost associated with the provision of additional transportation services. Yet, the individual benefits that accompanied such an arrangement would last only so long as competitors remained ignorant of the matter. Once they discovered the subterfuge, they would have little choice but to match the lower rates, officially or unofficially, spelling the end of the arrangement, regardless of whether it was called a cartel, a pool, or a traffic association.

Unlike some countries, such as Germany, pools were legally unenforceable in the United States. Because Fink and his associates lacked the legal authority to enforce their rate schedules, their most potent weapon was their ability to authorize all of the members of the association to lower their rates to match those of any carrier who attempted to undercut the cartel price. As such, Fink insisted that the rates established by the Eastern Trunk Line Association could be maintained only by "the intelligence and good faith of the parties composing it."[74] That good faith was sorely lacking, particularly after Jay Gould re-emerged onto the national railroad stage in 1880 with plans to assemble what amounted to a new trunk line connecting the east coast to the Midwest. By then, the Eastern Trunk Line Association had proved increasingly ineffective at managing competition.[75]

Across the Atlantic

In common with several other North American rail systems—most famously the Canadian Pacific Railway—the PRR's influence extended well out to sea. Unfortunately, the incorporation of the PRR and the completion of the company's main line across Pennsylvania coincided with Philadelphia's rapid decline as a transatlantic shipping port. The packet lines, with their regularly scheduled European voyages, generally departed from New York. That city's ship owners were quicker to adopt steam propulsion than their Philadelphia rivals, increasing their advantage. Bad luck was also a factor, as the Liverpool & Philadelphia Steamship Company, established in 1850 as the Quaker City's leading oceanic carrier, suffered several tragic accidents. In March 1854, only two weeks after the PRR completed its Horseshoe Curve route over the Alleghenies, the *City of Glasgow* disappeared in mid-Atlantic, and none of the 479 people on board were ever seen again. During the winter of 1857, when ice trapped a Liverpool & Philadelphia ship in the Delaware River, company officials relocated their western terminus to New York. With that move, Philadelphians no longer had access to regularly scheduled transatlantic steamship service.[76]

During the 1860s and the 1870s, the PRR's managers sought to divert additional trade to Philadelphia by providing an outlet for eastbound bulk commodities such as grain, oil, meat, and lumber. Despite the steady loss of the grain trade to New York and Baltimore, civic boosters and to a lesser extent PRR executives still clung to the old dream of reestablishing Philadelphia as a major grain port. The rapid rise of oil production in northwestern Pennsylvania, along with the growth of European refining capacity and the development of the oceangoing tanker, promised further transatlantic traffic. Livestock could be brought to Philadelphia, slaughtered, packed in ice, and dispatched to Europe, and American forests could supply the European market. All of those resources, PRR officials hoped, would reach Philadelphia over the rails of the PRR.

Europe offered considerable bounty in return. The American population was built largely through immigration, but perhaps never more so than in the half-century that followed the Civil War. Immigration increased steadily, from 143,439 during the 1820s to 599,125 in the decade that followed. The Irish potato famine and aftermath of the failed 1848 liberal revolutions in Europe caused a surge in immigration, with 1,713,251 arrivals in the 1840s and 2,598,214 during the next decade. The Civil War barely slowed the pace of immigration, with an additional 2,314,825 people arriving on U.S. soil during the 1860s. The economic malaise of the 1870s likewise did little to stem the tide, as 2,812,191 people, mainly Europeans, departed their homelands—although that was but a modest precursor of the influx that would occur in the late nineteenth and early twentieth centuries. With the exception of some timberlands in Michigan, the property of the Grand Rapids & Indiana, the PRR received no public land grants to sell to prospective settlers. The PRR's executives were nonetheless anxious to direct the westward flow of immigrant traffic to their lines. During the 1850s, even before the PRR controlled the railroads through New Jersey, the company stationed agents at the New York docks, ready to sell tickets to newly arrived immigrants. In general, however, PRR executives relinquished that city's oceangoing trade to others. They concentrated instead on their native city of Philadelphia.[77]

The efforts of PRR executives to influence transatlantic shipping began on the eve of the Civil War. In September 1859, Thomson may have been one of the incorporators of the Philadelphia & Crescent Navigation Company, which proposed to offer service between Philadelphia and Liverpool. By May 1862, PRR officials had agreed to subscribe to $200,000 in Philadelphia & Crescent stock, on the condition that others would match the investment. The most likely source of additional funding was the city of Philadelphia, the same entity that had underwritten a substantial portion of the cost of the PRR's initial construction. Civic boosters on the Philadelphia Board of Trade pressured the city's Select and Common Councils to support the Philadelphia & Crescent venture, and to encourage PRR officials to make good their offer. Councilman David Salomon, a Philadelphia cotton broker whose business had suffered greatly since the onset of the Civil War, even volunteered to serve as one of the PRR's Philadelphia city directors, largely so he could pressure the other board members to inaugurate steamship service.[78] In the summer of 1863, the Philadelphia Select and Common Councils approved a measure that would place any dividends on the city's PRR stock in excess of 6 percent into a special fund that would underwrite PRR support of the construction of a ship for transatlantic service. That was a substantial concession in light of wartime dividends that peaked at 30 percent in May 1864. Municipal support meshed well with Thomson's efforts to construct the Delaware Extension, bringing PRR tracks directly to dock facilities along the Delaware River. The board of directors established a Special Committee on Steamship Lines and offered inducements—including free wharfage—to any company that would offer regular service across the Atlantic. However, wartime issues took precedence, and local interest temporarily subsided.[79]

By 1865, the maturation of the iron-hulled, propeller-driven steamship greatly facilitated movement across the Atlantic Ocean, promising increased merchandise traffic, additional business and pleasure travel, and more immigration. Ever larger steamships came into service, with their increased capacity drawing them toward the New York market. Larger also meant a greater draft, and some of the new vessels could not transit the Delaware River to Philadelphia. With the war over, PRR managers were again interested in compensating for such disadvantages by subsidizing regular steamship service to Europe, something that the city had lacked since 1857. During the spring of 1866, the board agreed to authorize a subsidy of $10,000 per month to any company willing to offer scheduled service between Philadelphia and Liverpool. The directors later voted to invest up to $500,000 in any independent European shipping line that might establish service over that route.[80]

While Philadelphia city officials worried about the ongoing absence of direct transatlantic steamship service, PRR executives were more concerned about the maritime activities of the other major railroad serving the city. In 1869, the directors of the Philadelphia & Reading agreed to build a fleet of iron-hulled steamships to transport coal from Port Richmond to coastal ports, particularly in New England. By 1874, their fleet had reached fourteen ships, offering the company a distinct strategic advantage over the PRR. By then, however, Thomson had sought to mimic the Reading's maritime operations. During 1870, Thomson and Scott began discussions with Captain Thomas Henderson, the last surviving partner of one of the best-known shipping lines to ply the Atlantic. In 1856, Henderson had joined forces with two Scottish brothers, Nicol and Robert Handyside, to form the Anchor Line (not to be confused with the trade name of the Erie & Western Transportation Company on the Great Lakes). By 1859, the Anchor Line was offering scheduled service between Glasgow and New York, and the two PRR executives now attempted to persuade Henderson to shift the North American arrival port to Philadelphia. That was asking a great deal, inasmuch as New York offered far better port facilities as well as a much stronger demand for transatlantic shipping services. Thomson and Scott alienated Henderson with their insistence that they control the company's operations and finances, and the captain spurned their offer.[81]

Having failed in their efforts to establish control over a European shipping line, Thomson elected to underwrite a new, American-based firm that would offer service between Philadelphia and Liverpool. The use of American-built ships and American crews was certain to increase operating costs, but it was a necessary component of an effort to obtain a federal mail subsidy from Congress. In June 1870, the Committee on Steamships recommended that the PRR commit to 60 percent of the estimated $2 million investment that would be required to start such an operation. That November, the PRR board of directors approved the creation of the American Steamship Company of Philadelphia, more commonly referred to simply as the American Line. Pennsylvania Railroad officials agreed to purchase $400,000 of the initial $700,000

stock offering and to guarantee the entire $1.5 million bond issue. Somewhat after the fact, on February 7, 1871, the Pennsylvania legislature passed a bill enabling the PRR to invest in the American Line. PRR board members Washington Butcher, John Rice, Josiah Bacon, and Edward C. Knight became directors of the American Steamship Company, while the presidency went to the PRR's second vice president, Herman J. Lombaert. Tragically, that was to be Lombaert's last position with the Pennsylvania Railroad. By January 1872, exhausted by the stress associated with railway management, he was forced to take a leave of absence. He officially resigned his duties in December, was declared mentally incompetent, and was virtually bedridden for the remaining thirteen years of his life.[82]

Within a few months of the formation of the American Steamship Company, PRR personnel were also involved in another transatlantic line, the International Navigation Company, better known as the Red Star Line. The new company owed its origins to the shipping firm of Peter Wright & Sons, one of the pioneers in the development of oceangoing oil tankers. In May 1871, Clement A. Griscom, a Philadelphia ship broker representing Wright & Sons, obtained a Pennsylvania charter for the International Navigation Company. In contrast to the American Line, International would use foreign ships and foreign crews, largely as an economy measure. PRR and Empire Line officials were well acquainted with Griscom and the other principals of both Wright & Sons and International, thanks to their mutual involvement in oil transportation. Most of the support for the venture came from the Pennsylvania Railroad, in the form of a $1 million bond guarantee and the purchase of $1.5 million in stock. Many of the stockholders in the new company were PRR veterans, including William Leech, the Empire Line's Joseph D. Potts, the Union Line's Henry H. Houston, and Tom Scott, who counted Griscom as a close personal friend.[83]

Griscom, in collaboration with Thomson, soon developed plans to begin regular Red Star Line steamship service to Antwerp, as a Continental counterpart to the American Line service to Liverpool. On the recommendation of King Leopold, the Belgian Parliament chartered a subsidiary of the International Navigation Company, the Société Anonyme de Navigation Belge-Américaine, likewise referred to as the Red Star Line. While nominally a Belgian company, American investors owned about ninety-eight percent of its stock, with Griscom, Scott, and Houston serving as the American representatives on the board of directors. Peter Wright & Sons continued to manage the service and, given their expertise in oil transportation, it was hardly surprising that the first new ship of the Red Star Line was an oil tanker, the *Vaderland*.[84] Of even greater value was the Red Star Line's mail contract, in which the Belgian Parliament provided a $100,000 annual subsidy for the Antwerp-to-Philadelphia service.[85]

Despite the depression of the 1870s, and thanks in large measure to the Belgian subsidy, the two Red Star Line companies proved quite successful under Griscom's joint management. Red Star ships disgorged a torrent of immigrants, who were often disembarked, processed, and put on board special PRR trains within an hour. Red Star Line agents in eastern Europe sold through ship and rail tickets all the way to Chicago, eliminating the possibility that con artists at the Philadelphia docks might try to take advantage of the new arrivals. The through ticketing arrangements accordingly proved quite popular, accounting for steady growth in the number of immigrants that the Red Star Line landed in Philadelphia—from 3,174 in 1874 to 7,093 in 1875, rising to more than 30,000 in 1880 and above 40,000 in 1881. Those numbers were admittedly a fraction of the arrivals into New York, but it was valuable passenger traffic for the Pennsylvania Railroad nonetheless.[86]

Eastbound, trains delivered bulk cargoes to Girard Point along a branch line constructed in 1874. At Girard Point, the International Navigation Company built a slaughterhouse and facilities for the transshipment of grain, coal, and other products. In 1881, the PRR established a subsidiary, the Girard Point Storage Company, to purchase the Girard Point operations and to build a second grain elevator. Augmenting the PRR's much smaller 1863-vintage grain warehouse at the foot of Prime Street, the new Girard Point facilities gave the PRR ownership of approximately half of the grain storage capacity in Philadelphia.[87]

While the combined Red Star Line operations of the International Navigation Company and the So-

ciété Anonyme de Navigation Belge-Américaine were generally successful, the same could not be said for the American Line. Outside investor support for the venture could best be described as lukewarm. Nonetheless, the American Steamship Company contracted with the Philadelphia firm of William Cramp & Sons for four steamships, the *Pennsylvania*, the *Ohio*, the *Indiana*, and the *Illinois*. Three of those four states had no access to salt water, but the names were deeply symbolic, as they referred to the states that lay along the route of the Pennsylvania Railroad main line between Philadelphia and Chicago. At $520,000 apiece, the ships came close to exhausting the company's $2.2 million initial capitalization. Although they had tendered the lowest bid, Cramp & Son's architects had seriously underestimated the cost of construction, ensuring that the total would eventually go much higher, with the completion of the ships delayed by as much as a year. American Line managers refused to charter foreign-flagged vessels, in order to provide interim service, as that practice would have jeopardized their efforts to obtain a federal mail subsidy. Instead, International Navigation provided British ships, until the American Line vessels could be completed. On August 12, 1872, such problems were mostly forgotten, however, as the *Pennsylvania* slid down the ways at the Cramp & Sons shipyard and into the Delaware River. The *Ohio* entered the river in October, followed by the *Indiana* in March 1873 and the *Illinois* that June.[88]

In some respects, the coordinated rail-ship service provided by the PRR and the American Line was a great success. In November 1875, the *Illinois* transported beef, mutton, poultry, and oysters, along with eight tons of ice, from Philadelphia to Liverpool. Many PRR executives hoped that even larger cargoes would move by rail from midwestern farms before proceeding to Europe. Other shipments were less successful. The summer of 1875 produced a bumper crop of peaches, inspiring a plan to collect them by rail, rush the fruit to the Philadelphia docks, and ship them to Liverpool, packed in ice. The ice had melted before the *Ohio* had completed half of its voyage, and the cargo, now turned to mush, was unloaded and dumped into a pile that soon attracted what was probably the largest assemblage of fruit flies in the history of the British Isles.[89]

And then there were the accidents. In May and June of 1873, on its maiden voyage between Philadelphia and Queenstown, Ireland, the *Pennsylvania* lost three of its four propeller blades, and limped in under sail. The following winter, as the *Pennsylvania* made a westward trip across the Atlantic, the ship encountered a series of gales that delayed the ship's arrival in Philadelphia by nearly a week. Even worse, a wave roared over the bridge, carrying away the wheelhouse and with it the captain, the first mate, the second mate, and two others. Had it not been for the presence of Captain Cornelius L. Brady, traveling as a passenger, the ship might never have survived. In March 1874, a wave destroyed the wheelhouse on the *Ohio*, fortunately with no loss of life. A few months later, the ship caught fire. That incident, which left portions of the deck in ruins, occurred only a month after the *Illinois*, outbound from Philadelphia, demolished four canal boats floating in the Delaware River. The *Abbotsford* ran aground in Cummoes Bay, Wales, in July 1875. Although by some miracle everyone on board survived, it had to be sold for salvage.[90]

The American Line's financial performance was equally disheartening. The company's backers had proven unsuccessful in their efforts to obtain a federal mail subsidy, but they continued to bear the costs of American ships that were more expensive to operate than their British-flagged counterparts. As there was no longer any need to preserve the national identity of the American Line, the firm's managers leased two British-flagged vessels, the *Abbotsford* and the *Kenilworth*, permitting regular weekly sailings. Even worse, the inauguration of transatlantic service coincided almost precisely with the Panic of 1873 and subsequent depression, which greatly reduced both freight and passenger traffic. During 1873, American Line ships had completed fourteen round-trip voyages, earning the company a net income of $427.50. With the inclusion of interest charges, the company had lost nearly $90,000. The following year proved even less satisfactory, with losses totaling nearly $50,000, even before interest payments. The sinking of Philadelphia's sole floating drydock in February 1875 forced the American Line to send ships north to New York for repairs, further increasing expenses.[91]

As the deficits piled up, PRR directors debated whether, and under what circumstances, to abandon their commitment to the American Steamship Company. On Christmas Eve 1873, the board appropriated $150,000 for the struggling carrier. Another contribution, of $50,000, followed in December 1874. There were limits, however. In January 1876, American Line officials requested that the PRR board appropriate $1.3 million to build two new steamships, which they insisted should be available when prosperity returned. The PRR directors refused the request, but a short time later nonetheless provided sufficient funds for the American Line to continue to service its debt. The PRR board ultimately concluded that the American Line was generating enough extra business for the Pennsylvania Railroad to make the losses bearable, but some type of reorganization was necessary. By the spring of 1877, PRR officials had agreed to accept one thousand shares of essentially worthless American Steamship Company stock in exchange for the half-million dollars owed to the railroad. The paper transaction did little to salvage the steamship concern, and by 1882 the American Line had lost a cumulative total of more than half a million dollars.[92]

Another economic recession during the 1880s, combined with the necessity of immediate repairs to the *Pennsylvania* and its sister ships, convinced the PRR interests that they had little choice other than to dissolve the American Steamship Company. Since their inception, the American Line and the International Steamship Company (Red Star Line) had offered complementary shipping schedules between Philadelphia and European ports. Since January 1874 Peter Wright & Sons had jointly managed both firms, in the interests of economy. A decade later, PRR officials brokered an arrangement that would consolidate the two companies. The Red Star Line traded $725,000 worth of stock to the PRR, in exchange for the *Pennsylvania*, the *Ohio*, the *Indiana*, the *Illinois*, and the American Line's other assets. As part of the arrangement, Clement Griscom, the vice president of International Navigation, became a PRR director.[93]

The PRR was by no means out of the transatlantic shipping business, however. The railroad still owned a large block of International Navigation stock and regularly appointed representatives to that company's board of directors. PRR directors approved International Navigation's acquisition of the Inman Steamship Company, in 1886, and guaranteed the financing for two vessels that were built and operated by the new subsidiary. That assistance, coupled with a mail subsidy enacted by Congress in 1891, ensured the financial success of International Navigation, but with little benefit for Philadelphia. During the 1890s, the Pennsylvania legislature rejected requests to dredge the Delaware River, and International Navigation's managers had little choice other than to transfer their larger ships to New York.[94]

The PRR's role in maritime commerce did not end until 1902, when J. P. Morgan presided over the merger of the International Navigation Company into his steamship trust, the International Mercantile Marine Company. PRR officials were not represented on the board of the new company. By 1904, the White Star Line's J. Bruce Ismay had replaced Clement Griscom as president of the new conglomerate. Ismay also transferred the corporate headquarters to New York, in some respects symbolizing the end of Philadelphia's century-long struggle to maintain its position as a port city. After 1915 Philadelphia was again bereft of transatlantic passenger service.[95]

The Pennsylvania Railroad's thirty-year involvement with transatlantic commerce was not a stunning success, but it was not a complete failure, either. The railroad did lose a considerable sum on the hapless American Steamship Company, perhaps $1 million in all. Given that most of those losses occurred during the depression-addled 1870s, however, the steamship company's performance was no worse than might have been expected. The American and Belgian companies that composed the Red Star Line did considerably better, thanks in large part to the Belgian mail subsidy, but their performance was hardly exhilarating.[96]

To the undoubted dismay of the Philadelphia merchants and politicians who pressured PRR executives to invest in steamship service, the companies did not restore the glory days of the city's port. Thomson, Scott, and the other PRR executives who were involved in the American Line and the Red Star Line probably never expected any such mercantile resurrection. Instead, they were content to use PRR funds to support marginal steamship operations so long as they could offer an outlet for grain, oil, livestock, and other bulk commodities that traveled east over the PRR. If

the lines could bring in immigrants who would quickly board westbound PRR passenger trains, then so much the better. By the 1880s, however, PRR executives no longer had much use for Philadelphia's steamship operations. The 1871 lease of the United New Jersey Railroad & Canal Companies, in tandem with the development of the terminal facilities at Harsimus Cove, provided the PRR with excellent access to New York Harbor. After 1880, the railroad dispatched more freight to New York, with its superb steamship connections, than to the city that gave it birth.

"You Can Now Stop with Safety": Stockholder Rebellion and the Limits of Expansion

By the time the Panic of 1873 and its aftermath had spread over the nation, J. Edgar Thomson had presided over the affairs of the Pennsylvania Railroad for more than twenty years. As an engineer-manager, he had long sought to strengthen the PRR by reinvesting profits in the company, rather than milking them for financial gain. During the early 1850s, Thomson's efforts to seize control over the PRR's operations and finances, and his insistence on the use of bonded debt, had turned the board into a swirling mass of conspiratorial factions, ultimately making Thomson president of the company. In the decades that followed, Thomson spent many millions on new routes, new tracks, new cars and locomotives, and myriad other projects to increase the capacity of the physical plant and to protect the PRR's access to the South and the West. His policies had created one of the strongest companies in the United States and had won him the respect of financial analysts and the general public alike. Thomson nonetheless appreciated the necessity of maintaining dividends at a sufficient rate to placate existing stockholders and to attract new investment. He was successful for a time, and between 1863 and 1872 investors earned an average 9.2 percent return on their PRR stock, accompanied by supplemental dividends in 1864 (30 percent), 1867 (5 percent) and 1868 (5 percent).[97]

The Panic of 1873 upset that delicate balance and ended Thomson's dreams of expansion. Expenditures on operations and on the physical plant had generated a floating debt of nearly $16 million, with only $4.4

million in the corporate treasury. Thomson's efforts to place $35 million in mortgage bonds on the London market soon ran afoul of the spreading financial malaise. When the PRR board met on November 7, 1873, the directors preserved the railroad's badly depleted cash reserves by agreeing to pay the semiannual dividend in scrip, with a promise that it could be converted to cash in seventeen months. The board drained the sinking fund, and the PRR sold the securities of its subsidiaries, arranged short-term loans, and generally hoped that the economy would rebound quickly.[98]

The economy did not recover, and PRR stockholders grew increasingly restive. Where Thomson's expansionary acquisitions had once seemed aggressive and visionary, they now appeared misguided and imprudent. His investments in other railroads, in steamship lines, and in coal lands, which had once symbolized his concern for the PRR's well-being, now appeared an extension of his greed and self-aggrandizement. Tom Scott, whose charm, personality, charisma, and deep political connections had served the railroad well, came under even more intense scrutiny. Scott's tactics had induced the repeal of the tonnage tax, kept the Baltimore & Ohio out of Pittsburgh, and facilitated the expansion of the PRR system. Yet, they also included financial speculations in companies that were closely tied to the PRR, with attendant accusations of conflicts of interest. By the end of 1873, PRR investors had learned of the role that Scott and, to a lesser degree, Thomson, had played in the fast freight lines, the South Improvement Company, the Southern Railway Security Company, and such improvident western connections as the Texas & Pacific.

On March 10, 1874, for the first time in more than two decades, Thomson faced serious opposition to his leadership. The rebellion did not come from the board of directors, for Thomson had long since controlled appointments to the board and had generally bent the directors to his will. Instead, the unrest appeared at the company's annual meeting, from dissident stockholders. George H. Earle, Sr., rose, addressed the shareholders, and demanded greater transparency from Thomson, Scott, and the board. Earle had established a reputation for confrontation, and he was a formidable opponent to the PRR's management. Born in 1823, at age fifteen he apprenticed as a machinist at

Matthias Baldwin's workshops in Philadelphia. He later studied law. In 1848, Earle toured Europe and was purportedly an eyewitness to the democratic revolutions then sweeping the continent. He recounted that he was twice arrested on erroneous suspicions that he was either a gunrunner or a spy, but that he was quickly released. The greater danger supposedly occurred in Paris, when palace guards opened fire on protestors gathered at the Ministry of Foreign Affairs, where, he claimed, he was nearly killed. In 1849, following his return to the United States, he began practicing law in Philadelphia, and as he had learned German while in Europe, he specialized in cases involving German immigrants. His real passion, however, was abolitionism. He defended several runaway slaves, often in cooperation with Charles Gibbons, the state senator from Philadelphia who in 1846 had opposed municipal funding for the Pennsylvania Railroad, and whose political career had been destroyed as a result. Like Gibbons, Earle was a member of the Society for Promoting the Abolition of Slavery. Family legend held that when a mob surrounded Pennsylvania Hall in Philadelphia, setting it on fire to protest an abolitionist meeting being held there, Earle did his best to fend off the crowd—receiving for his trouble a severe head wound. As that event had occurred in 1838, when Earle was fifteen years old, his attendance was unlikely. The story nonetheless indicated his reputation as a zealous defender of the abolitionist cause. During the Civil War, Philadelphia's growing indebtedness induced Earle to play an active role in two organizations, the Reform Committee and the Committee of One Hundred, that intended to restore fiscal responsibility to the Quaker City. He died in 1907, far short of seeing his grandson, George Howard Earle III, elected governor of Pennsylvania in 1934—only the second Democratic governor in the commonwealth since the end of the Civil War.[99]

On March 10, 1874, Earle attempted to apply his principles of fiscal restraint to the Pennsylvania Railroad. He insisted that the stockholders create an investigating committee, whose members, none of them connected to the railroad's management, would determine the true financial standing of the company and evaluate Thomson's handling of the PRR's affairs. Until the committee completed its work, Earle insisted, neither the officers nor the directors of the PRR should be authorized to issue additional stocks or bonds, or to lease or purchase any additional subsidiary companies. The shareholders approved Earle's resolution, and Philadelphia Mayor William S. Stokley, as chairman of the annual meeting, appointed the members of the investigating committee. Philadelphia attorney William A. Stokes served as chair. John A. Wright, the ironmaker who in 1851 had persuaded Thomson to challenge the authority of the Merrick/Patterson faction on the PRR board, was also on the committee, but Earle was not.[100]

Over the next six months, the seven members of the investigating committee examined the PRR's finances in minute detail. The resulting 240-page report constituted a resume of the PRR's first quarter century of operations, as well as an evaluation of Thomson's long tenure as president. The committee members concluded that the Pennsylvania Railroad was, on balance, a financially stable and well-managed company. Under Thomson's guidance, the Pennsylvania system had grown to become the largest railroad in the United States, encompassing 8.4 percent of the nation's total rail mileage and 10.5 percent of all of the capital invested in the railroads. In the preceding decade, the PRR's annual freight earnings had nearly doubled, from $10.4 million to $19.6 million, with an even more gratifying increase in net freight earnings, from $2.5 million to $7.7 million. The report valued the PRR's physical plant at nearly $95 million, well above its $48.5 million book value, thus increasing the value of stockholders' equity from $73.1 million to almost $119 million.[101]

The situation was not entirely rosy, however. The report issued by the committee also reduced the value of the PRR's holdings in subsidiaries by almost $4 million, with Pittsburgh, Cincinnati & St. Louis Railway (Pan Handle) stock declared a total loss. The committee members also denigrated PRR investments in the Philadelphia & Erie, asserting their "opinion that this road is worth but little more than its bonded debt . . . which renders its common stock worthless and the preferred stock dependent altogether on future increase of trade."[102]

The members of the investigating committee were even more critical of efforts by Thomson, Scott, and their allies to expand the PRR's influence to the west of the Mississippi, in advance of local demand. "The building of railroads in the West," committee members observed, "is acknowledged to have gone beyond the ability of the country to make them profitable"— particularly as those "roads have been carried to the extreme verge of population."[103] As for the Indianapolis & Vincennes and the Cairo & Vincennes, the rump ends of Thomson's plan to expand southward along the Mississippi River, the committee adjudged the PRR's $1.3 million investment to be "indefensible."[104] The report ultimately demanded that PRR executives limit the railroad's territory to the area north of the Ohio and Potomac rivers and east of the Mississippi.[105]

While acknowledging Thomson's Herculean efforts to protect the Pennsylvania Railroad by guaranteeing secure southern and western connections, the committee members asserted that the time for expansion had ended. "The trade centers in the West reached by your systems of railway are surely great enough, and the responsibilities assumed sufficiently great, to satisfy the most ambitious," they noted. "You can now stop with safety, and your interests will be best taken care of by carefully nursing these western investments; limiting their expansion or extension, unless the local demands require it, and hoping for the time when, by some arrangement, it will not be necessary for you to employ so much capital in holding these roads."[106]

When addressing the issue of investments by Pennsylvania Railroad managers in companies that operated over PRR rails, the members of the investigating committee showed considerable tact and restraint. Despite widespread criticisms that freight forwarders, particularly the Union Line and the Empire Line, had drained the PRR of its most profitable traffic while enriching executives, the committee members concluded, "The transportation companies are, therefore, a necessary product of the peculiar character of western traffic, and are indispensable to every well-managed trunk line between East and West to fully meet the wants of the public. . . . It is a kind of work which a private corporation can do, but which one like the Pennsylvania Railroad Company cannot do well."[107] The underlying problem was one of perception, claimed the members of the committee, who were "aware of the strength of public prejudice and the almost insuperable difficulty in convincing the stockholders that such [fast freight] companies do not make more than their share of gains."[108] Nonetheless, the committee insisted that PRR officials focus on the core business of transportation and leave behind all efforts to offer service to Europe in the form of the American Steamship Company and the International Navigation Company.

More broadly, the report reflected the tensions inherent in the growing separation of ownership and management. The members of the investigating committee believed that the directors had the best interests of the stockholders at heart, but that they were not sufficiently familiar with the complexities of railroading to resist the influence of Thomson, Scott, and other executives. Given the "meagre and incomplete reports of the directors of railroads made to the stockholders," ordinary investors lacked the information necessary to rein in management.[109] The directors, therefore, were "almost wholly influenced in their action by the views of the President, and the power of the corporation quietly and surely glides into his hands."[110]

More than two decades earlier, first Herman Haupt and then Thomson had asserted that they knew far more about railroading than the members of the board of directors. As such, they were the ones who should exercise authority over matters that traditionally had been left to the discretion of the owners, such as the authorization of large expenditures, negotiations with other companies, and long-term decisions involving routes and rates. Thomson had been correct in the sense that his strategic vision had transformed the Pennsylvania Railroad from a local carrier to a major trunk-line railroad. Scott and other senior PRR executives had contributed to that success as well. Yet, the greatest strengths of managers like Thomson and Scott—their independence and determination—were also their greatest weaknesses. "Strong men, with their natural self-reliance, and from their more intimate knowledge of the particular interests of the company, are apt to assume the infallibility of their own judgment," the committee members suggested. Under those circumstances, there was a "tendency in the leading officials and managers of railroad companies to act as if the property they manage was their own."[111] Thomson, they emphasized, was above reproach, but if

a lesser man, a dishonest man, might take his place—"what havoc and destruction of values might result."[112]

The larger difficulty, the committee members suggested, was that the Pennsylvania Railroad had become too large and too complex for any one executive, no matter how talented, to manage. "The operations of your Company," they suggested, "have now reached the point where your committee think it has passed the power of any one man to manage its interests with that personal oversight and care which they demand."[113] The members of the investigating committee suggested a solution in the form of four salaried directors, one an expert in finance and the others knowledgeable in railroad operations, with one of them charged with overseeing Lines West. The four paid directors would constitute an executive council, chaired by the PRR president yet answerable only to the stockholders, and not management. In effect, they would enable the railroad's owners to counterbalance the president and the vice presidents who held seats on the board.[114]

By the time the investigating committee issued its report, J. Edgar Thomson was dead. Plagued by coronary disease late in life, in April 1874 he suffered a heart attack. On April 22, he attended his final meeting of the board of directors. A month later, on May 27, he suffered a second heart attack and died, in office, at the age of sixty-seven. He had no children, but he adopted his wife's niece, Charlotte Francis Foster, who had lived in the Thomson household since the death of her father, vice president William B. Foster, Jr., in 1860. Most of his estate went to a benevolent fund to care for the daughters of men who had lost their lives in PRR service.[115] In seeming tribute to the stability of the bureaucratic organization that he had created, the PRR's stock declined only one and a quarter points. As a writer for the *Railroad Gazette* observed in 1882, "The test of strength on the part of any organization is what becomes of it, and what becomes in its development by its first principles on the decease of its originators."[116] The system that Thomson had created, and the people whom he had molded, would soldier on without him.

For Tom Scott, the PRR's new president, and other senior executives, the stockholders' committee report merely reinforced policies that they were already beginning to implement. Chastened by the Panic of 1873, they had determined that the Pennsylvania Railroad was badly overextended. As such, they concluded that the best, indeed the only feasible, course of action involved the consolidation of the company's existing operations, coupled with renewed efforts to refine the organizational structure. The *Annual Report* for 1874 affirmed that "the Board have concluded to adopt as general policy that no further extension of lines should be made or obligations assumed by your Company.... The best energies of your Board and its officers will hereafter be devoted to the development of the resources of the lines now controlled."[117]

PRR managers also increasingly refrained from direct financial involvement in companies affiliated with the railroad. On September 23, 1874, the board resolved "that the officers of this Company will be expected to devote their time to the duties of the official positions they hold with the Company, and shall not be at liberty to accept official positions with corporations other than those controlled by this Company."[118] By June 1875, persistent rumors that PRR executives were speculating in company stock caused the board to make a further clarification to the new conflict-of-interest guidelines. They asserted that any "Director who directly or indirectly speculates in the rise or fall, from time to time, in the stock of this Company, or gives information for that purpose for the benefit of others, is not worthy of his position in this Board." Executives and other employees engaged in such practices would be immediately fired, as "their services would no longer be required by this Company, in order that they may be enabled to devote their whole time to such speculation."[119]

In other respects, however, little changed in the aftermath of the stockholders' revolt. The directors had elected Scott as president—and he remained as president—because he was Thomson's handpicked successor, not because he met with the approval of investors. John King, a Baltimore & Ohio vice president, suggested as much in a letter to B&O president John Garrett. "I learn from the most reliable sources," King noted, "that if the question of a successor to Mr. Thomson had been left alone to the stockholders, Mr. Scott would probably not have been selected; but the Board saw fit to elect him."[120]

Scott preserved his own power over the board and secured a measure of respite from the demands of the shareholders by simply buying them off, in the form of a 6 percent cash dividend. Investors, particularly those based in Europe, had little desire to supervise the operations of a large and technically complex organization, and they were perfectly willing to trade control for a guaranteed return. Had Scott, like Thomson, been the beneficiary of the long, sustained period of postwar economic growth, he probably could have maintained such an arrangement as long as he wished. The same Panic of 1873 that had goaded dissident shareholders into action soon deepened into one of the worst economic depressions in the nation's history, however. Under those circumstances, Scott's efforts to maintain his uneasy truce with investors led to a far more serious rupture between management and labor, as he was about to confront the limits of the PRR's power in the face of a national economic cataclysm.[121]

The Great Strike of 1877

In 1877, everything fell apart. In addition to declining revenues and the rate war with Standard Oil over the future of the Empire Line, PRR officials confronted the first great outbreak of labor violence and class conflict in the United States. Prior to 1877, the evolution of large-scale business enterprises, whether they were railroads, textile mills, or steelworks, had brought about the separation of owners, managers, and workers into distinct occupational groups and social classes. Members of the working class possessed little financial security and could expect to find themselves unemployed whenever the economy turned sour. European nations also experienced the pangs associated with industrialization, and it was there that the earliest manifestations of class conflict appeared. A series of uprisings rocked Europe in 1848, and in that heady atmosphere Karl Marx published the *Communist Manifesto*—one of the most influential calls to arms for the creation of a new economic order. A generation later, the short-lived Paris Commune that blossomed in the spring of 1871 raised the specter of a new era of political and economic radicalism.

Irrespective of their social class, most of the people who lived in the United States neither anticipated nor wanted such a dramatic upheaval. In a land possessed of at least the rhetoric of unlimited opportunity and freedom for all those who worked for it, individual progress within the system seemed far preferable to a radical overthrow of the system. Upward social mobility was indeed more common in the United States than in Europe, even if it tended to be intergenerational. Parents were willing to endure long hours, low wages, and poor working conditions, secure in the knowledge that their children could look forward to a better life. Workers moved from job to job with considerable frequency and alternated between periods of employment and unemployment—factors that undermined their ability to participate in union activity. The continuing influx of new immigrants, many of whom had little experience with industrialization or urban life, created a replacement labor pool that perpetually undermined efforts of more highly skilled workers to organize.

Business owners and managers, while scoffing at the ideas of Marx and other radicals, nonetheless acknowledged that the development of class consciousness was a very real possibility. As such, they gathered around them a formidable range of allies, ranging from the media to all three branches of government to police forces, both public and private. The capitalist class also began to offer employees, particularly skilled workers, access to a wide variety of social welfare programs. On the PRR, those initiatives included benefits for workers injured or killed on the job and—in later years—recreational programs, company hospitals, pension plans, and stock options. More broadly, PRR managers emphasized that they considered skilled train service employees more as partners than as workers. Whether train crews actually believed that rhetoric—and it was probable that most did not—enginemen in particular could take considerable pride in their status, their high pay, and their relative freedom from managerial oversight.

Despite executive efforts to dampen down class conflict, the depression that began in 1873 exacerbated disputes between managers and workers. By the spring of 1876, almost everyone in Pennsylvania had heard stories of labor unrest, and almost everyone was familiar with the Molly Maguires. Philadelphia & Reading president and Schuylkill County special prosecutor Franklin B. Gowen skillfully portrayed the Mollies as a merciless band of radical Irish terrorists. According to Gowen, they were responsible for coordinating strikes in the anthracite fields and had orchestrated a string of murders of mine superintendents and other representatives of capital. In reality, few of the Mollies were guilty of the charges against them, but they soon fell victim to the climate of hysteria that characterized labor relations in the anthracite fields. Given the sensational testimony that emerged at their trial—much of it provided by James McParland, an undercover Pinkerton agent—many Pennsylvanians could be forgiven for fearing that class violence was about to erupt in their state.[122]

By the 1870s, labor unions proved more popular among railway workers than organizations such as the Molly Maguires. Most early unions represented skilled workers, offering access to social and recreational activities as well as informal apprenticeship programs in which experienced enginemen mentored their younger colleagues. They also provided disability and death benefits, at a time when insurance companies refused to write policies for workers engaged in such a dangerous occupation as railroading. Until the late 1870s, their leaders and rank-and-file members rarely challenged managerial authority, and the experience of skilled PRR employees was no exception. The preeminent operating union, the Brotherhood of Locomotive Engineers, emerged on the Michigan Central in 1863 and spread to the PRR the same year. The Brotherhood of Locomotive Fireman dated to 1873, but it remained a weak union for more than a decade, owing in part to ongoing conflicts with the BLE. That dispute was not resolved until 1906, when the BLF amended its constitution to allow enginemen as members, creating the Brotherhood of Locomotive Firemen and Enginemen. In 1868, employees on the Illinois Central organized the Order of Railroad Brakemen of America. Other attempts to organize brakemen, through the Brakemen's Brotherhood and the Trainmen's Union, proved largely unsuccessful, until the creation of the Brotherhood of Railroad Brakemen in 1883. That organization became the Brotherhood of Railroad Trainmen three years later.[123]

The development of early unions accelerated after 1873, in tandem with the declining fortunes of the Pennsylvania Railroad. As the nation's economic malaise deepened, PRR investors suffered accordingly. In the years following the Civil War, many of the PRR's shareholders, especially those living in Europe, had been critical of the financial ventures orchestrated by Thomson, Scott, and other executives. Their displeasure had culminated in the 1874 report of the stockholders' investigating committee. Since 1868, however, Thomson and Scott had tempered the concerns of investors by paying them a steady 10 percent annual dividend, and that reliable return overcame a great many criticisms. The aftermath of the Panic of 1873 curtailed revenues and forced Scott, now the railroad's president, to take drastic action. On May 1, 1875, the board reduced the dividend to 8 percent a year, causing an immediate drop in the value of PRR securities, from $55 to $51 a share. The price continued to decline steadily, and by mid-February 1877 had reached a low of 40-7/8. The 30 percent decline since May 1875 represented a loss to investors of more than $61 million. On May 1, 1877, as the PRR's finances continued to worsen, the board further reduced the dividend to 6 percent, now paid in quarterly installments for the benefit of small investors. By the close of trading on the following day, PRR stock had declined to 35-7/8 per share. In the weeks that followed, the price continued to fall, to $32 a share, less than two-thirds of par.[124]

Under such conditions, Scott, his fellow executives, and the board agreed that they had little choice but to cut labor costs. The reductions began on Lines West, with a 10 percent decrease for all employees effective December 1, 1873. On December 26, members of the Brotherhood of Locomotive Engineers walked off the job, claiming that Scott had promised them that the PRR would not cut their wages, regardless of economic conditions. By December 31, most enginemen had returned to work, but the same tensions were already beginning to affect the eastern portion of the system. On December 24, the board approved a pay cut for both managers and workers on Lines East, effective on the first day of the new year. Six days later, Thomson, in poor health and only a few months before his death, met with PRR enginemen, promising that he would rescind the wage cuts once the depression ended. The economic crisis continued, however, and by January 1, 1875, the company, now under Scott's leadership, increased the workweek for shop forces and track employees to six ten-hour days—equivalent to a further 10 percent pay cut, in addition to the one that they had suffered a year earlier.[125]

The year 1877 began badly for PRR workers, with another 10 percent wage reduction for Lines West employees taking effect on January 1. On May 18, 1877, the directors agreed to impose a further wage reduction on all employees and managers earning more than ten cents per hour (a dollar a day), as of June 1. Even though Scott later denied it, it is probable that he agreed to make those reductions in concert with the other eastern trunk lines during rate negotiations that consumed a fair portion of the winter and spring of the year. At least one senior PRR executive, third vice president Alexander Cassatt, warned that the continued wage cuts might provoke labor militancy. According to worker lore, later printed in Pittsburgh newspapers, Cassatt told general manager Frank Thomson that train crews could no longer afford to buy butter for their bread. In a reply worthy of Marie Antoinette, whose equally fictitious reference to cake doubtless underlay the quotation, Thomson allegedly answered, "Butter! What do they want with butter, let them make dip!"[126] In all probability, Thomson never told his employees to make do with beef drippings, but many workers accepted the story as fact, and as evidence that PRR managers were utterly contemptuous of their employees.

The cumulative effect of the wage reductions was severe, with the wages of train crews declining by 19 percent since 1873. PRR longshoremen in New Jersey had seen their wages fall from twenty cents an hour to fifteen, a 25 percent reduction even before the June 1 cuts, which further lowered their wages to a mere 13¼ cents per hour. Wages for shop workers declined even more precipitously, by fully 27 percent. Including the 1877 cuts, the wages for clerks had fallen from $80 a month to $45 since 1873. Scott and the board nonetheless attempted to avoid layoffs and provide at least a basic income for low-paid workers by shifting a disproportionately large share of the wage reductions to higher-paid operating employees. Rather than gain the loyalty of the workforce, the skewed decreases had the opposite effect. Train service employees, particularly enginemen, were furious that they had been singled out to bear what they perceived as an unfair share of the railroad's burdens.[127]

Yet wage cuts alone did not cause the strikes of 1877. After all, in 1857 PRR managers had reduced the pay of train crews between 10 and 25 percent, and no serious labor unrest had developed. The 10 percent cut on Lines West in December 1873 had caused a brief strike, but it had ended quickly, without spreading to the rest of the system.[128] By 1877, however, skilled PRR train-service employees were increasingly outraged at the rules that managers had articulated in an effort to improve the railroad's efficiency. Prior to the economic depression of the 1870s, many skilled workers had imagined themselves stakeholders in the governance of industrial enterprise. That attitude was hardly unique to the railroads, and it was perhaps best exemplified by the efforts of machinist Terence Powderly to shape the Knights of Labor into a union that represented all skilled workers, allied with management to control the process of production. By the 1870s, however, the railroads—and, increasingly, other large business enterprises, as well—witnessed the separation of ownership from management, and management from labor. Henceforth, workers, no matter how skilled, would have little control over managerial functions; they would have to be content to trade their labor for an hourly wage. Whatever steps managers took to increase the efficiency and the profitability of the companies that they represented would be for their benefit, and that of the shareholders, and not the workers. Rather than solicit the advice of employees, executives would simply tell them what to do, and expect them to obey.

In that context, enginemen, firemen, conductors, and brakemen perceived the actions of PRR managers as efforts to reduce their control over the workplace, not just the size of their pay envelopes. Temporary wage cuts, ostensibly to meet the contingencies of the depression, seemed part of a new effort by executives to treat workers as disposable commodities to be ruthlessly exploited and, if possible, replaced by lower-cost labor. Pennsylvania Railroad Division General Superintendent G. Clinton Gardner acknowledged the PRR's policy of "filling vacancies at lower rates with a promise of advance, as experience has attained, [which] is doubtless greatly to the interests of the Company," rather than recruiting or retaining more highly skilled employees.[129] Gardner further enraged train crews by echoing Scott's call for force reductions, "dispensing with those who are not absolutely necessary or likely to be of great value to us in the future."[130] While those

comments were shared only with other PRR executives, Gardner's attitudes provided a reflection of company policies.

When PRR managers, particularly those on the Middle and Pittsburgh divisions, implemented new work rules, they provided a catalyst for worker rebellion. Many employees were upset at the classification system, which separated the job categories of enginemen, firemen, brakemen, and conductors into subclasses. PRR managers, including Gardner, insisted that such segmentation allocated labor more efficiently and increased the likelihood of promotion. Workers, however, believed that that division of labor allowed executives to more closely regulate their work while paying top-tier wages to only a small portion of the skilled worker pool.

On November 25, 1876, the PRR extended the policy, formerly limited to the Middle Division, of assigning crews to locomotives as they became available. For the first time, enginemen and firemen at Philadelphia, Harrisburg, Altoona, and Pittsburgh could expect to receive whatever locomotive the dispatcher assigned to them, and not the specific locomotive that they were accustomed to operate. Those dispatching procedures might be efficient, but they also deprived train crews of regular schedules, made it far more difficult for them to spend time at home with their families, and required them to undertake as many as a third more trips in order to continue earning the same pay. The workers certainly believed that they had been ill used, but their complaints did not take into account the vast scope of the PRR system. The railroad had, in effect, grown too large and too complex for the old, informal dispatching and labor-relations methods to continue.[131]

Those informal methods had traditionally included face-to-face conferences with senior PRR executives. By May 22, 1877, enginemen in Newark, New Jersey, organized a meeting in order to develop a response to the wage reductions, and their counterparts in Jersey City followed suit a day later. During the first week of June, a delegation consisting of several dozen of the railroad's most highly skilled workers met with Scott in his office in Philadelphia—hardly neutral territory. Apparently mesmerized by Scott's personality, the force of his arguments, fear for their jobs, or a combination of all three, the delegation agreed that the wage cuts were an unfortunate necessity. Other members of the Brotherhood of Locomotive Engineers were less accommodating, however, and at May 28 meetings in Jersey City and Newark, they discussed the possibility of a strike. In the end, most enginemen decided to remain on the job, if for no other reason than the presence of a New Jersey state law—passed the previous year in response to a strike on the Central of New Jersey—that provided criminal penalties for any train crew who chose to block a railway with their train.[132]

The labor uprisings of 1877, and the worst strike in the history of the Pennsylvania Railroad, began not with train crews, but with New Jersey longshoremen. On June 1, more than a hundred employees refused to report for work, threatening the PRR's operations in the New York area. PRR managers attempted to bribe them with a half-cent-an-hour wage increase, which most refused. Executives then endeavored to use clerks as replacement workers. Those clerks now bore a triple burden, mocked by the strikers as they attempted to shift heavy cargoes, derided by them as scabs, and all of that accompanying their own wage cuts.[133]

Existing fraternal unions responded only weakly to the situation, and the Brotherhood of Railway Conductors threatened to expel any member who engaged in such unseemly behavior as striking. In frustration, Pittsburgh, Fort Wayne & Chicago employees organized the Trainmen's Union, primarily under the leadership of a twenty-four-year-old brakeman, Robert A. Ammon. Eschewing the traditionally fragmented craft-based organization of existing unions, the Trainmen's Union accepted all skilled railway employees, ranging from engine crews to shop workers. A former insurance agent and hotelier, Ammon had been a brakeman for less than a year, and was hardly a typical railroad employee. Nevertheless, within days Ammon had signed up perhaps five hundred PRR and B&O employees in Pittsburgh alone. The new union set a strike date for June 27 on the Fort Wayne, as well as the Pan Handle and the Allegheny Valley Railroad. The strike soon collapsed, however, owing to disagreements within the new union, as well as to vigilance by railroad managers who had learned of the event from loyal employees and paid informants who had infiltrated the organization. The PRR also fired any known

TU member, including Ammon and Samuel A. Muckle, the union's Pittsburgh Division president, using the excuse of necessary force reductions in response to depressed economic conditions. The two hundred or so individuals who gathered on the day of the strike were technically no longer PRR employees, and police soon dispersed them. Those isolated incidents gave the PRR little cause to rescind its wage reductions, encouraging other carriers to follow suit.[134]

One of those railroads was the Baltimore & Ohio. To a greater extent than any eastern trunk line save the Erie, the B&O had been buffeted by the economic disaster of the 1870s. When the B&O board voted, on July 11, to mimic the PRR by reducing wages by 10 percent, effective five days later, it caught no one by surprise. It did, however, induce the full horrors of the strikes of 1877 and the beginnings of the age of industrial and class warfare in the United States.[135]

On July 16 Baltimore & Ohio train crews began leaving their posts in central Baltimore and at nearby Camden Junction. The important railroad hub of Martinsburg, West Virginia, soon became the focal point for strikers who abandoned their trains, effectively blockading a large portion of railroad. The governor of West Virginia called on the militia to restore order and, by the morning of July 17, soldiers had killed one striker. Two days later, federal troops arrived and broke the strike at Martinsburg, but labor militancy quickly spread to other locations on the Baltimore & Ohio.[136]

By July 19, worker unrest had reached the Pennsylvania Railroad as well. Unlike their B&O counterparts, PRR employees in and near Pittsburgh claimed that they understood the necessity of wage cuts and were willing to accept the loss in pay. What aggravated them more, they said, was the cavalier attitude of local PRR managers. "The officials of the road, and Mr. Scott, all treated us all right," Robert Ammon recalled. "It was only the little under-officials who treated us like dogs."[137] On July 16, the same day that striking crewman blockaded the B&O, PRR Pittsburgh Division superintendent Robert Pitcairn added to the workers' unease. Not satisfied with the pay cuts, he attempted to reduce costs still further by ordering double-heading on all trains operating between Pittsburgh and Derry. The order made perfect sense, operationally, to railroad managers, because two engines on those mountain grades could handle the same number of cars as a single engine on the gentler terrain east of Derry. Pitcairn accordingly gave little thought to the labor unrest that might result from what he considered a purely operational decision, and he apparently never contacted President Scott regarding the matter. From the workers' perspective, however, double-heading increased both the effort and the danger associated with operating trains over the Alleghenies. The change also halved the number of conductors, brakemen, and flagmen, and demoted many conductors to flagman status, reducing both their authority and their earnings. Employees with low seniority would lose their jobs entirely. The number to be laid off was not that large—fifty or sixty, in all—but the insult and the uncertainty that Pitcairn's order engendered was enough to rouse far more workers into action.[138]

Pitcairn's timing could not have been worse, given the events that were transpiring on the Baltimore & Ohio. On July 19, the date that the new rules took effect, PRR flagman Augustus Harris refused to work on a double-headed train out of Pittsburgh. The remainder of the crew quickly joined the wildcat strike, one that neither Ammon nor the Trainmen's Union had planned. The president of the TU's Pittsburgh Division was at home, asleep, when the strike began. PRR chief clerk David Watt had available some twenty-five other operating employees, yet they too refused to work. The dispatcher attempted to use yard crews to man the trains, further enraging the strikers. At that point the dissidents, numbering no more than a few dozen men, pulled the pins from the link-and-pin couplers and used them as clubs to threaten the replacement crews who were attempting to move trains out of the yard. A substitute brakeman, hit with an expertly thrown iron coupling link while attempting to add a cabin car to the train, gave up his labors and retreated to the comparative safety of a nearby passenger coach. By 10:00 A.M., the strikers had effectively blockaded the yards at Pittsburgh, with eastbound trains unable to depart. As trains arrived in Pittsburgh throughout the day, other crews joined the strikers, swelling their ranks into the hundreds. Workers attempted to cultivate public sympathy for their cause by allowing passenger trains to arrive and depart

more or less on schedule. When Watt attempted to throw a switch and allow one freight train to depart, however, striker Thomas McCall interposed himself between the chief clerk and the switch stand and, in the ensuing scuffle, struck his superior in the face. Watt, now sporting a black eye, telegraphed Robert Pitcairn. The division superintendent, traveling eastbound, disembarked at Lewistown and headed back to Pittsburgh.[139]

Throughout the afternoon of July 19, telegraphers relayed frantic messages back and forth across Pennsylvania. Yet, there were few senior executives in Philadelphia to read them. Scott was at Andalusia, the former home of Nicholas Biddle, having dinner with his daughter and son-in-law. First vice president George Brooke Roberts was at his summer home in Cape May, and ill. Frank Thomson, the general manager of Lines East, was in Long Branch, New Jersey. That left third vice president Alexander J. Cassatt. Cassatt believed that the Pittsburgh strikers would soon capitulate. When they did not, he boarded a train and headed west.

Even before Pitcairn and Cassatt could reach Pittsburgh, Watt had requested additional assistance from Pittsburgh mayor William McCarthy, only to encounter the full depth of local hostility to the Pennsylvania Railroad. The violence was more severe in Pittsburgh than in railroad towns like Altoona, Fort Wayne, or Terre Haute, a seeming paradox that bespoke the added willingness of urban residents to vent their frustration on the PRR and its competitors. In part, urban residents were furious that their cities were polluted with locomotive smoke, tired of their streets being occupied by trains, and infuriated that any animals, friends, or children foolish enough to wander onto the railroad's domain paid for that carelessness with their lives. Most Americans were willing to accept the noise, the smoke, and even the danger as necessary costs associated with progress. Still, in a city where massive freight and passenger trains rumbled down Liberty Street and other urban thoroughfares, injecting danger into densely packed communities, some workers and townspeople were apt to engage in violent reprisals.[140]

The annoying and dangerous presence of trains notwithstanding, Pittsburgh residents had far more obvious reasons to despise the Pennsylvania Railroad and its Philadelphia managers. For decades, PRR executives had prevented the Baltimore & Ohio from obtaining access to Pittsburgh, preserving their near-monopoly on rail services in southwestern Pennsylvania. The PRR's rate structure discriminated against local shippers in favor of more competitive long-haul traffic.[141] That rate discrimination only compounded the economic effects of the 1870s recession, which had thrown thousands of Pittsburghers out of work and so crippled the city's finances that, only days before the strike began, the city had laid off half of its police force. Crime soared as unemployed laborers attempted to support themselves and their families by any means necessary. Many people blamed the Pennsylvania Railroad, the great looming presence in the city, for all of those problems.[142]

Mayor McCarthy's response to Watt was accordingly both succinct and disappointing—he had few policemen to spare, and he was himself too ill to become involved in the dispute. Like many of his constituents, McCarthy was no friend of the Pennsylvania Railroad, and he held a particularly strong loathing for the company's executives. "I knew who and what Pennsylvania railroad officers were," he later recalled; "that they were imperious and dictatorial, and I could have no influence upon them whatever."[143] McCarthy accordingly supplied fewer than a dozen officers, who were clearly overmatched by the growing contingent of strikers, now accompanied by rock-throwing youths anxious for a little excitement. Several police traveled by train to Torrens, about three miles east of Pittsburgh, in order to assist trainmaster David Garrett, who was attempting to dispatch livestock to the east. The same train also brought an even larger number of strikers, who soon joined what was fast becoming a mob. While Garrett was able to send the livestock train east, through the ruse of claiming that he was only moving it to a siding, it would be the last regular train to move through Pittsburgh for the next three weeks.

By late afternoon, both in Torrens and in Pittsburgh proper, the intimidation by the increasingly restless mob—many of whom had no direct connection to the PRR—gave disgruntled employees an excuse to leave their trains, without acknowledging that they were voluntarily joining the ranks of the strikers. It would not have mattered much, in any event, with even those train crews willing to work finding themselves stymied by the yard switches that were under the control of the mob.[144]

With McCarthy reluctant to commit any more police officers to the suppression of the strike, Watt accepted the mayor's suggestion that he request assistance from Robert H. Fife, the sheriff of Allegheny County. By 11:00 P.M., Pitcairn had arrived in the city, joining Fife, Watt, and Major General Alfred L. Pearson, the commander of the Sixth Division of the Pennsylvania National Guard. The railroad executives, and Pearson, encouraged Sheriff Fife to deputize a posse of local citizens to quell the disturbance. Fife had good reason to doubt the allegiance of the local citizenry, and instead he requested the authority to use National Guard troops. Governor John F. Hartranft was traveling in the West, in Scott's private car. He could do little in response to Fife's plea, except return to Pennsylvania as rapidly as possible. In Hartranft's absence, Adjutant General James W. Latta authorized Pearson to mobilize three regiments of infantry and a battery of artillery, including Colonel Presley N. Guthrie's Eighteenth Regiment.[145]

By noon the next day, roughly two-thirds of Guthrie's soldiers had assembled at Torrens. It was a remarkable feat, considering that notices in the morning newspapers, along with word-of-mouth, were the only methods of providing notification, and that the mob had prevented many from responding. The 326 soldiers now faced more than 1,200 people, fewer than half of whom were striking PRR employees. As Guthrie waited anxiously for reinforcements, a train arrived from Pittsburgh carrying additional demonstrators, some of them rabble-rousers bent on little more than inciting violence. By the evening of July 20, the crowd numbered almost five thousand. Even with the arrival of fifty men from the Nineteenth Regiment and a further twenty-five from an artillery battery, Pearson was outnumbered ten to one. He believed that he could not disperse the protestors without ordering his troops to open fire, with the attendant loss of life.[146]

Nor could Pearson be certain that his soldiers would obey such an order. Local guardsmen were inclined to sympathize with the strikers, and on some occasions they stacked their weapons and openly fraternized with them.[147] Individuals from both groups, after all, were Pittsburghers, and part of the working class, worlds apart from the Philadelphia elites who governed the Pennsylvania Railroad, cut wages, imposed restrictive work rules, and dictated discriminatory rates to the residents of western Pennsylvania. One local observer, thirty-one-year-old Wilson Howell Carpenter, a partner in a steam-pump manufacturer, the Epping-Carpenter Company, noted, "The sympathy of the people and the troops were entirely with the strikers, [and] many of the soldiers openly declared they would not fire on them and turned out with the greatest reluctance."[148] One soldier emphasized, "They may call on me, and they may call pretty damn loud before they will clear the tracks."[149]

Doubting the loyalty of his men, Pearson requested the assistance of 1,200 soldiers from Major General Robert M. Brinton's First Division, based in Philadelphia. Local PRR officials—Vice President Cassatt, Fort Wayne vice president William Thaw, and general counsel John Scott among them—seconded the suggestion, and began to make the necessary transportation arrangements. Mayor McCarthy argued against the demand for troops, but in vain. "The troops were brought here unnecessarily," he later recalled, and he suggested that their use would be "disgracing the city" and "would end in bloodshed, which would be unnecessary."[150] By the time that he made those remarks, at legislative hearings into the Pittsburgh riots, McCarthy had the benefit of perfect hindsight. At the time, however, the mayor seemed personally offended at the judgment of PRR officials that his police force was inadequate. McCarthy simply refused to meet with Cassatt, leaving the PRR executives to their own devices.

More than a decade after the Civil War, Tom Scott was again arranging for the rapid mobilization of troops by rail, many of whom were veterans of the war, as well. Only about half of the number requested were available for embarkation at Philadelphia early on the morning of Saturday, July 21. Their ranks were further thinned when PRR train crews refused to move the Gray Invincibles, finding it unacceptable that an African American regiment should be used to control white workers. The six hundred who remained rode through the night, by the site of the previous year's

Centennial Exhibition, and past a long line of block signal towers, both of them showpieces of the progressive Pennsylvania Railroad. The trains stopped in the state capital long enough to take on board two Gatling guns before heading west toward Pittsburgh.[151]

The arrival of Philadelphia forces in Pittsburgh transformed the strike from a dispute between labor and capital to one that set the eastern and western portions of the state against one another. The trouble began in the huge yard and shop facilities that lay along Liberty Street between Twenty-Sixth Street and Twenty-Eighth Street, some blocks northeast of downtown. Early in the afternoon of July 21, General Brinton's Philadelphia Guard reached Pittsburgh. Their timing was inauspicious, as many factory workers, having finished their half day of Saturday labor, were drawn to the site of the unrest. Brinton and at least one prominent Pittsburgh industrialist urged restraint, suggesting that the troops stand down until Monday morning, when many of the city's residents would be back at work. Brinton's commander, General Pearson, was unsure as to a course of action, and sought Cassatt's advice. Cassatt, more than any other executive on the scene, was determined to safeguard PRR property and to retake possession of the railroad yards from the strikers. The PRR's third vice president never ordered either Pearson or Brinton to commit troops to the fray, but according to some accounts, he strongly intimated that something had to be done to restore order and protect PRR facilities.[152]

Based on Cassatt's inaccurate assurance that PRR train crews were willing to resume work as soon as the tracks were clear, Brinton ordered his troops to fix bayonets and capture the Twenty-Eighth Street crossing. The strikers, accompanied by what PRR officials called "the idle and vicious classes" of the city, attacked the troops, seizing their rifles, while a hail of rocks and coal lumps rained down from all sides. Several people in the crowd began shooting at the soldiers, who responded in kind, even though there was no clear order to fire. Volley after volley rang out, killing at least ten people, perhaps as many as twenty, with between thirty and seventy people badly wounded.[153]

The massacre at Twenty-Eighth Street turned a tense situation into a nightmare. The crowd, enraged at the deaths, demanded vengeance and looted local gun shops for weaponry. Soldiers from the local Pittsburgh militia wisely threw down their weapons and fled, lest their neighbors punish them for the actions of Brinton's Philadelphia troops. Some demonstrators procured a rope and a coffin, which they intended for General Pearson. The hapless Sheriff Fife went into hiding, lending credence to widespread reports that he had fallen victim to the mob. Cassatt, who had been watching the shooting from a cupola that formed a kind of aerie above the nearby shops, departed for the comparative safety of the PRR passenger station. He probably did not hold himself responsible for the deaths that he had just witnessed, but many Pittsburghers considered him guilty, and he would soon be reviled in the popular press.[154]

Shortly before 11:00 P.M., someone, perhaps a teenager bent on incendiary destruction, set fire to a freight car. Volunteers were more than willing to release the hand brake and push it down the grade through the yard. It derailed at a switch near Twenty-Eighth Street and was soon joined by half a dozen cars laden with coke. Oil-filled tank cars added to the conflagration. While comparatively few people were actively starting fires, a far greater number took advantage of the chaos to loot whatever they could carry from the PRR shops, nearby stores, and the hundreds of boxcars that filled the yards. The flames spread to the PRR shop buildings, first the sand house, then the Twenty-Eighth Street engine house. The fire department was undermanned, owing to the same financial crisis that had idled half the police force, and they were no match for the mob that intimidated them and severed their hoses—and they were certainly no match for the fire itself. Two blocks away, General Brinton and his six hundred frightened troops huddled inside the Twenty-Sixth Street engine house, certain that they were soon to be roasted alive.[155]

The fires at Twenty-Eighth Street distracted the mob, and they were probably what saved General Brinton's National Guard. At 2:00 A.M., the moonlight revealed to the anxious soldiers that the rioters had seized a cannon from the Pittsburgh Guard, probably with scant resistance, and had emplaced it to fire on the engine house. The Philadelphia troops inside opened fire, killing or wounding eleven. They kept firing through the night, any time volunteers appeared

who were foolish enough, or drunk enough, to attempt to bring their sole artillery piece into action. At dawn, the mob once again attempted to roll burning freight cars down on the Twenty-Sixth Street engine house. Guardsmen slowed their progress by throwing wheels on the tracks, but they still came too close. Rioters pushed cars loaded with whiskey almost up to the shop complex, and then set them on fire. The machine shop was soon ablaze and, one by one, the other buildings succumbed to the flames. By 8:00 A.M. on Sunday, July 22, the roundhouse had begun to burn, forcing General Brinton to order his troops to retreat.[156]

The soldiers abandoned their artillery pieces, taking with them only their small arms and their Gatling guns. Each man carried no more than a half-dozen rounds of ammunition. As they marched toward the federal Allegheny Arsenal, they passed the conflagration at Twenty-Eighth Street, a certain indication of what fate would have awaited them had they tarried longer at their improvised fortification. The crowd was at first overawed by the display of military force, but that fear quickly turned to renewed anger and a desire to exact revenge for the carnage of the previous day. Brinton's troops soon came under fire from snipers on street corners and in houses, shops, and even a police station. The soldiers finally arrived at the arsenal, half expecting to find it under the control of the protesters. To their relief, fewer than two dozen troops had safeguarded the vulnerable structure, and its thirty-six thousand guns, against a rather desultory attack by the rioters on the previous night. General Brinton left behind his dead and wounded, and retreated toward Sharpsburg, leaving Pittsburgh in the hands of the mob. The twenty-odd Philadelphia soldiers who had been assigned to guard the ammunition stored at the Union Depot escaped only because sympathetic locals provided them with civilian clothing, allowing them to slip out of the city undetected.[157]

Mayor McCarthy belatedly realized that his city teetered on the brink of destruction, and he attempted to restore order, but to no avail. Looters emptied whatever freight cars remained undamaged in the PRR yards, helping themselves to everything from alcohol to Bibles. The fires continued to spread, elements of the mob steadfastly refusing to allow firemen to save any structure belonging to the Pennsylvania Railroad.

Figure 48. During the night of Saturday, July 21, 1877, General Robert M. Brinton's Philadelphia National Guard troops took shelter inside the PRR engine house at Twenty-Sixth and Liberty Streets. Two blocks away, rioters pushed burning freight cars out of a PRR yard and toward the engine house and nearby structures. By early morning, the buildings were ablaze, forcing Brinton and his troops to flee.

Pennsylvania Historical and Museum Commission, Pennsylvania State Archives.

By early Sunday afternoon, the fire had reached Fifteenth Street and was rapidly approaching Union Depot. The adjacent hotel began to evacuate guests and furnishings alike. Shortly thereafter, an arsonist torched a passenger car sitting under the depot's train shed, while others set fire to the stationmaster's office. After consuming the depot and the train shed, the fire next devoured the Adams Express Company building and the Pan Handle freight station. A huge grain elevator caught fire nearby, and bystanders prevented firemen from saving it—even though it was not PRR property, it nonetheless operated in concert with the railroad, representing the evils of concentrated monopoly capital. The violence subsided quickly thereafter, in part because local residents had vented their frustrations against the Pennsylvania Railroad, and in part because there was nothing left to burn. On Monday morning, United States Army troops arrived from Ohio, entering a city that was quiet, and in ashes.[158]

Even as order was restored in Pittsburgh, the violence spread to other cities on the PRR system. Trainmen's Union organizer Robert Ammon had passed through Pittsburgh shortly before the strike began, settling at his home in Allegheny City. He negotiated what amounted to a mutual non-interference agreement with Mayor Ormsby Phillips and watched as the city across the river burned, yet he took no part in the rioting. Instead, he began to incite union activism along the Fort Wayne. His supporters entrenched themselves around the Allegheny City depot and seized control over the telegraph lines to the west. Ammon effectively took over management of the Fort Wayne, dispatching passenger trains on regular schedules. Freights were parked on sidings well removed from the city, guarded by strikers to keep them from falling into the hands of looters and arsonists. On July 24, Governor Hartranft finally arrived in Allegheny City from the West, and acceded to Ammon's request that he speak to the strikers from the rear platform of the train's observation car before continuing on his journey.[159]

East of Pittsburgh, the situation at Altoona became increasingly tense. Early on the morning of July 21, strikers at the PRR's sprawling shop and yard complex had allowed General Brinton's six hundred Philadelphia Guard troops to continue their journey west.

Later that day, after they received word of the deaths in Pittsburgh, workers at Altoona were determined to prevent any additional troops from passing through the city. On Sunday morning, another westbound troop train pulled into Altoona, to add a second locomotive for the trip over the Alleghenies. Yard crews blockaded the helper locomotive inside the roundhouse. They then dumped the fires and drained the water from all other available engines, removing their side rods for good measure. A detachment of soldiers made a halfhearted attempt to liberate at least one functioning locomotive before cheerfully surrendering their weapons and sitting down to breakfast with the strikers. Their commanders then agreed to reboard the train and return to Philadelphia. As the train approached Harrisburg, some soldiers jumped off, afraid that it might be overtaken by protestors in the state capital. A lieutenant changed into civilian clothes and negotiated a surrender of sorts to the Harrisburg mob, who joyously welcomed the deserters to the city, providing them with food at a local hotel before putting them on another train bound for Philadelphia.

The strike also spread to other locations along the PRR and its subsidiaries. Strikers blockaded the tracks at Harrisburg and Columbia, and demonstrations broke out at Jersey City, Johnstown, Indianapolis, and Fort Wayne. On July 22, Pan Handle employees at Columbus, Ohio, went on strike, demanding not merely a reversal of the recent 10 percent pay cut but the restoration of the wages that they had received in 1874. On July 24, strikers closed the shops at Fort Wayne and at Sunbury, Pennsylvania. Even more serious conflicts erupted in Chicago and St. Louis, on the outer fringes of the PRR system.[160]

By July 23, crews had struck the PRR's southwestern connection, the independent Terre Haute & Indianapolis Railroad. President William Riley McKeen sympathized with the strikers, and offered blanket amnesty to all those who returned to work. He successfully maintained the persona of a benevolent town father who abhorred the growing intrusion of the PRR into his native community of Terre Haute. In reality, McKeen was closely allied with PRR executives and with such key public officials as Indianapolis mayor John Caven and Indiana governor James D. Williams. Together, they made arrangements to crush the strike

Figure 49. Robert Ammon, head of the dissident Trainmen's Union, organized strikers on the Pittsburgh, Fort Wayne & Chicago. For a brief period of time, he also oversaw operations on the PRR's principal western subsidiary, dispatching passenger trains, but preventing freights from going through.

Library of Congress, Prints & Photographs Division, LC-USZ62-99142.

should the employees refuse McKeen's offer. In the end, the strike lasted barely a day and involved neither violence nor the destruction of property. A relieved McKeen praised the loyalty of his workforce and, late in his life, he nostalgically if inaccurately reminisced that there had never been any labor trouble on his railroad.[161]

In contrast to the demonstrations that roiled Pittsburgh, the PRR's home city remained remarkably free of violence. Philadelphians, unlike their neighbors to the west, had always been generally supportive of the Pennsylvania Railroad. Philadelphia mayor William S. Stokley also proved far more adept than his counterpart in Pittsburgh at protecting PRR facilities. Stokley presided over the city's fifty-nine thousand shares of PRR stock. He also possessed a reputation as a no-nonsense mayor who would brook no opposition to his authority and who—unlike Mayor McCarthy in Pittsburgh—was eager to cooperate with PRR and

military officials to restore law and order. On Friday, July 20, as General Brinton's troops began to assemble for their long trip west, Stokley met with Scott and Police Chief Kennard H. Jones. Jones was well suited to the task at hand, thanks to his extensive network of confidential informants and his willingness to use physical force to discourage agitation and to extract confessions. The three men also benefited from the lax organization and lack of leadership among Philadelphia operating employees.[162]

By Sunday, many Philadelphia firemen and brakemen had decided to walk off of the job, and demanded the suspension of all train service in the city. In contrast to his hardnosed actions in Pittsburgh, Scott soon agreed, buying time for reinforcements to arrive. Despite Scott's conciliatory tone, sporadic violence erupted in Philadelphia. Unlike Sheriff Fife in Pittsburgh, however, Police Chief Jones had access to ample reserves of manpower.[163] On July 22, he used six hundred police to push back an estimated five hundred people who were menacing the West Philadelphia depot. When General Winfield Scott Hancock took command of operations in the city on the following day, he supervised 1,300 regular policemen, 2,000 volunteer police, 400 armed firemen, 1,325 soldiers, 2,000 veterans held in reserve, and a gunboat on the Delaware River. That show of force was sufficient to keep protests to a minimum. Scott accordingly abandoned his earlier leniency, informing a delegation of strikers that they could be fired, and readily replaced. By Tuesday afternoon, July 24, trains were once again moving through Philadelphia.[164]

By the evening of Wednesday, July 25, the upheavals had begun to subside on the Pennsylvania Railroad and throughout the United States. On July 26, two thousand militia and regular Army troops, ordered into action by President Rutherford B. Hayes, were poised to reopen the PRR route into Pittsburgh. By the time they reached that beleaguered city, their ranks had grown to nine thousand, with Governor Hartranft issuing orders from a command post in a PRR business car. The same day, when Robert Ammon called for the delivery of cars containing coal and food, his influence over the strikers disappeared. Despised now by both management and labor, Ammon was arrested on July 30, charged with inciting a riot. He doubtless felt ill used, and he protested that he had merely been attempting to protect PRR property. He was later released on bail and indicted, but he was never put on trial. On July 27 Superintendent Pitcairn again refused demands for a 20 percent wage increase, but PRR officials were offering $200 bonuses for enginemen who demonstrated their loyalty to the company. The following day Governor Hartranft's troops arrived in Pittsburgh, and the PRR was reopened as far west as Altoona. Other troops lifted the blockades at Columbus and Terre Haute, while a full-scale police and military occupation restored a semblance of order in Chicago. On July 29, troops liberated the railroad facilities at St. Louis from the strikers, the Altoona shops reopened, and freight traffic finally began moving east out of Pittsburgh. The strike was over.[165]

As late as the middle of August, however, rumors continued to circulate that the strike would be reawakened, fueled by stories that shots had been fired at

a "troop train from Altoona" or reports of "an engine with Flues and Fire-box filled with powder obstructing the track in the Tunnel." "This part of the story," General Superintendent Gardner noted, "probably had its origin in the fact that an Engine was stolen from Altoona by a crowd of men and boys and run up the mountain it was thought either for the purpose of letting it run down in the face of the train with soldiers or of obstructing the tunnel."[166]

The 1877 Strikes in Retrospect

On July 20, the day after the strike began on the Pennsylvania Railroad, the Trainmen's Union held a rally in Pittsburgh. The attendees unanimously adopted a series of resolutions and created a committee of five employees to present them to PRR management. The five men were typical of the skilled workers who had dedicated a considerable portion of their lives to the difficult and dangerous business of railroading. Simon Hawk hired on as a fireman in 1863, earning a promotion to engineman two years later. Martin Robinson joined the PRR the same year as a brakeman, and he became a flagman in 1872. William Gardner (no relation to PRR general superintendent G. Clinton Gardner) had been a brakeman since 1869. George Miller was hired in 1872, five years before the strikes began. David Snyder had the least experience, having begun his career as a brakeman only two years prior to the cataclysmic events of 1877.

Of the petitioners' seven demands, only one dealt with wages. In addition to requesting a reversal of the wage cuts, they asked that all laid-off and fired employees be restored to duty, that the classification system be abolished, and that each yard and road engine be provided with a full complement of crewmen, without double-heading. The employees also pledged to protect PRR property to the extent possible "as long as This Trouble Exists." The committee announced its refusal to operate any more troop trains and even more audaciously saw fit to "demand Emphatically The Removal of Frank Thompson [sic]," the general manager of Lines East.[167]

The five PRR employees submitted the petition to third vice president Alexander Cassatt and Pittsburgh

Division superintendent Robert Pitcairn. Both executives were outraged at the audacity of the strikers' demands. Cassatt insisted that "they proposed to take the road out of our hands," while Pitcairn "told them I could not possibly send such a paper to Mr. Scott."[168] James McCrea, superintendent of the Middle Division, informed the committee that he lacked the authority to consider their demands, and "had not the slightest doubt that these or any others they propose would not be considered until law and order had first been restored, and business of the Road [kept] moving in [the] same manner prior to this demonstration."[169] General Superintendent Gardner was even more blunt in his assessment of the situation. "My views are, should we find any of our employees joining any such Trade Union, that they should be dismissed at once." He noted, "The only question in my mind was whether it was politic for us to act as the B&O RR did" in crushing the strike with an overwhelming show of military force.[170] Instead, Gardner limited his request for assistance to "two good detectives," along with the authority to "arrest quite a number of citizens as well as P.R.R. Employees."[171]

The employees' petition, as well as McCrea's and Gardner's comments, indicated the growing chasm that separated skilled workers and management on the Pennsylvania Railroad. Hawk and his comrades believed—or at least asserted—that they had the right to participate in the governance of the Pennsylvania Railroad. In that sense, they were not so much employees as colleagues, working in partnership with management. Thirty years later, after the 1892 Homestead strike, the 1894 Pullman strike, and other labor-management conflicts had convulsed the American workplace, that attitude seemed to many to be naive, outdated, even dangerous and antithetical to American values. Yet the notion of joint employee-employer governance was not so much unrealistic as it was the legacy of an economy innocent of big business, and of a time when skilled workers and owner-proprietors were one and the same individuals. In the aftermath of the 1877 strike, however, even skilled workers had few illusions regarding who controlled the workplace, and the process of production.

Scott, McCrea, Gardner, and other PRR executives saw things differently, perhaps more realistically, but certainly in a manner that took into account the wrenching transformations that industrialization had induced in the American workplace. They valued skilled employees, but only insofar as they could contribute to efficient production. They doubtless claimed to support individual initiative and autonomy, but were not willing to allow those characteristics to interfere with routine, order, and system. Above all, they were not willing to allow workers—no matter how highly skilled—to share a measure of control over the process of production. The Pennsylvania Railroad, like other sprawling, complex, hierarchical organizations, depended on consistent operating methods and on the continual exchange of data between local officials and top corporate officers. In denying Simon Hawk's demands for a share of corporate governance, PRR executives were doing nothing less than asserting that they, and they alone, could establish and maintain uniform procedures while controlling the flow of information throughout the system.

PRR executives won that battle, but at considerable cost. The idea of worker governance lay in ruins, but so did a substantial swath of Pittsburgh. Four soldiers and at least twenty rioters and onlookers lay dead. Virtually all of the PRR facilities between Twenty-Eighth Street and the Union Depot had been reduced to ashes. The PRR's shops were virtually destroyed, as was the Union Depot and hotel, along with dozens of other buildings. The rails were so badly warped by the heat, and so many ties destroyed by the flames, that PRR crews took a week—until July 30—to restore some semblance of service. The losses included 126 locomotives and 1,600 freight and passenger cars, many of which had been looted before being burned.[172]

Pennsylvania Railroad officials estimated that more than $2 million worth of company property had been destroyed in the riots at Pittsburgh. When combined with freight claims and service interruptions, the loss increased to $5 million. Other estimates placed the toll as high as $7.5 million. Whatever the precise amount, they helped persuade the board of directors to cancel the August and November dividend payments that year. On July 23, 1877, after the company announced the first suspension, PRR stock hit a new low of $26 a share, barely half of par.

In an attempt to recoup their losses, PRR officials audaciously attempted to extract payment from Allegheny County and the Commonwealth of Pennsylvania. By October 1879, the State Supreme Court ruled that the county was liable for damages, owing to ineffective efforts at law enforcement. Allegheny County had no money available, and local politicians gave their support to a Pittsburgh Riot Claims Bill in the General Assembly, promising more than $3 million in payments to the company. Despite the brazen nature of the bill, the PRR's lobbyists might have been successful had it not been for the torrent of opposition over the PRR's role in the South Improvement Company oil transportation cartel. The legislation went nowhere, and led to widespread accusations of influence peddling and bribery. In the ensuing investigation, former State Treasurer William H. Kemble, one of the PRR's chief lobbyists, laconically observed, "I know the Constitution has a lot of stuff in it that none of you live up to, and I'm no better than other people."[173] Even though his railroad had suffered at the hands of rioters, Reading president Franklin Gowen quickly volunteered to help prosecute anyone connected with the scandal, largely as a mechanism for hobbling the PRR. Despite Gowen's best efforts, Kemble and his associates escaped with little more than a token condemnation. PRR officials were more successful in their efforts to sue Allegheny County. In January 1880, in an out-of-court settlement, the county paid $1.6 million, along with far smaller amounts to other affected companies.[174]

The embers from the 1877 riots had barely cooled before PRR executives, government officials, and the general public struggled to make sense of the appalling destruction and loss of life. PRR officials insisted that outsiders had caused most of the damage. In an open letter to the *New York Herald*, Scott claimed that fewer than 5 percent of the Pittsburgh rioters were actually PRR employees. That figure seems absurdly low, yet most observers suggested that well over half of those who rampaged through the city were clearly not directly affiliated with the railroad, and that they were the ones who caused most of the destruction. In the aftermath of the strikes—which he called a crisis "almost as serious as that which prevailed at the outbreak of the Civil War"—Scott insisted that "the conduct of

the rioters [was] entirely inconsistent with the idea that this movement could have been directed by serious, right-minded men bent on improving the condition of the laboring classes."[175] The *New York World*—which Scott owned—predictably condemned the strike, blaming the violence on "the hands of men dominated by the devilish spirit of Communism."[176] Other PRR officials noted the destructive influence of "mobs of roughs and tramps" in several cities, claiming that "in Chicago the communists made a formidable demonstration."[177] Bystanders thought that they detected the presence of steel workers, upset over their own experience with layoffs and wage reductions, and identifiable by their pasty skin, a pallor allegedly induced by years inside the mills. Some suspected day laborers, who were dissatisfied with their lot in life, anxious to strike back against the amorphous forces of capitalism and to pick up some loot along the way. Several observers assigned responsibility to the Irish or to African Americans, many of whom served as replacements for striking workers.[178] Wilson Carpenter was the only one who gave primacy to PRR employees, forming the bulk of "the idle crowd, among whom were many strikers and a few bad characters," that soon degenerated into "a mob of howling demons."[179]

The common denominator in most of the violence seems to have been a large and highly mobile army of what were variously described as "tramps," "hoboes," "riff-raff," or "ne'er-do-wells." Many had been gainfully employed prior to the 1870s recession, but now traveled the rails, homeless, wandering from city to city, impotent in the new industrial age, their skills devalued, and nursing a deep grudge against the large and impersonal corporations that had exploited their labor, paid them starvation wages, and kept them at work for long hours under dangerous conditions. According to observers—and this reflected their largely upper-class or middle-class status—honest and conscientious workingmen rarely started the violence. Instead, they claimed, a small group of agitators, whether intending to improve the lot of the workingman or trying to destroy capitalism, caused the disaffected elements to coalesce and whipped many into an emotional frenzy. Teenagers, many of whom were also unemployed workers, then took over, damaging property and hurling missiles at police and soldiers. Those forces of law and order overreacted, perhaps in a justifiable panic, perhaps exhorted into action by PRR managers. Once the shooting began, the mob mentality took over, and the underlying army of the unemployed swung into action, looting buildings and railroad cars in the wake of the more incendiary hardcore strikers.[180]

In the aftermath of the 1877 strikes, middle-class and upper-class Americans condemned the violence and expressed their concern at the possibility that radical European political and economic philosophies had migrated across the Atlantic. As elite citizens of a capitalistic democracy, they saw attacks on capitalism as attacks on democracy itself. Since 1846, particularly since the end of the Civil War, Pennsylvania Railroad managers had developed considerable experience with their workforce. They knew, perhaps better than most, that the vast majority of their workers wanted to improve their lot within the system, not to destroy it. They could take but scant comfort in that belief, however, for they were genuinely shocked at the scope of the destruction and at the depths of worker resentment.

By the end of the decade, moreover, the officers and employees of the Pennsylvania Railroad had lost the two managers who had guided the company for a quarter of a century. In October 1878, barely four years after Thomson's death, Scott suffered the first of a series of strokes. Many years earlier, in 1855, he had been riding in the cab of a PRR locomotive. The engine had derailed, and then tipped over, pitching Scott headfirst to the ground. The resulting concussion had permanently affected his mobility. Coupled with the stresses associated with running the Pennsylvania Railroad, a recurrence of his illness, decades later, was not unexpected. With his speech slurred and his left side partly paralyzed, he yielded responsibility for the Pennsylvania Railroad to his first vice president, George Brooke Roberts. Public reports that Scott had caught "a severe cold" were probably meant to reassure anxious investors. By the end of the month, the board had excused the president from further administrative responsibilities, and in early November he embarked on a long trip to Europe and the Middle East in a futile attempt to restore his shattered health. It would be the first, and the last, vacation of his life.

Scott's travels abroad may have distanced him from the controversies surrounding his role in the Texas & Pacific and in his willingness to grant favorable rates to Standard Oil, but he could not avoid other, more personal tragedies. At the end of April, his former assistant and longtime lobbyist, Samuel S. Moon, died at the age of fifty-six. Less than a month later, on May 22, 1879, he lost his thirteen-year-old son, Thomas A. Scott, Jr. When Tom Scott returned to the United States, on September 10, his health had scarcely improved. On May 1, 1880, he submitted his resignation to the board, to take effect at the beginning of June. The following month, Roberts—who had effectively been running the company for the previous eighteen months—assumed the presidency. Scott, never fully able to separate himself from the company that he had helped to build, retained an office down the hall from the one that he had occupied for only six years. In less than a year, Tom Scott was dead. He was fifty-seven years old.[181]

Following the deaths of Thomson and Scott, and in the aftermath of the 1874 stockholders' investigating committee report and the 1877 strikes, a new generation of executives created a very different Pennsylvania Railroad, one in which they faced new limits on managerial authority. Roberts and his successors were no less willing than Scott had been to exploit workers and deprive them of any measure of control over the workplace, but they no longer risked wage reductions or sweeping and peremptory changes in work rules. During the 1880s, they instead began to buy off skilled workers, in much the same manner that Thomson and Scott had once bought off shareholders. In years to come, PRR officials would offer their most valued employees—primarily train crews—job security, relatively high wages, a pension plan, and the ability to adjudge themselves superior to the other, less skilled individuals who worked for the railroad. In exchange, skilled workers agreed to renounce violence, avoid strikes, and relinquish control over the process of production to management.

Roberts and his fellow executives were more comfortable with movement and with machinery than with people—they were all engineers, after all—and they accordingly sought engineering solutions to the problems that faced the Pennsylvania Railroad as the nineteenth century drew to a close. By making the railroad operate more efficiently, they believed, they could cut costs without reducing wages. Through continued growth, the PRR could generate ever-increasing profits, placating workers and investors alike. For the next two decades, a cadre of skilled engineers guided the Pennsylvania Railroad through an era of system building, in which they sought engineering solutions to what were, in many cases, actually human problems.

During the early 1900s, when the managerial quest for system and order drew to a close, many of the executives and workers who had been involved in the 1877 strikes were nearing the end of their careers, and their lives. A third of a century had passed since the convulsive events of 1877, which now seemed to fade into a distant memory. But PRR executives still remembered, still kept an accurate accounting of the fates of the five men who had constituted the committee of employees. The company's 1910 inquiry confirmed that Simon Hawk had left the PRR in 1881 and resided in Pine Run, Pennsylvania. Martin Robinson, who had retained his job as conductor even after the strike, lost it in 1884 when his engine, running light, backed into another train. The others were gone. George Miller was promoted to engineman in 1881, but died three years later. William Gardner became a conductor in 1880, yet his poor eyesight caused his transfer to the Altoona shops, then to a series of jobs as clerk, assistant weighmaster, yardmaster, and passenger conductor. He died in 1909. David Snyder became a flagman in 1883, then assistant yardmaster in 1887, before his death in 1898.[182] As for James McCrea, the Middle Division superintendent who "had not the slightest doubt that these [demands] or any others they prepared would not be considered until law and order had been first restored, and business on the Road [kept] moving," he was now president of the Pennsylvania Railroad.

Chapter 12

Order

1877–1899

Jay Gould was back from the wilderness. He had gained considerable notoriety during the first few years after the Civil War, winning control of the Erie from Cornelius Vanderbilt and quickly forming alliances with railroads in Ohio, Indiana, and Illinois. His actions had very nearly deprived the PRR of its western connections, inducing J. Edgar Thomson to take swift and decisive action by gaining control over the Pittsburgh, Fort Wayne & Chicago and the Columbus, Chicago & Indiana Central. Thomson's strategic decisions had beaten back the Gould threat, marking the beginning of a great period of the PRR's expansion.

Blocked at every turn, Gould soon fell from grace. There was widespread speculation that an 1869 attempt by Gould to corner the gold market had ended badly. In the end, he may in fact have made money on the venture, but the episode tarnished his reputation for invincibility. Gould clearly failed in his efforts to gain control over the Cleveland & Pittsburgh and the Atlantic & Great Western as western connections for the Erie. Even worse, in March 1872, investors in the Atlantic & Great Western forced him to relinquish both a seat on the board and the presidency of the Erie. Gould kept a low profile during the next few years, yet he never really disappeared. Instead, he plotted a return to power on a truly continental scale. He aimed

for nothing less than to be the first person to control a railroad empire that stretched from the Atlantic to the Pacific, a goal that not even Tom Scott had been able to achieve.[1]

Gould exploited a period of extreme instability in the railroad network. In the aftermath of the rate wars of the 1870s, few believed that pools had been successful at dampening down cutthroat competition. Following the creation of the Eastern Trunk Line Association in 1877, officials such as Albert Fink, the head of its Executive Committee, made confident pronouncements about his ability to set rates administratively—but even Fink acknowledged that there was no way to force the railroads to comply with his rulings. Earlier than many of his contemporaries, Gould intuitively grasped that the solution to the rate wars lay in the creation of cohesive, self-sustaining systems with access to all major markets, and beholden to no other carrier for traffic. Gould again belied his popular reputation as a reckless and unscrupulous financier, moving very carefully, and very quietly, in his efforts to piece together an integrated rail network.[2]

As the nation reeled under the aftereffects of the Panic of 1873, Gould began to lay the foundations for his transcontinental system. J. Edgar Thomson, Tom Scott, and the other members of the PRR investment consortium were badly overextended in the West,

Figure 50. The *Washington Limited Express*, making a steady fifty-five miles per hour on the Pennsylvania Railroad's immaculately groomed right of way circa 1896. While scenes like this endowed the Pennsylvania Railroad with the aura of invincibility, by the end of the nineteenth century the railroad was in a vulnerable position. Overbuilding and competition among the northeastern railroads had pushed rates so low that PRR executives found it difficult to bring order to their industry, or to fund new construction. Within the next few years, the PRR would rely on both inter-firm agreements and federal regulation to ensure rate stability.

Library of Congress, Prints & Photographs Division, LC-USZ62-89495.

bringing them under increased criticism from their more cautious shareholders. One by one, Gould picked off the railroads that they could no longer control. In 1874, the Union Pacific fell into the Gould orbit. The UP did not reach either Chicago or St. Louis, and Gould depended on three carriers (the Chicago, Burlington & Quincy Railroad; the Chicago, Rock Island & Pacific Railroad; and the Chicago & North Western Railway) to reach those gateway cities. Much like the PRR and the other members of the Eastern Trunk Line Association, the three granger railroads had formed a cartel, the Iowa Pool, setting rates at a level that Gould found unacceptable. Gould invested in two of the three companies, but Charles E. Perkins, the Burlington's recently appointed vice president, blocked his efforts and

began building alliances between his company and the PRR. In frustration, Gould resolved to de-escalate his involvement in the Union Pacific, instead concentrating his efforts on the Southwest. By 1881, he had invested in the Kansas Pacific Railroad (and merged it with the UP), had bought out Tom Scott's interest in the Texas & Pacific Railway, and had garnered the Missouri Pacific Railroad; the Missouri, Kansas & Texas Railroad; the St. Louis, Iron Mountain & Southern Railway; and the International & Great Northern Railroad.

East of the Mississippi, Gould played an even more dangerous game. The lynchpin of his empire was the Wabash Railway (after 1879, the Wabash, St. Louis & Pacific Railway), with a route angling northeastward between Kansas City and Toledo. Frustrated in his efforts to regain control over the Erie, he attempted to build another link between tidewater and the Great Lakes. Gould coveted the principal anthracite carriers, both as a source of revenues and as a means of access to east coast ports. He set his sights on the Jersey Central, and by February 1881 had finagled a seat on that company's board of directors. According to credible rumors, he soon began buying Reading stock, as well. More significant, Gould's investments in the Delaware, Lackawanna & Western, linking Hoboken, New Jersey, and Binghamton, New York, narrowed the gap between the eastern and western portions of his network. In August 1880, Gould and his allies incorporated the New York, Lackawanna & Western Railway, intending to extend the route from Binghamton west to Buffalo. In a very few months, Gould had come perilously close to accomplishing what no other railroader, not even J. Edgar Thomson and Tom Scott, had been able to achieve—a coast-to-coast rail empire.

It was not to be. Gould's house of cards fell as quickly as it rose. The system peaked in 1882, but a recession that began two years later, although comparatively mild, caught Gould overextended, and he had little choice other than to divest many of his holdings. By 1890, he retained only the Missouri Pacific, the Texas & Pacific, the International & Great Northern, and some short lines in Texas and Arkansas that were later organized as the St. Louis Southwestern Railway. His only other significant asset was the Wabash, which his son, George Gould, would later use as part of his own unsuccessful attempt at empire building.

Gould's brief return to power exerted a profound influence on the northeastern railroads. In 1880, Gould's machinations touched off another rate war, one that did not end until 1884. For a time, eastbound grain rates were as low as eight cents per hundredweight, less than a seventh of the level that had prevailed in 1873. After an all-too-brief period of stability, rates plummeted again, until the advent of another compromise in November 1885. Despite his best efforts, Albert Fink was powerless to stop the chaos. He held on as best he could, but several times threatened to resign. Finally, in June 1889 he did quit his $25,000-a-year post, sending letters of resignation to the presidents of all four trunk lines. Fink emphasized that his

action "was not due to any trouble in the Trunk Line Association," but industry experts knew better. When the New York Times headlined the story of his departure as "Mr. Albert Fink Is Tired," much the same could have been written about the efforts of traffic associations to control rates.[3]

Jay Gould was not the only railroader who reacted to the failure of pools and other traffic agreements by attempting to create a self-sustaining network. The first great period of consolidations had occurred during the 1850s, interrupted only by the economic depressions late in the decade, followed by the onset of the Civil War. The second wave of realignments began soon after Appomattox, and subsided in the aftereffects of the Panic of 1873. By 1875, PRR executives were overseeing 4,447 route miles, very much in line with conventional wisdom that suggested that any system that exceeded 5,000 miles was too large to be managed effectively.[4] However, the Gould-induced consolidations of the 1880s put the two previous periods to shame. For the first time, the New York Central extended its direct control west of Buffalo, becoming a large system. The PRR grew as well, from almost 4,500 miles to more than 7,000 miles. Railroaders now believed that it was possible to supervise as much as ten thousand miles of line, and they devised new organizational structures accordingly. When railroad officials did turn to system building, they did so with a vengeance.[5]

Perhaps ironically, given his role as the instigator of the new era of system building, Jay Gould posed relatively few problems for the PRR. Unlike the Vanderbilt family, whose members scrambled frantically to protect their western connections from the financier's onslaught, PRR executives had long since secured control over the PRR's lines in Ohio, Indiana, and Illinois. In 1880, as the great era of system building began, the PRR's route structure was essentially complete, and there was not much left to do. During the 1880s, the nation's rail mileage more than doubled, but the PRR system grew by only a little more than 10 percent—a testament to the pioneering efforts of Thomson, Scott, and others in the immediate postwar period, as well as an indication of the relative maturity of the northeastern railway network.[6] On Lines East, the most obvious gap lay in the short stretch of track between Philadelphia and Baltimore, operated by a company that was friendly to, but by no means the subject of, the PRR. Less significantly, the PRR lacked the New York Central's access to Lake Ontario. West of Pittsburgh and Erie, William Riley McKeen's independent Terre Haute & Indianapolis Railroad constituted the chief impediment to control over the route to St. Louis, and even he was a staunch PRR ally.[7]

Gould's indirect effects on the Pennsylvania Railroad were considerable, nonetheless. The PRR's strong position circa 1880 did not mean that the company would emerge unaffected—or unscathed—by the quest for order in the railroad business. The greatest danger came from two companies, the Reading and the Baltimore & Ohio, that had long been rivals of the PRR. Those two companies labored under the management of Franklin B. Gowen and John W. Garrett, one an adept financier and the other an experienced railroader, but individuals who each showed increasing signs of mental instability. During the 1880s, Gowen, Garrett, and their associates placed the PRR on the defensive. The resulting changes to the PRR's rail network, its finances, and its organizational structure were comparatively mild compared with the transformation of other American railroads—but they were significant nonetheless.

The New York Central, in contrast, was roiled by Gould's activities, as well as by the death of Cornelius Vanderbilt and public disapprobation at the concentration of wealth in the hands of the Vanderbilt family. Most notably, Gould forced the Vanderbilts to consolidate their network of affiliated railroads, albeit slowly, in a manner that mimicked what the Pennsylvania Railroad had already accomplished. During the late 1860s, Gould's efforts to secure western connections had badly frightened Cornelius Vanderbilt, who had responded by investing in several midwestern carriers, most notably the Lake Shore & Michigan Southern and the Toledo, Wabash & Western Railway (later part of the Wabash, St. Louis & Pacific Railway). Yet, unlike Thomson, Vanderbilt held back from a more formal consolidation, doubtless believing that Gould's rapid fall from grace, in 1872, protected the New York Central's western connections. While he retained his holdings in the Lake Shore, Vanderbilt disposed of most of the remainder.[8]

After Cornelius Vanderbilt died in January 1877, his son William Henry Vanderbilt took control of the NYC, only a short time before Jay Gould began another empire-building crusade. Unlike many of his contemporaries, and against all evidence to the contrary, the younger Vanderbilt believed—or at least hoped—that the Eastern Trunk Line Association would prove effective at stabilizing rates. Jay Gould labored under no such illusions. Between 1876 and 1878, Gould combined two elements of his agenda—seeking a connection to Detroit, and disposing of his interest in the failing Atlantic & Pacific Telegraph Company. He acquired holdings in both the Michigan Southern Railroad and the Canada Southern Railroad, carriers that paralleled a significant portion of the NYC system, and he informed Vanderbilt that he was willing to make a deal. The Western Union Telegraph Company (in which Vanderbilt was heavily invested) would buy out Atlantic & Pacific at a handsome profit, and in exchange, Gould would allow Vanderbilt to gain control over the two railroads. By 1878, in tandem with Vanderbilt family investments in the Lake Shore & Michigan Southern, the NYC operated two routes linking Buffalo and Chicago.[9]

Vanderbilt's acquisitions, no matter how reluctant, were nonetheless expensive. He had inherited from his father something like four hundred thousand shares of NYC stock, representing nearly 45 percent of the company. His holdings represented a vast pool of investment capital. In the aftermath of the 1870s depression, they also gave reporters and politicians ample opportunity to characterize Vanderbilt as someone who singlehandedly dominated the railroad business. During the spring of 1879, such accusations surfaced in the New York legislature, where an investigating committee led by Alonzo B. Hepburn criticized the NYC's involvement in pools and rebating. The negative characterizations reached their apex in October 1882, when Vanderbilt uttered an oft-quoted phrase—"The public be damned"—to freelance newspaper reporter Clarence Dresser. Although the quotation was taken badly out of context, Dresser and his more sensationalistic colleagues experienced little difficulty in portraying Vanderbilt as a malefactor of great wealth.[10]

By the time that Vanderbilt committed one of the greatest blunders in the history of public relations, he had already disposed of a large portion of his New York Central stock. In 1879, he relied on John Pierpont Morgan, then a largely unknown figure in financial circles, to sell the shares without flooding the market and depressing their value. Vanderbilt remained as NYC president, but his family's control over the company was much diluted. After 1879, the Vanderbilt family and a growing cadre of professional managers continued the policy of investing in other lines. By 1884, the NYC controlled, through the Lake Shore & Michigan Southern, the Pittsburgh & Lake Erie Railroad and its route from Youngstown to Pittsburgh. In 1882, the Vanderbilt interests gained control over one of their most important midwestern outlets, the Cleveland, Columbus, Cincinnati & Indianapolis Railway (the Bee Line). Seven years later, Morgan assisted in the addition of the Cincinnati, Indianapolis, St. Louis & Chicago Railway, with the two companies merging to form the Cleveland, Cincinnati, Chicago & St. Louis Railway (the Big Four). The addition of the Big Four essentially completed the NYC's route structure, nearly two decades after comparable developments on the PRR. Even then, the NYC's principal subsidiaries, such as the Lake Shore and the Big Four, continued to operate as largely autonomous entities with little central oversight.[11]

Despite the Vanderbilts' system-building efforts, their interests remained exceedingly vulnerable to Jay Gould's strategy. The most ominous threat came from the financier's plans to create what amounted to a fifth U.S. trunk line, using the Delaware, Lackawanna & Western and the New York, Lackawanna & Western to reach Buffalo, with the New York, Chicago & St. Louis Railroad (better known as the Nickel Plate Road) promising an extension westward toward Toledo and Chicago. New York Central officials retaliated by refusing to interchange traffic with the Lackawanna, but that strategy deprived their company of anthracite traffic and threatened them as much as it did Jay Gould. By some mechanism, the Vanderbilt interests sought to block Gould, forge alliances with other anthracite carriers, gain additional bituminous coal traffic, and establish better access to east coast ports.

The resulting New York Central strategy relied heavily on two accomplished but increasingly unreliable railway executives—John W. Garrett of the Baltimore & Ohio and Franklin B. Gowen of the Reading. Together, Vanderbilt, Garrett, and Gowen developed a three-pronged strategy to expand the joint influence of the Reading and the NYC, generally at the expense of the Pennsylvania Railroad. One goal, in tandem with Garrett, was to establish a line linking New York, Philadelphia, Baltimore, and Washington. That objective ultimately backfired on both Gowen and Garrett, inducing the PRR to gain control over its longstanding southern connection, the Philadelphia, Wilmington & Baltimore Railroad. Second, the Reading would be extended from its western terminus at Williamsport, north to a connection with the New York Central and perhaps as far west as Buffalo—enabling Vanderbilt to tap the northeastern anthracite region, as well as the bituminous coal fields of north-central Pennsylvania, while providing Gowen with coveted trunk-line status. Finally, the two executives would cooperate on the construction of a new rail route across southern Pennsylvania, paralleling the PRR. The latter two goals likewise proved disappointing for Gowen and for Vanderbilt. Once aroused, PRR officials fought back vigorously to defend their interests. Yet, the internecine battles between the PRR, the Reading, the NYC, and the B&O so threatened the stability of the northeastern railroads that investors—represented by financier J. Pierpont Morgan—had little choice other than to intervene in an effort to bring order out of the chaos.

The resurrected Jay Gould was in some respects a throwback to a freewheeling and morally ambiguous era of railroading, one that might have sat comfortably with Tom Scott. Yet, by the 1880s, Gould's piratical approach was badly out of step with the tenor of the times. Neither the Vanderbilts nor their chief investment banker, J. P. Morgan, had much patience with Gould, or with his efforts to destabilize the railroads. Gowen and Garrett were suspicious of the interloper, even if they were willing to work with him from time to time. Had he lived, Scott would have been a formidable adversary for Gould during the 1880s. Yet, Scott would have been the wrong individual to guide the Pennsylvania Railroad through the last two decades of the nineteenth century. An executive who lacked any significant engineering training, and who governed

Figure 51. In their battle to prevent the construction of a competing rail route across southern Pennsylvania, PRR executives confronted three businessmen of considerable renown. (top left) William Henry Vanderbilt (1821–1885) was a competent railroad executive, but lacked the respect afforded to his father—who seemed to take great pleasure in berating his son. The younger Vanderbilt was probably best known for his comment "the public be damned"—although taken out of context, it indelibly labeled him as unscrupulous and paternalistic. He served as president of the New York Central between 1877 and 1883 and attempted to fend off such challenges as the West Shore Line while extending the Beech Creek Railroad into the PRR's traditional territory. Two years after leaving the NYC presidency, he died of a stroke, before a horrified Robert Garrett—an event that helped push the B&O president, never a match for his more talented father, toward a nervous breakdown. (top right) Franklin B. Gowen (1836–1889) was a brilliant attorney, a gifted orator, an inveterate foe of organized labor, and the accomplished president of the Philadelphia & Reading. Yet, he was plagued by demons, and by 1880 his control over the Reading—and his mental faculties—had begun to unravel. (right) J. Pierpont Morgan (1837–1913) maintained stability by brokering a truce among the warring factions—an act that symbolized the growing authority of investment bankers over the railroads.

(top left) Library of Congress Prints & Photographs Division, LC-USZ62-137871; (top right) Historical Society of Pennsylvania, Society Portrait Collection; (right) Library of Congress Prints & Photographs Division, LC-USZ62-94188.

the company through shrewdness and the force of his personality, would be no match for the rapidly escalating complexity of the railroad business. What the PRR needed was a president as unlike Scott as it would be possible to imagine. What the PRR needed was someone like George Brooke Roberts.

George Brooke Roberts

George Roberts was born in 1833 into modest affluence at Pencoyd Farm, his family's estate in Montgomery County, and he died there sixty-four years later. Although one historian has suggested that Roberts was "the first of a presidential series drawn from wealthy upper-class backgrounds," the fifth individual to head the PRR grew up on a working farm, one that had been in his family for five generations.[12] His cousins, Algernon Sidney and Percival, ran the nearby Pencoyd Iron Works, later a component of United States Steel. After graduating from the Lower Merion Academy, Roberts enrolled in the Rensselaer Polytechnic Institute at age fifteen and graduated in 1849, completing a three-year course of study in only two years. He was unable to find a position on a New York railroad, and so relied on his family connections in Philadelphia. His uncle, Algernon S. Roberts, had been a strong supporter of the 1846 Pennsylvania Railroad charter and served as a director of the Harrisburg, Portsmouth, Mount Joy & Lancaster. Algernon's pull enabled his nephew to secure a position on the PRR, surveying the line over the Allegheny Mountains. At some point during his labors, he contracted typhoid, which permanently weakened his heart.[13]

George Roberts spent much of the following decade traversing Pennsylvania as a locating engineer for numerous railroads, including the Sunbury & Erie. In 1862, with Tom Scott involved in military and political matters, Thomson created for Roberts the position of assistant to the president, a sort of engineering chief-of-staff. Roberts served as a liaison with the Philadelphia & Erie, and based on his success there, the board in 1869 appointed him fourth vice president, in charge of new construction. He became second vice president in 1873, supervising accounting, transportation, and traffic. When Tom Scott assumed the presidency in 1874, Roberts became first vice president, responsible for negotiating the complex financial arrangements associated with the acquisition of subsidiary lines, particularly those west of Pittsburgh.[14]

When ill health forced Scott to retire in May 1880, the presidency went to Roberts, then only forty-seven years of age. As the first vice president, Roberts was next in line of succession, but senior PRR officials had also demonstrated a long tradition of stepping outside the linear promotion process. In particular, each outgoing president generally chose his successor, as Thomson had done with Tom Scott. Scott's protégé, third vice president Alexander J. Cassatt, was seemingly the natural choice to succeed his mentor as the PRR's president. However, many newspaper editors, public officials, and private citizens were opposed to Cassatt, blaming him for the violence that had occurred during the 1877 Pittsburgh riots. The directors were perhaps reluctant to place in charge of their company a man widely condemned as the instigator, but public resentment regarding Cassatt was probably a minor consideration in their decision.

More important, the directors had become increasingly nervous about Scott's expansionist vision, his forays into the West, and his questionable business dealings with Andrew Carnegie and other associates. In the aftermath of the Panic of 1873 and the 1874 report of the stockholders' investigating committee, they preferred to concentrate on the PRR's core transportation business, in its traditional territory north of the Ohio River and east of St. Louis and Chicago. Even though he played a far smaller role in the PRR's overexpansion than did Scott, Cassatt was inextricably linked to the actions of the Scots-Irish president.

While Cassatt had been negotiating rate agreements, clearing the tracks in Pittsburgh, and testifying before government bodies, Roberts had been responsible for remedying the financial and engineering problems that Scott had created, particularly on Lines West. Scott specialized in relations between the PRR and outside entities—including allied and competing carriers and governmental bodies—but Roberts was more of an internalist. Although he was an Episcopalian, he descended from a long Quaker lineage. Cautious and conservative, the bland and restrained Roberts seemed the antithesis of Scott's ebullient and

Figure 52. George Brooke Roberts (1833–1897) served as the fifth president of the Pennsylvania Railroad following Tom Scott's retirement in 1880. He had worked closely with his predecessor, and he saw the dangers that Scott's speculative ventures had posed to the stability of the company. As president, Roberts avoided such excesses of personal capitalism, relying instead on his engineering expertise to build the PRR into an orderly and smoothly functioning railroad system.

Pennsylvania Historical and Museum Commission, Pennsylvania State Archives.

manipulative persona. He seemed, in fact, rather like J. Edgar Thomson, considered by many to be the greatest president that the Pennsylvania Railroad had ever known.[15]

As Thomson's protégé, Roberts had some large shoes to fill, and fill them he did. He fended off a new round of challenges from rival trunk lines and financial interlopers. He equipped the Pennsylvania Railroad to accommodate a flood of new traffic, as the railroads finally became such efficient carriers of freight that they could best their old nemesis, the Erie Canal. He accelerated the coordination of Lines East and Lines West into a single great system that blanketed the northeastern United States. Thanks to his purchase of the Philadelphia, Wilmington & Baltimore Railroad in 1881, the Pennsylvania Railroad became the largest railroad, the largest transportation enterprise, and the largest corporation in the world.

Rivalry with the Reading

Roberts stepped into the PRR presidency at a time of renewed conflict with the railroad's longtime adversary, the Reading. During much of the nineteenth century, even as J. Edgar Thomson, Tom Scott, and their fellow PRR executives waged war against the three great rival trunk lines, they also battled a serious threat nearer to home. Chartered in 1833, the Reading built north from Philadelphia along the valley of the Schuylkill River, paralleling the Schuylkill Navigation canal. The company benefited from the anthracite boom, hauling millions of tons of hard coal to its extensive terminal facilities at Port Richmond, on the Delaware River, a short distance north of Philadelphia. In 1856, the Reading's control over the Lebanon Valley Railroad had enabled the company to offer service between Philadelphia and Harrisburg, in competition with the PRR. By the time of the Civil War, the Reading was the dominant carrier in Pennsylvania, with greater revenues and more robust profits than the PRR. J. Edgar Thomson's 1871 lease of the United New Jersey Railroad & Canal Companies, along with the acquisition of the lines that became part of the Pennsylvania Company, enabled the PRR to surpass the Reading's performance. Yet, the Reading remained a formidable competitor to the PRR, with its executives capable of forming alliances with other carriers to further invade PRR territory or—perhaps the ultimate nightmare—create another trunk line between tidewater and the Midwest.

The history of the Reading was inescapably intertwined with the career of its most influential president, Franklin B. Gowen. Intelligent, eloquent, and mercurial, Gowen charmed and bullied his way through the world of nineteenth-century railroading. John D. Rockefeller described him best, as "our brilliant and resourceful Gowen, this wonderfully resourceful man, who electrified audiences in Philadelphia with his great schemes," and, even more succinctly, as "an able and erratic gentleman."[16] From an early age, Gowen seemed to have nurtured a calculated resentment against the Pennsylvania Railroad and its executives. As early as 1866, Gowen, then a thirty-year-old attorney for the Reading, used his considerable oratorical skills to trounce the PRR's counsel in a case before the Pennsylvania Supreme Court. In a stunning legal victory, Gowen prevented the PRR from denying the Reading and the Atlantic & Great Western access to the Catawissa Railroad, a critical link between the oilfields of northwestern Pennsylvania and New York. It was something of a pyrrhic victory, however, as the delays associated with the case contributed to the bankruptcy of the A&GW and its withdrawal from the project.

Despite that setback, Gowen's reputation soared, and within three years he was president of the Reading. Gowen was determined to bring order to the anthracite fields by any means necessary. He copied the holding company model that Tom Scott had developed, establishing the Philadelphia & Reading Coal & Iron Company.[17] Gowen oversaw the first price-fixing agreements to control anthracite production. He had little tolerance for labor agitation, crushed incipient unions, and took a hard line against the 1877 strikes. Most famously—infamously, to some—he waged a vendetta against the Mollie Maguires, which he regarded as little better than a terrorist organization. Juries, swayed by Gowen's powerful oratory, saw little conflict of interest in his simultaneous roles as Schuylkill County special prosecutor and as an executive of both a railroad and a coal company.[18]

Gowen helped the Reading survive the financial crisis of the 1870s, although at considerable long-term cost to the company. With its double-tracked main line and its impressive engineering standards, the Reading had been very expensive to construct—a situation that in turn mandated high fixed charges. Unlike the locally financed PRR, the Reading's insatiable need for capital soon outstripped the abilities of capitalists in the United States. The Reading thus became the first American railroad to fall under the sway of British financiers. During the 1870s, the London investment-banking firm, McCalmont Brothers & Company, owned a controlling interest in the Reading, and generally gave Gowen free reign in its management. That may have been a mistake, for Gowen soon accumulated a $7 million floating debt—doubly dangerous because it was unsecured by any of the railroad's assets, and because it floated back and forth between the Reading Rail Road and the Reading Coal & Iron Company.

In May 1880, the financial crisis of the 1870s, in tandem with Gowen's rather unorthodox accounting methods, drove the Reading into bankruptcy and severed the long-standing relationship between Gowen and the McCalmonts. At the Reading's March 1881 shareholders' meeting, Gowen was unceremoniously booted from the presidency, yet he remained as a receiver of the bankrupt company. Despite his best efforts—including an impassioned and widely hailed speech at the Philadelphia Academy of Music in which he warned of the dangers of foreign control over the Reading—he was unable to reestablish his authority.

Behind the scenes, however, Gowen experienced considerably more success in his negotiations with New York Central president William H. Vanderbilt. According to the *New York Times*, Gowen, with his winning personality and his extraordinary persuasive abilities, convinced Vanderbilt to join forces with him, extending the New York Central's influence into Pennsylvania. Persuasive though Gowen may have been, it was almost certainly Vanderbilt who took the initiative, largely because he saw the Reading as a mechanism to invade territories that had traditionally been the domain of the Pennsylvania Railroad. To achieve that goal, he needed Gowen's cooperation—and Gowen, overseeing a bankrupt railroad, eagerly sought an alliance with the NYC. In July 1881, Vanderbilt invited Gowen to Saratoga Springs, and the two men agreed to terms.[19]

Following the Saratoga Springs meeting, Vanderbilt acquired a large block of Reading securities and, in January 1882, placed Gowen back in charge of the company. Augustus Schell, a New York attorney and a friend of the Vanderbilt family, carried with him to the Reading's annual shareholders' meeting sufficient proxies, representing the NYC interests, to decide who would control the company. He told no one of Vanderbilt's intentions to support Gowen, however. PRR executives, suspecting that Vanderbilt was willing to support Gowen, accordingly refused an option to purchase a large block of Reading shares. "The reason that the Pennsylvania officers declined to buy out Vanderbilt was that Gowen was a good enough president for them," noted the *New York Times*. "They did not want to interrupt him in his career as a wrecker."[20]

Pennsylvania Railroad officials soon had reason to regret their nonchalance, for Gowen's alliance with Vanderbilt threatened their interests and likewise imperiled the stability of the entire northeastern railroad network. Vanderbilt's involvement, in tandem with the seemingly intractable legal morass associated with the Reading reorganization, persuaded the McCalmonts to divest their holdings in the company. The British investors, who had generally sought stable profitability, yielded to American speculators anxious for a rapid return on their investment. At the same time, the Reading's receivership (the company did not emerge from reorganization until February 1883) seemed to have loosened what few restraints Gowen had ever imposed on himself, and increased his combative attitude toward the Pennsylvania Railroad.[21]

The Fight for the Philadelphia, Wilmington & Baltimore

As one part of their expansionist strategy, Gowen and Vanderbilt planned to extend their influence southward. Despite the Reading's dominance of the anthracite trade and the NYC's superb access to Manhattan, the two executives lacked a direct north–south route connecting the major cities along the Atlantic seaboard.

That absence became all the more acute after 1871, when Thomson gained control over the United Railroad & Canal Companies of New Jersey, eliminating the PRR's dependence on the Reading as a partner in the prewar "Allentown Route" to New York. Yet, while Gowen and Vanderbilt looked to the south, their colleague B&O president John W. Garrett looked to the north. Even though the Philadelphia, Wilmington & Baltimore Railroad carried B&O traffic north to Philadelphia, Garrett envisioned his own secure connection to the Quaker City. Gowen, Vanderbilt, and Garrett cooperated in the development of a new line—the "Bound Brook Route"—linking Baltimore to New York. They succeeded, but at considerable cost to the B&O.

By the late 1870s, the PRR depended more than ever on access to the Philadelphia, Wilmington & Baltimore route between Baltimore and Philadelphia. Despite the collapse of the Southern Railway Security Company, the traffic potential of the South continued to increase, and so too did the value of the new Baltimore & Potomac line to Washington. The PRR's secure link to Baltimore, via Harrisburg and the Northern Central Railway, was certainly adequate for western traffic, but it was inconvenient for freight and passengers traveling along the east coast. Most of the owners of the PW&B were Bostonians, and they had little stake in the fight between the port cities of Philadelphia and Baltimore, and little interest in the trunk-line rate wars that routinely pitted the PRR against the B&O. They were willing to haul freight from either carrier, with equal access for all and discrimination toward none. That proved to be an exceptionally profitable strategy, and the PW&B weathered the depression of the 1870s with relatively few problems. Thanks to the efforts of Samuel Morse Felton and other capable executives, the company managed to pay hefty dividends, while maintaining one of the best physical plants of any railroad in the United States—equal to if not surpassing that of the PRR itself.

John W. Garrett shattered the equilibrium when he attempted to extend the B&O's reach from Baltimore north to Philadelphia, and on to New York. That was an extraordinarily unwise move given the B&O's weak financial condition, and Garrett's motives remain a mystery. He may have feared that the PRR would pro-gressively deny the B&O access to east coast ports, reducing the Baltimore railroad to the status of a regional carrier. Badly stung by Thomson's success in building the Baltimore & Potomac Railroad into Washington, Garrett may also have sought a measure of revenge by extending the B&O to New York and negating much of the advantage that the United Companies lease had given to the PRR. By the late 1870s, moreover, Garrett was losing control over his mental faculties, and he was suffering from what was at best acute exhaustion or at worst the onset of some form of mental illness.[22]

Regardless of his reasons, Garrett's dream was to create a route between Baltimore and Jersey City, constructed to the highest possible engineering standards. More than anyone else, Garrett was aware of the B&O's shaky financial condition, making the construction of an entirely new line an exceedingly unwise proposition. As a temporary expedient, he sought to forge alliances that would carry B&O trains between Philadelphia and New York, avoiding the United Companies lines that had been under PRR control since 1871. The Jersey Central already possessed a line linking Jersey City with Allentown and the anthracite regions, passing through Bound Brook, New Jersey, along the way. The owners of the North Pennsylvania Railroad, awash with profits from the anthracite trade, had sponsored the construction of the Delaware & Bound Brook Railroad, incorporated in 1874, linking the tracks of the Jersey Central at Bound Brook with the Delaware River. The Delaware River Branch of the North Pennsylvania Railroad extended the tracks through the Keystone State, to Jenkintown and a connection with the North Pennsylvania line between Bethlehem and Philadelphia. Initially, all three companies were locally controlled, and operated without the B&O's influence. Linked together, however, the three railroads offered Garrett the possibility of extending the B&O's influence north to New York—with the one notable and, as events transpired, crucial stretch of track in Philadelphia that composed the Junction Railroad.

PRR officials attempted to prevent the completion of the Bound Brook Route, but to no avail. In late 1875 and early 1876, Delaware & Bound Brook workmen were attempting to install a crossing with the PRR's Mercer & Somerset Railroad near Hopewell, New

Jersey. PRR crews stationed a locomotive to block the site, triggering a brief confrontation known as the "Hopewell Frog War"—a reference to the device that enabled wheels from one set of tracks to cross those of another. Local residents were firmly on the side of the Delaware & Bound Brook, a company that promised to end the PRR's monopoly. So, too, were the courts, which permitted construction to continue. On May 1, 1876—just in time for the Centennial Exhibition in Philadelphia—the first passenger trains rolled along the Bound Brook Route between Philadelphia and Communipaw, New Jersey, opposite New York. Through fares were set at $2.65, ten cents lower than the PRR rate.[23]

Thanks to the "New Route," as the line was also known, Garrett could move traffic between Washington and New York without it ever touching PRR rails. For the first time since leasing the United Companies in 1871, the PRR faced competition along the route between Philadelphia and New York. Of equal concern to the PRR's executives, the Bound Brook Route ended the PRR's monopoly over service to such intermediate New Jersey points as Newark, Elizabeth, and Trenton, affording shippers in those cities access to two competing railroads. Only New Brunswick was still captive to the PRR.

Reading president Franklin Gowen also employed the Bound Brook Route in order to strike back at the PRR. Gowen eagerly sought a closer affiliation with the North Pennsylvania Railroad in order to gain access to its new connection to New York. Several North Pennsylvania directors had recently resigned from the board or died, and their successors were anxious to establish an alliance with the Reading. In February 1879, the Reading completed a new connection with the North Pennsylvania Railroad in North Philadelphia, making it easier to ship anthracite to New York over the Bound Brook Route rather than the PRR-controlled Delaware & Raritan Canal. Sugar refiner Edward C. Knight, president of the Delaware & Bound Brook, was a close friend of Gowen's. In May 1879 the two executives had little difficulty negotiating the Reading's lease of both the Delaware & Bound Brook Railroad and the North Pennsylvania Railroad. The Reading did not yet have control over the Jersey Central (and would not do so until 1883), but Gowen none-

theless used his new acquisitions to great advantage. He accused PRR officials of indiscriminate rate cutting and then slashed tariffs on the Bound Brook Route in response. By October 1879, another new connection, this time with the subsidiary Philadelphia, Germantown & Norristown Railroad, permitted passenger trains traveling over the Bound Brook Route to reach that company's terminus at Ninth and Green Streets, much closer to the city center than the PRR's station in West Philadelphia.[24]

For all of his success, however, Gowen's strategy depended on Garrett's willingness to funnel B&O traffic to his lines at Philadelphia. Again working through Knight, Gowen suggested to a highly receptive Garrett that the B&O might like to participate in the Bound Brook Route. However, Garrett soon confronted the terms of the 1860 agreement to build the Junction Railroad through West Philadelphia. All B&O traffic destined for New York from Baltimore and points west would travel north over the Philadelphia, Wilmington & Baltimore, and then over the Junction Railroad, in order to reach the Reading. The PRR, the Reading, and the PW&B each owned a one-third interest in the line, but the B&O did not. Furthermore, a critical one-mile section of the Junction Railroad, between Thirty-Fifth Street and a tunnel underneath Market Street, consisted of an existing stretch of track owned by the PRR. In 1866, PRR executives had audaciously suggested that they, and they alone, controlled that vital segment of the Junction Railroad. The courts disagreed, but PRR officials continued to insist that only the three railroads that were part owners of the Junction Railroad—a group that did not include the B&O—could operate over its tracks. In April 1879, the companies that composed the Bound Brook Route sued for open access to the Junction Railroad. They won a partial victory. In October 1880, the court maintained the B&O's right of access, but permitted PRR officials to restrict operations over the one-mile piece of line solely to PRR locomotives and train crews. On December 1, 1880, with the issue apparently resolved, Garrett shifted the B&O's New York passenger traffic to the Bound Brook route, followed a month later by freight.

Under orders from management, PRR employees did their best to create impediments for B&O traffic.

Pennsylvania Railroad trains moved expeditiously across the Junction Railroad, while B&O trains destined for the Bound Brook Route suffered interminable delays. One B&O train, carrying a congressional delegation to New York, was held for more than five hours. Freight suffered similar treatment, even if it was less vocal in its complaints. Explanations for the delays included crew shortages, emergency maintenance, defective equipment, unexpectedly high traffic levels, or any number of other, obviously fabricated excuses. It took another lawsuit to resolve the issue, again in favor of the B&O.[25]

With the Bound Brook Route giving Garrett access to New York, the B&O's president turned his attentions to the missing link in the chain between Baltimore and Philadelphia. Thus far, the PW&B had provided a connection between the two cities, but there was no guarantee that that company would remain so accommodating—or would continue to be free from the influence of the Pennsylvania Railroad. Garrett was therefore determined to buy the PW&B. His poorly conceived efforts to do so cost him dearly, nearly wrecking his dreams of a route between Washington and New York, and ultimately plunging his company into bankruptcy.

Colonel Henry S. McComb, the freewheeling railroad promoter who had been involved in efforts by Thomson and Scott to establish a Cairo, Illinois-to-New Orleans rail line parallel to the Mississippi River, was the instigating force behind the battle for the PW&B. During the 1860s and 1870s, in addition to soliciting support from PRR officials, McComb had enjoyed a wide and varied railroad career. He was among the original stockholders of Crédit Mobilier, the company responsible for building the Union Pacific. In 1872, he had a falling out with his business associates, accusing them of liberally supplying members of Congress with Crédit Mobilier stock in exchange for political favors. McComb's statements triggered a congressional investigation and made him many enemies. By 1877, moreover, the Illinois Central had defeated his ambitious plans for a Mississippi Valley route, and Colonel McComb turned his attentions northward and eastward.[26]

McComb's plan, to create an alternate, back-door route between Baltimore and Philadelphia, hinged on his efforts to acquire the Delaware Western Railroad,

a twenty-mile line running from Wilmington, Delaware, northwest to Landenberg, Pennsylvania. As early as 1870, McComb was on the board of directors of its predecessor company, the Wilmington & Western Railroad. By 1879, he was buying stock in the Delaware Western, with the idea of inducing a bidding war between the PRR and the B&O.

In March 1880, McComb met with Tom Scott, whom he knew well from their mutual involvement in the Union Pacific, the Texas & Pacific, and other ventures. McComb's timing was impeccably poor. Although the nation was emerging from the depression of the 1870s, little cash was available for speculative ventures, and PRR executives had no wish to trigger a ruinous rate war with the B&O. The Texas & Pacific fiasco and the collapse of other investments, in tandem with the 1877 strikes, had left Scott a broken and dispirited man. Eighteen months before meeting with McComb, Scott had suffered a massive stroke, and remained in poor health. First vice president George Roberts, who also attended the meeting, probably made most of the important decisions.

Scott and Roberts were polite, but evasive. They were willing to purchase McComb's share of the Delaware Western, but only if the maverick financier demonstrated a willingness to assist them in obtaining control over the Philadelphia, Wilmington & Baltimore. In his diary, McComb noted that the two PRR executives promised to "take care of" the Delaware Western, a pledge that could be interpreted as either gentlemanly or threatening. McComb, dissatisfied with the results of the meeting, soon attempted to interest the New York Central in his prize, also with disappointing results. Within a week, McComb upped the ante, endeavoring to charter the Baltimore & Northeastern Railroad as a Baltimore outlet for the Delaware Western. By the end of March, he was making inquiries about the purchase of the West Chester & Philadelphia, which, in conjunction with the other two companies, would have created a roundabout connection between Baltimore and Philadelphia.[27]

During late April and early May, McComb met with Garrett, followed by New York Central president William H. Vanderbilt and Reading president Franklin B. Gowen. The three executives were no more anxious to trigger a rate war and a frenzy of overbuilding than Scott and Roberts had been. Gowen was particularly reluctant, as he had a pretty fair idea of his railroad's shaky financial condition, with the Reading filing for bankruptcy less than a month later. Determined to bring the issue to a head, McComb trooped back to the PRR's headquarters in Philadelphia. On May 21, 1880, he told George Roberts that the construction of the Baltimore & Northeastern would proceed unless the PRR bought out his investments. On May 1, Scott had submitted his resignation, and in another ten days, Roberts knew, he would be the next president of the Pennsylvania Railroad. The PRR's quintessential organization man stared across his desk at an individual who might charitably be described as something of a loose cannon. Roberts knew blackmail when he saw it, and he wanted nothing to do with McComb's schemes. The PRR president probably no longer perceived of McComb as much of a threat, in any event, as the promoter had concluded that the West Chester & Philadelphia was too expensive to acquire, with the better-financed PW&B soon establishing control over the line.[28]

By the end of the year, however, McComb had regrouped, and constituted more of a threat to the PRR's interests than ever before. This time, McComb's timing was perfect. The New York Central was emerging from a bruising rate war, but it faced a threat from the New York, West Shore & Buffalo Railway, whose promoters envisioned a line that would parallel the NYC from Jersey City to Buffalo. Vanderbilt, in conjunction with the Reading interests and with industrialists Andrew Carnegie and Henry Clay Frick, was developing plans to extend the NYC's influence into southern Pennsylvania. Four days before Christmas, when McComb again met with Vanderbilt, the NYC president was receptive to extending his railroad's reach to the south. He agreed to underwrite half of the cost of McComb's Philadelphia-to-Baltimore railroad. In turn, Garrett promised to fund 20 percent, and he suggested that the Jersey Central was good for another 15 percent. Despite his battles with the NYC, Jay Gould was also heavily invested in the project, along with such traditional associates as Sidney Dillon and Russell Sage. Given the Jersey Central's participation in the Bound Brook Route, Gould saw in McComb's plan an opportunity to gain access as far south as Washington.[29]

The support from Vanderbilt, Garrett, and Gould dramatically increased the likelihood that McComb would be able to bring his plans to fruition, a possibility that struck fear into the hearts of the Boston capitalists who controlled the PW&B. Something similar had happened once before. During the early 1860s, the owners of the West Chester & Philadelphia, in conjunction with the Philadelphia & Baltimore Central Railroad, threatened to create a route that very roughly paralleled the PW&B alignment south of Philadelphia. Samuel Morse Felton and other PW&B officials had neutralized that threat by gaining control over the Philadelphia & Baltimore Central and then building a new connection (the Chester Creek Railroad) that left the West Chester & Philadelphia an isolated local carrier of scant value to its owners—and, incidentally, made that bereft company a target for Henry McComb. Now, with McComb and his allies poised to build between Baltimore and Philadelphia, they again threatened the profitability of the PW&B. Nathaniel Thayer, the PW&B's largest investor, collaborated with executives to devise a solution to the McComb threat. Together, they developed a plan to sell their company to the same railroads that were supporting McComb's plans, obviating the necessity of building the new line.

Once they possessed the opportunity to buy the PW&B, Garrett, Gowen, and Gould quickly cast McComb aside. Major New York investors, anxious to prevent a rate war that was certain to follow the construction of a duplicate line, contributed funds to the project. Gould, along with Sage and Dillon, helped to secure the participation of John Jacob Astor, August Belmont, and the banking house of Drexel & Company. The organizers of the consortium offered to give the PRR an essentially meaningless one-third share of the Philadelphia, Wilmington & Baltimore, but first vice president Alexander Cassatt remained aloof.[30]

Despite Cassatt's initial reluctance to buy into the PW&B, the PRR soon gained control over that company. During February, Thayer promised Garrett and his allies that he could persuade his fellow PW&B stockholders to sell at $70 a share, with a deadline of March 15, 1881. By some mechanism, Roberts became aware of the arrangement.[31] On March 7, under Cassatt's direction, the PRR offered Thayer and his fellow investors $78 a share, and soon persuaded them to part with their 39 percent stake in the PW&B. After Cassatt promised the same price for any and all stock made available by April 1, the shares came rolling in. By the deadline, the PRR had acquired 92 percent of the Philadelphia, Wilmington & Baltimore. After both the board of directors and the shareholders unanimously approved a $20 million increase in the PRR's stock, Roberts and Cassatt purchased 217,819 of the 235,901 PW&B shares, at a total cost of a little under $17 million.[32]

The transaction had cost the PRR dearly, yet its executives considered it to be worth every penny. For more than fifty years, the PRR displayed the cancelled check used to purchase the stock, in recognition of the role that the acquisition played in the destiny of the Pennsylvania Railroad. President Roberts gained a reputation as a savvy negotiator and a worthy successor to Thomson and Scott. Cassatt's involvement in the purchase largely redeemed his reputation within the PRR, following his hard-line reaction to the Pittsburgh strikers in 1877. The PRR gained undisputed control over a route linking the nation's political and economic capitals, and solidified its position as the preeminent railroad system in the northeast. With the PW&B acquisition, the PRR also became the nation's leading industrial employer, as well as the largest business corporation in the world.[33]

Once in control of the PW&B, Pennsylvania Railroad officials solidified their supremacy over the B&O in the Philadelphia-to-Washington market. Outmaneuvered by Roberts and Cassatt, the aging and ailing Garrett had little choice other than to buy the Delaware Western, in 1883, and to use its charter to construct a new route between Baltimore and Philadelphia. During the summer of 1884, Roberts acted as Garrett had feared and prohibited B&O passenger trains from using the PW&B, denying access to the Philadelphia and New York markets. Within months Garrett was dead, with his son Robert assuming the presidency of the B&O. By 1886, two years after John Garrett's death, the B&O had built a line that ran from the Canton district of Baltimore, parallel to the PW&B, to a crossing of the Schuylkill River south of Gray's Ferry, along the east bank of the river, past a station at Twenty-Fourth and Chestnut Streets, and through a tunnel to reach a junction with the Reading.

There was one serious problem, however, in that the B&O's new route required that cars be ferried across Baltimore harbor, between Locust Point and Canton. In 1895, the B&O mimicked the Union Railroad, building its own shortcut underneath Baltimore. By that time, electric traction was available, allowing the B&O to avoid the operation of steam locomotives through the Howard Street Tunnel. The B&O was soon able to offer "Royal Blue Line" service that matched or exceeded the PRR passenger trains in both speed and amenities. Despite the success of its passenger service and its innovative use of electric locomotives, the B&O's alignment between Washington and Philadelphia was distinctly inferior to the PW&B/Baltimore & Potomac route. Even without including the cost of the Howard Street Tunnel, the B&O spent $17.8 million on its new line between Baltimore and Philadelphia, considerably more than Roberts and Cassatt had paid the PW&B shareholders. Thanks to John W. Garrett's ill-advised decision to extend the B&O to Baltimore, and to the cost of the Howard Street Tunnel, the B&O entered receivership in 1883 and, along with the Erie, remained among the weakest of the four eastern trunk lines.[34]

Railroading on the Delmarva Peninsula

The 1881 purchase of the Philadelphia, Wilmington & Baltimore gave the PRR access to a web of rail lines through the largely pastoral countryside of the Delmarva Peninsula. Lightly built single-track branches and connecting steamboats calling at isolated ports seemed worlds apart from the PRR main line across Pennsylvania. Even under PRR supervision, the carriers that served the Eastern Shore of Chesapeake Bay never met the expectations of promoters who envisioned an artery of commerce connecting New York and Philadelphia with Hampton Roads and southeastern Virginia. Nevertheless, the Delmarva routes were an important generator of traffic, particularly during harvest season.

Local entrepreneurs developed many of the rail routes through the Delmarva Peninsula long before the PRR took control of the PW&B. The earliest project dated to 1836 and the incorporation of the Delaware Railroad Company. The company lay dormant until 1849, when Delaware State Supreme Court Chief Justice Samuel M. Harrington became involved in the venture. By 1853, he had obtained support from the PW&B, as well as lottery funds from the state of Delaware. The PW&B leased the railroad in 1855, and by 1859 tracks had reached Delmar, at the Maryland state line. Southward progress stopped there, halted by the reluctance of Maryland legislators to grant a corresponding charter in their state, and by the Civil War. After 1865, PW&B officials concentrated on the development of local agricultural branches to the Eastern Shore points of Centreville, Oxford, and Cambridge, Maryland. Additional lines reached the Atlantic Ocean at Rehoboth and Franklin City.[35]

South of Delmar, the Eastern Shore Railroad continued the route of the Delaware Railroad. The Eastern Shore was a Maryland corporation, chartered in 1833, and its promoters intended to follow the western side of the Delmarva Peninsula, bypassing Delaware territory and eventually connecting to Philadelphia. As such, they did their best to prevent the Delaware Railroad from entering the state. Even at that early date, they harbored grand visions of a line to the southern tip of the peninsula, where steamboats would convey traffic to Norfolk. From there, the Portsmouth & Roanoke Railroad stood ready to funnel traffic to the interior of southern Virginia and, by connections with other carriers, offered access to much of the South. As with the Delaware Railroad, the project faded; it would not be revived until 1853. By that time, the promoters of the Eastern Shore had curtailed their plans and agreed to make peace with their Delaware rivals. From a connection with the Delaware Railroad at Delmar, workmen began building south, but the Civil War interrupted construction. Not until November 1866 did rails reach the edge of Tangier Sound and the newly created port of Crisfield.

Shortly afterward, Samuel Harlan, Jr., and others incorporated the Eastern Shore Steamboat Company. The new firm was an extension of their involvement in Harlan, Hollingsworth & Company, a Wilmington, Delaware, manufacturer of ships and railway equipment. For the next several decades, the Eastern Shore Steamboat Company controlled the Eastern Shore Railroad, as a useful mechanism for collecting and distributing traffic from the interior of the Delmarva

Peninsula. As with the Delaware lines, however, PW&B personnel oversaw the operation of the Maryland company. At first, business was hardly promising. Crisfield proved poorly sited for passenger steamers to Norfolk, and there was little traffic with the postwar South in any event. Freight traffic, although modest, grew steadily, as oysters and produce—especially peaches—made their way to northern markets.[36]

By the late 1870s, the brothers Uriah Hunt Painter and William Painter were developing plans to extend rail service farther down the Delmarva Peninsula, to a more suitable port. Uriah Painter had gained considerable renown as a Civil War correspondent, but his railroading efforts probably benefited far more from his experience as clerk of the House Committee on Post Offices and Post Roads, and from the resulting connections with virtually everyone with influence in Washington. He later went into the timber business in Delaware, and was generally involved in a great many regional projects. The Painter brothers obtained the Maryland and Virginia charters for the Peninsula Railroad, with rights to lay tracks from a junction with the Eastern Shore Railroad at Kings Creek, Maryland, and southward toward Cape Charles. Aside from a few miles of line between Kings Creek and Pocomoke City, little action resulted.[37]

The Painters were typical of the small-scale local entrepreneurs who allied themselves with the Pennsylvania Railroad, after beginning projects that they often could not bring to fruition. When they had reached the limits of their abilities, officials affiliated with the PRR often intervened, so long as the plans held merit. Such was the case with the Peninsula Railroad and the other transportation arteries in the region. Two capitalists, each of whom possessed far greater resources than the Painters, stepped in to complete their work. One was Erie, Pennsylvania, businessman William Lawrence Scott, who had long been allied with the PRR. Scott had been the primary promoter of the Erie & Pittsburgh Railroad, and had also arranged its lease to the PRR in March 1870. He provided an equally valuable service by buying out the recalcitrant bondholders of the Columbus, Chicago & Indiana Central and enabling PRR officials to solidify their control over that key western subsidiary. Scott was by no means a Pennsylvania Railroad partisan, however: he served as a director of several railroads hostile to the PRR—necessary, in his view, to maintain his rights as a shipper. He was primarily interested in the region's railroads as a mechanism to develop his real estate holdings at the southern end of the Delmarva Peninsula.[38]

The other key instigator was the PRR's first vice president, Alexander J. Cassatt. In 1882, Cassatt temporarily left the employ of the PRR and oversaw the consolidation of the Delmarva Peninsula's rail lines,

south of Delmar, into the New York, Philadelphia & Norfolk Railroad. He became that company's president in 1885, but he maintained his ties with his former employer and after a short hiatus resumed his post on the PRR board of directors. In addition to his close connections with Pennsylvania Railroad officials, Cassatt also took advantage of the PRR's recent acquisition of the Philadelphia, Wilmington & Baltimore. In 1883, managers from the two companies agreed to devote 20 percent of the revenues derived

Figure 53. The Pennsylvania Railroad dominated transportation on the Delmarva Peninsula through a series of alliances with local carriers. One of the most important was the New York, Philadelphia & Norfolk Railroad, which extended the PRR's traffic as far south as Cape Charles, Virginia. The NYP&N operated a variety of ferries, tugs, and car floats to transport freight and passengers to Norfolk and other destinations. The name of the steamship *Pennsylvania*, shown here circa 1905, reflected the extensive maritime services that the PRR and its subsidiaries operated on Chesapeake Bay, as well as on the Great Lakes and around New York Harbor.

Detroit Publishing Company Photograph Collection, Library of Congress, Prints & Photographs Division, LC-D4-33854.

from interchange traffic with the New York, Philadelphia & Norfolk to the payment of interest on that company's bonds. The combined PRR/PW&B support facilitated an expansion of the Delmarva Peninsula lines. Together, Cassatt and William Scott elected to bypass Cherrystone, the port at the northern end of the traditional route to Hampton Roads. During the summer of 1883, Scott bought a large estate at the southern tip of the Delmarva Peninsula, and soon transferred most of the property to the New York, Philadelphia & Norfolk for use as the new Cape Charles yards. Cassatt then took over, organizing the dredging of a harbor (at the expense of the federal government) and the development of the marshlands into a ferry terminal. The entire route was completed in 1884, and by 1885 both fast passenger steamboats and car ferries were plying the waters of Chesapeake Bay. Initially, through Pullmans ran onto car ferries, allowing passengers to travel to Norfolk, and even as far as Florida, without detraining. That service lasted only until 1887, forcing travelers to walk onto the steamboats, but tugboats and car floats continued to convey freight cars directly to Norfolk.[39]

The New York, Philadelphia & Norfolk more than lived up to the expectations of its promoters, and additional construction and consolidation completed the rail network on the Delmarva Peninsula. In addition to the north–south spine between Wilmington and Cape Charles, lateral ribs branched off into the countryside. Mainly built or acquired between 1890 and 1905, the routes served numerous locations along Chesapeake Bay, reaching the Atlantic Ocean at Rehoboth, Delaware, and Ocean City and Franklin City, Maryland.[40] Although the PRR and its PW&B subsidiary developed a virtual monopoly over rail traffic on the Delmarva Peninsula, the two companies owned relatively few lines outright. Aside from the Delaware Railroad and the New York, Philadelphia & Norfolk, most of the other carriers remained nominally independent, with either the PRR or the PW&B owning enough stock to afford a measure of control.

Only when traffic demands warranted, or when there was a danger that the independent companies might fall under the sway of the Baltimore & Ohio or some other competing system, did PRR officials authorize outright acquisition. For a brief period, the

B&O offered service across the Delmarva Peninsula, by train to Bay Ridge, then ferry across Chesapeake Bay to Claiborne, then train again (along the Baltimore & Eastern Shore Railroad) to Salisbury and Ocean City. PRR officials quickly gained control over the Baltimore & Eastern Shore, which became the nucleus of the Baltimore, Chesapeake & Atlantic, ending the B&O's access to the Delmarva Peninsula.[41]

The Eastern Shore was heavily indented with bays and channels, ensuring that independent steamboat operators carried freight, passengers, and excursionists to Baltimore and other points on the opposite side of Chesapeake Bay. As such, managers from the PRR and its subsidiaries were never able to translate their rail monopoly into high rates. Between 1894 and 1905, the PRR bought out most of the independent steamship lines, largely to maintain rail tariffs. During the 1870s, the Delaware Railroad acquired many of the branches on the Eastern Shore (to Centreville, Oxford, and Cambridge, Maryland), with a general merger taking place in 1899. On the opposite side of the peninsula, the routes to Lewes and Rehoboth, and to Franklin City, which in 1883 became the Delaware, Maryland & Virginia Railroad, likewise passed to the PRR the following year. The last independent line, the Queen Anne's Railroad, with a route cutting across the peninsula, came under direct PRR control in 1905 as part of the Maryland, Delaware & Virginia Railway.[42]

Regardless of the precise ownership status of the Delmarva lines, Philadelphia, Wilmington & Baltimore officials, in consultation with their PRR colleagues, were responsible for the coordination of operations, as well as long-term strategic decisions. By the early twentieth century, the PRR's Delmarva subsidiaries operated a wide range of steamship services, ranging from Cape Charles–Norfolk car floats to sightseeing cruises, to small steamboats that nosed their way into hundreds of landing stages along the rivers that fed into both sides of Chesapeake Bay.[43] For many decades, the region retained a pastoral quality, as trains and steamboats gathered produce for northern markets, and sent work-weary city dwellers to be refreshed by the cool ocean breezes at a growing number of resorts.[44]

The Reading vs. the Pennsylvania Railroad, in Eastern Pennsylvania

Given that both the PRR and the Reading maintained their headquarters in Philadelphia, it was hardly surprising that the two companies contested for dominance in the Quaker City. The most visible rivalry erupted in the center of the city when each company constructed landmark passenger terminals. That competition with the Reading forced PRR officials to confront an issue that would trouble the PRR for most of its history—how to balance the PRR's operational needs with the convenience of the city's traveling public.

With the completion of the Philadelphia & Columbia Railroad in 1834, passenger cars reached the heart of Philadelphia, in conjunction with the City Railroad, the Northern Liberties & Penn Township Railroad, or the Southwark Rail-Road. Since the 1850s, many PRR executives, most notably Herman Haupt, had favored efficiency over proximity to the city center. He, and others, had advocated a station site west of the Schuylkill River in order to avoid the use of horses along the City Railroad. In October 1864, the PRR completed a new station at Thirtieth and Market Streets in West Philadelphia, and then abandoned passenger service into the city proper. The construction of the West Philadelphia ("Centennial") Station near the same site reinforced the aversion of PRR executives to offering service into the center of the city.

By the 1880s, however, Philadelphia's commercial center and its passenger terminals moved closer to each other, as the two embodiments of middle-class public space—railway stations and department stores—assumed grandiose proportions.[45] In 1876, when John Wanamaker opened his "Grand Depot" department store (located, fittingly enough, in a former PRR freight station at Thirteenth and Market Streets), he shifted Philadelphia's commercial hub farther west, away from the Delaware River. The construction of a new City Hall at the intersection of Broad and Market Streets had the same effect.

PRR and Reading officials reacted to Philadelphia's urban growth by erecting massive new passenger terminals, with the PRR striking first. In August 1879, the board approved the construction of the new Broad Street Station, just west of City Hall. George Roberts, at that time the PRR's first vice president, took charge of the project. He selected the Philadelphia architectural and engineering firm of Wilson Brothers, whose personnel were well known to him. The company's partners, Henry A., John A., and Joseph M. Wilson, were the grandsons of Major John Wilson, who had surveyed the Philadelphia & Columbia Railroad, and the sons of William Hasell Wilson, who had also contributed his engineering talents to the PRR. In the summer of 1874, a few years before work began on Broad Street Station, the board had given William H. Wilson charge of the PRR's newly created Real Estate Department, and he was in an excellent position to work with his three sons.[46] The Wilson brothers had already collaborated on numerous PRR projects, including the Baltimore & Potomac depot in Washington and new stations on the Main Line, west of Philadelphia. In August 1874, the board granted Joseph Wilson a leave of absence in order to assist in preparations for the 1876 Centennial Exhibition. He continued to receive a monthly retainer from the PRR, while working largely on the PRR's facilities at the exhibition grounds.[47]

Under the guidance of Roberts and the Wilson brothers, construction crews erected a magnificent Victorian Gothic edifice at the corner of Fifteenth and Filbert Streets, opposite City Hall. The station was an imposing pile of brick and granite, with a 176-foot-high clock tower that was nevertheless overshadowed by the nearby statue of William Penn atop City Hall. The station's headhouse stretched for 193 feet along Fifteenth Street, and for 122 feet to the west along Filbert Street. Two train sheds extended farther west, toward the Schuylkill River. The facility also included a new freight station at Fifteenth and Market Streets. After spending $4.3 million on construction, PRR officials opened Broad Street Station on December 5, 1881, eighteen months after Roberts had become the PRR's president.[48]

From the west, passenger trains crossed the Schuylkill River over a temporary replacement for the 1805-vintage Market Street Permanent Bridge, which had succumbed to fire in 1875. They avoided city streets by entering Broad Street Station on an iron elevated line that gave way to a stone viaduct as the tracks approached the station.[49] The combined structure, more than two thousand feet in length, was properly known as the Filbert Street Extension, but locals eventually referred to it as the "Chinese Wall." When the station opened, the area to the north of Filbert Street was an industrial zone, where the presence of noisy and smoky locomotives mattered little. By the early twentieth century, however, the city's commercial interests had become increasingly vocal in their protests over the rail traffic, as well as the viaduct and the low, dank street tunnels that led under it—all of which prevented commercial development along the north side of Market Street, occupied valuable real estate, and restricted access to northwestern Philadelphia. For many years they did their best to force the PRR to demolish the structure.[50]

From the perspective of PRR operating officials, Broad Street Station soon became a major bottleneck. In March 1881, six months before the station opened, the PRR purchased the Philadelphia, Wilmington & Baltimore Railroad, along with its subsidiary, the West Chester & Philadelphia Railroad. There seemed little reason to retain the small West Chester & Philadelphia depot at Thirty-First and Chestnut Streets in West Philadelphia, and after January 1, 1882, the PRR began routing trains from both of its new acquisitions across the Schuylkill River, over the Filbert Street Extension, and into Broad Street Station—immediately filling it to capacity. As more and more people moved to the outskirts of Philadelphia, they traveled to work along the PRR Main Line, the Chestnut Hill Branch, and other routes, ending their commute at an increasingly congested Broad Street Station. By 1886, more than a million people a month were using the facility.

In response to the overcrowding, workers repeatedly enlarged the facilities at Broad Street Station. In 1889, the freight station was removed from the site, banished to a new facility at Seventeenth and Market Streets.[51] By 1893, Philadelphia architect Frank Furness had overseen the construction of a new ten-story addition, blending its High Victorian motifs with the Victorian Gothic of the original structure. Furness was an imaginative and flamboyant architect with a flair for the dramatic. His original designs proved too extravagant for the more conservative PRR managers, who demanded modifications. The remodeled and expanded station was spectacular, nonetheless. The extended headhouse dwarfed the original structure, extending as far south as Market Street. The additional space enabled PRR officials to move the company's general offices from their location at 233 South Fourth Street to the station, where they remained until 1930. A massive vaulted train shed replaced the two earlier, smaller ones. Covering an area measuring 306 feet by 595 feet, and extending to a height of 108 feet, it was by far the largest single-span train shed in the world. West of the Schuylkill River, two short tunnels created grade separations that permitted north–south traffic to flow without interference from the east–west main line.[52]

Reading Rail Road officials soon sought to match the PRR's Broad Street Station. During the late 1880s, Reading president Austin Corbin attempted to consolidate the Reading's three outdated Philadelphia passenger facilities into one grand terminal that would rival Broad Street Station. In 1890, Archibald A. McLeod succeeded Corbin, and he obtained a municipal franchise to move the Reading's main terminal from Ninth and Green Streets, a few blocks south and west, to be closer to the central business district. Construction on the new Reading Terminal began in July 1891 and was completed in January 1893. In the planning stages, it was larger than the PRR's original 1881 Broad Street Station, but that facility's expansion in 1892 and 1893 allowed PRR officials to claim the largest station in the city. Size notwithstanding, Reading Terminal was conveniently located at Twelfth and Market Streets, just east of City Hall. More important, the Reading possessed a direct route through North Philadelphia, as well as a four-mile advantage in distance over the PRR in the highly competitive Philadelphia–New York passenger service. Unlike Broad Street Station, demolished in 1952, the Reading Terminal still survives, as part of the Pennsylvania Convention Center, home of the Reading Terminal Market.

The conflict between the PRR and the Reading also extended into Philadelphia's suburbs, and beyond. Between 1881 and 1884, the PRR board authorized the construction of several lines paralleling the Reading. One irritant to the Reading was the Chestnut Hill branch in suburban Philadelphia, less than seven miles long and, on a cost-per-mile basis, one of the

Figure 54. (top) The opening of Broad Street Station in 1881 marked the return of PRR passenger service to Center City Philadelphia. From West Philadelphia, trains crossed the Schuylkill River and traveled along the Filbert Street Extension, visible in the right background of the photo, before stopping underneath a low peaked-roof train shed. The original Victorian Gothic station soon proved inadequate for rising passenger levels, and in 1892 and 1893 architect Frank Furness designed a High Victorian addition that would be built along the south side of the original structure (at the left edge of the photo). (bottom) The new Broad Street Station, with its massive arched trainshed, was completed at virtually the same time as the Reading Terminal, located a few blocks to the east. Philadelphia's ornate City Hall, under construction between 1871 and 1901, is at the right edge of the photograph, across the street from the PRR's terminus.

(top) Temple University Libraries, Urban Archives, Philadelphia, Pennsylvania.(bottom) Detroit Publishing Company Photograph Collection, Library of Congress Prints & Photographs Division, LC-D4-12941.

most expensive stretches of track that the PRR ever constructed. That line, like its Reading counterpart that dated to the 1850s, was devoted primarily to serving one of the more prestigious residential suburbs of Philadelphia. The PRR's venture was in conjunction with director Henry H. Houston's 1884 plan to construct a planned residential community, Wissahickon Heights. While most senior PRR executives resided in the affluent Main Line suburbs to the west of Philadelphia, Chestnut Hill also became one of the city's most desirable residential areas, and the community generated considerable commuter traffic for both the PRR and the Reading.[53]

Competition for Anthracite

The duplication of facilities represented by the Chestnut Hill branch was but a sideshow compared with efforts by PRR executives to invade the heart of the Reading's territory by building a parallel line up the Schuylkill Valley. To some degree, President Roberts was retaliating against the Reading's involvement in the Bound Brook Route. Yet, conflicts over anthracite long antedated the Bound Brook line, or even the Roberts presidency. In the decade that followed the end of the Civil War, J. Edgar Thomson's associate Isaac J. Wistar was responsible for managing the PRR's anthracite properties, as well as its Pennsylvania Canal Company subsidiary. The PRR invested more than $5 million in the anthracite business, but the results were less than satisfactory. Despite improvements to the PRR-owned canals along the North Branch and the main stem of the Susquehanna River, the independent Susquehanna & Tide Water Canal controlled access to Chesapeake Bay. In 1872 the Reading leased the Susquehanna & Tide Water Canal, blocking the PRR's water route to the south. Pennsylvania's 1874 constitution prohibited all transportation companies, including the PRR, from making additional investments in mining properties, although it left untouched the PRR's existing holdings. The depression that began that year had a more deleterious effect, causing many of the PRR's shareholders to question whether their company had any business being involved in coal mining. As the economy recovered, PRR executives

were determined to place their anthracite properties on a stable and profitable footing, but they faced two recurring problems. First, the Reading dominated the carriage of anthracite to tidewater, and its executives were bound to oppose the PRR's plans. Second, anthracite prices were notoriously unstable, and unless someone could bring order to the coalfields, no one was likely to make much of a profit.

Reading president Franklin B. Gowen was the key to the anthracite trade. Gowen made several attempts to cartelize the anthracite business, although his actions promised scant benefit for the PRR. In 1873, he brokered a settlement among the major anthracite coal carriers, including the Reading; the Lehigh Valley; the Delaware, Lackawanna & Western; the Jersey Central; and the Delaware & Hudson, assigning each a share of the anthracite trade and specifying what rates they might charge. The PRR, with little anthracite traffic, did not join the 1873 cartel. When Gowen's cartel collapsed in August 1876, PRR executives professed little concern. By November 1877, a combination of economic crisis and labor unrest had pushed anthracite prices to record lows, encouraging the carriers to seek a new cartel agreement. In December, no less a personage than President Tom Scott participated in the discussions, the first time that a PRR executive had attended. In January 1878, the new cartel agreement gave the PRR a minuscule 7¼ percent share of the anthracite traffic, befitting the company's minor involvement in the hard coal trade. Moreover, in October 1878, when representatives from the Lehigh Valley refused to accept their quota, the cartel again collapsed.[54]

With the chronic instability and ultimate failure of the cooperative anthracite price-fixing agreements, PRR officials possessed a powerful incentive to increase their market share through competitive system building. The most immediate problem was that the PRR lacked convenient access to tidewater. Even though anthracite could reach New York markets, relying in part on the PRR-controlled Belvidere Delaware Railroad, such shipments required the cooperation of the Lehigh Valley. The only alternative was to send the coal west to Sunbury, south to Harrisburg, and then east again to Philadelphia. Direct access to the anthracite fields, from the south, would be a much better option. What made the situation all the more frustrating was that those coalfields contained more than one billion tons of recoverable coal—or so eminent mining engineer Joseph Smith Harris informed the PRR's board of directors in October 1880.[55]

With so much coal available, with the economy recovering from the depression of the 1870s, and with the Reading cooperating with the Jersey Central and the Baltimore & Ohio to build the Bound Brook Route between Philadelphia and New York, PRR officials possessed an irresistible temptation to take action. In the railroad's 1882 *Annual Report*, President George Roberts noted that the Schuylkill Valley generated more local traffic than any other comparable region of Pennsylvania, and that the Reading's dominance in that area deprived the PRR of its rightful share of those revenues. Roberts need hardly have mentioned that the real prize lay in the anthracite fields that were located barely a hundred miles from Philadelphia. Capturing that market would certainly constitute a fair measure of revenge for the Reading's involvement in the creation of the Bound Brook Route. In a convoluted turnabout, PRR executives pledged to build a new rail line along the Schuylkill River in order to protect the coal lands that an earlier generation of managers had acquired in order to protect the operations of the Pennsylvania Canal Company.[56]

Construction on the first segment of the route to the anthracite fields began late in 1881. In June 1883, PRR interests incorporated the Pennsylvania Schuylkill Valley Railroad as a consolidation of several existing companies.[57] Workers built rapidly through Norristown and Phoenixville, reaching Reading in November 1884. In December 1884, in a bid to halt further construction, Reading officials organized yet another pooling arrangement, but offered the PRR only 8 percent of total production. That quota translated to 2.4 million tons, a 22 percent reduction over what the railroad had transported the year before. Not surprisingly, PRR officials rejected the offer, and sent construction crews back into the field. By November 1886, they had extended tracks to Pottsville. Additional construction to New Boston Junction (Newton) provided access to the Lehigh Valley Railroad, with trackage rights to the anthracite fields in the vicinity of Hazleton, as well as a connection with the PRR line along the North Branch of the Susquehanna River to Wilkes-Barre.[58]

The PRR's Schuylkill Valley route, built within a stone's throw of the Reading, was one of the few examples of needless overbuilding on the system, threatening to destabilize rates on anthracite traffic.[59] Unfortunately for Roberts, the Reading—through the Philadelphia & Reading Coal & Iron Company—already controlled the region's most valuable anthracite properties. As such, the PRR would forever be fighting for anthracite traffic. The Pennsylvania Railroad line, as the second to be built up the valley, was well engineered but followed a less-than-ideal route. As a result, the PRR's anthracite transportation costs to Philadelphia fluctuated between 54.4 and 61.0 cents per ton, depending on routing, compared with 44.7 cents for the Reading.[60] Given high construction, operation, and maintenance costs, PRR officials were anxious to recoup their investment by hauling as much hard coal as possible, at exceedingly low rates. J. P. Morgan and his associates, heavily invested in the area's rail and mining operations, took no pleasure at the prospect of a rate war between the PRR and the Reading—a conflict that was certain to involve the other anthracite carriers as well.

By the time the Pennsylvania Schuylkill Valley Railroad entered service, Morgan had already intervened in the longstanding dispute between the PRR and Reading. More significantly, he had also imposed restraint on William H. Vanderbilt and his fellow New York Central investors. Since the 1870s, the PRR and the New York Central had emerged as by far the two strongest trunk lines. Their executives engaged in vicious rate wars, as they competed for long-haul traffic. Yet, despite their competitiveness, PRR and NYC executives each had refrained from invading the territory of the other. During the early 1880s, however, the establishment of the Bound Brook Route and the construction of the Pennsylvania Schuylkill Valley had involved the NYC in the escalating conflict between the PRR and the Reading. Once the PRR had invaded his railroad's territory, Gowen was eager for revenge, and he was anxious to enlist Vanderbilt's assistance. The NYC president, determined to replace the Lackawanna connection that he had lost to Jay Gould, considered Gowen a useful, albeit temporary ally. Together,

Gowen and Vanderbilt attacked the PRR's territory to both the north and the south. In their efforts to tap the bituminous coal reserves of north-central Pennsylvania, while simultaneously building a new railroad across the southern part of the state, Vanderbilt and Gowen triggered an open conflict between the nation's two leading trunk lines. In bringing about a peace between the PRR and the NYC, Morgan emerged as the only winner, enhancing his reputation while serving notice that, henceforth, bankers would play an ever more important role in the affairs of the railroads.

The West Shore, the Beech Creek, and the South Penn: Bankers and Railroaders

The conflict between the Pennsylvania Railroad and the New York Central began as an act of unscrupulous promotion that amounted to little better than extortion. For many decades, the NYC had operated a route from Manhattan north along the east bank of the Hudson River, and then west from Albany to Buffalo and, by way of the Lake Shore & Michigan Southern, to Chicago. Under the management of the Vanderbilt family, the NYC was an efficient and generally prosperous company, yet one that labored under the competition from the nearby Erie Canal and the Great Lakes. Given the high volume of water traffic flowing across New York—to say nothing of the freight carried by the Erie and the other trunk lines—there was little need for a new rail route through the region. Yet, two groups of promoters assembled a new rail link between New York and Cleveland, Ohio, with plans to proceed farther west to Chicago.

One threat to the NYC's interests emerged from the New York, West Shore & Buffalo Railway. The western side of the Hudson River, as far north as Albany, suffered from poor rail service and limited access to the NYC tracks on the opposite shore. During the 1870s, local entrepreneurs had attempted to build along the west shore, but with little success. In 1881, German-born financier Charles F. Woerishoffer joined forces with Edward F. Winslow (a cousin of Edward Winslow, of banking house Winslow, Lanier & Company), developing an audacious plan to complete the route and to extend it west to Buffalo, creating a new trunk line. One

of Woerishoffer's biographers noted that the financier "had the German ideas of open fight, and he attacked everything indiscriminately."[61] That seemed an apt description, for Woerishoffer and his associates proposed nothing less than to take on William H. Vanderbilt and the New York Central. They envisioned a 425-mile long, double-track railroad from Weehawken, New Jersey, to Buffalo, New York, paralleling the NYC for virtually the entire distance. In February 1880, the two entrepreneurs incorporated the West Shore, piecing together a series of railroads, dating back to the railway boom of the immediate post–Civil War period. The route followed the west shore of the Hudson River to Albany, and then turned east along the south bank of the Mohawk River (the NYC followed the north side) to Utica and points west. Woerishoffer and Winslow recruited sleeping car magnate George M. Pullman, along with one of Pullman's vice presidents, Horace Porter. Pullman and the Vanderbilt family had something of a history, and had not been on the best of terms since the NYC executives had subsidized efforts by Webster Wagner to develop sleeping cars. Wagner, as Pullman's chief competitor, had recently signed a contract with the New York Central, giving the Wagner Palace Car Company the exclusive right to operate sleeping cars throughout the NYC system. The West Shore project would afford Pullman the coveted opportunity to route his cars into the NYC's territory.[62]

At Buffalo, the promoters of the West Shore planned to link up with the New York, Chicago & St. Louis Railroad, organized in February 1881 and better known as the Nickel Plate Road. Midwestern speculators, including coal and iron magnate Samuel Thomas, banker George I. Seney, and attorney Calvin S. Brice, had established a route that again closely paralleled the NYC, between Buffalo and Chicago. Although consisting of only a single track, the line was built to commendable engineering standards, with low grades, broad curves, and long stretches of straight track. Jay Gould was keenly interested in the progress of the Nickel Plate, which he anticipated would bridge the gap between the Wabash at Toledo and the Lackawanna at Buffalo. William H. Vanderbilt was equally determined to gain control of the company, both to keep it out of Gould's hands and to ensure that he could maintain the NYC's rates on midwestern traffic.[63]

Vanderbilt had few illusions regarding the purpose of the two new lines. In August 1884, he told a reporter from the *New York Tribune* that "the West Shore was built as a blackmailing scheme, just as the Nickel Plate was."[64] Vanderbilt believed that he had little choice other than to neutralize both threats. The Nickel Plate was easily, if not inexpensively, dealt with. In October 1882, only days after the route entered service, Vanderbilt used more than $6.5 million of the Lake Shore & Michigan Southern's resources to purchase a controlling interest in the upstart line. The West Shore was somewhat more problematic. Now that the Nickel Plate was in the NYC camp, the company lacked an outlet west of Buffalo. In the long term, moreover, the West Shore's promoters would have experienced considerable difficulty in competing against the well-capitalized New York Central, and they probably never intended to. Instead, it is likely that they wanted to create a strong enough threat to the NYC's interests so that Vanderbilt would agree to buy them out at a healthy profit.

Pennsylvania Railroad executives had little reason to support the construction of either the Nickel Plate or the West Shore. A second, competing railroad along the entire NYC mainline would have harmed Vanderbilt, but it would also have forced rates on all of the trunk lines, the PRR included, to ruinously low levels. Furthermore, prior to Vanderbilt's incursions into Pennsylvania there is scant evidence to suggest that PRR officials invested in or otherwise supported the West Shore. Pennsylvania Railroad managers did agree to some through passenger services in conjunction with the West Shore, and allowed that company temporarily to use PRR facilities at Jersey City, but there was nothing unusual about that. Vanderbilt was nonetheless furious at the West Shore–Nickel Plate combination, and he blamed the PRR, at least in part, for the threat to his railroad's interests.[65]

Vanderbilt retaliated—if that is the proper word, for it was difficult to determine where retaliation left off and a realistic appraisal of the NYC's interests began—by supporting two incursions into the PRR's territory. One project involved an invasion of the PRR's bituminous coal territory in north-central Pennsylvania, along with a proposal to extend the Reading to Buffalo. The other development, one that

was more spectacular, but ultimately less destructive of the PRR's interests, led to the construction of a new mainline railroad across southern Pennsylvania.

Both endeavors depended on the participation of the Reading and its ambitious president, Franklin Gowen. The Reading's 1880 bankruptcy did little to dampen Gowen's enthusiasm for westward expansion, and he soon enlisted Vanderbilt's aid in an attempt to extend the Reading west to Lake Erie. In return, Vanderbilt and his NYC associates hoped that Gowen could improve their access to northeastern Pennsylvania's anthracite fields, while giving them a link to markets in Philadelphia. More importantly, Vanderbilt and Gowen each hoped that they could divert bituminous coal production in north-central Pennsylvania away from the PRR.

The origins of the projected line to north-central Pennsylvania, what became the Beech Creek Railroad, dated to the years just prior to the Civil War. In 1859, mining interests in Tioga County, Pennsylvania, had organized the Fall Brook Coal Company, under the control of George J. Magee. By 1877, they controlled several railroads that stretched north to a connection with the Erie at Corning, New York, and then to the New York Central main line at Lyons, midway between Syracuse and Rochester. By the end of the decade, however, Tioga County's mines were both depleted and affected by labor agitation. The New York Central interests accordingly decided to build west into Clearfield County, long a bastion of the PRR, in order to tap the coal reserves there. In 1882, Vanderbilt and his associates joined forces with Magee and other mine operators by incorporating the Clearfield Bituminous Coal Company. The new firm acquired thirty-three thousand acres of coal lands in Clearfield and Centre counties, and laid plans to link those properties to the existing Fall Brook Coal Company lines that connected Tioga County with the New York Central.[66]

The cooperation between Gowen and Vanderbilt was linked to the NYC president's efforts to control Jay Gould. Traditionally, the NYC had carried westbound anthracite traffic coming off of the Delaware, Lackawanna & Western Railroad to Buffalo and points beyond. Following Gould's August 1880 announcement that he intended to extend the Lackawanna to Buffalo, Vanderbilt intended to starve the upstart of revenue. Accordingly, he was anxious to shift anthracite traffic from the Lackawanna to the Reading, yet he lacked convenient access to his new ally. With the support of the NYC, the Fall Brook Coal Company restarted construction on the Jersey Shore, Pine Creek & Buffalo Railway, an unbuilt line dating to 1870.[67] With the completion of the Pine Creek route, Vanderbilt would possess a direct rail connection between the NYC and the Reading at Williamsport, Pennsylvania. Vanderbilt would then be able to send shipments, including lucrative anthracite traffic, between the Great Lakes and Philadelphia, bypassing both the Lackawanna and the PRR. To Gowen's great delight, the Reading would be able to use the Pine Creek line and a friendly connection with the Buffalo, New York & Philadelphia Railway (the former Buffalo & Washington Railway) to reach Lake Erie, at Buffalo, transforming the Reading from a regional anthracite carrier to a major eastern trunk line.[68]

There was a second, even more immediate threat to the PRR. The Fall Brook Coal Company, with the support of the New York Central interests, built a second railroad, stretching from Jersey Shore Junction, on the Pine Creek, west to the Clearfield District coalfields. Originally incorporated as the Susquehanna & South Western Railroad, and soon renamed the Beech Creek, Clearfield & South Western Railroad, the new line was built to the engineering standards of the 1880s and possessed grades that were far more favorable than the PRR route from Tyrone into the Clearfield District. Vanderbilt kept a careful eye on the Beech Creek, assigning his son Cornelius as vice president and treasurer. His son-in-law Hamilton McKown Twombly was on the Beech Creek board, as were NYC vice president Charles Clark and future NYC president Chauncey M. Depew. By January 1883, Beech Creek officials had signed an agreement for the interchange of coal traffic with the New York Central, as well as the Reading. In 1884, the first year of operations, the Beech Creek carried two hundred thousand tons of coal. Two years later, the company was reorganized as the Beech Creek Railroad.[69]

Even as they were challenging the PRR's dominance in north-central Pennsylvania, Vanderbilt and Gowen were preparing to unseat the PRR from its vir-

tual monopoly over transportation in the southern part of the state. Gowen was the more enthusiastic supporter of the South Penn project, which he perceived as yet another mechanism to extend the Reading's influence to the west. His efforts were warmly welcomed by a group of Pittsburgh industrialists, including Andrew Carnegie, who craved lower freight rates. Vanderbilt was more cautious, yet he was not above an attempt to extract a measure of revenge for what he perceived as the PRR's role in the West Shore. In the end, Vanderbilt was the most realistic of the lot, and he was willing to abandon Gowen and his allies in order to maintain harmonious relations with the Pennsylvania railroad.

From the earliest days of the PRR, residents of southwestern Pennsylvania had complained bitterly at the company's rate policies, which favored long-haul through traffic over the needs of local shippers. They were likewise angry at the efforts of Tom Scott and other PRR executives to deny the B&O and the allied Pittsburgh & Connellsville access to Pittsburgh. That line was now in service, and had been since 1871, but it offered a roundabout journey between Pittsburgh and New York, and was not competitive with the PRR. As such, Pittsburghers (as well as people living in areas of western Pennsylvania south of the PRR main line) had long supported a competing rail route through the region.

As early as 1838, Hother Hagé, acting on the instructions of the state Canal Commissioners, had completed surveys through the area. In 1839 and 1840, Charles L. Schlatter had also surveyed "Mr. Hagé's Route," but indicated that steep grades might require the use of a turnpike in lieu of a railroad. Marked improvements in the abilities of railway locomotives soon made the project feasible. In 1849, local interests had attempted to organize the Duncannon, Landisburg & Broad Top Railroad, with the legislature approving the charter in 1854. The company went through several name and route changes, from the pragmatically descriptive Sherman's Valley & Broad Top Railroad to the absurdly grandiose Pennsylvania Pacific Railway, before being renamed the South Pennsylvania Railroad on April 1, 1863.[70]

Harrisburg native and South Penn president James Worrall, a civil engineer who had assisted Hagé in laying out the proposed railroad and turnpike route between Chambersburg and Pittsburgh, was tireless in his efforts to begin construction. Most of the South Penn's directors lived in Reading, and they may well have anticipated that the railroad would convey that region's coal to the mills in the Pittsburgh area. The London investment-banking house of McCalmont Brothers & Company, the same firm that held a controlling interest in the Reading, owned a substantial block of South Penn shares. The McCalmonts had also financed the East Pennsylvania Railroad, a line that composed a portion of the joint PRR–Reading Allentown Route to New York established during the 1850s. The McCalmonts never paid more than a token portion of their South Penn subscription, and they sold most of their Reading holdings following the 1880 bankruptcy.[71]

With the Reading in a precarious financial state during the early 1880s, it was the Vanderbilt interests who provided the instigating force behind the revitalization of the South Penn. In 1881, William H. Vanderbilt's son-in-law, Hamilton Twombly, began paying for a survey for a railroad across southern Pennsylvania. During 1882 and 1883, Vanderbilt and Gowen organized a syndicate, consisting of some twenty-five investors, who collectively pooled $15 million to underwrite the cost of construction. Rather than render themselves liable for the entire amount of a stock subscription, the syndicate permitted its members to pay incremental assessments, based on the need for construction funds. Any investor could abandon the syndicate at any time, confident that he would lose no more than the sum that he had already invested. The syndicate consisted of four groups of investors—those connected with the New York Central; those who were associated with the Reading; Pittsburghers who were anxious for an investment opportunity, or lower freight rates, or both; and others, mainly from New York, who were hoping for a quick profit.[72]

The New York Central interests dominated the management of the syndicate and made most of the critical decisions regarding the construction of the South Penn. William H. Vanderbilt, his son William K. Vanderbilt, and Twombly pooled their resources, as did Augustus Schell, the individual who had served as Vanderbilt's intermediary in reestablishing Gowen in

the Reading presidency. George Magee was already a close ally of the NYC, thanks to his oversight of the Fall Brook Coal Company. All told, they contributed the bulk of the funds necessary to fund the construction of the South Penn, perhaps $5 million in all. Despite their NYC affiliations, and the obvious potential for the South Penn to upset the competitive balance with the PRR, they were investors on their own account, and the New York Central did not provide direct financial support for the venture.[73]

After the Vanderbilt interests, the two largest individual subscribers were Dr. David Hostetter ($2 million) and Ralph Bagaley ($1.2 million).[74] Both men owned considerable tracts of coking coal lands in the Connellsville Region, and they hoped that the South Penn would free them of dependence on the PRR and improve their access to Pittsburgh markets. Hostetter, who had made his fortune as a patent-medicine manufacturer, was the individual who had financed the Columbia Conduit Company pipeline to connect the oilfields of northwestern Pennsylvania with refineries in Pittsburgh and the rails of the Baltimore & Ohio. Bagaley was the publisher of the *Pittsburgh Chronicle*, a newspaper that had long criticized the PRR's freight rates and service. He was also a close personal friend of George Westinghouse, Jr., and in 1869 he had been one of the original incorporators of the Westinghouse Air Brake Company—in tandem with several PRR executives, individuals who were now firmly opposed to Bagaley's decision to invest in the South Penn.[75]

The highest-profile supporter of the South Penn may well have been Andrew Carnegie. He contributed $1 million, while his partner Henry Phipps invested half of that. Coke magnate Henry Clay Frick put up $250,000, with his associate Edmund M. Ferguson adding the same amount. Of all the investors, Carnegie and his allies were the most intensely interested in the potential of the South Penn as a functioning railroad. Since the 1850s, Carnegie had used the Pennsylvania Railroad and his connections with J. Edgar Thomson, Tom Scott, and other PRR executives to lay the foundations for his business career. In November 1872, Carnegie had formed Carnegie, McCandless & Company in order to construct a giant new Bessemer steel plant at Braddock, Pennsylvania. In order to curry favor with PRR executives, Carnegie elected to name the mill in Thomson's honor.[76] In October 1872 Carnegie wrote to Thomson, his letter dripping with praise, "There is not one of our party who is not delighted that an opportunity has arisen through which expression can be given, however feebly," noting that the name of the new mill reflected "the regard they honestly entertain for your exalted character & career."[77]

The 1875 opening of the Edgar Thomson Steel Works completed Carnegie's transformation from a partner with PRR executives into a shipper on PRR rails.[78] While every executive and investor associated with the E. T. Works desired to control costs, Carnegie was particularly incensed at what he considered to be excessively high railroad rates, especially those charged by the Pennsylvania Railroad.[79] Carnegie's early and close association with the Pennsylvania Railroad actually increased the intensity of his dislike for that organization. He had read the internal correspondence of PRR executives, seen the company's balance sheets, and knew full well about the willingness of railroad managers to grant rebates and to practice long-haul/short-haul price discrimination. As a steelmaker, Carnegie knew how to acquire proprietary information from the railroads, often by bribing freight agents. Officially, Carnegie paid the PRR far more than did his competitors located on other trunk lines. Unofficial rates were another matter entirely, however, and the rebates that Carnegie received from the PRR created something approaching transportation equity in the steel business. Yet, Carnegie was livid at any hint of PRR favoritism toward his competitors.[80]

In 1881, an incensed Carnegie demanded, in his words, "justice" for his company.[81] Under Carnegie's relentless pressure, PRR officials reduced rates for Carnegie Brothers & Company, Ltd., and for the H. C. Frick Coke Company, but not to the extent that the steelmaker wished. As Carnegie himself grudgingly admitted, the PRR had to charge such high rates, particularly on coke traffic between Connellsville and Pittsburgh, because there was no backhaul; that is, no offsetting shipment that would prevent the necessity of having the cars travel empty half of the time. The rate issue became more serious in 1884, when newly appointed PRR general freight agent John S. Wilson increased coke tariffs by 20 percent and refused to guarantee the favorable rates that Carnegie had earlier obtained for steel shipments. "We appeal to you first as we did to Mr. Cassatt," Carnegie wrote ominously to second vice president Frank Thomson in January 1884; "failing equal treatment here we appeal again to Mr. Roberts, failing here we appeal to the Directors, failing here we send a circular to every shareholder & failing here, we make our appeal to the great public whose opinion no corporation these days can successfully withstand."[82] Despite the implicit threat of unfavorable publicity and possible legislative sanction, President Roberts and other PRR executives refused to lower the rates that Wilson had established.[83]

Given his desire to force the PRR to lower its rates, Carnegie was receptive to Vanderbilt's entreaties. The NYC president suggested that the Reading and the South Penn, in collaboration with the Jersey Central, could form a new route between Jersey City and Pittsburgh. At Pittsburgh, the Vanderbilt interests had already invested some $10 million in the Pittsburgh & Lake Erie Railroad (organized in 1875) and its subsidiary, the Pittsburgh, McKeesport & Youghiogheny Railroad, providing Carnegie with routes south to the coking facilities at Connellsville and north to the mills at Youngstown, Ohio. At Youngstown, the Lake Shore & Michigan Southern could send traffic to points as far west as Chicago.[84]

Many of the smaller investors, like Carnegie and Hostetter, hoped that the South Penn would increase competition and lower rates in southwestern Pennsylvania. Several of the syndicate members had close ties to the oil and steel industries. They included Henry W. Oliver, head of the Oliver Iron & Steel Company, and Benjamin Franklin Jones, founder of the Jones & Laughlin Steel Corporation. Oliver Hazard Payne was an ironmaker and an oil refiner who invested half a million dollars, while also looking after the million dollars contributed by John D. Rockefeller and his brother, William Rockefeller. Like Hostetter and the Rockefellers, glassmaker Mark W. Watson was an investor in both the South Penn and its proposed northern outlet, the Pittsburgh & Lake Erie. John W. Chalfant was a Pittsburgh banker and iron manufacturer who also supported the construction of several other railroads in the region.[85]

Other investors in the syndicate were closely connected to the Reading, and they anticipated that the South Penn could provide that company with access to Pittsburgh and perhaps even help elevate it to trunk-line status. Franklin Gowen contributed $100,000. Edward Collings Knight invested about $200,000, but did not take an active role in the management of the project. After following in his father's footsteps as a merchant, Knight had opened a sugar refinery, the direct progenitor of the American Sugar Refining Company. That firm was at the center of the so-called "Sugar Trust," that led to the Supreme Court's 1895 ruling in *United States v. E. C. Knight Co*, a decision that sharply narrowed the ability of the Justice Department to prosecute antitrust cases. Knight had served as a director of the North Pennsylvania Railroad since 1859, was elected as president of the Jersey Central in 1876, controlled the Delaware & Bound Brook Railroad, and was instrumental in putting together the Bound Brook Route as an alternative to the PRR's lines between Philadelphia and New York. An ally of Franklin Gowen, Knight was on the Reading board of directors between 1882 and 1884. So, too was Henry Lewis, who contributed $100,000. Another contributor, J. V. Williamson, was involved in the coal and iron industries in the Reading area. John Kean, a New Jersey resident who had been one of the initial investors in both the Camden & Amboy and the Jersey Central, was anxious to ally the latter company with both the Reading and the South Penn.[86]

A final group of investors had no interest in the transportation potential of the South Penn, viewing the project merely as a speculative venture. They included New York financiers James Boorman Colgate of J. B. Colgate & Company, William Collins Whitney and his brother-in-law Henry F. Dimock, as well as Charles L. Borie and his son Beauveau Borie, Reading investors who represented the brokerage firm of C. & H. Borie. Abram S. Hewitt, a New York industrialist and politician, gave further weight to the New York City interest in the project. Also anxious to turn a profit were former California banker Darius Ogden Mills and Philadelphia publisher Joshua B. Lippincott. Stephen B. Elkins controlled substantial investments in coal and railroads, and would later, as a U.S. senator, sponsor several key pieces of Progressive era railway regulation.

The members of the South Penn syndicate organized the American Construction Company in order to build the new line. Surveying commenced in the fall of 1883, with construction beginning the following summer. Engineering expertise and construction methods had improved considerably since the PRR completed its line through the Alleghenies a third of a century earlier, yet the South Penn reflected few of those advancements. Work proceeded in fits and starts, and engineers almost continuously resurveyed large segments of the railroad, in part to cut costs and in part to ensure that the South Penn provided access for the businesses owned by syndicate members. The final alignment roughly paralleled Charles Schlatter's southern route, from Harrisburg southwest to Bedford, then west to Somerset and northwestward through New Stanton, terminating at a connection with the Pittsburgh, McKeesport & Youghiogheny just south of Braddock.[87]

Continual disagreements among the South Penn's investors virtually crippled construction efforts. Because they had organized a syndicate, rather than a partnership or a corporation, decisions made by the majority of investors were not binding on the others, and it soon became a case of every man for himself. Gowen, who sought access to Pittsburgh, favored the construction of a modern, double-track railroad with broad curves and low grades. So, too, did South Penn chief engineer Robert H. Sayre, a veteran of the Lehigh Coal & Navigation Company and the Lehigh Valley Railroad. Vanderbilt was disinclined to attempt to mimic the quality of the Pennsylvania Railroad main line, however, and in all likelihood he envisioned selling the South Penn to the PRR for its nuisance value. As such, Vanderbilt and his fellow New York Central investors doled out money as sparingly as possible. They preferred a single-track railroad that would terminate at a connection with the Baltimore & Ohio at Somerset rather than continue all the way to Pittsburgh.[88]

In the end, Vanderbilt's restrained approach prevailed—to the dismay of Sayre, an experienced engineer who had little patience with the financiers who dictated construction practices to him. Workers built massive cuts and fills, began boring nine tunnels, and laid the stone piers for a railroad bridge across the Susquehanna River at Harrisburg. Yet, the South Penn was to be a single-track railroad, hardly competitive with the nearby multiple-tracked PRR. Whereas the PRR contended with a single summit crossing at

Gallitzin, the South Penn faced an undulating saw-tooth profile with multiple summits and a maximum elevation that was more than 200 feet higher than on the PRR. Although the distance between Harrisburg and Pittsburgh was some twenty miles shorter via the South Penn than the PRR, the upstart line was unlikely to carry a significant amount of traffic. Perhaps predictably, a history of the New York Central indicated that the South Penn route "would avoid many of the [Pennsylvania Rail]road's heavy mountain grades and curves," while the Burgess and Kennedy official history of the PRR maintained that the South Penn had steeper grades and that "in no respect except length was it comparable with the Pennsylvania's main line." Both statements were probably true to some extent. What mattered, however, was the ruling grade in the prevailing direction of loaded traffic. That measure, critical for efficient and profitable operations, was decidedly in favor of the Pennsylvania Railroad.[89]

As work crews hacked their way across southern Pennsylvania, they were steadily completing a venture that stood to benefit no one. PRR officials correctly judged that the South Penn was a minimal threat, at best. They nonetheless concluded that they would have to buy the new line, if for no other reason than to prevent any possibility that it might someday interfere with the PRR's influence in southern Pennsylvania. In that context, Roberts and other PRR executives were anxious to halt work as soon as possible, and thus minimize the amount that they would have to pay to acquire the company. The more serious threat, Roberts knew, was the Beech Creek incursion into the northern Pennsylvania coalfields that had traditionally been PRR territory.

The South Penn's investors were having their doubts as well. The project threatened to exhaust the investment resources of Vanderbilt and the other syndicate members, with no appreciable result, and the Panic of 1884, while short in duration, nonetheless caused many of those investors to retrench. Aside from the problems associated with the South Penn, Vanderbilt was endeavoring to end the nuisance associated with the West Shore route along the Hudson River. He was certainly willing to give up the South Penn, and he would even consider relinquishing the Beech Creek, if in doing so he could rid himself of the West Shore.

In August 1884, William H. Vanderbilt initiated a compromise to resolve the competitive overbuilding in New York and Pennsylvania. Albert Fink, head of the Executive Committee of the Eastern Trunk Line Association, traveled to Saratoga Springs, New York. He was on vacation, or so he told reporters, but it was hardly coincidental that Vanderbilt was also there, or that George Roberts arrived a short time later. They discussed the stabilization of passenger rates in an attempt to end another war between the trunk lines. During the proceedings, Roberts later recalled, Vanderbilt took him aside and mentioned that he "wished to withdraw from the South Pennsylvania scheme, [and] wanted to know whether the Pennsylvania Railroad Company was willing to negotiate with him."[90] Roberts indicated that he might dispose of the PRR's West Shore holdings, and the two executives agreed to further discussions through the intermediary of Vanderbilt's son-in-law, Hamilton Twombly. During the months that followed, interested parties, including the Fall Brook Coal Company's George Magee, descended on Roberts's office, trying to get the best deal that they could. Magee agreed to allow the PRR to acquire the Beech Creek lines in Pennsylvania, so long as his interests in the Pine Creek route north into New York State would remain unmolested.[91]

Only the Reading interests seem to have been unaware of the negotiations between Vanderbilt and Roberts. Gowen in particular was determined to see the South Penn through to completion, regardless of the cost or consequences. He had once been a useful ally to the New York Central, but he was rapidly becoming a liability. By October 1884, the *New York Times* noted, with considerable understatement, "Mr. Vanderbilt and Mr. Gowen have had a falling out." Some months earlier, in January 1884, Gowen had selected George deBenneville Keim, also a member of the South Penn syndicate, as his replacement in the Reading presidency, believing that Keim would continue his policies. Very quickly, however, the *Times* reported that Gowen was "greatly disgusted" with Keim, who had fallen under Vanderbilt's influence. Gowen was not pleased with the results. "It is said that Mr. Vanderbilt's future policy will be more conciliatory to the Pennsylvania Railroad," Gowen lamented. "To this end it is announced that work on the

South Pennsylvania will not be pushed forward with rapidity."[92]

By the spring of 1885, the only remaining issue was the manner in which the PRR and South Penn factions would structure a settlement. In some countries, such as Japan, the central government might have intervened in the interest of national productivity. In Britain, managerial families might have worked out a gentlemen's agreement to ensure that everyone played fair. In Germany, the banks that had invested so heavily in transportation and manufacturing might have met to bring order out of chaos. During the late 1800s, however, federal and state law in the United States favored the financier, and not the family businessman or the central bank.[93]

Given the role that financiers played in corporate governance, it was hardly surprising that Vanderbilt used J. Pierpont Morgan, an investment banker of then-modest reputation, to negotiate a truce between the South Penn and the PRR. Like his father, Junius Spencer Morgan, J. P. Morgan was heavily involved in transatlantic finance. During the 1870s, he had cooperated with Anthony Drexel, placing the securities of the PRR and its affiliates in American and European markets. In 1879, however, J. P. Morgan moved away from the PRR and toward the New York Central. He negotiated with a consortium of investment bankers to market a large portion of the holdings of William H. Vanderbilt without flooding the market and weakening their value. Despite his close ties to the NYC, both J. P. Morgan and his father nonetheless continued their involvement in PRR securities issues. Perhaps better than any other financier, J. P. Morgan was able to utilize his connections within the twin realms of finance and railroading in order to mediate a settlement between the Pennsylvania Railroad and the New York Central.[94]

Morgan watched in dismay as the value of the New York Central stock that he and his fellow investors owned fell from $131 to $90 a share between 1880 and 1885. In March 1885, Morgan met with Vanderbilt in London, and they returned to the United States together. On board the ship, Vanderbilt agreed in principle to a settlement involving the South Penn, the Beech Creek, and the West Shore. Morgan then traveled to Philadelphia to secure the cooperation of President Roberts and other PRR senior executives.[95]

On July 20, 1885, Morgan welcomed aboard his yacht, the *Corsair*, Roberts, PRR second vice president Frank Thomson, and the New York Central's new president Chauncey M. Depew. Roberts later stressed that he "was not acting as President of the Pennsylvania Railroad Company," but there seemed little doubt that his personal investments and professional responsibilities were closely intertwined.[96] Morgan ensconced them in opulence for the better part of the day while the *Corsair*—whose name alone revealed a good deal about the financier's personality—cruised slowly along the Hudson River and down New York Bay, as far as Sandy Hook. Roberts proved the most recalcitrant, in part because he harbored a lingering suspicion of Vanderbilt. He also saw no reason why the PRR should have to pay for the South Penn, a line that was—as he told the *New York Times*—no more than "a number of poles in the earth . . . [and] a few furrows into hills."[97]

With darkness descending over the financial center of the western hemisphere, the great railroad builders trapped on a small vessel floating among a sea of commerce finally agreed on a plan. The PRR would pay up to $5.5 million for the South Pennsylvania Railroad. Depew also agreed to sell the Beech Creek line to Roberts, outraging the local interests who had initially promoted the line as an alternative to the PRR. In exchange, the NYC interests gained control over the West Shore. There remained a somewhat thorny problem in that Pennsylvania's 1874 constitution, enacted in the aftermath of the South Improvement Company scandal, prohibited any railroad incorporated in the commonwealth from acquiring a parallel or competing company. Roberts and Thomson devised a ludicrously transparent subterfuge. The Bedford & Bridgeport Railroad, a PRR subsidiary that could have connected with the South Penn, became the purchaser of record.[98]

On July 24, Twombly announced the terms of the *Corsair* compact, shocking members of the South Penn syndicate—most of whom were unaware that negotiations between the PRR and the New York Central had been taking place. Although George Magee acquiesced to Vanderbilt's decision to sell the Beech Creek to the PRR, not every member of the syndicate was as accommodating. The disagreements split precisely the Beech Creek's twelve-member board of directors, with five favoring the sale, five opposed, and two undecided, with one considering supporting the Vanderbilt interests and the other opposing them. Reading personnel were likewise slighted in the *Corsair* compact, causing President Keim, general traffic manager J. Lowrie Bell, and Reading shareholders J. V. Williamson and Beauveau Borie to oppose the agreement. Other syndicate members, including Hostetter, believed that the *Corsair* decision had deprived them of the annual returns—which they generously estimated at 10 percent—that they claimed the completed railroad would produce. Altogether, Vanderbilt's opponents controlled approximately $4 million of the $15 million invested in the syndicate, but it was not sufficient to alter the outcome of the agreement that Morgan had brokered.[99]

On August 25, a month after Morgan made public the announcement, Pennsylvania attorney general Lewis C. Cassidy sought an injunction to block the PRR's acquisition of the South Penn. Cassidy had little patience with the employment of the Bedford & Bridgeport Railroad as a dummy purchaser in an effort to comply with the terms of the 1874 constitution. He emphasized that the case was a way "to have the question finally determined whether a great railroad is simply a private corporation or an institution for the public good."[100] Cassidy's remarks spawned a torrent of rumors on Wall Street, with many speculators claiming that the Baltimore & Ohio had secretly persuaded the attorney general to initiate the suit in order to hamstring the PRR. More credible accounts suggested that Cassidy had taken action solely to advance his political career, noting that discussions regarding the settlement had been under way for many months prior to the filing of charges.[101] President Roberts counterattacked, telling reporters that it was ludicrous to consider the South Penn a competing railroad when it was in reality only a halfhearted construction project, with "no existence except on paper." He also suggested that Cassidy's rigid adherence to the letter of the law had "given a heavy blow to the amicable settlement of the railroad difficulties of the country" by stifling efforts to prevent "ruinous war between the lines" and "the building of uselessly competing roads."[102]

The justices of the state supreme court may not have shared Cassidy's interest in depicting the Pennsylvania

Railroad as an example of corporate tyranny, but they were likewise unconvinced by arguments by PRR attorneys that their company's charter antedated and thus superseded the new constitution. The *Corsair* compact clearly violated the law, and in October 1886 the court ruled that the PRR's Bedford & Bridgeport subsidiary could not take possession of the South Pennsylvania Railroad. The commonwealth's laws, they noted, allowed the PRR to build additional capacity, but not to acquire it from another company. In addition to preventing the PRR from acquiring the South Penn, the ruling likewise enjoined it from buying the Beech Creek. To the relief of local interests in Clearfield County, the New York Central leased the company in 1890, and it continued to compete against the PRR for coal traffic in north-central Pennsylvania.[103]

The informal resolution of the South Penn situation did little to cheer Franklin B. Gowen or his Reading associates, including President George deBenneville Keim. Despite his closer ties to Vanderbilt, Keim was caught unawares by the South Penn settlement. On Saturday, July 18, two days prior to the resolution of the dispute, Hamilton Twombly casually mentioned that the South Penn escapade was over and that the New York Central would no longer be supporting incursions into PRR territory. As a *New York Times* reporter reconstructed that brief and awkward meeting, "Mr. Keim asked Mr. Twombly what had been done to protect [the] Reading in the matter, and Mr. Twombly answered that nothing had been done."[104]

Morgan's truce between the PRR and the Vanderbilt interests ignored Gowen's expansionist plans as well as Andrew Carnegie's desire for lower rail rates, leaving both men livid with rage. Gowen remained active in the Reading's affairs, plotting his return to the presidency and continuing to advocate for the completion of the South Penn as a viable competitor to the PRR. He was a liability to both Vanderbilt and Morgan, and the financier made plain (through his ties to Drexel & Company) that the Reading would find it difficult to raise additional funds so long as Gowen was in a position of power. Despite his brief return to the Reading presidency in 1886, Gowen's career in railroading was over. He remained active in business and the law, but he became increasingly confused and despondent. In December 1889, he went to Washington to argue a case before the recently formed Interstate Commerce Commission. Gowen stopped at a hardware store, and then checked into Wormley's Hotel. The following afternoon, he locked the door to his room, unwrapped his purchase, loaded it, and put a bullet through his brain.[105]

Carnegie, who had much less at stake in the South Penn than Gowen, did not fall so far, nor so tragically, but he fell nonetheless. Even before the *Corsair* settlement, Carnegie had developed a fairly clear sense of his limited authority within the syndicate. He had naturally expected that his mills would provide the rails for the South Penn, but he lost the contract. To add to the insult, the low bidder turned out to be the Pennsylvania Steel Company, a firm with close ties to the Pennsylvania Railroad.[106]

Neither Morgan nor his NYC allies had informed Carnegie of the conference on board the *Corsair*, nor were the steelmaker's interests at issue. Carnegie believed that Vanderbilt and his New York Central allies had betrayed him and, in more pragmatic terms, the judicial ruling against the sale of the South Penn meant that he would be unlikely to recover his full investment. When the New York Central interests finally offered Carnegie sixty cents on the dollar for his South Penn holdings, the incensed Scotsman threatened to sue. As Henry Clay Frick observed, such a lawsuit would be unlikely to succeed, as none of the parties involved in the *Corsair* compact had signed their names to anything, and as that agreement had clearly violated Pennsylvania law.

Perhaps more important was the fact that Carnegie was no longer able to use the threat of the South Penn to exercise leverage against the PRR. Following the *Corsair* conference, he returned to his old habits of writing scathing invectives to PRR executives, excoriating them for their unfair actions in the matter of rates. Fuming with indignation, Carnegie presented self-righteous speeches to the Pennsylvania legislature, to the Franklin Institute, and at the dedication of the new Carnegie Library in Braddock, continually demanding additional regulation to protect the commonwealth from the rapaciousness of the Pennsylvania Railroad. In the spring of 1889, he testified before the General Assembly, demanding that legislators man-

date a reduction in railroad rates. Frick, who believed that labor costs constituted the gravest problem facing the Carnegie empire, warned his associate against politically intemperate attacks directed at the railroad that was their lifeline. "Our interests lie in the future of the P.R.R.," he wrote to Carnegie, but to no avail.[107] The PRR was able to exercise its political influence in Harrisburg to block rate regulation, but the incident was but a prelude to increasingly acrimonious battles between shippers and railroaders.[108]

The South Penn saga continued for the next half-century. Construction ceased on September 12, 1885, even though crews had completed nearly two-thirds of the heavy engineering work on the route. William H. Vanderbilt died of a stroke in December 1885, but his successors negotiated a settlement with the other South Penn investors, who recouped but a small portion of their original stake in the syndicate. In 1887, a group of Pittsburgh investors—led by David Hostetter and his son Bert—attempted to revive the South Penn but were unsuccessful. The Vanderbilt family, anxious to be done with the South Penn, ultimately offered the other syndicate members 60 percent of their original investment for their shares in the project. When the final accounting took place, the Vanderbilts had squandered as much as $4 million on the South Penn, with the other investors suffering a collective loss of perhaps $1.5 million.[109]

The South Penn never really did disappear, however. In 1899, then-president Alexander J. Cassatt suspended rebates and raised railroad rates in the northeast, under the "community of interest" plan. Carnegie, again incensed at what he considered to be unjust rates, dispatched crews to survey the route and prepare cost estimates. That, too, came to naught. Other carriers did use a small portion of the South Penn right of way, but most of the grade would never carry rail traffic.[110] The West Shore enjoyed more success, as New York Central officials soon integrated most of that railroad's tracks into its operations. New technology, in the form of the automobile, finally provided a use for the South Penn route. Between 1938 and 1940, crews used some of the roadbed, including six of the nine tunnels, to complete the nation's first superhighway, the Pennsylvania Turnpike.[111]

George Roberts and his fellow PRR executives demonstrated remarkable restraint throughout the entire South Penn incident. They elected not to provide any financial support to the West Shore, and likewise did not countenance the construction of parallel rail lines in an attempt to drive the NYC or the Reading to the bargaining table.[112] In the end, even Vanderbilt and his NYC allies saw the folly of the South Penn and were receptive to compromise. Only the outside investors, Carnegie among them, sought to continue construction at the expense of stability. The battle over the South Penn nonetheless rapidly assumed legendary status, as contemporary writers attempted to portray the contest as yet another example of unbridled robber-baron capitalism. With memories of Tom Scott and his holding companies still fresh in the minds of many, they could perhaps be forgiven for assuming that Pennsylvania Railroad executives were again attempting to control the business and the government of Pennsylvania.[113]

In fact, it was J. P. Morgan who dictated the outcome of the South Penn affair. His intervention secured peace between the PRR and the New York Central and helped to stabilize the market for railway securities. Yet, neither Morgan nor his fellow investment bankers were able to eliminate competitive overbuilding in the northeast. The officials of the four major trunk lines henceforth refrained from additional open warfare on the scale of the South Penn, but there were still plenty of independent promoters who exercised considerably less restraint. They included Henry S. Ives, whose association with the Cincinnati, Hamilton & Dayton, among other companies, sullied his reputation and led to his imprisonment. George Gould, the son of Jay Gould, was more reputable, and more careful, but he nonetheless helped to destabilize the nation's railroad network, in part by constructing the Western Pacific Railroad from Salt Lake City to California. In later years, the Van Sweringen brothers, Oris Paxton and Mantis James, picked up where Calvin Brice and Samuel Thomas had left off, reacquiring the Nickel Plate and making it the centerpiece of a budding railroad empire. For a time, each posed a threat to the interests of the Pennsylvania Railroad. With the resolution of the South Penn crisis, however, the established leaders of the great eastern trunk lines embarked upon a policy of negotiated consensus rather than open conflict.

Bessemer & Lake Erie

The conclusion of the South Penn incident failed to end the tensions between Andrew Carnegie and the Pennsylvania Railroad. By 1894, Carnegie was again ready to challenge the PRR's freight rates and anxious to build an alternate rail route for his coal and iron ore shipments. By then, however, he was no longer willing to entrust the New York Central, or any other independent railroad, as an ally. During 1896 and 1897, Carnegie embarked on a massive program of vertical integration, one that created a transportation empire of railroads and lake boats, under his control and free of the actions of the Pennsylvania Railroad. In 1896, he oversaw the consolidation of several existing switching lines that served the Edgar Thomson, Homestead, and Duquesne Works into the Union Railroad (not to be confused with the Union Railroad in Baltimore, a subsidiary of the PRR). With his own in-plant railway, Carnegie saved substantially on switching costs and was able to route freight over the PRR, the B&O, and whatever other competitor might enter the Pittsburgh region.[114]

Unfortunately for Carnegie, the B&O was unable to accommodate all of his traffic, and no other viable competitor was in the offing. By 1895, Carnegie had already made suggestions that he might move some steel production away from Pittsburgh. At the very least, he sought a better mechanism for bringing raw materials to the Monongahela Valley. He initially demonstrated lukewarm support for a barge canal that would link Lake Erie and the Ohio River before settling upon a railroad that would accomplish the same end.

In January 1896, Carnegie purchased the Pittsburgh, Shenango & Lake Erie Railroad, which operated a rail line between Butler, Pennsylvania, north of Pittsburgh, and the Lake Erie port of Conneaut, Ohio. It was not much of a railroad, and Conneaut was not much of a port, but the former could be rebuilt, and the latter had recently been dredged, courtesy of the Army Corps of Engineers, with the first ore boat arriving in 1892. An extension of some thirty miles would link the Pittsburgh, Shenango & Lake Erie route to the Union Railroad, Carnegie's in-plant system, at Bessemer, Pennsylvania. In April 1896, Carnegie incorporated the Butler & Pittsburgh Railroad Company in order to build the connection. A month later, a panicked PRR President Roberts granted Carnegie's demands for substantial rate reductions in exchange for the steelmaker's promise that he would not purchase any additional railroads. The upgrading of the Pittsburgh, Shenango & Lake Erie and the construction of the Butler & Pittsburgh went forward nonetheless, with Carnegie, Frick, and their associates funding virtually the entire cost of the project. In January 1897, the two Carnegie-owned railroads were consolidated as the Pittsburgh, Bessemer & Lake Erie Railroad, and that autumn construction crews completed work on the line. Renamed the Bessemer & Lake Erie in 1900, it soon repaid its $2 million cost by reducing substantially Carnegie's transportation expenditures.[115]

The Pittsburgh, Bessemer & Lake Erie was extraordinarily efficient, more so than the Pennsylvania Railroad, in large measure because it was owned by Carnegie (and later by U.S. Steel) and concentrated on the transportation of bulk commodities from Lake Erie to Pittsburgh. Yet, it lacked sufficient capacity to deliver all of the raw materials that Carnegie's blast furnaces required. Even so, Carnegie's railroad was sufficient to drive PRR executives to the bargaining table. In July 1898, President Frank Thomson, Roberts's successor, authorized further reductions in the rates for Carnegie Steel in exchange for Carnegie's promise that he would not extend the Pittsburgh, Bessemer & Lake Erie farther south to Frick's coking facilities at Connellsville. Not content with the new rates, Carnegie and Frick persuaded Thomson to approve substantial rebates, ensuring that their cost of transportation was well below the official charges. In granting the rate reductions and rebates, Thomson had reduced the PRR's revenues, but ensured that the railroad would retain 75 percent of the fifteen million tons of freight that Carnegie Steel shipped in 1896 alone. However, the rebates became a thorn in the side of PRR executives, and their attempts to eliminate them in 1899 would again provoke Carnegie's wrath.[116]

A Further Conflict with the Reading

The resolution of the South Penn affair dampened, but did not entirely eliminate, friction between the PRR and the Reading. In 1886, six years after the Reading's first bankruptcy, the firm again entered receivership. The Jersey Central also failed, and J. P. Morgan stepped in to sort out the mess. Morgan persuaded representatives from the PRR, the New York Central, and the Baltimore & Ohio that a bankrupt Reading would be in no one's best interest. Accordingly, all three of the Reading's rivals cooperated with J. P. Morgan & Company, assembling a $15 million reorganization plan that lowered the company's interest costs. In creating a two-tiered governing structure for the reorganized company, Morgan solidified his reputation as one of the nation's most innovative financiers. A voting trust oversaw financial matters, while a three-member committee, including Morgan, set corporate policy. One of the first acts of that committee was to divide traffic between the Reading and the PRR, and to reestablish the anthracite cartel. Morgan's 1886 pool allocated 3.5 million tons to the PRR, but the railroad again remained outside the cartel. With the continued instability in the anthracite trade, Reading officials renewed their efforts to control the situation.[117]

After preventing Franklin Gowen from regaining control over the Reading, Morgan chose an outsider and relative newcomer, Austin Corbin, as president of the company. Corbin had grown up in New Hampshire (the *New York Times* described him as "a Yankee of the Yankees"), received a law degree from Harvard, and became an Iowa banker. In 1865, at the age of thirty-eight and already wealthy, he moved to New York and established a bank there. He dabbled in railroads in the Midwest, and for a time was president of the Indianapolis, Bloomington & Western. He also supported the construction of the Elmira, Cortland & Northern Railroad, which he attempted unsuccessfully to sell to the promoters of the West Shore. Since 1880, he had presided over the rehabilitation of the Long Island Rail Road, a company that in 1900 would become part of the PRR system. Corbin was more of a financier than a railroader, however. He became interested in the Reading when he bought the company's bonds—selling at exceedingly low prices, owing to the bankruptcy—with the hope that he could have a voice in the reorganization proceedings. He had never made an enemy of Gowen, and so the Reading's former president found Morgan's choice of his replacement to be acceptable. Day-to-day operations were under the supervision of a largely unknown, yet supremely talented manager, Archibald Angus McLeod. Later, in 1890, a group of Philadelphia investors, led by department-store magnate John Wanamaker, battled with Morgan for control of the Reading, and installed McLeod as president. McLeod's efforts to impose order on the anthracite markets were even more ambitious than those that Gowen had employed.[118]

McLeod proved almost as confrontational toward the PRR as Gowen had been. To the dismay of PRR executives, McLeod moved quickly and aggressively to give his company direct rail access to New York and New England, as well as Lake Erie. In 1890, he launched construction on the Port Reading Railroad Company, which by 1892 had extended the Reading's reach from Bound Brook, New Jersey, to Port Reading, opposite Staten Island. In December 1891, the Reading leased the Lehigh Valley Railroad, another major anthracite carrier, with access to Buffalo. The following year, McLeod's attorneys devised a mechanism to reestablish the Reading's lease of the Jersey Central, first implemented in 1883, but voided by the New Jersey Court of Chancery three years later. In an effort to further stabilize anthracite traffic, McLeod formed an alliance with the Delaware, Lackawanna & Western Railroad, leading to growing accusations that he was attempting to mimic Gowen's efforts to monopolize the mining and shipment of hard coal.[119]

McLeod also extended the Reading's influence to New England and threatened to divert traffic away from the PRR and its principal northern connection, the New York, New Haven & Hartford Railroad. He established control over the Central New England & Western Railroad and the Poughkeepsie Bridge & Railroad Company, which he combined into the Philadelphia, Reading & New England Railroad on August 1, 1892. The bridge at Poughkeepsie, completed in December 1888, was a valuable prize, as it was the only rail crossing of the Hudson River south of Albany.[120] In order to gain access to Boston, McLeod bought twenty-four thousand shares of stock in the Boston & Maine,

and in 1893 became that company's president.[121] The Boston & Maine acquisition included a controlling interest in the New York & New England Railroad, linking Boston to Hopewell Junction. From there, the short Dutchess County Railroad provided access to the east end of the Poughkeepsie Bridge, as an alternative to the New Haven route between Simsbury, Connecticut, and Northampton, Massachusetts.[122]

Under McLeod's direction, the Reading's expansion established the "Poughkeepsie Bridge Route," an all-rail, inland competitor to the PRR/New Haven service. McLeod's new alignment enabled through traffic from Pennsylvania and points to the south and west, and destined for New England, to avoid the congestion of New York, as well as the water transfer across New York Harbor. By September 1892, McLeod's *New England Day Express* was offering all-rail service between Washington and Boston. From the national capital, passenger cars moved over the Baltimore & Ohio to Philadelphia, where they followed the Bound Brook Route to Bound Brook, then moved west over the Reading line to Easton, Pennsylvania. At Easton, the Lehigh & Hudson River Railway stretched north to a junction with the Central New England & Western, at Maybrook, New York. After crossing the Poughkeepsie Bridge, travelers joined the New Haven at Simsbury, Connecticut, for the trip to Northampton, Massachusetts, with the Boston & Maine Railroad completing the trip to Boston. Passenger service over the Poughkeepsie Bridge Route never lived up to expectations, however, largely because the indirect routing bypassed the largest city in the United States. Pennsylvania Railroad officials were nonetheless concerned that freight bound for New England might follow the Poughkeepsie Bridge Route, avoiding the cumbersome transfer in New York and depriving the PRR of substantial revenues.[123]

McLeod's ambitious maneuvering quickly transformed the Reading into a major regional railroad as well as the nation's dominant anthracite carrier.[124] More than 70 percent of the nation's anthracite traffic was now under McLeod's supervision. The Reading's power was temporary, however. McLeod's price-fixing policies alarmed legislators in New Jersey, New York, and Pennsylvania, as well as their counterparts in Congress. By 1893, the New Jersey courts had again ordered the Reading to relinquish the Jersey Central, reducing its share of the anthracite trade to little better than 40 percent. Even more ominously, McLeod had badly overextended the Reading's credit. He watched as the company again went bankrupt in February 1893. The Reading's collapse helped spawn a recession, second only to the Great Depression of the 1930s in its severity. In addition to the forced divestiture of the Jersey Central, the Reading lost control over the Delaware, Lackawanna & Western and the Philadelphia, Reading & New England. With them went the Reading's influence over the Poughkeepsie Bridge Route, as well as the short-lived *New England Day Express*.[125]

Amid the financial catastrophe, J. P. Morgan reasserted control over the Reading and extended his influence to encompass much of the railroad network in the United States. In the spring of 1893, McLeod resigned the presidency of the Boston & Maine and the Reading, as well as the Philadelphia & Reading Coal & Iron Company. Morgan, who had been a key player in the consortium of investors that had battled to keep McLeod out of New England, reorganized the Philadelphia & Reading Rail Road, which emerged from bankruptcy in 1896 as the Philadelphia & Reading Railway. Morgan's influence ensured that the new company would remain a regional anthracite carrier, whose new executives possessed no pretensions of acquiring trunk-line status. In the process, the financier reestablished the anthracite cartel, forming close relationships with the Jersey Central, the Delaware & Hudson, the Delaware, Lackawanna & Western, and the Lehigh Valley. Morgan and his fellow investment bankers had already put together what amounted to a community of interest, one that controlled 75 percent of the anthracite shipped to the east coast. With little more than 11 percent of the traffic, the PRR was the only significant anthracite carrier that was not yet included in the combination.[126]

Morgan, just hitting his stride as a financier, had succeeded admirably in his efforts to impose order on the anthracite business, but that was by no means the end of his difficulties. Labor militancy increasingly affected northeastern Pennsylvania, as did regulations banning child labor and mandating safer working practices. Demand for anthracite remained strong (production peaked in 1917, at more than 100 million

tons), but other fuels were poised to supplant the region's hard coal. The long, slow decline of the mining industry in northeastern Pennsylvania was less burdensome to the PRR than it was to the Reading and the other anthracite carriers. The corresponding increase in the use of bituminous coal, beginning late in the nineteenth century, would have more profound effects on the PRR's operations and corporate strategy.[127]

Conflict in the Southwest: Bringing the Vandalia to Heel

The economic crisis of the 1870s produced declining earnings, suspended dividends, and labor militancy across the Pennsylvania Railroad system, but the problems were especially severe on the Lines West of Pittsburgh and Erie. The Fort Wayne and the Pan Handle were crucial to the PRR's trunk-line business, yet they generated relatively little local traffic and produced far lower revenues, per mile, than routes to the east. The Pennsylvania Company constituted an effective mechanism for consolidating the PRR's midwestern investments, but the officials who managed that holding company exerted direct operational control over only a portion of the routes in Ohio, Indiana, and Illinois. More problematically, they could do relatively little to constrain the activities of the idiosyncratic local entrepreneurs who had helped to establish the carriers that later became a part of Lines West.

The financial structure of the companies that composed Lines West consisted of an almost impenetrable tangle of leases, bond guarantees, first, second, and third mortgages, other liens on various portions of the physical plant and equipment, and unsecured debt. Repeated receiverships had produced competing claims over corporate assets, some of which had not been fully resolved at the time of the Pennsylvania Company's development in 1870 and 1871. Some components were in respectable financial condition—most notably the Fort Wayne, thanks to Samuel J. Tilden's reorganization efforts during the 1860s. Others, particularly the Columbus, Chicago & Indiana Central, could easily have contributed entire chapters to textbooks on corporate bankruptcy law. Such financial imbroglios greatly increased the ability of bankers to sit on the boards of Lines West constituent companies. For the most part, however, they were second-tier investment bankers, such as those representing Winslow, Lanier & Company, and their function was to protect the rights of certain classes of investors, not to dictate corporate policy.

The Fort Wayne weathered the depression in reasonably good shape. A robust traffic mix, plus the generous terms of the PRR lease, enabled President George Washington Cass to reduce the company's bonded indebtedness and improve the physical plant with additional equipment, steel rail, and double-tracking. Even Cass's decision to serve as the president of the Northern Pacific Railroad, between 1872 and 1875, did little to threaten the Fort Wayne's financial stability.[128]

Other segments of the PRR system were not so fortunate. The Grand Rapids & Indiana Railroad was particularly hard-hit. The company had been in receivership between 1869 and 1871, emerging only when the PRR had organized the Continental Improvement Company and provided the resources to extend the line north to Traverse City, Michigan. With the depression threatening the company with another bankruptcy, the PRR intervened in 1875, buying the bonds of the GR&I and reorganizing the company in 1878.[129]

The depression produced a comparable effect on other, minor railroads. In April 1874, the Cairo & Vincennes Railroad—an independent company that nonetheless received assistance from the PRR—entered receivership. The Cleveland, Mt. Vernon & Delaware Railroad, the PRR's link between Columbus and Hudson, Ohio, defaulted in July 1874. The Ashtabula, Youngstown & Pittsburgh Railroad, leased by the Pennsylvania Company in January 1873 and completed later that year, failed in October 1877.

The Cleveland, Mount Vernon & Delaware Railroad was one small example of the complexity associated with corporate affairs on Lines West. Originally incorporated in 1851 as the Akron Branch of the Cleveland & Pittsburgh Railroad, it eventually opened a line between Hudson and Millersburg, Ohio, under the name of the Cleveland, Zanesville & Cincinnati Railroad. The company was in receivership between 1861 and 1864, at which time it came under the control of George Cass and became part of the Fort Wayne. In that manner the company, renamed the Cleveland,

Mount Vernon & Delaware, became part of the PRR system in 1869 and soon became a component of the Pennsylvania Company. By 1873, the company's investors had completed a route south to Columbus, but became embroiled in a dispute over whether to penetrate the coalfields of southern Ohio or to create a trunk line between Cleveland, Columbus, and Cincinnati.

In 1874, the Cleveland, Mount Vernon & Delaware fell victim to the Panic of 1873 and defaulted on its bonds. That unhappy situation affected two principal creditors—the PRR and a group of Dutch bondholders. The PRR board refused assistance, but attempted to mediate a settlement. Negotiations bogged down, and by 1877 the PRR had stopped paying interest on the company's bonds, many of which were in the hands of the Dutch investors. In 1880, the exasperated Dutch sued, taking the company into receivership. By 1885, the Cleveland, Mount Vernon & Delaware had been reorganized into the Cleveland, Akron & Columbus Railroad and, along with the Nickel Plate, it became part of Calvin Brice's midwestern rail empire, in competition with the PRR. Beginning in 1886, the PRR spent more than $2.2 million in repurchasing its subsidiary's stock. However, it was only after Brice's premature death in 1898 that the PRR was able to recapture control of the company. Even then, the Dutch investors controlled a substantial minority interest until 1911, when the PRR finally bought them out, at grossly inflated prices.[130]

The Pan Handle suffered the most serious effects from the depression. The Pittsburgh, Cincinnati & St. Louis was never a robust carrier, but its Achilles heel was Ben Smith's Columbus, Chicago & Indiana Central. In January 1869, Pan Handle and PRR officials had succeeded in keeping the CC&IC away from the Erie, but paid a high price for doing so, with the PRR guaranteeing that the Pan Handle would pay CC&IC investors a rental equivalent to 30 percent of gross earnings, with the PRR pledging to protect the Pan Handle's obligations. A year later, a modification to the lease agreement required the CC&IC to consolidate its outstanding mortgages—something that, PRR officials later argued, Smith and his associates failed to do. The PRR continued to guarantee the Pan Handle lease of the CC&IC, but did not specifically guarantee the new CC&IC bond issue.

Ben Smith's railroad had never been adequately capitalized, properly maintained, or efficiently managed, and its fortunes fell considerably during the 1870s. Its backdoor route to Chicago carried less traffic than the Fort Wayne line, and increased competition for St. Louis traffic reduced earnings on the route between Columbus and Indianapolis. In August 1874, the CC&IC's second mortgage bonds went into default. CC&IC officials, and many of the company's other investors, asserted that the 1869 lease amounted to a Pan Handle and a PRR guarantee of those bonds. Tom Scott denied that the PRR had ever made such a guarantee, but noted that the PRR owned $1,258,000 of the CC&IC bonds and would cease rental payments until its investment had been made good. Meanwhile, negotiations between PRR officials and CC&IC bondholders were not going well. By December 1874, PRR president Tom Scott and CC&IC president Benjamin E. Smith were at loggerheads, with the former demanding the creation of a new class of income bonds to replace the second mortgage bonds, and the latter refusing to do so. At the same time, the New York investors who controlled perhaps 40 percent of the CC&IC, and led by investment banker Charles W. Hassler, sued the PRR, demanding that that company live up to its supposed guarantee of the CC&IC bonds.[131]

From the perspective of PRR officials, the more serious problem was that the high rental payments guaranteed to the CC&IC were threatening the solvency of the Pan Handle. In order to protect the Pan Handle, and in retaliation for the CC&IC assertion in the matter of the bond guarantee, PRR officials demanded payment of the interest on their second mortgage bonds, forcing the CC&IC into receivership. By January 1875, in order to save their company, Pan Handle officials were attempting to repudiate the CC&IC lease. In February they filed suit in the United States Circuit Court for the District of Indiana, accusing CC&IC managers of failing to abide by the terms of the 1869 lease, owing to the company's high indebtedness and lack of a sinking fund. With the support of the PRR, the Pan Handle withheld its promised 30 percent rental payments. In response, CC&IC officials filed suit against the Pan Handle and the PRR, demanding fulfillment of the rental obligations.

As the lawsuits wound their way through the legal system, relations between the PRR, the Pennsylvania Company, the Pan Handle, and the CC&IC degenerated into near-chaos. PRR officials proposed several settlements that would have enabled CC&IC bondholders to recover most of their investments, but to no avail. CC&IC trustees, including William R. Fosdick and James A. Roosevelt, prepared a legal case, demanding that the PRR honor its alleged bond guarantees and make payment of the withheld rent. Financier J. F. D. Lanier seized a portion of the CC&IC, based on an 1865 ruling in a case involving bondholder rights on the New Castle & Richmond Railroad (later the Cincinnati, Logansport & Chicago Railway), one of the original constituent parts of the CC&IC. With ownership of the section of track between Richmond and New Castle in dispute, Pan Handle dispatchers were forced to reroute through trains.[132]

In July 1878, Judge John Marshall Harlan heard the first arguments in the Pan Handle's suit against the CC&IC, as the PRR endeavored to invalidate the 1869 lease. The following April, Harlan ruled that the lease was still valid under Ohio and Indiana law, and that the financial failings of the CC&IC were not a sufficient condition to enable the Pan Handle to withhold its contractually obligated rental payments. However, the judge agreed that the Pan Handle did have the right to demand that the CC&IC put its financial affairs in order, as provided for under the terms of the amended 1870 lease agreement. If that company did not implement a plan to reduce its debt load by the end of the year, then the Pan Handle could indeed break the lease. To the undoubted chagrin of the CC&IC bondholders, however, Judge Harlan did not address their right to compensation.[133]

In a separate ruling issued in August 1879, Judge Harlan addressed the suit filed by CC&IC investors in their attempt to reclaim the withheld rental payments, which by then had exceeded $3 million. He agreed that the CC&IC was entitled to the money, but only after the company had reduced its debt to acceptable levels. He further established that the payment would be $2.6 million, well below what CC&IC investors expected to receive, but well above what PRR officials were prepared to pay. With both sides threatening to appeal the verdict to the United States Supreme

Court, the various parties attempted to negotiate a resolution to the dispute.[134]

The legal battles involving the CC&IC continued into the next decade. By February 1880, the United States Circuit Court for Indiana ruled that the Pan Handle could not abrogate its lease of the CC&IC, but that the CC&IC had likewise failed to restructure its bonded indebtedness. The ruling, while not wholly favorable to the PRR, nonetheless enabled the reorganization of the CC&IC. In the midst of the declining revenues caused by an 1881 rate war, the PRR rectified some of the inefficient features of the southwestern portion of the Lines West organization. In 1883 the PRR transferred the bankrupt Columbus, Chicago & Indiana Central to two versions of the Chicago, St. Louis & Pittsburgh Railroad, one incorporated in Indiana and the other in Illinois. The two identically named companies were merged into one in 1884, and in 1890, the PRR combined that line, and several others, with the Pittsburgh, Cincinnati & St. Louis Railway to create the Pittsburgh, Cincinnati, Chicago & St. Louis Railway, still known as the Pan Handle.[135]

The financial problems associated with the CC&IC seriously affected Ben Smith's mental faculties. During the summer of 1877, his investment-banking house, Bartlit & Smith, fell victim to the financial panic. The same year, acting on his own authority, Smith issued $36,000 in Columbus & Indianapolis Central Railway bonds. The board of the parent company, the Columbus, Chicago & Indiana Central, eventually repudiated the debt. During the early 1880s, Smith failed in his efforts to develop a massive resort hotel at Rockaway Beach, New York. His fortune, reputation, and mental health all in tatters, Smith spent the remainder of his life in an insane asylum. Fortunately, PRR executives had long since recognized Smith's instability and had been careful to curtail his actions.[136]

By the early 1890s, on the eve of the great depression that was to prove fatal to so many railroads, the Pennsylvania Company had finally put its financial affairs in order. The Pennsylvania Railroad owned the Pennsylvania Company's stock, valued at $22.5 million, ensuring that the parent company would gain the benefit of the profits generated by its subsidiaries, and preventing key western lines from coming under the control of speculators or rival railroads. The Pennsylvania

Company's bonded debt was $20.8 million, of which the vast majority carried an extremely low interest rate of 4¼ percent. Even more gratifying, the Pennsylvania Company was now earning a respectable profit—$1.7 million in 1891, on gross earnings of $21.1 million. Few carriers could boast such impressive results.[137]

There was one piece missing from Lines West, however—the route between Indianapolis and St. Louis, still under the control of William Riley McKeen. The ongoing disputes regarding the Pan Handle and the CC&IC affected the PRR's relationship with the Terre Haute & Indianapolis Railroad and its western connection, the St. Louis, Vandalia & Terre Haute Railroad. Under the terms of the March 1868 agreement to issue Vandalia second mortgage bonds, McKeen footed only 20 percent of the cost to build the link to St. Louis, while Ben Smith and the CC&IC had agreed to pay 30 percent, with the Steubenville & Indiana and the Pan Handle each responsible for 25 percent. A month later, the combination of the latter two companies into the Pittsburgh, Cincinnati & St. Louis Railway gave the Pennsylvania Railroad a half-interest in the Vandalia Line, while the January 1869 Pan Handle lease of the CC&IC increased the PRR's share to 80 percent.[138]

Despite the overwhelming preponderance of the PRR's investment, McKeen controlled the expenditures and operations of the Vandalia Line. Under the terms of the 1868 agreement, the TH&I retained 70 percent of the Vandalia's gross earnings in order to offset operating costs. The remaining 30 percent would be distributed to all of the parties, in the same ratio as their investment in the Vandalia's second mortgage bonds. The participants had agreed to reimburse the TH&I for any Vandalia losses, according to the same ratio. McKeen and his fellow TH&I investors would suffer 20 percent of any losses incurred by the Vandalia, and reap only 20 percent of any profits—but they would get all of the revenues generated by traffic continuing along their line between Indianapolis and Terre Haute. That issue was of little consequence, so long as the TH&I was the only route linking those two cities. In September 1867, however, representatives from the Fort Wayne, the Bee Line, and the Cleveland, Columbus & Cincinnati Railroad had incorporated the Indianapolis & St. Louis Railroad as their link to the other route to St. Louis, the St. Louis, Alton & Terre Haute Railroad. After the PRR leased the Fort Wayne in July 1869, its officials frantically attempted to halt construction of the Indianapolis & St. Louis, but their counterparts on the Bee Line—affiliated as they were with the New York Central—would have none of it. The PRR now owned half of a route that paralleled the TH&I, yet the terms of the 1868 agreement required that all of the PRR's western traffic be routed over McKeen's railroad.

What PRR officials understandably viewed as needlessly inefficient duplication, McKeen saw as an opportunity. Using the TH&I's lease of the Vandalia Line to his advantage, McKeen poured money—80 percent of which was really the PRR's money—into his western outlet. In fairness to McKeen, the Vandalia Line badly needed new equipment and improvements to its physical plant. However, PRR officials asserted—with considerable justification—that McKeen was over-investing in the Vandalia Line, while authorizing favorable through rates to traffic connecting with the TH&I. In that manner, they complained, McKeen was able to draw traffic away from the Indianapolis & St. Louis (which was half-owned by the PRR), while forcing the PRR to bear 80 percent of the cost associated with the use of the Vandalia Line in order to cross-subsidize traffic on the TH&I. The cutthroat competition between the TH&I and the Indianapolis & St. Louis continued until April 1874, when the traffic declines associated with the economic depression persuaded all of the parties to agree on a traffic pool. A year later, the traffic pool evolved into the joint operation of the TH&I and the Indianapolis & St. Louis.[139]

The 1874 traffic pool resolved only one of the many disagreements between McKeen and PRR officials. In 1871, the formation of the Pennsylvania Company had enabled the PRR to more effectively organize and systematize its western operations. The same year, George Roberts, then the PRR's fourth vice president, with responsibility for western lines (and an officer of the Pennsylvania Company), became president of the St. Louis, Vandalia & Terre Haute. Yet, despite the PRR's 80 percent ownership of the Vandalia, Roberts failed to fill its board with PRR loyalists, stymied by an Illinois law requiring all of that company's directors to be state residents. What Roberts found even more frus-

trating was his inability to impose fiscal restraint and more efficient operating techniques on the Vandalia, or even to obtain accurate data from the TH&I personnel who were responsible for the line's operation. By 1871, PRR executives had devised sophisticated revenue and cost accounting mechanisms in the interest of increasing operating efficiency, yet those calculations depended on a reliable flow of information that the independent and occasionally irascible McKeen often failed to provide. Roberts next attempted to purchase a controlling interest in the TH&I, but McKeen outmaneuvered him by acquiring a large block of shares owned by the railroad's founder, Chauncey Rose.[140]

If the depression illustrated the dangers associated with McKeen's oversight of both the TH&I and the Vandalia, it also provided PRR officials with the opportunity to remedy the situation. In 1875, Pan Handle executives used their repudiation of the Columbus, Chicago & Indiana Central lease as an excuse to abrogate any responsibility for the CC&IC's 30 percent share of the Vandalia's losses, as provided in the 1868 contract. McKeen retaliated by declaring that he would no longer pay the specified 30 percent of the Vandalia's gross earnings to the CC&IC. McKeen's strategy affected the TH&I, as that company was due 20 percent of the 30 percent, but it hurt the PRR, with an 80 percent share, far more. Outraged PRR officials counterattacked, instructing Pittsburgh, Cincinnati & St. Louis officials to cease payment of its 50 percent share of the Vandalia's losses (that is, the portion that had originally been the responsibility of the Steubenville & Indiana and the Pan Handle Railway), and making the TH&I effectively responsible for any deficits that the Vandalia occurred while under McKeen's management. McKeen offered a compromise, in which the TH&I would be responsible for 28.6 percent of the Vandalia, with the remaining 71.4 percent assigned to the Pan Handle, but PRR executives refused to accept the arrangement.[141]

As the depression deepened, Pennsylvania Company officials attempted to shed their responsibility for the Fort Wayne's half of the essentially useless and financially troubled Indianapolis & St. Louis—an investment that had cost the Pan Handle, which inherited the Fort Wayne's share, more than $250,000 in

1876 alone. Even worse were the terms of the 1867 Indianapolis & St. Louis lease of the St. Louis, Alton & Terre Haute, which had guaranteed a minimum annual rental of $450,000. Beginning on June 1, 1878, the Pennsylvania Company began withholding rental payments, after the Alton line's directors refused to accept a reduced fee. In 1882, the PRR resolved the problem by relinquishing control of the Indianapolis & St. Louis, including that company's lease of the Alton Route, to Vanderbilt's Bee Line subsidiary, the Cleveland, Columbus, Cincinnati & Indianapolis Railway.[142]

Both Tom Scott and George Roberts, who now served as first vice president of the Pennsylvania Railroad, attempted to use similarly confrontational tactics to force the Terre Haute & Indianapolis to transfer its lease of the St. Louis, Vandalia & Terre Haute to the PRR. McKeen resisted the loss of control, but Roberts's ascension to the PRR presidency in June 1880 made him more insistent. McKeen allowed Pan Handle general manager Darius W. Caldwell, a veteran of the CC&IC, to serve as the general manager of the TH&I. Caldwell and another Pan Handle executive, Joseph Hill, soon implemented Lines West operating and financial accounting methods on the TH&I and on the Vandalia. The PRR likewise mined the TH&I of its most talented officers, continuing the decades-old practice of using its western affiliates as a mechanism for training and evaluating junior executives.[143]

For several decades, William McKeen had successfully protected local interests against the distant PRR organization, taking advantage of periodic conflicts between the great trunk lines. By the 1880s, however, competition had stabilized, as investors concluded that long-term financial success rested more with predictable organizational methods and not with maverick entrepreneurs or local rail magnates. Under such altered circumstances, the PRR was now in a position to dictate terms to the Terre Haute & Indianapolis. Aging, grief stricken at the death of his wife, and with his railroad affected by the 1881 rate war, McKeen agreed to sell his TH&I holdings to the PRR for $75 a share. Roberts nonetheless hesitated. He possessed grave concerns regarding the TH&I's financial condition, and he demanded a thorough auditing of that company's books as a condition for purchase. While

negotiations were taking place, Roberts expressed his dissatisfaction with McKeen's strategic decision making. As had been the case nearly a decade earlier, McKeen was seeking to increase the local traffic on the TH&I through leases and new construction, while Roberts perceived those moves as costly and unnecessary to the movement of PRR traffic to St. Louis.[144]

In 1887, frustrated at the PRR's delays, McKeen sold his holdings to a maverick young financier, Henry S. Ives, and the transaction soon changed the relationship between the PRR and the lines linking Indianapolis and St. Louis. McKeen may have been a nuisance, but he was a respectable one, and a person PRR executives trusted. Ives, in contrast, was young, headstrong, and unpredictable. His tactics offended more respectable Wall Street operatives and eventually landed him in New York's Ludlow Street Jail. The resulting *New York Times* headline—"This Time He Is Indicted"— fairly well summed up his credentials as a financier.[145]

Baltimore & Ohio president John W. Garrett was indirectly responsible for the meteoric rise and equally rapid fall of Henry Ives. Garrett had unwisely decided to extend the B&O's influence to Staten Island and, even with the use of the Bound Brook Route north of Philadelphia, the strategy crippled the railroad's finances. Garrett died in September 1884, and his son Robert inherited all of his father's eccentricities, and none of his talents. By early 1887, the heir to the B&O empire concluded that he needed to sell his large block of stock in the company.[146]

Ives immediately sensed an opportunity. Still in his twenties, he had already tricked seasoned Wall Street veterans into investing in a worthless telegraph company, in 1885, and he was stricken from the exchanges as a result. In 1886 he secured control over the Mineral Range Railroad, in Michigan, and then used that company as a base to acquire the Cincinnati, Hamilton & Dayton—a coup that temporarily redeemed his unsavory reputation in financial circles. The new acquisition, a well-managed company that was flush with cash, provided Ives with the opportunity to make a bid for the Terre Haute & Indianapolis. Together, the two roads would enable Ives to feed traffic to the B&O—crucial because Garrett had already lost control over the Ohio & Mississippi line linking Cincinnati and St. Louis. More important, the treasuries of the two companies could provide Ives with the funds that he needed to buy out Robert Garrett's share of the B&O.[147]

Ives used the treasury of the Cincinnati, Hamilton & Dayton to pay for a controlling interest in the Terre Haute & Indianapolis, and then drained the reserves of both railroads in order to make a bid for the B&O. Ives summarily canceled the traffic agreement between the Cincinnati, Hamilton & Dayton and the Cincinnati, Indianapolis, St. Louis & Chicago Railroad. For their own protection, the owners of the latter company sought an alliance with the Indianapolis & St. Louis and its parent company, the Bee Line. By 1889, the negotiations led to the creation of the Cleveland, Cincinnati, Chicago & St. Louis Railway—the "Big Four"—and that NYC-affiliated line quickly became the strongest competitor of the PRR's Lines West.[148]

George Roberts and other PRR executives were caught off guard by Ives's maneuverings, but they soon regrouped and fought back. On July 6, 1887, PRR attorneys filed suit against the Terre Haute & Indianapolis, attempting to abrogate that road's lease of the St. Louis, Vandalia & Terre Haute, and to claim the Vandalia Line for themselves. PRR officials also spoke with any Wall Street investor associated with Ives, warning of the consequences that would surely befall anyone who so blatantly violated the interests of the largest railroad in the world. On July 20, Garrett announced that Ives had failed to raise the funds necessary to exercise his option on the B&O stock. Ives's financial house of cards collapsed almost overnight, and on August 11 his investment bank, Henry Ives & Company, failed. By 1889, his appropriation of Cincinnati, Hamilton & Dayton funds landed him in Ludlow Street Jail. Although he was acquitted in 1890, he died four years later of tuberculosis.[149]

William McKeen regained the presidency of the Terre Haute & Indianapolis, but, thanks to Ives, he took control of a shattered railroad. In January 1888, his attorneys succeeded in beating back the PRR's attempt to invalidate the Terre Haute & Indianapolis lease of the Vandalia Line, but the railroad's weakened condition finally pushed McKeen into the arms of the Pennsylvania Railroad. Pennsylvania Company officials, including comptroller Thomas D. Messler, the accounting expert of Lines West, soon opened negoti-

ations with their counterparts on the Terre Haute & Indianapolis. They particularly wanted to work with John G. Williams, McKeen's chief legal counsel, who by 1888 was the vice president and general manager of the Terre Haute & Indianapolis. They had seen Williams in action during the fight over the Vandalia Line lease, and the PRR personnel knew talent when they saw it.[150]

By May 1890, PRR and Terre Haute & Indianapolis personnel had finally resolved the dispute, dating to the 1870s, as to which company would be responsible for the chronic operating losses on the Vandalia Line. McKeen signed promissory notes totaling nearly $800,000, yet his corporate treasury, well and truly raided by Ives, lacked the money to pay the Pan Handle the agreed-upon amount. Adding to those difficulties, McKeen did himself no favors when he pledged the TH&I's credit to the construction of the Indiana & Lake Michigan Railway, an extension of the Terre Haute & Logansport line from South Bend north to the port of St. Joseph on Lake Michigan. He also fulfilled the dream of Chauncey Rose, dating to 1861, to link Terre Haute to Peoria, Illinois. By acquiring the Terre Haute & Peoria Railroad in 1892, McKeen obtained a line from Terre Haute through Decatur to Peoria, but its poor construction and inadequate maintenance were not likely to add appreciably to the TH&I's bottom line.[151]

By 1892, McKeen was exhausted by years of legal and financial battles to keep the TH&I afloat, and he was ready for retirement. In May of the same year, the PRR's legal team was unable to persuade the justices of the United States Supreme Court to invalidate the Vandalia Line lease. Having failed in their legal gambit, PRR officials were now ready to deal seriously with McKeen. In addition to the vital link to St. Louis, they coveted the TH&I's leased Terre Haute & Logansport line north to Logansport, which would serve as a northern extension of the Jeffersonville, Madison & Indianapolis Railroad route between Louisville and Indianapolis.[152]

In August 1893, the Pennsylvania Company agreed to use a combination of cash and Pan Handle bonds to purchase McKeen's fourteen thousand shares of Terre Haute & Indianapolis stock at $75 a share—the same price that Roberts had refused a decade earlier. McKeen remained as president, largely as a figurehead, but Lines West personnel soon reorganized the TH&I's operating methods, bringing them into strict conformity with system practices. The PRR, through the Pennsylvania Company, had paid more than $1 million to retain secure access to St. Louis and to bring to heel the last of the maverick midwestern railway entrepreneurs.[153]

The PRR's timing was poor, however, and the severe depression that began only a few months after the sale hobbled the TH&I, the Vandalia Line, and the routes to St. Joseph and Peoria. After McKeen retired in 1895, Lines West first vice president James McCrea took his place and completed the transition to PRR control, imposing severe financial constraints in the process. The depression took its toll, however, and in 1896 the PRR placed the TH&I and its affiliated lines in receivership.[154] Effective January 1, 1905, the PRR consolidated the Terre Haute & Indianapolis; the St. Louis, Vandalia & Terre Haute; the Terre Haute & Logansport; the Logansport & Toledo; and the Indianapolis & Vincennes into the Vandalia Railroad.[155] John Williams, the savvy attorney who had fended off the PRR's attempts to break the Vandalia Line lease, became the general counsel for the newly organized company, his talents too valuable to be allowed to slip away.[156]

Organizational Changes on Lines West

Given the intricate ownership arrangements associated with the Pennsylvania Company and its subsidiaries, it was hardly surprising that coordination and organizational innovation on Lines West lagged behind similar developments on Lines East by perhaps a decade. The relative scarcity of traffic was partly to blame, as was the complex structure associated with the PRR's ownership of the Pennsylvania Company, and the Pennsylvania Company's control of its subsidiaries through leases, stock and bond purchases, and performance guarantees.

The principal component of the northwestern portion of Lines West, the Pittsburgh, Fort Wayne & Chicago, essentially ceased to exist as a separate entity following its 1869 lease to the PRR, a lease that was subsequently transferred to the Pennsylvania Company. The Fort Wayne retained only a token staff, necessary to process the PRR's lease payments and distribute them to investors. As such, Pennsylvania Company officials made all short-term operating and long-term strategic decisions governing the Fort Wayne, in collaboration with senior PRR executives. The situation was very different in the southwest, where the Pennsylvania Company controlled the Pittsburgh, Cincinnati & St. Louis Railway (the Pan Handle) and its affiliated lines through majority stock ownership. Pennsylvania Company officials were responsible for relations between the Pan Handle and other Lines West subsidiaries, particularly the interchange of traffic and the allocation of equipment. Strategic decisions involving the Pan Handle were also the responsibility of the Pennsylvania Company board of directors. Routine operating matters, however, remained under the control of Pan Handle officials.[157]

Through the 1880s, the management structure on Lines West evolved slowly from its origins during the previous decade. The president of the Pennsylvania Railroad served as president of the Pennsylvania Company. However, the first vice president of the Pennsylvania Company was for all intents and purposes in charge of Lines West, serving as chief executive officer. As on the PRR, additional Pennsylvania Company vice presidents held varying duties, including transportation, traffic, and accounting functions. They were assisted by the customary complement of staff officers, including the treasurer, the auditor, the secretary, the general counsel, the chief engineer, the general freight agent, the general passenger and ticket agent, and the purchasing agent. In many, but not all, cases, these positions overlapped. For example, the same executive served as the Pan Handle's ticket agent, as well as the general passenger and ticket agent for the Pennsylvania Company. Both of the firms shared the same secretary.[158]

Not until 1885, however, did Lines West possess a general manager.[159] He was the chief operating officer, reporting to the vice president in charge of the Transportation Department on Lines West, with duties equivalent to the general manager on Lines East. Even then, there was a difference. On Lines East, the general manager oversaw the general superintendents on each of the Grand Divisions and exercised additional control over the leased companies that were not yet part of the Grand Division structure. On Lines West, the same individual (James McCrea, initially, before he became fourth vice president in 1887) was simultaneously the general manager of the Pennsylvania Company and the Pan Handle. He had authority over traffic functions (the Passenger and Freight Departments), the Engineering Department, the Motive Power Department, and the Purchasing Department. Most important, McCrea and successive general managers supervised the Transportation Department. From there, the line of authority in the Transportation Department led downward through the customary complement of division superintendents and their personnel on each of the constituent Pennsylvania Company carriers.

In September 1890, the Pennsylvania Company administratively consolidated many of its southwestern lines, including the Pan Handle; the Chicago, St. Louis & Pittsburgh Railroad (the corporate successor to the Columbus, Chicago & Indiana Central); the Jeffersonville, Madison & Indianapolis Railroad; and the Cincinnati & Richmond Railroad, to form the Pittsburgh, Cincinnati, Chicago & St. Louis Railway, also known as the Pan Handle. The new Pan Handle's passenger cars wore the same Tuscan red livery that had become standard on Pennsylvania Railroad equipment, although the letterboards read "Pennsylvania Lines" rather than "Pennsylvania Railroad."[160] Freight cars and locomotives also carried Pennsylvania Lines lettering, or the heralds of affiliated railroads, such as the Grand Rapids & Indiana. Although the Lines West shops, such as those in Fort Wayne and in Columbus, Ohio, continued to manufacture and repair locomotives and rolling stock, the equipment visually resembled, and was certainly operationally compatible with, that employed on Lines East.

As part of the 1890 reorganization, Pennsylvania Company officials created two "Systems," analogous to the Grand Divisions on the Pennsylvania Railroad. Each System was supervised by a general superintendent, who in turn reported to the Lines West general manager. The old Pittsburgh, Fort Wayne & Chicago formed the core of the Northwest System, which extended from Pittsburgh through to Chicago. The

Southwest System, based on the Pan Handle companies, also possessed routes to Chicago, but its line due west from Pittsburgh stopped at Indianapolis. The independent Terre Haute & Indianapolis and its leased St. Louis, Vandalia & Terre Haute covered the remaining distance to St. Louis.[161]

Despite their organizational innovations, PRR executives were never entirely successful in their attempts to integrate the eastern and western portions of the system. In many respects, the lines west of Pittsburgh were considerably different than those to the east. In 1877, the PRR's Lines East consisted of 1,071 route miles, but Lines West spanned three times that distance—3,407 route miles. Yet, the western portion of the PRR system had fewer employees and, more important, generated a far lower volume of business than the east. The Southwest System proved particularly disappointing in that respect; its traffic never matched that of the Northwest System, much less that of Lines East. In 1873, for example, the Fort Wayne and the Cleveland & Pittsburgh (the two principal components of the Northwest System) collectively generated $5.4 million in net earnings, while the Pan Handle managed only $478,298 and the Columbus, Chicago & Indiana Central an anemic $233,183. Combined net earnings for all of the Pennsylvania Company subsidiaries totaled $8.7 million, well below the $9.4 million on the PRR proper. The situation was scarcely better in 1902, when the PRR's Lines East of Pittsburgh and Erie generated $37.6 million in net income, compared to $4.3 million on the Fort Wayne, and $2.6 million on the Pan Handle. The carriers operated directly by the Pennsylvania Company (which generated the bulk of the revenues on Lines West) garnered only $9.7 million in net income. The financial picture was clouded by the high level of rental payments that were guaranteed by the Pennsylvania Company and ultimately by the Pennsylvania Railroad—and much of that money, it should be noted, came back to the PRR, as an investor in the various Lines West subsidiaries. The more informative measure would probably be net earnings per mile—$10,353 on the PRR's Lines East, $9,213 on the Fort Wayne, and only $4,902 on the Pan Handle.[162]

Despite the ongoing efforts of PRR executives to generate additional business on Lines West, the bulk of the PRR's traffic moved comparatively short distances through the region that stretched from the far eastern edge of Ohio through the commonwealth of Pennsylvania. In that area, at least, the PRR was reasonably protected from water-carrier competition, as well as from the inroads of the other trunk lines. Traffic from the more westerly regions of the PRR was exceedingly vulnerable to competition from rival railroads and from lake boats, as well as from oceanic shipping. Even before the completion of the Panama Canal, Pittsburgh steel typically reached the west coast by first traveling east to an Atlantic seaport, and then continuing onward by ship, without ever gracing the rails of Lines West to Chicago or St. Louis.[163]

As such, the mix of traffic on Lines West was often different from that which prevailed on Lines East. The iron and coal regions of eastern Ohio in many ways resembled those of western Pennsylvania, and some lines, particularly between Pittsburgh and Cleveland, carried substantial quantities of raw materials. Farther west, however, the foothills of the Alleghenies gave way to farmland, with a much smaller industrial base. Traffic was particularly sparse on the southwestern portion of the system, and the St. Louis gateway never rivaled the importance of Chicago. By the early twentieth century, as Lines East executives attempted to cope with soaring traffic levels that threatened to inundate their facilities, their counterparts on Lines West struggled to generate additional business.

Furthermore, the tracks of the Northwest System, the Southwest System, and Lines East came together at one of the most congested locations in the United States. Hemmed in by rivers and hills, all three components of the PRR maintained separate freight facilities at Pittsburgh, greatly retarding the efficient exchange of traffic between Lines East and Lines West. The city's tremendous industrial growth during the late 1800s only added to the problem. By the beginning of the twentieth century, Pittsburgh accommodated more freight traffic than any other metropolitan area in the world. An even more serious crisis occurred during World War I, when the city's yards were jammed with traffic. In 1920, PRR executives had little choice other than to abandon the Pennsylvania Company model and bring Lines West more directly under their control. Many shippers, government officials, and railroad experts suggested that the move was long overdue.[164]

What critics of the PRR's organization and operations failed to appreciate, however, was that the PRR in 1920 was a far larger and more complex enterprise than it had been in 1870, when the Pennsylvania Company received its corporate charter. In 1873 the Pennsylvania Company controlled 2,943 route miles, with 803 of those miles (generally speaking, the core components of what later became the Northwest System) under direct operation and the remainder managed by the executives of the various constituent carriers. By 1898, the Pennsylvania Company's routes had increased to 4,353 miles, of which 1,777 miles were under direct operation. Through the late 1800s and into the early twentieth century, the Pennsylvania Company incrementally subsumed additional companies under its corporate umbrella. Its reach was greatest during the 1910s, when it controlled forty-one railroads, seven terminal or belt-line railroads, three improvement companies, and a steamship line. The Pennsylvania Company also held investments in dozens of other companies, a number of which were far more closely connected to the PRR than to Lines West. By 1920, the Pennsylvania Company had become something that J. Edgar Thomson and Tom Scott could never have envisioned, when they created that holding company fifty years earlier.[165]

Finance During the Era of System Building

The PRR's finances were badly buffeted by the depression of the 1870s. Not since 1852, when J. Edgar Thomson struggled to find the money necessary to complete the Mountain Division, had the Pennsylvania Railroad faced such stringent circumstances. The company's stockholders, who since 1868 had been accustomed to receiving annual dividend payments of 10 percent, certainly experienced some financial discomfort. In November 1873, the PRR paid its 5 percent dividend in scrip, rather than cash. At least that was a better performance than the Northern Central, which declined to pay any dividends at all. In May 1874, the PRR board voted to resume dividend payments at a rate of 10 percent annually, even though there was initially insufficient cash available to make good the pledge. The following year, the directors reduced dividends to a more modest 8 percent a year, prompting a quick decline in share prices. In May 1877, the dividend rate fell again, to 6 percent, and PRR stock soon dropped to about $35 a share, barely more than two-thirds of the par of $50. Three months later, still reeling from the Pittsburgh riots, the board suspended the scheduled dividend payment, causing stock prices to fall below $25. Not until October 1878 did dividend payments resume, at a rate of only 4 percent annually.[166]

The volatility of dividend payments created a substantial contingent of disgruntled shareholders, and their irritation was compounded by leases at the eastern and western edges of the system. During the heady, expansionist years of the late 1860s and early 1870s, Thomson and the board had been willing to pay virtually any price in order to secure control over such affiliates as the Fort Wayne; the Columbus, Chicago & Indiana Central; and the United Companies. In that sellers' market, the PRR provided extremely generous terms, paying CC&IC investors 30 percent of that railroad's earnings each year, to say nothing of guaranteeing a 12 percent annual return to Fort Wayne shareholders, and 10 percent to their counterparts who had invested in the United Companies. PRR shareholders could not help but notice that their company continued to make good those obligations, at a time when their own dividends were few and far between. The more serious problem was that the PRR had probably paid too much for its investments in subsidiary companies, particularly in light of the dramatic market declines that began in 1873. By 1878, the Pennsylvania Railroad was obligated to guarantee $180 million of the securities of its subsidiaries—more than the company itself was worth. The average interest on those obligations was 7.4 percent, well above prevailing market rates, and burdening the PRR with annual fixed charges of more than $13 million. The obvious solution would have been for the PRR to borrow money at 6 percent or less and use the funds to buy out the owners of stocks and bonds that earned as much as 12 percent, even if that meant paying a premium to investors who coveted their guaranteed high returns.[167]

At the March 1878 annual shareholders' meeting, President Scott proposed the creation of a trust fund that would purchase control of the securities that the PRR had guaranteed. Each month, the PRR would contribute $50,000 to a reserve account, up to 2 percent of the company's total equity capitalization. The trust managers (the PRR president, one of the vice presidents, and three directors) would then use those funds to buy stocks and bonds in the PRR's leased lines. The securities held in the trust would continue to earn interest, paid by the PRR, but those earnings would be retained by the trust and used to purchase additional subsidiary securities. Ultimately, some executives hoped, it might even be possible to use proceeds from the trust to retire the bulk of the PRR's bonded debt.[168]

PRR shareholders overwhelmingly approved the creation of the Trust of 1878, even though it annually siphoned off $600,000 that might otherwise have gone to dividends. In effect, they agreed with Scott that it would be wiser to forgo immediate returns, in the interest of long-term stability and enhanced earnings. The trust proved extraordinarily successful at reducing the PRR's fixed charges—so much so that in 1885 the annual contribution was lowered to 1 percent of net income prior to the payment of dividends. In addition, the trust solidified the PRR's control over the CC&IC, the Fort Wayne, the United Companies, and others, as the company increasingly moved from guaranteeing the payment of dividends and interest on the stocks and bonds of its subsidiaries to owning those companies outright.

The same desire for control led to the end of municipal ownership of PRR securities. Beginning in 1847, various local governments—including those of Philadelphia, the Northern Liberties, Spring Garden, and Allegheny County—had purchased more than $5.7 million in Pennsylvania Railroad stock, an amount that represented more than half of the company's initially authorized capitalization. That support was critical to the completion of the route between Harrisburg and Pittsburgh. Despite the large public investment, and even though the Philadelphia Select and Common Councils and the Commissioners of Allegheny County were entitled to appoint several PRR directors, actual control over the PRR remained firmly in the hands of corporate executives and private investors. The economic crisis that began in 1857 induced an amendment to the state constitution that barred further public subscriptions. Allegheny County was particularly affected by the downturn, not so much because of its PRR stock, but rather owing to unwise investments in many other railroads. As a result, the Allegheny County Commissioners distributed the PRR shares to the holders of otherwise-worthless county bonds, and the county's representatives left the PRR board. Philadelphia retained its large investment in PRR stock, and the Select and Common Councils continued to select directors—although they were individuals who typically cooperated closely with PRR executives. In the depressed economic conditions that followed the Panic of 1873, however, there were rumors that the city might sell its PRR stock to speculators such as Jay Gould, or to someone else who might threaten the long-established authority of PRR managers. In December 1879, the PRR board agreed to spend nearly $3 million to purchase the 59,149 shares of stock owned by the City of Philadelphia. The PRR's thirty-year status as a mixed enterprise was over.[169]

It was just as well that Scott had reduced the PRR's obligations, for his successor, George Roberts, was soon responsible for some very expensive projects. Chief among them was the acquisition of the Philadelphia, Wilmington & Baltimore, not through a lease or a securities guarantee, but rather through an outright cash purchase of the bulk of the outstanding shares. Although Roberts oversaw the construction of relatively few new lines, he invested heavily in improvements to the roadbed, locomotives, and cars. Between 1879 and 1896, the PRR spent more than $50 million on equipment and the physical plant—an amount that exceeded its total expenditures in those areas between 1846 and 1878. Real estate holdings more than doubled, from $9.9 million to $20.5 million. At the same time, the value of the PRR's investments in the securities of its subsidiaries increased from $54 million to $120 million, an amount that included, but was by no means limited to, the purchase of the PW&B. In addition to consuming more than $40 million in reinvested earnings, the improvements initiated by Roberts required $47.2 million raised from new stock offerings, along with $27.7 million worth of bonds and related debt instruments. It would have been far more difficult to raise such enormous sums had it not been for the financial restraints imposed by the Trust of 1878.[170]

Fortunately for Roberts, he presided over a railroad with a sterling reputation in financial circles, and investment bankers eagerly sought the PRR's business.[171] By the late 1880s, the most successful was Kuhn, Loeb & Company, the investment firm that Abraham Kuhn and Solomon Loeb had established in 1867. Under the aggressive leadership of Jacob Schiff, Loeb's son-in-law, the firm competed for the PRR account. In 1881 Kuhn, Loeb marketed the PRR's bonds for the first time. Over the next two decades, nearly $50 million in investment capital reached the Pennsylvania Railroad through Kuhn, Loeb. The PRR's business, along with that of the Union Pacific and the other companies controlled by Edward H. Harriman, established Kuhn, Loeb's reputation as one of the preeminent investment banking firms associated with the railroads, second only to J. P. Morgan. By the late 1890s, Kuhn, Loeb had replaced Tony Drexel (who died in 1893) as the PRR's investment banker of choice.[172]

For the next half-century, the rivalry between the Pennsylvania Railroad and the New York Central extended to the world of finance, with Kuhn, Loeb handling the affairs of one, and J. P. Morgan & Company those of the other. One was attuned to Philadelphia, and the other to New York and Wall Street. The Jewish families who managed Kuhn, Loeb were probably less welcome in the resolutely Protestant western Philadelphia suburbs that were home to so many senior PRR executives than the Protestants who worked for the House of Morgan. In practice, however, the nation's two leading banking houses, and their smaller rivals, jointly marketed large securities offerings for the PRR and other companies under what Morgan biographer Ron Chernow has called the "Gentleman Banker's Code."[173]

To satisfy the PRR's financial needs, Roberts increasingly turned to overseas capital markets, an area where Kuhn, Loeb possessed particularly strong connections. As late as 1871, Americans held more than 92 percent of PRR stock, with only 7.37 percent in the hands of foreign investors, most of whom were British. Foreign investment in the United States surged during the following decade, despite the economic conditions that followed the Panic of 1873. British investors in particular were attracted by the slow growth of the American money supply, as well as a deflationary spiral that was certain to benefit creditors. By 1885, the British had invested more in American railroads than in national debt, and by 1890 their holdings of American railway securities were in excess of £300 million. Those sweeping changes in transatlantic finance certainly affected the Pennsylvania Railroad. A consummate system builder, Roberts provided reassurance to conservative British investors, who felt that they no longer need worry about Tom Scott's speculative ventures. The level of foreign ownership of PRR stock increased to 29.8 percent in 1881, and to 47.5 percent by 1888. By 1890, foreign investors controlled more than half of the PRR's stock, a situation that was not notably different from the in-migration of capital that characterized the internal improvements of the early nineteenth century.[174]

British investors relished the sound management and financial stability that made the PRR such a safe investment, yet they often chafed at the reinvestments in tracks, structures, and equipment that made that stability possible. Foreign securities holders, particularly those from Britain, typically wanted a far larger share of the PRR's earnings distributed in the form of dividends. They believed that bonded debt should be used to finance additions to the physical plant—a request that threatened to undermine the railroad's long-standing policy of dividing current earnings more or less equally between dividends and reinvestment. As a consequence, Roberts had to plead for greater solidarity among the railroad's more conservative American stockholders, who were more concerned with long-term growth than with an immediate return on their investment.[175]

Yet, British investors exercised very little influence in the day-to-day operations of the Pennsylvania Railroad, in large measure because the existing directors refused to allow any British shareholders to sit on the PRR board. An 1884 editorial in the *Economist* acknowledged that the PRR was the "Greatest Railway Company in the World," yet lamented that "as to its future, that is largely with President Roberts; and even if the English shareholders desired a larger voice in the management, they could not get it."[176] In 1887, for example, British investors seeking higher dividends formed a shareholders' committee, but met with little success. More strident British critics simply labeled the

PRR's management style "autocratic." Yet, they rarely sold their PRR securities, suggesting that in the final analysis they were willing to yield administrative control to the professional managers who so diligently reinvested the railroad's income.[177]

In contrast, PRR executives, and American railroad experts in general, were increasingly critical of European investors. They alleged, often inaccurately, that foreigners wanted to acquire securities as a quick speculative venture, with correspondingly less interest in reinvested earnings or conservative management. As the Harvard-trained economist William Z. Ripley noted in 1914, "It is a deplorable feature of European investment—characteristic of several generations of experience—that interest is persistently manifested in speculative rather than conservative investment properties. Foreigners seem unable to learn the lesson that first-class American railway shares are often preferable to the bonds of second or third rate speculative or heavily over-capitalized enterprises."[178]

Yet, the British attitude toward American railway securities probably had less to do with their purported desire to earn lavish dividends than with larger changes in the global economy. By the end of the nineteenth century, the ruinous economic depression of the 1890s caused many British investors to dispose of their American investments. At the same time, the Boer War and the development of South African gold mines provided numerous alternative investment possibilities for British capital. Beginning around 1893, British purchases of American railway securities began to decline relative to British investments in American manufacturing firms and in British overseas colonies. At the same time, rates of return for British railway companies began to fall, and investors there seem to have taken that development as a sign to pull back from all railway investments, even though returns for American lines often held steady.[179]

The Beginnings of Railroad Regulation

Railroads constituted the nation's first big businesses, so it was hardly surprising that they also were the first to experience the expanded reach of the regulatory state. Just as governments, particularly at the local and state levels, competed against one another in their efforts to support railroad development, so too did they vie for the power to regulate the transportation enterprises that they had helped to create. Beginning as early as the 1830s, state governments in particular had employed legislative mechanisms to ameliorate the disruptive effects of railroad competition, safeguard the rights of investors, protect the lives of citizens, and control rates.[180]

Starting in the 1830s and 1840s, and paralleling legislative interest in canal regulation, state governments also assumed oversight of matters relating to railroad safety and finance. In 1832, Connecticut became the first state to establish a regulatory commission, charged with ensuring that railroads complied with the terms of their corporate charters. New Hampshire and Rhode Island each established regulatory agencies in 1844, one responsible for safety issues and the other charged with preventing discrimination in rates and terms of service. In 1869, under the leadership of Charles Francis Adams, Jr. (the great-grandson of President John Adams), the Massachusetts legislature created a Board of Railroad Commissioners. The board, and its counterparts in other states, have often been characterized as "sunshine commissions," whose members endeavored to shine the light of publicity on railroad operations, shaming managers into implementing reforms. Such voluntarism, Adams believed, would preclude the necessity for more activist government intervention in the railroad business.[181]

State legislators also attempted to protect passengers and shippers from what they considered to be unjust rates. Many corporate charters, including the one granted to the Pennsylvania Railroad, specified maximum rates. Such provisions, typically based on the language of turnpike and canal charters, were rarely effective. Part of the problem was that in many cases legislators sought to encourage the development of better transportation, and set rates at a level guaranteed to be remunerative. Even when statutes specified restrictive rates, railroad executives were usually able to employ creative accounting or some other subterfuge in order to thwart legislative intent. More broadly, rapid improvements in railway equipment and operating methods steadily lowered the cost of providing transportation, to a point where most carriers could

earn a healthy profit, even if their rates were set well below the level specified by state law. The larger issue was that charters rarely specified *minimum* tariffs, and thus could not protect PRR executives from ruinous rate wars that had roiled the railroads since the 1850s.[182]

Indiscriminate rate cutting on through routes, coupled with correspondingly higher rates on local service, encouraged western farmers to demand firmer legislative control over shipping costs. In 1867, Oliver H. Kelley oversaw the establishment of the National Grange of the Order of Patrons of Husbandry. While the Grange charter discouraged its members from engaging in direct political activism, the farmers who joined that organization often sought government intervention as a remedy for their difficulties. They had much to complain about, as they felt the burdens of a difficult climate, decreasing annual rainfall, and declining commodity prices, as well as the effects of an emerging global market for agricultural products. Farmers concentrated their inchoate unease on the railroads, which were vital to their survival but also symbolized eastern capital, greed, financial manipulation, industrialization, and other forces beyond their control.[183]

Farmers felt a particular antipathy toward the disparity between long-haul and short-haul rates. Railroads typically held rates to very low levels on lengthy routes linking major cities, owing largely to the pressure of rail and water carrier competition, although the increased efficiency associated with transporting large quantities of bulk products over long distances played a role as well. Because water carriers could carry grain more efficiently than the railroads, through traffic of necessity had to move at rates lower than the fully allocated cost of service (that is, variable cost plus the shipment's share of fixed costs), lest it be lost to the boats that plied the Great Lakes and the Erie Canal. No traffic pool, no matter how effective, had ever managed to set rates on the lake boats at a level high enough to enable the railroads to earn a profit solely on the long-distance transportation of bulk commodities. In many cases, competitive through traffic barely covered the variable costs associated with its transportation. As such, railway executives had little choice but to use captive local traffic to buy down a comparatively larger share of fixed costs. To reduce rates on local traffic in order to achieve parity with long-haul traffic would imperil the railroads' ability to cross-subsidize shipments that were unavoidably subject to water carrier competition. Raising rates on through traffic to match those applying to the short haul would strip the railroads of the long-haul shipments that, because of their sheer volume, paid down a substantial portion of fixed costs. In practice, moreover, long-haul/short-haul rate discrimination often worked to the benefit of both local farmers and through shippers. In many cases, low through rates secured the volume of traffic necessary for the railroads to offer any service at all, at any price, to marginal markets.[184]

Yet farmers and other shippers were uninterested in the economic principles that led to lower rates for longer hauls. Rather, farmers perceived only unfairness, and cast themselves in the role of victims. The Grangers and their allies reached the peak of their power during the early 1870s.[185] Beginning in 1871, the legislatures of Illinois, Iowa, Minnesota, and Wisconsin created "strong" railroad commissions vested with the power to establish railroad rates. Generally speaking, the laws required the railroads to carry local freight, within state limits, at per-mile rates that were no higher than those for through shipments. The carriers were generally quick to comply with the new state-mandated rate schedules, although not necessarily in the manner that the Grangers might have wished. Rather than lowering local tariffs, executives often raised long-haul rates. In some cases, they curtailed or suspended service on rural branch lines.

As such, a wide variety of individuals watched with interest as the railroads challenged the Granger Laws in court. In 1877, in *Munn v. Illinois* and seven related decisions (often referred to as the "Granger Cases"), the Supreme Court upheld the authority of states to regulate rates on any traffic that originated or terminated within their borders—even if it crossed state lines at some point in its journey.[186] Railroad attorneys argued forcefully that such a stipulation violated the Commerce Clause of the Constitution, which gave the federal government sole authority to regulate interstate commerce. In 1886, the Supreme Court clarified and narrowed the scope of the Granger Cases in *Wabash, St. Louis & Pacific Railroad Company v. Illinois*, ruling that state commissions possessed author-

ity over only that traffic that both originated and terminated in the state. For the moment, however, the federal government lacked authority over interstate traffic, where the problem lay not in the absence of competition, but rather in its excess. The rate wars that had rocked the railroads since the 1850s created rate instability and threatened their financial health, yet executives were unable to bring such practices to a halt.[187]

The *Wabash* decision was far from a watershed moment in the history of regulation, and many western farmers barely took notice of the restrictions that the judiciary had imposed on their strong state commissions. By the 1880s, intense trunk-line competition had lowered rates to a level that most farmers found acceptable, and the more radical regulatory demands of agrarian populism had begun to subside. Legislators in some of the granger states had already curtailed the power of their regulatory commissions, and many regulators had begun to heed the railroaders' warnings regarding the dangers associated with forcing rates on local traffic to unprofitable levels.[188] By the time of the *Wabash* case, the strongest support for reform came from food processors and urban merchants, who opposed long-haul/short-haul discrimination. In their rate negotiations with the railroads, they wished to replace the expense and uncertainty that accompanied court action with predictable administrative regulation.[189]

Business interests in the east, many of whom routinely shipped over the Pennsylvania Railroad, also played a significant role in the shaping of federal regulation. Their concern lay primarily in the unstable nature of railway rates, as well as the price discrimination—generally in the form of rebates—that the PRR and other railroads granted to favored shippers. The simmering criticism of rebates and other forms of favoritism boiled over in 1872, as a result of the short-lived South Improvement Company and its links between the railroads and favored oilmen, most notably John D. Rockefeller. The intense negative publicity that surrounded that venture produced legislative hearings at the state and federal levels, but legislators soon discovered that they had little power to punish Tom Scott or any of the other executives associated with the South Improvement pool. Pennsylvania Democrat James Herron Hopkins, a representative of the independent oilmen's virulently anti-Rockefeller (and anti-PRR) Producers' Union, and chairman of the House Commerce Committee, failed spectacularly in punishing anyone for anything. Most executives ignored their subpoenas and refused to testify. Vice President Cassatt did appear before the members of the committee, largely to inform them that because they lacked the power to regulate railroad rates, they did not even possess the authority to investigate perceived abuses in their application.[190]

While Hopkins and his supporters fulminated over Cassatt's explication of what was no more than the standard business position on the limits of congressional power, an increasing number of legislators put forth often-incompatible proposals for federal regulation of the railroads. In 1876, Hopkins introduced a bill to regulate interstate commerce, but he lost his reelection bid later that year. The chairmanship of the Commerce Committee, and the responsibility for Hopkins's bill, passed to Texas Democrat John H. Reagan. By 1878, the bill had become a mélange of anti-rebating provisions (which Hopkins had supported), prohibitions against long-haul/short-haul discrimination (which the Producers' Union had demanded), and a ban on pooling (which Reagan favored).[191]

By 1878, the Reagan bill had piqued the interest of New York merchants, who had never been happy about the system of port differentials that favored rival seaboard cities. They were particularly incensed at the creation of the Trunk Line Association in June 1877, under the authority of its commissioner, Albert Fink. The association had pooled westbound freight, allocating 25 percent to the PRR and 9 percent to the B&O, and permitting the NYC and the Erie 33 percent each, while setting the highest rates for traffic bound for New York, with one rate differential for Philadelphia and another for Baltimore freight. New York business and political leaders perceived that the pool and its associated differentials would erode their commercial advantages over Philadelphia and Baltimore. They organized the New York Cheap Transportation Association, soon renamed the New York Board of Trade & Transportation. Joining the chorus of protestors were the farmers and merchants in western New York, who, like their counterparts in southwest-

ern Pennsylvania, suffered the effects of long-haul/short-haul discrimination.[192]

In February 1879, the New York state legislature established a Special Committee on Railroad Transportation, chaired by Alonzo B. Hepburn, to investigate ratemaking practices. The members of the committee rejected the railroads' argument that New York was the most distant port from Chicago, and therefore the most expensive to service, as a justification for the port differentials. "We are of opinion, however, that our New York roads can afford to carry freight from the west to New York as cheaply as the other roads to their respective termini," insisted Hepburn, "and if they can afford to they ought to."[193] The members of the Hepburn Committee favored the creation of a three-member commission, "with power of investigation and recommendation," in order to pursue the matter further.[194] While the New Yorkers were unable to abolish the port differentials or to equalize trunk-line rates, they nonetheless made it impossible for Reagan to push forward a regulatory bill that appealed primarily to western farmers.[195]

By the early 1880s, the influence of the farmers, independent oilmen, and New York merchants had somewhat waned, replaced by growing concern, expressed by railroads and shippers alike, about the overall health of the railroads. Particularly after the PRR orchestrated the sale of the Empire Line's principal assets to Standard Oil in 1877, the independents were less willing to blame the railroads for discriminatory rates. In 1881, the New York Central broke the 1877 pool, partly in response to pressure from New York commercial interests, but principally in order to combat the expansionist vision of Jay Gould. At the same time, Albert Fink proved unable to control the wayward members of the Trunk Line Association, and he gave up in frustration. By 1884, as several American railroads went bankrupt, many railway officials had concluded that pools—even those managed by traffic associations—were incapable of sustaining railroad rates.

Railroad executives did their best to educate members of Congress on the importance of legislation that would preserve most forms of long-haul/short-haul discrimination, while employing the coercive power of the state to enforce traffic pools. As early as 1880, Tom Scott, along with NYC president William H. Vanderbilt, requested an opportunity to speak before the House Commerce Committee. Fink and Charles Francis Adams, both representing the Trunk Line Association, so successfully defended pooling in testimony before the committee that its members initially rejected the bill that Reagan had proposed. Such railroad input only grew stronger in the years that followed. In 1886, PRR vice president John P. Green wrote to Senator John Sherman expressing the common attitudes of railroad executives. Green insisted that the invalidation of long-haul/short-haul rate discrimination ran counter to the basic economics of railroading, and that the proposed act should provide for federal enforcement of pools, rather than their elimination.[196]

While opposed to the Reagan bill, PRR officials, along with their counterparts on other railroads, generally favored the more moderate regulatory approach embodied in a bill sponsored by Senator Shelby Cullom (Rep., Ill.) the chairman of the Senate Committee on Interstate Commerce. Cullom noted that by 1886, perhaps 75 percent of all rail traffic crossed state lines and was not well suited to control by state regulatory commissions. He believed that both Congress and the state legislatures were too politicized to establish effective policy in the matter of rates and terms of service. Cullom likewise suspected that the courts were apt to enforce the laissez-faire competitive models inherent in classical economic theory. Judges who were unwilling to recognize the existence of the railroads as a natural monopoly were, like legislators, ill equipped to manage competition. In Cullom's view, the only alternative lay in the creation of a national administrative capability, in the form of a regulatory body that possessed the authority to regulate rates—one similar to the commission established in 1873 in his native state of Illinois.[197]

The regulatory apparatus rapidly took shape between 1885 and 1887, even as the *Wabash* decision increased the urgency for a national approach to the issue of railroad regulation. The House approved the Reagan bill, but senators, railroad executives, and New York merchants gave their support to Cullom's version. The Senate overwhelmingly passed the Cullom bill, making plain their intent to impose regulation without attacking the railroads. By August 1886, a conference committee was at work attempting to reconcile the two divergent bills. The hybrid that emerged reflected the influence of both Reagan and Cullom, as well as of the varied interest groups that had helped to shape each version of the legislation. Reagan redeemed his pledge to prohibit pooling, while Cullom took satisfaction in the creation of an administrative commission. On February 4, 1887, President Grover Cleveland signed into law "An Act to Regulate Commerce."[198]

The Interstate Commerce Act, as it was commonly known, initiated a century of inconsistent and often schizophrenic federal regulation of the railroads. In 1887, there was no widespread belief that average rail charges were too high, and the act accordingly did not set a cap on rates. Instead, the legislation specified that all rates be "reasonable and just," yet provided precious little guidance on what that phrase actually meant. Railroads were required to post their tariffs and to provide at least a ten-day notice of all changes. Section Four of the act prohibited railroads from charging more for a short haul than for a long haul "under substantially similar circumstances and conditions"—language so vague as to defy interpretation. The railroads could not pool traffic or revenues, but they could—probably—establish rates collaboratively. Some features, such as the prohibition against pooling, seemed destined to increase both competition and instability. Other provisions, particularly the ambiguously worded prohibition against long-haul/short-haul discrimination, encouraged railroads to raise discounted long-haul rates, rather than decrease their more expensive short-haul counterparts.[199]

Most significantly, the act created a five-member Interstate Commerce Commission, with commissioners appointed by the President, with the advice of the Senate. The ICC possessed the authority to subpoena witnesses and records from railroads, shippers, and other parties. The agency also had the power to specify uniform accounting standards for reports filed with the commission, but did not yet have the authority to dictate how the railroads should maintain their internal accounts. The ICC was a strong regulatory commission in that its commissioners could do far more than merely offer advice and publicize abuses. Its decisions did not have the force of law, however, and the commission relied on the courts to implement sanctions against disobedient railroads or shippers. In the decades to come, Congress would add additional, often contradictory, regulatory mandates, making it extraordinarily difficult for even the most highly skilled and best-intentioned ICC bureaucrats to oversee the application of federal law to the railroads.[200]

The Interstate Commerce Commission in Action

For several years after its inception, many railroaders and shippers believed that the Interstate Commerce Commission might provide an effective administrative mechanism that could stabilize rates and reduce price discrimination. Thomas McIntyre Cooley, the agency's first chairman, possessed a superb knowledge of the law and of the operating requirements of the railroad business. In 1868, while a justice on the Michigan Supreme Court, he published *A Treatise on the Constitutional Limitations Which Rest upon the Legislative Power of the States of the American Union*, a book that soon became required reading for generations of law students. Prior to joining the ICC, he was a receiver for the bankrupt Wabash Railroad. Politically, he was a Mugwump, part of the small but influential group of reform-minded Republicans who sided with Democrat Grover Cleveland in the 1884 election rather than countenance the scandals associated with James G. Blaine. Cooley was one of the architects of the administrative state, believing that agencies such as the ICC could protect the public interest by routinizing the application of common law principles, free from interference by courts or legislatures.[201]

Cooley and his fellow commissioners did their best to be impartial, demanding concessions from both the railroads and their customers. Shippers were to accept the railroads' efforts to attain rate stability through collective ratemaking, while railway executives were to minimize rate discrimination. Yet, as Cooley and his fellow commissioners developed a better understanding of railway economics, they incrementally moved toward the positions adopted by the railroads, accepting arguments that differences in the cost of service justified discrimination based on haulage distance or the size of the shipment. In a June 1887 case involving the Louisville & Nashville, the commissioners deferred to the judgment of railroad executives with regard to what did or did not constitute long-haul/short-haul discrimination. Although the commissioners banned rebates, they acknowledged that carload traffic was inherently more efficient than less-than-carload lots, accepting rate differentials that continued to favor Standard Oil and other large shippers. Cooley nonetheless stood fast to his belief that in the absence of demonstrable differences in the cost of service, mere competitive pressures did not constitute a sufficient rationale for rate discrimination.[202]

The federal courts soon undermined the ICC's authority, however. While the Supreme Court in particular had little patience with legislative intervention—the justices had made that attitude quite clear in the *Wabash* decision—they regarded administrative agencies, likewise insulated from the legislative process, as a competitor in the shaping of public policy. ICC officials, led by Cooley, interpreted the vagueness inherent in the Interstate Commerce Act in order to advance their agency's administrative capabilities. The 1887 act had not explicitly granted to the ICC the power to set rates, but the commissioners nonetheless assumed that prerogative, based largely on the precedents established by strong state regulatory commissions. The Supreme Court, in contrast, saw ambiguity as anathema, with justices asserting that it was their responsibility to clarify ambiguous language. Furthermore, alterations in rates unavoidably entailed a redistribution of property, and the courts were not willing to cede their power to protect property rights to a regulatory body that the legislature had established.[203]

Whatever their motives, the courts emasculated the ICC, transforming it from a strong commission to little more than an investigative body. In 1889, a federal circuit court overturned an ICC directive, ruling that the commission's primary responsibility was to investigate and provide the facts that the judiciary could use to reach a decision. At virtually the same time, the Supreme Court ruled that the determination of "reasonable and just" rates was properly a judicial rather than a regulatory function.[204] In 1892, the court held that the Fifth Amendment protection against self-incrimination allowed railroad executives to refuse to testify regarding their company's rate structure. In 1897, the Supreme Court ruled that the ICC lacked the power to set rates, inasmuch as Congress had not explicitly granted that authority to the agency.[205] The same year, in the *Alabama Midland* case, the justices defied the ICC and permitted a railroad to charge a local tariff that was higher than through charges. By accepting the railroad's argument that such discrimination was necessary to meet competitive pressures, even in the absence of differences in the cost of service, the court destroyed the long-haul/short-haul rate discrimination provisions of the Act to Regulate Commerce.[206]

A further blow came in 1898 with the court's ruling in *Smyth v. Ames*. The justices unanimously overturned a Nebraska statute that set intrastate rates below the cost of service, on the grounds that such confiscatory policies violated the due process clause of the Fourteenth Amendment.[207] In requiring states to set rates at or above the cost of service plus a fair rate of return, the court had abandoned its earlier willingness (as demonstrated in the 1877 Granger Cases) to defer authority to state legislatures. However, in their assertion that they and they alone possessed the wisdom and restraint necessary to protect property rights, the justices also made emphatic their belief that the ICC had no power to interfere in such matters. In the court's view, the commissioners would have the ability to investigate perceived abuses, but not to remedy them. The matter of remedy, which invariably involved the reallocation of property, was a matter to be left solely to the judiciary.[208]

By the end of the nineteenth century the courts had consistently ruled that the judiciary, and not the administrative state, would be in charge of regulating the railroad business. Judicial attitudes reflected both a commitment to notions of laissez-faire individualism and an unwillingness to cede authority to the ICC or to state regulatory agencies. In the first instance the courts were mistaken, as a truly self-regulating free market, devoid of governmental constraints, had never existed in the United States—and, even if it had, the economic conditions of the late nineteenth century were so far removed from those of the Early Republic as to make their continuation untenable. The desire to retain power over the political economy was understandable, but unfortunate, as justices understood too

little about railroad operations and pricing policies, and the courts were too overwhelmed with cases to accurately parse the minutiae of interminable rate decisions. Railroad executives cheered certain rulings, particularly *Alabama Midland* and *Smyth v. Ames*, each of which dovetailed neatly with their rhetorical emphasis on the mastery of private capital over governmental meddling. In a larger sense, however, the judiciary left both railroaders and administrative regulators unable to exert authority over competitive patterns within the industry.

As the twentieth century dawned, the ICC resembled a national version of Charles Francis Adams's sunshine commission, its role confined chiefly to the collection and publication of statistical data. If such an agency struck railroad executives as unthreatening, it also seemed to them as an utterly impotent ally in their efforts to control interfirm competition. Absent legally enforceable pools, industry executives attempted to control rates through competitive system-building, and workers laid down more miles of track during the 1880s than in any other decade. In 1887, as Congress adopted the Act to Regulate Commerce, there was more new construction than in any prior year. Many of those routes had little economic value, and served merely as speculative ventures, or as efforts to undermine competitors' rates. The Interstate Commerce Act rendered pools both illegal and unenforceable, and the weakened ICC was not in a position to assist railroads with rate stabilization. It was hardly surprising, then, that the next decade saw a surge of railroad bankruptcies, following the Panic of 1893.

Pennsylvania Railroad executives had little need to engage in an orgy of new construction, and their company was in little danger of financial insolvency. They nonetheless asserted that unremunerative rates were starving the railroad of the income required for critical improvements to the physical plant, necessary in order to increase capacity. In the aftermath of the West Shore–South Penn debacle, and as the 1893 depression deepened, PRR and NYC officials vowed to rein in excess competition and competitive overbuilding. In April 1894, they signed a memorandum, widely referred to as a "peace agreement," in which they pledged to maintain comparable rates. They also promised to refrain from the construction of duplicate lines and from other attempts to invade each other's territory. Rebating continued nonetheless, as there was no legal mechanism for enforcing the compact.[209]

In the spring of 1895, PRR and NYC officials began to develop a more formal mechanism for controlling rates. By the summer, executives from the PRR and thirty other northeastern railroads agreed to establish the Joint Traffic Association, effective January 1, 1896. The association was not a pool, in that executives did not meet for the purpose of allocating railroad traffic. Instead, railroad officials agreed to create and fund a separate office, staffed by independent traffic experts, who employed techniques of statistical analysis to recommend economically optimal rates. There was a fine shade of distinction between pools and traffic associations, however, and the Joint Traffic Association was for all intents and purposes a cartel. The Supreme Court ruled as such in *United States v. Trans-Missouri Freight Association* (1897) and *United States v. Joint Traffic Association* (1898), holding that traffic associations violated the 1890 Sherman Act's prohibition against combinations in restraint of trade. The Supreme Court rulings had remarkably little effect on the railroads, however. Executives rapidly transformed their illegal traffic associations into legal rate bureaus, which continued to play an active role in the establishment of cooperative rates.[210]

The Economics of Freight Transportation

While the PRR and other carriers were free to set rates according to local competitive conditions, the rate bureaus established through rates and published tariff schedules, enabling railroad executives to maintain uniform prices. The rate bureaus continued the established practice of dividing all freight into one of two categories. Most high-value manufactured goods traveled under a system of *class rates*, so called because every conceivable product was assigned to one of several classes. Class rates typically applied to small and medium-sized shipments, which often constituted less-than-carload-lot (LCL) traffic. For more than a decade after its inception in 1846, the Pennsylvania Railroad posted only four classes of freight tariffs. First-class traffic included such high-value products as

dishes, clocks, and candy. Many agricultural commodities moved as second-class freight; oil was classified as third-class freight; and fourth class was reserved for iron and steel products, clay, soda ash, and oysters and clams (which, according to PRR rate sheets, would be transported "at owner's risk").[211] By the late 1880s, with the growing integration of the American railroad network, the PRR's freight classifications were frequently at odds with the equivalent systems on other railroads and could not readily accommodate long-distance shipments over multiple carriers. As early as 1882, traffic officials were making attempts, initially unsuccessful, to develop uniform freight classifications.

The pressure for greater uniformity increased following the passage of the Act to Regulate Commerce in February 1887. On April 1, 1887, the PRR and the other northeastern carriers adopted the Official Classification, for the area north of the Ohio River and east of Chicago and St. Louis. Railroads in other regions soon developed the essentially identical Southern Classification and the Western Classification. In Official Territory (also known as Eastern Territory or Trunk-Line Territory), a classification book assigned each of more than ten thousand commodities to one of six basic classes of freight. The classification book did not set rates, however. To calculate the cost of a shipment, an agent consulted the freight tariff. Railroad freight agents determined the rate through the simple process of identifying the class of the shipment in question, multiplying it by the weight of the shipment (usually expressed in hundreds of pounds, rather than in tons), multiplying it again by the distance traveled, and billing according to the appropriate freight tariff.[212]

In the decade following the 1887 Act to Regulate Commerce, the ICC and the courts affirmed that railroads could not be forced to transport products at a rate below the fully allocated cost of service, and that railroad executives could engage in price discrimination based on demonstrable differences in the expense associated with each shipment. As such, railroad officials found it imperative to categorize and justify even the most minute rate discrepancies, employing to that end four categories of rate differentials. The freight classifications established a system of *class differentials*, with rates varying according to the type of shipment.

Port differentials, first employed in 1858, levied progressively lower tariffs for shipments moving through Philadelphia and Baltimore, cities that were at a distance from the commercial center of New York. They persisted into the 1960s, despite periodic opposition from commercial interests in New York and Boston. The rate bureaus also oversaw *route differentials* (which provided a discount for traffic sent via indirect, slower routings), and *export differentials* (which discriminated on the basis of whether traffic bound for the east coast was destined for domestic consumption or export, and which were not folded into the port differentials until the 1930s). The differentials, although ostensibly based on variations in the cost of rail haulage and both coastal and transatlantic water service, were in reality designed to evenly allocate traffic among the various trunk lines and they thus embodied a certain degree of discriminatory pricing. After 1887, however, ICC officials rarely challenged established patterns of discrimination, asserting that shippers had grown accustomed to the rate structure and that the disruption of established competitive patterns would do more harm than good.[213]

Most freight traffic, particularly bulk commodities such as grain, coal, iron ore, and lumber, moved under a system of *commodity rates*. Unlike class rates, commodity rates were subject to negotiation between the shipper and the railroad (or railroads, in the case of an interline shipment). Rate bureaus conducted the negotiation process, with the input of traffic department officials of all of the railroads involved. When the shipper and the carrier agreed on a rate, it became legally binding for all comparable shipments over comparable routings. Any deviation from that posted rate would constitute discrimination and render the carriers liable to ICC sanction. ICC commissioners nonetheless granted the rate bureaus considerable leeway, questioning fewer than 5 percent of posted rates. More broadly, both the ICC and the federal courts recognized that rate bureaus embodied inherently monopolistic tendencies, but allowed them to remain intact. Shippers acknowledged that rate bureaus routinized the complex process of rate setting, and so confined their protests to the ICC to specific complaints regarding a particular tariff in dispute.[214]

The members of the Interstate Commerce Commission validated the railroads' rate practices in one other crucial respect. Even though they developed elaborate cost-accounting methods, railway executives often possessed little more than a hazy understanding of the fully allocated expense associated with moving a specific shipment from Point A to Point B. The basic difficulty was that railroads possessed extraordinarily high fixed costs and relatively low variable (also referred to as out-of-pocket or above-the-rails) costs. While executives could make certain assumptions regarding the percentage of fixed costs that should be assigned to a particular class of traffic (heavy coal trains obviously caused more damage to the physical plant than lightly laden express shipments), they could not allocate fixed costs with any degree of precision. It might be possible to imagine the American railroad landscape, with a seemingly endless variety of shipments traveling in tens of thousands of freight cars over hundreds of thousands of miles of track. Somewhere in that ocean of commerce, a single shipment, just one, might have been transported at a rate that reflected precisely its fully allocated cost of service—but, if so, it was only by the rarest of coincidences. All of the other cargoes were either subsidizing or being subsidized by some other source of traffic. Artificially low rates on bulk commodities, which were subject to water-carrier competition, were offset by higher rates on almost everything else, from passenger fares to high-value merchandise to less-than-carload-lot shipments to short-haul traffic. As such, it was correspondingly difficult to set rates according to the actual cost of service.

Given the difficulties of employing a cost-of-service pricing strategy, railroad traffic managers and rate bureaus instead set tariffs based on the value of service to the shipper. For the transportation of bulk cargoes, water carriers were (and remain) inherently more efficient than railroads. Railroad rates reflected the rail/water disparity, with bulk commodity tariffs set little higher than out-of-pocket costs.[215] In compensation, rate bureaus established substantial charges on high-value merchandise, based on the assumption that shippers were willing to pay a premium for speed. From the perspective of shippers, then, all rates embodied a tradeoff between transportation costs and inventory-in-transit costs—as the value of a cargo increased, the time spent en route became a critical factor and justified the added expense of railroad transportation.

Despite the legal prohibitions against long-haul/short-haul discrimination, ICC commissioners routinely countenanced another type of rate discrimination, based on the disparity between the cost of rail transportation and the value of that transportation to shippers. In permitting the railroads to continue their value-of-service pricing—a policy known as "umbrella ratemaking"—ICC officials concluded that it was both unavoidable and in the best interest of the American industrial economy. Farmers benefited from favorable rates on grain, while industrialists enjoyed reduced charges for coal, iron ore, and other basic commodities. Manufacturers paid high tariffs on finished products in order to cross-subsidize the transportation costs of the raw materials that fueled their factories. They rarely complained, however, as even high-value rates on manufactured goods constituted a small, and steadily declining, percentage of the final cost to the consumer.[216]

Yet, the inclusion of all shippers under an umbrella of steadily declining rates was predicated on continuing improvements in transportation efficiency. That happy circumstance was not destined to last into the twentieth century. As the law of diminishing returns leveled off the productivity gains of the late nineteenth century, rates stopped falling and shippers could no longer assuage their fears of discrimination with the certainty that next year's shipping costs would certainly be lower than those they were currently paying. In that context, shippers increased their demands that the ICC and state regulatory agencies protect them from the railroads. The result, during the first decade of the twentieth century, would be a series of laws that greatly strengthened the ICC, overriding judicial concerns regarding the expanded reach of administrative power and creating a far more adversarial relationship between the agency and the railroads that it regulated.

The Business of Moving Freight

The establishment of class and commodity rates, the development of rate differentials, and the shift to value-of-service pricing would have been of little conse-quence, had it not been for the growing sophistication of the Pennsylvania Railroad's traffic functions. During the late nineteenth century, PRR officials developed comprehensive traffic capabilities, as executives paid as much attention to the solicitation of freight as to its movement. Even as PRR transportation personnel were overseeing rapid gains in efficiency—permitting a steady decline in rates—their counterparts in traffic were becoming ever more adept at tailoring rates to particular classes of freight and even to specific shipments. There nonetheless remained considerable tension between the traffic officials who generated the railroad's business and the transportation personnel who moved those shipments to their destinations.

The depression of the 1870s caused PRR officials to devote increased attention to the solicitation of traffic. Following the creation of the Freight Department and the Passenger Department in 1873, the general freight and general passenger agents reported to both the general manager (whose primary duties involved transportation) and whichever vice president was responsible for traffic—although after 1874 only the latter had rate-making authority. Once the 1870s depression had ended, the growing volume in both the quantity of business and the variety of shipments caused PRR officials to increasingly differentiate between the business of hauling freight and the responsibilities of freight solicitation. In 1881, not long after George Roberts assumed the presidency, the board removed the Freight and Passenger departments from the supervision of the general manager. Thereafter, only the first vice president had authority over both transportation and traffic. At the same time, the board made subtle changes to the PRR's traffic administration. The general freight agents on each Grand Division became division freight agents. As in previous years, additional agents assisted with the heavy traffic demands associated with New York and New England. In June 1884, in response to the growing quantities of traffic interchanged with other railroads as well as the rapid increase in the coal and coke business, the board added the posts of through freight agent and coal freight agent. The following year, the Lines East general freight agent, who was in charge of local traffic, became the general freight traffic agent. As in earlier years, the Lines West of Pittsburgh and Erie possessed similar, although not identical, administrative mechanisms for the solicitation of traffic.[217]

The depression that began in 1893, like the one that had occurred two decades earlier, raised the profile of traffic officials. The final step in the development of the PRR's traffic organization occurred in March 1897, shortly after the death of President Roberts, when the board elevated the Traffic Department to vice presidential status. Sutherland M. Prevost, the new third vice president, was in charge of soliciting and developing traffic, and possessed the authority to set rates. His immediate subordinate was the freight traffic manager, who relieved Prevost of the burden of direct day-to-day supervision of the general (local) freight traffic agent, the through freight agent, the coal freight agent, the freight claim agent, and the manager of the Empire Line.[218] In addition, each of the PRR's five Grand Divisions employed a division freight agent, under the supervision of the assistant general freight agent. The five division freight agents (the number soon increased to eight, and then to ten) and their staffs were responsible for setting local rates, soliciting traffic, and encouraging industrial development in their area. Rate setting was not entirely under the control of the Traffic Department, however, as the maintenance of rates was the responsibility of the local agents, who were Transportation Department employees under the authority of the general manager.[219]

The solicitation of freight, observed one PRR executive, began with "a small army of men [who could] quote [the PRR's] prices anywhere and everywhere."[220] They were the freight agents, who were on the front lines of the battle to win traffic away from rival railroads. Local agents reported to the division freight agents, based at such key points as Philadelphia, Pittsburgh, Harrisburg, Altoona, Baltimore, and Wilmington. George D. Dixon, then the freight traffic manager, noted that the division freight agents had the "duty to keep in close touch with all the patrons of the road, from a commercial standpoint, looking after their interests, hearing their complaints, and adjusting local rates on their divisions, keeping themselves posted as to the business conditions prevailing, not only in their own territory, but in the surrounding territories."[221]

At the beginning of the twentieth century, the burden of traffic solicitation rested primarily on the shoulders of just 437 salesmen and managers. Most worked in on-line communities, but some were far removed from the PRR's operating territory, staffing off-line solicitation offices in cities such as Boston, Providence, New Haven, Toronto, and Atlanta.[222] Regardless of their location, freight solicitors relied on charm, diplomacy, and tact to win over shippers. Assistant general freight agent Robert C. Wright reflected on the changing role of the PRR's freight solicitors, noting that "modern conditions have entirely changed the scope of their work from what is still the general impression of the [independent] soliciting agent of former days, who at that time was largely the medium for securing traffic at cut rates and a spy on the operations of competitors."[223] Instead, Wright noted, "The Freight Solicitors of today are the medium of communication between the public and the carriers, and serve as the antennae by which the General Freight Department feels the public's requirements."[224] Contemporary economists, such as Emory R. Johnson and Grover G. Huebner, made much the same point when they asserted, "The personal equation has become of paramount importance. The solicitor must have the ability to pacify shippers who have real or supposed grievances. . . . He must be a ready and sympathetic listener, so that he may 'rejoice with them that do rejoice, and weep with them that weep.' "[225]

Amid all of the rejoicing and weeping, employees of the PRR Traffic Department developed a distinctive corporate culture. Traffic Department personnel constituted a tiny minority within the PRR system, literally outnumbered a hundred to one by their counterparts in the Transportation Department.[226] Wright emphasized that each member of the Traffic Department "has a dual duty before him—first, to the railroad company, his employer, and, second, to the shipping public, his patrons."[227] He also suggested that there were "three qualifications he must have: first he must be well informed; second, he must have a pleasing manner; third, he must have tact; and the greatest of these is tact," which he could use "as a lightning-rod to divert wrath from the railroad."[228]

In principle, senior PRR traffic executives, such as Julien L. Eysmans, Wright's successor, sought "the closest and most faithful cooperation between the Traffic and Operating [Transportation] Departments, both among officers and supervisory forces, in order that [the] Company shall never fail to hold its traditional place of leadership among its competitors."[229] In practice, however, the two departments engaged in an ongoing battle of wills, philosophies, and personalities. Traffic personnel were well-dressed, gregarious dealmakers who reveled in their ability to convince shippers to part with the money that ensured the railroad's profitability. They often looked with disdain on the begrimed, overall-clad laborers who could not seem to get freight to its destination as quickly, and in as good of a condition, as the shipper expected. Operating employees prided themselves on the mastery of a difficult and dangerous craft, and they had little patience for the suit-wearing salesmen with clean fingernails who, they believed, had probably never done a hard day's work in their lives.

Furthermore, "Transportation" alleged—or at least hinted—that "Traffic" employees were shallow and vainglorious, all style and no substance, and would promise prospective shippers everything under the sun, with little thought as to how the overburdened operating employees would actually make that possible. "There seems to be, however, and quite naturally," Wright observed, "a lack of understanding on the part of railroad men not directly connected with the Freight Traffic Department as to the character of work performed by what are known as a class as Freight Solicitors."[230] Traffic Department officials took pains to emphasize that they were not merely salesmen; instead, they were "engineers of sales and traffic service," who were every bit as important to the railroad as the civil, mechanical, and electrical engineers who maintained the tracks and bridges, developed locomotives and cars, and created signaling and communications systems.[231]

Traffic Department personnel at times remained aloof from their counterparts in transportation, and they often maintained closer relationships with each other and with shippers than with PRR employees in the Transportation Department. In 1900, traffic personnel on both Lines East and Lines West cooperatively established the Association of Freight Traffic Officers, followed three years later by the Association of Passenger Representatives of the Pennsylvania System. Each organization enabled traffic officials to

exchange information and develop coordinated marketing strategies, facilitating the selling of transportation services across the entire PRR system, from the eastern seaboard to the Midwest. Like the Association of Transportation Officers, the two traffic associations transcended the traditional divisional and hierarchical structure of the PRR's organization. Yet the two traffic groups were quite different from the ATO, in part because they included personnel from both Lines East and Lines West and—more significantly—because they embodied a more boisterous organizational culture. ATO officials were principally civil and mechanical engineers who met in order to share information and to consider technical questions in what amounted to an academic setting.

AFTO meetings were as much motivational rallies as anything else, where traffic officials discussed the PRR's history, developed a sense of camaraderie, and psyched themselves up for their next round of sales calls. The AFTO also sponsored some of the most lavish celebrations on the PRR, with rich foods and fine wines, liquors, and cigars. An AFTO chorus entertained the guests, generally by singing variants of popular vaudeville tunes of the day.[232] The songs celebrated the PRR's achievements, praised (and sometimes poked fun at) managers, and lambasted competing carriers, often with a dose of bawdy or racist humor thrown in for good measure. *Miss Bob White*, Willard Spenser's popular comic opera, contained a ditty, "The Watermelon," that became "The Tonnage Swellin'." The hit tune "In the Good Old Summertime" received new lyrics, becoming "On the Old Star Union Line."[233]

The dining and the entertainment were generally organized by AFTO personnel, but the invited guests included the railroad's senior managers, most of whom were associated with transportation functions. It seems likely that transportation personnel enjoyed the food, the wine, and the singing. Some, who had begun their careers as rodmen in the wilderness, and who dealt daily with the physically demanding and dangerous work associated with the PRR's operations, may have sat angrily through the meal, resentful of the traffic personnel who seemed to have much less taxing careers. More likely, however, transportation officials were content to relax and enjoy the antics of individuals who were critically important to the railroad's success but who—as they boasted to one another—probably did not have the fortitude to be a real railroader.

Passenger Travel

Pennsylvania Railroad officials also enhanced their passenger traffic capabilities during the late nineteenth century, as more and more people rode the rails. In 1881 slightly fewer than 19 million people traveled on the PRR's Lines East of Pittsburgh and Erie, covering more than 446 million miles in 371 passenger cars, with 116 baggage and mail cars handling express shipments. Their travel generated $10.2 million in passenger revenues (a little less than a third of the freight revenues that year), as well as $1.4 million in mail and express business. Passenger traffic had more than doubled by 1900, with nearly 42 million riders in 1,779 cars accruing more than 918 million passenger miles, and generating $19.1 million in revenues, augmented by $3.4 million in mail and express earnings.[234]

Even though passengers required considerable personal attention, the arrangement of the PRR's passenger traffic functions was generally similar to the one involving freight. The passenger traffic manager set ticket prices and schedules in collaboration with whichever vice president was in charge of transportation functions.[235] Those two executives were also responsible for working with the Passenger Department of the Trunk Line Association to establish procedures for through passenger ticketing, in a manner similar to the collaborative establishment of through freight rates. As was the case in freight service, the PRR maintained numerous passenger fares, whose complexity increased over time as managers attempted to maximize revenue through differentiations in service. For example, the number of ticket classes grew from thirty-eight in 1872 to seventy-five in 1893, including everything from excursion tickets to commuter fares.

The PRR's general passenger agent was the traffic official chiefly responsible for coordinating day-to-day operations across the railroad. James Robert Wood, the general passenger agent between 1881 and 1903, was an unusual employee in that he did not begin his career with the Pennsylvania Railroad. His first job

was instead on the Burlington & Missouri River Railroad, as secretary to the superintendent. After promotion to several more posts on that carrier (train master, general western passenger agent, general ticket agent, land agent, and then passenger agent), Wood worked for the Michigan Central, and then became general passenger agent of the Chicago, Burlington & Quincy. After joining the PRR, Wood took advantage of the growing standardization of the eastern railway network, enabling affluent passengers to avoid the common practice of changing trains repeatedly on long journeys. He introduced deluxe extra-fare "limited" trains—most notably the *Pennsylvania Limited*—that ran directly between major cities on a fast schedule and correspondingly attracted a well-heeled clientele.[236]

Wood and his successor, George W. Boyd, relied on the support of two assistant general passenger agents, one for local and the other for through traffic. District passenger agents, who were headquartered at Philadelphia, Pittsburgh, New York, Boston, Washington, Baltimore, Buffalo, Williamsport, and Reading, processed through passenger traffic. Five division ticket agents (two stationed in Philadelphia and the others in Pittsburgh, Williamsport, and Buffalo) took charge of local travel at key cities along the PRR. A European agent, stationed in Liverpool, and a passenger agent, in Southampton, coordinated transatlantic immigrant traffic.[237]

The accuracy and integrity of the passenger traffic accounts depended on employees scattered across the PRR system. Prior to the Civil War, conductors had accepted cash from passengers in exchange for travel, yet rarely issued tickets. Scalping was therefore commonplace, and a large portion of fares—more than 90 percent, according to some estimates—never reached the PRR's treasury. General ticket agent Lewis L. Houpt (Herman Haupt's brother) and his counterparts on other railroads had done their best to curtail such practices. Beginning in 1859, station agents were required to submit daily reports of passenger revenues, as well as a monthly summary of passenger ticket sales.[238]

Prior to 1876, however, PRR personnel could only calculate total passenger receipts and were unable to attribute revenue to specific trains or routes. The surge in traffic that accompanied the Centennial Exhibition forced managers to reorganize passenger functions. Freight crews, pressed into service as passenger trainmen, proved woefully unable to master either the rules of civility or the intricacies of the PRR's ticketing system and its forty-odd fare categories. Accordingly, the company recruited from outside the railroad industry, selecting personable young men who were used to working with the public. Max Riebenack, at that time the PRR's auditor of passenger receipts, and later the company's comptroller, recalled that the key qualifications were "gentlemanly appearance and deportment, as well as clerical ability."[239] After extensive training, they were subjected to a battery of tests, with those attaining the best scores assigned to premium runs.

The new train agents worked alongside conductors, with the former interacting with passengers and the latter overseeing the operation of the train. The train agents sold and collected tickets and prepared a report for every trip, providing a detailed accounting of the revenues generated by each train. A new corps of ticket receivers staffed large stations. In addition to collecting cash and redeemed tickets from the train agents (thus ensuring their integrity), the receivers prepared reports on passenger counts and ticket sales at their respective stations, while also noting the revenue generated by each route.[240] Passenger train personnel accordingly generated a number of forms, most significantly the Conductor's Report of Trains and the Ticket Receiver's Statement,[241] which indicated the number of passengers transported, the quantity of tickets collected, and onboard ticket sales. The auditor then employed the various reports to generate a weekly report of passenger earnings, supplied to the comptroller.[242]

In addition to the line officers and associated personnel who interacted with the public, the PRR also maintained seven passenger traffic staff departments, in charge of fares and rate divisions, the printing and issuance of tickets, ticket redemptions, advertising, special excursions, tours and conventions, and baggage (under the supervision of a general baggage agent and an assistant general baggage agent). The advertising agent played a particularly important role, as he was responsible for some ninety timetables, with more than a million and a quarter copies distributed each month.

Advertising agent Francis Nelson (Frank) Barksdale was primarily responsible for publicizing the PRR and generating additional passenger business. Born in Charlottesville, Virginia, he was the son of William Barksdale, a staunch secessionist and brigadier general in the Confederate Army, who died on the second day of the Battle of Gettysburg. Only ten years old when the war ended, Frank Barksdale later became a lawyer and a newspaper editor. He moved to Philadelphia in 1883 and promptly joined the PRR's Advertising Department. Barksdale relied heavily on the print media to sell the traveling public on the Pennsylvania Railroad. "Iteration is essential to effective advertising," Barksdale emphasized, "and the principle of keeping everlastingly at it is so generally recognized as the keystone of success that the daily newspaper is classed as the supreme medium for live advertising."[243] He also oversaw myriad promotional devices, ranging from souvenir travel guides to the more than two million flyers and posters distributed annually. Working with John Elfreth Watkins, a PRR executive who also served as curator of transportation at the Smithsonian, Barksdale arranged for the Camden & Amboy Rail Road's locomotive *John Bull*—the oldest on the PRR system—to be placed on display at the 1893 Columbian Exposition. Barksdale's office was ultimately responsible for developing the various iterations of the PRR's "Standard Railroad of the World" slogan.[244]

Barksdale also worked closely with the PRR's Tourist Bureau, established in 1887, that tapped into the new middle-class predilection for leisure travel. Its formation represented efforts by PRR officials to bypass independent tour operators and to incorporate their organizational capabilities into the company, as had occurred with the co-option of the independent freight forwarders many decades earlier. As the PRR's general passenger agent observed, the Tourist Bureau was created "for the purpose of diverting this class of traffic from the hands of private firms and middlemen into the hands of the railroad company itself."[245] PRR tourist agents guided package tours, which included rail and Pullman fare, hotel accommodations, meals, and even horse-drawn carriage excursions. In 1876, for example, the PRR publicized more than fourteen pages of excursions from New York City alone, to places such as Gettysburg, Niagara Falls, Montreal, and White Sulphur Springs, West Virginia. Other trips included grand tours of the West, winter sojourns to California, and even vacations as far away as Mexico City. Many of the tours included a matron, who would ensure the comfort and protect the modesty and virtue of female travelers. For special tours, involving presidents, foreign dignitaries, and similar VIPs, assistant general passenger agent George Boyd usually accompanied the train in order to ensure top-quality service. Frank Barksdale was often involved, as well, and he was responsible for arranging campaign tours for Presidents Benjamin Harrison and William McKinley, as well as a 1902 visit by Prince Henry of Prussia.[246]

Despite the growing sophistication of the PRR's passenger traffic organization, PRR officials were never as successful as their freight counterparts. The PRR's passenger counts and revenues increased at a far slower pace than freight traffic—a condition that was typical on most American railroads. It was, as it turned out, far more difficult to impose order on human passengers than on inanimate freight shipments. Even before travelers began to desert the railroads for the convenience of the private automobile, they were making plain their displeasure with what they considered to be unacceptably high rail fares. Boyd, Barksdale, and others could provide extraordinarily comfortable travel for those who could afford it, but most travelers were on a budget, and they paid more attention to ticket prices than to service amenities. No amount of advertising could disguise the fact that the economies of scale that inexorably drove down freight rates during the late nineteenth century did not exert the same salubrious influence on passenger fares—a situation that was to have important implications for regulation early in the next century.[247]

The Close of a Century

The era of competitive system-building, and the heady pace of expansion that accompanied it, came to an end after barely a decade. The Panic of 1893 portended a severe economic downturn, second only to the Great Depression of the 1930s in its severity. Railroad after railroad went bankrupt, with the list of the fallen including many of the PRR's traditional rivals, including

the Baltimore & Ohio, the Erie, and the Reading. By June 1894, 126 carriers were in receivership, representing a quarter of the capital invested in the national rail network. The carnage provided a clear indication that efforts by railroad executives to build self-sustaining systems—like earlier attempts to regulate competition through pools, rebates, and other mechanisms—had failed to bring order to the railroad network.[248]

The Pennsylvania Railroad suffered through the depression, but its conservative management policies ensured that the company was in little danger of bankruptcy. Throughout the PRR system, furloughs and deferred maintenance enabled reductions in expenditures to keep pace with declines in revenue. Between 1893 and 1894, gross earnings declined by $16.5 million (from $135 million to $118.5 million), while operating expenses fell by more than $13 million. In both years, the directors elected to pay the customary 5 percent dividend, although the special 2 percent distribution of 1893 was not repeated the following year. During the first year of the depression, the PRR's managers had been able to accumulate a surplus of almost $26.5 million. By the following year, that had dropped precipitously, to $895,100—but that was still a far cry from the financial disaster that was confronting the PRR's competitors. The frugality of PRR management came at a price, however, as deferred maintenance caused the physical plant to deteriorate. PRR executives also permitted marginal subsidiaries to fail, rather than risk having the contagion spread to the parent company. When a controlled line came to grief—and in 1896 the Grand Rapids & Indiana did just that—PRR officials allowed the company to slide into bankruptcy and reorganization.[249]

Just as the national economy was beginning to recover from the depression, Frank Thomson became the sixth president of the Pennsylvania Railroad, on February 3, 1897. Even though he was unrelated to J. Edgar Thomson, he was nonetheless a worthy successor for the leadership of what had become the largest private corporation in the world. Frank Thomson had developed track and roadbed standards, first as superintendent of the Eastern Division of the Philadelphia & Erie, and later as the general manager of Lines East. It was his idea to award premiums (prizes) for the best-maintained lines. He was particularly knowledgeable regarding signaling systems, air brakes, and automatic couplers—devices that promised to increase safety while improving the efficiency of transportation. He was thoroughly familiar with the PRR's operations, as well as the traffic requirements associated with freight and passenger service. While George Roberts managed the PRR, Thomson often took charge of negotiations with other railroads, attempting to maintain rate stability through pools and other cooperative arrangements. In 1871, he had supervised the national tour of Grand Duke Alexis, increasing both his knowledge of transportation logistics and his standing within the company. The tour had also enabled Thomson to indulge in one of his favorite pastimes, hunting. While an outdoorsman, Thomson was also a bookish intellectual. At a time when many Americans expressed concern at conflicts of interest, the *New York Times* observed that "his business connections have been for the most part restricted to the service of the company with which his name and career are so closely identified."[250] If that made him different from Tom Scott, Thomson was nonetheless something of a Scott protégé. In fact, it had been Scott who had seen Thomson's abilities, around the time of the Civil War, and had propelled him forward. The description of Thomson as having "the rare faculty of making friends, and no railroad man in America was more generally popular than he" could easily have applied to either executive.[251]

By May, 1899, Thomson had barely settled into his role as one of the most powerful executives in the United States when he set out on a tour of Lines West. He soon fell ill and cut short his trip, returning to Philadelphia under the excuse of a severe attack of indigestion. His doctors knew better. He suffered a series of heart attacks and died on June 5, 1899, a little more than two years into his presidency. As Thomson, who had not reached his fifty-eighth year of life, was being laid to rest, many PRR managers, employees, and investors were increasingly uneasy about the future prospects of their firm, shaken by recession and seemingly bereft of leadership. They need not have worried, however. When Thomson took office in 1897, a reporter had observed that "his advance to the Presidency will have no disturbing effect in any department. The well-

regulated machinery of the great system will continue to move as heretofore, under the guidance of strong hands."[252]

As the journalist had suggested, the "well-regulated machinery" of the Pennsylvania Railroad did indeed continue without interruption. Alexander J. Cassatt, who had been involved in the development of railroads on the Delmarva Peninsula, returned to the PRR as president. Under Cassatt's leadership, the PRR would experience an astonishing revival. The company's executives were able to stabilize rates, generate millions of dollars in additional revenue, attract additional millions in domestic and foreign capital, and undertake some of the most massive civil engineering projects in the history of the railroad industry. Much of the company's success at the dawn of the twentieth century could be credited to Cassatt's leadership, and to his connections in the arenas of banking and politics. He was finally able to impose a measure of order and stability on the northeastern railway network, a goal that had largely eluded George Roberts and Frank Thomson.

Yet, Cassatt's accomplishments at the beginning of the twentieth century did not so much reflect a change in corporate policy as the culmination of many years of work by Roberts, Thomson, and thousands of other executives and employees. Year in and year out, in times of prosperity and depression, they had been incrementally improving the railroad through the installation of new tracks, stronger bridges, signaling systems, air brakes, automatic couplers, telegraph lines, and better freight cars. The "well-regulated machinery" analogy was certainly apt, for the Pennsylvania Railroad *was* a machine, a vast assemblage of technological components that functioned as one. The engineers who ran that machine gloried in their ability to impose a mechanical order on the railroad's operations, even as senior executives experienced recurring disappointments in their efforts to bring organizational order to the railroad industry as a whole. The system that they created, from the late nineteenth century and into the twentieth, gave advertising agent Frank Barksdale ample opportunity to call the PRR "the standard railroad of the world."

Chapter 13

System

1889–1929

A gentle rain began to fall on Memorial Day 1889, soaking the hillsides east of Johnstown, above the South Fork of the Little Conemaugh River.[1] Through the night and into the next day, the downpour became more intense, filling the reservoir at the South Fork Fishing and Hunting Club. That lake, now a plaything for elite visitors, had once performed a more workaday role, supplying water to the Western Division of the Pennsylvania Canal. The section of canal to the west of Johnstown entered service in May 1831. However, as engineers such as Charles Treziyulney had predicted, there was often too little water available for boats to use the new route, particularly at higher elevations. In 1838, contractors had begun work on a dam to impound water and release it during the dry summer months. The project was not finished until 1852, only a decade before the canal was abandoned. In 1857, the PRR acquired the property, along with the rest of the Main Line of Public Works, but had little use for the reservoir. After 1875, when the club acquired the land, workers used whatever materials that lay near to hand to raise the height of the dam, greatly exceeding the limits of the initial design and creating a structure barely strong enough to hold back a normal complement of water.

The rains that arrived fourteen years later were far from normal, however. As the lake swelled, water roared through a sluiceway blocked with fish weirs and gates. The devices designed to provide fresh fare for the resort's kitchens now trapped logs and debris. With its intended egress blocked, the water now cascaded over the crest of the dam, eroding a depression in its midsection and threatening to topple the entire structure into the valley below. While one gang of men frantically dumped earth and rocks onto the fast-weakening dam, another worked at breakneck speed, excavating another discharge channel, but to no avail. Local residents and early-season holidaymakers sensed the futility of the situation and stood by in somber silence.[2]

At 3:10 P.M., the dam did not so much collapse as simply melt away, in an instant, discharging a torrent equal to Niagara on the valley below. When the flood reached the town of South Fork, it encountered the main stem of the Little Conemaugh, as well as the PRR's main line linking Philadelphia and Pittsburgh. The water sent a backwash up the valley to the east, tossing the iron Bridge No. 5 off of its abutments, severing the railroad's route. Extra 1165 East was waiting on a siding at South Fork, one of several trains delayed by the earlier erosion of portions of the rain-sodden roadbed. Engineman H. M. Bennett sensed that something truly awful was approaching down the valley of the South Fork. On his own initiative, he moved his train a short distance to the east, preventing its annihilation.

Figure 55. By the late nineteenth century, the PRR was not merely a railroad—it was a vast technological system, composed of machines and the people who operated them. Block signals, which
improved safety and increased operating efficiency, constituted one of the most visible elements of
that system. By the 1890s, when William Rau took this image of CY Tower at Beatty, Pennsylvania,
semaphores had replaced the disc signals that the PRR had installed in anticipation of the increased
traffic associated with the 1876 Centennial Exhibition. PRR signal engineers standardized equipment to the greatest possible extent—including the octagonal signal towers, which were fabricated
at the Altoona shops and then shipped, in segments, to the appropriate location.

*Photo by William H. Rau, Pennsylvania Historical and Museum Commission, Railroad Museum of
Pennsylvania.*

Bennett took shelter in SO Tower with Emma Ehrenfeld, one of several female telegraphers scattered across the PRR system. Both survived, although several other crewmen and many residents of the small town of South Fork did not.

Farther downstream, the sandstone Conemaugh Viaduct became a dam as trees and other debris blocked the eighty-foot arch. At around 3:30, the pressure eventually became too much and the last vestige of the Allegheny Portage Railroad gave way. The town of Mineral Point simply disappeared, along with its more than one hundred residents. Below Mineral Point, the crew of a PRR work train, sent to repair earlier flood damage along the river, watched in horror as the wave bore down on them, their lives spared only because centrifugal force pushed the wall of water to the opposite side of the valley. For the next mile, every trace of the Pennsylvania Railroad vanished, as rails, ties, and equipment joined the trees, rocks, and houses roiling through the floodwaters. Engineman John Hess raced the flood from Buttermilk Falls to East Conemaugh, using the whistle of his locomotive to sound a frantic warning before his train was submerged. Among those who heard him were passengers on the two sections of the *Day Express*, held at the East Conemaugh station until the tracks ahead were clear. Many fled to the hills; some reached safety, more than twenty were swept to their deaths, and those who stayed in the cars rode out the flood with little more than a good soaking.

Geography had blessed the city of Johnstown, nestled in a valley surrounded by coal-bearing mountains, with its proximity to navigable water on the western slope of the Alleghenies ensuring its status as the junction between the Allegheny Portage Railroad and the Western Division of the Pennsylvania Canal. Geography was now the city's curse. At 4:07 P.M., after traveling 13.3 miles in just under an hour, the water that roared down the Little Conemaugh swept through Johnstown. It struck Westmont Hill, the mountain that marked the end of the valley, directly across the main fork of the Conemaugh River from Johnstown itself. The ridge deflected the flood back into the community, with horrific results. After obliterating Johnstown, the water backed up against the railroad's four-track stone arch bridge across the Conemaugh River, creating a vast debris field, a solid mass of trees,

lumber, steel wire, railroad equipment, the bodies of the living, and the corpses of the dead. And then, at around 6:00 in the evening, the wreckage caught fire. The disaster, one of the worst in the nation's history, left more than 2,200 people dead and destroyed both communities and a significant portion of the Pennsylvania Railroad.

PRR officials swung into action to reopen the railroad and dispatch supplies to the survivors. One of the first on the scene was Pittsburgh Division superintendent Robert Pitcairn. Many local residents, already predisposed to dislike the PRR's transportation monopoly in the region, listed Pitcairn as one of those responsible for the violence that had occurred in Pittsburgh during the 1877 strikes. In the aftermath of the Johnstown Flood, critics noted his membership in the South Fork Fishing and Hunting Club, and held him personally responsible for the disaster. On May 31, however, Pitcairn did his best to alleviate the suffering that flowed past him. He had left Pittsburgh just before noon to inspect storm damage at Lilly, not far below the summit at Gallitzin. His train made it no farther than Sang Hollow, four miles downstream from Johnstown. There he saw first debris, and then people, being carried down the raging Conemaugh. Pitcairn, who had long harbored suspicions about the strength of the South Fork dam, immediately sensed what had happened. From the tower at Sang Hollow he telegraphed frantic messages to Pittsburgh, begging for help.

Newspaper reporters and photographers arrived in Johnstown even before the official rescue efforts were under way, all eager to satisfy the public's appetite for the grisly details of the tragedy. Not since the Civil War had cameras been able to depict such carnage; shutters opened, then closed, searing images onto glass plates, bearing witness. There were remnants of the *Day Express* at East Conemaugh, one car still miraculously upright, but with the locomotive askew and stripped of its stack and smokebox door, and the truck from a freight car ensnared in a clump of brush. In a pictorial study of an irresistible force meeting an immovable object, a gargantuan pile of shredded lumber was piled around the front end of a fifty-ton locomotive that remained perfectly in place. Railroad workers cleared silt from remarkably undamaged tracks, while in the background gondola cars lay one on top of another, stacked neatly by the floodwaters. There was a mangled tender, with only the number "477" to indicate its identity. The vast, flat expanse of Woodvale, once a company town, a modern planned community, was devoid of all human presence save for the shattered remains of the Gautier Steel Company and the tracks of the Pennsylvania Railroad, running arrow-straight through the mud. An upended house featured a tree protruding at right angles from one of the windows; a man scaling the trunk in a display of masculine bravado strikingly at odds with the town's impotence in the face of the flood, while far below him rested a locomotive tender bearing the initials "P.R.R." The photographs also showed the railroad's station at Johnstown, where the platform first served as a repository for hundreds of bodies, mostly unidentified, and later as a staging area for relief workers.

A substantial percentage of the Johnstown Flood photographs displayed traces of the Pennsylvania Railroad. In part, photographers wanted to capture the public's imagination, shocking them into the realization that something as seemingly invincible as a train could itself be annihilated by the onrushing water. But the preponderance of PRR images demonstrated just how strong a presence the railroad had maintained in the valley of the Little Conemaugh, and across Pennsylvania, just how thoroughly the company was integrated into the local economy, and just how much work would be necessary to restore the free flow of traffic through the area.

Johnstown was by far the worst, but by no means the only, site of damage along the Pennsylvania Railroad. The rains had wreaked havoc on PRR facilities throughout the state, affecting some 1,600 track miles. Crews had to replace twenty-one miles of track and six hundred thousand yards of fill, as well as numerous bridges and buildings.[3] It took four days—between Friday, May 31, and Monday afternoon, June 3—just to reestablish telegraphic communications. When messages again began flowing along the wires, senior officials learned that local managers, operating with minimal instructions or coordination, were already well under way with the task of rebuilding the railroad. Shop forces at Altoona equipped commissary and sleeping trains, which they dispatched over the

Middle and Pittsburgh Divisions. Bridge crews requisitioned all of the available timber stored at PRR facilities in Altoona, Philadelphia, Harrisburg, Wilmington, and Baltimore, but even that was not enough. Work crews relaid sidings in order to reach woodlots, rebuilt damaged sawmills, and cut whatever lumber they needed. Lines East general manager Charles E. Pugh telegraphed his Lines West counterpart, James McCrea, asking him to mobilize all of the men and materials at his disposal.

The first goal was to restore service between Philadelphia and Pittsburgh. With the line along the Little Conemaugh River virtually washed out of existence, PRR officials elected to use the Northern Central, the Philadelphia & Erie, and the Allegheny Valley as a temporary bypass. Even that would be problematic, as the flooding had destroyed four spans of the Philadelphia & Erie bridge across the West Branch of the Susquehanna River at Montgomery, near Williamsport. Vice president Frank Thomson personally took charge of its rebuilding. He collected a corps of carpenters and bridge builders and on the morning of Sunday, June 2, headed north from Harrisburg. The water at Montgomery did not subside for another two days, but by Saturday, June 8, a temporary bridge was in place, and the alternate route to Pittsburgh was open.

East of the Alleghenies, the Juniata River played havoc with the Middle Division of the main line, in some areas carving out fifteen-foot-deep gouges in the roadbed. Chief engineer William H. Brown directed the rebuilding of the bridges at Granville and Mayes, while the division's maintenance-of-way personnel, under the command of superintendent Oliver E. McClellan, tackled the washed-out embankments. By June 13, a single track was in service across the Middle Division. Work continued on various branch and secondary lines, including the Bald Eagle Valley Railroad, the tracks between Altoona and Hollidaysburg, the Susquehanna & Clearfield Branch, the Lewisburg & Tyrone Branch, and the Philadelphia & Erie between Driftwood and St. Mary's.

Yet, nothing could prepare PRR engineers for the destruction that lay along the Little Conemaugh. The railroad had lost three bridges, including the Conemaugh Viaduct that had once served the Allegheny Portage Railroad, along with dozens of buildings, 33 locomo-

Figure 56. In addition to its toll in human lives, the 1889 Johnstown Flood devastated Pennsylvania Railroad facilities and equipment along the valley of the Little Conemaugh River. This locomotive was one of thirty-three that were destroyed or simply disappeared beneath the floodwaters.

Pennsylvania Historical and Museum Commission, Railroad Museum of Pennsylvania.

tives, 18 passenger cars, and 315 freight cars.[4] The cost of the equipment was minor, however, compared with the loss of revenue, now that the main line between Philadelphia and Pittsburgh was out of commission.

As the floodwaters subsided, PRR crews worked quickly to restore rail service. Based on sporadic and incomplete reports of the calamity, general superintendent of motive power Theodore N. Ely gathered together as many shop workers as Altoona could spare—more than two thousand in all, few of whom had any experience in bridge and roadway construction—and headed for the site of the now-vanished Conemaugh Viaduct. The construction of a temporary trestle began on Friday, June 7. Under Ely's almost-

constant supervision, work proceeded around the clock, lighted by electric lamps and the flames from burning oil. By Wednesday, June 12, a 550-foot-long, 80-foot-high temporary wood structure was in place. Not until 1891 would construction crews complete a new three-track, double-arched stone viaduct at that location.

On June 9, the workers who had just finished replacing the Montgomery Bridge on the Philadelphia & Erie arrived on the scene. They set to work rebuilding the line between Mineral Point and Bridge No. 6, which the flood had also washed away. In many areas, their work was simply a matter of clearing mud and debris from the tracks; in others it involved re-grading the roadbed and installing new ties and rails. Between Mineral Point and AO Tower, however, the Little Conemaugh River changed its course, forcing the railroad to add two bridges to its main line. Some of the most serious difficulties emerged just east of AO Tower, at Bridge No. 6. The bridge was gone, along with more than two thousand feet of roadbed, and replacing it would be no easy task. By Wednesday, June 12, by dint of herculean effort, crews had installed a temporary trestle at the site, meeting the work crews from Lines West struggling toward them from Johnstown. The next day, a single track was open across the entire Pittsburgh Division.[5]

The situation at the great stone arch bridge in Johnstown was far worse, as it involved the interplay of brute force and public relations finesse. Damage control was the first order of business, and not merely in the sense of cleaning up the physical debris. The stone arch bridge in Johnstown became a public-relations nightmare for the PRR. Local residents who had once praised the indestructible bridge, both as a source of civic pride and a symbol of the PRR's commitment to the community, now directly blamed it for trapping the waterborne debris, exacerbating the death and destruction. The Citizens' Committee, responsible for restoring order in the city, hired explosives expert Arthur Kirk to blast loose the debris surrounding the bridge. Kirk, who soon earned the appellation "Prince of Dynamiters," grew increasingly frustrated with his inability to make meaningful progress. PRR executives watched nervously as Kirk shot off larger and larger charges, in close proximity to a bridge that was vital to continued railroad operations.

By the winter of 1890, Kirk had managed to clear the debris above the bridge, and now had orders from the Citizens' Committee to tackle the wreckage on the downstream side—and had armed himself with the four tons of dynamite that the committee had procured for his use. It was at that point that Superintendent Pitcairn "sent for Mr. Arthur Kirk and had a full talk with him." Kirk agreed to use extreme caution when blasting around the bridge site and to "be guided by any representative of the P.R.R. that we might appoint." He further mollified Pitcairn with his public assertions that the mass of debris would have formed at that location whether the stone arch bridge

had been there or not.[6] For his part, Pitcairn realized that the PRR could hardly interfere with removal operations. Even though an executive of the Cambria Iron Company—a major PRR shipper—served as chairman of the Citizens' Committee, Superintendent Pitcairn feared that "the Cambria people will not put themselves out of the way to defend us, and there will be a general howl from those who have lost friends and property at the obstruction placed by the P.R.R., [and] the statement that the stone bridge increased the loss of life and property will be raised again." Pitcairn's assessment that the PRR should do its best to "make friends with Mr. Kirk," and with the local community, indicated that in the years since the strikes of 1877, the PRR's executives had become far more conciliatory to local residents.[7]

For the Pennsylvania Railroad, Johnstown in 1889 was not Pittsburgh in 1877. The flood did not represent a dramatic break with the operating practices of the past. The restoration of the route through the valley of the Little Conemaugh nonetheless marked the beginning of a period in which the PRR began to rebuild its physical plant, pouring millions of dollars into betterment programs across the system in a frantic effort to maintain the free flow of traffic. For nearly fifty years, from the 1880s through the 1920s, PRR engineers and technicians struggled to increase efficiency and safety, while lowering transportation costs and rates. They enjoyed considerable success, yet increasingly confronted the law of diminishing returns.

In their efforts to enhance both efficiency and safety, PRR officials also comported their actions with the requirements imposed by the regulatory state. The ability of state regulatory agencies and ultimately the Interstate Commerce Commission (ICC) to validate specific technological devices suggests two divergent, but equally erroneous, assumptions. First, the power of the ICC in particular seemingly dictated equipment and operating methods to railroads like the PRR. In reality, however, railroaders did as much, if not more, to direct the pace and direction of technological change as did the regulators. Yet, railroad executives, who often boasted of their commitment to safety and efficiency, were well aware that state and federal legislators were always waiting in the background, ready to mandate policies and equipment if the private companies failed to take action.[8]

Second, given the tangible presence of new types of equipment, whose installation was often mandated by state or federal law, it would be tempting to assume that business historian Colleen Dunlavy's "structuring presence" of the state emerged in the railroad industry only with the installation of air brakes, automatic couplers, or block signals.[9] The government's structuring presence—reflected in the ability to encourage both the development and the regulation of the PRR—was in place well before any of those safety and performance-enhancing devices made their appearance. Safety appliances were highly visible—and often won the approval of skittish travelers and the politicians who represented them—but as manifestations of the authority of the state they were no more significant than the corporate charters, municipal investments, and rate regulations that preceded them.

In exploring the role of the PRR's technical experts in the creation of an efficient technological system, this chapter follows a somewhat different format than the others in this book. It is less chronological than topical, an approach that seems appropriate for several reasons. The devices designed to address specific operational and safety problems were often many decades in generation. To cite one example, automatic signaling systems debuted in the 1870s, but their pattern of development continued with little interruption through the 1920s. The same group of engineers, continually diminished and refreshed by retirement, death, new hires, and promotions, addressed the same basic questions in the same basic way. The delineators of the PRR's lifespan that so consumed senior executives—rate wars, financial upheavals, and long-term economic changes—were of far less importance to the individuals who ran the system. While never wholly disconnected from other facets of the PRR's operations, those functional specialists were to some degree isolated from them. The people who developed and maintained the PRR's standards were as individuals largely unknown. As a group, however, their contributions were vital to the financial success of the Pennsylvania Railroad, and even to the very survival of the company's employees and passengers. They were the functional specialists, the mid-level managers who resided

at the nexus between line and staff officers on the PRR's organization chart. This chapter is their story.

Building the System

In Philadelphia, on April 13, 1896, president George Brooke Roberts addressed the shareholders of the Pennsylvania Railroad, the grandest company in the world, on the occasion of its fiftieth birthday. At age sixty-three, Roberts was barely older than the firm that he managed. He could not know that his railroad would survive another seventy birthdays, but that he would see only one more of his own. All that he could say was that he controlled 138 subsidiary companies, with more than nine thousand miles of track, and that he directed $834 million in investment capital and the actions of more than a hundred thousand people. Each year, on average, those employees, and that capital, generated $135 million in gross revenues, almost a third of the amount of money that the federal government collected in 1890.[10]

Those statistics, heard by a relative few, and read later by many more in countless newspaper and magazine articles, were not the most obvious signs of the Pennsylvania Railroad's authority during the last decades of the nineteenth century. Anyone who worked on, traveled on, shipped on, or lived near the Pennsylvania Railroad knew full well its financial power, its technological prowess, and its sheer presence on the American landscape. Roberts, and the hundred thousand people who worked for him, created not just a railroad, but a massive technological system—a vast transportation machine whose parts functioned as one.

As with any machine, there were weak links and clogs within the system—what historian of technology Thomas Parke Hughes has referred to as "reverse salients." Hughes's military terminology aptly described the ongoing process of identifying and eliminating impediments to efficient operation, much as an experienced general would seek to reinforce bulges in his lines of defense. Roberts's soldiers were his employees, but his battlefield commanders were his engineers, the individuals who were experts at building and maintaining the physical plant, constructing locomotives and freight and passenger cars, and installing the brakes, couplers, and signaling systems that permitted ever-increasing volumes of traffic.[11]

The frantic rebuilding efforts that followed the 1889 Johnstown Flood were but a precursor to the ongoing investments and improvements that characterized the next two decades of the PRR's history. By the late 1880s, the PRR had developed a finely tuned Engineering Department, well suited to facilitating the flow of traffic through massive repair and betterment projects, and equally well suited to the task of providing senior executives with the practical knowledge necessary for managing the railroad's operations. The key to the PRR's success, indeed even to its very survival, was to provide sufficient physical capacity to allow ever-increasing volumes of traffic to move at ever-lower rates. That strategy, the legacy of Herman Haupt's vision for low unit costs, nonetheless had progressed far beyond what even he might have envisioned. The engineering works that made possible the greater efficiency included additional mainline tracks, bridges, cutoffs that shortened routes and avoided congested areas, flying junctions that kept trains moving by carrying one set of tracks over another, entirely new low-grade freight lines that bypassed major urban centers, track pans that enabled steam locomotives to scoop up water while still moving, and improved signaling and communications systems. The result, by the early years of the twentieth century, was a physical plant that staggered the imagination in terms of its sophistication and carrying capacity. But the cost was staggering, too, and that expense put a severe strain on the PRR's ability to raise capital, as the company turned to foreign sources, equipment-trust financing, anything that might generate funds while allowing at least some earnings to be diverted to dividends. The more frustrating problem, particularly for those engineers whose task it was to make the system function smoothly, was that it was never enough. Each improvement in physical plant and equipment, each gain in efficiency, was quickly overwhelmed by the onslaught of additional traffic, generated by the steadily decreasing rates that those same improvements had made possible.

One way to stay ahead of capacity involved simply adding more tracks. During the 1840s, chief engineer J. Edgar Thomson had designed the PRR as a double-track railroad, but a shortage of funds and a paucity of traffic had initially restricted the main line to a single track. In 1852, after the crisis over funding that catapulted Thomson into the presidency, the board authorized the installation of a second track. By the end of 1854, workers had installed double track on the entire distance between Altoona and Johnstown in order to cope with steep grades and increasing traffic. The short section between Harrisburg and the Rockville Bridge also became double track in 1854. By early 1856, the sections between Carr's Tunnel and Greensburg and between Irwin and Brinton's Station boasted a second track, followed by the section from Altoona to Tipton in February 1857. While some additional short pieces of second track entered service later that year, the national financial depression forced the board to temporarily curtail further work.[12]

By the end of 1862, in order to cope with wartime traffic, PRR crews had double-tracked virtually the entire 117-mile distance between Altoona and Pittsburgh, with the sole remaining bottleneck being the bridge over the Conemaugh River at Johnstown, which was not replaced until 1869. East of Altoona, double tracking was mostly complete by 1868, save for the bridges at Mount Union, Manayunk, and Rockville. By 1871, crews had replaced the first two bridges. The single-track span over the Susquehanna River, however, would remain in service until December 1877.[13]

Late in the nineteenth century, as traffic congestion increased, more tracks followed. Rather than incurring the expense of triple- or quadruple-tracking the entire line between Philadelphia and Pittsburgh, PRR engineers installed additional tracks at locations where grades or heavy traffic created serious bottlenecks. Virtually the entire distance between New York and Harrisburg featured four tracks by 1896, allowing for fast and slow trains in each direction. Of the 127 route miles between Harrisburg and Altoona, a fourth track had been installed on fifty-eight miles, and three tracks on another twenty-four. Of the remaining distance west to Pittsburgh, roughly a third possessed four tracks, another third, three tracks, and the remainder, only two. The route between Philadelphia and Washington was double-tracked, as was the Northern Central between Harrisburg and Baltimore, and the Fort Wayne between Pittsburgh and Crestline. By 1907, the PRR employed four tracks on virtually its entire main line, save for a short segment between Spruce Creek and Tyrone Forge.[14]

Track Pans

The construction and maintenance of what became a four-track (and, in some sections of New Jersey, a six-track) main line required enormous expenditures. One way to maintain optimal use of the PRR's facilities and reduce the need for even more trackage was simply to keep trains moving. Unfortunately, steam locomotives required fuel, water, and regular maintenance. There seemed little possibility of replenishing coal supplies or performing repairs while a train was in motion, but water was another matter. During the late 1850s, John Ramsbottom, the locomotive superintendent for the Northern Division of the London & North Western Railway at Crewe, sought a way for the crack *Irish Mail* to take water on the fly. By June 1860, he had developed and patented a scoop, attached to the underside of the tender, which the fireman could lower, at speed, into a long, shallow trough filled with water. The first application in the United States was in 1870, on the New York Central, at Montrose, New York. By November, the PRR had followed suit, with workers installing track pans at Sang Hollow, along the Conemaugh River on the Pittsburgh Division, near Johnstown.[15]

Track pans quickly appeared at numerous other locations throughout the PRR system, particularly in areas with high traffic volume and where grades would have increased the difficulty associated with restarting heavy trains that had stopped to take on water. In 1874, workers installed track pans on the Middle, Philadelphia, and New York Divisions. By 1929, the PRR operated some eighty track pans at twenty-seven sites, spaced perhaps thirty to forty-five miles apart, and representing a total of fifty-eight miles of troughs. Most of the pans conformed to a standard design, between 800 and 2,500 feet long, nineteen to twenty-six inches wide, and six inches deep. Despite the shallow depth, a skilled fireman could scoop up to a ton of water, while the train moved forward at as much as sixty miles an hour—giving him perhaps twenty seconds to lower and then raise the scoop. The track pans were

notoriously wasteful of water, and beginning in 1905 PRR officials spent some $30 million to build a series of dams, reservoirs, and pipelines in the mountains between Altoona and Johnstown. Some of the resulting water went to the shops and other buildings at Altoona, but much of it fed into the track pans. At its greatest extent, the PRR system included thirty-six reservoirs, with water—fourteen billion gallons in 1926 alone—flowing through 441 miles of pipelines.

By far the most elaborate set of track pans was located at Wilmore, between Gallitzin and South Fork. At 2,685 feet, the pans at Wilmore were the longest in the world, with a dedicated reservoir that supplied 1.5 million gallons of water a day. During World War II, even that was not enough, requiring PRR employees to pump water from a nearby creek. The facility grew to include a boiler house, three valve houses, a water treatment plant, a network of supply lines, and ten culverts that sluiced excess water away from the tracks.

Track pans both simplified and complicated operations on the Pennsylvania Railroad. They enabled dispatchers to keep trains moving, reducing congestion and the concomitant need for the installation of additional mainline tracks and sidings. In the face of competition from the New York Central, track pans enabled the PRR to cut as much as three hours off of the schedule of its premier New York–Chicago express trains. Unfortunately, track pans were also expensive to install and maintain. They could be sited only at locations where the tracks were level, and installation on curves, while possible, was quite problematic. During the winter months, the railroad used steam to prevent the pans from freezing. Even then, spray from passing trains coated everything nearby with sheets of ice, making life a misery for the section crews who had to chop it clear of the rails. Water spraying from the pans and from overfilled tenders eroded the roadbed and drenched passengers careless enough to leave their window open. Even worse, wintertime hoboes who rode the truss rods of freight cars or who traveled "blind baggage" (that is, between the tender and the door of the baggage or Railway Post Office car at the head of the train) were drenched, and then quickly froze to death.

Figure 57. In November 1870, PRR construction crews installed track pans at Sang Hollow, a few miles west of Johnstown. The pans, here seen on only one track, enabled locomotives to scoop up water without stopping, avoiding delays and increasing the number of trains that could travel over a given stretch of railroad. In the years that followed, the PRR used pans at twenty-six other locations on the system, representing a $30 million investment.

Pennsylvania Historical and Museum Commission, Railroad Museum of Pennsylvania.

Despite the expense, track pans increased operating efficiency, and the PRR kept many in service, so long as steam locomotives remained in common use. Some were phased out as early as the 1930s, thanks to more capacious tenders, as well as the electrification of the main line between New York, Washington, and Harrisburg. Railroad crews removed the Wilmore facility between 1953 and 1955. The last pans on the PRR, at

Hawstone, Pennsylvania, remained in use until 1956. By then, the advent of diesel locomotives had rendered the technology obsolete.

Rails of Steel

By the time of the Civil War, the railroads had established the basic standards for roadbed and track. A layer of stone ballast supported wooden crossties, set slightly less than two feet apart. Those ties in turn carried a pair of solid metal rails, which bore the enormous weight of locomotives, cars, and cargoes. In most respects, the design of railroad track has not changed, from that day to this. Mechanical engineers coped with increasing railway traffic by designing more capacious (and heavier) cars, and more powerful (and heavier) locomotives to haul them, forcing their civil engineering counterparts to increase the carrying capacity of tracks. They did so not by making radical changes in the track structure, but by incrementally increasing the weight (as expressed in pounds per yard) and strength of railroad rails.

The rapid expansion in the capacity of the PRR's physical plant was only possible because the PRR's engineers had access to one of the most remarkable products of the nineteenth century—steel.[16] In hindsight, steel offered such enormous advantages over iron, both in strength and in durability, that the decision to substitute one metal for another seemed ludicrously simple. During the 1860s, when J. Edgar Thomson became the first American railway executive to authorize the use of steel rails, the decision was far less straightforward. Steel rails were roughly twice as expensive as iron. They could not yet be manufactured in the United States and were subject to both the vagaries of the international marketplace and to high protective tariffs. Any railroad manager who elected to install steel rails would have to choose between dependence on an outside supplier and committing to the enormous capital investment necessary to vertically integrate into rail production. For the rest of the nineteenth century, steel rails failed at a remarkable rate, causing catastrophic accidents, subjecting the railroads to adverse publicity, and clogging the main lines with wrecks. Railroad executives and their counterparts in the steel

business all agreed that such failures were unacceptable. They disagreed, however, on the best solution for the problem, with PRR executives insisting on the right to design rails and oversee the fabrication process, and with steelmakers equally adamant that such practices would impede their use of efficient, mass-production manufacturing techniques. By the dawn of the twentieth century, railroad tracks had changed little, save in strength, from the designs of fifty years earlier. What had changed, and changed drastically, was the relationship of railroad executives to their suppliers.

By the time that the Pennsylvania Railroad was incorporated in 1846, the basic structure of railroad track was no longer in question, as it had been only a decade earlier. The early minutes of the board of directors contain few references to trackwork, for the simple reason that all of the engineers involved with the PRR's construction knew that the new line would consist of iron T-rails spiked to wooden ties. The forests of central and western Pennsylvania provided ample wood for the rough-hewn ties. The more serious issue concerned the source of supply for the iron rails. In 1847, conservative Philadelphia commercial interests still dominated the board, and the directors resolved to use Pennsylvania manufactured products wherever possible. One local source was David Reeves, who first began manufacturing rails at Phoenixville in 1846. The PRR's order for fifteen thousand tons of iron rail, at $15 per ton, enabled Reeves to establish a foundry and rolling mill in Lancaster County, and he began delivering rails in June 1848.[17]

In 1862, in response to the intense traffic demands associated with the Civil War, Thomson ordered 150 tons of steel rails from Britain and had them installed in the yards at Altoona and Pittsburgh. The first lot proved defective, but a second consignment of rails held up to the heavy traffic. By 1869, 146 miles of PRR track boasted steel rail, with use generally confined to curves and areas of particularly heavy traffic. Other components of the PRR system employed small quantities of steel rail as well, including the Pittsburgh, Fort Wayne & Chicago (six miles, installed in 1866) and the Northern Central (three and a quarter miles, installed during the same year). The independent Philadelphia, Wilmington & Baltimore Railroad also installed steel rail on thirty-five miles of track, in 1864, and by 1869 the company's directors had elected to use exclusively steel for replacement rails on the main line. By the late 1870s, the PW&B possessed a main line laid entirely with steel rails, one of the first railways in the United States to do so.

The years immediately following the Civil War witnessed a rapid increase in the quality of steel rails, along with a commensurate decline in price. Cost per ton fell from $166 in 1867 to $112 in 1872 and to only $59 in 1876. By the early 1870s, the Pennsylvania Railroad boasted 650 track-miles laid with steel rails, with perhaps a tenth that amount on secondary and branch lines. After 1877, trains traveled the entire distance between New York and Pittsburgh on steel rails.[18]

In authorizing the widespread adoption of steel rails, PRR officials took great pains to ensure that an adequate supply would be available, at a reasonable price. Imported steel rails were expensive, at roughly twice the cost of iron rails, and the price could rise whenever Congress enacted tariffs to protect steel producers in the United States. Thomson accordingly concluded that the PRR should integrate vertically into domestic rail manufacture, following the example of the London & North Western Railway, which in 1864 had constructed a Bessemer furnace at its Crewe works. He purchased the patent rights for the rails and, in partnership with Andrew Carnegie, set about to improve the manufacturing process.

Carnegie was also becoming interested in the Bessemer process, thanks in part to John Armstrong Wright, the ironmaker who had encouraged Thomson to lead the 1852 rebellion against president William C. Patterson and others on the PRR board of directors. Wright controlled the Freedom Iron Works (renamed the Freedom Iron Company in 1856), with its workers busily employed in manufacturing tires for PRR locomotive wheels. Carnegie invested in the company in 1861, with the firm's name changing to Freedom Iron & Steel four years later. Wright traveled to England in 1866, in order to observe the Bessemer method, and was so impressed that he made the commitment to produce steel at his Lewistown facility. Carnegie secured the American patent rights for a process, developed by British inventor Thomas Dodd, to bond steel facing to iron rails. He also established the American

Steeled Rail Company, with Tom Scott as one of the original investors. The PRR provided Carnegie with $20,000 to improve the Dodd process, and the Scotsman set to work expanding the manufacturing facilities at Freedom Iron & Steel. In early 1867, Carnegie sent an initial batch of semi-steel "Doddized" composite rails—the first manufactured in the United States—to Thomson. The following spring, the company produced its first true Bessemer steel.[19]

Even with Carnegie's support, however, Wright's venture into steel manufacturing ended in failure. Carnegie later observed that his ally "was quite right, but just a little in advance of his time."[20] The Doddized composite rails tended to delaminate, rendering them useless. Although Carnegie claimed that the rails provided "superior service [that] far more than compensated for the advance made by Mr. Thomson," the PRR president in fact noted that the experience had "impaired my confidence in this process" and informed Carnegie that "you may as well abandon the patent."[21] A second consignment of rails, manufactured with the new Bessemer furnaces, also fared badly. Carnegie requested additional money from the PRR, but Thomson refused.[22]

Carnegie's later ventures into steel manufacturing would prove somewhat more successful, but for now he yielded the field to the Pennsylvania Railroad. On September 22, 1865, Thomson and Scott were among the original incorporators of the Pennsylvania Steel Company, and they and their associates purchased the company's entire initial offering of $200,000 worth of stock.[23] Thomson also offered generous traffic agreements to the new company, including a 20 percent discount on the transportation of construction materials, as well as through rates, rather than higher local rates, on all raw materials and finished steel shipments. In return, Pennsylvania Steel Company executives agreed to ship exclusively via the Pennsylvania Railroad.[24]

William Sellers, another founder of Pennsylvania Steel, was closely connected to the Pennsylvania Railroad. He was a manufacturer of machine tools and a supplier to the Baldwin Locomotive Works. As president of the Franklin Institute between 1864 and 1867, Sellers would deliver an influential paper on the standardization of screw threads. The federal government accepted his recommendations in 1868, followed by the PRR the following year, ensuring their widespread adoption. The Sellers foundry produced iron turntables for PRR enginehouses, at one point completing them at a rate of one every four days. His firm, William Sellers and Company, would later manufacture the locomotive test plant installed at Altoona.[25]

The other major incorporator was Samuel Morse Felton, who had recently relinquished the presidency of the Philadelphia, Wilmington & Baltimore to become the first president of Pennsylvania Steel. Felton was responsible for naming the ninety-seven-acre site "Baldwin" in recognition of locomotive builder Matthias Baldwin—although in 1880 the location was renamed Steelton. Felton's son-in-law, Luther Bent, and then his son, Edgar C. Felton, served as general managers. Felton also recruited an experienced Sheffield steelmaker, William Butcher, and after Butcher left to establish the Midvale Steel Company, Felton replaced him with a Connecticut native, Alexander Lyman Holley. When the ship carrying a Bessemer converter from England sank off the Irish coast, Holley supervised the construction of a replacement, built in Philadelphia to the original specifications. On May 26, 1867, crews tapped the furnace at Baldwin for the first time.[26]

The Pennsylvania Steel facilities at Baldwin hardly constituted an integrated manufacturing facility. Workers sent steel ingots to the Cambria Iron Company in Johnstown for rolling into rails.[27] Rolling operations moved to Baldwin in 1868, but the Pennsylvania Steel Company did not add a blast furnace there until 1873. By then, in addition to manufacturing rails, the facility fabricated castings for switch frogs and other track components. Production expanded exponentially, from barely a thousand tons of rails in 1868 to 113,000 tons in 1880, earning a net income of $2 million. The true profitability of the company was difficult to measure, however, as Pennsylvania Steel sold rails and other track components to the PRR at below-market rates, and in turn received rebates for the transportation of iron ore, limestone, and coke.[28]

Whereas Carnegie Steel diversified into steel plate and structural steel, Pennsylvania Steel followed a different course and became an early adopter of open-hearth production methods, first employed at Steelton in 1884. Luther Bent was responsible for expanding

the operations of the Pennsylvania Steel Company. After obtaining high-quality, low-cost iron ore from a mine in Cuba, he negotiated a partnership with the Bethlehem Iron Company to jointly develop the mine and to establish a new steel mill at Sparrows Point, Maryland, served by a branch off of the Northern Central Railway and easily accessible by oceangoing ore vessels.[29] Production began in 1890, but by that time railroads had already installed steel rails on most of their important lines, and the great burst of competitive construction that had characterized the 1880s had largely ended. Even though periodic track renewals would always be necessary, the demand was certain to decline. The firm faltered and went bankrupt in 1893, a victim of the severe economic depression that began in that year.[30]

When investment banker J. P. Morgan created United States Steel in 1901, he consolidated most of the nation's steel manufacturing capacity into one company and was accordingly in a position to dictate rail prices to the Pennsylvania Railroad. In May 1901, some three months after the formation of U.S. Steel, rail manufacturers gave a clear indication of their dominance over the railroads. In response to what manufacturers considered to be unremunerative rail prices, which had dipped as low as $18 per ton during the 1890s, they formed a producers' cartel that set a rate of $28 per ton. The cartel remained in effect until 1915, substantially increasing the PRR's capital expenditures during that period, just as the ICC commissioners were becoming more reluctant to authorize higher railroad rates.[31]

In addition, U.S. Steel chairman of the board Elbert H. Gary indicated that he was willing to divert a substantial share of his company's traffic to the new rail system that George Gould was beginning to assemble. As a defensive strategy, PRR officials elected to acquire a substantial interest in both Pennsylvania Steel and the Cambria Steel Company (the former Cambria Iron Company), investing more than $20 million in the two firms. Their intent was to guarantee a supply of rails, independently of U.S. Steel, while simultaneously forcing Gary's company to accept the PRR's posted rates, without shifting production away from Pittsburgh or subsidizing the construction of competing rail lines.[32]

Both the Steelton and the Sparrows Point plants of Pennsylvania Steel continued to perform poorly, however, and PRR executives soon looked for an opportunity to exit the steel business. In March 1905, as Gould's rail empire was teetering on the brink of financial collapse, PRR and U.S. Steel officials negotiated what amounted to a truce. Railroad executives agreed to withdraw from the steel business, while U.S. Steel representatives vowed that they would no longer finance the construction of lines that might compete against the PRR. The next year, the commodities clause of the 1906 Hepburn Act prevented railroads from transporting any product that they mined or manufactured. Although PRR attorneys offered conflicting interpretations of the new legislation, some suggested that the commodities clause required the PRR to relinquish its investments in the steel business.

PRR board members likewise disagreed on what should be done with the steel companies. Director Henry Clay Frick insisted that they be sold as soon as possible. Frick had also been one of the founding directors of U.S. Steel, and he remained closely associated with that company, no doubt explaining why he was anxious to set adrift one of his competitors. Effingham B. Morris, president of the Girard Trust Company, and a PRR director since 1896, favored a continuation of PRR ownership. Morris, who was probably the individual who had initially supported the PRR's 1901 purchases of Pennsylvania Steel and Cambria Steel, was anxious to defend his earlier advice. Yet, by 1911, he admitted that PRR ownership hindered the competitive abilities of the two steel manufacturers. "Several of the larger systems of railroads frankly say they will not give either Pennsylvania Steel or Cambria Steel any orders at all," Morris acknowledged to PRR first vice president Samuel Rea, "because they belong to the Pennsylvania R.R. If the latter road is unwilling to treat these companies on any other than a strictly competitive basis and to give them work on a cost and percentage basis, as those other Railroads do with the U.S. Steel Corporation, then it seems to me the stock holdings of the P.R.R. had better be disposed of when a suitable opportunity occurs—if it ever does."[33] Eight years after the 1905 truce with U.S. Steel, he conceded that the investments in the two steel companies "have served their purpose and the original reason for their

purchase no longer exists."[34] Morris also emphasized that the "danger to the [Pennsylvania] Railroad from the predominance of the U.S. Steel Corporation is apparently lessening."[35] In all likelihood, Morris was referring to the activities of Charles M. Schwab, who in 1903 left U.S. Steel to take charge of the Bethlehem Steel Company, transforming the firm into a strong competitor.

By early 1914, as the Pennsylvania Steel Company continued to stagnate, Frick became more forceful in his demands that the PRR dispose of its holdings in both steel manufacturers. A decade earlier, Frick and the Mellon family had assisted William H. Donner in his efforts to establish the Union Steel Company— which they later sold to U.S. Steel, apparently at an inflated price. After leaving Union Steel, Donner became an investor and an executive at both Pennsylvania Steel and Cambria Steel. Frick persuaded the PRR board to grant Donner an option to buy the stock of both companies at a low, but reasonable cost. Before the option expired, World War I broke out in Europe, steel prices skyrocketed, and the two companies suddenly became very valuable properties. In the autumn of 1915, Donner exercised his options, relying largely on financing provided by the Mellon Bank of Pittsburgh (Richard B. Mellon, Andrew W. Mellon, and Richard King Mellon all would eventually serve on the PRR board). At the same time, PRR officials began selling additional shares, not covered by Donner's options. By February 1916, the Bethlehem Steel Company had purchased the remainder of the PRR's investments in the steel business. Effective July 1916, Bethlehem Steel took control of Sparrows Point and Steelton, ending the PRR's direct involvement in steel manufacturing.[36]

The Quality of Rails

Despite the problems at Pennsylvania Steel and Cambria Steel, the PRR's investments in those two companies at least permitted executives to exert some measure of control over the rail-manufacturing process. Outside suppliers were far less willing to accept the oversight of railroad managers. Yet, PRR executives rightly considered rails to be the single most important element of the company's technological system. PRR officials were accordingly determined to ensure the quality of railroad rails, regardless of which company supplied them. As early as 1868, president J. Edgar Thomson required rail manufacturers to drill, rather than punch, bolt holes at the end of each rail in order to reduce breakage. Within a few years, the PRR was sending inspectors into the mills to determine for themselves whether new rails were sound, and other American railroads soon copied this practice. Such inspections benefited both parties, because they prevented railroad accidents and the corresponding damage to the reputation of the mill that had rolled the rails.[37]

Rail testing was part of a broader effort to establish system-wide standards for materials and to evaluate the quality of products supplied by outside firms. By the early 1870s, PRR executives had located a Bureau of Experiments at Altoona, and then created the Department of Physical Tests in 1874. In November 1875, the PRR established a Chemical Laboratory and hired an academically trained chemist, Dr. Charles Dudley, to conduct a variety of chemical and metallurgical tests. One of the earliest functions of the Test Department involved the evaluation of broken rails in an effort to determine why they had failed in service. By 1876, Dudley had begun to examine rails that were worn, but sound, relating wearing qualities to such issues as traffic levels and the position of each rail in the track.[38]

By the 1870s, metallurgists and mechanical engineers had developed increasingly sophisticated scientific techniques to analyze both the composition and the strength of railroad rails. Dudley, in an 1878 report, emphasized that the life of rails could be doubled merely by changing their chemical composition. The next year, Dudley insisted that the PRR increase the carbon component of its rails. Test Department personnel began evaluating the metallurgical composition of rails as early as 1879 in an effort to clarify a situation that puzzled operating and maintenance-of-way officials.[39] With the exception of rails laid on the high side of a curve, softer rails actually lasted longer than harder ones, generally because they were less likely to spall or shatter.[40]

The research undertaken by Dudley and other Test Department officials collided with a growing debate among steelmakers regarding the optimal metallurgical composition of steel rails. During the 1870s, railroad demand for iron rails decreased precipitously, while purchases of steel rails increased at a corresponding rate. Any company that manufactured steel rails was likely to enjoy considerable success, while any firm that remained wedded to iron rail production was likely to fail. However, there was no clear distinction between the metallurgical definition of iron and that of steel. Representatives from firms that produced low-temperature steel (many with established capabilities in iron manufacturing) argued that carbon content established a metal as steel, while their counterparts in newer, high-temperature Bessemer steel-manufacturing facilities (including Carnegie's Edgar Thomson Steel Works) insisted that steel resulted solely from the complete melting, or fusion, of iron ore. The railroads, and the PRR in particular, ultimately validated the fusion definition of steel, largely because it produced a homogeneous product.[41]

The railroads' affirmation of the fusion process came at considerable cost, however. As metallurgists later discovered, rail rolled at excessively high temperatures was prone to cracking, spalling, shattering, and other potentially catastrophic defects. Those problems became far more serious during the first years of the twentieth century as PRR managers employed heavier cars and locomotives in order to improve the efficiency of the railroad's operations. The new equipment placed tremendous strains on rails, which began failing with appalling frequency. PRR executives demanded that steel mills improve the quality of their products and eliminate weak, brittle, and soft rails.[42]

Railroad officials associated with the American Society for Testing Materials (ASTM), the American Society of Civil Engineers (ASCE), and the recently organized American Railway Engineering and Maintenance of Way Association (AREMWA) led the efforts to address the growing rate of rail failures. Dudley enjoyed considerable respect among his peers, who elected him to the presidency of the ASTM in 1902, yet the PRR chemist was increasingly at odds with most of his colleagues. Dudley insisted that it was the shape, or profile, of the rail that was at fault, rather than the composition of the steel. Under his direction, the Test Department developed specifications for the heavier rails (as much as one hundred pounds per yard) that were necessary to accommodate heavier trains. Those criteria, which called for an exceptionally thin web, with a large head, ran counter to the accepted standard developed by the ASCE.[43]

The revised specifications brought Dudley and the Test Department into conflict with other PRR officials, with the steel producers who supplied the rails, and with newly established engineering professional organizations. William H. Brown, then the PRR's chief engineer of construction, insisted that metallurgical composition was the key issue, and that higher-carbon rails wore out more quickly than their older, low-carbon counterparts, regardless of rail profile. What was needed, Brown claimed, were rails that were characterized by greater "toughness" (that is, malleability), and not "hardness."[44] In 1898, the members of the PRR's Association of Transportation Officers ventured to suggest that the PRR adopt a more conventional profile, one that Dudley had not favored.[45] Lines West officials went further in their disagreement with Dudley's guidelines, and they preferred to follow the ASCE standards.[46] Steel manufacturers were even more vociferous in their opposition to the PRR's specifications for rail shape. They insisted, correctly, that rail profile had little to do with the high failure rates, and that Dudley's designs would actually increase the possibility of defects in the rail heads. Members of professional organizations such as the American Institute of Mining Engineers (AIME) also reacted with skepticism to Dudley's support of soft rails.[47] They questioned his methods and even the applicability of scientific analysis as a means of resolving problems on the railroads. Much to Dudley's chagrin, further tests by the mills, the railroaders, and metallurgists conclusively demonstrated that his support of soft rails had been grievously in error.[48]

Unlike Dudley, the railway officials who belonged to the American Society for Testing Materials, the American Railway Engineering and Maintenance of Way Association, and the American Society of Civil Engineers generally agreed that it was the quality of the steel, not the shape of the rail, that largely determined failure rates. As such, they enlisted the help of the American Institute of Mining Engineers to improve steel manufacturing techniques. Tests conducted by AIME and other engineering bodies demonstrated that excessively high rolling temperatures disrupted the steel's crystalline structure, causing serious weaknesses.[49]

In October 1901, PRR Test Department officials accepted the metallurgical explanation for rail failure, and contracts with the mills henceforth specified that rail would be rolled at 1,300 degrees Fahrenheit, as indicated by a dull red color of the steel. That stipulation produced two problems, however. The owners of independent steel mills objected to the presence of Test Department observers, fearing that they would interfere with the process of production or reveal proprietary information to their competitors, including the PRR-controlled Pennsylvania Steel Company. Second, "dull red" was an inherently subjective criterion, one that was hardly in accord with the techniques of scientific analysis. As an alternative to color, the PRR contracts included a shrinkage clause, specifying that thirty-foot-long rails, weighing one hundred pounds per yard, would shrink by no more than $5\frac{1}{8}$ inches. Shrinkage was a useful proxy for rolling temperature inasmuch as it could be precisely measured, and because it enabled independent steel manufacturers to retain complete control over the production process. The Test Department accordingly yielded control over rail manufacturing to outside firms, and—in a marked contrast to earlier efforts to inspect rail mills—company officials gave steelmakers the opportunity to influence rail design and composition. "We ask the mill men," PRR engineer of maintenance of way Joseph T. Richards acknowledged, "to come in and help us make good rail."[50]

The willingness of Test Department personnel to cede greater authority to the rail manufacturers did not end the problem of rail failures, however. Nickel-steel rails, first purchased in 1903, offered a possible solution, but managers judged that the much higher cost could not be justified, except in extreme applications. The PRR did not resolve the issue of rail failures until it began installing open-hearth steel rails, beginning in 1905. The willingness of smaller rail mills to experiment with open-hearth production had little to do with a commitment to technological innovation. Instead, those companies, such as Jones & Laughlin and Tennessee Coal & Iron, were less well integrated than U.S. Steel, and correspondingly less able to secure reliable supplies of high-grade Bessemer ores. Open-hearth furnaces could process lower-grade ore, and the $28-a-ton cartel price ensured that the higher production cost associated with the new methods were of little consequence.[51]

Despite the ascendancy of the open-hearth steel and the railroad industry's increased attention to rail quality, one type of defect continued to occur with alarming frequency. Transverse fissures were internal defects not visible during the manufacturing or installation process, creating weaknesses that were apparent only when the rail failed suddenly. In 1909 Test Department technicians began to microscopically examine rails that had failed in service in an effort to resolve the transverse-fissure problem. PRR officials embraced three responses to the problem of shattered rails, two internal and the other external to the company. Beginning in 1910, Motive Power Department personnel employed the PRR's Altoona locomotive test plant in an effort to design lighter, less destructive steam locomotives. Second, in 1919 their counterparts in the Test Department discovered patterns of small cracks in rails that, they claimed, proved that rail manufacturers were responsible for the problem. By 1923, however, ICC investigators had engaged in more exhaustive research, based on a larger sample of failed rails. They overruled PRR researchers, demonstrating that the small cracks were unrelated to the transverse fissure problem.

By the 1930s, PRR executives had concluded that they lacked the technical expertise necessary to prevent transverse fissures and other defects, and they likewise abandoned their efforts to evaluate rail quality. As early as the 1910s, independent rail-inspecting firms, such as Philadelphia-based William Webster, helped to maintain production standards while serving as a useful intermediary between the PRR and the steel manufacturers. Beginning in the 1930s, PRR officials employed Sperry Rail Service, with its specialized testing equipment, to evaluate installed rails across the system.[52]

Although the PRR Test Department had relinquished control over both the metallurgical composition of rails and the manufacturing process, railroad personnel continued to develop new rail profiles. Between 1898 and 1908 average locomotive and car weight

had grown by 50 percent, while speeds had increased as well, yet the PRR continued to rely, as it had done for several decades, on a standard rail weight of one hundred pounds per yard.[53] Chief engineer Alexander C. Shand, chief mechanical engineer Alfred W. Gibbs, and other members of the PRR Rail Committee insisted that these increased train weights mandated heavier rail. "My personal view of the whole subject," Shand noted, "is that the track as a whole has almost stood still for the last fifteen years, while at the same time the treatment of the track from heavier equipment, from greater volume of heavier equipment, and from speeds, has increased out of all proportion."[54] E. F. Kennedy, a metallurgical engineer at the Cambria Steel Company, seconded that assessment. Because "it is not possible to change the wheel loads and speeds," he claimed, "the only way to reduce stresses in the rail is to increase the section"—that is, to make the rail larger and heavier.[55] The engineers responsible for maintaining the PRR's physical plant, who lacked scientific training in metallurgy, disagreed with that assertion. Lines West consulting engineer Thomas H. Johnson explained, "The manufacturers favor the larger section, because the defects will be surrounded by a larger proportion of sound metal," while engineer of bridges John C. Bland maintained, "I cannot agree with the theory that the [heavier] rail should be called upon to do the work which a properly constructed track should do."[56]

Executive concerns regarding regulatory policy and the possibility of adverse publicity finally settled what might otherwise have been a strictly technical issue. "Considering the attitude of Mr. Howard, the Engineer of the Interstate Commerce Commission, on a number of passenger train accidents caused by broken rails," Shand observed, "it seems to me to be very unwise for us to postpone experimenting with a rail of a heavier section than 100 lbs. per yard."[57] Yet, Gibbs was careful to emphasize that Ivy Lee, the PRR's public-relations agent, "in his publicity articles will make it clear that the introduction of 120-pound rail is experimental only, [and] I think it will leave our hands absolutely free to subsequently abandon the use of rail heavier than 100 pounds."[58]

Progressively heavier loads nonetheless forced PRR officials to authorize the installation of more robust rail. In 1916, following experiments with 120-pound and 125-pound rail, the PRR introduced 130-pound rail, designed by the American Railway Engineering Association (AREA), as its system standard. By the early 1930s, the PRR's assistant chief engineer, Robert Faries, developed a 131-pound rail. Despite the seemingly insignificant one-pound weight differential, the new design was considerably taller and featured a thinner web and a smaller head profile—all designed to reduce the stresses induced by the cooling of a large mass of metal during manufacturing. In 1933, AREA adopted the 131-pound PS (Pennsylvania Standard) rail, replacing the existing 130-pound AREA specifications. By that time, the PRR's chief engineer, Thomas J. Skillman, had already worked with representatives from United States Steel and Bethlehem Steel to develop a far larger 152-pound rail, necessary to accommodate heavy, fast trains along the soon-to-be electrified line between New York and Washington, D.C. The new standard represented the heaviest rail ever used in regular mainline service in the United States.[59]

Safety Appliances

Railroading has always been a particularly dangerous occupation. By 1890, however, railway equipment had become larger and heavier, and more trains moved at faster speeds. The result was chronic carnage, as railroad accidents left some six thousand people dead each year, with another forty thousand injured. Frightened citizens read with horror the ghoulish accounts of derailments, collisions, and bridge collapses that appeared with distressing frequency in American newspapers. Yet, the mechanical equipment that had made trains larger and faster promised to make them safer as well. Air brakes could stop trains more quickly and safely, automatic couplers allowed brakemen to avoid being crushed between cars, and other safety appliances (principally uniformly positioned grab irons, steps and brake platforms) prevented often-fatal missteps. Automatic signaling systems offered the tantalizing possibility of removing human error from train operations. Railroad safety nonetheless depended as much on the success of efforts to educate workers and citizens about safer practices as it did on a technological

magic bullet that could reliably prevent death and dismemberment. For many decades, however, the promise of fail-safe mechanisms held a powerful lure for the public and for government regulators, if not necessarily for executives.

Public perceptions of accidents complicated efforts to develop a solution to the problem. Relatively few people perished in the types of spectacular catastrophes that merited a front-page newspaper headline. Instead, the vast majority of victims died one or two at a time, in accidents that were brutal but not necessarily newsworthy. The unfortunate victims may have been employees who paid for a moment's carelessness with their lives. Others were passengers who fell from trains, often while boarding or disembarking. Many more, including a heartbreaking number of children, were crossing or walking along tracks. Railroad executives, newspaper reporters, and members of the general public were often able to rationalize those sorts of small tragedies, attributing them to carelessness or stupidity or simple bad luck. The deaths of ordinary citizens along the right of way were particularly easy to dismiss, as the victims were by definition trespassers. The simple statement that a mutilated body was that of a tramp or vagrant was generally enough to render the death meaningless.[60]

Newspaper editors were nonetheless relentless in their demands that the railroads devote most of their attentions to preventing the types of mass-casualty accidents that constituted a relatively small proportion of the overall death toll. As such, railway executives felt considerable pressure to improve passenger-train safety, on the off chance that they might prevent a major disaster. The elimination of the more numerous smaller accidents constituted a far more difficult proposition. It was no surprise, therefore, that the PRR first applied safety equipment in the areas where it would be the most visible to the public and to regulators, and not where it would be most useful. Even though railway employees constituted the vast majority of accident victims, passenger trains were the first to become safer, through technological advances designed to preclude greater regulatory oversight of the PRR's operations.[61]

The Pennsylvania Railroad, given its size and its presence in the public eye, played a leadership role in the installation of safety appliances. Yet, as PRR executives sensed—and to the frustration of regulators and the public—money did not necessarily buy safety. Instead, the new technologies embodied a complex mix of cost considerations, patent law, public perceptions, government action, operating requirements, and labor relations. In the end, the PRR's executives, while by no means heartless, cared less about safety than they did about efficiency. Safety appliances saved lives but, of greater importance to PRR managers, they facilitated the operation of longer and heavier trains, with less risk that an accident might block the tracks and suspend the free flow of traffic. Safety worked only when the payoff came from better performance, not fewer casualties.

Air Brakes and Automatic Couplers

Air brakes exemplified the balance between enhanced safety and more efficient operations. In many popular accounts, George Westinghouse, Jr., invented the air brake, railroad managers rapidly appreciated the safety benefits associated with the device, and train operations became far less dangerous. The reality was far more complex. Westinghouse was by no means the only person to "invent" the air brake. The first patents for similar devices appeared in Britain in 1845, with installations beginning in 1860. In large measure, Westinghouse succeeded because he maintained control both over the patents for airbrake equipment and over the manufacturing and marketing of the device. In particular, Westinghouse developed a keen appreciation of the problem of interchangeability. He knew that his version of the air brake, if successful, would have to be adopted by railroads across the United States, to the absolute exclusion of the incompatible products developed by his competitors.

Westinghouse also benefited from impeccable timing in that he was able to exploit a sea change in American patent law. Earlier inventors of braking systems and other safety devices had often attempted to exploit the "doctrine of savings"—legal terminology for the full benefit that might accrue to the railroads from the new devices. Savings were difficult to calculate, however, particularly if they included estimates of the

value of forgone catastrophes. With multiple inventors developing similar devices more or less simultaneously, it was also difficult to determine who deserved the financial reward associated with the safety equipment. Even worse, improved safety and performance were generally the result of multiple, overlapping, symbiotic devices, ranging from air brakes to underframes. The allocation of the exact proportion of the savings to each component of railway equipment held the potential for endless judicial hairsplitting. Above all, railway officials perceived little economic incentive for the installation of air brakes (or any other safety device), if all of the benefits were simply passed on to a third party.

By the 1870s, however, members of Congress were increasingly sensitive to arguments put forth by railroad lobbyists (as well as their unlikely allies, the farmers) that inventors were little better than extortionists who deprived the public of full access to devices that could save time, money, and even human lives. Under such circumstances, the railroads provided a theoretical device with a practical application. They, and not the inventors, were responsible for ensuring public safety. The railroads accordingly benefited from new legislation and favorable court rulings that restricted royalties to more reasonable levels. Westinghouse was certainly not willing to relinquish control over his patents, but neither did he demand a "king's ransom." Furthermore, he refused to license production rights to any railroad or manufacturing company, ensuring control over quality, regulating the pace of technological diffusion, and—perhaps most important—preventing another inventor from making subtle changes to the air brake and patenting a competing device.[62]

Westinghouse depended on the railroads, however, and his early and close association with the Pennsylvania Railroad was vital to his efforts. In 1868, when Westinghouse began developing his air brake, he quickly formed an alliance with two PRR executives. One was William W. Card, a superintendent on the Pittsburgh, Cincinnati & St. Louis Railway (the Pan Handle), and the other was Pittsburgh Division superintendent Robert Pitcairn, an individual whose manifold responsibilities kept him connected to many aspects of the transportation business. In September,

Card allowed Westinghouse to install air brakes on a Pan Handle passenger locomotive. According to popular lore, the trial run, between Pittsburgh and Steubenville, provided an unexpected test of the new braking system. In an incident redolent with high drama, the engineman threw the test locomotive's air brake into emergency, preventing a collision with a horse and wagon. A short time later, in April 1869, Westinghouse received a patent for his air brake. That fall, Pennsylvania Railroad officials began air brake tests. While those initial experiments were initially unsuccessful, Westinghouse and PRR personnel soon resolved the problems. In October, the PRR hosted a special air brake–equipped demonstration train for the Master Mechanics' Association. The train operated between Pittsburgh and Altoona, over some of the most severe grades on the entire system. The following month, an air brake–equipped train ran through to Philadelphia for demonstrations before the PRR board of directors. In 1870, PRR officials chose the Westinghouse air brake as standard equipment on all passenger trains.

The close relationship between PRR officials and George Westinghouse extended to the incorporation of the company that bore his name. In September 1869, shortly after the first successful tests on the PRR, Westinghouse joined forces with Cassatt, Card, Pitcairn, Pan Handle purchasing agent George D. Whitcomb, PRR general superintendent Edward H. Williams, and Pittsburgh businessman Ralph Bagaley. Card and Pitcairn used PRR funds to underwrite the costs associated with Westinghouse's early experiments. They allowed the inventor to build his new Pittsburgh manufacturing facility adjacent to the PRR's shops. That cooperation did not prevent the emergence of disagreements, as both Westinghouse and PRR executives insisted on controlling the manufacture of the brakes. Railroad officials would have preferred to build air brakes at Altoona, under license, but Westinghouse refused.[63]

The Westinghouse apparatus initially relied on the application of compressed air to set the brakes. A failure of the locomotive's air compressor, or a leak in the brake line, rendered the system inoperable. In 1872, Westinghouse introduced the improved straight automatic air brake, employing a patented triple valve, allowing the brakes to be applied on all cars simultaneously, and preventing a broken air line from causing a brake failure.[64] His timing was fortuitous. In August 1871 the *Portland Express*, a passenger train on the Eastern Railroad of Massachusetts, was struck from behind by a train whose crew had been unable to apply the hand brakes in time. Charles Francis Adams, Jr., future president of the Union Pacific Railroad and grandson of President John Quincy Adams, was at that time in charge of the Massachusetts Board of Railroad Commissioners. He calmed public fears by insisting that rail travel was generally safe, but that technology and increased publicity would make it even more so. Like many reformers of his generation, Adams believed that cooperation and voluntarism would ensure railroad safety, and that railroad executives, once made aware of their failings, would quickly remedy them. As such, Adams favored so-called sunshine regulatory commissions, which exposed dangerous practices to the light of public scrutiny, without imposing direct governmental regulatory oversight.[65]

Railroad executives were not averse to increased safety, particularly when it promised to improve productivity. Their compliance with voluntary regulation, however, was largely based on their assessment that, should they not make small improvements voluntarily, state legislatures and regulatory commissions might mandate far more onerous safety requirements. Given the adverse publicity surrounding passenger train accidents, PRR executives concluded that investments in passenger train air brakes represented the best use of funds, not so much to improve safety, but rather to placate public opinion and government regulators. Air brake–equipped passenger trains also enabled PRR ticket agents to promote the enhanced safety of travel and to draw business away from competing railroads. Travelers readily appreciated the difference between air brake–equipped passenger trains (which they considered "safe") and "unsafe" trains that lacked such equipment. By the end of 1870, even before the tragedy in Massachusetts, two hundred passenger cars on the PRR sported air brakes, representing more than half of the national total.[66]

While the Westinghouse air brake found ready acceptance in PRR passenger service, success did not come so easily in freight operations. That situation was not simply an issue of technological inadequacy, as Westinghouse steadily improved the air brake design during the last decades of the nineteenth century. Other factors were at work. Pennsylvania Railroad passenger equipment generally remained on PRR rails, but freight cars did not. Transportation Department personnel experienced a persistent problem with air brake–equipped freight cars "disappearing," as other railroads temporarily incorporated them into their rolling stock fleets, avoiding the expense of upgrading their own cars. Furthermore, air brakes were of limited value unless they were applied to all (or at least a substantial proportion) of the cars in a train. That was not a difficulty in passenger service, because such trains were relatively short, and the cars usually remained as part of the same train. Freight service was much different, however, particularly when unequipped foreign-road rolling stock entered the mix. As such, the first widespread application of air brakes authorized by PRR executives involved fifty stock cars, converted in 1881. That was a logical choice, as stock cars frequently ran in dedicated trains, owing to the need to speed animals to the abattoirs, while pausing at regular intervals to provide feed and water. Stock trains also moved at relatively high speeds, increasing the importance of a reliable braking system. In June 1886, PRR shop crews added air brakes to one hundred refrigerator cars, again based on the principle that those cars, and the time-sensitive commodities that they contained, would travel in a group and not leave PRR rails.[67]

PRR officials soon discovered, to their chagrin, that air brakes often *reduced* productivity and retarded operations. Train crews who lacked instruction in the proper use of the new devices could stop too suddenly or release the brakes too rapidly, increasing the possibility of trains breaking in two, derailments, or damaged cargo. Yard crews had to hunt through a sea of freight equipment to find air brake–equipped cars and place them in a string immediately behind the locomotive. During the 1880s and into the 1890s, managers were appalled to discover that impatient crews, desperate to complete their runs in a timely manner, assembled cars in whatever order they found them, rendering the capital investment in air brakes essentially useless.[68]

Or worse. It took a skilled crew to control a train equipped with a mixture of air brakes and hand brakes, and their efforts were not always successful. At a little past one in the morning on May 11, 1905, near Harrisburg, Pennsylvania, an eastbound freight train braked suddenly in order to avoid a collision with a switch engine. The air brakes reacted almost instantly, and the hand brakes not at all. The train compressed like an accordion, flinging cars onto the adjacent tracks. Within seconds, the *Cleveland and Cincinnati Express* plowed into the wreckage, sending two cars toppling over an embankment. The situation, already bad enough, soon became much worse. The force of the collision, or perhaps an exploding boiler on the passenger locomotive, detonated ten tons of Judson Rock Creek Powder destined for the H. S. Kerbaugh Company in nearby Columbia. The explosion splintered through the wooden passenger cars, and set them alight. More than twenty people died, and over a hundred were injured. Some of the bodies were completely cremated, and others were so badly charred that they could be identified only by their watches and their jewelry. Theater magnate Samuel S. Shubert, horribly burned, lingered for two days in agony before succumbing to his injuries. His death alone ensured serious adverse publicity, as well as a larger than usual award settlement. Like most disasters, the Harrisburg wreck had multiple causes. Still, PRR executives could not help but notice that air brakes had helped the crew of the freight train avoid a comparatively minor collision with a switch engine, but had consigned two dozen people to a horrific death. At least until air brakes became universal, they occasionally created more problems than they solved.[69]

Air brakes were not the only pieces of equipment that promised to improve both safety and efficiency, nor were they the only devices to be embedded in a complex technological system involving railroads throughout the United States. The adoption of automatic couplers followed much the same pattern. As their name suggested, traditional link-and-pin couplers used an iron link, held in place by pins, to connect one car to another. They posed an extreme danger to train crews, who were often maimed or killed when coupling cars, accounting for more than a third of all of the employee accidents that occurred on American railroads between 1877 and 1887. While managers were sympathetic to the plight of injured workers, they possessed additional reasons for disliking link-and-pin couplers. Links could break, particularly when a heavy train was starting, or traveling upgrade—a problem exacerbated by the heavier equipment that accompanied rising traffic levels. On passenger trains, link-and-pin couplers increased the danger of telescoping, which, during a collision, would cause one car to lodge inside another, with a horrific toll in deaths and injuries. In the event of a labor uprising, train crews often hid the coupling pins, making it impossible for replacement workers to operate trains. The oval links could be thrown with alarming accuracy, and the pins themselves formed ideal clubs.[70]

As was the case with air brakes, however, PRR managers soon discovered the difficulties associated with translating the theoretical safety and efficiency of automatic couplers into reality. Once again, one individual—in this case, Eli Janney—has often been credited with "inventing" the automatic coupler. In reality, Janney's device was only one of hundreds of competing coupler models, most of which were incompatible. Perversely, the multiplicity of designs retarded the adoption of the automatic coupler until the railroads achieved uniformity and standardization. Like Westinghouse, Janney succeeded in large measure because he retained control over the device, while persuading railroad mechanical engineering associations to adopt his design to the exclusion of all others.

PRR officials were slow to adopt automatic couplers, in part because they lacked a close association with someone, like George Westinghouse, who could validate a specific design. In 1863, Ezra Miller, a mechanical engineer with the Chicago & North Western Railway, obtained his first patent for the platform coupler, so called because it integrated the coupler with the platform at the end of each passenger car. The system employed large levers, mounted on the end platform of each car, to disengage a hook that linked one car to another. Because passenger cars rarely strayed from their home rails, they were a natural first choice for conversion. Of greater concern to the traveling public, the Miller system greatly reduced the dangers of telescoping. The Erie began installing the Miller coupler on passenger equipment in 1866, and by 1874 some 574 railroads were using the new technology. However, the PRR was one of the last railroads in the United States to install the Miller platform coupler on its passenger equipment. That hesitancy produced unexpected benefits, however, by enabling the railroad to leapfrog to an even better design.[71]

In 1873, Janney patented the basic design of the automatic knuckle coupler, a device that remains the standard on all North American railroads today. The PRR's western subsidiaries, including the Pittsburgh, Fort Wayne & Chicago, were often the first to introduce new technologies to the PRR as a whole, and the Janney coupler was no exception. In 1874, Fort Wayne shop crews installed Janney couplers on eight passenger cars, and by 1878 its entire passenger fleet sported the new devices. On Lines East, passenger equipment still employed link-and-pin couplers, rather than the more modern Miller platform. Given the impending 1876 Centennial Exhibition in Philadelphia, PRR officials were reluctant to admit that their passengers traveled to Philadelphia on equipment that lacked a basic safety feature already in use on most other railroads across the United States. By the time that the exhibition closed, fifty-five Lines East passenger cars were equipped with Janney couplers. In 1878, the Pennsylvania Railroad adopted the Janney coupler as standard on all passenger equipment, one year after a comparable decision by Pennsylvania Company managers on Lines West. As with the Westinghouse air brake, the Pennsylvania Railroad gave its imprimatur to the Janney coupler, helping to ensure its acceptance on other carriers.[72]

Janney's coupler, however, was initially suitable only for passenger equipment. While PRR officials valued the greater safety associated with passenger train couplers, they were far more concerned with the problems that the link-and-pin coupler posed in freight service. Heavier cars and longer trains, combined with steep grades over the Alleghenies, increased the likelihood that links might snap under the strain, breaking the train apart and halting operations. As such, PRR executives demonstrated considerable interest in Janney's efforts to develop an improved freight-car coupler.

The adoption of the Janney coupler in freight service was more complicated than even the air brake. Beginning in the late 1870s, Janney oversaw the development of a freight-car version of his coupler, which he patented in 1882. Once again, he turned to PRR officials for their endorsement. John W. Cloud, the PRR's engineer of tests, evaluated the Janney freight-car coupler and gave it his approval.[73] As was the case with air brakes, however, PRR executives were initially reluctant to undertake the investment necessary to equip all of the company's freight cars with Janney couplers. Janney couplers and the older link-and-pin devices were incompatible (to reduce that difficulty, railroads often milled a slot in the knuckle of the Janney coupler, allowing them to mate with the older links). Of greater concern, the Janney design was not the only one on the market, and hundreds of others competed for supremacy. The Fort Wayne, the PRR's principal western subsidiary and an adopter of Janney passenger couplers, developed a freight-coupler design that would not mate with the Janney system. State legislatures and regulatory commissions only compounded the compatibility problem. Frustrated by the slow adoption rate, they often recommended wildly different designs and standards—Michigan alone favored seven different models.[74]

PRR managers could ensure uniformity on their own equipment, but could not control the decisions of officials on other railroads to install incompatible couplers on their freight cars, making interchange impossible and reducing, rather than increasing, the potential efficiencies associated with automatic couplers.[75] As was the case with air brakes, PRR executives tended to restrict the application of automatic couplers to special-purpose freight cars that operated in groups and were not interchanged with other railroads. In 1883, for example, the PRR applied the Janney coupler to one hundred stock cars.[76]

Several changes induced the widespread application of air brakes and automatic couplers to the PRR's freight equipment. Significantly, those changes had little to do with safety per se. As freight traffic increased late in the nineteenth century, PRR personnel endeavored to operate longer and heavier trains, on closer headways, in order to keep traffic flowing freely. The Motive Power Department provided more powerful locomotives, while shop forces at Altoona constructed heavier and more capacious freight cars. By the late 1880s, hand-operated brakes and link-and-pin couplers on PRR freight cars constituted a serious impediment to additional gains in productivity. PRR managers did not need to invent air brakes (or automatic couplers, for that matter) as a solution to that particular reverse salient—George Westinghouse and Eli Janney had done that for them. Instead, PRR executives came to appreciate that the new technologies could significantly increase productivity, while allowing them to emphasize to the public, and to regulators, that those devices would improve safety. Yet, increased productivity and enhanced safety were often at odds with one another. Air brakes and automatic couplers could have greatly increased safety on the PRR, but managers, anxious to run longer, faster, and more frequent trains, instead chose greater productivity on a railroad that was only marginally less dangerous than it had been prior to the installation of the new equipment.[77]

Trade groups such as the Master Car-Builders' Association (MCBA) enabled engineers from major railroads to jointly develop technical standards for air brakes and automatic couplers, as well as regulations governing the return of equipped cars to the railroad that owned them. The process of standardization began in 1869, when MCBA members first explored the possibility of establishing a uniform height for link-and-pin couplers. The full set of recommended practices did not emerge for another decade, and even then, the expense associated with converting cars to the new standards generally precluded their adoption. By 1879, furthermore, MCBA members, PRR officials, and their counterparts on other railroads had come to the conclusion that the link-and-pin coupler itself, and not merely its position on the car, was the most serious problem. The standards, no matter where they placed the coupler, could not protect employees from the high probability of injury or death, and of perhaps greater importance, they could not prevent increasingly heavy freight trains from breaking apart while en route, thus interfering with efficient operations.[78]

By the early 1880s, MCBA representatives were expressing concern that unless they agreed on designs for air brakes and automatic couplers, state legislatures would impose standards that railroad executives would find unacceptable. Before 1882, however, master mechanics representing smaller, financially weaker railroads had dominated the MCBA and, claiming poverty, opposed the more widespread application of safety appliances. A change in the MCBA's constitution, effective in 1882, allocated voting rights on the basis of the number of freight cars that each railroad owned. Because the PRR owned more cars than any other railroad in the nation, its managers, along with those representing other large railroads, were able to dominate discussions regarding air brake standards. In 1884, the MCBA established a testing program for automatic couplers, with the first trials scheduled for the following September. By 1885, however, the MCBA had endorsed a dozen designs—hardly a uniform standard.[79]

Edward B. Wall, superintendent of motive power for the PRR's Pan Handle subsidiary, and an MCBA member, was incensed at the organization's indecisiveness. "I think that it is almost imperative that we should adopt something, or else own up that we cannot," he insisted. Wall introduced a resolution calling on the association to approve the principle of a vertical-plane coupler: that is, one that allowed the faces of each coupler to slide up and down, as opposed to the link-and-pin, and similar designs, that principally allowed the coupler to swing only from side to side. "The great advantage of a vertical coupler," Wall noted, "is that, notwithstanding the inequalities of the track, [and] the different height of cars, you can couple with any kind of cars with a coupler that couples in a vertical plane." Significantly, Wall made no mention of crushed brakemen, mangled hands, or any of the other safety issues associated with the link-and-pin coupler. When the MCBA approved Wall's resolution, it narrowed the number of designs from twelve to nine, but that was still eight too many.[80]

The efforts of Master Car-Builders' Association personnel to endorse a single best practice in air brake design produced more rapid results and resolved the issue of automatic coupler standardization as well. In 1886, the same year that Westinghouse's original air brake patents expired, the MCBA conducted a series of air brake trials on the Chicago, Burlington & Quincy Railroad. By 1888, MCBA representatives had developed a set of recommended air brake standards, facilitating the installation of the devices on PRR freight equipment. There was just one problem, however. Because crews did not need to release hand brakes one car

at a time, freight trains could accelerate quickly, pulling out the slack between cars with astonishing rapidity. That situation reduced efficiency, however, inasmuch as couplers—both literally and figuratively the weak link in the system—shattered under the added stress and increased the incidence of train breaks. "It was never realized what an enormous evil the presence of this slack became on these long trains until these [air brake] trials were made," a frustrated MCBA official complained in 1887. "The tests, therefore, conclusively show that power train brakes cannot be successfully introduced, unless close couplings are used."[81] In 1887, despite continued foot-dragging by representatives from the smaller carriers, the members of the MCBA who represented the PRR and other larger railroads accordingly took prompt action to endorse the Janney design, which they renamed the "MCB Standard." The following year, Wall, PRR engineer of tests John Cloud, and Matthias N. Forney (a locomotive designer, a leading member of the MCBA, and the editor of the *Railroad Gazette*) persuaded Janney and his fellow investors to develop a more robust freight-car coupler based on his earlier passenger-car designs.[82]

With a standard automatic coupler profile, and with the assurance that the MCBA would pressure recalcitrant railroads to replace their link-and-pin couplers, PRR officials felt sufficiently confident to authorize the more widespread application of the Janney coupler on their freight equipment, in tandem with air brakes. By 1888, PRR executives had begun to specify air brakes on all new stock cars and boxcars used on Lines East, and in 1892 issued the same specifications for other classes of cars. Beginning in 1890, PRR shop forces installed air brakes on all of the cars that they repaired. Between January 1, 1888, and January 1, 1892, the number of air brake–equipped cars increased more than twenty-fold, from 486 to more than ten thousand. During the same period, just as PRR executives had elected to apply air brakes to most freight equipment, they also resolved to install automatic couplers, with the number of cars so equipped increasing from 436 to 12,076.[83]

In the case of air brakes and automatic couplers, effective federal safety legislation lagged behind railroad practice. In 1889, just two years after Congress created the Interstate Commerce Commission, that agency began publishing safety statistics, elevating local tragedies to a national political agenda. The Safety Appliance Act of 1893, enacted just after the PRR and other large carriers had committed to the widespread installation of safety appliances, mandated the installation of air brakes and automatic couplers on freight equipment.[84] There seemed to be ample reason for the new legislation, given that by 1893, less than 10 percent of the freight cars in service nationwide were equipped with air brakes. Railway managers were slow to comply with the law, which made safety a more important goal than operating efficiency. Executives argued, with some justification, that they needed more time to sort out issues involving the standardization of equipment and the interchange of cars, problems generally resolved through organizations such as the MCBA. The carriers requested, successfully, to delay the compliance date from 1898 to 1900. In 1903, Congress gave the ICC the authority to specify the minimum number of air brake–equipped cars in each train, but several more years would pass before air brakes and automatic couplers saw universal application.

By the beginning of the twentieth century, productivity demands ensured that the PRR, and most other large American railroads, would add air brakes and automatic couplers to substantially all of their freight cars, even in the absence of regulation. Railway officials had collectively embraced technologies that improved productivity. Engineering societies had sorted out the compatibility problems associated with equipment interchange, also largely in the absence of regulation. However, in the aftermath of the Safety Appliance Act, many ICC officials remained convinced that their quest for safety, not the railroads' demands for greater efficiency, had led to the installation of technologies that had saved countless lives. During the decades that followed, regulators attempted to extend their role as purveyors of safety, discounting claims by railway executives that expensive devices—such as automatic train stop systems—would do little to save lives.[85]

While there is ample evidence to suggest that federal safety legislation merely validated what the railroads were already doing, there were cases where the regulatory apparatus led, rather than followed. Railroaders were less willing to adopt safety appliances in

instances where they perceived no appreciable economic benefit, and where there was little need to standardize equipment across carriers. The most obvious example of that reluctance concerned safety hardware such as grabirons, ladders, and running boards. Nonstandard ladders did not affect interchangeability, but a brakeman who instinctively reached for an accustomed handhold only to grasp empty air paid the price for the lack of uniformity.

In the case of safety appliances, both Congress and the judiciary forced compliance on the railroads, to a much greater degree than had been the case with air brakes and automatic couplers. In 1908, the Supreme Court struck down the common-law concept of reasonable care, which favored the railroads, and replaced it with an assertion that the carriers had a responsibility to be proactive in their approach to safety issues.[86] In 1910, Congress further amended the Safety Appliance Act, giving the ICC the authority to specify the number and location of grabirons, ladders, and other safety appliances. Only then did the PRR and other railroads reconfigure their freight cars to make them safer, and compatible with national standards.

While the basic design of the automatic coupler changed little over the twentieth century, air brakes represented a more fluid technology, one that witnessed ongoing experimentation. Once again, Pennsylvania Railroad officials cooperated with Westinghouse and MCBA personnel in an effort to develop improved air brake designs. The impetus for innovation emerged largely from increased train lengths and weights, which overtaxed the ability of existing air brake equipment. In 1901, the PRR adopted a steel-underframe boxcar design, followed a year later by the first all-steel gondola. During the first decade of the twentieth century, the PRR built tunnels under the Hudson and East rivers as part of the New York Improvements. Company officials soon concluded that fire-prone wooden cars could not be used underground, and in 1902 they recommended the construction of a fleet of steel passenger cars. The new equipment promised greater safety and efficiency, but placed further demands on the existing air brake systems.

In 1902, PRR and Westinghouse engineers conducted tests at Absecon, New Jersey (on the Atlantic City Division of the West Jersey & Seashore Railroad, a PRR subsidiary), and the results encouraged West-inghouse personnel to design and manufacture a new, K-type air brake. The new system was soon obsolete, however, as it was difficult to maintain and could not cope with ever-longer trains. In 1909 PRR officials, along with their counterparts on other large railroads, requested that Westinghouse engineers develop a more robust air brake based on a series of trials on the Lake Shore & Michigan Southern (New York Central) at Toledo, Ohio. The resulting PC-type brake worked well for exceptionally heavy cars, but was ill suited to the majority of railroad equipment.[87]

In 1912, PRR Test Department personnel returned to Absecon for further tests. Railroad officials were anxious that air brakes could bring a steel passenger train to a rapid emergency stop, but they more prosaically wanted to ensure that routine (service) air brake applications be as efficient as possible. Using a test train composed of a K-2 Class Pacific and ten P-70 steel coaches, representatives from the Test Department and Westinghouse evaluated several combinations of brake shoes and brake rigging in 214 trial runs. Between February and May 1913, they conducted an additional 691 tests with a twelve-car train, in tandem with laboratory experiments at the American Brake Shoe & Foundry Company in Mahwah, New Jersey. Based on those tests, PRR and Westinghouse engineers developed several modifications to the braking system, the most important of which involved the use of clasp brakes, with two brake shoes on each wheel.[88]

By the early years of the twentieth century, PRR officials had largely relinquished control over the development of safety technology. The Absecon tests indicated that Westinghouse, and not the PRR, continued to take the lead in the development of air brake equipment. The Transportation Act of 1920 gave the ICC jurisdiction over safety issues and ensured that regulators would be able to dictate the design and use of air brakes. Between 1922 and 1924, ICC hearings revealed inadequacies with the K-type brake and caused some railroads, including the PRR, to supplement air brakes with brakemen, particularly on heavy trains moving down long, steep grades. Following a 1925 accident on the PRR, the ICC commissioners pressured the PRR to suspend the use of hand braking. The commissioners also requested that the American

Railway Association, the leading trade group, collaborate with Westinghouse on the development of a new air brake design. By 1925, ICC officials had become more receptive to the arguments made by railway executives that efficiency was as important a goal as safety. Yet, even with the ICC's new receptivity to efficiency considerations, the post-1920 landscape was vastly less favorable to PRR managers. They had ceded a large measure of control over the pace and direction of air brake technology to the regulatory state—a situation that would become even more apparent following the long and tortuous evolution of railway signaling systems.[89]

Controlling Trains, Controlling People: Building a Better Signal System

Like safety appliances, signaling systems promised to simultaneously improve safety and increase efficiency. Once again, however, those goals were occasionally at odds with one another. By the early 1870s, PRR executives acknowledged the threefold value of signals. First, they could make the railroad operate more efficiently, maximizing throughput by pushing as many trains as possible down a "pipeline" of fixed capacity. Second, they greatly reduced the chance of collisions, which, aside from their human toll, cost money in the form of both destroyed cargoes and equipment and delayed operations. Finally, signals offered substantial public-relations value, helping to convince nervous travelers and skeptical regulatory officials that replacing the human element with fail-safe technology could eliminate the hazards of rail travel. That was a myth; the human element would always remain, in the form of the people who installed, maintained, and operated the signals. The illusion of absolute safety persisted, however. In the 1870s, that perception provided the PRR with a powerful non-economic incentive to become an early adopter of railway signaling. Half a century later, during the 1920s, representatives of an increasingly powerful regulatory state demanded that the PRR adopt a new generation of "fail-safe" signaling systems, based largely on the desire to placate a fearful public. PRR officials did their best to avoid the new technologies, correctly asserting that their enormous expense would produce no appreciable gain in safety.

Even when they enjoyed the benefit of multiple tracks (which permitted unidirectional travel and virtually eliminated the possibility of head-on collisions) railroads depended heavily on signaling systems for the safe and efficient operation of trains. Then, as now, all signaling systems operated under some combination of the measurement of time or distance, based on the maxim that two objects cannot occupy the same space at the same time. Timetables, while not a signaling system per se, nonetheless constituted one of the earliest mechanisms for regulating train movement. If rigidly adhered to, timetables theoretically eliminated all possibility of collision by ensuring that a safe time interval separated one train from another. Timetables alone were not sufficient, however, because they could not accommodate unscheduled extra runs and delayed or disabled trains. In such instances, crewmen relied on written train orders that clearly specified when and where the train was to meet or overtake other traffic. Safe operation also depended on the localized, ad hoc signaling efforts of train crews (who employed flags or lanterns to warn approaching trains of an impending collision) and station agents (who used the telegraph to exchange information on the location of trains).

Following the Civil War, officials on heavily trafficked railroads began to regulate train movement by distance, rather than time. Block signaling systems divided a railroad into multiple sections, or blocks, with rules stipulating that no more than one train could occupy a single block at any given time. Observers, in the form of station agents or block tower operators, monitored the passage of trains in and out of each block and, using the telegraph, informed other block operators that a train from one block might be allowed to pass safely into another.

The advent of block signaling in the United States occurred in the aftermath of a March 7, 1865, rear-end collision on the Camden & Amboy Rail Road. Following the accident, which killed five Union soldiers and a train crewman, vice president Ashbel Welch worked with superintendent of telegraphs Robert Stewart to devise a safer operating system. Welch had visited Britain on several occasions, and had gained considerable experience with block signaling systems, which were a virtual necessity on heavily traveled lines. He established six blocks, averaging five miles in length, over the thirty miles that separated Kensington, Pennsylvania, and Trenton, New Jersey, followed soon thereafter by a twenty-six-mile expansion north to New Brunswick. In 1867, the newly created United Canal & Railroad Companies of New Jersey extended the block system to Jersey City.[90]

In 1871, the PRR leased the United Companies, and thereby acquired access to the pioneering block signaling system, which at that time protected some ninety route miles. Two years later, PRR officials copied the system for use on the Pittsburgh Division but sacrificed a measure of safety in the interest of increased capacity. They retained the existing use of a red signal for "stop" and a white signal for "clear," but added a green indication to signify "proceed with caution," thus allowing one train to enter a block before the preceding train had exited the other end.

While PRR officials clearly intended that the manual block signaling system increase operating efficiency, they were equally concerned about its public-relations value. The catalyst was the forthcoming 1876 Centennial Exhibition in Philadelphia, which created unprecedented traffic levels throughout the system, but nowhere more so than on the main line between Pittsburgh and Philadelphia. The PRR's preparations began in the autumn of 1874, when the company adopted a system-wide standard rulebook, replacing all of the diverse procedures in use on the various subsidiary companies. The standard rules in turn facilitated the implementation of the block system between Philadelphia and Pittsburgh. In 1874 the PRR converted the Philadelphia Division to block operation, followed in the summer of 1875 by both the Pittsburgh and the Middle Divisions. The board of directors authorized the construction of octagonal signal towers every six to ten miles to regulate the traffic flowing in and out of each block. Each tower was equipped with oil lights, with red, green, and white shutters, giving either a "stop," "proceed with caution," or a "proceed clear" indication. In later years, semaphores replaced the lanterns. The PRR's system was the most sophisticated in the United States, and it was more than a decade in advance of similar developments on other railroads. The widespread application of the block system improved the flow of Exhibition traffic along the main line, doing much to create the popular image of the PRR as a modern and progressive railroad. PRR officials prepared a travel guide, available to travelers heading by train to Philadelphia, that emphasized the safety associated with the block system. In assessing the degree to which the railroad had coped with Centennial traffic, however, PRR officials later concluded that the primary benefit of signals lay in added traffic capacity rather than enhanced safety.[91]

The block system could not prevent the possibility of collision, because it depended on the ability of tower operators to accurately collect and transmit information regarding the status of trains entering or leaving each block. Interlocking signals offered the first possibility to reduce, perhaps even eliminate, that human error. As their name suggested, mechanical interlocking devices allowed tower operators to throw levers that would set a train's route through a series of switches and signals, while automatically locking out conflicting routes. In 1856, John Saxby, a foreman on the London, Brighton & South Coast Railway, developed the technology to avoid a repeat of a serious accident that had resulted from a misrouted train. In 1863 he joined forces with John Farmer, and the two men made progressive improvements in the design and operation of their interlocking device. In October 1870, the United Companies again hosted the first application of a new signaling system in the United States. Ashbel Welsh, who was at that time president of the United Companies, ordered the installation of a Saxby & Farmer system near Trenton, New Jersey.[92] In 1875, G. O. Howell, the principal assistant signal engineer of the New Jersey Division of the PRR, which was by now controlling the United Companies, recommended the installation of a second Saxby & Farmer system at Newark Junction in order to accommodate Exhibition traffic. Ever sensitive to its public image, the PRR later donated that equipment to the Franklin Institute in Philadelphia, where visitors could marvel at the latest in American safety and efficiency.[93]

The Centennial Exhibition brought the PRR into partnership with George Westinghouse, enabling him to assert control over key aspects of signaling and train-control equipment. Mantua Junction, later known as "Zoo Tower" based on its proximity to the Philadelphia Zoological Gardens, controlled traffic from both the north and the west into Philadelphia. In preparation for the Centennial, PRR officials had hoped to install a Saxby & Farmer apparatus at that key location, but too few of the devices were available. The railroad's officials had to settle for an inferior product of Prall & Burr, which relied on a hydraulic system to actuate track switches, making it the first American-built interlocking system employed in railroad service. The Prall & Burr system worked well enough to attract the attention of George Westinghouse. Westinghouse had already succeeded admirably in marketing his air brake to the railroads, thanks to his control over patents and his unwillingness to license his technology to others, and he was determined to follow the same principles with signaling. Westinghouse replaced the Prall & Burr hydraulic actuation with a pneumatic (compressed air) system. While that change marked an undoubted improvement, Westinghouse experienced his greatest success only when he combined pneumatic interlocking equipment with two other innovations: the semaphore and automatic block signaling. By 1877 the PRR had become one of the first carriers in the United States to incorporate three-position lower-quadrant semaphores into its signaling system. The semaphore arm, when connected by rodding to an interlocking tower, afforded a clear visual indication of the occupancy status of the next block, and often the one beyond that, as well.[94]

The installation of the main-line signaling system produced corresponding alterations to the PRR's organizational structure. In 1879 officials established a Signal Department for Lines East, initially under the control of the Motive Power Department at Altoona. As soon as H. F. Cox took charge of the new Signal Department, he traveled to Europe to observe the latest in signaling equipment and methods. Semaphores had been in use in Britain since the 1840s, with some early applications in the United States as well. By delaying the adoption of semaphores for several decades (until traffic densities began to match those in Britain), the PRR benefited from one significant alteration in semaphore design. On the earliest semaphores, equipment failure might cause the semaphore arm to drop from the horizontal "stop" setting into a lowered

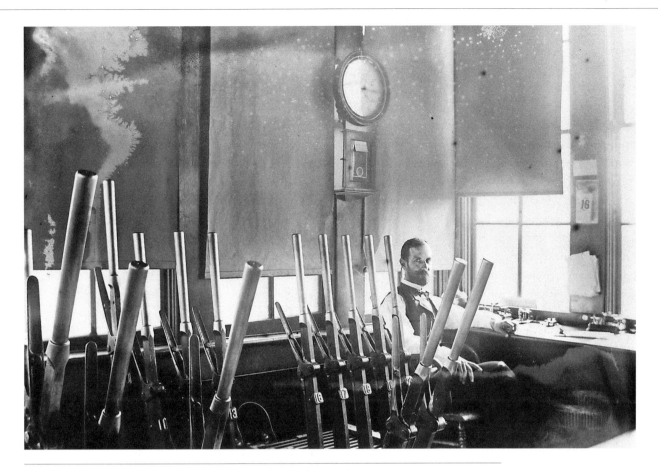

Figure 58. A PRR operator sits in the tower at Conestoga, Pennsylvania, circa 1905. The rods in the foreground composed a portion of an interlocking system that controlled both switches and signals. Once he had selected the route for each train, the tower operator threw the appropriate levers, eliminating any possibility that two trains could occupy the same track simultaneously. With their knowledge of signaling, telegraphy, and the rules governing train movements, tower operators could exert substantial control over the workplace. On repeated occasions, they walked off the job, particularly when they believed that PRR officials were prepared to adopt new technologies—such as the telephone or automatic block signals—that might challenge their livelihoods.

Pennsylvania Historical and Museum Commission, Railroad Museum of Pennsylvania.

"proceed" position. Later versions provided a more reliable alternative, using the upright vertical position for "proceed," while the default horizontal position indicated "stop."[95]

Even with the use of semaphores and interlocking devices, manual signaling systems were hardly failsafe. They still depended on the vigilance and training of tower operators, individuals who were often also responsible for receiving and transmitting telegraph messages and handling train orders. Most tower operators simply waited long enough for a train to clear a block, even if they had not received telegraphic confirmation to that effect from operators farther down the line, and then allowed a following train to proceed. The block system, moreover, did not readily accommodate traffic that moved at different speeds, one reason why the PRR's four-track main line included a "fast" and "slow" track for each direction of travel. Because the number of available blocks limited the line's carrying capacity, PRR signal engineers could increase that capacity simply by shortening blocks and moving towers closer together. That stratagem increased the likelihood of collisions, however, and required more towers and tower operators, thus increasing capital and labor costs. Tower operators also exhibited a sense of autonomy similar to that of train crews, inasmuch as they worked in locations far removed from managerial supervision, and could just as readily cripple operations through the simple expedient of walking off of the job.

Automatic block signals, which relied on track circuits, offered a potentially safer alternative to manual signaling. In an automatic system, signal engineers divided each line into a series of electrically isolated blocks. When a train ran over the gap separating two blocks, it would cause a momentary electrical short, rendering a positive indication that the train had left one block and entered another. William Robinson, a schoolteacher who had later invested in the oilfields of northwestern Pennsylvania, developed an electrically actuated automatic crossing gate, which debuted at the American Institute Fair in New York in 1870. He began adapting the device in order to make it compatible with block signaling, using the wheels of a train to complete the circuit. However, he soon realized that such a system was likely to create a great many false clear indications—a certain recipe for disaster. By 1872, he had perfected the closed track circuit, in which the wheels created a short circuit that indicated that the block was occupied and set the signals to "stop." The new system ensured that signaling errors would be false positives—irksome to operating personnel, perhaps, but far less dangerous than the alternative. He patented the system on August 20, 1872, and soon established the Union Electric Signal Company. Robinson demonstrated his automatic signal system at an exhibition in Erie, Pennsylvania. William A. Baldwin, the general superintendent of the Philadelphia & Erie, observed Robinson's invention, and encouraged its application along that PRR subsidiary. Alexander J. Cassatt, Frank Thomson, Robert Pitcairn, and other senior PRR executives traveled to Erie to see the automatic block signal system in operation. Convinced of its effectiveness, they soon ordered its use on the PRR main line.[96]

By the early 1880s, all of the elements of automatic signaling had coalesced on the Pennsylvania Railroad. After observing the Prall & Burr hydraulic interlock-ing system at the Centennial Exhibition, George Westinghouse had begun manufacturing an improved version. He soon recognized that the automatic signals offered a natural complement to interlocking technology, and he sought out Robinson's patents. By 1881, after purchasing a majority interest in the Robinson's Union Electric Signal Company, Westinghouse reorganized the firm as the Union Switch & Signal Company. He had purchased the most important patents relating to interlocking equipment, particularly those held by Saxby & Farmer, and established a factory at Swissvale, on the outskirts of Pittsburgh and adjacent to the PRR main line. In addition to supplying the Union Switch & Signal plant, the PRR served as a test bed for the company's new machinery, and the railroad's signal personnel worked closely with their counterparts at the firm.[97]

The construction of Philadelphia's Broad Street Station, in 1881, led to the installation of a large Union Switch & Signal interlocking plant, although without the use of track circuits. Numerous derailments resulted, and George D. Fowle, a PRR draftsman and signal expert, spent two weeks ensconced in the station's signal tower, grabbing whatever sleep he could on a cot set up next to the interlocking apparatus. Fowle was an amateur gymnast, and needed to be, as he frantically pulled lever after lever, to ensure that all of the routes into the station lined up correctly.[98] Cox and Fowle eventually resolved the difficulties, developing an interlocking apparatus that accommodated more than 260 trains a day—with arrivals and departures averaging one every two minutes during peak periods. In addition to the tower at Broad Street Station, towers located at Seventeenth Street, Twentieth Street, Thirtieth Street, and Thirty-Second Street regulated the flow of traffic in and out of the terminal. Another tower at Overbrook, four miles west of Broad Street Station, enabled passenger trains to move to the two outermost tracks, with the two center tracks reserved for freight trains. There was considerable redundancy in the system, as each tower covered overlapping stretches of line. A writer for *Railway World* noted approvingly that the interlocking apparatus "furnishes guarantees of safety approaching more nearly to perfection than could possibly be obtained by any other known arrangement." Moreover, and in yet another acknowledgment of the economic advantages of safety technology, the author observed that the new system "wholly dispenses with the numerous switchmen who would have been required, under old systems, to have conducted the complicated train movements." As an added bonus for PRR managers, the interlocking apparatus promised to simplify the assignment of blame for employee misconduct. "Any failure of a locomotive engineer to observe a danger signal quickly inflicts upon him the penalty of an exposure of his recklessness which does not involve danger to life or destruction of property, as his error can quickly be remedied, but not before the wrong-doing has been detected." As a result, "locomotive engineers [became] as careful to avoid disregard of a danger signal as a child whose fingers have been burned is to avoid fire." That analogy suggested that PRR enginemen were careless—or callous—enough to routinely misread signal indications, absent a definitive indication of their ineptitude. In later years, PRR studies indicated that train crews rarely made such mistakes, but managerial attitudes in the 1880s reflected an underlying premise that human error was the cause of most accidents, and that fallible people should be replaced with infallible technology.[99]

In 1882, contemporaneous with the installation of the interlocking system at Broad Street Station, Cox made another tour of Europe, to study signaling practices there, and the PRR shortly thereafter appointed him as the company's engineer of signals. Sometime during 1882, Signal Department engineers installed the first electrically operated pneumatic semaphores in the United States, replacing the mélange of colored balls and cubes that had been used prior to that time. In June 1883, the PRR reorganized the Signal Department independently of the Motive Power Department, with Cox now reporting to the chief engineer. Three years later, the PRR established a similar Signal Department on Lines West.[100]

In 1884 Union Switch & Signal and PRR engineers combined the three constituent elements of a modern, integrated automatic-signaling system: the interlocking apparatus, semaphores, and track circuits. Along a two-and-a-half-mile stretch of four-track main line separating East Liberty and Wilkinsburg, Pennsylvania (conveniently close to the US&S factory), signal

engineers installed track-detection circuits, semaphores, and two hydro-pneumatic interlocking plants, with fluid replacing the air used in earlier electro-pneumatic systems. By the end of the year, the PRR had sixty-five of the older electro-pneumatic semaphores in service as part of its automatic block system. The PRR at that time also employed 660 Saxby & Farmer–design interlocking mechanisms, most of them manufactured at Union Switch & Signal's Swissvale facility and representing nearly a third of that company's total output.[101]

With the new equipment, PRR officials were able to subdivide that short stretch of railroad into twenty blocks (five per main line track), equivalent to an average block length of just half a mile. In comparison to the six- to ten-mile-long blocks used in the 1870s, the US&S automatic block signaling system, at least theoretically and under ideal conditions, would permit the PRR to increase the number of trains over a given stretch of track between twelve and twenty times.[102]

Such impressive gains in productivity were largely illusory, however, and could rarely be achieved in actual practice. Any effort to keep traffic flowing smoothly through half-mile-long blocks required that all trains travel at precisely the same rate of speed. Should there be any deviation from that standard, the automatic signals would prevent accidents, but would do little to avoid congestion. Furthermore, with advanced signaling systems costing as much as $3,000 per mile to install, PRR officials could justify the expense only in areas of exceedingly high traffic density.

Faced with the high cost of automatic signaling systems, PRR managers used every conceivable stratagem to avoid their installation. By the early 1890s, Signal Department technicians were installing additional semaphore blades to the existing manual block system, giving enginemen a positive indication of the occupancy status of both the block that they were about to enter and the one lying beyond. In the event that the more distant signal indicated a clear block, enginemen would have no need to slacken speed and could keep trains moving with greater efficiency. PRR officials also authorized new operating practices that reduced many of the safety benefits associated with the PRR's 1870s-vintage manual block signaling. Under the permissive block system, tower operators waited a certain number of minutes after a train had passed them, and then permitted the following train to proceed without an absolute indication that the block was clear.[103]

Despite the additional semaphore blades and the adoption of permissive signaling, rising traffic levels overwhelmed the manual block system and at some key locations required the installation of expensive automatic block signaling. Although the automatic system permitted the PRR to eliminate many tower operators, the savings in labor costs was minimal in comparison with the expense of the new automatic equipment. It was not initially clear, furthermore, whether automatic signals increased safety to any appreciable degree. Under the manual block system, towermen could and did make mistakes, but automatic equipment could malfunction as well. PRR signal engineers lacked sufficient data to establish the likelihood of human error, but they concluded that the chance of a false clear indication under automatic signaling was no more than one in 635,151. Still, safety alone did not determine whether the PRR replaced manual blocks with a more expensive automatic signaling system. Instead, automatic block systems were installed only at critical locations, where it was imperative to keep trains moving, and where the cost of adding more tracks was prohibitive.[104]

Signal Department personnel initially employed automatic signals in congested yards and terminals, particularly in Philadelphia. More widespread applications followed, as the entire system experienced increasing traffic densities. Beginning in 1891, the Signal Department began installing automatic block signals from Jersey City south to Philadelphia and Wilmington, Delaware; from Philadelphia west to Paoli; and on the Pittsburgh Division. The depression that began in 1893 cut traffic levels and temporarily alleviated congestion, delaying more widespread use of automatic block signals. As the United States entered one on the worst economic crises in its history, the members of the ATO Committee on Interlocking and Block Signals recommended the curtailment of the new technology, lamenting that "the question of expense now makes it practically impossible of adoption."[105]

The economic recovery, late in the decade, caused a surge in traffic levels and congestion, leading to the rapid adoption of automatic block signals. By 1900, as *Railroad Gazette* editor Braman B. Adams observed, they were installed on "about 500 miles of track on lines which formerly were signaled by men; so there can be no question that, as far as safety goes, automatic signals are deemed fully as satisfactory as the manual system."[106] Thus, even at the dawn of the twentieth century, there was no clear consensus that automatic signals were any safer, or less prone to error, than their manual counterparts.

Speed and Signals

During the early twentieth century, an increase in the volume of traffic and the growing operation of preference freight trains encouraged PRR officials to place renewed emphasis on the development of more elaborate signaling systems. Preference freights accommodated time-sensitive, high-value commodities, and moved at speeds of twenty-five or even thirty miles per hour, at least double the rate at which bulk cargoes traveled. Even with a four-track main line, with fast and slow tracks in each direction, PRR dispatchers were struggling to accommodate a mix of low-grade freight, preference freight, express passenger trains, and locals, all of which moved at significantly different speeds. The problem was less severe on Lines West, as lighter traffic densities increased the likelihood that automatic block signaling would be used, albeit infrequently, to improve safety rather than increase efficiency. East of Pittsburgh, however, the PRR directors were forced to authorize the widespread application of automatic signaling in order to keep the traffic moving. By 1901, Signal Department personnel had installed automatic block signals along more than five hundred route miles, and many additional stretches of track received signals over the following decade.[107]

Signal development on both Lines East and Lines West tended to be slow, cautious, and conservative— hardly surprising, in that any mistakes carried with them a high probability of disaster. Signal Department personnel took considerable pride in the extensive experience and long tenure of their employees— only three men held the post of signal engineer between 1879 and 1937. The third and perhaps most important signal engineer was Alexander Holley Rudd, whose career coincided with the widespread application of the automatic block and related signaling systems.[108] Rudd joined the Pennsylvania Railroad in 1886, after graduating from Yale University at the age of nineteen. Unlike most other PRR personnel, whose intense culture of loyalty to the company rendered service on another railroad anathema, Rudd worked for the New York Central (1892–94), the New Haven (1894–1900), and the Delaware, Lackawanna & Western (1900–1902) before returning to the PRR in 1902. If Rudd had risen through one of the more traditional transportation functions, his absence from the PRR might well have crippled his career. Because his chances for promotion depended as much on his mastery of new and unfamiliar technologies as it did on adherence to PRR traditions, the breadth of his experience served him well.

In 1903, Rudd became assistant signal engineer, and the next year, in tandem with Pan Handle Pittsburgh Division superintendent Robert E. McCarty, embarked on a trip to Britain, to study signaling systems. After his return to the United States, Rudd and his Lines West counterpart, Frank Rhea, catalogued signaling equipment and operating methods across the entire system in preparation for the development of uniform standards. Rudd earned a promotion to signal engineer in 1907, at about the same time that PRR officials began conducting surprise checks to determine whether enginemen were responding quickly and reliably to signal indications. In 1920, following the consolidation of Lines East and Lines West into a single corporate structure, Rudd became the PRR's chief signal engineer. Rudd was innately conservative, reflective not only of his PRR experience but also of his understandable concern that new devices to control speeding trains might do more harm than good. In 1935, two years before his retirement, Rudd justified the "gradual and perhaps slow development and improvement" of signaling, emphasizing, "Our predecessors not only taught us what to do but, perhaps more important, what not to do, and why."[109]

On the eve of World War I, Rudd oversaw an expansion of the automatic block system, designed to cope with increasing congestion in the Philadelphia area. In 1913, the growth of suburban traffic from Broad Street Station west to Paoli induced PRR officials to electrify that section of track, a decision that marked the beginning of the end for semaphore signals. The towers that supported the overhead wires (more properly referred to as catenary) blocked the engineman's line of sight, obscuring the semaphore blades. The catenary also required large and bulky anchor bridges every three thousand to four thousand feet, further obstructing views. Yet, that problem created its own solution, as the anchor bridges were located at intervals that essentially matched the length of a block. It would be a simple matter, therefore, to install signals atop the anchor bridges and catenary towers in clear view of engine crews. In some cases the PRR employed traditional semaphores, but Signal Department personnel were already well aware that that technology was outdated. Semaphore arms had always been prone to freezing during winter storms, and their location atop the exposed catenary towers only exacerbated the problem.

Colored-light signals, originally developed by electric streetcar and interurban lines, offered a possible remedy for the defects associated with semaphores. Some systems employed colored lenses in front of multiple incandescent lamps, similar to a modern traffic light, while others used a single lamp set behind a rotating disk with lenses of different colors. The earliest systems employed ordinary incandescent bulbs, which had an effective range of no more than a hundred feet. By the early twentieth century, stronger bulbs and improved lenses had increased the range to more than two thousand feet, making such systems practicable for mainline railroad use.

The PRR's signal engineers initially displayed little interest in color-light signals because they concluded that, under certain atmospheric conditions—fog being the worst—train crews could not adequately differentiate between signal colors. Despite ongoing efforts to provide vision tests for PRR enginemen, some were color blind and unable to correctly read signal indications. In 1914, however, Dr. William Churchill of the Corning Glass Company, who had been working on signal systems for western railroads, offered Rudd another possibility. Position-light signals employed extremely bright bulbs and small, wide-angle lenses to project white light over very long distances. As their name suggested, it was the arrangement

Figure 59. By March 1938, when this photograph was taken, the PRR had applied position-light signals along much of its main line, such as here at Linden, New Jersey, with six tracks one of the busiest locations anywhere on the system. When workers electrified the tracks between New York and Washington, they typically incorporated both the catenary and the high-voltage carrier lines into the structure of the signal bridge.

Pennsylvania Historical and Museum Commission, Railroad Museum of Pennsylvania.

of the lights, not their color, that mattered. Just as the PRR had relied on the outside technical expertise of William Robinson and, later, Union Switch & Signal, Rudd now worked with Corning to perfect a special housing for the five-watt bulbs, as well as an egg-shaped lens that would maximize their brightness. Rudd astutely designed the signal heads in such a manner than a burned-out bulb would not prevent an engineman from reading the correct signal aspect.

By the summer of 1914, Rudd and his colleagues had concluded that position-light signals were clearly superior to color-light systems, despite their higher initial cost. In 1915 Signal Department personnel made the first test installations along a fifteen-mile stretch of

the Main Line between Overbrook and Paoli. In addition to the large signals mounted atop the catenary towers, workers also installed smaller "dwarf" signals, set close to the ground, to regulate low-speed switching movements.[110] Union Switch & Signal supplied the hardware, while PRR Signal Department employees performed the actual installation. Officials surveyed enginemen on the Philadelphia Division, and found that the vast majority—235 out of 254—favored position-light signals over semaphores. To the consternation of PRR executives, however, the automatic position-light signals did not eliminate the possibility of human error. Lights bright enough to be visible in the daytime tended to blur together at night, or in the fog, forcing tower operators to telephone one another to determine, on an entirely ad hoc basis, whether they should reduce the signal voltage.[111]

Outside of electrified territory, moreover, position-light signals required the installation of wires to supply electric current, retarding their adoption. The growth of the commercial electric grid, combined with improvements in batteries, gradually solved that problem, although more remote areas, such as the Horseshoe Curve area, retained semaphores and did not receive position-light signals until the 1940s. By the end of World War II, however, position-light signals protected 97 percent of the PRR's main and secondary lines.[112]

"A Change Came over the Spirit of Its Dreams": Public Policy and the Automatic Train Stop

While position-light signals offered an improvement over semaphores, they did not guarantee safety, particularly if rain, snow, or fog interfered with visibility. At worst, a missed signal could cause a serious accident. More commonly, however, it impeded the railroad's operations, as the rulebook required engine crews who could not clearly distinguish signals to treat them as an absolute stop indication. Far more frightening was the possibility that an engineman might be asleep, drunk, or incapacitated and thus unable to stop the train. Such dereliction of duty was comparatively uncommon, particularly on a railroad like the PRR, where engine crews were well trained and subjected to a high level of testing and discipline. Nevertheless, the horror of the rogue engineman captured the attention of the public and therefore attracted the scrutiny of politicians and regulators. Interstate Commerce Commission officials were especially determined to eliminate any possibility that human error might render a signaling system unsafe.

Railroad officials adhered to a different goal. In their pursuit of economic incentives, they were anxious to make changes in their signaling systems only in the interests of greater efficiency. Beginning in the 1890s, when members of the ATO had deplored the high cost of automatic block signaling, PRR executives had accurately, if pessimistically, concluded that advanced signaling systems were viable only in areas that experi-

enced considerable traffic congestion. PRR officials admitted that absolute safety was a laudable theoretical goal, but asserted correctly that it could never be achieved in actual practice. Safety, they discovered, depended as much on the control of policies, procedures, and human behavior as on "fail-safe" technology. New forms of training and organization promised to do far more than equipment to facilitate train operations and reduce—but never completely eliminate—the likelihood of catastrophe.

By the 1920s, the safety procedures advocated by PRR executives clashed with public opinion and regulatory activism, ensuring that regulatory policy took precedence over the efficient allocation of corporate resources. Safety-minded reformers and regulators saw no reason why the railroads should not develop devices that would eliminate human frailties and thus all possibility of human error. That the railroads would privately bear the expense associated with providing the public good of increased safety seemed irrelevant. Railroad executives had heard that message before—during the 1880s and 1890s, with air brakes and automatic couplers, for example—but that was an era of weak regulation, and a time when rising traffic levels provided an economic incentive for the adoption of technologies that incidentally increased safety. By the 1920s, however, the federal regulatory apparatus was far more powerful, with ICC commissioners able to dictate technological choices to the railroads. At the same time, increased highway competition siphoned away revenues, while precluding the increase in traffic that might otherwise have conditioned the adoption of a new generation of signaling systems.

It was in that context that the engineers in the PRR Signal Department assisted in the development of the automatic train stop. When added to automatic block-signaling systems, ATS offered additional protection, as it would bring the train to a halt whenever an engineman failed to respond to a signal indication. As early as 1880, engineers in the Motive Power Department (which at that time still oversaw signaling functions) experimented with the new devices. Mechanical engineer Axel Vogt and assistant engineer of motive power Joseph Wood attached a glass tube to the top of a locomotive cab and connected it to the air brake system. If an engineman passed a semaphore set to the "stop" position, a lever attached to the signal would break the glass tube, triggering the air brakes and halting the train. Unfortunately, the tube broke too readily during routine operations, stopping the train unnecessarily, and in 1883 PRR personnel discontinued their experiments.[113]

By the early twentieth century, with the spread of automatic block signaling, PRR signal engineers began to look again at the possibilities of ATS. Because ATS could not replace either fixed signals or train orders, Signal Department personnel instead developed the system for use in a few high-priority areas, where no price was too high to prevent an accident. The ultimate nightmare was the chance of a collision in one of the tunnels under the Hudson or East rivers. PRR engineers borrowed ATS designs that had been developed for subway and rapid-transit systems. In 1910, they installed mechanical trip stops, a more sophisticated version of the glass-tube device that Vogt and Wood had developed three decades earlier. Whenever a signal was set to "stop," a small lever mounted near the outside edge of the rail would swing into an upright position. If the engineman failed to obey the signal, his locomotive would pass over the upraised device, which would trigger a brake valve mounted on the truck. The equipment employed in the tunnels was doubly expensive—for it required the installation of both ATS *and* fixed signals—but it made the possibility of disaster exceedingly remote. The success of the tunnel installation persuaded PRR officials to reexamine the possibility that ATS might be used as a substitute for, rather than an addition to, fixed signals. Between 1912 and 1915, Signal Department engineers tested a variety of ATS devices, none of which performed adequately.[114]

While PRR executives emphasized that economic and technical constraints precluded the use of ATS as an economically viable substitute for fixed signals or train orders, public opinion and public policy framed the issue in terms of safety alone. Between 1896 and 1907, the passenger fatality rate increased by 50 percent, from sixteen to twenty-four deaths per billion miles traveled. Congress responded with a slew of legislative initiatives. In 1901, the Accident Report Act gave the ICC the authority to collect and disseminate accident data. The same year, signal expert Braman

Adams published *The Block System*, in which he used the existing PRR techniques as an exemplar for the rest of the railroad industry and hinted at the prospect of error-free rail travel. ICC officials soon joined the chorus, and the agency's 1903, 1904, and 1905 *Reports* stressed the importance of automatic block signaling and ATS, suggesting that Congress confer authority on the commissioners to mandate their installation. President Theodore Roosevelt said much the same thing in his 1904 and 1905 messages to Congress. In 1906, Congress authorized the ICC to investigate block signals and ATS systems. The ICC's Block Signal and Train Control Board, established in 1907, began a lengthy investigation, one that was hampered by the limited application of both automatic block signaling and ATS in actual practice. In 1907 Congress also passed the Hours of Service Act, designed in part to increase safety by limiting the number of hours that train crews, telegraphers, and dispatchers could work. Beginning in 1908, federal law made it far easier for employees and their families to prove that the railroads were at fault for accidents that resulted in injury, disability, or death. Two years later, an amended Accident Report Act required the railroads to report deaths and injuries, not merely the number of collisions and derailments.[115]

Such safety legislation had the perverse effect of making many railroads less safe. The federal mandate for reduced work hours, with no loss of pay, increased labor costs for telegraphers and tower operators, individuals who were critical to the success of the block system. Some railroads, such as the Illinois Central, reverted to the older and more dangerous system of train orders. Traffic density on the PRR generally precluded that possibility, at least during daylight hours. Nighttime was a different matter, however, and PRR officials closed many train order offices at night rather than bear the additional expense of staffing them around the clock.[116]

The terms of the Hours of Service Act may have been partly to blame for a spate of highly publicized accidents often caused by a failure to observe signals or by obstructions on the tracks. On August 13, 1911, near Fort Wayne, Indiana, four people died when the eastbound *Pennsylvania Special*, traveling too fast, derailed on a section of temporarily relocated track and crashed into a freight locomotive. Two years later, a PRR engineman paid with his life when he ignored a signal and rear-ended a passenger train that had stopped at the Tyrone, Pennsylvania, depot, injuring 150 passengers and tossing the Railway Post Office car into the station. In 1917, at Mount Union, Pennsylvania, a PRR freight slammed into the end of a stalled passenger train; twenty passengers died when the force of the collision telescoped one passenger car into another.[117]

Surely, the public believed, technology could halt the carnage caused by circumstance and human carelessness. Over the years, a steady stream of letters from frightened travelers, angry citizens, and crackpot inventors trickled into the PRR's Philadelphia offices, to be routed to the harried engineers of the Signal Department. The PRR received more than 1,500 suggestions from safety-conscious individuals, often with dollar signs in their eyes. One inventor, a circuit-riding preacher from Tennessee, offered a device that would spray oil on the rails whenever a train passed a stop signal, thus bringing it to a halt—unless, as Signal Engineer Rudd responded, the train happened to be going downhill. Another inventor acknowledged that his proposed solution was hardly fail-safe, but excused himself by noting that "God Almighty did not make this world 100 per cent perfect," either.[118]

Rudd and his PRR colleagues were less concerned about the comments coming from the general public than they were about those emanating from the Interstate Commerce Commission. ICC officials noted that many of the tragedies had occurred because train crews had failed to observe signals or train orders. They suggested that automatic train stop could have prevented the accidents, assuming that the railroads installed the equipment in tandem with, rather than in lieu of, automatic block signals—just like the PRR's small but expensive application under the Hudson and East rivers. Over the next five years the ICC's Block Signal and Train Control Board issued a series of reports, principally authored by Braman Adams and Charles C. Anthony, in 1907 the PRR's supervisor of signals at Altoona, and soon afterward the assistant signal engineer. Even though the reports refrained from recommending specific devices, they were favorable to the automatic block system, the most wide-

spread system in the United States at that time. By the time of the final report, in June 1912, the members of the PRR board of directors had also recommended the use of automatic-stop equipment in order to provide a further margin of safety.[119]

Railroad executives were generally opposed to the ICC's recommendations, but the response of PRR officials was different from most. Many managers, particularly those who represented carriers with low traffic densities, saw little need for either automatic block signaling or ATS. The PRR, with its high traffic densities, particularly on Lines East, was well suited for automatic block signaling, and by 1912 Signal Department personnel had already installed the necessary equipment on the railroad's principal routes. Anthony's role on the Block Signal and Train Control Board also suggested that any ICC recommendations would be consistent with established PRR practices. While PRR officials were willing to accept most of the ICC's recommendations, they nonetheless objected to two issues.

First, PRR personnel saw no need to install ATS—an expensive system that would do little to increase operating efficiency—merely to prevent the occasional stunning display of incompetence on the part of train crews. PRR officials conducted "surprise tests" of train crews to judge their reaction to signal indications. Enginemen and firemen objected vigorously to the surreptitious observation of their behavior, forcing the officials to adopt the more conciliatory terminology of "efficiency tests." Regardless of the nomenclature, executives boasted that by 1908, enginemen correctly read lineside signals 99.25 percent of the time. Even though the results indicated that an error had occurred in more than twenty of the 3,255 tests—a figure that might have led to a considerable number of accidents—PRR officials insisted that the excellent results proved that fail-safe ATS systems were unnecessary.[120]

Second, railroaders vigorously opposed the ICC's efforts to dictate safety and operating procedures to the carriers. For example, the federal Boiler Inspection Act of 1911, which gave the ICC the authority to assess the construction and maintenance standards of steam locomotives, seemed to many executives to constitute a particularly intrusive action by the regulatory state. Such intense governmental oversight, PRR officials feared, might well extend to every aspect of the railroad's activities. In a worst-case scenario, ICC officials—who understood few of the intricacies associated with the PRR's operations—might mandate the installation of ATS or some other expensive device that would do little or nothing to increase efficiency.[121]

To counter any possibility that the commissioners might seek to expand their authority, PRR officials took an increased interest in internal accident-awareness programs. By the spring of 1909, the supervisors of signals on almost every PRR division on Lines East (but not on Lines West, where the apprentice system still predominated) had established signaling training programs, with curricula that vastly exceeded in length and comprehensiveness the instruction received by employees on most other railroads. Beginning in the autumn of 1910, PRR managers established safety committees in the larger shop facilities, and the campaign to put employees in a "safety trend of mind" soon spread throughout the system. In 1911, PRR officials adopted the "Safety First" campaign that had been developed on the Chicago & North Western Railway the previous year. According to the PRR's publicity, the new methods reduced injuries and accidents by nearly two-thirds during 1911 alone. While train operations constituted only a small portion of the overall campaign, the railroad's message was clear—the ICC's efforts to prescribe specific types of safety equipment were unnecessary.[122]

PRR executives were nonetheless receptive to arguments that ATS and other types of safety equipment might improve operating efficiency. ATS offered the possibility of eliminating the fixed signals associated with the automatic block system, which were costly to install and maintain. As an ATO report noted, "It was the desire of our Executives to eliminate fixed signals, and it was the wish of our Operating Officers to eliminate train orders" on lines that were not yet equipped with signals. ATO officials admitted that their assumption that trains could be operated only with expensive signals or inefficient and potentially dangerous train orders might have represented a false dichotomy, "in view of our preconceived idea that the issue of train orders could only be eliminated by operating trains by the indications of fixed signals." An automatic-stop system could obviate train orders, without the capital

costs associated with signals, simply by halting trains whenever an engineman left a block without authorization. Even more enticing, the elimination of both fixed signals and train orders removed the human element from train operations, creating the ultimate in fail-safe technology.[123]

The potential of ATS remained largely unrealized, however. While the evidence is unclear, there seem to have been three problems associated with the early application of ATS as a mechanism to eliminate both signals and train orders. First, the ATS system proved extraordinarily expensive to develop and install, negating any cost savings associated with the elimination of fixed signals. ATS was simply not cost effective on light-density lines, precluding its adoption system-wide. A second, related difficulty was that ATS systems required a set of dedicated equipment equipped with a pickup shoe or some similar device that could "read" the restrictive signal indication. The problem, as representatives of the ATO admitted, "is the fact that, if the [fixed] signals are eliminated, no unequipped engine may be permitted to run over the line."[124] The presence of two locomotive pools—one suitable for ATS service and the other not—precluded standardization and the efficient assignment of motive power. Third, the operation of a train required considerably more finesse than simply starting and stopping the locomotive. Skilled enginemen brought their trains in, safely and on time, only because they possessed an intimate familiarity with every inch of track on their division, and because they were able to anticipate subtle alterations to the throttle and the air brake. An ATS system, even one that worked perfectly, could stop a train that had gone beyond the limits of its assigned block, but it could not gradually slow or accelerate a train in a manner that would prevent stalling on an ascending grade, or a runaway on a descent. Only an engineman could do that, and enginemen took a dim view of a technological system that would stop their train, without warning, in response to orders that they had never seen.

Over the next few decades, PRR and ICC officials argued over the merits of automatic block signaling, ATS, and federally mandated operating procedures. While many railroad executives were firmly opposed to any ICC-imposed requirements, PRR officials adopted a more conciliatory stance. With high traffic densities effectively mandating the widespread installation of automatic signals, and with the PRR in the forefront of signaling technology, the ICC was likely to give its imprimatur to the company's existing practices without imposing any significant new regulatory burdens. PRR managers were determined to avoid the forced installation of expensive ATS systems, which promised little additional safety and no increase in efficiency. However, either automatic signaling or ATS was preferable to ICC oversight of the PRR's operations. In that context, PRR executives were willing to employ mechanical devices as a substitute for the loss of managerial control to the regulatory state.[125]

The role of ATS as a substitute for ICC oversight came to a head during the 1920s. The Transportation Act of 1920 provided the ICC with the authority to mandate safety devices. Although its earlier recommendations had been voluntary, in 1922 the ICC issued order No. 13413, requiring the PRR and forty-eight other railroads to install automatic train control systems on at least one division, no later than February 1926. The ICC had been quite correct to support the adoption of block signaling, Rudd admitted, but it now was as if "a change came over the spirit of its dreams and for some time the automatic stop was the panacea for all evils."[126]

PRR executives insisted that compliance with the order would entail substantial costs, without any discernible corresponding benefit. The members of the ATO concluded that automatic-stop signals would not permit the elimination of fixed signals. They would not "provide for making efficiency checks of enginemen," and would have "no use except as a post-mortem and then of doubtful value" in investigative efforts to determine whether or not an engineman might be at fault in an accident. There was, ATO representatives concluded, no reason other than order No. 13413 to install automatic-stop systems.[127] "It should, therefore, seem the logical and sensible course," chief signal engineer Rudd emphasized, "to first extend and modernize our automatic block signal systems" rather than "proceed to 'paint the lily and gild the refined gold'" by installing ATS equipment.[128]

In response to the ICC order, the PRR conducted tests along fifty miles of the mostly single-track Lewis-town Branch. The PRR's ATS system, developed and installed by its traditional supplier, Union Switch & Signal, constituted a significant revision of the mechanical apparatus used in the Hudson and East River tunnels. Low-voltage 100 Hz alternating current carried the signal indication through the rails. A small pickup shoe mounted on the locomotive tender detected any interruption in the current, whether resulting from a stop signal or damaged track. The installation, completed in July 1923, facilitated evaluation of ATS in extremely difficult operating territory, while the remote location of the branch minimized the possibility of bad publicity should the system fail to function properly and delay trains or even cause accidents.[129]

PRR signal engineers soon learned that the inadvertent brake applications caused by the automatic stop system could seriously reduce productivity. They accordingly petitioned the ICC to permit the use of forestallers, which allowed crews to preempt the ATS equipment if they were certain that they were controlling the train properly. Train crews also disliked ATS, because it took control of the train out of their skilled and experienced hands, and they too were receptive to the forestaller. The cost of a completely automatic system would have been prohibitively expensive, both with respect to capital expenditures and in terms of the friction that it would engender among the ranks of skilled train crews, men who were no fools, and who saw no reason why they should sacrifice their prestige and dignity in the interest of foolproof operation.[130]

The ICC commissioners initially opposed the forestaller (because it allowed the possibility of human error), but relented in July 1924. By that time, the Lewistown Branch test installation had been in place for a year, and during that interval, Signal Department personnel worked to develop an alternative to ATS. As representatives from the Union Switch & Signal were installing the ATS apparatus, they mentioned to Rudd that it would be possible to modify the system by installing indicator lights in the locomotive cab, for minimal additional cost. Initially, the cab signals did little more than provide the engine crew with advance warning that the train's brakes were about to be applied automatically by the ATS equipment. Signal Department personnel soon augmented the cab signal indication with an in-cab whistle that would sound continuously until the crew responded to the signal by invoking the now-permitted forestaller feature. Failing that, the ATS would engage.[131]

PRR engineers insisted that in-cab position-light signals were actually safer than ATS, with or without the forestaller. The success of the ATS system depended on the selection of the correct stopping distance (that is, the maximum length that a braking train might conceivably travel, after passing a restrictive speed indication, before it would strike the train ahead of it). Trains varied considerably in length, weight, and speed, and a safe stopping distance for a slow, short freight train might well be insufficient for a fast passenger train. Stopping distances also differed from block to block, depending on grades and curvature. Both PRR and ICC officials could calculate the normal stopping distance for different types of trains under varying conditions. Those calculations, however, depended on the ability of the engineman to close the throttle once the ATS system had triggered the air brakes—and an incapacitated crewman was no more likely to shut off the power than he would be to apply the brakes. The ICC was either unwilling or unable to articulate a definitive stopping distance, creating further problems for Rudd. Furthermore, Rudd pointed out one aspect of the human equation that had apparently escaped the ICC's notice, and in doing so he criticized the forestaller feature that both the Signal Department and PRR train crews had supported. "With the permissive [forestaller] feature, a smart engineman may absolutely annul" the ATS system, Rudd noted, "even if he misreads his signal"— that is, he might grow so tired of false stops that he would preemptively override the ATS.[132]

Cab signals with whistle acknowledgers, Rudd emphasized, were far safer, and, more important, they promised to increase productivity, rather than decrease it. Whereas the ATS would engage only when a train passed a restrictive signal at each block limit, cab signals provided real-time information that mimicked the fixed position-light signals along the right of way. The cab signal would reflect any changes in the lineside signals, even if the engine was in the middle of the block, not yet within sight of the lineside signal at the block limit. That feature enabled an engineman to anticipate restrictive signal indications, slowing down before he reached the actual signal. Even better, from the PRR's perspective, a train could accelerate, mid-block, upon receiving a cab signal indication of a less restrictive block ahead, thus speeding train movements. Cab signals precluded any possibility that an engineman would misread conventional lineside signals that might be obscured by smoke, rain, or indeed the very bulk and speed of the locomotive that he was operating—both increasing the margin of safety and preventing crews from decelerating while "hunting" for a lineside signal. And, the cab-signal system, once perfected, would allow the PRR to dispense with lineside signals altogether, resulting in considerable cost savings.[133]

When the PRR and other railroads requested that the ICC allow cab signals in lieu of ATS or ATS/forestaller systems, the ICC initially refused. The possibility of operator error still existed, the commissioners argued, and it was hardly a fail-safe technology. In this instance, the PRR's long-standing tradition of discipline and control over the labor force yielded substantial dividends. An inexperienced "boomer" engineman on a lesser railroad might ignore an in-cab signal indication, but, Rudd argued, "Cab signals will, with the type and character of the men who run our trains, provide as much protection as the complex apparatus required for any system of [automatic] train control." The only way that the cab signaling system could possibly fail, Rudd insisted, would be "in the case of a train with the engineman gone suddenly crazy, and the fireman not knowing it."[134]

The ICC found Rudd's arguments persuasive. In 1927 and 1928, the commissioners conducted investigations and held hearings regarding the role of signaling systems in augmenting railroad safety. Several prominent commissioners, including former railway union official Frank McManamy and Joseph B. Eastman, quite possibly the most influential commissioner in the history of the agency, initially favored the mandated installation of ATS systems. However, Eastman in particular was receptive to arguments by PRR officials that cab signals represented a more efficient use of scarce resources. Following a 1929 accident on the Maryland Division, the ICC recommended that the PRR install cab signals in areas prone to fog. By early

1930, an in-cab signaling system (but not ATS) was in service between New York and Washington, and between Altoona and Pittsburgh.[135]

By the 1930s, ICC officials had ceased their insistence that the PRR and other railroads install ATS where safety alone was a consideration. Passenger rail travel began to decline during the 1920s owing to the proliferation of the automobile, reducing concerns over the risk to travelers. Automobiles were far more dangerous than trains, and railroad executives pointed to the carnage on the highways as evidence that their lines were safe enough, even without ATS. The Great Depression imposed financial constraints on the railroads, while reducing traffic levels and diminishing both the economic and the safety rationales associated

with automatic block signaling and ATS. On February 6, 1931, the commission permitted the PRR to employ cab signaling in all territories where it had previously required ATS. By that time, the PRR had installed ATS and cab signals on 645 route miles, with pick-up shoes on 1,100 locomotives, compared with 341 miles and more than a thousand locomotives and multiple-unit cars equipped solely with cab signals. Upon receipt of the ICC directive, shop forces immediately began to remove ATS equipment from locomotives, eliminating the earlier necessity of maintaining two separate motive power pools.[136]

In 1937—the same year that Alexander Rudd retired from his post as chief signal engineer, and as the PRR completed the installation of cab signals between

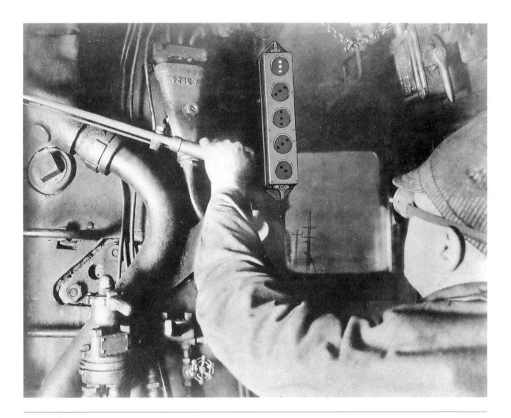

Figure 60. In a staged and heavily retouched publicity photo, a PRR engineman stares intently at the cab signal indicator. Small lights mimicked fixed trackside signals, indicating the occupancy status of the next block. Various three-light combinations indicated proceed, approach medium, approach slow, or absolute stop. Befitting a publicity photo, the three vertically arranged dots illuminated here indicate a clear block ahead. The limited view out of the front cab window, often obscured by smoke, steam, the bulk of the locomotive, and the engineman's safety goggles, illustrated the difficulty that crews sometimes experienced in reading lineside signals.

Temple University Libraries, Urban Archives, Philadelphia, Pennsylvania.

Philadelphia and Harrisburg—Congress passed the Signal Inspection Act. The law gave the ICC authority to mandate the installation of automatic block signaling, ATS, interlocking plants, and cab signals. The act also required the railroads to obtain ICC approval for the installation and operation of their signaling systems, while empowering the agency to set rules and standards for any carrier whose procedures did not pass regulatory muster. With executives using the depression as an excuse, most carriers failed to submit acceptable protocols to the ICC. In April 1939, the commission issued a set of uniform signaling guidelines.

The ICC rules, which took effect in September 1939, had relatively little effect on the PRR, a railroad that was already a leader in signaling systems. However, the ICC policies required the railroad to make signaling improvements along some of its lines. The resulting cost in turn encouraged signal engineers to more widely adopt a new type of train management in the form of centralized traffic control (CTC). CTC enabled a centrally located operator to throw switches and route trains over many miles of railroad, while providing a continuous indication of the occupancy status of each block. The New York Central was the first railroad in the United States to employ CTC, in 1927. The first installation on the PRR occurred in 1930, on a thirty-mile section of the old Vandalia Route in Indiana. That installation saved twelve minutes of dwell time in instances where two trains met. More significantly, CTC allowed the PRR to avoid the enormous capital expense associated with double-tracking that portion of the line. CTC installations spread rapidly thereafter, with long stretches of track receiving CTC just prior to World War II. The surge in wartime business prompted additional CTC installations. After 1945, however, a steady decline in freight and passenger traffic reduced the need for CTC, particularly in areas with multi-tracked main lines. During the postwar period, the PRR relied heavily on its low-tech infrastructure, while executives on other railroads—such as the New York Central—demonstrated a greater willingness to use more sophisticated devices and operating methods to control train movements.[137]

Neither automatic block signaling nor CTC was a fail-safe technology, however. Dispatchers could route trains incorrectly, and enginemen might fail to heed lineside signals. A series of postwar disasters persuaded both PRR and ICC officials to reexamine the issue of automatic train control. In February 1947, excessive speed caused the *Red Arrow* to derail near Gallitzin, Pennsylvania, killing twenty-four people. Four months later, the ICC issued new rules requiring railroads to install automatic block signals on any route where passenger trains would operate at speeds above fifty-nine miles per hour. Cab signaling or ATS was required on all lines where passenger train speeds exceeded seventy-nine miles per hour.[138]

A series of accidents in 1950 and 1951 dampened opposition from PRR officials regarding the new rules. On February 17, 1950, an engineman on the Long Island Rail Road, a PRR subsidiary, failed to obey a signal and caused a collision that killed thirty-one people. In September, the engineman on the *Spirit of St. Louis* ignored trackside signals, cab signal indications, and even the frantic warnings of crewmen on the ground, and his locomotive slammed into the rear of a stalled troop train. Thirty-three soldiers died, and 258 people suffered injuries. In November, another wreck on the Long Island Rail Road, again caused by crew error, led to seventy-seven deaths. In February 1951, eighty-five people died when the engineman on *The Broker* failed to obey a restrictive speed order. Two months later, on May 18, nine people lost their lives when the engineman on the eastbound *Red Arrow* ran past a stop signal, and his train struck the rear of the *Philadelphia Night Express* at Bryn Mawr, Pennsylvania.[139]

The negative publicity and potential legal ramifications associated with those accidents persuaded PRR officials to aggressively pursue both cab signaling and automatic speed control, as ATS was now generally known. Following the wreck of *The Broker*, a Middlesex County, New Jersey, grand jury handed down eighty-five indictments for manslaughter. On March 2, 1951, just hours after PRR attorneys entered pleas of not guilty, president James M. Symes announced that the railroad would spend $2 million (soon raised to $10 million) to equip much of the system with automatic train control. The ATC system, newly developed by Union Switch & Signal, was a refinement of ATS that would regulate train speeds as well as bring them to an emergency stop. With its high-density traffic, and in the aftermath of two horrific wrecks, the PRR's

Long Island Rail Road subsidiary was the first to receive ATC. Symes promised that the PRR would install ATC over an additional 1,100 route miles that hosted two-thirds of the railroad's total passenger mileage and carried three-fourths of all through passengers.[140]

By the mid-1950s, however, reduced freight and passenger traffic, coupled with the PRR's deteriorating financial condition, curtailed the adoption of ATC equipment. By 1955, traffic along the Northern Central between Baltimore and Harrisburg decreased to such an extent that PRR employees ripped out one of the two mainline tracks. They also removed the cab-signal system, the first to be installed, and now the first to be removed. In October 1956, PRR officials elected to suspend further installation of ATC. During the years that followed, as traffic levels continued to decline, the PRR deactivated cab signals and in many cases even removed the automatic block signaling apparatus. The rapid adoption of diesel locomotives during the 1950s permitted easy installation of a "deadman" control that would close the throttle and apply the brakes in the event that an engineman became incapacitated.[141] The deadman control had little effect on operating efficiency—and its value as a safety device was debatable—but it was inexpensive and did not interfere with managerial prerogatives regarding operating procedures. Its use, without corresponding reliance on either ATS or ATC, in effect validated Chief Signal Engineer Rudd's insistence that engine crews could be trusted, and that "the case of a train with the engineman gone suddenly crazy, and the fireman not knowing it" would be so rare as to be inconsequential.[142]

Telegraphy

As early as the 1850s, the PRR and other northeastern railroads were far larger, more complex, and more difficult to coordinate than any business that had heretofore existed. During the early nineteenth century, even the largest of the textile mills that dotted New England occupied no more than a few acres. Mill owners and managers could readily observe and coordinate all of the activity that took place in such a concentrated location. Railroads, by their very nature, extended over long distances, requiring managers to develop hierarchical organizational systems. Such managerial innovations, however, did not address the problems associated with physically transmitting information and instructions across the length and the breadth of a railroad network. George Washington Whistler's efforts to develop new operating methods for the Western Railroad of Massachusetts (in part to prevent a repeat of a horrific collision caused by poor dispatching) were certainly hampered by the lack of instantaneous communication.

The telegraph and its successors, the telephone and the radio, represented the technological triumphs of their respective eras and offered PRR executives the opportunity to rapidly and efficiently coordinate the railroad's operations. During the 1840s, several inventors developed telegraphic communication, belying later claims by Samuel F. B. Morse that he alone had perfected the new device. Their efforts held the potential to improve the safety and efficiency of railroad operations, yet railroad executives were initially reluctant to incorporate telegraphy into their operating routines. Moreover, as PRR managers soon learned, the telegraph, the telephone, and the radio were embedded in a complex social matrix that involved labor and government as much as it did copper wires and voices in the air.

Samuel Morse was an unlikely inventor. He was an itinerant artist, and perennially broke. In 1825, he was in Washington, D.C., painting a portrait, when he received a letter informing him that his wife was ill. By the time he returned home to New Haven, she had died. According to popular legend, the tragedy inspired him to develop a means of instantaneous communication. In reality, Morse was far more concerned with the disruptive tendencies associated with speculation in agricultural commodities, made possible by the absence of real-time information, and he thought that the telegraph could remedy that problem. Morse benefited from direct government support, and in 1843 he obtained a $30,000 congressional appropriation to build a telegraph line between Baltimore and Washington. He considered using a turnpike right of way, but preferred the Baltimore & Ohio's Washington Branch. Morse initially installed the wires in an underground trench, following British practice, but that method soon proved unworkable. On the verge of failure, Morse instead strung the wires from poles, and on May 24, 1844, he sent the famous "What hath God wrought?" message between the Capitol and the B&O's Mt. Clare Depot in Baltimore. The following year, Morse incorporated the Magnetic Telegraph Company in tandem with some politically powerful investors—chief among them former postmaster general Amos Kendall.[143]

The conventional wisdom, as business historian Alfred D. Chandler, Jr., has described, suggested that perspicacious railway managers immediately appreciated the potential of the new device.[144] In reality, those managers harbored justifiable suspicions toward telegraphy and were far slower to incorporate the new technology into their operating routines than were their counterparts in Britain.[145] Early telegraph lines were notoriously unreliable, prone to breaks and even to collapsing poles and wires, which would block railroad tracks and interrupt service. The B&O directors who had reluctantly assented to Morse's initial line had no interest in using the telegraph for dispatching purposes. In 1845, executives on the Camden & Amboy, soon to become the PRR's route to the New York area, declined Kendall's offer to string telegraph wire along the company's right of way.[146] In 1852, the directors of the Philadelphia, Wilmington & Baltimore Railroad, the PRR's gateway to the South, refused to approve the erection of additional telegraph lines, noting that the existing system "has caused much trouble at times—from poles falling across the track—distribution of poles & wires & the passing of telegraph hands on the road . . . and serious inconvenience to us in laying track and switches."[147]

Railway executives had other reasons to be cautious. In a few extreme cases, low-hanging telegraph wires injured or even killed railway workers. More commonly, periodic malfunctions in the independently owned telegraph system convinced railway executives that the technology was neither trustworthy nor under their control. They were unwilling to design operating routines that would of necessity require operations to be curtailed or suspended whenever the equipment underlying those operating methods failed. Railway managers could do little to remedy those problems, as they lacked control over the telegraph sys-

tem. They might also wonder whether the railroad or the telegraph company would be liable for accidents, whether telegraph operators would exercise sufficient care with the railroad's proprietary information, whether independent telegraph operators were sufficiently familiar with railroad operations to safely transmit train orders, and whether commercial traffic might take precedence over messages that were vital to the railroad's operations. Many states, after all, had laws requiring messages to be transmitted in the order that they were received, regardless of their importance to the railroad. PRR executives could doubtless envision a nightmare scenario in which trains blocked the line, unable to move in either direction, as an independent telegraph operator was busily engaged in the transmission of birthday greetings or the price of eggs in Lancaster. Furthermore, railroad managers saw little need for the telegraph. By the 1840s, they had developed an efficient and reasonably safe set of operating practices based on rigid adherence to the rule book and the timetable. Railway officials worried that telegraphy might confer unwarranted authority in the hands of employees, enabling them to bypass the rigid operating procedures that senior executives had carefully articulated in rule books. Like automatic signals, telegraphy would be used only in instances where less complicated and less expensive systems were simply incapable of coping with the volume of traffic.[148]

From the beginning of its corporate existence, the Pennsylvania Railroad had access to commercial telegraphy, yet for several years managers delayed incorporating the devices into their day-to-day operations. As with the B&O, and other carriers, the telegraph relied on the PRR only for a right of way and did not play a role in train operations. In 1845, a year prior to the incorporation of the PRR, Henry O'Rielly bought the rights to erect a telegraph line, on the Morse system, between Philadelphia, Harrisburg, and Pittsburgh, and on to Cincinnati and St. Louis.[149] O'Rielly had been the postmaster at Rochester, New York, and he was thus acquainted with Postmaster General Amos Kendall, who would later become one of the key investors in Morse's Magnetic Telegraph Company. In September, workers in Lancaster began erecting poles and wires, following the right of way of the Harrisburg, Portsmouth, Mount Joy & Lancaster toward the state capital. In early January, the line carried its first test message, but several days passed before anyone bothered to pay for the privilege of instantaneous communication. By September, the line had been extended east to Philadelphia along the state-owned Philadelphia & Columbia Railroad. Through the autumn, construction crews pushed the wire to the west, along the Cumberland Valley Railroad to Chambersburg and then along the turnpike to Bedford and Pittsburgh. In December, Pittsburghers sent their first telegraphic messages to Washington.[150]

By July 1848, O'Rielly and his associates felt secure enough to establish the Atlantic & Ohio Telegraph Company, the same firm that employed a young Andrew Carnegie as a telegraph operator at Pittsburgh. Yet, they had reason to regret their initial route through Carlisle and Bedford, in part because the lines were plagued by breaks and other malfunctions, and repair crews found it difficult to reach the areas west of Chambersburg that were accessible only by road. With the PRR well on the way to completion, its rail line promised superior access. On March 21, 1849, the PRR board accepted an offer from Atlantic & Ohio president James Kennedy Moorhead to move the Atlantic & Ohio lines to the PRR's route and "to erect Poles & Wires for a Telegraphic Communication along our line of Road through to Pittsburgh."[151] Atlantic & Ohio agreed to transmit PRR messages for free (and with priority over commercial traffic, President Merrick insisted), in exchange for open access to the PRR right of way.[152]

During the early 1850s, PRR executives began incorporating telegraphy into routine train operations, generally in advance of the other trunk lines, such as the Erie.[153] In contrast to the mutual animosity and mistrust that had characterized relationships during the 1840s, railroad executives and telegraph entrepreneurs were willing to cooperate with one another. Furthermore, the building of the Western Division and the necessity of moving merchandise, people, and construction supplies over an incomplete route taxed the ability of PRR employees to coordinate operations. In mid-1851, PRR managers began employing the Atlantic & Ohio line to locate the positions of trains on what was still a single-track railroad. Despite the terms of the contract, the PRR could use the Atlantic & Ohio telegraph line only during the day (as the telegraph company closed its offices at night), and even then only when there was no commercial traffic. At the end of 1851, superintendent of transportation Herman Haupt attributed passenger train delays to the nighttime closure of Atlantic & Ohio telegraph offices—a particularly serious problem given that the PRR officials had to schedule through trains to coordinate with the operations of the Allegheny Portage Railroad. More seriously, in the spring of 1852 two PRR trains collided owing to a mistake committed by an Atlantic & Ohio telegrapher. As work crews cleaned up the wreckage, the PRR's legal counsel suggested that the railroad had a strong case against the telegraph company.[154]

The initiation of through rail service between Philadelphia and Pittsburgh in December 1852 only exacerbated the problems. Dispatchers coped with the routing of trains over three railroads, while personnel at Pittsburgh sought instructions from Philadelphia as they struggled to transfer cargoes to and from the PRR's western rail and water connections.[155] Perhaps the most significant PRR employee at Pittsburgh was Tom Scott, who in December 1852 became the third assistant superintendent in charge of the Western Division. Shortly after his promotion, Scott requested and received permission from J. Edgar Thomson to extend the Atlantic & Ohio telegraph line to the PRR station. Scott also hired Andrew Carnegie as the PRR's first telegraph operator, famously starting the Scotsman's rapid upward ascent in the world of railroading. Other former Atlantic & Ohio telegraphers, including David McCargo and Robert Pitcairn, soon joined him. Scott was nonetheless mistrustful of his young clerk and prohibited Carnegie from sending train orders without his express approval. On one occasion, when Scott was out of the office, Carnegie dispatched trains on his own authority. Carnegie later boasted, in his self-serving *Autobiography*, that he had unclogged a congested PRR, but even he admitted that the superintendent was concerned at the usurpation of executive authority.[156]

In contrast to their counterparts on the Erie, PRR executives engaged in exhaustive research and debate prior to committing to telegraphic dispatching. In December 1852, as a result of the growing problems associated with the Atlantic & Ohio contract, the PRR board established a Committee on Telegraph. Over the next four months, the committee investigated the two leading systems, one patented by Morse, the other by Royal E. House. Unlike the Morse system of dots and dashes, House had developed a printing telegraph, one that typed legible characters on paper. The committee concluded that the House system was preferable, inasmuch as it greatly reduced the difficulty of training operators. In order to overcome nighttime train delays, the committee members suggested that each locomotive could be equipped with a House transmitter, which could wake telegraph operators by triggering a bell in the nearest station and then transmit an emergency message.[157]

The members of the Committee on Telegraph recommended that the PRR build its own telegraph line, internalizing communications functions and freeing the company from reliance on the Atlantic & Ohio. Despite the familiarity of PRR employees with the existing Morse system, the committee's recommendation favored the House equipment. By the spring of 1853, the legislature had authorized the PRR to erect a telegraph line connecting Philadelphia with Lancaster, Harrisburg, and Pittsburgh.

While the members of the Committee on Telegraph had initially supported the principle of the House system, they soon experienced difficulties in putting their recommendations into practice. Proponents of each system, anxious to secure both the royalties and the public-relations value associated with the use of their equipment along the PRR, offered competing performance claims. In April 1853, the PRR board hired an independent expert to determine the merits of each system. By January 1854, the Committee on Telegraph had reversed its earlier position, recommending the Morse system. The committee concluded that the House system was too expensive, and too technologically complex. Once telegraph operators mastered the Morse code, the absence of printed letters proved to be of little consequence. That decision greatly reduced the scope of the project, as the PRR could rely on the existing Atlantic & Ohio line east of Altoona.[158]

In September 1855, however, the board elected to dispense entirely with the services of the Atlantic & Ohio Telegraph Company and to build a new "line of

Telegraph from Philadelphia to Pittsburgh," a system that was "under the exclusive control of this Company."[159] The line would employ the Morse patents, with royalties paid at the rate of $10 per mile.[160] The PRR, with the permission of the Canal Commission, used the right of way of the Philadelphia & Columbia to carry the line to Philadelphia. By the end of April 1856, the PRR-controlled line was in operation over the entire system. A month later, the board established a set of operating procedures for the new Telegraph Department, subsumed under the control of the Transportation Department. In August 1858, the board approved the appointment of David Brooks, who had once overseen the Atlantic & Ohio's operations in Pittsburgh, as the first superintendent of telegraph. A year later, Brooks yielded that post to David McCargo, another Atlantic & Ohio veteran.[161]

Pennsylvania Railroad executives played an unwitting role in the development of Western Union, the company that dominated the telegraph business. In 1851, Hiram Sibley—like Henry O'Rielly, a native of Rochester, New York—organized the New York & Mississippi Valley Printing Telegraph Company, with rights to the House system. To a far greater extent than Morse or Kendall, Sibley appreciated the wisdom of establishing a close working relationship with the railroads. Sibley soon put together a network of telegraph lines in the Midwest, many of them along the railroads that would later become PRR subsidiaries, but he lacked a good connection to the east coast. Sibley's ally, Jeptha H. Wade, oversaw the creation of the Pennsylvania Telegraph Company to build a line between Pittsburgh and Philadelphia. Wade approached PRR directors Christian E. Spangler and George Howell, both members of the Committee on Telegraph, with a proposal to use the PRR right of way. Wade offered to provide House mechanisms in PRR facilities at Philadelphia, Lancaster, Harrisburg, and Pittsburgh. PRR personnel could send messages for free, but for no more than fifteen minutes at a time. In return, the PRR granted Wade the right to string wire along the PRR's poles (which railroad personnel had erected, and would continue to maintain) and agreed to transport Pennsylvania Telegraph Company personnel and equipment free of charge. In the event that the Pennsylvania Telegraph line malfunctioned, the company could transmit its messages over PRR wires. Spangler and Howell inexplicably accepted the lop-sided arrangement, and in May 1856 the PRR board gave its approval.[162]

Atlantic & Ohio officials were aghast that the PRR had given a critical advantage to a formidable competi-tor, and soon realized that they would have to come to some sort of an understanding with Sibley, Wade, and the New York & Mississippi Valley Printing Telegraph Company. In April 1856, a month before the PRR board granted them access to the right of way, Sibley, Wade, and Ezra Cornell, a longtime associate of Samuel Morse, created the Western Union Telegraph Company. The new firm took over the assets of the New York & Western Union Telegraph Company and soon gobbled up its competitors, as well. In January 1859, Atlantic & Ohio officials assented to a merger with Western Union.[163]

Within two years, in a nation torn apart by civil war, the telegraph proved beyond a doubt its role in railroad operations. J. Edgar Thomson lent the new superinten-dent of telegraph, David McCargo, and four experi-enced telegraph operators to the Union war effort. As traffic on the PRR soared to record levels, employees were no longer able to adhere rigidly to the rule book. Instead, they developed an informal set of dispatching practices (known as the "American system of dis-patching" or, more commonly, timetable-and-train order operation) that cobbled together rule books, time-tables, written train orders, and telegraphic messages. PRR managers had to acknowledge that telegraphy had become an integral part of everyday operations.[164]

Following the Civil War, Andrew Carnegie—who had always been adept at exploiting business opportu-nities associated with the railroads—parlayed his ex-pertise into the establishment of a new telegraph company. In 1867, Carnegie, probably backed, or at least encouraged, by Thomson and Scott, incorporated the Keystone Telegraph Company as a rival to West-ern Union. The PRR executives soon gave Keystone the right to erect poles and wires along the right of way across Pennsylvania in exchange for a small per-mile annual rental. Carnegie then opened negotiations with Pittsburgh businessman James L. Shaw, whose Pacific & Atlantic Telegraph Company was one of the few viable competitors to Western Union. Shaw agreed

to a merger between Keystone Telegraph and Pacific & Atlantic, trebling Carnegie's investment in the former firm. Not content with that quick profit, Carnegie de-termined to use the Pacific & Atlantic, in which he maintained a one-third interest, to compete against Western Union across the territory served by the PRR and its subsidiaries, and as far west as California.[165]

Carnegie's involvement with Keystone Telegraph represented far more than an attempt to exploit an in-sider advantage for personal profit. For all of their power, PRR executives were determined to keep West-ern Union from interfering with the railroad's opera-tions. Western Union officials, anxious to maximize revenues from commercial traffic, had imposed regula-tions that hindered managers on many railroads from effectively employing the telegraph as a dispatching tool—and, according to some critics, had contributed to accidents. When the PRR's directors had chosen, more than a decade earlier, to build a dedicated tele-graph line from Philadelphia to Pittsburgh, they had largely protected the company against Western Union. To be on the safe side, however, PRR executives in-sisted that any contract with outside telegraph com-panies—on subsidiary lines, for example—contain stipulations protecting the railroad's dispatching rights, in the event that Western Union might acquire the predecessor firms. More ominously, however, West-ern Union was for a time controlled briefly by William Henry Vanderbilt and for a much longer period by Jay Gould and his son George. In that context, Keystone Telegraph was not so much an insider investment scheme as a prudent safeguard against a Western Union monopoly of the telegraph network.[166]

The procedures for employing the telegraph were as important as the instrument itself, and PRR execu-tives soon developed voluminous rules and regulations for train dispatching. In 1874, with the telegraph in widespread use across the PRR system, executives pro-mulgated a new book of rules for the railroad's employ-ees. Signal engineer James B. Calvert has identified the 1874 manual as "the first modern rule book" in the United States because it eliminated the written rules governing delayed and extra trains in favor of tele-graphic dispatching. The 1874 rule book divided all trains into one of three categories: regular trains were listed in a printed employee timetable, and operated according to schedule; other trains traveled on the same schedule, as additional sections spaced closely behind one another, with green flags on the locomotive of all but the last section; and extras, with white-flagged locomotives, that ran according to train orders that dispatchers gave to train crews. The most significant change, however, involved the implementation of the double-order system of dispatching. While older methods gave train crews only the orders directly relating to their train, the double-order system gave them access to information regarding all of the other trains that they were scheduled to encounter. Should a dispatcher issue conflicting orders to several trains, crewmen were more likely to catch the error.[167]

During the 1880s, PRR officials took steps to develop standardized dispatching methods. Such practices would bring the railroad's newly acquired subsidiaries into conformity with the regulations developed on the Pennsylvania Railroad proper. As a result, operating employees hired from other railroads would require less training and be less likely to cause accidents by momentarily confusing the old dispatching rules with the current ones. PRR executives, including Lines West general manager James McCrea, Pittsburgh Division superintendent Robert Pitcairn, and Belvidere Division superintendent John A. Anderson, shared their expertise through professional organizations such as the General Time Convention. The convention developed a uniform time system (essential to accurate time-based dispatching) and a Standard Code of Train Rules, based in large part on PRR practice. Until 1894, however, each PRR Grand Division formulated its own rules and standards for telegraph operation, a situation that must have created considerable confusion. After that time, the general manager developed system-wide standards for the Telegraph Department, as overseen by the superintendent of telegraph. Individual division superintendents retained control of personnel and budgetary matters relating to the operation and maintenance of telegraph systems on their respective divisions.[168]

Expanding the Signal System: Telegraphy, Class, and Gender

By the early years of the twentieth century, PRR officials confronted two problems that were common to both communications and signaling—particularly as telegraphers and towermen were the same people. First, increasing traffic induced the railroad's executives, beginning around 1905, to expand the areas covered by block signaling—which in turn produced a shortage of block operators who were proficient in telegraphy. The 1907 Hours of Service Act only exacerbated the demand for skilled labor. Second, telegraphers and block operators enjoyed considerable workplace autonomy. Like enginemen, firemen, and conductors, the employees who sent telegraphic messages and operated the signaling system possessed an advanced skill, learned largely through an informal apprenticeship system, that was vital to railroad operations. Like train crews, telegraphers and block operators worked in isolated locations, largely free of direct managerial oversight. It was hardly surprising, therefore, that the development of labor organizations for telegraphers lagged only slightly behind the unionization of operating employees. After 1905, PRR managers sought to increase the number of skilled telegraphers and block operators without escalating wage rates or alienating their existing employees. Executives first attempted to break the apprenticeship system, through the establishment of a School of Telegraphy. When that stratagem produced disappointing results, managers next attempted to exploit a vast pool of female labor. Ultimately, however, the solution was technological, as PRR officials reduced the need for telegraphers by eliminating the telegraph in favor of the telephone.

During the Civil War, as the nation's telegraph network underwent rapid expansion, operators first developed workplace solidarity. In 1863, they founded the National Telegraphic Union, primarily as a benevolent and fraternal organization. Telegraphers became far more militant in 1869, when Western Union began hiring and training female operators. Western Union management underestimated the extent to which class consciousness would trump gender divisions, and male and female operators joined forces in an unsuccessful 1870 strike under the auspices of the Telegraphers' Protective League. The Brotherhood of Telegraphers, an affiliate of the Knights of Labor, launched another strike in 1883, with equally disastrous results.[169]

Out of the wreckage of the Brotherhood of Telegraphers came the Order of Railway (later, Railroad) Telegraphers (ORT), established in Cedar Rapids, Iowa, in 1886. By the end of the century, roughly half of the forty thousand railroad telegraphers in the United States were members. Commercial telegraphers followed suit in 1902, with the Commercial Telegraphers' Union of America (CTUA). Mimicking the relationship between the railroad operating brotherhoods and industrial unions, ORT was a far more moderate organization than the CTUA, functioning primarily as a benevolent association. In 1907 CTUA telegraphers went on strike, in response to Western Union's refusal to increase wages for San Francisco telegraphers who were still reeling from the earthquake the year before. Railroad telegraphers did not join the strike, but the ORT ordered its members to refuse all Western Union commercial transmissions. Western Union soon crushed the CTUA strike, and the ORT's lackluster support ensured that the PRR barely felt its effects.[170]

On the Pennsylvania Railroad, telegraphers had clashed with management as early as 1893, when a workers' committee met with the general manager of Lines East over a "misunderstanding" that resulted in a firing. Over the next decade, similar ad hoc committees aired grievances involving local working conditions.[171] The situation changed dramatically in 1903, when a telegraphers' committee demanded uniform system-wide rules regarding seniority and the advertising of vacant positions. The Lines East general manager reached an accord with the committee, but executives grew increasingly concerned at challenges to the long-standing prerogative of local division superintendents to hire, discipline, and fire at their own discretion, in conformity with local labor markets.[172]

The expansion of the block signaling system opened up new opportunities for the telegraphers in more ways than one. The new hires learned their trade by informally apprenticing with experienced block operators—a tradition that dated back to the earliest days of railroad telegraphy. The Order of Railroad Telegraphers bylaws, however, required that the union's president approve all new apprenticeships, and further provided that all "controversial matters" involving hiring and discipline would be handled through the workers' committees. PRR management may have condescendingly referred to those practices as a "ritual," but they constituted a very effective mechanism for controlling the supply of skilled workers, and thus their wages. After some block operators simply refused to accept any apprentices at all—making the operation of the newly expanded block signaling system effectively impossible—the PRR fired three of them. When a worker committee upheld the disciplinary action, its members were expelled from the Order of Railroad Telegraphers. The ORT banned another member in 1907, accusing him of being planted by PRR management for the purpose of opposing a Telegraphers' Eight Hour Law in the Maryland legislature. The more basic split in the union, however, seems to have reflected a simple disagreement over whether the ORT would accept the PRR's School of Telegraphy.[173]

In September 1907, with the shortage of block operators threatening to curtail operations, the railroad established a School of Telegraphy at Bedford, Pennsylvania, "for the purpose of educating young men to become Railroad Telegraph or Telephone Operators."[174] Graduates earned the promise of jobs on the PRR, with significant opportunity for promotion. Although the PRR had long maintained structured apprenticeship programs in various shop facilities, the School of Telegraphy was the first formal training program for operating employees, followed soon by the divisional signal schools. Students were expected to pay both an entrance fee and tuition, thus financing both their training and the opportunity to undermine their power in the workplace, as the School of Telegraphy combined education with a strong anti-union message. The school did not live up to expectations, however. Between six and eight months were required to train each telegrapher and, by September 1910, only 243 students had enrolled, of whom a mere 151 had graduated.[175]

To the dismay of PRR managers, the School of Telegraphy failed to create a plentiful supply of pliable telegraphers, but succeeded instead in antagonizing unionized employees. ORT was steadfast in its opposition to the School of Telegraphy, while expelled and disaffected employees, more conciliatory to the PRR's management, formed the Order of Railroad Telegraphers, Dispatchers, Agents, and Signalmen (ORT-DAS). In the undoubtedly biased estimation of Lines East general manager William Wallace Atterbury, the new organization maintained a membership of between six hundred and seven hundred telegraphers, with no more than a thousand remaining loyal to ORT.[176] While ORT leaders considered themselves the true representative for PRR telegraphers, management was equally certain that that organization "endeavored to create dissention and dissatisfaction among the employes of the Telegraph Department of the Pennsylvania Railroad."[177]

If communications and signaling technology could divide the labor force, it could also unite it, raising the very real possibility that PRR telegraphers, tower operators, dispatchers, signalmen, and signal maintainers might find common cause. In 1901, signalmen on the PRR's Middle Division, based at Altoona, complained that their wages of 14 cents an hour were well below the 24.6 cent rate paid on the New York Division. Under the leadership of H. G. Detwiler, they organized the Brotherhood of Railroad Signalmen of America (BRSA) and scheduled a meeting with John M. Wallis, the general superintendent of the Pennsylvania Railroad Grand Division. Wallis proved surprisingly conciliatory, perhaps because he was already overwhelmed with the growing congestion between Altoona and Pittsburgh—he was essentially forced to resign, little more than a year later, because he could not cope with the pressure. Other labor organizations were somewhat less helpful, as leadership of ORT (as well as the Brotherhood of Railroad Trainmen and the Car Builders' Union) refused to join the BRSA.[178] Rank-and-file employees were another matter, however. While some signalmen claimed membership in ORTDAS, others saw the wisdom of affiliating with the more radical (from the perspective of PRR executives) ORT, "on the ground that as the railway mileage operated under the block signaling system increased, the members of the two organizations [BRSA and ORT] were thrown into even closer contact, and that the Signalmen were the only ones, aside from the telegraphers, who were qualified to operate the plant."[179]

The growing traffic volumes that accompanied the outbreak of World War I redeemed the School of Telegraphy and transformed its function. While PRR executives had originally conceived the school as a way of wresting control over training functions from unionized workers, they now reinterpreted it as a mechanism for feminizing the occupation of telegraph operator. On a case-by-case basis, however, female telegraphers long antedated the School of Telegraphy. Elizabeth Cogley began her career with the Atlantic & Ohio Telegraph Company in Lewistown, Pennsylvania, in 1852. Three years later, she began working for the PRR, and was probably the first female telegrapher in the United States. In 1864 the PRR transferred her to Harrisburg—a clear acknowledgment of her skill, given that city's importance in funneling troops and war materiel to Union forces in Virginia. She remained with the PRR until her retirement in 1900. At isolated stations throughout the system, the wives of station agents frequently learned Morse code and transmitted messages when their husbands were engaged elsewhere. If widowed, they in some instances received managerial permission to remain as the sole station agent. As early as 1882, the PRR had employed women as tower operators, with the expectation that they would operate the telegraph key as a routine part of their job. One operator, Dolly Snyder, had signed on in 1904, only to lose her seniority when she joined her striking male counterparts during World War I.[180]

The labor shortages that accompanied World War I encouraged PRR executives to hire and train female telegraphers. In June 1917, the railroad moved the School of Telegraphy from Bedford to Philadelphia, and, as a PRR press release noted, "opened the course to girls and women, as well as men."[181] The new facility included fifty Morse units, as well as a model railroad. "Electrically operated, the tiny trains, looking like toys, are run on schedules as on a real railroad, and the student gets experience in multiple and single track operation," as the PRR's publicists emphasized.[182] By March 1918, the PRR employed ninety female telegraph operators on Lines East. An additional 138 were enrolled in the School of Telegraphy, where the assistant superintendent was also female. At that time, a federal agency, the United States Railroad Administration (USRA), had begun to oversee the operations of the railroads in the interest of wartime efficiency. In August 1918, the administration established a Women's Service Section (WSS) in an effort to protect both the workplace rights and the moral purity of female employees. WSS personnel acted as advocates for female telegraphers, albeit haphazardly and temporarily, strengthening their position within the PRR workforce.[183]

Figure 61. In 1907, PRR managers established a School of Telegraphy at Bedford, Pennsylvania. A more significant event occurred in 1917, when the railroad moved the school to Philadelphia and admitted female students. Women had already been dispatching telegraphic messages on the PRR, but not on a systematic basis. Even with the School of Telegraphy, PRR officials struggled to find enough skilled employees who could regulate train operations with the telegraph. The telephone was a much easier instrument to use, permitting even novice tower operators to communicate with one another.

Temple University Libraries, Urban Archives, Philadelphia, Pennsylvania.

Female telegraphers drew criticism from male employees on several levels. Their male counterparts believed, with considerable justification, that PRR executives were anxious to displace male telegraphers, particularly as women received lower pay than men. The PRR's predilection for hiring women tower operators whenever men went on strike—as happened at least fifteen times in 1917 alone—generated further animosity from male workers.[184] In addition to their pay, male telegraphers gained considerable satisfaction from their ability to control the destiny of hundred-ton locomotives and ten-thousand-ton trains, and did not believe that a woman would ever possess the constitutional prowess to perform what they considered to be an inherently masculine task. Train crews owed their lives to the correct transmission of train orders and often doubted the ability of a woman to operate telegraph and signal equipment. Social reformers, even those who applauded the entry of women into the railway workforce, expressed misgivings regarding the morality of female telegraphy. Like tower operators (and the same person would often perform both functions simultaneously) novice telegraphers often drew nighttime assignments at isolated locations—conditions deemed unsuitable for a virtuous woman.[185]

The end of the war, far more than the opposition of male workers, brought to an end the PRR's experiments with female telegraphy. The Transportation Act of 1920 dissolved the USRA and with it the WSS. Absent federal protection, and with returning veterans clamoring for a reduced number of jobs, PRR officials experienced little difficulty in removing female telegraphers from the payroll. By October 1920, the newly created Eastern Region employed only fifty-eight women telegraphers, and a lone female cadet remained in the School of Telegraphy.[186]

From Dots and Dashes to Voices in the Air: Telephony and Radio

By 1920, the PRR no longer needed women in its telegraphy school, and no longer required female telegraph operators, because its executives had substituted a technological fix for a gendered one. Since the 1870s, PRR managers had been terrified at the possibility that every employee who knew anything about operating the railroad's communication and signaling systems might go on strike simultaneously. That fear gave them added incentive to embrace a technological system that would enable them to create and maintain a much more malleable workforce, composed of employees who could easily be replaced. The telephone allowed women greater access to the still largely male preserve of railroad communications, replaced the "secret" code of dots and dashes with readily comprehensible speech, and dramatically reduced the leverage that skilled telegraphers had once possessed with PRR management.

PRR managers adopted the telephone slowly, and did so primarily to undermine worker autonomy, not to improve the efficiency or safety of the railroad's operations. In 1875, Alexander Graham Bell famously sent the first brief telephone message to his associate Thomas A. Watson. Two years later, in May 1877, Bell dispatched Watson and another assistant, Gardiner D. Hubbard, to demonstrate the new device in the PRR's Altoona shops. The system worked, but PRR executives elected to use the telephone to facilitate managerial communications, not to run trains. A short time after the Altoona demonstration, president Tom Scott ordered a line installed between his country house and the PRR's Centennial Station in West Philadelphia. The next circuit, installed a year or two later, linked

general manager Frank Thomson's home with his office, and with the office of general agent Charles E. Pugh. For the next fifteen years, however, executives continued to rely on the telegraph for system-wide communication. That situation did not change until 1893, when the PRR leased a telephone line from the American Telephone & Telegraph Company, linking Philadelphia, Jersey City, and New York. Pennsylvania Railroad officials did not, however, employ telephones to any appreciable degree where they would seem obviously applicable—that is, in train dispatching. Not until December 1897 did PRR officials test telephones for that purpose, on the South Fork Branch of the Pittsburgh Division. Telephone use was more common on Lines West, and Pittsburgh, Fort Wayne & Chicago dispatchers frequently relied on voice communication in yards, but not over the long distances between Pittsburgh and Chicago.[187]

The telephone was not as useful as it might first appear. For one thing, the PRR had perfected telegraphy over the preceding quarter century, while telephony remained an unproven technology. Phone conversations were problematic at best, owing to static and the loss of signal over long distances, and operators generally found telegraphic communications to be clearer and more reliable. Any failure in the phone system could shut down the railroad or even lead to catastrophic accidents. Whereas telegraphers wrote down the messages that they received, dispatchers who employed the telephone might not keep a written record—a failing that could result in erroneous train orders and would prevent managers from assigning blame in the event of a problem.[188]

Furthermore, PRR officials experienced the same difficulty with telephones as they did with telegraphic equipment and air brakes. Just as Samuel F. B. Morse could not be anointed as the sole "inventor" of the telegraph until he had bested his rivals in the courts, Bell did not have full legitimacy until he had beaten back challenges by Elisha Gray. Not until 1888 did the United States Supreme Court declare Bell to be the individual who had invented the telephone. In the case of telephony, PRR personnel struggled to resolve the critical issue of whether they should buy telephones from the American Bell Telephone Company, whether they might be able to manufacture them at Altoona, under license, or whether they could mimic Alexander Graham Bell's invention without running afoul of his patents. That issue became somewhat less serious in 1894, when several of Bell's key patents expired. By then, however, American Bell had developed a formidable organizational capability in long-distance telephone service, thanks in part to its network provider, the American Telephone & Telegraph Company, that precluded effective competition.[189]

The 1907 Hours of Service Act gave the PRR and other railroads a powerful incentive for rapidly installing telephones for use in train dispatching. The new law restricted dispatchers and block operators to no more than nine hours on duty, increasing the number of personnel required to maintain the same level of service. Skilled telegraphers were in short supply, expensive to train, and well represented by the Order of Railroad Telegraphers. As a result, railroads closed or curtailed the hours of many of their telegraph offices rather than bear the increased expense of staffing them with higher-wage labor. As was the case with the block system, however, traffic densities on the PRR were typically so high that executives had no choice other than to continue to staff telegraph offices while searching for methods that could reduce the number of skilled telegraphers that the law required.[190]

With the Hours of Service Act making the use of telephones all but unavoidable, PRR officials rapidly developed procedures for using the new equipment. In 1909, Lines East superintendent of telegraph John B. Fisher issued a pamphlet, *The Utility of Wires*, in which he articulated the basic arguments in favor of telephony. Significantly, he made no mention of the increased safety that might result from communication that employed the human voice rather than Morse code. Instead, Fisher noted that telephones would enable virtually anyone to be a dispatcher and would help to break the power of unions in the workplace.[191]

In the spring of 1910 PRR executives began to develop a system-wide policy governing telephones. They began by surveying various divisions on the extent of their telephone use, and their level of satisfaction with the new technology. The telephone was more expensive to install and maintain, divisional managers concluded, inasmuch as it required two wires, rather than the single line that carried telegraphic messages. The

increased complexity of the new equipment mandated a "higher grade of intelligence for supervision required to maintain [a] telephone system."[192]

Once installed, however, telephones were easier to use than telegraph keys. Telephones greatly increased operating efficiency by accommodating a far larger number of messages, and offered the further benefit "that handling business by telephone is not near as hard on the nerves as by telegraph." The telephone "eliminates [the] necessity for skilled labor," PRR officials noted, as "it only requires a month or two to enable persons to fit themselves for handling business by telephone, as against anywhere from 6 to 12 months, and even longer, by telegraph." The ease of telephone use enabled the PRR to retain and promote promising junior executives who lacked the basic telegraphy skill set. Telephony also served as an extension of the PRR's welfare capitalism by providing an additional "field to take care of intelligent unfortunates injured in the service"—something that was simply not possible with telegraphy, given the manual dexterity involved.[193]

PRR officials were somewhat more circumspect in their assertions that telephones could break the power of unions such as the Order of Railroad Telegraphers. In 1911, William Atterbury, then the fourth vice president, justified the expense (a little over six thousand dollars) associated with converting a portion of the Pittsburgh Division over to telephone dispatching, lamenting, "It is growing more difficult each year to obtain good, reliable telegraphers." But there was a sinister undertone in his rationale, foreshadowing the 1920s when then-President Atterbury would dedicate much of his time and effort to keeping the Pennsylvania Railroad free of independent labor unions. "With the possibility of labor trouble with telegraphers in this district," Atterbury noted, "the advantage of having both telephone and telegraph at our command for train operation cannot be estimated on a monetary basis."[194]

Within a few years after the adoption of the Hours of Service Act, PRR managers—like their counterparts on other carriers—made rapid advances in telephone use. By January 1910, PRR dispatchers used telephones on slightly less than a quarter of all routes east of Pittsburgh, some five hundred miles in all, with the highest incidence of telephone use occurring near

Philadelphia and Pittsburgh and on the more remote Cresson and Bedford Divisions. Six months later, the railroad had telephone wires in place along 1,100 miles of track. However, many dispatchers continued to rely on telegraphy, and the Philadelphia Terminal Division did not convert to telephones until 1917. System-wide, lines remained available for emergency telegraph dispatching use as late as the mid-1920s, although they were rarely used for that purpose. Instead, PRR officials authorized the installation of a duplex printing telegraph system. The devices, manufactured by the Morkrum Company of Chicago, were similar to that firm's better-known Teletype equipment. The new machines permitted the rapid transmission of routine statistical information and did not require skilled telegraphers to operate. The telegraphic lines that had once carried train orders across the system now carried some thirty-two million messages a year, none of them related to the PRR's day-to-day operations.[195]

World War I solidified the role of the telephone across all aspects of the PRR's operations. New hires—many of them women—possessed only rudimentary telegraph skills, and they found the telephone a far easier instrument to master. War-induced labor shortages also affected the crew callers, who at all hours of day or night would walk or bicycle to YMCAs, hotels, boarding houses, and private homes to inform train crews that they had been called for duty. Modesty and propriety prevented female employees from accepting that responsibility, but they could place a telephone call to the most disreputable of lodgings at even the smallest hour of the night. By war's end, most crew calling was literally just that, accomplished over wire rather than in person. By 1925, Altoona alone maintained 1,667 phone connections for the sole purpose of calling crews to duty.[196]

By 1931, the PRR maintained the largest privately owned company telephone system in the world, with 27,700 telephones, 141 exchanges, and more than 158,000 miles of wire. The PRR actually possessed three separate telephone networks. The first, and the one that was the most visible to the public, handled traffic with the outside world. More than 22,000 miles of trunk lines conveyed nearly a hundred million calls a year, everything from shippers' complaints to requests for passenger train departure times to last-minute calls from Penn Station in New York and Union Station in Chicago—both at conventional phone booths and on board luxury trains like the *Broadway Limited* and the *American*, which remained plugged into the phone lines until moments before departure. The system also accommodated some of the PRR's internal communications, linking the corporate offices in Philadelphia with all of the outposts of the PRR's vast empire. The PRR devoted a second, segregated system to accommodate interoffice calls entirely within large facilities.

The third and most vital system was entirely separate from the first two, accommodating the critical dispatching function. Each operating division maintained a dispatcher's office, a "quiet, very precise and methodical heart," the PRR's publicists noted, "for these men . . . are so expert and exact, as a result of long study and careful experience, that their work is carried forward with an almost uncanny calm and quiet and with absolute accuracy and dispatch."[197] Calm or not, they were indeed men; while women handled the bulk of the railroad network and private branch exchange calls, the PRR rarely, if ever, assigned them to train dispatching.

The chief train dispatcher supervised several dispatchers, each in charge of a specific section of the division. Train sheets allowed them to progressively track train movements across their territories. By selecting the appropriate lever on a large wall panel, they could communicate instantaneously with block operators at towers and depots, providing them with information regarding train routes. Tower operators used the dispatchers' telephone circuit to relay back to the dispatcher the exact time that a particular train had passed each tower. They also relied on a separate "message circuit" to send and receive information not directly connected to train dispatching. A third "general talking circuit," which extended to only the most important locations, allowed the division superintendent to quickly reach his key subordinates and could function as an emergency backup dispatchers' circuit when needed. Each division's superintendent of telegraph and signals kept the system in operation through frequent inspections and tests, maintaining complete redundancy with separate telephone lines on each side of the track.

The PRR also provided call boxes located at one-mile intervals along more than ten thousand route miles. Track telephones allowed train crews to communicate with tower operators, either as part of routine operations, or in cases of malfunctioning equipment or emergencies. In more serious cases, the tower operator could connect the crew at the track phone directly to the dispatcher. Maintenance-of-way crews carried portable telephones and long extension poles, which they could use to tap directly into the telephone lines at any location.

Even with call boxes at frequent intervals, train crews lacked instantaneous communication with dispatchers and tower operators. The first efforts to achieve wireless communication dated to 1881, when representatives from the Eastern Telegraph Company of England developed an induction transmission system. In the United States, Thomas Edison was experimenting with similar devices as early as 1885. Cost and reliability issues precluded widespread adoption until after World War I, however.

The first wireless communication system on the PRR premiered in October 1922, but for the amusement of travelers rather than the facilitation of operations. Passengers on the *Broadway Limited* were able to listen to Newark's WOR radio broadcasts using a conventional radio receiver. In 1924, technicians from the PRR and the American Radio Relay League experimented with the use of radio transmissions between company facilities (although not to train crews) as a backup measure, should the telephone wires be compromised. Two years later, the radio system enabled crewmen in the engine and the cabin car (the PRR did not use the more familiar nomenclature of "caboose") to communicate with each other, through the simple expedient of stringing copper wire along the tops of the freight cars. W. P. Hallstein, the supervisor of telegraph and signals, was quick to point out the impracticality of such a system, but trainmaster G. W. Bradley estimated that the phones had saved the crew at least an hour on their run. The potential of intra-train communication encouraged PRR personnel to experiment further with two-way radio communication, concluding that the technology was still too new to function satisfactorily in regular service.[198]

By 1937, however, technological developments encouraged PRR officials to collaborate with the Radio Corporation of America on further experiments, primarily on freight trains operating between Philadelphia and Harrisburg. The tests gradually minimized problems that included atmospheric distortion, interference from signal circuits, and restrictive clearances (which governed the size and placement of radio aerials). Even though the system worked well enough to allow crews in the engine and the cabin car to communicate with each other, and with dispatchers and tower operators, PRR technicians experimented with a different method. The system depended on the basic operating principles of cab signals, in that a telephone transmitter converted spoken words into electrical impulses, which were then sent through the tracks to a receiver coil suspended just above the rail.[199]

Following the quantum leap in radio technology that occurred during World War II, PRR officials concluded that radio offered the best communication choice. There was a problem in that the Federal Communications Commission exercised absolute control over the assignment of very high radio frequencies (VHF), which the agency allocated primarily to military and commercial broadcast use. In one of the weekly PRR staff meetings in September 1944, PRR executives complained that "the Federal Communications Commission said that there was no place on the radio for the railroads."[200] Because the PRR was unable to secure the required radio frequencies, technicians worked with General Electric and the Union Switch & Signal Company to develop an induction train telephone system, more commonly referred to as TrainPhone. TrainPhone employed rails or telephone lines as antennas to broadcast low-frequency signals to long antennas mounted on locomotives and cabin cars. By 1946 the PRR had installed TrainPhone equipment along 245 route miles and had equipped three hundred locomotives, ninety cabin cars, and thirteen towers with sending and receiving units. Unfortunately, high-voltage catenary interfered with TrainPhone equipment, and the system was useless in some of the PRR's most heavily trafficked territory.

In 1947, the FCC opened up a new portion of the radio spectrum, giving railroads access to the airwaves. The decision was initially of little value to the PRR, however. Because the company had been an innovative "first mover" in TrainPhone equipment, its officials had invested considerable resources in the development and application of a mechanism that soon became obsolete. However, with the PRR already committed to the TrainPhone, and with VHF radio still unproven in railroad service, officials concluded that it was best to continue down the technological path that they had already established. By January 1949, PRR personnel were moving forward with plans to apply TrainPhone equipment to 407 locomotives, 130 cabin cars, and 38 signal towers along 1,817 route miles. By July 1952, some 1,300 TrainPhone devices were in use on 916 locomotives and 230 cabin cars. A few unfortunate trainmen also lugged around the CarryPhone, a portable unit that weighed in at twenty-six pounds. Despite improvements in VHF radio technology, the PRR did not begin using radios on a regular basis until the mid-1960s, and relied on TrainPhone equipment as late as 1967.[201]

The Evolution of the Freight Car

In addition to their focus on the roadbed, safety appliances, signaling systems, and communication equipment, the PRR's system builders paid close attention to the freight cars that ran over their right of way. By carrying cargoes, freight cars earned money for the railroad. Unfortunately, they also cost money, both to build and to operate, particularly when they ran empty in one direction, absent a revenue-generating backhaul. For much of the PRR's history, car builders struggled to increase capacity while minimizing the tare (empty) weight of each car. For more than a hundred years, from 1846 until the years following World War II, the railroad freight car evolved gradually, as fixed four-wheel suspensions gave way to two-axle trucks, and as steel replaced wood. Cars also increased substantially in capacity, yet car types changed little. Flatcars, little more than wooden platforms atop wheels, were the simplest to construct, were easy to load and unload, and could accommodate bulky cargoes. The addition of sideboards transformed the flatcar into a gondola, which could transport coal, iron ore, and other mineral products. Hopper cars possessed higher sides, for greater

capacity, and drop bottoms that permitted faster unloading. The ubiquitous boxcar accommodated an extraordinary variety of cargoes, from grain to lumber, to machinery and automobiles—anything that required protection from the weather.

The earliest freight cars on the Pennsylvania Railroad were extraordinarily simple, both in design and in construction. In April 1848 the board authorized Chief Engineer Thomson to place contracts for seventy-five freight cars from the firm of Kimball & Gorton. By January 1850, the board had authorized the purchase of an additional 250 freight cars. They included 100 four-wheel freight cars (from Adam Johnson of Reading, Pennsylvania), 25 stock cars, and 108 more modern eight-wheel freight cars from Kimball & Gorton. By 1851, the PRR owned more than four hundred cars, nearly three-quarters of which were generic boxcars, along with nearly a hundred stock cars and a mere twenty-three "platform" (flat) cars. During the decades that followed, through war and economic expansion, the size and complexity of the freight car fleet increased steadily.[202]

By the early twentieth century, the Pennsylvania Railroad had assembled a massive collection of equipment, which peaked in 1919, at nearly three hundred thousand cars. In 1912 alone, the railroad ordered more than $20 million worth of freight cars, including six thousand boxcars and one thousand automobile cars. The following year, the PRR invested a further $16 million in its freight car fleet. PRR employees built equipment at the shops in Altoona, in addition to the thousands of cars that the PRR purchased from builders such as the Bethlehem Steel Corporation, the Pressed Steel Car Company, the Standard Steel Car Company, the Pullman Company, and American Car & Foundry. The contributions of those independent firms proved particularly important, as the PRR typically relied on outsiders for innovations, most notably in the area of steel construction.[203]

The Basic Boxcar

The ubiquitous boxcar was the most common type of railroad equipment in the United States, but the PRR was not a typical railroad. Particularly after the repeal

Figure 62. By the time of the Civil War, Pennsylvania Railroad freight equipment had advanced only marginally beyond what the company had used at the time it began operations. Most of the light two-axle cars were gone, replaced by cars riding on pairs of four-wheeled trucks. Still, the boxcar and platform (flat) car predominated. Their wooden construction and primitive trucks sharply limited their carrying capacity.

Pennsylvania Historical and Museum Commission, Railroad Museum of Pennsylvania.

in 1861 of the Pennsylvania tonnage tax, the company transported enormous quantities of steel, coal, and other bulk commodities, and relied heavily on flat, gondola, and hopper cars. But, the PRR also served the densest concentration of manufacturing in the United States, as well as the nation's most populous cities. As such, PRR freight trains accommodated a wide range of high-value finished products, almost all of which rode in boxcars. In 1853, the railroad had barely two hundred boxcars in service, yet that number increased rapidly to more than three thousand in 1880.[204]

A typical boxcar in service in 1880, dating perhaps to the time of the Civil War, weighed only ten tons, was twenty-seven feet long, and held twelve tons of cargo—anything from sawn lumber to barrels of flour to consignments of less-than-carload-lot (LCL) traffic. Wood was cheap and readily available, with oak (along with a little ash and hickory) used for sills, bolsters, and other structural members, and pine forming the car's sheathing. The more than 3,500 board feet of lumber that went into a typical boxcar cost the railroad no more than $87, well below the $150 worth of wrought iron and cast iron components. Even though each boxcar was a handcrafted item, labor represented less than 10 percent ($47.06) of the $556.82 cost of the car.[205]

By the late 1800s the average PRR boxcar was larger and more sturdily built, and accordingly more expensive, than its counterparts on other railroads. Many of the changes occurred thanks to chief of motive power Theodore N. Ely, who was a staunch advocate of larger cars. Seeking ways to move freight more efficiently, particularly after the depression of the 1870s, Ely insisted that more capacious boxcars represented a slightly higher initial cost, but that they produced substantial dividends in the form of increased cubic volume. Unfortunately, Ely's recommendations that boxcars should be wider and higher required the railroad to increase lineside clearances, a process that could prove more expensive than the new cars themselves. Cars could be made longer, but Ely himself concluded that a mere two-foot addition to average car length would force the railroad to increase siding and yard capacity by a third. Longer cars were also heavier cars, which in turn mandated better truck designs. And, as some PRR officials (most notably Lines West general manager Leonor F. Loree) argued, it was inefficient to manufacture cars larger than the average load that they were designed to carry.[206]

During the late 1800s and early 1900s, PRR executives also sought to increase the efficiency of freight operations by classifying boxcars. Classification fostered more predictable loading methods while enabling operating officials to precisely compute train weights—which would in turn assist them in selecting the most appropriate motive power. In 1879, PRR officials sought to apply the benefits of uniformity to manufacturing as well as transportation. They developed the first standardized boxcar designs, beginning with the Class XA. Through the end of the nineteenth century, however, the techniques of boxcar construction changed little. As the twentieth century dawned, steel would radically change the construction, if not the use, of boxcars. That transformation emanated from a very different type of equipment, one that formed the mainstay of the PRR's freight car fleet.[207]

From Cars for Coal to Cars of Steel

Coal constituted the single most important commodity that traveled over the Pennsylvania Railroad, and the cars that transported it were a vital part of the company's operations. Because coal was heavy and virtually indestructible, a variety of open-top gondola and hopper cars sufficed for its transportation. PRR mechanical engineers nonetheless devoted considerable time and effort to the improvement of coal car designs. In general, they faced four problems. First, coal demand fluctuated wildly according to the season of the year and the state of the industrial economy. The provision of sufficient cars to satisfy the maximum output of every on-line colliery would have taxed the PRR's capital reserves to their limit, so car shortages were an unavoidable aspect of the coal business. Second, whereas a boxcar might carry grain to tidewater and return west with manufactured goods, coal cars often carried loads in only one direction, with no backhaul. By the early twentieth century, PRR crews transported coal to lake ports and used the same equipment to bring iron ore southward, but the more efficient equipment utilization entailed the construction of cars sturdy enough to accommodate the greater density of ore. Third, the PRR's mechanical engineers struck a balance between the ease of unloading and the simplicity of construction and maintenance. Gondolas were little more than tubs on wheels, inexpensive to build and rugged in service. Unfortunately, they were slow and labor-intensive to unload, as crews shoveled out the coal by hand. Hopper cars (and their cousins, the drop-bottom gondola) emptied easily, but the door mechanisms were expensive to install, prone to damage, and in the case of wooden cars, interfered with the truss rods that stiffened the underframe. Furthermore, while gondolas could carry steel, lumber, and other products in addition to coal, hopper cars were generally unsuited for any service except coal, sand, rock, or iron ore. Finally, PRR mechanical engineers generally focused their skills most intently on efforts to reduce the tare weight of each car. As part of that process, they developed new designs and employed new materials that steadily increased the cubic capacity of cars used in coal service. The most important transformation involved the use of steel, a policy that in turn revolutionized the design of the PRR's entire freight-car fleet.

The earliest cars used in coal service, often referred to as "jimmies," were little more than boxes set atop pedestals that supported two axles and four wheels. In 1853, the PRR acquired an initial group of two hundred such cars, and the Reading owned an equal number, employed in the jointly operated service to the docks at Port Richmond. With limited capacity and poor riding qualities, the jimmies gradually gave way to gondolas, generally flatcars with sideboards that rested on a pair of independently pivoting four-wheel trucks.[208]

Until the early twentieth century, the PRR records did not differentiate between gondolas and hopper cars and, between 1862 and 1900, made no official distinction between flat and gondola cars, but the railroad nonetheless used many, if not most, gondolas to transport coal. In 1866, when the PRR rostered more than nine thousand freight cars (a total that did not include the equipment of freight forwarders that operated over the system), nearly four thousand of those were gondolas, the largest single component of the total.[209]

By 1869, PRR officials had begun to assign classification standards to the gondola fleet, beginning with the thirty-foot-long Class GA, which weighed nine and a half tons and could accommodate a fourteen-ton load. The car included hinged sides that swung outward, simplifying the unloading process. Because the bed of the hopper compartment was flat, much like the deck of a flatcar, shovel-wielding laborers were needed to remove all of the coal. By 1874, designers had incorporated a self-clearing feature on the Class GB, which featured a depressed center hopper to funnel discharging cargoes to a central area beneath the car—although some cleanup shoveling was necessary to fully empty the load. To compensate for the absence of truss rods, which would have interfered with the low-slung hopper bottom, PRR designers created an unusually short car, twenty-six feet long, with a hopper compartment that was two feet shorter than that. This car held a mere twenty tons, although the railroad progressively increased that capacity to thirty tons on the later Class GD. The same basic design re-

mained in production until 1902, with between fifteen thousand and twenty thousand in service.[210]

In 1895, Lines West personnel developed a far superior design, one that soon exerted a profound influence on Lines East as well. George L. Potter, the superintendent of motive power for the Northwest System of Lines West, was responsible for significant improvements in the PRR's hopper design. By the early 1890s, Potter had observed a variety of hopper cars belonging to other railroads as they sat in the freight yards near his office in Fort Wayne. He chose the best elements from each of the cars he saw and combined them into a master design, the Class GG, which was the first true hopper car on the Pennsylvania Railroad. The thirty-foot-long car could carry thirty-five tons—nearly double its tare weight—in two hopper compartments. The car could discharge its load in well under a minute and was the first car that was entirely self-clearing, and thus did not require shoveling.[211]

Yet, at the time they were built, the GG hopper cars were already on the verge of obsolescence. A composite of the best existing designs, they broke no new ground, and they represented the outer limits of wood's applicability in freight car construction. Officials on Lines East concluded that steel fabrication represented the only realistic solution to the capacity problem, yet they were reluctant to commit to full-scale construction. Their hesitancy was not for want of knowledge, for as early as 1887 PRR shop crews had used steel components to build some special-purpose cars, generally used to transport heavy coils of wire rope. Instead, managers shied away from the cost of a massive research and development program and the commitment to the tooling that would be necessary to build large numbers of steel cars at the Altoona shops. As a result, the development of steel hopper cars owed as much to outside innovators as it did to PRR personnel.[212]

Two steel manufacturers, Andrew Carnegie and Charles T. Schoen, were principally responsible for the initial development of steel freight cars. By the 1890s, Carnegie was seeking additional markets for steel, and in 1894 Carnegie Steel entered into a joint venture with the Fox Solid Pressed Steel Car Company to manufacture an all-steel flatcar. Hopper cars were a logical next step, and Keystone Bridge Company engineer J. B. Hardie, in tandem with Carnegie Steel executive Charles Taylor, designed a prototype that employed structural steel shapes. Hardie was particularly impressed with the wood GG hopper used on Lines West, largely because of its innovative self-clearing feature. The Keystone Bridge Company, a Carnegie firm and a longtime PRR supplier, built two steel cars and placed them on display at the 1896 Master Car-Builders' Association convention in Saratoga, New York. They then entered revenue service on the Carnegie-owned Pittsburgh, Bessemer & Lake Erie Railroad. The two cars initially generated little interest, primarily because traditionalists asserted, correctly, that chemical impurities in coal would leach out and corrode the metal.[213]

Schoen, a former journeyman cooper who made a small fortune as a spring manufacturer in Philadelphia, believed that he could improve the Carnegie design and, more importantly, bypass the steelmaker's patents. In 1888, Schoen had experienced an epiphany of sorts, believing that he could drastically lower the cost of building freight cars by substituting prefabricated steel panels for traditional piece-by-piece wood construction. He moved to Pittsburgh two years later, but neither investors nor railroad officials supported his endeavors.

Schoen's fortunes soon improved, thanks to the rapid increase in coal production that accompanied the nation's recovery from the depression of the 1890s. In 1888, Lines East personnel had used 16,827 hopper and gondola cars for the purpose of transporting coal. By 1896, the number had increased to 23,959, with a further eight thousand cars added over the following two years.[214] Under those circumstances, PRR officials anxiously sought any improvements that could increase coal-carrying capacity. In 1897, Schoen worked with Pennsylvania Railroad engineers to more or less simultaneously develop two all-steel car designs, the GM and the GL. The GM, which appears to have been developed largely by PRR personnel, was something of a throwback to earlier gondola designs. It contained two hoppers, each with a drop-bottom door, but the car lacked interior slope sheets and was not self-discharging, and it resembled a conventional gondola more than a true hopper car. Taking full advantage of

steel's tensile strength, the designers dispensed with conventional side sills, using the sides themselves as trusses. The car possessed a great virtue in that its tare weight was less than 31 percent of its rated load. The labor costs associated with emptying the car by hand canceled out the favorable load-to-weight ratio, and after production began in June 1898, only five of the cars ever entered service.[215]

The other design, the Class GL, proved far more successful, and served as a milestone in the development of freight cars. The car was a collaborative effort between Schoen and PRR officials representing both Lines East and Lines West. Like Carnegie Steel personnel, they essentially translated the Class GG wooden car into steel. The Schoen team also copied many elements of the Carnegie car, but substituted pressed steel for Carnegie's structural steel. Like the GG, the GL was self-clearing, which dramatically reduced labor costs. The car weighed 39,150 pounds empty, only slightly more than the GM (33,800 pounds), and was not that much heavier than the wooden GG (35,200 pounds). The GL had a slightly smaller cubic capacity than the gondola-like GM, but both cars were rated at fifty tons, mainly because of limitations in the weight-bearing abilities of the trucks.[216] In any case, the GL was vastly more efficient than the GG, which could carry only thirty-five tons. Because both classes of cars were the same length, Schoen and PRR mechanical engineers had effectively increased per-train haulage capacity by almost 43 percent with the GL design. The Schoen GL hopper car debuted at the 1897 Master Car-Builders' Association convention and soon attracted favorable attention. Although the car was developed largely for the PRR, Schoen's first order went to Carnegie's Pittsburgh, Bessemer & Lake Erie Railroad, with four hundred cars manufactured with Carnegie's rolled steel and six hundred fabricated with Schoen's pressed-steel manufacturing methods.[217]

Within a few months, the PRR's Lines West officials were sufficiently impressed to order two hundred cars, slightly larger than the Pittsburgh, Bessemer & Lake Erie equipment but otherwise virtually identical in design. In April 1898, Lines East ordered a thousand cars, at a cost of approximately $1 million, for service between Pittsburgh and the coal and ore terminals at the Lake Erie ports. "This is the largest single contract ever given for steel cars," noted the *New York Times*, "and the fact that it was placed by the Pennsylvania Railroad Company leads to the belief that other smaller lines will quickly adopt the use of steel cars."[218] They were the largest hopper cars built up to that time, and they could carry fifty-two tons of coal to the Great Lakes and return with fifty-five tons of denser iron ore—far more than the forty-ton limit of even the strongest wood hopper car. Within a short time, the PRR began rebuilding its coal-and ore-handling facilities, installing various types of mechanical systems that could load and unload lake boats as rapidly as the GL cars could bring in coal or take away ore.[219]

The GL ensured Charles Schoen's success as a manufacturer, while beginning the transformation of car-building from a highly skilled craft to something approaching assembly line status. In January 1899, the Schoen Pressed Steel Company merged with the Fox

Solid Pressed Steel Company, forming the Pressed Steel Car Company, which employed nearly twelve thousand workers. A month later, Schoen agreed to purchase all of his steel from Carnegie in exchange for the Scotsman's promise that he would not manufacture railway equipment. The Pressed Steel Car Company flourished, in large measure because Schoen applied mass-production techniques to freight car production. He was able to cut costs still further by de-skilling the work force. After a 1903 strike, Schoen fired most of his employees and replaced them with unskilled workers from eastern Europe. In 1909, under the leadership of the Industrial Workers of the World, they in turn struck over low wages and horrific working conditions. The subsequent Pressed Steel Strike (also known as the McKee's Rocks Strike) was one of the most violent in the United States, with eleven people dying in a riot and gun battle on August 22.[220]

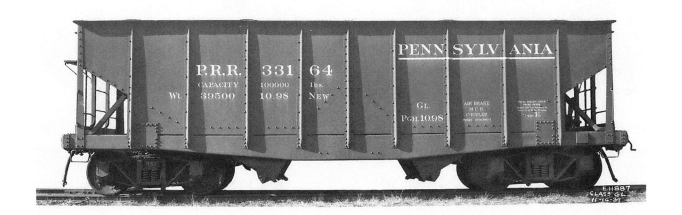

Figure 63. In October 1898, the Schoen Pressed Steel Company constructed the first Class GL hopper cars for the Pennsylvania Railroad. The design was not all that different from earlier Class GG wooden hopper cars. What set the new cars apart was their construction from pressed-steel components, which increased capacity and lowered the all-important ratio between dead weight and paying load. The earlier GG hoppers had required PRR locomotives to move 45.7 pounds of dead weight for every hundred pounds of coal. The new steel design lowered the ratio to 36.4 pounds for every hundred pounds of cargo.

Pennsylvania Railroad Negative Collection, Hagley Museum and Library.

The use of steel in freight car construction was only one of several factors that precipitated a surge in car orders during the earliest years of the twentieth century. As the nation recovered from the depression of the 1890s, the PRR experienced severe car shortages, with 1899 being a particularly bad year. PRR officials were desperate for new equipment, particularly if it promised to increase capacity. Yet, as with air brakes and automatic couplers, changes in freight car designs owed much to cooperation among executives representing multiple railroads. To a large degree, the car shortage problem stemmed from the manner in which railroads received compensation for cars that had strayed from their home rails. By the 1880s, with the standardization of rail gauge and equipment designs, it had become increasingly common for shipments to remain in the same car as they traveled over the tracks of several railroads from origin to destination. The railroad that owned and maintained the car possessed a strong incentive to retrieve its equipment as quickly as possible and return it to its property, where it could be used to generate additional revenue. Likewise, the other railroads had ample reason to keep the car as long as possible, using equipment that they did not own to augment their bottom line.

To alleviate the poaching problem, railroaders instituted a system of mileage charges that allowed the owning railroad to bill the other carriers based on the distance the car had traveled. The mileage basis did not address the tendency of shippers to retain cars for long periods, either because they were slow to load or unload them, or because they used the cars as warehouses on wheels. The problem was particularly acute in the coalfields, as mine owners were able to maintain a constant level of production by employing hopper cars to store large quantities of coal in anticipation of seasonal fluctuations in demand. Under the mileage system a car could remain in one location for months and—because it did not move—generate no income for the railroad that owned it. Accordingly, in 1902 the members of the American Railway Association, the dominant trade group, replaced the mileage basis with a per diem system. The change pleased the executives of many western railroads, where the long distances between city pairs had generated high mileage charges. In theory, the per diem system would have resolved the car shortage problem on the PRR, as the daily rental payments should have discouraged shippers from using cars for storage and should have encouraged other railroads to return cars to the PRR as quickly as possible. From the perspective of PRR officials, however, the per diem rates were set too low. As such, shippers, especially coal producers, often concluded that the daily charges were an acceptable cost of doing business and continued to store their cargoes in PRR-owned cars. Western railroads possessed a strong incentive to poach cars from the PRR and other equipment-rich northeastern carriers, not only to avoid the expense of purchasing and maintaining their own fleets but also to generate revenues (which were based on mileage) on shipments that covered half the continent, while paying the relatively minor daily fees. As such, the 1902 rules made the PRR's equipment shortage even worse, forcing the company to buy thousands of new cars as rapidly as possible.[221]

The Class GL steel hopper car provided a fortuitous solution to the PRR's most pressing equipment-shortage problem. By 1902 the railroad owned ten thousand GL hopper cars, and in 1905 ordered twenty thousand similar Class GP and GPa cars. Coke, lighter than coal, became an important commodity on the PRR at the beginning of the twentieth century, and the GPa cars accordingly came equipped with coke racks—basically slatted side extensions—to increase capacity. Similar steel fabrication methods were also used on the Class FL flatcar, followed shortly by the Class FM. In 1902, the PRR purchased its first steel gondolas, the Class GS. Beginning in 1908 the railroad differentiated between wooden and steel freight cars, recording each type separately.[222]

By 1909, with thousands of steel hopper cars in service, PRR personnel had begun to differentiate between the older generic gondola (Class G) and the new functionally differentiated hoppers (Class H). The first of the new class was the H21, a car that was substantially longer than the GL, and with four hopper bays instead of the earlier two. With a capacity of 2,508 cubic feet, the car was half again as large as the original GL and double the size of the wood GG. With their large cubic capacity, the new cars were ideally suited for hauling coke. Over the next decade, the PRR began equipping the cars with stronger trucks, increasing their capacity from forty to fifty tons, and facilitating their use in coal service. The PRR eventually rostered more than 39,000 H21 cars, along with 4,500 of the similar H22, and some remained in use until the 1970s.[223]

During World War I, officials from the USRA attempted to increase manufacturing and transportation efficiency through a series of standard locomotive and freight car designs. The preferred hopper model was a short, two-bay car that in many ways was a throwback to the older Class GL. Representatives from many of the carriers refused to accept their allotment of USRA cars, and one railroad was forced to comply by court order. PRR executives were able to persuade USRA officials that the materials earmarked for the standard-design cars would be better employed in the construction of H25 four-bay cars, using a design that was essentially identical to the H21. The PRR was one of thirteen railroads that refused to order USRA hopper cars, but it was the only one to receive such a consideration.[224]

By 1919, PRR car designers envisioned even more massive hopper cars, such as the H26, with a capacity of 105 tons, and the G23 gondola, with a capacity of 110 tons. Each of the cars rode on a pair of massive three-axle trucks, necessary to support a hopper car that weighed almost forty-two tons, and a gondola that weighed more than thirty-seven tons. The PRR's Altoona shops had built one prototype of each car immediately prior to World War I, but the USRA's control over the railroads prevented more widespread production. That may have been just as well, as the cars were too large for efficient use and probably would have required extensive track improvements if used in large numbers.[225]

During the early years of the twentieth century, the success of the GL hopper car was one of several factors that ensured the widespread use of steel on other types of freight equipment. By the end of the nineteenth century, all-wood boxcars were proving inadequate for the PRR's needs. They were neither strong nor capacious enough to accommodate increasing volumes of freight. More important, their underframes, even when supported by truss rods, were too weak to withstand the stresses caused by longer and heavier trains. As PRR designers increased the size and power of

steam locomotives, they unleashed forces that could tear trains apart, ripping draft gear loose from underframes and splintering wooden cars. At the same time, the cost of lumber escalated rapidly, as did wages for skilled woodworkers. When steelmakers improved the quality and reduced the price of their products, they correspondingly increased the feasibility of steel boxcar construction. Finally, the construction of the New York Improvements, with a series of tunnels linking New Jersey, Manhattan, and Long Island, precluded the use of fire-prone wooden passenger cars. PRR mechanical engineers assisted in the development of steel passenger cars, based in part on equipment used on the New York subways, and they were able to transfer their expertise to the construction of freight cars, as well.

Initially, PRR officials favored hybrid boxcar designs, retaining wood for the car body while utilizing structural steel for the load-bearing underframe. By 1901, the American Railway Association had developed new design standards for hybrid boxcars—thirty-six feet long; eight feet, six inches in width; and eight feet interior height, with a capacity of forty tons. PRR mechanical engineers responded with the Class XL boxcar, the first steel-underframe car on the railroad. With improved trucks, each car could accommodate fifty tons of cargo, an increase of 25 percent over all-wood designs. The XL also introduced standardized production methods that employed special-purpose steel presses and machine tools, greatly increasing manufacturing speed. The advent of steel underframes, combined with equipment shortages and the aging of the all-wood fleet, stimulated a rapid increase in orders for boxcars during the first years of the twentieth century. PRR shop forces built or purchased more than thirty-seven thousand XL boxcars between 1901 and 1913. The XL became the PRR's standard boxcar for the next decade, and as late as 1925 it represented more than half of the railroad's boxcar fleet.

Once PRR engineers had standardized the production of steel underframes, they were able to use the same design and production methods on other classes of cars. They included ventilated boxcars, Class RF refrigerator cars, and livestock cars, and by 1903, the PRR had 46,696 steel and steel-underframe cars in service. Beginning in 1906, in response to the small

Figure 64. The Class XL boxcar, first built in 1901, outwardly resembled earlier boxcar designs. There was a notable change, however, in that designers had replaced the wooden underframe and its associated truss rods with a steel underframe that could accommodate heavier loads and withstand the tremendous forces that a long freight train exerted on each car's draft gear.

Pennsylvania Railroad Negative Collection, Hagley Museum and Library.

but increasing production of motor vehicles, the Pennsylvania Railroad employed the XL underframe on automobile boxcars.[226]

Within a decade of their development, the composite steel-underframe boxcars were beginning to show signs of obsolescence. On the X23, first built in 1912, designers retained the customary wood sheathing but replaced the cars' wooden side trusses with steel, atop a steel underframe. The new equipment increased the standard length of the PRR's boxcars from thirty-six feet to forty feet, which would remain the standard for many decades to come. As with the XL design, the nearly seven thousand X23 boxcars were joined by similar cars, including more than three thousand R7 refrigerator cars and two thousand X24 automobile cars.

In 1913 the wooden sheathing of the X23 boxcar yielded to all-steel construction. Between 1915 and 1919, shop forces employed the same basic design in the construction of nearly ten thousand X25 cars. By 1919, representatives from the USRA had developed a series of standard boxcar designs, which proved more successful than their corresponding efforts with hoppers. The PRR and other eastern railroads with restrictive clearances utilized versions of this basic design, but with a lower car height, resulting in models such as the X26. Following the war, the Car Construction Committee of the American Railway Association developed a modified USRA design, one that the PRR copied in virtually every detail. The PRR variant of the USRA design evolved into the X29, the most common early steel boxcar on the railroad. Production began in 1924 and continued for the next decade.[227]

While wood and composite cars remained in service for many years to come, they were gradually phased out, either scrapped or converted to maintenance-of-way service. The onset of the Great Depression temporarily prolonged the life of many older cars, as cost-conscious executives were anxious to avoid the expense of more modern replacements. In 1936, however, the economy began to show signs of improvement, and the PRR board authorized the construction of ten thousand new steel freight cars. That decision consigned to destruction some thirty-two thousand wood and composite cars, including almost all of the remaining XL boxcars, automobile cars, and RF refrigerator cars.[228]

While PRR officials continued to make small, incremental improvements to hopper cars, boxcars, and other freight equipment, the basic designs changed little from the standards established by the H21 hopper car and the X29 boxcar. Forty-foot steel boxcars (with some fifty-foot variants for bulkier cargoes, including automobiles and furniture) remained the standard length on the PRR and other American railroads. For the next three decades, the railroads made few alterations to the basic boxcar design, in part because ICC rate schedules for LCL freight provided little financial incentive for concentrating shipments in fewer, larger cars. Since the late nineteenth century, mechanical engineers on the PRR and other railroads had succeeded admirably in reducing tare weights. Their efforts mattered little in the case of boxcars, however, as that equipment typically housed cargoes that were far smaller than the car's rated capacity. The resulting inefficiencies ensured that beginning in the 1920s, even as PRR designers were perfecting the X29, the railroad would experience considerable difficulty in competing against motor carriers for LCL traffic.

Improving the System

Freight cars and automatic signals, couplers and airbrakes, telegraphy and telephony—all were designed to make the Pennsylvania Railroad function more efficiently. That quest for efficiency began almost as soon as the PRR had been incorporated, and continued through the company's 1968 merger into the Penn Central. Yet, the last two decades of the nineteenth century witnessed the most rapid and sustained gains in efficiency in the history of American railroading. George Brooke Roberts and his system builders presided over one of the most productive periods in the history of the Pennsylvania Railroad. Lines East personnel moved almost four times the total freight ton-

nage in 1899 as they had in 1880, yet expenses barely doubled. Thanks to a heavy concentration of coal, iron ore, and steel traffic, the Pennsylvania Railroad, east of Pittsburgh and Erie, possessed the highest traffic density, as well as the lowest operating costs, per ton of freight, of any of the trunk lines. By the late 1880s the PRR routinely operated freight trains of nearly 2,500 tons, far heavier than most of its competitors. All told, the PRR and its subsidiaries handled something like an eighth of the nation's total freight tonnage. That remarkable performance facilitated the great surge in industrial expansion that remade the American landscape and the American economy.[229]

The PRR's growth depended mightily on a remarkable level of cooperation between the technical specialists who built the system and the personnel who operated it. That cooperation was in turn based on a mutual understanding that each employee was responsible for maximizing the performance measure known as the ton-mile, while minimizing the operating ratio. As its name suggested, the ton-mile represented the number of tons moved one mile over the railroad.[230] The PRR posted laudable growth in ton-miles thanks in large measure to the functionally specialized middle managers who deployed steel rails, track pans, automatic couplers, air brakes, signaling and communications systems, and more capacious freight cars in an effort to increase capacity and improve efficiency. Between 1870 and 1899, the PRR experienced a tenfold increase in ton-miles, from just over one billion to 10.9 billion.[231]

The impressive statistics nonetheless masked serious underlying problems. The ton-mile became the standard measure of performance in railroading largely because it was the easiest statistic to calculate. While executives in the railroad's Treasury and Accounting Departments were primarily responsible for long-term capital and financial accounting measures, cost accounting remained largely under the control of the Transportation Department. As such, transportation personnel used the ton-mile as a convenient measure to assess the relative performance of each operating division and its personnel. Division superintendents who posted high ton-mile figures, relative to expenditures, were deemed to be efficient and capable managers, worthy of promotion. Executives soon realized that their careers depended on their ability to move as much freight as possible.[232]

As a result, the reliance on the ton-mile as a measure of productivity favored explosive increases in traffic without a corresponding increase in earnings. The ton-mile was at heart an engineering criterion, and efforts to increase tonnage generally called for engineering solutions. Most PRR managers were trained in engineering, and were naturally predisposed to seek technological mechanisms for increasing efficiency and ton-mile rates. The problem was that the end result was supposed to be an increase in net earnings, not merely an increase in traffic.

And, it was in the area of net earnings that the PRR's performance appeared less promising. As traffic multiplied, competitive system building exerted a downward pressure on rates, which fell by more than 40 percent in just the five years between 1875 and 1880. During the thirty years between 1855 and 1884, rates fell from 3.0 cents to 0.7 cents per ton-mile, a decrease of 77 percent. Freight and passenger rates hit bottom in 1899, at 0.473 cents per ton-mile. More problematically, the PRR's profit, per ton-mile, had fallen by 70 percent, from just under one cent in 1870 to barely a third of a cent in 1899. Between 1870 and 1880, ton-miles tripled, and earnings doubled. During the next decade, ton-miles doubled, while earnings increased by just over 50 percent. As the final decade of the nineteenth century came to an end, ton-miles increased by half, while earnings rose by only a little more than 12 percent.[233]

For the PRR's accountants, the operating ratio (that is, the percentage of earnings consumed by operating expenses), rather than the level of ton-miles, provided a better measure of efficiency. The PRR's operating ratio was 51.7 in 1873, 54.1 in 1879, 68.1 in 1891, 70.0 in 1896, and 65.6 in 1900. The 1900 figure was well below that of the chronically troubled Erie (with an operating ratio of 71.7), but was nonetheless above that of the New York Central (62.4) and the Baltimore & Ohio (64.6). The PRR's operating ratio was not a precise measure of the company's performance, especially as some components of the system—most notably the United Railroads of New Jersey Grand Division—had substantially higher terminal costs and thus a disproportionately large operating ratio, compared to the re-

mainder of Lines East. Nonetheless, PRR executives were concerned about the generally upward trend of the operating ratio, as well as the unfavorable comparisons with other trunk lines. With progressively less money available to pay non-operating expenses, bond interest, and stock dividends, it seemed that massive increases in capital investments were not generating massive benefits for the company and its investors.[234]

By 1900, the PRR's executives were trapped in a vicious cycle, spending ever-larger sums to increase capacity and capture additional traffic, but knowing full well that increased capacity would only cause rates to decline even further. There were limits to the railroad's ability to generate capacity ahead of demand, however, and by the end of the nineteenth century, those limits had largely been reached. Although all railroads in the United States experienced that crisis of productivity, the PRR suffered more than most. Western railroads, despite their low traffic density, were able to amortize terminal costs over long line hauls between widely spaced city pairs. They also collected relatively undifferentiated agricultural commodities from a variety of locations and funneled them to a small number of gateway cities, such as Chicago or St. Louis. Eastern railroads accommodated a wide range of industrial, mineral, and agricultural items, and serviced a far larger number of communities en route. Because freight tended to travel shorter distances in the East than in the West, eastern railroads found it more difficult to distribute terminal costs over a long line haul. By the end of the nineteenth century, the Northeast became more urban, and its economy more diversified and consumer oriented. The region accordingly became less dependent on the PRR's traditional mainstays of coal, iron ore, and steel. As such, the variety of commodities multiplied, while the size of the average shipment declined considerably. Shippers now demanded—and were willing to pay for—premium service in fast preference trains that interfered with the PRR's traditional reliance on low-speed freight operations. In densely populated northeastern cities, freight shipments moved through congested terminal trackage, increasing switching costs.[235]

PRR engineers nonetheless succeeded remarkably well in overcoming the difficulties associated with northeastern railroading. Congestion was a fluid, rather

Figure 65. This frequently reproduced photograph, circa 1907, illustrates the severe congestion that affected the PRR during the early years of the twentieth century, yet the situation was not as dire as this image would suggest. The location, on the eastern slope of the Allegheny Mountains, near the Horseshoe Curve, had long been one of the busiest on the entire system. Furthermore, the train in the foreground is not in revenue service, but is instead composed of work equipment being used to clear a rockslide that formed but a temporary impediment to the PRR's operations. In general, technological improvements, such as the elaborate signal system that features prominently in the photograph, were capable of maintaining the free flow of traffic—but only so long as the PRR continued to earn sufficient revenues to pay the costs associated with building and maintaining the physical plant.

Library of Congress, Prints & Photographs Division, LC-USZ62-93787.

than a fixed, problem. Traffic levels varied according to the overall performance of the economy, declining in "dull" times and accelerating during periods of prosperity. Congestion also varied seasonally, becoming more acute during the autumn and into the winter, as western farmers rushed grain to eastern markets and as the demand for coal increased. As such, the simple passage of time would enable PRR crews to clear blockages and catch up to the temporary surge in freight traffic. Furthermore, PRR engineers continually identified choke points in the system, targeting them for improvements that would increase capacity. Especially severe bottlenecks existed only in a few relatively small areas, such as at Pittsburgh and on the eastern slope of the Alleghenies—and even then assumed crisis proportions for only a few years early in the twentieth century, peaking around 1903. In May of that year, the PRR introduced a new series of luxury "Blue Ribbon" passenger trains that traveled on accelerated schedules. Despite the burgeoning traffic levels, and amid the long slow freights carrying coal and steel, the *Chicago Limited*, the *New York Limited*, the *St. Louis Limited*, and all of the others generally managed to get through on time. So long as rates remained sufficiently remunerative, congestion was at worst only a temporary problem.

By the early years of the twentieth century, however, rates were declining faster than costs, progressively diminishing the revenues that PRR executives required to invest in the physical plant and equipment to create additional gains in efficiency. By the late 1800s, moreover, the pace of productivity was beginning to slow. The creation of through routes; the standardization of track gauge; the replacement of car ferries or wooden bridges with spans of steel and stone; and the installation of signal systems, couplers, air brakes, and steel rails had been hallmarks of late nineteenth-century railroading, and had dramatically lowered operating costs per ton-mile. By 1900, however, railroad executives could count on incrementally better cars and locomotives, but not on the stunning gains in efficiency that they had known in the past.[236]

More ominously, shippers and passengers had come to expect rapid improvements in service and corresponding decreases in rates, and they evinced little sympathy for the slowdown in productivity gains. They were more likely to excoriate the railroads for monopolizing the transportation sector of the economy, in seeming contravention of the public interest. Even though rates declined steadily as a percentage of the value of manufactured products, shippers insisted that rates were still too high in absolute terms—and the anti-corporatist impulses of the Progressive era provided them with powerful allies in local and national government.[237]

By the dawn of the twentieth century, PRR executives had begun to realize that their company was not rich enough, and could not build quickly enough, to unclog the system or to guarantee adequate profits. That was a remarkable admission for a corps of managers who were first and foremost civil engineers. Even more remarkable was their willingness to embrace cooperation with other railroads, with investment bankers, and with the federal government. Because they could no longer count on perpetual increases in efficiency, and because they could no longer build their way to prosperity, those associated with the Pennsylvania Railroad would find it necessary to place more reliance on cooperation than on competition. Henceforth, PRR executives would have to focus on order and on regulation, rather than on new construction.

Chapter 14

Regulation
1899–1910

During the closing years of the nineteenth century, the railroads were desperately in need of regulation. The flurry of competitive system building that had taken place during the 1880s had left many carriers in a weakened financial condition, unable to cope with the economic disaster that began in 1893. Despite the best efforts of Albert Fink and the Trunk Line Association, executives had failed to maintain rates, and one cartel arrangement after another succumbed to the insatiable demand to satisfy fixed costs by maximizing traffic. The Interstate Commerce Commission, far from providing order, had failed to satisfy the demands of shippers or railroaders, thanks in large measure to ongoing debates as to whether the courts or administrative agencies should exercise regulatory power.

Yet, if everyone agreed that something should be done, there was little consensus on how regulation should be implemented. Railway executives, in tandem with investment bankers, argued that they possessed both the insider knowledge and the financial tools that were necessary to stabilize rates and improve service. Acting in concert, they established "communities of interest" that went well beyond earlier pooling arrangements. Through shared stock ownership and overlapping boards of directors, the various communities of interest permitted managers to maintain

rates and avoid destructive competition. The result was a new wave of realignments, mimicking the consolidations that had occurred in the 1850s, in the decade after the Civil War, and during the 1880s.[1]

The resulting increase in both revenues and investor confidence enabled a new generation of executives to remake the American railroad system. To cope with surging traffic, construction crews straightened curves, lowered grades, dug tunnels, and built massive bridges, viaducts, fills, and terminals. The reconstruction of the railroads increased efficiency and reduced rates, ensuring that transportation expense would constitute an ever-decreasing share of the cost of agricultural and manufactured products.

Yet, the *fin de siècle* rail renaissance coincided with a growing public aversion to the big businesses that were largely responsible for the nation's economic growth. During a period of social and political transformation often referred to as the Progressive era, reformers attacked the types of collusive practices that railroad executives had employed to stabilize their business activities. Rather than allow railroaders and bankers to regulate each other, critics asserted that both national and state governments deserved a larger role in the regulation of the railroads. Those reformist impulses soon shaped the nature of railway regulation, particularly at the federal level. Whereas railway

Figure 66. As the son of an investment banker, Alexander J. Cassatt (1839–1906) enjoyed a life of wealth and privilege, with access to the highest echelons of economic and political power. He was also a talented engineer and a superb manager, with an eye for detail and procedure. Elevated to the PRR presidency in 1899, amid a new round of rate wars that followed the nation's recovery from a severe economic depression, Cassatt become one of the most influential leaders of the Pennsylvania Railroad.

George Grantham Bain Collection, Library of Congress, Prints & Photographs Division, LC-USZ62-104964.

executives had initially hoped that regulatory agencies such as the Interstate Commerce Commission might serve as a venue for mediated settlements of inter-corporate disputes, by 1906 they began to confront a legislative mandate that the ICC do as much to control the railroads as to coordinate them. To a greater degree than ever before, railway executives had to step out of their offices and their corporate boardrooms, and away from the familiar world of surveys, track charts, and the other paraphernalia associated with civil engineering. They found themselves speaking to an often-hostile press, testifying before Congress and the ICC, and engaging the services of public-relations experts. By the beginning of the twentieth century, railroaders were engaged in rebuilding the railroads while they were simultaneously rebuilding the reputation of the railroad industry.

Alexander J. Cassatt

While the Union Pacific's Edward Henry Harriman exemplified the new breed of railroad executives in the West, his eastern counterpart was surely Alexander Johnston Cassatt, between 1899 and 1906 the president of the Pennsylvania Railroad. Cassatt blended considerable engineering talent with a cultured sophistication that guided his business and social relationships with some of the most influential individuals in the United States. In some respects, Cassatt represented J. Edgar Thomson's engineering expertise and Tom Scott's gregarious charm, melded together in a single individual. Cassatt gave all of the outward appearance of an American aristocrat, with his townhouse on Rittenhouse Square in Philadelphia and his country estate in Haverford, and his indulgence in the gentleman's sport of thoroughbred horse racing. Yet, at the time of his death in 1906, he maintained a net worth of only some $5 million—a large sum perhaps, but as the *New York Times* observed, "As wealth is counted among great railroad magnates President Cassatt was not a remarkably rich man."[2]

On December 8, 1839, Alexander J. Cassat (later changed to Cassatt) was born in Pittsburgh, across the state and worlds away from the prestige and sophistication of Philadelphia. His father, Robert S. Cassat, was of Dutch Huguenot ancestry, and his mother had a Scots-Irish heritage, backgrounds that were both quite different from the English Quakers whose descendants proved so influential in Philadelphia. The elder Cassat became wealthy from manufacturing and banking, but even so, his children attended public schools. He was occasionally credited as being the first mayor of Allegheny City, but William Robinson, Jr., an individual closely connected with the PRR, preceded him in that office.[3] Robert Cassatt (as the family name was by then known) moved his wife and children to Philadelphia, established the banking house of Lloyd, Cassatt & Company in 1872, and enjoyed considerable financial success.[4]

The Cassatt family acquired all of the trappings of affluence, but theirs was new money, and they lacked the pedigree of established wealth. Conditioned perhaps by insecurity, Robert Cassatt retired early and pursued a life of leisurely sophistication. He was also determined to expose his children to a world of art and culture, and that meant taking them to Europe. At a time when the Grand Tour was a fashionable diversion for the well-to-do, the Cassatt family spent the first half of the decade of the 1850s in Europe. Young Mary Cassatt was enchanted by European art and blossomed into a renowned painter.[5]

Alexander Cassatt lacked his sister's artistic inclinations, but he was equally influenced by European art, culture, and science. When the Cassatt family returned to the United States, in 1855, he remained behind to study engineering at the institution later known as the Darmstadt University of Technology. Following his return to the United States, he attended the Rensselaer Polytechnic Institute, graduating in 1859 at the age of twenty. Although he possessed a degree in civil engineering, his training—including a thesis on the efficiency of water turbines—was more indicative of mechanical engineering expertise. Like Thomson, Cassatt went to Georgia to survey railroads, until the Civil War sent him back north to take a position as a PRR rodman. From there his rise was meteoric. Tom Scott spotted Cassatt's talents and became the young engineer's guardian and mentor, advancing him in steady increments toward the presidency. In 1864, after the PRR established control over the Philadelphia & Erie Railroad, Scott arranged for Cassatt to serve as the resident engineer of the new subsidiary's Middle Division. Shortly afterward, in the midst of the oil wars and surging northwestern Pennsylvania traffic, Scott placed Cassatt in charge of the Warren & Franklin Railroad, an important feeder to the Philadelphia & Erie.

Cassatt possessed a superb eye for detail, an excellent memory, and a thorough knowledge of the practical aspects of railroad operations. His aptitude in mechanical engineering served him well, and he worked as the superintendent of motive power and machinery for the Philadelphia & Erie and later for the PRR itself. Cassatt also demonstrated a talent for negotiation, and he took the lead in the efforts to lease the United Canal & Railroad Companies of New Jersey. After the PRR took control in 1871, Cassatt—still in his early thirties—became the first general manager of the newly created Lines East of Pittsburgh and Erie. His job was to coordinate and integrate the operations of the New Jersey routes, as well as the Philadelphia & Erie, with the PRR. Two years later, Cassatt moved his family into Cheswold, a large estate that symbolized his growing influence within the PRR and its affiliated organizations. His wife, Lois, was the niece of President James Buchanan, and likewise the niece of composer Stephen Foster and of long-dead PRR vice president William B. Foster, Jr. Cheswold was located near the train station in Haverford, one of the affluent suburbs that PRR officials were helping to develop along what was becoming known as the Main Line.[6]

Tom Scott gained the presidency in June 1874, and Cassatt rode his coattails into the office of third vice president, in charge of transportation and traffic. He soon became the point man for the PRR's efforts to control the downward spiral of rates following the Panic of 1873. Along with Scott, he met numerous times with representatives from the other trunk lines. Cassatt also played a major role in the management of the South Improvement Company and its efforts to stabilize the oil trade. Amid public furor over the PRR's role in the oil cartel, Cassatt testified numerous times before Congress, the Pennsylvania legislature, and the state supreme court. With considerable frankness, Cassatt insisted that overzealous competition had saddled the PRR with such low rates that the railroad had been unable to earn a profit from the oil

trade. Yet, he was careful to place most of the blame on John D. Rockefeller and Standard Oil, and not on Scott or other PRR personnel. Cassatt's public criticism of Standard Oil was more theatrical than real, however. In April 1879, he was probably responsible for convincing newly inaugurated Governor Henry M. Hoyt to quash efforts to extradite John D. Rockefeller and other Standard Oil officials from Ohio to force them to testify in Pennsylvania courts.[7]

During the 1877 strikes in Pittsburgh, Cassatt made what turned out to be a serious error in judgment, one that may have exacerbated the violence and probably set back his career. Even though Robert Pitcairn and some of the other PRR officials stationed in Pittsburgh had advised restraint, Cassatt was anxious to protect PRR property and reestablish normal operations. He instructed the Philadelphia militia to clear the PRR tracks through the city. The resulting gunfire claimed the lives of at least ten demonstrators, and ignited riots that destroyed a substantial portion of the PRR's rail facilities. Cassatt was not directly responsible for the carnage, nor is it reasonable to assume that any conciliatory actions on his part could have prevented an already tense situation from spiraling out of control. Many newspaper editors, particularly those who supported the rights of the working man, nonetheless cast Alexander J. Cassatt as one of the chief villains of the 1877 riots. The incident did not destroy his usefulness to the Pennsylvania Railroad, but it did tarnish his reputation, while creating something of a public relations problem for the company.

As the protégé of Tom Scott, Cassatt probably expected to succeed him in the presidency. Instead, when ill health forced Scott to retire in May 1880, the office went to George Brooke Roberts. While the members of the board were doubtless concerned at the public's assessment of Cassatt's role in the 1877 Pittsburgh riots, they were far more determined to avoid the injudicious expansion and dubious financial projects that Scott had implemented. Cassatt was far from a clone of Scott, but First Vice President Roberts seemed to embody the restraint, engineering expertise, and quiet confidence that characterized J. Edgar Thomson. With the directors giving a clear signal that they intended to adopt a more cautious and conservative approach to doing business, Cassatt had to content himself with Roberts's old post of first vice president. In view of his expertise in managing the PRR's operation and rates, however, Cassatt retained oversight of transportation and traffic, the duties that he had previously undertaken as third vice president, an office that was now temporarily eliminated.[8]

For the next two years, Roberts and Cassatt attempted to get along. Yet, one was an introverted blueblood Philadelphia Quaker and the other an extroverted French Huguenot and Scots-Irish son of a self-made man, hailing from the western part of the state. Little evidence exists to suggest overt confrontations between the president and the first vice president, but the tension was there nonetheless. In 1882, Cassatt and his fellow Pennsylvania Railroad executives came to a mutually amicable parting of the ways. Like other PRR managers, Cassatt found himself overwhelmed by the workload and the stress associated with running such an enormous and complex corporation. As he noted in his letter of resignation to the board of directors, "My only object in taking this step is to have more time at my disposal than any one occupying so responsible a position in railroad management can command."[9]

Cassatt never really left the Pennsylvania Railroad, however. He retained an office in Philadelphia, along with the board's assurance that he could return to management at any time. Beginning in September 1883, he served on the PRR board of directors and chaired the Road Committee, and could thus help to informally shape PRR policies. In 1885, he became the president of the New York, Philadelphia & Norfolk Railroad, a company that was closely affiliated with, and later a part of, the PRR. Cassatt pursued other projects as well, ranging from stock speculation to serving as president of the Intercontinental Railway Commission, responsible for developing a plan to link North, Central, and South America by rail. In his leisure time, Cassatt engaged in a variety of activities, most of them connected to horses. He hunted foxes, raised thoroughbreds at his Chesterbrook Farm, and was president of the Monmouth Park Racing Association, endeavoring to make that racetrack the premier facility in the United States. Cassatt served as president of the Lancaster Avenue Improvement Company, a firm that acquired and rehabilitated the old Lan-

caster Turnpike (today's Lancaster Avenue, U.S. Route 30) between West Philadelphia and Paoli. He was also the supervisor of roads for Lower Merion Township, ensuring that his affluent neighbors would have a smooth surface for their recreational carriage rides.[10]

During the late 1890s, Cassatt watched with interest as the nation's recovery from a severe economic depression produced ruinous rate wars and an overloaded physical plant. Following the untimely death of Frank Thomson in June 1899, the board of directors practically begged Cassatt to return to the PRR as its president, "apparently just in time," as the railroad's corporate history noted.[11] "It must be borne in mind," one executive acknowledged in 1906, "that, although he was not the next man in actual succession," he was by far the best candidate, owing to "his commanding personality," his continuing, if informal association with the Pennsylvania Railroad, and his combination of engineering and political skills.[12]

The Pennsylvania Railroad to which Cassatt returned in 1899 was a very different company from the one that he had left seventeen years earlier. There were more cars, more trains, more freight, and more passengers. Long stretches of the main line boasted four tracks, all of them crowded with traffic. Revenues had increased, and so had the complexity of operations. Perhaps most significantly, the PRR was more closely tied to the integrated national transportation network. Indeed, the actions of every carrier, no matter how geographically remote, affected all of the others. The maturing national economy could not help but affect the railroad that was better associated with industrialization than any other. With much of its revenue derived from raw materials, the demand and the price of basic commodities determined the health of the Pennsylvania Railroad. And, by the time that Alexander J. Cassatt assumed the presidency, coal had become the most important commodity of all.

An Empire of Coal

Coal was, without question, the single most significant product that the Pennsylvania Railroad transported. In tonnage, it vastly exceeded steel and iron-ore shipments—neither of which, incidentally, would have amounted to much, had it not been for the coal and coke that the PRR brought to the steel mills. The PRR depended heavily on the products of mines (principally coal, coke, and iron ore), which accounted for 63.3 percent of total tonnage by 1904.[13] In that year, coal traffic accounted for 56 percent of the total tonnage that moved across the Pennsylvania Railroad Grand Division. On Lines East, PRR locomotives hauled nearly five thousand cars of coal or coke per day, routing much of that traffic over the summit of the Alleghenies. As a result, the PRR enjoyed by far the highest traffic density (the ratio of revenue ton-miles to route miles) of any trunk line, roughly double that of either the B&O or the Erie.[14] PRR coal freight agent Robert H. Large understood, perhaps better than anyone else, the opportunities and the difficulties associated with such a staggering volume of coal traffic. "In some of our yards, for example Altoona," Large observed, "this work [of moving coal] goes on day in and day out, night in and night out, regardless of weather conditions, never ceasing except on the Sabbath, and, alas, not always then."[15]

In 1846, the incorporators of the Pennsylvania Railroad envisioned a route that would transport grain, not minerals, and coal traffic was slow to develop. Initially the problem was one of geography. Until well after the Civil War, most of Pennsylvania's coal output came from the anthracite fields in the northeastern portion of the state, not from the larger bituminous (soft) coal deposits that lay farther west. In 1860, for example, more than twenty-five thousand miners extracted nearly $12 million of anthracite from the hills of Pennsylvania, while fewer than five thousand of their counterparts pulled less than $3 million of soft coal from the ground. Anthracite producers typically ran large and efficient operations (even if working conditions were extraordinarily difficult and dangerous), while most bituminous mines were small and often seasonal in their output. Not until 1870 would Pennsylvania's soft coal production exceed its anthracite tonnage. Furthermore, despite the PRR's control over the Pennsylvania Canal Company, the Susquehanna Coal Company, and other related enterprises, its role in the anthracite market remained modest, and certainly not on par with that of the Reading, the Lehigh Valley, and other regional carriers.[16]

Bituminous coal was another matter entirely. Anthracite was concentrated in a compact area, and it represented less than a fifth of the commonwealth's total coal production and less than 1 percent of known reserves. Bituminous coal could be found under vast swaths of territory in central and southwestern Pennsylvania, some 14,200 square miles, representing a third of the total area of the state. Most of Pennsylvania's soft coal lay in four distinct regions. The North-Central Field lay principally in Bradford, Lycoming, and Tioga Counties, but the PRR's business there was generally restricted to the areas around Ralston, Pennsylvania, in Lycoming County, north of Williamsport.[17] The Broad Top Field, in Bedford, Fulton, and Huntingdon Counties, was something of a geological anomaly, located well to the east of the state's other principal bituminous deposits. That location, however, considerably reduced the distance and expense associated with moving coal to eastern markets and, as an added bonus, the coal was of exceptionally high quality. A third area of production, the Georges Creek Field (also known as the Cumberland Field), extended from Somerset County, Pennsylvania, and south into Allegany County, Maryland, west of Cumberland. It was readily accessible to the Baltimore & Ohio and the Western Maryland Railroad, but the PRR nonetheless captured some of the traffic. The largest and most important deposit was the Main Bituminous Field, which underlay much of southwestern Pennsylvania. It included the immensely valuable Pittsburgh Seam, which produced much of the coal and coke that fueled the area's burgeoning iron and steel industries. Although miners extracted bituminous coal from twenty-nine counties, the bulk of the production accordingly came from Cambria, Westmoreland, Allegheny, Fayette, Greene, and Washington Counties, the first three of which were also home to the tracks of the PRR main line. To its great good fortune, the Pennsylvania Railroad served what was once the richest mineral deposit, not only in Pennsylvania, or in the United States, but in the entire world.[18]

Although typically classified as "bituminous," much of Pennsylvania's coal was in fact semi-bituminous—and, despite the name, it was actually of a higher rank than regular bituminous coal, with carbon content closer to that of anthracite than that of poor-quality lignite. Geologists classified many of the region's bituminous deposits as steam coal, ideally suited for use in the fireboxes of railway locomotives, steamships, power plants, and similar applications. Other bituminous reserves, commonly referred to as metallurgical coal, could be readily converted into coke, the vital fuel for the region's burgeoning steel mills. Still other deposits possessed a chemical composition similar to that of cannel coal, and were ideally suited for conversion into the gas that illuminated eastern cities.

The railroads were collectively the single largest consumer of bituminous coal in the United States, representing approximately a quarter of total demand. During the last years of the nineteenth century and into the first years of the twentieth, as traffic levels increased and the PRR acquired ever more powerful locomotives, its coal consumption grew at a corresponding rate. Lines East purchased 3.6 million tons of coal in 1898, 4.7 million tons in 1900, 8.4 million tons in 1905, and 9.7 million tons in 1910. The PRR's ready access to steam coal deposits helped to substantially reduce operating costs. Non-railroad customers accounted for the remaining 75 percent of bituminous coal demand. Factories (other than iron and steel producers) used a quarter of total mine output, followed by slightly over 20 percent for the steel industry. Utilities consumed less than 10 percent, and no more than 5 percent was exported. Whatever the type, and wherever the location, bituminous coal deposits portended both massive shipments and equally impressive revenues for the Pennsylvania Railroad.[19]

Residents of southwestern Pennsylvania had long been aware of the bounty of coal in their midst, but poor transportation facilities restricted its use to local industries. The first mine in the region dated to 1785. In 1803, enterprising French merchants shipped coal from Pittsburgh, down the Ohio and Mississippi rivers, and then on to Philadelphia, as ship's ballast. A year later, western Pennsylvania coal traveled directly to tidewater for the first time, on an ark that floated down the Susquehanna River, from Clearfield County to Baltimore. Such routings could not compete with imported British coal (which also traveled as ballast) or with later anthracite production. As such, most southwestern Pennsylvania coal remained in the area, fueling the budding manufacturing

enterprises that produced iron, glass, and other products.[20]

The completion of the Main Line of Public Works did not greatly expand the reach of western Pennsylvania coal. In good years, the Western Division Canal carried perhaps two thousand tons of coal, virtually all of it destined for the manufactories at Pittsburgh. Such quantities were well below the anthracite traffic in the east (where many canal boats could easily accommodate a hundred tons, one-twentieth of the entire western traffic) and could not even keep pace with shipments along the Monongahela River, which had been rendered navigable by private capital.

Even though the Main Line of Public Works failed to stimulate the coal trade, other governmental actions had considerably more effect. In 1836, legislators created and funded the Geological Survey of Pennsylvania, with the intent of identifying the state's mineral resources. On June 16, 1836, on the same day that they authorized the Board of Canal Commissioners to eliminate the inclined planes on the Philadelphia & Columbia and Allegheny Portage railroads, legislators passed an act "to encourage the manufacture of iron with coke or mineral coal." The law, which facilitated the general incorporation of ironworks, undoubtedly benefited associates of then-Governor Joseph Ritner—including his brother George, who operated a foundry in Clearfield County. More important, however, the resulting increase in iron output strengthened the demand for coal, particularly in areas where charcoal was expensive or in short supply.[21]

The expected growth in coal traffic on the Main Line must have influenced subsequent efforts to eliminate the troublesome inclined planes, particularly on the Allegheny Portage Railroad. In January 1837, when principal engineer Charles DeHaas presented to the canal commissioners the results of his surveys across the Alleghenies, he emphasized that "bituminous coal must become an immense source of trade and revenue" for the proposed new line. Neither the canal commissioners nor the commercial interests in Philadelphia gave any credence to that prediction, yet it would soon loom large in the minds of a new generation of railroad owners and managers.[22]

The tonnage tax, a condition of the Pennsylvania Railroad's 1846 corporate charter, constituted the most serious impediment to efforts by PRR officials to develop bituminous coal traffic. Legislators intended that the tax, set at five mills per ton-mile on all freight transported more than twenty miles between March and December, would protect the state's investment in the Main Line of Public Works. Its effect was to make coal shipments effectively profitless to the PRR. In 1852, for example, local interests chartered the Huntingdon & Broad Top Mountain Railroad & Coal Company, intending to tap the isolated Broad Top Field in south-central Pennsylvania. They soon requested assistance from the PRR board, only to be told that the tonnage tax precluded the profitable transfer of coal traffic to the main line at Huntingdon. Under the circumstances, the first generation of PRR officials understandably assumed that their east–west mainline would carry little coal traffic.[23]

Public policy soon shifted in favor of the PRR, however. In 1853, members of the Pennsylvania legislature, anxious to stimulate economic growth in the western part of the state, amended the 1849 general incorporation law to liberalize the incorporation process for mining companies outside of the anthracite regions. More important, in May 1855 the legislature repealed the tonnage tax on coal and lumber shipments, leading to the rapid development of coal lands and a corresponding increase in traffic. By 1856, the Pennsylvania Railroad accommodated 190,344 tons of coal, representing 42 percent of the railroad's total tonnage. Yet, many managers were still convinced that the railroad was earning little if any profit from coal traffic, and they accordingly possessed scant desire to lower rates any further. In 1857, a frustrated Herman Haupt, then serving as a consultant to the PRR, emphasized that lower rates might attract an additional fifty thousand tons of coal traffic per year, without an appreciable increase in operating costs.[24]

Haupt's focus on the cost of transportation reflected his implicit assumption that demand for coal was relatively constant month to month (it was not), and PRR managers were not fully converted to his pricing philosophy until well after the Civil War. His arguments were nonetheless sufficiently persuasive as to induce several PRR officials to join Haupt in investing in Pennsylvania coal lands. Decades later, the PRR's critics would label such practices as conflicts of interest. While company managers undoubtedly expected to earn a profit from their participation in coal ventures, they were nonetheless equally determined to build a source of traffic for the PRR. The resulting policy of indirect investment continued to benefit the PRR for more than half a century. PRR vice president John P. Green recalled that in 1874, J. Edgar Thomson had "said to the gentlemen in the employ of our company, there is no reason at all why you should not put your money into the development of coal lands on the Lines of the Pennsylvania Railroad, because that is what the Pennsylvania Railroad is built for."[25]

The Westmoreland Coal Company, based in its eponymous county to the east of Pittsburgh, was among the first to take advantage of the legislature's repeal of the tonnage tax on coal. From the beginning, the company was closely connected to the Pennsylvania Railroad. In June 1854, a number of investors from Philadelphia, Pittsburgh, and Baltimore had established the firm in conformity with Pennsylvania's recently enacted supplement to the general incorporation law. They included James Magee, the Philadelphia merchant and manufacturer who eight years earlier had helped to organize the Pennsylvania Railroad, and who briefly held a seat on the company's board of directors. PRR chief engineer Herman Haupt was also among the incorporators, as was William Larimer, the treasurer of the Ohio & Pennsylvania Railroad.[26] In 1855, soon after the repeal of the tonnage tax on coal, Westmoreland officials placed pressure on the PRR to lower freight rates to Philadelphia. Larimer informed the PRR's directors, "If you will grant us a freight rate that will permit us to enter into a contract with the city gas works to supply it with coal your company will enjoy the benefits of earning on that tonnage. . . . Other sales would assuredly follow."[27] The argument was convincing, and the new rate of $6 a ton enabled Westmoreland to ship coal over the summit of the Alleghenies, to Philadelphia.[28]

At the same time, Westmoreland officials selected as company secretary a young William Jackson Palmer, a recent veteran of the ill-fated Hempfield Railroad in southwestern Pennsylvania. At the behest of his uncle, future Westmoreland president Francis H. Jackson, Palmer traveled extensively in Britain, observing coal mines and railroads. Upon his return, and probably thanks to James Magee's recommendation, Thomson selected Palmer as his personal assistant. The young man, still in his early twenties, spent the next few years supervising experiments to increase efficiency and reduce coal consumption on PRR locomotives, an activity that dovetailed neatly with his duties at Westmoreland.[29]

The Civil War and the beginning of the sustained postwar economic expansion immensely benefited both Westmoreland and the PRR. The coal company tapped new sources, including the Irwin Field, a deposit that was ideally suited to conversion into coal gas. By happy circumstance, the City of Philadelphia, which still held a substantial block of Pennsylvania Railroad stock, also owned the municipal gasworks, making the members of the Select and Common Councils natural allies of PRR and Westmoreland officials. In 1856, Westmoreland shipped ninety thousand tons of coal to fifty-eight gasworks. Output soared to 280,000 tons in 1869, virtually all of it sent east over the Pennsylvania Railroad. By 1871, Westmoreland officials had signed long-term contracts with Andrew Carnegie, ensuring that a large portion of the mines' output would travel along the PRR west to Pittsburgh, as well as east to tidewater. Westmoreland's principal competitor, the Penn Gas Coal Company, also generated substantial tonnage for the railroad. Well before Westmoreland acquired Penn Gas in 1905, the growing importance of kerosene and electric lighting reduced demand for coal gas, and the company began to shift its operations into West Virginia.[30]

Branches to the Coalfields

Although the PRR main line ran through coal country, only a tiny fraction of the state's reserves lay within ready reach of those tracks. To obtain access to the remainder, PRR personnel relied on a network of branch lines that ran up the valleys and wound around the hills of western Pennsylvania. During the earliest years of the PRR's existence, financial constraints forced company officials to concentrate their resources on the route between Harrisburg and Pittsburgh. The charter stipulation that limited branches to those counties traversed by the main line further constrained their ac-

tivities. As such, local interests developed most of the early coal branches, albeit generally in close cooperation with the PRR. That situation changed considerably after March 1861, when the General Assembly agreed to the repeal ("commutation") of the last vestiges of the tonnage tax, providing that the PRR invest $850,000 in uncollected tax revenues in local railroads. Of the proposed commutation lines (not all of which were built), most were well positioned to tap into the coal trade.

The Western Pennsylvania Railroad was one of the earliest recipients of commutation funds, even though the line ultimately proved more important as a mechanism to bypass Pittsburgh rather than to get coal to market. The project dated to 1853, when local interests in Butler and Lawrence Counties chartered the North-Western Railroad, which they envisioned as a line linking the PRR main line west of Johnstown to Cleveland, Ohio, in conjunction with the Cleveland & Mahoning Railroad. Despite financial support from the City of Philadelphia, and from several counties en route, they made little progress, and the company fell victim to the Panic of 1857. In 1859, the owners of the bankrupt railroad attempted to interest PRR officials in the line, but to no avail. The company was reorganized in 1860 as the Western Pennsylvania Railroad, and the following year received $250,000 in commutation funds. With PRR support, construction crews linked the main line at Torrance to the important community of Blairsville, on the Western Division Canal, and then extended the route northwesterly along the route of the canal to the Allegheny River near Freeport. Initially, the most important role of the Western Pennsylvania was to enable the PRR to move oil from northwestern Pennsylvania to Philadelphia, bypassing Pittsburgh. In later years, however, the route hosted considerable coal traffic and provided access to Indiana, Pennsylvania, along a branch that ran due north from Torrance and Blairsville.[31]

Communities such as Tyrone, Cresson, and Bellwood served as the termini of far more important coal branches. Tyrone provided access to the Bald Eagle Valley, which ran in a northeasterly direction through Centre County, separating Bald Eagle Mountain to the east from the front range of the Alleghenies to the west. That region of Pennsylvania, in Clearfield and Centre Counties, was home to the semi-bituminous deposits of the Clearfield District. In February 1857, local interests incorporated the Tyrone & Lock Haven Railroad, to build from Tyrone to a junction with the West Branch Division Canal, following the Bald Eagle Valley. The promoters soon gained the right to extend the line farther to the northeast, to a junction with the still incomplete Sunbury & Erie Railroad at Williamsport, and southwest to a junction with the terminus of the Juniata Division Canal at Hollidaysburg. Thanks to financial mismanagement, little work took place, and the company failed in 1860. By early 1861, however, the PRR was providing material for further construction. In April, Tom Scott oversaw the reorganization of the company as the Bald Eagle Valley Railroad, and served as one of its directors. That fall, the PRR offered direct financial assistance, using commutation funds to purchase $200,000 of the company's bonds.[32]

The Civil War greatly increased the interest of PRR executives in the Bald Eagle line. In addition to accelerating the demand for coal, Robert E. Lee's invasion of the North in September 1862 raised the frightening possibility that Confederate forces might sever the PRR main line through south-central Pennsylvania. When complete, the Bald Eagle Valley would offer an alternate route east, free from the effects of Confederate depredations. The PRR leased and then began operating the Bald Eagle Valley. By the spring of 1865, construction crews had completed the line from Vail (near Tyrone) to Lock Haven, on the route of the Sunbury & Erie—by now extended and renamed the Philadelphia & Erie. While the end of the Civil War removed any danger to the main line, the link through the Bald Eagle Valley nonetheless continued to provide an alternate route for traffic moving across Pennsylvania. In addition, the company tapped important coal deposits in the Snow Shoe Field, as well as ironworks at Bellefonte.[33]

At Vail, the Bald Eagle Valley connected with a much more extensive series of lines operated by the Cambria & Clearfield Railway. The company's easternmost segments traced their origins to the spring of 1856 and the organization of the Tyrone & Clearfield Railroad, under the leadership of a Bellefonte attorney

and judge, James Tracy Hale. Despite the initial reluctance of the PRR board to provide financial assistance, the company began construction and somehow survived the Panic of 1857. The PRR directors changed their policies, however, buying $75,000 of Tyrone & Clearfield securities, under the terms of the Commutation Act. After completing a route from Tyrone through Vail and on to Philipsburg, the company (reorganized in 1867 as the Tyrone & Clearfield Railway) constructed a network of branches interlacing the rich coal seams of Clearfield County.[34]

Farther west, a second network of coal branches connected with the main line at Bellwood and at Cresson. Charles Schlatter had once suggested that Ebensburg might be on the middle route between Philadelphia and Pittsburgh, but J. Edgar Thomson had chosen an alignment that was farther south. In May 1859, residents of the Cambria County seat organized the Ebensburg & Cresson Railroad to span the eleven miles to the PRR main line. By August 1861, the PRR was providing assistance under the terms of the Commutation Act, buying $66,500 of the company's bonds. By the time the line was completed in 1862, the PRR had leased the property. Three decades later, amid a rapid increase in coal production, the PRR extended the branch incrementally westward, as far as Black Lick, and a connection with another PRR branch that linked Indiana, Pennsylvania, to Blairsville, on the Western Pennsylvania Railroad.[35]

Bellwood, midway between Tyrone and Altoona, provided additional access to the coalfields. The Bell's Gap Railroad, chartered in May 1871, built a three-foot-gauge line from Bell's Mills (later, Bellwood) on the PRR main line northwest up Bell's Run to Lloydsville, with a later extension into the valley of Clearfield Creek, and on to Coalport. PRR officials were strong supporters of the line, which they envisioned as a mechanism to deliver coal to the shops at Altoona, as well as to the locomotives stationed there. Accordingly, PRR vice president Alexander J. Cassatt was a director of the Bell's Gap, and John Reilly, superintendent of transportation at Altoona, was the company's president. By the 1880s, a major coal producer, Berwind, White & Company had taken control, converted the line to standard gauge, and extended it farther north, to Irvona. At Irvona, the tracks met another branch, completed in 1886, that ran due south to the main line at Cresson. In 1885, Berwind, White incorporated another carrier, the Clearfield & Jefferson Railway, and in 1889 merged the two companies into the Pennsylvania & North Western Railroad. Under the ownership of what was by then known as the Berwind-White Coal Mining Company, construction crews pushed tracks farther north toward the Punxsutawney Field. Another outlet for coal followed the old Ebensburg & Cresson route from Cresson north to Ebensburg Junction. North of the junction, other branches extended north through Patton to connections with the Punxsutawney route at La Jose and McGees.[36]

Farther east, the Huntingdon & Broad Top Mountain benefited from the increase in coal traffic that followed the passage of the Commutation Act. In 1853, two years before the legislature removed the tonnage tax on coal, the company's owners had failed in their efforts to secure financial assistance from the PRR. The promoters of another line, the Bedford Railroad, also asked the PRR board for help in constructing what would eventually become a southerly extension of the Huntingdon & Broad Top Mountain, and likewise received nothing. After 1861, with $850,000 in commutation funds at their disposal, the PRR directors saw the matter differently, and purchased $100,000 of the Bedford's bonds. By 1872, the PRR had leased its successor company, the Bedford & Bridgeport Railroad, providing access to the Georges Creek (Cumberland) Field and ending the B&O monopoly on the area's coal traffic. The route was at best imperfect, however, as it relied on the independent Huntingdon & Broad Top Mountain, as well as the Cumberland & Pennsylvania Railroad, south of the state line.[37]

Herman Haupt must have been gratified. In the decades that followed his 1857 report to PRR officials, and as more and more trains nosed their way along a growing network of branch lines, the PRR's coal traffic increased substantially, from 704,754 tons in 1861 to 1,074,757 tons in 1865.[38] The growth in coal traffic continued steadily over the next few decades, reaching 4.7 million tons in 1875, despite the deepening recession. By 1880, as the United States had emerged from the aftereffects of the Panic of 1873, the PRR carried nearly 7.5 million tons of coal.[39]

Yet, the full flowering of the PRR's bituminous coal business did not occur until late in the nineteenth century. Between 1880 and 1900, large mining corporations began to rationalize bituminous production, and their investments stimulated a rapid increase in statewide output, from 16.6 million to 79.3 million tons, while employment in the fields more than tripled. Because it cost relatively little to dig for coal, the large producers never succeeded in eliminating small mining operations. As a result, annual and decadal production levels masked sharp fluctuations in both price and output. When the economy was prosperous and demand for coal was accordingly high, small fly-by-night operators quickly sunk mine shafts, and complained loudly when the PRR could not supply them with the occasional car necessary to accommodate their small output. In slack times, only the largest companies prospered, with their smaller competitors often throwing their supplies on the market at bargain prices, undercutting both colliery and railroad revenues.[40]

Most of the new bituminous production occurred in the Pittsburgh Seam of the Main Bituminous Field, a region well served by the Pennsylvania Railroad. The most important producer was undoubtedly the Berwind-White Coal Mining Company, a firm that by the end of the nineteenth century had far outstripped such earlier leaders as Westmoreland and Penn Gas. Charles F. Berwind began his career in 1861 as a clerk at the coal dealership operated by Robert Hare Powel, the son of the individual who sold a large portion of his West Philadelphia estate to the PRR. In 1869, Berwind began the partnership of Berwind & Bradley, reestablished in 1874 as Berwind, White & Company. The name change reflected the involvement of Allison White, a judge and member of Congress who resided in Lock Haven. The partners' initial base of operations was the Eureka Number 1 mine in Osceola Mills, in the southeastern part of Clearfield County. By 1885, the company operated eleven mines in Clearfield and Jefferson Counties.[41]

In 1886 the partners incorporated their firm as the Berwind-White Coal Mining Company. The company's literature emphasized that "purchasers may rely upon receiving prompt shipments and a superior quality of coal."[42] To ensure superior quality, company managers had the authority to shut any mine that did

Figure 67. Large mining firms, such as Westmoreland, Berwind-White, and Penn Gas, maintained bituminous coal production and delivery schedules, and gained an advantage over their smaller competitors, in part by owning fleets of gondola and hopper cars. Here, loaded Westmoreland cars sit near the Biddle Mine, waiting for PRR locomotive #114 to forward them to their destination, circa 1900.

Westmoreland Coal Company Photograph and Video Collection, Hagley Museum and Library.

not produce coal with adequate steaming qualities. Prompt shipments depended on the cooperation of the Pennsylvania Railroad. In order to secure that cooperation, beginning in 1888 Berwind-White officials (like their counterparts at Westmoreland and Penn Gas) purchased thousands of coal cars for their exclusive use. They also worked closely with PRR executives to secure the installation of sidings and spurs, and to ensure adequate car supplies and timely shipments. The willingness of PRR managers to cooperate became apparent following the 1889 Johnstown Flood.

With the PRR in disarray, President Roberts ordered his employees to seize all coal shipments in transit for use in PRR locomotives. Unlike their competitors, Berwind-White representatives were able to negotiate an exemption, and their coal supplies flowed uninterrupted to their customers.[43]

After Charles Berwind died in 1890, the presidency fell to his brother, Edward Julius Berwind. Edward developed the company's marketing capabilities and worked assiduously to persuade eastern factory owners to abandon anthracite in favor of the high-quality bituminous coal that his company supplied. He graduated from the United States Naval Academy and held a naval post in the administration of President Ulysses S. Grant. He was also closely associated with commercial maritime activity, in collaboration with J. P. Morgan, and he later served as a director of Morgan's International Mercantile Marine Company. As such, Edward Berwind was well positioned to sell coal to maritime users, and by the end of the nineteenth century, virtually every steamship that left the United States carried Berwind-White coal in its bunkers.[44]

The depletion of high-quality coal reserves in Clearfield County induced Edward Berwind to purchase sixty thousand acres of land in Cambria and Somerset Counties. In 1898 Berwind-White established its base of operations at the company town of Windber, Pennsylvania, located in Somerset County some ten miles southeast of Johnstown. That area of southern Pennsylvania had long been the province of the Baltimore & Ohio. For all of its tragic consequences, the 1889 Johnstown Flood produced the happy effect of draining the lake that blocked access to the South Fork of the Little Conemaugh River. Beginning in 1891, PRR construction crews laid tracks up the valley as far as Lovett. From there, Berwind-White paid for additional construction.[45] Tracks reached Scalp Level in 1897 and Windber the following year. By 1893, Berwind-White was already shipping more than 3.5 million tons per year from thirty mines. Much of Berwind-White's output traveled east over the PRR, to the piers at the PRR's Harsimus Cove, New Jersey, facility. There, Berwind-White maintained a fleet of tugs, barges, and lighters for local deliveries, as well as a contingent of oceangoing vessels, operated by the subsidiary Wilmore Steamship Company, to send coal to the Caribbean.[46]

Not surprisingly, Berwind-White quickly became the largest shipper of coal on the Pennsylvania Railroad, as well as the largest coal exporter in the United States. Many decades later, railroads would compete enthusiastically for what became known as "unit-train" cargoes, offering mine owners steep rate discounts for a steady stream of guaranteed business. However, those trainload shipments had long existed as the PRR moved vast quantities of Berwind-White coal to tidewater. "We have so developed and systematized our

business," Edward Berwind emphasized, "[that] we regularly supply about three hundred and fifty (350) cars of coal per day to be moved from a single point of shipment to a single destination—Harsimus. This enables the business to be moved in solid train loads, thus getting the maximum service out of the [PRR's] motive power and every expenditure incident to the movement, with the minimum use of tracks and no congestion of yards and terminals."[47]

Pennsylvania Railroad officials were willing to grant substantial concessions to Berwind-White in order to secure such a large volume of business. When the PRR built the Harsimus Cove terminal, executives set aside land for a coal pier, which they leased to Berwind-White for the bargain price of $108,000 a year. PRR crews then built transfer facilities at the pier, at a cost of just over $100,000. Berwind-White purchased the installation, with a ten-year, interest-free loan from the PRR, and received exclusive right of access. For many years, the Berwind-White facilities were the only privately owned, non-railroad piers on the New Jersey side of the Hudson River. One of the PRR's real-estate subsidiaries, the Manor Real Estate & Trust Company (which owned nearly nine thousand acres of coal lands, but did not engage in mining), brokered purchases and land swaps with the Wilmore Real Estate Company, the land-acquisition and management subsidiary of the Berwind-White Coal Mining Company. The PRR also provided one thousand cars exclusively for Berwind-White, augmenting the colliery's substantial fleet of privately owned equipment. Thanks to the efficiency of the Harsimus Cove piers, as well as the willingness of Berwind-White officials to ship entire trainloads of coal cars, cargoes could be transferred from railroad to ship in as little as six hours. Independent coal operators, who sent their output to the PRR's other New York facilities (at South Amboy and, after 1907, Greenville) and to the PRR's piers at Greenwich Point in Philadelphia, complained of delays as long as eight *days*. In addition, the PRR paid Berwind-White substantial drawbacks, partly in recognition of the economies of scale associated with large shipments, and partly to ensure that the PRR retained the colliery's business. Interstate Commerce Commission investigators later determined that that consideration netted Berwind-White more than a quarter of a million dollars each year, producing further howls of protest from smaller coal producers.[48]

The Keystone Coal & Coke Company never operated on so large a scale as Westmoreland or Berwind-White, but its close connection with the PRR illustrated both the benefits and the costs associated with joint investments in railroads and collieries. In 1902, Congressman George F. Huff, a former PRR official, oversaw the merger of several collieries near Greensburg, Pennsylvania. Cassatt & Company, the brokerage house that Robert Cassatt had established in 1872, owned a quarter of Keystone's stock, and Robert Kelso Cassatt, the son of the PRR president, served as the company's eastern sales agent. The railroad purchased much of the firm's output, and in 1905 Keystone supplied the PRR with more than 1.7 million tons of locomotive coal. The informal integration between Keystone and the PRR ensured dependable fuel supplies for the railroad at a reasonable cost.[49] The association also seemed to suggest a conflict of interest, and the owners of competing mining operations often claimed that the Pennsylvania Railroad showed undue favoritism toward Keystone.[50]

Thanks to producers such as Westmoreland, Penn Gas, Berwind-White, and Keystone, and many other firms, bituminous coal from western Pennsylvania proved an increasingly important traffic source for the Pennsylvania Railroad. In 1899, the PRR moved 16.4 million tons of coal. By 1903, the quantity had risen to 28.5 million tons, more than 48 percent of all the coal mined in Pennsylvania. More than seven million tons went to PRR piers at Canton (Baltimore), Maryland; Greenwich (Philadelphia); South Amboy, New Jersey; and Harsimus Cove for transfer to coastal shipping or for export.[51]

Coke from Connellsville

In addition to burgeoning coal production, the late nineteenth century also witnessed rapid growth in the manufacture and transportation of coke. The area south of Pittsburgh contained large deposits of bituminous coal with a high percentage of volatile matter. After being baked to remove impurities, the coal became coke, an ideal fuel for a growing number of Bessemer converters and open-hearth furnaces at locations such as Pittsburgh, Steubenville, Wheeling, and Youngstown. The best deposits lay in a narrow corridor, stretching from Latrobe, on the PRR main line, almost due south toward the intersection of Pennsylvania, West Virginia, and Maryland, an area roughly forty-two miles long and, on average, three and a half miles wide, typically referred to as the Connellsville District of the Pittsburgh Seam. At some point during the 1810s (the exact date is unclear), ironworkers in southwestern Pennsylvania began to experiment with coking coals. It was not until 1835, however, that they succeeded in using coke as fuel. In any event, they continued to prefer charcoal, drawn from the region's abundant forests. The coke industry did not begin to grow rapidly until the 1860s, and even as late as 1870, 70 percent of the nation's pig iron was smelted with anthracite coal or charcoal, not with coke.[52]

Perhaps more than any other individual, Henry Clay Frick took advantage of the potential of the Connellsville District. Frick began his career as a bookkeeper in the Westmoreland County whiskey distillery operated by his grandfather, Abraham Overholt. On and off the job, Frick was standing on top of some of the highest-quality coal deposits in the world. He was also in close proximity to the industries of Pittsburgh, as well as to the artery of transportation furnished by the Pennsylvania Railroad. In March 1871, while still in his early twenties, Frick established H. C. Frick & Company and bought 123 acres of coal lands, the first of many thousands. He soon developed close business relationships with leading Pittsburghers, including steelmaker Andrew Carnegie and banker Thomas Mellon, and in 1882 he cooperated with them to form the H. C. Frick Coke Company.[53]

Frick's timing was perfect. Demand for steel soared as the nation recovered from the Panic of 1873, and coke production increased in tandem. Between 1873 and 1875, Andrew Carnegie oversaw the construction of the Edgar Thomson Steel Works at Braddock. During the 1880s, Carnegie built additional blast furnaces and purchased the rival Homestead Steel Works, assuring his dominant position in the steel business. Carnegie, his allies, and his competitors oversaw a rapid increase in steel output, from 22,000 tons in 1867 to more than 26 million tons in 1906. The torrent of steel mandated an equally rapid increase in coke output, peaking in 1916 at nearly 22.5 million tons. Based on his contractual relationship with Carnegie, Frick became by far the largest coke producer in the United States. Even mill owners along the east coast found it more economical to use Connellsville coke than to tap nearby anthracite deposits.[54]

Despite its potential, several factors initially limited the PRR's involvement in the coking coal and coke trade. A substantial portion of the output of the mines in the vicinity of Connellsville went directly into nearby coking ovens, with little or no rail haul. In addition, PRR executives faced stiff competition from the B&O-affiliated Pittsburgh & Connellsville, whose tracks along the Youghiogheny River bisected the coking regions. In contrast, Pennsylvania Railroad tracks passed through Latrobe, a community located at the far northern end of the coking coal fields, and company officials initially demonstrated little interest in coke transportation.[55]

Pennsylvania Railroad executives were nonetheless badly stung by the arrival of the B&O's Pittsburgh & Connellsville connection in Pittsburgh in 1871, and responded by building a network of lines in southwestern Pennsylvania. The South-West Pennsylvania Railway was incorporated in March 1871, even as rival construction crews were putting the finishing touches on the Pittsburgh & Connellsville route. On May 2, Tom Scott presided over the formal organization of the South-West Pennsylvania in order to protect the PRR's interests and prevent the line from falling under B&O influence. He succeeded admirably, and became the first president of the new line, with other PRR officials dominating the company's board of directors. By April 1873, the route was in service, linking the PRR main line at Greensburg with Connellsville in the heart of the coking coal region. The PRR leased the company at that time and by 1880 had extended tracks south to Fairchance, at the southern end of the Connellsville District.[56]

Farther west, the PRR followed the Monongahela Valley southward, ultimately reaching coalfields deep in West Virginia. In April 1867, local interests had incorporated the Monongahela Valley Railroad, intending to build from Pittsburgh south to Waynesburg. Little activity occurred until February 1870, when

promoters renamed the company the Pittsburgh, Virginia & Charleston Railway. The Commonwealth of Pennsylvania soon provided financial assistance and, more important, the PRR bought control of the railroad. J. Edgar Thomson saw a triple role for his new acquisition. First, it could transport coal to Pittsburgh. Second, it would allow traffic moving off of the Pittsburgh, Cincinnati & St. Louis Railway (the Pan Handle) to bypass Pittsburgh, flowing south of the city and rejoining the main line farther to the east. His more immediate concern, however, was to blunt the B&O's incursion into southwestern Pennsylvania and prevent George Washington Cass, president of the Pittsburgh, Fort Wayne & Chicago, from forming an alliance with that rival trunk line.[57]

Construction began in 1873, fueled by generous PRR support, including a bond guarantee and direct financial aid. Track crews worked steadily southward, through Homestead, McKeesport, Monongahela City, and Donora, reaching West Brownsville in May 1881. Two years earlier, in May 1879, Pennsylvania Railroad officials had taken over the company's operations, incorporated into the PRR's Monongahela Division. In 1886, the PRR completed the Redstone Branch, linking the PV&C at West Brownsville Junction with the South-West Pennsylvania Railway at Redstone Junction, and providing a more efficient route for coal from the Connellsville District to reach Pittsburgh. During the years that followed, PRR construction crews built a web of branch lines through the region. Traffic levels surged, and by 1900 the line between Pittsburgh and Brownsville Junction was double tracked, with as many as four tracks in congested areas. Such investments soon displaced the B&O-affiliated Pittsburgh & Connellsville and other rivals, and as early as 1883 the PRR controlled 76 percent of all coke shipments in the Connellsville District.[58]

Further expansion occurred during the 1890s, as Pittsburgh industrialists requested that the PRR extend the tracks farther south, to Charleston, West Virginia. They made the same demand of the Pittsburgh & Lake Erie Railroad, which since 1887 was effectively under the control of the New York Central. Carnegie and Frick, who possessed resources that greatly exceeded those of the average Pittsburgh businessman, were prepared to take even more drastic action. By

December 1897, Carnegie offered to purchase from Andrew Mellon the newly incorporated Monongahela Southern Railroad, a short branch that extended from Monongahela Junction (Duquesne) to Mifflin Junction. The line, still in its preliminary stages, would have connected with Carnegie's Union Railroad, giving the steelmaker access to the coking fields south of Pittsburgh. Additional construction into West Virginia would have guaranteed Carnegie an almost limitless supply of coal, none of which need ever move over PRR rails. "When we get our own railroad through from mines to connection with trunk lines we can control matters, not till then," Carnegie emphasized. Frick, who had seen the disastrous results of Carnegie's involvement in the South Pennsylvania Railroad, was decidedly less enthusiastic about the construction of additional railroads through the region.[59]

During the system-building years of the 1880s, Carnegie's demand for secure transportation facilities might well have led to needlessly competitive overbuilding. By 1900, however, financier J. P. Morgan was anxious to maintain stability in both the steel and the railroad industries. Accordingly, in December 1900, under Morgan's guidance representatives from the PRR and the Pittsburgh & Lake Erie (NYC) joined forces to establish the Monongahela Railroad. The new company acquired some short stretches of the PRR's existing Pittsburgh, Virginia & Charleston Railway and South-West Pennsylvania Railway track, some thirty miles in all. More important, its managers took charge of an extension from Brownsville Junction south along the east bank of the Monongahela River to Martin, Pennsylvania.

Initially, Monongahela Railroad workers confined their activities to the construction of numerous spurs and branch lines in southwestern Pennsylvania, refraining from crossing into West Virginia. The depression that began in 1907 further delayed work on the route into the Mountaineer State. Construction resumed in 1911 and was largely completed the following year, although the line was not fully in service until 1914. A connection with the Buckhannon & Northern Railroad allowed trains to continue south, eventually reaching the area around Fairmont, West Virginia.[60] Eventually, the Monongahela operated something resembling a Q-shaped route, with a circle

through Brownsville Junction and Huron, Pennsylvania; Randall, West Virginia; Blacksville, Waynesburg, and Millsboro, Pennsylvania; and back to West Brownsville, with an extension from Randall through Morgantown and Fairmont to Loveridge, West Virginia. Even though the Monongahela never reached the West Virginia state capital, the Fairmont coalfields generated valuable traffic for both the PRR and the NYC.[61]

Although the PRR ultimately gained access to the coalfields of West Virginia, Thomson's vision of the PV&C as a low-grade bypass around the south side of Pittsburgh proved less successful. As early as June 1872, the PRR board authorized the construction of the Port Perry Bridge. The structure linked the main line, at Brinton's, near what would soon become the site of Carnegie's Edgar Thomson Works, with the PV&C tracks along the south bank of the Monongahela River, at Duquesne. The new link was designed to avoid the Grant's Hill Tunnel in downtown Pittsburgh, a major bottleneck for traffic flowing onto the Steubenville Extension and then westward on the Pan Handle. The Panic of 1873 delayed construction of the bypass line, which was not completed until 1879. After having spent more than half a million dollars on the project, the route still possessed unacceptably high grades and was of little use to the PRR. President George Roberts later authorized the rebuilding of the line, under the supervision of future president Samuel Rea—who had just returned to the PRR after a stint on the Pittsburgh & Lake Erie Railroad. By 1888, the PRR finally possessed a reasonably efficient route around the southern edge of Pittsburgh.[62]

Pocahontas and Flat Top

While the Pennsylvania Railroad benefited enormously from the rapid increase in bituminous coal production during the late 1800s, the company's managers sensed a serious problem. The undifferentiated nature of the commodity made it extraordinarily difficult for mine owners to control prices and retarded the ability of PRR executives to set and maintain stable and remunerative rates. The presence of coal in several states, including Pennsylvania, Virginia, West Virginia, Ohio, and Illinois, created further complica tions. Each state was anxious to maximize coal production and attain the resulting economic benefits. In the absence of a coordinated national energy policy, the legislatures of several states moved independently to boost coal production—just as they had unilaterally developed competing transportation routes to the west early in the century. The end result was the decentralization of coal production and an intense rivalry among coal-producing states that made control of prices and output levels largely impossible.[63]

The closing years of the nineteenth century witnessed the rapid expansion of bituminous coal production into north-central Pennsylvania and into West Virginia, areas where the PRR provided little, if any, service. Beginning in 1884, the New York Central's Beech Creek subsidiary began moving substantial quantities of coal out of the Clearfield District in north-central Pennsylvania, in competition with the PRR's Philadelphia & Erie.[64] While far less of a threat, the Erie also tapped coal deposits in Jefferson County, another area that had long been under the control of the Pennsylvania Railroad. The Buffalo, New York & Philadelphia Railroad and the Buffalo, Rochester & Pittsburgh Railway also competed for coal traffic, causing additional rate instability and leading to periodic and largely unsuccessful pooling efforts.[65]

The shift southward into West Virginia was even more pronounced. Even though it would be 1930 before the coal output of the Mountaineer State would surpass that of Pennsylvania, the West Virginia mines portended trouble for the PRR and for the coal trade in general. West Virginia succeeded in part because of inadequacies in the production and distribution of Pennsylvania coal. By the mid-1880s, steelmakers in both Pittsburgh and Chicago, as well as other coal consumers, were aghast at the high rates and poor service provided by the railroads that served southwestern Pennsylvania—and the PRR was the primary culprit. Rising labor costs played an even more important role, as miners in Ohio, Illinois, and southern Pennsylvania were increasingly successful in their demands for higher wages and improved working conditions. The first strike in the Monongahela Valley occurred as early as 1848. In the decades that followed, a growing number of labor organizations—including the American Miners' Association, established in 1861,

the Miners' and Laborers' Benevolent Association (1867), the Knights of Labor (1869), and the National Federation of Miners (1885)—became more militant and more successful at promoting the interests of workers. In 1883, the Amalgamated Association of Miners (the predecessor of the United Mine Workers of America) organized workers in the Irwin Field, home to Westmoreland and Penn Gas. The Pittsburgh region witnessed severe strikes in 1886, 1887, and again in 1889—part of more than seven hundred coal strikes across the United States between 1887 and 1894. In 1891, a strike in the Connellsville District led to the "Morewood Massacre," a clash between workers and National Guard troops that left seven people dead. Four more died in 1894 amid a strike and lockout. In September 1897, an even more serious incident at Lattimer, in northeastern Pennsylvania's anthracite fields, killed nineteen miners and wounded dozens more. Between 1897 and 1902, a series of strikes roiled the anthracite fields of northeastern Pennsylvania, and labor disputes affected the bituminous producers as well.[66]

The general public was increasingly critical of the violence, but even more outraged at the horrific tally of deaths in mining accidents. The adverse publicity encouraged mine owners to moderate their labor policies. The Lattimer Massacre also helped to revive the failing United Mine Workers of America. So, too did a July 1897 strike, called by UMW president Michael Ratchford, in a desperate attempt to save his union. The tactic succeeded, and in 1898 mine owners in Pennsylvania, Ohio, and Illinois recognized the UMW and agreed to collective bargaining.[67]

As the nineteenth century reached its end, many Pennsylvania coal producers were cautiously optimistic at the labor agreements, which they saw as a mechanism to equalize costs, and thus stabilize price and output levels. Their hopes were in vain, as the coal business became progressively more destabilized. In a desperate effort to maintain prices, owners styled themselves as part of the "Central Competitive Field," and attempted, albeit unsuccessfully, to allocate and maintain production quotas.[68]

Despite their cooperative efforts, Pennsylvania producers could do little to rein in their rivals in West Virginia. The coal deposits in West Virginia were a greater distance from the industrial northeast, and mine owners initially battled perceptions that the quality of their output was inferior to that of Pennsylvania's mines. West Virginia possessed two great advantages over Pennsylvania, however. First, despite their successes in the North, unions had been unable to penetrate West Virginia's coalfields, producing correspondingly lower labor costs. Second, the railroads that served the state—particularly the Norfolk & Western—developed innovative marketing and pricing strategies that made West Virginia coal competitive in a national market. Those developments quite naturally came at the expense of the Pennsylvania Railroad.

Virtually the entire state of West Virginia contained coal reserves, but the best were perversely the least accessible, in the rugged southwestern part of the state. That coal was of excellent quality, however, and converted into coke that had half the ash and only 5 percent more carbon than supplies from the Connellsville area. As early as 1750, travelers had observed coal outcrops on Flat Top Mountain, in the western part of what was then the colony of Virginia. Geologists later delineated the Flat Top–Pocahontas Field in McDowell and Mercer Counties, the New River Field, and the more westerly Kanawha Field. Prior to the Civil War, however, most of Virginia's coal came from more accessible mines near Richmond, and the unwillingness of legislators to fund transportation improvements in the western part of the state did little to improve matters.

The creation of West Virginia in 1863 accelerated the development of coal resources in the southern Appalachians. Coal production in West Virginia rose from 444,648 short tons in 1863, the first year of statehood, to 16.7 million tons by 1898. By 1879, 250 coke ovens were in use along the New River, a number that increased to 3,000 by 1902. Such numbers paled in comparison with the 26,000 Connellsville District coke ovens that were in operation in 1902, but West Virginia was showing impressive growth, nonetheless.[69] The increase could not have occurred, however, had it not been for the equally explosive growth of West Virginia's rail transportation facilities. A state that possessed 387 miles of track in 1870 had 1,433 miles in 1890 and 2,228 miles in 1900.[70]

The Baltimore & Ohio was well positioned to benefit from the development of the West Virginia coalfields, ensuring that it would be distinctly more prosperous in the twentieth century than it had been in the nineteenth. The B&O had been woefully undercapitalized, and its investors and employees faced extraordinary construction difficulties as they struggled to extend the line west to Wheeling. The Civil War demolished the railroad's physical plant, and by the early 1870s, Tom Scott and his colleagues in the Southern Railway Security Company had outmaneuvered B&O president John W. Garrett, restricting his access to the South. Garrett's expansionist efforts—the extension to Chicago, the Metropolitan Branch to Washington, the construction between Baltimore and Philadelphia, and the efforts to establish the Bound Brook route to New York—drained the corporate treasury and saddled the B&O with high fixed charges. By March 1896, the company was in receivership. As the nineteenth century came to a close, however, the B&O's salvation came welling up out of the ground, in the form of the vast sheets of coal that underlay Virginia and West Virginia. Ever since tracks reached Cumberland, Maryland, in 1842, coal had been a significant commodity on the B&O, but the southward shift of production made it more important than ever.[71]

The Pocahontas coal boom elevated the status of two other railroads that served the region. The Chesapeake & Ohio Railway dated to the period immediately following the Civil War, and to a consolidation of the Virginia Central and other Virginia railroads. In January 1873, construction crews completed a route that linked Richmond with the newly established town of Huntington, West Virginia, along the Ohio River. The community took its name from western railway entrepreneur Collis P. Huntington, who owned large tracts of coal land, and who also intended to make the C&O a part of a vast transcontinental empire. The Panic of 1873 doomed his efforts, and the C&O entered bankruptcy in 1878. Coal traffic revitalized the C&O and led to the construction of new routes to the coal piers at Newport News, Virginia, in 1881 and to Cincinnati in 1888. The railroad's main line ran along the New River, through the heart of one of the richest coalfields in the United States, and branch lines soon intertwined the New River Field and the adjacent Kanawha Field.[72]

The Norfolk & Western Railroad (later, Railway) also benefited from the increasing coal production in the Pocahontas region, and caused especially severe problems for the Pennsylvania Railroad. The N&W, organized in 1881, was a successor to William Mahone's Atlantic, Mississippi & Ohio Railroad. Philadelphia banker Clarence H. Clark and his associates had been responsible for the reorganization, and for constructing a link with the PRR, in the form of the Shenandoah Valley Railroad. They sought to transform the N&W from a regional carrier of agricultural commodities to a modern and efficient coal hauler. The individual in charge of that effort was N&W president Frederick J. Kimball, a veteran of the PRR's Philadelphia & Erie subsidiary and a partner in E. W. Clark & Company. Like PRR president George Roberts, Kimball was a meticulous civil engineer, and not a speculator. He systematized the N&W's operating practices, while keeping careful watch over the company's expenditures. In seeking new sources of revenue for the N&W, Kimball paid close attention to the expansion of coal production in West Virginia, particularly in the Flat Top–Pocahontas Field. By March 1883, the construction of seventy-five miles of new track enabled the N&W to move coal to tidewater, at Norfolk. The nearby Lamberts Point facility, opened the following year, gave the N&W one of the most elaborate coal terminals in the United States. By 1892, construction crews had extended the N&W from the Flat Top coalfields north to the Ohio River, at Kenova, West Virginia, and by 1901 the company offered service as far north as Columbus, Ohio, and as far west as Cincinnati.[73]

More important, Kimball and his associates developed innovative new methods for marketing coal, in an effort to stabilize price and output levels and overcome the distance advantage enjoyed by Pennsylvania producers. A June 1881 contract, the first between the N&W and the mine owners, revealed the extent to which each depended on the other. Officials of a mining consortium, the Southwest Virginia Improvement Company, agreed to ship coal solely over the N&W and to allow that railroad's representatives to set prices at the Lamberts Point piers. Rather than charge a fixed tariff, the N&W levied a floating rate, set at 70 percent of whatever revenue the coal might bring. The arrangement enabled N&W representatives to stabilize both coal output and transportation rates, as they could de-

cline to sell at unremunerative prices and, in extreme cases, could simply refuse to deliver cars and thus prevent mine owners from expanding production. Railroad control over coal marketing also acted as a check on quality and enabled sales agents to advertise West Virginia coal in northeastern markets.[74]

Subsequent agreements between the N&W and other coal producers established what amounted to a railroad-managed coal cartel. Under the terms of the August 1886 Coal Producers' Contract, the railroad retained its transportation monopoly, as well as a sales monopoly through the subsidiary Pocahontas Coal Company. All revenues derived from coal sales would go first to the N&W's general coal agent, who would then calculate the average price per ton that was due to the mine owners. With all mines receiving the same price, there was little incentive to cheat on the cartel. Thanks to the efforts of N&W managers, West Virginia coal operators were able to avoid conflict with one another. Instead, the entire region went to war against the commonwealth of Pennsylvania.[75]

With West Virginia coal threatening to flood the market, PRR officials increased their efforts to stabilize freight charges. An 1883 agreement equalized tidewater rates on coal from the PRR's Clearfield District and the B&O's Cumberland District. Similar accords followed in 1884 and 1885. In 1885, representatives from both the PRR and the B&O did their best to keep West Virginia coal off of the market, threatening a rate war if the N&W continued its initial large-scale shipments to Norfolk. Their efforts were futile, and the N&W's coal traffic grew from half a million tons in 1881 to more than seven million tons in 1894. Beginning in 1886, PRR and B&O officials attempted to make peace with their new competitor, through a traffic pool that gave small allotments to the N&W, as well as to the C&O. For the first time, the N&W was included in the system of port differentials that trunkline officials had established immediately prior to the Civil War, with the varying rates reflecting the added cost of coastal water transportation from more southerly ports to New York and New England.[76]

In April 1887, a month after passage of the Act to Regulate Commerce and the creation of the ICC, railroad managers abandoned the now-illegal traffic pools. In their stead, mine owners established the Seaboard

Steam Coal Association to allocate shipments. The association awarded 32.25 percent of the tidewater traffic to the PRR, 8.25 percent to the B&O, 11.5 percent to the N&W, 10.5 percent to the Beech Creek/NYC, and 9.5 percent to the C&O, with the remainder going to the Erie and the West Virginia Central. Subsequent agreements slightly altered the percentages, but the numbers were largely irrelevant, as every carrier fought to secure a larger-than-allocated share of the coal traffic. Regardless of whether the railroads or the producers attempted to maintain the cartel, the temptation to cheat was simply too strong. Pennsylvania Railroad executives were especially well positioned to shave rates, as their company possessed the lowest operating costs, per ton-mile, of any of the coal carriers. The owners of large collieries along the PRR, such as Westmoreland and Berwind-White, claimed that the posted rates prevented them from winning east coast contracts. They demanded, and usually received, substantial rebates. N&W officials accordingly alleged that the PRR was one of the worst offenders, but the simple reality was that all railroads undercut the rate and allocation structure, making a mockery of every attempt to achieve stability.[77]

What made the situation all the more serious for the PRR and its competitors was that coal prices fell steadily between 1865 and 1898, with particularly severe declines during the depression of the 1890s. Both the N&W and the B&O entered receivership, the former in 1895 and the latter in 1896, and the economic crisis claimed two anthracite carriers—the Reading and the Erie—as well. As the depression deepened, mine owners dissolved the Seaboard Steam Coal Association and expected railroad executives to again take charge of efforts to control excess competition.[78] In 1896, the railroaders created the Tidewater Bituminous Steam Coal Traffic Association, and established another round of traffic pools, now disguised as traffic associations, in compliance with the Act to Regulate Commerce. Those too collapsed, particularly after the bankruptcy of the Baltimore & Ohio induced that company's managers to offer substantial rebates.

The gradual erosion of the ICC's power by the courts further detracted from the railroads' efforts to achieve rate stability. In particular, the Supreme Court decisions in the 1897 *Trans-Missouri Freight Association* and the 1898 *Joint Traffic Association* cases invalidated traffic associations and other types of informal cartels. The replacement of traffic associations with rate bureaus mitigated many of the deleterious effects of the rulings, but seemed unable to control markets. Rates fell sharply in 1897, and conditions were even worse the following year. With the economy still recovering from the depression, and with traffic officials from all of the carriers willing to offer substantial sub rosa rebates, there seemed little possibility that the Pennsylvania Railroad or any of its competitors would receive the rates necessary to fund routine operations, much less the enhancement of the physical plant.[79]

By 1899, the growing conflicts among the PRR, the Beech Creek, the Baltimore & Ohio, the Chesapeake & Ohio, and the Norfolk & Western threatened the stability of the eastern railway network. Executives on bankrupt railroads were generally prone to rate cutting, but Baltimore & Ohio managers turned that process on its head. In December 1898, the receivers of the B&O sent a letter to the Interstate Commerce Commission, complaining that widespread rebating by the PRR and the NYC hampered their efforts to bring their company out of bankruptcy. B&O officials pledged to adhere faithfully to all posted rates, after January 1, 1899, and called upon the ICC "to investigate complaints of illegal rate cutting, and to put a stop to all illegal practices."[80] Given the ICC's limited authority, its commissioners had little opportunity to protect the B&O. The letter nonetheless infuriated PRR and NYC executives—in much the same manner that schoolchildren resent a tattletale—and they vowed to control rates on their terms, before the ICC could become involved.[81]

Despite the willingness of B&O managers to tell tales out of school, the inherent instability in coal rates was the more likely cause of the PRR's commitment to rate control. The PRR's coal freight agent, Robert Large, was particularly pessimistic regarding the PRR's inability to control coal rates. "The continued development in the Pocahontas fields of the Norfolk & Western Railway, and the New River and Kanawha fields of the Chesapeake & Ohio Railway, to say nothing of the development in the Cumberland, Meyersdale, Somerset and Fairmount regions of the Baltimore & Ohio Railroad," Large lamented, "all tend to make the situation a most complicated one."[82]

The Effort to Control Rates

Then, on June 9, 1899, Alexander Johnston Cassatt assumed the presidency of the Pennsylvania Railroad. As a skilled engineer who possessed a superb knowledge of railroad operations, Cassatt was intimately familiar with efforts by PRR personnel to increase operating efficiency. New and improved equipment enabled the company to transport ever-larger volumes of freight, at a steadily decreasing cost per ton-mile. In addition to his transportation skills, Cassatt had been heavily involved in the traffic side of the equation, and he had participated in numerous discussions with his counterparts on other railroads. Increased efficiency, he knew, was of little consequence so long as railroads routinely undercut each other's rates.

Now, as president, Cassatt insisted that rebates for favored shippers posed the greatest threat to rate stability. His predecessors, George Roberts and Frank Thomson, had authorized large rebates to Henry Clay Frick's coke operations (in 1892) and to Carnegie Steel (in 1896 and again in 1898) in order to prevent Carnegie from extending the Bessemer & Lake Erie to serve Frick's coke ovens. Cassatt had far less patience with the steelmaker. He had no sooner taken office than he announced an end to all of the rebates that Roberts and Thomson had negotiated.

Cassatt also attempted to protect the PRR's revenues by abolishing what many railroaders referred to as the "free pass evil." When he took office in 1899, a substantial percentage of the PRR's passengers rode without paying a cent. Annual passes that provided free rail travel had long been a perquisite on the railroads, and they did serve a legitimate function, particularly when employees used them while traveling on company business. Gradually, however, an ever-increasing group of individuals expected to receive free passes. Shippers hinted that a pass might encourage them to ship their products over a particular railroad. Officials associated with other railroads were issued passes as a professional courtesy. Many of the family members of managers on the PRR and other railroads likewise enjoyed free travel. So too did members of the clergy. The granting of free passes to reporters and politicians was a wise public-relations move, but smacked of influence peddling. And, there were extreme examples of the spread of the free pass ill. The

New York, New Haven & Hartford Railroad, a company in which the PRR owned some stock, issued a pass to "Admiral Dewey" (a fox terrier, and not the hero of the Spanish-American War), affixed to his collar, that enabled the dog to enjoy more than twenty-five thousand miles of free travel.[83]

Free passes cost the PRR considerable revenues, while exposing the company to accusations that executives were attempting to bribe legislators and buy off their critics. Members of Congress and various state legislatures spoke out against the practice and periodically proposed legislation to ban free passes, but with little practical result. Early in Cassatt's presidency, representatives from the trunk lines pledged to curtail passes. The *New York Times* labeled efforts to enforce the agreements as "farcical," suggesting that PRR officials were the only ones who had kept their promises. As a result, the railroad lost a substantial amount of business to its competitors. By the summer of 1902, PRR managers indicated that they did "not intend to be hoodwinked again by rival lines," and admitted that they were again issuing free passes. Within a short time, however, Cassatt concluded that the loss in passenger revenue, combined with growing public outrage over free passes, overshadowed the danger that freight business might be diverted to rival lines. By December 1905, Cassatt had ordered a sharp curtailment in the issuance of passes for the new year. As the *Times* observed, even his son, Robert Kelso Cassatt, had to pay his own way.[84]

Cassatt's battle to curtail rebates and free passes placed him in the public view to a greater extent than any president before him. Virtually every study of the Pennsylvania Railroad has characterized Cassatt as an innovative outsider, a savior who took the company's reins following the lackluster tenure of his predecessors, the overly cautious George Roberts and the short-lived Frank Thomson.[85] There is some truth in those assertions, for Cassatt was certainly a charismatic and influential individual. He was not much of an outsider, however, and his efforts to control rates were not terribly innovative. Instead, they were a calculated response to gathering political forces and a logical extension of the policies of those who had preceded him in the president's office.

Even before Cassatt became president, PRR executives were moving to control rates by curtailing rebates

Figure 68. Despite his affluence, his cultured upbringing, and his pursuit of the gentleman's hobbies of fox hunting and horse racing, Cassatt was at heart a skilled engineer and an experienced railroader. Although his clothes were hardly suited for the environment, he was as comfortable amid the detritus of a Pennsylvania Railroad yard as he was in the corporate boardroom—and probably felt more at ease in either location, compared with testifying in front of Congress or the Interstate Commerce Commission.

Pennsylvania Historical and Museum Commission, Pennsylvania State Archives.

and by employing traffic associations to formalize their relationships with other carriers. The plans that came to fruition under the Cassatt administration probably would have developed along similar lines even in his absence, although the new president's superb business, political, and social connections undoubtedly made the process function far more smoothly. By the time Cassatt assumed the presidency, he, in common with every other PRR executive, saw ample evidence that the railroad required massive investments in the physical plant and equipment in order to cope with surging traffic levels and growing congestion. Those investments would not be possible, Cassatt knew, unless the railroads found a way to stabilize rates. Higher rates would generate more money for betterments and would help to attract investment capital from Wall Street, and from Europe.

Cassatt's ability to maintain rates would be sharply limited, however, so long as other carriers granted rebates to their shippers.[86] Efforts to establish and maintain cartels were bound to fail, for all of the reasons that they had failed in the past. They were not legally enforceable, they challenged the prerogatives of the ICC, and they would likely be considered in violation of the antitrust provisions of the 1890 Sherman Act. Ownership was another matter entirely. In interpreting the Sherman Act, the courts did not consider mergers to be a combination in restraint of trade. As such, the law that Congress intended as a control over big business helped unleash a massive merger wave at the close of the nineteenth century in mining and manufacturing, as well as in transportation. There was, as yet, no law preventing the PRR from purchasing its competitors (that would come in 1914, with the Clayton Act). Given the political environment, the only way to prevent other railroads from undermining his efforts to control rebates, Cassatt determined, was to buy them.

Communities of Interest

For Cassatt, timing was everything as he attempted to restore rate stability. Roberts's cautious and careful management between 1880 and 1897 had given the PRR a superbly efficient physical plant, with the lowest operating cost per ton-mile of any of the major carriers. His conservative financial policies, and those of the PRR board, ensured that the company maintained the confidence of investors, and so possessed access to virtually unlimited capital. By the time that Cassatt assumed the presidency, the national economy had largely cast aside the aftereffects of the 1890s depression. Demand for coal was rising, and so, too were coal prices. The 1902 anthracite strike led to an increase in bituminous coal production, generating additional revenue for the Pennsylvania Railroad. The resulting surge in traffic made rebates less imperative and facilitated efforts at coordination in ways that would have been impossible only a few years earlier. Vice president John B. Thayer, who was the PRR executive most intimately associated with the setting of coal rates, acknowledged that Cassatt's efforts to prevent unremunerative rebates were "largely assisted by the tremendous volume of business thrown upon us by the increased prosperity."[87]

Moreover, Cassatt's efforts to assert control over rates were conditioned by profound changes in the nature of the relationships among railroad executives, investors, and investment bankers. During the 1880s,

the spate of competitive system building triggered by Jay Gould had overextended the credit of many railroads, including Gould's Wabash. In 1884, the Wabash entered receivership, as had countless railroads before it. Traditionally, bankruptcy judges had appointed receivers who were responsible for protecting the interests of investors. In this instance, however, Gould retained control of the Wabash and used receivership to reduce the railroad's fixed charges at the expense of bondholders. The federal courts acquiesced to the arrangement, accepting Gould's argument that the replacement of existing management and the breakup of his empire would imperil both the railroad's long-term financial viability and its service to shippers—in other words, that the Wabash and its allies were far more valuable as an integrated transportation system than as the sum of its individual parts.[88]

The shift in judicial philosophy, from the protection of investors to the promotion of system building, greatly increased the involvement of investment bankers in the railroad industry. As carrier after carrier entered receivership, investment bankers restructured their finances, generally by making dramatic reductions in debt. By the time that they had sorted out the bankruptcy wave of the 1890s, investment bankers had reduced the railroads' fixed charges, on average, by 27 percent. Total capitalization rarely decreased, however, and in some cases actually increased. What changed was the mix of debt and equity, and as one declined the other rose. Ultimately, the reorganizations replaced the mandatory obligations associated with bonded debt with the discretionary payments represented by stock dividends. Yet, owing to the increased use of financial instruments such as non-voting preferred stock, the shift from debt to equity rarely empowered shareholders, or enabled them to unseat entrenched management.[89]

Instead, those who gained power and influence in the aftermath of the 1890s reorganizations were the investment bankers. None proved more influential than J. P. Morgan. It was Morgan, as much as Cassatt, who sought closer cooperation among the eastern railroads, Morgan who provided a great deal of the advice and coordination needed to achieve that end, and Morgan who arranged much of the necessary financing—at considerable profit to himself. Long an experienced investment banker, Morgan went beyond the traditional role of marketing securities and devoted much of his time to planning and implementing corporate restructuring. He combined a number of ailing southern carriers—many of them formerly a part of the Southern Railway Security Company—into the Southern Railway, then went on to reorganize the Erie, the Reading, and the Northern Pacific, among others.[90]

For many American railroads, the depression of the 1890s had spelled an end to the financial autonomy of their managers. The investment bankers who had reorganized a record number of bankrupt carriers insisted on having representation on the boards of directors of the reconstituted companies in order to protect their interests and those of their clients. Bankers favored a centralized administrative structure to facilitate closer oversight of executive decisions, a policy that in many respects went against the preferences of professional railroad executives.[91]

Financiers, even those as powerful as J. P. Morgan, were rarely able to exert a lasting influence over the Pennsylvania Railroad or its operations, however. Their greatest obstacle, if it can be called that, was that the PRR never went bankrupt. That disappointing situation kept closed the door that financiers often used to gain control—as representatives of investors in reorganization proceedings, a role that they often parlayed into a seat on the board of directors. The PRR retained its decentralized operating structure, with divisional personnel overseeing day-to-day operations and central office staff setting long-term strategic policy. Some prominent Philadelphia and Pittsburgh bankers nonetheless served as PRR directors. The best known were probably Thomas A. Mellon (1856–64) and his son Andrew W. Mellon (1920–21) and grandson Richard King Mellon (1934–68), but Alexander Biddle (1874–99), Girard National Bank president Daniel B. Cummins (1878–87), Philadelphia National Bank presidents N. Parker Shortridge (1874–1915) and Benjamin B. Comegys (1887–1900), and Girard Trust Company president Effingham B. Morris (1896–1937) were also on the board.[92] They were commercial and not investment bankers, however. Instead, they were individuals who served as intermediaries to the business communities of the two most important cities served by the PRR, and they rarely, if ever, attempted to influence the railroad's strategy.

Morgan gained fame, wealth, and a measure of infamy by combining large railroads into even more massive "communities of interest" that—so critics alleged—monopolized transportation in the United States. While stopping well short of a formal merger, the various community-of-interest plans called for railroads, particularly those that, like the PRR, were in a strong financial position, to buy the stock of their weaker competitors. That shared stock ownership in turn permitted interlocking boards of directors, whose members were in a position to coordinate long-term corporate strategy even if they rarely attempted to influence day-to-day operations. More important, Morgan and his colleagues hoped that the communities of interest would succeed where pools, traffic associations, and rate bureaus had largely failed, by providing a reliable mechanism to set and enforce rates.[93]

Even though the financial chaos that followed the Panic of 1893 convinced Morgan of the desirability of the community-of-interest model, he was not able to bring his plans to fruition until after 1898, as the United States recovered from the depression and the economy flourished. The prosperity created something of a sellers' market, enabling executives and financiers to dictate rates to shippers. Of even greater importance, the surge of wealth enabled U.S. investors to repurchase some $250 million in railway securities from Europe. By 1901, Americans had repatriated about one-quarter of all the securities that had been held by European investors. The influx enabled financiers for the first time to buy and sell entire railway systems rather than mere blocks of securities. Moreover, repatriation, coupled with bankruptcy court rulings that favored entrenched managers and investment bankers, gave Morgan and his colleagues a freer hand in their efforts to create communities of interest.[94]

By 1906, Morgan and other investment bankers, most notably Kuhn, Loeb & Company, had brought together seven communities of interest, each representing more than twenty thousand miles of railroads. The PRR formed the basis of one community of interest, and the rival New York Central another. The lines controlled by James Jerome Hill (the Great Northern; the Northern Pacific; and the Chicago, Burlington & Quincy) dominated the Northwest, while Edward Harriman's roads (the Union Pacific, the Southern Pacific, and the Illinois Central) controlled traffic farther south. Jay Gould had died in 1892, but his son George controlled the remnants of his father's empire, organized into another community of interest. The Rock Island/Santa Fe group and Morgan's Southern Railway and affiliated lines rounded out a consortium that controlled two-thirds of the rail mileage in the United States. More sensationalistic, albeit inaccurate, accounts suggested that there were in truth only six great empires, but that their managers and financiers dominated more than 90 percent of the nation's track.[95]

Although the PRR and the New York Central headed rival communities of interest, executives from the two companies cooperated extensively in order to implement Morgan's plans. Morgan had made his reputation dealing in NYC securities, helping to guide that company through the transition from family to professional management. The process began in 1879, when William Henry Vanderbilt sold more than half of his NYC stock holdings, in part to raise money for expansion and in part to deflect public criticism of his power over the railroads. He died in 1885, and his son, Cornelius Vanderbilt II, took over the active management of the NYC and its subsidiaries. Although he was still a comparatively young man, Cornelius Vanderbilt II suffered a series of strokes, and on September 12, 1899, he succumbed to a massive cerebral hemorrhage at the age of fifty-five. His brother, William Kissam Vanderbilt, inherited oversight of the New York Central, but he gradually withdrew from the company's management. Instead, his brother-in-law, Hamilton McKown Twombly, became the leading force behind the New York Central.[96]

As the nineteenth century came to a close, a new cadre of professional NYC managers, unconnected with the Vanderbilt family, began to implement rate stability. They were particularly displeased that some elements of the New York Central system—particularly the Lake Shore & Michigan Southern and the New York, Chicago & St. Louis Railway (the Nickel Plate Road)—competed against one another and undercut each other's rates. In 1898, NYC managers purchased sufficient stock in both the Lake Shore and the Michigan Central Railroad to give them near-total control of both companies. The following year, the NYC bought a quarter of the Cleveland, Cincinnati, Chicago & St. Louis Railway (the Big Four), the company's principal extension into southern Ohio, Indi-

ana, and Illinois, roughly comparable to the PRR's Southwest System. The Lake Erie & Western Railway, linking Akron to Indianapolis and Peoria, also came under NYC control, as did the Boston & Albany railroad and its route to New England. Thereafter, the Lake Shore for all intents and purposes served as a holding company for the NYC's interests west of Buffalo, in much the same manner that the Pennsylvania Company functioned as the overall corporate umbrella for Lines West. Even so, as late as 1914, the NYC directly owned only about one-fifth of the system's total mileage, while the PRR's ratio was in excess of 50 percent.[97]

As the two dominant eastern trunk lines, the PRR and the NYC formed the logical centerpiece of Morgan's community-of-interest plans in the Northeast. Morgan and Cassatt agreed that the New York Central should establish control over the anthracite railroads that lay south of its established territory and along the northeastern fringes of the PRR's domain. As such, the NYC acquired substantial blocks of securities in the Erie; the Lehigh Valley; the Delaware, Lackawanna & Western; and the Reading, which in turn would control the Jersey Central. In exchange, the PRR would extend its sphere of influence to the south, into the Pocahontas bituminous region, through investments in the Baltimore & Ohio, the Chesapeake & Ohio, and the Norfolk & Western. In many cases, the NYC and the PRR made joint purchases of railroad company stock. In general terms, however, Cassatt—whose railroad was seriously threatened by the West Virginia coalfields—was more committed to the community of interest than were his counterparts on the New York Central.[98]

The Chesapeake & Ohio was the first target. Longtime C&O president Melville E. Ingalls, who had been one of the chief architects of the Joint Traffic Association, was also president of the Big Four and well known to NYC officials. Beginning in November 1899, the NYC's Hamilton Twombly oversaw a combined NYC and PRR acquisition of a 40 percent interest in the Chesapeake & Ohio, for a combined investment of $8,175,000. The arrangement was more in the line of a transfer than an outright purchase, as most of the securities had been in the possession of either the Vanderbilt interests or Drexel, Morgan & Company. Under the terms of a May 1901 agreement, each railroad received four seats on the C&O's board of directors. Cassatt and Morgan chose C&O general manager George W. Stevens to replace Ingalls as president, while PRR vice president John P. Green chaired the C&O finance committee. In June 1901, the PRR bought an additional $1.48 million in C&O stock, in that instance working through Kuhn, Loeb & Company. By then, the PRR had expended $5.57 million to acquire 26 percent of the C&O. Additional purchases followed in December.[99]

Morgan's reorganization of the Baltimore & Ohio, completed in July 1899, coincided with the PRR's efforts to include its southern rival in the community of interest.[100] The new B&O board included chairman William Salomon, representing Speyer & Company, as well as Jacob Schiff (representing Kuhn, Loeb) and western railroad executives James J. Hill and Edward H. Harriman. All of them readily agreed to support Morgan's efforts to develop the community of interest. In November 1899, Vice President Green began buying one hundred thousand shares of B&O preferred stock, worth more than $8.4 million, using Kuhn, Loeb & Company as an intermediary. In early 1900, Green oversaw the purchase of another one hundred thousand shares of preferred stock, giving the PRR about 20 percent of the B&O. Additional stock and bond acquisitions in 1901 and 1902 raised the PRR's investment to $65 million, representing perhaps 40 percent of the company.[101]

Cassatt was determined to apply PRR managerial and financial expertise to the B&O, a railroad that had been sorely lacking in both areas. In February 1900, PRR vice president Sutherland M. Prevost joined the B&O board of directors. John Green followed in November, and took responsibility for the B&O's financial matters. PRR executives Samuel Rea and James McCrea became B&O directors in May 1901. Aside from the contingent of PRR officials, most of the remaining members of the B&O board were pliant representatives from the banking houses of Speyer and Kuhn, Loeb.[102]

In May 1901, PRR officials demanded the resignation of B&O president John K. Cowen, along with general manager F. D. Underwood and assistant general manager Daniel Willard. Cassatt chose the fourth vice president of Lines West, Leonor F. Loree, as the new president of the B&O. Two other PRR executives (George L. Potter, the former general manager of Lines West, and former superintendent of telegraph Arthur Hale) filled the positions that Underwood and Willard had once occupied. By October, Frank D. Casanave, former general superintendent of the Pennsylvania Railroad Grand Division, had become the B&O's new superintendent of motive power. Loree and his fellow PRR transplants copied Cassatt's tactics, placing the B&O's rates on a stable basis and using the resulting increase in revenues to pay for substantial improvements to the company's track and equipment.[103]

The Norfolk & Western ultimately proved to be the most significant component of Cassatt's community of interest, in that it remained affiliated with the PRR for well over half a century, far longer than any other company. The N&W's aggressive expansion into the Flat Top region, as well as its marketing arrangements, had been responsible for much of the instability in coal rates. The company had entered receivership in 1895, giving N&W managers additional incentive to undercut PRR coal rates to tidewater.[104] Under those circumstances, Cassatt was determined to include the N&W in the community of interest in order to stabilize coal rates. Between February and May 1900, working through Kuhn, Loeb, the PRR invested some $13.5 million to buy approximately 30 percent of the securities of the Norfolk & Western. The purchases entitled Cassatt to appoint at first four and later six of the eleven members of the N&W board.[105] In 1901, additional purchases of $4.4 million brought the PRR's ownership stake to 40 percent.[106]

PRR officials soon endeavored to influence the N&W's policies, although far less intrusively than was the case on the B&O. Albert J. County, the PRR's vice president in charge of accounting and corporate work, would later note that his railroad's investment in the N&W "put the concern on its feet," enabling the company to modernize its operations.[107] PRR executives worked closely with their N&W counterparts to coordinate service and control coal prices and output levels, as well as transportation costs. In January 1900, the Tidewater Bituminous Steam Coal Traffic Association issued its annual rate schedule, the first since the implementation of the community of interest.

There was a significant difference from previous years in that the new tariffs now gave preference to the PRR rather than to the more southerly coal roads. A protest by N&W officials in December led to token adjustments, but nothing that would imperil the PRR's advantage. The resulting rate structure, with minor modifications, would last until World War I.[108]

However, at a time when longtime B&O personnel were accusing Leonor Loree and other PRR managers of behaving like an army of occupation, Pennsylvania Railroad executives were careful to emphasize that the N&W's "chief executives and operating officers . . . have always had a free hand from the Pennsylvania Railroad." Their actions did not constitute control, PRR managers emphasized, so much as the "policy of the Pennsylvania Railroad to conserve and assist railroads in providing experienced and active managers." As a result, they claimed, "The Pennsylvania management, plus the operating skill of local officers and the interest of local Directors, has brought the Norfolk & Western up from being a bankrupt road into a position of being a gold mine for its owners"—chief among them the Pennsylvania Railroad itself.[109]

The PRR's influence over the N&W enabled both companies to benefit from the traffic generated by the United States Steel Corporation. The managers of the new company were intent on rationalizing production, and they proposed to fuel their eastern mills with coal and coke from the Connellsville District, while employing the output of the Flat Top–Pocahontas Field at facilities in Ohio, Indiana, and Illinois. They soon set their sights on the Flat Top Coal Land Association, a firm that was closely affiliated with the N&W but still owned by E. W. Clark & Company and its allied investors. In June 1901, two months after the formal organization of U.S. Steel, a syndicate of investors, including Judge Elbert H. Gary, secured an option to purchase the Flat Top Association. Rather than accept a proposed minority interest in the project, N&W officials elected to assume sole control. By the end of December, the N&W interests had incorporated the Pocahontas Coal & Coke Company to buy the Flat Top lands, contingent on a major coal contract with U.S. Steel. Officially, PRR executives did no more than review the legal documents associated with the sale—but most experts concluded that Cassatt had brokered the entire arrangement.[110]

While rich in coal, the lands transferred to Pocahontas Coal & Coke were seriously overvalued, and it was unlikely that initial revenues would be sufficient to meet interest charges. Accordingly, the Pennsylvania Company and the Pan Handle jointly guaranteed a one-third share of the bonds of Pocahontas Coal & Coke, funding more than a million dollars' worth of interest payments between 1902 and 1913.[111] In return, the PRR received the exclusive right to transport coal originating on the N&W north to the Great Lakes. Construction crews soon began to double-track much of the PRR's branch between Columbus and Sandusky, Ohio, as well as the route from Columbus to Chicago in order to accommodate N&W coal traffic bound for the Great Lakes and the Midwest. Improvements to the Cumberland Valley Railroad, in part designed to blunt George Gould's efforts to use the Western Maryland as his extension to tidewater, enabled Pocahontas coal to flow north into Pennsylvania.[112]

Thanks in part to the effects of the Pocahontas Coal & Coke traffic, the close cooperation between the PRR and the N&W continued long after Cassatt's presidency and the formal end of the community of interest.[113] The two railroads interchanged traffic at numerous points in Virginia, Maryland, and Ohio. Gateways at Columbus, Ohio, and Hagerstown, Maryland, were particularly important, as they allowed traffic to bypass Pittsburgh. By the 1920s, PRR officials noted, they were "utilizing the N. & W. as a through route between the east and west."[114] As West Virginia's coal output increased steadily, PRR executives looked forward to "the long future, when its own [Pennsylvania] coal supplies may be measurably depleted or more or less displaced by those from other systems," such as the N&W.[115]

The Community of Interest, to the South and West

In addition to his efforts to stabilize rates on coal traffic moving to tidewater, Cassatt also worked to ensure that connections to the south and west would not disrupt the PRR's operations. South of Washington, he confronted a recurrence of the same problem that had plagued Tom Scott and J. Edgar Thomson some three decades earlier. During the 1870s, working through the Southern Railway Security Company, the two PRR executives had endeavored to establish friendly connections in the South while preventing the unnecessary duplication of the region's rail facilities. Thomson and Scott were particularly anxious to avoid the construction of a second line between Richmond and Washington. As a result, the PRR shared ownership of the critical route between those two cities. The northern portion of the line included the Alexandria & Washington Railroad (after 1887, the Alexandria & Washington Railway) and the Alexandria & Fredericksburg Railway. In 1890, the two companies merged into the Washington Southern Railway, operated by the PRR's Baltimore & Potomac Railroad.

South of Quantico, the independent Richmond, Fredericksburg & Potomac Railroad carried traffic on to Richmond. In 1880, the Richmond & West Point Terminal Railway & Warehouse Company rose from the ashes of the Southern Railway Security Company, but it too failed, entering receivership in 1892. Two years later, J. P. Morgan reorganized the firm as the Southern Railway. That company maintained a strong presence in the South, and the company's New Orleans–Richmond main line funneled considerable freight and passenger traffic to the PRR.[116]

The creation of the Southern Railway did little to stabilize the railroads south of Washington and Richmond, however. In the quarter-century that had elapsed since the collapse of the Southern Railway Security Company, Benjamin F. Newcomer and William T. Walters had pieced together some of its remnants into a system that stretched from Richmond south along the Atlantic seaboard. By 1898, the affiliated lines had been formally consolidated as the Atlantic Coast Line Railroad. The new company owned a substantial interest in the Richmond, Fredericksburg & Potomac, and relied on that carrier for access to Washington, in tandem with the Washington Southern. North of the national capital, the traffic generally followed the PRR's subsidiaries, the Baltimore & Potomac and the Philadelphia, Wilmington & Baltimore, consolidated in 1902 as the Philadelphia, Baltimore & Washington Railroad.

In 1900, Baltimore and Richmond financiers, under the leadership of investment banker John Skelton

Williams, incorporated the rival Seaboard Air Line Railroad, yet the company lacked a secure route between Richmond and Washington. Williams accordingly incorporated the Richmond & Washington Air Line Railway Company, to build a line parallel to that of the RF&P. North of the national capital, the promoters of the SAL envisioned a connection with the B&O and its affiliated Bound Brook Route, as far north as New York. The rivalry between the PRR–RF&P–ACL systems and those of the B&O–Richmond & Washington–Seaboard threatened to create better than a hundred miles of duplicate line between Washington and Richmond and drain away revenues badly needed to improve the RF&P.[117]

Cassatt mediated a settlement that gave the companies serving Washington and Richmond open access to the Richmond, Fredericksburg & Potomac. In September 1901, six railroads—the PRR, the ACL, the Seaboard, the B&O, the C&O, and the Southern—formed the Richmond-Washington Company, with each carrier sharing an equal interest in the new firm. The Richmond-Washington Company bought a controlling interest in the Richmond, Fredericksburg & Potomac and in the Washington Southern, with all of the members of the consortium enjoying equal access to the line between Richmond and Washington. With all of the traffic concentrated along a single route, RF&P officials possessed the wherewithal to improve their company's physical plant, adding new tracks and improving alignments by relocating long stretches of the right of way. In Alexandria, the massive new Potomac Yard, completed in 1906, facilitated the movement of traffic between the Northeast and the South, through the Washington gateway. The formation of the Richmond-Washington Company also enabled Cassatt to cooperate with B&O officials, within the community of interest, to build a new station in the nation's capital under the auspices of the Washington Terminal Company.[118]

To the west, the Hocking Valley Railway threatened to destabilize coal rates, exerting an influence that belied its short length. Since 1881, the Hocking Valley had operated a north–south mainline through Ohio, connecting Pomeroy, on the Ohio River, with the Lake Erie port of Toledo. The route also passed through some of the richest coal deposits in the state. As such, the Hocking Valley could transport coal to

Toledo at rates well below what the PRR could charge to send Pennsylvania coal to comparable lake ports. By 1903, J. P. Morgan & Company had gained control of the Hocking Valley, and the financier soon set out to remedy that rate imbalance. In June, Morgan lent five railroads—including the PRR and its Pan Handle subsidiary—the funds necessary to collectively acquire just over a quarter of the Hocking Valley's stock. Thereafter, Morgan and trunk-line managers could equalize rates on Great Lakes coal traffic.[119]

A Final Confrontation with Carnegie and Gould

While Cassatt's efforts to stabilize rates through the community of interest undoubtedly helped to stabilize the northeastern railroad network, his hard-line approach in the matter of rebates was fraught with peril. Like his predecessor, George Roberts, Cassatt had little patience with Andrew Carnegie's demands for preferential treatment. Roberts's intransigence had caused Carnegie to support the construction of the South Pennsylvania Railroad, and to build his own line—the Pittsburgh, Bessemer & Lake Erie—to the Great Lakes. Cassatt's creation of the community of interest produced similar consequences, leading Carnegie to lend his assistance in the construction of a fifth eastern trunk line, to the obvious detriment of the PRR interests.

By the beginning of the twentieth century, Carnegie and many of his fellow Pittsburgh businessmen were complaining about high rates and poor service on the PRR. In October 1900, Carnegie wrote a vitriolic letter to Carnegie Steel president Charles M. Schwab, in which he labeled the community of interest a "violation of the Constitution."[120] He pleaded with Cassatt, asserting that the cessation of rebates would ruin Carnegie Steel and other major shippers in the Pittsburgh area. In December, Carnegie met Cassatt in Pittsburgh, again demanding the restoration of rebates, and delivering a none-too-veiled threat that he might back the transcontinental ambitions of George Gould.

When Jay Gould died in 1892, his son had inherited much of his father's railroad empire, but little of his organizational skill. George Gould nonetheless oversaw a respectable system that included the Interna-

tional & Great Northern, the Missouri Pacific, the St. Louis Southwestern, the Texas & Pacific, and the Wabash. In conjunction with trackage rights over the Grand Trunk, Gould pieced together a route that stretched from El Paso, Texas, northeast to Buffalo, New York. In 1901, Gould added the Denver & Rio Grande and the Rio Grande Western to his empire, affording access to Salt Lake City. Determined to assemble a transcontinental rail empire, Gould in 1903 began the construction of the Western Pacific Railroad, destined to reach California in 1909. To the east, Gould intended to gain access to Pittsburgh and—he hoped—create a new trunk line by reaching tidewater at Baltimore.[121]

While Gould coveted access to Pittsburgh, it was his business associate, Wabash president (and former PRR executive) Joseph Ramsey, Jr., who suggested how that might be done. Ramsey recommended that Gould acquire the independent Wheeling & Lake Erie Railroad, which connected with the Wabash at Toledo and angled southeast to the Ohio River, with access to Wheeling and Steubenville. From Pittsburgh Junction (near Jewett, Ohio) the Wabash-Pittsburgh Terminal Railway would build a new line sixty miles east into Pittsburgh.[122] Carnegie's Union Railroad would provide access to the city's steel mills. As early as the spring of 1900, Ramsey began quietly buying property and lining up investor support in the Pittsburgh area. Carnegie hoped that Gould could break the PRR's control over railroad rates in southwestern Pennsylvania. He soon agreed to route a quarter of his western traffic over the Gould lines. John D. Rockefeller also appreciated the value of a new eastern trunk line to the Standard Oil Company, and he too established an alliance with Gould. Executives representing the Pittsburgh Coal Company also pledged to divert a substantial share of their business to the new line. On February 1, 1901, with Carnegie's backing, Gould established the Pittsburgh–Toledo Syndicate and began buying W&LE stock.[123]

Carnegie's desire to be free of the Pennsylvania Railroad ultimately threatened the entire steel industry. In addition to building the Pittsburgh, Bessemer & Lake Erie and supporting Gould's efforts to break the PRR's hold on Pittsburgh, Carnegie intended to build a new steel tube plant at Conneaut, Ohio, where the open waters of the Great Lakes would protect him from transportation monopolies. Morgan, already nervous about Carnegie's visions of a railroad empire, was aghast at the prospect, which threatened the National Tube conglomerate that the financier had organized in 1899. Wayne McVeagh, the PRR's chief legal counsel and a personal friend of Andrew Carnegie, attempted, and failed, to mediate a settlement to the dispute. By the autumn of 1900, Morgan had announced that "Carnegie is going to demoralize railroads just as he has demoralized steel" and set about to stop both threats.[124] In February 1901, only weeks after Carnegie had agreed to dispatch a substantial share of his traffic over the Wabash-Pittsburgh Terminal route, Morgan oversaw the creation of United States Steel. The new firm, not organized until April, was famously billed as the world's first billion-dollar corporation. Much of that capitalization was "water," however, and the company probably possessed less intrinsic worth than the Pennsylvania Railroad and its subsidiaries.[125]

The subsuming of the Carnegie Steel Company into U.S. Steel offered PRR officials a chance to bypass Andrew Carnegie's long-standing enmity toward their railroad. On February 26, the day after the incorporation of U.S. Steel, Cassatt wrote to Morgan, asking if he had any knowledge of the arrangements between Gould and Carnegie. Morgan, who knew full well of the agreement, disingenuously replied that he had no knowledge of any such cooperation. Vice president James McCrea soon uncovered the truth, however, and informed Cassatt of Gould's negotiations with both Carnegie and the Pittsburgh Coal Company.[126]

Cassatt did his best to thwart Gould's plans. He began buying W&LE stock, but was unable to wrest control of that carrier from Gould. PRR executives pressured the Pittsburgh City Council to deny Gould the authority to build a bridge into the city, to occupy city streets, to build a passenger terminal, or to operate locomotives fired with bituminous coal. Cassatt threatened to cease buying coal from the Pittsburgh Coal Company should its managers follow through with their proposal to ship over the Gould lines. PRR executives met repeatedly with NYC officials, and with financiers, including Morgan and Jacob Schiff, trying to devise a compromise that would keep Gould from reaching Pittsburgh. By June, the board of directors had authorized substantial additional investments

in the Pennsylvania Steel Company and the Cambria Steel Company, both to prevent U.S. Steel from monopolizing the rail market and to give Cassatt a bargaining chip in his negotiations with Morgan. Gould nearly buckled under the pressure and briefly considered selling the Wabash and the Wheeling & Lake Erie and retreating to the west side of the Mississippi River. By the middle of May, however, he had determined to resist the threats and entreaties of Cassatt, Morgan, and the others. Gould kept both railroads, and his construction crews crept ever closer to Pittsburgh.[127]

Gould's massive construction efforts required equally prodigious infusions of capital. Much of the money, he hoped, would come from West Virginia coal traffic. By December 1901, Gould had established the Little Kanawha Syndicate to purchase rail lines and coalfields in West Virginia. The first acquisition was the unfinished Little Kanawha Railroad, which Gould intended to link to his Wheeling & Lake Erie at Zanesville, Ohio.[128] Within weeks, Gould organized yet another investment consortium, designed to extend his reach to tidewater. Known as the Fuller Syndicate, for International Salt Company president Edward L. Fuller, the group first purchased the West Virginia Central & Pittsburgh Railway, a carrier that tied the Little Kanawha to a connection with the Baltimore & Ohio at Cumberland, Maryland.

Gould's coal railroads, stretching south and east of Pittsburgh, also offered the financier an opportunity to reach tidewater at Baltimore. The critical element would be the Western Maryland Railroad, a project that dated to the 1850s. By the 1870s, the Western Maryland operated a line as far west as Hagerstown, Maryland, and a connection to nearby Williamsport gave the company access to coal traffic off of the Chesapeake & Ohio Canal. With the Baltimore & Ohio under the influence of the PRR, the Western Maryland was also Gould's only mechanism for reaching Chesapeake Bay. In May 1902, the members of the Baltimore City Council voted to sell the city's interest in the Western Maryland to Gould and his allies in the Fuller Syndicate. They apparently sought to increase transportation competition and prevent the PRR, the B&O, or the Reading from buying the line.[129] Thanks to the acquisition of the Western Maryland, Gould had come tantalizingly close to achieving his dream of a coast-to-coast railroad empire.[130]

But not close enough. The eastern terminus of Gould's West Virginia Central was at Cumberland, Maryland, and the Western Maryland extended no closer than Cherry Run, fifty-nine miles away. Gould's surveyors were soon at work locating a line between the two communities. Until construction could be completed, however, the Baltimore & Ohio was the only railroad that bridged the gap. Cassatt's community of interest again proved its value to the PRR. After September 1, 1902, B&O president Leonor Loree refused to accept any of Gould's coal traffic. Gould owned both coal lands and railroads, yet lacked any effective mechanism for getting that coal to tidewater. The obvious solution was to extend the Western Maryland west to Cumberland, but that would take both time and money—and, without the coal revenues that Gould desperately needed, both commodities were in short supply.[131]

While Cassatt was willing to tolerate Gould's efforts to reach Pittsburgh, the PRR president simply could not countenance the development of a new eastern trunk line. The financier's purchase of the Western Maryland incensed Cassatt to the point of fury and led to a spectacular form of retribution. In May 1901, a year before Gould acquired the Western Maryland, Cassatt had telephoned vice president James Wood, asking his opinion regarding possible "retaliatory measures."[132] After a few days of deliberation, Wood presented Cassatt with six options for attacking the upstart financier. One involved the extension of the Eel River Railroad to Toledo, creating a PRR route that would essentially parallel Gould's Wabash between St. Louis and Lake Erie. Another possibility reflected the presence of a portion of George Gould's empire that, infuriatingly, lay literally on top of the Pennsylvania Railroad.[133]

In years past, Jay Gould had observed that the operation of telegraph lines along railroad rights of way could prove enormously profitable. However, the Western Union Telegraph Company dominated the communications sector, and that firm was under the control of the Vanderbilt family. In 1879 Congress passed the Butler Amendment, granting telegraph companies open access to railroad routes, and Gould

was quick to take advantage of the new law. He formed the American Union Telegraph Company and soon persuaded many railroads to abandon Western Union in favor of his new organization. PRR officials were particularly receptive, given the dual involvement of the Vanderbilts in the New York Central and in Western Union. Even better, Gould was willing to pay a high price for the right to string lines along the PRR—a $100,000 annual rental that perhaps represented a greater cost than his combined investments in American Union's wires, poles, and other equipment.[134]

At those rates, Gould could not make money off of his telegraphy contracts, nor did he expect to. Instead, he hoped to create a franchise war that would undermine Western Union and force William H. Vanderbilt to the bargaining table. The tactic worked, and in February 1881, Gould and his allies gained several seats on the board of Western Union, newly merged with American Union. In the process, Western Union inherited the recently negotiated American Union contract. Some six months later, on September 20, 1881, a supplemental contract permitted PRR officials to demand the removal of all Western Union equipment after twenty years. Following Jay Gould's death, control over Western Union—and the PRR contract—passed to his son.[135]

The Western Union's twenty-year agreement with the PRR lapsed in September 1901, just as George Gould was pushing the Wabash-Pittsburgh Terminal toward Pittsburgh. On September 24, four days after the expiration of the contract, Cassatt informed Gould that, should he proceed with his plans to reach Pittsburgh, all Western Union equipment would be removed from PRR property.[136]

The situation remained in flux for nearly another year, but Gould's imminent control over the Western Maryland goaded Cassatt into drastic action. A week after the City of Baltimore approved the sale of the Western Maryland, the PRR board agreed to terminate the contract with Western Union. By then, the Postal Telegraph-Cable Company, which John W. Mackay had organized in 1886 as a competitor to Western Union, was prepared to offer far better terms for access to the PRR right of way. On June 25, 1902, Cassatt signed a contract with Postal Telegraph and demanded that Western Union president Robert C.

Clowery remove all poles, wires, and other equipment from PRR property by December 1. On October 18, 1902, Western Union officials filed suit in the Western Pennsylvania United States Circuit Court at Pittsburgh, defending their right to occupy the PRR right of way. The PRR won the first round, but in the New Jersey United States Circuit Court, Judge Andrew Kirkpatrick held that the PRR was by 1866 federal law a post road, and that, as such, Cassatt was obliged to permit continued public access to the PRR right of way. On May 19, 1903, the United States Circuit Court of Appeals reversed that decision and ruled against Gould and Western Union.[137]

Gould vowed to appeal the ruling to the United States Supreme Court, but Cassatt preferred not to wait for the judicial proceedings to run their course. On May 21, 1903, PRR crews began removing the Western Union's equipment. Workmen initially attacked the poles with axes. When that proved too slow, they looped chains around the poles and used locomotives to drag them to the ground. They had no sooner cleared away the wreckage than Postal Telegraph-Cable Company crews rebuilt the lines with their own equipment. The fracas destroyed 60,000 poles and more than 1,500 miles of telegraph wire, with a loss to Western Union of perhaps $500,000.[138]

Although the courts ultimately acknowledged Cassatt's authority to expel Western Union from PRR property, observers were nonetheless aghast at his vitriolic reaction to Gould and decried Cassatt's willingness to "descend to about the level of primitive man."[139] J. P. Morgan, always concerned that unrestrained emotion could undermine efforts at stability, allegedly told Cassatt, "I do not like George Gould, but I do not like a man who destroys $5 million of vested property."[140] Even if Morgan had grossly overestimated the value of the Western Union's assets, he was right to be concerned that the larger confrontation between Cassatt and Gould would erode the value of all of the northeastern railroads. As one of Gould's key allies, John D. Rockefeller likewise had little desire to see the value of his railroad investments stripped away by a rate war between the PRR and the Wabash.

Rockefeller accordingly took the lead in mediating a truce between Gould and Cassatt. By January 1904, Gould had pledged that he would not use his investments in the Lackawanna, the Reading, and the Jersey Central as a mechanism for establishing an eastern terminus at New York or Philadelphia. In return, Cassatt abandoned his earlier efforts to prevent Gould from reaching tidewater at Baltimore. The PRR also ceased its delaying tactics in the Pittsburgh City Council, and that body promptly voted to allow the Wabash-Pittsburgh Terminal Railway to establish freight and passenger facilities in the city.[141] Cassatt pledged to make restitution for the full value of the Western Union property that he had ordered destroyed. The PRR further mollified Pittsburgh residents by investing more than $25 million in improvements in the area between 1902 and 1909.[142]

With Cassatt's capitulation, Gould was able to complete his line through Pittsburgh and to tidewater. By the summer of 1904 Gould and his associates had completed the Wabash-Pittsburgh Terminal into Pittsburgh. To the east, construction of the link between Cherry Run and Cumberland, under way since the summer of 1903, was completed in February 1906. By 1907, Gould was also promoting a line connecting the Wabash-Pittsburgh Terminal with the Western Maryland, at Cumberland, passing through the rich Connellsville coke region along the way.[143]

Even though Gould was in control of what the *New York Times* referred to as "a through and direct line from St. Louis through the richest parts of Illinois, Indiana, Ohio, the coal lands of western Virginia, and western Maryland to tidewater," his empire was on the brink of collapse.[144] No sooner had he completed his route to Pittsburgh than representatives from both the PRR and the B&O agreed to match his rates—and those two carriers had far greater reserves to last them through a rate war. The Wabash-Pittsburgh Terminal carried little freight traffic, and its passenger trains were virtually bereft of travelers. A further blow came in March 1905, when Elbert Gary, chairman of the board at U.S. Steel, promised to withdraw his support for Gould in exchange for a pledge by PRR executives to part with their investments in the Pennsylvania Steel Company and the Cambria Steel Company. To the east, Cassatt ordered the rebuilding of the PRR's Cumberland Valley Railroad between Harrisburg and a connection with the B&O at Martinsburg, West Virginia. He then pressured West Virginia coal producers to ship to tidewater over that route, starving the Western Maryland of revenue. Leonor Loree also used the B&O to buy three of the largest mining companies in West Virginia, both to keep them out of Gould's reach and to ensure that their output traveled over either the B&O or the PRR–Cumberland Valley route and not the Western Maryland. Absent the coal traffic that composed 70 percent of its income, the Western Maryland was soon in a precarious financial position.[145]

The enormous cost of the Pittsburgh extension, combined with its limited traffic potential, drained the resources of the Wabash and the other companies that made up the Gould system. The Panic of 1907 ended Gould's dreams of a transcontinental railroad network. In 1908, the Wheeling & Lake Erie, the Wabash-Pittsburgh Terminal Railway, and the Western Maryland all entered receivership. Three years later, the Wabash followed suit. Gould's plans had come to naught, but the shattered pieces of his empire remained in place. The financier lived until 1923, long enough to witness the disruptive effects of his proposed trunk line on the stability of the eastern railroad network.[146]

The Reading Joins the Community of Interest

George Gould's efforts to extend his empire to tidewater led to an expansion of the community of interest. In 1901, as described above, PRR officials accelerated their purchases of Chesapeake & Ohio, Baltimore & Ohio, and Norfolk & Western securities, in part to direct coal traffic away from the Gould roads. Their counterparts on the New York Central acquired a substantial share of the Lehigh Valley Railroad, blocking one of Gould's possible outlets to New York.[147] The Lehigh Valley purchase also meshed with efforts by Morgan and the Vanderbilt family to influence all of the anthracite carriers in northeastern Pennsylvania, stabilizing both transportation rates and hard-coal prices.[148]

Morgan's efforts to control the anthracite fields dovetailed with Cassatt's desire to keep Gould away from Philadelphia and led to the inclusion of the Reading in the community of interest. The Reading,

bankrupt in the 1890s, had by 1901 become a quite valuable property. Morgan's 1896 reorganization of the Reading Rail Road into the Reading Company had coordinated the mining, transportation, and marketing of anthracite. In 1901, the Reading acquired a controlling interest in the Jersey Central, establishing a secure access to New York Harbor. Gould coveted the Reading, because it provided an outlet to both New York and Philadelphia, and because it promised to generate badly needed traffic and revenues. In addition to gaining control of the Western Maryland route to Baltimore, Gould had negotiated a traffic agreement with the Reading that included access to New York.

Cassatt was understandably concerned that Gould might move to acquire the Reading, if for no other reason than to gain access to its Philadelphia terminal facilities, most notably the coal piers at Port Richmond. In March 1902, Cassatt first proposed to the NYC's Hamilton Twombly that their two companies divide the Reading between them. Twombly and NYC president William K. Vanderbilt were amenable to such an agreement ("share and share alike," Vanderbilt noted), but balked when Cassatt demanded that the Reading be allowed to send as much New York traffic as possible south to Philadelphia.[149] Vanderbilt perceived that an alliance of the PRR, the Reading, and the B&O might draw traffic away from the NYC's east–west main line. Cassatt was therefore quick to emphasize that he had "no disposition . . . to disturb the relations then existing between the Reading Railway Co. and the Baltimore & Ohio," regarding the allocation of traffic over the Bound Brook Route.[150]

Suitably reassured, the NYC interests agreed to cooperate with Cassatt in order to deprive Gould of access to the Reading. During the summer of 1902, the PRR's new fourth vice president, Samuel Rea, brokered a deal to purchase $43 million worth of Reading stock, to be split equally with the NYC. Rea and Cassatt were sensible of the reaction that was likely to accompany news that the PRR had joined forces with its long-standing rival. With the B&O already allied with the PRR, the inclusion of the Reading in the community of interest would create a virtual transportation monopoly in southeastern Pennsylvania. When a reporter for the *New York Times* suggested as much, first vice president John P. Green was quick to dismiss the allegation. "The story is a lie," he retorted, but Green and his PRR associates would have been foolish to further antagonize public opinion.[151] At the same time, the Pennsylvania constitution prohibited the merger of any parallel railroads chartered in the state. Accordingly, B&O president Leonor Loree took responsibility for buying slightly less than 40 percent of the Reading's shares through Kuhn, Loeb, with the B&O holding half of the stock. He assigned an equal amount to the New York Central's Lake Shore & Michigan Southern subsidiary, with independent local interests owning a substantial block, as well.[152]

When the news of the joint Reading purchase became public in January 1903, the B&O's involvement did little to calm the fears of Pennsylvanians or their elected officials. The two principal trunk lines had established a transportation duopoly in the east, with the PRR controlling all of the routes that led to Philadelphia, and the NYC dominating those serving New York. An editorial in the *Baltimore Herald* warned readers that "this tendency toward concentration . . . if not checked by some means . . . will not end until all the railroads in the country will be under one management and competition become an obsolete condition."[153]

New Routes to the Great Lakes

Even as he extended the PRR's influence to the south, under the terms of the community of interest, Cassatt also moved north, to Lake Erie and Lake Ontario. The cities along the southern shore of the Great Lakes were traditionally the domain of the NYC, but Cassatt's actions did not constitute a direct challenge to the Vanderbilt system. Instead, Cassatt was chasing the northward migration of the steel mills out of Pittsburgh. Conventional wisdom had generally suggested that it was far easier to bring the iron ore to the coal, rather than the coal to the iron ore—hence the survival of Pittsburgh mills, long after Michigan and Minnesota ores had replaced those mined in Pennsylvania. By the dawn of the twentieth century, however, new steel producers were putting that theory to the test, building lakeside mills that permitted the convenient shipment of Michigan and Minnesota iron ore by water, with coal arriving by rail.[154]

As early as 1895, Andrew Carnegie had suggested the possibility of shifting steel production out of Pittsburgh and toward the Great Lakes ports. To be sure, the Scotsman was speaking to an appreciative audience of Clevelanders, but industry insiders could not help but take notice of his attitudes. In 1899, officers of the Lackawanna Iron & Steel Company elected to relocate their operations from Scranton, where they had been based since 1840, to a new facility at Stony Point, south of Buffalo. The move brought the company within easier reach of their iron ore supplies and, as an added bonus, took them farther away from their recently unionized coal miners. The firm established extensive facilities and a company town at the site, soon renamed Lackawanna, New York. When Morgan orchestrated the creation of the U.S. Steel trust in 1901, Lackawanna Iron & Steel remained aloof, as the second-largest steel company in the world. Several other, smaller firms added to Buffalo's luster as a steel-producing center. The Buffalo & Susquehanna Iron Company's South Buffalo facility entered service in 1904. The New York Steel Company, incorporated in 1905, promised additional traffic.[155]

In 1900, in response to the development of steel production in New York, Cassatt sought a mechanism for bringing trainloads of coal to Buffalo. He found one in the Western New York & Pennsylvania Railway. That carrier had a long and convoluted history, only the barest details of which need be listed here. Given its eventual place in the PRR family, the company rather ironically owed its origins to the Erie Canal. Buffalo boomed following the canal's completion, yet its merchants chafed at the restrictions posed by winter, when the Great Lakes were frozen and the canal was out of service. With little loyalty to the state that had created the Erie Canal in the first place, they advocated a rail route south, into Pennsylvania. Such a line would also provide access to the coal and timber reserves in the northern part of the Keystone State.

There were many proposals to link northwestern Pennsylvania to Buffalo, but the earliest to assume tangible form was the Buffalo & Allegheny Valley Railroad. Incorporated in May 1853, its promoters intended to link Buffalo and Pittsburgh by way of Olean, New York. Little progress resulted, and the project lay dormant for the next twelve years. It was resurrected in 1865 as the Buffalo & Washington Railroad, which soon merged with the moribund Buffalo & Allegheny Valley to form the Buffalo & Washington Rail*way*. A year later, the company subsumed the Sinnemahoning Portage Railroad, a Pennsylvania-chartered company that was to build the line between a junction with the Philadelphia & Erie, at Emporium, and the New York state line, south of Olean. Construction proceeded slowly southward, with the company chronically short of funds, and might never have been completed had it not been for the efforts of Buffalo manufacturer Sherman S. Jewett. He solicited funds from New York investment banker Joseph Seligman, a German émigré whose banking house, J. & W. Seligman & Company, invested heavily in western railroads, as well as the New York elevated railway system. In 1871, with Seligman's support, the company was reorganized as the Buffalo, New York & Philadelphia Railway. By December 1872, construction crews had completed a line between Buffalo and Emporium.[156]

As the nation recovered from the effects of the Panic of 1873, a group of New York investors envisioned the Buffalo, New York & Philadelphia as a key component in a regional railroad empire that would link Pittsburgh with New York and New England via the Great Lakes ports of Buffalo and Rochester. They were not professional railroaders like J. Edgar Thomson or Tom Scott, nor were they even empire builders in the vein of Jay Gould. Instead, they merely sought speculative profits, particularly if they could buy a floundering company on the cheap. Joseph Seligman and his family dominated the New York interests. Another key player was Edward W. Clark, representing E. W. Clark & Company, the firm that had given Jay Cooke—progenitor of the Panic of 1873—his first job in the world of finance. Henry Post and Colonel Archer N. Martin represented another New York banking house, Post, Morton & Company.[157]

Seligman and the others were poised to take advantage of any available opportunities in railroad speculation, from moribund charters to lines that were in operation, but performing poorly. They were particularly interested in the routes leading to the oilfields in northwestern Pennsylvania—many of them lightly used after the oil boom had peaked. The Oil Creek & Allegheny Railway, the product of an 1868 consolida-

tion of several regional lines, had had a particularly unhappy existence.[158] The company, under the control of the Philadelphia & Erie, had once been critical to the PRR's involvement in the oil trade. By 1872, however, the region's output was dwindling, and the Philadelphia & Erie transferred its stake in the Oil Creek & Allegheny to the Allegheny Valley Railroad. By the end of 1875, the Oil Creek line was in foreclosure, and was snapped up by former Buffalo mayor William Fargo and his associate William G. Moorhead, individuals who were better known for their association with the Northern Pacific Railway. They in turn sold the line, now reorganized as the Pittsburgh, Titusville & Buffalo Railway, to the Seligman interests. In 1880, the members of the group gained control over the Buffalo, Chautauqua Lake & Pittsburgh Railway, giving them access to Lake Erie at Brocton, New York.[159] They soon incorporated the Buffalo, Pittsburgh & Western Railway to build from Brocton east to Buffalo, paralleling the Lake Shore & Michigan Southern. In January 1881, the two companies (the Pittsburgh, Titusville & Buffalo Railway and the Buffalo, Pittsburgh & Western Railway) merged to form the Buffalo, Pittsburgh & Western Rail*road*.[160]

Family patriarch Joseph Seligman died in 1880, but his son Isaac and his nephew Theodore soon took his place. During the early 1880s, the Seligman and Clark-Post-Martin groups were associated with George I. Seney and his associates, who were the backers of the Nickel Plate. When combined with the New York, West Shore & Buffalo Railway, the system promised to parallel the New York Central and its affiliates for virtually the entire distance between New York and Chicago. The effects on the New York Central—which were very much connected to the South Pennsylvania Railroad issue—were less important to the Seligmans than their vision of using the Buffalo, Pittsburgh & Western to give the West Shore access to Pittsburgh and to provide the Baltimore & Ohio with a route from Pittsburgh into New York and New England. To a substantial degree, their plan depended on the New Castle & Oil City Railroad linking New Castle and Stoneboro, Pennsylvania. The development of the line north of New Castle began in July 1864, with the incorporation of the New Castle & Franklin Railroad.[161] As events transpired, the Seligman interests were never able to piece together a complete route between Buffalo and Pittsburgh by way of Oil City, but for a time it appeared that they might have been able to do so.[162]

Even as the Vanderbilt interests were fending off the Nickel Plate/West Shore threat by buying those two companies, the Seligmans and their allies developed other plans for the Buffalo, Pittsburgh & Western Railroad. In 1881, they bought the Buffalo, New York & Philadelphia Railway (the more easterly route, between Buffalo and Emporium) from Sherman Jewett, and they soon sought a mechanism to connect their two properties. During 1881 and 1882, the Buffalo, Pittsburgh & Western built a line between Warren and Salamanca, New York, a city on the Erie's main line. Between 1882 and 1883, the Buffalo, New York & Philadelphia constructed a connecting route, the Olean & Salamanca Railroad, paralleling the Erie, between Salamanca and Olean. Trackage rights on the Philadelphia & Erie between Warren and Irvineton enabled the New York investors to jointly operate their two lines stretching south from Buffalo.[163]

The Seligman interests established control over yet another railroad, one that provided access to Rochester, New York. The route dated to March 1867 and the incorporation of the Northern Railroad & Navigation Company, but most of the construction took place under the aegis of a successor company, the Rochester, Nunda & Pennsylvania Railroad.[164] Initially, the principal target was a large tract of coal and timber land near Clermont, Pennsylvania, owned by one of the chief promoters of the enterprise. The resulting line was incomplete, poorly financed, and badly constructed, with portions laid to three-foot gauge. It fell victim to the depression of the 1870s and was reorganized in 1877 as the Rochester, Nunda & Pittsburgh Railroad. The new company limped on for a few more years, but came to grief in 1881.[165]

In February 1881, the Seligman syndicate acquired the Rochester, Nunda & Pittsburgh and folded it into a new corporation, the Rochester, New York & Pennsylvania Railroad. They rebuilt and completed the line, joining Olean to Rochester. For the northernmost portion of the route, they established the Genesee Valley Canal Railroad (so called because it possessed the right to lay rails along the towpath of the abandoned Genesee Valley Canal) and the Genesee

Valley Terminal Railroad, in order to gain access to industrial districts in Rochester and to ensure connections with the New York Central and the Erie. Within a short time, the Buffalo, New York & Philadelphia had leased the three railroads that composed the route between Olean and Rochester. In February 1883, the Buffalo, New York & Philadelphia Railway and the Buffalo, Pittsburgh & Western Railroad, along with the Olean & Salamanca Railroad and the Oil City & Chicago Railroad (the corporate successor to the New Castle & Franklin Railroad, the proposed link to Pittsburgh), merged into the Buffalo, New York & Philadelphia Rail*road*. The New York banking interests were well aware of the rivalry between the New York Central and the New York, West Shore & Buffalo, and they hoped that the Buffalo, New York & Philadelphia route to Rochester would appeal to either side as a means to reach Pittsburgh. The rivalry did not end until the autumn of 1885, when the Vanderbilts leased the West Shore.[166]

With three interconnected routes to the Great Lakes—one to Rochester and two to Buffalo—the New York investors set their sights to the south and acquired control over lines leading to New Castle, Pennsylvania, proximate to Pittsburgh. Their intent was to link the B&O at Pittsburgh with the Great Lakes, and with the Erie and New York Central routes heading east. Pennsylvania Railroad executives were obviously opposed to the development of such a system. They were even more concerned at the possibility that the Buffalo, New York & Philadelphia might serve as the western outlet for the Reading by way of the projected Jersey Shore, Pine Creek & Buffalo Railway (after 1884 the Pine Creek Railway) link between Williamsport and Port Allegany. It was that threat, as much as the intrusion of the New York Central's Beech Creek Railroad into the Clearfield District coalfields, that precipitated the conflict between the PRR and the NYC and led to the South Penn fiasco, as described in Chapter 12.[167]

The depression of the 1880s shattered the plans of the Seligman group. In May 1885, the Buffalo, New York & Philadelphia slid into receivership. J. P. Morgan, who was just establishing his reputation as a financier, stepped in to sort out the mess. By October 1887, he had reorganized the company as the Western New

York & Pennsylvania Railroad.[168] The Seligman interests nonetheless maintained their influence over the reorganized firm. The depression of the 1890s, even more severe than the one that had occurred during the previous decade, again led to receivership. As a result, in March 1895, the Western New York & Pennsylvania Railroad became the Western New York & Pennsylvania Rail*way*.[169]

The new company enjoyed some financial success, but hardly enough to attract the attention of PRR executives—until they learned of Buffalo's future as a steel center. By February 1900, credible rumors on Wall Street suggested that the PRR was buying large blocks of Western New York & Pennsylvania securities, mostly from European investors. PRR officials planned to merge the company with the Allegheny Valley, but the Western New York & Pennsylvania's New York investors opposed such a plan. In March, in a time-honored method of retaliation, PRR officials incorporated the Pennsylvania & Buffalo Connecting Railroad to form part of an alternate route between Buffalo and the tracks of the Philadelphia & Erie. With Cassatt already heavily invested in the community of interest, it is unlikely that the PRR would have spent copiously on a duplicate line with limited traffic potential. Cassatt's threat was nonetheless clear enough to put the Western New York & Pennsylvania investors in a more conciliatory mood. In April 1900, the PRR board approved the purchase of a controlling interest in the Western New York & Pennsylvania. By August, the new member of the PRR family, along with the Allegheny Valley, was being operated as the Buffalo & Allegheny Grand Division, and track crews were soon at work upgrading the lines to PRR standards.

In hindsight, Cassatt probably paid too much for the PRR's access to Buffalo and Rochester. While coal flowed north to the lakes in substantial quantities, and iron ore moved from Buffalo south to Pittsburgh, traffic in grain and in finished steel products was more apt to follow the New York Central, the Erie, or even the Erie Canal to the east coast. The presence of Cornelius Vanderbilt III and Hamilton Twombly on the board of directors of the Lackawanna Iron & Steel Company was emblematic of the problems that PRR officials would face in their efforts to exploit Buffalo's burgeoning industrial base.[170]

The PRR's other access to Lake Ontario, at Sodus Point, was hardly more favorable. During the Civil War, Northern Central Railway officials had negotiated trackage rights over the Philadelphia & Erie between Sunbury and Williamsport. On April 15, 1863, they leased the Elmira & Williamsport Railroad, a recently reorganized company with tracks that extended seventy-eight miles north to Elmira, New York. The same year, the Northern Central and the Erie Railway consented to the joint operation of the Buffalo, New York & Erie Railroad and its subsidiary, the Rochester & Genesee Valley Railroad, providing access to Rochester and Buffalo. That arrangement proved unsatisfactory, largely because of the need to break bulk at Elmira, as freight and passengers transferred between the Northern Central's standard gauge and the Erie's six-foot gauge. The 1863 agreement lasted only until 1866, when the Erie instead leased to the Northern Central the Elmira, Jefferson & Canandaigua Rail Road and its subsidiary, the Chemung Railroad. By 1868, the addition of a third rail enabled standard-gauge equipment to use the line.[171] The resulting route provided the Northern Central, and the PRR, with a link between Williamsport and Canandaigua. From Canandaigua, the New York Central's Auburn Branch provided onward connections, albeit through territory dominated by the New York Central and the Erie.[172]

The Sodus Point & Southern Rail Road offered more secure access to Lake Ontario, at the location of the largest calm-water port on the south side of the lake. Incorporated in 1852, construction began soon thereafter, and was suspended with almost equal alacrity. By 1872, construction crews were back at work, and in January 1873 they completed a line linking Sodus Point with Gorham, New York. At Stanley, little more than a mile from its southern terminus, the Sodus Point & Southern connected with the Elmira, Jefferson & Canandaigua, completing a through line between Williamsport and Lake Ontario.[173]

The Sodus Point & Southern (reorganized in 1875 as the Ontario Southern Railroad) was a poor prospect, but it appealed to Edward H. Harriman, who bought it on the cheap, as his first step on what was to be a stellar career in railroad finance and operations. In 1884, Harriman unloaded the company on the Northern Central, giving the PRR direct control over the entire line to Lake Ontario. Northern Central officials soon authorized the construction of a massive coal terminal at Sodus Point. The expansion of the docks a decade later increased the port's ability to process outbound shipments of Pennsylvania anthracite, much of which was destined for Canadian ports. Buffalo possessed far better facilities than Sodus Point, however, and the Lake Ontario port quickly lost ground to its Lake Erie rival. In 1882 the New York, Lackawanna & Western Railroad (the western extension of the Delaware, Lackawanna & Western) reached Buffalo, while the Lehigh Valley Railroad completed its own line in 1895, further reducing the value of the PRR's connection to Sodus Point.[174]

Benefits and Costs of the Community of Interest

Cassatt's community-of-interest plan was an immediate success, but one that was fraught with long-term consequences. As Cassatt, Morgan, and others envisioned, the overlapping ownership and interlocking directorates dampened down destructive competition among the eastern railroads. In 1900, for the first time in their history, the carriers were generally able to maintain posted coal rates. After 1900, the disruptive efforts of N&W managers to deliver coal to the New York market had ceased. The even more destabilizing efforts of George Gould met a quick end, thanks to the close cooperation between the PRR and the B&O. In other instances, however, the community of interest proved less successful—particularly in 1900, when westbound tariffs fell sharply, and in 1901, when the trunk lines slashed grain rates to extremely low levels. Such cases were the exception, however. According to economist William Z. Ripley, "The general situation in 1900 was more satisfactory than at any previous time in the history of railroading in the United States. With few exceptions the published rates were observed."[175]

In general, the stability and rising rates generated by the community of interest had a salubrious effect on the PRR's profitability. When Cassatt became president in 1899, average freight revenues stood at well under half a cent per ton-mile, with passenger revenues averaging less than two cents per mile. At the time of

his death in 1906, freight revenues had climbed to almost six cents per ton-mile, and passenger revenues, while growing at a smaller rate, were now in excess of two cents per mile.[176]

Rate stabilization made possible massive investments in the PRR's physical plant and equipment. In March 1903, Cassatt informed the shareholders that the railroad had already expended a quarter of a billion dollars over the previous five years, largely under his presidency, to upgrade equipment and the physical plant, and to purchase the securities of other railroads. He made it clear that he was not done yet, and that he planned to authorize an additional $67 million as soon as possible, just to keep pace with the increase in traffic. The PRR borrowed a large portion of that money, but the remainder came from the enhanced operating revenues that the community of interest had generated. Even the borrowed funds became easier to obtain, as rate stability convinced investors that the railroads remained a sound credit risk. The New York Improvements, particularly the massive Pennsylvania Station in Manhattan, constituted the most spectacular results of the increased investment. However, the additional revenues generated by the community of interest also made possible a plethora of other projects, all designed to increase the efficiency of the PRR's operations while speeding the flow of freight and passenger traffic.[177]

The costs associated with the community of interest were also substantial. In the first five months of 1900 alone, the PRR purchased $17.1 million in B&O stock (200,000 shares), $4.1 million in C&O stock (125,000 shares), and $13.5 million in N&W stock (260,000 shares), forcing the board of directors to authorize an emergency $20 million loan to obtain the necessary funds. The totality of the PRR's community-of-interest investments in the C&O, the B&O, the N&W, and the Reading cost the Pennsylvania Railroad in excess of $110 million, equivalent to more than a third of the PRR's total assets in 1898.[178] That enormous investment, in tandem with the money borrowed for improvements, taxed American and European capital markets and made future borrowing more difficult. Furthermore, each newspaper headline that announced the PRR's expenditure of millions of dollars in order to purchase the securities of another railroad, rather than to improve service, undermined Cassatt's efforts to portray the PRR as a modern and progressive company dedicated to the public welfare. Such purchases smacked of monopoly and made it more difficult for Cassatt and his successors to argue that the ICC's rate structure had left it starved for capital.

Cassatt and his fellow executives had, perhaps naively, asserted that the community of interest had created a level playing field, ensuring fair and just rates for all, with favoritism toward none. The PRR's 1902 *Annual Report* suggested that "the doing away with unjust discriminations and preferences between shippers, and the placing thereby of the transportation business of the country upon a stable basis, cannot fail to bring about better relations between the public and the railroad companies, and must also add largely to the value of railroad investments and to the security of the business interests which are dependent upon railway transportation."[179]

Many shippers, regulators, legislators, reporters, and citizens saw the matter somewhat differently, however. From coast to coast, competition seemed to be vanishing. Anthracite mines and railroads operated as one. Cassatt and Morgan had united virtually all of the railroads of the Northeast. Edward H. Harriman had pulled together the Union Pacific, the Southern Pacific, and the Illinois Central—and for good measure had worked with Morgan and James J. Hill to create the 1901 Northern Securities Company, a conglomeration of the Great Northern, the Northern Pacific, and the Chicago, Burlington & Quincy. Few Americans believed that the massive late-nineteenth century railroads were lacking in revenues or capital, and many observers confidently asserted that all competition had unnaturally disappeared from the transportation sector of the economy. Despite the rapidly declining fortunes of agrarian Populism, many western farmers continued to speak out against what they considered to be unjust discrimination and indefensibly high freight rates. In 1901, Frank Norris published *The Octopus: A California Story*, a sensationalistic and wildly inaccurate account of alleged depredations by the Southern Pacific Railroad.[180] Many easterners were equally outraged at the railroad policies that the ICC seemed unable to control. Ida M. Tarbell, whose

father's oil business had been ruined by the PRR-affiliated South Improvement Company, had become a popular muckraking journalist, railing against the abuses of large corporations. The 1904 publication of her magnum opus, *The History of the Standard Oil Company*, remains a watershed event in the development of the period of political and social transformation commonly referred to as the Progressive era.[181] In that context, efforts by Cassatt and Morgan to stabilize rates and rescue the railroads seemed both unjust and a threat to the nation's democratic, egalitarian political and economic ideals. Thanks in large measure to the community of interest, Cassatt and the Pennsylvania Railroad were about to experience a new burst of regulatory activism on the part of state and federal governments.

Capture and Control: The PRR and the ICC During the Progressive Era

During the first decade of the twentieth century, Congress greatly strengthened the Interstate Commerce Commission, transforming the agency from a fact-finding body to a powerful and independent administrative entity. The 1903 Elkins Act, the 1906 Hepburn Act, and the 1910 Mann-Elkins Act likewise altered the nature of the relationship between the Pennsylvania Railroad and the federal government. A simplistic analysis—one that in later years many PRR executives were quick to emphasize—suggested that the regulatory bureaucracy seized power from the private sector, reducing productive efficiency in an unrealistic attempt to achieve economic fairness.

The reality was far more complex, however. Governmental regulation of business has always embodied a mutual and often synergistic interdependency between the regulator and the regulated. Historians of public policy have long noted that tendency, but they have often disagreed as to the precise nature of the relationship. Some have suggested that government officials implemented regulation in order to serve the public interest, primarily by protecting farmers and other shippers from manipulative or otherwise unfair pricing practices established by the railroads. The resulting regulations might impair productive efficiency, but that was a worthwhile sacrifice in the interests of maintaining allocative efficiency—that is, in ensuring economic fairness for the broadest possible cross-spectrum of American society. In contrast, regulators might also have possessed less altruistic motivations, using administrative oversight to enhance their standing in society, at the expense of legislative and judicial bodies.[182]

At the opposite extreme, some economists and historians have detailed the ability of executives to "capture" the agencies assigned to regulate them. After all, they emphasize, insiders often comprehended the intricacies of their business affairs to a far more thorough degree than bureaucrats in Washington. In the capture model, railroad executives who lacked the organizational and legal tools necessary to control cutthroat competition endeavored to employ the federal government as a mediating body. Such practices may have produced problems for shippers, but they were necessary to preserve the financial stability of all of the railroads. The mere fact that the railroads benefited from regulation, therefore, did not necessarily indicate that that regulation was contrary to the public interest.[183]

Other historians give more authority to regulators, suggesting that, like humans, the governmental agencies that they head go through periods of immaturity, strength, and decline. According to the "life-cycle" theory, new regulatory agencies initially possess little power or influence. As regulators gain wisdom and confidence, and as Congress affords them greater administrative authority, the agency becomes powerful, relevant, and respected. Unfortunately, just as all life yields to decline and infirmity, regulatory agencies become ossified, hidebound by tradition, and ineffective—and, in the case of the ICC in 1995, would eventually perish.[184]

The relationship between the Pennsylvania Railroad and the Interstate Commerce Commission provided ample evidence to support both the capture and the life-cycle theories. During his presidency, Alexander Cassatt believed that government regulation, properly shaped, could encourage rate stability. He helped to draft the version of legislation that ultimately became the Elkins Act, and his close relationship with Theodore Roosevelt undoubtedly helped him to cap-

ture the ICC, at least to some degree. Yet, the capture theory fails to take into account the ICC's unwelcome intervention into certain aspects of the PRR's operations, from the community of interest to the allocation of coal cars. Likewise, few PRR executives voiced approval for the ICC's concurrent efforts to regulate safety or the hours and terms of service for railway workers. It likewise seems clear that ICC officials were becoming progressively more powerful and more confident during the early years of the twentieth century, often at the expense of executive autonomy.

Rather than choose between the capture and life-cycle theories, a more nuanced reading of the relationship between the PRR and the ICC would suggest that elements of both were at work. More precisely, the changing nature of the regulatory regime reflected a growing awareness—on the part of legislators, regulators, and executives—that neither the laws nor the courts were adequately equipped to mitigate the deleterious structural characteristics associated with the railroads. For more than half a century, railroaders had attempted to control destructive competition, relying successively on pools, fast freight lines, duplicate construction, system-building, traffic associations, rate bureaus, and communities of interest, while using inter-firm conferences, large shippers such as John D. Rockefeller, and affiliated executives such as the Empire Line's Joseph D. Potts as "eveners." All of those efforts had failed. In that context, for better or for worse, the ICC was the mediator of last resort.

The Elkins Act and the Effort to Control Rebates

The legislative history of the 1903 Elkins Act has certainly lent considerable support to assertions that regulatory agencies can fall under the sway of the very companies that they are supposed to control. The legislation was sponsored by Senator Stephen B. Elkins (Rep., W. Va.), an individual who was closely connected to the railroads. Elkins was a mine owner who represented a growing consensus among shippers that stable railroad rates were essential to the adequate maintenance of the railroads' physical plant and equipment, and thus to efficient service—an attitude that comported well with Cassatt's efforts to establish the community of interest.[185] In 1901, Elkins assumed the chairmanship of the Senate Committee on Interstate Commerce from Shelby Cullom, the individual who had been largely responsible for writing the 1887 Act to Regulate Commerce. While still in the chairmanship, Cullom had supported a sweeping regulatory bill, one that would have given the ICC the authority to set rates. Elkins, in contrast, narrowed the scope of the bill to the prohibition of rebates, something that railroaders, shippers, and regulators all deemed necessary. Neither shippers nor railroaders sought to radically increase the ICC's control over the railroads, however.[186]

In drafting the legislation, Elkins relied heavily on Cassatt and other PRR executives. Elkins and President Roosevelt met repeatedly with Cassatt, who suggested the basic principles that the bill should embody. The specific components of the bill apparently stemmed from a meeting between Cassatt and two Atchison, Topeka & Santa Fe officials, second vice president Paul Morton, and first vice president and general solicitor Edward D. Kenna. James A. Logan, the Pennsylvania Railroad's general counsel, largely wrote the actual bill. In a March 1902 interview, Logan emphasized his "faith in the integrity of governmental agencies; especially those of the dignity of the Interstate Commerce Commission," while suggesting that "not only the shipper but the carrier needs governmental help." Logan continued, "it seems to me the time has come when the government should reassume the right of a moderate control and supervision over the carriers."[187] Logan was careful to insist that shippers would benefit from a stable rate structure, but he also developed the argument that the railroads—long thought a bastion of economic power—were also threatened by competitive rate-cutting. Roosevelt, United States attorney general Philander C. Knox, and ICC chairman Martin A. Knapp then evaluated Logan's language, and suggested modifications.[188]

In February 1903, the Elkins bill sailed through Congress, with the unanimous approval of the Senate and only six dissenting votes in the House. While the act did not legalize pooling or other forms of cartel pricing, it nonetheless made it easier for railway executives to maintain agreed-upon rates. Prior to 1903, it had been lawful for managers to disregard their posted

rates, so long as they did not demonstrate undue favoritism for a particular shipper—that is, rebates and other forms of rate-cutting were permissible, so long as they applied equally to all. In addition to posting their rates (a stipulation of the 1887 act), the railroad executives now had to file their tariffs with the ICC and could not alter them without due notice. Any deviation from the posted rates became a criminal offense, with railroads and shippers alike liable for fines of up to $20,000 for each infraction.[189] The Elkins Act also ensured that corporations, and not merely individual freight agents, were now held responsible for violations. Federal courts possessed the authority to issue injunctions to compel the maintenance of just and reasonable rates, as determined by the ICC.[190]

Most observers praised the new law, which some "considered one of the best railroad measures so far enacted."[191] In 1905, Elkins claimed that his bill was an unqualified success, and he fittingly invoked the PRR in the process. "The Pennsylvania Railroad has not given a rebate since the act was passed," he asserted, "and they do not want to."[192] The confident official pronouncements nonetheless disguised the railroads' continued reliance on rebating. Posted rate sheets contained mysterious typographical errors, quickly corrected, that permitted some railroads to temporarily undercut their competitors. Freight agents made repeated mistakes in the classification of shipments, billing high-value freight at lower class rates. The underweighing of cargoes also occurred with distressing frequency.[193]

Over the next few years, the regulatory climate turned distinctly more hostile toward the Pennsylvania Railroad, as ratemaking authority slipped out of the control of Cassatt and other PRR executives. The events that followed conformed less to the "capture" theory of regulation, and more to a "life-cycle" paradigm, in which the ICC's weak infancy gave way to a vibrant and powerful maturity. More precisely, between 1901 and 1906, members of Congress became increasingly concerned that the existing regulatory regime was inadequate for the protection of shippers and the promotion of the stability of the railroads. In particular, they concluded that the ICC lacked adequate authority to resolve disputes between shippers and railroads, that the agency should possess the power to establish rates, and that the commissioners should be better able to coordinate the actions of a multitude of railroads.[194]

Theoretical considerations aside, by 1905 shippers were beginning to lose patience with railroaders' incessant demands for further rate stabilization. Their frustration had as much to do with cyclical changes in the American industrial economy as it did with the actions of railroad executives. The last third of the nineteenth century had been characterized by sustained deflation, largely as a result of rapid, complementary improvements in manufacturing and distribution processes. Rail rates had likewise fallen by about 50 percent, on average, a trend driven more by increased transportation efficiency than by rate wars and rebating. As the nation recovered from the 1893 depression, however, prices stabilized, and then began to creep upward. Rising labor and material costs had forced railroad executives to raise rates, a process facilitated by the creation of communities of interest. Manufacturers, who also faced higher prices for raw materials, had scant reason to blame the railroads for the inflationary spiral. Freight charges constituted a small, and in most instances a steadily decreasing, component of business expense. Yet, in light of the monopolistic overtones of the communities of interest, many shippers focused their wrath on the railroads, blaming them for the dislocations that were more properly attributable to secular changes in the economy as a whole.[195]

At some point, between the Elkins Act in 1903 and the Hepburn Act of 1906, the locus of regulatory power shifted away from the Pennsylvania Railroad and toward the Interstate Commerce Commission. Tensions between shippers and the railroaders had been apparent in the debates over the Elkins Act, but they became more noticeable as Congress considered legislation to grant additional powers to the ICC. While a great many factors influenced the congressional debate over legislation that became the 1906 Hepburn Act, growing public concern regarding the mismanagement of coal transportation loomed large among them. The shaping of railway regulation and the ICC's efforts to assign blame for a crisis in the coalfields were inextricably intertwined.

Managing Coal Transportation

Traffic managers on every railroad, including the PRR, struggled to provide sufficient gondola and hopper cars for the coal trade. Between 1888 and 1899, the number of coal-carrying cars on the PRR nearly doubled. By the beginning of the twentieth century, there were 129,455 PRR-owned hoppers and gondolas on Lines East alone—which, if placed end to end, would stretch more than 850 miles.[196] Yet, no matter how many cars the PRR placed in service, they were never enough. In spite of the PRR's investments, coal freight agent Robert H. Large complained that "it is rarely ever that we have sufficient cars available to meet the requirements of the trade," and that, no matter how much equipment the PRR put into service, "we will still hear the familiar sound of the [coal-mine] operator's voice crying out for some more cars."[197]

Mine owners and PRR officials blamed each other for the perennial shortages of hopper cars. Coal Freight Agent Large and other executives accurately accused the operators of employing the railroad's cars as a sort of rolling inventory, useful for storing coal until it could be delivered wherever and whenever it commanded the best price. They were also critical of small mines, many of which were open only during times of high demand. Large producers could fill cars almost immediately, while smaller operations might take days to load a single car. The owners of coal properties, in contrast, faulted the PRR for not building enough cars and for doing too little to increase main line and yard capacity—absent which the additional cars would have merely contributed to traffic congestion and brought the railroad's operations to a halt.

The car shortage resulted from three factors. First, railroad shops and independent car builders often could not complete equipment quickly enough to meet growing demand. Second, because coal was a bulk, low-value commodity that traveled at exceedingly low rates, with little profit margin per car, railroad executives were reluctant to allocate too large a share of capital to car construction. Most important, demand for coal tended to fluctuate wildly, according to the season and (for metallurgical coal, in particular) economic conditions. As such, PRR executives were often reluctant to invest in all of the cars that miners might require at peak periods of production.

As on other coal-carrying railroads, PRR officials used a rating system to determine the quota of cars assigned to each mine, based on some combination of the mine's potential capacity and its actual production.[198] Prior to 1906, each division superintendent was responsible for determining car quotas. In principle (under what ICC investigators referred to as a "theoretical system"), superintendents were aware of the typical output levels at each mine and assigned all available cars accordingly. In practice, however, they held back perhaps half of the available cars and waited for requests to arrive. In their testimony before the ICC and other regulatory bodies, PRR officials gave the indication that the remaining cars were allocated on a first-come, first-served basis, but that was clearly not the case. Preferred shippers, particularly those that filled large numbers of cars, tended to receive ample allotments, shortchanging the smaller producers. Other features of the rating system worked against the interest of small collieries. On Lines East, each mining company received a quota of cars based on the potential productive capacity of every mine under their control, rather than on actual output. As a result, the managers of companies that owned multiple mines could request a car allotment based on that theoretical capacity, and then shut down several shafts and concentrate their car supply on the remaining properties. The entire process remained a mystery to all but the well connected, and ICC observers suggested that "it was almost impossible for the shipper to ascertain accurately what was the system of car distribution, and whether it was faithfully carried out."[199]

The rating system provided large collieries with a powerful incentive to acquire their own fleets of coal cars. By using privately owned cars, mine owners could store coal for extended periods, in anticipation of higher prices, without paying the demurrage (rental) charges that applied to railroad-owned equipment. In addition, that company would have exclusive access to its own equipment, ensuring ample transportation capacity for any coal that it might produce. That was a particularly important benefit given the rating system employed by the PRR and other carriers. Division su-

perintendents assigned only PRR cars, without regard to the presence of private-owner equipment. In other words, a large company such as Westmoreland or Berwind-White would receive an allotment of PRR cars based (at least theoretically) on the output of its mines, and could then supplement that quota with its own equipment. Both parties benefited, with the PRR shifting a substantial portion of its capital costs to the collieries and mine owners certain of receiving adequate car allotments.[200]

The use of private-car fleets developed over many years. During the 1850s, Westmoreland purchased a group of twenty-four cars to move coal east, under the new lower rates made possible by the partial repeal of the tonnage tax. In 1861, as the Civil War intensified demand for coal, PRR officials cooperated with their counterparts on the Reading to ship coal from the Broad Top Field to the Port Richmond terminal. Shortly afterward, in April 1861, the PRR board encouraged companies such as Westmoreland and Penn Gas to buy coal cars for shipments traveling over the PRR-Reading route. By 1867, there were 2,536 private coal cars operating over the PRR, compared with 5,744 of the PRR's own "freight and coal" cars.[201]

The opening of new coalfields and the subsequent expansion in production that took place during the 1880s and 1890s increased the size of private-car fleets. By the early 1900s, they included 20,000 coal cars and 6,300 coke cars, equivalent to nearly a fifth as many hopper cars as the PRR maintained on its roster.[202] Berwind-White was a case in point, employing 3,286 of its own cars and making the company one of the largest private-equipment operators in the United States. In 1888, Berwind-White acquired an initial complement of five hundred cars from Robert Hare Powel & Company. An additional five hundred cars lettered for the subsidiary Bell's Gap Railroad joined the roster between 1899 and 1902. The 1902 anthracite strike created a shortage of hopper cars in the areas of Pennsylvania served by the PRR, increasing the willingness of large companies to buy their own cars. Between 1902 and 1907, Berwind-White purchased another 2,100 hopper cars, "at the earnest solicitation" of the Pennsylvania Railroad, Edward

Berwind noted.[203] Berwind-White likewise invested in 125 barges and several tugs, based at the PRR's Harsimus Cove facility, to expedite the delivery of coal to steamships and other customers.[204]

By the beginning of the twentieth century, many PRR officials were regretting that their predecessors had ever permitted the use of private-owner cars. During the 1850s, coal-company equipment rosters had begun modestly enough, with Westmoreland's small batch of two dozen cars, but the situation had rapidly grown out of control. By 1906, fifty-nine companies owned and operated more than twenty-six thousand cars over the PRR system. Unlike PRR equipment, which railroad crews could allocate to any convenient mine, private cars could be spotted only at the sidings of the colliery that owned them. The resulting increase in car miles and the concomitant loss in efficiency erased all of the benefits associated with shifting the capital cost for new cars to the mine owners—particularly as the PRR's increased reliance on equipment-trust financing was providing an additional mechanism to finance car acquisitions. PRR managers commissioned more than half a dozen reports on the subject, and all indicated that the railroad should take charge of its gondola and hopper cars. In hearings before the ICC, Lines East general manager William Wallace Atterbury asserted, "From a transportation standpoint I think every railroad man in the country would be glad to see the private car abolished," an opinion seconded by vice president John P. Green.[205] Another PRR vice president, James McCrea, reiterated a similar position to the ICC commissioners, testifying that, since 1904, PRR executives had been endeavoring to eliminate private-owner coal cars from the railroad.[206]

Private-car fleets also exacerbated the enmity that the proprietors of small collieries held toward the PRR. Railroad officials simply refused to accommodate private equipment unless the owner could guarantee a minimum quota of five hundred cars—representing an investment of perhaps $500,000. Mines with modest output lacked both private-car pools and a predictable supply of PRR equipment, and their production often suffered accordingly. Furthermore, small operators generally could not afford to maintain marketing capabilities in cities and ports remote from the coal-fields. The combination of equipment shortages and diminished marketing capabilities ensured that the owners of small mines continually struggled against their larger competitors. Understandably, if unfairly, they often blamed their problems on the Pennsylvania Railroad.[207]

The winter of 1905–6 tipped the balance of public opinion against the Pennsylvania Railroad. During 1905, mining engineer Phillip E. Womelsdorff made a thorough study of car-allocation procedures. He recommended sweeping changes, including the creation of an independent body, unconnected with the railroads or the mines, to determine ratings. As if to underscore Womelsdorff's concerns, the PRR soon experienced severe capacity problems. Track crews, struggling to keep pace with congestion on the main line, were unable to install spurs and sidings to serve newly opened mines—causing owners to charge discrimination. The additional trackage would have made little difference, in any event, as there were far too few cars to serve existing customers. For a six-week period in early 1906, PRR officials allocated cars only to the 122 largest mines on the system, owned by a mere forty-two companies. During that time, 379 mines received no cars at all. Because coal could not readily be stored at the mine head, the absence of cars accordingly meant a cessation of production at the smaller mines.[208]

Railroad officials were quick to point out that shipments to public utilities and other important customers had continued uninterrupted. The owners of small mines—many of which had only recently opened, in order to take advantage of a recent spike in demand—were nonetheless furious. They complained loudly to the media, their elected officials, and anyone else who would listen. Their anger resonated with a great many people who were already disturbed at the community of interest that Cassatt and Morgan had arranged to control coal rates. Something, they insisted, had to be done.

Coal Cars, Coal Lands, and ICC Oversight

The growing protests over the allocation of coal cars constituted but one element of an increasing public, legislative, and judicial hostility toward the railroads. In March 1904, in *Northern Securities Company v. United States*, the Supreme Court narrowly concluded that a collaborative agreement that tied together the Northern Pacific, the Great Northern, and the Chicago, Burlington & Quincy constituted a combination in restraint of trade. While the PRR's community of interest was organized along different lines, PRR officials could not help but regard the verdict with a certain degree of dread. Commensurately hostile action by Congress threatened to undo the gains that the Elkins Act had created and, by putting ratemaking authority under the control of a bureaucratic agency, make it difficult for railroaders to adjust their charges to suit changing business conditions. Many, although by no means all, merchants supported bills sponsored by Senator Joseph V. Quarles (Rep., Wisc.) and Representative Charles E. Townsend (Rep., Mich.) that would have given the ICC the authority to set absolute rates.[209]

Roosevelt was increasingly concerned at the level of support for the Quarles and Townsend Bills. While not an unabashed supporter of the railroads, the President nonetheless sensed the danger that ill-conceived legislation might pose to the American economy. Like many railroad executives, Roosevelt joined the fray, if for no other reason than to deflect what he considered to be unacceptable alternatives to moderate regulation. As the 1904 election campaign gathered momentum, candidate Roosevelt emphasized his support for enhanced ICC authority. Soon after the 1904 election, the House approved the Townsend Bill, legislation that would provide the commission with extensive rate-making authority. Although the legislation died a quick death in the Senate, it served notice that many members of Congress were no longer willing to countenance a weak regulatory apparatus. Roosevelt surmised that Congress would not assent to a sweeping overhaul of railroad regulation. Instead, as he made plain in his December 1905 message to Congress, he favored more incremental measures that would grant the ICC the more modest ratemaking authority that the commissioners had claimed, yet had been progressively denied by the courts. The ICC commissioners likewise voiced their displeasure for the alternatives offered by Quarles, Townsend, and their allies.[210]

Railroad executives initially exhibited little interest in the subsequent political maneuverings. By 1905, however, many officials were anxious to become involved in the legislative process, if for no other reason than to prevent Congress from favoring shippers, by giving the ICC stronger rate-setting provisions. Chief among those individuals were representatives from the Chicago, Burlington & Quincy; the Louisville & Nashville; the Southern; and the Pennsylvania Railroad.[211]

The most prominent voice came from Alexander J. Cassatt, whose status as the president of the nation's largest railroad often made him the de facto spokesman for the entire industry. He enjoyed a close political and personal relationship with Roosevelt, even though one was a Democrat and the other a Republican. Despite his political affiliations, Cassatt was closely tied to key GOP politicians, including political powerbroker Boies Penrose, the individual who held the Senate seat previously occupied by PRR ally J. Donald Cameron. Furthermore, Roosevelt relied on Cassatt's expertise and his connection to other railroad executives. In early 1905, Cassatt met repeatedly with Roosevelt at the White House. He also wrote a letter to the President suggesting amendments to the Elkins Act—incurring the ire of Progressive journalist Lincoln Steffens, who was outraged at the cozy relationship between the two presidents. Some of the changes, including the legalization of pooling and granting the ICC the authority to examine the railroads' financial accounts (devices that harkened back to Cassatt's role in maintaining the South Improvement Company cartel some three decades earlier) were beyond what even Roosevelt was willing to countenance. In general, however, both men were in accord on most of the substantive issues involving ICC authority to set maximum rates, subject to oversight by the judiciary. "Let the Government regulate us," Cassatt later told journalist James Creelman, in an interview in *Pearson's Magazine*. "For my part, and for my associates in the Pennsylvania Railroad Company, I am generally heartily in accord with the position taken by President Roosevelt, and we have been all along."[212] For his actions, Cassatt received the disapprobation of other railroad executives, some of whom hinted darkly that Cassatt had cut a deal with Roosevelt designed to spare the PRR from close regulatory scrutiny.[213]

With Roosevelt and Cassatt each emphasizing the need for moderate regulation that would favor the railroads, it was an easy matter for Cassatt to persuade Penrose and his allies to back a bill sponsored by William Peters Hepburn (Rep., Iowa), the chairman of the House Committee on Interstate and Foreign Commerce. Unlike the Quarles and Townsend Bills, Hepburn's contribution permitted the ICC merely to set maximum rates, but not to specify precisely what a railroad might charge for its services.[214]

Roosevelt's support for the Hepburn Bill caused concern among many congressional Democrats who feared that the pending legislation was too favorable to the railroads. Their concerns were unfounded. The timing of the ensuing congressional debates proved particularly unfortunate for Cassatt and his fellow PRR executives, as the hearings on the legislation provided a forum for criticism of the community of interest, and for the manner in which PRR officials allocated perennially scarce hopper cars. The public furor, while something of a short-lived tempest in a teapot, produced adverse publicity for the PRR, jeopardized Cassatt's health, and contributed to some of the more restrictive features of what became the Hepburn Act.[215]

The fireworks began on January 29, 1906, when Representative Oscar W. Gillespie (Dem., Tex.) introduced a resolution demanding that President Roosevelt order the ICC to investigate the community-of-interest arrangements among the PRR, the Baltimore & Ohio, the Chesapeake & Ohio, and the Norfolk & Western. The resolution called on Roosevelt to reveal to the House any information, drawn from ICC reports, that might indicate that the community of interest violated the antitrust provisions embodied in the Sherman Act. The notion that Cassatt and others were attempting to monopolize the railroad business had originated a year earlier, in the midst of efforts by railroad executives to dissuade Congress from granting the ICC broad authority to set rates. At the hearings, ICC commissioner Judson C. Clements testified that he believed that the PRR and other railroads were acting collusively. Congressman Gillespie, his imagination fired by the recent *Northern Securities* case, nonetheless let the matter lie fallow until he heard a complaint from the Red Rock Fuel

Company regarding inadequate car allocations. Officials from that West Virginia coal producer charged that the B&O, at the behest of PRR executives, refused to provide adequate service.

Gillespie then waited for a propitious "psychological moment" when most Republicans—the majority party at that time—were absent from the House chamber. As a reporter for the *New York Times* noted, "The men popularly credited with taking special care of the interests of those corporations were either absent or asleep."[216] Representative John Dalzell, a Republican from Pittsburgh, frantically attempted to block the resolution, but to no avail. Many House Democrats were as confused as their Republican counterparts, because Gillespie had neither cleared his actions with the Minority Leader, nor had he so much as spoken about the matter to more than a few of the other members of his party. The resolution nonetheless passed, and Pennsylvania Railroad stock promptly fell 2¼ points as a result. Wall Street investors had long assumed that the PRR's community of interest—which stopped short of majority control over other companies—was of an entirely different nature than the now defunct Northern Securities Company, and was thus more likely to pass legal muster. Now, they were not so sure.

On February 3, the ICC presented its report to Roosevelt, as directed, and the President soon transmitted it to Congress. Gillespie was far from satisfied. He asserted "that the response of the commission was an insult to the intelligence of the House." The aggrieved congressman then introduced an eight-part resolution calling on the ICC to determine whether railroads or their executives owned the securities of any mining companies, to establish whether any restraint of trade existed in the carriage of bituminous coal, to evaluate the railroads' systems for assigning cars, and to suggest improved methods for establishing quotas.[217]

The House Committee on Interstate and Foreign Commerce then reported Gillespie's resolution to the full House. It passed on February 23, with little opposition, but not before Congressman Charles H. Grosvenor (Rep., Ohio) expressed his pleasure "that the scope of this resolution is broad enough to give notice to certain gentlemen that Congress is not so childish in its knowledge of men and passing affairs that the puerile statement of a great railroad man [i.e., Cassatt], that his corporation does not own a controlling interest in certain other corporations—that it does not own a majority of stock—is no answer to the proposition that there is a combination, a community of interests and a community of management that bring that corporation [the PRR] and those which it dominates indirectly under the very ban that this resolution seeks to accomplish."[218]

Members of the Senate were hardly inactive during the winter of 1906. On February 8, South Carolina Democrat Benjamin Tillman addressed his fellow senators. Tillman was an unabashed populist and white supremacist, a man with a violent temper who in 1896 had gained the nickname "Pitchfork Ben" after threatening to skewer President Grover Cleveland with just such an implement. Like Congressman Gillespie, Tillman was sensitive to the complaints of the Red Rock Fuel Company. The senator observed that the ICC had required the B&O to cease and desist all discriminatory practices against the company, but that that railroad's officials—acting on the orders of Cassatt, Tillman was certain—had simply ignored the order. Senator Elkins, Tillman's most formidable adversary in the matter of railroad regulation, suggested that Red Rock managers could always petition the West Virginia courts for relief, but Tillman would have none of it.

Pitchfork Ben read into the record a letter from West Virginia Governor William M. O. Dawson. To Dawson, Cassatt's community-of-interest plan, and the PRR's investments in the Baltimore & Ohio, the Chesapeake & Ohio, and the Norfolk & Western, represented nothing less than a conspiratorial effort to hamstring the coal business in his state. "I have no doubt that an investigation will show that the Pennsylvania Railroad Company practically controls these three great trunk lines which traverse West Virginia, and which are the only means whereby the product of this State, including coal, can be shipped, either to the lakes in the West or other markets in the East," Dawson insisted. "Hence it is a fact that West Virginia today is in the grip of a railroad trust." In his letter, Dawson linked the PRR "trust" to the company's control of coal lands. "The Pennsylvania Railroad is very largely interested in the production or shipment of bi-

tuminous coal," Dawson argued, "and therefore the interests of West Virginia are subordinated to the interests of these others [such as the Commonwealth of Pennsylvania], and our railroads, upon which we are dependent as before stated, are controlled by an alien corporation practically in direct competition with us."[219] Tillman agreed wholeheartedly with Dawson's assessment, and he called on Congress to "prevent any monopoly of the Bituminous coal lands of the Atlantic slope by the Pennsylvania Railroad and its allies."[220]

Tillman, claiming that the Pennsylvania Railroad was "the head devil in the whole policy of monopoly," introduced a version of Gillespie's resolution into the Senate. On February 12, it passed unanimously.[221] Three weeks later, members of both chambers approved a joint resolution, ordering the ICC to investigate the railroads' monopolistic practices in the transportation of coal and oil. President Roosevelt condemned what was now called the Tillman-Gillespie-Campbell Resolution, suggesting that it "achieves very little and may achieve nothing."[222] Roosevelt also cautioned that the resolution would have little weight unless Congress also approved the Hepburn Bill currently under debate. He signed the order nonetheless, and by the end of March, the ICC had required the PRR, the Baltimore & Ohio, the Chesapeake & Ohio, the Norfolk & Western, and several other coal-carrying railroads to reveal any financial dealings pertaining to coal operations. It was by far the most sweeping and intrusive order in the nearly twenty-year history of the Interstate Commerce Commission.[223]

The ICC coal hearings began in Philadelphia on April 10, under the direction of ICC attorney William A. Glasgow, Jr. The PRR's coal traffic manager, Joseph G. Searles, acknowledged that until 1896, the Tidewater Bituminous Steam Coal Traffic Association (consisting of representatives from the PRR, the NYC, the B&O, the C&O, and the N&W) had fixed prices and assigned tonnage quotas to each member railroad. PRR Lines East general manager William Atterbury was considerably less loquacious. He professed ignorance of the increased demand for coal cars as a result of the 1902 anthracite strike—a difficult statement to credit, inasmuch as the PRR board of directors had promoted him to general manager, effective January 1, 1903, largely to reduce the congestion at Pittsburgh that had been caused by the corresponding increase in bituminous coal traffic. In response to probing questions by ICC investigators, Atterbury frequently replied, "I don't know."[224]

However, it was the PRR's less senior officials who offered the most damaging testimony. Many of them acknowledged that they had purchased, or had been given, shares in coal companies, although they often stopped short of suggesting a quid pro quo, in the form of favorable car allocations. Frank Casanave, who until 1901 was the general superintendent of the Pennsylvania Railroad Grand Division, held shares in several collieries. So too did Lines West second vice president Joseph Wood. The general superintendent of the United Railways of New Jersey Grand Division, Frank L. Sheppard, indicated that Edward Berwind had offered him stock, and further suggested that conventional wisdom held that PRR officials were heavily invested in the Berwind-White Coal Company. Pittsburgh Division trainmaster Edward Pitcairn (the son of superintendent Robert Pitcairn) and Cambria & Clearfield Division superintendent Ernest J. Cleave testified that mine owners had offered them free or steeply discounted shares of company stock in consideration for more favorable treatment. Michael Trump, the PRR's general superintendent of transportation, was given 200 shares of Atlantic Crushed Coke Company stock, worth $10,000. Tyrone Division trainmaster R. B. Freeman claimed to have received $100 Christmas presents from several coal companies. Assistant trainmaster Frederick Vrooman did considerably less well, with payouts limited to between five and twenty dollars apiece. George W. Clarke, a car distributor, got cigars, jewelry, and wine, as well as mysterious checks from various coal companies.[225]

Mine owners also admitted their willingness to solicit favorable treatment. Alfred Hicks, an officer with several coal and steel companies, testified that he had probably paid dividends to some of his PRR allies, but that he could not remember the precise details. "We did not have a very thorough system of bookkeeping," he acknowledged.[226] E. M. Gross, the Western manager of the Keystone Coal & Coke Company, named several PRR officials as recipients of bribes. ICC Commissioner Clements suggested that "it is a good thing to have friends in the Railroad," to which Gross replied, "Better to have friends than enemies."[227]

In the days that followed, revelation piled on top of revelation, and the accusations came perilously close to the president of the Pennsylvania Railroad. Cassatt's assistant, William A. Patton, admitted that he had received 6,140 shares of stock in various coal companies, worth some $307,000, for free.[228] Patton's chief clerk, J. N. Purviance, managed to acquire $38,500 in coal company stock, also at no cost to himself. In common with many other witnesses, Patton suggested that he had obtained those securities many years earlier, well before the growing public consensus that railroad ownership of coal lands constituted an unfair or monopolistic business practice. "Then it was not considered a crime," Patton argued, "as it appears to be now, for a railroad man to hold stock in a coal company."[229]

Although Alexander Cassatt's personal conduct seemed beyond reproach, his family's was not. The family investment-banking firm Cassatt & Company oversaw a multitude of coal investments. Robert Kelso Cassatt, the son of the PRR's president, was revealed to be the Eastern manager of the Keystone Coal & Coke Company. Richard Coulter, Jr., Keystone's secretary, testified that Robert Pitcairn and then-president Frank Thomson had received large consignments of company stock. There was little to corroborate Coulter's story, however, as Thomson was dead and Pitcairn, by now the resident assistant to the president at Pittsburgh, and weeks away from retirement, refused to appear before the ICC investigative committee. Congressman George Huff (Rep., Pa.), president of Keystone Coal & Coke, avoided a subpoena by remaining in his Greensburg office until 9:00 P.M. and then escaping through the basement.[230]

Executives from many other coal companies, particularly those who considered themselves ill used by the PRR, were eager to testify at the hearings. John Lloyd, a banker and mine owner, complained that his allocation of cars had declined once Keystone had begun operations. He claimed that he had endeavored to protect his interests by giving $25,000 to a PRR superintendent, justifying his conduct as "a good business move."[231] George E. Scott, representing the Puritan Coal & Coke Company, testified that the PRR had delivered only one car in twenty-three days, and that the PRR's general superintendent of transportation, Michael Trump, informed him that the PRR "intended to protect the Berwind-White Company at all costs."[232] John M. Jamison, president of the Jamison Coal & Coke Company, alleged that Richard L. O'Donnel, general superintendent of the Buffalo & Allegheny Valley Division, accepted coal company stock, as had superintendent of motive power Alfred W. Gibbs and George W. Clark, a car distributor at Altoona. O'Donnel, who appeared "pale and nervous" while giving his testimony, admitted that he received 1,045 shares in various coal companies, and that he had the opportunity to buy 322 more at "special" prices.[233] Morrisdale Coal Company official Frank H. Wigton asserted that PRR officials had granted rebates even after the passage of the Elkins Act—and the next day recanted his testimony, saying that the rebates had ended before the new law had gone into effect.[234] S. F. Potter, president of the Donohoe Coal & Coke Company, insisted that the PRR had delivered barely half of the cars that full output demanded. Potter was so incensed that he engaged in the not uncommon practice of dispatching an undercover operative to spy on a neighboring mine to count the number of cars that they received. "They shot at him," Potter complained, "and he was afraid to go back."[235]

The confrontational nature of the ICC hearings clearly caught Cassatt and other senior managers off guard. That spring, Cassatt was aging, tired, distraught from the death of his daughter, and anxious to raise capital from European investors in order to extend the PRR's tracks into Manhattan. William Glasgow, the ICC attorney, assured Cassatt that his presence would not be needed for some time. An appreciative Cassatt, convinced that he had nothing to hide, helpfully provided Glasgow with a complete accounting of all of the PRR's investments in coal companies and a list of their officers. Then, in early May, during a hiatus in the hearings, Cassatt sailed for Europe for his annual vacation.[236]

Before Cassatt had arrived in London, however, the *Philadelphia North American* was ready to publish rumors that the scandal would force him to resign in favor of Philadelphia & Reading president George F. Baer. Cassatt soon squelched those rumors, but he did not see the need to cut short his trip to Europe. By the end of the month, however, ICC chairman Martin Knapp had asked PRR first vice president John P. Green whether Cassatt might be willing to testify at the hearings. Green, reeling from the negative public-

ity, sent a cable to Cassatt, urging him to return to the United States in order to respond to the PRR's critics. The PRR president, who was already well aware of the drubbing that his company was taking at the hands of reporters, took the first available ship to New York. He arrived on June 3, where a special train was waiting to whisk him to Philadelphia.[237]

That evening, at his home in Haverford, Cassatt released his one and only public statement regarding the ICC investigation. The PRR's president was not pleased with media coverage of the scandal, stating "that the management deserved better treatment than it had received from the press, and particularly from the press of the company's home state." Cassatt emphasized that he had "rendered an immense service to the public" by ending rebates, abolishing free passes, and by refraining from overt attempts to influence Pennsylvania politics. The chief problem, he argued, was that increased coal output had outstripped the ability of PRR officials to place new cars in service. It was indeed tragic, he continued, that longtime enemies of the railroads—including the media and grandstanding politicians from both parties—should use that unfortunate situation to cast aspersions on the Pennsylvania Railroad and to continue their campaign to stir up "anti-corporation public sentiment."[238]

Cassatt had returned to a situation that, from the perspective of PRR officials, was deteriorating rapidly. The most damaging testimony occurred on June 6 and 7, when the assistants to three senior PRR officials admitted that they had accepted bribes from coal companies in order to steer the railroad's fuel orders to those concerns. Joseph Boyer, chief clerk to superintendent of motive power Alfred W. Gibbs, accepted bribes of eleven thousand shares of coal company stock and $46,000 in cash over a three-year period. M. K. Reeves, assistant to vice president Charles E. Pugh, received $40,000 from Representative Huff and Keystone Coal & Coke. Joseph K. Aiken, chief clerk in the superintendent's office of the Monongahela Division, boasted—"with an air of facetiousness," noted the *New York Times*—that his salary, which had ranged from $30 to $126 per month, had enabled him to purchase nearly $75,000 in coal company stocks.[239]

Despite all of the sensational revelations from shippers and PRR employees, the ICC hearings did not succeed in establishing any corporate wrongdoing.

Many witnesses altered their testimony, admitted that they were referring to alleged abuses that had occurred decades earlier, or acknowledged that they could not recall any instances of rebates after the 1903 Elkins Act had gone into effect. Even those individuals who claimed to have been offered or accepted bribes could furnish no proof to support their allegations, and none of them attempted to link their individual actions to PRR policy.

The publicity associated with the hearings was nonetheless devastating to the Pennsylvania Railroad, as *New York Times* headlines alternated between the damning ("Gifts to High and Low on Pennsylvania Road") and the farcical ("Congressman Huff Runs from Subpoena"). On May 17, amid increasingly sensational testimony before ICC representatives, second vice president Charles Pugh acknowledged that PRR officials discouraged the installation of new sidings at small mines, in the interest of efficiency. He insisted that he paid full value for all of the coal stocks that he owned, but when asked about similar investments by other PRR executives he said "I am not prepared to discuss the matter now. It is not a very serious matter, is it?" Then, after making what a reporter considered "a very deprecatory gesture," Pugh averred that "graft is a very common term nowadays," and matter-of-factly stated his opinion that "there are people who speak of almost everything as graft"—an assertion that might well have been true, but one that did little to improve the public image of the Pennsylvania Railroad.[240]

During the hearings, Cassatt launched an effort at damage control. On May 18, PRR officials announced that they would conduct an internal investigation of coal-car allocation practices, and on May 23 the board of directors convened a Special Committee of Inquiry. The committee issued a circular to more than 2,500 PRR personnel, requesting information on any employee who might be in a position to accept bribes for the unwarranted allocation of cars, the manipulation of company coal contracts, or any other unethical purpose.[241] "Apparently," the *Times* noted, "the housekeeping is to be a thorough one, and no one, high or low, is to be spared."[242] That was not precisely true, and Cassatt emphasized that the board of directors "would not sacrifice faithful and efficient officers to a manufactured and mistaken public opinion."[243] He showed

much less tolerance for Joseph Aiken and Joseph Boyer, whom he fired almost as soon as they had finished testifying.[244]

Cassatt did his best to act the role of an avuncular industrial statesman, attempting to reassure the public that conflicts of interest were limited to a few rogue employees. On June 10, Cassatt made public the information collected by the board's Special Committee of Inquiry, emphasizing that he did not hold any coal properties in his name. A week later, he hired an independent auditor to search through the PRR's books for any evidence of wrongdoing. On July 7, Cassatt issued a statement to all employees, ordering them to "divest themselves of any interests, direct or indirect, that they may have in the stocks of any coal companies . . . [and] in any companies or firms or with any individuals engaged in any other business where the holding of such interests might in any way conflict with their duty to the company or the company's duty to the public."[245] Given the interrelatedness of the PRR and the industrial economy of the Northeast, the complete elimination of conflicts of interest would be impossible, however. To a reporter from the *Times*, Cassatt confided that "to prohibit all officers and employees from holding stock of companies having business with the Pennsylvania Railroad Company would practically bar them from investing in the stocks of corporations located in the State of Pennsylvania, and a half dozen other states."[246]

The Hepburn Act and the End of the Community of Interest

In the midst of the ICC investigation into coal transportation and the community of interest, members of Congress were debating the Hepburn Bill. Populists such as Ben Tillman did their best to ensure that the 1906 legislation would not be as friendly to the railroads as the Elkins Act had been. In this instance, however, the furor over the coal bribes was a stroke of luck for railroad executives, as it deflected attention away from the more substantive regulatory matters under consideration. Moreover, the excesses of Tillman and his supporters alienated many elected officials and afforded moderates the opportunity to shape legislation that was less hostile to railroad interests. Roosevelt despised Tillman, but the senator's histrionics worked to the advantage of both the President and the railroad industry. Many conservative Republicans backed the Hepburn Bill rather than permit Tillman's version to pass Congress.[247]

Despite the bribery scandal, the 1906 Hepburn Act reflected Cassatt's influence, even if the final form of the legislation was not precisely what the PRR's president had envisioned. When the bill reached the House floor in February 1906, it encountered little opposition, passing by a vote of 347 to 7. In May, the Senate also gave its lopsided endorsement, approving the bill by a margin of 71 to 3. On June 29, 1906, President Roosevelt applied his signature. The Hepburn Act required rates to be "just, fair, and reasonable" (the Supreme Court had affirmed that concept eight years earlier, in *Smyth v. Ames*), but provided little guidance to the ICC on precisely how that was to be accomplished. The act gave the ICC jurisdiction over pipelines (except for those carrying oil or gasoline), express companies, sleeping car companies, and industrial railroads. It contained a Commodities Clause that prohibited railroads from transporting coal or other raw materials (except for wood products) from facilities that they owned. The ICC gained the power to specify standard accounting practices for the railroads. The act also embodied many of the concerns that had emerged in light of the inadequacies of the original 1887 Act to Regulate Commerce. Particularly after the 1897 *Alabama Midland* case, in which the Supreme Court effectively precluded the ICC's ability to enforce long-haul/short-haul provisions, railroad executives had often charged shippers whatever price they believed to be most remunerative.[248] In the unlikely event that the courts would later overturn those tariffs, the carrier could at least keep all of the revenue that they had earned prior to the judicial ruling. To remedy that situation, the Hepburn Act strengthened the ICC's ratemaking powers, giving the commissioners the authority to establish maximum rates, although only after they had received a complaint from a shipper. The act allowed the railroads to challenge adverse ICC decisions in the courts, but mandated that the rate remain in effect until the conclusion of the judicial proceedings—limiting the financial incentive for

railroads to use the courts to delay implementation of ICC rulings.[249]

While the Hepburn Act benefited the railroads to some degree, it was not so friendly as the Elkins Act, nor was it the solution which Cassatt had envisioned. As proponents of administrative regulation had long hoped, the new legislation made the ICC, and not the courts, the primary form of government oversight of the railroads. Shippers, who now enjoyed a relatively painless mechanism for seeking lower rates, readily approached the commissioners with their grievances. At the same time, railroad executives, confronted with the "just, fair, and reasonable" mandate, possessed a strong economic incentive to establish different classes of service in lieu of rate equalization, leading to endless and acrimonious debates between carriers and shippers. As a result, the number of formal complaints lodged with the ICC increased markedly, from sixty-five in 1905 to more than a thousand in 1909. Despite the increasing workload, the ICC accommodated those complaints on a case-by-case basis, without articulating a broad rate policy.[250]

The Hepburn Act, coupled with the damaging revelations of the ICC's coal bribery investigation, gave Cassatt little choice other than to dissolve the community of interest. To do otherwise, particularly in the aftermath of the *Northern Securities* case, would have risked further negative publicity, as well as considerable judicial and regulatory scrutiny. PRR officials claimed, with some justification, that the community of interest had achieved the desired goal of rate stabilization, but they privately acknowledged that such cooperative arrangements were no longer tenable. More broadly, a public-policy agenda, in the form of the Hepburn Act and a strengthened ICC, had taken precedence over earlier efforts by bankers and railroaders to regulate the industry through private channels.

As early as February 1906, Cassatt had informed New York Central officials that he intended to terminate the two railroads' joint control of the Chesapeake & Ohio. As vice president John Green observed, "Mr. Cassatt determined that it would be unwise for the Pennsylvania Railroad to permit Congress to convene [on December 6, 1906] with our company holding the Chesapeake & Ohio stock."[251] Beginning in early July 1906, the PRR incrementally sold all of its holdings in the C&O (more than $15.8 million worth), as well as the majority of its investments in the Norfolk & Western ($14.2 million) and the Baltimore & Ohio ($44 million). Rather than dump all of those securities on the market at more or less the same time, PRR officials contracted with Kuhn, Loeb & Company to take the entire amount and dispose of it more gradually. Kuhn, Loeb agreed to return a portion of the profits to the PRR, while railroad officials promised to make good any losses that the investment-banking house might suffer. Even though the Panic of 1907 prevented Kuhn, Loeb from disposing of the last of the securities until 1909, the PRR more than recouped its investment in the community of interest, enjoying an overall profit of $15 million—including $6.2 million on its N&W stock alone.[252]

Despite the sales, some elements of the community of interest survived. The Richmond-Washington Company proved effective at guaranteeing open access to the route between Washington and Richmond. Government officials and members of the public decried the PRR's efforts to bind together existing railroads into what they considered a transportation monopoly. Yet, they made few protests regarding the Richmond-Washington monopoly, created by Cassatt's ability to prevent the construction of a new and unnecessary parallel line.

Public criticism of the link between the Pennsylvania Railroad and the Norfolk & Western was more severe, but hardly insurmountable. In April 1909 the PRR reacquired from Kuhn, Loeb virtually all of the N&W stock that it had parted with some three years earlier. By 1910, additional purchases had given the PRR nearly one-half ownership in the N&W. With the Chesapeake & Ohio, the N&W's principal competitor, now operating independently, PRR managers apparently assumed that the federal government would tolerate the arrangement. That assumption proved incorrect, and in 1913 the Justice Department suggested that such a high degree of control was illegal. Rather than face a lawsuit, the PRR board sold some of the N&W shares, while converting N&W bonds into stock, thereby reducing the PRR's percentage of ownership. By the end of 1914, the PRR owned only 38 percent of the N&W. That share, however, was sufficient to generate substantial non-operating in-

come for the PRR, particularly during the dark years of the 1950s and 1960s, when the railroad's accountants relied heavily on the funds that the N&W dividends provided.[253]

If the long association between the Pennsylvania Railroad and the Norfolk & Western demonstrated the wisdom of Cassatt's community of interest, the resulting publicity helped bring to an end the president's career, and his life. By the end of June 1906, Joseph Whitaker Thompson, the United States attorney for the Eastern District of Pennsylvania, and Justice Department attorneys Alexander Simpson, Jr., and Charles Evans Hughes had decided to make an example out of one railroad executive by singling him out for prosecution. Despite his cooperation with the ICC, Cassatt was the obvious choice. Reporters, eager for salacious stories relating to one of the most powerful executives in the United States, suggested that Cassatt, if convicted of conspiracy, would receive a prison sentence. Even President Roosevelt averred that jail would offer more of a cautionary tale to other malefactors of great wealth than a series of fines.[254]

Cassatt was never even indicted, but the stress of hearings, combined with the demands associated with running the Pennsylvania Railroad, undermined his already fragile health. In July 1906 he traveled to Bar Harbor, Maine, in an attempt to rest and recuperate. Instead, he caught whooping cough from one of his grandchildren and did not return to Philadelphia until late September. He continued his convalescence at his home in Haverford, and in November moved to his townhouse on Rittenhouse Square. Although PRR officials repeatedly emphasized that their president was in good health, Cassatt worked but little from home, and those close to him saw that he was dying. On December 28, 1906, less than three weeks after celebrating his sixty-seventh birthday, Alexander J. Cassatt died. At that time, he was the oldest person to serve as president and, like three of his six predecessors, he died while still in office. Cassatt had succumbed to chronic heart disease, complicated by whooping cough, but, the *New York Times* noted, "Many men prominent in the railroad and financial worlds, who enjoyed intimate social or commercial relations with Mr. Cassatt, however, unhesitatingly assert that he really died of a broken heart due to the sensational revelations of grafting by officials of the Pennsylvania system made during the recent coal inquiry conducted by the Inter-State Commerce Commission."[255]

The Aftereffects of the Coal Hearings

Neither Cassatt's openness with investigators, nor his death, freed the Pennsylvania Railroad from increasing regulatory scrutiny. The ICC, strengthened by the provisions of the Hepburn Act, reduced the PRR's collaboration with large coal producers and brought to an end the company's investments in coal properties. On January 25, 1907, the ICC produced a summary of its hearings in its *Report on Discriminations and Monopolies in Coal and Oil*. The document criticized the Cassatt community-of-interest plan as being fundamentally destructive of competition. It also indicated that small mines suffered from pervasive discrimination in the matter of rates and car supply. Private-owner coal cars, which only the large mining operations could afford, exacerbated the problem, according to the ICC. Three weeks later, the internal investigation by the PRR board's Special Committee on the Ownership of Coal Stocks concluded that railroad officials had not demonstrated any favoritism in the purchase of coal or the allocation of equipment, and that only fourteen executives had received gifts of coal company stocks. Despite the near-absence of corruption among PRR personnel, commissioners and Congressmen alike were determined to establish barriers between the production and the transportation of coal.[256]

One proposed change involved the use of private-owner cars. In addition to Berwind-White and Westmoreland, nearly sixty other companies had invested heavily in more than twenty-six thousand coal cars that operated over the PRR, based on the understanding that that equipment not be factored into the rating system. After 1906, however, PRR officials responded to adverse public opinion by subtracting the size of the each company's hopper car fleet from their overall car allocation quota. In September 1906, PRR officials announced their intent to purchase the cars owned by Berwind-White and the Keystone Coal & Coke Company, reducing the railroad's car shortages and eliminating the possibility that private-car owners would receive a supplemental allotment of equipment.[257] The owners of large mining firms, which had already invested considerable sums in private cars, were hardly pleased. "The present [PRR] rule penalizes our enterprise in thus furnishing our own capital without reward," fumed Edward Berwind in 1906, "by denying us any right to participate in the distribution of our equipment."[258] Their opposition ensured that large private-owner fleets remained in service.

Despite protests by PRR officials and the owners of large mines, the ICC in 1907 ruled that the railroads were required to count privately owned cars in lieu of, rather than in addition to, railroad-owned cars as part of each mine's tonnage rating.[259] The new ICC regulations reduced but did not eliminate the incentive for companies to maintain private hopper cars. Particularly as the equipment had already been paid for, private-owner cars increased overall car availability and the likelihood that mines would receive adequate quotas. Large mining companies, such as Westmoreland and Berwind-White, retained their existing fleets but rarely purchased new cars.[260] By 1908, the ICC had nonetheless adopted additional car allocation rules that, according to the PRR's general counsel, were "to a greater or less degree, substantially differential [*sic*] from the regulation and practice of the Pennsylvania R.R. Co."[261]

The policies that the ICC adopted in the aftermath of the Hepburn Act hardly placated the owners of the smaller mines, however. By 1909, PRR fifth vice president William Atterbury warned President McCrea "that to-day there is a general feeling of unrest among our bituminous coal operators, with some definite complaints and the probability in the near future, as a result of a continuance, of general dissatisfaction and suits for damages."[262] Atterbury had already seen ample evidence that his predictions were coming true. In response to ongoing protests from Edward Berwind, PRR officials had placated the Berwind-White Coal Company by increasing its allotment of cars, stripping them from other mines. In March 1908, the infuriated owners of the Puritan Coal Mining Company filed suit against the PRR in the Court of Common Pleas of Clearfield County, Pennsylvania, successfully arguing that the PRR's favoritism had cost them more than a quarter of a million dollars in lost business. The PRR's attorneys eventually took the case to the United States Supreme Court, insisting that it was an administrative issue involving interstate commerce and that only the ICC, not the courts, held jurisdiction. The justices did not adhere to that view, and in April 1915 they affirmed the earlier ruling, awarding Puritan a substantial settlement. In April 1907, the owners of W. F. Jacoby & Company filed a complaint with the commission, claiming that the PRR had discriminated in the matter of car allocation at their Falcon No. 2 mine, again in favor of Berwind-White. That case, too, went before the Supreme Court, as did another instance of discrimination against the Clark Brothers Coal Mining Company.[263]

Car shortages continued into the second decade of the twentieth century. By 1912, the president of the Lackawanna Steel Company was complaining directly to the president of the Pennsylvania Railroad, "We are getting barely enough cars to keep us going at Buffalo."[264] The crisis became more acute after 1914, when the war in Europe increased demand for coal. Unusually severe winter weather in 1917, coupled with the shortage of hopper cars and general traffic congestion, contributed to the nationalization of the railroads, under the aegis of the United States Railroad Administration. When Congress returned the railroads to private ownership under the terms of the Transportation Act of 1920, legislators included the "open-top hopper law" (Part 1, Section 1), which codified earlier ICC rulings regarding the inclusion of mine-owned cars as part of the mine's quota. Private-car ownership remained legal, and some large companies maintained substantial rosters until after World War II. Westmoreland sold most of its hopper cars during the early 1940s, but Berwind-White retained a large fleet until the early 1960s.[265]

Exit from Anthracite

The sensational revelations that accompanied the 1906 coal hearings, coupled with the judicial interpretation of the Commodities Clause of the Hepburn Act, spelled an end to the PRR's rather limited involvement in the anthracite coal business. The departure was hardly a crippling blow, as the hard-coal industry was losing much of its luster for reasons that had little to do with public policy. For the previous decade, PRR officials had attempted to improve the profitability of their anthracite subsidiaries through reorganizations and additional investments, but with scant success. Shortly before Cassatt assumed the presidency, Samuel Rea, then the first assistant to president Frank Thomson, had recommended that, in the interests of greater efficiency, all of the PRR's anthracite operations be consolidated under unified management. Isaac J. Wistar, who for decades had presided over the PRR's anthracite and canal subsidiaries, cautioned against such a plan. Wistar asserted that labor unrest at one mine might spread to the others, and that "a trifling dispute with the mule drivers, or the slate pickers of one remote mine which could readily be closed for a year, might shut up our entire mining operation in several counties, and leave miles of cars idle on the sidings."[266] Likewise, Wistar noted, "Almost every legislature raises some sort of investigating Committee [and] If all our mining and purchasing operations were boiled down into one managing Company, the time of our principal officers would be largely occupied in keeping up with the investigations, inspections, &c. that are the constant subjects of legislative invention, and if their missiles should fail at one point, they might hit at another."[267] Under the circumstances, Rea reluctantly dropped his plan for consolidation.

When he became president, Cassatt nonetheless insisted that the PRR's anthracite properties be placed under consolidated management and given the capital necessary for expanded production. While each firm remained nominally independent, the Susquehanna Coal Company oversaw the operations of all of the others. As Rea, by then the third vice president, described the situation, Susquehanna had become the "'omnium-gatherum' of our entire anthracite business so far as mining, preparing and selling our own and the purchased coal is concerned."[268] Between 1894 and 1912, the PRR and its Northern Central subsidiary invested an additional $1.6 million in its various anthracite properties. In 1899, amid increasing coal prices, the PRR board authorized the construction of a massive new terminal complex at Greenville, New Jersey. The facilities included a pier to accommodate anthracite shipments, which the PRR promptly leased to the Susquehanna Coal Company. Nevertheless, the output of the PRR's anthracite mines remained small compared with that of the Reading and other anthracite carriers, and their affiliates, ensuring that the PRR's investment in the Pennsylvania Schuylkill Valley Railroad would never live up to its potential. More significantly, with eight carriers competing for the anthracite traffic, there was no possibility that the PRR could control either transportation or rates. In 1903, for example, the Pennsylvania Railroad transported barely 13 percent of the hard coal mined in Pennsylvania—not a bad result under the circumstances, but hardly the dominance that the company enjoyed in the bituminous regions to the west.[269]

In February 1906, the Supreme Court upheld ICC rules that severely constrained the ability of the railroads to cooperatively market coal.[270] A few months later, the Hepburn Act's Commodities Clause prohibited railroads from transporting raw materials that they mined or otherwise produced, except for those necessary to support their own operations. Justice Department attorneys soon attempted to pry apart railroads and coal companies. The first lawsuit came on June 12, 1907, against all of the principal anthracite carriers, although not against the PRR. On June 5, 1908, however, the Justice Department included the PRR in a new round of lawsuits, charging that the railroad's ownership of the Susquehanna Coal Company was a violation of the Hepburn Act. Although that case never proceeded to judgment, several others did. In a verdict involving the Delaware & Hudson, the United States Supreme Court affirmed the overall constitutionality of the Commodities Clause. The justices nonetheless narrowed the scope of the Hepburn Act's prohibition on the ownership of coal lands, drawing a distinction between direct and indirect ownership, and permitting railroads to mine coal so long as they turned it over to independent companies for sale.[271] As late as March 1911, based on the Supreme Court's ruling, First Vice President Rea suggested that the PRR could retain coal lands that might someday be needed to fuel the railroad's locomotives, while leasing the remainder to independent operators. "We should bring forward some of our subordinate companies and furnish them with the capital that will enable them to gather in and hold coal areas for the future needs of the Company, as a landlord and not an operator, and to sell later or lease in order to assure the traffic for the System," he suggested.[272]

Barely a week later, however, the Supreme Court, in the *Lehigh Valley* case, placed a stricter interpretation on the Commodities Clause and prohibited precisely the type of leasing arrangement that Rea had advocated. As such, the PRR board, on September 24, 1913, authorized the sale of the railroad's anthracite investments.[273] By the summer of 1917, the Susquehanna Collieries Company, a subsidiary of the Cleveland-based M. A. Hanna Company, had purchased the last of the PRR's anthracite properties. The Pennsylvania Railroad would continue to haul millions of tons of coal, but the company was no longer in the mining business.[274]

Publicity

The coal transportation hearings and the debate over the provisions of the Hepburn Act brought into sharp focus the importance of public relations to the railroads. Prior to 1906, despite their prominence and their centrality to the American economy, railway executives had given scant thought to their public image. Executives, who were experts in engineering or finance, often spoke with commendable frankness, uttering statements that reflected their understanding of the realities of railway operations, but that did not comport well with public opinion. William Henry Vanderbilt's infamous 1882 "the public be damned" quotation may have been the most memorable, but there were many others. In December 1906, Edward H. Harriman, in testimony before the ICC, acknowledged his desire to add the Santa Fe to his western rail empire. When asked if "it is only the restriction of the law that keeps you from taking it," Harriman blandly answered, "I would go on as long as I live."[275] Given the effectiveness of communities of interest in stabilizing rail rates, it was hardly a given that Harriman's plans contravened the public good. Such frank comments nonetheless scintillated newspaper readers and provided populist legislators with ample ammunition for their attacks on the railroads.

The same newspapers that detailed the embarrassing statements of railroad executives offered a means for railroaders to polish their tarnished reputations. More generally, the managers who headed large manufacturing and transportation corporations availed themselves of increasing literacy rates and the growing availability of national-circulation magazines to disseminate their message to the American public. Publicity, they reasoned, offered the best antidote to the activities of populist and pro-labor politicians.[276] As early as 1893, an executive from the Northern Pacific had suggested that "the time had come for a greater knowledge about corporation affairs on the part of those interested and the general public."[277] Many railroads established publicity bureaus, supplying statistics and other information to the newspapers. The president of the Southern Railway oversaw a Washington office to coordinate legislative affairs, with branches in most major cities. Railroad forces maintained elaborate card files detailing the professional and personal characteristics of the editors of even the smallest of small-town newspapers. Publicity bureau personnel in turn fed tailor-made information to the editors, always emphasizing the supposed wisdom and superiority of the railroad perspective. By 1909, industry officials had created the Special Committee on the Relations of the Railways to Legislation as a mechanism to shape pending federal legislation on the inspection of steam locomotive boilers.[278]

The Pennsylvania Railroad soon became a leader in efforts to create favorable publicity, thanks to several near-simultaneous developments. A series of horrific accidents called into question the PRR's commitment to the lives of its passengers. Many state legislators were contemplating the adoption of full-crew laws, ostensibly as a mechanism for increasing safety, as well as the creation of strong railroad commissions, to augment what they considered to be inadequate ICC regulation. By 1906, the damaging revelations in the coal hearings caused President Cassatt to become even more solicitous of public opinion. He cooperated with reporter and "yellow journalist" James Creelman for an article in *Pearson's Magazine* that would portray him in an exceedingly favorable light. Creelman bestowed upon Cassatt the mantle of an industrial statesman, suggesting that he was the only executive who was willing to place the public good ahead of crass considerations of profitability. Cassatt's desire to provide better service to New York caused him to courageously and selflessly wage war against the political corruption associated with the Tammany Hall machine, Creelman emphasized. The community of interest, the journalist asserted, was an attempt to make rates fair and equal for all, while improving the PRR's facilities, and did not represent a monopolistic effort to extort higher revenues from shippers. Cassatt's close ties to Roosevelt, far from symbolizing political cronyism, instead proved his commitment to the cause of regulation in the public interest. How unfortunate, Creelman suggested, that Cassatt's beneficent policies had been demonized by selfish and unenlightened critics.[279]

Even though newspapermen had not yet begun to reject such interviews as blatant propaganda—that would come later, around the time of World War I—many readers nonetheless saw little value in the hagiography that Creelman had provided. The editor of *Pearson's* acknowledged, "No article which we have published has brought upon us as much caustic comment as Mr. Creelman's story of the career of Mr. Cassatt, in connection with the wonderful development of the Pennsylvania Railroad."[280] Despite the criticism, the article demonstrated the value of public relations, with the editor acknowledging, "and yet, a half-year later, when sudden death forced a calm consideration of the public service accomplishments of Mr. Cassatt, many newspapers used the Pearson's Magazine story as the text upon which to build their obituary editorials," with the *New York World* reprinting the "article in full."[281] While not entirely inaccurate, the Creelman piece did much to create the Cassatt mystique that survived, to a certain extent, even into the early years of the twenty-first century.[282]

Other newspapers echoed Creelman's comments, and his favorable opinion of the PRR. In June 1906, the *Wall Street Journal* published an article entitled "A Study in Values" that offered a generally positive portrayal of the railroad. Its author rather condescendingly noted, "The Pennsylvania is too vast . . . to be grasped by the lay mind," and went on to educate readers as to the PRR's importance to the American industrial economy.[283] The increase in ton-miles during 1905 alone was the same as the entire business of the Wabash, the *Journal* noted, and twice that of the Reading. The implication, presumably, was that the executives of such a large and complex corporation were busily engaged in promoting the general welfare rather than in efforts to monopolize the railroads.

Yet, the media emphasis on the size, power, and the wealth of the Pennsylvania Railroad ran the risk of causing many citizens to feel that the company was too large and powerful, and that some of its riches should be redirected to serve the public good. Such a possibility loomed large in the mind of one of the pioneers of public relations, the individual who largely shaped the railroad's publicity campaigns. Ivy Ledbetter Lee, often referred to as the father of modern corporate publicity, was a moderately successful journalist and political adviser. Lee first took on public-relations work in 1903, soon joining forces with journalist George Parker. Lee's new career coincided with a growing national emphasis on the dissemination of information as a mechanism for rectifying criticism of allegedly abusive business practices. President Roosevelt called repeatedly for greater corporate publicity, which he believed "would tend to curb the evils of which there is just complaint and where the alleged evils are imaginary, would tend to show that such was the case."[284] Given the political environment, Lee had chosen a profession with significant growth potential. In 1905, he issued a "Declaration of Principles" in an effort to differentiate the emerging field of public relations from older, less reputable efforts by promoters and press agents. As such, business executives in many industries would have been familiar with Lee and his public-relations activities. Lee was also well positioned to defend Cassatt's community of interest, as the publicist believed that the stability of government-backed cartels would empower business executives to let loose the better angels of their nature, protecting the public interest from jungle-law competition. Lee's work with the PRR apparently fed his creative soul, for he regarded the railroad as a first-class operation, one that lived up to his rhetoric of a business that served the United States and its citizens.[285]

Lee, to a greater extent than many of the PRR managers to whom he reported, emphasized that publicity was to be a vital aspect of twentieth-century railroading. He noted that railway personnel, although well schooled in their craft, tended to provide the media with inaccurate information, factually correct data that might prove embarrassing to the company, or no information at all. Even worse, they might become enraged at reporters and throw them off of PRR property. Such ill-conceived and uncoordinated actions did the PRR no favors. As he had done in other industries, Lee advised PRR personnel to share information with the press, presenting their actions in the most favorable light possible rather than allowing muckraking reporters to reach their own conclusions. Lee and his corporate clients were painfully aware that many journalists misrepresented the facts, employed misleading statistics, and in some cases fabricated stories in order to sell papers. In that context, Lee saw himself as a crusader for truth, not as an apologist for the misdeeds of corporate America. His efforts, revolutionary for the time, deflected a great deal of media criticism from the PRR.[286]

During the spring of 1906, as the ICC investigation into coal shipments rapidly became a public-relations disaster, PRR management engaged Lee's services.[287] Initially, his role was limited to dampening down negative stories, at a time when PRR personnel were rarely willing to talk to reporters, much less provide them with detailed and accurate information. Lee was particularly adept at minimizing public criticism of accidents, such as the one that occurred on October 28, 1906.[288] A PRR passenger train that was nearing Atlantic City, New Jersey, derailed at the approach to a recently completed drawbridge over the Thoroughfare, the channel that separated the barrier island from the mainland. The first two cars plunged into the water, drowning fifty-three people in a gruesome disaster that seemed tailor-made for sensationalistic newspaper headlines. Work crews employed a crane in an attempt to retrieve one of the submerged cars, but only succeeded in driving it farther into the ooze at the bottom of the channel. In frustration, PRR officials discussed the possibility of splitting the car open with dynamite in an effort to extract as many bodies as possible. Some corpses, they acknowledged, had already drifted out to sea and would never be recovered.

As usual, PRR officials concentrated on repairing the damage and assessing culpability, and they refused to talk to the press. In the information vacuum, reporters interviewed anyone who was even remotely connected with the accident. An outside contractor opined that "the real trouble has been that the work [on the bridge] was a rush job and sufficient precautions were not taken," a comment that was bound to portray the PRR in an unfavorable light.[289] In a rapid effort at damage control, Lee issued what was probably the first press release in the history of American business, judiciously furnishing reporters with details of the disaster. Under the heading "Statement from the Road," the *New York Times* published Lee's message verbatim, with a subheading repeating his assertion that "the Rails on the Bridge Must Have Fitted Exactly."[290] That was not precisely true, and an internal PRR investigation concluded that a mechanical error had prevented the drawbridge from closing properly. Nevertheless, few newspaper editors criticized the railroad. Instead, they blamed a New Jersey state law that required bridge tenders to open the span on demand for even the smallest and most insignificant of fishing vessels.[291]

Another public relations challenge occurred on February 22, 1907, when the four-car *Pennsylvania Special* derailed near Mineral Point, east of Johnstown. Early newspaper reports were, as usual, both sensationalistic and inaccurate, suggesting that the entire train had plunged into the Conemaugh River, with many fatalities. The reality was bad enough, with more than fifty injured, including Ohio Congressman Beeman G. Dawes. Seven PRR employees were arrested for looting the wrecked cars. Reporters suggested that the train had been running late, and traveling too fast in order to make up lost time. Similar accidents were commonplace on such expresses, on both the PRR and the New York Central, they emphasized. "Absolutely no facilities were extended to many newspaper representatives who wanted to get news," complained a correspondent for the *New York Times*. "Attempts to get accurate details were hampered by the railroad officials."[292]

Initially, PRR officials speculated that a brake hanger had dropped down from one of the trucks on the tender and snagged the rails. Track workers suggested an alternate explanation, that the track itself had failed. Their version of events seemed to place just

as much blame on the PRR, but there was a difference. The train had derailed on a curve, along a section of track that had recently been equipped with experimental steel ties fabricated by U.S. Steel. The lateral stress caused by the train rounding the curve at high speed—no more than the permissible fifty miles an hour, PRR officials emphasized—caused the bolts that secured the rails to the ties to shear off. The PRR's investigating committee concluded that the engine on the train "was carefully inspected before it left the roundhouse, and was in perfect condition."[293] Even though there was a "lack of positive evidence as to the cause of this derailment," they emphasized that "the derailment was more serious than would have been the case with wooden ties."[294] By implication, it was the U.S. Steel track and not the PRR train that had caused the accident.

For the first time, Ivy Lee insisted that the report of the PRR's accident investigation committee be released to the newspapers. Happily for the Pennsylvania Railroad, editors reprinted large portions of the report, verbatim, suggesting that U.S. Steel was to blame for the wreck of the *Pennsylvania Special*. Particularly compelling was the PRR's announcement that it would immediately remove all steel ties in the interest of safety. Outraged U.S. Steel officials insisted that their ties had performed flawlessly on the company-owned Bessemer & Lake Erie Railroad, but to no avail. Thanks to Lee, the newspapers exonerated the Pennsylvania Railroad.[295]

PRR managers soon envisioned a much larger role for Ivy Lee. At a time when the company was under criticism for the community of interest and its links with coal producers, Cassatt and his fellow executives wanted to show the public that the Pennsylvania Railroad had done far more good than harm. It was important to emphasize that the higher rates associated with the community of interest were being used to enhance freight and passenger service, rather than lining the pockets of wealthy investors. Lee's article "Indirect Service of Railroads," in the November 1907 issue of *Moody's* magazine, emphasized the PRR's efforts in the "Encouragement of industries, aid to agriculture, distribution of immigrants, establishment of schools, payment of pensions to retired employees, beautifying of stations and station parks, [and] liberal contributions to the Railroad Y.M.C.A." Lee did not mention the PRR's traffic levels, its earnings, or the dividends paid to thousands of investors, for such statistics might have raised uncomfortable questions regarding Cassatt's insistence on higher rates. Instead, as the title of the article suggested, the PRR was to be praised for the intangible benefits that it produced for the nation. Lee encouraged his readers "to consider what transportation companies really do for the public, in addition to the direct service of transporting passengers and freight."[296]

Within a few years, the PRR had expanded the scope of Lee's efforts, and had given him considerably more autonomy as well. At the beginning of 1908, Lee became a full-time PRR employee, generally referred to as the railroad's publicity agent. Soon after he joined the PRR, Lee established a Publicity Bureau, the railroad's first system-wide mechanism for coordinating publicity. He was a fixture on the Pennsylvania Railroad, with an office in New York, a support staff, and a retainer of $10,000 a year. Lee was worth the expense, second vice president Samuel Rea asserted in 1910, because he "was well trained and always cautious . . . [and] he rarely made any breaks."[297]

Lee's primary function was to coordinate the actions of PRR personnel, ensuring that all information flowed through the proper channels. Beginning in March 1909, he developed standard procedures for the dissemination of information through press releases, replacing the older ad hoc methods. As the PRR's managers became more conscious of the toll that accidents exerted on the company's public image, Lee spent more and more time preparing press releases, "seeing to it that facts only are printed," and above all emphasizing "that upon occasions of wrecks it is impracticable for miscellaneous employes [sic] to give out information."[298] The dissemination of accurate and consistent information became even more important as senior PRR officials spent more and more of their time testifying before Congress and the ICC. "There was a time when railroad managers thought they were running a private business," Lee noted, "but they have come to find they are . . . running a business over which the public itself has assumed complete supervision and control."[299]

Information flowed both ways, and Lee saw his role as "interpreting the Pennsylvania Railroad to the pub-lic and interpreting the public to the Pennsylvania Railroad."[300] He observed that PRR employees had earned a reputation for being the least courteous of any major railroad. To the public, Lee emphasized that what appeared to be discourtesy was actually a single-minded devotion to safety and efficiency. Train crews, he stressed, were so focused on their demanding jobs that they had scant opportunity to engage in the social niceties. When discussing the issue with PRR personnel, Lee refrained from blaming either executives or employees. He acknowledged that the success of PRR managers in running an orderly and efficient railroad had perversely tarnished the railroad's public image. The desire to work safely and productively was to be commended, Lee emphasized, but those admirable traits should not come at the expense of friendly relations with passengers, shippers, and local communities.

As the uproar over the coal hearings and the community of interest subsided, Lee temporarily parted ways with the Pennsylvania Railroad. In October 1909, he received a leave of absence from the PRR, with his brother, James, taking his place, at the considerably lower salary of $3,000 per year. Now in the employ of Harris, Winthrop & Company, Lee spent much of his time in Europe, touring railways and evaluating their publicity efforts.

State Regulatory Activism

During the early years of the twentieth century, many states placed substantial restrictions on railroad operations. Much of the new regulatory activism at the state level stemmed from efforts by legislators to advance the interests of organized labor or else to demonstrate to their constituents that they were taking action against the presumed abuses that had been committed by railroad executives. In 1904, there were twenty-four state regulatory commissions in operation, but by the beginning of 1908 there were thirty-nine, most of which possessed the power to set intrastate rates. Whether through legislative action or commission ruling, many states controlled even the most mundane aspects of railroad operations, ranging from terminal facilities to the frequency and cost of passenger service to the installation of spurs and sidings. State legislators curried favor with railroad unions by restricting working hours, limiting train lengths, and imposing full-crew laws. Politicians generally emphasized that full-crew bills would increase safety, but most observers acknowledged that the more common motivation was to provide additional jobs for trainmen.[301]

Much of the legislative and commission activity involved restrictions on passenger fares. Over the last third of the nineteenth century, freight rates had declined substantially, while passenger fares had not. That unhappy circumstance had far more to do with the basic economics of railway transportation than with any desire on the part of railway executives to extort money from the traveling public. Decreases in freight rates, per ton-mile, had been driven by two factors—the increased capacity and efficiency of freight transportation, coupled with rapid growth in demand that resulted in a more intensive utilization of the physical plant. Passengers, however, were not amenable to more efficient loading, unloading, and haulage—particularly when the railroads, as common carriers, were required to operate trains on lightly patronized branch lines. Furthermore, passenger traffic had grown only modestly during the late nineteenth century, precluding efforts to use volume as a mechanism for lowering average cost per passenger mile.[302] Yet, by the early twentieth century, most citizens believed that they enjoyed a right to mobility—a situation that ironically stemmed in part from the railroads' efforts to increase passenger travel through advertising, the publication of promotional booklets, and the introduction of excursion fares. With railroad executives seemingly unwilling to reduce ticket prices as rapidly as they did freight tariffs, voters called for governmental policies that would facilitate their ability to travel.[303]

Beginning in 1906, legislators and members of state regulatory commissions in twenty-two states enacted laws limiting passenger fares. Eleven of those states—including Illinois, Indiana, Ohio, and New Jersey—imposed two-cent fares.[304] The New York legislature followed suit, before Governor Charles Evans Hughes vetoed the measure. The two-cent figure represented a politically comprehensible round number that rarely reflected the true cost of passenger service. Legislators

noted, correctly, that the railroads' variable cost of passenger transportation was generally below two cents per mile. However, they refused to acknowledge that variable costs, including locomotive and equipment maintenance and fuel and crew costs, accounted for only about a quarter of the total expense associated with the provision of passenger service. Because railroad accountants could not accurately assign a precise share of fixed costs to a particular class of service, they found it difficult to refute assertions that passenger trains consumed little more than their variable cost of service.[305]

For the PRR, the most serious threat emanated from the commonwealth of Pennsylvania, home to the bulk of the railroad's passenger mileage. In November 1906, in an attempt to forestall legislative action, PRR officials reduced maximum passenger rates to no more than two and a half cents per mile. Their efforts were for naught, however, and in his January 1907 inaugural address Governor Edwin S. Stuart called upon the members of the General Assembly to correct perceived abuses among the commonwealth's railroads. The new governor supported the creation of a state regulatory commission, and favored giving electric interurban railways the power of eminent domain and the right to carry freight, in competition with the steam railroads. Like his counterparts in many other states, Stuart also favored a two-cent passenger fare bill.[306]

Legislators responded enthusiastically to the governor's call to arms, while PRR executives did their best to educate the members of the General Assembly on the economics of passenger transportation. On February 26, fourth vice president John B. Thayer testified before the Pennsylvania Senate Railroad Committee, insisting that a two-cent fare would require offsetting increases in short-distance commuter fares, the curtailment of services, or the use of freight revenues to cross-subsidize passenger traffic. His arguments fell on deaf ears, and by March 26, both the House and the Senate had approved the legislation, which provided for fines of up to $1,000 for each offense. Ten days later, despite a written protest from James McCrea, the PRR's president, Governor Stuart signed the bill into law. In the next session of the General Assembly, legislators acknowledged that many of the railroads in the commonwealth had suspended local passenger service rather than incur the losses associated with the two-cent fare—an outcome that, despite earlier warnings from railroad officials, none of them had apparently anticipated.[307]

Representatives from the state's two leading railroads, the PRR and the Reading, soon challenged the constitutionality of the new fare law. Appearing before the Philadelphia County Court of Common Pleas, PRR officials presented testimony that was, according to a reporter for the *New York Times*, "nearly all heavily mathematical." Such evidence, while factually correct, did little to placate those who were convinced that the railroads had ample wealth to spare. In a refrain that would become distressingly familiar at both the state and the national levels, the law's defenders intimated that a large portion of the PRR's capitalization was "water"—that is, that a two-cent fare would be more than sufficient for the PRR to earn a profit on the actual worth of its facilities, if not necessarily on the supposedly inflated value of its securities. Vice president John Green vigorously refuted the allegation, but public suspicions remained, nonetheless.[308]

By September 1907, the Court of Common Pleas had overturned the two-cent fare law. The court accepted the PRR's argument that the fares would lower the net earnings on passenger service to 1.94 percent, far less than the 5.1 percent that the railroad had previously earned, and even further below the 6 percent that constituted the legal definition of a reasonable rate of return. Such confiscatory fares violated the due process clause of the Fourteenth Amendment to the federal Constitution, as well as the Pennsylvania state constitution. The court also ruled that the two-cent-fare law ran counter to the provisions of the PRR's 1846 corporate charter. The verdict marked a considerable victory for the PRR, as the court eschewed precedents in other states that suggested that unlawful confiscation applied only in situations where carriers had failed to earn any profit at all, regardless of capital costs. In November, the case reached the Pennsylvania Supreme Court, on appeal, and in January 1908 the justices upheld the lower court ruling. In defeat, Pennsylvania legislators vowed to repeal the law rather than take the matter to the United States Supreme Court. Within days, PRR officials announced that they would restore the old passenger rates, averaging perhaps two and a half cents per mile.[309]

In Pennsylvania, and in many other states, the courts and legislatures terminated the brief experiment with two-cent fares. PRR executives could take little comfort in their victory, however. The justices of the Pennsylvania Supreme Court had been sharply divided, four to three, over the issue. Even more frightening was the court's dissenting opinion, which held that "the power to supervise rate charges of a quasi public corporation, like a railroad corporation, is a police power of the State and that the Legislature has no authority to abridge it or to delegate it to a corporation [as in the PRR's 1846 charter, for instance] or to any other body."[310] The managers who represented the PRR and other railroads in the commonwealth had come perilously close to losing their authority to set intrastate rates for their services. In general terms, the three dissenting justices adopted the rationale of many reformers, who suggested that so long as the PRR's overall revenues were sufficiently remunerative, certain classes of service could be operated at little or no profit—or even at a loss—in order to better serve the public interest. More broadly, the short-lived fare fight reflected a growing, and inaccurate, public consensus that the railroads constituted limitless pools of wealth, some of which could be transferred through the mechanism of lower rates to presumably less-fortunate segments of American society. The growing efforts by legislatures and regulatory agencies to force the PRR and other railroads to cross-subsidize certain classes of service represented the ascendency of public opinion over economic rationality. So long as the railroads maintained a near-monopoly on transportation, cross-subsidization required little more than burdensome accounting practices, transferring revenues from lucrative services to those that were unremunerative. Within a few years, however, truck, bus, and automobile competition cut deeply into railroad revenues, ensuring that subsidized services imperiled the overall health of the railroad industry. Under those circumstances, regulatory insistence on lower passenger fares was one of many factors that contributed to the erosion of passenger rail service.

In the midst of their attempt to cap passenger fares, the members of the General Assembly implemented broader regulatory oversight of the PRR and the other railroads and public utilities that operated within the commonwealth. In May 1907, they created a State Railroad Commission, making Pennsylvania one of the last states to embrace the commission form of regulation. Most of the new state regulatory agencies that emerged during the early twentieth century were strong commissions that possessed the power to set intrastate rates, much like those that had first developed in the midwestern Granger states during the 1870s. Pennsylvania's version was a throwback to an earlier era of "sunshine" regulation. It was closely modeled on the 1869 Massachusetts Board of Railroad Commissioners, whose members envisioned that a body with the power to investigate, advise, and publicize would shame railroad executives into submission.

The duties of the Pennsylvania State Railroad Commission were many and varied, and included studying the effects of canal abandonment and preventing forest fires. Commissioners could do no more than inform the state attorney general should they uncover evidence of any illegal activity. The initial chairman of the three-member body was attorney Nathaniel Ewing, president of the Pennsylvania Bar Association and a former legal counsel for the PRR—and therefore a person unlikely to attack the railroads with any degree of vigor. Many of the commission's recommendations—such as one calling on the legislature to increase penalties for persons trespassing on railroad property—presumably generated little railroader opposition. The Massachusetts sunshine commission had developed in tandem with the maturation of the railroad network, but Pennsylvania's attempt came after the railroads were well established. Railroad executives had scant reason to respect its authority. Representatives from the carriers, the PRR and the Baltimore & Ohio in particular, simply disregarded many of the commission's rulings.[311]

The Mann-Elkins Act and the Matter of Rates

While the creation of the Pennsylvania State Railroad Commission initially created few problems for the Pennsylvania Railroad, federal regulation was another matter entirely. Cassatt had worked closely with Roo-

sevelt in order to shape the contours of both the 1903 Elkins Act and the 1906 Hepburn Act. The Hepburn Act emboldened reformers to a far greater extent than Cassatt had anticipated, however, leading to calls for additional regulation.

Within a few years, moreover, the two actors who had shaped the Hepburn Act passed from the scene. Alexander J. Cassatt, who died in December 1906, was no longer in a position to deflect adverse regulation, or to shape legislation in a manner that would best suit the interests of the Pennsylvania Railroad. His successor, James McCrea, the eighth president of the Pennsylvania Railroad, lacked Cassatt's political finesse, as well as his predecessor's easy access to the White House. Little more than two years later, on March 4, 1909, William Howard Taft took the oath of office as the twenty-seventh President of the United States. Roosevelt may have anointed Taft as his successor, but the two individuals possessed quite different personalities. Roosevelt was a politician and a consummate dealmaker. For all of his bluster regarding the malefactors of great wealth, he was willing to countenance many of the policies associated with big business, so long as capitalists agreed to mitigate their most egregious practices. In contrast, Taft was first and foremost a lawyer, not a politician. Unlike Roosevelt, he believed in enforcing the letter of the law and not in making deals with wayward industrialists.

Initially, many railroad executives believed that Taft's legal acumen and the presence of considerable legal talent in his cabinet would work in favor of the PRR and the other railroads. Beginning in the autumn of 1908, when it became clear that Taft would in all likelihood become the next President, railroad attorneys became far more aggressive in their attempts to challenge the ICC's administrative decisions in the courts. As the nation began to recover from the Panic of 1907, and as labor and material costs increased, railroad officials also became more vocal in their calls for corresponding rate increases. To their dismay, however, the railroads' combative stance aroused public opinion and alienated many members of Congress.[312]

At the same time, the courts were becoming more amenable to the concept of administrative regulation. The members of the established federal judiciary had traditionally taken a dim view of efforts to enhance the ICC's authority, but by 1910, the Supreme Court had become far more tolerant of the commission's role in the regulatory process. During the late 1800s, and into the earliest years of the twentieth century, the justices had generally adopted a conservative stance on issues that included health and safety legislation, child labor laws, and anti-trust policies. In many instances, their rulings seemed out of step with the progressive tenor of the times, and the justices soon confronted calls to curtail the court's power, perhaps through a constitutional amendment that would impose term limitations or other restrictions on judicial authority and autonomy. Faced with that discontent, the justices began to moderate their views. The ICC, an agency nearly a quarter-century old, now seemed less threatening to many on the court. Most notably, in 1910, the court largely abandoned its earlier assertion that the ICC should function primarily as an investigative body, with little policymaking authority. In *ICC v. Illinois Central Railroad*, the justices adopted what later became known as limited judicial review, reserving for themselves rulings on matters of law but allowing administrative agencies such as the ICC to develop a large and decisive body of rules that would permit routine policy decisions. The verdict validated the vision of those economists who sought to create an administrative state and permitted a gradual accretion of ICC power.[313]

During the first half of 1910, railroaders, shippers, legislators, and regulators debated the contours of what would become the third and final component of rate regulation during the Progressive era. They operated in the context of growing shipper discontent and growing judicial tolerance of the ICC. Shippers increasingly demanded that the ICC possess the authority to evaluate the reasonableness of proposed rate increases before they took effect. Given his legal expertise, Taft believed that effective regulation would be possible only when Congress had precisely delineated specific regulatory responsibilities and assigned them to the ICC, to the legislature, or to the courts, as appropriate. Furthermore, Taft supported the creation of a commerce court, a judicial body with oversight of ICC rulings.

Even though they no longer possessed the advantages of Cassatt's charm and persuasive abilities, PRR executives continued to meet with the President and members of Congress, in an effort to influence the legislative process. On January 3, 1910, McCrea and five other railroad presidents journeyed to the White House to meet with Taft and attorney general George W. Wickersham, a conference that had been arranged by J. P. Morgan. Wickersham had largely written the bill that was under discussion, in collaboration with Commerce Secretary Charles Nagel and Congressman Charles E. Townsend, the Michigan Republican who had been responsible for one of the pro-shipper predecessors of the Hepburn bill. They in turn relied heavily on suggestions from shippers, but less so from railroaders. As the *New York Times* noted, "The Attorney General was also discussing the matter all along with the lawyers for the big railroads, so that they were familiar with what was going on." That was a far cry from the Elkins Act seven years earlier, which was essentially drafted by PRR and Santa Fe attorneys. This time, McCrea and his colleagues offered suggestions to Taft, yet received only obstinacy in return. The *Times* headline—"Taft Yields Little to Railroad Men"—summarized the new political reality confronting the carriers.[314]

In its final form, the June 1910 Mann-Elkins Act represented a compromise between Taft's vision of a strong judicial presence in regulatory affairs and a desire among many members of Congress to greatly strengthen the ICC. The railroads escaped a proposed provision that would have given the ICC control over the issuance of securities—a power that the commission would not gain for another decade. The commission did, however, establish control over the telegraph and telephone industries. Most significantly, the Mann-Elkins Act shifted the burden of proof from shippers, who were no longer required to demonstrate that rates were unreasonable, to the railroads, whose executives now had to prove, to the satisfaction of the ICC commissioners, that their rates were not unjust. Shippers also gained the right to specify the routing of their shipments, thus preventing railroad executives from diverting freight from one carrier to another in order to maximize their railroad's line haul or to orchestrate a traffic pool. The legislation reestablished the prohibition against long-haul/short-haul discrimination, which had been largely nullified by the Supreme Court's ruling in the *Alabama Midland* case. In place of the problematic phrase "under substantially similar circumstances and conditions" contained in the 1887 Act to Regulate Commerce, the new law prohibited carriers from charging more for any combination of segments that constituted a longer route without the ICC's permission. As with earlier legislation, Congress had chosen not to provide the ICC with a precise definition of "reasonable and just" rates, forcing the commissioners to again navigate a course through the conflicting demands of the legislature, the judiciary, shippers, and the railroads.[315]

At Taft's insistence, the Mann-Elkins Act created a Commerce Court, which, the President hoped, would impose both judicial expertise and judicial restraint on the actions of the ICC commissioners. The plan proved unworkable, however, and railroad executives disliked what they regarded as another regulatory commission. Congress abolished the Commerce Court just three years later. With the extinction of the Commerce Court and the greater leeway afforded by the Supreme Court, the administrative apparatus created by the ICC was now firmly in command of the process of railway regulation.

Accounting for Efficiency

The passage of the Mann-Elkins Act coincided with a debate over two intertwined issues—rates and accounting practices—that were vital to efforts to earn a profit, attract additional capital, and improve the capacity and the efficiency of operations. The ICC's role in developing railway accounting practices, a power that it had gained under the terms of the Hepburn Act, impeded the PRR's ability to justify enhancements to the physical plant. The commission's simultaneous denial of rate increases caused further difficulties.

Prior to 1906, the Pennsylvania Railroad and the Interstate Commerce Commission employed similar accounting principles, in large measure because PRR executives had developed those methods. The individual most closely associated with that process was Thomas D. Messler, who developed his accounting expertise while employed on the New York & Erie between 1852 and 1856. Working under the direction of

Erie treasurer William E. Warren, Messler became acquainted with the Moran Brothers, a New York investment-banking firm. Moran Brothers was also involved in the merger of the Fort Wayne & Chicago, the Ohio & Pennsylvania, and the Ohio & Indiana railroads into the Pittsburgh, Fort Wayne & Chicago Rail Road, and maintained substantial holdings in the new company's securities. In 1856, the same year as the Fort Wayne merger, Moran Brothers insisted that the company's board of directors hire the twenty-three-year-old Messler as secretary and auditor. "The department over which he had supervision had been conducted theretofore with but little method and exactness," noted his son and biographer. "The accounts were seemingly in a hopeless tangle, and it was for him to unravel the mass by process of a reorganization of this department on the lines of modern railway accounting as then known to and practiced by the older railway companies in the East."[316]

Between 1856 and 1862, Messler developed the "Messler System" of accounting. In the aftermath of the Fort Wayne's 1859 bankruptcy and subsequent reorganization, and amid the escalating traffic demands associated with the Civil War, the Messler System became vital to the Fort Wayne's operations. In response to the growth in interchange traffic between railroads, Messler gave the Fort Wayne's accounting officers the authority to establish financial settlements with other carriers, as well as to collect all funds owed to the company. In order to limit the possibility of unauthorized expenditures or outright fraud, the Messler System required the signatures of three officials—a clerk, his supervisor, and the head of the department. Messler also charged all operating expenses to their originating departments, a practice that he later made standard on the PRR.[317]

By the time that the PRR leased the Fort Wayne in July 1869, Messler had been promoted to be the personal assistant to Fort Wayne president George W. Cass. The PRR's own president, J. Edgar Thomson, knew talent when he saw it, and arranged for Messler to join the Pennsylvania Railroad system. On July 1, 1871, Messler assumed his responsibilities as comptroller of the Pennsylvania Company, and by 1876 he had become the third vice president on Lines West. He also served as comptroller of several Lines West subsidiaries, including the Fort Wayne, the Pan Handle, and the Indianapolis & Vincennes. Given the organic growth of the western portion of the system, composed as it was of numerous existing companies cobbled together, Messler should not have been surprised to discover that each department maintained its own bookkeepers, auditors, and accounting standards. In practical terms, Lines West accountants were capable of summarizing the financial results of each railroad's operations, but they were unable to develop a real-time picture of operating costs. Messler accordingly placed each company's accounting methods on a standardized basis, routinized both interline freight accounts and internal funds transfers, and made certain that accountants, rather than auditors, were in charge of financial controls.[318]

In 1887, when Congress created the ICC, it gave that agency the authority to establish a uniform system of railway accounts. Regulators believed that the new accounting formats would permit more efficient administrative regulation and ensure accurate rate-making based on the value of rail service to shippers. It should be emphasized, however, that the commissioners only possessed the authority to proscribe standard accounting formats, but not the methods whereby the railroads developed those results. With the blessing of ICC chief statistician Henry Carter Adams, the commissioners selected as their standard the Messler System already employed on the PRR and on numerous other railroads in the United States.[319]

In 1894, the commissioners deviated from the Messler System, and for the first time stipulated that all railroads create a category for depreciation expense. Previously, rather than treat assets as depreciable, railroad accountants referred to capital consumption—that is, the erosion in the value of assets. New investments constituted capital formation, and after the deduction of capital consumption, the resulting measure—net capital formation—indicated the overall growth in the worth of a railroad's property. Rather than calculate depreciation rates that reflected the annual wear and tear on track and equipment, PRR managers had merely estimated the loss in value. Instead of a employing a separate depreciation account, the company deducted from net income both taxes and dividend payments, then placed whatever surplus remained in a surplus account (a "contingent fund," established in 1855) to pay for repairs and replacements. Any additional monies were used to finance additions to the physical plant and the acquisition of subsidiary lines. Such practices caused regulators to suspect that PRR officials were disguising high earnings by plowing them into the contingent fund and using the proceeds to purchase the stocks and bonds of other railroads. In any event, railroad managers generally ignored the ICC's 1894 depreciation directive, arguing with some justification that it was impossible to make consistent charges that reflected the loss of asset values. For one thing, investments were asynchronous—that is, they fluctuated wildly according to traffic levels and the state of the economy. Furthermore, given the rapid advancements in railroad technology, many assets might be rendered obsolete long before they were fully depreciated.[320]

Although PRR accountants rejected the ICC's depreciation policies, the railroad continued to affect the commissioners' efforts to develop new accounting standards. In 1896, Leonor Loree became general manager of Lines West. He recognized that the increased importance of the PRR's Traffic Department mandated additional revisions to the PRR's accounting system, through the separation of the expenses associated with the solicitation of business from those linked to the transportation of freight and passengers. After Cassatt tapped him to be president of the Baltimore & Ohio, as part of the community-of-interest plan, Loree subsequently applied his accounting methods to that carrier. Loree later served on the Chicago, Rock Island & Pacific Railroad and eventually became president of the Delaware & Hudson, further spreading his ideas.[321]

In *Smyth v. Ames* (1898) the Supreme Court ruled that neither the ICC nor a state regulatory commission could force railroads to set rates below the cost of service. The ICC commissioners accordingly contemplated the development of an accounting system that would indicate the expense associated with each class of traffic. Theirs was an impossible task, as even the most skilled railroad accountants could not determine the precise degree to which a particular car, carrying a specific load, eroded the value of the physical plant. ICC officials nonetheless attempted to differentiate the costs of initial construction, maintenance, betterments, and routine operations. As a model, they could look to the new accounting standards adopted in 1902 by U.S. Steel. That company was the first to list depreciation as an expense charged against income, strengthening the commissioners' determination to require railroads to establish depreciation accounts.[322]

The 1906 Hepburn Act authorized the ICC to evaluate the carriers' financial statements and to mandate uniform accounting methods (as opposed to the 1887 act's designation of uniform accounting formats). In recognition of the growing importance of traffic functions, the 1906 act created a new category of Traffic Expenses. The act also established a Bureau of Statistics and Accounts, headed by statistician Henry Adams. With the implementation of the Hepburn Act and the creation of the Bureau of Statistics and Accounts, Adams was more determined than ever before to implement his vision of accounting to achieve regulation, but he nonetheless continued to rely heavily on the input of industry executives. Among his sources was Frank Nay, the chief accounting officer on the Rock Island. The two men quite naturally agreed to copy the Rock Island's accounting methods, which, owing to Loree's influence, were essentially the same as those employed on the PRR.[323]

Railroad executives initially supported accounting uniformity, so long as the new policies promised to boost investor confidence and make capital more readily available. Many railroad managers—particularly PRR president James McCrea—were nonetheless strongly opposed to both the underlying rationale and the implementation of the accounting changes. McCrea and his fellow executives used accounts to determine the costs of operations and maintenance, and to attribute those expenditures as accurately as possible to particular classes of service. McCrea informed the commission of his displeasure with the new accounting standards, both because he believed that they allocated costs incorrectly, and because he insisted that large railroads should be given additional opportunity to suggest modifications to the ICC protocols.

McCrea had reason to be upset, as the ICC-mandated system of accounts retarded the PRR's ability to attract badly needed capital investment. Adams and other ICC officials had made one significant change

from the practices that Messler and Loree had developed. Prior to 1907, the PRR, like virtually every other railroad in the United States, had employed replacement-retirement-betterment accounting. That system, more often simply referred to as betterment accounting, took into consideration the physical, rather than the economic, consequences of the wearing out of assets. For example, should PRR construction crews lay a section of new track with rail weighing seventy-five pounds per yard, the railroad's accountants would capitalize that expense, but they would not establish a depreciation account for the asset. The rail would inevitably wear out, and require replacement. If workers replaced the worn seventy-five-pound rail with identical new rail, then the entire cost would be charged as a (replacement) expense. More commonly, however, the workers would install heavier rail, perhaps one hundred pounds per yard, in order to accommodate more robust cars and locomotives. In that event, 75 percent of the expense would be considered a replacement cost, without any addition to the railroad's capital, while the remainder (the betterment) was capitalized. However, the entire cost would be charged to operating expense, based on the railroads' not unreasonable assertion that the heavier rail was not an enhancement to the physical plant, but merely a necessary mechanism for accommodating heavier traffic with an equal degree of safety and efficiency.[324]

The ICC's position was that betterment accounting made it impossible to differentiate between operating costs and the costs associated with building and rebuilding the physical plant. They suspected that railroad executives were disguising high rates of return by assigning what were properly capital costs to operating expenses, artificially lowering net earnings. Furthermore, the commissioners were concerned about the safety implications associated with betterment accounting, given that in lean years railroad executives possessed a strong incentive to curtail the renewal of worn-out and potentially unsafe rail, bridges, and equipment in order to reduce the replacement and betterment costs that would otherwise be charged as operating expenses.[325]

ICC officials were sympathetic to the growing consensus by accountants at U.S. Steel and other industrial corporations that depreciation was an economic, not a physical, characteristic. That is, the commissioners intended to link the cost of each railroad's assets to the use of its facilities (or, more precisely, to operating revenues) rather than to an engineering assessment of when equipment was worn out or inadequate for elevated traffic levels. The new accounting standards proposed by the ICC mandated that the railroads could only charge the cost of maintaining the property in its original state to operating expenses. For example, if the PRR replaced rail weighing seventy-five pounds per yard with rail weighing one hundred pounds per yard, the ICC's new accounting guidelines mandated that 75 percent of the cost be charged to operating expense, and the remaining 25 percent (reflecting the difference in value between the lighter and the heavier rail) be applied to the capital account, to be depreciated over time. The one-quarter of the expense corresponding to the installation of the heavier rail could not be charged to operating expenses, as railroads had done in the past.[326]

ICC regulators insisted that mandatory depreciation schedules would benefit both investors and shippers. The imposition of uniform accounting rules, they asserted, would increase the margin of safety (i.e., the difference between the price of the stock and its actual value), and thus protect investors from unscrupulous or incompetent management. Yet, that benefit was of limited value to a company, like the PRR, that was conservatively capitalized and that possessed a sterling reputation in financial circles. Shippers, in the opinion of ICC officials, were the primary victims of the old accounting system, and thus the group most in need of protection. In the past, they alleged, the railroad practice of shifting capital costs to operating expense had produced a double burden on farmers, manufacturers, and other users of rail services. Bad enough, the ICC maintained, that shippers labored under the burden of the higher rates that resulted from operating expenses that were in reality capital expenditures. It was even worse that shippers were subsidizing railroad investors by increasing the value of the physical plant with a minimum of new capital investment. In that context, ICC officials argued, the accounting practices employed by the PRR and other railroads amounted to nothing less than a hidden tax on shippers, enacted by investors, outside the parameters of the democratic political process. ICC commissioners had articulated that argument in the *Central Yellow Pine Association* case of 1905, in which they criticized the PRR in particular for its presumed use of freight revenues to cross-subsidize capital expenditures. Yet, that was merely an administrative ruling, which the railroads soon challenged, and which was not resolved until May 1907, when the United States Supreme Court upheld the ICC position. In the meantime, the accounting standards imposed by the 1906 Hepburn Act afforded the ICC a far stronger mechanism for remedying what the commissioners perceived as an injustice to shippers.[327]

PRR officials, although willing to employ depreciation accounting, were nonetheless aghast at the ICC's policies regarding the allocation of betterment expenses. As President McCrea was quick to observe, railroad technology was not static, and as a result, neither were capital expenditures. It was not enough to reinvest income merely to maintain the railroad at the same standards that had existed a year or a decade earlier. "The PRR's efficiency and earning power are affected even less vitally by the failure to maintain the old property in good physical condition," he emphasized, "than by a failure to bring it up to the new and higher standard forced upon the railways by the conditions that confront them."[328] Stagnation was untenable, McCrea asserted, as the intense downward pressure on rates required the PRR to invest in ever more efficient equipment and operating methods.

The new depreciation accounting rules debuted in early June 1907, soon producing a vitriolic response from railway executives across the United States, many of whom erroneously believed that the standards applied to the physical plant rather than merely to equipment. Managers recognized elements of Pennsylvania Railroad practice in the new rules, and many held McCrea and other PRR executives responsible for the unwelcome changes. In reality, McCrea shared his colleagues' distaste for the new rules. He believed that the ICC practices constituted unwarranted government interference with managerial prerogatives, and with the sacrosanct relationship between investors and corporations. Neither he nor his fellow executives had ever questioned the ICC's newly legislated ability to mandate the integrity of railway accounting practices, but they vehemently denied the commission's right to anoint a specific accounting method, particularly one that was at variance with standard railroad practice. "But when questions of management arise connected with the disposition of the income of the Company and its application to the preservation of the property, and consequently the distribution of profits to the shareholders," McCrea complained, "these are entirely outside the domain of the accounting officers, and must be determined by the Boards of Directors and the Executive Officers in the discharge of the duties entrusted to them by the Board. These are questions, not of accounting, but of management."[329]

In addition to limiting managerial discretion, the ICC accounting rules made the PRR appear both far richer and far poorer than was actually the case. By shifting what had once been operating expenses to the capital account, the ICC's revisions artificially increased the PRR's net income, making it appear as if the railroad had suddenly become more prosperous—and a more promising target for reformers who were anxious to curtail what they insisted were excessively high rates and unwarranted profits. Those issues were particularly important in light of debates over corporate taxation. Since the 1890s, a growing number of politicians, journalists, and others had suggested that federal tariffs (which, along with taxes on alcohol and the sale of western land, constituted the national government's primary source of revenue) unduly burdened working-class and middle-class consumers, while leaving untaxed the vast pools of wealth generated by stocks and bonds. They proposed tariff reductions, coupled with taxes on both high personal incomes and on corporate profits. In 1907, the same year that the ICC developed the new depreciation rules, President Roosevelt gave his support to taxes on incomes, as well as to a measure that would require federal incorporation for companies engaged in interstate commerce. Supporters hoped that the tax, in addition to raising revenue, would force corporations to disclose additional financial data to investors, while limiting instances of overcapitalization and stock watering. The Corporate Excise Tax Act of 1909 levied a 1-percent tax on net income in excess of $5,000.[330] The PRR, and other corporations, would certainly be able to charge depreciation against net income, thus reducing tax

liability. With the tariff and tax situation still in flux during 1907 and 1908, there was nonetheless the possibility that the use of depreciation accounting as a substitute for replacement-retirement-betterment accounting might significantly raise the PRR's taxable income.

Simultaneously, the added capitalization mandated by the new depreciation schedules lowered return on investment, causing investors to shy away from what now seemed to be an unprofitable firm. As President McCrea observed, the "Capital account would necessarily be enormously increased," and the PRR would be "either burdened with debt or failing to earn a proper return on [the] capital invested, if not meeting absolute failure."[331] Many executives asserted that the replacement of betterment accounting with a standard monthly depreciation charge prevented them from curtailing expenditures, in the event of a financial crisis. By limiting the financial discretion of the board of directors, they became less able to offer dividends sufficient to attract investment capital.

By early 1908, as the short but severe Panic of 1907 continued to affect the national economy, railroad executives pushed back vigorously against the ICC. They blamed their declining net incomes on the new accounting standards, even though the recession was probably the determining factor. In March 1908, the *New York Times* reported that PRR executives had simply refused to obey the ICC's accounting directives. In the midst of the economic malaise, railway accountants were faced with a procrustean choice, whether to report high net incomes in order to placate investors and attract additional capital, or to suggest to the ICC that their net incomes were quite low, and that the railroads accordingly merited a rate increase. As a result, the railroads responded ineffectively to the ICC's policies, thanks in large measure to an acrimonious debate among executives representing various railroads as to the best alternative to the agency's depreciation accounting. Nor did it help that the PRR reported record earnings in 1907, undermining managerial efforts to suggest that the ICC's accounting standards had hobbled the company.[332]

The ICC did not fully implement the new depreciation rules until August 1909, provoking defiance from Lehigh Valley Railroad executives, an action that eventually sent the matter to the Supreme Court. By

1909, railway executives were no longer as concerned that the initial depreciation schedules might inflate expenditures in a manner that would frighten investors. Instead, the evolving protocols now seemed to understate expenses, risking the possibility that ICC officials would conclude that the railroads were financially sound and did not merit a rate increase. Following unsuccessful lawsuits by two shipping companies (the Goodrich Transportation Company and the White Star Line), the Kansas City Southern Railway took the matter to the courts in November 1911. In 1913, two years after Henry Adams retired from the ICC, the Supreme Court upheld the agency's right to dictate accounting practices to the railroads.[333] The ICC commissioners had succeeded in their efforts to apply to the transportation sector of the economy the depreciation standards that had been developed in manufacturing firms.[334] Unfortunately, such practices were injurious to conservatively financed and efficiently operated railroads, particularly those that plowed earnings back into the physical plant. And, few railroads were more efficiently run than the PRR. The ICC's depreciation-based accounting standards constituted a particularly devastating blow to any railroad that conservatively reinvested a large portion of its earnings back in the property. The PRR, which allocated $262 million in retained earnings to the betterment of its physical plant between 1887 and 1910, was particularly hard hit.[335]

By 1914, even the ICC commissioners could see that the railroads, under the post-1907 accounting methods, were unable to generate sufficient capital to undertake the betterments that the ICC had mandated. The growing political crisis in Europe, which later erupted into open warfare, reduced the railroads' ability to attract overseas capital. On July 1, 1914, the ICC responded with further revisions in accounting methods. Yet, the new practices did not differentiate clearly between costs for labor and materials, creating additional difficulties for the Pennsylvania Railroad. Under the new rules, neither workers nor managers knew the precise effect of wage rates, or wage increases, on income. Under those circumstances, both sides could argue with full righteous conviction regarding the justness of their cause. PRR executives insisted that high wage rates were threatening to drive the company into ruin, while employees asserted that the Pennsylvania Railroad was an extraordinarily rich corporation that could easily afford to increase their pay.[336]

More problematically, the ICC's post-1907 accounting methods proved unsuccessful in enabling the commissioners to determine the worth of the railroads and to establish "reasonable and just" rates that would guarantee a fair return on capital. The commissioners erred badly in their efforts to foster the railroaders' goal of calculating cost of service and the regulators' goal of establishing the value of the railroad network. Despite advances that had been made in other nations—such as the British railway accounting system, mandated by Parliament in 1911—the ICC succeeded in implementing methods that provided a reasonable measure of the cost of total service, but not the cost of each class of service. Furthermore, the commissioners failed even in their own goal of determining the productive value of the rail network, and instead determined only the cost of each railroad's assets. Under such circumstances, PRR executives lacked a clear understanding of precisely how much expense and revenue were associated with each type of traffic. They likewise found it increasingly difficult to persuade the ICC commissioners to set rates at a level that was appropriate to the value of service that the PRR provided. At a time when the Pennsylvania Railroad offered an increased range of specialized services, the ICC's accounting methods ensured that neither the commissioners nor PRR executives knew how much any of these services actually cost.[337]

The Changing Role of Statistics

While the Hepburn Act affected the PRR's cost-accounting methods, the ICC's growing emphasis on economic efficiency induced a more pervasive transformation in the railroad's employment of statistical data. Since the railroad's inception, PRR executives had developed increasingly sophisticated statistical controls, which they used to allocate expenses and revenues, determine rates, and regulate financial accounts. The freight congestion of the early twentieth century enhanced the importance of statistical data, as PRR officials sought to improve efficiency. What mattered in the end, however, was how the PRR's managers used those statistics, and how those uses evolved to suit the changing political environment in which the railroad operated. Initially, the PRR managers employed statistics as a kind of internal control to reduce congestion, decrease expenses, and standardize operations across the various divisions. As the regulatory state became more intrusive, however, executives redefined the role of statistics, using them externally as a public relations device to convince regulators and the general public alike that their requests for higher rates were not the result of wasteful practices or a desire for excessive profits.

While the PRR was an early leader in the development of system-wide cost accounting, until well into the twentieth century managers struggled to achieve consistency of information. The company's decentralized structure, with the concomitant autonomy of local managers, created significant variations in the collection and use of statistical data. Statistical operating controls (as opposed to financial or accounting measures) developed incrementally, on a division-by-division basis. In assessing the railroad's collection of statistical data, vice president Samuel Rea was undoubtedly correct in his assertion that the PRR's statistics were "the result of passing necessities rather than of thoughtful evolution."[338]

Virtually every component of the Pennsylvania Railroad generated statistics of one form or another. By the end of the nineteenth century, the Comptroller's Department had taken charge of preparing corporate statistics at the central office level. System offices collected "Statistics of Management," which affected such long-term policy decisions as major betterment expenditures and alterations in the relationships with subsidiary lines. At the same time, the general manager, the general superintendent of transportation, the superintendent of passenger transportation, the Passenger Department, the Freight Department, and the assistant to the president each collected and disseminated statistical data.

Out on the line, Transportation Department personnel collected data relating to train tonnage, engine availability, the number of trains dispatched, terminal delays, road delays, and the expenses associated with train movement. The Motive Power Department kept its own statistics on fuel cost and availability, material

stores, and shop productivity. Traffic Department officials calculated claims that resulted from loss, damage, and accidents, as well as changes in traffic patterns. Roughly half of the PRR's divisions maintained daily (and, in one case, weekly) records of the performance of individual freight crews. On many other divisions, however, as the members of the Association of Transportation Officers discovered, "no such statistics are kept, depending solely on the supervision of the local officials for the economical performance of this service."[339] Various departments prepared some statistics on an hourly, daily, weekly, monthly, or yearly basis, depending on their individual needs. Officers in one department often refused to share their statistical data with their counterparts in another. Traffic Department officials did not have access to statistics that classified freight tonnage according to commodities, and the Accounting Department did not even know how much it spent preparing statistical data for the system as a whole. And, there was a persistent duplication of effort—the Transportation Department, for example, maintained a statistician in the general manager's office, as did the general manager himself; both collected virtually identical data, "each case being practically independent of the other."[340] The resulting absence of coordination, Rea complained, meant that much of the available data was "susceptible of being erroneously applied."[341]

In an effort to better coordinate the flow of statistical data, comptroller Max Riebenack and some other PRR executives suggested the creation of a centralized "statistical bureau," one that would collect and disseminate information from across the system. Two serious obstacles hampered those efforts, however. The first was the perception that such an agency would require another layer of management, and entail considerable additional expense. Riebenack attempted to deflect that concern by noting that the PRR had long been a role model for all of the other railroads in the United States, if not the world, and he likewise "hoped that liberal views would prevail, and that the desire of our Company to lead in such matters the railroads of the country would be paramount in the eyes of the Executive Officers."[342]

The second difficulty associated with the creation of a centralized statistical capability related to the old adage that knowledge is power, and few departmental managers wanted to relinquish their control over statistical data. Riebenack even found it necessary to re-assure the general manager that "if such a [centralized statistical] bureau were organized and placed in my department, I would not for a moment think of cur-tailing any information that he now commands, and that he would have exactly the same use of the bureau as he now has of his own statistical force, although it would not adjoin his office."[343]

It was Vice President Rea, more than Comptroller Riebenack, who pushed most insistently for a central-ized statistical bureau. His opinions gained greater weight following the rulings in the *Trans-Missouri* and the *Joint Traffic* cases in 1897 and 1898. As railroad managers transformed their now-illegal traffic associa-tions into rate bureaus, they were careful to base rate, routing, and market-share decisions on statistical data that at least purported to show variations in the cost of service—rather than on the older model of infor-mal bargaining arrangements. At some time during the Frank Thomson administration (1897–99) Rea had recommended the appointment of a corporate statistician at the staff level who would develop sys-tem-wide statistical standards and act as a liaison among the PRR, the media, and the public. His supe-riors rejected that suggestion, asserting that "con-stantly increasing business" precluded the collection of system-wide statistical data.[344] In other words, PRR officials were so heavily engaged in their efforts to op-erate the railroad efficiently that they could not spare the time necessary to collect and interpret statistics.

Yet, Rea and other PRR officials turned that argu-ment on its head. A system-wide statistical bureau, they asserted, would serve to increase operating effi-ciency, and thus reduce the workload that confronted harried operating personnel. Rea was sympathetic to the argument that a statistical bureau might entail un-necessary additional work for PRR personnel, and that it might interfere with the prerogatives of local managers, but he was willing to accept the creation of an additional layer of bureaucracy in the interest of ef-ficiency. "So far as a Statistical Bureau is concerned, if it is going to satisfy a real need and is going to replace a duplication of work and eliminate separate statistical bureaus in each of the Departments, I am in favor of it," Rea emphasized, "but not otherwise."[345]

During 1909, a special committee, consisting of representatives from the Accounting, Transportation,

and Traffic Departments, as well as the Comptroller's office, discussed the establishment of a statistical bu-reau. In typical PRR fashion, the members of the com-mittee surveyed their counterparts on other railroads, some of which already maintained centralized statis-tical offices. One such carrier was the Union Pacific, whose president, Edward H. Harriman, had served alongside several PRR executives on the board of the Baltimore & Ohio as part of the community of interest.[346]

The Norfolk & Western, a company that was even more closely connected to the PRR, maintained one of the most advanced information-collection capabilities of any railroad, largely because of the company's role in managing the production and marketing of coal along its lines. In 1904, N&W and PRR officials had largely overseen the transformation of the Tidewater Bitumi-nous Steam Coal Traffic Association into a Bureau of Statistics, as a mechanism for allocating coal traffic and maintaining rates. While the Bureau of Statistics proved less effective than its members had hoped, it did contribute to making the N&W a leader in the collection and dissemination of statistical data. Nor-folk & Western officials were particularly interested in the development of mechanized office equipment, ranging from typewriters to accounting and calculat-ing machines that could accommodate the flow of data. The new devices were expensive and required specialized skills to operate, and they would be most effectively employed only if concentrated in one cen-tral location, and only if they could process standard-ized data sets. In 1909, accordingly, N&W managers informed their PRR counterparts that it was necessary "to establish a body of skilled but not high paid work-ers who will check the calculations and will operate mechanical devices for figuring, duplicating etc. and thus avoid the dispersal of [expensive] laborsaving de-vices which would be of limited use if distributed among the departments but which can be made of constant and economical use if brought together in one department."[347]

Based on the N&W model, PRR officials attempted to exploit economies of scale in the realm of data collec-tion and analysis. In November 1909, the members of the PRR's special committee issued a unanimous reso-lution approving the creation of a statistical bureau that would "centralize the preparation of statistical data, thereby avoiding duplication, where practicable, and curtailing expenses, and that desirable economies may be effected by its operation."[348]

The PRR's efforts to enhance operating efficiency by creating a statistical bureau soon ran headlong into the Progressive era, and to efforts by the federal government to employ a very different sort of efficiency for a very different purpose. Pennsylvania Railroad executives had no sooner decided to promote the "new" emphasis on efficiency through the centralized collation and dissemination of statistical data than they realized, to their horror, that that methodology was precisely what the Interstate Commerce Commission was attempting to impose on all of the railroads. Rea had sensed the danger as early as 1908, warning that any statistician "should also keep in touch with the present educational process through which we are going with the Interstate Commerce Commission."[349] Rea undoubtedly meant that the PRR's personnel should be familiar with the reporting requirements that the ICC had mandated, in the aftermath of the Hepburn Act. However, he was also concerned that the commissioners might demand that railroad officials use the data to prove that they were not wasting the nation's resources.

As the first decade of the twentieth century came to a close, regulators and politicians alike were increasingly convinced that railroads were operating inefficiently. They attributed the low rates of return that characterized the railroad industry to that presumed lack of efficiency, as well as to the longstanding charge that most railroads were overcapitalized, with significant amounts of watered securities. Progressives viewed increased efficiency as a panacea, one that would maintain railroad profits, permit steady decreases in rates, enhance safety, and provide labor with higher wages and shorter working hours. They argued that the most advanced techniques of statistical analysis would indicate where the railroads were wasting resources, and how those errors could be corrected. By 1910, executives on railroads such as the PRR had accepted the need for routinized statistics, in order to ensure the efficiency of their operations, while Progressives were determined to use those same statistics to prove that the railroads were inefficient.

The debate over efficiency reached a climax in the ICC *Eastern Rate* cases (also known as the *Advance Rate* cases) that began in 1910, and were not fully resolved until 1914. In 1903 and again in 1907 the PRR and the other trunk lines had raised commodity rates for bulk freight such as grain, coal, coke, and iron and steel products. In the spring of 1910, in the midst of rising raw material and labor costs, the eastern trunk lines filed an across-the-board increase in class rates on higher-value cargoes, a move that their western counterparts soon copied. The proposed rates affected only about 25 percent of total freight tonnage in the east, but the omnibus request represented a clear statement of unity on the part of railroad executives.

President Taft's unwillingness to acquiesce to pressure from railroad executives soon undermined whatever solidarity executives had hoped to achieve. On June 6, representatives from the western carriers met with Taft and agreed to withdraw their request for a rate increase. The following day, President McCrea and other eastern railroad presidents trooped to the White House as part of what a *New York Times* reporter referred to as "the picturesque business of private treaty making between the President of the United States and the Presidents of great railroad systems."[350]

The initial confrontation with Taft coincided with congressional negotiations involving the Mann-Elkins bill, and helped to influence the final version of the act. The pending Mann-Elkins legislation required the railroads to justify rate increases on the grounds of economic necessity. As such, executives asserted that the higher class rates were vital to the rights of investors and to the overall health of the railroad network. They nonetheless agreed to submit their proposed across-the-board rate increases to the ICC for approval, even though they were not legally required to do so until (and unless) the Mann-Elkins bill became law.[351]

The ICC rate hearings began in New York City in early September, and the railroaders were soon on the defensive. As contemporary economist William Z. Ripley observed, "All of the railway representatives traversed much the same ground, so widely scattering their effort that but superficial treatment of each point was possible. The shippers, on the other hand, evidently laid out their plan of campaign with more system and had correspondingly better results."[352] Many railroad executives, particularly the representatives from the

Baltimore & Ohio, acknowledged that they had little idea of the relationship between costs and revenues, particularly in the area of wages. PRR officials, including Frank C. Huff, the chief accountant to the general manager, did somewhat better, giving detailed estimates of how the rate increases, if granted, would raise revenues on Lines East by more than $3 million per year.[353]

Shippers were equally determined to avoid the rate increases, which they estimated would cost them between $30 million and $40 million per year. Shippers' attorney Louis D. Brandeis was particularly successful in presenting arguments that the railroads could save that much money, and more, simply by increasing the efficiency of their operations. During the rate hearings, Brandeis became increasingly impatient with—and antagonistic toward—railroad executives, as he subjected them to a withering barrage of questions regarding the supposed inefficiency of their companies. As the head of the nation's largest railroad, PRR president James McCrea was one of Brandeis's favorite targets. Unlike Baltimore & Ohio president Daniel Willard, who foolishly acknowledged that increased efficiency might obviate the necessity of a rate increase, McCrea held up well, and gave Brandeis but one opportunity for attack. The attorney exploited the PRR's penchant for systematized record keeping, questioning the railroad's minutely detailed analyses of the costs associated with locomotive repairs. Those expenditures, Brandeis suggested, represented traditions that had evolved incrementally over time, and not the potential savings that could accrue from more efficient practices.[354]

When the hearings began, Brandeis apparently intended to fight the railroads strictly on procedural grounds. As railroad executives provided testimony that was often ill informed or simply wrong, Brandeis changed his tactics to a broad-based attack on the perceived failings of railroad management.[355] On November 21, 1910, he dropped a bombshell, suggesting that more efficient management could generate additional income—more than $1 million per day, he suggested—without the need for rate increases. Brandeis's assertion was pure theatrics, and the million-dollar figure that he quoted was inaccurate, unsubstantiated, and meaningless. Nevertheless, as Brandeis had anticipated, his accusations fired the imagina-

tions of Progressive reformers, who believed that better management could ease conflicts among shippers, investors, executives, and workers, generating harmony by ensuring that efficiently operated railroads could provide benefits for all.[356]

ICC commissioners Franklin K. Lane and Charles A. Prouty were particularly sympathetic to Brandeis's position, and they used the data that the ICC had collected from the railroads to undermine calls for higher rates. Furthermore, many commissioners were no longer willing to accept claims made by railroad executives that it was impossible to accurately allocate costs among different classes of service, a condition that precluded cost-of-service pricing and instead mandated value-of-service pricing. Even though ICC officials had until quite recently supported precisely the type of value-of-service pricing that they now condemned, they believed that systematic new statistical controls should have enabled railroad managers to calculate a fair rate, based on the precisely defined cost of each shipment. The commissioners were particularly impressed by the ability of personnel at AT&T (a company that came under the ICC's jurisdiction as a result of the Mann-Elkins Act) to differentiate among various classes of service. State regulatory commissions had also made impressive, if not wholly accurate, efforts to separate freight and passenger expenditures, as a legacy of the two-cent-per-mile-fare movement during the first decade of the twentieth century.[357]

In February 1911, the ICC commissioners unanimously denied the railroads' proposed 1910 rate increase.[358] The decision served notice that the ICC and shippers intended to take full advantage of the expanded powers they had gained as a result of the Mann-Elkins Act.[359] The first of the *Eastern Rate* cases was perhaps not the disaster that PRR executives had feared, particularly as it did not affect the coal, coke, grain, and iron and steel products that were the mainstay of the PRR's business. It hardly boded well for the future, however. Executives had not anticipated the emotional resonance of Brandeis's arguments. Caught unprepared, they had made statements that were at times politically embarrassing, ill informed, contradictory, and occasionally incorrect. They had failed to drive home even the basic fact that they had presided over a sustained and substantial decrease in the basic cost of freight transportation. Above all, despite their interest in the efficiency of transportation, PRR managers did not expect that efficiency would become a topic for public discussion and ICC oversight.[360]

In the aftermath of the first *Eastern Rate* case, PRR executives again expanded the company's public-relations capabilities, and their efforts eventually helped to swing the tide in favor of rate increases. In December 1912, Ivy Lee returned from his European sojourn and quickly rejoined the PRR as President McCrea's executive assistant in charge of publicity—perhaps the first time that a publicist held an executive-level appointment. The position carried with it the princely salary of $10,000 a year, as well as an office in Philadelphia's Broad Street Station. Leaving his brother James in charge of routine publicity efforts on the PRR, Ivy Lee launched a campaign to educate the public on the need for more remunerative freight rates.

Even though he had been one of the pioneers of the carefully crafted press release, Lee concluded that such methods constituted a rather unsophisticated means of influencing public opinion. He soon developed a targeted campaign that tailored specific messages to ICC officials, politicians, newspaper editors, university faculty, railway employees, investors, and passengers. He launched a speaker's bureau and personally delivered a series of lectures at Harvard Business School and other venues. Lee oversaw the preparation of leaflets that were placed in PRR dining cars and placards that were displayed in railway stations. His most visible achievement may well have been an ongoing series of booklets, *Information for Employes and the Public.* The earliest issues of *Information* were distributed primarily to the PRR workforce, usually through railroad YMCA libraries, but by the 1920s the publication had evolved into a more sophisticated format, designed to appeal to shippers, passengers, and the general public.[361]

Lee's multifaceted approach emphasized the consistent message that the railroads were providing a vital public service, yet were prevented from receiving a fair rate of return. Intrusive governmental regulations, Lee asserted, had required them to improve their physical plant and increase safety by adopting steel passenger cars, installing signals, and eliminating grade crossings. According to Lee's arguments, the government was attempting to placate special interest groups—most no-

tably shippers (who received artificially low rates), the Post Office (which enjoyed scandalously low haulage charges), and organized labor (whose members luxuriated in unnaturally high wages)—by forcibly siphoning scarce resources from the hard-done-by railroads. Far from being wealthy, Lee emphasized, the railroads were in desperately poor financial circumstances.[362]

In addition to his efforts to educate the public on what he considered to be the economic realities of the railroads, Lee oversaw many other elements of the relationships among PRR executives, their employees, and government officials. In 1913, he suggested the creation of the Mutual Beneficial Association of Pennsylvania Railroad Employes, a benevolent organization for enginemen and other skilled workers, in part as an effort to undermine support for independent labor unions. Lee also helped to prepare executives such as vice president William Atterbury for appearances before various public bodies, including Congress and the ICC. When the Senate Commission on Industrial Relations (the Walsh Commission) called on Atterbury to testify on the PRR's treatment of its employees, Lee advised the full disclosure of every labor-management incident in the railroad's recent past. He learned that during the 1880s and 1890s, PRR officials had anticipated possible labor conflicts by stockpiling five thousand rifles in the attic of Broad Street Station—a revelation that was bound to suggest that the company maintained a somewhat antagonistic relationship with its workforce. Lee diffused the situation by releasing that information to the media before the Walsh Commission could do so, insisting that the PRR maintained the arsenal for the protection of its passengers, not for the suppression of its employees. The resulting press release was a typical example of Lee's involvement in the emerging field of propaganda. He avoided outright lying (the bane of the increasingly discredited field of press agentry), but spun his interpretation of the facts in a manner that rarely bore close scrutiny.[363]

Lee's public-relations campaign—undertaken even as he was defending John D. Rockefeller's Colorado Fuel & Iron Company in the aftermath of the April 1914 Ludlow Massacre—proved remarkably effective. As Lee had hoped, the public attitude toward the railroads at least partly shifted from scorn to pity.

Shippers, working through their local Chambers of Commerce, flooded the ICC with resolutions supporting the rate increase. By the autumn of 1914, the outbreak of war in Europe was increasing the demand for transportation, while inducing an increase in the costs of labor and supplies. In light of growing inflationary pressures on the American economy and the increasing difficulties that the railroads experienced in attracting capital, many ICC officials were rethinking their earlier hostility to higher rates. In December 1914, the commissioners granted the PRR a 5.48 percent increase on general freight—but not on coal, the railroad's largest single commodity, nor on parcel post shipments, which had begun on January 1, 1913, and were already proving wildly popular.[364]

The Pennsylvania Railroad emerged victorious in the latest chapter of the *Eastern Rate* cases, but the damage had already been done. In the aftermath of the Mann-Elkins Act, railroad executives dared to request a rate increase only when they could demonstrate that they were operating as efficiently as possible, and that forces beyond their control had caused an increase in their costs. Many shippers had not been convinced by Ivy Lee's emphasis on the poverty of the railroads. Even if they accepted that argument in the abstract, they were still likely to insist that higher rates should be borne by some other commodity, some other locale, or some other company, and not they.

Even if shippers failed to forestall a rate increase, they won through delay. Because railroads were forced to hold all rate increases in abeyance until the commissioners had decided on the matter, months or even years might pass before the new charges were put into effect. As a result, gains in revenues always lagged behind increases in costs. Executives on the PRR and other railroads were endlessly trying to catch up, and the resulting income shortfall left the company poorly prepared to accommodate the traffic demands associated with a European conflict that would soon become a world war.

In addition to indicating the enhanced ability of shippers to use the ICC as a weapon against the railroads, the *Eastern Rate* cases suggested that regulators, politicians, economists, and even the general public had begun to devise their own standards for efficient railroad operations. Many decades earlier, public capital had funded much of the initial construction of the Pennsylvania Railroad. Particularly after the 1861 repeal of the tonnage tax, however, executives such as J. Edgar Thomson and Tom Scott had operated largely outside the influence of the public regulatory apparatus and often with scant regard for public opinion. Only in rare instances, most notably after the South Improvement Company controversy and in the aftermath of the 1877 labor disputes, did legislators and the media lambaste the PRR and its officers. By the early twentieth century, PRR executives had long since weaned the company from direct governmental support. At the same time, Alexander Cassatt's successors, James McCrea and Samuel Rea, faced steadily increasing and indeed almost constant public scrutiny of the railroad's operations. The situation-dependent investigations of the late nineteenth century had generally been limited to criticism of managerial actions, and had stopped short of suggesting—much less dictating—how those managers should run the Pennsylvania Railroad. By the early twentieth century, however, a new group of reformers presumed that they, as outsiders, possessed a better understanding of how the railroads should be managed than did the railroaders themselves. That assertion, distressing to PRR managers, was particularly apparent in the development of scientific management, and in its application to the business of railroading.

The body of thought often referred to as scientific management antedated Louis Brandeis's impassioned remarks in the *Eastern Rate* hearings. His sensationalistic million-dollar-a-day claim nonetheless excited public opinion and persuaded many ICC commissioners that the railroads could and should be operated more efficiently. Within a year of Brandeis's testimony, dozens of articles on scientific management had appeared in the business press. The best-known book from that era was undoubtedly Frederick Taylor's *Principles of Scientific Management*, published in 1911, the same year that the ICC denied the railroads' request for higher rates. Despite his fame, Taylor was hardly typical of the extraordinary diversity of the field of scientific management, however. Of greater relevance to the PRR was the 1914 publication of Brandeis's *Other People's Money—And How the Bankers Use It*. Despite the title, the book criticized railroads as well as banks. Brandeis acknowledged that the PRR was, in general, a well-managed railroad, but he asserted that it suffered from "excessive bigness" that impaired its efficiency.[365] He seized on the community-of-interest plan that Cassatt and Morgan had developed as an example of the propensity of railroad executives, supposedly bloated with cash, to acquire other carriers, coal mines, and steelworks. In his view, such practices represented unbridled capitalistic greed and did nothing to improve the productivity of the national economy.

What made the Brandesian attacks on the railroads so ironic was that the Pennsylvania Railroad was already doing—and, for decades, had been doing—what Brandeis was advocating. In developing an efficient, smooth-running system, PRR managers had steadily increased efficiency and productivity. They created that increased productivity in part by accumulating an impressive body of statistics—information that Brandeis was ultimately able to use against them. Some historians have argued that in the aftermath of the *Eastern Rate* cases, railroad executives felt that they had to embrace the principles of scientific management.[366] That was not precisely true, for PRR executives had implemented some of the basic elements of scientific management, particularly those involving the standardization of operating practices, before 1910. After the *Eastern Rate* cases, and after Brandeis, the pressure to adopt other elements of scientific management became virtually irresistible. PRR managers had only recently developed a centralized mechanism for collecting and interpreting statistical data in order to improve the efficiency of the railroad's operations. Now, they were forced to use statistics to prove that they were operating efficiently.

The techniques of scientific management rarely lived up to the promises of their advocates, however, and particularly so in the railroad business. Railroads were not factories; they did not produce a standard product under observable and controlled conditions. The PRR's operations were subject to wide variations caused by undulating terrain, fluctuating traffic levels, and adverse weather conditions. As such, an essential component of efficiency, the concept of routine operations, was something of an oxymoron.

In the years after 1910, "scientific management" increasingly came to mean labor management, as companies attempted to extract as much productivity from labor as possible, through time-and-motion studies, the speedup of manufacturing, and the imposition of piece rates in lieu of hourly wages. Brandeis decried such efforts, which he believed unfairly victimized wage earners, but he could hardly stem the tide. Because the PRR's employees were an extraordinarily diverse lot, scattered across thousands of route miles, effective managerial supervision and control was largely impossible. Operating employees, represented by powerful unions, were effectively off limits to proponents of scientific management. So, too were the low-paid, largely seasonal workers engaged in track maintenance, an occupation that had proved difficult to mechanize. For the next two decades, the labor "problem" would continue to plague the PRR, and all of the other railroads, impeding managerial efforts to increase efficiency in the manner that Brandeis had demanded.[367]

After 1910, there was a very real possibility that regulatory officials might impose their own perceptions of efficiency on the Pennsylvania Railroad. In 1909, Samuel Rea and other PRR executives had supported the creation of a statistical bureau to "centralize the preparation of statistical data" in order to improve operating efficiency. Not long after the *Eastern Rate* hearings, Rea's assistant, Albert J. County, had warned his superior about "the Brandeis statements" concerning alleged inefficiencies and, more bluntly, about the "impertinent Governmental inquiries" that demanded statistical evidence showing that managers were committed to achieving greater efficiency. County was particularly averse to suggestions from PRR managers that the statistical bureau be renamed a "bureau of efficiency," as he believed that such language played right into Brandeis's arguments. "Beyond giving it a name in the organization," County complained, "no idea is conveyed of what it is intended to do," aside, perhaps, from convincing regulators, shippers, and the public that the PRR was being operated appropriately.[368]

County's opposition to the creation of a bureau of efficiency went beyond earlier concerns that such a centralized data-collection function might cause a turf war by interfering with carefully defined managerial authority within the Pennsylvania Railroad itself. Instead, the new threat came from outside and threatened the PRR's entire system of management. A bureau of efficiency, while it might suit the grand visions of a new Progressive order, held the potential to undermine the traditional and informal methods that the PRR had always employed to reach a consensus about any major issue. As County noted in 1914, "What they [the federal government] are attempting to accomplish through [a bureau of efficiency], we accomplish by either getting the views of the various Departments, or constituting a committee to take up the special subject." Those ad hoc methods of securing greater efficiency worked precisely because they took into account the traditions, fiefdoms, loyalties, and unique personal attributes that had been established informally within a highly bureaucratic organization.[369]

The seemingly simple word "efficiency" meant vastly different things to different people. PRR executives saw it as a way to make the system run more smoothly without challenging the closely guarded prerogatives of highly skilled managers. Even if Brandeis and other Progressives saw efficiency in much broader terms, as a method of creating economic and social harmony, their efforts appeared to PRR managers as nothing so much as an attempt by visionary elitists to replace practical railroading with pie-in-the-sky utopian visions.

The Value of the Railroads

The battle over rates and efficiency was part of a larger conflict to determine what the railroads were worth, both in terms of asset value and in terms of their importance to the national economy. With railroaders and shippers offering wildly differing assessments of the overall profitability of the railways, ICC officials began the monumental task of valuing the most capital-intensive business in the United States. In so doing, the commissioners hoped to be able to establish a fair rate of return on invested capital, and administratively determine "reasonable and just" rates.

For much of the nineteenth century, railroad investors, shippers, and government officials had expressed concerns about the dangers of "watered" stock—that is, a situation where a firm's capitalization vastly exceeded the value of its tangible physical assets. Stock-watering occurred when railroads traded shares for right of way, construction materials, or equipment, at above-market prices. Many unscrupulous railroad pro-

moters organized construction companies to build lines in exchange for railway securities, raking off a substantial profit from the difference between the payments and the actual cost of construction. More nefariously, promoters might divert the proceeds from stock sales to the income rather than the construction account, fooling investors into believing that the railroad was far more profitable than was actually the case. If stock had been watered, then a railroad was by definition overcapitalized, thus explaining why revenues translated into such a low rate of return on capital. In such circumstances, rate increases could hardly be justified.[370]

By the early twentieth century, however, there was very little water in railroad securities. Most of the earlier problems had been limited to speculative ventures, typically in western railroads, and did not affect the older and more established eastern carriers. Moreover, the seeming interminable sequence of railroad bankruptcies and reorganizations had typically wrung most of the water out of the industry's capitalization, often to the detriment of investors. Railroaders also made extensive investments in the physical plant and equipment, in amounts that often exceeded the initial cost of construction. As such, railroad officials were generally correct when they insisted that their companies represented massive pools of real capital, and not of water.

As a conservatively financed company, the PRR had been virtually immune from charges that its stock was watered, and the company's officials were especially determined to demonstrate that their railroad was worth what they said it was. President McCrea, testifying in Washington on October 12, 1910, during the *Eastern Rate* hearings, emphasized that "the Pennsylvania system east of Pittsburgh has cost very much more than capitalization represents." He insisted that "on the capitalization it has never paid a fair rate of return—less, in fact, than most other characters of investment, such as manufacturing, mining, and agriculture." McCrea was largely correct, as the PRR's rate of return on capital in 1909 was barely more than 5 percent. He was likewise accurate in his assertion that the ICC's accounting standards had penalized the railroad for "reinvestments in the property [that were] not capitalized."[371]

In their effort to determine whether railroad balance sheets represented real assets or water, regulators had long sought a mechanism to calculate the actual worth of the carriers. The original 1887 Act to Regulate Commerce had called for a valuation of railroad assets, but chief statistician Henry Adams had argued that the task was a practical impossibility. Nonetheless, railroad attorneys had on numerous occasions presented estimates of value to federal and state regulatory agencies, and to the courts, in order to justify rates, particularly in the aftermath of *Smyth v. Ames*. By 1901, moreover, Adams was beginning to reconsider the valuation question, thanks in large measure to changes in the financial community. His opinions reflected a growing consensus among accountants that the level of a carrier's bonded debt bore little resemblance to its true value. The only way to calculate the true worth of a railroad, and hence determine tariffs that would ensure a fair rate of return, would be to assess the worth of the physical plant. In 1903, the ICC's *Seventeenth Annual Report* had called for valuation legislation in order to assist in the determination of rates and as a mechanism for ensuring uniformity in state taxation. ICC officials were nonetheless reluctant to rely on the asset values provided by the carriers, preferring to conduct an independent audit of railroad property.[372]

During Senate deliberations over the Hepburn Act, Senator Robert M. La Follette (Rep., Wisc.) had introduced an amendment calling on the ICC to make a scientific determination of rates that would be based in part on the valuation of railroad properties, as well as on an assessment of the operating efficiency of the carriers. By 1908, President Roosevelt had joined those calling for a valuation of the railroads. Taft followed suit in his 1908 acceptance speech at the Republican national convention and in his 1911 message to Congress. During the election of 1912, both the Democratic and Progressive Parties advocated valuation legislation. In March 1913, Congress passed the Valuation Act, which charged the ICC with determining the original and the betterment costs associated with constructing and equipping all of the railroads in the United States. The monumental mandate more than doubled the size of the ICC's staff, as the commission proceeded to measure, photograph, and assign a value to virtually every item on the PRR and the nation's other railroads.[373]

Even though they believed that the entire valuation process would be a colossal waste of time and money,

railroad officials soon pledged to cooperate with the ICC. They had little reason not to, for they understood, better than anyone else, that their companies were far more capital-intensive than the railroads' critics were willing to acknowledge. President Rea served as the chairman of a valuation committee representing eighteen of the largest railroads in the United States. PRR assistant real estate agent Thomas W. Hulme received a leave of absence to serve as secretary of the Presidents' Conference Committee on the Valuation of Railroads. The PRR established separate Valuation Committees on Lines East and Lines West, each consisting of representatives from the Accounting, Engineering, and Real Estate Departments. In May 1915, in response to an ICC directive, the PRR, like all of the other railroads in the United States, began the preparation of a corporate family tree, showing the evolution of each predecessor company—something that remains a valuable resource for historians.[374]

The ICC established a Bureau of Valuation under the direction of commissioner Charles A. Prouty, and by 1917 the bureau employed some 1,600 people. By late 1921, ICC employees had largely completed their inventory work in the field. The number of Valuation Bureau employees soon shrank to six hundred, who spent years processing and interpreting the data. By then, however, the rise of motor carrier competition had transformed the transportation sector. While some of the information derived from the Valuation Act found its way into the text of the Transportation Act of 1920, the desire to accurately determine the value of the railroads had passed. ICC officials never completed their monumental task.[375]

Private and Public Regulation

By the end of December 1916, a decade had passed since Alexander J. Cassatt had died in office. As Europe entered the third year of what would only briefly be the bloodiest war in human history, American factories supplied the combatants and prepared the country for a conflict that it would enter barely three months later. The nation's railways experienced a surge in business, but few were burdened to a greater degree than the Pennsylvania Railroad. Carloads of coal, iron ore, steel, and manufactured products rumbled across the

PRR system. With increasing frequency, the traffic failed to move at all, occasionally forcing PRR managers to temporarily embargo freight at key locations. The congestion was principally the result of delays in unloading cars, particularly at docks, and not to problems on the main line. Yet, the congestion was chronic enough to bring about the temporary nationalization of all the carriers under the auspices of the United States Railroad Administration. To many reformers, particularly those who were in sympathy with organized labor, government control promised to remedy the inefficiency associated with private ownership.

The critics of the railroads were perhaps correct in their assertion that a more powerful regulatory state could enhance allocative efficiency by distributing to managers, workers, investors, shippers, and the general public a politically determined fair share of the national economic pie. The enhanced power and independence of the Interstate Commerce Commission, as expressed through the Hepburn and Mann-Elkins Acts, made such practices more likely.

Railroad executives reacted with scorn to the social engineering associated with the management of allocative efficiency. Their careers were built on productive efficiency—the ability of a company to transport the greatest possible quantity of freight and the greatest number of passengers at the lowest possible rates. When Cassatt became president in 1899, PRR executives had increased capacity and driven down costs to a degree that would have seemed impossible even a quarter of a century earlier.

To a large extent, however, they had done their jobs too well. The public had come to expect that rates would continue to decline precipitously, presumably forever. The law of diminishing returns ensured that rates did not keep falling, provoking a chorus of complaints from shippers who rarely acknowledged that transportation costs constituted only a small portion of their expense of doing business. At the same time, the enhanced capacity of the railroads required managers to solicit more and more business in order to chip away at fixed costs. The insatiable demand for traffic led to an orgy of system building in the 1880s, followed by bankruptcies in the 1890s. Rather than permit further instability among the railroads—chaos that would not have benefited anyone—railroaders and investment bankers took steps to regulate transportation. The community of interest that Cassatt helped to develop brought stability to the eastern railroads, but that victory came at considerable cost. Shippers, politicians, and journalists increasingly labeled such arrangements as monopolies, blamed them for rates that seemed unfairly high, and demanded that the government impose regulation on them. As Cassatt lay dying, he may have sensed that his vision of regulation was giving way to another, more intrusive version of regulation by Congress and the ICC. The full consequences of that transformation nonetheless would not be apparent for decades to come.

His critics notwithstanding, Cassatt's agenda of privately managed regulation had remade the Pennsylvania Railroad. The revenue generated by the community of interest, combined with the capital generated by investors, newly confident in the stability of the railroads, made possible a comprehensive program of expansion and upgrades. The New York Improvements, a massive plan to improve passenger and freight service in the nation's largest city, undoubtedly constituted the most spectacular manifestation of the new construction program. But across the PRR system, particularly on the Lines East of Pittsburgh and Erie, the railroad was transformed by new engineering projects. The work, a large portion of it completed after Cassatt's death, essentially created the physical plant that would serve the PRR through the remainder of its history. The traffic slowdowns that accompanied World War I were embarrassing and politically damaging to the PRR and its executives. They were inconsequential, however, compared with the congestion and chaos that would have resulted had not Alexander Cassatt launched the community of interest and rebuilt the Pennsylvania Railroad.

Chapter 15

Terminus

1917

Alexander Johnston Cassatt stood, larger than life, near the end of the arcade that formed the grand entryway of Pennsylvania Station in New York. He was close to the top of the stairs leading down to the vast expanse of the General Waiting Room, the largest indoor space in the city. Across from him stood another PRR president, Samuel Rea. Cassatt had been responsible for generating the financial resources necessary for building Penn Station, and for working with architect Charles Follen McKim on the design of the soaring aboveground structure. Rea had taken charge of the complex underground world of tracks, wires, and signals, a largely unnoticed realm that constituted the heart of what was more broadly known as the New York Improvements. They had cooperated on many other projects, as well, and together the two men had made much of the modern Pennsylvania Railroad.

The presence of the two PRR presidents, on opposite sides of the central axis of Penn Station, could never have taken place in reality, as Cassatt died in December 1906, nearly four years before the facility opened to the public. He was represented by a statue, one that literally was larger than life. It was unveiled on August 1, 1910, in what PRR officials termed an "unostentatious but dignified" ceremony. Attorney and board member Thomas De Witt Cuyler, chairman of the PRR's Memorial Committee, thought that no grand ceremony was necessary,

as "These massive walls and columns speak in their severe simplicity and majestic silence far more eloquently than human tongue could give utterance to." Rea, who was at that time the PRR's second vice president, spoke of Cassatt's statue as "a tribute to his genius."[1]

For the moment, the niche opposite Cassatt remained unoccupied. In March 1911, less than two years before he would become the ninth president of the Pennsylvania Railroad, Rea rejected a suggestion that it house a plaque bearing the names of all of the workers who had died while constructing the New York Improvements. The number was not large—certainly the list would have been far shorter than what some sensationalistic newspaper accounts had suggested—but it would have detracted from the grand neoclassical space that Cassatt had envisioned, and reflected badly on the PRR's public image as well. Ironically, and unintentionally, Rea preserved the space that would, nearly twenty years later, house his own likeness.

For more than a decade, between 1913 and 1925, Rea presided over the Pennsylvania Railroad, managing issues ranging from wartime nationalization to postwar changes in regulatory policy to increased highway competition and the beginnings of widespread electrification. For a PRR president, he lived an unusually long time after leaving office—more than three years. Following his death, the new president, William Wallace

Figure 69. For half a century after its opening in 1910, New York's Pennsylvania Station constituted a magnificent technological and architectural achievement. This view, looking generally southwest, depicts the station's principal façade along Seventh Avenue (to the left), with the less ornate Thirty-Third Street side tapering off into the right center distance. From the Seventh Avenue entrance, travelers walked along the arcade (between the two low-lying baggage courtyards and indicated by the small lunette windows, barely visible) in order to reach the General Waiting Room. Penn Station architect Charles Follen McKim added a massive cupola to the design, against Alexander Cassatt's objections, in order to give the waiting room a ceiling height of 150 feet. While clearly evident in this aerial view, it could not be seen from street level, maintaining the image of a long, low structure. Barely visible behind the cupola are the glass-and-steel groin vaults covering the concourse and, underneath, the tracks and platforms that were the heart of the PRR's operations in Manhattan. Barely visible behind the station (across Eighth Avenue) is the General Post Office, utilizing air rights over the PRR tracks leading west toward the tunnels under the Hudson River. The only other large structure in the area is the steeple of the Church of St. John the Baptist, where Father Capistran Claude complained vociferously about the dynamite blasts and the resulting rain of rocks that resulted from the excavation of the station's foundations. The absence of any other significant commercial development reflected the station's location in the low-rent Tenderloin District, at least a long city block away from the more fashionable neighborhoods on Broadway—a situation dictated by engineering considerations. Of equal concern to PRR executives, passengers possessed few local transportation options, as the Ninth Avenue Elevated (invisible in the distance) and the Sixth Avenue Elevated (behind the photographer) were a long way from the station. Without the development of commercial property and the construction of a subway under Seventh Avenue, Penn Station would not reach its full potential as a transportation hub. *Hagley Digital Images Collection, Hagley Museum and Library.*

Atterbury, commissioned a statue of Rea to be placed in the station that he had done so much to design and build. The sculptor was Adolph A. Weinman, the same artist who had immortalized Cassatt, and who had produced most of the ornamentation on what was, admittedly, the rather plain exterior of Penn Station. On April 9, 1930, as the nation was descending into the economic abyss of the Great Depression, director Effingham B. Morris presided at the dedication ceremony. The real guests of honor, however, were electrical engineer George Gibbs and civil engineer and bridge designer Gustav Lindenthal, the last surviving members of the board of engineers that had planned and coordinated the New York Improvements.[2]

During the first decade of the twentieth century, Cassatt, Rea, Gibbs, Lindenthal, and many others had created a new Pennsylvania Railroad, one that the company's founders could not possibly have envisioned in 1846. They poured hundreds of millions of dollars into massive improvement projects, while adding thousands of new cars and locomotives. Their ability to do so, only a few years after the crippling depression of the 1890s, was a testament to the financial solidity of the PRR system. And, in what was perhaps their most visible achievement, they created a massive new passenger station in the heart of the nation's largest city. Those PRR executives doubtless believed that the railroad's modernization would continue unabated for many decades to come. As such, they did not anticipate the radical transformations in regulatory policy and transportation dynamics that were about to sweep over their companies. In the century that lay ahead, their successors would confront the limits of their power and preside over the remorseless decline of their company. Even Penn Station, the edifice that Cassatt and Rea had labored so mightily to build, would succumb to the wrecking ball.[3] For the moment, however, Cassatt, Rea, and the others led the Pennsylvania Railroad to its greatest glory, orchestrating the construction of some of the most spectacular monuments in the history of transportation.

An Era of Rebuilding

After Alexander J. Cassatt assumed the presidency in 1899, he rebuilt the Pennsylvania Railroad. Many of the improvements that he oversaw, ranging from the Rockville Bridge over the Susquehanna River, to the tunnels under New York City, to Union Station in Washington, D.C., remain an integral part of the national transportation network. Those that have disappeared—most notably the Pennsylvania Station in Manhattan—did so because they were deliberately destroyed, and not because they were replaced with more capacious, efficient, or beautiful alternatives. By creating the community of interest, and by supporting the anti-rebating provisions of the 1903 Elkins Act, Cassatt was able to stabilize railroad rates and generate much of the capital needed for expansion. He also possessed the leadership necessary to prevail in negotiations with other railroad executives, politicians, and urban planners, while employing publicity in order to deflect criticism and project a positive image for the Pennsylvania Railroad.

For all of his individual accomplishments, however, Cassatt and his ambitious agenda were very much a part of the changing landscape of railroading at the dawn of the twentieth century. All across the United States, powerful executives were consolidating operations, raising additional capital, and transforming rambling nineteenth-century carriers into modern transportation systems. In 1898, far to the west, Edward Henry Harriman became chairman of the Executive Committee of the Union Pacific Railroad. While the Union Pacific was by no means a dilapidated carrier prior to Harriman's arrival, he nonetheless transformed the nation's first transcontinental railroad, turning it into an efficient carrier of freight and passengers by lowering grades, straightening curves, erecting new bridges, constructing entirely new bypass lines, installing signaling systems, upgrading ties and rails, and purchasing new locomotives and equipment.[4] Harriman also pulled together a coordinated transportation system in the West, establishing control over the Southern Pacific Company and the Illinois Central Railroad, and very nearly capturing the Northern Pacific and the Chicago, Burlington & Quincy, as well. Many of Harriman's competitors made similar investments, enhancing safety while dramatically increasing operating speeds and expanding transportation capacity.[5]

The activities of investment banks such as J. P. Morgan & Company and Kuhn, Loeb & Company made possible the betterment projects of Cassatt, Harriman, and their contemporaries. The late nineteenth and early twentieth centuries witnessed a vast exodus of railroad securities out of Europe, as overseas investors sold their holdings in American railroads. For the first time, financiers in the United States gained the opportunity to buy and sell entire railroad systems, and not merely blocks of securities. J. P. Morgan and his fellow bankers could orchestrate the creation of communities of interest while arranging the massive borrowing that was necessary to pay for a rebuilt railroad network.

Finally, Alexander Cassatt's commitment to revitalizing the Pennsylvania Railroad was shaped by one crucial reality—he had no other choice. Just as Cassatt became president, the PRR experienced the first of two serious episodes of traffic congestion. The blockages of 1899 primarily resulted from the lack of sufficient freight equipment, as the nation recovered from the Panic of 1893. Efforts to alleviate the problem required little more than the provision of additional freight cars, often paid for through equipment trust financing or by passing the associated capital costs to large coal shippers such as Westmoreland and Berwind-White.[6]

The crisis that took place in 1902 and 1903 was far more serious. Despite the acquisition of new freight cars, poor equipment utilization on Lines East rendered much of that investment meaningless. In the five years preceding 1903, the number of miles that a PRR freight car traveled each day fell nearly 35 percent, while locomotive mileage declined by 17 percent. Measuring from 1883, the results were even worse, with a 37.3 percent decrease in daily freight car average mileage. That meant that the PRR required nearly fifty thousand additional freight cars, representing a total investment of some $50 million, just to move the same quantity of freight.[7]

The crisis became apparent in one location more than any other. Pittsburgh, the city that served as a gateway between Lines East and Lines West, had long been a chokepoint on the PRR system. Three major components of the PRR—the main line east to Harrisburg, the Northwest System (Fort Wayne), and the Southwest System (Pan Handle) converged there, with further traffic pouring in from the lines through the Monongahela and Allegheny Valleys, and from Pitts-

burgh's vast industrial base. At the beginning of the twentieth century, more freight traffic passed through Pittsburgh than any other city in the world. Yet, all of the PRR's facilities were jammed into a series of river valleys surrounded by looming hills and urban sprawl. The surprise was not that operations at Pittsburgh virtually ground to a halt, but rather that PRR employees kept traffic moving as long as they did.

The trouble began in the spring of 1902, as a massive strike halted production in northeastern Pennsylvania's anthracite fields and produced a corresponding increase in the demand for bituminous coal from the western part of the state. As summer turned into fall, manufacturers and homeowners rushed to fill their coal bins prior to the onset of winter. The increased demand for coal exacerbated a surge in steel and merchandise traffic. PRR managers embargoed certain classes of freight into the Pittsburgh area, even though Pittsburgh Division superintendent Richard L. O'Donnel admitted that the very concept of an embargo was "extremely objectionable to every operative officer." He noted that the embargo had ripple effects as far away as Indianapolis and Milwaukee, and that "it was weeks afterwards before every agent knew that the embargo had been raised."[8] By mid-November, conditions were so severe that officials at the Homestead and Duquesne Works contemplated a suspension of production, owing to the lack of pig iron supplies.[9]

While shippers and railroaders alike were most concerned with freight congestion, PRR officials suffered the acute embarrassment of canceling the *Pennsylvania Limited*, the company's premier passenger train operating between Jersey City and Chicago. The train, equipped at a cost of more than half a million dollars, operated on a twenty-hour schedule—so fast that several hundred trainmen and yardmen were responsible for patrolling the right of way prior to its passage, and some trains waited in sidings for up to three hours to permit the *Limited* safe and uninterrupted travel. Cassatt and other PRR officials insisted "that the freight congestion must be broken at any cost," and reluctantly acknowledged "that the Pennsylvania special, the pride of the passenger department, must be sacrificed." The temporary cancellation of the PRR's finest passenger train was a blow to corporate pride, but, they admitted, "will do more toward relieving freight congestion than the abandonment of scores of local trains on divisions between New York and Chicago."[10]

Through dint of herculean efforts, PRR crews cleared the congestion, but both railroad officials and their customers were left badly shaken. The timing was especially unfortunate because George Gould was attempting to build to Pittsburgh, and on to tidewater. Pittsburgh's merchants and industrialists had long been opposed to the PRR's virtual transportation monopoly in their city. The congestion was the last straw, and many eagerly awaited Gould's arrival. Others called for investigations, regulations, or some other form of enhanced public supervision of the PRR.

In response to the congestion at Pittsburgh, Cassatt and the board of directors ordered substantial changes to the PRR's organization and personnel. As early as January 1902, the board had created a new position, superintendent of Pittsburgh terminals, whose oversight encompassed the entire Pittsburgh region, including portions of both Lines East and Lines West. Robert Pitcairn, the longtime superintendent of the Pittsburgh Division, accepted the less burdensome role of resident assistant to the president, with O'Donnel serving a brief stint as the new division superintendent. On Lines West, the allocation of operating responsibilities to two separate managers, the general superintendent of freight transportation and the general superintendent of passenger transportation, further eased the pressure.

By December 1902, as crews struggled to restore Pittsburgh to normal operations, Cassatt embarked on a rare purge of the senior officers who had failed to cope with the crisis. The bloodletting was extraordinarily swift, at a special board meeting that lasted less than fifteen minutes. O'Donnel, not even a year into his tenure as Pittsburgh Division superintendent, was to be replaced by Simon Cameron Long. John M. Wallis lost his position as general superintendent of the Pennsylvania Railroad Grand Division—"relieved at his own request," according to the polite language of the PRR's *Annual Report*.[11] The same fate befell general manager John B. Hutchinson. His replacement, William Wallace Atterbury, was a no-nonsense mechanical engineer. By the time he was thirty, he had

pulled himself up to the rank of superintendent of motive power for Lines East. In the autumn of 1902, Cassatt went to Pittsburgh in an effort to resolve the congestion. He was favorably impressed with Atterbury, at that time the general superintendent of motive power, and quickly advanced him several rungs on the ladder of succession.[12] A reporter for the *New York Times* summarized the promotions and demotions by suggesting that the board "made changes in the operating department of the company far more important than those which have ever attended any change in the Presidency, broke precedent in jumping young men over those supposed to be established for life, and arranged to transfer to other offices men in high positions."[13] An unnamed director put the matter rather more succinctly, emphasizing that "the notion that when a man gets a position on the Pennsylvania he is 'fixed for life,' no matter whether he is efficient or obliging or not, has got to be changed. The Pennsylvania has new conditions confronting it, and there will be some important changes in the Broad Street Station household."[14]

The "important changes" continued well into 1903, as the board reassigned hundreds of employees and brought in new talent from outside the company. Effective June 1, 1903, the board thoroughly reorganized the Transportation Department. With the worst of the crisis over, the elimination of the post of general superintendent of Pittsburgh terminals (in favor of the general agent at Pittsburgh) enabled superintendents to regain control over the respective divisions. To expedite operating functions, the board created two new Lines East offices, the superintendent of freight transportation and the superintendent of passenger transportation, each of whom reported to the general superintendent of transportation and, in turn, to the general manager. The Altoona Division disappeared into an enlarged Middle Division, with headquarters shifted from Harrisburg to the more critical location of Altoona. The Philadelphia Division acquired a small portion of the Middle Division, from Harrisburg to the Rockville Bridge, and its base was relocated from West Philadelphia to the state capital. Lines East officers also gained jurisdiction over the route between Philadelphia and Washington—an aftereffect of the November 1902 merger of the Baltimore & Potomac and the Philadelphia, Wilmington & Baltimore subsidiaries into the Philadelphia, Baltimore & Washington Railroad.[15]

There were corresponding changes in the PRR's traffic functions. The directors named John B. Thayer to the new office of fifth vice president. Thayer possessed authority over the Freight Department and the Passenger Department, as well as the Union Line Bureau and the Empire Line. Another new position, passenger traffic manager, oversaw the ongoing responsibilities of the general passenger agent and his staff—corresponding to the previously established positions of freight traffic manager and general freight agent. The board created another new post, general coal freight agent, to help coordinate the traffic that had been the single largest contributor to the congestion of the previous autumn.[16]

Although PRR officials cleared the congestion at the Pittsburgh gateway, similar problems continued to erupt at various points across Lines East. With the seasonal increase in coal traffic late in 1903, the situation again grew desperate, particularly on the lines leading to New York City. Trains filled all of the sidings on the Trenton Cutoff, and spilled over onto the eastbound main line for a distance of nearly ten miles. Even as late as February 1905, the PRR confronted a massive traffic snarl that had stranded thirty thousand cars at various points between Jersey City and Pittsburgh, with the worst congestion occurring on the Philadelphia Division.[17]

PRR officials continued to make changes to the railroad's organization and personnel, although never to the extent of late 1902 and early 1903. During 1906, the board split the office of general freight agent into two positions, one for through traffic and the other for local traffic. In April 1907, the PRR absorbed its Philadelphia & Erie subsidiary, with the former Philadelphia & Erie Grand Division becoming the Erie Grand Division. The United Railroads of New Jersey Grand Division similarly became the New Jersey Grand Division, while the existing Pennsylvania Railroad Grand Division was split into the Eastern and Western Pennsylvania Grand Divisions. A number of other, smaller changes took place at that time.[18]

Despite all of the refinements to the PRR's corporate structure, and even with the investment of many millions of dollars in expanded facilities, the congestion crisis never really disappeared until traffic levels plummeted following the Panic of 1907. PRR managers were undoubtedly frustrated at the ongoing blockages, but they were hardly in a state of panic. In time, additional investments in plant and equipment would have kept pace with rising traffic levels, reducing congestion to an episodic and temporary irritant. In no sense did they fear that they had reached the limits of what their engineering and organizational abilities could achieve. It was true that they were increasingly encountering the law of diminishing returns, as the great advances of the late nineteenth century—steel rail, signaling systems, airbrakes, automatic couplers, and the like—were giving way to more modest and more incremental improvements. The greatest effect of that situation, however, lay in the unwillingness of shippers to accept the simple reality that the era of steadily declining rates had ended, and hence their eagerness to turn to regulatory bodies for solace.[19]

The perception that PRR executives had lost the ability to manage innovation in the interest of operational efficiency stemmed from one unalterable circumstance that made the Pennsylvania Railroad unusual—indeed, almost unique—in the annals of railroading. The PRR's presence athwart the axis of industrial America ensured that the preponderance of its traffic would be in coal, iron ore, steel products, and other bulk commodities rather than compact, high-value merchandise. As such, the PRR Lines East of Pittsburgh and Erie possessed by far the heaviest traffic density (as measured by revenue ton-miles per mile of route) of any of the trunk lines and, with the exception of some local carriers that specialized in mineral transportation, the greatest density of any railroad in the United States.

The economic recovery that ended the depression of the 1890s only exacerbated the problem, as the PRR's freight density increased nearly 50 percent, from 3.2 million to 4.7 million tons per mile of road, between 1900 and 1906. In 1906, the PRR's traffic density was nearly thirteen times that of the Seaboard Air Line, six times that of the Southern Pacific, and almost four times that of the Union Pacific. It was 75 percent greater than the Norfolk & Western, a carrier whose principal role was to funnel bituminous coal to tidewater. Closer to home,

Lines East possessed a traffic density 78 percent higher than the Baltimore & Ohio, 72 percent greater than the Erie, and 86 percent larger than its most formidable competitor, the New York Central.[20]

The intensity of the PRR's traffic produced correspondingly large maintenance costs. In 1912, the PRR's maintenance-of-way expenditures were $5,437 per mile of line, more than five times that of the Chicago Great Western, a rural granger line, and—more significantly—twice that of the Erie or the Baltimore & Ohio, and 40 percent higher than the New York Central. The PRR's maintenance-of-equipment costs per mile were likewise the highest of any major railroad. Such figures did not indicate any inefficiency or incompetence on the part of PRR employees. Rather, they bespoke the constant pounding of trains laden with heavy bulk cargoes as they rolled across the system, every minute of every hour of every day of every year.[21]

The difference between the PRR, with the highest density of any trunk line, and the New York Central, with the lowest, was largely a product of geography, and not managerial preference. Over much of its distance, the NYC and its Lake Shore & Michigan Southern subsidiary paralleled the Hudson River, the Erie Canal, and the southern shore of Lake Erie. The famous "Water Level Route" may have provided passengers with a smooth and scenic ride, but it also ensured vigorous competition from water carriers. As such, NYC managers had initially shied away from grain, coal, iron ore, and other bulk commodities, inasmuch as they could not match the water rates. Shippers were willing to pay a premium for the transportation of high-value manufactured goods, however, and that traffic could bear the cost of rail transport. At the same time, the NYC possessed superb access to New York, which had long been the dominant commercial entrepôt in the United States. NYC trains distributed manufactured goods along a chain of major urban centers—Albany, Schenectady, Utica, Syracuse, Rochester, Erie, Cleveland, Toledo, and (indirectly) Detroit—that lay along the route between Manhattan and Chicago.[22]

The Pennsylvania Railroad, in contrast, was both protected and cursed by geography. As early as 1854, Herman Haupt had warned J. Edgar Thomson that the PRR should give preference to western connections that were sufficiently removed from both Lake Erie and the Ohio River to afford them some protection from water-carrier competition. The additional cost associated with transporting grain or other bulk cargoes north to a lake port or south to the Ohio River in effect negated the price advantage of boats, and facilitated the PRR's ability to earn a profit from the grain trade. However, the PRR's landlocked route ensured that Pittsburgh was the only major city between tidewater and Chicago. The port of Philadelphia, furthermore, was no match for New York with respect to the transshipment of finished goods. Philadelphia's exports generally originated solely within the commonwealth of Pennsylvania, with few derived from points farther west than the steel center of Youngstown, Ohio. As such, PRR managers eschewed the operation of fast merchandise freights largely because there were few high-value manufactured items for them to transport. That business was best left to the New York Central, whose route was better suited for merchandise traffic.[23]

The radical differences in the nature of Pennsylvania Railroad and New York Central traffic conditioned the managerial strategies of the two companies. By the beginning of the twentieth century, increases in transportation efficiency had enabled the NYC to win a large share of the grain trade, but the company still relied more heavily on merchandise traffic than did the PRR. The Vanderbilt interests, in cooperation with J. P. Morgan, were anxious to enlarge their western catchment basin by establishing greater control over their western subsidiaries, much as J. Edgar Thomson had done when he created Lines West several decades earlier. More significantly, the NYC incrementally developed a managerial ethos that emphasized rapid, flexible service, a situation that many decades later would vastly complicate the 1968 Penn Central merger.

Preference Freight

The business strategy of Pennsylvania Railroad executives was somewhat more complex, however, conditioned by the need to balance the unavoidable torrent of low-grade bulk freight with the growing appeal of higher-value "preference" freight, which moved at correspondingly higher speeds and rates. Aside from adding more tracks, heavier rails, and stronger bridges—all of which were designed to boost capacity—the only other way to reduce congestion involved running longer or faster trains. Logically, the faster that trains ran, the greater the number that could travel over a given stretch of railroad each day. Even a modest increase in average speed would greatly increase the railroad's capacity to carry traffic—what economists often refer to as high "throughput," the attempt to maximize the volume of material moving through a "pipeline" of fixed capacity. Faster trains nonetheless required additional locomotives (and additional crewmen), consumed more coal and water, required more repairs, and accelerated the rate of damage to track and equipment. While passengers were willing to pay a premium for speed, freight was unconcerned with its rate of progress. By the close of the nineteenth century, most freight trains carrying bulk cargoes such as grain or coal traveled at speeds of between eight and fifteen miles an hour. In that context, the PRR's massive investments in locomotives, cars, tracks, bridges, airbrakes, and automatic couplers were designed to increase train capacity rather than speed. The possibilities associated with increasing throughput by increasing speed were largely illusory, especially as overcrowding at freight terminals, and not delays in transit, accounted for the bulk of the congestion on the PRR and other railroads.

There were cases, however, where it was cost effective to move valuable or perishable freight with some degree of rapidity. Unfortunately, coal and other bulk commodities would, owing to their weight, continue to move at low speeds—no more than fifteen miles per hour, and often considerably less than that. The introduction of faster preference trains threatened to *reduce* the railroad's efficiency, as dispatchers attempted to cope with trains that were continually overtaking or falling behind one another. By the 1890s, the PRR's executives had not reached a consensus regarding the proper speed for freight trains. Members of the railroad's Association of Transportation Officers met in 1895 to consider the question, but discovered that they lacked the data necessary to perform an adequate cost-benefit analysis on the matter.[24]

Within a very few years, however, the increasing muscle of the federal regulatory apparatus had caused ATO members to revisit the issue of train speeds. The 1903 Elkins Act prevented railroads from granting rebates and increasingly forced them to compete in terms of service—including transit time—rather than price. "In these days of firm rates and absence of discrimination," assistant general freight agent Robert C. Wright noted in 1905, "traffic must be attracted by better facilities, better service, [and] better attention."[25] In practice, that meant preference freight trains. The members of the ATO suggested that expedited freight was a necessary evil. They acknowledged that "it might be argued that these trains are not at the present time, especially on certain divisions, an economical form of operation," and that "fast freight train service, particularly eastbound, is very expensive." Nevertheless, they suggested that "commercial conditions make such a fast freight train service a necessity."[26] Essentially, ATO officials conceded that preference freights acted as a "vital factor in building up territory and securing the locations of general industries," and as a mechanism for ensuring that "the railroad serves a diversity of traffic, without which the road would develop largely into a mineral-carrying road, and would then be subjected to the more serious fluctuations of that class of traffic."[27]

In May 1903, a month after passage of the Elkins Act, the members of the ATO had already recommended that trains carrying high-priority merchandise be sped up to match the pace of slow passenger trains, decreasing the number of train speeds from four (fast and slow passenger, fast and slow freight), to three. Three was still one too many, however, inasmuch as the railroad could provide only two tracks in each direction. ATO members acknowledged that faster preference freights meant that congestion "relief may be obtained [only] to a limited extent on the road."[28] Because the ATO's membership included a great many operating officials, they were sensitive to the havoc that preference freights were certain to create on each division through which they passed. To minimize the embarrassment, they insisted that "the Division accounts of the preference freight service should be kept entirely separate from ordinary freight service," ensuring that "the Superintendent shall not be hampered in his general showing by the extra demands of the special service."[29] ATO officials were, in effect, asserting that preference freights, while they might attract traffic and facilitate the movement of freight trains across the entire railroad, traveled out of sync with traditional traffic, and could reduce the efficiency of individual divisions through which they passed.[30]

The ATO's May 1903 recommendation came barely six months after the events of November 1902, when traffic through Pittsburgh had virtually ground to a halt. If anything, the Pittsburgh crisis indicated that all discussions of preference-freight operations were moot so long as the tracks were jammed with low-grade coal, iron-ore, and steel shipments. High-value freight could travel at reasonable speeds only if massive investments in new construction could clear the tracks of the slow-moving trains that carried bulk freight.

While NYC officials concentrated on solidifying their connections in the west, Cassatt and other PRR executives sought a mechanism for more efficiently moving and distributing bulk cargoes and establishing better connections to the export facilities in New York and to lucrative markets in New England. In part, that meant the provision of additional tracks, bridges, and freight bypass lines in order to speed the flow of traffic on the main line. Other railroad executives, such as Edward Harriman, employed similar strategies to increase the productivity of their railroads. For the PRR, however, most severe difficulties occurred not because freight moved too slowly over the main line, but rather because shipments backed up at east coast port facilities. Clogged yards in Philadelphia and New York created problems that spilled over onto the rest of the system. For Cassatt, therefore, the Pennsylvania Railroad's congestion problem was ultimately a terminal problem.[31]

Since assuming the presidency in 1899, Alexander Cassatt had authorized a growing slate of improvement projects, but the PRR's *Fifty-Sixth Annual Report*, published early in 1903, detailed a massive plan to rebuild the physical plant that topped anything that had come before. In an effort to clear congestion, Cassatt called for the completion of the four-track main line from Jersey City to Pittsburgh, with additional double-track bypass lines at critical locations. Replace-

ment bridges would be able to withstand the heaviest trains that the Transportation Department could throw at them, while expanded signaling systems would expedite the flow of traffic. New freight yards would permit the classification of trains flowing off routes designed to accommodate bulk freight, freeing the main line for passenger and high-speed merchandise freight service. A planned extension of the Allegheny Valley Railway would enable trains to pass far north of Pittsburgh, on a straight, flat route through the Alleghenies and on into Ohio. The list did not include projects that were already under way, including the provision of new passenger facilities at Pittsburgh, Washington, D.C., and, most ambitiously, in Manhattan. By themselves, few of the plans were entirely new, as PRR engineers had long planned for incremental capacity improvements. Put together in one package, however, the scope of Cassatt's agenda was truly breathtaking. And, at an estimated cost of $67 million—with tens of millions more for all of the other projects—Alexander Cassatt's improvements were going to be hideously expensive.[32]

"The Pennsylvania Is Spending More Money Than Any Other Railroad in the World"

All railroads are built of money, and the PRR was no exception. Cassatt's extraordinary improvements to the physical plant, coupled with the purchase of an increasing number of cars and locomotives, the cost of the community-of-interest acquisitions, and the refinancing of earlier loans required gargantuan investments. As Cassatt told a reporter for the *New York Times* in December 1902, "The Pennsylvania is spending more money than any other railroad in the world."[33] As a result, during the twenty years that followed the recovery from the depression of the 1890s, the PRR's book value increased by an astonishing 264 percent, from $397.4 million in 1896 to $1.05 billion in 1916.[34]

The massive increase in expenditures produced corresponding changes in the PRR's financing. Before 1900, the railroad's securities were backed by real assets, with bonds constituting a lien on the PRR's property. By the beginning of the twentieth century, however, the railroad was effectively mortgaged to the hilt, and it was no longer possible for Cassatt to authorize securities based on fixed assets. As a result, the company issued bonds backed only by its investments in subsidiary companies, by moveable equipment, or, even more problematically, by the potential for future annual income that would be generated by the PRR's operations. Particularly in the aftermath of the depression and railway bankruptcies of the 1890s, few investors would even consider such securities. However, the PRR's long-standing status as a financially sound and capably managed company largely exempted it from the doubt and scrutiny that might have attached to similar bonds issued by lesser railroads.[35]

Throughout its history, the Pennsylvania Railroad maintained a reputation for financial conservatism. The PRR's executives and directors eschewed speculative ventures, restricted dividends to a steady, predictable stream—typically 6 percent a year—and reinvested a substantial portion of earnings into the railroad's physical plant. In 1918, ICC commissioner George W. Anderson spoke approvingly of "the 'Pennsylvania Standard,' of which we have heard for many years. It is 'a dollar to the stockholders, and a dollar to the property.'"[36] What that meant, in practical terms, was that between 1887 and 1910, the board of directors reinvested $262 million on the Lines East of Pittsburgh and Erie.[37]

Thanks in large measure to their conservative financing, PRR executives prevented the railroad from gaining a reputation as an overvalued carrier with allegedly "watered" stock, in which the total capitalization greatly exceeded the company's actual value. The PRR stood in stark contrast to the Erie, particularly during the years when Jay Gould's machinations had solidified that carrier's reputation as the "Scarlet Woman of Wall Street." Even in 1903, long after Gould's death, the Erie had a book value of $150,000 per mile of road, while the PRR's value was a far more realistic $82,000 per mile. By 1906, the PRR's total capitalization was $110,000 per route mile—a relatively modest sum for a largely double- and quadruple-tracked railroad, particularly when only about $50,000 per mile represented the actual cost of the road, structures, and equipment, with the remainder composed of securities holdings in various other railroads. By 1916, book value had risen to $190,000 per mile on the lightly built Erie, but only $140,000 on the more sub-

stantially constructed PRR. Given that the PRR's earnings per mile exceeded those of the Erie, its relatively low capitalization provided compelling evidence, ICC regulators noted, that the Pennsylvania Railroad was worth what its accountants claimed.[38]

Such statistics, while portraying the PRR in an exceedingly favorable light, were in the final analysis largely meaningless. By the late nineteenth century, corporate accountants were moving away from assessing the worth of common stock according to its par value and to a new calculation based on the earning power of the company. In 1912, New York permitted corporations to issue no-par stock, and claims of stock watering soon fell by the wayside. Furthermore, railroad stocks were worth precisely what investors paid for them on Wall Street, at any given moment, and PRR shares usually sold at well above par. During the first dozen years of the twentieth century, investors collectively paid $43 million above par for newly issued PRR shares. That tribute to the railroad's financial solidity paid for a third of the cost of the New York Improvements, was not listed on the balance sheet as capital, and did not require the payment of additional dividends over and above those based on par value. In any event, allegations of stock watering and other financial irregularities, no matter how inaccurate and misleading, generally attached to companies such as the Erie and left PRR officials largely blameless.[39]

Despite its sterling reputation in financial circles, the massive improvement projects of the Cassatt years taxed the ability of PRR personnel to generate investment capital. First vice president John P. Green, the chief financial officer, had risen through the ranks of the PRR and had little experience outside of the company. Therefore, in May 1904, the board hired Henry Tatnall, president of Philadelphia's Franklin National Bank, as the sixth vice president, in charge of the Treasury Department. While it was rare for the PRR to recruit Transportation Department personnel from outside the company, the board frequently hired staff officers from other firms to perform nontraditional functions, and few tasks were more important than the generation of the capital that Cassatt required for his myriad improvements.[40]

Green and Tatnall had their work cut out for them as they sought new mechanisms for raising capital.

Overseas investors had long contributed to the financing of the Pennsylvania Railroad, and by 1890 they owned nearly half of the outstanding stock. Yet, they were increasingly relinquishing pride of place to domestic capital markets, particularly between 1895 and 1902. The maturation of the American economy coincided with the emergence of economic opportunities in such British colonies as South Africa, India, and Australia, leading to a reduction in European investment in American companies. Between 1896 and 1906 Europeans repatriated a quarter of a billion dollars in American railway securities.[41] The PRR was hardly immune from those changes, particularly as British shareholders had long complained about the PRR's conservative dividend policies. The proportion of PRR stock controlled by overseas investors fell from 52 percent in the mid-1890s to 19 percent in 1905. That decline reduced, but did not eliminate, the ability of investment bankers to place securities in overseas markets. PRR officials still sought overseas investors, and in 1905 the board agreed to list the railroad's securities on the stock exchanges in Berlin, Hamburg, and Frankfurt—a prelude to the company's appearance on the notoriously insular Paris Bourse the following year. The PRR's wider exposure slowed the decline in the percentage of foreign ownership, from 21.6 percent in 1902 to 20.2 percent by the end of 1906.[42]

Since the 1840s, the financial center of gravity of the United States had shifted from Philadelphia to New York, but the Pennsylvania Railroad retained at least a token connection to Philadelphia's capital markets until late in the century. During the 1880s, for example, Tony Drexel had been the railroad's Philadelphia capital connection, even if New York investment banker J. P. Morgan was the underlying authority in such matters. After Drexel's death in 1893, the PRR's Philadelphia managers gave up all pretense of reliance on local investment-banking talent in favor of New York investment bankers.[43] Foremost among them were Jacob Schiff and his partners in the New York house of Kuhn, Loeb & Company. Schiff, who was Solomon Loeb's son-in-law, effectively ran Kuhn, Loeb & Company, and he was the principal architect of the PRR's financing. Speyer & Company also placed considerable quantities of PRR securities. Although not in the same league as Schiff, James Joseph Speyer

was related to him by marriage and was an important financier in his own right. In 1837, his uncle had founded Philip Speyer & Company, known after 1876 simply as Speyer & Company. James Speyer possessed a particularly valuable connection in his younger brother Edgar, a German who moved to London, became a British citizen, and was in charge of Speyer Brothers, the family's British investment house. Edgar Speyer was well positioned to market PRR securities in Britain, and as the individual most responsible for financing the construction of the London Underground, he knew something of the scope of the PRR's New York Improvements.[44]

Unsurprisingly, given the PRR's growing reliance on New York investment bankers, the preponderance of stock ownership lay there as well. The PRR's stock was not listed on the New York Stock Exchange until 1900, unusually late for a railroad of any size. In May of that year, the PRR's directors acknowledged that New Yorkers, flush with the wealth generated in the boom economy of the late 1890s, were principally responsible for the massive repurchases of American securities that had once been held in Europe. "It is estimated that at least twenty-five per cent of the stock is now in New York hands," the PRR's directors noted in May 1900, "and the amount held is increasing daily, by reason of the fact that almost all the English stock that is sold is taken up by New York Parties."[45] Under those circumstances they were anxious to have the PRR's stock listed on Wall Street. Their decision soon proved correct, and by June 1903, one PRR director suggested that Philadelphia had relinquished the PRR to New York, and that it was "safe to say that control of Pennsylvania stock is now held in that city."[46]

Stocks and Bonds

In earlier periods of expansion, PRR officials had elected to blend debt and equity financing in a relatively equal ratio, but the new capital requirements of the early twentieth century led to an increased reliance on common stock rather than bonds.[47] By the end of the 1920s, the ratio of stocks to bonds stood at approximately 1.6 to 1, with the PRR's investors able to convert the majority of those bonds into stock at will.

That trend ran counter to normal industry practice, at a time when many American railroads were relying more heavily on debt issues.[48] The PRR's low leverage was both a cause of and caused by its financial conservatism. Foreign investors, in particular, were well acquainted with the Pennsylvania Railroad and knew that the company had survived the depression of the 1890s with its finances intact. As such, they possessed the confidence to risk their capital on equity.[49]

Between 1895 and 1902, a torrent of new common stock poured forth from the PRR's treasury, with the number of outstanding shares increasing from 2.6 million to 4.1 million. By 1905, an additional two million shares had been issued, with a like amount over the next four years.[50] The number of shares plateaued in 1914, at 9,985,314, and remained constant for the fourteen years thereafter. The vast majority of those shares—about 97 percent—were placed directly with investors, without reliance on Wall Street. Eighty percent of the shares went to existing PRR securities holders.[51]

The steady rise in the number of outstanding shares occurred in part because Pennsylvania Railroad executives were staunch advocates of convertible bonds, with large issues taking place in 1902 and again in 1905. Such instruments were hardly new. The PRR's first bond issue, in 1852, had given investors the opportunity for conversion into common stock. Many other railroads, including the Camden & Amboy, had been issuing convertible bonds since the 1830s.[52] Financiers relied heavily on convertible bonds during the period immediately following the Civil War, and they figured largely in the 1866–68 "Erie War" that pitted Cornelius Vanderbilt against Jay Gould, Jim Fisk, and Daniel Drew. That incident, and others like it, soured investors on convertible bonds. They did not redeem their reputation until 1901, when Edward Harriman of the Union Pacific used them to acquire the Southern Pacific and quite nearly the Northern Pacific, as well.[53]

The rapid growth in convertible bond issues was in part a mechanism to attract skittish investors, and in part an effort to protect the PRR's financial interests. Most of the securities used to finance Cassatt's ambitious betterment program, like those issued by other railroads, were not backed by a lien on the company's physical assets. Contemporary financial analysts suggested that, absent a guarantee of recompense, inves-

tors should purchase only bonds that would give them an equity stake in the firm.[54]

In addition to protecting the interests of investors, convertible bonds offered several key advantages to the PRR. They carried exceptionally low interest rates, typically 3½ percent. Investors were willing to accept such a low return because of their ability (at some specified future date) to exchange the bond for an equivalent amount of stock, at par, a figure that was generally well below the market price. Once they had converted their bonds to stock, moreover, investors removed a fixed charge from the PRR's books. Unlike bond interest, the PRR board was under no legal obligation to pay stock dividends. In practice, however, shareholders expected to receive their customary 6 percent annual dividend with the same certainty and regularity that might attach to the redemption of a bond coupon. Convertible issues were therefore particularly well suited for financing long-term projects, such as the various improvement plans, which would not generate their full revenue potential for many years to come. Ideally, betterments financed by convertible bonds would create a sort of sinking fund, as shareholder conversions gradually reduced fixed charges, while the rising earnings that resulted from the increased capacity simultaneously enabled additional dividends.[55]

The issuance of convertible bonds was also in keeping with a growing sense among some members of the national business community that the siren song of socialism, communism, or other radical economic philosophies could be muted through the simple expedient of turning more Americans into dedicated capitalists. As Vice President Green observed, "Where temporary issues of bonds have been made, there has been associated with them the right and privilege to convert the same into the stock of the Company, with the view of gradually eliminating the holders from the creditor list and making them partners in the property of the Company."[56] Those who owned a piece of the Pennsylvania Railroad, Green and other executives reasoned, would be less likely to demand that the government enact punitive restrictions against their company.

Between 1895 and 1915, as the PRR released many new stock and convertible bond issues, both the number of stockholders and the size of their holdings began to creep upward.[57] Until American Telephone & Telegraph flooded the market with its stock shortly after World War I, the PRR was second only to U.S. Steel in the number of shareholders of record. In 1895, the average American investor in the PRR owned seventy-eight shares of stock. By 1902, despite the large increase in total share capital, the size of the average holding had nearly doubled, to 147 shares. At the same time, however, the PRR's steady, predictable earnings attracted a great many middle-class investors, preventing the further concentration of stock in the hands of a few wealthy individuals. In 1915, the top ten individual and institutional shareholders owned just 5.40 percent of the Pennsylvania Railroad, compared with 21.78 percent for the Baltimore & Ohio, 28.03 percent for the New York Central, and 21.23 percent for the Erie.[58] During the summer of 1903 alone, the Pennsylvania Railroad added fifteen thousand new shareholders. By 1914, there were eighty-nine thousand shareholders in the Pennsylvania Railroad, a number that had increased to one hundred thousand by 1917. The PRR's management continued to boast that their fiscal prudence had maintained the stock's reputation as a reliable "widows and orphans" investment, and that women owned nearly half of the PRR's stock—although that particular situation had more to do with tax laws that encouraged affluent male investors to register their holdings in their wives' names.[59]

The widely dispersed nature of the PRR's shares assisted the company's executives in deflecting a growing torrent of criticism against the so-called money trust. One example came in July 1907, during testimony involving the two-cent-per-mile passenger fare. The Reading's legal counsel, John J. Johnson, helpfully set up PRR president James A. McCrea with the question, "Do your stockholders consist of bloated capitalists?" McCrea was obviously well prepared for just such a provocative query. "I think not sir," he replied, "forty-seven per cent. of the stockholders are women. In round figures, there are 45,000 stockholders. . . . Less than twenty stockholders hold 20,000 shares."[60] Such figures went a long way toward convincing the public that the PRR was a company owned by ordinary Americans rather than by supposed malefactors of great wealth.

In writing one of the several official histories of the PRR, Howard W. Schotter noted, "The Pennsylvania Railroad Company has never been controlled, directly or indirectly, by any group or groups of stockholders, nor has it ever been subject to so-called banker domination."[61] Schotter mentioned that even the largest stockholders typically owned less than one-quarter of 1 percent of the PRR's total outstanding stock, that no corporation owned as much as 1 percent of the shares.[62] As a large, capital-intensive firm, the PRR's stock was widely dispersed among a variety of institutional investors, ordinary Americans, Europeans, and, eventually, its own employees—making a repeat of Thomson's coordinated 1851–52 stockholder revolt all but impossible, and likewise preventing any financier from attempting to gain control over the company or corner the market in PRR securities. From whatever source, the net result was that a great many investors pooled their resources to underwrite one of the most capital-intensive businesses in history.

The great surge in Pennsylvania Railroad financing, like the community of interest and the improvement programs that were associated with it, began not long after Cassatt assumed the presidency. In 1873, the Pennsylvania legislature had set the railroad's equity ceiling at $151.7 million, but it took more than a quarter of a century for the company to actually issue that much stock. In 1901, after receiving permission from the legislature, the board and the stockholders voted to increase the PRR's equity ceiling by $100 million, to $251.7 million, with half of the additional shares to be issued immediately. During the spring of 1901, PRR stockholders of record took advantage of the opportunity to purchase the new shares at $60. For the first time, the railroad's stock sold at a premium, of 20 percent over par. That was still less than the market price, and well below the 1902 peak of $85.[63] A large portion of the additional capital went to the acquisition of outstanding minority interests in various PRR subsidiaries, including the Erie & Western Transportation Company (better known as the Anchor Line).[64]

By November 1902, the costs associated with new construction, particularly work on the New York Improvements, encouraged Cassatt to seek debt financing. Accordingly, bond value increased from $56.7 million in 1880 to $196.5 million in 1914. The bonds generally proved popular with investors, even though they carried relatively low interest rates, and even though few were secured by a lien on the PRR's assets. Between 1880 and 1914, the PRR issued only three sets of mortgage bonds, in 1893, 1895, and 1908. The remainder were convertible bonds or collateral bonds (so called because they used the value of the PRR's holdings in subsidiary companies as collateral, enabling the bonds to bear lower interest rates than would be the case had the subsidiaries themselves issued the securities). Whereas most newly issued shares went directly to existing PRR investors, the bonds were marketed by established investment bankers.[65]

The first issue was for $50 million, in 3¼ percent, ten-year bonds, payable in gold and convertible to stock. Once again, established shareholders had first choice to purchase the new bonds, in amounts up to a quarter of their existing holdings. The conversion option did not require the immediate issuance of new stock, but the likelihood that investors would avail themselves of that privilege would soon bring the PRR up against its equity ceiling. Moreover, in January 1903, the PRR had borrowed $35 million at 4¼ percent, mainly for immediate improvements at Pittsburgh, and the debt, which would come due in July, would have to be paid off. At the March 1903 annual meeting, therefore, the shareholders agreed to a further increase in equity, from $251.7 million to $400 million, with two-thirds of the amount to be issued immediately, and the remainder represented by the pending issuance of shares linked to convertible bonds. As usual, current investors were able to buy into the new equity issue at $60.[66]

The new round of financing encouraged the large, well-established investment-banking firms to cooperate closely with each other, and with PRR officials. Kuhn, Loeb & Company, the PRR's traditional banker, and J. P. Morgan, a house that was more closely associated with the New York Central, placed whatever remnants of the November 1902, $50 million bond issue had not gone to established PRR shareholders. The coming together of two traditional rivals caused much comment on Wall Street, but such cooperative arrangements were becoming increasingly common in the transportation and manufacturing sectors.[67] By that time, however, the Morgan and

Kuhn, Loeb firms were increasingly at odds with one another. The most publicized feud occurred because one supported James Jerome Hill and the other favored Edward Harriman in their 1901 battle to gain control over the Northern Pacific and the Chicago, Burlington & Quincy. More generally, Morgan was extremely reluctant to share top billing on any securities issue with any other investment-banking firm.

Another apportionment of PRR securities took place in May 1903 in a manner that would provoke considerable criticism of the railroad's finances. Company officials announced that they would offer $75 million of the PRR's recent $100 million stock issue to existing stockholders at $60. Kuhn, Loeb and Speyer & Company agreed to jointly purchase any unsold shares, at $58.75, but their commission would be calculated on the entire $75 million, regardless of how many shares they actually purchased. The arrangement with the investment bankers guaranteed that the railroad would sell the entire stock offering and quickly receive a guaranteed infusion of badly needed capital, regardless of how many shares were taken by existing investors. That seemed a wise policy at first, as a mini-depression that began during the spring of 1903 caused the PRR's stock to decline from almost $79 in January to less than $63 by May. That was still well above $60, however, and existing investors snapped up most of the $75 million issue. On Friday, June 26, the last day on which prospective investors could make the required 50 percent down payment, the overwhelmed clerks at Broad Street Station collected $21 million. One bank president observed that the success of the PRR's stock issue, in the midst of the economic downturn, constituted "one of the most remarkable financial achievements of modern times" and that it was a testament to the good credit of the railroad. Speyer and Kuhn, Loeb's Jacob Schiff agreed to take the unplaced shares at $60 rather than the $58.75 that they had earlier offered, in order that Cassatt would have sufficient funds to carry forward his improvement projects, and they made a great show of their generosity. In the end, however, the two bankers absorbed no more than a few thousand shares of PRR stock, while pocketing a $2.5 million commission on the entire transaction.[68]

Despite the rosy results associated with the May 1903 stock offering, share prices continued to decline, reaching a nadir of $55.375 in November 1903. Although Cassatt halted or delayed a few improvement projects, most continued, using the previously generated capital. The PRR did suspend new securities issues for more than a year, however, and when it turned again to the capital markets, it was for bonds rather than stock. In December 1904, the directors voted to increase the company's bonded debt by $50 million. In tandem with the March 1903 decision to increase debt by the same amount, the change enabled Cassatt to offer $100 million in ten-year, 3½ percent convertible bonds, with a portion of the proceeds being used to retire outstanding consolidated mortgage bonds. Speyer & Company had fallen on hard times, and despite the traditional PRR-NYC rivalry and the Harriman-Hill feud, Kuhn, Loeb and Morgan cooperated on the issue, under a March 1905 agreement. As with previous offerings, PRR shareholders were eligible to buy the bonds, up to a third of their holdings in the company. Few chose to do so, however, even after PRR stock prices surged back into the low seventies, and by May 1905 the PRR had placed barely $10 million with their existing investors. Morgan and Kuhn, Loeb were temporarily stuck with the bulk of the unsold bonds, most of which they did not place until after the effects of the Panic of 1907 had subsided. As a stopgap measure, PRR officials arranged with Kuhn, Loeb to market $50 million in eighteen-month Pennsylvania Company notes, guaranteed by the Pennsylvania Railroad, and bearing an effective interest rate of 5¼ percent.[69]

Based on the sluggish 1905 bond sales, PRR executives and American investment bankers concluded that the domestic capital market was fairly well saturated with PRR securities, and they accordingly placed renewed reliance on overseas markets. As declining British interest coupled with the urgent need to finance the New York Improvements and the other betterments of the Cassatt administration, the PRR turned to French investors. Cassatt spent May and June 1906 in Europe, blending his annual vacation with an effort to sell PRR securities on the Paris Bourse. By the middle of June, Kuhn, Loeb had placed a 3¼ percent loan for 250 million francs (equivalent to about $48 million) that was secured largely by the PRR's holdings in the Baltimore & Ohio, the Chesa-

peake & Ohio, and the Norfolk & Western. Kuhn, Loeb marketed the issue in conjunction with its French partner, Banque de Paris et des Pays-Bas, as well as with Crédit Lyonnais. Significantly, the loan represented the first time that an American railway company was listed on the Bourse. After compensating for discounts and commission fees, the effective rate on the loan was closer to 4½ percent, well below the rate of the earlier short-term 5¼ percent Pennsylvania Company notes. Much of the money would be used to buy new locomotives and freight cars and to begin work on the tunnels under the Hudson and East rivers as part of the New York Improvements.[70]

Between 1900 and 1906, Cassatt and his directors had authorized a truly gargantuan increase in the PRR's financial obligations, some $300 million in all.[71] The railroad's outstanding capital stock had increased from $129 million to $303 million, with nearly another $100 million authorized. Bonded debt more than doubled, from $88 million to $192 million. Some of the money went to the consolidation and refinancing of earlier securities issues. An additional $122 million was devoted to various improvement projects, augmented by $70 million in retained earnings. An even larger sum, $140 million, had been invested in the securities of the various railroads that constituted the community of interest, as well as to buying out minority shareholders in PRR-controlled subsidiaries. In spite of the massive expenditures, and thanks in part to the extensive borrowing, the PRR had maintained a steady stream of dividends—5 percent annually between 1893 and 1899, 6 percent between 1900 and 1905, and 7 percent beginning in November 1906. The stock therefore held its value well and frequently traded at least twenty points above par.

Yet, there were ominous signs that it was not merely the British investors who were disenchanted with the PRR's policy of holding down dividends in order to reinvest money in the property. The rapid increase in capital stock diluted the holdings of the existing shareholders and made the PRR a less-attractive investment. Following the one-third increase in stock in 1901, share values had held steady. A similar one-third increase two years later produced less salubrious results, and share prices remained flat for many years. More ominously, the massive improvements of the

Cassatt years consumed much of the money generated by the sale of the community-of-interest securities. Even the Pennsylvania Company and the Pan Handle had been milked, their dividend rates increased so that they could send more money to their owner, the Pennsylvania Railroad.

What frightened many investors was that the borrowing was not nearly over. When Cassatt informed reporters of the PRR's 250 million franc issue on the Bourse, he told them that the Pennsylvania Railroad would need an *additional* $90 million over the next two years to refinance maturing debt obligations and complete the various improvement projects—an amount that would be equivalent to $2.16 billion in 2010. His admission that the New York Improvements would probably cost at least $100 million, double the earliest estimates, was unlikely to provide any reassurance to investors, either. In that context, Cassatt's 1902 comment that the PRR was "spending more money than any other railroad in the world" seemed less a boast than a chilling warning of an infinity of debt that was to come.[72]

By early 1907, the steady increase in new securities issues had begun to sour investors on the company. Cassatt's death on December 28, 1906, produced barely a quiver on Wall Street, but his successor soon managed to alienate investors. On January 10, President McCrea, on his eighth day in office, announced that at the upcoming annual meeting he intended to ask the stockholders to approve a further $200 million increase in the PRR's capitalization—more than double what Cassatt had predicted just a few months earlier—with half in stock and the remainder in bonds. The amount was all the more shocking given that the PRR had recently realized some $50 million from the sale of the bulk of its community-of-interest holdings. In announcing the proposal, a reporter for the *New York Times* commented on "the apparently unending demands of the road for new capital." With the PRR poised to increase its capitalization to $800 million, the murmurs of concern that had surrounded the French franc loan now grew into a chorus of despair. Many investors were particularly appalled at the rather vague manner of the announcement, which gave few details as to how McCrea intended to raise or spend a sum that would have been the equivalent of nearly

$4.8 billion in 2010. When the stock markets opened the next day, PRR shares fell sharply in both London and New York. Despite their misgivings, shareholders fell obediently into line and assented to McCrea's demands—not that they had much choice, as Cassatt and then McCrea had been absolutely correct in their assertions that the PRR could not do without the additional funds. In February, Kuhn, Loeb agreed to place $60 million in new 5 percent short-term notes. A month later, PRR shareholders approved the $100 million increase in capital stock, from $400 million to $500 million.[73]

There was much worse to come. On September 4, 1907, John Thayer, the PRR's fourth vice president, boasted that his company was "hauling more freight than at any time in its history," predicting that record grain traffic might induce another car shortage. What was more, Thayer emphasized, "The outlook is splendid for a continuation of these conditions."[74] Thayer's optimism was sorely misplaced. Barely a month later, a failed attempt to corner the market for the stock of the United Copper Company brought about the collapse of the Knickerbocker Trust Company and led to a short but severe financial panic.

At first, President McCrea put a brave face on the crisis, but he later acknowledged that he would have to curtail or abandon many of the improvement projects. On November 1, McCrea predicted an "unsatisfactory outlook for raising new capital in 1908."[75] By mid-November, many shop workers at Altoona had been furloughed, and the workday for those that remained had been reduced to eight hours. Traffic and revenues had fallen precipitously by mid-January 1908, and on the PRR 60,000 freight cars sat idle, part of 413,000 nationwide. On January 25, the PRR's managers cut all employee wages by 10 percent. By March, the PRR had laid off still more personnel at Altoona and had closed the car shops at Hollidaysburg. In May, the board reduced the annual dividend from 7 percent to 6 percent. Less than two weeks later, vice president Samuel Rea, speaking in Boston, warned that "business conditions at present and those immediately in sight, do not warrant Wall Street's excessive optimism at this time."[76] Rea knew whereof he spoke, for PRR stock had fallen to less than $52 a share, its lowest level since the mid-1890s, and barely above par. Given the performance of many other securities, the PRR's investors could nonetheless count themselves lucky that they had weathered the Panic of 1907 relatively unscathed.[77]

While the effects of the Panic of 1907 lingered for nearly three years, the spring of 1908 brought some relief for the Pennsylvania Railroad. In late April, Kuhn, Loeb agreed to place $40 million in 4 percent, forty-year bonds (the remainder of the $100 million that McCrea had proposed in January of the previous year) at 96 percent of par. The banking house sold half of its allotment in New York in less than a minute. It took scarcely longer for Rothschild & Sons and Baring Brothers & Company to dispose of the other half on the London exchange. With the bonds selling so quickly, and at such a favorable rate, many Wall Street observers saw the surge of investor confidence as an indication that the panic was over.[78]

As the Pennsylvania Railroad, and the national economy, recovered from the Panic of 1907, new securities issues became more routinized. With the company completing many of its improvements, the newly generated funds were frequently used to refinance existing debts on both the PRR and its subsidiaries—often as part of an effort to simplify the railroad's corporate structure. In May 1908, the board authorized an additional $60 million bond issue. Ten months later, at the 1909 annual meeting, shareholders approved another $80 million increase in bonded debt. That October, the board made provision for the issue of previously authorized stock, solely for existing investors. Despite the ongoing dilution of shareholder equity, prices continued to climb out of the trough of late 1907, reaching a high of $75.625 in 1909.

Share prices fluctuated considerably thereafter, but the long-term trend was nonetheless downward. Investors had expected the PRR's reduction in dividends, from 7 percent to 6 percent, owing to the depressed economic conditions of 1907–08. They were less sympathetic regarding the April 1910 announcement that the economic recovery did not mandate a restoration of the old dividend rate, and share prices fell sharply, to about $66. As a *New York Times* reporter noted in May, "The stock has yielded ground grudgingly through all the recent declines, but yesterday its fall was relatively rapid and extensive." The newsman hinted that "one or two Directors have been named as

most anxious for an increase, but a case of revolt on the part of the Directors against the policy of a President of the Pennsylvania where the President stands for conservatism is almost inconceivable, and would certainly find no support with stockholders like the Pennsylvania's."[79]

While there was no revolt against the conservative dividend policy, many shareholders were nonetheless increasingly restive at the steady decline in stock prices. By the beginning of 1911, the directors voted in support of a $100 million increase in stock, and the shareholders gave their assent at the March annual meeting. Another issue followed in April 1913, for $45 million, and in response, the price of PRR shares fell below $58. It would be the PRR's last issue of stock until 1928. In July 1913, the PRR's Finance Committee, acting on the recommendation of President Rea, voted to move away from the railroad's long-standing reliance on equity issues. With shareholders demanding consistently high dividends, they concluded that bonds could be offered at a lower interest rate—particularly as bond interest was deductible from the newly instituted federal income tax, and stock dividends were not. As a result, Rea favored the creation of a new general mortgage, similar to the consolidated mortgage that the board had authorized in 1873. He also called for the refinancing of several of the PRR's principal subsidiaries—an action that dovetailed with the ongoing consolidation and simplification of the railroad's corporate structure.[80]

By 1913, however, investors were increasingly pessimistic, concluding that the ICC's rulings in the *Eastern Rate* cases would likely reduce corporate earnings, and their fears did little to improve the market for PRR securities. Yet, the railroad's problems were not solely the fault of the expanding regulatory state. The rapid pace of technological and organizational innovations that had emerged since the Civil War had begun to slow. Steel rail, air brakes, automatic couplers, signaling systems, standardized locomotives and rolling stock—to say nothing of the development of the line-and-staff business organization—had produced enormous gains in efficiency. By the early years of the twentieth century, there were no new technologies, and no new organizational methods, that could produce similar leaps in productivity, with correspondingly large declines in operating costs and rates. At a time when PRR executives needed more capital than ever, the return on their assets was steadily declining. For prospective investors, the issue was much simpler. Rising costs and reduced gains in efficiency progressively eroded the worth of PRR securities and made them less attractive investments. Yet, so long as dividend rates remained high, even astute investors might not have been aware of the company's growing capital crisis.

The souring of American investors on railway securities, combined with the saturation of domestic capital markets, led PRR officials and their investment bankers to again seek out foreign capital. British investment in American railway securities rebounded during the early years of the twentieth century, more than doubling between 1890 and 1913, from $1,458,000,000 to $3 billion. The PRR obtained a considerable share of that capital, in part by appealing to the interests of British investors of modest means. PRR officials worked with the company's British agents, the London Joint Stock Bank, Ltd., to issue dividend checks, in pounds, directly to Britons who coveted the small but predictable biannual payments. Large British firms, such as the "Shell" Transport and Trading Company and tobacco giant W. D. & H. O. Wills, Ltd., also owned substantial blocks of PRR securities. Despite the increased interest of PRR executives in overseas capital, British investors possessed ample alternative opportunities within the British Empire, and their overall holdings remained comparatively modest. By 1914, on the eve of World War I, American investors controlled the vast majority (some 85 percent) of PRR common stock, with only about $75 million in par value represented by foreigners.[81]

The onset of World War I brought a good deal of the PRR's foreign-held investments back to the United States while accelerating the railroad's demands for capital. The war transformed the United States from a debtor to a creditor nation and sent PRR securities westward across the Atlantic. In 1915, the PRR repurchased approximately $15 million in bonds, denominated in pounds sterling, from British investors, while the Pennsylvania Company issued $48.3 million in 4½ percent notes, enabling executives to repatriate some $37 million worth of the 1906 French franc loan.[82]

Despite the flurry of financial activity that accompanied the war, there were some underlying problems on Wall Street. One obvious difficulty was that all trading was either suspended or restricted between July 31, 1914, and April 1, 1915, largely in an effort to prevent Europeans from selling off all of their investments and depressing share prices. When limited trading resumed, PRR stock declined sharply to $51.25. It rallied to $60 by early 1917, and then fell again after the United States entered the war in April 1917. By 1918, with transportation in a shambles and the federal government in control of the railroads, shares had declined to $40.25, their worst showing since the crisis of 1877.[83]

The PRR's investment bankers were not having a much easier time of it. Throughout much of 1912 and into 1913, Representative Arsène Pujo (Dem., La.) had chaired a committee tasked with uncovering the "money trust," a great banking conspiracy that, he and his allies insisted, was manipulating the American economy and contravening the public interest. The members of the Pujo Committee found what they were looking for—or, at least, they claimed that they did—and their highly publicized report excoriated investment bankers such as J. P. Morgan and Jacob Schiff. The strain associated with the hearings may well have contributed to Morgan's death on March 31, 1913. Schiff survived until 1920, but was nonetheless badly shaken by the adverse publicity. In an effort to deflect criticism from his firm, he agreed to sharply reduce the standard 2½ percent commissions that Kuhn, Loeb and other banking houses earned through the sale of PRR securities. The effects of the Pujo Committee hearings lingered for the remainder of the decade and greatly complicated the efforts of PRR executives to raise additional capital.[84]

During early 1915, the PRR sold $49 million in 4½ percent bonds, a transaction that virtually exhausted the $100 million authorization established by the 1873 consolidated mortgage. Shortly thereafter, the board established the general mortgage that President Rea had advocated nearly two years earlier. Despite the growing reliance on debt, the terms of the general mortgage stipulated that the value of the outstanding bonds could not exceed the value of the outstanding stock, maintaining the PRR's extraordinarily low leverage. On May 7, 1915, Kuhn, Loeb made a public offering of $65 million of the consolidated mortgage bonds, bearing 4½ percent interest. A large portion of the money, along with that from the earlier $49 million sale of the consolidated mortgage bonds, was used to redeem $86.8 million worth of 3½ percent convertible bonds. The remainder went into the physical plant. The timing of the sale proved particularly fortuitous for the PRR, but not for Kuhn, Loeb. The following day, Americans received word of the sinking of the *Lusitania*, and securities prices tumbled. Kuhn, Loeb had underwritten the bonds, and the firm now faced the responsibility of disposing of them in a depressed market.[85]

Pennsylvania Railroad financing continued through the war, albeit interrupted by federal control over the railroads between December 1917 and February 1920. Kuhn, Loeb generally handled new securities issues, including a $20 million loan in July 1916 and a consignment of $60 million in mortgage bonds in March 1917, followed by another short-term loan in April. The board approved another $50 million, 5 percent bond issue in December 1918, which sold at only a small discount. In the realm of equity financing, shareholders agreed to a further $75 million increase in stock at the March 1917 annual meeting, although no additional shares were issued until 1928. More financing came in the form of a $50 million bond issue in April 1920, the first bond issue since the period of federal operation. The bonds carried an unusually high interest rate of 7 percent, indicative of the difficulties that PRR executives would experience as they attempted to secure capital during the postwar period. More significantly, the recently adopted Esch-Cummins Act (better known as the Transportation Act of 1920) gave the Interstate Commerce Commission authority over the issuance of new railroad securities.[86]

For better or for worse, the Pennsylvania Railroad had entered a new era of finance. After 1920, with both equity and debt issues proving increasingly problematic, the PRR relied more often on internal financing. The railroad's ratio of internal funds to gross assets increased from 17.0 percent in 1914 to 21.5 percent in 1920, and to 34.1 percent in 1929. Investment bankers, speculators, and dividend-seeking shareholders had never dominated the PRR to the same extent as many other railroads. That circumstance ensured that the company would barely feel the effects of the speculative ventures that roiled the railroads during the 1920s. Yet, internal financing also exempted the PRR from the constructive financial constraints that outsiders might have applied to the company. While internal financing enabled PRR executives to avoid some of the most deleterious effects associated with the decline of investor confidence in the railroads, it also masked the need to implement fundamental changes in the transportation sector of the economy.[87]

The Equipment Trust: Specialized Financing for Movable Capital

"The Pennsylvania Lines East of Pittsburg and Erie are the largest owners of freight equipment in the World," complained first vice president John P. Green in 1905, "and yet they are borrowers of cars" from other railroads. "The demand for additional cars upon our lines seems to be unquenchable," Green lamented, "and thirty to forty thousand cars simply melt out of sight almost as soon as they are built, and, like Oliver Twist, the operating and traffic officers are always 'crying for more.' "[88]

In order to quell the plaintive cries of PRR managers and shippers without loading the balance sheet with additional stock or general mortgage bonds, executives increasingly relied on equipment trusts. Equipment-trust financing offered PRR executives the opportunity to mortgage the railroad's moveable physical assets to outside investors. Unlike the railroad's fixed right of way, freight and passenger equipment was capable of movement, and in theory could be transferred to almost any railroad in the United States. Because equipment trust certificates constituted a first lien, cars and locomotives were beyond the reach of the railroad's bondholders. As a result, they were extraordinarily safe investments and rarely if ever went into default. Even for especially strong carriers such as the PRR, equipment trusts enabled executives to borrow funds at slightly lower rates than would normally apply to stock or bond issues, shaving perhaps half a percentage point off of the cost of capital. Born amid the financial exigencies of the 1870s, equipment-trust certificates assumed ever-greater importance as George Roberts,

Alexander Cassatt, and their successors attempted to attract desperately needed capital from every conceivable source.[89]

The first equipment trust dated to 1845, when the Schuylkill Navigation Company employed that technique to purchase barges. The greatest growth in equipment financing, however, occurred amid the traffic increases that followed the Civil War. In 1868, the Lehigh Coal & Navigation Company engaged Charles Gibbons, the same Philadelphia attorney who in 1846 had been so implacably opposed to municipal funding for the Pennsylvania Railroad, to develop the legal framework for the Railroad Car Trust of Philadelphia. Gibbons articulated what generally became known as the Philadelphia Plan, in which a trustee (typically a bank or a manufacturer) retained ownership in the equipment until the carrier paid off the entire outstanding principal and interest. The banks that issued equipment trust certificates typically provided 90 percent of the cost of the rolling stock, with the railroad contributing the remainder. Cars and locomotives purchased under equipment-trust financing were thus 90 percent leveraged, a substantially different circumstance than the fifty-fifty debt-to-equity ratio that applied to the PRR as a whole. Carriers like the PRR paid an annual interest charge equivalent to approximately 3 percent of the cost of the car, and made further payments of a tenth of the principal each year. Those amounts were not carried as debt, but were instead considered part of operating expense and charged against operating income. When the railroad had redeemed the equipment trust certificates, it owned the locomotive or rolling stock, free and clear.[90]

Railroads with weak credit were the earliest users of equipment trusts, but the depression of the 1870s imperiled the finances of even the PRR. In 1875, PRR officials developed a variant of the equipment trust whereby they paid for the equipment with both stock and trust certificates. The stock, held by the railroad, constituted the down payment, with the certificates issued to outside parties used to finance the balance of the acquisition. The trustee held title to the equipment and leased it to the PRR, with the lease payments gradually redeeming the trust certificates over a six-year period. Until then, the unpaid balance appeared on the PRR's books as a liability.[91]

The courts shaped the development of equipment-trust financing, both within the commonwealth of Pennsylvania and on the Pennsylvania Railroad. In contrast to other states, the Pennsylvania judiciary held that railroads could not use rolling stock (which they might move out of reach of creditors) as security for the issuance of mortgage bonds. Under that doctrine, railroad managers elected to vest ownership of the equipment in the hands of a third party trustee until they had completely paid off the purchase price. At the federal level, the Supreme Court ruled, in *United States v. New Orleans Railroad* (1870), that in the event of bankruptcy, "after acquired property"—that is, equipment owned directly by the railroad and purchased subsequent to the issuance of a mortgage—could be used to satisfy the demands of creditors. By maintaining third-party ownership, equipment trusts could shield some of a railroad's assets.[92]

The Roberts years, accompanied by the continual demand for more and larger equipment, witnessed a rapid increase in the creation of equipment trusts. One example was a $2.7 million allotment of Equipment Trust Gold Bonds issued in September 1889 and bearing an interest rate of 4 percent. Unlike earlier trust issues, the PRR officials in this instance dispensed with the practice of maintaining separate stock and trust accounts. Instead, they created a sinking fund to gradually retire the bonds. By 1896, the railroad had acquired nearly fifty-eight thousand cars, worth more than $30 million, through equipment trust financing. Roberts was suspicious of equipment-trust financing, however, and he did his best to restrain the practice during the final years of his presidency.[93]

After 1899, acute car shortages and the transition to steel-underframe and all-steel cars produced a surge in equipment-trust financing. Most of the monies generated from periodic offerings of stocks and bonds went immediately into rebuilding the physical plant, refinancing existing debts, and acquiring additional subsidiary securities, with little left over for cars and locomotives. The 1902 liberalization of per diem rates encouraged additional car construction, typically financed through trust certificates. Various trust instruments included many series of loans through the Pennsylvania Steel Equipment Improvement Trust (organized in 1905, with $10 million in capital), the

Pennsylvania Steel Rolling Stock Trust, the Pennsylvania Steel Freight Car Trust, and the Pennsylvania General Freight Equipment Trust. In 1906 alone, the PRR purchased nearly forty thousand cars through equipment-trust financing—a trend that continued with another major round of borrowing in 1913. By the end of 1914, the PRR had issued $102 million in equipment trust certificates.[94]

As was the case with the stocks and convertible bonds, investors were eager to buy the PRR's equipment trust certificates. Taken together, however, the repeated new securities issues and the increasingly creative manner in which the PRR acquired its capital portended problems for the years to come. While equipment trust certificates were a safe and reliable mechanism for funding car and locomotive purchases, they moved the railroad away from its traditionally even division between debt and equity. Equipment-trust certificates were popular with investors in large measure because, as the legal owners of the locomotives and rolling stock, they received payment from the railroads at a faster rate than their property depreciated.[95] By embracing equipment-trust financing, PRR executives avoided the restrictions associated with Pennsylvania law and the *New Orleans* case, but they also transferred many of the financial benefits associated with equipment depreciation to outside parties.

The People Who Rebuilt the Railroad

While bankers and a legion of investors provided the funds for rebuilding the Pennsylvania Railroad, the administration of that process fell to the company's engineering staff. As had been the case during earlier bursts of new construction, the PRR's organization chart swelled in order to accommodate the additional responsibilities. In November 1902, the board reestablished an independent Engineering Department, under the direct control of the second vice president, and separate from the Transportation Department. The following June, the directors created the new office of chief engineer of maintenance of way, to accommodate routine repairs now that a portion of the engineering staff had been sent off to supervise new construction. Despite the more modest traffic demands

on Lines West—generally resolved through the provision of a second mainline track, particularly on the Fort Wayne—organizational changes took place there, as well. At the beginning of 1903, the newly created offices of chief engineer of maintenance of way–Northwest System and chief engineer of maintenance of way–Southwest System assumed control over routine repairs. As such, they reported to their respective general superintendents, who in turn answered to general manager George L. Peck, head of the Transportation Department on Lines West. Chief engineer Thomas Rodd, freed of maintenance responsibilities, was able to focus on new construction.[96]

On the PRR's Lines East, the ultimate responsibility for rebuilding the railroad fell largely on the shoulders of two individuals, chief engineer William Henry Brown and vice president Samuel Rea. While presidents George Roberts and Alexander Cassatt had authorized the periodic rebuilding of the Pennsylvania Railroad, Brown was chiefly responsible for putting their plans into action. He was born in Lancaster County in 1836, and later became a PRR rodman. During the Civil War, he served as an assistant engineer of the United States Military Rail Roads, spending most of his time in Virginia. After the war, he went to the oilfields of northwestern Pennsylvania, working with the Oil Creek and the Philadelphia & Erie railroads. In 1869, he oversaw the expansion of the Altoona shops, and the following year he became resident engineer of the PRR's Middle Division. In 1881, in the middle of a lifetime of service to the Pennsylvania Railroad, he became chief engineer. His employment with the PRR was a family affair, as it was for many others, with one brother, Charles E. Brown, working for the auditor of merchandise traffic, and another, Theodore F. Brown, retiring in 1915 as the assistant auditor of the Union Line Bureau at Pittsburgh. His son, Frank Brown, was employed with the Philadelphia contracting firm of Drake & Stratton before becoming a partner in H. S. Kerbaugh & Company, which did considerable work for the PRR, while grandson Edwin Hobart Brown was a PRR electrical engineer.[97]

For nearly a third of a century, William Brown directed some of the PRR's most important construction projects. They included office buildings and stations in Harrisburg, Pittsburgh, and Philadelphia, where he oversaw construction of Broad Street Station and its associated Filbert Street Extension, better known as the "Chinese Wall." Brown was largely responsible for the rebuilding of the main line and the addition of third and fourth tracks in exceedingly difficult locations along Horseshoe Curve and to the west. He was responsible for elevating tracks in Pennsylvania and New Jersey above the level of surrounding streets, and he helped to coordinate the Pittsburgh Improvements. Brown built major bridges at New Brunswick and Trenton, New Jersey, and at Pittsburgh, Rockville, and Coatesville, Pennsylvania, and lesser structures at dozens of river crossings. All told, he was responsible for 133 line changes, 41 tunnels, 163 bridges, and 14 separate track elevations.[98]

Samuel Rea served as the linchpin in a small but talented professional network of technological practitioners. He was born in 1855 in Hollidaysburg, Pennsylvania, just as the Pennsylvania Railroad was bringing to an end the transfer of freight and passengers at that location, dooming the Allegheny Portage Railroad. In some respects Rea resembled Tom Scott, an individual who had also spent considerable time at Hollidaysburg, in that he was from a family of modest means, but with valuable political connections—his grandfather, John Rea, had been a member of the United States House of Representatives between 1803 and 1811. Unlike Scott, but in common with most of those who became top PRR executives, Rea developed extensive engineering experience. He began at age sixteen as a chainman, laying out branch lines near his hometown. The depression that began in 1873 cost him his position on the PRR and nearly terminated his railroad career. He worked at the Hollidaysburg Iron & Nail Company, accepted another brief stint with the PRR in 1875, and spent a portion of his time as assistant engineer for the Point Bridge, a highway span across the Monongahela River, completed in 1877. Rea returned to the PRR in 1879, and by 1883 he was principal assistant engineer, reporting to Joseph N. Du Barry, the third vice president, in charge of new rail lines. The flurry of new construction during the 1880s kept Rea extraordinarily busy. Yet, he felt that he had little opportunity for advancement, perhaps because of ongoing personality conflicts with Du Barry. Rea left the PRR in 1889 to become vice president of the Maryland Central Railroad and chief engineer of the Baltimore Belt Railroad—the B&O subsidiary

that was responsible for tunneling under the city in order to provide that carrier with an unbroken rail link between Washington and Philadelphia.[99]

In early 1892, the declining health of Vice President Du Barry afforded Rea the opportunity to return to the Pennsylvania Railroad. Alexander Cassatt—then in semi-retirement, but still closely connected to the PRR—arranged for Rea to become assistant to President Roberts, albeit at a lower salary than he had enjoyed while working for the Belt Line. Rea was primarily responsible for managing the details associated with constructing new rail lines, including real estate, financing, and the resolution of charter and other legal issues. The Panic of 1893 swept across the United States soon after Rea assumed his new post, and there was relatively little new construction for him to supervise. In June 1899, the board reestablished the office of fourth vice president for Rea, as an assistant to first vice president John P. Green, helping to keep track of the complex legal and financial arrangements that interconnected the various companies in the PRR system. Rea continued those duties after earning a promotion to third vice president in October 1905. The board of directors would later elect Rea to the presidency of the Pennsylvania Railroad, effective January 1, 1913.[100]

At the time of the Cassatt-era improvements, Rea possessed many valuable attributes. He was a highly proficient engineer, accustomed to the management of complex new construction projects. Of equal importance, he understood finance and accounting methods, a knowledge that was critical to the containment of costs. His experience with the Baltimore Belt, as well as research trips to Europe in 1887 and 1892, exposed him to some of the latest developments in underwater tunneling and electric propulsion. Above all, Rea radiated authority, as he stood, steely eyed, square jawed, and—at more than six feet in height—looming over his subordinates. In writing Rea's obituary, a reporter for the *New York Times* noted, "He would deal with tremendous problems and immense figures almost as with trifles, and while his associates often were struggling with a problem he would snap out his decision and the problem would be ended."[101]

William Brown and Samuel Rea were two of the best-known individuals associated with the PRR's burst of construction during the late nineteenth and early twentieth centuries, but they were not the only

Figure 70. (left) William Henry Brown (1836–1910) spent most of his life in the service of the Pennsylvania Railroad, and he was the company's chief engineer for a quarter of a century. He supervised many of the construction projects authorized by President Cassatt, most of which are still in use. He was probably best known as a staunch advocate of stone construction, creating bridges that could accommodate any level of traffic with no risk of collapse. (right) Samuel Rea (1855–1929, shown here circa 1905) was a superbly talented engineer who also mastered such diverse skills as finance and public relations. Perhaps his most important responsibility was the management of the New York Improvements, the PRR's complex and expensive effort to provide direct rail service to Manhattan and Long Island. His success in overseeing such a multifaceted and demanding project led to his elevation to the presidency in 1912. He retired in 1925 and enjoyed a retirement that lasted less than four years—still longer than that of any of his predecessors since 1852.

(left) Pennsylvania Historical and Museum Commission, Pennsylvania State Archives;(right) Library of Congress, Prints & Photographs Division, LC-USZ62-95435.

ones who played important roles in that process. Engineers, surveyors, site managers, and construction crews worked long hours to bring projects to fruition. Outside contractors contributed their expertise and their workers, augmenting the PRR's in-house capabilities. Architects and consulting engineers designed unique projects that lay outside the more routinized skills of PRR personnel. Those individuals—some famous, but many others undeservedly forgotten—swarmed across the right of way between Pittsburgh, Philadelphia, Washington, and New York, laying rail, building bridges, digging tunnels, and constructing some of the most magnificent structures ever designed.

Improvements at the Pittsburgh Gateway

Of all of the bottlenecks on the Pennsylvania Railroad system, Pittsburgh was by far the worst. Constrained by political and economic circumstance, Thomson and his fellow engineers had selected perhaps the least suitable location in the United States to site a major railroad hub. By the end of the 1870s, the tracks of the PRR main line, the Fort Wayne, the Pan Handle, the Allegheny Valley, and the Pittsburgh, Virginia & Charleston (the Monongahela Division) all intersected in or near Pittsburgh—to say nothing of a welter of branch lines, industrial spurs, and a network of tracks belonging to other railroads. Steep grades and sharp curves on many routes, some of them built to the engineering standards and traffic requirements of the 1840s and 1850s, further impeded efficient operations.

Beginning in the early 1880s, PRR engineers and construction crews added as many tracks as possible to the already crowded Pittsburgh Division main line and built numerous freight bypass routes around and through the city. One project, implemented between 1880 and 1883, created a new link between the Western Pennsylvania Railroad and the Pittsburgh Division, near Bolivar, allowing traffic interchanged between the PRR and the Fort Wayne to bypass Pittsburgh. As part of that project, beginning in 1883, crews rebuilt and double-tracked the Western Pennsylvania Railroad (later the Western Pennsylvania Division and then the Conemaugh Division).[102]

Between 1902 and 1904, the PRR completed a key link in its efforts to route traffic around Pittsburgh. The four-track Brilliant Branch (also known as the Brilliant Cutoff) diverged from the Pittsburgh Division main line at East Liberty and headed almost due north to a junction with the Allegheny Valley Railway at Brilliant. The line continued across the Allegheny River and terminated at a connection with the Western Pennsylvania, near Aspinwall. With the completion of the $3.6 million branch, freight traffic from points north and west of Pittsburgh (including eastbound trains off of the Fort Wayne) could bypass central Pittsburgh and its congestion. More ambitious proposals, such as a sixty-mile line extending J. Edgar Thomson's Allegheny Valley route west from Red Bank to a connection with the Fort Wayne, never came to fruition.[103]

Other improvements took place to the south and west of Pittsburgh. In 1886, PRR officials incorporated the Ohio Connecting Railway, to build a short link from the Fort Wayne, near Bellevue, across the Ohio River at Brunots Island and terminating at a junction with the Pan Handle at Elliot. The new line, opened in 1890, completed what amounted to a belt-line railway

around the city of Pittsburgh. Traffic off of the Fort Wayne could cross to the south side of the Ohio River, follow the Pan Handle and the Monongahela Division, cross over the Monongahela River at Port Perry, and rejoin the Pittsburgh Division for the trip east.[104]

The increased traffic flowing through and around Pittsburgh also mandated the construction of improved yard and terminal facilities. In 1884, the PRR opened an expanded Duquesne Freight Station, like the earlier structure located along the Monongahela River near the foot of Liberty Avenue but capable of accommodating a much larger volume of shipments. In August 1903, the PRR oversaw the completion of the Pittsburgh Union Stockyard on Herr's Island in the Allegheny River. A few months later, the facility became the Pittsburgh Union Stock Yards Company (soon renamed the Pittsburgh Joint Stock Yards Company) with the Baltimore & Ohio enjoying the right of access.

Human travelers reaped benefits as well, in the form of a new passenger station. In 1877, rioting Pittsburghers had burned down the old one, and it was not until 1898 that PRR officials opened negotiations with the city government, to finally replace the two-decade-old temporary station that had emerged from the ashes. They chose an architect who had attained national prominence as one of the designers of the 1893 Columbian Exposition in Chicago. Daniel H. Burnham had also done some work on the PRR's passenger stations in Chicago; Grand Rapids, Michigan; and Columbus, Ohio, so he would have been well known to the railroad's executives. Burnham's role in the creation of the 1893 "White City" had afforded him access to Charles Atwood's innovative design for the Exposition's Terminal Railroad Station—a structure that was based on the baths of ancient Rome. Yet, Burnham relied more heavily on older, established styles, blending his designs for Chicago office buildings with a massive vaulted train shed that was typical of late-nineteenth-century railway practice. The Rotunda and cab stand—a late design change—added an element of French Beaux Arts, with its squat, open-sided form distinctly at odds with the looming headhouse that lay behind it.[105]

In 1900, construction began on the new Pittsburgh Union Station, along Liberty Avenue, at Eleventh

Figure 71. For much of the nineteenth century, Pittsburgh residents had complained about the lack of adequate passenger facilities in their city, almost as often as they had criticized the PRR's virtual transportation monopoly in southwestern Pennsylvania. By 1898, PRR officials had concluded that the inefficient passenger facilities, including the tracks down Liberty Avenue, would have to be replaced. They hired Daniel Burnham, a Chicago architect well known for his work with the 1893 Columbian Exposition. The facility, completed in stages between 1901 and 1903, in turn inspired structures in Washington, D.C. (designed by Burnham), and New York (designed by Charles Follen McKim and his associates).

Library of Congress, Prints & Photographs Division, LC-DIG-det-4a17357.

Street. The waiting room opened the following year, but the thirteen-story office building that rested atop the station was not finished until 1902. In 1903, workers completed the installation of the train shed, which was similar to the one used at Philadelphia's Broad Street Station. As part of the Union Station project, the PRR erected a new bridge between Pittsburgh and Allegheny City and elevated the Fort Wayne tracks from the east end of the new bridge into downtown.

Despite public dismay regarding the PRR's November 1902 freight traffic congestion, and even as many residents eagerly awaited the arrival of George Gould's Wabash-Pittsburgh Terminal Railway, Pittsburghers finally enjoyed access to a long-desired Union Station. The name was something of a misnomer, however, as the station served only the PRR and its Lines West subsidiaries. Other carriers, including the B&O and the Wabash-Pittsburgh Terminal, used separate facilities. Even though many of its trains terminated at Union Station, the Fort Wayne also had its own terminus, located across the river in Allegheny City, with its clock conspicuously set to Central Time.[106]

The expansion of congested freight yards also occupied the attentions of PRR engineers. In 1885 and 1886, construction crews enlarged the centrally located Pittsburgh Yard, designed to process eastbound freight traffic. Farther west, near Rochester, Pennsylvania, they built an entirely new yard facility along the Fort Wayne. Construction on the Conway Yard began in 1884 and, after an expenditure of $1.5 million, traffic destined for points to the north, south, and west of Pittsburgh flowed far more smoothly. By the turn of the century, however, steadily increasing traffic was taxing the capacity of the Conway Yard. In 1900, operating officials recommended that gravity, rather than switch engines, be used to sort cars, a solution that they implemented in several other locations at more or less the same time.

Gravity yards, also known as summit yards, were the precursors to true hump yards. As their name suggested, summit yards relied on the natural undulations of the topography, with cars uncoupled at the top of a rise and allowed to roll gradually downhill to classification tracks located in a shallow depression. The PRR first employed gravity yards in 1899, one near Greensburg, on the South-West Pennsylvania Branch, and another at Honey Pot, southwest of Wilkes-Barre. The Conway Yard boasted what may well have been the first hump yard in the United States, where switch engines shoved cuts of cars up an artificial mound, increasing each car's subsequent descent and maximizing the distance that it would roll.[107] Initially, brakemen rode down the hump with each cut of cars, a labor-intensive and dangerous process. In 1906, however, the PRR installed Westinghouse electro-pneumatic retarders at the Hollidaysburg Yard, permitting the controlled braking of freight cars from a central location, and the practice soon spread to other hump yards.[108]

An even more impressive yard took shape fourteen miles east of Pittsburgh, near the mouth of Turtle Creek. With the completion of freight bypass lines to the north and the south of Pittsburgh, Turtle Creek became the junction between the east–west main line and the various routes to Chicago and St. Louis. As early as 1873, the PRR had purchased a large tract of

land in the area, but the Panic of 1873, the 1877 riots, and the 1889 Johnstown Flood had each delayed construction. The first facilities were completed in January 1891, with the yard entering service in April 1892. A hump yard for westbound traffic opened in November 1905, and the eastbound hump yard opened two years later. The facility was named for Robert Pitcairn, who for decades had attempted to facilitate operations in Pittsburgh while maintaining cordial relations with that city's residents.[109]

In addition to the construction of connecting lines, the laying of additional tracks, and the opening of major new facilities, the PRR directors authorized myriad other rebuilding projects, small only in comparison to the massive scale of the other improvements that were taking place in and around Pittsburgh. The easing of curves and gradients, the installation of new bridges (including the replacement of the Pan Handle span across the Monongahela River between 1902 and 1904), and the relocation of yard and industrial trackage sped traffic on its way. The elimination of grade crossings facilitated operations, reduced the possibility of accidents, and pleased local residents and civic leaders, but often resulted in protracted negotiations as to who would pay for the improved facilities. Perhaps the most notable change in that regard involved the completion in January 1906 of the Duquesne Way Elevated, a connection with the expanded Duquesne Freight Station, finally permitting the removal of tracks from Liberty Avenue.[110]

By 1908 the PRR had spent well over $25 million on its efforts to improve freight and passenger operations in Pittsburgh. Those changes, however, were barely sufficient to cope with the enormous traffic growth at the turn of the century—the number of PRR trains moving through the city more than doubled between 1903 and 1908. Even worse, the financial panic and recession that began in 1907 forced the curtailment of betterment projects in Pittsburgh and throughout the system. In combination with increasingly stringent state and federal rate regulations, the PRR was not well equipped to accommodate the surging traffic levels that accompanied World War I. The deficiencies were particularly apparent at Pittsburgh, which was again jammed with traffic until the end of the war brought a measure of relief.

From Pittsburgh east to the Susquehanna River,

PRR officials made relatively few changes to the route that J. Edgar Thomson and his assistants had surveyed half a century earlier. Beginning in 1881, construction crews were busily adding tracks to the Pittsburgh Division, west of Altoona, a process that was largely complete as the nineteenth century drew to a close. Perhaps their greatest challenge involved the installation of a third and a fourth track to the Horseshoe Curve. After coping with massive rocks, unstable soils, and a seemingly endless parade of freight and passenger trains, they completed the project in early 1900—and were even able to add a small park and flower garden for good measure. Farther west, the 1883 West Penn Extension, between Bolivar and Blairsville, required substantial expenditures to create an alternate route that was longer than the main line, all to reduce the eastbound grade from 0.99 percent to 0.40 percent. Still more projects were shelved, done in either by economic recession or by an unfavorable cost-benefit ratio.[111] The biggest exception occurred in 1904, when construction crews finished reinstalling rails on the abandoned grade of the New Portage Railroad, a project that had been under consideration since 1880 but was delayed by the economic downturn of the 1890s. Workers also improved the Petersburg Branch, built in sections between Hollidaysburg and Petersburg, between 1873 and 1900. The reuse of the former commonwealth-owned line, in tandem with the Petersburg Branch, created a relief route that bypassed the congestion at Altoona and along the Horseshoe Curve. The completion of the new double-track Gallitzin Tunnel on the PRR main line, built between 1901 and 1904, facilitated train movements between Altoona and Johnstown, and allowed the aging Allegheny Tunnel to be reduced to a single track.[112]

The Rockville Bridge

The Rockville Bridge across the Susquehanna River, just north of Harrisburg, had long been both a spectacular engineering achievement and an impediment to the PRR's operations. The first crossing, completed in 1849 under the direction of Herman Haupt, employed wooden trusses and carried only a single track. Over the next quarter of a century, PRR crews rebuilt much of the original main line, but did little more than repair the Rockville Bridge. During the summer of 1876, as travelers headed east toward the Centennial Exhibition in Philadelphia, their crossing of the Susquehanna River led them along the last stretch of single track and over the sole remaining wooden bridge on the entire PRR main line. One year earlier, however, PRR officials had begun to integrate the Northern Central Railway into their operations. In 1876, they rerouted most of the subsidiary's traffic over the Rockville Bridge, rather than the Northern Central's nearby Marysville Bridge. With that change, the congestion on the Rockville span became intolerable. Throughout much of 1877, construction crews from the Delaware Bridge Company built a second Rockville Bridge. The new structure doubled the number of tracks and was built of iron, rather than wood. During the 1880s and into the 1890s, however, steady increases in the weight of locomotives and cars, coupled with an increase in traffic, rendered the second Rockville Bridge obsolete.[113]

By 1900, much of the main line boasted four tracks, and the Rockville Bridge had again become a bottleneck. While the construction of a new four-track steel bridge was certainly feasible, PRR chief engineer William H. Brown had other ideas. Breaking with many of his contemporaries, Brown concluded that heavier trains called for the erection of stone arches, a technique that since Roman times had proved spectacularly successful at resisting the forces of compression. He harbored justifiable suspicions of iron bridges, many of which were poorly designed, or ill equipped to cope with steadily increasing axle loads. One example was the iron truss span that bridge engineers Charles Collins and Amasa Stone designed for a crossing of the Ashtabula River in northeastern Ohio. On December 29, 1876, the span collapsed under the weight of a Lake Shore & Michigan Southern passenger train. Nearly a hundred people died, and the list of casualties would eventually include Collins and Stone, each of whom committed suicide. The Ashtabula Horror and other, less spectacular failures presented William Brown with a compelling argument in favor of fail-safe stone construction.

During the 1880s, President Roberts elected to replace outdated iron truss bridges over the Conemaugh River at Johnstown and over Conestoga Creek, near

Lancaster. Brown initially planned to erect a stronger iron bridge at Johnstown, but—possibly at the suggestion of Pittsburgh Division superintendent Robert Pitcairn—he chose stone instead. The new four-track bridge entered service in 1887. Brown employed the same design techniques for the two-track span over Conestoga Creek, completed the following year. The solidity of stone-arch construction was amply demonstrated in 1889, when the Johnstown Flood piled tons of debris against the bridge at Johnstown. The bridge survived with only minor damage. Despite the unanticipated horror of the blazing debris field trapped against the bridge, Brown saw the incident as a vindication of the stone arch concept. Over the next two decades, particularly where river crossings were wide and shallow, Brown designed stone-arch bridges that would last virtually forever and accommodate even the heaviest of locomotives and cars. The more notable spans included those over the Raritan River at New Brunswick and over the Delaware River at Trenton; over the West Branch of Brandywine Creek at Coatesville, Pennsylvania; and a span across the Susquehanna River at Shock's Mill, as well as many smaller structures.[114]

Brown's longest and most visually stunning bridge was the one over the Susquehanna River at Rockville. In early March 1900, not long after Alexander Cassatt assumed the presidency, Brown solicited bids for a massive four-track, forty-eight-arch stone bridge that would stretch more than 3,800 feet across the Susquehanna. The winning bid went to outside contractors Drake & Stratton and H. S. Kerbaugh & Company, in which his son Frank Brown was a partner. Even though the PRR relied on its own labor force for routine construction and maintenance-of-way projects, its executives found it more cost effective to hire outside contractors for such large and complex projects. Specialized construction contractors maintained equipment that they could readily move from job site to job site. Likewise, they could transfer skilled employees as needed from one railroad's project to another. At that time, Drake & Stratton was also rehabilitating the PRR's Spruce Creek Tunnel near Altoona, which dated to 1850, while Kerbaugh was responsible for building the new PRR passenger station in Pittsburgh, along with realigning stretches of

the railroad's right of way through the Appalachians. Altogether, the two Philadelphia-based companies employed more than four thousand workers on various projects along the PRR.[115]

On May 1, 1900, work began on the third incarnation of the Rockville Bridge. As the Susquehanna River was quite shallow, it was relatively easy for workers to construct cofferdams that enabled skilled Italian stonemasons to lay some 220,000 tons of Pennsylvania sandstone that composed the visible facings of the bridge. They then filled the interior with concrete, using some 600,000 barrels of cement in the process. Work proceeded quickly, with only short interruptions during bitter winter weather. On March 30, 1902, the eastbound *Atlantic Express* became the first train to cross the new structure. Additional work to realign the approach tracks and construct "flying junctions" with the Northern Central continued into 1903.[116]

Not all of Brown's bridges were stone, however, and the chief engineer employed steel in locations where cost, the height of the bridge, or the inability to block a navigable channel precluded the use of stone arches—whatever was required to maintain the free flow of traffic. The Port Perry Bridge over the Monongahela River at Pittsburgh provided one example. Built between 1902 and 1903, the structure relied on steel trusses atop stone piers. Brown was less certain about the virtues of concrete. Even though the third Rockville Bridge consisted of a concrete core faced with a stone shell, Brown was, in general, suspicious of the new material.

After Brown retired in March 1906 at the mandatory age of seventy, his successor, Alexander C. Shand, proved more receptive to concrete. Stone bridges were expensive to construct, a problem that became more serious as the onset of World War I increased labor costs and restricted the immigration of European masons. Within a few years after Shand became chief engineer, he was substituting reinforced concrete for stone construction wherever possible. In 1913, he oversaw the construction of two small concrete slab bridges along the route between Havre de Grace and Baltimore, one over the Bush River and the other over the Gunpowder River. Later that year, construction crews completed a new bridge, with a stone exterior and a concrete core, on the Connecting Railway line over the

Figure 72. In the spring of 1900, as part of President Cassatt's massive betterment program, crews began building a new, four-track bridge across the Susquehanna River. While the PRR had been a leader in the development of iron and steel bridges, chief engineer William Henry Brown insisted that the new Rockville Bridge be constructed with a stone facing and a concrete core. It remains a symbol of the solidity and the expense of the civil engineering works the PRR implemented in order to cope with rising traffic levels and increased congestion. This view, taken from the west bank of the Susquehanna River, shows a train passing over the flying junction that provided a connection with the Northern Central Railway, whose tracks branch off to the right (south), toward Enola Yard.

Pennsylvania Historical and Museum Commission, Railroad Museum of Pennsylvania.

Schuylkill River, alongside the original bridge. A four-arch, all-concrete span at Gwynns Falls in Baltimore was placed in service the next year. By 1917, construction crews replaced the Cumberland Valley iron truss bridge at Harrisburg with a more modern structure, through the simple expedient of stripping off the ironwork, encasing the stone piers in concrete, and pouring concrete arches atop the hybrid piers. More than any other act, the entombment symbolized that the era of stone construction on the Pennsylvania Railroad was over.[117]

New Routes in the East

Aside from the difficulties at Pittsburgh, some of the most serious congestion on the Pennsylvania Railroad occurred in the region east of Harrisburg. Many routes—including the old Philadelphia & Columbia and the lines that later became part of the Philadelphia, Wilmington & Baltimore; the United Companies; and the Northern Central—had been built to the engineering standards of the early nineteenth century. By the early years of the twentieth century, Pennsylvania Railroad crews struggled to cope with a steady parade of freight trains that lumbered across Pennsylvania at no more than ten or fifteen miles an hour, interfering with the expeditious movement of passenger trains and preference manifests. In some cases, as in parts of New Jersey, the main line expanded to six tracks in order to accommodate the various classes of freight and passenger traffic. Elsewhere, however, existing operational complexity, urban congestion, and high real estate costs precluded that solution. As traffic levels soared, moreover, the addition of new tracks could do little to remedy the long-standing defects in grade and alignment.

Accordingly, Chief Engineer Brown planned a series of entirely new railroads east of Harrisburg that would provide an efficient mechanism for moving freight traffic. Engineers designed low-grade routes that, as their name suggested, possessed low gradients and, nearly equal in importance, steady ascents and descents that eliminated the "sawtooth" profile that so often complicated operations and required the use of helper locomotives. The new routes possessed generous engineering standards, with broad curves, grade-separated flying junctions, and other features designed to improve the flow of traffic. PRR managers intended to use the low-grade lines to haul bulk freight, freeing the existing main line for faster passenger and preference freight service.[118]

Most of the new low-grade routes were planned, and in some cases constructed, prior to the Cassatt administration. To a considerable degree, they were throwbacks to an earlier age of low-horsepower locomotives and small freight cars, and they were thus not in the forefront of emerging twentieth-century railway technology. In the period immediately following the Civil War, when J. Edgar Thomson had advocated the construction of the Allegheny Valley Railroad line along Red Bank Creek, he had envisioned a parade of slow-moving trains that plodded across western Pennsylvania at little more than a walking pace, carrying grain and other bulk cargoes at exceedingly low rates. As late as the 1920s, some PRR executives still considered the possibility of extending a low-grade route west into Ohio, but that particular fantasy never came to fruition.[119] Long before then—in fact, even as Cassatt settled into the president's office—more powerful locomotives and steel freight cars had increased both speed and carrying capacity, while substantially reducing operating costs. In the twentieth century, new equipment and better operating practices would do a far better job of alleviating congestion than the construction of entirely new railways.

Furthermore, the new routes for low-grade freight bore witness to the heavy traffic and the financial prowess of the Pennsylvania Railroad at the dawn of the twentieth century, but they were, in and of themselves, a money-losing proposition. Because the PRR would have to bear the burden of construction and maintenance costs on two lines, rather than one, the company was bound to experience an increase in operating expense per ton-mile, at least until traffic levels had grown to a level that could support both lines. To a certain degree, therefore, PRR officials authorized the construction of low-grade lines in anticipation of future demand, and did not expect them to earn a profit on their investment in the near term. More broadly, however, because low-grade traffic traveled at such low rates, managers did not anticipate that the new routes alone would ever recoup the massive investment required to build them. The PRR would make its money on the passengers and the high-value freight that traveled over the main line, but could do so only by shifting bulk freight to new routes that were, in and of themselves, never going to make a positive contribution to the railroad's net income.[120]

During the Civil War, prior to the construction of the Junction Railroad and the Connecting Railway, Philadelphia had constituted the most serious impediment to the flow of traffic between New York, Baltimore, Washington, and points west. Forty years later, Philadelphia was again a bottleneck, as trains overwhelmed the PRR's main yards, at Fifty-Second Street in West Philadelphia. Beginning in the late 1880s, a decade before Cassatt became president, PRR officials laid plans to link New York and the main line to the east of Harrisburg, bypassing Philadelphia entirely. The process culminated during the Cassatt years, as two more bypass lines (only one of which was completed) and a series of terminal improvements enabled traffic to flow more expeditiously through and around Philadelphia.

The Trenton Cutoff constituted the first major component of the plan to bypass Philadelphia. In December 1889, during the Roberts administration, the PRR incorporated the Trenton Cut-off Railroad Company. Construction crews completed the single-track line in January 1892, but surging traffic levels led to the installation of a second track the following year. The forty-five-mile-long Trenton Cutoff routed freight trains from Morrisville Yard, across the Delaware River from Trenton, New Jersey, and then southwest to Glen Loch,

Pennsylvania, on the east–west main line. The new tracks served few towns or industries, and generated little revenue for the PRR. However, the Cutoff shaved eight miles off of the distance between New York and Harrisburg. Of far greater importance, the route featured broad curves, low grades, and grade separations with other rail lines and major highways. The absence of passenger trains and the avoidance of terminal congestion ensured that through freight would move with few interruptions.[121]

East of the Susquehanna River, the PRR main line generally followed the route that the Philadelphia & Columbia and the Harrisburg, Portsmouth, Mount Joy & Lancaster railroads had established some seventy years earlier. Quadruple tracking, begun in 1873 in preparation for the Centennial Exhibition, spread west to Berwyn in 1887 and Paoli in 1893, handling an increasing number of commuter trains. By 1900, PRR crews had installed four tracks along the entire distance between Philadelphia and Harrisburg, save for bridges over Conestoga Creek, near Lancaster, and over the West Branch of the Brandywine Creek, at Coatesville.[122] Several minor line relocations, particularly in Lancaster and along the tracks between Philadelphia and Paoli, further improved operations, but could not fully compensate for the defects associated with the engineering practices of the early nineteenth century.[123] The problems were particularly severe in Lancaster County, where a combination of steep grades (between Swatara Creek and Elizabethtown), sharp curves (at Gap), and the two-track bridge across Conestoga Creek all impeded the efficient flow of traffic.

The Trenton Cutoff proved so successful that PRR officials soon planned to extend the route farther west. In November 1902, the PRR board approved plans for the Atglen & Susquehanna Branch, a new freight-only line between Atglen, midway between Downingtown and Lancaster on the main line, and Marysville, on the west bank of the Susquehanna River, just past the western end of the Rockville Bridge. Between Glen Loch (the western end of the Trenton Cutoff) and Atglen, the ten-and-a-half-mile-long Philadelphia & Thorndale Branch closely paralleled the old main line, but bypassed the congestion at Downingtown. West of Atglen, the line trended gradually toward the south-

west. The residents of Quarryville, the only town of any size along the route, could only gaze up at the PRR freight trains that bypassed their community, traveling on a high fill.[124] From Quarryville the new line turned to the northwest while dropping gradually to the level of the Susquehanna River at Creswell. The Atglen & Susquehanna then followed its namesake river, paralleling the Columbia & Port Deposit as far north as Shocks Mills. There, it crossed the Susquehanna on a massive fill and a 2,221-foot-long stone arch bridge. On the west bank of the river, the tracks continued north, joining the Northern Central Railway at Wago Junction (York Haven) and continuing north to the PRR main line at Marysville.[125]

The PRR constructed a new freight classification yard at Enola, Pennsylvania, the largest in the world, to anchor the western end of the new line. Completed in 1905 at a cost of more than $7 million (divided equally among the PRR, the Northern Central, the Philadelphia & Erie, and the Cumberland Valley), the four-mile-long yard at Enola could sort cars coming north from Baltimore and Washington over the Columbia & Port Deposit and the Northern Central, as well as those traveling east and west along the main line and the Trenton Cutoff/Atglen & Susquehanna route. Originally built to accommodate twenty thousand cars, the Enola yard eventually swelled to handle nearly three times that number.[126]

By the time that the Atglen & Susquehanna route opened on August 1, 1906, the PRR had spent nearly $20 million ($1 million of which was for the Shocks Mills Bridge and its approaches) and, according to some sensationalistic and wildly inaccurate accounts, nearly two hundred lives in building more than eighty miles of double-track railroad through some of the most difficult topography in southeastern Pennsylvania. Construction crews had moved more than twenty-two million cubic yards of earth and rock, built massive bridges and fills, and had even created an artificial lake by constructing a causeway across a bend of the Susquehanna River.

The investment produced a corresponding increase in efficiency and promised to relieve congestion for decades to come. In conjunction with the Trenton Cutoff, the Atglen & Susquehanna created a 140-mile-long route for low-grade freight, bypassing all of the congestion in Philadelphia, Lancaster, and Harrisburg. Whereas the original route between Philadelphia and Harrisburg had a ruling grade of 0.94 percent, the new line reduced it by more than half, to 0.4 percent. Most heavy freight traffic moved eastbound, to tidewater, and the project lowered the all-important ruling gradient in that direction from 0.7 percent to 0.3 percent. By removing through freights from the old main line, the PRR improved the flow of traffic for passenger, commuter, and local freight trains while avoiding expensive betterments to the former Philadelphia & Columbia and Harrisburg, Portsmouth, Mount Joy & Lancaster route. By 1906, a new generation of PRR executives and engineers had fulfilled at least a part of J. Edgar Thomson's 1867 promise to build a superbly engineered and highly efficient "railroad . . . to the Mississippi River . . . without materially interfering with the prospects of existing lines."[127]

Despite the success associated with the Trenton Cutoff and the Atglen & Susquehanna, PRR officials balked at the cost of providing other freight bypass routes in the east. As early as December 1902, PRR engineers considered building another bridge across the Susquehanna, north of Harrisburg, along with a cloverleaf loop track and flying junction, to improve the handling of coal traffic on the Northern Central. Owing to the enormous cost involved, the idea never got off the drawing board.

In 1903, President Cassatt advocated augmenting the Trenton Cutoff with a second, forty-mile-long low-grade line linking Morrisville, Pennsylvania, with Newark, New Jersey. In December 1905, PRR officials incorporated the Pennsylvania & Newark Railroad for that purpose. The following year, Congress assented to the construction by the PRR of a new bridge across the Delaware River, south of Trenton. The project fell victim to the Panic of 1907. By 1911, the PRR board had approved a modified plan, consisting of a new double-track freight line between Morrisville and Colonia, with additional tracks added to the existing main line between Colonia and Newark. By late 1916, however, PRR officials had suspended work on the project. Aside from the piers for the new double-track bridge across the Delaware River, the PRR had little to show for its efforts. Beset by high land costs, the project lay dormant throughout the 1920s, and the

electrification of the route between New York and Washington during the 1930s eventually rendered the Pennsylvania & Newark Railroad unnecessary.[128]

In April 1905, the board authorized studies for the construction of an alternate access to Philadelphia from the west, bypassing the commuter traffic and the undulating grade profile associated with the original Philadelphia & Columbia route through Paoli. Engineers accordingly drew up plans for the Darby Creek Low-Grade Line, a route along the Darby Creek Valley, linking Fifty-Fifth Street in Overbrook to Glen Loch. Preliminary studies suggested that the project would require a significant expansion of the Fifty-Second Street Yard in order to accommodate the additional traffic. Local residents objected to both the enlarged yard and to the construction of a new double-track freight line through what had become an affluent district of Philadelphia. They formed the Overbrook Association and lobbied vigorously against the plan. After repeated postponements, the PRR board voted in April 1907 to defer work on the proposed cutoff. The Panic of 1907 precluded construction, and even though PRR engineers revived the project in 1914, they soon abandoned it once again. As a result, PRR officials had to be content with some relatively minor line relocations in the Philadelphia suburbs.[129]

Although the PRR never built the Darby Creek line, the PRR board invested heavily in other projects designed to relieve congestion in the Philadelphia area. The vital Connecting Railway link through North Philadelphia swelled from its original two tracks to four (between 1882 and 1889) and then to six by 1918. Between 1912 and 1915, workers expanded the Connecting Railway Bridge across the Schuylkill River to a total of five tracks. Mantua Junction, some two miles west of Broad Street Station, served as the intersection of the PRR main line, the Connecting Railway route to New York, and the portion of the Junction Railroad that led to the Reading tracks at Belmont. Every train between Philadelphia and points west, as well as every train moving from Jersey City to Philadelphia and points south, passed through that congested location. By the 1880s, three signal towers were in use to control the flow of traffic. In March 1901, the PRR board approved a series of improvements for West Philadelphia, including the rebuilding of Mantua Junction.

The first component, built between 1901 and 1904, was the New York–Pittsburgh Subway—aptly named, for it enabled southbound trains from Jersey City to duck under the northernmost track of the east–west main line before joining the westbound tracks headed for Pittsburgh.[130]

The improvements at Mantua Junction would do little to speed the flow of passenger traffic, however, so long as trains continued to back in and out of Broad Street Station. That facility, whose Center City location was a mix of deference to the needs of Philadelphia travelers and defiance to the rival Reading, was now so congested that it threatened to bring operations in the city to a standstill. Accordingly, the PRR built two additional stations to the north and west of the city center. In June 1901, service began at a new station at Germantown Junction, thereafter known as North Philadelphia. Less than two years later, in March 1903, trains first used the new facility in West Philadelphia.[131] In May 1903, not long after the completion of the stations at North Philadelphia and West Philadelphia, the PRR introduced a fleet of luxury "Blue Ribbon" express passenger trains linking Jersey City with Philadelphia, Pittsburgh, Chicago, and St. Louis. To save time, the trains did not enter Broad Street Station but instead stopped at North Philadelphia before transiting the New York–Pittsburgh Subway at Mantua Junction and then heading west. Even though many of the trains traveling between Jersey City and Washington used the West Philadelphia station, there were a host of others—commuter service, the hourly "Clockers" between Philadelphia and New York, overnight trains to points west, and service to the Delmarva Peninsula, among others—ensuring that Broad Street Station remained an extraordinarily busy and congested facility.[132]

Freight traffic also assumed such proportions as to merit a new route through West Philadelphia. In November 1902, the directors approved the construction of the West Philadelphia Elevated Branch, better known simply as the High Line. When completed in 1904, a series of masonry arches and steel viaducts carried freight trains from Mantua Junction up and over the terminal facilities in West Philadelphia, to the western end of Arsenal Bridge. From there, trains could continue south toward Baltimore and Wash-

ington, or else cross the Schuylkill River to reach the docks, warehouses, and industrial facilities in South Philadelphia.[133]

Washington to New York

Some of the most comprehensive rebuilding efforts took place along the tracks linking New York and Washington, the trackage that in later years would become Amtrak's Northeast Corridor. Most of the main line north of Philadelphia was quadruple-tracked and elevated above the level of city streets. Lighter traffic levels south of Philadelphia restricted the use of third and fourth main line tracks to exceptionally busy areas. Highway crossings remained in many areas as well, although construction crews did elevate the tracks through Chester and Wilmington.[134]

Even though they never completed the Pennsylvania & Newark Railroad low-grade freight line, PRR engineers nonetheless made substantial changes between Jersey City and Philadelphia. The installation of additional tracks at critical locations, begun in preparation for the 1876 Centennial Exhibition in Philadelphia, continued incrementally over the next quarter-century, and by 1900 the entire distance boasted at least four tracks, with the exception of crossings of the Passaic, Raritan, Delaware, and Schuylkill rivers. By 1899, automatic block signals protected the entire distance between Philadelphia and Jersey City. The PRR board authorized numerous line relocations, either to reduce curvature or to raise the tracks above the level of the surrounding streets, generally at the insistence of municipal authorities. They included the elevation of the tracks in North Philadelphia (between 1891 and 1910) and in Bristol, Pennsylvania (between 1909 and 1911), as well as major projects at Jersey City (1891), at Elizabeth (1890–95), at Newark, Harrison, and Linden (mostly undertaken between 1901 and 1904), and at Rahway (1913). By 1901, the elevation of a five-mile stretch of right of way through New Brunswick had cost the PRR some $1.5 million. The line changes at Newark included a new bridge across the Passaic River, completed in 1899. In 1903, the construction of a new eighteen-span, four-track stone arch bridge across the Delaware River between Morrisville and Trenton resulted in further realignments and the concomitant elimination of grade crossings. A similar span, also completed in 1903, crossed the Raritan River at New Brunswick.[135]

The changes that occurred south of Philadelphia were somewhat less spectacular. Wilmington, Delaware, home to a large PRR shop facility, witnessed several improvements. In 1888, construction crews built the Shellpot Cutoff, including two bridges over the winding Christiana River, to provide a freight bypass around the city. The New Castle Cutoff, also dating to 1888, provided more direct access to the network of lines radiating down the Delmarva Peninsula. Beginning in 1902, workers elevated the PRR's tracks through Wilmington, at a cost of $2 million. A new passenger station opened in January 1907, while an expanded Edge Moor Yard accommodated growing freight traffic. South of Wilmington, a seventeen-span bridge over the Susquehanna River at Havre de Grace entered service in May 1906, replacing a single-track structure that dated to 1880.[136]

The PRR board of directors also authorized repeated improvements to facilities in Baltimore, but they could do little to remedy the increasingly inadequate Union and Baltimore & Potomac tunnels that carried trains under the city. The development of Baltimore's transportation infrastructure plodded along about as slowly as the horses that were still used to pull railroad cars through some parts of the city. The Philadelphia, Wilmington & Baltimore Railroad had completed its first dedicated passenger station in Baltimore in 1850, along President Street. The same year, the Baltimore & Susquehanna Railroad opened Calvert Station, a small facility that was quickly outdated. With the completion of the B&P and the Union Railroad tunnels in 1873, the PRR and the PW&B established a new joint facility, a simple board-and-batten structure that hardly merited its grandiose appellation of "Union Station."

In 1886, only a few years after its acquisition of the PW&B, the PRR constructed a second Union Station, more worthy of the name. Steadily increasing passenger traffic soon outstripped the capacity of the new depot. By 1898, PRR engineers had developed plans for the expansion and improvement of the Baltimore facilities, but the death of President Roberts the previous year and the short administration of Frank Thomson delayed action until Alexander Cassatt assumed the presidency. In 1902, Cassatt consolidated the PRR's principal subsidiaries south of Philadelphia—the Baltimore & Potomac Railroad and the Philadelphia, Wilmington & Baltimore Railroad—forming the Philadelphia, Baltimore & Washington Railroad. Cassatt also brought the B&O into the PRR's community of interest, raising the tantalizing possibility that the two companies might cooperate on the construction of a new union depot. Such plans ran afoul of the Maryland legislature, which denied the two railroads the necessary right of way, while growing federal scrutiny soon forced PRR executives to reduce their influence over the B&O. As a result, B&O passenger trains continued to use the Howard Street Tunnel, calling at the 1896-vintage Mount Royal Station and the much older Camden Station to the south of the PRR facilities. Baltimore's new station would be a Pennsylvania Railroad project, although the structure would also accommodate passenger trains from the PRR's Northern Central Railway subsidiary and from the independent Western Maryland Railway. As such, it was referred to as Union Station, and was not renamed Pennsylvania Station until 1928.[137]

The construction of Baltimore's Union Station lagged somewhat behind similar structures in Washington and New York. In 1908, the PRR accepted bids for the project, and the following year officials chose a design prepared by architect Kenneth M. Murchison. Before establishing his own studio, Murchison had worked with McKim, Mead & White, one of the most respected architectural firms in the United States, and the designers of Pennsylvania Station in New York. Murchison's Beaux Arts design borrowed elements from the Manhattan project, particularly the pink Milford granite employed on the exterior. The station itself more closely resembled the structure that Murchison had designed for the Delaware, Lackawanna & Western Railroad at Scranton, in collaboration with local architect Edward Langley and DL&W chief engineer Lincoln Bush, and completed in 1908. Bush also served as the consulting engineer on the Baltimore project, and he oversaw the installation of a train shed over the seven passenger tracks. The station building measured 275 feet long and 60 feet wide, a severely rectangular design that had more to do with engineering necessity than architectural aesthetics, as the building was surrounded by rail yards and postal and commissary tracks.

The new station opened in September 1911, yet many local residents soon considered it to be too small for Baltimore's needs. The completion of the rail tunnels under the Hudson River ensured the PRR's dominance over the B&O in the New York–Washington passenger market, but with the increased business came additional congestion at the Baltimore facility. Architects and engineers could do little to remedy the geographic constraints affecting the station site, in between the Union Tunnel and the Baltimore & Potomac Tunnels, well to the north of the central business district. Like its predecessor, the station was also inconveniently sited for trains traveling toward Harrisburg on the Northern Central Railway.[138]

Corresponding improvements to Baltimore's freight facilities were fairly modest, and there was to be no southerly equivalent to the Trenton Cutoff, or even Wilmington's more modest Shellpot Cutoff. In 1907, PRR officials proposed a freight bypass around the northeastern part of the city, but Maryland legislators prevented its construction. A plan to build through Canton and around the southeastern part of Baltimore—including a substantial tunnel underneath the harbor—also failed to pass legislative muster. As a stopgap solution, construction crews enlarged the B&P Tunnels, yet those three bores, along with the Union Tunnel, seriously impeded freight and passenger service through the city.[139]

Washington Union Station

Baltimore's Union Station, for all of its grandeur, paled in comparison with the facility forty miles to the south. The new Union Station at Washington was a source of pride for PRR officials and local residents, and it went a long way toward beautifying the national capital and enhancing the PRR's reputation in the city. Unlike Baltimore, Washington boasted a true union station, one that served the PRR, the B&O, and the railroads that entered the city from the south. As such,

the project indicated the success of Cassatt's community of interest in bringing rival railroads into cooperation with one another. PRR officials also worked closely with representatives from the federal government and the City Beautiful movement. All of the parties involved were acutely aware that Washington was symbolic of the United States as a whole, and not merely another community along the railroad's right of way. As such, and despite Cassatt's pronouncements that he was in charge of the station's design, PRR managers frequently discovered that aesthetic, political, and even patriotic considerations took precedence over engineering expertise.

As the nineteenth century came to a close, the urban fabric of Washington was more a national disgrace than a source of pride. In its broad outlines, the city followed the 1791 plan developed by Pierre Charles L'Enfant, but development had proceeded in a spectacularly haphazard fashion. The district referred to as Swampoodle, north of Capitol Hill, was a particularly noxious combination of boggy ground interspersed with slum dwellings. The nearby Baltimore & Ohio station at New Jersey Avenue and C Street brought steam locomotives virtually to the doorstep of the Capitol. The biggest disgrace, however, was the Mall, which was far from the grand public space that L'Enfant had envisioned. While the Mall was cluttered with unseemly intrusions, the worst culprit by far was the PRR's Baltimore & Potomac terminal at the intersection of Sixth and B Streets NW. The B&P approach to Washington was hardly ideal, with southbound trains crossing the Anacostia River, tunneling under Twelfth Street, and then following Virginia Avenue to the northwest, a route that required transiting the smoke-filled Virginia Avenue Tunnel and rounding a sharp detour known as "Dead Man's Curve." At Eighth Street and Virginia Avenue SW, the tracks curved to the southwest, along Maryland Avenue to the Long Bridge over the Potomac River. Thanks to the influence of Tom Scott and his Senate ally, Simon Cameron, the PRR secured a prime location on the Mall, at a site today occupied by the National Gallery of Art. The station was some six long blocks from the Capitol, but it was close to the business district and directly across the street from the city's best hotels. To reach the facility, trains followed a spur off of the main line, along Sixth Street, and then traveled north, across the Mall, to a train shed that was almost as long as the Mall was wide. While most Washingtonians accepted the intrusion as a necessary cost of improved transportation, an increasing number decried the sight of trains on the Mall. Local residents were even more incensed at the street running and numerous grade crossings that cluttered their city with B&O and B&P trains.[140]

Officials from both railroads likewise labored under the burden of outdated freight and passenger depots, cramped yards, and awkwardly located service facilities, which were no longer adequate for a rapidly growing

Figure 73. The PRR's Baltimore & Potomac Railroad station, built during the 1870s, was located at Sixth and B Streets, NW, on the Mall. Arriving trains skirted the southern edge of the city, and then crossed the Mall to a train shed located in the left distance, parallel to Sixth Street. The location, while convenient for travelers bound for nearby Capitol Hill, detracted from Pierre Charles L'Enfant's urban plan. The B&P tracks, as well as those used by the Baltimore & Ohio, crossed numerous streets at grade, while locomotives fouled the air with smoke. Civic leaders and members of Congress were determined to restore L'Enfant's vision. So, too, were influential architects and urban planners who were fascinated by the tenets of the City Beautiful movement. By 1900, Cassatt and other PRR officials were likewise anxious to improve the efficiency of operations through the city, and they were receptive to suggestions for a shared terminal facility.

Library of Congress, Prints & Photographs Division, LC-USZ62-101232.

city. As the nineteenth century came to an end, railroad
and municipal officials began to negotiate a settlement
that forced the carriers to eliminate grade crossings in
exchange for the right to build new terminals. The efforts of PRR executives to construct new facilities in
Washington required a special level of tact and diplomacy. Despite their long history of poor stewardship
of the Mall, local residents at least possessed a theoretical desire to make their city beautiful. Many chafed at
the railroad's intrusive presence; campaigned against
smoke, noise, and dangerous grade crossings; and regarded as unfair the authority of a private company to
use public land without compensation. At the same
time, many members of Congress were aware that their
predecessors had willingly granted the Baltimore & Potomac the right to occupy the Mall, and they accordingly had little taste for rescinding what they had so
freely given. Because it was the capital, the national
government, particularly members of the United States
Senate, played a far larger role than would have been the
case in Pittsburgh, Philadelphia, or New York, where
the War Department's supervision of navigable waterways constituted the only effective federal oversight.[141]

During the 1890s, the unique status of Washington as a federally managed city had helped to shape
the plans of PRR officials to establish more efficient
terminal facilities. In 1890, Congressman Louis Atkinson (Rep., Pa.), a reliable ally of the PRR, introduced a bill that would permit the Baltimore &
Potomac to construct additional trackage in Washington. The legislation, which had no bearing on the
B&P station, nonetheless intensified debates about
the railroad's place in the city. The bill passed easily in
January 1891, but the resulting controversy only became more intense.

Meanwhile, PRR officials were anxious to further
improve their Washington facilities, not to make the
city more beautiful, but rather to improve operating
efficiency. They were increasingly concerned at the activities of their competitors on the Baltimore & Ohio,
who were rapidly improving service along the eastern
seaboard by implementing *Royal Blue Line* passenger
service (in July 1890) and by constructing the Howard
Street Tunnel in Baltimore (completed in May 1895).
In the aftermath of the debates over the Atkinson bill,
PRR engineers worked with Senator James McMillan

(Rep., Mich.), chairman of the Committee on the District of Columbia, to reroute tracks through the city.
McMillan was thoroughly familiar with railroad operations, as he had co-founded the Detroit-based
Michigan Car Company some thirty years earlier. In
the spring of 1896, he introduced a bill embodying the
PRR's recommendations that the B&P station would
remain on the Mall, and should in fact be expanded.
In return, PRR officials agreed to place tracks in a
shallow cut, requiring the city to build humped bridges
in order to eliminate grade crossings. Citizens complained about what many considered a halfway measure, demanding that the tracks be buried deeper so
that the tops of the trains would be below street level.
PRR engineers balked at the added cost of the deeper
cuts and suggested that a roadbed at that level would
be inundated by a repeat of the floods that had occurred in 1889. Alternate versions called for elevated
access to the Mall over a series of viaducts. Despite
more than a year of discussions, the proposals went
nowhere.[142]

As was the case on so many parts of the PRR system, Cassatt's election to the presidency spurred rapid
action. Cassatt possessed impeccable political connections, and he was well suited to working with federal
officials. He also felt comfortable with a new generation of architects and city planners, individuals who
were seeking to apply to entire cities the City Beautiful
model that was so much a part of the 1893 Columbian
Exposition in Chicago. Like them, Cassatt thought in
terms of art and architecture, of massive projects that
demonstrated American industrial achievement while
invoking the glories of ancient Rome. Of even greater
importance, his community of interest brought together the two principal railroads that served Washington, and ensured an unprecedented level of
coordination between the PRR and the B&O.

Cassatt's presidency coincided with a new burst of
civic activism in Washington, the result of the Columbian Exposition, the national economic recovery, and
even the patriotism that surrounded the Spanish-
American War. In early 1900, Senator McMillan introduced two bills, one for the PRR and the other for
the B&O, that would authorize the reconstruction of
their terminal facilities. The PRR's version was essentially a resuscitation of the 1896–97 discussions, and

reflected the plans of the railroad's engineers. The senator echoed PRR statements, suggesting that Washington was rapidly becoming a bottleneck for north–south rail traffic, and that a replacement for the Long Bridge was badly needed. McMillan succeeded in pushing the two bills through the Senate, and the House passed similar versions. On February 12, 1901, President William McKinley signed both the PRR and the B&O bills into law.[143]

Congressional action seemingly settled the matter. Each railroad was to receive $1.5 million in local and federal funds in order to eliminate grade crossings.[144] Despite the PRR's growing influence over the B&O, under the community of interest that began in 1899, each railroad was to build its own terminal facility. The B&O terminal, estimated to cost $284,000, would be relocated to C Street and Delaware Avenue, closer to the Capitol. The PRR station, with a probable cost of $3.6 million, would remain on the Mall, and the site would in fact double in size. Trains would reach their respective stations over a series of unsightly embankments and viaducts that would cut across Washington. Despite the misgivings of some members of the Army Corps of Engineers, two new bridges, one for the PRR and the other for highway vehicles, would cut across the Potomac River. Most Washingtonians were hardly concerned at the effect that the bridges might have on navigation, but they were not pleased that a large portion of the PRR's expanded facilities would be built on land ceded by the federal government, with Garfield Park to be virtually destroyed.[145]

The public protests against the generous terms of the PRR bill, and in opposition to the viaduct and the continued occupation of the Mall, soon found supporters in Congress. In 1898, political and civic leaders met with President William McKinley, intending to build a monument to commemorate the centennial of the 1801 Organic Act that had officially marked the beginning of Washington's existence as a federal district. That conference helped provoke a more widespread reexamination of the city's future, and led to a growing consensus that L'Enfant's Mall should be freed of the unsightly B&P station. One of the most ardent supporters of an uncluttered Mall was Colonel Theodore A. Bingham, a military attaché to McKin-

ley, and later to Roosevelt, and his duties included oversight of Washington's civic spaces. In January 1900, Bingham prepared a report for the federal Office of Public Buildings and Grounds, calling for the replacement of the PRR and B&O stations. A strong supporter of L'Enfant's plan, Bingham envisioned Washington as a symbol of the nation's accomplishments as a democracy rather than as a commercial center. As such, he saw no reason why the city's grand public spaces should be cluttered with railroad tracks, stations, or other artifacts of commerce.[146]

By December 1900, even as the members of the House and the Senate were debating the PRR and B&O bills, interest groups had developed three radically different plans for the future of Washington. McMillan favored the addition of a new avenue to the L'Enfant plan in order to serve the PRR station that, under the terms of his soon-to-be-passed bill, would remain in its current location on the Mall. Bingham and his fellow members of the Army Corps of Engineers, who had already expressed concern at the construction of the two new bridges across the Potomac, were determined to clear the Mall of all private intrusions. The third group consisted largely of representatives from the American Institute of Architects who sought to apply the lessons of the 1893 Columbian Exposition and the City Beautiful movement to the national capital. Their annual convention, held in Washington in December 1900, gave them ample opportunity to critique both the McMillan and the Army Corps of Engineers agendas. Their plan called for a series of monumental buildings, particularly along the Pennsylvania Avenue axis that linked the White House to the Capitol. Moreover, the architects proved quite successful in their arguments that the McMillan plan was a politically motivated sop to the PRR, and that the Corps' version was based solely on cold and impersonal engineering calculations. They argued that they, and they alone, possessed both the objectivity and the artistic temperament necessary to shape Washington's destiny. Many members of the House Committee on the District of Columbia, the counterpart to McMillan's Senate committee, agreed with the Corps, while an increasing number of senators distanced themselves from McMillan and came to favor the architects' vision.[147]

Even though the McMillan plan became law in February 1901, the continuing debate ensured that the provisions of the two bills would be subjected to considerable discussion and revision. In March 1901, in response to growing criticism of his legislation, Senator McMillan established the Senate Park Improvement Commission of the District of Columbia, more commonly referred to as the McMillan Commission. Architects Daniel H. Burnham and Charles Follen McKim, landscape architect Frederick Law Olmsted, Jr., and sculptor Augustus Saint-Gaudens served on the McMillan Commission, and pressed for a comprehensive redevelopment of Washington on the City Beautiful model. The PRR station was not the only intrusion onto the Mall, but it was the most obvious impediment to the fulfillment of L'Enfant's vision, and its elimination became the prime target for the newly energized McMillan Commission.[148]

The growing influence of the City Beautiful movement ensured that a new PRR station on the Mall was no longer a realistic possibility. As early as May 1901, Burnham began pressuring Cassatt to build a combined PRR/B&O facility at a location near the intersection of Maryland and Virginia Avenues. Vice president Samuel Rea was particularly pessimistic about the validity of the PRR's continued occupancy of public land in so visible a location. More importantly, however, Rea and Cassatt welcomed the greater operating efficiency associated with a union station, one that would also accommodate the constellation of railroads that fanned out through the South. While PRR officials had long been interested in the railroad's southern connections, Cassatt's concern increased considerably in March 1900 when the Seaboard Air Line launched plans to create a second rail link between Washington and Richmond. Cassatt was anxious to avoid needless overbuilding and destructive competition, and he worked to mediate a settlement between the parties involved. Shared access to Washington's passenger and freight facilities would unavoidably be a part of any such agreement. Within a short time of taking office, therefore, Cassatt deemphasized efforts to protect the PRR's competitive position in Washington and instead focused on the integration of the city's transportation facilities.[149]

Once Cassatt had made the decision to build a shared terminal in Washington, much of what followed was a public-relations gambit. As part of their work for the McMillan Commission, Burnham, McKim, and Olmsted set sail for Europe to study the architectural achievements of other great capital cities. On July 10, 1901, Cassatt headed for Europe as well, partly on vacation, and partly in an effort to encourage the sale of PRR securities. The representatives from the McMillan Commission were ready to receive him. All three agreed that Burnham was the most eloquent and persuasive of the group, and on July 17 he stopped by Cassatt's hotel suite to welcome the PRR president to London. Given the discussions that had transpired over the previous few months, Cassatt could hardly have been surprised by Burnham's visit. Nor could he have been shocked to hear the architect's impassioned plea that the beauty of Washington—indeed, the good of the nation—required the mighty Pennsylvania Railroad to place civic duty ahead of profits. Cassatt, summoning deep reserves of magnanimity and altruism, agreed to the proposal. That, at least, was the story that everyone involved would later emphasize. In reality, Cassatt needed little convincing, as he had long since decided that the PRR would benefit from a combined terminal facility away from the Mall—an agenda that happily coincided with one of the principal goals of city planners.[150]

The B&O's cooperation was easily secured, thanks to the community of interest. In June 1901, Cassatt appointed Lines West fourth vice president Leonor Loree as president of the B&O. Even if Loree had not been allied with Cassatt, B&O officials were in no position to resist the public pressure that favored a union station. The company's franchise rights to enter the District of Columbia were due to expire in 1910, and it was up to Congress to decide whether to renew them.[151]

In December 1901, in keeping with the terms of the act that Congress had adopted that February, B&O officials incorporated a B&O subsidiary, the Washington Terminal Company, with Loree serving as president. In July 1904, the PRR assumed joint ownership with the B&O. Cassatt ensured that the PRR's southern connections were also included in the development of Washington's transportation system. In September 1901, thanks in large measure to the efforts of Cassatt and J. P. Morgan, the PRR, the B&O, the Seaboard, the Atlantic Coast Line, the Chesapeake &

Ohio, and the Southern Railway formed the Richmond-Washington Company, ensuring the coordination of traffic south of the Potomac River. The PRR retained ownership of the crucial Long Bridge but—consistent with the community-of-interest arrangements—granted the B&O and the various southern railways trackage rights to the new station.

While Washingtonians were delighted that Cassatt had agreed—with apparent generosity—to remove PRR facilities from the Mall, they were increasingly concerned about the details associated with the new union station. Chief among them was cost. The proposed site in Swampoodle, north of the Capitol, would require extensive filling and foundation work. Cassatt naturally anticipated that the federal government would pay part of the expense. Throughout much of 1901, however, the ongoing negotiations between PRR executives and the City Beautiful adherents had completely ignored the input of Congress. More to the point, the decision to build a shared terminal had rendered meaningless the provisions of the two McMillan bills that President McKinley had signed in February.

In April 1902, Senator McMillan introduced a new bill, one largely dictated by the PRR interests, that provided for the elimination of grade crossings and the construction of a joint terminal facility. The bill passed the Senate on May 15, but House members proved more obstinate. Some Representatives decried the bill as a giveaway to massive and wealthy corporations, some opposed the use of federal funds on city projects, and still others questioned the right of the McMillan Commission to shape Washington's urban fabric. McMillan's death on August 10, 1902, removed a powerful advocate for the legislation and threatened to turn the House debate into chaos. PRR officials, anxious to move the bill forward, indicated their willingness to compromise on some of the details of construction, particularly the elevation at which the tracks would approach the terminal. They also asserted, falsely, that they had not originally possessed any intrinsic desire to build an expensive new union station, and that they were merely trying to act in the best interests of the nation and its capital city. Their arguments prevailed, and by the end of February 1903, the House passed the union station bill, and President Roosevelt signed it into law. The new legislation re-quired the PRR and the B&O to jointly construct a station, "monumental in character," that would cost at least $4 million and, in return, each carrier was to receive $1.5 million in government funding.[152]

The station that resulted was indeed monumental, and easily exceeded the $4 million minimum cost that Congress had specified. Daniel Burnham was the obvious choice as architect, given his meeting with Cassatt in London and his work on the PRR's Union Station in Pittsburgh. At Pittsburgh, Burnham had relied heavily on the work of the late Charles Atwood, and he followed the same strategy in Washington. Peirce Anderson, chief designer at D. H. Burnham & Company, was responsible for the broad outlines of the design of the new Washington Union Station. His inspiration was the Baths of Diocletian in Rome. Anderson reinterpreted the Roman triumphal arch as a gateway to the capital city, placing three of them side by side to create an outthrust entrance portico. Six colossal statues based on those that graced the Arch of Constantine lined the attic level and stood watch over arriving and departing travelers.[153] Seven smaller arches lay to either side of the portico, and additional arches anchored porticos on each corner of the station.[154]

In designing the station, Anderson faced a severe challenge in that the nineteen platforms and twenty-nine tracks required an extremely wide passenger concourse, and therefore mandated an equally capacious headhouse. Initially, he envisioned a headhouse that would stretch the entire width of the concourse, some 760 feet in all. At Cassatt's suggestion, Anderson divided the headhouse into three unequal areas, much like the Baths of Diocletian. He significantly narrowed the general waiting room to a still-impressive 220 feet, with a vaulted roof that towered 96 feet above the floor. The station's interior was similarly majestic, continuing the theme of ancient Rome. Arches and arch-like lunette windows divided the various interior spaces, while thirty-six statues of legionnaires appeared on the mezzanine level. Doric and Ionic capitals topped columns and low-profile pilasters. More modest wings on either side of the waiting room corresponded to the open courtyards that had flanked the central portion of Diocletian's Baths. The ticket lobby, baggage room, and a covered carriage portico were to the left of the waiting room. At the opposite end of the headhouse, a dining room and a lunch counter kept travelers well fed. A presidential suite, with a separate entrance, safeguarded the Chief Executive during his travels in an effort to prevent a repeat of the 1881 assassination of President James A. Garfield in the Baltimore & Potomac station.

The concourse was gargantuan, 760 feet wide, 130 feet deep, and 44 feet in height. Here, too, Cassatt advised restraint, encouraging Anderson to lower the ceiling height in the concourse to a mere forty feet. Behind the station, twenty stub-end tracks accommodated the PRR and B&O trains headed for Baltimore, Philadelphia, New York, and points west. Nine through tracks enabled southbound trains to run underneath the station, pass through the First Street Tunnel beneath Capitol Hill, and skirt the south side of the Mall before crossing the Potomac River into Virginia.

Even though Union Station was to serve as the majestic gateway to the nation's capital, PRR executives were continually attempting to economize on the project. The initial bids for the construction of the headhouse and concourse came to $3.9 million, nearly a million dollars more than Burnham had initially anticipated. The cost cutting began immediately, followed by efforts to pressure contractors to reduce their charges. Cassatt was generally willing to pay for architectural niceties, but President McCrea was far more interested in economy than in architectural grandeur. The architects abandoned their attempts to sheathe the station in marble to match the Capitol. Light-colored granite from Bethel, Vermont, formed an acceptable substitute, and was certainly more luxurious than the limestone that PRR executives had suggested. On the interior, cement took the place of terra-cotta, and birch replaced mahogany. The swimming pool and the sauna disappeared, and officials of the Washington Terminal Company could do no better than to equip the presidential suite with wicker and rattan furniture.[155]

Railroad and civic officials had hoped to complete the new Union Station in time for the 1905 presidential inauguration, but work fell badly behind schedule. In 1903, following the eviction of Swampoodle's residents, construction crews began distributing the four million cubic yards of fill, representing eighty thousand hopper loads, necessary to raise the site's base elevation by forty feet. The Thompson-Starrett Company of New York won the construction contract, and soon began pouring the station's concrete foundations. Work progressed slowly, and the erection of the station proper did not begin until April 1905, weeks after the inauguration. Construction contractors were optimistic that B&O trains could begin using the station as early as May 1, 1907, but that deadline could not be met. The slow pace of construction was especially troubling because neither the PRR nor the B&O would receive its $1.5 million subsidy until the project was complete.

Finally, on October 27, 1907, the Washington Union Terminal hosted its first B&O passenger trains. Pennsylvania Railroad traffic began using the facility on November 17. Even then, several more years passed before railroad and municipal workers had finished building underpasses, repaving streets, completing the station façade, constructing streetcar tracks, and landscaping the plaza that lay in front of the headhouse. The final element of the project, the New York Avenue Bridge, was not completed until 1931.[156]

The construction of Union Station represented only one portion of the transformation of Washington's transportation infrastructure. Along with their design for the passenger terminal, D. H. Burnham & Company also drew up plans for a powerhouse and an express building. In addition to bearing half of the cost of the Terminal Company improvements, the PRR constructed a new six-mile-long route (officially known as the Magruder Branch) through the district, including a new trestle across the Anacostia River. The Washington Terminal Company built a massive viaduct and a series of bridges that led to the station, along with a coach yard and engine facilities at Ivy City. South of the station, two double-track tunnels, one 4,033 feet long and the other 898 feet long, permitted trains to pass under Capitol Hill and Massachusetts Avenue. Much of the original Baltimore & Potomac route south of the Mall, including a rebuilt tunnel under Virginia Avenue, remained in place as a freight bypass line. Three signal towers—A, C, and K—controlled train movements.

Despite the initial misgiving of Army Corps of Engineers officers, the construction of the badly needed rail and highway bridges was soon under way. On October 18, 1903, the collapse of one span of the Long Bridge left the bridge-tender floating lifeless in

Figure 74. When it opened in 1907, Washington Union Station was the largest railroad terminal in the world, and a suitable gateway to the national capital. It was also among the most expensive, with the station alone costing $5.3 million. Although Daniel Burnham took credit for the design, much of the work was actually done by one of his architects, Peirce Anderson. Inspired by the Baths of Diocletian, Anderson used three massive arches to provide access to the entrance portico and to the vaulted general waiting room that lay just beyond. Two large wings, adorned with additional arches, extended the headhouse to the full width of the passenger concourse, not visible in this photograph. Likewise invisible are the stub-end platforms, for northbound traffic, and the First Street Tunnel, which carried southbound passenger trains underneath Capitol Hill and to a new bridge across the Potomac River. The light-colored building to the left (west) of the station is the United States Post Office and District of Columbia Mail Depot, opened in 1914. The darker-colored building behind it, in the left background, is the Government Printing Office.

Library of Congress, Prints & Photographs Division, LC-DIG-npcc-31940.

the Potomac River and underscored the urgency to build a replacement span. The new Long Bridge, completed in August 1904, and located at Fourteenth Street, SW, some 150 feet to the northwest of its predecessor, was not really that new. All but two of the twelve spans were recycled from the second PRR crossing of the Delaware River at Trenton.[157]

South of the river, Cassatt's influence over the Richmond-Washington Company facilitated the construction of a massive new freight yard in Alexandria, Virginia. The facility, known as Potomac Yard, opened in August 1906. With a capacity of more than 6,700 cars, it served as the primary interchange between the PRR and the southern railway network. Potomac Yard afforded the B&O convenient access to the South for the first time since the 1870s, when the Southern Railway Security Company had temporarily placed the region under the PRR's influence.[158]

During the first decade of the twentieth century, the PRR and the B&O had remade Washington's railroad infrastructure while creating a transportation gateway that was truly suited for the capital city of the United States of America. The transformation had come at considerable cost, with most of the expense borne by the two carriers rather than by the federal or municipal governments. The station alone cost $5.3 million. The fills and bridges on the station approaches consumed $6 million, three times what had been expected. The First Street Tunnel and the Ivy City service facilities had been budgeted at $1.6 million apiece, but the former cost $2.2 million and the latter more than $4 million. The expense of the entire project nearly doubled, from $15 million to $28 million. Small wonder, then, that PRR chief engineer Alexander C. Shand declared that he was "disgusted with the amount of money expended."[159]

The Gateway to Manhattan

Yet, in terms of cost and achievement, nothing could compare with the New York Improvements. Long before the incorporation of the Pennsylvania Railroad, New York had become the leading commercial center in the United States. Prior to the Civil War, J. Edgar Thomson had been willing to turn traffic over to other carriers, as part of the Allentown Route that bypassed Philadelphia, rather than risk increasing the power of the New York trunk lines. The PRR's 1871 lease of the United Companies, at exceedingly generous terms, was necessary to give the PRR access to New York. Even then, the PRR came no closer than Jersey City. The closing of the final gap to Manhattan and Long Island consumed an extraordinary amount of money, but created a masterpiece of architecture and civil engineering.

"The railroad situation at New York is unique," the PRR's Samuel Rea noted in 1892. "A parallel does not exist. Here is a great seaport, with an aggregate population and of commercial importance second to none in the world, separated by the navigable waters of a river from all the rail transportation systems of its country, with but a single exception, namely, the New York Central System."[160] Rea's description was not entirely accurate. Other cities, such as San Francisco, faced similar impediments. Nor was the NYC the only carrier to reach Manhattan—the New York, New Haven & Hartford Railroad afforded access from New England. Like the executives of numerous other railroads, including the Erie, the Jersey Central, and the Lackawanna, Rea was nonetheless frustrated that the PRR's great rival could send cargoes along the "Water Level Route" by rail, and without breaking bulk, all the way to Manhattan. The NYC's passengers could likewise ride in comfort all the way to their destination at Grand Central Depot. By the time Rea voiced his complaint in 1892, NYC officials were planning an extensive rebuilding and expansion of their two-decade-old structure, an action that was certain to further solidify their dominant position in the New York passenger market.

PRR personnel, in contrast, dispatched freight and passenger traffic across New York Harbor in a veritable armada of ferries, tugs, barges, and other watercraft. For forty years, they struggled to develop a better system. Alexander J. Cassatt put it best when, on his ascension to the presidency of the Pennsylvania Railroad in 1899, he famously said (or at least was widely reported to have said) "that he had been unable to reconcile himself to the idea that a railroad system like the Pennsylvania should be prevented from entering the most important and populous city in the country by a river less than one mile wide."[161]

Yet the Hudson was no ordinary river. Its turbulent, Adirondack-fed, winter-ice-choked waters had frustrated all attempts to fling a bridge over them or, even more audaciously, to tunnel under them. By the end of the nineteenth century, ten railroads delivered 1,200 trains a day to the wrong side of the Hudson, forcing eighty million passengers a year to cross to Manhattan by ferry. The PRR's New York–bound passengers arrived by train at the Jersey City terminal, the former New Jersey Rail Road & Transportation Company facility at Exchange Place, dating to 1858. Between 1873 and 1874, not long after the Pennsylvania Railroad leased the United Companies, construction crews built a new station at the same site, with twelve tracks and four ferry slips. The structure lasted barely a decade before suffering extensive damage in a gas explosion and subsequent fire in August 1884.[162]

Over the next eight years, the PRR completed a number of repairs and improvements to the facility and the surrounding trackage. The former New Jersey Rail Road line into Exchange Place ran in the median of Railroad Avenue, crossing numerous side streets along the way, increasing congestion and giving Jersey City a reputation as the city with the most dangerous roads in the United States. PRR officials refused to bear the entire cost of elevating the tracks above street level, and they spent fifteen years in negotiations with the Jersey City Board of Public Works. In 1887, workers carved away another chunk of Bergen Hill in order to realign the route to the terminal, producing a new round of discussions about the elevation of other tracks in the area. The issue was not finally resolved until 1891, when the PRR constructed an elevated structure along Railroad Avenue.[163]

At the water's edge, PRR chief engineer William H. Brown supervised the construction of a massive new station. The facility was more utilitarian than beautiful, and it was notable for a small arch-roofed waiting room parallel to the river and, behind it, a massive arched train shed perpendicular to the water. It was the widest single-span train shed in the world, until it was eclipsed by the one at Broad Street Station in Philadelphia. Designed by bridge engineer Charles Conrad Schneider, the train shed was 256 feet wide and more than 652 feet long, covering twelve tracks and six platforms. Double-deck walkways provided speedy access to the ferries that called at the five slips. To accommodate the many train and engine movements—more than two thousand per day—engineers installed a Westinghouse electro-pneumatic interlocking system, at "A" Tower. More than one hundred signals regulated traffic in the area south and west of Exchange Place as part of the widespread installation of automatic block signaling along the lines between Jersey City, Philadelphia, and west as far as Paoli. By the time that work was completed in 1892, the PRR Jersey City terminal was larger than any other station in the area, larger even than the New York Central's Grand Central Depot in Manhattan.[164]

Whether they arrived at the Exchange Place terminal on a glamorous long-distance train, such as the *Pennsylvania Limited* or the *New York and Florida Special,* or on a lowly local run, most travelers continued across the Hudson River to Manhattan. With many eminent civil engineers insisting that neither a tunnel nor a bridge was practicable, the PRR continued to rely on a fleet of watercraft that transported passengers and freight across New York Harbor. The 1871 United Companies lease brought into the PRR family eight ferries, forty-three canal boats, and an equal number of barges and steamboats.[165] From Jersey City, the PRR offered service to termini at Cortlandt Street in Lower Manhattan and, farther north, at the foot of Desbrosses Street. The fleet grew larger in 1877, when PRR officials contracted with David Butterfield, the son of American Express Company vice president John Butterfield, to establish the Brooklyn Annex Ferry Company. In 1897, the PRR gained outright control of the firm, renaming it the Pennsylvania Annex Company. Massive ferries capable of accommodating as many as two thousand passengers, along with horses and wagons, crossed the Hudson every ten minutes during the day and four times an hour through the night. In 1897, the PRR established a ferry between Exchange Place and the foot of Twenty-Third Street, which soon became the primary crossing for long-distance passengers bound to or from Manhattan. At times, the PRR also operated ferry service to piers at Thirteenth Street and Thirty-Fourth Street. There were additional investments during the early years of the twentieth century, and throughout the remainder of its history the PRR was in some manner

Figure 75. Built between 1890 and 1892, the PRR's terminal at Exchange Place in Jersey City, New Jersey, was not a particularly beautiful structure, but it did provide an efficient mechanism for funneling passengers between ferries and trains. From right (north) to left, the slips served ferries to Desbroses Street, Cortlandt Street, and Brooklyn. Behind the massive twelve-track train shed lay intricate approaches, protected by automatic block signals and a Westinghouse interlocking system. Off to the right, north of the Jersey City Terminal, lay the PRR's sprawling Harsimus Cove freight yards, which dispatched cargoes to Manhattan, Long Island, and the Bronx, as well as along the Atlantic seaboard and overseas.

Pennsylvania Historical and Museum Commission, Pennsylvania State Archives.

associated with nearly twenty companies that provided shipping service in the New York area.[166]

Beginning in 1876, the PRR also offered service between Boston and Philadelphia (later extended to Washington), in cooperation with the New Haven. The train ferry *Maryland*, originally used by the Philadelphia, Wilmington & Baltimore to shift cars across the Susquehanna River at Havre de Grace, was rebuilt for the run between the Jersey City terminal and the New Haven's Harlem River piers at 130th Street. The service, which continued until 1912, offered an alternative to passenger trains operating over the short-

lived Poughkeepsie Bridge Route to the west. At times, the PRR even offered excursions up the Hudson River, enabling residents from Philadelphia and intermediate New Jersey points to ride the rails to Exchange Place and continue upriver to destinations such as West Point.[167]

Less noticeable, perhaps, was the fleet of PRR tugs, barges, lighters, scows, and car floats that carried freight across New York Harbor. For the last quarter of the nineteenth century, cargoes typically passed through the Meadows Yard, located in Kearney, before arriving at the Harsimus Cove facility, sited just north of the Jersey City terminal. Harsimus, whose construction—with PRR support—antedated the lease of the United Companies, included a granary operated by the New Jersey Warehouse & Guaranty Company, a stock yard managed by the Central Stock Yard & Transit Company, and coal piers that were under the supervision of the Berwind-White Coal Mining Company. Although a large portion of the freight was transferred to coastal or oceangoing vessels, much of the traffic, particularly produce, crossed the Hudson River. The PRR's freight facilities in Manhattan were far less extensive than those operated by the New York Central, but they nonetheless included piers at Battery Place, Morris Street, Cortlandt Street, and Twelfth Avenue at West Thirty-Fifth Street. The PRR's watercraft also traveled around the Battery to Long Island City or to the New Haven yards at Port Morris in the Bronx. Some freight, particularly coal, followed the East River into Long Island Sound for delivery to New England destinations, typically in conjunction with the New Haven. Most coal, however, was transferred to barges and other coastal vessels at South Amboy, while much of the high-grade fuel for ships' bunkers went through the Berwind-White facility at Harsimus Cove.[168]

The PRR's investments in its New York terminal facilities could not keep pace with the area's rapid growth. During the last three decades of the nineteenth century, the number of people living in New York City more than doubled, while the outlying counties grew at an even faster rate. In the city proper, the population increased from 942,292 in 1870 to more than 1.5 million two decades later. Despite the depression of the 1890s, the city's population rose by more than a third during that decade. A greater transformation occurred on January 1, 1898. After long and acrimonious debate, the state legislature combined ninety-six independent municipalities into Greater New York, instantly doubling the city's population to nearly 3.4 million. New Yorkers hoped that the consolidation might cure any number of urban ills, from poverty and overcrowding, to an inadequate water supply, to the disorganized transfer of freight and passengers across the Hudson River.[169]

Freight traffic in the New York area increased rapidly during the late nineteenth century, overtaxing the PRR's facilities at Harsimus Cove. While the Jersey City docks were ideally positioned for delivering shipments to Manhattan, lighters and car floats bound for Long Island crossed in front of the busy ferry terminal at Exchange Place. They then ran a gauntlet that included Jersey Central and Staten Island ferries, as well as hundreds of other freight and passenger vessels, including oceangoing steamships, making the transfer of freight both difficult and dangerous.[170]

Passenger traffic across the Hudson and East rivers also increased more rapidly than the growth in the area's population. By the turn of the century PRR ferries carried more than 8.2 million of the 70 million passengers who crossed the Hudson each year. Yet, that was less than half of the number who transited the East River. Many of those who worked in Manhattan preferred to live on Long Island, and their commute became considerably easier after the opening of the Brooklyn Bridge in 1883. The bridge alone could not accommodate the daily surge of commuter traffic, and various companies maintained a system of ferries rivaling those that operated on the Hudson. While PRR officials had no accurate count of the number of ferry passengers crossing the East River, they estimated that between nine and ten million (out of some 143 million) avoided the Brooklyn Bridge every year as they journeyed between Manhattan and Long Island. By 1907 Manhattan had attained a population density of 157 people per acre, providing ample incentive for the ongoing exodus to Brooklyn or to Queens, where the population densities were no more than three persons per acre. While streetcars and elevated railways carried many commuters to and from their Long Island homes, an increasing number headed farther east, riding the Long Island Rail Road to more distant communities.[171]

The Long Island Rail Road: From New England Gateway to Commuter Line

By the beginning of the twentieth century, the Long Island Rail Road had developed a flourishing commuter business, and the company soon became a part of the PRR empire and a key element in the New York Improvements. The company's origins dated to an 1834 charter issued by the New York State legislature.

At a time when New York was still a compact, walkable city, the promoters of the LIRR had no anticipation of commuter traffic. Instead, they envisioned rapid rail and water service between New York and Boston. They acquired the two-year-old Brooklyn & Jamaica Rail Road, and then built west to Greenport, near the northeastern tip of Long Island. From there, steamboats crossed Long Island Sound to Stonington, Connecticut, providing access to Boston while obviating the expense of building a rail line along the Connecticut shore north of New York City. The line to Greenport opened in 1844, but never lived up to expectations. Many passengers preferred the fast and comfortable vessels that plied the waters of Long Island Sound, making a direct voyage between Manhattan and Boston, and avoiding two ferry transfers and a lengthy rail trip. In 1848, the New York & New Haven Railroad completed the last link in a continuous rail line between New York and Boston, dooming the Long Island service. By 1850, the LIRR was bankrupt, and the company spent the next few decades in poor financial circumstances. In the westernmost portion of Long Island, commuter traffic generated predictable revenues. To the east, however, sparsely developed farmlands generated only modest seasonal business. Even worse, during the 1860s and 1870s, promoters engaged in a frenzy of speculative overbuilding, and in some cases three independent companies served essentially the same route. In 1876, manufacturer Conrad Poppenhusen and his family, backed by J. P. Morgan, gained control of the Long Island Rail Road and folded in many of the competing lines. The Poppenhusen empire collapsed the following year, leaving Drexel, Morgan & Company the dominant owner of a none-too-valuable railroad.[172]

Austin Corbin, a banker, real-estate developer, and railroad speculator, helped revive the fortunes of the Long Island Rail Road. He was responsible for developing the community of Manhattan Beach on Long Island, and his decision to ban Jews from his resort provided great fodder for his journalistic critics. His merciless dealings likewise earned him many enemies within the business community.[173] During the late 1870s, Corbin acquired several rail lines in the vicinity of Manhattan Beach and threatened to build a competing rail line alongside the LIRR. In November 1880, he and his fellow investors purchased enough LIRR stock, principally from J. P. Morgan, to give them control of the company. As the Long Island's president from the beginning of 1881 until his death in 1896, Corbin reorganized the company, imposing financial discipline, raising additional capital, and improving service.

Most LIRR commuters bound for Manhattan disembarked at Hunter's Point (Long Island City) in Queens, a facility that opened in 1861 and was rebuilt and expanded six times between 1870 and 1885. In 1890, the LIRR began construction of a massive new terminal complex, a structure that was consumed by fire in 1902. Less important was the terminal at Flatbush Avenue in Brooklyn, a mile inland from the East River. During the 1830s, when constructing the Brooklyn & Jamaica Rail Road through what was then largely open countryside, workers had laid rails alongside the route of the Brooklyn, Jamaica & Flatbush Turnpike. By the time of the Civil War, the railroad had relaid the tracks directly down the center of Atlantic Avenue, from the Flatbush Avenue terminal west to the Brooklyn city limits, a distance of about five miles. Between 1861 and 1877, municipal officials banned the use of steam locomotives within city limits, requiring passengers to ride behind plodding horses. Even during the Corbin years, when steam locomotives were again permitted, commuters faced a streetcar ride (later replaced by an elevated railroad) west of Flatbush Avenue. The opening of the Brooklyn Bridge in 1883 and the subsequent completion of the New York & Brooklyn Bridge Railway did little to alleviate the awkward connections at Flatbush Avenue.[174]

By 1900, the LIRR operated a dense rail network that encompassed more than 370 route miles, yet the company lacked direct rail access to Manhattan, the destination of most of its passengers. The absence of a rail link between Long Island and the mainland also affected Corbin's ambition to establish coordinated rail-water operations that would link New York with Europe. By 1896, construction crews had completed a line to Montauk Point, on the South Fork of the island, and were poised to begin the development of a deepwater port at Fort Pond Bay. Despite Corbin's insistence that the route would reduce the time needed for transatlantic crossings by as much as a day, the scheme failed, and the planned deepwater port at Montauk Point was never completed. Corbin nonetheless eagerly sought rail access to Manhattan, a dream shared by many of the commuters who rode the LIRR. That dream would not be fulfilled, however, until it meshed with the longstanding ambitions of PRR executives to reach Manhattan from the other direction, across the Hudson River.

Tunnel or Bridge: Antecedents to the New York Improvements

There were only two alternatives to the use of watercraft for the transportation of freight and passengers across New York Harbor. One was a tunnel, and the other, a bridge. During the late nineteenth century, most engineers dismissed a railway tunnel under the Hudson River as utterly impracticable for two reasons. The first was that a thick bed of silt lay at the bottom of the river, and any attempt to drive a tunnel through that quivering morass would be inviting disaster. A tunnel through the more solid strata that lay a hundred feet or more below the water would produce unacceptably steep grades and put the terminal far below the streets of Manhattan. The second problem, equally vexing, was that a tunnel from New Jersey, under the Hudson, and then under the East River to Long Island would be more than five miles in length. Steam locomotives would quickly fill the tunnels with smoke, asphyxiating crew and passengers alike.

Those who doubted the wisdom of a tunnel pointed to the sad experience of De Witt Clinton Haskin, who had gained both engineering expertise and a modest fortune while building railroads in California. He had observed James B. Eads's use of pneumatic caissons in order to excavate the foundations for the St. Louis Bridge, and he saw no reason why the same technique, turned on its side, could not burrow under the Hudson. In 1873, Haskin incorporated the Hudson Tunnel Railroad, proposing to dig a tunnel from Jersey City to Morton Street in Lower Manhattan. Earlier in the century, Marc Isambard Brunel had developed a shield for the construction of a tunnel under the River Thames, patenting the device in 1818. A tunnel shield, basically a hollow tube with a series of gates at the

front end, provided temporary support during the excavation process. Workers using hydraulic jacks would push the shield forward through the soft earth, removing the silt, clay, and gravel—a mixture typically referred to as "muck"—that oozed through the gates. As the shield advanced, laborers would line sections of the tunnel with bricks or cast-iron rings. The Thames Tunnel opened to foot traffic in 1843, proving the efficacy of the shield method of tunneling. Haskin was nonetheless anxious to avoid the complexity and expense associated with a shield, and he announced that he intended to rely solely on compressed air to support the tunnel during construction. Skeptics, unconvinced that the riverbed clays were sufficiently firm to eliminate the need for a shield, predicted disaster.[175]

PRR officials had shied away from direct involvement with Haskin, but they nonetheless watched his project with considerable interest. Construction began in 1879 and, for a time, workers made excellent progress. On July 21, 1880, their luck ran out, and a blowout flooded the tunnel and killed twenty people. Haskin attempted to keep the project going, but by 1887 he had conceded defeat. Between 1889 and 1891, British investors funded further work on Haskin's tunnel before they too abandoned the project. By 1891, as the last tunnel workers gave up in disgust, the PRR managers had also lost hope that trains could travel under the Hudson River.[176]

The failure of the Haskin tunnel coincided with a surge of interest in bridges. Construction on the Brooklyn Bridge began in 1870, and its steady progress convinced many engineers that a larger span could surmount the Hudson River as well. One of those experts was Gustav Lindenthal, a European émigré who worked briefly for the Keystone Bridge Company before serving as a consulting engineer, based in Pittsburgh. He was responsible for several major spans, including the Smithfield Street Bridge across the Monongahela River, completed in 1883, and the Seventh Street Bridge across the Allegheny River, opened the following year. It was during that time that he met Samuel Rea, then a principal assistant engineer to third vice president Joseph N. Du Barry, and the two men became close friends.[177]

In 1884, the year after the Brooklyn Bridge opened, Lindenthal advocated a suspension bridge spanning the Hudson, between Desbrosses Street and either Jersey City or Hoboken. The proposed structure was as massive as it was impracticable. A single main span would stretch for 2,850 feet, more than twice the corresponding distance on the Brooklyn Bridge. Somehow, trains would have to climb up to a deck that towered 135 feet above mean high tide. Even at a stiff 2.5 percent grade, that would require an approach more than a mile long—difficult on the New Jersey side, but virtually impossible in Manhattan. Assuming that they made it onto the structure, trains likely could not have coped with the flexing of the bridge deck—the same problem that, for a time, restricted trains moving across the Brooklyn Bridge to cable haulage. Even if the engineering challenges could have been surmounted, the cost—estimated at well over $50 million—was astronomical.[178]

Despite the impracticality of Lindenthal's design, PRR officials considered it a possible substitute for Haskin's disastrously failed tunnel project. In 1884, when Lindenthal first proposed a bridge over the Hudson River, Rea soon informed President Roberts of the plan. During the spring of 1887, Rea traveled to London and wrote an extensive report on that city's railroad terminals and its Underground lines. He was not yet convinced that a tunnel beneath the Hudson River was feasible, particularly in light of the failure of the Haskin project, but he was impressed with the grandeur of Charing Cross Station and hoped that a similar "grand terminal station with a bridge over the North River would indeed be the gateway to New York. We say a bridge, because the underlying strata of the North River will not permit the construction of a tunnel on admissible gradients for heavy traffic, and for fast trains, which of course would be essential requisites."[179] By default, if for no other reason, Lindenthal's bridge seemed the best way to reach Manhattan.

By 1890, Rea and Pennsylvania Railroad president George Brooke Roberts were among the incorporators of the North River Bridge Company (the use of "North" dated back to Dutch Colonial times, distinguishing the Hudson from the "South," or Delaware, River). Roberts had his doubts about the viability of the Lindenthal plan, but hoped that it might someday offer the PRR direct access to Manhattan. Rea, who was temporarily absent from the PRR while working

on the Baltimore Belt Line, was also dubious about the chances for success. He was nonetheless willing to lend his support, largely because of his friendship with Lindenthal. In addition to owning stock in the North River Bridge Company, Rea had helped overcome War Department opposition to the construction of a massive bridge across a navigable waterway. Despite the participation of Pennsylvania Railroad executives, the North River Bridge was not a PRR project. The terms of the federal charter required that all of the railroads serving New Jersey would have equal access rights. Furthermore, PRR officials were anxious to share the enormous cost with other carriers. Accordingly, Lindenthal suggested that the bridge would have fourteen tracks, ten for conventional railroad equipment, and the remainder for rapid transit. He estimated that nine hundred thousand railroad cars would be conveyed across the bridge each year, only two hundred thousand of which would be for the PRR.[180]

Within two years, however, Rea began to consider alternatives to the North River Bridge. In 1892, Cassatt arranged for Rea to return to the PRR, as an assistant to President Roberts, and suggested that Rea combine an already planned trip to Europe with a study of London's transportation infrastructure. The city's railways had changed markedly during the five years that had elapsed since Rea's 1887 visit. London's Metropolitan Railway, opened in 1863, had been the first of the subways, but it relied on steam rather than electric power. Even though the line was built at a shallow depth, with frequent openings for ventilation, passengers endured a hellish subterranean nightmare of smoke and soot. Rea observed that "the [initial] underground railways of the Metropolitan Companies in London, as at present operated, are dingy, smoky, dirty, and disagreeable, and certainly no one rides through them by choice."[181]

As Rea discovered, electricity proved the salvation of the Underground system. In 1884 and 1887, Parliament had enacted legislation that prohibited the use of steam locomotives in subways. When Rea arrived for his second visit in 1892, the change was notable. Two years earlier, the City & South London Railway opened a route, more than three miles long, including a section below the Thames. More important, it was the first Underground line to rely on electric power, permitting reliable operation and keeping the tunnels entirely free of smoke. "The real secret of the success of the [City & South London] system lies in the fact that the trains are propelled by electricity," Rea concluded, "and that the coal-burning locomotives are excluded from the tunnels."[182] The new electrified lines, Rea noted favorably, had gone deep, beneath building foundations and buried utilities. Even more enticingly, Rea arrived in London just as the success of the City & South London project was launching an underground railway boom that in turn spurred commercial development near stations.

Rea listened intently as the company's engineers, Benjamin Baker and James Henry Greathead, explained the details of the project to him. Greathead was particularly knowledgeable regarding the use of an improved tunnel shield that he had developed for the construction of the Tower Subway in 1869 and 1870.[183] Most of the City & South London route was built using the cut-and-cover method and did not require the use of a tunnel shield, but Greathead's techniques had proved that underwater tunneling was feasible.

Rea was entranced that the Underground system linked together many of the mainline surface railroad termini in London into a unified transportation system. His mind leaping three thousand miles across the Atlantic, Rea believed that the London system would work well in the American context, transferring passengers between the PRR's Jersey City rail terminal and various destinations in Manhattan. Rea felt that the City & South London line, "with its narrow tunnels, small cars and locomotives, does not impress one favorably when compared with the steam railways," but noted that "the engine builders state that they can furnish electric locomotives that will haul a train twice the size of those on the New York Elevated Railways, over grades of seventy feet per mile, at an *average speed of twenty-five miles per hour*."[184]

While his 1892 trip to London had by no means caused him to abandon his support for a bridge across the Hudson River, Rea nonetheless became considerably more open-minded regarding alternatives to such a massive and costly structure. In October 1892, after returning from his second trip to Europe, Rea wrote a lengthy report to President Roberts outlining five pos-

sible methods to reach Manhattan. Three of them "would furnish an indirect entrance, or . . . a *partial* solution to the problem," facilitating passenger travel without giving PRR trains direct access to the island. One option, preferred by Roberts, involved transferring cars across the river on fast-moving train ferries, to a Manhattan terminal at the foot of Thirty-Fourth Street. Another suggestion was the completion of one of the two Haskin tubes, with a cable similar to the one employed on the Brooklyn Bridge drawing conventional passenger trains under the river. A similar plan called for the construction of a new subway line from Jersey City to the Battery that would continue under the East River to a connection with the Long Island Rail Road at Flatbush Avenue in Brooklyn—an option that was strongly supported by LIRR president Austin Corbin. While each of the three proposals would alleviate the Jersey City terminal congestion to a degree, none was more than a stopgap solution. And, none of them were worthy of the public image of the mightiest railroad in the world. Pennsylvania Railroad executives, Rea emphasized, "should not be satisfied in simply doing something which any other railroad company may in a few years imitate."[185]

The two direct options were vastly more complex and expensive. The longest, at 31.5 miles, involved a new route that would depart from the existing main line near Rahway, New Jersey. After crossing Arthur Kill and Staten Island, it would plunge under the Narrows and onto Long Island. Trains would follow LIRR tracks to Hunter's Point, in Long Island City, and then bridge the East River before reaching a station on Madison Avenue between Thirty-Seventh and Thirty-Eighth Streets in Midtown, in close proximity to the New York Central's Grand Central Depot. Such a plan would have given travelers convenient, if somewhat indirect, access to Manhattan, while greatly simplifying the transfer of freight to Long Island and ultimately to New England. The Narrows route carried an estimated cost of more than $50 million, but its real disadvantage was its lengthy and roundabout access to Manhattan. Moreover, a tunnel under the Narrows would have presented the same engineering difficulties as one farther north and would have done little to alleviate the ferry traffic associated with New Jersey commuters.

Although he retained a favorable impression of the City & South London's tunnels, Rea's preferred alternative still involved a massive bridge—Lindenthal's bridge—that would carry trains into the heart of Manhattan, to a station at Broadway and Sixth Avenue, near Madison Square. Lindenthal's initial estimate of $50 million for the bridge kept increasing and, in conjunction with all of the other elements of the project, yielded a total price of $100 million—twice the cost of the route under the Narrows. Despite the expense, Rea considered Lindenthal's bridge "the best [method] yet evolved," and added, simply, "It solves the problem."[186]

The bridge plan was doomed from the start. Despite Rea's support, the bridge was even less practicable than it had been in 1884 when Lindenthal issued his first proposals. In 1891, the year before Rea traveled to London, the Board of Army Engineers had imposed two conditions that virtually ensured that the project would never come to fruition. One required that the bridge be raised an additional fifteen feet, to 150 feet above high tide, and the second ruled that a center pier would be a hazard to navigation, eliminating any chance that Lindenthal's impossibly long center span might be split into two, more manageable segments. Concerned about the growing cost and technical complexity of the bridge, President Roberts soon withdrew the PRR's active participation in the bridge project, although Roberts, Du Barry, Cassatt, Frank Thomson, and future PRR board members Henry Clay Frick and Percival Roberts, Jr., all offered technical and legal advice from time to time. The Panic of 1893, followed by the short-lived presidency of Frank Thomson (1897–99), caused work to be postponed indefinitely.[187]

Long Island to Manhattan

Even as PRR executives were struggling to determine the best method of crossing the Hudson River, a similar debate was taking place on the other side of Manhattan Island. Ironically, given the PRR's role in the New York Improvements, much of the discussion involved methods of connecting the Long Island Rail Road to the New York Central at the site of the Grand Central Depot. As early as the 1880s, advances in electrical equipment, combined with the allure of the Brooklyn Bridge, stimulated interest in a rail route between Long Island and Manhattan. Some promoters, who emphasized the virtues of a proven design, argued in favor of a second bridge across the East River at Blackwell's Island (today's Roosevelt Island), leading to Midtown, essentially along the route later followed by the 1909 Queensboro Bridge. Engineers suggested that the LIRR's conventional railroad equipment could not cross a suspension bridge, however, and used the cable-haulage system on the New York & Brooklyn Bridge Railway to bolster their argument.

In 1885, work began on the New Croton Aqueduct, a partly underground system designed to carry drinking water from Westchester County to the Bronx. The project suggested that a tunnel could likewise allow trains to cross from Long Island to Manhattan. In February 1885, a group of local promoters established the East River Tunnel Railroad Company, intending to link Queens with some point along a wide swath between Thirty-Fourth and Eighty-Sixth Streets in Manhattan. Austin Corbin, president of the Long Island Rail Road, was not listed among the incorporators, but he probably backed the project as a mechanism to connect the LIRR to Midtown. By August 1887, former Chicago mayor and New York area rapid-transit developer Walter S. Gurnee and his associates had incorporated another prospect, the New York & Long Island Railroad. Their plans were somewhat more specific, involving a tunnel and some surface running linking Long Island City to the vicinity of West Thirty-Eighth Street and Eleventh Avenue. Along the way, the tracks would connect with the NYC's West Side Line, with a branch to intersect De Witt Clinton Haskin's faltering Hudson Tunnel Railroad.[188]

If all of the proposed construction had come to pass, Corbin, Haskin, and their associates would have created a continuous rail route from New Jersey to Long Island, one that would have served much of Manhattan as well. While Corbin's plan differed substantially from each of Rea's alternatives, it promised a solution to the New York terminal problem at low cost to the Pennsylvania Railroad. While they by no means abandoned their interest in the North River Bridge Company, Rea, Roberts, Cassatt, and Frank Thomson, as well as J. P. Morgan and Standard Oil heir and corporate secretary Charles M. Pratt, supported Corbin's ambitious agenda. In 1891 Corbin invited Charles M. Jacobs, a British tunnel engineer who had worked with James H. Greathead on the City & South London Railway, to come to New York to construct the New York & Long Island Railroad tunnel under the East River. The following year, Corbin made changes to the alignment of the tunnels to facilitate a direct connection with the LIRR tracks in Long Island City.[189]

Fate dealt a cruel hand to both Corbin and his tunnels. Construction began in May 1892, as workers dug a shaft at Long Island City. That December, five workers died in a dynamite explosion that took place on the surface. The resulting lawsuits, combined with the onset of the Panic of 1893, soon brought a halt to construction. Even the financial backing of William Steinway, of piano fame, could not resurrect the project. Austin Corbin suffered horrific, and fatal, injuries in an 1896 carriage accident, and with him died his plans to transform Montauk into a deepwater port.[190]

Jacobs, the British tunnel engineer, long outlasted both Corbin and the New York & Long Island Railroad. Frustrated at the delays associated with the tunnel project, he soon went off on his own and established an engineering consultancy in New York, employing as his chief assistant a Welsh engineer, John Vipond Davies. In 1892, the owners of the East River Gas Company hired Jacobs and Davies to build a tunnel that would carry coal gas from a plant in Long Island City, under Blackwell's Island, to East Seventy-First Street in Manhattan, along almost the same route as Corbin's planned rail tunnel. The engineers ordered test borings at Blackwell's Island, but strong currents prevented them from doing so in either channel of the East River. Based on imperfect data, they concluded that it would be a relatively simple matter to drive a tunnel through bedrock, without the use of a shield. Instead, workers encountered a morass of mud and silt, much as Haskin had experienced underneath the Hudson River. The initial construction contractor failed, and Jacobs took charge of the project, belatedly introducing shields to cope with the unstable soil. The tunnel was completed in 1894, enhancing Jacobs's reputation as an expert in underwater excavation.[191]

The disappointments associated with the New York & Long Island Railroad did not by any means sour LIRR officials on the possibility of a tunnel under the East River at a different location. In addition to his efforts to reduce congestion at Hunter's Point, Austin Corbin had been concerned about the LIRR's other western terminus, at Flatbush Avenue in Brooklyn. Flatbush Avenue suffered from several problems, not the least of which was that it lay about a mile away from the East River and was thus hardly convenient for commuters who wished to reach Manhattan. Local residents objected to the line, originally a part of the Brooklyn & Jamaica Rail Road, that ran in the median of Atlantic Avenue. The tracks were some of the most dangerous in the United States, with more than fifty grade crossings manned by over one hundred watchmen.

Soon after he became LIRR president, Corbin attempted to replace the street running with an elevated structure, but property owners blocked his plans. They favored the lowering of the LIRR tracks into an open trench, a solution that Corbin considered unduly expensive. By June 1892, Corbin, aware of recent developments in electric traction, suggested the possibility of building a tunnel under Atlantic Avenue. The tunnel would also extend from Flatbush Avenue, beneath the westernmost portion of Brooklyn, under the East River to Lower Manhattan—particularly if he could get municipal authorities to pay a portion of the cost. Corbin's plan, like the one farther north, appealed to PRR executives, particularly if it could be extended an additional distance west, under the Battery and the Hudson River, to Jersey City. In 1896, Brooklyn civic leaders created the Atlantic Avenue Commission in an effort to negotiate a settlement with the Long Island Rail Road. The following year, Corbin's successor as LIRR president, William Henry Baldwin, Jr., and representatives from the city of Brooklyn agreed to split evenly the estimated $2.5 million cost of replacing the Atlantic Avenue tracks with a combination of subways and elevated structures. As yet, however, there was no agreement on the westward extension from Flatbush Avenue to Lower Manhattan.

The 1898 urban consolidation that transformed Brooklyn from an independent city into a borough of Greater New York placed both banks of the East River under a single political entity and made possible an expansion in the scope of the Atlantic Avenue Improvement. In early 1899, an amendment to the New York City charter permitted the granting of tunnel franchises. That June, the LIRR interests incorporated the New York & Long Island Terminal Railway Company (a separate entity from the more northerly proposed New York & Long Island Railroad), planning to build a tunnel from Flatbush Avenue to a terminus at Maiden Lane in the Financial District of Lower Manhattan, with a possible extension west into New Jersey. Under that scheme, the LIRR would remove its tracks from Atlantic Avenue, at a cost of $5 million, and build the East River tunnel, at an estimated cost of $10 million. In return, the railroad would receive the $1,250,000 that civic officials had promised in 1897. Very quickly, however, Baldwin reneged on his arrangement with the city, and on March 13, 1900, he withdrew the New York & Long Island Terminal Railway Company request for a tunnel franchise. While he still desired improved access to Manhattan, Baldwin now believed that he had found someone else to foot the bill.[192]

During the decades that followed the Civil War, New York's transportation infrastructure could not keep pace with the city's rapid growth. In 1875, New Yorkers created the Rapid Transit Commission, whose members advocated the construction of a series of elevated railways. While the Els were considerably faster than the horsecar lines that they replaced, they were noisy, smoky, and intrusive, hardly a source of municipal pride. By 1894, largely at the instigation of Mayor Abram S. Hewitt, the city had organized a Rapid Transit Railroad Commission in an effort to mimic subway projects in London and Glasgow. The commission possessed authority over all underground rapid transit lines, although not over mainline railways that carried long-haul traffic. In 1894, the commissioners selected a dynamic young engineer, William Barclay Parsons, to drive a line from City Hall to Grand Central, then north into Harlem and the Bronx. Disputes with local property owners delayed construction and forced a change in route. Even more serious arguments erupted over whether the Rapid Transit Railroad Commission would build the lines or merely issue a construction franchise to private contractors. The

commissioners decided on the latter course, and in February 1900 they signed Contract No. 1 with the Rapid Transit Construction Company. Construction contractor John B. McDonald was in charge of the firm, but the principal backing came from New York financier August Belmont, Jr. In April 1902, Belmont consolidated his holdings into the Interborough Rapid Transit Company, while acquiring various other surface and elevated transit lines. Many New Yorkers would soon condemn Belmont as a monopolist, but for the moment they were smitten with the allure of the subway.[193]

Even before the first section of the IRT entered service in October 1904, enthusiastic New Yorkers were so taken with the ease and novelty of the new transportation mode that they were planning a vast network of subterranean railway lines. During the summer of 1901, the Rapid Transit Railroad Commission negotiated Contract No. 2, again with the Belmont interests. The second subway would link City Hall and the Battery to Flatbush Avenue, more or less along the same route as the proposed LIRR tunnel.[194] As such, Baldwin was perfectly willing to allow the city to bear the entire $10 million cost of the tunnel that would shuttle his railroad's passengers under the East River. The LIRR, in turn, would construct only the Atlantic Avenue Improvement, while still receiving the $1,250,000 that constituted the city's share of the project. The first mayor of Greater New York, Robert Anderson Van Wyck, may have been a pliant puppet of the Tammany Hall political machine, but he nonetheless had no problem denouncing the LIRR proposal as a "species of dexterous jugglery" that was "little short of legal robbery."[195] In March 1901, Van Wyck vetoed the Atlantic Avenue Improvement bill, marking a new low in relations between city residents and the LIRR, and exacerbating the mutual enmity between Baldwin and Tammany politicians.[196]

The New York Improvements

As the nineteenth century gave way to the twentieth, a confluence of events had made possible the New York Improvements. After he became PRR president in June 1899, Alexander Cassatt began suppressing rebates and free passes, and brought the eastern railroads together in a community of interest. The resulting stabilization of revenues, combined with a surge in economic growth that began in December 1900, gave the PRR—already the wealthiest transportation company in the United States—the resources necessary to underwrite a massive construction project. The steady growth in freight and passenger traffic made conditions in New York increasingly unacceptable, as passengers, shippers, and civic leaders were more than happy to emphasize. Competing companies were anxious to improve their service to New York, building facilities that rivaled or even exceeded those offered by the PRR. In 1899 and 1900, the NYC rebuilt its Grand Central Depot—and between 1903 and 1913 would replace the facility with Grand Central Terminal. To the south, the Baltimore & Ohio's *Royal Blue* service was competitive with the PRR's trains between Washington, Philadelphia, and New York—so long as passengers on both carriers were required to complete their journey by ferry. With the 1898 consolidation of Brooklyn and Manhattan into the City of New York, a mechanism was in place to orchestrate the political maneuverings that were necessary to complete the project.

By the spring of 1900, Cassatt was ready to move forward with the New York Improvements, probably in advance of the PRR's directors. He was still uncertain as to precisely where the new tracks would go, where a Manhattan station might be located, and even whether the company would rely on a bridge or a tunnel to get past the Hudson River. Nevertheless, it was clear that he would depend heavily on the Long Island Rail Road, not only as a mechanism for gaining additional freight and passenger traffic on Long Island, but also as a means to interchange traffic with the New Haven route to Boston. Therefore, in May 1900, only weeks after William Baldwin announced that he was no longer interested in building a tunnel under the East River, the PRR spent nearly $6.8 million to acquire 56.6 percent of the LIRR's stock. Samuel Rea became an LIRR director, and, more importantly, PRR executives occupied all of the key managerial positions and integrated the operations of both companies.[197]

The PRR's control of the Long Island Rail Road soon created rumors that Cassatt intended to link the two carriers by rail. Cassatt obfuscated as long as he could, telling the media, and even the PRR's directors, that the LIRR merely offered a mechanism to distribute freight in Brooklyn, in conjunction with existing maritime operations. Baldwin likewise did his best to maintain the subterfuge. In October 1900, he suggested that the LIRR would build a separate tunnel on one of three possible routes, depending on the plans of the Board of Rapid Transit Railroad Commissioners. The following June, he suggested plans to alleviate congestion at Hunter's Point, Long Island City, by building a tunnel under the East River, to the vicinity of Fiftieth Street in Midtown. For that purpose, in June 1901 he helped to incorporate the Long Island Extension Railroad Company, along with Samuel Rea and half a dozen other PRR officials. Carefully staged negotiations between LIRR officials and August Belmont, Jr., established a route that would link Long Island City to Thirty-Third Street at Seventh Avenue, with a spur going as far north as Forty-Fifth Street. With New Yorkers talking excitedly about the LIRR tunnels—a project that neither Baldwin nor Cassatt ever intended to build—their interest was temporarily deflected from the actual plans being developed by PRR executives.[198]

Even as Cassatt was buying the Long Island Rail Road, he was making the final decision as to whether the PRR should bridge the Hudson River, or tunnel under it. By November 1899, Lindenthal was urging Cassatt to take over the North River Bridge Company as a PRR project. At first, Cassatt retained some hope that several of the other railroads terminating in New Jersey, particularly the Erie, the Jersey Central, the Lackawanna, and the Lehigh Valley, might join forces with the PRR to support Lindenthal's North River Bridge Company and build a union station in Manhattan. Even the NYC-controlled West Shore Railroad, with its tracks on the west bank of the Hudson River, might participate. If he had had his way, Cassatt would have positioned the joint facility in close proximity to the NYC's Grand Central Depot, with a LIRR tunnel at Forty-Second Street providing an onward connection to Long Island. In September 1900, Cassatt offered the other railroads a share of the project, suggesting that a consortium of investment bankers, including the Mercantile Trust Company and Kuhn, Loeb & Company, would provide the necessary resources.[199]

But it was not to be. As Samuel Rea recalled, Cassatt "waited a year on the other railroads to join in the project, but none of them evinced any desire to go into the scheme."[200] Engineers and executives on the other carriers, who possessed a fairly realistic understanding of the difficulties associated with a bridge, refused to participate. The only person who bothered to respond to the offer was George F. Baer, president of the Reading, and he respectfully declined the invitation. Because the federal charter of the North River Bridge Company gave all railroads open access to the structure, Baer and his colleagues were willing to allow the PRR to assume the entire cost of construction and then demand the use of the completed bridge—something that Cassatt was unwilling to countenance. The Vanderbilt associates were not merely disinterested—they were openly hostile to the North River Bridge proposal, as they saw no reason why they should relinquish the advantages associated with the NYC's superior entry into Manhattan. As a reporter later observed, "The interests of the various roads are hardly close enough to make the construction of a tunnel or bridge for joint use possible."[201] Even worse, the consortium of investment banks that Cassatt counted on for the project's financing judged the North River Bridge to be an exceedingly poor credit risk. Thus ended any possibility of rail access to Manhattan over the Hudson River.[202]

Despite their reticence, financiers harbored few illusions that Cassatt would give up. "The Pennsylvania Railroad," one of them told a reporter, "is bound to have this bridge built. It has decided that it needs an entrance [to Manhattan] and it is going to have it. . . . When the Pennsylvania Railroad undertakes to do a thing it always does it."[203] The unnamed banker very nearly had it right, but he erred in his assumption that Cassatt would continue the PRR's association with the North River Bridge Company.

The refusal of the other railroads to participate in the project coincided with Cassatt's interest in the latest European railway innovations. In July 1901, Cassatt sailed out of Philadelphia on his annual European vacation. By August, Samuel Rea had telegraphed the president, urging him to visit the most spectacular new train station in Europe. In May 1900, the Compagnie du Chemin de fer de Paris à Orléans had completed a new terminus near the heart of Paris. The Gare du Quai d'Orsay was a magnificent structure, with a soaring glass-roofed train shed. More significantly, trains approached the station through long tunnels that were unsuited for steam locomotive operation. Instead, engineers employed electricity along a distance of more than two miles. To an even greater degree than the B&O's Baltimore Belt Line electrification, the Gare d'Orsay demonstrated that a tunnel might be the best option for bringing the Pennsylvania Railroad into Manhattan.[204] Cassatt apparently thought as much, and suggested that the use of electric traction in a tunnel "might offer the solution to our problem."[205] His belief became a certainty after a meeting in London with tunnel expert Charles M. Jacobs. In September, the two engineers returned to the United States together, with much of their time at sea spent in discussions of the PRR's great new project. "Thereupon," Rea noted, "the Pennsylvania R.R. Co. proceeded to go into New York independently and by tunnel, as steam railroad operation by electricity had just then been demonstrated on the tunnel extension of the Orleans Ry. in Paris."[206]

During the autumn of 1901, Cassatt, Rea, Baldwin, Jacobs, and Davies developed a plan that combined elements of two of the proposals that Rea had suggested nearly a decade earlier. Freight traffic would follow a new line, from Waverly, New Jersey, east across Newark Bay to the new Greenville Yard in the southern part of Jersey City. Rather than send cars through a tunnel, under the Narrows, the PRR would rely on car floats for access to the LIRR's Bay Ridge Yard. From there, freight traffic could follow existing LIRR tracks north to the northern edge of Brooklyn, where a new line—the New York Connecting Railroad—would ultimately continue across the East River at Hell Gate to a connection with the New Haven at Port Morris in the Bronx. Passengers would follow a different route, deviating from the Jersey City main line at Harrison and traveling northeast on a new right of way across the Meadowlands before plunging under the Hudson River. The tracks would continue under Manhattan and the East River before joining the LIRR in Long Island City. From there, commuters could continue east to their homes on Long Island, while through passengers would ultimately be able to follow the

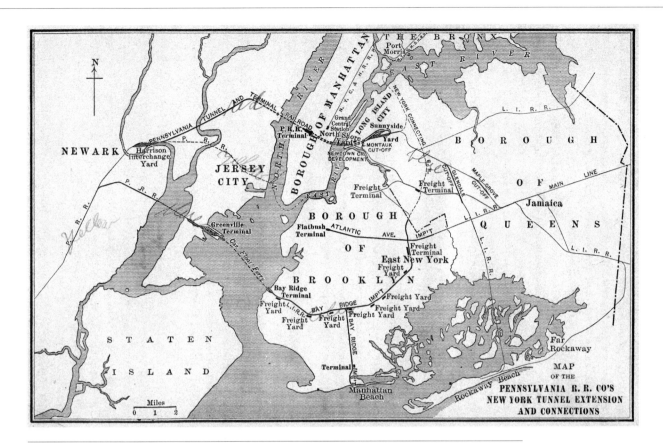

Figure 76. When they were completed in 1917, the New York Improvements revolutionized transportation in Greater New York, at a cost of some $140 million. Freight traffic left the main line at Waverly, New Jersey, and crossed Newark Bay to Greenville Yard. Carfloats carried the equipment to the Long Island Rail Road's Bay Ridge Yard in Brooklyn, where it could be sent to destinations on Long Island, or along the New York Connecting Railroad and across the Hell Gate Bridge to a connection with the New Haven at Port Morris. Passengers followed another new line, from Harrison, across the Meadowlands, and through twin tunnels under the Hudson River to Pennsylvania Station. Four more tunnels carried PRR and LIRR traffic beneath the East River to a connection with the vast LIRR suburban network, with some passenger trains continuing over the New York Connecting Railroad to destinations in New England. Sunnyside Yard, in Long Island City, serviced the thousands of passenger cars that passed through Penn Station each day. This "Map of the Pennsylvania R. R. Co.'s New York Tunnel Extension and Connections" originally appeared in Charles W. Raymond, *The New York Tunnel Extension of the Pennsylvania Railroad*, Paper No. 1150, *Transactions of the American Society of Civil Engineers*, vol. 68 (September 1910): 1–31, at 5.

New York Connecting Railroad to destinations in New England. The crown jewel in the entire project would be a massive new station that, Cassatt insisted, should be located along Fourth Avenue (today's Park Avenue) a short distance south of Grand Central Depot.

Very quickly, however, engineering considerations forced Cassatt to modify his plan to give PRR passen-

gers the grandest possible entrance into Manhattan. Davies, supported by Jacobs, informed Cassatt that the Fourth Avenue location was too near the East River and that a station at that site would require exceptionally steep grades for trains traveling to and from Long Island. With great reluctance, Cassatt agreed to relocate the Pennsylvania Station away from the fashionable area near Broadway and shift it toward

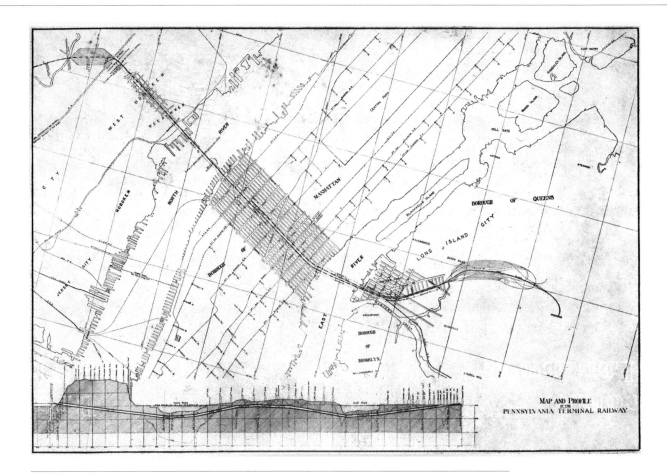

Figure 77. The core of the New York Improvements, shown here in plan and profile view, included a new route across the New Jersey Meadowlands (the Meadows Division, at upper left), twin single-track tunnels under Bergen Hill and the Hudson River (the North River Division) that continued under Manhattan to the site of Pennsylvania Station, just left of center. From there, four tracks continued east under the East River (the East River Division) before surfacing on Long Island and connecting with Long Island Rail Road tracks at Sunnyside Yard, just below center near the right side of the illustration. The profile view, at lower left, gives an indication of the steep grades and undulating course that the tracks followed in order to tunnel below the Hudson and East rivers, while providing access to Midtown Manhattan at a reasonable depth below street level.

Pennsylvania Historical and Museum Commission, Pennsylvania State Archives.

the Hudson River, placing it in a far less salubrious area known as the Tenderloin.[207]

The Pennsylvania Railroad to the Tenderloin, and the Hudson & Manhattan to Broadway

The Tenderloin lay in a kind of commercial ghetto between the financial district in Lower Manhattan and the desirable uptown areas around Grand Central Depot, Central Park, and the Upper East Side. In fact, it *was* a ghetto, a haunt of photographer and social reformer Jacob Riis just to the east of the area colorfully referred to as "Hell's Kitchen." In addition to housing a substantial portion of the city's African American population, the low-rent Tenderloin was well known for its bars, brothels, and gambling dens. In the long term, PRR officials hoped that the new station would act as a magnet for commercial development. Until that happened, the location was particularly inconvenient for commuters arriving on the Long Island Rail Road, and Cassatt could only hope that the city would move forward quickly with plans to connect Pennsylvania Station with the budding subway system. It was hardly the place where Cassatt would have wanted to site his grand edifice, had not engineering considerations forced him to do so.[208]

If there was one saving grace to the Tenderloin, it was that it offered some of the lowest real estate values in Manhattan. The area's unsavory reputation suggested that the PRR would be able to purchase the four blocks required for the station site for as little as $5 million—a bargain even in the first decade of the twentieth century. By October 1901, New York real estate speculator Douglas Robinson began buying property, very quietly, on behalf of the PRR. In December, the PRR interests incorporated the Stuyvesant Real Estate Company, a holding company designed to keep the railroad's name out of the public eye and thereby keep prices from skyrocketing. Robinson and the buyers who worked for Stuyvesant had scant hope of surreptitiously acquiring all of the parcels in the four-block area. Instead, they concentrated on the purchase of representative samples, from decrepit tenements to busy saloons, in order to establish baseline values for future condemnation proceedings.[209]

So much activity in so concentrated and undesirable an area was bound to attract attention, and the public soon learned of Cassatt's ambitious plans. On December 1, a reporter for the *New York Tribune* suggested that the PRR was behind efforts to buy land in the Tenderloin. He noted that the property was very near the proposed Manhattan anchorage of the North River Bridge, and so missed the full import of his discovery. Within days, a member of Kuhn, Loeb & Company had corrected the error, informing a journalist from the *New York Times* that the PRR would build a tunnel under the Hudson River and enter Manhattan on its own.

The story broke on the morning of December 11, 1901. With the disappearance of any pretense of secrecy, Cassatt was forced to release a statement to the press confirming that the Pennsylvania Railroad was moving forward with the project. The same day, Cassatt oversaw the incorporation of the Pennsylvania–New York Extension Railroad Company, the corporate entity responsible for the construction of the tunnels under the Hudson River.[210] Within weeks, Baldwin made a show of abandoning plans to build the Long Island Extension Railroad, and he promised to send LIRR trains into the PRR's Manhattan facility. On the day after Christmas, the Pennsylvania Railroad board of directors went through the formality of approving Cassatt's agenda for the New York Improvements, which he estimated would cost no more than $40 million.[211]

While PRR officials carried out the legal formalities, and as New Yorkers gossiped about the most mesmerizing construction project since the completion of the Brooklyn Bridge, representatives of other railroads were vocal in their opposition to Cassatt's decision to make the Hudson River tunnels solely a PRR project. In 1892, Samuel Rea had emphasized that "the railroad company that once gets control of such an entrance to New York will have much to say in, if not actually controlling, the railroad situation in the eastern part of the United States," and they had little reason to believe that the attitudes of PRR executives had mellowed during the nine years that followed.[212] New York Central managers were particularly angry, asserting that Cassatt would destabilize the relations between the eastern carriers. Representatives from the other carriers in New Jersey were also upset. None could afford to match the PRR's plans, and they feared that the new tunnel would seriously affect their passenger business.[213]

Cassatt was quick to offer his reassurances that he had no intention of either destabilizing the northeastern railroad network or of annihilating the PRR's smaller rivals. He suggested, rather condescendingly, perhaps, that the latest ferryboat designs permitted faster travel and would enable the other carriers to remain competitive with the PRR's tunnels. Cassatt was also quick to emphasize that unlike the other companies that served Jersey City, Hoboken, and Communipaw, the PRR carried mostly through traffic, rather than commuters. The PRR's station, he asserted, would be for passengers arriving from Philadelphia, Washington, Pittsburgh, and Chicago, and not from the New Jersey suburbs.[214] As Rea emphasized, the

PRR's station in Midtown was "built for the entire System and primarily for express and through passenger traffic; . . . most of our nearby commutation traffic will be handled downtown."[215]

Cassatt and Rea had good reason for their insistence that relatively few New Jersey commuters would use the PRR's proposed tunnels under the Hudson River. Ever since the construction of De Witt Clinton Haskin's long-suffering Hudson Tunnel Railroad had ground to a halt in 1892, various promoters had attempted to resurrect the project. The latest was William Gibbs McAdoo, who had enjoyed a short and spectacularly unsuccessful career as a street railway promoter in Tennessee before moving to New York in 1892. In October 1901, Charles Jacobs, at the same time as he was helping Cassatt and Rea determine the shape of the New York Improvements, took McAdoo on a tour of the defunct tunnel under the Hudson. McAdoo declared his intentions of completing one of Haskin's pair of tunnels. The project soon expanded to include two pairs of tunnels, as well as a Manhattan line north to Grand Central Depot.[216]

McAdoo solicited backing from Wall Street financiers and attorneys, including John Randolph Dos Passos, Jr., the titular head of the Hudson Tunnel Railroad Company and the individual who had introduced McAdoo to Charles Jacobs. McAdoo oversaw four interconnected companies (one in New York and one in New Jersey, for each of the two sets of tunnels), later consolidated as the Hudson & Manhattan Railroad. In 1902, construction resumed on the Haskin tunnels between Fifteenth Street in Jersey City and Morton Street in Manhattan, under the direction of chief engineer Jacobs and deputy chief engineer John Vipond Davies.[217]

Far from regarding the Hudson & Manhattan as a competitor, PRR officials welcomed the improved connections between their Jersey City terminal and Lower Manhattan. As early as May 1903, they had permitted McAdoo to build a Hudson & Manhattan station at Exchange Place, underneath the PRR's Jersey City terminal. Three years later, a second agreement enabled the Hudson & Manhattan to offer service to Newark, sharing the PRR right of way west of Jersey City. In March 1904, workers holed through the first of the Hudson Tubes, and Davies became the first person to walk underneath the Hudson River. Another eighteen months passed before the two headings of the parallel tunnel met, followed by additional work to prepare the route for operation. Not until February 1908 did paying passengers have the opportunity to mimic Davies's subterranean excursion. Construction crews were already at work on a second pair of tunnels located farther south, connecting Exchange Place with Cortlandt Street in Lower Manhattan. When the additional route opened in July 1909, traffic on the PRR's Cortlandt Street ferry fell by half. Pennsylvania Railroad agents gladly issued through tickets to Manhattan, speeding travelers to their destination and taking considerable pressure off of the ferry service. With the exception of the NYC and the New Haven, the PRR now enjoyed the most convenient New York service of any carrier.[218]

The Franchise

While the PRR's engineers were confident that they could drive a tunnel under the Hudson River, the company's managers were far less comfortable wading into the murky waters of New York politics. One of the great advantages to the North River Bridge Company had been its possession of a federal charter to cross from New York to New Jersey. The tunnel, which would in no way serve as an impediment to navigation, neither needed nor possessed that imprimatur. Instead, PRR officials were forced to secure separate franchises from each of the major political entities that lay in the path of the New York Improvements—the states of New Jersey and New York, as well as the city of Greater New York. In each instance, the PRR's representatives sought the most favorable terms, especially low rental rates and the permanent right of occupancy. In every venue, but particularly in the consolidated city, they faced considerable opposition.

Local and state politics proved extraordinarily divisive at a time when the traditional and highly localized spoils system (best represented by the powerful Tammany Hall machine) was on the wane. In its place emerged more progressive attitudes that ceded power to professionally trained experts who sought scientific and engineering solutions to larger regional problems.

Local ward bosses, particularly those Tammany Hall loyalists who dominated the Democratic Party, were another matter. They resented Cassatt's highly publicized refusal to bribe elected officials, to say nothing of his accusations that graft stood in the way of progress. Mostly, however, Tammany politicians feared the subordination of their local political expertise and control to the authority of regional planners who supported the PRR's New York Improvements.[219]

Reform politicians, including Republicans, Independents, and dissident Democrats, favored the project not only because it would improve their own economic opportunities, but also because they espoused regionalism over localism. New York City business interests, along with most newspaper editors, clearly approved of the PRR's plans. The members of the Merchants' Association of New York were particularly vocal in their disgust with Tammany Hall, their desire for political reform, and their support for Cassatt's efforts to improve the region's transportation. Decades earlier, commercial salesman William F. King had been the chief instigator for the formation of the Merchants' Association, largely in response to the system of freight differentials that eroded New York's advantages against Philadelphia and Baltimore. In his correspondence with Governor Benjamin Barker Odell, Jr., King stressed the "absolute necessity" of the New York Improvements, along with the enlargement of the Erie Canal, the construction of additional docking facilities, and channel dredging, "in order to maintain and develope the commercial supremacy of the City and State of New York."[220] The general public was caught in the middle, applauding the benefits that the New York Improvements could bring to their city, but concerned that the PRR's plans might interfere with traditional patterns of political patronage, real estate values, and labor conditions.[221]

In the midst of the intense political rivalry to establish who should rightfully control the future development of New York, Cassatt and his allies approached the three bodies that would determine the fate of the New York Improvements. One was the state legislature, heavily influenced by Senator Thomas C. Platt, a Republican political boss and power broker who was a reliable friend of corporate interests. The second was the Board of Aldermen, their number swollen to

seventy-six by the 1898 municipal consolidation, most of whom were Democrats closely tied to Tammany Hall. Their opponents were the Rapid Transit Railroad Commissioners, whose regional planners supported the reformers and correspondingly despised Tammany Hall. Produce merchant Alexander E. Orr, who had been president of the commission since its inception in 1894, was incensed by corruption, and particularly disgusted with Tammany Democrats.[222]

The individual who was best positioned to steer a course among the three political entities was Seth Low, the second mayor of Greater New York. His predecessor, Robert Anderson Van Wyck, the politician who had fulminated against the LIRR's refusal to build a tunnel under the East River, had carried political corruption several steps too far. After sensational revelations that Van Wyck had conspired to rig the price of ice, an indispensible commodity in the days before the widespread use of mechanical refrigeration, infuriated voters ran him out of office. Low, the president of Columbia University, campaigned on a "Fusion" ticket that brought together a diverse group of anti-Tammany voters. The same election gave Fusion candidates thirty-nine of the seventy-three seats then comprising the Board of Aldermen. After Low took office on January 1, 1902, he was by no means an uncritical ally of the Pennsylvania Railroad. However, he was an implacable foe of the Tammany Democrats, which was almost as good.[223]

The resulting negotiations between municipal officials and PRR representatives, while extraordinarily complex, revolved largely around a dispute between the Board of Aldermen and the Board of Rapid Transit Railroad Commissioners as to which body possessed the authority to negotiate the tunnel franchise. The aldermen had the right to issue railroad charters, while the transit commissioners were responsible for underground railway construction, under the terms of the 1894 Rapid Transit Act. Members of both bodies quite naturally claimed jurisdiction over the New York Improvements. Cassatt would have preferred to work with the transit commissioners rather than the Tammany-dominated city government. The aldermen nonetheless possessed one key power that the transit commissioners lacked—the authority to grant a franchise in perpetuity. Without such a perpetual franchise, Cassatt insisted, there was little point in proceeding with the project.[224]

The members of the Rapid Transit Railroad Commission, led by President Orr, possessed grave doubts about the wisdom of a perpetual franchise. So, too, did Seth Low. To a large degree, the mayor was trapped in his own rhetoric. In 1899 he had criticized the efforts of street railway promoters to monopolize transportation in New York, asserting that time limits were vital to the protection of the public interest. Despite Low's initial opposition to perpetual franchises, however, he soon came to agree with Cassatt's position on the issue. The mayor supported a bill in the state senate, sponsored by Oswego County Republican Nevada N. Stranahan, to modify the New York City charter and transfer jurisdiction over franchise negotiations from the Tammany-dominated Board of Aldermen to the Rapid Transit Railroad Commissioners. Livingston County Republican Otto Kelsey sponsored a similar bill in the state assembly. The legislation passed, giving the Rapid Transit Railroad Commissioners the authority to grant perpetual franchises. As a political compromise, the aldermen retained the right to approve or disallow whatever agreement that the commissioners negotiated in a straight up-or-down vote, but they would not be permitted to make any modifications to it.[225]

On May 5, 1902, Cassatt formally requested that the Board of Rapid Transit Railroad Commissioners grant the PRR a perpetual franchise, with fees to be renegotiated every twenty-five years. He promised that the PRR would construct as many as four single-track tunnels under the Hudson River, to a station that would cover the four blocks that separated Seventh and Ninth Avenues, and Thirty-First and Thirty-Third Streets. "As a station of adequate capacity cannot be built within the limits of two East and West streets," Cassatt insisted, "it is necessary that 32nd Street, between 7th and 9th Avenues, shall be closed." The new terminus would be built "in connection with the Subway Station at that point, so that passengers can be transferred from one line to the other." Cassatt, however, promised that he would not compete against the IRT or other subways for intra-city traffic.[226]

Once given the power to conduct the franchise negotiations, and freed of Tammany influences, Orr and

the other Rapid Transit Railroad Commissioners were generally willing to reach an amicable settlement with Cassatt. On June 15, the commissioners gave their approval to the franchise. In keeping with the terms of the Stranahan and Kelsey bills, they gave Cassatt everything that he requested. The PRR president in turn assented to a complex fee structure, destined to cost the PRR $2.5 million during the first quarter-century of the tunnel operations.[227]

The Board of Aldermen still possessed the authority to approve or reject the franchise that the Rapid Transit Commissioners had negotiated. The aldermen were anxious to preserve their power, and they were not willing to permit the Board of Rapid Transit Railroad Commissioners to dictate municipal policy. PRR vice president John Pugh Green sensed the "strong underlying jealousy" between the two bodies, and warned Cassatt of the need to operate "pretty carefully, so as not to get between the two."[228] Manhattan borough president Jacob A. Cantor was particularly vocal in his opposition to the perpetual nature of the franchise. So, too, was Timothy D. Sullivan, the political boss of the Bowery. Brooklyn borough president J. Edward Swanstrom—elected on the same Fusion ticket that brought Seth Low into office—was far more favorable to the PRR's interests, but his views were distinctly in the minority.[229]

On July 22, 1902, the Board of Aldermen dealt a crippling blow to the PRR's plans, rejecting the franchise by a vote of fifty-six to ten. Cassatt put a brave face on the defeat, pledging to renegotiate the agreement. Under the terms of the Stranahan and Kelsey bills, the aldermen lacked the authority to shape the second round of negotiations. Tammany leaders nonetheless made clear that they would again vote down whatever franchise agreement the Board of Rapid Transit Railroad Commissioners had negotiated, so long as it lacked adequate provisions for the protection of organized labor. The aldermen demanded such concessions as a union shop, an eight-hour day, and a ban on low-wage immigrant labor, stipulations that were similar to those already in place on the city's subway projects.[230]

Seth Low played peacemaker, attempting to mediate a settlement between the PRR and the aldermen. Yet, neither Cassatt nor Lowe was willing to accede to the demands by Tammany loyalists that the PRR do more to protect the rights of workers. Low's election had badly stung Tammany Hall, and its members were determined to regain the mayor's office. To do so, in the face of Fusion opposition, required the support of labor, particularly the Central Federated Union, an umbrella organization representing some 120 unions and 150,000 members. Low's hatred for Tammany Hall was thus tempered by his reluctance to alienate organized labor. Cassatt, meanwhile, was anxious to squelch rumors that he was planning to resurrect Austin Corbin's plan to establish a deep-water port at Montauk Point, imperiling the future of the laborers who made their living handling freight on the Hudson and East River docks. Such fears were baseless—Cassatt had no intention of diverting freight through the New York tunnels, but the accusations caused serious problems for the PRR nonetheless.[231]

Vice President Green, who was principally in charge of the negotiations with the aldermen, was willing to grant certain minor concessions, such as the installation of police and fire alarm cables in the tunnels, and permission for the Board of Health to supervise the underground workings. Green nonetheless believed that he was "largely wasting time in discussing a lot of detailed amendments which were suggested to the franchise."[232] The substantive issues, he observed, involved the reluctance of the aldermen to grant a franchise in perpetuity and their belief that the PRR should pay a larger franchise fee. Cassatt—who was vacationing in Bar Harbor, Maine, after an exhausting battle to encourage Congress to strengthen the Interstate Commerce Commission by adopting the Elkins Act—was not particularly concerned about the effect that labor concessions might have on the New York Improvements themselves. After all, prevailing wage rates in New York were already among the highest in the nation, and safety considerations restricted tunnel workers to no more than eight hours underground. As PRR officials emphasized, the State Court of Appeals had recently issued two rulings that allowed private contractors, similar to the ones who would be undertaking most of the work on the New York Improvements, to negotiate whatever wage rates they saw fit.[233]

The greater danger was that the Tammany labor policies, if accepted even once, might spread like a vi-

rus to the rest of the PRR system. In early August, Green warned Cassatt that "if the Penna. R. R. Co. agreed to this [labor provision] on the tunnel work, it would inevitably have the same question thrust at it from one end of its system to the other, and it was therefore simply impossible for us to agree to it."[234]

PRR officials were perfectly willing to play the political game on the labor issue. Cassatt made a confidential promise with Mayor Low that he would informally follow the terms of the labor clause, but refused to state so publicly. Instead, he issued a written statement supporting, in quite vague terms, the company's support for the welfare of the working man, a move that, Green suggested, might "help Mr. Cantor and others out a little in their relations with the labor vote."[235] Cantor, the Manhattan borough president, chose to appeal more directly to his constituents, however. After writing a caustic letter to President Cassatt excoriating PRR officials for their insensitivity to labor, he thoughtfully released his missive to the local press. Samuel Rea, now thoroughly incensed, composed a response to Cantor, a letter that PRR Legal Department personnel adjudged "rather undiplomatic" before returning the draft to Rea for revision.[236]

The franchise negotiations continued into the autumn. On September 3, Cassatt agreed to pay to the city an annual rental of nearly $40,000, even though he complained that "such a payment has never [before] been made to any city in this or any other country for such a purpose." He was nonetheless unwilling to budge on the labor question, which he called "unreasonable, arbitrary, and utterly unwarranted," and indicated that he could not possibly accept a franchise under those conditions.[237] Cantor, whom Green now accused of "playing the demagogue for all it is worth," was equally adamant in his refusal to abandon the labor provision, apparently "not because he thinks that it will do the laboring man any good, but because he wants to have the glory of compelling it to be inserted." Cassatt was equally rigid in his refusal to engage in "so entire a departure from [the PRR's] policy of the past [if Railroad officials were to] agree to arbitrate as to rates of wages and hours of labor."[238]

By the end of September Cassatt had had more than enough of Cantor, the labor question, and, it would appear, the New York Improvements themselves. Work in Manhattan had virtually ceased, pending resolution of the dispute. The future site of the station resembled a ghost town, with the PRR recruiting New York City policemen to replace the former tenants of the now-deserted buildings. It was, a reporter noted, "the most densely depopulated part of New York."[239] With the interminable delays costing the PRR more than a thousand dollars a day, Cassatt finally unleashed his ultimate weapon. The labor provision was a deal breaker, and Cassatt insisted that he "must resist the attempt to impose that condition, even to the point of declining to accept the franchise if inserted."[240]

On October 9, the Board of Rapid Transit Railroad Commissioners defied the Board of Aldermen and approved the franchise without the labor provision. Even though the commissioners had produced a franchise that was acceptable to Cassatt and his associates, the document was once again subject to approval by the aldermen. PRR officials waited anxiously for results of the November elections, hoping that Tammany Democrats would be turned out of office.[241]

Cassatt and his political allies unleashed a variety of strategies for overcoming aldermanic opposition. PRR officials informed newspaper reporters and editors that Tammany Hall corruption was impeding progress. The members of the Merchants' Association, staunch supporters of the PRR's plans, distributed a pamphlet that harshly criticized the labor provision. The document included protest coupons that could be clipped out and mailed to recalcitrant aldermen, whose names were included in the publication. The association also sent a letter to the Board of Aldermen supporting the PRR's position, as well as a request to Governor Odell, asking him to put additional pressure on the Tammany holdouts.[242]

By the middle of October, many aldermen were concerned that the steadfast Tammany opposition to the Pennsylvania Railroad might anger their constituents and cost them their reelection. As PRR officials informed the aldermen and the general public, the cancellation of the project would mean no jobs at all. A representative of the Knights of Labor was quick to emphasize, "It is not to labor's interest to deprive N. Y. City of this great project, simply because certain labor clauses are not contained therein," although he consoled himself by suggesting that worker solidarity

would prevail once construction was under way.[243] LIRR president William Baldwin, who understood New York politics as well as anyone, cautioned his PRR counterparts that they would need to "give a chance for many people to get down without serious injury to themselves," by providing an excuse to vote for the franchise without appearing to be selling out their labor constituency.[244] Acting on Baldwin's advice, PRR officials encouraged the defecting aldermen to excuse their votes by echoing the railroad's position that the labor clause was unconstitutional. By whatever methods, their efforts worked. On December 16, the Board of Aldermen approved the franchise. The vote was an uncomfortably close forty-one to thirty-six, but it was a victory for the PRR nonetheless.[245]

From the Meadows to Sunnyside

The massive construction effort went forward under the supervision of vice president Samuel Rea and a board of engineers. Various committees planned such matters as station design and construction, yard design, the installation of electrical equipment and signaling systems, and station operations. The members of the advisory committees reported to Rea, who assumed overall control of the New York Improvements. Rea in turn represented the views of the advisory committees at the meetings of the board of engineers, ensuring coordination among the planning and construction entities. The members of the board of engineers distilled the results of their meetings into a series of weekly reports to Rea, assessing progress to date and recommending further action as necessary. Ultimately, Cassatt and the PRR board of directors held the final authority over all aspects of the New York Improvements. In practice, however, Cassatt preferred to concentrate on the design of the station's public facilities, and left underground matters to Rea—who, based on his experiences in London and Baltimore, was well equipped to handle the responsibility. In addition to his role as a coordinator, Rea was also the individual who was primarily responsible for managing the expense of the project.[246]

On January 11, 1902, the board of engineers met for the first time, to consider the matter of the New York Improvements. Like Rea, all of the members were at

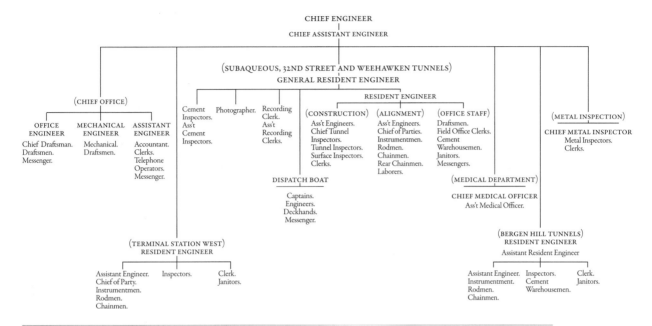

PENNSYLVANIA TUNNEL AND TERMINAL RAILROAD
PENNSYLVANIA RAILROAD TUNNELS
NORTH RIVER DIVISION

ENGINEERING STAFF ORGANIZATION

Figure 78. On the North River Division, chief engineer Charles M. Jacobs and his chief assistant engineer (Scottish tunnel expert James Forgie) supervised three residencies, each staffed by a resident engineer, and responsible for the tunnels under the Hudson River, Manhattan Island west of the station, and Bergen Hill (here listed as the "Subaqueous, 32nd Street, and Weehawken Tunnels"). Similar organization charts represented the East River Division, the Meadows Division, and the station site, with their respective chief engineers serving, with Jacobs, on the board of engineers. Vice president Samuel Rea held authority over the board of engineers, subject only to the jurisdiction of President Cassatt and the PRR board of directors. In addition to the staff officers on the divisions, line officers serving on advisory committees provided expertise that spanned the entire project—in many respects mimicking the line-and-staff organizational structure in place on the Pennsylvania Railroad as a whole. This organization chart originally appeared in Charles M. Jacobs, *The New York Tunnel Extension of the Pennsylvania Railroad, North River Division*, Paper No. 1151, *Transactions of the American Society of Civil Engineers*, vol. 68 (September 1910): 32–61, at 44.

the top of their profession. Charles W. Raymond, a West Point graduate and career Army officer, chaired the board. Raymond excelled at the design of harbor improvements, and his work at Philadelphia had undoubtedly impressed Cassatt and Rea. The greatest responsibility fell to experienced tunnel engineer Charles M. Jacobs, who served as chief engineer of the North River Division. Although he could not be present for the initial meeting, he would soon be overseeing the digging of two tunnels under the Hudson. Alfred Noble, chief engineer of the East River Division, was also no stranger to major engineering

works. He had directed the construction of five Mississippi River bridges, at Memphis, Alton, Bellefontaine, Leavenworth, and Thebes, as well as a bridge over the Ohio River at Cairo. Following the catastrophic 1900 Galveston hurricane, he helped to design a seawall that would protect the city from future disasters. Noble had served on two Nicaraguan canal commissions and had helped persuade the federal government to build across the Isthmus of Panama instead. Even as he worked on the New York Improvements, he served as a member of the Isthmian Canal Commission and the Board of Consulting Engineers,

Panama Canal. Gustav Lindenthal, doubtless still disappointed over the failure of his North River Bridge scheme, was on the board, but only until December 1903. PRR chief engineer William H. Brown was the only railroad employee, other than Rea, who served on the board of engineers. Brown had supervised the reconstruction of much of the trackage east of Pittsburgh, including the latest iteration of the Rockville Bridge over the Susquehanna River. He was well positioned to serve as chief engineer of the Meadows Division, which included aboveground work in New Jersey, from Meadows Yard northeast to the west portal of the Hudson River tunnels.[247]

William Brown, in charge of the Meadows Division, oversaw the most straightforward portion of the project. Beginning at a junction with the existing main line near Harrison (a site that was soon named Manhattan Transfer), construction crews moved more than 2.5 million cubic yards of earth in order to build an elevated right of way that stretched for more than three and a half miles across the marshy Meadowlands. Brown also supervised the erection of sixteen bridges, including a massive structure, with a swing span 110 feet long, over the Hackensack River.[248]

The North River Division, under the supervision of Charles Jacobs, began at the base of the New Jersey Palisades, in Hackensack. From there, twin tunnels extended west to the site of Pennsylvania Station, with their construction divided into three sections. The westernmost portion descended on a 1.3 percent grade,

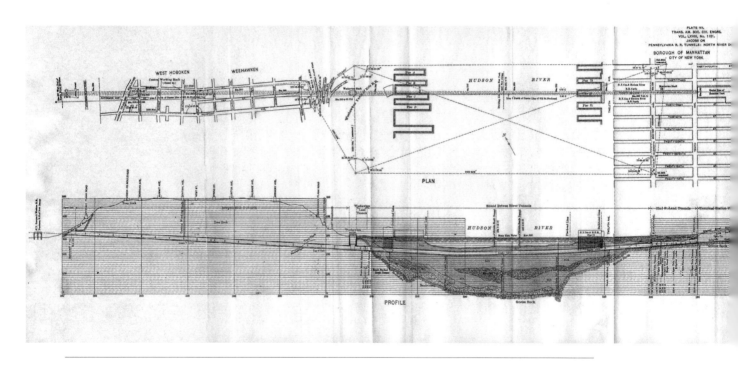

Figure 79. The North River Division constituted the most demanding component of the New York Improvements. After following the Meadows Division from Manhattan Transfer (Harrison) trains dove underground at what PRR engineers referred to as the Hackensack Portal, but which was more generally known as the Bergen Hill Portal, at the extreme left of this view. For construction purposes, PRR engineers designated the section through the trap rock of the New Jersey Palisades as the Bergen Hill Tunnels, extending 5,940 feet to a construction shaft adjacent to the Erie Railroad yards in Weehawken. The next section, 6,575 feet long, was known as the North River Tunnels, dug largely through the soft silt that composed the bed of the Hudson River, as far as the Manhattan Shaft, located near the intersection of Thirty-Second Street and Eleventh Avenue. From the Manhattan Shaft, a combination of tunnels and open cuts through the gneiss that underlay most of the island, in an area generally referred to as "Terminal Station—West," covered the remaining distance to Pennsylvania Station. These plan and profile views originally appeared in Charles W. Raymond, *The New York Tunnel Extension of the Pennsylvania Railroad*, following page 18.

traveling under Bergen Hill, the southern extremity of the Palisades. Tunnel crews worked inward from the Hackensack Portal (or, as it was more widely known, the Bergen Hill Portal) and from the base of a shaft sunk along the west bank of the Hudson River, near the Erie Railroad yards in Weehawken. Bergen Hill was composed largely of a mixture of igneous basalt (commonly known as trap rock) and sandstone. While the rock was difficult to penetrate, the resulting tunnels would be self-supporting, and would not require the use of a shield.

To the east of the Weehawken Shaft, however, the tunnel under the Hudson River ran through water-laden silt, well above bedrock. Based on his experience with the East River Gas Tunnel and the Hudson & Manhattan project, Jacobs knew full well that it would be impossible to construct the tunnels without the use of compressed air and shields at each working face. While Jacobs was confident that he could keep the Hudson River from flooding the workings, he was less certain about the stability of the completed tunnels that would for all intents and purposes be floating in a kind of quicksand. Accordingly, he proposed the use of screw piles, long tubes that would anchor the base of the tunnel to bedrock, creating a kind of bridge suspended in silt rather than air.

After rising on a gradual 0.5 percent incline, the tunnel's grade stiffened to 1.93 percent as it approached the Manhattan shoreline. A second shaft, 6,575 feet east of the Weehawken Shaft, near Thirty-Second Street and Eleventh Avenue in Manhattan, enabled workers to dig west under the Hudson River, toward New Jersey. In the opposite direction, a short stretch of tunnel ran through the gneiss that underlay most of Manhattan Island. Just beyond lay the massive excavations that would contain the subterranean yard trackage, between Ninth and Tenth Avenues and, to the east, the platforms of the station.

PRR engineers anticipated that four tracks would be necessary to connect Pennsylvania Station with Long Island in order to accommodate LIRR commuter trains and the movement of empty long-distance trains to and from servicing facilities in Long Island City. Two tunnels, each containing two tracks, would pass eastward, away from the station, before splitting into four single-track bores that plunged

steeply under the East River and then back up to the surface, near the LIRR Hunter's Point Terminal. At that location, a massive facility, Sunnyside Yard, would service both PRR and LIRR passenger equipment.

A Tunnel Under New York

On February 25, 1903, the year of planning and negotiations ended, and construction began. Workers commenced clearing the site of the Manhattan Shaft, although the excavation of its opposite number at Weehawken did not begin until June 11. Thereafter, laborers employed by the PRR's construction firm, the United Engineering & Contracting Company, dug steadily downward to the level of the tunnel. By the middle of December, they had completed the Manhattan Shaft, followed by the Weehawken Shaft in September 1904. From there, the O'Rourke Engineering Construction Company took over, pushing the tunnels under the Hudson. Tunneling on the New York side began on April 18, 1904, with work in New Jersey commencing as soon as the Weehawken Shaft was complete.

For the first few hundred feet toward the river, the tunnelers worked through rock, without the use of a shield. As the bedrock above them narrowed, they excavated four large chambers, one at each face, for the erection of the tunnel shields, and then pressed onward. At each shoreline, they contended with the further obstacle of the foundations for railroad piers—the New York Central on the Manhattan side, and the Erie, in New Jersey. Crews carefully cut away the minimum number of pilings, taking great care to shore up the structures on the surface.

Once the rock ran out, the mud began. In many cases, workers could employ hydraulic jacks to force their way forward, as the silt oozed through holes in the shield. Gangs of muckers kept the working face clear, shoveling up the mud that was the consistency of pudding and sending it to the surface. From time to time, small rocks and boulders impeded their progress and had to be pried, chipped, or blasted away. As each shield moved steadily toward the center of the river, workers installed the tunnel lining. The lining consisting of eleven semicircular segments and a "key segment" that locked together into a large cast-iron ring, thirty inches wide and two inches thick, producing a tunnel with an outside diameter of twenty-three feet. Initially, it took crews six hours to install one section, but with practice they reduced the time to thirty minutes. While the entire tunnel would eventually be lined with concrete, the cast-iron rings were strong enough to keep the mud at bay and to permit the shield to be pushed farther forward.

Tunnel crews were well rewarded for their work, and they earned every penny of their pay. Ordinary laborers made a respectable $1.75 per day, and everyone who worked in the tunnels was restricted to eight hours on duty—a shorter workday than was typical for the age. The dangers were considerable, however, and included injury or death from rockfalls and premature explosions. With the top of the tunnel so close to the bed of the Hudson River, workers faced the possibility of a blowout, in which escaping compressed air would blast upward, allowing mud and water to flood the tunnel. The more common danger was the bends, a potentially crippling or even lethal condition induced by too-rapid decompression, as tunnelers exited the air locks at the end of their shift.

Day by day, the tunnel crews dug slowly toward one another. On a good day they made fifteen or more feet. On a bad day, three. There were inevitable accidents, some more spectacular than others. In October 1904, water poured into one of the Manhattan headings, undermining the New York Central facilities just above. Four months later, on the other side of the river, irritated Erie Railroad officials watched as blasting in the PRR tunnel caused a sinkhole to appear in their Weehawken yards, claiming several freight cars.

Despite such embarrassing mishaps, tunnel workers made rapid progress. On September 10, 1906, the two crews working on the north tunnel met underneath the Hudson River. After more than two years of digging, with each heading traversing half a mile through unstable silt, the headings were one-sixteenth of an inch out of alignment. On October 9, 1906, Charles M. Jacobs led a delegation of engineers and journalists under the river, from Manhattan to Weehawken. Many of the reporters, unaccustomed to the heat, high air pressure, and generally claustrophobic conditions in the tunnel, underwent the journey with some trepidation. As a representative from the *New York Times* recalled,

"every one was glad to have it over with and even smoky Weehawken looked pleasant and inviting."[249] The same day, and only a few yards downriver, workers holed through the south tunnel. Much work remained to be done, but there seemed little doubt that the Pennsylvania Railroad would reach Manhattan.

Despite their success, Jacobs and his associates were becoming increasingly concerned about the alignment of the North River tunnels. By the spring of 1906, they had noticed that the tunnels were drifting, particularly in the vertical plane. Despite careful measurements, adjustments to the positions of the shields, and efforts to selectively weight the iron linings, the tunnels continued to rise and fall—up to several feet, in some instances. Jacobs was surprisingly lackadaisical about the problem, believing that the tunnels would stabilize in time. Rea, however, was alarmed at growing rumors within the engineering community that the tunnels might continue to sink, eventually sagging so much that they would remain, cracked, flooded, and abandoned, as a monument to the failure of the PRR's efforts to overcome the Hudson River.[250]

Jacobs, Rea, and the other tunnel engineers had made provision for the possibility that the tunnels might sink down in the silty ooze that underlay the Hudson. Every fifth tunnel segment contained a fitting at the bottom that enabled a screw-pile to be driven downward into bedrock. However, a vigorous debate soon emerged, with Jacobs and his staff insisting that the screw-piles would resolve the instability, and board of engineers chairman Charles Raymond, virtually alone, asserting that the resulting rigidity might place fatal stresses on the brittle cast iron rings. Not until November 1907, following minutely detailed measurements of the tunnels' oscillation, did Jacobs and the other engineers determine the source of the problem. At its mouth, the Hudson was a tidal river, and changes in the depth of the water also meant changes in weight. Rea, confident that the flexing of the tunnels was an acceptably routine event that would not worsen over time, eventually sided with Raymond. By June of 1908, thanks to Rea's recommendations, PRR officials had elected not to anchor the tunnels to bedrock with screw-piles.

The debate over the drifting of the Hudson tunnels was a minor issue compared with the unending series

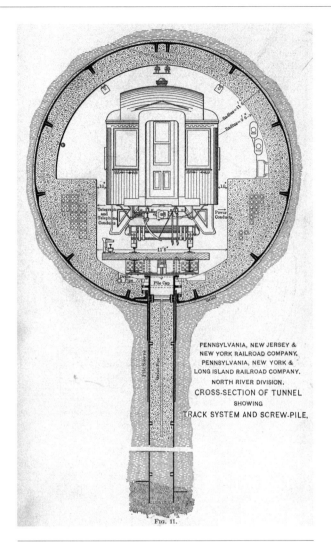

PENNSYLVANIA, NEW JERSEY &
NEW YORK RAILROAD COMPANY.
PENNSYLVANIA, NEW YORK &
LONG ISLAND RAILROAD COMPANY.
NORTH RIVER DIVISION.
CROSS-SECTION OF TUNNEL
SHOWING
TRACK SYSTEM AND SCREW-PILE.

Fig. 11.

Figure 80. North River Division chief engineer Charles M. Jacobs initially recommended the use of screw piles, long columns that would anchor the base of each tunnel to bedrock, forming a kind of bridge suspended in the silt of the Hudson River. As tunneling progressed, the shifting of the two tunnels seemed to indicate the necessity for screw piles. After considerable debate, however, PRR officials concluded that the tunnels would be sufficiently stable without further reinforcement. This cross-section originally appeared in Charles M. Jacobs, *The New York Tunnel Extension of the Pennsylvania Railroad, North River Division*, 58.

of Manhattan Island, the tracks curved to the north while descending steeply, at a 1.5 percent grade, in order to reach a sufficient depth to get under the East River. Traversing the same kind of silty ooze that lay under the Hudson, the four East River tunnels, A, B, C, and D, ran almost exactly underneath the LIRR ferry route between Manhattan and Long Island. On the opposite side, the line rose nearly as rapidly, at a 1.22 percent grade, in order to connect with the LIRR tracks in Long Island City.

On May 17, 1904, construction on the East River tunnels began with great promise and, at first, few problems. Near the intersection of Borden and East Avenues, workmen from the London contracting firm of S. Pearson & Son commenced excavations for the Long Island Shaft. Three weeks later, work began on the Manhattan Shaft. By autumn, crews in Long Island had reached the required depth and began digging toward Manhattan. Noble was anxious to keep all four tunnels progressing at a similar rate, and his decision to reassign workers from one heading to another ensured that progress continued sporadically through 1905 and into 1906. He also confronted several strikes and, much worse, pockets of sand and glacial till that slowed the progress of the shields to a crawl. The unstable soils caused cracks in more than a hundred cast-iron ring segments, causing workers to reinforce them with rods and turnbuckles and forcing engineers to substitute steel rings in areas of extreme stress. Blowouts occurred with distressing frequency, forcing construction crews to dump cement and three hundred thousand cubic yards of clay into the East River in an attempt to seal the riverbed. To reduce the risk of additional blowouts, engineers had to raise the air pressure in the tunnels, increasing the danger from the bends and so overtaxing the compressors that some headings had to be shut down for want of sufficient pressure. Work on the Manhattan heading of Tunnel C ceased entirely between March and October 1905, from December 1905 into the following January, and again from late March until July. By December 1905, digging on the Manhattan side of Tunnel A had come to a standstill, and would not resume for nearly a year. Not until October 1906, after both of the North River tunnels had been holed through, did work even begin on the Long Island end of Tunnel B. At the Man-

of disasters that was unfolding on the other side of Manhattan, underneath the East River. Alfred Noble and his managing engineer, Henry Japp, had their work cut out for them, thanks to the geography of that particular portion of New York. Near the eastern edge

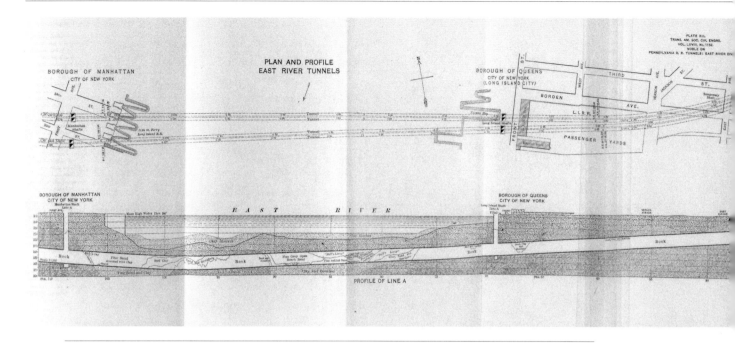

Figure 81. Alfred Noble, chief engineer of the East River Division, confronted a seemingly unending series of problems, including unstable soils, blowouts, inadequate air pressure, accidents, and unfavorable publicity, as his crews struggled to drive four parallel tunnels from Manhattan to Long Island City. By the time that they were finished, workers from the contracting firm of S. Pearson & Son had excavated 23,600 linear feet of tunnels. Because the tracks had to descend rapidly east of Pennsylvania Station, and then ascend just as quickly in order to reach the LIRR yards in Long Island City, the East River tunnels possessed some of the steepest grades on the entire PRR system. These plan and profile views originally appeared in Charles W. Raymond, *The New York Tunnel Extension of the Pennsylvania Railroad, North River Division,* following page 70.

hattan shoreline, the tunnels undermined the LIRR ferry terminal at the foot of Thirty-Fourth Street, rendering two of the four slips unsafe to operate.

All the while, workers were smothered by quicksand, crushed by falling timbers, burned, electrocuted, blown up, and killed by the bends. While the number was not appallingly large by the standards of the day— fourteen dead, as of the end of July 1906—the continuing troubles in the tunnels attracted unwelcome media scrutiny. Even as PRR officials were touting their successes on the Hudson side of Manhattan, they refused to release to the media any news of the conditions under the East River. In the absence of reliable information, newspaper reporters concocted sensational accounts of the proceedings, exaggerating the air pressure in the tunnels, overstating the number of deaths, and generally suggesting that the mighty

Pennsylvania Railroad had met its comeuppance at the hands of Mother Nature. Not until August 1906 did Henry Japp begin issuing public statements insisting that the risk of bends was low and that PRR engineers had no intention of abandoning the existing work in favor of a new tunnel location.[251]

In reality, the problems under the East River were annoying, but hardly insurmountable. By the autumn of 1906, even as many New Yorkers were growing suspicious that the East River tunnels were doomed to failure, construction crews began to hit their stride. Particularly on the Manhattan side, the sand gave way to firmer clay, enabling workers to push forward the shields with greater speed. Work progressed smoothly through 1907 and into the early months of 1908. On February 20, the two headings in Tunnel D met. Enthusiastic workers used compressed air to blow a toy train, a replica of the *Congressional Limited*, through a pipe linking the two sides of the tunnel. A similar scene took place on March 3, when the veterans of Tunnel B, not to be outdone, gave a rag doll a compressed-air ride between the two headings. The men in Tunnel C (who broke through on March 7) and Tunnel A (March 18), having lost the opportunity to send the first "train" and the first "person" under the East River, made do with hearty congratulations and two days of paid vacation. Despite all of the difficulties, Noble and Japp had managed to complete all four tunnels within a month of each other. The cost of the four East River tunnels, $13.8 million, was nonetheless significantly more than the $9.6 million spent under the Hudson River.[252]

There was still much work to be done on both sides of Manhattan Island. To the west, the digging of the Bergen Hill tunnels was taking longer than expected, thanks to the failure of the first construction contractor and the tough trap rock that confronted its successor. The southern tunnel was not holed through until April 13, 1908, a month after the last of the East River tunnels. The opening of the northern bore under Bergen Hill on May 7 was followed by a lavish celebratory dinner for North River Division chief engineer Charles Jacobs.[253]

On March 26, 1909, with the major design and construction work completed, Samuel Rea dissolved the board of engineers, although most of its members remained as advisers to the project. Belowground, workers poured the last of the concrete lining the East River tunnels in April 1909, and in the North River tunnels a month later. On June 21, Samuel Rea, Charles Jacobs, and other officials became the first people to ride under the Hudson River by automobile—as well as the last, until the opening of the Holland Tunnel in 1927. Within days, tracklaying had begun in both the Hudson and East River tunnels.

At 9:00 A.M. on November 18, 1909, a four-car passenger train left Philadelphia's Broad Street Station, headed for New York. PRR president James McCrea, Alexander Cassatt's successor, was on board, as was his son, James A. McCrea, general superintendent of the Long Island Rail Road. Vice President Rea was also present, along with a galaxy of other senior PRR executives. Less than two hours later, the train was in the yards at Harrison, New Jersey. After detaching two cars from the train, a steam locomotive pushed the remaining equipment—a diner and an observation car—toward Hackensack and the portal of the Bergen Hill tunnels. A few minutes later, the dignitaries reached Long Island. The celebration that followed, consisting primarily of lunch in the dining car, was a rather sedate affair compared with the raucous gatherings that had accompanied the holing through of the tunnels. After those earlier successes, the transit of passenger cars underneath Manhattan—the purpose for which the entire project had been undertaken—seemed a little anticlimactic. In any event, riding by rail under the great North River had probably lost some of its novelty, since over the past eighteen months many thousands of New Yorkers had made a similar journey through the tubes of the Hudson & Manhattan Railroad.[254]

Penn Station

Of the entire New York Improvements, it was clear that Pennsylvania Station was destined to be the most visible and the most awe-inspiring element. As one of the world's great rail terminals, Penn Station symbolized the power, wealth, and organizational mastery of the Pennsylvania Railroad. It represented a marriage of the twentieth century and antiquity, of engineering and art, and of utilitarianism and grandiose extravagance. Ironically, however, it enjoyed the briefest existence of any of the major components of the New York Improvements, succumbing to the wrecking ball barely half a century after its completion. The station's demise, although widely hailed as an act of desecration, albeit one that helped spawn the architectural preservation movement, brought an end to a building that was in many ways ill equipped for most of the people who used it.

The design of Penn Station owed a great deal to the artistic vision of President Cassatt, particularly to his European sojourns and his love of classical architecture. Cassatt had spent his teenage years in Europe, obtained much of his education there, and returned frequently to rest, visit family members, and promote the Pennsylvania Railroad. On one of those trips, in

August 1901, he had received Samuel Rea's telegram urging him to visit the Gare d'Orsay in Paris. Cassatt had been impressed by the combination of tunnels and electrification, hence his legendary recommendation that the PRR reach Manhattan through a tunnel, rather than over a bridge. Yet, Cassatt was even more interested in the exposed steel framework that lent a light, open, and airy feeling to the station's concourse.

During the summer of 1901, Cassatt was not the only notable American with an interest in architecture who was in Europe. In March, the McMillan Commission for the beautification of the national capital had retained the services of Daniel H. Burnham and Frederick Law Olmsted, Jr. The two leaders of Washington's City Beautiful movement soon sought the assistance of sculptor August Saint-Gaudens and architect Charles F. McKim. Their immediate task was to recreate Pierre L'Enfant's 1791 plan for the capital city, which included banishing the PRR's station from the Mall. In search of ideas, the members of the McMillan Commission visited Europe, spending most of their time in Paris and Rome. They had seen the Gare d'Orsay, with its exposed steel columns. In Rome, they visited the Coliseum and the Baths of Caracalla, and McKim in particular was awestruck by the majesty of the classical architecture.[255]

During the early years of the twentieth century, Charles McKim was at the height of his career. He had more than enough work to keep him busy, so he had little inclination to actively pursue such a major commission as the design of a new rail terminal in New York. Cassatt demanded a top-tier architect for the PRR's station, but he possessed neither the time nor the experience to personally make a selection. Instead, he relied on the suggestions of his officials, including Long Island Rail Road president William Baldwin. In December 1901, Baldwin recommended McKim's architectural firm, McKim, Mead & White, to Samuel Rea, and Rea in turn passed the recommendation on to Cassatt. Baldwin had assured Rea and Cassatt that McKim and his partners possessed ample experience with railroad structures, when in reality they did not. As such, Charles McKim might thus have had something of a shock when, in April 1902, while in Washington to discuss renovations to the White House, he received Cassatt's telegram summoning him to Philadelphia.[256]

On the morning of April 24, 1902, President Cassatt met with McKim at Broad Street Station. The architect offered a bid of $15 million for the New York station, and requested the customary 5 percent commission. Cassatt agreed, giving McKim authority over the design of the station above the level of the waiting room. Everything farther down, including the foundations, platforms, and retaining walls up to street level, would be the responsibility of Samuel Rea and his engineering staff.[257]

Even though he assigned the architectural work to McKim, Mead & White, Cassatt remained active in the station's design. He understandably demanded a magnificent edifice, one that would outshine anything that the New York Central, or any other rival for that matter, could provide. Cassatt also possessed a patrician attitude toward the station, which he saw as a monumental point of entrance for long-distance travelers arriving in Manhattan. As they disembarked from luxury trains such as the *Pennsylvania Special* (inaugurated in June 1902, and later renamed the *Broadway Limited*), passengers could make a grand procession across the concourse while porters labored behind the scenes to move mountains of steamer trunks. Daily commuters would not enjoy such a grand entrance to the city.

Cassatt's perception of the types of passengers who would use the new station reflected reality as much as snobbery or upper-class pretension. Like the New York Central, the PRR operated a large number of sleeping and parlor cars, over a hundred per day, in each direction, in and out of New York. As such, designers assumed that a substantial proportion of the estimated thirty thousand passengers who were expected to use the station each day would arrive and depart on luxurious long-distance trains. At a time when few people predicted the ubiquity of the automobile, there seemed no reason why long-distance rail travel should not increase steadily over the station's lifetime. Passengers on those trains often wanted—and were willing to pay for—the best possible facilities.[258]

Workers and shoppers headed into the city, or tired employees who wanted to go home at the end of a long day, cared far less for the vast public spaces. They wanted to get to and from their trains as quickly and as efficiently as possible, and PRR officials accordingly saw no reason to mix the twice-daily commuter rush with passengers who might be on their first visit to New York. Furthermore, the station's designers had ample reason to expect that commuter traffic would be relatively modest. While the LIRR boasted high ridership, white-collar workers typically headed downtown, where most of the city's corporate headquarters and other offices were located. At the time that Cassatt and McKim were designing the station, some theaters and department stores had been established in the area around Thirty-Fourth Street and Broadway, east of the site. The *New York Herald* had been at that location since 1894, but not until 1904 would the *New York Times* move to a new building at Forty-Second Street and Broadway, the area that then became Times Square. Farther east lay an upscale residential district, which was unlikely to generate much commuter traffic. To the west, the PRR shared the commutation business with several other steam railroads, as well as the Hudson & Manhattan. Much of the new line from Harrison to the Bergen Hill Portal ran across marshland, ensuring that there would be no new commuter suburbs in New Jersey. Even after the completion of the Hudson River tunnels and Penn Station, therefore, most of the office workers who traveled along the PRR would continue to detrain at Exchange Place and then take the ferries to Cortlandt Street to their jobs in the Financial District. Not until the 1920s and 1930s, with the ongoing shift of office space from the high-rent Financial District to cheaper real estate in Midtown, would commuters begin to flood Penn Station.[259]

In many respects, Charles McKim shared Cassatt's vision of a grand entrance to the metropolis, even if the two men differed as to the details. Even before McKim accepted the Penn Station commission, PRR executives had prepared a set of preliminary plans, largely drafted by John Vipond Davies, but with the broad outlines suggested by Cassatt. McKim incorporated some of Cassatt's elements, including a glass-roofed concourse, into his final design, but others he found unacceptable. Most disturbing to McKim was Cassatt's insistence that the station be topped with a large hotel, for the convenience of travelers. Such a plan would have been a natural extension of the erection of offices atop the PRR's Broad Street Station in Philadelphia and at Union Station in Pittsburgh, then under construction. More proximately, it would have

emulated William McAdoo's plans for the Hudson Terminal in Lower Manhattan. Located atop the Hudson & Manhattan Railroad, at the site later occupied by the World Trade Center, it was the largest office building in the world when it opened in April 1909. Despite such precedents, McKim warned that a towering edifice would detract from the monumental character of the building. He had a bitter hatred for the vertical, and he was determined to preserve an essentially horizontal design for the station. McKim was eventually able to persuade Cassatt to locate the hotel at another site, across the street. In reality, however, Cassatt needed little convincing. His engineers had already informed him that the weight of the proposed hotel would require dozens of additional support columns, forcing the elimination of at least two tracks—equivalent to nearly 10 percent of the station's capacity. McKim also refused to accept suggestions that the ceiling of the General Waiting Room be kept to the same three-story height as the rest of the building in order to reduce construction costs.[260]

Despite his love of antiquity, McKim faced the daunting task of incorporating modern railroad equipment and operating methods into his Beaux Arts neoclassical structure. Even though it covered four city blocks and measured 780 feet by 430 feet, the station nonetheless occupied a rather constrained site compared with other large urban termini. In most cities, the headhouse lay alongside or in front of the platforms and the train shed or canopy. At Penn Station, McKim was forced to locate the area intended for people above the space that would be occupied by trains. As such, he sought a mechanism to avoid the awkward transition from one setting to the other, and to gradually merge the human with the mechanical. McKim arranged the station in a series of incrementally descending units to lead travelers gradually from street level to the platforms, some forty-five feet underground.[261]

PRR officials expected that the station would be an extraordinarily busy place, by 1912 hosting one thousand trains on a typical weekday, and seventy-five million passengers per year.[262] McKim accordingly prepared a design that segregated arriving and departing travelers into separate areas of the facility, minimizing contact between each group. For McKim, the provision of multiple separate entrances for arriving and departing crowds paid homage to the Coliseum. So too did the squat appearance of the station, whose three-story height conformed to the architect's distaste for the vertical. The station bore a striking resemblance to the Baths of Caracalla, but the architect went one better, ensuring that the General Waiting Room was fully 20 percent larger than the Tepidarium that had inspired it.[263]

The construction of Penn Station began during the autumn of 1905, behind fencing that shielded the site from public view. Workers from the New York Contracting & Trucking Company began digging and blasting a massive hole in the Manhattan bedrock, first for the station yards and, the following spring, for the station itself. In the process of excavating the twenty-eight-acre site between Seventh and Tenth Avenues, workers relied largely on the cut-and-cover method, propping up streets, the Ninth Avenue elevated railway, and water and sewer pipes. Aside from a few spectacular and highly publicized explosions, the excavation went forward without incident, as construction trains hauled three million cubic yards of spoil to barges tied to piers in the Hudson River.

East of the site of Pennsylvania Station, the United Engineering & Contracting Company built the Crosstown Tunnels. Cassatt had been willing to bribe key opponents on the Board of Aldermen, but his conciliatory stance only went so far, and the Crosstown contract went to the firm controlled by state Senator Patrick H. McCarren, a Brooklyn native who refused to be bought by Tammany Hall. The Crosstown Tunnels skirted a seemingly endless maze of building foundations, buried utilities, and subway routes that were complete, under construction, or merely in the planning stages. Working from five shafts, tunnelers dug through bedrock, boulders, pockets of sand, and even long-forgotten underground streams. Not until January 1909 did crews finish the final excavations for the station yards, followed shortly afterward by the Crosstown Tunnels.[264]

Aboveground, Penn Station slowly rose from the bedrock of Manhattan. The George A. Fuller Construction Company secured the contract to erect the structural steel framework that would support the neoclassical façade that Charles McKim had designed. In the meantime, the architect's health declined rapidly, his misery further compounded by the June 1906

murder of Stanford White, the most talented of the firm's partners. White's killer, Harry K. Thaw, was the son of William Thaw, a one-time PRR board member, and before that, one of the private freight forwarders who had conducted operations over the railroad during the first years of its existence. In White's absence, McKim increasingly delegated work on Penn Station to William Symmes Richardson, who had joined the firm in 1895, and became a partner in 1906. Richardson was responsible for the interior design of the station and for coordinating the efforts of the architects and the engineers who worked on the structure. McKim died in September 1909; he, like Cassatt, did not live long enough to see his vision become reality.[265]

In the absence of the two progenitors of Penn Station, the laying of the cornerstone on August 10, 1908, was a rather subdued affair, with little ceremony or public notice. The exterior stonework along Seventh Avenue was in place by February 1909, with the remainder of the façade completed in July. By the spring of 1910, the station was largely finished, and test trains were running back and forth between Manhattan and Long Island. Service was delayed by several months, however, owing to the slow delivery of the all-steel electrified passenger equipment that would carry commuters through the East River tunnels.

On August 1, 1910, President McCrea led the PRR's directors and senior managers from Philadelphia, north to Manhattan, and up the stairs to the concourse and General Waiting Room. McCrea dedicated a statue of his predecessor, Alexander Cassatt, housed in a niche flanking the staircase leading down from the arcade. The official opening of Pennsylvania Station would not occur for more than another month, allowing workers to complete the final details, and engine crews and towermen to familiarize themselves with the facility's operations. Finally, at 3:36 A.M. on Thursday, September 8, the first Long Island Rail Road train left Penn Station. It carried only newspapers, to the disappointment of the visitors who had hoped to be passengers on the first revenue service. Within hours, amid widespread celebrations, many thousands of commuters and curious sightseers had the opportunity to ride through the East River tunnels to Long Island. Nearly three months passed before the first scheduled PRR passenger train departed from the station, at 12:02 A.M. on November 27. A new round of festivities erupted as PRR crews operated dozens of special trains that carried passengers under the Hudson. After a decade of work and the expenditure of $113 million—nearly a third of the cost of the Panama Canal—the gateway to Manhattan was open.[266]

Pennsylvania Station, the crowning jewel of the New York Improvements, was without doubt an impressive structure. The entire outside surface was covered in rose-colored granite, officially known as "Milford Pink" for the Massachusetts quarry where it originated. The main façade of the station, on Seventh Avenue, was lined with Doric columns.[267] The principal entrances on each side of the station included sculptures by Adolph Weinman—stone eagles and allegorical figures of Night and Day, leaning against a massive clock. The remaining walls, particularly those fronting Thirty-First and Thirty-Third Streets, were rather plain and austere, largely because of the decision to install sunken carriage drives that separated outbound passengers (on Thirty-First Street) from those headed from their trains into the city (on Thirty-Third Street).[268]

In the tradition of Classical design, the rather plain exterior gave way to a series of progressively more ornate interior spaces. From the Seventh Avenue entrance, on the east side of the station, travelers walked down a long arcade lined with fashionable shops that followed the route of the now vanished Thirty-Second Street. Extremely affluent travelers would probably have seen little of the arcade, however, as their chauffeurs would have taken them down the carriage drive to afford them a direct entrance to the side of the station.[269] On either side of the arcade, invisible to most visitors, large glass-roofed "train sheds" (more commonly referred to as baggage courtyards) allowed light to filter down to the platform level. The main baggage room was located underneath the arcade. From the baggage room, a series of passageways (along Seventh and Eighth Avenues, and connected by another corridor, parallel to Thirty-First Street) and elevators to track level enabled luggage to be deposited at the end of each platform without interfering with the movement of passengers. A vestibule marked the west end of the arcade and provided access to the station's lunch counter and dining room.[270]

Beyond the vestibule, a wide staircase led downward to the floor of the General Waiting Room, fifteen feet below street level. The massive space, 300 feet long and 110 feet wide, was by far the largest enclosed area in New York, and one of the most extensive in the world. The entire room was sheathed in what purported to be buff-colored travertine, imported from Italy and chosen as much for its superb wearing qualities as for its neutral palate. To either end of the long room, flanking the stairs that led downward from the side entrances on Thirty-First and Thirty-Third Streets, six Ionic columns—more elaborate than the Doric order used on the exterior—rose a modest thirty-one feet, a fifth of the height of the ceiling. Above the side entrances, beneath lunette windows, murals painted by artist Jules Guerin mapped out the PRR and LIRR territories. Lining the long walls, parallel to Seventh and Eighth Avenues, eight massive Corinthian columns, nearly sixty feet tall, supported the groin-vaulted ceiling that soared 147 feet above the floor. A cupola, necessary to contain such a high interior space, was evident in aerial views of Penn Station, but it was invisible from the street, and so did not detract from the long, low appearance of the structure. At the outer extremities of the General Waiting Room lay the various ancillary spaces—ticket counters, information booths, baggage-check facilities, and separate men's and ladies' waiting rooms.[271]

Travelers bound for their trains continued westward to a radically different space. The concourse, 315 feet long and 210 feet wide, was even larger than the General Waiting Room, although much of the space lacked a floor and was open to the tracks below. The design allowed sunlight to filter through onto the track level, while the glass blocks that composed the concourse floor provided additional platform illumination. It was here that McKim's architectural sensibilities, plus his undergraduate training in engineering, were most manifest. Because the station lay atop the platforms, McKim simply carried the steel columns that supported the floor of the concourse up to the ceiling. He made no attempt to disguise their industrial origins, and the latticework girders remained painted flat black for the remainder of the station's existence. Instead, McKim bent the overhead steelwork

Figure 82. When Pennsylvania Station opened to the public in 1910, the General Waiting Room was the largest interior space in New York City. While based on the ancient Roman Baths of Caracalla, the neo-classical décor was merely a façade covering a structural steel framework. Architect Charles Follen McKim orchestrated a transition from the plain Doric columns of the exterior to the Ionic order flanking the north and south entrances, ahead of and directly behind the photographer. Six massive Corinthian columns, grandest of all, lined the east and west sides of the room, but they were merely stone skins covering steel girders. Large lunette windows flooded the space with light and disguised the location of the floor, some fif-teen feet below ground. The murals that were positioned directly under the north and south windows gave little doubt that this station was the property of the Pennsylvania Railroad. The steps leading to the north (Thirty-Third Street) entrance (directly ahead) and to the arcade and the main Seventh Avenue entrance (to the right) suggested the descent that travelers made just to gain access to this level. To reach their trains, they would pass through the doorway to the left, to the concourse and then down to the platforms.

Pennsylvania Railroad Company Photographs, Hagley Museum and Library.

PENNSYLVANIA STATION
MAIN CONCOURSE AND STAIRWAYS TO PLATFORMS

Figure 83. The location of Pennsylvania Station atop—rather than beside or in front of—the tracks and station platforms presented Charles McKim with a formidable challenge. Instead of walking directly out into a traditional train shed, travelers would have to make a transition from the upper levels of the station down to the platform level. McKim elected to mimic the groin vaults of the General Waiting Room with the utilitarian steel shapes that supported the roof of the concourse. At right center, hidden in deep shadow, is the exit concourse that enabled arriving passengers to bypass the crush of travelers heading for their trains. The open well permitted light to shine down onto the platforms that lay more than forty feet below street level.

Pennsylvania Railroad Company Photographs, Hagley Museum and Library.

into a series of groin vaults, mimicking the covering of the General Waiting Room. Underneath the main concourse lay an exit concourse, a low-ceilinged space designed to funnel arriving passengers out of the station without interfering with those headed for their trains.[272]

The concourse served as a transitional space between the Beaux Arts exuberance of the public areas and the industrial efficiency of the tracks that lay below the station. Whereas the neoclassical design of the arcade and the General Waiting Room echoed the glories of ancient Rome, the concourse reflected a much more recent period of exuberance. The stark, yet celebratory industrial design of Joseph Paxton's 1851 Crystal Palace in London had helped influence the construction of later exhibition buildings, and ushered in a machine aesthetic in architecture. McKim's plans for the concourse refined that vision, but also anticipated later, more functional styles—one of the reasons that a future generation of Modernists praised the space as the only "authentic" part of Penn Station.[273] Ironically, however, by the time that McKim was planning the concourse, most experts in station design had already concluded that large, semi-enclosed train sheds were impracticable, and a relic of the nineteenth century. At the Washington Union Station, a virtually contemporaneous structure, architects Daniel Burnham and Peirce Anderson wisely chose small canopies over each platform rather than attempting to span all of the tracks with a single massive structure.

Both McKim and Cassatt thought it imperative to separate the PRR's long-distance travelers from the crush of twice-daily commuters. Long Island Rail Road passengers made do with a separate, smaller concourse, off to the side and on the same level as the exit concourse, which led in turn to two platforms serving tracks 18–21. Commuters, who arrived on tracks 20 and 21, walked a short distance along a narrow platform, and up one of many staircases to the LIRR concourse and the station's exits. In the original design, the space set aside for the use of the Long Island Rail Road resembled a subway station, surfaced with cement and tile, rather than travertine. While passengers arriving from Washington, Philadelphia, or Chicago partook of the grand public spaces, those who came from Babylon or Suffolk scuttled in and out of the station through low subterranean passageways, past a distinctly less prepossessing ticket office and waiting room, and through a dedicated entrance on Thirty-Third Street. The Long Island Rail Road concourse was low and dark, and lacking either heat or toilets. Within a year of the station's opening, however, construction crews were already at work, making the first in a series of improvements to the LIRR facilities. They added a new LIRR waiting room that was both

enclosed and heated. Two additional tracks were soon given over to LIRR traffic, with a further two later reassigned from the PRR to the LIRR. The baggage courtyard on the north side of the station received a floor, blocking light from entering the platform level, but permitting an expansion of the LIRR facilities. Somewhat less consideration was afforded to immigrants, who were excluded entirely from the station in favor of the existing facilities at Jersey City—a decision that seemed heartless, until one considered that Ellis Island was located adjacent to Communipaw, New Jersey, at a site that was well removed from Midtown Manhattan.[274]

From McKim's concourse, a series of stairways led downward toward the realm of vice president Samuel Rea and the PRR's engineers. The architectural majesty of the station's soaring above-ground spaces would have mattered little had it not been for the labyrinth of subterranean tracks, platforms, and signals that permitted the rapid arrival and departure of the trains. Initially, PRR officials planned to utilize standard-height platforms, with a surface set barely above the level of the rail. Very quickly, however, they elected to raise the platforms to the level of the passenger car floors, in order to speed loading and unloading, to minimize the descent from the concourse, and to reduce the possibility that passengers might try to cross the tracks from one platform to the other. From the depths of the station, trains traversed a maze of switches and signals, east toward Long Island or west through an open cut between Ninth and Tenth Avenues, and then under the Hudson River.

McKim's Pennsylvania Station was in many respects a brilliant design, but one that nonetheless possessed many compromises and flaws. The greatest difficulty, one that was hardly McKim's fault, was that the location of the platforms so far underground required considerable vertical movement. Elevators, although practicable for baggage, were too cramped and unreliable to facilitate the movement of a large number of people. The station was designed with forty-two hydraulic passenger elevators, but only eleven of them linked the platforms to the concourse level. Nearly twice as many—twenty-one in all—were reserved for passenger luggage. The remainder served the office wings that were located on either side of the Seventh Avenue entrance, and were not connected with the movement of passengers through the station. Escalators, a relatively new development, clashed with the neoclassical aura that McKim and Cassatt envisioned for the station. Thanks in part to cost-cutting measures implemented in the aftermath of the Panic of 1907, the station initially possessed only one escalator, allowing passengers to ascend some twenty-five feet from the Long Island Rail Road concourse to an exit off of Thirty-Fourth Street. As a result, most passengers trooped up and down a seemingly endless number of stairs. With porters often in short supply, passengers wheezed, groaned, and complained as they struggled with their luggage. Not until 1936 did the station's management cut an escalator into the center of the grand staircase that linked the arcade to the General Waiting Room. They added still more escalators in the years that followed, particularly on the lower levels of the station, greatly facilitating the movement of travelers and PRR personnel.

Other defects in the station's design were more difficult to countenance. The General Waiting Room and the concourse were both so large that they seemed to overwhelm the humans who passed through them. The station's interior arrangement proved confusing to many travelers, who often had difficulty finding a route out of the exit concourse and into the General Waiting Room. The later development of subway connections created additional problems, as it was relatively easy to get to the LIRR concourse, but not to the portions of the station that had been set aside for PRR passengers. The carriage drives entered and exited on Seventh Avenue, requiring the General Waiting Room to be set well back from the main entrance to the station—hence the long arcade, which covered the distance necessary to enable the carriage ramps to slope gradually downward to the principal level of the station. Many of the station's critics noted that that arrangement, coupled with the vast spaces, required passengers to walk a considerable distance in order to reach their trains. The concourse and the exit concourse that rested beneath it were not fully enclosed, and neither the architects nor PRR officials made any provision for heating those cavernous spaces. Blasts of cold air coming through the tunnels and up the open well in the concourse made waiting for a wintertime train an unpleasant proposition.[275] The groin-vaulted steel-and-glass roof of the concourse was plagued with leaks.

Penn Station was at best a hybrid of the neoclassical and the industrial, and at worst—as a later generation of Modernist architects emphasized—an outright fraud. From the outside, the completed building seemed to be constructed from massive blocks of pink granite, but it was merely a thin skin layered over the same steel framework that supported the skyscrapers that McKim so vociferously opposed. The six-story-tall interior Corinthian columns that harkened back to the Classical age were in reality a veneer that camouflaged the structural steel beams that supported the roof, while the vaulted and coffered ceiling was made of nothing more substantial than plaster. While the PRR's publicists emphasized the use of imported Italian travertine on the walls, most surfaces were in fact covered with colored concrete, mixed on site—a subterfuge that was admittedly commonplace on a great many monumental structures, both ancient and modern. Even then, the General Waiting Room and its ancillary structures were remarkably subdued, lacking the vibrant colors, lavish murals and mosaics, and omnipresent statuary that were more typical of contemporary neoclassical structures.[276]

In the final analysis, however, McKim's designs, especially for the areas antecedent to the concourse, may well have been too perfect. They were so highly refined, and such a tour de force of architectural skill, that even the slightest modification threatened to mar their aesthetic integrity. Such modifications were inevitable, thanks to the growth in commuter traffic and the concomitant decline in luxury long-haul passenger service. Despite pledges from PRR executives to maintain the character of McKim's vision, it was not long before the General Waiting Room and the other grand public spaces were cluttered with a variety of advertising placards, kiosks, and other impedimenta. The process culminated in 1957 with the erection of a massive new ticketing facility, the creation of industrial designer Lester C. Tichy, that was utterly at odds with McKim's intent. The severe functionality of the concourse and the areas that lay below it were far better suited to modification, and the periodic addition and removal of walls, floors, escalators, and passageways did little to mar the overall design.[277]

Despite its weaknesses, Penn Station represented a stunning engineering and artistic achievement, as PRR officials were determined to remind the American

people. The construction of the New York Improvements occurred when the Pennsylvania Railroad and
its competitors were coming under closer scrutiny
from politicians, regulators, journalists, and the general public. The monopolistic overtones of the community of interest, higher freight rates, and the damaging
testimony of the coal hearings all contributed to increasing hostility toward the railroads, a displeasure
that helped to shape regulatory policies. Under those
circumstances, PRR managers would have been foolish
not to emphasize the marvels associated with the Improvements, as well as the benefits that they would
bring to the traveling public and to the people of
New York.

Initially, the construction contractors who built the
New York Improvements had little patience with reporters who attempted to gain access to the tunnels.
The underground workings were a construction site,
after all, congested and potentially dangerous. The few
reporters who did manage to infiltrate the diggings
were therefore forcibly evicted, and ordered never to
return. In the absence of firsthand information, journalists fabricated accounts, based in large part on
fragmentary information, rumor, and innuendo. The
stories sold papers, but they also exaggerated whatever
problems workers had encountered, while overstating
the danger associated with the project. By the summer
of 1906, in particular, many newspaper readers could
be excused for believing that the construction of the
East River tunnels was descending into catastrophe.
In late June 1906, after a sinkhole collapsed part of the
LIRR's ferry slip at Hunter's Point, a *New York Times*
reporter visited the work site and attempted to talk to
the foreman. A gatekeeper yelled "That's a reporter.
Turn him back quick," before calling police to escort
the journalist off of the property.[278] Absent information from the foreman, the *Times* filled the remainder
of the column with an interview with members of the
Central Federated Union that was so closely linked to
Tammany Hall, giving workers an opportunity to
vent their rage against the construction contractors
and the PRR.

Journalist Ivy Ledbetter Lee joined the PRR in
1906 as a publicity consultant, and his arrival helped
spur a change in attitudes. Lee relied on carefully
crafted press releases to promote a positive image for

the Pennsylvania Railroad, and he encouraged PRR
officials to provide reporters with access to the New
York Improvements under controlled conditions. The
promenade through the north tunnel under the Hudson, in October 1906, was cause for one such tour,
and marked the first time that reporters had been permitted underground. PRR representatives led a carefully selected group of journalists through the air
lock, which one of them described as akin to a Coney
Island ride and another, something from "Twenty
Thousand Leagues Under the Sea, only smaller," and
into the tunnel.[279] There were some unpleasant moments, particularly when the PRR's assistant press
agent became unconscious in the air lock, but the reporters took everything in stride and provided favorable coverage of the PRR's conduct. Another
press junket accompanied the completion of the Bergen Hill tunnels.[280]

The need for favorable publicity was especially great
during the spring of 1906, given the sensational testimony of PRR officials during the ICC investigation
into coal stocks and car allocation. It was indeed fortuitous that McKim and his staff had recently completed the preliminary renderings of the exterior of
Penn Station. In mid-May, 1906, the PRR provided
leading newspapers with a three-page press release, including a description of the station and a set of exterior
and interior views. With the information came instructions that the papers were to wait until Sunday,
May 20, to run a special feature. Joseph Pulitzer was
eager to gain an advantage on his competitors, however, and on Wednesday, May 16, his *New York World*
published the story. Other papers in New York and
Philadelphia published articles the following day, even
as PRR executives were continuing to testify before
the ICC.[281] While Pulitzer and other newspaper owners had spoiled the PRR's plans for a dramatic Sunday
debut of the Penn Station design, the favorable publicity had nonetheless helped to distract attention from
the ICC hearings.[282]

More broadly, PRR executives wanted to use the
New York Improvements to demonstrate the PRR's
commitment to better service and to the development
of Greater New York, and not merely the accomplishments of the PRR's engineers. In 1904, two years before they hired Lee, the railroad's officials authorized a

display at the Louisiana Purchase Exposition in St. Louis. A large plaster model of one half of the proposed station was on display, illustrating the key features of the building. The highlight was a cross-section of one of the Hudson River tunnels, complete with a slice of a passenger car. From an engineering perspective, the exhibit was about as realistic as could be expected—the tunnel lining was saved, and in November 1906 it was the final segment installed in the south Hudson tunnel. Despite its intrinsic appeal, however, there was little sense of how the project would benefit ordinary Americans.[283]

By the beginning of 1907, with Lee on the PRR payroll, Samuel Rea was anxious to extract the greatest possible public relations value from the New York Improvements. He believed that the project, in addition to showcasing the railroad's engineering achievements, indicated that the PRR was a progressive corporation whose managers looked first and foremost to the public good. As such, he stressed, there was little need to increase the countervailing power of the government, and certainly no cause to allow regulatory agencies to dictate policies to the railroads. James McCrea had only recently become president, and while he was a capable engineer and executive, he lacked the personality and political savvy of his predecessor, Alexander Cassatt. Rea felt it necessary to remind him that the Pennsylvania Railroad was "constantly before the public, and looked upon as the saviour of Brooklyn in linking it with the railroad system of the Continent."[284]

At a time when Interstate Commerce Commission officials were beginning to question the massive costs of the New York Improvements and similar projects, Rea judged it unwise to stress financial data. Instead, he believed, the focus should be on the PRR's engineering achievements, as well as on the safety of the traveling public. In January 1907, for example, he emphasized that "from this time on" the PRR's managers "should endeavor to steer Messrs. Parker & Lee from emphasizing the fact of large expenditures, and rather point out the improvements which from time to time are being put into service. . . . Also in the New York tunnel extension to avoid using anything regarding risks in connection therewith, and only point out those portions which are at different times being completed. From now on we want its attractions advertised

from the point of view of the passenger traveling in a substantial, well-lighted, attractive tunnel."[285]

After Penn Station opened, the facility advertised itself, as traffic levels increased steadily. During the first decade of its operation, annual passenger counts rose from just under ten million to more than 36.5 million, equivalent to more than 114,000 travelers per day. In 1919, Penn Station surpassed Grand Central, and the NYC never regained the lead. Traffic continued to increase during the 1920s, to 65.6 million people in 1929, fell somewhat during the Great Depression, and then soared during the years of World War II, reaching an all-time peak of 109 million in 1945. Even then, at an average of 342,000 people per day, Penn Station was well under its maximum capacity of half a million daily passengers. Clearly, McKim's design had proven successful at accommodating vast crowds. As the decades passed, however, the composition of the station's users shifted in a way that neither McKim nor Cassatt had anticipated. In 1911, the PRR averaged 240 trains a day, with the LIRR operating 285, a nearly equal ratio. Suburban development sprawled over Long Island, thanks in part to the East River tunnels and to the LIRR's thick network of branch lines. Before long, more than two-thirds of the people using Penn Station passed through the cramped LIRR commuter facilities, and not the vast neoclassical spaces that McKim had used to awe affluent long-distance travelers.[286]

Steel and Electricity

The New York Improvements required the use of two complementary developments, steel passenger equipment and electric propulsion. Steel cars were a necessity for public relations, if not necessarily for operations, as the possibility of passengers trapped in a tunnel amid the flaming wreckage of wooden passenger cars was absolutely unthinkable. The lengthy tunnels likewise precluded the use of steam locomotives, and electric operation was the only viable alternative. While the New York Improvements undoubtedly accelerated the pace at which PRR executives adopted new equipment, they were by no means the sole determining factor. Other developments, particularly the desire to increase carrying capacity and reduce operating costs, mandated the adoption of the new technologies, for reasons that had little to do with the construction of Penn Station.

George Gibbs, an outside consultant to the PRR, played a crucial role in the adoption of both steel passenger cars and electric power. A supremely talented electrical engineer, Gibbs was associated with a great many rapid-transit and railway electrification projects during the early twentieth century. Even though Samuel Rea was in charge of the tracks, signals, and other aspects of the subterranean operations at Penn Station, he frequently deferred to Gibbs's expertise. During the early 1880s, shortly after graduating from the Stevens Institute of Technology, Gibbs found employment with Thomas Edison, who assigned him to the task of developing metering systems for the pioneering Pearl Street generating station. He later became chief of the Department of Tests for the Chicago, Milwaukee & St. Paul Railway, where his passion for passenger safety led him to develop steam heating and electric lighting systems for passenger cars, to replace fire-prone coal stoves and kerosene lamps. While still employed on that railroad, he paired with his brother Lucius to establish the Gibbs Electric Company.

George Gibbs benefited from the growing interest of railway officials in the application of electricity to propulsion. His association with Samuel M. Vauclain, of the Baldwin Locomotive Works, expanded his expertise in mechanical engineering, while his abilities as an electrical engineer soon brought him into contact with George Westinghouse, who later purchased Gibbs Electric. By 1900, Gibbs was in charge of Westinghouse's European operations and was a consultant on several major electrification projects, including the Mersey Tunnel and the Paris Métro. Most important, he was the first vice president of Westinghouse, Church, Kerr & Company, the New York–based contracting arm of the Westinghouse Electric Company. Since the late 1880s, the firm had supervised the electrification of a number of interurban rail lines. As such, Gibbs was thoroughly familiar with electricity and with railway operations. He was also acquainted with the Pennsylvania Railroad, as his cousin Alfred W. Gibbs, another Stevens graduate, had joined the PRR in 1879, and by 1903 he had become the general

superintendent of motive power on Lines East. In 1911, George Gibbs joined forces with another electrical engineer, E. Rowland Hill, to form the contracting firm Gibbs & Hill. Gibbs and his partner were not PRR employees, and were free to work on numerous other projects. For many years, however, they developed a close association with the PRR, and later maintained offices in leased space in Penn Station.[287]

In addition to designing the underground workings of Penn Station, Gibbs was involved in the construction of New York's subways, triggering his interest in steel passenger cars. Before the PRR's project was under way, Gibbs served as a consultant for August Belmont's Interborough Rapid Transit, in charge of electrical and signaling systems, as well as track standards. In 1901, Belmont asked Gibbs to design an all-steel subway car. Established car manufacturers were committed to wooden construction, however, and they resisted the IRT's plan for steel equipment. As a result, IRT officials had little choice other than to ignore Gibbs's plans for all-steel cars, opting instead for two steel-underframe prototypes, the *August Belmont* and the *John B. McDonald*. Belmont, in desperate need of equipment for the IRT, purchased hundreds of similar composite cars.

Even though they had initially been willing to accept a composite design, IRT officials soon decided that they would need to purchase all-steel cars. On the evening of August 10, 1903, a short circuit occurred in one of the motors of a train operating on the recently completed Line 2 Nord in Paris. A series of mistakes by the train crew caused a fire that engulfed the wood-bodied cars, killing eighty-four people. Like most disasters, the Paris Métro fire resulted from a combination of factors, but newspaper reports placed most of the blame on the wood car construction. Pressure from newspapers, government officials, and IRT riders therefore forced Belmont to approve Gibbs's design for an all-steel car. In December 1903, workers at the PRR's Altoona shops completed, at cost, a prototype car for the IRT. After testing on the Second Avenue Elevated, Gibbs redesigned the car, reducing weight through the use of pressed steel and aluminum panels. Belmont ordered a fleet of steel cars (often referred to as "Gibbs Cars") from American Car & Foundry. Soon afterward, the Long Island Rail Road placed an order for a set of steel cars, the Class MP-41, that were closely based on the Gibbs design. Any lingering doubts regarding the safety benefits of all-steel construction disappeared in 1905 when a subway fire incinerated five of the IRT's older composite cars.[288]

The introduction of steel passenger cars on the PRR to a large degree paralleled the developments on the IRT. In 1901, the same year that Gibbs developed the two prototypes for the IRT's composite cars, PRR officials authorized construction of the first steel-underframe freight equipment, the Class XL. That decision had little to do with safety. Instead, managers were concerned that conventional wooden underframes were not strong enough to withstand the drawbar pull of newer and more powerful locomotives, preventing the operation of longer freight trains. Steel underframes also enabled cars to carry more cargo, increasing the vital load-to-tare-weight ratio. Furthermore, as steelmakers lowered production costs and improved their fabrication techniques, they offered an alternative to increasingly scarce wood, as well as a mechanism for avoiding the escalating wage rates paid to skilled carpenters.

Nor was the PRR the only company interested in the new fabrication methods. Officials from the Louisville, New Albany & Chicago (the Monon); the Illinois Central; the Erie; the Santa Fe; and the Southern Pacific all experimented with steel or steel-underframe passenger cars. The Southern Pacific's prototype coach #1806, manufactured by the Pressed Steel Car Company of Pittsburgh, was the first all-steel mainline passenger car used in the United States, but its wooden interior perpetuated the risk of fire. Edward Harriman became an enthusiastic supporter of steel cars, and the companies that he controlled (the Southern Pacific, the Union Pacific, and the Illinois Central) soon acquired hundreds of all-steel cars.[289]

Like their counterparts on other railroads, PRR officials were anxious to employ steel as a method of decreasing the cost of passenger car construction, but the New York tunnels ensured that they were also concerned about the issue of safety. In October 1902, the members of the Mechanical and Electrical Advisory Committee for the New York Improvements examined the two composite cars that Gibbs had initially designed for the IRT. They dismissed the steel-underframe design as "entirely unsuitable" and insisted that

it was both too weak for mainline railroad service and too susceptible to fires caused by arcing between the electrified third rail and the truck-mounted pickup shoes. Accordingly, the committee recommended to President Cassatt "that designs should be begun at once for a passenger car to be built entirely of metal . . . [with] all parts of the car being constructed of incombustible materials."[290]

Beginning in 1904, Gibbs worked with PRR engineers William F. Kiesel, Jr., and Charles E. Barba to develop a design for an all-steel passenger coach. In June 1906, the railroad's shop forces completed a prototype, #1651, the sole member of the P-58 Class. In a masterstroke of public relations, the car made its inaugural run traveling from Altoona to Atlantic City, carrying delegates to the annual Master Car-Builders' Association convention. The car was then used in commuter service, trundling back and forth between Philadelphia's Broad Street Station and Paoli. At sixty-seven feet in length, the #1651 was shorter than a typical mainline passenger car, betraying elements of its IRT and LIRR heritage. Like the Southern Pacific coach, it was fire-resistant rather than fireproof, as it contained more than 1,500 pounds of wood. Nonetheless, PRR officials were confident enough to assert that in the future the railroad would order only steel cars, and that wood cars would be banished from all trains traveling under the Hudson and East rivers.[291]

PRR engineers soon began to develop two variants of the #1651, one for commuter runs and the other for mainline service. The P-54, first delivered in October 1910, became the backbone of the PRR's commuter fleets in New York and Philadelphia. While unpowered, Gibbs designed them so that they could be converted to self-propelled electric operation, like the IRT and the LIRR cars. A longer and more luxurious version of the #1651, the P-70, served as the PRR's principal long-distance passenger coach. In December, the Altoona shops completed the first P-70, with Altoona, the Pressed Steel Car Company, and the American Car & Foundry delivering several hundred more through 1908 and 1909.

Other car types followed in rapid succession. In November 1906, Altoona shop forces completed the PRR's first all-steel baggage car, followed by a Railway Post Office car in February 1907—minor accomplishments, given their simplicity in comparison to coaches. The Pullman Company, the firm that built and operated sleeping and parlor cars, likewise adopted all-steel construction, beginning in March 1907 with the sleeper *Jamestown*. By February 1910, PRR officials announced that they possessed 324 steel passenger cars, including 245 coaches, 21 combines, 10 diners, 29 baggage cars, 18 Railway Post Office cars, and one office car—a fleet that was still not large enough to eliminate wood cars from all of the trains that would soon be entering Penn Station. The LIRR was experiencing similar problems, as a shortage of steel cars forced the postponement of its scheduled May 1910 inauguration of service through the East River tunnels. Altogether, PRR officials estimated that they would require a thousand coaches, baggage cars, Railway Post Office cars, and dining cars, along with another five hundred Pullman sleeping and parlor cars, to fully equip all of the long-distance trains that would use Penn Station. By June, the PRR had more than seven hundred steel cars in service, with nearly two thousand more—including six hundred Pullman sleeping and parlor cars—on order. Even so, when Penn Station opened to PRR traffic in November, wooden Pullmans continued to run through the tunnels for a short time.[292]

The design and construction of steel passenger equipment was a relatively simple matter compared with electrification. The December 1902 municipal franchise stipulated "that the power to be used shall be electricity or other approved power not involving combustion in the tunnel."[293] That language merely confirmed what the PRR's engineers knew full well—that the New York Improvements would permanently bar steam locomotives from underneath the Hudson and East rivers.

As with steel cars, the PRR was hardly a pioneer in railroad electrification. Most of the other early experiments involved street railways, however, employing equipment that would never have been suitable in mainline service. As early as 1884, an electric street railway in Cleveland enjoyed modest success and was soon followed by similar examples in Toronto, Detroit, South Bend, Minneapolis, Kansas City, and New York. In 1883, electrical engineer Frank Julian Sprague began working with Thomas Edison at Menlo Park, and the next year he founded the Sprague Elec-

tric Railway & Motor Company. During 1885 and 1886, he experimented with electric traction on the Manhattan Elevated Railway, but his great triumph came in 1887 and 1888, when he electrified the Richmond Union Passenger Railway. Between 1892 and 1897, Sprague developed another critical element of electric railway equipment—a multiple-unit control that enabled one person to operate several locomotives or motorized cars simultaneously. In Britain, a corresponding success occurred with the electrification of the City & South London Railway between 1887 and 1890, an operation that Samuel Rea observed in 1892. As chief engineer of the Baltimore Belt Line, Rea was also familiar with the B&O's Howard Street Tunnel and associated electric operations. He returned to the PRR before the project was completed, however, and he was generally unconvinced that the B&O's locomotives were capable of pulling heavy trains into Manhattan at acceptable speeds on frequent headways—one of the reasons that he continued to support the North River Bridge.[294]

Pennsylvania Railroad officials also considered electrification for some of the company's rural branches, albeit on a much smaller scale than the B&O's efforts. In 1895, PRR engineers installed overhead wire to deliver 500-volt direct current to interurban-type equipment on the Burlington & Mount Holly Railroad & Transportation Company in New Jersey, over a distance of barely seven miles. The powerhouse burned down in 1901, ending electric operations.[295]

The New York, New Haven & Hartford conducted even more extensive experiments in an effort to cope with high passenger traffic densities and excessive terminal congestion. By the late 1890s, the success of Frank Sprague's Richmond installation had led to the construction of a growing number of longer-distance electric interurban railways connecting various towns. The new lines threatened the New Haven's revenues, causing that company's officials to buy out as many of the upstart competitors as possible. New Haven engineers also attempted to beat the interurbans at their own game, by electrifying eleven branch lines between 1894 and 1907. Initially, the New Haven used an overhead trolley line, but it later switched to a more reliable third-rail direct-current (DC) system. While the design worked satisfactorily, many passengers and local residents feared electrocution, or even some sort of poisoning from the electricity that supposedly leaked into the air. The hysteria reached its zenith in June 1906, when the Connecticut State Supreme Court ordered the New Haven to remove all of its third-rail equipment. In response, New Haven officials converted most of their routes to overhead wire.[296]

The great breakthrough occurred in Paris in May 1900, with the opening of the Gare du Quai d'Orsay, the same facility that gave Cassatt and others the architectural inspiration for Penn Station. Engineers from Compagnie Française Thomson-Houston, S.A. (the French subsidiary of General Electric), developed an electric system that was based in part on the B&O installation in Baltimore. The performance was much more impressive, however. Powerful electric locomotives, drawing 600-volt direct current from a third rail, pulled heavy passenger trains at more than twenty miles per hour, up grades as steep as 1.1 percent. Operating and maintenance costs were an astonishingly low twenty-six cents per mile. For the first time, PRR executives saw evidence that electric locomotives would be capable of delivering mainline passenger trains to Manhattan.[297]

Soon after the opening of the Gare d'Orsay, a series of events led all four of the major railroads that served or would serve Manhattan—the New York Central, the New Haven, the Long Island, and the PRR—to embrace electric power. In 1893, William J. Wilgus joined the NYC, and by 1899 he had risen to the rank of chief engineer for construction and maintenance of way. In that year he prepared a plan for improving Grand Central Depot and electrifying the company's lines into Manhattan, largely in order to improve operating efficiency. Such concerns faded into insignificance after January 8, 1902, when two New York Central trains collided in the smoke-darkened Park Avenue Tunnel leading to the station, killing seventeen people. Two weeks later, NYC officials attempted to quell the public outcry by promising the Board of Rapid Transit Railroad Commissioners that they would implement the 1899 Wilgus Plan. They had little choice in the matter, for in May 1903 the New York legislature banned steam locomotives south of the Harlem River after July 1, 1908.[298] As a result, NYC engineers pushed forward plans to rebuild Grand Central Depot into Grand Central Terminal (implemented in stages, between 1903 and 1913) and to electrify tracks as far north as North White Plains (in 1910) and Croton-Harmon (in 1913), using a 660-volt third-rail DC system. General Electric secured the contract for what was an unprecedented increase in the scale of railway electrification.[299]

By installing the first long-distance mainline electrification in the United States, the New Haven provided an example that more closely approximated the PRR's requirements. The New Haven used Grand Central as its New York terminus, and thus had to electrify its route into the city as well. A low-voltage DC system would have been a logical choice given its use on the NYC tracks, as well as on several New Haven branch lines. With the railroad's high traffic density, however, New Haven executives believed that it would be more efficient to change from electric to steam power at Stamford, Connecticut, well beyond the limits specified in the 1903 act. If successful at increasing train frequencies and reducing operating costs, electric service might be extended as far north as New Haven or even Boston.

After extensive study, New Haven engineers concluded that a low-voltage DC installation would not permit the reliable operation of heavy trains over such a long distance. Instead, they chose an 11,000-volt, single-phase alternating-current (AC) system. While General Electric manufactured some alternating-current components, the personnel of the Westinghouse Electric & Manufacturing Company were far more familiar with AC equipment. Because they could not send such high voltages through a ground-level third rail, electrical engineers relied on a catenary system, with wires suspended over the track.[300] Construction began in 1905, with electric service extended to New Rochelle in 1907, and to New Haven in 1914. The New Haven installation, which eventually encompassed nearly seven hundred track miles, represented a great advance beyond the NYC system. For the first time, a railroad had integrated electrified passenger, freight, and commuter operations over long distances, for reasons of operating efficiency and not merely compliance with state law.[301]

The New Haven electrification also marked the first key victory of AC locomotive propulsion. During the late 1800s, the "battle of the currents" pitted DC, championed by Thomas Edison, against alternating current, promoted by George Westinghouse and Nikola Tesla. The preferences continued even after 1896, when licensing agreements enabled General Electric (a product of the 1892 merger of Edison General Electric and the Thomson-Houston Company) and Westinghouse to build both types of equipment. Direct current offered a proven design, one that was extremely rugged, reliable, and inexpensive, and yet it suffered a severe voltage drop over long transmission distances. Alternating current was relatively new and untested, required more complicated equipment and therefore entailed a higher initial cost, and was more prone to malfunction. Alternating current offered far superior long-distance transmission capabilities, however, and a further advantage associated with the Tesla system was the ease of converting electrical energy to the rotational motion of the traction motors. Even better, if engineers could employ the same high-voltage alternating current to transmit power along the route and to distribute it to the locomotives, then they could greatly reduce the complexity of the installation.[302]

When Cassatt first announced plans for the New York Improvements, a low-voltage DC system seemed the obvious choice. Manhattan's streetcars and elevated lines employed direct current, drawn from overhead wires in the first instance, and a third rail in the second. The Hudson & Manhattan Railroad employed multiple-unit equipment, with self-propelled cars drawing power from a 650-volt DC electrified third rail. Belmont's Interborough Rapid Transit used a comparable 625-volt DC system that soon became standard on the entire New York City subway network. The New York Central's electrification project, virtually contemporaneous with the construction of Penn Station, likewise used direct current.

The Long Island Rail Road, more a rapid transit line than a true mainline railway, was the first of the PRR's New York lines to be electrified. Irrespective of the construction of Penn Station, electric power was an absolute necessity for the underground portions of the Atlantic Avenue Improvement, constructed between 1901 and 1905. Engineers utilized a 650-volt DC system to power thirty-eight miles of lines in Brook-

lyn and Queens. There seemed little reason not to extend electrification to the Hudson and East River tunnels, particularly as the two railroads would share the power plant at Hunter's Point in Long Island.[303]

The choice of electrical system was not so straightforward, however, as the battle of the currents soon affected the Pennsylvania Railroad and its equipment suppliers. The New York Central's DC electrification represented a collaborative effort involving three New York corporations. The Schenectady-based American Locomotive Company, the NYC's principal outside source of motive-power, furnished the locomotive bodies, while General Electric installed the electrical equipment. American Locomotive and GE each competed with a Pennsylvania firm that was closely tied to the Pennsylvania Railroad. Aside from the locomotives built at the Juniata Shops at Altoona, the PRR relied primarily on the Baldwin Locomotive Works, based in Philadelphia. Baldwin in turn maintained a close partnership with Westinghouse, a Pittsburgh manufacturer. Together, Baldwin and Westinghouse provided equipment for the LIRR's low-voltage DC and the New Haven's high-voltage AC electrification projects. PRR officials were loath to bypass two Pennsylvania firms in order to award the New York electrification contract to their NYC-affiliated rivals.

Even before Cassatt had announced the precise nature of the New York Improvements, PRR officials were developing plans to power the locomotives that would cross under the Hudson and East rivers. As early as September 1901, chief of motive power Theodore N. Ely asked representatives from Baldwin to develop specifications for electric locomotives for the New York Improvements. In March 1902, officials from Westinghouse, Church, Kerr & Company submitted a proposal for the electrical engineering work associated with the project. A month later George Westinghouse traveled with Cassatt between Philadelphia and New York, lobbying for the electrification contract. Within days, his contracting company had revised and resubmitted the Penn Station proposal.

On April 11, 1902, Westinghouse was assured of victory. Even though the PRR had not yet accepted the Westinghouse, Church, Kerr & Company bid, Cassatt appointed George Gibbs, that company's first vice president, to a post on the board of engineers for the New York Improvements. Gibbs, now the project's chief engineer of electric traction, was by no means captive to the Pennsylvania Railroad, and was free to work as a consultant with the Interborough Rapid Transit and even the New York Central. More important, he was bound to be highly favorable to Westinghouse and to AC electrification, and he was likely to steer other PRR officials in that direction.

With the Atlantic Avenue Improvement under way, in July 1902 LIRR officials became the first to officially employ Westinghouse, Church, Kerr & Company as their electrification contractor. Later that month, PRR officials approved in principle the electrification plans that Gibbs and his company had suggested—including a promise that the yet-to-be-developed locomotives could pull a five-hundred-ton train over severe grades at speeds of up to fifty-five miles per hour. The arrangement became official in January 1903, when the PRR contracted with Westinghouse, Church, Kerr & Company. For all intents and purposes, Gibbs was responsible for the underground portions of the New York Improvements. In addition to the electric locomotives, his duties included the coordination of all of the electrical, signaling, and track systems, as well as the installation of heating and ventilating equipment, passenger and freight elevators, and all the lighting for the tunnels and the station itself.[304]

Gibbs also chaired the PRR's Electric Locomotive Committee, responsible for selecting the most suitable motive power and propulsion system. The other members of the committee were all PRR employees, including chief mechanical engineer Axel S. Vogt, general superintendent of motive power on Lines West David F. Crawford, and his counterpart on Lines East, George's cousin Alfred W. Gibbs. The most critical task facing the members of the Electric Locomotive Committee was the development of a motive-power design that could meet the criteria that Gibbs had promised.

During 1905, PRR shop forces at Altoona built two experimental DC locomotives, No. 10001 and No. 10002. Westinghouse supplied, gratis, all of the electrical equipment, along with several engineers and technicians, in an attempt to win the PRR over to its products. Both locomotives were of the B+B type—

that is, they had two sets of twin driving axles, without any unpowered leading or trailing axles. One of the prototypes employed traction motors geared directly to the axles—a design that did not permit each wheel to move independently over rough or uneven track. The other prototype compensated for that deficiency with a quill drive. Under that system, each traction motor engaged with a hollow tube (the quill shaft), which surrounded the axle. The ends of the quill shaft transmitted power to the drive wheels through a series of drive cups. The axle-mounted drive wheels could rotate irrespective of the quill shaft, compensating for irregularities in the track. Unfortunately, the results of preliminary tests, conducted on the LIRR in September, were not encouraging. The absence of leading and trailing trucks caused both of the PRR locomotives to "hunt," or shift from side to side, causing lateral stresses on the rails and risking the possibility of derailment.

Alfred Gibbs was now in his element. Emphasizing the limits of his cousin's expertise, he declared that the locomotives' problems were mechanical, and not electrical, in nature and could be corrected only through a comparison with steam locomotive designs. During 1907, Baldwin and Westinghouse completed a third locomotive, No. 10003, in a 2-B configuration (that is, an unpowered two-axle lead truck and a pair of powered drive axles) in an effort to eliminate the tracking problems. While the nomenclature was different, the 2-B design embodied the same wheel arrangement as the 4–4–0 "American" locomotives that for more than half a century had proven their stability on railroads throughout the United States. Unlike the previous two experimental locomotives, the No. 10003 was designed for 11,000 volts AC, as used on the New Haven, and required a separate motor and generator set for the test runs. In November 1907, the PRR spent a quarter of a million dollars on the most expensive tests conducted in the history of railroading up to that time. Engineers evaluated all three units along a seven-mile stretch of track between Clayton and Franklinville, New Jersey, on the PRR's recently electrified West Jersey & Seashore Railroad subsidiary. By that time, the New Haven had acquired the first of its Baldwin-Westinghouse Class EP-1 electric locomotives, and PRR officials included one in their tests, along with two steam locomotives for comparison—one of which was a 4-4-0. When a locomotive passed over a section of track specially equipped with steel ties, the lateral forces drove a hardened steel ball into a recording plate at the end of the tie, providing a precise indication of how far the track had shifted to one side. As anticipated, the No. 10001 and No. 10002 produced unacceptably high levels of lateral sway, one of them actually distorting the straight track into a series of kinks. The New Haven locomotive was far more reliable, although it also had a tendency to hunt. No. 10003, however, produced spectacular results, with rapid acceleration and power that compared favorably with that of the steam locomotives.

Despite the success of the No. 10003, debates over whether production versions should be powered by low-voltage direct current or high-voltage alternating current imperiled the schedule of the electrification program. During the earliest meetings of the Electric Locomotive Committee, Gibbs apparently urged his fellow engineers to consider an installation similar to the one just announced by the New Haven. His arguments in favor of AC's superior long-distance transmission capabilities gained additional weight as PRR officials elected to relocate the proposed steam-to-electric transition from the mouth of the Bergen Hill tunnels to Manhattan Transfer, a more distant location in the New Jersey Meadowlands. Gibbs was probably the individual who advocated the construction of the Baldwin-Westinghouse No. 10003 and the 1907 testing of the New Haven EP-1. He also suggested that tunnel clearances be increased to permit the installation of high-voltage catenary. During the autumn of 1908, with the tunnels holed through and construction of Penn Station well under way, Gibbs and his associates were still undecided about the best type of current to use. They strung five miles of 11,000-volt AC catenary along a stretch of the Long Island Rail Road, but after extensive tests concluded that even though the electrical equipment worked well, the overhead power distribution system was too insubstantial to tolerate heavy use.

Vice President Rea, who bore the ultimate responsibility for completing the New York Improvements, lost patience with Gibbs and his extended search for the ideal electrical power. He acknowledged the potential of the New Haven installation, but argued that it would be dangerous to gamble on the performance of a new and largely untested system. "The New Haven rushed their electrification through on a system of electric traction different from their neighbors [the NYC], whose terminal and twelve miles of track they had to use," Rea emphasized.[305]

Rea was not the only one who was impatient. Railroad officials across the United States and Europe waited to see which system the PRR's engineers would validate. The long period of experimentation by the Electric Locomotive Committee was, as PRR assistant engineer B. F. Wood informed a meeting of the American Institute of Electrical Engineers, the single most significant factor responsible for delaying mainline railroad electrification in the United States.[306]

Gibbs and the other members of the Electric Locomotive Committee ultimately concluded that alternating current offered the better choice in theory, but that any unforeseen problems with the newer system might delay the opening of Penn Station, perhaps by years. On November 21, the committee's report recommended that the PRR adopt a 650-volt direct-current system for its first application of electric power to heavy-duty mainline service. In addition to its compatibility with both the LIRR and the Hudson & Manhattan, DC offered lower installation costs. Most important, DC was a proven system. From an engineering perspective, direct current was not the most efficient choice, but it was the safest one.

The selection of low-voltage direct current illustrated the perils of assuming a leadership position in a new and largely untested method of propulsion. Within a few years after the opening of Penn Station, additional research in Europe and the United States demonstrated that alternating current offered far greater advantages. By 1910, as the PRR was completing the installation of its DC apparatus, New Haven engineers had largely resolved the initial problems associated with its pioneering 11,000-volt AC system. William S. Murray, a consulting engineer on the New Haven, told the American Institute of Electric Engineers that his railroad represented the future of long-distance mainline electrification. He was correct, and when the Pennsylvania Railroad began a widespread electrification program in the 1920s and 1930s, officials chose high-voltage alternating current.

Once PRR officials committed to direct current, they rushed to order locomotives that would be ready in time for the opening of Penn Station. Based on the success of No. 10003, they elected to retain the 2-B wheel arrangement, but with two units permanently coupled back to back. The resulting 2-B+B-2 configuration represented precisely the same wheel arrangement as two 4–4-0 steam locomotives, one pointed forward and the other in reverse, permitting bidirectional operation. The PRR listed American-type locomotives as Class D, and logic dictated that the first of the new electrics be referred to as the Class DD-1. In 1909 and 1910, the Juniata Shops completed an initial order of twenty-four DD-1 locomotives, with nine

more delivered in 1911. All featured Westinghouse electrical equipment, including motors rated at 2,000 horsepower. The motors, which occupied most of the car body, drove the wheels through a huge jackshaft and the type of side rods more typically encountered on a steam locomotive.

The DD-1 design proved stunningly successful. A single locomotive had no difficulty pulling a thousand-ton train up the steep grades in the tunnels, and when traveling through the New Jersey Meadowlands a DD-1 could easily reach speeds of sixty miles an hour—handily beating the performance characteristics that Gibbs had promised at the beginning of the design process. On an average day, each loco-

Figure 84. A DD-1 electric locomotive pauses at Manhattan Transfer, near Harrison, New Jersey. The third rails that supplied low-voltage direct current are clearly visible. Until January 1933, when the PRR completed mainline electrification between New York and Philadelphia, all passenger trains traveling through the Hudson River tunnels into Manhattan paused here to change motive power. There was no highway access to the site, but most passengers bound for Lower Manhattan left their train here, transferring to the Hudson & Manhattan Railroad rather than travel to Pennsylvania Station in Midtown.

Pennsylvania Historical and Museum Commission, Railroad Museum of Pennsylvania.

motive traveled more than four hundred miles back and forth under the Hudson and East rivers, yet few malfunctioned. During their first four years of operation the DD-1 locomotives traveled some four million miles, yet suffered only forty-five breakdowns—an average of one every eighty-eight thousand miles. After an initial break-in period, maintenance costs averaged 3.51 cents per mile, a sixth of the cost for steam locomotives.[307]

For more than three decades, the PRR's fleet of DD-1 electric locomotives soldiered on, leaving the engine facilities at Sunnyside Yard, coupling onto passenger equipment, and dragging it under the East River to Penn Station. After pulling away from the platforms, the train plunged underneath the Hudson River and through the Bergen Hill tunnels, emerging in the New Jersey Meadowlands. At Manhattan Transfer, near Harrison, an isolated location accessible only by train, each DD-1 relinquished its charge to a more conventional steam locomotive for the trip to Philadelphia, Washington, Pittsburgh, St. Louis, or Chicago.

Millions of passengers changed at Manhattan Transfer, as well. In November 1911, when the Hudson & Manhattan Railroad completed a line between Lower Manhattan and Park Place in Newark, many long-distance travelers bound for Lower Manhattan detrained at Manhattan Transfer and rode through William McAdoo's Hudson Tubes (in cars painted Tuscan red, to match PRR equipment) to reach their destinations, without ever entering Penn Station.[308] Manhattan Transfer closed in 1937, four years after the PRR completed the electrification of the entire route between New York and Philadelphia. The site nonetheless assumed iconic status in the cultural history of New York, lending its name to a novel written by John Rodrigo Dos Passos (the illegitimate son of John Randolph Dos Passos, Jr., one of the major investors in the Hudson & Manhattan Railroad) and to a vocal jazz group.

Other Elements of the New York Improvements

Penn Station could not have functioned without a vast support network. Some of that system rested within the station itself in the form of space for PRR personnel, including a Railroad YMCA along Eighth Ave-

nue. A service station building, across Thirty-First Street from the passenger facilities, housed a heating plant, an incinerator, waterworks, and the hydraulics for the station elevators. Four towers controlled the complex interlocking apparatus that included 258 working levers and 86 spares, governing 144 switches and 231 signals. The signal systems were bi-directional, maximizing the efficiency of train movements. Block-occupancy detectors, introduced for the first time in the United States more or less simultaneously at Penn Station and at the Lackawanna's Hoboken terminal, enabled tower operators to follow the progress of each train through the tunnels.[309]

West of the station, occupying a space almost as large, was the new United States Post Office. The PRR transported 40 percent of the mail that reached New York, and mail-handling facilities were an essential element of the New York Improvements. As early as February 1903, Cassatt was engaged in negotiations for a building to be constructed atop the PRR tracks and platforms, to the west of Eighth Avenue. The plans for the Post Office depended on the exploitation of air rights. As part of the ongoing reconstruction of Grand Central Depot, NYC officials had taken advantage of the space that lay atop the underground right of way that lay just north of the station. By leasing the right to build structures "in the air" above the tracks, they maintained unimpeded railroad operations, while generating considerable additional revenue. However, the Congressmen who were responsible for Post Office appropriations insisted that the federal government should own the land underneath the building—an obvious impossibility given the presence of the PRR's tracks and platforms some forty feet below. Not until the summer of 1906 did Post Office officials agree to purchase the air rights, at a cost of $1.66 million. In 1908, McKim, Mead & White secured the contract for the building's design. They chose the same Milford Pink granite sheathing as employed on Penn Station, although the Eighth Avenue façade of the Post Office, with a broad stairway rising to an arcade of Corinthian columns, was considerably more ornate than its neighbor across the street. Despite its size and weight, the entire structure rested atop steel beams, twelve feet deep and four feet across, that spanned the PRR tracks. Opened just in time for the 1913 Christmas season, at a cost of $6 million, the new facility was capable of handling more than five million pieces of mail per day. Five conveyor belts moved mail sacks to and from the station platforms. Electric indicators kept track of train movements, enabling Post Office personnel to continue sorting letters until mere minutes prior to each train's departure.[310]

Given Penn Station's location in the undesirable Tenderloin district, ample opportunity existed for the railroad to coordinate real estate development in the area. PRR officials had predicted that office, retail, and entertainment establishments would migrate west, to the site of the new terminal. They were sorely disappointed, and for years the massive building loomed over the surrounding low-rent neighborhood. PRR officials watched with interest the implementation of projects associated with Grand Central and with the Hudson & Manhattan's Hudson Terminal. Unfortunately, the PRR lacked three key elements that were vital to the successful exploitation of the area's real estate potential. First, the station was not yet connected directly to the city's mass-transit system, precluding the easy distribution of workers and shoppers throughout Manhattan. Second, unlike the NYC's long southward approach to Grand Central, in a gradually descending shallow trench underneath Park Avenue, the PRR's deep tunnels ensured that—aside from the Post Office site—few additional air rights were available. High real estate costs also discouraged the PRR's managers from purchasing additional tracts of land in the Penn Station area.

Finally, the attitudes of PRR officials restricted their ability to develop the land surrounding Penn Station. PRR executives thought of themselves as railroaders, not real estate moguls. President James McCrea was particularly averse to involving the railroad in activities not directly connected to its core capabilities in transportation, and he initially attempted to sell off all of the Manhattan properties that were not necessary for the PRR's operations. Many civic leaders and newspaper editors criticized McCrea's unwillingness to improve the area around Penn Station, making pointed comparisons to the activities of the NYC and the Hudson & Manhattan. Samuel Rea was more solicitous of public opinion, and he suggested a number of proposals, including hotels, offices, depart-

ment stores, and apartments—some of which would be rented to PRR employees. Most of the suggestions came to naught. Even years after the deaths of Cassatt and McKim, Rea and some other PRR executives continued to adhere to their vision of a unified assemblage of structures around the nucleus of Penn Station. As such, they were reluctant to encourage commercial development at the expense of aesthetics—even going so far as to ban commercial advertising in the terminal. PRR officials also preferred not to relinquish authority to outside developers.[311]

The Hotel Pennsylvania constituted the only significant development orchestrated by the PRR that was not directly connected to the operation of Penn Station. Early in the station's design, both Cassatt and McKim had acknowledged that a hotel was a necessity for travelers. They agreed that structural and aesthetic considerations precluded placing the hotel atop the station proper, but made no immediate plans for off-site development. Finally, in September 1912, PRR interests incorporated the Pennsylvania Terminal Real Estate Company, and paid $1 million to acquire additional properties adjacent to the station. The first priority was a hotel site on Seventh Avenue between Thirty-Second and Thirty-Third Streets. However, it was not until the spring of 1916 that PRR officials assigned a contract with the George A. Fuller Company to build a hotel, designed by William S. Richardson of McKim, Mead & White. The Hotel Pennsylvania was in harmony with Penn Station, its limestone portico rising to precisely the same height as the Milford granite on the exterior of the railroad facility. When the hotel opened in January 1919, it was the largest in the world, with 2,200 rooms. Although PRR officials succeeded in establishing a hotel adjacent to Penn Station, after contributing $9.5 million to the project, they were unable to coordinate any additional commercial development.[312]

The largest ancillary facility for Penn Station lay across the East River, in Long Island City. PRR engineers had early on concluded that there was no realistic possibility of turning, servicing, or storing passenger equipment in the tunnels underneath Manhattan. Instead they planned to send empty trains farther east to the site of a massive new yard. That decision, along with the necessity of accommodating LIRR commuter trains, resulted in the construction of twice as many tunnels under the East River as under the Hudson. Work on Sunnyside Yard began early in 1907, and the facility was completed in the summer of 1910, at a cost of $4.6 million. Because much of the complex would be located on a swamp, workers moved 2.8 million cubic feet of soil in order to create a level and stable platform for fifty-three miles of track, covering 208 acres.[313] Seven rail and six street viaducts kept trains and highway vehicles moving efficiently. The North Yard housed commuter equipment, while the South Yard accommodated the cleaning, storage, and repair of the PRR's long-distance passenger fleet. Shop facilities performed minor repairs on both locomotives and passenger cars. The yards included PRR and Pullman Company commissaries to re-supply legions of dining and sleeping cars, and about half of the 2,500 workers there were employed by Pullman rather than the PRR. After passengers detrained at Penn Station, locomotives manned by PRR yard crews pulled the now-empty cars to Sunnyside, where they were turned on a balloon track. Car inspectors checked the equipment for defects, yard crews detached the diners and sleepers, then switched them to their respective commissary tracks, while an army of coach cleaners washed and swept the cars before restocking them for their next trip. Initially, the facility could accommodate more than 1,100 cars per day, with enough room available to nearly double that figure, if needed. By the 1940s, when the yard was operating at peak capacity, it serviced more than one hundred long-distance trains each day.[314]

Although seldom seen by travelers, new PRR and LIRR freight facilities constituted an important part of the New York Improvements. The tunnels under the Hudson and East rivers were never intended for freight, although they would later accommodate some coal traffic during World War I as a temporary emergency measure. In 1892, Samuel Rea had suggested the possibility of a tunnel across the Narrows, but no one was certain how trains might be propelled through it. By the time President Cassatt announced his plans for the New York Improvements, electrification had largely resolved the propulsion problem, but it did little to address the cost of another long underwater tunnel. Instead, Cassatt elected to modify Rea's proposal,

with car floats instead of locomotives, and water instead of rails. Rather than expand the crowded 1870s-vintage Harsimus Cove Yards, PRR engineers planned an entirely new facility more than three miles to the south, at Greenville. In 1880, the PRR had built the New York Bay Railroad, a short link from Waverly to a connection with the Jersey Central, at Oak Island Junction. Between 1901 and 1904, construction crews extended the line east across Newark Bay, on a mile-long trestle, and dumped twenty-two million cubic yards of fill—much of it removed from the tunnels and the foundations of Penn Station—on some 350 acres of marshland. When the new Greenville Yard opened in 1907, it constituted the largest integrated rail-water facility in the United States. Although built to accommodate four thousand cars, sufficient room was available to nearly triple that capacity. Three float bridges, rising and falling with the tide, enabled freight equipment to be shoved aboard car floats. Lighterage and warehouse piers permitted the manual transfer of cargoes from rail to water, while anthracite and bituminous coal docks supplemented the Berwind-White facilities at Harsimus Cove. Thereafter, Harsimus Cove served primarily for transferring freight, particularly produce that was bound for Manhattan, with Greenville accommodating export traffic and shipments destined for New England. A third facility, at South Amboy, continued to process coal shipments.[315]

Once aboard car floats at Greenville Yard, freight equipment crossed Upper New York Bay, well to the south of the congested areas around Communipaw, Jersey City, and Lower Manhattan. The freight arrived at the Long Island Rail Road's Bay Ridge Yard in South Brooklyn, opened in the spring of 1908. It then followed the LIRR's rebuilt Bay Ridge Branch—portions of which dated to 1876—east and north into Queens. At Fresh Pond Junction, freight passed onto the tracks of the New York Connecting Railroad, the final element of the New York Improvements.

A Gateway to New England

In addition to affording better access to the nation's largest city, the New York Improvements fulfilled the long-standing desire of PRR executives to expedite freight and passenger traffic destined for Boston and other New England points. They achieved that goal in 1917 with the completion of the Hell Gate Bridge linking Long Island and the Bronx. The Hell Gate Bridge made it possible to move traffic conveniently and expeditiously along all of the major cities of the eastern seaboard, from Washington to Boston. In the long run, however, the new route solidified the unhealthy relationship between the PRR and one of the weakest carriers in the Northeast, the New York, New Haven & Hartford Railroad.

The first efforts at linking the tracks of the PRR and the New Haven dated to 1892, when Samuel Rea's report to President Roberts suggested five possible mechanisms for reaching Manhattan. One route, by far the longest, called for a new double-track line across Staten Island, and then under the Narrows, by tunnel, to Long Island, with passenger trains traveling west across the Hudson River to a Midtown terminal. Freight and passenger trains bound for Boston would follow a different alignment, north through Queens, and then across the East River, at Hell Gate, to Wards Island and Randall's Island, and then to a connection with the New Haven at Port Morris. While a portion of the route, through Brooklyn, would utilize existing LIRR tracks, there was no corresponding route north through Queens. That problem was resolved in April 1892 with the incorporation of the New York Connecting Railroad—at that time intended to link the Long Island Rail Road to the New York Central. Rea's proposed tunnel under the Narrows never came to fruition, but the New York Connecting Railroad soon became a key element in Alexander Cassatt's plans to extend the PRR's influence to New England.

Gustav Lindenthal, who relished the opportunity to build a bridge at Hell Gate to match the one that he was planning to construct over the Hudson River, was a principal incorporator of the New York Connecting Railroad. As events transpired, however, it was another noted bridge engineer, Alfred P. Boller, who designed an eight-hundred-foot cantilever span for Hell Gate. Boller, a native of Philadelphia, was well known to PRR officials, as he had worked briefly on the Philadelphia & Erie Railroad during the 1860s. The principal guiding force behind the Connecting Railroad, Oliver W. Barnes, was even more closely as-

sociated with the PRR. He had joined the railroad in 1847, and by 1850 he was principal assistant engineer for the Western Division. In 1851, he laid out the town of Latrobe, Pennsylvania, named in honor of his friend, Baltimore & Ohio chief engineer Benjamin H. Latrobe. Barnes later served as the secretary of Crédit Mobilier before becoming associated with the New York Central Underground Railway Company, an ill-fated attempt to build an early subway system in Manhattan. He then served as chief engineer of the New York, Lake Erie & Western Railroad & Coal Company, and held the same position on the South Pennsylvania Railroad. He was also involved in the manufacture of iron and steel—accounting for his interest in the Hell Gate Bridge. His brother, William H. Barnes, was a longtime PRR director, but was probably not directly involved in the project. In 1894, Oliver Barnes and other New York Connecting Railroad officials conducted preliminary engineering surveys, and in 1897 and again in 1900 they obtained certain rights from the state legislature, including the authority to build the bridge. At that time, the New York Connecting Railroad remained a corporation that existed only on paper. By 1901, the company's investors nonetheless held a particularly valuable asset—War Department approval for the Hell Gate Bridge.[316]

By early 1900, Cassatt was willing to join forces with the New Haven in order to acquire the Long Island Rail Road and bring to fruition the New York Improvements. In the end, he elected to establish sole control over the LIRR, but the New Haven's participation would be vital for the proposed link to New England. In November 1901, J. Hampton Barnes, nephew of Oliver Barnes (and son of PRR director William Barnes) arranged to sell to the PRR a controlling interest in the New York Connecting Railroad. Cassatt quickly resold half of the PRR's stake to the New Haven.[317]

At the same time, rapid realignments in the structure of the New England railroads made cooperation with the New Haven all the more imperative. In 1900, New York Central officials cemented their long-standing relationship with the Boston & Albany Railroad, leasing that gateway across the Berkshires to New England. The lease carried with it a substantial block of New Haven shares, giving the NYC further influence in the distribution of the region's traffic. Financier J. P. Morgan, who enjoyed an enduring relationship with the NYC, also controlled a large number of New Haven securities and held a seat on that company's board of directors. In October 1903, he arranged for experienced New England railroad executive Charles Sanger Mellen to serve as president of the New Haven. Mellen soon began to create a smaller version of the PRR's community of interest. He established control over several regional railroads, including the New York, Ontario & Western; the Maine Central; and the Boston & Maine, as well as rapid transit and steamship lines. Like Cassatt, Mellen intended to use the newly consolidated system as an opportunity to stabilize rates and make substantial improvements in the New Haven's physical plant, and his plans included the more widespread adoption of electric traction. However, Cassatt worried that the New Haven's allies—particularly the New York, Ontario & Western—would provide Mellen with better access to the Poughkeepsie Bridge Route, an all-rail alternative to the water transfer at New York in competition against the PRR. "President Cassatt regarded [this] as unfriendly action on [the] part of the New Haven," Rea later recalled, "in hastily acquiring the N. Y., O. & W. Ry. trunk line without conference with [the] Pennsylvania at least."[318]

If the PRR could develop the New York Connecting Railroad as the preferred gateway to New England, it would largely neutralize the threat posed by the New Haven's acquisition of the New York, Ontario & Western, while transforming the New Haven from an adversary into an ally. Rea, in particular, emphasized that "this direct connection, bound by a valuable, jointly owned, connecting railroad, [would] make relations [with the New Haven] permanent as nothing else can." The PRR must not lose "the opportunity of tying New Haven traffic to it, but instead so permanently attach it to our System that even a change in ownership of the New Haven could not materially change conditions."[319] PRR officials accordingly sought closer cooperation with the New Haven and more secure access to New England. A year after taking office, Mellen invited Cassatt to invest in the New Haven and to take a seat on the company's board of directors.[320] In late December, the PRR directors agreed to buy ten thousand shares of

New Haven stock, double the amount that the NYC had acquired in the Boston & Albany lease three years earlier. By 1912, the PRR's holdings had increased to more than fifty thousand shares, representing 3.4 percent of the New Haven.[321]

Unfortunately, Mellen's version of the community of interest proved far less successful than the policies that Cassatt had put in place farther south. The New Haven's purchases of competing regional railroads suggested an effort to monopolize the area's transportation, and Mellen—along with Morgan—faced a grilling in front of the 1912–13 Pujo Committee investigation into the activities of Wall Street financiers. Interstate Commerce Commission and Justice Department officials were also sharply critical of Mellen's activities. By 1914, in an effort to fend off antitrust prosecution, Mellen had resigned the New Haven presidency and his successor, Charles Elliott, had signed a consent decree, pledging to divest virtually all of the company's acquisitions. More problematically, in creating his regional community of interest, Mellen had badly overextended the New Haven's credit, while acquiring some exceedingly weak carriers. The result was a financial crisis during the 1920s, followed by a 1935 bankruptcy that wiped out a large portion of the PRR's investments in the company. Throughout much of the twentieth century, therefore, the New Haven was in a parlous financial state, and in 1968 its ICC-mandated inclusion in the Penn Central was one of the factors that helped drag that company into ruin.

In 1903, as PRR and New Haven executives made preparations to build the New York Connecting Railroad, such problems lay many years in the future. Yet, they soon faced a repeat of the franchise battle that had slowed the construction of the tunnels under Manhattan. The company had been incorporated in 1892, six years prior to New York's municipal consolidation. While the company possessed War Department approval for the Hell Gate Bridge, it now required permission to build through the borough of Queens. On June 11, 1903, Connecting Railroad officials requested a franchise to do so, from the Board of Rapid Transit Railroad Commissioners. As Rea later recalled, the importance of establishing a New England gateway in close cooperation with the New Haven was so important that PRR officials felt justified "in making more than usual concessions at the start" to the city.[322]

The proposed price was far steeper than Rea could countenance, however. Harry C. Nichols, chief of the Bureau of Franchises, insisted on an up-front payment of $2,250,000, as well as annual fees for crossing city streets—most of which, it should be noted, were merely platted and not actually constructed. Representatives from the two sides spent more than a year in negotiations. Not until June 1904 did the commissioners approve a final agreement. Then, as with the tunnel franchise, they forwarded the document to the Board of Aldermen for an up-or-down vote.[323]

The wheel of political fortune, which had so favored the PRR during the battle for the tunnel franchise, now turned against the railroad. Seth Low had been a capable mayor, but he was often described as "colorless" and utterly lacking in charisma. He was also scrupulously honest—perhaps too much so, for his campaigns against liquor and other vices earned him the praise of straight-laced reformers but the enmity of far larger numbers of more morally fallible voters. In November 1903, George B. McClellan, Jr., son of the Civil War general, trounced Low at the polls. McClellan, who was closely allied with the Tammany machine, was not anxious to do any favors for the Pennsylvania Railroad.

With a mayor who was their ally rather than their opponent, the aldermen spent a leisurely ten months debating the franchise sent to them by the Board of Rapid Transit Railroad Commissioners. There was political posturing on both sides, with the aldermen claiming that they were protecting the citizenry from ruthless exploitation by a rapacious corporation, while PRR and New Haven officials expressed disgust that their gift to the city of improved transportation was being so brusquely criticized. Mayor McClellan and his allies on the Board of Aldermen insisted that the original franchise fee offer of $2,250,000 was too low, rather than too high, as PRR officials had claimed. The aldermen also sought to impose additional stipulations, including a requirement that the Hell Gate Bridge be modified to carry pedestrian and vehicle traffic as well as police and fire department communication lines, and that the railroad be allowed to charge no more than the city's standard five-cent subway fare

over the route—even though the line would be used strictly for through rather than local traffic.[324]

The delays proved so interminable that civic and business leaders, who sought better connections to New England and who saw through the aldermanic posturing, sued to force a vote on the franchise. Members of the New York Charter Revision Commission proposed that the municipal charter be amended to strip the franchise power from the politicians on the Board of Aldermen. They instead wished to delegate the franchise authority to the Board of Estimate and Apportionment, a body whose political composition encouraged a city-wide planning perspective.[325] In March 1905, a frustrated New York Supreme Court Justice William D. Dickey echoed the position of PRR officials. "The construction of this road would be a convenience and a benefit to many residents of Brooklyn," he emphasized. "The excuses for delay are fanciful, pretended, and have no merit."[326] Dickey thereupon issued a writ of mandamus, compelling the aldermen to vote on the franchise. The Board of Aldermen complied with the court order, but hardly in the manner that PRR executives might have wished. On April 18, they rejected the franchise and sent it back to the Board of Rapid Transit Railroad Commissioners for a further round of negotiations.

Cassatt and his associates, anxious to avoid repeating the long delays associated with the original tunnel negotiations, were determined to once and for all strip the aldermen of the power to approve or disallow railway franchises. Their unlikely ally was Senator Nathaniel A. Elsberg, a New York County Republican. Two years earlier, members of the Citizens' Union had criticized August Belmont's links to Tammany Hall, and his ability to exploit the terms of the 1894 Rapid Transit Act, in order to create a subway monopoly based on the IRT. In February 1903, Elsberg had responded to their concerns by introducing legislation (often referred to as the "Elsberg Rapid Transit Bill") that limited the length of franchises to twenty-five years, made it easier for the Rapid Transit Railroad Commissioners to revoke subway contracts, and provided for the separation of contracts for the construction and the operation of subways. The last provision aroused considerable opposition, for it reflected Elsberg's belief that the city government should run the subways. The bill also included a provision that would further clarify the terms of the 1902 Stranahan Rapid Transit Bill. Nevada Stranahan's legislation had stipulated that the aldermen could do no more than approve or reject whatever franchise agreement that the Rapid Transit Railroad Commissioners had negotiated. Elsberg was certain that an unholy alliance existed between Belmont and Tammany Hall's representatives on the Board of Aldermen. As such, his bill promised to eliminate entirely the aldermanic oversight of railway franchises, transferring the right of approval to the Board of Estimate and Apportionment. Despite the bill's many components, public reaction was shaped largely by the municipal-ownership provision, with conservative elements such as the *New York Times* labeling the legislation "a public outrage, a monstrous affront to the sane, responsible, and informed public opinion of this city, if this huge, crude, and ignorantly drawn measure were to be converted into law."[327] Most state legislators thought so as well, and by the end of April, the Elsberg bill had gone down to defeat.[328]

The subsequent legislative history of the new and varied incarnations of the original Elsberg bill proved extraordinarily complex. Alexander Orr, president of the Board of Rapid Transit Railroad Commissioners, had little patience with Elsberg's efforts to reduce the commission's power. Edward Morse Shepard, the Brooklyn Democrat who had lost the 1901 mayoral race to Seth Low, shared those attitudes. Shepard was the legal counsel for the commissioners, but he nonetheless saw considerable merit in the provision of the Elsberg bill that transferred franchise approval from the aldermen to the Board of Estimate and Apportionment. So, too, did Pennsylvania Railroad officials. Happily, Shepard was also the PRR's New York legal counsel, and he was well positioned to steer a version of the Elsberg bill through the state legislature.

Although Elsberg introduced bills in the 1904 session (they failed, again), his partial success came in 1905 as a result of intense lobbying by Shepard and his PRR backers. Republican power broker, senator, and key PRR ally Thomas Collier Platt testified before the New York Senate Cities Committee, echoing Elsberg's claim that the aldermen were too corrupt to be entrusted with the city's transportation future. Charles

Francis Murphy, since 1902 the leader of Tammany Hall, did his best to refute the charges, as he had in the past.[329]

By 1905, however, Murphy's opposition was little more than a pretense. In June 1904, the PRR had assigned the contract for excavation at the site of Pennsylvania Station to the New York Contracting & Trucking Company. The firm's president was John J. Murphy, brother of Charles Francis Murphy. Actual control of the company, however, lay with Alderman James E. Gaffney, a longtime adversary of the Pennsylvania Railroad. With what amounted to bribery transforming key Tammany politicians from adversaries to allies, aldermanic opposition to the New York Connecting Railroad franchise declined considerably.[330]

By the middle of April 1905, both houses of the legislature approved the Elsberg bill, transferring the final authority over the New York Connecting Railroad franchise to the Board of Estimate and Apportionment. Tammany stalwarts were predictably outraged, with Timothy P. "Little Tim" Sullivan—a former bootblack who, along with his cousin Timothy D. "Big Tim" Sullivan, controlled the Lower East Side—announcing that "this is the way the corporations want to punish the board [of Aldermen] because it wouldn't let the Pennsylvania Railroad steal a valuable franchise for the New York Connecting Road. We protected the city, and the company then went to Albany and got its obedient servants in the Legislature to pass the Elsberg bills."[331] Alderman Frank L. Dowling echoed those sentiments, suggesting that "the Pennsylvania Railroad owns the Legislature."[332] Pro-Tammany newspapers alleged "corruption in the New York Legislature," as "the Pennsylvania Railroad Company is said to have spent half a million dollars" to secure its right to build the New York Connecting Railroad.[333]

As expected, Mayor McClellan exercised his veto authority, arguing that the last vestiges of home rule were being usurped by state politicians who were at the PRR's beck and call. "The Pennsylvania Railroad Company but a few years ago acquired a foothold in this city, but it seems determined to exercise its power over public officials here as it has elsewhere. It has already made plain to me its ability to crush all opposition to its plans," he insisted.[334] Whether crushed by the PRR or more likely merely tired of Tammany posturing, the legislature in May 1905 overrode McClellan's veto. The aldermen soon threatened legal action, on the grounds that the law was in violation of the state constitution. In April 1906 the state courts finally gave their imprimatur to the transfer of power from the aldermen to the Board of Estimate and Apportionment. Some disgruntled aldermen vowed to appeal the case to the United States Supreme Court, but most privately conceded that their chances of success, in a solely intrastate political matter, were likely to be slim.[335]

Through the spring and into the summer of 1905, no one was entirely certain who possessed the power to award a construction franchise to the New York Connecting Railroad. By November, with the franchise still languishing before the Board of Rapid Transit Railroad Commissioners, Samuel Rea threatened to abandon the entire project, particularly if city officials followed through with their threats to regulate rates on a section of railroad that was clearly designed for interstate traffic. With work at a standstill, the protracted franchise negotiations continued into 1906.

By January, Cassatt had sweetened the deal, promising a ten-point improvement program that provided for the elimination of grade crossings and the conversion to electric power of all the LIRR lines within city limits.[336] He matched the carrot with a stick, however, and vowed to abandon the project if the franchise costs proved excessive. At the same time, the Rapid Transit Railroad Commissioners had accepted Cassatt's position that they lacked the authority to regulate rates on the New York Connecting Railroad, probably because their attorneys acknowledged that such regulation would contravene ICC authority. However, the commissioners held firm in their demands for the $2,250,000 up-front payment that Harry Nichols had originally demanded. That price, Cassatt made plain, was a deal breaker. Rather than risk the possibility that they might be blamed for terminating a project that would confer obvious commercial benefits on New York, the commissioners reduced the fee to a more modest $1,250,000, spread over twenty-five years.[337]

Despite Charles Murphy's willingness to trade an excavation contract for acquiescence to the Connecting Railroad franchise, the Tammany boss was still a force to be reckoned with in New York politics. In October 1905, newspaperman William Randolph Hearst announced that he was running for mayor on a platform that included municipal reform. Murphy and his associates orchestrated electoral fraud, ensuring McClellan's reelection and making the mayor more beholden to Tammany Hall than before. During the spring of 1906, McClellan again did his best to block the franchise, demanding that the Rapid Transit Railroad Commissioners restore the earlier conditions that were less favorable to the PRR. "I concede that the granting of this franchise will hasten the growth of the city," McClellan argued, "but for the present the benefit will be chiefly to the corporations securing the right."[338] Yet, even as he maintained a façade of fierce opposition to the PRR, McClellan was privately willing to yield ground to the railroad. In the face of widespread evidence of corruption (Tammany officials had attempted to dispose of unfavorable ballots by throwing them into the East River, for example), the PRR seemed less like a monopolistic threat to the public interest than a force for good government.[339]

By the spring of 1906, however, PRR officials were increasingly concerned at the terms of the latest incarnation of the Elsberg bill. Even as he was proposing to strip franchise authority from the aldermen, Elsberg was continuing to promote the 1903 Citizens' Union proposal to municipalize subway operations and impose time limits on subway operating contracts. In April 1905, the state senate resoundingly defeated the newest version of the "Elsberg Rapid Transit Bill" by a vote of forty to eight. President pro tem John Raines shook his fist at Elsberg, causing an uproar on the senate floor and forcing lieutenant governor M. Linn Bruce to plead for order. Senator Thomas F. Grady, one of Tammany's most eloquent orators, pointed out that Elsberg had earlier supported the granting of a perpetual franchise to the Pennsylvania Railroad for the route linking New Jersey to Long Island, but that he was now hypocritically attempting to impose restrictions that would discourage future entrepreneurs from building new subway lines. In the end, Senator Elsberg was the only legislator from Greater New York who supported his bill. He muttered darkly to reporters that "there are three great corporations against this bill, and the great unorganized public of New York City has not a representative to speak for their interests."[340]

One of those "three great corporations" was the IRT, but another was surely the Pennsylvania Railroad. PRR executives, despite their support for the other Elsberg bill, were vehemently opposed to *this* Elsberg bill, which they believed might hinder rather than help the construction of the New York Connecting Railroad. The members of the New York Chamber of Commerce shared that concern, and spoke forcefully against the legislation, noting that "the Elsberg Bill, as drawn, would so limit the power of the Board [of Rapid Transit Railroad Commissioners] that franchises could be granted only to railroads in tunnels intended to connect with trunk line steam railroads whose immediate termini are in another state." The New York Connecting Railroad, however, would be located entirely within the state of New York. "The obvious comment," concluded the Chamber's spokesman, "is that such provisions would preclude the Rapid Transit Commission from carrying out the plan of connecting the New-York, New Haven and Hartford Railroad and the Long Island Railroad by bridges over the East and Harlem Rivers."[341]

Representatives from the Chamber of Commerce were far more concerned, however, at an issue that had little immediate relevance for the PRR—namely, the provision that separated subway construction from ownership and suggested that the city's government might run the subway system. Their concerns, and those of other like-minded New Yorkers, led to a modification of the Elsberg bill that temporarily eliminated the provision of separate ownership and operation. The legislation passed the Senate on March 28, 1906, leaving "Elsberg in a rage," according to the *Times*, as the Republican from the Fifteenth District charged that his bill had been "emasculated."[342] By early April, the bill had passed the Assembly, with the construction and operation provisions restored. McClellan approved the measure, as did Governor Frank W. Higgins. In its final form, the Elsberg bill no longer contained restrictions that would preclude the granting of the PRR's much-desired charter. After a battle that lasted nearly three years, the Board of Rapid Transit Railroad Commissioners finally awarded a franchise for the construction of the New York Connecting Railroad on February 14, 1907.[343]

Even then, the struggle to allocate the franchise power was far from over. In December 1905, the Rapid Transit Railroad Commissioners had permitted August Belmont's IRT to swallow its chief competitor, the Metropolitan Street Railway. The following year, when William Randolph Hearst campaigned for governor, his platform included public ownership of New York's subway and surface transit companies as well as gas and electric services. Republican Charles Evans Hughes won the election, beating back Hearst's challenge by a mere fifty-eight thousand votes out of almost 1.5 million cast. Hughes was therefore aware that the public demanded transportation reforms. Once in office, he supported efforts to extinguish both the Board of Rapid Transit Railroad Commissioners and the New York State Railroad Commission. The June 1907 Page-Merritt bill created two Public Service Commissions, one for the First District (New York City) and the other for the Second District (the remainder of the state). The new system replaced the informal cooperative arrangements that had characterized the city's transportation politics with a more bureaucratic and more adversarial system. To the PRR's great advantage, however, the PSC undermined the Democrats who dominated New York City politics. By moving the forum for negotiations up the Hudson River to Albany, the Republican Party, always more conciliatory to the PRR's interests, would in future assume control of transportation policy.

With the franchise in hand, the construction of the New York Connecting Railroad became something of an anticlimax. Gustav Lindenthal was never able to build his North River Bridge, but in October 1904 he gained a measure of solace when he became consulting engineer and architect for the Hell Gate span. Lindenthal and his assistants soon developed three alternate bridge designs, each of which employed a center span approximately 850 feet long. In the fall of 1905, a realignment, necessary to avoid a state mental hospital on Wards Island, required Lindenthal to increase the center span to one thousand feet. He made additional modifications following the August 1907 Quebec Bridge disaster, when a cantilever span had collapsed into the St. Lawrence River while the bridge was under construction.[344]

Despite the planning, little construction was forthcoming. While Cassatt had been a strong supporter of the Hell Gate route, his successor, James McCrea, investigated other options. The delay induced by the franchise fight had enabled workers to make significant advances in other aspects of the New York Improvements, and the complexity of the North River and East River tunnels, in addition to the construction of Penn Station, taxed the PRR's engineering capabilities, as well as its finances. In the aftermath of the Panic of 1907, PRR officials pledged to carry on the Improvements, but they acknowledged that certain aspects of the project, such as the Connecting Railroad, would have to be postponed. In 1910, furthermore, a dispute erupted as officials of the three railroads that reached Manhattan directly—the PRR, the NYC, and the New Haven—met to discuss the effect that the Connecting Railroad would have on their ability to generate traffic. NYC executives were concerned that the new line would enhance the PRR's trunk-line status, while negating their recent efforts to penetrate New England through the lease of the Boston & Albany. Mellen, no doubt with strong prodding from J. P. Morgan and his allies on the NYC, was concerned that the PRR would usurp some of the New Haven's power in the New York and New England markets. In the end, however, Mellen pragmatically concluded that the PRR possessed adequate resources to invade New England on its own, and that he would be wise to have the railroad as an ally.[345]

Throughout the delays, Vice President Rea remained an advocate of the Hell Gate Bridge, pushing McCrea to begin construction. The PRR negotiated some contracts as early as August 1910, but major work did not begin until July 1912, with the erection of two massive towers that would eventually reach 220 feet in height. In January 1913, Rea ascended to the presidency, ensuring the completion of the project. However, another two years passed before steelworkers began erecting the superstructure of the bridge. Through 1914 and 1915, as Americans read of the growing carnage associated with the war in Europe, the two halves of the Hell Gate Bridge inched closer and closer to one another. By the end of September 1915, steelworkers had joined the two segments of the center arch. In March 1917,

Samuel Rea and Gustav Lindenthal presided over the dedication of the Hell Gate Bridge, at that time the largest single-arch span in the world. Freight service began shortly afterward, and not long after midnight on April 2, the first passenger trains crossed the structure, completing the principal portion of the New York Connecting Railroad.

From a junction with the New Haven, at Port Morris, the tracks crossed Bronx Kill via a bascule bridge, moving onto Randall's Island over a series of gradually ascending arches. Another bridge spanned Little Hell Gate, giving access to Wards Island and the northern portal of the Hell Gate Bridge. It was an impressive achievement, 1,017 feet long, with a deck 135 feet above mean high tide, and with the top of the arch 305 feet above the surface of the water. Once in Queens, the tracks descended on another long viaduct—the total length was some seventeen thousand feet, split more or less evenly on both sides of Hell Gate. Much of the remaining alignment lay atop earthen fill, satisfying local interests by eliminating grade crossings, but requiring construction crews to move 2.1 million cubic yards of material. At Sunnyside Junction the line split, with one segment, the first to be completed, swinging sharply west, affording passenger trains access to Sunnyside Yard, the East River tunnels, and Penn Station. The other branch, known as the Southern Division and completed in 1918, continued south to Fresh Pond Junction. There, freight traffic joined LIRR tracks for the trip south and west to the Bay Ridge Yard, with car floats continuing across Upper New York Bay to the Greenville Yard in New Jersey.[346]

Relative to its length, the New York Connecting Railroad was one of the most expensive construction projects undertaken by the PRR, on par with the facilities linking New Jersey and Long Island. The PRR and the New Haven each shouldered half of the $33 million cost, something that the New England carrier was ill equipped to do. Even for the PRR, the investment offered few immediate returns. Despite its potential as a freight gateway to New England, the Hell Gate Bridge carried mostly passenger trains, and with four tracks, it was never utilized at anything like full capacity. To an even greater extent than Penn Station—or, for that matter, the low-grade freight lines

Figure 85. In the spring of 1917, the opening of the Hell Gate Bridge on the New York Connecting Railroad marked the completion of the major elements of the New York Improvements. After spending more than $140 million, the Pennsylvania Railroad had created an infrastructure that would alleviate congestion at its New York facilities for decades to come. Gustav Lindenthal, the designer of the bridge, stands at center, with the white beard.

Library of Congress, Prints & Photographs Division, LC-USZ62-77070.

and the other Cassatt-era improvements—the Connecting Railroad represented construction well in advance of existing demand.

The Saga of the Subway

As they planned the New York Improvements, Cassatt, Rea, and their PRR and LIRR associates envisioned Penn Station as the nexus of a multifaceted urban passenger network that included long-distance trains, commuter traffic, and local transportation. In particular, they anticipated that subways would permit the rapid distribution of people to all parts of Manhattan. Indeed, they depended on convenient subway service in order to offset the disadvantages of the station's location, removed from the city's islands of commercial development. As construction crews began excavating the foundations for Penn Station, however, the nearest rapid transit lines were the elevated railways along Sixth Avenue and Ninth Avenue, operated by the Manhattan Railway Company.[347] Each was a long city block away from the nearest station entrance, and neither provided access to any of Manhattan's main commercial centers.

When the PRR board gave its assent to the New York Improvements, railroad officials had nevertheless assumed that a subway line along Seventh Avenue would be in operation soon after the completion of Penn Station.[348] Charles Raymond, the chairman of the board of engineers, believed that "the extension of the present subway down-town on the West side with direct connections to Brooklyn, and up-town from 42nd Street to the Bronx . . . will make the Pennsylvania Station a great centre for receiving and distributing passenger traffic between all the Boroughs of the City and outlying points."[349] That optimistic pronouncement soon ran headlong into the realities of New York City politics.

The construction of the New York subway system embodied a complex series of negotiations between technocrats and politicians, and between government and private enterprise. The Interborough Rapid Transit Company, controlled by August Belmont, Jr., first brought the benefits of the subway to Manhattan residents, but soon threatened to monopolize underground transportation. In 1900 and 1902, Belmont secured two initial subway franchises, Contract No. 1 and Contract No. 2, from the Board of Rapid Transit Railroad Commissioners. One line ran north to Harlem, the other east to Long Island, and neither was of any real value to the PRR. In March 1905, the commissioners proposed a massive $250 million system with nineteen routes, including subways underneath Seventh and Eighth Avenues, on either side of Penn Station, as well as a cross-town line along Thirty-Fourth Street. From the perspective of PRR officials, the most useful route was to be an adjunct to the existing IRT Harlem line, from Times Square along Seventh Avenue to the Battery. August Belmont was better positioned than anyone else to build the web of new lines, as part of his IRT system. He was certainly receptive to PRR demands for a route that would reach Penn Station, and the presence of attorney Thomas De Witt Cuyler on the boards of directors of both the PRR and the IRT ensured coordination between the two companies.[350]

The Rapid Transit Railroad Commissioners believed that they possessed ample reason to doubt Belmont's commitment to the public interest. By January 1903 the IRT had established control over the Manhattan Railway Company, including its Sixth Avenue and Ninth Avenue elevated lines. The Metropolitan Street Railway joined the Belmont empire in December 1905, and it seemed that the "Traction King" was poised to control all of Manhattan's rapid transit. The close cooperation between Belmont and Tammany Hall only made matters worse. A reporter for *McClure's* magazine summed up the public mood, warning readers of the "Giant Proportions of the New Belmont Monopoly."[351] The mergers, part of the same *fin de siècle* ordering of financial affairs that contributed to the PRR's community of interest, induced a bitter struggle between Belmont, his competitors, the Rapid Transit Railroad Commissioners, the aldermen, and the members of the Board of Estimate and Apportionment. The commissioners, anxious to prevent a monopoly, but lacking the statutory authority to mandate competition, descended into a kind of catatonic stupor, determined to delay the issuance of further franchises until they could be certain that Belmont would not gain control over them. They were willing to hold back some franchise rights, including those for an Eighth Avenue subway that would pass along the west side of Penn Station, for allocation to a competitive developer, should Belmont prove particularly obstreperous.[352]

Urban reformers were likewise determined to prevent the development of a transportation monopoly, even at the cost of the destruction of the Board of Rapid Transit Railroad Commissioners. When state legislators finally passed the Elsberg amendment to the Rapid Transit Act in 1906, they separated subway construction and operating contracts, and held out the possibility of municipal ownership, in case private companies were uncooperative. The next year, following the inauguration of Governor Charles Evans Hughes, the Page-Merritt bill replaced the Board of Rapid Transit Railroad Commissioners with a Public Service Commission. The new commissioners lacked the authority to authorize municipal construction and ownership, but they were determined to be far more adversarial in their interaction with any private contractor who might attempt to build a subway in the vicinity of Penn Station—or anywhere else in New York, for that matter.[353]

By the beginning of 1908, the members of the new Public Service Commission had issued the Triborough Subway Plan for a far-flung subway system that, once again, promised few benefits for the PRR. The PSC, in addition to reflecting the public antipathy toward monopoly, also embodied a reformist zeal to disperse the huddled masses away from the crowded slums of Manhattan, and into Long Island and the Bronx. Under those circumstances, the transportation of passengers to and from Penn Station possessed a distinctly secondary importance. That was one of the reasons why the members of a special Citizens' Committee, convened by the New York State Chamber of Commerce, were so deeply critical of the PSC's plans.[354]

As far as Rea and his associates were concerned, it would be best to entrust the Seventh Avenue line to Belmont, monopoly or no monopoly, as the subway king had already proven that he could get the job done. PSC members, anxious to disperse Manhattan's population and determined to avoid a Belmont transportation monopoly, found such suggestions unacceptable. "The Commission [was] paying too much attention to the clamor of the sensational newspapers," Gustav Lindenthal complained, noting that they "must have been obsessed by certain fixed ideas rather than by a real study of the transportation problem."[355] When Rea pushed for a Seventh Avenue subway, he discovered that he "could not find a man in New York, from Chairman [William R.] Wilcox of the Public Service Commission down who was willing to advocate this proposition, notwithstanding they could see that it involved the least outlay, but it seemed to favor the present [Belmont] subway interests, and every man of them was afraid politically to make such a suggestion."[356] An exasperated Rea even threatened to use PRR funds to establish a new subway company for the express purpose of constructing the Seventh Avenue line. "Of course we hoped that we never would be required to do this," he informed President McCrea, "and frankly we know that we never would be permitted to get into that situation even if we wanted to."[357]

By 1910, the subway situation was on the verge of descending into utter chaos. The 1909 municipal elections had provided the Tammany machine with a stinging rebuke, and anti-machine Fusion candidates gained control of the Board of Aldermen, the Board of Estimate and Apportionment, and four out of the five boroughs. Yet Tammany loyalist William J. Gaynor won the mayor's office, and continued the machine's long-standing alliance with Belmont and the IRT. The Fusionists, in contrast, agreed with the PSC policy of recruiting private capital to build the Triborough system, but not a single entrepreneur submitted a bid. Several dozen were willing to commit to the venture, but only if the city provided financing. Commissioner Wilcox, never a strong leader, seemed utterly demoralized by the chain of events.

Then, in November, William Gibbs McAdoo announced that he was prepared to save New York from the Belmont monopoly by building a subway that was connected to his Hudson & Manhattan Railroad. A significant portion of his system would duplicate the Triborough Plan, but the problem for the PRR was that McAdoo wanted to build underneath Sixth Avenue, one long block east of Penn Station. PSC officials, far from criticizing McAdoo for his unwillingness to connect with the PRR facility, were ecstatic that they had finally located someone who possessed the experience and the resources necessary to bring the Triborough system into being. August Belmont, who had little to fear from the PSC, was correspondingly nervous, concluding that McAdoo constituted a far more formidable opponent. Belmont soon submitted a rival plan, which included a Seventh Avenue subway, and correspondingly won the support of the Citizens' Committee of the New York Chamber of Commerce, particularly its newest member, Samuel Rea. The onslaught soon led McAdoo to withdraw from the fray. Having lost their potential savior, members of both the PSC and the Board of Estimate and Apportionment engaged in a series of acrimonious debates, uncertain whether they should permit Belmont to build the new lines and expand his monopoly, or else entrust the city's newest mass transit project to inexperienced and ill-financed newcomers.[358]

PRR officials did their best to convince the business community, elected officials, and members of the public that an IRT subway was preferable to no subway. For Rea and his associates, municipal concerns over competitive mass transit were decidedly secondary to the need to complete a line to Penn Station as quickly as possible. He begged Mayor Gaynor to consider the needs of "the people living in Long Island and New Jersey and all the travellers of the Pennsylvania R.R. whose convenience has been thoroughly disregarded by the Public Service Commission," emphasizing that "in the construction of subways the interests of the city should be considered first, instead of looking after competitive leasers."[359] Despite their efforts to influence the course of events, PRR officials could do little of value, Rea lamented, "except rely largely upon the moral support of public opinion" to demand that someone, preferably Belmont, be allowed to build a Seventh Avenue line.[360]

By January 1911, the disaster seemed complete. Edwin W. Winter, president of the Brooklyn Rapid Transit Company, an 1896 conglomerate of surface and elevated lines, offered yet another proposal for subway construction. None of the routes would serve Penn Station. Winter's company had established a virtual monopoly of the transit system in Brooklyn, and was in that respect hardly different from Belmont's domination in Manhattan. PSC officials nevertheless welcomed the new competitor against the IRT. In contrast, Rea and other PRR managers were aghast at the prospect of a new round of debate and delay.[361]

The PRR's salvation came from George McAneny, president of the borough of Manhattan. McAneny was a reformer, bitterly opposed to Tammany corruption. Unlike many of his associates, however, he had no innate dislike for business, and he was a protégé of Edward M. Shepard, the PRR's local legal counsel. McAneny was perfectly willing to work with anyone—even August Belmont—if he could improve the city and the lives of its inhabitants. He was also less concerned with dispersing the immigrants and the working poor into the suburbs than he was with creating an efficient, coordinated transportation system. Above all, McAneny was a dealmaker and a peacemaker, a man who knew how to get things done. His interests and tactics, therefore, meshed beautifully with the needs of the Pennsylvania Railroad. His great insight was that the BRT and the IRT, far from being mutually exclusive alternatives, could be made to work together. Soon after the BRT proposal became public,

McAneny chaired a new Transit Committee of the Board of Estimate and Apportionment, and that body soon usurped the PSC's control over subway planning. By June 1911, McAneny had issued a report that called for the creation of a dual contract system, with interlocking routes allocated more or less equally to the BRT and the IRT. McAneny was willing to award a profit guarantee to the BRT as the upstart competitor, but not to the established and already profitable IRT. Even though BRT officials quickly accepted the recommendations, Belmont balked.[362]

Rea, desperate to secure IRT participation in the dual contract proposal, met repeatedly with Mayor Gaynor, former Mayor Seth Low, and PSC officials, pressuring them to offer Belmont more generous terms. The PRR vice president also did his best to influence public opinion, informing journalists that "the [Penn Station] terminal is by design and use all that we expected it to be, but there is no doubt that it would be a material advantage to have subway rapid transit facilities, and it is a disgrace to the public authorities that they are not already in service."[363]

Many of the members of the PSC nonetheless remained convinced that Belmont was an unscrupulous monopolist, to whom the city's transit needs could not be safely entrusted. Commissioner Wilcox could do no better than propose the construction of a subterranean "moving sidewalk" beneath Thirty-Fourth Street that would link Penn Station to the proposed BRT line under Broadway. Rea, displeased at the prospect of PRR passengers transported by what amounted to a conveyor belt, rejected the suggestion. Another proposal, to build a set of platforms in the Crosstown Tunnels, at Fourth Avenue, was likewise rejected because it would have snarled traffic to and from Long Island, while rendering moot a significant portion of the PRR's investment in Penn Station.[364]

George McAneny was again responsible for resolving the impasse. A new round of negotiations began in November 1911, largely under the direction of Rea and his assistant, Albert J. County. By February 1912, McAneny had persuaded the members of the PSC to accept amended contract terms, which were considerably more generous to the IRT. The perceived favoritism induced a round of lawsuits, which were not resolved until June. In March 1913, IRT and BRT officials signed Contract No. 3 and Contract No. 4, the dual contracts that McAneny had envisioned more than two years earlier. Construction of the IRT's Seventh Avenue Subway between Times Square and Penn Station required another four years. On June 3, 1917, nearly seven years after its completion, Penn Station was finally integrated into the transportation system of Greater New York.[365]

Entr'acte

Very early on the morning of April 2, 1917, the first passenger trains crossed the Hell Gate Bridge, marking the official completion of the New York Improvements. That evening, President Woodrow Wilson addressed a joint session of Congress, informing his audience that "The world must be made safe for democracy." Within days, the United States had declared war against Germany and Austria-Hungary, joining a conflict that had raged in Europe since August 1914. As the nation mobilized, Pennsylvania Railroad personnel prepared to move a torrent of men and materiel to east coast ports. That was a very different role from the decades-old dream of conveying the western grain trade to Philadelphia, and one that doubtless would have discomfited many of the pacifist Quakers who had established the PRR more than seventy years earlier.[366]

The Pennsylvania Railroad was born amid a very different war, a struggle with Mexico that caused many Philadelphia Quakers to protest an act of imperialist aggression that was certain to benefit the slave-owning South. Those Quakers were long dead, as were all of the people who had created the Pennsylvania Railroad. Herman Haupt was the last to depart. Early in his long and varied career, he had served as the railroad's superintendent of transportation, general superintendent, chief engineer, and director. The principal designer of the PRR's organization had never been able to conform to the model of an organization man. He had left the PRR, then returned, left again, and afterward had drifted from place to place, and from job to job. On December 13, 1905, while walking through Manhattan to catch the PRR ferry to Jersey City, he suffered a mild heart attack. He was cared for by his son Louis

M. Haupt, a hydraulic engineer who had served on the first Isthmian Canal Commission, part of a project that would soon eclipse the New York Improvements as the greatest engineering achievement of the age. The following day, Louis Haupt escorted his father back to Philadelphia. They departed Lower Manhattan by ferry, only a few miles south of the subterranean world where at that moment construction crews were just beginning their efforts to tunnel under the Hudson River. Their train left Jersey City at 8:25 in the morning. Minutes later, Haupt leaned forward, as if to speak, and then fell into the arms of his son. Herman Haupt was eighty-eight years old, and, fittingly, he died on the Pennsylvania Railroad.[367]

The world that Haupt had known, the one that he had done so much to create, had passed away as well. From a single track linking Harrisburg to Duncansville, and Johnstown to Pittsburgh, the Pennsylvania Railroad had grown to encompass more than ten thousand miles in thirteen states. With the exception of Boston, its trains reached all of the major population centers in the Northeast, connecting Philadelphia, New York, Baltimore, and Washington to Pittsburgh, Erie, Buffalo, Cincinnati, Columbus, Cleveland, Indianapolis, Louisville, St. Louis, and Chicago. All-Pullman express trains thundered between Jersey City and Chicago in less time than it had taken to cross the commonwealth of Pennsylvania half a century earlier. Massive steam locomotives pulled long strings of cars—many of them made of steel, and equipped with automatic couplers and air brakes—that carried enormous tonnages of coal, iron, and steel along a four-track main line, at rates far lower than even Herman Haupt could have predicted. Gargantuan civil engineering works promised to increase transportation efficiency still further, by raising speeds and augmenting carrying capacity.

Yet, the Pennsylvania Railroad in many respects reached its apex just as Herman Haupt left it behind. The troubles began less than two years after his death, as the Panic of 1907 consumed the national economy. Its effects were short lived compared with the depressions of the 1870s and the 1890s, but they nonetheless caused the customary rounds of layoffs, salary reductions, deferred maintenance, and postponed or cancelled construction projects. What was different this time, however, was that the PRR, and the nation's other railroads, never fully recovered.

In many respects, 1907 was the last good year in the history of the Pennsylvania Railroad. President James McCrea would later point out that the PRR's gross earnings had reached a new record high in 1907, at $164.8 million, representing an increase of $16.6 million over the previous year. But, he also acknowledged that expenses had risen at an even faster rate, and were up more than $17.8 million. By the end of the decade, many operating officials and eminent economists had observed that the PRR and its competitors faced a steady decline in revenue per ton-mile, and that the railroads had to haul more and more freight just to maintain the same level of earnings. "The various economies in operation, heavier trainloads and the like," wrote transportation economist William Z. Ripley, "have not since 1906 yielded any greater profit from mere operation, with the ever increasing volume of business."[368] In and of itself, that was not too different from the situation that had characterized the last decades of the nineteenth century, as rapid increases in efficiency engendered a sustained decline in rates without jeopardizing overall profitability.[369]

What was different after 1907, however, was that the PRR, like other carriers, was confronting the law of diminishing returns in its operations. Following the incorporation of steel rail, stronger cars, signals, air brakes, and automatic couplers, there were no new innovations on the horizon—at least, none that could produce such large efficiency gains for such a relatively small initial investment. Many of the new construction projects—including the low-grade lines and the New York Improvements—had perversely the opposite effect, as they required massive up-front capital costs, but the resulting gains in efficiency would not be experienced for many years, and only as traffic levels increased. Not until the widespread adoption of diesel locomotives, during the decade that followed the end of World War II, would the railroads again experience the productivity boost that had been commonplace in the late 1800s.

Many Americans and, more to the point, officials representing the Interstate Commerce Commission continued to operate as if the railroad landscape would feature continually escalating productivity, coupled with steadily decreasing rates. The progressive vision of scientific management, most forcefully expressed by Louis Brandeis, suggested that the greater efficiency could fund everything from higher wages to increased safety, while continuing to generate returns that were sufficiently robust to satisfy investors and attract additional capital. That mantra had contributed to the passage of the Safety Appliance Act in 1893, the Hours of Service Act in 1907, and the Adamson Act in 1916. The latter two laws, in particular, substantially increased the railroads' labor costs, without a corresponding increase in labor productivity. At the same time, ICC regulators were progressively more reluctant to grant rate increases to the railroads, holding that profits should be derived from greater efficiency, not from additional charges to shippers. Even when railway officials could clearly demonstrate the burden of higher labor and material costs, the 1910 Mann-Elkins Act ensured that rate hikes would always lag months or even years behind the cost increases that had made them necessary.

The ICC's emphasis on efficiency in lieu of higher rates paled in comparison to a fundamental shift in regulatory policy. Prior to 1900, ICC officials, who at that time possessed quite limited ratemaking authority, had generally accepted the arguments of railway executives that they were entitled to allocate assets as they saw fit in order to ensure a reasonable rate of return for the company as a whole. So long as there was no overt evidence of discrimination based on the identity of the shipper or the distance that the freight traveled, railroad executives had the ultimate say in how those revenues would be spent.

During the early years of the twentieth century, however, ICC officials increasingly regulated the railroads' disposition of their retained earnings. Beginning with the *Eastern Rate* case in 1903, the commissioners broke with earlier policy, insisting that any monies reinvested in the physical plant, in order to increase efficiency or carrying capacity, were henceforth to be capitalized as additions to property, rather than charged against operating expenses. Subsequent ICC rulings, including the 1905 *Central Yellow Pine Association* case, as well as the uniform accounting standards imposed in the wake of the 1906 Hepburn Act, reinforced regulatory aversion to betterment expenditures. To the ICC's commissioners, the ability of railroad management to increase the value of the corporation (an activity that would certainly benefit shareholders) while simultaneously paying out dividends of 6 percent or better, indicated a measure of double-dipping and represented an unfair extortion of money from shippers and the general public in the form of unconscionably high rates. The PRR, which had reinvested $262 million in the company between 1887 and 1910, while maintaining respectable if not lavish dividends, became the ICC's prime example of corporate malfeasance. It struck regulators as inconceivable that of the $69 million expended on the New York Improvements prior to March 1908, the PRR's accountants had charged some $30 million against operating expenses.[370]

ICC officials, furthermore, were not alone in their belief that PRR executives were using infrastructure investments as a mechanism for protecting themselves against competition. A *New York Times* reporter described "the Pennsylvania's policy of maintaining for itself a practical monopoly of the railroad transportation within the State of Pennsylvania. To keep its position of advantage," the correspondent continued, "the road is compelled to supply new facilities as fast as the traffic grows under penalty of seeing other roads step in to share in the business, which the Pennsylvania management is unwilling to have happen if it can be prevented."[371] Many shippers were thus outraged that the PRR used their money to prevent the development of competitive transportation options that might have lowered their rates.

PRR officials, like their counterparts on other railroads, asserted that the reinvestment of retained earnings was not so much an attempt to increase the value of the property as it was to keep up with corresponding increases in demand. To maintain the physical plant to the same level as existed in, say, 1890 meant that weak bridges, lightweight rails, steep grades, curving tracks, and other bottlenecks would be incapable of handling the new normal level of traffic. In that context, *not* to improve would result not merely in stagnation, but ultimately in a diminution in the value of the railroad. Investors agreed, and despite occasional grumbling about the fifty-fifty split between dividends and reinvested earnings, they generally re-

spected the PRR's conservative financial policies. More important, they rewarded the company by subscribing to the multitude of stock and bond issues that were necessary to finance massive projects such as the New York Improvements. Under the new ICC policies, investors were understandably skittish about relinquishing their capital to the PRR and other railroads. With the ICC in effect forcing PRR officials to make a choice between paying dividends and reinvesting in the physical plant, many on Wall Street were concerned that improvement projects—which might take decades to reach capacity and fully amortize their construction costs—would be slow to generate an adequate return on investment.

The ICC's restrictions on retained earnings took effect as the recovery from the Panic of 1907, under way since June 1908, came to an end. By January 1910, the growth had stopped. For the next two years, the economy contracted, with the PRR laying off workers and canceling equipment orders. Stock prices exhibited considerable fluctuation, but trended steadily downward. Other companies felt the combined effects of the new ICC policies and the recession, and by 1912 total annual investment in the railroads was roughly a seventh of what it had been five years earlier. On the PRR, managers adopted a wait-and-see attitude, suspending work on such projects as the low-grade freight line across New Jersey and the proposed new yards to the west of Philadelphia.[372]

Even before the traffic demands associated with World War I had virtually paralyzed the eastern railroads, ICC officials concluded that the reduction in reinvested income and in new capital formation had adversely affected the railroads. With shippers expressing increasing concern that railway facilities might not be adequate for their needs, the commissioners in March 1914 contemplated a 5 percent rate hike for railroads operating east of the Mississippi River. Clifford Thorne, chairman of the Iowa State Railroad Commission, was relentless in his opposition to the increase, largely because he believed that if the eastern carriers proved successful, their western counterparts were certain to request a comparable decision from the ICC.[373] Thorne seized upon the ICC's determination to treat reinvested earnings as new investments rather than as operating expenses. "By a mere process of bookkeeping," he asserted, railroad executives could subsidize their shareholders at the expense of shippers, and "these gentlemen could increase their net corporate income far more than any decision of this commission could effect, with a continuation of present accounting methods and practices."[374]

Samuel Rea, whose management of the New York Improvements had led to his ascendency to the presidency of the Pennsylvania Railroad, was chief among the "gentlemen" that Thorne attacked so vigorously. "What the commissioners, the public, and the shippers have so far probably failed to appreciate," Rea emphasized, "is the cumulative result of legislative enactment and regulation, both State and Federal, dealing with almost every phase of railroad operations." Regulators, he stressed, were unwilling to acknowledge that railroad executives had requested higher rates because it had become inexorably more expensive to run a railroad, and not because they were rewarding investors with hidden dividends. "Railroad costs have been materially increased," Rea insisted, "and we cannot stop them."[375]

Many commercial interests supported the proposed rate advance, judging that a modest increase in their costs was far preferable to a poorly functioning railway network. Predictably, the editors of the *New York Times* urged the ICC to grant the higher tariffs, noting that otherwise "it cannot be long before the country in general must suffer from the reductions of dividends in both railways and industrial corporations."[376] More surprising was the reaction of Louis D. Brandeis, who allowed that "the net income and operating revenues of Eastern Railroads are smaller than is consistent with their assured prosperity and the welfare of the community."[377]

In December 1914, as Europe descended into the horrors of trench warfare, the ICC acquiesced to the railroads' argument. Rea deemed the resulting rate increase insufficient, as it applied to only about half of the PRR's traffic. While the commissioners had tacitly acknowledged that unremunerative tariffs jeopardized the national transportation infrastructure, they nonetheless confronted wide disparities in the financial health of the various carriers—a situation that during the 1920s would become the hotly debated "weak road/strong road" problem. The weaker carriers in the Northeast clearly deserved a rate increase, commis-

sioners believed, but perhaps the strongest railroad in the United States did not. As a result, the PRR's financial stability and conservative management practices worked against the company.[378]

So, too, did the willingness of PRR managers to pour hundreds of millions of dollars into massive betterments, many of which served only a small portion of the United States. In the aftermath of the ICC's 1906 hearings on monopolistic practices in the coal and oil industries, President Cassatt and his successors had emphasized their commitment to the public interest, manifested in such projects as the New York Improvements and Washington's Union Station. Local demand might have mandated the construction of those new facilities, but local resources would never be sufficient to pay for them. Their costs, of necessity, were distributed across the entire system, and were ultimately borne by shippers, through higher rates. PRR officials asserted, accurately, that such works did not and would not pay for themselves for decades, if ever.

By 1914, however, ICC regulators turned such rhetoric against the PRR. They advocated the compartmentalization of rates, so that each shipper paid for only the services that he used—no more and no less. In that context, the ability of PRR managers to cross-subsidize operations between freight and passengers, or between different communities and regions, amounted to nothing less than the unfair redistribution of property. In brief, ICC commissioners saw no reason why a furniture manufacturer in Fort Wayne, Indiana—someone who shipped no farther west than Chicago and no farther east than Pittsburgh—should be required to pay for the construction of a tunnel under the Hudson River that he would never use.[379]

The ICC's position on the allocation of the PRR's resources indicated that the commissioners possessed a far more limited understanding of the railroad business than did the firm's managers. Cassatt, McCrea, Rea, and others asserted that the entire company must function as one integrated network. Particularly in the absence of reliable data that might accurately show the precise cost of each unit of passenger and freight traffic, a substantial amount of cross-subsidization was necessary, and would always be necessary. ICC officials had by 1914 acknowledged that cost-accounting data could not delineate the expenditures associated with providing a particular service, and in that sense they were not wholly antithetical to the railroaders' position. The conflict lay instead in the determination of precisely *who* would allocate expenditures, and for what purpose. Railroad officials argued that as experts, they knew best how to distribute scarce resources, in order to construct and maintain an efficiently functioning transportation system. With equal conviction, regulators asserted that they and they alone possessed the objective detachment necessary to ensure economic fairness, and to equitably allocate scarce resources across American society. As the strongest of the strong railroads, the PRR could be expected to do its share to ensure equity through what amounted to the subsidization of weaker carriers, shippers, passengers, communities, and the public at large.

"Strong" did not mean "invincible," however, and the PRR would soon be buffeted by a series of crises—from global war to the rapid development of highway transportation—whose effects ICC regulators could not yet fully anticipate. In 1914, the disputes between executives and regulators largely involved a war of words, as representatives from both sides contested for the authority to determine whether "efficiency" reflected the prosperity of companies such as the PRR, or the harmonious interaction of interest groups within American society. The conflict in Europe soon transformed that war of words into a more internecine struggle to determine who possessed the right to shape the development of the transportation sector of the economy. Fundamental changes had come to the world of railroading and, as Samuel Rea observed, "we cannot stop them."

Notes

Introduction

1. Amtrak was sending the TurboTrain from the Department of Transportation High Speed Ground Transportation Test Center, in Pueblo, Colorado, to New York, where it was to be used in service between New York and Boston. *Columbus Citizen-Journal*, May 25, 1971.

2. W. Heyward Myers to William Wallace Atterbury, December 6, 1912, Penn Central Railroad Collection, M.G. 286, Pennsylvania Historical and Museum Commission, Pennsylvania State Archives, Harrisburg, Cassatt/McCrea papers, Box 31 (12–1861), folder 49/38.

3. "Historical Development of the Organization of the Pennsylvania Railroad," *Railroad Gazette* 14 (1882): 776–78, 793–94, 809–10, reprinted in Leland H. Jenks, "Early History of a Railway Organization," *Business History Review* 35 (Summer 1961): 153–79, at 179.

4. Relative position based on data relating to the PRR and its largest competitors, with PRR mileage and income statistics including the Pennsylvania Company, the umbrella company for most of the PRR's subsidiaries, west of Pittsburgh and Erie. Henry V. Poor, *Manual of the Railroads of the United States, 1874–75* (New York: H. V. & H. W. Poor, 1874), 79–87 (Philadelphia & Reading), 307–11 (New York Central & Hudson River), 315–24 (Erie), 449–58 (PRR), and 667–70 (Pennsylvania Company).

5. According to historian Leland H. Jenks, the PRR "was certainly in 1882 the largest private business concern in the world, with more than 30,000 employees on the 3,500 miles of main track which it owned, leased, and controlled east of Pittsburgh and Erie." Jenks, "Early History," 154.

6. The PRR's route mileage peaked in 1920, at 11,107. George H. Burgess and Miles C. Kennedy, *Centennial History of the Pennsylvania Railroad Company, 1846–1946* (Philadelphia: Pennsylvania Railroad, 1949), 534.

7. Alfred D. Chandler, Jr., *The Visible Hand: The Managerial Revolution in American Business* (Cambridge, Mass.: Belknap Press of Harvard University Press, 1977), 151; *Modern Railroads*, November 1956, 74; quoted in Dan Cupper, *Rockville Bridge: Rails Across the Susquehanna* (Halifax, Pa.: Withers Publishing, 2002), 80; Andrew Dow, *Dow's Dictionary of Railway Quotations* (Baltimore: Johns Hopkins University Press, 2006), 159 ("a nation").

8. *Railway Age Gazette* 56, no. 10 (March 6, 1914), 456–58, at 456.

9. Ibid.

10. David P. Morgan, *Trains*, July 1970, quoted in Dow, *Dictionary*, 160.

11. Colleen A. Dunlavy, *Politics and Industrialization: Early Railroads in the United States and Prussia* (Princeton, N.J.: Princeton University Press, 1994), 4.

Chapter 1. The Way West

1. In 1800, the town, then named Conemaugh, received a charter. It was incorporated in 1831, and at that time it had a population of 700. The name was changed to Johnstown in April 1834. J. J. McLaurin, *The Story of Johnstown: Its Early Settlement, Rise and Progress, Industrial Growth, and Appalling Flood on May 31st, 1889* (Harrisburg, Pa.: James M. Place, 1890), 35–38.

2. John Lauritz Larson, *Internal Improvement: National Public Works and the Promise of Popular Government in the Early United States* (Chapel Hill: University of North Carolina Press, 2001), 2–3.

3. Ibid., 35–36.

4. Ibid., 374–79; John R. Nelson, *Liberty and Property: Political Economy and Policymaking in the New Nation, 1789–1812* (Baltimore: Johns Hopkins University Press, 1987), 37–51.

5. Carter Goodrich, *Government Promotion of American Canals and Railroads, 1800–1890* (New York: Columbia University Press, 1960), 28–35; Ronald E. Shaw, *Canals for a Nation: The Canal Era in the United States, 1790–1860* (Lexington: University Press of Kentucky, 1990), 22–24; Larson, *Internal Improvement*, 59–62. For additional information on Gallatin's perspective on internal improvements, see Nelson, *Liberty and Property*, 116–27.

6. Robert G. Angevine, *The Railroad and the State: War, Politics, and Technology in Nineteenth-Century America* (Stanford, Calif.: Stanford University Press, 2004), 6–7; Shaw, *Canals for a Nation*, 23; Larson, *Internal Improvement*, 39–40, 50–51. See also Pamela L. Baker, "The Washington National Road Bill and the Struggle to Adopt a Federal System of

Internal Improvement," *Journal of the Early Republic* 22 (Fall 2002): 437–64, esp. 438–40.

7. Larson, *Internal Improvement*, 40–54; Richard R. John, *Spreading the News: The American Postal System from Franklin to Morse* (Cambridge, Mass.: Harvard University Press, 1995), 4–5, 108–9, 206–9.

8. Larson, *Internal Improvement*, 56.

9. George Rogers Taylor, *The Transportation Revolution, 1815–1860* (1951; Armonk, N.Y.: M. E. Sharpe, 1977), 19; Goodrich, *Government Promotion*, 24–26.

10. James Madison, Veto message to Congress, House of Representatives, March 3, 1817.

11. Larson, *Internal Improvement*, 64–69.

12. Business historian Colleen A. Dunlavy has argued convincingly that the supposed weakness of American government paradoxically increased the level of state involvement in the construction of internal improvements. In comparing railway development in Prussia and the United States, she demonstrates that Prussia's centralized and authoritarian government was able to develop a coherent national transportation network with comparatively little direct state oversight. In the United States, in contrast, the diffuse nature of political power associated with federalism encouraged competition among political entities and made private coordination of transportation development a more complex process, leading to a high level of government involvement. The devolution of control over internal improvements from the federal level to the state and local levels was part of that process. "And because greater formal representation and more distinct separation of powers allowed the state legislatures to dominate the policy-making process," Dunlavy observes, "a different dynamic drove the policy-making process in the United States, for the state legislatures proved, above all, more receptive to competing political demands." Dunlavy, *Politics and Industrialization: Early Railroads in the United States and Prussia* (Princeton, N.J.: Princeton University Press, 1994), 135.

13. "Indeed," as economic historian William J. Novak has observed, "anti-despotic governmental structures are frequently prerequisites for effective infrastructural governance and peripheral expansion." Novak, "The Myth of the 'Weak' American State," *American Historical Review* 113 (June 2008): 752–72, quotation at 767.

14. As historian John Lauritz Larson has written, "Few things a new American government might do at any level impinged on the people more directly, more unevenly, or more permanently than did public works of internal improvement. Therefore, few issues more fiercely tested the rhetoric of 'general welfare' and 'common good' that inevitably justified these public initiatives." Larson, *Internal Improvement*, 32. For a useful bibliographic overview of many of the canal projects, see Robert J. Kapsch, "Twenty-five Years of Canal History in the National Canal Museum's Canal History and Technology Proceedings: A Review," *Canal History and Technology Proceedings* 25 (2006): 97–157. For a contemporary account of early railway projects, see Frederick C. Gamst and Franz Anton Gerstner, *Early American Railroads: Franz Anton Ritter von Gerstner's Die innern Communicationen (1842–1843)* (Stanford, Calif.: Stanford University Press, 1997).

15. Because party labels in the early republic were so weak, I have used lowercase to refer to "federalists" and "republicans," except in cases of direct quotes. By the 1840s, when party identification mattered a great deal, I employ capitals, as in "Whigs" and "Democrats." In the aftermath of the hotly contested 1824 presidential election two identifiable parties emerged—the National Republicans, under John Quincy Adams, and the Democratic Republicans, linked to Andrew Jackson. Because the Jacksonian faction evolved into the more recent Democratic Party, later generations of writers frequently extended that nomenclature back into the Era of Good Feelings, when such was not the case.

16. Quoted in Philip S. Klein and Ari Hoogenboom, *A History of Pennsylvania*, 2nd ed. (University Park: Pennsylvania State University Press, 1980), 132.

17. Ibid., 132–39.

18. This concept reflects the work of the new institutionalist school, whose practitioners are more interested in the effects of government (and particularly the administrative state) on society and are correspondingly less concerned with more traditional studies of the way in which individuals and underlying social trends shaped governments. See, for example, Theda Skocpol, "Bringing the State Back In: Strategies of Analysis in Current Research," in Peter B. Evans, Dietrich Rueschemeyer, and Theda Skocpol, eds., *Bringing the State Back In* (Cambridge: Cambridge University Press, 1985), 3–37; Mark R. Wilson, "Law and the American State, from the Revolution to the Civil War: Institutional Growth and Structural Change," in Michael Grossberg and Christopher Tomlins, eds., *Cambridge History of Law in America, Vol. 2: The Long Nineteenth Century (1789–1920)* (Cambridge: Cambridge University Press, 2008), 1–35; Richard R. John, "Governmental Institutions as Agents of Economic Change: Rethinking American Political Development in the Early Republic, 1787–1835," *Studies in American Political Development* 11 (Fall 1997): 347–80, 697–705; John, "Ruling Passions: Political Economy in Nineteenth-Century America," in Richard R. John, ed., *Ruling Passions: Political Economy in Nineteenth-Century America* (University Park: Pennsylvania State University Press, 2006), 1–20, as well as other essays in that volume, which originally appeared in *Journal of Policy History* 18 (2006). I extend my appreciation to Richard R. John for his insights into new institutionalism.

19. Sean Patrick Adams, "Promotion, Competition, Captivity: The Political Economy of Coal," *Journal of Policy History* 18 (2006): 74–95; Adams, *Old Dominion, Industrial Commonwealth: Coal, Politics, and Economy in Antebellum America* (Baltimore: Johns Hopkins University Press, 2004); Andrew M. Schocket, *Founding Corporate Power in Early National Philadelphia* (DeKalb: Northern Illinois University Press, 2007).

20. As historian Pauline Maier has emphasized, "The [1787] Constitutional Convention's failure to grant Congress the explicit power to incorporate, and the torrent of opposition that greeted Congress's incorporation of the first Bank of the United States in 1791, served to establish the states as the primary creators of American corporations and the sites where arguments against corporations developed most fully." Maier, "The Revolutionary Origins of the American Corporation," *William and Mary Quarterly* 50 (January 1993): 51–84, at 52.

21. Ibid.; William J. Novak, "The American Law of Association: The Legal-Political Construction of Civil Society," *Studies in American Political Development* 15 (Fall 2001): 163–88; Schocket, *Founding Corporate Power*, 17–20.

22. "Business incorporation was viewed as a gift of the sovereign bestowed upon select groups of individuals as quid pro quo for the carrying out of certain important public tasks," writes historian William J. Novak. "Although it is common today [2001] to think of business corporations as quintessentially private enterprises, the business corporation first emerged in the nineteenth century as a distinctly public entity." Novak, "The American Law of Association," 181.

23. Schocket, *Founding Corporate Power*, 50, 110–11, 126, 140, 184–85.

24. By 1798, Massachusetts had permitted the general incorporation of public projects, such as aqueducts. New York adopted the first true general business incorporation law in 1811, largely in response to the depressed economic conditions induced by the 1807 Embargo Act and subsequent legislation. The principle of limited liability became more common, following its inclusion in an 1830 Massachusetts law. In Pennsylvania, limited incorporation provisions were included in many corporate charters issued prior

to 1819. During the financial panic that year, the Pittsburgh & Philadelphia Transportation Company (chartered in 1818) failed, leaving many creditors unsatisfied. That situation soured legislators on limited liability provisions for many years to come. Connecticut adopted a general incorporation law in 1837, and other northeastern states followed suit during the next two decades. In 1836, the Pennsylvania General Assembly permitted firms that smelted iron with anthracite to incorporate without a specific act of the legislature, although those provisions applied only to certain counties that lacked entrenched economic interests. This law was followed by supplements in 1849, 1850, 1851, and 1853 that exempted many agricultural processing firms from the necessity of obtaining a special charter. During the years that followed, the general incorporation laws were typically limited to specific enumerated industries (which legislators had targeted for development) and were also subject to restrictions (such as limited life) that made them unpalatable to entrepreneurs. State legislatures thus continued to do a brisk business in authorizing specific corporate charters. In 1873, Pennsylvania legislators enacted a general incorporation law for iron and steel firms. The 1874 law created a uniform incorporating process by replacing all of the earlier industry-specific general incorporation laws and by abolishing special acts of incorporation. Taylor, *The Transportation Revolution*, 240–43; Klein and Hoogenboom, *A History of Pennsylvania*, 306; Adams, *Old Dominion*, 171–78; Ronald E. Seavoy, "The Public Service Origins of the American Business Corporation," *Business History Review* 52 (Spring 1978): 30–60; Seavoy, *The Origins of the American Business Corporation, 1784–1855: Broadening the Concept of Public Service During Industrialization* (Westport, Conn.: Greenwood Press, 1982); Oscar Handlin and Mary F. Handlin, "Origins of the American Business Corporation," *Journal of Economic History* 5 (May 1945): 1–23; William G. Roy, *Socializing Capital: The Rise of the Large Industrial Corporation in America* (Princeton, N.J.: Princeton University Press, 1997), 78–114; Angelo T. Freedley, *The General Corporation Law of Pennsylvania (Approved 29th April, 1874) and Supplementary Acts, with Notes, Forms and Index* (Philadelphia: T. & J. W. Johnson, 1882).

25. Between 1821 and 1828, for example, the Bank of Pennsylvania subscribed to $4.6 million in internal-improvement loans and lent an additional $330,000 to the commonwealth between 1818 and 1820. Herman E. Krooss, "Financial Institutions," in David T. Gilchrist, ed., *The Growth of Seaport Cities, 1790–1825: Proceedings of a Conference Sponsored by the Eleutherian Mills–Hagley Foundation, March 17–19, 1966* (Charlottesville: University Press of Virginia, 1967), 104–38, at 114.

26. Louis Hartz, *Economic Policy and Democratic Thought: Pennsylvania, 1776–1860* (Cambridge, Mass.: Harvard University Press, 1948), 38–42, 46–48, 55, 82–83, 90, 96; Schocket, *Founding Corporate Power*, 138–70; John Majewski, *A House Dividing: Economic Development in Pennsylvania and Virginia Before the Civil War* (Cambridge: Cambridge University Press, 2000), 47; Randall M. Miller and William Pencak, eds., *Pennsylvania: A History of the Commonwealth* (College Station: Pennsylvania State University Press, 2002), 117, 123, 133–36, 164–65.

27. Much of the money went to the owners of completed routes, to buy down their debt, indicating that government support was not necessarily responsible for promoting construction in advance of settlement. However, inasmuch as turnpike companies earned notoriously low rates of return, such aid may well have had important long-term effects, by reducing the reluctance of investors to commit funds to enterprises of dubious profitability.

28. Hartz, *Economic Policy*, 294–95.

29. Larson, *Internal Improvement*, 71–73.

30. Everett S. Lee and Michael Lalli, "Population," in Gilchrist, ed., *The Growth of Seaport Cities*, 25–37, at 31; Gordon C. Bjork, "Foreign Trade," in Gilchrist, ed., *The Growth of Seaport Cities*, 60; Douglass C. North, *The Economic Growth of the United States, 1790–1860* (1961; New York: W. W. Norton, 1966), 49; Clifton Hood, "In Retrospect: Robert G. Albion's *The Rise of New York Port, 1815–1860*," *Reviews in American History* 27 (1999): 171–79; Hood, "Prudent Rebels: New York City and the American Revolution," *Reviews in American History* 25 (December 1997): 537–44. See also Daniel Joseph Hulsebosch, *Constituting Empire: New York and the Transformation of Constitutionalism in the Atlantic World, 1664–1830* (Chapel Hill: University of North Carolina Press, 2005), esp. 84–87, 98–101, 122–44; and Thomas M. Truxes, *Defying Empire: Trading with the Enemy in Colonial New York* (New Haven, Conn.: Yale University Press, 2008), esp. 22–23.

31. Auction sales became more common following the Treaty of Amiens in 1802. For the next decade, however, merchants employed auctions mainly to sell damaged goods. After the end of the War of 1812, British textile manufacturers instructed their New York agents to use auction sales in order to accommodate the new influx of cheap cloth. The 1817 liberalization of auction rules certainly increased New York's prominence in the transatlantic trade, but it also reflected the city's prominence in auction sales that had developed in the short time since 1815. Taylor, *The Transportation Revolution*, 11–12.

32. By 1821, New York controlled more than half of the reexport trade, and by 1860 the city's share had grown to almost 75 percent. Robert Greenhalgh Albion, with Jennie Barnes Pope, *The Rise of New York Port, 1815–1860* (New York: Charles Scribner's Sons, 1939, 1970), 1–2, 8–13, 32, 58–61; James Weston Livingood, *The Philadelphia–Baltimore Trade Rivalry, 1780–1860* (Harrisburg: Pennsylvania Historical and Museum Commission, 1947), 10–11; Christopher T. Baer, with Glenn Porter and William H. Mulligan, Jr., eds., *Canals and Railroads of the Mid-Atlantic States, 1800–1860* (Wilmington, Del.: Eleutherian Mills–Hagley Foundation, 1981), 6; Diane Lindstrom, *Economic Development in the Philadelphia Region, 1810–1850* (New York: Columbia University Press, 1978), 34–36. See also Gilchrist, ed., *The Growth of the Seaport Cities*; Allan R. Pred, *Urban Growth and the Circulation of Information: The United States System of Cities, 1790–1840* (Cambridge, Mass.: Harvard University Press, 1973); Taylor, *The Transportation Revolution*, 7, 180.

33. Larson, *Internal Improvement*, 73–80. The planning and construction of the Erie Canal is summarized in Peter L. Bernstein, *Wedding of the Waters: The Erie Canal and the Making of a Great Nation* (New York, W. W. Norton, 2005).

34. Guy Stevens Callender, "The Early Transportation and Banking Enterprises of the States in Relation to the Growth of Corporations," *Quarterly Journal of Economics* 17 (November 1902): 111–62; Shaw, *Canals for a Nation*, 30–45; Goodrich, *Government Promotion*, 36, 52–61; Taylor, *The Transportation Revolution*, 49. Bernstein, *Wedding of the Waters*, 190–91, 216.

35. The present value calculation presumes a base year of 1853 and use of the Federal Reserve Bank of Minneapolis CPI calculator, computed from the *Handbook of Labor Statistics*, http://www.minneapolisfed.org/community_education/teacher/calc/hist1800.cfm, accessed on July 6, 2010.

36. Goodrich, *Government Promotion*, 54–55; Taylor, *The Transportation Revolution*, 34, 161, 165.

37. Larson, *Internal Improvement*, 73–80; James D. Dilts, *The Great Road: The Building of the Baltimore and Ohio, the Nation's First Railroad, 1828–1853* (Stanford, Calif.: Stanford University Press, 1993), 14, 21.

38. The figures are based on Philadelphia corn prices of $1.13 per bushel, and a wagon freight rate of 30 cents per ton-mile (there are 35.7 bushels in a ton of corn). Taylor, *The Transportation Revolution*, 132–33; Richmond E. Myers, "The Development of Transportation in the Susquehanna River

Valley: A Geographical Study, 1700–1900" (Ph.D. diss., Pennsylvania State University, 1951), 217–20. For a comprehensive overview of Baltimore's commercial development during this period, see Gary Lawson Browne, *Baltimore in the Nation, 1789–1861* (Chapel Hill: University of North Carolina Press, 1980).

39. Avard L. Bishop, "Corrupt Practices Associated with the Building and Operation of the State Works of Pennsylvania," *Yale Review* 15 (1907): 391–411, at 392.

40. Livingood, *The Philadelphia–Baltimore Trade Rivalry*, 3–4, 17, 27, 32–38; Charles McCool Snyder, *The Jacksonian Heritage: Pennsylvania Politics, 1833–1848* (Harrisburg: Pennsylvania Historical and Museum Commission, 1958), 4–5; Baer, ed., *Canals and Railroads*, 3.

41. Based on the number of groundings, one of the most problematic obstructions was Bulkhead Shoal (or Bulkhead Bar), but the limiting factor was Mifflin Bar, with a depth at mean low water of seventeen feet. Systematic efforts to cut and maintain channels through those obstructions did not begin until 1888, with the project reaching fruition under the terms of the River and Harbor Act of 1899. United States, Army Corps of Engineers, *Annual Reports for the War Department for the Fiscal Year Ended June 30, 1899: Report of the Chief Engineers* (Washington, D.C.: Government Printing Office, 1899), Part 1, 164–65; Part 2, 1328–39.

42. Edgar P. Richardson, "The Athens of America: 1800–1825," in Russell F. Weigley, ed., *Philadelphia: A 300-Year History* (New York: W. W. Norton, 1982), 208–57, at 209.

43. Lindstrom, *Economic Development*, 38–39.

44. Thomas Pim Cope Diary, January 19, 1848, 120, http://triptych.brynmawr.edu/; see notes to Chapter 3 for a full description of the Cope Diary.

45. Cope Diary, vol. 8, March 4, 1846, 59.

46. As historian Diane Lindstrom has noted, "The city was trapped in a downward spiral—fewer imports, limited stock for nonlocal sale, smaller domestic commerce, and falling exports leading to still fewer imports." Lindstrom, *Economic Development*, 18–21, 24–40, quote at 40; Livingood, *The Philadelphia–Baltimore Trade Rivalry*, 24–25; Majewski, *A House Dividing*, 150.

47. Richardson, "The Athens of America," 209.

48. Livingood, *The Philadelphia–Baltimore Trade Rivalry*, 56; Avard Longley Bishop, "The State Works of Pennsylvania," *Transactions of the Connecticut Academy of Arts and Sciences* 13 (November 1907): 149–297, at 170; Taylor, *The Transportation Revolution*, 8; Myers, "The Development of Transportation," 209–15; Rhoda M. Dorsey, "Comment—Baltimore Foreign Trade," in Gilchrist, ed., *The Growth of Seaport Cities*, 62–67, at 66–67.

49. Taylor, *The Transportation Revolution*, 8.

50. Overall, Baltimore's greatest threat to Philadelphia occurred during the early 1820s. In 1810, for example, Philadelphia's exports were $86 per capita, considerably above those of Baltimore, at $68. By 1825, the positions were reversed, with Baltimore generating $62 per capita (in constant dollar terms) and Philadelphia trailing at $45. Yet, by 1830, Philadelphia had rebounded and was again ahead, by an impressive $74 to $38. Nicholas B. Wainwright, "The Age of Nicholas Biddle, 1825–1841," in Weigley, *Philadelphia: A 300-Year History*, 258–306, at 265–66; Livingood, *The Philadelphia–Baltimore Trade Rivalry*, 12–16, 26; Taylor, *The Transportation Revolution*, 186–87; Gordon C. Bjork, "Foreign Trade," in Gilchrist, ed., *The Growth of Seaport Cities*, 56; Dorsey, "Comment," 62–67.

51. The comparable numbers for the city of Philadelphia, excluding suburbs, in 1820, were 3 slaves and 7,579 free blacks, equivalent to 11.9 percent of the population.

52. Everett S. Lee and Michael Lalli, "Population," 30, 35; George Rogers Taylor, "Comment—Population," in Gilchrist, ed., *The Growth of Seaport Cities*, 38–46; Dorsey, "Comment," 62, 66; Browne, *Baltimore in the Nation*, 58–59, 97–102.

53. Lee and Lalli, "Population," 29–32; Robert A. Davidson, "Comment—New York Foreign Trade," in Gilchrist, ed., *The Growth of Seaport Cities*, 68–78, at 73.

54. In 1769, the American Society for Promoting Useful Knowledge merged with the American Philosophical Society, forming the American Philosophical Society for Promoting Useful Knowledge. Shaw, *Canals for a Nation*, 3; Darwin H. Stapleton, *The Transfer of Early Industrial Technologies to America* (Philadelphia: American Philosophical Society, 1987), 40–41; Myers, "The Development of Transportation," 1–16, 156–57.

55. Bishop, "The State Works of Pennsylvania," 158–60; Shaw, *Canals for a Nation*, 3–4; "William Weston and Early American Engineering," *Nature* 137 (1936): 733.

56. Legislators were unwilling to commit to a massive canal across the commonwealth, but they nonetheless appointed commissioners and allocated funds for several other projects. By April 1792, they had appropriated $25,000 for improving navigation along the Susquehanna River, $14,000 for the Conemaugh River, and precisely $150 for the Allegheny River. The expenditures were modest because they often involved no more than the elimination of rocks from otherwise navigable waterways. Such projects were likewise seldom controversial, as rivers were open to navigation by all, and as the small investment distributed benefits over a wide area. Joseph Stancliffe Davis, *Essays in the Earlier History of American Business Corporations, Number IV: Eighteenth Century Business Corporations in the United States* (Cambridge, Mass.: Harvard University Press, 1917), 149–52; Bishop, "The State Works of Pennsylvania," 160–61; Darwin H. Stapleton, "The Transfer of Early Industrial Technologies to America, With Especial Reference to the Role of the American Philosophical Society," *Proceedings of the American Philosophical Society* 135 (June 1991): 286–98, at 288–90; Archer Butler Hulbert, *Washington and the West, Being George Washington's Diary of September, 1784* (New York: Century Co., 1905), 192–93; Dilts, *The Great Road*, 17–18; Julius Rubin, "Canal or Railroad: Imitation and Innovation in the Response to the Erie Canal in Philadelphia, Baltimore, and Boston," *Transactions of the American Philosophical Society* 51 (1961): 1–106, at 19; Henry Simpson, *The Lives of Eminent Philadelphians, Now Deceased, Collected from original and Authentic Sources* (Philadelphia: William Brotherhead, 1859), 391–99.

57. J. Lee Hartman, "Pennsylvania's Grand Plan of Post-Revolutionary Internal Improvement," *Pennsylvania Magazine of History and Biography* 65 (1941): 439–57, at 443–55; Jay Veeder Hare, *History of the Reading* (Philadelphia, Reading Railway Dept., Young Men's Christian Association, 1909–14), 105–12; Robert McCullough and Walter Leuba, *The Pennsylvania Main Line Canal* (York, Pa.: American Canal and Transportation Center, 1973), 11.

58. The economic expansion that followed the end of the War of 1812 accelerated the pace of turnpike construction. By 1817, the Berks & Dauphin Turnpike, originally chartered in 1803, had connected Reading and Harrisburg. Commonwealth funds facilitated the construction of the Lancaster, Elizabethtown & Middletown Turnpike and the Middletown & Harrisburg Turnpike, both of which opened in 1818. The Downingtown, Ephrata & Harrisburg Turnpike, the York & Gettysburg Turnpike, and the Huntingdon, Cambria & Indiana Turnpike entered service the following year. Paul Marr, "The King's Highway to Lancaster: A Graph Theory Analysis of Colonial Pennsylvania's Road Network," *Journal of Transport History* 28 (March 2007): 1–20; Hartz, *Economic Policy*, 83–84; Donald C. Jackson, "Roads Most Traveled: Turnpikes in Southeastern Pennsylvania in the Early Republic," in Judith A. McGaw, ed., *Early American Technology: Making and Doing Things from the Colonial Era to 1850* (Chapel Hill:

University of North Carolina Press, 1994),197–239; Livingood, *The Phila-delphia–Baltimore Trade Rivalry*, 9, 27, 41–45.

59. Bishop, "The State Works of Pennsylvania," 164–67; Taylor, *The Transportation Revolution*, 133–34.

60. Adams, *Old Dominion*, 23–24, 52–61, 70–73; Alfred D. Chandler, Jr., "Anthracite Coal and the Beginnings of the Industrial Revolution in the United States," *Business History Review* 46 (Summer 1972): 141–81.

61. Luzerne County was established in 1786, from a portion of Northumberland County. The deposits there were later referred to as the Northern Anthracite Field. Schuylkill County, created in 1811, and Carbon County, established in 1843, were home to the Southern Anthracite Field and the Western and Eastern Middle Anthracite Fields, the latter of which also extended into Luzerne County. Prior to the American Revolution, only the Wyoming Valley experienced a significant degree of settlement by British colonists.

62. F. Charles Petrillo, *Anthracite and Slackwater: The North Branch Canal, 1828–1901* (Easton, Pa.: Center for Canal History and Technology, 1986), 10–16. Frederick Moore Binder, *Coal Age Empire: Pennsylvania Coal and Its Utilization to 1860* (Harrisburg: Pennsylvania Historical and Museum Commission, 1974), 8–10, 61–68; Myers, "The Development of Transportation," 106–10.

63. Cist also supported the construction of a canal between the Delaware and Susquehanna rivers. Petrillo, *Anthracite and Slackwater*, 16–21; H. Benjamin Powell, *Philadelphia's First Fuel Crisis: Jacob Cist and the Developing Market for Pennsylvania Anthracite* (University Park: Pennsylvania State University Press, 1978), 5–43; Binder, *Coal Age Empire*, 7.

64. Adams, "Promotion, Competition, Captivity," 78. For an account of White's business dealings, see Norris Hansell, *Josiah White, Quaker Entrepreneur* (Easton, Pa.: Canal History and Technology Press, 1992), esp. pp. 25–42.

65. These developments are extensively described in *A History of the Lehigh Coal and Navigation Company* (Philadelphia: William S. Young, 1840). See also Vince Hydro, "The Lehigh Coal and Navigation Company's Mauch Chunk Gravity Railroad," *Canal History and Technology Proceedings* 17 (1998): 1–50; Adams, *Old Dominion*, 67–68, 158–62; Schocket, *Founding Corporate Power*, 64, 73–74, 164–69; John H, White, Jr., "Inclined-Plane Railways," in *Encyclopedia of North American Railroads*, 535; John Hoffman, "Anthracite in the Lehigh Valley of Pennsylvania, 1820–1845," *United States National Museum Bulletin* 252 (1968): 91–141.

66. The first, modest efforts to improve the Schuylkill River began in April 1792, with the chartering of the Delaware & Schuylkill Canal Navigation. The incorporators elected to create a canal parallel to the Schuylkill River from Norristown southeast to the Northern Liberties district of Philadelphia, then east across the neck of the peninsula to the Delaware River. Construction proceeded by fits and starts, and even the use of a state-sanctioned lottery, in 1795, could not bring the project to fruition.

67. Edward Gibbons, "The Building of the Schuylkill Navigation System, 1815–1828," *Pennsylvania History* 57 (January 1990): 13–43; Stuart W. Wells, "'An Arduous and Novel Undertaking': Lock Navigation on the River Schuylkill," *Canal History and Technology Proceedings* 21 (2002): 35–61; Bishop, "The State Works of Pennsylvania," 153–55; H. Benjamin Powell, "Coal and Pennsylvania's Transportation Policy, 1825–1828," *Pennsylvania History* 38 (April 1971): 134–51; Schocket, *Founding Corporate Power*, 148–63; Adams, *Old Dominion*, 65–66, 158–62; Livingood, *The Philadelphia–Baltimore Trade Rivalry*, 100–107; Hare, *History of the Reading*, 220–38, 256–92, Henry Varnum Poor, *History of the Railroads and Canals of the United States* (New York: J. H. Schultz, 1860), 454–55.

68. For overviews of the development of Pennsylvania's anthracite fields, see Howard N. Eavenson, *The First Century and a Quarter of Ameri-*

can Coal Industry (Pittsburgh: Waverly Press, 1942), 138–54, and C. K. Yearly, Jr., *Enterprise and Anthracite: Economics and Democracy in Schuylkill County, 1820–1875* (Baltimore: Johns Hopkins Press, 1961), 23–93.

69. Binder, *Coal Age Empire*, 134; Chandler, "Anthracite Coal," 155; Lindstrom, *Economic Development*, 194–97.

70. Richardson, "The Athens of America," 234, 240–44.

71. Schocket, *Founding Corporate Power*, 3–15; Taylor, *The Transportation Revolution*, 10–11; Lindstrom, *Economic Development*, 40–54. See also Philip Scranton, *Endless Novelty: Specialty Production and American Industrialization, 1865–1925* (Princeton, N.J.: Princeton University Press, 1997); John K. Brown, *The Baldwin Locomotive Works, 1831–1915: A Study in American Industrial Practice* (Baltimore: Johns Hopkins University Press, 1995); Glenn Porter and Harold C. Livesay, *Merchants and Manufacturers: Studies in the Changing Structure of Nineteenth-Century Marketing* (Baltimore: Johns Hopkins University Press, 1971).

72. Richardson, "The Athens of America," 235. For details on the career of Stephen Girard, see George Wilson, *Stephen Girard: The Life and Times of America's First Tycoon* (Conshohocken, Pa.: Combined Books, 1995).

73. Ibid., 210

74. Powell, "Coal and Pennsylvania's Transportation Policy," 137–42. For an overview of Jacob Cist's involvement in internal improvements in Pennsylvania, see Powell, *Philadelphia's First Fuel Crisis*, 116–38.

75. Myers, "The Development of Transportation," 1–16.

76. Robert J. Kapsch, "Conewago Canal: First Canal of Pennsylvania," *Canal History and Technology Proceedings* 23 (2004): 5–43; Livingood, *The Philadelphia–Baltimore Trade Rivalry*, 28–32; *Report of the Governor and Directors, to the Proprietors of the Susquehanna Canal , at Their Semi-Annual Meeting, Held in the City of Baltimore, October 25, 1802* (Baltimore: Warner & Hanna, 1802); John Gibson, ed., *History of York County, Pennsylvania: From the Earliest Period to the Present Time, Divided into General, Special, Township and Borough Histories, with a Biographical Department Appended* (Chicago: F. A. Battey, 1886), 331–35; Myers, "The Development of Transportation," 1–16, 64, 114–15, 158–65.

77. Petrillo, *Anthracite and Slackwater*, 31; Myers, "The Development of Transportation," 87, 121–27.

78. In 1799, the Pennsylvania legislature specified criminal penalties for any person engaged in river improvements between Wright's Ferry (Wrightsville) and the Maryland state line. Two years later, however, the Pennsylvania legislature rescinded this policy, in compensation for the Maryland legislature's willingness to permit construction of the Chesapeake & Delaware Canal. The most serious threat to Philadelphia's interests came in April 1835, when residents of south-central Pennsylvania petitioned the General Assembly to charter the Susquehanna Canal Company, the Pennsylvania portion of a waterway linking Columbia with Baltimore. Philadelphians organized a town meeting and warned the legislature that such a canal would make the commonwealth's "public works tributary to a rival state," but the charter became law nonetheless. The Maryland legislature had already given its assent to the connecting Tidewater Canal Company, and by 1840 the Susquehanna & Tide Water Canal permitted safe navigation in both directions along the Susquehanna River. James W. Livingood, "The Canalization of the Lower Susquehanna," *Pennsylvania History* 8 (April 1941): 131–47, 146; Thomas C. Cochran, "Early Industrialization in the Delaware and Susquehanna River Areas: A Regional Analysis," *Social Science History* 1 (Spring 1977): 283–306; Livingood, *The Philadelphia–Baltimore Trade Rivalry*, 33.

79. Between 1811 and 1833, the Union Canal Company participated in something like fifty lotteries, awarding prizes in excess of $33 million. The company experienced relatively little financial benefit, however, and

cleared only between 5 and 10 percent of total lottery sales. Dean Aungst, *The Two Canals of Lebanon County* (Lebanon, Pa.: Lebanon County Historical Society, 1968), 20–21.

80. Hartman, "Pennsylvania's Grand Plan," 446–55; Hare, *History of the Reading*, 105–12.

81. Schocket, *Founding Corporate Power*, 66–67, 141–45; Livingood, *The Philadelphia–Baltimore Trade Rivalry*, 107–14; Bishop, "The State Works of Pennsylvania," 153–54, 161–64; Richard N. Pawling, "Geographical Influences on the Development and Decline of the Union Canal," *Canal History and Technology Proceedings* 2 (1983): 69–86; Dean M. Aungst, *The Union Canal and the Lehmans, 1828–1885* (Lebanon, Pa.: Lebanon County Historical Society, 1985).

82. Work on the Chesapeake & Delaware Canal resumed in 1824, and the canal opened to traffic five years later. Livingood, *The Philadelphia–Baltimore Trade Rivalry*, 81–99; Goodrich, *Government Promotion*, 41. For a more thorough account, see Ralph D. Gray, *The National Waterway: A History of the Chesapeake and Delaware Canal, 1760–1965* (Urbana: University of Illinois Press, 1967).

83. McCullough and Leuba, *The Pennsylvania Main Line Canal*, 8–10, 19.

84. Pennsylvania, House, "Report on Inland Navigation and Internal Improvement," *House Journal*, vol. 2, 1827–28, 670, quoted in James A. Ward, *Railroads and the Character of America, 1820–1887* (Knoxville: University of Tennessee Press, 1986), 58.

85. Quotation is from a report to the state legislature by canal commissioners Jacob Holgate and James Clarke, February 2, 1825, which appeared in *House Journal*, vol. 2, 1824–25, 284, and is quoted in Hartz, *Economic Policy*, 138, also published as *Report and Correspondence of the Commissioners for Promoting the Internal Improvement of the State* (Harrisburg: J. J. Wiestling, 1825), and printed in Mathew Carey, *To the Citizens of the Commonwealth of Pennsylvania*, vol. 1 (Harrisburg, Pa.: The Commonwealth, 1825), 47. Ward, *Railroads and the Character of America*, 58–62, 83–86, 116–20.

86. John Sergeant, *Niles Register*, September 24, 1825, quoted in Hartz, *Economic Policy*, 139.

87. Taylor, *The Transportation Revolution*, 361–62.

88. Cist and his allies pointed out that New York lacked significant coal deposits, and that residents of the Empire State would be so anxious to obtain Pennsylvania coal that they would willingly divert traffic away from the Erie Canal and southward into Pennsylvania. Binder, *Coal Age Empire*, 147–48.

89. Petrillo, *Anthracite and Slackwater*, 32.

90. Baer, ed., *Canals and Railroads*, 6; Bishop, "The State Works of Pennsylvania," 170–71; William Hasell Wilson and Solomon White Roberts, *Notes on the Internal Improvements of Pennsylvania* (Philadelphia: Railway World, 1879), 10.

91. The report noted that "A tunnel is a passage like a large well, dug horizontally through a hill or mountain, where there is not water enough to lock over it, or where the lockage-over would be too expensive," Report of the Commissioners, quoted in Wilson and Roberts, *Internal Improvements*, 12; George H. Burgess and Miles C. Kennedy, *Centennial History of the Pennsylvania Railroad Company, 1846–1946* (Philadelphia: Pennsylvania Railroad, 1949), 8–9; Bishop, "The State Works of Pennsylvania," 170–74; Petrillo, *Anthracite and Slackwater*, 32–33.

92. Report quoted in William Bender Wilson, *History of the Pennsylvania Railroad, with Plan of Organization, Portraits of Officials and Biographical Sketches*, vol. I (Philadelphia: Henry T. Coates & Co., 1899), 98.

93. Petrillo, *Anthracite and Slackwater*, 33.

94. The society's publications are inconsistent, variously using both "Improvement" and "Improvements" in the title.

95. W. Bernard Carlson, "The Pennsylvania Society for the Promotion of Internal Improvements: A Case Study in the Political Uses of Technological Knowledge, 1824–1826," *Canal History and Technology Proceedings* 7 (1988): 175–206, esp. pp. 181–83.

96. As Hartz has noted, "the aspirations of Philadelphia's merchant class were not identical with those of the state as a whole." Hartz, *Economic Policy*, 10.

97. Baer, ed., *Canals and Railroads*, 5; Schocket, *Founding Corporate Power*, 64–65.

98. There are numerous biographies of Carey, including Earl L. Bradsher, *Mathew Carey: Editor, Author, and Publisher: A Study in American Literary Development* (New York: Columbia University Press, 1912); Kenneth Wyer Rowe, *Mathew Carey: A Study in American Economic Development* (Baltimore: Johns Hopkins University Press, 1933); and James N. Green, *Mathew Carey: Publisher and Patriot* (Philadelphia: Library Company of Philadelphia, 1985). For Carey's role as a publisher, see Rosalind Remer, *Printers and Men of Capital: Philadelphia Book Publishers in the New Republic* (Philadelphia: University of Pennsylvania Press, 1996), esp. pp. 1–10, 35–38, 106–48.

99. Larson, *Internal Improvement*, 82–83; Julius Rubin, "An Imitative Public Improvement: The Pennsylvania Mainline," in Carter Goodrich, ed., *Canals and American Economic Development* (New York: Columbia University Press, 1961), 67–114, at 70–71; Stephen Noyes Winslow, *Biographies of Successful Philadelphia Merchants* (Philadelphia: James K. Simon, 1864), 144–49; Schocket, *Founding Corporate Power*, 104–7; David Kaser, *Messrs. Carey & Lea of Philadelphia: A Study in the History of the Book Trade* (Philadelphia: University of Pennsylvania Press, 1957); Louise Manly, *Southern Literature from 1579–1895: A Comprehensive Review, with Copious Extracts and Criticisms* (Richmond, Va.: B. F. Johnson, 1895), 126; Richardson, "The Athens of America," 248; Larson, *Internal Improvement*, 83.

100. *The First Annual Report of the Acting Committee of the Society for the Promotion of Internal Improvement in the Commonwealth of Pennsylvania* (Philadelphia: Joseph R. A. Skerrett, 1826), 8–9; Bishop, "The State Works of Pennsylvania," 175.

101. Richard I. Shelling, "Philadelphia and the Agitation in 1825 for the Pennsylvania Canal," *Pennsylvania Magazine of History and Biography* 62 (1938): 175–204.

102. Petrillo, *Anthracite and Slackwater*, 33.

103. *The First Annual Report of the Acting Committee*, 9, emphasis in the original.

104. Ibid., 8–9 (quote); Rubin, "Canal or Railroad," 20.

105. Boats typically traveled between three and five miles per hour, but their comparatively slow pace had little to do with equine stamina. Faster speeds would have created a bow wave that would have impeded the progress of other boats and, more importantly, eroded the canal banks. In practice, canal boats made even slower progress, averaging 1.8 miles per hour on the Erie Canal. Express "packet boats" carried passengers at an average of three or four miles an hour. Even with primitive wooden or strap-iron rails, horsecars could easily manage ten miles an hour, with the later introduction of locomotives permitting even faster travel.

106. Taylor, *The Transportation Revolution*, 138, 142; McCullough and Leuba, *The Pennsylvania Main Line Canal*, 15; Alfred D. Chandler, Jr., *The Visible Hand: The Managerial Revolution in American Business* (Cambridge, Mass.: Belknap, 1977), 83–86.

107. Rubin, "Canal or Railroad," 8, 29–31; John H, White, Jr., *American Locomotives: An Engineering History, 1830–1880,* rev. ed. (Baltimore: Johns Hopkins University Press, 1997), 239–43; Chapman Frederick Dendy Marshall, *A History of Railway Locomotives Down to the End of the Year 1831*

(1831; London: Locomotive Publishing, 1953), 139–41; Rubin, "Canal or Railroad," 22, 48; Robert E. Carlson, "British Railroads and Engineers and the Beginnings of American Railroad Development," *Business History Review* 34 (Summer 1960): 137–49, at 146.

108. *The First Annual Report of the Acting Committee*, 13.

109. Quoted in Rubin, "Canal or Railroad," 23.

110. Robert E. Carlson, "The Pennsylvania Improvement Society and Its Promotion of Canals and Railroads, 1824–1826," *Pennsylvania History* 31 (July 1964): 295–310, at 300–301; Rubin, "Canal or Railroad," 24; Wilson, *History of the Pennsylvania Railroad*, vol. I, 98.

111. Strickland had won the 1818 competition to design the Philadelphia headquarters of the second Bank of the United States. Fifteen years earlier, Strickland accepted an apprenticeship with the architect and engineer who had designed the first Bank of the United States, Benjamin Latrobe.

112. Strickland quoted in the Baltimore *American*, August 15, 1825, reprinted in Dilts, *The Great Road*, 27, emphasis in the original.

113. Carlson, "The Pennsylvania Improvement Society," 303–6; Pennsylvania Society for the Promotion of Internal Improvements in the Commonwealth, "Correct Information *on* the Subject of Railways," Philadelphia, February 25, 1825; Wilson and Roberts, *Internal Improvements*, 24.

114. Powell, "Coal and Pennsylvania's Transportation Policy," 135.

115. Albert Gallatin to James Trimble, May 5, 1825, in Henry Adams, ed., *The Writings of Albert Gallatin*, vol. 2 (Philadelphia: J. B. Lippincott & Co., 1879), 301.

116. Carlson, "The Pennsylvania Society for the Promotion," 183, 188.

117. Rubin, "Canal or Railroad," 25–26.

118. Ibid.; Dilts, *The Great Road*, 27–28; Petrillo, *Anthracite and Slackwater*, 35.

119. Acting Committee of the Pennsylvania Society for the Promotion of Internal Improvements, *Internal Improvement, Extracts from correspondence with William Strickland*, Philadelphia, December 21, 1825, quoted in Rubin, "Canal or Railroad," 28.

120. Rubin, "Canal or Railroad," 25; Dilts, *The Great Road*, 27.

121. Carlson, "The Pennsylvania Improvement Society," 299, quotation is from "Hamilton," "Internal Improvement—No. III, Canals and Railways," Philadelphia, November 28, 1825, quoted at 309–10.

122. Hartz, *Economic Policy*, 133–36.

123. Carey, *To the Citizens of the Commonwealth*, 47 (quote); Rubin, "Canal or Railroad," 25–26; Powell, "Coal and Pennsylvania's Transportation Policy," 136.

124. As H. Benjamin Powell has written, "The superabundance of coal in the state proved to be a decisive factor in the selection of a comprehensive canal system for the Commonwealth of Pennsylvania." Powell, "Coal and Pennsylvania's Transportation Policy," 144.

125. Powell, "Coal and Pennsylvania's Transportation Policy," 137–42; Petrillo, *Anthracite and Slackwater*, 34.

126. Josiah White, Erskine Hazard, and other investors in the Lehigh Coal & Navigation Company had repeatedly offered to construct a canal along the Delaware River to provide a better outlet for their anthracite. Other mine owners were reluctant to tie their fortunes to a private company and instead demanded that the commonwealth fund the construction of a public waterway. To the dismay of Lehigh Coal & Navigation officials, the canal commissioners built the Delaware Division to half the width of White and Hazard's canal, requiring expensive reloading at Easton. After the completion of the Delaware Division, White and Hazard complained repeatedly at the refusal of the commonwealth's Board of Canal Commissioners to increase the capacity of the canal or to authorize the construction of an outlet lock that would enable Lehigh Valley coal to more easily reach the Delaware & Raritan Canal route to New York City. Albright Zimmerman, "Problems of a State-Owned Delaware Division Canal," *Canal History and Technology Proceedings* 10 (1991): 115–48; McCullough and Leuba, *The Pennsylvania Main Line Canal*, 80–81. For a complete history of the Delaware Division, see Zimmerman, *Pennsylvania's Delaware Division Canal: Sixty Miles of Euphoria and Frustration* (Easton, Pa.: Canal History and Technology Press, 2002).

127. Powell, "Coal and Pennsylvania's Transportation Policy," 147–48; McCullough and Leuba, *The Pennsylvania Main Line Canal*, 20–22.

128. George Edward Reed, ed., *Pennsylvania Archives, Fourth Series*, vol. 5, *Papers of the Governors, 1817–1832* (Harrisburg: State of Pennsylvania/William Stanley Ray, 1900), 593.

129. McCullough and Leuba, *The Pennsylvania Main Line Canal*, 18–19; Petrillo, *Anthracite and Slackwater*, 37.

130. The Chesapeake & Ohio Canal would, if completed, channel western commerce toward Baltimore and away from Philadelphia. Lehman and his allies, however, were astute enough to sense that that company was making painfully slow progress through the difficult terrain along the Potomac River. They hoped that the Main Line of Public Works would be in operation long before the Maryland rival reached the Ohio River. The Chesapeake & Ohio Canal reached Cumberland, Maryland, in 1850, and went no farther. Carlson, "The Pennsylvania Society for the Promotion," 194–95.

131. Avard L. Bishop, "Corrupt Practices," 393; Rubin, "An Imitative Public Improvement," 93; Powell, "Coal and Pennsylvania's Transportation Policy," 135; Bishop, "The State Works of Pennsylvania," 178–80, 185–90, 199–201; Shelling, "The Pennsylvania Canal," 201–3; Wilson and Roberts, *Internal Improvements*, 13; McCullough and Leuba, *The Pennsylvania Main Line Canal*, 20–22.

132. Albright Zimmerman, "Governments and Transportation Systems: The Pennsylvania Example" (alternate title: "Governments and Transportation Systems: Pennsylvania as a Case Study"), *Canal History and Technology Proceedings* 6 (1987): 27–70, at 30–31.

133. As historian Avard L. Bishop (who was generally highly critical of the entire system of public works) has observed, "the Act of April 9th marked the inception of a complete change of policy," with legislators willing to sacrifice their earlier demands for an immediate cross-state route to the political pressure for myriad local feeders. Bishop, "Corrupt Practices," 393 (quote); Bishop, "The State Works of Pennsylvania," 185–90, 199–201; Petrillo, *Anthracite and Slackwater*, 39; McCullough and Leuba, *The Pennsylvania Main Line Canal*, 22–24.

134. McCullough and Leuba, *The Pennsylvania Main Line Canal*, 24–27; Bishop, "The State Works of Pennsylvania," 185–87, 199–201; Wilson and Roberts, *Internal Improvements*, 14–15.

135. From Athens, Pennsylvania, just to the south of the New York border, the privately owned Junction Canal, not completed until 1858, provided a connection to the Chemung Canal, and ultimately to the Erie Canal. While some traffic did follow that route, particularly during the Civil War, it was far less important than the section of the North Branch Division that carried anthracite southward out of the Wyoming Valley. Charles Patrillo, "The Junction Canal (1855–1871): Elmira, New York, to Athens, Pennsylvania," *Canal History and Technology Proceedings* 10 (1991): 181–211.

136. McCullough and Leuba, *The Pennsylvania Main Line Canal*, 30; Zimmerman, "Governments and Transportation Systems," 31–33.

137. Mathew Carey, *Brief View of the System of Internal Improvements of the State of Pennsylvania* (Philadelphia, 1831), quoted in Snyder, *Jacksonian Heritage*, 11.

138. Hartz, *Economic Policy*, 151; Goodrich, *Government Promotion*, 65–67; William Hasell Wilson, *The Columbia-Philadelphia Railroad and*

Its Successor (1896; edited and republished by Morris M. Green, Jr., ed., York, Pa.: American Canal & Transportation Center, 1985), 27–28; William A. Russ, Jr., "The Partnership Between Public and Private Initiative in the History of Pennsylvania," *Pennsylvania History* 20 (January 1953): 1–21, at 8; Majewski, *A House Dividing*, 116; Taylor, *The Transportation Revolution*, 45; Larson, *Internal Improvement*, 82–85; Bishop, "Corrupt Practices," 391; Bishop, "The State Works of Pennsylvania," 208–12, 225; Wilson and Roberts, *Internal Improvements*, 14; McCullough and Leuba, *The Pennsylvania Main Line Canal*, 24.

Chapter 2. Commonwealth

1. This and subsequent quotations are from Charles Dickens, *American Notes for General Circulation* (Boston: Ticknor and Fields, 1867), 3, 75–81. Dickens was not the first traveler to describe the Main Line of Public Works. One of the earliest was Philip H. Nicklin, who traveled the Main Line in 1835 and subsequently wrote *A Pleasant Peregrination Through the Prettiest Parts of Pennsylvania*, under the pseudonym Peregrine Prolix (Philadelphia: Grigg & Elliot, 1836). Unlike Dickens, he traveled along the Philadelphia & Columbia Railroad, and he noted that that line "is made of the best materials, and has cost the state a great sum; but it has some great faults" (p. 41). He nonetheless noted the changes that the railroad had produced along the route between Philadelphia and Lancaster, noting that "until the construction of the rail road, all the houses, mills, barns, bridges and roads were made of stone. Solidity was the particular characteristic of the State. The fashion has changed, and there is now an iron road and wooden bridges" (p. 40). He was far more impressed with the Allegheny Portage Railroad. In 1836, Philo E. Thompson kept a brief diary of a trip over the Philadelphia & Columbia, the Pennsylvania Canal, and the Allegheny Portage Railroad, as part of a 2,200-mile journey from Connecticut to Payson, Illinois. Thompson seemed moderately impressed with the trains (drawn by both horses and locomotives), inclined planes, and canal boats that sped him on his way, but he was more so with the increased settlement and prosperity that the Main Line had generated. He took a dim view of Pittsburgh, however, as "the blackest, nastiest place I ever saw. Buildings inferior, people generally of the lowest grade." Joel A. Tarr, ed., "Philo E. Thompson's Diary of a Journey on the Main Line Canal," *Pennsylvania History* 32 (July 1965): 295–304, quote at 300. Also see Leland D. Baldwin, "Charles Dickens in Western Pennsylvania," *Western Pennsylvania Historical Magazine* 19 (1936): 27–46. For a thorough survey of early travelers' accounts, see Robert McCullough and Walter Leuba, *The Pennsylvania Main Line Canal* (York, Pa.: American Canal and Transportation Center, 1973), 125–38.

2. William Hasell Wilson and Solomon White Roberts, *Notes on the Internal Improvements of Pennsylvania* (Philadelphia: Railway World, 1879), 15.

3. Not all of the members of the engineering corps were so talented, however, and some bordered on the incompetent. The worst was Henry G. Sargent, who, despite his experience on New York's Champlain Canal, so thoroughly mismanaged the Delaware Division Canal that the canal commissioners stripped him of his duties. James Dunlop Harris lacked the advantages of a West Point education, experience on the Erie Canal, or indeed any formal training whatsoever and, according to one biographer, "was to be no paragon representative of his profession." Yet, it was partisan political rancor among the canal commissioners, between supporters and opponents of President Andrew Jackson, that temporarily crippled Harris's career. *Canal Commissioners' Journal*, vol. 1, December 9, 1826, 99; May 2, 1827, 121–23; June 2, 1827, 176; September 10, 1827, 214, archived by the City of New Hope, Pennsylvania, at http://www.newhopepa.com/delawareriver/canal_comm_1.htm, accessed on July 8, 2010; Ronald E. Shaw, *Canals for a*

Nation: The Canal Era in the United States, 1790–1860 (Lexington: University Press of Kentucky, 1993, 1990), 65–66; Daniel Hovey Calhoun, *The American Civil Engineer: Origins and Conflict* (Cambridge, Mass.: Technology Press, Massachusetts Institute of Technology, 1960), 37; Wilson and Roberts, *Internal Improvements*, 17–18; Hubertis M. Cummings, "James D. Harris, Canal Engineer: Notes on His Papers and Related Canal Papers," *Pennsylvania History* 18 (October 1950): 31–45, quote at 35.

4. Geddes and Roberts found work surveying the Chesapeake & Ohio Canal, where they soon clashed with the West Point–trained engineers who had initially laid out the route. At the most basic level, Geddes and Roberts argued in favor of a fairly small canal prism—one that could be quickly and inexpensively built—while their West Point counterparts insisted on a larger and more substantial design. General Simon Bernard, the head of the Board of Engineers from Internal Improvements, had been one of Napoleon Bonaparte's engineers and had taken refuge in the United States following the Battle of Waterloo. When Bernard looked at Washington, D.C., he saw Paris, and envisioned the C&O Canal as a grand waterway linking the city to the provinces—to be built in the statist manner of engineering. Todd Shallat, "Building Waterways, 1802–1861: Science and the United States Army in Early Public Works," *Technology and Culture* 31 (January 1990): 18–50, 33–36; Shallat, "Engineering Policy: The U.S. Army Corps of Engineers and the Historical Foundation of Power," Public Historian 11 (Summer 1989): 7–27.

5. Wilson and Roberts, *Internal Improvements*, 16–17; Charles Beebe Stuart, *Lives and Works of Civil and Military Engineers of America* (New York: D. Van Nostrand, 1871), 109–11; F. Charles Petrillo, *Anthracite and Slackwater: The North Branch Canal, 1828–1901* (Easton, Pa.: Center for Canal History and Technology, 1986), 41.

6. Mathew Carey, *Appeal to the Wealthy of the Land, Ladies as Well as Gentlemen, on the Character, Conduct, Situation, and Prospects of Those Whose Sole Dependence for Subsistence Is on the Labour of Their Hands*, 3rd ed. (Philadelphia: L. Johnson, 1833), 10 (quote); George Rogers Taylor, *The Transportation Revolution, 1815–1860* (1951; Armonk, N.Y.: M. E. Sharpe, 1977), 289.

7. The 1832 cholera epidemic cut a similar swath of destruction on the Philadelphia & Columbia Railroad, killing dozens of workers. Fifty-seven Irish immigrants died of cholera and were buried at Duffy's Cut, in Chester County, supposedly the only mass grave on what would become the route of the Pennsylvania Railroad. William E. Watson, J. Francis Watson, John H. Ahtes III, and Earl H. Schandelmeier III have described the incident in detail in *The Ghosts of Duffy's Cut: The Irish Who Died Building America's Most Dangerous Stretch of Railroad* (Westport, Conn.: Greenwood Press, 2006). Unfortunately, such incidents were a routine occurrence on many early canal and railroad projects. During the 1820s, the intrepid female traveler Anne Newport Royall toured the Lehigh Navigation, accepted popular stereotypes of Irish laborers as lazy drunkards, and claimed that "on some of the canals, they die so fast, that they are thrown into the ground from four to six together, without coffins." Royall, *Mrs. Royall's Pennsylvania, or, Travels Continued in the United States*, vol. 1 (Washington, D.C.: Author, 1829), 126.

8. The portion of the Eastern Division between Harrisburg and Duncan's Island had a slightly larger prism than the other Main Line canals.

9. The 274-mile length of the canal portions of the Main Line of Public Works reflected the combined lengths of the Eastern Division (42.85 miles), the Juniata Division (127.32 miles), and the Western Division (104.25 miles). Two other short stretches of canals, the Allegheny Outlet (0.75 miles) and the Kittanning Feeder (14.00 miles), were also considered a part of the Main Line of Public Works, bringing the total canal length to 289 miles. Avard Longley Bishop, "The State Works of Pennsylvania,"

Transactions of the Connecticut Academy of Arts and Sciences 13 (November 1907): 149–297, at 199; McCullough and Leuba, *The Pennsylvania Main Line Canal*, 35, 83.

10. Wilson and Roberts, *Internal Improvements*, 40–41; McCullough and Leuba, *The Pennsylvania Main Line Canal*, 35–40.

11. Wilson and Roberts, *Internal Improvements*, 40–41; McCullough and Leuba, *The Pennsylvania Main Line Canal*, 41–47.

12. John Newton Boucher, ed., *A Century and a Half of Pittsburgh and Her People*, vol. 1 (New York: Lewis Publishing, 1908), 394–99; Wilson and Roberts, *Internal Improvements*, 44; Bishop, "The State Works of Pennsylvania," 198–99; McCullough and Leuba, *The Pennsylvania Main Line Canal*, 48–60.

13. The locks on the Union Canal were only eight and a half feet wide, compared with the fifteen feet that was the standard width on the Main Line of Public Works. McCullough and Leuba, *The Pennsylvania Main Line Canal*, 25; James Weston Livingood, *The Philadelphia–Baltimore Trade Rivalry, 1780–1860* (Harrisburg: Pennsylvania Historical and Museum Commission, 1947), 110.

14. Jay Veeder Hare, *History of the Reading* (Philadelphia: Reading Railway Dept., Young Men's Christian Association, 1909–14), 114.

15. Wilson and Roberts, *Internal Improvements*, 34.

16. *Encyclopedia of Contemporary Biography of Pennsylvania*, vol. 2 (New York: Atlantic Publishing & Engraving Co., 1889), 46; William Hasell Wilson, *Reminiscences of a Railroad Engineer* (Philadelphia: Railway World Publishing, 1896), 5–6; Wilson and Roberts, *Internal Improvements*, 3–7.

17. The young William Hasell Wilson gained valuable experience that he would put to use on the Pennsylvania Railroad. After working as a rodman on the Philadelphia & Columbia, Wilson served as an assistant engineer supervising the construction of a twenty-mile section of the line, before he had reached the age of twenty. By 1852, after spending more than a decade as a farmer, he resumed his engineering career and quickly found employment with the Pennsylvania Railroad. He became chief engineer of construction for the PRR in 1868, and he became president of the PRR's Philadelphia & Erie subsidiary five years later. His three sons followed in the footsteps of their father and their grandfather, and their generation represented the growing professionalization of American engineering. Each graduated from Rensselaer Polytechnic Institute before moving directly into supervisory positions on the Pennsylvania Railroad. William Hasell Wilson, *The Columbia-Philadelphia Railroad and Its Successor* (1896; edited and republished by Morris M. Green, Jr., ed., York, Pa.: American Canal & Transportation Center, 1985), 3–8; Henry Pettit, "Joseph Miller Wilson, A.M., C.E.," *Proceedings of the American Philosophical Society* 42 (May–December 1903): i–vi.

18. Wilson, *The Columbia-Philadelphia Railroad*, 8–10, 11–12; Hubertis Cummings, "Some Notes on the State-Owned Columbia and Philadelphia Railroad," *Pennsylvania History* 17 (January 1950): 39–49.

19. W. Uhler Hensel, "How the Pennsylvania Railroad Came Through Lancaster," *Journal of the Lancaster County Historical Society* 100 (Fall 1998): 272–85, at 274.

20. The line was most commonly known as the Philadelphia & Columbia Railroad, but it was also referred to as the "Columbia & Philadelphia Railroad" and occasionally as the "Columbia Railroad."

21. Bishop, "The State Works of Pennsylvania," 192–93; Wilson and Roberts, *Internal Improvements*, 19.

22. Wilson, *The Columbia-Philadelphia Railroad*, 10, 13–15; William Bender Wilson, *History of the Pennsylvania Railroad, with Plan of Organization, Portraits of Officials and Biographical Sketches*, vol. 1 (Philadelphia: Henry T. Coates & Co., 1899), 12–13.

23. In July 1833, the directors of the Southwark Rail-Road hired a young J. Edgar Thomson, future PRR president, as engineer, responsible for supervising the construction of the line. Wilson and Roberts, *Internal Improvements*, 25–26, 39; John C. Trautwine, Jr., "The Philadelphia and Columbia Railroad of 1834," *Philadelphia History* 2 (1925): 139–77, at 158–59; Hare, *History of the Reading*, 71, 99; Wilson, *History of the Pennsylvania Railroad*, vol. 1, 69, 307–8.

24. Wilson, *Internal Improvements*, 25–26; David W. Messer, *Triumph II: Philadelphia to Harrisburg, 1828–1998* (Baltimore: Barnard, Roberts & Co., 1999), 9, 14.

25. The cost was stunning as well, and the Reading was the most expensive railroad per mile ($140,000) in the United States. Henry Varnum Poor, *History of the Railroads and Canals of the United States* (New York: J. H. Schultz, 1860), 422.

26. While most coal traffic traversed the Reading main line to the Port Richmond terminal, passenger traffic and local merchandise traffic followed the west bank of the Schuylkill River a short distance to the base of the Belmont plane. From there, it traveled over the Philadelphia & Columbia, to the Reading depot at Broad and Cherry streets.

27. Frederick Moore Binder, *Coal Age Empire: Pennsylvania Coal and Its Utilization to 1860* (Harrisburg: Pennsylvania Historical and Museum Commission, 1974), 8–10, 61–68; Hare, *History of the Reading*, 1–22; C. K. Yearly, Jr., *Enterprise and Anthracite: Economics and Democracy in Schuylkill County, 1820–1875* (Baltimore: Johns Hopkins University Press, 1961), 159–61.

28. West Chester was just to the east of the two branches of the Brandywine River Valley, making it difficult for any railroad built through the town to continue directly to the west. Residents had to be content with branch-line status, incorporating the West Chester Railroad in 1831 and completing it the following year, connecting the town with the main line at West Chester Intersection, today's Malvern.

29. During 1882 and 1883, Pennsylvania Railroad construction crews built a new line through Lancaster, largely on Wilson's original right-of-way.

30. Hubertis M. Cummings, "Pennsylvania: Network of Canal Ports," *Pennsylvania History* 21 (1954): 260–73; Wilson and Roberts, *Internal Improvements*, 34; Wilson, *History of the Pennsylvania Railroad*, vol. 1, 61–64; Albright Zimmerman, "The Columbia and Philadelphia Railroad: A Railroad with an Identity Problem," *Canal History and Technology Proceedings* 3 (1984): 53–92, quotes at 58, 60–61.

31. Julius Rubin, "An Imitative Public Improvement: The Pennsylvania Mainline," in Carter Goodrich, ed., *Canals and American Economic Development* (New York: Columbia University Press, 1961), 67–114, at 103.

32. Wilson, *History of the Pennsylvania Railroad*, vol. 1, 100–101.

33. Darwin H. Stapleton, "Moncure Robinson: Railroad Engineer," in Barbara E. Benson, ed., *Benjamin Henry Latrobe and Moncure Robinson: The Engineer as Agent of Technology Transfer* (Greenville, Del., 1975), 37–44; Stapleton, "The Transfer of Early Industrial Technologies to America, With Especial Reference to the Role of the American Philosophical Society," *Proceedings of the American Philosophical Society* 135 (June 1991): 286–98, at 295; Richard B. Osborne, "Professional Biography of Moncure Robinson," *William and Mary Quarterly*, 2nd Ser., vol. 1, no. 4 (October 1921): 237–260; Moncure Robinson, "Letters of Moncure Robinson to His Father, John Robinson, of Richmond, Va., Clerk of Henrico Court," *William and Mary Quarterly*, 2nd Ser., vol. 8, no. 2 (April 1928): 71–95, and vol. 8, no. 3 (July 1928): 143–56.

34. As an experienced and widely traveled engineer, Robinson was certainly familiar with gravity-powered inclined-plane colliery railways in Britain, which used the weight of a loaded coal car traveling downhill to lift empty cars uphill to the mine entrance. He knew even more about a similar

railway that had recently opened much closer to home, in Pennsylvania. In 1823, William and Maurice Wurts had chartered the Delaware & Hudson Canal Company, and they soon encountered considerable difficulty in reaching anthracite deposits in northeastern Pennsylvania by water. By 1826, they had elected to build a gravity railroad over part of the route, with the tracks entering service in 1829. Similar designs appeared on long-distance railroads as well, including both ends of the Philadelphia & Columbia. The Baltimore & Ohio, with its planned all-rail route between tidewater and the Ohio River, used inclined planes to climb Parr's Ridge, separating the watersheds of the Patapsco and Potomac rivers. Most of those inclined planes were soon bypassed, or else the entire railroad was abandoned. There were some notable exceptions, however. The Delaware & Hudson continued to use inclined planes until the late 1800s. Nor was Robinson's reliance on inclined planes limited to the Allegheny Portage Railroad. He employed them on the Danville & Pottsville Railroad, a company that was chartered in 1826. By 1834, the Danville & Pottsville carried coal over Broad Mountain, between the valleys of Mahoney Creek and the Schuylkill River. The Chesterfield Railroad in Virginia, another coal carrier, under Robinson's supervision successfully employed inclined planes, rapidly becoming one of the most profitable companies in the United States. The Reading used the Mahoney plane until the 1930s, and the Jersey Central's Ashley planes remained in service until 1948.

35. Robinson estimated that a railroad line employing inclined planes could breast the summit in thirty-eight miles, but that a turnpike route would be at least fifty miles in length. Rubin, "An Imitative Public Improvement," 103; Stapleton, "Moncure Robinson," 37–44; Stapleton, "The Transfer of Early Industrial Technologies to America," 295; "Robinson, Moncure," *Dictionary of American Biography* 16 (New York, 1935), 48–49; Lorett Treese, *Railroads of Pennsylvania: Fragments of the Past in the Keystone Landscape* (Mechanicsburg, Pa.: Stackpole Books, 2003).

36. Wilson and Roberts, *Internal Improvements*, 28–29; Wilson, *History of the Pennsylvania Railroad*, vol. 1, 104–7, 114–15.

37. Wilson, *History of the Pennsylvania Railroad*, vol. 1, 104; McCullough and Leuba, *The Pennsylvania Main Line Canal*, 61–62.

38. Solomon Roberts was the nephew of Josiah White, the founder of the Lehigh Coal & Navigation Company canal. Solomon W. Roberts, "Obituary Notice of Edward Miller, Civil Engineer," Proceedings of the American Philosophical Society 12 (1871): 581–86; Wilson, *History of the Pennsylvania Railroad*, vol. 1, 104, 108; Rubin, "An Imitative Public Improvement," 103–4; Eugene S. Ferguson, ed., *Early Engineering Reminiscences (1815–1840) of George Escol Sellers* (Washington, D.C.: Smithsonian Institution, 1965), 154.

39. The other two contenders for the oldest railroad tunnel in the United States are the Bundy Hill Tunnel on the Norwich & Worcester Railroad (which opened in 1839 and is the oldest railroad tunnel still in use in the United States) and another, built by the New York & Harlem Railroad, which entered service in 1837. William D. Middleton, "Where Is America's Oldest Railroad Tunnel?" *Trains* 62 (May 2002): 60–65.

40. Wilson, *History of the Pennsylvania Railroad,* vol. 1, 104–7, 114–15.

41. The first train over the Allegheny Portage Railroad actually ran in November 1833, operated as a consideration to the returning Philadelphia delegation to a canal convention in Ohio. Wilson, *History of the Pennsylvania Railroad*, vol. 1, 107–8, 113; Solomon W. Roberts, *Reminiscences of the First Railroad Over the Allegheny Mountains, Read Before the Historical Society of Pennsylvania, April 8th, 1878* (Philadelphia: Railway World, 1879), 71; Ferguson, *Early Engineering Reminiscences*, 154.

42. Most of the early colliery railways that used inclined planes possessed a considerable advantage over the Allegheny Portage Railroad in that they relied on gravity to bring loaded coal cars from the mines to the nearest navigable waterway. Empty cars would be pulled upward either by horses or by the force of the descending equipment. On the Allegheny Portage, however, loaded cars moved in both directions, making such a system impossible.

43. Between 1843 and 1849, John A. Roebling, the engineer who would later gain great fame with the design of the Brooklyn Bridge, supervised the replacement of the hemp ropes with wire cables. While the new wire ropes, among the first to be used in the United States, greatly reduced the risk of accident, they did not eliminate the inconvenience or the expense associated with moving cars up and down the inclines. In late 1842 or early 1843, Roebling had installed a very short section of wire rope at the Hollidaysburg canal basin, used to draw section boats out of the water. Hubertis M. Cummings and Donald Sayenga, ed., "John August Roebling and the Public Works of Pennsylvania," *Canal History and Technology Proceedings* 3 (1984): 93–118, at 97–98 and 115n27; John D. Weinhold, "The Inclined Planes of the Allegheny Portage Railroad," *Canal History and Technology Proceedings* 17 (1998): 203–49, at 216–19; Roberts, *Reminiscences of the First Railroad*, 70; William Bender Wilson, "The Evolution, Decadence and Abandonment of the Allegheny Portage Railroad," in *Annual Report of the Secretary of Internal Affairs of the Commonwealth of Pennsylvania, 1898–99, Part IV: Railroad, Canal, Navigation, Telegraph and Telephone Companies, by William Bender Wilson, 1900*, 70–96, at 73.

44. George H. Burgess and Miles C. Kennedy, *Centennial History of the Pennsylvania Railroad Company, 1846–1946* (Philadelphia: Pennsylvania Railroad, 1949), 21.

45. After the Board of Canal Commissioners completed an alternate rail line through the mountains, most people referred to the original route as the "Old Portage Railroad," an appellation that nonetheless seemed to confer the grace and stature of antiquity on the original route. In 1929, Pennsylvania governor John S. Fisher unveiled a monument pieced together from the stone sleepers of the long-abandoned route, celebrating the construction project that had begun a century earlier. He referred to the inclined planes as the "Mother of the Pennsylvania Railroad," even though PRR executives were as anxious to bypass them as quickly as possible. Fisher's comments must have bemused fellow attendee Albert J. County, a PRR vice president, who later claimed that it was the failure of the "Old Portage, and not its success," that helped usher his employer into being. Despite abundant criticism from contemporary engineers, the completed Allegheny Portage Railroad nonetheless gained a reputation as an engineering marvel. In 1987, the American Society of Civil Engineers selected the Allegheny Portage Railroad as a National Historic Civil Engineering Landmark. The National Park Service has restored several structures, including Engine House No. 6 and the Lemon House tavern, as well as a portion of one of the inclined planes, incorporated into the Allegheny Portage Railroad National Historic Site. *Railway Age* 87, no. 14 (October 5, 1929): 811–12; Burgess and Kennedy, *Centennial History*, 10–12.

46. Frederick C. Gamst and Franz Anton Gerstner, *Early American Railroads: Franz Anton Ritter von Gerstner's Die innern Communicationen (1842–1843)* (Stanford, Calif.: Stanford University Press, 1997), 586.

47. The Allegheny Portage Railroad did own freight and passenger equipment, but many shippers deemed the supply to be insufficient.

48. "Message of Governor Porter, of Pennsylvania, to the Senate and House of Representatives of the Commonwealth of Pennsylvania," January 5, 1842, in *Hazard's United States Commercial and Statistical Register* 6 (January 12, 1842): 17–25, at 20. See also McCullough and Leuba, *The Pennsylvania Main Line Canal*, 151.

49. Wilson, *History of the Pennsylvania Railroad*, vol. 1, 116–17; Zimmerman, "The Columbia and Philadelphia Railroad," 69.

50. Roberts, *Reminiscences of the First Railroad*, 71–72.

51. Wilson, *History of the Pennsylvania Railroad*, vol. 1, 46; Wilson, *The Columbia-Philadelphia Railroad*, 20; Shaw, *Canals for a Nation*, 74; James M. Swank, *Progressive Pennsylvania: A Record of the Remarkable Industrial Development of the Keystone State* (Philadelphia: J. B. Lippincott, 1908), 150; William E. O'Connell, "The Development of the Private Railroad Freight Car, 1830–1966," *Business History Review* 44 (Summer 1970): 190–209, 191–94; Wilson, *History of the Pennsylvania Railroad*, vol. 1, 116, 125–26.

52. Gerstner, *Early American Railroads*, 568.

53. McCullough and Leuba, *The Pennsylvania Main Line Canal*, 88, provides a list of the dominant freight forwarders, based on 1841 listings in Isaac Harris's Pittsburgh business directory. They were the Western Transportation Line/Leech's Line (nineteen boats), the Patent Portable Boat Line (sixteen boats), the Reliance Portable Boat Line (fifteen boats), the United States Portable Boat Line (five boats), the Union Line (nine boats), the Mechanics' Independent Line (nine boats), Bingham's Line (seven boats), the Pennsylvania & Ohio Line (five boats), the Despatch Line (five boats), and several other smaller concerns.

54. Boucher, *A Century and a Half of Pittsburgh and Her People*, vol. 1, 400.

55. His principal firm was D. Leech & Company, a partnership of David Leech, William F. Leech, Robert S. Hays, George Black, and George W. Harris.

56. *Armstrong County Pennsylvania: Her People, Past and Present, Embracing a History of the County and a Genealogical and Biographical Record of Representative Families*, vol. 1 (Chicago: J. H. Beers & Co., 1914), 31, 135–36, 141–42.

57. John W. Jordan, *Encyclopedia of Pennsylvania Biography*, vol. 4 (New York: Lewis Historical Publishing, 1918), 1344; Rolland Harper Maybee, *Railroad Competition and the Oil Trade, 1855–1873* (1940; Philadelphia: Porcupine Press, 1974), 117–18.

58. Roberts, *Reminiscences of the First Railroad*, 73.

59. For one perspective on this issue, see Albright G. Zimmerman, "The Locomotive in the Garden of Pennsylvania, 1830–1850," *Canal History and Technology Proceedings* 14 (1995): 91–104.

60. Wilson, *History of the Pennsylvania Railroad*, vol. 1, 20–21.

61. Ibid., 12–14; Earl J. Heydinger, "The English Influence on American Railroads," *Railway and Locomotive Historical Society Bulletin* 91 (1954): 7–45.

62. John H. White, Jr., *American Locomotives: An Engineering History, 1830–1880, Revised and Expanded Edition* (Baltimore: Johns Hopkins University Press, 1997), 71–72.

63. Crews regarded the *Lancaster* as an extraordinary locomotive, with few mechanical problems. It remained in service until about 1850, and was scrapped in 1851. Ibid., 269–73.

64. Wilson, *History of the Pennsylvania Railroad*, vol. 1, 20–21, 106–7, 109–11, 121–23, 127, 130.

65. Roberts, *Reminiscences of the First Railroad*, 72.

66. Wilson, *History of the Pennsylvania Railroad*, vol. 1, 38–42.

67. Nicklin, *A Pleasant Peregrination*, 42.

68. Trautwine, "The Philadelphia and Columbia Railroad," 172–73; Gerstner, *Early American Railroads*, quote at 569, emphasis in the original.

69. In comparison, by the beginning of the 1860s, each train operating over the Philadelphia & Reading Rail Road (a line that transported coal almost exclusively) weighed, on average, 754 tons. McCullough and Leuba, *The Pennsylvania Main Line Canal*, 145; Thomas Weber, *The Northern Railroads in the Civil War, 1861–1865* (1952; Bloomington: Indiana University Press, 1999), 12.

70. "Annual Report of the Canal Commissioners of Pennsylvania, made to the Governor, December 2, 1834," in Samuel Hazard, ed., *The Register of Pennsylvania* 14 (December 13, 1834): 376–82, quote at 379; Wilson, *History of the Pennsylvania Railroad*, vol. 1, 106–7, 109–11, 121–23, 127, 130.

71. Wilson, *History of the Pennsylvania Railroad*, vol. 1, 130–31; McCullough and Leuba, *The Pennsylvania Main Line Canal*, 67.

72. The politicized appropriations process extended to the most mundane of contract and payment terms. Those who were financially powerful and politically well connected could expect prompt payment for their work. Small local contractors, particularly those who were out of political favor, called in vain for their rightful due, and they often faced the prospect of a long and costly lawsuit against the commonwealth. In 1854, for example, and near the end of the public operation of the Main Line of Public Works, legislators learned that the Canal Commission had simply ignored $149,377 in old debts, many of them owed to minor employees or small contractors who lacked the political influence necessary to secure payment. Louis Hartz, *Economic Policy and Democratic Thought: Pennsylvania, 1776–1860* (Cambridge, Mass.: Harvard University Press, 1948), 150–52, 160. For a long list of specific abuses associated with the construction and operation of Pennsylvania's internal improvements, see Bishop, "Corrupt Practices Associated with the Building and Operation of the State Works of Pennsylvania," *Yale Review* 15 (1907): 391–411.

73. By 1843, the Pittsburgh aqueduct, originally built of wood, was in such poor condition that Pittsburghers hired John Roebling to rebuild the structure as a wire-rope suspension bridge. It was a great success and established Roebling's reputation as a bridge engineer.

74. McCullough and Leuba, *The Pennsylvania Main Line Canal*, 141–42.

75. Bishop, "Corrupt Practices," 232; Charles McCool Snyder, *The Jacksonian Heritage: Pennsylvania Politics, 1833–1848* (Harrisburg: Pennsylvania Historical and Museum Commission, 1958), 13–14; Hartz, *Economic Policy*, 151–52, 156–59.

76. As historian Avard Longley Bishop has noted, the resulting "corruption thus imprinted upon the improvement system early in its history was not easily removed." Bishop, "The State Works of Pennsylvania," 229 (quote). In "Corrupt Practices," 411, Bishop suggested that the saga of Pennsylvania's internal improvements taught a valuable lesson: "Nor can the advocates of the extension of State enterprise into various fields of activity at present considered dangerously corruptible find much to substantiate their views by an examination of the same period."

77. A useful overview of those events is contained in Snyder, *Jacksonian Heritage*.

78. "Message of Governor Porter," January 5, 1842, 20.

79. Calhoun, *The American Civil Engineer*, 145–47; McCullough and Leuba, *The Pennsylvania Main Line Canal*, 150.

80. Hartz, *Economic Policy*, 151–52, 156–59.

81. Wilson, *The Columbia-Philadelphia Railroad*, 39; Wilson, *History of the Pennsylvania Railroad*, vol. 1, 142–43; Hartz, *Economic Policy*, 151–52, 157, 160.

82. Interestingly, there was one bureaucratic institution—the United States Army—that was well equipped to consistently produce highly trained and extraordinarily competent individuals. Although the Army was certainly politicized, it was never affected by patronage politics to the same degree as was state government. In addition, the national military was infused with an esprit de corps that was lacking in the operation of the Main Line or, for that matter, state militias. I extend my gratitude to Christopher T. Baer for his insights into operational practices on the Main Line of Public Works.

83. Solomon W. Roberts, "Reminiscences of the First Railroad over Allegheny Mountain," *Pennsylvania Magazine of History and Biography* 2 (1878): 370–93, at 384.

84. *House Journal, 1832–33*, vol. 2, 750, quoted in Hartz, *Economic Policy*, 157.

85. *House Journal, 1836–37*, vol. 2, 807, quoted in Hartz, *Economic Policy*, 157.

86. Wilson, *Reminiscences of a Railroad Engineer*, 8.

87. Wilson, "Evolution, Decadence and Abandonment," 77; Mc-Cullough and Leuba, *The Pennsylvania Main Line Canal*, 139.

88. Wilson, *The Columbia-Philadelphia Railroad*, 10–11, 38; Wilson, *History of the Pennsylvania Railroad*, vol. 1, 142–42, 151; Hartz, *Economic Policy*, 153–56.

89. Report upon the Public Works of a Select Committee, read in the Senate, February 4, 1854, quoted in Bishop, "The State Works of Pennsylvania," 243.

90. Burgess and Kennedy, *Centennial History*, 22–24; Wilson, *History of the Pennsylvania Railroad*, vol. 1, 50–55; John D. Denney, Jr., "Columbia on the Pennsy," *The Keystone* 27, no. 3 (Autumn 1994): 21–30, at 25; James B. McNair, *Simon Cameron's Adventures in Iron, 1837–1846* (Los Angeles: Fox Printing and Publishing, 1949), 49–55.

91. Paul J. Westhaeffer, *History of the Cumberland Valley Railroad, 1835–1919* (Washington, D.C.: Washington Chapter of the National Railway Historical Society, 1979), 4–7.

92. This bridge (not to be confused with the Rockville Bridge a few miles to the north, along the PRR main line) burned in December 1844. Rebuilt in 1846, it lasted until 1916, when the PRR replaced it with a concrete arch bridge. Burgess and Kennedy, *Centennial History*, 123–26; Westhaeffer, *History of the Cumberland Valley*, 7–19.

93. Richmond E. Myers, "The Development of Transportation in the Susquehanna River Valley: A Geographical Study, 1700–1900" (Ph.D. diss., Pennsylvania State University, 1951), 183–85.

94. Proposals to build a canal across the isthmus had existed even before the Revolutionary War. In 1802, the legislatures of Pennsylvania, Maryland, and Delaware had agreed to jointly support the project, which soon foundered. Prominent Philadelphians, including staunch internal-improvement advocates Mathew Carey and Joshua Gilpin, periodically called for the resumption of construction, and they were largely responsible for reviving the company in 1822. Livingood, *The Philadelphia–Baltimore Trade Rivalry*, 56–64, 81–99; Carter Goodrich, *Government Promotion of American Canals and Railroads, 1800–1890* (New York: Columbia University Press, 1960), 41. For a more thorough account, see Ralph D. Gray, *The National Waterway: A History of the Chesapeake and Delaware Canal, 1760–1965* (Urbana: University of Illinois Press, 1967).

95. Livingood, *The Philadelphia–Baltimore Trade Rivalry*, 116–33; Charles S. Roberts and David W. Messer, *Triumph VI: Philadelphia, Columbia, Harrisburg to Baltimore and Washington DC, 1827–2003* (Baltimore: Barnard, Roberts & Co., 2003), 21–22; Myers, "The Development of Transportation," 184–86; Poor, *Railroads and Canals of the United States*, 552.

96. Originally known as the York Road, the highway had been purchased by a group of investors, and it remained a private toll road until 1900. *New York Times*, May 5, 1900.

97. Samuel Hazard, ed., *Register of Pennsylvania*, January 31, 1829, 65; John Thomas Scharf, *History of Baltimore City and County, from the Earliest Period to the Present Day: Including Biographical Sketches of their Representative Men* (Philadelphia: Louis H. Everts, 1881), 343; Robert L. Gunnarsson, *The Story of the Northern Central Railway, from Baltimore to Lake Ontario* (Sykesville, Md.: Greenberg, 1991), 12–13.

98. On March 21, 1836, the Pennsylvania legislature chartered the York & Gettysburg Railroad, authorizing the company's promoters to link those two cities. That charter conflicted with the one granted to the York & Wrightsville Railroad in that both permitted the construction of a line between Wrightsville and York. Rather than engage in duplicate construction, the supporters of the two companies pooled their efforts, forming the Wrightsville, York & Gettysburg Railroad on February 27, 1837.

99. Because of the steep approaches on either side of the bridge, locomotives could not operate across the structure. The transfer of cars from one railroad to another was thus done by horse power. Livingood, *The Philadelphia–Baltimore Trade Rivalry*, 116–33; Roberts and Messer, *Triumph VI*, 21–22; Gunnarsson, *Northern Central Railway*, 22–27.

100. Christopher T. Baer has observed that "although decreasing ton-mile costs represented the economic bottom line and an impressive achievement of the antebellum era, Americans from the first were willing to pay for speed and convenience." Christopher T. Baer, with Glenn Porter and William H. Mulligan, Jr., eds., *Canals and Railroads of the Mid-Atlantic States, 1800–1860* (Wilmington, Del.: Eleutherian Mills–Hagley Foundation, 1981), 4.

101. Dickens, *American Notes*, 215.

102. Livingood, *The Philadelphia–Baltimore Trade Rivalry*, 133–37.

103. James D. Dilts, *The Great Road: The Building of the Baltimore and Ohio, the Nation's First Railroad, 1828–1853* (Stanford, Calif.: Stanford University Press, 1993), 16–18, 23–24, 32.

104. For a summary of the development of the Chesapeake & Ohio Canal, see Harlan D. Unrau, *Historic Resource Study: Chesapeake & Ohio Canal* (Hagerstown, Md.: United States Department of the Interior, National Park Service, 2007).

105. Ibid., 31–33.

106. Ibid., 27, 33–35.

107. The Cincinnati Southern Railway, a municipally owned line south to Chattanooga, built between 1869 and 1879, accounted for the bulk of Cincinnati's expenditures on internal improvements.

108. Carter Goodrich and Harvey H. Segal, "Baltimore's Aid to Railroads: A Study in the Municipal Planning of Internal Improvements," *Journal of Economic History* 13 (Winter 1953): 2–35; Dilts, *The Great Road*, 36–50.

109. Dilts, *The Great Road*, 45.

110. Pittsburgh was an attractive destination for the B&O, as that city would provide access to the Ohio River without a charter to enter Virginia, a state whose legislature was determined to support its own gateways to the west.

111. Erasmus Wilson, ed., *Standard History of Pittsburg, Pennsylvania* (Chicago: H. R. Cornell & Co., 1898), 131–33; Poor, *Railroads and Canals of the United States*, 490; Dilts, *The Great Road*, 48.

112. Goodrich and Segal, "Baltimore's Aid to Railroads," 22.

113. Wilson, *Standard History of Pittsburg*, 131–33; Poor, *Railroads and Canals of the United States*, 490; Dilts, *The Great Road*, 48.

114. Joseph S. Clark, Jr., "The Railroad Struggle for Pittsburgh: Forty-three Years of Philadelphia-Baltimore Rivalry, 1838–1871," *Pennsylvania Magazine of History and Biography* 48 (1924): 1–37, at 2–3.

115. Julius Rubin, "Canal or Railroad: Imitation and Innovation in the Response to the Erie Canal in Philadelphia, Baltimore, and Boston," *Transactions of the American Philosophical Society* 51 (1961): 1–106, at 16.

116. Albright Zimmerman, "Governments and Transportation Systems: The Pennsylvania Example" (alternate title: "Governments and Transportation Systems: Pennsylvania as a Case Study"), *Canal History and Technology Proceedings* 6 (1987): 27–70, at 33–34.

117. Snyder, *Jacksonian Heritage*, 75–81; Thomas Payne Govan, *Nicholas Biddle: Nationalist and Public Banker, 1786–1844* (Chicago: University of Chicago Press, 1959), 283–87; Goodrich, *Government Promotion*, 66–68; Zimmerman, "Governments and Transportation Systems," 36.

118. Nicholas Biddle to Joseph McIlvaine, January 23, 1836, quoted in Govan, *Nicholas Biddle*, 285.

119. Nicholas Biddle to McIlvaine, January 7, 1836, Biddle Papers, Manuscripts Division, Library of Congress, Washington, D.C., quoted in Walter Buckingham Smith, *Economic Aspects of the Second Bank of the United States* (Cambridge, Mass.: Harvard University Press, 1953), 179.

120. The proposed Gettysburg Railroad (or Gettysburg Extension, as it was sometimes called) was intended to connect to a route linking Gettysburg and Hagerstown, Maryland. This plan would have eventually created a roundabout, all-rail link between Philadelphia and Pittsburgh. In exchange for Maryland's concession that western trade be allowed to travel along this route to Philadelphia, legislators authorized a connection between the Eastern Division Canal at Columbia and the Susquehanna & Tidewater Canal at Wrightsville, allowing traffic from central Pennsylvania to reach Baltimore. As events transpired, however, B&O officials elected to locate the line along the south rather than the north bank of the Potomac River, bypassing Hagerstown and rendering the route to Gettysburg impracticable. The Franklin Railroad, chartered in 1832, offered a variant on this arrangement. By 1841, it had connected Chambersburg with Hagerstown, enabling a connection with a B&O branch line (completed in 1867) and the Western Maryland, which reached Hagerstown in 1872. That was, however, long after the PRR had completed a far more direct route between Philadelphia and Pittsburgh.

121. Legislators waited until 1838 to fund the final segment of the route, known as the Conneaut Division, a project that soon fell victim to the recession that followed the Panic of 1837.

122. Under the auspices of the private Erie Canal Company, the Conneaut Division reached Erie in 1844. Wilson and Roberts, *Internal Improvements*, 45–52; Goodrich, *Government Promotion*, 66–67; Shaw, *Canals for a Nation*, 78–81, 132; H. Benjamin Powell, "Coal and Pennsylvania's Transportation Policy, 1825–1828," *Pennsylvania History* 38 (April 1971): 134–51, at 146–48.

123. The Schuylkill Permanent Bridge succumbed to fire in 1875, and PRR crews quickly erected a temporary replacement structure. In 1881, as part of the construction of Broad Street Station, the PRR relocated its tracks to a new, rail-only span just north of Market Street. Shortly afterward, the City of Philadelphia erected a new Market Street Bridge, containing a roadway, walkway, and streetcar tracks. Edgar P. Richardson, "The Athens of America, 1800–1825," in Russell F. Weigley, ed., *Philadelphia: A 300-Year History* (New York: W. W. Norton, 1982), 208–57, at 231–32.

124. The Philadelphia & Reading Rail Road purchased the Columbia Bridge and the easternmost extremity of the Philadelphia & Columbia, using the route for access to the city. Wilson and Roberts, *Internal Improvements*, 38–39; Bishop, "The State Works of Pennsylvania," 196; Trautwine, "The Philadelphia and Columbia Railroad," 156–59; Zimmerman, "The Columbia and Philadelphia Railroad," 56–57.

125. DeHaas also considered an alternate route, without a tunnel, but at the expense of greater length. Weinhold, "The Inclined Planes of the Allegheny Portage Railroad," 220.

126. Wilson, *History of the Pennsylvania Railroad*, vol. 1, 138–42.

127. Peter Temin, *The Jacksonian Economy* (New York: Norton, 1969), 113–20.

128. The bill included funds for the Erie Extension, the North Branch Extension, the Sinnemahoning Extension (which would take the West

Branch Division some thirty-three miles past its current terminus at Farrandsville), and many other canal projects. Snyder, *Jacksonian Heritage*, 76, 130; Temin, *Jacksonian Economy*, 148–52.

129. Snyder, *Jacksonian Heritage*, 76, 130.

130. *A Further Report of the Survey of a Rail-Road from Chambersburg to Pittsburg, with an estimate of the cost of the work: Also, a further Report of the Survey of the Raystown Branch of the Juniata river, with an estimate of the cost of the work; by Hother Hagé, and the Report of Charles De Haas, Engineer, accompanied with a Survey and Estimate of the cost of constructing a McAdamized or Block road from Laughlinstown to Chambersburg, Read in the House of Representatives, January 28, 1839* (Harrisburg: Boas and Coplan, 1839); *Commemorative Biographical Encyclopedia of Dauphin County, Containing Sketches of Representative Citizens, and Many of the Early Scotch-Irish and German Settlers* (Chambersburg, Pa.: J. M. Runk & Co., 1896), 224; John Thomas Scharf and Thompson Wescott, *History of Philadelphia, 1609–1884*, vol. 3 (Philadelphia: L. H. Everts & Co., 1884), 2189–90.

131. As historian Charles McCool Snyder has suggested, the new Commissioners prepared for the upcoming elections, and "set to work to transform the improvements into a gigantic political machine for the cause of Antimasonry." Snyder, *Jacksonian Heritage*, 124–25.

132. *New York Times*, December 18, 1887.

133. Snyder, *Jacksonian Heritage*, 131.

134. *New York Times*, December 18, 1887.

135. *New York Times*, December 18, 1887 (quote); Snyder, *Jacksonian Heritage*, 131–35; Alexander Harris, *A Review of the Political Conflict in America: From the Commencement of the Anti-Slavery Agitation to the Close of Southern Reconstruction; Comprising also a Resume of the Career of Thaddeus Stevens: Being a Survey of the Struggle of Parties Which Destroyed the Republic and Virtualized Monarchized its Government* (New York: T. H. Pollock, 1876), 41–66, offers a biased and highly critical assessment of Steven's career, and his role in the Buckshot War. Hans L. Trefousse, *Thaddeus Stevens: Nineteenth-Century Egalitarian* (Chapel Hill: University of North Carolina Press, 1997), 57–66 provides a more balanced perspective.

136. The cessation of work on the Gettysburg Extension was conditioned more by economic and engineering realities than by political forces. The members of a committee of the Pennsylvania House of Representatives later concluded that "of all the works of doubtful expediency constructed by the State, in the opinion of your committee there is none so useless, so expensive or of as little value as the Gettysburg Railroad"—and few people had reason to doubt that assessment. Quoted in Wilson, *History of the Pennsylvania Railroad*, vol. 1, 389.

137. Westhaeffer, *History of the Cumberland Valley*, 39–41.

138. Burgess and Kennedy, *Centennial History*, 27; Cummings and Sayenga, "John August Roebling," 100–103.

139. Burgess and Kennedy, *Centennial History*, 27–28; Wilson and Roberts, *Internal Improvements*, 53–54.

140. Wilson, *History of the Pennsylvania Railroad*, vol. 1, 138–42.

141. Burgess and Kennedy, *Centennial History*, 28–33.

142. John Tyler, State of the Union Address, December 6, 1842.

143. Dickens, *American Notes*, quote at 53; Temin, *Jacksonian Economy*, 148–55.

144. Taylor, *The Transportation Revolution*, 375. For information on the problems associated with canal development in Ohio, Indiana, Illinois, and other states, see Harry N. Scheiber, *Ohio Canal Era: A Case Study of Government in the Economy, 1821–1861* (Athens: Ohio University Press, 1969), and John Lauritz Larson, *Internal Improvement: National Public Works*

and the Promise of Popular Government in the Early United States (Chapel Hill: University of North Carolina Press, 2001), 195–224.

145. William M. Gouge, *Niles' National Register*, September 3, 1842.

146. Investors were given the opportunity to trade their state bonds for stock certificates, without guaranteed interest payments, while commonwealth officials frantically attempted to find takers for $866,625 in notes backing an emergency loan.

147. The commonwealth passed on a total of five interest payments between 1842 and 1845. William Graham Sumner and Albert Galloway Keller, ed., *The Forgotten Man and Other Essays* (New Haven, Conn.: Yale University Press, 1918), 391–93; Snyder, *Jacksonian Heritage*, 155–57; Hartz, *Economic Policy*, 161; Zimmerman, "Governments and Transportation Systems," 37.

148. Govan, *Nicholas Biddle*, 311–12, 367, 392–93; Snyder, *Jacksonian Heritage*, 170, 177–78.

149. Construction crews completed the Shenango Division in May 1843. Work had begun on the Conneaut Division in 1838, but it fell victim to the depression that followed the Panic of 1837. Investors in the private Erie Canal Company (incorporated in March 1843, and not to be confused with the Erie Canal in New York) agreed to complete the Conneaut Division in exchange for the entire route between Beaver and Erie. They initially received only the Shenango and (incomplete) Conneaut divisions. In December 1844, the canal opened for service between Beaver and Erie, and on January 1, 1845, the Erie Canal Company received the Beaver Division as well as the French Creek Feeder. William Henry Moyer, "PRR's Navy, Part V: Pennsylvania Canals," *The Keystone* 42 (Summer 2009): 21–34.

150. Hartz, *Economic Policy*, 162–63.

151. Comments of Governor Pollock, 1857, quoted in Wilson, *History of the Pennsylvania Railroad*, vol. 1, 152.

152. As Job R. Tyson noted, in 1852, "It was an amphibious connection of land and water, consisting of two railways separated by a canal, and of two canals separated by a railway, happily elucidating the defects particular to both modes of transit, with the advantages of neither." This is certainly the most erudite, humorous, and oft-quoted criticism of the Main Line, but it should be remembered that its author was one of the organizers of the Pennsylvania Railroad, the company that put the state system out of business, and that Tyson's father-in-law, Thomas P. Cope, was a PRR director who declined to serve as the railroad's first president, owing to age and ill health. A more recent and dispassionate critic, economic historian Julius Rubin, likewise adjudged the state system as a "cumbrous mongrel line," while John Majewski has labeled it "a pronounced failure." Other scholars have offered even more sweeping criticisms. "The fact is that the state interventions were disasters," suggests economist Clifford F. Thies, "and it was from out of those disasters that there came a principled commitment, embodied in amendments to state constitutions, to laissez-faire." Job R. Tyson, *Letters on the Resources and Commerce of Philadelphia* (Philadelphia, 1852), 14; Rubin, "Canal or Railroad," 8; John Majewski, *A House Dividing: Economic Development in Pennsylvania and Virginia Before the Civil War* (Cambridge: Cambridge University Press, 2000), 113; Clifford F. Thies, "The American Railroad Network During the Early Nineteenth Century: Private Versus Public Enterprise," *Cato Journal* 22 (Fall 2002): 229–61, 230. During the early 1900s at a time of general interest in canal history (probably induced by the recent closure of many canals), Avard L. Bishop was the first historian to write a comprehensive history of the Main Line ("Corrupt Practices," in 1907), and he was highly critical of government operation. In excoriating state involvement in the economy, during the midst of the economic and political reforms of the Progressive Era, Bishop was thus making a clear statement against interventionism—just as Louis Hartz would later emphasize the accomplishments of Pennsylvania's

internal-improvement advocates in order to provide a pedigree for the statist policy solutions associated with the New Deal. See Zimmerman, "Governments and Transportation Systems," 42.

153. In addition to Job Tyson, who had links to the Pennsylvania Railroad, PRR historian William Bender Wilson wrote numerous accounts of the Main Line of Public Works and was generally critical of its operations and management.

154. See especially Hartz, *Economic Policy*. It should be emphasized, however, that Hartz and several of his contemporaries were ardent supporters of the New Deal of the 1930s. As such they were anxious to establish a historical pedigree for statist intervention into the economy, even when none existed.

155. Spiro G. Patton, "Canals in American Business and Economic History: A Review of the Issues," *Canal History and Technology Proceedings* 6 (1987): 3–25, at 12–13, makes reference to the works of historians Thomas C. Cochran, William R. Miller, Alfred D. Chandler, Jr., and Albert W. Niemi, Jr., particularly their assertions that canals failed to develop modern administrative and managerial practices.

156. Zimmerman, "The Columbia and Philadelphia Railroad," 61.

157. Historian William A. Russ, Jr., minimized the import of this massive cumulative deficit, insisting that "untold amounts of private wealth resulted from the public canals, making the loss of 59 millions a mere bagatelle." It would be equally misleading, however, to take at face value Julius Rubin's pessimistic estimates of the low economic development potential inherent in the canal. Russ, "The Partnership Between Public and Private Initiative in the History of Pennsylvania," *Pennsylvania History* 20 (January 1953): 1–21; Rubin, "Canal or Railroad," 15–16; Shaw, *Canals for a Nation*, 78. The present value calculation presumes a base year of 1835 and use of the Federal Reserve Bank of Minneapolis CPI calculator, computed from the *Handbook of Labor Statistics*, http://www.minneapolisfed.org/community_education/teacher/calc/hist1800.cfm, accessed on July 6, 2010; Hartz, *Economic Policy*, 47, 82, 149; Russ, "Partnership," 6; Majewski, *A House Dividing*, 9, 50–58.

158. The Pennsylvania Canal cost $8.3 million, at just over $30,000 per mile. Various estimates put the expense of the Portage Railroad at between $1.27 million and $1.83 million, representing a range of $35,000 to $50,000 per mile. The Philadelphia & Columbia Railroad consumed $4.2 million of the public treasury, at more than $50,000 per mile. According to Ephraim Banks, the auditor general of Pennsylvania, the railroad, fully equipped, may have cost as much as $5.3 million. Banks likewise estimated that by the end of 1853, the commonwealth had spent more than $11.1 million on the construction and operation of the Philadelphia & Columbia Railroad, while earning revenues of just over $9 million on that portion of the public works.

159. The return was scarcely better on other modes of transportation. By 1825, the commonwealth had invested more than $1.8 million in turnpike construction, yet received only $540 in dividends, a rate of return of 0.0003 percent. Rubin, "Canal or Railroad," 15, lists the initial construction cost of the Main Line of Public Works at $12.1 million, with a "total cost through 1857" of $16.5 million, owing to repairs and betterments, presumably including the New Portage Railroad that replaced the inclined planes. Wilson and Roberts, *Internal Improvements*, 44, lists the cost of the Main Line of Public Works at $15,624,714, while Bishop, "The State Works of Pennsylvania," 228, suggests that "the cost of the finished and unfinished improvements during the whole period of state ownership was $33,464,975." See also Cummings, "Some Notes," 48–49; Russ, "Partnership," 8; McCullough and Leuba, *The Pennsylvania Main Line Canal*, 28, 130.

160. Pennsylvania's state bond issues included $1.68 million between 1820 and 1825; $6,300,000 between 1825 and 1830; $16,130,000 between

1830 and 1835 (the period of the greatest expansion of the canal system, satisfying the demands of the Branch Men); and $3,167,000 between 1835 and 1838. Taylor, *The Transportation Revolution*, 372.

161. Hartz, *Economic Policy*, 149; Rubin, "Canal or Railroad," 15; Bishop, "The State Works of Pennsylvania," 229.

162. Rubin, "Canal or Railroad," 16, 33; Russ, "Partnership," 7, 9–10, 75, 81, 101; Taylor, *The Transportation Revolution*, 134, 137; Paul Marr, "Commodity Flow on the Pennsylvania Mainline System," *Canal History and Technology Proceedings* 21 (2002): 107–25, at 117. The 1829/1838 data are from Diane Lindstrom, *Economic Development in the Philadelphia Region, 1810–1850* (New York: Columbia University Press, 1978), 114–15. Despite the 1838 disparity between Main Line and New Orleans costs, Lindstrom has noted, "The failure to generate a substantial West-to-East trade with the completed Mainline system as late as 1839 can be explained by the fact that it cost far more to ship from Pittsburgh than from any costal port. Not until 1840—when special through rates were established—would most western exports to Philadelphia follow the Mainline instead of the circuitous route via New Orleans." Lindstrom, *Economic Development*, 113.

163. For an analysis of transportation patterns, see Marr, "Commodity Flow." In general, Marr adopts a positive view of the trade along the Pennsylvania system of public works, largely because he includes all of the canals—including the Delaware Division, which was responsible for a large portion of shipments, by weight.

164. Historian Catherine Reiser has correctly called the Western Division "a virtual life saver" for the region's iron interests, noting that "a local improvement would have been adequate to bring the needed supplies to Pittsburgh, but the undertaking was too costly for the iron interests to carry." Catherine Elizabeth Reiser, *Pittsburgh's Commercial Development, 1800–1850* (Harrisburg: Pennsylvania Historical and Museum Commission, 1951), 106.

165. In 1838, for example, New Orleans received 9,440 tons of Pittsburgh coal. The actual shipments of coal from Pittsburgh along the Ohio River were undoubtedly much higher, as additional coal was probably consigned to cities such as Cincinnati, Louisville, and St. Louis and thus never reached New Orleans. Howard N. Eavenson, *The First Century and a Quarter of American Coal Industry* (Pittsburgh: Baltimore Weekly Press, 1942), 389, 496–97.

166. During the construction of the Allegheny Portage Railroad, Moncure Robinson had suggested that the stationary steam engines installed on the western slope of the Alleghenies be more powerful than those on the east side in order to hoist eastbound coal cars over the summit. Lindstrom, *Economic Development*, 102; Eavenson, *The First Century*, 49; McCullough and Leuba, *The Pennsylvania Main Line Canal*, 99; Binder, *Coal Age Empire*, 159–60.

167. The experience of Philadelphia merchant Nathan Trotter was probably typical. During the years between 1803 and 1815, Trotter relied on turnpikes, shipping at least $200 worth of merchandise to each of ten communities to the north and west of Philadelphia, with none more distant than Harrisburg. The completion of public and private canals, along with the Philadelphia & Columbia Railroad, enabled Trotter to expand considerably the number of the towns that he served as well as their distance from Philadelphia. Between 1827 and 1831, he supplied at least $200 worth of goods to thirty-seven communities. Most of the new markets lay along the Union Canal, the Schuylkill Navigation, the Delaware Division, the Susquehanna Division, the North Branch Division, and the West Branch Division, and not the Main Line of Public Works. On the still-incomplete Main Line, Trotter's reach extended as far west as Huntingdon, but no farther. Trotter did manage to penetrate the Pittsburgh market during this period via the water route along the Atlantic seaboard, through the Gulf of Mexico, and up the Mississippi River. Even after the Allegheny Portage Railroad opened in 1834, Trotter seems not to have relied on that particular mode of transport, and his accounts for the period 1840–49 indicate that he sold an appreciable quantity of goods in only two cities to the west of the Allegheny Portage (Johnstown and Pittsburgh), but it is not clear whether shipments to the first of those communities traveled west from Philadelphia over the Main Line or east along the Western Division Canal from Pittsburgh. Elva Tooker, *Nathan Trotter: Philadelphia Merchant, 1787–1853* (Cambridge, Mass.: Harvard University Press, 1955), 121–28.

168. Given the record-keeping practices of the Canal Commission, which emphasized the careful accounting of disbursements and toll revenues rather than traffic carried, it is difficult to offer precise data on the quantities of freight that traveled over the Philadelphia & Columbia, the Pennsylvania Canal, and the Allegheny Portage Railroad. Traffic on the Allegheny Portage Railroad, weighed by commonwealth employees at the canal basin near the base of the inclined plane at Hollidaysburg, offered the best proxy for the success of the Main Line in moving freight across the state and showed slow but steady growth. In 1836, shortly after the route entered service, 29,740 tons of freight traveled westward across the railroad, while barely half that amount—15,439 tons—made the movement east. Between 1831 and 1835, the value of cargoes traveling eastbound over some portion of the Main Line was $1.8 million, little more than half of the $3.2 million in westbound shipments. The situation had scarcely improved between 1836 and 1840, with $7.0 million in freight moving westbound and only $4.3 million going east. Bishop, "The State Works of Pennsylvania," 248–49; Lindstrom, *Economic Development*, 102; Reiser, *Pittsburgh's Commercial Development*, 106–7, 219; Taylor, *The Transportation Revolution*, 162.

169. "Several proprietors of lines have thought it necessary to combine for the purpose of fixing high rates of freight during the first months of the season, when, by reason of the other routes not being open, ours is necessarily crowded," complained the canal commissioners in 1841. "The effects of this practice . . . are manifestly injurious to trade and prejudicial to the public interest, [and] it raises a suspicion of unfairness against us." *Annual Report of the Canal Commissioners for the Year Ending October 31, 1841*, 43, quoted in Reiser, *Pittsburgh's Commercial Development*, 94.

170. In 1855, late in the Main Line Canal era, it cost Leech & Company 1.1 cents to move a ton of freight the 395 miles between Philadelphia & Pittsburgh, compared with less than half a cent per ton for freight traveling the 350 miles between Albany and Buffalo. McCullough and Leuba, *The Pennsylvania Main Line Canal*, 146–47.

171. McCullough and Leuba, *The Pennsylvania Main Line Canal*, 148.

172. Roberts, *Reminiscences of the First Railroad*, 69.

173. Wilson, *History of the Pennsylvania Railroad*, vol. 1, 128, 143.

174. Bishop, "The State Works of Pennsylvania," 247.

175. In 1829, Anne Newport Royall saw the Lehigh Navigation and made a point of noting, "This is called the Lehigh Canal, which, including the cost expended on the Lehigh River, is rising $800,000! It has fifty locks! This was done by the enterprising Messrs. *White* & *Hazard* of 'The Lehigh Coal and Navigation Company,' at their private expense!!" Royall, *Mrs. Royall's Pennsylvania*, 101, emphasis in the original.

176. Lindstrom, *Economic Development*, 13–14, 19, 153, 173–74, 183–85.

Chapter 3. Community

1. Although largely superseded by more recent accounts of the Erie's history, the two most detailed accounts of the railroad's early years are still Edward H. Mott, *Between the Ocean and the Lakes: The Story of Erie* (New York: John S. Collins, 1899), 9–85, and Edward Hungerford, *Men of Erie: A Story of Human Effort* (New York: Random House, 1946), 6–69.

2. For a complete account of the various companies that were predecessors to the New York Central, see Frank Walker Stevens, *The Beginnings of the New York Central Railroad: A History* (New York: G. P. Putnam's Sons, 1926).

3. Rhoda M. Dorsey, "Comment—Baltimore Foreign Trade," in David T. Gilchrist, ed., *The Growth of Seaport Cities, 1790–1825: Proceedings of a Conference Sponsored by the Eleutherian Mills–Hagley Foundation, March 17–19, 1966* (Charlottesville: University Press of Virginia, 1967), 62–67, at 67.

4. William L. Raymond, *American and Foreign Investment Bonds* (Boston: Houghton Mifflin, 1916), 103.

5. Until 1856, various governments owned $6.8 million of the PRR's $12.4 million in stock. William G. Roy, *Socializing Capital: The Rise of the Large Industrial Corporation in America* (Princeton, N.J.: Princeton University Press, 1997), 92.

6. As historian William J. Novak has emphasized, the Commonwealth of Pennsylvania, the City of Philadelphia, and companies such as the Pennsylvania Railroad were equally a part of an integrated system of "self-rule through a great hierarchical chain of self-governing associations ranging from the body politic itself, through towns and counties, to corporations (municipal, civic, and business)." Novak, "The American Law of Association: The Legal-Political Construction of Civil Society," *Studies in American Political Development* 15 (Fall 2001): 163–88, 172–73.

7. James D. Dilts, *The Great Road: The Building of the Baltimore and Ohio, the Nation's First Railroad* (Stanford, Calif.: Stanford University Press, 1993), 320.

8. John Woolf Jordan, *A Century and a Half of Pittsburg and Her People*, vol. 3 (New York: The Lewis Publishing Company, 1908), 60–64; Erasmus Wilson, ed., *Standard History of Pittsburg, Pennsylvania* (Chicago: H. R. Cornell & Company, 1898), 83, 88, 93, 110, 112, 122, 131–32, 137–38, 211, 263, 791, 958.

9. Dilts, *The Great Road*, 321–23.

10. Douglas E. Bowers, "From Logrolling to Corruption: The Development of Lobbying in Pennsylvania, 1815–1861," *Journal of the Early Republic* 3 (Winter 1983): 439–74.

11. Karns was a staunch Whig (the party of the Philadelphia commercial elites) and he was accordingly well placed to warn Philadelphians of the plans of the B&O supporters. James Moore Swank, *Cambria County Pioneers: A Collection of Brief Biographical and Other Sketches Relating to the Early History of Cambria County, Pennsylvania* (Philadelphia: Allen, Lane & Scott, 1910), 90; Alexander Kelly McClure, *Old Time Notes of Pennsylvania: A Connected and Chronological Record of the Commercial, Industrial and Educational Advancement of Pennsylvania, and the Inner History of All Political Movements since the Adoption of the Constitution of 1838*, vol. 1 (Philadelphia: J. C. Winston, 1905), 127–28.

12. The spelling of his middle name seems to have varied between "Pim" and "Pym," with an approximately equal number of references for each. *Library of Congress Authorities* uses the preferred spelling of "Pim."

13. Urban historian Sam Bass Warner has accurately described Cope as "a good example of the old-style generalist, both in business and politics." Sam Bass Warner, *The Private City: Philadelphia in Three Periods of its Growth*, 2nd ed. (Philadelphia: University of Pennsylvania Press, 1987), 80.

14. Julianna R. Wood and Richard D. Wood, *Biographical Sketch of Richard D. Wood* (Philadelphia: Lippincott's Press, 1871), November 9, 1847, 304.

15. Biographical information on Thomas Cope is primarily from Eliza Cope Harrison, ed., *The Diary of Thomas P. Cope, 1800–1851* (South Bend, Ind.: Gateway Editions, 1978; hereafter cited as "Cope Diary"), and Henry Simpson, *The Lives of Eminent Philadelphians, Now Deceased, Collected from Original and Authentic Sources* (Philadelphia: William Brotherhead, 1859), 248–56. Cope's extensive diaries were essentially lost until the 1930s, when descendants rediscovered them in an outbuilding of a house in Maine and subsequently donated them to Haverford College. The Haverford College Libraries house the diaries (Ms. Coll. 975A-C) and other Cope business papers (Ms. Coll. 1013); see http://www.haverford.edu/library/special/aids/tpcope/. Harrison transcribed and published the diaries, but (understandably, given their length) left out many entries, including a number related to Cope's role in the Pennsylvania Railroad. Subsequent to Harrison's publication, Haverford College digitized the diaries in their entirety, and they are available via a keyword search at http://triptych.brynmawr.edu/. References to the Cope diaries are listed according to date of entry and Cope's pagination, not the pagination employed in Harrison's edited work. For a synopsis of the role of Quaker merchants in Philadelphia's economic development, see Andrew Dawson, *Lives of the Philadelphia Engineers: Capital, Class and Revolution, 1830–1890* (Aldershot: Ashgate, 2004), 89–92; E. Digby Baltzell, *Puritan Boston and Quaker Philadelphia: Two Protestant Ethics and the Spirit of Class Authority and Leadership* (Boston: Beacon Press, 1979); Baltzell, *Philadelphia Gentlemen: The Making of a National Upper Class*, rev. ed. (New Brunswick, N.J.: Transaction, 1989); *Biographies of Successful Philadelphia Merchants* (Philadelphia: James K. Simon, 1864), 181–85; Augustus C. Buell, *The Memoirs of Charles H. Cramp* (Philadelphia: J. B. Lippincott, 1906), 34–35; and Warner, *Private City*, 80–83.

16. Cope Diary, vol. 9, February 24, 1847, 1.

17. Cope Diary, vol. 7, June 4, 1845, 157.

18. Cope Diary, vol. 7, August 31, 1845, 187.

19. *Indiana (Pennsylvania) Republican*, quoted in George H. Burgess and Miles C. Kennedy, *Centennial History of the Pennsylvania Railroad Company, 1846–1946* (Philadelphia: Pennsylvania Railroad, 1949), 36.

20. Cope Diary, vol. 8, December 30, 1845, 32.

21. Quoted in Burgess and Kennedy, *Centennial History*, 36–37.

22. Philadelphia merchant Nathan Dunn, who had made his fortune in the China trade, had opened the Chinese Museum in 1838. He relocated his collection to London in 1842, leaving the building vacant for other public uses. Aaron Caplan, "Nathan Dunn's Chinese Museum" (B.A. thesis, University of Pennsylvania, 1986); John Rogers Haddad, *The Romance of China: Excursions to China in U.S. Culture, 1776–1876* (New York: Columbia University Press, 2008).

23. The "Tulip Mania" occurred in the Netherlands during 1636 and 1637, when speculators bought and sold tulip bulbs for exorbitant prices until the market collapsed, leaving many in ruins. Cope would have known a great deal about this relatively minor financial debacle, thanks to its description in Charles Mackay's *Extraordinary Popular Delusions and the Madness of Crowds*, published in 1841, a book that Cope must surely have read. Cope Diary, vol. 7, October 29, 1845, 206–7, October 30, 1845, 207 (quote); ibid., vol. 8, November 21, 1845, 7.

24. Cope Diary, vol. 8, December 11, 1845, 19–20; *Proceedings of the Meeting of the Citizens of the City and County of Philadelphia in Relation to the Great Pennsylvania Rail Road from Philadelphia via Harrisburg to Pittsburgh, with the Address of the Committee to the People of Pennsylvania* (Philadelphia: Steam Press, 1846).

25. Cope Diary, vol. 8, December 11, 1845, 19–20.

26. *Proceedings of the Meeting*, 6.

27. Ibid., 8, emphasis in the original.

28. Ibid., 11. The PRR's promoters also argued, "Experience has shown that when the amount of intercourse and business is large, and attracted from various distant points, the location of a canal and railroad between the same ultimate points, promotes the success of both."

29. Pauline Maier, "The Revolutionary Origins of the American Corporation," *William and Mary Quarterly* 50 (January 1993): 51–84.

30. Cope Diary, vol. 8, December 11, 1845, 21.

31. Joseph S. Clark, Jr., "The Railroad Struggle for Pittsburgh: Forty-Three Years of Philadelphia-Baltimore Rivalry, 1838–1871," *Pennsylvania Magazine of History and Biography* 48 (1924): 1–37, at 5, 34; Edward J. Davies II, "State Economic Policy and the Region in Pennsylvania, 1853–1895," *Business and Economic History* 21 (1992): 280–89, at 280; Bowers, "From Logrolling to Corruption," at 443–46, 451.

32. Bowers, "From Logrolling to Corruption," 443, 448, 456–59, 462.

33. Cope Diary, Vol. 8, February 16, 1846, 52 .

34. Ibid., March 4, 1846, 59–60.

35. Ibid., December 24, 1845, 30.

36. Cope Diary, vol. 9, March 18, 1847, 9.

37. McClure, *Old Time Notes of Pennsylvania*, 112, 235.

38. Cope Diary, vol. 8, December 30, 1845, 32.

39. Ibid., December 14, 1845, 22 (quote); John W. W. Loose, Lancaster County Historical Society, History of Masonic Lodge 43, Lancaster, Pennsylvania; http://www.lodge43.org/history.html, accessed on June 30, 2010.

40. Solomon W. Roberts, "An Obituary Notice of Charles B. Trego," Proceedings of the American Philosophical Society 14 (January–June 1875), 356–58; Cope Diary, vol. 8, December 24, 1845, 29.

41. Cope Diary, vol. 8, March 7, 1846, March 9, 1846, 61.

42. William Bender Wilson, *History of the Pennsylvania Railroad Company, with Plan of Organization, Portraits of Officials and Biographical Sketches*, vol. 2 (New York: Henry T. Coates & Co., 1899), 264; Cope Diary, vol. 8, January 19, 1846, 40; Burgess and Kennedy, *Centennial History*, 38.

43. In the earliest years of the railroad's construction and operation, the names "Pennsylvania" and "Pennsylvania Central" were used more or less interchangeably. Many years later, however, the Pennsylvania Railroad developed its own (inaccurate) legend regarding the origin of the longer version. During the early 1860s, the story went, William H. Holmes, a western passenger agent based in Chicago, decided that the rival New York Central should not be allowed to mislead travelers into believing that it was the only centrally located northern railroad. Accordingly, on his own initiative, Holmes renamed his employer the Pennsylvania Central Railroad and began issuing annual passes, seat checks, and promotional materials bearing that nomenclature. His initiative soon led to the "quite general use, in popular speech and writing, of the term Pennsylvania 'Central' Railroad, which was never at any time the correct corporate name of the Pennsylvania Railroad or any company associated with it." "Use of the Name Pennsylvania 'Central' Railroad," *Information for the Public and Employes [of the] Pennsylvania Railroad System, The Sesqui-Centennial, Philadelphia*, April 9, 1925, 23.

44. Baker had been involved in banking and in various canal and bridge projects in the Philadelphia area, and he was a co-founder of the city's Laurel Hill Cemetery, along with Henry Toland (a Philadelphia grocer and Robert Toland's brother) and Nicholas Biddle, the former president of the Second Bank of the United States. Bayard was the former United States district attorney for Delaware, and a future United States senator. Cope Diary, vol. 8, February 18, 1846, 52 (quote); Colleen McDannell, *Material Christianity: Religion and Popular Culture in America* (New Haven, Conn.: Yale University Press, 1998), 108.

45. Francis Rawn Shunk, Annual Message to the General Assembly, January 5, 1848, in *Pennsylvania Archives*, 4th Ser., vol. 7: *Papers of the Governors, 1845–1858* (Harrisburg, 1902), 208, quoted in Maier, "Revolutionary Origins," 59–60.

46. Cope Diary, vol. 8, February 19, 1846, 52, February 21, February 23, 1846, 54.

47. *Pittsburgh Chronicle*, February 14, 1846, reprinted in Reiser, *Pittsburgh's Commercial Development*, 154.

48. *Pittsburgh Chronicle*, April 9, 1846, reprinted in Reiser, *Pittsburgh's Commercial Development*, 154–55.

49. "Chinese" is probably a reference to the Chinese Museum, site of the first rally in support of the Pennsylvania Central. Ibid.,155.

50. Cope Diary, vol. 8, April 16, 1846, 75; Clark, "The Railroad Struggle for Pittsburgh," 10; Dilts, *The Great Road*, 318, 322.

51. Pennsylvania legislators were hardly alone in their efforts to select economic winners and losers by taxing one form of transportation in order to protect another. In New York, the legislature forbade the Utica & Schenectady Railroad from carrying freight along a route that paralleled the Erie Canal. Even after 1847, when legislators rescinded the ban, they still required the railroad to pay tolls to the state, in compensation for lost revenue on the state waterway. A similar provision applied to the connecting Syracuse & Utica Railroad, like the Utica & Schenectady destined to become a part of the New York Central. The state of New Jersey imposed a "transit duty" on freight and passengers entering or leaving the state on the Camden & Amboy Railroad, in exchange for the company's de facto monopoly on rail transportation. In 1833, when Maryland legislators granted the Baltimore & Ohio the authority to build a branch to Washington, they required the company to pay a fifth of all passenger revenues into the state treasury, equivalent to a surcharge of at least twenty-five cents for everyone who traveled over the new route. As business historian Colleen A. Dunlavy has observed, "Taxes on railroad traffic became, in effect, a way to ameliorate the disruptions brought on by technological change." Dunlavy, *Politics and Industrialization: Early Railroads in the United States and Prussia* (Princeton, N.J.: Princeton University Press, 1994), 77–83, quote at 77; Louis Hartz, *Economic Policy and Democratic Thought: Pennsylvania, 1776–1860* (Cambridge, Mass.: Harvard University Press, 1948), 52–53, 267–68; Frank Walker Stevens, *The Beginnings of the New York Central Railroad: A History* (New York: G. P. Putnam's Sons, 1926), 266–76; Poor, *History of the Railroads and Canals*, 397.

52. Clark, "The Railroad Struggle for Pittsburgh," 7–8; Cope Diary, vol. 8, February 27, 1846, 56.

53. The House approved the changes on April 17, in another close vote, fifty-one to forty-five.

54. Clark, "The Railroad Struggle for Pittsburgh," 10–11; Burgess and Kennedy, *Centennial History*, 37–39; Wilson, *History of the Pennsylvania Railroad*, vol. 1, 5.

55. In this instance, the members of the legislature acceded to Governor Shunk's insistence that the tonnage tax would constitute a first lien on the property, in the event of the PRR's bankruptcy.

56. Burgess and Kennedy, *Centennial History*, 39–40.

57. "An Act to Incorporate the Pennsylvania Railroad Company," April 13, 1846, reprinted in *Charter and Supplements of the Pennsylvania Railroad Company, with the Acts of Assembly and Municipal Ordinances Affecting the Company; Together with the By-Laws of the Board of Directors* (Philadelphia: Crissy & Markley, 1859), 3–5.

58. *Charter and Supplements*, 13. The legislature's supplement of February 17, 1854, removed that restriction, permitting the PRR to take any and all property that it required for construction through the power of eminent domain, but only in urban areas, where it was not possible to readily alter the route in order to avoid existing structures. "A Further Supplement to an Act to Incorporate the Pennsylvania Railroad Company," February 17, 1854, reprinted in *Charter and Supplements*, 35–36.

59. In October 1847, the company's directors reassured shareholders that the early "interest" payments were in keeping with the policies employed by other railroads, including those in Britain, Massachusetts, and

New York. By March 1848, a supplement to the charter permitted the company to change the 5 percent construction dividend to a 6 percent ordinary dividend, based on the paid-in capital (rather than the higher amount of the par value of the shares). Political economist George Heberton Evans, Jr., has labeled this "preferred" stock, by virtue of the guaranteed nature of the dividend payment. Many antebellum corporations avoided the use of the "preferred" terminology, however, and officially the PRR did not issue preferred stock. In May 1856, the board authorized payment of the first traditional dividend, at 4 percent. *Charter and Supplements*, 12; Evans, "The Early History of Preferred Stock in the United States," American Economic Review 19 (March 1929): 43–58, at 50–51.

60. Cope Diary, vol. 8, December 11, 1845, 21.

61. *The Pennsylvania Rail Road. Address of the Committee of Seven to the Citizens of Philadelphia, and of Pennsylvania, Appointed at a Town Meeting, held at Philadelphia, on the 28th of April, 1846* (Philadelphia: J. Harding, 1846); Edwin T. Freedley, *Philadelphia and Its Manufactures: A Hand-book Exhibiting the Development, Variety, and Statistics of the Manufacturing Industry of Philadelphia in 1857, Together with Sketches of Remarkable Manufactories and a List of Articles Now Made in Philadelphia* (Philadelphia: Edward Young, 1859), 117.

62. Cope Diary, vol. 8, April 28, 1846, 80–81 (quotes); Spiro G. Patton, "The Rivalry Between the Schuylkill Canal and the Reading Railroad for the Anthracite Trade," *Business and Economic History* 9 (1980): 139–42, at 140; C. Stuart Patterson, "Obituary Notices of Members Deceased: Frederick Frailey, LL.D.," Proceedings of the American Philosophical Society 40 (December 1901), i–ix; *New York Times*, September 24, 1901.

63. Isaac W. Norris, the principal of the latter firm, was one of the railroad's commissioners.

64. Cope Diary, vol. 8, June 5, 1846, 96, June 22, 1846, 99; "An Act to Incorporate the Pennsylvania Railroad Company," 3.

65. Cope Diary, vol. 8, June 22, 1846, 99 (quote), June 25, 1846, 99–100, June 27, 1846, 100, June 29, 1846, 101, July 8, 1846, 104, July 13, 1846, 105.

66. When Parliament passed the Importation Act of 1815, its intent was to protect domestic farmers from overseas competition. Over the next thirty years, the Corn Laws were the focus of debate between agrarian interests and the emerging community of industrialists, who favored cheaper food supplies for their workers. It should be noted that "corn" was a generic name applied to all grains, including wheat. Overall, however, the repeal of the Corn Laws was a relatively insignificant factor in the growth of American grain exports compared with the demand induced by industrialization in Britain and other western European countries, particularly during the 1850s. George Rogers Taylor, *The Transportation Revolution, 1815–1860* (1951; repr. Armonk, N.Y.: M. E. Sharpe, 1977), 195.

67. The first successful transatlantic cable did not enter service until 1866.

68. Cope Diary, vol. 8, July 20, 1846, 109; Taylor, *The Transportation Revolution*, 95.

69. The charter allowed the PRR to demand assessments of up to $5 per share, within any sixty-day period, with the purchaser to forfeit the stock if payments were more than six months in arrears. *Charter and Supplements*, 110.

70. Philadelphia was governed by a bicameral legislature, through the Common Council, established in 1691, and the Select Council, established in 1796. Both bodies were elected. Until 1839, the members of the Select Council chose the city's mayor, and they retained control over municipal executive appointments until 1885. In 1919, the Select and Common Councils were combined into the Philadelphia City Council. Finding Aid, Collection 1002, Philadelphia (Pa.) City Council, Petitions to the Select and Common Councils, Historical Society of Pennsylvania; available at http:// www.hsp.org/files/findingaid1002councilpetitions.pdf, accessed on July 25, 2010.

71. Cope Diary, vol. 8, June 5, 1846, 95–96.

72. Cope Diary, vol. 8, May 23, 1846, 91, July 15, 1846, 105–6, July 18, 1846, 107–8; *Art, Scenery and Philosophy in Europe: Being Fragments from the Port-Folio of the Late Horace Binney Wallace, Esq., of Philadelphia* (Philadelphia: Herman Hooker, 1855); "Obituary. The Late Horace Binney Wallace, Esq.," *American Law Register (1852–1891)* 1 (March 1853): 310–15.

73. McClure, *Old Time Notes of Pennsylvania*, 122; Charles Chauncey Binney, *The Life of Horace Binney, With Selections from His Letters* (Philadelphia: J. B. Lippincott, 1903), 245 (quote); Julius Rubin, "Canal or Railroad: Imitation and Innovation in the Response to the Erie Canal in Philadelphia, Baltimore, and Boston," *Transactions of the American Philosophical Society* 51 (1961): 1–106, at 22.

74. Binney also argued, "The result of the whole is that the subscribing, the borrowing, and the taxing, being none of them incident to the exercise of a power for the government of the city, for its welfare, cannot lawfully be exercised by the Councils." Binney, *The Life of Horace Binney* (Binney pamphlet dated ca. July 14, 1846, reprinted on p. 247).

75. Charles Wetherill, *History of the Religious Society of Friends Called by Some the Free Quakers, in the City of Philadelphia* (Philadelphia: The Society, 1894); J. Thomas Scharf and Thompson Westcott, *History of Philadelphia, 1609–1884*, vol. 2 (Philadelphia: L. H. Everts & Co., 1884), 1258–59.

76. Cope Diary, vol. 8, July 3, 1846, 102; Stephen Noyes Winslow, *Biographies of Successful Philadelphia Merchants* (Philadelphia: James K. Simon, 1864), 139–40.

77. Dawson, *Lives of the Philadelphia Engineers*, 95.

78. Cope Diary, vol. 8, July 1, 1846, 101–2, July 3, 1846, 103.

79. "Majority and Minority Reports of the Joint Committee of Councils," reprinted in J. Elfreth Watkins, *Pennsylvania Railroad Company, 1846–1896, in its Relation to the Pennsylvania State Canals and Railroads and the Consolidated System East and West of Pittsburgh* (unpublished ms., 1896, original at the Smithsonian Institution, with microfilm copies in the Pennsylvania Railroad Company Collection, call no. 1807/1810, Hagley Museum and Library, Wilmington, Delaware (hereafter cited as HML), and in the Pennsylvania State Archives, Harrisburg, with an additional microfilm copy in the author's possession, hereafter cited as "Watkins History"), "Appendix," 88–92.

80. "Majority and Minority Reports of the Joint Committee of Councils," reprinted in Watkins History, "Appendix," 88–92.

81. Cope Diary, vol. 8, July 3, 1846, 102; July 17, 1846, 107; Hartz, *Economic Policy*, 105.

82. Toland and Hinchman were, until 1845, two of the five Whigs representing the City of Philadelphia in the House of Representatives. *Biographical Sketch of Richard D. Wood*, vol. 1, September 28, 1846, 274; Cope Diary, vol. 8, September 28, 1846, 135, October 1, 1846, 136–37 (quote).

83. *Biographical Sketch of Richard D. Wood*, vol. 1, October 7, 1846, October 8, 1846, October 12, 1846, 275.

84. Cope Diary, vol. 8, September 28, 1846, 135, October 7, 1846, 140, October 10, 1846, 141–42; Binney, *The Life of Horace Binney*, 250.

85. *Biographical Sketch of Richard D. Wood*, vol. 1, October 14, 1846, 275.

86. Frank William Taussig, *The Tariff History of the United States: A Series of Essays* (New York: G. P. Putnam's Sons, 1888), 110–14; Taylor, *The Transportation Revolution*, 364–66; Charles McCool Snyder, *The Jacksonian Heritage: Pennsylvania Politics, 1833–1848* (Harrisburg: Pennsylvania Historical and Museum Commission, 1958), 187–203; Cope Diary, vol. 8, October 15, 1846, 142–43.

87. Such a clause was not unusual in an era when many citizens believed that city investments in private corporations might constitute an unconstitutional expansion of municipal power. As Hartz notes, "Between 1846 and 1860 the legislature enacted two general measures and thirty-five special measures expressly authorizing stock subscriptions by local governments." Hartz, *Economic Policy*, 88; Cope Diary, vol. 8, November 5, 1846, 147–48, November 13, 1846, 151; Burgess and Kennedy, *Centennial History*, 41–43; see also Scharf and Westcott, *History of Philadelphia*, Vols. 1 and 3.

88. Cope Diary, vol. 8, November 27, 1846, 156–57.

89. Cope Diary, vol. 8, December 4, 1846, 159; *Biographical Sketch of Richard D. Wood*, vol. 1, December 2 and 5, 1846, December 7, 1846, December 8, 1846, December 15, 1846, December 24, 1846, 279–81.

90. Cope Diary, vol. 8, December 9, 1846, 160 (quote, emphasis in the original).

91. As a founding member of the Young Men's Colonization Society, Cresson had already alienated the anti-colonization abolitionists in Philadelphia. Whatever his faults, he contributed enough to the PRR's future that in 1854 the company named the town of Cresson, Pennsylvania, in his honor. Cope Diary, vol. 8, November 28, 1846, 157 (quote), February 11, 1847, 185 ("Magnus Apostle" quote); Bruce Dorsey, "A Gendered History of African Colonization in the Antebellum United States," *Journal of Social History* 34 (Fall 2000): 77–103.

92. *Biographical Sketch of Richard D. Wood*, vol. 1, December 31, 1846, 281; "A Stockholder" [Joel Cook], *The Philadelphia National Bank: A Century's Record, 1803–1903* (Philadelphia: William F. Fell, 1903), 111.

93. Cope Diary, vol. 8, December 16, 1846, 161.

94. PRR Board of Directors (BOD) Minutes, HML, May 21, 1851, 451 (quote).

95. Cope Diary, vol. 8, December 29, 1846, 169 (quotes).

96. Cope Diary, vol. 8, December 29, 1846, 169 (quotes).

97. Burgess and Kennedy, *Centennial History*, 41–43; Wilson, *Standard History of Pittsburg*, 134–35.

98. Cope Diary, vol. 8, January 26, 1847, 177 ("private means"), January 30, 1847, 178 ("on velvet").

99. Cope Diary, vol. 8, December 16, 1846, 161 (quote), February 11, 1847, 184.

100. In June 1839, a Philadelphia ordinance provided for the popular election of the mayor. In the October elections, Swift won the most votes in a three-way race. In the absence of a clear majority, the law provided that the councils select the mayor, and they chose Swift (making him the last appointed mayor, and subsequently the first elected mayor in Philadelphia). In 1840, he did win a clear majority, and took office on the basis of the popular vote. Swift did not stand for reelection the following year, but he won reelection in 1845 and served until 1848. John Russell Young, ed., *Memorial History of the City of Philadelphia, from its First Settlement to the Year 1895*, vol. 1 (New York: New-York History Company, 1895), 499.

101. Cope Diary, vol. 8, February 11, 1847, 184–85, February 12, 1847, 185.

102. Ibid., February 14, 1847, 186, February 15, 1847, 186–87, February 18, 1847, 187–88 (quote, emphasis in the original). Note that the spelling of "Pittsburgh" was not fixed, even on maps and by the Post Office, until well into the 20th century—"Pittsburg" was a quite common variant.

103. Ibid., January 7, 1847, 171–72.

104. Ibid., February 20, 1847, 188–89.

105. Ibid., February 22, 1847, 1.

106. Ibid., January 15, January 16, 1847, 174.

107. Ibid., January 22, 1847, 176.

108. Cooper opposed the PRR bill as an apparent tactic to fuel his own gubernatorial ambitions, and he had already promised Gibbons the post of secretary of state. In any event, the Whigs nominated General James Irvine as their candidate, and he in turn lost the 1847 election to the incumbent Democratic governor and former secretary of the Canal Commission, Francis Shunk. Cope Diary, vol. 9, March 17, 1847, 8 (quotes).

109. Ibid., March 12, 1847, 6.

110. Ibid., March 27, 1847, 12.

111. Cope Diary, vol. 8, January 16, 1847, 525 (quote); vol. 9, June 12, 1847, 535.

112. Cope Diary, vol. 9, August 12, 1847, 537.

113. Ibid., November 20, 1847, 545.

114. Ibid., January 5, 1848, 115–16; Homer Tope Rosenberger, *The Philadelphia and Erie Railroad: Its Place in American Economic History* (Potomac, Md.: Fox Hills Press, 1975), 76–79, 97–98, 162–67.

115. Cope Diary, vol. 9, March 13, 1848, 140.

116. Ibid., March 16, 1848, 141; John P. Green, "Financing the Pennsylvania Railroad," n.d., ca. 1905, HML, Box 419, folder 556.

117. Cope Diary, vol. 9, November 20, 1847, 100.

118. PRR BOD Minutes, June 28, 1848, 97–102, HML.

119. Burgess and Kennedy, *Centennial History*, 41–42, 58.

120. It should be noted, however, that Henry Corbit, while not officially a city director, was a member of the Select and Common Councils as well as the PRR board. He resigned, effective May 17, 1847, owing to health problems associated with his 260-pound girth. Cope Diary, vol. 9, March 27, 1847, 12–13, May 12, 1847, 29; Burgess and Kennedy, *Centennial History*, 785–86.

121. As economic historian Carter Goodrich has observed, "Public and individual investors were thought of as sharing the overriding interest in the completion of a proposed improvement, and it was often believed that this common purpose would be better served under private leadership." Goodrich, *Government Promotion of American Canals and Railroads, 1800–1890* (New York: Columbia University Press, 1960), 290.

122. Of the $8,106,000 in paid-in capital, local governments held $5,750,000 and private interests $2,356,000. The City of Philadelphia, along with Butler and Lawrence Counties, also invested heavily in the North Western Railroad Company, a more northerly route between Blairsville and Allegheny City, that eventually (as the Western Pennsylvania Railroad) became an important PRR bypass line through the congested Pittsburgh area. By January 1, 1856, various government entities still held a majority of PRR stock—$6,750,000, compared with $4,855,000 in the hands of contractors and private investors. In 1880, the PRR board of directors authorized the purchase of the remaining 59,149 shares of stock held by the City of Philadelphia to prevent the railroad from coming under the control of New York financial interests. Several municipally appointed directors, including Alexander M. Fox, John Price Wetherill, Jr., and William L. Elkins, remained on the board, owing to their private investment interests, but no longer represented the public. PRR BOD Minutes, May 5, 1847, 20; Burgess and Kennedy, *Centennial History*, 54, 58, 71, 76, 85, 109–10, 382, 788.

123. As sociologist William G. Roy has observed, "Whereas state governments, as the chartering agencies, had a structural capacity to hold corporations accountable to the public, local governments were more likely to behave like private owners." Roy, *Socializing Capital*, 89.

124. Andrew M. Schocket, "Thinking About Elites in the Early Republic," *Journal of the Early Republic* 25 (Winter 2005): 547–55.

125. This is what business historian Pamela Walker Laird has aptly described as "pull." Laird, *Pull: Networking and Success Since Benjamin Franklin* (Cambridge, Mass.: Harvard University Press, 2006), 1–10, 22–24.

126. For the standard account of the transformation of American merchants to industrialists, see Glenn Porter and Harold C. Livesay, *Merchants*

and Manufacturers: Studies in the Changing Structure of Nineteenth-Century Marketing (Baltimore: Johns Hopkins University Press, 1971).

127. "Majority and Minority Reports of the Joint Committee of Councils," reprinted in Watkins History, "Appendix," 88–92.

128. Thomas Williams continued his combative ways for much of the remainder of his life. During the early 1860s, he was a staunch, if unsuccessful, critic of the PRR's efforts to repeal the tonnage tax. He was elected to Congress in 1862, and he later served as one of the prosecutors in the impeachment proceedings against President Andrew Johnson. See Burton Alva Konkle, "His Notable Speech on the Maintenance of the Constitution and the Union and the Climax in His Fight Against the Pennsylvania Railroad," in The Life and Speeches of Thomas Williams: Orator, Statesman, and Jurist, vol. 2 (Philadelphia: Campion & Company, 1905), 434–58.

129. Wilson, Standard History of Pittsburgh, 141 ("groaned"), 142 ("millstone"); George Thornton Fleming, History of Pittsburgh and Environs, vol. 2 (New York: American Historical Society, 1922), 164; David Cannadine, Mellon: An American Life (New York: Random House, 2008), 29.

130. Isaac F. Redfield et al., eds., The American Law Register, New Series, vol. 4: From November 1864 to November 1865 (Philadelphia: D. B. Canfield & Co., 1865), 681 (quote); Constitution of the Commonwealth of Pennsylvania (1838), Article XI, Sec. 1 (Amendment of 1857); John Majewski, A House Dividing: Economic Development in Pennsylvania and Virginia Before the Civil War (Cambridge: Cambridge University Press, 2000), 123.

131. Binney, The Life of Horace Binney, 254–55.

132. Ibid., 255.

133. Ibid., 247, 412–13.

134. McClure, Old Time Notes of Pennsylvania, 38–41, 185–86, 202–5, 212–13; Stephen Noyes Winslow, Biographies of Successful Philadelphia Merchants (Philadelphia: James K. Simon, 1864), 140; Burgess and Kennedy, Centennial History, 789; Warren F. Hewitt, "The Know-Nothing Party in Pennsylvania," Pennsylvania History 2 (April 1935): 69–85, 74.

135. Cope Diary, vol. 8, February 23, 1846, 54.

136. Cope Diary, vol. 8, February 28, 1846, 57.

137. McClure, Old Time Notes of Pennsylvania, 235–36; William Still, The Underground Railroad: A Record of Facts, Authentic Narrative, Letters, &c. (Philadelphia: Porter and Coates, 1872).

138. Dilts, The Great Road, 321–23; Cope Diary, vol. 8, May 6, 1846, 85 (quote).

139. The decision by the B&O board to build west to Wheeling, a route strongly favored by President Louis McLane, was extraordinarily complex and divisive. McLane's absence from the United States between July 1845 and October 1846 made the selection process even more difficult. See Dilts, The Great Road, 322–36.

140. J. H. Hollander, The Financial History of Baltimore (Baltimore: The Johns Hopkins Press, 1899), 322–24; John Thomas Scharf, History of Baltimore City and County, from the Earliest Period to the Present Day (Philadelphia: Louis H. Everts, 1881), 329–40; Wilson, Standard History of Pittsburgh, 142; Carter Goodrich and Harvey H. Segal, "Baltimore's Aid to Railroads: A Study in the Municipal Planning of Internal Improvements," Journal of Economic History 13 (Winter 1953): 2–35.

141. Tom Scott shepherded those bills through the General Assembly with sufficient persuasiveness to give rise to the apocryphal incident in which a senator, relieved that the passage of the two bills would temporarily exempt them from further contact with the PRR vice president, said, "Mr. Speaker, may we now go Scott free?" Legislative Record, February 14, 1867, 141–42, quoted in Clark, "The Railroad Struggle for Pittsburgh," 26.

142. Clark, "The Railroad Struggle for Pittsburgh," 12–32; Wilson, Standard History of Pittsburgh, 134–42.

143. Clark, "The Railroad Struggle for Pittsburgh," 33–34.

Chapter 4. Enterprise

1. George H. Burgess and Miles C. Kennedy, Centennial History of the Pennsylvania Railroad Company, 1846–1946 (Philadelphia: Pennsylvania Railroad, 1949), 785; Thomas Pim Cope Diary, January 19, 1848, 120, http://triptych.brynmawr.edu/, (hereafter cited as "Cope Diary;" see notes to Chapter 3 for a full description of the Cope Diary), vol. 9, March 17, 1847, 8 (quote).

2. Cope Diary, vol. 9, March 14, 1847, 6–7.

3. In 1844, Ellet had written a lengthy pamphlet to his fellow shareholders, explaining why the competing Reading Rail Road would never be able to carry anthracite at lower rates than the Schuylkill Navigation. Charles Ellet, An Address to the Stockholders of the Schuylkill Navigation Company in Reply to a Pamphlet Circulated by the Reading Rail Road Company (Philadelphia: Joseph and William Kite, 1845).

4. Julianna R. Wood and Richard D. Wood, Biographical Sketch of Richard D. Wood, vol. 1 (Philadelphia: Lippincott's Press, 1871), March 4 and 6, 1847, 287.

5. E. Digby Baltzell, Puritan Boston and Quaker Philadelphia: Two Protestant Ethics and the Spirit of Class Authority and Leadership (Boston: Beacon Press, 1979), 224, 482–83; Dawson, Lives of the Philadelphia Engineers, 94–102. Baltzell's list of "First Family Moneymakers" lists eleven Philadelphians born between 1766 and 1826 who would have been of age to participate in the creation and governance of the PRR. Aside from Merrick, they were Anthony Morris, John Harrison, Richard Worsam Meade, Nicholas Biddle, Francis M. Drexel, George Sechel Pepper, Adolph Edward Borie, Richard Peters, Samuel Wetherill II (son of John Price Wetherill), and Anthony Drexel. Biddle died in 1844, two years before the PRR's incorporation, while Peters was probably active in Philadelphia at that time. Drexel was not involved in the PRR's formation, but he later played an active role in its finances. Once established, however, the PRR contributed to the creation of new wealth in the city, and Baltzell's list of "Philadelphia Moneymakers Outside Fifty First Families" includes the names of PRR executives Thomas A. Scott and Alexander J. Cassatt, as well as Henry H. Houston and executives from the locomotive builders (who certainly benefited from PRR orders) Matthias Baldwin, Matthew Baird, and John H. Converse.

6. Cope described Merrick, quite succinctly, as "a scientific mechanic largely engaged, as a member of the firm Merrick & Towne, in the manufacture of machinery, & accustomed of course to the management of workmen. He is the planner of our Gas Works, esteemed the best in the Union, and visited Europe to gain a knowledge of the methods practised there, & is a gentleman of pleasant manners, a nephew of the late John Vaughn, Secretary to the American Philosophical Society & a member of the Franklin Institute, where he is highly respected." Cope Diary, vol. 9, March 31, 1847, 13–14.

7. As historian Edward Digby Baltzell has noted, "In that day, to move from the counting house of a well-established merchant into a factory was something of a social depredation, but Merrick was hardly bothered by such petty considerations." Baltzell, Philadelphia Gentlemen: The Making of a National Upper Class (1958; repr. Glencoe, Ill.: Free Press, 1989), 101.

8. Merrick was professionally well acquainted with Thomas Cope, as he was with most of the other leading merchant families in Philadelphia. In 1849, John Edmund Cope, the son of Thomas Cope's nephew, Herman Cope, married Helen Taylor Merrick, who was the daughter of Samuel Vaughan Merrick. Their daughter, Helen Vaughan Cope, in 1880 married Charles Matthew Lea, part of a family that included one of the PRR's founding directors, Thomas T. Lea. Charles Lea's grandmother was Frances Anne Carey, the daughter of publisher and Main Line of Public Works advocate Mathew Carey. In 1822, Isaac Lea married Frances Anne Carey,

the daughter of Mathew Carey and the sister of Henry C. Carey. By 1827, Lea had become a full partner in the firm. An enthusiastic supporter of municipal gas lighting, Merrick in 1836 prepared a report on the latest European advances in that field, and presented his findings to the Common and Select Councils. Despite the opposition of Horace Binney, Sr., and other "anti-gas" interests, the councils approved the proposal. Leland H. Cox, Jr., "Porter's Edition of *Instructions to Young Sportsmen*," in James L. W. West III, ed., *Gyascutus: Studies in Antebellum Southern Humorous and Sporting Writing* (Amsterdam: Rodopi, 1978), 81–102, at 88; Steven Conn, *Museums and American Intellectual Life, 1876–1926* (Chicago: University of Chicago Press, 1998), 248; Andrew Dawson, *Lives of the Philadelphia Engineers: Capital, Class and Revolution, 1830–1890* (Aldershot: Ashgate, 2004), 84, 98; Eugene S. Ferguson, ed., *Early Engineering Reminiscences (1815–1840) of George Escol Sellers* (Washington, D.C.: Smithsonian Institution, 1965), 3, 16, 19; Wood and Wood, *Biographical Sketch of Richard D. Wood*, vol. 1, March 16, 1847, 287 (quote).

9. Elizabeth M. Geffen, "Industrial Development and Social Crisis, 1841–1854," in Russell F. Weigley, ed., *Philadelphia: A 300-Year History* (W. W. Norton, 1982), 307–62, at 351.

10. Julius Rubin, "Canal or Railroad: Imitation and Innovation in the Response to the Erie Canal in Philadelphia, Baltimore, and Boston," *Transactions of the American Philosophical Society* 51 (1961): 1–106, at 22; Rudolph J. Walther, *Happenings in ye Olde Philadelphia, 1680–1900* (Philadelphia: Walther Printing House, 1925), 42.

11. Burgess and Kennedy, *Centennial History*, 43–44, 785; Stephen Noyes Winslow, *Biographies of Successful Philadelphia Merchants* (Philadelphia: James K. Simon, 1864), 121–29; Henry C. Conrad, *History of the State of Delaware*, vol. 3 (Wilmington, Del.: Author, 1908), 853; George Richmond et al., *Biographical Sketches of the Leading Citizens of Beaver County, Pennsylvania* (Buffalo, N.Y.: Biographical Publishing, 1899), 238; James Henry Lea and George Henry Lea, *The Ancestry and Posterity of John Lea, of Christian Malford, Wiltshire, England, and of Pennsylvania in America, 1503–1906* (Philadelphia: Lea Brothers & Co., 1906), 122.

12. In 1850, two years after he resigned as a PRR director, Wood purchased a controlling interest in the Cumberland Furnace, renaming it R. D. Wood & Co. He diversified into textiles and dyes, with considerable success, and soon created a flourishing manufacturing empire based in Millville, New Jersey. During the 1860s, he oversaw the construction of railroads linking Millville to Camden and to Cape May, New Jersey. His son, George Wood (who also served as a PRR director between 1891 and 1926), established a hobby farm, Wawa Dairy Farms. After World War II, with the decline of the northern textile industry, Wawa Dairy Farms saved the company from financial disaster and served as the genesis of a chain of convenience stores in the Philadelphia region. The standard family biography is Wood and Wood, *Biographical Sketch of Richard D. Wood*, 3 vols., R. D. Wood & Co. Records, 1858–1910 (Collection 1176), Historical Society of Pennsylvania, Philadelphia; William Bender Wilson, *History of the Pennsylvania Railroad Company, with Plan of Organization, Portraits of Officials and Biographical Sketches*, vol. 2 (New York: Henry T. Coates & Co., 1899), 14, 28–30; John Thomas Scharf and Thompson Wescott, *History of Philadelphia, 1609–1884*, vol. 3 (Philadelphia: L. H. Everts & Co., 1884), 2103; Stuart M. Blumin, *The Emergence of the Middle Class: Social Experience in the American City, 1760–1900* (Cambridge: Cambridge University Press, 1989), 210; Franklin Fire Insurance Company, *Semicentennial Celebration of the Franklin Fire Insurance Company of Philadelphia* (Philadelphia: J. B. Lippincott, 1879), 13; Baltzell, *Philadelphia Gentlemen*, 101.

13. *Second Annual Report of the Directors of the Pennsylvania Rail-Road Company, Oct. 31, 1848* (Philadelphia: Crissy & Markley, 1848), 12.

14. Alfred D. Chandler, Jr., *The Visible Hand: The Managerial Revolution in American Business* (Cambridge, Mass.: Belknap Press of Harvard University Press, 1977), 15–78.

15. James A. Ward, "Power and Accountability on the Pennsylvania Railroad, 1846–1878," *Business History Review* 49 (Spring 1975): 37–59.

16. PRR Board of Directors (BOD) Minutes, Pennsylvania Railroad Company Collection, call no. 1807/1810, Hagley Museum and Library, Wilmington, Delaware (hereafter cited as HML), April 21, 1847, 16; E. M. Boyle to Serano S. Pratt, December 31, 1906, Pennsylvania Railroad Company Collection, Box 144, folder 33; Burgess and Kennedy, *Centennial History*, 43–44.

17. Based on his intimate knowledge of the PRR's records, Christopher T. Baer is in agreement with my assessment that Lombaert was likely Merrick's choice. Baer has also identified Edward F. Gay (the final engineer on the state system), Solomon White Roberts (later the chief engineer for the Ohio & Pennsylvania Railroad, eventually a part of the Pittsburgh, Fort Wayne & Chicago Railway), William Milnor Roberts (one of the surveyors of the Union Canal, who gained an international reputation as a hydrological engineer and who conducted preliminary surveys for the Northern Pacific Railroad), or two individuals who later became associate chief engineers on the PRR, Edward Miller and William B. Foster, Jr., as likely candidates for the post. In his diary, Richard D. Wood mentions meeting with Charles Schlatter on March 16, 1847, to see "his survey of the route for the railroad to Pittsburg. He seems a pleasant fellow, and is seeking employment upon the Central Railroad," quite possibly as chief engineer. On April 8, Wood met with anthracite developer Lewis Mayer, who was promoting "S. Kneass as engineer of [the] Pennsylvania Railroad"—this could have been either Samuel H. Kneass or his younger brother Strickland Kneass, but most probably the former. Wood and Wood, *Biographical Sketch of Richard D. Wood*, vol. 1, April 13, 1847, 287, 289.

18. Cope Diary, vol. 9, April 6, 1847, 15 (quote); William Bender Wilson, *General Superintendents of the Pennsylvania Railroad Division, Pennsylvania Railroad Company* (Philadelphia: Kensington Press, 1900), 15.

19. Cope Diary, vol. 9, April 9, 1847, 16.

20. Ibid., April 8, 1847, 16.

21. Ibid., April 9, 1847, 16.

22. Wood and Wood, *Biographical Sketch of Richard D. Wood*, vol. 1, March 27, 1847, 289.

23. On April 13, the PRR board selected James E. Day and Israel Pemberton as the principal assistant engineers for the Western Division. On April 18, the PRR board selected Samuel H. Kneass and Hother Hagé as the principal engineers for the Eastern Division. Ibid., 290.

24. Cope Diary, vol. 9, April 6, 1847, 15, April 8, 1847, 15–16, April 9, 1847, 16 (quote).

25. Wilson, *History of the Pennsylvania Railroad*, vol. 1, 108, 113, 145, 250.

26. Ibid., vol. 2, 261–70; F. Charles Petrillo, *Anthracite and Slackwater: The North Branch Canal, 1828–1901* (Easton, Pa.: Center for Canal History and Technology, 1986), 84.

27. "Historical Development of the Organization of the Pennsylvania Railroad," *Railroad Gazette* 14 (1882): 776–78, 793–94, 809–10, in Leland H. Jenks, "Early History of a Railway Organization," *Business History Review* 35 (Summer 1961): 163–79, at 166.

28. James A. Ward, "John Edgar Thomson and the Cult of Personality on the Pennsylvania Railroad," *Railroad History* 177 (August 1997): 68–77, 70.

29. James A. Ward, *J. Edgar Thomson: Master of the Pennsylvania* (Westport, Conn.: Greenwood Press, 1980), 3–8.

30. Isaac J. Wistar, *Autobiography of Isaac Jones Wistar, 1827–1905*, vol. 2 (Philadelphia: Wistar Institute of Anatomy and Biology, 1914), 138.

31. Cope Diary, June 2, 1847, 40 (quote).

32. John N. Hoffman, *Girard Estate Goal Lands in Pennsylvania, 1801–1884*, Smithsonian Studies in History and Technology 15 (Washington, D.C.: Smithsonian Institution Press, 1972), 12, 48n40; Scharf and Wescott, *History of Philadelphia*, vol. 3, 2190–91.

33. PRR BOD Minutes, June 9, 1847, 30–31; Burgess and Kennedy, *Centennial History*, 45–47, 52–53; Ward, *Master of the Pennsylvania*, 13–44; *American Railroad Journal, and Advocate of Internal Improvements, vol. III, Pt. II, July, 1834, to January, 1835* (New York: D. K. Minor, 1835), 564; *The American Almanac and Repository of Useful Knowledge for the Year 1837* (Boston: Charles Bowen, 1836), 235; William Hasell Wilson, *Notes on the Internal Improvements of Pennsylvania* (Philadelphia: Railway World, 1879), 4.

34. Aaron W. Marrs, *Railroads in the Old South: Pursuing Progress in a Slave Society* (Baltimore: Johns Hopkins University Press, 2009); Cliff Schexnayder, "Herman Haupt: The Pennsylvania Railroad Experience," *Practice Periodical on Structural Design and Construction* 12 (February 2007): 9–15.

35. Technically, New York, instead of a canal commission, had two interrelated bodies, the Canal Board and the Canal Fund.

36. Daniel Hovey Calhoun, *The American Civil Engineer: Origins and Conflict* (Cambridge, Mass.: Technology Press of Massachusetts Institute of Technology, 1960), 63–64; Robert H. Hanson, *Safety—Courtesy—Service: History of the Georgia Railroad* (Johnson City, Tenn.: Overmountain Press, 1996), 1–6.

37. Colleen A. Dunlavy, *Politics and Industrialization: Early Railroads in the United States and Prussia* (Princeton, N.J.: Princeton University Press, 1994), 229; Calhoun, *The American Civil Engineer*, 183–85. Calhoun suggests that Thomson was "probably" the person who initiated the Baltimore meeting.

38. "His exertions in pushing the Georgia road through to Atlanta taught him that railroading was a great deal more than merely the knowledge of where to lay the crossties and rails," James Ward has explained. "Of paramount importance for a successful operation was the necessity to harmonize often antagonistic personalities and divergent points of view toward a common purpose." James A. Ward, "J. Edgar Thomson and the Georgia Railroad, 1834–1847," *Railroad History* 134 (Spring 1976): 4–33, at 5.

39. Thomson maintained ties to the Georgia Rail Road, however, and served as the company's resident engineer until 1852. Ward, "Thomson and the Georgia Railroad," 16–30.

40. Mark Aldrich, "Earnings of American Civil Engineers, 1820–1859," *Journal of Economic History* 31 (June 1971): 407–19; Ward, "Thomson and the Georgia Railroad," 18. For a comprehensive overview of engineers' salaries, see Calhoun, *The American Civil Engineer*, 167–73.

41. Cope Diary, vol. 9, April 9, 1847, 16 (quotes).

42. While Thomson thought highly of the Schlatter surveys, Schlatter himself was not so fortunate. Shortly after the organization of the engineer corps, Schlatter approached Thomas Cope, asking for a job. The engineer had apparently only recently returned from Maine, so he had not submitted an application. Cope supported his candidacy. Merrick, however, called Schlatter a "bag of wind" and refused to place him on the payroll. Schlatter later was involved in railroad engineering projects in New York and eventually became the chief engineer and vice president of the Brunswick & Western Railroad in Georgia (later a part of the Atlantic Coast Line). He died in 1886 at the age of seventy-nine. Cope Diary, vol. 9, April 9, 1847, 16; April 15, 1847, 18 (quote); *New York Times*, August 5, 1886; Anthony J. Bianculli, *Trains and Technology: The American Railroad in the Nineteenth Century*, vol. 4: *Bridges and Tunnels, Signals* (Newark, Del.: University of Delaware

Press, 2003), 35; Lucian Lamar Knight, *A Standard History of Georgia and Georgians*, vol. 6 (Chicago: Lewis Publishing, 1917), 2806.

43. In his report to the PRR board of directors, Thomson seemed positively apologetic that he would have to bypass the potentially rich traffic of southern Pennsylvania, as well as alienate the Cumberland Valley investors who hoped that their railroad would constitute a part of a through route across the state. Thomson nonetheless offered a measure of consolation to those bypassed by the Pennsylvania Railroad. "The facilities that rail-roads offer, for extending their benefits to remote districts, by means of lateral lines," Thomson observed, "constitute one of their chief advantages over canals, and should prevent the error, too frequently committed in locating leading routes, of turning from a direct course to accommodate local interests to the injury of the great object intended to be accomplished." *First Annual Report of the Chief Engineer of the Pennsylvania Railroad Company* (Philadelphia: John C. Clark, 1848).

44. *First Annual Report of the Chief Engineer.*

45. The Perry County interests later had their wishes at least partly fulfilled, and by 1889 the Perry County Railroad (later the Susquehanna River & Western Railroad) built along a portion of the proposed route, to a junction with the PRR at Duncannon. *First Annual Report of the Chief Engineer*; Harry Harrison Hain, *History of Perry County, Pennsylvania, Including Descriptions of Early and Pioneer Life from the Time of Earliest Settlement* (Harrisburg: Hain-Moore Co., 1922), 433–34.

46. *First Annual Report of the Chief Engineer.*

47. Ibid.

48. Paid-in capital is as of October 30, 1847, according to the treasurer's report, in the *First Annual Report of the Directors of the Pennsylvania Railroad Co. to the Stockholders, Oct. 30, 1847* (Philadelphia: Crissy & Markley, 1847), 21.

49. Under the agreement, PRR officials would control through rates, while Harrisburg, Portsmouth, Mount Joy & Lancaster personnel set local tariffs. *Second Annual Report of the Directors of the Pennsylvania Railroad*, 17.

50. David W. Messer, *Triumph IV: Harrisburg to Altoona, 1846–2001* (Baltimore: Barnard, Roberts & Co., 2001), 11.

51. *First Annual Report of the Chief Engineer.*

52. Messer, *Triumph IV*, 10–11.

53. This and subsequent paragraphs are drawn largely from *First Annual Report of the Chief Engineer* and from *Guide for the Pennsylvania Railroad with an Extensive Map; Including the Entire Route; With all its Windings, Objects of Interest, and Information Useful to the Traveller* (Philadelphia: T. K. and P. G. Collins, 1855), 12–23.

54. *First Annual Report of the Chief Engineer.*

55. Burgess and Kennedy, *Centennial History*, 47–49.

56. Dan Cupper, *Rockville Bridge: Rails Across the Susquehanna* (Halifax, Pa.: Withers Publishing, 2002), 5–7; "Biographical Sketch of Herman Haupt," in Watkins Collection, Smithsonian Institution, Box 2, folder 2; James J. D. Lynch, Jr., "Rockville Bridge Under the PRR—A Capsule History," *The Keystone* 31 (Winter 1998): 51–53; "Over the River: Crossing the Susquehanna at Rockville, An Interesting Story of Railroad Bridges," *Mutual Magazine*, April 1935, 15–17; James A. Ward, *That Man Haupt: A Biography of Herman Haupt* (Baton Rouge: Louisiana State University Press, 1973), 26–27; PRR BOD Minutes, March 21, 1849, 159; Burgess and Kennedy, *Centennial History*, 50, 53.

57. On January 1, 1861, the PRR gained complete control of the railroad through a 999-year lease, followed by a merger, part of a broader corporate simplification project, in 1917. PRR BOD Minutes, September 27, 1848, 114–18; February 1, 1861, 3–7; Burgess and Kennedy, *Centennial History*, 53, 81, 99–100, 554.

58. PRR BOD Minutes, August 15, 1849, 185–86.

59. James D. Dilts, *The Great Road: The Building of the Baltimore and Ohio, the Nation's First Railroad, 1828–1853* (Stanford, Calif.: Stanford University Press, 1993), 322–36, 358–81.

60. I extend my appreciation to Dave Cathell for his thoughts on the region's geography.

61. *First Annual Report of the Chief Engineer.*

62. Charles S. Roberts and Gary W. Schlerf, *Triumph I: Altoona to Pitcairn, 1846–1996* (Baltimore: Barnard, Roberts & Co., 1997), 276.

63. Ibid., 273.

64. In 1851, Western Division principal assistant engineer Oliver W. Barnes laid out the town of Loyalhanna, but on Thomson's suggestion renamed it Latrobe—a bit of professional courtesy to Benjamin H. Latrobe, an engineer whose association with the Baltimore & Ohio and Pittsburgh & Connellsville made him something of a thorn in the side of PRR supporters. John Newton Boucher, *History of Westmoreland County, Pennsylvania*, vol. 1 (New York: Lewis Publishing Co., 1906), 557.

65. This was at best a temporary solution, however, as it required PRR equipment to travel over the westernmost inclined plane before reaching the so-called Long Level, by far the longest flat section on the Portage Railroad at just over thirteen miles. PRR construction crews continued to build farther east, to a point some eight miles east of Johnstown. The new link, which opened in April 1852, bypassed Plane Number 1 and took advantage of the commonwealth's double-track Big Viaduct over the Little Conemaugh River, as well as the portion of the Long Level from that location farther east to South Fork. *Guide for the Pennsylvania Railroad*, 25–35; *Second Annual Report of the Chief Engineer*, in *Third Annual Report of the Directors of the Pennsylvania Rail-Road Company to the Stockholders, October 31, 1849* (Philadelphia: Crissy & Markley, 1850): 35–57, esp. 38–45.

66. PRR BOD Minutes, May 29, 1850, 289.

67. Wilson, *History of the Pennsylvania Railroad*, vol. 1, 153–57.

68. Ibid., 156–57; Wilson, *Internal Improvements*, 43.

69. Roberts and Schlerf, *Triumph I*, 277.

70. Frank Abial Flower, "General Herman Haupt," in Herman Haupt, *Reminiscences of General Herman Haupt* (Milwaukee: Wright & Joys, 1901), xiii–xvi; Ward, *That Man Haupt*, 18–19; Schexnayder, "Herman Haupt," 9–11; William Wallace Atterbury, "Brigadier General Herman Haupt, Director of Military Railroads of the United States in the Civil War," *Mutual Magazine*, August 1933, 15–19.

71. Flower, "General Herman Haupt," xvi.

72. Wilson, *History of the Pennsylvania Railroad*, vol. 2, 261–66; Flower, "General Herman Haupt," xvi; Jay V. Hare, *History of the Reading, Which Appeared as a Serial in* The Pilot *and* Philadelphia & Reading Railway Men, *Beginning May 1909—Ending February 1914* (Philadelphia: John Henry Stock & Co., 1966), 280–81.

73. PRR BOD Minutes, January 5, 1848; Ward, *That Man Haupt*, 24–25.

74. Calhoun, *The American Civil Engineer*, 182.

75. Charles F. O'Connell, "The United States Army and the Origins of Modern Management," (Ph.D. diss., Ohio State University, 1982), 243.

76. Cope Diary, January 8, 1848, 117.

77. PRR BOD Minutes, April 28, 1847, 17.

78. Ibid., October 24, 1849, 210; Ward, "Power and Accountability," 42.

79. Ibid., October 16, 1847, 50; Wood and Wood, *Biographical Sketch of Richard D. Wood*, vol. 1, April 28, 1847, 291; Cope Diary, January 8, 1848, 117 (quotes).

80. Cope Diary, March 29, 1848, 145 (quote).

81. Wood and Wood, *Biographical Sketch of Richard D. Wood*, vol. 1, May 31, 1848, 313–14.

82. Cope Diary, June 5, 1848, 172 (quote).

83. Burgess and Kennedy, *Centennial History*, 785.

84. PRR BOD Minutes, December 15, 1851, 20.

85. Military historian Charles F. O'Connell, Jr., has suggested, "The Army management model provided a conceptual and procedural framework that the officers advanced when there were no other equally suitable models available in the business community." O'Connell also emphasized (p. 112) that "though the Pennsylvania's organization was unique in the business community, the United States Army had recognized at least thirty years earlier that the division of management functions between line and staff officers yielded improved efficiency and economy." Although he found little evidence to suggest a direct transfer of military practice to the railroads, business historian Alfred D. Chandler, Jr., nonetheless observed that "the military model may, however, have had an indirect impact on the beginnings of modern business management," thanks to officers' familiarity with a hierarchical, bureaucratic organization. "Yet even for such officers," Chandler acknowledged, "engineering training was probably more important than bureaucratic procedures." Charles F. O'Connell, Jr., "The Corps of Engineers and the Rise of Modern Management, 1827–1856," in *Military Enterprise and Technological Change: Perspectives on the American Experience*, Merritt Roe Smith, ed. (Cambridge, Mass.: MIT Press, 1985), 87–116, at 116; Chandler, *Visible Hand*, 95.

86. John Lauritz Larson, *Internal Improvement: National Public Works and the Promise of Popular Government in the Early United States* (Chapel Hill: University of North Carolina Press, 2001), 45–46.

87. Daniel Walker Howe, *The Political Culture of the American Whigs* (Chicago: University of Chicago Press, 1979), 108–22, 136–39; Robert V. Remini, *Henry Clay: Statesman for the Union* (New York: W. W. Norton, 1991), 174–75, 225–33.

88. A more recent parallel can be found in the Federal-Aid Highway Act of 1956, also known as the National Interstate and Defense Highways Act, in which federal support for road construction was justified by issues of national security. Robert G. Angevine, *The Railroad and the State: War, Politics, and Technology in Nineteenth-Century America* (Stanford, Calif.: Stanford University Press, 2004), 29–35, 37–39; Larson, *Internal Improvement*, 126–48; Pamela L. Baker, "The Washington National Road Bill and the Struggle to Adopt a Federal System of Internal Improvement," *Journal of the Early Republic* 22 (Fall 2002): 437–64, at 443–48; Henry L. Abbott, "The Corps of Engineers," in Theo. F. Rodenbough and William L. Haskin, *The Army of the United States: Historical Sketches of Staff and Line, with Portraits of Generals-in-Chief* (New York: Maynard, Merrill & Co. 1896), 111–25; Forest G. Hill, *Roads, Rails and Waterways: The Army Engineers and Early Transportation* (Norman: University of Oklahoma Press, 1957); Dunlavy, *Politics and Industrialization*, 111–12, 228–34.

89. Prior to the early 1830s, Erie Canal veterans outnumbered West Point graduates on internal-improvement projects. Thanks in large measure to the General Survey Act, by the mid- to late 1830s the number of West Point engineers greatly exceeded those who had worked on the Erie Canal. Calhoun, *The American Civil Engineer*, 24–53; Keith W. Hoskin and Richard H. Macve, "The Genesis of Accountability: The West Point Connection," *Accounting, Organizations, and Society* 13 (1988): 37–73, 46; Angevine, *The Railroad and the State*, 10–13, 22; O'Connell, "The Corps of Engineers," 91–95.

90. Calhoun, *The American Civil Engineer*, 54–90, esp. 58–61, and 192–95. I thank Christopher Baer for his comments on the engineering profession.

91. Ibid.

92. The only exception might be the individuals responsible for maintaining steam locomotives on the Philadelphia & Columbia and Allegheny Portage railroads, as well as the stationary engines on the latter line. Those

skilled workers were typically classed as master mechanics, not as mechanical engineers, and certainly not as civil engineers.

93. As historian Daniel H. Calhoun has emphasized, "It may be said that the engineer role was specialized out of the executive role, and that an occasional reassimilation of the two roles was only to be expected." Calhoun, *The American Civil Engineer*, 73–78, 87–90, quote at 77.

94. Ibid., 88–89, 139, 195.

95. Ibid., 123–35; O'Connell, "The Corps of Engineers," 102; Dilts, *The Great Road*, 52–53.

96. Dilts, *The Great Road*, 62–63, 70–75.

97. Ward, *That Man Haupt*, 27; Hoskin and Macve, "The Genesis of Accountability," 60–62; Alfred D. Chandler, Jr., "The Railroads: Pioneers in Modern Corporate Management," *Business History Review* 39 (Spring 1965): 16–40, reprinted in Thomas K. McCraw, ed., *The Essential Alfred Chandler: Essays Toward a Historical Theory of Big Business* (Boston: Harvard Business School Press, 1988), 179–201, at 184–94.

98. Chandler, *Visible Hand*, 96–98.

99. Ibid., 99–100. Quotation is from *Organization of the Service of the Baltimore & Ohio R. Road, Under the Proposed New System of Management: Submitted by the President, to the Board, on the 10th of February, 1847, and by them Approved* (Baltimore: s.n., 1847).

100. Angevine, *The Railroad and the State*, 264n14.

101. As Keith Hoskin and Richard Macve have observed, in discussing the development of managerial hierarchies, "the crucial step lay not in the explicit invention of this particular *form* of organization, but in creating the framework of practices and accountabilities within which this organizational form became feasible." Keith W. Hoskin and Richard H. Macve, "The Pennsylvania Railroad, 1849 and the 'Invention of Management,'" Working paper, London School of Economics/Warwick Business School, draft of February 13, 2005, 4, emphasis in the original. They suggest, persuasively, that scholars who suggest that there was a direct transfer of managerial methods from the military to the railroads, as well as those who reject such a hypothesis, are missing the mark. They have adopted a "third perspective" that emphasizes "the new way they [West Point Cadets] had *learned to learn* at USMA [the United States Military Academy]." It was that learning strategy that most clearly transferred from the military to the railroads, as managers "*internalised* their self-awareness of their required performance." Ibid., 6, 10, emphasis in the original. I extend my gratitude to Hoskin and Macve for sharing the draft of their research. Military historian Charles F. O'Connell makes a similar point, suggesting that "West Point trained Haupt to accept bureaucratic values," and "As a trained engineer and military officer, Haupt viewed the managerial problems he faced through a particular intellectual prism. His response to these problems was based on the procedural and behavioral model he learned at West Point." O'Connell, "The United States Army," 255, 272.

102. O'Connell, "The United States Army," 246; Hoskin and Macve, "The Pennsylvania Railroad, 1849," 17–18, 69–70n26; Alfred D. Chandler, Jr., *Henry Varnum Poor: Business Editor, Analyst, and Reformer* (Cambridge, Mass.: Harvard University Press, 1956), 48–54.

103. PRR BOD Minutes, March 7, 1849, 155; Ward, "Herman Haupt and the Development of the Pennsylvania Railroad," *Pennsylvania Magazine of History and Biography* 95 (1971): 73–97, at 78.

104. O'Connell, "The United States Army," 246; Hoskin and Macve, "The Pennsylvania Railroad, 1849," 18–24, 36.

105. PRR BOD Minutes, June 6, 1849, 173, June 8, 1849, 174, August 20, 1849, 187–88.

106. O'Connell, "The United States Army," 249.

107. PRR BOD Minutes, August 22, 1849, 189, September 5, 1849, 199.

108. Ibid, December 5, 1849, 221–22, December 24, 1849, 231–32.

109. Ibid., January 19, 1850, 239; Ward, "Power and Accountability," 44–45.

110. As O'Connell has observed, "Even as he [Haupt] and the board struggled for control of the railroad, the employees learned to carry out their functions in peace. The staff level that Haupt represented served to insulate the line and lower level staff officers from the turmoil in Philadelphia." O'Connell, "The United States Army," 277n49.

111. PRR BOD Minutes, October 30, 1850, 341–42, O'Connell, "The United States Army," 250–52.

112. PRR BOD Minutes, November 7, 1850, 345, December 18, 1850, 366; Wilson, *General Superintendents*, 15; Hoskin and Macve, "The Pennsylvania Railroad, 1849," 19–20; O'Connell, "The United States Army," 259.

113. PRR BOD Minutes, January 8, 1851, 373–74; Ward, "Power and Accountability," 44–45.

114. Ibid., December 11, 1850, 361–62, January 15, 1851, 378, February 5, 1851, 394–95.

115. Herman Haupt, *Reply of the General Superintendent of the Pennsylvania Railroad, To a Letter From a Large Number of Stockholders of the Company, Requesting Information in Reference to the Management of the Road*, January 20, 1852 (Philadelphia: T. K. & P. G. Collins, 1852), 12, quoted in Ward, "Herman Haupt and the Development of the Pennsylvania Railroad," 88; O'Connell, "The United States Army," 257–58.

116. PRR BOD Minutes, November 7, 1850, 345; January 8, 1851, 373–74; May 2, 1851, 435–40 (quote); Christopher T. Baer and Craig A. Orr, "A Guide to the Records of the Pennsylvania Railroad Company and the Penn Central Transportation Company," vol. 6 (Accounting Department), HML.

117. J. Elfreth Watkins, *Pennsylvania Railroad Company, 1846–1896, in its Relation to the Pennsylvania State Canals and Railroads and the Consolidated System East and West of Pittsburgh* (unpublished ms., 1896, original at the Smithsonian Institution, with microfilm copies at HML and in the Penn Central Railroad Collection, M.G. 286, Pennsylvania Historical and Museum Commission, Pennsylvania State Archives, Harrisburg, with an additional microfilm copy in the author's possession, hereafter cited as "Watkins History"), vol. 2, "Organization and Departments," 2–4; O'Connell, "The United States Army," 260.

118. Hoskin and Macve, "The Pennsylvania Railroad, 1849," 22–25, 52–53; O'Connell, "The United States Army," 261–62.

119. O'Connell, "The United States Army," 260–61.

120. Haupt, "Reminiscences of Early History of the Pennsylvania Railroad Company," n.d., Hill Railway Library Collection, University of Washington Library, quoted in Ward, "That Man Haupt," 40; O'Connell, "The United States Army," 260–63.

121. Richard R. John, "Taking Sabbatarianism Seriously: The Postal System, the Sabbath, and the Transformation of American Political Culture," *Journal of the Early Republic* 10 (Winter 1990): 517–67.

122. Joel A. Tarr, ed., "Philo E. Thompson's Diary of a Journey on the Main Line Canal," *Pennsylvania History* 32 (July 1965): 295–304, at 299.

123. Albright Zimmerman, "Problems of a State-Owned Delaware Division Canal," *Canal History and Technology Proceedings*, 10 (1991): 115–48, at 131.

124. Cope Diary, vol. 9, January 5, 1848, 115–16.

125. *Third Annual Report, Pennsylvania Rail-Road Company, October 31, 1849*, 9, 19; Aaron W. Marrs, "Railroads and Time Consciousness in the Antebellum South," *Enterprise and Society* 9 (September 2008): 433–56.

126. John, "Taking Sabbatarianism Seriously," 562; *Prohibition of Sunday Traveling on the Pennsylvania Rail Road* (Philadelphia: Merrihew & Thompson, 1850), 3. For another example of the often contentious relations between the railroads and the Post Office, see Dunlavy, *Politics and Industrialization*, 181–85.

127. PRR BOD Minutes, November 14, 1849, 216.

128. Herman Haupt to Bernard Lorenz, June 16, 1852, PRR Letterbook at Historical Society of Pennsylvania, quoted in Ward, "Herman Haupt and the Development of the Pennsylvania Railroad," 79.

129. Conversely, in January 1852, the canal commissioners decided to suspend all canal traffic (except for passenger packet boats) and all local passenger trains on the Philadelphia & Columbia on Sundays. Ward, *That Man Haupt*, 29; PRR BOD Minutes, May 1, 1850, 283.

130. *Second Annual Report of the Chief Engineer*, 55.

131. The original spelling of the family name was "Houpt." Herman Haupt changed his name, while at West Point,'whereas his brother did not.

132. *Fourth Annual Report of the Directors of the Pennsylvania Railroad Co., December 31, 1850* (Philadelphia: Crissy & Markley, 1851), 56–59.

133. *Fifth Annual Report of the Directors of the Pennsylvania Railroad Co., February 2, 1852* (Philadelphia: Crissy & Markley, 1852), 55–64.

134. *Sixth Annual Report of the Directors of the Pennsylvania Railroad Co., February 7, 1853* (Philadelphia: Crissy & Markley, 1853), 56–76.

135. Robert L. Gunnarsson, *The Story of the Northern Central Railway, from Baltimore to Lake Ontario* (Sykesville, Md.: Greenberg, 1991), 12–28.

136. Haupt, *Reply to Stockholders*, 23n, quoted in Ward, "Herman Haupt and the Development of the Pennsylvania Railroad," 88–89.

137. *First Annual Report of the Directors of the Pennsylvania Railroad*, 10–11.

138. *Second Annual Report of the Directors of the Pennsylvania Rail-Road*, 12.

139. Herman Haupt, *Reply of the General Superintendent of the Pennsylvania Railroad, To a Letter From a Large Number of Stockholders of the Company, Requesting Information in Reference to the Management of the Road*, January 20, 1852 (Philadelphia: T. K. & P. G. Collins, 1852), 40.

140. Haupt, "Reply of the General Superintendent," quoted in Watkins History, "The Administration of President Patterson, 1851," 39.

141. *The American Railroad Journal*, March 27, 1852.

142. Haupt, *Reply of the General Superintendent*, 32.

143. *First Annual Report of the Directors of the Pennsylvania Railroad*, 10–11.

144. *Fifth Annual Report of the Directors of the Pennsylvania Railroad*, 7.

145. O'Connell, "The United States Army," 263.

146. Herman Haupt to Thomas Moore, October 6, 1851, quoted in PRR BOD Minutes, December 15, 1851, 20.

147. Herman Haupt to William C. Patterson, October 7, 1851, quoted in PRR BOD Minutes, December 15, 1851, 16.

148. PRR BOD Minutes, October 15, 1851, 15.

149. Ibid., 20.

150. Ibid.

151. Ibid., 20–21.

152. Herman Haupt, statement before the PRR board of directors, PRR BOD Minutes, October 22, 1851, 24.

153. Ibid., 24–39, quote at 25.

154. Ibid., 39–40.

155. PRR BOD Minutes, November 5, 1851, 54–55.

156. Ward, *That Man Haupt*, 42–43.

157. PRR BOD Minutes, October 29, 1851, 45.

158. Ibid., October 29, 1851, 50, November 26, 1851, 74, December 3, 1851, 84.

159. Ibid., November 5, 1851, 54.

160. Ibid., November 26, 1851, 76.

161. Ibid., November 5, 1851, 57, November 25, 1851, 71–77, December 26, 1851, 90–91; Ward, *That Man Haupt*, 43–44.

162. PRR BOD Minutes, June 5, 1850, 293, December 4, 1850, 357–60; Chandler, *Henry Varnum Poor*, 78.

163. *First Annual Report of the Directors of the Pennsylvania Railroad*, 14.

164. John P. Green, "Financing the Pennsylvania Railroad," n.d., ca. 1905, HML, Box 419, folder 556.

165. Watkins History, "Administration of President Patterson," 39.

166. Wright's first job after graduating from Dickinson College had been as an assistant on Hother Hagé's 1838 survey for a railroad or turnpike between Chambersburg and Pittsburgh.

167. Paul T. Fagley, "Forging Iron, Forging Steel, Forging Freedom: The Story of the Iron and Steel Industry at Burnham, Pennsylvania, from Freedom Forge to Standard Steel," *Canal History and Technology Proceedings* 14 (1995): 31–71, at 42–43.

168. The original "silk stocking" reference was probably to the "Silk Stocking Brigade," a Philadelphia militia unit organized by John Cadwalader during the American Revolution. Sam Bass Warner, *The Private City: Philadelphia in Three Periods of its Growth*, 2nd ed. (Philadelphia: University of Pennsylvania Press, 1987), 43.

169. Ward, "Herman Haupt and the Development of the Pennsylvania Railroad," 91–92.

170. Aldrich, "Earnings of American Civil Engineers," 413–19. Aldrich has observed that "first-ranked engineers' salaries were dependent upon cost per mile [a proxy for technical complexity] during the 1830's and on total project construction cost [a proxy for administrative complexity] in the 1850's" (418).

171. PRR BOD Minutes, December 26, 1851, 90–91, December 31, 1851, 95–96.

172. Haupt, *Reply of the General Superintendent*.

173. Burgess and Kennedy, *Centennial History*, 59–60.

174. Herman Haupt, "How J. Edgar Thomson Became President of the Pennsylvania Railroad Company (in 1852)," 5, quoted in Ward, *That Man Haupt*, 45.

175. Ward, *Master of the Pennsylvania*, 90.

176. Ward, "Herman Haupt and the Development of the Pennsylvania Railroad," 92–93; Alexander K. McClure, *Old Time Notes of Pennsylvania* (Philadelphia: John C. Winston Co., 1905), 135–36.

177. PRR BOD Minutes, December 26, 1851, February 3, 1852, 118–19.

178. Watkins History, vol. 2, "Organization and Departments," 13, 20–21; Ward, "Power and Accountability," 48–58.

179. It should also be noted that the records of much of what the directors discussed at board meetings has not survived. As Hagley Museum and Library archivist Christopher T. Baer has observed, most of what the directors considered went into the board file, only portions of which have been preserved. Additional information, including periodic reports from the general superintendent (after 1871, the general manager) pertaining to operating matters were archived in the general manager's files, and not included in the board files. Unfortunately, the general manager's files have been lost. It is clear, however, that board members were at least aware of the conduct of routine operating matters.

180. As urban historian Sam Bass Warner has emphasized, "The new habits of business taught the mid-nineteenth-century businessman that the city was not important to their daily lives, and in response these business leaders became ignorant of their city and abandoned its politics." Warner, *The Private City*, 85.

Chapter 5. Executive

1. PRR Board of Directors (BOD) Minutes, Pennsylvania Railroad Company Collection, call no. 1807/1810, Hagley Museum and Library, Wilmington, Delaware (hereafter cited as HML), August 11, 1852, 220.

2. Until the 1840s, when John A. Roebling installed wire ropes on the inclines, hemp ropes broke with considerable frequency. However, the Allegheny Portage Railroad employed safety cars, generally known as "bucks," that prevented cars from running away down an incline. Hubertis M. Cummings and Donald Sayenga, eds., "John August Roebling and the Public Works of Pennsylvania," *Canal History and Technology Proceedings*, vol. 3 (March 31, 1984): 93–118, at 115n27.

3. Accident originally reported in the *Hollidaysburg Register & Inquirer*, September 1, 1847, reprinted in Chris J. Lewie, *Two Generations on the Allegheny Portage Railroad: The First Railroad to Cross the Allegheny Mountains* (Shippensburg, Pa.: Burd Street Press, 2001), 88–89; *Fifth Annual Report of the Directors of the Pennsylvania Rail Road Company to the Stockholders, February 2, 1852* (Philadelphia: Crissy & Markley, 1852), 64.

4. Statement of George W. Carpenter, submitted in PRR BOD Minutes, January 6, 1858, 287 (quote); Joseph Jackson, *America's Most Historic Highway—Market Street—Philadelphia* (Philadelphia: John Wanamaker, 1926), 220–21.

5. Nathaniel Burt, *The Perennial Philadelphians: The Anatomy of an American Aristocracy* (1963; repr. Philadelphia: University of Pennsylvania Press, 1999), 190, quoted in Andrew Dow, *Dow's Dictionary of Railway Quotations* (Baltimore: Johns Hopkins University Press, 2006), 160.

6. Frederick C. Gamst and Franz Anton Gerstner, *Early American Railroads: Franz Anton Ritter von Gerstner's Die innern Communicationen (1842–1843)* (Stanford, Calif.: Stanford University Press, 1997), 562–63; George H. Burgess and Miles C. Kennedy, *Centennial History of the Pennsylvania Railroad Company, 1846–1946* (Philadelphia: Pennsylvania Railroad, 1949), 17, 83–84. William Bender Wilson, *History of the Pennsylvania Railroad Company, with Plan of Organization, Portraits of Officials and Biographical Sketches*, vol. 1 (New York: Henry T. Coates & Co., 1899), 44–45.

7. Herman Haupt, *Report of H. Haupt, Chief Engineer of the Pennsylvania Rail Road Company, with a Communication from the President of the Ohio & Pennsylvania Rail Road Company, of the Expediency of Aiding the Ohio and Indiana and the Fort Wayne and Chicago Rail Road Companies to Complete Their Roads* (Philadelphia: Crissy & Markley, 1854), 33.

8. *Charter and Supplements of the Pennsylvania Railroad Company, with the Acts of Assembly and Municipal Ordinances Affecting the Company* (Philadelphia: Crissy & Markley, 1859), 19. The PRR was permitted to charge a toll of up to three cents per passenger or baggage car mile and two cents per freight car mile. (The charter provided a strong incentive for the retention of two-axle freight cars, as the car-mile rate was computed on the assumption that each freight car had four wheels.) The company could also charge up to two and a half cents per passenger mile, three cents per ton-mile of freight. The distinction between tolls and rates was finally clarified in an 1865 Pennsylvania Supreme Court case, *Timothy Boyle v. Philadelphia and Reading Railroad Company*, but in general PRR officials referred to all charges for carriage as "rates." Rolland Harper Maybee, *Railroad Competition and the Oil Trade, 1855–1873* (1940; Philadelphia: Porcupine Press, 1974), 85–87.

9. *Second Annual Report of the Directors of the Pennsylvania Railroad Co. to the Stockholders* (Philadelphia: Crissy & Markley, 1848), 12.

10. PRR BOD Minutes, August 2, 1848, 106, August 9, 1848, 107, March 21, 1849, 157, August 2, 1849, 182–83, August 25, 1849, 195, December 5, 1849, 224, November 7, 1850, 343.

11. PRR BOD Minutes, February 20, 1850, 256.

12. Ibid., May 29, 1850, 290.

13. Thomson to R. Clinton Wright, December 10, 1852, quoted in Wilson, *History of the Pennsylvania Railroad*, vol. 1, 157–58.

14. Ibid., March 8, 1854, 440.

15. Ibid., March 22, 1854, 443; James A. Ward, *That Man Haupt: A Biography of Herman Haupt* (Baton Rouge: Louisiana State University Press, 1973), 29.

16. PRR BOD Minutes, June 19, 1850, 296, August 28, 1850, 311, September 11, 1850, 318, March 5, 1851, 410; *Statement of the Canal Commissioners, Relative to the Passenger Travel over the Philadelphia and Columbia Railroad* (Harrisburg: O. Barrett & Co., 1852), 6.

17. PRR BOD Minutes, August 28, 1850, 312.

18. PRR BOD Minutes, January 8, 1851, 375; Wilson, *History of the Pennsylvania Railroad*, vol. 2, 288–91; David R. Contosta, *A Philadelphia Family: The Houstons and Woodwards of Chestnut Hill* (Philadelphia: University of Pennsylvania Press, 1988), 3–11.

19. PRR BOD Minutes, May 2, 1851, 343–40, November 23, 1852, 273–74; Wilson, *History of the Pennsylvania Railroad*, vol. 1, 172; vol. 2, 271; J. Elfreth Watkins, *Pennsylvania Railroad Company, 1846–1896, in its Relation to the Pennsylvania State Canals and Railroads and the Consolidated System East and West of Pittsburgh* (unpublished ms., 1896, original at the Smithsonian Institution, with microfilm copies at HML and in the Penn Central Railroad Collection, M.G. 286, Pennsylvania Historical and Museum Commission, Pennsylvania State Archives, Harrisburg, with an additional microfilm copy in the author's possession, hereafter "Watkins History"), "Vol. II: Passenger Department," 10.

20. The freight roster grew rapidly after that point, and by the end of 1853, the PRR owned 1,012 four-axle boxcars, 109 two-axle boxcars, 119 stockcars, and other miscellaneous equipment. *Seventh Annual Report of the Directors of the Pennsylvania Railroad Co. to the Stockholders, February 6, 1854* (Philadelphia: Crissy & Markley, 1854), 55.

21. PRR BOD Minutes, April 5, 1848, 78; *Fifth Annual Report of the Directors of the Pennsylvania Railroad Co. to the Stockholders, February 2, 1852* (Philadelphia: Crissy & Markley, 1852), 63–64.

22. PRR BOD Minutes, May 5, 1852, 162.

23. Ward, *That Man Haupt*, 39–41.

24. A complete account of the controversy is contained in *Statement of the Canal Commissioners, Relative to the Passenger Travel over the Philadelphia and Columbia Railroad* (Harrisburg: O. Barrett & Co., 1852), quotations at 7.

25. PRR BOD Minutes, May 27, 1852, 175, June 15, 1852, 194; Ward, *That Man Haupt*, 33–37; "Clearfield County Comprehensive Plan, 2006 Update, Chapter 4: History, Resource Inventory & Comprehensive Plan," http://www.planning.clearfieldco.org/06Comp_Plan/06Chapter_4_History_Resource_Invent_Preservation_Plan.pdf, 31, accessed on June 26, 2010; *Commemorative Biographical Encyclopedia of Dauphin County, Pennsylvania Containing Sketches of Prominent and Representative Citizens, and Many of the Early Scotch-Irish and German Settlers* (Chambersburg, Pa.: J. M. Runk and Co., 1896).

26. Technically, the canal commissioners eliminated the drawback (a form of discount or rebate) that enabled passengers detraining at Dillerville to travel at a reduced fare, compare to the full trip between Philadelphia and Columbia. It is possible that the canal commissioners rescinded the drawbacks in retaliation for Thomson's August 16 letter "To the People of Pennsylvania." However, the Canal Commission's planed rate and service changes were published on July 23, in response to earlier criticisms of the commonwealth's policies.

27. PRR BOD Minutes, August 16, 1852, 220–22; Ward, *That Man Haupt*, 33–37; James A. Ward, "Herman Haupt and the Development of the Pennsylvania Railroad," *Pennsylvania Magazine of History and Biography* 95 (1971): 73–97, at 82–83.

28. *Statement of the Canal Commissioners*, 5.

29. PRR BOD Minutes, January 31, 1853, 301–2.

30. The PRR was nonetheless still prohibited from competing against Bingham & Dock for the mail and passenger trades. Three years later, the legislature repealed that provision, and permitted open bidding for passenger service, following the expiration of the Bingham & Dock contract, on August 16, 1856. On that date, the PRR gained a five-year contract to operate passenger and mail services on the Philadelphia & Columbia, and at that time purchased the remaining half interest in Bingham & Dock. PRR BOD Minutes, July 22, 1856, August 20, 1856, 172–73. "An Act Authorizing the Pennsylvania Railroad Company to Run their Cars over Connecting and Continuous Railroads," March 3, 1853, reprinted in *Charter and Supplements of the Pennsylvania Railroad Company, with the Acts of Assembly and Municipal Ordinances Affecting the Company; Together with the By-Laws of the Board of Directors* (Philadelphia: Crissy & Markley, 1859), 50–51; PRR BOD Minutes, October 27, 1852, 262, January 5, 1853, 289–90, March 23, 1853, 322.

31. Wilson, *History of the Pennsylvania Railroad*, vol. 1, 177.

32. As freight traffic increased, the PRR built another freight station two blocks to the west, at Fifteenth and Market. The building at Thirteenth and Market remained in service until 1874, when the PRR completed a large new freight terminal at Dock Street. Thereafter, the Thirteenth and Market building hosted an exhibition by the Franklin Institute, as well as religious revival meetings, before becoming the home of the first department store operated by John Wanamaker. PRR BOD Minutes, June 9, 1852, 189; David W. Messer, *Triumph III: Philadelphia Terminal, 1838–2000* (Baltimore: Barnard, Roberts and Co., 2000), 25–26; Wilson, *History of the Pennsylvania Railroad*, vol. 1, 172–77; Dorothy Gondos Beers, "The Centennial City, 1865–1876," in Russell F. Weigley, ed., *Philadelphia: A 300-Year History* (New York: W. W. Norton, 1982), 417–70, at 444.

33. The partnership of Clarke & Thaw dated to 1842, with the Pennsylvania & Ohio Transportation Company established the following year, when the partners began offering service over the Main Line of Public Works. *History of Allegheny County, Pennsylvania: Including its early Settlement and Progress to the Present Time: A Description of its Historic and Interesting Localities; its Cities, Towns and Villages; Religious, Educational, Social and Military History; Mining, Manufacturing and Commercial Interests; Improvements, Resources, Statistics, etc.; Also, Biographies of Many of its Representative Citizens* (Chicago: A. Warner & Co., 1889), 214, 228–29.

34. For several years, beginning in 1832, Clarke was a business associate of David Leech. The fact that the two forwarders were later in competition with one another (and still later were again allies) illustrates the fluidity of these partnerships.

35. PRR BOD Minutes, March 8, 1854, 439, May 23, 1855, 67, June 2, 1855, 68, June 15, 1855, 82, July 11, 1855, 87–88; Wilson, *History of the Pennsylvania Railroad*, vol. 1, 46.

36. Maybee, *Railroad Competition and the Oil Trade*, 111–12.

37. PRR BOD Minutes, May 13, 1857, 231, June 24, 1857, 239, November 11, 1857, 272.

38. The firm of Bingham & Dock was also known as Bingham's & Dock and, for a brief period in 1854 and 1855, as Bingham, Davis & Company. I extend my appreciation to Christopher T. Baer for clarifying the complex relationships among the members of the various transportation company partnerships.

39. The Post Office Acts of 1845 and 1851 provided the federal government with a monopoly on the carriage of letters for free. For some time, however, Adams continued to carry letters free of charge to established package shippers. There is no comprehensive scholarly history of Adams Express, and the best available account is probably Alexander Lovett Stimson, *History of the Express Business, Including the Origin of the Railway System in America, and the Relation of both to the Increase of New Settlements and the Prosperity of Cities in the United States* (New York: Baker & Godwin, 1881), esp. 51–59.

40. The New York Central maintained a similar cooperative relationship with the American Express Company, while the United States Express Company was tied to the Baltimore & Ohio and the Erie. The express companies were different from the fast freight lines that were a routine part of railroad operations in the 1860s and 1870s. The fast freight lines, such as the PRR's Empire Line and Star Union Line, were organizational innovations designed to overcome problems such as gauge breaks and the PRR's lack of direct control over western connections. By the 1880s, as the PRR and other trunk lines built integrated systems, managers internalized the operations of these formerly semi-autonomous lines (although the dedicated equipment pools and service often remained). Adams and the other express companies generally handled shipments that were much smaller in volume, much higher in value, and required specialized handling. Given the irregular nature of express shipments, it was generally not in the best interest of the carriers to internalize that particular function of their operations. In 1918, the United States Railroad Administration ordered those express companies to be combined into the American Railway Express Company in the interest of wartime efficiency. In 1920, with the return of railroad operations to private ownership, consolidated operations remained in force, and were reconstituted as the Railway Express Agency in 1929. PRR BOD Minutes, March 20, 1851, 416–17, November 12, 1851, 64, February 28, 1855, 55, March 14, 1855, 56, June 24, 1857, 239, February 19, 1867; Calvet M. Hahn, "Adams' Express and Independent Mail," Collectors Club Philatelist 69 (May–June 1990): 181–239; Richard R. John, *Spreading the News: The American Postal System from Franklin to Morse* (Cambridge, Mass.: Harvard University Press, 1995), 160, 254. For an account of the formation of the Adams Express Company and its links to the PRR, see Alvin Fay Harlow, *Old Waybills: The Romance of the Express Companies* (New York: D. Appleton–Century, 1934), esp. 62–63, 466. For additional information on the development of express companies, see Peter Z. Grossman, "The Market for Shares of Companies with Unlimited Liability: The Case of American Express," *Journal of Legal Studies* 24 (January 1995): 63–85; Grossman, "Golden Silence: Why the Express Chose Not to Incorporate," *Business and Economic History* 21 (1992): 300–306; Grossman, "The Dynamics of a Stable Cartel: The Railroad Express, 1851–1913," *Economic Inquiry* 34 (April 1996): 220–36; Grossman, *American Express: The Unofficial History of the People Who Built the Great Financial Empire* (New York: Crown, 1987); Reed Massengill, *Becoming American Express: 150 Years of Reinvention and Customer Service* (New York: American Express, 1999); and Emory R. Johnson and Grover G. Huebner, *Railroad Traffic and Rates*, vol. 2: *Passenger, Mail, and Express Services* (New York: D. Appleton, 1911), 259–323.

41. This is the point that business historian Alfred D. Chandler, Jr., has made forcefully, in such works as *The Visible Hand: The Managerial Revolution in American Business* (Cambridge, Mass.: Belknap Press, 1977) and *Strategy and Structure: Chapters in the History of the Industrial Enterprise* (Cambridge, Mass.: MIT Press, 1962), among other works. Chandler's assessment of the development of the PRR's organizational structure is correct in its broad outlines—an impressive achievement, particularly as he undertook his research before the bulk of the PRR's primary source documents were available to researchers. However, Chandler relied heavily on only a few of the PRR's organizational manuals, and thus missed the continually changing and ad hoc nature of the company's organization—a minor issue, given that he was interested in the broad outlines of management practice rather than on the corporate histories of specific enterprises. More problematically, Chandler and other new institutionalist scholars have often neglected the influence of the political realm on business structure and

strategy. For useful overviews of these issues, see Colleen A. Dunlavy, *Politics and Industrialization: Early Railroads in the United States and Prussia* (Princeton, N.J.: Princeton University Press, 1994), 5–12; William E. Leuchtenburg, "The Pertinence of Political History: Reflections on the Significance of the State in America," *Journal of American History* 73 (December 1986): 585–600; and Theda Skocpol, "Bringing the State Back In: Strategies of Analysis in Current Research," in Peter B. Evans, Dietrich Rueschemeyer, and Theda Skocpol, eds., *Bringing the State Back In* (Cambridge: Cambridge University Press, 1985), 3–37.

42. In that sense, the development of the PRR's organizational structure comports with the assessment of labor historian Walter Licht that the interaction of idiosyncratic actors was more significant than the quest for a rational bureaucracy. "Bureaucratic work organizations . . . emerged as part of a complex unfolding process involving people, conscious decision making, personal interests, and human conflict," he has argued—an assertion that applies equally well to the development of organizational structures as to labor–management relations. Licht, *Working for the Railroad: The Organization of Work in the Nineteenth Century* (Princeton, N.J.: Princeton University Press, 1983), 270–71; and Richard R. John, "Elaborations, Revisions, Dissents: Alfred D. Chandler, Jr.'s 'The Visible Hand' After Twenty Years," *Business History Review* 71 (Summer 1997): 151–200.

43. Watkins History, vol. 2, "Organization and Departments," 1, emphasis in the original.

44. Ibid.

45. Herman Haupt, *Reply of the General Superintendent of the Pennsylvania Railroad to a Letter From a Large Number of Stockholders of the Company Requesting Information in Reference to the Management of the Road* (Philadelphia, 1852), 8.

46. "Herman Haupt, the Board of Directors of the Penna. RR Co.," September 11, 1852, Letterpress copybook, Historical Society of Pennsylvania, Philadelphia, 265–67, quoted in Keith W. Hoskin and Richard H. Macve, "The Pennsylvania Railroad, 1849 and the 'Invention of Management,'" Working Paper, London School of Economics/Warwick Business School, 71n36.

47. Hoskin and Macve, "The Pennsylvania Railroad, 1849," 25–26.

48. There was a certain irony in the concentration of power in Thomson's hands, for he had chafed against just such an arrangement while he was subordinate to Samuel Merrick and William Patterson. As military historian Charles F. O'Connell has suggested, however, "The key difference was that with Thomson as president, potentially recalcitrant subordinates could be sure that their views would be heard by a professional engineer and railroader who was intimately well-acquainted with their problems." O'Connell, "The United States Army and the Origins of Modern Management" (PhD diss., Ohio State University, 1982), 267–68.

49. Wilson, *History of the Pennsylvania Railroad*, vol. 1, 91.

50. *Pennsylvania Railroad Company, Organization for Conducting the Business of the Road, Adopted by the Board of Directors, Nov. 23, 1852* (Philadelphia: Crissy & Markley, 1852); Leland H. Jenks, "Early History of a Railway Organization," *Business History Review* 35 (Summer 1961): 163–79; Watkins History, "Freight Department—Development of the Organization, 1846–1896," 6; Hoskin and Macve, "The Pennsylvania Railroad, 1849," 44–45, 54–56.

51. Wilson, *History of the Pennsylvania Railroad*, vol. 2, 265–66; James A. Ward, *J. Edgar Thomson, Master of the Pennsylvania* (Westport, Conn.: Greenwood Press, 1980), 98; Evelyn Foster Morneweck, *Chronicles of Stephen Foster's Family*, vol. 1 (Pittsburgh, Pa.: Davis & Warde, 1944), 255.

52. PRR BOD Minutes, December 18, 1850, 366, December 26, 1867, 284; Wilson, *History of the Pennsylvania Railroad*, vol. 2, 153, 157; *Sixth Annual Report of the Directors of the Pennsylvania Rail Road Company to the Stockholders, February 7, 1853* (Philadelphia: Crissy & Markley, 1855), 26–27; William Bender Wilson, *General Superintendents of the Pennsylvania Railroad Division, Pennsylvania Railroad Co.* (Philadelphia: Kensington Press, 1900), 5, 16.

53. Wilson, *History of the Pennsylvania Railroad*, vol. 1, 91, vol. 2, 271; Watkins History, "Organization and Departments," 4.

54. James William Putnam, *The Illinois and Michigan Canal: A Study in Economic History* (Chicago: University of Chicago Press, 1918), 126–27; F. Ellis and A. N. Hungerford, eds., *History of that Part of the Susquehanna and Juniata Valleys, Embraced in the Counties of Mifflin, Juniata, Perry, Union and Snyder, in the Commonwealth of Pennsylvania* (Philadelphia: Everts, Peck and Richards, 1886), 805; Wilson, *History of the Pennsylvania Railroad*, vol. 1, 91.

55. Wilson, *General Superintendents*, 27–31.

56. Samuel Richey Kamm, "The Civil War Career of Thomas A. Scott" (Ph.D. diss., University of Pennsylvania, 1940), 3–4; James A. Ward, "Power and Accountability on the Pennsylvania Railroad, 1846–1878," *Business History Review* 49 (Spring 1975): 37–59, at 54; Ward, "Herman Haupt and the Development," 80.

57. Wilson, *General Superintendents*, 20; Kamm, "The Civil War Career," 4–8; PRR BOD Minutes, December 1, 1852, 277; Joseph Frazier Wall, *Andrew Carnegie* (New York: Oxford University Press, 1970), 114–15.

58. *New York Times,* August 3, 1878; James Grant Wilson and John Fiske, eds., Appletons' Cyclopædia of American Biography, *vol. 5 (New York: D. Appleton, 1888), 335.*

59. *Wilson,* History of the Pennsylvania Railroad, vol. 1, 92.

60. Charles Frederick Carter, *When Railroads were Old and New* (1909) (quote); Wilson, *History of the Pennsylvania Railroad*, vol. 1, 92–93.

61. Watkins History, "Organization and Departments," 4.

62. Burgess and Kennedy, *Centennial History*, 85–86; Wilson, *History of the Pennsylvania Railroad*, vol. 1, 92–93, vol. 2, 266–67; George Stuart Patterson, "The Growth and Functions of the Legal Department," n.d., ca. 1905, HML, Box 419, folder 556; "Pennsylvania Railroad Company, Legal Department," Watkins History, "Vol. II: Legal Department," 30–31; Watkins History, "Administration of President Thomson," 26.

63. PRR BOD Minutes, September 29, 1847, 48.

64. Ibid., April 17, 1850, 277.

65. Ibid., May 29, 1850, 290.

66. Ibid., December 18, 1850, 364.

67. Ibid., October 9, 1850, 330, April 18, 1851, 429, June 21, 1851, 462.

68. J. Edgar Thomson to William S. Campbell, November 1, 1850, reprinted in Lewie, *Two Generations*, 103.

69. PRR BOD Minutes, December 4, 1850, 357–58. Interestingly, however, in the PRR's *Seventh Annual Report*, 36–40, published in February 1854, chief engineer Herman Haupt suggested that increasing traffic levels might soon require the PRR to construct a second complete line (as opposed to adding additional tracks to the existing main line) over the Allegheny mountains. "It will be much better," Haupt argued, "to construct a new road with inclined planes, to be used for ascending tonnage, than to widen the present road bed for a third track." Haupt readily conceded that his proposal would be impracticable for passenger traffic, but that the use of a single, long, inclined plane would be far more efficient than using steam locomotives to power trains up gradients that approached 2 percent. By the end of the 1860s, rapid improvements in the hauling capacity of conventional steam locomotives had rendered Haupt's argument irrelevant.

70. PRR BOD Minutes, December 4, 1850, 357–58.

71. *Statement of the Canal Commissioners*, 10.

72. The person in charge of the 1850 surveys was principal assistant engineer R. W. Clarke, son of former canal commissioner James Clarke.

73. Charles S. Roberts and Gary W. Schlerf, *Triumph I: Altoona to Pitcairn, 1846–1996* (Baltimore: Barnard, Roberts & Co., 1996), 61, 70.

74. The curve, more than any other site along the Pennsylvania Railroad—indeed along the tracks of any railroad—became a major tourist attraction. As early as 1855, the railroad published guidebooks that praised such engineering marvels as the Horseshoe Curve. The railroad first landscaped the area in 1879 so that travelers who had detrained at the nearby Kittanning Point station (and presumably a few intrepid hikers as well) could see the curve. Most of the PRR's long-distance passenger trains rounded the curve at night, but the PRR required conductors on the daytime trains to announce the curve to passengers. In the mid-1920s, the railroad placed a stone horseshoe at the curve. With the completion of the first paved road to the site, in 1932, most visitors arrived by road; eight years later the railroad demolished the Kittanning Point station and, in the same year, the New Deal–era National Youth Administration built a small visitors center. During the 1980s, the National Park Service and America's Industrial Heritage Project worked with the Altoona-based Railroader's Memorial Museum to build a new visitors center, which opened on April 25, 1992. Dan Cupper, *Horseshoe Heritage: The Story of a Great Railroad Landmark* (Halifax, Pa.: Withers, 1993), 4–6, 12–14, 17, 28–29, 45–47.

75. Of the eight hundred feet in the tunnel that were not lined, a two-hundred-foot-long section of weak sandstone collapsed in March 1856, closing the tunnel and necessitating additional lining.

76. Wilson, *History of the Pennsylvania Railroad*, vol. 1, 158–59; Burgess and Kennedy, *Centennial History*, 65.

77. Julius Rubin, "Canal or Railroad: Imitation and Innovation in the Response to the Erie Canal in Philadelphia, Baltimore, and Boston," *Transactions of the American Philosophical Society* 51 (1961): 1–106, at 16; Wilson, *History of the Pennsylvania Railroad*, vol. 1, 126.

78. Wilson, *History of the Pennsylvania Railroad*, vol. 1, 143; Avard Longley Bishop, "The State Works of Pennsylvania," *Transactions of the Connecticut Academy of Arts and Sciences* 13 (November 1907): 149–297, at 245; Roberts and Schlerf, *Triumph I*, 115–30.

79. William Freame Johnston, "Annual Message to the Assembly—1860," Harrisburg, January 1, 1850; George Edward Reed, ed., *Pennsylvania Archives, Papers of the Governors*, vol. 7 (1845–1858), 4th ser. (Harrisburg: William Stanley Ray, 1902), 358–400, at 385.

80. *Report of Robert Faries, Civil Engineer, on the Surveys to Avoid the Inclined Planes on the Allegheny Portage Railroad* (Harrisburg, 1851).

81. Wilson, *History of the Pennsylvania Railroad*, vol. 1, 142–47, 150; Cupper, *Horseshoe Heritage*, 28–29.

82. Roberts and Gay report to the Board of Canal Commissioners, 1852, quoted in Wilson, *History of the Pennsylvania Railroad*, vol. 1, 148.

83. Wilson, *History of the Pennsylvania Railroad*, vol. 1, 142–47, 150; Cupper, *Horseshoe Heritage*, 28–29.

84. The New Portage tunnel was not completed until December 1856. Originally named the Allegheny Tunnel, the PRR appropriated that name for the Summit Tunnel following the closure of the New Portage Railroad. By the 1870s, the PRR had re-laid rails on a portion of the New Portage as a coal-carrying branch line and referred to the reopened bore as the New Portage Tunnel. It later became a key component of a bypass line to the south of Altoona.

85. Roberts and Schlerf, *Triumph I*, 42–45.

86. Burgess and Kennedy, *Centennial History*, 60–61.

87. The board agreed that the bonds could be denominated in dollars at 6 percent interest, or in pounds sterling at 5 percent interest. When issued, the bonds were all denominated in dollars.

88. PRR BOD Minutes, May 31, 1852, 178–79; Burgess and Kennedy, *Centennial History*, 59–64; Howard W. Schotter, *The Growth and Development of the Pennsylvania Railroad Company: A Review of the Charter and Annual Reports of the Pennsylvania Railroad Company 1846 to 1926, Inclusive* (Philadelphia: Allen, Lane & Scott, 1927), 34–35.

89. For a discussion of the ease and low cost associated with chartering corporations in the United States, compared to Great Britain, see Dan Bogart and John Majewski "Two Roads to the Transportation Revolution: Early Corporations in the U.K. and the United States," working paper, http://www.nber.org/chapters/c11999.pdf, accessed on June 15, 2011.

90. Edwin J. Perkins, *American Public Finance and Financial Services, 1700–1815* (Columbus: Ohio State University Press, 1994); Richard E. Sylla, "The Origins of the New York Stock Exchange," in William N. Goetzmann and K. Geert Rouwenhorst, *The Origins of Value: The Financial Innovations That Created Modern Capital* (Oxford: Oxford University Press, 2005), 299–312; Sylla, "U.S. Securities Markets and the Banking System, 1790–1840," *Federal Reserve Bank of St. Louis Review* 80 (May/June 1998): 83–98; Kenneth A. Snowden, "Commentary," *Federal Reserve Bank of St. Louis Review* 80 (May/June 1998): 99–103.

91. Benjamin U. Ratchford, *American State Debts* (Durham, N.C.: Duke University Press, 1941), 79–80; George Rogers Taylor, *The Transportation Revolution, 1815–1860* (New York: Rinehart, 1951), 344; Sylla, "U.S. Securities Markets"; Snowden, "Commentary."

92. Taylor, *Transportation Revolution*, 375–77.

93. As political economist Robert E. Wright has observed, "Philadelphia's stock exchange was a fairly insignificant institution until the 1830s and not terribly important thereafter. It is important to note, however, that the exchange was but a small part of Philadelphia's securities *market*, which by 1830 boasted over a hundred regularly traded securities." Wright, *The First Wall Street: Chestnut Street, Philadelphia, and the Birth of American Finance* (Chicago: University of Chicago Press, 2005), 166–67, emphasis in the original.

94. Domenic Vitiello, with George E. Thomas, *The Philadelphia Stock Exchange and the City It Made* (Philadelphia: University of Pennsylvania Press, 2010), xii, 26–42; Alfred D. Chandler, Jr., *Henry Varnum Poor: Business Editor, Analyst, and Reformer* (Cambridge, Mass.: Harvard University Press, 1956), 74–75; Chandler, "Patterns of American Railroad Finance, 1830–50," *Business History Review* 28 (September 1954): 248–63, at 252–53.

95. Chandler, *Henry Varnum Poor*, 48, 75–77; Chandler, "American Railroad Finance," 256–61.

96. In 1817, brokers adopted a constitution for the New York Stock & Exchange Board. It became the New York Stock Exchange in 1863 amid the explosive growth of wartime government and private securities trading.

97. Many companies based outside of New York were not listed on the New York Stock Exchange in the antebellum period. As a Philadelphia firm, the PRR relied on that city's capital markets, as well as funds provided by overseas investors. The Baltimore & Ohio was likewise absent from Wall Street, in large measure because the Commonwealth of Maryland and the cities of Baltimore and Wheeling collectively owned nearly half of that company's stock. Sylla, "The Origins of the New York Stock Exchange," 299–312; Taylor, *Transportation Revolution*, 100, 320; Chandler, "American Railroad Finance," 261–63; Chandler, *Henry Varnum Poor*, 105–7.

98. William Z. Ripley, *Railroads: Finance & Organization* (New York: Longmans, Green, and Co., 1915), 227–80; Jonathan Barron Baskin, "The Development of Corporate Financial Markets in Britain and the United States, 1600–1914: Overcoming Asymmetric Information," *Business History Review* 62 (Summer 1988): 199–237, at 225–26; David L. Dodd: *Stock Watering: The Judicial Valuation of Property for Stock-Issue Purposes* (New York: Columbia University Press, 1930), 1–27.

99. Chandler, "American Railroad Finance," 248; Dunlavy, *Politics and Industrialization*, 234.

100. Through the 1830s, European interest in American railway securities was primarily limited to those of the Baltimore & Ohio, the Reading, and the Camden & Amboy. Leland H. Jenks, "Capital Movement and Transportation: Britain and American Railway Development," *Journal of Economic History* 11 (Autumn 1951): 375–88, at 376.

101. By 1853, for example, foreign investors (almost all of whom were European) owned 26 percent of the bonds issued by American railroad companies, but only 3 percent of their stock. Generally speaking, however, most experts—including financial analyst and publisher Henry Varnum Poor—suggested that a railroad's bonded debt should not compose more than half of total capitalization. Chandler, *Henry Varnum Poor*, 134–37; Baskin, "Corporate Financial Markets," 215–19; Mary A. O'Sullivan, "Finance Capital in Chandlerian Capitalism," *Industrial and Corporate Change* 19 (2010): 549–89, at 575.

102. Vitiello, *The Philadelphia Stock Exchange*, 89–90.

103. Mira Wilkins, *The History of Foreign Investment in the United States to 1914* (Cambridge, Mass.: Harvard University Press, 1989), 191; Taylor, *The Transportation Revolution*, 100–101; Chandler, *The Visible Hand*, 91; Chandler, *Henry Varnum Poor*, 80–84, 97, 103.

104. Wilkins, *Foreign Investment*, 78–81.

105. Burgess and Kennedy, *Centennial History*, 64–65. The purchaser is listed as "Charles Edward Fisher," but the name is probably incorrect. Dorothy R. Adler, *British Investment in American Railways, 1834–1898*, ed. Muriel E. Hidy (Charlottesville: University Press of Virginia, 1970), 57.

106. Apparently, neither Miller nor Thomson tried his luck in the French or Dutch exchanges. As historian Augustus Veenendaal has noted, "The Dutch market was not yet ready to buy American railroad securities," perhaps because investors in the Netherlands had earlier purchased Commonwealth of Pennsylvania improvement bonds, securities that had lost much of their value with the decline of the Main Line of Public Works. Augustus J. Veenendaal, Jr., *Slow Train to Paradise: How Dutch Investment Helped Build American Railroads* (Stanford, Calif.: Stanford University Press, 1996), 11, 58, 61–62, 155–56; Adler, *British Investment*, 55n–56n; Burgess and Kennedy, *Centennial History*, 64–65, 67–68.

107. Burgess and Kennedy, *Centennial History*, 69–70.

108. Ibid., 70–71; Schotter, *Growth and Development*, 41–42.

109. By about 1857, investment bankers were pressuring railroad executives to establish sinking funds for their bond issues, and the practice soon became commonplace. Chandler, *Henry Varnum Poor*, 135.

110. Burgess and Kennedy, *Centennial History*, 69–71, 298–99; *Eighth Annual Report of the Directors of the Pennsylvania Railroad Company to the Stockholders, February 5, 1855* (Philadelphia: Crissy & Markley, 1855), 4, 14.

111. The legislature chartered the West Chester Railroad in 1831. The line connecting West Chester to the Philadelphia & Columbia opened in 1832, and later became the PRR's Frazer Branch. The legislature chartered the Columbia & Octoraro in 1853, and renewed the charter in 1856, but the line was never built. "An Act, Extending the time for commencing the Columbia and Octoraro Railroad," No. 754, *Laws of the General Assembly of the State of Pennsylvania, Passed at the Session of 1857* (Harrisburg: A. Boyd Hamilton, 1857), 766; J. Thomas Scharf and Thompson Wescott, *History of Philadelphia, 1609–1884*, vol. 3 (Philadelphia: L. H. Everts & Co., 1884), 2179–80.

112. "An Act to incorporate the Lancaster, Lebanon, and Pine Grove railroad company," No. 185, *Laws of the General Assembly of the Commonwealth of Pennsylvania, Passed at the Session of 1852* (Harrisburg: Theo. Fenn & Co., 1852), 745.

113. PRR BOD Minutes, May 20, 1853, 344, June 24, 1853, 355–57, September 3, 1853, 373, December 21, 1853, 415–19, February 8, 1854, 431–32, March 8, 1854, 439.

114. PRR BOD Minutes, June 24, 1853, 355–56, March 8, 1854, 349, June 6, 1855, 78, May 14, 1856, 150; Burgess and Kennedy, *Centennial History*, 94.

115. In their communications with the canal commissioners, Thomson and his fellow PRR executives doubtless emphasized that they were on the verge of authorizing construction on the Lancaster, Lebanon & Pine Grove, and that that line would soon bypass the Philadelphia & Columbia. In a more confidential April 1854 report to the PRR board of directors, however, chief engineer Herman Haupt acknowledged that "the Lancaster, Lebanon and Pine Grove Rail Road, cannot possibly be finished as soon as it will be required, even if commenced immediately; serious inconveniences and losses will certainly be experienced for the want of it, before a car will be able to run upon this road." Haupt, *Report of H. Haupt*, 33–34.

116. Clifford F. Thies has suggested that "the Pennsylvania Railroad was organized in order to acquire the state works of Pennsylvania," an assessment that ignores both the motives of the PRR's incorporators and Thomson's increasing frustrations at the failure of the Main Line of Public Works to accommodate the efficient operation of the company that he represented. Thies, "The American Railroad Network During the Early Nineteenth Century: Private Versus Public Enterprise," *Cato Journal* 22 (Fall 2002): 229–61, 258.

117. John Lauritz Larson, *Internal Improvement: National Public Works and the Promise of Popular Government in the Early United States* (Chapel Hill: University of North Carolina Press, 2001), 5–6, 226–27, 233–40, 252–55.

118. Louis Hartz, *Economic Policy and Democratic Thought: Pennsylvania, 1776–1860* (Cambridge, Mass.: Harvard University Press, 1948), 149.

119. Hartz, *Economic Policy and Democratic Thought*, 162–64, 138–39; Robert McCullough and Walter Leuba, *The Pennsylvania Main Line Canal* (York, Pa.: The American Canal and Transportation Center, 1973), 153–54.

120. As under the terms of the earlier law, any purchaser would be required to maintain all of the canals as public highways, but there was also a provision that permitted the new owner to engage directly in freight transportation rather than to rely on the services of independent transporters.

121. PRR BOD Minutes, April 25, 1854, 454; Bishop, "The State Works of Pennsylvania," 249–54; McCullough and Leuba, *The Pennsylvania Main Line Canal*, 158. For an overview of the complex political situation in Pennsylvania during the 1850s, see John F. Coleman, *The Disruption of the Pennsylvania Democracy, 1848–1860* (Harrisburg: Commonwealth of Pennsylvania, 1975), esp. 46, 55–56, 76–77.

122. Warren F. Hewitt, "The Know Nothing Party in Pennsylvania," *Pennsylvania History* 2 (April 1935): 69–85, 75–77; Coleman, *Disruption of the Pennsylvania Democracy*, 61–79.

123. "Report to the Stockholders," May 23, 1855, in PRR BOD Minutes, June 6, 1855, 73–81, quotes at 77 ("forever maintaining"), 79 ("Portage Rail Road"), and 80 ("highest prospective value").

124. While they refused the offer, the canal commissioners awarded William Cameron and his associate Andrew P. Wilson the sole right to operate passenger cars over the Philadelphia & Columbia, beating out such political rivals as Jacob Dock and George Wolf. The Camerons, in concert with their brother James, had invested in the connecting Harrisburg, Portsmouth, Mount Joy & Lancaster Railroad, with William Cameron serving as a construction contractor. James Cameron was superintendent on that line, and in February 1839 he became superintendent of motive power on the Philadelphia & Columbia. He attracted significant partisan opposition, and the General Assembly authorized an investigation of his alleged mismanagement of the line. He resigned his post at the end of November. Some twenty years later, on July 21, 1861, James Cameron, then a colonel in New York's Seventy-Ninth Highlanders Regiment, died at the Battle of Bull Run. *New York Times*, July 1, 1879; James B. McNair, *Simon*

Cameron's Adventures in Iron, 1837–1846 (Los Angeles: Fox Printing and Publishing, 1949), 51–66.

125. Hartz, *Economic Policy and Democratic Thought*, 167

126. *Miscellaneous Documents Read in the Legislature*, 1854, 335, quoted in Hartz, *Economic Policy and Democratic Thought*, 166; Carter Goodrich, "The Revulsion Against Internal Improvements," *Journal of Economic History* 10 (November 1950): 145–69.

127. McCullough and Leuba, *The Pennsylvania Main Line Canal*, 159.

128. PRR BOD Minutes, June 6, 1855, 78; Ward, *Master of the Pennsylvania*, 110–14; Hartz, *Economic Policy and Democratic Thought*, 175–79; Hewitt, "The Know Nothing Party in Pennsylvania," 84; McCullough and Leuba, *The Pennsylvania Main Line Canal*, 159–64.

129. In 1858, the legislature exited the canal business, trading its remaining canals to the Sunbury & Erie Railroad in order to help that struggling company complete its line to Erie, Pennsylvania. Burgess and Kennedy, *Centennial History*, 95–96, 298.

130. William Henry Moyer, "PRR's Navy, Part V: Pennsylvania Canals," *The Keystone* 42 (Summer 2009): 21–34.

131. In April 1868, the PRR board approved plans to improve the railroad's alignment between Ardmore and Rosemont, a short distance to the west of Philadelphia. As part of the project, the PRR purchased seven tracts of land in the vicinity of Humphreysville, named for local farmer Thomas Humphryes. The 280 acres of land later became the site of Bryn Mawr, an upper-class commuter suburb. Wilson, *History of the Pennsylvania Railroad*, vol. 1, 45; David W. Messer, *Triumph II: Philadelphia to Harrisburg, 1828–1998* (Baltimore: Barnard, Roberts, and Co., 1999), 22–24; *Brief Title to Bryn Mawr in Lower Merion Township, Montgomery County, Pennsylvania* (Philadelphia: A. C. Bryson & Co., 1869).

132. In December 1860, the PRR leased the tracks between Dillerville and Harrisburg for 999 years.

133. PRR BOD Minutes, September 19, 1860, 515–17, November 28, 1860, 528–29, February 1, 1861, 3–7; Burgess and Kennedy, *Centennial History*, 100.

134. Constituent elements of the New Portage Railroad lived on, however. PRR crews tore up the rails in 1858 and shipped them west to the Pittsburgh, Fort Wayne & Chicago, where they carried trains of that PRR subsidiary the final eighty-two miles from Plymouth, Indiana, into Chicago. The stone block sleepers unearthed from the levels and the inclined planes buttressed the walls of the PRR shops at Altoona. The stone arch bridge, built as part of the original Allegheny Portage Railroad, continued in PRR service until 1889, when the Johnstown Flood washed it to oblivion. That double-track structure would not have lasted much longer in any case, since the PRR was rapidly widening its main line to accommodate a surge of traffic in the late 1800s. During the 1890s, the PRR reopened the New Portage tunnel at Gallitzin, then, in 1904, re-laid rails on the New Portage grade between Tunnel Hill and Duncansville, providing a secondary line west of Altoona, one that bypassed the Horseshoe Curve. That line remained in service until abandoned by Conrail in 1981. In 1964 Congress designated the area around Plane Number 6 a National Historic Site, and the Park Service restored the inclined plane and its attendant hoist house to their original condition. Twenty-three years later, in 1987, the American Society of Civil Engineers gave their imprimatur to the site, designating it a National Historic Civil Engineering Landmark. The Commonwealth of Pennsylvania reactivated its participation in the Portage Railroad In 1995, cooperating with Conrail to rebuild both the New Portage Tunnel and the nearby Allegheny Tunnel (the southernmost of the two ex-PRR bores through Tunnel Hill) to accommodate double-stack container equipment. Ward, *Master of the Pennsylvania*, 114; Wilson, *History of the Pennsylvania Railroad*, vol. 2, 152; Cupper, *Horseshoe Heritage*, 21, 28–29.

135. PRR BOD Minutes, February 11, 1863.

136. Moyer, "Pennsylvania Canals," 21–34.

137. Henry Varnum Poor, *History of the Railroads and Canals of the United States of America, Exhibiting their Progress, Cost, Revenues, Expenditures, & Present Condition* (New York: John H. Schultz, 1860), 453; Jay V. Hare, *History of the Reading, Which Appeared as a Serial in* The Pilot *and* Philadelphia & Reading Railway Men, *Beginning May 1909—Ending February 1914* (Philadelphia: John Henry Stock & Co., 1966), 58–59.

138. PRR BOD Minutes, May 29, 1850, 290.

139. Engineers' Club of Philadelphia, *Proceedings of the Engineers' Club of Philadelphia*, vol. 17 (Philadelphia: The Club, 1900), 202; Poor, *History of the Railroads*, 453; Hare, *History of the Reading*, 59–61.

140. Paul J. Westhaeffer, *History of the Cumberland Valley Railroad, 1835–1919* (Washington, D.C.: Washington Chapter of the National Railway Historical Society, 1979), 60–62.

141. Poor, *History of the Railroads and Canals*, 474, 484–85; Hare, *History of the Reading*, 35; Elizabeth M. Geffen, "Industrial Development and Social Crisis, 1841–1854," in Weigley, ed., *Philadelphia*, 306–62, at 323.

142. Poor, *History of the Railroads and Canals*, 474, 482–85.

143. Edward Hungerford, *Men of Erie: A Story of Human Effort* (New York: Random House, 1946), 106–22; Taylor, *Transportation Revolution*, 84.

144. The eight constituent companies were the Albany & Schenectady Railroad (the former Mohawk & Hudson Railroad); the Utica & Schenectady Railroad; the Syracuse & Utica Railroad; the Rochester & Syracuse Railroad (the product of an 1850 consolidation of the Auburn & Syracuse Railroad and the Auburn & Rochester Railroad); the Buffalo & Rochester Railroad (the 1850 merger of the Tonawanda Railroad and the Attica & Buffalo Railroad); the Schenectady & Troy Railroad; the Rochester, Lockport & Niagara Falls Railroad (the former Lockport & Niagara Falls Railroad); and the Buffalo & Lockport Railroad. The creation of the New York Central is described in great detail in Frank Walker Stevens, *The Beginnings of the New York Central Railroad: A History* (New York: G. P. Putnam's Sons, 1926), 350–87.

145. Douglas J. Puffert, *Tracks Across Continents, Paths Through History: The Economic Dynamics of Standardization in Railway Gauge* (Chicago: University of Chicago Press, 2009), 118–19.

146. Message of Gov. William Bigler, February 11, 1854, in George Edward Reed, ed., *Pennsylvania Archives, Fourth Series*, vol. 7: *Papers of the Governors, 1845–1858* (Harrisburg: William Stanley Ray, 1902), 689.

147. Burgess and Kennedy, *Centennial History*, 223.

148. Watkins History, "Vol. II, Western Pennsylvania Division," 3.

149. The Pennsylvania Supreme Court held that "the right of the judiciary to declare a statute void, and to arrest its execution, is one which, in the opinion of all courts, is coupled with responsibilities so grave that it is never to be exercised except in very clear cases." *Erie & North-East Railroad Co. v. Casey*, 26 Pa. 287, 300–301 (1856).

150. Edward J. Davies II, "State Economic Policy and the Region in Pennsylvania, 1853–1895," *Business and Economic History* 21 (1992): 280–89, at 283; John Elmer Reed, *History of Erie County, Pennsylvania*, vol. 1 (Topeka: Historical Publishing, 1925).

151. Taylor, *Transportation Revolution*, 164–65.

152. Poor, *History of the Railroads and Canals*, 361–97.

153. Taylor, *Transportation Revolution*, 16–67.

154. William Z. Ripley, *Railroads: Rates and Regulation* (New York: Longmans, Green, and Co., 1912; New York: Arno Press, 1973), 442. Citations in text refer to the Arno Press edition.

155. Donald J. Patton, "General Cargo Hinterlands of New York, Philadelphia, Baltimore, and New Orleans," *Annals of the Association of American Geographers* 48 (December 1958): 436–55.

156. *Seventh Annual Report*, 11.

157. George Brooke Roberts testimony, "Transportation Interests in the United States and Canada," Report No. 847, Senate, 51st Cong., 1st sess. (1890), 220, cited in Julius Grodinsky, *Jay Gould: His Business Career, 1867–1892* (Philadelphia: University of Pennsylvania Press, 1957), 322.

158. Burgess and Kennedy, *Centennial History*, 55–57, 65, 71–73.

159. Haupt to the PRR Board of Directors (resignation letter), September 11, 1852, Letterpress copybook, Historical Society of Pennsylvania, Philadelphia, 265–67, quoted in Hoskin and Macve, "The Pennsylvania Railroad, 1849," 71n36.

160. "A Stockholder" [Joel Cook], *The Philadelphia National Bank: A Century's Record, 1803–1903* (Philadelphia: William F. Fell, 1903), 122.

Chapter 6. Coordination

1. Gary Kinder, *Ship of Gold in the Deep Blue Sea* (New York: Vintage Books, 1999).

2. George Washington Van Vleck, *The Panic of 1857: An Analytical Study* (New York: Columbia University Press, 1943); Russell F. Weigley, "The Border City in the Civil War, 1854–1865," in Weigley, ed., *Philadelphia: A 300-Year History* (New York: W. W. Norton, 1982), 363–416, at 381.

3. Herman Haupt, "Report of the General Superintendent," January 1, 1852, in *Fifth Annual Report of the Directors of the Pennsylvania Railroad Co. to the Stockholders, February 2, 1852* (Philadelphia: Crissy & Markley, 1852), 54, emphasis in the original.

4. James A. Ward, *J. Edgar Thomson: Master of the Pennsylvania* (Westport, Conn.: Greenwood Press, 1980), 107; PRR Board of Directors (BOD) Minutes, Pennsylvania Railroad Company Collection, call no. 1807/1810, Hagley Museum and Library, Wilmington, Delaware (hereafter cited as HML), October 24, 1857, 263.

5. General superintendent Charles Minot resigned rather than implement McCallum's plan, permitting the bridge engineer to become the Erie's new general superintendent.

6. Alfred D. Chandler, Jr., *The Visible Hand: The Managerial Revolution in American Business* (Cambridge, Mass.: Harvard University Press, 1977), 101–5; Charles D. Wrege and Guidon A. Sorbo, Jr., "A Bridge Builder Changes a Railroad: The Story of Daniel Craig McCallum," *Canal History and Technology Proceedings* 24 (March 19, 2005): 183–218; Edward Hungerford, *Men of Erie: A Story of Human Effort* (New York: Random House, 1946), 139–43.

7. As Keith W. Hoskin and Richard H. Macve have demonstrated, beginning in 1849 Haupt developed the basic elements of a divisionally based line-and-staff management system, well before Daniel McCallum published his famous organization tree in 1854. Hoskin and Macve, "The Pennsylvania Railroad, 1849 and the 'Invention of Management,'" Working Paper, London School of Economics/Warwick Business School, draft of February 13, 2005, esp. pp. 14–16. Their findings are part of a growing consensus that Daniel McCallum's contributions to the development of railroad management were far less substantial than earlier historians—most notably Alfred Chandler—have suggested.

8. After many years of research, Charles Wrege and Guidon Sorbo, Jr., have located what is probably the only surviving copy of McCallum's organizational "tree," in the Library of Congress, and they have suggested that the artist responsible for the actual image, George Holt Henshaw, probably relied on the locally abundant *Salix caprea* (also known as the Goat Willow or Pussy Willow) as a model. Wrege and Sorbo, "A Bridge Builder Changes a Railroad," 197–99.

9. Beginning in December 1853, Poor had used the *American Railroad Journal* as a forum to condemn the anarchy associated with the Erie gauge war. He was particularly aghast at the notion that New York interests had conspired to destroy the Commonwealth of Pennsylvania and the Pennsylvania Railroad. The legislatively induced change of gauge at Erie, Poor insisted, was a sign of the backward and narrow-minded economic attitudes of many Pennsylvanians. The restrictions would do incalculable harm to western farmers and would not impede New York's ability to capture a large share of the western grain trade, most of which followed the Erie Canal. Even Pennsylvania would suffer, Poor argued, because investors would cringe at the commonwealth's provincialism. The state had already defaulted on its debts, Poor observed, and future investments were unlikely to fare any better. An infuriated Thomson had promptly written a sharp rebuttal, and the two men remained on poor terms. The *American Railroad Journal* was a publication based in New York, not in Philadelphia. Chandler, *Visible Hand*, 101–5; Alfred D. Chandler, Jr., *Henry Varnum Poor: Business Editor, Analyst, and Reformer* (Cambridge, Mass.: Harvard University Press, 1956), 190–91.

10. In March 1857, Lombaert's title changed from superintendent to general superintendent.

11. There is some uncertainty as to precisely when the board created the operating divisions. During the railroad's construction phase, predating 1852, the route was divided into the Eastern and Western Divisions, with the later addition of the Mountain Division. Early references to a particular division may reflect either construction or operational matters, or both. William Bender Wilson's *General Superintendents of the Pennsylvania Railroad Division, Pennsylvania Railroad Co.* (Philadelphia: Kensington Press, 1900), 31, lists March 1, 1857, as the date when the Eastern, Middle, and Western Divisions were established, with the Philadelphia Division created a few months later, following the purchase of the Main Line of Public Works.

12. Hoskin and Macve, "The Pennsylvania Railroad, 1849," 45–46.

13. As the PRR's new organization manual emphasized, "The Division Superintendents shall, on their respective Divisions (subject to the directions and approval of the General Superintendent), exercise all the powers delegated by the organization to the General Superintendent, for the control and the use of the road, its branches and connections, for the transportation of Freight and Passengers, including the movement of Motive Power thereon, whether engaged in the transportation of Freight or Passengers, or in the construction and repairing of the road, or the supply of fuel and materials. They shall also have general charge of all employees connected with Motive Power and Transportation on their respective divisions, and see that they perform the duties assigned them." *The Pennsylvania Rail Road Company, Organization for Conducting the Business of the Road, Adopted December 26, 1857* (Philadelphia, 1858).

14. Leland H. Jenks, "Early History of a Railway Organization," *Business History Review* 35 (Summer 1961): 163–79, at 161; Chandler, *Visible Hand*, 105–6.

15. According to noted business historian Alfred D. Chandler, Jr., the 1858 reorganization pioneered the "line-and-staff" concept, by which the managers on the line of authority were responsible for ordering men involved with the basic function of the enterprise, and other functional managers (the staff executives) were responsible for setting standards. Chandler, *Visible Hand*, 106.

16. Chandler (*Visible Hand*, 105) has suggested that the Legal Department was created in the organization that took effect on January 1, 1858. In reality, however, the board did not create a named "Legal Department" until 1869. In January 1854, the board appointed a solicitor at Pittsburgh. Four years later, the January 1, 1858, organization manual that Chandler cited listed three solicitors. Six months later, the number had increased to eleven district solicitors on the PRR, with an additional four district solicitors for the Philadelphia & Erie (the former Sunbury & Erie), after the PRR

gained control over that company. As the size and complexity of the legal staff increased, the PRR board then accorded it departmental status, in May 1869. Chandler also indicated that the 1858 structure included a "secretary's office," when the first secretary, Oliver Fuller, was actually appointed on April 5, 1847, contemporaneous with the initial organization of the company. Chandler's reference to the establishment of a "purchasing department" is also unclear. In May 1863, the board established the position of supply agent as part of the Transportation Department. Three years later, the PRR established the Supplying Department, which became the Purchasing Department in 1887. PRR BOD Minutes, May 24, 1858, 334–36; George Stuart Patterson, "The Growth and Functions of the Legal Department," n.d., ca. 1905, HML, Box 419, folder 556; J. Elfreth Watkins, *Pennsylvania Railroad Company, 1846–1896, in its Relation to the Pennsylvania State Canals and Railroads and the Consolidated System East and West of Pittsburgh* (unpublished ms., 1896, original at the Smithsonian Institution, with microfilm copies at HML and in the Penn Central Railroad Collection, M.G. 286, Pennsylvania Historical and Museum Commission, Pennsylvania State Archives, Harrisburg, with an additional microfilm copy in the author's possession, hereafter cited as "Watkins History"), vol. 2: "Legal Department—Pennsylvania Railroad Company, Legal Department," 30–31.

17. Hoskin and Macve, "The Pennsylvania Railroad, 1849," 41–42.

18. *Eleventh Annual Report of the Directors of the Pennsylvania Railroad Company, to the Stockholders, February 1, 1858* (Philadelphia: Crissy & Markley, 1858), 16; Watkins History, "Pennsylvania Railroad Division," 8–9; Wilson, *General Superintendents*, 19.

19. Scott also oversaw the Canal Department, with a resident engineer (soon changed to a chief engineer) in charge of operating and maintaining the properties that the PRR had acquired from the commonwealth. One year after the reorganization took effect, the board responded to the economic downturn associated with the Panic of 1857, as well as the temporary suspension of major new construction projects, by employing only one resident engineer, William Hasell Wilson, based in Altoona (as had been the case between March and December of 1857, after George W. Mowry, the resident engineer of the Eastern Division, resigned his post). Following the creation of the Canal Department in August 1857, the PRR employed both a resident engineer and a chief engineer & general superintendent (whose duties were soon combined in one office, the resident engineer & general superintendent) of the Canal Department, but those responsibilities were not directly connected to railroad matters. In the 1863 reorganization, new construction remained centralized, but the board assigned routine maintenance to a new Maintenance of Way Department, under the overall jurisdiction of a chief engineer, but decentralized with a resident engineer assigned to each of what were at that time three divisions. PRR BOD Minutes, December 18, 1850, 366, August 5, 1857, 250, December 8, 1858, 384, December 26, 1867, 284; William Bender Wilson, *History of the Pennsylvania Railroad Company, with Plan of Organization, Portraits of Officials and Biographical Sketches*, vol. 2 (New York: Henry T. Coates & Co., 1899), 153, 157; Alfred D. Chandler, Jr., "The Railroads: Pioneers in Modern Corporate Management," *Business History Review* 39 (Spring 1965): 16–40, reprinted in Thomas K. McCraw, ed., *The Essential Alfred Chandler: Essays Toward a Historical Theory of Big Business* (Boston: Harvard Business School Press, 1988): 179–201, at 195–96; Watkins History, "Organization and Departments," 5.

20. As Chandler has emphasized, that "constant flow of information was essential to the operation of these new large business domains," and it was people like Lombaert who "contributed substantially to the emergence of accounting out of bookkeeping." Chandler, *Visible Hand*, 109.

21. Hoskin and Macve, "The Pennsylvania Railroad, 1849," 32–33.

22. Chandler, in *Visible Hand* (109–20), lists three types of accounts—financial, capital and cost. As Chandler observes, however, railroad officials did not develop cost-accounting methods until the late 1860s, more than a decade after their financial and capital accounting methods.

23. First-class freight included high-value manufactured and agricultural products, such as butter, furniture, and tin ware. Alcohol, most fruit, groceries, ropes, and tobacco traveled as second-class freight. Bulkier items, ranging from bricks to iron ore to ironware, were classified as third-class freight, with lumber and grain moving as fourth-class freight. The data clearly indicated that the higher the class (and therefore the value of the commodity and the rate attached to it), the more likely it was to move from east to west. Conversely, lower-valued third- and fourth-class freight typically moved from west to east.

24. Chandler, *Visible Hand*, 109–11.

25. By the 1870s, therefore, PRR officials abandoned the use of the contingency fund, and instead maintained money in the railroad's surplus account, sufficient to fund replacements and betterments. Chandler, *Visible Hand*, 111–12.

26. Frank Abel Flower, "General Herman Haupt," in Herman Haupt, *Reminiscences of General Herman Haupt* (Milwaukee, Wisc.: Wright & Joys, 1901), xviii.

27. The Georgia Rail Road was also very lightly and cheaply constructed, at $17,000 per mile, compared with $54,000 for the Baltimore & Ohio. George Rogers Taylor, *The Transportation Revolution, 1815–1860* (New York: Rinehart, 1951), 54.

28. Watkins History, "John Edgar Thomson," 5.

29. "Seventh Annual Report of the Chief Engineer," *Seventh Annual Report of the Directors of the Pennsylvania Railroad Co. to the Stockholders, February 6, 1854* (Philadelphia: Crissy & Markley, 1854), 34.

30. "Seventh Annual Report of the Chief Engineer," 34, emphasis in the original, 1853 tonnage data at 71, 78.

31. Haupt was no longer formally connected with the PRR, having resigned his post as chief engineer in 1855 and his short-lived seat on the PRR board the following year. In spite of his increasingly frustrating involvement with the Hoosac Tunnel in Massachusetts, he nonetheless continued to advise J. Edgar Thomson and his directors while maintaining investments in several coal companies.

32. Herman Haupt, *The Coal Business on the Pennsylvania Railroad: A Communication Addressed to the President, Directors, and Stockholders of the Pennsylvania Railroad, on the Cost of Transportation* (Philadelphia: T. K. and P. G. Collins, 1857), 3–4.

33. Ibid., 19.

34. Henry Varnum Poor, *History of the Railroads and Canals of the United States of America, Exhibiting their Progress, Cost, Revenues, Expenditures, & Present Condition* (New York: John H. Schultz, 1860), 473–74.

35. New York Legislature, Assembly, Select Committee on the Pro Rata Freight Bill, *Testimony and Proceedings Taken and Heard Before the Select Committee Relative to the Pro Rata Freight Law* (Albany: Charles Van Benthuysen, 1860), 173 (quote); George H. Miller, *Railroads and the Granger Laws* (Madison: University of Wisconsin Press, 1971), 35–36.

36. *Testimony and Proceedings*, 172–74.

37. Ibid.

38. For an overview of the economic issues associated with railroad pricing policies, see Herbert Hovenkamp, "Regulatory Conflict in the Gilded Age: Federalism and the Railroad Problem," *Yale Law Journal* 97 (May 1988): 1017–72. Such pricing strategies, and the conflicts associated with them, began long before the Gilded Age.

39. As transportation economist William Z. Ripley later observed, "Grain was literally meandering toward the East instead of following a

direct route." William Cronon has described much the same practice, in relation to the "granger" roads to the west of Chicago. William Cronon, *Nature's Metropolis: Chicago and the Great West* (New York: W. W. Norton, 1991), 85–90; Rolland Harper Maybee, *Railroad Competition and the Oil Trade, 1855–1873* (Philadelphia: Porcupine Press, 1974), 88; William Z. Ripley, *Railroads: Rates and Regulation* (New York: Longmans, Green, and Co., 1912; repr. New York: Arno Press, 1973), 356–60, quotation at 359. All references to Ripley are to the Arno Press edition.

40. George H. Burgess and Miles C. Kennedy, *Centennial History of the Pennsylvania Railroad Company, 1846–1946* (Philadelphia: Pennsylvania Railroad, 1949), 341, 358–61; Emory R. Johnson and Grover G. Huebner, *Railroad Traffic and Rates,* vol. 1: *Freight Service* (New York: D. Appleton, 1911), 385–86.

41. *Seventh Annual Report,* 16.

42. The terms *rebate* and *drawback* have often been used interchangeably, but they were not the same. A rebate was an up-front reduction in the posted rate, offered at the time of shipment. Railroads that awarded drawbacks to favored shippers collected the posted rate and then refunded a portion of those charges—usually in a lump sum, once a month. Railroad traffic managers could offer rebates and drawbacks on the same shipment. As late as the 1870s, railroad executives were more likely to authorize drawbacks than rebates. By the late 1870s, however, rebates were more typical, and that term has often come to refer to all types of *sub rosa* rate reductions.

43. Hovenkamp, "Regulatory Conflict," 1035–44.

44. *Eighth Annual Report of the Directors of the Pennsylvania Railroad Co. to the Stockholders, February 5, 1855* (Philadelphia: Crissy & Markley, 1855), 13–14.

45. Chandler, *Visible Hand,* 125.

46. Chandler, *Visible Hand,* 142–44; Chandler, "The Coming of Big Business," in C. Vann Woodward, ed., *The Comparative Approach to American History* (New York: Basic Books, 1968), 220–37, at 234.

47. Chandler, *Henry Varnum Poor,* 150–51.

48. PRR BOD Minutes, November 2, 1857, 268.

49. Maybee, *Railroad Competition and the Oil Trade,* 81.

50. Ibid., 89–92.

51. Ibid., 92–95.

52. Ibid., 97–99.

53. *Report of the Investigating Committee of the Pennsylvania Railroad Company* (Philadelphia: Allen, Lane & Scott, 1874), 100–104.

54. Haupt's career after leaving the PRR was not a happy one. He accepted a truly worthy challenge, supervising the construction of the Hoosac Tunnel in Massachusetts. Construction on the four-mile tunnel lagged well behind schedule, ultimately taking twenty-two years to complete and costing far more than anticipated. Those delays were hardly Haupt's fault, as neither drilling techniques nor explosives technology was far enough advanced to surmount the virtually impervious granite of the Berkshires. Haupt received much of the blame, however, and was the target of several lawsuits—all of which undermined his effectiveness with the United States Military Railroad during the Civil War and led to his ouster on September 14, 1863. Following the Civil War, he was involved in several railroad projects, including the Shenandoah Valley Railroad and the Atlanta & Charlotte Air-Line, which were part of efforts by J. Edgar Thomson and Tom Scott to control the railroad network in the South, through the Southern Railway Security Company. Haupt was also the engineer for the Tide Water Pipe Company, the first successful long-distance pipeline in the United States. He died in 1905, at the age of 88. "Biographical Sketch of Herman Haupt," in Watkins Collection, Smithsonian Institution, Box 2, folder 2;

James A. Ward, *That Man Haupt: A Biography of Herman Haupt* (Baton Rouge: Louisiana State University Press, 1973), 44–46.

55. PRR BOD Minutes, March 7, 1861, 17; *Charter and Supplements of the Pennsylvania Railroad Company, with the Acts of Assembly and Municipal Ordinances Affecting the Company; Together with the By-Laws of the Board of Directors* (Philadelphia: Crissy & Markley, 1859), 18–19, 25.

56. *Seventh Annual Report,* 35, 579.

57. PRR, BOD Minutes, June 6, 1855, 80. Ward, *Master of the Pennsylvania,* 110–11.

58. Ward, *Master of the Pennsylvania,* 110–11.

59. Burgess and Kennedy, *Centennial History,* 92–93, 97; James A. Ward, "Herman Haupt and the Development of the Pennsylvania Railroad," *Pennsylvania Magazine of History and Biography* 95 (1971): 73–97, at 85; Ward, *Master of the Pennsylvania,* 111; *Charter and Supplements of the Pennsylvania Railroad,* 26–27, 56.

60. PRR BOD Minutes, January 21, 1857, 204–5, March 7, 1861, 17–18.

61. Ibid., March 7, 1861, 18; Ward, *Master of the Pennsylvania,* 114; Louis Hartz, *Economic Policy and Democratic Thought: Pennsylvania, 1776–1860* (Cambridge, Mass.: Harvard University Press, 1948), 268–69, 273–85.

62. James Pollock, "Annual Message to the Assembly," January 6, 1858, in George Edward Reed, ed., *Pennsylvania Archives, Fourth Series,* vol. 7: *Papers of the Governors, 1845–1858* (Harrisburg: William Stanley Ray, 1902), 937.

63. Pollock, "Annual Message to the Assembly," 937.

64. William A. Stokes, "Letter . . . to Honorable John Creswell, Jr., Speaker of the Senate of Pennsylvania on the Subject of the Tonnage Tax . . ." (Philadelphia, 1859), 5–6, 17, 28–29, quoted in Hartz, *Economic Policy and Democratic Thought,* 272.

65. PRR BOD Minutes, February 3, 1858, 295–96, May 24, 1858, 337.

66. Hartz, *Economic Policy and Democratic Thought,* 269, 273.

67. Burgess and Kennedy, *Centennial History,* 92–93, 97; Ward, *Master of the Pennsylvania,* 112–13.

68. *New York Times,* May 22, 1881.

69. Rockefeller developed a respect for Scott's abilities, particularly after the PRR executive graciously accepted defeat in the aftermath of failed efforts by the PRR's Empire Line affiliate to challenge Standard Oil during the 1870s. John D. Rockefeller, with William O. Inglis and David Freeman Hawke, *John D. Rockefeller Interview, 1917–1920* (Westport, Conn.: Meckler Publishing, in Association with the Rockefeller Archive Center, 1984), 238.

70. Huntington quoted in Richard White, "Information, Markets, and Corruption: Transcontinental Railroads in the Gilded Age," *Journal of American History* 90 (June 2003): 19–43.

71. Quoted in Henry Demarest Lloyd, *Wealth Against Commonwealth* (New York: Harper & Brothers, 1894), 147.

72. Robert Lamborn to William Jackson Palmer, March 22, 1867, Palmer Papers, quoted in James A. Ward, "Power and Accountability on the Pennsylvania Railroad, 1846–1878," *Business History Review* 49 (Spring 1975): 37–59, quote at 58.

73. Joseph S. Clark, Jr., "The Railroad Struggle for Pittsburgh: Forty-Three Years of Philadelphia-Baltimore Rivalry, 1838–1871," *Pennsylvania Magazine of History and Biography* 48 (1924): 1–37, at 22–23, 26 (quotation is from the *Legislative Record,* February 14, 1867, 141–42).

74. Historian Richard White, in offering a critical assessment of Scott, correctly suggests that "Tom Scott was, depending on the place and moment, a salaried manager, an investor, and a speculator." White, *Railroaded: The Transcontinentals and the Making of Modern America* (New York:

W.W. Norton, 2011), 232. For White's analysis of Scott's involvement in corruption and conflict-of-interest issues, see *Railroaded*, 3–9.

75. After analyzing myriad biographies of the two executives, historian James A. Ward has observed that the dominant paradigm was one of symbiosis, with each depending on the other, and with each providing the qualities that the other lacked. "Thomson became the arch engineer, the man who knew and thoroughly understood *things*," Ward notes, while Scott developed "an uncanny insight into and an affinity for *people*." Ward, "J. Edgar Thomson and Thomas A. Scott: A Symbiotic Partnership?" *Pennsylvania Magazine of History and Biography* 100 (1976): 37–65, quote at 46, emphasis in the original.

76. Isaac J. Wistar, *Autobiography of Isaac Jones Wistar, 1827–1905*, vol. 2 (Philadelphia: Wistar Institute of Anatomy and Biology, 1914), 136.

77. *New York Times*, May 22, 1881.

78. Samuel Richey Kamm, "The Civil War Career of Thomas A. Scott" (Ph.D. diss., University of Pennsylvania, 1940), 4–8; Joseph Frazier Wall, *Andrew Carnegie* (New York: Oxford University Press, 1970), 114–15.

79. PRR BOD Minutes, March 21, 1860, 480; Burgess and Kennedy, *Centennial History*, 92–93, 97; Ward, *Master of the Pennsylvania*, 112–13; Douglas E. Bowers, "From Logrolling to Corruption: The Development of Lobbying in Pennsylvania, 1815–1860," *Journal of the Early Republic* 3 (Winter 1983): 439–74, at 468–70; Kamm, "The Civil War Career," 17.

80. Burgess and Kennedy, *Centennial History*, 97–99, 343; Ward, *Master of the Pennsylvania*, 115–16, 465; Bowers, "From Logrolling to Corruption," 469–70; Kamm, "The Civil War Career," 15.

81. "An Act Exempting Coal and Lumber from the Tonnage Tax," May 7, 1855, reprinted in *Charter and Supplements of the Pennsylvania Railroad Company*, 56.

82. Kamm, "The Civil War Career," 12–14.

83. Ibid., 15; PRR BOD Minutes, March 7, 1861, 16–29.

84. Despite the promise of commutation assistance, three other companies—the Chambersburg & Allegheny Railroad, the Phillipsburg & Waterford Railroad, and the Fayette County Railroad—never got off of the drawing board.

85. PRR BOD Minutes, March 7, 1861, 16–27; Ward, *Master of the Pennsylvania*, 115–16; Hartz, *Economic Policy and Democratic Thought*, 269; Burgess and Kennedy, *Centennial History*, 106–8; Miller, *Railroads and the Granger Laws*, 36.

86. Alexander K. McClure, *Old Time Notes of Pennsylvania* (Philadelphia: John C. Winston Co., 1905), 481.

87. McClure, *Old Time Notes of Pennsylvania*, 486; Kamm, "The Civil War Career," 16–18.

88. Miller, *Railroads and the Granger Laws*, 36.

89. Ward, *Master of the Pennsylvania*, 116.

90. Andrew Carnegie, *Autobiography of Andrew Carnegie* (Boston: Houghton Mifflin, 1920), 68.

91. Ibid., 36–38, 42, 59.

92. Ibid., 63–65; Wall, *Andrew Carnegie*, 115–19.

93. McCargo died in 1902. John W. Jordan, *Encyclopedia of Pennsylvania Biography*, vol. 2 (New York: Lewis Historical Publishing, 1914), 430–32.

94. Carnegie, *Autobiography*, 69; David Nasaw, *Andrew Carnegie* (New York: Penguin Press, 2006), 56–59; Wall, *Andrew Carnegie*, 122–25.

95. For a good overview of the influence of PRR personnel on Carnegie's career, and his participation in what Pamela Walker Laird accurately labels "peer networks," see Pamela Walker Laird, *Pull: Networking and Success Since Benjamin Franklin* (Cambridge, Mass.: Harvard University Press, 2006), 25–31.

96. David Nasaw relied too heavily on Carnegie's inaccurate recollection of his career advancement. He suggests, echoing the *Autobiography*, that Carnegie gained his promotion to superintendent as a direct consequence of Scott's promotion. Likewise, even though both Carnegie and Nasaw make reference to the PRR's "Pittsburgh Division," the railroad did not use that nomenclature at that time. Wall offers the correct sequence of events. Carnegie, *Autobiography*, 84, 90–92; Nasaw, *Andrew Carnegie*, 63–65; Wall, *Andrew Carnegie*, 135, 143–44; PRR BOD Minutes, November 30, 1859, 452.

97. As Nasaw has noted, Carnegie "got less out of them than he should have . . . [and] would never again put himself in a position where he was responsible for supervising any of them." Nasaw, *Andrew Carnegie*, 68.

98. Biographer Joseph Frazier Wall has suggested that Carnegie's actions "reveal the basic philosophy that was to underlie Carnegie's business methods throughout his life: reduce prices by reducing cost," and cited as evidence Carnegie's authorization of reductions in passenger fares in order to increase the volume of traffic. Wall, *Andrew Carnegie*, 171–72.

99. Charles R. Morris, *The Tycoons: How Andrew Carnegie, John D. Rockefeller, Jay Gould, and J.P. Morgan Invented the American Supereconomy* (New York: Times Books, Henry Holt, 2005), 14.

100. Ward, "Herman Haupt and the Development," 80.

101. The Trenton Delaware Bridge Company received Pennsylvania and New Jersey charters in the spring of 1798, making the company the oldest constituent corporate entity in the PRR system. The bridge remained in service until 1875. David W. Messer and Charles S. Roberts, *Triumph V: Philadelphia to New York, 1830–2002* (Baltimore: Barnard, Roberts & Co., 2002), 64–65.

102. John Stevens, *Documents Tending to Prove the Superior Advantages of Railway and Steam Carriages over Canal Navigation* (New York: T. & J. Swords, 1812).

103. *Archibald Douglas Turnbull*, John Stevens: An American Record (New York: Century Co., 1927); W. Woodford Clayton and William Nelson, eds., *History of Bergen and Passaic Counties, New Jersey* (Philadelphia: Everts & Peck, 1882), 88; George Rogers Taylor, *The Transportation Revolution, 1815–1860* (New York: Rinehart, 1951), 58–59; Weigley et al., *Philadelphia: A 300-Year History*, 72–73, 231.

104. Wheaton J. Lane, *From Indian Trail to Iron Horse: Travel and Transportation in New Jersey, 1620–1860* (Princeton, N.J.: Princeton University Press, 1939), 253–57, 281–84; Burgess and Kennedy, *Centennial History*, 242–45.

105. The company was chartered under the archaic spelling, New Jersey Atlantick Railroad. Christopher T. Baer, William J. Coxey, and Paul W. Schopp, *The Trail of the Blue Comet: A History of the Jersey Central's New Jersey Southern Division* (Palmyra, N.Y.: West Jersey Chapter of the National Railway Historical Society, 1994), 16–17.

106. This was actually the second incarnation of the Delaware & Raritan Canal. In 1824, the New Jersey legislature had chartered the first Delaware & Raritan Canal, after the company's investors agreed to pay a $100,000 bonus into the state treasury. The company experienced difficulty in raising capital, with much of its stock being acquired by a New York speculator, Floyd S. Bailey. In addition, the Pennsylvania legislature prevented the canal from drawing any water from the Delaware River, making the project impracticable. While New Jersey legislators were debating the incorporation of the Camden & Amboy and the Delaware & Raritan Canal, they were also considering a bill to charter the New Jersey Atlantic Railroad, whose promoters envisioned a line from Jersey City through Newark, New Brunswick, and Trenton to Salem. At Salem, a connection would be made with the New Castle & Frenchtown Turnpike & Rail

Road Company and, they hoped, would eventually permit construction of a railroad south and west to New Orleans. The New Jersey legislature declined to take action on the proposal, however. Carter Goodrich, *Government Promotion of Canals and Railroads, 1800–1890* (Westport, Conn.: Greenwood Press, 1974), 123; Horace Jerome Cranmer, *The New Jersey Canals: State Policy and Private Enterprise, 1820–1832* (New York: Arno Press, 1978), 242, 252–53; Samuel Hazard, *Register of Pennsylvania*, vol. 2 (December 6, 1828), 324; Robert T. Thompson, *Colonel James Neilson: A Business Man of the Early Machine Age in New Jersey, 1784–1862* (New Brunswick, N.J.: Rutgers University Press, 1940); Baer, Coxey, and Schopp, *Trail of the Blue Comet*, 17.

107. *First Annual Report of the Delaware and Raritan Canal Company*, 10, quoted in Lane, *Indian Trail*, 260.

108. Lane, *Indian Trail*, 259.

109. Ward, *Master of the Pennsylvania*, 19.

110. Douglas J. Puffert, *Tracks Across Continents, Paths Through History: The Economic Dynamics of Standardization in Railway Gauge* (Chicago: University of Chicago Press, 2009), 101–2, 109–10.

111. Even though the *John Bull* was hardly the first locomotive to operate in the United States, the historian John White noted that it "was very likely the first engine to be set aside as a historic relic." After the 1871 lease of the United Companies, the PRR gained possession of the *John Bull*. Rather than sell or scrap the John Bull after its service life had ended, they preserved the locomotive and displayed it at various exhibitions, including the Centennial celebration in Philadelphia, and in 1885 sent it to the Smithsonian Institution in 1885. Wilson, *History of the Pennsylvania Railroad*, vol. 1, 225; Burgess and Kennedy, *Centennial History*, 246–47; John H. White, *American Locomotives: An Engineering History, 1830–1880*, rev. ed. (Baltimore: Johns Hopkins University Press, 1997), 251–52; Lane, *Indian Trail*, 286–88.

112. In 1833, the Camden & Amboy purchased the Union Line.

113. Lane, *Indian Trail*, 289–90.

114. The PRR acquired the Delaware & Raritan Canal in 1872 as the result of its lease of the Joint Companies, and it kept the canal in service until 1932. In 1836, Robert F. Stockton and the Stevens interests obtained a charter for the Belvidere Delaware Railroad along the New Jersey side of the Delaware River. Active work did not begin until 1848, however. In November 1855, the first train traversed the line from Trenton through Phillipsburg to Belvidere. At Phillipsburg, the Bel-Del connected with the Lehigh Valley Railroad, under the control of Asa Packer, but likewise supported by the Stockton and Stevens interests. Together, the Lehigh Valley and the Bel-Del enabled anthracite to be transported to Coalport, just east of Trenton, where it could be transferred to the Delaware & Raritan Canal for shipment to Philadelphia. The Camden & Amboy built several other branch lines in New Jersey, largely to placate local residents who chafed at that company's virtual transportation monopoly. One example was the Flemington Railroad & Transportation Company, which provided a twelve-mile branch between Lambertville and Flemington. The Camden & Amboy had guaranteed the bonds of the Belvidere Delaware, and when the new company experienced financial difficulties, it became a Camden & Amboy subsidiary. When the PRR leased the United Companies in 1871, the "Bel-Del" was part of the bargain, and it became the Belvidere Division of the United Railroads of New Jersey Grand Division. Albright G. Zimmerman, *Pennsylvania's Delaware Division Canal: Sixty Miles of Euphoria and Frustration* (Easton, Pa.: Canal History and Technology Press, 2002); Burgess and Kennedy, *Centennial History*, 247–48; Poor, *History of the Railroads and Canals*, 386–545; Lane, *Indian Trail*, 261–68, 390–92; Baer, Coxey, and Schopp, *Trail of the Blue Comet*, 18.

115. Baer, Coxey, and Schopp, *Trail of the Blue Comet*, 17–18.

116. The initial term of the monopoly was thirty years. Many legislators assumed that the termination date of the monopoly would be 1864, thirty years after the opening of the Camden & Amboy, while Camden & Amboy officials claimed that their railroad was not completed until 1839. In 1854, an amendment to the Camden & Amboy charter provided that monopoly privileges would expire on January 1, 1869. Lane, *Indian Trail*, 323–24, 356–59.

117. Wilson, *History of the Pennsylvania Railroad*, vol. 2, 218–21; Burgess and Kennedy, *Centennial History*, 243–46; Poor, *History of the Railroads and Canals*, 377 (quote).

118. Lane, *Indian Trail*, 323.

119. By 1860, New Jersey had collected $3,870,250 from the Joint Companies (in the form of transit duties and stock dividends) and garnered an additional $1,334,692 from the New Jersey Rail Road line between Jersey City and New Brunswick. Lane, *Indian Trail*, 410.

120. New Jersey collected additional revenues from the dividends on the $200,000 in stock held in the state treasury. Poor, *History of the Railroads and Canals*, 377 (quote).

121. Charles Sumner, "Railroad Usurpation in New Jersey," Speech in the Senate, on a Bill to Regulate Commerce among the Several States, February 14, 1865, in *The Works of Charles Sumner*, vol. 9 (Boston: Lee and Shepard, 1874), 237–65, quote at 261. See also Thomas Weber, *The Northern Railroads in the Civil War, 1861–1865* (Bloomington: Indiana University Press, 1999), 124.

122. Disputes regarding an equitable division of rates between the Joint Companies and the New Jersey Rail Road & Transportation Company dragged on for more than twenty years and led ultimately to their consolidation in 1867. Initially, the Camden & Amboy carried most of the traffic across New Jersey. During the Civil War, the Philadelphia & Trenton became the principal route for passengers. Freight continued to follow the Camden & Amboy, largely because of the absence of adequate transfer facilities at the New Jersey Rail Road's Jersey City terminus. The rectification of that problem would be one of the main factors leading to the PRR's 1871 lease of the United Companies, the 1867 successor to the Joint Companies. Burgess and Kennedy, *Centennial History*, 251–63; John Wall and Harold Gill, *History of Middlesex County, 1664–1920*, vol. 2 (New York: Lewis Historical Publishing, 1921), 40–44; Cranmer, *The New Jersey Canals*, 321; John O. Raum, *History of the City of Trenton, New Jersey* (Trenton, N.J.: W. T. Nicholson & Co., 1871), 339; Lane, *Indian Trail*, 362–69; Leslie E. Freeman, "The New Jersey Railroad and Transportation Co.," Railway & Locomotive Historical Society Bulletin 88 (May 1953): 100–159.

123. Baer, Coxey, and Schopp, *Trail of the Blue Comet*, 19.

124. Burgess and Kennedy, *Centennial History*, 252–53.

125. In 1863, construction crews built a more direct line between Dean's Pond (Monmouth Junction) to Trenton, bypassing Princeton. Even though Princeton residents were able to use a short shuttle train between Princeton and Princeton Junction, on the main line, there remained considerable lingering resentment toward the Camden & Amboy and its successor, the PRR.

126. Messer and Roberts, *Triumph V*, 15–16.

127. In 1842, the New Jersey legislature closed that loophole and stipulated that the transit duties would apply to all traffic moving between any point on the Delaware River and any point on the Raritan River. Lane, *Indian Trail*, 334–36.

128. The uproar in Kensington between 1840 and 1842 should not be confused with the far more serious nativist riots that erupted in Kensington and Southwark during the summer of 1844. Michael Feldberg, "Urbanization as a Cause of Violence: Philadelphia as a Test Case," in Allen F. Davis and Mark H. Haller, eds., *The Peoples of Philadelphia: A History of*

Ethnic Groups and Lower-Class Life, 1790–1940 (Philadelphia: Temple University Press, 1998), 59–61, 68.

129. Charles S. Roberts and David W. Messer, *Triumph VI: Philadelphia, Columbia, Harrisburg to Baltimore and Washington, D.C.* (Baltimore: Barnard, Roberts & Co., 2003), 36.

130. Burgess and Kennedy, *Centennial History*, 388–89; Wilson, *History of the Pennsylvania Railroad*, vol. 1, 305–7.

131. The company was chartered under the archaic spelling, Baltimore & Port Deposite Rail Road

132. The existing highway bridge across the Schuylkill, at Grey's Ferry, was something of a hazard to navigation in its own right. Because the bridge was built atop a series of pontoons, bridge tenders had to open a gap in the bridge every time a ship wished to pass. Burgess and Kennedy, *Centennial History*, 389–90; Wilson, *History of the Pennsylvania Railroad*, vol. 1, 292–302.

133. For the effects of early railroads on employment and economic development in Wilmington, see Bruce Seely, "Wilmington and Its Railroads: A Lasting Connection," *Delaware History* 19 (Spring/Summer 1980): 1–19.

134. The merger of the New Castle & Frenchtown Turnpike & Railroad Company into the Philadelphia, Wilmington & Baltimore did not take place until 1877. Also included in the 1877 consolidation were the Southwark Railroad and the New Castle & Wilmington Railroad, the latter company chartered in Delaware in 1839, and by 1852 operating between its two namesake cities. Wilson, *History of the Pennsylvania Railroad*, vol. 1, 293–308.

135. Ibid., vol. 1, 292–302; Burgess and Kennedy, *Centennial History*, 390–91; J. Thomas Scharf and Thompson Wescott, *History of Philadelphia, 1609–1884*, vol. 3 (Philadelphia: L. H. Everts & Co., 1884), 2340–41; *Memorial Biographies of the New-England Historic Genealogical Society*, vol. 6: *1864–1871* (Boston: The Society, 1905), 279–80.

136. The Pennsylvania Railroad Company, "Inspection of Physical Property by Board of Directors, November 10–11–12, 1948," 19–20, archived at http://www.railsandtrails.com/PRR/BOD1948/index.htm, accessed June 26, 2010; Wilson, *History of the Pennsylvania Railroad*, vol. 1, 294–96, 312.

137. Descriptions of the New York–Washington journey are available in Eugene S. Ferguson, ed., *Early Engineering Reminiscences (1815–40) of George Escol Sellers* (Washington, D.C.: Smithsonian Institution, 1965), 144–46; Herbert H. Harwood, Jr., *Royal Blue Line: The Classic B&O Train Between Washington and New York* (Baltimore: Johns Hopkins University Press, 2002), 14–15; and Charles P. Dare, *Philadelphia Wilmington and Baltimore Rail Road Guide: Containing a Description of the Scenery, Rivers, Towns, Villages, and Objects of Interest along the Line of Road; Including Historical Sketches, Legends, &c.* (Philadelphia: Fitzgibbon and Van Ness, 1856).

138. Arthur M. Johnson and Barry Supple, *Boston Capitalists and Western Railroads: A Study in the Nineteenth-Century Railroad Investment Process* (Cambridge, Mass.: Harvard University Press, 1967), 54–56.

139. Wilson, *History of the Pennsylvania Railroad*, vol. 1, 303–5, 310–11; Chandler, *Henry Varnum Poor*, 163–68; Leslie R. Tucker, *Major General Isaac Ridgeway Trimble: Biography of a Baltimore Confederate* (Jefferson, N.C.: McFarland, 2005), 63–86.

140. PRR, Office of the General Superintendent, "Memorandum on 'Contract System' of Operating the Philadelphia, Wilmington & Baltimore Railroad Prior to and During the Civil War," April 17, 1922, HML, Box 1351, folder 8.

141. Lane, *Indian Trail*, 323–25, 341–44, 407.

142. Robert L. Gunnarsson, *The Story of the Northern Central Railway, from Baltimore to Lake Ontario* (Sykesville, Md.: Greenberg Publishing, 1991), 12–28.

143. The Williamsport–Erie line effectively duplicated much of the route of the Sunbury & Erie Railroad. The promoters of the Sunbury & Erie, sensitive to the danger, attempted to block construction of the Susquehanna Railroad by claiming the best route through the Susquehanna Valley. The courts blocked that effort, but they enjoyed more success in the legislature. In May 1853, the Sunbury & Erie interests secured a modification to their company's charter, stipulating that the Susquehanna Railroad must place the line to Sunbury under contract within one year and complete it within three years. If the organizers of the Susquehanna Railroad failed to meet those objectives, then they would forfeit to the Sunbury & Erie the right to construct their railroad. The promoters of the Susquehanna Railroad had ample incentive to initiate construction as quickly as possible. Wilson, *History of the Pennsylvania Railroad*, vol. 1, 231, 238–39; Homer Tope Rosenberger, *The Philadelphia and Erie Railroad: Its Place in American Economic History* (Potomac, Md.: Fox Hills Press, 1975), 53–55; Gunnarsson, *Northern Central Railway*, 28–29.

144. The Wrightsville, York & Gettysburg Railroad was not included in the merger, but was nonetheless operated by the Northern Central until 1870, when the PRR assumed control.

145. At Sunbury, the Northern Central also connected with a carrier then known as the Shamokin Valley & Pottsville Railroad. Chartered as the Danville & Pottsville Railroad in 1826, the company became the Philadelphia & Sunbury Railroad in 1850. By that time, it had managed to construct a coal line from Sunbury east to Shamokin, with an extension to Mount Carmel completed in 1854. At Millersburg, some thirty miles north of Harrisburg., the Northern Central interchanged with another anthracite carrier, the Lykens Valley Railroad & Coal Company, which had been in operation since 1834. In 1863, the Northern Central acquired control of the Shamokin Valley & Pottsville. Wilson, *History of the Pennsylvania Railroad*, vol. 1, 231, 240; Burgess and Kennedy, *Centennial History*, 128–35; Poor, *History of the Railroads and Canals*, 503; Gunnarsson, *Northern Central Railway*, 38–40.

146. The disposition of the Erie Triangle (sometimes referred to as the Triangle Lands) occurred after the federal government intervened to settle a boundary dispute that involved Pennsylvania, New York, Massachusetts, and Connecticut. Pennsylvania was able to purchase the land in large measure because it abutted the Triangle Lands and because the state lacked access to Lake Erie.

147. The Susquehanna & Waterford Turnpike, chartered in 1812 and completed in 1824, linked the Susquehanna River, near the mouth of Anderson Creek in Clearfield County, with Waterford, where a connection with another turnpike provided access to Erie.

148. In 1831, crews began digging the Beaver & Erie Division of the Pennsylvania Canal, from the confluence of the Ohio and Beaver rivers north to Pulaski. Five years later, work commenced on the Shenango Division, which carried boats north as far as Conneaut Lake. In 1838, the Board of Canal Commissioners let contracts for the final segment to Erie as part of the Conneaut Division, but by 1843 the commonwealth had transferred the entire project to a private firm, the Erie Canal Company. The canal reached Erie the following year. A link between Erie and the east was more problematic, however. By 1835, the West Branch Division of the Pennsylvania Canal had reached Farrandsville, to the west of Lock Haven. Three years later, crews began work on an extension of the canal some thirty-three miles west to the mouth of Sinnemahoning Creek, but the commonwealth's financial problems soon brought construction to a halt. Rosenberger, *The Philadelphia and Erie Railroad*, 69; William James McKnight, *A Pioneer Outline History of Northwestern Pennsylvania* (Philadelphia: J. P. Lippincott, 1905), 211–17; Poor, *History of the Railroads and Canals*, 555–56.

149. Rosenberger, *The Philadelphia and Erie Railroad*, 23–24, 76, 81; Messer and Roberts, *Triumph V*, 10; John Hoffman, "Anthracite in the Lehigh Valley of Pennsylvania, 1820–1845," *United States National Museum Bulletin* 252 (1968): 91–141; Robert R. Goller, *The Morris Canal: Across New Jersey by Water and Rail* (Charleston, S.C.: Arcadia Publishing, 1999); Barbara N. Kalata, *A Hundred Years, a Hundred Miles: New Jersey's Morris Canal* (Morristown, N.J.: Morris County Historical Society, 1983).

150. In December 1824, the New Jersey legislature granted a charter to the Morris & Essex Canal & Banking Company to build a canal between Newark, on the Passaic River, and Phillipsburg, on the Delaware River, for the purpose of bringing northeastern Pennsylvania anthracite to New York markets. Most of the canal was completed by 1831, and the remainder opened in 1836. Both the circumstances and the motives surrounding the Biddle acquisition of the Morris Canal & Banking Company are unclear. With the destruction of the federally chartered Second Bank of the United States, Nicholas Biddle became the president of the United States Bank of Pennsylvania. As a state-chartered corporation, Biddle's new bank lacked the authority to operate in any other state. The acquisition of the Morris Canal & Banking Company (a New Jersey corporation) gave Biddle access to the Morris Canal Bank, based in Jersey City. The Morris Bank enabled Biddle to participate in the New York banking field and served as a vehicle for his investments in state internal-improvement loans in Michigan and Indiana.

151. In 1836 Nicholas Biddle arranged for the United States Bank of Pennsylvania to subscribe to $250,000 of Little Schuylkill & Susquehanna stock. The same year, the Little Schuylkill & Susquehanna leased the Morris Canal & Banking Company.

152. The story of these anthracite carriers is extraordinarily complex, with details found in Earl J. Heydinger, "Railroads of the First and Second Anthracite Coal Fields of Pennsylvania," *Bulletin of the Railway and Locomotive Historical Society* 105 (October 1961): 38–50, 106 (April 1962): 32–40, 107 (October 1962): 28–39, 108 (April 1963): 19–28, 109 (October 1963): 16–29, 110 (April 1964): 59–63; "The Formation of the Beaver Meadow Railroad and Coal Co.," http://himedo.net/TheHopkinThomasProject/TimeLine/BeaverMeadows/BeaverMeadowrRR/BeaverMeadowFormation.htm, accessed on June 15, 2011; "Railroad History of Catawissa Pennsylvania," http://caboosenut.com/railroad%20history.htm, accessed on June 15, 2011.

153. Curiously, that same day Ritner vetoed legislation to fund a collection of state-sponsored internal improvements, describing them as overly ambitious. However, the events were indicative of Ritner's fear that the massive internal-improvement bill was more than the state could afford, rather than a rejection of the concept of public works, in favor of private companies such as the Sunbury & Erie.

154. Rosenberger, *The Philadelphia and Erie Railroad*, 60–61; Richard Sylla, Jack W. Wilson, and Robert E. Wright, "Integration of Trans-Atlantic Capital Markets, 1790–1845," *Review of Finance* 10 (2006): 613–44.

155. Rosenberger, *The Philadelphia and Erie Railroad*, 119–32.

156. Charles S. Roberts and David W. Messer, *Triumph VII: Harrisburg to the Lakes, Wilkes-Barre, Oil City and Red Bank* (Baltimore: Barnard, Roberts & Co., 2004), 138; Poor, *History of the Railroads and Canals*, 429; *Historical and Biographical Annals of Columbia and Montour Counties, Pennsylvania, Containing a Concise History of the Two Counties and a Genealogical and Biographical Record of Representative Families*, vol. I (Chicago: J. H. Beers & Co., 1915), 44–45.

157. Rosenberger, *The Philadelphia and Erie Railroad*, 172–95.

158. The history of Philadelphia's investment in the Sunbury & Erie was somewhat complex. In February 1853, the Select and Common Councils approved assistance, but they soon rescinded the offer amid disputes over the composition of the railroad's board of directors. In January 1854, fol-

lowing a purge of the Sunbury & Erie's board, the councils again authorized the subscription. Philadelphia's investment authorized the Common and Select Councils to appoint three of the thirteen directors of the Sunbury & Erie. In 1904, the city sold its stock in what was by then the Philadelphia & Erie.

159. Rosenberger, *The Philadelphia and Erie Railroad*, 160, 196, 202–3, 209–11, 225.

160. The primary culprits were a consortium of investors who, in February 1856, incorporated the McKean & Elk Land & Improvement Company. The Kane family, including Judge John K. Kane and his son, Thomas Leiper Kane, were heavily involved in the venture, and they lent their name to the town of Kane, Pennsylvania. The Sunbury & Erie board did not commit to the final choice of alignment until May 1859. Rosenberger, *The Philadelphia and Erie Railroad*, 340–48.

161. Burgess and Kennedy, *Centennial History*, 146–53; Rosenberger, *The Philadelphia and Erie Railroad*, 251.

162. The Williamsport & Elmira Railroad traced its origins to 1831, as part of a project by Elmira commercial interests to build a line between Williamsport and Ralston, Pennsylvania, in order to gain access to bituminous coal deposits. By 1832, they had agreed to extend the route farther north, to the Pennsylvania border, and obtained a charter to that effect. By 1837, with financial support from the United States Bank of Pennsylvania, the company was able to complete a primitive line (with wooden rails innocent of even strap iron). The Williamsport & Elmira went bankrupt in 1849, but in 1850 nonetheless received a New York charter to build still farther to the north. Construction resumed in 1853, and by September 1854 the entire line was in service between Williamsport and the south side of Elmira. In 1860, the Williamsport & Elmira again entered receivership and was reorganized as the Elmira & Williamsport Railroad. The company's owners, unsuccessful in their efforts to join forces with the Reading, in order to establish through service between Philadelphia and Buffalo, evinced their willingness to join the PRR family. In April 1863, the Northern Central secured control of the company, under the terms of a 999-year lease. The Canandaigua & Elmira Rail Road began its corporate existence in May 1845 as the Canandaigua & Corning Railroad (the name change occurred in 1852). The Chemung Railroad was also incorporated in May 1845, in order to construct a broad-gauge line between the Erie main line, at Horseheads, and Watkins Glen, on Seneca Lake. After January 1, 1853, the Canandaigua & Elmira operated its own lines, as well as the Chemung Railroad, independently of the Erie. The Canandaigua & Elmira fell victim to the financial malaise of the 1850s and was reorganized in 1857 as the Elmira, Canandaigua & Niagara Falls Rail Road and again in 1859 as the Elmira, Jefferson & Canandaigua Rail Road. It was purchased by the Northern Central in 1872. Both segments eventually became part of the PRR's line to Sodus Point, New York, on Lake Ontario. The Canandaigua & Niagara Falls also went bankrupt and was reorganized in 1857 as the Niagara Bridge & Canandaigua Railroad. The New York Central leased that company the following year.

163. Jay V. Hare, *History of the Reading, Which Appeared as a Serial in* The Pilot *and* Philadelphia & Reading Railway Men, *Beginning May 1909—Ending February 1914* (Philadelphia: John Henry Stock & Co., 1966), 53–54, 63 (quote attributed to Reading Managers, January 1857, presumably in Reading BOD Minutes), 237–38; Poor, *History of the Railroads and Canals*, 429; Wilson, *History of the Pennsylvania Railroad*, vol. 1, 272; Gunnarsson, *Northern Central Railway*, 83–91.

164. *New York Times*, September 4, 1858.

165. On May 19, 1858, the commonwealth sold the North Branch Division, the Susquehanna Division, the West Branch Division, and the Delaware Division to the Sunbury & Erie. Six days later, the Sunbury & Erie

resold the canal to the North Branch Canal Company, which had been incorporated on April 21, 1858 (there was a previous incarnation of the North Branch Canal Company, chartered in July 1842, when Pennsylvania teetered on the verge of bankruptcy; it was designed to complete the North Branch Extension to the New York State Line, but little action resulted, and the state regained control of the project in 1851). On June 24, the North Branch Canal Company sold the more southerly stretch between Northumberland and Wilkes-Barre (sixty-four miles) went to the Wyoming Canal Company, reorganized in 1863 as the Wyoming Valley Canal Company. On January 1, 1869, the PRR's Pennsylvania Canal Company subsidiary purchased the Wyoming Canal Company, operating it as the Wyoming Division. The more northerly portion, between Wilkes-Barre and the New York state line (103 miles) remained a part of the North Branch Canal Company, reorganized in 1865 as the Pennsylvania & New York Canal & Railroad Company, a part of the Lehigh Valley Railroad. On June 26, 1858, the Sunbury & Erie sold the Susquehanna Division and the West Branch Division to the West Branch & Susquehanna Canal Company, also incorporated on April 21, 1858. On January 1, 1869, the Pennsylvania Canal Company leased the West Branch & Susquehanna Canal Company and bought the company on October 14, 1873. On July 10, 1858, the Sunbury & Erie sold the Delaware Division Canal to the Delaware Division Canal Company. In August 1866, the Lehigh Coal & Navigation Company leased the Delaware Division Canal Company.

166. The Sunbury & Erie paid that debt with $281,000 in Wyoming Canal Company bonds and $250 in cash.

167. Poor, *History of the Railroads and Canals*, 506–7; William Harry Moyer, "PRR's Navy, Part V: Pennsylvania Canals," *The Keystone* 42 (Summer 2009): 21–34; F. Charles Petrillo, *Anthracite and Slackwater: The North Branch Canal, 1828–1901* (Easton, Pa.: Center for Canal History and Technology, 1986), 91–104, 118–21.

168. Poor, *History of the Railroads and Canals*, 506; Wilson, *History of the Pennsylvania Railroad*, vol. 1, 248–56.

169. John Nathan Hoffman, *Girard Estate Coal Lands in Pennsylvania, 1801–1884* (Washington, D.C.: Smithsonian Institution Press, 1972), 62–67; Gunnarsson, *Northern Central Railway*, 73–74; Richmond E. Myers, "The Development of Transportation in the Susquehanna River Valley: A Geographical Study, 1700–1900" (Ph.D. diss., Pennsylvania State University, 1951), 244–46.

170. In February 1863 the Northern Central leased the Shamokin Valley & Pottsville for 999 years. Roberts and Messer, *Triumph VII*, 30; Gunnarsson, *Northern Central Railway*, 74–75.

171. Paul G. Marr, "The Wiconisco Canal," *Canal History and Technology Proceedings* 24 (March 19, 2005): 5–21.

172. On April 5, 1826, the Pennsylvania General Assembly granted a corporate charter to investors in the Dauphin & Susquehanna Coal Company. A year later, the company received authority to build either a canal or slackwater navigation for the transportation of anthracite. In April 1838, the legislature expanded that authority to include the construction of a railroad. As early as 1839, Edward Miller had surveyed a rail route linking the mines to the Susquehanna River, but construction on the line between Dauphin and the coal-mining town of Rausch Gap did not begin until 1850. From Rausch Gap (reached in 1852), the Dauphin & Susquehanna Coal Company built east to Auburn, and a junction with the Reading. Hare, *History of the Reading*, 79–81; Donald L. Rhoads, Jr., and Robert A. Heilman, *Railroads of Lebanon County, Pennsylvania: A Pictorial and Descriptive History* (Lebanon, Pa.: Lebanon County Historical Society, 2000), 16, 87, 177.

173. William Henry Egle, ed., *Notes and Queries, Historical, Biographical, and Genealogical: Chiefly Relating to Interior Pennsylvania, Third Series*, vol. 1 (Harrisburg: Daily Telegraph Print, 1887), 323.

174. Despite its disadvantages, the PRR carried substantial quantities of anthracite to western Pennsylvania, as well as north to central and western New York, including the various lake ports. During the late nineteenth century, the PRR accordingly accounted for about 10 percent of the anthracite traffic in the United States. PRR BOD Minutes, May 2, 1860, 489–90.

175. Lane, *Indian Trail*, 341–42.

176. At the same time, and after an investment of some $4 million, the Dauphin & Susquehanna Coal Company had failed to tap significant anthracite reserves. The company went bankrupt in 1857, and Reading officials were willing to purchase both the railroad (after 1859, it became the Schuylkill & Susquehanna Railroad) and its subsidiary, the Allentown Railroad, largely to prevent it from falling under the control of a rival carrier. The Reading board of directors approved the arrangement in July 1860 but did not assume formal control over the two railroads until August 1861. Hare, *History of the Reading*, 80–82; Poor, *History of the Railroads and Canals*, 501–2; Brandy M. Watts, "The Schuylkill & Susquehanna Railroad," http://www.stonyvalley.com/, accessed on June 17, 2011.

177. The Reading leased the East Pennsylvania Railroad in May 1869, but it held effective control well before that date. Poor, *History of the Railroads and Canals*, 390, 426, 439; Hare, *History of the Reading*, 165–71, 180.

178. Hare, *History of the Reading*, 165.

179. By 1866, a regular line of Silver Palace sleeping cars was operating over the Allentown Route, from Jersey City to Chicago. With the completion of the Connecting Railway, in 1867, the route became distinctly less popular. PRR BOD Minutes, January 19, 1859, 393–94; Hare, *History of the Reading*, 182–84; *New York Times*, July 28, 1867.

180. PRR BOD Minutes, December 28, 1859, 456–57.

181. "To the Select & Common Councils of the City of Philadelphia," in PRR BOD Minutes, October 24, 1855, 109.

182. David W. Messer, *Triumph III: Philadelphia Terminal, 1838–2000* (Baltimore: Barnard, Roberts & Co., 2000), 286.

183. The West Chester & Philadelphia, incorporated in 1848, had built a line from West Philadelphia, south a short distance along the west side of the Schuylkill River, and then southwest toward a connection with the Philadelphia & Baltimore Central Railroad's route to the Susquehanna River.

184. In 1866, the PRR extended its tracks to Greenwich Point, where it built its own coal and oil terminals. A new freight house opened eight years later, at Delaware Avenue and Dock Street, replacing the earlier facility at Thirteenth and Market. The year 1874 also witnessed the completion of the Girard Point Branch, to a new terminal at Girard Point, which was built and initially operated by the International Navigation Company, a firm that was closely allied with the PRR. In December 1875, the PRR purchased the Philadelphia Navy Yard, permitting further expansion. In 1882, construction crews built a line (the River Front Railroad) linking the waterfront facilities to the Philadelphia & Trenton, at Lehigh Avenue, completing a belt line around Philadelphia. PRR BOD Minutes, January 19, 1859, 392–94, December 28, 1859, 456–58, January 11, 1860, 463–64, May 16, 1860, 493–94, May 23, 1860, 498–99; *Fifteenth Annual Report of the Board of Directors to the Stockholders of the Pennsylvania Railroad Co., February 3, 1862* (Philadelphia: Crissy & Markley), 12–13; Wilson, *History of the Pennsylvania Railroad*, vol. 1, 69–75, 178; Messer, *Triumph III*, 286.

185. Burgess and Kennedy, *Centennial History*, 136–37; Gunnarsson, *Northern Central Railway*, 49.

186. Gunnarsson, *Northern Central Railway*, 29.

187. The PRR's 1846 corporate charter prohibited the company from owning the securities of another corporation. In March 1853, the legislature amended the charter, permitting the PRR to invest in railroads that operated outside Pennsylvania—this was primarily an effort to facilitate the PRR's

control of rail lines in Ohio and Indiana. However, the PRR did not yet have the right to invest in companies incorporated in Pennsylvania or doing business in Pennsylvania, as legislators deemed that such authority might give the PRR the opportunity to undermine competition.

188. Ward, "Symbiotic Partnership," 58–59.

189. Clayton Coleman Hall, *Baltimore: Its History and Its People*, vol. II (New York: Lewis Historical Publishing, 1912), 306, 165–69; Glenn Hoffman, *Building a Great Railroad: A History of the Atlantic Coast Line Railroad Company* (Jacksonville, Fla.: CSX Corporation, 1998), 1.

190. Brantz Mayer, *Baltimore Past and Present, with Biographical Sketches of its Representative Men* (Baltimore: Richardson & Bennett, 1871), 289–91.

191. Burgess and Kennedy, *Centennial History*, 135–39.

192. In 1861, Thomson purchased 28.26 percent of the outstanding Northern Central stock. Another major purchase, in January 1863, increased what was by then the PRR's stake in the Northern Central to 33.79 percent. For the remainder of the century, the PRR would own a minority interest in the company, but that was nonetheless sufficient to guarantee effective control. Gunnarsson, *Northern Central Railway*, 49.

193. Burgess and Kennedy, *Centennial History*, 530.

Chapter 7. Expansion

1. Edwin L. Moseley, "Long Time Forecasts of Ohio River Floods," *Ohio Journal of Science* 39 (July 1939): 220–31, 229; *Proceedings of the Fourth Annual Meeting of the Indiana State Medical Society* (Indianapolis: Elder & Harkness, 1853), 51.

2. According to economic historian Douglass C. North, "In the first two expansive periods analyzed here, 1815 to 1818 and 1832 to 1839, cotton was the key industry in both the boom and the subsequent collapse and readjustment. In the last period [the 1850s] the sources of expansion are more diffuse, but grain in the West played the most important role." North, *The Economic Growth of the United States, 1790–1860* (Englewood Cliffs, N.J.: Prentice-Hall, 1961), 71.

3. Ibid., 102–6, 142–43, 192, 207.

4. *First Annual Report of the Directors of the Pennsylvania Railroad Co. to the Stockholders* (Philadelphia: Crissy & Markley, 1847), 16.

5. Alfred D. Chandler, Jr., *Henry Varnum Poor: Business Editor, Analyst, and Reformer* (Cambridge, Mass.: Harvard University Press, 1956), 294n88; Frederick Albert Cleveland and Fred Wilbur Powell, *Railroad Promotion and Capitalization in the United States* (New York: Longmans, Green, and Co., 1909), 326; Jay Veder Hare, *History of the North Pennsylvania Railroad* (Philadelphia: Reading Co., 1944), 9; *New York Times*, June 12, 1896.

6. Thomas Sergant Fernon, "Report to J. Edgar Thomson, President of the Pennsylvania Railroad Company, Submitting Results of Observations Concerning the Tendencies of Trade Towards the Seaboard through the West, North of the Ohio River" (Philadelphia: The American Philosophical Society, 1852), 1.

7. Fernon, "Report to J. Edgar Thomson," 6, emphasis in the original.

8. Ibid., 5.

9. Ibid., 2–3, 41.

10. *Sixteenth Annual Report of the Board of Directors to the Stockholders of the Pennsylvania Rail Road Company, February 2, 1863* (Philadelphia: Crissy & Markley, 1863), 17.

11. *Charter and Supplements of the Pennsylvania Railroad Company, with the Acts of Assembly and Municipal Ordinances Affecting the Company; Together with the By-Laws of the Board of Directors* (Philadelphia: Crissy & Markley, 1859), 34–35.

12. *Twenty-Fourth Annual Report of the Board of Directors to the Stockholders of the Pennsylvania Railroad Co. to the Stockholders, February 21, 1871* (Philadelphia: E. C. Markley & Son, 1871), 17 (quotes); Howard W. Schotter, "Scope of the Pennsylvania Railroad System," July 2, 1937, Pennsylvania Railroad Company Collection, call no. 1807/1810, Hagley Museum and Library, Wilmington, Delaware (hereafter cited as HML), Box 219, folder 12.

13. Herman Haupt, *Report of H. Haupt, Chief Engineer of the Pennsylvania Rail Road Company, with a Communication from the President of the Ohio & Pennsylvania Rail Road Company, of the Expediency of Aiding the Ohio and Indiana and the Fort Wayne and Chicago Rail Road Companies to Complete Their Roads* (Philadelphia: Crissy & Markley, 1854), 31.

14. Dorothy R. Adler and Muriel E. Hidy, eds., *British Investment in American Railways, 1834–1898* (Charlottesville: University Press of Virginia, 1970), 90.

15. Haupt, *Report of H. Haupt*, 22.

16. *Sixth Annual Report of the Directors of the Pennsylvania Railroad Co. to the Stockholders, February 7, 1853* (Philadelphia: Crissy & Markley, 1853), 21.

17. The Pennsylvania & Ohio Canal, built between 1835 and 1840, connected the Ohio & Erie, at Akron, to New Castle, Pennsylvania, on the commonwealth's Beaver & Erie Canal. Another east–west feeder, the unsuccessful Sandy & Beaver Canal, linked the Ohio & Erie, at Bolivar, to Glasgow, Pennsylvania, on the Ohio River.

18. Ronald E. Shaw, *Canals for a Nation: The Canal Era in the United States, 1790–1860* (Lexington: University Press of Kentucky, 1990), 135–43; Victor M. Bogle, "Railroad Building in Indiana," *Indiana Magazine of History* 58 (September 1962): 211–32.

19. There was a certain irony in Jackson's rationalization for his veto of the Maysville Road bill. In the aftermath of President James Madison's 1817 veto of the Bonus Bill, on the grounds that the Constitution did not permit the federal government to fund internal improvements, supporters of better transportation had chopped national projects into state-by-state segments, reasoning that the federal government could lawfully fund projects that did not cross state lines. The trading of political favors (what later generations would come to call pork-barrel politics) would, in theory, assure that a sufficient number of legislators would vote to approve funds for each state's pet projects. The Maysville Road (and its parent firm, the Maysville, Washington, Paris & Lexington Turnpike Road Company) was just such a project, in that it was to form a portion of the interstate Cumberland Road. Jackson certainly knew that the specific bill under consideration was national in scope and, as such, his veto had more to do with his opposition toward federal involvement in transportation, and not merely his aversion to federal aid for a local improvement. Andrew Jackson, Message to the United States Congress, House of Representatives, Veto of Maysville Road Bill, 1830 (quote); Pamela L. Baker, "The Washington National Road Bill and the Struggle to Adopt a Federal System of Internal Improvement," *Journal of the Early Republic* 22 (Fall 2002): 437–64; George Rogers Taylor, *The Transportation Revolution, 1815–1860* (New York: Rinehart, 1951), 19–20; Robert G. Angevine, *The Railroad and the State: War, Politics, and Technology in Nineteenth-Century America* (Stanford, Calif.: Stanford University Press, 2004), 41–47, 51–53; John Lauritz Larson, *Internal Improvement: National Public Works and the Promise of Popular Government in the Early United States* (Chapel Hill: University of North Carolina Press, 2001), 5; Louis Hartz, *Economic Policy and Democratic Thought: Pennsylvania, 1776–1860* (Cambridge, Mass.: Harvard University Press, 1948), 12–13; Carter Goodrich, *Government Promotion of Canals and Railroads, 1800–1890* (Westport, Conn.: Greenwood Press, 1974), 41, 169.

20. Harry N. Scheiber, *Ohio Canal Era: A Case Study of Government and the Economy, 1820–1861* (Athens: Ohio University Press, 1969), 110–13, 130–33, 275–82.

21. Douglas J. Puffert, *Tracks Across Continents, Paths Through History: The Economic Dynamics of Standardization in Railway Gauge* (Chicago: University of Chicago Press, 2009), 110–11; Walter Rumsey Marvin, "Columbus and the Railroads of Central Ohio Before the Civil War" (Ph.D. diss., Ohio State University, 1953), 13, 24–26, 55–58, 95–98; Scheiber, *Ohio Canal Era*, 95–97.

22. Marvin, "Railroads of Central Ohio," 51, 57–68; Scheiber, *Ohio Canal Era*, 282–83.

23. Marvin, "Railroads of Central Ohio," 68, 105–12, 119–67.

24. William Alexander Taylor, *Centennial History of Columbus and Franklin County Ohio*, (Chicago: S. J. Clarke, 1909), vol. 1, 510–15, vol. 2, 211–13; Alfred E. Lee, *History of the City of Columbus, Capital of Ohio*, vol. 2 (New York: Munsell & Co., 1892), 320; Marvin, "Railroads of Central Ohio," 19, 31–32, 43–44, 71–73, 80–83, 105–6, 168–75.

25. Scheiber, *Ohio Canal Era*, 283–86.

26. J. V. Smith, *Report of the Debates and Proceedings of the Convention for the Revision of the Constitution of the State of Ohio, 1850–1851* (Columbus: S. Medary, 1851), 372 ("less important"), 402 ("through his house"), 496 ("what more?").

27. When the 1851 constitution took effect, several local governments had scheduled, but had not yet conducted, funding referenda. In 1852, the Ohio Supreme Court ruled that citizens had the right to vote on those proposals, and the decision made possible the granting of an additional $3 million in local railroad aid. Scheiber, *Ohio Canal Era*, 286–87, 297–98; "Ohio Constitutional Convention of 1850–1851," Ohio History Central, July 1, 2005, http://www.ohiohistorycentral.org/entry.php?rec=524, accessed on July 1, 2010.

28. "General Railroad Laws of Ohio, February 11, 1848," *Annual Report of the Commissioner of [the Ohio Department of] Railroads and Telegraphs, for the Year 1870*, vol. 1 (Columbus, Ohio: Nevins & Myers, 1870), 14–21, 23–25; Scheiber, *Ohio Canal Era*, 296; George Heberton Evans, Jr., "Preferred Stock in the United States, 1850–1878," *American Economic Review* 21 (March 1931): 56–62, at 58–59.

29. The CC&C–Columbus & Xenia–Little Miami route could move traffic from Cincinnati, Columbus, and points west to the northern Ohio town of Crestline. From there, traffic moved from a planned connection with the Ohio & Pennsylvania Railroad for travel east to Pittsburgh and Philadelphia. However, the CC&C continued still farther north to Cleveland. Given the Cleveland connections of Kelley and his fellow investors, it seemed logical that the western traffic would continue east, via Lake Erie and the Erie Canal, or over the tracks of the Erie or the collection of railroads that later became the New York Central. (In 1906, the NYC did in fact acquire the Cleveland, Cincinnati, Chicago & St. Louis Railway, known as the "Big Four," and the corporate successor to the CC&C, although it had established effective control two decades earlier.) Kelley's affinity for New York, rather than Cleveland, became even more apparent in April 1851 when he became president of the Cleveland, Painesville & Ashtabula Railroad, later to become the NYC's primary western connection to Chicago. With Kelley in charge of both the CC&C and the line between Cleveland and Ashtabula, the two companies soon coordinated their operations. Under the circumstances, the CC&C route was a useful, if temporary, adjunct to the PRR's western operations, but the CC&C was not likely to be a long-term ally. Harry N. Scheiber, "Alfred Kelley and the Ohio Business Elite, 1822–1859," *Ohio History* 87 (1978): 365–92, at 389–91; Marvin, "Railroads of Central Ohio," 112–16, 175–77, 181–202.

30. Scheiber, "Alfred Kelley," 391–92; Marvin, "Railroads of Central Ohio," 204–7, 213–14.

31. Marvin, "Railroads of Central Ohio," 178.

32. Ibid.,176–81; Erasmus Wilson, ed., *Standard History of Pittsburg, Pennsylvania* (Chicago: H. R. Cornell & Co., 1898), 142.

33. Initially, the Cleveland & Pittsburgh exchanged little freight at Alliance with the Ohio & Pennsylvania and the PRR. Grain from northern Ohio typically flowed north to Cleveland, and then east along Lake Erie and the Erie Canal. By 1858, Ohio beef also went to Cleveland, not Pittsburgh, for shipment east. In 1856, a shipment of iron ore traveled from Lake Champlain, by canal and lake boat, to Cleveland. There, using buckets and wheelbarrows, workers laboriously transferred the cargo into Cleveland & Pittsburgh cars. Most of the ore went south to the Ohio River, and then by boat to steel mills at Wheeling or Pittsburgh, without ever gracing PRR rails. By 1858, transfer crews had upgraded to whisky barrels, sawed in half and fitted with hoisting cables. Still they managed to load no more than ten or fifteen cars a day. By the end of the century, thirty years after the PRR had established control over the Cleveland & Pittsburgh, that number had increased tenfold. For the moment, however, Thomson was far more interested in obtaining access to another rapidly growing lake port.

By 1860, representatives from the Cleveland & Pittsburgh and the Ohio & Pennsylvania (by that time merged into the Pittsburgh, Fort Wayne & Chicago) agreed to pool traffic along the essentially parallel lines between Rochester and Alliance. The cordial relationship between the two railroads was not destined to last, however. In 1862, the owners of the Cleveland & Pittsburgh, anxious to avoid reliance on the Fort Wayne, initiated the construction of their own line between Rochester and Pittsburgh. In the process, the line that was surveyed so closely paralleled that of the Fort Wayne that the Cleveland & Pittsburgh's attorneys asked the courts to condemn more than twenty-three miles of the Fort Wayne's "surplus" right-of-way, within six and a half feet of the existing tracks. Fort Wayne officials, uncertain about the outcome of the case, arranged a consolidation between the two lines. Based on an 1862 agreement, which took effect on April 1, 1863, the two railroads created an executive committee consisting of the presidents and one director from each to oversee the operations of both companies. The coordinated system was able to make good use of duplicate main lines between Rochester and Alliance, Ohio. The Fort Wayne route was ten miles shorter, but the Cleveland & Pittsburgh had the advantage of easier grades, and the PRR later took advantage of that difference by assigning passenger trains and express freights to the former line, while reserving the Cleveland & Pittsburgh for trains carrying coal, ore, and other heavy, low-value cargoes. The Cleveland & Pittsburgh retained its separate identity until March 1918 as part of the transfer of properties from the Pennsylvania Company to the Pennsylvania Railroad. George H. Burgess and Miles C. Kennedy, *Centennial History of the Pennsylvania Railroad Company, 1846–1946* (Philadelphia: Pennsylvania Railroad, 1949), 183–84, 556; James Harrison Kennedy, *A History of the City of Cleveland: Its Settlement, Rise, and Progress, 1796–1896* (Cleveland: The Imperial Press, 1896), 321–28; Joseph Henderson Bausman and John Samuel Duss, *History of Beaver County, Pennsylvania and Its Centennial Celebration*, vol. 1 (New York: Knickerbocker Press, 1904), 255–56; J. Elfreth Watkins, *Pennsylvania Railroad Company, 1846–1896, in its Relation to the Pennsylvania State Canals and Railroads and the Consolidated System East and West of Pittsburgh* (unpublished ms., 1896, original at the Smithsonian Institution, with microfilm copies at HML and in the Penn Central Railroad Collection, M.G. 286, Pennsylvania Historical and Museum Commission, Pennsylvania State Archives, Harrisburg, with an additional microfilm copy in the author's possession, hereafter "Watkins History"), vol. 2, "Cleveland and Pittsburgh Division," 46–47, "Iron Ore and Coal Trade of the Lakes," 68–75.

34. Carl W. Condit, *Chicago, 1930–1970: Building, Planning, and Urban Technology* (Chicago: University of Chicago Press, 1974), 283.

35. Wilson, *Standard History of Pittsburg*, 83, 88, 93, 110, 112, 122, 131–32, 137–38, 211, 263, 791, 958; John Woolf Jordan, *A Century and a Half of Pittsburg and Her People*, vol. 3 (New York: Lewis Publishing Co., 1908), 60–64; Catherine Elizabeth Reiser, *Pittsburgh's Commercial Development, 1800–1850* (Harrisburg: Pennsylvania Historical and Museum Commission, 1951), 180–81.

36. William J. Watt, *The Pennsylvania Railroad in Indiana* (Bloomington: Indiana University Press, 1999), 23.

37. PRR Board of Directors (BOD) Minutes, HML, September 4, 1851.

38. Ibid., April 3, 1852, 151, April 28, 1852, 159, December 21, 1852, 283–84; Wilson, *Standard History of Pittsburg*, 142.

39. On April 11, 1853, the same day that the Ohio & Pennsylvania reached Crestline, the Pennsylvania legislature repealed the law, dating to February 1848, requiring all railroads to be constructed to standard gauge—which in turn enabled the break between standard and Ohio (4' 10") gauge to be set at Pittsburgh, rather than the Ohio border. Watkins History, vol. 2, "Western Pennsylvania Division," 3; Samuel Harden Church, *Corporate History of the Pennsylvania Lines West of Pittsburgh: Comprising Charters, Mortgages, Decrees, Deeds, Leases, Agreements, Ordinances, and Other Papers with Descriptive Text*, vol. 1, (Baltimore: Friedenwald Co., 1898), 93–96; Burgess and Kennedy, *Centennial History*, 60–64, 76–77, 176–77; Marvin, "Railroads of Central Ohio," 227.

40. The small town of Warsaw was a logical choice for the convention. The proposed route of the Fort Wayne & Chicago ran from Fort Wayne through Warsaw. From Warsaw, possible routes headed northwest to Chicago and due west toward Logansport, Indiana; Peoria, Illinois; and Burlington, Iowa.

41. Coverdale & Colpitts, *Corporate, Financial and Construction History of Lines Owned, Operated and Controlled to December 31, 1945*, vol. 3: *Lines West of Pittsburgh* (New York: Coverdale & Colpitts, 1947), 35.

42. Ibid., vol. 3, 8–42.

43. Haupt, *Report of H. Haupt*, 13.

44. Office of the Ohio & Indn. R.R. Co., January 7, 1853, reprinted in PRR BOD Minutes, February 2, 1853, 304.

45. PRR BOD Minutes, December 22, 1852, 285–86, April 13, 1853, 329–34, April 27, 1853, 340, August 17, 1853, 368; Burgess and Kennedy, *Centennial History*, 76–77, 176; Church, *Corporate History*, vol. 1, 94, 96–98; James A. Ward, *J. Edgar Thomson: Master of the Pennsylvania* (Westport, Conn.: Greenwood Press, 1980), 104.

46. *Report of H. Haupt*, 6–7.

47. Robinson quotations in *Report of H. Haupt*, 39 and 39, emphasis in the original.

48. Ibid., 11.

49. Ibid., 30.

50. Roberts quotation in ibid., 44.

51. Ibid., 17.

52. PRR BOD Minutes, May 3, 1854, 458, May 22, 1854, 462–63; Watt, *The Pennsylvania Railroad in Indiana*, 24; William Bender Wilson, *History of the Pennsylvania Railroad Company, with Plan of Organization, Portraits of Officials and Biographical Sketches*, vol. 2 (New York: Henry T. Coates & Co., 1899), 261–67.

53. Church, *Corporate History*, vol. 1, 98–99; Ward, *Master of the Pennsylvania*, 104; Burgess and Kennedy, *Centennial History*, 176.

54. Burgess and Kennedy, *Centennial History*, 176–77.

55. The PRR repaid Thomson in 1862, giving him $47,000 in bonds of the Pittsburgh, Fort Wayne & Chicago Railway, the corporate successor to the three railroads linking Pittsburgh and Chicago. PRR BOD Minutes, March 31, 1856, 140, August 18, 1862, 203–5; William Hasell Wilson, *The Columbia-Philadelphia Railroad and Its Successor* (1896; York, Pa.: American Canal and Transportation Center, 1985); Wilson, *History of the Pennsylvania Railroad*, vol. 2, 173–74.

56. PRR BOD Minutes, June 14, 1856, 157–58.

57. Alvin F. Harlow, *Old Waybills: The Romance of the Express Companies* (New York: D. Appleton-Century Co., 1934), 62–63; Allen Johnson, ed., *Dictionary of American Biography* (New York: Charles Scribner's Sons, 1920); Thomas C. Cochran, *Railroad Leaders, 1845–1890: The Business Mind in Action* (Cambridge, Mass.: Harvard University Press, 1953); *New York Times*, March 22, 1888.

58. PRR BOD Minutes, February 2, 1853, 304–6, March 17, 1858, 308–11, April 14, 1858, 317–20; Burgess and Kennedy, *Centennial History*, 177–78; Ward, *Master of the Pennsylvania*, 104–5; Church, *Corporate History*, vol. 1, 99–106; Watt, *The Pennsylvania Railroad in Indiana*, 26.

59. Burgess and Kennedy, *Centennial History*, 178–79.

60. Charles S. Roberts and David W. Messer, *Triumph VIII: Pittsburgh, 1749–2006* (Baltimore: Barnard, Roberts & Co., 2006), 25–26; Wilson, *History of the Pennsylvania Railroad*, vol. 1, 161.

61. Burgess and Kennedy, *Centennial History*, 83, 101, 109, 291.

62. Roberts and Messer, *Triumph VIII*, 26–27, 96.

63. Taylor, *The Transportation Revolution*, 238.

64. James Franklin Doughty Lanier, *Sketch of the Life of J. F. D. Lanier* (New York: Hosford and Sons, 1870); Chandler, *Henry Varnum Poor*, 88; Watt, *The Pennsylvania Railroad in Indiana*, 27.

65. *New York Times*, July 21, 1869.

66. Thomson's suggestion, one that Poor favored, was to limit a railroad's bonded debt to no more than one-half of total capitalization. Bonds in excess of that amount would be replaced by preferred stock, which carried a guaranteed return, but without voting rights (although, under the Thomson plan, the holders of preferred stock would be able to select one director). As Thomson, Poor, and others emphasized, preferred stock might be safer and more remunerative than second or third mortgage bonds. Chandler, *Henry Varnum Poor*, 136–37.

67. Watt, *The Pennsylvania Railroad in Indiana*, 26–27.

68. George H. Burgess and Miles C. Kennedy, *Centennial History of the Pennsylvania Railroad Company, 1846–1946* (Philadelphia: Pennsylvania Railroad, 1949), 178–84, 195–96; James A. Ward, *J. Edgar Thomson, Master of the Pennsylvania* (Westport, Conn.: Greenwood Press, 1980), 144; Church, *Corporate History*, vol. 1 (Baltimore: Friedenwald Co., 1898), vol. 1, 92–113.

69. Watt, *The Pennsylvania Railroad in Indiana*, 36, 74.

70. The account that follows will emphasize, in considerable detail, the development of the companies east of Cincinnati and Columbus, as they were the ones in which PRR officials played the most active role. Farther west, toward Indianapolis and St. Louis, local promoters exerted more influence, only later bringing what were effectively complete railroad systems into the PRR network. Their activities accordingly mandate a more summary overview, both here and in later chapters. The information in the following sections is largely drawn from Coverdale & Colpitts, *Corporate, Financial and Construction History*, vol. 3; J. C. Morris, ed., *Thirty-Fifth Annual Report of the Commissioner of Railroads and Telegraphs to the Governor of the State of Ohio for the Year 1902, December 31, 1902, Part II: History of the Railroads of Ohio* (Springfield, Ohio: Springfield Publishing Co., 1902); Marvin, "Railroads of Central Ohio"; Christopher T. Baer, "A General Chronology of the Pennsylvania Railroad Company Predecessors and

Successors and Its Historical Context," http://www.prrths.com/Hagley/ PRR_hagley_intro.htm; Victor M. Bogle, "Railroad Building in Indiana, 1850–1855," *Indiana Magazine of History* 58 (September 1962); the PRR corporate genealogy described in the Interstate Commerce Commission Valuation Reports, 1915–18, ed. Robert T. Netzlof, available at http:// rnetzlof.pennsyrr.com/corphist/index.html; and Samuel Harden Church, *Corporate History of the Pennsylvania Lines West of Pittsburgh:, Comprising Charters, Mortgages, Decrees, Deeds, Leases, Agreements, Ordinances, and Other Papers with Descriptive Text* (Baltimore: Friedenwald Co., 1898–1906). The Church history consists of twelve volumes, plus an index (volume 13), issued between 1898 and 1906. Church compiled three additional volumes between 1918 and 1926—a different volume 13, plus volume 14 and 15, sixteen volumes in all.

71. Henry Wadsworth Longfellow, "Catawba Wine," *The Complete Poetical Works of Longfellow* (Cambridge, Mass: Houghton Mifflin, 1920), 196–97.

72. Taylor, *The Transportation Revolution*, 71–73; North, *Economic Growth*, 192.

73. B&O officials routinely handed westbound freight to Ohio River steamboats rather than to the Central Ohio in an attempt to capture the corresponding eastbound traffic and keep it away from the PRR. Such practices contributed to the Central Ohio's financial difficulties. Marvin, "Railroads of Central Ohio," 230–68; James D. Dilts, *The Great Road: The Building of the Baltimore and Ohio, the Nation's First Railroad, 1828–1853* (Stanford, Calif.: Stanford University Press, 1993), 322–36.

74. "Marietta & Cincinnati Railroad," Ohio History Central, July 1, 2005, http://www.ohiohistorycentral.org/entry.php?rec=750, accessed on June 25, 2010; *Cincinnati, Washington & Baltimore R. Co. v. Hoffines*, Ohio Supreme Court, December 10, 1889, in J. C. Thomson, ed., *The American and English Railroad Cases: A Collection of all the Railroad Cases in the Courts of Last Resort in America and England*, vol. 40 (Northport, N.Y.: Edward Thompson Co., 1890), 229.

75. *An Act to Incorporate the Hempfield Rail Road Company, with the Supplements Thereto, and the Act of the Virginia Legislature, Granting the Right of Way Through that State* (Philadelphia: John C. Clark, 1853).

76. Fernon, "Report to J. Edgar Thomson," 6.

77. PRR BOD Minutes, September 21, 1852, 238–39, February 2, 1853, 307–8.

78. *Album of Genealogy and Biography, Cook County, Illinois, with Portraits*, 13th ed. (Chicago: La Salle Book Co., 1900), 96.

79. Julianna R. Wood and Richard D. Wood, *Biographical Sketch of Richard D. Wood*, vol. 2 (Philadelphia: Lippincott's Press, 1871), February 4, 1853, 51.

80. *Sharpless v. the Mayor of Philadelphia*, 21 Penn. 147 (1853), at 169.

81. Hartz, *Economic Policy*, 113–22; "Supreme Court of Pennsylvania at Pittsburg, September, 1853. Sharpless et al vs. The Mayor, &c., of Philadelphia," American Law Register (1852–1891) 2 (November 1853): 27–43.

82. PRR BOD Minutes, June 30, 1852, 208–10, September 21, 1852, 238–39, January 31, 1853, 302, February 2, 1853, 307–8, March 23, 1853, 322, April 13, 1853, 330–31, April 25, 1853, 338; Ward, *Master of the Pennsylvania*, 106; Burgess and Kennedy, *Centennial History*, 77–79, 87–88, 188.

83. The merger was also planned to include the Chartiers Valley Railroad, providing a connection to Pittsburgh. Allegheny County provided $150,000 in assistance to the Chartiers Valley, with the City of Pittsburgh contributing an equal amount. PRR BOD Minutes, November 12, 1856, 188–89 (quote), November 24, 1856, 192–93; Wilson, *Standard History of Pittsburg*, 142.

84. PRR BOD Minutes, December 23, 1857, 282, January 6, 1858, 288; John E. Pixton, Jr., "Faith *vs.* Economics: The Marietta and Cincinnati

Railroad, 1845–1883," *Ohio Historical Quarterly* 66 (January 1957): 1–10, quote at 3.

85. John Hulme, "To the President and Directors of the Pennsylvania Rail Road Company," February 15, 1858, in PRR BOD Minutes, February 17, 1858, 301–4.

86. In 1882, the B&O finally acquired the Marietta & Cincinnati. The company never completed its extension from Marietta north to Bellaire, although the PRR later occupied a portion of the route. In 1871, the B&O also gained control of the Hempfield Railroad's route between Wheeling and Washington, Pennsylvania, renaming it the Wheeling, Pittsburgh & Baltimore Railroad. Dilts, *The Great Road*, 447n9; Pixton, "Faith *vs.* Economics," 2–4; John F. Stover, *History of the Baltimore and Ohio Railroad* (West Lafayette, Ind.: Purdue University Press, 1987), 147–48; Marvin, "Railroads of Central Ohio," 238.

87. John Stirling Fisher and Chase Mellen, *A Builder of the West: The Life of General William Jackson Palmer* (Caldwell, Id.: Caxton Printers, 1939), 21–25, 50; Marvin, "Railroads of Central Ohio," 228.

88. Hulme, "To the President and Directors," 301–4.

89. William Henry Perrin, *History of Delaware County and Ohio* (Chicago: O. L. Baskin & Co., 1880), 255; *Thirty-Eighth Annual Report of the Commissioner of Railroads and Telegraphs to the Governor of the State of Ohio for the Year 1905* (Springfield, Ohio: Springfield Publishing Co., 1906), 59, 77.

90. Burgess and Kennedy, *Centennial History*, 77; Howard W. Schotter, *The Growth and Development of the Pennsylvania Railroad Company: A Review of the Charter and Annual Reports of the Pennsylvania Railroad Company 1846 to 1926, Inclusive* (Philadelphia: Allen, Lane & Scott, 1927), 39–40.

91. The PRR later acquired a section of the original Springfield, Mt. Vernon & Pittsburgh, linking Delaware, Ohio, and Loudonville, Ohio. The route between Springfield and Delaware came under the control of the New York Central, but caused no serious harm to the PRR's strategic interests. PRR BOD Minutes, June 22, 1855, 83–84, December 26, 1855, 119, March 19, 1856, 138, March 31, 1856, 139–40, June 25, 1856, 160; Burgess and Kennedy, *Centennial History*, 77; Ward, *Master of the Pennsylvania*, 106; "An Act to Incorporate the Springfield and Mansfield Railroad Company," March 21, 1850; George B. Wright, ed., *Annual Report of the Commissioner of Railroads and Telegraphs, for the Year 1870*, vol. 1 (Columbus, Ohio: Nevins and Myers, 1870), 385–87; Coverdale & Colpitts, *Corporate, Financial and Construction History*, vol. 3, 273–87; Marvin, "Railroads of Central Ohio," 225, 228.

92. Marvin, "Railroads of Central Ohio," 264.

93. Henry Howe, *Historical Collections of Ohio, in Three Volumes: An Encyclopedia of the State*, vol. 2 (Columbus, Ohio: Henry Howe & Son, 1891), 268, 611; Lee, *History of the City of Columbus*, 268; Taylor, *Centennial History of Columbus*, vol. 1, 355–56.

94. PRR BOD Minutes, December 3, 1853, 404–5, February 22, 1854, 437; Marvin, "Railroads of Central Ohio," 228–29.

95. Marvin, "Railroads of Central Ohio," 164–65.

96. Ibid., 262–63.

97. Marvin, "Railroads of Central Ohio," 259, 265.

98. George Thornton Fleming, *History of Pittsburg and Environs*, vol. 2 (New York: American Historical Society, 1922), 160–62.

99. Thomas Cushing, *History of Allegheny County, Pennsylvania, Including its Early Settlement and Progress to the Present Time; a Description of its Historic and Interesting Localities; its Cities, Towns and Villages; Religious, Educational, Social and Military History; Mining, Manufacturing and Commercial Interests, Improvements, Resources, Statistics, etc.; also, Biographies of Many of its Representative Citizens*, vol. 2 (Chicago: A Warner,

854 Notes to Pages 268–274

1889), 214–15; Fleming, *History of Pittsburg and Environs*, vol. 2, 112–13, 162–63, 202; John Newton Boucher, *History of Westmoreland County, Pennsylvania*, vol. 1 (New York: Lewis Publishing Co., 1906), 270; Edward Payson Cowan, *Memorial Volume, James Kennedy Moorhead* (Pittsburgh: Jos. Eichbaum & Co., 1885).

100. PRR BOD Minutes, February 8, 1854, 432; Wilson, *Standard History of Pittsburg*, 142.

101. Walter Rumsey Marvin, "The Steubenville and Indiana Railroad: The Pennsylvania's Middle Route to the Middle West," *Ohio Historical Quarterly* 66 (January 1957): 11–21, at 11–12, 19.

102. E. Elza Scott, "An Historical Sketch of Richard 'Graybeard' Wells and His Pioneer Farm and Family," http://www.brookecountywvgenealogy.org/richardwells.html, accessed on June 14, 2010; Mary Donaldson Sinclair, *Pioneer Days* (Steubenville, Ohio: D. J. Sinclair, 1962), 55–56, 155–57.

103. J. H. Newton, G. G. Nichols, and A. G. Sprankle, eds., *History of the Pan-Handle, West Virginia, Being Historical Collections of the Counties of Ohio, Brooke, Marshall and Hancock, West Virginia* (Wheeling: J. A. Caldwell, 1879), 350–51.

104. Tom Scott's ability to cause mischief on the Steubenville & Indiana was limited by the short duration of his vice presidency. Elected to that office in May 1857, he was replaced by Joseph D. Potts, another PRR stalwart, in January 1858. Samuel Richey Kamm, "The Civil War Career of Thomas A. Scott" (Ph.D. diss., University of Pennsylvania, 1940), 6–7; Samuel Harden Church, *Corporate History of the Pennsylvania Lines West of Pittsburgh:, Comprising Charters, Mortgages, Decrees, Deeds, Leases, Agreements, Ordinances, and Other Papers with Descriptive Text*, vol. 3 (Baltimore: Friedenwald Co., 1899), 22–30; Burgess and Kennedy, *Centennial History*, 188–89; Marvin, "The Steubenville and Indiana Railroad," 17–18, 20.

105. The details were far more complex, particularly as there were numerous other creditors. In September 1859, the Harrison County Court of Common Pleas, responding to a suit by the Baltimore investors, appointed PRR ally Thomas Jewett as receiver. His brother Hugh was at the same time the receiver of the Central Ohio Railroad, which had also succumbed to bankruptcy in 1859. At a February 1864 foreclosure sale, Thomson, prominent New York attorney Henry M. Alexander, and former Ohio attorney general George Wythe McCook purchased the S&I for $1.9 million. In January 1867, the PRR board finally resolved the S&I's outstanding debts and provided for a new $6 million mortgage to upgrade the line. The agreement never took effect, however, and the Steubenville & Indiana bankruptcy was not formally discharged until 1870. Two years earlier, on April 30, 1868, Thomson oversaw a merger of the S&I into the Pittsburgh, Cincinnati & St. Louis Railway, with the PRR firmly in control of the company. Well before 1868, however, PRR and Steubenville & Indiana officials had made provisions to operate through service between Pittsburgh and the west. In May 1864, as part of the proposed S&I reorganization, the company purchased a 50 percent stake in the portion of the Central Ohio Railroad line linking Newark and Columbus. In January of the following year, the Jewett brothers, one representing the S&I and the other the Central Ohio, agreed to jointly operate the line. That was just as well, as the Central Ohio soon fell under the influence of the Baltimore & Ohio. Bankrupt since 1859, it was reorganized in January 1866 and leased to the B&O in November of that year, giving the PRR's archival access to Columbus and later to Chicago, as well. PRR BOD Minutes, January 9, 1867, 96; Marvin, "Railroads of Central Ohio," 269.

106. In the process, John S. King and Ambrose W. Thompson, who had earlier agreed to construct the railroad in exchange for $500,000 in bonds, transferred their contract to William Thaw of the Western Transportation Company. The precise details were both convoluted and contentious, and they are described in great detail in *McElrath, et al. versus The Pittsburg and Steubenville Railroad Company et al.*, in P. Frazer Smith, ed., *Pennsylvania State Reports, vol. LV, Comprising Cases Adjudged in the Supreme Court of Pennsylvania*, vol. 5 (Philadelphia: Kay & Brother, 1868), 189–209; PRR BOD Minutes, April 15, 1857, 223.

107. Burgess and Kennedy, *Centennial History*, 190–91.

108. Ibid., 192; Coverdale & Colpitts, *Corporate, Financial and Construction History*, vol. 3, 364–65.

109. Church, *Corporate History*, vol. 3, 1–2, 8–21; Burgess and Kennedy, *Centennial History*, 107, 189–92, 324–25; Ward, *Master of the Pennsylvania*, 178; PRR BOD Minutes, August 20, 1856, 170.

110. Burgess and Kennedy, *Centennial History*, 192; Coverdale & Colpitts, *Corporate, Financial and Construction History*, vol. 3, 364–65.

111. Linda A. D. Olsen, "The Panhandle Division: An Early History," *The Keystone* 23 (Winter 1990): 9–10. See also Thomas M. Olsen, Linda A. D. Olsen, and James J. D. Lynch, *The Panhandle Division Main Line, 1942* (Steubenville, Ohio: Public Library of Steubenville and Jefferson County, 1999).

112. Marvin, "Railroads of Central Ohio," 216, 271–78, 296–97; Wylie J. Daniels, *The Village at the End of the Road: A Chapter in Early Indiana Railroad History* (Indianapolis: Indiana Historical Society, 1938), 57–65.

113. PRR BOD Minutes, February 17, 1854, 433. Marvin, "Railroads of Central Ohio," 288–90.

114. The cooperation became even closer in 1864, when the Indianapolis, Pittsburgh & Cleveland and the Bellefontaine & Indiana merged into the Bellefontaine Railway, still known as the Bee Line. In May 1868, the Bellefontaine merged with its primary eastern connection, the CC&C, to create the Cleveland, Columbus, Cincinnati & Indianapolis Railway. In 1889, the line became part of the Cleveland, Cincinnati, Chicago & St. Louis Railway (the "Big Four"), a system that was closely tied to the New York Central. Daniels, *The Village at the End of the Road*, 85; Marvin, "Railroads of Central Ohio," 216–20, 227, 292–94.

115. Marvin, "Railroads of Central Ohio," 293–94.

116. Taylor, *Centennial History of Columbus*, vol. 1, 364–66.

117. The gauge break would not last for long, however. As early as April 1856, the directors of the Steubenville & Indiana had agreed to widen their tracks to Ohio gauge, principally in order to connect with the Cleveland & Pittsburgh Railroad. That decision permitted uninterrupted Ohio-gauge service from Pittsburgh to Indianapolis, and west as far as Terre Haute, Indiana. Marvin, "Railroads of Central Ohio," 278–88, 293–94, 297–301.

118. Biographical information regarding Benjamin E. Smith is extraordinarily difficult to obtain, largely because his eventual insanity dissuaded the publication of the same type of praise-laden biographies that are generally available for his contemporaries. Smith's primary investment south of Columbus was the Mineral Railroad (later the Columbus & Hocking Valley Railroad), which he helped organize in 1865. The Hocking Valley eventually carried coal north to Lake Erie, and its activities meshed with Smith's investments in southern Ohio. The company, which eventually became the Hocking Valley Railway, many years later came under the control of the Chesapeake & Ohio Railway. Edward H. Miller, *The Hocking Valley Railway* (Athens: Ohio University Press, 2007), 14–12, 33; Marvin, "Railroads of Central Ohio," 303–9.

119. *The Governors of Ohio* (Columbus: Ohio Historical Society, 1954); Richard H. Abbott, *Ohio's War Governors* (Columbus: Ohio State University Press, 1962).

120. Richard T. Wallis, *The Pennsylvania Railroad at Bay: William Riley McKeen and the Terre Haute & Indianapolis Railroad* (Bloomington: Indiana University Press, 2001), 2–5.

121. In 1859, Cleveland, Columbus & Cincinnati officials broke their alliance with the Little Miami and the Columbus & Xenia in favor of a

Cincinnati-to-Cleveland route that involved the Cincinnati, Hamilton & Dayton; the Sandusky, Dayton & Cincinnati Railroad (the former Mad River & Lake Erie, after 1858); and the Springfield, Mt. Vernon & Pittsburgh (which the CC&C would purchase in 1861). In 1860, CC&C officials severed their ties to the Columbus & Xenia, largely because of the latter railroad's support for the Steubenville & Indiana (which drew traffic toward the PRR at Pittsburgh, and away from the CC&C route to Cleveland). As a result, representatives from the Little Miami and the Cincinnati, Hamilton & Dayton agreed to form a traffic pool on their parallel lines. Marvin, "Railroads of Central Ohio," 207–10, 223–25.

122. Marvin, "Railroads of Central Ohio," 158–59.

123. Most of the original Eaton & Hamilton route, to the southeast of Richmond Junction, was now relegated to the status of a branch line. The Dayton & Western Railroad leased a short portion of the Richmond & Miami in order to maintain access to Richmond. The Eaton & Hamilton (the Ohio company) also relied on the Richmond & Miami for access to Richmond. In November 1864, the Eaton & Hamilton (the Indiana company) leased the Richmond & Miami. Frazer E. Wilson, *History of Darke County, Ohio, from Its Earliest Settlement to the Present Time*, vol. 1 (Milford, Ohio: Hobart Publishing Co., 1914), 389–90, 491; Marvin, "Railroads of Central Ohio," 309.

124. Following the 1859 bankruptcy of the New York & Erie Rail Road, the company was reorganized in 1861 as the Erie Railway.

125. In March 1863, the Columbus & Xenia leased the Dayton & Western (including that carrier's access to Richmond over the Richmond & Miami), creating a through route between Columbus and Richmond (via Xenia and Dayton) that was roughly parallel to, and to the south of, the line established by the Columbus & Indianapolis and the Richmond & Covington route through Bradford.

126. By December 1864, as discussed above, the more northerly Bellefontaine & Indiana and Indianapolis, Pittsburgh & Cleveland railroads responded to the new competitive threat with a merger of their own, creating the Bellefontaine Railway (the Bee Line) and drifting ever closer to the Lake Shore interests and, ultimately, a formal association with the New York Central. Marvin, "Railroads of Central Ohio," 309–10.

127. The promoters of the Logansport & Pacific Railway (organized in March 1853 as the Logansport & Pacific Railroad, and soon renamed) were also interested in a connection with the Peoria & Oquawka Railroad (incorporated in 1849, with an intended destination of Oquawka, Illinois, on the Mississippi River, north of Burlington, Iowa).

128. Coverdale & Colpitts, *Corporate, Financial and Construction History*, vol. 3, 366–67.

129. The Cincinnati & Chicago Railroad was the product of a May 1854 merger between the Cincinnati, Cambridge & Chicago Short Line Railway and the Cincinnati, New Castle & Michigan Railroad, both incorporated in 1853. By 1854, the Cincinnati & Chicago was offering through service to Cincinnati, in conjunction with the Richmond & Miami Railroad, the Eaton & Hamilton Railroad, and the Cincinnati, Hamilton & Dayton Railroad.

130. Coverdale & Colpitts, *Corporate, Financial and Construction History*, vol. 3, 366–67.

131. Ibid., 367–68.

132. Leander J. Monks, ed., *Courts and Lawyers of Indiana*, vol. 2 (Indianapolis: Federal Publishing Co., 1916), 586, 749.

133. Benjamin Homans, *The United States Railroad Directory, for 1856* (New York: B. Homans, 1856), 104, 130.

134. The promoters of the Illinois company planned to meet at Logansport the tracks of the Lake Erie, Wabash & St. Louis Railroad, whose supporters intended to build a direct line from Toledo southwest to the Illinois state line near Danville, Illinois, with the Toledo & Illinois Railroad continuing westward toward the Mississippi River, at Quincy, Illinois, and Keokuk, Iowa. In 1865, they were merged into the Toledo, Wabash & Western Railway and became an integral part of the Wabash system.

135. During the 1860s, the line through Peoria went through several incarnations before ending up partly in the PRR camp. In September 1862, New York banker John Stewart Kennedy organized the Toledo, Logansport & Burlington Rail*way*, to assume control over the Indiana portion of the route, between Logansport and State Line. By the spring of 1864, the original Peoria & Oquawka line in Illinois had been divided, with the portion west of Peoria reorganized as the Peoria & Burlington Railroad, later a part of the Chicago, Burlington & Quincy Railroad. The section to the east of Peoria was reincarnated as the Toledo, Peoria & Warsaw Railway. By October 1868, that company had completed a new alignment across Illinois, linking Peoria with Warsaw, across the Missouri River from Keokuk, Iowa. A few months later, the Toledo, Peoria & Warsaw, in conjunction with the Columbus, Chicago & Indiana Central Railway, the Des Moines Valley Railroad, and the Wabash & Western Railway, jointly organized the Keokuk & Hamilton Bridge Company to provide access to Iowa and ultimately the eastern end of the Union Pacific, at Omaha, Nebraska. PRR officials—particularly J. Edgar Thomson and Tom Scott—were now very much interested in the potential of that route, and the PRR board accordingly invested $150,000 in the Toledo, Peoria & Warsaw. Thomson and Scott also invested personally in the Keokuk & Hamilton Bridge Company, along with such business associates as Benjamin Smith and Andrew Carnegie.

The eventual disposition of the route between Logansport and the Mississippi River was extraordinarily complex, with the eastern third (in Indiana) going to the PRR, the middle third (between the Illinois border and Peoria) coming under the control of the Toledo, Peoria & Western, and the western third (from Peoria to the Missouri River) passing to the Chicago, Burlington & Quincy. The basic outlines are as follows:

In Indiana: In September 1854, the Logansport & Pacific Railway (i.e., the portion of the route in Indiana) became the Logansport, Peoria & Burlington Railway. That name was in turn changed to the Toledo, Logansport & Burlington Rail*road* in June 1858 (and then to the Toledo, Logansport & Burlington Rail*way*, in September 1862). It was that Indiana company that became a part of the Columbus & Indiana Central Railway and later passed to the PRR.

In Illinois (east of Peoria): In February 1861, the Peoria & Oquawka was renamed the Logansport, Peoria & Burlington Railroad. The March 1863 division of that line caused the portion east of Peoria to retain the same name. In May 1864, the company was reorganized as the Toledo, Peoria & Warsaw Railway. In December 1865, that company gained control of the Mississippi & Wabash Railroad. The Toledo, Peoria & Warsaw (the line from Peoria west to the Mississippi River) went bankrupt in 1874. In December 1879, the company's creditors established the Toledo, Peoria & Western Railroad, and they acquired control of the Toledo, Peoria & Warsaw the following May. The Wabash, St. Louis & Pacific Railway, then part of Jay Gould's expanding western rail empire, immediately leased the Toledo, Peoria & Warsaw. The Wabash went bankrupt in 1883 and lost control of the Toledo, Peoria & Western. In 1893, the PRR and the Chicago, Burlington & Quincy purchased jointly a controlling interest in the Toledo, Peoria & Western.

In Illinois (west of Peoria): In February 1861, the Peoria & Oquawka was renamed the Logansport, Peoria & Burlington Railroad. The March 1863 division of that line caused the portion west of Peoria to become the Peoria & Burlington Railroad. This is the portion that eventually became part of the Chicago, Burlington & Quincy.

Information is from PRR BOD Minutes, March 17, 1858, 311 (quote); Grant, *Follow the Flag*, 15–19, 63–69; Watt, *The Pennsylvania Railroad in Indiana*, 87; Christopher T. Baer's PRR Chronology; and the "Lists and Family Trees of North American Railroad Companies," http://laurent.aublette.free.fr/en/intro_en.html, accessed on April 25, 2010.

136. The only portion of the original Eaton & Hamilton/Richmond & Miami/Cincinnati, Logansport & Chicago/Cincinnati & Chicago (the names are as of the spring of 1854) route to Chicago that remained under the control of the Cincinnati, Hamilton & Dayton was the Ohio segment of the Eaton & Hamilton, reorganized in May 1866 as the Cincinnati, Richmond & Chicago Railroad. It, too, would eventually pass to the Pennsylvania Railroad, but not until the 1880s. Coverdale & Colpitts, *Corporate, Financial and Construction History*, vol. 3, 368.

137. Based on his extensive examination of the minutes of the various companies involved, Christopher Baer has observed that the Chicago & Great Eastern bonds remained in New York, eventually coming under the control of investment bankers such as William R. Fosdick, James Alfred Roosevelt (Theodore Roosevelt's uncle), and Adrian G. Iselin (who during the 1870s, after the PRR gained control of the successor company, the Columbus, Chicago & Indiana Central, still merited a seat on that company's board of directors, along with Benjamin Smith and William Dennison—although it should be noted that the directors had little influence on corporate policy and served principally to oversee the allocation of lease and interest payments). *New York Times*, July 11, 1868; Edward Vernon, ed., *American Railroad Manual* (New York: American Railroad Manual Co., 1873), 422–23; Marvin, "Railroads of Central Ohio," 310.

138. The company was chartered under the archaic spelling, Lawrenceburgh & Indianapolis Rail-Road.

139. Federal Writers' Project, United States Works Progress Administration, *Indiana: A Guide to the Hoosier State* (New York: Oxford University Press, 1941), 453.

140. Unlike the inclined planes on the Philadelphia & Columbia and the Allegheny Portage Railroad, designers did not employ a cable hoisting mechanism. Until 1848, horses raised and lowered the cars. In that year, workers installed a cogwheel system that worked well, until it was replaced in 1868 by the powerful locomotive *Reuben Wells*, specially designed for the Madison incline. Despite steady improvements in motive power technology, the incline continued to tax the nerve of operating crews, particularly on descents. Daniels, *The Village at the End of the Road*, 17–18; Phil Anderson, *Pioneer Railroad of the Northwest: History of the Jeffersonville, Madison and Indianapolis Railroad* (Madison, Ind.: Jefferson County Historical Society, 2005), 4–7, 23–26; Freda L. Bridenstine, *The "Madison and Indianapolis": Indiana's First Railroad* (Madison, Ind.: Jefferson County Historical Society, n.d.), 1–27.

141. Daniels, *The Village at the End of the Road*, 18–45; Anderson, *Pioneer Railroad*, 8–10; Bridenstine, *The "Madison and Indianapolis,"* 28–47.

142. Technically, the company was at that time known as the Madison, Indianapolis & Peru Railroad, following a merger, effective January 1, 1854, between the Madison & Indianapolis and the Peru & Indianapolis Railroad. The merger was dissolved in November 1855.

143. Daniels, *The Village at the End of the Road*, 69–70, 86; Anderson, *Pioneer Railroad*, 19–20.

144. Wallis, *The Pennsylvania Railroad at Bay*, 3–4.

145. Brough was also largely responsible for providing the railroads serving Indianapolis with equal access to the city. The Indianapolis Union Railway Company, organized in December 1849, constructed the first union depot in the United States.

146. Wallis, *The Pennsylvania Railroad at Bay*, 5–7; Daniels, *The Village at the End of the Road*, 78–82, 99–104; Anderson, *Pioneer Railroad*, 14.

147. In 1877, the Evansville & Crawfordsville became part of the Chicago & Eastern Illinois Railroad. It was never affiliated with the PRR system. Wallis, *The Pennsylvania Railroad at Bay*, 5–8.

148. Ibid., 5–7.

149. Transshipment was necessary at Dunkirk, given the Erie's six-foot track gauge. After June 1864, following the completion of the Atlantic & Great Western to Dayton, the Erie relied on the A&GW—Cincinnati, Hamilton & Dayton—Ohio & Mississippi broad-gauge route to St. Louis. Wallis, *The Pennsylvania Railroad at Bay*, 10–11.

150. Fisher and Mellen, *A Builder of the West*, 61–62.

151. *New York Times*, June 11, 1875, January 31, 1880; *Pennsylvania Railroad Co. v. St. Louis, Alton & Terre Haute Railroad Co.*, 118 U.S. 290 (1886).

152. Wallis, *The Pennsylvania Railroad at Bay*, 12.

153. Evelyn Foster Morneweck, *Chronicles of Stephen Foster's Family*, vol. 2 (Pittsburgh, Pa.: Davis & Warde, 1944), 517–18.

154. Details of trip based on descriptions provided in *Excursion Trip of the Directors and Officers of the Pennsylvania R.R. Co., October 3, 1859* (Philadelphia: s.n., 1859) (a souvenir booklet presented to the participants), quotes at 3.

155. Richmond E. Myers, "The Development of Transportation in the Susquehanna River Valley: A Geographical Study, 1700–1900" (Ph.D. diss., Pennsylvania State University, 1951), 123, 127.

156. *Excursion Trip of the Directors and Officers*, 26.

Chapter 8. Conflict

1. As historians George Rogers Taylor and Irene D. Neu observed, the war's "military requirements merely reinforced a movement which was gathering momentum in any case." Taylor and Neu, *The American Railroad Network, 1861–1890* (Urbana: University of Illinois Press, 2003), 6.

2. Thomas Weber, *The Northern Railroads in the Civil War, 1861–1865* (Bloomington: Indiana University Press, 1999), 59–60.

3. In contrast, Thomson's personal assistant, William Jackson Palmer, was an ardent abolitionist who, in December 1859, nearly lost his life when rioters disrupted an antislavery convention in Philadelphia. John Stirling Fisher and Chase Mellen, *A Builder of the West: The Life of General William Jackson Palmer* (Caldwell, Id.: Caxton Printers, 1939), 63–64.

4. James A. Ward, *J. Edgar Thomson, Master of the Pennsylvania* (Westport, Conn.: Greenwood Press, 1980), 124–25.

5. The PRR's officers nonetheless harbored enough anxiety about the course of the war that they made plans for removing the corporate records from Philadelphia should Confederate armies threaten that city. Reminisces of Bayard Butler, in Frank J. Firth to J. Elfreth Watkins, March 19, 1897; Theodore N. Ely to Watkins, June 23, 1897; both in Watkins Collection, Smithsonian Institution, Box 2, folder 2.

6. Robert L. Gunnarsson, *The Story of the Northern Central Railway, from Baltimore to Lake Ontario* (Sykesville, Md.: Greenberg Publishing, 1991), 49.

7. Harold R. Manakee, *Maryland in the Civil War* (Baltimore: Maryland Historical Society, 1961), 24–29.

8. Samuel Richey Kamm, "The Civil War Career of Thomas A. Scott" (Ph.D. diss., University of Pennsylvania, 1940), 27; Manakee, *Maryland in the Civil War*, 30–38; Leslie R. Tucker, *Major General Isaac Ridgeway Trimble: Biography of a Baltimore Confederate* (Jefferson, N.C.: McFarland, 2005), 99–110.

9. The PRR did not yet control the PW&B, but it did depend heavily on that line for freight and passenger traffic south of Philadelphia. Ward,

Master of the Pennsylvania, 126–27; Manakee, *Maryland in the Civil War*, 47–49; Weber, *The Northern Railroads*, 35–36.

10. "Undaunted, Carnegie climbed back into the cab and gave the signal for the train to move on," writes Carnegie biographer Joseph Frazier Wall. "With blood streaming down his face, Carnegie could sense the full drama of bringing the first troops into Washington since it had been isolated by Secessionist mobs in Baltimore." Joseph Frazier Wall, *Andrew Carnegie* (New York: Oxford University Press, 1970), 160.

11. As Nasaw has observed, Carnegie (who later hired a substitute in order to avoid the draft) was anxious to convince Americans that he had seen "combat" and that—like so many others—he had been wounded in the cause of liberty and Union. Nasaw, *Andrew Carnegie* (New York: Penguin Press, 2006), 72.

12. Ivan E. Frantz, Jr., "The Pennsylvania Railroad and the Civil War," *The Keystone* 38, no. 3 (Autumn 2005): 9–28; Herbert C. Archdeacon, "Two Civil War Railroaders," *The Keystone* 38, no. 3 (Autumn 2005): 29–31; Ward, *Master of the Pennsylvania*, 127; Kamm, "The Civil War Career," 34, 41–42.

13. Weber, *The Northern Railroads*, 37.

14. Despite its indirect nature, the Allentown Route, in tandem with the Northern Central, bypassed the difficult interchange and gauge break at Philadelphia. Unfortunately for Cameron, it also alienated Joint Companies officials, who were anxious to maintain the Camden & Amboy's state-sanctioned monopoly (an appeal to states rights' doctrine that would have resonated with Cameron's enemies in the Confederacy) and who were correspondingly no friends of the Republicans in Lincoln's administration.

15. Ward, *Master of the Pennsylvania*, 128–29; Kamm, "The Civil War Career," 38, 46–47, 50, 66–82, 84.

16. Christopher R. Gabel, *Railroad Generalship: Foundations of Civil War Strategy* (Fort Leavenworth, Kans.: U.S. Army Command and General Staff College, 1997), 7–14; Weber, *The Northern Railroads*, 134–37.

17. Weber, *The Northern Railroads*, 137–42.

18. General Benjamin Franklin Butler referred to those former slaves as "contrabands" in order to bypass the terms of the 1850 Fugitive Slave Act and reassure Northern whites that the intent of war was an effort to restore the Union, not to abolish slavery.

19. Herman Haupt, *Reminiscences of General Herman Haupt* (Milwaukee, Wisc.: Wright & Joys, 1901), 49.

20. For a thorough account of Haupt's Civil War experiences, see Haupt, *Reminiscences*, and Weber, *The Northern Railroads*, 137–68.

21. "Biographical Sketch of Herman Haupt," in Watkins Collection, Smithsonian Institution, Box 2, folder 2; Ivan E. Frantz, Jr., "The Pennsylvania Railroad and the Civil War," *The Keystone* 38 (Autumn 2005): 9–28, at 15; Herbert C. Archdeacon, "Two Civil War Railroaders," *The Keystone* 38 (Autumn 2005): 29–33, at 30–31.

22. Gabel, *Railroad Generalship*, 14–20.

23. Frantz, "The Pennsylvania Railroad and the Civil War"; Archdeacon, "Two Civil War Railroaders."

24. Later PRR presidents tended to be Republican, as well. The exceptions were Alexander J. Cassatt (president between 1899 and 1906) and Samuel Rea (1913–25), who were Democrats.

25. Kamm provides an alternate explanation for Scott's second trip west. In that version, both Stanton and his former law partner, Peter H. Watson, were so disappointed with Scott's performance that Watson threatened to resign his post in the War Department—causing Stanton to send Scott west until tempers had cooled. Kamm, "The Civil War Career," 2, 83–124.

26. Ibid., 130–31.

27. Dan Cupper, *Rockville Bridge: Rails Across the Susquehanna* (Halifax, Pa.: Withers Publishing, 2002), 15; George H. Burgess and Miles C. Kennedy, *Centennial History of the Pennsylvania Railroad Company, 1846–1946* (Philadelphia: Pennsylvania Railroad, 1949), 138–39; Paul J. Westhaeffer, *History of the Cumberland Valley Railroad, 1835–1919* (Washington, D.C.: Washington Chapter of the National Railway Historical Society, 1979), 65–84.

28. Kamm, "The Civil War Career," 134–39; Weber, *The Northern Railroads*, 130–33.

29. PRR Board of Directors (BOD) Minutes, Pennsylvania Railroad Company Collection, call no. 1807/1810, Hagley Museum and Library, Wilmington, Delaware (hereafter cited as HML), April 1, 1863, 295 (quote), April 6, 1864, 379; Russell F. Weigley, "The Border City in the Civil War, 1854–1865," in Weigley, ed., *Philadelphia: A 300-Year History* (New York: W. W. Norton, 1982), 307–416, at 408–9; Frederick M. Binder, "Philadelphia's Free Military School," *Pennsylvania History* 17 (October 1950): 281–91.

30. Kamm, "The Civil War Career," 164–75; Frantz, "The Pennsylvania Railroad and the Civil War"; Archdeacon, "Two Civil War Railroaders"; Weber, *The Northern Railroads*, 181–86.

31. J. Elfreth Watkins, *Pennsylvania Railroad Company, 1846–1896, in its Relation to the Pennsylvania State Canals and Railroads and the Consolidated System East and West of Pittsburgh* (unpublished ms., 1896, original at the Smithsonian Institution, with microfilm copies at HML, and in the Penn Central Railroad Collection, M.G. 286, Pennsylvania Historical and Museum Commission, Pennsylvania State Archives, Harrisburg, with an additional microfilm copy in the author's possession, hereafter "Watkins History"), vol. 2, "Maintenance of Way—Steel Rails," 55–60; Weber, *The Northern Railroads*, 70.

32. In February 1869, workers finished a new iron bridge over the Conemaugh River, completing the uninterrupted double track between Altoona and Pittsburgh. Ward, *Master of the Pennsylvania*, 129–31; Watkins History, "Pennsylvania Railroad Division," 16, 19; Weber, *The Northern Railroads*, 63, 230–31.

33. Frederick Moore Binder, *Coal Age Empire: Pennsylvania Coal and Its Utilization to 1860* (Harrisburg: Pennsylvania Historical and Museum Commission, 1974), 128–29; Weber, *The Northern Railroads*, 62, 222; John K. Brown, *The Baldwin Locomotive Works, 1831–1915: A Study in American Industrial Practice* (Baltimore: Johns Hopkins University Press, 1995), 24–25, 260n81.

34. The level of troop transport could be highly variable—in 1864, it accounted for only 3.5 percent of the PRR's revenues, but the figure rose to 18 percent in 1865 as Union soldiers were being mustered out of service. Weber, *The Northern Railroads*, 84.

35. The PRR's principal subsidiaries also flourished during the war. Despite wartime demands for materials and labor, the Northern Central was able to double-track its entire main line between Baltimore and York by the end of 1865. The profits were even more gratifying, and the Northern Central's net income in 1864 was larger than its gross income had been in 1860 and 1861. The Philadelphia & Erie (the former Sunbury & Erie) handled substantial traffic in oil and other commodities, even though its main line was not completed until the autumn of 1864. The Pittsburgh, Fort Wayne & Chicago, though still an affiliated line and not yet a subsidiary, experienced considerable success, albeit largely as the result of eastbound agricultural shipments, not troop transportation. On the PW&B, only later a PRR subsidiary, passenger traffic more than doubled and freight traffic increased by almost four times. Frantz, "The Pennsylvania

Railroad and the Civil War"; Archdeacon, "Two Civil War Railroaders"; Ward, *Master of the Pennsylvania*, 131–32; Burgess and Kennedy, *Centennial History*, 310–11; Weber, *The Northern Railroads*, 49–50, 67–68, 221–22.

36. William Bender Wilson, *History of the Pennsylvania Railroad Company, with Plan of Organization, Portraits of Officials and Biographical Sketches*, vol. 1 (New York: Henry T. Coates & Co., 1899), 244–45, 339; Weber, *The Northern Railroads*, 68.

37. Burgess and Kennedy, *Centennial History*, 453–54; William Bender Wilson, *History of the Pennsylvania Railroad*, vol. 2, 35–36, 39–40; Weber, *The Northern Railroads*, 182, 232; Alexander K. McClure, *Old Time Notes of Pennsylvania*, vol. 1 (Philadelphia: John C. Winston, 1905), 152–53.

38. Kamm, "The Civil War Career," 191.

39. In January 1859, William Hasell Wilson was the only resident engineer on the PRR, based at Altoona and with supervision over the Maintenance-of-Way Department. In April 1861, he became the PRR's chief engineer, a position he retained through the end of 1867. By June 1862, the PRR fielded assistant engineers on the Eastern and Western Divisions, as well as an assistant engineer of surveys and construction and an assistant engineer of fuel and iron.

40. Watkins History, "Pennsylvania Railroad Division," 15–16; ibid., "Pittsburgh Division," 15.

41. Watkins History, vol. 3, "Organization and Departments," 5–6.

42. D. S. Newhall, "Purchasing Supplies," n.d., ca. 1905, HML, Box 419, folder 556.

43. Watkins History, "Organization and Departments," 5; ibid., "Freight Department—Development of the Organization, 1846–1896," 7.

44. "Engineering Department of P.R.R., 1847 to Date," n.d., ca. 1905, HML, Box 609, folder 22; PRR BOD Minutes, October 12, 1867, 176–77, February 24, 1875, 446; *Encyclopedia of Contemporary Biography of Pennsylvania*, vol. 2 (Bethlehem: Historical Society of Pennsylvania, 1868); Watkins History, "Organization and Departments," 7.

45. *Leland H. Jenks*, "Early History of a Railway Organization," *Business History Review* 35 (Summer 1961): 153–79, at 167; Wilson, *History of the Pennsylvania Railroad*, vol. 2, 271–72.

46. Lewis Neilson, "The Growth and Functions of the Executive Department of the Pennsylvania Railroad Company," n.d., ca. 1905, HML, Box 419, folder 556, 2.

47. Supervision of the Transportation Department was particularly fluid, residing with the third vice president (Cassatt, 1874–80), then the first vice president (Cassatt, 1880–82), then the second vice president (Thomson, 1882–88), then the first vice president (Thomson, 1888–97), then the second vice president (Pugh, 1897–1911), and then the fourth vice president (Atterbury, 1911–12), when the equivalent title became vice president in charge of operations, a post that Atterbury held until November 1924. In some instances, junior officers served as protégés to the vice president who was in charge of the Transportation Department, before assuming that post themselves—for example, Third Vice President Pugh worked under Frank Thomson between 1893 and 1897 before being promoted to second vice president, while Fifth Vice President Atterbury was mentored by Pugh between 1909 and 1911, prior to assuming control over transportation. Neilson, "Executive Department."

48. The one exception that proved the rule was the presidency of Walter S. Franklin (1948–54) whose experience in traffic functions was exceptionally valuable during a time of contracting business. Franklin also possessed impeccable connections among the Philadelphia gentry, and his brother Philip A. S. Franklin had been the president of the International Mercantile Marine Company.

49. "Railroad Organization," *Railroad Gazette* 12 (1880): 358–59, quoted in Jenks, "Early History," 155.

50. Jenks, "Early History," 170.

51. Weber, *The Northern Railroads*, 108–9.

52. Charles Sumner, "Railroad Usurpation in New Jersey," Speech in the Senate, on a Bill to Regulate Commerce among the Several States, February 14, 1865, in *The Works of Charles Sumner*, vol. 9 (Boston: Lee and Shepard, 1874), 237–65, quote at 265. See also Weber, *The Northern Railroads in the Civil War*, 124.

53. Christopher T. Baer, William J. Coxey, and Paul W. Schopp, *The Trail of the Blue Comet: A History of the Jersey Central's New Jersey Southern Division* (Palmyra, N.J.: West Jersey Chapter of the National Railway Historical Society, 1994), 55–56.

54. The chief sponsor of the National Railway bill was Congressman Thaddeus Stevens (Republican, Pa.), a reliable ally of the PRR. Baer, Coxey, and Schopp, *Trail of the Blue Comet*, 55–56; Weber, *The Northern Railroads*, 96–97, 108–26, 266n5.

55. Burgess and Kennedy, *Centennial History*, 261–62.

56. The route ran along the PW&B to its Philadelphia station, now located at Broad Street and Prime Street (Washington Avenue), then back along the PW&B to a connection with the Delaware Extension (much of which was over the tracks of the West Chester & Philadelphia at that location), then north to the PRR yards in West Philadelphia, along the completed northern segment of the Junction Railroad, onto the Reading mainline, then north to West Falls, and along the Reading's Port Richmond Branch to an intersection with the Philadelphia & Trenton.

57. Wilson, *History of the Pennsylvania Railroad*, vol. 1, 188–89, 307–8; Burgess and Kennedy, *Centennial History*, 104–5, 401–2; David W. Messer, *Triumph III: Philadelphia Terminal, 1838–2000* (Baltimore: Barnard, Roberts & Co., 2000), 316.

58. Messer, *Triumph III*, 109–10.

59. Frank A. Wrabel, "Terminals, Tunnels and Turmoil," *The Keystone* 28 (Spring 1995): 30–31; Burgess and Kennedy, *Centennial History*, 236, 241.

60. Since 1835, Powel had been one of the supporters of the West Philadelphia Railroad as a bypass for the Belmont Plane. Completed in 1850, it became the PRR's route west out of Philadelphia.

61. Of more immediate concern to Patterson and his fellow PRR directors, however, was the inability of the PRR to own land for terminal facilities. That restriction forced Patterson and his associates to buy the land in their own name—only to discover that the PRR's charter prohibited the use of more than thirty acres of land in West Philadelphia. *Sixth Annual Report of the Directors of the Pennsylvania Railroad Co. to the Stockholders, February 7, 1853* (Philadelphia: Crissy & Markley, 1853), 18–19.

62. PRR BOD Minutes, May 12, 1851, 441–43, November 3, 1851, 51, April 7, 1852, 153; Messer, *Triumph III*, 12; Wilson, *History of the Pennsylvania Railroad*, vol. 1, 180–82; *Seventh Annual Report of the Directors of the Pennsylvania Railroad Co. to the Stockholders, February 6, 1854* (Philadelphia: Crissy & Markley, 1854), 14.

63. Messer, *Triumph III*, 12, 21, 27.

64. Wilson, *History of the Pennsylvania Railroad*, vol. 1, 314–17.

65. Anthony J. Bianculli, *Trains and Technology: The American Railroad in the Nineteenth Century*, vol. 4: *Bridges and Tunnels, Signals* (Newark: University of Delaware Press, 2003), 46–48.

66. John F. Stover, *History of the Baltimore and Ohio Railroad* (West Lafayette, Ind.: Purdue University Press, 1987), 141–53.

67. T. J. Stiles, *The First Tycoon: The Epic Life of Cornelius Vanderbilt* (New York: Alfred A. Knopf, 2009), 381–86, 403–9, 412–13, 421–37; Rolland Harper Maybee, *Railroad Competition and the Oil Trade, 1855–1873*

(Philadelphia: Porcupine Press, 1974), 32–33; Frank Walker Stevens, *The Beginnings of the New York Central Railroad: A History* (London: G. P. Putnam's Sons, 1926), 350–87.

68. The classic indictment of Gould and other nineteenth-century business executives is Matthew Josephson, *The Robber Barons: The Great American Capitalists, 1861–1901* (New York: Harcourt, Brace, 1934). Recent scholarship has taken issue with the inaccurate characterization of Jay Gould as an unscrupulous "robber baron," and has likewise disagreed with more nuanced assessments by Alfred D. Chandler, Jr., and others that suggest that Gould was a parasitic speculator rather than a constructive manager. As historian and Gould biographer Maury Klein has noted, "Gould left the [Erie and] other companies much stronger than he had found them, [and] created large, stable properties where none had existed before." Maury Klein, "Jay Gould: A Revisionist Interpretation," *Business and Economic History* 15 (1986): 55–68, quotation at 59; Richard R. John, "Turner, Beard, Chandler: Progressive Historians," *Business History Review* 82 (Summer 2008): 227–40, at 235–36; Richard Sylla, "Chandler on High Technology Industries from the 1880s to the 1990s: A Comment," Capitalism and Society 1 (2006): 1–7; and Mary A. O'Sullivan, "Finance Capital in Chandlerian Capitalism," *Industrial and Corporate Change* 19 (2010): 549–89, at 583–84.

69. Charles Francis Adams, Jr., "A Chapter of Erie," in *Chapters of Erie and Other Essays* (Boston: Fields, Osgood & Co., 1871), 1–99; Maury Klein, *The Life and Legend of Jay Gould* (Baltimore: Johns Hopkins University Press, 1986), 88–102; Edward Hungerford, *Men of Erie: A Story of Human Effort* (New York: Random House, 1946), 158–70; Maybee, *Railroad Competition and the Oil Trade*, 32–33, 148, 155–58.

70. Harold F. Williamson and Arnold D. Daum, *The American Petroleum Industry, 1859–1899: The Age of Illumination* (Evanston, Ill.: Northwestern University Press, 1959), 11–13, 63–81.

71. Ibid.,165–69.

72. The three companies were the Franklin & Warren Railroad (1851, renamed the Atlantic & Great Western Railroad Company of Ohio in 1853), the Erie & New York City Railroad (1851), and the Meadville Railroad (1857, renamed the Atlantic & Great Western Railroad Company of Pennsylvania the following year).

73. Maybee, *Railroad Competition and the Oil Trade*, 3–5.

74. In 1865, the AG&W extended tracks eastward along the Allegheny River, from Franklin to Oil City.

75. Maybee, *Railroad Competition and the Oil Trade*, 5–7, 13–14, 16–19; Lorett Treese, *Railroads of Pennsylvania: Fragments of the Past in the Keystone Landscape* (Mechanicsburg, Pa.: Stackpole Books, 2003), 256; Burgess and Kennedy, *Centennial History*, 171. See also Paul Ellsworth Felton, "A History of the Atlantic and Great Western Railroad" (Ph.D. diss., University of Pittsburgh, 1943); William Reynolds, with Peter K. Gifford and Robert D. Ilisevich, eds., *European Capital, British Iron and an American Dream: The Story of the Atlantic and Great Western Railroad* (Akron, Ohio: University of Akron Press, 2002).

76. Maybee, *Railroad Competition and the Oil Trade*, 33.

77. Ibid., 22–25.

78. In 1864–65, Pittsburgh's refining capacity was approximately 4,500 barrels per day, compared with that of New York at 3,100 barrels, Cleveland at 750 barrels, and the oil region itself at 2,160 barrels. Maybee, *Railroad Competition and the Oil Trade*, 197; Williamson and Daum, *The American Petroleum Industry*, 169, 192, 289–91.

79. Charles S. Roberts, *Triumph VIII: Pittsburgh, 1749–2006* (Baltimore: Barnard, Roberts & Co., 2006), 13, 133–37; Wilson, *History of the Pennsylvania Railroad*, vol. 1, 212–13.

80. By January 1871, the PRR had also extended tracks from Kiski Junction northwest to Butler, Pennsylvania, fulfilling at least a part of the

original vision of the promoters of the North Western Rail Road. PRR BOD Minutes, May 27, 1862, 181–82.

81. Maybee, *Railroad Competition and the Oil Trade*, 199–200.

82. Homer Tope Rosenberger, *The Philadelphia and Erie Railroad: Its Place in American Economic History* (Potomac, Md.: Fox Hills Press, 1975), 381.

83. PRR BOD Minutes, November 11, 1861, 121–23.

84. By 1873, the PRR had also guaranteed $10 million of that company's bonds. Maybee, *Railroad Competition and the Oil Trade*, 34–37; Wilson, *History of the Pennsylvania Railroad*, vol. 1, 257; Burgess and Kennedy, *Centennial History*, 155–57; Ward, *Master of the Pennsylvania*, 135; Rosenberger, *The Philadelphia and Erie Railroad*, 406–8.

85. Maybee, *Railroad Competition and the Oil Trade*, 37–38, 74–75.

86. The NYC initially lacked a route into the oilfields. In 1864, however, local interests incorporated the Cross Cut Railroad, to build between Corry (the northern terminus of the Oil Creek Railroad) and the New York state line. From there, the Buffalo & Oil Creek Cross Cut Railroad, incorporated in 1865, would take traffic north to Brocton and a connection with the Buffalo & State Line Railroad (after 1867, the Buffalo & Erie Railroad, and after 1869 the Lake Shore & Michigan Southern). After a long and complex series of corporate reorganizations, the two companies in 1895 became a part of the Western New York & Pennsylvania Railway, and five years later the PRR leased the company. Paul V. Pietrak, Joseph G. Streamer, and James A. Van Brocklin, *The History of the Western New York & Pennsylvania Railway Company and Its Predecessors and Successors* (Hamburg, N.Y., 2000), 3(4–5).

87. The Oil City & Pithole linked Oil City and Irvineton, while the Farmers Railroad connected Oil City to Petroleum Centre. Maybee, *Railroad Competition and the Oil Trade*, 39–45, 167–72; Burgess and Kennedy, *Centennial History*, 171–75; Williamson and Daum, *The American Petroleum Industry*, 172–76.

88. The new company's directors included individuals from the PRR's competitors, including Alexander S. Diven, vice president of the New York & Erie, and Charles H. Lee, representing the Lake Shore & Michigan Southern.

89. The Atlantic & Great Western maintained sole control over a third outlet via its branch line from Meadville to Franklin. Under the terms of its original contract with the Oil Creek Railroad, however, A&GW officials had agreed that rates on the Franklin Branch would be at least as high as those charged on the Oil Creek—that is, the same fifty cents per barrel.

90. In 1876, following a foreclosure, the Oil Creek & Allegheny River Railway was reorganized as the Pittsburgh, Titusville & Buffalo Railway and later became a constituent of the Western New York & Pennsylvania Railway. Maybee, *Railroad Competition and the Oil Trade*, 39–45, 167–75; Burgess and Kennedy, *Centennial History*, 171–75; Pietrak, Streamer, and Van Brocklin, *Western New York & Pennsylvania Railway Company*, 3(13).

91. Burgess and Kennedy, *Centennial History*, 162–64.

92. Until 1870, there was no direct connection at Pittsburgh between Allegheny Valley tracks and those of the PRR, and the first Allegheny Valley passenger trains did not enter Pittsburgh's Union Station until 1872. Maybee, *Railroad Competition and the Oil Trade*, 200–201; Roberts, *Triumph VIII*, 28.

93. This was the combined Cross Cut Railroad and Buffalo & Oil Creek Cross Cut Railroad, mentioned in an note 86 above.

94. *Twenty-First Annual Report of the Board of Directors of the Pennsylvania Railroad Co. to the Stockholders, February 15, 1868* (Philadelphia: E. C. Markley & Son, 1868), 18–19.

95. As Thomson suggested in the PRR's *Twenty-First Annual Report* for 1867, "Instead of changing locomotives at the end of each day's service

as at present, the trains under this system will be provided with double crews, alternating their time on duty until their destination is completed and the return trip accomplished." *Twenty-First Annual Report*, 19; Rosenberger, *The Philadelphia and Erie Railroad*, 499, 538.

96. *Twenty-First Annual Report*, 20.

97. Ibid., 20.

98. Ibid., 20.

99. Technically, the commonwealth accepted $3.5 million in Allegheny Valley second mortgage bonds, in exchange for the $4 million in Philadelphia & Erie second mortgage bonds that replaced the $3.5 million in Sunbury & Erie bonds that that company had issued, in order to acquire portions of the canal system from the state. However, there was at least a theoretical possibility that the commonwealth might demand repayment of both the original Sunbury & Erie and the replacement Philadelphia & Erie bond issues, totaling $7.5 million. The agreement thus satisfied that combined amount. Burgess and Kennedy, *Centennial History*, 165–66.

100. The delay in opening occurred because striking workers threatened to demolish the summit tunnel if their demands were not met. Operating results were still not encouraging, and the PRR forced the Allegheny Valley Railroad into receivership ten years later. In 1892, the PRR reorganized the Allegheny Valley Railroad as the Allegheny Valley Rail*way*, and leased the company in 1900. *New York Times*, April 14, 1875; Wilson, *History of the Pennsylvania Railroad*, vol. 1, 360–64; Burgess and Kennedy, *Centennial History*, 87, 149, 167–69.

101. Thomson intended that the Allegheny Valley low-grade line would be extended to connect with the Pittsburgh, Fort Wayne & Chicago route across Ohio, but the Panic of 1873 prevented construction. PRR officials resurrected the idea in 1903 when they incorporated the Pennsylvania-Western Railway Company, to build a line from Enon, Pennsylvania (located south of New Castle, near the Ohio border), some seventy miles east to Red Bank, Pennsylvania. This line would have essentially paralleled the Western Allegheny Railroad, but with much lower grades. It would have also served as the easternmost portion of a low-grade line through northwestern Pennsylvania and northeastern Ohio, but the cost proved prohibitive, and nothing more was done. Office of Chief of Corporate Work, "North Penn Coal Company—Western Allegheny Railroad Company," November 4, 1937, HML, Box 218, folder 17; Burgess and Kennedy, *Centennial History*, 170.

102. Testimony of H. H. Houston before the Committee of Investigation appointed by the Legislature of Pennsylvania, at the Session of 1867 Relating to Fast Freight Transportation Companies Operating Upon Railways in Pennsylvania, in *The Pennsylvania System of Fast Freight Lines, as Exemplified by Union Line and the Empire Line, Operating Between the Atlantic Cities and the Great West over the Pennsylvania and Philad'a & Erie Railroads, and the Western Railways Connecting Therewith* (Philadelphia, 1867), 53–55.

103. William Z. Ripley, *Railroads: Rates and Regulation* (New York: Longmans, Green, 1912), 443.

104. Testimony of J. Edgar Thomson, in *The Pennsylvania System of Fast Freight Lines*, 50 (quote); William E. O'Connell, "The Development of the Private Railroad Freight Car, 1830–1966," *Business History Review* 44 (Summer 1970): 190–209, at 194–97.

105. Taylor and Neu, *The American Railroad Network*, 69; Maybee, *Railroad Competition and the Oil Trade*, 118–20.

106. Taylor and Neu, *The American Railroad Network*, 67–68; Testimony of H. H. Houston, in *The Pennsylvania System of Fast Freight Lines*, 53–54.

107. Maybee, *Railroad Competition and the Oil Trade*, 114–15, 121–22.

108. As early as January 1863, well before the chartering of the Western Insurance & Transportation Company, Cass, in conjunction with William Thaw, had already established a Union Transportation Company to offer through freight service from Illinois, Indiana, and Ohio to New York—and that was probably the origin of the later Star Union Line moniker. Testimony of William Thaw, in *The Pennsylvania System of Fast Freight Lines,*, 17–32; Wilson, *History of the Pennsylvania Railroad*, vol. 2, 291; Maybee, *Railroad Competition and the Oil Trade*, 121–22; PRR BOD Minutes, December 9, 1863, 342–43, December 23, 1863, 351.

109. Prior to the Civil War, PRR officials also possessed veto power over the rates charged by affiliated transporters, such as Leach & Company and Clarke & Thaw. In 1867, and in response to probing questions from the Pennsylvania legislature, Thaw asserted that the Union Line served a great many railroads. Many of those lines were either Pennsylvania Railroad subsidiaries or friendly connections. The list included, in addition to the PRR itself, the Camden & Amboy; the Fort Wayne; the Pittsburgh, Columbus & Cincinnati; the Little Miami and Columbus & Xenia Railroad; the Columbus, Piqua & Indianapolis; the Bellefontaine Line (Crestline–Indianapolis); the Jeffersonville Railroad; the Evansville & Crawfordsville Railroad; the Louisville & Nashville; the Louisville & Memphis; the Terre Haute & Richmond; and the Terre Haute, Alton & St. Louis Railroad. However, the Union Line also operated its equipment over the Louisville & Nashville and several western railroads that were unconnected with the PRR. Testimony of William Thaw, in *The Pennsylvania System of Fast Freight Lines*, 17–32 (quotes); Emory R. Johnson and Grover G. Huebner, *Railroad Traffic and Rates*, vol. 1: *The Freight Service* (New York: D. Appleton, 1911), 244–45.

110. Taylor and Neu, *The American Railroad Network*, 58–59; Douglas J. Puffert, *Tracks Across Continents, Paths Through History: The Economic Dynamics of Standardization in Railway Gauge* (Chicago: University of Chicago Press, 2009), 135–36.

111. Wilson, *History of the Pennsylvania Railroad*, vol. 2, 66–67.

112. Barnes had joined the PRR engineer corps in 1848 and assisted in surveying the route down the western slope of the Alleghenies. In 1858, he became the assistant superintendent of the Pittsburgh, Fort Wayne & Chicago, and he continued to occupy that post even as served as president of the Empire Line.

113. Wilson, *History of the Pennsylvania Railroad*, vol. 2, 24–25; Maybee, *Railroad Competition and the Oil Trade*, 114–15, 122–23.

114. Burgess and Kennedy, *Centennial History*, 172, 325–29; Maybee, *Railroad Competition and the Oil Trade*, 124–28, 241–42; Testimony of Joseph D. Potts, in *The Pennsylvania System of Fast Freight Lines,* 74–83; John H. White, *The American Railroad Freight Car: From the Wood-Car Era to the Coming of Steel* (Baltimore: Johns Hopkins University Press, 1993), 366, 378–79; O'Connell, "The Development," 199.

115. PRR BOD Minutes, September 20, 1865, 479–80, February 6, 1867, 103, February 19, 1868, 204; *New York Times*, December 21, 1909; William Harry Moyer, "The PRR's Navy, Part IV: The Great Lakes," *The Keystone* 41 (Autumn 2008): 13–51.

116. Watkins History, vol. 2, "Iron Ore and Coal Trade of the Lakes," 74–77.

117. Walter Thayer, "Transportation on the Great Lakes," *Annals of the American Academy of Political and Social Science* 31 (January 1908): 126–38; Maybee, *Railroad Competition and the Oil Trade*, 127–28; Moyer, "The Great Lakes," 15, 25–27, 30–31.

118. In 1877, the PRR demanded that Empire Line investors sell most of their assets to John D. Rockefeller's Standard Oil, but the investors retained ownership of the Erie & Western, which subsequently became an

independent company, although one that was largely owned by individuals closely connected with the PRR. In November 1899, the Erie & Western's president offered to sell the company to the PRR. By early 1900, the PRR and the Northern Central Railway, a PRR subsidiary, owned virtually all of the Erie & Western's stock. At that time, crews replaced the Anchor Line logo (an anchor tilted forty-five degrees to the right) on all of the company's ships with the PRR keystone logo. In 1914, Interstate Commerce Commission officials ruled that railroad operation of Great Lakes shipping violated the terms of the Panama Canal Act, which prohibited railroads from offering maritime service that competed directly with rail routes. PRR service stopped at the end of the 1915 shipping season. In March 1916, the Great Lakes Transit Corporation took over the operation of the boats, once again under the oversight of James C. Evans. The Erie & Western Transportation Company was not formally dissolved until November 8, 1924. Moyer, "The Great Lakes," 32–36.

119. Williamson and Daum, *The American Petroleum Industry*, 529.

120. Some evidence suggests that the Grand Trunk Railway used similar cars beginning in 1862. Williamson and Daum, *The American Petroleum Industry*, 180–81; Samuel T. Pees and Richard Senges, "The Densmore Brothers and America's First Successful Railway Oil Tank Car, 1865," *Oil-Industry History* 5 (2004): 3–17; White, *The American Railroad Freight Car*, 365–67.

121. *The Derrick's Hand-Book of Petroleum: A Complete Chronological and Statistical Review of Petroleum Developments from 1859 to 1898*, vol. 1 (Oil City, Pa.: Derrick Publishing Co., 1898), 964–65.

122. White, *The American Railroad Freight Car*, 366.

123. White, *The American Railroad Freight Car*, 367–79; O'Connell, "The Development," 199; Williamson and Daum, *The American Petroleum Industry*, 181–83. Maybee indicates, based on a document in the William Thaw Papers, that the Empire Line possessed three hundred "tank cars" as of October 1865. That seems far too early for cylindrical iron tanks, suggesting that those "tank cars" were probably Densmore-type vat cars. Despite the failure of the Empire Line's efforts to convert a boxcar to oil service, PRR executives did not readily abandon the notion that tank cars could be used to transport commodities other than oil. In 1868, for example, Tom Scott suggested that iron tank cars could be filled with coal for the backhaul from the east coast. Maybee, *Railroad Competition and the Oil Trade*, 241–42.

125. Burgess and Kennedy, *Centennial History*, 172, 325–29; Richard Burg, "The Early Oil Trade and 'A' Series Tank Cars on the Pennsylvania Railroad, 1859–1929," *The Keystone* 15 (March 1982): 4–9; Testimony of Joseph D. Potts, in *The Pennsylvania System of Fast Freight Lines*, 74–83; White, *The American Railroad Freight Car*, 366, 378–79; O'Connell, "The Development," 199.

126. Refiners did not widely employ tank cars for the distribution of refined products until the 1880s, well after the new equipment had proved its worth in crude oil shipments.

127. Williamson and Daum, *The American Petroleum Industry*, 528–33.

128. Ibid., 434, 530–31.

129. In 1865, for example, the Pennsylvania legislature prohibited the storage of more than twenty-five barrels of crude or refined petroleum within the city limits of Philadelphia, unless the fire marshal granted a special exemption. Ibid., 43–60, 85, 190, 317.

130. Maybee, *Railroad Competition and the Oil Trade*, 51–52.

131. Ibid., 55–57, 181–82; Earl J. Heydinger, "Railroads of the First and Second Anthracite Coal Fields of Pennsylvania, Group VI: The Little Schuylkill," *Bulletin of the Railway and Locomotive Historical Society* 108 (1963): 19–28.

132. Maybee, *Railroad Competition and the Oil Trade*, 55.

133. The westernmost portion of the new route was to include the Western Railroad (Franklin to Bellefonte), with the Lewisburg, Centre & Spruce Creek Railroad (Bellefonte to Milton) composing the eastern end. While neither section was constructed in its intended form, a portion of the alignment became the Lewisburg & Tyrone Railroad, a PRR subsidiary. Farther east, A&GW intended to rely on the Morris & Essex Railroad, which they leased in November 1865. Jay V. Hare, *History of the Reading, Which Appeared as a Serial in* The Pilot *and* Philadelphia & Reading Railway Men, *Beginning May 1909—Ending February 1914* (Philadelphia: John Henry Stock & Co., 1966).

134. That situation arose because, in October 1860, the Catawissa had acquired trackage rights over the Sunbury & Erie, between Milton and Williamsport, for a period of twenty years. Even though the Sunbury & Erie had shortly afterward been reorganized as the Philadelphia & Erie and had then been leased by the PRR (on January 1, 1862), the trackage rights contract was still valid, and it was included under the terms of the A&GW lease of the Catawissa. Hare, *History of the Reading*, 156–57.

135. The issue hinged on the language of the April 1861 act that permitted "any railroad companies to enter into contracts for the use or lease of any other railroads. . . . Provided, That the roads of the companies so contracting or leasing shall be directly, or by means of intervening railroads, connected with each other." PRR attorneys argued that the difference in gauge between the Atlantic & Great Western and the Catawissa made a "connection" impossible.

136. The Reading leased the Catawissa Railroad in 1872 and soon ended the through traffic agreement. The only alternative was a roundabout route along the Philadelphia & Erie and the Northern Central to Sunbury, along the Shamokin Valley & Pottsville Railroad (after 1863, a subsidiary of the Northern Central) to Mount Carmel, and on the Lehigh Valley and the Jersey Central to Communipaw. Maybee, *Railroad Competition and the Oil Trade*, 51–75; Marvin W. Schlegel, *Ruler of the Reading: The Life of Franklin B. Gowen, 1836–1889* (Harrisburg: Archives Publishing, 1947), 10–11, 49; Hare, *History of the Reading*, 157–58.

137. Maybee, *Railroad Competition and the Oil Trade*, 181–82.

138. Ibid., 130–31. Maybee lists a rate of $3.57 a barrel and a total gross income of $122.80 for a forty-barrel car. This arithmetic is clearly incorrect, and the context suggests that the correct rate should be $3.07 per barrel.

139. Ibid., 126–31.

140. As the PRR was the largest single stockholder in the Philadelphia & Erie, it was naturally a foregone conclusion that those shares would be voted in favor of the changes. The PRR did not yet own a majority of Philadelphia & Erie stock, however, and so Thomson would have to contend with the other large investor, the City of Philadelphia. Under intense pressure from Tom Scott, the city councils consented to those modifications, which substantially lowered rental payments based on the premise that they would enable Philadelphia to compete more effectively for oil at Great Lakes traffic. The City of Philadelphia retained its 45,000-share investment in the Philadelphia & Erie until November 1907, when it sold the securities to Drexel & Company for $2.6 million—representing a loss of $3.5 million.

141. Charles S. Roberts and David W. Messer, *Triumph VII: Harrisburg to the Lakes, Wilkes-Barre, Oil City and Red Bank, 1827–2004* (Baltimore: Barnard, Roberts & Co., 2004), 145.

142. In *The Pennsylvania System of Fast Freight Lines*: Testimony of John S. Hilles, 33–35, Testimony of J. P. Cranford, 39–40, Testimony of George Webb, 40–41, Testimony of Joseph Montgomery, 41.

143. Management scholar William E. O'Connell has observed, "The flat rate per car prompted the fast freight lines to solicit high value freight from which, under the concept of value of service pricing, they could exact higher rates. This left the railroads to handle the low value and, therefore, low revenue freight for their own accounts." O'Connell, "The Development," 196.

144. *Report of the Investigating Committee of the Pennsylvania Railroad Company* (Philadelphia: Allen, Lane & Scott, 1874), 119–25; Maybee, *Railroad Competition and the Oil Trade*, 268; White, *The American Railroad Freight Car*, 132.

145. *New York Times*, April 7, 1875; James Page, *Letter to the Stockholders of the Pennsylvania Railroad Company* (Philadelphia: Collins, 1863), 18 (quote).

146. PRR BOD Minutes, January 28, 1863, 259.

147. Maybee, *Railroad Competition and the Oil Trade*, 119; Reports of the Majority and Minority of the Committee Appointed Feb. 4, 1861, to Examine the Condition and Policy of the Pennsylvania Railroad Company (Philadelphia: Collins, 1862).

148. *Report of the Investigating Committee*, 119–25.

149. Testimony of John S. Hilles, in *The Pennsylvania System of Fast Freight Lines*, 33–35 (quote).

150. Perhaps the best assessment of the efficacy of the PRR's fast freight lines came from the fear that they engendered in executives on other railroads. In 1866, at the Atlantic Trunk Line Convention in New York, Baltimore & Ohio president John W. Garrett introduced a resolution calling for a ban on fast freight lines, lest his company, already weakened by the Civil War, be placed at a further competitive disadvantage. The resolution failed, despite support from the Erie's representatives, causing executives on each of the trunk lines more forcefully to protect their interests by augmenting their freight line capabilities. Despite that competition, however, railroad executives appreciated the advantages that fast freight companies could offer in the coordination of interline service. Accordingly, they established a series of cooperative freight lines, pooling equipment and facilities. The Red Line, established in 1866, offered service between Boston, New York, and Chicago; the Blue Line covered many of the same termini but ran through Canada; while the Green Line served the South. By the late 1870s, in the aftermath of the depression that occurred during that decade, most of the fast freight lines were cooperative in nature. Like the PRR's Union and Empire Lines, they remained in service until the time of the First World War, when the United States Railroad Administration prohibited the competitive solicitation of traffic in the interests of wartime efficiency. Maybee, *Railroad Competition and the Oil Trade*, 133–35; Taylor and Neu, *The American Railroad Network*, 71–75; Williamson and Daum, *The American Petroleum Industry*, 346.

151. Ripley, *Railroads: Rates and Regulation*, 18.

Chapter 9. Empire

1. In 1860, the PRR listed $13.2 million in paid-in capital, along with $16.2 million in funded debt, nearly half of which had been issued to pay for the purchase of the Main Line of Public Works. The Reading, in contrast, listed $11.5 million in paid-in capital, plus $12.1 million in funded debt. However, the PRR operated 423 route miles, compared with the Reading's 173, indicating that the Reading had a much higher per-mile capitalization than the PRR. Henry Varnum Poor, *History of the Railroads and Canals of the United States of America, Exhibiting their Progress, Cost, Revenues, Expenditures, & Present Condition* (New York: John H. Schultz, 1860), 272–87, 469–74, 482–85.

2. The Reading carried substantial freight tonnage, despite its relatively short length, because the vast majority of its traffic consisted of anthracite. Frederick Moore Binder, *Coal Age Empire: Pennsylvania Coal and Its Utilization to 1860* (Harrisburg: Pennsylvania Historical and Museum Commission, 1974), 140–41; Stuart W. Wells, "'An Arduous and Novel Undertaking': Lock Navigation on the River Schuylkill," *Canal History and Technology Proceedings* 21 (March 23, 2002): 35–61, at 52.

3. Alfred D. Chandler, Jr., *The Visible Hand: The Managerial Revolution in American Business* (Cambridge, Mass.: Belknap Press of Harvard University Press, 1977), 151.

4. George H. Burgess and Miles C. Kennedy, *Centennial History of the Pennsylvania Railroad Company, 1846–1946* (Philadelphia: Pennsylvania Railroad, 1949), 178–84; James A. Ward, *J. Edgar Thomson, Master of the Pennsylvania* (Westport, Conn.: Greenwood Press, 1980), 144; Samuel Harden Church, *Corporate History of the Pennsylvania Lines West of Pittsburgh, Comprising Charters, Mortgages, Decrees, Deeds, Leases, Agreements, Ordinances, and Other Papers with Descriptive Text*, vol. 1 (Baltimore: Friedenwald Co., 1898), 92–113; *A Compilation of the Laws, Deeds, Mortgages, Leases, and Other Instruments, and Minutes of Proceedings Affecting the Pittsburgh, Fort Wayne, and Chicago Railway Company* (New York: John Polhemus, 1875), 13–19.

5. *A Compilation of the Laws . . . Affecting the Pittsburgh, Fort Wayne, and Chicago*, 159.

6. PRR Board of Directors (BOD) Minutes, Pennsylvania Railroad Company Collection, call no. 1807/1810, Hagley Museum and Library, Wilmington, Delaware (hereafter cited as HML), April 1, 1868, 215–17, December 16, 1868, 257, November 2, 1869, 323–36.

7. A separate company, the Pan Handle Railroad, was also incorporated in 1868, to build a branch from the Panhandle Railway main line to Wheeling.

8. Samuel Harden Church, *Corporate History of the Pennsylvania Lines West of Pittsburgh, Comprising Charters, Mortgages, Decrees, Deeds, Leases, Agreements, Ordinances, and Other Papers with Descriptive Text*, vol. 3 (Baltimore: Friedenwald Co., 1899), 30–34; Burgess and Kennedy, *Centennial History*, 192.

9. PRR executives did not gain control over the route to Keokuk until nearly a century later, when in 1960 they purchased a half-interest in the Toledo, Peoria & Western, in tandem with the Santa Fe. William B. Dana, ed., *The Merchants Magazine and Commercial Review*, vol. 58 (New York: William B. Dana, 1868), 465; Paul H. Stringham, *Toledo, Peoria & Western: Tired, Proven, and Willing* (Peoria, Ill.: Deller Archive, 1993); Robert W. Jackson, *Rails Across the Mississippi: A History of the St. Louis Bridge* (Urbana: University of Illinois Press, 2001), 65–70.

10. Richard T. Wallis, *The Pennsylvania Railroad at Bay: William Riley McKeen and the Terre Haute & Indianapolis Railroad* (Bloomington: Indiana University Press, 2001), 18–19, 27–29.

11. As of late 1868, those lines were the Buffalo & Erie Railroad, the Lake Shore Railway, the Cleveland & Toledo Railroad, and the Michigan Southern & Northern Indiana Railroad.

12. Julius Grodinsky, *Jay Gould: His Business Career, 1867–1892* (Philadelphia: University of Pennsylvania Press, 1957), 56–58.

13. William J. Watt, *The Pennsylvania Railroad in Indiana* (Bloomington: Indiana University Press, 2000), 45; Grodinsky, *Jay Gould*, 58–63.

14. Maury Klein, *The Life and Legend of Jay Gould* (Baltimore: Johns Hopkins University Press, 1986), 93–95; *The Railway News and Joint Stock Journal* 12 (November 6, 1869), 476.

15. Rolland Harper Maybee, *Railroad Competition and the Oil Trade, 1855–1873* (Philadelphia: Porcupine Press, 1974), 157.

16. *Twenty-Second Annual Report of the Board of Directors of the Pennsylvania Railroad Co. to the Stockholders,* February 16, 1869 (Philadelphia: E. C. Markley & Son, 1869), 16 (quote, emphasis in the original); Maybee, *Railroad Competition and the Oil Trade*, 140–41.

17. Maybee, *Railroad Competition and the Oil Trade*, 140–41.

18. Ward, *Master of the Pennsylvania*, 145.

19. Church, *Corporate History*, vol. 3, 86–87.

20. *Twenty-Second Annual Report*, 16–17.

21. Church, *Corporate History*, vol. 3, 85–94; Burgess and Kennedy, *Centennial History*, 194–95, 198–99; Ward, *Master of the Pennsylvania*, 144–47; *Report of the Investigating Committee of the Pennsylvania Railroad Company* (Philadelphia: Allen, Lane & Scott, 1874), 38; Watt, *The Pennsylvania Railroad in Indiana*, 45.

22. Gould controlled the proxies, but apparently not much of the stock itself. During the mid-1800s it was possible to buy the voting rights to the stock from investors, who retained ownership of the shares and were entitled to continue to receive dividends. Grodinsky, *Jay Gould*, 65.

23. Maybee, *Railroad Competition and the Oil Trade*, 159–60; Klein, *Jay Gould*, 93–94; Grodinsky, *Jay Gould*, 65.

24. Douglas J. Puffert, "The Standardization of Track Gauge on North American Railways, 1830–1890," *Journal of Economic History* 60 (December 2000): 933–60, at 952; Puffert, *Tracks Across Continents, Paths Through History: The Economic Dynamics of Standardization in Railway Gauge* (Chicago: University of Chicago Press, 2009), 142–45.

25. Watt, *The Pennsylvania Railroad in Indiana*, 45; Klein, *Jay Gould*, 93–94.

26. Ward, *Master of the Pennsylvania*, 147–49; Burgess and Kennedy, *Centennial History*, 195–99; Church, *Corporate History*, vol. 1, 112–13; *Report of the Investigating Committee*, 38.

27. The classic account of Chicago's growth is contained in William Cronon, *Nature's Metropolis: Chicago and the Great West* (New York: W. W. Norton, 1991).

28. After 1867, the Ohio & Mississippi Railway.

29. The Alton Route moniker (like the Vandalia Route, in its early years) was simply shorthand for the railroad's corporate title—it should not be confused with the Alton Railroad, after 1947 a part of the Gulf, Mobile & Ohio Railroad.

30. Watt, *The Pennsylvania Railroad in Indiana*, 28–32, 48–49.

31. In 1889, the railroad became a portion of the Cleveland, Cincinnati, Chicago & St. Louis ("Big Four") Railroad, after 1906 a subsidiary of the New York Central.

32. The 1862 agreement was between the Indianapolis & Cincinnati and the Terre Haute & Richmond, the predecessor company of the Terre Haute & Indianapolis. Wallis, *The Pennsylvania Railroad at Bay*, 13–14.

33. Thomson was to have been a party to the agreement but, perhaps assuming that Cass and the Fort Wayne would adequately represent the PRR's interests, ultimately declined to participate. Samuel Harden Church, *Corporate History of the Pennsylvania Lines West of Pittsburgh, Comprising Charters, Mortgages, Decrees, Deeds, Leases, Agreements, Ordinances, and Other Papers with Descriptive Text*, vol. 6 (Baltimore: Friedenwald Co., 1899), 614–16; Burgess and Kennedy, *Centennial History*, 203–4; Wallis, *The Pennsylvania Railroad at Bay*, 14–15.

34. Wallis, *The Pennsylvania Railroad at Bay*, 15–16.

35. As soon as the TH&I, with the support of the PRR, refused to lease the St. Louis, Alton & Terre Haute, that company's owners had little choice other than to sign a lease with the remaining five members of the consortium.

36. Wallis, *The Pennsylvania Railroad at Bay*, 26.

37. Because the members of the PRR board were still cautious and conservative regarding the expenditure of company monies on western expansion, Thomson funded the project indirectly through the four railroads that connected Pittsburgh with Terre Haute—that is, the Pan Handle; the Steubenville & Indiana; the Columbus, Chicago & Indiana

Central; and the Terre Haute & Indianapolis. Based on the March 1868 guarantee provided by those four railroads, the St. Louis, Vandalia & Terre Haute issued $2.6 million in second mortgage bonds, with the PRR buying the $1.6 million portion that Thomson had ensured would be guaranteed by its Steubenville & Indiana and Pan Handle subsidiaries. Under the agreement, the CC&IC guaranteed 30 percent of the financing, the Steubenville & Indiana 25 percent, the Pan Handle 25 percent, and Terre Haute & Indianapolis 20 percent. Wallis, *The Pennsylvania Railroad at Bay*, 19–21.

38. Burgess and Kennedy, *Centennial History*, 205–6; Wallis, *The Pennsylvania Railroad at Bay*, 19.

39. In 1880, the Indianapolis, Cincinnati & Lafayette Railroad was reorganized as the Cincinnati, Indianapolis, St. Louis & Chicago Railway, commonly known as the "Big Four." In 1889, the company merged with the Cleveland, Columbus, Cincinnati & Indianapolis Railway and the Indianapolis & St. Louis Railway to form the Cleveland, Cincinnati, Chicago & St. Louis Railway (still known as the Big Four, and part of the New York Central).

40. Wallis, *The Pennsylvania Railroad at Bay*, 16.

41. Ibid., 53, 89, 112–16.

42. Burgess and Kennedy, *Centennial History*, 206–12.

43. Freda L. Bridenstine, "The Madison and Indianapolis Railroad" (M.A. thesis, Butler University, 1931), reprinted as *The "Madison and Indianapolis": Indiana's First Railroad* (Madison, Ind.: Jefferson County Historical Society, n.d.), 55.

44. Burgess and Kennedy, *Centennial History*, 212–16.

45. For an overview of Cairo's unrealized potential as a rail hub, see Fred W. Ash, "Submerged Ambitions," *Railroad History* 196 (Spring–Summer 2007): 6–21.

46. In 1870, and acting through the association, McComb and his allies acquired control over the Mississippi Central Railroad and the San Antonio & Mexican Gulf Railroad—which he bought from the federal government in a foreclosure sale. By 1871, McComb had joined forces with Tom Scott in the ill-fated Texas & Pacific venture.

47. Information on McComb is from John F. Stover, "Colonel Henry S. McComb, Mississippi Rail-road Adventurer," *Journal of Mississippi History* 17 (1955): 177–90; Stover, *History of the Baltimore and Ohio Railroad* (West Lafayette, Ind.: Purdue University Press, 1987), 154; Mark R. Wilson, "The Extensive Side of Nineteenth-Century Military Economy: The Tent Industry in the Northern United States During the Civil War," *Enterprise & Society* 2 (June 2001): 297–337; and Burgess and Kennedy, *Centennial History*, 217–18.

48. In January 1872, the St. Louis & Iron Mountain and the Cairo, Arkansas & Texas merged, forming the St. Louis, Iron Mountain & Southern Railway.

49. PRR BOD Minutes, April 28, 1869, 289; Burgess and Kennedy, *Centennial History*, 216–18; Watt, *The Pennsylvania Railroad in Indiana*, 48, 82–83; Jean Strouse, *Morgan: American Financier* (New York: Harper Perennial, 2000), 196–97.

50. *Laws of the General Assembly of the State of Pennsylvania, Passed at the Session of 1862* (Harrisburg: A Boyd Hamilton, 1862), 12–13; PRR BOD Minutes, October 8, 1862, 216–17, April 1, 1863, 294–95; Church, *Corporate History*, vol. 1, 569–72; Burgess and Kennedy, *Centennial History*, 223.

51. William Reynolds, Peter H. Gifford, and Robert D. Ilisevich, *European Capital, British Iron, and an American Dream: The Story of the Atlantic and Great Western Railroad* (Akron, Ohio: University of Akron Press, 2002), 43–53.

52. Burgess and Kennedy, *Centennial History*, 223–25.

53. *New York Times*, September 21, 1891.

54. Church, *Corporate History*, vol. 1, 468–76; Burgess and Kennedy, *Centennial History*, 223–25.

55. On January 1, 1873, the Pennsylvania Company took control of the railroad, later renamed the Pittsburgh, Youngstown & Ashtabula Railroad. The opening of the line four months later unfortunately coincided with a severe economic depression that severely curtailed coal and iron ore traffic. After the economy recovered, however, iron ore traffic increased steadily, thanks to Ashtabula's convenient access to Youngstown. Samuel Harden Church, *Corporate History of the Pennsylvania Lines West of Pittsburgh:, Comprising Charters, Mortgages, Decrees, Deeds, Leases, Agreements, Ordinances, and Other Papers with Descriptive Text*, vol. 2 (Baltimore: Friedenwald Co., 1898), 265–89; Burgess and Kennedy, *Centennial History*, 225–27; J. Elfreth Watkins, *Pennsylvania Railroad Company, 1846–1896, in its Relation to the Pennsylvania State Canals and Railroads and the Consolidated System East and West of Pittsburgh* (unpublished ms., 1896, original at the Smithsonian Institution, with microfilm copies at HML and in the Penn Central Railroad Collection, M.G. 286, Pennsylvania Historical and Museum Commission, Pennsylvania State Archives, Harrisburg, with an additional microfilm copy in the author's possession, hereafter referred to as the "Watkins History"), vol. 2, "Iron Ore and Coal Trade of the Lakes," 72–73.

56. The 1871 Mansfield, Coldwater & Lake Michigan Rail*road* was a merger of the Mansfield, Coldwater & Lake Michigan Rail*way* (an Ohio company) and the Ohio & Michigan Railway (a Michigan Company), each of which had been chartered in 1870. The merger was arranged in December 1870 but the new company was not organized until the following year.

57. In 1877, George Cass and Tom Scott arranged for the companies (including the Toledo & Woodville) to be transferred to the North Western Ohio Railway, a company that had been organized the previous year. In 1891, the North Western Ohio became part of the Toledo, Walhonding Valley & Ohio Railroad, and then the Toledo, Columbus & Ohio River Railroad, in 1911. During the 1920s, the line to Toledo served as the beginnings of a PRR route to Detroit, virtually the last major expansion project that the PRR undertook. The short western end of the route was operated briefly by the Grand Rapids & Indiana and then became part of the Allegan & South Eastern Railroad. Church, *Corporate History*, vol. 2, 1–31; Burgess and Kennedy, *Centennial History*, 227–29.

58. Lake Carriers' Association, "History of the Iron Ore Trade," *Annual Report of the Lake Carriers' Association, 1910* (Detroit, Mich.: P. N. Bland, 1911), 101–17; George G. Tunell, "Lake Transportation and the Iron-Ore Industry," *Journal of Political Economy* 5 (December 1896): 23–39; Watkins History, "Iron Ore and Coal Trade," 68–75.

59. *Charter and Supplements of the Pennsylvania Railroad Company, with the Acts of Assembly and Municipal Ordinances Affecting the Company; Together with the By-Laws of the Board of Directors* (Philadelphia: Crissy & Markley, 1859), 25–75.

60. "An Act Regulating Railroad Companies," February 19, 1849, reprinted in *Charter and Supplements of the Pennsylvania Railroad Company*, 79–89.

61. Illinois passed a general railroad incorporation law in 1849, followed by New York in 1850 and Ohio and Indiana in 1852. The Pennsylvania General Assembly did not enact a true general railroad incorporation law until April 1868, however. Edward J. Davies II, "State Economic Policy and the Region in Pennsylvania, 1853–1895," *Business and Economic History* 21 (1992): 280–89, at 284; Sean Patrick Adams, "Different Charters, Different Paths: Corporations and Coal in Antebellum Pennsylvania and Virginia," *Business and Economic History* 27 (Fall 1998): 78–90, 82; Alfred D. Chandler, Jr., *Henry Varnum Poor: Business Editor, Analyst, and Reformer* (Cambridge, Mass.: Harvard University Press, 1956), 192.

62. One major exception was the Lehigh Coal & Navigation Company, which both mined and transported anthracite.

63. Sean Patrick Adams, *Old Dominion, Industrial Commonwealth: Coal, Politics, and Economy in Antebellum America* (Baltimore: Johns Hopkins University Press, 2004), 170–78.

64. James C. Bonbright and Gardiner C. Means, *The Holding Company: Its Public Significance and its Regulation* (New York: McGraw-Hill, 1932), 58.

65. Watt, *The Pennsylvania Railroad in Indiana*, 49–50; John Bell Rae, *The Development of Railway Land Subsidy Policy in the United States* (New York: Arno Press, 1979), 80–81.

66. Burgess and Kennedy, *Centennial History*, 199–202.

67. Watt, *The Pennsylvania Railroad in Indiana*, 50; Burgess and Kennedy, *Centennial History*, 200–202.

68. Ida M. Tarbell, *The History of the Standard Oil Company* (New York: McClure, Phillips & Co., 1904), 79; Bonbright and Means, *The Holding Company*, 59–60.

69. *Laws of the General Assembly of the State of Pennsylvania Passed at the Session of 1873* (Harrisburg: Benjamin Singerly, 1873), 955–56; Calvin G. Beitel, *A Digest of the Corporations Chartered by the Legislature of Pennsylvania, Between the Years 1700 and 1873 Inclusive: Giving the Dates of Acts of Incorporation, with the Several Supplements Thereto, with a Reference to the Pages of the Pamphlet Laws, where they may be Found* (Philadelphia: J. Campbell & Son, 1874), 209–10, 270–71, 275. For a complete list of subsidiaries, see Coverdale & Colpitts, *Corporate, Financial and Construction History of Lines Owned, Operated and Controlled to December 31, 1945*, vol. 4, *Affiliated Lines, Miscellaneous Companies, and General Index* (New York: Coverdale & Colpitts, 1947).

70. In 1871, the principals of the Reading also incorporated the Excelsior Enterprise Company. It was renamed the National Company in 1872 and in 1896 became the Reading Company, overseeing both the Philadelphia & Reading Railroad and the Philadelphia & Reading Coal and Iron Company. E. G. Campbell, *The Reorganization of the American Railroad System, 1893–1900* (New York: Columbia University Press, 1938), 107–8; Bonbright and Means, *The Holding Company*, 62; Marvin W. Schlegel, *Ruler of the Reading: The Life of Franklin B. Gowen, 1836–1889* (Harrisburg: Archives Publishing, 1947), 34–36.

71. Salomon Frederik van Oss, *American Railroads as Investments: A Handbook for Investors in American Railroad Securities* (New York: G. P. Putnam's Sons, 1893), 262; Chandler, *Visible Hand*, 541n24, gives an estimate of fifty thousand to fifty-five thousand employees for the system as a whole, with perhaps two-thirds of those on Lines East. Chandler's estimate, based on James Dredge, *The Pennsylvania Railroad: Its Organization, Construction, and Management* (London: John Wiley and Sons, 1879), and Henry V. Poor, *Manual of Railroads of the United States for 1878* (New York: H. V. Poor, 1878), seems accurate. The PRR did not release employment figures (which, in any event, would have been kept by the various operating divisions and subsidiary companies, and not the central office) at that time, and so the precise number of employees is impossible to determine with any degree of precision. As with all railroads, the number of employees varied greatly according to the season (a large share of track maintenance took place during the warmer months) and according to economic conditions.

72. "An Act to Incorporate the Pennsylvania Company," May 7, 1870, in Church, *Corporate History*, vol. 1, 11–12.

73. "Capital Stock Issues of the Pennsylvania Company," December 5, 1936, Pennsylvania Railroad Company Collection, call no. 1807/1810, HML, Box 219, folder 10; William Bender Wilson, *History of the Pennsylvania Railroad Company, with Plan of Organization, Portraits of Officials*

and Biographical Sketches, vol. 2 (New York: Henry T. Coates & Co., 1899), 24–26; PRR BOD Minutes, February 1, 1871, 441–44; David R. Contosta, *A Philadelphia Family: The Houstons and Woodwards of Chestnut Hill* (Philadelphia: University of Pennsylvania Press, 1992), 15, 40; *Men and Women of America: A Biographical Dictionary of Contemporaries* (New York: L. R. Hamersly & Co., 1910), 97.

74. The earliest preferred-stock issues were generally employed as a temporary expedient in order to raise funds for construction. During the 1860s, Samuel Tilden, along with Thomson and other investors, relied on preferred stock to lower the heavy debt load of the bankrupt Pittsburgh, Fort Wayne & Chicago. During the 1860s, the overuse of preferred stock had damaged its reputation. In addition to the Pennsylvania Company preferred stock, several of the PRR's subsidiaries, including the Philadelphia & Erie, the Allegheny Valley, the Cumberland Valley, and the Columbus, Chicago & Indiana Central, among others, had issued preferred stock on their own account. The Pennsylvania Railroad held many of those preferred stocks as part of its investments in various subsidiaries. The PRR proper did not issue preferred stock, however—even though its original 1846 stock offering carried a guaranteed interest rate during the construction phase. George Heberton Evans, Jr., "The Early History of Preferred Stock in the United States," American Economic Review 19 (March 1929): 43–58, at 58; Evans, "Preferred Stock in the United States, 1850–1878," American Economic Review 21 (March 1931): 56–62; Jonathan Barron Baskin, "The Development of Corporate Financial Markets in Britain and the United States, 1600–1914: Overcoming Asymmetric Information," *Business History Review* 62 (Summer 1988): 199–237, at 219–20; Chandler, *Henry Varnum Poor*, 137.

75. The Pennsylvania Company paid fixed annual rentals to its subsidiaries, such as the Fort Wayne. In return, the Pennsylvania Company held the securities of those subsidiaries, and collected all net income in excess of the rental payments. In order to fund improvements, subsidiaries issued "special betterment stock," likewise held by the Pennsylvania Company. The Pennsylvania Company in turn deposited the special betterment stock with a trust company, such as Girard. The Girard Trust Company, knowing that the betterment stock was ultimately guaranteed by a lien against the Pennsylvania Railroad, then issued its own trust certificates (in $1,000 denominations, and paying 3½ percent interest) that were in turn backed by the stock of the subsidiary company. The Pennsylvania Company could then sell the Girard trust certificates on the open market and transfer the proceeds to its subsidiaries. John P. Green, "Financing the Pennsylvania Railroad," n.d., ca. 1905, HML, Box 419, folder 556; Burgess and Kennedy, *Centennial History*, 219–21.

76. Lines East is employed here in its geographic sense, as encompassing all trackage east of Pittsburgh and Erie. In terms of corporate organization, Lines East encompassed only the PRR proper and the lines leased to the PRR, most notably the Philadelphia & Erie and, later, the United New Jersey Railroad & Canal Company (the successor to the Joint Companies). The PRR controlled additional carriers, such as the Northern Central and the Cumberland Valley (and, eventually, the Philadelphia, Wilmington & Baltimore) through stock ownership. Those companies maintained separate boards of directors, although their directors frequently overlapped with those on the PRR. They thus remained organizationally separate from the PRR's Lines East corporate structure. E-mail from Christopher T. Baer, January 2010.

77. Henry V. Poor, *Manual of the Railroads of the United States for 1874–75* (New York: H. V. Poor, 1874), 667–70.

78. The PRR's other fast freight affiliate, the Empire Line, continued in service, as it still played a vital role in drawing oil shipments away from the New York Central and the Erie. By the late 1870s, Thaw, Houston, and the others who had received Pennsylvania Company stock for their share of the Union Line in turn traded those securities for PRR stock—largely because the PRR board was concerned that the heirs of those initial investors might be less loyal to the railroad and sell a part interest in the Pennsylvania Company to potentially hostile outside interests. Beginning in 1887, Lines West and Lines East jointly managed the operations of the Union Line Bureau. William Z. Ripley, *Railroads: Rates and Regulation* (New York: Longmans, Green, and Co., 1912; repr. New York: Arno Press, 1973), 443.

79. Craig Sanders, *Limited, Locals, and Expresses in Indiana 1838–1971* (Bloomington: Indiana University Press, 2003), 109–10.

80. J. Edgar Thomson to William Mahone, December 30, 1865, Papers of General William Mahone, Petersburg, Virginia, quoted in Nelson Morehouse Blake, *William Mahone of Virginia: Soldier and Political Insurgent* (Richmond: Garrett & Massie, 1935), 76.

81. *Twenty-Fifth Annual Report of the Board of Directors of the Pennsylvania Railroad Co. to the Stockholders, February 20, 1872* (Philadelphia: E. C. Markley & Son, 1872), 16.

82. William Thaw was president of the Pennsylvania Company from June 1, 1870 until January 20, 1871. He was succeeded by Tom Scott, who attained the PRR presidency on June 3, 1874.

83. Church, *Corporate History*, vol. 1, 1–10; *By-Laws and Organization for Conducting the Business of the Pennsylvania Company, As Approved by the Board of Directors, October 12th 1876, to take effect November 1st, 1876* (Philadelphia: Review Printing House, 1877); Chandler, *Visible Hand*, 176–77.

84. James M. Symes, the PRR's president between 1954 and 1960, also spent much of his career on Lines West and its successor, the Western Region. Poor, *Manual of the Railroads . . . for 1874–75*, 385–88; *New York Times*, February 9, 1891; *Engineering Journal* 65 (March 1891), 139; Chandler, *Visible Hand*, 176–77.

85. For a brief period, between January and August 1874, McCullough was simultaneously the first vice president and the general manager, but he relinquished the latter post to James D. Layng, a veteran of the Ohio & Pennsylvania, the Steubenville & Indiana, and the Fort Wayne—but who nonetheless spent the later stages of his career as an executive with the New York Central. Mitchell C. Harrison, *New York State's Prominent and Progressive Men: An Encyclopedia of Contemporaneous Biography*, vol. 1 (New York: The Tribune Association, 1900): 226–27.

86. Information regarding Thomas Jewett's stroke is from http://boards.ancestry.com/thread.aspx?mv=flat&m=286&p=surnames.jewett, accessed on June 28, 2011.

87. Poor, *Manual of the Railroads . . . for 1874–75*, 655, 666, 694; James Grant Wilson and John Fiske, eds., *Appletons's Cyclopedia of American Biography*, vol. 3 (New York: D. Appleton & Co., 1888), 433–34.

88. *New York Times*, September 30, 1885.

89. Christopher T. Baer, William J. Coxey, and Paul W. Schopp, *The Trail of the Blue Comet: A History of the Jersey Central's New Jersey Southern Division* (Palmyra, N.Y.: West Jersey Chapter of the National Railway Historical Society, 1994), 50–58.

90. Burgess and Kennedy, *Centennial History*, 266–70.

91. In May 1872, the Camden & Amboy, the Delaware and Raritan Canal Company, and the New Jersey Rail Road (the Joint Board of Directors of the United Canal & Railroad Companies of New Jersey) were consolidated as the United New Jersey Railroad & Canal Company. *Report of the Investigating Committee*, 38.

92. Puffert, "The Standardization of Track Gauge," 953; Puffert, *Tracks Across Continents*, 144; David W. Messer and Charles S. Roberts, *Triumph V: Philadelphia to New York, 1830–2002* (Baltimore: Barnard, Roberts & Co., 2002), 33, 65–66, 105, 350.

93. Carl W. Condit, *The Port of New York: A History of the Rail and Terminal System from the Beginnings to Pennsylvania Station* (Chicago: University of Chicago Press, 1980), 166.

94. In part, however, the losses attributed to the New Jersey lines were an accounting device, based on the allocation of earnings per mile of track. Thus, the United Railroads of New Jersey Grand Division bore the entire cost of terminal operations at Harsimus Cove and other New York locations, even if the freight processed there came from parts of the PRR system well outside of New Jersey. Wilson, *History of the Pennsylvania Railroad*, vol. 1, 222–23; Ward, *Master of the Pennsylvania*, 151–53; Burgess and Kennedy, *Centennial History*, 240.

95. Samuel Rea, *Pennsylvania Railroad New York Tunnel Extension—Historical Outline: Remarks of Mr. Samuel Rea, Second Vice-President, at the Annual Dinner to the President, Given by the Board of Directors of the Pennsylvania Railroad Co., December 15, 1909* (Philadelphia: Allen, Lane & Scott, 1909), 6 (quote).

96. There was a third option, although one that was not yet complete during the immediate postwar period. The Columbia & Port Deposit Railroad, a company that traced its origins to 1857, was constructing a line along the Susquehanna River, from Columbia south to a junction with the PW&B at Port Deposit, Maryland. Construction did not begin until 1867, however, and the line, barely forty miles long, was still incomplete a decade later. The PRR acquired the line, often referred to as the "Port Road," in 1877.

97. James D. Dilts, *The Great Road: The Building of the Baltimore and Ohio, the Nation's First Railroad, 1828–1853* (Stanford, Calif.: Stanford University Press, 1993), 151–59.

98. Wilson, *History of the Pennsylvania Railroad*, vol. 1, 276–92, 332–33.

99. Clayton Colman Hall, ed., *Baltimore: Its History and Its People*, vol. 1, *History* (New York: Lewis Historical Publishing, 1912), 492–93; Wilson, *History of the Pennsylvania Railroad*, vol. 1, 333–35.

100. Burgess and Kennedy, *Centennial History*, 275.

101. Hall, *Baltimore*, 306; Herbert H. Harwood, *Impossible Challenge: The Baltimore and Ohio Railroad in Maryland* (Baltimore: Barnard, Roberts & Co., 1979), 146–47; *Railroad Company v. Maryland*, 88 U.S. 21 Wall, 456 (1874); Joshua Dorsey Warfield, *The Founders of Anne Arundel and Howard Counties, Maryland: A Genealogical and Biographical Review from Wills, Deeds and Church Records* (Baltimore: Kohn & Pollock, 1905), 287–88.

102. Dian Olson Belanger, "The Railroad in the Park: Washington's Baltimore & Potomac Station, 1872–1907," *Washington History* 2 (Spring 1990): 4–27; Wilson, *History of the Pennsylvania Railroad*, vol. 1, 333–36; Burgess and Kennedy, *Centennial History*, 272–76; Ward, *Master of the Pennsylvania*, 150; Harwood, *Impossible Challenge*, 146.

103. Jacob Harry Hollander, *The Financial History of Baltimore* (Baltimore: Johns Hopkins University Press, 1899), 322–24; Hall, *Baltimore*, 494–95.

104. Initially, the Baltimore & Susquehanna relied on the B&O tracks along Pratt Street for access to dock facilities in Baltimore. In 1840, the Baltimore & Susquehanna built its own line to Baltimore's Inner Harbor. Robert L. Gunnarsson, *The Story of the Northern Central Railway, from Baltimore to Lake Ontario* (Sykesville, Md.: Greenberg Publishing, 1991), 30–33.

105. John Thomas Scharf, *History of Baltimore City and County, from the Earliest Period to the Present Day: Including Biographical Sketches of their Representative Men* (Philadelphia: Louis H. Everts, 1881), 353–55; Gunnarsson, *Northern Central Railway*, 98–99.

106. Wilson, *History of the Pennsylvania Railroad*, vol. 1, 262, 277–78; Hall, *Baltimore*, 488–89; Charles S. Roberts and David W. Messer, *Triumph*

VI: *Philadelphia, Columbia, Harrisburg to Baltimore and Washington, D.C., 1987–2003* (Baltimore: Barnard, Roberts & Co., 2003), 229.

107. *Twenty-Fifth Annual Report*, 21.

108. Maybee, *Railroad Competition and the Oil Trade*, 236–39; Harold F. Williamson and Arnold D. Daum, *The American Petroleum Industry, 1859–1899: The Age of Illumination* (Evanston, Ill.: Northwestern University Press, 1959), 298; Allan Nevins, *Study in Power: John D. Rockefeller, Industrialist and Philanthropist*, vol. 1 (New York: Charles Scribner's Sons, 1953), 80.

109. Williamson and Daum, *The American Petroleum Industry*, 291–92.

110. Nevins, *Study in Power*, vol. 1, 60.

111. Maybee, *Railroad Competition and the Oil Trade*, 220–24, 229; Nevins, *Study in Power*, vol. 1, 61.

112. Maybee, *Railroad Competition and the Oil Trade*, 197, 220–24, 229; Williamson and Daum, *The American Petroleum Industry*, 298–300.

113. Williamson and Daum, *The American Petroleum Industry*, 301–3; Nevins, *Study in Power*, vol. 1, 58–65; Burton J. Hendrick, *The Age of Big Business: A Chronicle of the Captains of Industry* (New Haven, Conn.: Yale University Press, 1919), 14; Testimony of W. H. Doane and "Contract Between the South Improvement Company and the Pennsylvania Railroad," January 18, 1872, in *A History of the Rise and Fall of The South Improvement Company, Report of The Executive Committee of the Petroleum Producers' Union, Embracing the Reports of the Sub-Committees on Transportation, Legislation, Investigation, and Treasurer's Report*, Oil City, Pa. (Lancaster, Pa.: Wylie & Griest, 1872), 45, 97–102; Ron Chernow, *Titan: The Life of John D. Rockefeller, Sr.* (New York: Vintage Books, 1998), 134–36, 142–43; Maybee, *Railroad Competition and the Oil Trade*, 255–63.

114. Williamson and Daum, *The American Petroleum Industry*, 303–5.

115. PRR BOD Minutes, April 1, 1868, 214.

116. Tarbell, *A History of the Standard Oil Company*, 48 (quote).

117. Williamson and Daum, *The American Petroleum Industry*, 309–10, 334.

118. Ibid., 343–46.

119. Tarbell, *A History of the Standard Oil Company*, 48; Nevins, *Study in Power*, vol. 1, 95.

120. Nevins, *Study in Power*, vol. 1, 97–98.

121. Rockefeller made these comments, very late in his life, in a series of interviews with *New York World* reporter William O. Inglis. The interviews were an attempt to repair the damage to Rockefeller's reputation, caused by the publication of Ida Tarbell's exposé, *The History of the Standard Oil Company*, in 1904. As such, Rockefeller was anxious to blame Scott, or indeed anyone other than himself, for the furor surrounding the South Improvement Company. John D. Rockefeller, with William O. Inglis and David Freeman Hawke, *John D. Rockefeller Interview, 1917–1920* (Westport, Conn.: Meckler Publishing, in Association with the Rockefeller Archive Center, 1984), 28 ("scheme"), 362 ("represented the views").

122. Williamson and Daum, *The American Petroleum Industry*, 347–48.

123. John Thomas Scharf and Thompson Westcott, *History of Philadelphia, 1609–1884*, vol. 3 (Philadelphia: L. H. Everts & Co., 1884), 2025; Maybee, *Railroad Competition and the Oil Trade*, 285–92, 298, 300, 327; Nevins, *Study in Power*, vol. 1, 103–5, 109–10.

124. Rockefeller, *Interview*, 480.

125. Maybee, *Railroad Competition and the Oil Trade*, 303, 306; Nevins, *Study in Power*, vol. 1, 106.

126. Nevins, *Study in Power*, vol. 1, 106.

127. Ibid., 106–7.

128. Williamson and Daum, *The American Petroleum Industry*, 349–50.

129. Maybee, *Railroad Competition and the Oil Trade*, 304–12.

130. "Extracts from the Testimony of W. G. Warden," Washington, D.C., March 30, 1872, in Tarbell, *History of the Standard Oil Company*, 306.

131. Scott, seconded by Empire Line president Joseph D. Potts, suggested (according to Peter Watson's congressional testimony, reprinted in *A History of the Rise and Fall of the South Improvement Company*), that "You can't succeed unless the producers are taken care of." The phrase "taken care of" is open to multiple interpretations, ranging from the avuncular to the sinister. Nevins, *Study in Power*, vol. 1, 108; Williamson and Daum, *The American Petroleum Industry*, 350.

132. Williamson and Daum, *The American Petroleum Industry*, 350.

133. Tarbell, *A History of the Standard Oil Company*, 79.

134. Maybee, *Railroad Competition and the Oil Trade*, 327–29, 380.

135. Tarbell, *A History of the Standard Oil Company*, 72–73 (quotes); *A History of the Rise and Fall of the South Improvement Company*, 9–11.

136. Tarbell, *A History of the Standard Oil Company*, 79; Chernow, *Titan*, 138–40.

137. Nevins, *Study in Power*, vol. 1, 45–46.

138. Maybee, *Railroad Competition and the Oil Trade*, 175–81; Williamson and Daum, *The American Petroleum Industry*, 183–89, 364; J. T. Henry, *The Early and Later History of Petroleum, With Authentic Facts in Regard to Its Development in Western Pennsylvania* (Philadelphia: James B. Rodgers Co., 1873), 531–33.

139. In February 1875, for example, PRR officials demonstrated their ability to block pipeline construction. The Columbia Conduit Company erected a pipeline over Western Pennsylvania Railroad (PRR) tracks at Powers Run, Pennsylvania. The courts had denied the company the right of eminent domain and, absent that authority, nothing prevented PRR employees from simply ripping up the portion of the pipeline that crossed the railroad's right of way. Maybee, *Railroad Competition and the Oil Trade*, 353–54.

140. Maybee, *Railroad Competition and the Oil Trade*, 353–57; Williamson and Daum, *The American Petroleum Industry*, 351–52.

141. Williamson and Daum, *The American Petroleum Industry*, 351.

142. Nevins, *Study in Power*, vol. 1, 124.

143. Maybee, *Railroad Competition and the Oil Trade*, 347, 362–65; Williamson and Daum, *The American Petroleum Industry*, 351. For Cornelius Vanderbilt's perspective on the South Improvement Company, see T. J. Stiles, *The First Tycoon: The Epic Life of Cornelius Vanderbilt* (New York: Alfred A. Knopf, 2009), 519–22.

144. This was the Buffalo & Jamestown Railroad, incorporated in 1872. The company built only as far south as Kennedy, New York, and a connection with the Atlantic & Great Western, never reaching Titusville. In 1880, the Erie leased the company, recently reorganized as the Buffalo & Southwestern Railroad. Paul V. Pietrak, Joseph G. Streamer, and James A. Van Brocklin, *The History of the Western New York & Pennsylvania Railway Company and Its Predecessors and Successors* (Hamburg, N.Y.: s.n. 2000), 3(15).

145. Maybee, *Railroad Competition and the Oil Trade*, 337–53, 357.

146. Nevins, *Study in Power*, vol. 1, 128.

147. Rockefeller, *Interview*, 362.

148. Nevins, *Study in Power*, vol. 1, 126; Tarbell, *A History of the Standard Oil Company*, 90; Chernow, *Titan*, 141–42; *A History of the Rise and Fall of The South Improvement Company*, 17.

149. Maybee, *Railroad Competition and the Oil Trade*, 360; Burgess and Kennedy, *Centennial History*, 162–67.

150. Williamson and Daum, *The American Petroleum Industry*, 364–66.

151. Ibid., 360–66.

152. Maybee, *Railroad Competition and the Oil Trade*, 366–69, 375, 391; Williamson and Daum, *The American Petroleum Industry*, 352–60.

153. Quoted in Gabriel Kolko, *Railroads and Regulation, 1877–1916* (Princeton, N.J.: Princeton University Press, 1965), 22.

154. Quoted in Tarbell, *A History of the Standard Oil Company*, 103; Maybee, *Railroad Competition and the Oil Trade*, 376–77.

155. Mahlon H. Hellerich, "The Origin of the Pennsylvania Constitutional Convention of 1873," *Pennsylvania History* 34 (April 1967): 158–86.

156. Mahlon H. Hellerich, "Railroad Regulation in the Constitutional Convention of 1873," *Pennsylvania History* 26 (January 1959): 35–53.

157. Hellerich, "Railroad Regulation," 42–43; Samuel T. Wiley, ed., *Biographical and Portrait Cyclopedia of the Nineteenth Congressional District, Pennsylvania, Containing Biographical Sketches of Prominent and Representatives Citizens of the District* (Philadelphia: C. A. Ruoff, 1879), 165–68, 267–68; Abram Douglas Harlan, *Pennsylvania Constitutional Convention, 1872 and 1873: Its Members and Officers and the Results of Their Labors* (Philadelphia: Inquirer Book and Job Print, 1873), 60, 73.

158. Hellerich, "Railroad Regulation," 42–43; Harlan, *Pennsylvania Constitutional Convention*, 63, 65–66, 88–89; *New York Times*, May 6, 1873.

159. Harlan, *Pennsylvania Constitutional Convention*, 22–23.

160. Hellerich, "Railroad Regulation in the Constitutional Convention of 1873," 47–53.

161. In later years, many states adopted progressively more liberal general incorporation laws, with Delaware's 1899 version symbolizing a "race to the bottom," in which corporate affairs took precedence over the public interest. In 1874, however, the intent of Pennsylvania's legislators was to reduce political influence peddling and encourage competition in the interest of lower costs, and not to attract corporate headquarters from other states. For a discussion of the effects of general incorporation laws, see, for example, William G. Roy, *Socializing Capital: The Rise of the Large Industrial Corporation in America* (Princeton, N.J.: Princeton University Press, 1997) and Naomi R. Lamoreaux, *The Great Merger Movement in American Business, 1895–1904* (New York: Cambridge University Press, 1985). Pennsylvania passed a general *railroad* incorporation law in 1868, largely in response to the PRR's efforts to prevent the B&O-affiliated Pittsburgh & Connellsville from building to Pittsburgh. Connecticut passed the first general incorporation law in 1837, followed by Virginia (1860), California (1863), Arizona (1866), Maryland (1868), and Illinois (1872). Other states followed the same model, after 1874, including New York and New Jersey (1875), Maine (1876), Rhode Island (1893), Delaware (1899), Massachusetts (1902), and Alabama (1903). Adolf Augustus Berle and Gardiner Coit Means, *The Modern Corporation and Private Property* (New Brunswick, N.J.: Transaction, 1991, 1932), 127; Angelo T. Freedley, *The General Corporation Law of Pennsylvania (Approved 29th April, 1874) and Supplementary Acts, with Notes, Forms and Index* (Philadelphia: T. & J. W. Johnson, 1882).

162. Wilson, *History of the Pennsylvania Railroad*, vol. 2, 301–8.

163. As historian Robert Harrison has observed, "The Pennsylvania Railroad and other large companies might employ or assist members both during and after their service in the legislature, since it was not clear that their patronage was connected with any particular action or vote on the part of the recipient." Robert Harrison, "The Hornets' Nest at Harrisburg: A Study of the Pennsylvania Legislature in the Late 1870s," *Pennsylvania Magazine of History and Biography* 103 (July 1979): 334–55, at 342–44, 347 (quote).

164. Carmen DiCiccio, *Coal and Coke in Pennsylvania* (Harrisburg: Pennsylvania Historical and Museum Commission, 1996), 9; F. Charles Petrillo, *Anthracite and Slackwater: The North Branch Canal, 1828–1901* (Easton, Pa.: Center for Canal History and Technology, 1986), 13.

165. Petrillo, *Anthracite and Slackwater*, 125–34, 141–42, 151.

166. Ibid., 207–9.

167. Isaac J. Wistar, *Autobiography of Isaac Jones Wistar, 1827–1905*, vol. 2 (Philadelphia: Wistar Institute of Anatomy and Biology, 1914), 119–24.

168. Wistar, *Autobiography*, 132–33.

169. At their greatest extent, in 1872, the canals operated by the PRR Canal Department covered the distance between Columbia and Hollidaysburg (173 miles), from Clark's Ferry (Duncan's Island) to Farrandsville (112 miles) and from Northumberland to Wilkes-Barre (64 miles), and the Wiconsico Canal (12 miles). In May 1858, the commonwealth sold the North Branch Division to the Sunbury & Erie Railroad, with the property then resold to the North Branch Canal Company. In June, the two portions of the canal were again sold. The section between Northumberland and Wilkes-Barre (64 miles) went to the Wyoming Canal Company. That firm entered receivership in 1861, and was reorganized as the Wyoming Valley Canal Company in 1863. In 1865, the more northerly portion of the North Branch Division, between Wilkes-Barre and the New York state line (103 miles), was transferred to the Pennsylvania & New York Canal & Railroad Company, under the control of the Lehigh Valley Railroad. It was abandoned in 1882. In 1871, the Erie & Pittsburgh Railroad purchased the Erie Canal Company route between Erie and the Ohio River at Beaver. The Erie Canal (not to be confused with the profitable Erie Canal across New York) carried little traffic, but it was worth acquiring for its nuisance value. It was largely abandoned in 1871 following the collapse of an aqueduct over Elk Creek.

170. Petrillo, *Anthracite and Slackwater*, 189–209, 215–19; Petrillo, "The Pennsylvania Canal Company (1857–1926): The New Main Line Canal—Nanticoke to Columbia," *Canal History and Technology Proceedings*, vol. 6 (March 28, 1987): 83–112, at 94–97, 96–98. For details regarding canal operations during the late nineteenth century, see Gerald Smeltzer, *Canals Along the Lower Susquehanna (1796 to 1800)* (York, Pa.: Historical Society of York County, 1963).

171. Petrillo, "The Pennsylvania Canal Company," 101.

172. Wistar, *Autobiography*, 133–34.

173. The Lykens Valley Coal Company was incorporated in June 1836. It should not be confused with the Lykens Valley Railroad & Coal Company (incorporated in April 1830), which was a transportation, and not a mining firm. The Summit Branch Railroad dated to 1846, and the Mineral Railroad & Mining Company to 1864. Between 1866 and 1880, the Summit Branch Railroad leased and operated the Lykens Valley Railroad & Coal Company, and during the 1870s established control over the Lykens Valley Coal Company, as well. In 1880, the Northern Central leased the Lykens Valley Railroad & Coal Company. The Susquehanna Coal Company was chartered in April 1867 as the Pittston Railroad & Coal Company, and changed its name in February 1869. The PRR owned directly two-thirds of the stock of Susquehanna Coal, with the remainder controlled by the Pennsylvania Canal Company. Wistar, *Autobiography*, 134–35, 140. Coverdale & Colpitts, *Corporate, Financial and Construction History*, vol. 1, 128–35; William Hasell Wilson, *Notes on the Internal Improvements of Pennsylvania* (Philadelphia: Railway World, 1879), 56–59; William Henry Moyer, "PRR's Navy, Part V: Pennsylvania Canals," *The Keystone* 42 (Summer 2009): 21–34; Eliot Jones, *The Anthracite Coal Combination in the United States, With Some Account of the Early Development of the Anthracite Industry* (Cambridge, Mass.: Harvard University Press, 1914), 85, 125–26; Gunnarsson, *Northern Central Railway*, 77–78.

174. Sunbury, on the Philadelphia & Erie, was the junction with the Danville, Hazleton & Wilkesbarre Railroad, paralleling the Wyoming Valley Canal Company for much of the distance. Begun in 1859 as the Wilkesbarre & Pittston Railroad, by December 1871 the line was open between Sunbury and Tomhicken, where a connection with the Lehigh Valley provided access to Hazleton. In February 1872, the PRR leased the Danville,

Hazleton & Wilkesbarre, which immediately became part of a routing that took anthracite over the Lehigh Valley, the Belvidere-Delaware Railroad, and the recently leased United New Jersey Railroad & Canal Companies. The Belvidere-Delaware was a subsidiary of the United Companies, and within weeks, the PRR was operating both lines as part of the United Railroads of New Jersey Grand Division. In order to reach Wilkes-Barre, the PRR relied on the North & West Branch Railroad, incorporated in 1871 as part of an effort to link Wilkes-Barre with Williamsport. Construction began in 1880, and despite an 1881 reorganization was completed between Catawissa and Wilkes-Barre in 1882, along the old towpath of the Wyoming Division Canal. The Danville, Hazleton & Wilkesbarre was initially operated as part of the Eastern Division of the Philadelphia & Erie, but in 1873 became the separate Sunbury Division. By 1875, in the midst of the economic recession, the PRR allowed the Danville, Hazleton & Wilkesbarre to fall into receivership, owing to a dispute over the terms of the 1872 lease. The company was reorganized in 1878 as the Sunbury, Hazleton & Wilkesbarre Railroad. In 1900, the North & West Branch combined with the Sunbury, Hazleton & Wilkesbarre and several other lines to form the Schuylkill & Juniata Railroad, a PRR subsidiary. One other significant component of the Schuylkill & Juniata was the Sunbury & Lewistown Railroad, linking Selinsgrove Junction on the Northern Central with Lewistown on the PRR main line. PRR officials intended that the line would expedite the movement of anthracite from northeastern Pennsylvania to furnaces near Lewistown, as well as at locations farther west. In addition, iron ore from the Juniata Valley could move east toward Danville. The route never lived up to expectations, however.

175. Charles S. Roberts and David W. Messer, *Triumph VII: Harrisburg to the Lakes, Wilkes-Barre, Oil City and Red Bank, 1827–2004* (Baltimore: Barnard, Roberts & Co., 2004), 30, 60, 63; Howard W. Schotter, *The Growth and Development of the Pennsylvania Railroad Company: A Review of the Charter and Annual Reports of the Pennsylvania Railroad Company 1846 to 1926, Inclusive* (Philadelphia: Allen, Lane & Scott, 1927), 154–56.

176. Henry V. Poor, *Manual of the Railroads of the United States, 1881* (New York: H. V. Poor, 1881), 270; Watkins History, "Administration of President Thomson, 1873," 165.

177. Ironically, during the late 1860s, before the PRR had become heavily invested in coal lands, Pennsylvania Canal Company president Isaac Wistar had urged J. Edgar Thomson to support legislation that would have prohibited railroads from owing collieries. Thomson declined to pursue the matter, however. On December 31, 1873, the day before the new constitution went into effect, the PRR acquired $1 million in Susquehanna Coal Company stock, nearly doubling the PRR's investment in that company. Wistar, *Autobiography*, 134; Jones, *The Anthracite Coal Combination*, 124.

178. *Report of the Investigating Committee*, 136.

179. In 1854, the Philadelphia & Baltimore Central (a Pennsylvania-chartered company) absorbed the Baltimore & Philadelphia Railroad, its Maryland-chartered counterpart.

180. In 1865, Samuel Morse Felton resigned the presidency of the PW&B, owing to ill health. He soon accepted a new set of responsibilities, becoming president of both the PRR-affiliated Pennsylvania Steel Company and of the Philadelphia & Baltimore Central. In 1868, under Felton's guidance, the Philadelphia & Baltimore Central leased the Chester Creek Railroad. When completed in April 1869, the Chester Creek linked Baltimore Junction to a connection with the Philadelphia, Wilmington & Baltimore at Lamokin, Pennsylvania. Philadelphia & Baltimore Central construction crews also built west to Octoraro, Maryland, on the eastern bank of the Susquehanna River, where they established a second connection with the PW&B. John Thomas Scharf, *History of Delaware, 1609–1888*, vol. 1 (Philadelphia: L. J. Richards & Co., 1888), 425–26; Scharf and Wescott, *History*

of Philadelphia, vol. 3 (Philadelphia: L. H. Everts & C., 1884), 2197–98; Wilson, *History of the Pennsylvania Railroad*, vol. 1, 327–30.

181. The Washington & Maryland Line Railroad was chartered in Pennsylvania in April 1857. In February 1858, the Maryland legislature chartered the Columbia & Port Deposit Railroad. In 1860, the Pennsylvania Company was renamed the Columbia & Maryland Line Railroad in 1860. Four years later it was consolidated with the Maryland company, under the common name of the Columbia & Port Deposit Railroad.

182. The PW&B's acquisition of the Philadelphia & Baltimore Central isolated the West Chester & Philadelphia and reduced it to the status of a local carrier. During the late 1870s, railroad promoter Henry S. McComb attempted to establish control over the West Chester & Philadelphia, as part of his efforts to create a route between Philadelphia and Baltimore, paralleling the PW&B. In 1880, PW&B officials acquired the West Chester & Philadelphia, in order to blunt the McComb threat. In 1881, when the PRR gained control over the PW&B, those lines became part of the PRR system, as did the West Chester & Philadelphia and its subsidiary, the West Chester Railroad. PRR BOD Minutes, January 9, 1867, 97, June 13, 1877, 412.

183. In May 1893, the Philadelphia, Wilmington & Baltimore (at that time controlled by the PRR) leased the Columbia & Port Deposit. *Columbia Spy*, September 21, 1867, April 17, 1869, November 5, 1870, January 28, 1871, February 25, 1871; Burgess and Kennedy, *Centennial History*, 375–76; Wilson, *History of the Pennsylvania Railroad*, vol. 1, 193. I extend my appreciation to Christopher Baer for his insights into the history of the Columbia & Port Deposit, the Philadelphia & Baltimore Central, and the West Chester & Philadelphia railroads.

184. Chandler, *The Visible Hand*, 155.

185. Howard W. Schotter, "Scope of the Pennsylvania Railroad System," July 2, 1937, HML, Box 219, folder 12.

186. Schotter, "Scope of the System," 14–15.

187. The figure is from 1936. Schotter, "Scope of the System," 19.

188. Richard E. Sylla, *The American Capital Market, 1846–1914: A Study of the Effects of Public Policy on Economic Development* (New York: Arno Press, 1975), 1–70; Gerald Berk, *Alternative Tracks: The Constitution of American Industrial Order, 1865–1917* (Baltimore: Johns Hopkins University Press, 1994), 32–35. Considerable debate has emerged as to the timing and the causes of the development of American financial markets. Some scholars, most notably Alfred D. Chandler, Jr., have asserted that the burgeoning railroad industry essentially created Wall Street. Others, such as Richard Sylla, have shown that other factors, particularly federal banking policies, principally those enacted during the Civil War, played a critical role in determining the scope and character of American finance capital. Chandler likewise suggested that New York did not attain its financial dominance until the period after the Civil War, with Vincent Carosso suggesting that the American investment-banking sector as a whole was weak, prior to 1860, while Sylla, Gerald Berk, Edwin J. Perkins, and others have set the date several decades earlier. For a cogent summary of these debates, see O'Sullivan, "Finance Capital."

189. When the Civil War began, PRR officials were already well acquainted with Jay Cooke. In 1833, his sister, Sarah, had married William G. Moorhead, one of the leading businessmen in Pittsburgh. Moorhead, in conjunction with his brother, J. Kennedy Moorhead, had established the Washington Packet Line, operating over the Main Line of Public Works, and they invited Cooke to join them as a clerk. In 1857, William G. Moorhead became the president of the Sunbury & Erie Railroad. PRR officials were also familiar with Cooke's role in refinancing some of the leftover portions of the state's canal system that the PRR had not purchased, including the Delaware Division, the Wyoming Division, and the West Branch Divi-

sion. Before the war, they had also worked with the financier, through E. W. Clark & Company. Ellis Paxon Oberholtzer, *Jay Cooke: Financier of the Civil War*, vol. 1 (Philadelphia: George W. Jacobs, 1907), 40–43, 99–100, 112. See also M. John Lubetkin, *Jay Cooke's Gamble: The Northern Pacific Railroad, the Sioux, and the Panic of 1873* (Norman: University of Oklahoma Press, 2006).

190. Dorothy R. Adler and Muriel E. Hidy, eds., *British Investment in American Railways, 1834–1898* (Charlottesville: University Press of Virginia, 1970), 144–45.

191. Chandler, *Henry Varnum Poor*, esp. 205–25 and 247–50; Richard White, "Information, Markets, and Corruption: Transcontinental Railroads in the Gilded Age," *Journal of American History* 90 (June 2003): 19–43.

192. Chandler, *Henry Varnum Poor*, 220–25.

193. In the railroad industry as a whole, in 1855, debt represented only 39 percent of total capitalization. Debt did not exceed equity until 1872. Berk, *Alternative Tracks*, 49.

194. Stephen J. Lubben, "Railroad Receiverships and Modern Bankruptcy Theory," *Columbia Law Review* 89 (September 2004): 1420–75, at 1433–35.

195. Schotter, *Growth and Development*, 65–66, 72–73.

196. Mira Wilkins, *A History of Foreign Investment in the United States to 1914* (Cambridge, Mass.: Harvard University Press, 1989), 473, 490; Adler, *British Investment*, 74, 147, 153.

197. Burgess and Kennedy, *Centennial History*, 300.

198. Ibid., 303.

199. Ibid., 70, 298–301; Schotter, *Growth and Development*, 65–66, 72–73.

200. Burgess and Kennedy, *Centennial History*, 300–302; Schotter, *Growth and Development*, 56–58, 66–72.

201. Burgess and Kennedy, *Centennial History*, 303–4.

202. Chandler, *The Visible Hand*, 155. Even before the Civil War, investment bankers had underwritten securities issues, but only in the sense that they promised to make a good-faith effort to find buyers. The novelty of the arrangement with Jay Cooke stemmed from the banker's willingness to take the bonds up front, regardless of whether he could immediately find buyers for them—a form of underwriting that became progressively more common by the late nineteenth century. I extend my appreciation to economic and business historian Edwin J. Perkins for his insights into underwriting practices.

203. PRR BOD Minutes, March 26, 1873, 150–53; Vincent P. Carosso and Rose C. Carosso, *The Morgans: Private International Bankers, 1854–1913* (Cambridge, Mass.: Harvard University Press, 1987), 224–25.

204. David Nasaw suggests, probably correctly, that Carnegie invented the tale of Baring Brothers' initial acceptance of the bonds, followed by their subsequent refusal, to cover the fact that he was demanding too high a price for the securities. PRR BOD Minutes, January 24, 1872, 26–34, April 23, 1873, 156–60; Nasaw, *Andrew Carnegie* (New York: Penguin Press, 2006), 126–28; Joseph Frazier Wall, *Andrew Carnegie* (New York: Oxford University Press, 1970), 282–86; Carosso, *The Morgans*, 708–709n14; Adler, *British Investment*, 206.

205. Carosso, *The Morgans*, 709n14.

206. Morgan's placement of New York Central securities in London reawakened the interest of European investors in American railways following the Panic of 1873. Leland H. Jenks, "Capital Movement and Transportation: Britain and American Railway Development," *Journal of Economic History* 11 (Autumn 1951): 375–88, at 377.

207. The NYC affiliation did not end the Morgan family association with the PRR, to be sure. In 1884, for example, Drexel & Company and

Drexel, Morgan oversaw the marketing of $3 million in 4¼ percent PRR bonds, in the United States, while J. S. Morgan & Company sold a portion of the bonds on the London market. Carosso, *The Morgans*, 709n14; Campbell, *The Reorganization of the American Railroad System*, 146–47.

208. Chandler, *The Visible Hand*, 155; Dan Rottenberg, *The Man Who Made Wall Street: Anthony J. Drexel and the Rise of Modern Finance* (Philadelphia: University of Pennsylvania Press, 2001), 80; Domenic Vitiello, with George E. Thomas, *The Philadelphia Stock Exchange and the City It Made* (Philadelphia: University of Pennsylvania Press, 2010), 92–93.

209. Chandler, *The Visible Hand*, 155; Wilkins, *Foreign Investment*, 470; Carosso, *The Morgans*, 223, 242–43, 248.

210. Burgess and Kennedy, *Centennial History*, 302–4.

211. Schotter, *Growth and Development*, 106–7.

212. After London, Asiatic & American failed, F. Boykett took over much of its business, including the PRR accounts. During the 1880s, Boykett yielded to T. W. Powell, of the Heseltine & Powell firm. Burgess and Kennedy, *Centennial History*, 304–6, 350; PRR BOD Minutes, February 2, 1874, May 2, 1874, May 7, 1874; Wilkins, *Foreign Investment*, 115, 875n3; Dolores Greenberg, *Financiers and Railroads, 1869–1889: A Study of Morton, Bliss & Company* (Newark: University of Delaware Press, 1980), 80; Schotter, *Growth and Development*, 107–9.

213. PRR BOD Minutes, May 2, 1874, 284–85, May 15, 1874, 286–94.

214. PRR BOD Minutes, February 2, 1874, 255–59, May 2, 1874, 284–85, May 15, 1874, 286–94, August 10, 1875, 54–62, December 3, 1875, 101–2.

215. William Z. Ripley, *Railroads: Finance and Organization* (New York: Longmans, Green, and Co., 1915), 456–57.

216. As Alfred D. Chandler, Jr., has observed, "In the years after the Civil War, external relations were becoming as critical to the successful operation of the new large railroads as were the development of internal organization and controls before the war." Chandler, *The Visible Hand*, 121.

217. Ibid., 125–29.

218. It should be noted that, over the years, the supervision of the general manager and the oversight of the Transportation Department shifted from office to office. The responsibilities tended to follow specific individuals, in this case Alexander J. Cassatt. Under the 1873 organization, he was the general manager, reporting directly to President Thomson, and shared transportation responsibilities with second vice president George Brooke Roberts, who also supervised the Accounting Department. Following the death of J. Edgar Thomson and the board's selection of Tom Scott as president, Frank Thomson replaced Cassatt as general manager of Lines East, allowing Cassatt to be promoted to third vice president—taking with him the traffic and transportation functions that had formerly been under the control of the general manager. In 1880, Cassatt was promoted to first vice president, bypassing the office of the second vice president and its oversight of accounting functions. With his authority over transportation traveling with him to his new post, there was no longer any need for the office of third vice president, which the board abolished. In addition to gaining oversight over the Transportation and Traffic Departments, Cassatt also retained the traditional first vice presidential duties associated with maintaining relationships with affiliated lines. Cassatt temporarily left the PRR in 1882, and Frank Thomson (who since 1874 had filled Cassatt's old post as general manager) took charge of transportation matters, but as the second vice president, not as the first vice president—at least until 1888, when he became first vice president and Transportation and Traffic oversight moved up the corporate ladder with him.

219. D. S. Newhall, "Purchasing Supplies," n.d., ca. 1905, HML, Box 419, folder 556.

220. In 1861, the board began to expand the PRR's legal functions, appointing a general counsel as an assistant to the Philadelphia district solici-

tor. Two years later, the board increased the centralization of legal functions, appointing an assistant secretary to oversee the eleven district solicitors. In May 1877, the board assigned three general counsels (one in Philadelphia, one in Pittsburgh, and one in New Jersey) to assist the general solicitor, a system that remained in place until 1881. Wilson, *History of the Pennsylvania Railroad*, vol. 2, 301–8; George Stuart Patterson, "The Growth and Functions of the Legal Department," n.d., ca. 1905, HML, Box 419, folder 556; "Historical Development of the Organization of the Pennsylvania Railroad," *Railroad Gazette* 14 (1882): 776–78, 793–94, 809–10, in Leland H. Jenks, "Early History of a Railway Organization," *Business History Review* 35 (Summer 1961): 163–79, at 168; Watkins History, vol. 2, "Freight Department," 7; "Legal Department," 31–32.

221. Wilson, *History of the Pennsylvania Railroad*, vol. 2, 173–74.

222. The three Grand Divisions and the other affiliated lines were primarily administrative, rather than operating, entities. In terms of day-to-day operations, it was more efficient to operate the portion of the Northern Central north of Harrisburg (the Susquehanna Division) in unison with the Eastern Division of the Philadelphia & Erie (renamed the Williamsport Division in 1909), with the same division superintendent managing both sections. In 1914, coincident with the PRR's lease of the Northern Central, the Susquehanna Division was formally merged into the Williamsport Division. Similarly, between 1875 and 1883, the portion of the Northern Central, south of Harrisburg (the Baltimore Division) shared a division superintendent with the Baltimore & Potomac. Gunnarsson, *Northern Central Railway*, 100, 146.

223. After 1875, the West Jersey system shared the same general manager as the PRR. The Philadelphia, Wilmington & Baltimore Railroad (acquired by the PRR in 1881) and the West Jersey & Seashore Railroad (an 1896 consolidation of existing lines) were also kept outside of the Grand Division structure. Beginning in 1883, and following the PRR's purchase of the Philadelphia, Wilmington & Baltimore, that subsidiary shared officers with the Baltimore & Potomac.

224. Neilson, "Executive Department"; Chandler, *The Visible Hand*, 178.

225. The position of superintendent of transportation had been reestablished in April 1870, when Cassatt became general superintendent.

226. On May 1, 1869, the post of general ticket agent was renamed general passenger and ticket agent, and it was changed again on April 1, 1872, to general passenger agent. On March 1, 1873, the board added an assistant general passenger agent and a general baggage agent, and assigned a general ticket agent to each Grand Division. Watkins History, vol. 2, "Passenger Department," 10.

227. "Historical Development," in Jenks, "Early History," 170 (quote); Chandler, *The Visible Hand*, 107.

228. Watkins History, "Pennsylvania Railroad Division," 20–21; Watkins History, "Freight Department," 7; PRR BOD Minutes, June 29, 1874, 312–15; Chandler, *Visible Hand*, 120–21, 128–30.

229. Effective August 1, 1874, the post of chief engineer of maintenance-of-way was abolished in favor of the title engineer maintenance-of-way. William H. Brown occupied that post between August 1, 1874, and December 31, 1881, when he was promoted to chief engineer. At that time, the position of engineer maintenance-of-way became vacant, with the corresponding duties being undertaken by the assistant chief engineer in charge of maintenance-of-way. Other new posts included the principal assistant engineer, maintenance-of-way, United Railroads of New Jersey Grand Division (created January 1, 1872), the principal assistant engineer, maintenance-of-way, PRR Grand Division (created January 1, 1878), and the principal assistant engineer, maintenance-of-way, Philadelphia & Erie Grand Division (created September 1, 1881). Watkins History, "Engineers, Maintenance of Way Department, Pennsylvania Railroad,

with Periods of Service, 1867–1897;" Wilson, *History of the Pennsylvania Railroad*, vol. 2, 174–75.

230. After Wilson retired in 1884, the comparable position became real estate agent.

231. The position of conveyancer (1877–81) and then chief conveyancer (1881–84), in charge of deeds and titles, was initially a part of the Legal Department, and was not transferred to the Real Estate Department until 1884. PRR BOD Minutes, June 29, 1874, 312–25. Watkins History, "Organization and Departments," 10; Wilson, *History of the Pennsylvania Railroad*, vol. 2, 156–61; Benjamin W. Carskaddon, "Functions and Growth of the Real Estate Department," n.d., ca. 1905, HML, Box 419, folder 556.

232. "Historical Development," in Jenks, "Early History," 169–70.

233. Wilson, *History of the Pennsylvania Railroad*, vol. 2, 190–91, 261–62.

234. Watkins History, vol. 2, "Maintenance of Way—Development of Track Standards," 64–66; Watkins, "Engineers, Maintenance of Way Department."

235. Watkins History, "Development of Track Standards," 64–69.

236. Some senior PRR executives began their careers in the Maintenance-of-Way Department, assigned to a division, and then entered the Special Apprentice Program at the Altoona shops, established in 1871. Those apprenticeships combined hands-on mechanical engineering experience with schooling in many aspects of the PRR's operations, and were quite different from the apprenticeships undertaken by machinists, boilermakers, and others who would expect to spend their entire careers as part of the working class. After completing the Special Apprenticeship Program, the best prospects ascended through the ranks of the Motive Power Department. William Wallace Atterbury followed that route to the presidency, but it was far more common for individuals with that type of training to rise no higher than a senior staff position, perhaps as mechanical engineer. Alexander J. Cassatt also rose through the ranks of the Motive Power Department, although prior to the establishment of the Special Apprentice Program. J. Aubrey Tyson, "The Making of Railway Officials," *Munsey's Magazine* 30 (March 1904): 868–72; *Railway World* 50 (December 14, 1906): 1076.

237. "Historical Development," in Jenks, "Early History," 178.

238. I extend my deep gratitude to Christopher Baer, whose knowledge of the PRR's organizational structure is unparalleled, for his insights into the promotion process. "Engineering Department of P.R.R., 1847 to Date," n.d., ca. 1905, HML, Box 609, folder 22.

239. Even though he rose through the ranks of the Transportation Department, William Wallace Atterbury nonetheless possessed a comprehensive view of the company, particularly in areas such as labor matters and public relations.

240. Those who followed the Thomson model included George Brooke Roberts (1880–97) and Roberts's protégé, Samuel Rea (1913–25). Rea proved himself with the management of the New York Improvements at the beginning of the twentieth century. The comparable Philadelphia Improvements, carried out mostly during the 1920s, produced a worthy successor to Rea, in the form of executive vice president Elisha Lee, but Lee died unexpectedly in August 1933. The suspension of large construction projects after 1929 effectively ended that path of promotion.

241. Those who followed the Scott model included Frank Thomson (1897–99) and Alexander J. Cassatt (1899–1906); Cassatt's protégé, William Wallace Atterbury (1925–35); and Atterbury's protégé, Martin W. Clement (1935–48). James McCrea (1907–12), James M. Symes (1854–1960), and Allen J. Greenough (1960–68) also followed that avenue of promotion.

242. The multigenerational nature of the advancement process made the PRR somewhat unique among American railroads. In 1898, an official of the Lehigh Valley Railroad suggested that "there was generally only one generation of managing engineers on a railroad." That was generally not true on the PRR. J. Shirley Eaton, "Educational Training for Railway Service," U.S. Department of the Interior, *Report of the Commissioner of Education, 1898–99* (Washington, D.C., 1900), 87, quoted in Stuart Morris, "Stalled Professionalism: The Recruitment of Railway Officials in the United States, 1885–1940," *Business History Review* 47 (Autumn 1973): 317–34, at 325.

243. Christopher T. Baer and John Dziobko, Jr., *The Pennsy in the 1960s: The Final Decade* (Kutztown, Pa.: Kutztown Publishing, 2008), 7–8.

244. William Bender Wilson, *Robert Pitcairn, 1836–1909, In Memoriam* (Holmsburg, Pa.: privately printed, 1913); Wilson, *History of the Pennsylvania Railroad*, vol. 2, 116–19.

245. "Historical Development of the Organization of the Pennsylvania Railroad," *Railroad Gazette* 14 (1882): 776–78, 793–94, 809–10, in Leland H. Jenks, "Early History of a Railway Organization," *Business History Review* 35 (Summer 1961): 163–79, at 174.

246. Watkins History, "Conclusion," 2.

247. "Historical Development," in Jenks, "Early History," 166.

248. Jenks, "Early History," 166–67n13.

249. The author was anonymous, but economist and sociologist Leland H. Jenks has suggested that it was prolific contributor Charles L. Condit, whose rapid output may have produced some errors of observation and interpretation. "Historical Development," in Jenks, "Early History," 175, Jenks's identification of Condit at 162.

250. *Thirty-First Annual Report of the Board of Directors of the Pennsylvania Railroad Co. to the Stockholders, March 25, 1878* (Philadelphia: E. C. Markley & Son, 1878), 189–90; Jenks, "Early History," 160–61.

251. As Leland Jenks has suggested, "There was a functional division of authority, in which the line of demarcation was faint. In practice there was a dual responsibility for both efficiency and economy, a system of counteracting forces, in which the general superintendent was the occasional arbiter." Jenks, "Early History," 162.

252. Chandler, *Visible Hand*, 130–32.

253. Burgess and Kennedy, *Centennial History*, 186–87, 218–19.

Chapter 10. Connections

1. Information on the American tour of Grand Duke Alexis is drawn from *His Imperial Highness the Grand Duke Alexis in the United States of America During the Winter of 1871–72* (Cambridge, Mass.: Riverside Press, 1872), quotations in this and the following paragraphs at 143 ("our act of emancipation"), 154 ("untold numbers"), 161–62 ("asked many questions"); Helen Cody Wetmore, *Last of the Great Scouts: The Life Story of Col. William F. Cody "Buffalo Bill,"* 2nd ed. (London: Methuen & Co., 1903), 195–97; and *New York Times*, November 20, 1871, November 23, 1871, November 25, 1871, December 4, 1871, January 4, 1872, January 13, 1872, January 14, 1872.

2. The earliest elements of various plans to connect the anthracite region of northeastern Pennsylvania to Boston and the rest of New England dated to 1854 and the incorporation of the South Mountain Railroad. The project lay dormant until after the Civil War, and the 1871 incorporation of the Poughkeepsie Bridge Company, to span the Hudson River at that location. By 1873, J. Edgar Thomson, Tom Scott, and Andrew Carnegie had invested $100,000 in the bridge company. Thomson was also an investor in the South Mountain & Boston Railroad, a line that would extend the Harrisburg–Portland, Pennsylvania (the crossing of the Delaware River) route of the South Mountain Railroad north and east to the Massachusetts state line. A third carrier, the Massachusetts Central Railroad, was to cover the remaining distance to Boston. The financial panic of 1873 brought a quick

end to that project, and by 1874 the PRR interests had withdrawn. A successor company, the Pennsylvania, Poughkeepsie & New England Railroad, was likewise unsuccessful. The Poughkeepsie Bridge did not enter service until the beginning of 1889. James A. Ward, *J. Edgar Thomson, Master of the Pennsylvania* (Westport, Conn.: Greenwood Press, 1980), 182–83; *New York Times*, January 24, 1880.

3. The primary account of the 1874 trip to Florida is from Richard Lathers and Alvan Francis Sanborn, eds., *Reminiscences of Richard Lathers: Sixty Years of a Busy Life in South Carolina, Massachusetts and New York* (New York: Grafton Press, 1907), 313–17, quote at 313. Also *New York Times*, September 5, 1873, April 5, 1895, December 3, 1900; Henry V. Poor, *Manual of the Railroads of the United States, 1876–77* (New York: H. V. and H. W. Poor, 1876); Clarence V. Roberts, *Early Friends Families of Upper Bucks: With Some Account of their Descendents* (Philadelphia, 1925; repr. Baltimore: Genealogical Publishing, 1975), 105–6, Daniel Hodas, *The Business Career of Moses Taylor: Merchant, Finance Capitalist, and Industrialist* (New York: New York University Press, 1976); *Genealogical and Family History of Southern New York and the Hudson River Valley*, vol. 3 (New York: Lewis Historical Publishing, 1914), 1412–13.

4. For a thorough overview of corruption in the postwar railroad industry, particularly with respect to the transcontinental lines, see Richard White, *Railroaded: The Transcontinentals and the Making of Modern America* (New York: W.W. Norton, 2011).

5. By the time that courts had finally resolved the last of the claims, in 1880, the estate was valued at $823,000. William B. Foster, Jr., the original associate engineer of the PRR's Eastern Division (and Thomson's brother-in-law) had two children, William and Charlotte Francis. Following Foster's death in 1860, Thomson was appointed guardian of Foster's two children. He in turn adopted his niece, Charlotte Frances Foster. Evelyn Foster Morneweck, *Chronicles of Stephen Foster's Family*, vol. 2 (Pittsburgh, Pa.: Davis & Warde, 1944), 515–19; Joanne O'Connell, "Understanding Stephen Collins Foster: His World and Music," (Ph.D. diss., University of Pittsburgh, 2007), 400.

6. James A. Ward, "Power and Accountability on the Pennsylvania Railroad, 1846–1878," *Business History Review* 49 (Spring 1975): 37–59, at 50; Ward, "J. Edgar Thomson and Thomas A. Scott: A Symbiotic Partnership?" *Pennsylvania Magazine of History and Biography* 100 (1976): 37–65, at 45; Ralph and Muriel Hidy, *Pioneers in Big Business, 1882–1911: History of the Standard Oil Company (New Jersey)* (1955), 118–20, 202, 543; Ida M. Tarbell, *The History of the Standard Oil Company* (New York: McClure, Phillips & Co., 1904), 59–61, 90–92, 170; Morneweck, *Chronicles*, 519.

7. The supposed dichotomy between the Thomson and Scott investment strategies appears in virtually every account of the two executives, from contemporary newspaper and magazine articles, the writings of James Ward, and, more recently, Richard White's "Information, Markets, and Corruption: Transcontinental Railroads in the Gilded Age," *Journal of American History* 90 (June 2003): 19–43.

8. Perhaps the only truly speculative venture unconnected to the PRR was Thomson's investment in the European & North American Railroad, a proposed line between St. Johns, New Brunswick, and Portland, Maine. The project, designed to minimize the length of the ocean voyage between Europe and the United States, proved unsuccessful, but a portion of the route eventually bore the tracks of the Maine Central Railroad. Jay V. Hare, *History of the Reading, Which Appeared as a Serial in* The Pilot *and* Philadelphia & Reading Railway Men, *Beginning May 1909–Ending February 1914* (Philadelphia: John Henry Stock & Co., 1966), 215.

9. David D. Colton to Collis Huntington, May 3, 1877, in *Ellen Colton v. Leland Stanford et al.* in Superior Court of the State of California

in and for the County of Sonoma, 1883, XII, 7496, quoted in Ward, "Power and Accountability," 58.

10. Historian James A. Ward has indicated that "Thomson and Scott also knew, as did their board, that their manifold ventures outside the company gave them greater clout within it. As the 'Philadelphia parties' became more influential on the state and national level, it became progressively more difficult to oppose their policies within the confines of the road's board room." Such clout, Ward noted, "was also partially due to the financial prominence of both men outside the company." Ward, "Power and Accountability," 56, 58.

11. Ibid., 50.

12. Business historian Alfred D. Chandler, Jr., has drawn a distinction between speculators, such as Jay Gould, and managers, such as J. Edgar Thomson. "The speculators differed from the managers and the investors; they had no long-term interest in their enterprise," Chandler writes. "Their profits came instead from exploiting ancillary operations such as construction and express companies, from obtaining land and mineral rights along the line of the road, and, most often, from making money by manipulating the price of the roads' securities." However, as Julius Grodinsky and Maury Klein, among others, have indicated, Gould was an innovative railroad manager who by no means fit the cartoonish stereotype of a "robber baron." Likewise, Scott and even Thomson—archetypes of Chandler's dispassionate professional managers—were engaged in many of the practices that Chandler has labeled "speculative," particularly when they involved business opportunities that were connected to the PRR, but not a part of the railroad's core operations. Thus, the evidence suggests that the distinction between "manager" and "speculator" is something of a false dichotomy—or, at the very least, that the boundary between the two groups was extraordinarily indistinct and permeable. Chandler, *The Visible Hand: The Managerial Revolution in American Business* (Cambridge, Mass.: Belknap Press of Harvard University Press, 1977), 146–47.

13. George H. Burgess and Miles C. Kennedy, *Centennial History of the Pennsylvania Railroad Company, 1846–1946* (Philadelphia: Pennsylvania Railroad, 1949), 65; Dan Cupper, *Rockville Bridge: Rails Across the Susquehanna* (Halifax, Pa.: Withers, 2002), 7–9; Cupper, *Horseshoe Heritage: The Story of a Great Railroad Landmark* (Halifax, Pa.: Withers, 1993), 14; PRR Board of Directors (BOD) Minutes, Pennsylvania Railroad Company Collection, call no. 1807/1810, Hagley Museum and Library, Wilmington, Delaware, November 2, 1857, 269, January 6, 1858, 286; William Bender Wilson, *History of the Pennsylvania Railroad Company, with Plan of Organization, Portraits of Officials and Biographical Sketches*, vol. 1 (New York: Henry T. Coates & Co., 1899), 160.

14. Victor C. Darnell, "The Haupt Iron Bridge on the Pennsylvania Railroad," *Journal of the Society for Industrial Archeology* 14 (1988): 35–50.

15. Beautiful it may have been, but its single track was an impediment to the efficient flow of traffic, and the PRR replaced it with a double-track span in 1868 and 1869. Ibid., 35, 39, 47.

16. Ibid., 39, 50. By the 1870s, the 1851-design modular bridges could no longer accommodate the steady increase in train weights. Many were reused as pedestrian or carriage bridges over PRR tracks and, for that reason, several survived into the twenty-first century. One was reinstalled as a vehicular bridge near Ronks, Pennsylvania, and remained in service until 2002. Another span, relocated to the Church Road crossing of the PRR mainline at Ardmore, Pennsylvania, remained in place until 2006. Both have been removed and taken to the Railroad Museum of Pennsylvania at Strasburg for restoration. A third iron bridge is at the Railroaders Memorial Museum in Altoona. I extend my appreciation to Kurt R. Bell and Bradley K. Smith of the Pennsylvania Historical and Museum Commission, Railroad Museum of Pennsylvania.

17. Biographical data on Jacob Linville from *Proceedings of the American Society of Civil Engineers* 33 (August 1907): 744–50. Linville quotation is unattributed.

18. Joseph Frazier Wall, *Andrew Carnegie* (New York: Oxford University Press, 1970), 188–89, 227–29.

19. David Nasaw, *Andrew Carnegie* (New York: Penguin, 2006), 75–79, 82, 100–104; Wall, *Andrew Carnegie*, 229–30.

20. Nasaw, *Andrew Carnegie*, 80, 102–4; Robert W. Jackson, *Rails Across the Mississippi: A History of the St. Louis Bridge* (Urbana: University of Illinois Press, 2001), 29–34.

21. Jackson, *Rails Across the Mississippi*, 62.

22. The Illinois legislature had chartered the Keokuk & Hamilton Bridge Company in 1857, but the company was apparently not organized for another eleven years.

23. *Keokuk & Hamilton Bridge Co. v. People of the State of Illinois* (175 U.S. 626, 1900); Gouverneur K. Warren, *Report on the Bridging of the Mississippi River between St. Paul Minnesota and St. Louis Missouri* (Washington, D.C.: U.S. Government Printing Office, 1878), 72–74, 77–80, 87, 90–96, 110–11, 113–15, 117–21, 122–23, 131–35, 140–57, 197. I would like to extend my gratitude to Jack Brown for alerting me to this source.

24. Nasaw, *Andrew Carnegie*, 116, 134–35; Wall, *Andrew Carnegie*, 270–77; Jackson, *Rails Across the Mississippi*, 55, 69–70. For additional information on the development of the Eads Bridge, as well as Jacob Linville's role in that process, see John A. Kouwenhoven, "The Designing of the Eads Bridge," *Technology and Culture* 23 (October 1982): 535–68.

25. For several years after the St. Louis Bridge opened in 1874, the railroad companies serving St. Louis engaged in protracted negotiations involving bridge tolls and the provision of freight terminal facilities on the west side of the Mississippi River, with some railroads and investors (including individuals affiliated with the PRR) threatening to boycott the bridge. In 1889, Jay Gould established a regional operating entity, the Terminal Railroad Association of St. Louis, in order to control the only available river crossing, at the Eads Bridge, and regulate rail access through St. Louis. In so doing, he protected the interests of his railroads, the Missouri Pacific and the Wabash, but to the detriment of the PRR. Under threat of judicial sanction, the Terminal Railroad Association admitted the St. Louis, Vandalia & Terre Haute Railroad (PRR) in 1902. Coverdale & Colpitts, *Corporate, Financial and Construction History of Lines Owned, Operated and Controlled to December 31, 1945*, vol. 4: *Affiliated Lines, Miscellaneous Companies, and General Index* (New York: Coverdale & Colpitts, 1947), 4, 416; David Reiffen and Andrew N. Kleit, "Terminal Railroad Revisited: Foreclosure of an Essential Facility or Simple Horizontal Monopoly?" *Journal of Law and Economics* 33 (October 1990): 419–38, at 427–29; Mary L. Azcuenaga, "Essential Facilities and Regulation: Court or Agency Jurisdiction?" *Antitrust Law Journal* 58 (1989): 879–86; Abbott B. Lipsky, Jr., and J. Gregory Sidak, "Essential Facilities," *Stanford Law Review* 51 (May 1999): 1187–1249; Richard T. Wallis, *The Pennsylvania Railroad at Bay: William Riley McKeen and the Terre Haute & Indianapolis Railroad* (Bloomington: Indiana University Press, 2001), 34–35; *United States v. Terminal Railroad Association*, 224 U.S. 383 (1912); *United States v. Terminal Railroad Association*, 236 U.S. 194 (1915); Jackson, *Rails Across the Mississippi*, 116, 121–23, 214.

26. *Reports of Explorations and Surveys, to Ascertain the Most Practicable and Economical Route for a Railroad from the Mississippi River to the Pacific Ocean* (Washington, D.C.: Beverly Tucker, 1855).

27. William Robinson Petrowski, *The Kansas Pacific: A Study in Railroad Promotion* (New York: Arno Press, 1981), 7–15.

28. Ibid., 63–89, 102–23; George L. Anderson, *Kansas West* (San Marino, Calif.: Golden West Books, 1963), 11–15.

29. Petrowski, *Kansas Pacific*, 115–16, 125, 128–29.

30. On July 1, 1866, the partnership was dissolved and reconstituted as Shoemaker, Miller & Company, reflecting the participation of Edward Miller, former chief engineer of the Pennsylvania Railroad. Solomon W. Roberts, "Obituary Notice of Edward Miller, Civil Engineer," *Proceedings of the American Philosophical Society* 12 (1871): 581–86; Petrowski, *Kansas Pacific*, 167, 183.

31. *Testimony Taken by the United States Pacific Railway Commission*, 50th Cong., 1st sess., 4875, quoted in Petrowski, *Kansas Pacific*, 162.

32. Petrowski, *Kansas Pacific*, 125, 171–72, 186; Anderson, *Kansas West*, 21–255; John Stirling Fisher and Chase Mellen, *A Builder of the West: The Life of General William Jackson Palmer* (Caldwell, Id.: Caxton Printers, 1939), 117–18, 126–32.

33. Petrowski, *Kansas Pacific*, 142–53, 179–81, 195–99.

34. Palmer joined forces with Scott to charter a "Tom Scott" holding company, the Union Improvement Company, to build the Denver & Rio Grande as far south as the Mexican border. Another Tom Scott venture, the Empire Contract Company, was to continue the line south to Mexico City. Palmer soon encountered financial difficulties and lost the strategic Ratón Pass to the Atchison, Topeka & Santa Fe. Fortuitously, the mineral wealth of southwestern Colorado enabled Palmer to redirect his railroad to the west. The Rio Grande never extended farther south than Santa Fe, New Mexico. In September 1880, however, the Mexican government awarded Palmer a franchise to build the Ferrocarril Nacional Mexicano (Mexican National Railway), a three-foot-gauge line linking Mexico City to Nuevo Laredo, completed in 1888. The Texas Mexican Railway provided a link between Laredo and the Gulf of Mexico, at Corpus Christi, Texas. In 1909, the Ferrocarril Nacional Mexicano, recently converted to standard gauge, became part of the Ferrocarriles Nacionales de México (the National Railways of Mexico, more commonly known as NdeM). As of this writing, the route is operated by Kansas City Southern de México. Fisher and Mellen, *A Builder of the West*, 195–96; Robert Greenleaf Athearn, *The Denver and Rio Grande Western Railroad, Rebel of the Rockies* (Lincoln, Nebr.: Bison Books, 1977), reprint of *Rebel of the Rockies: A History of the Denver and Rio Grande Western Railroad* (New Haven, Conn.: Yale University Press, 1962); William D. Middleton, George M. Smerk, and Roberta L. Diehl, eds., *Encyclopedia of North American Railroads* (Bloomington: Indiana University Press, 2007), 696–97.

35. The Kansas Pacific was still useful as a western connection, assuming that traffic destined for the PRR had some way to reach St. Louis from Kansas City. The North Missouri Railroad, incorporated in 1851, possessed a main line from St. Louis north to Ottumwa, Iowa, as well as a branch line to Kansas City. In 1871, the company completed a bridge across the Missouri River at St. Charles, with the cost contributing to its bankruptcy three months later. In August 1871, Scott and James Eads oversaw the reorganization of the North Missouri Railroad as the St. Louis, Kansas City & Northern Railway. By May 1872, PRR officials had also negotiated a traffic-sharing agreement with the Chicago & Alton to employ that carrier as their joint connection with the Kansas Pacific. The PRR cancelled the arrangement two years later, when Jay Gould gained control of the Kansas Pacific. In 1879, the St. Louis, Kansas City & Northern merged with the Wabash Railway, forming the Wabash, St. Louis & Pacific Railway, the centerpiece of Gould's empire. J. A. Dacus and James W. Buel, *A Tour of St. Louis; Or, the Inside Life of a Great City* (St. Louis: Western Publishing, 1878), 164–67; Jackson, *Rails Across the Mississippi*, 123–24, 184; *New York Times*, May 6, 1882.

36. J. Edgar Thomson to William Jackson Palmer, January 17, 1869, quoted in Petrowski, *Kansas Pacific*, 210.

37. Petrowski, *Kansas Pacific*, 209–12.

38. Julius Grodinsky, *Jay Gould: His Business Career, 1867–1892* (Philadelphia: University of Pennsylvania Press, 1957), 115–16.

39. *Railroad Gazette*, February 11, 1871, 467 (quote), reprinted in Grodinsky, *Jay Gould*, 116; Maury Klein, *Union Pacific: Birth of a Railroad, 1862–1893* (New York: Doubleday, 1987), 97–107, 275–77; White, *Railroaded*, 105.

40. Ward, *Master of the Pennsylvania*, 191, 200–204; Klein, *Union Pacific*, 286–87; Wall, *Andrew Carnegie*, 286–90; Nasaw, *Andrew Carnegie*, 123–24.

41. Andrew Carnegie, *Autobiography of Andrew Carnegie* (Boston: Houghton Mifflin, 1920), 164.

42. Wall, *Andrew Carnegie*, 286–89; Scott Reynolds Nelson, *Iron Confederacies: Southern Railways, Klan Violence, and Reconstruction* (Chapel Hill: University of North Carolina Press, 1999), 146; James A. Ward, "John Edgar Thomson and the Cult of Personality on the Pennsylvania Railroad," *Railroad History* 177 (Autumn 1997): 68–77, at 71.

43. Jackson, *Rails Across the Mississippi*, 173–74; James Grant Wilson and John Fiske, eds., *Appleton's Cyclopedia of American Biography*, vol. 2 (New York: D. Appleton and Company, 1888), 429.

44. Wall, *Andrew Carnegie*, 279.

45. The line was never built, but the Iowa Contracting Company was somehow connected with the Missouri, Iowa & Nebraska Railroad, which ran from Centerville, Missouri (south and a little west of St. Louis) north to Alexandria, where it connected with the Mississippi Valley & Western Railroad that provided a link to Keokuk. Both Andrew Carnegie and Benjamin Smith were directors of the Missouri, Iowa & Nebraska, but in 1880 it was leased to the Wabash. Henry V. Poor, *Manual of the Railroads of the United States for 1874–75* (New York: H. V. Poor, 1874), 200; *Poor's Manual of Railroads*, vol. 18 (New York: Poor's Railroad Manual Co., 1885), 977–78.

46. The German Banking firm of Sulzbach Brothers, which had based its substantial investment in the railroad on Thomson's implied support for the project, lost a substantial sum of money. In November 1875, more than a year after Thomson's death, Sulzbach Brothers sued Thomson's estate for $125,000.

47. State of Iowa, *Nineteenth Annual Report of the Board of Railroad Commissioners for the Year Ending June 30, 1896* (Des Moines: F. R. Conaway, 1896), 207.

48. At some point the Milwaukee Road extended tracks north to Jackson Junction, on the MILW line west to Rapid City, South Dakota Jackson, *Rails Across the Mississippi*, 125–26; Wall, *Andrew Carnegie*, 280–82, 295–97; Nasaw, *Andrew Carnegie*, 120, 130.

49. Jackson, *Rails Across the Mississippi*, 174–76.

50. H. Craig Miner, *The St. Louis–San Francisco Transcontinental Railroad: The Thirty-Fifth Parallel Project* (Lawrence: University Press of Kansas, 1972), 1–13, 17–19, 26–27, 40; Solomon W. Roberts, "Obituary Notice of Edward Miller, Civil Engineer," *Proceedings of the American Philosophical Society* 12 (1871): 581–86.

51. The Pacific Railroad Company of Missouri (the 1849 company) later became part of the Missouri Pacific Railroad.

52. In January 1867, the Atlantic & Pacific bought the Southwest Pacific Railroad (the former Southwest Branch). In 1872, the A&P leased the Pacific Railroad of Missouri (later, the Missouri Pacific) and the St. Louis & Gulf Railroad, creating—at least on paper—through routes between St. Louis and Sabine Point, Texas, and Santa Barbara, California. Miner, *The St. Louis–San Francisco*, 40–45, 48–51, 58, 60–63, 85–86.

53. Senator John Scott introduced aid petitions from both the Atlantic & Pacific and the Texas & Pacific on the same day, December 10, 1874. Neither was successful.

54. Jackson, *Rails Across the Mississippi*, 150, 189; Douglas L. Lowell, "The California Southern Railroad and the Growth of San Diego," Pt. 1, *Journal of San Diego History* 31 (Fall 1985); Miner, *The St. Louis–San Francisco*, 58, 87–88; Julius Grodinsky, *Transcontinental Railway Strategy, 1869–1893: A Study of Businessmen* (Philadelphia: University of Pennsylvania Press, 1962), 22–23, 34–35, 166–69.

55. Cerinda W. Evans, *Collis Potter Huntington,* vol. 1 (Newport News, Va.: Mariners' Museum, 1954), 246–50.

56. C. Vann Woodward, *Reunion and Reaction: The Compromise of 1877 and the End of Reconstruction* (Boston: Little, Brown, 1966), 69–71; Virginia H. Taylor, *The Franco-Texan Land Company* (Austin: University of Texas Press, 1969); S. G. Reed, *A History of the Texas Railroads and of Transportation Conditions Under Spain and Mexico and The Republic and The State* (Houston: St. Clair Publishing, 1941), 93–94, 101–3, 356–60.

57. Reed, *A History of the Texas Railroads*, 358–61.

58. Taylor, *The Franco-Texan Land Company*, 60, 75–80, 86–87; Woodward, *Reunion and Reaction*, 72–73; White, Railroaded, 105.

59. Taylor, *The Franco-Texan Land Company*, 99–105, 294; Woodward, *Reunion and Reaction*, 73–74; Reed, *A History of the Texas Railroads*, 362.

60. In 1851, the Missouri legislature chartered the Iron Mountain Railroad, whose incorporators proposed to transport ore from Iron Mountain, Missouri, to the Mississippi River at Belmont, Missouri, opposite the northern end of the Mobile & Ohio Railroad, some twenty miles south of Cairo, Illinois. Groundbreaking occurred in 1853, but full-scale construction did not begin for another three years. By 1858, Iron Mountain construction crews, building south from St. Louis, had reached Pilot Knob, Missouri. The Civil War halted further activity and plunged the company into bankruptcy. Reorganized in 1867 as the St. Louis & Iron Mountain Railroad, construction again proceeded, in a southwesterly direction, and in November 1872 reached the Arkansas state line and a junction with the Cairo, Arkansas & Texas Railroad. That line was originally the Cairo & Fulton Railroad, chartered in Arkansas in 1853 and in Missouri in 1854. Following the Civil War it completed a line from Bird's Point, Missouri, opposite Cairo, Illinois, to Texarkana. In 1872, that company was reorganized as the Cairo, Arkansas & Texas. By January 1873, trains were operating from St. Louis as far south as Argenta (North Little Rock), across the Arkansas River from Little Rock. Rails reached Texarkana in January 1874. In May 1874 the St. Louis & Iron Mountain and the Cairo, Arkansas & Texas Railroad merged into the St. Louis, Iron Mountain & Southern Railway. Fred W. Ash, "Submerged Ambitions," *Railroad History* 196 (Spring–Summer 2007): 6–21, at 10–14; "Cairo and Fulton Railroad, The Encyclopedia of Arkansas History and Culture," http://encyclopediaofarkansas.net/encyclopedia/entry-detail.aspx?entryID=2422, accessed August 5, 2011.

61. Leo E. Huff, "The Memphis and Little Rock Railroad During the Civil War," Arkansas Historical Quarterly 23 (Autumn 1964): 260–70; Jackson, *Rails Across the Mississippi*, 123–24, 184; Dacus and Buel, *A Tour of St. Louis*, 147–55; Iron Mountain chronology from the Missouri Pacific Historical Society, http://mopac.org/history_stlims.asp, accessed on June 27, 2010.

62. Reed, *A History of the Texas Railroads*, 364–65.

63. J. Edgar Thomson to Andrew Carnegie, November 3, 1873, Andrew Carnegie, Personal Miscellaneous Papers, Manuscripts and Archives Division, New York Public Library, quoted in Nasaw, *Andrew Carnegie*, 154.

64. Ward, *Master of the Pennsylvania*, 205–8; Ward, "Symbiotic Partnership," 62–64; Wall, *Andrew Carnegie*, 299–306.

65. In their officially sanctioned corporate history of the Pennsylvania Railroad, George H. Burgess and Miles C. Kennedy give scant mention to the California & Texas Railway Construction Company affair, acknowl-

edging in a footnote, "None of these activities seems to have interfered with the performance of Colonel Scott's duties to the Pennsylvania." Burgess and Kennedy, *Centennial History*, 348.

66. Woodward, *Reunion and Reaction*, 76–77, 82–83.

67. Lewis B. Lesley, "A Southern Transcontinental Railroad into California: Texas and Pacific Versus Southern Pacific, 1865–1885," *Pacific Historical Review* 5 (March 1936): 52–60.

68. White, *Railroaded*, 106–7, 118–30; *New York Times*, January 27, 1876.

69. *New York Times*, January 30, 1877.

70. Huntington to associates, March 16, 1878, quoted in Evans, *Huntington*, 256–57.

71. White, *Railroaded*, 106–8, 118–30.

72. As historian Richard White has observed, "it was astonishing that in the very year of the Crédit Mobilier, Scott, dragging the corpse of a similar construction company, persuaded creditors that he could induce Congress to offer him essentially the same arrangement that had plunged the Union Pacific and Congress into scandal." White, *Railroaded*, 94; Taylor, *The Franco-Texan Land Company*, 102–3; Woodward, *Reunion and Reaction*, 76–77, 82–83; Evans, *Huntington*, 256–60.

73. *New York Times*, January 26, 1875.

74. White, *Railroaded*, 121.

75. Woodward, *Reunion and Reaction*, 131–42; White, *Railroaded*, 108–9, 119–21.

76. Woodward, *Reunion and Reaction*, 78–81, 90–91.

77. *New York Times*, January 26, 1876.

78. Ibid., 94–98, 113–16; White, *Railroaded*, 124.

79. *New York Times*, January 12, 1877.

80. Taylor, *The Franco-Texan Land Company*, 105; Woodward, *Reunion and Reaction*, 128–32; White, *Railroaded*, 124–25; *New York Times*, January 5, 1877, January 6, 1877, January 12, 1877, January 15, 1877, January 22, 1877, January 25, 1877, January 30, 1877, February 14, 1877.

81. Woodward, *Reunion and Reaction*, 131–42; White, *Railroaded*, 119–22.

82. John Hope Franklin, *Reconstruction After the Civil War*, 2nd ed. (Chicago: University of Chicago Press, 1994), 206–10; Michael W. Fitzgerald, *Splendid Failure: Postwar Reconstruction in the American South* (Chicago: Ivan R. Dee, 2007), 204–5.

83. The *Pennsylvania* was equipped with adjustable-gauge trucks, and was well suited to long-distance travel over a variety of routes prior to the standardization of track gauge. In an era when governments did not yet provide transportation to presidents, governors, and other key officials, the lending of private railway cars was relatively commonplace as an act of professional courtesy, and it did not necessarily entail political favors or any other type of quid pro quo. Robert V. Bruce, *1877: Year of Violence* (Indianapolis: Bobbs-Merrill, 1959), 49–50; Shelton Stromquist, *A Generation of Boomers: The Pattern of Railroad Labor Conflict in Nineteenth-Century America* (Urbana: University of Illinois Press, 1987), 18.

84. For the debate concerning Scott's role in the Compromise of 1877, see Allan Peskin, "Was There a Compromise of 1877?" *Journal of American History* 60 (June 1973): 63–75, and C. Vann Woodward. "Yes, There Was a Compromise of 1877," *Journal of American History* 60 (1973): 215–23.

85. *A Compilation of the Laws, Deeds, Mortgages, Leases, and Other Instruments, and Minutes of Proceedings, Affecting The Pittsburgh, Fort Wayne and Chicago Railway Company* (New York: John Polhemus, 1875), 267–73; William J. Watt, *The Pennsylvania Railroad in Indiana* (Bloomington: Indiana University Press, 2000), 5, 26–27, 45, 74, 95.

86. Gould also purchased the International & Great Northern Railroad and the Missouri-Kansas Texas Railroad (in 1880), and the St. Louis,

Iron Mountain & Southern (in 1883), denying the PRR interests an eastern connection to the Texas & Pacific. Taylor, *The Franco-Texan Land Company*, 175–76.

87. Ibid., 176.

88. Woodward, *Reunion and Reaction*, 236–37; Evans, *Huntington*, 262–64.

89. John Bell Rae, *The Development of Railway Land Subsidy Policy in the United States* (New York: Arno Press, 1979), 277.

90. *New York Times*, December 31, 1881; Evans, *Huntington*, 262–63; Grodinsky, *Transcontinental Railway Strategy*, 35.

91. Nathaniel Mason Pawlett, *A Brief History of the Roads of Virginia, 1607–1840* (Charlottesville: Virginia Highway & Research Council, 1977, rev. 2003); Thomas Sergant Fernon, *Report to J. Edgar Thomson, President of the Pennsylvania Railroad Company, Submitting Results of Observations Concerning the Tendencies of Trade Towards the Seaboard through the West, North of the Ohio River* (Philadelphia: The American Philosophical Society, 1852), 25; James F. Doster, "Vicissitudes of the South Carolina Railroad, 1865–1878: A Case Study in Reconstruction and Regional Traffic Development," *Business History Review* 30 (June 1956): 175–95.

92. As historian Maury Klein has observed, "The prevailing attitude toward railroads in the South considered them to be localized enterprises whose primary purpose was three-fold: profitmaking; developing the commerce and other economic activity of its principal terminus; and developing the economic resources of the region tributary to the road." Klein, "Southern Railroad Leaders, 1865–1893: Identities and Ideologies," *Business History Review* 42 (Autumn 1968): 288–310, quote at 294.

93. The North witnessed similar, politically motivated impediments to the free flow of commerce—as witnessed by the 1853–1854 Erie "gauge war" and the steamboat interests who in 1856 demolished the Rock Island Bridge Company span across the Mississippi River. Those were isolated incidents, however, and more pragmatic northerners attempted to profit from the growth of the railroad network rather than engage in quixotic battles to halt the growing interdependency of the national economy. For many northern entrepreneurs and industrialists, an integrated regional transportation system was in fact vital to their economic interests. Long-distance, efficient rail routes were essential to the success of John D. Rockefeller in oil, Andrew Carnegie in steel, Cyrus McCormick in agricultural equipment, Gustavus Swift and Philip Danforth Armour in meatpacking, and Aaron Montgomery Ward in retailing. Those executives were but the most visible leading edge of a series of northern industrial, urban business communities that stretched from Pittsburgh to Cleveland, and from Detroit to Chicago. Those executives were not afraid that through railroads might bypass their communities, but feared, instead, that without a vibrant railroad system, their businesses and their communities might wither and die. Their massive, vertically integrated enterprises depended on the economies of scale that the railroads made possible. Their factories required enormous quantities of raw materials and produced mountains of manufactured products, and much of that traffic traveled by rail. That commerce, in tandem with the flood of grain from the west, underwrote the survival of competing trunk lines such as the PRR, companies that poured money into their physical plant and equipment, in order to drive down rates by operating as efficiently as possible. George Rogers Taylor and Irene D. Neu, *The American Railroad Network, 1861–1890* (Urbana: University of Illinois Press, 2003), 78–81; Douglas J. Puffert, "The Standardization of Track Gauge on North American Railways, 1830–1890," *Journal of Economic History* 60 (2000): 933–60.

94. Klein, "Southern Railroad Leaders," 301–2.

95. Nelson, *Iron Confederacies*, 83–84.

96. The company was originally chartered under the antiquarian spelling of the Richmond, Fredericksburg & Potowmac Railroad.

97. Fairfax Harrison, *A History of the Legal Development of the Railroad System of Southern Railway Company* (Washington, D.C.: Southern Railway Co., 1901), 1478–81.

98. Richard E. Prince, *Seaboard Air Line Railway: Steamboats, Locomotives, and History* (Bloomington: Indiana University Press, 2000), 8–9.

99. John B. Mordecai, *A Brief History of the Richmond, Fredericksburg and Potomac Railroad* (Richmond: Old Dominion Press, 1940), 42; Herbert H. Harwood, *Impossible Challenge: The Baltimore and Ohio Railroad in Maryland* (Baltimore: Barnard, Roberts & Co., 1979), 61, 96–97, 104, 144; Wilson, *History of the Pennsylvania Railroad*, vol. 1, 336–37.

100. Carrol H. Quenzel, "The Manufacture of Locomotives and Cars in Alexandria in the 1850's," *Virginia Magazine of History and Biography* 62 (April 1954): 181–89; Wilson, *History of the Pennsylvania Railroad*, vol. 1, 346–51.

101. Harrison, *Southern Railway Company*.

102. Harwood, *Impossible Challenge*, 104, 146.

103. The B&O controlled two railroads (the Winchester & Potomac and the Winchester & Strasburg) that provided a route south from the B&O main line at Harpers Ferry. The Orange, Alexandria & Manassas continued the route south, from Strasburg to Harrisonburg, completed in 1868. The Valley Railroad was a southerly extension of that line. Work on the Valley Railroad ended in 1883, and the line extended only between Harrisonburg and Staunton, Virginia. For a comprehensive overview of Mahone's railroad career, see Nelson Morehouse Blake, *William Mahone of Virginia: Soldier and Political Insurgent* (Richmond: Garrett & Massie, 1935).

104. Richard G. Lowe, *Republicans and Reconstruction in Virginia, 1856–1870* (Charlottesville: University Press of Virginia, 1991), 150–51.

105. Ibid., 121–41.

106. Ibid., 157–58, 173–74.

107. Robert A. Brock, *Virginia and Virginians: Eminent Virginians . . . History of Virginia from Settlement of Jamestown to Close of Civil War*, vol. 1 (Richmond: H. H. Hardesty, 1888), 241–42; *New York Times*, July 15, 1869; Lowe, *Republicans and Reconstruction*, 143–44, 166–67, 172–78.

108. James Brown Scott, *Judicial Settlement of Controversies Between States of the American Union: An Analysis of Cases Decided in the Supreme Court of the United States* (Union, N.J.: The Lawbook Exchange, 2002), 489–90; Burgess and Kennedy, *Centennial History*, 279–80; Harrison, *Southern Railway Company*, 475.

109. Kevin M. Levin, "William Mahone, the Lost Cause, and Civil War History," *Virginia Magazine of History and Biography* 113 (2005): 378–412; Blake, *William Mahone*, 156–95.

110. Harrison, *Southern Railway Company*, 475.

111. Blake, *William Mahone*, 120.

112. John F. Stover, "The Pennsylvania Railroad's Southern Rail Empire," *Pennsylvania Magazine of History and Biography* 81 (1957): 28–38, at 28; Mark W. Summers, *Railroads, Reconstruction, and the Gospel of Prosperity: Aid Under the Radical Republicans, 1865–1877* (Princeton, N.J.: Princeton University Press, 1984), 176.

113. As historian Herbert H. Harwood, Jr., has noted, "There is clear evidence that some time in the early 1870s a physical and emotional decline began; by the time he died in 1884 Garrett was a severely depressed recluse." Harwood, *Impossible Challenge*, 99–104, 112–14, quote at 112.

114. Harwood, *Impossible Challenge*, 104, 144–46; Charles M. Blackford, *Legal History of the Virginia Midland Railway Co., and of the Companies which Built its Lines of Road* (Lynchburg, Va.: J. P. Bell & Co., 1881), 30–34, 50–55, 201; Harrison, *Southern Railway Company*, 453–76.

115. Specifically, while the Commonwealth of Virginia had invested in the portion of the line that lay south of the Potomac, it could not legally invest in the portion that lay within the District of Columbia—that section had been financed, in part, through a bond guarantee from the City of Washington. Harrison, *Southern Railway Company*, 1489–96.

116. *Congressional Globe*, June 17, 1870, 4531.

117. Ibid., 4532.

118. By 1870, the Long Bridge was badly deteriorated, and Baltimore & Potomac crews soon rebuilt the structure, atop stone piers. Additional repairs and modifications were made in 1877, 1881, 1884–85, 1894, and 1896–97. Ivan E. Frantz, Jr., "The Pennsylvania Railroad and the Civil War," *The Keystone* 38:3 (Autumn 2005), 21–22; Mordecai, *A Brief History of the Richmond, Fredericksburg and Potomac*, 42; Wilson, *History of the Pennsylvania Railroad*, vol. 1, 337–38; Herbert Charles Bell, *History of Venango County, Pennsylvania—Its Past and Present* (Chicago: Brown, Runk & Co., 1890), 788–91.

119. Wilson, *History of the Pennsylvania Railroad*, vol. 1, 345, 353 (quote).

120. Harwood, *Impossible Challenge*, 174–78; Harrison, *Southern Railway Company*, 483–98.

121. Harrison, *Southern Railway Company*, 1488–89, 1500–1501.

122. The legal and financial issues associated with the Alexandria & Washington Railroad were not finally resolved until 1887, when the PRR purchased the company and reorganized it as the Alexandria & Washington Railway. In 1890, the company was consolidated with the Alexandria & Fredericksburg, forming the Washington Southern Railway. Harrison, *Southern Railway Company*, 1496, 1501–2; Wilson, *History of the Pennsylvania Railroad*, vol. 1, 353; Mordecai, *Brief History*, 43.

123. Wilson, *History of the Pennsylvania Railroad*, vol. 2, 344–45.

124. Mordecai, *Brief History*, 43–44; Alfred Crosby Brown, *The Old Bay Line, 1840–1940* (New York: Bonanza Books, 1977).

125. *Twenty-Fourth Annual Report of the Pennsylvania Railroad Co. to the Stockholders, February 21, 1871* (Philadelphia: E. C. Markley & Son, 1871), 24.

126. PRR BOD Minutes, November 27, 1872, 113–14; Harrison, *Southern Railway Company*, 1501.

127. In 1884, key PRR allies William T. Walters and Benjamin F. Newcomer (described in the next section) purchased a substantial block of RF&P securities, in order to ensure more harmonious relations between the two companies. *Acts and Joint Resolutions Passed by the General Assembly of the State of Virginia, at Its Session of 1870–1871* (Richmond: James E. Goode, 1871), 141–45; John F. Stover, *The Railroads of the South, 1865–1900: A Study in Finance and Control* (Chapel Hill: University of North Carolina Press, 1955), 99–121; Harrison, *Southern Railway Company*, 1487; Harwood, *Impossible Challenge*, 176; Mordecai, *Brief History*, 45–46.

128. Glenn Hoffman, *Building a Great Railroad: A History of the Atlantic Coast Line Railroad Company* (CSX Corporation, 1998).

129. As historian Glenn Hoffman has noted, it was thanks to the two Baltimoreans and the capital that they controlled that "some of the homey practices of locally owned railroads were replaced with more impersonal, business-like policies." Ibid., 3–8, quote on 8.

130. Ibid., 13.

131. *Organization and Charter of the Southern Railway Security Company* (New York[?]: Southern Railway Security Co., 1871).

132. Hoffman, *Building a Great Railroad*, 14; C. K. Brown, "The Southern Railway Security Company: An Early Instance of the Holding Company," *North Carolina Historical Review* 6 (April 1929): 158–70.

133. Herman Haupt, *Reminiscences of General Herman Haupt* (Milwaukee: Wright & Joys, 1901), xxxiv.

134. Nelson, *Iron Confederacies*, 141–43; John H. White, Jr., "America's Most Noteworthy Railroaders," *Railroad History* 154 (1986): 9–15; *New York Times*, November 26, 1910; Frank Abial Flower, "General Herman Haupt,"

in Haupt, *Reminiscences*, xxxiv; Brown, "The Southern Railway Security Company," 160–61.

135. Stover, "Southern Rail Empire." 31; Howard W. Schotter, *The Growth and Development of the Pennsylvania Railroad Company: A Review of the Charter and Annual Reports of the Pennsylvania Railroad Company 1846 to 1926, Inclusive* (Philadelphia: Allen, Lane & Scott, 1927), 110–11.

136. Howard Douglas Dozier, *A History of the Atlantic Coast Line Railroad* (Boston: Houghton, Mifflin, 1920), 128–29; Hoffman, *Building a Great Railroad*, 16–17.

137. Stover, "Southern Rail Empire," 32–34.

138. Hoffman, *Building a Great Railroad*, 16–17; Harrison, *Southern Railway Company*, 80–96; Blake, *William Mahone*, 120, 139.

139. Alvin Fay Harlow, *Old Waybills: The Romance of the Express Companies* (New York: D. Appleton–Century, 1934), 66–67.

140. Hoffman, *Building a Great Railroad*, 16–17; Harrison, *Southern Railway Company*, 639–773; Stover, "The Pennsylvania Railroad's Southern Rail Empire," 34–37.

141. During the 1830s, as construction crews were building the Cumberland Valley Railroad, Baltimore & Ohio engineers were planning to build along the north bank of the Potomac River, through Hagerstown, on their way to the Ohio River at Wheeling. In keeping with that proposed route, promoters chartered the Franklin Rail-road Company in Pennsylvania in March 1832 and in Maryland five years later. Although the company's founders envisioned the line as an extension of the B&O route to Baltimore, members of the Pennsylvania legislature believed that it could also serve to direct traffic north, to the Main Line of Public Works. Accordingly, in March 1839, they appropriated $100,000 to purchase two thousand shares of stock in the enterprise. In 1838, workers began building south from Chambersburg, and the first train reached Hagerstown in February 1841. It was not much of a railroad, with horses drawing cars slowly along a track that consisted of strap iron atop wooden sills. Even worse, B&O officials altered their route, electing to cross to the south bank of the Potomac at Harpers Ferry, and leaving Hagerstown without a rail connection to Baltimore. In 1867, the Baltimore & Ohio constructed a branch line to Hagerstown, and the terminus of what was by then the Cumberland Valley Railroad and a part of the PRR system. Wilson, *History of the Pennsylvania Railroad*, vol. 1, 396–97; Paul J. Westhaeffer, *History of the Cumberland Valley Railroad, 1835–1919* (Washington, D.C.: Washington Chapter of the National Railway Historical Society, 1979), 39–46.

142. Andrew S. McCreath, *The Mineral Wealth of Virginia Tributary to the Lines of the Norfolk and Western and Shenandoah Valley Railroad Companies* (Harrisburg: Lane S. Hart, 1884), 1–3; Westhaeffer, *Cumberland Valley*, 131–40; Joseph T. Lambie, *From Mine to Market: The History of Coal Transportation on the Norfolk and Western Railway* (New York: New York University Press, 1954), 11–19.

143. The thirteen railroads were the Alexandria & Fredericksburg; the Richmond & Petersburg; the Wilmington & Weldon; the Wilmington, Columbia & Augusta; the Richmond & Danville; the North Carolina; the Charlotte, Columbia & Augusta; the Atlanta & Richmond Air-Line; the Western & Atlantic; the East Tennessee, Virginia & Georgia; the Memphis & Charleston; the Cheraw & Darlington; and the Northeastern.

144. Quotations from Memphis *Avalanche*, reprinted in *Philadelphia North American*, January 1, 1872, and *New York Herald*, March 11, 1872, both in Grodinsky, *Transcontinental Railway Strategy*, 23.

145. James F. Doster, "Vicissitudes of the South Carolina Railroad, 1865–1878: A Case Study in Reconstruction and Regional Traffic Development," *Business History Review* 30 (June 1956): 175–95.

146. Hoffman, *Building a Great Railroad*, 25–28, 32–36; Allan Nevins, *Study in Power: John D. Rockefeller: Industrialist and Philanthropist*, vol. 1

(New York: Charles Scribner's Sons, 1953), 370–75; Brown, "Southern Railway Security Company," 165–69.

147. Harrison, *Southern Railway Company*, 25–54, 97–111, 685–696; Maury Klein, *The Great Richmond Terminal: A Study in Businessmen and Business Strategy* (Charlottesville: University Press of Virginia, 1970), 35–36, 86–96, 253–84; Hoffman, *Building a Great Railroad*, 45–72.

148. Wilson, *History of the Pennsylvania Railroad*, vol. 1, 396–97; Westhaeffer, *Cumberland Valley*, 39–46; Lambie, *From Mine to Market*, 1–15.

149. Nelson, *Iron Confederacies*, 72–73, 86; Klein, "Southern Railroad Leaders," 295; Stover, "Southern Rail Empire," 32.

150. John W. Wyatt, address to the Florida legislature, in John Wallace, *Carpetbag Rule in Florida: The Inside Workings of the Reconstruction of Civil Government in Florida After the Close of the Civil War* (Jacksonville, Fla.: Da Costa Printing and Publishing, 1888), 156–57, emphasis in the original.

151. Canter Brown, Jr., *Florida's Black Public Officials, 1867–1924* (Tuscaloosa, Ala: University of Alabama Press, 1998), 10, 145–48; Paul Ortiz, *Emancipation Betrayed: The Hidden History of Black Organizing and White Violence in Florida From Reconstruction to the Bloody Election of 1920* (Berkeley, Ca.: University of California Press, 2005), 17–19; Nelson, *Iron Confederacies*, 163–69.

152. Nelson, *Iron Confederacies*, 153–78.

153. According to Chauncey Depew, president of the New York Central between 1885 and 1898, "Scott selected as editor of the New York World one of the most brilliant journalistic writers of his time, William H. Hurlburt. When it became known, however, that the World belonged to Colonel Scott, Hurlburt's genius could not save it." The *New York World*, established in 1860, thrived only after Joseph Pulitzer became its editor in 1883. It ceased publication in 1931. Chauncey M. Depew, *My Memories of Eighty Years* (New York: Charles Scribner's Sons, 1924), 244 (quote); James Melvin Lee, *History of American Journalism* (Boston: Houghton Mifflin, 1917), 370–71; Grodinsky, *Jay Gould*, 14. I gratefully acknowledge Christopher T. Baer's perspective on *Iron Confederacies* and that book's interpretation of Tom Scott and the SRSC.

154. Stover, *Railroads of the South*, 37–38, 129–34, 279–82; Klein, "Southern Railroad Leaders," 305.

155. See, for example, Dozier, *A History of the Atlantic Coast Line Railroad*, 122–27.

156. See, for example, Richard J. Orsi, *Sunset Limited: The Southern Pacific Railroad and the Development of the American West, 1850–1930* (Berkeley: University of California Press, 2005).

157. Herbert H. Harwood, Jr., *Royal Blue Line: The Classic B&O Train Between Washington and New York* (Baltimore: Johns Hopkins University Press, 1990), 112–13.

158. Douglas J. Puffert, *Tracks Across Continents, Paths Through History: The Economic Dynamics of Standardization in Railway Gauge* (Chicago: University of Chicago Press, 2009), 149–53.

Chapter 11. Limits

1. Alexander K. McClure, *Old Time Notes of Pennsylvania*, vol. 2 (Philadelphia: John C. Winston Co., 1905), 380–81.

2. After the completion of Broad Street Station, in 1881, the Centennial Station was used primarily as office and storage space. It succumbed to fire in April 1896.

3. David W. Messer and Charles S. Roberts, *Triumph III: Philadelphia Terminal, 1838–2000* (Baltimore: Barnard, Roberts & Co., 2000), 28, 73–74, 94–96.

4. Messer and Roberts, *Triumph III*, 12–13; Steven W. Usselman, *Regulating Railroad Innovation: Business, Technology, and Politics in America, 1840–1920* (Cambridge: Cambridge University Press, 2002), 249–51, 295.

5. Wilson also designed the Main Building, in collaboration with architect John McArthur, Jr., and civil engineer Henry Pettit, as well as bridges spanning the PRR tracks, at Fortieth Street and at Forty-First Street. His father, William Hasell Wilson, had been a civil engineer who worked for the PRR, and his grandfather, Major John Wilson, had been the surveyor for the route of the Philadelphia & Columbia Railroad. His brothers, John and Henry, also worked for the PRR.

6. The building's provenance is unclear, however, and it may not have been the Japanese Building, or even associated with the exhibition at all. Greg Prichard, a Wayne, Pennsylvania, historian, believes that the structure may actually have been Catalogue Building #2, one of the locations where exhibition attendees could purchase official visitors' guides—see Wayne History Online, http://www.waynepa.com/history/trains/waynestation/; Messer and Roberts, *Triumph III*, 196; George H. Burgess and Miles C. Kennedy, *Centennial History of the Pennsylvania Railroad Company, 1846–1946* (Philadelphia: Pennsylvania Railroad, 1949), 353–57; Domenic Vitiello, "Engineering the Metropolis: William Sellers, Joseph M. Wilson, and Industrial Philadelphia," *Pennsylvania Magazine of History and Biography* 126 (April 2002): 273–303.

7. The inauguration of the Continental Fast Freight Line enabled the B&O to establish competitive through service to St. Louis. During 1873, the year of the panic, the B&O opened the Metropolitan Branch, a cutoff between Washington, D.C., and Point of Rocks, Maryland, creating a direct route between the national capital and the west. Farther south, Garrett's decision to provide assistance to the Washington City, Virginia Midland & Great Southern Railroad indicated his desire to compete against the network that Tom Scott had created under the auspices of the Southern Railway Security Company.

8. PRR Board of Directors (BOD) Minutes, Pennsylvania Railroad Company Collection, call no. 1807/1810, Hagley Museum and Library, Wilmington, Delaware (hereafter cited as HML), December 27, 1876, 319–20.

9. Harold F. Williamson and Arnold R. Daum, *The American Petroleum Industry: The Age of Illumination, 1859–1899* (Evanston, Ill.: Northwestern University Press, 1959), 371–95.

10. Richard Burg, "The Early Oil Trade and 'A' Series Tank Cars on the PRR, 1859–1929," *The Keystone* 15 (March 1982): 4–9; Ida Tarbell, *The History of the Standard Oil Company* (New York: McClure, Phillips & Co., 1904), 24; Herbert C. Bell, ed., *History of Northumberland County, Pennsylvania* (Chicago: Brown, Runk & Co., 1891); Samuel P. Bates, *History of Erie County, Pennsylvania* (Chicago: Warner, Beers & Co., 1884), 430–44.

11. Emory R. Johnson and Grover G. Huebner, *Railroad Traffic and Rates*, vol. 1: *Freight Service* (New York: D. Appleton, 1911), 244; Williamson and Daum, *The American Petroleum Industry*, 185–87, 398.

12. Allan Nevins, *Study in Power: John D. Rockefeller, Industrialist and Philanthropist*, vol. 1 (New York: Charles Scribner's Sons, 1953), 182–85.

13. Williamson and Daum, *The American Petroleum Industry*, 396–400.

14. Ibid., 401–2.

15. Ibid., 402–5; Nevins, *Study in Power*, vol. 1, 197–200.

16. Williamson and Daum, *The American Petroleum Industry*, 352, 405–409; Nevins, *Study in Power*, vol. 1, 204–5.

17. Nevins, *Study in Power*, vol. 1, 218–20, 228–29.

18. Ibid., 218–25.

19. Johnson and Huebner, *Railroad Traffic and Rates*, vol. 1, 244; Nevins, *Study in Power*, vol. 1, 186–89. See also "Kewanee Oil Company, 100 Years of Beginning: A History of the Company, 1871–1971," Fred F. Randolph Papers, University of Tulsa, McFarlin Library, Special Collections Department, Box 1, Folder 15.

20. Williamson and Daum, *The American Petroleum Industry*, 396–414.

21. Alexander J. Cassatt, *Pennsylvania v. Pennsylvania Railroad*, in U.S. House of Representatives, Committee on Manufactures, *Report on Investigation of Trusts*, 50th Cong., 1st sess., House Report No. 3112 (Washington, D.C.: U.S. Government Printing Office, 1888), 196, quoted in Williamson and Daum, *The American Petroleum Industry*, 416.

22. Nevins, *Study in Power*, vol. 1, 232–35.

23. Ibid., 229.

24. Williamson and Daum, *The American Petroleum Industry*, 398–99, 423.

25. Ron Chernow, *Titan: The Life of John D. Rockefeller, Sr.* (New York: Vintage Books, 1998), 200–201; Nevins, *Study in Power*, vol. 1, 231–35.

26. Chernow, *Titan*, 200–201; Nevins, *Study in Power*, vol. 1, 231–35; *The Derrick's Hand-Book of Petroleum: A Complete Chronological and Statistical Review of Petroleum Developments from 1859 to 1898* (Oil City, Pa.: Derrick, 1989), 969.

27. John D. Rockefeller, with William O. Inglis and David Feeeman Hawke, *John D. Rockefeller Interview, 1917–1920* (Westport, Conn.: Meckler Publishing, in Association with the Rockefeller Archive Center, 1984), 427.

28. Rockefeller biographer Ron Chernow has suggested, "Once again, the railroads balked at investing in rolling stock that couldn't also transport general freight, so Rockefeller stepped boldly into the breach." That was not precisely true. While the PRR did not own tank cars, its closely held subsidiary, the Empire Line, certainly did. Rockefeller's motivation for acquiring tank cars had less to do with the balking of railroad executives and more to do with his desire to blunt the efforts of Potts and other Empire Line officials to protect the independent producers by engaging in refining. Chernow, *Titan*, 170.

29. Williamson and Daum, *The American Petroleum Industry*, 424–25; Nevins, *Study in Power*, vol. 1, 240–41.

30. *Rockefeller Interview*, 1597.

31. The National Storage Company, which owned and operated Empire's terminal at Communipaw, New Jersey, was not included in the settlement. The company's stockholders, including Potts and soon-to-be PRR president George Brooke Roberts, retained their control over the firm, which operated as an independent entity between 1877 and 1881. In 1881, the National Transit Company (a subsidiary of Standard Oil) purchased the National Storage Company, and the facilities at Communipaw were later acquired by the Lehigh Valley Railroad. The PRR retained the New York Harbor lighterage operations of the National Storage Company. In February 1900, the PRR bought out the Erie & Western Transportation Company at a cost of $2.65 million. The Erie & Western eventually ran afoul of the 1912 Panama Canal Act, which prohibited railroads from operating water carrier subsidiaries that might compete with rail routes. By the end of 1915, the Great Lakes Transit Corporation had purchased the assets of the Anchor Line. Thereafter, the PRR retained its ships only in those areas where maritime operations were ancillary to rail service—primarily in New York Harbor and on Chesapeake Bay. *New York Times*, February 25, 1900; PRR BOD Minutes, September 17, 1877, 467–69.

32. Nevins, *Study in Power*, vol. 1, 246–47, 367–70, 375.

33. Burg, "The Early Oil Trade," 8–9.

34. In 1878, Rockefeller consolidated his transportation holdings under the banner of the Union Tank Line. By then, Standard Oil controlled 3,000 of the 3,200 tank cars in service in the United States. In 1891, Union Tank Line became part of the Standard Oil Trust. Its cars were available to all shippers; however, it granted a substantial rebate to units of the trust.

Standard Oil divested its holdings in Union Tank Car in 1911, following the Supreme Court's ruling in the *Standard Oil* case. The name was changed to Union Tank Car Company in 1919. It has remained an independent company, with UTLX reporting marks. UTLX, "Company History," http://www.utlx.com/history.html, accessed on June 28, 2010; Nevins, *Study in Power*, vol. 1, 248–49, 258–59, 275–76; Williamson and Daum, *The American Petroleum Industry*, 427–28.

35. Williamson and Daum, *The American Petroleum Industry*, 400, 410–12.

36. According to Rockefeller, "I think possibly Mr. Benson was more like the type of uneducated Englishman in his tenacity and inability to modify as the evidences which would convince other men were presented." *Rockefeller Interview*, 604.

37. The oil shipments typically followed the Catawissa Railroad, the Little Schuylkill Railroad, and the Reading to Philadelphia, or else the Catawissa and the Jersey Central to Bayonne, New Jersey. Within a few years, the Tide Water line had been extended to the east coast, eliminating the rail haulage. Frank Abial Flower, "General Herman Haupt," in Herman Haupt, *Reminiscences of General Herman Haupt* (Milwaukee: Wright & Joys, 1901), xxxiv–xxxvi; Williamson and Daum, *The American Petroleum Industry*, 438–46; Nevins, *Study in Power,* vol. 1, 345–48.

38. Williamson and Daum, *The American Petroleum Industry*, 445–46; Marvin W. Schlegel, *Ruler of the Reading: The Life of Franklin B. Gowen, 1836–1889* (Harrisburg: Archives Publishing, 1947), 183.

39. In 1888, the Tide Water Pipe Company became the Tide Water Oil Company, with the new name reflecting its acquisition of refineries at Bayonne, New Jersey, and at other locations.

40. *New York Times*, February 21, 1883 (quote); Williamson and Daum, *The American Petroleum Industry*, 452–56.

41. The 1884 agreement was in force until 1905, but was adhered to only until 1893.

42. Williamson and Daum, *The American Petroleum Industry*, 451, 456–58.

43. Both quotations from *New York Times*, June 21, 1876.

44. *New York Times*, June 20, 1876, June 21, 1876, June 28, 1876, July 8, 1876, July 11, 1876 (quote).

45. *New York Times*, December 28, 1878, September 26, 1879; Gerald D. Nash, "Origins of the Interstate Commerce Act," *Pennsylvania History* 24 (July 1957): 181–90; Williamson and Daum, *The American Petroleum Industry*, 431.

46. Both quoted in Robert Harrison, "The Hornets' Nest at Harrisburg: A Study of the Pennsylvania Legislature in the Late 1870s," *Pennsylvania Magazine of History and Biography* 103 (July 1979): 334–55, at 335–36.

47. Ibid.,340.

48. Williamson and Daum, *The American Petroleum Industry*, 107, 427–28.

49. William Z. Ripley, *Railroads: Rates and Regulation* (New York: Longmans, Green, and Co., 1912, repr. New York: Arno Press, 1973), 20–21; Larry Lowenthal, "The Second Critical Period of the New York State Canal System," *Canal History and Technology Proceedings* 18 (1999): 57–85, at 58.

50. Ripley, *Railroads: Rates and Regulation*, 356–61.

51. Ibid., 361.

52. *Twenty-Eighth Annual Report of the Pennsylvania Railroad Co. to the Stockholders, March 9, 1875* (Philadelphia: E. C. Markley & Son, 1875), 42.

53. *New York Times*, February 27, 1875; Alfred D. Chandler, Jr., *The Visible Hand: The Managerial Revolution in American Business* (Cambridge, Mass.: Belknap Press of Harvard University Press, 1977), 126,

137–38; D. T. Gilchrist, "Albert Fink and the Pooling System," *Business History Review* 34 (Spring 1960): 24–49, at 33–34.

54. John F. Stover, *History of the Baltimore and Ohio Railroad* (West Lafayette, Ind.: Purdue University Press, 1987), 141–53; Ripley, *Railroads: Rates and Regulation*, 362.

55. Quoted in Williamson and Daum, *The American Petroleum Industry*, 401.

56. PRR BOD Minutes, June 9, 1875, 30–33; Ripley, *Railroads: Rates and Regulation*, 22.

57. Chandler, *Visible Hand*, 138.

58. *New York Times*, April 6, 1877, May 16, 1877.

59. Ripley, *Railroads: Rates and Regulation*, 360–61.

60. The CB&Q share for a routing via the PRR would be 4.9 cents: $(145 \div (145 + 899)) \times (0.30 + 0.047) = 0.0486$.

61. Robert W. Harbeson, "The North Atlantic Port Differentials," *Quarterly Journal of Economics* 46 (August 1932): 644–70.

62. Harbeson, "North Atlantic Port Differentials," 651–52.

63. The two- and three-cent-per-hundredweight differentials applied to commodity rates, representing perhaps 75 percent of all the freight transported on American railroads. With reference to class rates, the situation was somewhat more complicated. The class rate structure consisted of six classes of freight, with differentials adjusted according to the value of the cargo. While the Philadelphia differential was two cents per hundredweight on all six classes of eastbound export freight, the westbound (import) differential was set at 6–6–2–2–2–2, from highest- to lowest-value cargoes. For Baltimore, all six classes of freight carried a three-cent differential below New York, with westbound differentials set at 8–8–3–3–3–3. Ex-lake grain (that is, grain carried on lake boats to Buffalo or a similar point, and then transferred to freight cars) destined for either Philadelphia or Baltimore moved at one-half of one cent per hundredweight below New York rates. When the Interstate Commerce Commission convened in 1887, the commissioners left the differentials in place—Thomas McIntyre Cooley, the first chairman of the ICC, had in 1882 been part of a committee that had made significant adjustments in the application of differentials, and he continued to favor their use. In 1899, in response to protests from New York merchants (resulting in *New York Produce Exchange v. Baltimore & Ohio Railroad Company*, 7 ICC 612 [1898]), the railroads cut in half the differentials on grain, flour, iron, and steel. Between 1877 and 1930, the differentials applied uniformly to both domestic shipments and to freight destined for export. After about 1897, railroads began to offer drastically lower rates on commodities intended specifically for export, a practice affirmed by the ICC in 1899. Following an Interstate Commerce Commission ruling in 1930 (the *Eastern Class Rate Investigation*, 164 ICC 314), the differentials applied solely to export traffic. Harbeson, "North Atlantic Port Differentials," 646–47; Ripley, *Railroads: Rates and Regulation*, 409.

64. Harbeson, "North Atlantic Port Differentials," 669–70.

65. Ripley, *Railroads: Rates and Regulation*, 24.

66. Robert V. Bruce, *1877: Year of Violence* (Indianapolis: Bobbs-Merrill, 1959), 40–42; Chandler, *The Visible Hand*, 138; Burgess and Kennedy, *Centennial History*, 359–60; Gilchrist, "Albert Fink," 34.

67. The development of rate bureaus was part of the development of continuous management—a phrase introduced by historian Robert H. Wiebe to describe the feedback loop wherein bureaucratic experts made continual adjustments to all of the interdependent variables associated with the oversight of complex systems. See Wiebe, *The Search for Order, 1877–1920* (New York: Hill and Wang, 1967), 145, and Brian Balogh, *A Government Out of Sight: The Mystery of National Authority in Nineteenth-Century America* (Cambridge: Cambridge University Press, 2009), 350–51,

369–71. Henry Fink, *Regulation of Railway Rates on Interstate Freight Traffic*, 2nd ed. (New York: Evening Post Job Print, 1905), 24–37.

68. Chandler, *The Visible Hand*, 115–17.

69. *New York Times*, June 18, 1889; Maury Klein, *History of the Louisville & Nashville Railroad* (Lexington: University Press of Kentucky, 2002), 165; Gilchrist, "Albert Fink," 27–30.

70. Johnson and Huebner, *Railroad Traffic and Rates*, vol. 1, 297; Chandler, *The Visible Hand*, 138–41; Thomas K. McCraw, *Prophets of Regulation: Charles Francis Adams, Louis D. Brandeis, James M. Landis, Alfred E. Kahn* (Cambridge, Mass.: Harvard University Press, 1984), 47–49; *New York Times*, June 9, 1877; Gilchrist, "Albert Fink," 41.

71. Albert Fink, *The Railroad Problem and Its Solution: Argument of Albert Fink before the Committee on Commerce of the U.S.D. House of Representatives, in Opposition to the Bill to Regulate Interstate Commerce, January 14, 15, and 16, 1880* (New York, 1882), 21, quoted in Chandler, *The Visible Hand*, 140.

72. George Rogers Taylor and Irene D. Neu, *The American Railroad Network, 1861–1890* (Urbana: University of Illinois Press, 2003), 2.

73. Chandler, *The Visible Hand*, 141–44.

74. Fink, *The Railroad Problem*, 21, quoted in Chandler, *The Visible Hand*, 140.

75. Chandler, *The Visible Hand*, 141–43.

76. William Henry Moyer, "PRR's Navy, Part V: Transatlantic Shipping Lines," *The Keystone* 44 (Summer 2011): 18–68, at 18–20, 21.

77. Harvard University Library Open Collections Program, "Aspiration, Acculturation, and Impact: Immigration to the United States, 1789–1930," http://ocp.hul.harvard.edu/immigration/dates.html, accessed on June 28, 2010.

78. Salomon, unsuccessful in his mission, resigned from the board in February 1864 after serving less than a year.

79. PRR BOD Minutes, April 4, 1860, 482, April 17, 1861, 42–43, May 28, 1862, 184–85, March 23, 1863, 289, April 1, 1863, 296–97, September 2, 1863, 324, December 9, 1863, 346–49, February 3, 1864, 360–61; *Prospectus of the Philadelphia and European Steamship Company. At Present Under the charter of the Philadelphia and Crescent Navigation Company* (Philadelphia: Jackson, 1859); *Publications of the American Jewish Historical Society, Number 27* (Baltimore: The Lord Baltimore Press, 1920), 402–3; Burgess and Kennedy, *Centennial History*, 787; Julianna R. Wood and Richard D. Wood, *Biographical Sketch of Richard D. Wood*, vol. 2 (Philadelphia: Lippincott's Press, 1871), December 7, 1863, 274; Moyer, "Transatlantic Shipping Lines," 20–21.

80. PRR BOD Minutes, March 21, 1866, 39–40, January 23, 1867, 101–2.

81. PRR BOD Minutes, May 15, 1867, 133–34, September 18, 1867, 171, October 27, 1868, 246–49; William Henry Flayhart III, *The American Line (1871–1902)* (New York: W. W. Norton, 2000), 15–17; Dorothy Gondos Beers, "The Centennial City, 1865–1876," in Russell F. Weigley, ed., *Philadelphia: A 300-Year History* (New York: W. W. Norton, 1982), 417–70, at 430.

82. PRR BOD Minutes, June 30, 1870, 403, October 24, 1870, 411–14, November 1, 1870, 419–20, November 23, 1870, 423–24, March 27, 1871, 453–54, April 4, 1871, 455; Flayhart, *The American Line*, 17–19; Burgess and Kennedy, *Centennial History*, 786–88.

83. PRR BOD Minutes, July 17, 1872, 79–81; Flayhart, *The American Line*, 79–83; Moyer, "Transatlantic Shipping Lines," 24–25.

84. Although capable of carrying oil, the *Vaderland* also provided accommodations for eight hundred steerage passengers, along with thirty in first class. The ship proved unsatisfactory as a tanker (mainly owing to concerns regarding the transportation of passengers on a vessel prone to fire) and the ship spent most of its career carrying grain.

85. Flayhart, *The American Line*, 84–96; Moyer, "Transatlantic Shipping Lines," 25–26, 32.

86. Flayhart, *The American Line*, 102.

87. Ibid., 88, 96; James J. D. Lynch, Jr., "Grain, Girard Point and the Pennsylvania Railroad," *High Line* 6 (Autumn 1985 and Winter 1985).

88. Flayhart, *The American Line*, 19–23, 32–35, 39, 52; Moyer, "Transatlantic Shipping Lines," 26–29.

89. Flayhart, *The American Line*, 57–60.

90. Ibid., 37, 42–53, 57.

91. Ibid., 39–41, 53–56, 60–61; Moyer, "Transatlantic Shipping Lines," 26–29.

92. PRR BOD Minutes, December 24, 1873, 241, December 9, 1874, 412–13, February 23, 1876, 157, March 22, 1876, 173; Flayhart, *The American Line*, 64–66, 74–78; Moyer, "Transatlantic Shipping Lines," 30–31.

93. Flayhart, *The American Line*, 40–41, 78, 111–12; Moyer, "Transatlantic Shipping Lines," 33–35.

94. Moyer, "Transatlantic Shipping Lines," 35, 40–44.

95. Flayhart, *The American Line*, 325–54; Moyer, "Transatlantic Shipping Lines," 52, 68.

96. Flayhart, *The American Line*, 78.

97. James A. Ward, "Power and Accountability on the Pennsylvania Railroad, 1846–1878," *Business History Review* 49 (Spring 1975): 37–59, at 52.

98. James A. Ward, *J. Edgar Thomson, Master of the Pennsylvania* (Westport, Conn.: Greenwood Press, 1980), 209–10.

99. Pliny Earle, *The Earle Family, Ralph Earle and his Descendants* (Worcester, Mass.: Charles Hamilton, 1888); John Thomas Scharf and Thompson Westcott, *History of Philadelphia, 1609–1884*, vol. 2 (Philadelphia: L. H. Everts, 1884), 1477.

100. *Report of the Investigating Committee of the Pennsylvania Railroad Company* (Philadelphia: Allen, Lane & Scott, 1874), 3–4.

101. Ibid., 104, 115; Ward, *Master of the Pennsylvania*, 210–11, 216; Burgess and Kennedy, *Centennial History*, 314–15, 341.

102. *Report of the Investigating Committee*, 13.

103. Ibid., 61.

104. Ibid., 75.

105. Burgess and Kennedy, *Centennial History*, 329–35; Chandler, *The Visible Hand*, 154.

106. *Report of the Investigating Committee*, 70.

107. Ibid., 121, 123–24.

108. More broadly, the report expressed the "fear that the property of the company may be used by officials and favored employees for their own personal benefit." In order to eliminate that "evil," committee members insisted "that purity of management can only be obtained when the Directors, officials, and employees are free from any complications which may affect the interest of your road, and that such rules are established and carried into practice as will prevent such persons from in any way using the road or the Company for their own profit." Ibid., 160–61.

109. Ibid., 159.

110. "The problem was," the report suggested, "how to place all needed restrictions on your agents [i.e., the directors who represented the stockholders] without affecting their ability to produce the best possible results, with a proper reservation of the rights and obligations of ownership." Ibid., 166, 169.

111. Ibid., 160.

112. Burgess and Kennedy, *Centennial History*, 332.

113. *Report of the Investigating Committee*, 167.

114. In advocating for the establishment of salaried directors who were experts in railroad operations and management, the members of the inves-

tigating committee were incorporating long-standing suggestions by reformers in the financial press, most notably Henry Varnum Poor. The committee members acknowledged that Pennsylvania law forbade directors from receiving salaries, but suggested that the law could be changed. *Report of the Investigating Committee*, 174–79; Alfred D. Chandler, Jr., *Henry Varnum Poor, Business Editor, Analyst, and Reformer* (Cambridge, Mass.: Harvard University Press, 1956), 160–63.

115. *Pennsylvania State Reports*, vol. 92 (Philadelphia: Kay & Brother, 1881), 408; Ward, *Master of the Pennsylvania*, 98.

116. *Railroad Gazette* 14 (1882): 776–78, 793–94, 809–810, quoted in Leland H. Jenks, "Early History of a Railway Organization," *Business History Review* 35 (Summer 1961): 163–79, at 167.

117. *Twenty-Eighth Annual Report*, 43 (quote); Chandler, *The Visible Hand*, 154; Ward, *Master of the Pennsylvania*, 211.

118. PRR BOD Minutes, January 27, 1875, 437–38. Scott fixed January 1, 1875, as the deadline for PRR officers to dispose of their outside interests. Given the difficulty of selling the securities in the midst of a recession, the board extended the deadline to July 1, 1875.

119. PRR BOD Minutes, June 9, 1875, 29–30.

120. John King to John Garrett, July 16, 1874, B&O Railroad Papers, Box 62, quoted in Ward, "Power and Accountability," 54–55.

121. Ward, "Power and Accountability," 55.

122. Schlegel, *Ruler of the Reading*, 62–152.

123. Shelton Stromquist, *A Generation of Boomers: The Pattern of Railroad Labor Conflict in Nineteenth-Century America* (Urbana: University of Illinois Press, 1987), 107–11; John C. Paige, *A Special History Study: Pennsylvania Railroad Shops and Works, Altoona, Pennsylvania* (Washington, D.C.: United States Department of the Interior, National Park Service, 1989), 73–74; "A Historical Sketch of the Brotherhood of Locomotive Firemen and Enginemen," *Brotherhood of Locomotive Firemen and Enginemen's Magazine* 48 (June 1910): 843–50.

124. Bruce, *Year of Violence*, 32–34, 50.

125. PRR BOD Minutes, November 7, 1873, 219–21, December 24, 1873, 243.

126. Pennsylvania General Assembly, *Report of the Committee Appointed to Investigate the Railroad Riots in July, 1877* (Harrisburg: Lane & Hart, 1878), 818–19.

127. *Year of Violence*, 41–43, 51–52; PRR BOD Minutes, May 18, 1877, 396.

128. PRR Labor Chronology, Engine and Train Service Employees, 1–2, HML, Box 877, folder 4.

129. G. Clinton Gardner to Frank Thomson, Gardner Letterbook, January 22, 1878, 288–91; HML, Box 423, folder 2.

130. Gardner to Theodore N. Ely, Gardner Letterbook, April 9, 1877, 220–22.

131. Bruce, *Year of Violence*, 50.

132. Ibid., 48–51; *New York Times*, May 29, 1877.

133. Bruce, *Year of Violence*, 51–52.

134. PRR Labor Chronology; Bruce, *Year of Violence*, 60–63, 124.

135. Bruce, *Year of Violence*, 63–65.

136. Ibid., 74–100.

137. *Report of the Committee Appointed to Investigate the Railroad Riots*, 674.

138. PRR Labor Chronology; Bruce, *Year of Violence*, 115–17; Philip S. Foner, *The Great Labor Uprising of 1877* (New York: Monad Press, 1977), 56–57.

139. PRR Labor Chronology; Bruce, *Year of Violence*, 118–24.

140. Bruce, *Year of Violence*; David O. Stowell, *Streets, Railroads, and the Great Strike of 1877* (Chicago: University of Chicago Press, 1999). Bruce

and Stowell are not alone in their examination of the deleterious effects of the railroads—and their noisy, smoky, and dangerous trains—on the urban fabric. For example, see Joel A. Tarr and David Stradling, "Environmental Activism, Locomotive Smoke, and the Corporate Response: The Case of the Pennsylvania Railroad and Chicago Smoke Control," *Business History Review* (Winter 1999): 677–704; Stradling, *Smokestacks and Progressives: Environmentalists, Engineers, and Air Quality in America, 1881–1951* (Baltimore: Johns Hopkins University Press, 1999); and Christine Meisner Rosen, "'Knowing' Industrial Pollution: Nuisance Law and the Power of Tradition in a Time of Rapid Economic Change, 1840–1864," *Environmental History* 8 (October 2003): 1–33. The trains belonging to the various railroads that served Pittsburgh certainly blocked streets and caused accidents and fatalities, but the city had relatively little street running compared with other urban centers. It is important to emphasize, moreover, that public attitudes during the late nineteenth century were very different from those of the early twenty-first century. Most Pittsburghers were willing to tolerate noise, smoke, and other inconveniences as a necessary sign of progress. After all, the city's steel mills and other factories contributed a fair amount of pollution as well, and they were left untouched by the violence. Not until the late 1940s and into the 1950s did Pittsburgh civic leaders come to terms with the environment in the smokiest city in the United States.

141. According to many Pittsburghers, PRR executives also exploited (and, through discriminatory rate policies, often contributed to) the financial distress of under-funded local railroads. When those local railroads went bankrupt, PRR officials were waiting in the wings to reorganize the company as a valuable feeder to the PRR system.

142. Small wonder then, that, as labor historian Philip S. Foner has observed, "by 1877, hatred of the Pennsylvania Railroad had permeated all classes in Pittsburgh." Foner, *The Great Labor Uprising*, 55 (quote), 57–58.

143. *Report of the Committee Appointed to Investigate the Railroad Riots*, 832.

144. Bruce, *Year of Violence*, 121–25, 134.

145. Ibid., 130–34. See also Steven Patrick Schroeder, "The Elementary School of the Army: The Pennsylvania National Guard, 1877–1917" (Ph.D. diss., University of Pittsburgh, 2006).

146. Bruce, *Year of Violence*, 135–37.

147. The same type of fraternizing also occurred on the Baltimore & Ohio at Pittsburgh and Martinsburg, again compelling the state militias to call on reinforcements from the eastern part of the state.

148. Douglas L. Mahrer, ed., "The Diary of Wilson Howell Carpenter: An Account of the 1877 Railroad Riots," *The Keystone* 30 (Autumn 1991): 46–52.

149. Quoted in Bruce, *Year of Violence*, 140.

150. *Report of the Committee Appointed to Investigate the Railroad Riots*, 832.

151. PRR Labor Chronology; Bruce, *Year of Violence*, 137–38; Foner, *The Great Labor Uprising*, 60.

152. In later testimony, Brinton noted, "I asked permission of General Pearson to clear the streets, and to follow the crowd to the arsenal, and he, more in his manner than anything else, appealed to Mr. Cassatt, and Mr. Cassatt said, I have nothing to do with the movements of the troops, I know nothing about that whatever." *Report of the Committee Appointed to Investigate the Railroad Riots*, 899.

153. *Report of the Committee Appointed to Investigate the Railroad Riots*, 10, 380, 592; PRR Labor Chronology, 3; Bruce, *Year of Violence*, 138–47; Foner, *The Great Labor Uprising*, 62–64.

154. *Report of the Committee Appointed to Investigate the Railroad Riots*, 174–85.

155. Bruce, *Year of Violence*, 154–58.

156. Ibid., 156–58.

157. Ibid., 165–68.

158. Ibid., 168–80.

159. Ibid., 126–27, 184–85; Foner, *The Great Labor Uprising*, 68–69.

160. The strike also affected several PRR-affiliated lines (including the Philadelphia & Erie and the Erie & Pittsburgh), as well as the Erie; the Philadelphia & Reading; the Chicago, Alton & St. Louis; the Canada Southern; New York Central affiliates the Lake Shore & Michigan Southern and the Cleveland, Columbus, Cincinnati & Indianapolis; and the Ohio & Mississippi. Dan Cupper, *Rockville Bridge: Rails Across the Susquehanna* (Halifax, Pa.: Withers, 2002), 20–21; Bruce, *Year of Violence*, 185–87, 206–7.

161. Richard T. Wallis, *The Pennsylvania Railroad at Bay: William Riley McKeen and the Terre Haute & Indianapolis Railroad* (Bloomington: Indiana University Press, 2001), 47–55, Foner, *The Great Labor Uprising*, 95–101.

162. Philip English Mackey, "Law and Order, 1877: Philadelphia's Response to the Railroad Riots," *Pennsylvania Magazine of History and Biography* 96 (April 1972): 183–202.

163. Pittsburgh employed 120 policemen, while Philadelphia—a city little more than five times its size—had 1,300 on its roster.

164. Bruce, *Year of Violence*, 195–96; Foner, *The Great Labor Uprising*, 192.

165. Bruce, *Year of Violence*, 280–91, 305; Foner, *The Great Labor Uprising*, 74–77; Walter Licht, *Working for the Railroad: The Organization of Work in the Nineteenth Century* (Princeton, N.J.: Princeton University Press, 1983), 136–37, 262.

166. Gardner to Pugh, Gardner Letterbook, August 13, 1877, 262–64.

167. Simon Hawk et al., resolution to James McCrea, July 24, 1877, Penn Central Railroad Collection, M.G. 286, Pennsylvania Historical and Museum Commission, Pennsylvania State Archives, Harrisburg (hereafter PHMC), Cassatt/McCrea papers, Box 38 (12–1799), folder 48/35.

168. Cassatt and Pitcairn quoted in *Report of the Committee to Investigate the Railroad Riots*, 70 ("send a paper"), 699 ("out of our hands").

169. James McCrea to Thomas A. Scott, July 25, 1877, PHMC, Cassatt/McCrea papers, Box 38 (12–1799), folder 48/35.

170. Gardner to Frank Thomson, Gardner Letterbook, June 30, 1877, 252–54.

171. Gardner to Pugh, Gardner Letterbook, July 25, 1877, 260–61.

172. Damage on the rest of the system was far less severe, mainly limited to PRR facilities at Allegheny, Altoona, Harrisburg, and Philadelphia.

173. *New York Times*, April 22, 1880.

174. *New York Times*, January 24, 1879, February 6, 1879, March 6, 1879, March 7, 1879, March 20, 1879, March 21, 1879, April 4, 1879, April 10, 1879, April 19, 1879, April 23, 1879, April 25, 1879, May 21, 1879, May 28, 1879, May 29, 1879, May 30, 1879, June 6, 1879, August 12, 1879, August 29, 1879, August 30, 1879, August 31, 1879, January 3, 1880, January 20, 1880, January 22, 1880, March 9, 1880, March 11, 1880, March 12, 1880, August 29, 1880, November 21, 1880; Burgess and Kennedy, *Centennial History*, 372–73; Bruce, *Year of Violence*, 299–300.

175. Thomas A. Scott, "The Recent Strikes," *North American Review* 125 (September 1877): 351–62, quotes at 352 and 357.

176. *New York World*, July 22, 1877, quoted in Philip S. Foner, *History of the Labor Movement in the United States,* vol. 1: *From Colonial Times to the Founding of the American Federation of Labor* (New York: International Publishers, 1947), 468.

177. PRR Labor Chronology, 16.

178. Bruce, *Year of Violence*, 120, 134–35, 171.

179. Mahrer, ed., "Diary of Wilson Howell Carpenter," 49.

180. Bruce, *Year of Violence*, 143, 154.

181. *Philadelphia Public Ledger*, May 23, 1879; PRR BOD Minutes, May 1, 1880, 28–31; *New York Times*, May 22, 1881. I thank Christopher T. Baer for alerting me to the short obituary notice of Thomas A. Scott, Jr., and for information on the death of Samuel Moon, the latter contained in his "General Chronology of the Pennsylvania Railroad Company," for April 29, 1879, http://www.prrths.com/Hagley/PRR1879%20Aug%2006.pdf, and for the reference to the "severe cold," October 30, 1878, http://www.prrths.com/Hagley/PRR1878%20June%2006.pdf.

182. W. Heyward Myers to William Wallace Atterbury, March 22, 1910, PHMC, Cassatt/McCrea papers, Box 38 (12–1799), folder 48/35.

Chapter 12. Order

1. Maury Klein, *The Life and Legend of Jay Gould* (Baltimore: Johns Hopkins University Press), 1986), 115–26.

2. Ibid., 232–33.

3. *New York Times*, June 18, 1889 (quotes); Klein, *Jay Gould*, 272–73; Alfred D. Chandler, *The Visible Hand: The Managerial Revolution in American Business* (Cambridge, Mass.: Belknap Press of Harvard University Press, 1977), 140–42; *Railway Age* 96, no. 17 (April 28, 1934): 631; William Z. Ripley, *Railroads: Rates and Regulation* (New York: Longmans, Green, and Co., 1912; repr. New York: Arno Press, 1973), 22–23.

4. Mileage figures include 1,504 miles on Lines East, plus 2,943 miles controlled by the Pennsylvania Company, and are based on data from Henry V. Poor, *Manual of the Railroads of the United States for 1874–75* (New York: H. V. & H. W. Poor, 1874), 450, 669.

5. William Z. Ripley, *Railroads: Finance and Organization* (New York: Longmans, Green, 1915), 456–57.

6. In 1880, the Pennsylvania Railroad (Lines East) operated 1,875.6 route miles, and the Pennsylvania Company 3,546.7. In 1890, the PRR had expanded to 2,500.7 route miles, and the Pennsylvania Company had contracted slightly, to 3.490.4 miles. The system as a whole increased from 5,422.3 route miles in 1880 to 5,991.1 route miles in 1890. Henry V. Poor, *Manual of the Railroads of the United States, 1881* (New York: H. V. & H. W. Poor, 1881), 281; Poor, *Manual of the Railroads of the United States, 1891* (New York: H. V. & H. W. Poor, 1891), 853.

7. Chandler, *The Visible Hand*, 145–48, 167–71.

8. Ibid., 150–51, 157–58.

9. Klein, *Jay Gould*, 199–205.

10. John Steele Gordon, "The Public Be Damned," *American Heritage* 40 (September-October 1989).

11. *Investigation of Railroads, Holding Companies, and Affiliated Companies: Report of the Committee on Interstate Commerce: Railroad Combination in the Eastern Region, Part 1 (Before 1920)*, 76th Cong., 3rd sess. (Washington, D.C.: U.S. Government Printing Office, 1940) (hereafter referred to as "Wheeler Report"), 4–6; Chandler, *The Visible Hand*, 157–58, 160–61; Jean Strouse, *Morgan: American Financier* (New York: Harper Perennial, 2000), 196–97.

12. Edward Digby Baltzell, *Philadelphia Gentlemen: The Making of a National Upper Class* (1958; rept. New Brunswick, N.J.: Transaction, 1989), 114.

13. David G. Loth, *Pencoyd and the Roberts Family* (New York: s.n., 1961), 37–42; Baltzell, *Philadelphia Gentlemen*, 77, 121, 196.

14. Roberts retained his engineering responsibilities while serving as second vice president and first vice president. After 1874, and with the contractions that followed the Panic of 1873, the board abolished the separate Engineer Department in charge of new projects, and the head of the Transportation Department (Roberts) had oversight over all routine (maintenance-of-way) engineering work, as well as what little new work was

undertaken. *New York Times*, January 31, 1897; George H. Burgess and Miles C. Kennedy, *Centennial History of the Pennsylvania Railroad Company, 1846–1949* (Philadelphia: Pennsylvania Railroad, 1949), 350–51, 385–87, 798; William Bender Wilson, *History of the Pennsylvania Railroad Company, with Plan of Organization, Portraits of Officials and Biographical Sketches*, vol. 2 (New York: Henry T. Coates & Co., 1899), 246–47; Richard T. Wallis, *The Pennsylvania Railroad at Bay: William Riley McKeen and the Terre Haute & Indianapolis Railroad* (Bloomington: Indiana University Press, 2001), 67; Loth, *Pencoyd and the Roberts Family*, 42–48.

15. Burgess and Kennedy, *Centennial History*, 387, 454, 456; James A. Ward, "J. Edgar Thomson and Thomas A. Scott: A Symbiotic Partnership?" *Pennsylvania Magazine of History and Biography* 100 (1976): 37–65, 54–56.

16. John D. Rockefeller, with William O. Inglis and David Freeman Hawke, *John D. Rockefeller Interview, 1917–1920* (Westport, Conn.: Meckler Publishing, in Association with the Rockefeller Archive Center, 1984), 563 ("able and erratic"), 604 ("brilliant and resourceful").

17. The Philadelphia & Reading Coal & Iron Company did not follow the Tom Scott model precisely, as it owned most of the coal properties directly, rather than through additional corporate intermediaries.

18. Marvin Wilson Schlegel, *Ruler of the Reading: The Life of Franklin B. Gowen* (Harrisburg: Archives Publishing Company of Pennsylvania, 1947), 11; Robert V. Bruce, *1877: Year of Violence* (1959; repr. Chicago: Ivan R. Dee, 1989), 41; C. K. Yearly, Jr., *Enterprise and Anthracite: Economics and Democracy in Schuylkill County, 1820–1875* (Baltimore: Johns Hopkins University Press, 1961), 185–89, 207–13.

19. Julius Grodinsky, *Jay Gould: His Business Career, 1867–1892* (Philadelphia: University of Pennsylvania Press, 1957), 361–62.

20. *New York Times*, July 26, 1885 (quote).

21. James L. Holton, *The Reading Railroad: History of a Coal Age Empire*, vol. 1 (Laury's Station, Pa.: Garrigues House, 1989–92), 226; Stuart Daggett, *Railroad Reorganization* (Cambridge, Mass.: Harvard University Press, 1908; repr. New York: Augustus M. Kelley, 1967), 98; Schlegel, *Ruler of the Reading*, 212–30.

22. Herbert H. Harwood, Jr., *Royal Blue Line: The Classic B&O Train Between Washington and New York* (Baltimore: Johns Hopkins University Press, 2002), 27–28.

23. Through service was a cooperative effort by the Jersey Central, the Delaware & Bound Brook, and the North Pennsylvania. In a conciliatory gesture, PRR officials permitted trains traveling over the Bound Brook Route to use the PRR's trackage in Philadelphia to access the exhibition grounds. Jay Veeder Hare, *History of the North Pennsylvania Railroad* (Philadelphia: Reading Co., 1944), 19–24; David W. Messer and Charles S. Roberts, *Triumph V: Philadelphia to New York, 1830–2002* (Baltimore: Barnard, Roberts and Co., 2002), 30–31; Lorett Treese, *Railroads of New Jersey: Fragments of the Past in the Garden State Landscape* (Mechanicsburg, Pa.: Stackpole Books, 2006), 17.

24. The Reading had leased the Philadelphia, Norristown & Germantown in December 1870. Schlegel, *Ruler of the Reading*, 179–80.

25. The courts could do nothing to prevent PRR officials from rerouting freight traffic, in order to punish all of the railroads associated with the Bound Brook Route. They prevented any eastbound freight from transferring onto the Reading at Harrisburg. As a result, the prewar Allentown Route—already lightly used, since the PRR had leased the United Companies in 1871—faded into obscurity. *New York Times*, July 23, 1879, October 29, 1880; Harwood, *Royal Blue Line*, 25–27; Schlegel, *Ruler of the Reading*, 180; Jay V. Hare, *History of the Reading, Which Appeared as a Serial in* The Pilot *and* Philadelphia & Reading Railway Men, *Beginning May 1909—Ending February 1914* (Philadelphia: John Henry Stock & Co., 1966), 101–4.

26. John F. Stover, "Colonel Henry S. McComb, Mississippi Railroad Adventurer," *Journal of Mississippi History* 18 (July 1955): 177–90, at 179; John F. Stover, *History of the Baltimore and Ohio Railroad* (West Lafayette, Ind.: Purdue University Press, 1987), 154; Mark R. Wilson, "The Extensive Side of Nineteenth-Century Military Economy: The Tent Industry in the Northern United States During the Civil War," *Enterprise & Society* 2 (June 2001): 297–337.

27. John Thomas Scharf, *History of Delaware, 1609–1888*, vol. 2 (Philadelphia: L. J. Richards & Co., 1888), 749–59; Henry S. McComb Diary, Hagley Museum and Library, Wilmington, Delaware (hereafter cited as HML), accession no. 0699, various entries, March 4–March 31, 1880.

28. McComb Diary, April 27, 1880, April 30, 1880, May 3, 1880.

29. Harwood, *Royal Blue Line*, 28; Grodinsky, *Jay Gould*, 326–29.

30. *New York Times*, February 19, 1881; Burgess and Kennedy, *Centennial History*, 403–7; Grodinsky, *Jay Gould*, 328.

31. One of the most commonly repeated stories was that Garrett attended a dinner party in Boston and injudiciously bragged that he was about to gain control of the PW&B, and that one of the guests soon informed Roberts. It is more likely, however, that PW&B shareholders, well aware that the B&O and the PRR interests each desired their railroad, kept Roberts appraised of developments.

32. Burgess and Kennedy, *Centennial History*, 401–7; Harwood, *Royal Blue Line*, 29.

33. As part of the purchase of the PW&B, the PRR also gained that company's one-third interest in the Junction Railroad. The Reading sold its share of the Junction Railroad to the PRR in 1898, making that short yet vital connecting link entirely a PRR property. In 1902, as part of President Cassatt's corporate simplification program, the PRR consolidated the Philadelphia, Wilmington & Baltimore with the Baltimore & Potomac, forming the Philadelphia, Baltimore & Washington Railroad (PB&W).

34. *New York Times*, February 11, 1887; Burgess and Kennedy, *Centennial History*, 401–7, 498; Frank A. Wrabel, "Terminals, Tunnels and Turmoil," *The Keystone* 28 (Spring 1995): 24–25, 35; Harwood, *Royal Blue Line*, 56.

35. The Old Dominion Steamship Company controlled and operated three railroads, used in conjunction with steamship service between the Atlantic side of the Virginia portion of the Delmarva Peninsula and New York. In 1883, the three railroads were consolidated as the Delaware, Maryland & Virginia Railroad. The Junction & Breakwater Railroad began at a junction with the Delaware Railroad, at Harrington, and continued to Lewes, Delaware (in 1869), and Rehoboth (in 1878). Two allied companies, the Breakwater & Frankford Railroad (chartered in Delaware) and the Worcester Rail Road (chartered in Maryland) laid rails from a junction with the Junction & Breakwater at Georgetown, Delaware, and reached Franklin City, Virginia, in 1876. In May 1883, all three companies were merged into the Delaware, Maryland & Virginia Railroad. The Philadelphia, Wilmington & Baltimore purchased the company in 1885, and control passed to the Philadelphia, Baltimore & Washington Railroad when that company was established in 1902. The Delaware, Maryland & Virginia merged into the PB&W in 1956. Burgess and Kennedy, *Centennial History*, 395–98; Wilson, *History of the Pennsylvania Railroad*, vol. 1, 324–26.

36. Burgess and Kennedy, *Centennial History*, 398–400; Clayton Colman Hall, *Baltimore: Its History and Its People*, vol. 1 (New York: Lewis Historical Publishing, 1912), 498; James Murray, *History of Pocomoke City, Formerly New Town: From Its Origin to the Present Time* (Baltimore: Curry, Clay & Co., 1888), 108–9; *New York Times*, July 12, 1885, July 3, 1901.

37. *New York Times*, October 21, 1900; Samuel T. Wiley and Winfield Scott Garner, eds., *Biographical and Portrait Cyclopedia of Chester County,*

Pennsylvania, Comprising a Historical Sketch of the County (Philadelphia: Gresham Publishing, 1893), 791–93.

38. *New York Times*, September 21, 1891.

39. Burgess and Kennedy, *Centennial History*, 488, 558; Herbert H. Harwood, *Impossible Challenge: The Baltimore & Ohio Railroad in Maryland* (Baltimore: Barnard, Roberts & Co., 1979), 159–60; Wilson, *History of the Pennsylvania Railroad*, vol. 1, 324–27; William Harry Moyer, "The PRR's Navy, Part III: Chesapeake Bay Area," *The Keystone* 40 (Winter 2007): 11–49.

40. The various lines included the Baltimore & Eastern Shore Railroad (Claiborne to Salisbury, Maryland, incorporated in 1886 and completed in 1890) and the Wicomico & Pocomoke Railroad (Salisbury to Ocean City, incorporated in 1848 and completed in 1876), which in 1894 were merged into the Baltimore, Chesapeake & Atlantic Railway. The Queen Anne & Kent Railroad, chartered in 1856, built lines from Massey to Centreville and Chestertown. The Delaware & Chesapeake Railway (chartered in 1854 as the Maryland & Delaware Rail Road, and reorganized in 1878) owned a line from Clayton to Oxford. The Cambridge & Seaford Rail Road, chartered in 1882) built between its namesake cities. The three companies (Queen Anne & Kent, Delaware & Chesapeake, and Cambridge & Seaford) were folded into the Delaware Railroad in 1899. In 1856, Maryland chartered the Kent County Rail Road. Construction proceeded slowly, and by 1870 the company had opened a line from Massey, Maryland (a junction on the Queen Anne & Kent Railroad), west to Kennedyville, with additional extensions in the years that followed. The Smyrna & Delaware Bay Railroad, chartered in 1865, carried the route east to Woodland Beach, Delaware, a short distance south of Bombay Hook, across Delaware Bay from Bayside, New Jersey. By 1873, Jay Gould had taken charge of the project, as well as two New Jersey companies, the New Jersey Southern Railroad (the former Raritan & Delaware Bay Railroad) and the Vineland Railway. Together, Gould envisioned a route from New York to Baltimore—albeit one that would require water crossings of New York Bay, Delaware Bay, and Chesapeake Bay. The plan succumbed to the Panic of 1873. Ten years later, the New Jersey Southern merged the Kent County and the Smyrna & Delaware Bay into the Baltimore & Delaware Bay Railroad. The PRR bought the company in 1901, but abandoned the lightly used line east of Massey. The remainder became part of the Delaware Railroad in 1902. The Maryland, Delaware & Virginia Railway was established in 1905 as the reorganization of the Queen Anne's Railroad (Love Point, Maryland, to Lewes, Delaware, completed between 1898 and 1902). The Baltimore, Chesapeake & Atlantic owned all of the stock in the Maryland, Delaware & Virginia. Burgess and Kennedy, *Centennial History*, 488; Christopher T. Baer, William J. Coxey, and Paul W. Schopp, *The Trail of the Blue Comet: A History of the Jersey Central's New Jersey Southern Division* (Palmyra, N.Y.: West Jersey Chapter of the National Railway Historical Society, 1994), 78, 81–82, 86–93, 110, 128–30; Coverdale & Colpitts, *Corporate, Financial and Construction History of Lines Owned, Operated and Controlled to December 31, 1945*, vol. 2: *Lines East of Pittsburgh* (New York: Coverdale & Colpitts, 1947), 349–426.

41. Harwood, *Impossible Challenge*, 159–60.

42. PRR officials used a variety of mechanisms to control the lines on the Delmarva Peninsula. The PRR controlled the New York, Philadelphia & Norfolk through interlocking directors and the assignment of PRR officials to the company's operations. The PRR did not acquire majority stock ownership in the New York, Philadelphia & Norfolk until 1908. On December 14, 1920, the PRR leased the company as the Norfolk Division, but Interstate Commerce Commission approval (required by the Transportation Act of 1920) delayed the formal takeover until November 1, 1922. The PRR controlled the Baltimore, Chesapeake & Atlantic through stock owned by the PRR and by three of its subsidiaries.

43. Two companies operated the bulk of the Chesapeake Bay steamship services. The Maryland, Delaware & Virginia controlled the Weems Steamboat Company and the Chester River Steamboat Company. The Baltimore, Chesapeake & Atlantic Railway controlled the Choptank Steamboat Company, the Eastern Shore Steamboat Company, the Maryland Steamboat Company, and the Wheeler Transportation Company, which operated multiple steamship routes linking Baltimore and other Western Shore points to Maryland's Eastern Shore. The New York, Philadelphia & Norfolk operated service across the mouth of Chesapeake Bay, from Cape Charles to Norfolk and the surrounding area, as well as to Old Point Comfort, at the tip of the York-James Peninsula. The Delaware, Maryland & Virginia Railroad also operated a few steamship routes on the Atlantic side of the Delmarva Peninsula, linking Chincoteague Island to the mainland at Franklin City, Virginia. Burgess and Kennedy, *Centennial History*, 421–22; Davis, *End of the Line*, 103–7. For a thorough account of railroad ferry operations on Chesapeake Bay, see Moyer, "The PRR's Navy, Part III"; John D. Denny, Jr., "When the Pennsylvania Railroad Sailed the Chesapeake, Weather and Tide Permitting," *The Keystone* 40 (Winter 2007): 50–76; Robert H. Burgess and H. Graham Wood, *Steamboats Out of Baltimore* (Cambridge, Md.: Tidewater Publishers, 1968); and David C. Holly, *Tidewater by Steamboat: A Saga of the Chesapeake: The Weems Line on the Patuxent, Potomac, and Rappahannock* (Baltimore: Johns Hopkins University Press, 1991).

44. For many years, the PRR subsidized what were generally unprofitable freight and passenger services on Chesapeake Bay, in order to draw traffic to the rail operations. The 1915 Panama Canal Act prohibited railroads from operating water carriers that directly paralleled or competed with rail service, causing Interstate Commerce Commission officials to order the suspension of many Chesapeake Bay routes. Petitions from area residents, who were in danger of losing service, caused the ICC to relent, and most routes remained intact. However, the rapid growth of highway travel during the 1920s greatly reduced water traffic and led to the reorganization of the Delmarva Peninsula railroads. The Maryland, Delaware & Virginia entered bankruptcy and in 1923 was split into three components and sold at foreclosure. Some of the rail lines were scrapped, and those that were still profitable went to a newly incorporated PRR subsidiary, the Baltimore & Eastern Railroad. Another new PRR subsidiary, the Baltimore & Virginia Steamboat Company, acquired some of the steamships, docks, and routes along the Potomac and Rappahannock rivers. In 1926, the PRR forced the Baltimore, Chesapeake & Atlantic into bankruptcy. In 1928, most of the BC&A steamship services were sold to the Baltimore & Virginia Steamboat Company, while the BC&A's rail operations, as well as the ferry service between Baltimore and Claiborne, Maryland, went to the Baltimore & Eastern Railroad. The Great Depression sharply curtailed the remaining Chesapeake Bay operations, with the Baltimore & Virginia Steamboat Company entering bankruptcy in 1932. The opening of the Chesapeake Bay Bridge-Tunnel in 1964 marked the end of service between Cape Charles and Norfolk (service to Old Point Comfort had ended in 1953), but other PRR water service continued through the 1968 Penn Central merger. Moyer, "The PRR's Navy, Part III," 22–49.

45. For information on the representation of middle-class space in department stores and railway stations (with particular links to women's history), see John Henry Hepp IV, *The Middle-Class City: Transforming Space and Time in Philadelphia, 1876–1926* (Philadelphia: University of Pennsylvania Press, 2003); Jack Simmons, *The Victorian Railway* (New York: Thames and Hudson, 1991); Susan Porter Benson, *Counter Cultures: Sales-*

women, Managers, and Customers in American Department Stores, 1890–1940 (Urbana: University of Illinois Press, 1986); and Amy Richter, "Tracking Public Culture: Women, the Railroad, and the End of the Victorian Public" (Ph.D. diss., New York University, 2000).

46. By 1870, John A. Wilson was the PRR's chief engineer of maintenance of way, and in April of that year the board of directors appointed him as chief engineer of low-grade lines. Joseph Wilson was engineer of bridges and buildings.

47. In January 1876, John and Joseph Wilson, in conjunction with Frederick G. Thorn, established the architectural firm of Wilson Brothers & Company, primarily to design buildings for the Centennial Exhibition.

48. David W. Messer, *Triumph III: Philadelphia Terminal, 1838–2000* (Baltimore: Barnard, Roberts & Co., 2000), 15, 25–27, 29, 35–37, 40. Hepp, *The Middle-Class City*, 49–55. The PRR records contain few surviving references to the construction of Broad Street Station in 1881 or to its expansion in 1893–94. For some examples, see A. J. Latta to William H. Brown, September 7, 1884, Pennsylvania Railroad Company Collection, call no. 1807/1810, HML, Box 1471, folder 4; General Superintendent to Brown, July 8, 1892, HML, Box 1471, folder 6; Brown to S. M. Prevost, August 9, 1893, HML, Box 1470, folder 36; General Manager to Brown, September 18, 1894, HML, Box 1470, folder 38.

49. Wilson Brothers & Company designed the structure, with the ironwork provided by William Sellers & Company, a local firm with longstanding ties to the PRR.

50. Messer, *Triumph III*, 13, 44–45.

51. The PRR also maintained a large freight terminal, completed in 1887, between Forty-Ninth and Fiftieth Streets in West Philadelphia, near the former site of the Centennial Exhibition. The area around the station became the Fifty-Second Street Yards, the principal site for the classification of freight traveling between western points and Philadelphia.

52. In 1903, the PRR built a second bridge across the Schuylkill River, parallel to the original, and by 1910 had widened it to four tracks. Burgess and Kennedy, *Centennial History*, 431–33; Messer, *Triumph III*, 14–16.

53. Houston and his PRR allies originally intended to extend the route to Phoenixville, Pennsylvania—hence the incorporation of the Germantown, Norristown & Phoenixville Railroad. By 1882, Houston had curtailed his ambitions, and the line became the Philadelphia, Germantown & Chestnut Hill Railroad. The Panic of 1893 forced Houston to curtail plans to extend the Chestnut Hill line to additional lands that he owned at Roxborough. George Woodward, Houston's son-in-law, later expanded the Wissahickon Heights development and changed its name to St. Martin's. David R. Contosta, *Suburb in the City: Chestnut Hill, Philadelphia, 1850–1990* (Columbus: Ohio State University Press, 1992), 2–3, 78–83, 98, 107–8, and Contosta, *A Philadelphia Family: The Houstons and Woodwards of Chestnut Hill* (Philadelphia: University of Pennsylvania Press, 1992), 25–27. See also Willard S. Detweiler, Jr., *Chestnut Hill: An Architectural History* (Philadelphia: Chestnut Hill Association, 1969); Robert Fishman, *Bourgeois Utopias: The Rise and Fall of Suburbia* (New York: Basic Books, 1989), 142–48.

54. Schlegel, *Ruler of the Reading*, 44, 153.

55. PRR Board of Directors (BOD) Minutes, HML, October 1, 1880.

56. In 1872, the PCC abandoned the portion of the Juniata Division canal west of Williamsburg. The section from Petersburg to Williamsburg was abandoned in 1874, as was the West Branch Division between Lock Haven and Farrandsville. The portion of the Juniata Division between Huntington and Petersburg was withdrawn from service in 1877. Sections of both the West Branch and Juniata Divisions remained in service, carrying local traffic. In 1882, service ended on the North Branch Division,

north of Nanticoke. Even as late as 1888, however, the remaining canals carried a respectable six hundred thousand tons of anthracite. The severe rainstorms of 1889 (the same ones that caused the Johnstown Flood) damaged the canals beyond repair, at a time when rapid improvements in railroad operating efficiency made the canals less competitive. The PCC soon abandoned the West Branch Division, west of Loyalsock Creek, as well as the entire Wiconsico Division and all but fourteen miles of the Juniata Division. A flood in May 1894 led to the abandonment of the Reading-controlled Susquehanna & Tide Water Canal, preventing anthracite and other cargoes from reaching Chesapeake Bay by water. On December 11, 1900, the last boatload of anthracite reached its destination, and the PCC officially abandoned the last of its canal network in April 1901. The Pennsylvania Canal Company was not formally dissolved until 1926. F. Charles Petrillo, "The Pennsylvania Canal Company (1857–1926): The New Main Line Canal—Nanticoke to Columbia," *Canal History and Technology Proceedings* 6 (1987): 83–112, at 98–107.

57. These were the Philadelphia, Norristown & Phoenixville Railroad; the Phoenixville & West Chester Railroad; and the Phoenixville, Pottstown & Reading Railroad. The Reading & Pottsville Railroad was added in 1885.

58. Burgess and Kennedy, *Centennial History*, 413–14; Messer, *Triumph III*, 210–11; Eliot Jones, *The Anthracite Coal Combination in the United States, With Some Account of the Early Development of the Anthracite Industry* (Cambridge, Mass.: Harvard University Press, 1914), 47–48.

59. As Alfred D. Chandler, Jr., correctly observes, such overbuilding was more properly construction ahead of demand, rather than a complete waste of resources: "In time, however, most of the new roads became fully used. Many redundancies were temporary ones." Chandler, *The Visible Hand*, 148.

60. The cost data are from 1913–14, but the disparity would probably have been similar in previous years. Jones, *The Anthracite Coal Combination*, 137–38.

61. Henry Clews, *Twenty-Eight Years in Wall Street* (New York: Irving Publishing, 1887), 427.

62. *New York Times*, November 4, 1882, May 25, 1883; Albro Martin, "Crisis of Rugged Individualism: The West Shore–South Pennsylvania Railroad Affair, 1880–1885," *Pennsylvania Magazine of History and Biography* 93 (April 1969): 218–43, at 222–24; Herbert H. Harwood, Jr., *The Railroad That Never Was: Vanderbilt, Morgan, and the South Pennsylvania Railroad* (Bloomington, Ind.: Indiana University Press, 2010), 20–23.

63. *New York Times*, April 8, 1893, January 12, 1903; Grodinsky, *Jay Gould*, 364; Chandler, *The Visible Hand*, 161.

64. Vanderbilt did in fact purchase the Nickel Plate, in 1882. The West Shore completed its route between Weehawken and Buffalo but went bankrupt in June 1884. Vanderbilt bought the company in 1885. D. T. Gilchrist, "Albert Fink and the Pooling System," *Business History Review* 34 (Spring 1960): 24–49, at 44–45.

65. Martin, "Rugged Individualism," 227; Harwood, *The Railroad That Never Was*, 22–23.

66. Harwood, *The Railroad That Never Was*, 76–80.

67. The Jersey Shore had been connected with the efforts by Buffalo investors to complete a line (the Buffalo & Washington Railway) between Buffalo and a junction with the Philadelphia & Erie, at Emporium. In 1867, the Buffalo interests, with the cooperation of Reading officials, had explored the possibility of building east from Port Allegany through Coudersport to Williamsport and a connection with the Reading. Renamed the Pine Creek Railway in 1884, the carrier provided a possible route south through the Grand Canyon of Pennsylvania to Newberry, and a connection with the Reading, to the west of Williamsport.

68. Grodinsky, *Jay Gould*, 364; Schlegel, *Ruler of the Reading*, 236; Paul V. Pietrak, Joseph G. Streamer, and James A. Van Brocklin, *The History of the Western New York & Pennsylvania Railway Company and Its Predecessors and Successors* (Hamburg, N.Y.: s.n., 2000), 2(8)–2(9).

69. *New York Times*, July 19, 1885; Joseph T. Lambie, *From Mine to Market: The History of Coal Transportation on the Norfolk and Western Railway* (New York: New York University Press, 1954), 83–84.

70. William H. Shank, *Vanderbilt's Folly: A History of the Pennsylvania Turnpike* (York, Pa.: American Canal and Transportation Center, 1973), 17–18; Harwood, *The Railroad That Never Was*, 14–18.

71. *Annual Report of the Auditor General of the State of Pennsylvania and of the Tabulations and Deductions from the Reports of the Railroad, Canal & Telegraph Companies for the Year 1873* (Harrisburg: Benjamin Singerly, 1874), 587–94; David W. Messer and Charles S. Roberts, *Triumph IV: Harrisburg to Altoona, 1846–2001* (Baltimore: Barnard, Roberts & Co., 2001), 306–7.

72. Harwood, *The Railroad That Never Was*, 39–41.

73. Martin, "Rugged Individualism," 229–30; *New York Times*, June 9, 1885, October 1, 1888. Harwood, *The Railroad That Never Was*, 40–48, provides descriptions of the syndicate members. The composition of the syndicate changed over time, and there was apparently never a single master list of subscribers. For a version of the subscriber list, see Henry E. Wallace, ed., *Manual of Statistics: Stock Exchange Hand-Book*, vol. 11, January 1, 1889 (New York: Investors Publishing, 1889), 220. Another version appears in the *New York Times*, October 14, 1885. Schlegel, *Ruler of the Reading*, 244, suggests that Magee was involved in the venture, and one subscriber list indicates a $50,000 investment by a "G. L. Magee," which is probably a misprint for "G. J. Magee." It could also be a misprint for "C. L. Magee," and thus a reference to Christopher L. Magee, a Pittsburgh political boss and powerbroker, although that seems unlikely. Other subscriber lists omit the Magee name entirely—for example, *New York Times*, October 14, 1885.

74. In later years, Ralph Bagaley changed the spelling of his last name to "Baggaley." Harwood, *The Railroad That Never Was*, 46.

75. Gowen, *Ruler of the Reading*, 243; Martin, "Rugged Individualism," 235.

76. It is not clear to what extent PRR executives supported Carnegie's early ventures in the steel business. During the early 1870s, Tom Scott probably contributed some capital, and Thomson may have been one of the initial investors. Mary A. O'Sullivan, "Finance Capital in Chandlerian Capitalism," *Industrial and Corporate Change* 19 (2010): 549–89, at 578–79; Thomas J. Misa, *A Nation of Steel: The Making of Modern America, 1865–1925* (Baltimore: Johns Hopkins University Press, 1995), 134–35; Joseph Frazier Wall, *Andrew Carnegie* (New York: Oxford University Press, 1970), 308–11.

77. Andrew Carnegie to J. Edgar Thomson, October 30, 1872, Carnegie Steel Papers, Historical Society of Western Pennsylvania, Library and Archives Division, Pittsburgh, Box 1, folder 3, quoted in Wall, *Andrew Carnegie*, 145.

78. One of Carnegie's first priorities was to come to terms with the Pennsylvania Steel Company, a company that was closely affiliated with the Pennsylvania Railroad. In addition to convincing the PRR to purchase rail from a company that competed against its own subsidiary, Carnegie also demanded admission to the Bessemer Association, a cartel composed of the ten leading American steel manufacturers. Executives from Pennsylvania Steel, along with their counterparts from the PRR and the other nine members of the Bessemer Association, were unwilling to risk the possibility that Carnegie could undercut the prices that the cartel had established. Accordingly, in June 1875, the association granted a share of the rail market to Carnegie, ensuring the success of the Edgar Thomson Works. Wall, *Andrew Carnegie*, 169–70.

79. "From the moment the first rail rolled out of the mill at E.T.," Carnegie biographer Joseph Frazier Wall has suggested, "Carnegie carried on a relentless war against the railroads to reduce the cost of transportation. On this subject he was almost paranoiac." Wall, *Andrew Carnegie*, 506.

80. *New York Times*, July 26, 1885, July 31, 1885.

81. "Justice" is from Carnegie to Alexander J. Cassatt, March 5, 1881, Letterbook, 1881–1883, Andrew Carnegie Papers, United States Steel Corporation, Pittsburgh, quoted in Wall, *Andrew Carnegie*, 507.

82. Carnegie to Frank Thomson, January 23, 1884, Letterbook, 1884, Carnegie Papers, United States Steel, quoted in Wall, *Andrew Carnegie*, 509.

83. David Nasaw, *Andrew Carnegie* (New York: Penguin Press, 2006), 252.

84. *New York Times*, June 9, 1885; Messer and Roberts, *Triumph IV*, 308.

85. *New York Times*, June 9, 1885, July 19, 1885, July 26, 1885, July 31, 1885, August 1, 1885, August 26, 1885, November 7, 1888, April 11, 1911. Schlegel, *Ruler of the Reading*, 244.

86. Knight was also closely allied with the PRR, serving as one of the Philadelphia city directors between 1861 and 1863, and again as a director, on his own account, between 1864 and 1874. Several years after PRR executives pursued their efforts to create a transatlantic maritime service, they selected Knight as president of the American Steamship Company. Jay Veeder Hare, *History of the North Pennsylvania Railroad* (Philadelphia: Reading Co., 1944), 24, 29; Burgess and Kennedy, *Centennial History*, 787; American Historical Company, American Biography: A New Cyclopedia, vol. 6 (New York: American Historical Society, 1919), 56–57.

87. Messer and Roberts, *Triumph IV*, 308; Harwood, *The Railroad That Never Was*, 52–64, 85–87.

88. Harwood, *The Railroad That Never Was*, 81–89; Martin, "Rugged Individualism," 231; *New York Times*, January 5, 1907.

89. Misa, *A Nation of Steel*, 135; Wall, *Andrew Carnegie*, 510–11; Burgess and Kennedy, *Centennial History*, 410; Harwood, *The Railroad That Never Was*, 60–62.

90. *New York Times*, October 3, 1885.

91. *New York Times*, August 28, 1884.

92. *New York Times*, October 1, 1884 (quotes).

93. Alfred D. Chandler, Jr., with Takashi Hikino, *Scale and Scope: The Dynamics of Industrial Capitalism* (Cambridge, Mass.: Belknap Press of Harvard University Press, 1990), 395, 398, 415–19, 501.

94. E. G. Campbell, *The Reorganization of the American Railroad System, 1893–1900* (New York: Columbia University Press, 1938), 146–47.

95. The negotiations are described in detail in Harwood, *The Railroad That Never Was*, 90–100.

96. *New York Times*, October 3, 1885.

97. *New York Times*, August 30, 1885 (quote); Ron Chernow, *The House of Morgan: An American Banking Dynasty and the Rise of Modern Finance* (New York: Atlantic Monthly Press, 1990), 54–57.

98. Burgess and Kennedy, *Centennial History*, 411; Harwood, *The Railroad That Never Was*, 94–96.

99. *New York Times*, July 19, 1885, August 1, 1885, August 26, 1885; Schlegel, *Ruler of the Reading*, 258–59.

100. *New York Times*, August 26, 1885.

101. *New York Times*, August 27, 1885.

102. *New York Times*, August 30, 1885.

103. Martin, "Rugged Individualism," 237–38.

104. *New York Times*, July 24, 1885.

105. In 1896, a decade after he had forced Gowen out of the Reading, J. P. Morgan rescued the company from another bankruptcy and solidified his reputation as one of the world's greatest financiers. *New York Times*,

December 15, 1889, December 17, 1895; Schlegel, *Ruler of the Reading*, 286–87.

106. Harwood, *The Railroad That Never Was*, 68–69.

107. Frick to Carnegie, August 9, 1889, quoted in Wall, *Andrew Carnegie*, 519.

108. In 1897, Carnegie finally extracted a measure of revenge against the PRR, when he established the Pittsburgh, Bessemer & Lake Erie Railroad, enabling the steelmaker to transport iron ore from the Lake Erie port of Conneaut, Ohio, to his mills near Pittsburgh. In 1900, the company was renamed the Bessemer & Lake Erie Railroad. It became a component of United States Steel, upon that company's formation in 1901. Wall, *Andrew Carnegie*, 514–19; Nasaw, *Andrew Carnegie*, 252–55, 336–38.

109. Schlegel, *Ruler of the Reading*, 278; Harwood, *The Railroad That Never Was*, 105–12.

110. For a few years after 1899, the Pittsburgh, Westmoreland, & Somerset Railroad used a short portion of the South Penn grade, along with one of the line's tunnels. In 1904, the B&O acquired a portion of the old South Penn right of way through its subsidiary, the Fulton, Bedford & Somerset Railroad.

111. Alvin F. Harlow, *The Road of the Century: The Story of the New York Central* (New York: Creative Age Press, 1947), 321–36; reprinted in B. A. Botkin and Alvin F. Harlow, eds., *A Treasury of Railroad Folklore: The Stories, Traditions, Ballads and Songs of the American Railroad Man* (New York: Crown Publishers, 1953), 142–44; Burgess and Kennedy, *Centennial History*, 408–12; Shank, *Vanderbilt's Folly*, 25–35; Martin, "Rugged Individualism," 238–40 Harwood, *The Railroad That Never Was*, 113–34.

112. The construction of the PRR's rail route along the Schuylkill Valley, parallel to the Reading main line, was primarily a response to the Reading's involvement in the Bound Brook Route, rather than a reaction to the South Penn, and the Pennsylvania Schuylkill Valley Railroad was not a part of the South Penn negotiations.

113. According to historian Albro Martin, "As spice for the popular writings that pass for histories of railroad 'tycoonery' in the eighties, however, the myth that the Pennsylvania seized the West Shore in direct warfare against the Central seems to have been too good not to be true." Martin, "Rugged Individualism," 242.

114. Kenneth Warren, *Triumphant Capitalism: Henry Clay Frick and the Industrial Transformation of America* (Pittsburgh: University of Pittsburgh Press, 1996), 73, 189–92.

115. Wall, *Andrew Carnegie*, 612–20; Nasaw, *Andrew Carnegie*, 518–20.

116. Misa, *A Nation of Steel*, 167–68; Wall, *Andrew Carnegie*, 619–22; Nasaw, *Andrew Carnegie*, 519–20.

117. In a lengthy article, legal historian Stephen J. Lubben is highly critical of efforts by Morgan and other financiers to reorganize bankrupt railways during the late nineteenth and early twentieth centuries. The gist of Lubben's argument is that Morgan, and others, collected lavish fees while preserving too high a level of shareholder equity, even when creditors had not been fully compensated. As such, he notes, receiverships generally failed to restore railroads to financial health, and frequently led to another bankruptcy at a later date. Lubben's points are well taken, but they ignore the reality that many bankrupt roads were chronically weak carriers, without the route structure and traffic density enjoyed by companies such as the PRR and the NYC—this was the gist of the so-called weak-road/strong-road problem that the Interstate Commerce Commission confronted during the 1920s. Stephen J. Lubben, "Railroad Receiverships and Modern Bankruptcy Theory," *Cornell Law Review* 89 (September 2004): 1420–75; Jones, *The Anthracite Coal Combination*, 48–49.

118. *New York Times*, January 25, 1891, February 20, 1896, June 5, 1896 (quote).

119. Baer, Coxey, and Schopp, *The Trail of the Blue Comet*, 124–25, 153.

120. During the early 1870s, J. Edgar Thomson and Tom Scott had invested in the Poughkeepsie Bridge Company, as well as in the associated South Mountain & Boston Railroad, but the Panic of 1873 ended their involvement in the project. In July 1892, the Poughkeepsie Bridge Company was reorganized as the Poughkeepsie Bridge & Railroad Company, in preparation for its merger with the Central New England & Western Railroad. *New York Times*, July 16, 1892.

121. McLeod also tried, but failed, to gain control over the Old Colony Railroad, with a network of branch lines south and east of Boston. The New Haven leased the company in May 1893.

122. In the early 1880s, Jay Gould had attempted to gain control of the New York & New England through the mechanism of his associate Cyrus W. Field. The PRR's George Brooke Roberts and Erie president Hugh J. Jewett were also on the company's board, ensuring adequate traffic connections with the major trunk lines. By the end of the decade, as Gould's empire collapsed, the New York & New England featured many of the same investors who had been associated with the Reading interests in the effort to construct the South Pennsylvania Railroad. They included John D. Rockefeller (whose partner Jabez Bostwick was president of the New York & New England), but his brother William Rockefeller, like J. P. Morgan, was on the board of the directors of the rival New Haven. The New Haven leased the New York & New England in 1898. Grodinsky, *Jay Gould*, 333–36.

123. *New York Times*, September 7, 1893; David W. Messer and Charles S. Roberts, *Triumph II: Philadelphia to Harrisburg, 1828–1998* (Baltimore: Barnard, Roberts & Co., 1999), 253–54; Messer and Roberts, *Triumph IV*, 315–18.

124. As historian E. G. Campbell has noted, "McLeod had taken a little line entirely dependent on coal trade, controlling less than 1,200 miles of track with no terminals, and transformed it into one of the major systems of the East, with a terminal on the Great Lakes and another on New York Harbor, controlling almost 4,000 miles of trunk line." Campbell, *The Reorganization of the American Railroad System*, 112.

125. Messer and Roberts, *Triumph II*, 254.

126. *New York Times*, April 5, 1893, May 24, 1893; Campbell, *The Reorganization of the American Railroad System*, 112–28, 176–89, 276.

127. Thomas Dublin and Walter Licht, *The Face of Decline: The Pennsylvania Anthracite Region in the Twentieth Century* (Ithaca, N.Y.: Cornell University Press, 2005).

128. William J. Watt, *The Pennsylvania Railroad in Indiana* (Bloomington: Indiana University Press, 2000), 69.

129. In 1895, the Grand Rapids & Indiana Rail*road* defaulted on its bonds, enabling the PRR to reorganize the company through foreclosure. The Grand Rapids and Indiana Rail*way*, organized in 1896, never generated appreciable revenues or profits.

130. Henry V. Poor, *Manual of the Railroads of the United States, 1888* (New York: H. V. & H. W. Poor, 1888), 418–19; Augustus J. Veenendaal, Jr., *Slow Train to Paradise: How Dutch Investment Helped Build American Railroads* (Stanford, Calif.: Stanford University Press, 1996), 107–9; Burgess and Kennedy, *Centennial History*, 489.

131. The information on the CC&IC is from the *Commercial and Financial Chronicle*, September 5, 1874, 247, September 19, 1874, 295, October 3, 1874, 350, December 19, 1874, 638, January 16, 1875, 61, March 13, 1875, 258, April 3, 1875, 326, May 1, 1875, 426–27, July 8, 1875, 14 and the *Railroad Gazette*, August 1, 1874, 298, August 29, 1874, 337, September 19, 1874, 367–69, October 10, 1874, 398, October 31, 1874, 429, November 7, 1874, 437, December 26, 1874, 507.

132. *James Pullan v. The Cincinnati and Chicago Air-Line Railroad Company, et al.*, Circuit Court, District of Indiana, June Term, 1865.

133. *New York Times*, April 29, 1879.

134. *New York Times*, August 7, 1879.

135. Watt, *The Pennsylvania Railroad in Indiana*, 69–74; *New York Times*, April 29, 1879, September 30, 1881, February 12, 1882.

136. *New York Times*, September 30, 1885.

137. Salomon Frederik van Oss, *American Railroads as Investments: A Handbook for Investors in American Railroad Securities* (New York: G. P. Putnam's Sons, 1893), 262–66.

138. Wallis, *The Pennsylvania Railroad at Bay*, 24.

139. Ibid., 32–38.

140. Ibid., 34–43.

141. Ibid., 41–43.

142. Ibid., 42, 56–57.

143. Ibid., 63–64.

144. Ibid., 66–70, 73–76.

145. *New York Times*, February 22, 1889.

146. Harwood, *Royal Blue Line*, 36–38.

147. Wallis, *The Pennsylvania Railroad at Bay*, 77–78.

148. Ibid., 88.

149. Ibid., 90–95, 108.

150. Ibid., 105–8.

151. Ibid., 109–26.

152. The PRR had controlled the Jeffersonville, Madison & Indianapolis since 1871. In 1882, Lines West officials negotiated trackage rights over the Indianapolis, Peru & Chicago Railroad (later the Lake Erie & Western Railroad) between Indianapolis and a junction with the ex–Indiana Central route at Kokomo, Indiana. The connect link was in poor condition, however, and the TH&I-controlled line between Terre Haute and Logansport offered a far better alternative. Wallis, *The Pennsylvania Railroad at Bay*, 131–33.

153. Technically, the Pan Handle, the Steubenville & Indiana, and the Columbus, Chicago & Indiana Central (all PRR subsidiaries) provided financing for the new line, and their securities were in turn guaranteed by the PRR, with the Vandalia leased to the Terre Haute & Indianapolis. Samuel Harden Church, *Corporate History of the Pennsylvania Lines West of Pittsburgh: Comprising Charters, Mortgages, Decrees, Deeds, Leases, Agreements, Ordinances, and Other Papers with Descriptive Text*, vol. 6, (Baltimore: Friedenwald Co., 1899), 613–14, vol. 11 (1905), 529–31; Burgess and Kennedy, *Centennial History*, 203–6.

154. In 1898, the PRR cast adrift the Indiana & Lake Michigan Railway, and that line, never generating much traffic, came under the control of the Michigan Central Railroad (NYC). The final significant piece to be added to the PRR's midwestern system extended from Logansport northeast to Butler, Indiana. Originally incorporated in 1853 as the Auburn & Eel River Valley Rail Road, the company went through several name changes and fell into the orbit of the Wabash Railroad, part of Jay Gould's empire. By 1900, the successor company was bankrupt and its lease to the Wabash invalidated. In 1901, the PRR acquired the line for $1.5 million and reincorporated it as the Logansport & Toledo Railway. At that time, George J. Gould (the son of Jay Gould) was satisfying his transcontinental railway ambitions by pushing his Wabash-Pittsburgh Terminal Railway into the heart of PRR territory, at Pittsburgh. PRR officials considered retaliation, by building a link between Logansport and Toledo, paralleling the Wabash for the entire distance between Toledo and St. Louis. Instead, they settled for establishing coordinated through service with the Lake Shore & Michigan Southern, with a connection at Butler.

155. The Vandalia Railroad subsidiary encompassed most of the routes west of Indianapolis—that is, everything other than the Pan Handle lines from Richmond to Indianapolis, from Richmond to Chicago via Logansport, from Logansport west to the Illinois border at Effner, and from Bradford, Ohio, north to Logansport, as well as the Fort Wayne tracks to Chicago. As part of a general corporate simplification, the Vandalia Railroad became a part of the Pan Handle on January 1, 1917.

156. Wallis, *The Pennsylvania Railroad at Bay*, 91, 136–47, 153–61.

157. See, for example, Henry V. Poor, *Manual of the Railroads of the United States for 1876–77* (New York: H. V. & H. W. Poor, 1876), 630.

158. Poor, *Manual of Railroads, 1881*, 285, 537, 540.

159. The position of general manager was actually a simultaneous appointment with the Pennsylvania Company and the two components of the route to St. Louis, the Chicago, St. Louis & Pittsburgh Railroad, and the Pittsburgh, Cincinnati & St. Louis Railway.

160. Some sources suggest that Pan Handle passenger equipment received Tuscan red paint only after the 1890 consolidation, but it is quite possible that a similar color had been in use since the 1860s. The color standard had certainly been established by 1879. Charles Blardone, Jr., and Peter Tilp, *Pennsylvania Railroad Passenger Car Painting and Lettering* (Upper Darby, Pa.: Pennsylvania Railroad Historical and Technical Society, 1988), 13.

161. Watt, *Pennsylvania Railroad in Indiana*, 81, 86; Christopher T. Baer, "Pennsylvania Railroad Company: Operating Department, 221,235, HML.

162. Poor, *Manual of the Railroads . . . for 1874–75*, 451, 670; *Poor's Manual of the Railroads of the United States*, vol. 36 (New York: Poor's Railroad Manual Co., 1903), 699, 754, 763–64, 773, 775.

163. Chandler, *The Visible Hand*, 541n24; Ripley, *Railroads: Rates and Regulation*, 641.

164. The PRR's solution to the problem of coordination was to transfer the railroad operations of the Pennsylvania Company to the Pennsylvania Railroad, and then to create four (later reduced to three) regions, akin to a multidivisional corporation. On January 1, 1918, the Pennsylvania Company turned over operating and managerial responsibilities to the PRR proper. World War I and the period of government control that lasted from 1917 until 1920 delayed the full implementation of the consolidation and decentralization plan, but in 1920 the PRR adopted a four-region plan that placed Pittsburgh in the middle of the new Central Region. The Pennsylvania Company ceded control of all of its equipment and most of its securities to the PRR. In 1928, the Pennsylvania Company relinquished its charter powers as an operating entity and remained in existence solely as an investment company. Howard W. Schotter, "Brief Sketch of History, Pennsylvania Company," 4, June 10, 1937, HML, Box 203, folder 8; Burgess and Kennedy, *Centennial History*, 221–22.

165. Poor, *Manual of the Railroads . . . for 1874–75*, 668–69; Church, *Corporate History*, vol. 1, 3–5.

166. PRR BOD Minutes, November 7, 1873, 219–21, May 2, 1874, 283–84, May 15, 1874, 286–87, May 1, 1877, 386–87, August 1, 1877, 446, October 28, 1878, 158–59.

167. Burgess and Kennedy, *Centennial History*, 380–81.

168. Howard W. Schotter, *The Growth and Development of the Pennsylvania Railroad Company: A Review of the Charter and Annual Reports of the Pennsylvania Railroad Company 1846 to 1926, Inclusive* (Philadelphia: Allen, Lane & Scott, 1927), 179–83.

169. *Thirty-First Annual Report of the Board of Directors of the Pennsylvania Railroad Co. to the Stockholders, March 25, 1878* (Philadelphia: E. C. Markley & Son, 1878), 74–79; *Thirty-Second Annual Report of the Board of Directors of the Pennsylvania Railroad Co. to the Stockholders* (Philadelphia: E. C. Markley & Son, 1879), 35–39; Burgess and Kennedy, *Centennial History*, 41–42, 58, 380–82; Schotter, *Growth and Development*, 184.

170. Burgess and Kennedy, *Centennial History*, 439–43.

171. "Competition to sponsor the [Pennsylvania Railroad] company's securities was keen," banking historian Vincent Carosso has emphasized.

"Roberts demanded and received the highest prices obtainable for the Pennsylvania's bonds, knowing that if Drexel & Co. didn't take them, other rival bankers stood ready to do so." Vincent P. Carosso and Rose C. Carosso, *The Morgans: Private International Bankers, 1854–1913* (Cambridge, Mass.: Harvard University Press, 1987), 721n120.

172. Soon after his father's death, Anthony Drexel, Jr., retired from the banking business, leaving J. P. Morgan in control of two interrelated banking houses, J. P. Morgan & Company in New York and Drexel & Company in Philadelphia. During the 1880s and 1890s, Speyer & Company also marketed securities for the PRR. Dan Rottenberg, *The Man Who Made Wall Street: Anthony J. Drexel and the Rise of Modern Finance* (Philadelphia: University of Pennsylvania Press, 2001), 165. Chandler, *The Visible Hand*, 155; Veenendaal, *Slow Train to Paradise*, 63; Vincent P. Carosso, *Investment Banking in America: A History* (Cambridge, Mass.: Harvard University Press, 1970), 27, 33, 52–53; Carosso, *The Morgans*, 721n120.

173. Morgan biographer Ron Chernow has suggested that Junius Morgan imported this concept of gentlemanly cooperation from the British financial community. In 1912, the hearings of the House Banking and Currency Committee, better known as the Pujo Committee, recast this code of conduct as something akin to a conspiracy to dominate the U.S. economy and contributed to J. P. Morgan's death a year later. Chernow, *House of Morgan*, 11–13, 149–56, 197, 258.

174. Most of the foreign investment originated from Britain. As of November 1, 1895, American investors held 51.1 percent of the PRR's stock, British investors held 47.4 percent, and investors from other nations made up the remaining 1.5 percent. Mira Wilkins, *A History of Foreign Investment in the United States to 1914* (Cambridge, Mass.: Harvard University Press, 1989), 198; Dorothy R. Adler and Muriel E. Hidy, eds., *British Investment in American Railways, 1834–1898* (Charlottesville: University Press of Virginia, 1970), 176; Burgess and Kennedy, *Centennial History*, 440–41; Gerald Berk, *Alternative Tracks: The Constitution of American Industrial Order, 1865–1917* (Baltimore: Johns Hopkins University Press, 1994), 35.

175. Burgess and Kennedy, *Centennial History*, 440–41.

176. *Economist* 42 (March 22, 1884): 352–53, quoted in Adler, *British Investment*, 176.

177. Overall, as Wilkins writes, "A distinction should be made, moreover, between the foreign investors' exercise of influence and their exercise of control. The evidence is overwhelming that foreign investors had opportunity to influence and frequently did influence American railroad developments. By influence, I mean the investor had the ability to change outcomes within certain very important limits and constraints. By contrast, control—the overall ability to formulate the strategies and tactics of a U.S. railroad enterprise—seems to have been exercised, but seldom over long periods." Wilkins, *Foreign Investment*, 210, 227–28; Dolores Greenberg, *Financiers and Railroads: A Study of Morton, Bliss & Company, 1869–1889* (Newark: University of Delaware Press, 1980), 114–15; Adler, *British Investment*, 175–76, 199–200.

178. Ripley, *Railroads: Finance and Organization*, 9.

179. The rate of foreign ownership of PRR stock declined from 52 percent in 1890 to 48 percent in 1893, 47 percent in 1894, 45 percent in 1897, 43 percent in 1898, 36 percent in 1899, and 29 percent in 1900. Mira Wilkins notes that stock prices increased considerably in 1900, causing many European investors to sell out. Leland H. Jenks, "Capital Movement and Transportation: Britain and American Railway Development," *Journal of Economic History* 11 (Autumn 1951): 375–88, at 377; Wilkins, *Foreign Investment,* 730–31n69; A. W. Currie, "British Attitudes toward Investment in North American Railroads," *Business History Review* 34 (Summer 1960): 194–216, at 210–13.

180. Colleen A. Dunlavy, *Politics and Industrialization: Early Railroads in the United States and Prussia* (Princeton, N.J.: Princeton University Press, 1994), 69–97.

181. Robert L. Rabin, "Federal Regulation in Historical Perspective," *Stanford Law Review* 38 (May 1986): 1189–1326, at 1201n25; Thomas K. McCraw, *Prophets of Regulation: Charles Francis Adams, Louis D. Brandeis, James M. Landis, Alfred E. Kahn* (Cambridge, Mass.: Belknap Press of Harvard University Press, 1984), 1–56.

182. George Rogers Taylor, *The Transportation Revolution, 1815–1860* (Armonk, N.Y.: M. E. Sharpe, 1977), 88–89; George H. Miller, *Railroads and the Granger Laws* (Madison: University of Wisconsin Press, 1971), 24–32, 42–49.

183. Rabin, "Federal Regulation," 1199–1206. For an overview of the Granger Laws, see Berk, *Alternative Tracks*, 155, 77–88; Miller, *Railroads and the Granger Laws*; and Solon Buck, *The Granger Movement: A Study of Agricultural Organization and Its Political, Economic, and Social Manifestations, 1870–1880* (Lincoln: University of Nebraska Press, 1965).

184. The role of rate discrimination in enabling service is discussed at length in Arthur T. Hadley, *Railroad Transportation: Its History and Laws* (New York: G. P. Putnam's Sons, 1885), 116–17; and Ripley, *Railroads: Rates and Regulation*, 217–21.

185. Despite their rural, agrarian roots, the Grangers attracted considerable support from easterners who were likewise displeased at rate discrimination. In 1873, for example, delegates from Pennsylvania and New York attended a Granger conference in Chicago, largely in response to the preferential long-haul rates charged by the PRR, the New York Central, and the Erie. Berk, *Alternative Tracks*, 79.

186. In addition to *Munn v. Illinois*, the cases were *Chicago, Burlington & Quincy Railroad v. Iowa*; *Peik v. Chicago & North Western Railway*; *Winona & St. Paul Railroad v. Blake*; and several others.

187. While the *Wabash* decision prevented state regulatory commissions from regulating interstate rates by statute, they retained the ability to do so through common law. That process was likely to be expensive and unrewarding, however. Through the late 1800s, classical economic theory emphasized the virtue of competition in a free market, and economists, legislators, and jurists were often slow to understand that railroads represented both a natural monopoly and an extraordinarily capital-intensive industry. But the time of the 1873 decision in the *Slaughter-House Cases*, however, the Supreme Court was beginning to recognize both the presence and the economic justification for natural monopolies. McCraw, *Prophets of Regulation*, 57–62; Rabin, "Federal Regulation," 1208–10; Herbert Hovenkamp, "Regulatory Conflict in the Gilded Age: Federalism and the Railroad Problem," *Yale Law Journal* 97 (May 1988): 1017–72, esp. pp. 1026–30, 1045–46, 1057–58, and 1061–65.

188. The increased radicalism of the farmers, particularly those individuals associated with the Texas-based Farmers Alliance, eroded their political effectiveness in the national arena. Furthermore, as Robert Rabin has suggested, "The political forces that coalesced to pass the Granger Laws had no broader vision of a restructured economic system," and their efforts could not accommodate other political interests, nor could they adapt to the new institutional models developed during the late 1800s. Rabin, "Federal Regulation," 1205.

189. Political scientist Stephen Skowronek traces the development of administrative (or bureaucratic) regulation during the late nineteenth and early twentieth centuries. He is not at all certain that the new administrative state is in any way preferable to an older nineteenth-century system based on political parties (which provided an orderly mechanism for distributing political spoils), and the courts (which protected property rights, and thus ensured the growth of capitalist enterprises). However, the political economy of the United States in the early to mid-nineteenth century

was far more complex than Skowronek suggests. The party system, in particular, was far more inchoate, and his "courts and parties" analysis leaves out a great many interest groups. Nor does his model acknowledge the development of strong administrative capabilities, early in the nineteenth century, in such key institutions as the military, the Patent Office, and the Post Office. Nonetheless, his analysis of the period after 1887 remains both perceptive and informative. For a critique of Skowronek's arguments, see Richard R. John, "Ruling Passions: Political Economy in Nineteenth-Century America," in John, ed., *Ruling Passions: Political Economy in Nineteenth-Century America* (University Park: Pennsylvania State University Press, 2006), 1–20, at 3–8. Skowronek, *Building a New American State: The Expansion of National Administrative Capacities, 1877–1920* (Cambridge: Cambridge University Press, 1982), 127–28.

190. *New York Times*, June 28, 1876.

191. Reagan was not ideologically opposed to pooling, and he later supported government-managed pools as a mechanism to ensure rate stability and protect the financial health of the railroad industry. Instead, Reagan was responding to his constituents' outrage over the Southern Railway and Steamship Association's control over traffic in Texas, and elsewhere in the South. Skowronek, *Building a New American State*, 125–27, 140–43; *New York Times*, December 28, 1878.

192. The disaffection of the New York commercial interests increased substantially as the nineteenth century came to a close, thanks to the terms of the 1877 Seaboard Differential Agreement. The agreement had set the port differentials at fixed amounts, measured in cents per hundredweight rather than as a percentage of the rail rate. As rates declined steadily in the late nineteenth century, deflation tended to increase the differentials as a percentage of the overall rate and magnify the advantages accruing to the competing ports of New York and Philadelphia. Ripley, *Railroads: Rates and Regulation*, 404–6.

193. *Report of the Special Committee on Railroads, Appointed Under a Resolution of the Assembly, February 28, 1879, to Investigate Alleged Abuses in the Management of Railroads Chartered by the State of New York* (Albany: Weed, Parsons & Co., 1880), 38.

194. Ibid., 76.

195. *New York Times*, September 26, 1879.

196. Ari A. Hoogenboom and Olive Hoogenboom, *A History of the ICC: From Panacea to Palliative* (New York: Norton, 1976), 12–13; Skowronek, *Building a New American State*, 128–29, 143–44.

197. Skowronek, *Building a New American State*, 145–47; Rabin, "Federal Regulation," 1206–8; Ripley, *Railroads: Rates and Regulation*, 442.

198. Skowronek, *Building a New American State*, 146–50.

199. *New York Times*, June 4, 1887; Skowronek, *Building a New American State*, 149; Ripley, *Railroads: Rates and Regulation*, 443; Hoogenboom, *A History of the ICC*, 17–19.

200. McCraw, *Prophets of Regulation*, 61–63; Hoogenboom, *A History of the ICC*, 7–20; Chandler, *The Visible Hand*, 141–44, 172.

201. Berk, *Alternative Tracks*, 100–4; Hoogenboom, *A History of the ICC*, 19–32.

202. As Herbert Hovenkamp has observed, "Already in the 1890's, the Commission realized two things about the railroads that had escaped both Congress and the Supreme Court. First, in the absence of minimum and maximum rate regulation [which the 1887 act had not bestowed upon the ICC], pooling was essential to preserve the financial integrity of the railroads." (The other realization had to do with efforts by railway executives to achieve interfirm coordination). Hovenkamp, "Regulatory Conflict," 1041; Gerald Berk, "Adversaries by Design: Railroads and the American State, 1887–1916," *Journal of Policy History* 5 (1993): 335–54, at 338, 342; Berk, *Alternative Tracks*, 105.

203. Rabin, "Federal Regulation," 1210; Skowronek, *Building a New American State*, 150–60; Hovenkamp, "Regulatory Conflict," 1059.

204. *Chicago, Milwaukee & St. Paul Railway v. Minnesota*, 134 U.S. 418 (1889).

205. *ICC v. Cincinnati, New Orleans & Texas Pacific Railway*, 167 U.S. 479 (1897)—under ICC nomenclature, the case was also referred to as the *Maximum Freight Rate Case*, or as the *Cincinnati Freight Bureau Case*. Eliot Jones, *Principles of Railway Transportation* (New York: Macmillan, 1924), 225–27.

206. *ICC v. Alabama Midland Railway*, 168 U.S. 144 (1897); Berk, *Alternative Tracks*, 107.

207. *Smyth v. Ames*, 169 U.S. 466 (1898).

208. Hoogenboom, *A History of the ICC*, 21–25, 30–32; Skowronek, *Building a New American State*, 150–60; Rabin, "Federal Regulation," 1209–15.

209. Wheeler Report, Part I, 16–17.

210. John Lewson, *Monopoly and Trade Restraint Cases*, vol. 2 (Chicago: T. H. Flood & Co., 1908), 612–13; Gabriel Kolko, *Railroads and Regulation, 1876–1916* (Princeton, N.J.: Princeton University Press, 1965), 72–83; "Railroad Rate Bureaus and the Anti-Trust Laws," *Columbia Law Review* 46 (November 1946): 990–1004; Henry Fink, *Regulation of Railway Rates on Interstate Freight Traffic*, 2nd ed. (New York: Evening Post Job Print, 1905), 37–39.

211. Tariff information is from a PRR bill of lading from August 13, 1858. John H. White, *The American Railroad Freight Car: From the Wood-Car Era to the Coming of Steel* (Baltimore: Johns Hopkins University Press, 1993), 39; PRR BOD Minutes, July 23, 1851, 480; Emory R. Johnson and Grover G. Huebner, *Railroad Traffic and Rates*, vol. 1: *Freight Service* (New York: D. Appleton, 1911), 331.

212. Albro Martin, *Enterprise Denied: Origins of the Decline of American Railroads, 1897–1917* (New York: Columbia University Press, 1971), 40–41; Johnson and Huebner, *Railroad Traffic and Rates*, vol. 1, 331–43; George D. Dixon, "Freight Traffic," n.d., ca. 1905, HML, Box 419, folder 556; Gilchrist, "Albert Fink and the Pooling System," 35; "Railroad Rate Bureaus and the Anti-Trust Laws," *Columbia Law Review* 46 (November 1946): 990–1004, at 993; R. W. Harbeson, "The North Atlantic Port Differentials," *Quarterly Journal of Economics* 46 (August 1932): 644–70; Johnson and Huebner, *Railroad Traffic and Rates*, vol. 1, 387–404.

213. *The New York Harbor Case*, 47 ICC 643 (1917); Keith D. Revell, "Cooperation, Capture, and Autonomy: The Interstate Commerce Commission and the Port Authority in the 1920s," *Journal of Policy History* 12 (2000): 177–214; Revell, *Building Gotham: Civic Culture and Public Policy in New York City, 1898–1938* (Baltimore: Johns Hopkins University Press, 2003); Anthony Patrick O'Brien, "The ICC, Freight Rates, and the Great Depression," *Explorations in Economic History* 26 (1989): 73–98; Hovenkamp, "Regulatory Conflict in the Gilded Age," 1017–72.

214. The unofficial governmental tolerance of rate bureaus continued for more than half a century, until the 1948 Reed-Bulwinkle Act gave them official legal standing.

215. That was particularly true for the eastern trunk lines, which faced competition from Great Lakes shipping. Beginning in May, rail rates declined precipitously and then rose steeply after September, when ice closed the lakes to navigation.

216. Mark H. Rose, Bruce E. Seely, and Paul F. Barrett, *The Best Transportation System in the World: Railroads, Trucks, Airlines, and American Public Policy in the Twentieth Century* (Columbus: Ohio State University Press, 2006).

217. In October 1882, the PRR added an assistant general freight agent, renamed the local freight agent in 1885. J. Elfreth Watkins, *Pennsylvania*

Railroad Company, 1846–1896, in Its Relation to the Pennsylvania State Canals and Railroads and the Consolidated System East and West of Pittsburgh (unpublished ms., 1896, original at the Smithsonian Institution, with microfilm copies at HML and in the Penn Central Railroad Collection, M.G. 286, Pennsylvania Historical and Museum Commission, Pennsylvania State Archives, Harrisburg [hereafter PHMC], with an additional microfilm copy in the author's possession, hereafter referred to as "Watkins History"), vol. 2, "Freight Department," 8.

218. Those individuals were appointed by the president and not by the vice president with authority over traffic functions. There were corresponding positions in the Accounting Department—namely, the auditor of freight receipts, the auditor of passenger receipts, the auditor of coal freight receipts, the auditor of the Union Line, the auditor of the Empire Line, the auditor of canal and coal companies, and the auditor of disbursements.

219. Johnson and Huebner, *Railroad Traffic and Rates*, vol. 1, 67–69, 346; James Peabody, *Railway Organization and Management* (Chicago: LaSalle Extension University, 1916), 169–70; Leland H. Jenks, "Early History of a Railway Organization," *Business History Review* 35 (Summer 1961): 163–79, at 176; Watkins History, vol. 2, "Organization and Departments," 19–21; Wilson, *History of the Pennsylvania Railroad*, vol. 2, 43–44, 59–60, 64–66, 84–85.

220. Julien L. Eysmans, "'Sales Engineering' in Railroad Work: Relations Between the Traffic and Operating Departments of the Pennsylvania," *Information for the Public and Employes [of] The Pennsylvania Railroad System*, April 1925, 17–22.

221. Dixon, "Freight Traffic."

222. Dixon, "Freight Traffic."

223. Robert C. Wright to George D. Dixon, June 11, 1914, PHMC, Rea Papers, Box 57 (12–1887), folder 82/8.

224. Wright to Dixon, June 11, 1914, PHMC, Rea Papers, Box 57 (12–1887), folder 82/8.

225. Johnson and Huebner, *Railroad Traffic and Rates*, vol. 1, 319–20; Frederick J. McWade, "The Handling of Baggage," n.d., ca. 1905, HML, Box 419, folder 556.

226. By 1925, for example, there were 198,000 Operating Department (as the Transportation Department was known beginning in 1912) employees on the PRR, compared with fewer than two thousand in Traffic. Eysmans, "Sales Engineering."

227. Robert C. Wright, "Freight Solicitation," n.d., ca. 1905, HML, Box 419, folder 556.

228. Ibid.

229. Ibid. Eysmans served as the general freight agent and, later, the general traffic manager and vice president in charge of traffic.

230. Wright to Dixon, June 11, 1914, PHMC, Rea Papers, Box 57 (12–1887), folder 82/8.

231. Ibid.

232. PRR traffic officials apparently had a long history of participation in such boisterous entertainment. In 1855, at a meeting of passenger agents, general ticket agent Lewis L. Houpt composed a festive poem, although there is no record as to whether it was ever set to music: "Each ambitious bottle holder / Sought to pass a resolution / But it happened very often / That the mover and the motion / Both were laid beneath the table / When they woke they found that real pain / Had resulted from the champagne." *New York Times*, October 13, 1901.

233. *New York Times*, April 16, 1901, Steven W. Usselman, *Regulating Railroad Innovation: Business, Technology, and Politics in America, 1840–1920* (Cambridge: Cambridge University Press, 2002), 368–69.

234. Henry V. Poor, *Manual of the Railroads of the United States, 1882* (New York: H. V. & H. W. Poor, 1882), 271–73; *Poor's Manual of the Rail-*

roads of the United States, vol. 34 (New York: H. V. and H. W. Poor, 1901), 674–75.

235. The first vice president (1881–82), the second vice-president (1882–88), the first vice-president (1888–97), and then the third vice president.

236. Wood was promoted to passenger traffic manager in 1903, retaining that post until his retirement in 1913. PRR, *Information for Employes and the Public*, May 31, 1917, 8.

237. George W. Boyd, "The Development of Passenger Business," n.d., ca. 1905; Emory R. Johnson and Grover G. Huebner, *Railroad Traffic and Rates*, vol. 2: *Passenger, Mail, and Express Services* (New York: D. Appleton, 1911), 1–17, 167–68, 187; Max Riebenack, "Railway Statistics as Applicable to Earnings of Passenger Trains," *Publications of the American Statistical Association*, vol. 3: *1892–1893* (Boston: W. J. Schofield, 1893), 519–32, at 525.

238. As late as 1853, the PRR employed passenger waybills, and it was apparently one of the last railroads in the United States to switch to conventional paper tickets. *New York Times*, October 13, 1901.

239. Riebenack, "Railway Statistics," 523.

240. After the exhibition, the PRR retained the ticket receivers, but replaced the train agents with conductors trained in accounting methods.

241. Technically, the "Statement of Mileage for all Passenger Business of Trains Reported at [the] Ticket Receiver's Office, at [*name of city*] for [*dates*]."

242. Johnson and Huebner, *Railroad Traffic and Rates*, vol. 2, 54, 65–66, 71, 75; Riebenack, "Railway Statistics"; Samuel Anderson, "Miscellaneous Receipts and Accounts," n.d., ca. 1905; A. J. Gillingham, "Passenger Receipts," n.d., ca. 1905, HML, Box 419, folder 556.

243. Francis (Frank) N. Barksdale, "Advertising Ancient and Modern," n.d., ca. 1905, HML, Box 419, folder 556.

244. Michael E. Zega, "PRR's Colonel Frank N. Barksdale, Inventor of the Limited Booklet," *Railroad Heritage* 1 (Spring 2000): 12–13; *The Caduceus of Kappa Sigma* 31, no. 5 (February 1916): 500–1.

245. Boyd, "Passenger Business."

246. See, for example, *The Centennial Exhibition and the Pennsylvania Railroad* (s.l.: Rand, McNally & Co., 1876), 33–47, and *Florida Winter Pleasure Tours Under the Personally-Conducted System of the Pennsylvania Railroad, Season of 1896* (Philadelphia: Allen, Lane & Scott, 1895); with information regarding the presidential tours from *The Caduceus of Kappa Sigma*.

247. Johnson and Huebner, *Railroad Traffic and Rates*, vol. 2, 1–17, 21, 37, 188, 194–96; *Scranton Tribune*, April 6, 1897; *Altoona Mirror*, December 31, 1912.

248. Campbell, *The Reorganization of the American Railroad System*, 268–69; Stephen J. Lubben, "Railroad Receiverships and Modern Bankruptcy Theory," *Columbia Law Review* 89 (September 2004): 1420–75, at 1429.

249. Campbell, *The Reorganization of the American Railroad System*, 267–70.

250. *New York Times*, February 28, 1897 (quote); Burgess and Kennedy, *Centennial History*, 453–54.

251. *New York Times*, June 6, 1899.

252. *New York Times*, February 28, 1897.

Chapter 13. System

1. In 1889, Memorial Day was May 30, a Thursday. In 1968 Congress changed the observance of Memorial Day to the last Monday in May.

2. The best account of the disaster is undoubtedly David McCullough, *The Johnstown Flood* (New York: Simon & Schuster, 1968), esp. pp. 51–55, 59, 76, 85, 103–122, 174–204, 239–40. Also useful is Paula and Carl Degen, *The Johnstown Flood of 1889: The Tragedy of the Conemaugh* (Philadelphia:

Eastern Acorn Press, 1984), and Edwin P. Alexander, *The Pennsylvania Railroad: A Pictorial History* (New York: W. W. Norton, 1947), 228–30, reprinted in B. A. Botkin and Alvin F. Harlow, eds., *A Treasury of Railroad Folklore: The Stories, Traditions, Ballads and Songs of the American Railroad Man* (New York: Crown, 1953), 26–28.

3. Most of the following description of the rebuilding efforts is from J. Elfreth Watkins, *Pennsylvania Railroad Company, 1846–1896, in its Relation to the Pennsylvania State Canals and Railroads and the Consolidated System East and West of Pittsburgh* (unpublished ms., 1896, original at the Smithsonian Institution, with microfilm copies in the Pennsylvania Railroad Company Collection, call no. 1807/1810, Hagley Museum and Library, Wilmington, Delaware [hereafter cited as HML], and in the Penn Central Railroad Collection, M.G. 286, Pennsylvania Historical and Museum Commission, Pennsylvania State Archives, Harrisburg [hereafter cited as PHMC], with an additional microfilm copy in the author's possession, hereafter referred to as the "Watkins History"), "The Great Flood of 1889," 75–90.

4. William Bender Wilson, *History of the Pennsylvania Railroad Company, with Plan of Organization, Portraits of Officials and Biographical Sketches*, vol. 1 (New York: Henry T. Coates & Co., 1899), 160–64.

5. Charles S. Roberts and Gary W. Schlerf, *Triumph I: Altoona to Pitcairn, 1846–1996* (Baltimore: Barnard, Roberts & Co., 1997), 216.

6. Robert Pitcairn to William H. Brown, February 5, 1890, HML, Box 1452, folder 330.3.

7. Ibid.

8. Regulatory historian Thomas K. McCraw aptly summarizes the threat of government action as a "gun behind the door," even if "the gun was more useful cocked than fired." McCraw, *Prophets of Regulation: Charles Francis Adams, Louis D. Brandeis, James M. Landis, Alfred E. Kahn* (Cambridge, Mass.: Belknap Press of Harvard University Press, 1984), 35.

9. Colleen A. Dunlavy, *Politics and Industrialization: Early Railroads in the United States and Prussia* (Princeton, N.J.: Princeton University Press, 1994), 4 (quote), 202–34.

10. *New York Times*, January 31, 1897.

11. For the concept of reverse salients, see, for example, Thomas Parke Hughes, *Networks of Power: Electrification in Western Society, 1880–1930* (Baltimore: Johns Hopkins University Press, 1983); Hughes, *American Genesis: A Century of Invention and Technological Enthusiasm* (New York: Viking, 1989); and Hughes, Trevor Pinch, and Wiebe Bijker, eds., *The Social Construction of Technological Systems: New Directions in the Sociology and History of Technology* (Cambridge, Mass.: MIT Press, 1987).

12. Wilson, *History of the Pennsylvania Railroad*, vol. 1, 160.

13. David W. Messer, *Triumph IV: Harrisburg to Altoona, 1846–2001* (Baltimore: Barnard, Roberts and Co., 2001), 12–13.

14. PRR Board of Directors (BOD) Minutes, HML, November 2, 1857, 269; January 6, 1858, 286; George H. Burgess and Miles C. Kennedy, *Centennial History of the Pennsylvania Railroad Company, 1846–1946* (Philadelphia: Pennsylvania Railroad, 1949), 65, 438; Dan Cupper, *Rockville Bridge: Rails across the Susquehanna* (Halifax, Pa.: Withers Publishing, 2002), 7–9; Wilson, *History of the Pennsylvania Railroad*, vol. 2, 160; Cupper, *Horseshoe Heritage: The Story of a Great Railroad Landmark* (Halifax, Pa.: Withers Publishing, 1992), 14; Messer, *Triumph IV*, 13.

15. Information relating to track pans is from James Alexander, Jr., "The Wilmore Track Pans," *Milepost*, February 1993; Alexander, "Scooping Water in the Age of Steam, *Milepost*, April 1992; *Trains*, May 1993, available online at http://jimquest.com/writ/trains/pans/scoop.htm, retrieved August 8, 2010; H. W. Schotter, *The Growth and Development of the Pennsylvania Railroad Company: A Review of the Charter and Annual Reports of the Pennsylvania Railroad Company 1846 to 1926, Inclusive* (Philadelphia:

Allen, Lane & Scott, 1927), December 1927, E. E. Russell Tratman, *Railway Track and Track Work* (New York: McGraw-Hill, 1909); Anthony J. Bianculli, *Trains and Technology: The American Railroad in the Nineteenth Century,* vol. 3: *Track and Structures* (Newark: University of Delaware Press, 2003), 196–97; Roberts and Schlerf, *Triumph I*, 199–200, 251–52; David W. Messer and Charles S. Roberts, *Triumph V: Philadelphia to New York, 1830–2002* (Baltimore: Barnard, Roberts & Co., 2002), 133; Watkins History, vol. 2, "Steam Locomotives," 108–11.

16. As Jeremy Atack and Jan K. Brueckner note, approvingly, pioneering economic historian Albert Fishlow asserted that "steel rails were the single most important technological innovation adopted by the railroads." Atack and Brueckner, "Steel Rails and American Railroads, 1867–1880," *Explorations in Economic History* 19 (1982): 339–59; "Productivity and Technological Change in the Railroad Sector, 1840–1910," in the National Bureau of Economic Research Conference on Research in Income and Wealth, vol. 30, *Output, Employment, and Productivity in the United States After 1800* (New York: NBER, 1966), 583–646.

17. Wilson, *History of the Pennsylvania Railroad*, vol. 1, 90.

18. Atack and Brueckner have provided a sophisticated regression analysis of the factors that induced the widespread adoption of steel rails between 1867 (when the first domestically produced rails became available) and 1880. They argue, convincingly, "that a simple cost-minimization view of the adoption of steel rails is unsupportable for the period 1867–1880." There is considerable merit in their argument, which acknowledges "the inertia which undoubtedly characterized the decisions of many railroads." However, they adopt a relatively simplistic and exclusionary definition of "cost-minimization," one that largely ignores the labor costs generated by the periodic replacements of iron rails, the lost revenue associated with delayed trains affected by broken iron rails or by periodic track closures associated with programmed iron-rail replacement, and the costs (including detrimental public relations) induced by accidents attributable to defective iron rails. Atack and Brueckner, "Steel Rails and American Railroads," 340–42, 347 (quotes); William Z. Ripley, *Railroads: Rates and Regulation* (New York: Longmans, Green, and Co., 1912; repr. New York: Arno Press, 1973), 17.

19. In October 1864, Carnegie established the Cyclops Iron Company, in order to provide components for Piper & Shiffler (later the Keystone Bridge Company). Paul T. Fagley, "Forging Iron, Forging Steel, Forging Freedom: The Story of the Iron and Steel Industry at Burnham, Pennsylvania, from Freedom Forge to Standard Steel," *Canal History and Technology Proceedings* 14 (March 11, 1995): 31–71, at 42–47; Joseph Frazier Wall, *Andrew Carnegie* (New York: Oxford University Press, 1970), 249.

20. Andrew Carnegie, *Autobiography of Andrew Carnegie* (Boston: Houghton Mifflin, 1920), 185.

21. Ibid., 186 ("superior service"); J. Edgar Thomson to Andrew Carnegie, March 15, 1867, Carnegie Steel Papers, Historical Society of Western Pennsylvania, Library and Archives Division, Pittsburgh, Pennsylvania, Box 44, folder 3, quoted in Wall, *Andrew Carnegie*, 257 ("impaired my confidence," "abandon").

22. The disagreement between Thomson and Carnegie over the merits of the Dodd process encouraged the young entrepreneur to move from bridge building into steel manufacturing, and to likewise increasingly distance himself from the Pennsylvania Railroad. With Thomson refusing to purchase any more of Carnegie's Dodd-process steel rails, the Scotsman marketed rails to the PRR's competitors. Carnegie had little success, however, as other railroads were equally unimpressed by the test results. With the failure of the Dodd process, Carnegie acquired the American patent rights for the Webb process for bonding a steel head to an iron rail, but this was likewise an impracticable technology. Wilson, *History of the Pennsyl-*

vania Railroad, vol. 1, 203; David Nasaw, *Andrew Carnegie* (New York: Penguin Press, 2006), 101–2; Wall, *Andrew Carnegie*, 255–59; Jeanne McHugh, *Alexander Holley and the Makers of Steel* (Baltimore: Johns Hopkins University Press, 1980), 222–23.

23. The first direct purchases of Pennsylvania Steel Company stock by the PRR apparently did not take place until 1871. *Investigation of Railroads, Holding Companies, and Affiliated Companies: Report of the Committee on Interstate Commerce: Railroad Combination in the Eastern Region, Part 1 (Before 1920)*, 76th Cong., 3rd sess. (Washington, D.C.: U.S. Government Printing Office, 1940) (hereafter referred to as "Wheeler Report"), 109.

24. The PRR proper did not invest in the Pennsylvania Steel Company until 1871, when the railroad acquired six thousand shares, valued at $600,000. PRR BOD Minutes, December 13, 1865, 5–7; Thomas J. Misa, *A Nation of Steel: The Making of Modern America, 1865–1925* (Baltimore: Johns Hopkins University Press, 1995), 21; David Jackson, "Pennsylvania Steel, 1867–1916," *The Keystone* 31 (Winter 1998): 41–50, at 41; "Pennsylvania Steel Company, Cambria Steel Company," November 20, 1937, HML, Box 219, folder 13.

25. Jackson, "Pennsylvania Steel," 41; Bruce Sinclair, "At the Turn of a Screw: William Sellers, the Franklin Institute, and a Standard American Thread," *Technology and Culture* 10 (January 1969): 20–34; John C. Paige, *A Special History Study: Pennsylvania Railroad Shops and Works, Altoona, Pennsylvania* (Washington, D.C.: United States Department of the Interior, National Park Service, 1989); J. Leander Bishop, *A History of American Manufactures from 1608 to 1860*, vol. 2 (Philadelphia: Edward Young & Co., 1864), 549; Burgess and Kennedy, *Centennial History*, 404–5; Jackson, "Pennsylvania Steel," 41.

26. The Cambria Iron Company was founded in 1852, almost simultaneous with the arrival of the PRR in Johnstown, but initially experienced little success. The Morill Tariff of 1861 sharply curtailed U.S. demand for imported British iron and steel, and enabled Cambria and other domestic producers to attain profitability as the first large integrated rail mill east of Pittsburgh. In 1869, Cambria installed Bessemer converters (the sixth steel mill in the United States to do so), and the company rolled its first steel rails in 1871. John Newton Boucher, *The Cambria Iron Company, Reprinted from the Fifteenth Annual Report of the Bureau of Industrial Statistics, Pennsylvania* (Harrisburg: Meyers Printing, 1888); Jackson, "Pennsylvania Steel," 41–44; Mark Reutter, *Sparrows Point: Making Steel: The Rise and Ruin of American Industrial Might* (New York: Summit Books, 1988), 22–23.

27. The Cambria Iron Company was organized in August 1852. Two years later, the company rolled its first iron rails, and within a few years generated more than 10 percent of the annual rail output in the United States. By the mid-1870s, it was the nation's largest iron and settle producer. Sharon Brown, "The Cambria Iron Company of Johnstown, Pennsylvania," *Canal History and Technology Proceedings* 7 (March 26, 1988): 19–46.

28. Jackson, "Pennsylvania Steel," 44–46.

29. The branch line, owned by the Pennsylvania Steel Company, was the Baltimore & Sparrows Point Railroad. It was completed in 1889. The B&O also possessed rail access to the Sparrows Point facility. Robert L. Gunnarsson, *The Story of the Northern Central Railway, from Baltimore to Lake Ontario* (Sykesville, Md.: Greenberg Publishing, 1991), 105.

30. Jackson, "Pennsylvania Steel," 48–49. For a complete account of the Sparrows Point facility, see Reutter, *Sparrows Point*.

31. Misa, *A Nation of Steel*, 151–52.

32. The PRR made the purchases through Drexel & Company, representing a little more than 50 percent of Cambria Steel's outstanding stock, and slightly more than 70 percent of Pennsylvania Steel. The PRR retained a bare majority of Pennsylvania Steel (most of which was actually held by the Pennsylvania Company, not the PRR directly) and sold the remaining

20 percent stake to the Reading Iron Company, a subsidiary of the Reading Company. The PRR did not rely exclusively on Pennsylvania Steel and Cambria Steel for its rails, however, placing orders for 1908 delivery with United States Steel (71,500 tons), Lackawanna Steel (10,600 tons), as well as Pennsylvania Steel (30,500 tons) and Cambria Steel (30,000 tons). Wheeler Report, Part 1, 51–52, 109–12; Jackson, "Pennsylvania Steel," 49–50, "Pennsylvania Steel Company, Cambria Steel Company," PRR Press Release, May 11, 1908, HML, Box 145, folder 1; Memo to A. J. County, February 26, 1915, HML, Box 145, folder 6.

33. Effingham B. Morris to Samuel Rea, December 4, 1911, HML, Box 145, folder 6.

34. Morris to William H. Donner, February 26, 1913, quoted in Wheeler Report, Part 1, 113.

35. Morris to Rea, December 4, 1911, HML, Box 145, folder 6.

36. *New York Times*, December 13, 1902, October 9, 1912; Wheeler Report, Part 1, 54–56, 109–15; Jackson, "Pennsylvania Steel," 49–50, "Pennsylvania Steel Company, Cambria Steel Company."

37. Steven W. Usselman, *Regulating Railroad Innovation: Business, Technology, and Politics in America, 1840–1920* (Cambridge: Cambridge University Press, 2002), 221–23, 360–67; "Departments of Chemical and Physical Tests (Historical)," 252, HML.

38. "Departments of Chemical and Physical Tests," 29–30.

39. By 1913, of the fifty staff in the chemical department, seven were chemists whose primary function was to evaluate the conformity of rails to existing standards, while another five chemists were engaged in developing new specifications. "Departments of Chemical and Physical Tests," 29–30.

40. Usselman, *Regulating Railroad Innovation*, 221–22.

41. Misa, *A Nation of Steel*, 29–39.

42. Ibid., 143–44.

43. Usselman, *Regulating Railroad Innovation*, 360; Misa, *A Nation of Steel*, 145–46.

44. "Departments of Chemical and Physical Tests," 7–9.

45. As early as 1875, division superintendents had met with officials in the Motive Power Department in an effort to standardize locomotive designs and develop the types of locomotives that best suited operating characteristics on various parts of the railroad. The delegates to those meetings soon turned their attention to other technological issues that seemed amenable to standardization, including signaling systems. Following the catastrophic strikes of 1877, they focused, albeit temporarily, on labor relations issues. In May 1879, PRR executives established the ATO as an official organization, composed, as historian Steven Usselman has described, of the "assistant superintendents of motive power, general agents, engineers of maintenance of way, and principal assistant engineers from the various divisions and subsidiary lines," organized into "three standing committees: maintenance of way, motive power, and conducting transportation." The ATO fostered a spirit of professional and intellectual camaraderie by allowing PRR engineers, freed of direct oversight by the central office, to develop solutions to system-wide problems that cut across divisional boundaries and the demarcations of career specialization. The initial incarnation of the ATO lasted only until 1880, but the organization was reconstituted in 1893. By the 1890s, ATO officials were involved in a wide variety of technical issues, ranging from signals to telephones to air brakes to the design and composition of rails. Usselman, *Regulating Railroad Innovation*, 189–91.

46. Ibid., 233, 360.

47. In 1919, the American Institute of Mining Engineers became the American Institute of Mining and Metallurgical Engineers.

48. Usselman, *Regulating Railroad Innovation*, 222–23, 237–38.

49. Misa, *A Nation of Steel*, 143–45.

50. Ibid., 150–154, quote at 154.

51. Ibid., 152–54; Usselman, *Regulating Railroad Innovation*, 221–23, 360–67; "Departments of Chemical and Physical Tests," 252; Alfred W. Gibbs to William Wallace Atterbury, October 11, 1913, PHMC, Rea Papers, Box 32 (12–1862), folder 50/11.

52. Mark Aldrich, *Death Rode the Rails: American Railroad Accidents and Safety, 1828–1965* (Baltimore: Johns Hopkins University Press, 2006), 72, 186, 205–208, 258–60.

53. PRR Press Release, May 11, 1908, HML, Box 145, folder 1; Samuel Rea memorandum RE: Bethlehem Steel Company, November 25, 1912, HML, Box 145, folder 6; *New York Times*, February 19, 1916; Rea to Atterbury, October 21, 1913, PHMC, Rea Papers, Box 32 (12–1862), folder 50/11.

54. Gibbs to Atterbury, October 11, 1913, PHMC, Rea Papers, Box 32 (12–1862), folder 50/11.

55. E. F. Kennedy to Gibbs, October 13, 1913, PHMC, Rea Papers, Box 32 (12–1862), folder 50/11.

56. Thomas H. Johnson to Gibbs, October 7, 1913 ("The manufacturers favor"); J. C. Bland (Engineer of Bridges) to Gibbs, October 8, 1913 ("I cannot agree"); both in PHMC, Rea Papers, Box 32 (12–1862), folder 50/11.

57. Alexander C. Shand to Gibbs, October 3, 1913, PHMC, Rea Papers, Box 32 (12–1862), folder 50/11.

58. Shand to Atterbury, October 11, 1913, PHMC, Rea Papers, Box 32 (12–1862), folder 50/11.

59. In 1918, chief engineer Alexander C. Shand and chief mechanical engineer Alfred W. Gibbs had proposed testing two-hundred-pound rail, but there is no record that this was ever done. "Minutes of meeting of Rail Committee of the Pennsylvania Railroad," September 30, 1912; Gibbs to Atterbury, June 8, 1916; Shand and Gibbs to Rea, May 2, 1918; all in PHMC, Rea Papers, Box 32 (12–1862), folder 50/11; *Railway Age* 91 (August 8, 1931): 205–6; 94 (April 29, 1931): 627–34.

60. Aldrich, *Death Rode the Rails*, 97.

61. James W. Ely, Jr., *Railroads and American Law* (Lawrence: University Press of Kansas, 2001), 211; Aldrich, *Death Rode the Rails*, 4–5, 108–12, 196–97, 244–50.

62. Steven W. Usselman and Richard R. John, "Patent Politics: Intellectual Property, the Railroad Industry, and the Problem of Monopoly," *Journal of Policy History* 18 (2006): 96–125, at 113–14.

63. John H. White, *The American Railroad Passenger Car* (Baltimore: Johns Hopkins University Press, 1978), 551; Steven W. Usselman, "Air Brakes for Freight Trains: Technological Innovation in the American Railroad Industry, 1869–1900," *Business History Review* 58 (Spring 1984): 30–50; Usselman, *Regulating Railroad Innovation*, 134–38; Francis Ellington Leupp, *George Westinghouse: His Life and Achievements* (Boston: Little, Brown, 1918), 65, 73.

64. The PRR installed the first such equipment in 1875, and it replaced the older pressure air brake as standard equipment three years later.

65. McCraw, *Prophets of Regulation*, 17–31; Usselman, *Regulating Railroad Innovation*, 120–21, 131–35; Aldrich, *Death Rode the Rails*, 71–72.

66. Aldrich, *Death Rode the Rails*, 72–78.

67. Usselman, *Regulating Railroad Innovation*, 289.

68. Burgess and Kennedy, *Centennial History*, 717; Usselman, *Regulating Railroad Innovation*, 276–79.

69. *New York Times*, May 12, 1905, May 14, 1905; Mark Aldrich, "Regulating Transportation of Hazardous Substances: Railroads and Reform, 1883–1903," *Business History Review* 76 (Summer 2002): 267–97; "The Great Dynamite Wreck," *The Keystone* 37 (Winter 2004).

70. Aldrich, *Death Rode the Rails*, 82–85, 108–10; Charles H. Clark, "The Development of the Semiautomatic Freight-Car Coupler, 1863–1893," *Technology and Culture* 13 (April 1972): 170–208.

71. In contrast, the Philadelphia, Wilmington & Baltimore was one of the first railroads in the United States to install Miller couplers, albeit before it was part of the PRR system. White, *The American Railroad Passenger Car*, 562–64, 567; Aldrich, *Death Rode the Rails*, 27–28; Clark, "The Development," 180–83.

72. John H. White, *The American Railroad Passenger Car* (Baltimore: Johns Hopkins University Press, 1978), 562–64, 567; John H. White, *The American Railroad Freight Car: From the Wood-Car Era to the Coming of Steel* (Baltimore: Johns Hopkins University Press, 1993), 511; Clark, "The Development," 186–89.

73. White, *The American Railroad Passenger Car*, 562–64; Clark, "The Development," 191.

74. By 1886, four states had passed legislation mandating some form of automatic coupler, but as historian Charles H. Clark has noted, "Of the thirty-five separate couplers which were acceptable to the railroad commissioners of these four states, not a single device was legal in all of them." Clark, "The Development," 197.

75. White, *The American Railroad Freight Car*, 498–502.

76. Ibid., 562–64; Usselman, *Regulating Railroad Innovation*, 289.

77. Aldrich, *Death Rode the Rails*, 78, 244–50.

78. Usselman, *Regulating Railroad Innovation*, 121–22; Clark, "The Development," 182–85.

79. Clark, "The Development," 193–99.

80. In addition to the Janney design, they included the Cowell, Archer, Ames, United States, Mitchell, Wilson & Walker, Conway Ball, and Gifford. *American Engineer and Railroad Journal* 68 (May 1894): 232–33 (quotes).

81. Master Car-Builders' Association, *Report of the Proceedings of the Twenty-First Annual Convention* (New York, 1887), 189, quoted in Clark, "The Development," 200.

82. Usselman, "Air Brakes for Freight Trains," 41–45; Usselman, *Regulating Railroad Innovation*, 137, 192–95, 276–79; Clark, "The Development," 199–203.

83. Usselman, *Regulating Railroad Innovation*, 289.

84. The 1893 act had encouraged the installation of grab irons and other safety devices on freight cars, but the widespread application of uniformly positioned grab irons, as well as ladders and running boards, would have to await the passage of an amendment to the law in 1910. Hotboxes (caused by insufficient lubricant in solid-bearing trucks) remained a problem, causing train detentions in order to cool down overheated journal boxes and, in some cases, causing catastrophic failure. The PRR and other railroads had installed roller bearings to some passenger cars and steam locomotives; these were like air brakes and couplers, the areas that offered the greatest public relations value and the greatest gains in operating efficiency, respectively. Freight equipment lagged behind, and as late as the early 1950s, hotboxes cost the PRR some $4 million per year in damaged equipment and delayed trains. The Association of American Railroads did not prohibit solid bearings in new car construction until 1966, and a ban on their use on existing cars in interchange service did not take effect until 1980, long after both the Pennsylvania Railroad and the Penn Central had ceased to exist. White, *The American Railroad Passenger Car*, 519; Jeff Wilson, "Modeler's Guide to Freight Car Trucks," *Model Railroader* (December 2003): 72–77.

85. Usselman, *Regulating Railroad Innovation*, 276–79; Ely, *Railroads and American Law*, 217–18; Aldrich, *Death Rode the Rails*, 16, 111–12; Clark, "The Development," 204–8.

86. *St. Louis, Iron Mountain & Southern Railway Company v. Taylor*, 210 U.S. 281 (1908).

87. Aldrich, *Death Rode the Rails*, 195.

88. PRR Test Department, *Brake Tests: A Report of a Series of Road Tests of Brakes on Passenger Equipment Cars Made at Absecon, New Jersey, in 1913* (Altoona: Pennsylvania Railroad Company, 1913); Aldrich, *Death Rode the Rails*, 195.

89. Aldrich, *Death Rode the Rails*, 250–52.

90. James B. Calvert, "Notes on Pennsylvania Railroad Operation and Signaling," October 10, 2000, revised June 20, 2005, http://mysite.du.edu/~jcalvert/railway/prr/prrsig.htm, accessed June 20, 2010.

91. Usselman, *Regulating Railroad Innovation*, 125, 293–300; Pennsylvania Railroad, *The Centennial Exhibition and the Pennsylvania Railroad, 1776–1876* (Chicago: Rand, McNally, 1876). For a description of the PRR's manual block-signaling practices, see Braman B. Adams, *The Block System of Signaling on American Railroads: The Methods and Appliances Used in Manual and Automatic Block Signaling* (New York: Railroad Gazette, 1901), 7–24.

92. As signal engineer and signaling historian James B. Calvert has suggested, "These Saxby and Farmer plants were the reason that American signals and signal towers resemble their British prototypes, and that the semaphore signal became standard American practice, as it was in Britain." Calvert, "Notes on Pennsylvania Railroad Operation and Signaling."

93. Brian Solomon, *Railroad Signaling* (St. Paul, Minn.: MBI Publishing, 2003), 23–26.

94. Usselman, *Regulating Railroad Innovation*, 133–38; Usselman, "Air Brakes for Freight Trains"; Usselman, "From Novelty to Utility: George Westinghouse and the Business of Innovation During the Age of Edison," *Business History Review* 66 (1992): 251–304; Calvert, "Notes on Pennsylvania Railroad Operation and Signaling."

95. Solomon, *Railroad Signaling*, 19–23, 39, 42–43.

96. Ibid., 33–34; Usselman, *Regulating Railroad Innovation*, 129–30.

97. Usselman, *Regulating Railroad Innovation*, 133–38, 307; Usselman, "Air Brakes for Freight Trains"; Usselman, "From Novelty to Utility"; Calvert, "Notes on Pennsylvania Railroad Operation and Signaling"; Solomon, *Railroad Signaling*, 34–35.

98. In 1887, the PRR rewarded Fowle for his efforts, appointing him signal engineer, with the same duties (although a slightly different title), than H. F. Cox, the outgoing engineer of signals.

99. *Railway World* 8 (August 26, 1882), 797–801, quotes at 799; *Journal of the Railway Signal Association* 6 (1909), 425.

100. *Signal Engineer* 1 (June 1908), 28.

101. Cupper, *Rockville Bridge*, 68; Solomon, *Railroad Signaling*, 39; Calvert, "Notes on Pennsylvania Railroad Operation and Signaling"; Watkins History, vol. 2, "Semaphore Signals."

102. Calvert, "Notes on Pennsylvania Railroad Operation and Signaling." For a description of the PRR's automatic-block system, see Adams, *The Block System*, 129–39.

103. Usselman, *Regulating Railroad Innovation*, 301.

104. Ibid., 126; Adams, *The Block System*, 167.

105. "Report of the Committee on Interlocking and Block Signals," October 24, 1893, ATO files, HML, Box 1, folder 16, quoted in Usselman, *Regulating Railroad Innovation*, 309.

106. Adams's five hundred miles somewhat overstated the application of automatic block signals, as he was referring to track miles, not route miles. By the beginning of 1901, the PRR had installed automatic signals along only 146 route miles of Lines East (compared with 788 miles protected by manual block signaling), as well as thirty-five miles on Lines West, compared with 349 miles of manual block. Adams, *The Block System*, 165 (quote), 169–70.

107. Usselman, *Regulating Railroad Innovation*, 282–83, 301–2, 311–12.

108. Rudd was a descendent of Alexander Lyman Holley, who in 1865 played a critical role in designing the production facilities of the Pennsylvania Steel Company. Jackson, "Pennsylvania Steel," 44.

109. *New York Times*, January 15, 1904; *Information for Employees and the Public*, January 29, 1917, 2; Alexander H. Rudd, "The Evolution of Cab Signals," *Mutual Magazine*, June 1935, 11–18. Rudd biographical information is from Calvert, "Notes on Pennsylvania Railroad Operation and Signaling."

110. Additional installations took place on the New York Division during 1917 and 1918.

111. The PRR solved this problem by halving the number of lights on each signal head. Edward Waytel, "The First Position Light Signals and Subsequent Developments," *The Keystone* 14 (December 1981): 4–12; Solomon, *Railroad Signaling*, 56–59.

112. Waytel, "The First Position Light Signals and Subsequent Developments."

113. Rudd, "The Evolution of Cab Signals," 12; Michael W. Savchak, "A History of Cab Signaling and Automatic Train Control on the PRR," *The Keystone* 39 (Autumn 2006): 11–39, at 11.

114. Savchak, "A History of Cab Signaling," 11–13.

115. As economic historian Mark Aldrich has observed, "Between 1901, with the passage of the first Accident Report Act, and 1912, when the Block Signal Board delivered its final report, the carriers' safety record had been under almost continuous public assault." Aldrich, "Public Relations and Technology: The 'Standard Railroad of the World' and the Crisis in Railroad Safety, 1897–1916," *Pennsylvania History* 74 (Winter 2007): 74–104, at 77–83, quote at 83; Usselman, *Regulating Railroad Innovation*, 315; Adams, *The Block System*, with an extensive description of PRR practice at 7–24 and 129–39.

116. Aldrich, *Death Rode the Rails*, 185; Usselman, *Regulating Railroad Innovation*, 315–25.

117. Robert C. Reed, *Train Wrecks: A Pictorial History of Accidents on the Main Line* (New York: Superior Publishing, 1968), 65, 80–81, 115–16.

118. Rudd, "The Evolution of Cab Signals," 12.

119. Usselman, *Regulating Railroad Innovation*, 320.

120. Ibid., 313; Aldrich, "Public Relations and Technology," 94–95.

121. Usselman, *Regulating Railroad Innovation*, 316.

122. Railway Signal Association, *Index to Signal Literature*, vol. 1: *October 1910* (Bethlehem, Pa.: Times Publishing Co., 1911), 172–74; *New York Times*, January 28, 1912; Aldrich, "Public Relations and Technology," 96.

123. ATO, "Report of the Committee on Telegraph, Telephone, and Signals," October 1, 1923, HML.

124. Ibid.; Solomon, *Railroad Signaling*, 137.

125. Usselman, *Regulating Railroad Innovation*, 315–26.

126. Aldrich, *Death Rode the Rails*, 246–48; Alexander H. Rudd, "Comments at the Meeting of the Signal Section of the American Railway Association," September 1924, quoted in *Railway Age* 77 (1924): 645.

127. ATO, "Report of the Committee on Telegraph, Telephone, and Signals," October 1, 1923, HML (quote); Solomon, *Railroad Signaling*, 137–39.

128. Rudd, "Comments at the Meeting."

129. *Railway Age* 120 (July 15, 1922): 120; *Railway Age* 120 (August 4, 1923): 218–19; Savchak, "A History of Cab Signaling," 15–17.

130. *Railway Age* 89 (August 9, 1930): 277–79.

131. Rudd, "The Evolution of Cab Signals," 12–18; Ed Waytel, "Cab Signals," *The Keystone* 13, no. 4 (December 1980): 4–10.

132. Rudd, "Comments at the Meeting."

133. *Railway Age* 77 (1924): 645–46; *Railway Age* 78 (March 28, 1925): 841–42; *Railway Age* 89 (August 9, 1930): 277–79; Duffy, *Electric Railways*, 202; Aldrich, *Death Rode the Rails*, 248–50.

134. Rudd, "Comments at the Meeting."

135. *Railway Age* 89 (August 9, 1930): 277–79; Savchak, "A History of Cab Signaling," 27.

136. *Railway Age* 93 (December 31, 1932): 982–83; *Railway Age* 99 (July 20, 1935): 94; *Railway Age* 99 (August 17, 1935): 210–12; Rudd, "The Evolution of Cab Signals," 12–18; Aldrich, *Death Rode the Rails*, 249.

137. *Railway Age* 90 (January 24, 1931): 230–31; Robert Charles Williams, "The Maintainers of Safety and Efficiency: The Brotherhood of Railroad Signalmen, 1900–1940" (M.A. thesis, University of Delaware, 2008), 13–14.

138. Rather than install the required equipment, however, many railroads merely reduced train speeds to the levels specified by the ICC. Savchak, "A History of Cab Signaling," 32–33.

139. Joel Rosenbaum, "The Wreck of *The Broker*," *The Keystone* 38, no. 3 (Autumn 2005): 42–50; Savchak, "A History of Cab Signaling," 32–35.

140. PRR officials made no provision for applying speed-control equipment to freight locomotives, partly for economic reasons, and in part because longer and heavier trains were more difficult to regulate with the new technology. Speed control would do nothing to prevent an errant freight locomotive from striking a passenger train, causing a serious accident. *Railway Age* 130 (March 12, 1951): 93–94.

141. In September 1958, a Jersey Central commuter train ran through an open drawbridge and into Newark Bay, killing forty-eight people and prompting the New Jersey Board of Public Utilities to mandate the installation of deadman controls on all passenger locomotives operating within the state. Unlike ATS, however, the deadman version of automatic speed control did not prevent a careless engineman from overrunning a stop signal.

142. Savchak, "A History of Cab Signaling," 35–39.

143. James D. Dilts, *The Great Road: The Building of the Baltimore & Ohio, the Nation's First Railroad, 1828–1853* (Stanford, Calif.: Stanford University Press, 1993), 293–96. Richard R. John, *Network Nation: Inventing American Telecommunications* (Cambridge, Mass.: Belknap Press of Harvard University Press, 2010), 24–89.

144. For example, see Alfred D. Chandler, Jr., *The Visible Hand: The Managerial Revolution in American Business* (Cambridge, Mass.: Belknap Press of Harvard University Press, 1977), 89, 98, 103. Joseph Frazier Wall, writing in 1970, well before the publication of *The Visible Hand*, correctly assessed the limited receptivity of early railroad executives to the telegraph, noting that "the railroad industry, with a few notable exceptions, had been unbelievably slow in realizing the significance of the telegraph." Wall, *Andrew Carnegie*, 215.

145. As Benjamin Schwantes has observed, British railways tended to have higher traffic densities and greater levels of capitalization than their U.S. counterparts, factors that tended to encourage the adoption of telegraphy. Benjamin Sidney Michael Schwantes, "Fallible Guardian: The Social Construction of Railroad Telegraphy in Nineteenth-Century America" (Ph.D. diss., University of Delaware, 2008), 8–9, 38–44.

146. Schwantes, "Disinterest and Distrust: The Ambivalent Relationship Between Railroad Managers and Telegraph Entrepreneurs in Antebellum America," paper presented at the 2007 Business History Conference, Cleveland, Ohio, June 1, 2007, 11–14.

147. Philadelphia, Wilmington & Baltimore Railroad Company, Minute Book of the Stockholders and Board of Directors, vol. 2, April 13, 1852, 142, HML; quoted in Schwantes, "Fallible Guardian," 55; John, *Network Nation*, 76.

148. Schwantes, "Fallible Guardian," 12.

149. "O'Rielly" is the preferred spelling of the last name, even though most accounts list him as "O'Reilly." John, *Network Nation*, 440n58.

150. James D. Reid, *The Telegraph in America: Its Founders, Promoters, and Noted Men* (1879; repr. New York: Arno Press, 1974), 152–62; John, *Network Nation*, 82–87.

151. PRR BOD Minutes, March 21, 1849, 156.

152. PRR BOD Minutes, March 29, 1849, 156, November 14, 1849, 217; Robert Luther Thompson, *Wiring a Continent: The History of the Telegraph in the United States, 1832–1866* (Princeton, N.J.: Princeton University Press, 1947), 99, 137; Schwantes, "Fallible Guardian," 86–87; "An Act to Incorporate the Woodbury and Broad Top Turnpike or Plank Road Company [and] . . . Authorizing the Pennsylvania Railroad Company to Construct a Line of Telegraph along their Road . . . ," May 11, 1853, reprinted in *Charter and Supplements of the Pennsylvania Railroad Company, with the Acts of Assembly and Municipal Ordinances Affecting the Company* (Philadelphia: Crissy & Markley, 1859), *Charter and Supplements of the Pennsylvania Railroad Company*, 52–53.

153. The PRR's use of the telegraph, albeit limited, indicates that the company's managers were at least as proactive as the Erie's Daniel McCallum (who did not become general superintendent until May 1854).

154. As Schwantes has noted, it is not clear whether the PRR pursued legal action against the A&O for recovery of damages. Schwantes, "Fallible Guardian," 87–88; Thompson, *Wiring a Continent*, 209.

155. Schwantes, "Fallible Guardian," 68.

156. "Pennsylvania Railroad System. Telegraph Department," n.d., ca. 1895, J. Elfreth Watkins Collection, Smithsonian Institution, Box 2, folder 4; Schwantes, "Fallible Guardian," 70–73.

157. PRR BOD Minutes, April 7, 1852, 153, April 21, 1852, 157, December 15, 1852, 280; Schwantes, "Fallible Guardian," 87–90; Reid, *The Telegraph in America*, 455–62.

158. PRR BOD Minutes, April 6, 1853, 327, January 4, 1854, 422; Schwantes, "Fallible Guardian," 89–90.

159. PRR BOD Minutes, September 19, 1855, 102 (quote); Schwantes, "Fallible Guardian," 89–90.

160. PRR BOD Minutes, August 23, 1855, 92, September 19, 1855, 102.

161. Wilson, *History of the Pennsylvania Railroad*, vol. 2, 176–77.

162. Thompson, *Wiring a Continent*, 296, 397; Reid, *The Telegraph in America*, 174–78, 476–77; Alvin F. Harlow, *Old Wires and New Waves: The History of Telegraph, Telephone, and Wireless* (New York: D. Appleton-Century Co., 1936), 254–57; John, *Network Nation*, 92–97.

163. After lengthy negotiations, Western Union leased the Atlantic & Ohio, effective April 15, 1864.

164. The effect of the Civil War was equally noticeable on the PRR's western outlets. In 1860, Fort Wayne personnel began using the telegraph to regulate train operations, although only during the day. Beginning in 1863, Fort Wayne officials implemented routinized dispatching methods. Ivan E. Frantz, Jr., "The Pennsylvania Railroad and the Civil War," *The Keystone* 38, no. 3 (Autumn 2005): 9–28; Herbert C. Archdeacon, "Two Civil War Railroaders," *The Keystone* 38, no. 3 (Autumn 2005): 29–31; James A. Ward, *J. Edgar Thomson, Master of the Pennsylvania* (Westport, Conn.: Greenwood Press, 1980), 127; Samuel Richey Kamm, "The Civil War Career of Thomas A. Scott" (Ph.D. diss., University of Pennsylvania, 1940), 34, 41–42; Schawantes, "Fallible Guardian," 13–14, 111–62.

165. Even though Carnegie was able to recruit ex-PRR telegraph experts, including David Brooks and David McCargo, and despite support from Tom Scott, Pacific & Atlantic was no match for Western Union, a company with forty times the capital. By 1872, Carnegie had begun selling his investments in the Pacific & Atlantic to Western Union, and the two

companies were formally consolidated in January 1874. Ward, *Master of the Pennsylvania*, 184–85; "Pennsylvania Railroad System. Telegraph Department"; Wall, *Andrew Carnegie*, 212–21; Nasaw, *Andrew Carnegie*, 107–8.

166. Schwantes, "Fallible Guardian," 183–84.

167. Calvert, "Notes on Pennsylvania Railroad Operation and Signaling"; Schwantes, "Fallible Guardian," 202–3.

168. "Pennsylvania Railroad System. Telegraph Department"; Schwantes, "Fallible Guardian," 213–25.

169. Melodie Andrews, "'What the Girls Can Do': The Debate over the Employment of Women in the Early American Telegraph Industry," *Essays in Economic and Business History* 8 (1990): 109–20. Thomas C. Jepsen, *My Sisters Telegraphic: Women in the Telegraph Office, 1846–1950* (Athens: Ohio University Press, 2000), 148–54.

170. In Los Angeles, the 1907 CTUA strike illustrated a certain degree of friction between male and female union members—in one instance a male operator showed his displeasure toward a female operator who crossed the picket lines by sending her telegraphic messages accusing her of being a scab and a whore. Thomas C. Jepsen, *Ma Kiley: The Life of a Railroad Telegrapher* (El Paso: Texas Western Press, 1997), 37–42. Other reactions were possible, as well—in the "Great Strike" of 1883, striking female telegraphers received baskets of lilies, symbolizing the purity of their cause. During the strike, Western Union offered free cigars to entice scabs, something that would not tempt female strikers, who were seen as both morally virtuous and incorruptible. Edwin Gabler, *The American Telegrapher: A Social History, 1860–1890* (New Brunswick, N.J.: Rutgers University Press, 1988), 143, 172, 199. See also Archibald M. McIsaac, *The Order of Railroad Telegraphers: A Study in Trade Unionism and Collective Bargaining* (Princeton, N.J.: Princeton University Press, 1933), and Vidkunn Ulriksson, *The Telegraphers: Their Craft and Their Unions* (Washington, D.C.: Public Affairs Press, 1953).

171. Telegraphers did not organize workers' committees on Lines West until January 1918.

172. "Chronology of Relations with Telegraph Department Employes," 3, HML, Box 877, folder 20.

173. Ibid.

174. In 1860, the Baltimore & Ohio was probably the first American railroad to open a telegraph school, in Pittsburgh, one that accepted both men and women. It is interesting to note that even though the PRR's 1907 School of Telegraphy apparently taught telephony from the beginning, technology was not reflected in the name. "Pennsylvania Railroad School of Telegraphy," October 1, 1910, PHMC, Cassatt/McCrea papers, Box 57 (12–1818), folder 84/8.

175. PRR press release, October 8, 1910, PHMC, Cassatt/McCrea papers, Box 57 (12–1818), folder 84/8.

176. Out of approximately 3,900 employees in the Telegraph Department on Lines East.

177. "Chronology of Relations with Telegraph Department Employes," 3, HML, Box 877, folder 20.

178. The BRSA became affiliated with the American Federation of Labor in 1914; Williams, "The Maintainers of Safety," 91–108.

179. "Chronology of Relations with Telegraph and Signal Department Employes and the Regulations Governing Working Conditions," 9, HML, Box 877, folder 18.

180. Jepsen, *Ma Kiley*, 11–12; Jepsen, *My Sisters Telegraphic*, 6, 80; Janet F. Davidson, "Women and the Railroad: The Gendering of Work During the First World War Era, 1917–1920" (Ph.D. *diss.*, University of Delaware, 1999), 240–41.

181. PRR press release, June 22, 1917, PHMC, Rea Papers, Box 57 (12–1887), folder 84/8.

182. Ibid.

183. PRR, Lines East, "Statement Showing by Grand Divisions and by Occupations Number of Women Employes on March 1, 1918," HML, Box 987, folder 12. United States Railroad Administration, *General Order No. 27: Wages of Railroad Employees* (Washington, D.C.: U.S. Government Printing Office, May 25, 1918); Davidson, "Women and the Railroad," 46–47, 62.

184. Davidson, "Women and the Railroad," 238–51.

185. Ibid., 72–85, 228–38.

186. Pennsylvania System, Eastern Region, "Statement Showing by Divisions and Occupations Number of Women Employes on October 1, 1920," HML, Box 987, folder 12.

187. Schwantes, "Fallible Guardian," 236–39.

188. Association of Transportation Officers, "Report of Committee on Telegraph," November 22, 1897, HML, Box 407, folder 8; Schwantes, "Fallible Guardian," 236–39.

189. Association of Transportation Officers, "Report of Committee on Telegraph," November 22, 1897, HML, Box 407, folder 8; Schwantes, "Fallible Guardian," 236–39.

190. Schwantes, "Fallible Guardian," 233–34; Aldrich, *Death Rode the Rails*, 185.

191. Schwantes, "Fallible Guardian," 234–35; Usselman, *Regulating Railroad Innovation*, 306–7.

192. "Memorandum: Some of the Advantages and Disadvantages of Telephone in Place of Telegraph," April 11, 1910, PHMC, Cassatt/McCrea papers, Box 56 (12–1817), folder 82/26.

193. "Memorandum: Some of the Advantages and Disadvantages of Telephone in Place of Telegraph," April 11, 1910, PHMC, Cassatt/McCrea papers, Box 56 (12–1817), folder 82/26; Usselman, *Regulating Railroad Innovation*, 305.

194. Atterbury to James McCrea, December 20, 1911, PHMC, Cassatt/McCrea papers, Box 56 (12–1817), folder 82/26.

195. Memorandum: Some of the Advantages and Disadvantages of Telephone in Place of Telegraph," April 11, 1910, PHMC, Cassatt/McCrea papers, Box 56 (12–1817), folder 82/26; Pennsylvania Railroad Information, "The Wire System of a Great Railroad," HML, Box 1414, folder 34, pp. 16–18; *Railway Age* 90 (April 4, 1931); *Railway Signal Engineer* 11 (August 1918): 263; Frank H. Bernhard, ed., *EMF Electrical Year Book* (Chicago: Electrical Trade Publishing Co., 1921), 734; Schwantes, "Fallible Guardian," 241.

196. *Railway Age* 90 (April 4, 1931).

197. Pennsylvania Railroad Information, "The Wire System of a Great Railroad," 10.

198. *Railway Age* 73 (October 21, 1922): 769; *Railway Age* 76 (May 31, 1924): 1335; *Railway Age* 80 (May 8, 1926): 1271; Vincent Reh, *Railroad Radio: Hearing and Understanding Railroad Radio Communications and Systems* (Grand Isle, Vt.: Byron Hill, 1996), 6–8.

199. One system (developed in cooperation with the Union Switch & Signal Company) used both rails to transmit signals, while the other (developed in cooperation with General Electric) employed a loop system by using one rail in conjunction with a lineside wire suspended from telephone poles and connected to the track at regular intervals. "Two-Way Train Radio," *Mutual Magazine*, January 1938, 18–19, 35; *Railway Age* 103 (December 25, 1937): 824.

200. Minutes of Monday Staff Meeting, September 29, 1944, PHMC, Box 26 (9–1622), folder 011.301.

201. "Two-Way Train Radio," *Mutual Magazine*, January 1938, 18–19, 35; "Automatic Signals and Train Control Devices: Pennsylvania Railroad Makes Big Investment and Extensive Installations in Signal Protection,"

Mutual Magazine, October 1926, 12, 25; "Address of General C. D. Young, Vice-President in Charge of Purchases, Stores and Insurance of the Pennsylvania Railroad, at Mount Union College, Alliance, Ohio, on October 18, 1946, on the Occasion of the Celebration of Mount Union's 100th Anniversary," HML, Box 45 (9–1641), folder 110.01; *Railway Age* 126 (January 22, 1949): 52, 127 (October 8, 1949): 63; Reh, *Railroad Radio*, 8–11.

202. PRR BOD Minutes, April 5, 1848, 78, April 28, 1848, 82, January 30, 1850, 246, May 29, 1850, 290; Mike Schafer and Brian Solomon, *Pennsylvania Railroad* (Osceola, Wis.: MBI Publishing, 1997), 81.

203. The Pennsylvania Railroad, "Information for the Press," October 12, 1912, January 24, 1913, both in HML, Box 145, folder 1; *Philadelphia Public Ledger*, January 24, 1913.

204. White, *The American Railroad Freight Car*, 123.

205. Ibid., 125; Burgess and Kennedy, *Centennial History*, 771–72.

206. White, *The American Railroad Freight Car*, 194–96.

207. The PRR employed the following classification system: A, tank cars; F, flatcars; G, gondolas; H, hopper cars; K, stock cars; R, refrigerators; X, boxcars and automobile cars; N, cabin cars (the PRR did not use the term "caboose").

208. Ian S. Fischer, "Wooden Gondola Cars of the Pennsylvania System," *The Keystone* (Spring 1986): 9–37, at 9.

209. George D. Dixon, "Freight Traffic," n.d., ca. 1905, HML, Box 419, folder 556.

210. White, *The American Railroad Freight Car*, 184–86, 306, 321–22, 325–27, 335–37, 346–47, 358; Fischer, "Wooden Gondola Cars," 11.

211. White, *The American Railroad Freight Car*, 184–86, 306, 321–22, 325–27, 335–37, 346–47, 358; Martin Robert Karig III, *Coal Cars: The First Three Hundred Years* (Scranton, Pa.: University of Scranton Press, 2007), 48; "Steel Car Development," *American Engineer and Railroad Journal*, October 1903, 352; Fischer, "Wooden Gondola Cars," 14.

212. "Steel Car Development," 352.

213. The corrosion problem would not be fully resolved until the introduction of CorTen steel in the 1930s. In 1915, the PRR began using copper-bearing steel in hopper car construction in order to reduce corrosion. Karig, *Coal Cars*, 41; Fischer, "Wooden Gondola Cars," 14.

214. The figures do not include the equipment owned by equipment trust firms, totaling about forty thousand cars in each of those years, car type not specified.

215. *Poor's Manual of Railroads of the United States for 1900*, vol. 33 (New York: Poor's Railroad Manual Co., 1901), 669; "Steel Car Development," 352.

216. As with the Class GM, the Class GL cars rode on trucks that Schoen designed in collaboration with PRR mechanical engineer Axel S. Vogt.

217. "Steel Car Development," 352–54.

218. *New York Times*, April 17, 1898.

219. "Steel Car Development," 352–54.

220. Mitchell Charles Harrison, *Prominent and Progressive Americans: An Encyclopaedia of Contemporaneous Biography*, vol. 1 (New York: Tribune Association, 1902), 300–301; Karig, *Coal Cars*, 42; Bianculli, *Trains and Technology: The American Railroad in the Nineteenth Century*, vol. 3, 104; *New York Times*, February 19, 1899, August 17, 1909, September 16, 1909.

221. *American Railway Association: Historical Statement, Present Activities*, August 15, 1921; John Richard Felton, "The Utilization and Adequacy of the Freight Car Fleet," *Land Economics* 47 (August 1971): 267–73, at 268–69; Yehuda Grunfeld, "The Effect of the Per Diem Rate on the Efficiency and Size of the American Railroad Freight-Car Fleet," *Journal of Business* 32 (January 1959): 52–73.

222. Karig, *Coal Cars*, 63.

223. White, *The American Railroad Freight Car*, 472, 591–97; Burgess and Kennedy, *Centennial History*, 775–76; Karig, *Coal Cars*, 63–64, 254, 262–63.

224. Al Westerfield, "Billboard Reefers and Other Disasters: How Government Regulation Affected Car Building," in Anthony W. Thompson, ed., *Symposium on Railroad History*, vol. 4 (Wilton, Calif.: Signature Press, 1996), 35–46, at 40.

225. *Railway Age* 66 (June 18, 1919): 1461–66.

226. There is evidence to suggest that in 1877, the Milton Car Company, in Pennsylvania, built a boxcar with an iron or steel underframe for the Empire Line, to the design of Frederick J. Kimball. Because the Empire Line was already operating metal-frame tank cars, it would be a logical next step to apply the same methods to boxcar construction. White, *The American Railroad Freight Car*, 567–98; Gary C. Rauch and Robert L. Johnson, "The XL Box Car and Related Classes," *The Keystone* 33, no. 2 (Summer 2000): 13–25; Al Westerfield, "PRR XL Box Cars and Related Classes," *The Keystone* 33, no. 2 (Summer 2000): 28–43; Burgess and Kennedy, *Centennial History*, 771–72.

227. Ted Culotta, "Essential Freight Cars, 35: The X29 Boxcar: Pt. I," *Railroad Model Craftsman*, January 2007, 90; Culotta, "Essential Freight Cars, 36: The X29 Boxcar: Pt. II," *Railroad Model Craftsman*, February 2007, 90; Gary Rauch and Robert Johnson, "PRR Class X29 Boxcars and Related Classes (X28, X28a, X30, K8)," *The Keystone*, December 1976, 2.

228. Burgess and Kennedy, *Centennial History*, 769–74; Walker D. Hines, *War History of American Railroads* (New Haven, Conn.: Yale University Press, 1928), 275; Rauch and Johnson, "The XL Box Car," 25; *Railway Age* 76 (June 17, 1924): 1661–63.

229. *Poor's Manual of Railroads, 1900*, 670–80.

230. The use of the ton-mile as a performance measure came in part from the efforts of Albert Fink, the Louisville & Nashville Railroad executive who later headed the Joint Executive Committee of the Eastern Trunk Line Association. In the decade or so following the end of the Civil War, Fink had developed the mechanisms of cost accounting, using those statistical measures to augment the somewhat older techniques of financial and capital accounting. Fink had developed four measures of accounting for transportation costs. Two of those—interest charges and the maintenance of bridges, buildings, and the right of way—did not vary according to the volume of business. Station and terminal expenses rose in tandem with traffic levels, but not according to the number of trains that a railroad operated. The most significant category—"Movement Expenses"—depended on the volume of traffic. It was a relatively simple matter to calculate movement expenses as a function of the number of train miles on a particular division, or even on a railroad as a whole. That measure was of limited usefulness, however, as trains rarely operated a full capacity, and as cars often moved heavily laden in one direction and empty in the other. As Fink and other managers emphasized, the most reliable performance measure was the number of tons moved multiplied by the number of miles traveled. The maximization of ton-miles, rather than train-miles, became the goal of a railroad's operating personnel. Likewise, a railroad's costs were best measured by adding together the movement expenses, the station expenses, the maintenance-of-way expenses, and the interest charges, per ton-mile. Chandler, *The Visible Hand*, 115–20.

231. *Poor's Manual of Railroads, 1900*, 675.

232. For an excellent overview of the ton-mile issue, see Usselman, *Regulating Railroad Innovation*, 335–37.

233. *Poor's Manual of Railroads, 1900*, 675.

234. Henry V. Poor, *Manual of the Railroads of the United States for 1874–75* (New York: H. V. Poor, 1874), 340; Henry V. Poor, *Manual of the Railroads of the United States for 1892* (New York: H. V. and H. W. Poor,

1892), 838; *Poor's Manual of the Railroads of the United States*, vol. 13 (New York: H. V. and H. W. Poor, 1897), 587; *Poor's Manual of the Railroads of the United States*, vol. 34 (New York: H. V. and H. W. Poor, 1901), 48, 96, 124, 675.

235. White, *The American Railroad Freight Car*, 12–15; Usselman, *Regulating Railroad Innovation*, 342–43; William Cronon, *Nature's Metropolis: Chicago and the Great West* (New York: W. W. Norton, 1991), 83–92.

236. This situation was true of all of the carriers, not merely the PRR. As transportation economist William Z. Ripley observed in 1912, "The various economies in operation, heavier trainloads and the like, have not since 1906 yielded any greater profit from mere operation, with the ever increasing volume of business. In other words, the increase in the margin between cost of operation and revenue per train mile,—measuring profitableness per unit of movement—has not kept pace with the augmentation of the size of the unit,—the trainload." Ripley, *Railroads: Rates and Regulation*, 99.

237. Charles W. Raymond, "The New York Tunnel Extension of the Pennsylvania Railroad," n.d., ca. 1907, 40, HML, Box 146, folder 9; Burgess and Kennedy, *Centennial History*, 461.

Chapter 14. Regulation

1. William Z. Ripley, *Railroads: Finance and Organization* (New York: Longmans, Green, 1915), 456–57; Gerald Berk, *Alternative Tracks: The Constitution of American Industrial Order, 1865–1917* (Baltimore: Johns Hopkins University Press, 1994), 155.

2. *New York Times*, December 29, 1906.

3. William Bender Wilson, *History of the Pennsylvania Railroad Company, with Plan of Organization, Portraits of Officials and Biographical Sketches*, vol. 2 (New York: Henry T. Coates & Co., 1899), 18, credits Robert Cassat as the first mayor. Leland D. Baldwin, *Pittsburgh: The Story of a City, 1750–1865* (Pittsburgh: University of Pittsburgh Press, 1937), 241, and other sources, correctly list Robinson as the first mayor of Allegheny City, in 1840.

4. In 1877, the partnership became Cassatt & Company. In 1940, Cassatt & Company merged with Merrill, Lynch. John D. Farlin, "Charles E. Merrill: The Father of Main Street Brokerage," *Journal of the North American Management Society* 3 (2008): 3–12. The standard biography of Cassatt is Patricia Talbot Davis, *End of the Line: Alexander J. Cassatt and the Pennsylvania Railroad* (New York: Neale Watson, 1978).

5. *New York Times*, June 18, 1899.

6. Biographical information is from Davis, *End of the Line*, 9–44.

7. Allan Nevins, *Study in Power: John D. Rockefeller, Industrialist and Philanthropist*, vol. 2 (New York: Charles Scribner's Sons, 1953), 305–15; Ron Chernow, *Titan: The Life of John D. Rockefeller, Sr.* (New York: Random House, 1998), 201–2, 212.

8. George H. Burgess and Miles C. Kennedy, *Centennial History of the Pennsylvania Railroad Company, 1846–1946* (Philadelphia: Pennsylvania Railroad, 1949), 455–56.

9. *New York Times*, June 18, 1899.

10. *New York Times*, December 5, 1890, June 18, 1899; Davis, *End of the Line*, 91–102, 114–25.

11. Burgess and Kennedy, *Centennial History*, 455–56.

12. E. M. Boyle to Sereno S. Pratt, December 31, 1906, Pennsylvania Railroad Company Collection, call no. 1807/1810, Hagley Museum and Library, Wilmington, Delaware (hereafter HML), Box 144, folder 33.

13. Manufactured items were next highest, at 20.1 percent of total tonnage, and that traffic was heavily influenced by the output of on-line steel mills, and indirectly by the mineral trade as well. By comparison, agricultural and forest products each accounted for just over 5 percent of tonnage.

14. The PRR's high traffic density also ensured that the railroad labored under a commensurately higher maintenance-of-way expense, per route mile, relative to other carriers. George D. Dixon, "Freight Traffic," n.d., ca. 1905, HML, Box 419, folder 556; William Z. Ripley, *Railroads: Rates and Regulation* (New York: Longmans, Green, and Co., 1912; repr. New York: Arno Press, 1973), 60.

15. Robert H. Large, "The Development of Coal in the State of Pennsylvania and Its Relation to the Earnings of the Pennsylvania Railroad," n.d., ca. 1905, HML, Box 419, folder 556.

16. Carmen DiCiccio, *Coal and Coke in Pennsylvania* (Harrisburg: Pennsylvania Historical and Museum Commission, 1996), 31–32, 62–63.

17. Deposits in Bradford County, in the far north of Pennsylvania, were better served by the Lehigh Valley and other railroads approaching via New York State, while the New York Central and the Erie reached deep into Tioga County.

18. These are commonly accepted names, but there are alternates, including the Mountain Field, north and east of Ebensburg, and the more westerly Black Lick and Indiana Fields. Once past the summit of the Alleghenies, the PRR main line ran through the rich bituminous coal deposits of the vast Windber Field, the Westmoreland Field, the Irwin Gas Field, and—most important of all—the Pittsburgh Field. The Allegheny Valley was proximate to several fields (Butler, Sagamore, Low Grade Division, and Clarion) in Butler, Armstrong, and Clarion Counties. In northern Pennsylvania, the lines that became part of the Western New York & Pennsylvania provided access to the Overmont Field in McKean County. Farther north lay the Snowshoe Field, in Clearfield and Centre Counties, and the Moshannon Field in Clearfield County. For an excellent overview of coalfields in western Pennsylvania, eastern Ohio, and northern West Virginia, see the "Coalfields of the Appalachian Mountains," based on accounts compiled from the *Pittsburgh Post-Gazette* and other sources, available at http://www.coalcampusa.com, accessed on June 22, 2010; and DiCiccio, *Coal and Coke in Pennsylvania*, 2, 11–13. See also Howard N. Eavenson, "The Early History of the Pittsburgh Coal Bed," *Western Pennsylvania History* 22 (September 1939): 165–76, at 165: "During the 179 years in which it has been mined, there has been produced from the Pittsburgh Coal Bed in the four states of Maryland, Pennsylvania, West Virginia, and Ohio a greater value, at mine prices, than has ever been yielded by any single mineral deposit in the world's history."

19. "Pennsylvania Railroad Lines East of Pittsburgh and Erie: Statement Showing Total Quantity of Bituminous Coal Purchased," April 5, 1909, revised March 15, 1910, and December 13, 1911; Samuel Rea, "Fuel Supply Along Conemaugh Division," August 27, 1909, both in HML, Box 135, "Coal Lands"; Joseph T. Lambie, *From Mine to Market: The History of Coal Transportation on the Norfolk and Western Railway* (New York: New York University Press, 1954), 70–71.

20. DiCiccio, *Coal and Coke in Pennsylvania*, 16–17.

21. James M. Swank, *Introduction to a History of Ironmaking and Coal Mining in Pennsylvania* (Philadelphia, 1878), 71.

22. DeHaas report to the Board of Canal Commissioners, January 14, 1837, quoted in Wilson, *History of the Pennsylvania Railroad*, vol. 2, 139–40; Catherine Elizabeth Reiser, *Pittsburgh's Commercial Development, 1800–1850* (Harrisburg: Pennsylvania Historical and Museum Commission, 1951), 54, 194–95, 205–24.

23. PRR Board of Directors (BOD) Minutes, HML, September 28, 1853, 390; Sean P. Adams, *Old Dominion, Industrial Commonwealth: Coal, Politics, and Economy in Antebellum America* (Baltimore: Johns Hopkins University Press, 2004), 172.

24. Herman Haupt, *The Coal Business on the Pennsylvania Railroad: A Communication Addressed to the President, Directors, and Stockholders of*

the Pennsylvania Railroad, on the Cost of Transportation (Philadelphia: T. K. and P. G. Collins, 1857).

25. *Transportation of Coal: Hearings before a Subcommittee of the Committee on Naval Affairs*, United States Congress, 63rd Cong., 3rd sess., 1915, 329.

26. In 1854, Haupt and other PRR principals also incorporated the Allegheny Railroad & Coal Company and the Clearfield Coal & Lumber Company. During the mid-1860s, Thomson, Scott, and other PRR executives established the Foster Coal & Iron Company, largely to provide support for the family of Vice President William B. Foster, Jr., following his untimely death in March 1860. Westmoreland acquired Foster Coal & Iron in 1870. By the late 1800s, the Westmoreland Coal Company was under the control of the Hutchinson family of Philadelphia. DiCiccio, *Coal and Coke in Pennsylvania*, 35; John William Leonard, ed., *Who's Who in Finance and Banking: A Biographical Dictionary of Contemporaries, 1920–1922* (New York: Who's Who, 1922), 351; Evelyn Foster Morneweck, *Chronicles of Stephen Foster's Family*, vol. 2 (Pittsburgh, Pa.: Davis & Warde, 1944), 519.

27. Dan Rottenberg, *In the Kingdom of Coal: An American Family and the Rock That Changed the World* (New York: Routledge, 2003), 34–35.

28. DiCiccio, *Coal and Coke in Pennsylvania*, 35; Frederick Moore Binder, *Coal Age Empire: Pennsylvania Coal and Its Utilization to 1860* (Harrisburg: Pennsylvania Historical and Museum Commission, 1974), 127–28.

29. James A. Ward, *J. Edgar Thomson: Master of the Pennsylvania* (Westport, Conn.: Greenwood Press, 1980), 100–101; John Stirling Fisher and Chase Mellen, *A Builder of the West: The Life of General William Jackson Palmer* (Caldwell, Id.: Caxton Printers, 1939), 24, 50–59.

30. The Westmoreland Coal Company is still in business but ironically no longer operates in Pennsylvania. Binder, *Coal Age Empire*, 38; William Jasper Nicolls, *The Story of American Coals* (Philadelphia: J. B. Lippincott, 1904), 104, 266; Corporate history of the Westmoreland Coal Company, available at http://www.westmoreland.com/about.asp?topic=history, accessed on May 6, 2009.

31. Burgess and Kennedy, *Centennial History*, 107–10.

32. PRR BOD Minutes, March 6, 1861, 13–14, August 21, 1861, 69; Wilson, *History of the Pennsylvania Railroad*, vol. 1, 51.

33. Much of the coal traveled over the Bellefonte & Snow Shoe Railroad. Originally incorporated in 1839, as the Allegheny & Bald Eagle Railroad, Coal & Iron Company, construction lagged for nearly two decades. In 1859, in addition to adopting its new name, the Bellefonte & Snow Shoe completed a link between Snow Shoe and Snow Shoe Intersection (on the Bald Eagle Valley) and assumed operations of the Tyrone & Lock Haven Railroad, which spanned the short distance between the Bald Eagle Valley tracks at Milesburg and the nearby community of Bellefonte. Wilson, *History of the Pennsylvania Railroad*, vol. 1, 206–8; David W. Messer, *Triumph IV: Harrisburg to Altoona, 1846–2001* (Baltimore: Barnard, Roberts and Co., 2001), 191.

34. Wilson, *History of the Pennsylvania Railroad*, vol. 1, 51; Clement Ferdinand Heverly, *History of the Towandas, 1770–1886, Including the Aborigines, Pennamites and Yankees, Together with Biographical Sketches and Matters of General Importance Connected with the County Seat* (Towanda, Pa.: Reporter-Journal Printing Co., 1886), 256–57; PRR BOD Minutes, April 28, 1858, 328, December 8, 1858, 359, June 25, 1862, 191–92.

35. Wilson, *History of the Pennsylvania Railroad*, vol. 1, 51; Charles S. Roberts and Gary W. Schlerf, *Triumph I: Altoona to Pitcairn, 1846–1996* (Baltimore: Barnard, Roberts & Co., 1997), 180.

36. George W. Hilton, *American Narrow Gauge Railroads* (Stanford, Calif.: Stanford University Press, 1990), 485; Roberts, *Triumph IV*, 193, 200.

37. Wilson, *History of the Pennsylvania Railroad*, vol. 1, 51.

38. Henry V. Poor, *Manual of the Railroads of the United States for 1868–69* (New York: H. V. and H. W. Poor, 1868), 229.

39. Henry V. Poor, *Manual of the Railroads of the United States, 1881* (New York: H. V. & H. W. Poor, 1881), 263.

40. DiCiccio, *Coal and Coke in Pennsylvania*, 31–32, 62–63.

41. Richard Burg, "When Empty Return to Windber, P.R.R.," *The Keystone* 19 (August 1986): 7–24, at 7.

42. Berwind, White & Company prospectus, 1874, quoted in National Park Service, Historic American Engineering Record, "Photographs, Written Historical and Descriptive Data, Eureka No. 40, Berwind-White Coal Mining Company," Historic American Engineering Record No. PA-184 (hereafter referred to as HAER), 12.

43. Ibid., 12–13.

44. Ibid., 10–14.

45. Berwind-White officials apparently requested that the PRR pay for the line, known as the Scalp Level Railroad, but the PRR board refused. Instead, the PRR directors agreed to purchase the line (which cost $300,000 to build and another $173,000 to equip), using the revenues derived from the transportation of Berwind-White coal. In 1902, the PRR merged the Scalp Level Railroad with the PRR's South Fork Railroad Company.

46. Margaret M. Mulrooney, *A Legacy of Coal: The Coal Company Towns of Southwestern Pennsylvania* (Washington, D.C.: Historic American Buildings Survey, Historic American Engineering Record, National Park Service, 1989), 51–53, 87; Roberts and Schlerf, *Triumph I*, 208; Lambie, *From Mine to Market*, 81; HAER, 13–14, 17–18.

47. In 1906, however, the ICC had branded such discounts as discriminatory, since they were not available to small shippers. Edward J. Berwind to Alexander J. Cassatt, March 27, 1906, Penn Central Railroad Collection, M.G. 286, Pennsylvania Historical and Museum Commission, Pennsylvania State Archives, Harrisburg (hereafter referred to as PHMC), Cassatt/McCrea Papers, Box 45 (12–1806), folder 55/66.

48. *Transportation of Coal: Hearings before a Subcommittee of the Committee on Naval Affairs*, 110–11, 323; Jim Panza and Richard Burg, "The Berwind Hopper Cars," *Railroad Model Craftsman*, October 1986, 74.

49. The PRR owned a few small soft-coal producers, mainly on Lines West, but their primary function was to provide fuel for steam locomotives and stationary applications, and not for sale.

50. *Report on Discriminations and Monopolies in Coal and Oil*, United States House, 59th Cong., 2nd sess., 1907, 63; John N. Boucher, *History of Westmoreland County, Pennsylvania*, vol. 1 (New York: Lewis Publishing, 1906), 1–5; *Freight: The Shippers' Forum* 5 (June 1906), 309.

51. DeHaas report, 5, 8.

52. Binder, *Coal Age Empire*, 75–84; DiCiccio, *Coal and Coke in Pennsylvania*, 27–28, 39, 74.

53. Frick's association with Mellon began as a result of the Panic of 1873, at a time when the budding coke magnate was desperate for capital. In 1881, while in New York on his honeymoon, Frick met Carnegie and soon joined forces with him. For information on Frick's early career, see Kenneth Warren, *Triumphant Capitalism: Henry Clay Frick and the Industrial Transformation of America* (Pittsburgh: University of Pittsburgh Press, 1996), 1–20.

54. DiCiccio, *Coal and Coke in Pennsylvania*, 67–69.

55. Kenneth Warren, *Wealth, Waste, and Alienation: Growth and Decline in the Connellsville Coke Industry* (Pittsburgh: University of Pittsburgh Press, 2001), 23–28.

56. Warren, *Wealth, Waste, and Alienation*, 26–28.

57. Charles S. Roberts and David W. Messer, *Triumph VIII: Pittsburgh, 1749–2006* (Baltimore: Barnard, Roberts & Co., 2006), 304–6.

58. *Thirty-Seventh Annual Report of the Board of Directors of the Pennsylvania Railroad Company to the Stockholders* (1884), 31–32.

59. Andrew Carnegie to Henry Clay Frick, December 1, 1897, Frick Papers, Frick Art and Historical Center, Pittsburgh, Pennsylvania, quoted in Warren, *Wealth, Waste, and Alienation*, 75.

60. In July 1915, the Monongahela Railroad merged with the Buckhannon & Northern Railroad, forming the Monongahela Rail*way.*

61. In 1926, ownership in the Monongahela Railway was redistributed, with the PRR, the Pittsburgh & Lake Erie, and the B&O each holding a one-third share in the company. Warren, *Wealth, Waste, and Alienation*, 130–31.

62. Roberts, *Triumph VIII*, 30–31. *Trains* 71, no. 9 (September 2011): 56–57 contains a map that depicts this route.

63. Sean Patrick Adams, "Promotion, Competition, Captivity: The Political Economy of Coal," *Journal of Policy History* 18 (2006): 74–95, at 76.

64. The Beech Creek (originally the Beech Creek, Clearfield & South Western Railroad, and reorganized in 1886 as the Beech Creek Railroad) was closely connected to the Vanderbilt interests, and was leased by the NYC in 1890.

65. Lambie, *From Mine to Market*, 82–84.

66. DiCiccio, *Coal and Coke in Pennsylvania*, 55–58, 131–34.

67. Warren, *Wealth, Waste, and Alienation*, 69–70, 100.

68. DiCiccio, *Coal and Coke in Pennsylvania*, 103–4, 135.

69. James Morton Callahan, *The Semi-Centennial History of West Virginia, With Special Articles on Development and Resources* (Wheeling?: The Semi-Centennial Commission of West Virginia, 1913), 184, 353; Philip Mallory Conley, *History of the West Virginia Coal Industry* (Charleston, W.Va.: Education Foundation, 1960), 223–29; Warren, *Wealth, Waste, and Alienation*, 148–49.

70. Warren, *Wealth, Waste, and Alienation*, 148–49.

71. E. G. Campbell, *The Reorganization of the American Railroad System, 1893–1900* (New York: Columbia University Press, 1938), 128–44, 207–14.

72. Huntington eventually relinquished control over the C&O to a consortium of northeastern railroad and financial interests, led by J. P. Morgan and William Kissam Vanderbilt (the son of William Henry Vanderbilt, who had succumbed to a stroke in 1885). They chose Melville E. Ingalls, the president of the NYC-allied Cleveland, Cincinnati, Chicago & St. Louis ("Big Four") Railroad, to head the reorganized Chesapeake & Ohio. Ingalls, along with general manager George W. Stevens, rebuilt the railroad's physical plant, including a new, low-grade line linking Clifton Forge, Virginia, to Richmond.

73. Lambie, *From Mine to Market*, 22, 30–34, 111–33.

74. Ibid., 34–45.

75. Most mines, it should be noted, were quite closely connected to the N&W. While the railroad did not own any coal lands directly, many of its investors—including E. W. Clark & Company—organized the Flat Top Coal Land Association, which controlled most of the land in the regions and leased mining rights to many smaller companies. Such railroad-managed cartels were by no means unique to the N&W. The Chesapeake & Ohio sold directly all of the coal mined along its route. On the Baltimore & Ohio, four mining companies, many of them linked to the railroad's management, controlled nearly 95 percent of total coal shipments. In northern Pennsylvania, the Clearfield Bituminous Coal Corporation regulated price and output levels in the mines along the New York Central's Beech Creek subsidiary. On the Pennsylvania Railroad, the Coal Sales Department was responsible for all coal purchases on Lines East, as well as for coordinating shipments from mines across Pennsylvania. The PRR also depended heavily on the market power of such large shippers as Westmoreland, Berwind-White, and Penn Gas, companies that had a long tradition of close cooperation and even interlocking ownership with the PRR. The Pennsylvania Railroad's executives nonetheless possessed less power over coal production, marketing, and pricing than any of their competitors, largely because of the presence of so many small collieries in southwestern Pennsylvania. The B&O's access to large portions of the Pittsburgh Seam also complicated efforts by PRR managers to control output, rates, and shipments. Lambie, *From Mine to Market*, 47–52, 160.

76. Ibid., 81–86, 135–36.

77. Ibid., 84–110, 161.

78. Mine owners replaced the Seaboard Steam Coal Association with the Bituminous Coal Trade Association, but the new entity made no attempt to make or enforce pooling arrangements.

79. Quotas varied, but the PRR typically received slightly under half of the available tonnage. Lambie, *From Mine to Market*, 164–82.

80. Receivers of the Baltimore & Ohio Railroad to the Chairman of the Interstate Commerce Commission, December 20, 1898, quoted in *Investigation of Railroads, Holding Companies, and Affiliated Companies: Report of the Committee on Interstate Commerce: Railroad Combination in the Eastern Region, Part 1 (Before 1920)*, 76th Cong., 3rd sess. (Washington, D.C.: U.S. Government Printing Office, 1940) (hereafter referred to as "Wheeler Report"), 19 (Exhibit C-8).

81. Wheeler Report, Part 1, 17–19.

82. Large, "The Development of Coal in the State of Pennsylvania."

83. *New York Times*, July 24, 1904.

84. *New York Times*, April 27, 1900, July 24, 1902 (quotes), September 28, 1902, January 12, 1905, December 14, 1905, January 4, 1906, January 7, 1906; Davis, *End of the Line*, 181–82.

85. See, for example, the characterization of Cassatt in Burgess and Kennedy, *Centennial History*, and in such popular accounts as Davis, *End of the Line*, and Jill Jonnes, *Conquering Gotham: a Gilded Age Epic: The Construction of Penn Station and Its Tunnels* (New York: Penguin, 2007). In reality, both Roberts and Frank Thomson were highly capable managers. Thomson, in particular, was largely responsible for the PRR's track and roadbed standards. Both were well suited to the engineering requirements of the late nineteenth century, but Cassatt clearly excelled in his relations with the press, members of Congress, and the public.

86. It should be emphasized that Cassatt was not opposed to rebates, per se. After all, during the 1870s, he had agreed with other PRR executives that rebates were necessary in order to secure the business of Standard Oil—and, unlike his colleagues, he had frankly admitted as much to legislative investigation committees. Years later, as president, he was still willing to authorize rebates in some instances. In December 1901 and January 1902, for example, Interstate Commerce Commission hearings produced evidence to suggest that Cassatt had approved substantial reductions in tariffs on dressed beef between Chicago and tidewater. Cassatt obviously considered that arrangement to be in the PRR's best interest. Rebates on coal traffic were another matter entirely. They eroded the PRR's longstanding dominance in coal transportation and, he believed, had to be stopped. Frank Parsons, *The Heart of the Railroad Problem: The History of Railway Discrimination in the United States, the Chief Efforts at Control and the Remedies Proposed, with Hints from Other Countries* (Boston: Little, Brown, 1906), 77.

87. John B. Thayer testimony, Interstate Commerce Commission Docket 869, at 1834, quoted in Lambie, *From Mine to Market*, 189.

88. Berk, *Alternative Tracks*, 51–60.

89. As political scientist Gerald Berk has observed, "The scope of railroad reorganization went well beyond the temporary reduction of fixed costs to systematic effort to externalize the cost of economic uncertainty

and instability onto outside shareholders." Historian Brian Balough has echoed Berk's comments, asserting that in the matter of receiverships, "Courts provided the tools through which national system builders were able to reduce costs that the market had imposed on their risky ventures without sacrificing management's longer-term ambitions. The government helped to wring the risk out of system building—or at least lower its costs." Less compelling is Berk's suggestion that "Wabash and its children acquainted Americans with a defining feature of the modern corporation: the legal separation of ownership from managerial control." In truth, many carriers—including the PRR—had maintained that separation since the 1850s, well before the Wabash's 1884 receivership. Berk, *Alternative Tracks*, 47–51, 65–72, quotes at 65 and 72; Balogh, *A Government Out of Sight: The Mystery of National Authority in Nineteenth-Century America* (Cambridge: Cambridge University Press, 2009), 336.

90. Berk, *Alternative Tracks*, 62–65.

91. Alfred D. Chandler, Jr., *The Visible Hand: The Managerial Revolution in American Business* (Cambridge, Mass.: Belknap Press of Harvard University Press, 1977), 185–87; Mary A. O'Sullivan, "Finance Capital in Chandlerian Capitalism," *Industrial and Corporate Change* 19 (2010): 549–89, at 566–67. Economic sociologists Frank Dobbin and Timothy J. Dowd link the growing influence of Morgan and other financiers over the railroad industry to the Supreme Court's ruling, in the *Trans-Missouri* case, that any effort by railroads to cooperate on rates and traffic shares would run afoul of the 1890 Sherman Act. As a result, Dobbin and Dowd emphasized, "When railroads abandoned the buying and selling strategies associated with the cartel, in 1897, they embraced the strategies prescribed by the financiers." Morgan and his associates had seen ample evidence of the damage that cutthroat competition (what Dobbin and Dowd refer to as the "predatory model") had done to the railroad industry and, with the cooperative model undermined by the courts, they steered the industry toward a finance model. They provide a compelling argument, and one very much in keeping with the Chandlerian overview. It should be emphasized, however, that bankers were involved in railroad governance even before the Civil War. They often occupied seats on the boards of directors of railroads, and other major American companies, as a means of protecting their own investments as well as those of their clients. Likewise, financiers were mediating rate wars between the PRR and the other eastern trunk lines as early as 1875, well before *Trans-Missouri*. In addition, because Dobbin and Dowd selected as their sample the railroads of Massachusetts, many of which were local or regional carriers of no great consequence, their data underestimated the influence of large and economically powerful railroads like the PRR, with executives who were capable of dictating terms to other lines. Furthermore, New England was unusual in that it was largely closed to outside investors, even though New Englanders were more than willing to invest in railroads throughout the United States—the Philadelphia, Wilmington & Baltimore being an obvious example. Dobbin and Dowd, "The Market That Antitrust Built: Public Policy, Private Coercion, and Railroad Acquisitions, 1825–1922," *American Sociological Review* 65 (October 2000): 631–57. For another perspective on this issue, see Peter Tufano, "Business Failure, Judicial Intervention, and Financial Innovation: Restructuring U.S. Railroads in the Nineteenth Century," *Business History Review* 71 (Spring 1997): 1–40.

92. Richard King Mellon continued to serve on the board of directors of the Penn Central until April 1969. Burgess and Kennedy, *Centennial History*, 786–90.

93. Chandler, *Visible Hand*, 171–74.

94. Ibid., 171; Ripley, *Railroads: Finance and Organization*, 7–10; Berk, *Alternative Tracks*, 69–70.

95. Chandler, *Visible Hand*, 174–75; Berk, *Alternative Tracks*, 155. The 90 percent claim is from John Moody, *The Truth About the Trusts: A Description and Analysis of the American Trust Movement* (New York: Moody Publishing, 1904), 429–50.

96. *New York Times*, September 13, 1899.

97. Wheeler Report, Part 1, 24–26; William Z. Ripley, *Railroads: Finance and Organization*, 417, 474–78.

98. Robert B. Carson, *Main Line to Oblivion: The Disintegration of New York Railroads in the Twentieth Century* (Port Washington, N.Y.: National University Publications, Kennikat Press, 1971), 39–44; Burgess and Kennedy, *Centennial History*, 460–61; Chandler, *The Visible Hand*, 173.

99. Wheeler Report, Part 1, 20–21, 73–78; *New York Times*, July 12, 1914, November 4, 1920; Carson, *Main Line to Oblivion*, 38; Lambie, *From Mine to Market*, 186.

100. The New York banking houses of Kuhn, Loeb & Company and Speyer & Company handled the financial details of the reorganization, but Morgan was the guiding force in the process.

101. Wheeler Report, Part 1, 21–24, 85–91.

102. Ibid., 24.

103. In December 1903, Loree resigned the B&O presidency in order to become president of the Chicago, Rock Island & Pacific Railroad. After that date, the PRR continued to own B&O stock, but had relatively little direct influence on the company's management. Burgess and Kennedy, *Centennial History*, 458–62; Chandler, *Visible Hand*, 173; *New York Times*, June 2, 1901, April 28, 1903.

104. In September 1896, the Norfolk & Western Rail*road* was reorganized as the Norfolk & Western Rail*way*.

105. The four initial PRR directors were Samuel Rea, Sutherland M. Prevost, John P. Green, and James McCrea. The remaining two were W. H. Barnes and N. Parker Shortridge. Many of these individuals also held seats on the boards of the B&O and the C&O, ensuring continuity of oversight.

106. Wheeler Report, Part 1, 21, 79–84; Lambie, *From Mine to Market*, 187–88.

107. Albert J. County to Howard W. Schotter, October 31, 1936, HML, Box 203, folder 1.

108. In 1904, the Tidewater Bituminous Steam Coal Traffic Association became the Bureau of Statistics of the Tidewater Bituminous Steam Coal Traffic, giving the impression that the entity was an information agency, and not a rate-setting arm of the railroads. As PRR vice president John B. Thayer observed, "We can make the most positive statement that that association, so far as the enforcement of percentages was concerned, or the restraint of traffic, in that way fell to the ground; and it continued merely as a statistical bureau in charge of a man without power." *Transportation of Coal: Hearings before a Subcommittee of the Committee on Naval Affairs*, 336; Lambie, *From Mine to Market*, 177–82.

109. "Norfolk & Western Railway: How it has developed under cooperative management with the Pennsylvania Railroad," n.d., HML, Box 203, folder 1.

110. Lambie, *From Mine to Market*, 237–51.

111. The N&W guaranteed the remaining two-thirds, and between 1902 and 1913 made good $2,066,000 in interest payments to Pocahontas Coal & Coke.

112. Lambie, *From Mine to Market*, 237–51.

113. Burgess and Kennedy, *Centennial History*, 459, 526; Chandler, *Visible Hand*, 173; Richard Saunders, Jr., *Merging Lines: American Railroads, 1900–1970* (DeKalb: Northern Illinois University Press, 2001), 30–31; "P.R.R. Consolidations and Leases, etc.," 1923, HML, Box 219, folder 4;

Wood, Struthers & Co., "Norfolk & Western Railway Company: Some Account of the Remarkable Development of This Prosperous Enterprise of the South and Middle West," October 1917, HML, Box 168, folder 14.

114. "Memorandum respecting relations between the Pennsylvania and Norfolk & Western Systems," October 18, 1920, HML, Box 215, folder 14.

115. Samuel Rea to T. Dewitt Cuyler, December 23, 1912, HML, Box 218, folder 14.

116. Campbell, *The Reorganization of the American Railroad System*, 145–60; Maury Klein, *The Great Richmond Terminal: A Study in Businessmen and Business Strategy* (Charlottesville: University Press of Virginia, 1970), 280–84.

117. John B. Mordecai, *A Brief History of the Richmond, Fredericksburg and Potomac Railroad* (Richmond: n.p., 1940), 51–52, 57–59.

118. Burgess and Kennedy, *Centennial History*, 490–91, 498–500, "Career of Samuel Rea, Ninth President of the Pennsylvania Railroad," *Pennsylvania Railroad: Information for the Public and Employes*, October 1925, 10; Wheeler Report, Part 1, 50–51, 101; *New York Times*, September 1, 1901.

119. Wheeler Report, Part 1, 50.

120. Carnegie to Schwab, October 9, 1900, Andrew Carnegie Papers, Library of Congress, vol. 78, quoted in Joseph Frazier Wall, *Andrew Carnegie* (New York: Oxford University Press, 1970), 776–77.

121. David Nasaw, *Andrew Carnegie* (New York: Penguin Press, 2006), 582.

122. Gould's efforts to reach Pittsburgh are described in great detail in Howard V. Worley, Jr., and William N. Poellot, Jr., *The Pittsburgh & West Virginia Railway: The Story of the High and Dry* (Halifax, Pa.: Withers Publishing, 1989), especially 35–78.

123. H. Roger Grant, *"Follow the Flag": A History of the Wabash Railroad Company* (DeKalb: Northern Illinois University Press, 2004), 94–96; Wheeler Report, Part 1, 28–30.

124. From Frederick Lewis Allen, *The Great Pierpont Morgan*, 134, quoted in Wall, *Andrew Carnegie*, 784.

125. Nasaw, *Andrew Carnegie*, 582–88.

126. Wheeler Report, Part 1, 28–32.

127. Ibid.; Grant, *"Follow the Flag,"* 94–105.

128. The Zanesville, Marietta & Parkersburg Railroad, incorporated in December 1901, was to form the Ohio portion of the route.

129. Other sources suggest that "the Pennsylvania was not interested or it was outbid" for the Western Maryland. A connection between the Western Maryland and the Reading, at Shippensburg, Pennsylvania, gave Gould access to Philadelphia and New York. Wheeler Report, Part 1, 36.

130. Carter Goodrich and Harvey H. Segal, "Baltimore's Aid to Railroads: A Study in the Municipal Planning of Internal Improvements," *Journal of Economic History* 13 (Winter 1953): 2–35, at 33–34.

131. To Gould's dismay, B&O officials even refused to forward coal shipments off of the West Virginia Central to the Western Maryland. In June 1904, Gould sued the B&O, and won. In February 1905, the U.S. Circuit Court at Baltimore ordered the B&O to transfer coal shipments off of the West Virginia Central to the Western Maryland, at Cherry Run. The decision also required the B&O to allow the Western Maryland to occupy some segments of the Chesapeake & Ohio Canal right of way in order to construct its extension to Cumberland. Paul J. Westhaeffer, *History of the Cumberland Valley Railroad, 1835–1919* (Falls Church, Va.: Washington Chapter, National Railway Historical Society, 1979), 238–50.

132. Transcript of telephone conversation, May 18, 1901; Green to Cassatt, May 19, 1901, quoted in Wheeler Report, Part 1, 33, 290–91.

133. Wheeler Report, Part 1, 33–34.

134. The June 1879 Butler Amendment to an Army appropriations bill permitted railroads to operate telegraph lines, even if such a privilege had not been specifically granted to them by corporate charter. In return, railroad executives agreed to abide by the terms of the National Telegraph Act of 1866, which, among other provisions, permitted any telegraph company to string wires along any corridor—including railroad lines—that Congress had designated as a national post road. The Butler Amendment thus broke the exclusive right-of-way contracts that Western Union had pioneered. Richard R. John, *Network Nation: Inventing American Telecommunications* (Cambridge, Mass.: Belknap Press of Harvard University Press, 2010), 95–96, 116, 164–70.

135. Julius Grodinsky, *Jay Gould: His Business Career, 1867–1892* (Philadelphia: University of Pennsylvania Press, 1957), 269–87; Christopher H. Sterling, Phyllis W. Bernt, Martin B. H. Weiss, *Shaping American Telecommunications: A History of Technology, Policy, and Economics* (Mahwah, N.J.: Lawrence Erlbaum Associates, 2006), 44–45.

136. George B. Oslin, *The Story of Telecommunications* (Macon, GA: Mercer University Press, 1999), 261.

137. *New York Times*, September 24, 1901, October 19, 1902, May 20, 1903.

138. Nearly a decade later, in December 1912, the Supreme Court ruled that the PRR was not in fact a post road, and that Cassatt had had every right to remove Western Union equipment from PRR property—not that it made much difference, at that point. *New York Times*, May 22, 1903; Grant, *"Follow the Flag,"* 96; Burgess and Kennedy, *Centennial History*, 515–16; Davis, *End of the Line*, 157–61.

139. Quoted in Grant, *"Follow the Flag,"* 96.

140. The quotation is from Davis, *End of the Line*, 159, but the original source is not indicated.

141. The Wabash-Pittsburgh Terminal had gained the right of access to Pittsburgh in February 1903, after several members of the City Council bought shares in the enterprise. The construction of a bridge across the Monongahela River, along with freight and passenger facilities within city limits, remained under debate, until the truce.

142. *New York Times*, January 16, 1904.

143. Grant, *"Follow the Flag,"* 97; Westhaeffer, *History of the Cumberland Valley Railroad*, 250.

144. *New York Times*, January 16, 1904.

145. Wheeler Report, Part 1, 54–56.

146. In June 1905, the NYC interests (working through the Pittsburgh & Lake Erie), the PRR, and the B&O acquired the Little Kanawha Railroad and its associated companies, giving the carriers one hundred thousand acres of coal lands and preventing Gould from resurrecting his transcontinental ambitions. The Wabash emerged from receivership in 1915, followed by the Wheeling & Lake Erie in 1916 and the Wabash-Pittsburgh Terminal Railway (reorganized as the Pittsburgh & West Virginia Railway) in 1917. Gould's Missouri Pacific entered receivership in 1915, and (like the Wabash) was reorganized by Kuhn, Loeb. The Western Pacific also went bankrupt in 1915, and in 1917 Gould lost control over the Denver & Rio Grande. Grant, *"Follow the Flag,"* 105; Wheeler Report, Part 1, 56–59, 70.

147. Between February 1892 and August 1893, the Reading had leased the Lehigh Valley—an arrangement that ended when the Reading went bankrupt. During the Reading's receivership, and following the company's reorganization, the Lehigh Valley was largely controlled by Philadelphia investors, and not by J. P. Morgan and his New York associates. After a series of purchases in 1903 and 1904, the Lake Shore & Michigan Southern; the Erie; the Delaware, Lackawanna & Western; the Reading; and the

Jersey Central jointly owned slightly less than 30 percent of the Lehigh Valley's outstanding stock.

148. Wheeler Report, Part 1, 43–44, 93–95.

149. Hamilton Twombly and the Vanderbilts were also concerned at the high price of Reading Company stock.

150. Alexander J. Cassatt to William K. Vanderbilt, October 25, 1902, HML, Box 217, folder 12.

151. *New York Times*, July 19, 1902; Wheeler Report, Part 1, 45–50.

152. Alexander J. Cassatt to William K. Vanderbilt, October 25, 1902; Vanderbilt to Cassatt, October 29, 1902 (quote); Cassatt to Vanderbilt, November 1, 1902; Vanderbilt to Cassatt, November 5, 1902; Vanderbilt to Cassatt, November 10, 1902; Cassatt to George F. Baer, November 25, 1902; "Memorandum of Purchase of Reading Company's Stocks," July 21, 1927; all in HML, Box 217, folder 12; Burgess and Kennedy, *Centennial History*, 460; *New York Times*, January 9, 1903; Wheeler Report, Part 1, 97–100.

153. *Baltimore Herald*, January 9, 1903 (quote); Wheeler Report, Part 1, 45–50.

154. Between 1866 and 1884, iron ore rates on the Great Lakes had declined from $6.00 per ton to $1.35 per ton, thanks to improvements in shipping and cargo handling methods, while shipments had risen from 278,796 tons to 2,518,693 tons in 1884. By the early 1880s, mining engineers had discovered and were beginning to develop the massive iron ore deposits in the Mesabi Range, in northern Minnesota. 1886, a consortium of investors that included John D. Rockefeller, Marshall Field, and Cyrus McCormick acquired large reserves in the Mesabi Range. The consortium soon negotiated a delivery agreement with Andrew Carnegie, president of the Carnegie Steel Company. In 1897, Rockefeller organized the Bessemer Steamship Company to fulfill the terms of the contract. Carnegie, rather than depend on the Bessemer Company, incorporated his own carrier, the Pittsburgh Steamship Company, the following year. The two firms soon operated more than twenty massive ore boats—by far the largest vessels that had yet operated on the Great Lakes. The older, steam-powered unloaders could not keep pace with these massive vessels, and in 1899 George H. Hulett worked with the Carnegie Steel Company to attack that reverse salient, developing the Hulett unloader. Within a decade, a ton of iron ore could traverse a thousand miles across the Great Lakes for seventy-eight cents. Lake Carriers' Association, "History of the Iron Ore Trade," *Annual Report of the Lake Carriers' Association, 1910* (Detroit, Mich.: P. N. Bland, 1911); George G. Tunell, "Lake Transportation and the Iron-Ore Industry," *Journal of Political Economy* 5 (December 1896): 23–39.

155. Josephus N. Larned, *A History of Buffalo, Delineating the Evolution of the City*, vol. 1 (New York: Progress of Empire State Co., 1911), 272–86; Warren, *Triumphant Capitalism*, 186–87, 196–97.

156. Paul V. Pietrak, Joseph G. Streamer, and James A. Van Brocklin, *The History of the Western New York & Pennsylvania Railway Company and Its Predecessors and Successors* (Hamburg, N.Y.: s.n. 2000), 2(1)–2(7), 4(1); Charles S. Roberts and David W. Messer, *Triumph VII: Harrisburg to the Lakes, Wilkes-Barre, Oil City and Red Bank* (Baltimore: Barnard, Roberts and Co., 2004), 250–51. Also useful is the "Corporate Genealogy: Western New York & Pennsylvania," maintained by Robert T. Netzlof, based on Interstate Commerce Commission valuation reports, at http://rnetzlof.pennsyrr.com/corphist/wny_p.html.

157. Pietrak, Streamer, and Van Brocklin, *The Western New York & Pennsylvania Railway Company*, 4(1)–4(2); John M. Gresham, ed., *Biographical and Portrait Cyclopedia of Fayette County, Pennsylvania* (Chicago: John M. Gresham & Co., 1889), 511.

158. The constituent companies involved in the 1868 mergers included the Oil Creek Railroad, the Warren & Franklin Railway, the Farmers Railroad, and the Reno Railroad.

159. The New York Central developed the route under the aegis of a Pennsylvania corporation, the Cross Cut Railroad (incorporated in May 1864), and its New York counterpart, the Buffalo & Oil Creek Cross Cut Railroad (incorporated in July 1865). In October 1866, the New York company leased its Pennsylvania connection and soon completed a line between Corry, Pennsylvania, and Brocton, New York—and a connection with the Buffalo & Erie Railroad (after 1869 the Lake Shore & Michigan Southern Railway) to Buffalo. The Buffalo & Oil Creek Cross Cut was reorganized into the Buffalo, Corry & Pittsburgh Railroad, but it went bankrupt and was liquidated in December 1872. The following January, the Allegheny Valley interests acquired the property, retaining it until 1879. At that time, the New York portion of the line (the original Buffalo & Oil Creek Cross Cut) became the Dunkirk, Chautauqua Lake & Pittsburgh Railroad, while the Pennsylvania portion (the former Cross Cut) became the Corry & State Line Railroad. By May 1879, these two companies had merged to form the Buffalo, Chautauqua Lake & Pittsburgh Railway.

160. The consolidation also incorporated several smaller carriers, including the Salamanca, Bradford & Allegheny River Railroad; the Salamanca, Bradford & Allegheny River Railroad Company of New York; and the Titusville & Oil City Railway. See "Pennsylvania Railroad Chautauqua Branch," Western New York Railroad Archive, http://wnyrails.org/railroads/prr/prr_chaut.htm, accessed on June 22, 2010.

161. Owing largely to financial problems, construction crews did not reach Stoneboro until 1874. South of New Castle, the line depended on the New Castle & Beaver Valley Railroad (leased by the Pittsburgh, Fort Wayne & Chicago in 1865) and the Fort Wayne proper to reach Pittsburgh. The larger problem lay to the east and north of Stoneboro, as the only connection with Oil City consisted of the tracks of the Jamestown & Franklin Railroad (part of the Lake Shore & Michigan Southern, and affiliated with the New York Central). The Seligman and Clark, Post, and Martin interests proposed a parallel line, the Oil City & Chicago Railroad, to close the gap, but they never completed the project.

162. Pietrak, Streamer, and Van Brocklin, *The Western New York & Pennsylvania Railway Company*, 3(18)–3(22)–3(25), 4(2)–4(3).

163. In January 1881, a merger between the Buffalo, Pittsburgh & Western and the Salamanca; the Bradford & Allegheny River Railroad; and the Titusville & Oil City Railway formed the Buffalo, Pittsburgh & Western Railroad. Roberts and Messer, *Triumph VII*, 253–54; Pietrak, Streamer, and Van Brocklin, *The Western New York & Pennsylvania Railway Company*, 4(2).

164. The Rochester, Nunda & Pennsylvania Railroad was affiliated with two other companies, the Rochester, Nunda & Pennsylvania Extension Railroad and the Northern Extension of the Rochester, Nunda & Pennsylvania Railroad.

165. Pietrak, Streamer, and Van Brocklin, *The Western New York & Pennsylvania Railway Company*, 5(1)–5(3); Roberts and Messer, *Triumph VII*, 254.

166. The BR&P connected with the NYC at Rochester, and with the West Shore at Genesee Junction, a short distance to the south. Roberts and Messer, *Triumph VII*, 254–55; Pietrak, Streamer, and Van Brocklin, *The Western New York & Pennsylvania Railway Company*, 3(26), 5(4)–5(11).

167. Pietrak, Streamer, and Van Brocklin, *The Western New York & Pennsylvania Railway Company*, 2(8)–2(9).

168. There were actually two companies, the Western New York & Pennsylvania Railroad of New York and the Western New York & Pennsylvania Railroad of Pennsylvania. They were soon combined into one corporate entity.

169. Pietrak, Streamer, and Van Brocklin, *The Western New York & Pennsylvania Railway Company*, 4(4)–4(5).

170. *New York Times*, February 15, 1902; American Iron and Steel Association, *The Iron and Steel Works of the United States*, 15th ed. (Philadelphia: Allen, Lane & Scott, 1902), 86.

171. In May 1872, the Northern Central acquired outright control over the Elmira, Jefferson & Canandaigua Rail Road and the Chemung Railroad, removing them from the Erie's influence.

172. Following the cancellation of the 1863 lease three years later, the PRR did not again obtain direct access to Buffalo and Rochester until 1900, when it purchased a controlling interest in the Western New York and Pennsylvania Railway. Burgess and Kennedy, *Centennial History*, 422–23, 482–87; Wilson, *History of the Pennsylvania Railroad*, vol. 1, 246–48; Robert L. Gunnarsson, *The Story of the Northern Central Railway, from Baltimore to Lake Ontario* (Sykesville, Md.: Greenberg, 1991), 83–91.

173. Gunnarsson, *Northern Central Railway*, 105.

174. In 1886, the PRR and the Northern Central oversaw the consolidation of the Elmira, Jefferson & Canandaigua; the Sodus Bay & Southern; and the Chemung Railroad to form the Elmira & Lake Ontario Railroad. In 1913, the PRR leased the Northern Central for ninety-nine years, with the Northern Central continuing to exercise sole ownership of all of the stock of the Elmira & Lake Ontario. Roberts and Messer, *Triumph VII*, 29; Wilson, *History of the Pennsylvania Railroad*, vol. 1, 246–48, 271–74; J. Elfreth Watkins, *Pennsylvania Railroad Company, 1846–1896, in its Relation to the Pennsylvania State Canals and Railroads and the Consolidated System East and West of Pittsburgh* (unpublished ms., 1896, original at the Smithsonian Institution, with microfilm copies at HML and PHMC, with an additional microfilm copy in the author's possession, hereafter referred to as the Watkins History), vol. 2, "Iron Ore and Coal Trade of the Lakes," 77.

175. Lambie, *From Mine to Market*, 72, 180; Ripley, *Railroads: Rates and Regulation*, 435–36.

176. Burgess and Kennedy, *Centennial History*, 461.

177. John P. Green, "Financing the Pennsylvania Railroad," n.d., ca. 1905, HML, Box 419, folder 556.

178. In 1905, the PRR's investments in the community of interest included the following (the first number is the total capitalization of the company; the second number is PRR holdings): B&O preferred ($59,973,800; $21,480,000); B&O common ($124,558,000; $30,293,300); C&O common ($62,799,100; $10,130,000); N&W preferred ($22,000,000; $5,500,000); N&W common ($64,469,200; $20,330,000).

179. The Pennsylvania Railroad Company, *Fifty-Sixth Annual Report of the Board of Directors to the Stockholders, for the Year 1902* (March 1903), 26.

180. Historian Richard J. Orsi has demonstrated the extent to which Norris—and many subsequent authors—misinterpreted the 1880 Mussel Slough incident, to the detriment of the Southern Pacific. Frank Norris, *The Octopus: A California Story* (Garden City, N.Y.: Doubleday, 1901); Orsi, *Sunset Limited: The Southern Pacific Railroad and the Development of the American West, 1850–1930* (Berkeley: University of California Press, 2005), esp. 92–104.

181. The various chapters had appeared earlier, in serial form, in *McClure's* magazine. Ida M. Tarbell, *The History of the Standard Oil Company* (New York: McClure, Phillips & Co., 1904).

182. See, in particular, the writings of Charles Francis Adams and Louis Brandeis, as well as Thomas K. McCraw, *Prophets of Regulation: Charles Francis Adams, Louis D. Brandeis, James M. Landis, Alfred E. Kahn* (Cambridge, Mass.: Belknap Press of Harvard University Press, 1984), 1–142, and Herbert Hovenkamp, "Regulatory Conflict in the Gilded Age: Federalism and the Railroad Problem," *Yale Law Journal* 97 (May 1988): 1017–72, at 1020–26; and Stephen Skowronek, *Building a New American State: The Expansion of National Administrative Capacities, 1877–1920* (Cambridge: Cambridge University Press, 1982).

183. The best-known proponent of the capture thesis is undoubtedly Gabriel Kolko, in *Railroads and Regulation, 1876–1916* (Princeton, N.J.: Princeton University Press, 1965). Kolko is correct in his assertion that railroad executives (including many PRR officials) attempted to shape the contours of the regulatory state, and that some aspects of regulation benefited the railroads. However, Kolko did not acknowledge that the railroads were one of many competing interest groups that together affected the shape of regulatory policy. Nor does he admit that regulations that benefited the railroads could also prove constructive for American society as a whole, or that the railroad executives possessed valid economic reasons (as opposed to stereotypical "robber-baron" Machiavellianism) for pursuing their policies. Essentially, as Herbert Hovenkamp has observed, "In Kolko's mind, every dispute became pure politics. *Railroads and Regulation* is a book about railroad lobbying, not about railroad economics." Hovenkamp, "Regulatory Conflict," 1024. Gerald Berk, with his emphasis on "liberal positivism," would seem to fall into the capture school as well, not so much because railroaders dictated regulatory policy to the ICC, but because they set the language through which those policies would be discussed. "By early in the new century," Berk has suggested, "the ICC had capitulated to the terms of the debate laid down by the railroads and the Supreme Court." In other words, railroaders and a conservative court had deemphasized discussions of economic fairness, replacing them with an insistence that restrictive ICC rate regulations were confiscatory and interfered with constitutional property rights. Berk, *Alternative Tracks*, 155–56.

184. McCraw, *Prophets of Regulation*, 44.

185. PRR officials were certainly sympathetic to Elkins's legislative agenda. In 1902, for example, fourth vice president Samuel Rea requested that U.S. attorney general Philander C. Knox control rates in order to protect the public interest. Knox's response, reflecting the previous fifteen years of judicial interpretations of the 1887 Act to Regulate Commerce, was that the federal government had precious little authority in the matter, and that new legislation might well be necessary.

186. *New York Times*, January 5, 1911; Skowronek, *Building a New American State*, 250.

187. *Railroad Gazette* 34 (March 21, 1902): 208.

188. *New York Times*, March 26, 1903.

189. The imposition of fines replaced the earlier sanction of unjustment (that is, of refunding to aggrieved shippers the difference between a just rate and the rate that they actually paid), as the older system had proven utterly unworkable. The Elkins Act also repealed the option of imprisonment as a sanction, a provision that had been added in 1889. Ripley, *Railroads: Rates and Regulation*, 458.

190. Hovenkamp, "Regulatory Conflict," 1067; Skowronek, *Building a New American State*, 250; Ripley, *Railroads: Rates and Regulation*, 207, 493–94.

191. Parsons, *The Heart of the Railroad Problem*, 111.

192. Elkins quoted in ibid., 111; Kolko, *Railroads and Regulation*, 94–101, 117; James W. Ely, *Railroads and American Law* (Lawrence: University Press of Kansas, 2002), 225.

193. Ripley, *Railroads: Rates and Regulation*, 185–209.

194. Skowronek, *Building a New American State*, 250–51.

195. Ripley, *Railroads: Rates and Regulation*, 42–43, 411, 488.

196. *Poor's Manual* lists the 1888 and 1899 numbers as the total of "Freight, Gondola" and "Freight, Coal" cars. Naturally, gondolas had uses other than the carriage of coal, so it is impossible to know precisely how many cars were in coal service at any given time. The 1905 figure (125,579) includes 42,662 cars on the Lines West of Pittsburgh and Erie. The PRR's Susquehanna Coal Company owned an additional 1,397 cars, assigned to anthracite service. *Poor's Manual of the Railroads of the United States*, vol.

33 (New York: H. V. and H. W. Poor, 1900), 669; *Transportation of Coal: Hearings before a Subcommittee of the Committee on Naval Affairs*, 1915, 357.

197. Large, "The Development of Coal in the State of Pennsylvania," 7.

198. Prior to 1906, the two halves of the PRR system employed somewhat different mechanisms for allocating cars. As the railroad's superintendent of freight transportation observed, "The system of rating mines west of Pittsburgh is based exclusively on capacity to ship . . . while the system east of Pittsburgh is based partly upon ability to ship . . . and partly on the mining capacity." On Lines East, where most coal production occurred, PRR officials determined the capacity of each mine, expressed as a percentage of total coal output on each operating division. Mines received a comparable percentage of available cars, with monthly reports suggesting instances where quotas should be reassessed. The system was somewhat different on Lines West, where coal composed a smaller portion of total freight tonnage. Personnel on each division forwarded to the general superintendent a daily report of car requests and car availability. Every mine received a tonnage rating, based on the average of three days' worth of maximum possible output. Train conductors were responsible for delivering available cars to mines, proportional to their tonnage rating, and relaying the number of cars delivered to the division trainmaster. The trainmaster also received daily reports from the mine owners, indicating the number of cars that had been left on their sidings—information that enabled the trainmaster to verify the information that the conductors had provided and to prevent those conductors from accepting bribes to take cars from one mine's quota and leave them on another mine's sidings. Each week, the division superintendents forwarded car supply information to the general superintendent of freight transportation, who was responsible for determining that allotment percentages were roughly equal across each division. Every two weeks, PRR officials prepared a summary report to ensure that each mine continued to receive its established quota of hopper cars. R. M. Patterson to James McCrea, PHMC, Cassatt/McCrea Papers, Box 45 (12–1806), folder 55/66. Patterson suggested that "to have divisions so closely inter-related as those of our Lines East and West of Pittsburgh on a different basis for the distribution of coal cars is, in my judgment, unwise, and I may add that, as a result of this investigation, lack of uniformity can be advocated neither from the standpoint of differences in conditions nor from that of the difficulty in both getting together on the same basis." Large, "The Development of Coal in the State of Pennsylvania," 7; James J. Turner to James McCrea, February 28, 1907, PHMC, Cassatt/McCrea Papers, Box 45 (12–1806), folder 55/66.

199. *Transportation of Coal: Hearings before a Subcommittee of the Committee on Naval Affairs*, 368.

200. As partial compensation for the equipment cost, the PRR provided a rebate of six mills per ton-mile for all coal shipped in privately owned cars. This concession did not cover the mines' full cost, however, and mine owners regarded the difference as an expense necessary to secure adequate car supplies. Burg, "When Empty," 18.

201. Rottenburg, *In the Kingdom of Coal*, 34–35; *Poor's Manual of Railroads for 1868–69*, 229.

202. Large, "The Development of Coal in the State of Pennsylvania," 7. Large's numbers are supported by ICC figures, indicating 125,579 PRR cars (Lines East and West) and 26,102 private-owner cars. *Transportation of Coal: Hearings before a Subcommittee of the Committee on Naval Affairs*, 357.

203. In encouraging Berwind-White, the Keystone Coal & Coke Company, and other large shippers to buy their own hopper cars, Cassatt was endeavoring to shift the capital cost of the new equipment from the PRR to its shippers. At the same time, because he could bundle the PRR's car orders with those from the coal companies, Cassatt could obtain more favorable terms from hopper car manufacturers. Edward J. Berwind to Alexander J. Cassatt, March 27, 1906, PHMC, Cassatt/McCrea Papers, Box 45 (12–1806), folder 55/66.

204. *New York Times*, June 13, 1906, June 20, 1906; Panza and Burg, "The Berwind Hopper Cars," 74–76.

205. *Transportation of Coal: Hearings before a Subcommittee of the Committee on Naval Affairs*, 1915, 370.

206. *New York Times*, June 8, 1906.

207. *New York Times*, April 11, 1906.

208. *Transportation of Coal: Hearings before a Subcommittee of the Committee on Naval Affairs*, 358–59, 362.

209. Kolko, *Railroads and Regulation*, 102–7.

210. Skowronek, *Building a New American State*, 255; Kolko, *Railroads and Regulation*, 107–16.

211. Kolko, *Railroads and Regulation*, 114–20, 129.

212. *New York Times*, May 19, 1906; James Creelman, "All Is Not Damned," *Pearson's Magazine* 15 (June 1906): 543–54, quotation at 551–52.

213. *New York Times*, January 13, 1905, February 5, 1905; Davis, *End of the Line*, 176–77.

214. Kolko, *Railroads and Regulation*, 128–31.

215. Skowronek, *Building a New American State*, 255–56.

216. *New York Times*, January 31, 1906.

217. *New York Times*, February 7, 1906.

218. *New York Times*, February 24, 1906.

219. *New York Times*, February 9, 1906 (quote); Kolko, *Railroads and Regulation*, 136–37.

220. *Congressional Record*, February 12, 1906, 2428.

221. *New York Times*, February 13, 1906.

222. *New York Times*, March 8, 1906.

223. *New York Times*, March 7, 1906

224. *New York Times*, April 6, 1906, April 11, 1906, April 12, 1906 (quote).

225. *New York Times*, April 14, 1906, May 19, 1906, May 25, 1906, *Philadelphia Public Ledger*, May 17, 1906, May 18, 1906.

226. *New York Times*, April 14, 1906.

227. *New York Times*, May 19, 1906 (quote), May 25, 1906.

228. The Patton family was related to Tom Scott, by marriage, and had invested in coal and iron development in central Pennsylvania. The family contributed their name to the town of Patton, Pennsylvania, home of my paternal grandparents.

229. *New York Times*, May 24, 1906.

230. *New York Times*, May 17, 1906, May 25, 1906.

231. Quoted in Thomas Latimer Kibler, *The Commodities' Clause: A Treatise on the Development and Enactment of the Commodities' Clause and its Construction When Applied to Inter-State Railroads Engaged in the Coal Industry* (Washington, D.C.: John Byrne & Co., 1916), 58.

232. *New York Times*, May 25, 1906.

233. *Philadelphia Public Ledger*, May 18, 1906.

234. *New York Times*, May 17, 1906, May 25, 1906.

235. *New York Times*, June 8, 1906.

236. Davis, *End of the Line*, 184.

237. *New York Times*, May 17, 1906, June 4, 1906.

238. *New York Times*, June 4, 1906.

239. *New York Times*, June 7, 1906, June 8, 1906 (quote).

240. *New York Times*, May 19, 1906 ("Gifts"), May 25, 1906 ("Huff"); *Philadelphia Public Ledger*, May 18, 1906 ("almost everything").

241. PRR BOD Minutes, July 2, 1906, 214–17, July 9, 1906, 218–19.

242. *New York Times*, June 9, 1906.

243. *New York Times*, June 4, 1906.

244. *New York Times*, June 8, 1906.

245. *New York Times*, July 8, 1906.

246. *New York Times*, June 4, 1906.

247. Kolko, *Railroads and Regulation*, 136–44.

248. Also in 1897, the Supreme Court, in *ICC v. Cincinnati, New Orleans & Texas Pacific Railway*, 167 U.S. 479, had ruled that the determination of rates was a legislative rather than an administrative function.

249. Kolko, *Railroads and Regulation*, 127–51; Ripley, *Railroads: Rates and Regulation*, 472.

250. Ari A. Hoogenboom and Olive Hoogenboom, *A History of the ICC: From Panacea to Palliative* (New York: Norton, 1976), 53, 55, 59; Ely, *Railroads and American Law*, 226–27; McCraw, *Prophets of Regulation*, 59; Kolko, *Railroads and Regulation*, 151–52.

251. John P. Green memorandum, n.d., ca. November 1906, quoted in Wheeler Report, Part 1, 63 (Exhibit C-103).

252. In September 1906, the PRR purchased an additional $10.7 million in B&O stock. Kuhn, Loeb sold the PRR's stake in the B&O to the Oregon Short Line Railroad, a subsidiary of the Union Pacific. In 1913, in an arrangement brokered by Kuhn, Loeb & Company, the PRR traded its remaining B&O investments for stock in the Southern Pacific. The Supreme Court had ruled in December 1912 that the combined ownership of the Union Pacific and the Southern Pacific (part of the Harriman System) violated the Sherman Act, and ordered the former railroad to dispose of its investments in the latter. The Southern Pacific was certainly not a competitor of the PRR, and as it did not connect with the PRR, it was not likely to direct much traffic to the railroad. Instead, the PRR saw the Southern Pacific as a sound investment, one that was likely to yield substantial dividends. In addition, PRR executives were understandably concerned that, if they did not agree to the trade, the Supreme Court might well order them to divest the PRR's investments in the B&O. In 1918 the PRR sold nearly half of its investment in the Southern Pacific, then worth slightly more than $32 million. As a result of its Southern Pacific holdings, the PRR found itself in the oil business after the SP distributed the stock of its Pacific Oil Company subsidiary as a dividend. In 1913, the Justice Department argued that the continued B&O and NYC control of the Reading was a violation of the Sherman and Clayton Acts. However, both companies retained most of their Reading holdings. Wheeler Report, Part 1, 63–67, 90–91, 100; PRR BOD Minutes, July 2, 1906, 217–18, July 9, 1906, 219–20; "Southern Pacific Company Stock Held by the Pennsylvania System," January 11, 1919, HML, Box 215, folder 14; PRR Treasury Department, "Exchange of B. & O. Stock for Southern Pacific Co," September 24, 1937, HML, Box 219, folder 6; *New York Times*, June 26, 1906, July 25, 1906, September 4, 1906.

253. Wheeler Report, Part 1, 66–67, 82–84.

254. *New York Times*, June 25, 1906.

255. *New York Times*, September 23, 1906, September 25, 1906, October 28, 1906, October 29, 1906, December 23, 1906, December 29, 1906 (quote); Davis, *End of the Line*, 195–98.

256. *New York Times*, February 14, 1907.

257. *Hillsdale Coal & Coke Company v. Pennsylvania Railroad Company*, 19 ICC 356 (1910). *New York Times*, June 22, 1906, June 23, 1906, September 7, 1906; Lambie, *From Mine to Market*, 215, 231.

258. Edward J. Berwind to Alexander J. Cassatt, March 27, 1906, PHMC, Cassatt/McCrea Papers, Box 45 (12–1806), folder 55/66.

259. *Railroad Commission of Ohio v. Hocking Valley Railway Company*, 12 ICC 398 (1907), and *Traer v. Chicago & Alton Railroad Company*, 13 ICC 451 (1908). The Supreme Court upheld the "Hocking Valley—Traer Rule" in *Interstate Commerce Commission v. Illinois Central Railroad Company*, 215 U.S. 452 (1910), and in the *Assigned Car Cases*, 274 U.S. 564 (1927).

260. Al Westerfield, "Billboard Reefers and Other Disasters: How Government Regulations Affected Car Building," in Anthony W. Thompson, ed., *Symposium on Railroad History*, vol. 4 (Wilton, Calif.: Signature Press, 1996), 35–46, at 36–37.

261. George V. Massey to James McCrea, September 24, 1908, PHMC, Cassatt/McCrea Papers, Box 45 (12–1806), folder 55/66.

262. William Wallace Atterbury to James McCrea, October 26, 1909, PHMC, Cassatt/McCrea Papers, Box 45 (12–1806), folder 55/66.

263. *Pennsylvania Railroad Company v. Puritan Coal Mining Company*, 237 U.S. 121 (1915); *Pennsylvania Railroad Company v. W. F. Jacoby & Company*, 242 U.S. 89 (1916); *Pennsylvania Railroad Company v. Clark Brothers Coal Mining Company*, 238 U.S. 456 (1915).

264. E.A.S. Clarke to James McCrea, September 4, 1912, PHMC, Cassatt/McCrea Papers, Box 45 (12–1806), folder 55/66.

265. William E. O'Connell, Jr., "The Development of the Private Railroad Freight Car, 1830–1966," *Business History Review* 44 (Summer 1920): 190–209, 203; Panza and Burg, "The Berwind Hopper Cars," 76; Burg, "When Empty," 20.

266. Isaac J. Wistar to Samuel Rea, June 12, 1899, HML, Box 135, "Coal Lands."

267. Wistar to Rea, February 17, 1899, HML, Box 135, "Coal Lands."

268. Rea to James McCrea, February 17, 1909, PHMC, Cassatt/McCrea Papers, Box 52 (12–1813), folder 76/12.

269. Rea to Wistar, February 6, 1899; Max Riebenack to Rea, May 15, 1899; Rea to John P. Green, May 23, 1899; Rea to Wistar, June 5, 1899; Morris Williams to Wistar, June 9, 1899; all in HML, Box 135, "Coal Lands"; *Decisions of the Interstate Commerce Commission of the United States*, vol. 35: *June, 1915 to July, 1915* (Washington, D.C.: U.S. Government Printing Office, 1915), 244–45, 320–22; "Anthracite coal business, year 1906," PHMC, Cassatt/McCrea Papers, Box 52 (12–1813), folder 72/16.

270. Interstate Commerce Commission v. Chesapeake & Ohio Railway Company, *128* Fed. 59 (1904); *New York, New Haven & Hartford Railroad Company v. Interstate Commerce Commission*, 200 U.S. 361 (1906).

271. *United States v. Delaware & Hudson Company, et al.*, 213 U.S. 366 (1909); Lambie, *From Mine to Market*, 256–58.

272. Morris Williams to John B. Thayer, December 5, 1907, PHMC, Cassatt/McCrea Papers, Box 52 (12–1813), folder 72/16; Samuel Rea to James McCrea, March 27, 1911, HML, Box 135, "Coal Lands" (quote).

273. Prior to the sale, the board merged the various anthracite companies into the Susquehanna Coal Company, which had for years coordinated their production and marketing efforts.

274. *United States v. Lehigh Valley Railroad Company*, 220 U.S. 257 (1911); "Decision of United States Supreme Court in the Lehigh Valley R.R. Case," April 4, 1911; PRR BOD Minutes, September 24, 1913, 86, September 26, 1917, 144–45; Samuel Rea to H. Tatnall, February 18, 1911; HML, Box 135; *New York Times*, September 27, 1913, July 14, 1914; *New York Sun*, April 4, 1911; Eliot Jones, *The Anthracite Coal Combination in the United States, with Some Account of the Early Development of the Anthracite Industry* (Cambridge, Mass.: Harvard University Press, 1914), 210–11.

275. Cattle Raisers *Association of* Texas v. Missouri, Kansas & Texas *Railway* Company 12 ICC 1 (1906), quoted in Ripley, *Railroads: Rates and Regulation*, 491.

276. Richard S. Tedlow, *Keeping the Corporate Image: Public Relations and Business, 1900–1950* (Greenwich, Conn.: JAI Press, 1979), 18.

277. *The Independent*, February 2, 1893, quoted in Karen Miller Russell and Carl O. Bishop, "Understanding Ivy Lee's Declaration of Principles: U.S. Newspaper and Magazine Coverage of Publicity and Press Agentry, 1865–1904," *Public Relations Review* 35 (2009): 91–101, quote at 96.

278. Ripley, *Railroads: Rates and Regulation*, 496–98; Mark Aldrich, "Public Relations and Technology: The 'Standard Railroad of the World' and the Crisis in Railroad Safety, 1897–1916," *Pennsylvania History* 74 (Winter 2007): 74–104, at 85.

279. Creelman, "All Is Not Damned," 543–54.

280. "Inside with the Publishers," *Pearson's Magazine*, April 1907, 477.

281. Ibid.

282. For example, see Jonnes, *Conquering Gotham*, which characterizes Cassatt and the PRR as noble warriors fighting against political corruption in New York.

283. *New York Times*, June 9, 1906, June 11, 1906, June 17, 1906; *Wall Street Journal*, June 29, 1906.

284. *Washington Post*, August 24, 1902, quoted in Russell and Bishop, "Declaration of Principles," 96.

285. Russell and Bishop, "Declaration of Principles," 91–101; Marvin N. Olasky, "Ivy Lee: Minimizing Competition Through Public Relations," *Public Relations Quarterly* 32 (Fall 1987): 9–15; Burton St. John III, "The Case for Ethical Propaganda within a Democracy: Ivy Lee's Successful 1913–1914 Railroad Rate Campaign," *Public Relations Review* 32 (2006): 221–28.

286. Aldrich, "Public Relations and Technology," 83–85.

287. Michael Schudson, *Discovering the News: A Social History of American Newspapers* (New York: Basic Books, 1981), 134–35; Shirley Harrison and Kevin Moloney, "Comparing Two Public Relations Pioneers: American Ivy Lee and British John Elliot," *Public Relations Review* 30 (June 2004): 205–15; Karen Miller Russell and Carl O. Bishop, "Understanding Ivy Lee's Declaration of Principles: U.S. Newspaper and Magazine Coverage of Publicity and Press Agentry, 1865–1904," *Public Relations Review* 35 (June 2009): 91–101; Tedlow, *Keeping the Corporate Image*, 9–10.

288. According to historian of journalism Ray E. Hiebert, Lee's first service to the PRR came in the aftermath of a passenger train derailment at Gap, Pennsylvania. Breaking with traditional railroad practice, Lee insisted that the PRR release the full details of the accident. A near-simultaneous incident on the New York Central produced a much more guarded response from that railroad's executives, who stonewalled media representatives. Reporters accordingly heaped praise on the PRR, lauding the openness of company management, while likewise excoriating the NYC's secrecy. Hiebert's account, cited by many other scholars, does not appear in either the PRR records or contemporary newspaper accounts. The incident was probably not terribly serious, and it would hardly have cemented Lee's reputation as a consultant to the PRR. Hiebert, *Courtier to the Crowd: The Story of Ivy Lee and the Development of Public Relations* (Ames: Iowa State University Press, 1966), 56–57.

289. *New York Times*, October 29, 1906.

290. *New York Times*, October 30, 1906.

291. Edgar A. Haine, *Railroad Wrecks* (New York: Cornwall Books, 1993), 58–60.

292. *New York Times*, February 23, 1907, February 24, 1907 (quote), February 26, 1907, February 28, 1907.

293. *New York Times*, February 25, 1907.

294. *New York Times*, February 27, 1907.

295. *New York Times*, February 27, 1907, February 28, 1907; Aldrich, "Public Relations and Technology," 84.

296. Ivy Lee, "Indirect Service of Railroads," *Moody's Magazine* 2 (November 1907): 580–84, at 580.

297. After Lee left the PRR, taking residence in London, the railroad hired his brother, J. W. Lee, at a considerably lower salary of $3,000 per year. Samuel Rea to E. B. Thomas, March 14, 1910 (quote), HML, Box 145, folder 1; Roland Marchand, *Creating the Corporate Soul: The Rise of Public Relations and Corporate Imagery in American Big Business* (Berkeley: University of California Press, 1998), 42–43.

298. The Pennsylvania Railroad, Lines East and West of Pittsburgh, "Notice to the Press, Relative to Method of Making Public Details of Accidents," May 26, 1909, HML, Box 145, folder 1.

299. Hiebert, *Courtier to the Crowd*, 47, 55–59, 65, 93 (reprint of quotation in frontispiece of Ivy Lee, *Publicity for Public Service Corporations* [New York, 1916]).

300. Hiebert, *Courtier to the Crowd*, 59.

301. Ely, *Railroads and American Law*, 261; Ripley, *Railroads: Rates and Regulation*, 628–31.

302. Transportation economists Emory R. Johnson and Grover G. Huebner, writing in 1911, suggested that four factors contributed to relatively high passenger fares: the absence of the type of third-class services used in Europe, the preponderance of Pullman fares (made necessary by long distances that required overnight travel), and competition from electric interurban railways, which tended to increase the average length of steam rail passenger trips. Johnson and Huebner, *Railroad Traffic and Rates*, vol. 2: *Passenger, Mail, and Express Services* (New York: D. Appleton, 1911), 229.

303. Ripley, *Railroads: Rates and Regulation*, 429–30.

304. In most cases, the bills exempted short-distance commuter fares from the two-cent stipulation. Likewise, railroads were generally able to offer profitable long-distance passenger service at or below two cents per mile—even though PRR officials found it necessary to drop the $10 extra fare that applied to the limiteds operating between the east coast and the Midwest.

305. *New York Times*, June 14, 1907, September 5, 1907, October 3, 1907, November 15, 1907, September 4, 1908, March 9, 1909, March 10, 1909; Ripley, *Railroads: Rates and Regulation*, 430, 630.

306. *New York Times*, November 2, 1906.

307. *New York Times*, February 27, 1907, March 27, 1907, April 4, 1907, April 6, 1907.

308. *New York Times*, March 31, 1907, April 1, 1907, July 12, 1907.

309. The Perry County Court reached a similar conclusion, in a case involving the Susquehanna River & Western Railroad. Another case, in the Pittsburgh Court of Common Pleas, involved the Pittsburgh & Lake Erie Railroad and the Pittsburgh, McKeesport & Youghiogheny Railroad. *New York Times*, July 13, 1907, July 14, 1907, September 11, 1907, September 20, 1907, November 12, 1907, December 13, 1907, January 24, 1908, January 21, 1908, January 26, 1908, December 9, 1908, December 28, 1908.

310. Quoted in the *New York Times*, January 21, 1908.

311. Arthur U. Ayres, "The Pennsylvania State Railroad Commission," *Quarterly Journal of Economics* 26 (August 1912): 792–97.

312. Skowronek, *Building a New American State*, 261; Ripley, *Railroads: Rates and Regulation*, 557–58.

313. *ICC v. Illinois Central Railroad*, 215 U.S. 452 (1910); Robert L. Rabin, "Federal Regulation in Historical Perspective," *Stanford Law Review* 38 (May 1986): 1189–1326, at 1232–36; Skowronek, *Building a New American State*, 266–67.

314. *New York Times*, January 4, 1910.

315. Kolko, *Railroads and Regulation*, 185, 188–95; David H. Burton, *Taft, Holmes, and the 1920s Court: An Appraisal* (Madison, N.J.: Fairleigh Dickinson University Press, 1998), 81–82; Skowronek, *Building a New American State*, 261–67; Ripley, *Railroads: Rates and Regulation*, 566–71, 580–87; Isaiah Leo Sharfman, *Railway Regulation: An Analysis of the Underlying Problems in Railway Economics, from the Standpoint of Government Regulation* (Chicago: LaSalle Extension University, 1915), 216–19.

316. Remsen Varick Messler, *A History Or Genealogical Record of the Messler (Metselaer) Family* (Chicago: The Lakeside Press, 1903), 59.

317. William E. Hooper, "The Accounting System Prescribed for Railroads by the Interstate Commerce Commission," Annals of the American Academy of Political and Social Science 63 (January 1916): 222–31; Messler, *A History Or Genealogical Record,* 59–61.

318. Ibid.

319. Adams and other ICC officials also relied on the advice of other railway officials, including the PRR's John Riebenbach. Jan R. Heier, "America's Railroad Depreciation Debate, 1907 to 1913: A Study of Divergence in Early Twentieth Century Accounting Standards," *Accounting Historians Journal* 33 (January 2006): 89–124, at 91–92.

320. Melville J. Ulmer, "Trends and Cycles in Capital Formation by United States Railroads, 1870–1950," Occasional Paper 43 (New York: National Bureau of Economic Research, 1954); Heier, "America's Railroad Depreciation Debate," 91; Chandler, *Visible Hand,* 111–15; *New York Times,* June 15, 1907.

321. Paul Miranti, Jr., "The Mind's Eye of Reform: The ICC's Bureau of Statistics and Accounts and a Vision of Regulation, 1887–1940," *Business History Review* 63 (Autumn 1989): 469–509; Hooper, "The Accounting System Prescribed for Railroads," 223.

322. Heier, "America's Railroad Depreciation Debate," 90–91.

323. Ripley, *Railroads: Rates and Regulation,* 48; Miranti, "Mind's Eye of Reform," 487.

324. Heier, "America's Railroad Depreciation Debate," 93–95.

325. Ibid., 97–100.

326. Hooper, "The Accounting System Prescribed for Railroads," 230.

327. The *Central Yellow Pine Association* case involved a rate increase of two cents per hundredweight, implemented in April 1903 on lumber moving from the southeast to the Ohio River and points to the north. Keith D. Revell, *Building Gotham: Civic Culture and Public Policy in New York City, 1898–1938* (Baltimore: Johns Hopkins University Press, 2003), 64–69; *Railroad Gazette* 41, no. 23 (December 7, 1906): 155; *Illinois Central Railroad Company v. Interstate Commerce Commission,* 206 U.S. 441 (1907); *New York Times,* September 16, 1907; Philadelphia News Bureau, May 29, 1907, press release, HML, Box 151, "Railroad Accounting."

328. James McCrea to Martin A. Knapp, October 4, 1907, HML, Box 151, "Railroad Accounting."

329. James McCrea to James S. Harlan, July 5, 1907, HML, Box 151, "Railroad Accounting."

330. The Payne-Aldrich Tariff provided the corresponding reduction in tariffs, although Congress did not reduce duties to the extent that many supporters of the corporate income tax had anticipated. The individual income tax was implemented in the aftermath of the 1913 ratification of the Sixteenth Amendment to the Constitution. Marjorie E. Kornhauser, "Corporate Regulation and the Origin of the Corporate Income Tax," *Indiana Law Journal* 66 (Winter 1990): 53–136.

331. James McCrea to Martin A. Knapp, October 4, 1907, HML, Box 151, "Railroad Accounting."

332. *New York Times,* March 2, 1908, March 3, 1908, March 4, 1908; Heier, "America's Railroad Depreciation Debate," 101–14.

333. *Kansas City Southern Railway Company v. United States,* 231 U.S. 423 (1913).

334. As accounting historian Jan R. Heier has observed, the commissioners "saw most other industries embracing economic depreciation and became unrelenting on this issue, wavering little from its basic theory. Such regulations, as the railroads and the press felt, penalized the efficient and well-run railroad." Heier, "America's Railroad Depreciation Debate," 119.

335. Revell, *Building Gotham,* 66.

336. The traffic crisis of the World War I years, coupled with the period of federal control under the United States Railroad Administration, tem-

porarily superseded accounting considerations. In 1923, however, the ICC mandated the application of depreciation accounts to the railroads' physical plant. Opposition from railroad executives continued for the next ten years, and in 1933, at the nadir of the Great Depression, the ICC permitted the railroads to retain replacement-retirement-betterment accounting standards for track and structures. During the mid-1950s, with the PRR and other railroads in decline, accounting firm Arthur Andersen became a forceful advocate for depreciation accounting. However, the ICC did not prohibit betterment accounting for the physical plant until 1983, only twelve years before the agency itself was abolished. Hooper, "The Accounting System Prescribed for Railroads," 227; Heier, "America's Railroad Depreciation Debate," 119–21.

337. Hooper, "The Accounting System Prescribed for Railroads," 227–31.

338. Samuel Rea to James McCrea, January 8, 1908, HML, Box 145, folder 3.

339. "Report of the Committee of Conducting Transportation on 'A general study of the conditions governing the operations of local freight trains,'" October 5, 1915, HML, Box 420, folder 596–97.

340. Max Riebenack to Samuel Rea, February 8, 1910, HML, Box 145, folder 3.

341. Samuel Rea to James McCrea, January 8, 1908, HML, Box 145, folder 3.

342. Max Riebenack to Samuel Rea, February 8, 1910, HML, Box 145, folder 3. The more pragmatic Rea had insisted that "so far as a Statistical Bureau is concerned, if it is going to satisfy a real need and is going to replace a duplication of work and eliminate separate statistical bureaus in each of the Departments, I am in favor of it, but not otherwise." Samuel Rea to M. Riebenack, January 10, 1910, HML, Box 145, folder 3.

343. Samuel Rea to M. Riebenack, January 10, 1910, HML, Box 145, folder 3.

344. Max Riebenack, "Memorandum for A. J. County," May 13, 1909, HML, Box 145, folder 3.

345. Samuel Rea to Max Riebenack, January 10, 1910, HML, Box 145, folder 3.

346. "Proceedings of the Meeting of the Special Committee Composed of Representatives of the Accounting, Transportation and Traffic Departments to Consider the Question of the Establishment of a Bureau of Statistics," October 28, 1909, HML, Box 145, folder 3.

347. Rea underlined this passage before forwarding the letter to his assistant, Albert J. County, an individual who often handled sensitive public-relations and regulatory affairs issues. William G. MacDowell to Samuel Rea, June 25, 1909, HML, Box 145, folder 3.

348. The Association of Transportation Officers did not handle this matter, probably because the discussions involved close collaboration between the Transportation and Traffic Departments. "Proceedings of the Meeting of the Special Committee Composed of Representatives of the Accounting, Transportation and Traffic Departments to Consider the Question of the Establishment of a Bureau of Statistics," November 11–12, 1909, HML, Box 145, folder 3.

349. Samuel Rea to James McCrea, January 8, 1908, HML, Box 145, folder 3.

350. *New York Times,* June 8, 1910.

351. As Paul J. Miranti, Jr., has observed, "Anticipating the Mann-Elkins Act's requirement of justifying requested rate increases and eager for greater efficiency in the hearing process, the railroads shifted the focus of their petitions away from the adequacy of particular rates to the adequacy of overall rates." Miranti, "Mind's Eye of Reform," 488–89; *New York Times,* October 13, 1910.

352. Ripley, *Railroads: Rates and Regulation,* 596.

353. *New York Times*, September 8, 1910.

354. Ripley, *Railroads: Rates and Regulation*, 596–600; Albro Martin, *Enterprise Denied: Origins of the Decline of American Railroads, 1897–1917* (New York: Columbia University Press, 1971), 206–7; Oscar Kraines, "Brandeis' Philosophy of Scientific Management," *Western Political Quarterly* 13 (March 1960): 191–201, at 194; Miranti, "Mind's Eye of Reform," 491, 498.

355. According to public law scholar Oscar Kraines, when the hearings began, "Brandeis had no thought at the time of introducing the subject of scientific management [for] he had supposed that the leading railroads were efficient." Kraines, "Brandeis' Philosophy," 192.

356. *New York Times*, September 8, 1910, September 10, 1910.

357. Ripley, *Railroads: Rates and Regulation*, 596–600; Martin, *Enterprise Denied*, 206–7; Kraines, "Brandeis' Philosophy," 194; Miranti, "Mind's Eye of Reform," 491, 498.

358. *In Re Advances in Rates by Carriers in Official Classification Territory* (*Advances in Rates, Eastern Case*), 20 ICC 243 (1911); *Advances in Rates, Western Case*, 20 ICC 307 (1911).

359. Ripley, *Railroads: Rates and Regulation*, 594–96.

360. Martin, *Enterprise Denied*, 217–8.

361. Scott M. Cutlip, *The Unseen Power: Public Relations, a History* (Hillsdale, N.J.: Lawrence Erlbaum Associates, 1994), 45–54.

362. "Framing the Pennsylvania's messages with facts," Burton St. John has observed, Lee's "campaign strategy centered on the premise that the citizenry would support a railroad rate hike if it became aware of the dire economic reality of the railroads." St. John, "The Case for Ethical Propaganda," 225.

363. Lee resigned his post as executive assistant, effective January 1, 1915, but continued to work with the PRR as a consultant. Hiebert, *Courtier to the Crowd*, 60–69, 90–91: Marion R. Fremont-Smith, *Governing Nonprofit Organizations: Federal and State Law and Regulation* (Cambridge, Mass.: Harvard University Press, 2004), 68; Olasky, "Ivy Lee," 11–12.

364. Martin, *Enterprise Denied*, 217–18, 290; St. John, "The Case for Ethical Propaganda," 225; *New York Times*, March 10, 1914, March 11, 1914, April 3, 1914, October 1, 1914, October 24, 1914, December 17, 1914, December 20, 1914.

365. Louis D. Brandeis, *Other People's Money—And How the Bankers Use It* (New York: F. A. Stokes, 1914), 126.

366. Kraines, "Brandeis' Philosophy," 195.

367. Ripley, *Railroads: Rates and Regulation*, 598–99.

368. Albert J. County to Rea, February 11, 1914, HML, Box 145, folder 3.

369. "It is pretty hard for a[n efficiency] bureau of this kind to avoid friction and be useful," County emphasized, "unless the men are appointed for life and they are officered by men of tact as well as persistence." County to Rea, February 11, 1914, HML, Box 145, folder 3.

370. David L. Dodd, *Stock Watering: The Judicial Valuation of Property for Stock-Issue Purposes* (New York: Columbia University Press, 1930), 8–27, 231–41, 297–305; Ripley, *Railroads: Finance and Organization*, 227–80.

371. *New York Times*, October 13, 1910.

372. By 1907, fifteen states had made at least a partial determination of the worth of railroad property within their borders, typically for tax assessment purposes. Progressive era "gas-and-water socialism" had also included the valuation of privately owned utilities that were acquired and operated by municipal governments. Henry Hull, "The Federal Valuation Act," *Columbia Law Review* 17 (November 1917): 585–92; T. P. Artaud, "A Review of the Federal Valuation of Railroads," *Yale Law Journal* 32 (November 1922): 37–52; Berk, *Alternative Tracks*, 157.

373. Hoogenboom and Hoogenboom, *A History of the ICC*, 54–55, 81; Miranti, "Mind's Eye of Reform," 490.

374. *New York Times*, April 25, 1913, May 28, 1913, July 1, 1913.

375. Artaud, "Federal Valuation of Railroads," 44–49.

Chapter 15. Terminus

1. William Couper, ed., *History of the Engineering, Construction and Equipment of the Pennsylvania Railroad Company's New York Terminal and Approaches* (New York: Isaac H. Blanchard, 1912), 19 (quotes); *New York Times*, July 27, 1910, August 2, 1910.

2. *New York Times*, April 10, 1930.

3. While most of the aboveground portions of Penn Station disappeared and were replaced by Madison Square Garden, the underground heart of the facility survived, largely without alteration. So, too, did the statue of Samuel Rea, which was removed and stands today in front of 2 Penn Plaza, near the corner of Seventh Avenue and Thirty-Second Street, not too far from the facilities that he helped to develop. Cassatt's statue went farther astray, initially to the Rensselaer Polytechnic Institute (his alma mater), and then transferred to the Railroad Museum of Pennsylvania. Jill Jonnes, *Conquering Gotham: A Gilded Age Epic: The Construction of Penn Station and Its Tunnels* (New York: Viking, 2007), 314.

4. Maury Klein, *Union Pacific: The Rebirth, 1894–1969* (New York: Doubleday, 1989), 48–68.

5. For Harriman's career, see Lloyd J. Mercer, *E. H. Harriman: Master Railroader* (Boston: Twayne, 1985) and Maury Klein, *The Life and Legend of E. H. Harriman* (Chapel Hill: University of North Carolina Press, 2000). For Harriman's contemporary, James Jerome Hill of the Great Northern, see Albro Martin, *James J. Hill and the Opening of the Northwest* (New York: Oxford University Press, 1976).

6. William Z. Ripley, *Railroads: Finance and Organization* (New York: Longmans, Green, 1915), 166.

7. ATO, "The Decreasing Average Mileage of Our Freight Equipment and Engines," 1904, Pennsylvania Railroad Company Collection, call no. 1807/1810, Hagley Museum and Library, Wilmington, Delaware (hereafter cited as HML), Box 415, folder 303; Steven W. Usselman, *Regulating Railroad Innovation: Business, Technology, and Politics in America, 1840–1920* (Cambridge: Cambridge University Press, 2002), 340–41.

8. Comments of Richard L. O'Donnel, "Report of the Proceedings of the Joint Meeting of the Traffic and Transportation Officers," December 1, 1903, 134, HML, Box 407, folder 13.

9. *New York Times*, November 15, 1902, November 19, 1902, November 24, 1902, February 6, 1903.

10. *New York Times*, February 1, 1903.

11. The Pennsylvania Railroad Company, *Fifty-Sixth Annual Report of the Board of Directors to the Stockholders, for the Year 1902* (March 1903), 27.

12. George H. Burgess and Miles C. Kennedy, *Centennial History of the Pennsylvania Railroad, 1846–1946* (Philadelphia: Pennsylvania Railroad, 1949), 589–90.

13. *New York Times*, December 21, 1902.

14. Ibid.

15. The Philadelphia, Wilmington & Baltimore had leased the Baltimore & Potomac, effective November 1, 1891. On June 1, 1902, the Philadelphia, Wilmington & Baltimore (soon to become the Philadelphia, Baltimore & Washington) took over the operation of the Columbia & Port Deposit Railway. There were other changes in the divisional structure during the early years of the twentieth century. On August 1, 1900, the Western New York & Pennsylvania and the Allegheny Valley railroads were assigned to the new Buffalo & Allegheny Grand Division (renamed the Northern Grand Division in 1912). In August 1914, the PRR leased the Northern Central Railway and assigned it, along with the Erie Grand Division, to the new Central Grand Division. Between May 1916 and January

1918, the portion of the Northern Central south of Harrisburg was assigned to the Baltimore Grand Division. Thereafter, it became part of the Southern Grand Division, in conjunction with the Philadelphia, Baltimore & Washington. *New York Times*, May 28, 1903; Christopher T. Baer, "Pennsylvania Railroad Company: Operating Department—Grand/General Divisions," 1, HML.

16. *New York Times*, May 28, 1903.

17. Frederic Abendschein, "The Atglen & Susquehanna: Lancaster County's Low Grade," *The Keystone* 27, no. 4 (Winter 1994): 14.

18. Baer, "Pennsylvania Railroad Company: Operating Department—Grand/General Divisions," 1, HML.

19. Usselman, *Regulating Railroad Innovation*, 346–47.

20. It should be noted that these figures are expressed in terms of miles of line, and not miles of track, understating the density of heavily trafficked single-track lines. Even allowing for the multi-track main line, however, the PRR possessed extraordinarily high traffic densities. Ripley, *Railroads: Finance and Organization*, 75.

21. Ibid.

22. While the NYC enjoyed excellent access to Manhattan, the company was nonetheless at a significant disadvantage against the PRR. The PRR owned directly more than half of the system's total mileage. For the NYC, the ratio was one mile in five. As a result, PRR executives could distribute the enormous costs of local terminal improvements over a much larger revenue base. Ripley, *Railroads: Finance and Organization*, 417.

23. Donald J. Patton, "General Cargo Hinterlands of New York, Philadelphia, Baltimore, and New Orleans," *Annals of the Association of American Geographers* 48 (December 1958): 436–55.

24. Usselman, *Regulating Railroad Innovation*, 282–84, 342; Emory R. Johnson and Grover G. Huebner, *Railroad Traffic and Rates*, vol. 1: *The Freight Service* (New York: D. Appleton, 1911), 254, 280.

25. Robert C. Wright, "Freight Solicitation," n.d., ca. 1905, HML, Box 419, folder 556.

26. Superintendent, New York Division, to President and members of the ATO, October 31, 1899, HML, Box 414, folder 182–187.

27. ATO, "Report of the Joint Committee . . . on 'Considering the General Freight Movement of the Pennsylvania Railroad, Do Preference Freights Pay?'" March 25, 1904, HML, Box 407.

28. ATO, "Report of the Joint Committee . . . on 'Preference Freights,'" May 6, 1903, HML, Box 407.

29. Ibid.

30. The financial downturn that began in 1907 temporarily suspended the debate regarding train speeds, but the subsequent economic recovery again brought the issue to the fore. In early January 1911, the PRR experimented with increased train speeds. According to president James McCrea, the experiment was a failure, and he cautioned his counterpart on the Wabash against speeding up freight trains. "Some of our competitors quickly learned what was being done, promptly posted their Soliciting Agents, improved their own service, gave our customers so much cause for complaint against us, and took away so much business that, on the first of April, by mutual consent, we had to go back to our old practices. In light of these experiences," he noted, "the proposed reduction in time would probably lose to the Pennsylvania Railroad Company the benefit of its good road, equipment and organization." McCrea and other PRR officials in fact favored reductions in average train speeds, judging that the Operating Department could handle evenly paced traffic more economically. In June 1912, they suggested that the railroad increase freight transit times between Chicago and New York from sixty to eighty or even eighty-four hours. George D. Dixon, head of the Traffic Department, brushed aside those operational goals, warning his superiors that the PRR could not increase

travel times without "very seriously interfering with the business, to say nothing of the criticisms we would receive." Dixon noted, "We have very serious competition with the different water lines, whose time is most regular, and any lengthening out of our time would make their routes, with lower rates, much more attractive." The overbuilt nature of the northeastern railway network compounded the problem, Dixon observed. While both the PRR and the New York Central generated sufficient preference freight business to fill entire trains, other, weaker carriers (such as the Erie and the Baltimore & Ohio) typically augmented their partially filled preference trains, using cars filled with low-priority freight. On those routes, low-value freight moved at preference speeds, forcing the PRR to maintain comparable travel times for all of its freight in order to remain competitive. James McCrea to F. A. Delano, April 29, 1911, Penn Central Railroad Collection, M.G. 286, Pennsylvania Historical and Museum Commission, Pennsylvania State Archives, Harrisburg (hereafter PHMC), Cassatt/McCrea Papers, Box 57 (12–1818), folder 85/1 (first quote); George D. Dixon to William Wallace Atterbury, June 22, 1912, PHMC, Cassatt/McCrea Papers, Box 57 (12–1818), folder 85/13 (second quote).

31. Ripley, *Railroads: Finance and Organization*, 478.

32. *Fifty-Sixth Annual Report of the Pennsylvania Railroad Company* (1902), 23–25.

33. *New York Times*, December 21, 1902.

34. The 1896 figures for the Pennsylvania Railroad include $83,655,840 in bonded debt, $183,556,000 in debt guarantees (mainly for Lines West subsidiaries), and $130,192,500 in outstanding stock. The 1916 figures include $23,290,000 in equipment-trust certificates, $240,177,469 in bonded debt, $286,864,180 in debt guarantees, and $499,265,700 in stock. In 1906, the comparable figures were $71,018,000 in equipment-trust certificates, $188,471,320 in bonded debt, $332,563,663 in debt guarantees, and $305,951,350 in outstanding stock, for a total of $898,004,333. Economist William Z. Ripley listed the PRR (Lines East) total capitalization, as of June 30, 1906, as $1,674,416,000, a figure that was swollen by the PRR's community-of-interest holdings. Burgess and Kennedy, *Centennial History*, 802–5; Ripley, *Railroads: Finance and Organization*, 69.

35. Christopher T. Baer and Craig A. Orr, "A Guide to the Records of the Pennsylvania Railroad Company and the Penn Central Transportation Company," vol. 6 (Financial Department), HML.

36. Government Control and Operation of Railroads, Hearing before the Committee on Interstate Commerce, United States Senate, 65th Cong., 2nd sess. (Washington, D.C.: U.S. Government Printing Office, 1918), 552.

37. Ripley, *Railroads: Finance and Organization*, 240.

38. Government Control and Operation of Railroads, Hearing before the Committee on Interstate Commerce, United States Senate, 65th Cong., 2nd sess., 865; Ripley, *Railroads: Finance and Organization*, 66.

39. Ibid., 275; David L. Dodd, *Stock Watering: The Judicial Valuation of Property for Stock-Issue Purposes* (New York: Columbia University Press, 1930), 8–27, 231–41, 297–305. I am indebted to economic and business historian Edwin J. Perkins for bringing this issue to my attention.

40. Nelson, "Executive Department," 3; Baer and Orr, "Guide to the Records of the Pennsylvania Railroad Company."

41. The 1896–1906 repatriation represented only a temporary interruption in the influx of British capital prior to World War I. British investment in American railroads increased from $486 million in 1876 to $1.7 billion in 1898 to $3.0 billion in 1913. In comparison, in 1898 total investment in American railroads was $5.2 billion. Lance Edwin Davis, Robert E. Gallman, *Evolving Financial Markets and International Capital Flows: Britain, the Americas, and Australia, 1865–1914* (Cambridge: Cambridge University Press, 2001), mentioned in Mary A. O'Sullivan, "Finance Capital in

Chandlerian Capitalism," *Industrial and Corporate Change* 19 (April 2010): 549–89, at 574.

42. Leland H. Jenks, "Capital Movement and Transportation: Britain and American Railway Development," *Journal of Economic History* 11 (Autumn 1951): 375–88, at 377; Mira Wilkins, *A History of Foreign Investment in the United States to 1914* (Cambridge, Mass.: Harvard University Press, 1989), 730–31n69; A. W. Currie, "British Attitudes Toward Investment in North American Railroads," *Business History Review* 34 (Summer 1960): 194–216, at 210–13; PRR Board of Directors (BOD) Minutes, HML, February 8, 1905, 224–25; Stephen J. Lubben, "Railroad Receiverships and Modern Bankruptcy Theory," *Columbia Law Review* 89 (September 2004): 1420–75; Dorothy R. Adler and Muriel E. Hidy, eds., *British Investment in American Railways, 1834–1898* (Charlottesville: University Press of Virginia, 1970), 200; Ripley, *Railroads: Finance and Organization*, 5–10.

43. As Perkins has observed, an increase in the number of shares held by New York investors did not necessarily indicate that the PRR's capital was being concentrated in that city. It was common for shares to be registered under "street names" with New York investment-banking houses to disguise their true ownership. Perkins, personal communication with author, June 2010.

44. *New York Times*, May 23, 1903.

45. PRR BOD Minutes, May 23, 1900, 460.

46. *New York Times*, December 2, 1900, June 28, 1903 (quote); PRR BOD Minutes, May 23, 1900, 460–62, 467, December 12, 1900, 64–69.

47. The PRR did not issue preferred stock, although several of its subsidiaries (including the Pennsylvania Company) had. For a time, the PRR also owned large blocks of preferred stock in other carriers as part of the community of interest.

48. In the American railroad industry as a whole, the level of outstanding stock was $5.8 billion in 1900, compared to $4.9 million in bonds. Between 1900 and 1914, debt had more than doubled, to $10.1 billion, while equity had risen by less than half, to $8.7 billion. The comparable figures in 1929 were debt, $12.2 billion and stocks, $9.9 billion. That was a stock-to-bond ratio of 0.8, compared to 1.6 for the PRR. Jim Cohen, "Private Capital, Public Credit and the Decline of American Railways, 1840–1940," *Journal of Transport History* 31 (June 2010): 42–68, at 45–46.

49. John P. Green, "Financing the Pennsylvania Railroad," n.d., ca. 1905, HML, Box 419, folder 556.

50. Between 1896 and 1906, the PRR's total capital stock grew from $129.3 million to $305.9 million. Burgess and Kennedy, *Centennial History*, 441, 504–5.

51. Jonathan Barron Baskin, "The Development of Corporate Financial Markets in Britain and the United States, 1600–1914: Overcoming Asymmetric Information," *Business History Review* 62 (Summer 1988): 199–237, at 218; Burgess and Kennedy, *Centennial History*, 802–3.

52. Philadelphia & Reading Rail Road bonds were among the first to be convertible into stock, helping to establish substantial British investor control of that company. Jenks, "Capital Movement and Transportation," 376; Yumiko Morii, "A Comparative Analysis of Corporate Finance in the United States and Japan from 1880 to 1930" (Ph.D. diss., Florida International University, 2008), 33–37.

53. Alfred D. Chandler, Jr., "Patterns of American Railroad Finance, 1830–50," *Business History Review* 28 (September 1954): 248–63, at 250–51; Ripley, *Railroads: Finance and Organization*, 156–62.

54. Baskin, "Corporate Financial Markets," 215–16.

55. "While they did not technically increase the expenses of the road," historian Albro Martin has noted, "the six percent dividend was psychologically almost as much of an obligation to the Pennsylvania in 1904 as interest on first-mortgage bonds was to ordinary railroads." Albro Martin,

Enterprise Denied: Origins of the Decline of American Railroads, 1897–1917 (New York: Columbia University Press, 1971), 105.

56. Green, "Financing the Pennsylvania Railroad." As Perkins has noted, many of the members of the New York Stock Exchange were reluctant to place securities in the hands of individuals that they considered too unsophisticated to be capitalists. Along with executives at AT&T, PRR officials encouraged employees to become investors. It should be emphasized, however, that the PRR's policies applied to train crews (enginemen, firemen, conductors, and brakemen), shop workers, clerks, and other skilled employees. Perkins, personal communication with the author, June 2010.

57. According to Frank J. Warne, a labor activist who earned an economics degree from the University of Pennsylvania, "The reason the Pennsylvania Railroad has such a large number of stockholders is simply this: When they purchased the stock of a subsidiary company, they issued against it a bond which permits the holder of that bond to transfer it back for stock in the Pennsylvania Railroad. The New York Central and most companies when they buy the subsidiary issue a collateral bond, which can not be turned into stock of the parent company, and that explains why the Pennsylvania Railroad to-day has such a large number of separate and individual stockholders." Government Control and Operation of Railroads, Hearing before the Committee on Interstate Commerce, United States Senate, 65th Cong., 2nd sess., 1091–92.

58. The largest PRR stockholders in 1915 were: Henry Clay Frick, New York, 151,327 shares, valued at $7,566,350 ($50 par); Duveen Brothers, New York, 68,518, $3,425,900; Trustee Adams Express Company, New York, 63,200, $3,160,000; Girard Trust Company, Trustee, under the will of J. J. Emery, Philadelphia, 52,512, $2,625,600; Mary M. Emery, Cincinnati, 50,500, $2,525,000; Mutual Life Insurance Company, New York, 35,000, $1,750,000; Direction der Disconto-Gesellschaft, London, 34,484, $1,724,200; Morton F. Plant, New York, 32,000, $1,600,000; W. W. Astor, New York, 31,339, $1,566,950; and Fahnestock and Co., New York, 27,660, $1,383,000.

The ten largest investors owned collectively 546,540 shares, with a value of $27,327,000. In 1915, there were 10,129,150 shares of PRR stock outstanding (Burgess and Kennedy, *Centennial History*, 803, indicates 9,985,314 shares outstanding in 1915), worth $506,457,858. For the Erie, the four largest stockholders (and six of the top ten) were London-based investment firms. For the Baltimore & Ohio, the largest stockholder by far was Deutsche Bank, with nearly 185,000 shares. Government Control and Operation of Railroads, Hearing before the Committee on Interstate Commerce, United States Senate, 65th Cong., 2nd sess. 1091–92.

59. The great bull market of the 1920s more than doubled the number of shareholders, and as of December 31, 1936, despite the deleterious effects of the Great Depression, the PRR had 218,720 stockholders. They represented every state and sixty-five foreign countries, with the average stockholder owning sixty shares. The fifty largest shareholders owned just 7 percent of the company. Howard W. Schotter, "Scope of the Pennsylvania Railroad System," July 2, 1937, HML, Box 219, folder 12; *Railway Age Gazette* 56, no. 10 (March 6, 1914), 456–58; Ripley, *Railroads: Finance and Organization*, 620–21; Gardiner C. Means, "The Diffusion of Stock Ownership in the United States," *Quarterly Journal of Economics* 44 (August 1930): 561–600, at 594.

60. *New York Times*, July 13, 1907.

61. Schotter, "Scope of the Pennsylvania Railroad System."

62. The assertion that no single *corporate* investor owned more than 1 percent of the PRR's stock did not apply to at least one *individual* investor, Henry Clay Frick, who in 1915 controlled just over 1.5 percent of the PRR's stock—but even that was a comparatively low figure.

63. PRR stock possessed a par value of $50 per share, as was typical for the Philadelphia stock market, while shares sold on Wall Street typically had a par value of $100. For simplicity's sake, all share prices are listed relative to a $50 par, and should be doubled to determine their New York price. The peak of $85 meant that the share price on Wall Street was actually listed at $170.

64. Howard W. Schotter, *The Growth and Development of the Pennsylvania Railroad Company: A Review of the Charter and Annual Reports of the Pennsylvania Railroad Company 1846 to 1926, Inclusive* (Philadelphia: Allen, Lane & Scott, 1927), 267–68.

65. Morii, "Comparative Analysis," 37–39.

66. The PRR possessed a great advantage in its ability to sell a $50 par share at $60. The extra $10 could be invested in the railroad without being listed on the books as capitalization. Between 1902 and 1913, the PRR raised an additional $43 million through that mechanism. *New York Times*, November 18, 1900, March 27, 1901, January 7, 1903, January 24, 1903, January 25, 1903, March 11, 1903; PRR BOD Minutes, December 26, 1900, 81–82, March 27, 1901, 141–48, March 25, 1903, 187–94; Schotter, *Growth and Development*, 278, 283–84; Ripley, *Railroads: Finance and Organization*, 275.

67. As banking historian Vincent P. Carosso has observed, in 1885, 1888, and again in 1889, the three firms had cooperated in arranging financing for PRR subsidiaries and affiliated lines, including the Western Pennsylvania Railroad and the Philadelphia & Erie. Nonetheless, as Carosso has suggested, "none of J. P. Morgan & Co.'s joint managements prompted more comment than New York press reports that the firm and Kuhn, Loeb had agreed to cosponsor the Pennsylvania Railroad's proposed $50 million offering of 3½ percent convertible bonds." Carosso, *The Morgans: Private International Bankers, 1854–1913* (Cambridge, Mass.: Harvard University Press, 1987), 501, 721–22n120.

68. *New York Times*, June 28, 1903 (quote), June 30, 1903, July 1, 1904; Schotter, *Growth and Development*, 283–84.

69. *New York Times*, May 9, 1905; PRR BOD Minutes, March 29, 1905, 272–79; Schotter, *Growth and Development*, 289; Morii, "Comparative Analysis," 38.

70. *New York Times*, May 12, 1906, May 16, 1906, June 20, 1906, June 25, 1906, September 27, 1906; Schotter, *Growth and Development*, 292; Wilkins, *Foreign Investment*, 196, 729n50, 731n70, Carosso, *Investment Banking in America*, 84.

71. Similar financial developments were taking place on the PRR's subsidiaries. In October 1901 the PRR board authorized the Pennsylvania Company to issue $19 million in new stock, virtually the same amount that was already outstanding. By the end of 1902, the amount had doubled again, from $40 million to $80 million. Even that was insufficient, and in the spring of 1904 the Pennsylvania Company took on a short-term loan of $50 million, repayment of which required another $20 million increase in capital stock. Another loan, for $20 million, followed in April 1906. Other subsidiaries witnessed a similar growth in their capitalization. In September 1903, the PRR directors gave their approval for an increase in the Northern Central's stock, from $12 million to $20 million. A month later, Kuhn, Loeb agreed to place $10 million in Long Island Rail Road bonds, for improvements to the commuter line that the PRR had acquired three years earlier. Kuhn, Loeb placed the same amount of Philadelphia, Baltimore & Washington bonds, facilitating construction on the company that had been created the previous year, from the merger of the Baltimore & Potomac and the Philadelphia, Wilmington & Baltimore. The funds raised by the various stock and bond issues contributed mightily to equipment purchases and to betterments to the physical plant, all across the PRR system. *New York Times*, October 30, 1903; PRR BOD Minutes, October 30, 1901, 269–72, September 23, 1903, 319–23.

72. *New York Times*, June 13, 1906, June 19, 1906; Burgess and Kennedy, *Centennial History*, 504–5.

73. *New York Times*, January 11, 1907, January 12, 1907, February 20, 1907.

74. *New York Times*, September 5, 1907.

75. *New York Times*, November 2, 1907.

76. *New York Times*, May 12, 1908.

77. *New York Times*, January 17, 1908, March 2, 1908, March 3, 1908, April 23, 1908, April 28, 1908; PRR BOD Minutes, May 1, 1908, 178–80; *Railway Age Gazette* 56, no. 10 (March 6, 1914): 456–58.

78. *New York Times*, April 22, 1908, April 23, 1908, April 27, 1908, April 28, 1908; Schotter, *Growth and Development*, 309.

79. *New York Times*, April 29, 1910, May 1, 1910 (quote).

80. *New York Times*, March 10, 1909, November 2, 1909, January 12, 1911, April 10, 1913; PRR BOD Minutes, May 1, 1908, 178–80, October 28, 1908, 264–67, November 1, 1909, 12–14, January 11, 1911, 346–47, April 9, 1913, 444–46; Burgess and Kennedy, *Centennial History*, 582–83; Morii, "Comparative Analysis," 40–41.

81. Wilkins, *Foreign Investment*, 198, 217, 730–31n69.

82. Schotter, *Growth and Development*, 339–40.

83. Share prices listed in Christopher T. Baer, "A General Chronology of the Pennsylvania Railroad Company Predecessors and Successors and its Historical Context," for 1914, 1917, and 1918, http://www.prrths.com/Hagley/PRR_hagley_intro.htm.

84. Ron Chernow, *The House of Morgan: An American Banking Dynasty and the Rise of Modern Finance* (New York: Grove, 1990), 149–56; Jean Strouse, *Morgan: American Financier* (New York: Harper Perennial, 2000), 659–82

85. *New York Times*, January 29, 1915, January 31, 1915, February 18, 1915, May 8, 1915, June 2, 1915; PRR BOD Minutes, January 27, 1915, 434–35, February 10, 1915, 444–45, May 12, 1915, 13–15; Schotter, *Growth and Development*, 339–40; Carosso, *Investment Banking in America*, 220; Wilkins, *Foreign Investment*, 729–30n55.

86. *New York Times*, December 21, 1918, April 8, 1918; PRR BOD Minutes, July 12, 1916, 343, March 28, 1917, 50–51, 1917, April 11, 1917, 60–63, December 20, 1918, 123–24, April 7, 1920, 494.

87. Morii, "Comparative Analysis," 41–42. The PRR's shift away from external financing in some respects runs counter to the argument made by Alfred D. Chandler, Jr., in *The Visible Hand*, that railroads were fundamentally different from manufacturing enterprises in that the former relied on outside financing (as labored under the banker dominance that accompanied it), while the latter were largely self-financed, except perhaps when they elected to move into distribution. As several historians have suggested, outside dominance, either by restrained investment bankers or allegedly reckless speculators, might not have been such a bad thing. Richard Sylla writes of the "external financial discipline for entrenched corporate managers" that such attacks provided (Sylla, "Chandler on High Technology Industries from the 1880s to the 1990s: A Comment," Capitalism and Society 1 [2006]: 1–7, quote at 6). For a discussion of this issue, see O'Sullivan, "Finance Capital," esp. 583–86.

88. Green, "Financing the Pennsylvania Railroad"; ATO, "The Decreasing Average Mileage of Our Freight Equipment and Engines"; Usselman, *Regulating Railroad Innovation*, 340–41.

89. Green, "Financing the Pennsylvania Railroad."

90. Arthur S. Dewing, "Railroad Equipment Obligations," *American Economic Review* 7 (June 1917): 353–76; Green, "Financing the Pennsylvania Railroad."

91. Burgess and Kennedy, *Centennial History*, 379–80, 442.

92. *United States v. New Orleans Railroad*, 79 U.S. 362 (1870).

93. Burges and Kennedy, *Centennial History*, 506.

94. By 1917, the PRR was paying an average return of just over 4.35 percent on its securities, compared with 4.05 percent on its equipment trust obligations. Dewing, "Railroad Equipment Obligations," 357; Burgess and Kennedy, *Centennial History*, 379, 442, 506, 585; Grant Gilmore, *Security Interests in Personal Property*, vol. 1 (Union, N.J.: The Lawbook Exchange, 1999), 744–46; *Moody's Manual of Railroads and Corporation Securities, 1915* (New York: Moody Manual Co., 1915), 1420–21; PRR BOD Minutes, May 10, 1899, 208–14.

95. As one railroad economist noted, "The railroad obligates itself to pay off its certificates more rapidly than the security behind them declines in value." Dewing, "Railroad Equipment Obligations," 370.

96. Baer, "General Chronology," November 1, 1902, January 1, 1903.

97. *New York Times*, June 26, 1910; PRR, *Information for Employees and the Public*, September 30, 1915, 3.

98. In 1874, only three years before the completion of the second Rockville Bridge, Brown became the PRR's engineer of maintenance of way, a position that he held until 1881, when he became chief engineer. Between April 1, 1893, and November 1, 1902, he was chief engineer of construction, and then chief engineer again from that date until his retirement in 1906. I extend my appreciation to Christopher T. Baer for clarifying Brown's career information.

99. *Engineering Reminiscences: Address by Samuel Rea, Retired President, Pennsylvania Railroad, before the Franklin Institute of Philadelphia at the Presentation of the Franklin Medal, May 12, 1926* (Philadelphia: Franklin Institute, 1926); Burgess and Kennedy, *Centennial History*, 533–34.

100. Burgess and Kennedy, *Centennial History*, 533–34; Lewis Neilson, "The Growth and Functions of the Executive Department of the Pennsylvania Railroad Company," n.d., ca. 1905, HML, Box 419, folder 556; John Woolf Jordan, *Encyclopedia of Pennsylvania Biography*, vol. 1 (New York: Lewis Historical Publishing Co., 1914), 518–20.

101. *New York Times*, March 29, 1929.

102. Charles S. Roberts and David W. Messer, *Triumph VIII: Pittsburgh, 1749–2006* (Baltimore: Barnard, Roberts and Co., 2006), 119.

103. Ibid., 32, 63.

104. *New York Journal*, November 29, 1911; Burgess and Kennedy, *Centennial History*, 428–29, 492; Roberts and Messer, *Triumph VIII*, 31–32.

105. Titus M. Karlowicz, "Architecture of the World's Columbian Exposition" (Ph.D. diss., Northwestern University, 1965); Sally A. Kitt Chappell, "Urban Ideals and the Design of Railroad Stations," *Technology and Culture* 30 (April 1898): 354–75.

106. Although later generations of PRR officials promised to erect a new station at the site, the only significant changes occurred during the late 1940s and early 1950s, with the realignment of some trackage and the replacement of the massive—and badly corroded—train shed with more modest platform canopies. The station endures, as of this writing, while its more grandiose counterpart on Broad Street in Philadelphia has long since succumbed to the wrecking ball. Roberts, *Triumph VIII*, 32–33, 98–100, 207; Chappell, "Urban Ideals."

107. The PRR also opened hump yards at Altoona at the Edge Moor Yard, near Wilmington, Delaware, and at Cambridge, Ohio, at approximately the same time.

108. John A. Droege, *Freight Terminals and Trains, Including a Revision of Yards and Terminals* (New York: McGraw-Hill, 1912), 13, 61–97.

109. Roberts and Messer, *Triumph VIII*, 31.

110. Henry Brownfield Scott, *Sesqui-Centennial and Historical Souvenir of the Greater Pittsburgh* (Pittsburgh, 1908), 79–80.

111. One example was a proposed line along the west bank of the Susquehanna River linking the main line at Aqueduct (near Duncannon) to Selinsgrove Junction, at the western terminus of the Sunbury & Lewistown. The Northern Central did benefit, however, from the construction of a new freight yard at Northumberland opened in 1911.

112. Since the 1870s, the PRR had been using a portion of the New Portage Railroad, including the tunnel at Gallitzin (originally referred to as the Allegheny Tunnel, and renamed the New Portage Tunnel by the PRR). The tunnel was in poor repair, carried only a single track, and was not suitable for mainline operations. In 1898, PRR crews rebuilt the tunnel and installed a second track. David W. Messer, *Triumph IV: Harrisburg to Altoona, 1846–2001* (Baltimore: Barnard, Roberts and Co., 2001), 146–48; Roberts and Schlerf, *Triumph I: Altoona to Pitcairn, 1846–1996* (Baltimore: Barnard, Roberts and Co., 1997), 100–101, 131–32, 141, 245, 248.

113. *Railway World* 5 (June 7, 1879): 532.

114. Roberts and Schlerf, *Triumph I*, 239, Dan Cupper, *Rockville Bridge: Rails Across the Susquehanna* (Halifax, Pa.: Withers Publishing, 2002), 6, 27–28, 35.

115. Cupper, *Rockville Bridge*, 28–44, 49.

116. Flying junctions, like modern freeway interchanges, enabled one set of tracks to cross over or under another, prior to joining a new route. They were particularly useful on multi-track railroads such as the PRR, as they enabled, for example, a train from Baltimore to Pittsburgh, moving north on the Northern Central, to cross under the eastbound tracks of the PRR main line, before switching onto the westbound main line. Ibid., 30–60.

117. Ibid., 65.

118. Most of the traffic on the low-grade lines, at least initially, consisted of eastbound coal shipments and, westbound, the movement of empty cars, especially those that had carried iron and steel products to tidewater.

119. For information on the so-called Sam Rea Line into Ohio, see Ed Waytel, "The 'Sam Rea Line'," *The Keystone* 19, no. 2 (Summer 1986): 25–34.

120. Economist William Z. Ripley summarized the situation in 1912: "Notwithstanding the extraordinary density of traffic on this extra two track [low-grade] line, it probably does not meet the fixed charges on cost of construction of the line. Yet the new double track was absolutely necessary, regardless of its profitableness, in order to relieve congestion on the old four tracks. In other words, the demands of the service forced an expenditure which in and of itself was not financially self-supporting. But the profit of the old line would be sufficiently enhanced to take care of the whole. A resolutely conservative policy of finance becomes imperative under such circumstances." Ripley, *Railroads: Rates and Regulation*, 62.

121. *New York Times*, July 28, 1892; Burgess and Kennedy, *Centennial History*, 428; Michael Bezilla, *Electric Traction on the Pennsylvania Railroad, 1895–1968* (University Park: Pennsylvania State University Press, 1980), 94–95.

122. The PRR west of Dillerville (Lancaster) was actually two two-track lines, one (the original Harrisburg, Portsmouth, Mount Joy & Lancaster) via Elizabethtown and the other via Columbia, which also carried Columbia & Port Deposit Railroad traffic along the Susquehanna River. The two lines came together at Royalton for the last few miles into Harrisburg.

123. Other realignments, including the proposed elimination of a sharp curve at Berwyn, fell victim to the Panic of 1907 and were never implemented.

124. Quarryville residents instead relied on an extant PRR branch from Lancaster

125. David W. Messer, *Triumph II: Philadelphia to Harrisburg, 1828–1998* (Baltimore: Barnard, Roberts, and Co., 1999), 274–78.

126. Between 1906 and 1911, the PRR and the Northern Central also built a new classification yard at Northumberland, Pennsylvania, replacing

overcrowded facilities at Sunbury and Williamsport. It was smaller than the Enola Yard, but it was an impressive facility nonetheless. As a related project, construction crews upgraded the line between Sunbury and Williamsport to double track. ATO, "Report of the Joint Committee . . . on 'Preference Freights,'" May 6, 1903, HML, Box 407; Frederich Abendschein, "The Atglen & Susquehanna: Lancaster County's Low Grade," *The Keystone* (Winter 1994): 10–25; Cupper, *Rockville Bridge*, 61; Robert L. Gunnarsson, *The Story of the Northern Central Railway, from Baltimore to Lake Ontario* (Sykesville, Md.: Greenberg, 1991), 111.

127. Messer, *Triumph II*, 44, 278. Thomson quote is from *Twenty-First Annual Report of the Board of Directors of the Pennsylvania Railroad Co. to the Stockholders, February 15, 1868* (Philadelphia: E. C. Markley & Son, 1868), 20.

128. Cupper, *Rockville Bridge*, 62–63; Burgess and Kennedy, *Centennial History*, 544; *The High Line* 17 (1999); David W. Messer and Charles S. Roberts, *Triumph V: Philadelphia to New York, 1830–2002* (Baltimore: Barnard, Roberts and Co., 2002), 60.

129. Messer, *Triumph II*, 278; David W. Messer, *Triumph III: Philadelphia Terminal, 1838–2000* (Baltimore: Barnard, Roberts and Co., 2000), 100–101.

130. PRR BOD Minutes, March 27, 1901,150–51; Messer, *Triumph III*, 90,109, 163, 199.

131. Even after the completion of Broad Street Station, the PRR had not entirely abandoned service west of the Schuylkill River. The 1876-vintage West Philadelphia (Centennial) Station was used mainly for storage, and it burned down in 1896. Instead, local residents relied on a far smaller facility on Powelton Avenue, completed in 1882.

132. Messer, *Triumph III*, 14–15.

133. PRR BOD Minutes, November 26, 1902, 39; Messer, *Triumph III*, 286–88.

134. Roberts and Messer, *Triumph VI: Philadelphia, Columbia, Harrisburg to Baltimore and Washington, D.C., 1827–2003* (Baltimore: Barnard, Roberts and Co., 2003), 43.

135. Messer and Roberts, *Triumph V*, 33, 41, 65–66, 81, 105–6, 149.

136. The 1880 bridge consisted of new spans, installed between 1874 and 1880, on the existing piers, which had supported the first bridge, opened in 1866. When the 1906 bridge entered service, PRR officials offered the old bridge to anyone who wanted it, free of charge, in order to avoid the expense of demolishing the earlier structure. Cecil and Harford Counties (the two counties that bordered that stretch of the Susquehanna River) both refused the offer. Private investors later bought the span and spent a modest sum converting it into a toll highway bridge. In 1923, the Commonwealth of Maryland bought the bridge for $585,000. That purchase price, coupled with tolls charged between 1910 and 1923, ensured that the owners of the private toll bridge earned $1,364 for each dollar that they had invested in the project. The current U.S. Route 40 and I-95 bridges have replaced the original highway bridge, but the piers, completed in 1866, are still standing in the Susquehanna River as of this writing. Roberts and Messer, *Triumph VI*, 77–78, 96; Maryland State Roads Commission, *A History of Road Building in Maryland* (Baltimore: Maurice Leeser Co., 1959), 132–33.

137. Frank A. Wrabel, "Terminals, Tunnels and Turmoil," *The Keystone* 28 (Spring 1995): 12–15, 21–22, 36–37; Roberts and Messer, *Triumph VI*, 287.

138. Wrabel, "Terminals, Tunnels and Turmoil," 36–41, 47–48, 50; *Railway Age* 98, no. 18 (May 4, 1935): 686–90.

139. As of this writing, the B&P Tunnels and, to a lesser extent, Union Tunnel, constitute the most serious impediment to Amtrak's Northeast Corridor operations. Roberts and Messer, *Triumph VI*, 322–23.

140. Dian Olson Belanger, "The Railroad in the Park: Washington's Baltimore & Potomac Station, 1872–1907," *Washington History* 2 (Spring 1990): 4–27. Currently, the best published sources of information regarding the design and construction of the Washington Union Station come from two biographies of Daniel Burnham: Thomas S. Hines, *Burnham of Chicago: Architect and Planner* (New York: Oxford University Press, 1974), esp. 139–57; and Charles Moore, *Daniel H. Burnham: Architect, Planner of Cities*, 2 vols. (Boston: Houghton Mifflin, 1921), esp. vol. 1, 129–88 and 197–229, and vol. 2, 6–13, and from Carol M. Highsmith and Ted Landphair, *Union Station: A History of Washington's Grand Terminal*, 2nd ed. (Washington, D.C.: Union Station Venture, 1998). At the time of this writing, William Wright is completing a dissertation on the station, "Now Arriving Washington: Union Station and Life in the Nation's Capital," and much of his work is archived at http://www.washingtonunionstation.com/.

141. Belanger, "The Railroad in the Park."

142. Wright, "Now Arriving Washington," 49–53; Belanger, "The Railroad in the Park," 24.

143. Wright, "Now Arriving Washington," 53–59.

144. The federal government and the District of Columbia would share the $1.5 million payment to the B&O, while the federal government would assume sole responsibility for the payment to the PRR (as the Mall was federal property).

145. Roberts and Messer, *Triumph VI*, 361.

146. Norris Galpin Osborn, *Men of Mark in Connecticut: Ideals of American Life Told in Biographies and Autobiographies of Eminent Living Americans*, vol. 2 (Hartford: William R. Goodspeed, 1906), 75–76.

147. Wright, "Now Arriving Washington," 64–67.

148. Michael J. Bednar, *L'Enfant's Legacy: Public Open Spaces in Washington, D.C.* (Baltimore: Johns Hopkins University Press, 2006), 48–55.

149. Wright, "Now Arriving Washington," 74–77.

150. *New York Times*, November 13, 1901; Wright, "Now Arriving Washington," 61–74.

151. Wright, "Now Arriving Washington," 53–54.

152. Ibid., 90–100.

153. The station's statuary was the product of Louis Saint-Gaudens, a capable sculptor in his own right, even if he was not so well known as his brother, Augustus.

154. Descriptions of the station in this and subsequent paragraphs are generally from Wright, "Now Arriving Washington," 101–15 and 209–23; and Burgess and Kennedy, *Centennial History*, 499–500.

155. In 1910, the directors of the Washington Terminal Company approved $500 to furnish the room, most of which went toward a set of ordinary wicker and rattan furniture. The cheap furnishings in any event proved unable to accommodate the girth of President William Howard Taft. Not until the administration of Franklin Delano Roosevelt, in 1939, did the federal government authorize $16,000 to rehabilitate and refurnish the suite. It became a USO lounge during World War II. Highsmith and Landphair, *Union Station*, 64, 72; Wright, "Now Arriving Washington," 110–15, 171.

156. Wright, "Now Arriving Washington," 172–97.

157. Roberts and Messer, *Triumph VI*, 332, 362–69; Highsmith and Landphair, *Union Station*, 47–50; Burgess and Kennedy, *Centennial History*, 499–500.

158. Roberts and Messer, *Triumph VI*, 370.

159. Wright, "Now Arriving Washington," 202–3.

160. Samuel Rea, *Pennsylvania Railroad New York Tunnel Extension—Historical Outline: Remarks of Mr. Samuel Rea, Second Vice-President, at the Annual Dinner to the President, Given by the Board of Directors of the*

Pennsylvania Railroad Co., December 15, 1909 (Philadelphia: Allen, Lane & Scott, 1909), 58, quoted in Keith D. Revell, *Building Gotham: Civic Culture and Public Policy in New York City, 1898–1938* (Baltimore: Johns Hopkins University Press, 2003), 19.

161. Charles W. Raymond, "The New York Tunnel Extension of the Pennsylvania Railroad," Paper No. 1150; *Transactions of the American Society of Civil Engineers*, vol. 68 (September 1910): 1–31, at 9, 38, 40, HML, Box 146, folder 9, 1.

162. In addition to the PRR, the companies were the B&O, the Reading, and the Lehigh Valley, all of which shared the Jersey Central at Communipaw; the Erie; the New York, Ontario & Western Railroad; the New York, Susquehanna & Western Railway (which also terminated in Jersey City); the Delaware, Lackawanna & Western in Hoboken; and the New York, West Shore & Buffalo Railway at Weehawken. Jonnes, *Conquering Gotham*, 13.

163. Burgess and Kennedy, *Centennial History*, 434.

164. Carl W. Condit, *The Port of New York: A History of the Rail and Terminal System from the Beginnings to Pennsylvania Station* (Chicago: University of Chicago Press, 1980), 49–50, 152–65; William Harry Moyer, "The PRR's Navy—Part I, New York Area," *The Keystone* 39 (Winter 2006): 7–64, at 43–44.

165. Although the PRR's Ferry Department was responsible for maritime operations in the New York area, the company leased the franchise rights to operate the ferries from the Associates of the Jersey Company. That company was established in 1804 as a mechanism for developing the town of Jersey (later, Jersey City). The PRR controlled the company through majority stock ownership and leased the ferry rights in 1877, retroactive to 1875.

166. Moyer, "The PRR's Navy—Part I," 7–64.

167. Condit, *Port of New York*, 49–51; Moyer, "The PRR's Navy—Part I," 10–11, 30–31, 33, 40, 44–45.

168. Condit, *Port of New York*, 110–11; 166–67.

169. Revell, *Building Gotham*, 1–3; Condit, *Port of New York*, 105, 127.

170. Moyer, "The PRR's Navy—Part I," 50; Condit, *Port of New York*, 167, 377n23.

171. The numbers were 4,621,653 to Cortlandt Street, 1,815,650 to Desbrosses Street, 1,568,062 to Twenty-Third Street, and 247,588 to the Pennsylvania Annex, for a total of 8,252,953. "Statement Showing Rail Passengers Crossing the Various Jersey City Ferries of the Pennsylvania Railroad for the Year Ending March 31st, 1902," PHMC, Cassatt/McCrea papers, Box 17 (12–1778), folder 32/63; Raymond, "The New York Tunnel Extension"; Revell, *Building Gotham*, 3.

172. The corporate history of the LIRR during the nineteenth century is extremely complex. Information from this and subsequent paragraphs is from Peter Ross, *A History of Long Island from Its Earliest Settlement to the Present Time*, vol. 1 (New York: Lewis Publishing, 1902), 285–304; Vincent F. Seyfried, *The Long Island Rail Road: A Comprehensive History*, 7 vols. (Garden City, N.Y.: Exposition Press, 1961–75); Ron Ziel and George H. Foster, *Steel Rails to the Sunrise:* The Long Island Railroad (New York: Duell, Sloan and Pearce, 1965); Condit, *Port of New York*, 40–44; and "The Long Island Railroad Celebrates 100th Anniversary," *Mutual Magazine* (July 1934): 23–28; *New York Times*, October 28, 1877.

173. *Coney Island and the Jews: A History of the Development and Success of this Famous Seaside Resort, together with a Full Account of the Recent Jewish Controversy* (New York: G. W. Carleton & Co., 1879).

174. Eugene L. Armbruster, *The Ferry Road on Long Island* (New York: self-published, 1919), 13.

175. William Charles Copperthwaite, *Tunnel Shields and the Use of Compressed Air in Subaqueous Works* (New York: D. Van Nostrand, 1906), 1–11.

176. For information on the work on the Haskin tunnel, see S. D. V. Burr, *Tunneling Under the Hudson River: Being a Description of the Obstacles Encountered, the Experience Gained and the Plans Finally Adopted for Rapid and Economical Prosecution of the Work* (New York: J. Wiley, 1885); Brian J. Cudahy, *Rails Under the Mighty Hudson: The Story of the Hudson Tubes, the Pennsy Tunnels and Manhattan Transfer* (New York: Fordham University Press, 2002), 11–13; Condit, *Port of New York*, 249–50; Jonnes, *Conquering Gotham*, 15–20. Both Jonnes and Revell use the last name "Haskins," but this spelling (based, apparently, on several contemporary sources) is incorrect.

177. Ame A. Jakkula, "A History of Suspension Bridges in Bibliographical Form," *Bulletin of the Agricultural and Mechanical College of Texas,* 4th Series, Vol. 12, No. 7 (July 1, 1941).

178. *American Biography: A New Cyclopedia*, vol. 5 (New York: The American Historical Society, 1919), 194–97; Condit, *Port of New York*, 256–57.

179. Samuel Rea, *The Railways Terminating in London, with a Description of the Terminal Stations, and the Underground Railways* (New York: Engineering News Publishing, 1888), 32.

180. The Charter of the North River Bridge Company, July 11, 1890; "true and correct list of the stockholders," September 20, 1900; Gustav Lindenthal to Samuel Rea, March 16, 1897; Lindenthal to the Board of Directors of the North River Bridge Company, March 11, 1897; all in HML, Box 157, folder 7; Condit, *Port of New York*, 257–58; "Career of Samuel Rea, Ninth President of the Pennsylvania Railroad," *Pennsylvania Railroad: Information for the Public and Employes*, October 1925, 4; Burgess and Kennedy, *Centennial History*, 533–34.

181. "Report of Samuel Rea to George Roberts on the System of Underground Transit in London, England," October 15, 1892, in Rea, *Historical Outline*, 53–54.

182. Ibid., 53–54.

183. The Greathead-Barlow shield was a considerable improvement over the one developed by Marc Isambard Brunel for the construction of the Thames Tunnel.

184. "Report of Samuel Rea," 27–36, emphasis in the original.

185. Rea to Roberts, October 5, 1892, 81 (quotes, emphasis in the original); "Report of Samuel Rea"; Messer and Roberts, *Triumph V*, 256.

186. Rea to Roberts, October 5, 1892, 60, 78 (quote); Jonnes, *Conquering Gotham*, 41–43.

187. It was Cassatt who suggested that the North River Bridge Company initiate condemnation proceedings at the site of the New Jersey approach to the proposed bridge. Even though no actual construction was forthcoming, the evictions would at least test the validity of the new charter. The case went all the way to the Supreme Court, which decided in favor of Lindenthal and the North River Bridge Company. Rea, *Historical Outline*, 8–11.

188. *New York Times*, August 6, 1887.

189. Ziel and Foster, *Steel Rails to the Sunrise*, 73; Richard S. Tedlow, Courtney Purrington, and Kim Eric Bettcher, "The American CEO in the Twentieth Century: Demography and Career Path," Harvard Business School working paper 03-097 (2003); Condit, *Port of New York*, 263.

190. William H. Baldwin, Jr., the new president of the LIRR, was less committed to the tunnel under Blackwell's Island. The owners of the New York & Long Island Railroad, after unsuccessfully attempting to sell their franchise to the PRR, eventually found a buyer in subway magnate August

Belmont, Jr. Work on the tunnels did not resume until 1905, long after PRR executives had made their own arrangements for reaching Long Island. Although completed in 1907, the "Steinway Tunnels," as they were popularly called, did not enter service until 1915, as part of the Flushing Line of Belmont's Interborough Rapid Transit system. Much of the information on the New York & Long Island Railroad is derived from work by Joseph Brennan at Columbia University (http://www.columbia.edu/~brennan/beach/chapter22.html), accessed on April 30, 2010, and by David Rogoff, *Electric Railroads* 29 (April 1960) (http://www.nycsubway.org/articles/steinwaytunnels.html), both accessed on January 15, 2010; and Seyfried, *Long Island Rail Road*, vol. 7, 76–77.

191. August Belmont, Jr., founder of the Interborough Rapid Transit Company, was a director of the East River Gas Company. *New York Times*, July 15, 1894, July 17, 1894; Charles M. Jacobs, *A General Report on the Initiation and Construction of the Tunnel Under the East River, New York, to the President and Directors of the East River Gas Company* (New York, 1894); Revell, *Building Gotham*, 21.

192. James B. French, "The Atlantic Avenue Improvement of the Long Island Railroad in Brooklyn, N.Y.," *Transactions of the Association of Civil Engineers of Cornell University* 12 (1903–04): 1–12; *New York Times*, March 11, 1900.

193. Benson Bobrick, *Labyrinths of Iron: Subways in History, Myth, Art, Technology, and War* (New York: Quill, 1981, 1986), 217–64.

194. In 1902, August Belmont, Jr., incorporated the Interborough Rapid Transit Company as the umbrella organization for the various subway contracts, as well as a number of elevated lines.

195. *New York Times*, March 15, 1901.

196. Construction on the Atlantic Avenue Improvement began in December 1901, and the new route entered service four years later. With the LIRR relying on the completion of what later became the Interborough Rapid Transit, the company never extended its tracks west of Flatbush Avenue.

197. As one of the conditions for its access to Manhattan, the PRR implemented the Atlantic Avenue Improvement, removing Long Island Rail Road tracks from that thoroughfare onto elevated and depressed rights of way, eliminating more than ninety grade crossings in the process. Raymond, "New York Tunnel Extension," 7; Ziel and Foster, *Steel Rails to the Sunrise*, 8–36; Burgess and Kennedy, *Centennial History*, 473–81.

198. *New York Times*, June 19, 1901, October 21, 1901, December 4, 1901; French, "The Atlantic Avenue Improvement."

199. *New York Times*, June 26, 1901; Jonnes, *Conquering Gotham*, 38–39.

200. Samuel Rea to E. H. McHenry, February 27, 1907, HML, Box 142, folder 10.

201. *New York Times,* December 14, 1901.

202. The North River Bridge Company should not be confused with the New York & New Jersey Bridge Company, which would have bridged the Hudson at the level of Midtown, slightly north of the North River Bridge. The company's promoters never received a congressional charter. As late as the 1920s, long after the PRR had completed the Hudson tunnels, Lindenthal was still promoting his bridge, plaintively asserting "the pressure for the bridge is increasing all the time, particularly from automobile owners." The closest approximation to the project was the George Washington Bridge, designed by Lindenthal's protégé Othmar Ammann and completed in 1931. Located near the northern tip of Manhattan Island, the bridge took advantage of bluffs on either side of the Hudson River and did not require the long approaches that had been one of the principal defects associated with the North River Bridge. Samuel Rea to George B. Roberts,

"The Question of the Entrance into New York City for Railroads that Terminate on the West Side of the Hudson River," October 5, 1892; "Remarks of Mr. Samuel Rea, Second Vice-President, at the Annual Dinner to the President Given by the Board of Directors of the Pennsylvania Railroad Co.," December 15, 1909; both reprinted in *Historical Outline*, 8–11; Gustav Lindenthal to Samuel Rea, November 14, 1910, HML, Box 142, folder 1; Jonnes, *Conquering Gotham*, 45–46, 53–54; Revell, *Building Gotham*, 26; Condit, *Port of New York*, 265; Othmar Ammann, "General Conception and Development of Design," in *George Washington Bridge Across the Hudson River at New York, N.Y., Transactions of the American Society of Civil Engineers* 97 (1933): 1–65.

203. *New York Times*, June 26, 1901.

204. Condit, *Port of New York*, 213–19.

205. According to Rea's recollection of events, Cassatt sent a telegram to his fourth vice president, informing him that the Gare d'Orsay might serve as a useful model for the New York Improvements. The cable, if it existed, seems to have disappeared, and is not in any known archived collection of PRR materials. Yet, it seems odd that PRR personnel would have discarded so historically significant a document. It is also puzzling that Cassatt was in Paris the previous year, four months after the Gare d'Orsay opened, but seems not to have visited the station, or at least made no mention of it. It is possible that Rea's recollection of the events leading to the initiation of the New York Improvements was not precisely accurate. Rea, *Historical Outline*, 20.

206. Rea to E. H. McHenry, February 27, 1907 (quote), HML, Box 142, folder 10; Burgess and Kennedy, *Centennial History*, 534.

207. Cassatt was not the only one to suffer disappointment during the autumn of 1901. In September, Rea informed Gustav Lindenthal that PRR officials were no longer interested in his North River Bridge. Lindenthal soon wrote back, insisting vigorously that a tunnel was virtually impossible and frantically offering to scale down the scope of the bridge, but to no avail. The board of directors did not officially adopt the name "Pennsylvania Station" for the new passenger facility until March 1909, although the phrase was in common use long before that date.

208. Raymond, "New York Tunnel Extension," 42.

209. Jonnes, *Conquering Gotham*, 67–72, 79–81, 84–86.

210. The Pennsylvania–New York Extension Railroad Company replaced the Long Island Extension Railroad Company, the firm that the PRR and LIRR interests had incorporated in June 1901. Because the project crossed a state boundary, the PRR eventually created two corporations—the Pennsylvania, New Jersey & New York Railroad (in February 1902) and the Pennsylvania, New York & Long Island Railroad (in April 1902), with Cassatt serving as president of both entities. The state line was an arbitrary political demarcation, and the two companies lasted only until June 1907, when they were merged into the Pennsylvania Tunnel & Terminal Railroad. In July 1928 the PRR leased the Pennsylvania Tunnel & Terminal Railroad for 999 years. "Pennsylvania Tunnel and Terminal Railroad Company," September 1961, HML, Box 258, folder 2.

211. PRR BOD Minutes, December 26, 1901, 309–10, *New York Times*, December 11, 1901, December 12, 1901, December 13, 1901, December 14, 1901; Jonnes, *Conquering Gotham*, 86–91.

212. Rea to Roberts, October 5, 1892, 81 (quotes).

213. *New York Times,* December 13, 1901, December 14, 1901.

214. *New York Times,* December 14, 1901.

215. Rea to Samuel Hopkins, September 8, 1911, HML, Box 139, folder 42.

216. John J. Broesamle, *William Gibbs McAdoo: A Passion for Change, 1863–1917* (Port Washington, N.Y.: Kennikat Press, 1973), 17–20.

217. J. Vipond Davies, "The Hudson and Manhattan Tunnels," *Proceedings of the American Electric Railway Association* (Albany: J. B. Lyon, 1911): 236–45.

218. Hudson & Manhattan service to Park Place, Newark, began in November 1911. Much of the information on the Hudson & Manhattan Railroad is from John Vipond Davies, "The Tunnel Construction of the Hudson and Manhattan Railroad Company," *Proceedings of the American Philosophical Society* 49 (July 1910): 164–78; William G. McAdoo, *Crowded Years: The Reminiscences of William G. McAdoo* (Boston: Houghton Mifflin, 1931); Anthony Fitzherbert, *The Public Be Pleased: William G. McAdoo and the Hudson Tubes* (New York: Electric Railroaders' Association, 1964), 1–8; and Broesamle, *William Gibbs McAdoo*, 19–23.

219. Revell, *Building Gotham*, 39–40.

220. William F. King to Benjamin Barker Odell, November 28, 1902, PHMC, Cassatt/McCrea papers, Box 17 (12-1778), folder 32/63 (quote); Merchants' Association of New York, *In Memory of William F. King* (New York: Merchants' Association, 1909), 28–35.

221. Rea noted, "We have had comparatively little sympathy or help from the political element or from our railroad friends, and we have had to rely upon our own efforts, warmly seconded by the public." Samuel Rea to James McCrea, February 15, 1907, HML, Box 142, folder 25; Revell, *Building Gotham*, 37–49.

222. Revell, *Building Gotham*, 39–40.

223. Ibid., 41.

224. *New York Times*, March 21, 1902, March 22, 1902.

225. *New York Times*, March 24, 1902, March 25, 1902, March 26, 1902, March 27, 1902, April 12, 1902; Revell, *Building Gotham*, 39–40; Jonnes, *Conquering Gotham*, 99–109.

226. Alexander J. Cassatt to the President and the Board of Rapid Transit Railroad Commissioners, May 5, 1902, PHMC, Cassatt/McCrea papers, Box 17 (12-1778), folder 32/63.

227. Cassatt to Alexander Orr, April 25, 1902; John P. Green to Cassatt, July 25, 1902; Green to Cassatt, July 29, 1902; all in PHMC, Cassatt/McCrea papers, Box 17 (12-1778), folder 32/63; *New York Times*, June 6, 1902, June 17, 1902; Raymond, "New York Tunnel Extension," 13–19; Jonnes, *Conquering Gotham*, 109–10.

228. Green to Cassatt, August 6, 1902 (quote), PHMC, Cassatt/McCrea papers, Box 17 (12-1778), folder 32/63; Revell, *Building Gotham*, 39–42; Condit, *Port of New York*, 269–70.

229. In a manner that mimicked Cassatt's official pronouncements, the borough president noted that "the Pennsylvania Railroad Company has established a reputation for fair dealing with its employees." J. Edward Swanstrom to William H. Farley, October 13, 1902, PHMC, Cassatt/McCrea papers, Box 17 (12-1778), folder 32/63.

230. *New York Times*, July 24, 1902, July 27, 1902, July 30, 1902, August 6, 1902, September 4, 1902.

231. *New York Times*, July 23, 1902, July 24, 1902.

232. Rea to Cassatt, July 29, 1902, PHMC, Cassatt / McCrea papers, Box 17 (12-1778), folder 32/63.

233. William H. Baldwin, Jr. to Cassatt, December 8, 1902, PHMC, Cassatt/McCrea papers, Box 17 (12-1778), folder 32/63; John P. Green to Cassatt, August 6, 1902, PHMC, Cassatt/McCrea papers, Box 17 (12-1778), folder 32/63.

234. Green to Cassatt, August 6, 1902, Cassatt/McCrea papers, PHMC, Box 17 (12-1778), folder 32/63.

235. Jacob Cantor to Cassatt, August 14, 1902; Green to Cassatt, August 6, 1902 (quote); both in PHMC, Cassatt/McCrea papers, Box 17 (12-1778), folder 32/63.

236. A. S. (possibly Alan H. Strong) to Rea, August 16, 1902, PHMC, Cassatt/McCrea papers, Box 17 (12-1778), folder 32/63.

237. Cassatt to Charles V. Fornes, September 3, 1902, PHMC, Cassatt/McCrea papers, Box 17 (12-1778), folder 32/63.

238. Green to Cassatt, September 5, 1902, PHMC, Cassatt/McCrea papers, Box 17 (12-1778), folder 32/63.

239. *New York Times*, August 3, 1902.

240. Cassatt to Abram S. Hewitt, September 28, 1902 (quote); Cassatt to Alexander E. Orr, October 8, 1902; both in PHMC, Cassatt/McCrea papers, Box 17 (12-1778), folder 32/63.

241. Timothy L. Woodruff to Frank Platt, October 19, 1902, PHMC, Cassatt/McCrea papers, Box 17 (12-1778), folder 32/63; *New York Times*, October 3, 1902, October 10, 1902; Condit, *Port of New York*, 270.

242. Merchants' Association of New York, "Protest Against the Demand for an Eight-Hour Labor Clause in the Pennsylvania Tunnel Franchise," October 2, 1902; William F. King to Benjamin B. Odell, Jr., November 28, 1902; William F. King to Cassatt, December 5, 1902; Cassatt to King, December 6, 1902; all in PHMC, Cassatt/McCrea papers, Box 17 (12-1778), folder 32/89; *New York Times*, December 4, 1902, December 9, 1902, December 17, 1902.

243. Resolution, Office of the Recording Secretary, Order of Knights of Labor, October 16, 1902, PHMC, Cassatt/McCrea papers, Box 17 (12-1778), folder 32/63.

244. William H. Baldwin, Jr., to Rea (telephone message), December 12, 1902, PHMC, Cassatt/McCrea papers, Box 17 (12-1778), folder 32/63.

245. J. Edward Swanstrom to The Pennsylvania Railroad Company, December 17, 1902; Cassatt to Swanstrom, December 24, 1902; both in PHMC, Cassatt/McCrea papers, Box 17 (12-1778), folder 32/63; *New York Times*, November 14, 1902.

246. President Cassatt put his engineering expertise to good use as well, personally suggesting that concrete "benches" be located along the side of each tunnel to serve as a conduit for electrical cables and as a sidewalk for track workers. Raymond, "New York Tunnel Extension," 34.

247. Alfred Noble biography, n.d. (ca. 1908); HML, Box 145, folder 24; Condit, *Port of New York*, 276–77; PRR BOD Minutes, April 23, 1902.

248. Construction details are generally from Raymond, "New York Tunnel Extension"; Charles M. Jacobs, "North River Division," Paper No. 1151; Alfred Noble, "East River Division," Paper No. 1152; E. B. Temple, "Meadows Division and Harrison Transfer Yard," Paper No. 1153; F. Lavis, "The Bergen Hill Tunnels," Paper No. 1154; B. H. M. Hewett and W. L. Brown, "The North River Tunnels," Paper No. 1155; B. F. Cresson, Jr., "The Terminal Station-West," Paper No. 1156; George C. Clarke, "The Site of the Terminal Station," Paper No. 1157; James H. Brace and Francis Mason, "The Cross-Town Tunnels," Paper No. 1158; and Brace, Mason, and S. H. Woodard, "The East River Tunnels," Paper No. 1159; all in *Transactions of the American Society of Civil Engineers*, vol. 68 (September 1910): 1–478; Raymond, "The New York Tunnel Extension, The Pennsylvania R.R. Co., Meadows Division," HML, Box 146, folder 9A; and Condit, *Port of New York*, 294–311.

249. *New York Times*, October 10, 1906.

250. Jonnes, *Conquering Gotham*, 178, 191–92, 199–201, 221–22, 255–59, gives a good account of the screw-pile controversy.

251. *New York Times*, June 30, 1906, July 2, 1906, July 3, 1906, August 17, 1906, September 7, 1906.

252. *New York Times*, March 19, 1908.

253. *New York Times*, April 12, 1908, May 8, 1908; Jonnes, *Conquering Gotham*, 268–69.

254. *New York Times*, November 19, 1909.

255. Jonnes, *Conquering Gotham*, 147.

256. Ibid., 139–42.

257. Alexander Cassatt to Charles McKim, April 24, 1902, PHMC, Cassatt/McCrea papers, Box 15 (12–1776), folder 32/14.

258. Condit, *Port of New York*, 274; Hilary Ballon, *New York's Pennsylvania Stations* (New York: W. W. Norton, 2002), 54–55.

259. Most commuters preferred to live on Long Island, particularly on the North Shore, rather than in the more industrial and working-class neighborhoods in New Jersey. However, PRR trains carried considerable local traffic from Newark, Elizabeth, and New Brunswick into Manhattan, and Princeton (reached by a short branch off of the main line) was a prestigious suburb. The PRR also operated trains over the New York & Long Branch Railroad to resort towns on the Jersey Shore. At the time that Penn Station opened, most of the travelers who used the service had summer homes in the area and spent the workweek in Manhattan. I thank Christopher Baer for his thoughts on commutation traffic and the anticipated early traffic mix at Penn Station.

260. Condit, *Port of New York*, 279; Ballon, *New York's Pennsylvania Stations*, 42–43, 54; Jonnes, *Conquering Gotham*, 166.

261. Ballon, *New York's Pennsylvania Stations*, 53–55.

262. The estimate was four hundred trains from the PRR, and the remainder from the LIRR. "New York Tunnel Extension Railroad Line," 1908, HML, Box 145, folder 19.

263. Ballon, *New York's Pennsylvania Stations*, 53–55, 65–66.

264. *New York Times*, April 25, 1905; Messer and Roberts, *Triumph V*, 258–59.

265. Condit, *Port of New York*, 278.

266. Roberts and Messer, *Triumph V*, 261.

267. Technically, the columns were of the Tuscan order, a variant of the Doric.

268. Station descriptions are from Condit, *Port of New York*, 283–93; Ballon, *New York's Pennsylvania Stations*, 55–78; and Steven Parissien, *Pennsylvania Station: McKim Mead and White* (London: Phaidon Press, 1996).

269. Pedestrians entering the station off of either Thirty-First or Thirty-Third Street crossed a short bridge over the carriage drive before descending to the level of the General Waiting Room.

270. Ballon, *New York's Pennsylvania Stations*, 60–62.

271. Ibid., 62–67.

272. Ibid., 67–73.

273. Particularly after the end of World War II, many architectural critics praised the naked latticework of the concourse as the only authentic part of the station, and even that was as much the design of engineers from Westinghouse as it was of Charles Follen McKim. Even though most of the station's users probably did not share the Modernist's disdain for the aesthetic trickery of the General Waiting Room and its associated public spaces, such elite criticisms did no favors for the activists who in the early 1960s were attempting to save the building from demolition.

274. Not long after Penn Station opened, World War I and increasingly stringent immigration criteria caused a sharp reduction in immigration, and the elimination of emigrant trains. Ballon, *New York's Pennsylvania Stations*, 36.

275. In 1929 and 1930, crews installed curtain walls in the exit concourse and a floor over the open areas of the concourse, both to reduce updrafts and to protect travelers from the catenary that was being installed as part of the conversion of the route between New York and Washington to electric propulsion. Little more than a decade later, the new floor served its most important purpose, when it accommodated the unprecedented crush of wartime travel.

276. One comparison is the Library of Congress Building (currently known as the Thomas Jefferson Building), opened in 1897.

277. I extend my deep appreciation to Christopher Baer for his insights into the design and remodeling of Penn Station. In addition to having had the privilege of using the original Penn Station (which was demolished the year before I was born), he has extensively studied the vast quantity of blueprints and architectural drawings relating to the project. He has also assisted in the development of several models of the station and has served as an adviser to a project (by the Hagley Model Railroad Group) to create a 1:87 model of Penn Station for a 2004 exhibit on the station at the Hagley Museum and Library—see *The Keystone Modeler* 15 (October 2004): 11–20.

278. *New York Times*, July 2, 1906.

279. *New York Times*, October 10, 1906.

280. Jonnes, *Conquering Gotham*, 249, 264–68.

281. See, for example, *Philadelphia Public Ledger*, May 17, 1906.

282. Jonnes, *Conquering Gotham*, 202–4.

283. Usselman, *Regulating Railroad Innovation*, 246–47, 348–51.

284. Rea to McCrea, February 15, 1907, HML, Box 142, folder 25.

285. Rea to J. B. Thomas, January 24, 1907, HML, Box 145, folder 1.

286. Condit, *Port of New York*, 308–9; Ballon, *New York's Pennsylvania Stations*, 93.

287. David B. Sloan, *George Gibbs, M.E., D. ENG. (1861–1940), E. Rowland Hill, M.E., E.E. (1872–1948), Pioneers in Railroad Electrification* (New York: Newcomen Society in North America, 1957); George Gibbs biography, n.d., ca. 1908, HML, Box 145, folder 24; George Gibbs Obituary, *Transactions of the American Society of Civil Engineers* 105 (1940): 1840–44.

288. Fortunately, there were no passengers on board, and therefore no fatalities. Later that year, a short circuit caused another fire, in a loaded train, but with far less damage to the equipment and, aside from a panicked stampede out of the subway, no injuries to passengers. *New York Times*, March 30, 1905, December 30, 1905.

289. John H. White, *The American Railroad Passenger Car* (Baltimore: Johns Hopkins University Press, 1978), 131–32, 135.

290. Report of Mechanical & Electrical Advisory Committee to Cassatt, October 15, 1902, PHMC, Cassatt/McCrea Papers, Box 16 (12–1777), folder 32/43.

291. *New York Times*, August 12, 1906.

292. While wooden cars were soon removed from the trains using Penn Station, and soon afterward from most long-distance service, wooden cars remained in branchline service until 1928. In some instances, steel cars saved lives, as in a July 1913 wreck near Tyrone, Pennsylvania, with only one fatality. In cases where steel cars were intermixed with wood equipment, travel was even more dangerous because the steel cars could telescope into the weaker wooden ones. *New York Times*, November 13, 1906; White, *The American Railroad Passenger Car*, 136–40, 632; "The Passing of the Wooden Passenger Car from This Railroad," July 1928, HML, Box 1414, folder 34.

293. Quoted in Condit, *Port of New York*, 271.

294. Ibid., 176–200.

295. Michael C. Duffy, *Electric Railways, 1880–1990* (London: The Institution of Electrical Engineers, 2003), 37; Bezilla, *Electric Traction on the Pennsylvania Railroad*, 4–5, 59–60, 74.

296. Condit, *Port of New York*, 200–208.

297. Ibid., 213–19.

298. Josef W. Konvitz, "William J. Wilgus and Engineering Projects to Improve the Port of New York, 1900–1930," *Technology and Culture* 30 (April 1989): 398–425.

299. *Scientific American*, October 29, 1904, 297–98; William D. Middleton, *When the Steam Railroads Electrified* (Milwaukee: Kalmbach, 1974), 37–71.

300. On the twelve miles of shared NYC/New Haven track between Woodlawn and Grand Central, the New Haven locomotives drew electric power from the NYC's 660-volt third-rail DC system.

301. Middleton, *When the Steam Railroads Electrified*, 72–85.

302. Ibid., 74–76.

303. Information on the New York electrification in this and subsequent paragraphs is drawn from Middleton, *When the Steam Railroads Electrified*, 112–31; Bezilla, *Electric Traction*, 33–53; and Condit, *Port of New York*, 312–32.

304. A few of these responsibilities were later removed from the company's purview, including track, signaling, and electric distribution systems, with the Union Switch & Signal Company winning the contract for signal work. Mechanical and Electrical Advisory Committee, New York Extension to Cassatt, December 3, 1902, PHMC, Cassatt/McCrea papers, Box 16 (12–1777), folder 32/43.

305. Rea to McCrea, September 23, 1908, HML, Box 142, folder 10.

306. Bezilla, *Electric Traction*, 34–39, 91–92.

307. Ibid., 47–49, 53; Duffy, *Electric Railways*, 89, 284; Paul T. Warner, *Motive Power Development on the Pennsylvania Railroad System, 1831–1924* (Philadelphia: Pennsylvania Railroad, 1924), 74–75.

308. Many commuters, however, continued to ride on the PRR to Exchange Place in Jersey City, before transferring to ferries or the Hudson & Manhattan Railroad

309. Condit, *Port of New York*, 303–5.

310. The Post Office was later extended, covering the PRR's tracks as far west as Ninth Avenue. *New York Times*, February 14, 1903, March 9, 1906, June 29, 1906, December 28, 1913; Ballon, *New York's Pennsylvania Stations*, 85–86.

311. Ibid.

312. In 1921, PRR officials signed an agreement with the Equitable Life Assurance Society to construct an office building on PRR-owned land, between Thirty-First and Thirty-Second Streets, opposite Penn Station's Seventh Avenue façade. The few remaining parcels under PRR ownership were generally too small to permit further development. Ballon, *New York's Pennsylvania Stations*, 85–92.

313. Even so, the yard was not large enough to accommodate PRR and LIRR traffic, and the facility was expanded on four separate occasions. It eventually encompassed more than four hundred acres.

314. Nicholas Kalis, "Sunnyside: The World's Greatest Passenger Railroad Yards," *The Keystone* 29 (Spring 1996): 15–62; *Railway Age* 87, no. 12 (September 21, 1929): 671–74; Messer and Roberts, *Triumph V*, 259.

315. Messer and Roberts, *Triumph V*, 211–13, 236; Moyer, "The PRR's Navy—Part 1," 50–51, 56–64.

316. *New York Times*, October 24, 1900, December 11, 1912; Condit, *Port of New York*, 332–35, 395n12. See also *Guide for the Pennsylvania Railroad, Including the Entire Route with all Its Windings, Objects of Interest, and Information Useful to the Traveller* (Philadelphia: T. K. and P. G. Collins, 1855); Fletcher M. Green, "Origins of the Credit Mobilier of America," *Mississippi Valley Historical Review* 46, no. 2 (September 1959): 238–251; Wallace B. Katz, "The New York Rapid Transit Decision of 1900: Economy, Society, Politics," Historic American Engineering Record Survey Number HAER NY-122, pp. 2–144 (Washington, D.C.: National Park Service), available at http://www.nycsubway.org/articles/haer-nyrapid.html, accessed on June 21, 2010.

317. Othmar H. Ammann, "The Hell Gate Arch Bridge and Approaches of the New York Connecting Railroad over the East River in New York City," *Transactions of the American Society of Civil Engineers* 82 (1918): 852–1039, at 1000.

318. Rea to McCrea, August 9, 1909, HML, Box 142, folder 10 (quote); Ripley, *Railroads: Finance and Organization*, 464–73.

319. Rea to McCrea, September 23, 1908, HML, Box 142, folder 10.

320. After Cassatt's death, James McCrea served as the PRR representative on the New Haven board, followed in turn by Samuel Rea. In 1910, additional purchases of New Haven stock, arranged through the Adams Express Company, enabled the PRR to appoint another representative (Philadelphia attorney and PRR director Thomas De Witt Cuyler) to the New Haven board.

321. PRR BOD Minutes, December 28, 1904, 183; Burgess and Kennedy, *Centennial History*, 413, 526–27; *Investigation of Railroads, Holding Companies, and Affiliated Companies: Report of the Committee on Interstate Commerce: Railroad Combination in the Eastern Region, Part 1 (Before 1920)*, 76th Cong., 3rd sess. (Washington, D.C.: U.S. Government Printing Office, 1940), 51, 105–7.

322. Rea to McCrea, September 23, 1908, HML, Box 142, folder 10.

323. *New York Times*, March 24, 1904; Condit, *Port of New York*, 334–35.

324. *New York Times*, April 10, 1905, November 17, 1905.

325. The Board of Aldermen included the five borough presidents, the board president, and sixty-seven aldermen from the assembly districts in the five boroughs, and there was little to keep the aldermen from pursuing a strictly local political agenda. The Board of Estimate and Apportionment consisted of three at-large officials (the mayor, the comptroller, and the president of the Board of Aldermen) and the five borough presidents. The key lay in the voting structure, with the three at-large members each receiving three votes, the presidents of Manhattan and Brooklyn two votes apiece, and the presidents of Queens, Richmond, and the Bronx one vote apiece. That structure enabled the at-large members to impose their citywide planning vision on the relatively less powerful local interests, represented by the borough presidents. Revell, *Building Gotham*, 41, 44–48.

326. *New York Times*, March 23, 1905.

327. *New York Times*, April 21, 1903.

328. *New York Times*, February 26, 1903, April 21, 1903, April 22, 1903, April 23, 1903, April 24, 1903; Clifton Hood, *722 Miles: The Building of the Subways and How They Transformed New York* (Baltimore: Johns Hopkins University Press, 1993), 129.

329. *New York Times*, March 10, 1904, March 29, 1905.

330. *New York Herald*, June 21, 1904; Revell, *Building Gotham*, 44–48.

331. *New York Times*, April 14, 1905.

332. Ibid.

333. *The Public*, May 13, 1905, 90.

334. *New York Times*, April 29, 1905.

335. *New York Times*, April 11, 1905, April 19, 1905, April 15, 1905, April 29, 1905, May 3, 1905, May 5, 1905, May 25, 1905, November 17, 1905.

336. The construction of the tunnels under the Hudson and East rivers, and the station in Manhattan, were four components of the plan. The other six points involved the electrification of all LIRR tracks in Brooklyn and Queens, the completion of the Atlantic Avenue Improvement, the construction of new passenger and freight terminals at Flatbush Avenue, the completion of the New York Connecting Railroad link between Long Island and Port Morris in the Bronx, the construction of the Glendale Cutoff to provide easier access to Rockaway Beach, permission for the Hudson & Manhattan Railroad to extend its service from Jersey City west to Newark, the construction of new transfer facilities at Greenville, and the upgrading of the LIRR branch line to Bay Ridge in Brooklyn. While Cassatt's offer was intended to mollify the members of the Board of Rapid Transit Rail-

road Commissioners, he and other PRR and LIRR officials had long planned to do most of the projects that he listed.

337. *New York Times*, January 22, 1906, January 23, 1906, January 24, 1906, February 2, 1906, February 9, 1906, March 2, 1906; Condit, *Port of New York*, 272–73.

338. *New York Times*, March 23, 1906.

339. Revell, *Building Gotham*, 47.

340. *New York Times*, April 5, 1905.

341. Report of the Committee on Internal Trade and Improvements, February 27, 1906, Proceedings of the Chamber of Commerce, New York Chamber of Commerce, *Forty-Eighth Annual Report of the Corporation of the Chamber of Commerce of the State of New-York, for the Year 1905–1906* (New York: The Chamber, 1906), 131.

342. *New York Times*, March 29, 1906.

343. *New York Times*, March 29, 1906, April 12, 1906, April 21, 1906, April 25, 1906, April 27, 1906, February 15, 1907.

344. Messer and Roberts, *Triumph V*, 322.

345. Ibid.

346. Ibid., 321–23; William G. Thom, "Constructing the New York Connecting: Last Act of an Ambitious Plan," *The Keystone* 30 (Winter 1997): 41–47; Robert C. Sturm, *New York Connecting Railroad: Long Island's Other Railroad* (Long Island Sunrise Chapter NRHS, 2006), 35–36.

347. Both lines were built during the 1870s, the Sixth Avenue line by the Metropolitan Elevated Railway, and the Ninth Avenue line by the New York Elevated Railroad. They were leased by the Manhattan Railway in 1879 and later became part of the Interborough Rapid Transit Company.

348. George Gibbs to Rea, September 4, 1908, HML, Box 145, folder 27.

349. Raymond, "New York Tunnel Extension," 42.

350. Coal magnate Edward J. Berwind, a close ally of the PRR, was also on the IRT board. *Directory of Directors in the City of New York*, vol. 1903 (New York: Directory of Directors Co., 1915), 834; *New York Times*, November 3, 1922; Hood, *722 Miles*, 120–21. James Blaine Walker, *Fifty Years of Rapid Transit* (New York: Law Printing Co., 1918), also provides an account of events.

351. Ray Stannard Baker, "The Subway 'Deal': How New York Built Its New Underground Railroad," *McClure's* 24 (March 1905): 451–69 (quote).

352. Hood, *722 Miles*, 124–25.

353. Ibid., 126–32.

354. Ibid., 135–40.

355. Gustav Lindenthal to Rea, November 14, 1910, HML, Box 142, folder 1.

356. Rea to McCrea, September 2, 1908, HML, Box 145, folder 27.

357. Ibid.

358. Hood, *722 Miles*, 143–50, Revell, *Building Gotham*, 108–10; Broesamle, *William Gibbs McAdoo*, 37–40.

359. Rea to William J. Gaynor, November (?), 1910, HML, Box 142, folder 1.

360. Rea to Joseph P. Day, November 12, 1910, HML, Box 142, folder 1 (quote); Revell, *Building Gotham*, 110–11.

361. Hood, *722 Miles*, 150–51.

362. Ibid., 151–61. See also William R. Willcox, *Dual System of Rapid Transit for New York City* (New York: New York Public Service Commission, 1912); Revell, *Building Gotham*, 112–13.

363. Rea to George G. Bass, September 7, 1911, HML, Box 145, folder 27. Bass was the associate editor of the Boston News Bureau.

364. *New York Times*, April 30, 1911, July 22, 1911, August 7, 1911, October 12, 1911, November 17, 1911, November 18, 1911, November 30, 1911, January 16, 1912, January 31, 1912, February 29, 1912.

365. Another year passed before the Seventh Avenue line was extended south to Lower Manhattan. In 1932, the Independent Subway System completed a line under Eighth Avenue on the other side of Penn Station. *New York Times*, June 30, 1912, June 4, 1912; Hood, *722 Miles*, 157–58.

366. *New York Times*, April 3, 1917.

367. *New York Times*, December 15, 1905.

368. Ripley, *Railroads: Rates and Regulation*, 99.

369. *New York Times*, March 3, 1908. The total included only Lines East. In 1907, Lines West had gross earnings of $110.3 million. For a perspective on this issue, see Ripley, *Railroads: Rates and Regulation*, 96–100.

370. Revell, *Building Gotham*, 64–66; *New York Times*, March 3, 1908. As the commissioners phrased their argument, "Assuming that the stockholder is only entitled to extract from the public a certain amount for the performance of the service, he clearly has no right to both receive that amount in dividends, and add to the productive value of his property." In the "Matter of Proposed Advances in Freight Rates," 9 ICC 382 (1903), quoted in Revell, *Building Gotham*, 65.

371. *New York Times*, January 11, 1907.

372. Ari A. Hoogenboom and Olive Hoogenboom, *A History of the ICC: From Panacea to Palliative* (New York: Norton, 1976), 57; Revell, *Building Gotham*, 71. Information on economic cycles is from the National Bureau of Economic Research, "U.S. Business Cycle Expansions and Contractions," archived at http://www.nber.org/cycles/cyclesmain .html#announcements.

373. Thorne also acted in behalf of railroad commissions in Kansas, Nebraska, Missouri, Oklahoma, and North and South Dakota.

374. *New York Times*, March 10, 1914.

375. *New York Times*, March 11, 1914.

376. *New York Times*, March 26, 1914.

377. *New York Times*, May 1, 1914.

378. *New York Times*, December 20, 1914; Revell, *Building Gotham*, 67–68.

379. Revell, *Building Gotham*, 67–68.

Index

American Express Company, 314, 837n.40
American Line. *See* American Steamship Company
American Philosophical Society, 14, 814n.54
American Railway Engineering and Maintenance of Way Association, 571
American Railway Express Company, 837n.40
American Revolution, 1, 5
American Society of Civil Engineers, 571–72
American Society for Promoting Useful Knowledge, 14–15, 96, 814n.54
American Society for Testing Materials, 571
American Steamship Company, 469–71
American System, 25, 26, 129
American Telephone & Telegraph Company, 608–9, 716
American Union Telegraph Company, 655
Amiens, Treaty of, 813n.31
Ammon, Robert, 480, *487*
Amtrak (National Railroad Passenger Corporation), vii, 736
Anabaptists, 1–2
Anchor Line (Glasgow–New York), 469
Anchor Line (Great Lakes). *See* Erie & Western Transportation Company
Anderson, Peirce, 743–45, 780
Annual Report (PRR, 1870), 437
Annual Report (PRR, 1871), 359
Annual Report (PRR, 1872), 350
Annual Report (PRR, 1874), 476
Annual Report (PRR, 1882), 515
anthracite (hard coal): vs. bituminous production, 630, 636–37; blast-furnace use of, 44; cartels and, 501, 514–18, 527–29, 657; coordination of movement of, 130–31; cost of, 18; and development of holding companies, 345–47; ignition of, 17; iron smelting with, 44, 73–74, 813n.24; legislative support for production, 8–9, 344; manufacturing fostered by, 18; Philadelphia's industrial economy driven by, 18–19, 78, 243; production of, 18; PRR involvement in, 234, 237, 373–76, 377, 678–79; strike (1902), 641, 647, 707; role in westward transportation patterns, 8, 16–22, 27, 31, 33, 815n.61. *See also* Wyoming Valley
Anti-Masons, 56, 60, 64, 66–68, 156, 823n.131
arks (flat-bottom scows), 20
Army Corps of Topographical Engineers, 62
Arsenal Bridge, 237, 298–99, *300*, 736, 408
assistant superintendents, 164–68. *See also individual superintendents*
Association of Freight Traffic Officers, 552–53
Association of Transportation Officers of the Pennsylvania Railroad, 397, 552, 572, 588, 591, 594–95, 711–12
Atglen & Susquehanna Branch, 734–35
Atlantic Avenue Improvement, 755–56, 788–89. *See also* Long Island Rail Road; New York Improvements
Atlantic & Great Western Railroad, 861nn.133–34; bankruptcy of, 501; broad gauge of, 856n.149; construction of, 304–5; leased to Gould, 333; oil trade dominated by, 305, 309, 313, 360–61, 859n.89; Philadelphia & Reading's traffic

agreement with, 321; in receivership, 322, 333; uniform-gauge route established by, 305
Atlantic, Mississippi & Ohio Railroad, 438, 440, 442–44. *See also* Norfolk & Western
Atlantic & Ohio Telegraph Company, 166, 212, 287–88, 601–2
Atlantic & Pacific Railroad, 418–19
Atlantic & Pacific Telegraph Company, 496
Atterbury, William Wallace: and attitudes toward telephone dispatching, 609; early career of, 708
Attica & Buffalo Railroad, 77, 841n.144
Auburn & Port Clinton Railroad, 235, 374
Auburn & Rochester Railroad, 77, 841n.144
Auburn & Syracuse Railroad, 77, 841n.144
auction sales, 9–10, 813n.31
automatic train control. *See* signals
automatic train stop. *See* signals

Backwoodsman (locomotive), 53
Bacon, George Vaux, 109
Bacon, Josiah, 403
Baer, Christopher T., 822n.100, 831n.17, 835n179, 856n137
Bagaley, Ralph, 519, 576
Baird, Matthew, 420, 830n.5
Baird, Thomas, 112
Baker, Benjamin, 753
Baker, Evan, 274
Baker, George N., 88, 91, 827n.44
Bald Eagle Valley Railroad, 634
Baldwin, Matthias W., 53, 78, 92, 107, 414, 830n.5. *See also* Baldwin Locomotive Works
Baldwin, William A. (Philadelphia & Erie superintendent), 586
Baldwin, William Henry, Jr. (LIRR president), 755–58, 761, 766, 774, 916n.190
Baldwin Locomotive Works: employees' shares in PRR, 92; location/operations of, 569; and PRR, 292; reputation of, 53; and Sellers, 568; and Westinghouse, 788–90
Baltimore: as commercial center and port, 11–16, *16*, 77, 814n.50; growth of, 13, 77; internal improvements in, 63; PRR facilities in, 358, 737–38; roads connecting to, 12, 16; slaves and free blacks in, 13; suburbs of, 13; Susquehanna Valley routes, 59–61, 822n.94, 822nn.98–100; wheat/flour trade in, 12–13. *See also* Baltimore & Potomac Tunnels
Baltimore American, 62
Baltimore & Ohio Railroad, xiv; accounting controls at, 133; Army vs. civil engineers for, 131–32; arrival in Wheeling, 189; bankruptcy, 507; bridges built by, stone vs. wooden, 132; charter of, 62, 64, 80–81, *85*, 86–90, 100, 116, 131, 827n.53; and competition for bituminous coal traffic, 643–44; construction of, 63, 75, 120; competition with PRR, 326; inclined planes for, 820n.34; and inclusion in the community of interest, 649–51; management/organization of, 133–34; opening of, 75; organization of, 138; Pennsylvania threatened by, 25; Philadelphia threatened by, 76; PRR's rivalry with, 189, 303, 326, 356–57, 434–35,

503–5; public/private support of, 62–64; route of, 63, 103–4, 189, 822n.110, 823n.120, 830n.139; surveys for, 62; taxes on, 827n.51; and United States Express Company, 837n.40; Wheeling terminus of, 120, 189. *See also under* Garrett, John W.
Baltimore & Port Deposit Rail Road, 222. *See also* Philadelphia, Wilmington & Baltimore Railroad
Baltimore & Potomac Railroad (B&P): construction of, 357–59, 415, 437; and the Long Bridge, 435–36; merger with PW&B, 652, 870n.223, 883n.33, 910n.15 (*see also* Philadelphia, Baltimore & Washington Railroad); organization of, 388, *391*; PRR dependence on, 404, 430; routes of, 356–57, 507; terminal at Sixth and B Streets NW (Washington), 738, *739*; Washington Southern Railway operated by, 652
Baltimore & Potomac station (Washington), 357, *739*, 740–41; James A. Garfield assassinated in, 744
Baltimore & Potomac Tunnels, 358, 737–38, 915n.139
Baltimore & Susquehanna Railroad: charter of, 141; construction of, 61, 225, *231*, 237–38; funding of, 61; incorporation of, 59–60; opening of, 61; surveys for, 59. *See also* Northern Central Railway
Baltimore & York Turnpike (*formerly* York Road), 60, 822n.96
Baltzell, Edward Digby, 830n.5, 830n.7
Bank Act (1836), 65–66
Bank Act (1840), 69
Bank of Pennsylvania, 26, 813n.25
Bank of the United States: design of, 817n.111; incorporation of, 812n.20
Bank War, 64–66, 175, 226
banks: internal improvements underwritten by, 8, 65, 813n.25; specie payments by, 69–70. *See also individual banks*
Banks, Ephraim, 824n.158
Barclay, Richard D., 347, 363, 439, 441
Barksdale, Francis Nelson, 554–56
Barnes, J. Hampton, 795
Barnes, Oliver W., 795, 833n.64
Barnes, William H., 315–16, 348, 795, 860n.112, 902n.105
Bayard, James A., Jr., 88, 827n.44
Beaver Division, *34*, 65, 824n.149
Beaver & Erie Canal (Erie Extension), *35*, 65, 70
Bedford Railroad, 211
Beech Creek Clearfield & South Western Railroad. *See* Beech Creek Railroad
Beech Creek Railroad, 516–24
Bee Line, 272, 274, 337, 339, 497, 532–35, 854n.114, 855n.126, 863n.39, 882n.160
Bellefontaine Railway. *See* Bee Line
Bellefontaine & Indiana Railroad, 272–73
Bell's Gap Railroad, 634, 667
Belmont, August, Jr., 756–57, 784, 788, 797–98, 800, 803–5. *See also* Interborough Rapid Transit Company; subways
Benson, Byron D., 455, 459–60

House Committee on Roads and Canals, 129
Houston, Henry Howard: and the American
Steamship Company, 469–70; background
of, 155; and development of Chestnut Hill,
512, 514; as a director of the Indianapolis &
Vincennes, 342; and the Empire Line, 316; as
general freight agent for PRR, 155, 161, *168*,
313, 315; and holding companies, 347, 420; at
Leech & Company, 155; as a member of the
Philadelphia elite, 830n.5; through-freight
cost-benefit analysis by, 161; and tour of west-
ern lines, 281; and the Union Line, 348, 350;
and the Western Transportation Company,
270
Houston, Sam, 155
Howard Street Tunnel (B&O), 507
Howell, G. O., 584
Howell, George, 100, 143–44, 148, 602–3
Hubley, Edward B., 68
Hudson & Manhattan Railroad, 762, 773–75,
788, 790, *791*, 792–93, 804, 918n.218
Hudson River Railroad, 186, 303. *See also* New
York Central & Hudson River Railroad
Hudson Tubes. *See* Hudson & Manhattan
Railroad
Hudson Tunnel Railroad, 751, 754, 762. *See also*
Haskin, De Witt Clinton; Hudson & Man-
hattan Railroad
Huff, George F., 638, 67–74
Hughes, Charles Evans, 676, 684, 800, 803
Hughes, Thomas P., 563
hump yards, 729
Hunter's Point (Long Island Rail Road), 750,
753, 755, 757, 769, 782, 788
Huntingdon & Broad Top Mountain Railroad,
632–35
Huntingdon, Cambria & Indiana Turnpike,
814n.58
Huntington, Collis P., 406, 414, 419–26, 428

Illinois: financial crisis in, 69
Illinois & St. Louis Bridge Company ("Eads
Bridge"), 412
*The Impolicy of Building Another Railroad
Between Washington and New York* (S. M.
Felton), 298
Improvement Act (1821), 20
inclined planes: accidents on, 150, 172, 836n.2;
on the Allegheny Portage Railroad, 31, 38,
46–49, *48*, 53, 58, 68; on the Danville &
Pottsville Railroad, 232; elimination of, 66;
on the Philadelphia & Columbia Railroad, *37*,
44, 53, 66; Moncure Robinson on, 46,
819–20nn.34–35
incorporation, business: by Congress, 812n.20;
early state laws on, 812–13n.24; and eminent
domain, 8; industry-specific, 813n.24; and limited liability, 8, 812–13n.24; as public vs. private, 812n.22; in transportation, scope of, 8. *See
also* corporate charters; free incorporation laws
Indiana: financial crisis in, 69
Indiana Central Railway, 273–75
Indianapolis & Bellefontaine Railroad, 272–73
Indianapolis & St. Louis Railroad, 338–39, 350,
532–34

Indianapolis & Vincennes Railroad, 341–42, 350,
352, 421, 474
Indiana Republican, 82
individualism: republican, 52
Industrial Heritage Project, 839n.74
Information for Employees and the Public, 698
Ingersoll, Charles J., 28, 30
Insurance Company of North America, 92, 108
Interborough Rapid Transit Company, 756, 784,
788–89, 803. *See also* August Belmont, Jr.;
subways
Internal Improvement Act (1821), 23
internal-improvement bill (1838), 66–67, 823n.128
Internal Improvement Convention (Harrisburg,
Pa., 1825), 29–30
internal-improvement convention (Brownsville,
1835), 63
Internal Improvement Fund Act (1826), 32
internal improvements: and federalism, 3, 5–7, 14,
23; and national planning, 4–6, 10; in Pennsylvania, 15, 22–27; and the War of 1812, 6, 10
Internal Improvements Commission, 24, 27, 29,
62
International Mercantile Marine Company, 472,
637
International Navigation Company, 469–72
Interstate Commerce Commission: actions of,
546–48; and the development of the administrative state, 546–47; coal hearings, 671–74,
677–78, 680; and development of accounting
standards, 689–93; establishment of, 544–
46; judicial opposition to, 546–47, 686–87;
and limited judicial review, 687; Penn Central bankruptcy blamed on, xii; in the Progressive Era, 663–64; and railroad valuation,
701–2; and safety, 562, 573, 581–82, 591–98;
as a stabilizing force in the railroad industry,
625, 627
*Interstate Commerce Commission v. Alabama
Midland*, 547, 675
*Interstate Commerce Commission v. Illinois
Central Railroad*, 687
iron: growth of trade in, 73–74; smelting of, 17
(*see also* anthracite); tariff on, 92
Irvine, James, 829n.108
Ives, Henry S., 526, 534–35

J. & M. Brown, 107
Jack's Narrows (near Mt. Union, Pa.), 2
Jackson, Andrew: in the Bank War, 64–66, 175,
226; at the Battle of New Orleans, 6; Demo-
cratic Republicans' emergence under, 812n.15;
presidential victory of, 8, 33, 36, 64
Jackson–Clay men (Amalgamation Party), 8
Jacobs, Charles M., 755, 758–59, 762, 767–71,
773. *See also* New York Improvements
Janney, Eli, 578–80
Jay Cooke & Company, 380, 416, 418, 442, 451
Jefferson, Thomas, 1; on federal support for road
and canal construction, 4
Jeffersonville, Madison & Indianapolis Railroad,
278, 340, 349
Jenks, Leland H., 811n.5
Jersey Central. *See* Central Railroad of New
Jersey

Jewett, Hugh J., 267, 342, 352, 462, 466, 854n.105
Jewett, Sherman S., 659
Jewett, Thomas L., 266–67, 271, 273, 315, 328, 352,
414, 854n.105
John Bull (locomotive), 216, 554
John E. Thayer & Brother, 223
Johnson, Andrew, 830n.128
Johnson, Jane, 103
Johnston, William F., 172, 181
Johnstown (*formerly* Conemaugh, Pa.): charter/
incorporation of, 811n.1 (Ch. 1); flood in, 3,
557–62; settlement of, 3
Johnstown Flood (1889), 47, 559–60, *561*, 637,
729–30, 841n.134
Joint Companies, 217–25, 235–36, 283, 297–99,
301, 353–54, 846n.114, 846n.122. *See also*
Camden & Amboy Rail Road; Delaware &
Raritan Canal Company; United New Jersey
Railroad & Canal Companies
Joint Traffic Association, 548
Jones, Samuel, 47
Junction Canal, *35*, 817n.135
Junction Railroad, 293–94, 296, 298–301,
300–301, 324–25, 355, 402, 459, 503–5, 733,
735, 883n.33
Juniata Division Canal, 2; acquired by PRR, 184;
construction of, 41, 56; length of, 818n.9;
route of, 33, *34*, *35*, *39*, 41
Juniata River, 2, 3; and the cross-state route pro-
posal, 15

Kansas Pacific Railway, 403, 413–17, 494,
873n.35
Karns, Samuel D. ("Captain"), 80–81, 826n.11
Keating, William H., 107
Kelley, Alfred, 249–50, 262, 851n.29
Kelley, Oliver H., 542
Kennedy, E. F., 573
Kennedy, John Stewart, 855n.135
Kennedy, Miles C., 111, 522
Kennedy, William M., 139
Keokuk bridge, 275, 280, 332, 410–12, 417
Keokuk Bridge Company. *See* Keokuk bridge
Keystone Bridge Company (*formerly* Piper &
Shiffler), 355, 409–10, 412–13, 616
Keystone Coal & Coke Company, 638, 672–73,
677, 906n.203
Keystone Telegraph Company, 603
Kiesel, William F., Jr., 785
Kiskiminetas River, 41, 51
Kittanning Feeder, 818n.9
Kneass, Samuel H., 831n.17, 831n.23
Kneass, Strickland, 296, 831n.17
Knight, Edward C., 371, 469, 504, 521, 886n.86
Knight, Jonathan, 131–32
Knights of Labor, 479, 604, 641, 766
Know-Nothings, 95
Kuhn, Loeb & Company, 650, 658, 676, 706,
714, 717–20, 722, 758, 761

labor/workforce: dangers to, viii–ix, xiii; vs.
management, xii–xiii; number of employees,
ix; overview of, xiii; prestige/ security of, x,
xiii. *See also* strikes
Lafayette, Marquis de, 26

Acknowledgments

The completion of this, the first half of a two-volume history of the Pennsylvania Railroad, has been a long and arduous task. Whatever I have accomplished has been possible—to use the oft-quoted phrase attributed to Isaac Newton—only because I have been standing on the shoulders of giants. While I have not made a systematic analysis of the issue, I imagine that more words have been written, and continue to be written, about the PRR than any other railroad in the United States, and perhaps the world. I owe a particular debt of gratitude to the many individuals whose love of the railroad industry and passion for the PRR has led them to preserve written records, photographs, and artifacts, often rescuing them from oblivion at times when the conventional wisdom suggested that such repositories of history were nothing more than detritus from a failed company in a dying industry. Many historians and railroad enthusiasts have written books and articles profiling various aspects of the PRR's history and operations, examining in detail sources and topics that I would not otherwise have been able to include in this volume. It would be difficult to surpass Richard T. Wallis's account of the PRR's development of the Vandalia Route, Michael Bezilla's coverage of the railroad's electrification, or James A. Ward's biographies of J. Edgar Thomson and Herman Haupt. They, and many others, have prepared a path for me to follow, and I thank them profusely.

Even today, nearly two decades after completing graduate school at The Ohio State University, I still owe an enormous debt of gratitude to the faculty who guided me through my doctoral studies, and who helped to lay the foundation for my academic career. Chief among them is Mansel G. Blackford, who was quite possibly the world's best dissertation adviser. Had it not been for him, my career and this book would not have been possible. K. Austin Kerr and William R. Childs, also on my dissertation committee, are both superbly knowledgeable regarding the political economy of the railroads, continue to offer their advice and support. David Sicilia and his family have welcomed me into their home, proximate to the National Archives, and I thank them for their generous hospitality.

Many thanks go to those at my home institution of Southern Polytechnic State University, including a series of department chairs, from Charlie Weeks to La Juana Cochrane to Julie Newell, who have put up with my seemingly endless research agenda. Thanks, too, to my colleagues in the Social and International Studies Department, who have taken in stride my angst at the progress of the manuscript. At a university with teaching obligations of four or five classes a semester, located in one of two states that do not make provision for faculty sabbaticals, reassigned time has come through the generosity of Dean Alan Gabrielli and Dean Thomas Nelson, and their support is greatly appreciated. Interlibrary loan has been a lifeline to books from across the United States, and I give a special thanks to Southern Polytechnic State University Library director Joyce Mills and her extraordinarily talented staff, including Li Chen, Mark Kirkley, Yongli Ma, Ann Mills, Steven Vincent, and Aaron Wimer.

Resources related to the Pennsylvania Railroad are located in repositories across the United States, and research for this project would not have been possible without the assistance of many dedicated librarians and archivists. In particular, I extend my thanks to Joseph-James Ahern, Senior Archivist at the University of Pennsylvania Archives; Randy Elliott, at the Allen County/Fort Wayne Historical Society; Paul T. Fagley, Cultural Educator at the Greenwood Furnace State Park; Nicole Joniec, at the Library Company of Philadelphia; Sheri Hamilton and Susan J. Beates at the Drake Well Museum; Cynthia Ostroff at the Yale University Library; Brenda Galloway-Wright, Ann Mosher, and Adam Feldman at the Urban Archives, Temple University; Joseph Shemtov and Elsa Varela, at the Free Library of Philadelphia; Cory Gooch and Robin Held at the Frye Art Museum, Seattle; Hillary S. Kativa, at the Historical Society of Pennsylvania; Erin Rushing, Digital Images Librarian, Smithsonian Institution Libraries; David A. Pfeiffer at the National Archives and Records Administration, College Park; David Haberstich, Curator of Photography and Reference Coordinator at the National Museum of American History, Smithsonian Institution; and Richard Burkert, President of the Johnstown Area Heritage Association.

The Railroad Museum of Pennsylvania, at Strasburg, houses a stupendous collection of physical artifacts, documents, and photographs pertaining to the PRR. All of the staff members there, particularly Kurt Bell and Bradley K. Smith, have been exceptionally generous with their time and advice. The bulk of the PRR's written records are distributed among eight libraries and archives, with one of the largest collections at the Pennsylvania Historical and Museum Commission in Harrisburg. Associate Archivist Michael D.

Sherbon has made extraordinary efforts to locate documents and photographs, as have Archivist Brett M. Reigh and other staff members. The other extensive collection of PRR materials is located at the Hagley Museum and Library in Wilmington, Delaware, an institution that houses one of the preeminent collections of business history in the United States. The Hagley Library has provided generous financial support for this project, in keeping with their mission to disseminate a broader knowledge of business history to the widest possible audience. Roger Horowitz and the indefatigable Carol Lockman have arranged housing, dealt with crises, and provided a friendly ear on my repeated visits. Jon M. Williams, the Andrew W. Mellon Curator of Prints and Photographs at the Hagley, as well as Archivist Judy Stevenson, Curator Kevin Martin, and Archival Specialist Barbara D. Hall, have scoured the collections for book illustrations, and I have also benefited from the assistance of Terry Snyder and Lynn Catanese. Reference Archivist Marjorie McNinch has been superb in her role as the liaison between me and all of the archival boxes that lay behind the door to the stacks. She has endured a torrent of call slips, offered invaluable assistance, and waited patiently while I made my best effort to look at just one more document before closing time. And, I extend special thanks to Stephen Shisler, who has retrieved countless manuscript boxes for me, and then returned them to their rightful abodes.

Most of the researchers who have worked at the Hagley Library and virtually all of those who have studied the history of the Pennsylvania Railroad have benefited from the knowledge, wisdom, and counsel of Assistant Curator Christopher T. Baer. I have lost count of the number of books relating to the PRR, railroad history, and business history in general that have listed his name in the acknowledgments, but they must number in the hundreds. His encyclopedic knowledge of the PRR's records is unsurpassed. He has helped to rescue a vast array of documents from destruction and, working with Craig Orr, Michael Nash, and others, has processed and catalogued the records, preparing a series of scope and content notes that neatly encapsulate the key elements of the PRR's history. Much of that process is described in Christopher T. Baer, "Salvaging History," *Railroad History*

192 (Spring–Summer 2005): 76–87. Chris has devoted immense effort to the creation of "A General Chronology of the Pennsylvania Railroad Company, Predecessors and Successors and Its Historical Context," available at http://www.prrths.com/Hagley/PRR_hagley_intro.htm. His PRR chronology is an invaluable resource for anyone studying the PRR, or indeed any aspect of railroad history in the United States. I have spoken and corresponded with Chris on numerous occasions, and he has always been exceedingly generous with his advice, and wonderfully patient and tolerant of my slow and halting climb up the vast learning curve that the PRR's history represents. Many other authors, I suspect, have had the same experience. Chris has also read various drafts of the book manuscript, and he has provided extraordinarily perceptive and substantive comments that have altered my thinking on aspects of the PRR's history and operations. His input has made this book immeasurably better, in so many ways, and I thank him profusely.

Many other individuals have read part or all of the lengthy manuscript, and their feedback is much appreciated. Correspondence with Jim Cohen at the City University of New York, and with John K. (Jack) Brown at the University of Virginia, has sharpened my understanding of finance, organizational practices, networking, and insider dealing. Keith Hoskin at the University of Warwick and Richard Macve at the London School of Economics have been most generous with their research into managerial practices. Edwin J. Perkins, Emeritus Professor at the University of Southern California, has given me new perspective on the issues of banking and finance. Richard R. John at the Columbia University School of Journalism has shared his extraordinary knowledge of the politics of the Early Republic, as well as his perceptive analyses of the role of business and technology in society. Mark H. Rose at Florida Atlantic University has read through at least two iterations of the manuscript and I am grateful for his close attention to matters large and small.

More than merely reading the manuscript, Mark has been a wonderful colleague and friend throughout the years of research and writing. It was he who first suggested that I undertake this work, and he who provided advice and support at every step of the process. As one of the editors of the University of Pennsylvania Press book series that includes this work, he has been a tireless advocate. Richard John and Pamela Laird, who serve with Mark as co-editors of the series, have also been extraordinarily supportive, particularly at those times when it seemed as if the project would never be finished.

It has been a delight and a privilege to work with Robert Lockhart, my editor at the University of Pennsylvania Press. He has been extraordinarily patient with my efforts, which have taken much more time and produced a book that is far longer than either of us had initially anticipated. I am fairly certain that I am not the first author to miss a deadline, but I doubt that many other authors have been fortunate enough to work with an editor who has been as understanding; he trusted in the hope that I would complete the book, eventually. Thanks, too, to his hardworking and extraordinarily capable editorial assistant, Julia Rose Roberts. As project editor, Noreen O'Connor-Abel has moved the manuscript right through the production process, responding almost immediately to my queries, while tolerating my own delays (unavoidable, to be sure) in reviewing the material. As copyeditor, Joyce Ippolito was alert to details while always preserving the intent and the spirit of my prose. Carol Roberts, who has provided the index for this volume, has done an exemplary job of identifying hundreds of names and places, while deftly categorizing the more abstract concepts and themes.

My greatest debt of gratitude goes to all of my friends and relations, who have suffered through this seemingly interminable process right along with me. I honor my mother, Helen R. Churella, and the memory of my father, Albert A. Churella, for raising me right, and for encouraging my career aspirations. Thanks to my two dear fur children, Walnut, now departed, who occasionally tolerated my innate inferiority to her and to all things dog, and to Chancey, the good-natured goofball. As stress relievers, they have no equal. Above all, above everything, I cherish the bond that I share with my muse, my inspiration, and the love of my life, my wife, Marianne Holdzkom. I would be a poor person indeed without her. Love ya, sweetie.